World Map: Physical

ARCTIC OCEAN

Svalbard
Norwegian Sea
N. Cape
Novaya Zemlya
Severnaya Zemlya
New Siberian Is.

North Sea
L. Ladoga
Ural Mts.
West Siberian Plain
Yenisey
Lr. Tunguska
Lena
Aldan
Kamchatka

North European Plain
Ob
Irtysh
Sayan Mts.
Stanovoy Ra.
Sea of Okhotsk

Europe
Volga
Don
Danube
Carpathians
Blanc 4808
Apennines
Pic d'Aneto 404
Black Sea
Caucasus
Elbrus 5642
Aral Sea
Syrdarya
Amudarya
Balkhash
Altai
Gobi Desert
Amur
Sakhalin
Hokkaido
Sea of Japan
Japan
Mt. Fuji 3776

Mediterranean Sea
Anatolia
Mt. Ararat 5165
Caspian Sea
Elburz
Zagros
Tian Shan
Pamirs
Tarim Basin
Qilian Shan
Hwang-ho
Korea
Yellow Sea

Dead Sea -403
Euphrates
Tigris
Hindu Kush
K2 8611
Karakoram
Kunlun Shan
Plateau of Tibet
North China Plain
East China Sea

Isthmus of Suez
The Gulf
Sulaiman Ra.
Indus
Thar Desert
Mt. Everest 8848
Himalaya
Gongga Shan 7556
Yangtze
China
Si

Libyan Desert
Hoggar
Red Sea
Arabia
Rub' al Khali
Ganges
India
Deccan
W. Ghats
E. Ghats
Bay of Bengal
Salween
Indo China
Hainan
Taiwan
PACIFIC
Wake

hara
Tibesti
L. Chad
Nile
White Nile
Blue Nile
Arabian Sea
Socotra
C. Guardafui
Mekong
Philippine Is.
Mariana Is.
Guam
Mariana Trench 11022
Marshall Is.

el
Ethiopian Highlands
Somali Peninsula
C. Comorin
Ceylon
South China Sea
Kinabalu 4101
Celebes Sea
Caroline Is.

ne
Mt. Cameroon 4095
L. Turkana
Mt. Kenya 5199
Seychelles
INDIAN
Str. of Malacca
Sumatra
Borneo
Celebes
Moluccas
Gilbert Is.
Nauru

uinea
Congo Basin
Congo
Lake Victoria
Kilimanjaro 5895
Tanganyika
OCEAN
Sunda Is.
Java Sea
Java
Banda Sea
New Guinea
Poncak Jaya 5029
Bismarck Arch.
Solomon Is.
Ellice Is.

Kasai
L. Malawi
Zambezi
Comoros
7450 Java Trench
Timor
Torres Str.
C. York
Coral Sea
New Hebrides
Fiji Is.

Cubango
Mozambique Chan.
Madagascar
Pic Boby 2658
Mauritius
Réunion
Cocos
Hamersley Ra.
MacDonnell Ra.
Great Barrier Reef
New Caledonia

Kalahari Desert
Orange
Drakensberg
Australia
Great Victoria Desert
Great Dividing Range

Cape of Good Hope
C. Leeuwin
Great Australian Bight
Murray
Darling
Mt. Kosciuszko 2237
Tasman Sea
North I.
New Zealand

Crozet Is.
Kerguelen
Bass Str.
Tasmania
Aoraki Mt. Cook 3753
South I.

SOUTHERN OCEAN

Queen Maud Land
Enderby Land
Queen Mary Coast
Wilkes Land
South Magnetic Pole
Antarctica
Victoria Land
Ross Sea

East from Greenwich

Projection: Hammer Equal Area

Copyright: George Philip Ltd.

PHILIP'S

ENCYCLOPEDIC
WORLD
ATLAS

COMPREHENSIVE EDITION

A–Z COUNTRY BY COUNTRY TEXT
KEITH LYE

NAME FORMS
For ease of reference, both English and local name forms appear in the atlas.
Oceans, seas and countries are shown in English throughout the atlas; country
names may be abbreviated to their commonly accepted form (e.g. Germany, not
The Federal Republic of Germany). Conventional English forms are also used for
place names on the smaller-scale maps of the continents. However, local name forms
are used on all the larger-scale country-by-country maps. For countries which do
not use a Roman script, place names have been transcribed according to the systems
adopted by the British and US Geographic Names Authorities. For China, the Pin Yin
system has been used, with some more widely known forms appearing in brackets,
as with Beijing (Peking). For major place names, both English and local forms appear
in the index, the English version being cross-referenced to the local form.

Published in Great Britain in 2000
by George Philip Limited,
a division of Octopus Publishing Group Limited,
2–4 Heron Quays, London E14 4JP

Copyright © 2000 George Philip Limited

Cartography by Philip's

ISBN 0–540–07929–4

A CIP catalogue record for this book is available from the British Library.

Printed in Spain

Details of other Philip's titles and services can be found on our website at:
www.philips-maps.co.uk

Philip's is proud to announce that its World Atlases
are now published in association with The Royal
Geographical Society (with The Institute of British
Geographers).

The Society was founded in 1830 and given a
Royal Charter in 1859 for 'the advancement of
geographical science'. It holds historical collections
of national and international importance, many of
which relate to the Society's association with and
support for scientific exploration and research
from the 19th century onwards. It was pivotal
in establishing geography as a teaching and research
discipline in British universities close to the turn of
the century, and has played a key role in geographical
and environmental education ever since.

Today the Society is a leading world centre
for geographical learning – supporting education,
teaching, research and expeditions, and promoting
public understanding of the subject.

The Society welcomes those interested in
geography as members. For further information,
please visit the website at: www.rgs.org

PHILIP'S
ENCYCLOPEDIC
WORLD
ATLAS

COMPREHENSIVE EDITION

A–Z COUNTRY BY COUNTRY
PLUS COMPLETE WORLD ATLAS

IN ASSOCIATION WITH
THE ROYAL GEOGRAPHICAL SOCIETY
WITH THE INSTITUTE OF BRITISH GEOGRAPHERS

CONTENTS

INDEX TO COUNTRY MAPS

WORLD MAPS

INDEX TO WORLD MAPS

WORLD STATISTICS: Countries

This alphabetical list includes all the countries and territories of the world. If a territory is not completely independent, then the country it is associated with is named. The area figures give the total area of land, inland water and ice.

Units for areas and populations are thousands. The population figures are 1998 estimates. The annual income is the Gross National Product per capita in US dollars. The figures are the latest available, usually 1997.

Country/Territory	Area km^2 Thousands	Area $miles^2$ Thousands	Population Thousands	Capital	Annual Income US $
Afghanistan	652	252	24,792	Kabul	600
Albania	28.8	11.1	3,331	Tirana	750
Algeria	2,382	920	30,481	Algiers	1,490
American Samoa (US)	0.20	0.08	62	Pago Pago	2,600
Andorra	0.45	0.17	75	Andorra La Vella	16,200
Angola	1,247	481	11,200	Luanda	340
Anguilla (UK)	0.1	0.04	11	The Valley	6,800
Antigua & Barbuda	0.44	0.17	64	St John's	7,330
Argentina	2,767	1,068	36,265	Buenos Aires	8,750
Armenia	29.8	11.5	3,422	Yerevan	530
Aruba (Netherlands)	0.19	0.07	69	Oranjestad	15,890
Ascension Is. (UK)	0.09	0.03	1.5	Georgetown	–
Australia	7,687	2,968	18,613	Canberra	20,540
Austria	83.9	32.4	8,134	Vienna	27,980
Azerbaijan	86.6	33.4	7,856	Baku	510
Azores (Portugal)	2.2	0.87	238	Ponta Delgada	–
Bahamas	13.9	5.4	280	Nassau	11,940
Bahrain	0.68	0.26	616	Manama	7,840
Bangladesh	144	56	125,000	Dhaka	270
Barbados	0.43	0.17	259	Bridgetown	6,560
Belarus	207.6	80.1	10,409	Minsk	2,150
Belgium	30.5	11.8	10,175	Brussels	26,420
Belize	23	8.9	230	Belmopan	2,700
Benin	113	43	6,101	Porto-Novo	380
Bermuda (UK)	0.05	0.02	62	Hamilton	31,870
Bhutan	47	18.1	1,908	Thimphu	390
Bolivia	1,099	424	7,826	La Paz/Sucre	950
Bosnia-Herzegovina	51	20	3,366	Sarajevo	300
Botswana	582	225	1,448	Gaborone	4,381
Brazil	8,512	3,286	170,000	Brasília	4,720
British Antarctic Terr. (UK)	1,709	660	0.3	–	–
Brunei	5.8	2.2	315	Bandar Seri Begawan	15,800
Bulgaria	111	43	8,240	Sofia	1,140
Burkina Faso	274	106	11,266	Ouagadougou	240
Burma (= Myanmar)	677	261	47,305	Rangoon	1,790
Burundi	27.8	10.7	5,531	Bujumbura	180
Cambodia	181	70	11,340	Phnom Penh	300
Cameroon	475	184	15,029	Yaoundé	650
Canada	9,976	3,852	30,675	Ottawa	19,290
Canary Is. (Spain)	7.3	2.8	1,494	Las Palmas/Santa Cruz	–
Cape Verde Is.	4	1.6	399	Praia	1,010
Cayman Is. (UK)	0.26	0.10	35	George Town	20,000
Central African Republic	623	241	3,376	Bangui	320
Chad	1,284	496	7,360	Ndjaména	240
Chatham Is. (NZ)	0.96	0.37	0.05	Waitangi	–
Chile	757	292	14,788	Santiago	5,020
China	9,597	3,705	1,236,915	Beijing	860
Christmas Is. (Australia)	0.14	0.05	2	The Settlement	–
Cocos (Keeling) Is. (Australia)	0.01	0.005	1	West Island	–
Colombia	1,139	440	38,581	Bogotá	2,280
Comoros	2.2	0.86	545	Moroni	450
Congo	342	132	2,658	Brazzaville	660
Congo (Dem. Rep. of the)	2,345	905	49,001	Kinshasa	110
Cook Is. (NZ)	0.24	0.09	20	Avarua	900
Costa Rica	51.1	19.7	3,605	San José	2,640
Croatia	56.5	21.8	4,672	Zagreb	4,610
Cuba	111	43	11,051	Havana	1,300
Cyprus	9.3	3.6	749	Nicosia	13,420
Czech Republic	78.9	30.4	10,286	Prague	5,200
Denmark	43.1	16.6	5,334	Copenhagen	32,500
Djibouti	23.2	9	650	Djibouti	850
Dominica	0.75	0.29	78	Roseau	3,090
Dominican Republic	48.7	18.8	7,999	Santo Domingo	1,670
Ecuador	284	109	12,337	Quito	1,590
Egypt	1,001	387	66,050	Cairo	1,180
El Salvador	21	8.1	5,752	San Salvador	1,810
Equatorial Guinea	28.1	10.8	454	Malabo	530
Eritrea	94	36	3,842	Asmara	570
Estonia	44.7	17.3	1,421	Tallinn	3,330
Ethiopia	1,128	436	58,390	Addis Ababa	110
Falkland Is. (UK)	12.2	4.7	2	Stanley	–
Faroe Is. (Denmark)	1.4	0.54	41	Tórshavn	23,660
Fiji	18.3	7.1	802	Suva	2,470
Finland	338	131	5,149	Helsinki	24,080
France	552	213	58,805	Paris	26,050
French Guiana (France)	90	34.7	162	Cayenne	10,580
French Polynesia (France)	4	1.5	237	Papeete	7,500
Gabon	268	103	1,208	Libreville	4,230
Gambia, The	11.3	4.4	1,292	Banjul	320
Georgia	69.7	26.9	5,109	Tbilisi	840
Germany	357	138	82,079	Berlin/Bonn	28,260
Ghana	239	92	18,497	Accra	370
Gibraltar (UK)	0.007	0.003	29	Gibraltar Town	5,000
Greece	132	51	10,662	Athens	12,010
Greenland (Denmark)	2,176	840	59	Nuuk (Godthåb)	15,500
Grenada	0.34	0.13	96	St George's	2,880
Guadeloupe (France)	1.7	0.66	416	Basse-Terre	9,200
Guam (US)	0.55	0.21	149	Agana	6,000
Guatemala	109	42	12,008	Guatemala City	1,500
Guinea	246	95	7,477	Conakry	570
Guinea-Bissau	36.1	13.9	1,206	Bissau	240
Guyana	215	83	820	Georgetown	690
Haiti	27.8	10.7	6,781	Port-au-Prince	330
Honduras	112	43	5,862	Tegucigalpa	700
Hong Kong (China)	1.1	0.40	6,707	–	22,990
Hungary	93	35.9	10,208	Budapest	4,430
Iceland	103	40	271	Reykjavik	26,580
India	3,288	1,269	984,000	New Delhi	390
Indonesia	1,905	735	212,942	Jakarta	1,110
Iran	1,648	636	64,411	Tehran	4,700
Iraq	438	169	21,722	Baghdad	2,000
Ireland	70.3	27.1	3,619	Dublin	18,280
Israel	27	10.3	5,644	Jerusalem	15,810
Italy	301	116	56,783	Rome	20,120
Ivory Coast (Côte d'Ivoire)	322	125	15,446	Yamoussoukro	690
Jamaica	11	4.2	2,635	Kingston	1,560
Japan	378	146	125,932	Tokyo	37,850
Jordan	89.2	34.4	4,435	Amman	1,570
Kazakstan	2,717	1,049	16,847	Astana	1,340
Kenya	580	224	28,337	Nairobi	330
Kerguelen Is. (France)	7.2	2.8	0.7	–	–
Kermadec Is. (NZ)	0.03	0.01	0.1	–	–
Kiribati	0.72	0.28	85	Tarawa	920
Korea, North	121	47	21,234	Pyŏngyang	1,000
Korea, South	99	38.2	46,417	Seoul	10,550
Kuwait	17.8	6.9	1,913	Kuwait City	17,390
Kyrgyzstan	198.5	76.6	4,522	Bishkek	440
Laos	237	91	5,261	Vientiane	400
Latvia	65	25	2,385	Riga	2,430
Lebanon	10.4	4	3,506	Beirut	3,350
Lesotho	30.4	11.7	2,090	Maseru	670
Liberia	111	43	2,772	Monrovia	770
Libya	1,760	679	4,875	Tripoli	6,510
Liechtenstein	0.16	0.06	32	Vaduz	33,000
Lithuania	65.2	25.2	3,600	Vilnius	2,230
Luxembourg	2.6	1	425	Luxembourg	45,360
Macau (China)	0.02	0.006	429	Macau	7,500
Macedonia	25.7	9.9	2,009	Skopje	1,090
Madagascar	587	227	14,463	Antananarivo	250
Madeira (Portugal)	0.81	0.31	253	Funchal	–
Malawi	118	46	9,840	Lilongwe	220
Malaysia	330	127	20,993	Kuala Lumpur	4,680
Maldives	0.30	0.12	290	Malé	1,080
Mali	1,240	479	10,109	Bamako	260
Malta	0.32	0.12	379	Valletta	12,000
Marshall Is.	0.18	0.07	63	Dalap-Uliga-Darrit	1,890
Martinique (France)	1.1	0.42	407	Fort-de-France	10,000
Mauritania	1,030	412	2,511	Nouakchott	450
Mauritius	2.0	0.72	1,168	Port Louis	3,800
Mayotte (France)	0.37	0.14	141	Mamoundzou	1,430
Mexico	1,958	756	98,553	Mexico City	3,680
Micronesia, Fed. States of	0.70	0.27	127	Palikir	2,070
Moldova	33.7	13	4,458	Chişinău	540
Monaco	0.002	0.0001	32	Monaco	25,000
Mongolia	1,567	605	2,579	Ulan Bator	390
Montserrat (UK)	0.10	0.04	12	Plymouth	4,500
Morocco	447	172	29,114	Rabat	1,250
Mozambique	802	309	18,641	Maputo	90
Namibia	825	318	1,622	Windhoek	2,220
Nauru	0.02	0.008	12	Yaren District	10,000
Nepal	141	54	23,698	Katmandu	210
Netherlands	41.5	16	15,731	Amsterdam/The Hague	25,820
Netherlands Antilles (Neths)	0.99	0.38	210	Willemstad	10,400
New Caledonia (France)	18.6	7.2	192	Nouméa	8,000
New Zealand	269	104	3,625	Wellington	16,480
Nicaragua	130	50	4,583	Managua	410
Niger	1,267	489	9,672	Niamey	200
Nigeria	924	357	110,532	Abuja	260
Niue (NZ)	0.26	0.10	2	Alofi	–
Norfolk Is. (Australia)	0.03	0.01	2	Kingston	–
Northern Mariana Is. (US)	0.48	0.18	50	Saipan	11,500
Norway	324	125	4,420	Oslo	36,090
Oman	212	82	2,364	Muscat	4,950
Pakistan	796	307	135,135	Islamabad	490
Palau	0.46	0.18	18	Koror	5,000
Panama	77.1	29.8	2,736	Panama City	3,080
Papua New Guinea	463	179	4,600	Port Moresby	940
Paraguay	407	157	5,291	Asunción	2,010
Peru	1,285	496	26,111	Lima	2,460
Philippines	300	116	77,736	Manila	1,220
Pitcairn Is. (UK)	0.03	0.01	0.05	Adamstown	–
Poland	313	121	38,607	Warsaw	3,590
Portugal	92.4	35.7	9,928	Lisbon	10,450
Puerto Rico (US)	9	3.5	3,860	San Juan	7,800
Qatar	11	4.2	697	Doha	11,600
Réunion (France)	2.5	0.97	705	Saint-Denis	4,500
Romania	238	92	22,396	Bucharest	1,420
Russia	17,075	6,592	146,861	Moscow	2,740
Rwanda	26.3	10.2	7,956	Kigali	210
St Helena (UK)	0.12	0.05	7	Jamestown	–
St Kitts & Nevis	0.36	0.14	42	Basseterre	5,870
St Lucia	0.62	0.24	150	Castries	3,500
St Pierre & Miquelon (France)	0.24	0.09	7	Saint Pierre	–
St Vincent & Grenadines	0.39	0.15	120	Kingstown	2,370
Samoa	2.8	1.1	224	Apia	1,170
San Marino	0.06	0.02	25	San Marino	20,000
São Tomé & Príncipe	0.96	0.37	150	São Tomé	330
Saudi Arabia	2,150	830	20,786	Riyadh	6,790
Senegal	197	76	9,723	Dakar	550
Seychelles	0.46	0.18	79	Victoria	6,850
Sierra Leone	71.7	27.7	5,080	Freetown	200
Singapore	0.62	0.24	3,490	Singapore	32,940
Slovak Republic	49	18.9	5,393	Bratislava	3,700
Slovenia	20.3	7.8	1,972	Ljubljana	9,680
Solomon Is.	28.9	11.2	441	Honiara	900
Somalia	638	246	6,842	Mogadishu	500
South Africa	1,220	471	42,835	C. Town/Pretoria/Bloem.	3,400
Spain	505	195	39,134	Madrid	14,510
Sri Lanka	65.6	25.3	18,934	Colombo	800
Sudan	2,506	967	33,551	Khartoum	800
Surinam	163	63	427	Paramaribo	1,000
Svalbard (Norway)	62.9	24.3	4	Longyearbyen	–
Swaziland	17.4	6.7	966	Mbabane	1,210
Sweden	450	174	8,887	Stockholm	26,220
Switzerland	41.3	15.9	7,260	Bern	44,220
Syria	185	71	16,673	Damascus	1,150
Taiwan	36	13.9	21,908	Taipei	12,400
Tajikistan	143.1	55.2	6,020	Dushanbe	330
Tanzania	945	365	30,609	Dodoma	210
Thailand	513	198	60,037	Bangkok	2,800
Togo	56.8	21.9	4,906	Lomé	330
Tokelau (NZ)	0.01	0.005	2	Nukunonu	–
Tonga	0.75	0.29	107	Nuku'alofa	1,790
Trinidad & Tobago	5.1	2	1,117	Port of Spain	4,230
Tristan da Cunha (UK)	0.11	0.04	0.33	Edinburgh	–
Tunisia	164	63	9,380	Tunis	2,090
Turkey	779	301	64,568	Ankara	3,130
Turkmenistan	488.1	188.5	4,298	Ashkhabad	630
Turks & Caicos Is. (UK)	0.43	0.17	16	Cockburn Town	5,000
Tuvalu	0.03	0.01	10	Fongafale	600
Uganda	236	91	22,167	Kampala	320
Ukraine	603.7	233.1	50,125	Kiev	1,040
United Arab Emirates	83.6	32.3	2,303	Abu Dhabi	17,360
United Kingdom	243.3	94	58,970	London	20,710
United States of America	9,373	3,619	270,290	Washington, DC	28,740
Uruguay	177	68	3,285	Montevideo	6,020
Uzbekistan	447.4	172.7	23,784	Tashkent	1,010
Vanuatu	12.2	4.7	185	Port-Vila	1,290
Vatican City	0.0004	0.0002	1	–	–
Venezuela	912	352	22,803	Caracas	3,450
Vietnam	332	127	76,236	Hanoi	320
Virgin Is. (UK)	0.15	0.06	13	Road Town	–
Virgin Is. (US)	0.34	0.13	118	Charlotte Amalie	12,000
Wake Is.	0.008	0.003	0.3	–	–
Wallis & Futuna Is. (France)	0.20	0.08	15	Mata-Utu	–
Western Sahara	266	103	280	El Aaiún	300
Yemen	528	204	16,388	Sana	270
Yugoslavia	102.3	39.5	10,500	Belgrade	2,000
Zambia	753	291	9,461	Lusaka	380
Zimbabwe	391	151	11,044	Harare	750

WORLD STATISTICS: Cities

This list shows the principal cities with more than 500,000 inhabitants (only cities with more than 1 million inhabitants are included for Brazil, China and India). The figures are taken from the most recent census or estimate available, and as far as possible are the population of the metropolitan area, e.g. greater New York, Mexico or Paris. All the figures are in thousands. Local name forms have been used for the smaller cities (e.g. Kraków).

	Population thousands
Afghanistan	
Kabul	1,565
Algeria	
Algiers	2,168
Oran	916
Angola	
Luanda	2,418
Argentina	
Buenos Aires	11,256
Córdoba	1,208
Rosario	1,118
Mendoza	773
La Plata	642
San Miguel de Tucumán	622
Mar del Plata	512
Armenia	
Yerevan	1,248
Australia	
Sydney	3,770
Melbourne	3,217
Brisbane	1,489
Perth	1,262
Adelaide	1,080
Austria	
Vienna	1,595
Azerbaijan	
Baku	1,720
Bangladesh	
Dhaka	6,105
Chittagong	2,041
Khulna	877
Rajshahi	517
Belarus	
Minsk	1,700
Homyel	512
Belgium	
Brussels	948
Benin	
Cotonou	537
Bolivia	
La Paz	1,126
Santa Cruz	767
Bosnia-Herzegovina	
Sarajevo	526
Brazil	
São Paulo	16,417
Rio de Janeiro	9,888
Salvador	2,211
Belo Horizonte	2,091
Fortaleza	1,965
Brasília	1,821
Curitiba	1,476
Recife	1,346
Pôrto Alegre	1,288
Manaus	1,157
Belém	1,144
Goiânia	1,004
Bulgaria	
Sofia	1,116
Burkina Faso	
Ouagadougou	690
Burma (Myanmar)	
Rangoon	2,513
Mandalay	533
Cambodia	
Phnom Penh	920
Cameroon	
Douala	1,200
Yaoundé	800
Canada	
Toronto	4,344
Montréal	3,337
Vancouver	1,831
Ottawa-Hull	1,022
Edmonton	885
Calgary	831
Québec	693
Winnipeg	677
Hamilton	643
Central African Rep.	
Bangui	553
Chad	
Ndjaména	530
Chile	
Santiago	5,067
China	
Shanghai	15,082
Beijing	12,362
Tianjin	10,687
Hong Kong (SAR)*	6,502
Chongqing	3,870
Shenyang	3,860
Wuhan	3,520
Guangzhou	3,114
Harbin	2,505
Nanjing	2,211
Xi'an	2,115
Chengdu	1,933
Dalian	1,855
Changchun	1,810
Jinan	1,660
Taiyuan	1,642
Qingdao	1,584
Fuzhou, Fujian	1,380
Zibo	1,346
Zhengzhou	1,324
Lanzhou	1,296
Anshan	1,252
Fushun	1,246
Kunming	1,242
Changsha	1,198
Hangzhou	1,185
Nanchang	1,169
Shijiazhuang	1,159
Guiyang	1,131
Ürümqi	1,130
Jilin	1,118
Tangshan	1,110
Qiqihar	1,104
Baotou	1,033
Hefei	1,000
Colombia	
Bogotá	6,004
Cali	1,985
Medellín	1,970
Barranquilla	1,157
Cartagena	812
Congo	
Brazzaville	937
Pointe-Noire	576
Congo (Dem. Rep.)	
Kinshasa	1,655
Lubumbashi	851
Mbuji-Mayi	806
Costa Rica	
San José	1,220
Croatia	
Zagreb	931
Cuba	
Havana	2,241
Czech Republic	
Prague	1,209
Denmark	
Copenhagen	1,362
Dominican Republic	
Santo Domingo	2,135
Santiago	691
Ecuador	
Guayaquil	1,973
Quito	1,487
Egypt	
Cairo	9,900
Alexandria	3,431
El Giza	2,144
Shubra el Kheima	834
El Salvador	
San Salvador	1,522
Ethiopia	
Addis Ababa	2,112
Finland	
Helsinki	532
France	
Paris	9,319
Lyon	1,262
Marseille	1,087
Lille	959
Bordeaux	696
Toulouse	650
Nice	516
Georgia	
Tbilisi	1,300
Germany	
Berlin	3,470
Hamburg	1,706
Munich	1,240
Cologne	964
Frankfurt	651
Essen	616
Dortmund	600
Stuttgart	587
Düsseldorf	571
Bremen	549
Duisburg	535
Hanover	524
Ghana	
Accra	949
Greece	
Athens	3,097
Guatemala	
Guatemala	1,167
Guinea	
Conakry	1,508
Haiti	
Port-au-Prince	1,255
Honduras	
Tegucigalpa	813
Hungary	
Budapest	1,885
India	
Bombay (Mumbai)	12,572
Calcutta (Kolkata)	10,916
Delhi	7,207
Madras (Chennai)	5,361
Hyderabad	4,280
Bangalore	4,087
Ahmadabad	3,298
Pune	2,485
Kanpur	2,111
Nagpur	1,661
Lucknow	1,642
Surat	1,517
Jaipur	1,514
Coimbatore	1,136
Vadodara	1,115
Indore	1,104
Patna	1,099
Madurai	1,094
Bhopal	1,064
Vishakhapatnam	1,052
Varanasi	1,026
Ludhiana	1,012
Indonesia	
Jakarta	11,500
Surabaya	2,701
Bandung	2,368
Medan	1,910
Semarang	1,366
Palembang	1,352
Tangerang	1,198
Ujung Pandang	1,092
Bandar Lampung	832
Malang	763
Padang	721
Pakanbaru	558
Samarinda	536
Banjarmasin	535
Surakarta	516
Iran	
Tehran	6,750
Mashhad	1,964
Esfahan	1,221
Tabriz	1,166
Shiraz	1,043
Ahvaz	828
Qom	780
Bakhtaran	666
Karaj	588
Iraq	
Baghdad	3,841
Diyala	961
As Sulaymaniyah	952
Arbil	770
Al Mawsil	664
Kadhimain	521
Ireland	
Dublin	952
Israel	
Tel Aviv-Yafo	1,502
Jerusalem	591
Italy	
Rome	2,775
Milan	1,369
Naples	1,067
Turin	962
Palermo	698
Genoa	678
Ivory Coast	
Abidjan	2,500
Jamaica	
Kingston	644
Japan	
Tokyo-Yokohama	26,836
Osaka	10,601
Nagoya	2,152
Sapporo	1,757
Kyoto	1,464
Kobe	1,424
Fukuoka	1,285
Kawasaki	1,203
Hiroshima	1,109
Kitakyushu	1,020
Sendai	971
Chiba	857
Sakai	803
Kumamoto	650
Okayama	616
Sagamihara	571
Hamamatsu	562
Kagoshima	546
Funabashi	541
Higashiosaka	517
Hachioji	503
Jordan	
Amman	1,300
Az-Zarqā	609
Kazakstan	
Almaty	1,150
Qaraghandy	573
Kenya	
Nairobi	2,000
Mombasa	600
Korea, North	
Pyŏngyang	2,639
Hamhung	775
Chŏngjin	754
Chinnampo	691
Sinŭiju	500
Korea, South	
Seoul	11,641
Pusan	3,814
Taegu	2,449
Inchon	2,308
Taejŏn	1,272
Kwangju	1,258
Ulsan	967
Sŏngnam	869
Puch'on	779
Suwŏn	756
Anyang	590
Chŏnju	563
Chŏngju	531
Ansan	510
P'ohang	509
Kyrgyzstan	
Bishkek	584
Latvia	
Riga	846
Lebanon	
Beirut	1,900
Tripoli	500
Libya	
Tripoli	1,083
Lithuania	
Vilnius	580
Macedonia	
Skopje	541
Madagascar	
Antananarivo	1,053
Malaysia	
Kuala Lumpur	1,145
Mali	
Bamako	800
Mauritania	
Nouakchott	735
Mexico	
Mexico City	15,048
Guadalajara	2,847
Monterrey	2,522
Puebla	1,055
León	872
Ciudad Juárez	798
Tijuana	743
Culiacán Rosales	602
Mexicali	602
Acapulco de Juárez	592
Mérida	557
Chihuahua	530
San Luis Potosí	526
Aguascalientés	506
Moldova	
Chişinău	700
Mongolia	
Ulan Bator	627
Morocco	
Casablanca	3,079
Rabat-Salé	1,344
Fès	735
Marrakesh	621
Mozambique	
Maputo	2,000
Nepal	
Katmandu	535
Netherlands	
Amsterdam	1,101
Rotterdam	1,076
The Hague	694
Utrecht	548
New Zealand	
Auckland	997
Nicaragua	
Managua	864
Nigeria	
Lagos	10,287
Ibadan	1,365
Ogbomosho	712
Kano	657
Norway	
Oslo	714
Pakistan	
Karachi	9,863
Lahore	5,085
Faisalabad	1,875
Peshawar	1,676
Gujranwala	1,663
Rawalpindi	1,290
Multan	1,257
Hyderabad	1,107
Paraguay	
Asunción	945
Peru	
Lima-Callao	6,601
Callao	638
Arequipa	620
Trujillo	509
Philippines	
Manila	9,280
Quezon City	1,989
Davao	1,191
Caloocan	1,023
Cebu	662
Zamboanga	511
Poland	
Warsaw	1,638
Lódz	825
Kraków	745
Wroclaw	642
Poznań	581
Portugal	
Lisbon	2,561
Oporto	1,174
Romania	
Bucharest	2,060
Russia	
Moscow	9,233
St Petersburg	4,883
Nizhniy Novgorod	1,425
Novosibirsk	1,400
Yekaterinburg	1,300
Samara	1,200
Omsk	1,200
Chelyabinsk	1,100
Kazan	1,100
Ufa	1,100
Volgograd	1,003
Perm	1,000
Rostov	1,000
Voronezh	908
Saratov	895
Krasnoyarsk	869
Togliatti	689
Simbirsk	678
Izhevsk	654
Krasnodar	645
Vladivostok	632
Yaroslavl	629
Khabarovsk	618
Barnaul	596
Irkutsk	585
Novokuznetsk	572
Ryazan	536
Penza	534
Orenburg	532
Tula	532
Naberezhnyye-Chelny	526
Kemerovo	503
Saudi Arabia	
Riyadh	1,800
Jedda	1,500
Mecca	630
Senegal	
Dakar	1,571
Sierra Leone	
Freetown	505
Singapore	
Singapore	3,104
Somalia	
Mogadishu	1,000
South Africa	
Cape Town	2,350
East Rand	1,379
Johannesburg	1,196
Durban	1,137
Pretoria	1,080
West Rand	870
Port Elizabeth	853
Vanderbijlpark-Vereeniging	774
Soweto	597
Sasolburg	540
Spain	
Madrid	3,029
Barcelona	1,614
Valencia	763
Sevilla	719
Zaragoza	607
Málaga	532
Sri Lanka	
Colombo	1,863
Sudan	
Omdurman	1,267
Khartoum	925
Khartoum North	879
Sweden	
Stockholm	1,744
Göteborg	775
Switzerland	
Zürich	1,175
Bern	942
Syria	
Aleppo	1,591
Damascus	1,549
Homs	644
Taiwan	
Taipei	2,653
Kaohsiung	1,405
Taichung	817
Tainan	700
Panchiao	544
Tajikistan	
Dushanbe	524
Tanzania	
Dar-es-Salaam	1,361
Thailand	
Bangkok	5,572
Togo	
Lomé	590
Tunisia	
Tunis	1,827
Turkey	
Istanbul	7,490
Ankara	3,028
Izmir	2,333
Adana	1,472
Bursa	1,317
Konya	1,040
Gaziantep	930
Icel	908
Antalya	734
Diyarbakir	677
Kocaeli	661
Urfa	649
Kayseri	648
Manisa	641
Hatay	561
Samsun	557
Eskisehir	508
Balikesir	501
Turkmenistan	
Ashkhabad	536
Uganda	
Kampala	773
Ukraine	
Kiev	2,630
Kharkiv	1,555
Dnipropetrovsk	1,147
Donetsk	1,088
Odesa	1,046
Zaporizhzhya	887
Lviv	802
Kryvyy Rih	720
Mariupol	510
Mykolayiv	508
United Kingdom	
London	8,089
Birmingham	2,373
Manchester	2,353
Liverpool	852
Glasgow	832
Sheffield	661
Nottingham	649
Newcastle	617
Bristol	552
Leeds	529
United States	
New York	16,329
Los Angeles	12,410
Chicago	7,668
Philadelphia	4,949
Washington, DC	4,466
Detroit	4,307
Houston	3,653
Atlanta	3,331
Boston	3,240
Dallas	2,898
Minneapolis-St Paul	2,688
San Diego	2,632
St Louis	2,536
Phoenix	2,473
Baltimore	2,458
Pittsburgh	2,402
Cleveland	2,222
San Francisco	2,182
Seattle	2,180
Tampa	2,157
Miami	2,025
Newark	1,934
Denver	1,796
Portland (Or.)	1,676
Kansas City (Mo.)	1,647
Cincinnati	1,581
San Jose	1,557
Norfolk	1,529
Indianapolis	1,462
Milwaukee	1,456
Sacramento	1,441
San Antonio	1,437
Columbus (Oh.)	1,423
New Orleans	1,309
Charlotte	1,260
Buffalo	1,189
Salt Lake City	1,178
Hartford	1,151
Oklahoma	1,007
Jacksonville (Fl.)	665
Omaha	663
Memphis	614
El Paso	579
Austin	514
Nashville	505
Uruguay	
Montevideo	1,378
Uzbekistan	
Tashkent	2,107
Venezuela	
Caracas	2,784
Maracaibo	1,364
Valencia	1,032
Maracay	800
Barquisimeto	745
Ciudad Guayana	524
Vietnam	
Ho Chi Minh City	4,322
Hanoi	3,056
Haiphong	783
Yemen	
Sana	972
Aden	562
Yugoslavia	
Belgrade	1,137
Zambia	
Lusaka	982
Zimbabwe	
Harare	1,189
Bulawayo	622

* SAR = Special Administrative Region of China

WORLD STATISTICS: Physical Dimensions

Each topic list is divided into continents and within a continent the items are listed in order of size. The bottom part of many of the lists is selective in order to give examples from as many different countries as possible. The figures are rounded as appropriate.

World, Continents, Oceans

	km²	miles²	%
The World	509,450,000	196,672,000	–
Land	149,450,000	57,688,000	29.3
Water	360,000,000	138,984,000	70.7
Asia	44,500,000	17,177,000	29.8
Africa	30,302,000	11,697,000	20.3
North America	24,241,000	9,357,000	16.2
South America	17,793,000	6,868,000	11.9
Antarctica	14,100,000	5,443,000	9.4
Europe	9,957,000	3,843,000	6.7
Australia & Oceania	8,557,000	3,303,000	5.7
Pacific Ocean	179,679,000	69,356,000	49.9
Atlantic Ocean	92,373,000	35,657,000	25.7
Indian Ocean	73,917,000	28,532,000	20.5
Arctic Ocean	14,090,000	5,439,000	3.9

Ocean Depths

Atlantic Ocean	m	ft
Puerto Rico (Milwaukee) Deep	9,220	30,249
Cayman Trench	7,680	25,197
Gulf of Mexico	5,203	17,070
Mediterranean Sea	5,121	16,801
Black Sea	2,211	7,254
North Sea	660	2,165
Indian Ocean	**m**	**ft**
Java Trench	7,450	24,442
Red Sea	2,635	8,454
Pacific Ocean	**m**	**ft**
Mariana Trench	11,022	36,161
Tonga Trench	10,882	35,702
Japan Trench	10,554	34,626
Kuril Trench	10,542	34,587
Arctic Ocean	**m**	**ft**
Molloy Deep	5,608	18,399

Mountains

Europe		m	ft
Elbrus	Russia	5,642	18,510
Mont Blanc	France/Italy	4,807	15,771
Monte Rosa	Italy/Switzerland	4,634	15,203
Dom	Switzerland	4,545	14,911
Liskamm	Switzerland	4,527	14,852
Weisshorn	Switzerland	4,505	14,780
Taschorn	Switzerland	4,490	14,730
Matterhorn/Cervino	Italy/Switzerland	4,478	14,691
Mont Maudit	France/Italy	4,465	14,649
Dent Blanche	Switzerland	4,356	14,291
Nadelhorn	Switzerland	4,327	14,196
Grandes Jorasses	France/Italy	4,208	13,806
Jungfrau	Switzerland	4,158	13,642
Grossglockner	Austria	3,797	12,457
Mulhacén	Spain	3,478	11,411
Zugspitze	Germany	2,962	9,718
Olympus	Greece	2,917	9,570
Triglav	Slovenia	2,863	9,393
Gerlachovka	Slovak Republic	2,655	8,711
Galdhöpiggen	Norway	2,468	8,100
Kebnekaise	Sweden	2,117	6,946
Ben Nevis	UK	1,343	4,406
Asia		**m**	**ft**
Everest	China/Nepal	8,848	29,029
K2 (Godwin Austen)	China/Kashmir	8,611	28,251
Kanchenjunga	India/Nepal	8,598	28,208
Lhotse	China/Nepal	8,516	27,939
Makalu	China/Nepal	8,481	27,824
Cho Oyu	China/Nepal	8,201	26,906
Dhaulagiri	Nepal	8,172	26,811
Manaslu	Nepal	8,156	26,758
Nanga Parbat	Kashmir	8,126	26,660
Annapurna	Nepal	8,078	26,502
Gasherbrum	China/Kashmir	8,068	26,469
Broad Peak	China/Kashmir	8,051	26,414
Xixabangma	China	8,012	26,286
Kangbachen	India/Nepal	7,902	25,925
Trivor	Pakistan	7,720	25,328
Pik Kommunizma	Tajikistan	7,495	24,590
Demavend	Iran	5,604	18,386
Ararat	Turkey	5,165	16,945
Gunong Kinabalu	Malaysia (Borneo)	4,101	13,455
Fuji-San	Japan	3,776	12,388
Africa		**m**	**ft**
Kilimanjaro	Tanzania	5,895	19,340
Mt Kenya	Kenya	5,199	17,057
Ruwenzori	Uganda/Congo (D.R.)	5,109	16,762
Ras Dashan	Ethiopia	4,620	15,157
Meru	Tanzania	4,565	14,977
Karisimbi	Rwanda/Congo (D.R.)	4,507	14,787
Mt Elgon	Kenya/Uganda	4,321	14,176
Batu	Ethiopia	4,307	14,130
Toubkal	Morocco	4,165	13,665
Mt Cameroon	Cameroon	4,070	13,353
Oceania		**m**	**ft**
Puncak Jaya	Indonesia	5,029	16,499
Puncak Trikora	Indonesia	4,750	15,584
Puncak Mandala	Indonesia	4,702	15,427
Mt Wilhelm	Papua New Guinea	4,508	14,790
Mauna Kea	USA (Hawaii)	4,205	13,796
Mauna Loa	USA (Hawaii)	4,170	13,681
Mt Cook (Aoraki)	New Zealand	3,753	12,313
Mt Kosciuszko	Australia	2,237	7,339
North America		**m**	**ft**
Mt McKinley (Denali)	USA (Alaska)	6,194	20,321
Mt Logan	Canada	5,959	19,551
Citlaltepetl	Mexico	5,700	18,701
Mt St Elias	USA/Canada	5,489	18,008
Popocatepetl	Mexico	5,452	17,887
Mt Foraker	USA (Alaska)	5,304	17,401
Ixtaccihuatl	Mexico	5,286	17,342
Lucania	Canada	5,227	17,149
Mt Steele	Canada	5,073	16,644
Mt Bona	USA (Alaska)	5,005	16,420
Mt Whitney	USA	4,418	14,495
Tajumulco	Guatemala	4,220	13,845
Chirripó Grande	Costa Rica	3,837	12,589
Pico Duarte	Dominican Rep.	3,175	10,417
South America		**m**	**ft**
Aconcagua	Argentina	6,960	22,834
Bonete	Argentina	6,872	22,546
Ojos del Salado	Argentina/Chile	6,863	22,516
Pissis	Argentina	6,779	22,241
Mercedario	Argentina/Chile	6,770	22,211
Huascaran	Peru	6,768	22,204
Llullaillaco	Argentina/Chile	6,723	22,057
Nudo de Cachi	Argentina	6,720	22,047
Yerupaja	Peru	6,632	21,758
Sajama	Bolivia	6,542	21,463
Chimborazo	Ecuador	6,267	20,561
Pico Colon	Colombia	5,800	19,029
Pico Bolivar	Venezuela	5,007	16,427
Antarctica		**m**	**ft**
Vinson Massif		4,897	16,066
Mt Kirkpatrick		4,528	14,855

Rivers

Europe		km	miles
Volga	Caspian Sea	3,700	2,300
Danube	Black Sea	2,850	1,770
Ural	Caspian Sea	2,535	1,575
Dnepr (Dnipro)	Black Sea	2,285	1,420
Kama	Volga	2,030	1,260
Don	Volga	1,990	1,240
Petchora	Arctic Ocean	1,790	1,110
Oka	Volga	1,480	920
Dnister (Dniester)	Black Sea	1,400	870
Vyatka	Kama	1,370	850
Rhine	North Sea	1,320	820
N. Dvina	Arctic Ocean	1,290	800
Elbe	North Sea	1,145	710
Asia		**km**	**miles**
Yangtze	Pacific Ocean	6,380	3,960
Yenisey–Angara	Arctic Ocean	5,550	3,445
Huang He	Pacific Ocean	5,464	3,395
Ob–Irtysh	Arctic Ocean	5,410	3,360
Mekong	Pacific Ocean	4,500	2,795
Amur	Pacific Ocean	4,400	2,730
Lena	Arctic Ocean	4,400	2,730
Irtysh	Ob	4,250	2,640
Yenisey	Arctic Ocean	4,090	2,540
Ob	Arctic Ocean	3,680	2,285
Indus	Indian Ocean	3,100	1,925
Brahmaputra	Indian Ocean	2,900	1,800
Syrdarya	Aral Sea	2,860	1,775
Salween	Indian Ocean	2,800	1,740
Euphrates	Indian Ocean	2,700	1,675
Amudarya	Aral Sea	2,540	1,575
Africa		**km**	**miles**
Nile	Mediterranean	6,670	4,140
Congo	Atlantic Ocean	4,670	2,900
Niger	Atlantic Ocean	4,180	2,595
Zambezi	Indian Ocean	3,540	2,200
Oubangi/Uele	Congo (Dem. Rep.)	2,250	1,400
Kasai	Congo (Dem. Rep.)	1,950	1,210
Shaballe	Indian Ocean	1,930	1,200
Orange	Atlantic Ocean	1,860	1,155
Cubango	Okavango Swamps	1,800	1,120
Limpopo	Indian Ocean	1,600	995
Senegal	Atlantic Ocean	1,600	995
Australia		**km**	**miles**
Murray–Darling	Indian Ocean	3,750	2,330
Darling	Murray	3,070	1,905
Murray	Indian Ocean	2,575	1,600
Murrumbidgee	Murray	1,690	1,050
North America		**km**	**miles**
Mississippi–Missouri	Gulf of Mexico	6,020	3,740
Mackenzie	Arctic Ocean	4,240	2,630
Mississippi	Gulf of Mexico	3,780	2,350
Missouri	Mississippi	3,780	2,350
Yukon	Pacific Ocean	3,185	1,980
Rio Grande	Gulf of Mexico	3,030	1,880
Arkansas	Mississippi	2,340	1,450
Colorado	Pacific Ocean	2,330	1,445
Red	Mississippi	2,040	1,270
Columbia	Pacific Ocean	1,950	1,210
Saskatchewan	Lake Winnipeg	1,940	1,205
South America		**km**	**miles**
Amazon	Atlantic Ocean	6,450	4,010
Paraná–Plate	Atlantic Ocean	4,500	2,800
Purus	Amazon	3,350	2,080
Madeira	Amazon	3,200	1,990
São Francisco	Atlantic Ocean	2,900	1,800
Paraná	Plate	2,800	1,740
Tocantins	Atlantic Ocean	2,750	1,710
Paraguay	Paraná	2,550	1,580
Orinoco	Atlantic Ocean	2,500	1,550
Pilcomayo	Paraná	2,500	1,550
Araguaia	Tocantins	2,250	1,400

Lakes

Europe		km²	miles²
Lake Ladoga	Russia	17,700	6,800
Lake Onega	Russia	9,700	3,700
Saimaa system	Finland	8,000	3,100
Vänern	Sweden	5,500	2,100
Asia		**km²**	**miles²**
Caspian Sea	Asia	371,800	143,550
Lake Baykal	Russia	30,500	11,780
Aral Sea	Kazakstan/Uzbekistan	28,687	11,086
Tonlé Sap	Cambodia	20,000	7,700
Lake Balqash	Kazakstan	18,500	7,100
Africa		**km²**	**miles²**
Lake Victoria	East Africa	68,000	26,000
Lake Tanganyika	Central Africa	33,000	13,000
Lake Malawi/Nyasa	East Africa	29,600	11,430
Lake Chad	Central Africa	25,000	9,700
Lake Turkana	Ethiopia/Kenya	8,500	3,300
Lake Volta	Ghana	8,500	3,300
Australia		**km²**	**miles²**
Lake Eyre	Australia	8,900	3,400
Lake Torrens	Australia	5,800	2,200
Lake Gairdner	Australia	4,800	1,900
North America		**km²**	**miles²**
Lake Superior	Canada/USA	82,350	31,800
Lake Huron	Canada/USA	59,600	23,010
Lake Michigan	USA	58,000	22,400
Great Bear Lake	Canada	31,800	12,280
Great Slave Lake	Canada	28,500	11,000
Lake Erie	Canada/USA	25,700	9,900
Lake Winnipeg	Canada	24,400	9,400
Lake Ontario	Canada/USA	19,500	7,500
Lake Nicaragua	Nicaragua	8,200	3,200
South America		**km²**	**miles²**
Lake Titicaca	Bolivia/Peru	8,300	3,200
Lake Poopo	Peru	2,800	1,100

Islands

Europe		km²	miles²
Great Britain	UK	229,880	88,700
Iceland	Atlantic Ocean	103,000	39,800
Ireland	Ireland/UK	84,400	32,600
Novaya Zemlya (N.)	Russia	48,200	18,600
Sicily	Italy	25,500	9,800
Corsica	France	8,700	3,400
Asia		**km²**	**miles²**
Borneo	South-east Asia	744,360	287,400
Sumatra	Indonesia	473,600	182,860
Honshu	Japan	230,500	88,980
Celebes	Indonesia	189,000	73,000
Java	Indonesia	126,700	48,900
Luzon	Philippines	104,700	40,400
Hokkaido	Japan	78,400	30,300
Africa		**km²**	**miles²**
Madagascar	Indian Ocean	587,040	226,660
Socotra	Indian Ocean	3,600	1,400
Réunion	Indian Ocean	2,500	965
Oceania		**km²**	**miles²**
New Guinea	Indonesia/Papua NG	821,030	317,000
New Zealand (S.)	Pacific Ocean	150,500	58,100
New Zealand (N.)	Pacific Ocean	114,700	44,300
Tasmania	Australia	67,800	26,200
Hawaii	Pacific Ocean	10,450	4,000
North America		**km²**	**miles²**
Greenland	Atlantic Ocean	2,175,600	839,800
Baffin Is.	Canada	508,000	196,100
Victoria Is.	Canada	212,200	81,900
Ellesmere Is.	Canada	212,000	81,800
Cuba	Caribbean Sea	110,860	42,800
Hispaniola	Dominican Rep./Haiti	76,200	29,400
Jamaica	Caribbean Sea	11,400	4,400
Puerto Rico	Atlantic Ocean	8,900	3,400
South America		**km²**	**miles²**
Tierra del Fuego	Argentina/Chile	47,000	18,100
Falkland Is. (E.)	Atlantic Ocean	6,800	2,600

THE WORLD
AND
CONTINENTS

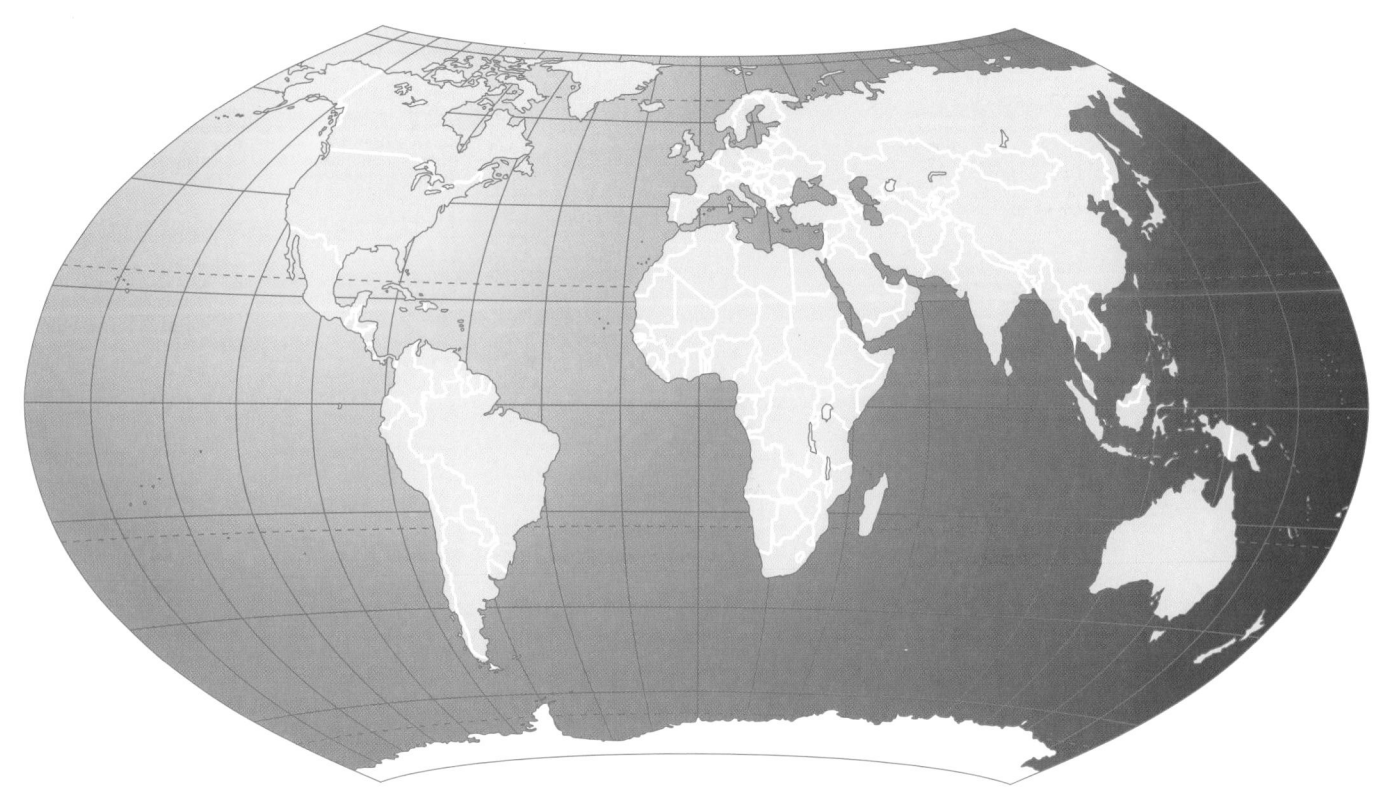

WORLD : Political

Beaufort Sea
Parry Is.
Queen Elizabeth Is.
Ellesmere I.
Banks I.
Victoria I.
Devon I.
Baffin Bay
Baffin I.
Davis Str.
GREENLAND
(Denmark)
Nuuk
Denmark Str.
ICELAND
Reykjavík
Norwe
Arctic Circle
Sea
Faroe Is.
(Den.)
Bering Strait
St. Lawrence I.
ALASKA
(U.S.A.)
Yukon
Fairbanks
Anchorage
G. of Alaska
Kodiak I.
Mackenzie
Great Bear L.
Yellowknife
Great Slave L.
Hudson Bay
Churchill
Aleutian Is. (U.S.A.)
Queen Charlotte Is.
Edmonton
Calgary
Nelson
CANADA
Schefferville
Vancouver
Vancouver I.
L. Winnipeg
Winnipeg
Seattle
Portland
Missouri
UNITED STATES
OF AMERICA
L. Superior
Ottawa
Québec
Montréal
Newfoundland
St. John's
Minneapolis
Milwaukee
L. Michigan
L. Huron
Detroit
Toronto
Boston
Halifax
Salt Lake City
Denver
CHICAGO
Cleveland
Pittsburgh
NEW YORK
PHILADELPHIA
Baltimore
Washington D.C.
SAN FRANCISCO
Sacramento
Colorado
Kansas City
St. Louis
Cincinnati
LOS ANGELES
San Diego
Phoenix
Dallas
Memphis
Atlanta
Mississippi
El Paso
Ciudad Juárez
Houston
New Orleans
Jacksonville
Bermuda
(U.K.)
Guadalupe I.
(Mexico)
Monterrey
Gulf of Mexico
G. of California
Miami
BAHAMAS
MEXICO
Havana
CUBA
León
Guadalajara
MÉXICO
Puebla
Turks & Caicos Is.
(U.K.)
Cayman Is. (U.K.)
HAITI
DOMINICAN REP.
JAMAICA
Port-au-Prince
Kingston
Santo Domingo
PUERTO RICO
Virgin Is. (U.S.A.)&(U.K.)
ANTIGUA & BARBUDA
ST. KITTS & NEVIS
GUADELOUPE (Fr.)
DOMINICA
MARTINIQUE (Fr.)
ST. LUCIA
ST. VINCENT & THE GRENADINES
BARBADOS
GRENADA
TRINIDAD & TOBAGO
NETH. ANTILLES
Revilla Gigedo Is.
(Mexico)
Belmopan
BELIZE
GUATEMALA
Guatemala
HONDURAS
Tegucigalpa
San Salvador
EL SALVADOR
NICARAGUA
Managua
Caribbean Sea
Barranquilla
San José
COSTA RICA
Panamá
PANAMA
Caracas
VENEZUELA
Orinoco
Georgetown
Paramaribo
Cayenne
GUYANA
SURINAM
FRENCH GUIANA
Clipperton I.
(Fr.)
Medellín
Cali
BOGOTÁ
COLOMBIA
Coco I.
(C.Rica)
Malpelo
(Colombia)
Galápagos
(Ecuador)
Quito
ECUADOR
Guayaquil
Iquitos
Negro
Japurá
Manaus
Amazon
Belém
Fortaleza
Fernando de Noronha
(Brazil)
Natal
Recife
BRAZIL
PERU
LIMA
Callao
Salvador
Brasília
L. Titicaca
La Paz
BOLIVIA
Sucre
Arequipa
Belo Horizonte
SÃO PAULO
RIO DE JANEIRO
Antofagasta
PARAGUAY
Asunción
Santos
Curitiba
Tucumán
Pôrto Alegre
Córdoba
Paraná
Rio Grande
Valparaíso
SANTIAGO
Rosario
URUGUAY
BUENOS AIRES
Montevideo
Talcahuano
ARGENTINA
Bahía Blanca
CHILE
Chiloé I.
Falkland Is.
(U.K.)
Punta Arenas
Tierra del Fuego
C. Horn
Scotia Sea
South Georgia
(U.K.)
South Sandwich Is.
(U.K.)
Drake Passage
South Orkney Is.
South Shetland Is.
Bellingshausen Sea
Weddell Sea
Antarctic Circle
Amundsen Sea
Antarctica
West from Greenwich
NORTH ATLANTIC OCEAN
SOUTH ATLANTIC OCEAN
Azores
(Port.)
São Paulo
(Brazil)
Ascension I.
(U.K.)
St. Helena
(U.K.)
Trindade
(Brazil)
Tristan da Cunha
(U.K.)
Gough I.
(U.K.)
UNITED KINGDOM
Glasgow
Dublin
IRELAND
LONDON
FRANCE
Bordeaux
PORTUGAL
Lisbon
Madrid
SPAIN
Tangier
Rabat
Casablanca
Marrakesh
MOROCCO
Madeira
(Port.)
Canary Is.
(Sp.)
El Aaiun
WESTERN SAHARA
MAURITANIA
Nouakchott
Timbuktu
MALI
CAPE VERDE IS.
Dakar
SENEGAL
GAMBIA
Bamako
BURKINA FASO
Ouagadougou
GUINEA-BISSAU
Bissau
GUINEA
Conakry
Freetown
SIERRA LEONE
IVORY COAST
GHANA
Yamoussoukro
Monrovia
LIBERIA
Abidjan
Accra
Gulf of G
International Date Line
Midway Is.
Hawaiian Is.
(U.S.A.)
Honolulu
Oahu
Hawaii
Tropic of Cancer
PACIFIC OCEAN
Palmyra Is.
(U.S.A.)
Kiritimati
Howland I. (U.S.A.)
Baker I. (U.S.A.)
Jarvis I.
(U.S.A.)
Equator
Abariringa
KIRIBATI
Phoenix Is.
Malden I.
Starbuck I.
Tokelau Is.
(N.Z.)
Penrhyn Is.
Marquesas Is.
Wallis & Futuna
(Fr.)
SAMOA
AMERICAN SAMOA
Manihiki
Flint I.
FRENCH POLYNESIA
Tuamotu Is.
Society Is.
Tahiti
FIJI
TONGA
Niue
(N.Z.)
Cook Is.
(N.Z.)
Tubuai Is.
Pitcairn I.
(U.K.)
Ducie I.
Tropic of Capricorn
Rapa
Easter I.
(Chile)
Sala-y-Gomez
(Chile)
San Felix
(Chile)
San Ambrosio
(Chile)
Juan Fernández
(Chile)
Kermadec Is. (N.Z.)
Chatham Is.
(N.Z.)

Projection: *Hammer Equal Area*

10 **11** **12** **13** **14** **15** **16** **17** **18**

A R C T I C   O C E A N

Svalbard *(Norw.)*

Severnaya Zemlya   Laptev Sea   East Siberian Sea   New Siberian Is.   Wrangel I.   **A**

gian   *Sea*   Barents   Sea   Novaya Zemlya   Kara Sea   Norilsk   Arctic Circle

Murmansk   Salekhard   Yenisey   Verkhoyansk   Lena   Magadan   Bering Sea

NORWAY   SWEDEN   FINLAND   Arkhangelsk   Ob   R U S S I A   Yakutsk   Okhotsk   Sea of   Petropavlovsk-   **B**
Oslo   Helsinki   Tomsk   Krasnoyarsk   Irkutsk   Okhotsk   Kamchatskiy

rth   DENMARK   Stockholm   EST.   ST.PETERSBURG   Perm   Yekaterinburg   L. Baikal   Sakhalin   Komsomolsk   International Date Line
ea   Copenhagen   LATVIA   Kazan   Omsk   Novosibirsk   Ulan Ude   Khabarovsk
Hamburg   POLAND   LITH.   Volga   MOSCOW   Samara   Chelyabinsk   Barnaul   Amur   Vladivostok   Sapporo
Amsterdam   NETH.   Minsk   BELARUS   Saratov   Astana   Qaraghandy   Ulan Bator   Harbin   JAPAN
Brussels   Berlin   Prague   Warsaw   Kiev   Irtysh   KAZAKSTAN   MONGOLIA   Changchun   SHENYANG   NORTH   Pyŏngyang   TŌKYŌ
PARIS   LUX.   GERMANY   Vienna   SLOVAK   UKRAINE   Volgograd   L. Balkhash   BEIJING   TIANJIN   KOREA   SEOUL   PACIFIC
Lyons   SW.   AUSTRIA   Budapest   REP.   Odessa   Astrakhan   Aral   Almaty   Bishkek   Ürümqi   SOUTH   Osaka
Milan   ITALY   HUNG.   ROMANIA   Bucharest   Sea   KYRGYZSTAN   C H I N A   Lanzhou   Taiyuan   KOREA   Kitakyūshū   OCEAN
Marseilles   YUG.   Belgrade   BULGARIA   Black Sea   GEORGIA   UZBEKISTAN   Tashkent   Hwang-ho   Nanjing   SHANGHAI   **C**
Barcelona   Rome   ALB.   Sofia   ISTANBUL   Ankara   ARM.   Baku   Samarkand   Dushanbe   Xi'an   Wuhan
Naples   Sardinia   GREECE   TURKEY   İzmir   AZER.   TURKMENISTAN   TAJIKISTAN   Chengdu   CHONGQING   East China   Fuzhou
Algiers   Sicily   Athens   Tabriz   Ashkhabad   Kābul   TIBET   Lhasa   Sea   Taipei
Tunis   MALTA   CYPRUS   Beirut   SYRIA   Damascus   TEHRĀN   Mashhad   AFGHANISTAN   Islamabad   KASHMIR   Kunming   GUANGZHOU   RYUKYU Is.
TUNISIA   Crete   Jerusalem   ISR.   Baghdād   Esfahān   Lahore   NEPAL   Katmandu   Hainan   HONG KONG   TAIWAN
Tripoli   JORDAN   Amman   IRAQ   I R A N   KUWAIT   Shīrāz   PAKISTAN   DELHI   BHU.   South   Volcano Is.   Tropic of Cancer
Benghazi   Alexandria   Kanpur   New Delhi   Rangoon   China   *(Japan)*
GERIA   CAIRO   BAHRAIN   QATAR   Abu Dhabi   KARACHI   Ahmadābād   KOLKATA   DACCA   BURMA   Sea   Marcus I.   *(Japan)*
L I B Y A   EGYPT   Riyadh   U.A.E.   Muscat   Ganges   (Calcutta)   BANGLA-   MYANMAR   Hanoi   Wake I.
Aswān   Mecca   SAUDI   OMAN   MUMBAI   Nagpur   DESH   VIET-   *(U.S.A.)*
NIGER   Red Sea   ARABIA   Arabian   (Bombay)   Bay of   NORTHERN   20
CHAD   Omdurman   Asmara   Saná   Sea   Hyderābad   Bengal   THAILAND   NAM   MANILA   MARIANAS
Niamey   Khartoum   ERITREA   YEMEN   Bangalore   CHENNAI   BANGKOK   PHILIPPINES   *(U.S.A.)*   MARSHALL IS.
Kano   L. Chad   SUDAN   DJIBOUTI   Aden   (Madras)   Andaman Is.   CAMBODIA   GUAM   **D**
NIGERIA   Ndjamena   Addis Ababa   G. of Aden   Socotra   Lakshadweep Is.   *(India)*   Phnom   Ho Chi Minh   *(U.S.A.)*   FEDERATED STATES
Abuja   CENTRAL   *(Yemen)*   *(India)*   Penh   City   Yap   Truk   Pohnpei
Ibadan   CAMEROON   AFRICAN   ETHIOPIA   SOMALI   Nicobar Is.   PALAU   Caroline Is.
Lagos   Douala   REP.   SRI LANKA   *(India)*   OF MICRONESIA
TOGO   BENIN   Yaoundé   Bangui   UGANDA   MALDIVES   Colombo   MALAYSIA   Medan   SABAH
EQUATORIAL   Libreville   GABON   Kisangani   Kampala   KENYA   Equator   Kuala Lumpur   BRUNEI   Gilbert Is.
uinea   GUINEA   CONGO   L. Turkana   I N D I A N   PEN. MALAYSIA   SARAWAK   NAURU   KIRIBATI
SÃO TOMÉ   DEM.REP.OF THE   RWANDA   Nairobi   SINGAPORE   Borneo   0
& PRÍNCIPE   CONGO   Kigali   *(Zaïre)*   Victoria   SEYCHELLES   OCEAN   Banjarmasin   IRIAN   New
Brazzaville   Kinshasa   BURUNDI   L.   Mombasa   Chagos Arch.   Palembang   Sumatra   JAYA   Ireland
CABINDA   Bujumbura   Kananga   Dodoma   Zanzibar   *(U.K.)*   I N D O N E S I A   PAPUA   New
(Angola)   Tanganyika   Dar es Salaam   Amirante   Diego Garcia   JAKARTA   Ujung Pandang   NEW   Britain
Luanda   TANZANIA   Is.   Bandung   Surabaya   GUINEA   SOLOMON
Lubumbashi   Aldabra Is.   Cocos Is.   Christmas I.   Java   Port   IS.   **E**
ANGOLA   COMOROS   *(Austral.)*   *(Austral.)*   Timor   Arafura Sea   Moresby   Santa Cruz I.   TUVALU
Benguela   Mayotte   *(Fr.)*   Cargados Carajos   C. York
ZAMBIA   Malawi   Agalega Is.   Darwin   VANUATU
Lusaka   MALAWI   *(Fr.)*   MADAGASCAR   Rodriguez   Cairns   FIJI
Lilongwe   Antananarivo   RÉUNION   MAURITIUS   Great   Townsville   Suva
ZIMBABWE   MOZAMBIQUE   *(Fr.)*   Australian   20
NAMIBIA   Harare   Bight   Port Hedland   Alice Springs   NEW
Bulawayo   Tropic of Capricorn   A U S T R A L I A   Rockhampton   CALEDONIA   *(Fr.)*
Windhoek   BOTSWANA   Mozambique Channel   Geraldton   Brisbane
Gaborone   Pretoria   Amsterdam I.   Kalgoorlie-   Lord Howe I.
SOUTH   Johannesburg   SWAZILAND   *(Fr.)*   St.Paul I.   Boulder   Newcastle   *(Austral.)*   **F**
AFRICA   LESOTHO   Maputo   *(Fr.)*   Perth   Adelaide   Sydney   Norfolk I.
Cape Town   Durban   Fremantle   Darling   Canberra   *(Austral.)*
C. of Good Hope   Port Elizabeth   Prince Edward Is.   Crozet Is.   Melbourne   Tasman   Auckland
(S.Africa)   *(Fr.)*   Kerguelen   Tasmania   Sea   NEW   North I.
(Fr.)   McDonald Is.   Heard I.   Hobart   ZEALAND
Bouvet I.   *(Austral.)*   *(Austral.)*   Christchurch   Wellington   40
(Norw.)   South I.
O U T H E R N   O C E A N   Stewart I.   Bounty Is.   Dunedin   *(N.Z.)*
Antipodes Is.   *(N.Z.)*
Campbell I.   Auckland Is.   *(N.Z.)*   Macquarie Is.   *(N.Z.)*   **G**
(Austral.)

c   t   i   c   a

East from Greenwich   20   40   60   80   100   120   140   160   180   Ross Sea   **H**

10 **11** **12** **13** **14** **15** **16** **17** **18**

Hanoi ● Capital Cities

AFRICA : Physical

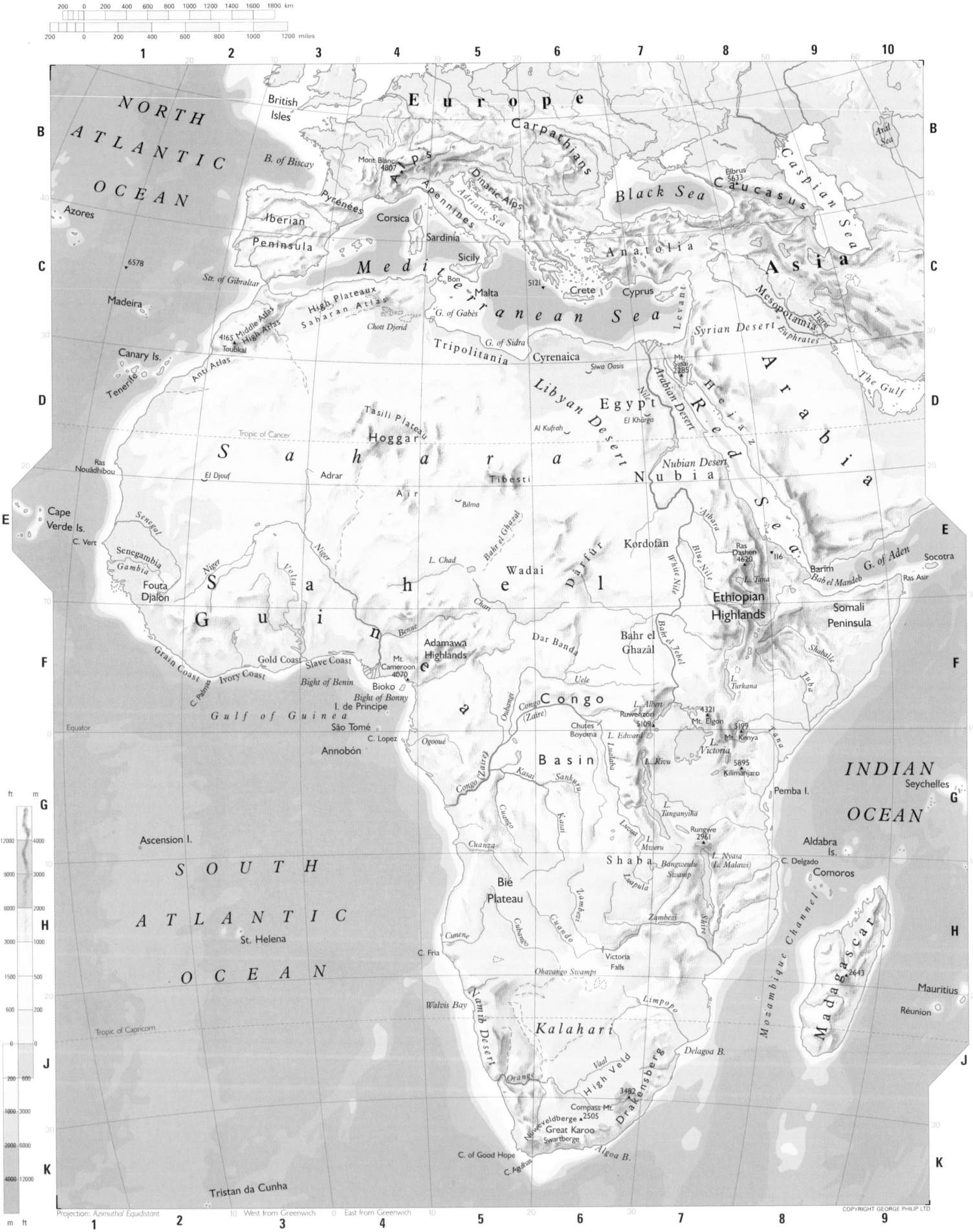

200   0   200   400   600   800   1000   1200   1400   1600   1800 km
200   0   200   400   600   800   1000   1200 miles

1   **2**   **3**   **4**   **5**   **6**   **7**   **8**   **9**   **10**

NORTH ATLANTIC OCEAN

British Isles

E u r o p e

Carpathians

Azores

Alps
Mont Blanc 4807
B. of Biscay
Pyrénées
Dinaric Alps
Black Sea
Caucasus
Elbrus 5633
Caspian Sea
Aral Sea

Iberian Peninsula
Corsica
Apennines
Adriatic Sea
Anatolia
Asia

6578

Sardinia
Sicily

Madeira
Str. of Gibraltar
High Plateaux
Saharan Atlas
C. Bon
Malta
Crete
Cyprus
5121
Mesopotamia
Tigris
The Gulf

Canary Is.
Middle Atlas 4165
High Atlas
Toubkal
G. of Gabès
Chott Djerid
Medite rranean Sea
Levant
Syrian Desert Euphrates

Tenerife
Anti Atlas
Tripolitania
Cyrenaica
G. of Sidra
Libyan Desert
Egypt
Siwa Oasis
Nile
Mt. Sinai 2285
Arabian Desert
Hejaz
A r a b i a

Ras Nouâdhibou
Tropic of Cancer
Hoggar
Tasili Plateau
Al Kufrah
El Khārga
Nubian Desert
Red Sea

S a h a r a
Adrar
Tibesti
Nubia
Kordofân
Ras Dashen 4620
116
Barim
G. of Aden
Socotra

El Djouf
Air
Bilma
N u b i a
Atbara

Senegal
Niger
Volta
Niger
L. Chad
Bahr el Ghazal
Wadai
Darfur
White Nile
Blue Nile
L. Tana
Bab el Mandeb
Ras Asir

Cape Verde Is.
C. Vert
Senegambia
Gambia
Fouta Djalon
S a h e l
Chari
Sahel
Ethiopian Highlands
Somali Peninsula

G u i n e a
Benue
Adamawa Highlands
Dar Banda
Bahr el Ghazâl
Uele
L. Turkana
Shabelle

Grain Coast
Gold Coast
Slave Coast
Ivory Coast
C. Palmas
Bight of Benin
Mt. Cameroon 4070
Bioko
Bight of Bonny
I. de Principe
C o n g o
Oubangi
Congo (Zaïre)
Chutes Boyoma
L. Albert
Ruwenzori 5109
4321
Mt. Elgon
Mt. Kenya 5199
Juba

Gulf of Guinea
São Tomé
C. Lopez
Equator
Ogooué
Congo (Zaïre)
B a s i n
Kasai
Sankuru
L. Edward
Lualaba
L. Kivu
L. Victoria
5895
Kilimanjaro
INDIAN OCEAN

Annobón
Cuango
Kwilu
L. Tanganyika
Pemba I.
Seychelles

Ascension I.
Cuanza
L. Mweru
Rungwe 2961
Aldabra Is.

SOUTH ATLANTIC OCEAN
S h a b a
Bangweulu Swamp
L. Nyasa (L. Malawi)
C. Delgado
Comoros

Bié Plateau
Zambezi
Luapula
Shire

St. Helena
Cunene
Cubango
Cuando
Zambezi
Victoria Falls
Mozambique Channel

C. Fria
Okavango Swamps
Limpopo
Madagascar 2643

Walvis Bay
Namib Desert
K a l a h a r i
Mauritius
Réunion

Tropic of Capricorn
Delagoa B.

Orange
Vaal
High Veld
Drakensberg
Algoa B.

C. of Good Hope
Nieuveldberge
Compass Mt. 2505
Great Karoo
Swartberge
3482

C. Agulhas

Tristan da Cunha

ft   m
12000 4000
9000 3000
6000 2000
3000 1000
1500 500
600 200
0
200 600
1000 3000
2000 6000
4000 12000
m   ft

Projection: Azimuthal Equidistant   West from Greenwich   East from Greenwich
COPYRIGHT GEORGE PHILIP LTD.

1   **2**   **3**   **4**   **5**   **6**   **7**   **8**   **9**

4

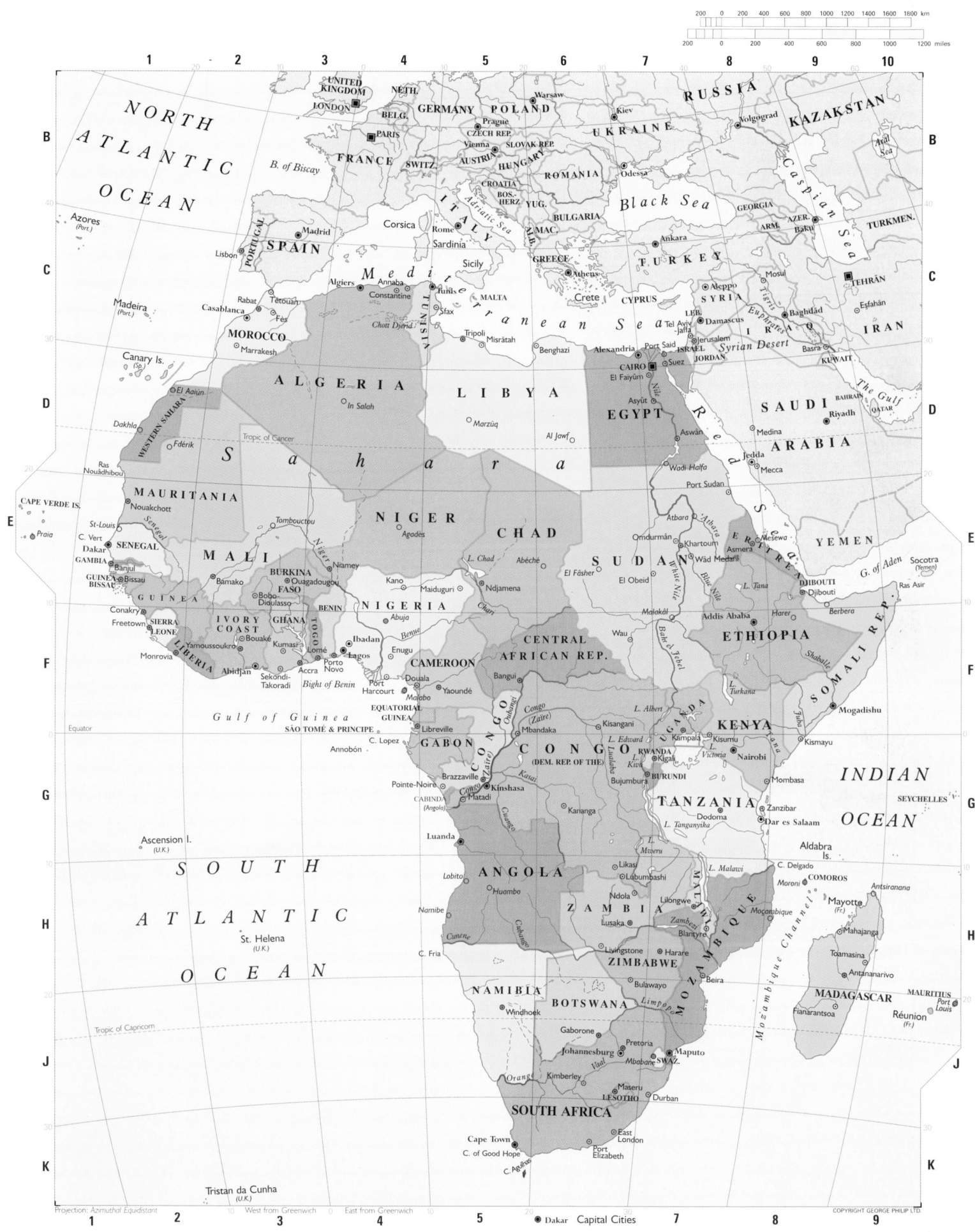

200 0 200 400 600 800 1000 1200 1400 1600 1800 km
200 0 200 400 600 800 1000 1200 miles

| | 1 | 2 | 3 | 4 | 5 | 6 | 7 | 8 | 9 | 10 | |

B NORTH ATLANTIC OCEAN

UNITED KINGDOM · LONDON · NETH · BELG · Warsaw · GERMANY · POLAND · Kiev · RUSSIA · KAZAKSTAN · Volgograd · Aral Sea **B**
Prague · CZECH REP · Vienna · SLOVAK REP · UKRAINE · Odessa · Caspian Sea
FRANCE · SWITZ · AUSTRIA · HUNGARY · ROMANIA · Black Sea · GEORGIA · AZER · Baku · TURKMEN

B. of Biscay · CROATIA · BOS · HERZ · YUG · BULGARIA · Ankara · ARM · TURKEY

Azores (Port.) · PORTUGAL · Madrid · SPAIN · Corsica · Rome · ITALY · Adriatic Sea · N.B. · MAC · GREECE · Athens · TURKEY · Mosul · TEHRAN
C Lisbon · Madeira (Port.) · Sardinia · Sicily · Crete · CYPRUS · SYRIA · Aleppo · Baghdad · Eṣfahān · IRAN **C**
Algiers · Annaba · Mediterranean Sea · MALTA · LEB · Tel Aviv-Jaffa · Damascus · IRAQ · Basra · KUWAIT
Casablanca · Rabat · Tétouan · Fès · Tunis · Constantine · Sfax · Tripoli · Misrātah · Benghazi · Alexandria · Port Said · ISRAEL · JORDAN · Jerusalem · Suez · Syrian Desert · BAHRAIN · The Gulf
Canary Is. (Sp.) · MOROCCO · Marrakesh · Chott Djerid · TUNISIA · CAIRO · SAUDI · Riyadh · QATAR **D**
D Dakhla · WESTERN SAHARA · El Aaiún · ALGERIA · In Salah · LIBYA · EGYPT · El Faiyûm · Asyût · Aswân · Medina · ARABIA
Ras Nouâdhibou · Fdérik · Tropic of Cancer · Marzûq · Al Jawf · Wadi Halfa · Jedda · Mecca

Sahara

E CAPE VERDE IS. · St-Louis · MAURITANIA · Nouakchott · Tombouctou · NIGER · Agadès · CHAD · Port Sudan · Atbara · Omdurmân · Khartoum · Mesewa · Asmera · ERITREA · YEMEN · Socotra (Yemen) **E**
Praia · C. Vert · Dakar · SENEGAL · Sénégal · MALI · Niger · Niamey · L. Chad · Abéché · El Fâsher · SUDAN · Wâd Medanî · DJIBOUTI · G. of Aden · Ras Asir
GAMBIA · Banjul · Bamako · BURKINA FASO · Ouagadougou · Kano · Maiduguri · Ndjamena · El Obeid · White Nile · Blue Nile · L. Tana · Djibouti · Berbera
GUINEA-BISSAU · Bissau · GUINEA · Bobo-Dioulasso · BENIN · NIGERIA · Abuja · Chari · Malakâl · Addis Ababa · Harer · SOMALI REP

F Conakry · Freetown · SIERRA LEONE · IVORY COAST · GHANA · Kumasi · TOGO · Ibadan · Enugu · Benue · CAMEROON · CENTRAL AFRICAN REP · Wau · Bahr el Jebel · L. Turkana · ETHIOPIA · Shabeelle · Mogadishu **F**
Monrovia · Yamoussoukro · Bouaké · Porto Novo · Lagos · Douala · Bangui · Ubangi · Malabo · Yaoundé · Kisangani · UGANDA · Kampala · Kisumu · KENYA · Kismayu
LIBERIA · Abidjan · Sekondi-Takoradi · Accra · Bight of Benin · Port Harcourt · EQUATORIAL GUINEA · Congo (Zaïre) · L. Albert · L. Edward · L. Victoria · Nairobi
Gulf of Guinea · SÃO TOMÉ & PRÍNCIPE · Libreville · Mbandaka · RWANDA · Kigali · Kisumu · Mombasa
Equator · C. Lopez · GABON · CONGO · CONGO (DEM. REP. OF THE) · Kasai · L. Kivu · BURUNDI · Bujumbura

G Ascension I. (U.K.) · Annobón · Pointe-Noire · Brazzaville · Kinshasa · Lualaba · TANZANIA · Dodoma · Zanzibar · L. Tanganyika · Dar es Salaam · INDIAN OCEAN · SEYCHELLES **G**
CABINDA (Angola) · Matadi · Kananga · Cuango · L. Mweru
Luanda · Lobito

H SOUTH ATLANTIC OCEAN · Luanda · Likasi · Lubumbashi · L. Malawi · C. Delgado · COMOROS · Moroni · Antsiranana · Mayotte (Fr.) **H**
St. Helena (U.K.) · Huambo · ANGOLA · Ndola · Lilongwe · MALAWI · Blantyre · Mozambique · Mahajanga
Namibe · Cunene · ZAMBIA · Lusaka · Zambezi · MOZAMBIQUE · Toamasina
C. Fria · Livingstone · Harare · Beira · MADAGASCAR · MAURITIUS · Port Louis · Antananarivo

J NAMIBIA · Bulawayo · ZIMBABWE · Limpopo · Mozambique Channel · Fianarantsoa · Réunion (Fr.) **J**
Windhoek · BOTSWANA · Gaborone · Pretoria · Johannesburg · Maputo · SWAZ · Mbabane
Tropic of Capricorn · Orange · Vaal · Kimberley · Maseru · LESOTHO · Durban · East London

K Tristan da Cunha (U.K.) · Cape Town · C. of Good Hope · SOUTH AFRICA · Port Elizabeth · C. Agulhas **K**

Projection: Azimuthal Equidistant · West from Greenwich · East from Greenwich · ● Dakar Capital Cities · COPYRIGHT GEORGE PHILIP LTD.

| 1 | 2 | 3 | 4 | 5 | 6 | 7 | 8 | 9 |

AFRICA : Climate and Natural Vegetation

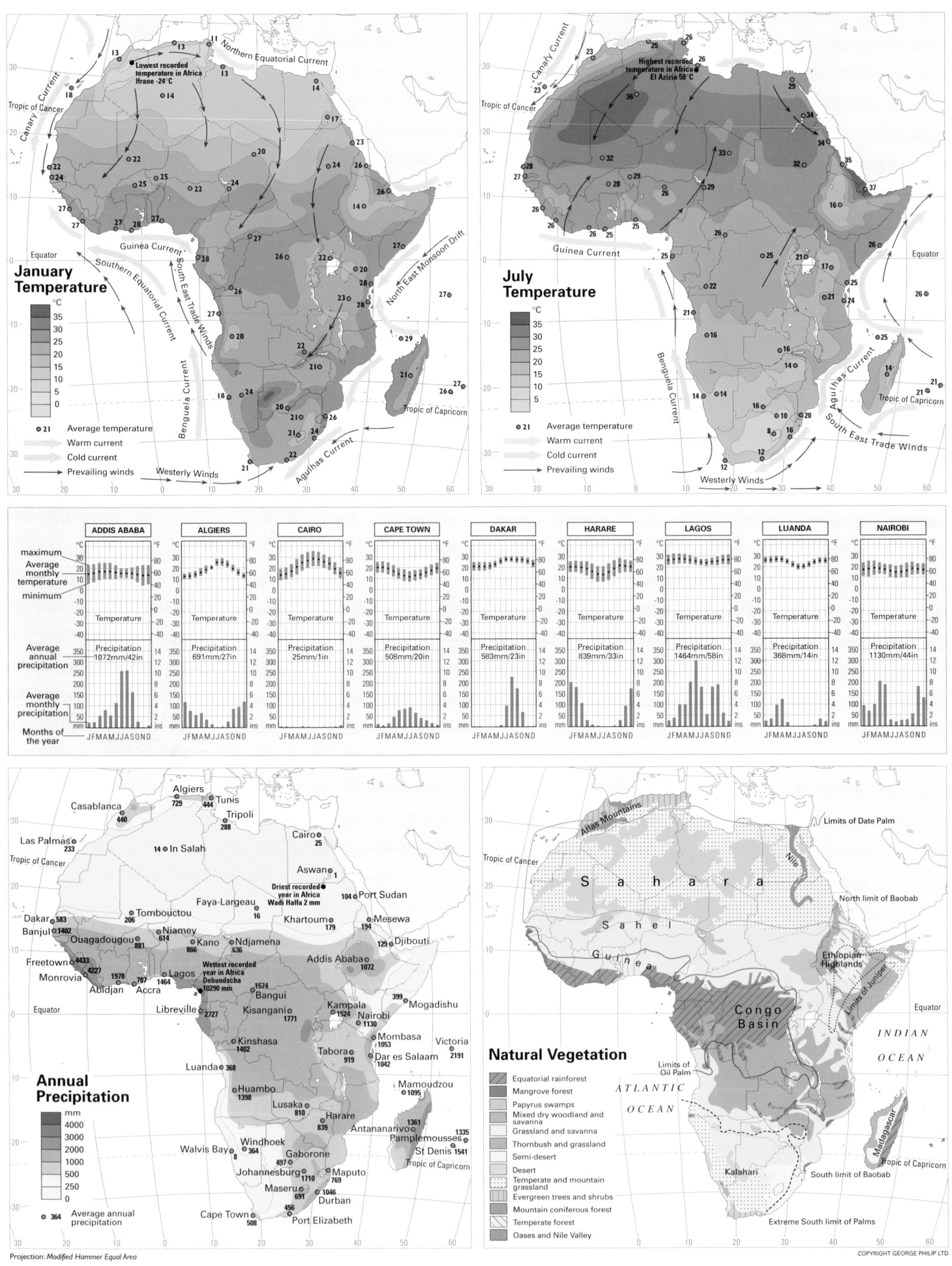

January Temperature

°C
35
30
25
20
15
10
5
0

⊙ 21 Average temperature
Warm current
Cold current
→ Prevailing winds

Lowest recorded temperature in Africa Ifrane -24°C

Northern Equatorial Current
Canary Current
Tropic of Cancer
Guinea Current
Southern Equatorial Current
South East Trade Winds
Benguela Current
North East Monsoon Drift
Equator
Westerly Winds
Agulhas Current
Tropic of Capricorn

July Temperature

°C
35
30
25
20
15
10
5

⊙ 21 Average temperature
Warm current
Cold current
→ Prevailing winds

Highest recorded temperature in Africa El Azizia 58°C

Canary Current
Tropic of Cancer
Guinea Current
Benguela Current
South East Trade Winds
Agulhas Current
Equator
Tropic of Capricorn
Westerly Winds

	ADDIS ABABA	ALGIERS	CAIRO	CAPE TOWN	DAKAR	HARARE	LAGOS	LUANDA	NAIROBI
maximum / Average monthly temperature / minimum	Temperature	Temperature	Temperature	Temperature	Temperature	Temperature	Temperature	Temperature	Temperature
Average annual precipitation / Average monthly precipitation	Precipitation 1072mm/42in	Precipitation 691mm/27in	Precipitation 25mm/1in	Precipitation 508mm/20in	Precipitation 583mm/23in	Precipitation 839mm/33in	Precipitation 1464mm/58in	Precipitation 368mm/14in	Precipitation 1130mm/44in
Months of the year	JFMAMJJASOND	JFMAMJJASOND	JFMAMJJASOND	JFMAMJJASOND	JFMAMJJASOND	JFMAMJJASOND	JFMAMJJASOND	JFMAMJJASOND	JFMAMJJASOND

Annual Precipitation

mm
4000
3000
2000
1000
500
250
0

⊙ 364 Average annual precipitation

Algiers 729
Tunis 444
Casablanca 440
Tripoli 288
Las Palmas 233
Cairo 25
Tropic of Cancer
Aswan 1
14 In Salah
Driest recorded year in Africa Wadi Halfa 2 mm
104 Port Sudan
Faya-Largeau 16
Tombouctou 206
Khartoum 179
Mesewa 194
Dakar 583
Niamey 614
Kano 866
Ndjamena 636
Djibouti 129
Banjul 1402
Ouagadougou 881
Freetown 4433
Abidjan 1978
Accra 787
Lagos 1464
Bangui 1574
Addis Ababa 1072
Monrovia 4227
Kisangani 2727
Kampala 1524
Nairobi 1771
Mogadishu 399
Libreville 2727
Kinshasa 1402
Tabora 919
Mombasa 1053
Dar es Salaam 1042
Victoria 2191
Luanda 368
Mamoudzou 1095
Huambo 1398
Lusaka 810
Harare 839
Antananarivo 1361
Pamplemousses 1335
Windhoek 364
Gaborone 497
St Denis 1541
Walvis Bay 8
Johannesburg 1710
Maputo 769
Maseru 691
Durban 1046
Cape Town 508
Port Elizabeth 456

Wettest recorded year in Africa Debundscha 10290 mm

Equator
Tropic of Capricorn

Projection: Modified Hammer Equal Area

Natural Vegetation

Equatorial rainforest
Mangrove forest
Papyrus swamps
Mixed dry woodland and savanna
Grassland and savanna
Thornbush and grassland
Semi-desert
Desert
Temperate and mountain grassland
Evergreen trees and shrubs
Mountain coniferous forest
Temperate forest
Oases and Nile Valley

Atlas Mountains
Limits of Date Palm
Tropic of Cancer
Sahara
Sahel
Nile
North limit of Baobab
Guinea
Ethiopian Highlands
Limits of Juniper
Limits of Oil Palm
Congo Basin
Equator
INDIAN OCEAN
ATLANTIC OCEAN
Kalahari
South limit of Baobab
Madagascar
Tropic of Capricorn
Extreme South limit of Palms

COPYRIGHT GEORGE PHILIP LTD

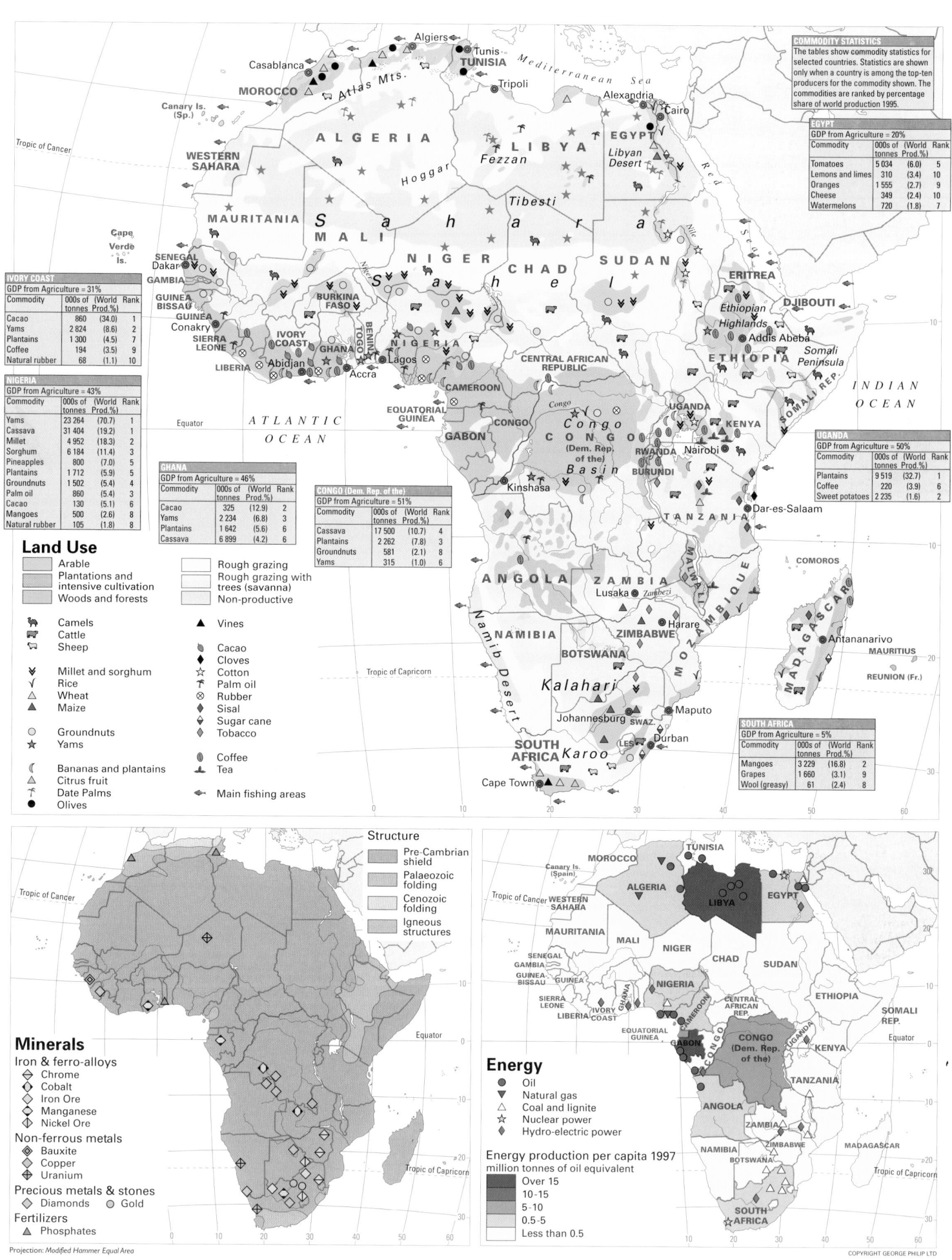

COMMODITY STATISTICS

The tables show commodity statistics for selected countries. Statistics are shown only when a country is among the top-ten producers for the commodity shown. The commodities are ranked by percentage share of world production 1995.

EGYPT
GDP from Agriculture = 20%

Commodity	000s of tonnes	(World Prod.%)	Rank
Tomatoes	5 034	(6.0)	5
Lemons and limes	310	(3.4)	10
Oranges	1 555	(2.7)	9
Cheese	349	(2.4)	10
Watermelons	720	(1.8)	7

IVORY COAST
GDP from Agriculture = 31%

Commodity	000s of tonnes	(World Prod.%)	Rank
Cacao	860	(34.0)	1
Yams	2 824	(8.6)	2
Plantains	1 300	(4.5)	7
Coffee	194	(3.5)	9
Natural rubber	68	(1.1)	10

NIGERIA
GDP from Agriculture = 43%

Commodity	000s of tonnes	(World Prod.%)	Rank
Yams	23 264	(70.7)	1
Cassava	31 404	(19.2)	1
Millet	4 952	(18.3)	2
Sorghum	6 184	(11.4)	3
Pineapples	800	(7.0)	5
Plantains	1 712	(5.9)	5
Groundnuts	1 502	(5.4)	4
Palm oil	860	(5.4)	3
Cacao	130	(5.1)	6
Mangoes	500	(2.6)	8
Natural rubber	105	(1.8)	8

GHANA
GDP from Agriculture = 46%

Commodity	000s of tonnes	(World Prod.%)	Rank
Cacao	325	(12.9)	2
Yams	2 234	(6.8)	3
Plantains	1 642	(5.6)	6
Cassava	6 899	(4.2)	6

CONGO (Dem. Rep. of the)
GDP from Agriculture = 51%

Commodity	000s of tonnes	(World Prod.%)	Rank
Cassava	17 500	(10.7)	4
Plantains	2 262	(7.8)	3
Groundnuts	581	(2.1)	8
Yams	315	(1.0)	6

UGANDA
GDP from Agriculture = 50%

Commodity	000s of tonnes	(World Prod.%)	Rank
Plantains	9 519	(32.7)	1
Coffee	220	(3.9)	6
Sweet potatoes	2 235	(1.6)	2

SOUTH AFRICA
GDP from Agriculture = 5%

Commodity	000s of tonnes	(World Prod.%)	Rank
Mangoes	3 229	(16.8)	2
Grapes	1 660	(3.1)	9
Wool (greasy)	61	(2.4)	8

Land Use

- Arable
- Plantations and intensive cultivation
- Woods and forests
- Rough grazing
- Rough grazing with trees (savanna)
- Non-productive

- Camels
- Cattle
- Sheep
- Millet and sorghum
- Rice
- Wheat
- Maize
- Groundnuts
- Yams
- Bananas and plantains
- Citrus fruit
- Date Palms
- Olives
- Vines
- Cacao
- Cloves
- Cotton
- Palm oil
- Rubber
- Sisal
- Sugar cane
- Tobacco
- Coffee
- Tea
- Main fishing areas

Minerals

Iron & ferro-alloys
- Chrome
- Cobalt
- Iron Ore
- Manganese
- Nickel Ore

Non-ferrous metals
- Bauxite
- Copper
- Uranium

Precious metals & stones
- Diamonds
- Gold

Fertilizers
- Phosphates

Structure
- Pre-Cambrian shield
- Palaeozoic folding
- Cenozoic folding
- Igneous structures

Energy

- Oil
- Natural gas
- Coal and lignite
- Nuclear power
- Hydro-electric power

Energy production per capita 1997
million tonnes of oil equivalent
- Over 15
- 10–15
- 5–10
- 0.5–5
- Less than 0.5

Projection: Modified Hammer Equal Area

COPYRIGHT GEORGE PHILIP LTD

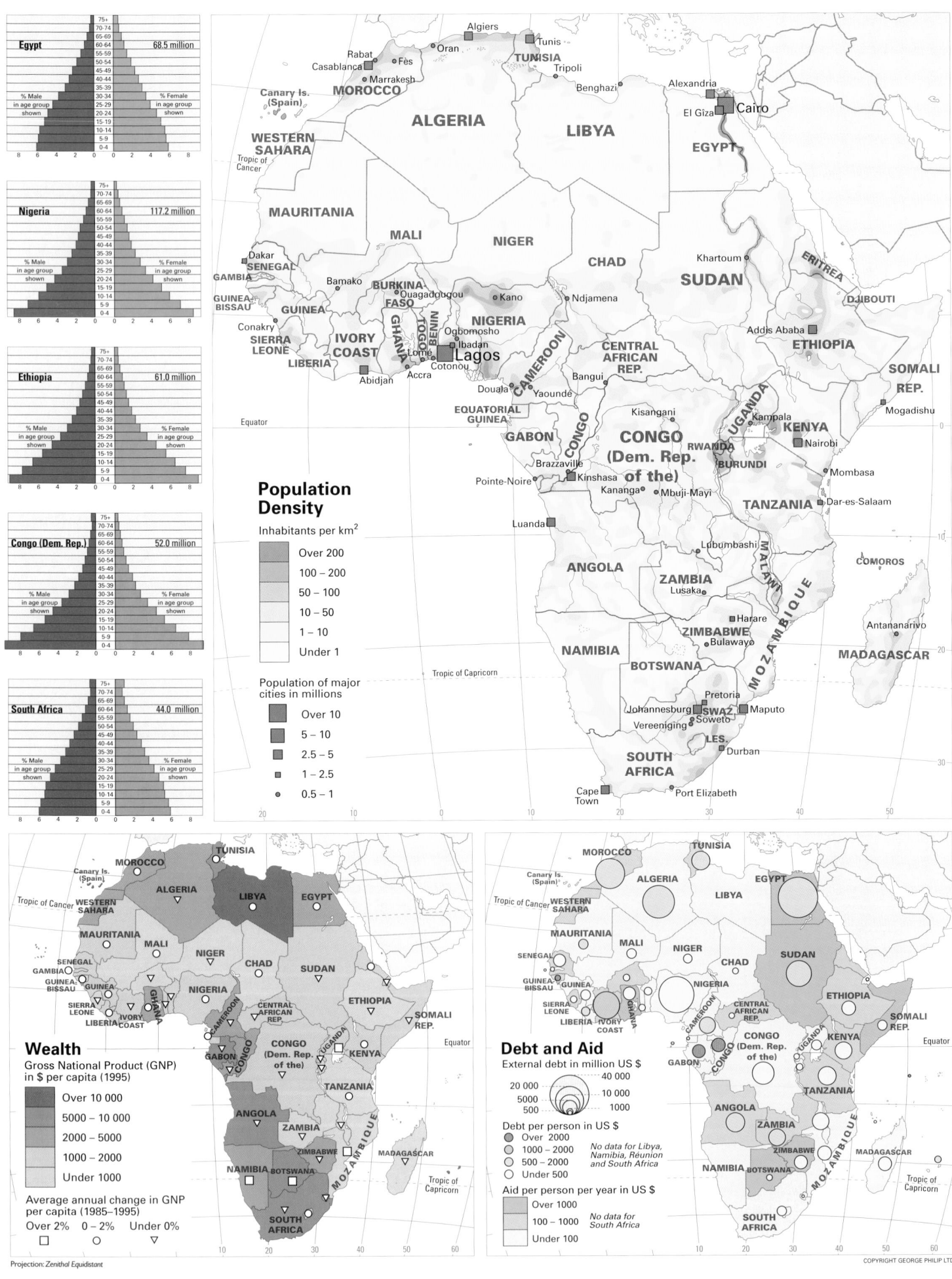

Egypt 68.5 million

% Male in age group shown | % Female in age group shown

Nigeria 117.2 million

% Male in age group shown | % Female in age group shown

Ethiopia 61.0 million

% Male in age group shown | % Female in age group shown

Congo (Dem. Rep.) 52.0 million

% Male in age group shown | % Female in age group shown

South Africa 44.0 million

% Male in age group shown | % Female in age group shown

Population Density

Inhabitants per km²

- Over 200
- 100 – 200
- 50 – 100
- 10 – 50
- 1 – 10
- Under 1

Population of major cities in millions

- Over 10
- 5 – 10
- 2.5 – 5
- 1 – 2.5
- 0.5 – 1

Equator

Tropic of Cancer

Tropic of Capricorn

Wealth

Gross National Product (GNP) in $ per capita (1995)

- Over 10 000
- 5000 – 10 000
- 2000 – 5000
- 1000 – 2000
- Under 1000

Average annual change in GNP per capita (1985–1995)

Over 2% | 0 – 2% | Under 0%

Projection: Zenithal Equidistant

Debt and Aid

External debt in million US $

- 40 000
- 20 000
- 10 000
- 5000
- 500 — 1000

Debt per person in US $
- Over 2000
- 1000 – 2000
- 500 – 1000
- Under 500

No data for Libya, Namibia, Réunion and South Africa

Aid per person per year in US $
- Over 1000
- 100 – 1000
- Under 100

No data for South Africa

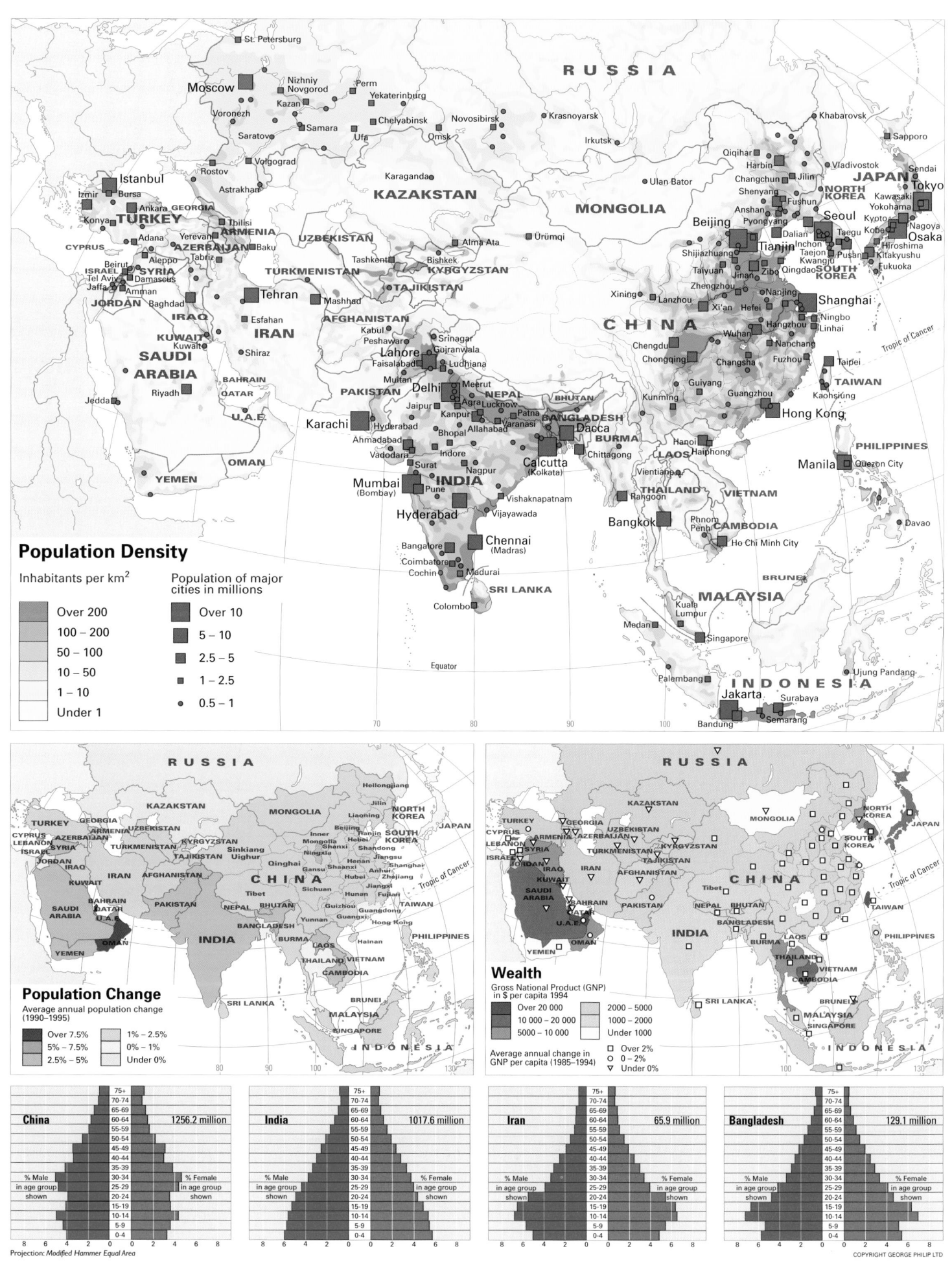

Population Density

Inhabitants per km²

	Over 200
	100 – 200
	50 – 100
	10 – 50
	1 – 10
	Under 1

Population of major cities in millions

■	Over 10
■	5 – 10
■	2.5 – 5
■	1 – 2.5
•	0.5 – 1

Population Change

Average annual population change (1990–1995)

	Over 7.5%
	5% – 7.5%
	2.5% – 5%
	1% – 2.5%
	0% – 1%
	Under 0%

Wealth

Gross National Product (GNP) in $ per capita 1994

	Over 20 000
	10 000 – 20 000
	5 000 – 10 000
	2000 – 5000
	1000 – 2000
	Under 1000

Average annual change in GNP per capita (1985–1994)

□	Over 2%
○	0 – 2%
▽	Under 0%

China	1256.2 million
India	1017.6 million
Iran	65.9 million
Bangladesh	129.1 million

% Male in age group shown   % Female in age group shown

75+
70-74
65-69
60-64
55-59
50-54
45-49
40-44
35-39
30-34
25-29
20-24
15-19
10-14
5-9
0-4

8 6 4 2 0 2 4 6 8

Projection: Modified Hammer Equal Area

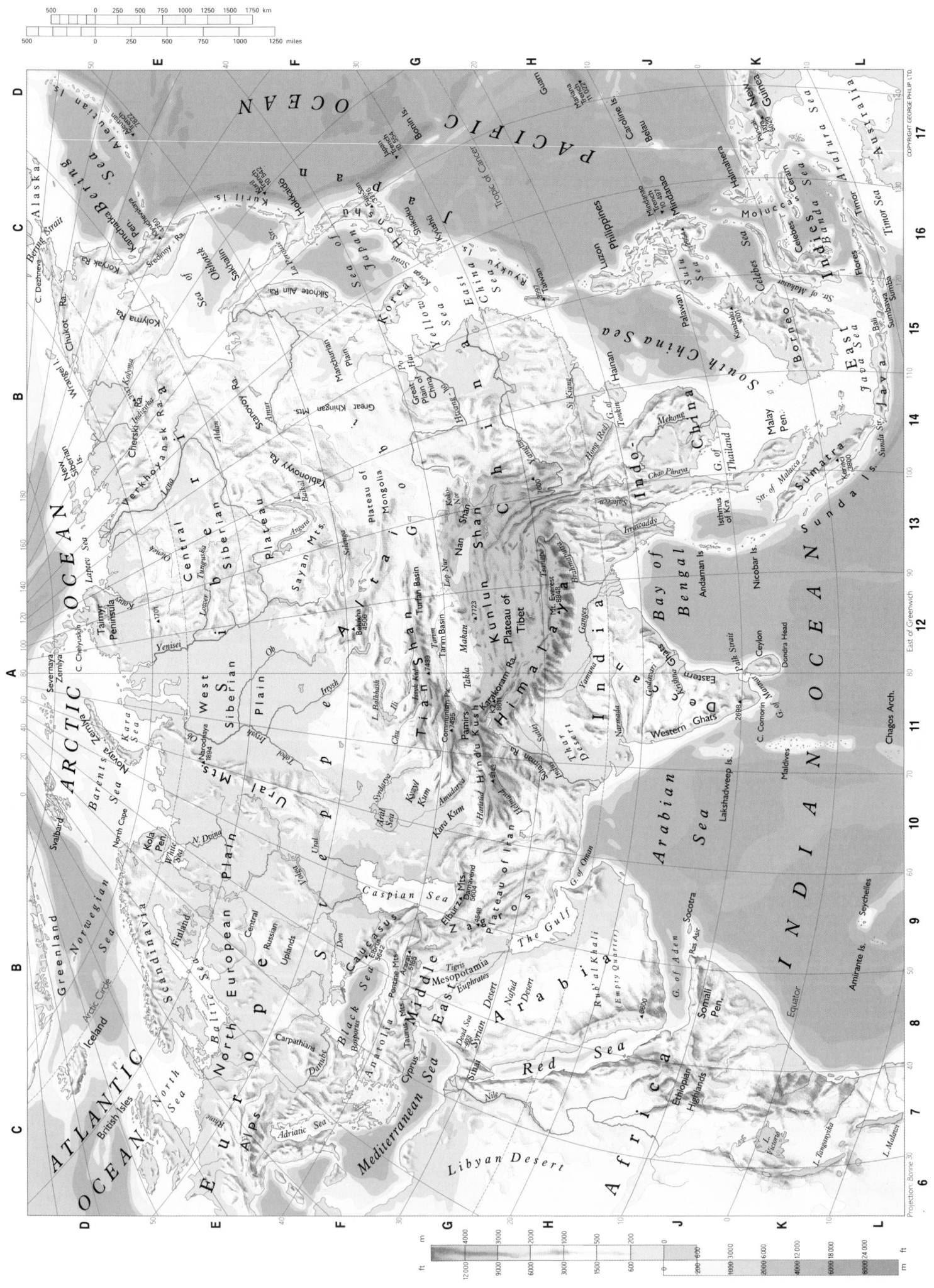

500   0   250 500 750 1000 1250 1500 1750 km

500   0   250   500   750   1000   1250 miles

Projection: Bonne

m   4000 3000 2000 1000 500 200 0
ft   12000 9000 6000 3000 1500 600   200-600 1000 3000 2000 6000 4000 12000 6000 18000 8000 24000   m
                                                                                                                ft

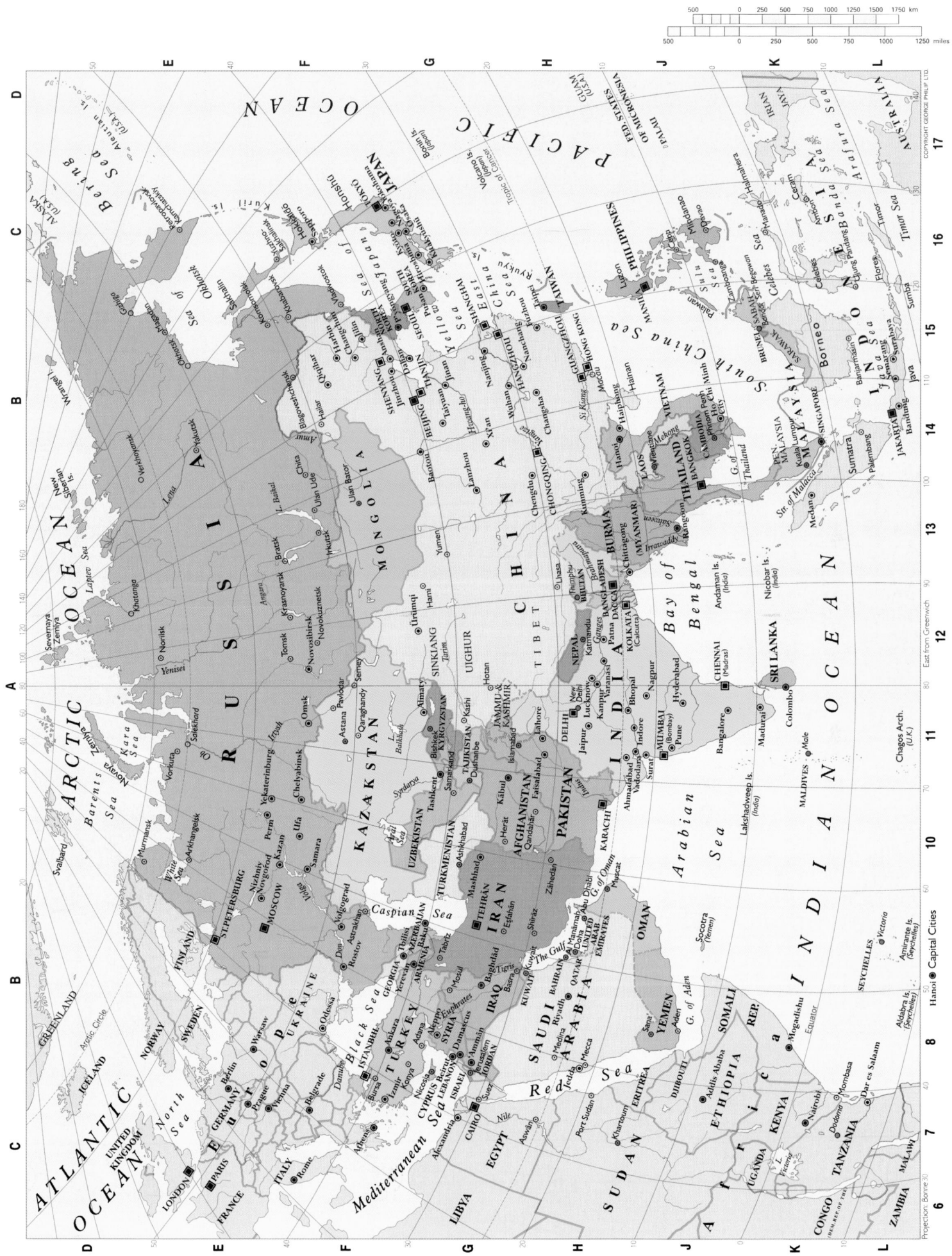

500 0 250 500 750 1000 1250 1500 1750 km
500 0 250 500 750 1000 1250 miles
ARCTIC OCEAN
PACIFIC OCEAN
INDIAN OCEAN
ATLANTIC OCEAN
R U S S I A
C H I N A
MONGOLIA
KAZAKSTAN
UZBEKISTAN
TURKMENISTAN
KYRGYZSTAN
TAJIKISTAN
AFGHANISTAN
PAKISTAN
I N D I A
NEPAL
BHUTAN
BANGLADESH
BURMA (MYANMAR)
THAILAND
LAOS
VIETNAM
CAMBODIA
MALAYSIA
SINGAPORE
I N D O N E S I A
PHILIPPINES
TAIWAN
JAPAN
NORTH KOREA
SOUTH KOREA
SRI LANKA
MALDIVES
IRAN
IRAQ
SYRIA
TURKEY
JORDAN
ISRAEL
LEBANON
CYPRUS
SAUDI ARABIA
YEMEN
OMAN
UNITED ARAB EMIRATES
QATAR
BAHRAIN
KUWAIT
GEORGIA
ARMENIA
AZERBAIJAN
EGYPT
SUDAN
ETHIOPIA
ERITREA
DJIBOUTI
SOMALI REP.
KENYA
TANZANIA
UGANDA
E u r o p e
A f r i c a
Caspian Sea
Black Sea
Red Sea
Mediterranean Sea
Arabian Sea
Bay of Bengal
South China Sea
East China Sea
Yellow Sea
Sea of Japan
Sea of Okhotsk
Bering Sea
Laptev Sea
Kara Sea
Barents Sea
TIBET
SINKIANG
UIGHUR
JAMMU & KASHMIR
MOSCOW
BEIJING
TOKYO
SEOUL
NEW DELHI
DELHI
TEHRĀN
BANGKOK
MANILA
JAKARTA
HONG KONG
SHANGHAI
KOLKATA (Calcutta)
MUMBAI (Bombay)
CHENNAI (Madras)
KARACHI
ISTANBUL
CAIRO
Tropic of Cancer
Arctic Circle
Equator
Hanoi ● Capital Cities
COPYRIGHT GEORGE PHILIP LTD.
Projection: Bonne
East from Greenwich

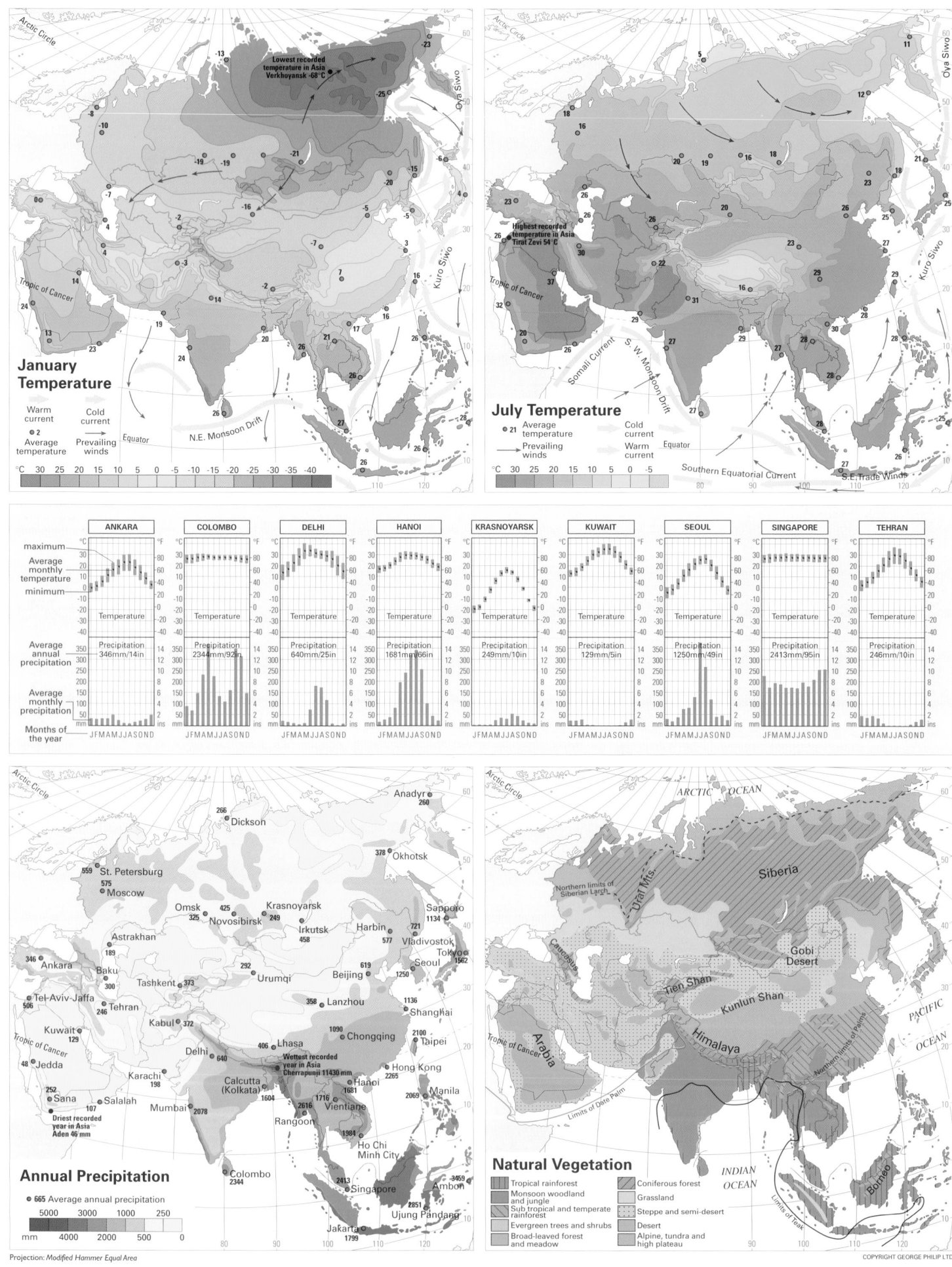

January Temperature

Warm current
Cold current
● 2 Average temperature
Prevailing winds
Equator
N.E. Monsoon Drift
Tropic of Cancer
Arctic Circle
Oya Siwo
Kuro Siwo
Lowest recorded temperature in Asia Verkhoyansk -68°C

°C 30 25 20 15 10 5 -5 -10 -15 -20 -25 -30 -35 -40

July Temperature

● 21 Average temperature
Prevailing winds
Cold current
Warm current
Equator
Tropic of Cancer
Arctic Circle
Oya Siwo
Kuro Siwo
Highest recorded temperature in Asia Tirat Zevi 54°C
Somali Current
S.W. Monsoon Drift
Southern Equatorial Current
S.E. Trade Winds

°C 30 25 20 15 10 5 0 -5

	ANKARA	COLOMBO	DELHI	HANOI	KRASNOYARSK	KUWAIT	SEOUL	SINGAPORE	TEHRAN
maximum									
Average monthly temperature									
minimum									
	Temperature	Temperature	Temperature	Temperature	Temperature	Temperature	Temperature	Temperature	Temperature
Average annual precipitation	Precipitation 346mm/14in	Precipitation 2344mm/92in	Precipitation 640mm/25in	Precipitation 1681mm/66in	Precipitation 249mm/10in	Precipitation 129mm/5in	Precipitation 1250mm/49in	Precipitation 2413mm/95in	Precipitation 246mm/10in
Average monthly precipitation									
Months of the year	JFMAMJJASOND	JFMAMJJASOND	JFMAMJJASOND	JFMAMJJASOND	JFMAMJJASOND	JFMAMJJASOND	JFMAMJJASOND	JFMAMJJASOND	JFMAMJJASOND

Annual Precipitation

● 665 Average annual precipitation

Anadyr 260
Dickson 266
St. Petersburg 559
Moscow 575
Okhotsk 378
Omsk 325
Novosibirsk
Krasnoyarsk 425
Irkutsk 249
458
Harbin 577
Sapporo 1134
Vladivostok 721
Tokyo 1562
Astrakhan 189
Ankara 346
Baku
Tashkent 300
Urumqi 373
292
Beijing
Lanzhou 358
619
Seoul 1250
Shanghai 1136
Tel-Aviv-Jaffa 506
Tehran 246
Kabul 372
Lhasa 406
Chongqing 1090
Taipei 2100
Kuwait 129
Delhi 640
Wettest recorded year in Asia Cherrapunji 11430 mm
Hong Kong 2265
Jedda 48
Karachi 198
Calcutta (Kolkata) 1604
Hanoi 1681
Manila 2069
Sana 252
Salalah 107
Mumbai 2078
Vientiane 1716
2616
Driest recorded year in Asia Aden 46 mm
Rangoon 1984
Ho Chi Minh City
Colombo 2344
Singapore 2413
Ambon 3459
2851
Ujung Pandang
Jakarta 1799

mm 5000 4000 3000 2000 1000 500 250 0

Natural Vegetation

Tropical rainforest
Monsoon woodland and jungle
Sub tropical and temperate rainforest
Evergreen trees and shrubs
Broad-leaved forest and meadow
Coniferous forest
Grassland
Steppe and semi-desert
Desert
Alpine, tundra and high plateau

ARCTIC OCEAN
Siberia
Ural Mts.
Northern limits of Siberian Larch
Caucasus
Gobi Desert
Tien Shan
Kunlun Shan
Himalaya
Arabia
Tropic of Cancer
Limits of Date Palm
Limits of Teak
Northern limits of Palms
Borneo
INDIAN OCEAN
PACIFIC OCEAN

Projection: Modified Hammer Equal Area

COPYRIGHT GEORGE PHILIP LTD

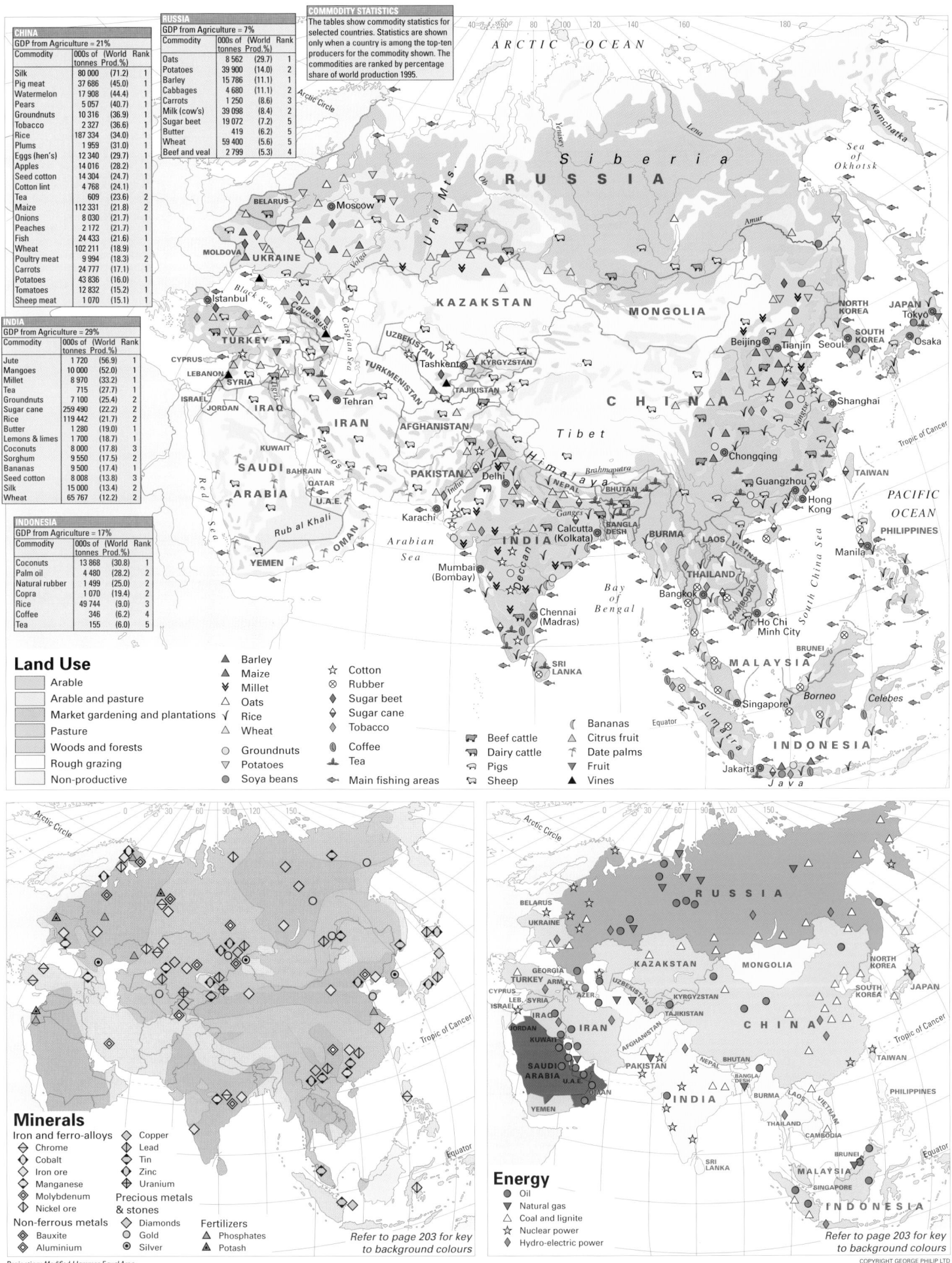

CHINA
GDP from Agriculture = 21%

Commodity	000s of tonnes	(World Prod.%)	Rank
Silk	80 000	(71.2)	1
Pig meat	37 686	(45.0)	1
Watermelon	17 908	(44.4)	1
Pears	5 057	(40.7)	1
Groundnuts	10 316	(36.9)	1
Tobacco	2 327	(36.6)	1
Rice	187 334	(34.0)	1
Plums	1 959	(31.0)	1
Eggs (hen's)	12 340	(29.7)	1
Apples	14 016	(28.2)	1
Seed cotton	14 304	(24.1)	1
Cotton lint	4 768	(24.1)	1
Tea	609	(23.6)	2
Maize	112 331	(21.8)	2
Onions	8 030	(21.7)	1
Peaches	2 172	(21.7)	1
Fish	24 433	(21.6)	1
Wheat	102 211	(18.9)	1
Poultry meat	9 994	(18.3)	2
Carrots	24 777	(17.1)	1
Potatoes	43 836	(16.0)	1
Tomatoes	12 832	(15.2)	1
Sheep meat	1 070	(15.1)	1

INDIA
GDP from Agriculture = 29%

Commodity	000s of tonnes	(World Prod.%)	Rank
Jute	1 720	(56.9)	1
Mangoes	10 000	(52.0)	1
Millet	8 970	(33.2)	1
Tea	715	(27.7)	1
Groundnuts	7 100	(25.4)	2
Sugar cane	259 490	(22.2)	2
Rice	119 442	(21.7)	2
Butter	1 280	(19.0)	1
Lemons & limes	1 700	(18.7)	1
Coconuts	8 000	(17.8)	3
Sorghum	9 550	(17.5)	2
Bananas	9 500	(17.4)	1
Seed cotton	8 008	(13.8)	3
Silk	15 000	(13.4)	2
Wheat	65 767	(12.2)	2

INDONESIA
GDP from Agriculture = 17%

Commodity	000s of tonnes	(World Prod.%)	Rank
Coconuts	13 868	(30.8)	1
Palm oil	4 480	(28.2)	2
Natural rubber	1 499	(25.0)	2
Copra	1 070	(19.4)	2
Rice	49 744	(9.0)	3
Coffee	346	(6.2)	4
Tea	155	(6.0)	5

RUSSIA
GDP from Agriculture = 7%

Commodity	000s of tonnes	(World Prod.%)	Rank
Oats	8 562	(29.7)	1
Potatoes	39 900	(14.0)	2
Barley	15 786	(11.1)	1
Cabbages	4 680	(11.1)	2
Carrots	1 250	(8.6)	3
Milk (cow's)	39 098	(8.4)	2
Sugar beet	19 072	(7.2)	5
Butter	419	(6.2)	5
Wheat	59 400	(5.6)	5
Beef and veal	2 799	(5.3)	4

COMMODITY STATISTICS
The tables show commodity statistics for selected countries. Statistics are shown only when a country is among the top-ten producers for the commodity shown. The commodities are ranked by percentage share of world production 1995.

Land Use

- Arable
- Arable and pasture
- Market gardening and plantations
- Pasture
- Woods and forests
- Rough grazing
- Non-productive

▲ Barley	☆ Cotton		☾ Bananas
▲ Maize	⊗ Rubber	🐄 Beef cattle	△ Citrus fruit
ⱽ Millet	◆ Sugar beet	🐄 Dairy cattle	⚘ Date palms
△ Oats	◇ Sugar cane	🐖 Pigs	▼ Fruit
√ Rice	◇ Tobacco	🐑 Sheep	▲ Vines
△ Wheat	◉ Coffee		
○ Groundnuts	⚖ Tea		
▽ Potatoes	⬄ Main fishing areas		
● Soya beans			

Minerals

Iron and ferro-alloys
- ◈ Chrome
- ◈ Cobalt
- ◈ Iron ore
- ◈ Manganese
- ◈ Molybdenum
- ◈ Nickel ore

Non-ferrous metals
- ◈ Bauxite
- ◈ Aluminium

- ◇ Copper
- ◈ Lead
- ◈ Tin
- ◈ Zinc
- ◈ Uranium

Precious metals & stones
- ◇ Diamonds
- ◈ Gold
- ◉ Silver

Fertilizers
- △ Phosphates
- ▲ Potash

Refer to page 203 for key to background colours

Projection: *Modified Hammer Equal Area*

Energy

- ● Oil
- ▼ Natural gas
- △ Coal and lignite
- ☆ Nuclear power
- ◆ Hydro-electric power

Refer to page 203 for key to background colours

100 0 200 400 600 800 1000 1200 1400 km
100 0 200 400 600 800 1000 miles

B **A** **B**

C Asia **C**
ARCTIC OCEAN Greenland
St. Lawrence I.
C. Dezhneva
C. Prince of Wales
Bering Strait Axel Heiberg I.
Barrow Pt. Ellesmere I.
Parry Is. Sverdrup Is. Kane Basin
Beaufort Sea Queen Elizabeth Is. Mt. Forel 3380
Nunivak I. Brooks Ra. M'Clure Strait Melville I. Bathurst Iceland
Bering Sea Melville I. Devon I. Denmark Strait
Yukon Banks C. Bathurst Viscount Melville Sd. Lancaster Sd. Bylot I. Baffin Bay
Mt. McKinley 6194 Porcupine Somerset Disko I. Davis Strait
Alaska Peninsula Alaska Range Victoria I. Prince of Wales Boothia Pen. Baffin Island
Kodiak I. Mt. St. Elias 5489 Mackenzie Mts. Gulf of Boothia Cumberland Sd. Cape Farewell
D Gulf of Alaska Mt. Logan 5959 Great Bear L. Arctic Circle Melville Pen. Foxe Basin Frobisher B. Labrador Sea **D**
Stikine Nahanni Mackenzie Back Foxe Channel C. Chidley
Alexander Archipelago Skeena Great Slave L. Southampton I. Hudson Strait Hamilton Inlet
Queen Charlotte Islands L. Athabasca Dubawnt C. Wolstenholme Ungava Peninsula Coast of Labrador
Queen Charlotte Str. Fraser Peace Reindeer L. Nelson C. Henrietta Maria Str. of Belle Isle
E Mt. Waddington 3994 Mt. Robson 3954 Athabasca Churchill James Bay Eastmain Laurentian Plateau Newfoundland **E**
Vancouver I. Selkirk Mts. Saskatchewan L. Winnipeg Belcher Is. St. Lawrence Gulf of St. Lawrence C. Race
Juan de Fuca Str. Great Hudson Bay Great Lakes Cape Breton
C. Flattery Mt. Rainier 4392 Rocky Mountains Missouri L. Superior Mt. Washington 1917 P.I. Edward Sable I.
F Coast Range Cascade Range Columbia Plains Mississippi L. Michigan L. Huron L. Ontario Niagara Falls Appalachian Mts. Hudson B. of Fundy C. Cod Nova Scotia **F**
C. Blanco Mt. Shasta 4317 Snake L. Erie Long I. Nantucket I.
C. Mendocino Sacramento Sierra Nevada Platte Missouri Ohio Cumberland Plateau Tennessee Allegheny Mts. C. Charles Chesapeake B.
San Joaquin 4418 Great Basin Wasatch Ra. Great Salt Lake Arkansas Ozark Plateau Blue Ridge Mts. C. Hatteras Bermuda
G Mt. Whitney Death Valley 86 Mt. Elbert 4399 Colorado Plateau Red Alabama Mississippi Florida NORTH ATLANTIC OCEAN **G**
PACIFIC OCEAN Grand Canyon Blanca Peak 4378 Sargasso
Guadalupe Colorado Gila Bahamas Sea
Tropic of Cancer Lower California Rio Grande Mississippi River Delta
H C. San Lucas Western Sierra Madre Mexican Plateau Eastern Sierra Madre Gulf of Mexico Florida Strait Hispaniola 9200 **H**
Clarion Fracture Zone Gulf of California C. Corrientes Cuba Puerto Rico
Revilla Gigedo Is. Santiago Gulf of Campeche Yucatán Yucatán Channel Greater Jamaica Antilles
Popocatepetl 5452 Orizaba 5700 Yucatán Peninsula Yucatán Basin Cayman Trough Caribbean Sea
Balsas Isthmus of Tehuantepec G. of Honduras Colombian Basin
J G. de Tehuantepec Guatemala Trench C. Gracias a Dios Sierra Nevada de Santa Marta 5800 G. of Venezuela **J**
Central America G. of Darién Maracaibo
G. of Panamá Andes Cord. de Mérida

ft m
9000 3000
6000 2000
3000 1000
1500 500
600 200
0 0
200 600
1000 3000
2000 6000
4000 12000
6000 18000
8000 24000
m ft
Projection: Bonne

7 120 **8** 110 West from Greenwich **9** 100 **10** 90 **12** 70
11 80

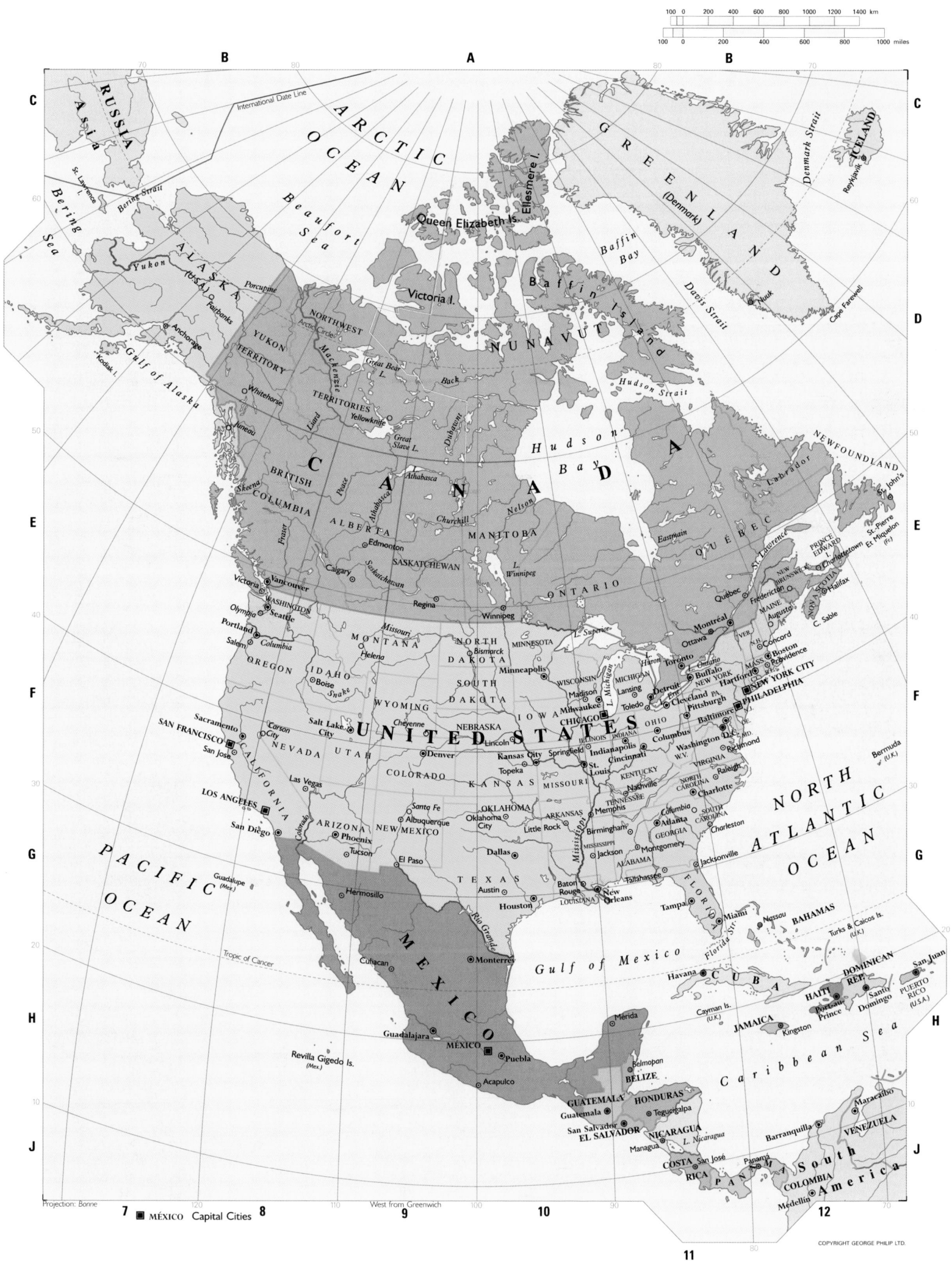

100 0 200 400 600 800 1000 1200 1400 km
100 0 200 400 600 800 1000 miles

B   A   B

RUSSIA
Asia
St. Lawrence
Bering Strait

ARCTIC OCEAN

International Date Line

Queen Elizabeth Is.
Ellesmere I.

GREENLAND
(Denmark)

Denmark Strait

Reykjavik **ICELAND**

C

Bering Sea

Beaufort Sea

Baffin Bay

60

ALASKA
(U.S.A.)
Yukon
Fairbanks
Porcupine

Victoria I.

Baffin Island

Davis Strait

Nuuk

Cape Farewell

D

Anchorage
Kodiak I.
Gulf of Alaska

NORTHWEST
Arctic Circle
YUKON
TERRITORY
Whitehorse
Juneau
Mackenzie
Great Bear L.
TERRITORIES
Yellowknife
Back

NUNAVUT

Hudson Strait

NEWFOUNDLAND

50

Liard
Great Slave L.
Dubawnt

C A N A D A

Hudson Bay

Labrador

St. John's

St-Pierre
Et Miquelon (Fr.)

E

Skeena
BRITISH
COLUMBIA
Fraser
Peace
Athabasca
ALBERTA
Athabasca
Churchill
Nelson
MANITOBA
L. Winnipeg
ONTARIO
Eastmain
St. Lawrence
QUÉBEC
PRINCE EDWARD I.
Charlottetown
NOVA SCOTIA
Halifax
C. Sable

Victoria
Vancouver
Calgary
SASKATCHEWAN
Saskatchewan
Regina
Winnipeg
Québec
Fredericton
NEW BRUNSWICK
MAINE
Augusta

WASHINGTON
Seattle
Olympia
Portland
Salem
Columbia
OREGON

MONTANA
Missouri
Helena
IDAHO
Boise
Snake
WYOMING

NORTH DAKOTA
Bismarck
SOUTH DAKOTA
MINNESOTA
Minneapolis
WISCONSIN
Madison
Milwaukee
L. Superior
L. Michigan
L. Huron
MICHIGAN
Lansing
Detroit
Toledo
Cleveland
L. Ontario
Toronto
Buffalo
L. Erie
NEW YORK
PA.
Pittsburgh
Ottawa
Montréal
VER.
Concord
MASS.
N.Y.
Hartford CT.
Boston
Providence
NEW YORK CITY
PHILADELPHIA
N.J.

40

Sacramento
SAN FRANCISCO
San Jose
Carson City
Salt Lake City
NEVADA
UTAH
UNITED STATES
Cheyenne
NEBRASKA
Lincoln
IOWA
ILLINOIS
INDIANA
CHICAGO
OHIO
Columbus
W.V.
Baltimore
MD.
Richmond
Washington D.C.

F

LOS ANGELES
San Diego
CALIFORNIA
Las Vegas
COLORADO
Denver
Santa Fe
ARIZONA
Phoenix
Tucson
NEW MEXICO
Albuquerque
Colorado
El Paso
KANSAS
Topeka
Kansas City
St. Louis
MISSOURI
Springfield
KENTUCKY
Nashville
TENNESSEE
Memphis
VIRGINIA
NORTH CAROLINA
Raleigh
Charlotte
Cincinnati
Indianapolis

30

Bermuda (U.K.)

NORTH ATLANTIC OCEAN

G

PACIFIC OCEAN

Guadalupe (Mex.)

OKLAHOMA
Oklahoma City
ARKANSAS
Little Rock
Dallas
TEXAS
Austin
Houston
Baton Rouge
LOUISIANA
New Orleans
MISSISSIPPI
Jackson
ALABAMA
Montgomery
Birmingham
GEORGIA
Atlanta
Columbia
SOUTH CAROLINA
Charleston
Jacksonville
FLORIDA
Tallahassee
Tampa
Miami

20

Tropic of Cancer

Hermosillo
M E X I C O
Monterrey
Rio Grande

Gulf of Mexico

Florida Str.
Nassau
BAHAMAS
Turks & Caicos Is. (U.K.)
Havana
C U B A
Cayman Is. (U.K.)
JAMAICA
Kingston
HAITI
Port-au-Prince
DOMINICAN REP.
Santo Domingo
San Juan
PUERTO RICO (U.S.A.)

H

Culiacán
Revilla Gigedo Is. (Mex.)
Guadalajara
MÉXICO
Puebla
Acapulco
Mérida
BELIZE
Belmopan

Caribbean Sea

Maracaibo
Barranquilla
VENEZUELA

10

GUATEMALA
Guatemala
San Salvador
EL SALVADOR
HONDURAS
Tegucigalpa
NICARAGUA
L. Nicaragua
Managua

J

COSTA RICA
San José
PANAMA
COLOMBIA
Medellín
South America

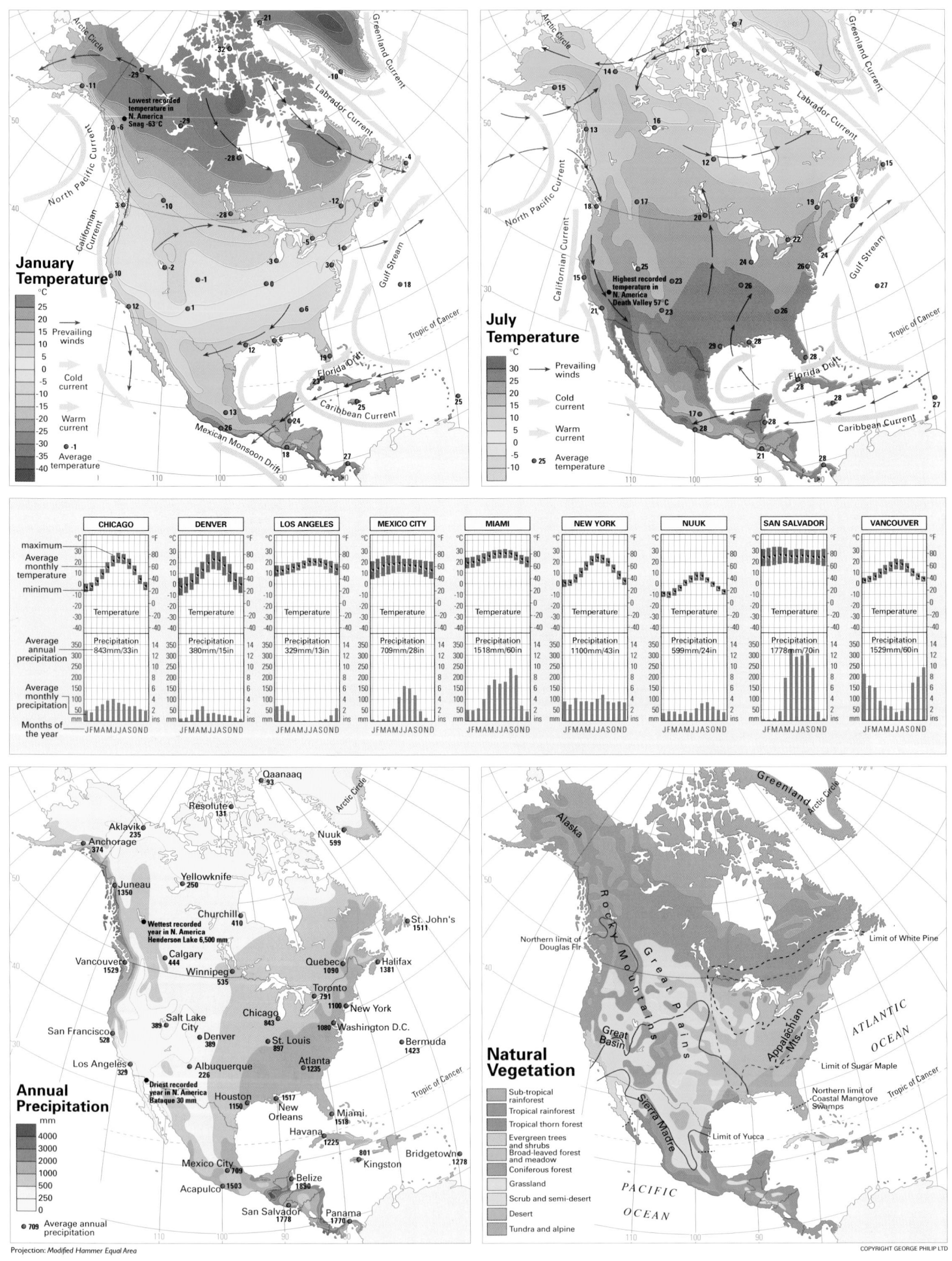

January Temperature

°C
- 25
- 20
- 15
- 10
- 5
- 0
- -5
- -10
- -15
- -20
- -25
- -30
- -35
- -40

→ Prevailing winds
⟹ Cold current
⟹ Warm current
• -1 Average temperature

Lowest recorded temperature in N. America Snag -63°C

July Temperature

°C
- 30
- 25
- 20
- 15
- 10
- 5
- 0
- -5
- -10

→ Prevailing winds
⟹ Cold current
⟹ Warm current
• 25 Average temperature

Highest recorded temperature in N. America Death Valley 57°C

	CHICAGO	DENVER	LOS ANGELES	MEXICO CITY	MIAMI	NEW YORK	NUUK	SAN SALVADOR	VANCOUVER
maximum / Average monthly temperature / minimum	Temperature	Temperature	Temperature	Temperature	Temperature	Temperature	Temperature	Temperature	Temperature
Average annual precipitation	Precipitation 843mm/33in	Precipitation 380mm/15in	Precipitation 329mm/13in	Precipitation 709mm/28in	Precipitation 1518mm/60in	Precipitation 1100mm/43in	Precipitation 599mm/24in	Precipitation 1778mm/70in	Precipitation 1529mm/60in
Average monthly precipitation / Months of the year	JFMAMJJASOND	JFMAMJJASOND	JFMAMJJASOND	JFMAMJJASOND	JFMAMJJASOND	JFMAMJJASOND	JFMAMJJASOND	JFMAMJJASOND	JFMAMJJASOND

Annual Precipitation

mm
- 4000
- 3000
- 2000
- 1000
- 500
- 250
- 0

• 709 Average annual precipitation

Qaanaaq 93
Resolute 131
Aklavik 235
Anchorage 374
Nuuk 599
Juneau 1350
Yellowknife 250
Churchill 410
Wettest recorded year in N. America Henderson Lake 6,500 mm
St. John's 1511
Calgary 444
Vancouver 1529
Winnipeg 535
Quebec 1090
Halifax 1381
Salt Lake City 389
Chicago 843
Toronto 791
New York 1080
Washington D.C.
San Francisco 528
Denver 389
St. Louis 897
Bermuda 1423
Los Angeles 329
Albuquerque 226
Atlanta 1235
Driest recorded year in N. America Bataque 30 mm
Houston 1150
New Orleans 1517
Miami 1518
Havana 1225
Mexico City 709
Belize 1890
Bridgetown 1278
Acapulco 1503
Kingston 801
San Salvador 1778
Panama 1770

Natural Vegetation

- Sub-tropical rainforest
- Tropical rainforest
- Tropical thorn forest
- Evergreen trees and shrubs
- Broad-leaved forest and meadow
- Coniferous forest
- Grassland
- Scrub and semi-desert
- Desert
- Tundra and alpine

Greenland
Alaska
Rocky Mountains
Great Plains
Great Basin
Appalachian Mts.
Sierra Madre
ATLANTIC OCEAN
PACIFIC OCEAN

Northern limit of Douglas Fir
Limit of White Pine
Limit of Sugar Maple
Northern limit of Coastal Mangrove Swamps
Limit of Yucca

Projection: Modified Hammer Equal Area

COPYRIGHT GEORGE PHILIP LTD

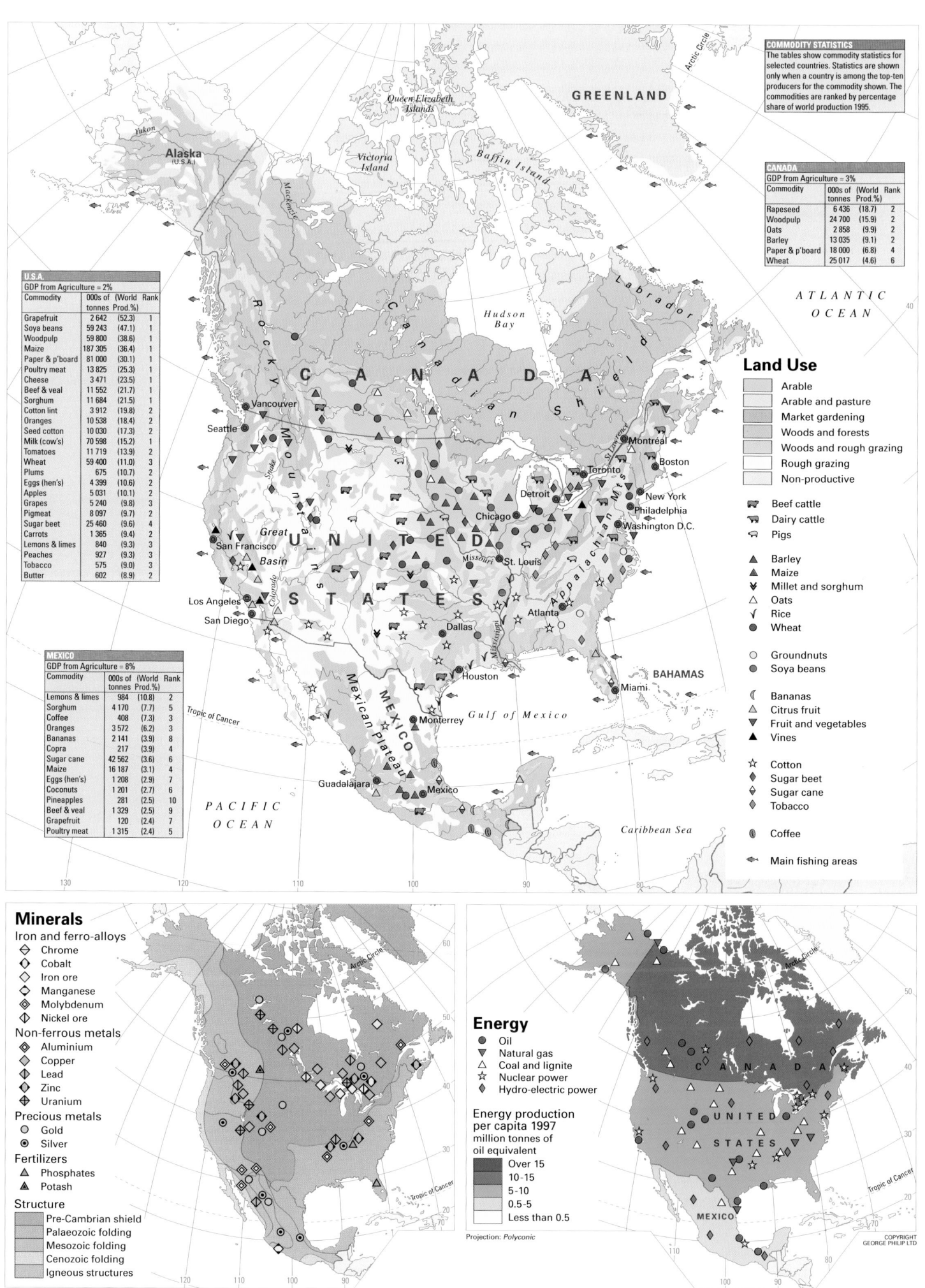

GREENLAND

COMMODITY STATISTICS
The tables show commodity statistics for selected countries. Statistics are shown only when a country is among the top-ten producers for the commodity shown. The commodities are ranked by percentage share of world production 1995.

CANADA
GDP from Agriculture = 3%

Commodity	000s of tonnes	(World Prod.%)	Rank
Rapeseed	6 436	(18.7)	2
Woodpulp	24 700	(15.9)	2
Oats	2 858	(9.9)	2
Barley	13 035	(9.1)	2
Paper & p'board	18 000	(6.8)	4
Wheat	25 017	(4.6)	6

U.S.A.
GDP from Agriculture = 2%

Commodity	000s of tonnes	(World Prod.%)	Rank
Grapefruit	2 642	(52.3)	1
Soya beans	59 243	(47.1)	1
Woodpulp	59 800	(38.6)	1
Maize	187 305	(36.4)	1
Paper & p'board	81 000	(30.1)	1
Poultry meat	13 825	(25.3)	1
Cheese	3 471	(23.5)	1
Beef & veal	11 552	(21.7)	1
Sorghum	11 684	(21.5)	1
Cotton lint	3 912	(19.8)	2
Oranges	10 538	(18.4)	2
Seed cotton	10 030	(17.3)	2
Milk (cow's)	70 598	(15.2)	1
Tomatoes	11 719	(13.9)	2
Wheat	59 400	(11.0)	3
Plums	675	(10.7)	2
Eggs (hen's)	4 399	(10.6)	2
Apples	5 031	(10.1)	2
Grapes	5 240	(9.8)	3
Pigmeat	8 097	(9.7)	2
Sugar beet	25 460	(9.6)	4
Carrots	1 365	(9.4)	2
Lemons & limes	840	(9.3)	3
Peaches	927	(9.3)	3
Tobacco	575	(9.0)	3
Butter	602	(8.9)	2

MEXICO
GDP from Agriculture = 8%

Commodity	000s of tonnes	(World Prod.%)	Rank
Lemons & limes	984	(10.8)	2
Sorghum	4 170	(7.7)	5
Coffee	408	(7.3)	3
Oranges	3 572	(6.2)	3
Bananas	2 141	(3.9)	8
Copra	217	(3.9)	4
Sugar cane	42 562	(3.6)	6
Maize	16 187	(3.1)	4
Eggs (hen's)	1 208	(2.9)	7
Coconuts	1 201	(2.7)	6
Pineapples	281	(2.5)	10
Beef & veal	1 329	(2.5)	9
Grapefruit	120	(2.4)	7
Poultry meat	1 315	(2.4)	5

Land Use

- Arable
- Arable and pasture
- Market gardening
- Woods and forests
- Woods and rough grazing
- Rough grazing
- Non-productive

- Beef cattle
- Dairy cattle
- Pigs

- ▲ Barley
- ▲ Maize
- ⅄ Millet and sorghum
- △ Oats
- ⋎ Rice
- ● Wheat

- ○ Groundnuts
- ● Soya beans

- ☾ Bananas
- △ Citrus fruit
- ▽ Fruit and vegetables
- ▲ Vines

- ☆ Cotton
- ◆ Sugar beet
- ◆ Sugar cane
- ◆ Tobacco

- ◉ Coffee

- ➤ Main fishing areas

Minerals

Iron and ferro-alloys
- ◇ Chrome
- ◇ Cobalt
- ◇ Iron ore
- ◇ Manganese
- ◈ Molybdenum
- ◇ Nickel ore

Non-ferrous metals
- ◈ Aluminium
- ◇ Copper
- ◆ Lead
- ◆ Zinc
- ⊕ Uranium

Precious metals
- ○ Gold
- ◉ Silver

Fertilizers
- △ Phosphates
- ▲ Potash

Structure
- Pre-Cambrian shield
- Palaeozoic folding
- Mesozoic folding
- Cenozoic folding
- Igneous structures

Energy
- ● Oil
- ▼ Natural gas
- △ Coal and lignite
- ☆ Nuclear power
- ◆ Hydro-electric power

Energy production per capita 1997
million tonnes of oil equivalent

- Over 15
- 10-15
- 5-10
- 0.5-5
- Less than 0.5

Projection: Polyconic

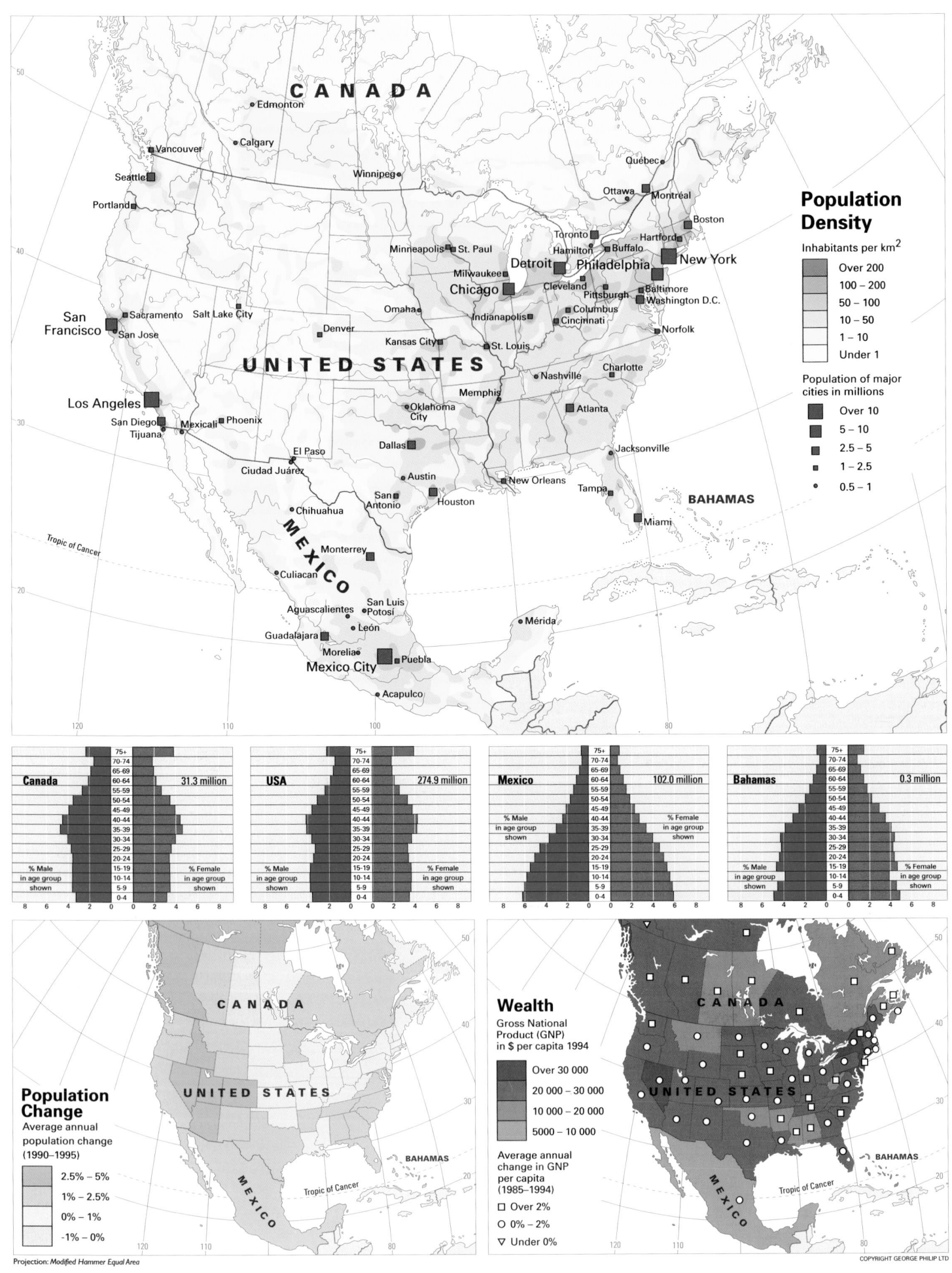

Population Density

Inhabitants per km²

Over 200
100 – 200
50 – 100
10 – 50
1 – 10
Under 1

Population of major cities in millions

Over 10
5 – 10
2.5 – 5
1 – 2.5
0.5 – 1

CANADA
Edmonton
Calgary
Vancouver
Seattle
Portland
Winnipeg
Québec
Ottawa
Montréal
Boston
Hartford
Toronto
Hamilton
Buffalo
New York
Minneapolis
St. Paul
Detroit
Philadelphia
Milwaukee
Cleveland
Baltimore
Chicago
Pittsburgh
Washington D.C.
Omaha
Columbus
Indianapolis
Cincinnati
San Francisco
Sacramento
San Jose
Salt Lake City
Denver
Kansas City
St. Louis
Norfolk
UNITED STATES
Nashville
Charlotte
Los Angeles
Memphis
San Diego
Phoenix
Oklahoma City
Atlanta
Tijuana
Mexicali
El Paso
Dallas
Jacksonville
Ciudad Juárez
Austin
New Orleans
Tampa
BAHAMAS
San Antonio
Houston
Chihuahua
MEXICO
Miami
Monterrey
Culiacan
San Luis Potosí
Aguascalientes
Mérida
León
Guadalajara
Morelia
Mexico City
Puebla
Acapulco
Tropic of Cancer

Canada — 31.3 million
USA — 274.9 million
Mexico — 102.0 million
Bahamas — 0.3 million

Age groups: 75+, 70-74, 65-69, 60-64, 55-59, 50-54, 45-49, 40-44, 35-39, 30-34, 25-29, 20-24, 15-19, 10-14, 5-9, 0-4

% Male in age group shown | % Female in age group shown

Population Change

Average annual population change (1990–1995)

2.5% – 5%
1% – 2.5%
0% – 1%
-1% – 0%

CANADA
UNITED STATES
MEXICO
BAHAMAS
Tropic of Cancer

Wealth

Gross National Product (GNP) in $ per capita 1994

Over 30 000
20 000 – 30 000
10 000 – 20 000
5000 – 10 000

Average annual change in GNP per capita (1985–1994)

Over 2%
0% – 2%
Under 0%

CANADA
UNITED STATES
MEXICO
BAHAMAS
Tropic of Cancer

Projection: Modified Hammer Equal Area

COPYRIGHT GEORGE PHILIP LTD

Venezuela 23.6 million

| 75+ |
| 70-74 |
| 65-69 |
| 60-64 |
| 55-59 |
| 50-54 |
| 45-49 |
| 40-44 |
| 35-39 |
| % Male / 30-34 / % Female |
| in age group / 25-29 / in age group |
| shown / 20-24 / shown |
| 15-19 |
| 10-14 |
| 5-9 |
| 0-4 |

8 6 4 2 0 2 4 6 8

Population Density

Inhabitants per km²

Over 200	10 – 50
100 – 200	1 – 10
50 – 100	Under 1

Wealth

Gross National Product (GNP) in $ per capita 1994–1995

Over 20 000	2000 – 5000
10 000 – 20 000	1000 – 2000
5000 – 10 000	Under 1000

Average annual change in GNP per capita (1985–1995)

□ Over 2%   ○ 0 – 2%   ▽ Under 0%

Projection: Modified Hammer Equal Area

Population of major cities in millions

■ Over 10	■ 1 – 2.5
■ 5 – 10	● 0.5 – 1
■ 2.5 – 5	

Brazil 173.8 million

| 75+ |
| 70-74 |
| 65-69 |
| 60-64 |
| 55-59 |
| 50-54 |
| 45-49 |
| 40-44 |
| 35-39 |
| % Male / 30-34 / % Female |
| in age group / 25-29 / in age group |
| shown / 20-24 / shown |
| 15-19 |
| 10-14 |
| 5-9 |
| 0-4 |

8 6 4 2 0 2 4 6 8

Argentina 37.2 million

| 75+ |
| 70-74 |
| 65-69 |
| 60-64 |
| 55-59 |
| 50-54 |
| 45-49 |
| 40-44 |
| 35-39 |
| % Male / 30-34 / % Female |
| in age group / 25-29 / in age group |
| shown / 20-24 / shown |
| 15-19 |
| 10-14 |
| 5-9 |
| 0-4 |

8 6 4 2 0 2 4 6 8

COPYRIGHT GEORGE PHILIP LTD

SOUTH AMERICA : Physical

100 0 200 400 600 800 1000 1200 1400 km
100 0 200 400 600 800 1000 miles

A

Tropic of Cancer

Yucatán Channel
Cuba
Greater
Gulf of Campeche
Yucatán Peninsula
Turks & Caicos Is.
Hispaniola
9200
Puerto Rico
NORTH

B

Isthmus of Tehuantepec
G. de Honduras
Jamaica
Antilles
Guadeloupe
Dominica
Martinique
St. Lucia
Barbados
St. Vincent
ATLANTIC

Guatemala Trench
Coco
L. Nicaragua
Caribbean Sea
Lesser Antilles
I. Margarita
Grenada
Tobago
Trinidad
OCEAN

Panama Canal
C. de la Aguja
Sierra Nevada de Santa Marta
5800
Maracaibo
Cord. de Merida

C

G. of Darién
Gulf of Panamá
Llanos
Orinoco
Guiana Highlands
Mt. Roraima 2810
C. Orange

C. de San Francisco
Cordillera Occidental
Cordillera Central
Cordillera Oriental
Magdalena
Guaviare
Meta
Sierra Pacaraima
Serra Tumucumaque
Branco
Caurimare
Essequibo
Equator

Cotopaxi 5897
Chimborazo 6267
Caquetá
Negro
Amazon
Marajó I.

D

Galapagos Is.
G. of Guayaquil
Pta. Pariñas
Pta. Negra
Napo
Putumayo
Japurá
Amazon
Tocantins
Parnaíba
C. de São Roque

Marañón
Ucayali
Juruá
Purus
Madeira
Tapajós
Xingu
Araguaia
São Francisco
Plat. of Borborema

Huascarán 6768
S e l v a s
Roosevelt
Aripuanã
Tres Pilos
Arinos

E

Chile Peru Trench
Chincha Alta
L. Titicaca
Madre de Dios
Guaporé
Mamoré
Plateau of Mato Grosso
Brazilian Highlands

Bolivian Plateau
Nevada Ancohuma 6550
L. de Poopó

PACIFIC
Abrolhos Bank

F

Tropic of Capricorn
San Félix
San Ambrosio
Atacama Desert
8050
Cerro Ojos del Salado 6863
Gran Chaco
Paraguay
Paraná
Iguaçu Falls
Serra do Mar
Uruguay
Serra da Mantiqueira
Pico da Bandeira 2890
C. Frio

OCEAN
Andes
Salinas Grandes
Pilcomayo

G

Arch. de Juan Fernández
Mt. Aconcagua 6960
Sierra de Córdoba
L. Mar Chiquita
Saladó
Entre Ríos
Paraná
L. dos Patos

Pampas
Río de la Plata

Colorado
Bahía Blanca
SOUTH

Chile Rise
Chiloé I.
Negro
G. San Matías
Valdés Peninsula 40
Argentine Basin
ATLANTIC

H

Chonos Archipelago
Mte. San Valentín 4058
Taitao Peninsula
Chubut
Gulf of San Jorge
6212
OCEAN

Gulf of Penas
Patagonia
Wellington I.
Madre de Dios I.
West Falkland
Falkland Is.
East Falkland

Magellan's Str.
Santa Inés I.
Tierra del Fuego
Staten I.
South Georgia

Canal Cockburn
Canal Beagle
C. Horn

Projection: Lambert's Azimuthal Equal Area

60 West from Greenwich 50

COPYRIGHT GEORGE PHILIP LTD.

ft / m elevation scale:
12000 / 4000
9000 / 3000
6000 / 2000
3000 / 1000
1500 / 500
600 / 200
0 / 0
200 / 600
1000 / 3000
2000 / 6000
4000 / 12000
6000 / 18000
8000 / 24000
m / ft

100 0 200 400 600 800 1000 1200 1400 km

100 0 200 400 600 800 1000 miles

1 **2** **3** **4** **5** **6** **7**

90 80 70 60 50 40

Tropic of Cancer

A

Havana
CUBA
BAHAMAS
Turks & Caicos Is.
(U.K.)

20

HAITI **DOMINICAN REP.** San Juan Virgin Is. (U.K.)
Port-au-Prince PUERTO RICO (U.S.A.) **ST. KITTS & NEVIS** **ANTIGUA & BARBUDA**

MEXICO
JAMAICA Kingston Basse-Terre **GUADELOUPE** (Fr.)
DOMINICA MARTINIQUE (Fr.)
Fort-de-France **ST. LUCIA**

B

GUATEMALA **BELIZE**
HONDURAS
Tegucigalpa
Guatemala
San Salvador **NICARAGUA**
EL SALVADOR Managua

Caribbean Sea
Castries
Aruba Curaçao **ST. VINCENT** Kingstown **BARBADOS** Bridgetown
GRENADA St. George's

N O R T H

A T L A N T I C

O C E A N

COSTA San José
RICA **P A N A M A** C. de la Aguja
Panama G. of Darién Barranquilla **Maracaibo** Caracas Port of Spain **TRINIDAD & TOBAGO**
Gulf of Panamá Cartagena Barquisimeto Valencia
Cúcuta San Cristóbal Orinoco Ciudad Guayana

C

10

Medellín Bucaramanga **VENEZUELA** **GUYANA** Georgetown Paramaribo Cayenne
Bogotá **SURINAM** C. Orange
Cali **FRENCH GUIANA**

COLOMBIA **RORAIMA** *Branco* **AMAPÁ**

Magdalena

Galapagos Is. (Ecuador)
Quito Equator *Amazon* Marajó I. Belém

D

0

ECUADOR *Napo* *Japurá*
Guayaquil *Putumayo* Manaus Santarém São Luís
G. of Guayaquil Iquitos *Marañón* **AMAZONAS** *Amazon* **PARÁ** Fortaleza
Juruá *Madeira* *Tapajós* **MARANHÃO** Teresina C. de São Roque
Purus *Xingu* RIO G. DO NORTE Natal
Chiclayo *Ucayali* **CEARÁ** PARAÍBA
Trujillo *Acre* Pôrto Velho **PIAUÍ** Campina Grande
Chimbote **RONDÔNIA** *Parnaíba* PERNAMBUCO Recife

E

10

PERU *Madre de Dios* **B R A Z I L** ALAGOAS Maceió
Callao **LIMA** **MATO GROSSO** SERGIPE Aracaju
Cuzco *Mamoré* **GOIÁS** **BAHÍA** Salvador
L. Titicaca Cuiabá DIS. FED Brasília *São Francisco*
Arequipa La Paz **BOLIVIA** Goiânia TOCANTINS
Cochabamba Santa Cruz **MINAS GERAIS**
Iquique Sucre *Paraguay* **MATO GROSSO DO SUL** Belo Horizonte ESPÍRITO SANTO

F

20

Antofagasta Salta **PARAGUAY** Ribeirão Prêto Juiz de Fora Vitória
Pilcomayo Asunción **PARANÁ** **SÃO PAULO** Campos
San Félix (Chile) San Miguel de Tucumán **SÃO PAULO** R. DE J. Niterói
San Ambrosio (Chile) Resistencia Corrientes *Uruguay* Campinas **RIO DE JANEIRO**
Salado SANTA CATARINA Curitiba

G

P A C I F I C

Córdoba Santa Fe RIO GRANDE DO SUL Pôrto Alegre
San Juan Paraná Pelotas
Arch. de Juan Fernández (Chile) Viña del Mar Mendoza **A R G E N T I N A** Rosario **URUGUAY**
Valparaíso Montevideo
SANTIAGO **BUENOS AIRES**
Talca La Plata *Rio de la Plata*

O C E A N Concepción
Bahía Blanca Mar del Plata
Valdivia *Colorado*
Puerto Montt *Negro* Viedma

Comodoro Rivadavia
Gulf of San Jorge

Gulf of Penas
C H I L E *Chubut*

S O U T H

A T L A N T I C

O C E A N

H

West Falkland **FALKLAND IS.** (U.K.)
Magellan's Str. Stanley
Punta Arenas East Falkland
Tierra del Fuego
C. Horn South Georgia (U.K.)

Tropic of Capricorn

30

40

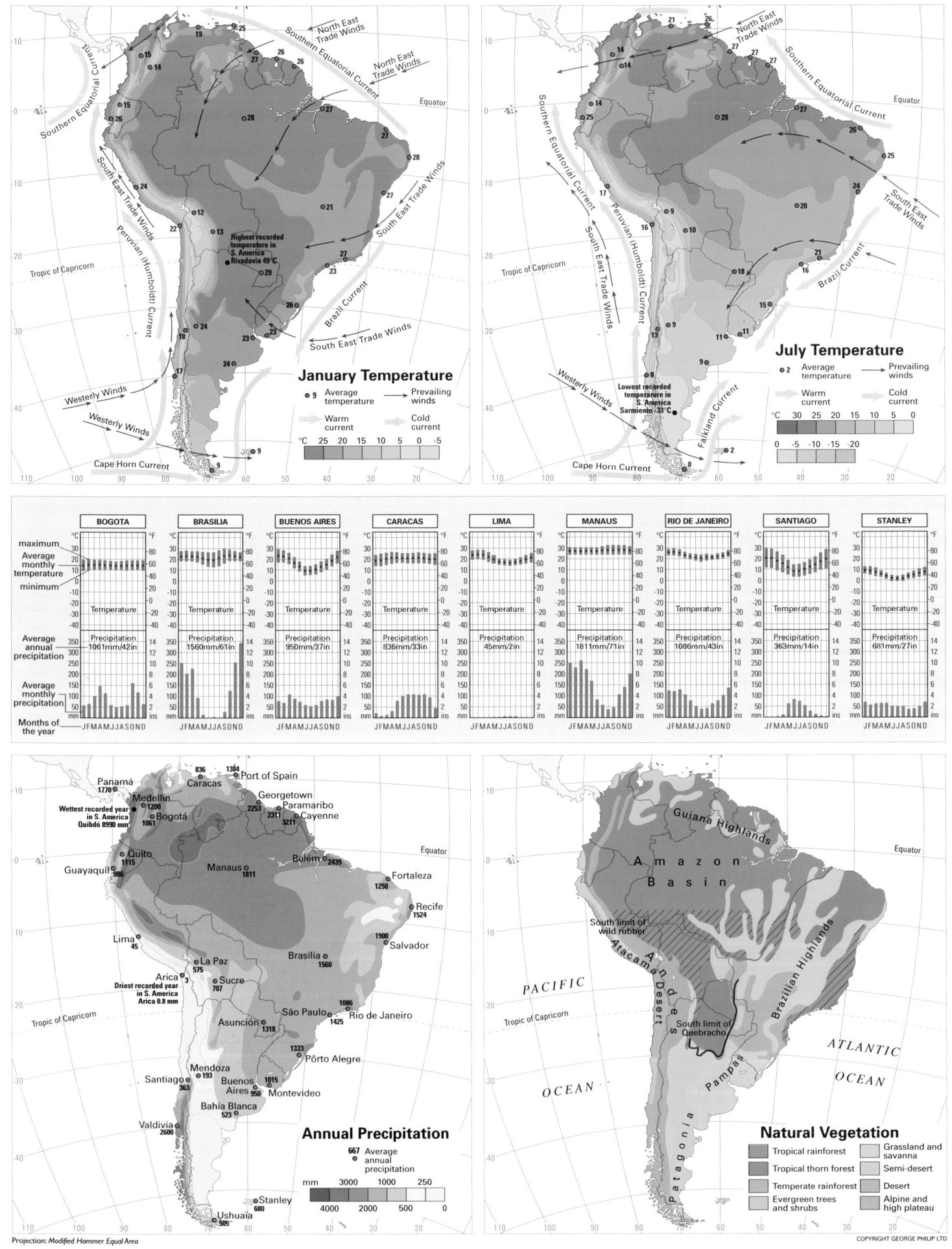

January Temperature

Average temperature ● 9
Prevailing winds →
Warm current →
Cold current →

°C 25 20 15 10 5 0 -5

Highest recorded temperature in S. America Rivadavia 49 °C

July Temperature

Average temperature ● 2
Prevailing winds →
Warm current →
Cold current →

°C 30 25 20 15 10 5 0
0 -5 -10 -15 -20

Lowest recorded temperature in S. America Sarmiento -33 °C

Climate graphs

BOGOTA	BRASILIA	BUENOS AIRES	CARACAS	LIMA	MANAUS	RIO DE JANEIRO	SANTIAGO	STANLEY

maximum
Average monthly temperature
minimum

Temperature (each graph)

Average annual precipitation:
- BOGOTA: Precipitation 1061mm/42in
- BRASILIA: Precipitation 1560mm/61in
- BUENOS AIRES: Precipitation 950mm/37in
- CARACAS: Precipitation 836mm/33in
- LIMA: Precipitation 45mm/2in
- MANAUS: Precipitation 1811mm/71in
- RIO DE JANEIRO: Precipitation 1086mm/43in
- SANTIAGO: Precipitation 363mm/14in
- STANLEY: Precipitation 681mm/27in

Average monthly precipitation

Months of the year: JFMAMJJASOND

Annual Precipitation

Panamá 1770
Caracas 836
Port of Spain 1384
Medellín 1200
Bogotá 1061
Georgetown 2253
Paramaribo 2311
Cayenne 3211
Wettest recorded year in S. America Quibdó 8990 mm
Quito 1115
Guayaquil 986
Manaus 1811
Belém 2439
Fortaleza 1250
Recife 1524
Lima 45
1900
Salvador
La Paz 575
Brasília 1560
Arica 3
Sucre 707
Driest recorded year in S. America Arica 0.8 mm
São Paulo 1425
Rio de Janeiro 1086
Asunción 1318
Pôrto Alegre 1333
Mendoza 193
Santiago 363
Buenos Aires 950
Montevideo 1015
Bahía Blanca 523
Valdivia 2600
Stanley 680
Ushuaia 505

667 ● Average annual precipitation

mm 3000 1000 250
4000 2000 500 0

Natural Vegetation

Guiana Highlands
Amazon Basin
Brazilian Highlands
Andes
Atacama Desert
Pampas
Patagonia
South limit of wild rubber
South limit of Quebracho

PACIFIC OCEAN
ATLANTIC OCEAN
Equator
Tropic of Capricorn

- Tropical rainforest
- Tropical thorn forest
- Temperate rainforest
- Evergreen trees and shrubs
- Grassland and savanna
- Semi-desert
- Desert
- Alpine and high plateau

Projection: Modified Hammer Equal Area

COPYRIGHT GEORGE PHILIP LTD

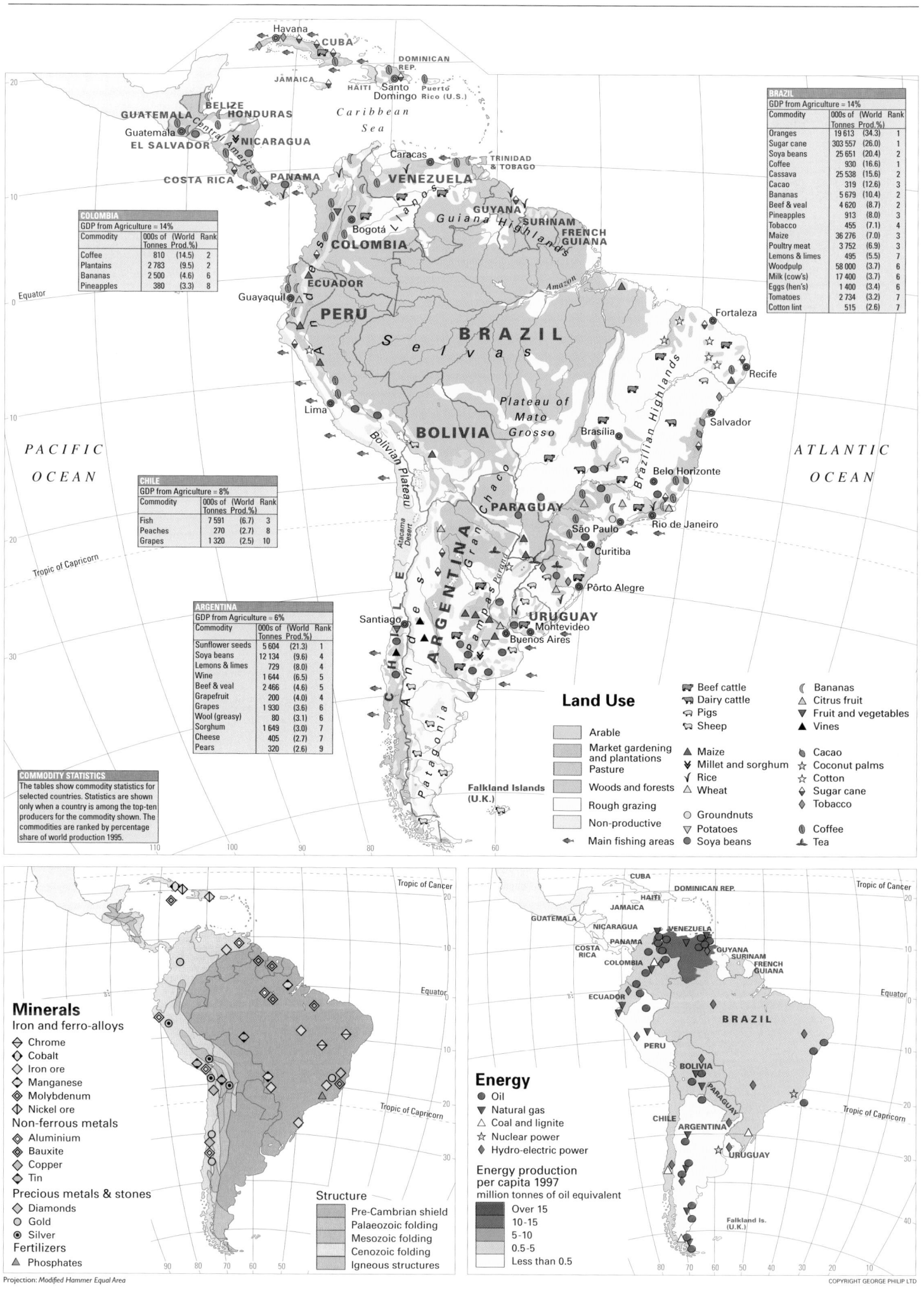

COLOMBIA
GDP from Agriculture = 14%

Commodity	000s of Tonnes	(World Prod.%)	Rank
Coffee	810	(14.5)	2
Plantains	2 783	(9.5)	2
Bananas	2 500	(4.6)	6
Pineapples	380	(3.3)	8

BRAZIL
GDP from Agriculture = 14%

Commodity	000s of Tonnes	(World Prod.%)	Rank
Oranges	19 613	(34.3)	1
Sugar cane	303 557	(26.0)	1
Soya beans	25 651	(20.4)	2
Coffee	930	(16.6)	1
Cassava	25 538	(15.6)	2
Cacao	319	(12.6)	3
Bananas	5 679	(10.4)	2
Beef & veal	4 620	(8.7)	2
Pineapples	913	(8.0)	3
Tobacco	455	(7.1)	4
Maize	36 276	(7.0)	3
Poultry meat	3 752	(6.9)	3
Lemons & limes	495	(5.5)	7
Woodpulp	58 000	(3.7)	6
Milk (cow's)	17 400	(3.7)	6
Eggs (hen's)	1 400	(3.4)	6
Tomatoes	2 734	(3.2)	7
Cotton lint	515	(2.6)	7

CHILE
GDP from Agriculture = 8%

Commodity	000s of Tonnes	(World Prod.%)	Rank
Fish	7 591	(6.7)	3
Peaches	270	(2.7)	8
Grapes	1 320	(2.5)	10

ARGENTINA
GDP from Agriculture = 6%

Commodity	000s of Tonnes	(World Prod.%)	Rank
Sunflower seeds	5 604	(21.3)	1
Soya beans	12 134	(9.6)	4
Lemons & limes	729	(8.0)	4
Wine	1 644	(6.5)	5
Beef & veal	2 466	(4.6)	5
Grapefruit	200	(4.0)	4
Grapes	1 930	(3.6)	6
Wool (greasy)	80	(3.1)	6
Sorghum	1 649	(3.0)	7
Cheese	405	(2.7)	7
Pears	320	(2.6)	9

COMMODITY STATISTICS
The tables show commodity statistics for selected countries. Statistics are shown only when a country is among the top-ten producers for the commodity shown. The commodities are ranked by percentage share of world production 1995.

Land Use
Arable; Market gardening and plantations; Pasture; Woods and forests; Rough grazing; Non-productive; Main fishing areas

Beef cattle; Dairy cattle; Pigs; Sheep; Bananas; Citrus fruit; Fruit and vegetables; Vines; Maize; Millet and sorghum; Rice; Wheat; Cacao; Coconut palms; Cotton; Sugar cane; Tobacco; Groundnuts; Potatoes; Soya beans; Coffee; Tea

Minerals
Iron and ferro-alloys: Chrome, Cobalt, Iron ore, Manganese, Molybdenum, Nickel ore
Non-ferrous metals: Aluminium, Bauxite, Copper, Tin
Precious metals & stones: Diamonds, Gold, Silver
Fertilizers: Phosphates

Structure
Pre-Cambrian shield; Palaeozoic folding; Mesozoic folding; Cenozoic folding; Igneous structures

Energy
Oil; Natural gas; Coal and lignite; Nuclear power; Hydro-electric power
Energy production per capita 1997 million tonnes of oil equivalent: Over 15; 10-15; 5-10; 0.5-5; Less than 0.5

Projection: Modified Hammer Equal Area

COPYRIGHT GEORGE PHILIP LTD

23

AUSTRALIA & OCEANIA : Physical and Political

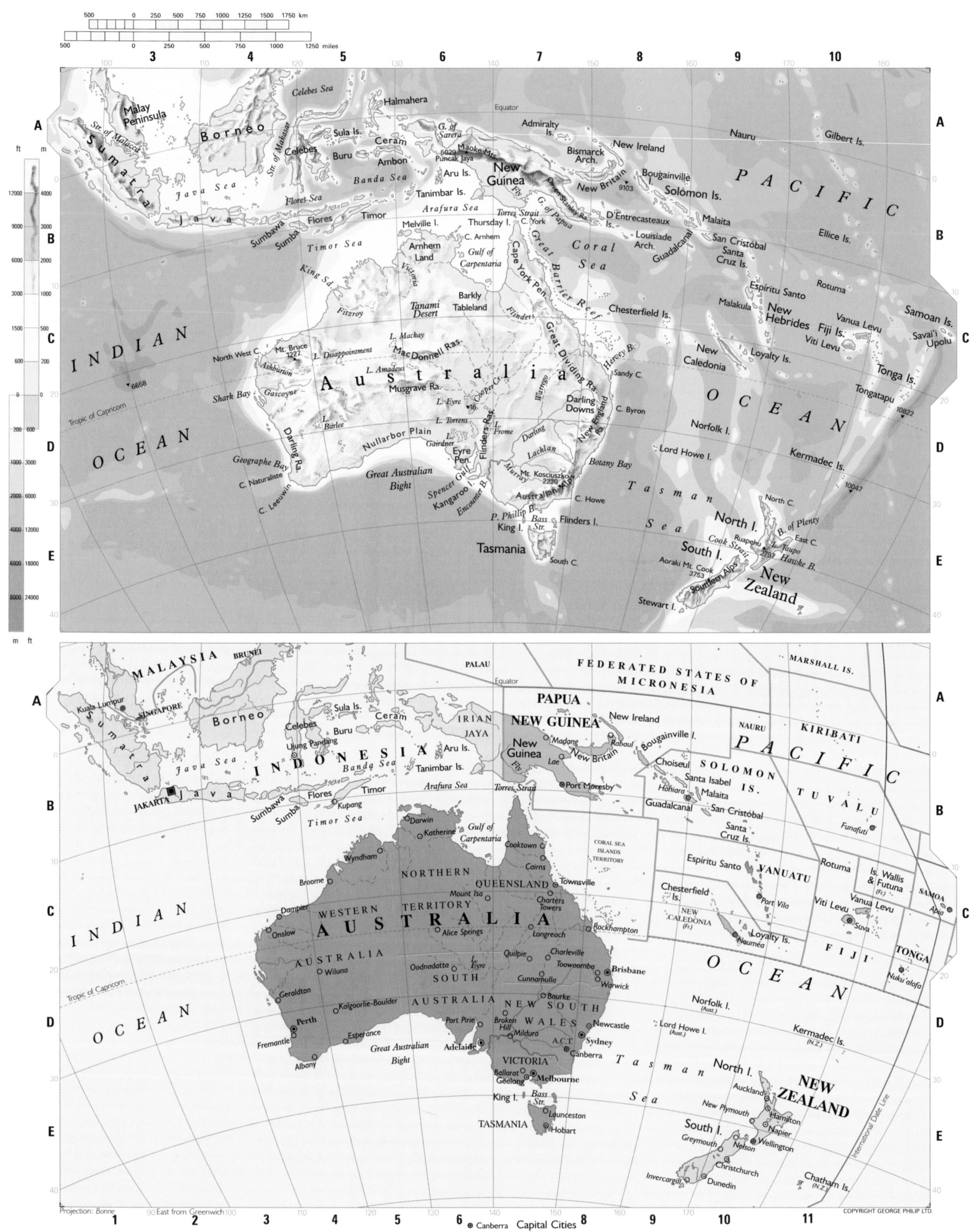

Equator
Tropic of Capricorn
Celebes Sea
Halmahera
Malay Peninsula
Str. of Malacca
Sumatra
Borneo
Celebes
Sula Is.
Ceram
Buru
Ambon
Banda Sea
Java Sea
Java
Flores Sea
Flores
Sumbawa
Sumba
Timor
Timor Sea
Aru Is.
Tanimbar Is.
Arafura Sea
New Guinea
Admiralty Is.
Bismarck Arch.
New Ireland
New Britain
Bougainville I.
Solomon Is.
Nauru
Gilbert Is.
PACIFIC OCEAN
INDIAN OCEAN
Torres Strait
Gulf of Carpentaria
Coral Sea
Great Barrier Reef
Arnhem Land
Great Dividing Ra.
Tanami Desert
Barkly Tableland
Australia
MacDonnell Ras.
Musgrave Ra.
L. Eyre
Nullarbor Plain
Great Australian Bight
Tasman Sea
Tasmania
Bass Str.
King I.
Norfolk I.
Lord Howe I.
Kermadec Is.
North I.
South I.
New Zealand
Cook Strait
Stewart I.
Fiji Is.
Tonga Is.
Samoan Is.
New Caledonia
Loyalty Is.
New Hebrides
Ellice Is.
MALAYSIA
BRUNEI
SINGAPORE
Kuala Lumpur
JAKARTA
INDONESIA
PALAU
FEDERATED STATES OF MICRONESIA
MARSHALL IS.
KIRIBATI
NAURU
PAPUA NEW GUINEA
Port Moresby
SOLOMON IS.
Honiara
TUVALU
VANUATU
Port Vila
FIJI
Suva
TONGA
SAMOA
NEW ZEALAND
Wellington
AUSTRALIA
WESTERN AUSTRALIA
NORTHERN TERRITORY
QUEENSLAND
SOUTH AUSTRALIA
NEW SOUTH WALES
VICTORIA
TASMANIA
A.C.T.
Canberra
Perth
Darwin
Adelaide
Melbourne
Sydney
Brisbane
Hobart
Auckland
Christchurch
International Date Line
Projection: Bonne
East from Greenwich
Canberra Capital Cities
COPYRIGHT GEORGE PHILIP LTD.

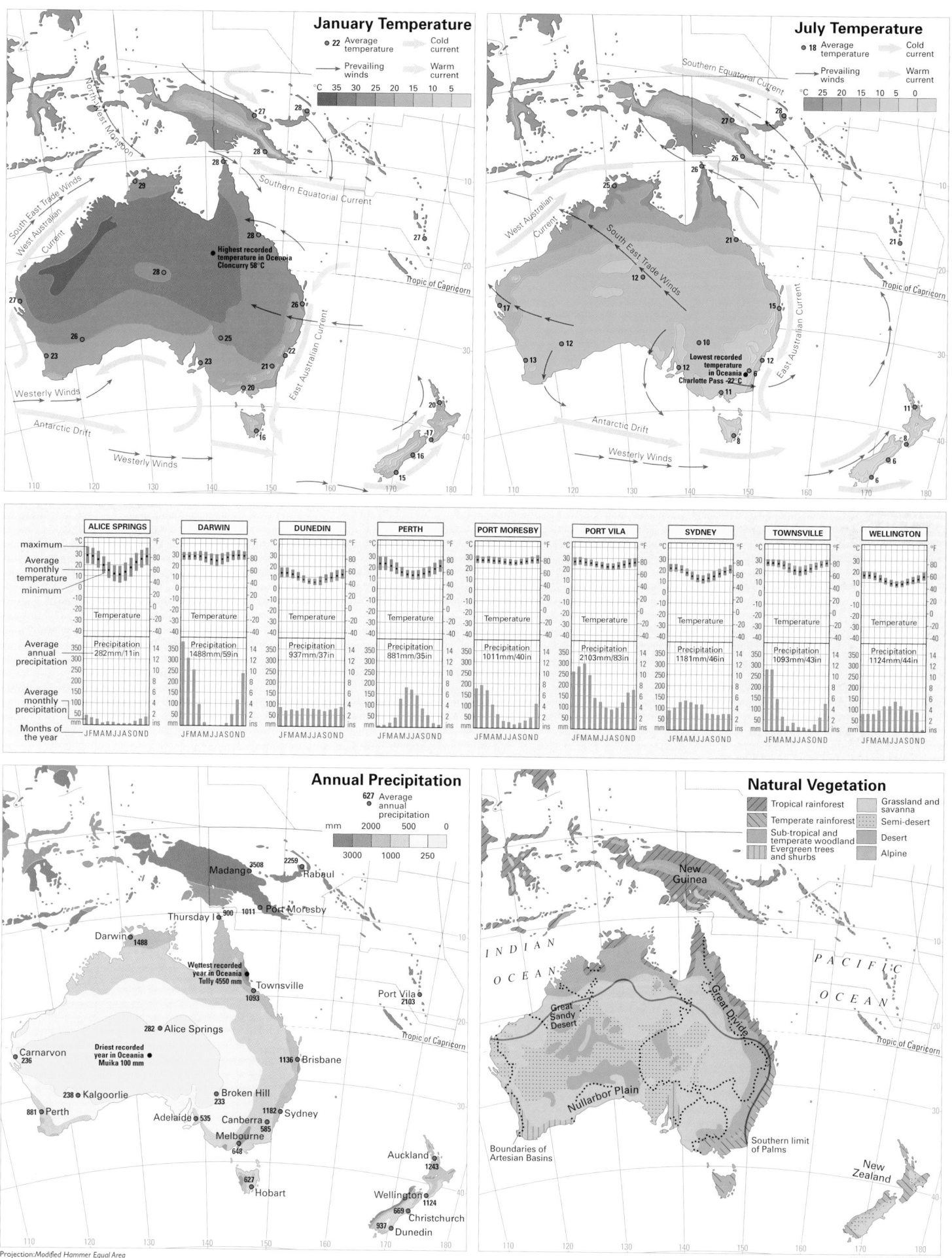

January Temperature

- ● 22 Average temperature
- → Prevailing winds
- ⇨ Cold current
- ⇨ Warm current

°C 35 30 25 20 15 10 5

North-West Monsoon

South East Trade Winds

West Australian Current

Southern Equatorial Current

Tropic of Capricorn

Highest recorded temperature in Oceania Cloncurry 58°C

East Australian Current

Westerly Winds

Antarctic Drift

Westerly Winds

27 28 28 28 29 28 27 28 26 27 26 25 23 23 22 21 20 16 17 16 15

July Temperature

- ● 18 Average temperature
- → Prevailing winds
- ⇨ Cold current
- ⇨ Warm current

°C 25 20 15 10 5 0

Southern Equatorial Current

West Australian Current

South East Trade Winds

Tropic of Capricorn

Lowest recorded temperature in Oceania Charlotte Pass -22°C

East Australian Current

Antarctic Drift

Westerly Winds

28 27 26 26 25 21 21 12 17 15 10 13 12 12 12 6 11 8 11 6 6

Climate graphs

	ALICE SPRINGS	DARWIN	DUNEDIN	PERTH	PORT MORESBY	PORT VILA	SYDNEY	TOWNSVILLE	WELLINGTON
Precipitation	282mm/11in	1488mm/59in	937mm/37in	881mm/35in	1011mm/40in	2103mm/83in	1181mm/46in	1093mm/43in	1124mm/44in

maximum — Average monthly temperature — minimum

Average annual precipitation

Average monthly precipitation

Months of the year: JFMAMJJASOND

Annual Precipitation

- ● 627 Average annual precipitation

mm 2000 500 0
3000 1000 250

Madang 3508
Rabaul 2259
Thursday I. 500 / 1011 Port Moresby
Darwin 1488
Wettest recorded year in Oceania Tully 4550 mm
Townsville 1093
Port Vila 2103
Alice Springs 282
Carnarvon 236
Driest recorded year in Oceania Muika 100 mm
Brisbane 1136
Kalgoorlie 238
Broken Hill 233
Perth 881
Adelaide 535 / Canberra / Sydney 1182
Melbourne 585 / 648
Hobart
Auckland 1243
Wellington 1124
Christchurch 669
Dunedin 937

Tropic of Capricorn

Projection: Modified Hammer Equal Area

Natural Vegetation

- ▨ Tropical rainforest
- ▧ Temperate rainforest
- ▥ Sub-tropical and temperate woodland / Evergreen trees and shrubs
- ░ Grassland and savanna
- ⦂ Semi-desert
- ▦ Desert
- ▤ Alpine

New Guinea

INDIAN OCEAN

PACIFIC OCEAN

Great Sandy Desert

Great Divide

Nullarbor Plain

Tropic of Capricorn

Boundaries of Artesian Basins

Southern limit of Palms

New Zealand

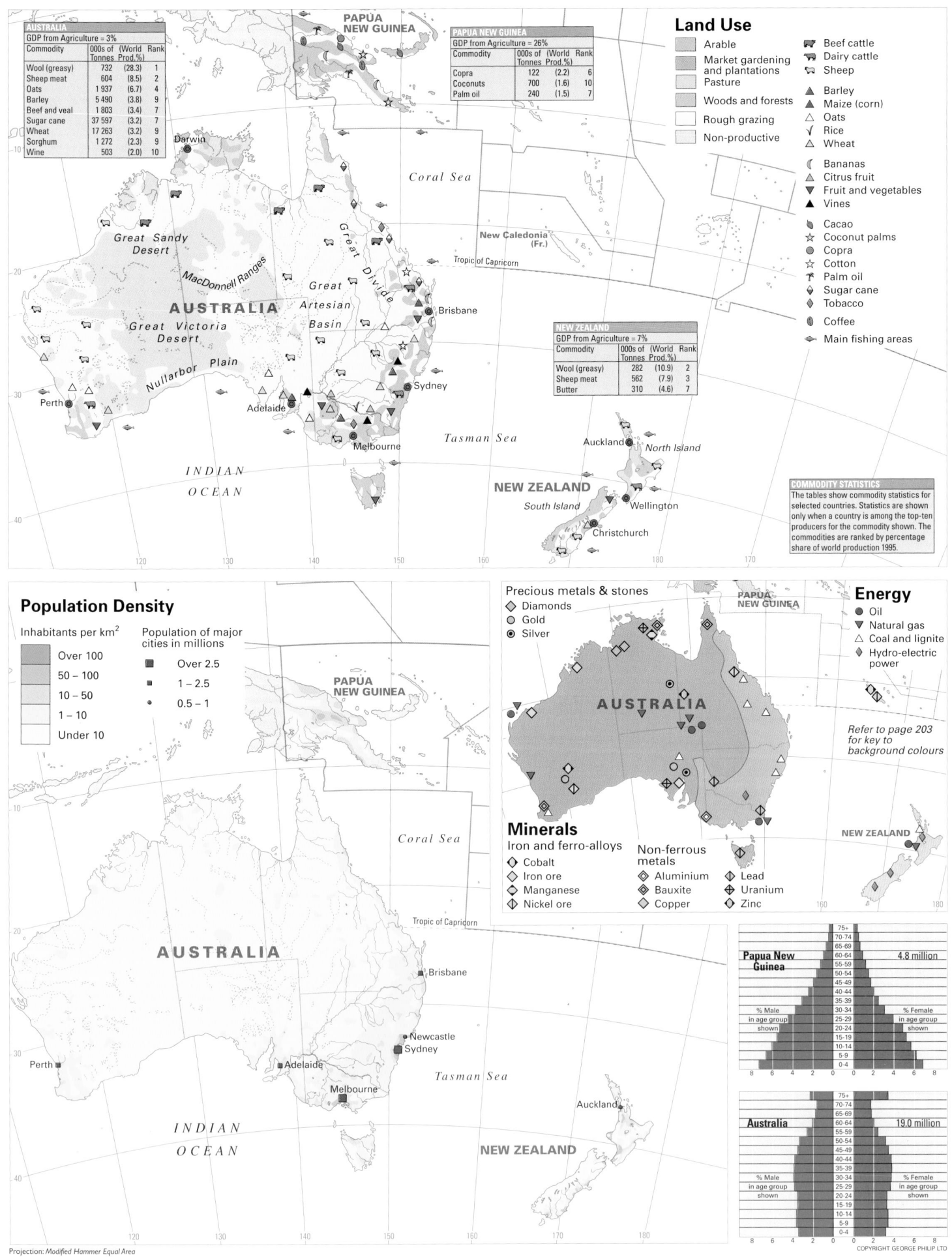

Land Use

- Arable
- Market gardening and plantations
- Pasture
- Woods and forests
- Rough grazing
- Non-productive

- 🐂 Beef cattle
- 🐄 Dairy cattle
- 🐑 Sheep

- ▲ Barley
- ▲ Maize (corn)
- △ Oats
- √ Rice
- △ Wheat

- ◖ Bananas
- △ Citrus fruit
- ▽ Fruit and vegetables
- ▲ Vines

- ◗ Cacao
- ☆ Coconut palms
- ● Copra
- ☆ Cotton
- ⊤ Palm oil
- ◇ Sugar cane
- ◆ Tobacco
- ◖ Coffee

- 🐟 Main fishing areas

AUSTRALIA

GDP from Agriculture = 3%		
Commodity	000s of Tonnes	(World Prod.%) Rank
Wool (greasy)	732	(28.3) 1
Sheep meat	604	(8.5) 2
Oats	1 937	(6.7) 4
Barley	5 490	(3.8) 9
Beef and veal	1 803	(3.4) 7
Sugar cane	37 597	(3.2) 7
Wheat	17 263	(3.2) 9
Sorghum	1 272	(2.3) 9
Wine	503	(2.0) 10

PAPUA NEW GUINEA

GDP from Agriculture = 26%		
Commodity	000s of Tonnes	(World Prod.%) Rank
Copra	122	(2.2) 6
Coconuts	700	(1.6) 10
Palm oil	240	(1.5) 7

NEW ZEALAND

GDP from Agriculture = 7%		
Commodity	000s of Tonnes	(World Prod.%) Rank
Wool (greasy)	282	(10.9) 2
Sheep meat	562	(7.9) 3
Butter	310	(4.6) 7

COMMODITY STATISTICS
The tables show commodity statistics for selected countries. Statistics are shown only when a country is among the top-ten producers for the commodity shown. The commodities are ranked by percentage share of world production 1995.

Population Density

Inhabitants per km²
- Over 100
- 50 – 100
- 10 – 50
- 1 – 10
- Under 10

Population of major cities in millions
- ■ Over 2.5
- ▪ 1 – 2.5
- • 0.5 – 1

Minerals

Iron and ferro-alloys
- ◇ Cobalt
- ◇ Iron ore
- ◇ Manganese
- ◈ Nickel ore

Non-ferrous metals
- ◈ Aluminium
- ◈ Bauxite
- ◇ Copper
- ◈ Lead
- ⊕ Uranium
- ◇ Zinc

Precious metals & stones
- ◇ Diamonds
- ◎ Gold
- ◉ Silver

Energy
- ● Oil
- ▼ Natural gas
- △ Coal and lignite
- ◆ Hydro-electric power

Refer to page 203 for key to background colours

Papua New Guinea	4.8 million
75+	
70-74	
65-69	
60-64	
55-59	
50-54	
45-49	
40-44	
35-39	
% Male in age group shown	30-34 / % Female in age group shown
	25-29
	20-24
	15-19
	10-14
	5-9
	0-4
8 6 4 2	0 2 4 6 8

Australia	19.0 million
75+	
70-74	
65-69	
60-64	
55-59	
50-54	
45-49	
40-44	
35-39	
% Male in age group shown	30-34 / % Female in age group shown
	25-29
	20-24
	15-19
	10-14
	5-9
	0-4
8 6 4 2	0 2 4 6 8

Projection: Modified Hammer Equal Area

COPYRIGHT GEORGE PHILIP LTD

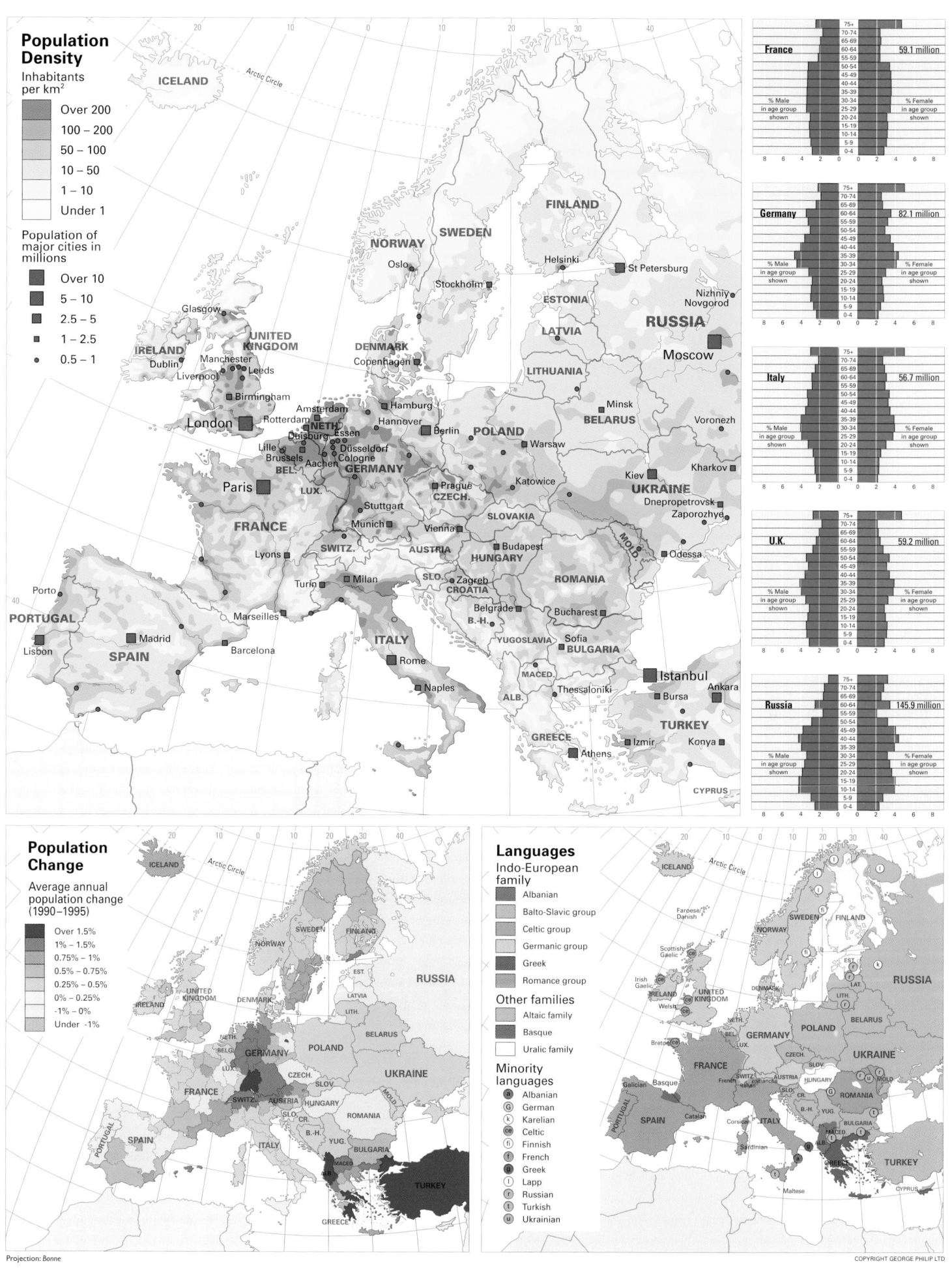

Population Density

Inhabitants per km²

- Over 200
- 100 – 200
- 50 – 100
- 10 – 50
- 1 – 10
- Under 1

Population of major cities in millions

- Over 10
- 5 – 10
- 2.5 – 5
- 1 – 2.5
- 0.5 – 1

France 59.1 million

Germany 82.1 million

Italy 56.7 million

U.K. 59.2 million

Russia 145.9 million

% Male in age group shown   % Female in age group shown

Population Change

Average annual population change (1990–1995)

- Over 1.5%
- 1% – 1.5%
- 0.75% – 1%
- 0.5% – 0.75%
- 0.25% – 0.5%
- 0% – 0.25%
- -1% – 0%
- Under -1%

Languages

Indo-European family

- Albanian
- Balto-Slavic group
- Celtic group
- Germanic group
- Greek
- Romance group

Other families

- Altaic family
- Basque
- Uralic family

Minority languages

- (a) Albanian
- (G) German
- (k) Karelian
- (ce) Celtic
- (f) Finnish
- (fr) French
- (g) Greek
- (l) Lapp
- (r) Russian
- (t) Turkish
- (u) Ukrainian

Projection: Bonne

EUROPE : Physical

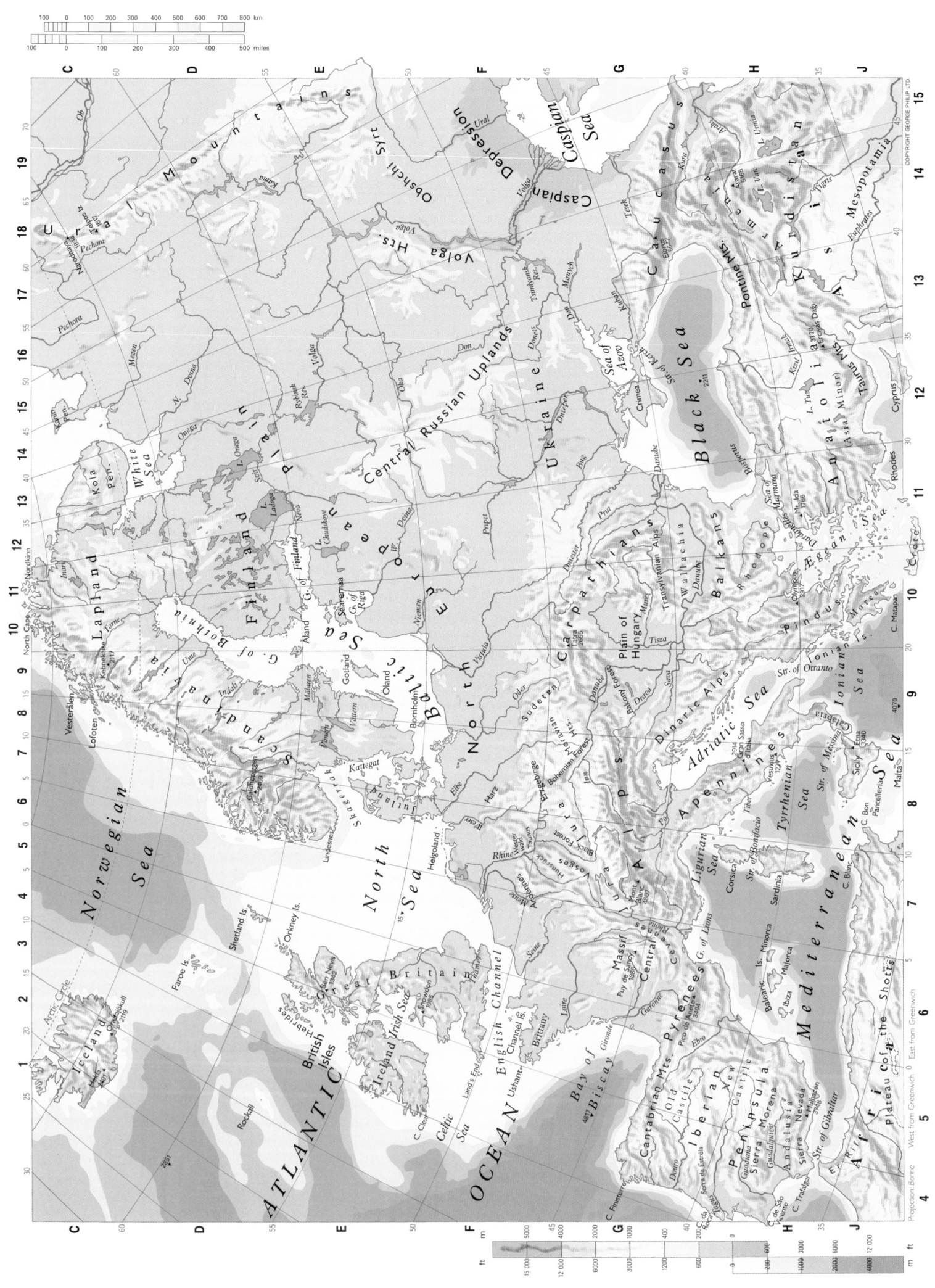

Norwegian Sea
North Sea
Baltic Sea
White Sea
Black Sea
Caspian Sea
Sea of Azov
Mediterranean Sea
Adriatic Sea
Tyrrhenian Sea
Ionian Sea
Ægean Sea
Ligurian Sea
Celtic Sea
Irish Sea
ATLANTIC OCEAN
Bay of Biscay
English Channel
G. of Bothnia
G. of Finland
G. of Riga
G. of Lions
Kattegat
Skagerrak
Iceland
Faroe Is.
Shetland Is.
Orkney Is.
British Isles
Great Britain
Ireland
Hebrides
Lapland
Scandinavia
Finland
Kola Pen.
Jutland
Ural Mountains
Caspian Depression
Obshchi Syrt
Volga Hts.
Central Russian Uplands
North European Plain
Ukraine
Carpathians
Transylvanian Alps
Plain of Hungary
Wallachia
Balkans
Rhodope
Pindus
Dinaric Alps
Alps
Apennines
Pyrenees
Massif Central
Cantabrian Mts.
Iberian Peninsula
Old Castile
New Castile
Sierra Morena
Sierra Nevada
Str. of Gibraltar
Plateau of the Shotts
Africa
Caucasus
Pontine Mts.
Armenia
Kurdistan
Mesopotamia
Anatolia (Asia Minor)
Taurus Mts.
Crimea
Cyprus
Crete
Rhodes
Sicily
Malta
Corsica
Sardinia
Balearic Is.
Str. of Otranto
Str. of Messina
Str. of Bonifacio
Volga
Don
Dnieper
Danube
Rhine
Elbe
Vistula
Oder
Loire
Seine
Garonne
Ebro
Tagus
Pechora
Mezen
N. Dvina
W. Dvina
L. Ladoga
L. Onega
L. Chudskoye
Projection: Bonne
COPYRIGHT GEORGE PHILIP LTD.

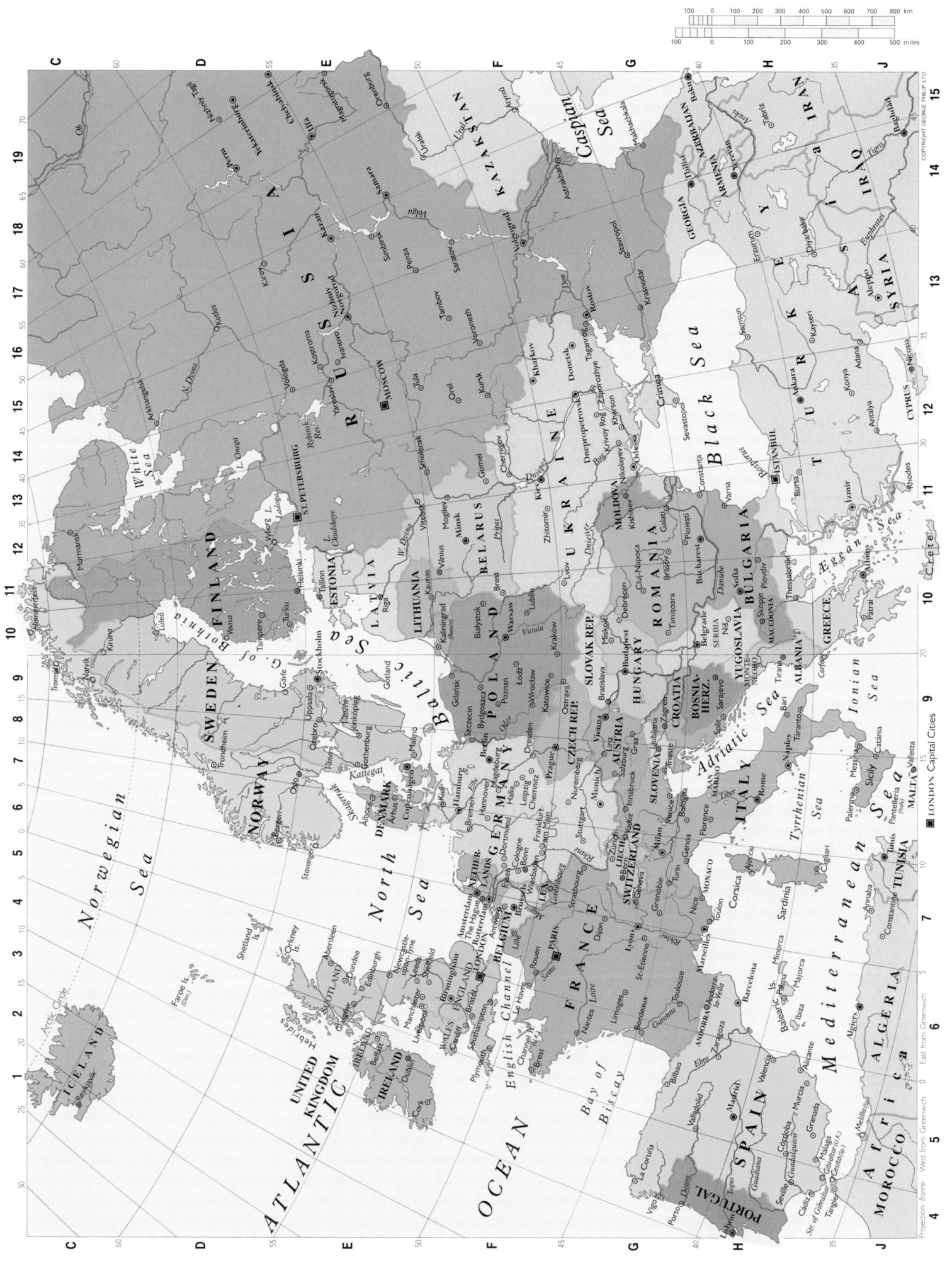
ICELAND
Reykjavik
Norwegian Sea
NORWAY
SWEDEN
FINLAND
Helsinki
Stockholm
Oslo
White Sea
G. of Bothnia
Baltic Sea
North Sea
UNITED KINGDOM
IRELAND
Dublin
LONDON
English Channel
ATLANTIC OCEAN
Bay of Biscay
FRANCE
PARIS
SPAIN
Madrid
PORTUGAL
Lisbon
DENMARK
Copenhagen
NETHERLANDS
BELGIUM
GERMANY
Berlin
POLAND
Warsaw
CZECH REP.
Prague
SLOVAK REP.
AUSTRIA
Vienna
HUNGARY
Budapest
SWITZERLAND
ITALY
Rome
Adriatic Sea
Tyrrhenian Sea
Ionian Sea
Mediterranean Sea
SLOVENIA
CROATIA
BOSNIA-HERZ.
YUGOSLAVIA
ALBANIA
MACEDONIA
GREECE
Athens
Aegean Sea
BULGARIA
Sofia
ROMANIA
Bucharest
MOLDOVA
UKRAINE
Kiev
BELARUS
Minsk
LITHUANIA
LATVIA
ESTONIA
RUSSIA
MOSCOW
ST. PETERSBURG
Black Sea
Caspian Sea
KAZAKSTAN
GEORGIA
ARMENIA
AZERBAIJAN
TURKEY
Ankara
ISTANBUL
CYPRUS
SYRIA
IRAQ
IRAN
ALGERIA
MOROCCO
TUNISIA
MALTA
Africa
Asia
■ LONDON Capital Cities
COPYRIGHT GEORGE PHILIP LTD
Projection: Bonne
West from Greenwich
East from Greenwich
km
miles

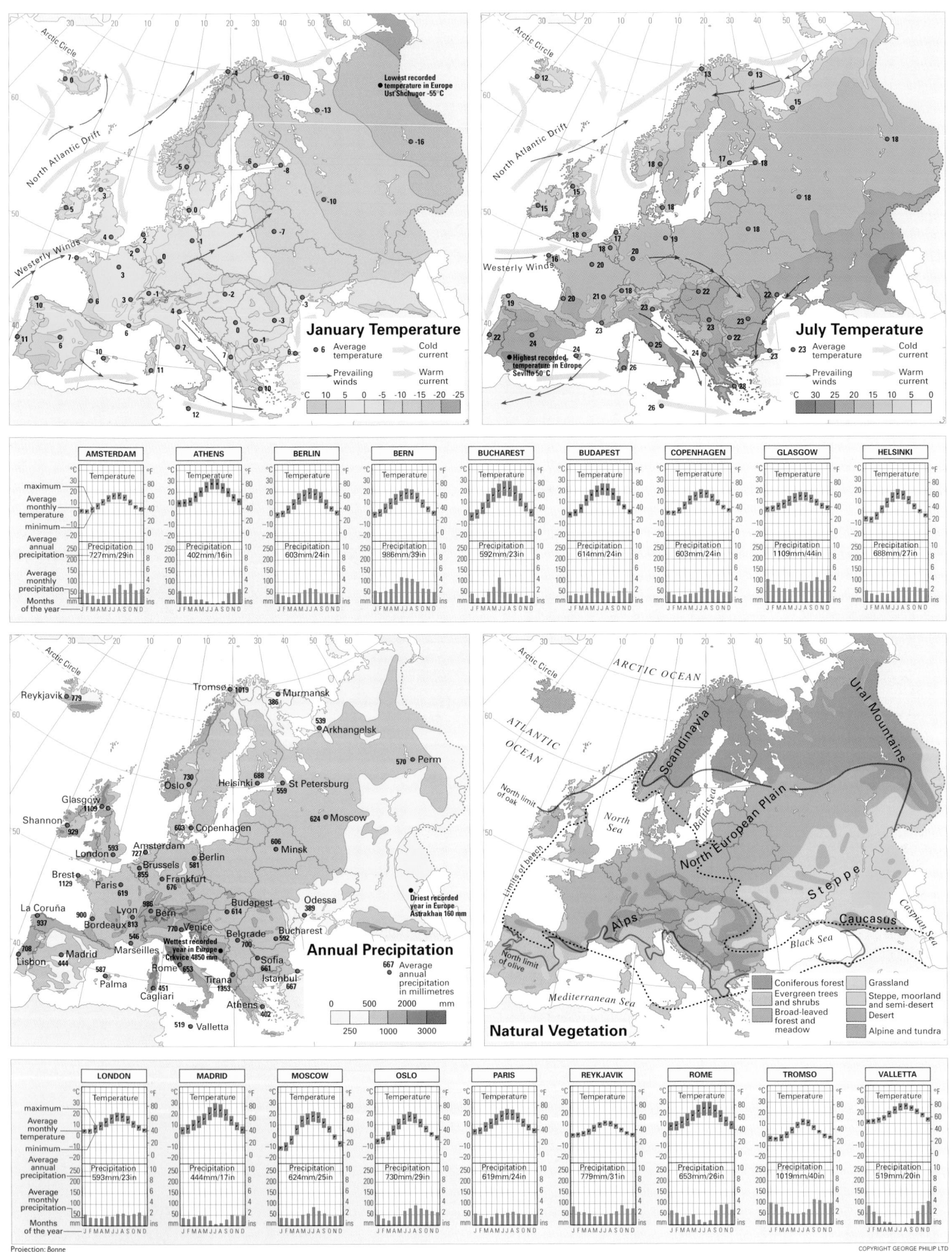

January Temperature
- 6 Average temperature
- Prevailing winds
- Cold current
- Warm current

°C 10 5 0 -5 -10 -15 -20 -25

Lowest recorded temperature in Europe Ust'Shchugor -55°C

July Temperature
- 23 Average temperature
- Prevailing winds
- Cold current
- Warm current

°C 30 25 20 15 10 5 0

Highest recorded temperature in Europe Seville 50°C

Annual Precipitation
- 667 Average annual precipitation in millimetres

0 500 2000 mm
250 1000 3000

Driest recorded year in Europe Astrakhan 160 mm

Wettest recorded year in Europe Crkvice 4850 mm

Natural Vegetation
- Coniferous forest
- Evergreen trees and shrubs
- Broad-leaved forest and meadow
- Grassland
- Steppe, moorland and semi-desert
- Desert
- Alpine and tundra

North limit of oak
North limit of beech
North limit of olive

Scandinavia, Ural Mountains, North European Plain, Steppe, Alps, Caucasus, Baltic Sea, North Sea, Black Sea, Caspian Sea, Mediterranean Sea, Arctic Ocean, Atlantic Ocean

Climate graphs (top row): AMSTERDAM, ATHENS, BERLIN, BERN, BUCHAREST, BUDAPEST, COPENHAGEN, GLASGOW, HELSINKI

- AMSTERDAM — Precipitation 727mm/29in
- ATHENS — Precipitation 402mm/16in
- BERLIN — Precipitation 603mm/24in
- BERN — Precipitation 986mm/39in
- BUCHAREST — Precipitation 592mm/23in
- BUDAPEST — Precipitation 614mm/24in
- COPENHAGEN — Precipitation 603mm/24in
- GLASGOW — Precipitation 1109mm/44in
- HELSINKI — Precipitation 688mm/27in

Climate graphs (bottom row): LONDON, MADRID, MOSCOW, OSLO, PARIS, REYKJAVIK, ROME, TROMSO, VALLETTA

- LONDON — Precipitation 593mm/23in
- MADRID — Precipitation 444mm/17in
- MOSCOW — Precipitation 624mm/25in
- OSLO — Precipitation 730mm/29in
- PARIS — Precipitation 619mm/24in
- REYKJAVIK — Precipitation 779mm/31in
- ROME — Precipitation 653mm/26in
- TROMSO — Precipitation 1019mm/40in
- VALLETTA — Precipitation 519mm/20in

Projection: Bonne

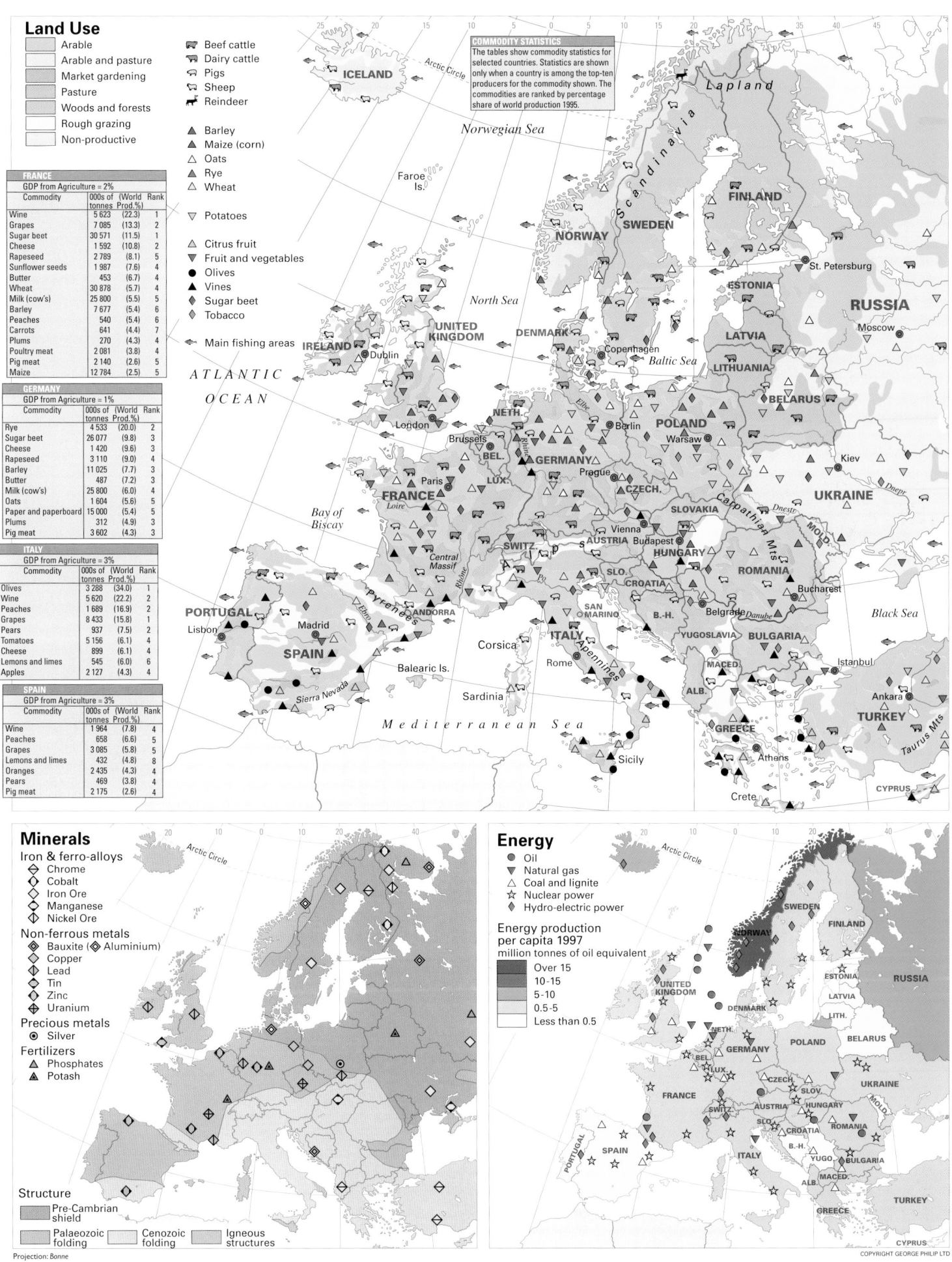

Land Use

- Arable
- Arable and pasture
- Market gardening
- Pasture
- Woods and forests
- Rough grazing
- Non-productive

- Beef cattle
- Dairy cattle
- Pigs
- Sheep
- Reindeer

- Barley
- Maize (corn)
- Oats
- Rye
- Wheat

- Potatoes

- Citrus fruit
- Fruit and vegetables
- Olives
- Vines
- Sugar beet
- Tobacco

- Main fishing areas

COMMODITY STATISTICS
The tables show commodity statistics for selected countries. Statistics are shown only when a country is among the top-ten producers for the commodity shown. The commodities are ranked by percentage share of world production 1995.

FRANCE
GDP from Agriculture = 2%

Commodity	000s of tonnes	(World Prod.%)	Rank
Wine	5 623	(22.3)	1
Grapes	7 085	(13.3)	2
Sugar beet	30 571	(11.5)	1
Cheese	1 592	(10.8)	2
Rapeseed	2 789	(8.1)	5
Sunflower seeds	1 987	(7.6)	4
Butter	453	(6.7)	4
Wheat	30 878	(5.7)	4
Milk (cow's)	25 800	(5.5)	5
Barley	7 677	(5.4)	6
Peaches	540	(5.4)	6
Carrots	641	(4.4)	7
Plums	270	(4.3)	4
Poultry meat	2 081	(3.8)	4
Pig meat	2 140	(2.6)	5
Maize	12 784	(2.5)	5

GERMANY
GDP from Agriculture = 1%

Commodity	000s of tonnes	(World Prod.%)	Rank
Rye	4 533	(20.0)	2
Sugar beet	26 077	(9.8)	3
Cheese	1 420	(9.6)	3
Rapeseed	3 110	(9.0)	4
Barley	11 025	(7.7)	3
Butter	487	(7.2)	3
Milk (cow's)	25 800	(6.0)	4
Oats	1 604	(5.6)	5
Paper and paperboard	15 000	(5.4)	5
Plums	312	(4.9)	3
Pig meat	3 602	(4.3)	3

ITALY
GDP from Agriculture = 3%

Commodity	000s of tonnes	(World Prod.%)	Rank
Olives	3 288	(34.0)	1
Wine	5 620	(22.2)	2
Peaches	1 689	(16.9)	2
Grapes	8 433	(15.8)	1
Pears	937	(7.5)	2
Tomatoes	5 156	(6.1)	4
Cheese	899	(6.1)	4
Lemons and limes	545	(6.0)	6
Apples	2 127	(4.3)	4

SPAIN
GDP from Agriculture = 3%

Commodity	000s of tonnes	(World Prod.%)	Rank
Wine	1 964	(7.8)	4
Peaches	658	(6.6)	5
Grapes	3 085	(5.8)	5
Lemons and limes	432	(4.8)	8
Oranges	2 435	(4.3)	4
Pears	469	(3.8)	4
Pig meat	2 175	(2.6)	4

Minerals

Iron & ferro-alloys
- Chrome
- Cobalt
- Iron Ore
- Manganese
- Nickel Ore

Non-ferrous metals
- Bauxite (Aluminium)
- Copper
- Lead
- Tin
- Zinc
- Uranium

Precious metals
- Silver

Fertilizers
- Phosphates
- Potash

Structure
- Pre-Cambrian shield
- Palaeozoic folding
- Cenozoic folding
- Igneous structures

Projection: Bonne

Energy

- Oil
- Natural gas
- Coal and lignite
- Nuclear power
- Hydro-electric power

Energy production per capita 1997
million tonnes of oil equivalent
- Over 15
- 10-15
- 5-10
- 0.5-5
- Less than 0.5

COPYRIGHT GEORGE PHILIP LTD

POLAR REGIONS

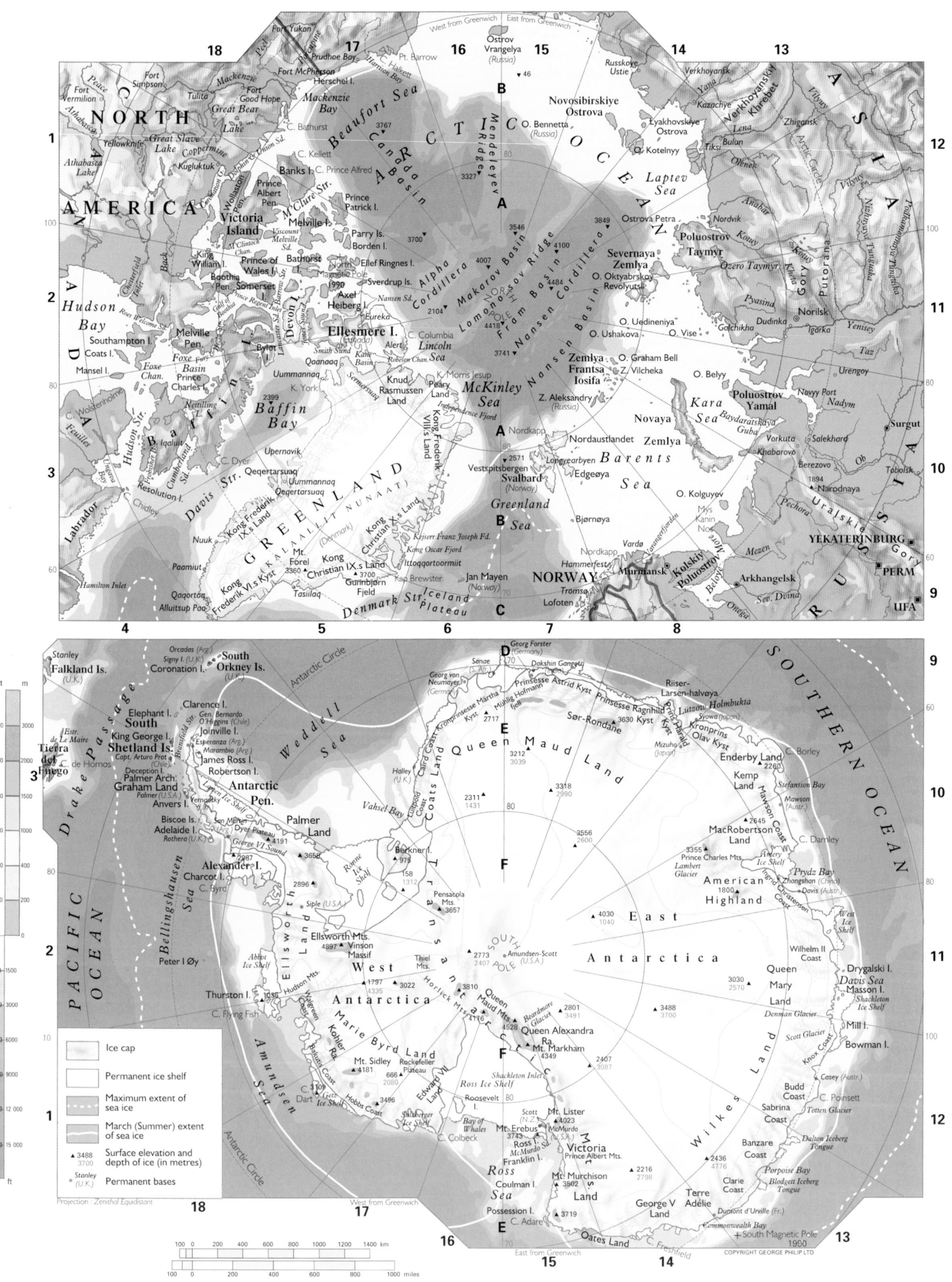

A–Z
COUNTRY
BY
COUNTRY

SETTLEMENTS

▣ **PARIS**   ▣ **Berne**   ◉ **Livorno**   ◎ Brugge   ◎ Algeciras   ○ *Frejus*   ○ *Oberammergau*   ○ *Thira*

Settlement symbols and type styles vary according to the scale of each map and indicate the importance
of towns on the map rather than specific population figures

∴ Ruins or archaeological sites   ⌣ Wells in desert

ADMINISTRATION

───── International boundaries

─ ─ ─ ─ International boundaries
(undefined or disputed)

┄┄┄┄ Internal boundaries

Country names

NICARAGUA

Administrative
area names

LOUISIANA

International boundaries show the *de facto* situation where there are rival claims to territory

COMMUNICATIONS

───── Principal roads

───── Other roads

─┤┄┄├─ Road tunnels

⌣ Passes

✈ Airfields

───── Principal railways

─ ─ ─ Railways
under construction

───── Other railways

─┤┄┄├─ Railway tunnels

┄┄┄┄┄ Principal canals

PHYSICAL FEATURES

───── Perennial streams

─ ─ ─ Intermittent streams

⬭ Perennial lakes

⬭ Intermittent lakes

Swamps and marshes

Permanent ice
and glaciers

▲ 8848 Elevations in metres

▼ 8500 Sea depths in metres

1134 Height of lake surface
above sea level in metres

Introduced in December 1992, this flag uses the colours of the Mujaheddin ('holy warriors') who fought against Afghanistan's socialist government from the 1970s. The flag bears the new national arms of the country.

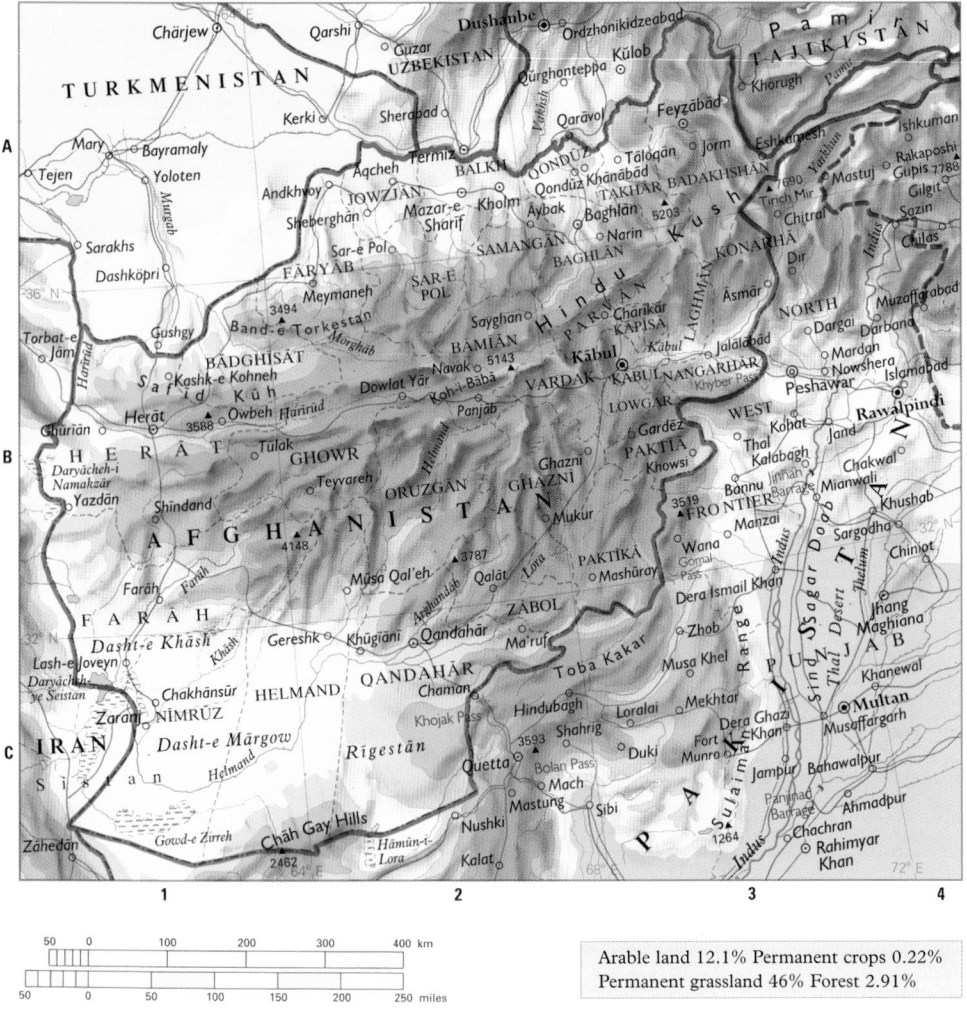

Arable land 12.1% Permanent crops 0.22%
Permanent grassland 46% Forest 2.91%

History

In ancient times, Afghanistan was invaded by Aryans, Persians, Greeks and Macedonians, and warrior armies from central Asia. Arab armies introduced Islam in the late 7th century. Afghanistan has always occupied a strategic position since the Khyber Pass was both the gateway to India and the back door to Russia. The modern history of the country began in 1747, when the various tribes in the region united for the first time, though a civil war was fought between 1819 and 1835 as rival factions struggled for power. In 1839, British troops invaded Afghanistan to reduce Russian influence. Over the following 80 years, Britain fought three Anglo-Afghan wars to maintain control of the region. The British finally withdrew in 1921, when Afghanistan became independent.

Politics

In 1964, Afghanistan adopted a democratic constitution, but the country's ruler, King Zahir, and the legislature failed to agree on reforms. In 1973, Muhammad Daoud Khan, the king's cousin, seized power and abolished the monarchy. He ruled as president until 1978, when he was killed during a left-wing coup. The new regime's socialist policies, which conflicted with Islam, provoked a rebellion. On Christmas Day 1987, Soviet troops invaded Afghanistan to support the left-wing regime. The subsequent Soviet occupation led to a bitter and protracted civil war. Various Muslim groups united behind the banner of the Mujaheddin ('holy warriors') to wage a guerrilla campaign, financed by the United States and aided by Pakistan. Soviet forces were forced to withdraw in 1989. By 1992, the Mujaheddin had defeated the left-wing regime. One of the Muslim factions, called the Taliban ('students'), emerged as the dominant group. By the end of the century, they controlled 90% of the land. However, in the north, ethnic and religious minorities, who feared Taliban domination held out.

Geography

The Republic of Afghanistan is a landlocked country. The three main physical regions are the central highlands, the south-western lowlands and the northern plains. The central highlands, comprising most of the Hindu Kush and its foothills, with several snow-capped peaks rising to more than 6,400 m [21,000 ft], cover nearly three-quarters of the country. Most Afghans live in the deep, narrow valleys of the highlands.

Much of the land in the south-west is desert, although the restoration of canals has brought fertility to parts of the Helmand River valley. The plains and hill country in the north, near the borders of Turkmenistan, Uzbekistan and Tajikistan, contain most of the country's limited agricultural land.

Climate

The height of the land and the country's remote position have a great effect on the climate. In winter, northerly winds bring cold, snowy weather to the mountains, but summers are hot and dry.

Economy

Afghanistan is one of the world's poorest countries. About 60% of the people make a living by farming. Many people are semi-nomadic, moving around with their herds of sheep and other animals. Wheat is the chief crop. Afghanistan has many mineral deposits, but most are undeveloped. Natural gas is produced, together with some coal, copper, gold, precious stones and salt. There are few factories. The main exports are karakul skins (which are used to make hats and jackets), cotton, dried fruit and nuts, fresh fruit and natural gas.

AFGHANISTAN (KABUL)

The climate of Afghanistan is governed more by altitude than by latitude. From December to March, air masses come from the continental north, bringing cold weather and snow on the mountains. June to September is hot and dry, with the east getting rain from a weakened monsoon. The temperature at Kabul, at 2,000 m [6,000 ft], ranges from −5°C to 25°C [23–77°F]. There are over 10 hours of sunshine daily, May to August.

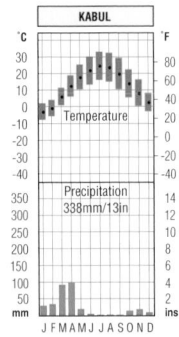

AREA
652,090 sq km
[251,772 sq mls]
POPULATION
24,792,000
CAPITAL (POPULATION)
Kabul (1,565,000)
GOVERNMENT
Islamic republic
ETHNIC GROUPS
Pashtun ('Pathan') 52%,
Tajik 20%, Uzbek 9%,
Hazara 9%, Chahar 3%,
Turkmen 2%, Baluchi 1%
LANGUAGES
Pashto, Dari/Persian
(both official), Uzbek
RELIGIONS
Islam (Sunni Muslim 74%,
Shiite Muslim 25%)
CURRENCY
Afghani = 100 puls

Albania's official name, Shqiperia, means 'Land of the Eagle', and the black double eagle was the emblem of the 15th-century hero Scanderbeg. A star placed above the eagle in 1946 was removed in 1992 when a non-Communist government was formed.

Geography

The Republic of Albania lies in the Balkan Peninsula. It faces the Adriatic Sea in the west and is bordered by Yugoslavia (Serbia and Montenegro), Macedonia and Greece. About 70% of the land is mountainous, with the highest point, Korab, reaching 2,764 m [9,068 ft] on the Macedonian border. Most Albanians live in the west on the coastal lowlands. This is the main farming region. Albania lies in an earthquake zone and severe earthquakes occur occasionally.

Climate

The coastal areas of Albania have a typical Mediterranean climate, with fairly dry, sunny summers and cool, moist winters. The mountains have a severe climate, with heavy winter snowfalls.

History

In ancient times, Albania was part of a region called Illyria. In 167 BC, it became part of the Roman Empire. When the Roman Empire broke up in 395, much of Albania became part of the Eastern Roman, or Byzantine, Empire. The country was subsequently conquered by Goths, Bulgarians, Slavs and Normans, although southern Albania remained part of the Byzantine Empire until 1204. In the 14th century, much of Albania became part of the Serbian Empire. In the 15th century, a leader named Scanderbeg, now regarded as a national hero, successfully led the Albanians against the invading Ottoman Turks. But after he died in 1468, the Turks took over the country. Albania became part of the Ottoman Empire until 1912, when Albania declared its independence.

Italy invaded Albania in 1939, but German forces took over the country in 1943. At the end of World War II, an Albanian People's Republic was formed under the Communist leaders who had led the partisans against the Germans. Pursuing a modernization programme on rigid Stalinist lines, the regime of Enver Hoxha at various times associated politically and often economically with Yugoslavia (up to 1948), the Soviet Union (1948–61) and China (1961–77), before following a fiercely independent policy. After Hoxha died in 1985, his successor, Ramiz Alia, continued the dictator's austere policies, but by the end of the decade, even Albania was affected by the sweeping changes in Eastern Europe.

Politics

In 1990, the more progressive wing of the Communist Party, led by Ramiz Alia, won the struggle for power. The new government instituted a wide programme of reform, including the legalization of religion, the encouragement of foreign investment, the introduction of a free market for peasants' produce, and the establishment of pluralist democracy. The Communists comfortably retained their majority in elections in April 1991, but the government was brought down two months later by a general strike. An interim coalition 'national salvation' committee took over, but collapsed within six months. Elections in 1992 finally brought to an end the last Communist regime in Europe when the non-Communist Democratic Party won power. In 1997, amid a financial crisis caused by the collapse of fraudulent pyramid-selling schemes, fresh elections took place which returned a socialist-led government to power.

Economy

Albania is Europe's poorest country. In the early 1990s, agriculture employed 56% of the people. The land was divided into large collective and state farms, but private ownership has been encouraged since 1991. Major crops include fruits, maize, olives, potatoes, sugar beet, vegetables and wheat. Livestock farming is also important.

Albania has some mineral reserves, such as chromite, copper and nickel, which are exported. The country also has some oil, brown coal and hydroelectricity, and a few heavy industries.

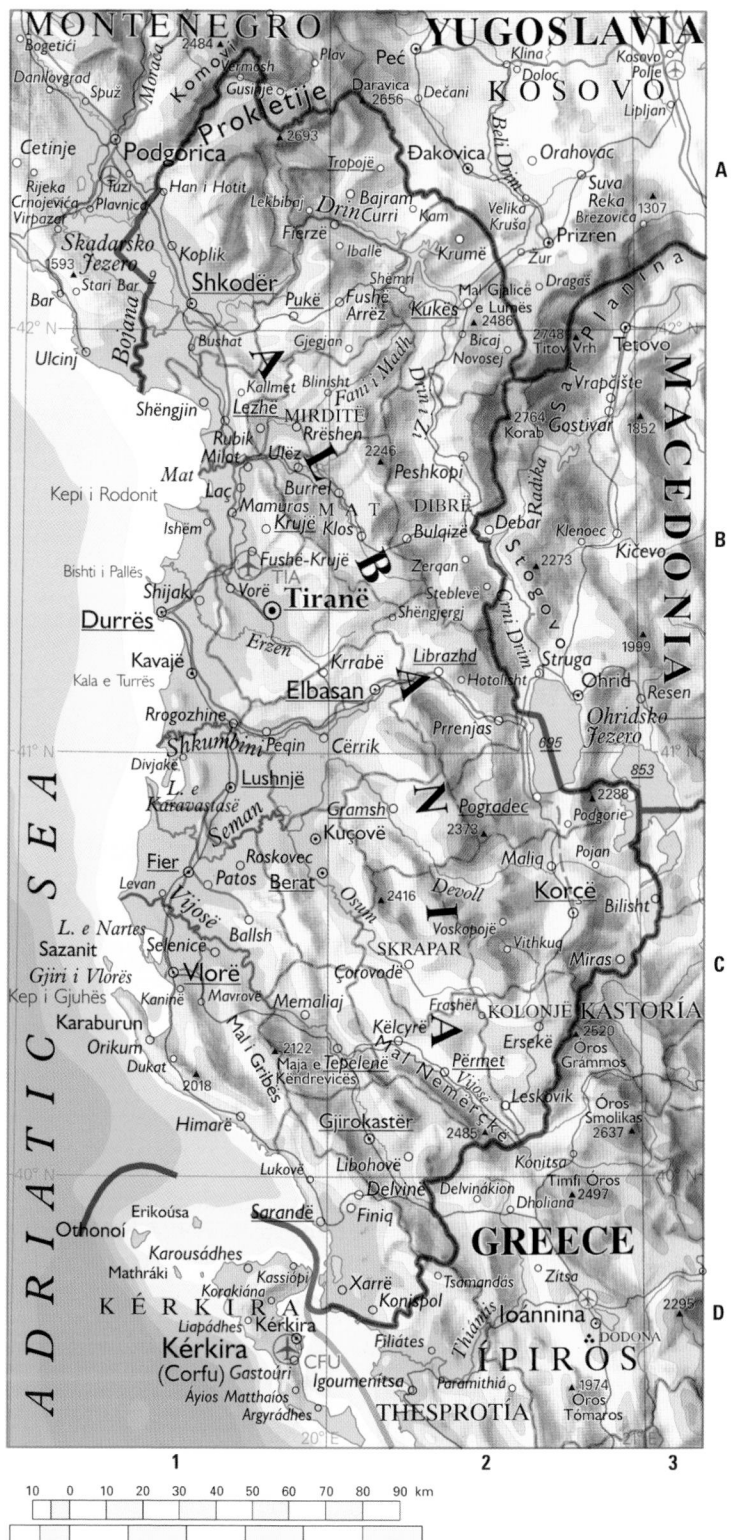

AREA
28,750 sq km [11,100 sq mls]
POPULATION
3,331,000
CAPITAL (POPULATION)
Tirana (Tiranë, 251,000)
GOVERNMENT
Multiparty republic
ETHNIC GROUPS
Albanian 98%, Greek 1.8%,

Macedonian, Montenegrin, Gypsy
LANGUAGES
Albanian (official)
RELIGIONS
Many are non-believers; of the believers, 65% follow Islam and 33% follow Christianity (Orthodox 20%, R. Catholic 13%)
CURRENCY
Lek = 100 qindars

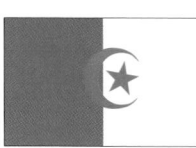

The star and crescent and the colour green on Algeria's flag are traditional symbols of the Islamic religion. The liberation movement which fought for independence from French rule from 1954 used this flag. It became the national flag when Algeria became independent in 1962.

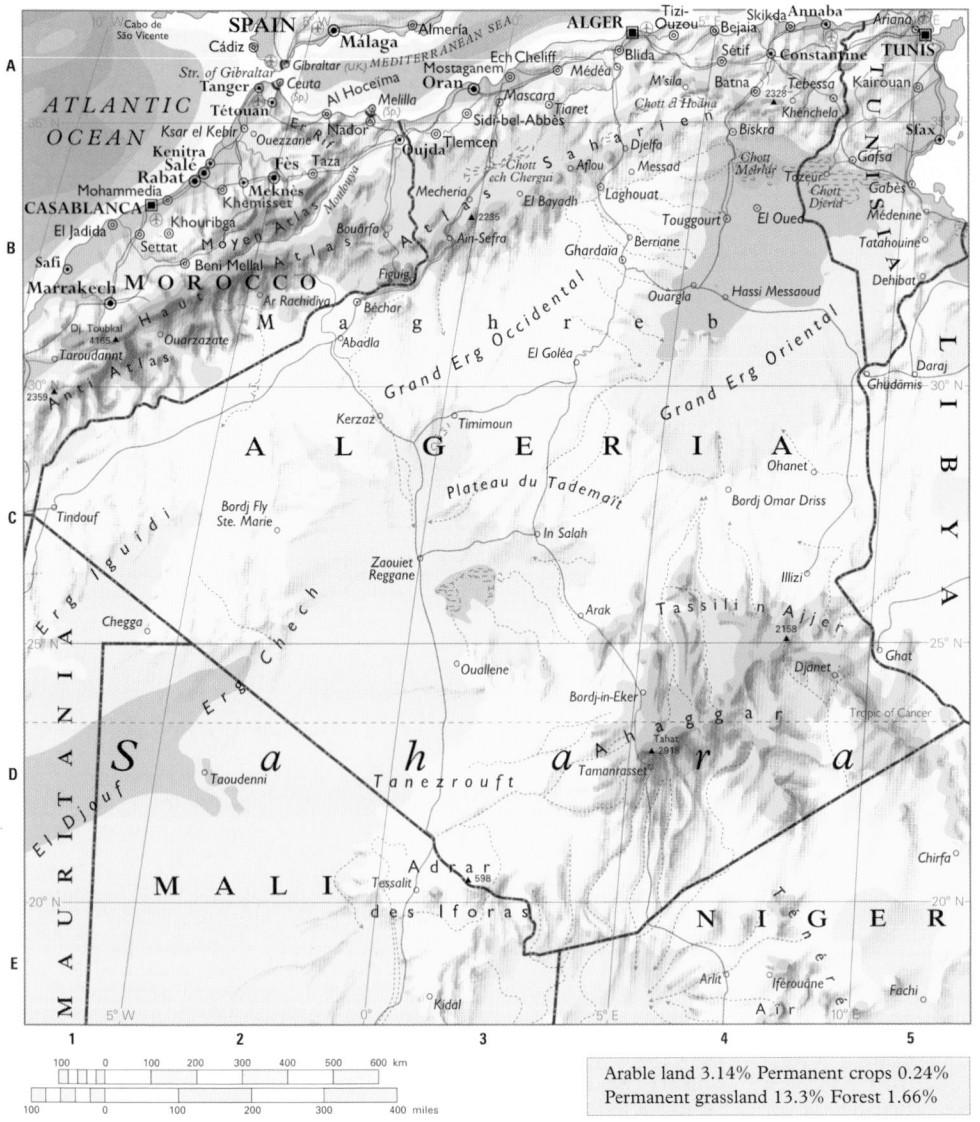

Arable land 3.14% Permanent crops 0.24%
Permanent grassland 13.3% Forest 1.66%

History

In early times, the region came under such rulers as the Phoenicians, Carthaginians, Romans and Vandals. Arabs invaded the area in the AD 600s, converting the local Berbers to Islam and introducing Arabic. Inter marriage has made it difficult to distinguish Arabs from Berbers by ancestry, though Berber dialects are still spoken. A law, effective from July 1998 making Arabic the only language allowed in public life, met with much opposition in Berber-speaking areas.

Politics

Like its neighbours Morocco and Tunisia, Algeria experienced French colonial rule and colonization by settlers. Algeria achieved independence in 1962, following years of bitter warfare between nationalist guerrillas and French armed forces. After independence, the socialist FLN (National Liberation Party) formed a one-party government. Opposition parties were permitted in 1989 and, in 1991, a Muslim party, the FIS (Islamic Salvation Front) won an election. The FLN cancelled the election results and declared a state of emergency. Terrorist activities mounted and, between 1991 and 1999, about 100,000 people were killed. A proposal to ban political parties based on religion was approved in a referendum in 1996. In 1999, Abdelaziz Bouteflika, the candidate who was thought to be favoured by the army, was elected president, although his victory appeared hollow, because his six opponents withdrew prior to the election, alleging fraud.

Economy

Algeria is a developing country, whose main income comes from its two main natural resources, oil and natural gas, which were discovered in the Sahara in 1956. Its natural gas reserves are among the world's largest. Since independence, oil and gas have accounted for around two-thirds of the country's total revenues and more than 90% of the exports. Algeria's crude oil refining capacity is the biggest in Africa. Other manufactured products include cement, iron and steel, textiles and vehicles. While most larger industries are state-owned, much of light industry is under private control.

Agriculture employs about 16% of the population. Barley, citrus fruits, dates, potatoes and wheat are the major crops. Cattle, goats and sheep are raised by Berber nomads, who live in the north-east. Many people work abroad due to the high level of unemployment.

Geography

The People's Democratic Republic of Algeria is Africa's second largest country after Sudan. Most Algerians live in the north, on the fertile coastal plains and hill country. South of this region lie high plateaux and ranges of the Atlas Mountains. Four-fifths of Algeria is in the Sahara, the world's largest desert. Most people in the Sahara live at oases, where springs and wells supply water.

Climate

The coast has a Mediterranean climate, with warm and dry summers and mild and moist winters. The northern highlands have warmer summers and colder winters. The arid Sahara is hot by day and cool at night. The yearly rainfall is less than 200 mm [8 in].

ALGERIA (ALGIERS)

Algiers is exposed to the maritime influences of the Mediterranean Sea, but is sheltered from the Sahara to the south by the Atlas Mountains. The temperature range is very small: annual 13°C [23°F]; diurnal 6°C [11°F]. Frosts have not been recorded. Rainfall has a winter maximum typical of the Mediterranean region, with amounts varying greatly from year to year. The mountains to the south are often snow-covered in winter.

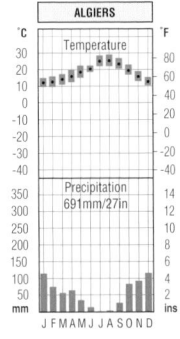

AREA	ETHNIC GROUPS
2,381,740 sq km	Arab 83%, Berber 16%
[919,590 sq mls]	LANGUAGES
POPULATION	Arabic (official),
30,481,000	Berber, French
CAPITAL (POPULATION)	RELIGIONS
Algiers (Alger, 1,722,000)	Sunni Muslim 98%
GOVERNMENT	CURRENCY
Socialist republic	Algerian dinar = 100 centimes

AMERICAN SAMOA – SEE PACIFIC OCEAN, PAGES 174–178;
ANDORRA – SEE SPAIN, PAGES 206–208

The flag is based on the flag of the MPLA (the Popular Movement for the Liberation of Angola) during the independence struggle. The emblem includes a star symbolizing socialism, one half of a gearwheel to represent industry, and a machete symbolizing agriculture.

Geography

The Republic of Angola is a large country, more than twice the size of France, on the south-western coast of Africa. Most of the country is part of the plateau that forms most of southern Africa, with a narrow coastal plain in the west.

Angola has many rivers. In the north-east, several rivers flow northwards to become tributaries of the River Congo, while in the south, some rivers, including the Cubango (Okavango) and the Cuanda, flow south-eastwards into inland drainage basins in the interior of Africa.

Climate

Angola has a tropical climate, with temperatures of over 20°C [68°F] all year round, though upland areas are cooler. The coastal regions are dry, increasingly so to the south of Luanda, but the rainfall increases to the north and east. The rainy season is between November and April. Tropical forests flourish in the north, but the vegetation along the coast is sparse, with semi-desert in the south.

History

Bantu-speaking peoples from the north settled in Angola around 2,000 years ago. In the late 15th century, Portuguese navigators, seeking a route to Asia around Africa, explored the coast and, in the early 16th century, the Portuguese set up bases.

Angola became important as a source of slaves for Brazil, Portugal's huge colony in South America. After the decline of the slave trade, Portuguese settlers began to develop the land. The Portuguese population increased gently in the 20th century.

In the 1950s, local nationalists began to demand independence. In 1956, the MPLA (Popular Movement for the Liberation of Angola) was founded with support from the Mbundu and mestizos (people of African and European descent). The MPLA led a revolt in Luanda in 1961, but it was put down by Portuguese troops.

Other opposition groups developed. In the north, the Kongo set up the FNLA (Front for the Liberation of Angola), while, in 1966, southern peoples, including many Ovimbundu, formed UNITA (National Union for the Total Independence of Angola).

Politics

The Portuguese agreed to grant Angola independence in 1975, after which rival nationalist forces began a struggle for power. A long-running civil war developed between the government forces, which received aid from the Soviet Union and Cuba, the FNLA in the north and UNITA in the south. As the war developed, both the FNLA and UNITA turned to the West for support, while UNITA received support from South Africa. FNLA guerrilla activity ended in 1984, but UNITA took control of large areas. Economic progress was hampered not only by the vast spending on defence and security, but also by the MPLA government's austere Marxist policies.

In 1991, a peace accord was agreed and multiparty elections were held, in which the MPLA, which had renounced Marxism-Leninism and was liberalizing the economy, won a majority. However, UNITA's leaders rejected the election result and civil war resumed in 1994. In 1997, a coalition government was formed, but the UNITA leader, Jonas Savimbi, failed to participate. Full-scale civil war was resumed in 1999.

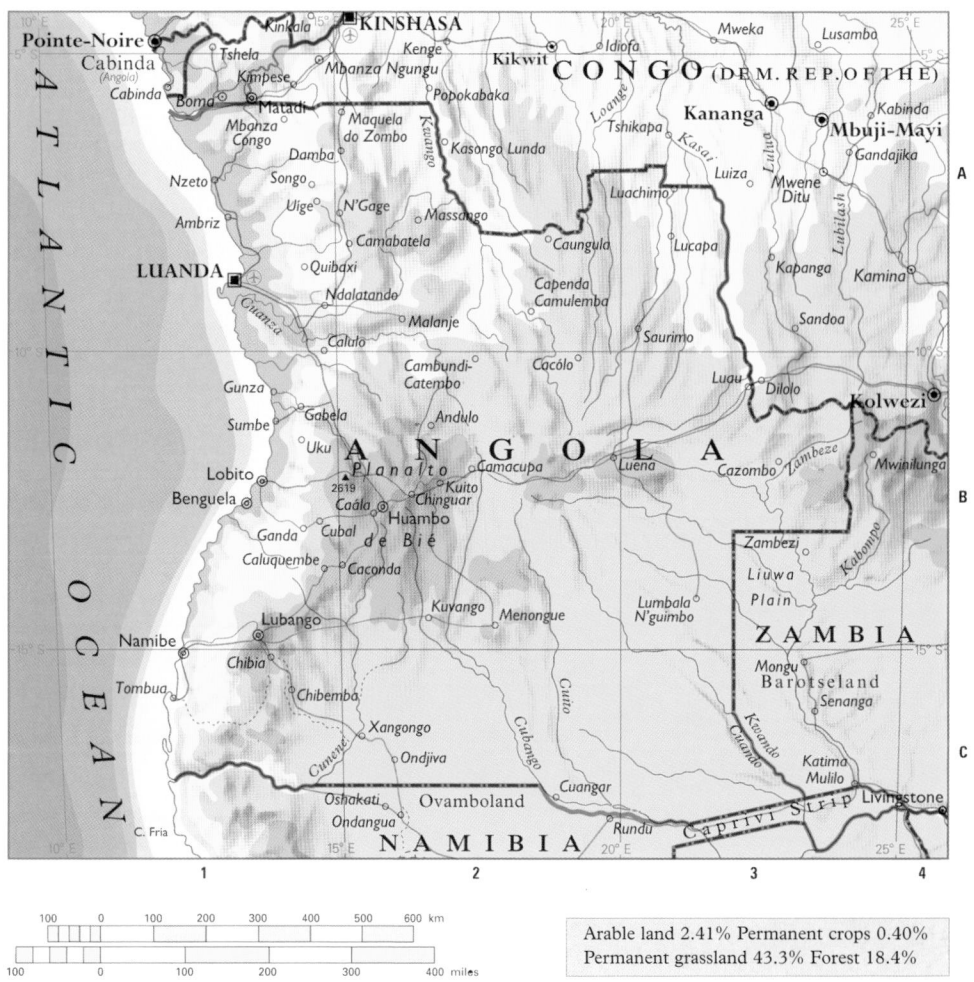

Arable land 2.41% Permanent crops 0.40%
Permanent grassland 43.3% Forest 18.4%

Economy

Angola is a developing country, where 70% of the people are poor farmers, although agriculture contributes only about 9% of the gross domestic product. The main food crops include cassava, maize, sweet potatoes and beans, while bananas, coffee, palm products, seed cotton and sugar cane are grown for export. Cattle are the leading livestock, but sheep and goats are raised in drier areas.

Despite the poverty of most of its people and its low per capita GNP ($260 in 1997), Angola has much economic potential. It has oil reserves near Luanda and in the enclave of Cabinda, which is separated from Angola by a strip of land belonging to the Democratic Republic of Congo. Oil and mineral fuels are the leading exports. Other resources include diamonds (the second most important export), copper and manganese. Angola also has a growing industrial sector. Manufactures include cement, chemicals, processed food and textiles.

AREA	Kongo 13%, Luimbe-Nganguela
1,246,700 sq km	5%, Nyaneka-Humbe 5%,
[481,351 sq mls]	Chokwe, Luvale, Luchazi
POPULATION	**LANGUAGES**
11,200,000	Portuguese (official)
CAPITAL (POPULATION)	**RELIGIONS**
Luanda (2,250,000)	Christianity (Roman Catholic
GOVERNMENT	69%, Protestant 20%),
Multiparty republic	traditional beliefs 10%
ETHNIC GROUPS	**CURRENCY**
Ovimbundu 37%, Mbundu 22%,	Kwanza = 100 lwei

ANGUILLA – SEE CARIBBEAN SEA, PAGES 71–76;
ANTIGUA AND BARBUDA – SEE CARIBBEAN SEA, PAGES 71–76

ARGENTINA

The 'celeste' (sky blue) and white stripes were the symbols of independence around the city of Buenos Aires, where an independent government was set up in 1810. It became the national flag in 1816. The gold May Sun was added two years later.

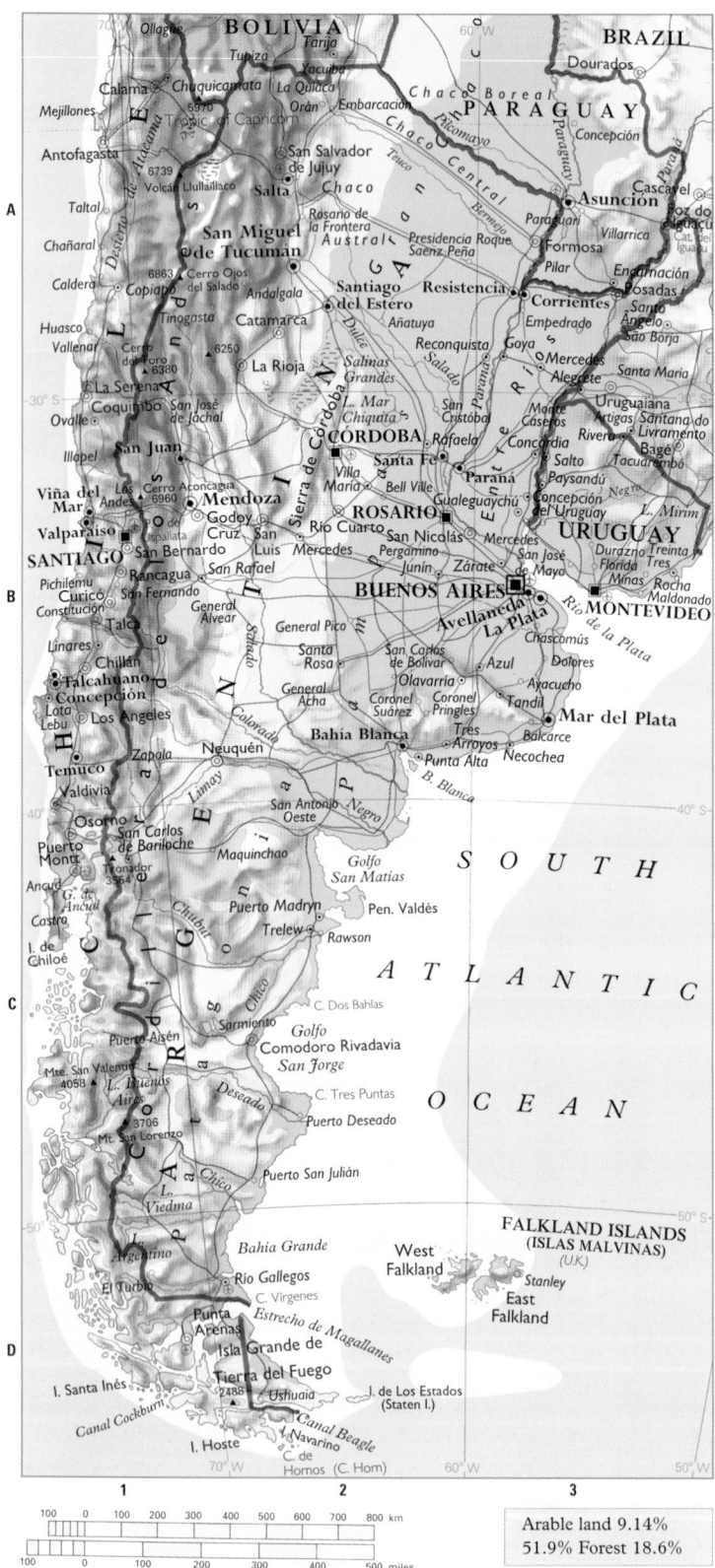

Arable land 9.14%
51.9% Forest 18.6%

Geography

The Argentine Republic, the largest of South America's Spanish-speaking countries, is less than a third of the size of Brazil. Its western boundary lies in the Andes, which includes basins, ridges and peaks of more than 6,000 m [19,685 ft] in the north. South of latitude 27°S, the ridges merge into a single high cordillera, where Aconcagua, at 6,960 m [22,834 ft], is the tallest mountain in the western hemisphere. In the south, the Andes are lower, with glaciers and volcanoes. Eastern Argentina is a series of alluvial plains, stretching from the Andean foothills to the sea. The Gran Chaco in the north slopes down to the Paraná River, from the high desert in the Andean foothills to lowland swamp forest. Between the Paraná and Uruguay rivers is Mesopotamia, a fertile region. Further south are the pampa grasslands, which are damp and fertile near Buenos Aires and drier, but still productive, elsewhere. To the south, the pampa gives way to the dry, windswept plateaux of Patagonia that extend towards Tierra del Fuego.

Climate

The climate varies from subtropical in the north to temperate in the south. Rainfall is abundant in the north-east, but is lower to the west and south. Patagonia is a dry region, crossed by rivers that rise in the Andes.

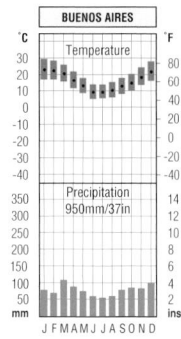

ARGENTINA (BUENOS AIRES)

Argentina, which stretches from the tropics almost into Antarctica, with the Andes to the west and lying between the two oceans, experiences a number of climates. The north is subtropical, with temperatures around 20°C [68°F] in June and 25°C [77°F] in January. The south is temperate, with May to August above freezing, and 10°C [50°F] in January or February. Rainfall is heaviest in the subtropical north-east.

History

The first inhabitants of Argentina were Native Americans, though population densities were low by comparison with most of the rest of South America. In the pampa and in Patagonia, the people were nomadic hunters and gatherers, but farming communities existed in the north-west and the north-eastern forests. Spanish explorers first reached the coast in 1516, landing on the shores of the Rio de la Plata. They were soon followed by others in search of gold and silver. European settlement in Argentina, a name meaning 'land of silver', was concentrated at first in the north-west around Salta and San Miguel de Tucumán, which had strong links to Peru. This area is unusual today in retaining a large mestizo (mixed Amerindian and Spanish) population, a remnant of colonial times. Buenos Aires was founded in 1580. When it was accepted that the new Spanish territory lacked mineral wealth, the Spaniards began to develop agriculture by introducing cattle, horses and sheep. Before long, the settlements in the north-west began to develop economically by supplying animals, cloth and food to the mining settlements in Peru.

In 1776, Argentina, Paraguay, Uruguay and southern Bolivia were disengaged from Peru to form a separate viceroyalty, with its administrative centre at Buenos Aires which became a major trading city. In 1810, Buenos Aires declared itself independent and set up a government to administer the United Provinces of the Rio de la Plata, as the region was called, but Uruguay, Bolivia and Paraguay eventually broke away. In 1812, an Argentine general, José de San Martín, began an armed struggle against Spain and, in 1816, representatives of the Argentine provinces officially declared the country's independence. The new nation was then named the United Provinces of La Plata. In 1817, San Martín led an expedition across the Andes and defeated the Spaniards in Chile. His forces went on to conquer the Spaniards in Peru. Following independence, the people in Buenos Aires were in conflict with rural landowners, who wanted more control over their affairs. Following a period of dictatorship between 1829 and 1852, the country adopted a new constitution in 1853. This constitution, based largely on that of the USA, gave the provinces the right to control their own affairs. At first, Buenos Aires refused to enter the confederation, but it joined in 1862, becoming capital of the country, which had been renamed Argentina in 1860.

Early prosperity, based on stock raising and farming, combined with stable government, was boosted from 1870 by a massive influx of European immigrants, particularly Italians and Spaniards, for whom Argentina was a real alternative to the United States. They settled lands recently cleared of Native Americans and often organized by huge land companies. Britain provided much of the capital and some of the immigrants, especially people from Wales, who are still identifiable in Patagonia today, speaking their own language. Development of a good railway network to the ports, plus steamship services to Europe, and, from 1877, refrigerated vessels, helped to create the strong meat, wool and wheat economy that carried Argentina through its formative years and into the 20th century. Before the Great Depression in the 1930s, Argentina was one of the world's more prosperous nations.

Politics

The collapse in the economy during the Great Depression led to a military coup in 1930. This started a long period of military intervention in the politics of the country. During World War II, Argentina openly favoured Germany, Italy and Japan, though it declared war on the Axis powers in March 1945. In 1943, another coup enabled Colonel Juan Peron, the minister of labour, to win popular support, because he then strengthened the unions and helped urban workers to obtain higher wages and better working conditions. Peron was elected president in 1946 and his second wife, Eva, served as his assistant until her death in 1952. Peron greatly increased government expenditure and, as the economic situation worsened, he restricted civil rights. Peron began his second term in 1952, but he lost the support of the Roman Catholic Church after he restricted its authority. In 1955, Peron fled the country after a rebellion by the armed forces. Elections were held in 1958, but another coup occurred in 1962. A series of military and civilian governments then held power until 1972. In 1973, a supporter of Peron, Hector Jose Campora, was elected president, but he resigned later in the year when Peron returned to Argentina. Peron was elected president, but following his death in 1974, his third wife, Isabel, took office. By then the economy was out of control. Soaring inflation and terrorism by extremist groups became widespread. Isabel Peron was arrested in 1976 and a military government was established.

The period from 1976 – the so-called 'dirty war' – saw the torture, wrongful imprisonment and murder ('disappearance') of up to 15,000 people by the military. Up to 2 million people fled the country. In 1982, the government, blamed for the poor state of the economy, launched an invasion of the Falkland Islands, which they had claimed since 1820. Britain regained the islands, which Argentines call Islas Malvinas, by sending an expeditionary force. Argentina's President Galtieri

resigned. Constitutional government was restored in 1983 under President Raul Alfonsin, leader of the Radical Party, though the army remained influential. Argentina's economic problems – with their classic Latin American causes of reliance on certain commodities, big borrowing and maladministration – were inherited by his Peronist successor, Carlos Menem, in 1989. His austerity programme took Argentina through inflation rates of 3,084% and 2,314% down to 85% by 1991. This was stable money by previous standards. Menem also granted pardons to some of the people who had been imprisoned and he launched a privatization programme, selling off many government businesses to private owners.

For much of the decade, the economy boomed. Menem was re-elected in 1995, but, having completed two successive terms, he was forced to stand down in 1999 after the onset of a severe economic depression. Menem's chosen successor, Edward Duhalde, was defeated by the conservative Fernando de la Rua, who headed the Alianza Party, an alliance of centre and centre-left parties. One of the new president's main problems was how to gain support for his programme of fiscal austerity while his Justicialist (Peronist) Party opponents controlled the Congress. In 1999, Argentina and Britain signed an agreement concerning the Falkland Islands, the first since 1982. Under the agreement, Argentines were allowed to visit the Falkland Islands and erect a memorial to their war dead, while Argentina agreed to allow flights from the Falkland Islands to Chile.

Economy

According to the World Bank, Argentina is an 'upper-middle-income' developing country. It is one of the richest countries in South America in terms of natural resources, especially its fertile farmland, while its population – though remarkably urban, with 87% living in cities and towns – is not growing at anything like the rates seen in most of Africa and Asia. (In the 1990s, the rate of population increase was about 1.2% per annum, as compared with the world average of 1.57%.)

Argentina's population, predominantly European and predominantly middle-class, nevertheless relies on an economic base that is mainly agricultural. The richest farmland is found in the pampa and Mesopotamia, where the chief products are beef, maize and wheat. Sheep are raised in drier parts of the country, while other crops include citrus fruits, cotton, flax, grapes, potatoes, sorghum, sugar cane, sunflower seeds and tea. Many of the farms in Argentina are huge and mechanized. The owners of most of the large estates rent land to tenant farmers. However, many of the small farms in the north produce little more than what the farmers' families need to survive.

Oilfields in Patagonia and the Piedmont make Argentina almost self-sufficient in oil and natural gas, although much of the country's electricity supply is produced by hydroelectric plants. The country lacks the coal, iron ore and most of the minerals needed for industry, though some deposits of iron ore, lead, uranium and zinc are also mined. The chief industries are based on food products, such as beef, beer, flour, sugar, vegetable oil, wine, wool and hides. Other industries include the manufacture of cars, electrical equipment and textiles. Most consumer goods, such as food and household equipment, are produced in Argentina. However, many manufactures, including machinery, iron and steel and other items needed for production, together with transport equipment and chemical products, are imported. More than two-thirds of the country's factories are situated in or around Buenos Aires. Cordoba and Rosario are other industrial cities. Service industries, including transport and banking, which are heavily dependent on agriculture, employ more than half of the population.

The Pampas

'Pampa', or 'pampas', is a South American Quechua Indian term describing a flat featureless expanse. Although the term is applied to other flat areas in South America, including the desert in northern Chile, pampa is the most commonly used name for the broad grassy plains of central Argentina, between the Gran Chaco to the north and Patagonia to the south. From west to east, they stretch between the eastern flanks of the Andes to the Atlantic Ocean. Covering an area of about 760,000 sq km [295,000 sq mls], the Argentine pampa represents, geologically, outwash fans of rubble, sand, silt and clay, eroded from the Andes, washed down by torrents and redistributed by wind and water. Fine soils cover huge expanses of the pampa, providing good deep soils in the well-watered areas, such as the Buenos Aires region in the east. But where rainfall and ground water are lacking, scrub and sandy desert are the result, such as the dry pampa in the west, including most of La Pampa Province, which is largely barren, with sandy deserts and large saline areas.

Spanish settlers introduced horses and cattle, and later the best areas of pampa were enclosed for cattle ranching and cultivation. Now the pampas are almost entirely converted to rangelands growing turf grasses, or to huge fields producing alfalfa, maize, wheat and flax.

AREA	ETHNIC GROUPS
2,766,890 sq km	European 85%,
[1,068,296 sq mls]	Mestizo, Amerindian
POPULATION	**LANGUAGES**
36,265,000	Spanish (official)
CAPITAL (POPULATION)	**RELIGIONS**
Buenos Aires	Christianity
(10,990,000)	(Roman Catholic 92%)
GOVERNMENT	**CURRENCY**
Federal republic	Peso = 10,000 australs

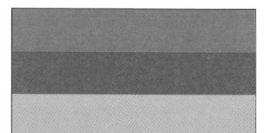

Armenia's flag was first used between 1918 and 1922, when the country was an independent republic. It was readopted on 24 August 1990. The red represents the blood shed in the past, the blue the land of Armenia, and the orange the courage of the people.

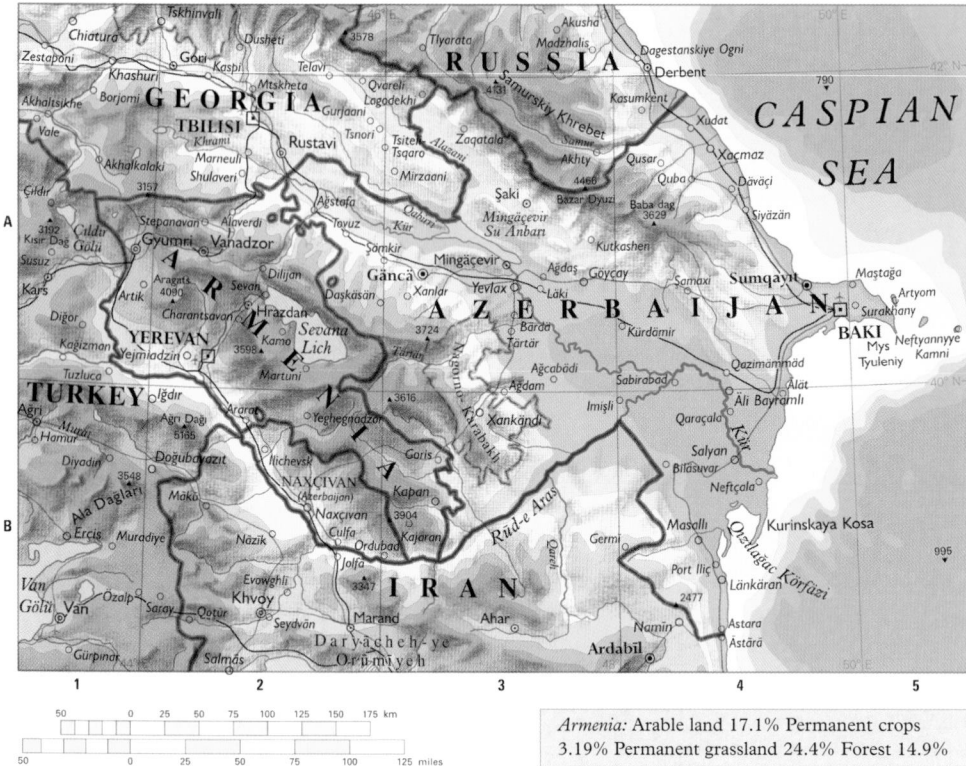

Armenia: Arable land 17.1% Permanent crops 3.19% Permanent grassland 24.4% Forest 14.9%

I, the Turks deported many Armenians, fearing they would support Russia. An independent Armenian republic was set up in the area held by Russia in 1918, but the western part of historic Armenia remained in Turkey, and another area was held by Iran.

In 1920, Armenia became a Communist republic. In 1922, it became, with Azerbaijan and Georgia, part of the Transcaucasian Republic within the Soviet Union. But the three territories became separate Soviet Socialist Republics in 1936. After the break-up of the Soviet Union in 1991, Armenia became an independent republic. Fighting broke out over Nagorno-Karabakh, an area enclosed by Azerbaijan where the majority of the people are Armenians. In 1992, Armenia occupied the territory between itself and Nagorno-Karabakh. A cease-fire in 1994 left Armenia in control of about 20% of Azerbaijan's land area.

The World Bank classifies Armenia as a 'lower-middle-income economy'. Conflict with Azerbaijan in the early 1990s damaged the economy, but since 1991 the government has encouraged free enterprise, by selling farmland and government-owned businesses.

Geography and Climate

The Republic of Armenia is a landlocked country, mostly consisting of a plateau, criss-crossed by faults. Movements along the faults cause earth tremors and occasionally major earthquakes. Armenia's highest point is Mount Aragats, at 4,090 m [13,149 ft].

The height of the land gives rise to severe winters and cool summers. The highest peaks are snow-capped, but the total yearly rainfall is low.

History, Politics and Economy

In the 19th century, Armenians suffered hardships under Turkish rule. The Turks killed hundreds of thousands of people. During World War

AREA	ETHNIC GROUPS
29,800 sq km	Armenian 93%, Azerbaijani 3%,
[11,506 sq mls]	Russian, Kurd
POPULATION	**LANGUAGES**
3,422,000	Armenian (official)
CAPITAL (POPULATION)	**RELIGIONS**
Yerevan	Christianity
(1,226,000)	(Armenian Apostolic)
GOVERNMENT	**CURRENCY**
Multiparty republic	Dram = 100 couma

AZERBAIJAN

Geography and Climate

Azerbaijan lies in south-west Asia, facing the Caspian Sea to the east. It includes the Naxçivan Autonomous Republic, an area cut off from the rest of Azerbaijan by Armenian territory. The Caucasus Mountains border Russia in the north.

Azerbaijan has hot summers and cool winters, with low rainfall on the plains and much higher rainfall in the highlands.

History and Politics

After the Russian Revolution of 1917, attempts were made to form a Transcaucasian Federation made up of Armenia, Azerbaijan and Georgia. When this failed, Azerbaijanis set up an independent state. But Russian forces occupied the area in 1920. In 1922, the Communists set up a Transcaucasian Republic consisting of Armenia, Azerbaijan and Georgia under Russian control. In 1936, the areas became separate Soviet Socialist Republics within the Soviet Union. Following the break-up of the Soviet Union in 1991, Azerbaijan became independent. Economic progress was slow, partly because of the conflict with Armenia over the enclave of Nagorno-Karabakh, a region in Azerbaijan where the majority of people are Armenians. A cease-fire in 1994 left Armenia in control of about 20% of Azerbaijan's area.

Economy

In the mid-1990s, the World Bank classified Azerbaijan as a 'lower-middle-income' economy. Yet, by the late 1990s, the oil reserves in the Baku area on the Caspian Sea, and in the sea itself, held great promise. Oil extraction and manufacturing, including oil refining and the production of chemicals, machinery and textiles, are now the most valuable activities.

AREA	ETHNIC GROUPS
86,600 sq km	Azerbaijani 83%, Russian 6%,
[33,436 sq mls]	Armenian 6%, Lezgin, Avar,
POPULATION	Ukrainian, Tatar
7,856,000	**LANGUAGES**
CAPITAL (POPULATION)	Azerbaijani (official)
Baku (Baki, 1,081,000)	**RELIGIONS**
GOVERNMENT	Islam
Federal multiparty	**CURRENCY**
republic	Manat = 100 gopik

ARUBA – SEE CARIBBEAN SEA, PAGES 71–76;
ASCENSION – SEE ATLANTIC OCEAN, PAGES 41–43

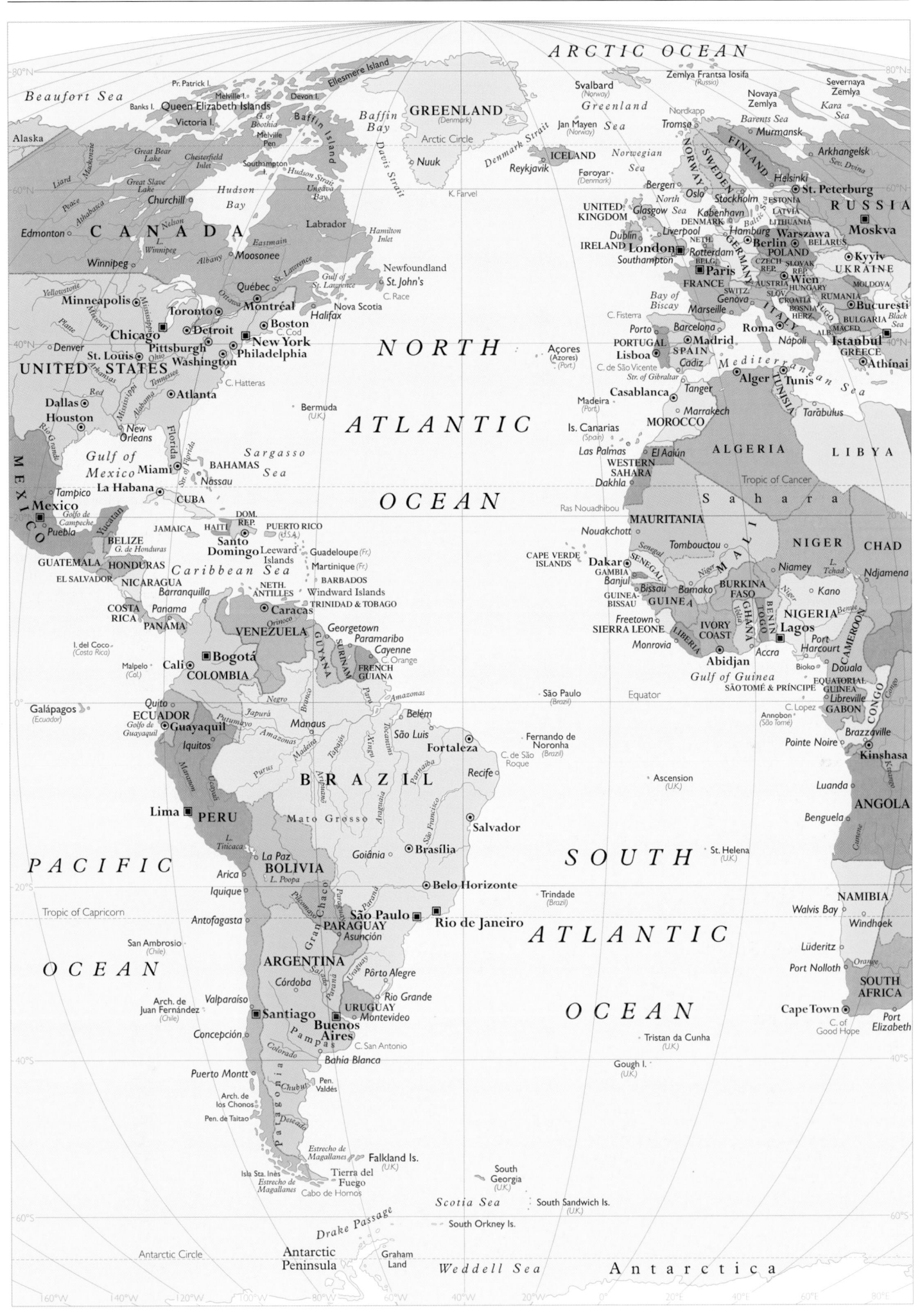

ARCTIC OCEAN

Beaufort Sea

Pr. Patrick I.
Ellesmere Island
Melville I.
Banks I. Queen Elizabeth Islands
Devon I.
Baffin Bay
GREENLAND (Denmark)
Svalbard (Norway)
Zemlya Frantsa Iosifa (Russia)
Severnaya Zemlya
Novaya Zemlya

Alaska
G. of Boothia
Victoria I.
Melville Pen.
Southampton
Baffin Island
Arctic Circle
Nuuk
Greenland
Jan Mayen (Norway)
Nordkapp
Tromsø
Murmansk
Barents Sea
Kara Sea

Great Bear Lake
Chesterfield Inlet
Hudson Strait
Davis Strait
Reykjavík
ICELAND
Norwegian Sea
Sev. Dvina
Arkhangelsk

Liard
Great Slave Lake
Hudson Bay
Ungava Bay
Denmark Strait
Føroyar (Denmark)
Bergen
North Sea
Oslo
Stockholm
NORWAY SWEDEN FINLAND
Helsinki
St. Peterburg
RUSSIA

Edmonton
Peace
Athabasca
Churchill
CANADA
Nelson
Labrador
Eastmain
K. Farvel
UNITED KINGDOM
Glasgow
København
DENMARK
Baltic Sea
ESTONIA
LATVIA
LITHUANIA
Moskva

Winnipeg
L. Winnipeg
Albany
Moosonee
Hamilton Inlet
Dublin
IRELAND
Liverpool
Southampton
NETH.
Hamburg
Berlin
Warszawa
POLAND
BELARUS
Kyyiv
UKRAINE

Yellowstone
Québec
St. Lawrence
Newfoundland
St. John's
London
Paris
BELG.
GERMANY
CZECH REP.
SLOVAK.
AUSTRIA
SLOV.
RUMANIA
MOLDOVA

Minneapolis
Missouri
Toronto
Montréal
Nova Scotia
C. Race
FRANCE
SWITZ.
Genova
ITALY
CROATIA
BOSNIA
HERZ.
YUGO
Bucureşti
Black Sea

Chicago
Detroit
Boston
C. Cod
New York
Halifax
Bay of Biscay
Marseille
Roma
Napoli
BULGARIA
MACED.
Istanbul

Denver
St. Louis
Pittsburgh
Washington
Philadelphia
Porto
Barcelona
Madrid
SPAIN
Athínai
GREECE

UNITED STATES
Ohio
Tennessee
Atlanta
C. Hatteras
Açores (Azores) (Port.)
PORTUGAL
Lisboa
Cádiz
C. de São Vicente
Str. of Gibraltar
Mediterranean Sea

Dallas
Houston
Mississippi
Alabama
Madeira (Port.)
Casablanca
Tanger
Alger
TUNISIA
Tunis

New Orleans
Red
Rio Grande
Florida
Bermuda (U.K.)
Is. Canarias (Spain)
Las Palmas
El Aaiún
MOROCCO
Marrakech
Tarābulus

MEXICO
Gulf of Mexico
Miami
Str. of Florida
BAHAMAS
Nassau
Sargasso Sea
NORTH ATLANTIC OCEAN
ALGERIA
LIBYA
WESTERN SAHARA
Dakhla
Sahara
Tropic of Cancer

Tampico
La Habana
CUBA
Ras Nouadhibou
Nouakchott
MAURITANIA

Mexico
Golfo de Campeche
Puebla
JAMAICA
HAITI
DOM. REP.
PUERTO RICO (U.S.A.)
Santo Domingo
Leeward Islands
Guadeloupe (Fr.)
CAPE VERDE ISLANDS
Tombouctou
MALI
NIGER
CHAD
Ndjamena

BELIZE
G. de Honduras
GUATEMALA
HONDURAS
Martinique (Fr.)
BARBADOS
Dakar
SENEGAL
Niamey

EL SALVADOR
NICARAGUA
Barranquilla
Caribbean Sea
NETH. ANTILLES
Windward Islands
TRINIDAD & TOBAGO
GAMBIA
Banjul
BURKINA FASO
BENIN
L. Tchad
Kano

COSTA RICA
Panama
PANAMA
Caracas
Orinoco
Georgetown
Paramaribo
Cayenne
GUINEA-BISSAU
Bissau
GUINEA
Bamako
GHANA
TOGO
NIGERIA
Benue
Lagos

I. del Coco (Costa Rica)
VENEZUELA
GUYANA
SURINAM
FRENCH GUIANA
C. Orange
Freetown
SIERRA LEONE
IVORY COAST
LIBERIA
Accra
Port Harcourt

Malpelo (Col.)
Cali
Bogotá
COLOMBIA
Monrovia
Abidjan
Bioko
Douala
CAMEROON

Galápagos (Ecuador)
Quito
ECUADOR
Golfo de Guayaquil
Guayaquil
Negro
Branco
Amazonas
Equator
Gulf of Guinea
SÃO TOMÉ & PRÍNCIPE
EQUATORIAL GUINEA
Libreville
GABON
CONGO

Iquitos
Japurá
Manaus
Belém
São Paulo (Brazil)
C. López
Annobon (São Tomé)
Brazzaville

Marañón
Amazonas
Purus
Madeira
Tapajós
Xingu
Tocantins
São Luís
Fernando de Noronha (Brazil)
C. de São Roque
Luanda
Kinshasa

Lima
PERU
Ucayali
Araguaia
BRAZIL
Fortaleza
Recife
Ascension (U.K.)
Benguela
ANGOLA

La Paz
BOLIVIA
Mato Grosso
Goiânia
Brasília
São Francisco
Salvador
SOUTH
St. Helena (U.K.)

PACIFIC
Arica
Iquique
L. Titicaca
L. Poopa
Gran Chaco
Paraguay
Belo Horizonte
Trindade (Brazil)
NAMIBIA
Walvis Bay

OCEAN
Tropic of Capricorn
Antofagasta
PARAGUAY
Asunción
Paraná
São Paulo
Rio de Janeiro
ATLANTIC
Windhoek

San Ambrosio (Chile)
ARGENTINA
Córdoba
Pôrto Alegre
Salado
Uruguay
OCEAN
Lüderitz
Port Nolloth
Orange

Arch. de Juan Fernández (Chile)
Valparaíso
URUGUAY
Rio Grande
Montevideo
Tristan da Cunha (U.K.)
SOUTH AFRICA

Santiago
Concepción
Buenos Aires
Pampas
C. San Antonio
Gough I. (U.K.)
Cape Town
C. of Good Hope
Port Elizabeth

Puerto Montt
Colorado
Bahía Blanca
Pen. Valdés
Chubut

Arch. de los Chonos
Pen. de Taitao
Deseado

Patagonia
Estrecho de Magallanes
Falkland Is. (U.K.)
South Georgia (U.K.)

Isla Sta. Inés
Estrecho de Magallanes
Tierra del Fuego
Cabo de Hornos
Scotia Sea
South Sandwich Is. (U.K.)

Drake Passage
South Orkney Is.

Antarctic Circle
Antarctic Peninsula
Graham Land
Weddell Sea
Antarctica

250 0 250 500 750 1000 1250 1500 1750 2000 km
250 0 250 500 750 1000 1250 miles

ATLANTIC OCEAN

ASCENSION

Ascension is a volcanic island of 88 sq km [34 sq mls], with a single high peak, Green Mountain (859 m [2,817 ft]), surrounded by ash and lava plains. The climate is cool and damp enought to support a farm which supplies vegetables for the local community of 1,500. Ascension has no native population. Administered from St Helena since 1922, its inhabitants are British, St Helenian or American.

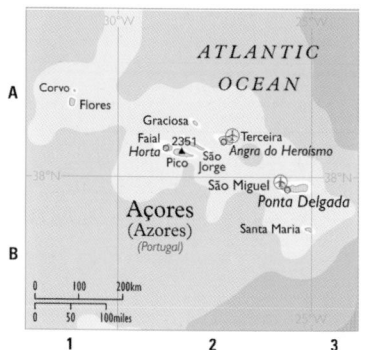

AZORES

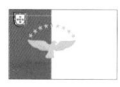

The Azores is a group of nine large and several small islands in the North Atlantic Ocean. Part of the Mid-Atlantic Ridge, the islands are of relatively recent volcanic origin. The Azores have been Portuguese since the mid-15th century and, since 1976, they have been governed as three districts of Portugal, which form an autonomous region. Farming and fishing are the main occupations and tourism is growing.

AREA	CAPITAL
2,247 sq km [868 sq mls]	Ponta Delgada
POPULATION	**CURRENCY**
240,000	Por. escudo = 100 centavos

BERMUDA

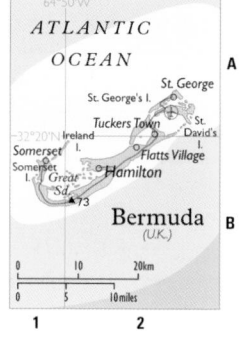

Bermuda comprises some 150 small islands, the coral caps of ancient volcanoes rising from the floor of the North

AREA	CAPITAL
53 sq km [20 sq mls]	Hamilton
POPULATION	**CURRENCY**
62,000	Berm. dollar = 100 cents

Atlantic Ocean. Uninhabited when discovered in 1503 by the Spaniard Juan Mermúdez, the islands were taken over by the British over a century later, with slaves brought from Virginia. Bermuda is Britain's oldest overseas territory, but it has a long tradition of self-government. Tourism is the mainstay of the economy, but the islands are a tax haven for overseas companies.

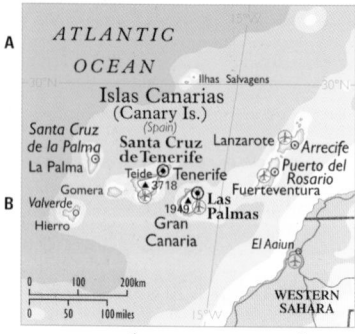

CANARY ISLANDS

The Canary Islands contain seven large islands and many small volcanic islands situated off southern Morocco. The climate is subtropical, being dry at sea level, but wetter on the mountains. Claimed by Portugal in 1341, they were ceded to Spain in 1479. Since 1927, they formed two Spanish provinces. Tourism is a major occupation. Farming is important, as are food and fish processing, and boat building.

AREA	CAPITAL
7,273 sq km [2,807 sq mls]	Las Palmas/Santa Cruz
POPULATION	**CURRENCY**
1,700,000	Spanish peseta

CAPE VERDE

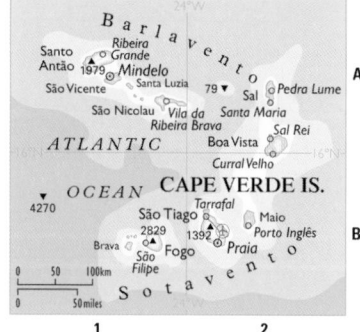

The Republic of Cape Verde consists of ten large and five small islands, divided into the Barlavento (windward) and Sotavento (leeward) groups. They are volcanic and mainly mountainous, with steep cliffs and rocky headlands.

The highest point is on the island of Fogo, an active volcano, which reaches 2,829 m [9,281 ft]. The climate is tropical, being hot for most of the year and mainly dry at sea level. The higher ground is cooler.

Portuguese since the 15th century, and used chiefly as a provisioning station and assembly point for slaves in the trade from West Africa, Cape Verde included Portuguese Guinea (now Guinea-Bissau) until 1879, when the mainland territory was separated. It was populated with slaves from Africa, and people from African and European origin.

Cape Verde became an overseas territory of Portugal in 1951 and fully independent in 1975. Linked with Guinea-Bissau in the fight against colonial rule, its socialist, single-party government flirted with union in 1980. But in 1991, the ruling party was soundly trounced in the country's first multiparty elections by a newly legalized opposition party, the Movement for Democracy (MPD). In the presidential elections, the MPD candidate, Antonio Mascarenhas Monteiro, was elected with 72% of the vote. He was re-elected unopposed in 1996.

Poor soils and lack of water at the lower levels on the islands have inhibited development. But bananas, beans, coffee, fruit, groundnuts, maize and sugar cane are grown on the wetter, higher ground, when they are not ruined by endemic droughts, such as the one that killed 75,000 people in 1900. Cape Verde's exports comprise fish and fish preparations and bananas, but the country has to import much of the food it needs. The only significant minerals are salt and *pozzolana*, a volcanic rock used to make cement.

Much of the country's income comes from foreign aid and remittances which are sent home by the 600,000 Cape Verdeans who work abroad. In the last severe drought (1968–82), about 40,000 people emigrated to Portugal alone. Tourism is still in its infancy – the number of tourists reached 37,000 in 1996. Economic problems, including high unemployment levels, have been compounded by the arrival of thousands of Angolan refugees.

AREA	CAPITAL
4,030 sq km [1,556 sq mls]	Praia
POPULATION	**CURRENCY**
399,000	C. Verde escudo = 100 centavos

FALKLAND ISLANDS

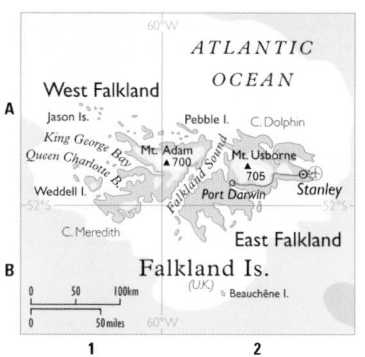

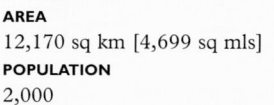

The Falkland Islands, or the Islas Malvinas, as they are called in Argentina, which lies 40 km [300 mls] to the west, consist of two main islands, and more than 200 small ones.

The windswept islands were discovered in 1592 by the English navigator John Davis. The Falklands were first occupied nearly 200 years later by the French (East) in 1764 and the British (West). The French interest, bought by Spain in 1770, was assumed by Argentina in 1806. The British, who had withdrawn in 1774, returned in 1832. They dispossessed the Argentinian settlers and founded a settlement of their own – one that became a colony in 1892. In 1982, Argentinian forces invaded the islands, but two months later, the United Kingdom regained possession. In 1999, a formal agreement between Britain and Argentina permitted Argentinians to visit the islands. The economy is dominated by sheep-farming. The prospect of rich offshore oil and natural gas reserves remains enticing, but may be uneconomic to extract and export.

AREA	CAPITAL
12,170 sq km [4,699 sq mls]	Stanley
POPULATION	CURRENCY
2,000	F. Islands pound = 100 pence

GREENLAND

Greenland is regarded by geographers as the world's largest island. It is almost three times larger than the second largest island, New Guinea, but an ice sheet, the world's second largest after Antarctica, covers more than 85% of its area. Settlement is confined to the rocky coast. The warmer south-west coast, where the capital Nuuk (Godthaab) is situated, has more than seven months with average temperatures below freezing.

Greenland became a Danish possession in 1380 and an integral part of the Danish kingdom in 1953. It was taken into the European Economic Community (EEC) in 1973, despite a majority of Greenlanders voting against this. In 1979, after another referendum, home rule was introduced, with full internal self-government in 1981. In 1985, Greenland withdrew from the EEC, halving the Community's land area.

Greenland still relies heavily on Danish aid and Denmark is its main trading partner. The chief rural occupations are sheep-rearing and fishing, with shrimps, prawns and molluscs being exported. The only major manufacturing industry is fish canning, which has drawn many Inuit to the towns. Few Inuit now follow the traditional life of nomadic hunting. Most Greenlanders live precariously between the primitive and the modern. Yet a nationalist mood prevails, buoyed by rich fish stocks, lead and zinc from Uummannaq in the north-west, untapped uranium in the south and, possibly, oil in the east. In addition, an adventure-oriented tourist industry is expanding. In 1997, the nationalist resurgence was evident when Greenland made Inuit name forms official.

AREA	CAPITAL
2,175,600 sq km [838,999 sq mls]	Nuuk (Godthaab)
POPULATION	CURRENCY
59,000	Danish krone

MADEIRA

Madeira is the largest of the group of volcanic islands lying 550 km [350 mls] west of the Moroccan coast and 900 km [560 mls] south-west of the national capital, Lisbon. Porto Santo and the uninhabited Ilhas Selvagens and Desertas complete the group, with a total area of 813 sq km [314 sq mls], of which Madeira contributes 745 sq km [288 sq mls].

With a warm climate and fertile soils, the Madeira Islands are known for their rich exotic plant life. The abundance of species is all the more surprising because rainfall is confined to the winter months.

The present name, meaning 'wood', was given by the Portuguese when they first saw the forested islands in 1419. The forests were largely destroyed and a farming industry was established. Spain held the islands between 1580 and 1640, while Britain occupied the islands twice early in the 19th century.

Major crops include bananas, maize, mangos, oranges and sugar cane. Grapes are grown to make the islands' best-known product, Madeira wine. Fishing is important, as also is tourism – the islands are a famous winter resort.

AREA	CAPITAL
813 sq km [314 sq mls]	Funchal
POPULATION	CURRENCY
300,000	Euro; Spanish peseta = 100 céntimos

ST HELEN

T ISTA I DA UNHA

The national flag was adopted in 1901. It includes the British Union Flag, revealing Australia's historic links with Britain. In 1995, the Australian government put the flag used by the country's Aboriginal people, not shown, on the same footing as the national flag.

Geography

The Commonwealth of Australia, the world's sixth largest country, is also a continent. It is primarily a land of low- to medium-altitude plateaux that form monotonous landscapes. The edges of the plateaux are more diverse, especially in the east, where gorges and waterfalls occur between the Great Dividing Range and the coast. Stunning gorge scenery is also found in the Hamersley Range and Kimberley Plateau.

Eastern Australia is the zone of greatest relief, highest rainfall, most abundant vegetation and largest population. Much of the region shows signs of volcanic activity in the relatively recent geological past and the young basaltic outcrops support nutrient-rich soils in contrast to the nutrient-poor, heavily weathered soils in the rest of Australia. The Great Dividing Range extends from the Cape York Peninsula to Victoria, while the mountains of Tasmania are its southernmost extension. The range contains many sub-ranges, one of which, the Snowy Mountains, contains Australia's highest peak, Mount Kosciuszko, which reaches 2,230 m [7,316 ft] above sea level.

Between the eastern highlands and the western plateaux lie the Carpentaria, central and Murray lowlands. The central lowlands drain to the internal river systems supplying Lake Eyre, or to the Bulloo system, or, through great inland deltas, to the Darling River. The parallel dune ridges of this area form part of the great continent-wide set of dune ridges extending in a huge anti-clockwise arc, eastwards through the Great Victoria Desert, northwards through the Simpson Desert and westwards to the Great Sandy Desert. All of these, though inhospitable, are only moderately arid, allowing widespread, if sparse, vegetation cover.

Ancient rocks form the western half of Australia. The area has little surface water and is essentially a landscape of worn-down ridges and plateaux, with depressions with sandy deserts and occasional salt lakes.

The Great Barrier Reef

When coral is alive it sways gently in the sea's currents, but when it dies it forms hard coral 'limestone' rock. The Great Barrier Reef, off the coast of Queensland in the Coral Sea and the world's biggest, is a maze of some 2,500 reefs exposed only at low tide, ranging in size from a few hundred hectares to 50 sq km [20 sq mls], and extending over an area of 250,000 sq km [100,000 sq mls]. The closest parts of the Great Barrier Reef are about 16 km [10 mls] from the coast, while other parts are 160 km [100 mls] out at sea.

The section extending for about 800 km [500 mls] north of Cairns forms a discontinuous wall of coral, through which narrow openings lead to areas of platform or patch reefs. South of Cairns, the reefs are less continuous, and extend further from the coast. Between the outer reef and the coast are many high islands, remnants of the mainland. These are coral cays, developed from coral sand on reefs and known locally as low islands, they are usually small and uninhabited, exceptions being Green Island and Heron Island.

A tourist attraction with more than 400 types of coral and over 1,500 species of fish, the modern reefs have evolved in the last 20,000 years, over older foundations exposed to the atmosphere during former low sea levels. Coral is susceptible to severe damage from tropical cyclones and also to damage by crown-of-thorns starfish, which feed on the living coral polyps. Scientists have not yet found the reason for

Climate

Only 10% of Australia has an average yearly rainfall of over 1,000 mm [39 in]. These areas include the tropical north, where Darwin is situated, the north-east coast, and the south-east, where Sydney is located. The interior is dry, and water evaporates quickly in the heat.

The wettest part of the continent is the east coast of Queensland where the average annual rainfall reaches as much as 3,810 mm [150 in]. The coast is sometimes hit by typhoons.

AUSTRALIA – DARWIN

The wettest areas of Australia are the north, the east coast, Tasmania in the south-east, and the south-west tip of the continent. The northern half of Australia lies in the tropics. For example, Darwin has high temperatures that drop only very slightly during the dry winter. However, the monsoon brings much rain in the high sun period between December and March. Conditions during summer may be oppressive due to high humidity.

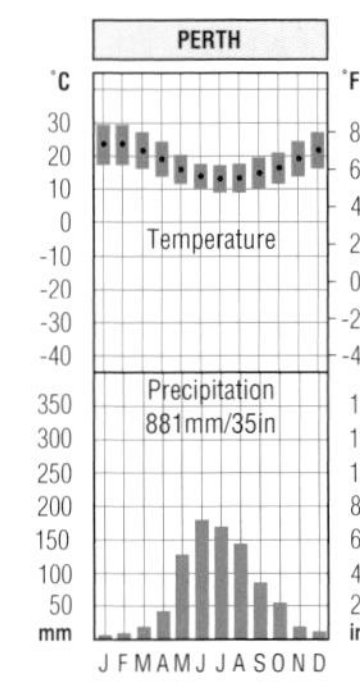

PERTH

The vast interior of Australia is very hot and dry. There are no great areas of high land that could form a barrier to the rain-bearing winds, or a relief to the high temperatures. Along the southern coast rainfall is slightly higher than in the interior. There is higher rainfall in the extreme south-west around Perth, which experiences a Mediterranean-type climate of hot, dry summers and warm, wet winters.

SYDNEY

In the south-east, annual rainfall is high, with a maximum from April to June. Rain falls on 12–13 days each month. The vast valleys inland of the Great Divide, in the lee of the rain-bearing winds, are drier. Temperatures are moderate, with winter night frosts in the south and the interior. Snow falls on the uplands of the south-east and Tasmania. Frosts are unknown in Sydney, the lowest temperatures being 2–4°C [36–39°F].

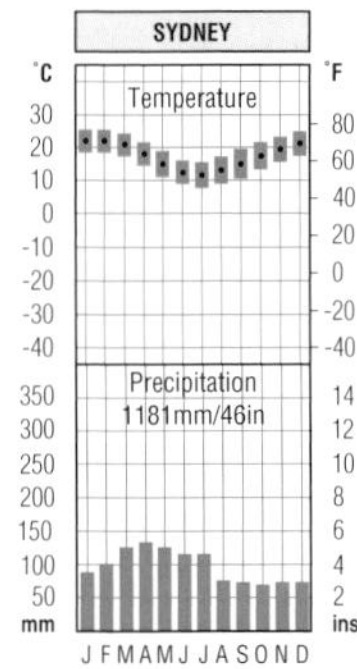

Vegetation

Luxuriant forests grow on the humid margins of Australia. They include the great jarrah forests of tall eucalyptus hardwoods in the extreme south-west of Western Australia; the temperate rainforests in Tasmania and on humid upland sites north through New South Wales to the Queensland border; and the tropical and subtropical rainforests found in the wetter areas along the coast, from the McIllwraith Range in the north to the vicinity of Mallacoota Inlet in the south.

Some rainforest areas are maintained as managed forests, others are in national parks, but most of the original cover has been cleared for agriculture, particularly for dairying and cattle fattening, and also for sugar- and banana-growing, north of Port Macquarie. The most adap-

History

The Aboriginal people of Australia entered the continent from South-east Asia over 40,000 years ago. Fires, lit for hunting and allowed to burn uncontrolled, altered much of the vegetation, but the Aboriginal people understood their environment, protecting vital areas of natural food supply, restricting the use of certain desert waterholes which tradition taught would be reliable in a drought, and developing a resource-use policy which was aimed at living with nature.

European exploration began in 1606, when Willem Jansz, a Dutch navigator, sailed along the west coast of the Cape York Peninsula, thinking it was New Guinea. In 1642, another Dutchman, Abel Janszoon Tasman, circumnavigated Australia without sighting the mainland. But he did visit Van Diemen's Land, which was later renamed Tasmania in his honour. Other Dutch sailors who sighted the continent were unimpressed by its arid character and the hostility of its inhabitants. However, in 1770, the British Captain, James Cook, sighted the fertile east coast. He claimed the region for Britain and named it New South Wales. Between 1801 and 1803, a British navigator, Matthew Flinders, sailed around Australia, charting its coastline and proving that it was one landmass. He suggested that the area, which was known as New Holland, be renamed Australia after *Terra Australis* (Southern Continent), the name used for the supposed continent before its discovery. The name change took place in 1817.

European settlement in Australia began in 1788 as a penal colony at Botany Bay, in New South Wales. The settlement at this bay, which had been visited by Captain Cook, was the beginning of the city of Sydney. In 1813, the crossing of the Blue Mountains was the first of many expeditions to open up the grasslands beyond the Great Dividing Range. Other settlements were quickly established in Tasmania in 1803 and Queensland in 1824. The 1830s saw an increasing number of free, assisted immigrants arriving from Britain and also the beginning of the exploration of the interior. But Australia's population remained small until the 1851 gold rush in New South Wales brought a large influx of fortune hunters. Most of the prospectors were disappointed, but many stayed on, having earned less than they needed to buy their return ticket. As a result, Australia's population rose from about 400,000 in 1850 to 1,100,000 in 1860.

During the 19th century, the continent became divided into the colonies of New South Wales, Queensland (1859), South Australia (1836), Tasmania (1825), Victoria (1851) and Western Australia (1829). The area which now forms Northern Territory was under the control of South Australia. During the colonial period, the state seaports of Sydney, Brisbane, Adelaide, Hobart, Melbourne and Perth became established as the dominant manufacturing, commercial, administrative and legislative centres of their respective states. None of them has since relinquished these positions.

In 1901, the former colonies, which were redesignated as states, came together to create the Commonwealth of Australia with a federal constitution and Melbourne as its temporary capital. Trade between the states became free. External affairs, defence and immigration policy became federal responsibilities, though health, education, transport, mineral, agricultural and industrial development remained firmly in the hands of each state. Only gradually did powers of taxation give the federal government the opportunity to develop national policies.

The federal capital established at Canberra, in the new Australian Capital Territory, grew from a tiny settlement in 1911 to become a great seat of administration and learning, and the largest inland regional commercial centre. Building began in 1923 and a federal parliament opened in Canberra in 1927. The federal government's territorial responsibilities included the Northern Territory, which has been self-governing since 1978.

Immigration has changed the ethnic character of Australia since 1960. Australia now has Greek, Italian, Lebanese, South-east Asian, Turkish and Yugoslav communities alongside Aboriginal, British, Irish, Chinese, Dutch and German communities, though the culture remains strongly British in flavour. Almost 60% of the Australian population lives in Sydney, Melbourne, Adelaide, Brisbane, Perth and Hobart. Migration within states from inland rural areas to capital cities or coastal towns has left rural communities with ageing populations, while the new mining towns have young populations. The most rapid growth, outside mining towns, has been in coastal towns, which provide retirement homes and lifestyles differing from those of the cities.

From 1788, European settlement upset the ecological balance through the widespread clearing of coastal forests, overgrazing of inland pastures, and the introduction of exotic species, especially the destructive rabbit. But Europeans have also brought the technology which has enabled the mineral, water and soil resources of Australia to be developed. Soon after 1788, small-scale manufacturing began to supply domestic goods and machinery to the colonial community. Inevitably, manufacturing grew in the colonial seaport capitals, especially Sydney and Melbourne, which now have more than 60% of all manufacturing industries (though only 40% of the total population).

Much of Australia's growth since the beginning of European settlement has been related to the exploitation of mineral resources, which has led directly to the founding, growth and often eventual decline of the majority of inland towns. Broken Hill and Mount Isa are copper-, lead-, silver- and zinc-producing centres, while Kalgoorlie, Bendigo, Ballarat and Charters Towers all grew in the 19th-century gold rushes.

Today, less glamorous minerals support the Australian economy. In Western Australia, the great iron ore mines of Mount Tom Price, Mount Newman and Mount Goldsworthy are linked by new railways to special ports at Dampier and Port Hedland. Offshore are the oil and gas fields of the north-western continental shelf. Railways are vital for bulk freight, especially mineral ores, coal and wheat. However, most cattle and sheep are carried by 'road trains' – powerful units pulling several trailers. A rapidly improving highway system links all the major cities and towns, providing easy mobility for a largely car-owning population. Although 90% of all passenger transport is by road, air services provide much inter-state travel. Australia is also well-served by local broadcasting and television. The radio remains a lifeline for remote settlements dependent on the flying doctor or aerial ambulance, and for others when bush or forest fires threaten isolated communities.

Politics

Australia's close ties with Britain were evident during World Wars I and II, when Australia considered itself automatically on the side of Britain when the wars broke out. About 59,000 Australians died in World War I (the highest number of deaths in proportion to the total number of troops among all the Allies) and more than 29,000 died in battle or in prison camps in World War II.

After World War II, Australia began to redefine its global role and it began to play an increasingly important part in Asia and the Pacific region. In 1950, it helped to create the Colombo Plan for economic development in southern and south-eastern Asia. In 1952, it signed the ANZUS treaty, a mutual defence treaty with New Zealand and the United States. This led to Australia sending troops to Vietnam between 1964 and 1975, though, from 1966, Australia's involvement in the war and its alliance with the US, became a matter of heated debate.

Marsupials

Marsupials are mammals that give birth to their young at an early stage of development and attach them to their milk glands for a period, often inside a pouch (marsupium). Once widespread around the world, they have mostly been ousted by more advanced forms, but marsupials continue to flourish in Australia, New Guinea and South America.

Best known are the big red and grey kangaroos that range over the dry grasslands and forests of Australia. Standing up to 2 m [6.5 ft] tall, they are grazers that now compete for food with cattle and sheep. Bounding at speed they can clear fences of their own height. Wallabies – small species of the same family – live in the forests and mountains.

Australia has many other kinds of marsupials, though several have died out since the coming of Europeans. Tree-living koalas live exclusively on eucalyptus leaves. Heavily built wombats browse in the undergrowth like large rodents, and the fierce-sounding Tasmanian Devils are mild scavengers of the forest floor.

AUSTRALIA

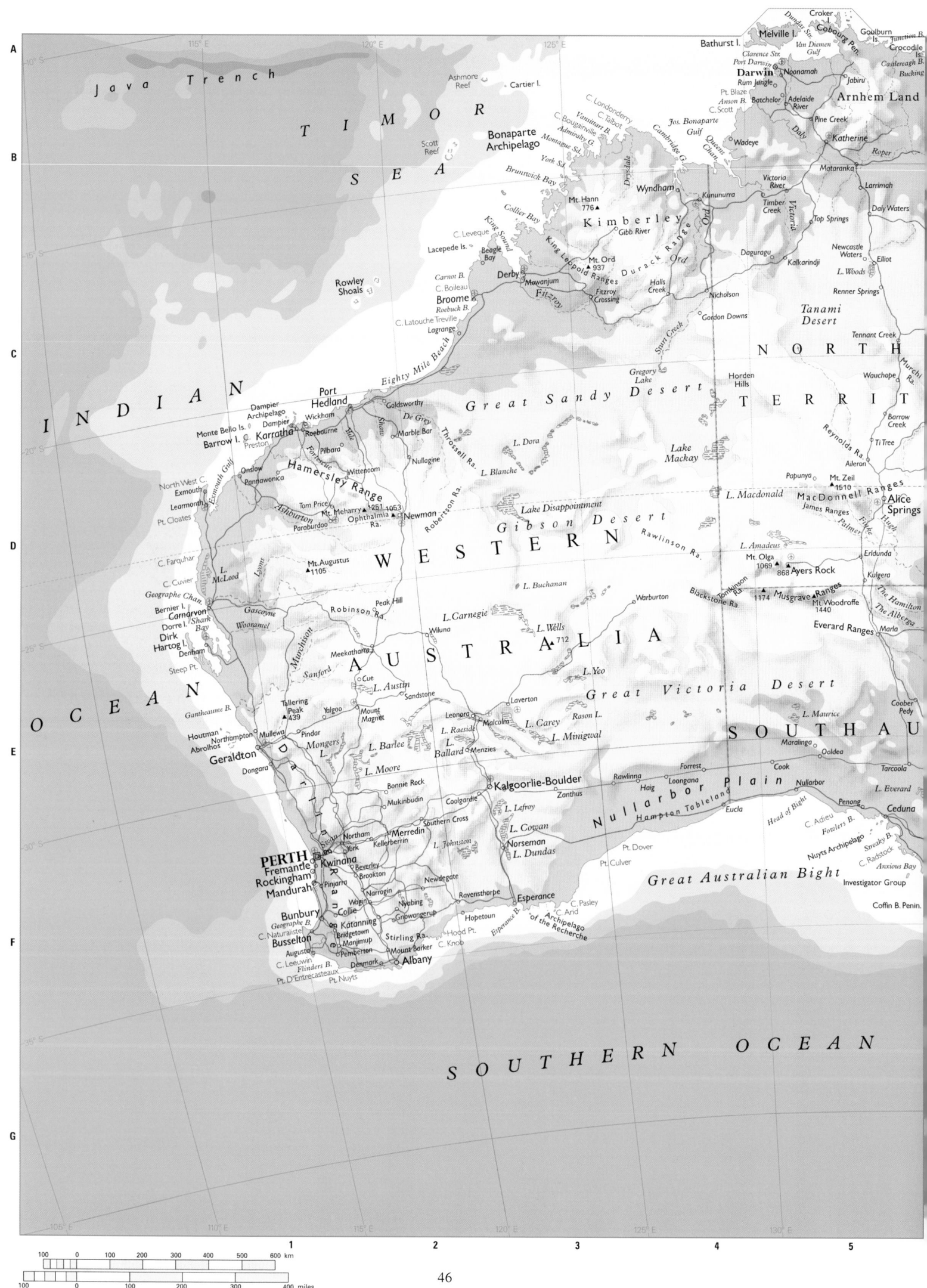

Java Trench

TIMOR SEA

Ashmore Reef · Cartier I.

Bathurst I.

Croker I.
Cobourg Pen.
Goulburn Is.
Crocodile Is.
Castlereagh B.
Bucking

Melville I.
Dundas Str.
Van Diemen Gulf

Clarence Str.
Port Darwin
Darwin
Rum Jungle
Noonamah

Pt. Blaze
Batchelor
Adelaide River
Jabiru
Arnhem Land

C. Londonderry
C. Talbot
Anson B.
C. Scott
Pine Creek
Daly

Vansittart B.
C. Bougainville
Admiralty G.
Montague Sd.

Bonaparte Archipelago
Jos. Bonaparte Gulf
Cambridge G.
Queens Chan.
Wyndham
Kununurra

Katherine
Roper
Matarankа
Larrimah

York Sd.
Brunswick Bay
Victoria River

Daly Waters
Top Springs
Timber Creek

Scott Reef

Mt. Hann 776
K i m b e r l e y
Gibb River

Newcastle Waters
L. Woods
Elliot

Victoria

C. Leveque
King Sound
Mt. Ord 937
King Leopold Ranges
Durack Range
Ord

Daguragu
Kalkarindji
Renner Springs

Lacepede Is.
Beagle Bay
Collier Bay

Halls Creek

Carnot B.
Derby
Mowanjum
Fitzroy Crossing

Nicholson
Tanami Desert
Tennant Creek

C. Boileau
Broome
Roebuck B.

Gordon Downs

C. Latouche Treville
Lagrange

Surt Creek

N O R T H

Eighty Mile Beach

Gregory Lake
Horden Hills

Wauchope
Murchi Ra.

T E R R I T

Port Hedland
Goldsworthy
Great Sandy Desert

Barrow Creek

Dampier Archipelago
Wickham
De Grey
Marble Bar

Reynolds Ra.
Ti Tree

Monte Bello Is.
Dampier
Roebourne
L. Dora

Lake Mackay

Barrow I. **Karratha**
Preston
Pilbara
Nullagine
L. Blanche

Papunya
Mt. Zeil 1510

North West C.
Exmouth
Hamersley Range
Wittenoom

L. Macdonald
MacDonnell Ranges
Alice Springs

Learmonth
Tom Price
Robertson Ra.

James Ranges
Palmer
Finch

Pt. Cloates
C. Farquhar
Ashburton
Mt. Meharry 1251 · 1053
Ophthalmia Ra.
Newman

Gibson Desert
L. Amadeus
Erldunda

C. Cuvier
Paraburdoo
Robertson Ra.
Rawlinson Ra.

Mt. Olga 1069
868 Ayers Rock
Kulgera

L. McLeod
Mt. Augustus 1105
W E S T E R N

Blackstone Ra.
Musgrave Ranges
Mt. Woodroffe 1440
Marla

Geographe Chan.
Lyons
L. Buchanan

1174
The Hamilton

Bernier I.
Carnarvon
Gascoyne
Peak Hill
Warburton

Everard Ranges
The Alberga

Dorre I.
Shark Bay
Robinson Ra.

Dirk Hartog I.
Denham
Wooramel
L. Carnegie

A U S T R A L I A
L. Wells 712

Steep Pt.
Murchison
Meekatharra
Wiluna

Great Victoria Desert
L. Maurice
Coober Pedy

Sanford
Cue
L. Yeo

S O U T H A U
Maralinga
Marla

Houtman Abrolhos
L. Austin
Sandstone

Forrest
Cook
Tarcoola

Northampton
Tallering Peak 439
Yalgoo
Mount Magnet

Rawlinna
Loongana
Ooldea

Mullewa
Pindar
Leonora
Malcolm
L. Raeside
L. Carey
Rason L.

Haig
Nullarbor
L. Everard

Geraldton
Dangara
L. Barlee
Menzies
Zanthus

Nullarbor Plain
Hampton Tableland
Eucla
Penong
Ceduna

Bonnie Rock
L. Moore
L. Ballard
Kalgoorlie-Boulder

C. Adieu
Fowlers B.
Nuyts Archipelago
Streaky B.

Mukinbudin
Coolgardie
L. Lefroy

Pt. Dover
Head of Bight
C. Radstock
Anxious Bay

Southern Cross
L. Cowan

Pt. Culver
Investigator Group

PERTH
Northam
York
Kellerberrin
Merredin
L. Johnston
Norseman
L. Dundas

Great Australian Bight
Coffin B. Penin.

Fremantle
Kwinana
Beverley
Brookton
Newdegate

Rockingham
Pinjarra
Narrogin

Mandurah
Wagin
Collie
Gnowangerup
Ravensthorpe
Esperance
C. Pasley
C. Arid
Archipelago of the Recherche

Bunbury
Geographe B.
Katanning
Nyabing
Hopetoun
Esperance B.

Busselton
Bridgetown
Manjimup
Stirling Ra.
Hood Pt.
C. Knob

C. Naturaliste
Augusta
Pemberton
Mount Barker

C. Leeuwin
Flinders B.
Denmark
Albany

Pt. D'Entrecasteaux
Pt. Nuyts

I N D I A N

O C E A N

S O U T H E R N   O C E A N

| 1 | 2 | 3 | 4 | 5 |

100 0 100 200 300 400 500 600 km

100 0 100 200 300 400 miles

46

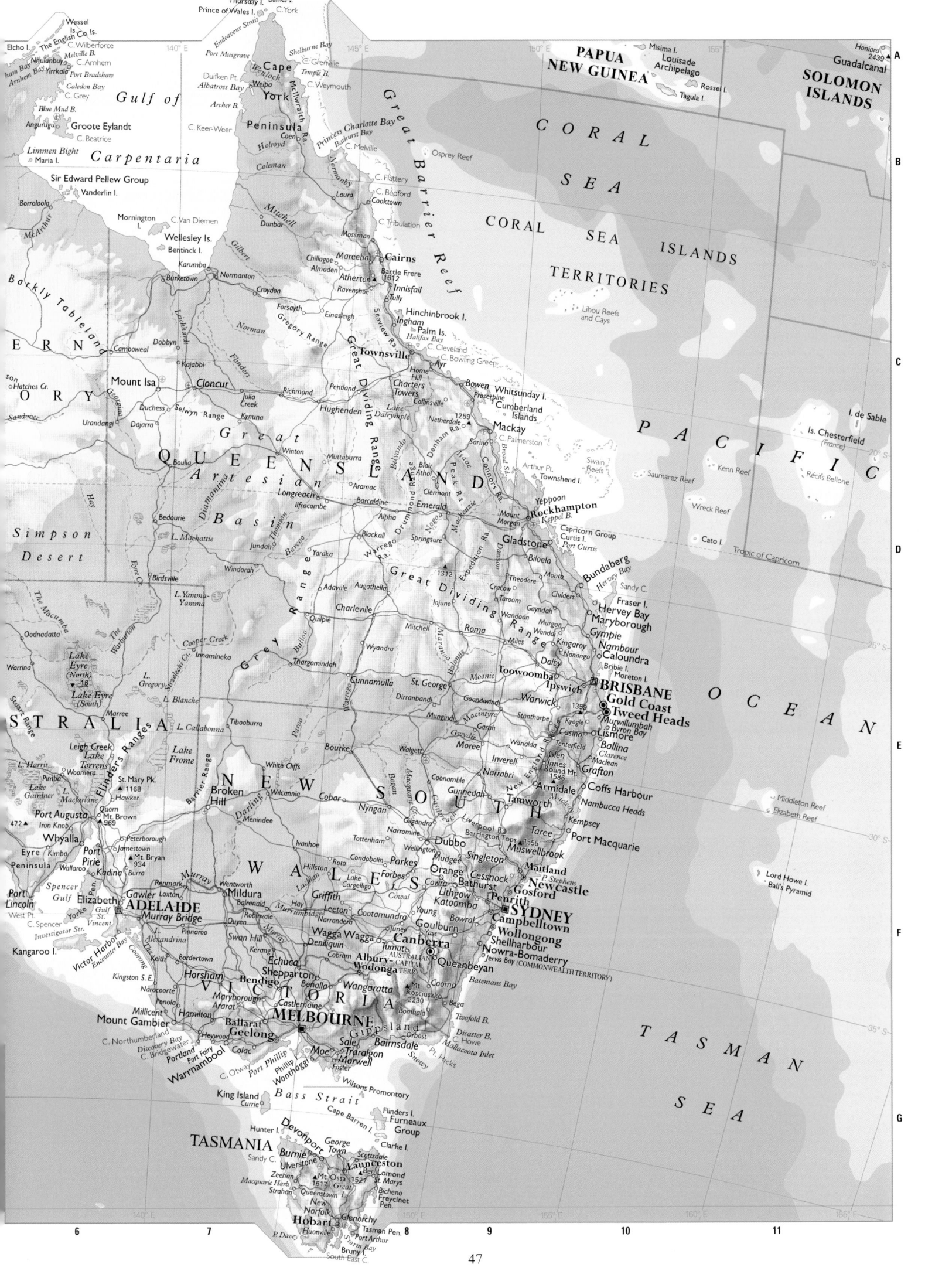

A

Wessel
Is. Co. Is.
Elcho I.
The English Co. Is.
Nhulunbuy C. Wilberforce
ham Bay Melville B.
Arnhem Bay Yirrkala C. Arnhem
Port Bradshaw
Blue Mud B. Caledon Bay
C. Grey
Limmen Bight Groote Eylandt
Maria I. C. Beatrice

Gulf of
Carpentaria

Borroloola
M.Arthur
Sir Edward Pellew Group
Vanderlin I.

Mornington I. C. Van Diemen
Wellesley Is. Bentinck I.

PAPUA
NEW GUINEA

Misima I.
Louisade
Archipelago
Rossel I.
Tagula I.

SOLOMON
ISLANDS

Honiaro 2439
Guadalcanal

C O R A L

S E A

CORAL SEA ISLANDS

TERRITORIES

Osprey Reef

Lihou Reefs
and Cays

I. de Sable

Is. Chesterfield
(France)

Récifs Bellone

PACIFIC

Wreck Reef

Cato I.

Middleton Reef

Elizabeth Reef

Lord Howe I.
Ball's Pyramid

OCEAN

T A S M A N

S E A

47

Several other factors contributed to a reassessment by Australians of their role in the world and their relationship with Britain. These included the changes in Australia's population after World War II, when the country was seriously underpopulated, Britain's membership in the European Economic Community (now the European Union) which began in 1973, and changes in Australia's trade directions, with Japan and the United States replacing Europe as the country's chief trading partners. In 1986, the Australia Act abolished the remaining legislative, executive and judicial controls of the British parliament.

In 1999, a referendum was held on whether the country should remain a constitutional monarchy, with the British monarch as its head of state, or become a republic. The Australian Labor Party and much of the Liberal-National Party favoured the republican option. However, the issue put at the referendum meant that the president would have been chosen by the parliament. Hence, many people who favoured republicanism voted 'no' to the proposal, since they wanted a direct vote for the president. Only 45% of Australians voted in favour of change, and Australia remained a constitutional monarchy.

Another problem Australia faces is the status of the Aboriginal people who, for many years, were an unseen and unheard part of the population. However, in the 1960s, Aboriginal militants working on stations in the outback drew attention to their working conditions and achieved equal pay for black and white workers. In 1967, a large majority supported proposals in a constitutional referendum to grant the Aboriginals the right to vote. In 1971, they were included on the official census for the first time. This enabled them to vote and to receive social service benefits. Aboriginal campaigns for land rights began in the late 1960s, and they first proved successful in Northern Territory in 1976. In 1985, the title for Australia's best-known tourist attraction, Uluru (Ayers Rock), was handed to the traditional Aboriginal owners of the area. Campaigns for land rights continued through the 1990s, following a 1992 High Court ruling that Australia was not an 'empty land' when Europeans first arrived in 1788.

The country's leading political parties are the conservative Liberal Party, the Australian Labor Party, which is supported by the trade unions, and the National Party, which represents the rural population, including farmers.

Economy

Australia is a prosperous country, with a per capita GNP in 1997 of US $20,650, which was about the same as the per capita GNP of the United Kingdom. Crops can grow on only about 6% of the country, though dry pasture covers another 58%. Apart from the empty and largely unusable desert areas in Western Australia and the Simpson Desert, extensive cattle or sheep production dominates all of Australia, north and west of a line from Penong in South Australia, through Broken Hill in New South Wales to Bundaberg in Queensland, and east of a line from Geraldton to Esperance in Western Australia. Cattle and sheep populations in this zone are sparse, while individual pastoral holdings are large, with some covering more than 400,000 hectares (1 million acres).

Some of the Aboriginal people live by hunting and gathering in Arnhem Land and on the fringes of the deserts. But nearly all of them now live close to government settlements or mission stations. Many work as stockmen and seasonal agricultural workers, while thousands more have migrated to country towns or cities.

The intensive pastoral zones support the bulk of sheep and cattle of Australia. Wool, mutton and beef production is still the basic industry. The country is the world's largest producer of wool and third in lamb and mutton. Wheat is cultivated in combination with sheep-raising over large tracts of the gentle inland slopes of the coastal ranges. Along the east coast are important cattle, dairy and sugar cane industries. Sugar cane production is especially important between Brisbane and Cairns. Irrigated areas also support cotton, rice, fruit and vegetable crops, largely for home consumption. Wine production around Perth, Adelaide, central Victoria and eastern New South Wales has expanded in recent decades, producing vintages of international renown.

Australia's mineral wealth is phenomenal. In 1995, it produced 38% of the world's diamonds, 14% of the world's manganese ore, 11% of the world's gold and uranium, 9% of the world's iron ore, 8% of the world's nickel, 7% of the world's silver and 4–5% of the world's aluminium, lead, tin and zinc. In the east, the coal mines of central Queensland and eastern New South Wales are linked by rail to bulk-loading facilities at Sarina, Gladstone, Brisbane, Newcastle, Sydney and Port Kemble, which enable this high-grade cooking coal to be shipped to worldwide markets. Bauxite mining has led to the development of new settlements at Nhulunby and Weipa on the Gulf of Carpentaria, with associated refineries at Kwinana, Gladstone and Bell Bay.

Rum Jungle, south of Darwin, became well known as one of the first uranium mines, but deposits further east in Arnhem Land are now being exploited. Meanwhile, new discoveries of ore bodies continue to be made in the ancient rocks in the western half of the country. Natural gas from Cooper Basin, just south of Innamincka on Cooper Creek, is piped to Adelaide and Sydney, while oil and gas from the Bass Strait and brown coal from the Yallourn-Morwell area have been vital to the industrial growth of Victoria. Fossil fuels are supported by hydro-electric power from projects in western Tasmania and the Snowy Mountains.

Although Australia's prosperity was based on farming and mining, manufacturing is now the leading economic activity. It accounted for nearly 16% of the gross domestic product in 1994–5, as compared with 3.3% from agriculture and 4.4% from mining. Many of Australia's factories concentrate on assembly work or light manufacturing, including the production of consumer products for domestic consumption. Leading manufactures include chemicals, clothing, processed food, metals, including iron and steel, paper, textiles and transport equipment. But Australia imports many producer goods, including machinery, construction equipment and other goods involved in production.

The leading sources of imports are the United States, Japan, the United Kingdom, Germany and China. Australia's leading exports include food and live animals, mineral fuels and lubricants, basic manufactures and metal ores and metal scrap. Major export destinations are Japan, South Korea, New Zealand, the United States, China, Singapore and Taiwan.

Australian Territories

Australia is responsible for a number of other territories. In the Indian Ocean, Britain transferred sovereignty of Heard Island and McDonald Island (both 1947), and further north the Cocos (Keeling) Islands (1955) and Christmas Island (1958). Australia also has jurisdiction over the Ashmore and Cartier Islands in the Timor Sea, the Coral Sea Islands Territory, and Norfolk Island in the south-west Pacific – while Lord Howe Island and Macquarie Island are administered by New South Wales and Tasmania, respectively. Of all these, only the Cocos Islands (600), Christmas Island (2,300), Norfolk Island (2,000) and Lord Howe Island (300) have permanent populations. The Coral Sea Islands Territory, which became an Australian territory in 1969, covers a sea area of about 1,000,000 sq km [386,100 sq mls], but its scattered reefs and islands are totally uninhabited apart from a meteorological station on Willis Island.

The country is also in charge of the largest sector of Antarctica, a continent protected from military and nuclear pollution under international agreement since 1991. A member of ANZUS since 1951, Australia has reviewed its own defence position since New Zealand banned US Navy nuclear warships in 1985.

AREA	Aboriginal 1.5%,
7,686,850 sq km	Asian 1.3%
[2,967,893 sq mls]	**LANGUAGES**
POPULATION	English (official)
18,613,000	**RELIGIONS**
CAPITAL (POPULATION)	Christianity (Roman
Canberra (325,000)	Catholic 26%, Anglican 24%,
GOVERNMENT	others 20%), Islam,
Federal constitutional monarchy	Buddhism, Judaism
ETHNIC GROUPS	**CURRENCY**
White 95%,	Australian dollar = 100 cents

According to legend, the colours on Austria's flag date back to a battle in 1191, during the Third Crusade, when an Austrian duke's tunic was stained with blood, except under his swordbelt, where it remained white. The flag was officially adopted in 1918.

Geography

The Republic of Austria is a landlocked country in the heart of Europe. About three-quarters of the land is mountainous, and tourism and winter sports are major activities in this scenic country. Northern Austria contains the valley of the River Danube, which rises in Germany and flows to the Black Sea, and the Vienna Basin. This is Austria's main farming region.

Southern Austria contains ranges of the Alps, which rise to their highest point at Grossglockner, at 3,797 m [12,457 ft] above sea level.

Climate

The climate of Austria is influenced both by westerly and easterly winds. The moist westerly winds bring rain and snow. They also moderate the temperatures. However, dry easterly winds bring very cold weather during the winter, and hot weather during the summer.

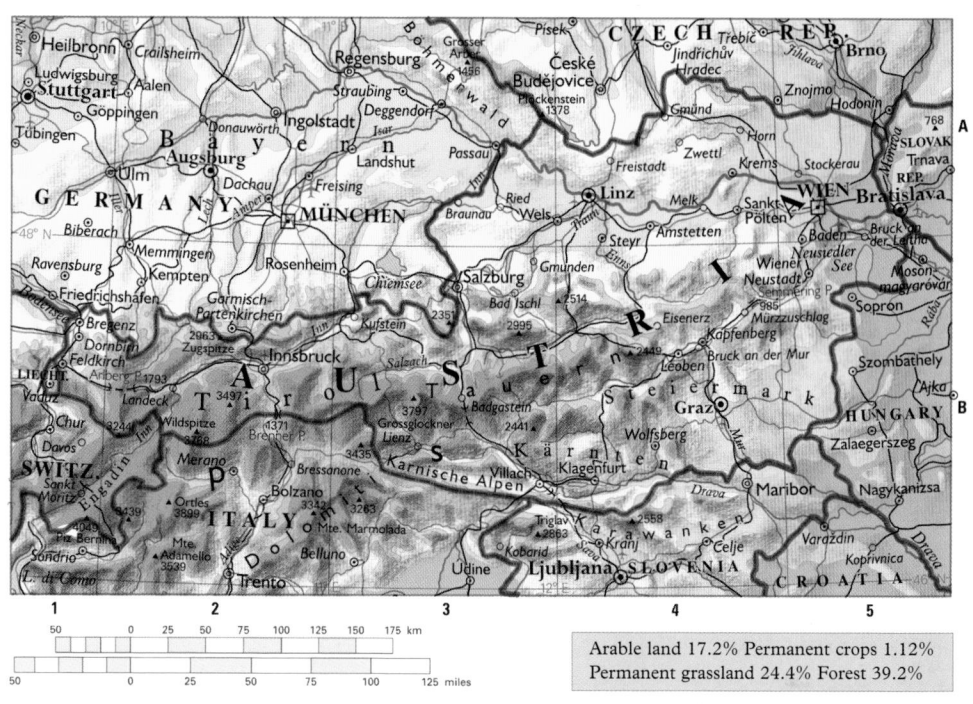

Arable land 17.2% Permanent crops 1.12%
Permanent grassland 24.4% Forest 39.2%

AUSTRIA (VIENNA)

Western Alpine regions have an Atlantic-type climate, while eastern lowlands are continental. The airflow is mainly from the west, which has twice the rainfall of the east at over 1,000 mm [40 in]. Winters are cold, and on the mountains there are glaciers and permanent snow in great depths. In Vienna, the January temperature is below freezing and is around 20°C [68°F] in July. From June to August, it is wetter and warmer.

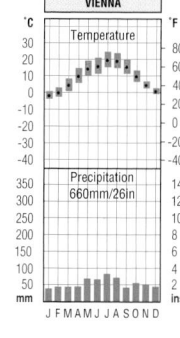

Austria has been neutral since 1955 but, unlike Switzerland, it has not been frightened to take sides on certain issues. In 1994, two-thirds of the people voted in favour of joining the European Union and the country became a member on 1 January 1995. However, Austria became a centre of controversy in 1999, when the extreme right-wing Freedom Party, led by Jörg Haider, who had described Nazi Germany's employment policies as 'sound', came second in national elections to the ruling Social Democratic Party. In February 2000, a coalition government was formed consisting of equal numbers of ministers from the conservative People's Party, which had come third in the elections, and the Freedom Party. This led to widespread protests throughout the EU and beyond.

History

Following the collapse of the Roman Empire, of which Austria, south of the Danube formed a part, the area was invaded and settled by waves of Asian, Germanic and Slav peoples. In the late 8th century, Austria came under the rule of Charlemagne, but in the 10th century, the area was overrun by groups of Magyars.

In 955, the German king Otto I brought Austria under his rule, and in 962 it became part of what later became known as the Holy Roman Empire. German emperors ruled the area until 1806, when the Holy Roman Empire broke up. The Habsburg ruler of the Holy Roman Empire became Emperor Francis I of Austria. In 1867, Austria and Hungary set up the powerful dual monarchy of Austria-Hungary.

Austria-Hungary was allied to Germany in World War I, but the defeated empire collapsed in 1918. Austria's present boundaries derive from the Versailles Treaty which was signed in France in June 1919. In 1933, the Christian Socialist Chancellor Engelbert Dollfuss ended parliamentary democracy and ruled as a dictator. However, he was assassinated in 1934 because he opposed the Austrian Nazi Party's aim of uniting Austria and Germany.

The *Anschluss* (union with Germany) was achieved by the German invasion in March 1938. Austria became a province of the Third Reich called Ostmark until the defeat of the Axis powers in 1945.

Politics

After World War II, Austria was occupied by the Allies – Britain, France and the United States – and it paid reparations for a 10-year period. Finally, after agreeing to be permanently neutral, Austria became an independent federal republic in 1955.

Economy

Austria is a prosperous country. It has plenty of hydroelectric power, some oil and gas, and reserves of lignite (brown coal). However, these do not meet the country's needs, and fossil fuels are imported.

The country's leading economic activity is manufacturing metals and metal products, including iron and steel, vehicles, machinery, machine tools and ships. Vienna is the main industrial centre, though factories are found throughout the country. Many factories contain craft industries, making such things as fine glassware, jewellery and porcelain.

Crops are grown on 18% of the land and another 24% is pasture. Dairy and livestock farming are the leading activities. Major crops include barley, potatoes, rye, sugar beet and wheat.

AREA	Turkish, German
83,850 sq km [32,374 sq mls]	**LANGUAGES**
POPULATION	German (official)
8,134,000	**RELIGIONS**
CAPITAL (POPULATION)	Christianity
Vienna (Wien, 1,560,000)	(Roman Catholic 78%,
GOVERNMENT	Protestant 6%), Islam
Federal republic	**CURRENCY**
ETHNIC GROUPS	Euro; Schilling =
Austrian 93%, Yugoslav 2%,	100 Groschen

AZERBAIJAN – SEE ARMENIA, PAGE 40; AZORES – SEE ATLANTIC OCEAN, PAGES 41–43; BAHAMAS – SEE CARIBBEAN SEA, PAGES 71–76; BAHRAIN – SEE GULF STATES, PAGES 113–114

Bangladesh adopted this flag in 1971, following the country's break from Pakistan. The green is said to represent the fertility of the land. The red disc is the sun of independence. It commemorates the blood shed during the struggle for freedom.

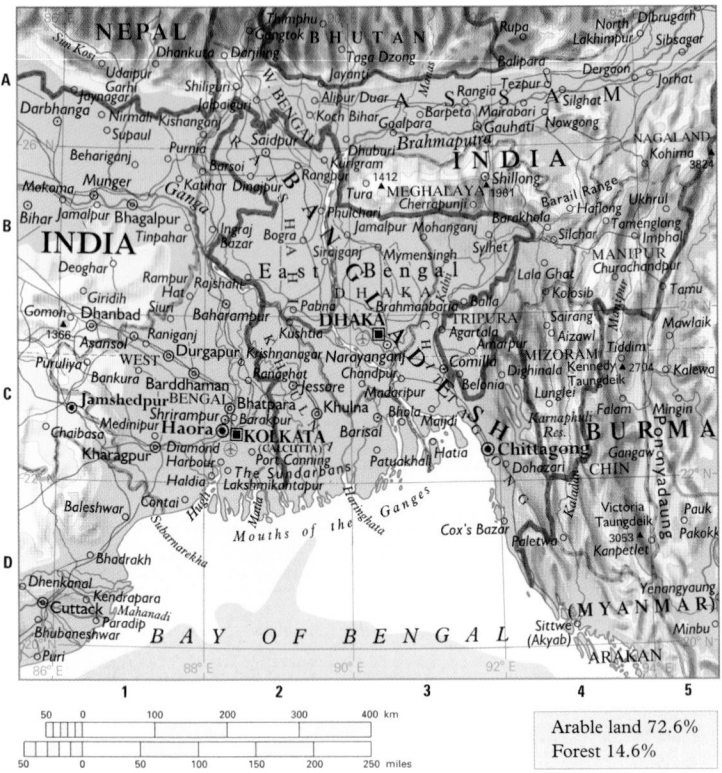

Arable land 72.6%
Forest 14.6%

Geography

The People's Republic of Bangladesh is one of the world's most densely populated countries. Apart from the hilly regions in the far north-east and south-east, most of the land is flat and covered by fertile alluvium spread over the land by the Ganges, Brahmaputra and Meghna rivers. These rivers overflow when they are swollen by the annual monsoon rains. Floods also occur along the coast, 575 km [357 mls] long, when tropical cyclones (the name for hurricanes in this region) drive sea-water inland. These periodic storms cause great human suffering. The world's most devastating tropical cyclone ever recorded occurred in Bangladesh in 1970, when an estimated 1 million people were killed.

Climate

Bangladesh has a tropical monsoon climate. Dry northerly winds blow during the winter, but, in summer, moist winds from the south bring monsoon rains. Heavy monsoon rains cause floods and in 1998, around two-thirds of the entire country was submerged, causing extensive damage.

BANGLADESH (DHAKA)

The Ganges delta has a monsoon climate. From June to September winds blow from the south over the Bay of Bengal, bringing heavy rain, over 240 mm [10 in] per month. On occasions, winds are so strong they pile seawater up against the outflowing river, bringing flood devastation. April is the hottest month and temperatures remain high through the monsoon season, though with little sunshine. January is the coldest month.

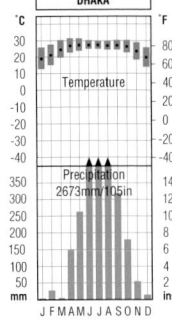

Vegetation

Most of Bangladesh is cultivated, but forests cover about 16% of the land. They include bamboo forests in the north-east and mangrove forests in the swampy Sundarbans region in the south-west, which is a sanctuary for the Royal Bengal tiger.

History

For 300 years after the mid-8th century AD, Buddhist rulers governed eastern Bengal, the area that now makes up Bangladesh. In the 13th century, Muslims from the north extended their rule into Bengal and, in 1576, the area became part of the Muslim Mughal Empire which was ruled by the emperor Akbar. This empire, which also included India, Pakistan and Afghanistan, began to break up in the early 18th century. Europeans, who had first made contact with the area in the 16th century, began to gain influence.

The East India Company, chartered by the English government in 1600 to develop trade in Asia, became the leading trade power in Bengal by the mid-18th century. In 1757, following the defeat of the nawab of Bengal in the Battle of Plessey, the East India Company effectively ruled Bengal. Discontent with the company led to the Sepoy Rebellion in 1857. In 1958, the British government took over the East India Company and its territory became known as British India.

Politics

In 1947, British India was partitioned between the mainly Hindu India and the Muslim Pakistan. Pakistan consisted of two parts, West and East Pakistan, which were separated by about 1,600 km [1,000 mls] of Indian territory. Differences developed between West and East Pakistan, since people in the east felt themselves victims of ethnic and economic discrimination by the Urdu- and Punjabi-speaking peoples of the west. In 1971, resentment turned to war when Bengali irregulars, aided by Indian troops, established the independent nation of 'Free Bengal', with Sheikh Mujibur Rahman as head of state. The Sheikh's assassination in 1975 – in one of the four military coups in the first 11 years of independence – led finally to a takeover by General Zia Rahman, who created an Islamic state before he, too, was assassinated in 1981. General Ershad took over in a coup in 1982. He resigned as army chief in 1986 to become a civilian president.

By 1990, protests from supporters of his two predecessors toppled Ershad from power and, after the first free parliamentary elections since independence, a coalition government was formed in 1991. Many problems arose in the 1990s, including the increasing strength of Muslim fundamentalism and the consequences of cyclone damage. In 1996, Sheikh Hasina Wajed, daughter of the country's first president, was elected prime minister, while a former Chief Justice, Shahabuddin Ahmed, was elected president unopposed.

Economy

Bangladesh is one of the world's poorest countries. Its economy depends mainly on agriculture, which employs more than half of the people. Rice is the chief crop and Bangladesh is the world's fourth largest producer.

Other important crops include jute, sugar cane, tobacco and wheat. Jute processing is the leading manufacturing industry and jute is the leading export. Other manufactures include leather, paper and textiles. Some 60% of the internal trade is carried by boat.

AREA	**ETHNIC GROUPS**
144,000 sq km	Bengali 98%, tribal groups
[55,598 sq mls]	**LANGUAGES**
POPULATION	Bengali, English
125,000,000	(both official)
CAPITAL (POPULATION)	**RELIGIONS**
Dhaka	Islam 87%, Hinduism 12%,
(6,105,000)	Buddhism, Christianity
GOVERNMENT	**CURRENCY**
Multiparty republic	Taka = 100 paisas

BARBADOS – SEE CARIBBEAN SEA, PAGES 71–76

In September 1991, Belarus adopted a red and white flag, replacing the flag used in the Soviet era. In June 1995, following a referendum in which Belarussians voted to improve relations with Russia, it was replaced with a design similar to the old flag, but without the hammer and sickle.

Geography

The Republic of Belarus, or Belorussia as it is also known, is a landlocked country in Eastern Europe. It was formerly part of the Soviet Union. The land is low-lying and mostly flat. In the south, much of the land is marshy. This area contains Europe's largest marsh and peat bog, the Pripet Marshes. A hilly region extends from north–east to south–west and includes the highest point in Belarus, situated near the capital Minsk. This hill reaches a height of 342 m [1,122 ft] above sea level. Over 1,000 lakes, mostly small, dot the landscape. Forests cover large areas. Belarus and Poland jointly control a remnant of virgin forest, which contains a herd of rare wisent (European bison). This is the Belovezha Forest, which is known as the Bialowieza Forest in Poland.

Climate

The climate of Belarus is affected by both the moderating influence of the Baltic Sea and continental conditions to the east. The winters are cold and the summers warm.

History

Slavic people settled in what is now Belarus about 1,500 years ago. In the 9th century, the area became part of the first East Slavic state, Kievan Rus, which became a major European power in the 10th and 11th centuries. But, in the 13th century, Mongol invaders captured the eastern part of Kievan

Arable land 29.8% Permanent crops 0.67%
Permanent grassland 14.1% Forest 33.7%

Rus, while Germanic tribes threatened from the west. Belarus allied itself with Lithuania, which also became a powerful state. In 1386, the Lithuanian Grand Duke married the queen of Poland and Lithuanian-Polish kings ruled both countries until 1569, when Lithuania with Belarus merged with Poland. In the 18th century, Russia took most of eastern Poland, including Belarus. Yet the people of Belarus continued to maintain their individuality.

Following the Russian Revolution of 1917, a Communist government replaced tsarist rule in Russia, and, in March 1918, Belarus became an independent, non-Communist republic. However, later that year, Russian Communists invaded Belarus, which they renamed Byelorussia, a name derived from the Russian words *Belaya Rus*, or White Russia. They established a Communist government there in 1919, and, in 1922, the country became a founder republic of the Soviet Union. In 1939, Russia occupied what is now western Belarus, which had been part of Poland since 1919. Nazi troops occupied the area between 1941 and 1944, during which one in four of the population died. In 1945, Byelorussia became a founding member of the United Nations.

Politics

In 1990, the Byelorussian parliament declared that its laws took precedence over those of the Soviet Union. On 25 August 1991, many observers were very surprised that this most conservative and Communist-dominated of parliaments declared its independence. This quiet state of the Soviet Union played a supporting role in its deconstruction and the creation of the Commonwealth of Independent States (CIS). In September 1991, the republic changed its name back from the Russian form of Byelorussia to Belarus, its Belorussian form.

The Communists retained control in Belarus after independence. A new constitution introduced in 1994 led to presidential elections that brought Alyaksandr Lukashenka to power. This enabled economic reform to get underway, though the country remained pro-Russian. Lukashenka favoured a union with Russia and, in 1999, signed a union treaty committing the countries to setting up a confederal state. However, observers regarded the treaty as largely symbolic, while Russia insisted that there must be a referendum before any actual merger takes place.

Economy

The World Bank classifies Belarus as an 'upper-middle-income' economy. Like other former republics of the Soviet Union, it faces many problems in turning from Communism to a free-market economy.

Under Communist rule, many manufacturing industries were set up, making such things as chemicals, lorries and tractors, machine tools and textiles. Farming is important and major products include barley, eggs, flax, meat, potatoes and other vegetables, rye and sugar beet. Leading exports include machinery and transport equipment, chemicals and food products.

AREA	Russian, Polish
207,600 sq km [80,154 sq mls]	**LANGUAGES**
POPULATION	Belarussian, Russian
10,409,000	(both official)
CAPITAL (POPULATION)	**RELIGIONS**
Minsk (1,700,000)	Christianity (mainly
GOVERNMENT	Belarussian Orthodox, with
Multiparty republic	Roman Catholics in the west)
ETHNIC GROUPS	**CURRENCY**
Belarussian 80%,	Belarussian rouble = 100 kopecks

BELGIUM

Belgium's national flag was adopted in 1830, when the country won its independence from the Netherlands. The colours came from the arms of the province of Brabant, in central Belgium, which rebelled against Austrian rule in 1787.

Belgium/Luxembourg: Arable land 23.7% Permanent crops 0.52% Permanent grassland 21% Forest 21.3%

Geography

The Kingdom of Belgium is a densely populated country situated in western Europe. Behind the coastline on the North Sea, which is 63 km [39 mls] long, lie its coastal plains. Some low-lying areas, called polders, are protected from the sea by dykes (or sea walls).

Central Belgium consists of low plateaux and the only highland region is the Ardennes in the south-east. The Ardennes, reaching a height of 694 m [2,277 ft], consists largely of moorland, peat bogs and woodland. The country's chief rivers are the Schelde, which flows through Tournai, Gent (or Ghent) and Antwerp in the west, and the Sambre and the Meuse, which flow between the central plateau and the Ardennes. The river valleys are fertile.

Climate

The moderating effects of the sea give much of Belgium a temperate climate, with mild winters and cool summers. Moist winds from the Atlantic Ocean bring significant amounts of rainfall throughout the year, especially in the Ardennes. During January and February, much snow falls in the Ardennes, where temperatures are more extreme than in the rest of the country. Brussels has mild winters and warm summers. The highland regions are much cooler.

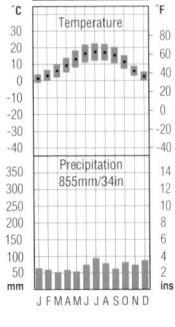

BELGIUM (BRUSSELS)

Belgium has a cool, temperate, maritime climate with weather systems moving eastwards from the Atlantic. Rainfall is heavy in the higher Ardennes plateau with snow from January to February. At Brussels, no month has a mean temperature below freezing and summer is warm. Temperatures over 30°C [86°F] have been recorded from May to September. Temperatures are lower at all seasons in the higher land to the south of the country.

History

Due to its strategic and stormy position, Belgium has often been called the 'cockpit of Europe'. In the Middle Ages, the area was split into small states, but, with the Netherlands and Luxembourg, it was united and made prosperous by the dukes of Burgundy in the 14th and 15th centuries. Later, at various times, Belgium, came under Austrian, Spanish and French rule.

From 1815, following the Napoleonic Wars, Belgium and the Netherlands were united as the 'Low Countries' but, in 1830, a National Congress proclaimed independence from the Dutch. In 1831, Prince Leopold of Saxe-Coburg became Belgium's king.

The division between Belgium and the Netherlands rested on history rather than geography. Belgium was a mainly Roman Catholic country while the Netherlands was mainly Protestant. Both were neutral in foreign policy, but both were occupied by the Nazis from 1940 until September 1944.

After World War II, Belgium achieved rapid economic progress, first through collaboration with the Netherlands and Luxembourg, which formed a customs union called Benelux, and later as a founder member of what is now the European Union. In 1960, Belgium granted independence to the Belgian Congo (now the Democratic Republic of the Congo) and, in 1962, its supervision of Ruanda-Urundi (now Rwanda and Burundi) was ended.

Politics

Belgium has always been an uneasy marriage of two peoples: the majority Flemings, who speak a language closely related to Dutch, and the Walloons, who speak French. The dividing line between the two communities runs east–west, just south of Brussels, although the capital is officially bilingual.

Since the inception of the country, the Flemings have caught up and overtaken the Walloons in cultural influence as well as in numbers. In 1971, the constitution was revised and three economic regions were established: Flanders (Vlaanderen), Wallonia (Wallonie) and Brussels, all shown on the administrative map on page 53. However, tensions remained and some experts predicted the break-up of the nation. In 1993, Belgium adopted a federal system of government, with each of the three regions being granted its own regional assembly.

Elections under this system were held in 1995. The number of deputies in the federal Chamber of Representatives was reduced from 212 to 150, while the number of members in the Senate was reduced from 184 to 71. The regional assembly of Flanders had 118 deputies, while the assemblies of Brussels and Wallonia each had 75.

Economy

Belgium is a major trading nation, with a highly developed economy. It imports most of the materials it needs for manufacturing, because it lacks minerals, except for coal. The textile industry, which has existed since medieval times in the towns of Flanders, Gent and Bruges,

BELGIUM

remains important. The steel industry, which was once situated in the Sambre-Meuse Valley, contained the main coalfield, but newer plants lie near the coast in Flanders. Chemicals, chemical products and processed foods are other leading manufactures.

Agriculture employs only 2.5% of the workforce, as compared with 24% in industry, but intensive farming methods produce most of the food needed by the country. Barley and wheat are the chief crops, followed by flax, hops, potatoes and sugar beet. However, the most valuable activities are dairy farming and livestock production.

AREA	Walloon 32%), Italian,
30,150 sq km [11,780 sq mls]	French, Dutch, Turkish,
POPULATION	Moroccan
10,175,000	**LANGUAGES**
CAPITAL (POPULATION)	Dutch, French,
Brussels (Brussel or	German (all official)
Bruxelles, 952,000)	**RELIGIONS**
GOVERNMENT	Christianity
Federal constitutional monarchy	(Roman Catholic 88%), Islam
ETHNIC GROUPS	**CURRENCY**
Belgian 91% (Fleming 55%,	Euro; Belg. franc = 100 centimes

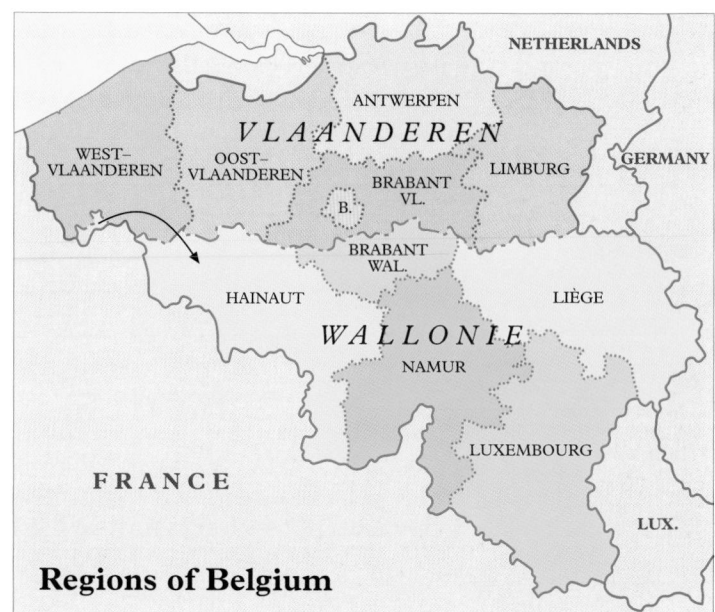

Regions of Belgium

LUXEMBOURG

Geography

The Grand Duchy of Luxembourg is one of the smallest and oldest countries in Europe. The north belongs to an upland region which includes the Ardennes in Belgium and Luxembourg, and the Eiffel Highlands in Germany. This scenic region contains the country's highest point, a hill in the north which reaches 565 m [1,854 ft] above sea level. The southern two-thirds of Belgium, which is geographically part of French Lorraine, is a hilly or rolling plateau called the Bon Pays or Gut Land ('Good Land'). This region contains rich farmland, especially in the fertile Alzette, Moselle and Sûre (or Sauer) river valleys in the south and east.

Climate

Luxembourg experiences a temperate climate. The south of the country has warm summers and autumns, when grapes ripen in sheltered south-eastern valleys. Winters are sometimes severe, particularly in the Ardenne region, where snow can cover the land for some weeks.

LUXEMBOURG (LUXEMBOURG)

Luxembourg receives a reasonable amount of rain, sometimes snow, falling evenly throughout the year on about 200 days. The total is greater on the higher lands in the north. January is the coldest month with an average at freezing-point. The daytime temperatures exceed 20°C [68°F] from June to August. While the highest recorded temperature is 37°C [99°F], the lowest has reached –20°C [–4°F] on a number of occasions.

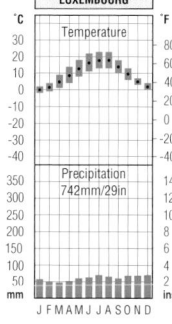

Vegetation

Forests cover about a fifth of Luxembourg, mainly in the north, where deer and wild boar are found. Farms cover about 25% of the land and pasture covers another 20%.

History

Luxembourg became an independent state in AD 963 and a duchy in 1354. In the 1440s, Luxembourg came under the House of Burgundy and, in the early 16th century, under the rule of the Habsburgs. From 1684, it came successively under France (1684–97), Spain (1697–1714) and Austria until 1795, when it reverted to French rule. In 1815, following the defeat of France, Luxembourg became a Grand Duchy under the Netherlands. This was because the Grand Duke

was also the king of the Netherlands. In 1890, when Wilhelmina became queen of the Netherlands, Luxembourg broke away because its laws did not permit a woman to rule. The Grand Duchy then passed to Adolphus, Duke of Nassau-Weilburg. But, in 1912, Luxembourg's laws were changed to allow Marie Adélaïde of Nassau to become the ruling grand duchess. Her sister Charlotte succeeded in 1919, but she abdicated in 1964 in favour of her son Jean.

Germany occupied Luxembourg in World Wars I and II. In 1944–5, northern Luxembourg was the scene of the Battle of the Bulge. Following World War II, the economy recovered rapidly.

Politics

In 1948, Luxembourg joined Belgium and the Netherlands in a union called Benelux and, in the 1950s, it was one of the six founders of what is now the European Union. The country's capital, which is a major financial centre, contains the headquarters of several international agencies, including the European Coal and Steel Community and the European Court of Justice.

Economy

Luxembourg has iron-ore reserves and is a major steel producer. It also has many high-technology industries, producing electronic goods and computers. Steel and other manufactures, including chemicals, glass and rubber products, dominate the country's exports. Other major activities include tourism and financial services.

Half the total land area is farmed, though agriculture employs only around 3% of the workforce. Major crops include barley, fruits, oats, potatoes and wheat. Cattle, sheep, pigs and poultry are reared.

AREA	**ETHNIC GROUPS**
2,590 sq km	Luxembourger 71%,
[1,000 sq mls]	Portuguese 10%, Italian 5%,
POPULATION	French 3%, Belgian 3%
425,000	**LANGUAGES**
CAPITAL (POPULATION)	Letzeburgish/Luxembourgian
Luxembourg	(official), French, German
(76,000)	**RELIGIONS**
GOVERNMENT	Christianity (R. Catholic 95%)
Constitutional monarchy	**CURRENCY**
(Grand Duchy)	Euro; Lux. franc = 100 centimes

BELIZE – SEE GUATEMALA, PAGE 110

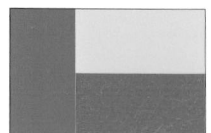

The colours on this flag, used by Africa's oldest independent nation, Ethiopia, symbolize African unity.Benin adopted this flag after independence in 1960. A flag with a red (Communist) star replaced it between 1975 and 1990, after which Benin dropped its Communist policies.

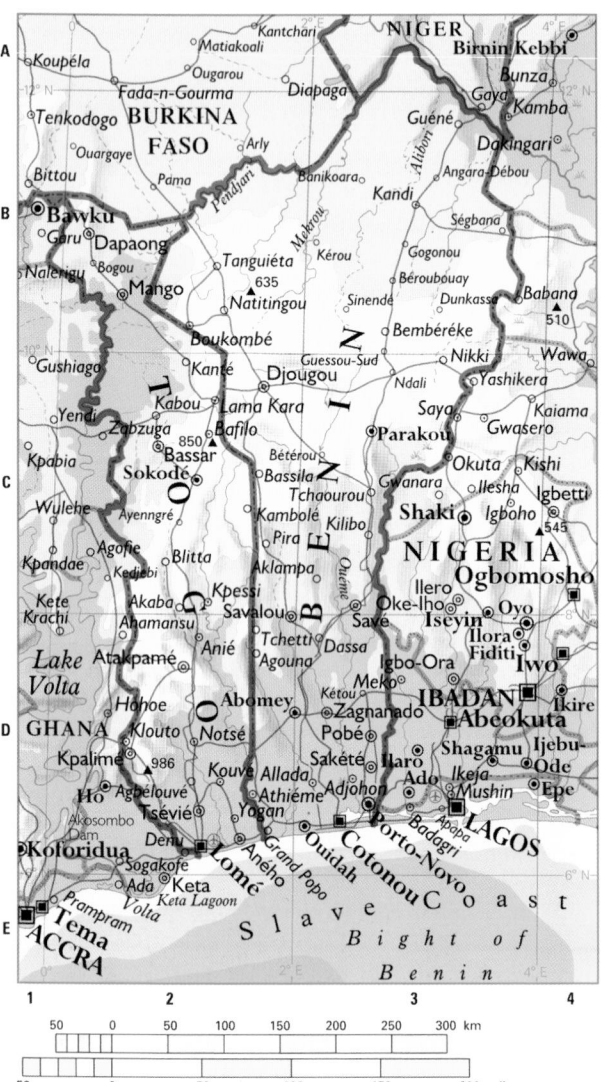

Geography and Climate

The Republic of Benin is one of Africa's smallest countries. It extends north–south for about 620 km [390 mls]. Lagoons line the short coastline, and the country has no natural harbours.

Benin has a hot, wet climate. The average annual temperature on the coast is about 25°C [77°F], and the average rainfall is about 1,330 mm [52 in]. The inland plains are wetter than the coast.

History and Politics

The ancient kingdom of Dahomey had its capital at Abomey. In the 17th century, the kings of Dahomey became involved in supplying slaves to European slave traders, including the Portuguese who shipped many Dahomeans to the Americas, particularly to Portugal's huge territory of Brazil.

After slavery was ended in the 19th century, the French began to gain influence in the area. Benin became self-governing in 1958 and fully independent in 1960. After much instability and many changes of government, a military group took over in 1972. The country, renamed Benin in 1975, became a one-party socialist state. Socialism was abandoned in 1989, and multiparty elections were held in 1991 and 1996.

Economy

Benin is a poor developing country. Agriculture employs more than half of the people, though many live at subsistence level, making little contribution to the economy. Benin produces some petroleum, but industry is on a small scale. The main exports include cotton, crude petroleum, palm oil and palm kernels. Cocoa, coffee, groundnuts (peanuts), tobacco and shea nuts are also grown for export.

AREA	**ETHNIC GROUPS**
112,620 sq km	Fon, Adja, Bariba, Yoruba, Fulani
[43,483 sq mls]	**LANGUAGES**
POPULATION	French (official), Fon, Adja, Yoruba
6,101,000	**RELIGIONS**
CAPITAL (POPULATION)	Traditional beliefs 60%,
Porto-Novo (179,000)	Christianity 23%, Islam 15%
GOVERNMENT	**CURRENCY**
Multiparty republic	CFA franc = 100 centimes

TOGO

Geography and Climate

The Republic of Togo is a long, narrow country in West Africa. From north to south, it extends about 500 km [311 mls]. Its coastline on the Gulf of Guinea is only 64 km [40 mls] long, and it is only 145 km [90 mls] at its widest point.

Togo has year-round high temperatures. The main wet season runs from March to July, with a minor wet season in October and November.

History and Politics

Togo became a German protectorate in 1884. In 1919, Britain took over the western third of Togo, while France took over the eastern two-thirds. In 1956, the people of British Togoland voted to join Ghana, while French Togoland became an independent republic in 1960.

A military regime took power in 1963, and in 1967 General Gnassingbé Eyadéma became head of the government and suspended the constitution. A new constitution was adopted in 1992 and multi-party elections were held in 1994. However, in 1998, paramilitary police prevented the completion of the count in presidential elections when it became clear that Eyadéma had been defeated. Eyadéma continued in office and the main opposition parties boycotted the general elections in 1999.

Economy

Togo is a poor developing country. Farming employs 65% of the people, but most farmers grow little more than they need to feed their families. Major food crops include cassava, maize, millet and yams. The chief export crops are cocoa, coffee and cotton. But the leading export is phosphate rock, which is used to make fertilizers. Togo's small-scale manufacturing and mining industries employ about 6% of the people.

AREA	Tem-Kabre 26%,
56,790 sq km [21,927 sq mls]	Gurma 16%
POPULATION	**LANGUAGES**
4,906,000	French (official), Ewe,
CAPITAL (POPULATION)	Kabiye
Lomé (590,000)	**RELIGIONS**
GOVERNMENT	Traditional beliefs 50%,
Multiparty republic	Christianity 35%, Islam 15%
ETHNIC GROUPS	**CURRENCY**
Ewe-Adja 43%,	CFA franc = 100 centimes

BERMUDA – SEE ATLANTIC OCEAN, PAGES 41–43;
BHUTAN – SEE NEPAL, PAGE 164

BOLIVIA

This flag, which has been Bolivia's national and merchant flag since 1888, dates back to 1825 when Bolivia became independent. The red stands for Bolivia's animals and the courage of the army, the yellow for its mineral resources, and the green for its agricultural wealth.

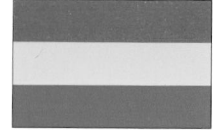

Geography

The Republic of Bolivia is a landlocked country in central South America. The Andes in the west rise to a height of 6,542 m [21,464 ft] at Nevado Sajama. To the east lies the Altiplano, a high plateau that contains part of Lake Titicaca in the north and Lake Poopó in the south, while to the east lies the majestic Cordillera Real. More than half of all Bolivians live on the Altiplano. Eastern Bolivia is a vast lowland plain, drained by the headwaters of the River Madeira. The south-east is semi-arid, the centre is tropical savanna, while the north-east is forested.

Climate

The Bolivian climate is greatly affected by altitude, with the Andean peaks permanently snow-covered, while the eastern plains remain hot and humid.

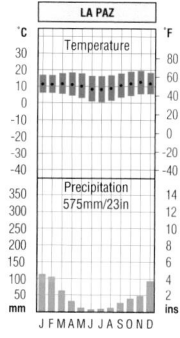

BOLIVIA (LA PAZ)

Although within the tropics, La Paz lies at 3,625 m [11,893 ft] on the Bolivian plateau where altitude affects temperatures. The annual range is small (1°C [33°F]), but temperatures rise rapidly by day and fall sharply at night; the diurnal range is very large (10–15°C [50–59°F]), with frequent night frosts in winter. Rainfall, often thundery, occurs mainly in the summer. From April to October, rain falls on less than 10 days per month.

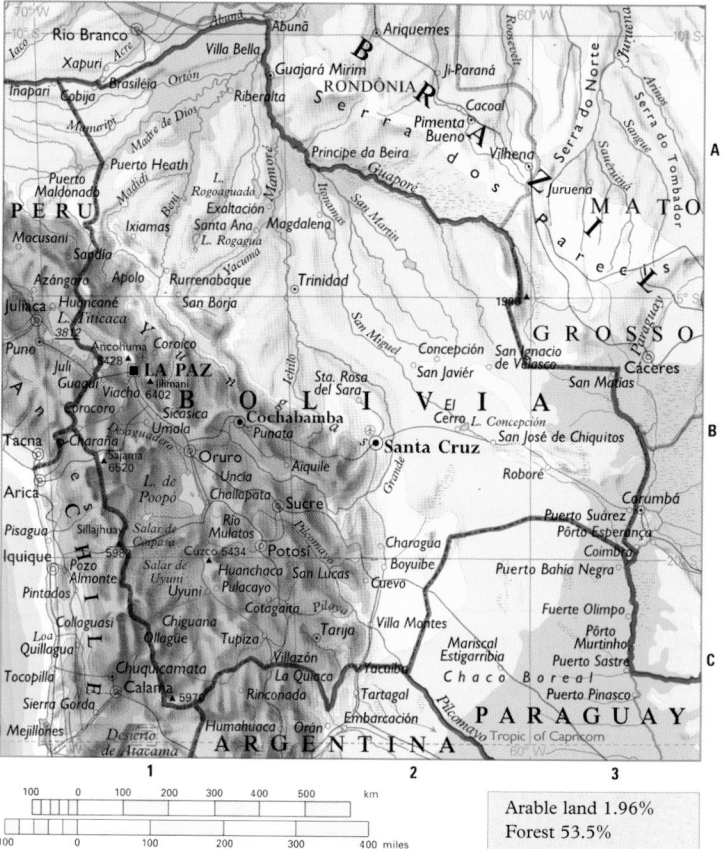

Arable land 1.96%
Forest 53.5%

History

American Indians have lived in Bolivia for at least 10,000 years. The main groups today are the Aymara and Quechua people.

When Spanish soldiers arrived in the early 16th century, Bolivia was part of the Inca empire. Following the defeat of the Incas, Spain ruled from 1532 to 1825, when Antonio José de Sucre, one of revolutionary leader Simón Bolívar's generals, defeated the Spaniards. Since independence, Bolivia has lost much territory to its neighbours. In 1932, Bolivia fought with Paraguay for control of the Gran Chaco region. Bolivia lost and most of this area passed to Paraguay in 1938.

Politics

Following the Chaco War, Bolivia entered a long period of instability. It had ten presidents, six of whom were members of the military, between 1936 and 1952, when the Revolutionary Movement replaced the military. The new government launched a series of reforms, which included the break-up of large estates and the granting of land to Amerindian farmers. Another military uprising occurred in 1964, heralding another period of instability. Elections were held in 1980, but the military again intervened until 1982, when civilian government was restored. Presidential elections were held in 1989, 1993 and 1997, when General Hugo Bánzer Suárez, who had ruled the country as a dictator in the 1970s, became president. Since the 1980s, Bolivia has followed free-enterprise policies, including privatization of formerly government-owned enterprises.

Economy

Bolivia is one of the poorest countries in South America. It has several natural resources, including tin, silver and natural gas, but the chief activity is agriculture, which employs 47% of the people. Potatoes, wheat and a grain called *quinoa* are important crops on the Altiplano, while bananas, cocoa, coffee and maize are grown at the lower, warmer levels. Manufacturing is on a small scale, and the chief exports are mineral ores, especially tin. However, experts believe that the main (and illegal) export may be coca, which is used to make the drug cocaine. The government is trying to stamp out this growing industry.

The Altiplano

A high, rolling plateau 3,600 m [12,000 ft] above sea level on the Peruvian border of Bolivia, the Altiplano stretches 400 km [250 mls] north to south between the eastern and western cordilleras of the Andes. Surrounded by high, snow-capped peaks, at its north end lies Lake Titicaca, the highest navigable body of water in the world. To the south are smaller lakes, and an extensive salt flat. Though tropical in latitude, the Altiplano is cold and bleak, yet over half the population of Bolivia, including many native Indians, make it their home.

The natural vegetation of the Altiplano is grassland with low trees and shrubs, merging at high levels to the harsh scrubland of the puna, the name for the higher and bleaker parts of the Altiplano. Summer rains and winter snows supply enough moisture to support pasture, and herds of llama and alpaca are raised as pack animals, while also providing meat and wool for peasant farmers. The northern part of the Altiplano contains various urban centres, such as Puno and Juliaca in the Lake Titicaca basin, and La Paz, which lies in a chasm that cuts the floor of the Altiplano. The arid conditions in the southern part of the Altiplano are hostile to human settlement, though the area is rich in minerals.

AREA
1,098,580 sq km [424,162 sq mls]
POPULATION
7,826,000
CAPITAL (POPULATION)
La Paz (1,126,000)
GOVERNMENT
Multiparty republic
ETHNIC GROUPS
Mestizo 31%,
Quechua 25%,
Aymara 17%, White 15%
LANGUAGES
Spanish, Aymara,
Quechua (all official)
RELIGIONS
Christianity
(Roman Catholic 94%)
CURRENCY
Boliviano = 100 centavos

BOSNIA-HERZEGOVINA

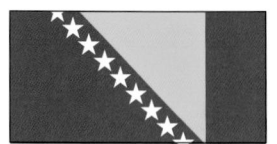

Bosnia-Herzegovina adopted a new flag in 1998, because the previous flag was thought to be synonymous with the wartime Muslim regime. The blue background and white stars represent the country's links with the EU, and the triangle stands for the three ethnic groups in the country.

Arable land 11.8% Permanent crops 3.92% Forest 39.2%

Geography

The Republic of Bosnia-Herzegovina is one of the five republics to emerge from the former Federal People's Republic of Yugoslavia. Much of the country is mountainous or hilly, with an arid limestone plateau in the south-west. The River Sava, which forms most of the northern border with Croatia, is a tributary of the River Danube. Because of the country's odd shape, the coastline is limited to a short stretch of 20 km [13 mls] on the Adriatic coast.

Climate

A Mediterranean climate, with dry, sunny summers and moist, mild winters, prevails only near the coast. Inland, the weather becomes more severe, with hot, dry summers and bitterly cold, snowy winters. The north experiences the most severe weather.

History

Slavs settled in the area that is now Bosnia-Herzegovina around 1,400 years ago. In the late 15th century, the area was taken by the Ottoman Turks. In 1878, the dual monarchy of Austria-Hungary gained temporary control over Bosnia-Herzegovina and it formally took over the area in 1908. The assassination of Archduke Francis Ferdinand of Austria-Hungary in Sarajevo, in June 1914, was the catalyst that led to the start of World War I. In 1918, Bosnia-Herzegovina became part of the Kingdom of the Serbs, Croats and Slovenes, which was renamed Yugoslavia in 1929. Germany occupied Yugoslavia during World War II, and Bosnia-Herzegovina came under the control of a puppet regime in Croatia. A Communist government took over in Yugoslavia in 1945, and a new constitution in 1946 made the country a federal state, with Bosnia-Herzegovina as one of its six constituent republics.

Under Communist rule, Bosnia-Herzegovina was a potentially ex-

plosive area because of its mixture of people, including Bosnian Muslims, Orthodox Christian Serbs and Roman Catholic Croats, as well as Albanian, gypsy and Ukrainian minorities. The ethnic and religious differences started to exert themselves after the death of Yugoslavia's president Josip Broz Tito in 1980, and the increasing indications that Communist economic policies were not working.

Politics

Free elections were held in 1990 and non-Communists won a majority, with a Muslim, Alija Izetbegovic, as president. In 1991, Croatia and Slovenia declared themselves independent republics and seceded from Yugoslavia. Bosnia-Herzegovina held a referendum on independence in 1992. While most Bosnian Serbs boycotted the vote, the Muslims and Croats voted in favour and Bosnia-Herzegovina proclaimed its independence. War then broke out.

At first, the Muslim-dominated government allied itself uneasily with the Croat minority, but it was at once under attack by local Serbs, supported by their co-nationals from beyond Bosnia-Herzegovina's borders. In their 'ethnic cleansing' campaign, heavily equipped Serb militias drove poorly-armed Muslims from towns they had long inhabited. By early 1993, the Muslims controlled less than a third of the former federal republic, and even the capital, Sarajevo, became disputed territory, with constant shelling.

The Muslim-Croat alliance rapidly disintegrated and refugees approached the million mark. Tougher economic sanctions on Serbia in April 1993 had little effect on the war in Bosnia. A small United Nations force attempted to deliver relief supplies to civilians and maintain 'safe' Muslim areas to no avail.

Finally, in 1995, the warring parties agreed to a solution to the conflict – the Dayton Peace Accord. This involved dividing the country into two self-governing provinces, one Bosnian Serb and the other Muslim-Croat, under a central, unified, multi-ethnic government. Elections were held in 1996 and 1998 under this new arrangement.

Economy

The economy of Bosnia-Herzegovina, the least developed of the six republics of the former Yugoslavia, apart from Macedonia, was shattered by the war during the early 1990s. Before the war started, manufactures were the main exports, including electrical equipment, machinery and transport equipment, and textiles.

Farm products include fruits, maize, tobacco, vegetables and wheat, but the country has to import food.

AREA	Croat 17%
51,129 sq km [19,745 sq mls]	**LANGUAGES**
POPULATION	Serbo-Croatian
3,366,000	**RELIGIONS**
CAPITAL (POPULATION)	Islam 40%, Christianity
Sarajevo (526,000)	(Serbian Orthodox 31%,
GOVERNMENT	Roman Catholic 15%,
Transitional	Protestant 4%)
ETHNIC GROUPS	**CURRENCY**
Muslim 49%, Serb 31%,	Convertible mark = 100 paras

The black-and-white zebra stripe in the centre of Botswana's flag symbolizes racial harmony.
The blue represents rainwater, because water supply is the most vital need in this dry country.
This flag was adopted in 1966, when Botswana became independent from Britain.

Geography

The Republic of Botswana is a landlocked country which lies in the heart of southern Africa. The majority of the land is flat or gently rolling, with an average height of about 1,000 m [3,280 ft]. More hilly country lies in the east. The Kalahari, a semi-desert area covers much of Botswana.

Most of the south has no permanent streams. But large depressions occur in the north. In one, the Okavango River, which flows from Angola, forms a large delta, an area of swampland. Another depression contains the Makgadikgadi Salt Pans. During floods, the Botletle River drains from the Okavango Swamps into the Makgadikgadi Salt Pans.

Climate

Temperatures are high in the summer months (October to April), but the winter months are much cooler. In winter, night-time temperatures sometimes drop below freezing point. The average annual rainfall ranges from over 400 mm [16 in] in the east to less than 200 mm [8 in] in the south-west.

Gaborone, the capital of Botswana, lies in the wetter eastern part of the country, where most of the people live. The rainy season occurs during summer, between the months of November and March. Frosts sometimes occur in parts of the east when the temperature drops below freezing.

History

The earliest inhabitants of the region were the San, who are also called Bushmen. They had a nomadic way of life, hunting wild animals and collecting plant foods.

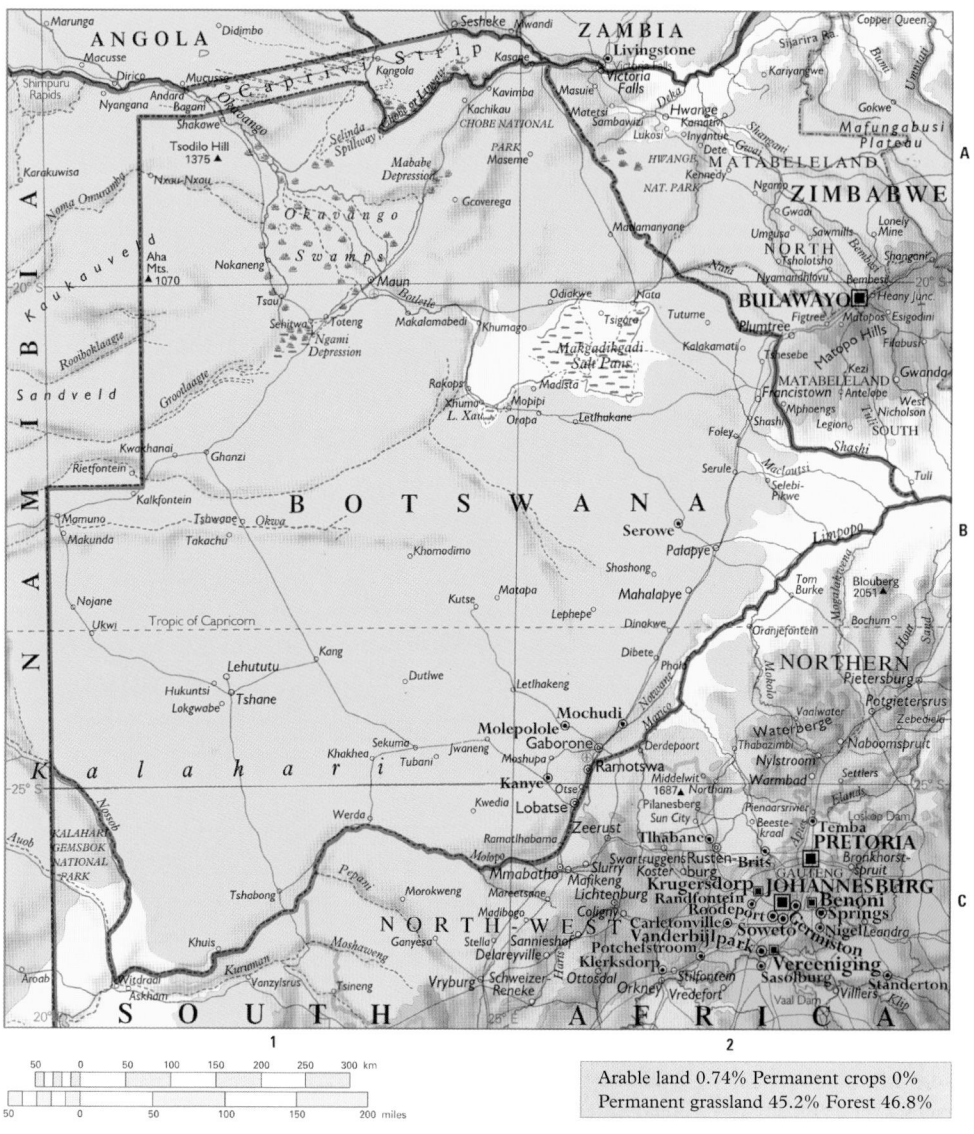

Arable land 0.74% Permanent crops 0%
Permanent grassland 45.2% Forest 46.8%

The Tswana, who speak a Bantu language, now form the majority of the population. They are cattle owners, who settled in eastern Botswana more than 1,000 years ago. Their arrival led the San to move into the dry Kalahari region. Today, the San form a tiny minority of the population. Most of them live in permanent settlements and work on cattle ranches.

Politics

Britain ruled the area as the Bechuanaland Protectorate between 1885 and 1966. When the country became independent, it adopted the name of Botswana. Since then, unlike many African countries, Botswana has been a stable multiparty democracy.

Under its first president, Sir Seretse Khama, who died in 1980, and his successor, Sir Ketumile Masire, who served from 1980 until 1998, when he retired in favour of Festus Mogae, the economy was steadily diversified. Despite a very long drought, the economy expanded during the 1980s and 1990s, which enabled it to finance wide-ranging social programmes, together with the creation of huge national parks and game reserves, which has led to a very rapid expansion of tourism.

Economy

In 1966, Botswana was one of Africa's poorest countries, depending on meat and live cattle for its exports. But the discovery of minerals, including coal, cobalt, copper and nickel, has helped to diversify the economy. The mining of diamonds at Orapa, starting in 1971, was the chief factor in transforming the economy. By 1997, Botswana had become the world's leading producer, overtaking Australia and the Democratic Republic of the Congo. By 1994, diamonds accounted for about 80% of Botswana's exports, followed by copper-nickel matte, textiles and meat products. Another major source of income comes from tourists, the majority of whom come from South Africa, which continues to have a great influence on Botswana.

The development of mining and tourism has reduced the relative importance of farming, though agriculture still employs about a fifth of the population. The most important type of farming is livestock raising, particularly cattle, which are mostly reared in the wetter east. Crops include beans, maize, millet, sorghum and vegetables. Industry is still on a small scale.

AREA	ETHNIC GROUPS
581,730 sq km	Tswana 75%, Shona 12%,
[224,606 sq mls]	San (Bushmen) 3%
POPULATION	**LANGUAGES**
1,448,000	English (official), Setswana
CAPITAL (POPULATION)	**RELIGIONS**
Gaborone	Traditional beliefs 49%,
(133,000)	Christianity 50%
GOVERNMENT	**CURRENCY**
Multiparty republic	Pula = 100 thebe

The green on the flag symbolizes Brazil's rainforests and the yellow diamond its mineral wealth. The blue sphere bears the motto 'Order and Progress'. The 27 stars, arranged in the pattern of the night sky over Rio de Janeiro, represent the states and the federal district.

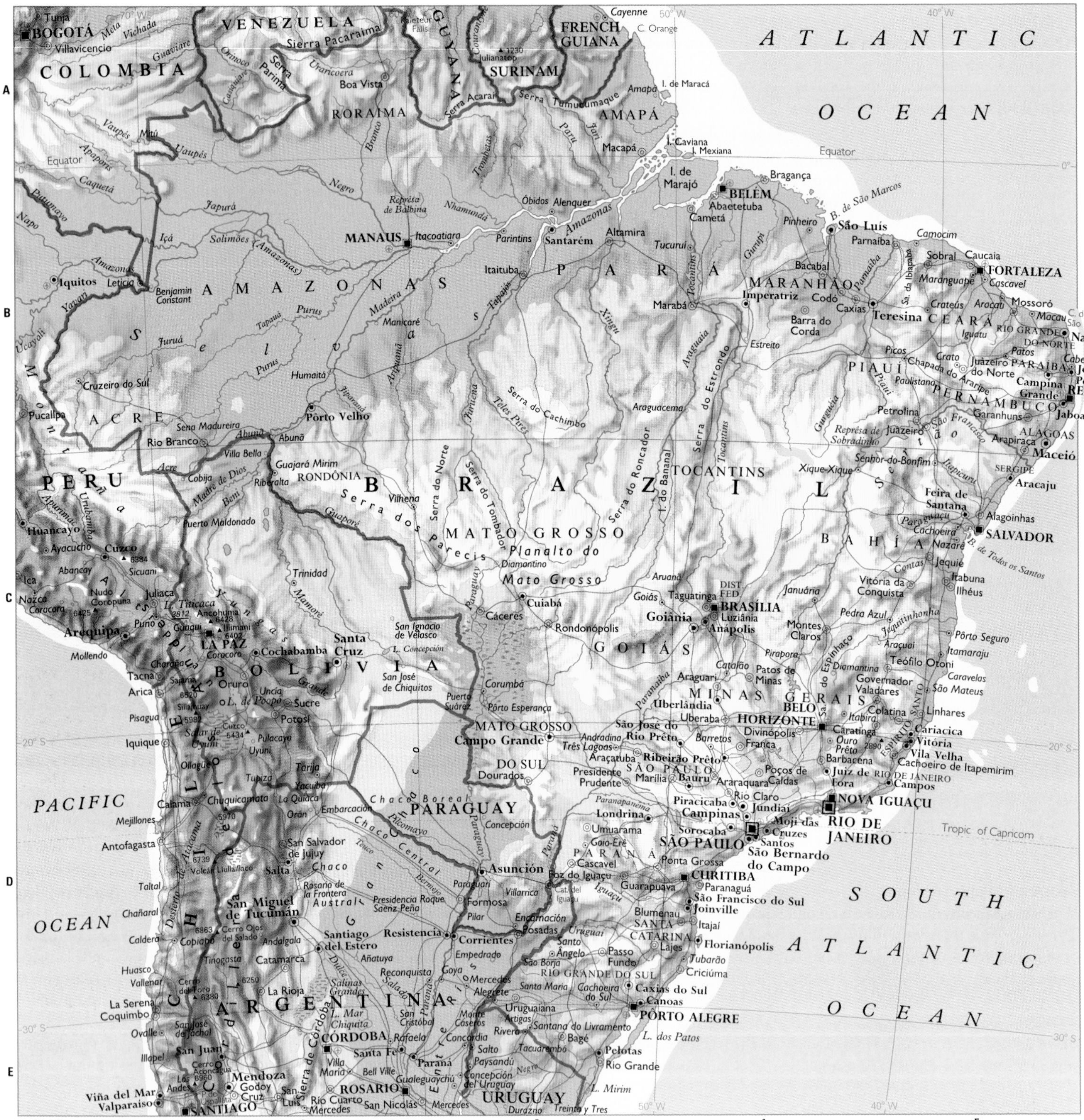

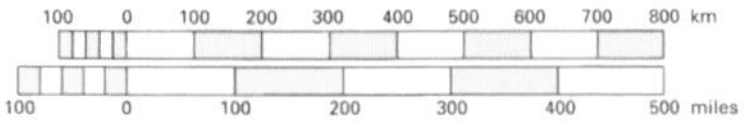

Arable land 5.11% Permanent crops 0.89%
Permanent grassland 21.9% Forest 57.7%

Geography

The Federative Republic of Brazil is the world's fifth largest country. Structurally, it has two main regions. In the north is the vast Amazon basin, once an inland sea and now drained by a river system that carries one-fifth of the world's running water. The largest area of river plain is in the upper part of the basin, along the frontiers with Bolivia and Peru. Downstream, the flood plain is relatively narrow.

The Brazilian Highlands make up the country's second main region. It consists largely of hard crystalline rock dissected into rolling uplands.

It includes the heartland (Mato Grosso) and the whole western flank of the country from the bulge to the border with Uruguay. The undulating plateau of the northern highlands carries poor soils. The typical vegetation is thorny scrub which, in the south, merges into wooded savanna. Conditions are better in the south, where rainfall is more reliable. More than 60% of the country's population live in the four southern and south-eastern states, which are the most developed part of Brazil, though they account only for 17% of Brazil's total area.

Climate

Manaus has high temperatures all through the year. The rainfall is heavy, though the period from June to September is drier than the rest of the year. The capital, Brasília, and the city Rio de Janeiro also have tropical climates, with much more marked dry seasons than Manaus. The far south has a temperate climate. The north-eastern interior is the driest region, with an average annual rainfall of only 250 mm [10 in] in places. The rainfall is also unreliable and severe droughts are common in this region.

BRAZIL – BRASÍLIA

Brazil lies almost entirely within the tropics. The north-ern half of the country is dominated by the Amazon Basin and, excluding the highlands in the south-east, there are no mountains. Monthly temperatures are very high – over 25°C [77°F] – with very little annual variation. Brasília has only a 4°C [39°F] difference between July and October. The hottest part of the country is in the north-east. Frosts often occur in the eastern highlands and the extreme south.

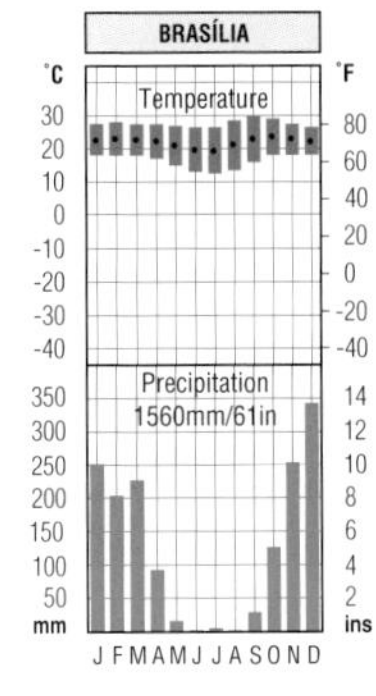

RIO DE JANEIRO

Rio de Janeiro experiences a high rainfall and a marked dry season from May to August – rain falls on only about 20 days from June to August – but not so marked as inland. Most of Brazil has moderate rainfall, but there are very heavy precipitation totals at the mouth and in the headwaters of the Amazon, and on the south-east coast below the highlands. There is an arid zone in the north-east. In Rio de Janeiro, the sun shines for 5–7 hours per day.

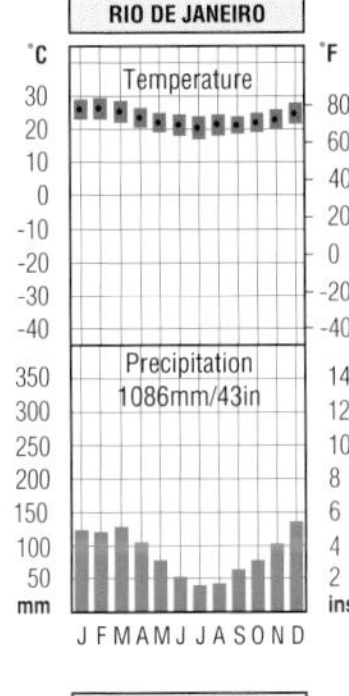

MANAUS

At Manaus, in the centre of the Amazon Basin, there is little difference between the temperature of the warmest month, October (29°C [84°F]), and the coolest, April (27°C [81°F]). Temperatures are not extremely high and the highest recorded was 37°C [99°F]; the lowest was 18°C [64°F]. Rainfall totals are high, especially December to March, with a distinct dry season from June to September, when rain falls, on average, only 5–10 days per month.

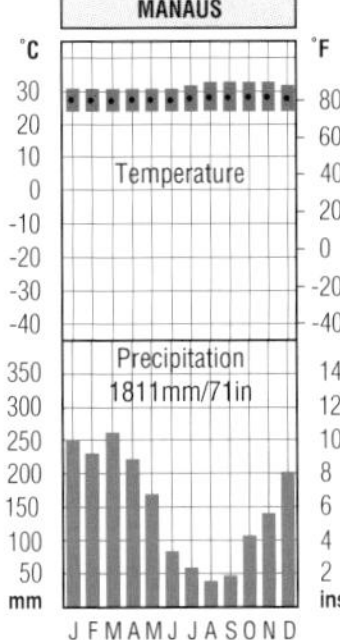

Vegetation

The Amazon basin contains the world's largest rainforests, which the Brazilians call the *selvas*. The forests contain an enormous variety of plant and animal species. But many species are threatened by loggers and others who want to exploit the forests. Forest destruction is also ruining the lives of the last surviving groups of Amazonian Indians.

Forests grow on the north-eastern coasts, but the dry interior has large areas of thorny scrub. The south-east contains fertile farmland and large ranches.

History

The Portuguese explorer Pedro Alvarez Cabral claimed Brazil for Portugal in 1500. While Spain was occupied in western South America, the first Portuguese colonists arrived in the north-eastern the 1530s. They were followed by other settlers, missionaries, explorers and prospectors who gradually penetrated the country during the 17th and 18th centuries. They encountered many groups of Amerindians, some of whom lived semi-nomadic lives, hunting, fishing and gathering fruits, while others lived in farming villages, growing cassava and other crops.

The Portuguese enslaved many Amerindians who were used for plantation work, while others were driven into the interior. The Portuguese also introduced about 4 million African slaves, notably in the sugar-cane-growing areas in the north-east. For many decades

Rio de Janeiro and São Paulo

Much of Brazil's population is concentrated in a small, highly developed 'corner' in the south-east of the country. Rio de Janeiro, discovered by the Portuguese in 1502, lies in a mag-nificent setting, stretching for 20 km [12 mls] along the coast between mountain and ocean. Though no longer the capital, it remains the focus of Brazil's cultural life, attracting visitors with the world's greatest pre-Lent festival at carnival time.

São Paulo, its early growth fuelled by the coffee boom of the late 19th century, is the most populous city in the southern hemisphere. Estimates state that the 1985 total of 15.5 million will have increased to 22.1 million by the year 2000. In both cities the gap between rich and poor is all too evident, the sprawling shanty towns (favelas) standing in sharp contrast to sophisticated metropolitan centres.

following the early settlements, Brazil was mainly a sugar-producing colony, with most plantations centred on the rich coastal plains of the north-east. These areas later produced cotton, cocoa, rice and other crops. In the south, colonists penetrated the interior in search of slaves and minerals, especially gold and diamonds. The city of Ouro Preto in Minas Gerais was built and Rio de Janeiro grew as a port for the area.

Initially little more than a group of rival provinces, Brazil began to unite in 1808, when the Portuguese royal court, seeking refuge from Napoleon's armies which had invaded Portugal in 1807, transferred from Lisbon to Rio de Janeiro. The eldest son of King Joas VI of Portugal was chosen as the 'Perpetual Defender' of Brazil by a national congress. In 1822, he proclaimed the independence of the country and was chosen as the constitutional emperor with the title of Pedro I. He became increasingly unpopular and was forced to abdicate in 1831. He was succeeded by his five-year-old son, Pedro II, who officially took office in 1841. Pedro's liberal policies included the gradual abolition of slavery (1888).

During the 19th century. Sao Paulo state became the centre of a huge coffee-growing industry. While the fortunes made in mining helped to develop Rio de Janeiro, profits from coffee were invested in the city of Sao Paulo. Immigrants from Italy and Germany settled in the south, introducing farming in the fertile valleys, in co-existence with the cattle ranchers and gauchos of the plains. The second half of the 19th century saw the development of the wild rubber industry in the Amazon basin, where the city of Manaus, with its world-famous opera house, served as a centre and market. Although Manaus lies 1,600 km [1,000 mls] from the mouth of the Amazon, rubber from the hinterland could be shipped out directly to world markets in ocean-going steamers. Brazil enjoyed a virtual monopoly of the rubber trade until the early 20th century, when Malaya began to compete, later with massive success.

The Amazon

Though not the world's longest river – 6,430 km [3,990 mls] – the Amazon is the mightiest, discharging 180,000 cu m/sec [6,350,000 cu ft/sec] into the Atlantic, more than four times the volume of its nearest rival, the Congo. The flow is so great that silt discolours the water up to 200 km [125 mls] out to sea.

The Amazon starts its journey in the Andes of Peru – only 150 km [95 mls] from the Pacific – at Lake Villafro, head of the Apurimac branch of the Ucayali, which then flows north to join the other main headstream, the Marañón. Navigable to ocean-going vessels of 6,600 tonnes up to the Peruvian jungle port of Iquitos, some 3,700 km [2,300 mls] from the sea, it then flows east – briefly forming the Peru-Colombian border – before entering Brazil. Here it becomes the Solimões, before joining the Negro (itself 18 km [11 mls] wide) at Manaus.

Along with more than 1,000 significant tributaries, seven of them more than 1,600 km [1,000 mls] long, the Amazon drains the largest river basin in the world – about 7 million sq km [2.7 million sq mls] – nearly two-fifths of South America and an area more than twice the size of India.

Regions of Brazil

Politics

A new constitution came into force in October 1988 – the eighth since Brazil became independent from Portugal in 1822. The constitution transferred powers from the president to the congress and paved the way for a return to democracy. In 1989, Fernando Collor de Mello was elected to cut inflation and combat corruption. But he made little progress and in 1992, with inflation soaring, his vice-president, Itamar Franco, took over as president. He served until 1994 when the Social Democrat Fernando Henrique Cardoso, a former finance minister, was elected president. Cardoso won a second term starting in 1999.

Today the country comprises 23 states, each with its own directly elected governor and legislature, three territories and the Federal District of Brasília, Brazil's capital since 1960. In 1991, Brazil, Argentina, Paraguay and Uruguay set up Mercosur, an alliance aimed at creating a free trade zone.

Economy

The United Nations has described Brazil as a 'Rapidly Industrializing Country', or RIC. Its total volume of production is one of the largest in the world. But many people, including poor farmers and residents of the *favelas* (city slums), do not share in the country's fast economic growth. Widespread poverty, together with high inflation and unemployment, cause political problems.

By the early 1990s, industry was the most valuable activity, employing 25% of the people. Brazil is among the world's top producers of bauxite, chrome, diamonds, gold, iron ore, manganese and tin. It is also a major manufacturing country. Its products include aircraft, cars, chemicals, processed food, raw sugar, iron and steel, paper and textiles.

Brazil is one of the world's leading farming countries and agriculture employs 28% of the people. Coffee is a major export. Other leading products include bananas, citrus fruits, cocoa, maize, rice, soya beans and sugar cane. Brazil is also the top producer of eggs, meat and milk in South America.

Forestry is a major industry, though many people fear that the exploitation of the rainforests, with 1.5% to 4% of Brazil's forest being destroyed every year, is a disaster for the entire world.

Brazil's exports reflect its mixed economy. The leading items include iron and steel, non-electrical machinery and apparatus, mineral ores, motor vehicles, wood pulp, paper and paper products, coffee, sugar and confectionery, and aluminium and related products. Imports include machinery, chemicals and chemical products, and mineral fuels. Brazil's leading trading partners are the United States and Argentina.

A federal system was adopted for the United States of Brazil in the 1881 constitution and Brazil became a republic in 1889. Until 1930, the country experienced very strong economic expansion and prospered, but social unrest in 1930 resulted in a major revolt. From then on the country was under the control of President Getulio Vargas, who established a strong corporate state similar to that of fascist Italy, although Brazil entered World War II on the side of the Allies. Democracy, often corrupt, prevailed from 1956, 1964 and 1985. In between there were five military presidents of illiberal regimes.

The Amazon Rainforest

The world's largest and ecologically most important rainforest was still being destroyed at an alarming rate in the late 1990s, with somewhere between 1.5% and 4% disappearing each year in Brazil alone. Opening up the forest for many reasons – logging, mining, ranching, peasant resettlement – the Brazilian authorities did extremely little in real terms when confronted with a catalogue of indictments: decimation of a crucial world habitat; pollution of rivers; destruction of thousands of species of fauna and flora, especially medicinal plants; and the brutal ruination of the lives of the last remaining Amerindian tribes.

Once cut off from the rest of the world by impenetrable jungle, hundreds of thousands of Indians have been displaced in the provinces of Rondonia and Acre, principally by loggers and landless migrants, and in Para by mining, dams for HEP and ranching for beef cattle. It is estimated that five centuries ago the Amazon rainforest supported some 2 million Indians in more than 200 tribes; today the number has shrunk to a pitiful 50,000 or so, and many of the tribes have disappeared altogether.

A handful have been relatively lucky. The Yanomani, after huge international support, won their battle in 1991 for a reserve three times the size of Belgium – but for the majority of tribes a traditional life style has vanished forever.

AREA	Mestizo 12%,
8,511,970 sq km	African American 11%,
[3,286,472 sq mls]	Japanese 1%,
POPULATION	Amerindian 0.1%
170,000,000	**LANGUAGES**
CAPITAL (POPULATION)	Portuguese (official)
Brasília (1,596,000)	**RELIGIONS**
GOVERNMENT	Christianity
Federal republic	(Roman Catholic 88%)
ETHNIC GROUPS	**CURRENCY**
White 53%, Mulatto 22%,	Real = 100 centavos

BRUNEI – SEE MALAYSIA, PAGES 154–155

This flag, first adopted in 1878, uses the colours associated with the Slav people. The national emblem, incorporating a lion – a symbol of Bulgaria since the 14th century – was first added to the flag in 1947. It is now added only for official government occasions.

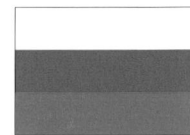

Geography

The Republic of Bulgaria is a country in the Balkan Peninsula, facing the Black Sea in the east. There are two main lowland regions. The Danubian lowlands in the north consists of a plateau that descends to the Danube, which forms much of the boundary with Romania. The other lowland region is the warmer valley of the River Maritsa, where cotton, fruits, grains, rice tobacco and vines are grown.

Separating the two lowland areas are the Balkan Mountains (Stara Planina), rising to heights of over 2,000 m [6,500 ft]. North of the capital city, Sofia, the Balkan Mountains contain rich mineral veins of iron and nonferrous metals. In south-facing valleys overlooking the Maritsa Plain, plums, tobacco and vines are grown. A feature of this area is Kazanluk, from which attar of roses is exported worldwide to the cosmetics industry. South and west of the Maritsa Valley are the Rhodope (or Rhodopi) Mountains, which contain lead, zinc and copper ores.

Climate

Summers are hot and winters are cold, but seldom severe. Rainfall is moderate all through the year.

Arable land 36.2% Permanent crops 1.97%
Permanent grassland 16.3% Forest 35.1%

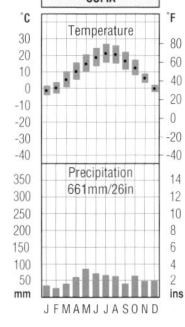

BULGARIA (SOFIA)

Bulgaria has hot summers, cold winters and moderate rainfall, with a summer maximum. This is changed by the influence of nearby seas and mountains. Eastern and southern lowlands have a much drier, warmer summer. Varna, on the coast, is usually 3–4°C [5–7°F] warmer than Sofia. The Danube lowlands are colder in winter with winds coming in from the continental interior. Temperatures are lower in the mountains.

History

Most of the Bulgarian people are descendants of Slavs and nomadic Bulgar tribes who arrived from the east in the 6th and 7th centuries. A powerful Bulgar kingdom was set up in 681, but the country became part of the Byzantine Empire in the 11th century.

Ottoman Turks ruled Bulgaria from 1396 and ethnic Turks still form a sizeable minority in the country. In 1879, Bulgaria became a monarchy, and in 1908 became fully independent. Bulgaria was an ally of Germany in World War I (1914–18) and again in World War II (1939–45). In 1944, Soviet troops invaded Bulgaria. After the war, the monarchy was abolished and the country became a Communist ally of the Soviet Union.

Politics

In the period after World War II, and especially under President Zhikov from 1954, Bulgaria became all too dependent on the Soviet Union. In 1990, the Communist Party held on to power under increasing pressure by ousting Zhikov, renouncing its leading role in the nation's affairs and changing its name to the Socialist Party, before winning the first free elections since the war, albeit unconvincingly and against confused opposition. With improved organization, the Union of Democratic Forces defeated the old guard in the following year

and began the unenviable task of making the transition to a free-market economy. Subsequent governments faced numerous problems, including inflation, food shortages, rising unemployment, strikes, a large foreign debt, a declining manufacturing industry, increased prices for raw materials, and a potential drop in the recently expanding tourist industry. In addition, there was the nagging worry of a sizeable Turkish minority, disaffected with mismanaged attempts at forced assimilation.

Economy

According to the World Bank, Bulgaria in the 1990s was a 'lower-middle-income' developing country. Bulgaria has some deposits of minerals, including brown coal, manganese and iron ore. Manufacturing is the leading economic activity, though problems arose in the early 1990s, because much industrial technology was outdated. The main products are chemicals, processed foods, metal products, machinery and textiles. Manufactures are the leading exports. Bulgaria trades mainly with countries in Eastern Europe.

Wheat and maize are the chief crops of Bulgaria. Fruit, oilseeds, tobacco and vegetables are also important and these are grown in the south-facing valleys overlooking the Maritsa Plain. Livestock farming, particularly the rearing of dairy and beef cattle, sheep and pigs, is important.

AREA	Gypsy 3%, Macedonian,
110,910 sq km [42,822 sq mls]	Armenian, Romanian,
POPULATION	Greek
8,240,000	**LANGUAGES**
CAPITAL (POPULATION)	Bulgarian (official), Turkish
Sofia (Sofiya, 1,117,000)	**RELIGIONS**
GOVERNMENT	Christianity (Eastern
Multiparty republic	Orthodox 87%), Islam 13%
ETHNIC GROUPS	**CURRENCY**
Bulgarian 86%, Turkish 10%,	Lev = 100 stotinki

This flag was adopted in 1984, when Upper Volta was renamed Burkino Faso. The red, green and yellow colours used on this flag symbolize the desire for African unity. This is because they are used on the flag of Ethiopia, Africa's oldest independent country.

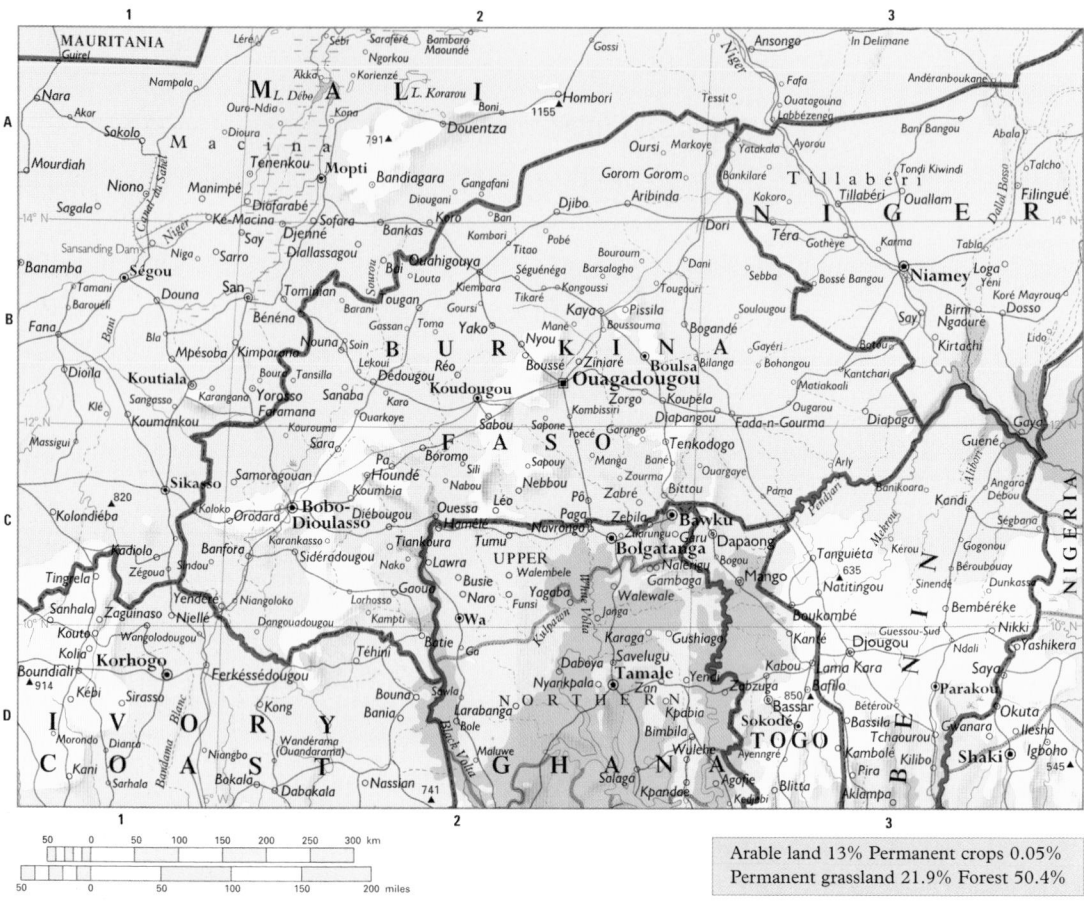

Arable land 13% Permanent crops 0.05%
Permanent grassland 21.9% Forest 50.4%

Geography and Climate

The Democratic People's Republic of Burkina Faso is a landlocked country, a little larger than the United Kingdom, in West Africa. But Burkina Faso has only one-sixth of the population of the UK.

Burkina Faso consists of a plateau, between about 300 m and 700 m [650–2,300 ft] above sea level. The plateau is cut by several rivers. Most of the rivers flow south into Ghana or east into the River Niger. During droughts, some of the rivers stop flowing, becoming marshes.

Burkina Faso has three main seasons. From October to February, it is relatively cool and dry. From March to April, it is hot and dry, while it is hot and humid from May to September.

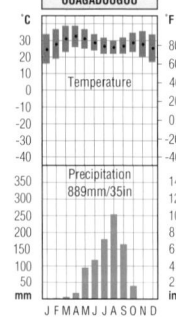

BURKINA FASO (OUAGADOUGOU)

The country's capital city, Ouagadougou, situated in central Burkino Faso, experiences uniformly high temperatures throughout the year. Most of the rain falls during the summer between May and September, but the rainfall is extremely erratic and droughts are common. The average annual rainfall in Ouagadougou is around 900 mm [35 in], with as much as 830 mm [33 in] falling between May and September.

Vegetation

The northern part of the country is covered by savanna, consisting of grassland with stunted trees and shrubs. It is part of a region called the Sahel, where the land merges into the Sahara Desert. Overgrazing of the land and deforestation (that is, the chopping down of trees to clear land) are common problems here.

Woodlands border the rivers and parts of the south-east region are swampy. The south-east contains the 'W' National Park, which

Burkina Faso shares with Benin and Niger, and the Arly Park. A third wildlife area is the Po Park situated south of Ouagadougou.

History and Politics

The people of Burkina Faso are divided into two main groups. The Voltaic group includes the Mossi, who form the largest single group, and the Bobo. The other main group is the Mande family. Burkina Faso also contains some Fulani herders and Hausa traders, who are related to the people of northern Nigeria. In early times, the ethnic groups in Burkina Faso were divided into kingdoms and chiefdoms. The leading kingdom, which was ruled by an absolute monarch called the Moro Naba, was that of the Mossi. It has existed since the 13th century.

The French conquered the Mossi capital of Ouagadougou in 1897 and they made the area a protectorate. In 1919, the area became a French colony called Upper Volta.

After independence in 1960, Upper Volta became a one-party state. But it was unstable – military groups seized power several times and a number of political killings took place. In 1984, the country's name was changed to Burkina Faso. Elections were held in 1991 – the first time in more than ten years – but the military kept an important role in the government.

Economy

Burkina Faso is one of the world's 20 poorest countries and has become extremely dependent on foreign aid. Approximately 90% of the people earn their living by farming or by raising livestock. Grazing land covers around 37% of the land and farmland covers around 10%.

Most of Burkina Faso is dry with thin soils. The country's main food crops are beans, maize, millet, rice and sorghum. Cotton, groundnuts and shea nuts, whose seeds produce a fat used to make cooking oil and soap, are grown for sale abroad. Livestock are also an important export.

The country has few resources and manufacturing is on a small scale. There are some deposits of manganese, zinc, lead and nickel in the north of the country, but there is not yet a good enough transport route there. Many young men seek jobs abroad in Ghana and Ivory Coast. The money they send home to their families is important to the country's economy.

AREA	**ETHNIC GROUPS**
274,200 sq km	Mossi 48%, Mande 9%,
[105,869 sq mls]	Fulani 8%, Bobo 7%
POPULATION	**LANGUAGES**
11,266,000	French (official), Mossi, Fulani
CAPITAL (POPULATION)	**RELIGIONS**
Ouagadougou	Traditional beliefs 45%,
(690,000)	Islam 43%, Christianity 12%
GOVERNMENT	**CURRENCY**
Multiparty republic	CFA franc = 100 centimes

BURMA (MYANMAR)

The colours on Burma's flag were adopted in 1948 when the country became independent from Britain. The socialist symbol, added in 1974, includes a ring of 14 stars representing the country's 14 states. The gearwheel represents industry and the rice plant symbolizes agriculture.

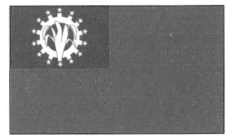

Geography and Climate

The Union of Burma is now alternatively known as the Union of Myanmar; its name was changed in 1989. Mountains border the country in the east and west, with the highest mountains in the north. Burma's highest mountain is Hkakabo Razi, which is 5,881 m [19,294 ft] high. Between these ranges is central Burma, which contains the fertile valleys of the Irrawaddy and Sittang rivers. The Irrawaddy delta on the Bay of Bengal is one of the world's leading rice-growing areas. Burma also includes the long Tenasserim coast in the south-east.

Burma has a tropical monsoon climate. There are three seasons. The rainy season runs from late May to mid-October. A cool, dry season follows, between late October and the middle part of February. The hot season lasts from late February to mid-May, though temperatures remain high during the humid rainy season.

History and Politics

Many groups settled in Burma in ancient times. Some, called the hill peoples, live in remote mountain areas where they have retained their own cultures. The ancestors of the country's main ethnic group today, the Burmese, arrived in the 9th century AD.

Britain conquered Burma during the 19th century and made the country a province of British India. In 1937, the British granted Burma limited self-government. Japan conquered Burma in 1942, but the Japanese were driven out in 1945. Burma became fully independent in 1948.

Revolts by Communists and various hill people led to instability in the 1950s. In 1962, Burma became a military dictatorship and, in 1974, a one-party state. Attempts to control minority liberation movements and the opium trade led to repressive rule. The National League for Democracy led by Aung San Suu Kyi won the elections in 1990, but the military ignored the result and continued their repressive rule. They earned Burma the reputation for having one of the world's worst records on human rights. Burma's internal political problems helped to make it one of the world's poorest countries. Its admission to ASEAN (Association of South-east Asian Nations) in 1997 may have implied regional recognition of the regime, but the European Union continued to voice its concern over human rights abuses.

Economy

Agriculture is the main activity, employing 64% of the people. The chief crop is rice. Groundnuts, maize, plantains, pulses, seed cotton, sesame seeds and sugar cane are other farm products. Forestry is important and teak is a major product. Fish and shellfish are also produced. Burma's varied natural resources are mostly underdeveloped, but the country is famous for its precious stones, especially rubies. The country also has sufficient oil and natural gas to meet most of its needs. Manufacturing is small-scale and mainly geared to supplying the home market. Major products include fertilizers, processed food and textiles.

Until 1964, Burma was the world's leading rice producer, but it had slipped to seventh place by 1995. Rice, however, remains a leading export, together with such products as teak, pulses and beans, and rubber. Despite the country's repressive reputation, the number of tourists visiting Burma began to increase in the late 1990s.

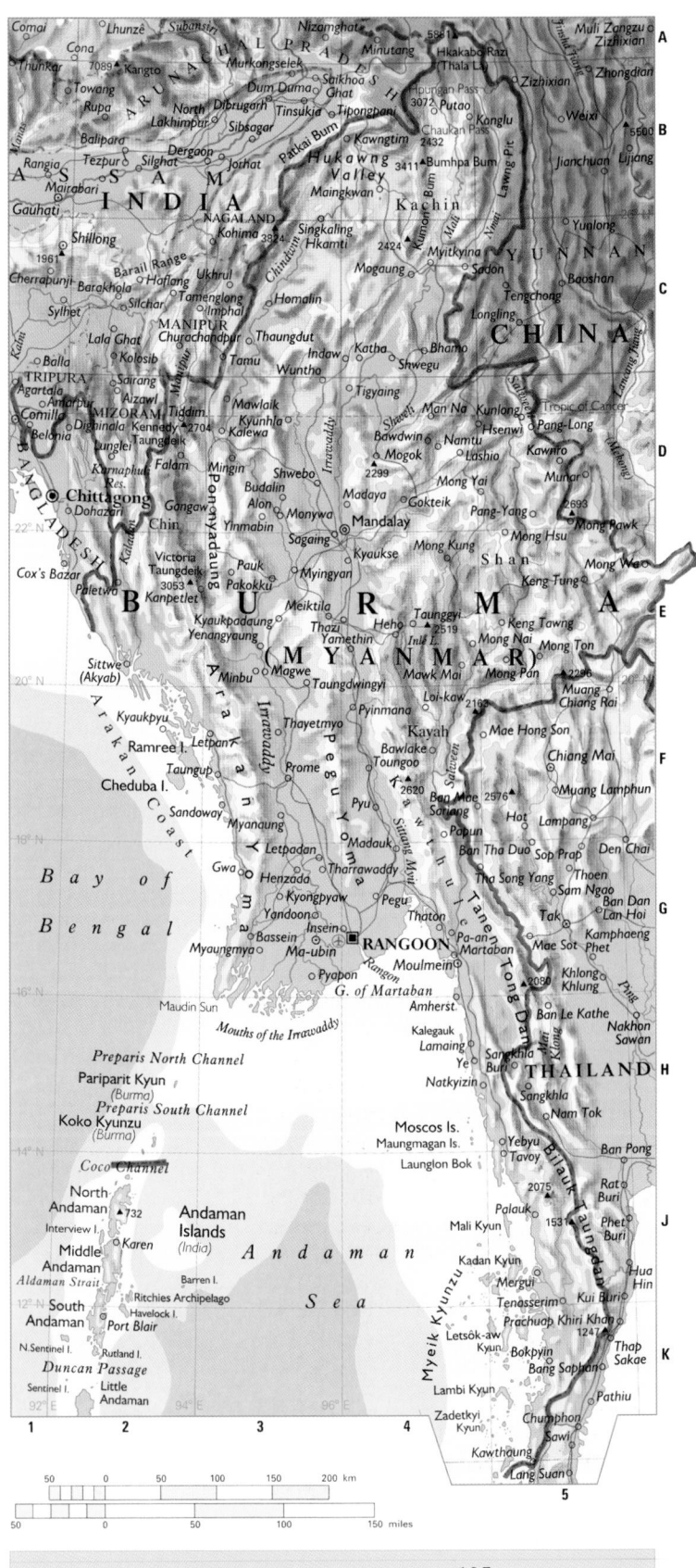

AREA	Mon 2%, Kachin 1%
676,577 sq km	**LANGUAGES**
[261,228 sq mls]	Burmese (official),
POPULATION	Shan, Karen,
47,305,000	Rakhine, Mon,
CAPITAL (POPULATION)	Kachin, English,
Rangoon	Chin
(2,513,000)	**RELIGIONS**
GOVERNMENT	Buddhism 89%,
Military regime	Christianity,
ETHNIC GROUPS	Islam
Burman 69%, Shan 9%,	**CURRENCY**
Karen 6%, Rakhine 5%,	Kyat = 100 pyas

BURUNDI – SEE RWANDA, PAGE 195

CAMBODIA

Red is the traditional colour of Cambodia. The blue symbolizes the water resources that are so important to the people, three-quarters of whom depend on farming for a living. The silhouette is the historic temple at Angkor Wat.

Arable land 21.6%
Forest 69.1%

Geography

The Kingdom of Cambodia is a country in South-east Asia. Low mountains border the country except in the south-east. But most of Cambodia consists of plains drained by the River Mekong, which enters Cambodia from Laos in the north and exits through Vietnam in the south-east. The north-west contains Tonlé Sap (or Great Lake). In the dry season, this lake drains into the River Mekong. But in the wet season, the level of the Mekong rises and water flows in the opposite direction from the river into Tonlé Sap – the lake then becomes the largest freshwater lake in Asia.

Climate

Cambodia has a tropical monsoon climate, with high temperatures all through the year. The dry season, when winds blow from the north or north-east, runs from November to April. During the rainy season, from May to October, moist winds blow from the south or south-east. The high humidity and heat often make conditions unpleasant. The rainfall is heaviest near the coast, and rather lower inland.

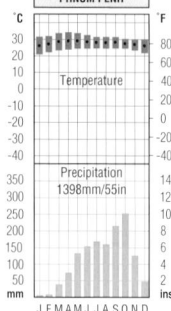

CAMBODIA (PHNOM PENH)

Phnom Penh is situated in the southern region of Cambodia. It experiences a tropical climate with uniformly high temperatures throughout the year. The average temperature in January is about 25.6°C [78°F], while that recorded in July is 28.9°C [84°F]. Rainfall is slightly lower here than on the coast with most falling between May and November. The average annual amount has been recorded at 1,398 mm [55 in].

PHNOM PENH

Temperature

Precipitation
1398mm/55in

History

Early civilizations in what is now Cambodia included the kingdom of Funan, which developed in the south around AD 100. Another kingdom, called Chenla, had developed north of Funan by around 600, but it broke up in the 8th century. The Tonlé Sap lowlands in the north-west were the cradle of the Hindu-Buddhist Khmer empire, which lasted from 802 to 1431. Its zenith came in the reign of

Suryavarman II (1113–50), who built the great funerary temple of Angkor Wat. Together with Angkor Thom, the Angkor site contains the world's largest group of religious buildings. The wealth of the kingdom rested on fish from the lake and rice from the flooded lowlands, for which an extensive system of irrigation channels and strong reservoirs was developed. Thai forces captured Angkor in 1431 and forests covered the site. Following its rediscovery in 1860, it has been gradually restored and is now a major tourist attraction.

Cambodia was under French rule from 1863 as part of Indo-China until it achieved independence in 1954. In a short period of stability during the late 1950s and 1960s, the country developed its small-scale agricultural resources and rubber plantations. It remained predominantly rural, but achieved self-sufficiency in food, with some exports.

Politics

Despite its claims of neutrality in the struggles between Communist and non-Communist groups in South-East Asia, South Vietnam and the United States argued that North Vietnam had bases in Cambodia during the Vietnam War. In 1969, US planes bombed North Vietnamese targets in Cambodia. In 1970, King Norodom Sihanouk was overthrown and Cambodia became a republic. Under assault from South Vietnamese troops, the Communist Vietnamese withdrew deep into Cambodia. US raids ended in 1973, but fighting continued as Cambodia's Communists in the Khmer Rouge fought against the government. The Khmer Rouge, led by Pol Pot, were victorious in 1975. They began a reign of terror, murdering government officials and educated people. Up to 2 million people were estimated to have been killed. After the overthrow of Pol Pot by Vietnamese forces in 1979, civil war raged between the puppet government of the People's Republic of Kampuchea (Cambodia) and the US-backed government of Democratic Kampuchea, a coalition of Prince Sihanouk, the Khmer Liberation Front, and the Khmer Rouge, who, from 1982, claimed to have abandoned their Communist ideology.

Devastated by war and denied almost any aid, Cambodia continued to decline. It was only the withdrawal of Vietnamese troops in 1989, sparking a fear of a Khmer Rouge revival, that forced a settlement. In October 1991, a UN-brokered peace plan for elections in 1993 was accepted by all parties. A new constitution was adopted in September 1993, restoring democracy and the monarchy. Sihanouk again became king. However, the Khmer Rouge continued hostilities and were banned in 1994. In 1997, Hu Sen, the second prime minister, engineered a coup against Prince Norodom Ranariddh (Sihanouk's son), the first prime minister Ranariddh went into exile but returned in 1998. Elections in 1998 resulted in victory for Hu Sen, but Ranariddh alleged electoral fraud. A coalition government was formed in December 1998, with Hu Sen as prime minister, and Ranariddh becoming Chairman of the National Assembly.

Economy

Cambodia is a poor country. Until the 1970s, farmers produced most of the food needed by the people. By 1986, it was only able to supply 80% of its needs. Farming is the main activity and rice, rubber and maize are major products. Manufacturing is almost non-existent.

AREA	ETHNIC GROUPS
181,040 sq km	Khmer 94%, Chinese 3%,
[69,900 sq mls]	Cham 2%, Thai, Lao,
POPULATION	Kola, Vietnamese
11,340,000	**LANGUAGES**
CAPITAL (POPULATION)	Khmer (official)
Phnom Penh	**RELIGIONS**
(920,000)	Buddhism 88%, Islam 2%
GOVERNMENT	**CURRENCY**
Constitutional monarchy	Riel = 100 sen

CAMEROON

Cameroon uses the colours that appear on the flag of Ethiopia, Africa's oldest independent nation. These colours symbolize African unity. The flag is based on the tricolour adopted in 1957. The design with the yellow liberty star dates from 1975.

Geography and Climate

The Republic of Cameroon in West Africa got its name from the Portuguese word *camarões*, or prawns. This name was used by Portuguese explorers who fished for prawns along the coast. Behind the narrow coastal plains on the Gulf of Guinea, the land rises to a series of plateaux. In the north, the land slopes down towards the Lake Chad basin. The mountain region in the south-west of the country includes Mount Cameroon, a volcano which erupts from time to time. The vegetation varies greatly from north to south. The deserts in the north merge into dry and moist savanna in central Cameroon, with dense tropical rainforests in the humid south.

The rainfall is heavy, especially in the highlands. The rainiest months near the coast are from June to September. The rainfall decreases to the north and the far north has a hot, dry climate. Temperatures are high on the coast, whereas the inland plateaux are cooler.

CAMEROON (DOUALA)

Rainfall at Douala is at its heaviest during the months of July, August and September when the south-west monsoon is at its strongest and steadiest, and temperatures hardly vary. Sunshine levels are relatively low, averaging only 3 hours per day. Rainfall on the seaward slopes of Cameroon Peak is even heavier and often exceeds 9,000 mm [350 in] in places.

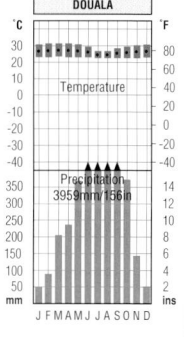

History

Among the early inhabitants of Cameroon were groups of Bantu-speaking people. (There are now more than 160 ethnic groups, each with their own language.) In the late 15th century, Portuguese explorers, who were seeking a sea route to Asia around Africa, reached the Cameroon coast. From the 17th century, southern Cameroon was a centre of the slave trade, but slavery was ended in the early 19th century. In 1884, the area became a German protectorate.

Politics

Germany lost Cameroon during World War I (1914–18). The country was then divided into two parts, one ruled by Britain and the other by France. In 1960, French Cameroon became the independent Cameroon Republic. In 1961, after a vote in British Cameroon, part of the territory joined the Cameroon Republic to become the Federal Republic of Cameroon. The other part joined Nigeria. In 1972, Cameroon became a unitary state called the United Republic of Cameroon. It adopted the name Republic of Cameroon in 1984, but the country had two official languages. In 1995, partly to placate the English-speaking people, Cameroon became the 52nd member of the Commonwealth.

Economy

Like most countries in tropical Africa, Cameroon's economy is based on agriculture, which employs 73% of the people. The chief food crops include cassava, maize, millet, sweet potatoes and yams. The country also has plantations to produce such crops as cocoa and coffee for export.

Cameroon is fortunate in having some oil, the country's chief export, and bauxite. Although Cameroon has few manufacturing and processing industries, its mineral exports and its self-sufficiency in food production make it one of the wealthier countries in tropical Africa. Another important industry is forestry, ranking second among the exports, after oil. Other exports, in order of importance, are cocoa, coffee, aluminium and cotton.

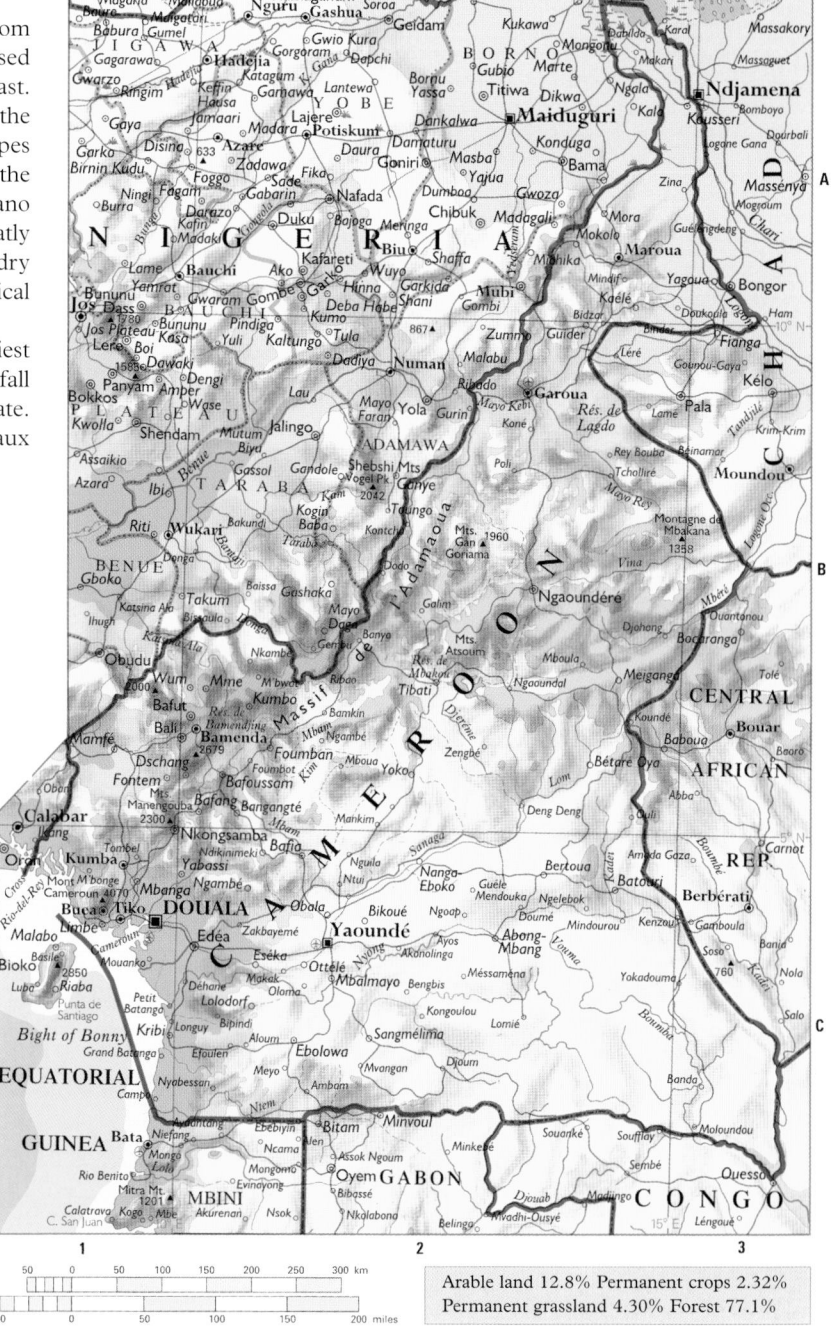

Arable land 12.8% Permanent crops 2.32%
Permanent grassland 4.30% Forest 77.1%

AREA	Bamum 19%, Duala,
475,440 sq km	Luanda and Basa 15%,
[183,567 sq mls]	Fulani 10%
POPULATION	**LANGUAGES**
15,029,000	French and English (both official)
CAPITAL (POPULATION)	**RELIGIONS**
Yaoundé (750,000)	Christianity 53%,
GOVERNMENT	traditional beliefs 25%,
Multiparty republic	Islam 22%
ETHNIC GROUPS	**CURRENCY**
Fang 20%, Bamileke and	CFA franc = 100 centimes

Canada's flag, with its simple 11-pointed maple leaf emblem, was adopted in 1965 after many attempts to find an acceptable design. The old flag, used from 1892, was the British Red Ensign, but this flag became unpopular with Canada's French community.

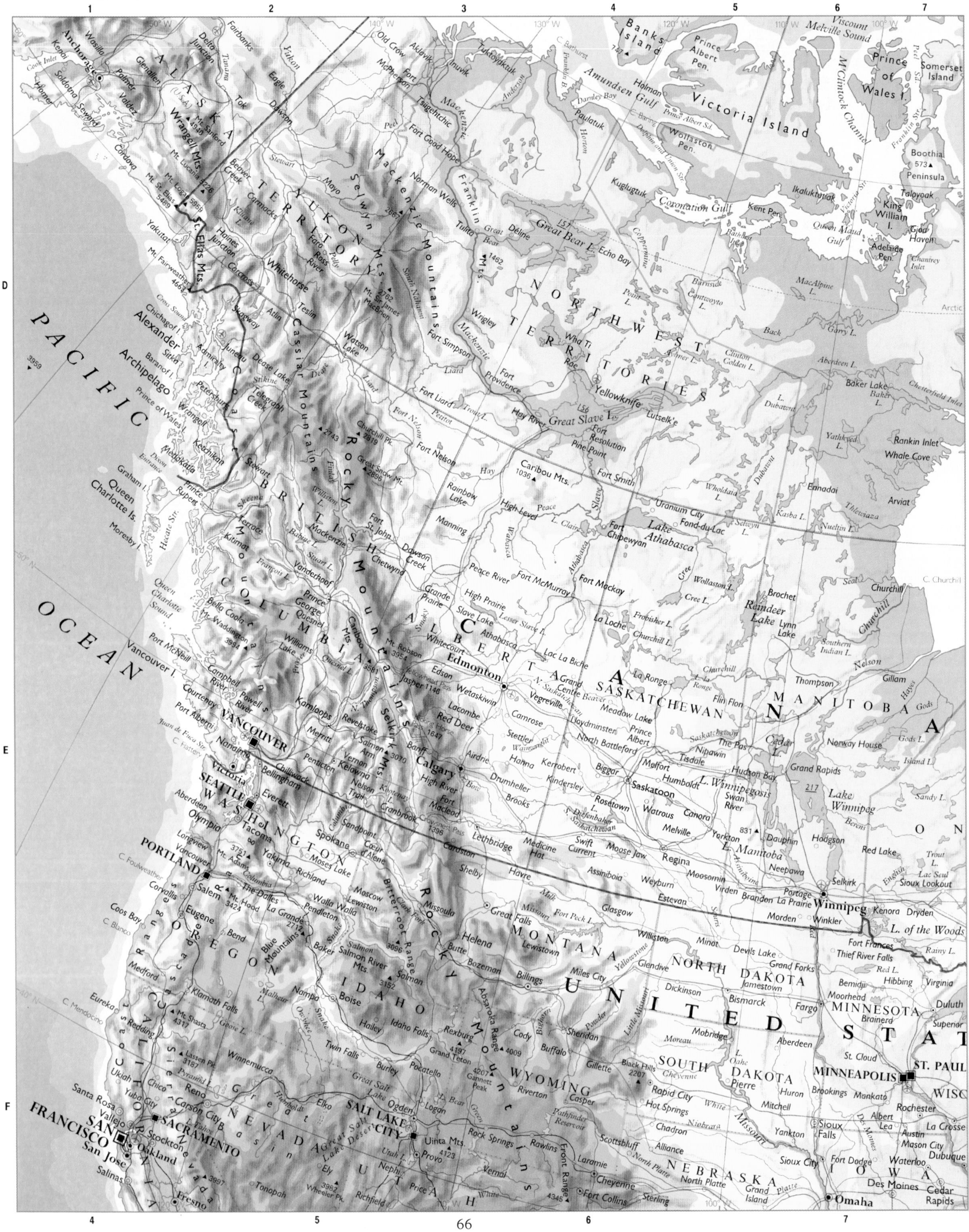

Arable land 4.93% Permanent crops 0.01%
Permanent grassland 3.03% Forest 53.6%

100 0 100 200 300 400 500 600 km
100 0 100 200 300 400 miles

NORTHERN CANADA
Continuation northwards on same
scale as main map

Geography

A vast confederation of ten provinces and three territories, Canada is the world's second largest country after Russia, with an even longer coastline – about 250,000 km [155,000 mls]. It is sparsely populated because it contains vast areas of virtually unoccupied mountains, cold forests, tundra and polar desert in the north and west. About 80% of the population of Canada lives within about 300 km [186 mls] of the southern border. Yet Canada is a land of great beauty and variety.

Western Canada includes the Pacific Ranges and coastlands. This region includes much of British Columbia, the Queen Charlotte Islands, Vancouver Island, and the south-western part of Yukon Territory. In the Yukon Territory stands Canada's highest peak, Mount Logan, which reaches 5,959 m [19,551 ft] in the St Elias Mountains, near the Alaskan border. Glaciers cover many mountains in the St Elias Mountains and glaciation has left its mark along the coast, where it has carved deep fiords.

East of the Pacific Ranges lie the Rocky Mountains. These two highland regions form part of the huge cordillera that stretches from Alaska to Mexico. The magnificent scenery in the Rockies is crowned by Mount Robson, which reaches 3,954 m [12,972 ft] in eastern British Columbia. East of the Rocky Mountains lie vast interior plains extending north to the Arctic Ocean. The southern part of the interior plains are grassy prairies, though the land has been largely transformed by farming. The interior plains are rich in minerals and fossil fuels.

East of the interior plains lies a region called the Canadian Shield, a horseshoe-shaped area curving from the Arctic Ocean, around Hudson Bay to the coast of Labrador. It is a region of ancient rocks that formed the ancient core of North America. North of the Canadian Shield, almost entirely within the Arctic Circle, lie Canada's Arctic Islands.

South of the Canadian Shield are Canada's most populous regions: the lowlands north of lakes Erie and Ontario, and the St Lawrence River lowlands, where more than half of the nation's people live. The far south-east of Canada contains part of the Appalachian Mountains, which extend through the eastern United States.

Climate

Canada has a cold climate. In winter, temperatures fall below freezing point throughout most of Canada. But the south-western coast has a relatively mild climate. Along the Arctic Circle, mean temperatures are below freezing for seven months a year. By contrast, hot winds from the Gulf of Mexico warm southern Ontario and the St Lawrence River lowlands in summer. As a result, southern Ontario has a frost-free season of nearly six months.

The coasts of British Columbia are wet, with an average annual rainfall of more than 2,500 mm [98 in] in places. By contrast, the prairies are arid or semi-arid, with an average annual rainfall of 250 to 500 mm [10–20 in]. The rainfall in south-eastern Canada ranges from around 800 mm [31 in] in southern Ontario to about 1,500 mm [59 in] on the coasts of Newfoundland and Nova Scotia. Heavy snow falls in eastern Canada in winter.

Vegetation

Forests of cedars, hemlocks and other trees grow on the western mountains, with firs and spruces at the higher levels. The mountain forests provide habitats for bears, deer and mountain lions, while the sure-footed Rocky Mountain goats and bighorn sheep roam above the tree line (the upper limit of tree growth).

The interior plains were once grassy prairies. While the drier areas are still used for grazing cattle, the wetter areas are used largely for growing wheat and other cereals. North of the prairies are the boreal forests which, in turn merge into the treeless tundra and Arctic wastelands in the far north. The lowlands in south-eastern Canada contain forests of deciduous trees, such as beech, hickory, oak and walnut.

CANADA – QUÉBEC

The effect of the Great Lakes is felt in the Ontario Peninsula, resulting in slightly warmer winters than in Québec. But the temperatures in northern Canada are extreme: along the Arctic Circle, the mean monthly temperatures are below freezing for much of the year. In Québec, rainfall is moderate all year with no marked peak, and with a reasonable amount of snow. Québec has an average of about 1,053 mm [41 in] of rain each year.

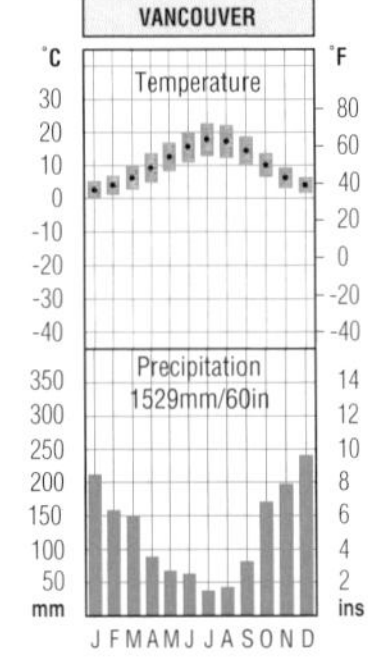

VANCOUVER

West of the Rockies, and to a lesser extent on the eastern coast, the nearby ocean changes the expected climate. At Vancouver, rainfall is high with a maximum occurring between October and March. There is little snow, with just over 50 frost days. Summers are cool, with no mean temperatures above 18°C [64°F], the record being 34°C [93°F] in August. Temperatures in winter decline a little to the north along this coastal fringe.

EDMONTON

The July temperature is about 17°C [63°F], but that of December is nearly –14°C [6°F], an annual range of over 30°C [54°F]. But high summer temperatures are recorded in these areas, over 30°C [54°F] having been recorded in all months, April to September. Rainfall is low with a maximum from June to August, and there is little snowfall. On average there are over 210 frost days. Westwards into the Rockies, the snow can reach great depths.

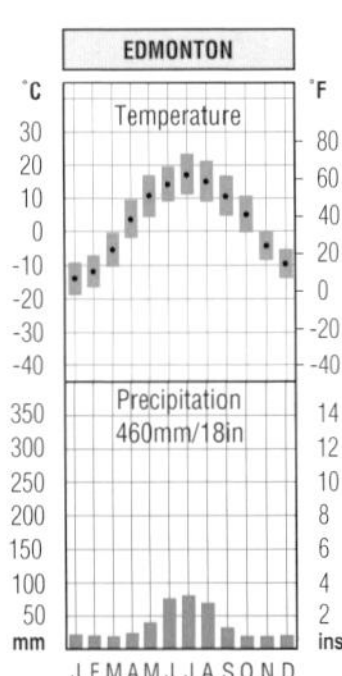

The Tundra

Beyond their habitable southern rims, northern Canada and Alaska, are thinly populated and bleak. The subarctic zone contains the vast boreal (northern) forests, which are also called the taiga. Winters are long, cold and snowy, while summers are cool. The dominant trees are needleleaf evergreens, including such trees as fir, pine and spruce, which are specially adapted to the climate. For example, their conical shapes prevent overloading by snow, their thick trunks protect them against the cold, and their shallow roots absorb moisture from the soil, even when the subsoil is frozen solid. Many small mammals, such as beavers, mice and hares, live in the forests, while larger mammals include bears, caribou, foxes, moose and wolves. But the number of species is small compared with the mild deciduous forests.

To the north, conditions become more severe and the boreal forest dies out, replaced by tundra. Only 11,000 years ago, the tundra was covered by ice sheets. Glaciation has scoured the surface bare in many areas and new soils have not yet had time to form. In other places, only the top 60 cm [24 in] of soil thaws in summer, while the subsoil (permafrost) is permanently frozen. Winters are long and bitterly cold. Summers are brief and cool. Even in the southern parts of the tundra, the season of plant growth is only 70 to 80 days. Precipitation is light – usually less than 250 mm [10 in] a year, and much falls as snow. Except in areas of snow drifts, snow is seldom deep, but it provides cover for vegetation and burrowing animals.

The treeless tundra supports low grasses, lichens, mosses and spindly shrubs, providing food for migrating reindeer and resident animals, such as hares, lemmings, voles and other small browsers and grazers. Their numbers are augmented each summer by hosts of migrant birds, including ducks, geese, swans, waders and others that fly in from temperate latitudes to feed on the vegetation and on the swarms of insects that fill the air over vast swampy areas. Beyond the Canadian tundra lie Arctic lands, some of which are permanently covered by glaciers and small ice caps. In the seas around the northernmost islands, such animals as polar bears and seals feed on fish, spending much of their lives on the sea ice.

History

Canada's first people, ancestors of the Native Americans, or the Indians, arrived in North America from Asia around 40,000 years ago. Later arrivals were the Inuit (Eskimos), who also came from Asia. Norse voyagers and fishermen were probably the first to visit Canada, but John Cabot's later discovery of North America in 1497 led to the race to annex lands and wealth, with France and Britain the main contenders. Jacques Cartier's discovery of the St Lawrence River in 1534 gave France a head start. From their settlements near Québec, explorers, trappers and missionaries pioneered routes, penetrating into northern North America. With the hope of finding a North-west Passage to China and South-east Asia, the French followed the St Lawrence and Niagara rivers deep into the heartland of the continent.

Discovering the Great Lakes, they then moved north, west and south in their search for trade. From the fertile valley of the upper St Lawrence, French

Provinces of Canada

influence spread north through the boreal forests and over the tundra. To the west and south, they reached the prairies, exploring further into the Rocky Mountains and down the Ohio and Mississippi rivers. In 1763, after a series of wars that gave Britain brief control of the whole of North America, French-speaking communities were already scattered widely across the interior. Many of the southern settlements became American after 1776, when the United States declared independence from Britain, while the northern ones became part of a British colony.

British settlers had long been established on the Atlantic coast in fishing communities, farming the land where possible. In the 1780s, a new wave of English-speaking settlers – the United Empire Loyalists – moved north into Nova Scotia, New Brunswick and Lower Canada. With further waves of immigration from Britain, English speakers soon dominated fertile land between lakes Huron and Erie. From there, they spread westwards. Restricted to the north by the boreal forests and tundra and to the south by the United States, they spread through Québec into Upper Canada (now Ontario), the only province on the Canadian shores of the Great Lakes. Mostly English-speaking settlers continued westwards to establish settlements on the prairies, finally crossing the Rocky Mountains to link with embryo settlements along the Pacific coast. Hence, the St Lawrence lowlands and pockets of settlement on the Canadian Shield remained French in language and culture. The bulk of Canada, to the east and west, became predominantly English.

Canada's topography and immense scale inhibited the development of a single nation. The union of British Upper Canada and French Lower Canada was sealed by the confederation of 1867, when, as the newly named provinces of Ontario and Québec, they were united with the maritime core of Nova Scotia and New Brunswick. Three years later, the settlement on the Red River entered the confederation as Manitoba and, in the following year, the Pacific colonies of Vancouver Island and British Columbia, now united as a single province, completed the link from sea to sea. Prince Edward Island joined in 1873, the prairie provinces of Alberta and Saskatchewan in 1905, and Newfoundland in 1949.

Though self-governing in most respects from the time of confederation, Canada remained technically subject to the British Imperial parliament until 1931.

The creation of the British Commonwealth in 1931 made Canada a sovereign nation under the crown. Canada is now a constitutional monarchy. Under the Constitution Act of 1982, Queen Elizabeth II is head of state and a symbol of the close ties between Canada and Britain. The British monarch is represented by an appointed governor-general, but the country is ruled by a prime minister, and an elected, two-chamber parliament.

Canada combines the cabinet system with a federal form of government, with each province having its own government. The federal government can reject any law passed by a provincial legislature, though this seldom happens in practice. The territories are self-governing, but the federal government plays a large part in their administration.

Politics

The promotion of Canadian unity across so wide a continent has been the aim of successive governments for more than 200 years. Yet with the population spread out along a southern ribbon of settlement, about 4,000 km [2,500 mls] long but rarely more than 300 km [186 mls] wide, Canada has made this objective difficult to achieve.

Transcontinental communications have played a critical role. From the eastern provinces, the Canadian Pacific Railway crossed the Rockies to reach Vancouver in 1885. Later, a second route, Canadian National, was pieced together, and the Trans-Canada Highway links the extreme east and west of the country. Transcontinental air routes link the major centres, and local air traffic is especially important in the boreal forests, mountains and tundra. Modern telecommunications have enabled all parts of the confederation – even the most remote parts of the Arctic territories – to be linked. Even so, the vastness is intimidating. The country spans six time zones – at noon in Vancouver, it is 3:00 PM in Toronto and 4:30 PM in St John's, Newfoundland.

A constant hazard to Canadian nationhood is the proximity of the United States. Though benign, with shared British traditions, the prosperous giant to the south has often seemed to threaten the survival of Canada through economic dominance and cultural annexation. The two countries have the largest bilateral trade flow in the world. Economic co-operation was further enhanced in 1993 when Canada, the United States and Mexico set up NAFTA (North American Free Trade Agreement).

A constant problem facing those who want to maintain the unity of Canada is the persistence of French culture in Québec, which has fuelled a separatist movement seeking to turn the province into an independent French-speaking republic. More than 5 million of the 7.5 million Québeckers are French speakers. In 1994, Québeckers voted the separatist Parti Québécois into provincial office. The incoming prime minister announced that the independence for Québec would be the subject of a referendum in 1995. In that referendum, 49.4% voted 'Yes' (for separation) while 50.5% voted 'No'.

Provincial elections in 1998 resulted in another victory for the Parti Québécois. But while the separatist party won 75 out of the 125 seats in the provincial assembly, it won only 43% of the popular vote, compared with 44% for the anti-secessionist Liberal Party and 12% for the floating Action Démocratique de Québec. Also significant was a ruling by Canada's highest court that, under Canadian law, Québec does not have the right to secede unilaterally. The court ruled that, should a clear majority of the people in the province vote by 'a clear majority' to a 'clear question' in favour of independence, the federal government and the other provinces would have to negotiate Québec's secession.

Other problems involve the rights of the aboriginal Native Americans and the Inuit, who together numbered about 470,000 in 1991. In 1999, a new Inuit territory was created. Called Nunavut, it is made up of 64% of the former North-west Territories, and covers 2,201,400 sq km [649,965 sq mls]. The population in 1991 was about 25,000, 85% of whom were Inuit. Nunavut, whose capital is Iqaluit (formerly Frobisher Bay), will depend on future aid, but its mineral reserves and the prospects of an ecotourist industry hold out promise for the future.

Economy

Canada is a highly developed and prosperous country. Rich in natural resources, including oil and natural gas, a wide range of minerals, forests and rich farmland, its economy has traditionally been based on selling commodities – raw materials and farm produce. Up to 78% of the population now live in cities and towns, and manufacturing and service industries play a major role in the economy. Resource-based industries now employ only 5% of the workforce, as compared with 16% in manufacturing and nearly three-quarters in service industries.

Although farmland covers only 8% of the country, Canadian farms are highly mechanized and productive. The leading farm products are beef cattle, milk, pigs and wheat. Also important are barley, chickens and eggs, maize and canola, which is used to make cooking oil. More than three-quarters of Canada's farmland is situated in the prairie provinces of Alberta, Manitoba and Saskatchewan. These provinces produce most of the country's grains, while beef cattle ranching is also important. The other main farming region is the St Lawrence lowlands in the east. Québec is the leading milk-producing province, while Ontario ranks second. The Atlantic provinces are known for their potatoes and dairy farming, while British Columbia produces eggs and poultry, fruits, livestock and milk. The fishing industry dates back to the early days of European settlement, but overfishing now threatens production in the Grand Banks, one of the world's finest fishing areas, off the coast of Newfoundland.

Forestry is a major industry. British Columbia, Québec and Ontario are the leading timber-producing provinces. Cheap hydroelectric power, coupled with improved transmission technology, has encouraged the further development of wood pulp and paper industries, even in the remote parts of the northern forests of Québec and Ontario. It has also stimulated industry and commerce in the south.

Canada is one of the world's leading exporters of minerals. Petroleum and natural gas are the most important products taken from the ground, with Alberta being the leading producer. The country is also the world's top exporter of asbestos, potash, uranium and zinc, and a major producer of copper, gold, iron ore and nickel. Ontario is the leading province for producing metal ores. British Columbia produces copper and is the leading coal producer, while Québec is a major producer of iron ore and gold.

The processing of fuels, minerals and other produce for export form the basis of Canada's manufacturing industries. Other industries include food processing, chemicals and pharmaceuticals, the manufacturing of transport equipment, including cars, trucks and aircraft, and paper products. Other products include metal products, electrical equipment, wood products, and computers and software.

Service industries account for 70% of the country's gross domestic product. They include community, business and personal services, followed by finance, insurance and real estate. Tourism is also important and Canada attracts visitors from all over the world.

Canada's economy is based on foreign trade, and leading exports are machinery and transport equipment, mineral fuels, food (especially wheat), timber, newsprint and paper products, and wood pulp. The share of commodities has fallen from nearly 60% in 1980 to 35% in the late 1990s, while the share of manufacturing has increased. Canada's leading trading partner is the United States. Canada's exports to the United States rose from 15% of the gross domestic product in 1989 to 30% in 1998. Manufacturing accounted for half of the increase.

Saint-Pierre et Miquelon

The last fragment of the once-extensive French possessions in North America outside the Caribbean, Saint-Pierre et Miquelon comprises two main islands and some small rocky islets, about 16 km [10 mls] off the south coast of Newfoundland. The total area of the islands is 242 sq km [93 sq mls]. The population is 6,390, almost 90% of whom live on Saint-Pierre and the rest on Miquelon. The administrative and commercial centre is Saint-Pierre (see map on page 67).

The islands contain areas of marshes, peat bogs, small lakes and bare hills (called Mornes) that rise to the highest point on the archipelago. This is the Morne de la Grande Montagne, which reaches 240 m [787 ft]. The coast is very scenic. Temperatures vary from about –10°C [–14°F] in winter to 20°C [68°F] in summer, while the average annual rainfall is about 1,500 mm [59 in]. The forests that once covered the islands have been largely cleared, giving them a bare appearance.

The islands were originally settled by seafarers from western France in the early 17th century. After being exchanged several times between France and Britain, Saint-Pierre and Miquelon finally became a French colony in 1816. Today the people speak French and most are Roman Catholics. The territory became a French overseas department in 1976 and, like Martinique, Guadeloupe, French Guiana and Réunion, it enjoyed the same status as the departments in Metropolitan France. In 1985, however, it became a 'territorial collectivity', a status already held by Mayotte, an island which formerly belonged to the Comoros in the Indian Ocean. Like Mayotte, it sends one deputy to the National Assembly in Paris and one senator to the Senate. A Prefect represents the French government in the territory.

The majority of people depend on fishing. Frozen and dried fish are the main exports. Other economic activities include fox and mink farming and tourism. Much land is barren rock but some vegetables are grown and animals are raised. But the economy of the islands depends on subsidies from France.

AREA	
9,976,140 sq km [3,851,788 sq mls]	Ukrainian 2%, Native American (Amerindian/Inuit) 1.5%, Chinese
POPULATION 30,675,000	**LANGUAGES** English and French (both official)
CAPITAL (POPULATION) Ottawa (1,010,000)	**RELIGIONS** Christianity (Roman Catholic 47%, Protestant 41%), Judaism, Islam, Hinduism
GOVERNMENT Federal multiparty constitutional monarchy	
ETHNIC GROUPS British 34%, French 26%, German 4%, Italian 3%,	**CURRENCY** Canadian dollar = 100 cents

CANARY ISLANDS – SEE ATLANTIC OCEAN, PAGES 41–43;
CAPE VERDE – SEE ATLANTIC OCEAN, PAGES 41–43

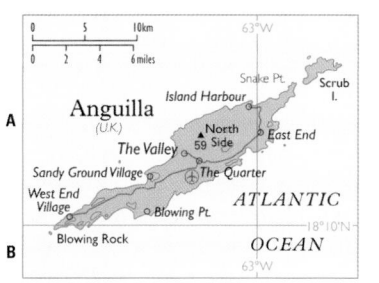

ANGUILLA

AREA	CAPITAL
96 sq km	The Valley
[37 sq mls]	CURRENCY
POPULATION	East Caribbean
11,000	dollar

Formerly part of St Kitts and Nevis, Anguilla, the most northerly of the Leeward Islands, officially became a British dependency (now a British overseas territory) in 1980. A new constitution was adopted in 1982. The main source of revenue is now tourism.

ANTIGUA AND BARBUDA

AREA	CAPITAL
440 sq km	St John's
[170 sq mls]	CURRENCY
POPULATION	East Caribbean
64,000	dollar

A former British dependency in the Caribbean, Antigua and Barbuda became independent in 1981. Tourism is the main industry, though sugar is an important product. Around 98% of the people live on Antigua, 2% on Barbuda, while the third island, Redonda, is uninhabited.

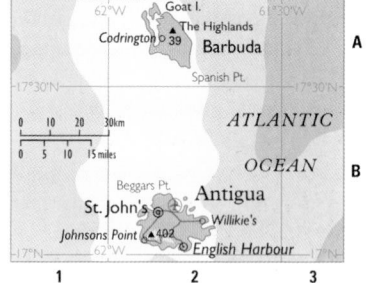

BAHAMAS

The Bahamas is a coral-limestone archipelago comprising 29 inhabited islands, plus more than 3,000 cays, reefs and rocks, centred on the Grand Bahama Bank off eastern Florida and Cuba. The Bahamas has developed close ties with the United States.

More than 90% of the 3.6 million visitors a year are Americans. Tourism now accounts for 70% of the gross domestic product and involves about 40% of the workforce. Off-shore banking, financial services and a large 'open registry' merchant fleet also offset imports (including most foodstuffs), providing the country with a relatively high standard of living.

The remainder of the non-administrative population works mainly in the traditional areas of fishing and agriculture, notably citrus fruit production.

The Bahamas has been a democracy since 1973 when it became independent from Britain. Relations with the United States were strained when it was used as a tax haven for drug traffickers in the 1980s, with government ministers implicated in drug-related corruption.

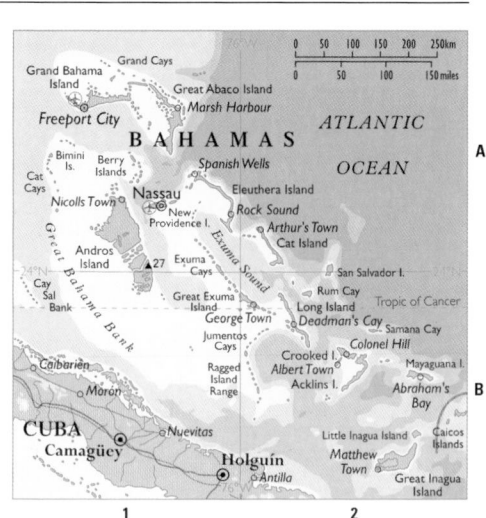

AREA	CAPITAL
13,880 sq km	Nassau
[5,359 sq mls]	CURRENCY
POPULATION	Bahamian dollar
280,000	= 100 cents

CARIBBEAN SEA

BARBADOS

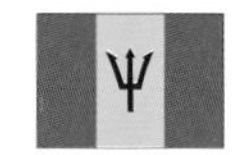

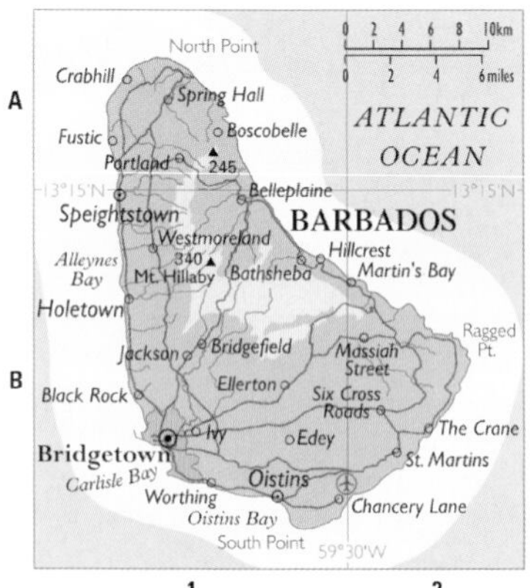

The most eastern Caribbean nation, and first in line for the seasonal hurricanes that batter the region, Barbados is underlain by limestone and capped with coral. Mt Hillaby, which reaches 340 m [1,115 ft], the highest point, is fringed by marine terraces marking stages in the island's emergence from the sea.

AREA	CAPITAL
430 sq km	Bridgetown
[166 sq mls]	**CURRENCY**
POPULATION	Barbados dollar
259,000	= 100 cents

Barbados became British in 1627, and it became independent as a constitutional monarchy in 1960. However, in the late 1990s, there was discussion about changing the constitution and turning the country into a republic.

The economy was based on sugar production, using African slave labour. Cane plantations take up most of the cropped land, but sugar now contributes 13% of domestic exports – far less than previously. Manufactures make up the leading exports, but tourism is the growth sector and the most valuable activity for this relatively prosperous, but very overcrowded, island. Despite political stability and advanced welfare and education services, emigration is high, notably to the United States and United Kingdom.

CAYMAN ISLANDS

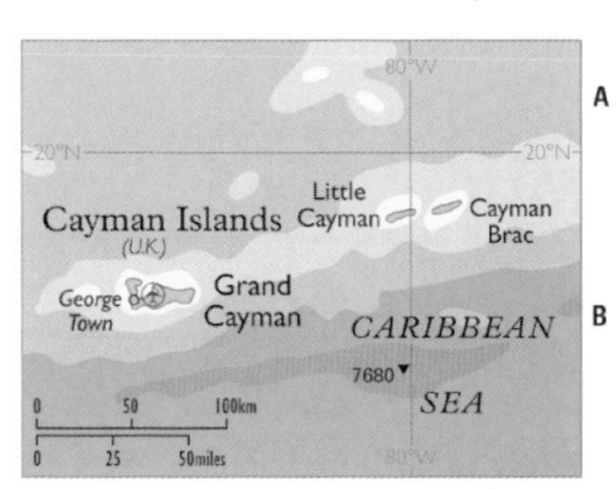

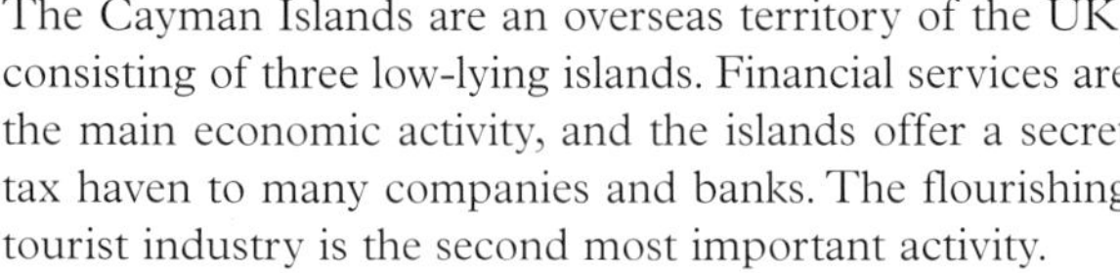

The Cayman Islands are an overseas territory of the UK, consisting of three low-lying islands. Financial services are the main economic activity, and the islands offer a secret tax haven to many companies and banks. The flourishing tourist industry is the second most important activity.

AREA	CAPITAL
259 sq km	George Town
[100 sq mls]	**CURRENCY**
POPULATION	Cayman Island
35,000	dollar = 100 cents

DOMINICAN REPUBLIC

Second largest of the Caribbean nations in both area and population, the Dominican Republic shares with Haiti the island of Hispaniola, with the Dominican Republic occupying the eastern two-thirds. Of the steep-sided mountains that dominate the island, the country includes the northern Cordillera Septentrional, the huge Cordillera Central, which rises to Pico Duarte, at 3,175 m [10,414 ft] the highest peak in the Caribbean, and the southern Sierra de Baoruco. Between them and to the east lie fertile valleys and lowlands, including the Vega Real and the coastal plains where the main sugar plantations are found.

Typical of the Caribbean region, the climate is hot and humid throughout the year close to sea level, while cooler conditions prevail in the mountains. Rainfall is heavy, especially in the north-east.

Christopher Columbus 'discovered' the island and its Amerindian population, soon to be decimated, on 5 December 1492. The city of Santo Domingo, now the capital and chief port, was founded by Columbus' brother Bartholomew four years later and is the oldest in the Americas. For long a Spanish colony, Hispaniola was initially the centrepiece of their empire, but was later to become a poor relation. In

1795, it became French, then Spanish again in 1809. But in 1821, when it was called Santo Domingo, it won its independence. Haiti held the territory from 1822 until 1844 when, on restoring sovereignty, it became the Dominican Republic. Growing American influence culminated in occupation between 1916 and 1924. This was followed by a period of corrupt dictatorship. From 1930 until his assassination in 1961, the country was ruled by Rafael Trujillo, one of Latin America's best-known dictators, who imprisoned or killed many of his opponents.

A power struggle developed between the military, the upper class, those who wanted the country to become a democracy and others who favoured making it a Communist regime. Juan Bosch became president in 1962, but was ousted in 1963. Bosch supporters tried to seize power in 1965, but were met with strong military opposition. This led to US military intervention in 1965. Since 1966, a young democracy has survived violent elections under the watchful eye of the Americans.

The World Bank describes the Dominican Republic as a 'lower-middle-income' developing country. In the 1990s, industrial growth that exploited the country's huge hydroelectric potential, mining and tourism has augmented the traditional agricultural economy, though the country is far from being politically stable. Agriculture is a major activity. Leading crops include avocados, bananas, beans, mangos, oranges, plantains, rice, sugar cane and tobacco. Gold and nickel are mined. Sugar refining is a major industry, with the bulk of the production exported to the United States. Leading exports are ferronickel, sugar, coffee, cocoa and gold. The island's main trading partner is the United States.

AREA	ETHNIC GROUPS
48,730 sq km	Mulatto 73%,
[18,815 sq mls]	White 16%,
POPULATION	Black 11%
7,999,000	**LANGUAGES**
CAPITAL (POPULATION)	Spanish (official)
Santo Domingo	**RELIGIONS**
(2,135,000)	Roman Catholic 93%
GOVERNMENT	**CURRENCY**
Multiparty republic	Peso = 100 centavos

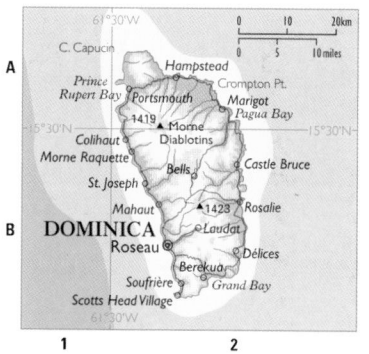

DOMINICA

The Commonwealth of Dominica, a former British colony, became independent in 1978. The island has a mountainous spine and less than 10% of the land is cultivated. However, agriculture employs over 60% of the people. The manufacturing of coconut-based soap is important, but much food has to be imported.

The future of Dominica depends a good deal on the development of luxury tourism.

AREA	CAPITAL
751 sq km [290 sq mls]	Roseau
POPULATION	CURRENCY
78,000	Franc, pound, E. Car. dollar

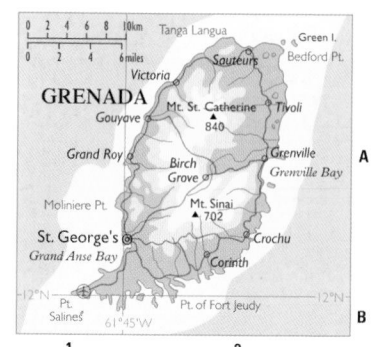

GRENADA

The most southerly of the Windward Islands in the Caribbean Sea, Grenada became independent from the UK in 1974. A military group seized power in 1983, when the prime minister was killed. US troops intervened and restored order and constitutional government.

Since the invasion, the island has been reliant on aid. Grenada is the world's leading producer of nutmeg.

AREA	CAPITAL
344 sq km [133 sq mls]	St George's
POPULATION	CURRENCY
96,000	Eastern Caribbean dollar

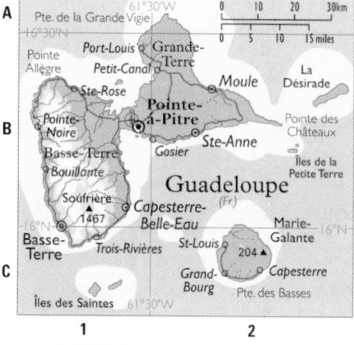

GUADELOUPE

Guadeloupe is a French overseas department which includes seven Caribbean islands, the largest of which is Basse-Terre. French aid has helped to maintain a reasonable standard of living for the people.

Food is the biggest import, much of it coming from France, while bananas are the chief export. Despite French aid and thriving tourism, unemployment remains high.

AREA	CAPITAL
1,710 sq km [660 sq mls]	Basse-Terre
POPULATION	CURRENCY
416,000	French franc

HAITI

The Republic of Haiti occupies the western third of Hispaniola, the Caribbean's second largest island. The land is mainly mountainous, with a long, indented coast. Most of the country is centred around the Massif du Nord, with the narrow Massif de la Hotte forming the southern peninsula. The climate is hot and humid. The northern highlands have an average annual rainfall of about 2,000 mm [79 in], more than twice as much as on the southern coast.

Ceded to France in 1697, Haiti developed as a sugar-producing colony. For nearly two centuries, since a slave revolt made it the world's first independent black state in 1804, it has been bedevilled by military coups, government corruption, ethnic violence and political instability, including a period of US control from 1915 to 1934.

The violent regime of François Duvalier ('Papa Doc'), president from 1957, was especially brutal, but that of his son, Jean Claude ('Baby Doc'), president from 1971, was little better – both used their murderous private militia, the Tontons Macoutes, to conduct a reign of terror. In 1986, popular unrest finally forced Duvalier to flee the country, and the military took over. After another period of political chaos, the country's first multiparty elections were held in December 1990. A radical Roman Catholic priest, Father Jean-Bertrand Aristide, won the election on a platform of sweeping reforms. But the military again seized power in September 1991. The military agreed to step down in 1994 and Aristide returned as president at the end of 1994. In 1995, René Préval was elected president, but violence and poverty still prevail. In 1999, Préval dissolved parliament, announcing he would rule by decree. Haiti has few natural resources. Coffee is the only significant cash crop. Two-thirds of the population lives at or below the poverty line, subsisting on agriculture and fishing. The country has few industries.

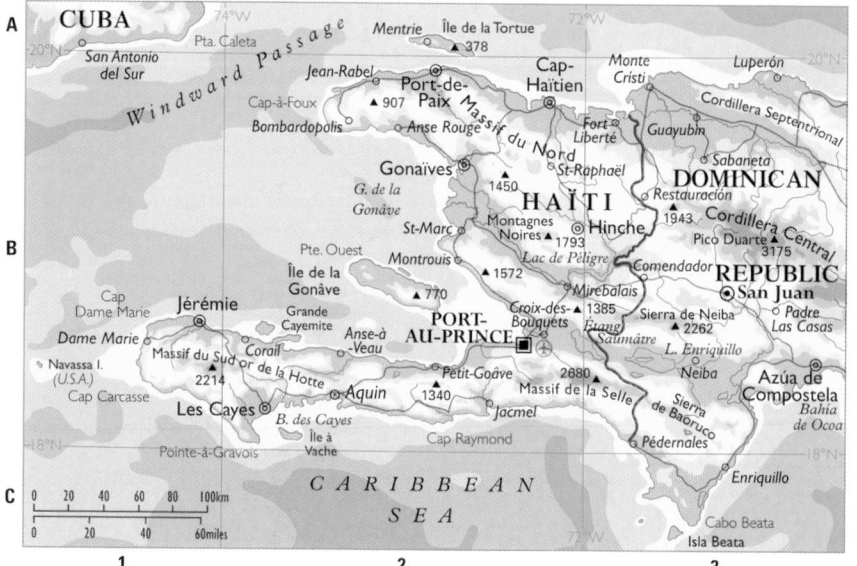

AREA	ETHNIC GROUPS
27,750 sq km	Black 95%, Mulatto 5%
[10,714 sq mls]	LANGUAGES
POPULATION	French (official),
6,781,000	Creole
CAPITAL (POPULATION)	RELIGIONS
Port-au-Prince (1,402,000)	Roman Catholic 80%,
GOVERNMENT	CURRENCY
Multiparty republic	Gourde = 100 centimes

JAMAICA

Third largest of the Caribbean islands, half of Jamaica lies above 300 m [1,000 ft]. The country has a central range culminating in Blue Mountain Peak, at 2,256 m [7,402 ft], from which it slopes westwards. The 'cockpit' country in the north-west of the island is an inaccessible limestone area. The climate is hot and humid, with moist south-east trade winds bringing rain to the mountains.

Britain took over Jamaica in 1655 and, with sugar as its staple product, the colony became a prized imperial possession. The African slaves imported to work on the plantations were the forefathers of much of the present population. But the plantations disappeared and the sugar market collapsed in the 19th century. Jamaica became independent in 1962 and economic problems arose under Michael Manley's socialist government in the 1970s. Some progress was made in the 1980s under the pragmatic leadership of Edward Seaga. Manley returned as prime minister in 1989, but he was succeeded in 1992 by Percival Patterson. Jamaica's problems include drug trafficking, violent crime and economic difficulties. Riots in 1999 were caused by price and tax increases, including a 30% rise in the cost of petrol. Jamaica's chief resource is bauxite, most of which is exported as ore and about one-fifth as alumina. Tourism and bauxite production, the two most important industries, comprise two-thirds of the foreign earnings.

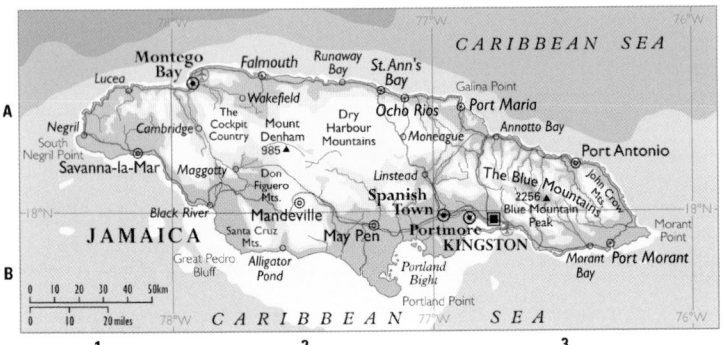

AREA 10,990 sq km [4,243 sq mls]	East Indian 3%, White 3% **LANGUAGES**
POPULATION 2,635,000	English (official), Creole, Hindi,
CAPITAL (POPULATION) Kingston (644,000)	Spanish, Chinese **RELIGIONS**
GOVERNMENT Constitutional monarchy	Protestant 70%, Roman Catholic 8%
ETHNIC GROUPS Black 76%, Afro-European 15%,	**CURRENCY** Dollar = 100 cents

MARTINIQUE

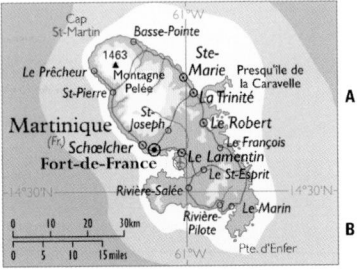

Martinique comprises three groups of volcanic islands and the intervening lowlands. The highest peak is Mount Pelée, notorious for its violent eruption in 1902 when, in minutes, it killed all the inhabitants of St Pierre (estimated at 28,000) except one – a prisoner saved by the thickness of his cell. The climate is hot and humid. The heaviest rains often occur in the hurricane season (July–November).

Colonized by France from 1635, Martinique has been French ever since, apart from brief British interludes. It became an overseas department in 1946 and, like Guadeloupe, it was made an administrative region in 1974.

Tourism is the chief industry. Sugar cane is the chief crop although the main farm exports are bananas, rum and pineapples. Manufactures include cement, food processing and oil refining. The crude oil comes from Venezuela, and refined oil is the second most valuable export after bananas. French aid is very important. Making up about 70% of the GDP, it helps to provide jobs and maintain a higher standard of living than on Guadeloupe.

AREA 1,100 sq km [425 sq mls]	**CAPITAL** Fort-de-France
POPULATION 407,000	**CURRENCY** French franc

MONTSERRAT

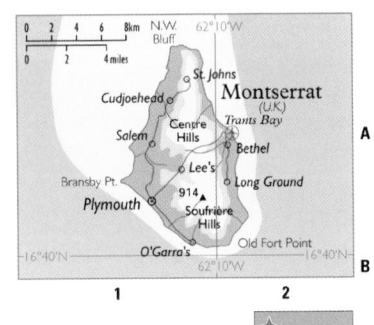

Montserrat is a British overseas territory in the Caribbean. The climate is tropical and hurricanes often cause damage. Intermittent eruptions of the Soufrière Hills volcano between 1995 and 1998 led to the emigration of many inhabitants and the virtual destruction of the capital, Plymouth.

AREA 1,100 sq km [39 sq mls]	**CAPITAL** Plymouth
POPULATION 12,000	**CURRENCY** Eastern Caribbean dollar

NETHERLANDS ANTILLES  ARUBA

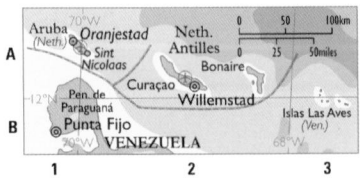

The Netherlands Antilles consists of two different island groups: one off the coast of Venezuela, and the other at the northern end of the Leeward Islands, some 800 km [500 mls] away. With Aruba, they formed part of the Dutch East Indies, attaining internal self-government in 1954. Curaçao is politically dominant in the federation, accounting for nearly 45% of the area and 80% of the population. By Caribbean standards, most people are well off. They enjoy the benefits of an economy buoyed by tourism, offshore banking and oil refining (from Venezuela), mostly for export to the Netherlands and more important than the traditional orange liqueur.

Aruba is a flat limestone island, the most western of the Lesser Antilles, some 68 km [42 mls] west of Curaçao. It was incorporated into the Netherlands Antilles in 1845, but, in 1977, the people voted in a referendum for autonomy. With Dutch agreement in 1981, Aruba separated from the Netherlands Antilles in 1986.

NETHERLANDS ANTILLES	**ARUBA**
AREA 993 sq km [383 sq mls]	**AREA** 193 sq km [75 sq mls]
POPULATION 210,000	**POPULATION** 69,000
CAPITAL Willemstad	**CAPITAL** Oranjestad

PUERTO RICO

The Commonwealth of Puerto Rico is the easternmost of the islands in the Greater Antilles. The land is mountainous, with a narrow coastal plain. Cerro da Punta, at 1,338 m [4,389 ft], is the highest peak. The climate is hot and wet, though rainstorms are short in many places.

Ceded by Spain to the United States in 1898, Puerto Rico became a self-governing commonwealth in free association with the United States after a referendum in 1952. Puerto Ricans are US citizens, but they pay no federal taxes, nor do they vote in US congressional or presidential elections. In 1991, Puerto Ricans narrowly rejected a proposal to guarantee 'the island's distinct cultural identity', a result interpreted as a move towards statehood. But in 1998, 50.2% of the people voted for maintaining the status quo, rather than asking for statehood.

Flat land for agriculture is scarce. It is mainly devoted to cash crops, such as bananas, coffee, sugar, tobacco, tropical fruits, vegetables and various spices. However, the island is now the most industrialized and urbanized in the Caribbean – nearly half the population lives in the San Juan area. Manufacturing and tourism are growing industries. The rising standard of living, while low in US terms, is the highest in Latin America outside the tax havens. The chief exports are chemicals and chemical products, machinery and food.

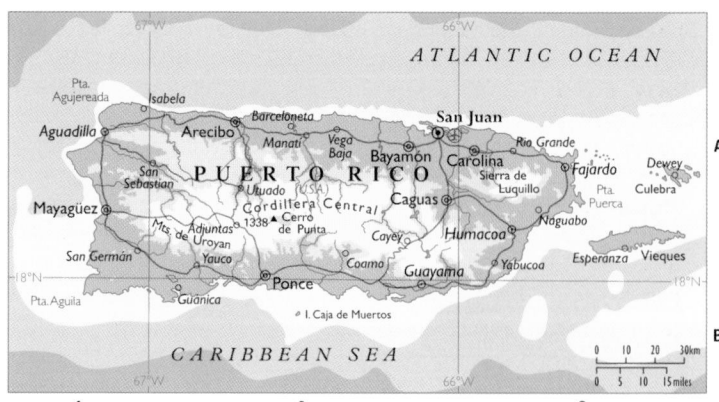

AREA	ETHNIC GROUPS
8,900 sq km [3,436 sq mls]	Spanish 99%, African American
POPULATION	LANGUAGES
3,860,000	Spanish and English (both official)
CAPITAL	CURRENCY
San Juan	US dollar = 100 cents

ST KITTS AND NEVIS

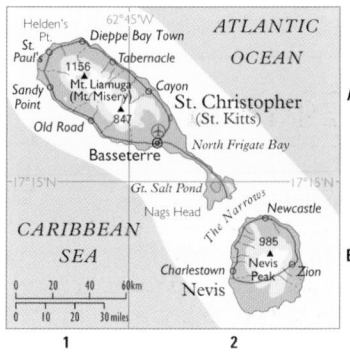

The Federation of St Kitts and Nevis comprises two well-watered volcanic islands, with mountains rising to around 1,000 m [3,300 ft]. The islands were the first in the Caribbean to be colonized by Britain (1623 and 1628), and they became an independent country in 1983. In 1998, a vote for the secession of Nevis fell short of the two-thirds required. Tourism has replaced sugar as the main earner.

AREA	CAPITAL
360 sq km [139 sq mls]	Basseterre
POPULATION	CURRENCY
42,000	East Caribbean dollar

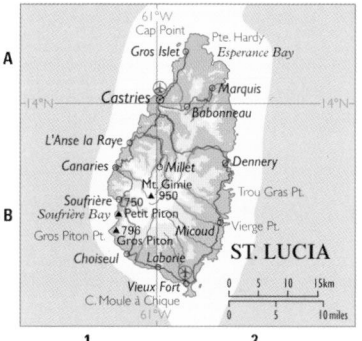

ST LUCIA

St Lucia is a mountainous forested island of extinct volcanoes, graphically represented on its flag. To the south of its highest point of Mt Gimie, at 950 m [3,116 ft] above sea level, lies Qualibou, an area containing 18 volcanic domes and seven craters. In the west are the Pitons, rising from the sea to more than 750 m [2,460 ft]. Temperatures in St Lucia are high, and the rainfall is heavy. The rainiest months are likely to occur during the hurricane season, which runs from July to November. St Lucia boasts a huge variety of plant and animal life.

First settled by the British in 1605, St Lucia changed hands between Britain and France 14 times before being formally ceded to Britain in 1814. Self-governing as an 'Associated State of the UK' from 1967, it gained independence as a member of the Commonwealth in 1979.

Though not poor, St Lucia is still over-dependent on bananas, which are vulnerable to hurricanes and disease. Other agricultural products are coconuts and cocoa, but clothing makes up the second largest export, and the free port of Vieux Fort has attracted modern industries. Cruise liners deliver tourists to Castries, and the Grande Cul de Sac Bay to the south is one of the deepest tanker ports in the Americas. It is used mainly for trans-shipment of oil.

AREA	CAPITAL
610 sq km	Castries
[236 sq mls]	CURRENCY
POPULATION	E. Caribbean
150,000	dollar

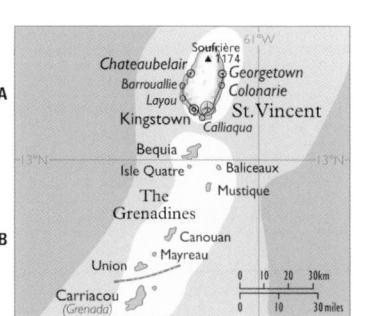

ST VINCENT AND THE GRENADINES

St Vincent and the Grenadines comprises the main island, which makes up 89% of the area and contains 95% of the population, and the northern Grenadines, of which the largest are Bequia, Mustique and Canouan. St Vincent is a mountainous, volcanic island which receives heavy rainfall. Soufrière, at 1,174 m [3,851 ft], is an active volcano.

'Discovered' in 1498, St Vincent was settled in the 16th century and became a British colony in 1783, after a century of conflict with France, often supported by the Caribs – the last of whom were deported to Honduras after the Indian War of 1795–7. The colony became self-governing in 1969 and independent in 1979. Less prosperous than its Commonwealth neighbours, it has wealthy pockets, notably Mustique and Bequia, whose beautiful clean waters have fostered tourism.

AREA	CAPITAL
388 sq km [150 sq mls]	Kingstown
POPULATION	CURRENCY
120,000	East Caribbean dollar

CARIBBEAN SEA

TRINIDAD AND TOBAGO

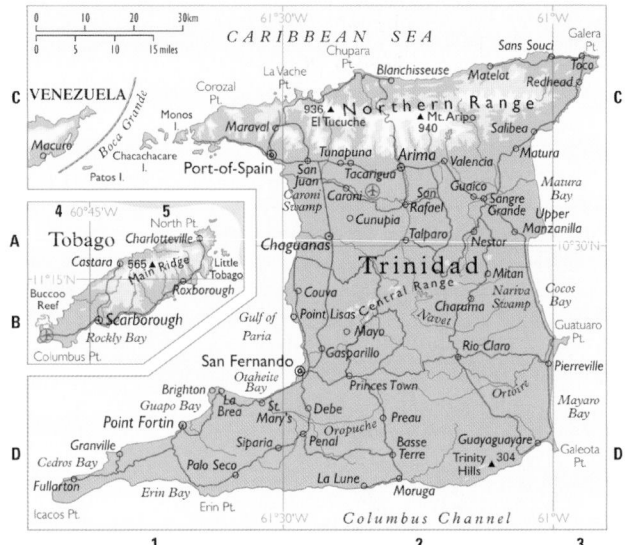

The Republic of Trinidad and Tobago contains Trinidad, a rectangular island situated just 16 km [10 mls] off Venezuela's Orinoco delta, and Tobago, a detached extension of its Northern Range of hills, lying 34 km [21 mls] to the northeast. Trinidad's highest point is Mount Aripo, at 940 m [3,085 ft] in the rugged, forested Northern Range. Temperatures are high throughout the year and the rainfall is heavy, with the wettest months from June to November.

'Discovered' by Christopher Columbus in 1498, Trinidad was later planted by Spanish and French settlers before becoming British in 1797. Black slaves worked the plantations until emancipation in 1834, when Indian and Chinese indentured labourers were brought in. Indian influence is strong in some villages, while African culture dominates in others. Spain, the Netherlands and France competed for Tobago before it came under British control in 1814. It joined Trinidad to become a single colony in 1899. Independence came in 1962, and a republic was established in 1976. Trinidad experienced a sharp change in 1986 when, after 30 years, the People's National Movement was defeated and the National Alliance for Reconstruction coalition took office. Later, after four years of PNM rule, a coalition took over in 1995, but the country continued to face economic problems and high unemployment.

Oil was the lifeblood of the nation's economy throughout the 20th century, giving the island a relatively high standard of living. Falling prices in the 1980s had a severe effect, only partly offset by the growth of tourism and continued revenues from asphalt – the other main natural resource – and gas. The country's chief exports in 1995 included refined petroleum, crude petroleum, anhydrous ammonia, iron and steel and methanol.

AREA	White 1%, Chinese 1%
5,130 sq km [1,981 sq mls]	**LANGUAGES**
POPULATION	English (official)
1,117,000	**RELIGIONS**
CAPITAL	Christian 40%,
Port-of-Spain	Hindu 24%, Muslim 6%
ETHNIC GROUPS	**CURRENCY**
Black 40%, East Indian	Trinidad and Tobago
40%, Mixed 18%,	dollar = 100 cents

TURKS AND CAICOS ISLANDS

The Turks and Caicos Islands are a group of 30 islands, eight of them inhabited, lying at the eastern end of the Grand Bahama, north of Haiti. They are composed of low, flat limestone terrain, with scrub, marsh and swamp providing little space for agriculture.

Previously claimed by France and Spain, the islands have been British since 1766. They were administered from Jamaica until 1959 when they became a separate Crown Colony (though since 1998, they have been described, in common with other former colonies, as a British overseas territory). Tourism and finance have recently overtaken fishing as the main economic activities. More than 70,000 tourists visited the islands in 1994. Over half of the people live in rural areas, but farming is mainly at subsistence level. Dried, frozen and processed fish remain the chief exports. Offshore banking facilities are also expanding.

AREA	**CAPITAL**
430 sq km [166 sq mls]	Cockburn Harbour
POPULATION	**CURRENCY**
16,000	US dollar = 100 cents

VIRGIN ISLANDS, UK

The British Virgin Islands comprise four low-lying islands and 36 islets and cays. The largest island, Tortola, contains more than three-quarters of the total population, around a third of whom live in the capital Road Town on the south-east side of Tortola. The climate is pleasant. Road Town has an average annual rainfall of 1,090 mm [43 in].

The islands were 'discovered' by Christopher Columbus in 1493. Dutch from 1648 but British since 1666, they are now a British overseas territory, enjoying, since 1977, a strong measure of self-government. Tourism is the chief source of income. It accounts for 75% of all economic activity.

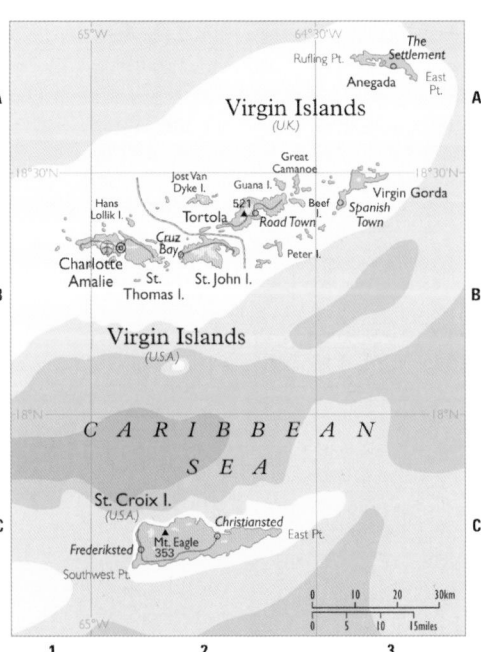

AREA	**CAPITAL**
153 sq km	Road Town
[59 sq mls]	**CURRENCY**
POPULATION	US dollar
13,000	

VIRGIN ISLANDS, US

The US Virgin Islands comprise 68 islands, the three largest being St Thomas, St Croix and St John. The islands, excluding St Croix, are rugged and hilly. The highest point, Crown Mountain on St Thomas, reaches 474 m [1,556 ft].

The United States purchased the islands from Denmark in 1917 for the sum of US $25 million. From 1973, the citizens have elected a delegate to the House of Representatives.

Tourism is the main industry and airborne day-trippers from the US are attracted by the duty-free shops of St Thomas. The islands have the highest density of hotels and condominiums in the Caribbean.

AREA	**CAPITAL**
340 sq km	Charlotte
[130 sq mls]	Amalie
POPULATION	**CURRENCY**
118,000	US dollar

CENTRAL AFRICAN REPUBLIC

The red, yellow and green colours on this flag were originally used by Ethiopia, Africa's oldest independent nation. They symbolize African unity. The blue, white and red recall the flag of France, the country's colonial ruler. This flag was adopted in 1958.

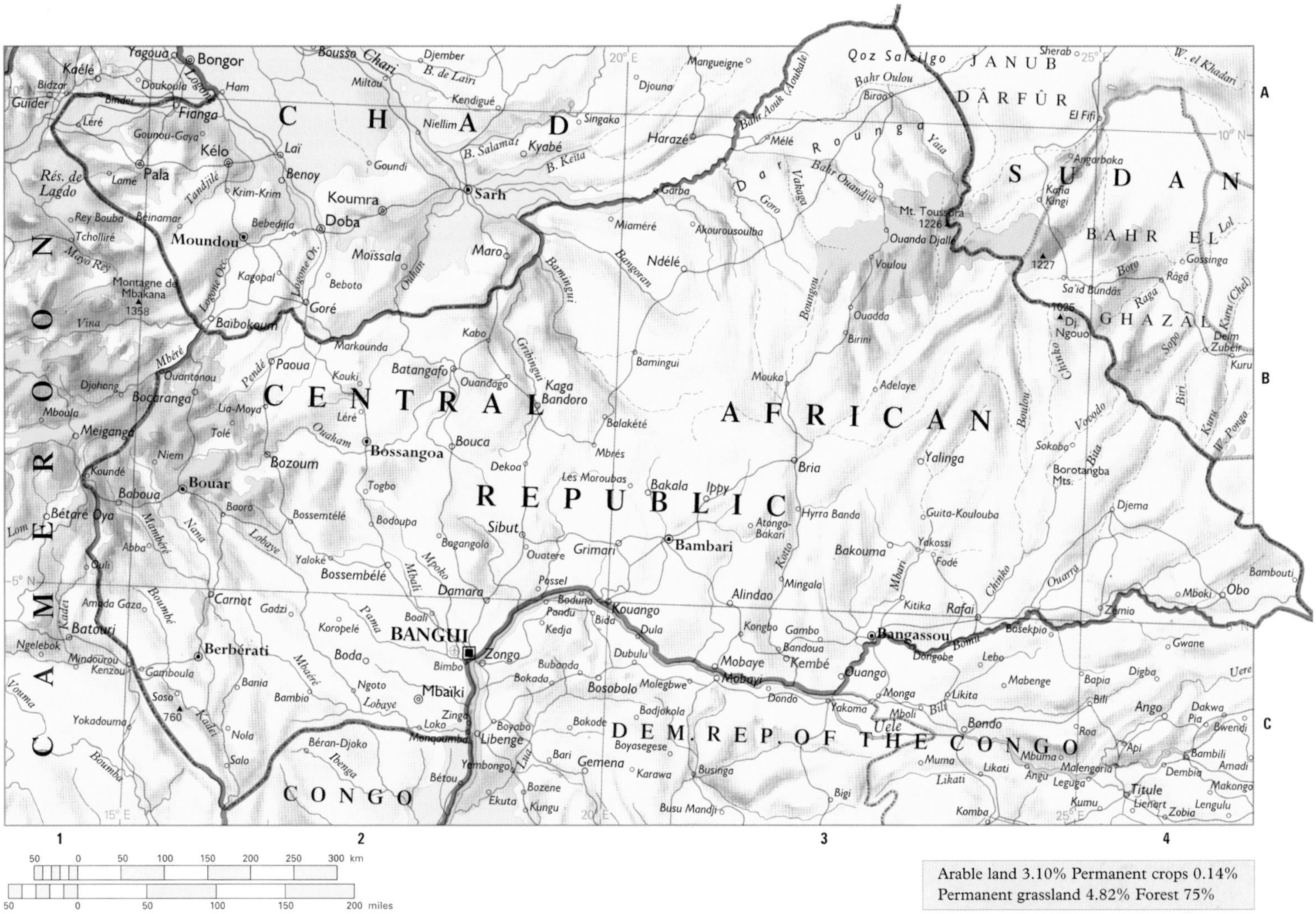

Arable land 3.10% Permanent crops 0.14%
Permanent grassland 4.82% Forest 75%

Geography

The Central African Republic is a landlocked country in central Africa. It consists mostly of a plateau lying between 600 m and 800 m [1,970 ft to 2,620 ft] above sea level. The Oubangi drains the south, while the Chari (or Shari) River flows from the north to the Lake Chad basin.

Climate

The climate is warm throughout the year, with an average yearly rainfall totalling 1,574 mm [62 in]. The north is drier, with an average yearly rainfall total of about 800 mm [31 in].

History and Politics

Little is known of the early history of the area. Between the 16th and 19th centuries, the population was greatly reduced by the slave trade. The country is still thinly populated. Although it is larger than France in area, France has 18 times as many people.

France set up an outpost at Bangui in 1899 and ruled the country as a colony from 1894. Known as Ubangi-Shari, the country was ruled by France as part of French Equatorial Africa until it gained independence in 1960.

The Central African Republic became a one-party state in 1962, but army officers seized power in 1966. The head of the army, Jean-Bedel Bokassa, made himself emperor in 1976. The country was renamed the Central African Empire, but after a brutal and tyrannical reign, Bokassa was overthrown by a military group in 1979. As a result, the monarchy was abolished and the country again became a republic.

The country adopted a new, multiparty constitution during 1991.

Elections were held in 1993. An army rebellion in 1996 was finally put down in 1997 with assistance from French troops.

Economy

The World Bank classifies the Central African Republic as a 'low-income' developing country. Over 80% of the people are farmers – most of them producing little more than they need to feed their families. The main crops are bananas, maize, manioc, millet and yams. Coffee, cotton, timber and tobacco are also produced for export.

Diamonds, the only major mineral resource, are the most valuable single export. Manufacturing is on a very small scale. Products include beer, cotton fabrics, footwear, leather, soap and sawn timber. The Central African Republic's development has been greatly impeded by its remote position, its poor transport system and its untrained workforce. The country is heavily dependent on aid, especially from France.

AREA	Ngbandi 11%, Azande 10%,
622,980 sq km [240,533 sq mls]	Sara 7%, Mbaka 4%
POPULATION	**LANGUAGES**
3,376,000	French and Sango (both official)
CAPITAL (POPULATION)	**RELIGIONS**
Bangui (706,000)	Traditional beliefs 57%,
GOVERNMENT	Christianity 35%,
Multiparty republic	Islam 8%
ETHNIC GROUPS	**CURRENCY**
Banda 29%, Baya 25%,	CFA franc = 100 centimes

Chad's flag was adopted in 1959 as the country prepared for independence in 1960. The blue represents the sky, the streams in southern Chad, and hope. The yellow symbolizes the sun and the Sahara in the north. The red represents national sacrifice.

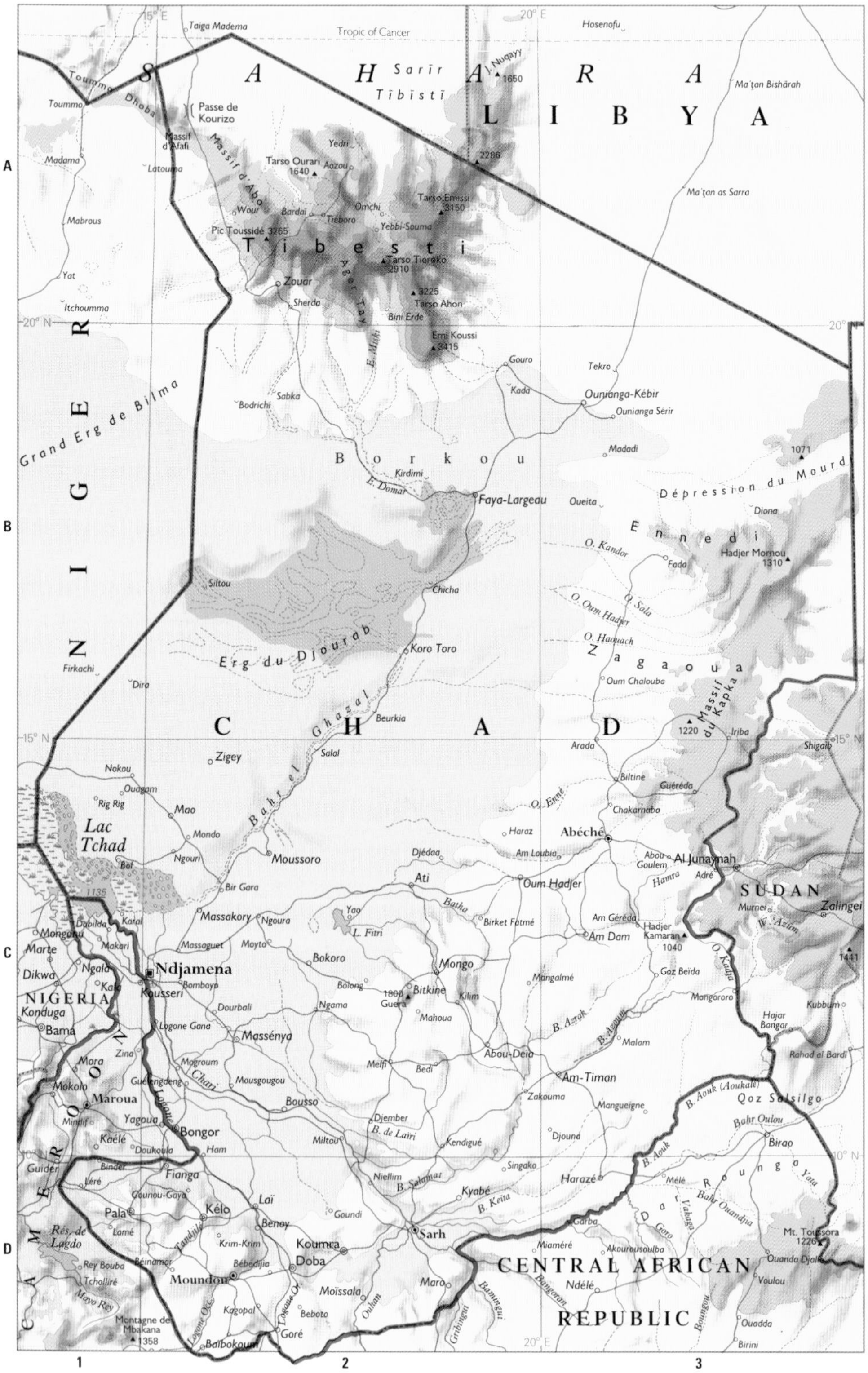

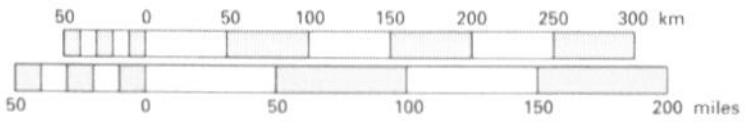

of the Sahara Desert. The mountains contain Chad's highest peak, Emi Koussi, at 3,415 m [11,204 ft] above sea level.

Chad has a hot, tropical climate, with a marked dry season from between November and April. The south of the country is wetter, with an average yearly rainfall of around 1,000 mm [39 in]. The burning-hot desert in the north has an average yearly rainfall of less than 130 mm [5 in].

History and Politics

Chad straddles two worlds. The north is populated by Muslim Arab and Berber peoples, while black Africans, who follow traditional beliefs or who have converted to Christianity, live in the south.

Southern Chad was part of the Kanem empire, which was founded in about AD 700. Other smaller kingdoms developed around Kanem. French explorers were active in the area in the late 19th century. France finally made Chad a colony in 1902.

After becoming independent in 1960, Chad has been hit by ethnic conflict. In the 1970s, civil war, frequent coups and intervention in the north by Libya, retarded the country's economic development. Chad and Libya agreed a truce in 1987 and, in 1994, the International Court of Justice ruled that Libya had no claim on the Aozou Strip in the far north.

A rebel group, named the Patriotic Salvation Movement, seized power in 1990 and its leader, Idriss Déby, became head of state. In 1991, a law was made permitting political parties, provided they are not based on regionalism, tribalism or intolerance. Following presidential elections in 1996, in which Déby was re-elected, a new constitution was approved in a referendum in 1997.

Economy

Hit by drought and civil war, Chad is one of the world's poorest countries. Farming, fishing and livestock raising employ 83% of the people. Groundnuts, millet, rice and sorghum are major food crops in the wetter south, but the most valuable crop in export terms is cotton. Other exports include live animals, including cattle. The country has few natural resources and few manufacturing industries.

Geography and Climate

The Republic of Chad is a landlocked country in north-central Africa. It is Africa's fifth largest country and is more than twice as big as France, which once ruled it as a colony. The land consists largely of desert and rocky plateaux and most people live in the fertile south.

Southern Chad is crossed by rivers that flow into Lake Chad, on the western border. Beyond a large depression, north-east of Lake Chad, are the Tibesti Mountains which rise steeply from the sands

AREA	
1,284,000 sq km [495,752 sq mls]	Sudanic Arab 26%, Teda 7%, Mbum 6%
POPULATION	**LANGUAGES**
7,360,000	French and Arabic (both official)
CAPITAL (POPULATION)	
Ndjamena (530,000)	**RELIGIONS**
GOVERNMENT	Islam 40%, Christianity 33%, traditional beliefs 27%
Transitional	
ETHNIC GROUPS	**CURRENCY**
Bagirmi, Kreish and Sara 31%,	CFA franc = 100 centimes

CHILE

Chile's flag was adopted in 1817. It was designed in that year by an American serving in the Chilean army who was inspired by the US Stars and Stripes. The white represents the snow-capped Andes, the blue the sky, and the red the blood of the nation's patriots.

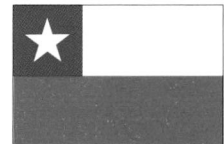

Geography

The Republic of Chile stretches about 4,260 km [2,650 mls] from north to south, although the maximum east–west distance is only about 430 km [267 mls]. The high Andes Mountains form Chile's eastern borders with Argentina and Bolivia. To the west are basins and valleys, with coastal uplands overlooking the shore. In the south, the land has been worn by glaciers and the coastal uplands are islands, while the inland valleys are arms of the sea. Most people live in the central valley, which contains the capital, Santiago.

Climate

Chile is divided into three main climate zones. The north has an arid climate, but temperatures are moderated by the cold Peru Current. Central Chile has a Mediterranean climate. The south is cool and stormy.

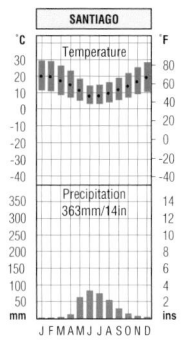

CHILE (SANTIAGO)

Chile has a great variety of climates because of its latitudinal extent and the high Andes in the east. Rainfall increases southwards from the deserts in the north. For example, Antofagasta has an annual average rainfall of 14 mm [0.6 in]. Central Chile has a Mediterranean-type climate, with hot, dry summers and mild, moist winters. The climate of Chile's capital, Santiago, is typical of central Chile, with average temperatures of 21°C [69°F] in January and 9°C [48°F] in July. The average annual rainfall is 360 mm [14 in], of which 280 mm [11 in] falls between May and August. By contrast, southern Chile has a cool, changeable and often stormy, wet climate.

History

Amerindian people reached the southern tip of South America at least 8,000 years ago. In 1520, the Portuguese navigator Ferdinand Magellan became the first European to sight Chile, but the country became a Spanish colony in the 1540s. Under Spain, the economy in the north was based on mining, while huge ranches, or *haciendas*, were set up in central Chile. After Chile became independent in 1818, mining continued to flourish in the north, while Valparaiso developed as a port exporting produce from central Chile to California and Australia. Industrial growth, fuelled by revenue from nitrate exports, began in the early 20th century, though many people did not benefit from the country's growing prosperity.

Politics

After World War II, Chile faced economic problems, partly caused by falls in world copper prices. A Christian Democrat was elected president in 1964, but was replaced by Salvador Allende Gossens in 1970. Allende's administration, the world's first democratically elected Marxist government, was overthrown in a CIA-backed coup in 1973. General Augusto Pinochet Ugarte took power as a dictator, banning all political activity in a repressive regime. A new constitution took effect from 1981, allowing for an eventual return to democracy. Elections took place in 1989. President Patrico Aylwin took office in 1990, but Pinochet secured continued office as commander-in-chief of the armed forces. Eduardo Frei was elected president in 1993 and he was succeeded by a socialist, Ricardo Lagos, who narrowly defeated a conservative candidate in January 2000. In 1999, General Pinochet, who was visiting Britain for medical treatment, was faced with extradition to Spain to answer charges that he had presided over acts of torture when he was Chile's dictator, but was allowed to return to Chile in February 2000.

Economy

The World Bank classifies Chile as a 'lower-middle-income' developing country. Mining is important. Minerals dominate Chile's exports. But the most valuable activity is manufacturing; products include processed foods, metals, iron and steel, wood products and textiles.

Agriculture employs 18% of the people. The chief crop is wheat, while beans, fruits, maize and livestock products are also important. Chile's fishing industry is one of the world's largest.

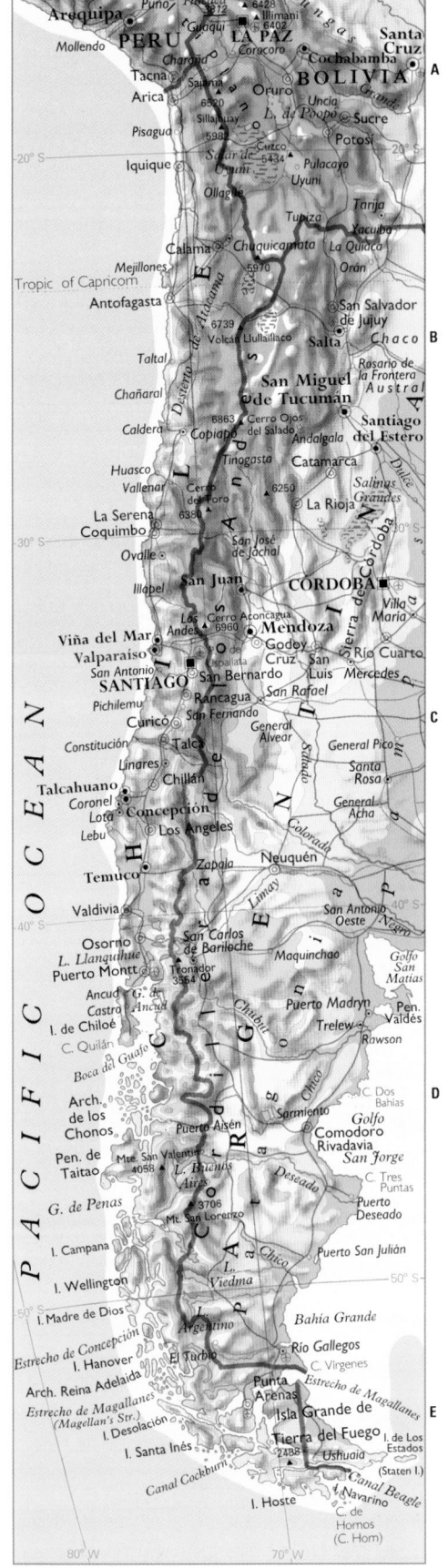

AREA	**ETHNIC GROUPS**
756,950 sq km [292,258 sq mls]	Mestizo 92%, Amerindian 7%
POPULATION	**LANGUAGES**
14,788,000	Spanish (official)
CAPITAL (POPULATION)	**RELIGIONS**
Santiago (5,077,000)	Christianity (Roman Catholic 81%)
GOVERNMENT	**CURRENCY**
Multiparty republic	Peso = 100 centavos

China's flag was adopted in 1949, when the country became a Communist People's Republic. Red is the traditional colour of both China and Communism. The large star represents the Communist Party programme. The smaller stars symbolize the four main social classes.

Geography

By far the most populous country in the world, though India is steadily closing the gap, the People's Republic of China is the world's third largest country after Russia and Canada. Before the development of modern transport systems, the vast size of China often hampered communications between the country's centre and the peripheries. Distances between the major cities are huge. By rail, the distance from Beijing to Guangzhou, for example, is 2,324 km [1,450 mls].

Mountains and plateaux alternate with basins and alluvial plains across China. Soil erosion, caused mainly by deforestation, has devastated many mountain areas. Most of the people live in the eastern lowlands. Manchuria, in the north, comprises a wide area of gently undulating country, originally grassland, but now an important agricultural area. The loess lands of the north-west occupy a broad belt from the great loop of the Huang He into the Shanxi and Henan Provinces. Here, valley sides, hills and mountains are blanketed in loess – a fine-grained, unstratified soil deposited by the wind during the last Ice Age. Within this region, the loess plateaux are deeply incised by gorges and ravines.

By contrast with the loess lands, the landscape of the North China Plain is very flat. Further south, the Chang Jiang (Yangtze) Delta is a region of large lakes. Here, low-lying land is traversed by a large network of canals and other, often ancient, man-made works. Far inland in the Chang Jiang Basin, and separated from the middle Chang Jiang Basin by gorges, lies the Red Basin of Sichuan Province. High mountains surround the basin to the north, west and south. The mountains of the Qin Ling ranges, in particular, protect the basin from cold winter winds.

The Qin Ling ranges are an important boundary between the relatively harsh environments of the north and the more productive lands of the south. A second major line, which follows the Da Hingaan Ling mountains and the eastern edge of the high Tibetan Plateau, divides the intensively cultivated lands of eastern China from the mountains and arid steppes of the interior. In the north, this boundary is marked by the Great Wall of China. Western China includes the Junggar Pendi (Dzungarian Basin), the Turpan (or Turfan) Depression, the Takla Makan (Taklimakan) Desert, and the high, windswept plateau of Tibet edged by the Himalayas.

China's two major rivers are the Chang Jiang and Huang He, the world's third and seventh longest, respectively. The Chang Jiang has a catchment basin almost twice as large as that of the Huang He and it is a major transport artery. The Huang He, or Yellow River, has been called 'China's Sorrow' because it has, throughout history, been responsible for frequent and disastrous floods. However, since 1949, the introduction of flood prevention schemes has greatly reduced the incidence of flooding.

Climate

The climate of China is influenced by the air masses of Asia, the Pacific Ocean and the mountains in the west. During the winter, the cold, dry Siberian air flows southwards, while during the summer, tropical Pacific air brings relatively high temperatures and rain. Summer temperatures within eastern China are high, with very little difference between the north and the south. The average annual rainfall ranges from more than 2,000 mm [80 in] in the south to desert conditions in the north-west. Tibet has extremely cold winters and low precipitation.

CHINA (BEIJING)

Beijing has a climate representative of much of north-eastern China. Winters are bitterly cold and average temperatures are below freezing from December to February. Precipitation in winter is small, but light snow and frost are common, while strong winds sometimes bring unpleasant dust storms. Summers are warm and wet, though droughts may occur. The average annual rainfall in Beijing is 620 mm [24 in]. In July and August, rainfall totals around 380 mm [15 in].

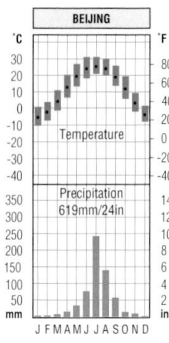

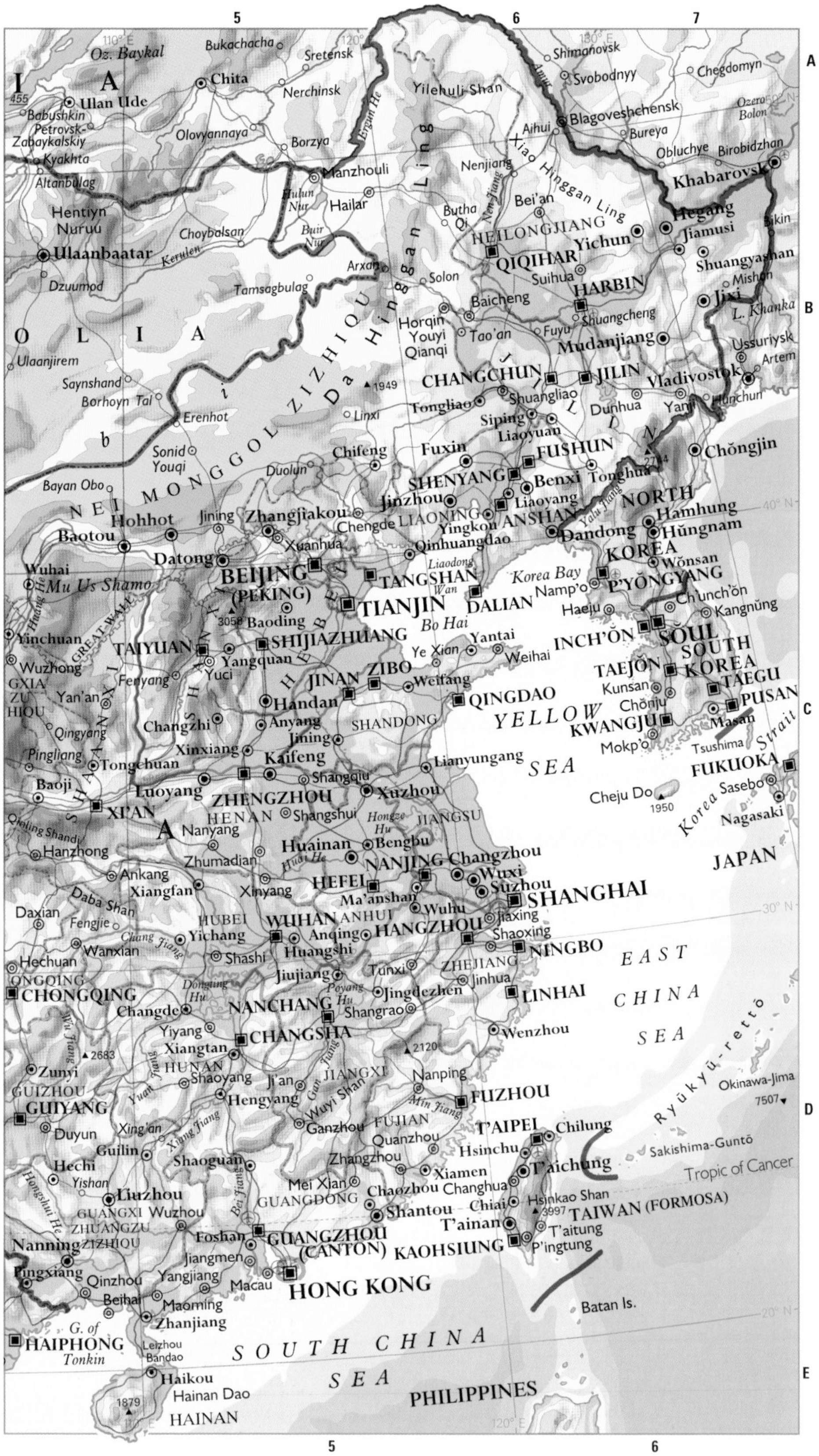

Vegetation

Because of its huge size and varied altitudes, China contains almost every type of vegetation, ranging from deserts and grasslands to boreal forests (or taiga – an extension of the forests of Siberia) near the north-eastern border with Russia, temperate forests with deciduous trees in east-central China, tropical forests in the far south-east, including Yunnan Province and the island of Hainan, together with mangrove swamps along the shores of the South China Sea. Broadly, China can be divided into two main vegetation regions: the dry north-west and the humid south-east.

History

China has one of the world's oldest civilizations, going back more than 3,500 years. Early Chinese civilization arose along the inland margins of the North China Plain, in a markedly harsher – especially in terms of winter temperatures – environment than that of other great civilizations of the Old World. The Shang Dynasty, noted for its fine craftsmanship in bronze, flourished in northern China from 1630–1122 BC. The Shang civilization was followed by many centuries of political fragmentation, and it was not until the 3rd century BC that China was unified into a centrally administered empire. Under the Qin (Ch'in) Dynasty (221–206 BC), the Great Wall of China was completed, while Chinese armies pushed southwards beyond the Chang Jiang (Yangtze River), reaching the southern Chinese coast in the vicinity of Canton (now Guangzhou). Under the Han Dynasty (206 BC–AD 220), the Chinese empire covered a vast area.

In succeeding centuries, there was a gradual movement of people from the north to the warmer, more productive lands of the south. This slow migration was greatly accelerated by incursions of barbarian nomads into northern China, especially during the Song (or Sung) Dynasty (AD 960–1279). By the late 13th century, the southern lands, including the Chiang Jiang Valley, probably contained between 70% and 80% of the Chinese population.

During the Han, T'ang and Song Dynasties, a remarkably stable political and social order evolved within China. Major distinguishing features of Chinese civilization came to include Confucianism, whereby the individual was subordinated to family obligations and to state service, the state bureaucracy, members of which were recruited by public examinations, and the benign rule of the emperor – the 'Son of Heaven'. Great advances were made in the production of porcelain, silk, metals and lacquerware, while gunpowder, the compass and printing were among several Chinese inventions which reached the West in medieval times. But the economy of pre-modern China was overwhelmingly agricultural, and the peasant class accounted for most of the population.

Despite the geographical diversity and size of the territory, China, during pre-modern times, experienced long periods of unity and cohesion rarely disturbed by invasion. Two important dynasties, the Yuan (1279–1368) and

Arable land 9.92% Permanent crops 0.35%
Permanent grassland 42.9% Forest 14%

the Qing (or Ch'ing, 1644–1912), were established by the Mongols and Manchus, respectively. But almost invariably, alien rulers found it necessary to adopt Chinese methods of government, and the Chinese cultural tradition was preserved intact.

In the 18th century, China experienced rapid population growth and living standards began to fall. By the early 19th century, the government was weak and corrupt, and the country suffered famines and political unrest. British victory in the Opium War (1839–42) was followed by the division of China into spheres of influence for the major imperialist powers, and by the establishment of treaty ports, controlled by Western countries, along the Chinese coast and the Chang Jiang.

Meanwhile, the disintegration of imperial China was hastened by peasant uprisings, such as the Taiping rebellion (1850–64), and by the defeat of China in the Sino-Japanese War of 1894–5. Belated attempts were made to arrest the decline of the Chinese Empire, but, in 1912, following an uprising in Wuhan, the last of the Chinese emperors abdicated and a republic was proclaimed.

Although the republican administration in Peking (Beijing) was regarded as the legitimate government, real power rested with army generals and provincial governors. Rival generals, or warlords, raised private armies and plunged China into a long period of internal disorder. Alternative solutions were offered by two political parties. One was the Kuomintang (or Chinese Nationalist Party) formed by Sun Yatsen, a Western-educated physician, and later led by the Kuomintang's military leader Chiang Kai-Shek. The other was the Communist Party, which had been founded in 1921 by Mao Zedong (Mao Tse-tung) and 11 others. In 1931, Japan seized Manchuria and, in 1937, full-scale warfare broke out between the countries. In the bitter fighting which followed, the Communists under Mao Zedong, gained the support of the peasantry and proved adept practitioners of guerrilla warfare.

The defeat of Japan in 1945 was followed by a civil war which cost 12 million lives. The Communists routed the Nationalist armies, forcing them to take refuge on the island of Taiwan, where they established a government under Chiang Kai-Shek. On the mainland, the Chinese People's Republic was established on 1 October 1949.

Politics

Under Communist rule, the instability that afflicted China before World War II was virtually eliminated and living standards for the people greatly improved, especially in rural areas where land was seized from private landowners and redistributed among the peasants. By 1957, virtually all economic activities were under government control. However, many of the subsequent changes in Chinese society brought great suffering. In 1958, the government launched the country's Second Five-Year Plan, which was called the 'Great Leap Forward'. Based on Mao's belief that human effort could overcome all obstacles, the plan aimed to speed economic development by increasing the work force and the number of hours worked.

One of the salient features of Communist society was the organization of the rural population into about 50,000 communes – self-sufficient units of varying sizes which were intended to increase the efficiency of agriculture. The communes also ran rural industries and were responsible for the administration of schools and clinics. Labour was organized on a vast scale to tackle public works, such as water conservation, flood control and land reclamation. In manufacturing, machinery was operated continuously, without any time for maintenance, and people were encouraged to increase steel production by using backyard furnaces. The end products were often useless. The Great Leap Forward proved to be an economic disaster, causing food shortages and a real fall in industrial production. Famine and disease caused the deaths of an estimated 20 million people. A split developed between the revolutionaries who wanted to build a classless society in which everyone worked for the common good, and the moderates who believed that China's future depended on real economic development.

In 1966, Mao gave his support to the radicals, triggering off a period called the Cultural Revolution. The radicals attacked party and government officials who were deemed to be counter-revolutionary. Universities were closed between 1966 and 1970, and students were organized into groups called Red Guards. The Red Guards rampaged through the country destroying property, demonstrating and seizing control of many provincial and city governments. The Cultural Revolution caused such upheaval that, in 1967, Mao had to use the army to restore order. By 1969, things were returning to normal, though deep political differences between the radicals and the moderates remained.

In international affairs, China began to fall out with the Soviet Union in 1956, criticizing its policy of co-existence with the West. In 1960, the Soviet Union stopped all technical aid to China and, in 1963, all relations between the countries were broken off when the Soviet Union signed a nuclear-test ban treaty with the United Kingdom and the United States. It was only in 1989, shortly before the abandonment of Communism in the Soviet Union, that relations began to improve. By contrast, relations with Western nations improved from the 1970s. In 1971, the United Nations agreed to admit the People's Republic of China instead of Taiwan (the Republic of China). Relations with the United States also improved following a visit to China by President Richard M. Nixon in 1972.

Mao Zedong, chairman of the Communist Party, and Zhou Enlai, the prime minister, both died in 1976. A struggle for power then ensued between the moderates led by Hua Guofeng and the radicals led by Mao's widow, Jiang Qing. Hua prevailed and became prime minister and chairman of the Communist Party. Jiang Qing and her three main supporters, who were known as the 'Gang of Four', were imprisoned. In 1977, Deng Xiaoping, a moderate who had been removed from office during the Cultural Revolution, became deputy prime minister and vice-chairman of the Communist Party. In 1980, Hua resigned as prime minister and, in 1981, he resigned as chairman of the Communist Party. Deng then became the most powerful leader in China. He set about reforming the economy, reducing government control over business, abolishing the commune system and permitting private ownership of the land. China also encouraged foreign investment and free enterprise in developing new industries in 'special economic zones' in eastern coastlands of China. People began to migrate to these zones in search of jobs.

However, economic reforms were not matched by political changes. In 1986, students began to call for political reforms and more freedom

---

Tibet

With an average elevation of 4,500 m [14,750 ft] and an area of 1.2 million sq km [460,000 sq mls], Tibet is the highest and most extensive plateau in the world. It is a harsh, hostile place, and most of its population of just over 2 million people live in the relatively sheltered south of the country.

For much of its history, Tibet has been ruled by Buddhist priests – *lamas* – as a theocracy. The Dalai Lama, a title passed on in successive incarnations from a dying elder to a newborn junior, usually dominated from Lhasa. Between 1720 and 1911 Tibet was under Chinese control, and was reabsorbed by Chinese forces in 1950, after the establishment of the People's Republic of China the previous year. At first, Tibet retained the right to regional self-government and was guaranteed freedom of worship. But from 1956, China tightened its control and the Dalai Lama fled to India in 1959. He was followed by more than 100,000 refugees. A brutal process of Chinese acculturation began and, in 1961, a report of the International Commission of Jurists accused China of genocide. An 'Autonomous Region of Tibet', called Xizang in Chinese, was proclaimed in 1965, but during the Cultural Revolution (1966–76) many Tibetan shrines and monasteries were destroyed.

After Mao's death in 1976, liberalization policies led to monasteries being rebuilt. Reforms led to a massive influx of Chinese immigrants. This influx, and China's control over religious life further threatened Tibetan culture. For example, in 1995, when the Dalai Lama, who had been awarded the Nobel Peace Prize in 1989, selected the new incarnation of the Panchen Lama, the second-ranking leader of his sect, China arrested the boy and enthroned another in his place.

of speech. In 1987, the secretary of the Communist Party, Hu Yaobang, who had liberal views on freedom of speech and political reform, was removed from office. When he died in April 1989, students held demonstrations to honour him. Large crowds collected in Tiananmen Square in central Beijing, where military parades were held, and also in some other cities. The students called for more democracy, but they were crushed by the armed forces who killed hundreds of protesters. After the suppression of the demonstrations, many students were arrested and Zhao Ziyang, the prime minister, was dismissed from office because of his support for the pro-democracy movement. A hard line faction within the Communist Party *Politburo* appointed Jiang Zemin as secretary-general, who became Deng's favoured successor. From the late 1980s, Deng gradually withdrew from politics as his health deteriorated and he finally died in 1997 at the age of 92.

Other important developments in the 1990s included the return to China of the former British territory of Hong Kong in 1997, and also the formerly Portuguese territory of Macau in 1999. Hong Kong, a small territory but one of the economic success stories of eastern Asia after World War II, seemed bound to contribute substantially to the continuing economic development of south-eastern China. China would also like to restore Taiwan to its status as a Chinese province, but, in 1999, the Taiwanese President Lee Teng-hui angered President Jiang Zemin by declaring that relations between Taiwan and China should be on a 'special state-to-state' basis. This was at odds with China's 'one nation' policy, whereby China and Taiwan should be regarded one country with two equal governments. With the United States prepared to defend the island in the event of Chinese aggression, it seemed unlikely that Taiwan would be prepared to reunite with mainland China in the near future.

Against all the optimism surrounding the country's economic prospects at the start of the 21st century, China remains a developing country, and it needs high economic growth rates in order to provide employment for its already huge and growing population. However, its policies aimed at limiting population growth have achieved much success – in 1999, the Chinese government claimed that its birth control policies had reduced the number of births by 338 million between 1978 and 1998. As a result, at the turn of the century, the government seemed prepared for a gradual relaxation of its one-child policy, easing the penalties for having a bigger family. China's admission to the World Trade Organization, which was finally negotiated with the United States in 1999, was another important step and China's share of world trade seemed likely to increase.

So far the benefits of economic growth have been unevenly felt – it has been confined mainly to the east, while much of the vast interior remains untouched. However, evidence for China's commitment to continuing economic reform was provided in 1998 by the appointment of Zhu Rongji as prime minister, replacing the conservative Li Peng. Zhu, an economist and protégé of Deng Xiaoping, had, as deputy prime minister, already been in overall charge of the economy. He was also associated with programmes of modernizing the economy, ensuring gradual growth in the prosperity of the Chinese people, though he had shown little interest in political reform. However, providing that the country's leaders continue to follow their pragmatic path, many experts predict a major economic and also, eventually, a political blossoming for China in the 21st century.

Economy

Since the 1970s, economic reforms have allowed market forces to operate alongside public ownership. Technocrats, who solve problems and push forward the economic reforms, have become increasingly important in government. These new leaders have encouraged foreign investment, especially in special economic zones in eastern China, and the promotion of the country's potential for tourism. The reforms have led to rapid economic growth. Between 1978 and 1997, economic growth rates reached 8% to 10% per annum. The economy continued to expand in the late 1990s, when other countries in eastern Asia suffered economic setbacks. China's total gross national product (GNP) of US $1,055,372 in 1997 placed it seventh among the world's largest economies, after the United States, Japan, Germany, France, the

> ### Hong Kong and Macau
> Hong Kong and Macau are Special Administrative Regions of China, which were formerly ruled by Britain and Portugal respectively. The island of Hong Kong, off the coast of south-eastern China, became British under the Treaty of Nanjing (1842). The Kowloon Peninsula on the mainland was added in 1860 and another mainland area called the 'New Territories' was added in 1898. On 1 July 1997, Hong Kong was returned to China, which agreed to allow it to enjoy full economic autonomy and to pursue its capitalist path for at least 50 years. Hong Kong is a small territory covering only 1,071 sq km [413 sq mls], with a population of about 6 million. However, in 1997, it was the world's biggest container port, the world's biggest exporter of clothes and the tenth biggest trader. Its economy had been so successful since the end of World War II that its huge neighbour stood to increase its export earnings by more than 25%, when the handover occurred. The fortunes of this dynamic, densely populated community have been based on manufacturing, banking and commerce, with the sheltered waters between Kowloon and Hong Kong island providing one of the world's finest natural deep-water harbours. Yet Hong Kong has few natural resources and its prosperity has rested on the ingenuity and hard work of its people.
>
> Nearby Macau was a Portuguese colony from 1557 until December 1999, when it, too, became a Special Administrative Region of China. From the 16th to the 18th centuries, it was a trading centre for silk, gold, spices and opium, but was overtaken in importance by Hong Kong in the 19th century. With an area of 16 sq km [6 sq mls] and a population of about 490,000, Macau lies on a peninsula at the head of the Canton (Pearl) River, 64 km [40 mls] west of Hong Kong and connected to China by a narrow isthmus. The main industries are textiles and tourism, and the territory is heavily reliant on the Chinese mainland for food, water and raw materials.

United Kingdom and Italy. However, with its population of more than 1.2 billion, its per capita GNP was only $860, which placed it among the world's poorer developing countries.

In the mid-1990s, despite moves towards industrialization, agriculture still employed 53% of the population, while mining and manufacturing employed another 17%. The collectivization of agriculture through the creation of communes was replaced from 1978 by household enterprises, numbering more than 230 million in 1996, together with town and village enterprises, co-operatives and some state farms, where workers are paid wages. These changes led to a rise in national production and agricultural output doubled in the 1980s.

While less than 3% of the country can be cultivated, China has practised intensive farming for thousands of years and, as a result, the country is largely self-sufficient in food. However, the threat of floods and drought remain, despite government initiatives in soil conservancy, afforestation, together with irrigation and drainage projects. The crops grown vary according to the climate. The warm south-east has a long growing season and two to three crops can be grown on the same plot of land in a single year. Major crops in the area include rice, tea and sweet potatoes. In the north, with its cooler climate and shorter growing season, wheat is the chief crop, together with maize and sorghum. Western China is largely arid and barren and crops are grown only around isolated oases. However, nomadic pastoralists, such as the Uighurs in Xinjiang, raise goats, horses and sheep.

China leads the world in the production of rice, sweet potatoes and wheat. It also ranks among the top five producers of bananas, barley, natural rubber, sesame seed, sorghum, soya beans, sugar cane and tea. Livestock are also important. China leads the world in producing eggs, goats, horses and mules. It also ranks among the top five producers of beef and veal, cattle, poultry meat, sheep and wool.

Forestry remains important. China's total roundwood production in 1996 made it the world's second largest producer after the United States.

Regions of China

(Map of China showing regions and neighbouring countries)

RUSSIA

KAZAKSTAN

MONGOLIA

HEILONGJIANG

KYRGYZSTAN

JILIN

XINJIANG UYGUR ZIZHIQU (SINKIANG A.R.)

NEI MONGGOL ZIZHIQU (INNER MONGOLIA A.R.)

LIAONING

NORTH KOREA

BEIJING SHI

TIANJIN SHI

HEBEI

SHANXI

SHANDONG

SOUTH KOREA

QINGHAI

NINGXIA HUIZA ZIZHIQU (A.R.)

SHAANXI

HENAN

JIANGSU

JAPAN

XIZANG ZIZHIQU (TIBET A.R.)

ANHUI

SHANGHAI SHI

NEPAL

BHUTAN

SICHUAN

CHONGQING SHI

HUBEI

ZHEJIANG

INDIA

BANGLADESH

GUIZHOU

HUNAN

JIANGXI

FUJIAN

YUNNAN

GUANGXI ZHUANGZU ZIZHIQU (A.R.)

GUANGDONG

TAIWAN

HONG KONG (S.A.R.)
MACAU

BURMA (MYANMAR)

VIETNAM

THAILAND

LAOS

HAINAN

PHILIPPINES

- - - - - Disputed international boundary
(A.R.) = Autonomous Region
(S.A.R.) = Special Administrative Region

China has massive natural resources. Coal is found in most of the country's provinces, and China leads the world in coal production. In the 1950s, coal accounted for more than 90% of the country's total energy supply. However, China is now a major producer of oil. Oil and gas contribute 19% of the energy supply, as compared with coal, 75%, and hydroelectric power, 6%. China has other large mineral deposits. It leads the world in producing antimony, iron ore, tin and tungsten, and ranks among the top five producers of bauxite, copper, lead, manganese ore, molybdenum, phosphates, salt and zinc ore.

With its massive reserves of coal and iron ore, China is a major producer of steel, ranking second only in the world to Japan. Manufacturing now plays a major part in China's economy. Besides steel, China also manufactures tools and machinery for new factories, cement, chemicals and fertilizers, military equipment and transport equipment, including locomotives, lorries and tractors. The leading consumer goods include processed food and textiles, bicycles, radios and sewing machines. China still has many cottage industries in rural areas. Many of them produce such items as silk and cotton textiles.

The rapid growth of the manufacturing sector since 1978 has not been without problems, including the clash between market forces and the rigid political controls of the Communist Party, such as the collapse of some out-of-date, government-owned enterprises that can no longer compete with new, technologically advanced factories. However, inefficient state enterprises still survive, together with corruption, bureaucracy and environmental pollution, including the use of coal which causes severe air pollution, while water supplies are polluted by industrial effluents and untreated sewage. But the march

of industrialization in the east seems irresistible and foreign investment and trade are increasing. Another major change that has resulted from the economic reforms is the increase in the internal migrant population, which was estimated at 21 million in 1990. Many of the migrants were looking for seasonal work or jobs in the new industries being established in the special economic zones. Under Communism, everyone had a job. However, in the new China, urban unemployment had increased to an estimated 3% by 1996, although many believed that the real percentage of people out of work was much higher.

Prior to 1997, when Britain returned Hong Kong to China, the country's overseas trade accounted for less than 3% of the world total. In 1995, the leading exports were manufactures, including machinery and transport equipment, metal products, rubber and textiles. Other important items include food and live animals, chemicals and chemical products, and mineral fuels and lubricants. Leading trading partners are Japan, Hong Kong, the United States, Taiwan and South Korea.

AREA	ETHNIC GROUPS
9,596,960 sq km	Han Chinese 92%,
[3,705,386 sq mls]	55 minority groups
POPULATION	**LANGUAGES**
1,236,915,000	Mandarin Chinese (official)
CAPITAL (POPULATION)	**RELIGIONS**
Beijing	Atheist 50%,
(Peking, 12,362,000)	Confucian 20%
GOVERNMENT	**CURRENCY**
Single-party	Renminbi yuan = 10 jiao =
Communist republic	100 fen

COLOMBIA

The yellow on Colombia's flag depicts the land, which is separated from the tyranny of Spain by the blue, symbolizing the Atlantic Ocean. The red symbolizes the blood of the people who fought to make the country independent. The flag has been used since 1806.

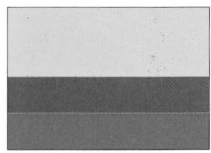

Geography

The Republic of Colombia, in north-western South America, is the only country in the continent to have coastlines on both the Pacific and the Caribbean Sea. Colombia also contains the northernmost ranges of the Andes Mountains.

Climate

There is a tropical climate in the lowlands. But the altitude greatly affects the climate of the Andes. The capital, Bogotá, which stands on a plateau in the eastern Andes at about 2,800 m [9,200 ft] above sea level, has mild temperatures throughout the year. The rainfall is heavy, especially on the Pacific coast.

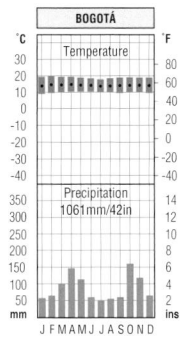

COLOMBIA (BOGOTÁ)

Colombia is split by the northern Andes. The altitude of these mountains changes the tropical climate of the country, lowering temperatures and increasing the amount of rainfall, with permanent snow at the higher levels. Elsewhere, temperatures are high with very little annual variation. Rainfall is high on the Pacific coast, but it is drier on the Caribbean coast and in the Magdalena Valley, which both experience dry seasons.

History

Amerindian people have lived in Colombia for thousands of years. Today, however, only a small proportion of the people are of unmixed Amerindian ancestry. Mestizos (people of mixed white and Amerindian ancestry) form the largest group, followed by whites and mulattos (people of mixed European and African ancestry).

Spaniards opened up the area in the early 16th century and they set up a territory known as the Viceroyalty of the New Kingdom of Granada, which included Colombia, Ecuador, Panama and Venezuela. In 1819, the area became independent, but Ecuador and Venezuela soon split away, followed by Panama in 1903.

The Drugs Trade

Colombia is notorious for its illegal export of cocaine, and reliable estimates class the drug as the country's most lucrative source of foreign exchange as kilo after kilo feeds the insatiable demand from the USA and, to a lesser extent, Western Europe. In addition to the indigenous crop, far larger amounts of leaf are smuggled in from Bolivia and Peru for refining, processing and 're-export'. US agencies estimated that in 1987 retail sales of South American cocaine totalled US $22 billion.

Violence, though focused on the drug capitals of Medellín and Cali, is endemic, with warfare between rival gangs and between producers and the authorities on an almost daily basis. Assassinations of civil servants, judicial officials, police officers or anyone attempting to investigate, control or end the rule of the multimillionaire drug barons are commonplace.

In 1990, as part of US President George Bush's US $10.6 billion 'war on drugs', the governments of three Andean states – Colombia, Bolivia and Peru – joined forces with the US Drug Enforcement Agency in an attempt to clamp down on the production and distribution of cocaine. But while early results from Bolivia were encouraging, the situation in Colombia hardened, despite the brave attempts of politicians, administrators and police to break the socio-economic stranglehold of the drug cartels. Throughout the 1990s, the country was faced with terrorism caused by rival drug-producing groups and also by the activities of two left-wing guerrilla groups.

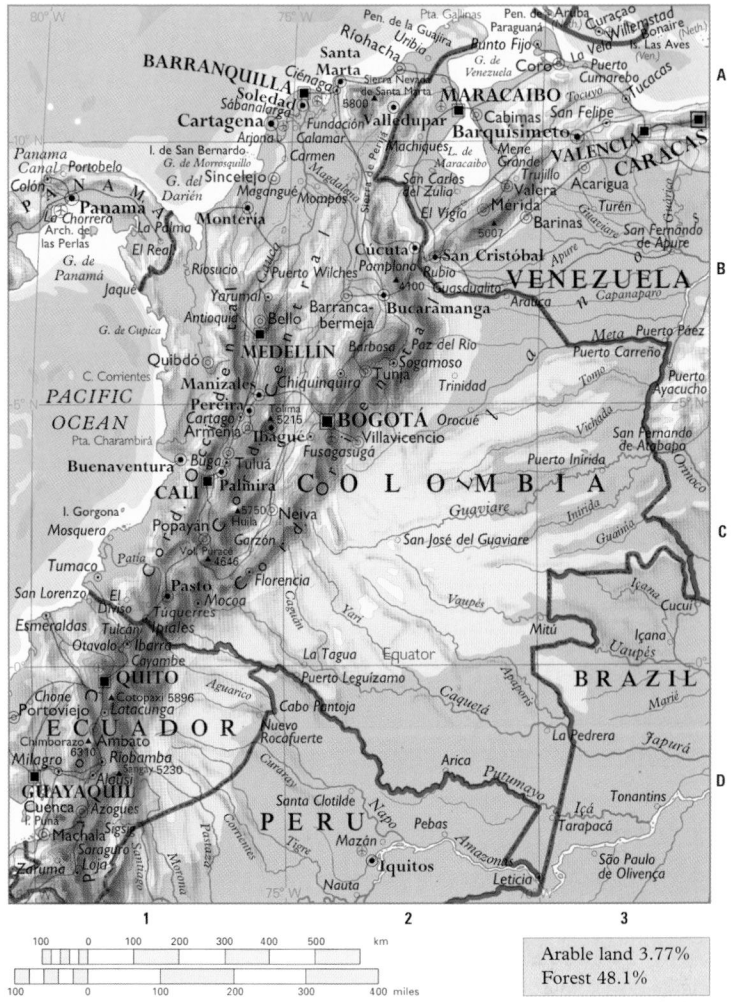

Arable land 3.77%
Forest 48.1%

Politics

Colombia's recent history has been very unstable. Rivalries between political parties led to civil wars in 1899–1902 and 1949–57, when the parties formed a coalition. Coalition government ended in 1986. Colombia's problems include the illicit drug industry and violent guerrilla activity. In 1999, Andrés Pastrana, a Conservative who was elected president in 1998, appealed for a huge increase in US military aid.

Economy

The World Bank classifies Colombia as a 'lower-middle-income' developing country. Agriculture is important and coffee is the leading export crop. Other crops include bananas, cocoa, maize and tobacco. Mining and manufacturing are becoming more important in the economy. Colombia exports coal and oil, and it also produces emeralds and gold. Manufacturing is based mainly in Bogotá, Cali and Medellín.

AREA	**ETHNIC GROUPS**
1,138,910 sq km	Mestizo 58%, White 20%,
[439,733 sq mls]	Mulatto 14%, Black 4%
POPULATION	**LANGUAGES**
38,581,000	Spanish (official)
CAPITAL (POPULATION)	**RELIGIONS**
Bogotá	Christianity
(5,026,000)	(Roman Catholic 93%)
GOVERNMENT	**CURRENCY**
Multiparty republic	Peso = 100 centavos

COMOROS – SEE INDIAN OCEAN, PAGES 122–123

Congo's red flag, with the national emblem of a crossed hoe and mattock (a kind of pick-axe), was dropped in 1990, when the country officially abandoned the Communist policies it had followed since 1970. This new flag was adopted in its place.

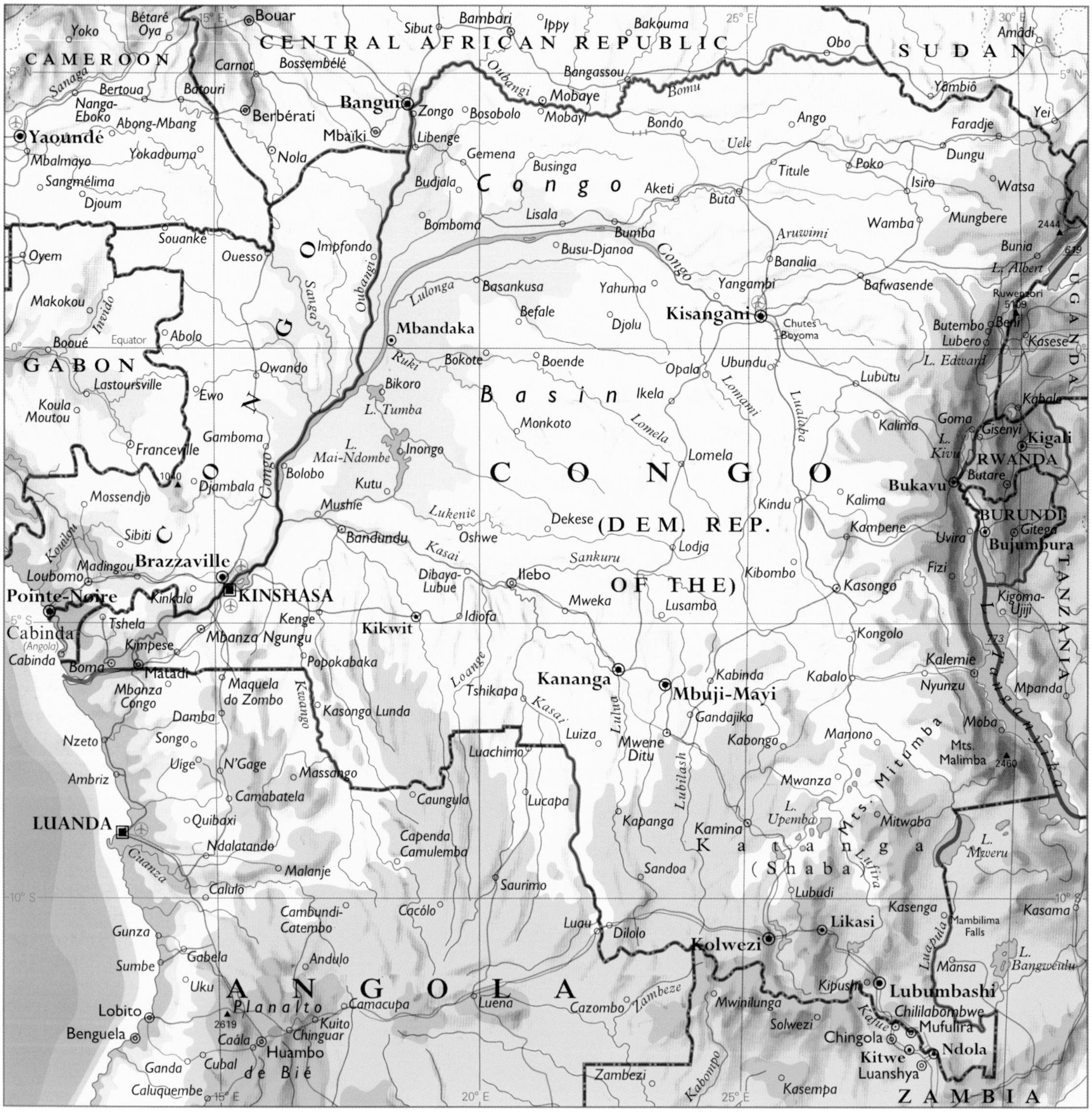

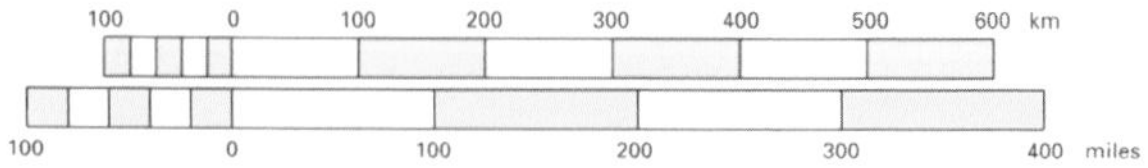

| Congo: Arable land 0.42% Permanent crops 0.07% Forest 58.3% |
| Congo (Dem. Rep. of the): Arable land 3.21% Permanent crops 0.27% Forest 76.7% |

Geography and Climate

The Republic of Congo lies on the River Congo in Africa. The Equator runs through the centre of the country. Congo has a narrow coastal plain on which its main port, Pointe Noire, stands. Behind the plain are uplands through which the River Niari has carved a valley. To the east lies Malebo (formerly Stanley) Pool, a large lake where the River Congo widens. Central Congo consists of high plains, while the north has large swampy areas in the valleys of rivers that flow into the River Congo and its tributary, the Oubangi.

Most of the country has a humid, equatorial climate, with rain all through the year. The coastal plain is drier and cooler than the rest of the country, because the cold Benguela current flows northwards along the coast.

History and Politics

Between the 15th and 18th centuries, part of Congo probably belonged to the huge Kongo kingdom, whose centre lay to the south. Portuguese explorers reached the coast of Congo in the 15th century and the area soon became a trading region, the main commodities being slaves and ivory. The slave trade continued until the 19th century. European exploration of the interior did not occur until the late 19th century. The area came under French protection in 1880. It became known as Middle Congo, a country within French Equatorial Africa, which also included Chad, Gabon, and Ubangi-Shari (now called Central African Republic). Congo remained under French control until 1960.

Congo became a one-party state in 1964 and a military group took over the government in 1968. In 1970, Congo declared itself a Communist country, though it continued to seek aid from Western countries. The government officially abandoned its Communist policies in 1990. Multiparty elections were held in 1992 and the former military leader, Denis Sassou-Nguesso, was defeated by Pascal Lissouba. However, in 1997, Sassou-Nguesso, assisted by his personal militia and also by troops from Angola, launched an uprising which overthrew Lissouba, who fled the country, taking refuge in Burkina Faso. But forces loyal to Lissouba fought back, starting a civil war which caused some 250,000 people to flee their homes. By 1999, malnutrition was widespread, especially among children of the refugees.

Economy

The World Bank classifies Congo as a 'lower-middle-income' developing country. Agriculture employs about 60% of the people, though many farmers produce little more than they need to feed their families. The chief food crops include bananas, cassava, maize, plantains, rice and yams. Cash crops include cocoa, coffee and sugar cane.

Congo's main exports are oil and oil products, which account for over 80% of the exports. The industrial sector is small but growing.

AREA	Mboshi 12%, Mbete 5%
342,000 sq km	**LANGUAGES**
[132,046 sq mls]	French (official),
POPULATION	Kongo, Teke
2,658,000	**RELIGIONS**
CAPITAL (POPULATION)	Christianity (Roman Catholic
Brazzaville (938,000)	54%, Protestant 25%, African
GOVERNMENT	Christians 14%), traditional
Military regime	beliefs 5%
ETHNIC GROUPS	**CURRENCY**
Kongo 52%, Teke 17%,	CFA franc = 100 centimes

CONGO (DEMOCRATIC REPUBLIC OF THE)

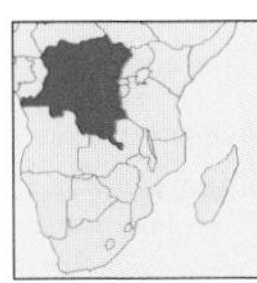

The Democratic Republic of the Congo adopted a new flag in 1997 after Laurent Kabila rose to power. The blue represents the UN's role in securing independence for the country, and the six small stars represent the original provinces of the independent state.

Geography

The Democratic Republic of the Congo, formerly known as Zaïre, is the world's 12th largest country. Much of the country lies within the drainage basin of the huge River Congo. The river reaches the sea along the country's coastline, which is 40 km [25 mls] long. Mountains rise in the east, where the country's borders run through lakes Tanganyika, Kivu, Edward and Albert. These lakes lie on the floor of an arm of the Great Rift Valley.

Climate

The equatorial region has high temperatures and heavy rainfall throughout the year. In the subtropical south, where the town of Lubumbashi is situated, there is a marked wet and dry season.

History

Pygmies, who lived by hunting and gathering, were the first inhabitants of what is now the Democratic Republic of the Congo. But around 2,000 years ago the area was gradually settled by the technologically far more advanced Bantu-speaking people, who used iron tools and farmed the land. The pygmies, unable to compete, gradually moved into remote parts of the northern rainforests, while such Bantu-speaking peoples as the Kongo, Kuba, Luba and Lunda later founded large, powerful kingdoms.

The Portuguese reached the coast in the late 15th century and, soon afterwards, the slave trade began when Europeans bought slaves from coastal chiefs. The slave trade weakened the African kingdoms which lay in the interior. European exploration of the interior began in the late 19th century and, in 1908, the country, then called Congo Free State, became the personal property of King Leopold II of Belgium. The king's agents treated the local people badly, employing forced labour, and, in 1908, the Congo Free State became a Belgian colony, which was renamed Belgian Congo.

Politics

The Belgian Congo became independent in 1960 and was renamed Zaïre in 1971. Ethnic rivalries caused instability until 1965, when the country became a one-party state, ruled by President Mobutu. The government allowed the formation of political parties in 1990, but elections were repeatedly postponed. In 1996, fighting broke out in eastern Zaïre, as the Tutsi-Hutu conflict in Burundi and Rwanda spilled over. Laurent Kabila, an outspoken opponent of Mobutu, led an uprising spearheaded by Tutsis who lived in Zaïre and eventually took power in Kinshasa in 1997. A rebellion against Kabila broke out in 1998. Rwanda and Uganda supported the rebels, while Angola, Chad, Namibia and Zimbabwe sent troops to assist Kabila. A cease-fire was signed in 1999 by six African heads of state, including Kabila, and later by rebel leaders. However, the rebels controlled large areas and more fighting broke out as various groups sought to occupy strategic areas before the arrival of UN observers.

Economy

The World Bank classifies the Democratic Republic of the Congo as a 'low-income' developing country, despite its abundant mineral reserves. The country is the world's leading producer and exporter of diamonds. It also has offshore oil deposits and petroleum ranks as the second most valuable export, followed by copper. Coffee is also exported, while other cash crops include cocoa, cotton, palm products, rubber and tea. Agriculture employs 65% of the people, although many farmers live at subsistence level. Food crops include bananas, cassava, groundnuts, maize, plantains, rice, sugar cane and yams. Manufactures include beer and other beverages, bicycles, cement, leather, metals, processed food, rubber, tobacco, textiles, vehicles and wood products.

AREA	Ngale 6%, Rundi 4%, Teke,
2,344,885 sq km	Boa, Chokwe, Lugbara, Banda
[905,365 sq mls]	**LANGUAGES**
POPULATION	French (official),
49,001,000	tribal languages
CAPITAL (POPULATION)	**RELIGIONS**
Kinshasa (3,804,000)	Christianity (Roman
GOVERNMENT	Catholic 48%, Protestant 29%),
Single-party republic	indigenous Christian churches
ETHNIC GROUPS	17%), traditional beliefs 3%,
Luba 18%, Kongo 16%,	Islam 1%
Mongo 14%, Rwanda 10%,	**CURRENCY**
Azande 6%, Bandi and	Congolese franc

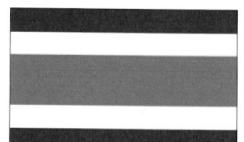

Costa Rica's flag is based on the blue-white-blue pattern used by the Central American Federation (1823–39). This Federation consisted of Costa Rica, El Salvador, Guatemala, Honduras, and Nicaragua. The red stripe, which was adopted in 1848, reflects the colors of France.

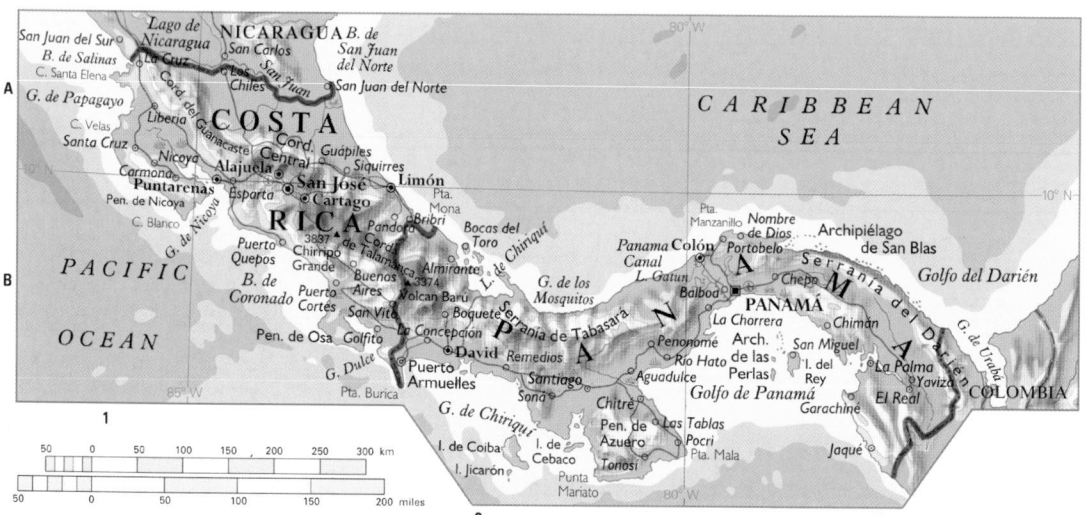

Geography and Climate

The Republic of Costa Rica in Central America has coastlines on both the Pacific Ocean and also on the Caribbean Sea. Central Costa Rica consists of mountain ranges and plateaux with many volcanoes. The Meseta Central, where the capital, San José is situated, and the Valle del General in the southeast, have rich, volcanic soils and are the most thickly populated parts of Costa Rica. The highlands descend to the Caribbean lowlands and the Pacific Coast region, with its low mountain ranges.

The coolest months are December and January. The northeast trade winds bring heavy rain to the Caribbean coast. There is less rainfall in the highlands and on the Pacific coastlands.

History and Politics

Christopher Columbus reached the Caribbean coast in 1502 and rumors of treasure attracted many Spaniards to settle in the country. Spain ruled the country until 1821, when Spain's Central American colonies broke away to join Mexico in 1822. In 1823, the Central American states broke with Mexico and set up the Central American Federation. Later, this large union broke up and Costa Rica became fully independent in 1838. From the late 19th century, Costa Rica experienced a number of revolutions, with both periods of dictatorship and democracy. In 1948, following a revolt, the armed forces were abolished. Since 1948, Costa Rica has enjoyed a long period of stable democracy, which many in Latin America admire and envy.

Economy

Costa Rica is classified by the World Bank as a "lower-middle-income" developing country and one of the most prosperous countries in Central America. There are high educational standards, and a high life expectancy of 73.5 years.

The country's resources include its forests, but it lacks minerals apart from some bauxite and manganese. Manufacturing is increasing. The United States is Costa Rica's chief trading partner. Tourism is a fast-growing industry.

AREA	Black and Mulatto 3%,
19,730 sq mi [51,100 sq km]	East Asian (mostly
POPULATION	Chinese) 3%
3,605,000	**LANGUAGES**
CAPITAL (POPULATION)	Spanish (official)
San José (1,186,000)	**RELIGIONS**
GOVERNMENT	Christianity
Multiparty republic	(Roman Catholic 81%)
ETHNIC GROUPS	**CURRENCY**
White 85%, Mestizo 8%,	Colón = 100 céntimos

PANAMA

Geography and Climate

The Republic of Panama forms an isthmus linking Central America to South America. The Panama Canal, which is 50.7 mi [81.6 km] long, cuts across the isthmus.

Panama has a tropical climate. Temperatures are high, though the mountains are much cooler than the coastal plains. The main rainy season is between May and December.

History and Politics

Christopher Columbus landed in Panama in 1502 and Spain took control of the area. In 1821, Panama became a province of Colombia.

In 1903, Colombia refused a request by the United States to build a canal. Panama revolted against Colombia, and became independent. The United States began to build the canal, which opened in 1914, and they administered the Panama Canal Zone, a strip of land along the canal. But many Panamanians resented US influence and, in 1979, the Canal Zone was returned to Panama. Control of the Canal itself was handed over by the USA to Panama on December 31, 1999.

Panama's government has changed many times since independence, and there have been periods of military dictatorships. In 1983, General Manuel Antonio Noriega became Panama's leader. In 1988, two US grand juries in Florida indicted Noriega on charges of drug trafficking. In 1989, Noriega was apparently defeated in a presidential election, but the government declared the election invalid. After the killing of a US marine, US troops entered Panama and arrested Noriega, who was convicted by a Miami court of drug offences in 1992. Elections in 1994 were won by the Democratic Revolutionary Party, led by Ernesto Pérez Balladares.

Economy

The World Bank classifies Panama as a "lower-middle-income" developing country. The Panama Canal is an important source of revenue, generating jobs in commerce, trade, manufacturing, and transport. The main activity is agriculture, which employs 27% of the people.

AREA	Black and Mulatto 20%,
29,761 sq mi [77,080 sq km]	White 10%, Amerindian 8%,
POPULATION	Asian 2%
2,736,000	**LANGUAGES**
CAPITAL (POPULATION)	Spanish (official)
Panama City (452,000)	**RELIGIONS**
GOVERNMENT	Christianity (Roman Catholic
Multiparty republic	84%, Protestant 5%), Islam 5%
ETHNIC GROUPS	**CURRENCY**
Mestizo 60%,	Balboa = 100 centésimos

CROATIA

Croatia adopted a red, white and blue flag in 1848. Under Communist rule, a red star appeared at the centre. In 1990, the red star was replaced by the present coat of arms, which symbolizes the various parts of the country.

Geography

The Republic of Croatia was one of six republics making up the former Communist country of Yugoslavia until it became independent in 1991. The region bordering the Adriatic Sea is called Dalmatia. It includes the coastal ranges, which contain large areas of bare limestone, reaching 1,913 m [6,276 ft] at Mount Troglav. Other highlands lie in the north-east. Most of the rest of the country consists of the fertile Pannonian Plains, which are drained by Croatia's two main rivers, the Drava and the Sava.

Climate

The coastal area has a typical Mediterranean climate, with hot, dry summers and mild, moist winters. Inland, the climate becomes more continental. Winters are cold, while temperatures often soar to 38°C [100°F] in the summer months.

History

Slav people settled in the area around 1,400 years ago. In 803, Croatia became part of the Holy Roman Empire and the Croats soon adopted Christianity. Croatia was an independent kingdom in the 10th and 11th centuries. In 1102, the king of Hungary also became king of Croatia, creating a union that lasted 800 years. In 1526, much of Croatia and Hungary came under the Ottoman Turks following Hungary's defeat in the Battle of Mohács. At about the same time, the Austrian Habsburgs gained control of the rest of Croatia. In 1699, the Habsburgs drove out the Turks and Croatia again came under Hungarian rule. In 1809, Croatia became part of the Illyrian provinces of Napoleon I of France, but the Habsburgs took over in 1815.

In 1867, Croatia became part of the dual monarchy of Austria-Hungary and in 1868 Croatia signed an agreement with Hungary guaranteeing Croatia some of its historic rights. During World War I, Austria-Hungary fought on the side of the defeated Axis powers, and, in 1918, the empire was broken up. Croatia declared its independence and joined with neighbouring states to form the Kingdom of the Serbs, Croats and Slovenes. The Croats hoped to achieve regional autonomy, but the Serbs enforced a centralized system based on Belgrade. Serbian domination provoked Croatian opposition. In 1929, the king changed the country's name to Yugoslavia and began to rule as a dictator. He was assassinated in 1934 by a Bulgarian employed by a Croatian terrorist group, provoking more hostility between Croats and Serbs.

Germany occupied Croatia in World War II. Croatia was declared an independent state, though, in reality, it was ruled by the invaders. After the war, Communists took power in Yugoslavia, with Josip Broz Tito as its leader. Tito held Yugoslavia together until his death in 1980, but in the 1980s, economic and ethnic rivalries, including a deterioration in relations with Serbia, threatened stability. In the early 1990s, Yugoslavia split into five nations, one of which was Croatia which declared itself independent in 1991.

Politics

After Serbia supplied arms to Serbs living in Croatia, war broke out between the two republics, causing great damage, large-scale movements of refugees and disruption of the economy, including the vital tourist industry. Rivalry between the Croats and Serbs goes back centuries – Croatia was politically linked with Hungary and, therefore, to Western Europe and the Roman Catholic church, from 1102 to 1918. The rivalry was fuelled in World War II by the setting up in Croatia and much of Bosnia-Herzegovina of a puppet Fascist regime by Germany, with the support of Croatian Catholics.

Arable land 19.7% Permanent crops 2.09% Forest 37.6%

In 1992, the United Nations sent a peace-keeping force to Croatia, effectively ending the war with Serbia. However, in 1992, war broke out in Bosnia-Herzegovina and Bosnian Croats occupied parts of that country. But in 1994, Croatia helped to end the Croat-Muslim conflict in Bosnia-Herzegovina and, in 1995, after retaking some areas occupied by Serbs, it contributed to the drawing up of the Dayton Peace Accord, which ended the civil war. Croatia's arch-nationalist president, Franco Tudjman, died in December 1999. In January 2000, Tudjman's Croatian Democratic Union was defeated in a general election by a more liberal, westward-leaning alliance of Social Democrats and Social Liberals. In February, Stipe Mesic, the last head of state of the former Yugoslavia before it disintegrated in 1991, was elected president.

Economy

The wars of the early 1990s disrupted Croatia's economy, which had been quite prosperous before the disturbances. Tourism on the Dalmatian coast had been a major industry. Croatia also had major manufacturing industries, and manufactures remain the chief exports. Manufactures include cement, chemicals, refined oil and oil products, ships, steel and wood products. Major farm products include fruits, livestock, maize, soya beans, sugar beet and wheat.

AREA	Serb 12%, Bosnian
56,538 sq km [21,824 sq mls]	**LANGUAGES**
POPULATION	Serbo-Croatian
4,672,000	**RELIGIONS**
CAPITAL (POPULATION)	Christianity (Roman
Zagreb (931,000)	Catholic 77%, Eastern
GOVERNMENT	Orthodox 11%),
Multiparty republic	Islam 1%
ETHNIC GROUPS	**CURRENCY**
Croat 78%,	Kuna = 100 lipas

CUBA

Cuba's flag, the 'Lone Star' banner, was designed in 1849, but it was not adopted as the national flag until 1901, after Spain had withdrawn from the country. The red triangle represents the Cuban people's bloody struggle for independence.

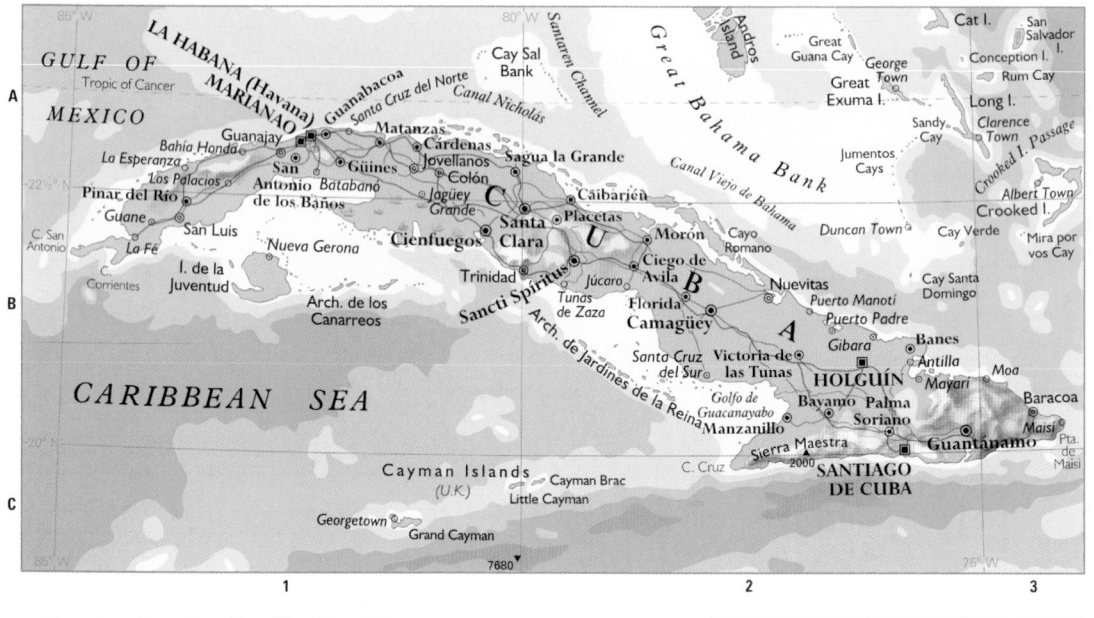

Arable land 24% Permanent crops 6.65%
Permanent grassland 27% Forest 23.7%

Geography

The Republic of Cuba is the largest island country in the Caribbean Sea. It consists of one large island, Cuba, the Isle of Youth (Isla de la Juventud) and about 1,600 small islets. Mountains and hills cover about a quarter of Cuba. The highest mountain range, the Sierra Maestra in the south-east, reaches 2,000 m [6,562 ft] above sea level. The rest of the land consists of gently rolling country or coastal plains, crossed by fertile valleys carved by the short, mostly shallow and narrow rivers.

Climate

Cuba lies in the tropics. But sea breezes moderate the temperature, warming the land in winter and cooling it in summer.

CUBA (HAVANA)

Cuba experiences uniformly high temperatures throughout the year: 22°C [72°F] in January, and 28°C [82°F] during August. The highest temperature ever recorded in Cuba is 36°C [97°F], with the lowest at 10°C [50°F]. Rainfall is heavier on the northern side of the island and falls in a marked wet season which runs from May to October – this season may also experience hurricanes, which often cause widespread devastation.

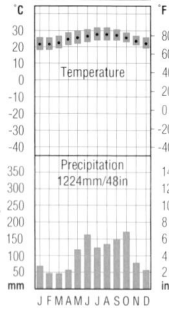

History

Christopher Columbus discovered the island in 1492 and Spaniards began to settle there from 1511. Spanish rule ended in 1898, when the United States defeated Spain in the Spanish-American War. The United States ruled Cuba from 1898 until 1902, when the people elected Tomás Estrada Palma as president of the independent Republic of Cuba, though American influence remained strong. In 1933, an army sergeant named Fulgencio Batista seized power and ruled as dictator. However, under a new constitution, he was elected president in 1940, serving until 1944. He again seized power in 1952 and became dictator, but, on 1 January 1959, he fled Cuba following the overthrow of his regime by a revolutionary force led by a young lawyer, Fidel Castro. Many Cubans who were opposed to Castro left the country, settling in the United States. Groups of exiles mounted anti-Castro campaigns.

Politics

The United States opposed Castro's policies, so he turned to the Soviet Union for assistance. In 1961, Cuban exiles attempting an invasion were defeated. In 1962, the US learned that nuclear missile bases armed by the Soviet Union had been established in Cuba. The US ordered the Soviet Union to remove the missiles and bases. After a few days, during which many people feared that a world war might break out, the Soviet Union agreed to American demands.

Cuba's relations with the Soviet Union remained strong until 1991, when the Soviet Union was broken up. The loss of Soviet aid greatly damaged Cuba's economy. Castro continued the country's left-wing policies, despite the isolation of his Marxist regime and the disruption of trade, which severely affected the economy of a country that had been highly dependent on oil and aid from the Soviet Union. The new situation undermined Castro's considerable social achievements, but, in February 1993, elections showed a high level of support for his left-wing policies. In 1998, hopes of a thaw in relations with the United States were raised when the US government announced that it was lifting the ban on flights to Cuba. The Pope, making his first visit to Cuba, criticized the 'unjust and ethically unacceptable' US blockade on Cuba.

Economy

Sugar cane remains Cuba's outstandingly important cash crop, accounting for more than 60% of the country's exports. It is grown on more than half of the island's cultivated land and Cuba is one of the world's top ten producers of the product. Before 1959, the sugar cane was grown on large estates, many of them owned by US companies. Following the Revolution, they were nationalized and the Soviet Union and Eastern European countries replaced the United States as the main market. The other main crop is tobacco, which is grown in the north-west. Cattle raising, milk production and rice cultivation have also been encouraged to help diversify the economy, and the Castro regime has devoted considerable efforts to improving the quality of rural life, making standards of living more homogeneous throughout the island.

Cuba is also a significant producer of minerals. Minerals and concentrates rank second to sugar among the exports, followed by fish products, tobacco and tobacco products, especially the famous cigars, citrus fruits and other agricultural products. Since the collapse of the Communist governments in Eastern Europe and the Soviet Union, Cuba has sought to increase its trade with Latin America and China.

AREA	**ETHNIC GROUPS**
110,860 sq km	White 66%, Mulatto 22%,
[42,803 sq mls]	Black 12%
POPULATION	**LANGUAGES**
11,051,000	Spanish (official)
CAPITAL (POPULATION)	**RELIGIONS**
Havana	Christianity (Roman Catholic
(La Habana, 2,241,000)	40%, Protestant 3%)
GOVERNMENT	**CURRENCY**
Socialist republic	Cuban peso = 100 centavos

CYPRUS

This flag became the official flag when the country became independent from Britain in 1960. It shows an outline map of the island, with two olive branches. Since Cyprus was divided, the separate communities have flown the Greek and Turkish flags.

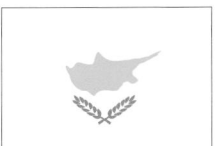

Geography

The Republic of Cyprus is an island nation which lies in the north-eastern Mediterranean Sea. Cyprus has scenic mountain ranges, including the Kyrenia Range in the north and the Troodos Mountains in the south, which rise to 1,951 m [6,401 ft] at Mount Olympus. The island also contains fertile lowlands, including the broad Mesaoria Plain.

Climate

Cyprus experiences hot, dry summers and mild, wet winters. Summers are hotter than those in the western Mediterranean since Cyprus lies close to the hot mainland of south-western Asia.

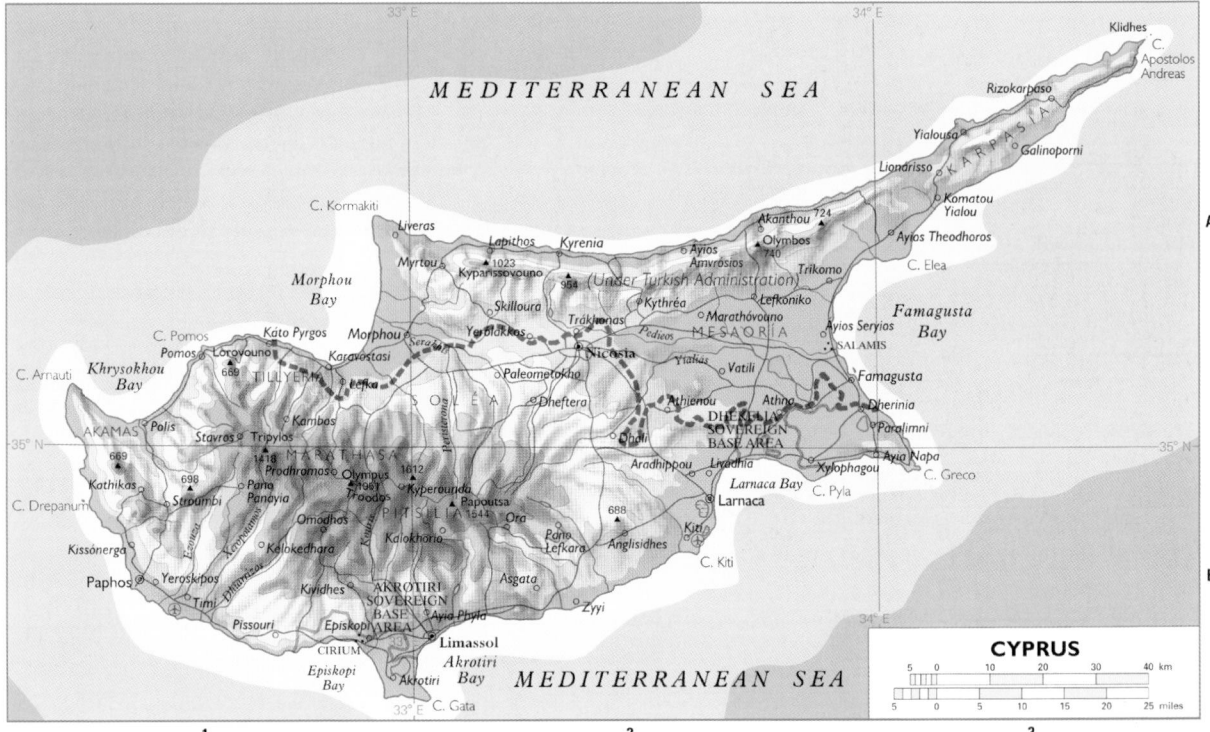

History and Politics

Greeks settled on Cyprus 3,200 years ago. In the 1570s, the island became part of the Turkish Ottoman Empire. In 1878, it was leased to Britain, who annexed it in 1914 and made it a colony in 1925. In the 1950s, Greek Cypriots, led by Archbishop Makarios, began a campaign for union with Greece. A guerrilla force called EOKA attacked the British who exiled Makarios. Cyprus became independent in 1960, but Britain retained two military bases.

The constitution of Cyprus provided for power-sharing between the Greek and Turkish Cypriots. When this proved unworkable, fighting broke out. In 1974, Makarios was overthrown and Turkey invaded northern Cyprus. Many Greek Cypriots fled from the north, which, in 1983, was proclaimed an independent state called the Turkish Republic of Northern Cyprus. In 1998, the north proposed that the Greeks and Turks join a confederation in which both sides keep sovereignty over their areas, but this was rejected by the Greek and Cypriot leaders.

Economy

The chief minerals are asbestos and chromium. However, the most valuable activity is tourism. Industry employs 37% of the workforce and manufactures include cement, clothes, footwear, tiles and wine. In the early 1990s, the United Nations reclassified Cyprus as a developed country, though the economy of the Turkish-Cypriot north lags behind that of the Greek-Cypriot south.

AREA	CAPITAL (POPULATION)
9,250 sq km [3,571 sq mls]	Nicosia (189,000)
POPULATION	CURRENCY
749,000	Cyprus pound = 100 cents

MALTA

The Republic of Malta comprises two main islands, Malta and Gozo, a smaller island, Comino and two tiny islets.

Malta has hot, dry summers and mild, wet winters. The sirocco, a hot wind from North Africa, may raise temperatures in the spring.

During World War I (1914–18), Malta was an important naval base. In World War II (1939–45), Italian and German aircraft bombed the islands. In recognition of the bravery of the Maltese, the British King George VI awarded the George Cross to Malta in 1942. In 1953, Malta became a base for NATO (North Atlantic Treaty Organization). The country became independent in 1964, and a republic in 1974. In 1979, Britain's military agreement with Malta expired, and Malta ceased to be a military base. In the 1980s, the people declared Malta a neutral country. Malta applied to join the European Union in the 1990s, but the application was scrapped when the Labour Party won the elections in 1996. But, following its election defeat in 1998, the bid for EU membership was renewed.

The World Bank has classified Malta as an 'upper-middle income' developing country. It lacks natural resources, but most of the people work in commercial shipbuilding, manufacturing and the tourist industry.

Manufactures include chemicals and processed food. Farming is extremely difficult, due to rocky soils. Crops include barley, fruits, potatoes and wheat.

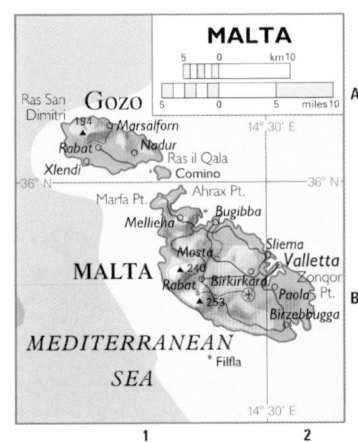

AREA	CAPITAL (POPULATION)
316 sq km [122 sq mls]	Valletta (102,000)
POPULATION	CURRENCY
379,000	Maltese lira = 100 cents

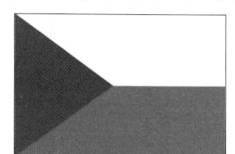

After independence, on 1 January 1993, the Czech Republic adopted the former flag of Czechoslovakia. It features the red and white of Bohemia in the west, together with the blue of Moravia and Slovakia. Red, white and blue are the colours of Pan-Slavic liberation.

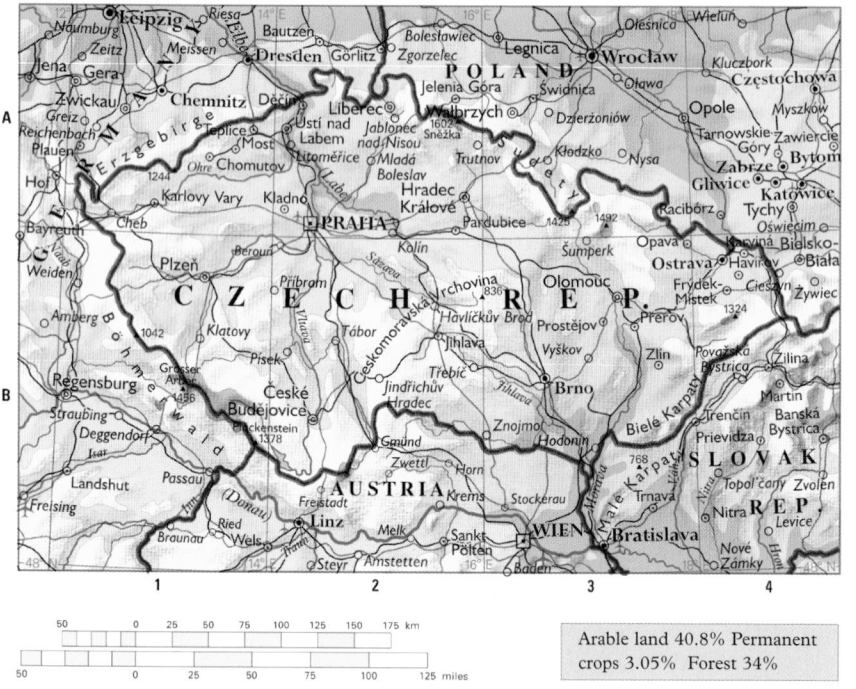

Arable land 40.8% Permanent crops 3.05% Forest 34%

German culture was dominant until the late 18th century. However, although Austria continued to rule Bohemia and Moravia, Czech nationalism continued to grow throughout the 19th century. During World War I, Czech nationalists advocated the creation of an independent nation. At the end of the war, when Austria-Hungary collapsed, the new republic of Czechoslovakia was founded. The 1920s and 1930s were generally a period of stability and economic progress, but problems arose concerning the country's minority groups. Many Slovaks wanted a greater degree of self-government, while Germans living in Sudetenland, in western Czechoslovakia, were unhappy under Czech rule.

In 1938, Sudetenland was turned over to Germany and, in March 1939, Germany occupied the rest of the country. By 1945, following the Nazi defeat, a coalition government, including Czech Communists, was formed to rule the country. In 1948, Communist leaders seized control and made the country an ally of the Soviet Union in the Cold War. In 1968, the Communist government introduced reforms, which were known as the 'Prague spring'. However, Russian and other East European troops invaded and suppressed the reform group.

Geography

The Czech Republic is the western three-fifths of the former country of Czechoslovakia. It contains two regions: Bohemia in the west and Moravia in the east. Mountains border much of the country in the west. The Bohemian basin in the north-centre is a fertile lowland region, with Prague, the capital city, as its main centre. Highlands cover much of the centre of the country, with lowlands in the south-east. Some rivers, such as the Elbe (Labe) and Oder (Odra) flow north into Germany and Poland. In the south, rivers flow into the Danube Basin.

Climate

The climate of the Czech Republic is influenced by its landlocked position in east-central Europe. The country experiences a humid continental climate, with warm summers and cold winters. Rainfall is generally higher in summer, with occasional thunderstorms.

CZECH REPUBLIC (PRAGUE)

Prague has a climate that is transitional between the severe continental conditions experienced in Russia, and the mild and wet conditions of Western Europe. The weather is often changeable. Summers are warm and sunny, although hot spells frequently end in thunderstorms. Spring and summer are the wettest seasons, while the precipitation in winter is low. Bitterly cold spells occur during winter when easterly winds blow.

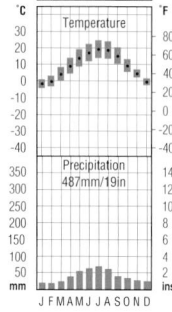

History

The ancestors of the Czech people began to settle in what is now the Czech Republic around 1,500 years ago. Bohemia, in the west, became important in the 10th century as a kingdom within the Holy Roman Empire. In the 13th century, craftworkers and merchants from Germany settled there, adding to the region's prosperity. By the 14th century, Prague was one of Europe's major cultural cities. Religious wars in the first half of the 15th century led many Czech people to become Protestants. From 1526, the Roman Catholic Habsburgs from Austria began to rule the area, but, in 1618, a Czech Protestant rebellion started the Thirty Years' War. From 1620, most Czechs were made to convert to Catholicism and adopt German as their language.

Politics

When democratic reforms were introduced in the Soviet Union in the 1980s, the Czechs also demanded change. In 1989, the Federal Assembly elected Václav Havel, a noted playwright and dissident, as the country's president and, in 1990, free elections were held. The smooth transition from Communism to democracy was called the 'Velvet Revolution'. The road to a free-market economy was not easy, with resulting inflation, falling production, strikes and unemployment, though tourism has partly made up for some of the economic decline. Political problems also arose when Slovaks began to demand independence. Finally, on 1 January 1993, the more statist Slovakia broke away from the free-market Czech Republic. However, the split was generally amicable and border adjustments were negligible. The Czechs and Slovaks maintained a customs union and other economic ties.

Economy

Under Communist rule the Czech Republic became one of the most industrialized parts of Eastern Europe. The country has deposits of coal, uranium, iron ore, magnesite, tin and zinc. Manufactures include such products as chemicals, iron and steel and machinery, but the country also has light industries making such things as glassware and textiles for export. Manufacturing employs about 40% of the Czech Republic's entire workforce.

Farming is important. The main crops include barley, fruit, hops for beer-making, maize, potatoes, sugar beet, vegetables and wheat. Cattle and other livestock are raised. Under Communist rule, the land was owned by the government. But the private ownership of the land is now being restored. The country was admitted into the Organization for Economic Co-operation and Development (OECD) in 1995.

AREA	Slovak 3%, Polish,
78,864 sq km [30,449 sq mls]	German, Silesian, Gypsy,
POPULATION	Hungarian, Ukrainian
10,286,000	**LANGUAGES**
CAPITAL (POPULATION)	Czech (official), Moravian
Prague (Praha, 1,213,000)	**RELIGIONS**
GOVERNMENT	Christianity (Roman
Multiparty republic	Catholic 39%, Protestant 4%)
ETHNIC GROUPS	**CURRENCY**
Czech 81%, Moravian 13%,	Czech koruna = 100 haler

DENMARK

Denmark's flag is called the Dannebrog, or 'the spirit of Denmark'. It may be the oldest national flag in continuous use. It represents a vision thought to have been seen by the Danish King Waldemar II before the Battle of Lyndanisse, which took place in Estonia in 1219.

Geography

The Kingdom of Denmark is the smallest country in Scandinavia. It consists of a peninsula, called Jutland (or Jylland), which is joined to Germany, and more than 400 islands, 89 of which are inhabited.

The land is flat and mostly covered by rocks dropped there by huge ice-sheets during the last Ice Age. The highest point in Denmark is on Jutland and is only 173 m [568 ft] above sea level.

Climate

Denmark has a cool but pleasant climate, except during cold spells in the winter when The Sound between Sjælland and Sweden may freeze over. Summers are warm. Rainfall occurs throughout the year.

History

Danish Vikings terrorized much of Western Europe for about 300 years after AD 800. Danish kings ruled England in the 11th century. Control of the entrances to the Baltic Sea contributed to the power of Denmark in the Middle Ages, when the kingdom dominated its neighbours and expanded its territories to include Norway, Iceland, Greenland and the Faroe Islands. The link with Norway was broken in 1814, and with Iceland in 1944. But Greenland and the Faroes retained connections with Denmark. The granite island of Bornholm, off the southern tip of Sweden, also remains a Danish possession. This island was occupied by Germany in World War II, but it was liberated by the Soviet Union and returned to Denmark in 1946. Denmark was also occupied by Germany in 1940, but it was liberated in 1945. The Danes then set about rebuilding their industries and restoring their economy.

Politics

Denmark is a generally comfortable mixture of striking political opposites. The Lutheran tradition and the cradle of Hans Christian Andersen's fairy tales co-exist with open attitudes to pornography and one of the highest illegitimacy rates in the West. A reputation for caring and welfare services, which necessitates high taxation, is somewhat dented by the high suicide rate.

The country is also one of the 'greenest' of the developed nations, with a pioneering Ministry of Pollution that has real power to act – in 1991, it became the first government anywhere to fine industries for emissions of carbon dioxide, the primary 'greenhouse' gas. At the same time, Denmark has Europe's highest rate of deaths from cancer.

Denmark gets on well with its neighbours. It joined the North Atlantic Treaty Organization in 1949, and in 1973 it joined the European Economic Community (now the European Union). However, it remains one of the European Union's least enthusiastic members and was one of the four countries that did not adopt the euro, the single EU currency, when it was introduced on 1 January 1999. In 1972, in order to join the EEC, Denmark had become the first Scandinavian country to break away from the other major economic grouping in Europe, the European Free Trade Association (EFTA), but it continued to co-operate with its five Scandinavian partners through the consultative Nordic Council which was set up in 1953.

Denmark granted home rule to the Faroe Islands in 1948, although in 1998, the government of the Faroes announced plans for independence. In 1979, home rule was also granted to Greenland, which demonstrated its new-found independence by withdrawing from the European Union in 1985. Denmark is a constitutional monarchy, with a hereditary monarch, and its constitution was amended in 1953 to allow female succession to the throne.

Arable land 55.9% Permanent crops 0.05% Forest 10.5%

Economy

Denmark has few mineral resources and no coal, though there is now some oil and natural gas from the North Sea. A century ago, Denmark was a poor farming and fishing country, but the country has been transformed into one of Europe's wealthiest industrial nations. The first steps in the process were taken in the late 19th century, with the introduction of co-operative methods of processing and distributing farm produce, and the development of modern methods of dairy farming and pig and poultry breeding. Farming now employs only 4% of the workforce, but it is highly scientific and productive.

From a firm agricultural base, Denmark has developed a wide range of industries. Some, including brewing, meat canning, fish processing, pottery, textiles and furniture making, use Danish products, but others, such as shipbuilding, oil refining, engineering and metal-working, depend on imported raw materials. Copenhagen is the chief industrial centre and draws more than a million tourists each year. At the other end of the scale is Legoland, the famous miniature town of plastic bricks, built at Billand, north-west of Vejle in eastern Jutland. It was here that Lego was created before it became the world's best-selling construction toy and a prominent Danish export. The country's main exports are machinery, meat, pharmaceuticals, furniture and textiles.

AREA	ETHNIC GROUPS
43,070 sq km [16,629 sq mls]	Danish 97%
POPULATION	**LANGUAGES**
5,334,000	Danish (official)
CAPITAL (POPULATION)	**RELIGIONS**
Copenhagen	Christianity (Lutheran 91%,
(København, 1,353,000)	Roman Catholic 1%)
GOVERNMENT	**CURRENCY**
Parliamentary monarchy	Krone = 100 øre

DJIBOUTI – SEE SOMALIA, PAGE 202;
DOMINICA – SEE CARIBBEAN SEA, PAGES 71–76;
DOMINICAN REPUBLIC – SEE CARIBBEAN SEA, PAGES 71–76

Ecuador's flag was created by a patriot, Francisco de Miranda, in 1806. The armies of Simón Bolivar, the South American general, won victories over Spain, and flew this flag. At the centre is Ecuador's coat of arms, showing a condor over Mount Chimborazo.

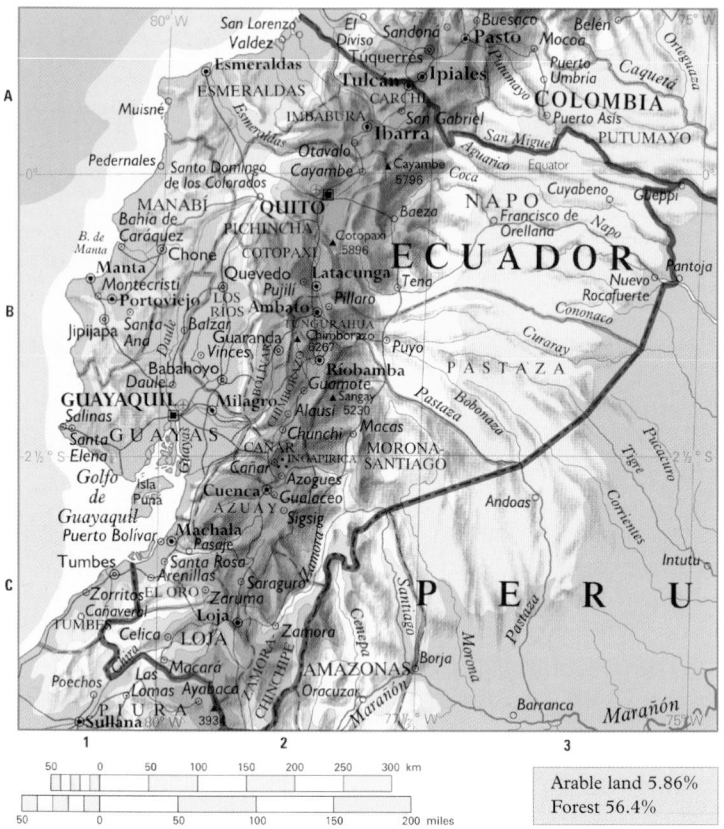

Arable land 5.86%
Forest 56.4%

Geography

The Republic of Ecuador straddles the Equator on the west coast of South America. Three ranges of the high Andes Mountains form the backbone of the country. Between the towering, snow-capped peaks of the mountains, some of which are volcanoes, lie a series of high plateaux, or basins. Nearly half of Ecuador's population lives on these plateaux.

West of the Andes lie the flat coastal lowlands, which border the Pacific Ocean and average 100 km [60 mls] in width. The eastern alluvial lowlands, often called the Oriente, are drained by headwaters of the River Amazon.

Climate

The climate in Ecuador is greatly influenced by the altitude. The coastal lowlands are hot, despite the cooling effect of the cold offshore Peru Current. The Andes have spring-like temperatures throughout the year, while the eastern lowlands are hot and humid. The rainfall is heaviest in the eastern lowlands and the northern coastal lowlands.

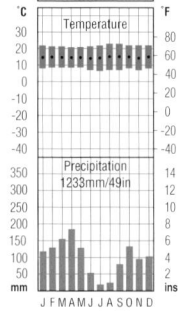

ECUADOR (QUITO)

Ecuador lies on the Equator but is bisected by the Andes, where temperatures are moderated by the altitude. Temperatures on the coastal lowlands range from 23–25°C [73–77°F]. But in Quito, which stands at 2,500 m [8,200 ft] above sea level, average temperatures are around 14–15°C [57–59°F], though days are warm and nights are often chilly. Permanent snowfields and glaciers lie not far from Quito in the high Andes.

History

The Inca people of Peru conquered much of what is now Ecuador in the late 15th century. They introduced their language, Quechua, which is widely spoken today. In 1532 a colony was founded by the Spaniards in the territory, which was then called Quito. The country became independent in 1822, following the defeat of a Spanish force by an army led by General Antonio Jose de Sucre in a battle near Quito. Ecuador became part of Gran Colombia, a confederation which also included Colombia and Venezuela. Ecuador became a separate nation in 1830. The 19th century was very unstable and presidents and dictators came and went. This instability continued into the 20th century.

In 1832, Ecuador annexed the volcanic Galapagos Islands, which lie 970 km [610 mls] west of Ecuador, of which they form a province. The archipelago, which contains six main islands and more than 50 smaller ones, later became world-famous through the writings of Charles Darwin, who visited the islands in 1835. His descriptions of the unique endemic flora and fauna gave him crucial evidence for his theory of natural selection.

Politics

The failure of successive governments to tackle the country's many social and economic problems caused great instability in Ecuador throughout the 20th century. A war with Peru in 1941 led to loss of territory and border disputes flared up again in 1995, though the two countries eventually signed a peace treaty in January 1998.

Military regimes ruled the country between 1963 and 1966 and again from 1976 to 1979. However, under a new constitution introduced by the second of these military juntas and approved by a national referendum, civilian government was restored. Civilian governments have ruled Ecuador since multiparty elections in 1979. But the volatile character of politics here was evident throughout the 1980s and 1990s. For example, a state of emergency, albeit of short duration, was declared in 1986 and, in 1995, the vice-president was forced to leave the country after accusations that he had bribed opposition deputies.

In 1996, the president was deposed on the grounds of mental incompetence and, in 1998, accusations of fraud marred the victory of President Jamil Mahaud of the centre-right Popular Democracy Party. In January 2000, Mahaud was toppled from power following huge demonstrations by Ecuadorian Amerindians against the president's economic policies and a military coup. Gustavo Noboa, the vice-president, took over as head of state.

Economy

The World Bank classifies Ecuador as a 'lower-middle-income' developing country. Agriculture employs 30% of the people. Bananas, cocoa and coffee are all important export crops. Other products in the hot coastal lowlands include citrus fruits, rice and sugar cane, while beans, maize and wheat are important in the highlands. Cattle are raised for dairy products and meat, while fishing is important in the coastal waters. Forestry is a major activity. Ecuador produces balsa wood and such hardwoods as mahogany. Mining is important and oil and oil products now play a major part in the economy. Ecuador started to export oil in the early 1970s and is a member of the Organization of Petroleum Exporting Countries. Manufactures include cement, Panama hats, paper products, processed food and textiles. Major exports are food and live animals, and mineral fuels. Ecuador's main trading partners are the United States and Colombia.

AREA	and Amerindian) 40%,
283,560 sq km [109,483 sq mls]	Amerindian 40%,
POPULATION	White 15%, Black 5%
12,337,000	**LANGUAGES**
CAPITAL (POPULATION)	Spanish (official), Quechua
Quito (1,101,000)	**RELIGIONS**
GOVERNMENT	Christianity
Multiparty republic	(Roman Catholic 92%)
ETHNIC GROUPS	**CURRENCY**
Mestizo (mixed White	Sucre = 100 centavos

EGYPT

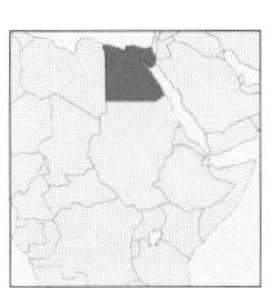

A flag consisting of three bands of red, white and black, the colours of the Pan-Arab movement, was adopted in 1958. The present design has a gold eagle in the centre. This symbolizes Saladin, the warrior who led the Arabs in the 12th century.

Geography

The Arab Republic of Egypt is Africa's second largest country by population after Nigeria, though it ranks 13th in area. Most of Egypt is desert. Almost all the people live either in the Nile Valley and its fertile delta or along the Suez Canal, the artificial waterway between the Mediterranean and Red Seas. This canal shortens the sea journey between the United Kingdom and India by 9,700 km [6,027 mls]. Recent attempts have been made to irrigate parts of the Western Desert and thus redistribute the rapidly growing Egyptian population into previously uninhabited regions.

If not for the valley of the River Nile, Egypt would be sparsely populated. Egypt's other main regions are the Western and Eastern Deserts, which are parts of the vast Sahara, and the Sinai Peninsula in the north-east.

The Western Desert includes almost three-quarters of Egypt and consists of low vales and scarps, mainly of limestone. A number of depressions are below sea level and in some of them the prospect of tapping artesian water holds out hope for future development.

The Eastern Desert between the Nile and the Red Sea, is a much dissected area, and parts of the Red Sea Hills rise to more than 2,000 m [6,560 ft] above sea level. Beyond the Gulf of Suez and the Suez Canal, the Sinai Peninsula is largely mountainous and rugged. It contains the highest of Egypt's mountains – Gebel Katherina, which reaches 2,637 m [8,650 ft] – and is almost entirely uninhabited.

Climate

Egypt, one of the world's hottest and sunniest countries, has a desert climate. The northern Mediterranean region, which extends south from the coast for about 80 km [50 mls], has the highest rainfall, with between 100 and 200 mm [4–8 in] a year. The rainfall occurs in winter and is brought by depressions coming from the west. Summers are hot, though sea breezes bring relief in the daytime. In winter, the weather is mostly warm and sunny, though northerly winds sometimes lower temperatures.

South of Cairo (El Qâhira), average annual rainfall is about 25 to 50 mm [1–2 in], though, in reality, years may pass without significant rainfall until a freak storm occurs, sometimes causing local flooding. Winter days are warm and sunny, though nights are sometimes chilly. In the Nile Valley, because of the high humidity, mists and fog sometimes occur in the early morning but they soon clear as the sun rises in the sky. The heat in the summer is intense, though the low humidity makes conditions more bearable. In parts of the Sinai Peninsula, snow sometimes falls in winter but it seldom lasts more than a day or two.

Arable land 3.12% Permanent crops 0.39%
Permanent grassland 0% Forest 0.03%

EGYPT (CAIRO)

Cairo experiences a desert climate with sparse rainfall that occurs mostly between November and March. Winters are warm, with average temperatures of around 13°C [55°F] in January. Summers may be extremely hot. Between March and June, the Nile Valley, including Cairo, is often affected by a hot, dry and dusty wind that blows from the Sahara. Called the *khamsin*, it often raises dust and sand that reduce visibility.

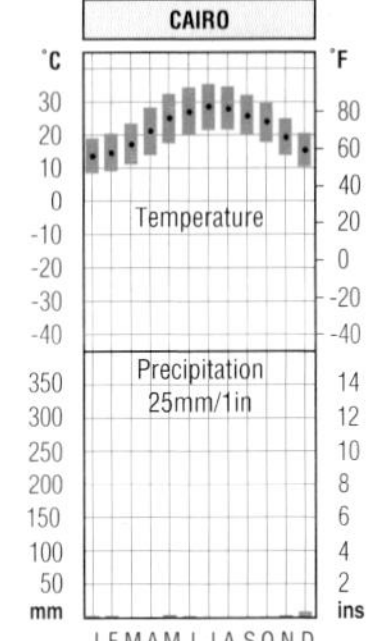

Vegetation

The Nile Valley forms a long, green ribbon of farmland, dotted with date palm trees, the most characteristic plant in northern Africa and south-western Asia. Bamboo and reeds also grow in the Nile Valley and the northern Mediterranean strip is rich in plants in spring.

But, dry landscapes, with sand dunes (called *erg* in Arabic), plains of loose gravel (*reg*) and areas of bare rock (*hammada*) cover most of the country. The Western Desert is devoid of plant life except around oases, the most important of which are Khârga, Dakhla, Farâfra, Bahariya and Siwa. Thorny shrubs and acacia trees grow in the Eastern Desert. The number of shrubs and trees increases in the Red Sea Hills.

EGYPT

History

The Nile Valley was one of the cradles of civilization. The dependable annual flooding of the great river each summer and the discovery of the art of cultivating wheat and barley fostered simple irrigation techniques and favoured co-operation between the farmers. City life began, and the foundations of writing, arithmetic, geometry and astronomy were laid. Great temples, magnificent statuary and pyramid tombs preserved in the dry climate in the valley remain as memorials to this early civilization.

Ancient Egypt was founded 5,000 years ago and thrived for about 2,000 years. The Egyptian civilization began in 3100 BC, when King Menes of Upper Egypt conquered Lower Egypt, creating a united nation under a central government. Menes established the first of more than 30 dynasties that ruled Ancient Egypt. The Old Kingdom, which began in 2686 BC, is known as the Pyramid Age. The first Step Pyramid was built at Saqqarah in about 2650 BC, followed by the great pyramids at El Giza which were built between 2600 and 2500 BC. The Middle Kingdom began in 1991 BC and continued until 1786 BC. It was a time of territorial expansion, trade and a flowering of the arts. Towards the end of the Middle Kingdom, settlers from Asia spread into the Nile Delta and, in 1670 BC, they seized power. In the New Kingdom, which began in 1554 BC, the Egyptians drove out the immigrants and founded a major empire extending into south-western Asia.

Ancient Egypt began to decline around 1070 BC. It lost its overseas territories and succumbed to a series of invaders, including Nubians, Assyrians and Persians. In 332 BC, Egypt became part of the empire of Alexander the Great, who founded the city of Alexandria, which later became Egypt's capital and one of the great cultural centres of the ancient world. In 30 BC, Egypt became part of the Roman Empire. Muslim Arabs invaded Egypt between AD 639 and 642. They introduced their language, Arabic, and their religion, Islam, which gradually began to replace Coptic Christianity. Their influence was so great that most Egyptians now regard themselves as Arabs.

Egypt became an important part of the Islamic Empire. At first, it was ruled from Damascus by caliphs of the Ummayad Dynasty and later from Baghdad by the Abbasid caliphs. Between 969 and 1171, Egypt was ruled by the Fatimid Dynasty. They claimed descent from Fatima, daughter of the Prophet Muhammad, and they were members of the Shiite minority of Muslims. However, in 1171, Saladin, the general who led Muslim armies against the Crusaders, overthrew the Fatimids and restored the Sunni form of Islam to Egypt. His descendants formed the Ayyubid Dynasty which ruled Egypt until 1250.

In 1250, the Mamelukes, who had served as the sultan's guards, revolted and Mameluke rule continued until 1517, when the Ottoman Turks invaded Egypt from Syria. However, the Mamelukes retained power as regional governors, or *beys*.

In 1798, Napoleon Bonaparte's French army invaded Egypt, but the Ottomans, with British assistance, drove them out in 1801. By 1805, Muhammad Ali, a Turkish officer sent to drive the French out of Egypt, became the country's ruler. His period in power was marked by reforms aimed at modernizing the country. After Muhammad Ali's death in 1849, his son gave the French a contract to build the Suez Canal, which opened in 1869. Britain became increasingly involved in Egypt after buying Egypt's shares in the Canal in 1875. In 1882, British troops intervened and defeated the Egyptian army in the battle of At Tall al-Kabir.

In the late 19th century, Britain effectively ruled Egypt. During World War I the Ottoman Turks, to whose empire Egypt nominally belonged, were allies of Germany. In 1914, Britain declared Egypt a protectorate. In 1919, Egyptian nationalists called for independence which was achieved in 1922 when Egypt became a constitutional monarchy. But Britain retained the right to keep troops in the country.

In World War II, German and Italian armies invaded Egypt in an attempt to capture the strategic Suez Canal, but they were halted at the Battle of El Alamein and subsequently driven out of North Africa. After World War II, Egyptian leaders tried unsuccessfully to remove British troops from their country. In 1948, when the State of Israel was established, Egyptian and other forces launched an attack on the Israelis, but the Israelis were victorious, and the United Nations finally brought the war to an end in 1949.

Politics

In 1952, following a military revolution led by General Muhammad Naguib, the monarchy was abolished and Egypt became a republic. Naguib became president, but he was overthrown in 1954 by Colonel Gamal Abdel Nasser. President Nasser sought to develop Egypt's economy, and he announced a major project to build a new dam at Aswan to provide electricity and water for irrigation. When Britain and the United States failed to provide finance for building the dam, Nasser seized the Suez Canal Company in July 1956. In retaliation, Israel, backed by British and French troops, invaded the Sinai Peninsula and the Suez Canal region. However, under international pressure, they were forced to withdraw. Construction of the Aswan High Dam began in 1960 and it was fully operational by 1968.

In 1967, Egypt lost territory to Israel in the Six-Day War and Nasser tendered his resignation, but the people refused to accept it. After his death in 1970, Nasser was succeeded by his vice-president, Anwar el-Sadat. In 1973, Egypt launched a surprise attack in the Sinai Peninsula, but its troops were finally forced back to the Suez Canal. In 1977, Sadat began a peace process when he visited Israel and addressed the Knesset (Israel's parliament). Finally, in 1979, Egypt and Israel signed a peace treaty under which Egypt regained the Sinai Peninsula. However, extremists opposed contacts with Israel and, in 1981, Sadat was assassinated. He was succeeded as president by Hosni Mubarak.

While Egypt has played an important role in foreign affairs, it has continued to face several problems at home. Despite economic progress, most people remain poor, while some groups dislike what they see as increasing Western influence and would like to return to the fundamental values of Islam. In the 1990s, attacks on foreign visitors caused a decline in the valuable tourist industry, despite government attempts to curb the activities of Islamic extremists. In 1997, 58 foreign tourists were killed by Islamic terrorists near Luxor. In 1999, Mubarak was attacked while he was campaigning for his fourth six-year term as president. However, he suffered only a minor wound. Despite such occasional incidents, tourism is showing signs of recovery.

Economy

Egypt is Africa's second most industrialized country after South Africa, but it remains a developing country. The majority of the people are poor. Farming employs 34% of the workers. Most *fellahin* (peasants) grow such food crops as beans, maize, rice, sugar cane and wheat, but cotton is the chief cash crop. Egypt depends increasingly on the Nile. Its waters are seasonal, and control and storage have become essential in the last 100 years. The Aswan High Dam is the greatest of the Nile dams, and the water behind it in Lake Nasser is making desert reclamation possible. The electricity produced at the dam has also been important in the development of industry.

Most industrial development has come about since World War II. Textiles, including the spinning, weaving, dyeing and printing of cotton, wool, silk and artificial fibres, form the largest industry. Other products derive from local agricultural and mineral raw materials and include sugar refining, milling, oil-seed pressing, and the manufacture of chemicals, glass and cement. Egypt also has iron and steel, oil refining and car assembly industries, while many consumer goods, such as radios, TV sets and refrigerators, are also made. The chief exports are oil and oil products, followed by cotton yarn, textiles and clothing.

AREA	**ETHNIC GROUPS**
1,001,450 sq km	Egyptian 99%
[386,660 sq mls]	**LANGUAGES**
POPULATION	Arabic (official), French, English
66,050,000	**RELIGIONS**
CAPITAL (POPULATION)	Islam (Sunni Muslim 94%),
Cairo	Christianity (mainly Coptic
(El Qâhira, 9,656,000)	Christian 6%)
GOVERNMENT	**CURRENCY**
Republic	Pound = 100 piastres

EL SALVADOR – SEE GUATEMALA, PAGES 110–111;
EQUATORIAL GUINEA – SEE GABON, PAGE 103;
ERITREA – SEE ETHIOPIA, PAGE 98

ESTONIA

Estonia's flag was used between 1918 and 1940, when the country was an independent republic. It was readopted in June 1988. The blue is said to symbolize the sky, the black Estonia's black soil, and the white the snow that blankets the land in winter.

Geography

The Republic of Estonia is the smallest of the three states on the Baltic Sea, which were formerly part of the Soviet Union, but became independent in the early 1990s. Estonia consists of a generally flat plain which was covered by ice-sheets during the Ice Age. The land is strewn with moraine (rocks deposited by the ice).

The country is dotted with more than 1,500 small lakes. Water, including the large Lake Peipus (Ozero Chudskoye) and the River Narva, makes up much of Estonia's eastern border with Russia. Estonia has more than 800 islands, which together comprise about a tenth of the country. The largest island is Saaremaa (Sarema).

Climate

Despite its northerly position, Estonia has a fairly mild climate due to its proximity to the sea. This is because sea winds tend to warm the land during winter and cool it in summer. Winters are cold, with temperatures in January ranging from −7°C to −2°C [19–28°F]. In July, temperatures range from 16°C to 18°C [61–64°F]. The precipitation ranges from about 500 to 700 mm [20–28 in].

History

The ancestors of the Estonians, who are related to the Finns, settled in the area several thousand years ago. Divided into several separate states, they were vulnerable to Viking attacks, but in the early 13th century, German crusaders, known as the Teutonic Knights, introduced Christianity. Germany took control of the southern part of Estonia and Denmark took control of the north. The Danes sold the north to the Germans in 1324 and Estonia became part of the Holy Roman Empire. By the 17th century, much of Estonia consisted of large estates owned by German noblemen. However, in 1561, Sweden took over northern Estonia and Poland ruled the south. Sweden controlled the entire country from 1625 until 1721 but, following the victory of Peter the Great over Sweden in 1721, the area became part of the Russian Empire. German nobles still had estates there until 1919, though the Estonian serfs who worked for them were freed in 1816. The serfs were granted the right to own land in 1868 and some of them became successful landowners. A national revival in the 19th century culminated on 24 February 1918, when Estonia declared its independence. A democratic form of government was established in 1919. However, a fascist coup in 1934 ended democratic rule.

Politics

In 1939, Germany and the Soviet Union agreed to take over large areas of eastern Europe, and it was agreed that the Soviet Union would take over Estonia. The Soviet Union forcibly annexed the country in 1940. Germany invaded Estonia in 1941, but the Soviet Union regained control in 1944 when the country became the Estonian Soviet Socialist Republic. Many Estonians opposed Soviet rule and were deported to Siberia. About 100,000 Estonians settled in the West.

Resistance to Soviet rule was fuelled in the 1980s when the Soviet leader Mikhail Gorbachev began to introduce reforms and many Estonians called for independence. In 1990, the Estonian parliament declared Soviet rule invalid and called for a gradual transition to full independence. The Soviet Union regarded this action as illegal, but finally the Soviet State Council recognized the Estonian parliament's proclamation of independence in September 1991, shortly before the Soviet Union itself was dissolved in December 1991.

Since independence, the Estonians have sought to increase their links with Europe. It was admitted to the Council of Europe in 1993; it is also a member of the NATO Partnership for Peace, an associate member of the European Union since 1995, and, since 1999, a member of the World Trade Organization. But despite the fact that it had the highest standard of living among the 15 former Soviet republics, Estonia has found the change to a free-market economy hard-going.

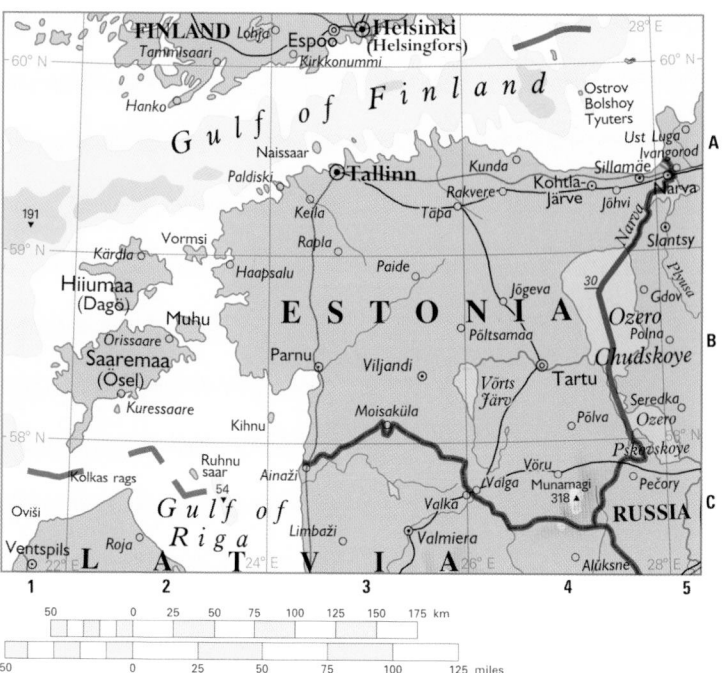

In January 1992, the combination of food shortages and an energy crisis forced the resignation of prime minister Edgar Savissar, who enjoyed wide popular and parliamentary support. A co-founder of the Popular Front, the country's pro-democracy movement, he was held responsible for a recession which appeared to have hit Estonia far harder than the other two Baltic states to the south.

Other problems facing Estonia include crime, rural under-development and the status of its non-Estonian citizens, including Russians who make up about 30% of the population. In the country's first free elections in 1992, only Estonians were permitted to vote and all Russians were excluded. Tension on this issue continued through the 1990s as dual citizenship was outlawed, while restrictions were placed on Russians applying for Estonian citizenship. In the mid-1990s, Russia described Estonia's citizenship policies as discriminatory against ethnic Russians. In 1996, Estonia dropped the requirement that candidates for local office pass an Estonian language test.

Economy

Manufacturing is the most valuable activity. The timber industry is among the most important industries, alongside metal-working, shipbuilding, clothing, textiles, chemicals and food processing. Food processing is based primarily on extremely efficient dairy farming and pig breeding, but oats, barley and potatoes are suited to the cool climate and the average soils. Like the other two Baltic states, Estonia is not rich in natural resources, though its oil shale is an important mineral deposit; enough gas is extracted to supply St Petersburg, Russia's second largest city. The leading exports are mineral fuels and chemical products, followed by food, textiles and cloth, and wood and paper products. Finland and Russia are the leading trading partners.

AREA	Russian 30%, Ukrainian 3%,
44,700 sq km [17,300 sq mls]	Belarussian 2%, Finnish 1%
POPULATION	**LANGUAGES**
1,421,000	Estonian (official), Russian
CAPITAL (POPULATION)	**RELIGIONS**
Tallinn (435,000)	Christianity (Lutheran, with
GOVERNMENT	Orthodox and Baptist
Multiparty republic	minorities)
ETHNIC GROUPS	**CURRENCY**
Estonian 62%,	Kroon = 100 sents

ETHIOPIA

The tricolour flag of Ethiopia first appeared in 1897. The central pentangle was introduced in 1996, and represents the common will of the country's 68 ethnic groups, and the present sequence was adopted in 1914.

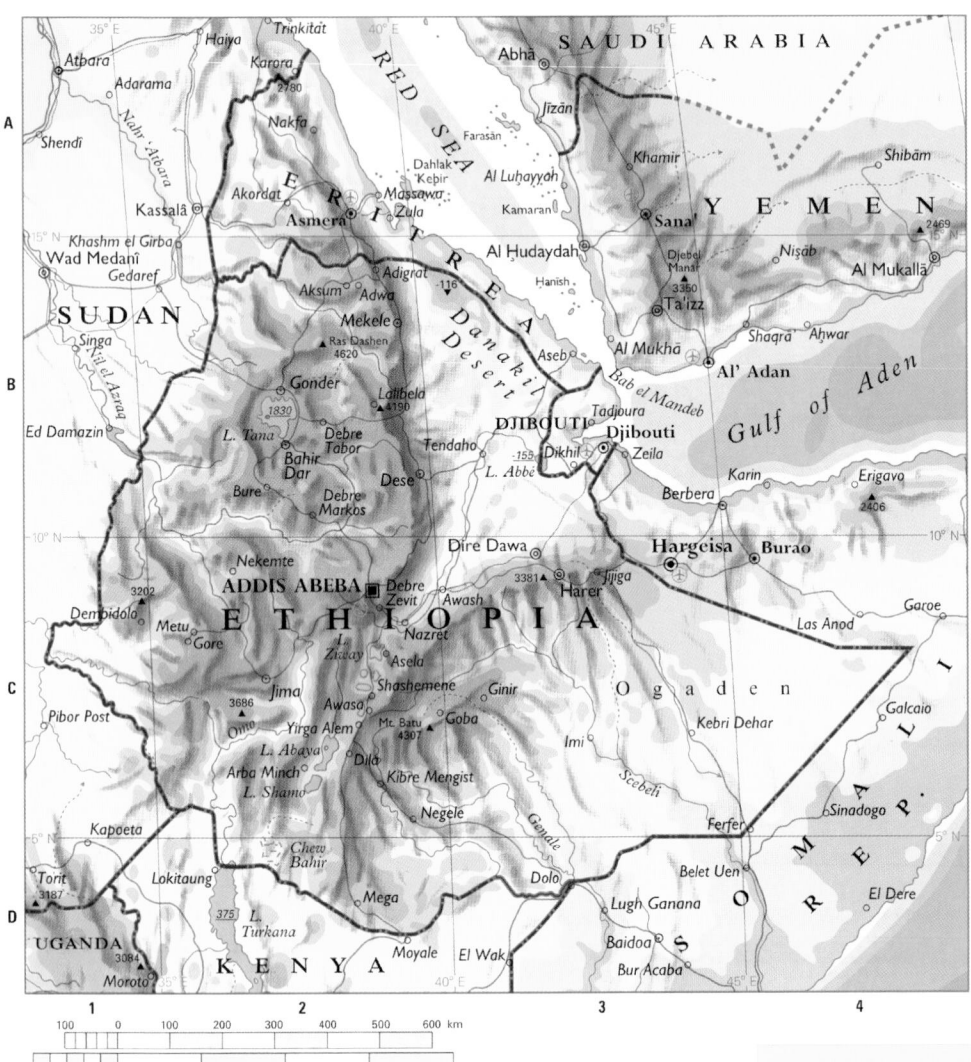

20°C [68°F]. The rainfall is generally more than 1,000 mm [39 in]. But the lowlands bordering the Eritrean coast are hot.

History

Ethiopia was the home of an ancient monarchy, which became Christian in the 4th century. In the 7th century, Muslims gained control of the lowlands, but Christianity survived in the highlands. In the 19th century, Ethiopia resisted attempts to colonize it. Italy invaded in 1935, but Ethiopian and British troops defeated the Italians in 1941.

Politics

In 1952, Eritrea, on the Red Sea coast, was federated with Ethiopia. But in 1961, Eritrean nationalists demanded their freedom and began a struggle that ended in their independence in 1993. Relations with Eritrea gradually soured and border clashes occurred in 1998 and 1999. Ethnic diversity in Ethiopia has led to demands by minorities for self-government. As a result, in 1995, Ethiopia was divided into nine provinces, each with its own regional assembly.

Economy

Having been afflicted by drought and civil war in the 1970s and 1980s, Ethiopia is now one of the world's poorest countries. Agriculture is the main activity. Coffee is the leading cash crop and export, followed by hides, skins and pulses.

Geography and Climate

Ethiopia is a landlocked country in north-eastern Africa. The land is mainly mountainous, though there are extensive plains in the east and south. The highlands are divided into two blocks by an arm of the Great Rift Valley. North of the Rift Valley, the land is especially rugged, rising to 4,620 m [15,157 ft] at Ras Dashen. South-east of Ras Dashen is Lake Tana, source of the River Abay (Blue Nile).

The climate in Ethiopia is greatly affected by the altitude. Addis Abeba, at 2,450 m [8,000 ft], has an average yearly temperature of

AREA	Tigrinya 9%, Guage 3%,
1,128,000 sq km	60 others
[435,521 sq mls]	**LANGUAGES**
POPULATION	Amharic (official),
58,390,000	280 others
CAPITAL (POPULATION)	**RELIGIONS**
Addis Abeba (2,316,000)	Ethiopian Orthodox 53%,
GOVERNMENT	Sunni Muslim 31%,
Federation of nine provinces	animist beliefs 11%
ETHNIC GROUPS	**CURRENCY**
Amharic 38%, Galla 35%,	Birr = 100 cents

ERITREA

Geography

The State of Eritrea consists of a hot, dry coastal plain, with a mountainous central area. Most people live in the cooler highland area.

Politics and Economy

Eritrea, an Italian colony from the 1880s, was part of Ethiopia from 1952–93, when it became a fully independent nation. National reconstruction was hampered by conflict with Yemen over three islands in the Red Sea, while in 1998 and 1999, clashes with Ethiopia flared up along the countries' borders.

Farming and nomadic livestock rearing are the main activities in this poor, war-ravaged country. Eritrea has a few manufacturing industries, based mainly in Asmera.

AREA	**ETHNIC GROUPS**
94,000 sq km	Tigrinya 49%, Tigre 32%, others
[36,293 sq mls]	**LANGUAGES**
POPULATION	Arabic, English,
3,842,000	Tigrinya, Tigre,
CAPITAL (POPULATION)	**RELIGIONS**
Asmera	Coptic Christian 50%,
(367,500)	Muslim 50%
GOVERNMENT	**CURRENCY**
Transitional government	Nakfa

FALKLAND ISLANDS – SEE ATLANTIC OCEAN, PAGES 41–43; FIJI – SEE PACIFIC OCEAN, PAGES 174–178

FINLAND

The flag of Finland was adopted in 1918, after the country had become an independent republic in 1917, following a century of Russian rule. The blue represents Finland's many lakes. The white symbolizes the blanket of snow which masks the land in winter.

Geography and Climate

The Republic of Finland is a beautiful country in northern Europe. Part of the country lies north of the Arctic Circle, in the 'Land of the Midnight Sun'. Here the sun shines for 24 hours a day for extended periods of time in summer, especially in June.

In the south, behind the coastal lowlands where most Finns live, lies the Lake District, a region of sparkling lakes worn out by ice-sheets in the Ice Age. The thinly populated northern uplands cover about two-fifths of the country.

Helsinki has warm summers, but the average temperatures between the months of December and March are below freezing point. Snow covers the land in winter. The north has less precipitation than the south, but is much colder.

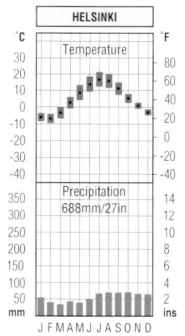

FINLAND (HELSINKI)

Finland's winters are long and harsh. A third of the country is north of the Arctic Circle where temperatures can reach −30°C [−22°F]. Snow may lie for up to six months, never clearing from north-facing slopes. Helsinki has four or five months below 0°C [32°F]. The seas and lakes nearly always freeze in winter. Summers can be hot. Rainfall is low, decreasing northwards and falling from late summer to winter, often as snow.

History and Politics

Between 1150 and 1809, Finland was under Swedish rule. The close links between the countries continue today. Swedish remains an official language in Finland and one of the legacies of this period is a Swedish-speaking minority of 6% of the total population. In some localities on the south and west coasts, Swedish speakers are in the majority and Åland, an island closer to the Swedish coast than to Finland, is a self-governing province. Many towns use both Finnish and Swedish names. For example, Helsinki is Helsingfors, and Turku is Åbo in Swedish. Finnish bears little relation to the Swedish or any other Scandinavian language. It is closest to Magyar, the language of Hungary.

In 1809, Finland became an independent grand duchy of the Russian Empire, though the Russian tsar was its grand duke. Nationalist feelings developed during the 19th century, but in 1899 Russia sought to enforce its culture on the Finns. In 1903, the Russian governor suspended the constitution and became dictator, though following much resistance, self-government was restored in 1906. Finland proclaimed its independence in 1917, after the Russian Revolution and the collapse of the Russian Empire and, in 1919, it adopted a republican constitution. During World War I, the Soviet Union declared war on Finland and took the southern part of Karelia, where 12% of the Finnish people lived. Finland allied itself to Germany and Finnish troops regained southern Karelia. But at the end of the war, Russia regained southern Karelia and other parts of Finland. It also had to pay massive reparations to the Soviet Union.

After World War II, Finland pursued a policy of neutralism acceptable to the Soviet Union and this continued into the 1990s until the collapse of the Soviet Union. Finland also strengthened its links with other north European countries and became an associate member of the European Free Trade Association (EFTA) in 1961. Finland became a full member of EFTA in 1986, in a decade when its economy was growing at a faster rate than that of Japan.

In 1992, along with most of its fellow EFTA members, Finland, which had no longer any need to be neutral, applied for membership of the European Union (EU). In 1994, the Finnish people voted in favour of joining the EU and the country officially joined on 1 January 1995. On 1 January 1999, Finland adopted the euro, the single EU currency.

Economy

Forests are Finland's most valuable resource, and forestry accounts for about 35% of the country's exports. The chief manufactures are wood products, pulp and paper. Since World War II, Finland has set up many other industries, producing such things as machinery and transport equipment. Its economy has expanded rapidly, but there has been a large increase in the number of unemployed people.

AREA	**ETHNIC GROUPS**
338,130 sq km	Finnish 93%, Swedish 6%
[130,552 sq mls]	**LANGUAGES**
POPULATION	Finnish, Swedish (both official)
5,149,000	**RELIGIONS**
CAPITAL (POPULATION)	Christianity
Helsinki (525,000)	(Evangelical Lutheran 88%)
GOVERNMENT	**CURRENCY**
Multiparty republic	Euro; Markka = 100 penniä

The colours of this flag originated during the French Revolution of 1789. The red and blue are said to represent Paris, while the white represented the monarchy. The present design was adopted in 1794, and is meant to symbolize republican principles.

Geography

The Republic of France is the largest country in Western Europe. The scenery is extremely varied. The Vosges Mountains overlook the Rhine Valley in the north-east, the Jura Mountains and the Alps form the borders with Switzerland and Italy in the south-east, while the Pyrenees straddle France's border with Spain. The only large highland area entirely within France is the Massif Central between the Rhône-Saône Valley and the basin of Aquitaine. This dramatic area, covering one-sixth of the country, has peaks rising to more than 1,800 m [5,900 ft]. Volcanic activity dating back 10 to 30 million years ago appears in the form of steep-sided volcanic plugs. Older rocks, such as limestone, provide soil for agriculture, while coal measures have been mined for centuries at St-Etienne and Le Creusot.

Brittany (Bretagne) and Normandy (Normande) form a scenic hill region. Fertile lowlands cover most of northern France, including the densely populated Paris Basin. Another major lowland area, the Aquitanian Basin, is in the south-west, while the Rhône-Saône Valley and the Mediterranean lowlands are in the south-east.

Climate

The climate of France varies from west to east and from north to south. The west comes under the moderating influence of the Atlantic Ocean, giving generally mild weather. To the east, summers are warmer and winters colder. The climate also becomes warmer as one travels from north to south. The Mediterranean Sea coast experiences hot, dry summers and mild, moist winters. The Alps, Jura and Pyrenees mountains have snowy winters. Winter sports centres are found in all three areas. Large glaciers occupy high valleys in the Alps.

FRANCE – PARIS

The climate is influenced by the Atlantic, the Mediterranean and the continent. With no mountain barriers, the Atlantic regime extends far inland, giving mild weather with much wind and rain, but little snow. To the east the climate gets warmer, but with colder winters. Towards the mountains and to the south, rainfall increases, with permanent snow above 3,000 m [12,000 ft]. At Paris, low rainfall is distributed evenly all year.

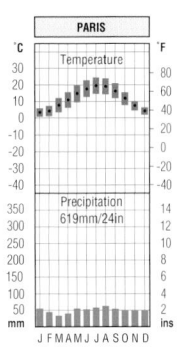

BORDEAUX

Winters are mild and summers warm; the average temperature for January is 5°C [41°F], and for June to September 18–21°C [64–70°F]. Rain falls fairly evenly all year, with a slight maximum in November and December. Rain falls on over 160 days in the year. Snow is common and there may be 20–35 days with frost each year. The annual amount of sunshine exceeds 2,000 hours, with over seven hours daily from April to October.

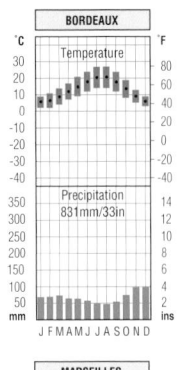

MARSEILLES

The Mediterranean climate extends over the south-east, pushing northwards into the Rhône Valley, mountain foothills, and over Corsica. The winters are very mild. Summers are dry and the rain falls mainly from September to March but on only around 75 days per year. One feature of the area is its peculiar winds, notably the Mistral, a cold, dry and strong wind which blows southwards during winter and spring, causing crop damage.

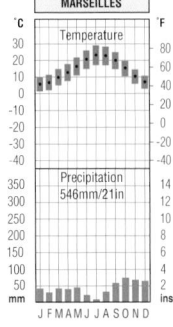

History

The Romans conquered France (then called Gaul) in the 50s BC. Roman rule began to decline in the fifth century AD and, in 486, the Frankish realm (as France was called) became independent under a

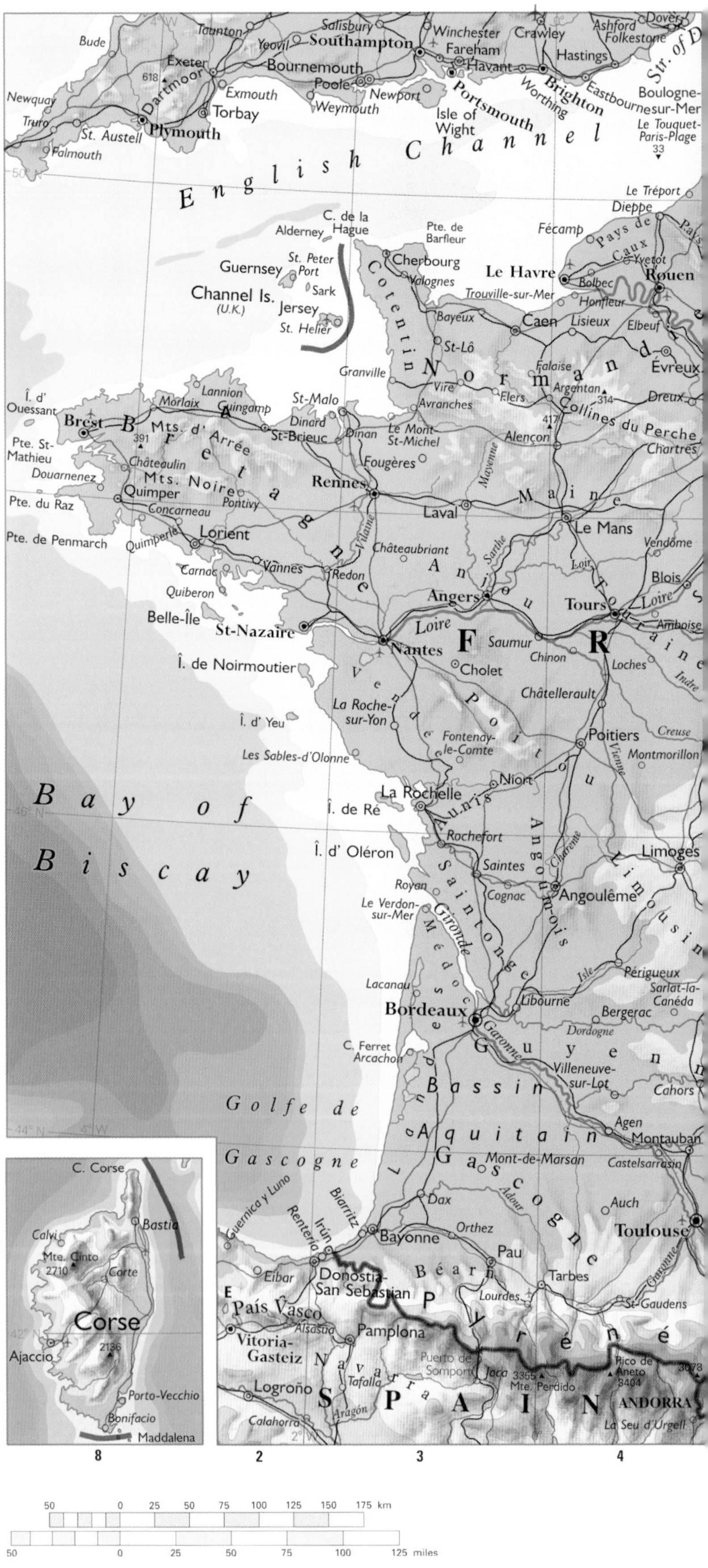

Christian king, Clovis. In 800, Charlemagne, who had been king of the Franks since 768, became emperor of the Romans. Through conquest, his empire extended from central Italy to Denmark, and from eastern Germany to the Atlantic Ocean. However, in 843, the empire was divided into three parts and the area of France contracted.

After the Norman invasion of England in 1066, large areas of France came under English rule. By 1453, after the Hundred Years' War, France drove most of the English out. In this war, the French kings lost much power to French nobles, but Louis XI, who reigned from 1461 to 1483, laid the foundations for absolute rule by French kings.

France developed into a powerful monarchy between the 16th and 18th centuries. The monarchy was supported by a large bureaucracy, which maintained a standing army and collected taxes. In 1786, a new land tax was proposed and opposition to this and other measures was a major factor that triggered off the French Revolution (1789–99). In 1792, France was declared a republic. However, in 1799, an army officer and military genius, Napoleon Bonaparte, took power and founded the First Empire in 1804. He fought a series of brilliant military campaigns, building up a vast French empire. But, to maintain control over the empire, France's resources became overstretched and Napoleon's armies were finally defeated at the Battle of Waterloo in 1815. The monarchy was restored after Napoleon's downfall, but revolutionaries founded the Second Republic in 1848.

A nephew of Napoleon, Louis Napoleon Bonaparte, was elected president in 1848, but he seized power in 1851 and established the Second Empire. In 1852, he took the title of Napoleon III. In 1870, France, concerned at the growing power of Prussia, declared war, but it met with defeat the following year. At the end of the war, France was forced to give up most of Alsace and part of Lorraine to the new German Empire, an issue that remained a bone of contention between the two countries. Following the defeats in the Franco-Prussian War, the French revolted and the Third Republic was established.

France grew in strength in the later 19th century, founding a major overseas empire in Africa and Asia. But its growing economy was shattered during World War I, when millions of French military personnel were slaughtered in a series of major battles. The rise of Hitler in Germany in the 1930s led to serious unrest in France. Finally, in September 1939, France and Britain declared war on Germany, following Germany's invasion of Poland. In 1945, at the end of the war, Charles De Gaulle, leader of the Free French, formed a provisional government, but he resigned as president in 1946 when the National Assembly supported a new constitution, creating the Fourth Republic. De Gaulle opposed the constitution because it did not provide strong executive powers.

Politics

France faced many problems in the 1940s and 1950s. With aid from the United States, it began to revive its economy, but Communist-led strikes often crippled production. France also faced growing support for independence movements in its overseas empire. After a bitter war, France withdrew from French Indochina in 1954 and then faced a long and costly struggle in Algeria, which finally ended when Algeria became independent in 1962. The threat to French power in Algeria caused considerable unrest in France in the 1950s and, in 1958, De Gaulle was recalled to power as prime minister. His government prepared a new constitution, establishing the Fifth Republic. It gave the president greater executive powers and reduced the power of parliament. The Electoral College elected De Gaulle as president for a seven-year term.

De Gaulle set about giving independence to many of its overseas territories and worked to make France a major player in an alliance of western European nations. In 1957, France had become a founder member of the European Economic Alliance (EEC) and, in 1963, De Gaulle opposed British membership, considering that Britain's links with the United States would give it too much influence in Europe's economy. However, De Gaulle's popularity waned in the late 1960s when huge student demonstrations and workers' strikes paralyzed the country. De Gaulle resigned as president in 1969. His successor, Georges Pompidou, changed course in foreign affairs by re-establishing closer contacts with the United States and supporting the entry of Britain into the EEC. After the death of Pompidou in 1974, the Gaullist Party, which had backed both De Gaulle and Pompidou, was weakened by internal divisions. But France continued, under a variety of governments, of the right and the left, to become a prosperous and dynamic country.

French life is still focused on Paris, where the traditional luxury industries, such as perfumes, thrive alongside commerce, light and heavy industry and services of all kinds. Virtually all the major French enterprises have their headquarters in Paris, whose metropolitan area contains about a sixth of the country's population. Modern economic

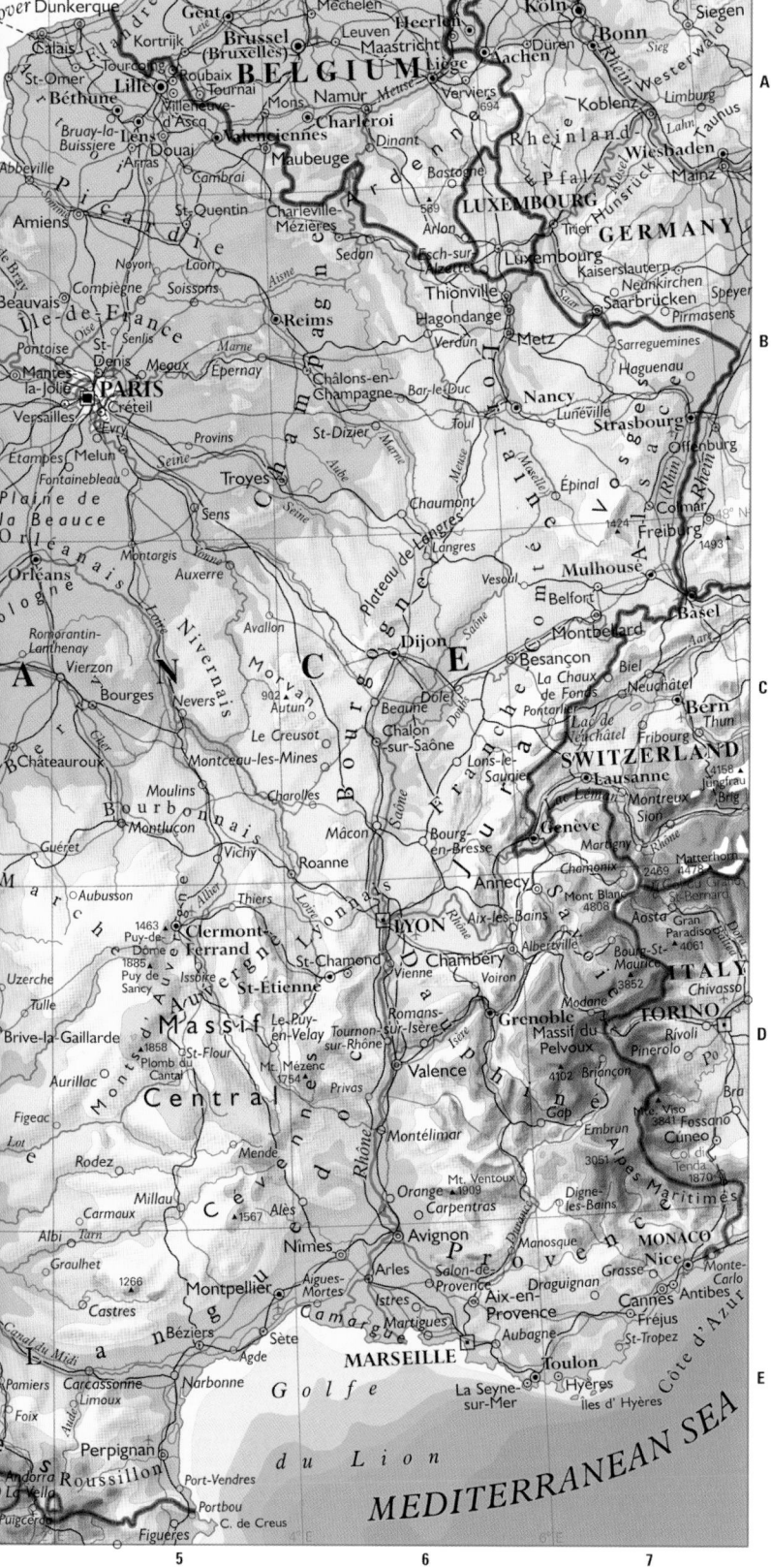

Arable land 33.3% Permanent crops 2.13%
Permanent grassland 19.3% Forest 27.3%

planning has been pursued and consumer industries have prospered. However, some critics say that there is still an inadequate provision for social services, including housing. Since 1945, many people have argued about the poor standard of housing, both rural and urban, much of which is obsolete and without basic amenities. Rapid urban growth has resulted in overcrowding and even the growth of poorly built new districts to house immigrants, especially those from Spain and North Africa. The 4 million underprivileged workers from the Maghreb became a major political issue in the 1990s, leading to political successes in some areas for the extreme right. In France, as in most other countries, there also remains a disparity between the richer and the poorer regions. Other problems faced by France included unemployment, pollution and the growing number of elderly people.

A socialist government under Lionel Jospin was elected in 1997. He increased the minimum wage, shortened the working week, and took France into the European single currency on 1 January 1999. The high social security taxes and inflexible labour laws seem likely to continue, but, at the turn of the century, the economy was continuing to grow and inflation was negligible.

Economy

France is one of the world's most developed countries. It has the world's fourth largest economy, after the United States, Japan and Germany, and it had a high per capita gross national product of US $26,300 in 1997. Before World War II, agriculture was the mainstay of the economy, although it now contributes only 2.6% of the gross domestic product, as compared with a 22% contribution by manufacturing.

However, France remains the largest producer of farm products in Western Europe. It produces most of the food it needs and it is a leading food exporter. Wheat is the single most important crop. Apples, barley, grapes, maize, oats and rapeseed are other leading crops. Livestock, including beef and dairy cattle, sheep, pigs and poultry are also important. Fishing and forestry are also significant activities.

Besides its fertile soils, France's other natural resources include large deposits of iron ore and bauxite, together with coal, some petroleum and natural gas, and potash, but it has to import petroleum and petroleum products. In 1997, about 73% of the country's electricity supply came from nuclear power stations, while hydroelectric plants contributed another 20%. France was the European Union's biggest exporter of electricity in 1997.

France is one of the world's leading manufacturing nations. While Paris is the leading manufacturing centre, many other cities and towns throughout the country have factories. France ranks fourth among the world's producers of cars and eighth among the producers of commercial vehicles. The country is also known for its aircraft, both military and commercial. It also produces aerospace equipment, many kinds of weapons and electronic goods, including computers, radios and television sets. Other products include chemicals, industrial machinery, iron and steel, machine tools, medicines, textiles and timber, wood pulp and paper. The food processing industry is well known, especially for its cheeses, such as Brie and Camembert, and its top-quality wines from such areas as Alsace, Bordeaux, Burgundy, Champagne and the Loire valley.

The leading exports of France are machinery and transport equipment, followed by agricultural products, chemical products and plastics. The country's leading trading partners are Germany, Italy and Belgium-Luxembourg, all of which are fellow members of the European Union.

Regions of France

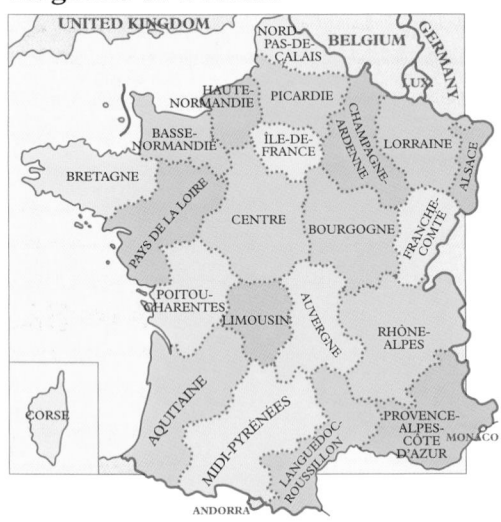

Corsica

Annexed by France from Genoa in 1768 – months before the birth of Napoleon Bonaparte – Corsica (or Corse) lies 168 km [105 mls] from France and 11 km [7 mls] from Sardinia. Corsica is divided into two departments of France, with its administrative centre at Ajaccio on the west coast. Roughly oval in shape, it is 190 km [118 mls] long and half as wide, with a population of 240,178.

Most of the island is formed of rugged mountains, some reaching to over 2,710 m [8,890 ft]. Only about a quarter of Corsica provides rough grazing for sheep and goats; another quarter is in forests with evergreen oak and cork oak to 650 m [2,000 ft], then chestnuts with beech followed by pines to the tree line, between 1,600 and 2,000 m [5,000–6,000 ft]. During winter there is heavy snow on the mountains. Only 2% of the island is cultivated, mainly in the valleys, on terraced hillsides or on the discontinuous fringe of alluvial lowland along the coasts. Fishing is important and industries include tunny and lobster canning, chiefly at Ajaccio and Bastia – though tourism is now the principal earner. Separatist terrorist movements are still sporadically active in some areas.

AREA
551,500 sq km
[212,934 sq mls]
POPULATION
58,805,000
CAPITAL
(POPULATION)
Paris (9,469,000)
GOVERNMENT
Multiparty republic
ETHNIC GROUPS
French 93%,
Arab,
German
LANGUAGES
French (official),
Breton,
Occitan
RELIGIONS
Roman Catholic
86%, Islam 3%
CURRENCY
Euro; Franc =
100 centimes

MONACO

The tiny Principality of Monaco consists of a narrow strip of coastline and a rocky peninsula on the French Riviera. Like the rest of the Riviera, it has mild, moist winters and dry, sunny summers. Average temperatures range from 10°C [50°F] in January to 24°C [75°F] in July. The average annual rainfall is about 800 mm [31 in].

The Genoese from northern Italy gained control of Monaco in the 12th century and, from 1297, it has been ruled for most of the time by the Genoese Grimaldi family. Monaco attracted little attention until the late 19th century when it developed into a major tourist resort. World attention was focused on Monaco in 1956 when Prince Rainier III of Monaco married the actress Grace Kelly. Their son, Prince Albert, is the heir apparent. The country's wealth comes mainly from banking, finance, gambling and tourism. Attractions include three casinos and such sporting events as the Monte Carlo Rally and the Monaco Grand Prix. The territory has a marine museum, a zoo and botanical gardens, while its Grand Theatre presents some of the world's finest musicians. Manufactures include chemicals, electronic goods and plastics.

AREA	CAPITAL
1.5 sq km [0.6 sq mls]	Monaco
POPULATION	**CURRENCY**
32,000	French franc

FRENCH GUIANA – SEE GUYANA, PAGE 115;
FRENCH POLYNESIA – SEE PACIFIC OCEAN, PAGES 174–178

GABON

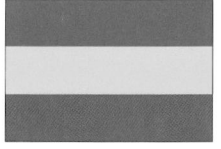

Gabon's flag was adopted in 1960 when the country became independent from France. The central yellow stripe symbolizes the Equator which runs through Gabon. The green stands for the country's forests. The blue symbolizes the sea.

Geography

The Gabonese Republic lies on the Equator in west-central Africa. In area, it is a little larger than the United Kingdom, with a coastline 800 km [500 mls] long. Behind the narrow, partly lagoon-lined coastal plain, the land rises to hills, plateaux and mountains divided by deep valleys carved by the River Ogooué and its tributaries.

Climate

Most of Gabon has an equatorial climate, with high temperatures and humidity throughout the year. The rainfall is heavy and the skies are often cloudy.

History and Politics

Gabon became a French colony in the 1880s, but it achieved full independence in 1960. In 1964, an attempted coup was put down when French troops intervened and crushed the revolt. In 1967, following the death of the first president, Léon Mba, Bernard-Albert Bongo, who later renamed himself El Hadj Omar Bongo, became president. He made Gabon a one-party state in 1968, but opposition parties were legalized in 1991. Bongo was re-elected in 1993 and 1998.

Economy

Gabon's abundant natural resources include its forests, oil and gas deposits near Port Gentil, together with manganese and uranium. These mineral deposits make Gabon one of Africa's wealthier countries. But agriculture still employs about 75% of the population, most farmers producing little more than they need to support their families.

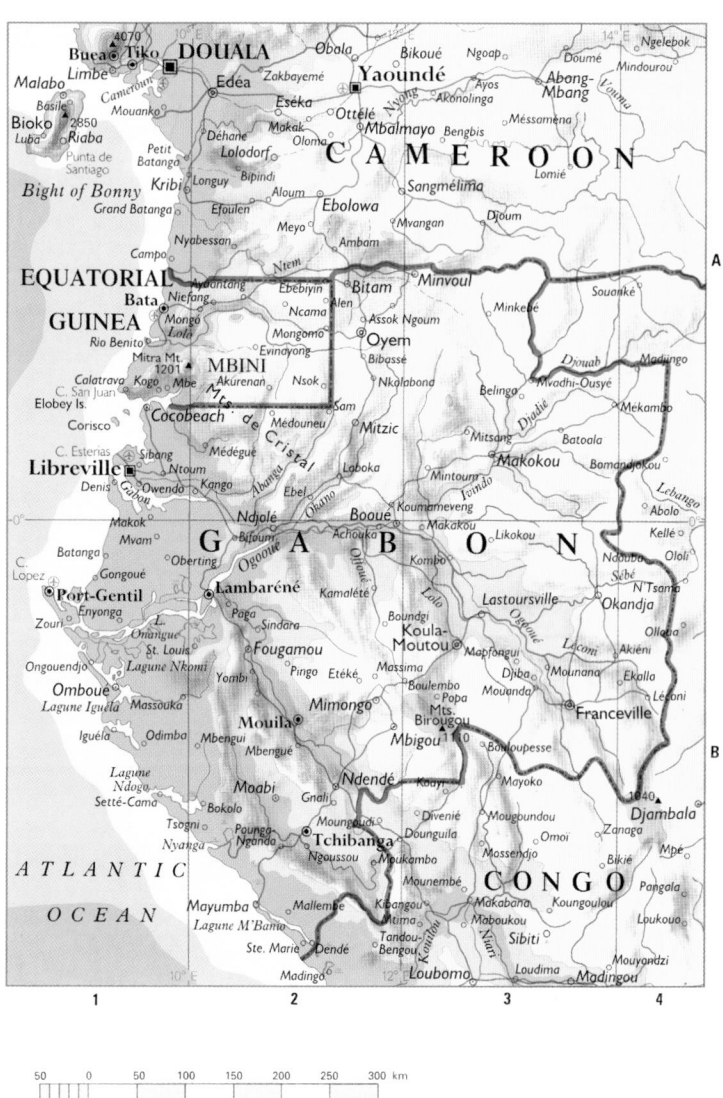

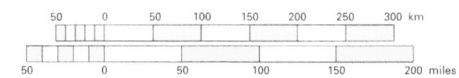

AREA	Mbete 14%, Punu 12%
267,670 sq km [103,347 sq mls]	**LANGUAGES**
POPULATION	French (official), Bantu languages
1,208,000	**RELIGIONS**
CAPITAL (POPULATION)	Christianity (Roman Catholic
Libreville (418,000)	65%, Protestant 19%, African
GOVERNMENT	churches 12%), traditional
Multiparty republic	beliefs 3%, Islam 2%
ETHNIC GROUPS	**CURRENCY**
Fang 36%, Mpongwe 15%,	CFA franc = 100 centimes

EQUATORIAL GUINEA

Geography and Climate

The Republic of Equatorial Guinea is a republic in west-central Africa. It consists of a mainland territory which makes up 90% of the land area, called Mbini (or Rio Muni), between Cameroon and Gabon, and five offshore islands in the Bight of Bonny, the largest being Bioko. The island of Annobon lies 560 km [350 mls] south-west of Mbini. Mbini consists mainly of hills and plateaux behind the coastal plains.

The climate is hot and humid with significant rainfall which diminishes inland. There is a dry season between December and February.

History and Politics

Portuguese navigators reached the area in 1471. In 1778, Portugal granted Bioko, together with rights over Mbini, to Spain.

In 1959, Spain made Bioko and Mbini provinces of overseas Spain. In 1963, it gave the provinces a degree of self-government. Equatorial Guinea became independent in 1968. The first president, Francisco Macias Nguema, proved to be a tyrant. He was overthrown in 1979 and a group of officers, led by Lt.-Col. Teodoro Obiang Nguema Mbasogo, set up a Supreme Military Council to rule the country. Elections were held in the 1990s, though the president continued to rule in a semi-dictatorial manner despite protests by opposition parties.

Economy

Equatorial Guinea is a poor country. Agriculture employs around 60% of the people, though many farmers live at subsistence level, making little contribution to the economy. The main food crops are bananas, cassava and sweet potatoes, but the chief cash crop is cocoa, grown on Bioko. Oil and gas are produced off Bioko. In the mid-1990s, oil and wood products were the leading exports, followed by cocoa.

AREA	Bubi 10%,
28,050 sq km [10,830 sq mls]	Ndowe 4%
POPULATION	**LANGUAGES**
454,000	Spanish (official),
CAPITAL (POPULATION)	Fang, Bubi
Malabo (35,000)	**RELIGIONS**
GOVERNMENT	Christianity 89%,
Multiparty republic (transitional)	traditional beliefs 5%
ETHNIC GROUPS	**CURRENCY**
Fang 83%,	CFA franc = 100 centimes

GAMBIA, THE – SEE SENEGAL, PAGE 198

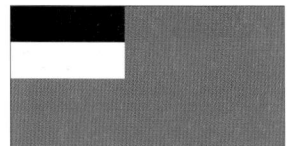

Georgia's flag was first used between 1917 and 1921. It was readopted when Georgia became independent. The wine-red colour represents the good times of the past and the future. The black symbolizes Russian rule and the white represents hope for peace.

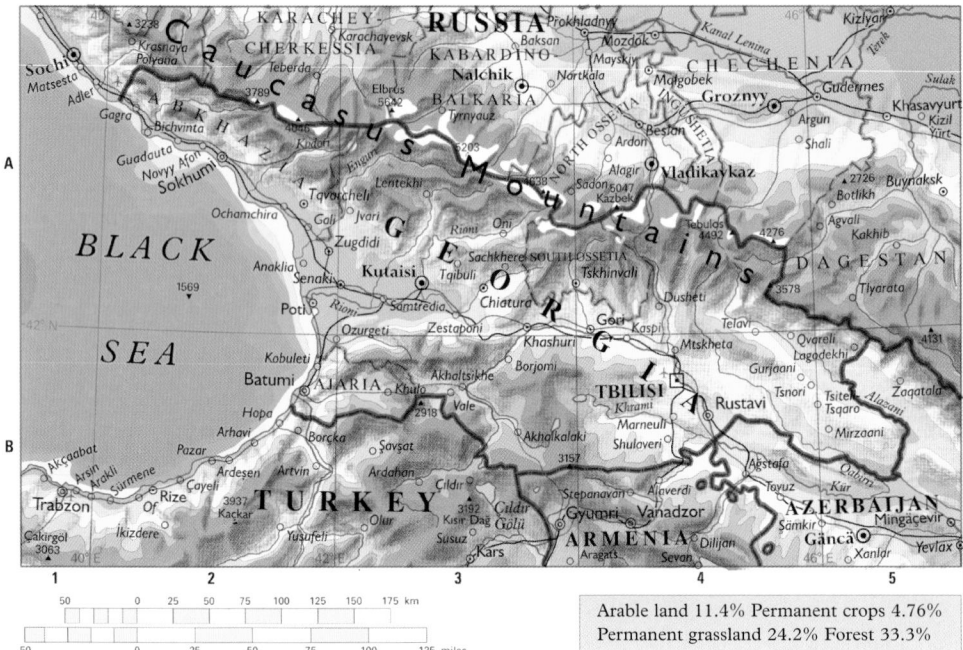

Arable land 11.4% Permanent crops 4.76%
Permanent grassland 24.2% Forest 33.3%

Geography

Georgia is a country on the borders of Europe and Asia, facing the Black Sea. The land is rugged with the Caucasus Mountains forming its northern border. The highest mountain in this range, Mount Elbrus (5,642 m [18,506 ft]), lies over the border in Russia.

Lower ranges run through southern Georgia, through which pass the borders with Turkey and Armenia. The Black Sea coastal plains are in the west. In the east a low plateau extends into Azerbaijan. The main river in the east is the River Kura, on which the capital Tbilisi stands.

Climate

The Black Sea plains have hot summers and mild winters, when the temperatures seldom drop below freezing point. The rainfall is heavy, but inland Tbilisi has moderate rainfall, with the heaviest rains in the spring and early summer.

GEORGIA (TBILISI)

Nestling between the Caucasus and the mountains of Armenia, Tbilisi is sheltered from the winter cold of central Asia and the heavy rain of the Black Sea coast. The sparse rainfall is effective in spring but evaporates quickly in the summer heat. Rain falls on about 70 days per year. The winters are less severe than expected in a continental location; temperatures rarely fall below freezing in December and January.

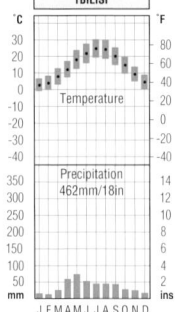

History

The first Georgian state was set up nearly 2,000 years ago and, by the 3rd century BC, most of what is now Georgia was united as a single kingdom. For much of its history, Georgia was ruled by various conquerors. For example, between about 60 BC and the 11th century, the area was ruled successively by Romans, Persians, Byzantines, Arabs and Seljuk Turks. Christianity was introduced in AD 330 and most Georgians are now members of the Georgian Orthodox Church. Georgia freed itself from foreign rule in the 11th and 12th centuries, but Mongol armies invaded in the 13th century. From the 16th to the 18th centuries, Iran and the Turkish Ottoman Empire struggled for control of the area.

In the late 18th century, Georgia sought the protection of Russia and, by the early 19th century, became part of the Russian Empire. After the Russian Revolution of 1917, Georgia declared itself independent and was recognized by the League of Nations. However, Russian troops invaded in 1921, making Georgia a Communist republic. From 1922, Georgia, Armenia and Azerbaijan were linked, forming the Transcaucasian Republic. But, in 1936, the territories became separate republics within the Soviet Union. Renowned for their longevity, the people of Georgia are famous for producing Josef Stalin, who was born in Gori, 65 km [40 mls] north-west of the capital Tbilisi. Stalin ruled the Soviet Union from 1929 until his death in 1953.

Politics

A maverick among the Soviet republics, Georgia was the first to declare its independence after the Baltic states (April 1991) and deferred joining the Commonwealth of Independent States (CIS) until 1993.

In 1991, Zviad Gamsakhurdia, a non-Communist who had been democratically elected president of Georgia in 1990, found himself holed up in Tbilisi's KGB headquarters, under siege from rebel forces. They represented widespread opposition to his government's policies, ranging from the economy to the imprisonment of his opponents. Gamsakhurdia had also been in conflict with the minority in South Ossetia, in north-central Georgia, one of the country's three regions where nationalists had demanded the right to set up their own governments. The others are Abkhazia in the north-west, which proclaimed its sovereignty in 1994, and Adjaria (or Adzharia) in the south-west. In January 1992, following the break-up of the Soviet Union, Gamsakhurdia fled the country and a military council took power.

In March, Eduard Shevardnadze, former Soviet Foreign Minister, was named head of state and was elected, unopposed, later that year. Shevardnadze was re-elected in 1995, taking 74.9% of the votes cast, defeating five other candidates. However, supporters of the deposed president Gamsakhurdia carried on intermittent armed conflict, and in 1998 an attempt was made to assassinate Shevardnadze.

Economy

Georgia is a developing country. Agriculture is important – major products include barley, citrus fruits, grapes for wine-making, maize, tea, tobacco and vegetables. Food processing and silk and perfume-making are other important activities. Sheep and cattle are reared.

Barite (barium ore), coal, copper and manganese are mined, and tourism is a major industry on the Black Sea coast. Georgia's mountains have huge potential for generating hydroelectric power, although most of the country's electricity is generated in Russia or Ukraine.

AREA	Ossetes 3%, Greek 2%,
69,700 sq km [26,910 sq mls]	Abkhazian 2%, others 3%
POPULATION	**LANGUAGES**
5,109,000	Georgian (official)
CAPITAL (POPULATION)	**RELIGIONS**
Tbilisi (1,279,000)	Christianity (Georgian Orthodox
GOVERNMENT	65%, Russian Orthodox 10%,
Multiparty republic	Armenian Orthodox 8%),
ETHNIC GROUPS	Islam 11%
Georgian 70%, Armenian 8%,	**CURRENCY**
Russian 6%, Azerbaijani 6%,	Lari

This flag, adopted by the Federal Republic of Germany (West Germany) in 1949, became the flag of the reunified Germany in 1990. The red, black and gold colours date back to the Holy Roman Empire. They are associated with the struggle for a united Germany from the 1830s.

Geography

The Federal Republic of Germany is the fourth largest country in Western Europe, after France, Spain and Sweden. The North German Plain borders the North Sea in the north-west and the Baltic Sea in the north-east. Rivers draining the plain include the Weser, Elbe and Oder.

The central highlands contain plateaux and highlands, including the Harz Mountains, the Thuringian Forest (Thüringer Wald), the Ore Mountains (Erzgebirge), and the Bohemian Forest (Böhmerwald) on the Czech border. South Germany is hilly, but the land rises in the south to the Bavarian Alps, which contain Germany's highest peak, Zugspitze, at 2,963 m [9,721 ft] above sea level. The Black Forest (Scharzwald) overlooks the River Rhine to the west. The Black Forest contains the source of the Danube.

A third kind of country is provided by the downfaulted basins filled with softer deposits, notably the Upper Rhine Plain between Basel and Mainz. Earth movements and eruptions produced another element, such as volcanic mountains at Vogelsberg and hot mineral springs that gave rise to famous spas. Here is Germany at its most picturesque, with castles on wooded heights, looking down over vineyards to clustered villages of half-timbered houses.

Climate

North-west Germany has a mild climate, but the Baltic coastlands are cooler. To the south, the climate becomes more continental, especially in the highlands. The precipitation is greatest on the uplands, many of which are snow-capped in winter.

Arable land 33.8% Permanent crops 0.60%
Permanent grassland 15.1% Forest 30.6%

GERMANY – BERLIN

The climate of northern Germany is affected by weather from the Atlantic. January and February are the only months with mean temperatures just below 0°C [32°F], and summers are warm. Rainfall is moderate, 500–750 mm [20–30 in], falling in all months. Humidity is high with fog in the autumn. Winter can be overcast. Snow lies for long spells inland and in the hills. When the winds blow from Scandinavia, very cold weather follows.

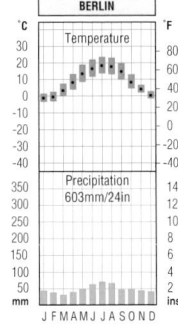

HAMBURG

Average temperatures, from December to March, are low and frost is usual on over 50 days in this period. Summers are pleasantly warm, the highest recorded temperatures being 34–35°C [93–95°F] in July and August, the averages being 16–17°C [61–62°F]. Moderate rainfall is evenly distributed all year with a slight peak in July and August. Rain falls on nearly 200 days in the year. Fog is frequent and winter sunshine totals are low.

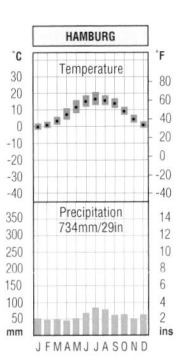

GERMANY

MUNICH

In the south it is a little warmer in the summer and slightly colder in winter. It is also wetter, Munich receiving nearly twice as much rain as Berlin. Further south it is even wetter with more snow. Rainfall is heavier in the summer months. The coming of spring is much earlier in the Rhine Valley and the south. The Föhn wind gets its name from this area. It is a dry warm wind that blows northwards from the Alps, mainly in the summer.

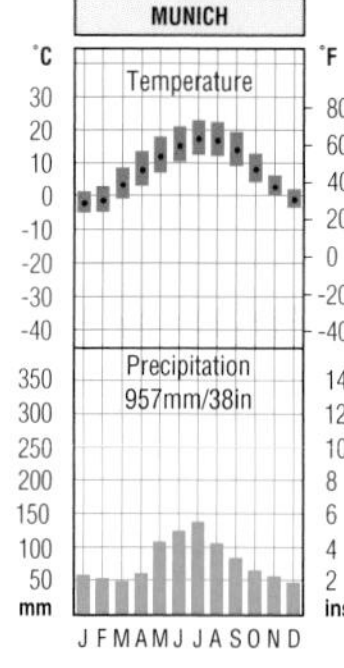

Vegetation

The North German Plain contains large areas of heathland, with such plants as grasses, heather, mosses and lichens. The most common trees in the forests of central and southern Germany are pine, beech (on the higher mountain slopes) and oak. The common oak grows throughout the country, while the Durmast oak is found mainly in the east. The western oak forests also contain hornbeam. Plantations of spruce are important commercially. More tolerant to extreme cold than beech, spruce are found up to the tree line in the southern mountains. Alder grows in river valleys, often with poplar and willow. Industrial pollution is the cause of acid rain, which has damaged many trees.

History

Around 3,000 years ago, various tribes from northern Europe began to settle in what is now Germany, occupying the valleys of the Rhine and the Danube. The Romans called this region Germania after the

The Reunification of Germany

In 1945, a devastated Germany was divided into four zones, each occupied by one of the victorious powers: Britain, France, the USA and the Soviet Union. The division was originally a temporary expedient (the Allies had formally agreed to maintain German unity), but the Russians published a constitution for the German Democratic Republic in 1946. The split solidified when the Russians rejected a currency reform common to all three Western zones. The German Federal Republic – 'West Germany' – was created in 1949.

Throughout the years of the Cold War, as NATO troops faced Warsaw Pact tanks across the barbed wire and minefields of the new frontier, the partition seemed irrevocable. Although both German constitutions maintained hopes of reunification, it appeared that nothing short of total war could bring it about. The West, with three-quarters of the population, rebuilt war damage and prospered. The East was hailed as the industrial jewel of the Soviet European empire, though some of its people were prepared to risk being shot to escape westwards.

By the late 1980s, it was clear that the Soviet Empire was crumbling. In the autumn of 1989, thousands of East Germans migrated illegally to the West across the newly open Hungarian border and mass demonstrations in East German cities followed. At first, the government issued a stream of threats, but when it became clear that there would be no Soviet tanks to enforce its rule, it simply packed up. With the frontiers open, the 'successful' East German economy was a catastrophic shambles, a scrapyard poisoned by uncontrolled pollution, with bankruptcy imminent. The choice facing German leaders in 1990 was starkly simple: either unite East and West, or accept virtually the entire Eastern population as penniless refugees.

The West German government, led by Chancellor Helmut Kohl, acted quickly, often bullying the weaker Easterners. The Western Deutschmark became the common currency, and on 3 October 1990 – more than 45 years after Germany had lost the war – the country was formally reunited. However, the costs of restructuring the economy of the East are high, and the German people will be paying for many years.

Germani, the name of one of the tribes. Other tribes included the Franks, Goths and Vandals. The Romans attempted to conquer the tribes in AD 9, but they were defeated in a battle in the Teutoburg Forest. In the 5th century, the Germanic tribes attacked the Roman Empire and plundered Rome. The western part of the Roman Empire split up into several kingdoms, the largest of which was the Kingdom of the Franks.

In 486, Clovis, a Frankish king, extended his rule to include Gaul (now France) and western Germany, introducing Christianity and other Roman practices. A later Frankish ruler, Charlemagne, came to power in 768 and established his capital at Aachen. He expanded the territory, uniting many tribes into his empire. He became emperor of the Romans in 800 but, in 843, his empire was split into three, the eastern part being what is now Germany. From 962, much of the German Empire became part of what was later known as the Holy Roman Empire under King Otto II of Germany. The Holy Roman Empire was never entirely German. Some Germans lived outside its boundaries, while many non-German areas, such as Italy and parts of eastern Europe, lay within it.

In 1517, a German monk, Martin Luther, began to criticize many of the practices and teachings of the Roman Catholic Church. A Protestant movement called the Reformation soon attracted much support in Germany. By the early 17th century, the people of Germany were deeply divided by political and religious rivalries. The Thirty Years' War, which began in 1618 and lasted for 30 years, ravaged much of the country. The conflict was partly a struggle between Protestants and Roman Catholics, but it was also a battle between certain princes and the emperor, a member of the royal Austrian Habsburg family. At the end of the war, Germany had lost territory to France and Sweden, while Germany itself was split into hundreds of states and free cities. It took almost 200 years for Germany to recover from this disastrous war.

In the 17th century, the Hohenzollern family began to assume importance in eastern Germany. Its rise to power began with Frederick William, who became ruler of Brandenburg in 1648. His son, Frederick I, became the king of Prussia. The Hohenzollerns gradually extended their power and built up a professional civil service and army. Between 1740 and 1768, Frederick II (the Great) made Prussia a great power.

During the Napoleonic wars, some German states allied themselves with France, and Prussia stayed out of the wars until 1806. Following defeats by Napoleon, Prussia lost its territories west of the Elbe, but Prussia helped to defeat Napoleon's armies at the battles of Leipzig (1813) and Waterloo (1815). Following the Napoleonic wars, Prussia gained the Rhineland, Westphalia and much of Saxony.

German nationalism increased during the 19th century. In the early 1860s, the Prussian king, Wilhelm I, appointed Otto von Bismarck as prime minister in order to resolve a constitutional crisis about army reforms. Bismarck set about strengthening Prussian power through three short wars that led to the annexation of territory. One conflict led to the acquisition of Schleswig-Holstein from Denmark, while another led to the annexation of territory from Austria. The third was the Franco-Prussian War (1870–1), following which victorious Germany was granted Alsace and part of Lorraine. In 1871, Wilhelm I was crowned the first Kaiser of the new German Empire and Bismarck became the chancellor and head of government. Bismarck sought to consolidate German power and avoid conflict with Austria-Hungary and Russia, but he was forced to resign in 1890 when Frederick III's son, Wilhelm II, wanted to establish his own authority and extend Germany's influence in the world. Wilhelm's ambitions led Britain and France to establish the Entente Cordiale in 1904, while Britain and Russia signed a similar agreement in 1907. This left Europe divided, with Germany, Austria-Hungary and Italy forming the Triple Alliance.

Germany and its allies were defeated in World War I, which ended on 11 November 1918. Germany became a republic and lost territories, including Alsace, the German part of Lorraine, Poland, some of Silesia and part of West Prussia. Overseas, it lost its colonies. Germany's humiliation under the terms of the Versailles Treaty caused much resentment, which was made worse by an economic collapse in 1922 and 1923. Support grew for the Nazi Party and its leader Adolf

Berlin

Like defeated Germany itself, Berlin was formally divided between the four victorious powers – despite the fact that it was located in Prussia, 160 km [100 mls] inside Soviet-occupied eastern Germany. In June 1948, in an attempt to bring the whole city under their control, the Soviets closed all road and rail links with the West. The Western Allies supplied the city by a massive airlift; in October 1949 the blockade was abandoned, but Berlin's anomalous situation remained a potential flashpoint, and provoked a series of diplomatic crises – mainly because it offered an easy escape route to the West for discontented East Germans.

In August 1961, alarmed at the steady drain of some of its best-trained people, the East German authorities built a dividing wall across the city. Over the years, the original improvised structure – it was thrown up overnight – became a substantial barrier of concrete and barbed wire, with machine-gun towers and minefields; despite the hazards, many still risked the perilous crossing, and hundreds of would-be refugees – often youngsters – died in the attempt.

The Berlin Wall, with its few heavily guarded crossing points, became the most indelible symbol of the Cold War. When the East German government collapsed in 1989, the Wall's demolition became the most unambiguous sign of the Cold War's ending. When East Germany joined the West, it was agreed that Berlin would become the formal capital of the unified state in the year 2000 – until that time, both Berlin and the quiet Rhineland city of Bonn were to be joint capitals. The renovated Reichstag with its spectacular glass dome, the work of the British architect Sir Norman Foster, was officially opened in April 1999.

Federal structure of Germany

Hitler, who became chancellor in 1933. Hitler's order to invade Poland in 1939 triggered off World War II. Hitler's armies were finally defeated in 1945 and the country was left in ruins. Germany was obliged to transfer to Poland and the Soviet Union 114,500 sq km [44,200 sq mls], situated east of the Oder and Neisse rivers, nearly a quarter of the country's pre-war area. The German-speaking inhabitants were expelled – as were most German-speaking minorities in the countries of Eastern Europe – and the remainder of Germany was occupied by the four victorious Allied powers. In 1948, West Germany, consisting of the American, British and French zones, was proclaimed the Federal Republic of Germany with its provisional capital at Bonn, while the Soviet zone became the German Democratic Republic with its capital in East Berlin.

Politics

The post-war partition of Germany into the democratic West Germany and a Communist East Germany, together with its geographical position, made it a central hub of the Cold War which ended in the collapse of Communism in the late 1980s and early 1990s. In Germany, it ended with the reunification of Germany on 3 October 1990. West Germany, initially under constraints imposed by the Allies, had become a showpiece of the West through its phenomenal recovery and sustained growth – the so-called *Wirtschaftswunder* ('economic miracle'). It also played a major part, together with France, in the revival of Western Europe through the development of the European Community (now the European Union). By contrast, although East Germany had achieved the highest standard of living in the Soviet bloc, it was short of the levels of the European Union members.

Following reunification, when the new country adopted West Germany's official name, the Federal Republic of Germany, massive investment was needed to rebuild the East's industrial base and transport system. This meant increased taxation. In addition, the new nation found itself funnelling aid into Eastern Europe – Germany led the European Union in recognizing the independence of Slovenia and Croatia and then the former Soviet republics. All this took place against the background of a continued downturn of world trade. There were also social effects. While Germans in the West resented added taxes and the burden imposed by the East, easterners resented what many saw as the overbearing and patronizing attitudes of westerners. There was also concern of a revival of the far right, and neo-Nazis and other right-wingers have protested against the increasing numbers of immigrant workers.

Reunification appeared in the late 1990s to be the beginning rather than the end of a chapter in German history. The creation of a unified state proved to be a much more complicated, expensive and lengthy undertaking than anyone had envisaged when the Berlin Wall came down. In 1998, the centre-right government of Helmut Kohl, who had presided over reunification, was defeated by the left-of-centre Social Democratic Party (SPD) which was led by Gerhard Schröder. An SPD-Green Party coalition was set up, but it faced problems, including a record rate of unemployment and a sluggish economy. However, in 1999, allegations against former Chancellor Kohl of using secret bank accounts to finance his party proved damaging to his former ruling party, the Christian Democratic Union.

Economy

Despite the problems associated with reunification, Germany has the world's third largest economy after the United States and Japan. The foundation of the 'economic miracle' that led to Germany's astonishing post-war recovery was manufacturing.

Germany's industrial strength was based on its coal reserves, though oil-burning and nuclear generating plants have become increasingly important since the 1970s. Lower Saxony has oilfields, while southern Germany also obtains power from hydroelectric plants. The country has supplies of potash and rock salt, together with smaller quantities of copper, lead, tin, uranium and zinc. The leading industrial region is the Ruhr, which produces iron and steel, together with major chemical and textiles industries. Germany is the world's third largest producer of cars, while other manufactures include cameras, drugs, electronic equipment, fertilizers, processed food, plastics, scientific instruments, ships, tools and wood and pulp products.

Agriculture employs 2.4% of the workforce, but Germany imports about a third of its food. Products include barley, fruits, grapes, oats, potatoes, rye, sugar beet, vegetables and wheat. Beef and dairy cattle are raised, together with pigs, poultry and sheep. Chief exports are machinery and transport equipment and chemicals and chemical products. Germany's major trading partners include France, the Netherlands, Italy, the United States and the United Kingdom.

AREA	Yugoslav 1%, Italian 1%,
356,910 sq km	Greek, Polish, Spanish
[137,803 sq mls]	**LANGUAGES**
POPULATION	German (official)
82,079,000	**RELIGIONS**
CAPITAL (POPULATION)	Christianity (Protestant,
Berlin (3,472,000)	mainly Lutheran 45%,
GOVERNMENT	Roman Catholic 37%),
Federal multiparty republic	Islam 2%
ETHNIC GROUPS	**CURRENCY**
German 93%, Turkish 2%,	Euro; Deutschmark = 100 Pfennig

Ghana's flag has red, green and yellow bands like the flag of Ethiopia, Africa's oldest independent nation. These colours symbolize African unity. The black star is a symbol of African freedom. Ghana's flag was adopted when the country became independent in 1957.

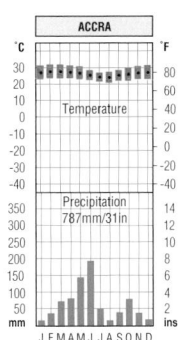

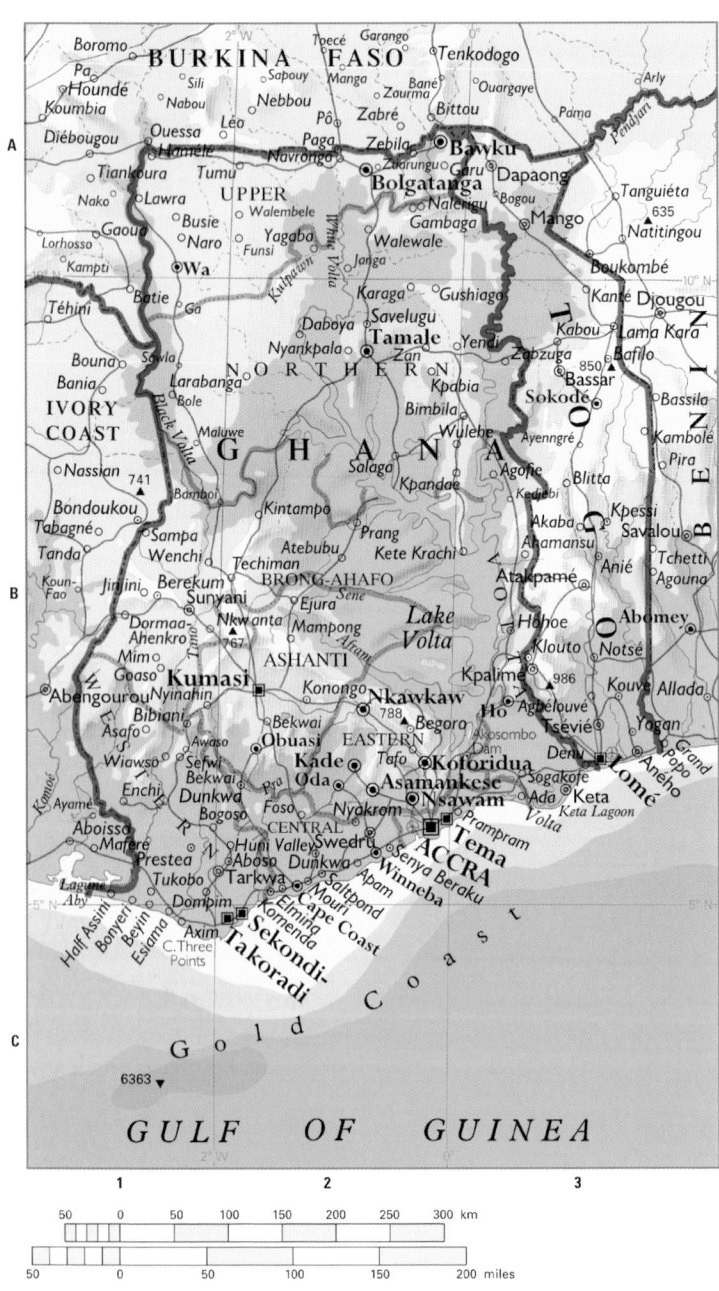

50	0	50 100 150 200 250 300 km

50	0	50 100 150 200 miles

GHANA (ACCRA)

The climate of coastal regions is similar to much of the Guinea coast, with high temperatures, high humidity and a double maximum of rainfall associated with two passages of the intertropical rainbelt. However, the total rainfall is less than that of coastal regions to the east and west of Ghana, a feature attributed to the presence of a local upwell of cooler water offshore. The total yearly rainfall can be as low as 300 mm [12 in].

History

Portuguese explorers reached the area in 1471 and named it the Gold Coast. The area became a centre of the slave trade in the 17th century. The slave trade was ended in the 1860s and the British gradually took control of the area.

The country became independent in 1957, when it was renamed Ghana. Ghana was a great African empire which flourished to the north-west of present-day Ghana between the AD 300s and 1000s. This name was chosen to celebrate the fact that Ghana was the first country in the Commonwealth to be ruled by black Africans.

Politics

After independence in 1957, attempts were made to develop the economy by creating large state-owned manufacturing industries. But debt and corruption, together with falls in the price of cocoa, the chief export, caused economic problems. This led to instability and frequent coups. In 1981, power was invested in a Provisional National Defence Council, led by Flight-Lieutenant Jerry Rawlings.

The government steadied the economy and introduced several new policies, including the relaxation of government controls. In 1992, a new constitution was introduced which allowed for multiparty elections. Rawlings was re-elected later that year, and again in 1996. In the later 1990s, the economy steadily expanded, largely as a result of the government following World Bank policies, which led to an expansion of foreign investment.

Economy

The World Bank classifies Ghana as a 'low-income' developing country. Most people are poor and farming employs 59% of the population. Food crops include cassava, groundnuts, maize, millet, plantains, rice and yams. But cocoa is the most valuable export crop. Timber and gold are also exported. Other valuable crops include tobacco, coffee, coconuts and palm kernels.

Many small factories produce goods, such as beverages, cement and clothing, for local consumption.

The aluminium smelter at Tema, a port near Accra, is the country's largest factory. Electricity for southern Ghana is produced from a hydroelectric station at the Akosombo Dam. There are plans to construct around 600 km [378 mls] of pipeline which will form part of the West African Gas Pipeline Project. It is hoped that this will lessen the dependence of electricity production on hydroelectric stations.

Geography

The Republic of Ghana faces the Gulf of Guinea in West Africa. This hot country, just north of the Equator, was formerly called the Gold Coast. Behind the thickly populated southern coastal plains, which are lined with lagoons, lies a plateau region in the south-west.

Northern Ghana is drained by the Black and White Volta Rivers, which flow into Lake Volta. This lake, which has formed behind the Akosombo Dam, is one of the world's largest artificially created lakes.

Climate

Ghana has a tropical climate. A cool offshore current reduces temperatures on the coast, and the north is hotter. The heaviest rains occur in the south-west. Northern and eastern Ghana have marked dry seasons.

Vegetation

Rainforests grow in the south-west. To the north, the forests merge into savanna (tropical grassland with some woodland). More open grasslands dominate in the far north.

AREA	Mossi 16%, Ewe 12%,
238,540 sq km [92,100 sq mls]	Ga-Adangame 8%, Gurma 3%
POPULATION	**LANGUAGES**
18,497,000	English (official), Akan, Mossi
CAPITAL (POPULATION)	**RELIGIONS**
Accra (1,781,000)	Christianity 62%,
GOVERNMENT	traditional beliefs 21%,
Multiparty republic	Islam 16%
ETHNIC GROUPS	**CURRENCY**
Akan 54%,	Cedi = 100 pesewas

Blue and white became Greece's national colours during the war of independence (1821–9). The nine horizontal stripes on the flag, which was finally adopted in 1970, represent the nine syllables of the battle cry 'Eleutheria i thanatos' ('Freedom or Death').

Geography

The Hellenic Republic, as Greece is officially called, lies at the southern end of the Balkan Peninsula. Olympus, at 2,917 m [9,570 ft], is the highest peak. Nearly a fifth of the land area is made up of around 2,000 islands, mainly in the Aegean Sea, east of the main peninsula, but also in the Ionian Sea to the west. Only 154 are inhabited. The island of Crete is structurally related to the main Alpine fold mountain system to which the mainland Pindos Range belongs.

Climate

Low-lying areas in Greece have mild, moist winters and hot, dry summers. The east coast has more than 2,700 hours of sunshine a year and only about half of the rainfall of the west. The mountains have a more severe climate, with snow on the higher slopes in winter.

History and Politics

Crete was the centre of the Minoan civilization, an early Greek culture, between about 3000 and 1450 BC. The Minoans were followed by the Mycenian culture which prospered on the mainland until about 1100 BC.

In about 750 BC, the Greeks began to colonize the Mediterranean, creating wealth through trade. The city-state of Athens reached its peak in the 400s BC, but in 338 BC Macedonia became the dominant power. In 334–331 BC, Alexander the Great conquered south-western Asia. Greece became a Roman province in 146 BC and, in AD 365, part of the Byzantine Empire. In 1453, the Turks defeated the Byzantine Empire. But between 1821 and 1829, the Greeks defeated the Turks. The country became an independent monarchy in 1830.

After World War II (1939–45), when Germany had occupied Greece, a civil war broke out between Communist and nationalist forces. This war ended in 1949. A military dictatorship took power in 1967. The monarchy was abolished in 1973 and democratic government was restored in 1974. Greece joined the European Community in 1981. But despite efforts to develop the economy, Greece remains one of the poorest nations in the European Union. In 1998, it failed to qualify for the adoption of the euro.

In 1999, Greece and Turkey co-operated when major earthquakes struck in both countries. This led to an improvement in relations between these rival nations.

Economy

Manufacturing is important. Products include processed food, cement, chemicals, metal products, textiles and tobacco. Greece also mines lignite (brown coal), bauxite and chromite.

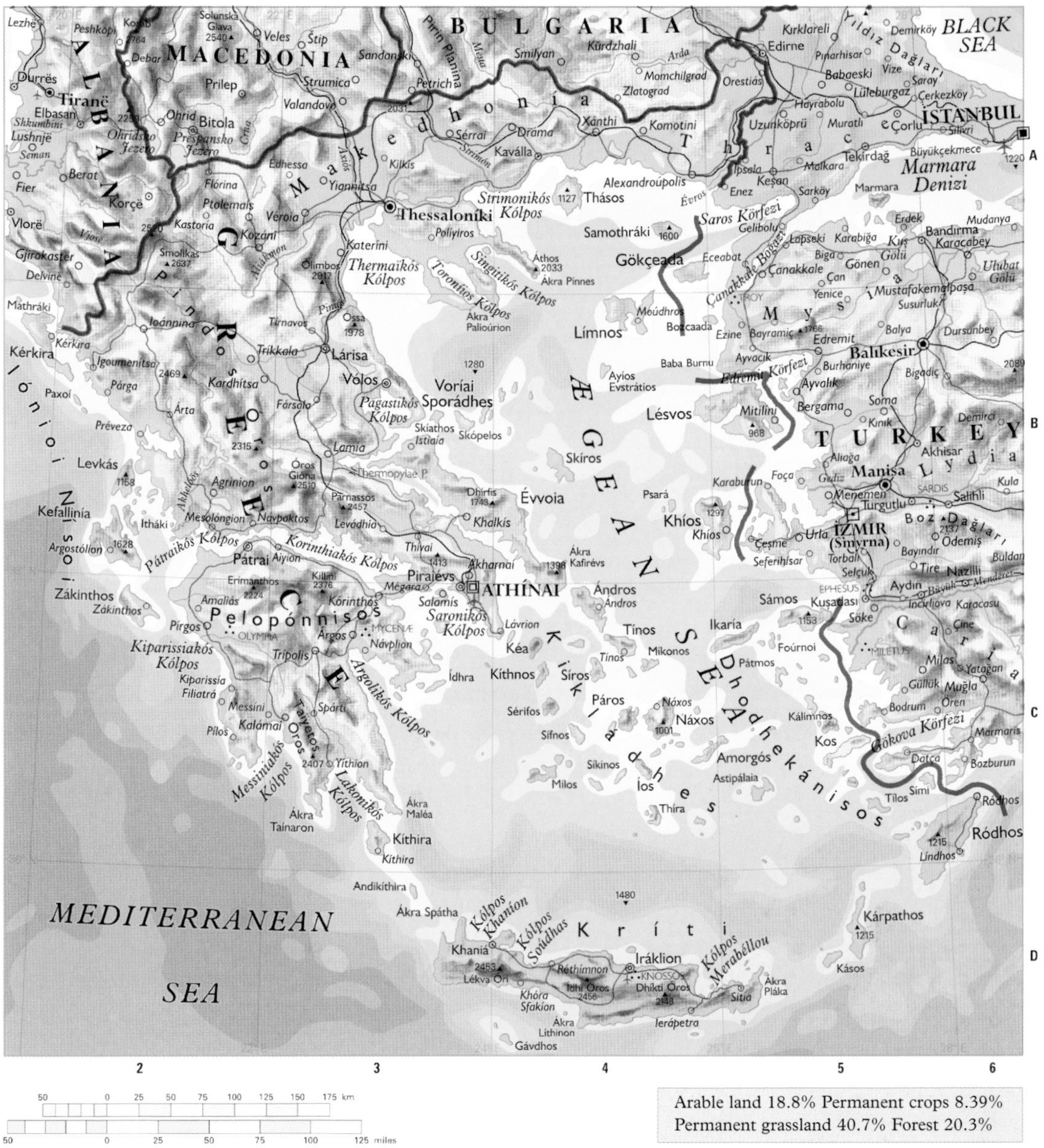

Arable land 18.8% Permanent crops 8.39%
Permanent grassland 40.7% Forest 20.3%

Farmland covers about a third of the country, and grazing land another 40%. Major crops include barley, grapes for wine-making, dried fruits, olives, potatoes, sugar beet and wheat. Poultry, sheep, goats, pigs and cattle are raised. The vital tourist industry is based on the warm climate, the beautiful scenery, especially on the islands, and the historical sites dating back to the days of classical Greece.

AREA	Macedonian 2%,
131,990 sq km [50,961 sq mls]	Turkish 1%,
POPULATION	Albanian, Slav
10,662,000	**LANGUAGES**
CAPITAL (POPULATION)	Greek (official)
Athens (Athínai, 3,097,000)	**RELIGIONS**
GOVERNMENT	Christianity
Multiparty republic	(Eastern Orthodox 97%)
ETHNIC GROUPS	**CURRENCY**
Greek 96%,	Drachma = 100 lepta

GREENLAND – SEE ATLANTIC OCEAN, PAGES 41–43;
GRENADA – SEE CARIBBEAN SEA, PAGES 71–76;
GUADELOUPE – SEE CARIBBEAN SEA, PAGES 71–76;
GUAM – SEE PACIFIC OCEAN, PAGES 174–178

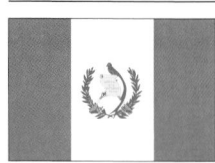

Guatemala's flag was adopted in 1871, but its origins go back to the days of the Central American Federation (1823–39), which was set up after the break from Spain in 1821. The Federation included Costa Rica, El Salvador, Guatemala, Honduras and Nicaragua.

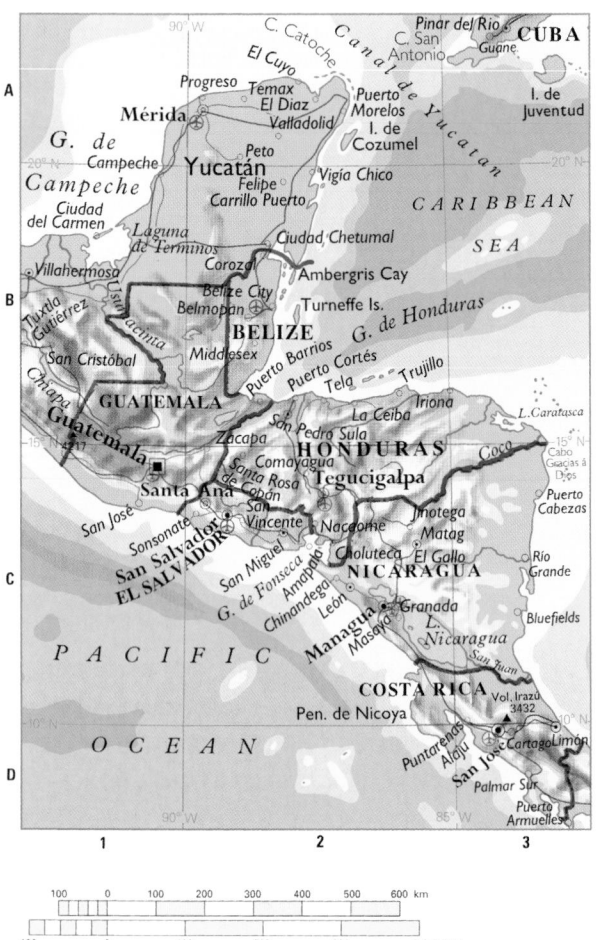

Geography and Climate

The Republic of Guatemala in Central America contains a thickly populated, fertile, mountain region. The mountains run in an east–west direction and contain many volcanoes, some of which are active. Volcanic eruptions and earthquakes are common. South of the mountains lie the thinly-populated Pacific coastlands.

Guatemala lies in the tropics. The lowlands are hot and wet, but the central mountain region is cooler and drier.

History and Politics

In 1823, Guatemala joined the Central American Federation. It became fully independent in 1839 but has since been plagued by instability and periodic violence.

Guatemala has a long-standing claim over Belize, but this was reduced in 1983 to the southern fifth of the country. Violence became widespread in Guatemala from the early 1960s, because of conflict between left-wing groups, including many Amerindians, and government forces. A peace accord was signed in December 1996, ending a war that had lasted 36 years and claimed around 200,000 lives.

Economy

The World Bank classifies Guatemala as a 'lower-middle-income' developing country. Agriculture employs nearly half of the population and coffee, sugar, bananas and beef are the leading exports.

AREA	Hispanic and Amerindian) 45%,
108,890 sq km [42,042 sq mls]	White 5%, Black 2%, others, including
POPULATION	Chinese 3%
12,008,000	**LANGUAGES**
CAPITAL (POPULATION)	Spanish (official), Mayan languages
Guatemala City (1,814,000)	**RELIGIONS**
GOVERNMENT	Christianity (Roman Catholic 75%,
Republic	Protestant 25%)
ETHNIC GROUPS	**CURRENCY**
Amerindian 45%, Ladino (mixed	Guatemalan quetzal = 100 centavos

BELIZE

Geography and Climate

Behind the swampy coastal plain in the south, the land rises to the low Maya Mountains, which reach a height of 1,120 m [3,674 ft] at Victoria Peak. The north is mostly low-lying and swampy.

Belize has a tropical, humid climate. Temperatures are high all year and the average yearly rainfall ranges from 1,300 mm [51 in] in the north to over 3,800 mm [150 in] in the south.

History and Politics

From 1862, Belize (then called British Honduras) was a British colony. Full independence was achieved in 1981, but Guatemala, which had claimed the area since the early 19th century, opposed Belize's independence and British troops remained to prevent a possible invasion. In 1983, Guatemala reduced its claim to the southern fifth of Belize. Improved relations in the early 1990s led Guatemala to recognize Belize's independence and, in 1992, Britain agreed to withdraw its troops from the country.

Economy

The World Bank classifies Belize as a 'lower-middle-income' developing country. Its economy is based on agriculture. Sugar cane is the chief commercial crop and export. Other crops include bananas, beans, maize and rice. Forestry and tourism are other important activities.

AREA	Garifuna (Black-Carib Indian)
22,960 sq km [8,865 sq mls]	7%, White 4%, East Indian 3%
POPULATION	**LANGUAGES**
230,000	English (official), Creole,
CAPITAL (POPULATION)	Spanish
Belmopan (4,000)	**RELIGIONS**
GOVERNMENT	Christianity (Roman Catholic
Constitutional monarchy	58%, Protestant 29%),
ETHNIC GROUPS	Hinduism 2%
Mestizo (Spanish-Indian) 44%,	**CURRENCY**
Creole 30%, Mayan Indian 11%,	Belize dollar = 100 cents

EL SALVADOR

Geography and Climate

The Republic of El Salvador is the only country in Central America without a coast on the Caribbean Sea. The country has a narrow coastal plain along the Pacific Ocean. Behind the coastal plain, the coastal range is a zone of rugged mountains, including volcanoes, overlooking a densely populated inland plateau. Beyond the plateau, the land rises to the sparsely populated interior highlands.

The coast has a hot, tropical climate. Inland, the climate is moderated by altitude. Rain falls nearly every day between May and October.

History and Politics

Amerindians have lived in El Salvador for thousands of years. The ruins of Mayan pyramids built between AD 100 and 1000 are still found in the western part of the country. Spanish soldiers conquered the area in 1524 and 1525, and Spain ruled until 1821. In 1823, all the Central American countries, except for Panama, set up a Central American Federation. But El Salvador withdrew in 1840 and declared its independence in 1841. El Salvador suffered from instability throughout the 19th century. The 20th century saw a more stable government, but from 1931 military dictatorships alternated with elected governments and the country remained poor.

In the 1970s, El Salvador was plagued by conflict as protesters demanded that the government introduce reforms to help the poor. Kidnappings and murders committed by left- and right-wing groups caused instability. A civil war broke out in 1979 between the US-backed, right-wing government forces and left-wing guerrillas in the FMLN (Farabundo Marti National Liberation Front). In 12 years, more than 750,000 people died and hundreds of thousands were made homeless. A cease-fire was agreed on 1 February 1992 and presidential elections were held in 1993 and 1999.

Economy

El Salvador is classified as a 'lower-middle-income' economy. Coffee is the main export, followed by sugar and cotton. Fishing is important.

AREA	and Amerindian) 89%,
21,040 sq km [8,124 sq mls]	Amerindian 10%,
POPULATION	White 1%
5,752,000	**LANGUAGES**
CAPITAL (POPULATION)	Spanish (official)
San Salvador (1,522,000)	**RELIGIONS**
GOVERNMENT	Christianity (Roman Catholic
Republic	94%)
ETHNIC GROUPS	**CURRENCY**
Mestizo (mixed White	Colón = 100 centavos

HONDURAS

Geography and Climate

Honduras is a republic in Central America. The northern coast extends for more than 600 km [373 mls]. The Pacific coast in the south-east is only about 80 km [50 mls] long.

The climate is tropical, though the uplands are cooler than the coastal plains. The rainiest months are November to May. In October 1998, Honduras and Nicaragua were hit by Hurricane Mitch, which caused floods and mudslides. The death toll was about 7,000.

History and Politics

In the 1890s, American companies developed plantations in Honduras to grow bananas. The companies exerted great political influence and the country became known as a 'banana republic'. Instability continued to mar the country's progress and American aid was crucial. During the 1980s, Honduras allowed US-backed 'Contra' rebels from Nicaragua to operate in Honduras against Nicaragua's left-wing Sandinista government. A cease-fire was signed in Nicaragua in 1988, after which the 'Contra' bases were closed down. Since 1980, civilian governments have ruled Honduras, but the military retains much influence.

Economy

Honduras is a developing country – one of the poorest in the Americas. It has few resources besides some silver, lead and zinc. Agriculture dominates the economy. Bananas and coffee are the leading exports, and maize is the main food crop.

Honduras is the least industrialized country in Central America. Manufactures include processed food, textiles, and a wide variety of wood products.

AREA	Amerindian 7%, Black
112,090 sq km [43,278 sq mls]	(including Black Carib) 2%,
POPULATION	White 1%
5,862,000	**LANGUAGES**
CAPITAL (POPULATION)	Spanish (official)
Tegucigalpa (739,000)	**RELIGIONS**
GOVERNMENT	Christianity (Roman Catholic
Republic	85%)
ETHNIC GROUPS	**CURRENCY**
Mestizo 90%,	Honduran lempira = 100 centavos

NICARAGUA

Geography and Climate

The Republic of Nicaragua is the second largest country in Central America. In the east is a broad plain which is drained by rivers that flow from the Central Highlands. The fertile western Pacific region contains volcanoes, many of which are active, and earthquakes are common.

Nicaragua has a tropical climate and there is a marked wet season from May to October. In October 1998, Hurricane Mitch caused great devastation in Nicaragua, causing at least 1,800 deaths.

History and Politics

In 1502, Christopher Columbus claimed the area for Spain, which ruled Nicaragua until 1821. By the early 20th century, the United States had considerable influence in the country and, in 1912, US forces entered Nicaragua to protect US interests. From 1927 to 1933, rebels under General Augusto César Sandino tried to drive US forces out of the country. In 1933, US marines set up a Nicaraguan army, the National Guard, to help defeat the rebels. Its leader, Anastasio Somoza Garcia, had Sandino murdered in 1934. From 1937, Somoza ruled as a dictator.

In the mid-1970s, people began to protest against Somoza's rule. Many joined a guerrilla force, called the Sandinista National Liberation Front, named after General Sandino. The rebels defeated the Somoza regime in 1979. In the 1980s, the US-supported forces, called the 'Contras', launched a campaign against the Sandinista government. The US government opposed the Sandinista regime, under Daniel José Ortega Saavedra, claiming it was a Communist dictatorship. The National Opposition Union, a coalition, defeated the Sandinistas in elections in 1990. In 1996, the Sandinistas were again defeated. Leader of the Liberal Alliance Party, Arnoldo Alemán, became president.

Economy

Agriculture is the main activity, employing nearly half of the people. Coffee, cotton, sugar and bananas are grown for export, while rice is the main food crop.

AREA	Black 9%, Amerindian 4%
130,000 sq km [50,193 sq mls]	**LANGUAGES**
POPULATION	Spanish (official),
4,583,000	Misumalpan
CAPITAL (POPULATION)	**RELIGIONS**
Managua (974,000)	Christianity (Roman Catholic
GOVERNMENT	91%, others 9%)
Multiparty republic	**CURRENCY**
ETHNIC GROUPS	Córdoba oro (gold córdoba) =
Mestizo 77%, White 10%,	100 centavos

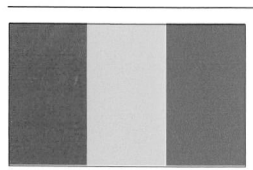

GUINEA

Guinea's flag was adopted when the country became independent from France in 1958. It uses the colours of the flag of Ethiopia, Africa's oldest nation, which symbolize African unity. The red represents work, the yellow justice and the green solidarity.

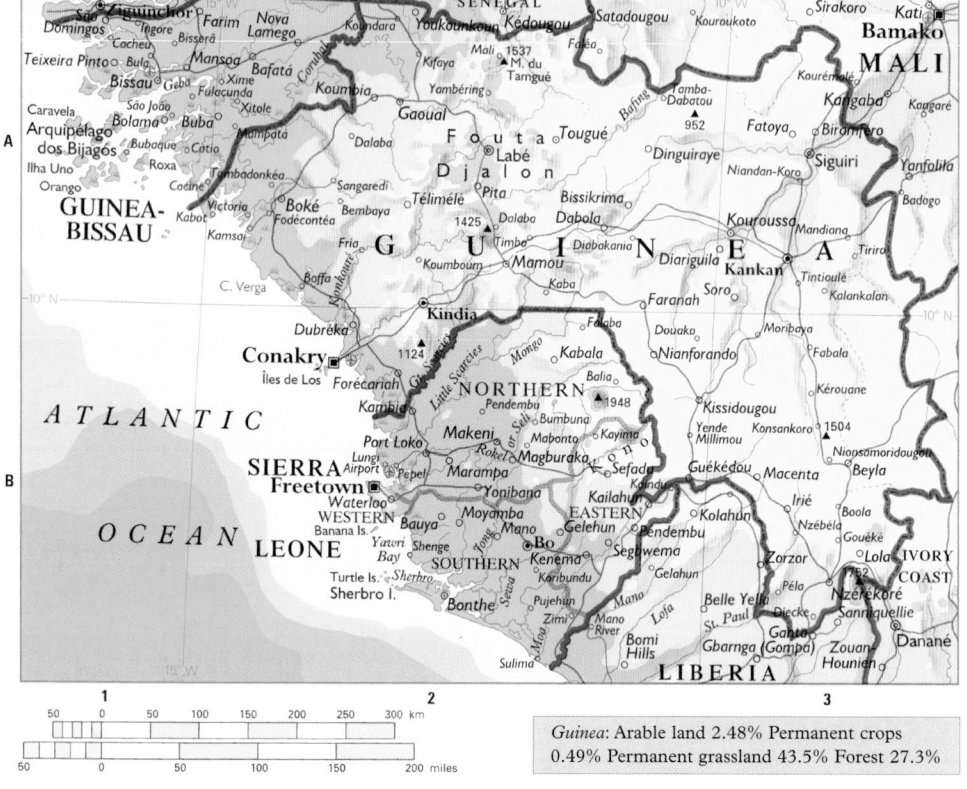

Guinea: Arable land 2.48% Permanent crops
0.49% Permanent grassland 43.5% Forest 27.3%

Geography and Climate

The Republic of Guinea faces the Atlantic Ocean in West Africa. A flat, swampy plain borders the coast. Behind this plain, the land rises to a plateau region called Fouta Djalon. The Upper Niger Plains, named after one of Africa's longest rivers, the Niger, which rises there, are in the north-east.

Guinea has a tropical climate and Conakry, on the coast, has heavy rains and cooler temperatures between May and November. During the dry season, hot, dry harmattan winds blow south-westwards from the Sahara Desert. The Fouta Djalon is cooler than the coast. The driest region is the north-east. This region and the south-eastern highlands experience greater temperature variations than on the coast.

History and Politics

Portuguese explorers arrived in the mid-15th century and the slave trade began soon afterwards. From the 17th century, other European slave traders became active in Guinea. France became involved in the area in the mid-19th century and, in 1891, it made Guinea a French colony.

Guinea became independent in 1958. The first president, Sékou Touré, followed socialist policies, though most people remained poor. Touré had to introduce repressive policies to hold on to power. After his death in 1984, military leaders took over. Colonel Lansana Conté became president and his government introduced free enterprise policies. Conté was elected president in 1993 and 1998.

Economy

The World Bank classifies Guinea as a 'low-income' developing country. It has several natural resources, including bauxite (aluminium ore), uranium, diamonds, gold and iron ore. Bauxite and alumina (processed bauxite) account for 90% of the value of the exports.

AREA	Susu 11%, Kissi 7%,
245,860 sq km [94,927 sq mls]	Kpelle 5%
POPULATION	**LANGUAGES**
7,477,000	French (official), Fulani,
CAPITAL (POPULATION)	Malinke
Conakry (1,508,000)	**RELIGIONS**
GOVERNMENT	Islam 85%, traditional
Multiparty republic	beliefs 5%
ETHNIC GROUPS	**CURRENCY**
Fulani 40%, Malinke 26%,	Guinean franc = 100 cauris

GUINEA-BISSAU

Geography and Climate

The Republic of Guinea-Bissau is a small country in West Africa. The land is mostly low-lying, with a broad, swampy, coastal plain and many flat offshore islands, including the Bijagós Archipelago.

The country has a tropical climate, with one dry season from December to May and a rainy season from June to November.

History, Politics and Economy

Portugal appointed a governor to administer Guinea-Bissau and the Cape Verde Islands in 1836, but in 1879 the territories separated and Guinea-Bissau became a colony, then called Portuguese Guinea. Development was slow, partly because the territory did not attract settlers on the same scale as the African colonies of Angola and Mozambique.

In 1956, African nationalists in Portuguese Guinea and Cape Verde founded the African Party for the Independence of Guinea and Cape Verde (PAIGC). Because Portugal seemed determined to hang on to its overseas territories, the PAIGC began a guerrilla war in 1963. By 1968, it held two-thirds of the country. In 1972, a rebel National Assembly, elected by the people in the PAIGC-controlled areas, voted to make the country independent as Guinea-Bissau.

Following independence in 1975, Guinea-Bissau's leaders favoured union with Cape Verde. This objective was abandoned in 1980, following a military coup. The country ceased to be a one-party state in 1991 and elections were held in 1994. In 1998 an army rebellion sparked a civil war. This ended in victory for the army rebels in May 1999 with Chief Brigadier Ansumane Mane heading an 'interim' government.

Guinea-Bissau is a poor country. Most farming is at subsistence level. Major crops include beans, coconuts, groundnuts and maize.

AREA	23%, Malinke 12%,
36,120 sq km [13,946 sq mls]	Mandyako 11%, Pepel 10%
POPULATION	**LANGUAGES**
1,206,000	Portuguese (official),
CAPITAL (POPULATION)	Crioulo
Bissau (145,000)	**RELIGIONS**
GOVERNMENT	Traditional beliefs 54%,
Interim government	Islam 38%
ETHNIC GROUPS	**CURRENCY**
Balante 27%, Fulani (or Peul)	CFA franc = 100 centimes

BAHRAIN

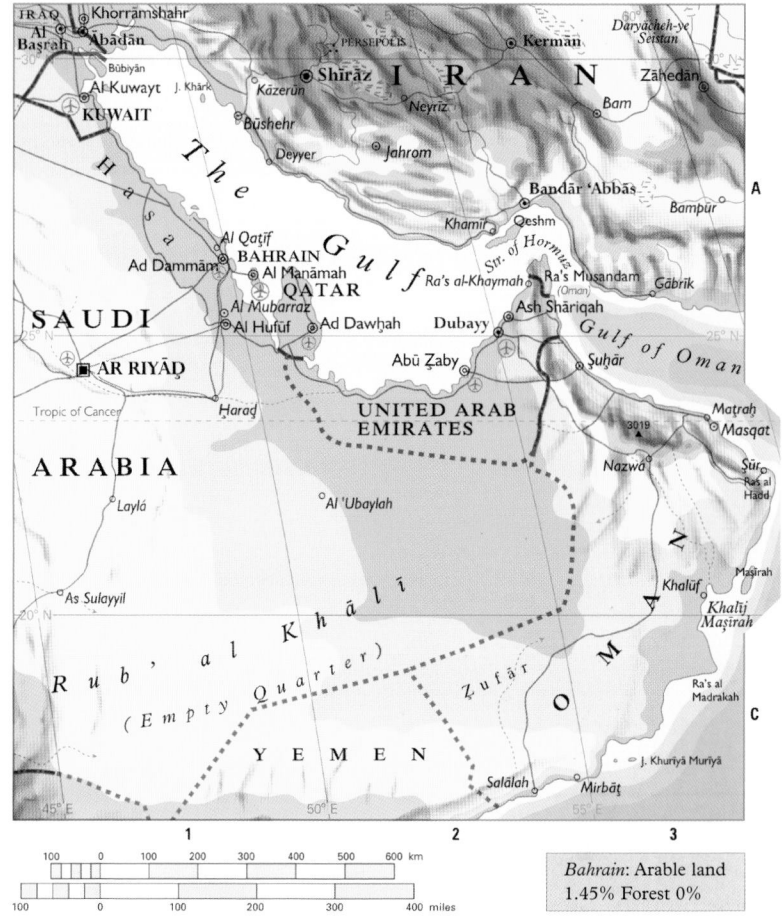

The Emirate of Bahrain, whose flag dates from about 1932, consists of the island of Bahrain and 34 smaller islands. A causeway links the island of Bahrain to the Saudi Arabian mainland. Most of the land is desert, but there are freshwater springs on the north coast of Bahrain island. Summers are hot and humid, with average temperatures of 33°C [91°F] in July, while winters are mild, with average January temperatures of about 17°C [63°F].

Bahrain has long been a centre of trade, but was largely undeveloped until the discovery of oil in 1932. The Al Khalifa Arabs took over Bahrain from Persia in 1728, and have ruled ever since. Bahrain became a British protectorate in 1861. Britain withdrew from the Gulf region in 1971 and Bahrain became independent.

In 1973, Bahrain adopted a new constitution, creating a National Assembly with 30 elected members. However, relations between the Al Khalifa family and the National Assembly proved unsuccessful and the National Assembly was dissolved in 1975. Since then, the country has been ruled by the Emir and a cabinet, headed by a prime minister, whom he appoints. Bahrain faces several problems. Tension between the Sunni and the majority Shiite population, who favour the establishment of an Islamic republic, has been apparent since before independence. During the First Gulf War, Iran responded to Bahrain's support for Iraq by reiterating claims to the territory. In 1996, relations with Iran again deteriorated when Iran was accused of supporting an underground Shiite organization, Hezbollah Bahrain. In 1997, relations improved when Bahrain received a visit from Iran's foreign minister. Throughout the 1990s, a dispute with Qatar rumbled on over Qatar's claims to the Hawar Islands, an oil- and natural gas-rich group which Bahrain controlled and planned to develop with tourist facilities.

The people of Bahrain enjoy one of the highest standards of living in the Gulf region. The adult literacy rate is 85%, while free medical care is available. The country's prosperity is based on oil, which accounted for 60% of the exports in 1995. However, when production waned in the 1970s, Bahrain diversified into other sectors: its aluminium-smelting plant is the Gulf's largest non-oil industrial complex, while banking, communications and leisure are also important. Bahrain is now a major banking and financial centre, serving the Gulf region. Construction, fishing, manufacturing and transport have all been developed in recent years.

Bahrain: Arable land 1.45% Forest 0%

AREA	Indian and Pakistani 25%,
678 sq km [262 sq mls]	other Arab 4%,
POPULATION	European 3%
616,000	**LANGUAGES**
CAPITAL (POPULATION)	Arabic (official),
Manama (Al Manámah, 143,000)	English
GOVERNMENT	**RELIGIONS**
Monarchy (emirate) with a cabinet	Muslim (Shiite majority) 85%,
appointed by the Emir	Christian 7%
ETHNIC GROUPS	**CURRENCY**
Bahraini Arab 68%, Persian,	Bahrain dinar = 1,000 fils

KUWAIT

The State of Kuwait, whose flag dates from 1961, consists of a mainland area and several offshore islands at the head of the Gulf. Kuwait City lies on a fine natural harbour called Kuwait Bay. Kuwait is a low-lying country covered mostly by desert scrub. Average annual rainfall is around 125 mm [5 in] and most rain occurs between November and March. Winters are mild, but summers are hot, with average temperatures of 33°C to 35°C [91°F to 95°F] between June and September. Inland, the high humidity makes conditions extremely uncomfortable.

The area was thinly populated until about 1710, when people from Arabia arrived. They built the port that later became Kuwait City and elected the head of the Al Sabah family as their ruler. The family rules the country today. British interest in the area began in the late 18th century. In 1899, Britain became responsible for the territory's defence and, in 1914, it became a British protectorate. Drilling for oil began in 1936 and oil was produced commercially in 1946. Kuwait soon became a prosperous oil exporter and became independent in 1961.

In August 1990, Iraq invaded Kuwait, claiming that it was legally part of Iraq. When Iraq refused to withdraw, a US-led multinational force invaded on 17 January 1991, expelling the Iraqis, but not before they had set fire to more than 500 oil wells, causing massive pollution, and destroying almost all industrial and commercial installations. Kuwait's revenge was directed mainly at the huge contingent of Palestinian, Jordanian and Yemeni immigrant workers, who were seen as pro-Iraq. In 1994, Iraq recognized Kuwait's independence and boundaries. A partly elected National Council was established in 1990, and, in 1999, proposals were made to give women the vote and permit them to run for office.

The economy is based on oil, which accounted for 95% of the exports in 1995. Kuwait has about 10% of the world's known reserves. The country has a small fishing fleet but, otherwise, most food is imported. The shortage of water has inhibited the development of industries. About three-quarters of Kuwait's drinking water is either imported or produced from sea water in desalination plants.

AREA	non-Kuwaiti Arab
17,820 sq km [6,880 sq mls]	36%, various Asian 20%
POPULATION	**LANGUAGES**
1,913,000,000	Arabic 78%, Kurdish 10%,
CAPITAL (POPULATION)	Farsi 4%
Kuwait City (Al Kuwayt, 189,000)	**RELIGIONS**
GOVERNMENT	Muslim 90% (Sunni 63%),
Constitutional monarchy	Christian 8%, Hindu 2%
ETHNIC GROUPS	**CURRENCY**
Kuwaiti Arab 44%,	Kuwaiti dinar = 1,000 fils

OMAN

The Sultanate of Oman occupies the south-eastern corner of the Arabian Peninsula. It also includes the tip of the Musandam Peninsula, overlooking the Strait of Hormuz. The fertile coastal plain along the Gulf of Oman, called Al Battinah, is backed by mountains. Inland are deserts, including part of the Rub' al Khali (Empty Quarter). While most of the coast along the Arabian Sea is barren, the south-east province of Zufar (also called Dhofar) has tropical vegetation. The south-east has an average annual rainfall of up to 630 mm [25 in], but most of Oman has less than 150 mm [6 in]. In summer, temperatures may reach 54°C [129°F], but winters are mild to warm.

Oman was an important trading area in ancient times. The Portuguese conquered its ports in the early 16th century, but local Arabs forced them out in 1650. The Al Bu Said family came to power in the 1740s and has ruled the country ever since. British influence dates back to the end of the 18th century, when the two countries entered into the first of several treaties. The country became independent in 1971.

Until 1970, Oman was a backward country compared to its oil-rich Gulf neighbours. However, when, with British collusion, Sultan Said bin Taimur was deposed by his son, Qaboos, Oman made substantial strides. It saw an end to the civil war against Yemen-backed separatist guerrillas in the province of Zufar and enjoyed an expanding economy based on oil reserves far larger than expected when production began in 1967. An absolute ruler, Qaboos forewent the prestigious projects favoured by Arab leaders to concentrate on social programmes. Even so, by 1995, only one in three adults was literate, while defence and security were taking nearly 18% of the gross national product.

The World Bank classifies Oman as an 'upper-middle-income' developing country. Oil accounts for over 90% of Oman's export revenues. Huge natural gas deposits were discovered in 1991 that were equal to all the finds of the previous 20 years. Although less than 1% of the land is cultivated, agriculture provides a living for half of the people. Major crops include alfalfa, bananas, coconuts, dates, tobacco and wheat.

AREA	**ETHNIC GROUPS**
212,460 sq km [82,031 sq mls]	Omani Arab 74%, Pakistani 21%
POPULATION	**LANGUAGES**
2,364,000	Arabic (official), Baluchi, English
CAPITAL (POPULATION)	**RELIGIONS**
Muscat (Masqat, 350,000)	Islam (Ibadiyah) 86%,
GOVERNMENT	Hinduism 13%
Monarchy with consultative	**CURRENCY**
council	Omani rial = 100 baizas

QATAR

The State of Qatar occupies a low, barren peninsula which juts out from the Arabian peninsula into the Gulf. The land is mostly stony desert, with some barren salt flats. There is a lack of freshwater supplies and much of the drinking water is distilled sea water, produced in desalination plants.

From May to September it is extremely hot, with temperatures soaring to 49°C [120°F], but winters are mild to warm. Average annual rainfall total seldom exceeds 100 mm [4 in]. Most rain falls in winter.

During the mid-19th century, members of the Al-Thani family became the leaders of Qatar and this remains the ruling family today. The Ottoman Turks took over in the late 19th century, but the peninsula became a British protectorate in 1916. Oil exploration began in 1930 and oil was struck in 1939, although commercial exploitation did not begin until 1949.

Qatar became independent in 1971 when it chose not to unite with the United Arab Emirates. In 1982, Qatar, Bahrain, Kuwait, Oman, Saudi Arabia and the United Arab Emirates united to form the Gulf Co-operation Council, which is concerned with such matters as defence and economic development. In 1995, Qatar signed a security pact with the United States. A bloodless coup also occurred in 1995, when the heir apparent, Sheikh Hamad, deposed his father, Sheikh Khalifa bin Hamad Al-Thani, while Khalifa was abroad.

The high standard of living in Qatar derives from oil revenue, which accounts for more than 80% of the country's export revenues. Money from oil sales has been used to diversify the economy. Industries have been set up, while wells have been dug to develop agriculture. The economy is heavily dependent on an immigrant workforce, notably from the Indian subcontinent and poor states in south-western Asia.

AREA	**ETHNIC GROUPS**
11,000 sq km [4,247 sq mls]	Southern Asian 34%, Qatari 20%
POPULATION	**LANGUAGES**
697,000	Arabic (official)
CAPITAL (POPULATION)	**RELIGIONS**
Doha (Ad Dawhah, 243,000)	Sunni Muslim 92%, Christian,
GOVERNMENT	Hindu
Constitutional absolute	**CURRENCY**
moncarchy	Qatar riyal = 100 dirhams

UNITED ARAB EMIRATES

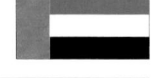

The United Arab Emirates (UAE) is largely flat, stony or sandy desert, with occasional oases. Average annual rainfall is less than 130 mm [5 in]. In summer (May to September), temperatures may soar to 49°C [120°F] with high humidity on the coast. Winters are warm to mild.

European contact began in the 16th century when trading posts were set up along the coast. The Arab states which now form the UAE began to develop in the 18th century. In 1820, conflict between the states led Britain to force the states to sign the first of a series of truces. This led the region to become known as the Trucial States. Oil was discovered in 1958. The Trucial States became independent in 1971 when six of the seven Trucial States – Abu Dhabi, Ajman, Dubai, Fujairah, Sharjah and Umm-al-Qaiwain – opted to form a single country called the United Arab Emirates, with Ras al-Khaimah joining in 1972. Instead of joining to form nine states, Bahrain and Qatar chose independence.

The economy is based on oil production, and oil makes up more than 90% of the country's exports. Because of its mineral wealth, the UAE has one of the highest per capita GNPS in Asia. However, many of the people are immigrants from southern Asia, south-western Asia and northern Africa, including Egypt. Less than 1% of the land is farmed, but such crops as dates are grown at oases. Some desert nomads herd camels, goats and sheep. Fishing is important along the coast. The country has four international airports.

AREA	**ETHNIC GROUPS**
83,600 sq km [32,278 sq mls]	Arab 87%, Indo-Pakistani 9%,
POPULATION	Iranian 2%
2,303,000	**LANGUAGES**
CAPITAL (POPULATION)	Arabic (official), English
Abu Dhabi (Abū Zāby, 928,000)	**RELIGIONS**
GOVERNMENT	Muslim 95%, Christian 4%
Federation of seven emirates,	**CURRENCY**
each with its own government	Dirham = 100 fils

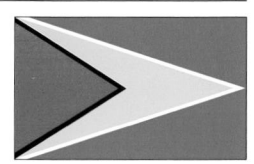

Guyana's flag was adopted in 1966 when the country became independent from Britain. The colours symbolize the people's energy in building a new nation (red), their perseverance (black), minerals (yellow), rivers (white), and agriculture and forests (green).

Geography and Climate

Guyana faces the Atlantic Ocean in north-eastern South America. The coastal plain is flat and mainly below sea level. Dykes (sea walls) prevent flooding. Inland is a hilly region which rises to the Pakaraima Mountains, part of the Guiana Highlands, in the west. Other highlands are in the south. Guyana has several grand waterfalls, including the King George VI Falls (488 m [1,601 ft]).

The climate is hot and humid, although temperatures are lower in the highlands in the west and south. The rainfall is heavy, occurring on more than 200 days a year.

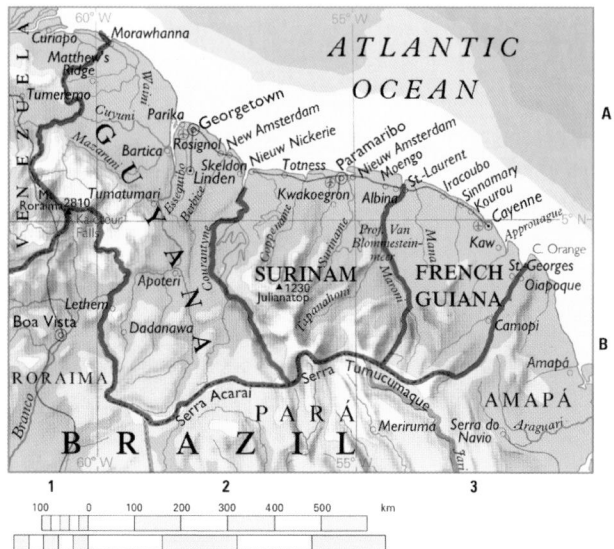

AREA
214,970 sq km [83,000 sq mls]
POPULATION
820,000
CAPITAL (POPULATION)
Georgetown (200,000)
GOVERNMENT
Multiparty republic
ETHNIC GROUPS
Asian Indian 49%, Black 36%,
Mixed 7%, Amerindian 7%,
Portuguese, Chinese
LANGUAGES
English (official)
RELIGIONS
Christianity (Protestant 34%,
Roman Catholic 18%),
Hinduism 34%, Islam 9%
CURRENCY
Guyana dollar = 100 cents

Politics and Economy

British Guiana became independent in 1966. A black lawyer, Forbes Burnham, became the first prime minister. Burnham died in 1985 and was succeeded by Hugh Desmond Hoyte. Hoyte was defeated in presidential elections in 1993 by the East Indian Cheddi Jagan. Following Jagan's death in 1997, his wife Janet was elected president. She retired in 1999.

Guyana is a developing country. Its resources include gold, bauxite, forests and fertile soils. Agriculture employs 27% of the people. Sugar cane and rice are the leading crops.

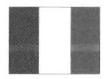

FRENCH GUIANA

Geography and Climate

French Guiana is the smallest country in mainland South America. The coastal plain is swampy in places, but dry areas are cultivated. Inland lies a plateau, with the low Tumachumac Mountains in the south. Most of the rivers run north towards the Atlantic Ocean.

French Guiana has high temperatures throughout the year. Rainfall is heavy, especially between December and June, but it is dry between August and October.

History, Politics and Economy

The area became a French colony in the late 17th century, and in the 1790s was used by France as a penal settlement for political prisoners. In 1946, French Guiana became an overseas department of France, and in 1974 also became an administrative region. An independence movement developed in the 1980s, but most of the people want to retain links with France and continue to obtain financial aid for development.

AREA	Chinese 14%,
90,000 sq km	French 10%,
[34,749 sq mls]	Haitian 7%
POPULATION	**LANGUAGES**
162,000	French (official)
CAPITAL	**RELIGIONS**
(POPULATION)	Christianity
Cayenne (42,000)	(Roman
GOVERNMENT	Catholic 80%,
Overseas department	Protestant 4%)
of France	**CURRENCY**
ETHNIC GROUPS	French franc =
Creole 42%,	100 centimes

SURINAM

Geography and Climate

The Republic of Surinam lies between French Guiana and Guyana in north-eastern South America. The once swampy coastal plain has been drained and now consists of farmland.

Surinam has a humid climate. Temperatures are high all year round.

History, Politics and Economy

In 1667, Britain handed Surinam to the Dutch in return for New Amsterdam (now the state of New York). Slave revolts hampered development and in the early 19th century Britain and the Netherlands disputed the ownership of the area. The British gave up their claims in 1813. Slavery was abolished in 1863, and Indian and Indonesian labourers were introduced to work on plantations. Surinam became independent in 1975, but the economy was weakened when thousands of skilled people emigrated to the Netherlands. In 1992, the government negotiated a peace agreement with the *boschneger*, descendants of African slaves, who had launched a struggle against the government. But instability continued and, in 1993, the Netherlands stopped its

financial aid after an EC report stated that Surinam had failed to reform the economy and control inflation.

AREA	Indonesian 14%, Black 9%,
163,270 sq km [63,039 sq mls]	Amerindian 3%, Chinese 3%,
POPULATION	Dutch 1%
427,000	**LANGUAGES**
CAPITAL (POPULATION)	Dutch (official), Sranantonga
Paramaribo (201,000)	**RELIGIONS**
GOVERNMENT	Christianity (Roman Catholic
Multiparty republic	23%, Protestant 19%,
ETHNIC GROUPS	Hinduism 27%, Islam 20%
Asian Indian 37%, Creole	**CURRENCY**
(mixed White and Black) 31%,	Surinam guilder = 100 cents

HAITI – SEE CARIBBEAN SEA, PAGES 71–76;
HONDURAS – SEE GUATEMALA, PAGES 110–111

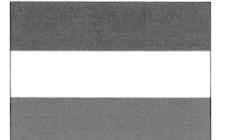

Hungary's flag was adopted in 1919. A state emblem was added in 1949 and removed in 1957. The colours of red, white and green had been used in the Hungarian arms since the 15th century. The tricolour design became popular during the 1848 rebellion against Habsburg rule.

Arable 51.4% Permanent crops 2.44% Forest 19.1%

Geography

The Hungarian Republic is a landlocked country in central Europe. The land is mostly low-lying and drained by the Danube (Duna) and its tributary, the Tisza. Most of the land east of the Danube belongs to a region called the Great Plain (Nagyalföld), which covers about half of Hungary.

West of the Danube is a hilly region, with some low mountains, called Transdanubia. This region contains the country's largest lake, Balaton. In the north-west is a small, fertile and mostly flat region called the Little Plain (Kisalföld).

Climate

Hungary lies far from the moderating influence of the sea. As a result, summers are warmer and sunnier, and the winters colder than in Western Europe.

HUNGARY (BUDAPEST)

The plains of Hungary have warm summers and cold winters with snow between 30 and 40 days. At Budapest, maximum temperatures exceed 20°C [68°F] from May to September, with the minimum below freezing from December to February. A double maximum of rainfall occurs. The first is in summer when convectional storms are most active. The second in November is a feature of the climate to the south-west.

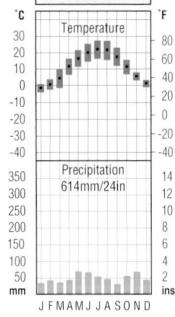

History

Magyars first arrived in the area from the east in the 9th century. In the 11th century, Hungary's first king, Stephen I, made Roman Catholicism the official religion. Hungary became a powerful kingdom, but in 1526 it was defeated by Turkish forces, who later occupied much of Hungary. In the late 17th century, the Austrian Habsburgs conquered Hungary. In 1867, Austria granted Hungary equal status in a 'dual monarchy', called Austria-Hungary. In 1914, a Bosnian student killed the heir to the Austria-Hungary throne. This led to World War I, when Austria-Hungary fought alongside Germany. Defeat in 1918

led to nearly 70% of its territory being apportioned by the Treaty of Versailles to Czechoslovakia, Yugoslavia and Romania. Some 2.6 million Hungarians live in these countries today. The government hoped to regain these territories by siding with Hitler's Germany in World War II, but the result was the occupation of the Red Army in late 1944. Elections were held in 1945 and, in 1946, the country was declared a republic. Although the smallholders had won a clear majority of the votes in the 1945 elections, the Communists gradually took control even after failing to win a majority of the votes cast in new elections in 1947.

Politics

Hungary became a Communist state in 1949, with a constitution based on that of the Soviet Union. The first leader of the Communist government was Mathias Rákosi, who was replaced in 1953 by Imre Nagy. Nagy sought to relax Communist policies and was forced from office in 1955. He was replaced by Rákosi in 1956 and this led to a major uprising in which many Hungarians were killed or imprisoned. Nagy and his co-workers were executed for treason in 1958.

Janos Kádár came to power in the wake of the suppression, but his was a relatively progressive leadership, including an element of political reform and a measure of economic liberalism. However, in the late 1970s, the economic situation worsened and new political parties started to appear.

Kádár resigned in 1989 and the central Committee of the Socialist Workers' Party (the Communist Party) agreed to sweeping reforms, including the introduction of a pluralist system and a democratic parliament, which had formally been little more than a rubber-stamp assembly. The trial of Imre Nagy and his co-workers was declared unlawful and their bodies were reburied with honour in June 1989.

In 1990, Hungarians voted into office a centre-right coalition headed by the Democratic Forum. In 1994, the Hungarian Socialist Party (made up of ex-Communists) won a majority and governed in coalition with the Alliance of Free Democrats. However, in elections in 1998, no single party won a majority. Victor Orbán, leader of the centre-right Federation of Young Democrats–Hungarian Civic Party (Fidesz-MPP), was asked to form a government. In 1999, Hungary joined NATO.

Economy

Before World War II, Hungary's economy was based mainly on agriculture. But the Communists set up many manufacturing industries. The new factories were owned by the government, as also was most of the land. However, from the late 1980s, the government has worked to increase private ownership. This change of policy caused many problems, including inflation and high rates of unemployment.

Manufacturing is the most valuable activity. The major products include aluminium made from local bauxite, chemicals, electrical and electronic goods, processed food, iron and steel, and vehicles.

AREA	Gypsy, German, Croat,
93,030 sq km [35,919 sq mls]	Romanian, Slovak
POPULATION	**LANGUAGES**
10,208,000	Hungarian (official)
CAPITAL (POPULATION)	**RELIGIONS**
Budapest (1,909,000)	Christianity (Roman Catholic
GOVERNMENT	64%, Protestant 23%,
Multiparty republic	Orthodox 1%), Judaism 1%
ETHNIC GROUPS	**CURRENCY**
Magyar (Hungarian) 98%,	Forint = 100 fillér

ICELAND

Iceland's flag dates from 1915. It became the official flag in 1944, when Iceland became fully independent. The flag, which uses Iceland's traditional colours, blue and white, is the same as Norway's flag, except that the blue and red colours are reversed.

Geography

The Republic of Iceland, in the North Atlantic Ocean, is closer to Greenland than Scotland. Iceland sits astride the Mid-Atlantic Ridge, the geological boundary between Europe and North America. The island is slowly getting wider as the ocean is stretched apart by the forces of plate tectonics.

Iceland has around 200 volcanoes and eruptions are frequent. An eruption under the Vatnajökull ice-cap in 1996 created a subglacial lake which subsequently burst, causing severe flooding. Geysers and hot springs are other volcanic features. During the thousand years that Iceland has been settled, between 150 and 200 volcanic eruptions have occurred. Ice-caps and glaciers cover about one-eighth of the land. The only habitable regions are the coastal lowlands.

Climate

Although it lies far to the north, Iceland's climate is moderated by the warm waters of the Gulf Stream. The port of Reykjavik is ice-free all the year round.

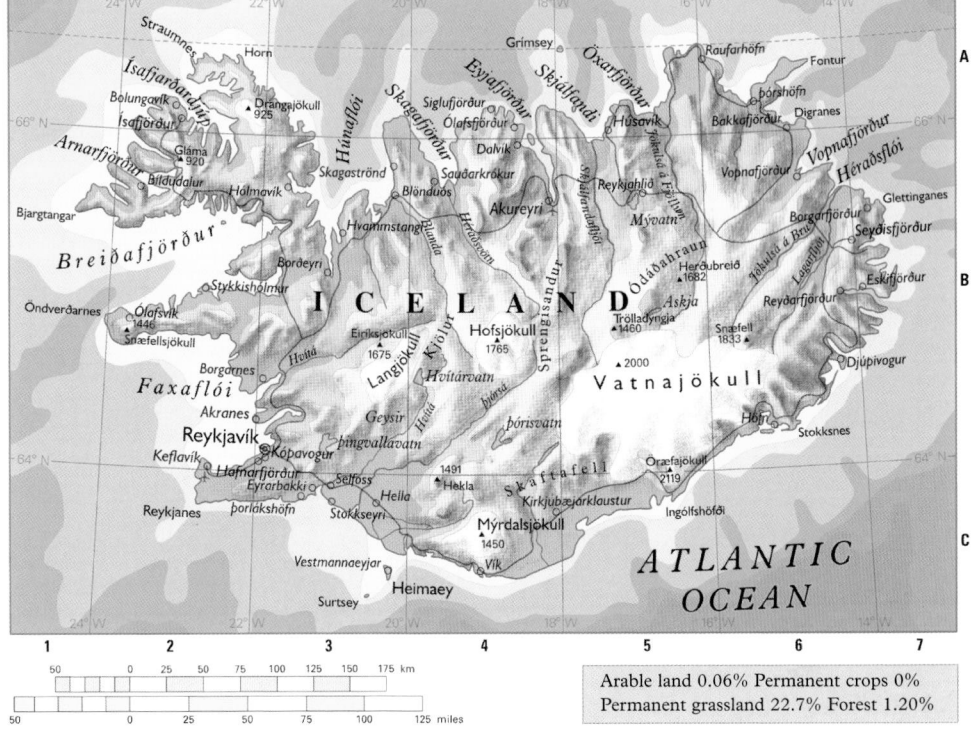

Arable land 0.06% Permanent crops 0%
Permanent grassland 22.7% Forest 1.20%

ICELAND (REYKJAVIK)

Due to the influence of the Gulf Stream, Iceland is relatively warm. The coldest month at Reykjavik, January, is normally 0°C [32°F], while the warmest month is July at 12°C [54°F]. Precipitation falls on 200 days a year, 65 of them as snow. There is very high rainfall on the south coast, exceeding 800 mm [32 in], with half of this in the north. Sunshine levels are low, being 5–6 hours from May to August. Gales are frequent.

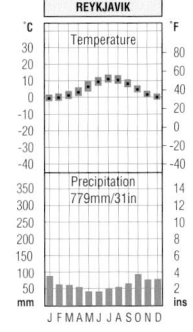

History

Norwegian Vikings colonized Iceland in the AD 870s and the population grew as more settlers arrived from Norway, and from the Viking colonies in the British Isles. In 930, the settlers founded the oldest, and what is thought to be the world's first, parliament (the *Althing*). One early settler was Eric the Red, a Viking who sailed to Greenland in about 982 and founded another colony there in about 985.

Iceland was an independent country until 1262 when, following a series of civil wars, the Althing recognized the rule of the king of Norway. When Norway united with Denmark in 1380, Iceland came under the rule of Danish kingdoms. Life on Iceland was never easy. The Black Death, which swept the island in 1402, claimed two-thirds of the population, while, in the late 18th century, volcanic eruptions destroyed crops, farmland and livestock, causing a famine. Then, during the Napoleonic Wars in the early 19th century, food supplies from Europe failed to reach the island and many people starved.

When Norway was separated from Denmark in 1814, Iceland remained under Danish rule. In the late 19th century, the invention of motorized craft, which changed the fishing industry, led to mounting demands for self-government. In 1918, Iceland was acknowledged as a sovereign state, but remained united with Denmark through a common monarch. During World War II, when Germany occupied Denmark, British and American troops landed in Iceland to protect it from invasion by the Germans. Finally, following a referendum in which 97% of the people voted to cut all ties with Denmark, Iceland became a fully independent republic on 17 June 1944.

Politics

Fishing, on which Iceland's economy is based, is a major political issue. From 1975, Iceland extended its territorial waters to 200 nautical miles, causing skirmishes between Icelandic and British vessels. The issue was resolved in 1977 when Britain agreed not to fish in the disputed waters. Another problem developed in the late 1980s when Iceland reduced the allowable catches in its waters, because overfishing was causing the depletion of fishing stocks, especially of cod. The reduction of the fish catch led to a slowdown in the economy and, eventually, to a recession, though the economy recovered in the mid-1990s when the conservation measures appeared to have been successful. In the late 1990s, Iceland had outstanding disputes over fishing rights with Norway, Russia, the Faroe Islands and Canada.

Iceland has no armed forces of its own. However, it joined the North Atlantic Treaty Organization (NATO) in 1949 and, under a NATO agreement, the United States maintains a base on the island.

Economy

Iceland has few resources besides the fishing grounds which surround it. Fishing and fish processing are major industries which dominate Iceland's overseas trade. Barely 1% of the land is used to grow crops, mainly root vegetables and fodder for livestock. However, 23% of the country is used for grazing sheep and cattle. Iceland is self-sufficient in meat and dairy products. Vegetables and fruits are grown in greenhouses heated by water from hot springs. Manufacturing is important. Products include aluminium, cement, clothing, electrical equipment, fertilizers and processed foods.

AREA	Danish 1%
103,000 sq km [39,768 sq mls]	**LANGUAGES**
POPULATION	Icelandic (official)
271,000	**RELIGIONS**
CAPITAL (POPULATION)	Christianity (Evangelical
Reykjavik (103,000)	Lutheran 92%,
GOVERNMENT	other Lutheran 3%,
Multiparty republic	Roman Catholic 1%)
ETHNIC GROUPS	**CURRENCY**
Icelandic 97%,	Króna = 100 aurar

The Indian flag was adopted shortly after the country gained independence from Britain in 1947. The saffron (orange) represents renunciation, the white represents truth, and the green symbolizes mankind's relationship with nature. The central wheel represents dynamism and change.

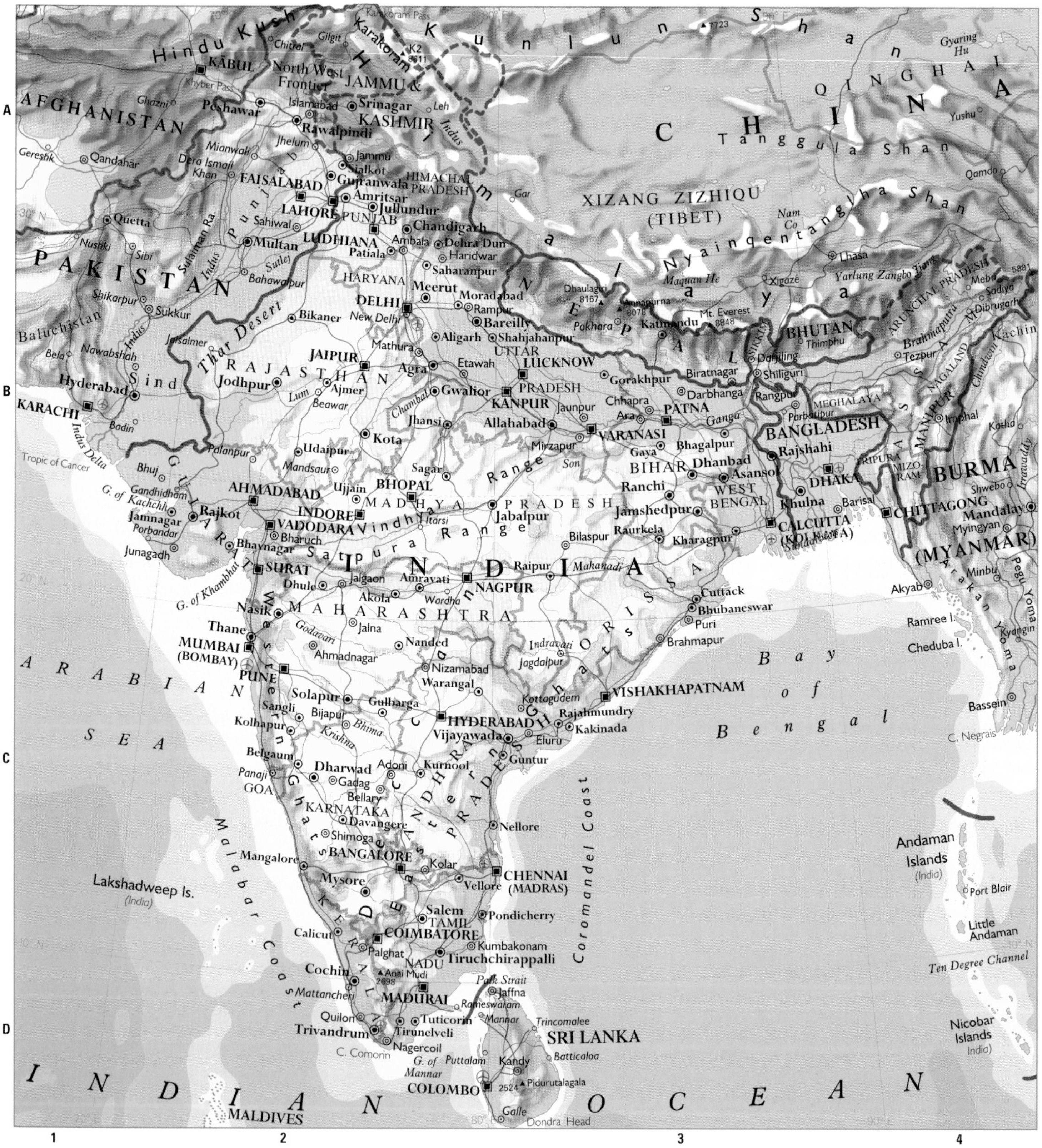

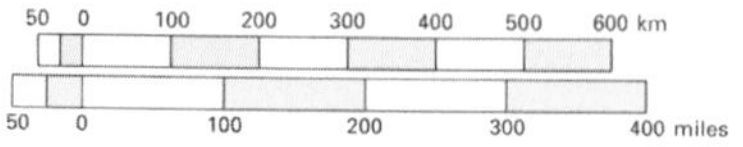

Arable land 55.9% Permanent crops 1.19%
Permanent grassland 3.83% Forest 23%

Geography

The Republic of India, the world's seventh largest country, extends from high in the Himalayas, through the Tropic of Cancer, to the warm waters of the Indian Ocean at Cape Comorin. In 1999, the population was reported to have topped the 1 billion mark. India is the world's second most populous nation after China, and the largest democracy.

The foothills of the Himalayas, the world's youngest and highest mountain range, form a stunning backdrop for northern India, rising abruptly from the plains in towering ranks. The Himalayas include Kanchenjunga, India's highest peak at 8,598 m [28,208 ft] above sea level on the Sikkim-Nepal border. In the north-west, harsh dry highlands, sparsely occupied by herders, stretch northwards to the everlasting snows of the Karakoram Range in Kashmir. Beyond lie alpine meadows, lakes and woodlands, often grazed in summer by seasonally migrant flocks from lower villages. The Vale of Kashmir is a fertile land, claimed by both India and Pakistan. In the east lies the high plateau of Meghalaya ('abode of the clouds'), Assam, where the slopes of the Himalayas are ablaze with rhododendrons and magnolias, and the forested ridges of Nagaland, Manipur and Nizoram.

The great plains form a continuous strip from the Punjab eastwards. The fertile soils of the Punjab have provided prosperity for the Sikh farmers of the Punjab and Haryana states. Somewhat similar landscapes extend east to the plains surrounding Delhi, the third largest city which stands on the banks of the Jumna (Yamuna) river. The vast and fertile northern plains, India's most densely populated and developed region, are drained by the Indus, Ganges and Brahmaputra rivers, all of which rise in the snowy highlands to the north. To the east again lie the lowlands of Uttar Pradesh, which are crisscrossed by the Ganges and Jumna rivers and their many tributaries. Along the border with Nepal lie the *terai*, or foothill plains.

Near the Bangladesh border, the Ganges begins to divide into distributary streams, while still receiving tributaries from the north and west. West Bengal consists largely of rice- and jute-growing lands flanking the distributary streams that flow south to become the Hoogly, on which Calcutta, India's largest city, is situated. The Sundarbans, a World Heritage site of mangrove and swamp forests at the seaward margin of the Ganges Delta, extend eastwards into Bangladesh.

South-west of the Punjab Plains lies the Great Indian, or Thar, Desert. Its western fringes are in Pakistan, but it contains a broad tract of dunes in the north-western lowlands of Rajasthan, India's largest state. The desert ranges from perennially dry wastelands of shifting sands to areas capable of cultivation in wet years. Rajasthan rises in a series of steps to the jagged, bare range of brightly coloured sandstone ridges, the Aravallis, that extend north-eastwards and end at Delhi.

South and west of the Aravallis lie the cotton-growing lands of tropical Gujerat, where Ahmadabad is the chief city. Between the gulfs of Khambat and Kachchh is the low peninsular plateau of Kathiawar. Between this plateau and the Pakistan border stretches the desert salt marsh of the Rann of Kachchh. Formerly an arm of the Arabian Sea, this region is still occasionally flooded by exceptionally heavy rains. South-east of the Aravallis is an area of transition between the great plains of the north and the uplands and plateaux of southern India. First come the Chambal badlands – wastelands south of Agra which have been partly reclaimed – and then rough hill country extending south-eastwards to Rewa. The Son River provides a lowland corridor through the hills south of Rewa. Eastwards again the hills are forested around Ambikapur and Lohardaga. Industrial development becomes important around the coalfields of the Damodar Valley, centred on Asanol.

South of the Chambal River and of Indore, the sandy plateau of the north gives way to forested hills, split by the broad corridors of the Narmada and Tapi rivers. Tribal lands persist in the Satpura Range, and the Ajanta Range to the south is noted for primitive cave paintings near Aurangabad. From here to the south, the soils are mainly volcanic. Mumbai (formerly Bombay), India's second largest city, lies on the coastal lowlands by a broad estuary, among rice fields dotted with low lava ridges. Fishing villages line the shore, while inland rise the stepped, forested slopes and pinnacles of peninsular India's longest mountain range, the Western Ghats (Sahyadri). South of Goa, formerly a Portuguese enclave which retains a Portuguese atmosphere, to Trivandrum in the south, the coast is a kaleidoscope of farms, orchards and fishing villages. Here the Ghats are edged with granite, gneiss, sandstone and schist, and clad in dense rainforest.

To the east, the peninsula is drier, with rolling plateaux given over to such dry crops as millet and pulses. The central plateau, called the Deccan, is bordered in the east by the Eastern Ghats, which meet the Western Ghats in the southern Nilgiri Hills. The longest rivers in southern India, including the Godavari, Krishna and Cauvery, drain eastwards from the Western Ghats and empty into the Bay of Bengal. Shorter rivers flow westwards down the slopes of the Western Ghats into the Arabian Sea.

Climate

India has three seasons. The weather during the cool season, which extends from October to February, is mild in the northern plains, but southern India remains hot, though temperatures are a little lower than for the rest of the year. Temperatures on the northern plains sometimes soar to 49°C [120°F] during the hot season from March to the end of June. The monsoon season starts in the middle of June and continues into September. At this time, moist south-easterly winds from the Indian Ocean bring heavy rains to India. Darjeeling in the north-east has an average annual rainfall of 3,040 mm [120 in], but parts of the Great Indian Desert in the north-west have only 50 mm [2 in] of rain a year. The monsoon rains are essential for India's farmers. If they arrive late, crops may be ruined. If the rainfall is considerably higher than average, floods may cause great destruction.

INDIA (DELHI)

The summer rains, typical of the Indian monsoon, arrive later and are less intense at Delhi than in lower parts of the Ganges Valley. From November to May, it is sunny and temperatures increase rapidly until the arrival of the rains in June. During the rainy season the temperature is uniformly hot. The latter part of the year is sunny, dry and cooler. Night temperatures from December to February are usually below 10°C [50°F].

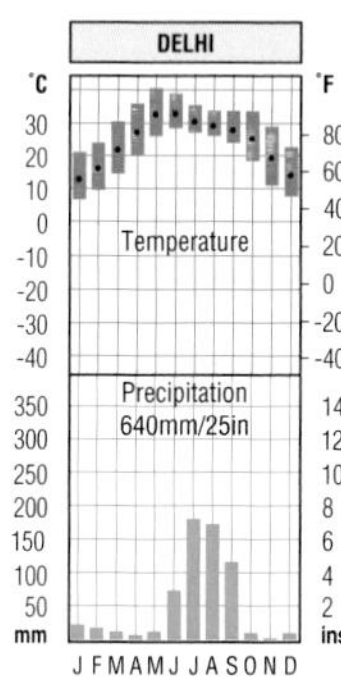

Vegetation

India has a wide range of vegetation types. Palm trees abound on the southern Deccan Plateau, with bamboo, rosewood, ironwood and teak in the Western Ghats. By contrast, the vegetation in the Great Indian Desert is very limited. In uncultivated parts of the northern plains, there are forests of many kinds of trees, of which the sal (*Shorea robusta*) is typical. The north-east, including Assam, has luxuriant plant life, with broadleaved forests and bamboo. The Himalayan foothills have an equally varied vegetation, with such trees as alders, birches, junipers, laurels, maples, rhododendrons and dwarf willows. The mountains have a range of vegetation zones depending on the altitude.

The Himalayas

The Earth's highest mountain range, with an average height of 6,100 m [20,000 ft], the Himalayas are structurally part of the high plateau of Central Asia. The range stretches over 2,400 km [1,500 mls] from the Pamirs in the north-west to the Chinese border in the east. There are three main ranges: Outer, Middle and Inner; in Kashmir, the Inner Himalayas divide into five more ranges, including the Ladakh Range and the Karakorams. The world's highest mountain, Mt Everest (8,848 m [29,029 ft]), is on the Tibet-Nepal border; next highest is K2 (8,611 m [28,251 ft]) in the Karakorams, and there are a further six peaks over 8,000 m [26,250 ft].

The name comes from the Nepalese words *him* ('snows') and *alya* ('home of'), and the mountains are very much revered in Hindu mythology as the abode of gods. Recently, the hydroelectric potential of the range has inspired more secular reverence: enormous quantities of energy could be tapped, although certainly at some cost to one of the world's most pristine environments.

The Himalayas began to rise over 50 million years ago, as two continental plates, the Indian and the Eurasian, collided. As the Indian plate moved northwards, it tended to underride the Eurasian plate, squeezing up the intervening sediments on the floor of the now vanished Tethys Sea into a fold mountain range. The northwards movement of the Indian plate continues, which accounts for the frequent earthquakes in the region. The process is further thickening what is already about the thickest part of the Earth's crust. In parts of the Himalayas, the crust is 90 km [56 mls] deep, as compared to an average continental thickness of 35 to 40 km [22–25 mls].

History

India's early settlers were scattered across the subcontinent in Stone Age times. The first of its many civilizations began to flourish in the Indus Valley in what is now Pakistan and western India around 4,500 years ago, and in the Ganges Valley from about 1500 BC, when Aryan people arrived in India from central Asia. The earlier, darker-skinned people, the Dravidians, moved southwards, ahead of the Aryans, and their descendants are now the main people in southern India.

In 326 BC, the armies of Alexander the Great conquered north-western India, but the area was soon reconquered by Indians. In 321 BC, after Alexander's death, the Maurya Empire, named after its first leader, Chandragupta Maurya, was founded in India. Its most famous ruler was Emperor Asoka, who built up a huge, though loosely held empire with its centre at Pataliputra (modern Patna). However, military conquest ceased after Asoka, a Hindu, converted to Buddhism. After the death of Asoka in 232 BC, the empire broke up into smaller areas. Buddhism became the common religion of India, but Hinduism finally became the majority religion by around AD 800.

In about AD 120, the Scythians occupied northern India and founded the Kushan Dynasty, but from 320 to about 500, northern India was ruled by the native Indian Gupta Dynasty. This period saw a great revival in the arts, learning and science. Another Hindu-Buddhist civilization developed in southern India at the same time. The southern Indians were a sea-faring people and they spread their culture into South-east Asia. From about 450, India was conquered by many invaders who introduced their cultures. Important among these was the arrival of Muslim armies from Arabia in the 8th century, and other armies from Persia and Afghanistan in the 11th century. Islam became an important religion in the north-west. A Muslim sultanate established in Delhi in 1206 continued until 1526. The Tartar armies of Tamerlane, a Muslim conqueror from central Asia, raided India in 1398 and briefly occupied Delhi. Another central Asian leader, Babar, a descendant of Tamerlane and Genghis Khan, invaded India in 1526 and founded the Mogul Dynasty. A new religion, Sikhism, which combined elements of Hinduism and Islam, emerged during Mogul rule and it became especially strong in Punjab.

The Mogul Empire began to decline in the 18th century as the British East India Company was gradually taking control of India.

Kashmir

Until Indian independence in August 1947, Kashmir's mainly Muslim population was ruled, under British supervision, by a Hindu maharaja. Independence obliged the maharaja to choose between Pakistan or India; hoping to preserve his own independence, he refused to make a decision. In October, a ragtag army of Pathan tribesmen invaded from newly created Pakistan. Looting industriously, the Pathans advanced slowly, and India had time to rush troops to the region. The first Indo-Pakistan war resulted in a partition that satisfied neither side, with Pakistan holding one-third and India the remainder, with a 60% Muslim population. Despite promises, India has refused to allow a plebiscite to decide the province's fate. Two wars in 1965 and 1972 failed to alter greatly the 1948 cease-fire lines.

During the late 1980s, Kashmiri nationalists in the Indian-controlled area began a violent campaign in favour of either secession to Pakistan, or local independence. India responded by flooding Kashmir with troops and accusing Pakistan of intervention. During the 1990s, Pakistani-backed guerrillas attempted to break India's hold on the Srinagar Valley, Kashmir's most populous region, and tension increased following the testing of nuclear devices by India and Pakistan in 1998.

In 1999, armed troops occupied strategic positions on the Indian side of the cease-fire line. India said that the troops were Pakistani soldiers, while Pakistan claimed that they were Muslim rebels with local support in Kashmir. Fighting ensued, arousing fears of a war between India and Pakistan. In July, most of the forces had withdrawn from Indian-held Kashmir, but tension continued as militants sporadically attacked Indian forces.

Vasco da Gama had reached Calicut in southern India in 1498 and, for a period, the Portuguese were in control of the ports along the west coast of India. The Portuguese were followed by traders from the Netherlands, France and England. The British East India Company was formed in 1600 and, by 1757, following the victory by one of the company's military leaders, Robert Clive, in the Battle of Plassey, it became the leading power in India. In the first half of the 19th century, the Company extended its rule into Afghanistan, Burma and Nepal, together with Punjab and Kashmir. But, under the India Act of 1858, the British government took over the territories occupied by the East India Company, which then became known as British India.

An independence movement began in India after the Sepoy Rebellion (1857–9) and, in 1885, the Indian National Congress was founded. It was initially a debating society but it developed into a political movement advocating self-government. In 1906, Indian Muslims, concerned that Hindus formed the majority of the members of the Indian National Congress, founded the Muslim League. In 1920, Mohandas K. Gandhi, a former lawyer, became leader of the Indian National Congress which soon became a mass movement. Gandhi's policy of non-violent disobedience proved highly effective, and in response Britain began to introduce political reforms. In the 1930s, the Muslim League, led by Muhammad Ali Jinnah, called for the establishment of a Muslim state, called Pakistan.

Politics

In 1946, after the end of World War II, Britain offered independence to India providing that it could agree on a form of government. But differences between the religious groups delayed progress until, in 1947, it was agreed that British India be partitioned into the mainly Hindu India and the Muslim Pakistan. Both countries became independent in August 1947, but the events were marred by mass slaughter as Hindus and Sikhs fled from Pakistan, and Muslims flocked to Pakistan from India. In the boundary disputes and reshuffling of minority populations that followed, some 1 million lives were lost. Since 1947–8, events have done little to promote good relations between the countries.

India's first prime minister was Jawaharlal Nehru, a close associate of Gandhi, who was assassinated in 1948 by a Hindu extremist who hated him for his tolerant attitude towards Muslims. The country adopted a new constitution in 1948 making the country a democratic republic within the Commonwealth, and elections were held in 1951 and 1952. The government sought to develop the economy and raise living standards at home, while, on the international stage, Nehru won great respect for his policy of non-alignment and neutrality. But he was criticized in 1961 when India invaded three small Portuguese colonies – Damao (now Daman), Diu and Goa – and integrated them into India. In mid-1987, Goa was made India's 25th state, while Daman and Diu remained a territory.

India also came into conflict with China during armed border disputes in 1959 and 1962, when a cease-fire was agreed. This conflict shattered the people's confidence in neutrality, though it was the disputed status of Kashmir that became India's thorniest security problem. The border disputes led to an increase in defence spending and this, in turn, slowed down India's economic development.

Following Nehru's death in 1964, Lal Bahadur Shastri, a cabinet member under Nehru, became prime minister. He led India during a dispute with Pakistan that led to border fighting. After Shastri's death in 1966, Nehru's daughter, Mrs Indira Gandhi, took office. Her Congress Party lost support because of food shortages, unemployment and other problems. In 1971, India helped the people of East Pakistan achieve their independence from West Pakistan to become Bangladesh. India tested its first atomic bomb in 1974, but it pledged to use nuclear power for peaceful purposes only. In 1975, Mrs Gandhi was found guilty of using illegal methods during the parliamentary elections in 1971. Mrs Gandhi refused to resign and governed by emergency rule, imposing censorship on the press. The government passed measures that made Mrs Gandhi's actions in 1971 legal and the Supreme Court overthrew her conviction.

In 1977, Mrs Gandhi lost her seat in parliament and her Congress Party was defeated by the Janata Party, a coalition led by Morarji R.

Desai. Disputes in the Janata Party led to Desai's resignation in 1979 and, in 1980, Congress-I (the I standing for Indira) won the elections. Mrs Gandhi again became prime minister, but her government faced many problems, especially those arising from communal conflict. One problem was that many Sikhs wanted more control over the Punjab, and Sikh radicals began to commit acts of violence to draw attention to their cause. In 1984, armed Sikhs occupied the sacred Golden Temple, in Amritsar. In response, Indian troops attacked the temple, causing much damage and deaths. This led to further violent acts and, in October, 1984, two of Mrs Gandhi's Sikh guards assassinated her.

Mrs Gandhi's son, Rajiv, was chosen to succeed his mother as prime minister, but, in 1989, Congress lost its majority in parliament and Rajiv resigned as prime minister. He was succeeded by Vishwanath Pratap Singh, of the National Front, a coalition of opposition parties. Singh resigned in 1990 and was succeeded by Chandra Shekhar of the socialist Janata Party. During elections in 1991, Rajiv Gandhi was assassinated by Tamil extremists. But Congress went on to win the elections and P. J. Narasimha Rao became prime minister. Congress was defeated at elections in 1996 and a series of short-lived coalition governments ruled until fresh elections were held in 1998 and 1999, and Atal Behari Vajpayee of the Bharatiya Janata Party (Hindu nationalists) became prime minister, leading a 24-party coalition called the National Democratic Alliance.

India is a vast country with an enormous diversity of cultures and problems of organization. It has more than a dozen major languages, each with a rich literature, and many minor languages. Hindi, the national language, and the Dravidian languages of the south (Kannada, Tamil, Telugu and Malayam) are Indo-European. Sino-Tibetan languages are spoken in the north and east, while smaller groups speak residual languages in forested hill refuges. Ethnic origins also differ and the mosaic of religions adds variety – and potential conflict.

Hinduism is all-pervasive, though the country is officially secular and Buddhism is slowly reviving in the country of its origin – the Buddha was born on the borders of India and Nepal. Jainism is strong in the merchant towns around Mt Abu in the Aravallis hills north of Ahmadabad. Islam has contributed many mosques and monuments, the Taj Mahal being the best known. The forts of Delhi, Agra and many other northern cities, together with the ghost city of Fatehpur Sikri, near Agra, are Islamic relics of the Mogul period. Despite the formation of Pakistan, India retains a large Muslim minority. Now it is the turn of the Punjab's militant Sikhs who seek separation. Christian influences include elaborate Roman Catholic churches and many schools and colleges set up by various denominations. The British also left their mark. Mumbai (Bombay) and Calcutta both have some notable Victoriana, while the capital New Delhi is a planned Edwardian city.

Cultural differences are further complicated by huge gaps in the standards of living between labourers, prosperous farmers, the educated urban middle classes and slum dwellers. India's complex society always appears on the verge of collapse into chaos. But despite its size, population and potential for division, it manages to remain intact.

Economy

According to the World Bank, India is a 'low-income' developing country. While it ranked 15th in its total gross national product in 1997, its per capita GNP of US $370 placed it among the world's poorest countries. Despite initiatives, including the Green Revolution, its socialist policies have failed to raise the living standards of the poor. In the 1990s, the government introduced private enterprise policies to stimulate growth.

India ranks fifth in the world in total farm area and agriculture employs about 60% of the people. About 80% of farmland is devoted to growing grains, such as rice, wheat, millet and sorghum, and pulses, such as beans and chickpeas. India ranks second only to China in rice and wheat production, it leads the world in millet production, and it ranks second in producing sorghum. India also leads the world in producing bananas, hemp, jute, lemons and limes, mangos and tea. India has more cattle and buffaloes than any other country. But, because they are sacred to Hindus, these animals are not killed for meat except by Muslims and Christians. Water buffaloes are important as sources of milk, while the hides of dead animals are used to make

Administrative regions of India

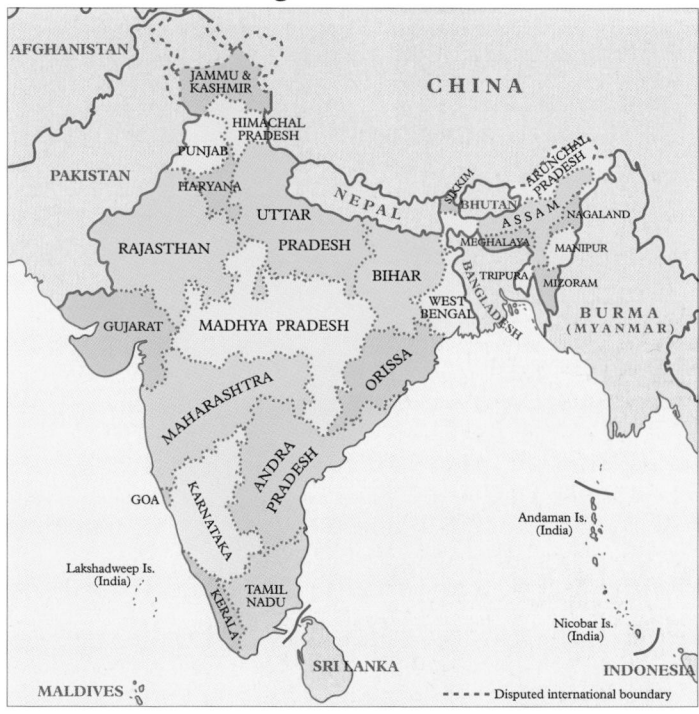

leather. India is also a major sheep and poultry producer.

India's mineral resources include coal and petroleum. It also has large deposits of bauxite, chromite, iron ore, manganese, and many smaller deposits of other minerals. Many of its minerals are used in domestic industries. In 1947, India was already a partially industrialized country and it has made great strides during a succession of five-year plans that provided explicitly for both nationalized and private industry. The Damodar coalfield around Asanol has been developed and several new fields opened. The Tata family's steel city of Jamshedpur, itself now diversified by other industries, has been complemented by new state plants and planned towns in Durgapur and other places, in collaboration with Britain, Germany and the former Soviet Union. Major engineering factories have been built at Bangalore, Vishakhapatnam and elsewhere, including the ill-fated Bhopal, where a major industrial accident occurred in 1984. Oil refineries have been set up at Barauni in the north-east and also near Mumbai, for new fields developed in the north-west. Several nuclear power stations are now in operation and the country's massive hydroelectric potential is being developed, but not without controversy about the effect of new dams on the environment. Small-scale and high-tech electronic industries are also important.

Clothing and textile industries employ more workers than any other industries. Other industries produce cement, chemicals, dyes, medicines, fertilizers, food products, paper, sugar, sewing machines, tractors, transport equipment and wood products. India also imports rough diamonds and exports jewellery. Major exports include agricultural and allied products, cut and polished diamonds, including jewellery, garments, machinery, transport equipment, metal products, iron and steel, and electronic components. Leading trading partners include the United States, Germany and Japan.

AREA	other (mainly Mongoloid) 3%
3,287,590 sq km	**LANGUAGES**
[1,269,338 sq mls]	Hindi 30% and English
POPULATION	(both official), Telugu 8%,
984,000,000	Bengali 8%, Marati 8%,
CAPITAL (POPULATION)	Urdu 5%, Tamil, many
New Delhi (part of Delhi,	local languages
301,000)	**RELIGIONS**
GOVERNMENT	Hinduism 83%, Islam (Sunni
Multiparty federal republic	Muslim) 11%, Christianity 2%,
ETHNIC GROUPS	Sikhism 2%, Buddhism 1%
Indo-Aryan (Caucasoid) 72%,	**CURRENCY**
Dravidian (Aboriginal) 25%,	Rupee = 100 paisa

INDIAN OCEAN

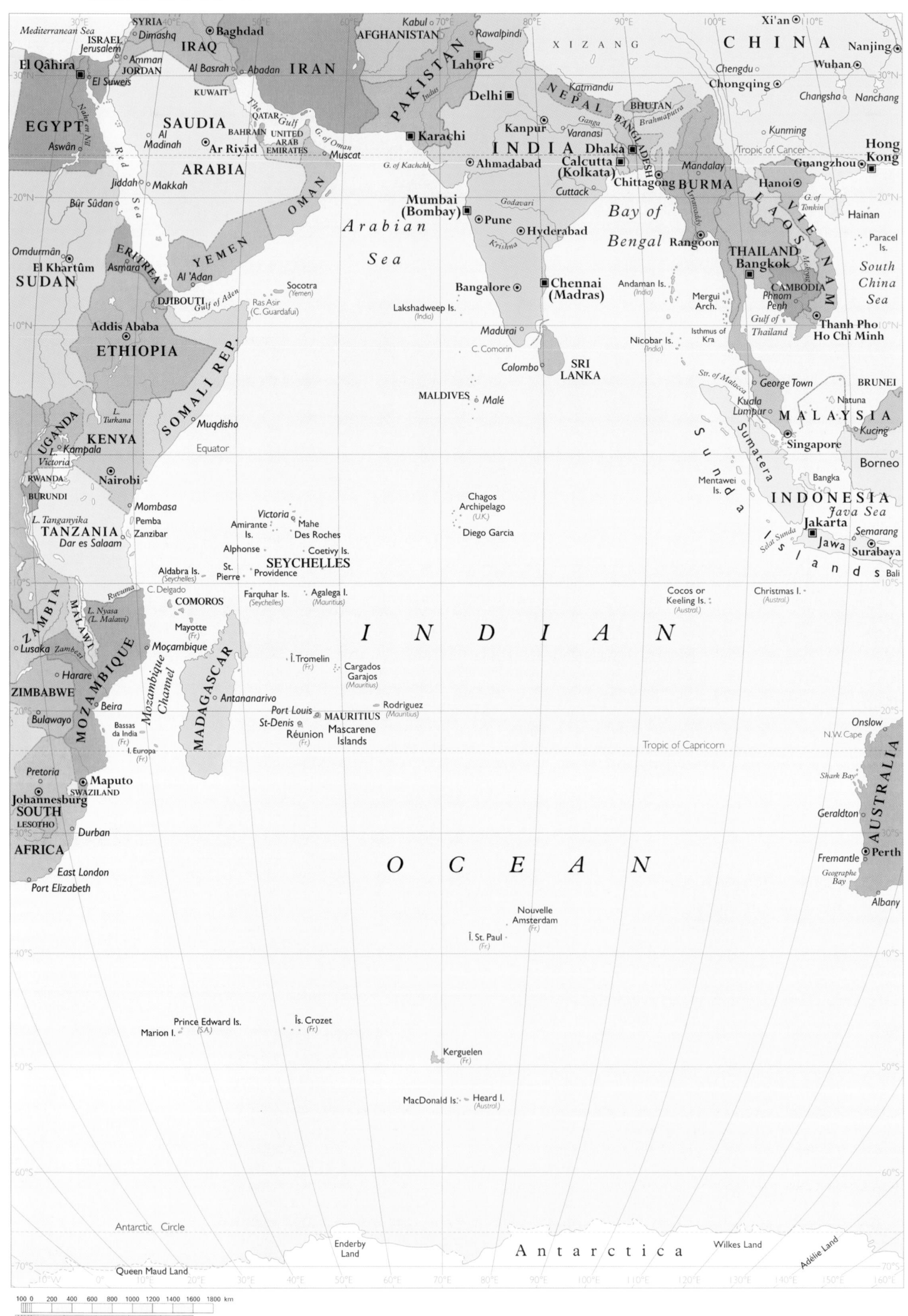

Mediterranean Sea
SYRIA
ISRAEL
Jerusalem
Dimashq
Amman
JORDAN
El Qâhira
El Suweis
EGYPT
Aswân
Bûr Sûdan
Jiddah
Makkah
SUDAN
El Khartûm
Omdurmân
Addis Ababa
ETHIOPIA
UGANDA
Kampala
RWANDA
BURUNDI
L. Tanganyika
TANZANIA
Dar es Salaam
ZAMBIA
Lusaka
ZIMBABWE
Bulawayo
Harare
Pretoria
Johannesburg
SOUTH
AFRICA
Maputo
SWAZILAND
LESOTHO
Durban
East London
Port Elizabeth

IRAQ
Baghdad
Al Basrah
Abadan
KUWAIT
Al Madinah
Ar Riyâd
ARABIA
SAUDIA
BAHRAIN
QATAR
UNITED ARAB EMIRATES
OMAN
YEMEN
Al 'Adan
ERITREA
Asmara
DJIBOUTI
Gulf of Aden
Ras Asir (C. Guardafui)
SOMALI REP.
KENYA
Nairobi
Mombasa
Pemba
Zanzibar
L. Turkana
L. Victoria
Muqdisho
Equator

AFGHANISTAN
Kabul
Rawalpindi
Lahore
Delhi
Karachi
IRAN
The Gulf
G. of Oman
Muscat
PAKISTAN
Indus
Ahmadabad
G. of Kachchh
Mumbai (Bombay)
Pune
Hyderabad
Bangalore
Chennai (Madras)
INDIA
Kanpur
Varanasi
Ganga
NEPAL
Katmandu
Calcutta (Kolkata)
BHUTAN
BANGLADESH
Dhaka
Chittagong
Godavari
Krishna
Madurai
C. Comorin
Colombo
SRI LANKA
MALDIVES
Malé
Lakshadweep Is. (India)
Arabian Sea
Socotra (Yemen)

XIZANG
Chengdu
CHINA
Xi'an
Nanjing
Wuhan
Chongqing
Changsha
Nanchang
Kunming
Tropic of Cancer
Hong Kong
Guangzhou
Hanoi
Hainan
G. of Tonkin
Paracel Is.
South China Sea
Brahmaputra
Mandalay
Irrawaddy
BURMA
Rangoon
Cuttack
Bay of Bengal
Andaman Is. (India)
Mergui Arch.
Nicobar Is. (India)
Isthmus of Kra
THAILAND
Bangkok
Gulf of Thailand
CAMBODIA
Phnom Penh
Thanh Pho Ho Chi Minh
LAOS
VIETNAM
Mekong

Str. of Malacca
George Town
Kuala Lumpur
MALAYSIA
Kucing
Singapore
Sumatera
BRUNEI
Natuna
Borneo
Bangka
INDONESIA
Java Sea
Jakarta
Jawa
Semarang
Surabaya
Bali
Mentawei Is.
Sunda Islands
Selat Sunda

Victoria
Mahe
Amirante Is.
Des Roches
Alphonse
Coetivy Is.
SEYCHELLES
Providence
St. Pierre
Aldabra Is. (Seychelles)
C. Delgado
Farquhar Is. (Seychelles)
Agalega I. (Mauritius)
COMOROS
Mayotte (Fr.)
Moçambique
Ruvuma
L. Nyasa (L. Malawi)
MALAWI
MOZAMBIQUE
Mozambique Channel
Zambezi
Beira
Bassas da India (Fr.)
I. Europa (Fr.)
MADAGASCAR
Antananarivo
Î. Tromelin (Fr.)
Cargados Garajos (Mauritius)
Port Louis
St-Denis
Réunion (Fr.)
MAURITIUS
Rodriguez (Mauritius)
Mascarene Islands

Chagos Archipelago (U.K.)
Diego Garcia

INDIAN

Cocos or Keeling Is. (Austral.)
Christmas I. (Austral.)

OCEAN

Tropic of Capricorn

Onslow
N.W. Cape
Shark Bay
AUSTRALIA
Geraldton
Fremantle
Perth
Geographe Bay
Albany

Nouvelle Amsterdam (Fr.)
Î. St. Paul (Fr.)

Prince Edward Is. (S.A.)
Marion I.
Îs. Crozet (Fr.)

Kerguelen (Fr.)

MacDonald Is.
Heard I. (Austral.)

Antarctic Circle

Queen Maud Land
Enderby Land
Antarctica
Wilkes Land
Adélie Land

100 0 200 400 600 800 1000 1200 1400 1600 1800 km
100 0 200 400 600 800 1000 miles

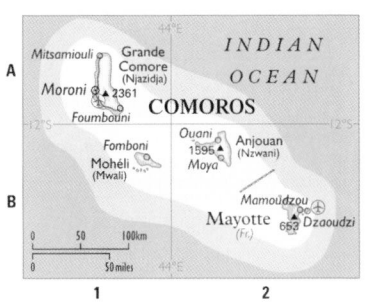

COMOROS

The Federal Islamic Republic of the Comoros is an island nation at the northern end of the Mozambique Channel. Formerly French, the territory became independent in 1974, but Mayotte, the fourth and eastern-most of the large islands, seceded and became a French Territorial Collectivity. In 1997, two other islands, Anjouan and Mohéli, announced their secession, but the government refused to accept these acts and tried to negotiate greater autonomy for the islands. In 1999, the military overthrew the elected president. Comoros is poor and depends on subsistence agriculture.

AREA	CAPITAL
2,230 sq km [861 sq mls]	Moroni
POPULATION	CURRENCY
545,000	Com. franc = 100 centimes

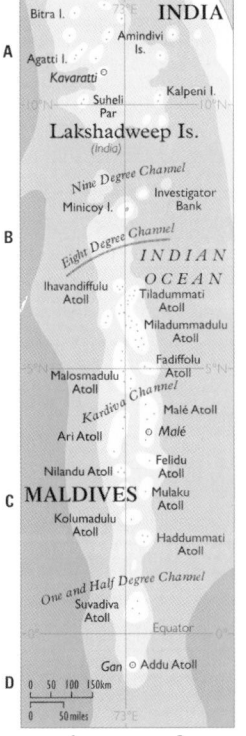

MALDIVES

The Republic of the Maldives comprises some 1,900 small, low-lying islands and atolls, 202 of which are inhabited. They are scattered along a broad north–south line, starting about 650 km [400 mls] west-south-west of the southern tip of India.

Sri Lanka settled the islands in about 500 BC. For a time under Portuguese and, later, Dutch rule, they became a British protectorate in 1887. They achieved independence in 1965. The country became a republic when the sultan was deposed in 1968. The chief crops are bananas, coco-nuts, mangos, sweet potatoes and spices, but much food is imported. Fishing is important, but tourism has displaced it as the mainstay of the economy.

AREA	CAPITAL
298 sq km [115 sq mls]	Malé
POPULATION	CURRENCY
290,000	Rufiyaa = 100 laari

MAURITIUS

The Republic of Mauritius consists of the main island situated 800 km [500 mls] east of Madagascar, Rodrigues and several small islands. The main island, fringed with coral reefs, rises to a high lava plateau. The climate is tropical with heavy rains in winter. French from 1715, and British from 1810, the territory gained independence as a constitutional monarch, in 1992. The islands suffer tensions between the Indian majority, who are descended from contract workers brought in after the end of slavery in 1834, and the Creole minority.

Sugar-cane plantations cover extensive areas of Mauritius and, although the sugar industry has declined, sugar is still exported. Tea and tobacco are also grown. The expansion of textiles and clothing, together with growth in tourism, have to some extent off-set the decline in sugar, although Mauritius remains heavily in debt.

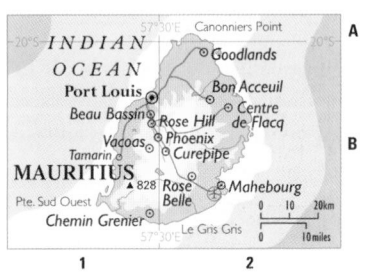

AREA	CAPITAL
1,860 sq km	Port Louis
[718 sq mls]	CURRENCY
POPULATION	Maur. rupee
1,168,000	= 100 cents

RÉUNION

Réunion, which lies south-west of Mauritius, has a mountainous, wooded centre, which is surrounded by a fertile coastal plain. The climate is similar to Mauritius. French since 1638, it became a French Department in 1946, though there is increasing pressure on France for independence.

Sugar cane dominates the economy, though vanilla, perfume oils and tea also produce revenue. Tourism is the big hope for the future, but unemployment is high and the island relies on French aid.

AREA
2,510 sq km
[969 sq mls]
POPULATION
705,000
CAPITAL
St-Denis

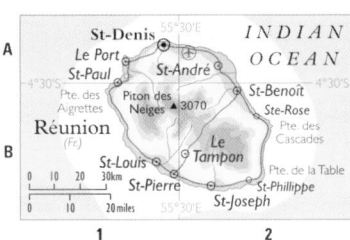

SEYCHELLES

The Republic of Seychelles includes a group of four large and 36 small granitic islands, plus a wide scattering of coralline islands, 14 of them inhabited, lying to the south and west. French from 1756 and British from 1814, the islands gained their independence in 1976. A year later, a coup resulted in the setting up of a one-party socialist state that several attempts failed to remove. Multiparty elections were held in 1992 and France-Albert René, who had been elected president unopposed in 1979 and 1984, was re-elected president under a new constitution adopted in 1993. René was again re-elected president in 1998.

Experiencing a tropical oceanic climate, the Seychelles produces copra, cinnamon and tea, although rice is imported. Fishing and luxury tourism are the two main industries.

Formerly part of the British Indian Ocean Territory, Farquhar, Des Roches and Aldabra (famous for its unique wildlife) were returned to the Seychelles in 1976. The British Indian Ocean Territory now consists only of the Chagos Archipelago, with Diego Garcia, the largest island, supporting a US Navy base.

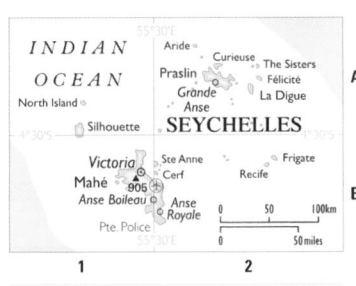

AREA	CAPITAL
455 sq km	Victoria
[176 sq mls]	CURRENCY
POPULATION	Seych. rupee
79,000	= 100 cents

This flag was adopted in 1945, when Indonesia proclaimed itself independent from the Netherlands. The colours, which date back to the Middle Ages, were adopted in the 1920s by political groups in their struggle against Dutch rule.

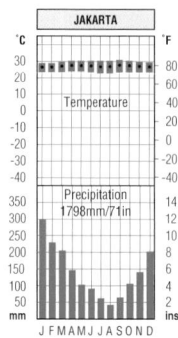

Geography

The Republic of Indonesia is an island nation in South-east Asia. In all, Indonesia contains about 13,600 islands, less than 6,000 of which are inhabited. Three-quarters of the country is made up of five main areas: the islands of Sumatra, Java and Sulawesi (Celebes), together with Kalimantan (southern Borneo) and Irian Jaya (western New Guinea). These five areas also contain 80% of the population. Java is especially densely populated. Although it covers only 7% of the land area, it contains more than half of the country's people. Most of the islands stand on the continental shelves and have extensive coastal low-lands, though Sulawesi and the chain of islands between Java and Irian Jaya rise from deep water. All are mountainous, because this is a region of great crustal activity. More than 200 volcanoes, including Krakatoa (Pulau Rakata) are scattered along the arc formed by Sumatra, Java and the Lesser Sunda Islands. However, the highest peak is Puncak Jaya, which reaches 5,029 m [16,499 ft] above sea level.

Climate

Indonesia straddles the Equator and has a hot and humid climate. Only Java and the Sunda Islands have a relatively dry season. There are also many variations caused by the exposure of the islands to the monsoon system. From December to March, the moist prevailing wind blows from mainland Asia to Indonesia. Between mid-June and October, the prevailing wind brings dry air from Australia.

INDONESIA (JAKARTA)

Temperatures in Jakarta are almost constantly high all year round. Daytime temperatures reach 29°C to 31°C [84–88°F], only cooling to around 23°C [73°F] at night. This is due to its location on the shores of the hot Java Sea, the uniform intensity of the midday sun and the duration of daylight, with an average of more than 6 hours of sunshine a day. Rainfall is heaviest in summer, most falling in thunderstorms.

History

The first major empire in the area was the maritime power of Sri Vijaya, centred on Palembang. It held sway from the 8th to the 13th centuries. In the 14th century, it was replaced by the kingdom of Madjapahit, which was centred on east-central Java. European influences grew from the 16th century and the area came under the domination of the Dutch East India Company. The Dutch government took over the islands in 1799. Freedom movements starting in the early 20th century found full expression under Japanese occupation in World War II, and Indonesia declared its independence when Japan surrendered in 1945. After four years of intermittent fighting, the Dutch recognized the country as a sovereign state in 1949.

Politics

Indonesia's first president, the anti-Western Achmed Sukarno, plunged his country into chaos and poverty, while costly military adventures drained the treasury. In 1962, Indonesian troops invaded Dutch New Guinea (Irian Jaya), and between 1963 and 1966 Sukarno attempted to destabilize the fledgling Federation of Malaysia through incursions into northern Borneo. In 1967, Sukarno was toppled by General Suharto, following Sukarno's suppression of an allegedly Communist-inspired uprising that cost 80,000 lives. Suharto's military regime, with US assistance, brought a period of relatively rapid economic growth, but was characterized by corruption. Nationalist demonstrations led the Portuguese to leave their colony of East Timor in 1975. Later that year, Indonesian troops invaded East Timor against the opposition of local nationalists, who demanded independence. But the Indonesian government maintained control through repressive policies.

A depression in 1997 hit the economies of most nations in eastern Asia, including Indonesia. In 1998, the country was on the brink of civil war and, in May, President Suharto was forced to stand down. He was succeeded by his deputy, Bacharuddin Jusuf Habibie. In June 1999, Habibie's ruling Golkar Party was defeated and, in October, the parliament elected Abdurrahman Wahid as president, and Megawati Sukarnoputri (daughter of President Sukarno) as vice-president.

In August 1999, the people of East Timor voted in favour of independence, though their victory was marred by violence instigated by anti-independence militias backed by government forces. Following this vote, secessionist groups in Aceh province, in northern Sumatra, also called for an independence referendum, while unrest caused by the Free Papua Movement occurred in Irian Jaya. To add to Indonesia's problems, Muslim-Christian clashes, unconnected with secessionist aspirations, broke out in the Moluccas at the end of 1999.

Economy

According to the World Bank, Indonesia is a 'lower-middle-income' developing country. The country has fertile soils and agriculture employs more than half of the population. Rice is the chief food crop, but bananas, cassava, coconuts, groundnuts, maize, spices and sweet potatoes are also important. The chief cash crops, most of which are grown on large plantations, include coffee, palm oil, rubber, sugar cane, tea and tobacco. Fishing is another important source of food. Forests cover much of the land and forest products, including valuable tropical hardwoods, are important products.

Indonesia has very important mineral reserves, including oil, and Indonesia is a member of OPEC (Organization of Petroleum Exporting Countries). Other minerals include bauxite, coal, iron ore, nickel and tin. Manufacturing has increased greatly since the 1970s, especially on the island of Java. Oil and natural gas refining is a major industry, together with the manufacture of steel, aluminium, cement, fertilizers, paper and textiles. The chief exports include oil and natural gas, wood products, manufactured goods, rubber and coffee.

AREA	Madurese 4%,
1,904,570 sq km [735,354 sq mls]	more than 300 others
POPULATION	**LANGUAGES**
212,942,000	Bahasa Indonesian (official),
CAPITAL (POPULATION)	others
Jakarta (11,500,000)	**RELIGIONS**
GOVERNMENT	Islam 87%, Christianity 10%
Multiparty republic	(Roman Catholic 6%),
ETHNIC GROUPS	Hinduism 2%, Buddhism 1%
Javanese 39%, Sundanese 16%,	**CURRENCY**
Indonesian (Malay) 12%,	Indonesian rupiah = 100 sen

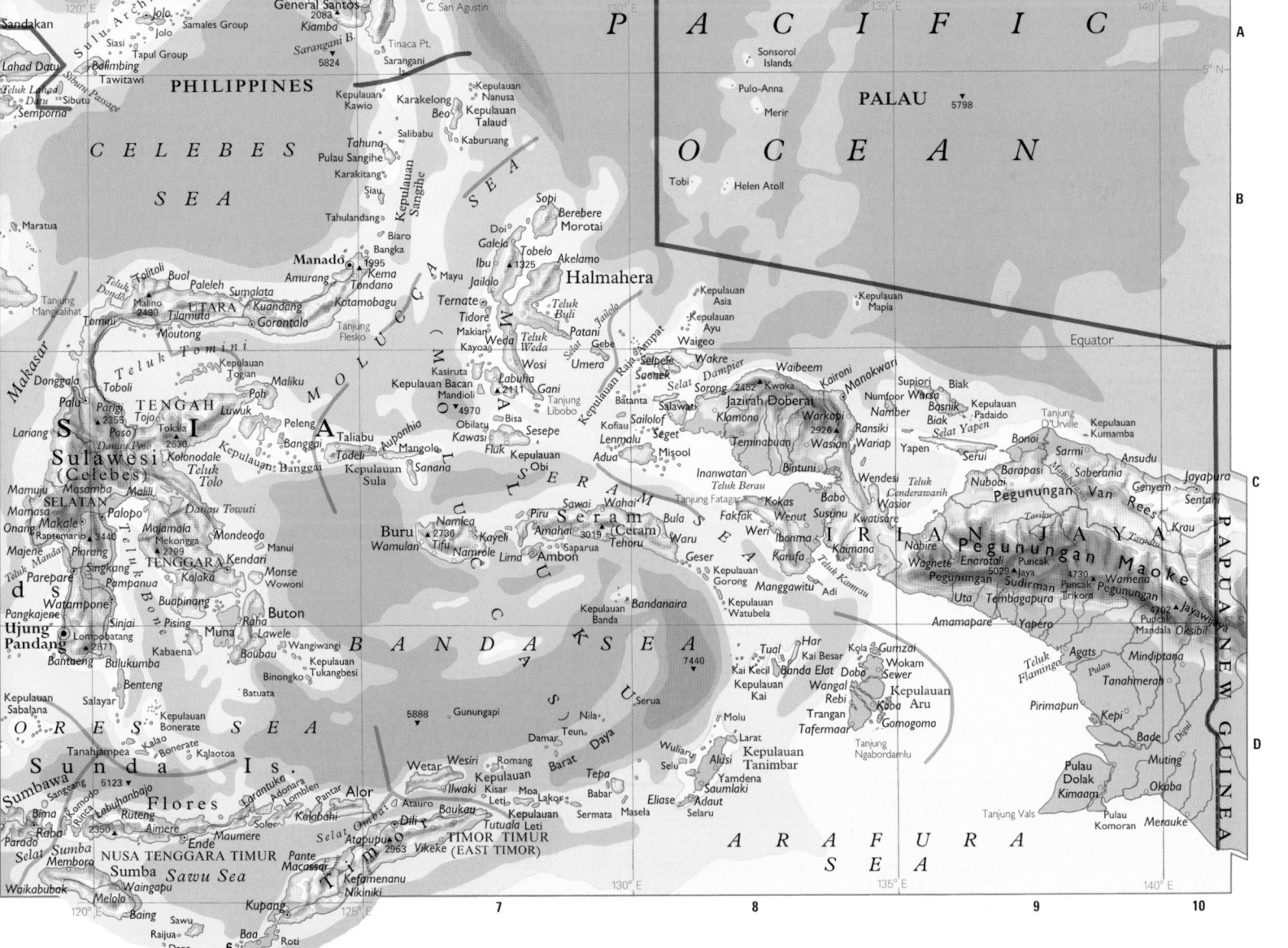

IRAN

Iran's flag was adopted in 1980 by the country's Islamic government. The white stripe contains the national emblem, which is the word for Allah (God) in formal Arabic script. The words Allah Akbar (God is Great) is repeated 11 times on both the green and red stripes.

Geography and Climate

The Republic of Iran contains a barren central plateau which covers about half of the country. It includes the Great Salt Desert (Dasht-e-Kavir) and the Great Sand Desert (Dasht-e-Lut). The Elburz Mountains, which border the plateau to the north, contain Iran's highest peak, Damavand, which reaches 5,604 m [18,386 ft]. North of the Elburz Mountains are the fertile, densely populated lowlands around the Caspian Sea, which have a mild climate with abundant rainfall. Bordering the plateau to the west are the Zagros Mountains, whose high plateaux are the summer retreats of the Bakhtiars and Kurds.

The Zagros Mountains separate the central plateau from the Khuzistan Plain, a region of sugar plantations and oil fields, which extend to the Iraqi border. The Khuzistan Plain has Iran's most important petroleum deposits and it was the target of the Iraqi invasion in 1980.

Much of Iran experiences a severe, dry climate, with hot summers and cold winters. In Tehran, rain falls on only about 30 days in the year and the annual temperature range is more than 25°C [45°F]. The climate in the lowlands, however, is generally milder.

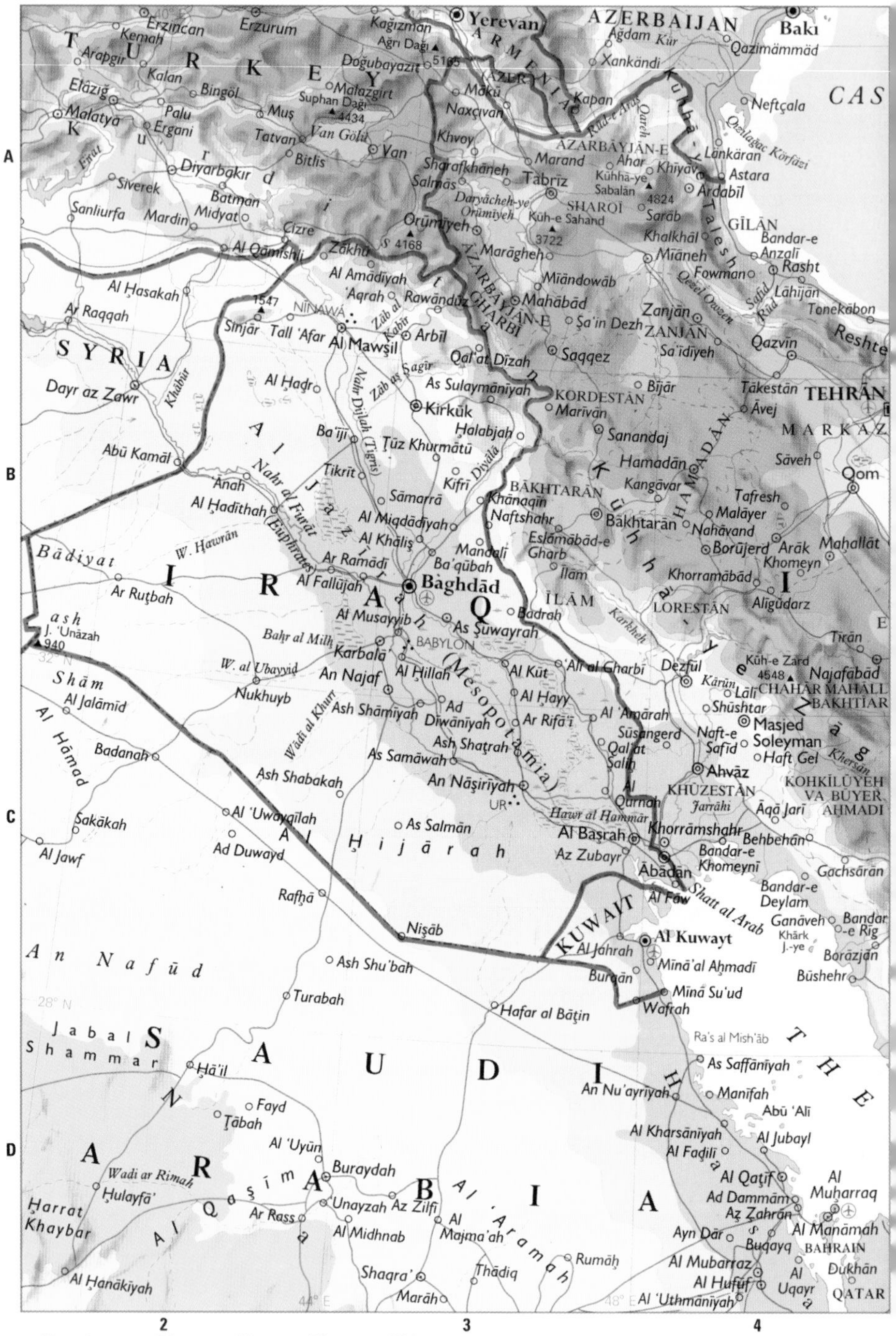

History and Politics

Iran was called Persia until 1935. Ancient Persia was a powerful empire. It flourished from 550 BC, when its king, Cyrus the Great, conquered the Medes, to 331 BC, when the empire was then conquered by Alexander the Great.

Arab armies introduced Islam in AD 641 and they made Iran a great centre of learning. But the area split up into a number of small kingdoms in the 10th century. Seljuk Turks conquered Iran in the 11th century, but, in 1220, Mongol armies seized the region. Mongol power declined in the 15th century and Iran was ruled by the Turkish Safavid Dynasty from 1501 to 1722 and by the Qajars, a Turkoman group, from 1794 until 1925.

Britain and Russia competed for influence in the area in the 19th century, and in the early 20th century the British began to develop the country's oil resources. In 1925, the Pahlavi family took power. Reza Khan became shah (king) and worked to modernize Iran. The Pahlavi Dynasty ended in 1979 when a religious leader, Ayatollah Ruhollah Khomeini, made Iran an Islamic republic. In 1980–8, Iran and Iraq fought over disputed borders. Khomeini died in 1989 but his views and anti-Western attitudes continued to exert influence around the world. Arab leaders in the Gulf saw his revolution as a threat to their oil-rich governments, but other Arab states were less hostile.

The 1980–8 war led to a great reduction in Iran's vital oil production, but output returned to its mid-1970s levels by 1994. In 1997, the election of a liberal, Mohammad Khatami, as president heralded a move away from extreme Islamic fundamentalism, though the conservative faction, led by the spiritual leader Ayatollah Al Khamenei, still retained great power. However, in February 2000, the supporters of Khatami's reformist programme for a government accountable to the people, a society based on the rule of law, and a political system based on a separation of powers, won a resounding electoral victory.

Economy

Iran's prosperity is based on its oil production and oil accounts for 75% of the country's exports. However, the economy was severely damaged by the Iran–Iraq war in the 1980s. Oil revenues have been used to develop a growing manufacturing sector, but agriculture still accounts for about 25% of the gross domestic product, even though farms cover only a tenth of the land. The main crops are wheat and barley. Livestock farming and fishing are other important activities.

Iran: Arable 10.1% Permanent crops 0.99% Forest 6.97%

AREA	Kurdish 9%, Gilaki 5%,
1,648,000 sq km [636,293 sq mls]	Luri, Mazandarani,
POPULATION	Baluchi, Arab
64,411,000	**LANGUAGES**
CAPITAL (POPULATION)	Farsi/Persian (official),
Tehran (6,750,000)	Kurdish
GOVERNMENT	**RELIGIONS**
Islamic republic	Islam 99%
ETHNIC GROUPS	**CURRENCY**
Persian 46%, Azerbaijani 17%,	Rial = 100 dinars

126

IRAQ

Iraq's flag was adopted in 1963, when the country was planning to federate with Egypt and Syria. It uses the four Pan-Arab colours. The three green stars symbolize the three countries. Iraq retained these stars even though the union failed to come into being.

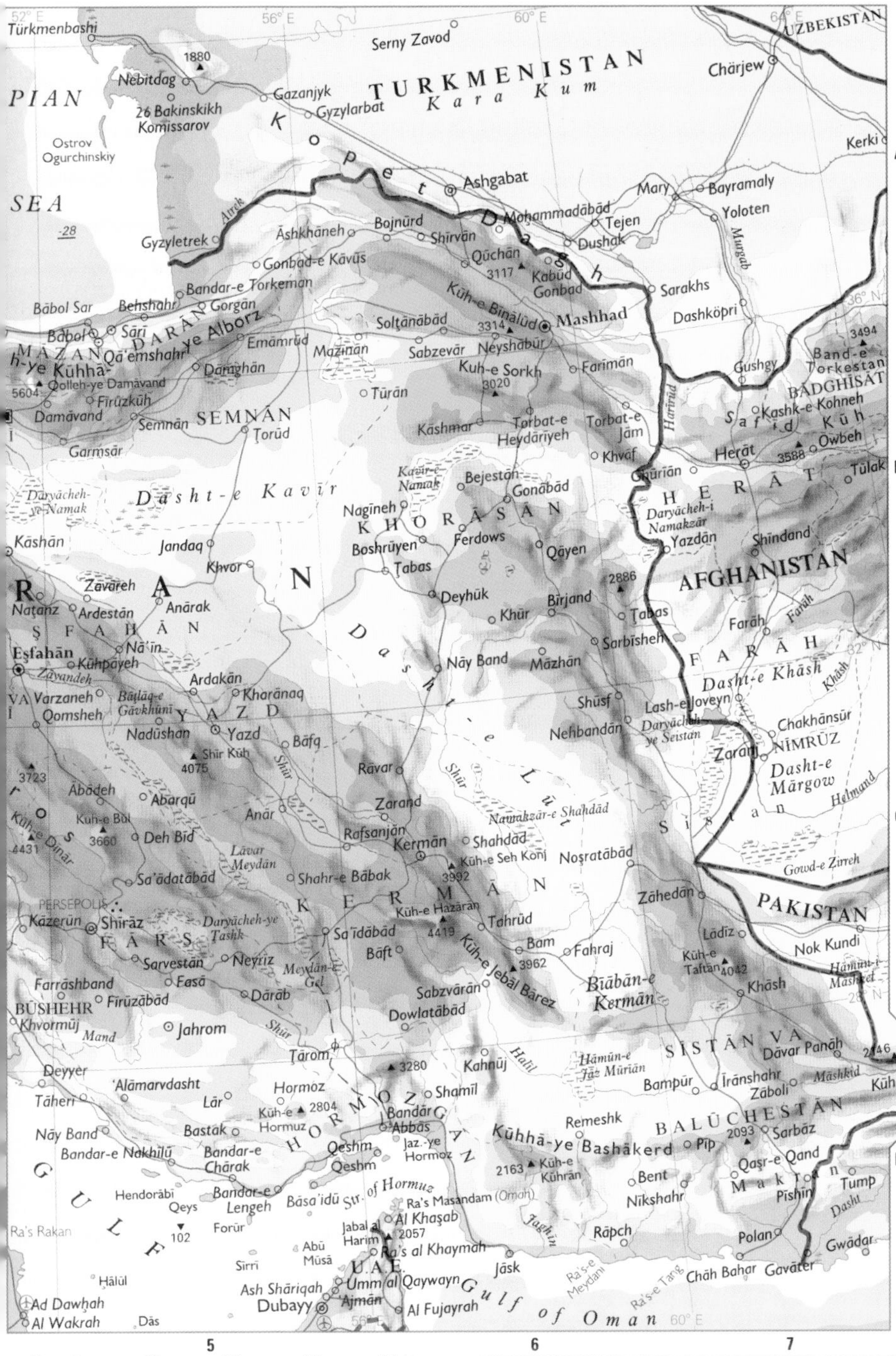

History and Politics

Mesopotamia was the home of several great civilizations, including Sumer, Babylon and Assyria. It later became part of the Persian Empire. Islam was introduced in AD 637 and Baghdad became the brilliant capital of the powerful Arab empire. However, Mesopotamia declined after the Mongols invaded it in 1258. From 1534, Mesopotamia became part of the Turkish Ottoman empire. Britain invaded the area in 1916. In 1921, Britain renamed the country Iraq and set up an Arab monarchy. Iraq finally became independent in 1932.

By the 1950s, oil dominated Iraq's economy. In 1952, Iraq agreed to take 50% of the profits of the foreign oil companies. This revenue enabled the government to pay for welfare services and development projects. But many Iraqis felt that they should benefit more from their oil.

Since 1958, when army officers killed the king and made Iraq a republic, the country has undergone turbulent times. In the 1960s, the Kurds, who live in northern Iraq, Iran, Turkey, Syria and Armenia, asked for self-rule. The government rejected their demands and war broke out. A peace treaty was signed in 1975, but conflict continued.

In 1979, Saddam Hussein became Iraq's president. Under his leadership, Iraq invaded Iran in 1980, starting an eight-year war. During this war, Iraqi Kurds supported Iran and the Iraqi government attacked Kurdish villages with poison gas.

In 1990, Iraqi troops occupied Kuwait, but an international force drove them out in 1991. Since 1991, Iraqi troops have attacked Shiite Marsh Arabs and Kurds. In 1996, the government aided the forces of the Kurdish Democratic Party in an offensive against the Patriotic Union of Kurdistan, a rival Kurdish faction. In 1998, Iraq's failure to permit UNSCOM, the UN body charged with disposing of Iraq's deadliest weapons, access to all suspect sites led to Western bombardment of military sites. Periodic bombardment and economic sanctions continued, but Iraq was allowed to export a limited amount of oil in exchange for food and medicines. In 1999, the Security Council lifted all limits on how much oil Iraq could export, but concern continued about the effect of sanctions on civilians.

Economy

Civil war, Gulf War damage, UN sanctions and economic mismanagement have all contributed to economic chaos in the 1990s. Oil remains Iraq's main resource, but a UN trade embargo in 1990 halted oil exports. Farmland, including pasture, covers around a fifth of the land. Products include barley, cotton, dates, fruit, livestock, wheat and wool, but Iraq still has to import food. Industries include oil refining and the manufacture of petrochemicals and consumer goods.

Iraq: Arable land 12% Permanent crops 0.46%
Permanent grassland 9.15% Forest 4.28%

Geography and Climate

The Republic of Iraq is a south-west Asian country at the head of the Gulf. Deserts cover western and south-western Iraq, with part of the Zagros Mountains in the north-east, where farming can be practised without irrigation. Western Iraq contains a large slice of the Hamad, or Syrian, Desert, but essentially comprises lower valleys of the rivers Euphrates (Nahr al Furat) and Tigris (Nahr Dijlah). The region is arid, but has fertile alluvial soils. The Euphrates and Tigris join south of Al Qurnah, to form the Shatt al Arab. The Shatt al Arab's delta is an area of irrigated farmland and marshes. This waterway is shared with Iran; it was the alleged cause of the First Gulf War.

The climate of Iraq varies from temperate in the north to subtropical in the south and east. Baghdad, in central Iraq, has cool winters, with occasional frosts, and hot summers. Rainfall is generally low.

AREA	Turkmen, Persian, Assyrian
438,320 sq km [169,235 sq mls]	**LANGUAGES**
POPULATION	Arabic (official),
21,722,000	Kurdish (official in
CAPITAL (POPULATION)	Kurdish areas)
Baghdad (3,841,000)	**RELIGIONS**
GOVERNMENT	Islam 96%, Christianity 4%
Republic	**CURRENCY**
ETHNIC GROUPS	Iraqi dinar = 20 dirhams
Arab 77%, Kurdish 19%,	= 1,000 fils

Ireland's flag was adopted in 1922 after the country had become independent from Britain, though nationalists had used it as early as 1848. Green represents Ireland's Roman Catholics, orange the Protestants, and the white a desire for peace between the two.

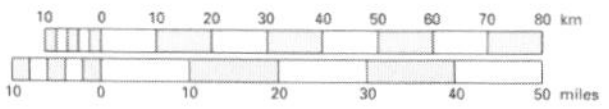

Arable land 19.1%	Permanent crops 0.04%
Permanent grassland 44.6%	Forest 4.65%

Vegetation

Forests cover approximately 5% of Ireland. Much of the land is under pasture and a very small percentage of land is set aside for crops.

History

Most Irish people are descendants of waves of immigrants who settled on the island over a long period. Celts settled in Ireland from about 400 BC. They were followed later by the Vikings, Normans and the English.

Vikings raided Ireland from the 790s and in the 8th century they established settlements. But Norse domination was ended in 1014 when they were defeated by Ireland's king, Brian Boru. The Normans arrived in 1169 and, gradually, Ireland came under English influence. Much of Ireland's history after that time was concerned with the struggle against British rule and, from the 1530s, the preservation of Roman Catholicism.

In 1801, the Act of Union created the United Kingdom of Great Britain and Ireland. But Irish discontent intensified in the 1840s when a potato blight caused a famine in which a million people died and nearly a million emigrated. Britain was blamed for not having done enough to help but, as the years went by, it introduced a number of reforms, improving the lot of the rural community. In the late 19th century, demands were made for home rule, but the British parliament defeated home rule bills in 1886 and 1892. In 1905, Arthur Griffith, a journalist, founded a movement advocating self-government for Ireland. It was called *Sinn Féin*, a name meaning 'We Ourselves'.

Geography and Climate

The Republic of Ireland occupies five-sixths of the island of Ireland. The country consists of a large lowland region surrounded by a broken rim of low mountains. The lowlands include peat bogs, where the peat (formed of partly decayed plants) is dug up and used as fuel. The uplands include the Mountains of Kerry where Carrauntoohill, Ireland's highest peak at 1,041 m [3,415 ft], is situated. The River Shannon is the longest in the British Isles. It flows through three large lakes, loughs Allen, Ree and Derg.

Ireland has a mild, damp climate influenced by the warm Gulf Stream current. The effects of this are greatest in the west. Dublin in the east is cooler than places on the west coast. Rain occurs all year.

Another organization which operated in secret, the Irish Republican Brotherhood, was also active in the early 20th century and its supporters became known as republicans. In 1914, the British parliament passed a home rule bill, but it was agreed to postpone its implementation until the end of World War I. In 1916, republicans launched what was called the Easter rebellion in Dublin, but the uprising was crushed. In 1918, the republicans took over the Sinn Féin movement. They won a majority of Ireland's seats in the British parliament, but instead of going to London, they set up the *Dáil Éireann* (House of Representatives) in Dublin and declared Ireland an independent republic in January 1919.

In 1920, the British parliament passed the Government of Ireland

IRELAND

The Troubles

The Anglo-Irish Treaty of 1921 established southern Ireland – Eire – as an independent state, with the six northern Irish counties, and their Protestant majority, remaining part of the United Kingdom (though Eire's constitution claimed authority over the whole island). Northern Ireland (Ulster) was granted local self-government from the Stormont parliament in Belfast. However, the Protestant majority (roughly two-thirds of the population) systematically excluded the Catholic minority from power and often from employment, despite occasional attacks from the near-moribund IRA – the Irish Republican Army, which had done most of the fighting that led to Eire's independence.

In 1968, inspired by the Civil Rights movement in the southern states of the USA, northern Catholics launched a civil rights movement of their own. But Protestant hostility threatened a bloodbath, and in August 1969 British Prime Minister Harold Wilson deployed army units to protect Catholics from attack.

Within a short period, the welcome given by Catholics to British troops turned to bitterness; the IRA and many of the Catholic minority came to see them as a hostile occupying force, and there were deaths on both sides. Protestant extremists were quick to form terrorist organizations of their own. In 1971, the British introduced internment without trial for suspected IRA terrorists, removing some of the main security risks from the streets but provoking violent protest demonstrations. In 1972, British troops killed 13 demonstrators in Londonderry, claiming to have been fired upon: the claims were vigorously denied by the demonstrators.

In an attempt to end the alienation of the Catholics, Britain negotiated an agreement with Protestant politicians to share power in an executive composed of both communities, but the plan collapsed after dissatisfied Protestants staged a general strike. The British government responded by suspending the Stormont parliament and ruling Northern Ireland direct from Westminster. The failure of power-sharing encapsulated the British policy dilemma in Ulster: the Catholics, or most of them, wanted to join the Irish Republic; the Protestants, virtually without exception, did not. Each side bitterly distrusted the other, and long years of sectarian killing only increased the distrust.

The violence continued throughout the 1970s and 1980s, despite a series of political initiatives that included an Anglo-Irish agreement giving the Republic a modest say in Ulster's affairs. Among the conflict's victims were several British politicians, as well as soldiers, policemen, and thousands of ordinary men and women. Armed troops patrolling the streets and almost daily reports of sectarian murders became a way of life. But with the increasing war-weariness of the people, a joint declaration on Northern Ireland was agreed between Britain and Ireland in 1993. Further proposals for a settlement in 1995 led to a resumption of terrorism by the IRA, but talks later resumed to produce a framework for power-sharing which was subsequently approved by referenda in 1998.

Act, partitioning Ireland. The six Ulster countries accepted the Act, but fighting broke out in southern Ireland. The Irish Republican Army attacked British army and government buildings, while Britain replied with repressive measures. In 1921, a treaty was agreed allowing southern Ireland to become a self-governing dominion, called the Irish Free State, within the British Commonwealth. One Irish group, led by Michael Collins and later by William T. Cosgrave, accepted the treaty and the Irish Free State came into being in 1921. But another group, led by Eamon de Valera, wanted complete independence. Civil war occurred between 1922 and 1923. Cosgrave, leader of the Cumann na nGaedheal Party, served as president of the Executive Council that governed the Irish Free State between 1922 and 1932, when it was defeated by Fianna Fáil, a party set up by de Valera who had left Sinn Féin. De Valera cut most ties between the Irish Free State and Britain.

Politics

The Irish Free State was neutral during World War II. In 1949, John A. Costello, leader of Finna Gael (formerly the Cumann na nGaedheal Party) cut all remaining ties with Britain and declared southern Ireland to be an independent republic. Ireland has subsequently played an independent role in Europe. It joined the European Economic Community (now the European Union) in 1973 and, unlike Britain, it adopted the euro, the single currency of the EU, in 1999.

However, the government of Ireland has worked with British governments in attempts to solve the problems of Northern Ireland. In 1998, it supported the creation of a Northern Ireland Assembly, the setting up of north–south political structures and the amendment of the 1937 constitution by removing from it the republic's claim to Northern Ireland. A referendum showed strong support for the proposals and the amendments to the constitution. The 1998 Good Friday Agreement in Northern Ireland, which aimed to end the long-standing conflict, met with much support, but in 1999 it ran into difficulties, including the refusal of the underground Irish Republican Army to give up its weapons.

Economy

Agriculture was the traditional mainstay of the economy, although fishing, home crafts and local labouring were also important extra sources of income in the poorer western areas. A marked contrast exists between the richest and poorest rural areas. The eastern central lowland and the south-east, particularly the lowland areas of Wicklow and Wexford, contain splendid large farms, with pastures supporting fine-quality cattle, sheep and, in some areas, racehorses. From Wexford, too, rich farmland extends through the valleys and lowlands westwards to the counties of Tipperary and Limerick, and from Waterford to Cork and Killarney. North of the Shannon, in Clare and east Galway, there is intensive sheep and some cattle production. To the north, farming is mixed – with dairying, meat production and, in some areas, specialization on such crops as potatoes and barley. Little wheat is grown – oats are better suited to the damp summer climate.

Aided by EU grants, farming is now relatively prosperous. The number of people working on the land continues to decline, because of the introduction of machinery, the union of small farms into larger ones, and the increased number of jobs in the towns. Industrialization was confined, until recent years, to the north-east, especially Belfast. This meant that southern Ireland had an essentially agrarian economy, with industries mainly confined to food processing and beverage-making.

Manufacturing is now the leading activity, with high-tech industries producing such products as chemicals and pharmaceuticals, electronic equipment, machinery, paper and textiles. The leading exports include machinery and transport equipment, chemical products and food products. Ireland's main trading partners are the United Kingdom, Germany and France. Prosperity during the 1960s was followed by a slowdown, caused partly by high government spending. However, a new spirit of co-operation in the 1980s and 1990s brought strong growth.

AREA	**ETHNIC GROUPS**
70,280 sq km	Irish 94%
[27,135 sq mls]	**LANGUAGES**
POPULATION	Irish and English (both official)
3,619,000	**RELIGIONS**
CAPITAL (POPULATION)	Christianity (Roman Catholic
Dublin	93%, Protestant 3%)
(1,024,000)	**CURRENCY**
GOVERNMENT	Euro; Irish pound
Multiparty republic	= 100 new pence

Israel's flag was adopted when the Jewish state declared itself independent in 1948. The blue and white stripes are based on the tallit, a Hebrew prayer shawl. The ancient, six-pointed Star of David is in the centre. The flag was designed in America in 1891.

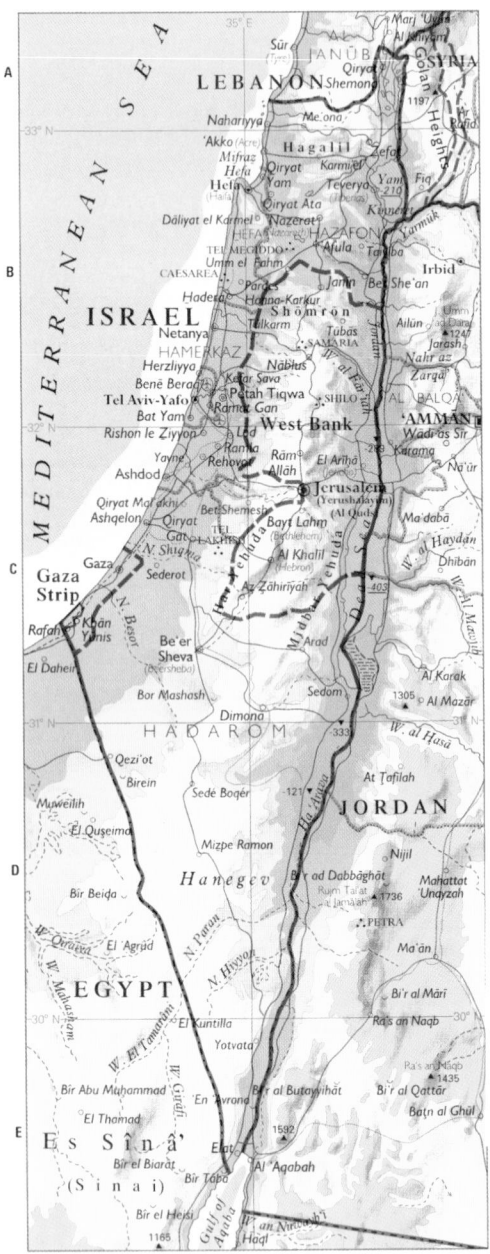

Geography

The State of Israel is a small country in the eastern Mediterranean. It includes a fertile coastal plain, where Israel's main industrial cities, Haifa (Hefa) and Tel Aviv–Jafo are situated. Inland lie the Judaeo-Galilean highlands, which run from northern Israel to the northern tip of the Negev Desert in the south. To the east lies part of the Great Rift Valley which runs through East Africa into Asia. In Israel, the Rift Valley contains the River Jordan, the Sea of Galilee and the Dead Sea, whose shoreline is 403 m [1,322 ft] below sea level, the world's lowest point on land.

Climate

Israel has hot, dry, sunny summers. Winters are mild and moist on the coast, but the total annual rainfall decreases from west to east and also from north to south, where the Dead Sea region has only 70 mm [2.5 in] a year.

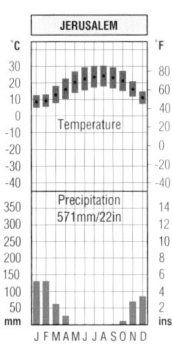

ISRAEL (JERUSALEM)

East of the Mediterranean Sea, the annual rainfall amount decreases inland and the length of the summer dry season increases to more than five months, which last from May through to September. At over 700 m [2,250 ft], Jerusalem has lower temperatures and a greater range of temperatures than the coastal regions of Israel. The average temperature in January is 12.8°C [55°F], while in July an average of 28.9°C [84°F] is experienced. To the south, the rainfall decreases rapidly in the rocky desert around the Dead Sea. Sunshine levels are high. In Jerusalem there is an average daily sunshine total of over 9 hours, ranging from 6–12 hours.

History

Israel is part of a region called Palestine. Some Jews have always lived in the area, though most modern Israelis are descendants of immigrants who began to settle there from the 1880s. Britain ruled Palestine from 1917. Large numbers of Jews escaping Nazi persecution arrived in the 1930s, provoking an Arab uprising against British rule. In 1947, the UN agreed to partition Palestine into an Arab and a Jewish state. Fighting broke out after Arabs rejected the plan. The State of Israel came into being in May 1948, but fighting continued into 1949. Other Arab-Israeli wars were fought in 1956, 1967 and 1973. The Six Day War in 1967 led to the acquisition by Israel of the West Bank, which had been formerly under Jordanian administration, along with East Jerusalem. At the same time, Israel also occupied the Gaza Strip and the Sinai Peninsula from Egypt and the Golan Heights from Syria. In 1982, Israel invaded Lebanon to destroy the stronghold of the PLO (Palestine Liberation Organization), but they left in 1985.

Politics

Hopes of a Middle Eastern peace settlement were first raised in 1978, when Israel signed a treaty with Egypt which led to the return of the Sinai Peninsula to Egypt in 1979. However, conflict continued between Israel and the PLO. In 1993, the PLO and Israel agreed to establish Palestinian self-rule in two areas: the Gaza Strip and the town of Jericho on the West Bank. The agreement was extended in 1995 to include more than 30% of the West Bank. Israel's prime minister, Yitzhak Rabin, who had been seeking a 'land for peace' settlement, was assassinated in 1995 and his successor, Simon Peres, was narrowly defeated in elections in 1996. Peres was succeeded as prime minister by the right-wing Binyamin Netanyahu, who favoured a more hardline policy towards the Palestinians. As a result, the peace process stalled.

In May 1999, Netanyahu was defeated in national elections by his challenger, the left-wing Ehud Barak, who promised to resume the peace process. But many problems remained, including the extension of Jewish settlements in the occupied areas and attacks on Israel by the militant Islamic group, the Hezbollah, based in southern Lebanon. These attacks caused an escalation of the conflict in southern Lebanon in early 2000.

However, Barak continued the peace process by agreeing to extend Palestinian control over 40% of the West Bank and also provided a 'safe passage' road route for Palestinians to travel between the Gaza Strip and the West Bank. Negotiations with Syria also began, concerning the future of the occupied Golan Heights.

Economy

Since 1948, the State of Israel has developed rapidly and its citizens now enjoy a high standard of living. The leading activity is manufacturing, and products include chemicals, electronic equipment, fertilizers, military equipment, plastics, processed food, scientific instruments and textiles. Israel produces potash, while cotton, fruits, grain, poultry and vegetables are major farm products. Machinery and transport equipment, cut diamonds and chemicals are exported.

AREA
26,650 sq km [10,290 sq mls]
POPULATION
5,644,000
CAPITAL (POPULATION)
Jerusalem (591,000)
GOVERNMENT
Multiparty republic
ETHNIC GROUPS
Jewish 82%, Arab and others 18%
LANGUAGES
Hebrew and Arabic (both official)
RELIGIONS
Judaism 82%, Islam 14%,
Christianity 2%,
Druse and others 2%
CURRENCY
New Israeli sheqel = 100 agorat

ITALY

The Italian flag is based on the military standard carried by the French Republican National Guard when Napoleon invaded Italy in 1796, causing great changes in Italy's map. It was finally adopted as the national flag after Italy was unified in 1861.

Geography

The Republic of Italy is famous for its history and traditions, its art and culture, and beautiful scenery. Northern Italy is bordered in the north by the Alps, with their many climbing and skiing resorts. The Alps overlook the northern plains – Italy's most fertile and densely populated region – drained by the River Po. Generally lower than the Alps, the Apennines, which form the backbone of southern Italy, reach their highest peaks – almost 3,000 m [9,800 ft] – in the Gran Sasso Range overlooking the the central Adriatic Sea, near Pescara. Limestones are the most common rocks. Between the mountains, however, are long, narrow basins, some with lakes, others as farms.

Southern Italy contains a string of volcanoes, stretching from Vesuvius, near Naples (Nápoli), through the Lipari Islands, to Mount Etna on Sicily. Traces of volcanic activity are found throughout Italy. Ancient lava flows cover large areas and, where they have weathered, they produce fertile soils. Italy is still subject to earthquakes and volcanic eruptions. Sicily is the largest island in the Mediterranean. Sardinia, also part of Italy, is more isolated from the mainland and its rugged, windswept terrain and lack of resources have set it apart.

Climate

Milan (Milano), in the north, has cold, often snowy winters. But the summer months are warm and sunny. Rainfall is plentiful, with brief but powerful thunderstorms in summer. Southern Italy has mild, moist winters and warm, dry summers.

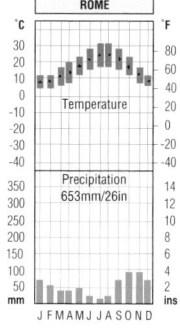

ITALY (ROME)

Summers are warm with June to September averages of over 20°C [68°F], but the winters can be cold, with very low averages, and sub-zero temperatures having been recorded from November to March. There are over 2,500 hours of sunshine per year, ranging from only 3 hours in December, to 8–10 hours from May to September. Rain falls mainly in the winter and, in all, on only about 65 days per year.

History and Politics

Magnificent ruins throughout Italy testify to the glories of the ancient Roman Empire, which was founded, according to legend, in 753 BC. It reached its peak in the AD 100s. It finally collapsed in the 400s, although the Eastern Roman Empire, also called the Byzantine Empire, survived for another 1,000 years.

In the Middle Ages, Italy was split into many tiny states. They made a huge contribution to the revival of art and learning, called the Renaissance. Cities, such as Florence (Firenze) and Venice (Venézia), testify to the artistic achievements of this period.

In 1800, present-day Italy was made up of several political units including the Papal States (a large area in central Italy ruled by the Roman Catholic Church), while a substantial part of the north-east was occupied by Austria. The struggle for unification – the *Risorgimento* – began early in the 19th century, but little progress was made until an alliance between France and Piedmont (then part of the Kingdom of Sardinia) drove Austria from Lombardy in 1859. Tuscany, Parma and Modena joined Piedmont-Lombardy in 1860, and the Papal States, Sicily, Naples – including most of the southern peninsula – and Romagna were brought into the alliance. King Victor Emmanuel II was proclaimed ruler of a united Italy the following year. Venetia was acquired from Austria in 1866 and Rome was finally annexed in 1871. Since then, Italy has been a unified state, though the pope and his successors disputed the takeover of the Papal States. This dispute was not resolved until 1929, when Vatican City was established as a fully independent state.

Since unification, the population has doubled, and though the rate of increase is notoriously slow today, the rapid growth of population, in a poor country attempting to develop its resources, forced millions of Italians to emigrate during the first quarter of the 20th century. Italy's short-lived African Empire enabled some Italians to settle overseas, but it did not substantially relieve the population pressure. Now there are immigrant Italians to be found on all the inhabited continents. Especially large numbers settled in the United States, South America and Australia, and more recently, large numbers of Italians have moved for similar reasons into northern Europe.

In 1915, during World War I, Italy entered the war alongside the Allies. After the war, Italy was given nearly 23,000 sq km [9,000 sq mls] of territory that had belonged to Austria-Hungary, including Trentino and Trieste, but it was far less than Italy had hoped to gain. In 1922, Benito Mussolini became prime minister of Italy and, from 1925, he ruled as a dictator, with the title *Il Duce*. Many of his internal policies proved successful, but he pursued an aggressive foreign policy, aimed at increasing Italy's status in the world. In 1936, Italian forces invaded Ethiopia, while military personnel were sent to support the rebellion of General Francisco Franco in Spain. In 1939, Italy agreed to fight alongside Germany in the event of war, though it did not enter the war in June 1940. During the war, Italy lost much of its colonial empire to the Allies and, in late 1943, Italy declared war on Germany. German forces then took control and installed Mussolini as head of a puppet government. Mussolini was captured and shot by partisans in 1945, when he tried to escape to Switzerland.

Italy became a republic in 1946 following a referendum, and Allied troops left the country in 1947. Since then, the Christian Democrats resisted the opposition of the Communist Party to pursue a strongly pro-Western and European policy. However, no single government

Regions of Italy

was able to face up to the country's many social problems, including corruption at high levels of society, and changes of the mostly weak coalition governments were frequent, leading to instability.

Italy became a founder member of the North Atlantic Treaty Organization in 1949, and of the European Economic Community (EEC, now the European Union) in 1957. After the establishment of the EEC, Italy's economy began to expand. However, much of the economic development took place in the great triangular plain of Lombardy, betwen the Alps and the Apennines, which has long been Italy's most productive region, both agriculturally and industrially. By contrast, central Italy between the Po Valley and the Tiber, is less developed. It represents a transition zone between the developed north and the poor agrarian south, which is known as the Mezzogiorno.

The Mezzogiorno displays, albeit in a less severe form, many of the characteristics of the developing world, with its heavy dependence on its peasant farms, which are too small to lend themselves to modern techniques, although there are some large estates. The eight regions of the Mezzogiorno cover some 40% of Italy's land area (including Sicily and Sardinia), but they contribute only about a quarter of the gross domestic product. The birth rate is also much higher in the south and overpopulation is always a threat. But, the situation is eased because many poor southerners are forced to migrate to northern cities or to other parts of the European Union. But migration tends to take away the younger and more active members of the population, leaving the older people behind. Italy also faces urban problems, caused by the rapid growth of such cities as Naples when young people leave rural areas and settle in city slums. The problems of the Mezzogiorno are no longer a problem only for Italy, because the stability and prosperity of the country is now a matter for the entire European Union.

Overall, however, Italy has made enormous progress since World War II. By the late 1990s, it had the world's sixth largest economy and, on 1 January 1999, it adopted the euro, the single unit of currency of the European Union. In 1992, the old political establishment was driven from office and several prominent leaders were accused of links to organized crime and some were imprisoned. In 1996, the left-wing Olive Tree alliance led by Romano Prodi took office, but Prodi was forced to resign in 1998 following his rejection of demands made by his Communist allies. He was replaced as prime minister by Massimo D'Alemo, the first former Communist to occupy that role. However, D'Alemo's attempts to create a two-party system in Italy failed in 1999. After his coalition failed, he, too, resigned as prime minister, though he continued in office leading a new coalition government. However, he resigned again in April 2000, following right-wing victories in regional elections. Such events suggested that Italy's problems of political instability were far from over.

Economy

Only 50 years ago, Italy was a mainly agricultural society. Today it is a major industrial power, with the world's sixth largest economy. Apart from natural gas in the Po Valley, it lacks mineral resources, and has to import most of the fuels and other materials used in its industries. Manufactures include cars, chemicals, food products, machinery, steel, televisions, textiles and clothing, and wine. Major crops include grapes for wine-making, and olives, which are used to make olive oil. Other crops include citrus fruits, maize, rice, sugar beet and wheat. Cattle, pigs, poultry and sheep are raised, but Italy imports meat. Leading exports include machinery and transport equipment, chemicals, textiles and clothing. Italy's main trading partners are Germany, France, the United Kingdom and the United States.

AREA	French, Albanian,
301,270 sq km [116,320 sq mls]	Ladino, Slovenian,
POPULATION	Greek
56,783,000	**LANGUAGES**
CAPITAL (POPULATION)	Italian 94% (official)
Rome (Roma, 2,688,000)	**RELIGIONS**
GOVERNMENT	Christianity
Multiparty republic	(Roman Catholic) 83%
ETHNIC GROUPS	**CURRENCY**
Italian 94%, German,	Euro; Lira = 100 centesimi

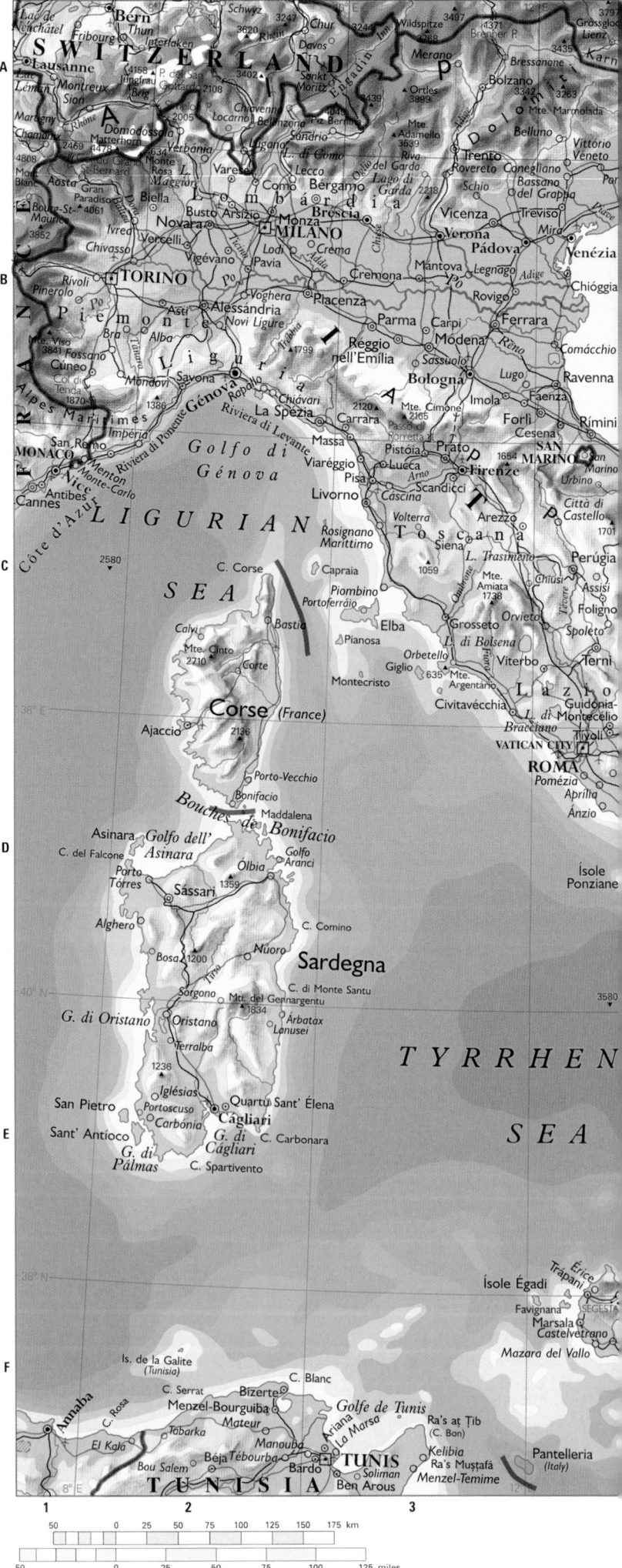

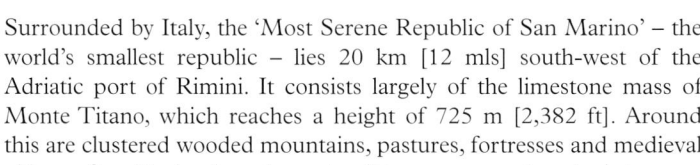

SAN MARINO

Surrounded by Italy, the 'Most Serene Republic of San Marino' – the world's smallest republic – lies 20 km [12 mls] south-west of the Adriatic port of Rimini. It consists largely of the limestone mass of Monte Titano, which reaches a height of 725 m [2,382 ft]. Around this are clustered wooded mountains, pastures, fortresses and medieval villages. San Marino has pleasant, mild summers and cool winters.

The republic was named after St Marinus, the stonemason saint who is said to have first established a community here in the 4th century AD. San Marino has been independent since 1885 and a republic since the 14th century. It has a friendship and co-operation treaty with Italy dating back to 1862. It uses Italian currency, but issues its own stamps, which are an important source of revenue. The state is governed by an elected council and has its own legal system. It has no armed forces and the police are 'hired' from the Italian constabulary. Most of the people live in the medieval city of San Marino, which receives more than 3 million tourists a year. The chief occupations are tourism, limestone quarrying and the making of ceramics, textiles and wine. The de facto customs union with Italy makes San Marino an easy conduit for the illegal export of lira and certain kinds of tax evasion for Italians.

AREA	GOVERNMENT
61 sq km	Republic
[24 sq mls]	ETHNIC GROUPS
POPULATION	San Marinese, Italian
25,000	LANGUAGES
CAPITAL	Italian (official)
San Marino	CURRENCY
(2,395)	Italian lira

VATICAN CITY

Vatican City State, the world's smallest independent nation, is an enclave on the west bank of the River Tiber in Rome. It forms an independent base for the Holy See, the governing body of the Roman Catholic Church. It consists of 44 hectares [109 acres] and includes St Peter's Square, St Peter's Basilica and Vatican Palace. Summers are warm, but winters can be cold. The average annual rainfall is about 650 mm [26 in] and most of the rain occurs in winter. Vatican City has more than 2,500 hours of sunshine a year.

The popes have been prominent patrons of the arts, and the treasures of the Vatican, including Michelangelo's frescoes in the Sistine Chapel, attract tourists from all over the world. Similarly, the Vatican Library contains a priceless collection of manuscripts from both pre-Christian and Christian times. The popes have lived in the Vatican since the 5th century, apart from a brief period at Avignon, France, in the 14th century. Sustained by investment income and voluntary contributions, it is all that remains of the Papal States which, until 1870, occupied most of central Italy. In 1929, Benito Mussolini recognized the independence of the Vatican City, in return for papal recognition of the kingdom of Italy. Since the 1960s, the Vatican has played an important role in some areas of international diplomacy.

The population, which includes the country's only armed force of 100 Swiss Guards, is made up entirely of unmarried males. The Commission appointed by the Pope to administer the affairs of the Vatican also has control over a radio station, the Pope's summer palace at Castel Gandolfo, and several churches in Rome. Vatican City has its own newspaper, police and railway station, and it issues its own stamps and coins.

AREA	POPULATION
0.44 sq km [0.17 sq mls]	About 1,000

Italy: Arable land 28.3% Permanent crops 9.57% Permanent grassland 15.4% Forest 23%

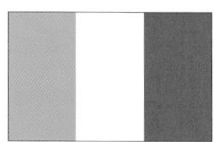

This flag was adopted in 1960 when the country became independent from France. It combines elements from the French tricolour and the Pan-African colours. The orange represents the northern savanna, the white peace and unity, and the green the forests in the south.

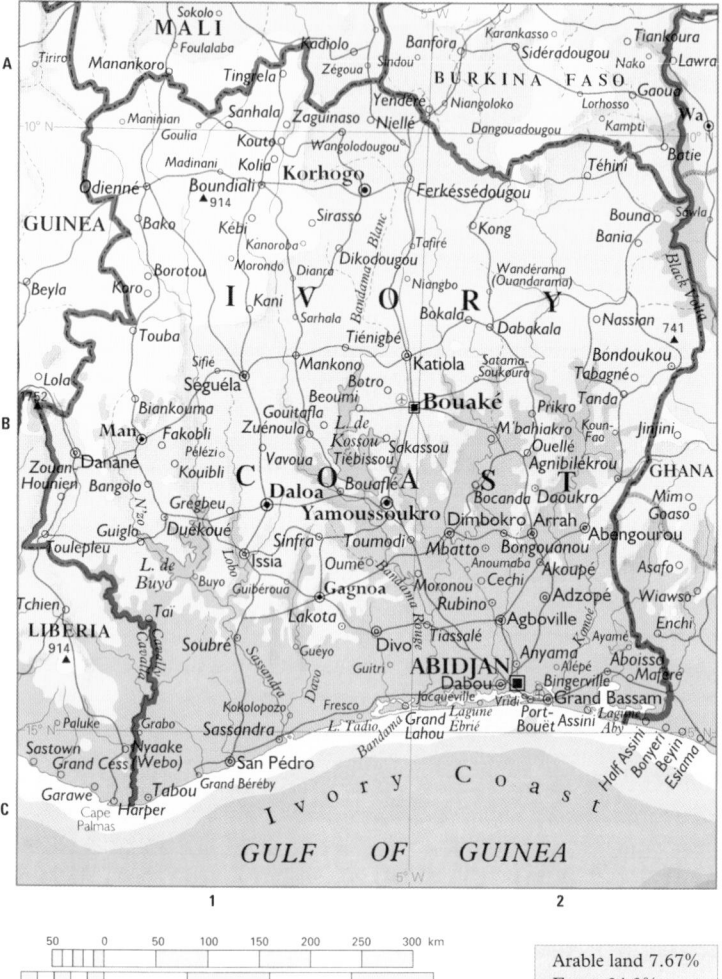

Arable land 7.67%
Forest 34.3%

Geography

The Republic of the Ivory Coast, in West Africa, is officially known as Côte d'Ivoire. The south-east coast is bordered by sand bars that enclose lagoons, on one of which the former capital and chief port of Abidjan is situated. But the south-western coast is lined by rocky cliffs. Behind the coast is a coastal plain, but the land rises inland to high plains. The highest land is an extension of the Guinea Highlands in the north-west, along the borders with Liberia and Guinea. The rivers run generally north–south.

Climate

Ivory Coast has a hot and humid tropical climate, with high temperatures throughout the year. The south of the country has two distinct rainy seasons: between May and July, and from October to November. Inland, the rainfall decreases. Northern Ivory Coast has a dry season and only one rainy season. As a result, the forests in central Ivory Coast thin out to the north, giving way to savanna.

IVORY COAST (ABIDJAN)

The uniform high temperature and humidity and the double rainfall maxima are features of the climate of the West African coast as far west as Liberia. The total rainfall amount increases steadily westwards as the south-west summer monsoon winds have a longer sea track. Heavier, more prolonged rainfall occurs in May and June, when the intertropical rainbelt moves northwards ahead of the monsoon.

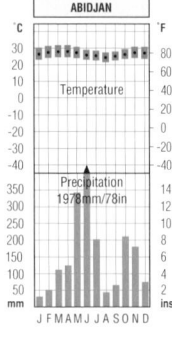

History

The region that is now Ivory Coast came under successive black African rulers until the late 15th century, when Europeans, attracted by the chance to trade in slaves and such local products as ivory, began to establish contacts along the coast. French missionaries reached the area in 1637 and, by the end of the 17th century, the French had set up trading posts on the coast. In 1842, France brought the Grand-Bassam area under its protection and Ivory Coast became a French colony in 1893. From 1895, it was ruled as part of French West Africa, a massive union which also included Benin, Burkina Faso, Guinea, Mali, Mauritania, Niger and Senegal. In 1946, Ivory Coast became a territory in the French Union. The port of Abidjan was built in the early 1950s, but the country achieved autonomy in 1958.

Politics

Ivory Coast became fully independent in 1960. Its first president, Félix Houphouët-Boigny, became the longest serving head of state in Africa with an uninterrupted period in office that ended with his death in 1993. Houphouët-Boigny was a paternalistic, pro-Western leader, who made his country a one-party state. In 1983, the National Assembly agreed to move the capital from Abidjan to Yamoussoukro, Houphouët-Boigny's birthplace. Visitors to Abidjan, where most of the country's Europeans live, are usually impressed by the city's general air of prosperity, but the cost of living for local people is high and there are great social and regional inequalities. Despite its political stability since independence, the country faces such economic problems as variations in the price of its export commodities, unemployment and high foreign debt.

Following the death of Houphouët-Boigny in 1993, the Speaker of the National Assembly, Henri Konan Bédié, proclaimed himself president. He was re-elected president in 1995. In view of the country's apparent stabilities, it surprised most observers when 11 leading members of the opposition were jailed in 1999 for public order offences. In December 1999, an army mutiny led to the overthrow of Bédié and a new administration was set up by General Robert Guei.

Economy

In terms of such indices as gross national product and international trade figures, Ivory Coast is one of Africa's more prosperous countries. Its free-market economy has proved attractive to foreign investors, especially French firms, while France has given much aid, especially for basic services and education. Its economy is based on agriculture, which employs about three-fifths of the people. The chief farm products are cocoa, coffee, cotton and cotton cloth, which together make up nearly half of the value of the total exports. Other exports include bananas, palm oil, pineapples and tropical woods. Food crops include cassava, maize, plantains, rice, vegetables and yams.

The country has few worked minerals, but manufacturing is growing. Manufactures include processed farm products, timber and textiles. Ivory Coast imports crude petroleum for its refineries.

AREA	Voltaic 16%, Malinke 15%,
322,460 sq km [124,502 sq mls]	Southern Mande 10%
POPULATION	**LANGUAGES**
15,446,000	French (official),
CAPITAL (POPULATION)	Akan, Voltaic
Yamoussoukro (120,000)	**RELIGIONS**
GOVERNMENT	Islam 38%, Christianity 28%,
Multiparty republic	traditional beliefs 17%
ETHNIC GROUPS	**CURRENCY**
Akan 41%, Kru 17%,	CFA franc = 100 centimes

JAMAICA – SEE CARIBBEAN SEA, PAGES 71–76

Japan's flag was officially adopted in 1870, though Japanese emperors had used this simple design for many centuries. The flag shows a red sun on a white background. The geographical position of Japan is also expressed in its name 'Nippon' or 'Nihon', meaning 'source of the Sun'.

Geography

Japan is an island nation in north-eastern Asia. It is a constitutional monarchy, with an emperor as its head of state.

Japan contains four large islands. In order of size, they are Honshu, Hokkaido, Kyushu and Shikoku. These islands make up more than 98% of the country. But Japan also has thousands of small islands, including the Ryukyu island chain which extends south of Kyushu towards the island of Taiwan.

The four main islands are mainly mountainous, while many of the small islands are the tips of volcanoes rising from the sea bed. Japan has more than 150 volcanoes, about 60 of which are active. Volcanic eruptions, earthquakes and tsunamis (destructive sea waves triggered by underwater eruptions and earthquakes) often occur. For example, an earthquake in 1995 killed over 5,000 people in Kobe. This is because the islands lie on an unstable part of the Earth where the land is constantly moving.

Throughout Japan, complex folding and faulting has produced an intricate mosaic of landforms. Mountains and forested hills alternate with small basins and coastal lowlands, covered by alluvium which has been deposited there by the short rivers that rise in the uplands. Most of the people live on the coastal plains. One densely populated zone stretches from the Kanto Plain, where Tokyo is situated, along the narrow plains that border the southern coasts of Honshu, to northern Kyushu.

The pattern of landforms is further complicated by the presence of volcanic cones and calderas. The highest mountain in Japan, the majestic cone of Fuji-san (3,776 m [12,388 ft]), is a long dormant volcano which last erupted in 1707. It is considered sacred, and is visited by thousands of pilgrims every year.

Climate

The climate of Japan varies greatly. Hokkaido in the north has cold, snowy winters. At Sapporo, temperatures below –20°C [4°F] have been recorded from between December and March. Summers are warm, with temperatures often exceeding 30°C [86°F]. Rain falls all year.

Tokyo has higher rainfall and temperatures than the rest of the country. The southern islands of Shikoku and Kyushu in the south have warm temperate climates. Summers are hot. Winters are mild.

JAPAN – TOKYO

Despite its maritime location, Tokyo has a large annual range of temperature (23°C [70°F]) due to the seasonal reversal of wind, blowing from the cold heart of Asia in winter and from the warm Pacific in summer. Winter is usually sunny, but cold, dry, north-westerly winds often blow, and frosts may occur as late as April. Summer in Tokyo is wet, hot and humid. In August it is usually over 30°C [86°F] during the day.

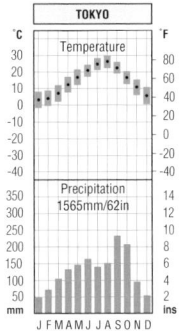

History

The Ainu may have been the first people to have settled in Japan. Scientists do not agree about their origins, some suggesting that they are related to European or Asian groups, and others suggesting they are related to Australian Aborigines. Today the Ainu, who are ethnically and culturally different from the Japanese, number only about 15,000, most of whom live in Hokkaido. Many have intermarried with Japanese. But, most modern Japanese are descendants of early immigrants who arrived in successive waves from the Korean Peninsula and other parts of the Asian mainland, though some may also have come from the islands to the south. Anthropologists have found evidence that people with a hunting and gathering culture had reached the islands around 6,500 years ago. This culture is named *Jomon*, or 'cord pattern',

after the ropelike patterns on their pottery. A new agricultural society, called the *Yayoi*, replaced the Jomon in the 3rd century BC. Under this new society, most people lived in farming villages.

The earliest zone of settlement included the northern part of Kyushu island and the coastlands of Setonaikai (Inland Sea). By the 5th century AD, Japan was divided among numerous clans, of which the largest and most powerful was the Yamato. The Yamato ruled from the area which now contains the city of Nara. They controlled most of central Japan, together with parts of southern Korea. Shinto, a polytheistic religion based on nature worship, was already practised, and the Japanese imperial dynasty already established. The chiefs of the Yamato clan are regarded as the ancestors of the Japanese imperial family.

The 5th century AD was also a time when new ideas and technology reached Japan from China. The Japanese adopted the Chinese system of writing and Chinese methods of calculating the calendar. Confucianism was also introduced from China and, in about 552, Buddhism reached Japan from Korea and China. In 646, the imperial court introduced a programme to adopt Chinese methods of government and administration. Under the so-called Taika Reform, Japan was divided into provinces, districts and villages. Also introduced was a central system of taxation and a land distribution programme. Early cities, modelled on the capital of T'ang-dynasty China, were built at Nara in 710 and, in 794, at Heian, which was later known as Kyoto. Kyoto remained the seat of Japan's imperial court until 1868.

The adoption of the Chinese system of centralized, bureaucratic government was relatively short-lived and, in the 9th century, the emperor and his court fell under the control of a powerful noble family called the Fujiwaras. The Fujiwara family ruled Japan for about 300 years. During this period, the emperors lost real power although they remained the official rulers, while the *daimyo*, the feudal lords who ruled great estates, became more and more powerful.

From the early 12th century onwards, political power passed increasingly to military aristocrats. Government was conducted in the name of the emperor by warrior leaders called *shoguns*. Civil warfare between rival groups of feudal lords was endemic over long periods, but, under the rule of the Tokugawa shoguns, between 1603 and 1867, Japan enjoyed a great period of peace and prosperity. Society was rigidly stratified, with military families (the feudal lords and their retainers, or *samurai*) forming a powerful elite. During the shogun era, a code of conduct was developed for the samurai. Called *bushido* ('the way of the warrior'), it stressed military skills and fearlessness, as well as frugality, kindness, honesty and filial piety. But, above all, the samurai's supreme obligation was to his feudal lord.

Japan's isolated position afforded the country some security. But they were threatened by the Mongol emperor Kublai Khan in 1274. His armies landed on Kyushu but withdrew because of an approaching typhoon. Kublai Khan attacked again in 1281, but this time his fleet was destroyed by a typhoon. The Japanese called this typhoon *kamikaze* ('divine wind'), the name used for the suicide pilots of World War II. European contact began when Portuguese sailors reached Japan in 1543. In 1549, a Spanish priest arrived and began to convert the Japanese to Christianity. His work was continued by other Spanish and Portuguese missionaries. Besides missionaries, Dutch and English traders arrived in the early 17th century. In the 1630s, the Japanese, fearing European conquest, ordered all Christian missionaries to leave the country, and forced Japanese converts to give up their faith. This led Japan to embark on a lengthy period of enforced isolation from the rest of the world. Japanese who lived abroad were not allowed to return, while no Japanese person was allowed to leave the country. The only Europeans allowed to stay were Dutch traders, who had not been involved in Christian missionary work. The Japanese allowed the Dutch to maintain a single trading station based on a small island in Nagasaki harbour. They permitted one Dutch ship to visit this station every year.

Arable land 10.6% Permanent crops 1.12%
Permanent grassland 1.76% Forest 66.4%

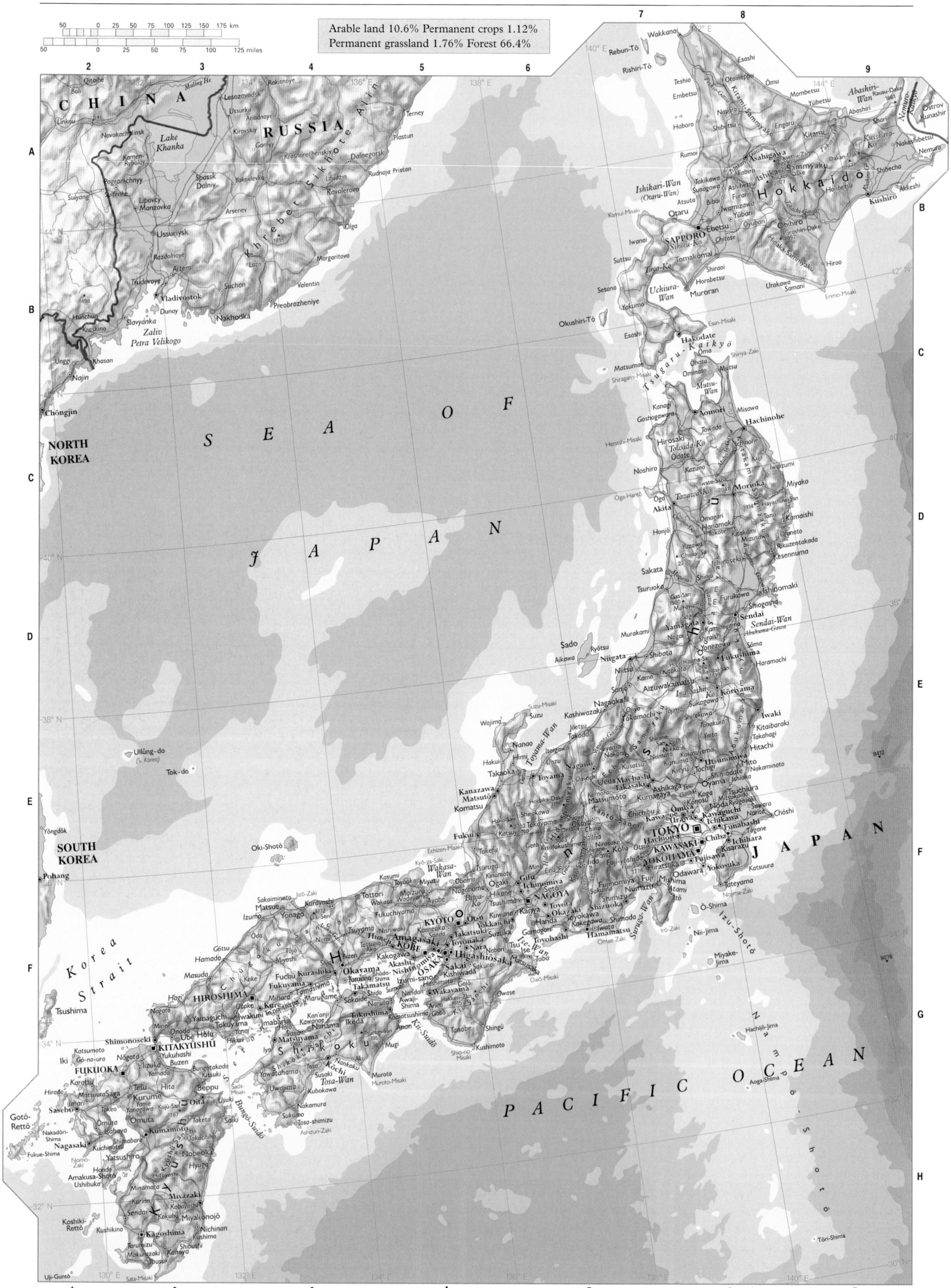

50   0 25 50 75 100 125 150 175 km
50   0 25 50 75 100   125 miles

CHINA

RUSSIA

Khrebet Sikhote Alin'

Lake Khanka

Vladivostok

NORTH KOREA

SOUTH KOREA

Korea Strait

SEA OF JAPAN

Hokkaidō

SAPPORO

Hakodate

Tsugaru Kaikyō

Aomori

Hachinohe

Hirosaki

Akita

Morioka

Sendai

Niigata

Fukushima

Kōriyama

Sado

Kanazawa

Toyama

Nagaoka

TOKYO

KAWASAKI

YOKOHAMA

KYŌTO

KŌBE

OSAKA

NAGOYA

HIROSHIMA

Okayama

Takamatsu

Shikoku

KITAKYŪSHŪ

FUKUOKA

Nagasaki

Kumamoto

Kagoshima

Miyazaki

PACIFIC OCEAN

JAPAN

The policy of seclusion could not be maintained indefinitely. In the early 19th century, the United States became concerned about the mistreatment of American sailors who had been shipwrecked in Japan. In 1853, a mission led by Commodore Matthew C. Perry of the US Navy arrived at Edo (now Tokyo) with four warships. He demanded that diplomatic relations be restored, that all ports be opened to Western trade, and that shipwrecked Americans should be well treated. In 1854, Perry returned to Edo Bay and the government agreed to sign a treaty with the United States. The treaty provided for a US diplomat to reside in Japan and for the United States to have trading rights in two Japanese ports, Hakodate and Shimoda. Britain, the Netherlands and Russia soon signed similar agreements.

Most treaties gave foreigners the right of extra-territoriality, whereby foreigners were allowed to live in Japan, where they were subject to the laws of their own countries, not to the laws of Japan. They were called 'unequal treaties', because they gave foreigners powers that were not granted to the Japanese in return. The capitulation of the shogun to Perry's demands prepared the way for the overthrow of the now weak Tokugawa shogunate in 1867. In 1868, the Meiji Restoration restored the emperor's traditional powers.

That same year, the capital of Japan was moved from Kyoto to Edo (Tokyo). Emperor Mutsuhito, who adopted the title *Meiji*, a title meaning 'enlightened rule', reigned from 1867 to 1912. The Meiji period was marked by the adoption of Western ideas and technology. The Japanese set up an educational system and a telegraph network. They began to build railways and introduced modern systems of banking and taxation. They also abolished the samurai and established a modern army and navy.

In 1889, Japan introduced its first constitution under which the emperor became head of state and supreme commander of the army and navy. The emperor appointed government ministers, who were responsible to him. The constitution also allowed for a parliament, called the Diet, with two houses. The 1890s saw the revision of the unequal treaties and Westerners gave up the right to extra-territoriality.

From the 1890s, Japan also began to build up an overseas empire. In 1894–5, Japan fought China over the control of Korea, which had been under Chinese control for centuries. Japan was victorious and, under the Treaty of Shimonoseki (1895), Japan took Taiwan. Korea was made an independent territory, thus leaving it open to Japanese influence. Rivalry with Russia led to the Russo-Japanese War (1904–5). The causes of the war included the conflicting interests of both countries in Korea and Manchuria. With the help of President Theodore Roosevelt, peace was negotiated after a year of heavy fighting. Under the Treaty of Portsmouth (named after Portsmouth, New Hampshire, where it was signed), Japan gained the Liaodong peninsula, which Russia had leased from China, while Russia recognized the supremacy of Japan's interests in Korea. The Treaty of Portsmouth established Japan as a world power. It also demonstrated for all the world that an Asian power could take on and defeat a European power.

In World War I, Japan supported the Allies and it seized German holdings in the Shandong peninsula, as well as taking Micronesian islands in the western Pacific Ocean, namely the Caroline, Mariana and Marshall groups. After the war, Japan's foreign policy strongly supported the maintenance of world peace, and Japan became a founding member of the League of Nations in 1920. However, many problems arose in the 1920s, including the earthquake that struck Tokyo and Yokohama in 1923, and the world depression in the late 1920s. The growing strength of the Japanese military was demonstrated by the army's seizure of Manchuria in 1931. They made Manchuria a puppet state called Manchukuo, and extended their influence into other parts of northern China. In Japan, nationalists threatened those civilian politicians who opposed the military. In 1932, Japanese nationalists assassinated the prime minister. Japan left the League of Nations in 1933 after that institution had condemned its actions in Manchuria.

During the 1930s, and especially after the outbreak of war between Japan and China in 1937, militarist control of Japan's government grew steadily. By the end of 1938, when Japan controlled most of eastern China, militarists began to talk of bringing all of eastern Asia under Japanese control. In September 1939, Japan occupied the northern part of French Indo-China and, later that month, signed an agreement

The Japanese Boom

In 1945 Japan lay in ruins, with its major cities in ashes – two of them dangerously radioactive. Its smouldering ports were choked with the sunken remnants of its merchant marine fleet, and its people were demoralized. Less than two generations later, the Japanese economy was second only to that of the USA. Its high-technology products dominated world markets, while Japanese banks and private investors owned huge slices of industry and real estate on every continent.

The far-sighted American Occupation authorities deserve some of the credit. Realizing that industrial recovery could go hand in hand only with political development, they wrote a new constitution for Japan. As a link with the past, the Emperor kept his place, but as a constitutional monarch answerable to a democratically elected Diet, with women given full voting rights for the first time. Trade unions, with the right to strike, were established, and land reform eliminated politically subservient tenants. By 1950, 90% of farmland was owner-cultivated. Great industrial conglomerates were broken into smaller units, and education was enormously expanded. Most ordinary Japanese accepted the reforms; they remembered the pain the old ways had brought.

The Korean War in 1950 gave the slowly recovering Japanese economy a tremendous boost. Japanese factories, well paid in American dollars, provided much of the steel, vehicles and other equipment the war demanded. When the Occupation formally ended in 1952, Japan was clearly on the way up. The American military presence, guaranteed by treaty, continued, but caused no resentment; on the contrary, safe beneath the US defence umbrella, Japan could devote its resources to productive industry, not armaments.

The Japanese owed the first stage of their transformation to the Americans; the rest, they did themselves. Carefully planned economic policies, directed by the Ministry of Trade and Industry (MITI) – nicknamed 'Japan Inc.'s Corporate Headquarters' – directed investment to key industries. First, the metal, engineering and chemical industries were rationalized and modernized. With the education system producing a steady stream of graduates, already trained in the industrial disciplines their future employers required, results were soon appearing. In the 1950s and 1960s efficient Japanese steel-makers consistently undersold European and American rivals, while producing better-quality steel. 'Made in Japan', once a sneering joke to describe shoddy goods, was taking on an entirely new commercial meaning.

Japan's major weakness was its near-total lack of natural resources; but foresight and planning made up for them. After the 1970s oil crisis, it was clear that the costs of heavy industry were going to rise unprofitably high; besides, the pollution they had brought was reaching dangerous levels. MITI switched resources to automobiles and electronics. Soon, Japan began to capture and dominate these markets, too.

By the 1980s, Japan's trading partners were becoming alarmed. Noting that trade with Japan was largely a one-way street – Japan's home market is still hard to penetrate – they built protective walls of tariffs and duties. Japan responded with its usual flexibility: it bought factories within its rivals' walls, and traded from there. The Tokyo stock market survived a serious 'crash' in the spring of 1992 – testament to the strength of the national economy. Even so, Japan's colossal trade surpluses in the early 1990s were causing resentment and danger to the world economic system. In 1997, Japan, and much of eastern Asia, entered into a period of economic recession. Drastic measures were taken to restore confidence and, by the turn of the century, the economy was reported to be slowly growing again. However, Japan faces several long-term problems, including the squeezing of the economy by an ageing population needing expensive social services, and also by competition with other dynamic developing countries.

with Italy and Germany, which assured their co-operation in building a 'new world order', while acknowledging Japan's leadership in Asia.

In 1941, Japanese troops entered southern Indochina, causing mounting tension with the United States. Then, in December 1941, it launched a surprise attack on the American naval base of Pearl Harbor, in Hawaii. This action drew the United States into World War II. The Japanese soon conquered large areas in South-east Asia and the South Pacific, but after their defeat in the naval Battle of Midway in 1942, their power began to decline.

In 1945, American bombers attacked Japan and, on 6 August, the first atomic bomb was dropped on Hiroshima. The USSR declared war on Japan and invaded Manchuria and Korea. On 9 August, the Americans dropped a second atomic bomb on Nagasaki. On 2 September, World War II ended when Japan officially surrendered.

Politics

At the end of the war, Japan lost all the territories it had gained in mainland Asia, together with most of the islands it had governed in the Pacific, including the Bonin Islands, Iwo Jima, the Kuril Islands, southern Sakhalin, the Ryukyu Islands and Taiwan. This reduced Japan to its four main islands, plus a few small nearby islands. However, the United States returned the northern Ryukyu Islands to Japan in 1958, the Bonin Islands and Iwo Jima in 1968, and the southern Ryukyu Islands in 1972. Russia still occupies southern Sakhalin. It has also refused to give up the four small islands at the southern end of the Kuril Islands, which were historically ruled by Japan. These islands have become a matter of dispute between Japan and Russia.

The Allies occupied Japan in August 1945. Most of the occupation forces were Americans, led by General Douglas MacArthur, who, with his advisers, drafted a new democratic constitution in 1946. Under the constitution, power was transferred from the emperor to the people. The army and navy were abolished and the country renounced war as a political weapon. The emperor, who had been regarded as divine ruler, became a constitutional monarch. MacArthur also introduced many economic reforms that laid the foundations for Japan's remarkable post-war recovery, which transformed it into the world's second largest economic power.

From 1949, the Americans began to ease their control over Japan. In 1951, Japan signed a Treaty of Peace with 48 nations, not including the Soviet Union, together with a peace treaty with the United States that permitted the US to have military bases in Japan until Japan was able to undertake its own defence. The peace treaty went into effect on 28 April 1952 and the Allied occupation ended on that day. Japan became a member of the UN in 1956, when the Soviet Union and Japan agreed to end the state of war between them.

In 1955, members of rival Japanese parties came together to form the conservative Liberal-Democratic Party. This party controlled Japan's government until the 1990s, when a series of coalition governments were formed. A true opposition party emerged in the late 1990s, when the Democratic Party of Japan united with several small parties. The economy began to slow down in the early 1990s and, in 1997, the country underwent a serious economic crisis. Its banking system was saddled with large loans. Bankruptcies and unemployment were rising, while stock prices and the exchange rates for the yen were falling. The crisis caused fears that Japan's deteriorating economy threatened financial markets around the world. The government was forced to take drastic steps, including massive increases in public spending, the provision of financial support for small companies, income tax cuts and the reform of the banking system, to restore consumer and investor confidence. In the 1998 elections, the Liberal-Democratic Party lost seats and was forced into a coalition government with the small Liberal Party. The Democratic Party took the second largest number of seats.

Economy

Japan's natural resources are limited and the country has to import many of the materials, including fuels, that it requires for manufacturing. Yet the country has the world's second largest economy after the United States. Its gross national product is more than twice as large as the GNP of Germany and more than four times that of China. The most important sector of the economy is manufacturing which

has grown enormously in the last 50 years. Japan's success is owed to several factors, including its use of the latest technology, its skilled and hard-working labour force, its vigorous export policies and the comparatively small governing expenditure on defence. About 77% of the population lives in cities and towns where most of the manufacturing industries are situated. Increasing urbanization has created housing shortages and the cities inevitably suffer from pollution. Another problem is the growing number of people of pensionable age. As a result, the retirement age is being progressively raised from 60 years to 65 by 2013. Unemployment in early 1999 stood at 4.6%, the highest rate since records began in 1953.

Japan has reserves of a variety of minerals, but most deposits are too small to be mined economically. Minerals include coal, copper, lead, manganese, silver, tin and zinc. Some petroleum is produced off Honshu, but it accounts for less than 1% of the country's needs. Such minerals as bauxite, copper and petroleum, together with the coking coal and iron ore needed to make steel, are imported for use in manufacturing. Imported petroleum and natural gas are the most important fuels used in generating electricity. Coal and hydroelectric power are also used and nuclear power stations have become increasingly important. By 1996, Japan had 19 nuclear power plants, with six more under construction. However, parliament passed new legislation to tighten inspections of nuclear facilities after a major accident at a uranium processing plant at Tokaimura, north-east of Tokyo, in September 1999. Experts described this accident as the second worst after the one at Chernobyl (Chornobyl), in Ukraine, in 1986.

Manufacturing accounts for 25% of Japan's gross domestic product. The leading manufacturing sector involves the production of transport equipment. Japan leads the world in producing ships, accounting for 62% of world production in 1996. Its annual production of around 8 million cars a year makes it the world's leading car producer, while it ranks second only to the USA in the production of commercial vehicles. Japan also manufactures machinery, electrical appliances and electronic equipment. Japan is the world's top producer of steel, much of which is exported.

Agriculture accounts for 2% of the gross domestic product and employs about 5% of the workforce. Because so much of the land is rugged, only a small percentage is cultivated. But through intensive farming and the use of terracing and irrigation, Japan produces nearly three-quarters of the food it needs. Rice is the leading staple crop, though its consumption is declining. Japan ranks eighth in the world in the production of rice. It is grown on about half of the country's farmland. Other major crops include fruits, soya beans, sugar beet, tea, tobacco and wheat. Mulberry bushes are cultivated to produce food for silkworms. Before 1945, Japan lacked animal proteins. However, in the last 50 years, livestock farming has become increasingly important. Today, dairy products, eggs and meat are consumed in increasingly large quantities. Traditionally, fish were the main source of protein.

Japan has a highly developed and modern transport system, with a modern road, rail and air system, together with coastal shipping. Japan's high-speed electric trains are famous and the undersea Seikan Tunnel, which was opened to traffic in 1988 connecting Honshu and Hokkaido, is one of the world's longest. The world's longest undersea road tunnel, spanning Tokyo Bay, was opened in 1997.

The United States accounts for about 25% of Japan's total trade and Japan is the second most important trading partner of the United States after Canada. Japan's other major trading partners include China, South Korea and Taiwan.

AREA	Korean, Ainu
377,800 sq km	**LANGUAGES**
[145,869 sq mls]	Japanese (official)
POPULATION	**RELIGIONS**
125,932,000	Shintoism 93%,
CAPITAL (POPULATION)	Buddhism 74%,
Tokyo (26,836,000)	Christianity 1% (most
GOVERNMENT	Japanese consider themselves
Constitutional monarchy	to be both Shinto and Buddhist)
ETHNIC GROUPS	**CURRENCY**
Japanese 99%, Chinese,	Yen = 100 sen

JORDAN

The green, white and black on this flag are the colours of the three tribes who led the Arab Revolt against the Turks in 1917. Red is the colour of the Hussein Dynasty. The star was added in 1928. Its seven points represent the first seven verses of the sacred book, the Koran.

Geography and Climate

The Hashemite Kingdom of Jordan is an Arab country in south-western Asia. The Great Rift Valley in the west contains the River Jordan and the Dead Sea, which Jordan shares with Israel. The Great Rift Valley is part of a huge gash in the Earth's crust, which runs south through East Africa to Mozambique. East of the Rift Valley is the Transjordan Plateau, where most Jordanians live. To the east and south lie vast areas of desert. Jordan has a short coastline on an arm of the Red Sea, the Gulf of Aqaba. The country's highest peak, Jabal Ramm, reaches 1,754 m [5,755 ft] in the south.

About 90% of Jordan has a desert climate, with an average annual rainfall of less than 200 mm [8 in]. Summers are hot, but winters may be cold, with snow on higher areas. The north-west is the wettest area, with an average annual rainfall of up to 800 mm [31 in] in higher areas.

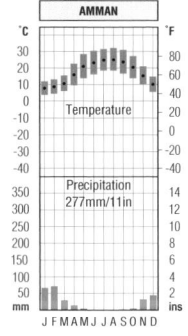

JORDAN (AMMAN)

The Jordan Valley marks the eastern limit of the true Mediterranean region, and although Amman lies only a short distance east of Jerusalem, it has a much lower rainfall and a longer dry season. Rain is almost unknown from May to September. Amman's semi-arid climate is transitional between the Mediterranean type and the true desert to the east. Temperatures are similar on average to those of Jerusalem, but summer days are hotter.

History

Jordan's early history is closely linked with that of Israel. It was first settled by Semitic peoples about 4,000 years ago, and was later conquered by Egyptian, Assyrian, Chaldean, Persian and Roman forces. The area fell to the Muslim Arabs in AD 636 and the Arab culture they introduced survives to this day.

By the end of the 12th century, Christian crusaders controlled parts of western Jordan, but they were driven out by the great Muslim warrior Saladin in 1187. The Egyptian Mamelukes overthrew Saladin's successors in 1250. The Mamelukes ruled until 1517, when the area was conquered by the Ottoman Turks. Jordan stagnated under the rule of the Ottoman Turks, but the opening of a railway in 1908 stimulated the economy. Arab and British forces defeated the Turks during World War I and, after the war, the area east of the River Jordan was awarded to Britain by the League of Nations.

Politics

In 1921, Britain created a territory called Transjordan, east of the River Jordan. In 1923, Transjordan became self-governing, but Britain retained control of its defences, finances and foreign affairs. This territory became fully independent as Jordan in 1946.

Jordan has suffered from instability arising from the Arab-Israeli conflict since the creation of the State of Israel in 1948. After the first Arab-Israeli War (1948–9), Jordan acquired the fertile West Bank, which was officially incorporated into the state in 1950. This crucial area, which included East Jerusalem, was lost to Israel in the 1967 war and Jordan subsequently carried the burden of Palestinian refugees on its own territory. In the 1970s, Palestinian guerrillas using Jordan as a base became a challenge to the authority of the government of King Hussein, who had become king in 1953. After a short civil war, the Palestinian leadership fled the country.

In 1988, King Hussein suddenly renounced all responsibility for the West Bank – a recognition that the Palestine Liberation Organization, and not the long-suffering Jordan, was the legitimate representative of the Palestinian people. Nevertheless, Palestinians still formed a majority of the population. The refugees, numbering around 900,000, placed a huge burden on an already weak economy. Jordan

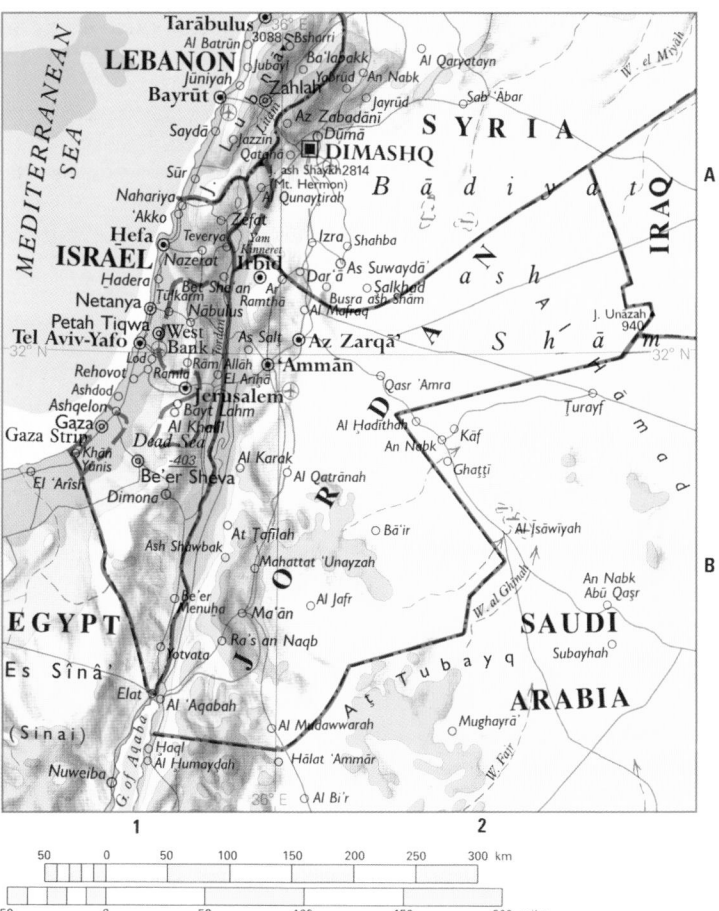

was further undermined by the 1991 Gulf War when, despite its official neutrality, the pro-Iraq, anti-Western stance of the Palestinians in Jordan did nothing to improve prospects of trade and aid deals with Europe and the United States, while Jordan's vital economic links with Israel had already been severed. The ban on political parties was removed in 1991, and martial law was lifted after 21 years. Multiparty elections were held in 1993 and, in 1994, Jordan and Israel signed a peace treaty, ending a state of war which had been going on for more than 40 years. The treaty restored some land in the south to Jordan.

Jordan's King Hussein, who had commanded great respect for playing an important role in Middle Eastern affairs, died in 1999. He was succeeded by his eldest son who became King Abdullah II.

Economy

Jordan lacks natural resources, apart from phosphates and potash, and the country's economy depends substantially on aid. The World Bank classifies Jordan as a 'lower-middle-income' developing country. Because of the dry climate, under 6% of the land is farmed or used as pasture. Major crops include barley, citrus fruits, grapes, olives, vegetables and wheat.

Jordan has an oil refinery and manufactures include cement, pharmaceuticals, processed food, fertilizers and textiles. The main exports are phosphates, fertilizers, potash, fruits and vegetables.

AREA	ETHNIC GROUPS
89,210 sq km [34,444 sq mls]	Arab 99% (50% Palestinians)
POPULATION	**LANGUAGES**
4,435,000	Arabic (official)
CAPITAL (POPULATION)	**RELIGIONS**
Amman (1,300,000)	Islam 93%, Christianity 5%
GOVERNMENT	**CURRENCY**
Constitutional monarchy	Jordan dinar = 1,000 fils

Kazakstan's flag was adopted on 4 June 1992, about six months after it had become independent. The blue represents cloudless skies, while the golden sun and the soaring eagle represent love of freedom. A vertical strip of gold ornamentation is on the left.

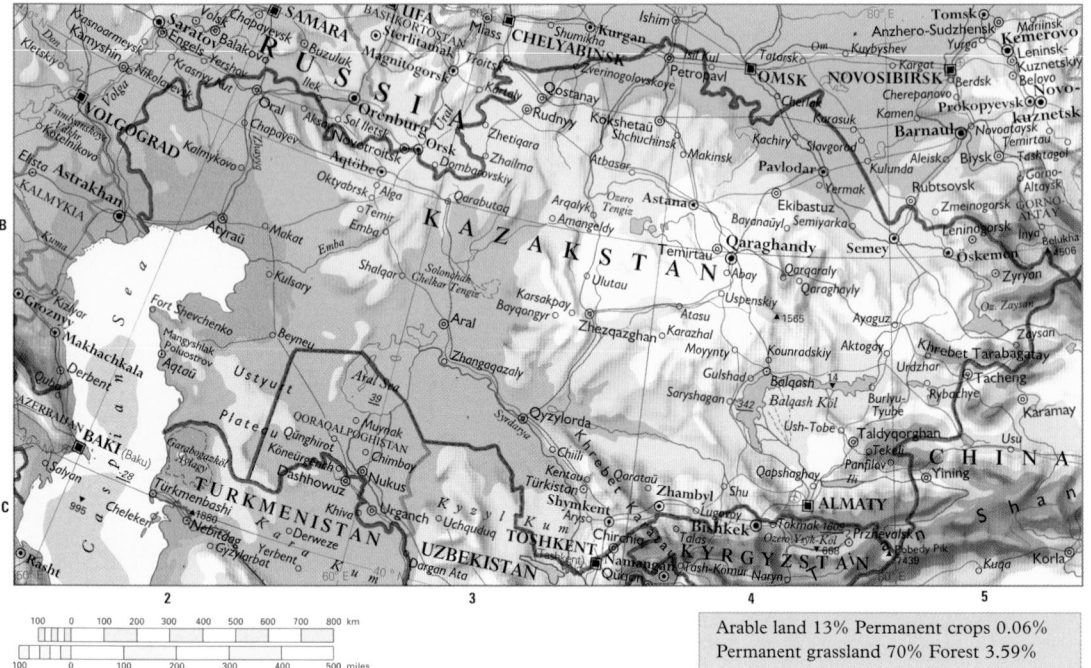

Arable land 13% Permanent crops 0.06%
Permanent grassland 70% Forest 3.59%

Geography

Kazakstan is a large country in west-central Asia. In the west, the Caspian Sea lowlands include the Karagiye Depression, which reaches 132 m [433 ft] below sea level. The lowlands extend eastwards through the Aral Sea area. The north contains high plains, but the highest land is along the eastern and southern borders. These areas include parts of the Altai and Tian Shan mountain ranges.

Eastern Kazakstan contains several freshwater lakes, the largest of which is Lake Balkhash (Balqash Köl). The water in the rivers has been used for irrigation, causing ecological problems. For example, the Aral Sea, deprived of water, shrank from 66,900 sq km [25,830 sq mls] in 1960, to 33,642 sq km [12,989 sq mls] in 1993. Areas which once provided fish have dried up and are now barren desert.

Climate

The climate reflects Kazakstan's position in the heart of Asia, far from the influence of the oceans. Winters are cold and snow covers the land for about 100 days, on average, at Alma Ata (Almaty). Rainfall is generally quite low.

KAZAKSTAN (ALMA ATA)

Kazakstan is a large country in the centre of Asia and its climate is markedly continental. The summers are warm and the winters cold, the annual temperature range being 30°C [54°F]. Half the year will experience frost (at Alma Ata) and snow lies for about 100 days. Rainfall is low with only around 250 mm [10 in] in the north and twice this amount in the south, with desert and semi-desert conditions covering large areas.

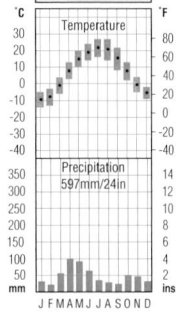

History

From the late 15th century, the Kazaks built up a large nomadic empire ruled by khans. But Kazak power declined in the 17th century. In the early 18th century, Russia became influential in the area. In 1731, the Kazaks in the west accepted Russian rule to gain protection from attack from neighbouring peoples. By the mid-1740s, Russia ruled most of the region and, in the early 19th century, Russia abolished the khanates. They also encouraged Russians and Ukrainians to settle in Kazakstan.

After the Russian Revolution of 1917, many Kazaks wanted to make their country independent. But the Communists prevailed and in 1936 Kazakstan became a republic of the Soviet Union, called the Kazak Soviet Socialist Republic. During World War II, and also after the war, the Soviet government moved many people from the west into Kazakstan. From the 1950s, people were encouraged to work on a 'Virgin Lands' project, which involved bringing large areas of grassland under cultivation.

Politics

Reforms in the Soviet Union in the 1980s led to the break-up of the country in December 1991. Kazakstan kept contacts with Russia and most of the other republics in the former Soviet Union by joining the Commonwealth of Independent States (CIS), and in 1995 Kazakstan announced that its army would unite with that of Russia. In December 1997, the government moved the capital from Alma Ata to Aqmola (later renamed Astana), a town in the Russian-dominated north. It was hoped that this move would bring some Kazak identity to the area.

Under Soviet rule, Kazakstan was a dumping ground and test bed – the Soviet missile- and rocket-launching site at Baykonur (Bayqongyr) suffered great environmental damage, including the shrinking of the Aral Sea by 70%. But Kazakstan has emerged as a powerful entity, wealthier and more diversified than other Asian republics. It could provide the 'new order' between East and West. It is the only former Soviet republic whose ethnic population is almost outnumbered by another group (the Russians), and its Muslim revival is relatively muted. Its first elected president, Nursultan Nazarbayev, a former Communist leader, introduced many reforms, including a multiparty system.

Economy

The World Bank classifies Kazakstan as a 'lower-middle-income' developing country. Livestock farming, especially sheep and cattle, is important, and major crops include barley, cotton, rice and wheat. The country is rich in mineral resources, including coal and oil reserves, together with bauxite, copper, lead, tungsten and zinc. Manufactures include chemicals, food products, machinery and textiles. Oil is exported via a pipeline through Russia. However, to reduce dependence on Russia, Kazakstan signed an agreement in 1997 to build a new pipeline to China. Other exports include metals, chemicals, grain, wool and meat.

AREA	German 6%, Ukrainian 5%,
2,717,300 sq km	Uzbek, Tatar
[1,049,150 sq mls]	**LANGUAGES**
POPULATION	Kazak (official); Russian,
16,847,000	the former official language,
CAPITAL (POPULATION)	is widely spoken
Astana (280,000)	**RELIGIONS**
GOVERNMENT	Mainly Islam, with a
Multiparty republic	Christian minority
ETHNIC GROUPS	**CURRENCY**
Kazak 40%, Russian 38%,	Tenge

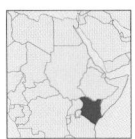

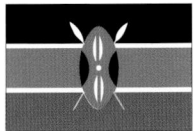

Kenya's flag dates from 1963, when the country became independent. It is based on the flag of KANU (Kenya African National Union), the political party which led the nationalist struggle. The Masai warrior's shield and crossed spears represent the defence of freedom.

Geography

The Republic of Kenya is a country in East Africa which straddles the Equator. It is slightly larger in area than France. Behind the narrow coastal plain on the Indian Ocean, the land rises to high plains and highlands, broken by volcanic mountains, including Mount Kenya, the country's highest peak at 5,199 m [17,057 ft].

Crossing the country is an arm of the Great Rift Valley. On the floor of this steep-sided valley are several lakes, including Baringo, Magadi, Naivasha, Nakuru and, on the northern frontier, Lake Turkana (formerly Lake Rudolf).

Climate

The Equator passes through Kenya just north of the snow-capped Mount Kenya. While the climate is tropical, it is very much affected by altitude, especially in the south-western highlands. This region is distinctly cooler than the hot and humid coast.

The average annual rainfall is between 1,000 mm and 1,300 mm [39–51 in]. However, the rainfall is variable. Only about 15% of Kenya has a reliable annual rainfall of 800 mm [31 in].

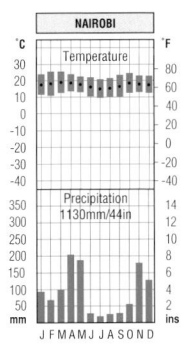

KENYA (NAIROBI)

Nairobi lies in the south-western highlands, at a height of 1,820 m [5,971 ft] above sea level. Temperatures here have been recorded at about 10°C [50°F] lower than those in Mombasa. The main rains occur during April and May, with a lesser rainy season in November and December.

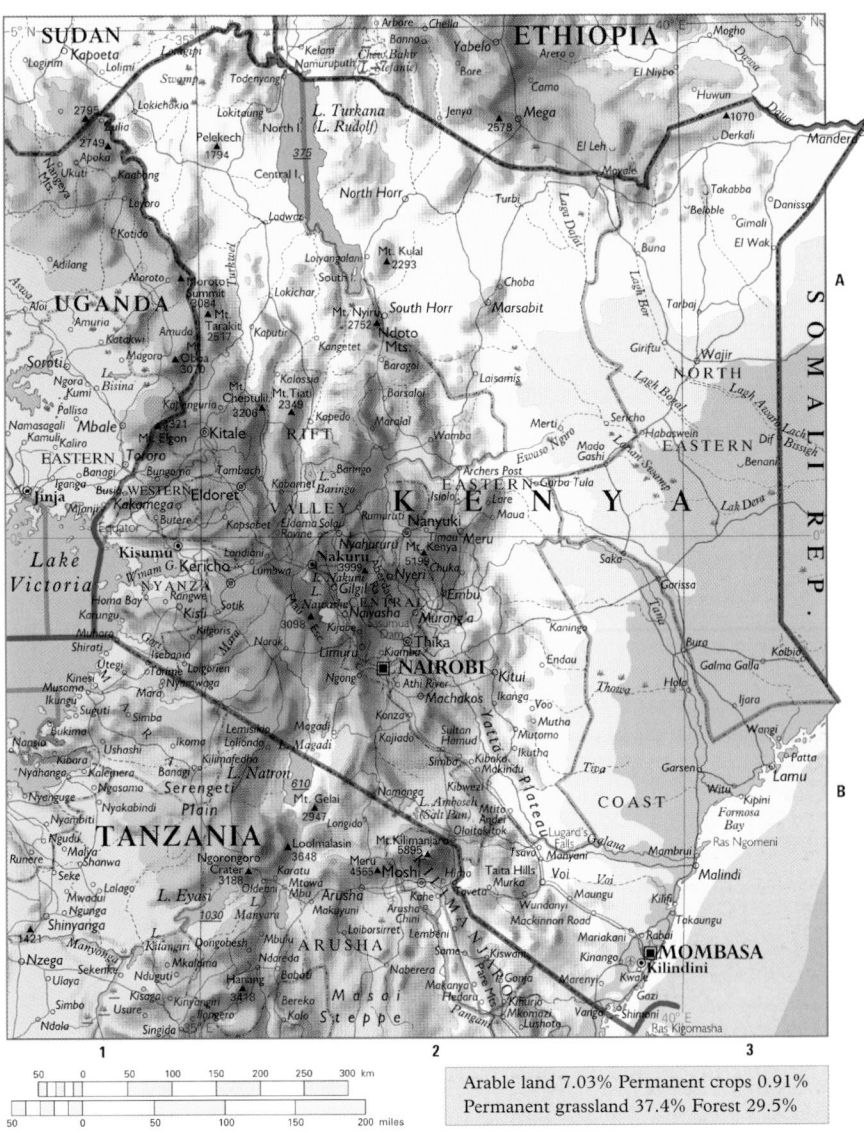

Arable land 7.03% Permanent crops 0.91%
Permanent grassland 37.4% Forest 29.5%

History

The Kenyan coast has been an important trading centre for more than 2,000 years. Early Arab traders carried goods from eastern Asia and exchanged them for items from the local people. The Portuguese explorer Vasco da Gama reached the coast in 1498. Later, the Portuguese competed with the Arabs for control of the coast.

The British took control of the coast in 1895 and soon extended their influence inland. Many Britons set up large farms in Kenya. However, opposition to British rule mounted in the 1940s, and, in 1953, a secret movement called Mau Mau launched an armed struggle. Mau Mau was defeated, but Kenya gained its independence in 1953.

Politics

Many Kenyan leaders felt that the division of the population into 40 ethnic groups might lead to instability. They argued that Kenya should have a strong central government and, as a result, Kenya has been a one-party state for much of the time since independence. Multiparty democracy was restored in the early 1990s and elections were held in 1992 and 1997, each resulting in a victory for the ruling president Daniel Arap Moi.

In the 1960s, attempts by Kenya, Tanzania and Uganda to collaborate collapsed because of the deep differences between the political and economic policies of the countries. However, hopes were revived in 1999, when a new East African Community was created. It aims to establish a customs union, a common market, a monetary union, and, ultimately, a political union.

Economy

According to the United Nations, Kenya is a 'low-income' developing country. Agriculture employs about 80% of the people, but many Kenyans are subsistence farmers, growing little more than they need to support their families. The chief food crop is maize. Bananas, beans, cassava and sweet potatoes are also grown. The main cash crops and leading exports are coffee and tea. Manufactures include chemicals, leather and footwear, processed food, petroleum products and textiles.

By the standards of tropical Africa, Kenya has a stable economy, even allowing for a thriving black market and the usual reliance on aid.

AREA	Luo 13%, Kamba 11%,
580,370 sq km [224,081 sq mls]	Kalenjin 11%
POPULATION	**LANGUAGES**
28,337,000	Swahili and English (both official)
CAPITAL (POPULATION)	**RELIGIONS**
Nairobi (2,000,000)	Christianity (Catholic 27%,
GOVERNMENT	Protestant 19%, others 27%),
Multiparty republic	traditional beliefs 19%, Islam 6%
ETHNIC GROUPS	**CURRENCY**
Kikuyu 21%, Luhya 14%,	Kenya shilling = 100 cents

KIRIBATI – SEE PACIFIC OCEAN, PAGES 174–178

KOREA, NORTH

The flag of the Democratic People's Republic of Korea (North Korea) has been flown since Korea was split into two states in 1948. The colours are traditional ones in Korea. The design, with the red star, indicates that North Korea is a Communist country.

Geography

The Democratic People's Republic of Korea occupies the northern part of the Korean Peninsula which extends south from north-eastern China. Mountains form the heart of the country, with the highest peak, Paektu-san, reaching 2,744 m [9,003 ft] on the northern border.

Climate

North Korea has a fairly severe climate, with bitterly cold winters when winds blow from across central Asia, bringing snow and freezing conditions. In summer, moist winds from the oceans bring rain.

History

The early history of the Korean peninsula is covered in the article on South Korea on page 143. North Korea came into being in 1945 when the peninsula, which had been a Japanese colony since 1910, was partitioned. Soviet forces occupied the north, while US troops controlled the south.

Politics

Soviet occupation led to a Communist government being established in 1948 under the leadership of Kim Il Sung. He initiated a Stalinist regime in which he assumed role of dictator, and a personality cult developed around him. He became the world's most durable Communist leader.

The Korean War began in June 1950 when North Korean troops invaded the south. North Korea, aided by China and the Soviet Union, fought with South Korea, which was supported by troops from the United States and other UN members. The war ended in July 1953. An armistice was signed but no permanent peace treaty was agreed upon. After the war, North Korea adopted a hostile policy towards South Korea in pursuit of its policy of reunification. At times, the situation grew so tense that it became a matter of international concern.

The ending of the Cold War in the late 1980s eased the situation and both North and South Korea joined the United Nations in 1991. The two countries made several agreements, including one in which they agreed not to use force against each other.

As Communism collapsed in the Soviet Union, however, North Korea remained as isolated as ever, pursuing the overriding principle of self-reliance.

In 1993, North Korea began a new international crisis by announcing that it was withdrawing from the Nuclear Non-Proliferation Treaty. This led to suspicions that North Korea, which had signed the Treaty in 1985, was developing its own nuclear weapons. Kim Il Sung, who had ruled as a virtual dictator from 1948 until his death in 1994, was succeeded by his son Kim Jong Il. In the late 1990s, increasing uncertainty surrounding North Korea's nuclear capabilities cast unease over the region as a whole.

Economy

North Korea has considerable resources, including coal, copper, iron ore, lead, tin, tungsten and zinc. Under Communism, North Korea has concentrated on developing heavy, state-owned industries. Manufactures include chemicals, iron and steel, machinery, processed food and textiles. Agriculture employs about a third of the people and rice is the leading crop. Economic decline and mismanagement, aggravated by three successive crop failures caused by floods in 1995 and 1996, and a drought in 1997, led to famine on a large scale.

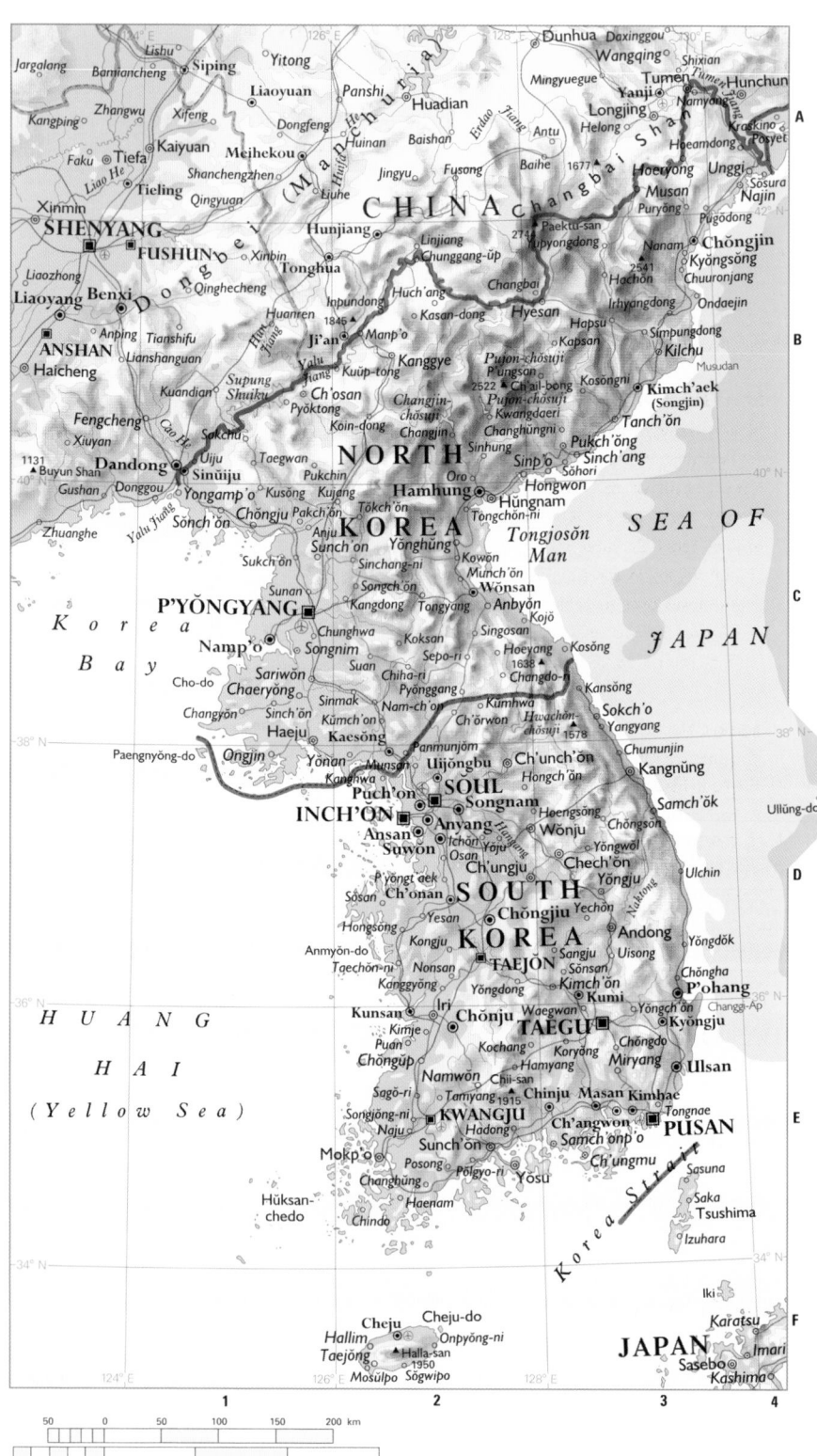

AREA	ETHNIC GROUPS
120,540 sq km [46,540 sq mls]	Korean 99%
POPULATION	**LANGUAGES**
21,234,000	Korean (official)
CAPITAL (POPULATION)	**RELIGIONS**
P'yŏngyang (2,639,000)	Traditional beliefs 16%, Chondogyo 14%,
GOVERNMENT	Buddhism 2%, Christianity 1%
Single-party people's republic	**CURRENCY**
	North Korean won = 100 chon

KOREA, SOUTH

South Korea's flag, adopted in 1950, is white, the traditional symbol for peace. The central 'yin-yang' symbol signifies the opposing forces of nature. The four black symbols stand for the four seasons, the points of the compass, and the Sun, Moon, Earth and Heaven.

Geography

The Republic of Korea, as South Korea is officially known, occupies the southern part of the Korean Peninsula. Mountains cover much of the country. The southern and western coasts are major farming regions. Many islands are found along the west and south coasts, the largest of which is Cheju-do, which contains South Korea's highest peak, Halla-san, which rises to 1,950 m [6,398 ft].

Climate

Like North Korea, South Korea is chilled in winter by cold, dry winds blowing from central Asia. Snow often covers the mountains in the east. The summers are hot and wet, especially in July and August.

SOUTH KOREA (SEOUL)

North-westerly winds from central Asia give cold, dry weather in winter and night temperatures from December to March are usually below freezing. Snow lies on western mountain slopes east of Seoul. Summer is hot and wet, causing coastal sea fog in spring as warmer air from the south moves over the cold water surface. In July and August it rains on average every other day. During winter it rains less than 5 days a month.

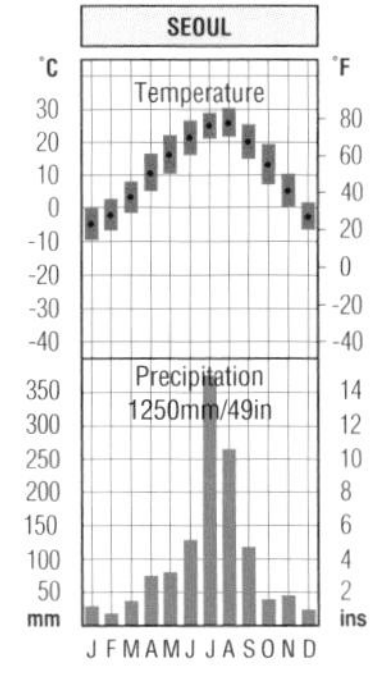

History

In the last 2,000 years, China has had a great influence on the people of Korea. The Chinese conquered the north in 108 BC and ruled until they were thrown out in AD 313. Mongol armies attacked Korea in the 13th century, but in 1388, a general, Yi Songgye, founded a dynasty of rulers which lasted until 1910.

From the 17th century, Korea prevented foreigners from entering the country. Korea was often called the 'Hermit Kingdom' until 1876, when Japan forced it to open some of its ports. Soon, the United States, Russia and some European countries were trading with Korea. In 1910, Korea became a Japanese colony.

After Japan's defeat in World War II (1939–45), North Korea was occupied by troops from the Soviet Union, while South Korea was occupied by United States forces. Attempts to reunify Korea failed and, in 1948, a National Assembly was elected in South Korea. This Assembly created the Republic of Korea, while North Korea became a Communist state. North Korean troops invaded the South in June 1950, sparking off the Korean War (1950–3).

Politics

The story of South Korea after the civil war was a very different one from that of the North, though the South was hardly a Far Eastern oasis of liberalism. While land reform based on smallholdings worked well enough to produce some of the world's highest rice yields (and self-sufficiency in food grains), the real economic miracle came in industrial expansion which started in the early 1960s. Initiated by a military government – one of several bouts of army rule since the inauguration of the republic – and based on slender natural resources, the country utilized its cheap, plentiful but well-educated labour force to transform the economy. The original manufacturing base of textiles remained important, but South Korea became a world leader in footwear, shipbuilding, consumer electronics, toys and vehicles.

The country's dynamism had to be linked to more liberal policies and, in 1988, a new constitution came into force, enabling presidential elections to be held every five years. Evidence of the new spirit of democracy came in 1997 when, in presidential elections, Kim Dae-jung, leader of past pro-democracy campaigns, narrowly defeated Hoi-chang, the governing party's candidate. In foreign affairs, a major breakthrough had occurred in 1991 when both North Korea and

South Korea were admitted as full members of the United Nations. The two countries signed several agreements, including one in which they agreed not to use force against each other, but tensions between them continued. In 1998, North Korea launched what was at first thought to be a medium-range missile across Japan into the Pacific Ocean. This initially caused great anxiety throughout the region, but it was thought later that the 'missile' was, in fact, a satellite.

Economy

The World Bank classifies South Korea as an 'upper-middle-income' developing country. It is also one of the world's fastest growing industrial economies. Resources include coal and tungsten. South Korea's main manufactures are processed food and textiles. Since partition, heavy industries have been built up, making chemicals, fertilizers, iron and steel, and ships. South Korea has also developed the production of computers, cars and televisions. In late 1997, however, dramatic expansion of the economy was halted by a market crash which affected many of the booming economies of Asia. In an effort to negate the economic and social turmoil that resulted, tough reforms were demanded by the International Monetary Fund. An agreement was reached to restructure much of the short-term debt faced by the government.

Farming remains important in South Korea. Rice is the chief crop, together with fruit, grains and vegetables. Fishing is also important.

The Korean War

Hastily divided in 1945 between a Soviet-occupied North and an American-occupied South, Korea was considered by most Western strategists an irrelevance to the developing Cold War. But when the heavily armed North invaded the South in June 1950, US President Truman decided to make a stand against what he saw (mistakenly) as Moscow-organized aggression. A Soviet boycott of the UN allowed US troops – assisted by contingents from Britain, Canada, France and other allies – to fight under the UN flag, and under General Douglas MacArthur they went on the offensive. American seapower permitted a landing far behind North Korean lines, and soon the Northerners were in retreat.

With some misgivings, Truman ordered his forces north of the 38th parallel, the former partition line. But as US troops neared the Chinese frontier in November 1950, hundreds of thousands of Chinese 'volunteers' surged across the Yalu River and threatened to overwhelm them. The UN troops retreated far southwards in disarray, until a 1951 counter-attack slowly pushed back up the country, and the combatants became entrenched along the 38th parallel in a bitter war of attrition that endured until an armistice was negotiated in 1953. Not until 1991, almost 40 years later, were North and South able to agree to a tentative non-aggression pact.

AREA	**LANGUAGES**
99,020 sq km [38,232 sq mls]	Korean (official)
POPULATION	**RELIGIONS**
46,417,000	Buddhism 28%,
CAPITAL (POPULATION)	Christianity
Seoul (Soul, 11,641,000)	(Protestant 19%,
GOVERNMENT	Roman Catholic 6%)
Multiparty republic	**CURRENCY**
ETHNIC GROUPS	South Korean won =
Korean 99%	100 chon

KUWAIT – SEE GULF STATES, PAGES 113–114

Kyrgyzstan's flag was adopted in March 1992. The flag depicts a bird's-eye view of a 'yurt' (circular tent) within a radiant sun. The 'yurt' recalls the traditional nomadic way of life. The 40 rays of the sun stand for the 40 traditional tribes.

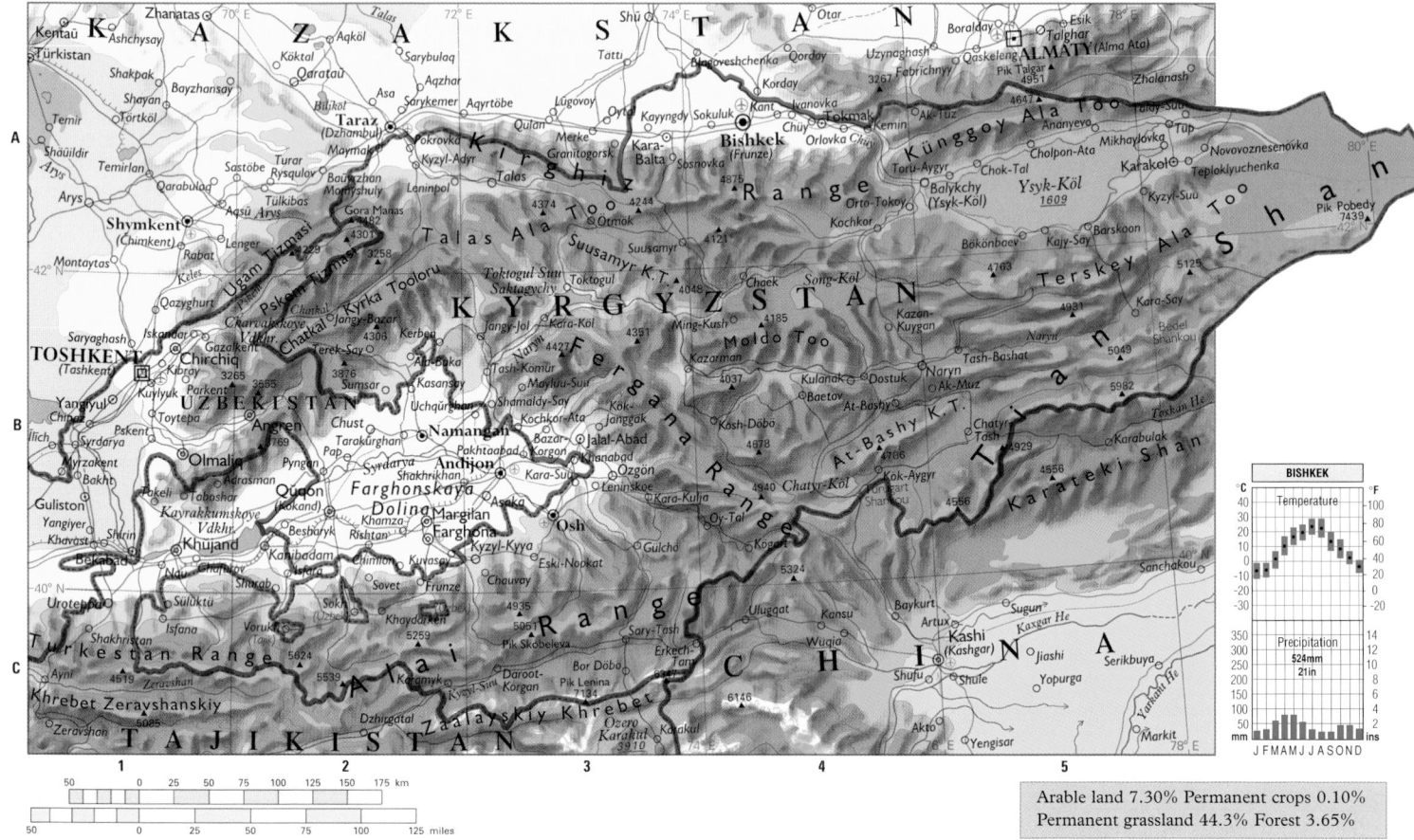

Arable land 7.30% Permanent crops 0.10%
Permanent grassland 44.3% Forest 3.65%

Geography and Climate

The Republic of Kyrgyzstan, or Kirghizia as it is also known, is a landlocked country between China, Tajikistan, Uzbekistan and Kazakstan. The country is mountainous, with spectacular scenery. The highest mountain, Pik Pobedy in the Tian Shan Range, reaches 7,439 m [24,406 ft] above sea level in the east. Less than a sixth of the country is below 900 m [2,950 ft]. The largest of the country's many lakes is Lake Issyk Kul (Ysyk-Köl) in the north-east. Its shoreline is 1,609 m [5,279 ft] above sea level.

The lowlands of Kyrgyzstan have warm summers and cold winters. But the altitude influences the climate in the mountains, where the January temperatures plummet to −28°C [−18°F]. Far from any sea, Kyrgyzstan has a low annual rainfall.

History

The area that is now Kyrgyzstan was populated in ancient times by nomadic herders. Mongol armies conquered the region in the early 13th century. They set up areas called khanates, ruled by chieftains, or khans. Islam was introduced in the 17th century.

China gained control of the area in the mid-18th century, but, in 1876, Kyrgyzstan became a province of Russia and Russian settlement in the area began.

Politics

In 1916, Russia crushed a rebellion among the Kyrgyz, and many subsequently fled to China. In 1922, the area became an autonomous *oblast* (self-governing region) of the newly formed Soviet Union but, in 1936, it became one of the Soviet Socialist Republics. Under Communist rule, nomads were forced to work on government-run farms, while local customs and religious worship were suppressed. However, there were improvements in education and health.

In 1991, Kyrgyzstan became an independent country following the break-up of the Soviet Union. The Communist Party was dissolved, but

the country maintained ties with Russia through an organization called the Commonwealth of Independent States. Kyrgyzstan adopted a new constitution in 1994 and parliamentary elections were held in 1995. However, in the late 1990s, Kyrgyzstan's president Askar Akayev, once regarded as the most democratically minded politician in Central Asia, introduced a series of constitutional changes and other measures which gave greater powers to himself and limited press freedom. Kyrgyzstan also has the potential for an ethnic tinderbox, with its large Russian minority (who held positions of power in the days of the Soviet Union), disenchanted Uzbeks, and an influx of Chinese Muslim immigrants.

Economy

In the early 1990s, when Kyrgyzstan was working to reform its economy, the World Bank classified it as a 'lower-middle-income' developing country. Agriculture, especially livestock rearing, is the chief activity. The chief products include cotton, eggs, fruits, grain, tobacco, vegetables and wool. However, food must be imported. Industries are mainly concentrated around the capital Bishkek. Manufactures include machinery, processed food, metals and textiles. Exports include wool, chemicals, cotton and metals.

AREA	Uzbek 13%, Ukrainian 3%,
198,500 sq km [76,640 sq mls]	German 2%, Tatar 2%
POPULATION	**LANGUAGES**
4,522,000	Kyrgyz (official),
CAPITAL (POPULATION)	Russian,
Bishkek (584,000)	Uzbek
GOVERNMENT	**RELIGIONS**
Multiparty republic	Islam
ETHNIC GROUPS	**CURRENCY**
Kyrgyz 52%, Russian 22%,	Som = 100 tyiyn

LAOS

Since 1975, Laos has flown the flag of the Pathet Lao, the Communist movement which won control of the country after a long struggle. The blue stands for the River Mekong, the white disc for the Moon, and the red for the unity and purpose of the people.

Geography

The Lao People's Democratic Republic is a landlocked country in South-east Asia. Mountains and plateaus cover much of the country. The highest point is Mount Bia, which reaches 2,817 m [9,242 ft] in central Laos.

Most people live on the plains bordering the River Mekong and its tributaries. This river, one of Asia's longest, forms much of the country's north-western and south-western borders. A range of mountains called the Annam Cordillera runs along the eastern border with Vietnam.

Climate

Laos has a tropical monsoon climate. Winters are dry and sunny, with winds blowing in from the north-east. The temperatures rise until April, when the wind directions are reversed and moist south-westerly winds reach Laos, heralding the start of the wet monsoon season.

History

From the 9th century AD, Lao and Tai people set up a number of small states ruled by princes. But the area that is now Laos was united in 1353 in a kingdom called Lan Xang ('land of a million elephants'). Apart from a period of Burmese rule between 1574 and 1637, the Lan Xang ruled Laos until the early 18th century. In 1713, the region was divided into three separate kingdoms – Champasak, Vientiane and Louangphrabang – which became vassals of Siam (now Thailand).

In the 19th century, Chao Anou, the king of Vientiane, united his kingdom with Vietnam in an attempt to break Siamese domination, but he was defeated and Vientiane became a Siamese province. In the late 19th century, however, France gradually gained control of all Siamese territory east of the River Mekong.

Politics

France made Laos a protectorate in the late 19th century and ruled it as part of French Indo-China, a region which also included Cambodia and Vietnam. After France's surrender to Germany in 1945, Japanese forces moved into Indo-China. They allowed the French to continue as puppet rulers until 1945, when they interned all French authorities and military units. A Free Laos movement set up a government, but it collapsed when the French returned in 1946.

Under a new constitution, Laos became a monarchy in 1947 and, in 1949, the country became a self-governing state within the French Union. After full independence in 1954, Laos suffered from instability caused by a power struggle between royalist government forces and a pro-Communist group called the Pathet Lao. The Pathet Lao took power in 1975 after two decades of chaotic civil war in which the royalist forces were supported by American bombing and Thai mercenaries, while the Patriotic Front Pathet Lao was assisted by North Vietnam. The king, Savang Vatthana, abdicated in 1975, and the People's Democratic Republic of Laos was proclaimed. Over 300,000 Laotians, including technicians and other experts, as well as farmers, and members of ethnic minorities, fled the country. Many opponents of the government who remained were sent to re-education camps.

Communist policies brought isolation and stagnation under the domination of the Vietnamese government in Hanoi, who had used Laos as a great supply line in their war against the United States. In 1986, the Laotian Politburo embarked on its own version of *perestroika*, opening up its doors to tourists and also opening up trade links with its neighbours, notably China and Japan. In 1997, Laos became a member of the Association of South-east Asian Nations (ASEAN).

Arable land 3.79% Permanent crops 0.11%
Permanent grassland 3.47% Forest 54.4%

Also important was the development of the hydroelectric power potential from the River Mekong and the export of electricity to Thailand, earning Laos the title of the 'battery of South-east Asia'.

Most enterprises are now outside state control while the government works to develop alternative crops to opium. But political reform towards a multiparty democracy seems a forlorn hope.

Economy

Laos is one of the world's poorest countries. Agriculture employs about 76% of the people, as compared with 7% in industry and 17% in services. Rice is the main crop, and timber and coffee are both exported. But the most valuable export is electricity, which is produced at hydroelectric power stations on the River Mekong and is exported to Thailand. Laos also produces opium. In the early 1990s, Laos was thought to be the world's third biggest source of this illegal drug.

AREA	Mon-Khmer 17%, Tai 8%
236,800 sq km [91,428 sq mls]	**LANGUAGES**
POPULATION	Lao (official), Khmer,
5,261,000	Tai, Miao
CAPITAL (POPULATION)	**RELIGIONS**
Vientiane (449,000)	Buddhism 58%,
GOVERNMENT	traditional beliefs 34%,
Single-party republic	Christianity 2%, Islam 1%
ETHNIC GROUPS	**CURRENCY**
Lao 67%,	Kip = 100 at

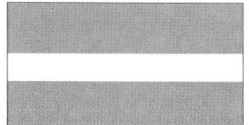

The burgundy and white Latvian flag, which dates back to at least 1280, was revived after Latvia achieved its independence in 1991. According to one legend, the flag was first made from a white sheet which had been stained with the blood of a Latvian hero.

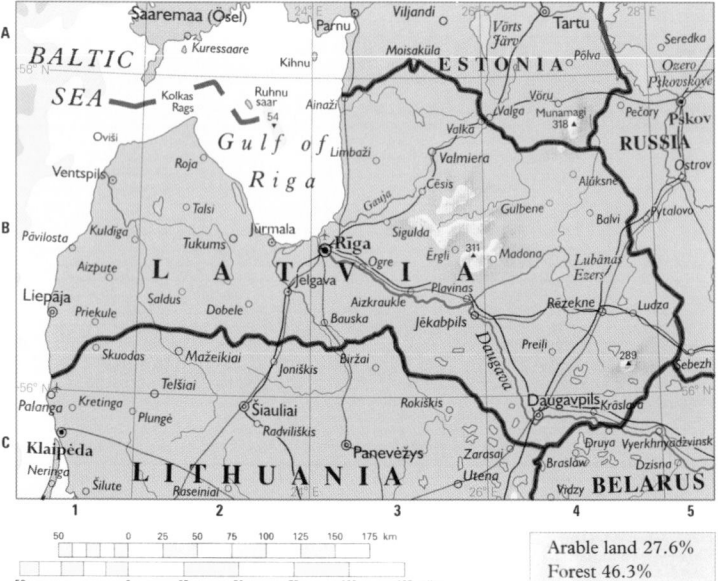

Arable land 27.6%
Forest 46.3%

Geography

The Republic of Latvia is one of three states on the south-eastern corner of the Baltic Sea which were ruled as parts of the Soviet Union between 1940 and 1991. Latvia consists mainly of flat plains separated by low hills, composed of moraine (ice-worn rocks). The moraine was dumped there by ice-sheets during the Ice Age. The country's highest point is only 311 m [1,020 ft] above sea level. Small lakes and peat bogs are common. The country's main river, the Daugava, is also known as the Western Dvina.

Climate

Air masses from the Atlantic influence the climate of Latvia, bringing warm and rainy conditions in summer. Winters are cold, The average temperature range is 16°C to 18°C [61–64°F] in July, and –7°C to –3°C [19–27°F] in January.

LATVIA (RIGA)

Riga has warm summers and cold winters, with rain or snow in all months. June to August are the warmest months with temperatures over 15°C [59°F], and sub-zero averages from December to March. Temperature extremes are just over 34°C [93°F] and –29°C [–20°F]. On average, rain falls on a third of the days in the second half of the year, but the total is relatively light. It can be overcast for long periods.

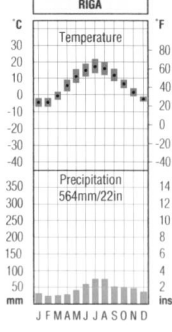

History

The ancestors of most modern Latvians settled in the area about 2,000 years ago. Between the 9th and 11th centuries, the region was attacked by Vikings from the west and Russians from the east. In the 13th century, German invaders took over, naming the country Livland, or Livonia in Latin.

In 1561, Latvia was partitioned and most of the land came under Polish or Lithuanian rule. A Germany duchy was also established there. In 1621, the Swedish king Gustavus II Adolphus took over Riga. In 1629, the greater part of the country north of the Daugava (Western Dvina) River was ceded to Sweden, though the south-east remained under Lithuanian rule. But, in 1710, Peter the Great took control of Riga and, by the end of the 18th century, all of Latvia was under Russian control, although the German landowners and merchants continued to exercise considerable power. The 19th century saw the rise of Latvian nationalism and calls for independence became increasingly frequent in the early 20th century, as German and Russian power declined.

After the Russian Revolution of March 1917, the Latvian National Political Conference demanded independence, but Germany occupied Riga in September. However, after the November Revolution, the Latvian National Political Conference proclaimed the country's independence on 18 November 1918. Russia and Germany, which had both tried to maintain control, finally recognized Latvia's independence in 1920. In 1922, Latvia adopted a democratic constitution and the elected government introduced land reforms. However, a coup in May 1934 ended this period of democratic rule. In 1939, Germany and the Soviet Union agreed to divide up much of eastern Europe. Soviet troops invaded Latvia in June 1940 and Latvia was made a part of the Soviet Union. But German forces invaded the area in 1941 and held it until 1944, when Soviet troops reoccupied the country. Many Latvians opposed to Russian rule were either killed or deported.

Politics

Under Soviet rule, many Russians settled in Latvia and many Latvians feared that the Russians would become the dominant ethnic group. From the mid-1980s, when Mikhail Gorbachev was introducing reforms in the Soviet Union, Latvian nationalists campaigned against Soviet rule. In the late 1980s, the Latvian government ended absolute Communist rule and voted to restore the banned national flag and anthem. It also proclaimed Latvian the country's official language.

In 1990, Latvia established a multiparty political system. In elections in March, candidates in favour of separation from the Soviet Union won two-thirds of parliamentary seats. The parliament declared Latvia independent on 4 May 1990, though the Soviet Union declared this act illegal. However, the Soviet government recognized Latvia's independence in September 1991, shortly before the Soviet Union itself was dissolved. Latvia held its first free elections to its parliament (the Saeima) in 1993. Voting was limited only to people who were citizens on 17 June 1940 and their descendants. This meant that about 34% of Latvian residents were unable to vote. In 1994, Latvia restricted the naturalization of non-Latvians, including many Russian settlers, who were not allowed to vote or own land. However, in 1998, the government agreed that all children born since independence should have automatic citizenship, regardless of the status of their parents.

Economy

The World Bank classifies Latvia as a 'lower-middle-income' country. In the 1990s, it faced problems in transforming its government-run economy into a free-market one. The country lacks natural resources apart from land and forests, and has to import many raw materials.

Its industries cover a wide range, with products including electronic goods, farm machinery, fertilizers, processed food, plastics, radios, washing machines and vehicles. But Latvia produces only about a tenth of the electricity it needs. The rest has to be imported from Belarus, Russia and Ukraine. Farm products include barley, dairy products, beef, oats, potatoes and rye.

AREA	Belarussian 4%, Ukrainian 3%,
64,589 sq km [24,938 sq mls]	Polish 2%, Lithuanian, Jewish
POPULATION	**LANGUAGES**
2,385,000	Latvian (official), Russian
CAPITAL (POPULATION)	**RELIGIONS**
Riga (840,000)	Christianity (including
GOVERNMENT	Lutheran, Russian Orthodox
Multiparty republic	and Roman Catholic)
ETHNIC GROUPS	**CURRENCY**
Latvian 53%, Russian 34%,	Lats = 10 santimi

LEBANON

Lebanon's flag was adopted in 1943. It uses the colours of Lebanese nationalists in World War I (1914–18). The cedar tree on the white stripe has been a Lebanese symbol since Biblical times. Because of deforestation, only a few of Lebanon's giant cedars survive.

Geography and Climate

The Republic of Lebanon is a country on the eastern shores of the Mediterranean Sea. Behind the coastal plain are the rugged Lebanon Mountains (Jabal Lubnán), which rise to 3,088 m [10,131 ft]. Another range, the Anti-Lebanon Mountains (Al Jabal ash Sharqi), form the eastern border with Syria. Between the two ranges is the Bekaa Valley, a fertile farming region.

The Lebanese coast has hot, dry summers and mild, wet winters. Inland, onshore winds bring heavy rain to the western slopes of the mountains in the winter months, with snow at the higher altitudes.

History and Politics

The Phoenicians, who probably settled in the area that is now Lebanon around 5,000 years ago, were traders and explorers who founded city-states along the coast. From about 800 BC the area came under waves of invaders – Egyptians, Hittites, Assyrians, Babylonians and Persians. The armies of the Macedonian general Alexander the Great seized the area in 332 BC and the Romans took control in 64 BC, leaving behind them many structures that still stand today. Christianity was introduced in AD 325. In 395, the area became part of the Byzantine Empire. However, Muslim Arabs occupied the area in the early 7th century, converting many people to Islam, although Christian worship continued in the mountains.

European Crusaders arrived in Lebanon in about 1100 and the area became a battlefield between Christian and Muslim armies. Around 1300, the Muslim Mamelukes of Egypt drove the last of the Crusaders out of the area. In 1516, Lebanon was taken over by the Turkish Ottoman Empire, whose capital was Istanbul, in western Turkey. Turkish rule continued until World War I, when British and French forces defeated the Ottoman Turks, whose empire collapsed. France took over Lebanon's political affairs from 1922.

France ruled Lebanon until 1944 and, for three decades, the country was relatively peaceful and prosperous by Middle Eastern standards. Its association with France had bequeathed a distinct Gallic flavour, though with so many racial and religious groups, the population was truly cosmopolitan. Beirut, the dominant city, was both the centre of international commerce (the Lebanese are, after all, descendants of the Phoenicians) and an elegant playground of the wealthy.

All that changed after March 1975, when this beautiful country saw sporadic conflict spiral into fierce civil war between Christians, Muslims and Druses, who practise a secret religion related to Islam. The complex politics of the ensuing years proved almost as unfathomable as Lebanon sank into a seemingly permanent state of chaos. Assassinations, bombings and kidnappings became routine as numerous factions – Maronite Christians, Druses, Sunni and Shiite Muslims, including fundamentalists backed by Iran – fought for control.

The situation was complicated by a succession of interventions by Palestinian refugees, the Syrian army, Western and then UN forces as the country became a patchwork of occupied zones and 'no-go areas'. The core religious confrontation has deep roots. In 1860, thousands of Maronites, who are aligned to the Roman Catholic Church, were murdered by Druses, who are so tangential to other Islamic sects that they are not now regarded as Muslims, and Muslim tolerance to Christian power after independence lasted only until 1958.

Although it was not directly involved, Lebanon was destabilized by the Arab-Israel War of 1967 and by the exile of the PLO leadership to Beirut in 1970. By 1990, the Syrian army had crushed the two-year revolt of Christian rebels against the Lebanese government, but peace

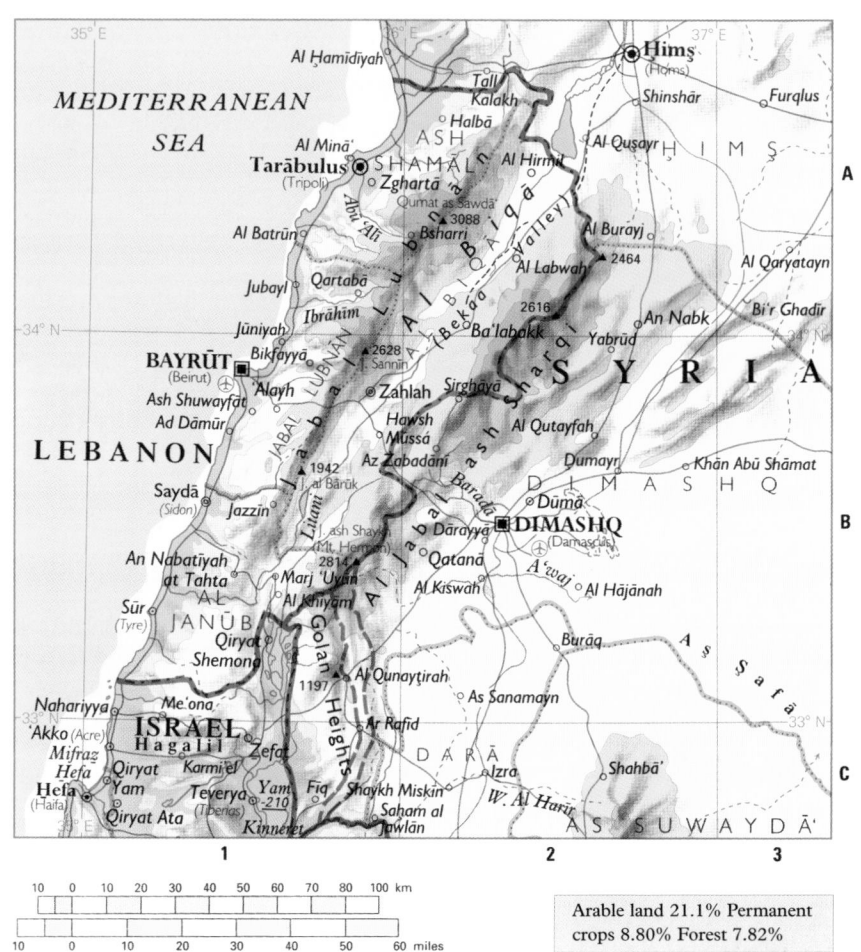

Arable land 21.1% Permanent crops 8.80% Forest 7.82%

proved fragile and a solution elusive. In 1996, Israeli forces launched a sustained attack on the pro-Iranian Hezbollah positions in southern Lebanon, resulting in heavy civilian casualties. Sporadic fighting continued in southern Lebanon in 1997 and it again flared up in early 2000 when Israel was seeking a general peace agreement with Syria.

Economy

Civil war almost destroyed valuable trade and financial services which, together with tourism, had been Lebanon's chief source of income. The manufacturing industry, formerly another major activity, was also badly hit and many factories were damaged.

Manufactures include chemicals, electrical goods, processed food and textiles. Farm products include fruits, vegetables and sugar beet. The relative stability of the economy in the 1990s led to an annual growth rate of the gross national product of 4.9% between 1990 and 1997. By 1997, Lebanon's per capita GNP of US $3,350 placed it among the 'upper-middle-income' developing countries.

AREA	Palestinian 12%), Armenian 5%,
10,400 sq km [4,015 sq mls]	Syrian, Kurdish
POPULATION	**LANGUAGES**
3,506,000	Arabic (official)
CAPITAL (POPULATION)	**RELIGIONS**
Beirut (Bayrūt, 1,500,000)	Islam 58%,
GOVERNMENT	Christianity 27%, Druse
Multiparty republic	**CURRENCY**
ETHNIC GROUPS	Lebanese pound =
Arab (Lebanese 80%,	100 piastres

LESOTHO – SEE SOUTH AFRICA, PAGES 203–205

Liberia was founded in the early 19th century as an American colony for freed slaves who wanted to return to Africa. Its flag was adopted in 1847, when Liberia became independent. The 11 red and white stripes represent the 11 men who signed Liberia's Declaration of Independence.

Geography

The Republic of Liberia is a country in West Africa. Behind the coastline lies a narrow coastal plain. Beyond, the land rises to a plateau region, with the highest land along the border with Guinea.

Climate

Liberia has a tropical climate with high temperatures and humidity throughout the year. The rainfall is abundant all year, but there is a particularly wet period from June to November.

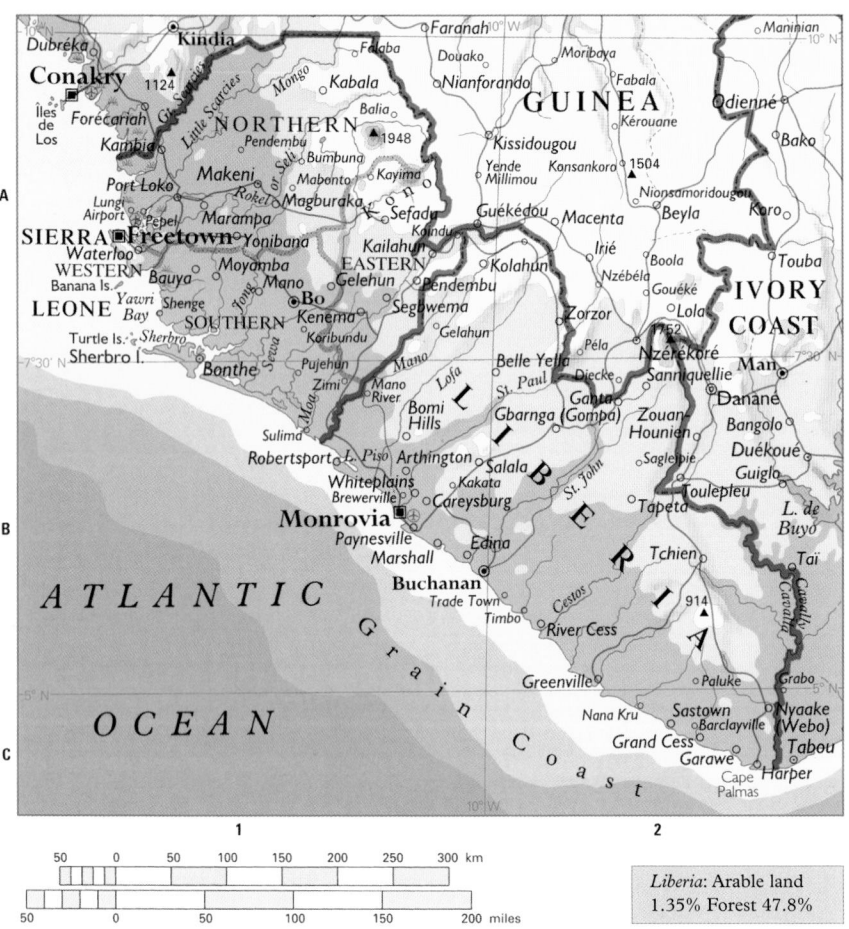

Liberia: Arable land 1.35% Forest 47.8%

History and Politics

In the late 18th century, some white Americans in the United States wanted to help freed black slaves to return to Africa. They set up the American Colonization Society in 1816, which bought land in what is now Liberia.

In 1822, the Society landed former slaves at a settlement on the coast which they named Monrovia. In 1847, Liberia became a fully independent republic with a constitution much like that of the United States. For many years, the Americo-Liberians controlled the government and US influence was strong. In 1980, a military force composed of locals killed the Americo-Liberian president, and an army sergeant, Samuel K. Doe, became president. Civil war between various ethnic groups erupted in 1989. Peace-keeping forces from other West African countries intervened and a cease-fire was agreed in 1995, when a Council of State, composed of former warlords, was set up. In 1997, one of the warlords, Charles Taylor, was elected president.

Economy

Agriculture employs 70% of the people, but many families live at subsistence level, making little or no contribution to the economy. Major food crops include cassava, fruits, rice and sugar cane. Rubber is grown on plantations and cocoa and coffee are leading cash crops. The country's chief natural resources are forests and iron ore deposits, though gold and diamonds are also mined. Liberia has an oil refinery, but manufacturing is small-scale. Chief exports are rubber, timber, diamonds, gold and coffee.

AREA	Grebo 9%, Gio 8%,
111,370 sq km	Kru 7%, Mano 7%
[43,000 sq mls]	**LANGUAGES**
POPULATION	English (official)
2,772,000	**RELIGIONS**
CAPITAL (POPULATION)	Christianity 68%,
Monrovia (490,000)	Islam 14%,
GOVERNMENT	traditional beliefs and
Multiparty republic	others 18%
ETHNIC GROUPS	**CURRENCY**
Kpelle 19%, Bassa 14%,	Liberian dollar = 100 cents

SIERRA LEONE

Geography

The Republic of Sierra Leone contains broad, largely swampy coastal plains, with plateaux and uplands in the north-east.

Climate

The climate is tropical, with heavy rainfall. In the north, it is dry between December and March. In the south, it is dry between January and February.

History and Politics

A former British territory, Sierra Leone became independent in 1961 and a republic in 1971. It became a one-party state in 1978, but in 1991 people voted for the restoration of democracy. A military group seized power in 1992 and a civil war caused destruction in 1994–5. Elections in 1996 were followed by another military coup. In 1998, the West African Peace Force restored the deposed President Ahmed Tejan Kabbah, but further conflict in 1999 forced Kabbah to enter into a peace agreement with the main rebel leader, Foday Sankoh.

Economy

The World Bank classifies Sierra Leone among the 'low-income' economies. Agriculture provides a living for 70% of the people, though farming is mostly at subsistence level. Food crops include cassava, maize and rice, the staple food. The most valuable exports include diamonds, bauxite and rutile. The country has few manufacturing industries.

AREA	Temne 32%,
71,740 sq km [27,699 sq mls]	Limba 8%
POPULATION	**LANGUAGES**
5,080,000	English (official)
CAPITAL (POPULATION)	**RELIGIONS**
Freetown (505,000)	Traditional beliefs 51%,
GOVERNMENT	Islam 39%,
Single-party republic	Christianity 9%
ETHNIC GROUPS	**CURRENCY**
Mende 35%,	Leone = 100 cents

LIBYA

Libya's flag was adopted in 1977. It replaced the flag of the Federation of Arab Republics which Libya left in that year. Libya's flag is the simplest of all world flags. It represents the country's quest for a green revolution in agriculture.

Geography

The Socialist People's Libyan Arab Jamahiriya, as Libya is officially called, is a large country in North Africa. Most people live on the Mediterranean coastal plains in the north-east and north-west. The Sahara, the world's largest desert, occupying 95% of Libya, reaches the Mediterranean coast along the Gulf of Sidra (Khalij Surt). The Sahara is virtually uninhabited except around scattered oases. The land rises towards the south, reaching 2,286 m [7,500 ft] at Bette Peak on the border with Chad.

Climate

The coastal plains in the north-west and north-east of Libya experience hot summers. Winters are mild with some rain. Inland, the average yearly rainfall drops to around 100 mm [4 in] or less. Daytime temperatures are high but nights are cool.

Vegetation

Shrubs and grasses grow on northern coasts, with some trees in wetter areas. Few plants grow in the desert, except at oases where date palms provide protection from the hot sun.

History

Libya's first known inhabitants were the Berbers. From the 7th century BC to the 5th century AD, Libya came under the Carthaginians, Greeks and Romans. The Romans left superb ruins, but the Arabs, who invaded the area in AD 642, imposed their culture, including their religion, Islam. From 1551, Libya was part of the Ottoman empire. Italy took control in 1911, but lost the territory in World War II. Libya became an independent kingdom in 1951.

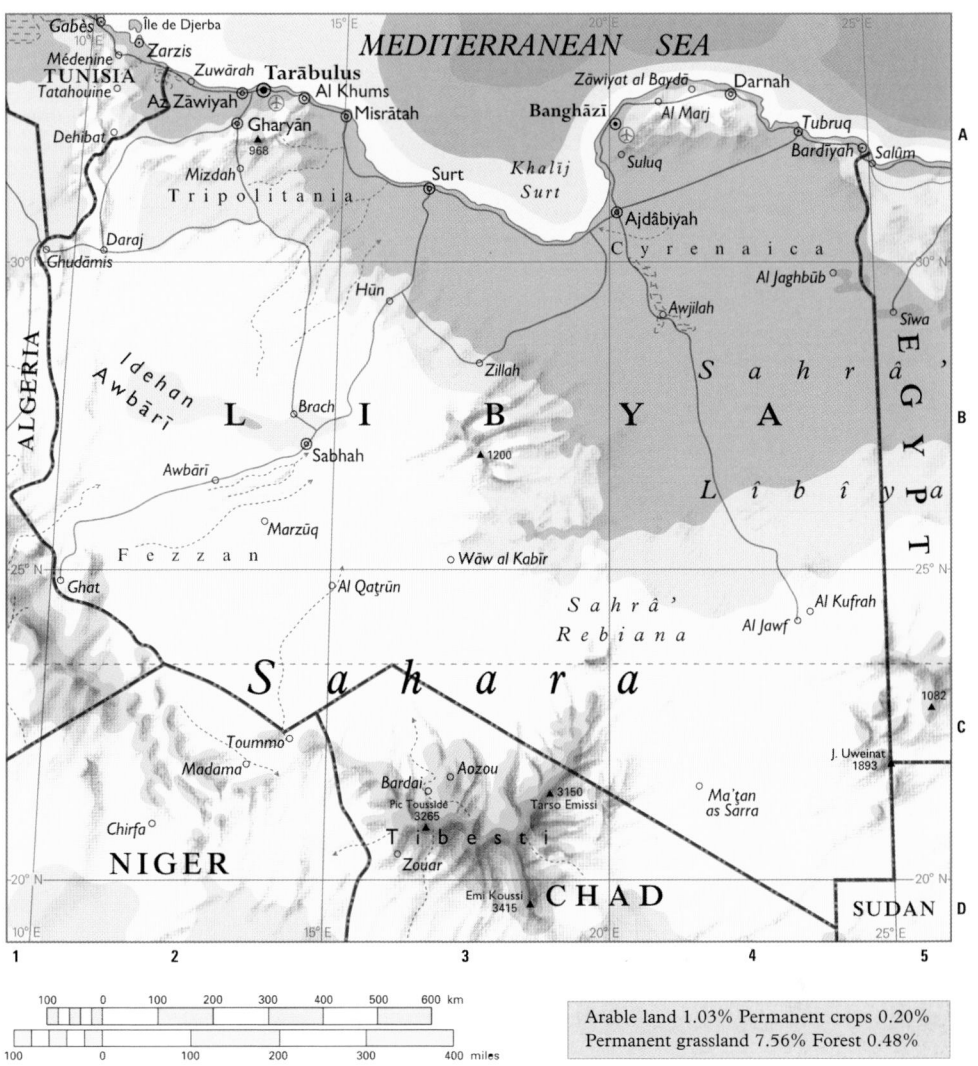

Arable land 1.03% Permanent crops 0.20%
Permanent grassland 7.56% Forest 0.48%

Politics

In 1969, a military group headed by Colonel Muammar Gaddafi deposed the king and set up a military government. Under Gaddafi, the government took control of the economy and used money from oil exports to finance welfare services and development projects. However, although Libya appears to be democratic, political parties are not permitted. Gaddafi has attracted international criticism for his support for radical movements, such as the PLO (Palestine Liberation Organization) and various terrorist groups. In 1986, his policies led the United States to bomb installations in the capital and in Benghazi. Libya has disputes with its neighbours, including Chad, where it sent troops to intervene in a civil war. In 1994, the International Court of Justice ruled against Libya's claim for territory in the Aozou Strip in northern Chad.

In 1999, Gaddafi sought to restore good relations with the outside world by surrendering for trial two Libyans suspected of planting a bomb on a PanAm plane, which exploded over the Scottish town of Lockerbie in 1988. He also accepted Libya's responsibility for the shooting of a British policewoman in London in 1984. This act led to the restoration of diplomatic relations between Libya and Britain.

Economy

The discovery of oil and natural gas in 1959 led to the transformation of Libya's economy. Formerly one of the world's poorest countries, it has become Africa's richest in terms of its per capita income. However, it remains a developing country because of its dependence on oil, which accounts for nearly all of its export revenues.

Agriculture is important, although Libya has to import food. Crops include barley, citrus fruits, dates, olives, potatoes and wheat. Cattle, sheep and poultry are raised. Libya has oil refineries and petrochemical plants. Other manufactures include cement, processed food and steel. The government has invested money from its oil revenues in developing the economy, providing services for the people, and improving farmland. One of its most ambitious projects is the 'Great Man-Made River' which involves tapping subterranean water from rocks beneath the Sahara and piping it to the dry, populated areas in the north. However, the water in the aquifers is non-renewable and will eventually run dry.

AREA	ETHNIC GROUPS
1,759,540 sq km	Libyan Arab and Berber 89%,
[679,358 sq mls]	others 11%
POPULATION	**LANGUAGES**
4,875,000	Arabic (official)
CAPITAL (POPULATION)	**RELIGIONS**
Tripoli (Tarābulus, 990,000)	Islam
GOVERNMENT	**CURRENCY**
Single-party socialist state	Libyan dinar = 1,000 dirhams

LIECHTENSTEIN – SEE SWITZERLAND, PAGE 213

This flag was created in 1918 when Lithuania became an independent republic. After the Soviet Union annexed Lithuania in 1940, the flag was suppressed. It was revived in 1988 and again became the national flag when Lithuania became fully independent in 1991.

Arable land 35.4%
Forest 30.9%

Geography

The Republic of Lithuania is the southernmost of the three Baltic states which were ruled as part of the Soviet Union between 1940 and 1991. Much of the land is flat or gently rolling. The highest point is a hill, north-east of Vilnius, which reaches 288 m [945 ft] above sea level. From the south-east, the land slopes down to the fertile central lowland, which is used primarily for raising cattle, pigs and poultry. In the west is an area of forested sandy ridges, dotted with lakes. South of Klaipeda, sand dunes separate a large lagoon from the Baltic Sea.

Most of the land is covered by moraine (ice-worn rocks) which was deposited there by ice-sheets during the Ice Age. Hollows in the moraine contain about 3,000 lakes. The longest of the many rivers is the Neman, which rises in Belarus and flows through Lithuania to the Baltic Sea.

Climate

Winters are cold. January's temperatures average –3°C [27°F] in the west and –6°C [21°F] in the east. Summers are warm, with average temperatures in July of 17°C [63°F]. The average rainfall in the west is about 630 mm [25 in]. Inland areas are drier.

History

The Lithuanian people were united into a single nation in the 12th century and developed into a powerful kingdom. Its first great ruler was Mindaugas who became king in 1251. In the 13th century, the region was attacked by German crusaders called the Teutonic Knights, but by the 14th century, Lithuania ruled a territory which extended nearly as far as Moscow in the east and the Black Sea in the south. In 1386, Lithuania united with Poland and the two countries became a single state in 1569. This state collapsed in the 18th century and, by 1795, Lithuania came under the control of Russia. Despite rebellions in 1833 and 1863, Lithuania failed to regain its independence.

Nationalism became a major issue in the late 19th century. In 1905, a conference of elected representatives called for self-government, which Russia refused to grant. German troops occupied Lithuania during World War I and, in February 1918, Lithuania declared its independence from Germany and Russia. Although fighting with Russia continued after the end of World War I, Lithuania established a democratic form of government, and in 1920, Russia and Lithuania signed a peace treaty. However, Poland occupied Vilnius from 1920 until 1939, having incorporated it into Poland in 1923. In 1926, a coup overthrew the democratic regime in Lithuania.

In 1939, Germany and the Soviet Union agreed to divide up much of eastern Europe. Lithuania and Vilnius were ceded to the Soviet Union in 1940 and a government acceptable to the Soviet Union was set up. But German forces invaded the area in 1941 and held it until 1944, when Soviet troops reoccupied the country. Many Lithuanian guerrillas fought against Soviet rule between 1944 and 1952. Thousands of Lithuanians were killed and many sent to labour camps.

Politics

From the mid-1980s, while Mikhail Gorbachev was introducing reforms in the Soviet Union, several non-Communist movements developed, calling for independence for Lithuania. From 1988, Lithuania led the way among the three Baltic states in the drive to shed Communism and regain nationhood. In 1989, the parliament in Lithuania declared that Soviet laws were invalid unless they had been approved by the Lithuanian parliament and that Lithuanian should be the official language. It also restored religious freedom and the freedom of the press, abolishing the monopoly of power held by the Communist Party and establishing a multiparty system.

Following elections to parliament in February 1990, in which pro-independence candidates won more than 90% of the seats, Lithuania declared itself independent on 11 March 1990, a declaration that was rejected by the Soviet leaders. This resulted in the occupation of most of the capital by Soviet troops and a crippling economic blockade. After negotiations to end the sanctions failed, Soviet troops moved into Lithuania in January 1990 and 14 people were killed when the troops fired on demonstrators. Finally, on 6 September 1991, the Soviet government recognized Lithuania's independence.

Parliamentary elections in 1992 were, surprisingly, won by the Lithuanian Democratic Labour Party (which was made up of former Communists). Russian troops withdrew from the country in 1993, but the government faced mounting problems as it sought to privatize the economy. In 1996, following new parliamentary elections, a coalition government was set up by the conservative Homeland Union and the Christian Democratic Party. In 1998, an independent, Valdas Adamkus, a Lithuanian–American who had fled the country in 1944, was elected president. By the turn of the century, the government was seeking closer ties with the West. Lithuania also had better relations with Russia than the other two Baltic states, partly because ethnic Russians make up a lower proportion of the population than in Estonia and Latvia.

Economy

The World Bank classifies Lithuania as a 'lower-middle-income' developing country. Lithuania lacks natural resources, but manufacturing, based on imported materials, is the most valuable activity. Products include chemicals, electronic goods, processed food and machine tools. Dairy and meat farming are important, as also is fishing. The main exports are textiles, chemicals, mineral products and machinery. Russia and Germany are Lithuania's leading trading partners.

AREA	Russian 9%, Polish 7%,
65,200 sq km [25,200 sq mls]	Belarussian 2%
POPULATION	**LANGUAGES**
3,600,000	Lithuanian (official),
CAPITAL (POPULATION)	Russian, Polish
Vilnius (576,000)	**RELIGIONS**
GOVERNMENT	Christianity
Multiparty republic	(mainly Roman Catholic)
ETHNIC GROUPS	**CURRENCY**
Lithuanian 80%,	Litas = 100 centai

LUXEMBOURG – SEE BELGIUM, PAGES 52–53

MACEDONIA

Macedonia's flag was introduced in August 1992. The emblem in the centre of the flag was the device from the war-chest of Philip of Macedon; however, the Greeks claimed this symbol as their own. In 1995, Macedonia agreed to redesign their flag, as shown here.

Geography

The Republic of Macedonia is a country in south-eastern Europe, which was once one of the six republics that made up the former Federal People's Republic of Yugoslavia. This landlocked country is largely mountainous or hilly. The highest point is Mount Korab, which reaches 2,764 m [9,068 ft] above sea level on the border with Albania. Most of the country is drained by the River Vardar and its many tributaries. In the south-west, Macedonia shares two large lakes – Ohrid and Prespa – with Albania and Greece. Forests of beech, oak and pine cover large areas, especially in the west.

Climate

Macedonia has hot summers, though highland areas are cooler. Winters are cold and snowfalls are often heavy. The climate is fairly continental in character and precipitation occurs throughout the year. Average temperatures in Skopje range from 1°C [34°F] in January to 24°C [75°F] in July. The average annual precipitation in the city is 550 mm [21 in].

History

Until the 20th century, Macedonia's history was closely tied to that of a larger area, also called Macedonia, which included parts of northern Greece and south-western Bulgaria. The region reached its peak in power at the time of Philip II (382–336 BC) and his son Alexander the Great (336–323 BC), who conquered an empire that stretched from Greece to India. After Alexander's death, the empire was split up by Macedonian generals and it gradually declined. The area became a Roman province in the 140s BC and part of the Byzantine Empire from AD 395. In the 6th century, Slavs from eastern Europe attacked and settled in the area, followed by Bulgars from central Asia in the late 9th century. The Byzantine Empire regained control in 1018, but Serbs took Macedonia in the early 14th century.

However, in 1371, the area was conquered by the Ottoman Turks who ruled for more than 500 years. The Ottoman Empire began to collapse in the late 19th century. In 1913, at the end of the Balkan Wars, the area was divided between Bulgaria, Greece and Serbia.

Politics

As a result of the division of the area known as Macedonia, Serbia took the north and centre of the region, Bulgaria took a small area in the south-east, and Greece gained the south. At the end of World War I, Serbian Macedonia became part of the Kingdom of the Serbs, Croats and Slovenes, which was renamed Yugoslavia in 1929. Yugoslavia was conquered by Germany during World War II, but when the war ended in 1945 the Communist partisan leader Josip Broz Tito set up a Communist government. Tito maintained unity among the diverse peoples of Yugoslavia but, after his death in 1980, the ethnic and religious differences began to reassert themselves. In the early 1990s, Yugoslavia broke apart into five sovereign republics. Macedonia declared its independence on 18 September 1991 and it subsequently avoided the civil war that shattered other parts of the former Yugoslavia.

However, Macedonia ran into problems concerning recognition. Greece, worried by the consequences for its own Macedonian region, vetoed any acknowledgement of an independent Macedonia on its borders. It considered Macedonia to be a Greek name. It also objected to a symbol on Macedonia's flag, which was associated with Philip of Macedon, and a reference in the country's constitution to the desire to reunite the three parts of the old Macedonia.

Macedonia adopted a new clause in its constitution rejecting any Macedonian claims on Greek territory and, in 1993, the United Nations accepted the new republic as a member under the name of The Former Yugoslav Republic of Macedonia (FYROM).

By the end of 1993, all the countries of the European Union, except

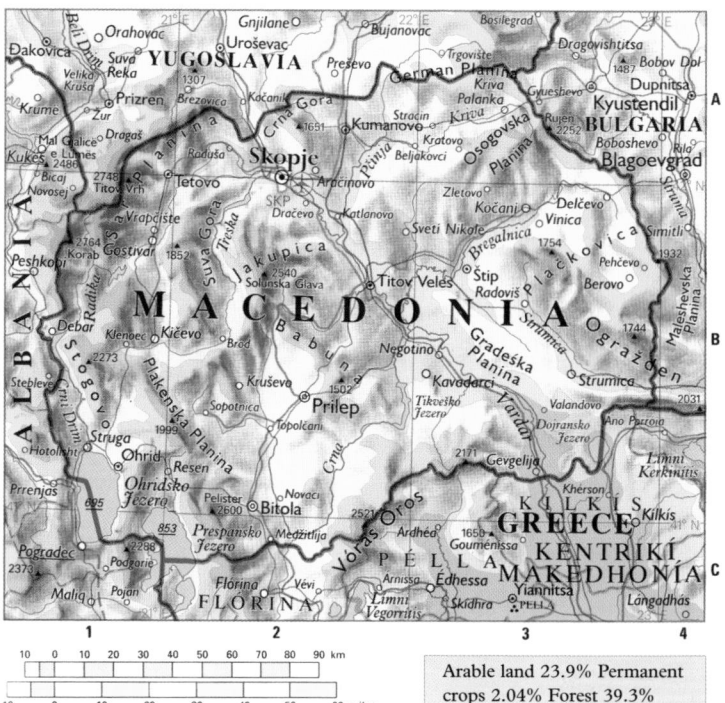

Arable land 23.9% Permanent crops 2.04% Forest 39.3%

Greece, were establishing diplomatic relations with the FYROM. Greece barred Macedonian trade in 1994, but lifted the ban in 1995. In 1999, Macedonia faced new problems, caused by the crisis in Kosovo, Yugoslavia, where Serbian ethnic cleansing was taking place against the Albanian-speaking people. NATO air attacks on Yugoslav military targets led to a large influx of about 250,000 refugees into Macedonia.

Economy

According to the World Bank, Macedonia ranks as a 'lower-middle-income' developing country. Manufactures dominate the country's exports. Macedonia mines coal, but has to import all its oil and natural gas. Chromium, copper, iron ore, lead, manganese, uranium and zinc are also mined. Manufactures include cement, chemicals, cigarettes, cotton fabric, footwear, iron and steel, refrigerators, sulphuric acid, tobacco products and wool yarn.

Agriculture employs 9% of the population, as compared with 23% in manufacturing and mining. Most other people work in service industries, including government and defence. About a quarter of the land is farmed and major crops include cotton, fruits, including grapes, maize, potatoes, tobacco, vegetables and wheat. Cattle, pigs, poultry and sheep are also raised, and the country produces most of its basic food needs. Forestry is another important activity in some areas.

The country's main exports are manufactures, machinery and transport equipment, food products, raw materials and chemicals. The leading trading partners include Germany, Russia and Italy.

AREA	Turkish 5%, Romanian 3%,
25,710 sq km	Serb 2%
[9,927 sq mls]	**LANGUAGES**
POPULATION	Macedonian (official),
2,009,000	Albanian
CAPITAL (POPULATION)	**RELIGIONS**
Skopje	Christianity (mainly Eastern
(541,000)	Orthodox, with Macedonian
GOVERNMENT	Orthodox and Roman Catholic
Multiparty republic	communities), Islam
ETHNIC GROUPS	**CURRENCY**
Macedonian 65%, Albanian 21%,	Dinar = 100 paras

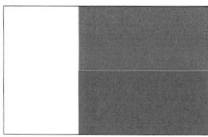

The colours on this flag are those used on historic flags in South-east Asia. It was from this region that the ancestors of many Madagascans came around 2,000 years ago. This flag was adopted in 1958, when Madagascar became a self-governing republic under French rule.

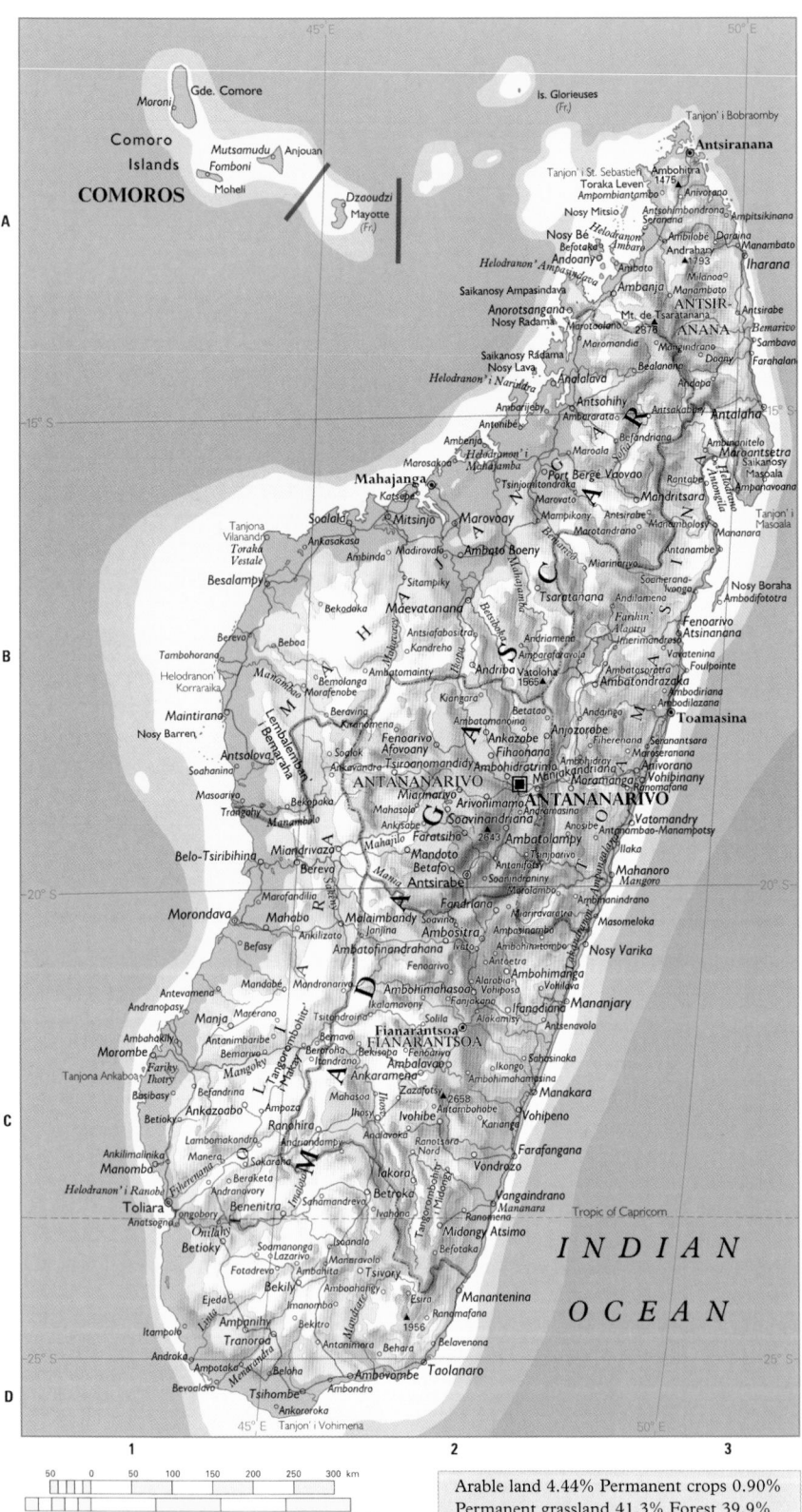

Arable land 4.44% Permanent crops 0.90%
Permanent grassland 41.3% Forest 39.9%

Geography and Climate

The Democratic Republic of Madagascar, in south-eastern Africa, is an island nation, which has a larger area than France. Behind the narrow coastal plains in the east lies a highland zone, mostly between 610 m and 1,220 m [2,000–4,000 ft] above sea level. Some volcanic peaks, such as Tsaratanana in the north, rise above this level. The highlands are Madagascar's most densely populated region. Broad plains border the Mozambique Channel in the west.

Temperatures in the highlands are moderated by the altitude. The winters (from April to September) are dry, but heavy rains occur in summer. The eastern coast-lands are warm and humid. The west is drier, and the south and south-west are hot and dry.

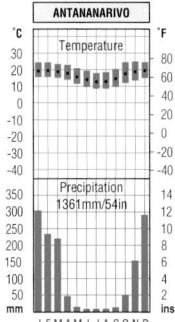

MADAGASCAR (ANTANANARIVO)

Apart from the east coast, which has rain at all seasons, Madagascar has a summer rainy season and a winter dry season. Antananarivo's high altitude moderates temperatures. In February tropical cyclones may affect the island. On a few occasions temperatures have exceeded 30°C [86°F].

History and Politics

People from South-east Asia began to settle on Madagascar around 2,000 years ago. Other immigrants from Africa and Arabia settled on the coasts. The Malagasy language is of South-east Asian origin, though it included words from Arabic, Bantu languages and European languages. The first Europeans to reach Madagascar were Portuguese. Later, the island, which was ruled by powerful monarchs, became a haven for pirates. France made contacts with the island in the 1860s. Finally, French troops defeated a Malagasy army in 1895 and Madagascar became a French colony. In 1960, it achieved full independence as the Malagasy Republic.

In 1972, army officers seized control and, in 1975, under the leadership of Lt-Commander Didier Ratsiraka, the country was renamed Madagascar. Parliamentary elections were held in 1977, but Ratsiraka remained president of a one-party socialist state. The government resigned in 1991 following large demonstrations. In 1992–3, Ratsiraka was defeated by opposition leader Albert Zafy. But Ratsiraka returned to power following presidential elections in 1996.

Economy

Madagascar is one of the world's poorest countries. The land has been badly eroded because of the cutting down of the forests and overgrazing of the grasslands. Farming, fishing and forestry employ about 80% of the people.

The country's food crops include bananas, cassava, rice and sweet potatoes. Coffee is the leading export. Other exports include cloves, sisal, sugar and vanilla. There are few manufacturing industries and mining is unimportant at present.

AREA	Betsileo 11%, Tsimihety
587,040 sq km	7%, Sakalava 6%
[226,656 sq mls]	**LANGUAGES**
POPULATION	Malagasy, French
14,463,000	(both official)
CAPITAL (POPULATION)	**RELIGIONS**
Antananarivo (1,053,000)	Christianity 51%,
GOVERNMENT	traditional beliefs 47%,
Republic	Islam 2%
ETHNIC GROUPS	**CURRENCY**
Merina 27%,	Malagasy franc
Betsimisaraka 15%,	= 100 centimes

MADEIRA – SEE ATLANTIC OCEAN, PAGES 41–43

MALAWI

The colours in Malawi's flag come from the flag of the Malawi Congress Party, which was adopted in 1953. The symbol of the rising sun was added when Malawi became independent from Britain in 1964. It represents the beginning of a new era for Malawi and Africa.

Geography and Climate

The Republic of Malawi in southern Africa is a small, landlocked and oddly shaped country, which is nowhere more than 160 km [100 mls] wide. Its dominant physical feature is Lake Malawi, which is drained in the south by the River Shire, a tributary of the Zambezi. The highest point is Mulanje, which reaches 3,000 m [9,843 ft] in the south-east.

While the low-lying areas of Malawi are hot and humid all year round, the uplands have a pleasant climate. Lilongwe, at about 1,100 m [3,609 ft] above sea level, has a warm and sunny climate. Frosts sometimes occur in July and August, in the middle of the long dry season. The wet season extends from November to May. Wooded savanna and tropical grasslands cover much of the country, with swampy vegetation in many river valleys.

History and Politics

The Bantu-speaking ancestors of the people of Malawi, who first reached the area around 2,000 years ago, introducing an iron age culture, developed kingdoms in the region. In the first half of the 19th century, two other Bantu-speaking groups, the Ngoni (or Angoni) and the Yao invaded the area. The Yao took slaves and sold them to Arabs who traded along the coast. In 1859, the British missionary-explorer David Livingstone reached the area and was horrified by the cruelty of the slave trade. In 1875, the Free Church of Scotland established a mission in the area, while Scottish businessmen worked to found businesses to replace the slave trade. The British made treaties with local chiefs on the western banks of what was then called Lake Nyasa and, in 1889, the area was made the British Protectorate of Nyasaland.

In 1953, Britain made the protectorate part of the Federation of Rhodesia and Nyasaland. This included Northern Rhodesia (now Zambia) and Southern Rhodesia (Zimbabwe). The people of Nyasaland opposed the creation of the federation, fearing domination by the white minority community in Southern Rhodesia. In 1958, Dr Hastings Kamuzu Banda, a doctor educated in the United States, took over the leadership of the opposition to the federation and also to the continuance of British rule. Faced with mounting protests, especially in Nyasaland and Northern Rhodesia, Britain dissolved the federation in 1963. During 1964, Nyasaland became fully independent as Malawi, the name of a kingdom that existed in the area in the 16th century. Banda became the country's first prime minister and, in 1966, after the country adopted a new constitution, making the country a republic. Banda became the first president.

Malawi's recent history was largely dominated by Banda who declared Malawi a one-party republic in 1966 and himself president for life in 1971. However, his autocratic regime differed from most of black Africa in being conservative and pragmatic – hostile to its socialist neighbours, but friendly with South Africa. At first, his austerity programme and agricultural policies seemed to have wrought an economic miracle, but a swift decline in the 1980s, combined with the problems arising from the arrival of a million refugees from war-torn Mozambique, led to a return to poverty, despite massive aid packages. Another immediate and ongoing problem was the high incidence of AIDS, which put pressure on the country's limited welfare services. Mounting political dissent led to the restoration of a multiparty system in 1993. In national elections in 1994, Banda and his party were defeated and Bakili Muluzi became president. Banda was arrested and charged with murder, but he died in 1997.

Economy

The overthrow of Banda led to a restoration of political freedoms, and the abolition of school fees and school uniforms has nearly doubled school enrolment. However, Malawi remains one of the world's poorest countries. Reforms in the 1990s included the encouragement of small farmers to diversify their production, but free enterprise and privatization have angered some farmers who have suffered from the ending of subsidies. The country lacks mineral resources, and manufacturing and tourism are on a small scale. The country's game reserves, with their limited wildlife, do not compare with those of its neighbours.

Although fertile farmland is limited, agriculture dominates the economy, employing more than 80% of the labour force. Tobacco is the leading export, followed by tea, sugar and cotton. The main food crops include cassava, groundnuts, maize, rice and sorghum. Many farmers raise cattle, goats and other livestock.

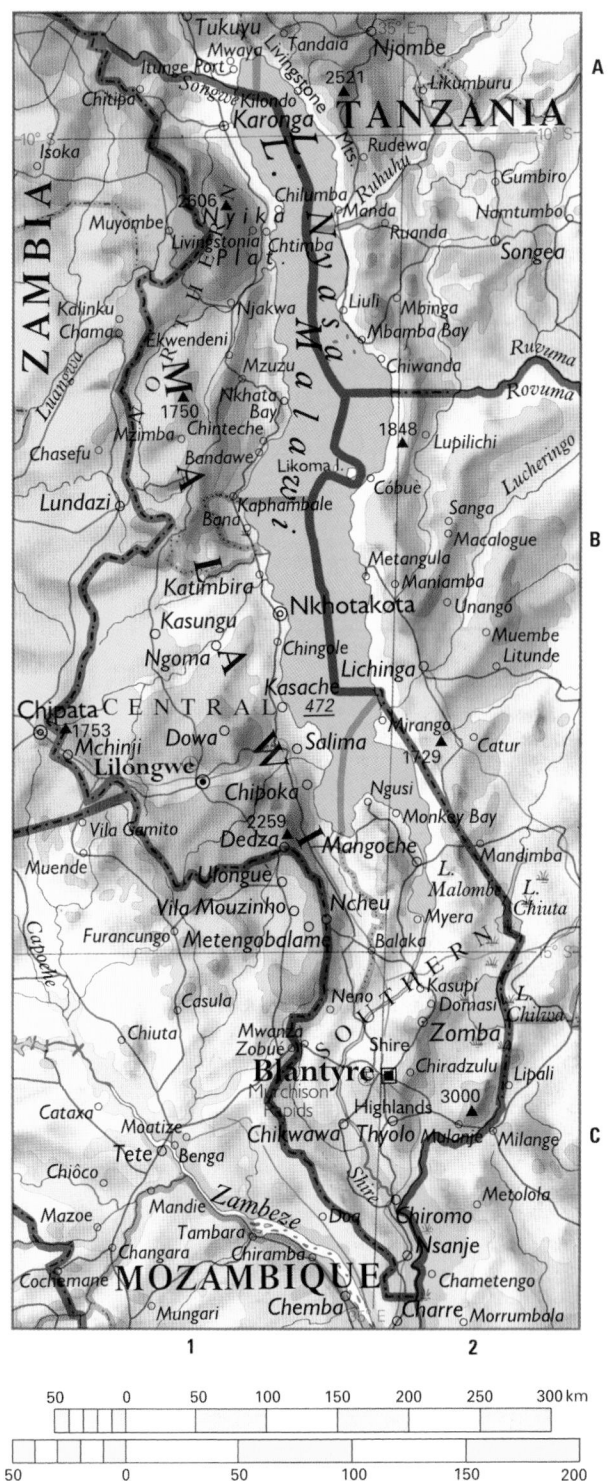

AREA	Yao 13%, Ngoni 7%
118,480 sq km	**LANGUAGES**
[45,745 sq mls]	Chichewa and English
POPULATION	(both official)
9,840,000	**RELIGIONS**
CAPITAL (POPULATION)	Christianity
Lilongwe (395,000)	(Protestant 34%,
GOVERNMENT	Roman Catholic 28%),
Multiparty republic	traditional beliefs 21%,
ETHNIC GROUPS	Islam 16%
Maravi (Chewa, Nyanja,	**CURRENCY**
Tonga, Tumbuka) 58%,	Kwacha =
Lomwe 18%,	100 tambala

This flag was adopted when the Federation of Malaysia was set up in 1963. The red and white bands date back to a revolt in the 13th century. The star and crescent are symbols of Islam. The blue represents Malaysia's role in the Commonwealth.

Arable land 5.55% Permanent crops 17.6%
Permanent grassland 0.86% Forest 67.9%

Geography

The Federation of Malaysia consists of two main parts. Peninsular Malaysia consists of 11 states and a federal territory (Kuala Lumpur), with two states (Sabah and Sarawak) and a federal territory (Labuan) in northern Borneo. The Malay peninsula is dominated by fold mountains with a north–south axis. The most important is the Main Range, which runs from the Thai border to the south-east of Kuala Lumpur, reaching 2,182 m [7,159 ft] at its highest point, Gunong Kerbau. South of the Main Range lies the flat, poorly drained lowlands of Johor. The short rivers have built up a margin of lowlands around the coast.

Northern Borneo has a mangrove-fringed coastal plain, backed by hill country, with east–west fold mountains in the interior. The most striking mountain, and Malaysia's highest point, is the granite peak of Mount Kinabalu, in Sabah, which reaches 4,101 m [13,455 ft].

Climate

Malaysia has a hot equatorial climate. Temperatures are high all year, though the mountains are much cooler than lowland areas. Rainfall is heavy throughout the year.

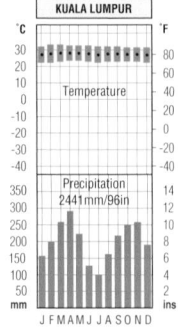

MALAYSIA (KUALA LUMPUR)

Kuala Lumpur experiences uniform temperature throughout the year. The length of daylight and the intensity of the noonday sun varies little from season to season and the sea is always very warm. The daytime temperature is about 32°C [90°F]. Rainfall is high at all seasons, but with a double maximum around the equinoxes, when the tropical rainbelt lies close to the Equator. Rain falls on over 200 days in the year.

History

The ancestors of the Malays probably reached the Malay peninsula from China around 4,000 years ago. The peninsula later became a crossroads for sea traders from China and India. Hinduism and Buddhism were introduced from India in the 9th century AD. An early golden age of Malay political power came in the 15th century with the rise of the Kingdom of Malacca (now Melaka), on the south-western

coast of the Malay peninsula. Malacca controlled the important sea routes and attracted traders from all parts of Asia. Arab traders introduced Islam and, in 1414, Malacca's ruler became a Muslim. Many of the people on the peninsula soon embraced Islam, which remains the official religion of Malaysia today.

The first Europeans to reach the area were the Portuguese and Malacca became a Portuguese possession in 1511. The Dutch, who had been trading in the area during the early 17th century, took Malacca in 1641, and many people from the Dutch-controlled Sulawesi and Sumatra settled in the peninsula, adding to the region's complex ethnic mix. The British, who had been seeking a suitable trading post in South-east Asia, took over Malacca in 1794 and, though Malacca was returned to the Dutch in 1814, it became British in 1824. Through the activities of Stamford Raffles, an agent for the British-owned East India Company, the British occupied Singapore in 1819 and made it a British territory in 1824. In 1826, the British founded the Straits Settlement, which consisted of Penang (now Pinang), Malacca and Singapore. In 1867, the Straits Settlement became a British colony. British rule was gradually extended, with Sabah and Sarawak becoming a British protectorate in 1888. In 1896, Negeri Sembilan, Penang, Perak and Selangor became the Federated Malay States. Under British rule, the economy developed and thousands of Chinese and Indian workers came to work on the rubber plantations.

Japan occupied what is now Malaysia and Singapore during World War II, but British rule was restored in 1945 following Japan's defeat. In the late 1940s and the 1950s, Communists, inspired by the Chinese revolution, fought the British, but guerrilla warfare ended with the independence of the Federation of Malaya in 1957. In 1963, Malaya joined with Singapore, and what is now Sabah and Sarawak, to form the nation of Malaysia, with Tunku Abdul Rahman of the Alliance Party as prime minister. Brunei was invited to join, but no agreement was achieved on entry terms. But, from the start, arguments between Singapore and the Malaysian government occurred, causing Singapore to withdraw in 1965, and become an independent sovereign state.

Politics

One of the problems faced by the new nation was its great ethnic and religious diversity, with Malays of Chinese and Indian origin, many brought in by the British to work the tin mines and rubber plantations. There are also a number of Eurasians, Europeans and aboriginal peoples, notably in Sabah and Sarawak. This patchwork has caused tensions, especially between the Muslim Malays and the politically dominant, mainly Buddhist, Chinese. But while riots did break out in 1969, it never escalated into serious armed conflict, nor did it prevent economic development.

In foreign affairs, Malaysia faced attacks by Indonesia, which objected to Sabah and Sarawak joining Malaysia. Indonesia's policy of 'confrontation' forced Malaysia to increase its defence expenditure. Malaysia was also reluctant to have dealings with Communist countries, but at the same time it was keen to remain independent of the Western bloc and was aware of the need for South-east Asian nations to work together. From 1967, it was playing a major part in regional affairs, especially through its membership of ASEAN (Association of South-east Asian Nations), together with Indonesia, the Philippines, Singapore and Thailand. (Later members of ASEAN include Brunei in 1984, Vietnam in 1995, Laos and Burma (Myanmar) in 1997, and Cambodia in 1999.)

From the 1970s, Malaysia achieved rapid economic progress, especially under the leadership of Dr Mahathir Mohamad, who became prime minister in 1981. Mahathir encouraged the development of industry in order to diversify the economy and reduce the country's reliance on agriculture and mining. For example, the first Malaysian car, the *Proton Saga*, went into production in 1985. In the early 1990s, manufacturing accounted for about 20% of the gross domestic product. By 1996, its share of the GDP had risen to nearly 35%. However, together with most of the 'economic tigers' in Asia's eastern rim, Malaysia was hit by an economic recession in 1997–8. In response to the crisis, the government ordered the repatriation of many temporary foreign workers and initiated a series of austerity measures aimed at restoring confidence and avoiding the chronic debt problems affecting some other Asian countries. In 1998, the economy shrank by about 5%.

During the economic crisis, differences developed between Mahathir Mohamad and his deputy prime minister and finance minister, Anwar Ibrahim. Anwar wanted Malaysia to work closely with the International Monetary Fund (IMF) to promote domestic reforms and strict monetary and fiscal policies. By the summer of 1998, he had gone further, attacking corruption and nepotism in government. Mahathir, who was suspicious of international 'plots' to undermine Malaysia's economy, put much of the blame for the crisis on foreign speculators. He sacked Ibrahim from the government and also from the ruling United Malays National Organization (UMNO). Anwar was later convicted of conspiracy and charged with sexual misconduct. He was jailed for six years.

In late 1999, Mahathir called a snap election to consolidate his power and strengthen his mandate to deal with the economy. With the economy appearing to be rebounding from recession, Mahathir's coalition retained its two-thirds majority in parliament. But many Malays voted for the conservative Muslim Parti Islam. This meant that Mahathir had to rely more on the Chinese and Indian parties in his coalition. The opposition also gained strength by forming a united front at the 1999 elections, together with other groups, including one formed by Anwar Ibrahim's wife, who was fighting to establish her husband's innocence.

Economy

The World Bank classifies Malaysia as an 'upper-middle-income' developing country. Its per capita gross national product of US $4,680 in 1997 was second only to that of Singapore among the members of ASEAN. Manufacturing is the most important sector of the economy and it accounts for a sizeable proportion of the exports. During the 1970s, the economy was stimulated by the arrival of electronics companies from Japan and the United States, whose managements were attracted by Malaysia's social and political stability, its efficient workforce and favourable economic climate. The manufacture of electronic equipment is now a major industry, and, by 1994, Malaysia ranked second in the world in producing radios and fifth in television receivers. Other electronic products include clocks, semiconductors for computers, stereo equipment, tape recorders and telephones. Other major industrial products include chemicals, petroleum products, plastics, processed food, textiles and clothing, rubber and wood products. Partly because of industrialization, Malaysia is becoming increasingly urbanized. By 1997, about 55% of the population lived in cities and towns.

In 1996, manufacturing employed 26% of the workforce, as compared with agriculture which employed 16%. Malaysia leads the world in the production of palm oil, and, in the mid-1990s, it ranked third in producing natural rubber. Malaysia also ranked fifth in the production of cocoa beans, the commercial cultivation of which began only in the 1950s. Other important crops include apples, bananas, coconuts, pepper, pineapples and many other tropical fruits, rice (Malaysia's chief food crop), sugar cane, tea and tobacco. Some farmers raise livestock, including cattle, pigs and poultry. The country's rainforests contain large reserves of timber, and wood and wood products, including plywood and furniture, play an important part in the economy.

The mining of tin originally laid the foundations of industry in Malaysia, but its relative importance has declined and, by the mid-1990s, the country had slipped to eighth place in the world among tin ore producers. Malaysia also has some bauxite, copper, gold, iron ore and ilmenite (an ore from which titanium is obtained). Since the 1970s, the production of oil and natural gas has steadily increased.

The expansion of Malaysia's economy has depended on its ability to expand its export markets. By the mid-1990s, the country's leading exports were machinery and transport equipment, which accounted for about 55% of the value of the exports. Other exports included manufactures, mineral fuels, animal and vegetable oils, inedible raw materials and food.

AREA	groups 62%, Chinese 30%,
329,750 sq km	Indian 8%
[127,316 sq mls]	**LANGUAGES**
POPULATION	Malay (official), Chinese, Iban
20,993,000	**RELIGIONS**
CAPITAL (POPULATION)	Islam 53%, Buddhism 17%,
Kuala Lumpur (1,145,000)	Chinese folk religionist 12%,
GOVERNMENT	Hinduism 7%, Christianity 6%
Federal constitutional monarchy	**CURRENCY**
ETHNIC GROUPS	Ringgit (Malaysian dollar)
Malay and other indigenous	= 100 cents

BRUNEI

The Negara Brunei Darussalem (or State of Brunei, Abode of Peace, as it is officially known) was a British protectorate until its independence in 1984. Lying on the north coast of Borneo, most of the land is flat and covered by dense rainforest. Temperatures are high all through the year. The average annual rainfall on the coast is 2,500 mm [98 in].

Britain took Brunei in the 19th century in order to protect the shipping lanes between India and China. In 1888, the territory became a British protectorate. Oil and natural gas found in offshore waters have made Brunei a prosperous state and the Sultan is said to be among the world's richest men. Oil, natural gas and oil products make up around 90% of the country's exports. Japan is Brunei's leading export market, but ASEAN nations account for nearly half of the country's imports.

AREA	**CAPITAL**
5,770 sq km [2,228 sq mls]	Bandar Seri Begawan
POPULATION	**CURRENCY**
315,000	Brunei dollar (BND) = 100 cents

MALDIVES – SEE INDIAN OCEAN, PAGES 122–123

The colours on Mali's flag are those used on the flag of Ethiopia, Africa's oldest independent nation. They symbolize African unity. This flag was used by Mali's African Democratic Rally prior to the country becoming independent from France in 1960.

Arable land 2.05% Permanent crops 0%
Permanent grassland 24.6% Forest 9.83%

History

From the 4th to the 16th centuries, Mali was part of three major black African cultures – ancient Ghana, Mali and Songhai. Reports on these empires were made by Arab scholars who crossed the Sahara to visit them. One major centre was Timbuktu (Tombouctou), in central Mali. In the 14th century, this town was a great centre of learning in history, law and the Muslim religion. It was also a trading centre and stopping point for Arabs and their camel caravans. At its height, the Mali Empire was West Africa's richest and most powerful state. France ruled the area, which was then known as French Sudan, from 1893. The country became independent as Mali in 1960, after attempts to create a union with Senegal had failed.

Politics

The first socialist government was over-thrown in 1968 by an army group led by Moussa Traoré. But his repressive military, single-party regime did little for the country, despite pressure from the aid donor nations to liberalize the economy. Moussa Traoré was finally ousted by a military group in 1991. Multiparty democracy was restored in 1992 and Alpha Oumar Konaré was elected president. The new government agreed a pact providing for a special administration for the Tuareg minority in the north.

Economy

Mali is one of the world's poorest countries and 70% of the land is desert or semi-desert. Only about 2% of the land is used for growing crops, while 25% is used for grazing animals. Despite this, agriculture employs more than 80% of the people, many of whom still subsist by nomadic livestock rearing. Farming is hampered by water shortages, and the severe droughts in the 1970s and 1980s led to a great loss of animals and much human suffering. The farmers in the south grow millet, rice, sorghum and other food crops to feed their families. The chief cash crops are cotton (the main export), groundnuts and sugar cane. Many of these crops are grown on land which is irrigated with river water. Only a few small areas in the south are worked without irrigation, while the barren deserts in the north are populated only by a few poor nomads.

Geography

The Republic of Mali is a landlocked country in northern Africa. The land is generally flat, with the highest land in the Adrar des Iforas on the border with Algeria. Today, the only permanent rivers are in the south. The main rivers are the Sénégal, which flows westwards to the Atlantic Ocean to the north of Kayes, and the Niger, which makes a large turn, called the Niger Bend, in south-central Mali.

Climate

Northern Mali is part of the Sahara, with a hot, practically rainless climate. But the south has enough rain for farming. In the south-west of the country, unpleasant weather is experienced when dry and dusty harmattan winds blow from the Sahara Desert.

MALI (BAMAKO)

Bamako, situated in the south-west region of the country, experiences a tropical climate. There is a distinct rainy season that occurs between May and October. The average annual rainfall amount has been recorded at around 1,120 mm [45 in]. Temperatures are very constant and relatively high throughout the year, ranging from an average of 24.4°C [76°F] in January to 26.7°C [80°F] in July.

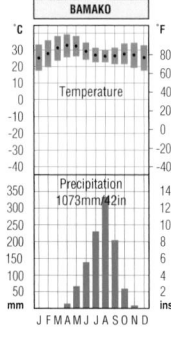

AREA	14%, Senufo 12%, Soninke 9%,
1,240,190 sq km [478,837 sq mls]	Tuareg 7%, Songhai 7%, Malinke
POPULATION	(Mandingo or Mandinke) 7%
10,109,000	**LANGUAGES**
CAPITAL (POPULATION)	French (official), Voltaic languages
Bamako (746,000)	**RELIGIONS**
GOVERNMENT	Islam 90%, traditional beliefs 9%,
Multiparty republic	Christianity 1%
ETHNIC GROUPS	**CURRENCY**
Bambara 32%, Fulani (or Peul)	CFA franc = 100 centimes

MALTA – SEE CYPRUS, PAGE 91;
MARSHALL ISLANDS – SEE PACIFIC OCEAN, PAGES 174–178;
MARTINIQUE – SEE CARIBBEAN SEA, PAGES 71–76

MAURITANIA

The Islamic Republic of Mauritania adopted its flag in 1959, the year before it became fully independent from France. It features a yellow star and crescent. These are traditional symbols of the national religion, Islam, as also is the colour green.

Geography

The Islamic Republic of Mauritania in north-western Africa is nearly twice the size of France., though France has more than 28 times as many people. Over two-thirds of the land is barren, most of it being part of the Sahara, the world's largest desert. Apart from a few nomads, most Mauritanians live in the south, either on the plains bordering the Senegal River in the south-west or on the tropical savanna in the south-east. The highest point, Kediet Ijill, reaches 915 m [3,002 ft] above sea level. It is an area rich in haematite (high-quality iron ore).

Climate

The amount of rainfall and the length of the rainy season increase from north to south. Much of the land is desert, with dry north-east and easterly winds all year. But south-westerly winds bring summer rain to the south.

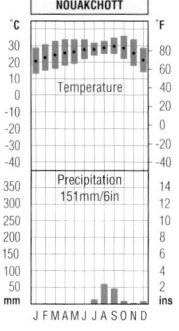

MAURITANIA
(NOUAKCHOTT)

Nouakchott is situated in the south of the country, where south-westerlies bring rain in summer. Sunshine hours and temperatures are very high, every month having recorded over 40°C [104°F]. The monthly temperature ranges from 30°C [86°F], from August to October, to 20°C [68°F] in January.

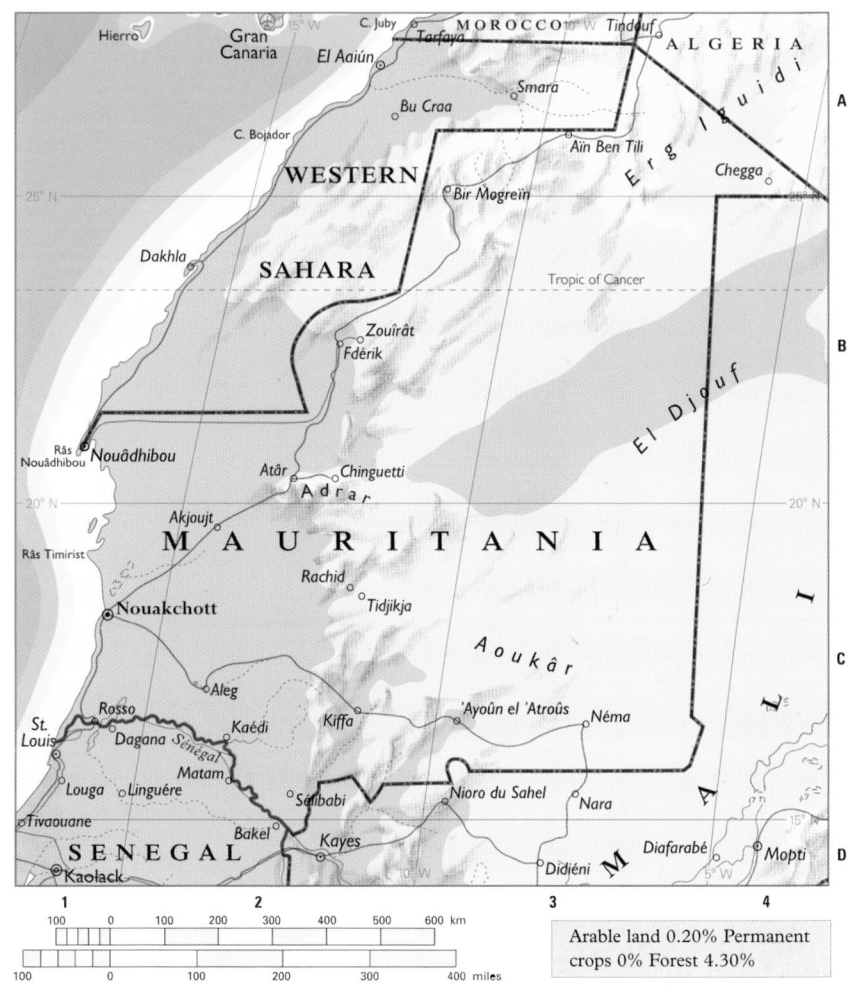

Arable land 0.20% Permanent crops 0% Forest 4.30%

History

From the 4th to the 16th centuries, parts of Mauritania belonged to two great African empires – ancient Ghana and Mali. Portuguese explorers arrived in the 1440s. But European contact did not begin in the area until the 17th century when trade in gum arabic, a substance obtained from an acacia tree, became important. Britain, France and the Netherlands were all interested in this trade.

France set up a protectorate in Mauritania in 1903, attempting to exploit the trade in gum arabic. The country became a territory of French West Africa and a French colony in 1920. French West Africa was a huge territory, which included present-day Benin, Burkina Faso, Guinea, Ivory Coast, Mali, Niger and Senegal, as well as Mauritania. In 1958, Mauritania became a self-governing territory in the French Union and it became fully independent in 1960.

Politics

In 1961, Mauritania's political parties were merged into one by the president, Mokhtar Ould Daddah, who made the country a one-party state. In 1976, Spain withdrew from Spanish (now Western) Sahara, a territory bordering Mauritania to the north. Morocco occupied the northern two-thirds of this territory, while Mauritania took the rest. But Saharan guerrillas belonging to POLISARIO (the Popular Front for the Liberation of Saharan Territories) began an armed struggle for independence. In 1979, Mauritania withdrew from the southern part of Western Sahara, which was then occupied by Morocco.

Following independence, Mauritania became a one-party state in 1965 and, from 1978, it was ruled by a series of military regimes. In 1991, the country adopted a new constitution when the people voted to create a multiparty democracy. In 1992, an army colonel, Maaouiya Ould Sidi Ahmed Taya, who had served as leader of a military administration since December 1984, was elected president. However, subsequent legislative elections in 1992 were boycotted by opposition parties who alleged fraud. Taya was re-elected in 1997.

Economy

The World Bank classifies Mauritania as a 'low-income' developing country. Agriculture employs 69% of the people, though the majority live at subsistence level. Many are still cattle herders who drive their herds from the Senegal River through the Sahelian steppelands, coinciding with the seasonal rains. However, droughts in the 1980s greatly reduced the domestic animal populations, forcing many nomadic farmers to seek help in urban areas. Farmers in the south-east grow such crops as beans, dates, millet, rice and sorghum. Fishing has recently become important. The government has expanded the fishing industry and some of the world's leading fishing grounds lie off the coast.

The country's chief natural resource is iron ore and the vast reserves around Fderik provide a major source of revenue. Besides iron ore, Mauritania's other leading exports include fish and cephalopods. Other exports include animal products, dates and gum arabic.

AREA	Wolof 7%, Tukulor 5%,
1,030,700 sq km [397,953 sq mls]	Soninke 3%, Fulani 1%
POPULATION	**LANGUAGES**
2,511,000	Arabic (official),
CAPITAL (POPULATION)	Wolof,
Nouakchott (600,000)	French
GOVERNMENT	**RELIGIONS**
Multiparty Islamic republic	Islam 99%
ETHNIC GROUPS	**CURRENCY**
Moor (Arab-Berber) 70%,	Ouguiya = 5 khoums

MAURITIUS – SEE INDIAN OCEAN, PAGES 122–123

Mexico's flag dates from 1821. The stripes were inspired by the French tricolour. The emblem in the centre contains an eagle, a snake and a cactus. It is based on an ancient Aztec legend about the founding of their capital, Tenochtitlán (now Mexico City).

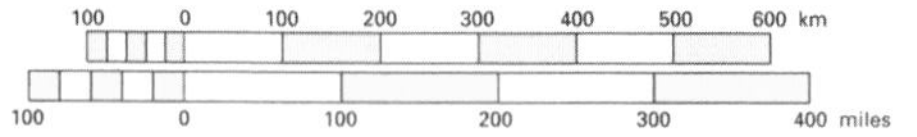

Arable land 12.1% Permanent crops 0.83%
Permanent grassland 39% Forest 25.5%

Geography

The United Mexican States, as Mexico is officially named, is the world's most populous Spanish-speaking country. Mountain ranges and plateaux cover about two-thirds of the land, with extensive coastal plains, especially along the Gulf of Mexico. The chief natural region is the Plateau of Mexico, which is bordered by two ranges: the Sierra Madre Occidental and the Sierra Madre Oriental. The southern part of the Plateau of Mexico is dotted with volcanoes, many of which are active. The volcanoes include the snow-capped Citlaltépetl (also called Orizaba), which reaches 5,700 m [18,701 ft], and Popocatépetl, which stands close to Mexico City.

Besides frequent volcanic activity, this region is also prone to many earthquakes. Earthquakes occur as a relatively small plate, underlying the Pacific Ocean west of south-western Mexico and Central America, sinks down in occasional jerky movements beneath the south-western tip of the North American plate. Such a plate movement, with its epicentre 400 km [250 mls] west of Mexico City, triggered the 1985 earthquake, measured at 8.1 on the Richter scale, that led to about 10,000 deaths in the capital. The massive damage was attributed to the fact that Mexico City stands on thick silt deposits formed on an old lake floor. Regions between Mexico City and the epicentre were relatively undamaged.

Mexico also contains two large peninsulas: the isolated Baja (Lower) California in the north-west with its mountainous core, and the Yucatan Peninsula, a low, flat limestone plateau in the south-east. Southern Mexico contains two highland regions broken only by the low, narrow isthmus of Tehuantepec: the Southern Uplands, which include the Sierra Madre del Sur, and the Chiapas Highlands which extend to the border with Guatemala in Central America.

Climate

The climate is especially affected by the altitude. There are three main altitudinal climatic zones. The *tierra caliente* (hot land) includes regions up to 910 m [3,000 ft], the *tierra templada* (temperate land) extends from 910 m to 1,800 m [3,000–6,000 ft], while the *tierra fria* (cold land) lies above 1,800 m [6,000 ft]. The highest peaks in the tierra fria are always snow-capped. The effects of altitude are evident by comparing the dry, sunny climate of the resort of Acapulco with the much cooler Mexico City, which lies at about 2,300 m [7,546 ft] above

MEXICO

sea level. Most rainfall occurs in summer. More than 70% of the country is arid. Northern Mexico contains deserts and semi-deserts, where many kinds of cactus plants are found, though mountains with higher rainfall are forested.

MEXICO – MEXICO CITY

The tropical climate at Mexico City lacks a winter season. The weather is cool and dry, except during the rainy season, which runs from May through to September. The annual median temperature is 18°C [64°F]. The warmer months are July and August, when temperatures average around 21°C [70°F]. Night frosts occur during December, and sudden temperature changes are usual.

ACAPULCO

Acapulco, on the Pacific coast, has high rainfall in the form of storms. Around 1,500 mm [59 in] falls in a year but on only 70 days – 50 of them between June and September. Practically no rain falls from February to April. On average there are over 7 hours of sunshine each day with over 9 hours in the rainless months. The climate is hot, every day recording over 30°C [86°F], but this falls towards 20°C [68°F] at night.

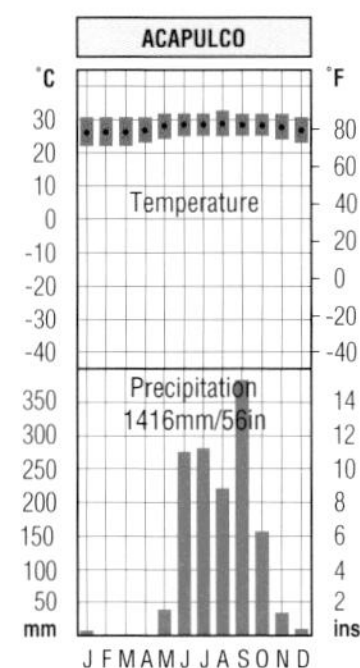

Vegetation

The vegetation of Mexico ranges from deserts in the north to rainforests in the south. The country also has areas of tropical grassland. The high mountains contain zones of vegetation which vary according to the altitude.

History

The Pre-Colombian civilizations that flourished for centuries before the Spanish conquest still play a strong role in fostering Mexican national identity. The Olmecs, the classical cultures of Teotihuacán, the Zapotecs and the Toltecs all left remarkable architectural monuments, though the most outstanding culture in Mexico and Central America was that of the Maya. The Maya civilization flourished from the 3rd to the 10th centuries and extended from the Yucatán Peninsula to Honduras. The magnificent ruins left by the Maya and other cultures in Mexico and Central America now attract visitors from all over the world.

However, the culture that was at its height when Mexico succumbed to the Spanish *conquistadores* was that of the Aztecs. The Aztecs invaded central Mexico during the 13th century and founded their island-city of Tenochtitlán in Lake Texcoco in 1325. During the 15th century, they conquered neighbouring states and drew tribute from an empire that extended from the Pacific to the Gulf of Mexico and into northern Central America. Spain conquered the Aztecs in 1519–21. In the early 17th century, the Spaniards drained Lake Texcoco in order to expand the new capital of Mexico City.

Spain ruled Mexico until the country gained its independence in 1821. In the 1830s and 1840s, Mexico lost land to the United States. The mid-19th century was a time of upheaval and, in 1862, British, French and Spanish troops arrived in Mexico after the government stopped payments on its national debts. The British and Spanish troops soon left, but the French invaded Mexico City in 1863. In 1864, Maximilian, brother of the emperor of Austria, was proclaimed emperor. But Mexican forces regained power in 1867, and Maximilian was shot. Between 1876 and 1880, and also from 1884 to 1911, Mexico was ruled as a dictatorship by Porfirio Diaz, a mestizo general. This time of relative stability led to an expansion of Mexico's economy. However, the peasants received few of the benefits, while the big landowners, businessmen and foreign investors prospered.

Politics

Between 1910 and 1921, violent revolutions caused chaos. Reforms were introduced in the 1920s and, in 1929, the Institutional Revolutionary Party (PRI) was formed. The PRI won every election from 1929 until 1997, when opposition parties gained a majority in the Chamber of Deputies. However, the PRI leader, Ernesto Zedillo Ponce de Leon, who had been sworn in as the country's president in 1994, remained in office. In November 1999, in a further step towards democracy, the PRI held its first primary election for president. This replaced the previous practice when the incumbent president nominated his successor. Following a campaign that resembled the primary elections in the United States, the experienced Francisco Labastida was elected as the party's presidential candidate for the election scheduled for July 2000. The chances of success for the opposition parties were weakened when they failed to agree on a single presidential candidate.

Mexico faces many problems, including unemployment, poverty and rapid urbanization. The country's recent history has been marked by massive migrations of people. Many have moved from rural areas to cities, especially the capital, which has become one of the world's largest urban areas. Others have emigrated illegally to the United States, where they hope to enjoy higher living standards. Other problems faced by Mexico in the 1990s were demands by Native American groups in the south, such as the Zapatista National Liberation Army and the Popular Revolutionary Army, for increased rights for indigenous peoples and greater democracy in the country.

Economy

The World Bank classifies Mexico as an 'upper-middle-income' developing country. Until the mid-20th century, agriculture and mining dominated the economy, but manufacturing is now the leading activity. Mexico has also been a major oil exporter since the 1970s. Oil revenues have brought many benefits, but Mexico has found it hard to repay its loans whenever the world prices of oil have fallen.

In the 1990s, despite its growing economy, Mexico suffered from severe financial crises. Hope for the future lies in increasing co-operation with the United States and Canada through NAFTA (North American Free Trade Association), which came into being on 1 January 1994. Many believe that, through NAFTA, Mexico will have the chance to attract more foreign investment, reduce the national debt, raise living standards, and enable it to tackle the problem of illegal emigration to the United States.

Agriculture employs about 24% of the workforce. Crops are grown on 12% of the land area, with the best farmland being on the fertile volcanic soils on the southern part of the Plateau of Mexico. The main food crops include beans, maize and rice, while major cash crops include coffee, cotton, fruits and vegetables. Farm animals are raised throughout the country.

Mexico is the world's leading silver producer. It also mines copper, gold, lead, zinc and other minerals. Mexico City is the main industrial centre, but new factories, called *maquiladoras*, have been built near the United States border. Many of them assemble goods, such as car parts and electrical goods, for US companies. Craft products, including silver jewellery, glassware, pottery and textiles, are important, especially for sale to tourists. Tourism is a major activity in Mexico, with visitors attracted by both the ancient ruins and the seaside resorts.

AREA	Amerindian 30%,
1,958,200 sq km [756,061 sq mls]	European 9%
POPULATION	**LANGUAGES**
98,553,000	Spanish (official)
CAPITAL (POPULATION)	**RELIGIONS**
Mexico City (15,643,000)	Christianity
GOVERNMENT	(Roman Catholic 90%,
Federal republic	Protestant 5%)
ETHNIC GROUPS	**CURRENCY**
Mestizo 60%,	New peso = 100 centavos

MICRONESIA, FED. STATES OF – SEE PACIFIC OCEAN, PAGES 174–178;
MOLDOVA – SEE ROMANIA, PAGES 188–189;
MONACO – SEE FRANCE, PAGES 100–102

MONGOLIA

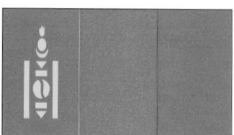

Mongolia's flag contains blue, the national colour, together with red for Communism. The traditional Mongolian golden 'soyonbo' symbol represents freedom. Within this, the flame is seen as a promise of prosperity and progress.

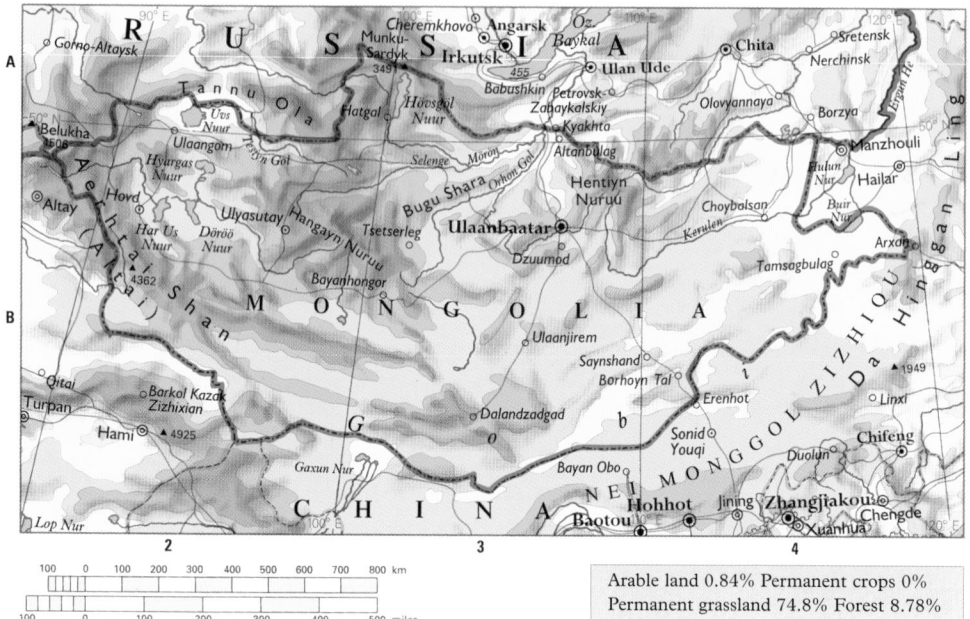

Arable land 0.84% Permanent crops 0%
Permanent grassland 74.8% Forest 8.78%

Geography

The State of Mongolia, which is sandwiched between China and Russia, is the world's largest landlocked country. High plateaux cover most of Mongolia. The highest plateaux are in the west, between the Altai Mountains (or Aerhtai Shan) and the Hangayn Mountains (or Hangayn Nuruu).

The Altai Mountains contain the country's highest peaks, which reach 4,362 m [14,311 ft] above sea level. The land descends towards the east and south, where part of the huge Gobi Desert is situated.

Climate

Because of its remote position, Mongolia has an extreme continental climate, with long, bitterly cold winters and short, warm summers. The average annual rainfall ranges from no more than 500 mm [20 in] in the highlands to 125 mm [5 in] in lowland areas.

MONGOLA (ULAN BATOR)

Ulan Bator lies on the northern edge of a vast desert plateau in the heart of Asia. Winters are bitterly cold and dry. During the summer, the temperatures are moderated by the height of the land above sea level. A large diurnal temperature range of over 15°C [27°F] occurs all year. Rain falls almost entirely in summer, the amount varying greatly from year to year, and decreasing to the south.

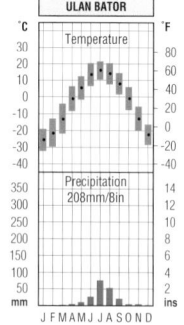

History

In the 13th century, the great Mongol conqueror Genghis Khan united the Mongol people, created a ruthless army, and founded the largest land empire in history. Under his grandson, Kublai Khan, the Mongol empire stretched from Korea and China, across Asia into what is now Iraq. In the north-west, Mongol rule extended beyond the Black Sea into eastern Europe. Learning flourished under Kublai Khan, but, after his death in 1294, the empire broke up into several parts. It was not until the late 16th century that Mongol princes reunited Mongolia. During their rule, they introduced Lamaism (a form of Buddhism).

In the early 17th century, the Manchu leaders of Manchuria took over Inner Mongolia. They later conquered China in 1644 and Outer Mongolia some 40 years later. Present-day Mongolia then became a remote Chinese province with little contact with the outside world.

Outer Mongolia broke away from China following the collapse of the Qing (or Ch'ing) Dynasty in 1911, and the Mongols appointed a priest, called the Living Buddha, as their king. Legally, Outer Mongolia remained Chinese territory, although China and Russia agreed to grant it control over its own affairs in 1913. Russian influence increased and, in 1921, Mongolian and Russian Communists took control of Outer Mongolia. In 1924, they proclaimed the Mongolian People's Republic.

Politics

Mongolia became an ally of the Soviet Union which was set up in 1922. Its support was particularly significant from the 1950s, when the Soviet Union was in dispute with Mongolia's neighbour, China. The Soviet Union helped to develop Mongolia's mineral reserves so that, by the late 1980s, minerals had overtaken agriculture as the country's main source of revenue.

In 1990, the people, influenced by reforms taking place in the Soviet Union, held demonstrations, demanding more freedom. Free elections in June 1990 resulted in victory for the Communist Mongolian People's Revolutionary Party (MPRP). But the new government began to move away from Communist policies, launching into privatization and developing a free-market economy. The 'People's Democracy' was abolished in 1992 and democratic institutions were introduced.

However, the MPRP was defeated in elections in 1996 by the opposition Mongolian Democratic Union coalition. In office, the Democratic Union ran into economic problems and, in the presidential elections of 1997, the MPRP candidate, Natasagiyn Babagandi, defeated the Democratic Union nominee. Further problems occurred in July 1998 when parliament passed a no-confidence vote concerning bank privatization. The government resigned and the crisis was finally ended in December when Janlaviyn Narantsatsralt, mayor of Ulan Bator, was approved as prime minister.

Economy

The World Bank classifies Mongolia as a 'lower-middle-income' developing country. Many people were once nomads, moving around with their herds of animals. Under Communist rule, most people were moved into permanent homes on government-owned farms. Livestock and animal products remain important, but the Communists developed mining and manufacturing. By 1996, mineral products accounted for nearly 60% of the country's exports. Minerals produced in Mongolia include coal, copper, fluorspar, gold, molybdenum, tin and tungsten. The leading manufactures are textiles and metal products. Chemicals, clothing, food and wood products are also important.

AREA	**ETHNIC GROUPS**
1,566,500 sq km	Khalkha Mongol 79%,
[604,826 sq mls]	Kazak 6%
POPULATION	**LANGUAGES**
2,579,000	Khalkha Mongolian (official),
CAPITAL (POPULATION)	Kazak
Ulan Bator	**RELIGIONS**
(Ulaanbaatar, 619,000)	Tibetan Buddhist (Lamaist)
GOVERNMENT	**CURRENCY**
Multiparty republic	Tugrik = 100 möngös

MONTSERRAT— SEE CARIBBEAN SEA, PAGES 71–76

MOROCCO

Morocco has flown a red flag since the 16th century. The green pentagram (five-pointed star), called the Seal of Solomon, was added in 1915. This design was retained when Morocco gained its independence from French and Spanish rule in 1956.

Geography

The Kingdom of Morocco lies in north-western Africa. Its name comes from the Arabic Maghreb-el-Aksa, meaning 'the furthest west'. Behind the western coastal plain the land rises to a broad plateau and the ranges of the Atlas Mountains. The High (Haut) Atlas contains the highest peak, Djebel Toubkal, at 4,165 m [13,665 ft]. Other ranges include the Anti Atlas in the south, the Middle (*Moyen*) Atlas and the Rif Atlas (or Er Rif) in the far north.

Climate

The Atlantic coast of Morocco is cooled by the Canaries Current. Inland, summers are very hot and dry and winters are mild. Between the months of October and April, south-westerly winds from the Atlantic Ocean bring rainfall, and snow frequently falls on the High Atlas Mountains.

History

The original people of Morocco were the Berbers. But in the 680s, Arab invaders introduced Islam and the Arabic language. By the early 20th century, France and Spain controlled Morocco, but the country became an independent kingdom in 1956.

Politics

Although Morocco is a constitutional monarchy, King Hassan II ruled the country in a generally authoritarian way between coming to the throne in 1961 and his death in 1999. His successor, King Mohamed VI, faced a number of problems, including finding a solution to the future of Western Sahara.

Economy

Morocco is classified as a 'lower-middle-income' developing country. It is the world's third largest producer of phosphate rock, which is used to make fertilizer. One of the reasons why Morocco wants to keep Western Sahara is that it, too, has large phosphate reserves. Farming employs 44% of Moroccans. Chief crops include barley, beans, citrus fruits, maize, olives, sugar beet and wheat. Processed phosphates are exported, but most of Morocco's manufactures are for home consumption. Fishing and tourism are important.

Morocco: Arable land 19.3% Permanent crops 1.49% Permanent grassland 47.1% Forest 20.1%

AREA	ETHNIC GROUPS
446,550 sq km	Arab 70%, Berber 30%
[172,413 sq mls]	**LANGUAGES**
POPULATION	Arabic (official), Berber,
29,114,000	French
CAPITAL (POPULATION)	**RELIGIONS**
Rabat (1,220,000)	Islam 99%, Christianity 1%
GOVERNMENT	**CURRENCY**
Constitutional monarchy	Moroccan dirham = 100 centimes

WESTERN SAHARA

Western Sahara is a disputed territory in north-western Africa. It is mostly barren, though it contains large reserves of phosphates. Spain claimed the area in the early 16th century, though it was under Moroccan control until 1860, when Spain took over.

In 1958, it became a Spanish province called the Province of Spanish Sahara.

In 1976, Spain withdrew. Morocco took the northern two-thirds of the territory, which became known as Western Sahara, while Mauritania took the rest. However, local Saharans in POLISARIO (Popular Front for the Liberation of Saharan Territories) formed a government in exile and called for the establishment of an independent Sahrawi Arab Democratic Republic. POLISARIO also launched a guerrilla war against Moroccan and Mauritanian forces. Hit by the conflict, Mauritania withdrew in 1979, and Morocco took over the entire territory. A cease-fire was declared in 1991, but a proposed referendum on the territory's future was repeatedly delayed owing to the lack of agreement between Morocco and POLISARIO on an electoral register.

AREA	CAPITAL
266,000 sq km [102,700 sq mls]	El Aaiún
POPULATION	**CURRENCY**
230,000	Morr. dirham = 100 centimes

Mozambique's flag was adopted when the country became independent from Portugal in 1975. The green stripe represents fertile land, the black stands for Africa and the yellow for mineral wealth. The badge on the red triangle contains a rifle, a hoe, a cogwheel and a book.

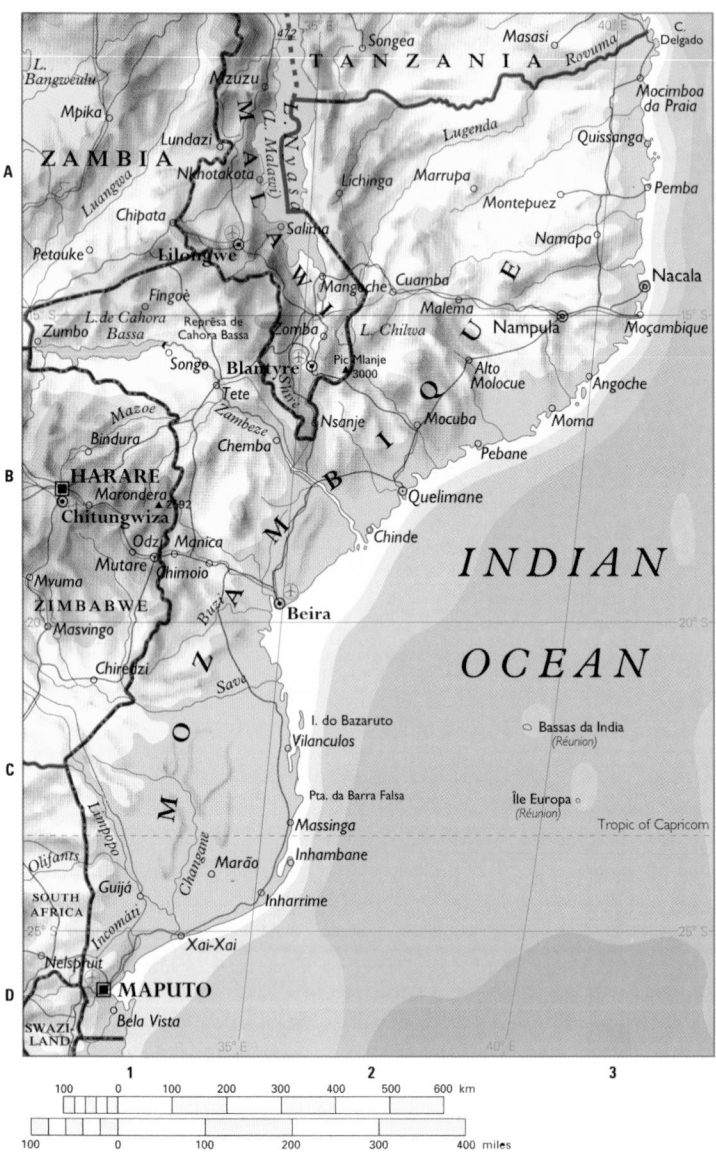

Geography

The Republic of Mozambique borders the Indian Ocean in south-eastern Africa. The coastal plains are narrow in the north but broaden in the south and they make up nearly half of the country. Inland lie plateaux and hills, which make up another two-fifths of Mozambique, with highlands along the borders with Zimbabwe, Zambia, Malawi and Tanzania.

Climate

Most of Mozambique has a tropical maritime climate, with two main seasons. The hot, wet season runs from November to March, with a dry, milder season between April and October. The rainfall varies,

being greatest on the north-western highlands and lowest on the south-eastern lowlands. Temperatures in the lowlands vary from between 20°C to 30°C [79–86°F] in January, and 11°C to 15°C [52–59°F] in January. The interior highlands are much cooler and generally less humid.

History

Arab traders began to operate in the area in the 9th century AD, and Portuguese explorers arrived in 1497. The Portuguese set up trading stations in the early 16th century and the area became a source of slaves. In 1885, when the European powers divided Africa, Mozambique was recognized as a Portuguese colony. But black African opposition to European rule gradually increased. In 1961, the Front for the Liberation of Mozambique (FRELIMO) was founded to oppose Portuguese rule. In 1964, FRELIMO launched a guerrilla war, which continued for ten years. Mozambique became independent in 1975, when FRELIMO, which followed Marxist-Leninist policies, took over the government.

Politics

After independence, Mozambique became a one-party state. Its government aided African nationalists in Rhodesia (now Zimbabwe) and South Africa. But the white governments of these countries helped an opposition group, the Mozambique National Resistance Movement (RENAMO) to lead an armed struggle against Mozambique's government. The civil war, combined with severe droughts, caused much human suffering in the 1980s. In 1989, FRELIMO declared that it had dropped its Communist policies and ended one-party rule. The war officially ended in 1992 and multiparty elections in 1994 were won by FRELIMO, whose leader, Joaquim A. Chissano, became president. RENAMO's leader, Afonso Dhlakama, accepted the election results and stated that the civil war would not be resumed. This led to a period of relative stability. In 1995, Mozambique became the 53rd member of the Commonwealth, joining its English-speaking allies in southern Africa.

Economy

By the early 1990s, Mozambique was one of the world's poorest countries. Battered by civil war, which had killed around a million people and had driven 5 million from their homes, combined with devastating droughts and floods, the economy collapsed. However, by the end of the century, economists were praising Mozambique for its economic recovery. Although 80% of the people are poor, support from the World Bank and other international institutions, privatization and rescheduling of the country's foreign debts, led to an expansion of the economy and the bringing down of inflation to less than 10% by 1999. However, massive floods at the start of 2000 killed and made thousands homeless, devastating the economy for many years to come.

Agriculture is important. Crops include cassava, cotton, cashew nuts, fruits, maize, rice, sugar cane and tea. Fishing is important and shrimps, cashew nuts, sugar and copra are exported. Despite its large hydroelectric plant at the Cahora Bassa Dam on the River Zambezi, manufacturing is small-scale. Electricity is exported to South Africa.

MOZAMBIQUE (MAPUTO)

Maputo is located on the coast of Mozambique, and lies south of the Tropic of Capricorn. The winters here are dry with average temperatures of around 18°C [64°F] recorded in June and July. The south is drier than the rest of the country and Maputo has an average annual rainfall total of 760 mm [30 in]. This compares with 1,520 mm [60 in] at Sofala, which is situated in central Mozambique.

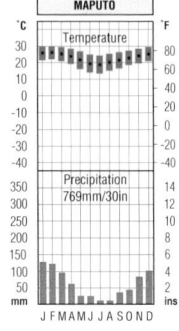

AREA	Malawi 12%, Shona 11%, Yao
801,590 sq km [309,494 sq mls]	4%, Swahili 1%, Makonde 1%
POPULATION	**LANGUAGES**
18,641,000	Portuguese (official), many others
CAPITAL (POPULATION)	**RELIGIONS**
Maputo (2,000,000)	Traditional beliefs 48%,
GOVERNMENT	Christianity (Roman Catholic
Multiparty republic	31%, others 9%), Islam 13%
ETHNIC GROUPS	**CURRENCY**
Makua 47%, Tsonga 23%,	Metical = 100 centavos

NAMIBIA

Namibia adopted this flag in 1990 when it gained its independence from South Africa. The red diagonal stripe and white borders are symbols of Namibia's human resources. The green and blue triangles and the gold sun represent the country's resources.

Geography

The Republic of Namibia was formerly ruled by South Africa, which called it South West Africa. The country became independent in 1990. The coastal region contains the arid Namib Desert, mostly between 900 m and 2,000 m [2,950–6,560 ft] above sea level, which is virtually uninhabited. Inland is a central plateau, bordered by a rugged spine of mountains stretching north–south.

Eastern Namibia contains part of the Kalahari, a semi-desert area which extends into Botswana. The Orange River forms Namibia's southern border, while the Cunene and Cubango Rivers form parts of the northern borders.

Climate

Namibia has a warm and largely arid climate. Average daily temperatures range from about 24°C [75°F] in January to 20°C [68°F] in July. The average annual rainfall ranges from about 500 mm [20 in] in the north to 25 mm to 150 mm [1–6 in] in the south. Most of the rain falls in summer.

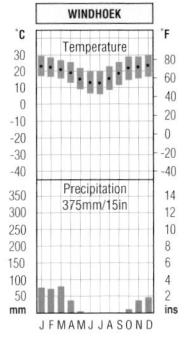

NAMIBIA (WINDHOEK)

Windhoek stands at a height of around 1,700 m [5,500 ft] above sea level on the Namibian Plateau and it is very well isolated from the effects of the cold Benguela Current. Windhoek has an average annual rainfall total of 360 mm [14 in], often occurring during thunderstorms in the hot summer months. However, the rainfall can be unreliable. The climate here is warm and sunny, but frosts may occur during the winter.

History

The earliest people in Namibia were the San (also called Bushmen) and the Damara (Hottentots). Later arrivals were people who spoke Bantu languages. They migrated into Namibia from the north and included the Ovambo, Kavango and Herero. From 1868, Germans began to operate along the coast and, in 1884, Germany annexed the entire territory which they called German South West Africa. In the 1890s, the Germans forcibly removed the Damara and Herero from the Windhoek area. About 65,000 Herero were killed when they revolted against their eviction.

In 1915, South African troops took over the territory. In 1920, the League of Nations gave South Africa a mandate to govern the country. But South Africa ruled it as though it were a South African province.

Politics

After World War II, many people challenged South Africa's right to govern the territory. A civil war began during the 1960s between African guerrillas and South African troops. A cease-fire in Namibia's long-running civil war was agreed in 1989 and the country became independent in 1990. After independence, the government pursued a policy of 'national reconciliation'. An area on Namibia's coast, called Walvis Bay (Walvisbaai), remained part of South Africa until 1994, when South Africa transferred it to Namibia. Elections in 1994 resulted in victory for the ruling South West African People's Organization (SWAPO) and Sam Nujoma was re-elected president.

Namibia's Caprivi Strip, a geographical oddity which European powers gave to Germany in the late 19th century so it would have access to the River Zambezi, became the scene of a rebellion in 1999. A small band of rebels tried, unsuccessfully, to seize the regional capital, Kutima Mulilo, as part of an attempt to make the Caprivi Strip independent. The Strip is populated mainly by Lozi people, who resent SWAPO rule. Lozi separatists also live in Botswana and Zambia.

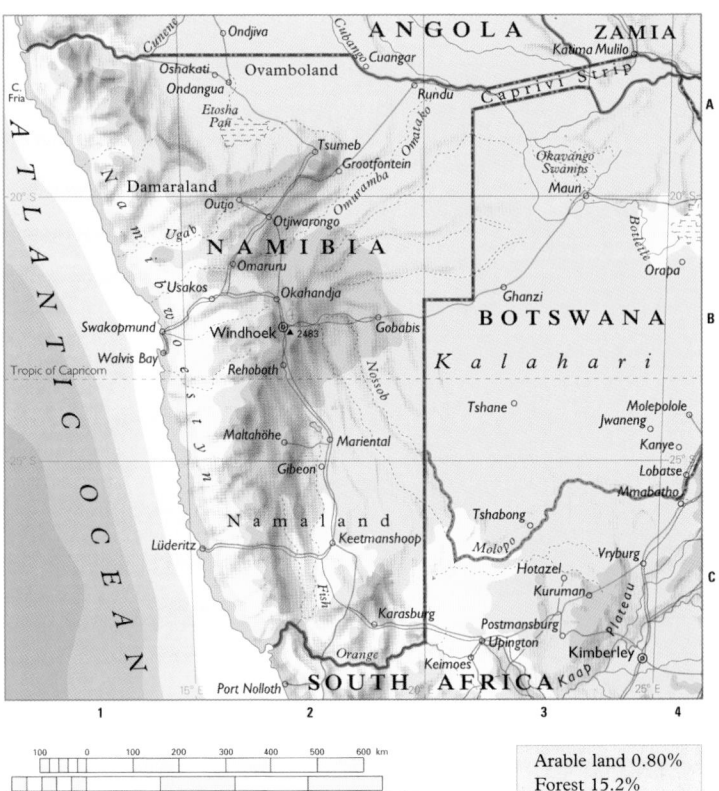

Arable land 0.80%
Forest 15.2%

Economy

Namibia has important mineral reserves, including diamonds, zinc, uranium, copper, lead and tin. Mining is the most valuable economic activity and, by the mid-1990s, minerals accounted for as much as 90% of the exports, with diamonds making up over half the total revenue from minerals.

Farming employs around two out of every five Namibians, although many farmers live at subsistence level, making little or no contribution to the economy. Because most of the land in Namibia has too little rainfall for arable farming, the principle agricultural activities are cattle and sheep raising. However, livestock raising has been hit in the last 20 years by extended droughts that have depleted the number of farm animals. The chief crops are maize, millet and vegetables.

Fishing in the Atlantic Ocean is also important, though overfishing has reduced the yields of Namibia's fishing fleet. The country has few manufacturing industries apart from jewellery-making, some metal smelting, the processing of farm products, such as karakul pelts (sheepskins that are used to make fur coats), and textiles. Tourism is developing, especially in the Etosha National Park in northern Namibia, which is rich in wildlife.

AREA	ETHNIC GROUPS
825,414 sq km [318,434 sq mls], including Walvis Bay, a former South African territory	Ovambo 50%, Kavango 9%, Herero 7%, Damara 7%, White 6%, Nama 5%
POPULATION	**LANGUAGES**
1,622,000	English (official), Ovambo
CAPITAL (POPULATION)	**RELIGIONS**
Windhoek (126,000)	Christianity 90% (Lutheran 51%)
GOVERNMENT	**CURRENCY**
Multiparty republic	Namibian dollar = 100 cents

NAURU – SEE PACIFIC OCEAN, PAGES 174–178

This Himalayan kingdom's uniquely shaped flag was adopted in 1962. It came about in the 19th century when two triangular pennants – the royal family's crescent moon symbol and the powerful Rana family's sun symbol – were joined together.

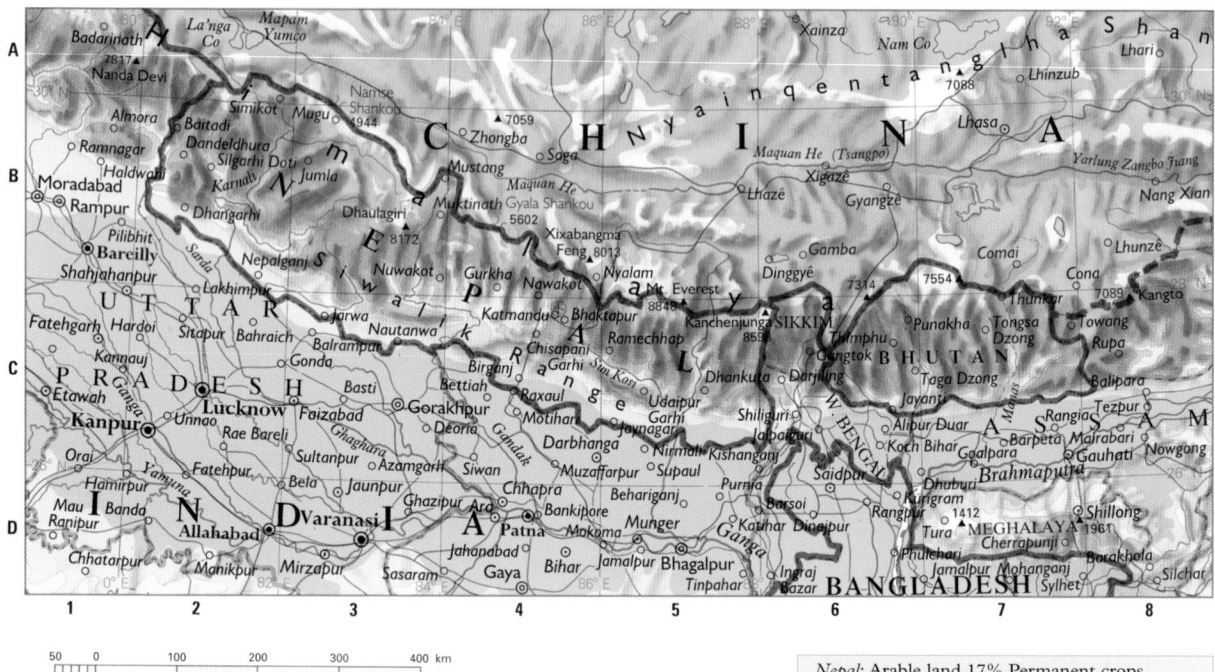

AREA
140,800 sq km
[54,363 sq mls]
POPULATION
23,698,000
**CAPITAL
(POPULATION)**
Katmandu
(535,000)
GOVERNMENT
Constitutional
monarchy
ETHNIC GROUPS
Nepalese 53%,
Bihari 18%, Tharu
5%, Tamang 5%,
Newar 3%
LANGUAGES
Nepali (official)
RELIGIONS
Hindu 86%,
Buddhist 8%,
Muslim 4%
CURRENCY
Nepalese rupee
= 100 paisa

Nepal: Arable land 17% Permanent crops
0.21% Permanent grassland 14.6% Forest 42%

Geography and Climate

More than three-quarters of the Kingdom of Nepal lies in the Himalayan mountain heartland, culminating in Mount Everest (or Chomolongma in Nepali), at 8,848 m [29,029 ft]. The far lower Siwalik Range overlooks the Ganges plain. The huge differences in altitude give Nepal a wide variety of climatic and vegetation regions, ranging from tropical forest to polar conditions on the ice-covered mountain tops.

History, Politics and Economy

Nepal was united by the Gurkhas in the late 18th century, but until 1951, when it was opened up to foreigners, it was a patchwork of feudal valley kingdoms where local leaders displayed more allegiance to their clans than to the state. However, in 1951, the monarchy was re-established. A brief period of democracy ended with the return of autocratic royal rule in 1960 under King Mahendra.

Mass demonstrations followed the return of autocratic rule, and

King Mahendra's son, Birendra, was forced in 1990 to concede a new constitution incorporating pluralism and basic human rights. In May 1991, the first democratic elections for 32 years took place and were won by the centrist Nepali Congress Party. From 1994, the country was ruled by a coalition led by the Marxist-Leninist Party. However, in 1999, the Nepali Congress Party returned to power.

Nepal is one of the world's poorest countries, with a per capita gross national product of US $210 in 1997. Agriculture employed over 80% of the workforce, accounting for two-fifths of the gross domestic product. Export crops include herbs, jute, rice, spices and wheat. Tourism, which is centred around the high Himalaya, has grown in importance since 1951, when the country first opened to foreigners. The government is highly dependent on aid to develop the infrastructure and set up small businesses. There are also plans to exploit the hydroelectric potential offered by the Himalayan rivers.

BHUTAN

Geography and Climate

The Kingdom of Bhutan is a mountainous, isolated country located between India and Tibet.

The climate is similar to that of Nepal, being dependent on altitude and affected by monsoon winds.

History

Bhutan became a separate state in the early 17th century when a Tibetan lama became its spiritual and temporal ruler. In 1907, Bhutan became a monarchy when Ugyen Wangchuk, a powerful local governor, made himself king and set up the country's first effective central government.

Politics

In 1910, Britain took control of Bhutan's foreign affairs, but it did not interfere with internal affairs. The monarch of Bhutan, King Jigme Singye Wangchuk, who came to the throne in 1972, is both head of state and government. However, under a 1949 treaty, India

took responsibility for Bhutan's foreign affairs and, later, took control of its defence.

Economy

Bhutan is a low-income developing country. Agriculture employs 90% of the workforce and barley, rice and wheat are the chief crops. People living in the mountains raise cattle and yaks. Economic development depends largely on harnessing the country's hydroelectric potential.

AREA	**ETHNIC GROUPS**
47,000 sq km [18,147 sq mls]	Bhutanese, Nepali
POPULATION	**LANGUAGES**
1,908,000	Dzongkha (official)
CAPITAL (POPULATION)	**RELIGIONS**
Thimphu (30,000)	Buddhism 75%, Hindu
GOVERNMENT	**CURRENCY**
Constitutional monarchy	Ngultrum = 100 chetrum

The flag of the Netherlands, one of Europe's oldest, dates from 1630, during the long struggle for independence from Spain which began in 1568. The tricolour became a symbol of liberty which inspired many other revolutionary flags around the world.

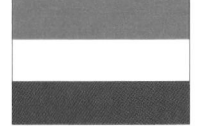

Geography

The Kingdom of the Netherlands is one of the 'Low Countries'. The others are Belgium and Luxembourg. The Netherlands lies at the western end of the North European Plain, which extends to the Ural Mountains in Russia. Except for the far south-eastern corner, the Netherlands is flat, and about 40% lies below sea level at high tide. To prevent flooding, the Dutch have built dykes (sea walls) to hold back the waves. Large areas which were once under the sea, but which have been reclaimed, are called polders.

The Netherlands is often inaccurately called Holland. This name refers only to the two north-western provinces, where less than 40% of the population lives. The Netherlands is Europe's most crowded country, yet the east and south are relatively sparsely populated. The figure for Zuid-Holland province is about 1,080 per sq km [2,800 per sq ml].

The greatest density of population is in the urban areas of Randstad Holland, a 50 km [31 mls] diameter horseshoe region, with Dordrecht at the centre of the loop. This area includes many major cities, such as Hilversum, Utrecht, Dordrecht, Rotterdam, The Hague ('s-Gravenhage), Leiden, Haarlem and Amsterdam. Nearly all this crucial area lies well below sea level.

Climate

Because of its position on the North Sea, the Netherlands has a temperate climate. Winters are mild, with rain coming from the Atlantic depressions which pass over the country. North Sea storms often batter the coasts. Storm waves have periodically breached the dykes, causing flooding and sometimes loss of life.

Arable land 27.1% Permanent crops 0.83%
Permanent grassland 31% Forest 10.3%

NETHERLANDS (AMSTERDAM)

Amsterdam has a climate typical of the coastal margins of north-west Europe. Daily and annual temperature range is small. Winters are mild with wind and rain from Atlantic depressions. No monthly minimum temperature is below freezing. The prevailing westerly winds keep summers cool. Rainfall increases from a spring minimum to a maximum in late summer and autumn, falling on about 130 days per year.

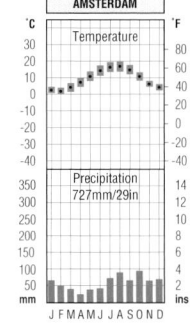

Vegetation

Plant and animal life in this densely populated country have been highly modified by human activity. Seen from the air, most of the Netherlands is made up of richly cultivated fields, mainly rectangular in shape, with water-filled ditches between them, along which farmers travel by boat. Control of water to prevent flooding is a major problem. Without the protection of dykes and sand dunes, around two-fifths of the land would be flooded. To prevent soil erosion, the sand dunes that line much of the coast are planted with marram grass and, where possible, trees. Salt-resistant plants also grow along the coast, while woodland covers about a fifth of the land area.

History

Roman armies led by Julius Caesar conquered the Low Countries in 58 BC. Roman rule continued until the 5th century AD when the area came under the Franks, but when the Frankish Empire was divided in the 9th century, the Low Countries became part of the East Frankish Kingdom.

From the 12th century, the region became increasingly prosperous and this led to the growth of trading towns, which attracted the interest of the rulers of France and Germany. Despite the efforts of nobles to maintain the independence of the Low Countries, the region came under the French dukes of Burgundy in the 14th century. In 1516, Charles V, who inherited the Low Countries from the dukes of Burgundy in 1506, became king of Spain and the area came under Spanish control. In the 16th century, the Protestant Reformation movement gained influence in the Low Countries. The Roman Catholic monarchy tried to suppress Protestantism and conflict broke out in 1568 when William I of Orange, outraged at Spain's behaviour towards Protestants, led a revolt against the rule of Philip II of Spain. The revolt began to falter in 1579, when nobles in what is now Belgium returned to Spanish control, but the Protestants in the northern provinces continued their revolt. The Dutch declared themselves independent in 1581, though the struggle continued until the end of the Thirty Years' War in 1648, when Spain finally recognized Dutch independence.

The 17th century saw a great expansion of Dutch sea power. Dutch explorers, such as Abel Janszoon Tasman, were active in opening up new lands, and expanding trade. The rapid growth of the East India Company made the Netherlands the leading power in what is now Indonesia, while other traders operated in other parts of Asia, including Sri Lanka and Japan. In addition, the Dutch West India Company was active in western Africa and the Americas. For a time, the huge expansion of trade developed by these companies made Amsterdam the world's leading commercial centre.

Between 1652 and 1674, the Netherlands maintained its superiority at sea after fighting three naval wars with England. However, the situation was reversed between 1701 and 1714 when the Dutch lost control of the seas to Britain, a setback which curtailed Dutch trade. During the American Revolutionary War (1775–84), the Dutch supported the Americans, but the Dutch were again defeated by Britain in a naval war between 1780 and 1784. The weakened Netherlands was conquered by France in 1795, while Britain occupied much of the country's overseas territories. In 1806, the brother of Napoleon I, Louis, became king of the country which became the Kingdom of Holland. However, the French were driven out in 1813.

After the Napoleonic Wars, the Congress of Vienna reorganized the countries of Europe. Belgium, Luxembourg and the Netherlands were united to form the Kingdom of the Netherlands. William VI, prince of Orange, became William I of the Netherlands and Grand Duke of Luxembourg. Internal differences caused the break-up of the kingdom. Belgium broke away in 1830, and in 1839 Belgium and the Netherlands were recognized as separate monarchies. When Queen Wilhelmina ascended to the throne in 1890, Luxembourg ended its ties with the Dutch royal family because its laws did not permit a female ruler.

The Netherlands was neutral in World War I, but German troops invaded the country on 10 May 1940. Much of the Dutch fleet escaped and served with the Allies. The people suffered greatly during the occupation and around three-quarters of the country's Jews were murdered, while many other people were forced to work in German factories. By the end of the war, about 270,000 Netherlanders had been killed or had died of starvation.

Politics

After World War II, the Netherlands began to play a major part in European affairs. In 1948, it joined with Belgium and Luxembourg to form an economic union called Benelux and, in 1949, it abandoned its traditional neutrality when it became a member of the North Atlantic Treaty Organization. The country's economic recovery was rapid, and the economy received a further stimulus when it became a founder member of the European Economic Community (EEC) in 1957. The Maastricht Treaty, which transformed the EEC into the European Union, was signed in the Dutch city of Maastricht in 1991. On 1 January 1999, the Netherlands became one of the 11 countries to adopt the euro, the single currency of the European Union.

Because of ill health, Queen Wilhelmina abdicated in favour of her daughter, Juliana, in 1948. Juliana reigned until 1980 when she, in turn, abdicated in favour of her daughter, Beatrix. The Netherlands is a constitutional monarchy with a parliament which consists of two chambers. The 75 members of the First Chamber are elected by members of the Provincial States, the representative bodies of the 12 provinces, while the 150-member Second Chamber is directly elected. The Hague is the seat of the government, the parliament and the High Court, but Amsterdam is the national capital.

In 1949, after much fighting, the Dutch recognized the independence of its largest overseas possession, Indonesia. In 1954, Surinam and the Netherlands Antilles were granted self-government. In 1962, the Dutch handed over Netherlands New Guinea to the United Nations, which handed it over, as Irian Jaya, to Indonesia in 1963. Surinam became fully independent in 1975, leaving the Netherlands with only two remaining overseas territories, Netherlands Antilles and Aruba, which had been part of Netherlands Antilles until it broke away in 1986.

Partly because of its policies of economic co-operation with other European nations, the Netherlands is now one of Europe's most prosperous countries, with well-developed social services and government-funded health care. However, its high standard of living also owes much to its domestic policies and the determination of its people.

The truth of the old saying that 'God created the world but the Dutch created Holland' was again demonstrated after the North Sea storm of January 1953. During this storm, waves penetrated the coastal defences in the south-western delta region, flooding about 4.3% of the country, destroying or damaging more than 30,000 houses and killing 1,800 people. The Dutch response to the disaster was typical. Within three weeks, a commission of enquiry had recommended the Delta Plan, a huge project to protect the delta region. Completed in 1986, it involved the construction of massive dams and floodgates, which can be closed during severe storms. However, global warming, with its predicted rise in sea levels and increasing frequency of storms, may provide the Netherlands with its greatest challenge of how it can hang on to the land it has so laboriously wrested from the sea.

Economy

The Dutch economy is one of the strongest economies in Europe. Despite its comparatively small size, its economy is the world's 12th largest, with a total gross national product in 1997 of US $403,057 million. The Netherlands is a highly industrialized country and manufacturing and commerce are the most valuable activities. Mineral resources include china clay, which is abundant, natural gas from the North Sea, and coal, though commercial mining ceased in 1965. However, the country has to import many of the materials needed by its manufacturers. The emphasis of modern industry is on oil, steel, chemicals and electrical engineering. The products are wide-ranging, including aircraft, chemical products, electronic equipment, machinery, textiles and vehicles. In the area south of Rotterdam, the Dutch have constructed a vast port and industrial area, Europoort. Together with Rotterdam's own facilities, the complex is the largest and busiest in the world.

Agriculture employs only 3% of the workforce, but, through the use of scientific techniques, yields are high. The use of the land varies. In the west, the concentration on bulb farming is marked near Haarlem in soils of clay mixed with sand. There, too, glasshouse cultivation, combined on a number of holdings with the growing of flowers and vegetables out-of-doors, is widespread. The Dutch cut and sell more than 3 billion flowers a year. Much of the produce is exported, some of it by air to London and other north European cities.

Some soils are better suited to pastoral farming and dairy farming is the leading farming activity, with milk, cheese and butter production. Gouda has a famous cheese market and the well-known red-coated, round Edam cheeses come from northern areas. In the areas above sea level, farming is varied, with a combination of cattle and crops. Major food crops include barley, potatoes, sugar beet and wheat.

The Netherlands is one of the world's leading trading nations. Its chief exports include machinery and transport equipment, food, chemicals and chemical products, petroleum products, iron and steel and clothing. The main trading partners are Germany, Belgium-Luxembourg, France and the United Kingdom.

AREA	Indonesian, Turkish,
41,526 sq km	Moroccan, German
[16,033 sq mls]	**LANGUAGES**
POPULATION	Dutch (official), Frisian
15,731,000	**RELIGIONS**
CAPITAL (POPULATION)	Christianity
Amsterdam (1,100,000)	(Roman Catholic 34%,
GOVERNMENT	Dutch Reformed Church 17%,
Constitutional monarchy	Calvinist 8%), Islam 3%
ETHNIC GROUPS	**CURRENCY**
Netherlander 95%,	Euro; Guilder = 100 cents

NETHERLANDS ANTILLES – SEE CARIBBEAN SEA, PAGES 71–76;
NEW CALEDONIA – SEE PACIFIC OCEAN, PAGES 174–178

NEW ZEALAND

New Zealand's flag was designed in 1869 and adopted as the national flag in 1907 when New Zealand became an independent dominion. The flag includes the British Blue Ensign and four of the five stars in the Southern Cross constellation.

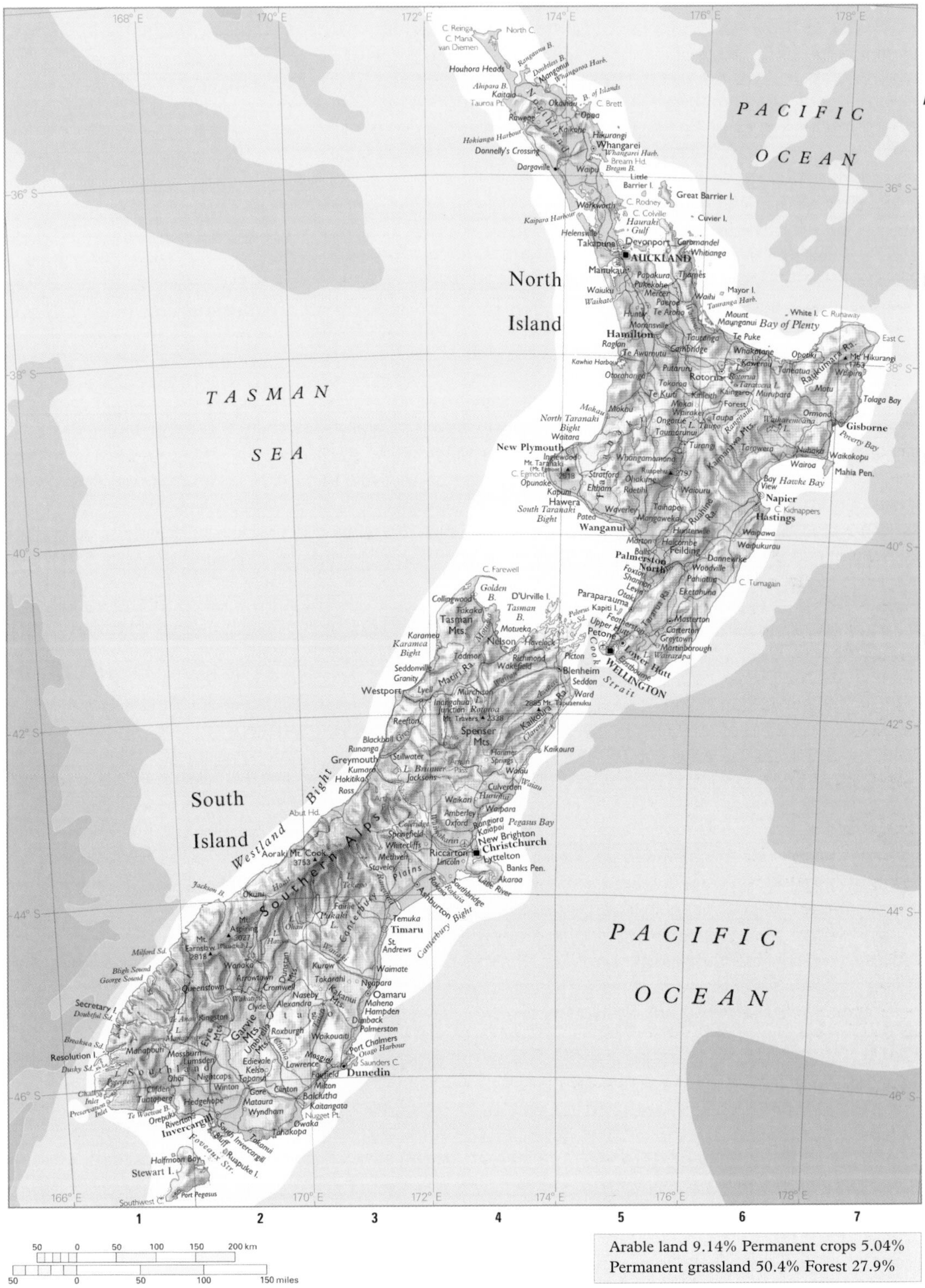

Geography

New Zealand lies about 1,600 km [994 mls] south-east of Australia. It consists of two main islands and several other small ones. Geologically part of the Circum-Pacific Mobile Belt of tectonic activity (the 'Pacific ring of fire'), New Zealand is mountainous and partly volcanic. Many of the highest mountains, including the Southern Alps, which contain the country's highest peak, Mount Cook (Aoraki) at 3,753 m [12,313 ft], were thrust up from the seabed in the past 10 to 15 million years. Much of North Island was formed by volcanic activity even more recently, mainly in the past 4 million years. Minor earthquakes are common and there are several areas of volcanic and geothermal activity, especially on North Island.

About 75% of New Zealand lies above the 200 m [650 ft] contour, but in the south-east, rivers have cut broad, fertile valleys between low ranges. New Zealand's only extensive lowland area is the Canterbury Plains.

Climate

Auckland in the north has a warm, humid climate throughout the year. Wellington has cooler summers, while in Dunedin, in the south-east, temperatures sometimes dip below freezing in winter. The rainfall is heaviest on the western highlands.

Vegetation

Because of New Zealand's isolation, almost 90% of the country's indigenous plants are peculiar to the country.

However, much of the original vegetation has been destroyed and only small areas of the kauri forests have survived. Mixed evergreen forest grows on the west side of South Island. Along the Southern Alps, the false beech is the chief forest tree. New Zealand also has large plantations of introduced species, including the radiata pine, which covers large areas on the Volcanic Plateau on North Island, together with willows and poplars which have been planted in areas suffering from soil erosion.

History

Evidence suggests that early Maori settlers who came from islands to the north arrived in New Zealand, which they called Aotearoa, more than 1,000 years ago. The Dutch navigator Abel Janszoon Tasman reached the area in 1642, but, after several of his men were killed

Arable land 9.14% Permanent crops 5.04%
Permanent grassland 50.4% Forest 27.9%

by Maoris, he made no further attempt to land. His discovery was not followed up until 1769, when the British Captain James Cook rediscovered the islands and thoroughly charted them. Cook like Tasman recorded the presence of Maoris, who were Polynesians, and hunted and farmed from well-defended coastal settlements.

Sealing gangs, whalers and traders, mainly from Australia, were New Zealand's first European inhabitants, closely followed by missionaries and farmers from Britain and Australia. By the early 1830s, about 2,000 Europeans had settled there. New Zealand remained a lawless frontier territory with no legal government until 1840 when the Treaty of Waitangi signed by Maori chiefs and Captain William Hobson of the British Navy (who became New Zealand's first governor) made

New Zealand a British colony. In return, the Treaty gave rights and privileges of British subjects to the Maori people. The following decades saw the arrival of thousands of new settlers from Britain and, by the mid-century, there were more than 30,000 of them. New Zealand set up its first elected House of Representatives in 1852.

Though their relationships with the Maoris, who at this stage outnumbered them by two to one, were generally good, difficulties over land ownership led to conflict between 1845 and 1872. Thereafter, the Maori population declined, partly as a result of contracting European diseases, while the numbers of Europeans continued to increase. British settlers found a climate slightly warmer than their own, with longer growing seasons but variable rainfall – crippling droughts sometimes occurred in dry areas.

From 1884, when the first Merino sheep were introduced from Australia, New Zealand became predominantly a land of sheep, the grassy lowlands, especially on South Island, providing year-round forage. Huge flocks were built up, mainly for wool and tallow production. From the lowlands, they spread into the hills – the 'high country' – which was cleared of native bush and sown with European grasses for pasture. North Island proved more difficult to turn into farmland, later proving its value for dairying.

New Zealand's early prosperity was finally established when the export of frozen mutton and lamb carcasses began in 1882. Soon, a steady stream of chilled meat and dairy products, and later of fruit, was crossing the oceans to established markets in Britain – New Zealand is still the world's second largest producer of lamb. Wheat and other cereals were also grown. High productivity was maintained by applications of fertilizers, mainly based on phosphate mined on Nauru.

Politics

In 1893, New Zealand became the first country in the world to give women the vote. In 1907, New Zealand became a self-governing dominion in the British Empire (now the British Commonwealth) and New Zealanders fought alongside the Allies against Germany, Italy and Japan in both World Wars. In 1952, New Zealand signed the ANZUS treaty, a mutual defence pact with Australia and the United States. Troops from New Zealand served in the Korean War (1950–3) and a few units later served in the war in Vietnam.

New Zealand Territories

New Zealand comprises not just the two main islands, together with Stewart Island in the south, Chatham Island to the east, and a number of uninhabited outlying islands, but also territories further out in the Pacific. They include the Kermadec Islands to the north, which were annexed to New Zealand in 1887. The Kermadec Islands, the site of an isolated meteorological station, have no separate administration.

Tokelau Islands, north of Samoa, consist of three atolls, with a total land area of 12 sq km [4.6 sq mls] and a population of 1,500. Administrative control of Tokelau was transferred by Britain to New Zealand in 1925. Formal sovereignty was transferred to New Zealand in 1948 but New Zealand's laws are extended to Tokelau only with the consent of its people.

The Cook Islands, between American Samoa and French Polynesia, became a British protectorate in 1888 and were annexed to New Zealand in 1901. Since 1968, the islands have been a self-governing territory in 'free association' with New Zealand. The Cook Islands cover an area of 235.4 sq km [91 sq mls], with a population of 19,000. The capital is Avarua.

Niue, between Tonga and the Cook Islands, was visited by Captain Cook in 1774. It became a British protectorate in 1900 and was annexed to New Zealand in 1901. Since 1974, Niue, the world's largest raised coral island, has had the same status as the Cook Islands, with internal self-government in association with New Zealand. Niue covers an area of 258 sq km [100 sq mls] and has a population of 2,200. Its capital is Alofi.

The Cook Islands and Niue islanders have full citizenship of New Zealand, which controls their defence and contributes aid. (See Pacific Ocean map, page 174.)

The Maoris

'Strong, raw-boned, well-made, active people, rather above than under the common size . . . of a very dark brown colour, with black hair, thin black beards, and . . . in general very good features.' So Captain James Cook described the Maoris he met in New Zealand in 1770. Of Polynesian stock, the Maoris settled (mainly in North Island) from about AD 800 to 1350. A warlike people, living in small fortified settlements, they cultivated kumaras (sweet potatoes) and other crops, hunted seals and moas (large flightless birds, now extinct) and gathered seafoods.

The Maoris befriended the early European settlers; readily accepting British sovereignty, Christianity and pacification, they rebelled only as more and more of their communal land was bought for the settlers' use. Given parliamentary representation from 1876, they eventually integrated fully. Now Maoris form about 9% of New Zealand's population, still living mostly in North Island. Though socially and politically equal in every way to whites, they are still over-represented in the poorer, unskilled sections of the population, separated more by poverty and lack of opportunity than by colour from the mainstream of national life.

After World War II, New Zealand diversified its economy. Though agricultural products remain the chief exports, fishing and forestry were developed, along with geothermal energy and hydroelectricity. The timber and forest products found valuable overseas markets. The country also began to develop its tourist potential.

However, after Britain joined the European Economic Community (now the European Union) in 1973, New Zealand's exports to Britain shrank from 70% to 10%. Along with its re-evaluation of its defence position through ANZUS, it also had to reassess its economic strategy. This has involved seeking new markets in Asia, cutting subsidies to farmers, privatization and cutting back on its extensive welfare programmes in the 1990s. The rights of Maoris and the preservation of their culture are other major political issues in New Zealand. In 1998, New Zealand completed a NZ $170 million settlement with the Ngai Tahu group on South Island in compensation for forced land purchases in the 19th century. The government expressed its profound regret for past suffering and for injustices that had impaired the development of the Ngai Tahu.

Economy

New Zealand's economy has traditionally depended on agriculture, although manufacturing now employs twice as many people as agriculture. Meat and dairy products are the most valuable agricultural products. In 1995, New Zealand ranked seventh among the world's leading butter producers. In 1997, New Zealand had about 47 million sheep, 3.6 million dairy cattle and 4.7 million beef cattle. Major crops include barley, fruits, potatoes and other vegetables, and wheat. Fishing is also important. The chief manufactures are processed food products, including butter, cheese, frozen meat and woollen products. Food and live animals make up 45% of New Zealand's exports. The country's chief trading partners are Australia, Japan and the United States.

AREA
268,680 sq km
[103,737 sq mls]
POPULATION
3,625,000
CAPITAL (POPULATION)
Wellington (329,000)
GOVERNMENT
Constitutional monarchy
ETHNIC GROUPS
New Zealand European 74%,
New Zealand Maori 10%,
Polynesian 4%
LANGUAGES
English and Maori
(both official)
RELIGIONS
Christianity (Anglican 21%,
Presbyterian 16%,
Roman Catholic 15%)
CURRENCY
New Zealand dollar = 100 cents

NICARAGUA – SEE GUATEMALA, PAGES 110–111

NIGER

This flag was adopted shortly before Niger became independent from France in 1960. The orange stripe represents the Sahara in the north and the green represents the grasslands in the south. Between them, the white stripe represents the River Niger, with a circle for the sun.

Geography

The Republic of Niger is a landlocked nation in north-central Africa. The northern plateaux lie in the Sahara, while north-central Niger contains the rugged Aïr Mountains, which reach a height of 1,900 m [6,232 ft] above sea level. The rainfall in the mountains – averaging around 175 mm [7 in] per year – is sufficient in places to permit the growth of thorny shrub. However, severe droughts since the 1970s have crippled the traditional lifestyle of the nomads in northern and central Niger as the Sahara has slowly advanced south. The southern region has also been hit by droughts.

The south consists of broad plains. The Lake Chad Basin lies in south-eastern Niger on the borders with Chad and Nigeria. The only permanent rivers are the Niger and its tributaries in the south-west. The narrow Niger Valley is the country's most fertile and densely populated region. Yet Niger, a title which comes from a Tuareg word meaning 'flowing water', seems scarcely appropriate for a country which consists mainly of hot, arid, sandy, and stony basins.

Climate

Niger has a tropical climate and the south has a rainy season between June and September. The rainfall decreases in both quantity and reliability from south to north.

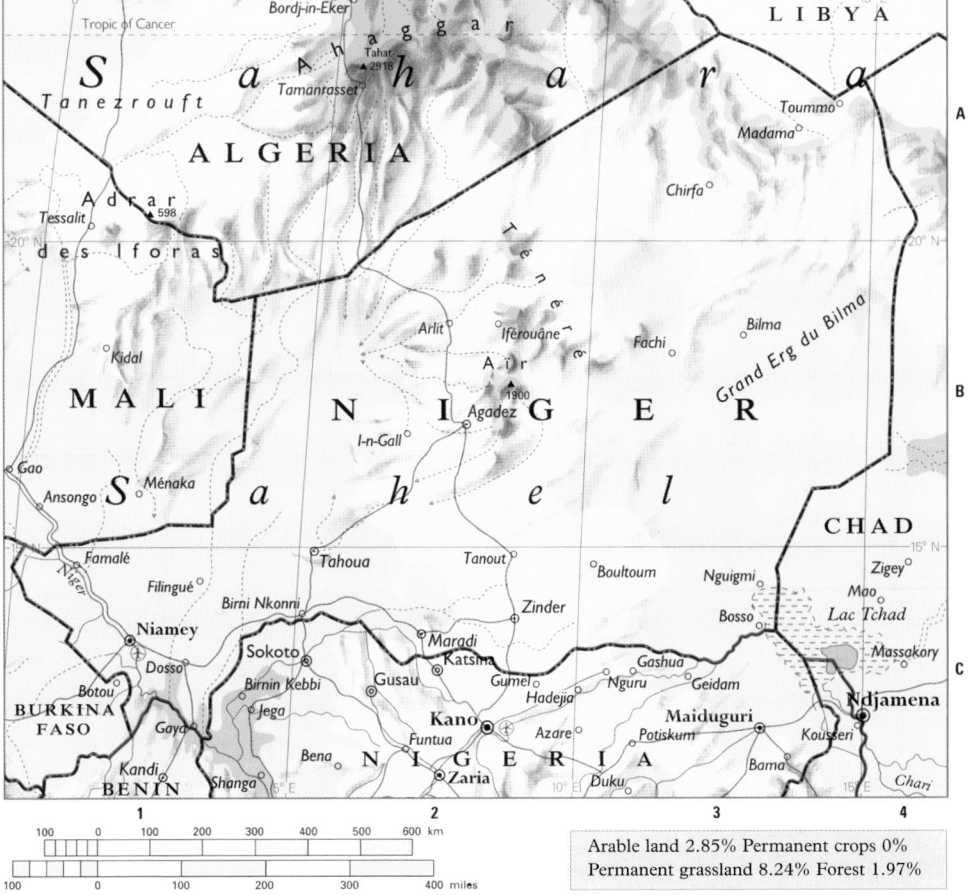

Arable land 2.85% Permanent crops 0%
Permanent grassland 8.24% Forest 1.97%

NIGER (NIAMEY)

The climate of southern Niger is similar to other places within the vast tropical grassland belt of northern Africa – the Sahel. From November to April, the hot, dry harmattan wind blows from the Sahara, the skies are clear and there is no rain. Between March and May the intensity of the sun increases rapidly. But in June, the intertropical rainbelt reaches the region, and the increasing cloud and rain give rise to cooler conditions.

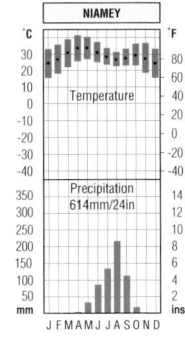

History

Nomadic Tuaregs settled in the Aïr Mountains around 1,000 years ago. By the 15th century they had built an empire based on Agadez. At around that time, the Zerma-Songhai people founded the Songhai Empire along the River Niger and conquered the Tuaregs, but in the late 16th century Songhai was defeated by a Moroccan army.

Later on, the Hausa and then the Fulani set up kingdoms in the region. European explorers reached Niger in the early 19th century. France became involved in West Africa in the late 19th century and it gained control of Niger in 1900. In 1906, France put down a Tuareg uprising and, between 1922 and 1958, it ruled Niger as part of a huge territory called French West Africa. In 1958, Niger became an autonomous republic and, in 1960, it finally became fully independent.

Politics

Since independence, Niger has been badly hit by severe droughts which have caused extensive damage and suffering. Food shortages and the collapse of the traditional nomadic way of life of some of

Niger's people have caused political instability. In 1974, a group of army officers, led by Lt.-Col. Seyni Kountché, overthrew the country's first president, Hamani Diori, and seized control of the government, suspending the constitution. Kountché died in 1987, and in 1989 civilian rule was restored. A multiparty constitution was adopted in 1992, but the military once again seized power in 1996. The coup leader, Col. Ibrahim Barre Mainassara, was elected president later that year, but he was assassinated in 1999 and replaced by Daouda Malam Wanke.

Economy

Niger's chief resource is uranium and it is the fourth largest producer in the world. Some tin and tungsten are also mined, although other mineral resources are largely untouched.

Despite its resources, Niger is one of the world's poorest countries. Farming employs 85% of the population, though only 3% of the land can be used for crops and 7% for grazing. Food crops include beans, cassava, millet, rice and sorghum. Groundnuts and cotton are major cash crops.

AREA	Zerma-Songhai 21%,
1,267,000 sq km	Tuareg 11%,
[489,189 sq mls]	Fulani (or Peul) 10%
POPULATION	**LANGUAGES**
9,672,000	French (official),
CAPITAL (POPULATION)	Hausa,
Niamey	Songhai
(398,000)	**RELIGIONS**
GOVERNMENT	Islam 98%
Multiparty republic	**CURRENCY**
ETHNIC GROUPS	CFA franc =
Hausa 53%,	100 centimes

Nigeria's flag was adopted in 1960 when Nigeria became independent from Britain. It was selected after a competition to find a suitable design. The green represents Nigeria's forests. The white in the centre stands for peace.

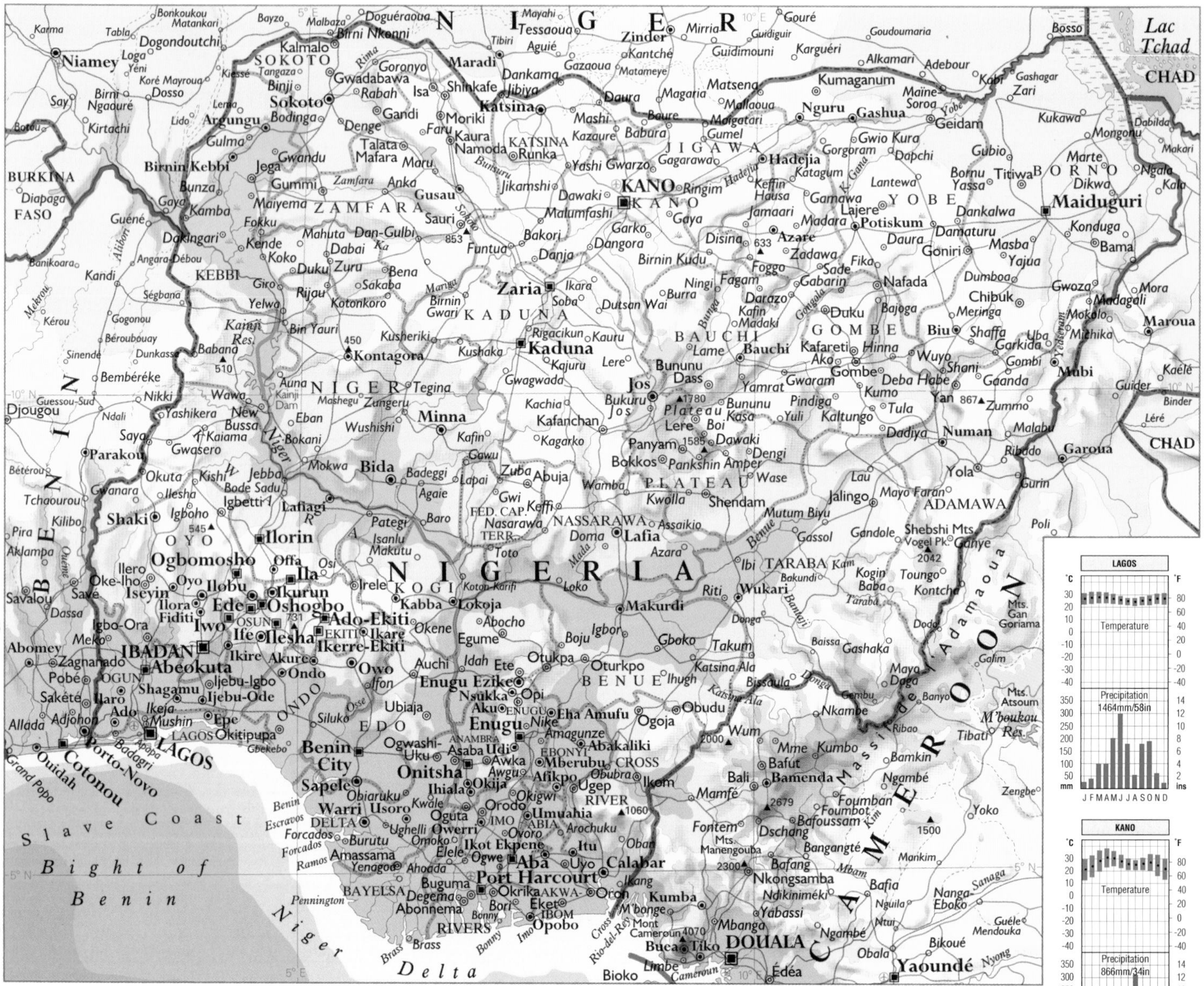

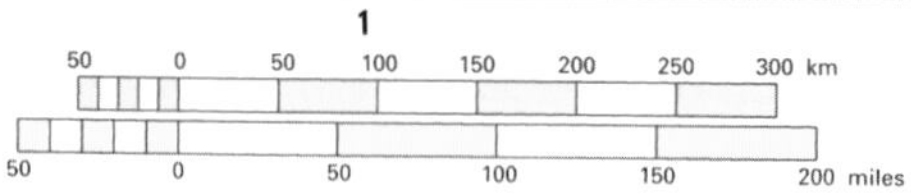

Arable land 33.1% Permanent crops 2.78%
Permanent grassland 43.9% Forest 12%

Geography

The Federal Republic of Nigeria is the most populous nation in Africa. The country's main rivers are the Niger and Benue, which meet in central Nigeria. North of the two river valleys are high plains and plateaux. The Lake Chad Basin is in the north-east, with the Sokoto plains in the north-west. Southern Nigeria contains hilly uplands and broad coastal plains, including the swampy Niger Delta. Highlands form the border with Cameroon.

Climate

The south of the country has high temperatures and rain all year. Parts of the coast have an average annual rainfall of 3,800 mm [150 in]. The north has a marked dry season and higher temperatures than the south.

Vegetation

Behind the mangrove swamps along the coast are rainforests, though extensive areas have been cleared by farmers. The north contains large areas of savanna (tropical grassland with scattered trees) with forests along the rivers. Open grassland and semi-desert occur in drier areas.

NIGERIA – LAGOS

The coastal belt of Nigeria experiences uniformly high temperatures and humidity throughout most of the year. The coolest months of the year are July and August, when the monsoon brings oceanic air from beyond the Equator. Even then the lowest recorded temperature is 16°C [61°F]. There are two periods of heavy rain: the long rains with a maximum during June, and the short rains with a maximum during October, with rain falling on every other day during the month. Humidity in Lagos remains high and sunshine levels are relatively low.

KANO

The north of Nigeria also experiences high temperatures and humidity most of the year. Average annual rainfall is generally less than 1,000 mm [39 in]. For example, Kano, in north-central Nigeria, has an average annual rainfall of 870 mm [34 in]. But during the marked dry season, from October to April, the average rainfall totals only 26 mm [1 in]. Heaviest rains occur from July to September. The hottest period of the year is from March to June; the coolest from December to January.

AFRICA

NIGERIA

History

Among the earliest civilizations that grew up in Nigeria was the Nok (500 BC to AD 200). The Nok civilization, which flourished in a valley near the confluence of the Benue and Niger Rivers, was named after a village where black Africa's oldest sculptures, made from terracotta, were first excavated. Northern Nigeria became part of the kingdom of Kanem in the 8th century, while the kingdom of Bornu developed later in what is now north-eastern Nigeria. Powerful Hausa states grew up from AD 1000 and, later, some of them became part of the Songhai Empire which flourished in the region in the 15th and 16th centuries.

Two civilizations in southern Nigeria were known for their superb art. Ife was a major Yoruba culture, which developed around 1,000 years ago. It produced terracotta and bronze sculptures. The other was Benin, which flourished between Lagos and the Niger delta in the 15th and 17th centuries. Benin sculptures, including its famous brasses, were discovered by the Portuguese, who used Benin as a slave trading centre in the late 15th century. Benin declined when it fought wars with other African states that traded slaves with Europeans on the coast.

The slave trade continued and Britain competed with other nations for control of the trade. However, Britain outlawed slavery in 1807. Soon afterwards, British traders began to trade in the agricultural products of the region. In 1851, Britain made Lagos a base from which they could continue their efforts to stop the slave trade. During the second half of the 19th century, Britain gradually extended its influence over Nigeria. By 1914 it ruled the entire country.

Politics

Nigeria became independent in 1960 and a federal republic in 1963. A federal constitution dividing the country into regions was necessary because Nigeria contains more than 250 ethnic and linguistic groups, as well as several religious ones. Local rivalries have long been a threat to national unity. In 1967, in an attempt to meet the demands of more ethnic groups, the country's four regions were replaced by 12 states. The division of the Eastern Region provoked an uprising. In May 1967, the governor of the Eastern Region, Colonel Odumegwu Ojukwu, proclaimed it an independent republic called Biafra. Civil war continued until Biafra's surrender in January 1970.

After the end of the war, the country's revenues were enhanced by its oil exports. But oil did not bring stability. Instead, political problems continued and the country had only nine years of civilian government between independence in 1960 and 1998. In 1998, Nigeria's military dictator, General Sani Abacha, died. He was succeeded by General Abdulsalam Abubakar, who pushed ahead with a timetable to hold state and national elections, culminating in the election of a president in 1999. The successful candidate was a former military leader, Olusegun Obasanjo, who set about tackling corruption. However, the difficulties he faced in maintaining national unity were highlighted when ethnic riots broke out between Yorubas and Hausas in suburbs of Lagos. By 1999, Nigeria was divided into 36 states and the federal territory of Abuja.

Economy

Although blessed with many natural resources, including oil reserves, metals, forests and fertile farmland, Nigeria has a low per capita GNP of US $260 (1997) which makes it a low-income developing economy.

Agriculture employs 43% of the people and Nigeria is one of the world's leading producers of cocoa beans, groundnuts (peanuts), palm oil and kernels, and natural rubber. The leading food crops include beans, cassava, maize, millet, plantains, rice in river valleys or on irrigated land, sorghum and yams. Goats, poultry and sheep are raised throughout the country, but most of the cattle are concentrated in the northern tropical savanna region. Besides oil and tin, Nigeria produces some coal, gold, iron ore, lead, natural gas and zinc. Industry is increasing and manufactures include cement, chemicals, fertilizers, processed food, metal products, textiles and timber. The country also has oil refineries, as well as motor car assembly plants and steel mills. In the mid-1990s, crude petroleum accounted for about 98% of the total value of Nigeria's exports. Other exports include cocoa, rubber, urea and ammonia, and fish. Manufactures, including machinery and transport equipment, are leading imports.

Democracy and Africa's future

In the early 1950s, most of Africa was under colonial rule. The great flush of optimism that followed decolonization in the 1950s and 1960s did not bring the rewards of peace, unity and prosperity that many African leaders had envisaged. Instead, ancient divisions between ethnic and religious groups caused civil conflict, the collapse of elected democracies, and their replacement by corrupt and incompetent dictatorships.

Nigeria, whose large oil reserves appeared to assure it a prosperous future, is a case in point. Nigerians are divided into more than 250 ethnic groups, and the people are further divided by religion. Strong but mostly corrupt and inefficient military administrations have sought to maintain the unity of the country, at the expense of human rights.

In such countries as Burundi and Rwanda, the ancient rivalries between the Hutu majority and the Tutsi overlords expressed itself in blood-letting on an appalling scale. Elsewhere, rival groups were backed by Western or Soviet aid, and civil wars became bloody reflections of the Cold War. The collapse of the Soviet Union in the early 1990s led many to hope for an end to the civil war in Angola, which had long been a scene of a proxy West/East conflict. However, ethnic rivalries proved even stronger than ideological ones and the Angolan war continued into the 21st century.

Yet, from the late 1980s, there were promising signs that new hope had reached the world's poorest continent. In many countries, dictators were succumbing quite peacefully to popular demands for multiparty elections. Instead of the coup d'etat being the only way to change governments, politicians were again being chosen through the ballot box. The transition to democracy was not always smooth. For example, Sierra Leone's President Ahmed Tejan Kabbah was elected in 1996 and deposed in 1997. He returned to office in 1998 only after a Nigerian-led intervention force mounted an offensive against the military junta.

Democracy does not provide all the answers for Africa's problems, including its poverty, high debts and the periodic collapses in the prices for many African commodities. In this context, moves in 1999 by Western powers to cancel debts providing that the African governments ensured the beneficiaries were social matters, such as education and health, were very significant. In Mozambique, a country shattered by civil war and natural disasters, including droughts and floods, policies designed to diversify the economy and attract foreign investment brought many material benefits in the late 1990s.

Yet, even as new initiatives provide reason for hope, so too new dangers threaten. In eastern and southern Africa, health workers are faced with a major challenge – the control of AIDS. For example, in Botswana, Namibia, Swaziland and Zimbabwe, between a fifth and a quarter of people aged 15–49 are afflicted by HIV or AIDS. In Botswana, a country which has been successful in both political and economic terms, children born early in the 21st century will have a life expectancy of 40 years. Without AIDS, it would have been around 70 years.

AREA	Fulani 11%, Ibibio 6%
923,770 sq km [356,668 sq mls]	**LANGUAGES**
POPULATION	English (official),
110,532,000	Hausa, Yoruba, Ibo
CAPITAL (POPULATION)	**RELIGIONS**
Abuja (339,000)	Christianity (Protestant 26%,
GOVERNMENT	Roman Catholic 12%),
Federal republic	Traditional beliefs 19%,
ETHNIC GROUPS	Islam 43%
Hausa 21%, Yoruba 21%,	**CURRENCY**
Ibo (or Igbo) 19%,	Naira = 100 kobo

NORTHERN MARIANA ISLANDS – SEE PACIFIC OCEAN, PAGES 174–178

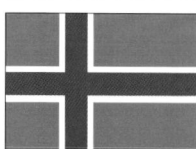

This flag became the national flag of Norway in 1898, although merchant ships had used it since 1821. The design is based on the Dannebrog, the flag of Denmark, the country which ruled Norway from the 14th century until the early 19th century.

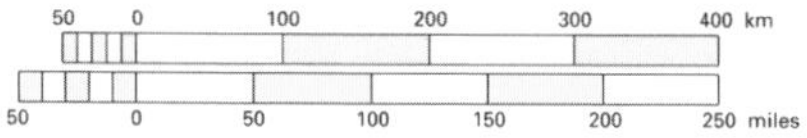

The configuration of Norway's jagged coastline, which is the longest in Europe, helps to explain the ease with which the Norwegians took to the sea in early times and why they have remained a seafaring nation. The *vidda* are cut by long, narrow, steep-sided fjords on the west coast, whose spectacular scenery attracts a large number of cruise liners. The largest of the fjords, which were worn out by the great northern ice sheet, is Sognefjord, which is 203 km [127 mls] long and less than 5 km [3 mls] wide. It is the longest inlet in Europe and is the best known of Norway's fjords. Inland, the moving ice eroded deep valleys which now contain ribbon lakes.

About 150,000 islands, some of which are no more than rocky reefs, lie along the coast. The largest group, the Lofoten Islands, lie above the Arctic Circle. These islands, known as the skerryguard, protect the mainland shore of Norway from the battering of Atlantic breakers and provide sheltered leads of water for ferries and fishing boats.

Communications along the country's coast were until recently much easier by boat than by land. The two island groups, the Svalbard and the Jan Mayen Islands, are possessions of Norway in the Arctic Ocean.

Arable land 2.94% Permanent crops 0%
Permanent grassland 0.42% Forest 27.1%

Climate

The warm North Atlantic Drift, the northern extension of the Gulf Stream, which flows off the coast of Norway, moderates the country's climate, with milder winters and cooler summers. Nearly all the country's ports remain ice-free throughout the year. However, inland, away from the moderating effects of the sea, the climate becomes more severe. Winters are bitterly cold and snow covers the land for at least three months a year.

Geography

The Kingdom of Norway forms the western part of the mountainous Scandinavian Peninsula. It is a rugged country in which communication is difficult. The landscape is dominated by rolling plateaux, the *vidda*, which are generally between 300 m and 900 m [1,000–3,000 ft] high, but some peaks rise from 1,500 m to 2,500 m [5,000–8,000 ft] in the area between Oslo, Bergen and Trondheim. In the far north, the summits are around 1,000 m [3,000 ft] lower. The highest areas retain permanent icefields, as in the Jotunheimen Mountains above Sognefjord. The mountains were uplifted during three mountain-building periods over the last 400 million years. Intrusions of volcanic material accompanied uplifting and folding and there are great masses of granites and gneisses – the source of Norway's mineral wealth.

Norway has few large areas of flat land, but in the east the *vidda* are broken by the deep valleys of rivers flowing to the lowlands of southern Norway, focused on Oslo. During the last Ice Age, the land was covered by the great northern ice sheet. When it melted about 10,000 years ago, it left behind large deposits of glacial moraine, well represented around Oslo in the Raa moraine.

NORWAY (OSLO)

The warm waters and cyclones of the North Atlantic give the western coastlands of Norway a warm maritime climate of mild winters and cool, wet summers. Rain is heavy on the coast but lighter inland and northwards. Inland winters are more severe and summers warmer. At Oslo, snow usually begins in November, lying until late March. Sunshine from November to January is only about one hour, but from April to August it is 6–8 hours.

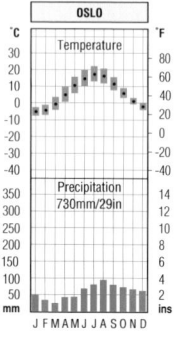

Vegetation

Landscapes dominated by bare rock exist in places where ice stripped away the soil during the Ice Age. Icefields still occur in some higher areas, but Norway also has large forests of pine and spruce, which flourish in the broad, glaciated valleys. Pines and spruce grow up to 850 m [2,800 ft] in the east and up to 700 m [2,300 ft] in the area around Trondheim. Birch forest extend from about 900 m to 1,900 m [3,000–3,900 ft]. Higher up, dwarf birch occur in the willow zone. Wild berries, including blueberries and cranberries, grow in all regions.

History

The sea has always been a major influence in Norwegian life. From about AD 800, Vikings from Norway roamed the northern seas, raiding and founding colonies around the coasts of Britain, Iceland and even North America. In about 900, Norway was united under Harold I, the country's first king, and Christianity was introduced under Olav II in the late 10th century. Viking power ended in the late 11th century. In 1380, Norway was united with Denmark, when Margaret, wife of Norway's King Haakon VI and daughter of the king of Denmark, began to rule Denmark as its regent. In 1388, Swedish noblemen chose Margaret to rule Sweden and, in 1397, the three countries were united. Sweden broke away from the union in 1523 and, in 1526, Denmark, which had become increasingly powerful, made Norway a Danish province.

In 1813, towards the end of the Napoleonic Wars, Sweden defeated Denmark, an ally of France. In 1814, Denmark ceded Norway to Sweden, though Denmark retained Norway's island colonies of Greenland, Iceland and the Faroe Islands. Norway wanted independence, but Sweden defeated the Norwegians and made them accept Charles XIII of Sweden as their ruler in November 1814. Norway finally ended its union with Sweden in 1905. The Norwegians then chose as their king a Danish prince, who took the title Haakon VII. At the time of independence, Norway had one of the world's largest merchant fleets, and its industries, powered mainly by hydroelectricity, were increasing.

Norway was neutral in World War I, but it lost about half of its merchant fleet, which was used for carrying cargo for the Allies. Norway sought to maintain its neutrality in World War II, but German troops invaded the country in 1940. In 1945, however, the Germans surrendered and Haakon VII returned to Norway in triumph.

Scandinavia

There are several possible definitions of the term Scandinavia. In the narrow geographical sense it refers to the peninsula shared by Norway and Sweden; in a broader cultural and political sense it includes the five countries of the Nordic Council – Norway, Sweden, Denmark, Finland and Iceland. These five countries are sometimes collectively known as Norden. Two other terms are also in use: Fennoscandia refers to Finland and the Scandinavian peninsula, while Baltoscandia refers to the regions that surround the Baltic Sea. Of the five countries of Norden, all, except Finland, have related languages, and all have a tradition of parliamentary democracy. Finland and Iceland are republics, while Denmark, Norway and Sweden are constitutional monarchies.

There are also strong historical links between the countries, beginning in the 8th century when their ancestors, the Norsemen, colonized large parts of northern Europe. All have at different times been governed together, Sweden and Finland separating in 1809, Norway and Sweden in 1905, and Denmark and Iceland as recently as 1944.

Because of their northerly position and exposure to Atlantic weather systems, Scandinavia has a cool, wet climate, not favourable to crops. But, due to long hours of daylight in the northern summer, crops are grown north of the Arctic Circle.

Scandinavians were once among the poorest peoples of Europe, but during the last century they have become among the richest, making use of limited natural resources, and seizing opportunities provided by their maritime position to become major shipping and fishing nations.

Of Norway's Arctic territories, Svalbard, an archipelago half as big as Denmark and situated halfway between the North Pole and the Arctic Circle, is the largest. It was claimed at various times by Norway, Britain and the Netherlands. However, in 1920, a treaty signed in Paris recognized Norwegian sovereignty and, in 1925, the islands were officially incorporated into the kingdom of Norway.

The volcanic Jan Mayen Island, which lies north-north-east of Iceland, was named after the Dutch whaling captain Jan Jacobsz May. Though uninhabited, it was used by seal trappers and other hunters, and, in 1921, Norway established a meteorological and radio station there. It was officially incorporated into Norway in 1929, but its only residents today are the 30 or so staff at a weather station.

Politics

After World War II, Norwegians worked to rebuild their economy and their merchant fleet. The economy was boosted in the 1970s, when Norway began producing petroleum and natural gas from wells in the North Sea. Rapid economic growth has ensured that Norwegians are among the most prosperous people in Europe. Few people are wealthy, because taxation is high, but few are very poor, and an advanced welfare system provides good services even to the most isolated communities. The majority of the people now own their homes and many families have second homes on the shores of fjords or lakes. Norway is by far Europe's biggest donor of foreign aid per capita, with a figure of 1.1% of the gross national product, as compared with the Organization for Economic Co-operation and Development (OECD) target of 0.7%.

Norway has played an important role in Europe. In 1949, it became a member of the North Atlantic Treaty Organization, though it did not allow NATO bases or nuclear weapons on its soil for fear of provoking its neighbour, the Soviet Union. During 1960, Norway and six other countries formed an economic union called the European Free Trade Association (EFTA). Norway refused to join the European Economic Community (EEC) when Britain, Denmark and Ireland decided to join on 1 January 1973. However, it continued to work with its Scandinavian neighbours through the Nordic Council, even after Sweden and Finland left EFTA to join the European Union in 1995.

In 1994, Norwegians again voted against membership of the European Union, with 52.4% voting against joining. Some Norwegians feared that membership would involve a loss of their hard-won sovereignty, while people working in agriculture and fishing anticipated massive cuts in government subsidies. There were also fears that Norway might lose control over its natural resources, including fish, oil, natural gas and metals, while others believed that EU membership might undermine Norway's cradle-to-grave welfare system.

Economy

Norway's chief resources and exports are oil and natural gas which come from wells under the North Sea. Farmland covers only 3% of the land. Dairy farming and meat production are the chief activities, though Norway has to import food. Using cheap hydroelectric power, Norway has set up many industries. Manufactures include petroleum products, chemicals, aluminium, wood pulp and paper, machinery, clothing and furniture. Fuel and fuel products make up more than half of the total value of exports, followed by machinery and transport equipment, metals and metal products, and food products.

AREA	**ETHNIC GROUPS**
323,900 sq km	Norwegian 97%
[125,050 sq mls]	**LANGUAGES**
POPULATION	Norwegian (official),
4,420,000	Lappish, Finnish
CAPITAL (POPULATION)	**RELIGIONS**
Oslo (714,000)	Christianity (Lutheran 88%)
GOVERNMENT	**CURRENCY**
Constitutional monarchy	Krone = 100 ore

OMAN – SEE GULF STATES, PAGES 113–114

Top map:

RUSSIA

Ulaanbaatar
MONGOLIA
Vladivostok
Sea of Okhotsk
Kamchatka
Bering Sea
Aleutian Islands
Alaska (U.S.A.)
Anchorage
CANADA

Beijing
CHINA
Sŏul
KOREA
JAPAN
Tōkyō
Shanghai
Sea of Japan
East China Sea
Kurílskiye Ostrova (Kurile Is.)

Vancouver
Seattle
Portland
Montréal
Chicago
Washington
New York
San Francisco
UNITED STATES
ATLANTIC OCEAN
Los Angeles

Hong Kong
Taipei
TAIWAN
Ryūkyū-retto (Ryukyu Is.)
International Date Line
PACIFIC
Tropic of Cancer
Honolulu
Hawaiian Is. (U.S.A.)
MEXICO
Mexico
Gulf of Mexico
CUBA

BURMA
Hanoi
THAILAND
VIETNAM
Bangkok
CAMBODIA
South China Sea
PHILIPPINES
Manila
Guam (U.S.A.)
NORTHERN MARIANAS (U.S.A.)
MARSHALL ISLANDS
OCEAN
BELIZE
HONDURAS
GUATEMALA
EL SALVADOR
NICARAGUA
COSTA RICA
PANAMA

Kuala Lumpur
BRUNEI
MALAYSIA
Singapore
Borneo
PALAU
FED. STATES OF MICRONESIA (U.S.A.)
Micronesia
NAURU
Kiritimati
Polynesia
COLOMBIA
Equator
Galápagos
Quito
ECUADOR

Jakarta
INDONESIA
PAPUA NEW GUINEA
Melanesia
KIRIBATI
TUVALU
Tokelau Is. (N.Z.)
Îs. Marquises
Lima
PERU

Timor Sea
SOLOMON ISLANDS
Wallis and Futuna Is. (Fr.)
SAMOA AMER. SAMOA
Îs. de la Société
Îs. Tuamotu

Coral Sea
VANUATU
FIJI
Cook Islands (N.Z.)
Niue (N.Z.)
Tahiti
FRENCH POLYNESIA
Tropic of Capricorn

NEW CALEDONIA (France)
TONGA
Pitcairn Is. (U.K.)
CHILE
Santiago

AUSTRALIA
Brisbane
Perth
Sydney
Adelaide
Melbourne
Tasmania
INDIAN OCEAN
Auckland
Tasman Sea
NEW ZEALAND
I. de Pascua (Easter I.) (Chile)
ARGENTINA

Cabo de Hornos
Falkland Is.

Scale:
500 0 500 1000 1500 2000 2500 3000 3500 4000 km
500 0 500 1000 1500 2000 2500 miles

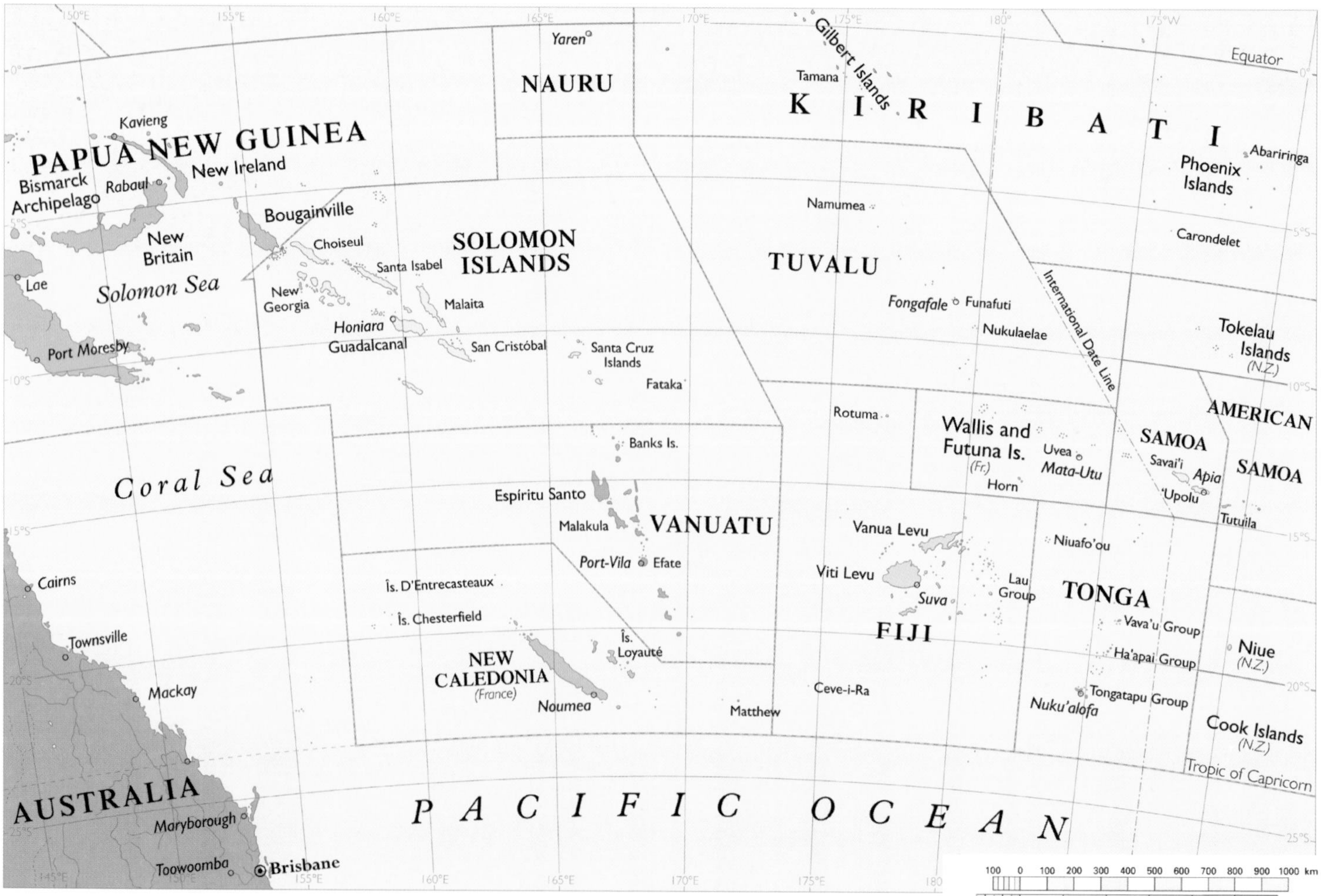

Bottom map:

NAURU
Yaren
Gilbert Islands
Tamana
KIRIBATI
Equator
Abariringa

Kavieng
PAPUA NEW GUINEA
New Ireland
Bismarck Archipelago
Rabaul
Phoenix Islands
Carondelet

New Britain
Bougainville
Choiseul
Santa Isabel
SOLOMON ISLANDS
Namumea
TUVALU

Lae
Solomon Sea
New Georgia
Malaita
Honiara
Guadalcanal
San Cristóbal
Santa Cruz Islands
Fongafale Funafuti
Nukulaelae
International Date Line
Tokelau Islands (N.Z.)

Port Moresby
Fataka
Rotuma
Wallis and Futuna Is. (Fr.)
Uvea Mata-Utu
Horn
SAMOA
Savai'i
Apia
'Upolu
AMERICAN SAMOA
Tutuila

Coral Sea
Banks Is.
Espíritu Santo
Malakula
VANUATU
Vanua Levu
Niuafo'ou
Viti Levu
Lau Group
TONGA
Niue (N.Z.)

Cairns
Port-Vila Efate
Suva
FIJI
Vava'u Group
Ha'apai Group

Îs. D'Entrecasteaux
Îs. Chesterfield
Ceve-i-Ra
Nuku'alofa
Tongatapu Group

Townsville
Îs. Loyauté
NEW CALEDONIA (France)
Noumea
Matthew
Cook Islands (N.Z.)

Mackay
Tropic of Capricorn

AUSTRALIA
Maryborough
PACIFIC OCEAN

Toowoomba
Brisbane

Scale:
100 0 100 200 300 400 500 600 700 800 900 1000 km
100 0 100 200 300 400 500 600 miles

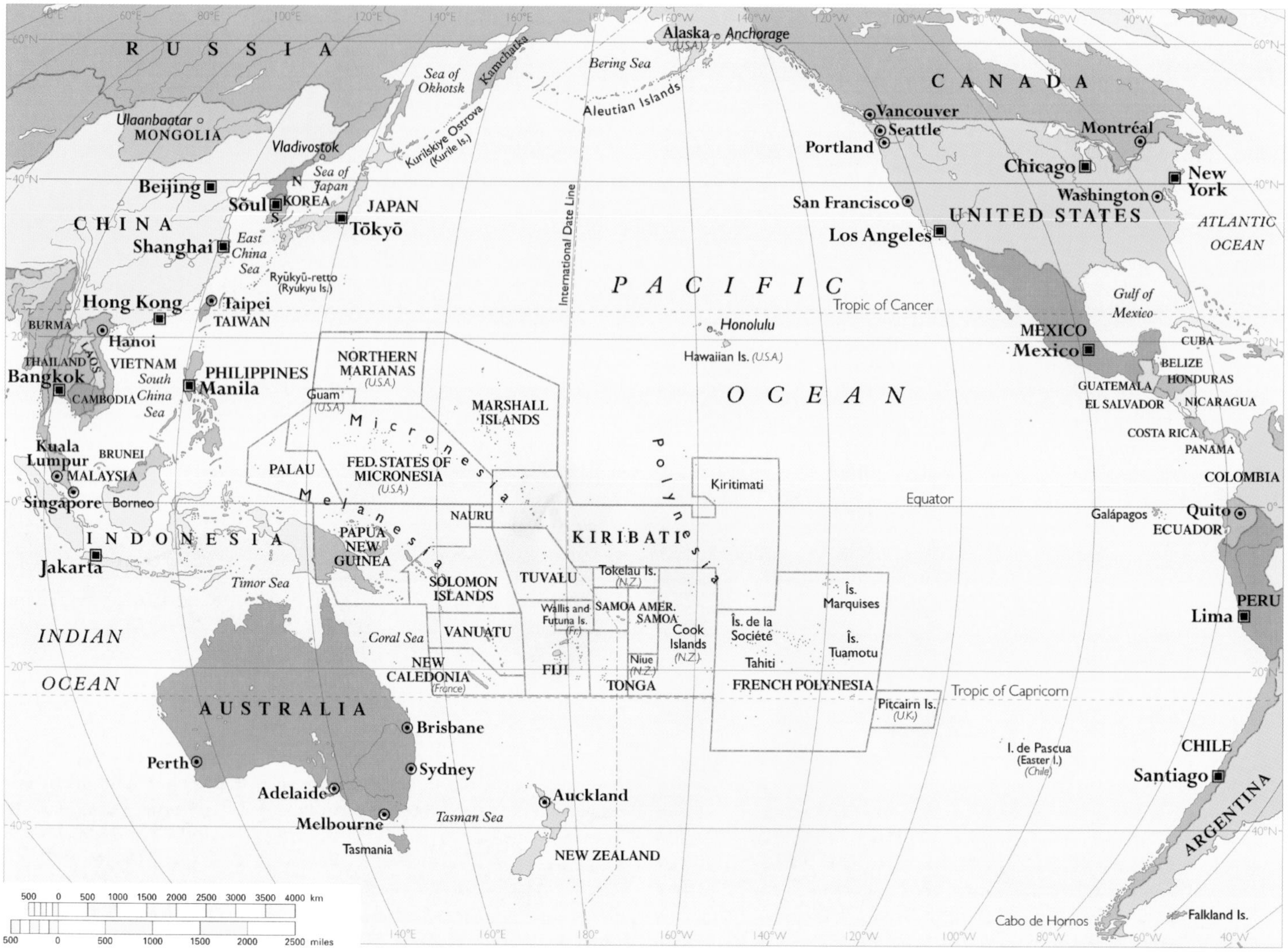

AMERICAN SAMOA

A self-governing 'unincorporated territory' of the United States, American Samoa, in the south-central Pacific Ocean, consists of two volcanic islands and two atolls. Assistance by the United States has given its people a standard of living ten times that of Samoa.

AREA	CAPITAL
200 sq km [77 sq mls]	Pago Pago
POPULATION	**CURRENCY**
62,000	US dollar

FEDERATED STATES OF MICRONESIA

The Federated States of Micronesia, a former US territory in the western Pacific, became fully independent in 1991, though the United States will keep control of defence and security until 2001. The main export is copra. Fishing and tourism are also important.

AREA	CAPITAL
705 sq km [272 sq mls]	Palikir
POPULATION	**CURRENCY**
127,000	US dollar

FIJI

The Republic of the Fiji Islands (Fiji's official name since 1998) comprises more than 800 Melanesian islands. The larger ones are volcanic and mountainous and surrounded by coral reefs. The rest are low coral atolls. Easily the biggest are Viti Levu, with the capital of Suva on its south coast, and Vanua Levu, which is just over half the size of the larger island. The climate is tropical, with south-east trade winds blowing throughout the year. Heavy rains occur, especially between November and May. Tropical forests cover much of the land.

The Dutch navigator, Abel Janszoon Tasman reached the islands in 1643, while Captain James Cook visited one of the southern islands in 1774. Following conflict between various Fijian tribes in the 19th century, a local chief named Cacobau asked Britain to make Fiji a colony. Fiji became a colony in 1874 and remained so until 1970.

Fiji suffers today from its colonial past. Until the late 1980s, Indian workers brought in by the British to work on the sugar plantations outnumbered the native Fijians, but were second-class citizens in terms of electoral representation, economic opportunity and land ownership. However, they played an important part in the economy. The constitution adopted on independence was intended to ease racial tension, but military coups in 1987 overthrew the recently elected (and first) Indian-majority government, suspended the constitution and set up a Fijian-dominated republic outside the Commonwealth. The country returned to civilian rule in 1990 and Fiji rejoined the Commonwealth in 1997. However, with a new constitution guaranteeing Melanesian

political supremacy, many Indians had already emigrated before the 1992 elections, taking their valuable skills with them. A new constitution was introduced in 1998. Elections in 1999 led to victory for the Fiji Labour Party, led by an Indian, Mahendra Chaudhry. His two deputies were both Melanesians, and the defeated prime minister, Sitiveni Rabuka, who had led the 1987 coup, resigned, stating that this time he would not cause trouble.

Agriculture is the mainstay of the economy. Sugar cane, copra and ginger are the main cash crops, and fish and timber are also exported. Manufactures include beer, cement and cigarettes. The leading markets for Fiji's exports are Australia, the United Kingdom, the United States and Japan. Imports come from Australia, New Zealand, the United States and Japan. Tourism is important, though the tourist industry received a massive setback due to the political turmoil in the 1980s.

AREA
18,270 sq km [7,054 sq mls]
POPULATION
802,000
CAPITAL
Suva
CURRENCY
Fiji doll. = 100 cents

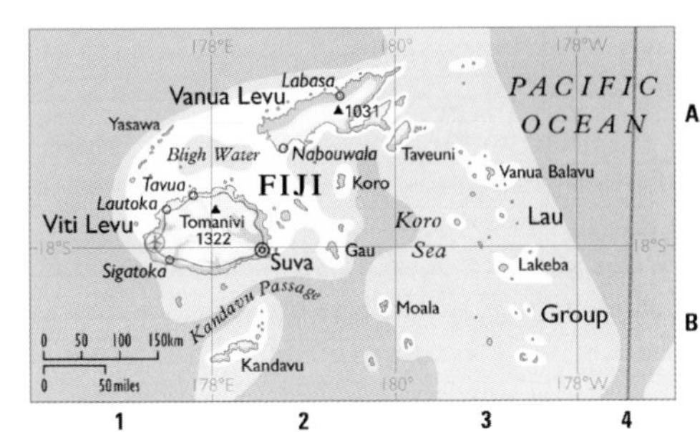

FRENCH POLYNESIA

French Polynesia consists of 130 islands, scattered over 4 million sq km [1.5 million sq mls]. Tahiti is the largest island. The territory became a French protectorate in 1843 and an Overseas Territory in 1958. In 1984, the islands gained increased autonomy and a territorial assembly. The high standard of living comes largely from links with France, including a substantial military presence. France began stationing personnel there in 1962, and started nuclear testing at Mururoa –

recent underground tests took place there in 1995–6. Tourism has also improved the original subsistence agriculture and fishing economy.

AREA	CAPITAL
3,941 sq km [1,520 sq mls]	Papeete
POPULATION	**CURRENCY**
237,000	Euro; French franc

GUAM

Guam, a strategically important 'unincorporated territory' of the USA, is the largest of the Mariana Islands in the Pacific Ocean. It is composed of a coralline plateau. Populated for more than 3,000 years, it was charted by Ferdinand Magellan in 1521, colonized by Spain from 1688, but ceded to the United States after the 1896–8 war, and occupied by the Japanese in 1941–4. It is now of great strategic importance to the United States. Exports include textiles, beverages,

tobacco and copra, but most food is imported. Guam is also a major tourist destination, and enjoys a relatively high standard of living.

AREA	CAPITAL
541 sq km [209 sq mls]	Agana
POPULATION	**CURRENCY**
149,000	US dollar

PACIFIC OCEAN

KIRIBATI

The Republic of Kiribati (pronounced Kiri-bass, the closest that the Gilbertese language can get to Gilberts) comprises three groups of coral atolls – 16 islands which used to form the Gilbert Islands, 8 Phoenix Islands, and 11 of the Line Islands – plus the higher and volcanic Banaba (formerly Ocean Island). The largest island, Kiritimati Atoll (formerly Christmas Island), in the east, covers more than half of the area of the country. (Kiritimati, which was used for British and US nuclear tests from 1957 until 1962, is the Gilbertese version of the word 'Christmas'.) Though the land area is relatively small, the islands are scattered over 5 million sq km [2 million sq mls] of the Pacific, straddling both the Equator and the International Date Line. Temperatures are high and the rainfall is generally abundant.

Together with the Ellice Islands, which broke away as Tuvalu in 1975, becoming independent in 1978, the (mainly Micronesian) Gilbert and the Polynesian Ellice Islands were a British protectorate from 1892, and a colony from 1916. Some of the Line and Phoenix Islands were added later. The islands were occupied by Japan during World War II, but were recaptured after the battle of Tarawa in 1943. In 1976, the Gilbert and Ellice Islands separated into two. The Gilbert Islands became fully independent in 1979 as the Republic of Kiribati.

Few of the coral islands rise more than 4 m [13 ft] above sea level, though bananas, breadfruits, coconuts and papayas are harvested, with taro (babai) cultivated in deep pits to provide the staple vegetable.

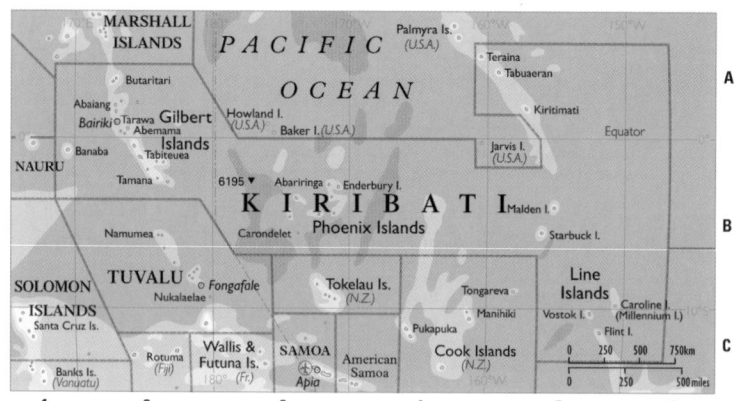

Following the exhaustion of Banaba's phosphate deposits in 1980, the leading exports are copra, and fish and fish preparations – fishing and the making of canoes are an important part of life in Kiribati.

Kiribati remains heavily dependent on foreign aid and its future, both medium-term economic, and long-term environmental (due to possible rising sea levels caused by global warming), is bleak. Kiribati's difficulties are compounded by an overcrowding problem that forced the resettlement of some 4,200 people in the 1990s.

AREA	CAPITAL
728 sq km [281 sq mls]	Tarawa
POPULATION	**CURRENCY**
85,000	Australian dollar

MARSHALL ISLANDS

The Republic of the Marshall Islands comprises an archipelago of 31 coral atolls, 5 single islands and about 1,150 islets in two chains – the eastern and western. The capital is situated on Majuro Atoll in the eastern chain. The chief atoll in the western chain is Kwajalein. The islands also include the former US nuclear testing sites of Bikini and Enewatak. The climate is hot and humid, with the rainy season between May and November.

A German protectorate from 1886, the Marshall Islands were occupied by Japan in World War I and, after the war, Japan was granted a League of Nations mandate to rule the islands. Occupied by Allied forces in 1944, the islands became part of the UN Territory of the Pacific Islands in 1947, administered by the United States. In 1986, the islands became a republic 'in free association' with the United States.

The United Nations recognized the termination of the Trusteeship in 1990 and the new country became a member of the United Nations in 1991. The republic then became a sovereign state, with responsibility for its foreign affairs, although not for its defence and security until 2001. The economy, based on agriculture and tourism, is heavily supported by aid from the United States, which still retains a missile site on the island of Kwajalein. A plan to produce high-quality black pearls, employing thousands of workers, was announced in 1999.

AREA	CAPITAL
181 sq km [70 sq mls]	Dalap-Uliga-Darrit
POPULATION	**CURRENCY**
63,000	US dollar

NAURU

Nauru is the world's smallest republic, located in the western Pacific Ocean, close to the Equator. Formerly ruled by Australia, Nauru became independent in 1968. Its prosperity is based on phosphate mining, but the reserves are running out.

AREA	CAPITAL
21sq km [8 sq mls]	Yaren
POPULATION	**CURRENCY**
12,000	Australian dollar

NEW CALEDONIA

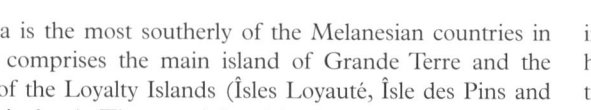

New Caledonia is the most southerly of the Melanesian countries in the Pacific. It comprises the main island of Grande Terre and the dependencies of the Loyalty Islands (Îsles Loyauté, Îsle des Pins and the Bélep archipelago). The remaining islands, many of them coral atolls, are small and uninhabited.

A French possession since 1853 and a French Overseas Territory from 1958, New Caledonia split with France on the question of independence. The Kanaks, the indigenous Melanesian people but numbering under half of the population, support independence, while the less numerous French settlers, many of whom fled Algeria after it gained independence, are against it. In the 1990s, an agreement for increased autonomy helped to ease the tension. But, in 1998 France announced an agreement with local Melanesians that a vote on independence should be postponed for 15 years. New Caledonia is rich in minerals.

AREA	CAPITAL
18,580 sq km [7,174 sq mls]	Nouméa
POPULATION	**CURRENCY**
192,000	French franc

NORTHERN MARIANA ISLANDS

The Commonwealth of the Northern Mariana Islands comprise all 17 Mariana Islands except for Guam, the most southerly. Part of the US Trust Territory of the Pacific from 1947, its people voted in the United Nations plebiscite for Commonwealth status in union with the United States. The US approved the change in 1976, and internal self-government followed in 1978. In 1986, the islanders, most of whom live on Saipan, were granted US citizenship. Fishing is important but tourism, which is growing rapidly, seems to be the key to the future. The number of tourists rose from 130,000 in 1984 to 676,000 in 1995.

AREA	CAPITAL
477 sq km [184 sq mls]	Saipan
POPULATION	**CURRENCY**
50,000	US dollar

PALAU (BELAU)

The Republic of Palau comprises an archipelago of six Caroline groups in the Caroline Islands, totalling 26 islands and more than 300 islets, varying in terrain from mountain to reef. Palau was part of the US Trust Territory of the Pacific Ocean, which was established in 1947. In 1978, it voted to break away from the Federated States of Micronesia and a new, self-governing constitution became effective in 1981. The territory then entered into 'free association with the United States', providing sovereign-state status. However, in 1983, the proposal was rejected in a referendum, because the US refused to accede to a 92% vote in a 1979 referendum that would have made it a nuclear-free zone. On 1 October 1994, Palau finally became an independent republic and, in December 1994, it joined the United Nations. Palau relies heavily on US aid. Other activities include tourism and subsistence agriculture.

AREA	CAPITAL
458 sq km [177 sq mls]	Koror
POPULATION	**CURRENCY**
18,000	US dollar

PITCAIRN

Pitcairn Island is a British overseas territory in the Pacific Ocean about halfway between New Zealand and Panama. This isolated island rises steeply from the sea to an elevation of about 250 m [820 ft] and the climate is mild and wet. The Pitcairn Island Group also includes the uninhabited islands of Henderson, Ducie and Oeno. Uninhabited until 1790, it was occupied by nine mutineers from HMS *Bounty*, together with some men and women from Tahiti. The present population lives in Adamstown on Pitcairn, which comes under the administration of the British High Commissioner in Wellington, New Zealand.

AREA	CAPITAL
48 sq km [19 sq mls]	Adamstown
POPULATION	**CURRENCY**
60	New Zealand dollar = 100 cents

SAMOA

The Independent State of Samoa, which was known as Western Samoa until its name was officially changed in July 1997, comprises two large volcanic islands, seven small islands and a number of islets. The main islands of Upolo and Savai'i both have central mountainous regions, surrounded by coastal lowlands and coral reefs. Upolu contains two-thirds of the country's population. Samoa has a tropical climate, but the south-east trade winds moderate the climate. Temperatures seldom fall below 24°C [75°F], or rise above 29°C [85°F]. The coolest months are May to November, while the rainy season extends from December to April. The south and east coasts receive the most rainfall.

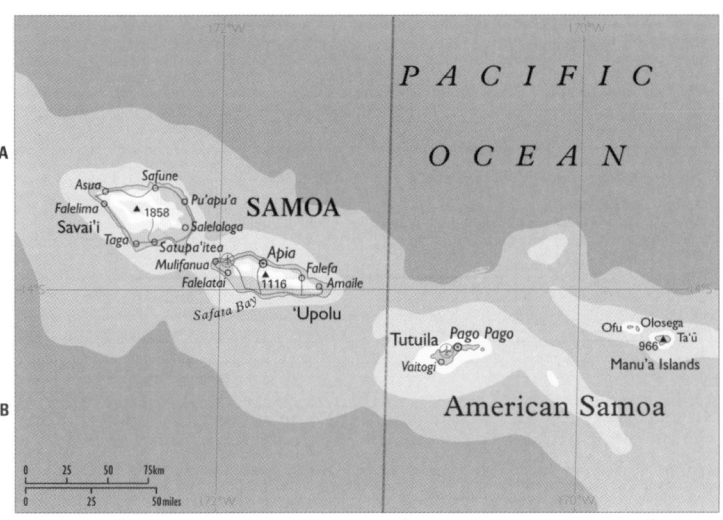

The first European contacts occurred in the 18th century but, following the establishment of a Christian mission on Savai'i in the 1830s, missionaries, as well as whaling and trading ships began to visit the islands. In 1899, Germany and the United States took control, with Germany taking Western Samoa. Ruled by New Zealand from 1920 – first under a League of Nations mandate and later a United Nations trusteeship – the islands achieved independence as a parliamentary democracy in 1962. Before 1991, when the first elections under universal suffrage were held, the 49-member Legislative Assembly was elected exclusively by *matai* (heads of Samoan family groups).

Agriculture employs more than 60% of the workforce. The chief food crops are bananas, breadfruit, coconuts, mangos, papayas, pineapples and taro, while some farmers raise cattle, chickens and pigs. Besides its fertile soils, Samoa's other resources are its forests and fish. With aid from the United Nations, fishing has become an important activity. The few industries are powered mainly by hydroelectricity. Samoa's exports include coconut oil, coconut cream and copra, which together made up 70% of the value of the exports in 1995.

Other important sources of revenue are remittances from Samoans working overseas, together with foreign aid. Tourism is growing. More than 70,000 foreign tourists visited the country in 1996. Many come to see the home of the writer Robert Louis Stevenson, which is now the official home of Samoa's head of state.

AREA	CAPITAL
2,840 sq km [1,097 sq mls]	Apia
POPULATION	**CURRENCY**
224,000	Tala = 100 sene

PACIFIC OCEAN

SOLOMON ISLANDS

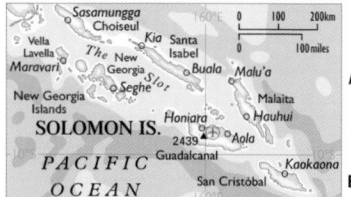

The Solomon Islands represent part of the drowned outermost crustal fold of the ancient Australian continent. New Caledonia lies on an inner fold, nearer the mainland. The main islands in the Solomon Islands are volcanic in origin and the mountains are covered by dense forests. The northern islands have a tropical marine climate, but the south is cooler.

The southern Solomons became British in 1893, while Germany ceded islands in the north in 1900. During World War II, Japan occupied the islands, which became the scene of fierce fighting, notably the battle of Guadalcanal. Known as the British Solomons, the islands won independence in 1978. Since then, the Solomons have faced many economic problems, while ethnic violence broke out in 1999.

The coastal plains are used for subsistence farming. While coconut products and cocoa are exported, forestry and fishing are the main industries, accounting for four-fifths of the exports.

AREA	CAPITAL
28,370 sq km [10,954 sq mls]	Honiara
POPULATION	**CURRENCY**
441,000	Solomon Island dollar = 100 cents

TONGA

The Kingdom of Tonga comprises more than 170 islands, 36 of which are inhabited. They are a mixture of coralline outcrops and higher volcanic outcrops. The largest island, Tongatapu, contains nearly two-thirds of the population.

Dutch navigators visited the islands in the early 17th century, and British missionaries converted most people to Christianity in the early 19th century. Tonga became a British protectorate in 1900. Tonga is a monarchy and the king rules with a prime minister and cabinet. From 1965, the ruler has been King Taufa'ahau Tupou IV, whose line goes back a thousand years. He presided over the islands' transition from British protectorate to independent Commonwealth country in 1970. Tonga became a member of the United Nations in 1999.

Most Tongans live off their own produce, which includes fish, tapioca and yams. While the government owns all the land, men are entitled to rent areas to grow food – a policy that is now under pressure with Tonga's young population. The main exports include squash, fish and vanilla beans. Tourism is developing – Tonga received 100,000 foreign visitors in 1996.

AREA	CAPITAL
750 sq km [290 sq mls]	Nuku'alofa
POPULATION	**CURRENCY**
107,000	Pa'anga = 100 seniti

TUVALU

Tuvalu, formerly the Ellice Islands, consists of nine coral atolls, none of which rise more than 4.6 m [15 ft] above sea level. Britain took control of the islands in the 1890s and, in 1916, joined them to the Gilbert Islands to form a colony called the Gilbert and Ellice Islands. The two groups were separated in 1975 and the Ellice Islands were renamed Tuvalu. The country became independent in 1978. The people depend on subsistence farming, the raising of pigs and poultry, and fishing.

Exports include clothing and footwear, copra and fruits. Foreign exchange also comes from the sale of elaborate postage stamps.

AREA	CAPITAL
24 sq km [9 sq mls]	Fongafale
POPULATION	**CURRENCY**
10,000	Australian dollar

VANUATU

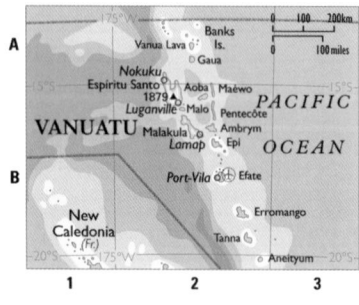

The Republic of Vanuatu is an archipelago of 30 large islands and 70 islets, the majority of which are mountainous and volcanic, with coral beaches, reefs, forests and limited coastal cultivation. The climate is tropical, but moderated by the influence of the oceans and the trade winds.

The islands were visited by the Portuguese in 1696 and rediscovered by the French in 1768. They were charted by Captain James Cook in 1774, who named the islands New Hebrides. In 1888, France and Britain agreed on joint supervision and, from 1906, the islands were ruled as an Anglo-French condominium. The islands became independent as Vanuatu in 1980. The Francophone Espiritu Santo, the largest island, attempted to secede from Vanuatu, whose government was anglophone, and politics have remained unstable. Agriculture is the main activity and Vanuatu exports copra, beef and veal, timber and cocoa.

AREA	CAPITAL
12,190 sq km [4,707 sq mls]	Port-Vila
POPULATION	**CURRENCY**
185,000	Vatu (VUV)

WALLIS AND FUTUNA

The Wallis and Futuna Islands comprise three main islands and many islets. In a 1959 referendum, the Polynesian islanders voted in favour of a change from a dependency to a French Overseas Territory. French aid remains vital to an economy based on subsistence agriculture.

AREA	CAPITAL
200 sq km [77 sq mls]	Mata-Utu
POPULATION	**CURRENCY**
15,000	French franc

PAKISTAN

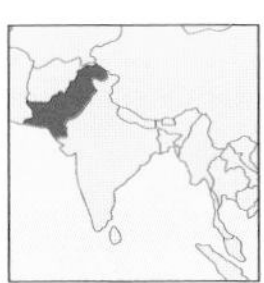

Pakistan's flag was adopted in 1947, when the country became independent from Britain. The colour green, the crescent Moon and the five-pointed star are all traditional symbols of Islam. The white stripe represents the other religions in Pakistan.

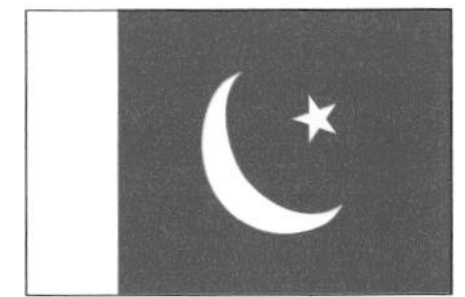

Geography

The Republic of Pakistan contains mountains, fertile plains and rocky deserts. The Karakoram range, which contains K2, the world's second highest mountain at 8,611 m [28,251 ft], lies on the border with China in northern Jammu and Kashmir – disputed areas, occupied by Pakistan but claimed by India. Other mountains rise in the west. The Thar (or Great Indian) Desert straddles the border with India in the south-east. The arid Baluchistan Plateau lies in the south-west.

Like Egypt, most of the terrain in Pakistan is inhospitable, and, just as Egypt is the gift of the Nile, so Pakistan is the gift of the River Indus and its tributaries. Irrigation is vital both in the Punjab in eastern Pakistan, 'the land of five rivers' (the Indus, Jhelum, Beas, Ravi and Sutlej), and on the dry plains that flank the Indus between Khairpur and Hyderabad. The stations at Tarbela, on the Indus, and Mangla, on the Jhelum, are among the world's biggest earth- and rock-filled dams.

Climate

The mountains have cold, snowy winters. But most of Pakistan has hot summers and cool winters. Rainfall is sparse over much of the country.

PAKISTAN (KARACHI)

The summer monsoon rains decrease in intensity from the Indian peninsula westwards into Pakistan, leaving much of the Indus lowland arid. Rain falls on approximately 20 days in the year, half of these in July and August. Karachi is hot all year but, being on the coast, has a smaller temperature range than inland. Summer rains are thundery. Small amounts of winter rain are brought by low-pressure systems from the west.

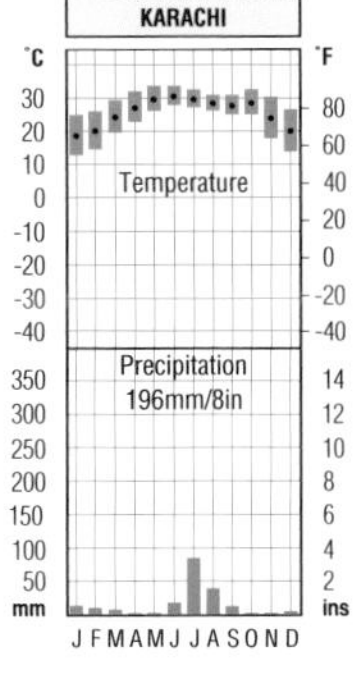

Vegetation

Forests grow on mountain slopes, but most of Pakistan is covered by dry grassland and low bushes, with only occasional trees, apart from forest plantations and the many fruit orchards in farming areas. Plants that are adapted to surviving in dry conditions grow in semi-arid areas. Wild animals found in the northern mountains include bears, leopards and wild sheep. Crocodiles and wild boars are found in the delta region.

History

Pakistan was the site of the Indus Valley civilization which developed about 4,500 years ago. Two major archaeological sites, at Harappa, in the Ravi valley south of Faisalabad, and at Mohenjo-Daro, south-west of Sukkur, are the remains of large, well-planned cities. The Indus Valley civilization, which developed a system of weights and measures and a type of writing using pictographs, broke up into smaller cultures around 1700 BC. Historians believe that its break-up may have been caused by changes in the courses of the rivers.

The region that is now Pakistan was subsequently conquered by successive waves of people from south-western and central Asia. The Aryans reached the area by about 1500 BC and, in time, they settled across northern India. From the 6th century BC, the area was conquered by the Persians, and then, in 326 BC, it was occupied by the armies of Alexander the Great. Soon afterwards it became part of the Maurya Empire until that empire began to break up around 230 BC. It was then invaded successively by Bactrians, Scythians, Afghans and Parthians, until it became part of the Kushan Empire between about AD 50 and the mid-3rd century.

Islam was introduced in AD 711 by Muslims who had sailed across the Arabian Sea. In about AD 1000, Turkish Muslims invaded from the north and founded a kingdom that included the entire Indus Valley, with its capital at Lahore. Between 1206 and 1526, the area was part of the Delhi Sultanate, which included northern India. In 1526, it became part of the Mogul Empire which was founded by Babar, a Muslim ruler from Afghanistan. Under the Mogul Empire, a new religion emerged, which became especially strong in Punjab. This religion, called Sikhism, combined elements of Hinduism and Islam. The Mogul Empire began to decline in the 18th century as the British East India Company was taking control of India. In the 1840s, the Company gained areas in Punjab and Sind. In 1858, when the British government took over from the British East India Company, the region, which became known as British India, included all of what is now Pakistan.

Politics

From the early 20th century, the Muslim League and the Indian National Congress sought greater self-government for British India. In the 1930s, the Muslim League, led by Muhammad Ali Jinnah, called for the creation of a Muslim state called Pakistan, a name that means 'land of the pure' in Urdu. On 14 August 1947, Pakistan became an independent nation, with India gaining independence the following day. The partition of British India was accompanied by slaughter as Hindus and Sikhs fled from Pakistan and Muslims fled from India.

In 1948, India and Pakistan went to war over Kashmir (officially the Indian state of Jammu and Kashmir). At the end of the war, Pakistan was left in control of the area to the west of the 1949 cease-fire line, with India in control to the east. The Kashmir problem was partly religious – with a mainly Muslim population ruled by a Hindu maharaja who had acceded to India. But there was also a strategic issue, namely that the five rivers that rise in or pass across Kashmir or the neighbouring state of Himachal Pradesh are vital to Pakistan's economy. This region has remained a disputed zone, with fighting breaking out periodically. The present boundary is a truce line established in 1972, following further conflict in 1971.

When Pakistan became independent, it consisted of two parts: West and East Pakistan. Following a bitter civil war and Indian military intervention, East Pakistan broke away from the western wing in 1971 to become Bangladesh. However, neither nation has enjoyed stability or sound government since the civil war. The nation that is now Pakistan has been subject to military rule and martial law, interspersed with periods of fragile democracy, generally resting on army consent.

Following the resignation of President Mohammad Yahya Khan, after the civil war in 1971, Zulfiquar Ali Bhutto became president. Under a new constitution in 1973, which provided for a head of state and a prime minister as the head of the government, Bhutto resigned as president to become prime minister. But the military thought him to be too pro-Western in his policies and, in 1977, following his party's victory in elections, he was overthrown by an army coup. The coup was led by General Mohammad Zia ul-Haq, who became president in 1978. Bhutto was convicted of the murder of a political opponent while he was serving as prime minister and he was executed in 1979.

Elections were held in February 1985 and martial law was ended in December 1985. Zia ul-Haq dismissed the prime minister, the cabinet and the parliament in 1988, but in August that year he was killed in a plane crash. Ghulam Ishaq Khan, leader of the Senate, became the acting president. In November 1988, elections brought Benazir Bhutto, daughter of the former prime minister and leader of the Pakistan People's Party (PPP), to power as prime minister. In August 1990, President Ishaq Khan dismissed Benazir Bhutto and her cabinet, accusing the government of corruption. He dissolved the National Assembly and declared a state of emergency.

Elections in 1990 resulted in victory for a coalition group, the Islamic Democratic Alliance. The leader of the chief party in the coalition, Nawaz Sharif of the Pakistan Muslim League, became prime minister. In further elections in 1993, following the resignations of the president and prime minister, the PPP won the most seats and Benazir Bhutto

PAKISTAN

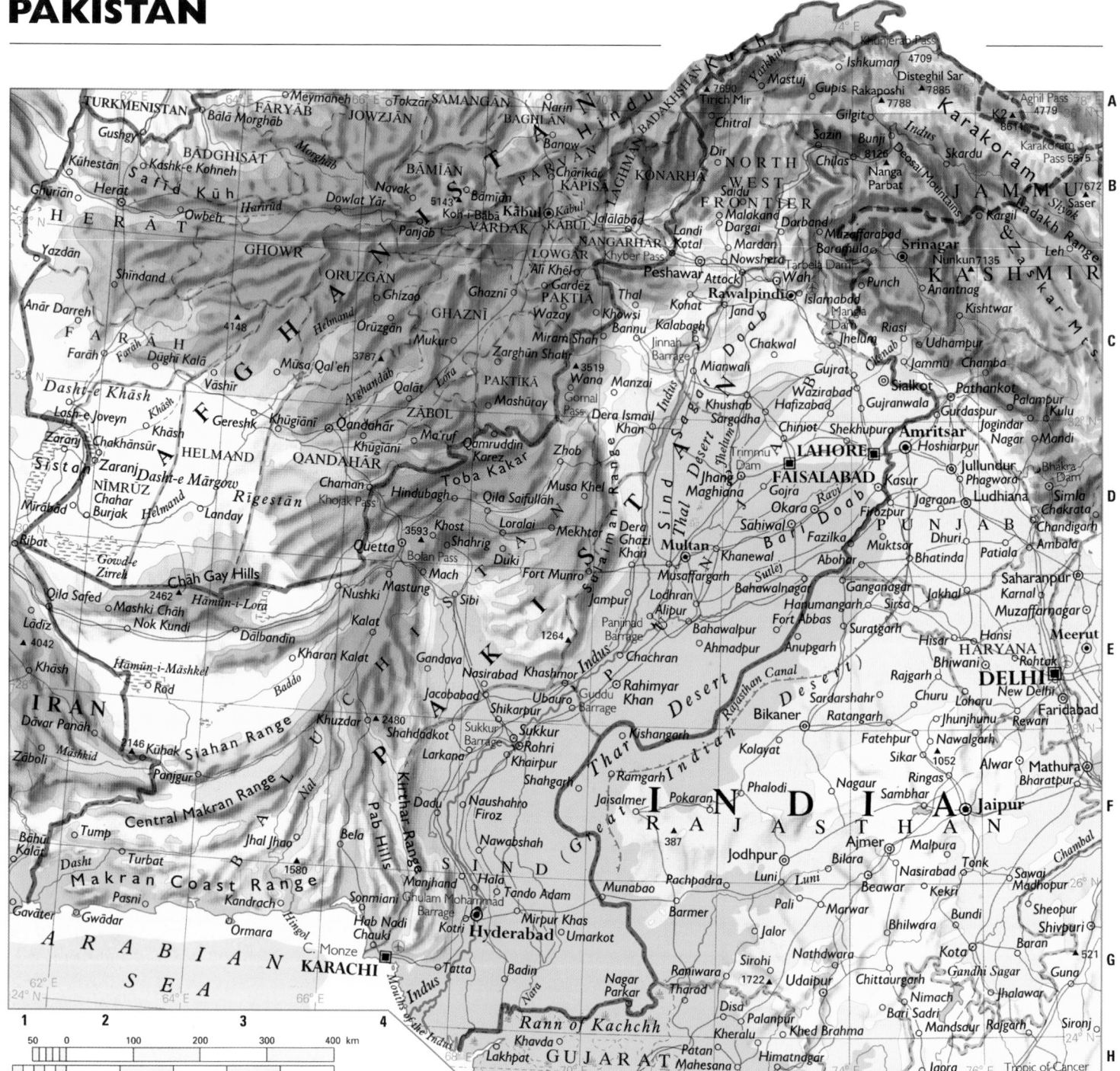

again became prime minister. History repeated itself in the late 1990s. In 1996, President Farooq Leghari dismissed Benazir Bhutto and her cabinet. Further elections in 1997 restored Nawaz Sharif as prime minister. But in October 1999, a military coup occurred. Martial law was declared, Nawaz Sharif was arrested and charged with kidnapping, attempted murder, hijacking and terrorism, and General Prevez Musharraf proclaimed himself the country's 'chief executive'.

In May 1998, nuclear tests carried out first by India and then by Pakistan created fears of a nuclear war in Kashmir. However, clashes in Kashmir continued during 1999 without the use of nuclear weapons.

Economy

According to the World Bank, Pakistan is a 'low-income' developing country, with a per capita gross national product of US $490 in 1997. Agriculture, which employs around 47% of the workforce, is the most important sector of the economy, accounting for nearly one-fourth of the country's gross domestic product. Major crops, grown mostly on irrigated land, include cotton, fruits, rice, sugar cane, vegetables and wheat. Goats and sheep are important in mountainous areas. Cattle and water buffaloes are mainly important as beasts of burden, though they also provide meat, milk and hides. Fishing for sardines, sharks, shrimps and other sea food is important in the Arabian Sea.

Some chromite, gypsum, iron ore, limestone and rock salt are mined and manufacturing industries employ approximately 9% of the workforce. Manufacturing has increased substantially since Pakistan became independent in 1947. Leading manufactures include bicycles, car tyres, cement, industrial chemicals, cotton yarn, fertilizers, processed food products, especially flour and sugar, and jute and cotton textiles. Textiles and ready-made garments are major exports. Pakistan's major trading partners include the United States, Japan and Germany.

AREA	ETHNIC GROUPS
796,100 sq km	Punjabi 60%, Sindhi 12%,
[307,374 sq mls]	Pushtun 13%, Baluch, Muhajir
POPULATION	**LANGUAGES**
135,135,000	Urdu (official), many others
CAPITAL (POPULATION)	**RELIGIONS**
Islamabad	Islam 97%, Christianity,
(204,000)	Hinduism
GOVERNMENT	**CURRENCY**
Federal republic	Pakistan rupee = 100 paisa

PALAU – SEE PACIFIC OCEAN, PAGES 174–178;
PANAMA – SEE COSTA RICA, PAGE 88

PAPUA NEW GUINEA

Papua New Guinea's flag was first adopted in 1971, four years before the country became independent from Australia. It includes a local bird of paradise, the 'kumul', in flight, together with the stars of the Southern Cross. The colours are those often used by local artists.

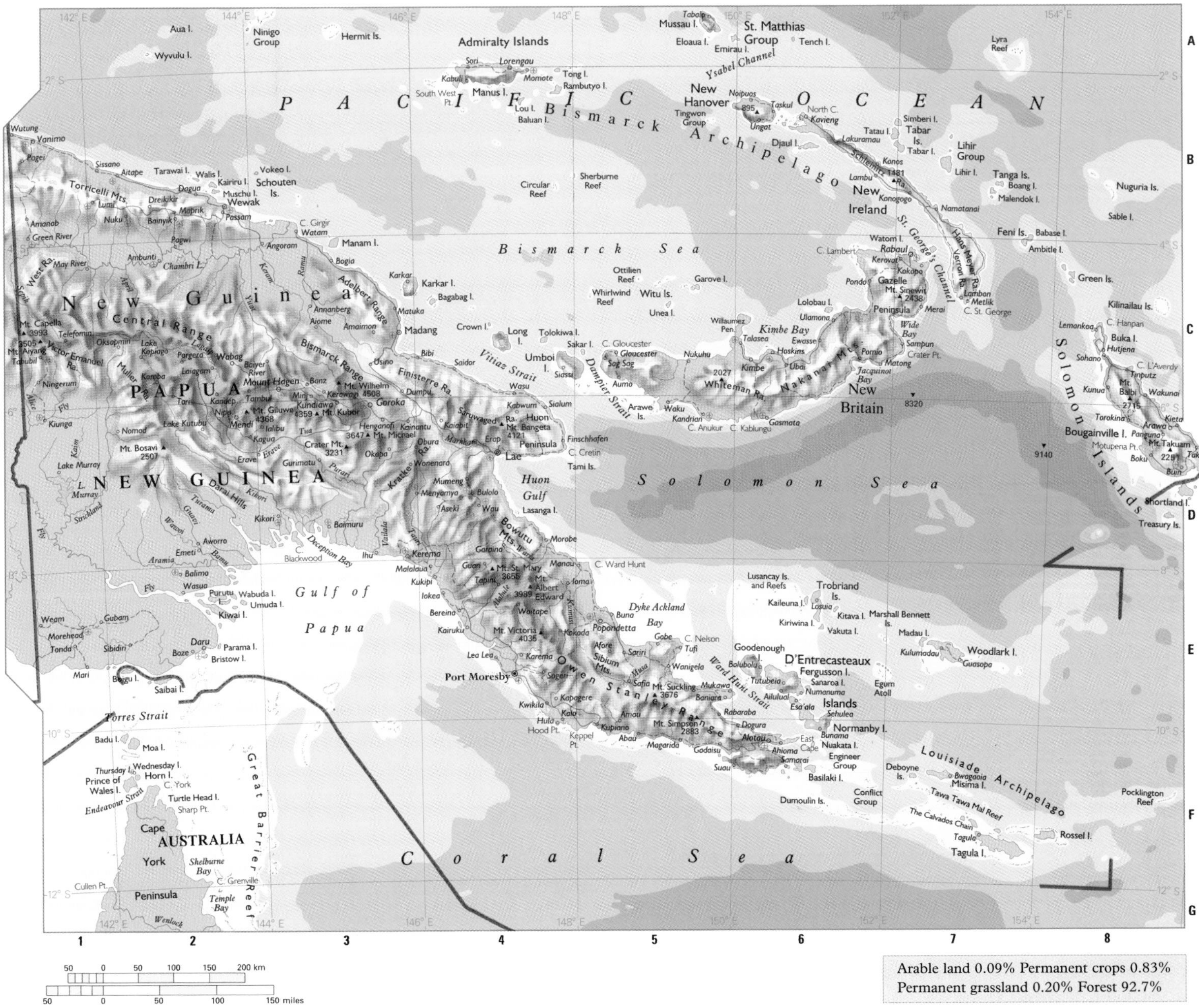

Arable land 0.09% Permanent crops 0.83%
Permanent grassland 0.20% Forest 92.7%

Geography and Climate

Papua New Guinea is part of a Pacific island region called Melanesia. It includes the eastern part of New Guinea, the Bismarck Archipelago, the northern Solomon Islands, the D'Entrecasteaux Islands and the Louisiade Archipelago. The land is largely mountainous.

The climate is tropical. It is hot all year with most rain occurring during the monsoon season (December–April), when north-westerly winds blow. Winds blow from the south-east during the dry season.

History, Politics and Economy

The Dutch took western New Guinea (now part of Indonesia) in 1828. In 1884, Germany took north-eastern New Guinea and Britain took the south-east. In 1906, Britain handed the south-east over to Australia. It then became known as the Territory of Papua. When World War I broke out in 1914, Australia took German New Guinea. In 1921, the League of Nations gave Australia a mandate to rule the area, which was named the Territory of New Guinea.

Japan invaded New Guinea in 1942, but the Allies reconquered in 1944. In 1949, Papua and New Guinea combined into the Territory of Papua and New Guinea. The country became independent in 1975.

Since independence, the government has worked to develop mineral reserves. At one of the most valuable mines on Bougainville, in the northern Solomon Islands, people demanded a larger share in profits, causing conflict. The mine was closed and the Bougainville rebels proclaimed the island independent. But this secession was not recognized internationally. An agreement to end the conflict was signed in 1998. Local autonomy was granted to Bougainville in 2000.

The World Bank classifies Papua New Guinea as a 'lower-middle-income' developing country. Agriculture employs most of the people.

AREA	**ETHNIC GROUPS**
462,840 sq km	Papuan 84%, Melanesian 1%
[178,703 sq mls]	**LANGUAGES**
POPULATION	English (official), many others
4,600,000	**RELIGIONS**
CAPITAL (POPULATION)	Protestant 58%, Roman Catholic
Port Moresby (174,000)	33%, traditional beliefs 3%
GOVERNMENT	**CURRENCY**
Constitutional monarchy	Kina = 100 toea

The front (obverse) side of Paraguay's tricolour flag, which evolved in the early 19th century, contains the state emblem, which displays the May Star, commemorating liberation from Spain in 1811. The reverse side shows the treasury seal – a lion and staff.

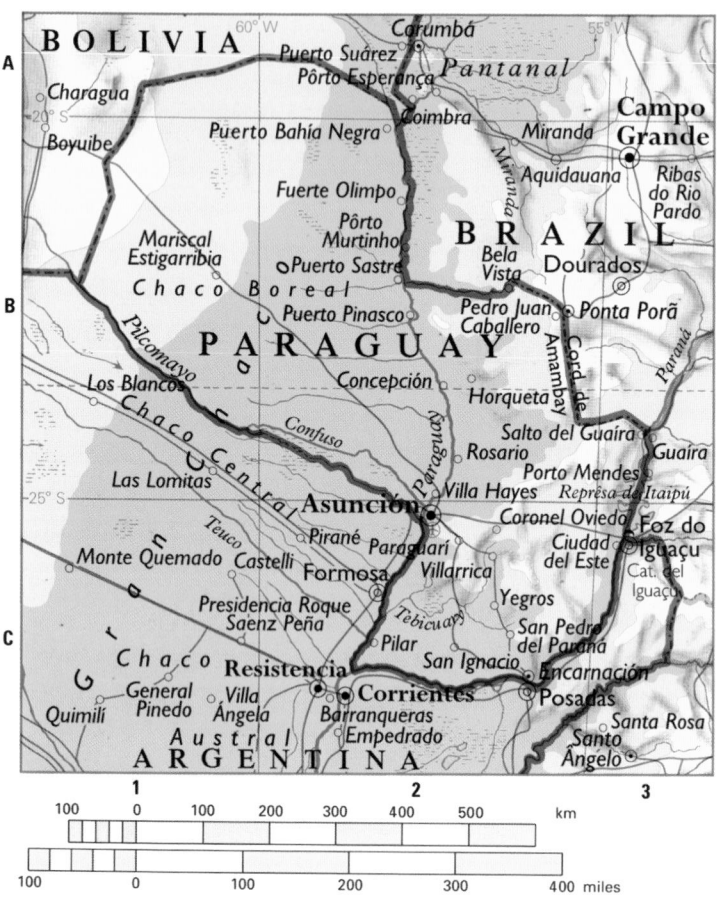

	1			2			3

```
100    0    100   200   300   400   500      km
100    0         100        200       300      400 miles
```

Geography and Climate

The Republic of Paraguay is a landlocked country in South America. Rivers form most of its borders. They include the Paraná in the south and the east, the Pilcomayo (Brazo Sur) in the south-west, and the Paraguay in the north-east. West of the River Paraguay is a region known as the Chaco, which extends into Bolivia and Argentina. The Chaco is mostly flat, but the land rises to the north-west. East of the Paraguay is a region of plains, hills and, in the east, the Paraná Plateau region.

Northern Paraguay lies in the tropics, while the south is subtropical. Most of the country has a warm, humid climate. The Chaco is the driest and hottest part of the country. Rainfall increases to the Paraná Plateau in the south-east.

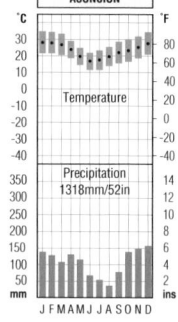

PARAGUAY (ASUNCIÓN)

In South America, between 20°S and 30°S, there is a prominent summer wet season. Rain is often heavy, yielding as much as 20 mm [0.8 in] a day in Asunción. Summers throughout the plains of Paraguay are very hot and humid, but winters are mild and relatively dry. Much of the winter rain is associated with surges of cold air from the Southern Ocean, which can give surprisingly low temperatures, especially in the south.

History

The Guarani, an Amerindian people, were the indigenous people of what is now Paraguay. Spanish and Portuguese explorers reached the area in the early 16th century and, in 1537, a Spanish expedition built a fort at Asunción, which later became the capital of Spain's colonies in south-eastern South America. The Spaniards were attracted by the potential labour supply of the Guarani and the chance to find a short cut to the silver mines of Peru. From the late 16th century, Jesuit missionaries arrived to convert the Guarani to Christianity and to protect them against those who wanted to exploit them as cheap labour. Complaints against the Jesuits' power led to their expulsion in 1767.

From 1766, Paraguay formed part of the Rio de la Plata Viceroyalty, with its capital at Buenos Aires. However, this proved unpopular and Paraguay broke free in 1811, achieving its independence from Buenos Aires in 1813. For more than a century, the country struggled for nationhood and was torn by destructive internal strife and conflict with neighbouring states: between 1865 and 1870, war against Brazil, Argentina and Uruguay cost the country more than half of its 600,000 people and much of its territory. Some territory was regained after the Chaco Wars against Bolivia between 1920 and 1935, and, in 1947, a period of civil war was followed by a spell of political and economic stability. At a time when most other South American countries were attracting European settlers and foreign capital for development, Paraguay remained isolated and forbidding.

Politics

In 1954, General Alfredo Stroessner seized power and assumed the presidency. During his dictatorship, there was considerable economic growth, particularly in the 1970s, with an emphasis on developing hydroelectricity. By 1976, Paraguay was self-sufficient in electrical energy since the completion of the Aracay complex. A second hydroelectric project, the world's largest, started production in 1984, at Itaipu. This was a joint US $20 billion venture with Brazil to harness the Paraná. Paraguay was then generating 99.9% of its electricity from water power. However, demand slackened and income declined, making it difficult for Paraguay to repay foreign debts incurred on the projects. High inflation and balance of payments problems followed.

Stroessner's regime was an unpleasant variety of nepotism. He ruled with an increasing disregard for human rights during nearly 35 years of fear and fraud until his supporters deposed him in 1989. Three elections were held in the 1990s, but the fragility of democracy was demonstrated in 1998, when the newly elected president, Raul Cubas Grau, was threatened with impeachment after issuing a decree freeing his former running mate, General Lino Oviedo, who had been imprisoned for attempting a coup against the previous president, Juan Carlos Wasmosy. In March 1999, Paraguay's vice-president, an opponent of Cubas, was assassinated and the Congress impeached Cubas, who resigned and fled to Argentina. The head of the Senate, Luis Gonzalez, then assumed the presidency.

Economy

The World Bank classifies Paraguay as a 'lower-middle-income' developing country. Agriculture and forestry are the leading activities, employing 48% of the population. The country has very large cattle ranches, while crops are grown in the fertile soils of eastern Paraguay. Major exports include cotton, soya beans, timber, vegetable oils, coffee, tannin and meat products.

The country has abundant hydroelectricity and it exports power to Argentina and Brazil. Its factories produce cement, processed food, leather goods and textiles. Paraguay has no major mineral or fossil fuel resources.

AREA	ETHNIC GROUPS
406,750 sq km	Mestizo 90%, Amerindian 3%
[157,046 sq mls]	**LANGUAGES**
POPULATION	Spanish, Guaraní (both official)
5,291,000	**RELIGIONS**
CAPITAL (POPULATION)	Christianity (Roman Catholic
Asunción (945,000)	96%, Protestant 2%)
GOVERNMENT	**CURRENCY**
Multiparty republic	Guaraní = 100 céntimos

PERU

Peru's flag was adopted in 1825. The colours are said to have been inspired by a flock of red and white flamingos which the Argentine patriot General José de San Martín saw flying over his marching army when he arrived in 1820 to liberate Peru from Spain.

Geography

The Republic of Peru lies in the tropics in western South America. A narrow coastal plain borders the Pacific Ocean in the west. Inland are ranges of the Andes Mountains, which rise to 6,768 m [22,205 ft] at Mount Huascarán, an extinct volcano. The Andes also contain active volcanoes, windswept plateaux, broad valleys and, in the far south, part of Lake Titicaca, the world's highest navigable lake. To the east the Andes descend to a hilly region and a huge plain. Eastern Peru is part of the Amazon basin.

Climate

The coastal region is arid and chilled by the cold offshore Peru Current. In the Andes, temperatures are moderated by the altitude. The eastern lowlands are hot and humid.

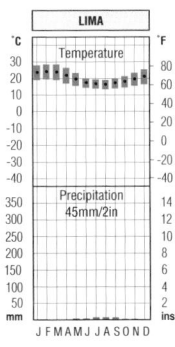

PERU (LIMA)

Lima lies a short distance inland, but its climate is typical of the coastal plain. Midday temperatures are a little higher than those on the coast, which is affected by the cold Peru Current. Most of the Peruvian coast, has a desert climate. However, the northern coast often has very heavy rainfall which is caused when the cold Peru Current retreats during a climatic phenomenon known as El Niño.

History

Amerindian people probably reached the area about 12,000 years ago. Several civilizations developed in the Andes region. By about AD 1200, the Inca were established in southern Peru. In 1500, their empire extended from Ecuador to Chile. The Spanish adventurer Francisco Pizarro visited Peru in the 1520s. Hearing of Inca riches, he returned in 1532. By 1533, he had conquered most of Peru.

In 1820, the Argentinian José de San Martín led an army into Peru and declared the country to be independent. However, Spain still held large areas. In 1823, the Venezuelan Simón Bolívar led another army into Peru and, in 1824, one of his generals defeated the Spaniards at Ayacucho. The Spaniards surrendered in 1826. Peru suffered much instability throughout the 19th century.

Politics

Instability continued into the 20th century. When civilian rule was restored in 1980, a left-wing group called the Sendero Luminoso, or the 'Shining Path', began guerrilla warfare against the government. In 1990, Alberto Fujimori, son of Japanese immigrants, became president. In 1992, he suspended the constitution and dismissed the legislature. The guerrilla leader, Abimael Guzmán, was arrested in 1992, but instability continued. In 1996, Tupac Amaru (MRTA) rebels seized the Japanese ambassador's residence, taking hostages and demanding the release of guerrilla prisoners. The stalemate ended in April 1997, when Peruvian troops attacked and freed the remaining 72 hostages.

A new constitution was introduced in 1993, giving increased power to the president, who faced problems in rebuilding the economy. To add to Peru's problems, in 1991 the country suffered the worst cholera outbreak in the Americas in the 20th century. This resulted in some 2,500 deaths, while the worst El Niño in the 20th century caused a severe drought and failure of the fish harvest in 1997. However, in 1998, a border dispute with Ecuador, which had dated back to a war in 1942, was finally settled when Peru and Ecuador signed a peace agreement.

Economy

The World Bank classifies Peru as a 'lower-middle-income' developing country. Agriculture employs 35% of the people and major food crops include beans, maize, potatoes and rice. Coffee, cotton and sugar are the chief cash crops. Many farms are small and the farmers live at subsistence level. Other farms are co-operatives, where farmers own and operate the farm as a group. Fishing is important, except in years when El Niño wrecks the industry.

Peru is one of the world's main producers of copper, silver and zinc. Iron ore, lead and oil are also produced, while gold is mined in the highlands. Most manufacturing is small-scale. Larger plants produce such things as chemicals, clothing and textiles, paper products, processed food and steel. The country's leading exports are copper and copper products, fish meal, zinc products, coffee, oil and lead products.

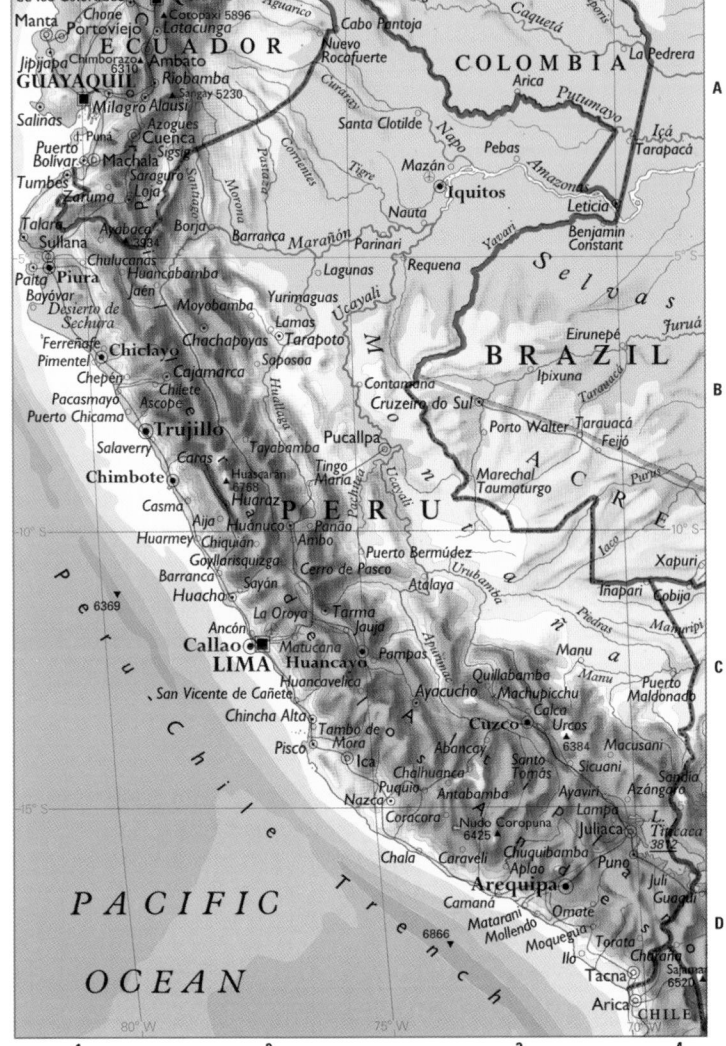

Arable land 2.93%
Forest 66.3%

AREA	Mestizo 32%, White 12%,
1,285,220 sq km [496,223 sq mls]	Aymara 5%
POPULATION	**LANGUAGES**
26,111,000	Spanish and Quechua
CAPITAL (POPULATION)	(both official), Aymara
Lima (Lima-Callao, 6,601,000)	**RELIGIONS**
GOVERNMENT	Christianity (Roman Catholic
Transitional republic	93%, Protestant 6%)
ETHNIC GROUPS	**CURRENCY**
Quechua 47%,	New sol = 100 centavos

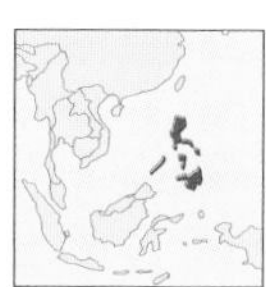

This flag was adopted in 1946, when the country won its independence from the United States. The eight rays of the large sun represent the eight provinces which led the revolt against Spanish rule in 1898. The three smaller stars stand for the three main island groups.

Geography

The Republic of the Philippines is an island country in south-eastern Asia. It includes about 7,100 islands, of which 2,770 are named and about 1,000 are inhabited. Luzon and Mindanao, the two largest islands, make up more than two-thirds of the country. The land is mainly mountainous and lacks large lowlands. The country lies in an unstable region and earthquakes are common. The islands also have several active volcanoes, one of which is the highest peak, Mount Apo, at 2,954 m [9,692 ft] above sea level.

Climate

The country has a tropical climate, with high temperatures throughout the year. The dry season runs from December to April. The rest of the year is wet. The high rainfall is associated with typhoons which periodically strike the east coast.

PHILIPPINES (MANILA)

The islands in the southern Philippines have an equatorial climate, but the northern and central islands have a tropical monsoon climate, with a marked dry season. Manila has a typical monsoon climate. Of the average annual rainfall of 2,085 mm [82 in], around 1,930 mm [76 in] occurs between May and November. December to April is the dry season. Between August and October, much of the rain comes from typhoons (hurricanes).

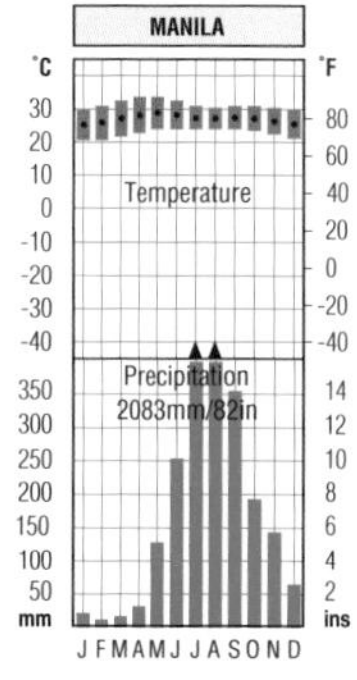

History

The earliest people to settle in the Philippines were probably Negritos, small groups of whom are still found in remote mountain areas. But most modern Filipinos are descendants of people who probably came from the Asian mainland more than 30,000 years ago. Little is known about the early history of the islands. However, most people were probably hunters and gatherers, except in the interior of northern Luzon, where the Igorot people built spectacular irrigated rice terraces contouring the mountain slopes. Most people practised animism, a mixture of monotheism and polytheism, and contacts with traders from China and Indonesia never led to the adoption of Buddhism or Hinduism. However, things changed from the 15th century, with the introduction of Islam to the southern islands.

The first European to reach the Philippines was Ferdinand Magellan in 1521. He was killed in a battle with local warriors and his round-the-world voyage was completed without him. Spanish explorers claimed the region in 1565 when they established their first permanent settlement on Cebu. Manila was founded in 1571. The Spaniards regarded their new territory as a stepping stone to the Spice Islands to the south, but their motives for colonization were not entirely commercial. Soon after the conquest of the islands, they converted most people (except for the Muslims on Mindanao and Sulu) to Roman Catholicism.

The economy grew from the late 18th century when the islands were opened up to foreign trade. Public education began in the 1860s, but in 1892 a secret revolutionary society was formed. Called Katipunan, it launched a revolt against Spanish rule in 1896. The revolt was put down and the rebel leader Emilio Aguinaldo left the country.

In April 1898, the United States declared war on Spain and the first major engagement was the destruction of all the Spanish ships in Manila Bay. Aguinaldo returned to the Philippines and formed an army which fought alongside the Americans. On 12 June, Aguinaldo proclaimed the Philippines an independent nation. A peace treaty between Spain and the United States was signed in December 1898 and the United States took over the government of the Philippines. However, Aguinaldo still wanted independence and fighting took place between 1899 and 1901, when Aguinaldo was captured.

Politics

The Philippines became a self-governing US Commonwealth in 1935 and the Act guaranteed the territory full independence after a ten-year transitional period. However, Japanese troops occupied the islands between 1942 and 1945, and the Philippines finally achieved independence on 4 July, 1946 though ties with the United States remained strong. The new country faced many problems, both economic and political. For example, the army had to put down a Communist rebellion between 1949 and 1954.

From 1946 until 1971, the country was governed under a constitution that was similar to that of the United States, with the president serving one four-year term in office. In 1971, constitutional changes were proposed, but before the new constitution had been ratified, President Ferdinand Marcos declared martial law in 1972. In 1977, the main opposition leader, Benigno Aquino Jr, was sentenced to death. He was allowed a stay of execution and went to the United States for medical treatment. Martial law was lifted in 1981, but Aquino was shot dead on his return to the Philippines in 1983.

Following presidential elections in 1986, Marcos was proclaimed president by the parliament, but the elections were proved to be fraudulent and his opponent, Corazon Aquino, Benigno Aquino's widow, became president. Having lost the support of the public and important figures in the church and armed forces, and charged with corruption, Marcos fled the country and a new constitution was introduced in 1987, restricting the president to one six-year term in office.

Attempts to overthrow Corazon Aquino failed, but she decided not to run for re-election in 1992 and was succeeded by Fidel Ramos, who had been her defence minister. Ramos was succeeded in 1998 by Joseph Estrada, a former film star. The economy, lacking any real natural resources, remains weak. Levels of unemployment and emigration among Filipinos remains high, though the Philippines did not suffer as much from the economic recession of 1997–8 as many other countries in eastern Asia. Attempts to end a guerrilla war waged by the Muslim Moro Islamic National Liberation Front ended in a peace agreement in 1996. However, Muslim demands for independence continued, with sporadic fighting on Mindanao and adjacent islands.

Economy

The Philippines is a developing country with a lower-middle-income economy. Agriculture employs 40% of the workforce. Rice and maize are the main food crops, while bananas, cassava, coconuts, coffee, cocoa, fruits, sugar cane, sweet potatoes and tobacco are also important. Farm animals include water buffaloes, goats and pigs. Forests cover nearly half of the land and forestry is a valuable industry. Sea fishing is also important and shellfish are obtained from inshore waters.

While agriculture accounted for 22% of the gross domestic product in 1995, manufacturing accounted for 23% of the GDP. Manufactures include chemicals, clothing and footwear, food products, petroleum and coal products. The chief exports include electronics, garments and coconut oil. Some coal, copper, gold, nickel and silver are mined. The leading trading partners are the United States, Japan and Singapore.

AREA	Ilocano 10%,
300,000 sq km	Hiligaynon Ilongo 9%, Bicol 6%
[115,300 sq mls]	**LANGUAGES**
POPULATION	Pilipino (Tagalog) and English
77,736,000	(both official), Spanish, others
CAPITAL (POPULATION)	**RELIGIONS**
Manila (Metro Manila,	Christianity (Roman Catholic
9,280,000)	84%, Philippine Independent
GOVERNMENT	Church or Aglipayan 6%,
Multiparty republic	Protestant 4%), Islam 4%
ETHNIC GROUPS	**CURRENCY**
Tagalog 30%, Cebuano 24%,	Philippine peso = 100 centavos

PHILIPPINES

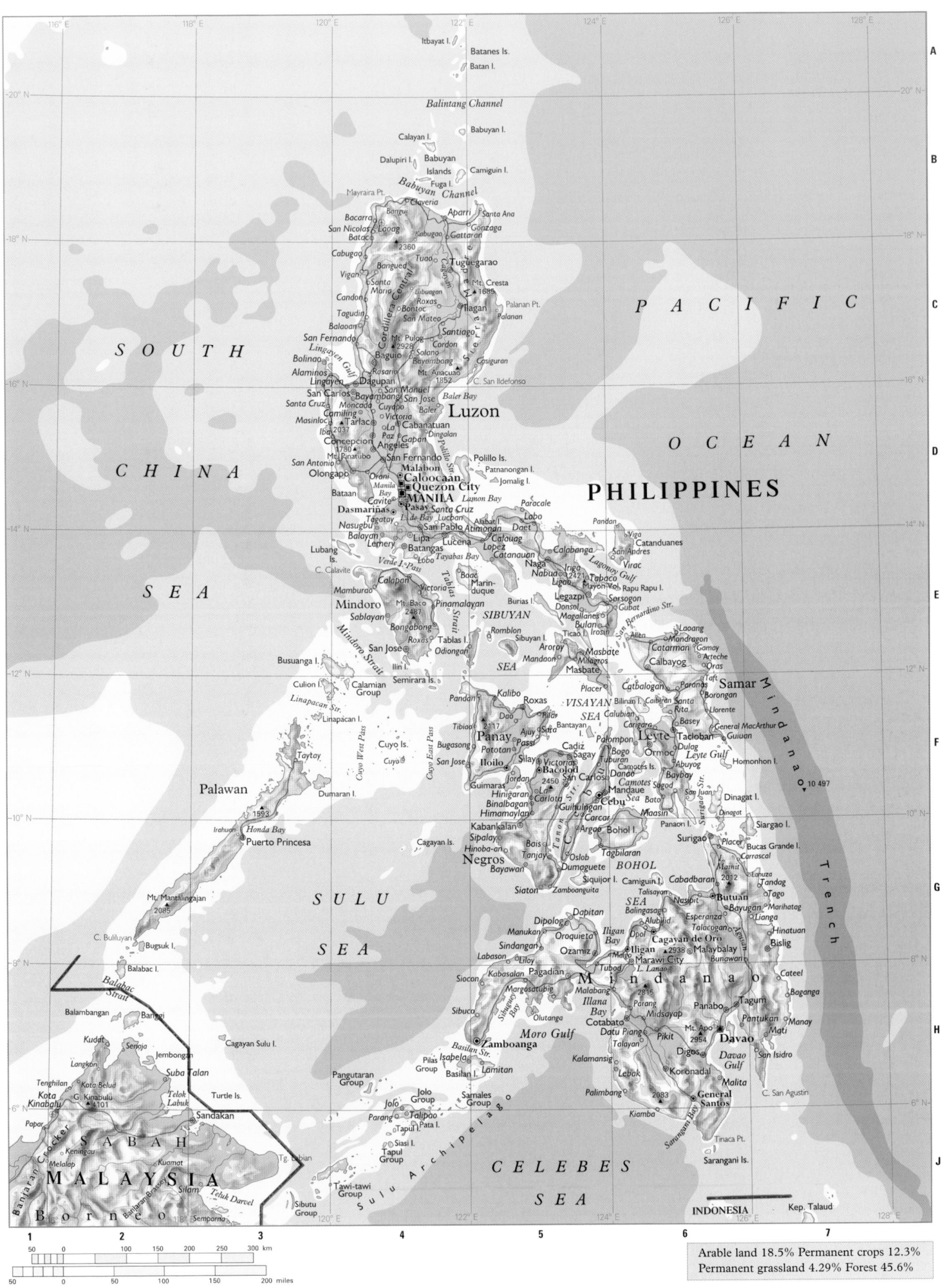

Arable land 18.5% Permanent crops 12.3%
Permanent grassland 4.29% Forest 45.6%

PITCAIRN – SEE PACIFIC OCEAN, PAGES 174–178

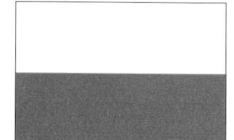

POLAND

Poland's flag was adopted when the country became a republic in 1919. Its colours were taken from the 13th-century coat of arms of a white eagle on a red field. This coat of arms still appears on Poland's merchant flag.

Arable land 47% Permanent crops 1.12%
Permanent grassland 13.3% Forest 28.9%

Geography

The Republic of Poland faces the Baltic Sea in north-central Europe. Behind the lagoon-fringed coast is a broad plain. Much of the soil is infertile, being made up of stony moraine (rock deposited by ice-sheets during the Ice Age). The plains of central Poland are more fertile.

The land rises to a plateau region in the south-east of the country. The Sudetey Highlands straddle the border with the Czech Republic. Part of the Carpathian Range lies on the south-eastern border with the Slovak Republic.

Climate

Poland's climate is influenced by its position in Europe. Warm, moist air masses come from the west, while cold air masses come from the north and east. Summers are warm, but winters are cold and snowy.

History

Poland's boundaries have changed several times in the last 200 years, partly as a result of its geographical location between the powers of Germany and Russia. It disappeared from the map in the late 18th century, when a Polish state called the Grand Duchy of Warsaw was set up. But in 1815, the country was partitioned, between Austria, Prussia and Russia. Poland became independent in 1918, but in 1939 it was divided between Germany and the Soviet Union. The country again became independent in 1945, when around 6 million people, or a massive 17% of its total population were lost, when Poland gave up territory to the Soviet Union and, in compensation, gained parts of Germany as far as the River Oder. As a result, Poland lost poor

agricultural land in the east and gained an important industrial region in the west, including in the south-west Silesia and the former German city of Breslau (now called Wroclaw), in the north-west the Baltic port of Stettin (now Szczecin), and in the north the other port of Danzig (now Gdánsk).

Acquisition of a length of Baltic coastline gave Poland an opportunity to develop maritime interests. Today the Polish fleets operate worldwide.

Politics

Communists took power in 1948, but opposition mounted and became focused through an organization called Solidarity.

Solidarity was led by a trade unionist, Lech Walesa. A coalition government was formed between Solidarity and the Communists in 1989. In 1990, the Communist Party was dissolved and Walesa became president. But Walesa faced many problems in turning Poland towards a market economy. Solidarity dividing in 1990 over personality and the speed of reform, and the adoption of its reforms was interrupted in 1993, when the former Communists won the parliamentary elections. In 1995, the ex-Communist Aleksander Krasniewski defeated Walesa in presidential elections, but he continued the westward-looking policies of his predecessor. Parliamentary elections in 1997 resulted in defeat for the reformed Communist government and the return of a right-wing coalition dominated by the Solidarity trade union. This coalition resumed the implementation of its reform programme, including changes in the country's administrative structure and a reform of the country's pension system. In 1999, Poland joined NATO and appeared to be on the fast track to becoming a member of the European Union.

Economy

Poland has large reserves of coal and deposits of various minerals which are used in its factories. Manufactures include chemicals, processed food, machinery, ships, steel and textiles. Major crops include barley, potatoes, rye, sugar beet and wheat. Machinery, metals, chemicals and fuels are the country's leading exports.

AREA	Ukrainian 1%,
312,680 sq km [120,726 sq mls]	German 1%
POPULATION	**LANGUAGES**
38,607,000	Polish (official)
CAPITAL (POPULATION)	**RELIGIONS**
Warsaw (Warszawa, 1,638,000)	Christianity
GOVERNMENT	(Roman Catholic 94%,
Multiparty republic	Orthodox 2%)
ETHNIC GROUPS	**CURRENCY**
Polish 98%,	Zloty = 100 groszy

PORTUGAL

Portugal's flag was adopted in 1910 when the country became a republic. The green represents Henry the Navigator (1394–1460), who sponsored many Portuguese explorers. The red symbolizes the monarchy. The shield reflects Portugal's leading role in world exploration.

Geography

The Republic of Portugal shares the Iberian Peninsula with Spain. It is the most westerly of Europe's mainland countries. The land rises from the coastal plains on the Atlantic Ocean to the western edge of the huge plateau, or *Meseta*, which occupies most of the Iberian Peninsula. In central Portugal, the Sera da Estrela contains Portugal's highest point, at 1,993 m [6,537 ft]. Portugal also contains two autonomous regions, the Azores and Madeira Island groups.

Climate

The climate is moderated by winds blowing from the Atlantic Ocean. Summers are cooler and winters are milder than in other Mediterranean lands.

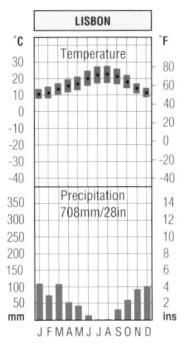

PORTUGAL (LISBON)

The west coast of the Iberian Peninsula has the oceanic variety of a Mediterranean climate with cooler summers, milder winters and a smaller temperature range than in true Mediterranean lands. Sunshine at Lisbon is abundant, averaging 7.5 hours a day all year. Frosts are rare, and temperatures over 30°C [86°F] have been recorded from March to September, and over 40°C [104°F] in July and August. Most rain falls in the winter half of the year, with July and August being virtually rainless. The severity of the summer drought decreases from south to north.

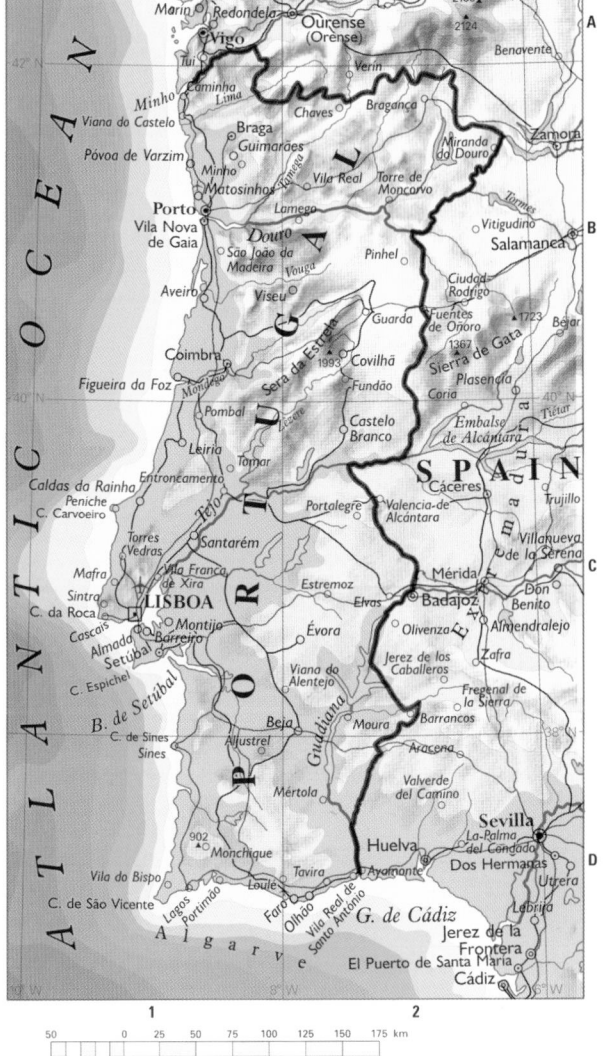

History

The Romans completed their conquest of the Iberian Peninsula, including Portugal, around 2,000 years ago and Christianity was introduced in the 4th century AD. The Romans called Portugal *Lusitania*. Following the collapse of the Roman Empire in the 5th century, Portugal was conquered by the Visigoths, who were Christians, but in the early 8th century, the Iberian Peninsula was conquered by Muslim Moors. The Christians strove to drive out the Muslims and, by the mid-13th century, they had retaken Portugal and most of Spain.

In 1143, Portugal became a separate country, independent from Spain. In the 15th century, the Portuguese, who were skilled navigators, led the 'Age of Exploration', pioneering routes around Africa onwards to Asia. Portugal set up colonies in Africa and Asia, though the biggest prize was Brazil in South America. Portugal became wealthy through trade and the exploitation of its colonies, but its power began to decline in the 16th century, when it could no longer defend its far-flung empire. Spain ruled Portugal from 1580 to 1640, when Portugal's independence was restored by John, Duke of Braganza, who took the title of John IV. England supported Portuguese independence and several times defended it from invasion or threats by Spain and its allies. However, in 1822, Portugal suffered a major blow when it lost Brazil. Portugal became a republic in 1910, but its first attempts at democracy led to great instability. Portugal fought alongside the Allies in World War I.

Politics

A coup in 1926 brought an army group to power. They abolished the parliament and set up a dictatorial regime. In 1928, they selected António de Oliviera Salazar, an economist, as minister of finance. He became prime minister in 1932 and ruled as a dictator from 1933. After World War II, when other European powers began to grant independence to their colonies, Salazar was determined to maintain his country's empire. Colonial wars flared up and weakened Portugal's economy. Salazar suffered a stroke in 1968 and died two years later. His successor, Marcello Caetano, was overthrown by another military coup in 1974 and the new military leaders set about granting independence to Portugal's colonies. Free elections were held in 1978 and full democracy was restored in 1982, when a new constitution abolished the military Council of the Revolution and reduced the powers of the president.

Portugal joined the European Community (now the European Union) in 1986, and on 1 January 1999 it became one of the 11 EU countries to adopt the euro, the single currency of the EU. However, although its economy was growing strongly in the late 1990s, Portugal remains one of the EU's poorer members, with the comparatively low per capita gross national product of US $10,450 in 1997.

Economy

Agriculture and fishing were the mainstays of the economy until the mid-20th century. But manufacturing is now the most valuable sector. Textiles, processed food, paper products and machinery are important manufactures. Major crops include grapes for wine-making, olives, potatoes, rice, maize and wheat. Cattle and other livestock are raised and fishing catches include cod, sardines and tuna.

AREA	Cape Verdean, Brazilian,
92,390 sq km	Spanish, British
[35,670 sq mls]	**LANGUAGES**
POPULATION	Portuguese (official)
9,928,000	**RELIGIONS**
CAPITAL (POPULATION)	Christianity (Roman
Lisbon (Lisboa, 2,561,000)	Catholic 95%, other
GOVERNMENT	Christians 2%)
Multiparty republic	**CURRENCY**
ETHNIC GROUPS	Euro; Escudo
Portuguese 99%,	= 100 centavos

PUERTO RICO – SEE CARIBBEAN SEA, PAGES 71–76; QATAR – SEE GULF STATES, PAGES 113–114; REUNION – SEE INDIAN OCEAN, PAGES 122–123

ROMANIA

Romania's flag, adopted in 1948, uses colours from the arms of the provinces, which united in 1861 to form Romania. A central coat of arms, added in 1965, was deleted in 1990 after the fall of the Communist regime under the dictator Nicolae Ceaucescu.

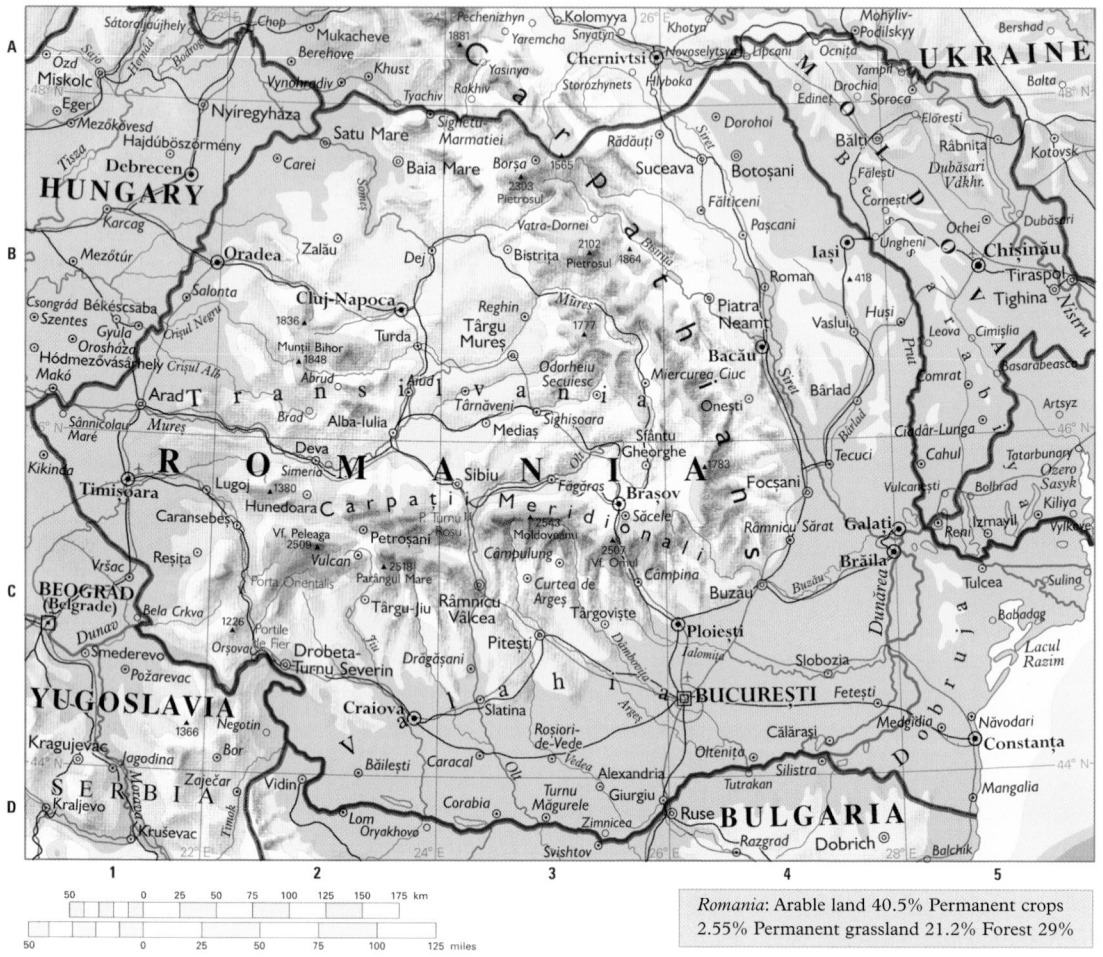

Romania: Arable land 40.5% Permanent crops 2.55% Permanent grassland 21.2% Forest 29%

lowlands and the plateaux. In the mountains, the vegetation changes with the altitude. Oaks are the dominant trees up to about 800 m [2,600 ft] above sea level, while beeches predominate between 800 m and 1,400 m [2,600–4,600 ft]. Conifers grow from between 1,400 m and 1,800 m [4,600–5,900 ft]. At the highest levels there are alpine and sub-alpine pastures. By contrast, the Danube Delta, a massive marshland region, contains large regions of reeds, which form floating or fixed islands of decaying vegetation, while feather grass and other steppe species grow on sandy areas.

History

Around 2,300 years ago, Romania was called Dacia, after the local Dacian people. But after the Romans conquered the area in AD 106, the Dacians embraced Roman culture and the Latin language so completely that the region then became known as Romania. After the fall of the Roman Empire, Romania was invaded many times. The first step towards the creation of the modern state occurred in the 14th century when two principalities (states ruled by princes) were formed: Walachia (or Valachi) in the south and Moldavia in the east. But they were conquered by the Ottoman Turks around 1500.

From the late 18th century, the Turkish Empire began to break up. The modern history of Romania began in 1861 when Walachia and Moldavia united. After World War I (1914–18), Romania, which had fought on the side of the victorious Allies, obtained large areas, including Transylvania, where most people were Romanians. This almost doubled the country's size and population. In 1939, Romania lost territory to Bulgaria, Hungary and the Soviet Union. Romania fought alongside Germany in World War II, and Soviet troops occupied the country in 1944. Hungary returned northern Transylvania to Romania in 1945, but Bulgaria and the Soviet Union kept former Romanian territory when King Michael was forcibly removed from the throne. During the 1950s, the Soviet Union maintained a tight control over their satellite. But in the 1960s, Romania's Communist Party, led by Gheorghe Gheorghiu-Dej, began to oppose Soviet control. This policy was carried on by Nicolae Ceaucescu, who became the Communist Party chief after the death of Gheorghiu-Dej in 1965.

Under Ceaucescu, Romania began to develop industries based on the oil and natural gas reserves on the flanks of the Transylvanian Alps. However, Ceaucescu's rule was one of the most odious in the Communist world. Corrupt and self-seeking, he nevertheless won plaudits from the West for his independent stance against Soviet control – including a knighthood from Queen Elizabeth II. But while he distanced Romania from Soviet foreign aims, he pursued a strict Stalinist approach on the domestic front. The remorseless industrialization and urbanization programmes of the 1970s caused a severe debt problem and, in the 1980s, he modified his policies, cutting imports and diverting output to exports. But while Romania achieved the

Geography and Climate

Romania is a country on the Black Sea in eastern Europe. Eastern and southern Romania form part of the Danube River Basin. The delta region, near the mouths of the Danube, where the river flows into the Black Sea, is one of Europe's finest wetlands. The southern part of the coast contains several resorts.

The country is dominated by a great arc of fold mountains, the Carpathians, which curve around the plateaux of Transylvania in central Romania. The southern arm of the mountains, which rise to 2,543 m [8,341 ft] at Mount Moldoveanu, is known as the Transylvanian Alps. On the Yugoslav border, the River Danube (Dunav/Dunărea) has cut a gorge – the Iron Gate (Portile de Fier) – whose rapids are tamed by the building of a huge dam.

Romania has hot summers and cold winters. The rainfall is heaviest in spring and early summer, when thundery showers are common.

ROMANIA (BUCHAREST)

In general, central Europe has a large seasonal range of temperature and a summer rainfall maximum. Winter depressions, which bring much rain to north-west Europe, are mostly prevented from reaching the east by high pressure. At Bucharest, the heaviest rains fall as thundery showers in spring and early summer, when the air warms rapidly. Romania is one of the sunniest parts of Europe.

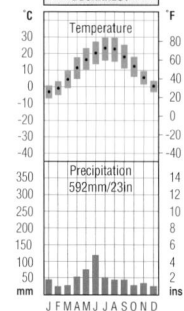

Vegetation

Forests cover large areas, creating fairy-tale landscapes in Transylvania and the Carpathians, while farmland dominates in the Danubian enviable status of a net creditor, its people – brainwashed by incessant propaganda – were reduced from self-sufficiency to subsistence and shortages, with food and energy both savagely rationed.

Meanwhile, with many of his relations in positions of power, Ceaucescu built ghetto-like 'agro-industrial' housing complexes, desecrating some of the country's finest architecture and demolishing thousands of villages in the process. In December 1989, mass anti-government demonstrations were held in Timisoara and protests spread across Romania. Security forces fired on crowds, causing many deaths. But after army units joined the protests, Nicolae Ceaucescu and his wife Elena fled from Bucharest on 22 December. Both were executed on Christmas Day on charges of genocide and corruption.

Politics

A provisional government of the National Salvation Front (NSF), which had been founded only on 22 December 1989, took control of the government. Much of the old administrative apparatus was dismantled, the Communist Party was dissolved, and religion was re-legalized. In May 1990, under Ion Iliescu, the NSF won Romania's first free elections since World War II by a huge majority – a result that international observers judged flawed but not fraudulent.

A new constitution enshrining pluralist democracy, human rights and a market economy was passed by parliament in November 1991. Though not special by contemporary eastern European standards, it was a far cry from the despotic rule of Nicolae Ceaucescu. However, the NSF contained many old-guard Communists and its credibility sank further when Iliescu used miners to curb anti-government demonstrations. Strikes and protests continued, not only against the new authorities, but also against the effects of a gradual but nevertheless marked switch to a market economy, which had caused food shortages, rampant inflation and increasing unemployment. In addition, foreign investment was sluggish, deterred by the political instability. Presidential elections in 1996 led to defeat for Iliescu and victory for Emil Constantinescu of the centre-right Democratic Convention of Romania (CDR). The CDR also emerged as the largest

party in parliamentary elections. This made Romania the last country in eastern Europe, apart from the rump Yugoslavia, to replace a regime that was closely associated with Communism with a democratic regime.

One problem faced by Romania concerns the independent nation of Moldova on the country's eastern border. Two-thirds of Moldovans speak Romanian, the country's official language. Some people on both sides of the border favour reunification. This led to conflict after the break-up of the Soviet Union in 1991. Another problem facing Romania concerns the status of the Hungarian ethnic minority in the west.

Economy

According to the World Bank, Romania is a 'lower-middle-income' economy. Under Communist rule, industry, including mining and manufacturing, became more important than agriculture. Oil and natural gas are the chief mineral resources, but the aluminium, copper, lead and zinc industries use domestic supplies, and the iron and steel industry relies on imported ores. Besides metals, Romania also manufactures cement, processed food, petroleum products, textiles and wood products. Agriculture employs nearly a third of the workforce. Crops include fruits, maize, potatoes, sugar beet and wheat. Sheep are the chief livestock. Romania's leading exports include textiles, mineral products, chemicals, machinery and footwear. The country's chief trading partners include Germany, Italy, Russia and France.

AREA	Hungarian 7%, Gypsy 2%
237,500 sq km [91,699 sq mls]	**LANGUAGES**
POPULATION	Romanian (official),
22,396,000	Hungarian
CAPITAL (POPULATION)	**RELIGIONS**
Bucharest (Bucuresti, 2,061,000)	Christianity (Romanian
GOVERNMENT	Orthodox 87%, Roman Catholic
Multiparty republic	5%, Greek Orthodox 4%)
ETHNIC GROUPS	**CURRENCY**
Romanian 89%,	Romanian leu = 100 bani

MOLDOVA

Geography and Climate

The Republic of Moldova is a small country sandwiched between Ukraine and Romania. It was formerly one of the 15 republics that made up the Soviet Union. Much of the land is hilly and the highest areas are near the centre of the country.

Moldova has a moderately continental climate, with warm summers and fairly cold winters when temperatures dip below freezing point. Most of the rain comes in the warmer months.

History

In the 14th century, the Moldavians formed a state called Moldavia. It included part of Romania and Bessarabia (now the modern country of Moldova). The Ottoman Turks took the area in the 16th century, but in 1812 Russia took over Bessarabia. In 1861, Moldavia and Walachia united to form Romania. Russia retook southern Bessarabia in 1878.

After World War I (1914–18), all of Bessarabia was returned to Romania, but the Soviet Union did not recognize this act. From 1944, the Moldovan Soviet Socialist Republic was part of the Soviet Union.

Politics

In 1989, the Moldovans asserted their independence and ethnicity by making Romanian the official language and, at the end of 1991, Moldova became independent. Moldova is ethnically complex. It combines the Moldavian part of Ukraine with the larger Bessarabia – the section of Romania between the Prut and Nistru (Dnister) rivers. Its majority Moldovan population is ethnically Romanian, and there are people on both sides who favour reunification. This is opposed by Russians, Ukrainians and, in the south, by the Gagauz, the Christian Orthodox Turks. In 1992, fighting occurred between Moldovans and

Russians in Trans-Dnestr, the mainly Russian-speaking area east of the River Dnestr, and a joint Moldovan-Russian peace-keeping force was established to restore order.

In 1994, Moldova adopted a new constitution making the country a democratic republic. On 1 January, 1997, a former Communist, Petru Lucinschi, became president. In parliamentary elections in 1998, the Party of the Moldovan Communists (PCM) won the highest share of the votes. However, it was forced into opposition by the creation of a loose centre-right coalition named the Alliance for Democratic Rights.

Economy

Moldova is a fertile country in which agriculture remains central to the economy. Major products include fruits, maize, tobacco and wine.

There are few natural resources within Moldova, and the government imports materials and fuels for its industries. Light industries, such as food processing and the manufacturing of household appliances, are gradually expanding.

AREA	**ETHNIC GROUPS**
33,700 sq km	Moldovan 65%, Ukrainian 14%,
[13,010 sq mls]	Russian 13%, Gagauz 4%,
POPULATION	Jewish 2%, Bulgarian
4,458,000	**LANGUAGES**
CAPITAL (POPULATION)	Moldovan/Romanian (official)
Chişinău	**RELIGIONS**
(700,000)	Christianity (Eastern Orthodox)
GOVERNMENT	**CURRENCY**
Multiparty republic	Leu = 100 bani

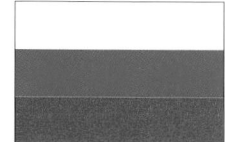

In August 1991, Russia's traditional flag, which had first been used in 1699, was restored as Russia's national flag. It uses colours from the flag of the Netherlands. This flag was suppressed when Russia was part of the Soviet Union.

Geography and Climate

Russia is the world's largest country. About 25% lies west of the Ural Mountains (Uralskie Gory) in European Russia, where 80% of the population lives. It is an indication of the size of the former Soviet Union that, having shed nearly a quarter of its area with the departure of the 14 republics in 1991, the remaining Russian Federation (as the country is also officially called) remains by far the largest country in the world.

Diversity certainly characterizes Russia's landforms. Within its borders are rugged peaks and salt flats, glaciers and deserts, marshes and rolling hills, as well as broad level plains. In the west, the North European Plain occupies the greater part of European Russia, as well as much of Ukraine, all of Belarus and the three Baltic states. On the eastern side of the plain are the Ural Mountains, an ancient, heavy eroded range that forms the geographical divide between Europe and

SMALL ADMINISTRATIVE
SUB-DIVISIONS
WITHIN RUSSIA

1 Adygea
2 Karachey-Cherkessia
3 Kabardino-Balkaria
4 North Ossetia
5 Ingushetia
6 Chechenia
7 Dagestan
8 Mordvinia
9 Chuvashia
10 Mari El
11 Tatarstan
12 Udmurtia
13 Khakassia

Asia. The Urals have few peaks rising above 1,600 m [5,248 ft]. The eastern slopes of the Ural Mountains merge into the West Siberian lowland, the largest plain in the world, with extensive low-lying marshes. The plains of Russia are surrounded on the south and east by mountain ranges. In the south, the Caucasus Mountains on the borders of Azerbaijan and Georgia contain Russia's highest peak, Mount Elbrus, which rises 5,642 m [18,506 ft] above sea level. In the east, the Altai (Altay) and Sayan ranges extend into Mongolia, while beyond Lake Baykal, the world's deepest lake, and the River Lena are the East Siberian ranges in the eastern extremity of the Asian landmass. The Kamchatka Peninsula is geologically unstable – being part of the

'Pacific ring of fire' – and earthquakes and volcanic eruptions are very common.

Much of Russia's landscape bears the imprint of the last Ice Age in the form of chaotic drainage systems, extensive marshlands, lakes and moraines in lowland areas, and cirques and U-shaped valleys in the mountains. Over half of the total area has permafrost – permanently frozen ground which may extend hundreds of metres in depth. The rivers that flow across the Russian plains are among the longest and most languid in the world. Drainage in European Russia forms a radial pattern, with the hub in the Central Uplands west of Moscow. The Volga, Europe's longest river at 3,700 km [2,300 mls], flows from

Arable land 7.72% Permanent crops 0.12%
Permanent grassland 5.17% Forest 45.4%

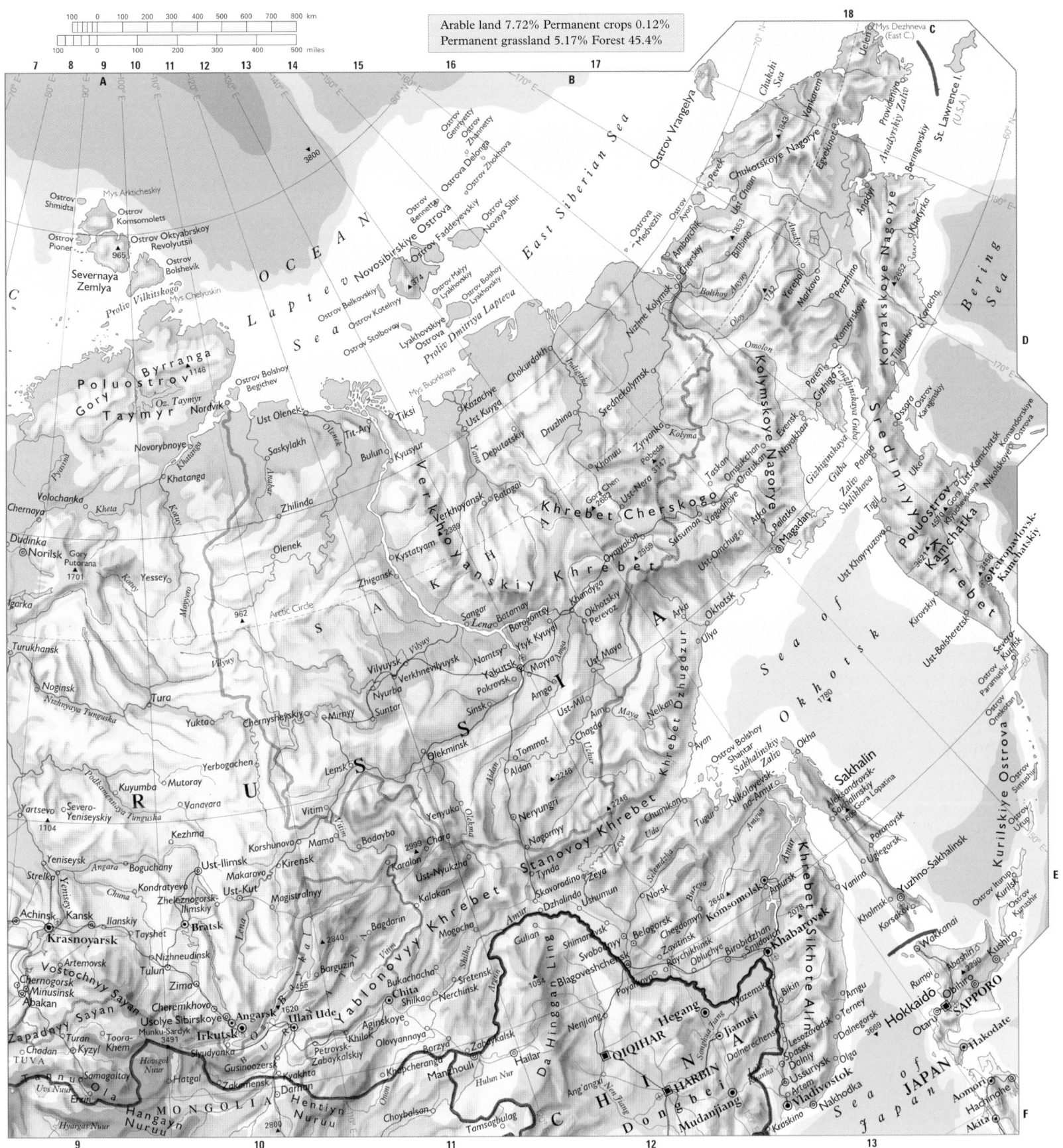

RUSSIA

this area south to the landlocked Caspian Sea, the world's largest inland body of water. The main rivers in Siberia flow north to the Arctic. They include the Yenisey-Angara, the Ob-Irtysh and the Lena, which are, respectively, the fifth, sixth and 11th longest in the world. Another major river in eastern Siberia, the Amur, is formed by the joining of the Argun and Shilka rivers. The Amur forms much of Russia's border with China before turning north and emptying into the Tatar Strait, a stretch of water separating Siberia from Sakhalin Island.

Moscow has a continental climate with cold and snowy winters and warm summers. Krasnoyarsk in south-central Siberia has a harsher, drier climate, but it is not as severe as parts of northern Siberia.

RUSSIA – MOSCOW

Despite a large temperature range and cold winters, Moscow has a less extreme continental climate than more easterly regions. Prevailing westerly winds and an absence of mountains allow the Atlantic Ocean to extend its influence deep into the continent. Rainfall is uniform, with a slight summer maximum. Winters are cloudy with frequent snow and a very small daily variation in temperature.

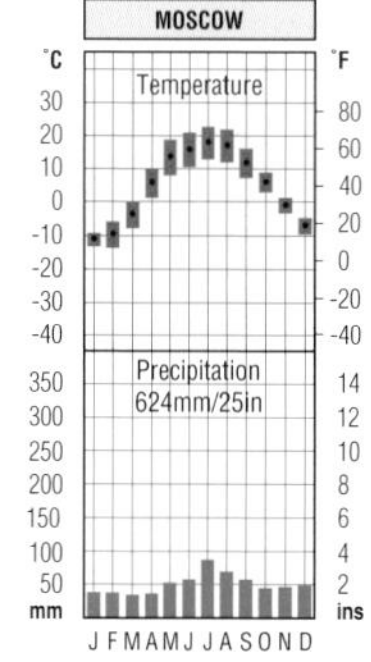

KRASNOYARSK

The climate of Krasnoyarsk is harsh. There are sub-zero temperature averages for seven months, October to April, with low records exceeding –30°C [–22°F]. Summers are not too warm, though a temperature of over 40°C [104°F] has been measured in July. The annual range of temperature is 36°C [65°F]. Snow lies on the ground for over six months of the year, but the amounts are not great. The rainfall total is low.

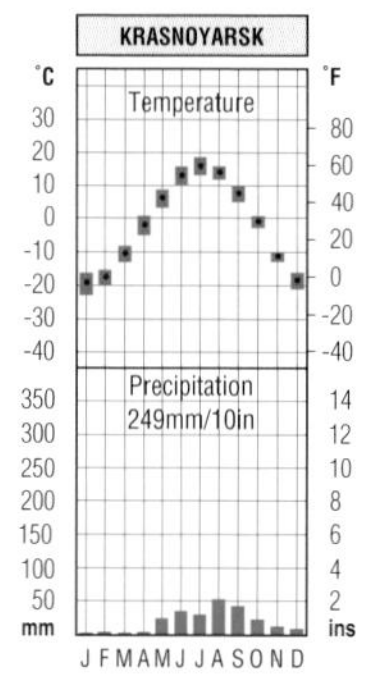

VLADIVOSTOK

The prevailing winds in winter from the north-west give low temperatures to Vladivostok. Temperatures below –20°C [–4°F] have been recorded from November to March. Snow usually lies from mid-December to mid-February. There are many foggy days in May to July, making the sunshine totals lower in summer than winter. Rainfall is low, with the monthly total exceeding 100 mm [4 in] from July to September.

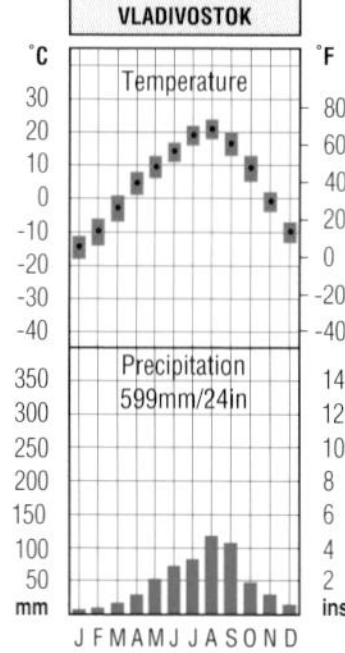

Vegetation

Extending latitudinally across Russia, and corresponding to the major climatic belts, are a series of sharply differentiated natural zones. These zones can also be seen as vertical bands on high mountains. The first of these zones is the tundra, which stretches north of the Arctic Circle from the Norwegian border to the Kamchatka Peninsula. Climatic conditions here restrict plant growth and soil formation, so that the region well deserves its name 'bald mountain top', the meaning of the term tundra in the Sami (Lapp) language. Stunted shrubs, mosses, lichens and berry-bearing bushes growing in thin, infertile soils form the vegetation cover, supporting the herds of reindeer which, for hundreds of years, have formed the basis of the local people's economy.

Extending south of the tundra, and occupying about 60% of the country, are the coniferous forests of fir, pine, silver fir, cedar and Siberian larch, that make up a region called the taiga. This is the world's largest forest covering an area more than three times that of the Amazonian rainforest. Marshes are common in the taiga, especially in western Siberia. The wildlife of the taiga includes fur-bearing animals, such as ermine, sable and beaver.

In the west and east, the coniferous forests merge into zones of mixed forests, the third main vegetation zone. These forests contain coniferous trees together with such broad-leaved trees as beech, horn-

beam, maple and oak. Much of this mixed forest has been cleared for farming.

The fourth main vegetation zone is the steppe, which is sandwiched between the forests to the north, and the semi-deserts and deserts of the central Asian republics to the south. Hardly any of the natural grassland vegetation of the steppes has survived, since vast expanses have been brought under the plough. The soils of the steppe are chernozems, or black earths. They are the most fertile in the world.

History

The present size of Russia is a product of a long period of evolution. In the 9th century AD, a state called Kievan Rus was formed at the junction of the forest and the steppe in what is now Ukraine. As time went by, other states were formed further to the north. All were eventually united under the principality of Muscovy. In the 13th century, Mongol armies from the east penetrated the forests and held sway over the Slavic peoples there. It was only in the 16th century that the Mongol yoke was thrown off as the Slavs, under Ivan the Terrible (1530–84), began to advance across the steppes.

This signalled the beginning of a period of expansion from the core area of Slavic settlement to the south, east and west. Expansion across Siberia was rapid and the first Russian settlement on the Pacific, Okhotsk, was established in 1649. Progress across the open steppe was slower but, by 1696, Azov, the key to the Black Sea, was secured. A series of struggles in the 17th and 18th centuries against the Swedes and the Poles resulted in the addition of the Gulf of Finland, the Baltic coast and part of Poland to the growing Russian Empire, while, in the 19th century, the Caucasus, Central Asia and new territories in the Far East were added.

Russia had been a centralized state throughout its history, although many Russians began to demand reforms in the 19th century. A major historic landmark, and indeed a major event in world history, took place towards the end of World War I. This was the 1917 Russian Revolution, when Tsar Nicholas II was forced to abdicate and a Bolshevik (Communist) government was established under Vladimir Lenin (1870–1924). The years following the Revolution witnessed many changes, including the establishment of the Union of Soviet Socialist Republics (also called the USSR or the Soviet Union) in 1922. The most dramatic and far-reaching changes took place from the 1930s, when Joseph Stalin (1879–1953) instituted central planning of the economy, collectivized agriculture and began a period of rapid industrialization. After Stalin's death, the Soviet leaders modified some

Lake Baykal
With a lowest point of 1,620 m [5,315 ft], Lake (Oz) Baykal in southern Siberia is the world's deepest lake. Also the largest in Eurasia – at 636 km [395 mls] long by an average width of 48 km [30 mls] – it measures some 31,500 sq km [12,160 sq mls] more than the area of Belgium. It is so deep that it is the world's largest body of fresh water and indeed contains no less than a fifth of the fresh water contained in all the world's lakes. Its volume of 23,000 cu km [5,520 cu mls] is as much as the five Great Lakes of North America combined.

Situated in a deep tectonic basin, and fed by 336 rivers and streams, it acts as a reservoir for only one river: the Angara, which flows north to join the Yenisey. Though renowned for its purity and endemic lifeforms (65% of its 1,500 animal species and 35% of its plant species are unique to Lake Baykal), industrial plants have caused increasing pollution since the 1960s.

The graben fault that hosts the arc-shaped lake was caused by gigantic upheavals in the Earth's crust some 80 million years ago. When the climate turned wetter, about 25 million years ago, the lake began to fill – and it is still getting larger. When the sarma wind blows from the north-west, it generates waves over 5 m [16.5 ft] high. Located 80 km [50 mls] from the Mongolian border, Baykal drains an area of 540,000 sq km [208,500 sq mls] – 13% more than the area drained by all five of North America's Great Lakes.

policies, but they remained true to the principles of Communism until Mikhail Gorbachev changed the face of Russia in the 1980s.

The state that the Communists inherited in 1917 was not merely large, but was also made up of peoples of very diverse ethnic, religious and cultural backgrounds. Among the varied peoples – speaking more than 100 languages – the Slavs, consisting of the Russians, Ukrainians and Belarussians, were the most numerous. Other groups include the Turkic and Persian peoples of Central Asia, Finno-Ugrians, Mongols and many others. Under Soviet rule, the ethnic diversity of the nation was recognized by the existence of federal republics (of very disparate size), autonomous republics and regions set up to recognize smaller ethnic groups. Although Russia is inhabited throughout, the greatest concentration of people has, traditionally, been in the European part. It was here that the first Russian towns, with their fortresses (kremlins) and onion-domed churches, were founded. Outside this settled core, there were towns and cities which the Russians acquired during their expansion, or themselves established on the frontiers.

After the Revolution, changes took place in the distribution of the population so that the former pattern of a small highly populated core and 'empty' periphery began to break down. Today, the settled area extends into southern Siberia and, in a narrow band, across to the Pacific Ocean. As a result, a far higher proportion of the Russian population is to be found east of the Ural Mountains than before the Revolution, and even before World War II. The redistribution was actively encouraged by a regime committed to a policy of developing the east. Migration to the towns and cities has also been marked since 1917, so that, by 1997, some 73% of the population lived in cities and towns. The capital Moscow, like the other cities of the North European Plain, is a mixture of old and new, but Moscow is also a blend of European and Asian styles and cultures.

Under Communism, the country was transformed from an underdeveloped nation into a powerful industrial one. In 1917, most industrial development was concentrated in a few centres in the European part of the country, including Moscow, St Petersburg and the Donbas region of the Ukraine. As in many other parts of the world, industrialization was initially based on the iron and steel industry. In the 1930s, heavy national investment went into expanding production in the already existing industrial areas of European Russia, and establishing industry in central and eastern Russia. For example, new, large integrated steel mills were built in the southern Urals and on the Kuzbas coalfield in western Siberia. The shift away from coal as a basis for industrial development to alternative energy sources took place later in the Soviet Union than in many other countries. From the 1960s, however, petroleum and natural gas industries began to develop rapidly and the same was true of industries based on hydroelectric power. Hydroelectric power was especially important in building up industry in eastern Siberia, where massive installations on the River Angara provided energy for aluminium production. Although the introduction of large-scale industry into formerly backward areas helped to even out levels of development, regional imbalances remained large. The pre-revolutionary foci of development continued to attract a large proportion of available investment and this has meant that, of the regions developed since the Revolution, only western Siberia can be said today to have a well-developed, mature industrial structure.

While overall industrial production forged ahead, agriculture was the 'Achilles heel' of the Soviet economy and, in several years from the mid-1960s, foreign grain had to be imported. Soviet farms were of two types: collective (kolkhozi) and state (sovkhozi). The former were, according to the definition, democratically run producers' co-operatives which, in return for a grant of land, delivered some of their produce to the state. In theory free to run their affairs, they were always subject to government interference. The state farms were state-owned and state-managed. While the greater part of the total Soviet agricultural output came from collective and state farms, a large share of market garden produce and some livestock products originated on the so-called personal plots.

In the drive for economic development, the Soviet government neglected the consumer sector. For example, growth rates in textiles, food industries and wood processing lagged behind those for iron and steel production. The paucity of consumer goods, often compounded by gross inefficiencies in the state distribution system, was obvious in the size of queues that formed whenever any scarce product came on sale. Another indication was the existence of a flourishing black market.

During Stalin's rule, a conscious policy to restrict foreign trade and maximize self-sufficiency was pursued. With the formation of COMECON (the eastern trading bloc) and the realization that much of Western technology would be useful to its own continued development, the Soviet Union revised its policy. By the 1980s, the Soviet Union had begun to trade with most countries of the world, though its share of the total turnover of world trade was small.

Politics

The 1980s was a time of change when Mikhail Gorbachev sought to introduce economic and political reforms necessitated by the failures of Communist economic policies. Two Russian words, which seemed to sum up Gorbachev's efforts at reform, became well known internationally. They were glasnost, meaning 'openness', and perestroika, meaning 'restructuring'. When the Soviet Union broke up in December 1991, the consequence of growing unrest, mounting nationalism and acute economic problems were experienced and Russia maintained contact with 11 of the 15 former Soviet republics through a loose confederation called the Commonwealth of Independent States (CIS).

Despite Gorbachev's brave efforts at reform, his successor Boris Yeltsin inherited an economy in crisis, bogged down by lumbering and often obstructive bureaucracy, inept use of resources and an inefficient transport system. After the abolition of price controls sent the cost of basic commodities rocketing, the early 1990s saw food shortages worsen and unemployment rise. However, despite these many difficulties, which also included a rise in corruption and crime, the people backed the government's programme of reforms in a referendum in 1993 and returned Yeltsin as president in July 1996, defeating his Communist opponent Gennady Zyuganov in the second round of voting.

The Kuril Islands (Kurilskiye Ostrova)

A chain of 56 windswept, volcanically active islands extending 1,200 km [750 mls] between the end of Russia's Kamchatka Peninsula and the tip of Japan's northern island of Hokkaido, the Kurils separate the Sea of Okhotsk from the Pacific Ocean. With a total area of 15,600 sq km [6,000 sq mls], the islands have a stormy, foggy climate – the consequence of a cold offshore current, which comes from the Arctic.

When they were first visited by the Dutch in 1634, the islands were sparsely populated by a people called the Ainu, who are related to the Ainu of Hokkaido, Japan. Russian fur traders founded a station on the islands in 1795 and Russia claimed the northern islands in 1830. The Kurils were ceded to Japan in 1875 when Japan traded the Russians the southern half of Sakhalin Island for the Kurils. At the end of World War II, Soviet forces seized the islands, giving the Soviet Union ice-free northern access to the Pacific Ocean. However, the Japanese still regard the southern section, consisting of Etorofu, Kunashir, Shikotan and the Habomai islets, as theirs, referring to them as the 'northern territories' and allotting 7 February as a national day in their honour.

Although there are rich fishing grounds in the territorial waters and the possibility of mineral wealth, it is indeed a matter of honour rather than economics for Tokyo. The Soviets offered to return Shikotan and the Habomai islands in 1956, but the Japanese held out for all four, and the offer was withdrawn. While the advent of Gorbachev and glasnost made little difference, the deconstruction of the Soviet Union has: Boris Yeltsin's Russia, desperate for substantial Japanese aid and co-operation, found the islands a stumbling block to assistance. However, more than half of the population who have moved there since 1945 are Russian, and in a 1991 poll the islanders voted 4–1 to remain under Moscow's control.

Republics of Russia

1 KABARDINO-BALKARIA
2 NORTH OSSETIA
3 INGUSHETIA
4 CHECHENIA
5 ADYGEA
6 KARACHEY-CHERKESSIA
- - - Republic boundary
······ Autonomous okrug boundary

However, Yeltsin, who was known to be in poor health, resigned on 31 December 1999 and appointed the prime minister Vladimir Putin as the acting president. Putin, who was elected president by a landslide in March 2000, faced many problems. Besides finding solutions to the country's profound economic problems, Putin also has to maintain national unity in a country consisting of 21 republics, six territories and 49 provinces. Fighting began in the secessionist Chechen Republic during the 1990s and flared up into full-scale war in 1999 and 2000, when Russian troops occupied the capital Groznyy with much loss of life.

Economy

In the early 1990s, the break-up of the Soviet Union and the ongoing government policies to privatize agriculture and industry threw Russia's economy into disarray and, according to World Bank data, the country was ranked as a 'middle-income' economy. Russia was admitted to the Council of Europe in 1997, essentially to discourage instability in the Caucasus region. More significantly still, Boris Yeltsin was invited to attend the G7 summit in Denver in 1997. The summit became known as the 'Summit of Eight' and it appeared that Russia would thereafter be included in future meetings of the world's most powerful economies.

Industry is the most valuable activity and manufacturing and mining account for 31% of the gross national product, as compared with nearly 9% from agriculture. Under Communism, manufacturing in the Soviet Union was much less efficient than in the West and the emphasis was firmly on heavy industry. But today, light industry, producing a wide range of consumer goods, is becoming increasingly important. Mining remains important and the country's massive resources include oil and natural gas. Russia ranks first in natural gas production and third in oil. It also ranks among the world's top ten producers of chromite, coal, copper, diamonds, gold, phosphate rock, iron ore, molybdenum, nickel, potash, silver, tin ore, tungsten and uranium. Other natural resources include vast forests, which supply coniferous wood and wood pulp, and it has great hydroelectrical potential.

Agriculture employs approximately 14% of the workforce. Grains are very important and Russia remains one of the world's top producers of barley, oats, rye and wheat. The country is also a major producer of butter, cattle, cheese, eggs, milk, pigs, potatoes and other vegetables, sheep, sunflower seeds and wool. However, Russia periodically has to import the food that it needs. Fishing is also very important and Russia ranks sixth among the world's leading fishing nations.

In 1997, Russia had the world's 12th largest economy. The leading exports include fuels and lubricants, metals, machinery and transport equipment, chemicals, precious metals and wood products. Before the break-up of the Soviet Union, much of the country's foreign trade was with its satellite countries in eastern Europe, but, although these countries remain important, the leading trading partners in 1996 included Germany, Italy, the United States, the United Kingdom. China and Switzerland.

The Trans-Siberian Railway

The world's longest line, the Trans-Siberian Railway (formerly called the Great Siberian Railway), runs for 9,310 km [5,785 mls] from Moscow to Vladivostok and Nakhodka on the Sea of Japan. Construction began as part of a new development programme for Siberia. The Siberian section, starting at Chelyabinsk in the southern Urals, was built between 1881 and 1905, with an extension to Lake Baykal in 1917. The railway has played a crucial role in the settlement and industrialization of Siberia and it was used in both World Wars to transport troops and supplies. Since the 1920s, the Trans-Siberian Railway has been linked to other railways in the region.

Today, the complete journey from the capital to the Pacific coast, involving 92 stops in eight time zones, takes more than seven days. It has become a route much used by the adventurous tourists, some of whom do not complete the entire trip and, instead, change on to other lines. One route takes tourists from the Trans-Siberian Railway through Mongolia and into China.

AREA	Ukrainian 3%, Chuvash 1%,
17,075,000 sq km	more than 100 other
[6,592,800 sq mls]	nationalities
POPULATION	**LANGUAGES**
146,861,000	Russian (official),
CAPITAL (POPULATION)	many others
Moscow	**RELIGIONS**
(Moskva, 9,233,000)	Christianity (mainly Russian
GOVERNMENT	Orthodox, with Roman Catholic
Federal multiparty	and Protestant minorities),
republic	Islam, Judaism
ETHNIC GROUPS	**CURRENCY**
Russian 82%, Tatar 4%,	Russian rouble = 100 kopeks

RWANDA

Rwanda's flag has the red, yellow and green colours used on the flag of Ethiopia, Africa's oldest independent nation. These three colours symbolize African unity. The 'R' distinguishes Rwanda's flag from the flag of Guinea. Rwanda adopted this flag in 1961.

Geography and Climate

The Republic of Rwanda is a small, landlocked country in east-central Africa. Lake Kivu (Lac Kivu) and the River Ruzizi in the Great African Rift Valley form the country's western border.

Kigali, the capital of Rwanda, stands on the central plateau of Rwanda. Here, temperatures are moderated by the altitude. The rainfall is abundant, but much heavier rain falls on the western mountains. The floor of the Great Rift Valley is warmer and drier than the rest of the country.

History and Politics

The Twa, a pygmy people, were the first known people to live in Rwanda. About 1,000 years ago, a farming people, the Hutu, settled in the area, gradually displacing the Twa.

From the 15th century, a cattle-owning people from the north, the Tutsi, began to dominate the Hutu, who had to serve the Tutsi overlords.

Germany conquered the area, called Ruanda-Urundi, in the 1890s. But Belgium occupied the region during World War I (1914–18) and ruled it until 1961, when the people of Ruanda voted for their country to become a republic, called Rwanda. This decision followed a rebellion by the majority of Hutu people against the Tutsi monarchy. About 150,000 deaths resulted from this conflict. Many Tutsis fled to Uganda, where they formed a rebel army. Burundi became independent as a monarchy, though it became a republic in 1966. Relations between Hutus and Tutsis continued to cause friction. Civil war broke out in 1994, and in 1996 the conflict spilled over into the Democratic Republic of the Congo (then Zaïre), where Tutsis clashed with government troops. The Tutsi uprising in eastern Zaïre eventually led to the overthrow of President Mobutu and his replacement by Laurent Kabila in 1997. In the late 1990s, the International Criminal Tribunal for Rwanda launched investigations into people suspected of genocide.

Economy

According to the World Bank, Rwanda is a 'low-income' developing country, with a low per capita GNP of only US $210 (1997). Agriculture employs 90% of the people, but many farmers live at subsistence level, contributing little to the economy. The chief food crops include bananas, beans, cassava, plantains, potatoes, sorghum and sweet potatoes, and some farmers raise cattle and other livestock. The chief cash crop is coffee, which is also the leading export, followed by tea and hides and skins. Rwanda also produces pyrethrum, which is used to make insecticide. The country produces some cassiterite (tin ore) and wolframite (tungsten ore), but manufacturing is small-scale. Manufactures include beverages, cement and sugar.

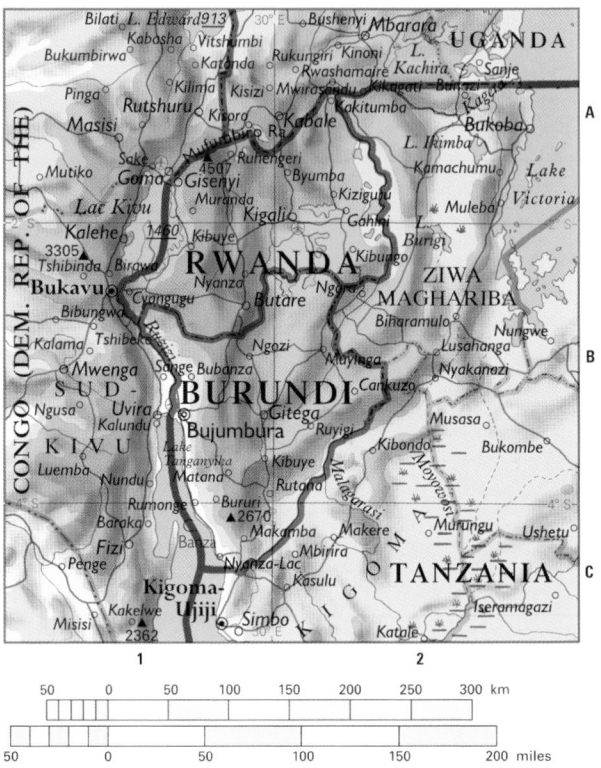

AREA	LANGUAGES
26,340 sq km	French, English,
[10,170 sq mls]	Kinyarwanda
POPULATION	(all official)
7,956,000	**RELIGIONS**
CAPITAL (POPULATION)	Christianity 74%
Kigali (235,000)	(Roman Catholic 65%),
GOVERNMENT	traditional beliefs 17%,
Republic	Islam 9%
ETHNIC GROUPS	**CURRENCY**
Hutu 90%, Tutsi 9%,	Rwanda franc
Twa 1%	= 100 centimes

BURUNDI

The Republic of Burundi is a small country in mainland Africa. Part of the Great African Rift Valley, which runs throughout eastern Africa into south-western Asia, lies in western Burundi.

Bujumbura, the capital city, lies on the shore of Lake Tanganyika. It has a warm climate. A dry season occurs from June to September, but other months are fairly rainy. The mountains and plateaux to the east are cooler and wetter, but rainfall generally decreases to the east.

Germany conquered the area that is now Burundi and Rwanda in the late 1890s. The area was taken by Belgium during World War I (1914–18). In 1961, the people of Urundi voted to become a monarchy, while the people of Ruanda voted to become a republic. The two territories became fully independent as Burundi and Rwanda in 1962, but rivalries between the Hutu and Tutsi led to periodic outbreaks of fighting. The Tutsi monarchy ended in 1966 and Burundi became a republic. Instability continued with coups in 1976, 1987, 1993 and 1996, with periodic massacres of thousands of people.

Burundi is one of the world's ten poorest countries. About 92% of the people are farmers, who mostly grow little more than they need to feed their own families. The main food crops are beans, cassava, maize and sweet potatoes. Cattle, goats and sheep are raised, while fish are an important supplement to people's diets. However, Burundi has to import food. Coffee is by far the most valuable export, followed by tea, cotton and hides and skins. Burundi has some peat and nickel deposits, but manufacturing is small-scale.

AREA	ETHNIC GROUPS
27,830 sq km	Hutu 85%, Tutsi 14%, Twa 1%
[10,745 sq mls]	**LANGUAGES**
POPULATION	French and Kirundi (both official)
5,531,000	**RELIGIONS**
CAPITAL (POPULATION)	Christianity 85% (Catholic 78%),
Bujumbura (300,000)	traditional beliefs 13%
GOVERNMENT	**CURRENCY**
Republic	Burundi franc = 100 centimes

ST HELENA – SEE ATLANTIC OCEAN, PAGES 41–43;
ST KITTS & NEVIS, ST LUCIA, ST VINCENT AND
THE GRENADINES – SEE CARIBBEAN SEA, PAGES 71–76;
SAN MARINO – SEE ITALY, PAGES 131–133;
SAO TOME & PRINCIPE – SEE ATLANTIC OCEAN, PAGES 41–43

Saudi Arabia's flag was adopted in 1938. It is the only national flag with an inscription as its main feature. The Arabic inscription above the sword means 'There is no God but Allah, and Muhammad is the Prophet of Allah'.

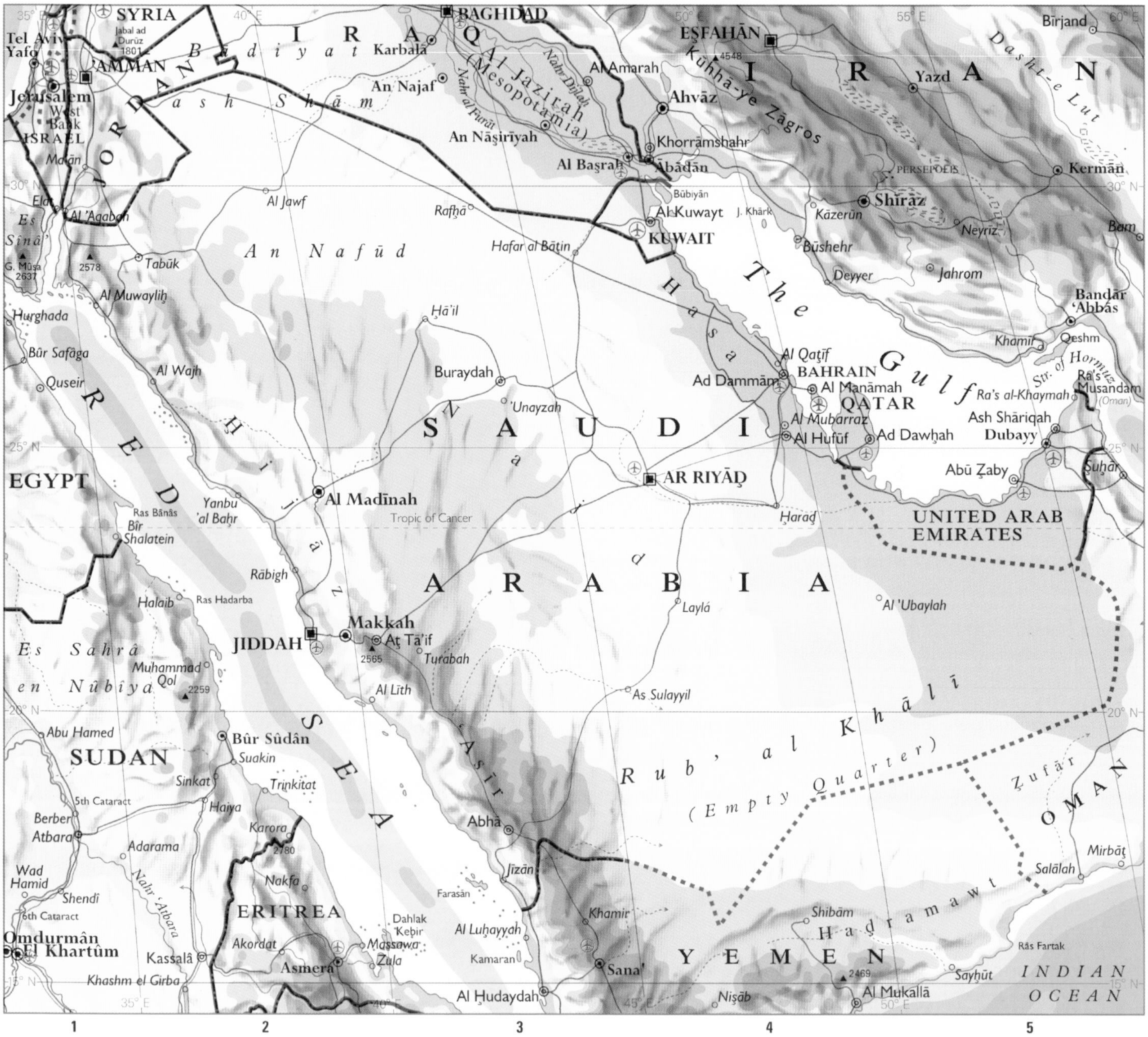

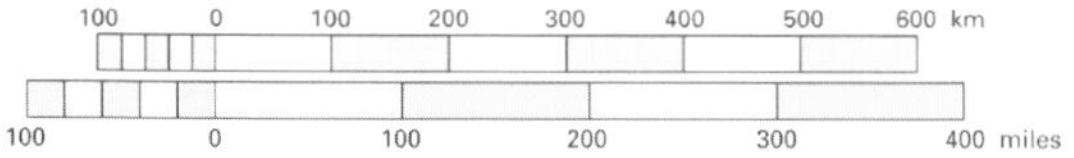

Arable land 1.72% Permanent crops 0.05%
Permanent grassland 55.8% Forest 0.84%

Geography and Climate

The Kingdom of Saudi Arabia occupies about three-quarters of the Arabian Peninsula. The heart of the state consists of the province of Najd, within which there are three main groups of oases. Najd is enclosed on its east side by an arc of sandy desert, which broadens out into the two great dune seas of Arabia. The An Nafūd lies in the north. To the south, the Rub' al Khāli, or 'Empty Quarter', the largest expanse of sand in the world, covers an area of 647,500 sq km [250,000 sq mls]. Many of the Bedouin nomads are found here, still trading and herding.

To the west, Najd is separated from the border hills along the Red Sea by fields of rough basaltic lava. The northern part of the highland region, called the Hejaz (Hijāz), consists of low rocky mountains rising steeply from the sea. But in the southern section, towards the border with Yemen, the coastal strip is well supplied with water, and a high storage dam has been built inland from Jizān in the far south-west. The hills of Asir in the south-west benefit from the summer monsoon and

are terraced in order to grow grain and fruits in the orchards.

Saudi Arabia has a hot, dry climate. In the summer, the temperatures are extremely high, though the nights are cool.

SAUDI ARABIA (RIYADH)

In the interior of Saudi Arabia the diurnal temperature range is much greater than in the coastal regions. During the summer, daytime temperatures frequently exceed 40°C [100°F], but fall sharply at night. At over 400 m [1,300 ft] above sea level, Riyadh has unusually cold winters for its latitude, with no rain between June and October. Most rain falls as short, heavy showers in spring. Frosts have been recorded in January and February.

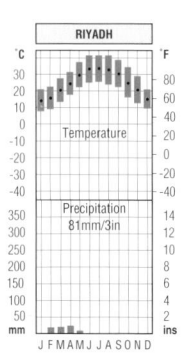

SAUDI ARABIA

History

Groups of Bedouin nomads have lived in the interior of Arabia for thousands of years. Other groups founded trade centres along the caravan routes, or traded around the margins of the peninsula. They included the Sabaeans, who traded in frankincense, myrrh and spices in the south-west around 2,700 years ago, and the Nabataeans who controlled the north-western trade routes from the 5th century BC to the 2nd century AD.

Saudi Arabia contains the two holiest places in Islam – Mecca (or Makkah), the birthplace of the Prophet Muhammad in AD 570, and Medina (Al Madinah) where Muhammad and his followers went in 622 when Muhammad met with opposition from people in Mecca. Muhammad died in 632 and soon afterwards his successors, called caliphs, conquered a large empire beyond Arabia. The Muslim Empire began to break up in the mid-700s and Arabia was split into small areas ruled by warring groups.

In the mid-15th century, the Saud Dynasty established control over a small area near present-day Riyadh. In the mid-18th century, the Saudi ruler established an alliance with a religious leader, Muhammad Ibn Abd al-Wahhab, who wanted to restore strict observance of Islam. The Wahhabi movement swept across Arabia and the Saud family took over areas converted to the Wahhabi beliefs. By the early 19th century, they had taken Mecca and Medina, and the Ottoman governor of Egypt attacked to halt their expansion. By the late 19th century, most of the Arabian Peninsula was under the rule of Ottoman Turks and tribal chiefs, and leading members of the Saud family fled into exile.

Politics

In 1902, a young member of the Saud family, Abd al-Aziz Ibn Saud, led a force from Kuwait, where he had been living in exile, and captured Riyadh. From 1906, the Saud family gradually won control over the territory held by their ancestors and extended their land following the defeat of the Ottoman Empire in World War I. After further conquests in the 1920s at the expense of the Rashidis and Hashemites, Ibn Saud proclaimed the country the Kingdom of Saudi Arabia in 1932. Frontiers with neighbours to the south and east remained ill-defined, but this mattered little until the discovery of vast reserves of oil.

In 1932, Saudi Arabia was a poor, isolated country, but from 1933 the oil industry began when Ibn Saud's government granted Standard Oil of California the right to explore for oil. Other companies later became involved and the first major discovery was made in 1938,

Mecca (Makkah)

Mecca, the holiest city of Islam, was a centre of pilgrimage long before the birth of the Prophet Muhammad. Its chief sanctuary, then as now, was the Ka'ba, a building that houses a striking black stone of probable meteoric origin, said to have been given to the patriarch Abraham by the Archangel Gabriel.

In 632, shortly before his death, the Prophet undertook his own final pilgrimage to the city; the pilgrimage to Mecca – the Hajj – remains the fifth of the Five Pillars of Islam, and every Muslim is expected to make it at least once in a lifetime.

Mecca is also part of the Second Pillar, the duty of prayer, for it is towards the Ka'ba (now enclosed by Mecca's Great Mosque) that Muslims face five times daily when they pray.

At the start of the 20th century, Mecca was a provincial town in the Ottoman Empire. Today, with a population of more than 600,000, it is the capital of the Western Province (formerly Hejaz) of Saudi Arabia. Despite development of various industries, its chief business remains the Hajj. Over 1.5 million pilgrims visit it during the month of pilgrimage (the Muslim month of Dhu al-Hijjah). Most of them travel through the port of Jiddah, situated 70 km [43 mls] to the west on the Red Sea coast. Non-Muslims (infidels) are excluded from the city and any intruders face heavy penalties. An early description of the city was written by the explorer Sir Richard Burton, who visited it in 1853 disguised as a Muslim from Afghanistan. Although Burton was not the first non-Muslim to reach the city, his account was the most accurate up to that date.

though full-scale production did not begin until after the end of World War II. Saudi Arabia eventually became the world's leading oil exporter and its export revenues brought enormous benefits. Oil revenues were used to finance educational and social programmes, and its five-year development plans have launched colossal industrial and domestic projects and the expansion of a private industrial base. In addition, Saudi Arabia became highly influential in the Arab world where it played a major role in supplying development aid.

Ibn Saud died in 1953 and was succeeded by his son, Saud, while Saud's brother Faisal became prime minister. Saud proved to be a poor manager of the country's economy, although Faisal proved to be an adept politician. In 1962, Saudi Arabia supported the royalist forces in Yemen (Sana), while Egypt supported the Yemeni military who had established a republic. War with Egypt seemed possible, but the tension was defused when Egypt withdrew its forces from Yemen in 1967. Saud, who had been suffering ill health, abdicated in 1964 in favour of his brother Faisal. In 1967, Saudi Arabia supported Egypt, Jordan and Syria in the Six-Day War against Israel. Although it did not send troops, it gave aid to the Arab combatants.

In March 1975, King Faisal was assassinated by one of his nephews. King Khalid, Faisal's half-brother, succeeded him. Khalid served as prime minister and he appointed another half-brother, Prince Fahd, as deputy prime minister. When Khalid died in 1982, Fahd became king. When Fahd suffered a stroke in 1995, he appointed his half-brother, Crown Prince Abdullah Ibn Abdulaziz, to act on his behalf. Although he is assisted by a Consultative Council, the monarch holds executive and legislative powers and is also the imam (supreme religious ruler). Saudi Arabia is an absolute monarchy with no formal constitution.

Progress in Saudi Arabia has not always been smooth. In the mid-1980s, world oil prices slumped dramatically, disrupting many of the projects started in the boom years. Instead, the country put more emphasis on developing human resources through management and technical training. Meanwhile expenditure on defence is high, even by the profligate standards of the region. The country's position as the West's staunchest Middle Eastern ally has often conflicted with its other role as the guardian of Islam's holy places. Despite its large donations to poorer Arab nations (Saudi Arabia is by far the world's largest donor by percentage of gross national product), its commitment to the cherished Arab cause of a Palestinian state has at times seemed weak.

While supporting Iraq against the Shiite Iran in the First Gulf War in the 1980s, Saudi Arabia then invited Western forces to protect it against possible Iraqi aggression following the invasion of Kuwait in 1990. In 1991, Saudi aircraft and troops played a significant role in the quick victory of the Allies over Iraq's Saddam Hussein.

Economy

Saudi Arabia has about 25% of the world's known oil reserves, and oil and oil products make up 85% of its exports. Agriculture employs 48% of the people, including nomadic herders who rear various animals. Crops grown in the south-western highlands and at oases include fruits, vegetables and wheat. The rearing of animals by nomads is a leading activity, as also is the production of dairy products, eggs and poultry. Since the mid-20th century, modern irrigation and desalination schemes have greatly increased crop production. The government encourages the development of agriculture and manufacturing as a means of diversifying the economy. Manufactures include cement, glass, industrial chemicals, food products and refined petroleum. Petroleum and petrochemicals dominate exports, while machinery, transport equipment and food products are the chief imports.

AREA	**ETHNIC GROUPS**
2,149,690 sq km [829,995 sq mls]	Arab (Saudi 82%, Yemeni 10%,
POPULATION	other Arab 3%)
20,786,000	**LANGUAGES**
CAPITAL (POPULATION)	Arabic (official)
Riyadh (Ar Riyād, 2,000,000)	**RELIGIONS**
GOVERNMENT	Islam 99%, Christianity 1%
Absolute monarchy with	**CURRENCY**
consultative assembly	Saudi riyal = 100 halalas

This flag was adopted in 1960 when Senegal became independent from France. It uses the three colours that symbolize African unity. It is identical to the flag of Mali, except for the five-pointed green star. This star symbolizes the Muslim faith of most of the people.

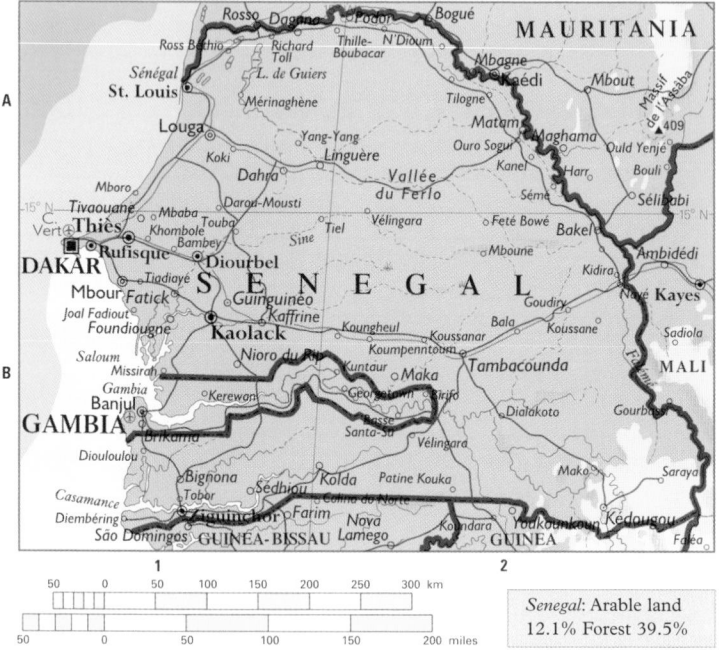

Senegal: Arable land 12.1% Forest 39.5%

Geography and Climate

The Republic of Senegal is situated on the north-west coast of Africa. The volcanic Cape Verde (Cap Vert), on which Dakar stands, is the most westerly point in Africa. Plains cover most of Senegal, though the land rises gently in the south-east.

Dakar has a tropical climate, with a short rainy season between July and October when moist winds blow from the south-west.

History and Politics

In 1882, Senegal became a French colony, and from 1895 it was ruled as part of French West Africa, the capital of which, Dakar, developed as a major port and city.

In 1959, Senegal joined French Sudan (now Mali) to form the Federation of Mali. Senegal withdrew in 1960 to become the separate Republic of Senegal. Its first president, Léopold Sédar Senghor, was a noted African poet. He continued in office until 1981, when he was succeeded by the prime minister, Abdou Diouf. Diouf was re-elected president in 1983, 1988 and 1993. In 1998, parliament passed a law making him president for life. Also in 1998, Senegal, together with Guinea, sent troops into Guinea-Bissau to put down a rebellion.

Senegal and The Gambia have always enjoyed close relations despite their differing French and British traditions. In 1981, Senegalese troops put down an attempted coup in The Gambia. In 1982, the two countries set up a defence alliance, called the Confederation of Senegambia, but this confederation was dissolved in 1989.

Economy

According to the World Bank, Senegal is a 'lower-middle-income' developing country. It was badly hit in the 1960s and 1970s by droughts, which caused starvation. Agriculture still employs 81% of the population, though many farmers produce little more than they need to feed their families. Food crops include groundnuts, millet and rice. Phosphates are the country's chief resource, but Senegal also refines oil which it imports from Gabon and Nigeria. Dakar is a busy port and has many industries. Senegal exports fish products, groundnuts, oil products and phosphates.

AREA	**ETHNIC GROUPS**
196,720 sq km	Wolof 44%, Fulani-Tukulor 24%,
[75,954 sq mls]	Serer 15%
POPULATION	**LANGUAGES**
9,723,000	French (official), tribal languages
CAPITAL (POPULATION)	**RELIGIONS**
Dakar	Islam 94%, Christianity 5%,
(1,729,000)	traditional beliefs and others 1%
GOVERNMENT	**CURRENCY**
Multiparty republic	CFA franc = 100 centimes

GAMBIA, THE

Geography and Climate

The Republic of The Gambia is the smallest country in mainland Africa. It consists of a narrow strip of land bordering the River Gambia. The Gambia is almost entirely enclosed by Senegal, except along the short Atlantic coastline.

The Gambia has hot and humid summers, but winter temperatures (from November to May) drop to around 16°C [61°F]. In the summer, moist south-westerlies bring rain, which is heaviest on the coast.

History and Politics

English traders bought rights to trade on the River Gambia in 1588, and in 1664 the English established a settlement on an island in the river estuary. In 1765, the British founded a colony called Senegambia, which included parts of The Gambia and Senegal. In 1783, Britain handed this colony over to France.

During the 1860s and 1870s, Britain and France discussed the exchange of The Gambia for some other French territory. No agreement was reached and Britain made The Gambia a British colony in 1888. It achieved full independence in 1965 and became a republic in 1970. Relations between the French-speaking Senegalese and the English-speaking Gambians form a major political issue. In 1981, an attempted coup in The Gambia was put down with the help of Senegalese troops. In 1982, The Gambia and Senegal set up a defence alliance, called the Confederation of Senegambia, though this alliance

was later dissolved in 1989. In July 1994, a military group overthrew the president, Sir Dawda Jawara, who fled into exile. Captain Yahya Jammeh, who took power, was elected president in 1996.

Economy

Agriculture employs more than 80% of the people. The main food crops include cassava, millet and sorghum, but groundnuts and groundnut products are the chief exports. Tourism is a growing industry.

AREA	or Malinke) 40%, Fulani (also
11,300 sq km [4,363 sq mls]	called Peul) 19%, Wolof 15%,
POPULATION	Dyola 10%, Soninke 8%
1,292,000	**LANGUAGES**
CAPITAL (POPULATION)	English (official), Mandinka, Fula
Banjul (171,000)	**RELIGIONS**
GOVERNMENT	Islam 95%, Christianity 4%,
Military regime	traditional beliefs 1%
ETHNIC GROUPS	**CURRENCY**
Mandinka (also called Mandingo	Dalasi = 100 butut

SEYCHELLES – SEE INDIAN OCEAN, PAGES 122–123;
SIERRA LEONE – SEE LIBERIA, PAGE 148

SINGAPORE

Singapore's flag was adopted in 1959 and it was retained when Singapore became part of the Federation of Malaysia in 1963. The crescent stands for the nation's ascent. The stars stand for Singapore's aims of democracy, peace, progress, justice and equality.

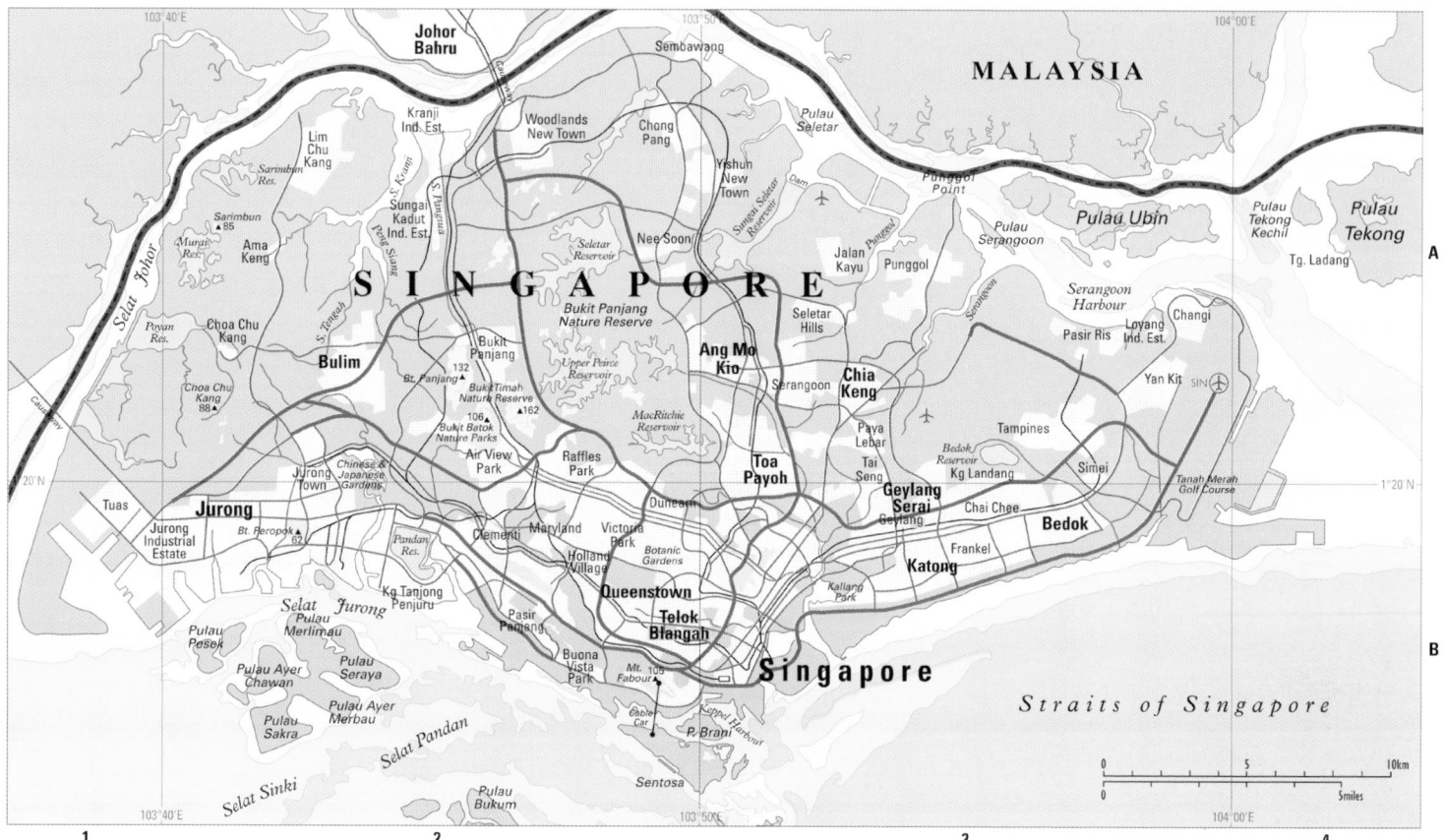

Geography and Climate

The Republic of Singapore is an island country at the southern tip of the Malay Peninsula. It consists of the large Singapore Island and 58 small islands, 20 of which are inhabited.

Singapore has a hot and humid climate, typical of places near the Equator. Temperatures are high and rainfall is heavy through the year.

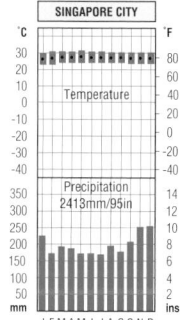

SINGAPORE (SINGAPORE CITY)

Uniformly high temperatures, averaging 27°C [80°F], high humidity and heavy rain all year round are typical of a place situated very close to the Equator and surrounded by water. Daytime temperatures are usually above 30°C [86°F]. Rain is often intense and thunder occurs on average 40 days a year. Rainfall varies greatly from year to year, the highest recorded being more than twice the lowest. Rain falls on over 180 days per year.

Vegetation

Rainforest once covered Singapore, but forests now grow on only 5% of the land. Today, about 50% of Singapore is built-up. Most of the rest consists of open spaces, including parks, granite quarries and inland waters. Farmland covers 4% of the land and plantations of permanent crops make up 7%.

History

According to legend, Singapore was founded in 1299. It was first called Temasak ('sea town'), but was named Singapura ('city of the lion') when an Indian prince thought he saw a lion there. Singapore soon became a busy trading centre, but Javanese raiders destroyed it in 1377.

In 1819, Sir Thomas Stamford Raffles, agent of the British East India Company, made a treaty with the Sultan of Johor which allowed the British to build a settlement on Singapore Island. Singapore soon became the leading British trading centre in South-east Asia. Japanese forces seized the island in 1942, but British rule was restored in 1945.

Politics

In 1963, Singapore became part of the Federation of Malaysia, which included Malaya and the territories of Sabah and Sarawak on the island of Borneo. But, in 1965, Singapore became an independent country.

The People's Action Party (PAP) has ruled Singapore since 1959. Its leader, Lee Kuan Yew, served as prime minister from 1959 until 1990, when he resigned and was succeeded by Goh Chok Tong. Under the PAP, the economy has expanded rapidly, although some people consider that the PAP's rule has been dictatorial and oversensitive to criticism.

Economy

The World Bank classifies Singapore as a 'high-income' economy. Its highly skilled workforce has created one of the world's fastest growing economies. Trade and finance are leading activities and manufactures include chemicals, electronic products, machinery, metal products, scientific instruments, ships and textiles. Singapore has a large oil refinery and petroleum products and manufactures are the main exports.

AREA	**LANGUAGES**
618 sq km [239 sq mls]	Chinese, Malay,
POPULATION	Tamil and English
3,490,000	(all official)
CAPITAL (POPULATION)	**RELIGIONS**
Singapore City (2,874,000)	Buddhism, Taoism and
GOVERNMENT	other traditional beliefs 54%,
Multiparty republic	Islam 15%, Christianity 13%,
ETHNIC GROUPS	Hinduism 4%
Chinese 78%,	**CURRENCY**
Malay 14%, Indian 7%	Singapore dollar = 100 cents

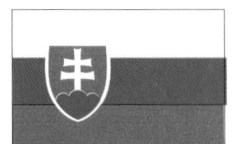

This flag, using the typical red, white and blue Slavonic colours, dates back to 1848. The Slovak Republic adopted it in September 1992, prior to independence on 1 January 1994. The three blue mounds in the shield represent three mountain ranges.

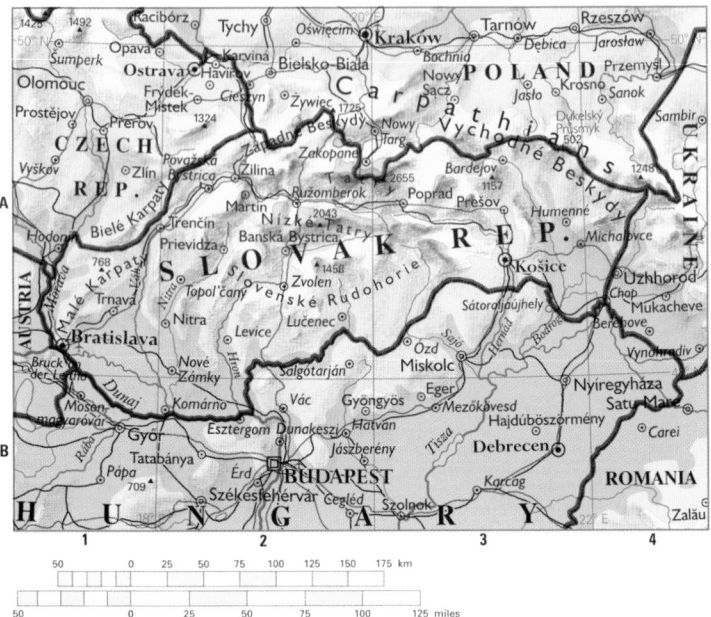

Geography

The Slovak Republic, or Slovakia, is a mainly mountainous country, with part of the Carpathian system that divides the Slovak Republic from Poland in the north. The highest peak is in the scenic Tatra (Tatry) Mountains on the Polish border, where Gerlachovsky Stit reaches 2,655 m [8,711 ft] above sea level. Forests cover much of the mountain slopes and there are also extensive areas of pasture. The south-western Danubian lowlands form a fertile lowland region. The Danube (Dunaj) forms part of the southern border with Hungary. Most of the country's rivers flow south from the northern mountains to the Danube Basin.

Climate

The climate is transitional between the milder conditions of western Europe, which are influenced by air masses from the Atlantic, and the continental conditions of Russia to the east. The conditions in Kosice in the eastern part of the country are fairly typical. Here, average temperatures range from −3°C [27°F] in January to 20°C [68°F] in July. Kosice has an average annnual rainfall of 600 mm [24 in], the wettest months being July and August. The mountains have a more extreme climate and snow or rain occurs throughout the year.

History

Slav peoples settled in the region in the 5th century AD. In the 9th century, the region, together with Bohemia and Moravia in what is now the Cezch Republic, became part of the Greater Moravian Empire. Hungarians conquered this empire in 907 and ruled the area for nearly a thousand years. Religious wars in the 15th century led many Czech nobles to settle in what is now the Slovak Republic. Then, in 1526, Hungary was defeated by the Turkish Ottomans and, soon afterwards, the Ottomans occupied much of eastern and central Hungary. As a result, the centre of Hungarian power shifted into Slovakia.

Slovak nationalism developed from the late 18th century, but it was kept under check by the Hungarians. In 1867, Hungary and Austria were united to form the dual monarchy of Austria-Hungary. Under Hungary, the Slovaks suffered from enforced 'Magyarization'. At the end of World War I, Austria-Hungary collapsed and the Czechs and Slovaks united to form a new nation called Czechoslovakia. However, the dominant status of the Czechs, who largely controlled the economy and government of the new country, led to much Slovak resentment, and support for Slovak nationalism increased. In 1938, Hungary forced Czechoslovakia to give up several areas with large Hungarian populations. These areas included Kosice in the east.

In 1939, fearing that it might be divided up between Germany, Poland and Hungary, Slovakia declared itself independent, but the country was soon conquered by Germany. At the end of World War II, Slovakia again became part of Czechoslovakia. In 1948, Communists seized control of the government. In the late 1960s, many Czechs and Slovaks, led by Alexander Dubcek, tried to reform the Communist system. This movement, known as 'the Prague Spring' or 'socialism with a human face', was put down in 1968 by Soviet and other troops. However, demands for democracy re-emerged in the 1980s, when the Soviet leader Mikhail Gorbachev launched a series of reforms in the USSR.

Politics

At the end of November 1989, Czechoslovakia's parliament abolished the Communist Party's sole right to govern. In December, the Communist Gustáv Hável, who had been head of the party since the removal of Alexander Dubcek, resigned. Non-Communists led by the playwright and dissident Václav Havel formed a new government. Non-Communists won a majority in elections in June 1990.

However, in elections in 1992, the Movement for Democratic Slovakia, led by Vladimir Meciar, campaigned for Slovak independence and won a majority in Slovakia's parliament. In September 1992, the Slovak National Council approved a new constitution for the Slovak Republic, which came into existence on 1 January 1993.

The Slovak Republic, which became a member of the OECD (Organization for Economic Co-operation of Development) in 1997, maintained close contacts with its former partner, although occasional diplomatic spats occurred. However, Slovak independence raised national aspirations among the Magyar-speaking community. Relations with Hungary were not helped in 1996, when the Slovak government initiated eight new administrative regions which the Hungarian minority claimed under-represented them politically. The government also made Slovak the only official language. The government's autocratic rule, human rights record and apparent tolerance of organized crime led to mounting international criticism. In 1998, Meciar's party was defeated in a general election by a four-party coalition and Mikulas Dzurinda, leader of the centre-right Slovak Democratic Coalition, replaced Meciar as prime minister. In April 2000, Meciar was arrested and charged with abuse of power and fraud.

Economy

Before 1948, the Slovak Republic's economy was based on farming, but Communist governments developed manufacturing industries, producing such things as chemicals, machinery, steel and weapons. Since the late 1980s, many state-run businesses have been handed over to private owners.

Farming employs about 12% of the people. Major crops include barley, grapes for wine-making, maize, sugar beet and wheat.

Manufacturing employs around 33% of workers. Bratislava and Kosice are the chief industrial cities. The armaments industry is based at Martin, in the north-west. Products include ceramics, machinery and steel.

AREA	groups of Czechs, Germans,
49,035 sq km	Gypsies, Poles, Russians
[18,932 sq mls]	and Ukrainians
POPULATION	**LANGUAGES**
5,393,000	Slovak (official), Hungarian
CAPITAL (POPULATION)	**RELIGIONS**
Bratislava (451,000)	Christianity (Roman Catholic
GOVERNMENT	60%, Protestant 6%,
Multiparty republic	Orthodox 3%)
ETHNIC GROUPS	**CURRENCY**
Slovak, Hungarian, with small	Koruna = 100 halierov

SLOVENIA

Slovenia's flag, which was based on the flag of Russia, was originally adopted in 1848. Under Communist rule, a red star appeared at the centre. This flag, which was adopted in 1991 when Slovenia proclaimed its independence, has a new emblem, the national coat of arms.

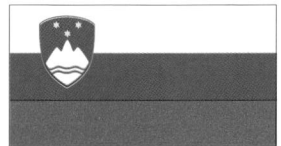

Geography

The Republic of Slovenia was one of the six republics which made up the former Yugoslavia. Much of the land is mountainous and forested. The highest peak is Mount Triglav in the Julian Alps (Julijske Alpe), an extension of the main Alpine ranges in the north-west. Mount Triglav reaches 2,863 m [9,393 ft] above sea level. Ski resorts and impressive mountain scenery make the region a tourist attraction. Much of central and eastern Slovenia is hilly. The River Sava which flows through central Slovenia is a tributary of the Danube, as also is the Drava in the north-east.

The central area also contains a limestone karst region, with numerous underground streams and cave networks. The Postojna Caves, south-west of Ljubljana, are among the largest in Europe. The country has a short coastline on the Adriatic Sea.

Climate

The short coast of Slovenia has a mild Mediterranean climate. Inland, the climate is more continental. The mountains are snow-capped in winter. Eastern Slovenia has cold winters and hot summers. Rain occurs in every month in Ljubljana. Late summer is the rainiest season.

Vegetation

Forests cover about half of Slovenia. Mountain pines grow on higher slopes, with beech, oak and hornbeam at lower levels. The Karst region is largely bare of vegetation because of the lack of surface water. Farmland covers about a third of Slovenia.

History

The ancestors of the Slovenes, the western branch of a group of people called the South Slavs, settled in the area around 1,400 years ago. An independent Slovene state was formed in AD 623, but the area came under Bavarian-Frankish rule in 748. In 1278, the Austrian royal family of the Habsburgs took control of the region which, apart from a short period of French rule between 1809 and 1815 (during the Napoleonic wars), remained under Austrian control until 1918, when the dual monarchy of Austria-Hungary collapsed.

In 1918, at the end of World War I, Slovenia became part of a new country called the Kingdom of the Serbs, Croats and Slovenes, which was renamed Yugoslavia in 1929. Slovenia was invaded by Germany and Italy in 1941 and was partitioned between them and Hungary. At the end of the war, however, Slovenia again became one of the six republics that made up the Federal Republic of Yugoslavia.

In the late 1960s and early 1970s, some Slovenes called for the secession of their federal republic from Yugoslavia, but the dissidents were removed from the Communist Party by President Josip Broz Tito, whose strong rule maintained the unity of his country.

Politics

After Tito's death in 1980, the federal government in Belgrade found it increasingly difficult to maintain the unity of the disparate elements of the population. It was also weakened by the fact that Communism was increasingly seen to have failed in Eastern Europe and the Soviet Union. In 1990, as Communist governments were collapsing in other parts of Eastern Europe, Slovenia held multiparty elections and a non-Communist coalition was formed to rule the country.

In June 1991, Slovenia and neighbouring Croatia proclaimed their independence, but these acts were not accepted by the central government. However, after a few days of fighting between the Slovene militia and Yugoslav forces, Slovenia, the most ethnically homogenous of Yugoslavia's six component parts, found ready support from Italy and Austria (which had Slovene minorities of about 100,000 and 80,000, respectively), as well as Germany, which was an early supporter of Slovene independence. After a three-month moratorium, during which there was a negotiated, peaceful withdrawal, Slovenia

became independent on 8 October 1991. It was fortunate in avoiding the civil conflict that plagued other parts of the former Yugoslavia.

Slovenia's independence was recognized by the European Community in 1992. Multiparty elections were held and Milan Kucan (a former Communist) of the Party of Democratic Reform became president, while Janez Drnovsek, of the centre-left Liberal Democratic Party, became prime minister, heading a coalition government. In 1996, Kucan was re-elected president and, when the Liberal Democrats emerged as the party with the largest number of seats in the National Assembly, Drnovsek continued in office as prime minister and pushed ahead with the development a market economy. Slovenia became an associate member of the European Union in 1996.

Economy

The reform of the economy, formerly run by the government, and the fighting in areas to the south have caused problems for Slovenia, although it remains one of the fastest growing economies in Europe, with a per capita gross national product of US $9,680 in 1997. At the turn of the century, Slovenia was expected to be among the first countries to join an expanded European Union.

Manufacturing is the principal activity. Manufactures include chemicals, machinery and transport equipment, metal goods and textiles. Slovenia mines some iron ore, lead, lignite and mercury. The leading crops are maize, potatoes and wheat. Slovenia's chief exports include machinery and transport equipment, other manufactures, chemicals, food products and mineral fuels. Slovenia's leading trading partners include Germany, Italy, Croatia, France and Austria.

AREA	ETHNIC GROUPS
20,251 sq km	Slovene 88%, Croat 3%,
[7,817 sq mls]	Serb 2%, Bosnian 1%
POPULATION	**LANGUAGES**
1,972,000	Slovene (official),
CAPITAL (POPULATION)	Serbo-Croat
Ljubljana	**RELIGIONS**
(280,000)	Christianity (mainly Catholic)
GOVERNMENT	**CURRENCY**
Multiparty republic	Tolar = 100 stotin

SOLOMON ISLANDS – SEE PACIFIC OCEAN, PAGES 174–178

This flag was adopted in 1960, when Italian Somaliland in the south united with British Somaliland in the north to form Somalia. The colours are based on the United Nations flag and the points of the star represent the five regions of East Africa where Somalis live.

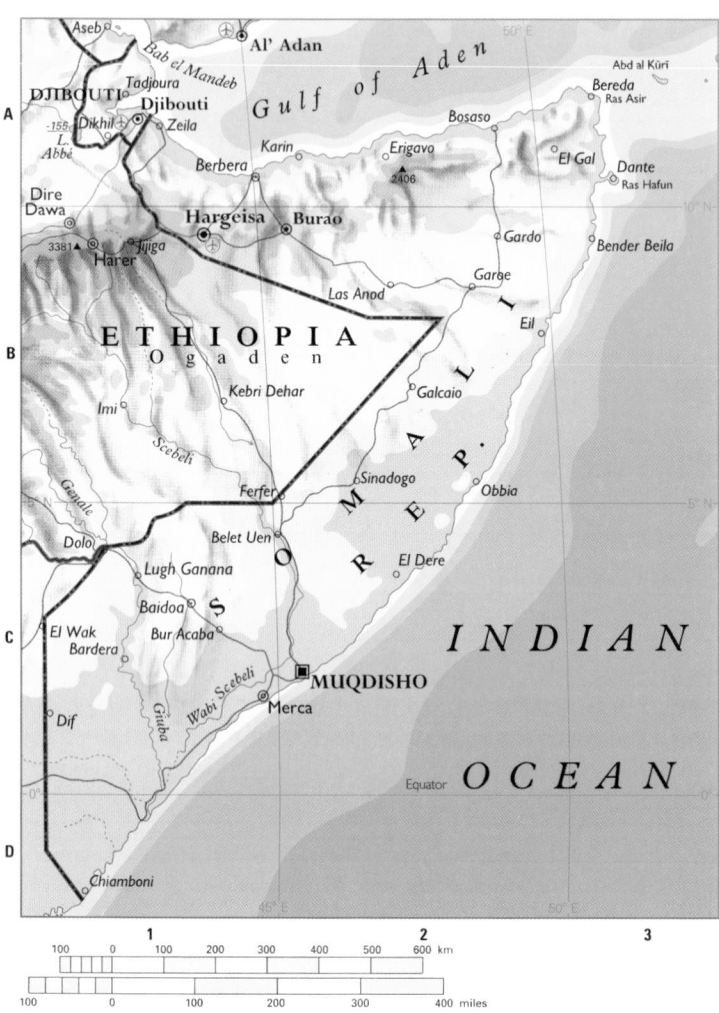

Geography and Climate

The Somali Democratic Republic, or Somalia, lies in a region known as the 'Horn of Africa'. The most mountainous part is in the north, behind the narrow coastal plains that border the Gulf of Aden.

Rainfall is light. The wettest regions are the south and the northern

mountains, but droughts often occur. Temperatures are high on the low plateaux and plains. Frosts occur on high northern mountain slopes.

History, Politics and Economy

European powers became interested in the Horn of Africa in the 19th century. In 1884, Britain made the northern part of what is now Somalia a protectorate, while Italy took the south in 1905. Somali was thus divided into five areas: the two Somalilands, Djibouti (taken by France in the 1880s), Ethiopia and Kenya. Many Somalis have since longed for reunification in a Greater Somalia.

Italy entered World War II in 1940 and invaded British Somaliland. However, British forces conquered the region in 1941 and ruled both Somalilands until 1950, when the United Nations asked Italy to take over the former Italian Somaliland for ten years. In 1960, both Somalilands became independent and united to become Somalia.

Economic problems since independence led a military group to seize power in 1969. In the 1970s, Somalia supported an uprising of Somali-speaking people in the Ogaden region of Ethiopia. But Ethiopian forces prevailed and, in 1988, Somalia signed a peace treaty with Ethiopia. The fighting weakened Somalia's economy. More problems occurred when people in the north fought to secede from Somalia. In 1991, they set up the 'Somaliland Republic'. The new state was recognized neither internationally nor by Somalia's government. Fighting continued and US troops sent in by the UN in 1993 had to withdraw in 1994. By 1999, Somalia was divided into three regions – the north, north-east and south, and had no effective national government.

Somalia is a developing country whose economy has been shattered by drought and war. Catastrophic flooding in 1997 further damaged the infrastrucure, destroying any hope of recovery. Many Somalis are nomads who raise livestock. Live animals and meat are major exports.

AREA	**ETHNIC GROUPS**
637,660 sq km [246,201 sq mls]	Somali 98%, Arab 1%
POPULATION	**LANGUAGES**
6,842,000	Somali and Arabic (both official),
CAPITAL (POPULATION)	English, Italian
Mogadishu (Muqdisho,1,000,000)	**RELIGIONS**
GOVERNMENT	Islam 99%
Single-party republic, military	**CURRENCY**
dominated	Somali shilling = 100 cents

DJIBOUTI

Geography and Climate

The Republic of Djibouti in eastern Africa is situated where the Red Sea meets the Gulf of Aden. Behind the coastal plain on the northern side of the Gulf of Tadjoura is a highland region, the Mabla Mountains.

Djibouti has a very hot climate. Summer temperatures of more than 44°C [112°F] have been recorded. It rains about 26 days every year.

History, Politics and Economy

Islam was introduced into the area which is now Djibouti in the 9th century AD. The conversion of the Afars led to conflict between them and the Christian Ethiopians who lived in the interior. By the 19th century, the Issas, who are Somalis, had moved north and occupied much of the land of the Afars. France gained influence in the second half of the 19th century and, in 1888, set up a territory called French Somaliland. The capital of the territory, Djibouti, became important when the Ethiopian emperor, Menelik II, decided to build a railway to it from Addis Ababa, making it the main port handling Ethiopian trade.

In 1967, the people voted to retain their links with France, though most of the Issas favoured independence. The country was renamed

the French Territory of the Afars and Issas, but it was named Djibouti when it became fully independent in 1977.

Djibouti became a one-party state in 1981, but a new constitution was introduced in 1992, permitting four parties that must maintain a balance between the ethnic groups in the country. But in 1992 and 1993, the Afars launched an uprising which was put down by government troops. A peace agreement was signed in 1994.

Djibouti is a poor country. Its economy is based mainly on money it gets for use of its port and the railway that links it to Addis Ababa.

AREA	**ETHNIC GROUPS**
23,200 sq km [8,958 sq mls]	Issa 47%, Afar 37%, Arab 6%
POPULATION	**LANGUAGES**
650,000	Arabic and French (both official)
CAPITAL (POPULATION)	**RELIGIONS**
Djibouti (383,000)	Islam 96%, Christianity 4%
GOVERNMENT	**CURRENCY**
Multiparty republic	Djibouti franc = 100 centimes

SOUTH AFRICA

South Africa's flag was first flown in 1994 when the country adopted a new, non-racial constitution. It incorporates the red, white and blue of former colonial powers, Britain and the Netherlands, together with the green, black and gold of black organizations.

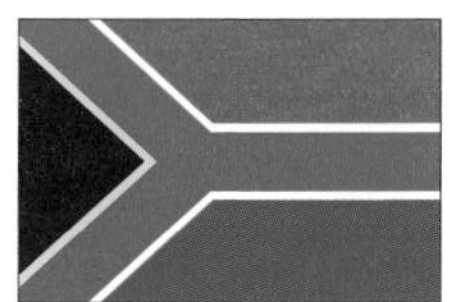

Geography

The Republic of South Africa is geologically very ancient, with few deposits less than 600 million years old. The country can be divided into two main regions – the interior plateau, the southern part of the huge plateau that makes up most of southern Africa, and the coastal fringes. The interior consist of two main parts. Most of the Northern Cape Province and Free State are drained by the Orange River and its right-bank tributaries that flow over level plateaux, varying in height from 1,200–2,000 m [4,000–6,000 ft]. The Northern Province is occupied by the Bushveld, an area of granites and igneous intrusions.

The Fringing Escarpment divides the interior from the coastal fringe. This escarpment makes communication within the country very difficult. In the east, the massive basalt-capped rock wall of the Drakensberg, at its most majestic near Mont-aux-Sources and rising to more than 3,000 m [over 10,000 ft], overlooks KwaZulu-Natal and Eastern Cape coastlands. In the west there is a similar, though less well developed, divide between the interior plateau and the coastlands. The Fringing Escarpment also parallels the south coast, where it is fronted by a series of ranges, including the folded Cape Ranges.

Climate

Most of South Africa has a mild, sunny climate. Much of the coastal strip, including the city of Cape Town, has warm, dry summers and mild, rainy winters, just like the Mediterranean lands in northern Africa. Inland, large areas are arid.

SOUTH AFRICA – JOHANNESBURG

In winter the air is very dry and the sky almost cloudless on the High Veld. The large diurnal range of temperature often exceeds 15°C [59°F]. Summer is the rainy season, when north-easterly winds bring moist air from the Indian Ocean. Rainfall is more abundant and the winter dry season shorter than in western areas at the same latitude. From May to September it usually rains on 1–3 days per month.

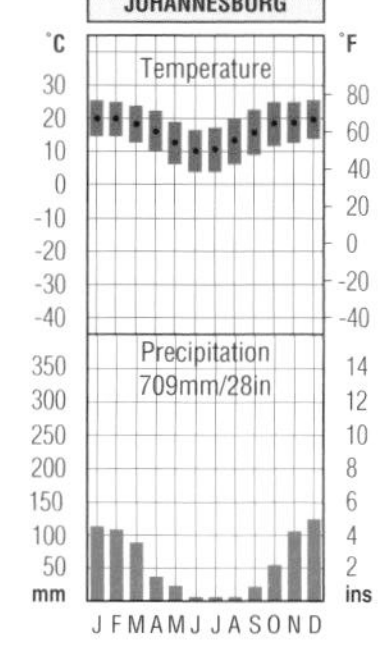

CAPE TOWN

The south-western corner of South Africa has a different climate from the rest of the country. It lies far enough south to be affected by westerly winds which bring rain in winter. The dry summers and wet winters resemble those of the Mediterranean, but it is cooler in summer due to the cold Benguela Current flowing northwards along the coast. From October to February, there are over 10 hours of sunshine per day.

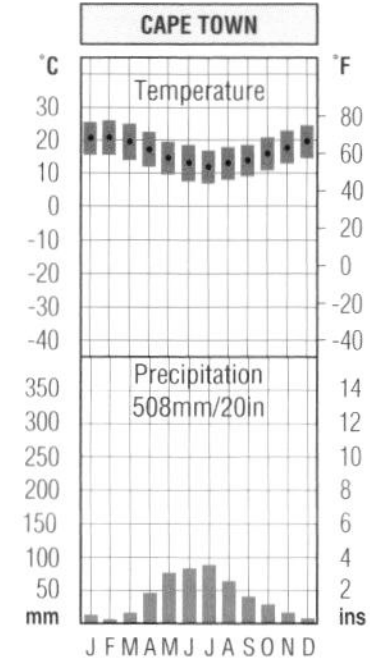

History

Early inhabitants were the Khoisan (also called Hottentots and Bushmen). However, the majority of the people today are Bantu-speakers from the north who entered the country, introducing a cattle-keeping, grain-growing culture. Arriving via the plateaux of the north-east, they continued southwards into the well-watered zones below the Fringing Escarpment of KwaZulu-Natal and Eastern Cape. By the 18th century, these people had reached the south-east. They formed large groups, including the Zulu, Xhosa, Sotho and Tswana.

Simultaneously with this advance, a group of Europeans was establishing a supply base for the Dutch East India Company on the site of present-day Cape Town. The first group was led by Jan van Riebeeck who founded the base in 1652. In 1657, some Company employees set up their own farms and were known as Boers (farmers). After Britain

took over the Cape Town settlement in the early 19th century, many Boers, who resented British rule, began to move inland to develop their own Afrikaner culture. Beginning in 1836, this migration was known as the Great Trek. Their advance was channelled in the south by parallel coastal ranges, and eventually black and white met near the Kei River. To the north, once the Fringing Escarpment had been overcome, the level plateau surfaces allowed a rapid spread northwards, with the Boers founding the Transvaal in 1852 and Orange Free State in 1854.

In 1870, diamonds were found near the site where Kimberley now stands. Both the British and the Boers claimed the area, but Britain annexed it in 1871. In 1880, the Boers rebelled and defeated the British in the First Boer War. In 1886, gold was discovered in the Witwatersrand in what is now Gauteng. Many immigrants, called *uitlanders* (foreigners), flooded to the area. Most of them were British and, to maintain their control, the Boers restricted their freedom. Tension developed, culminating in the Second Boer War (1899–1902). The Boer republics of Orange Free State and Transvaal then surrendered and became British colonies. Meanwhile, British forces had overcome Zulu resistance to European settlement. By 1898, all opposition had been suppressed and the black people had lost their independence.

Politics

In 1906, Transvaal was granted self-rule, followed by Orange Free State in 1907. The other two parts of the country, Cape Colony and Natal, already had self-rule. In 1910, the entire country was united as the Union of South Africa, a self-governing country within the British Empire. During World War I, two Boer generals led South African forces against Germany. In German South West Africa (now Namibia), General Louis Botha conquered the Germans, while General Jan Christiaan Smuts led Allied forces in German East Africa (now Tanzania). In 1920, the League of Nations gave South Africa control over South West Africa, under a trusteeship agreement. In 1931, Britain granted South Africa full independence as a member of the Commonwealth of Nations.

The Rise and Fall of Apartheid

From its 1948 institution, apartheid ('separate development') meant not only racial segregation but also massive racial discrimination. Over the next generation, a whole body of apartheid law was created. Key measures deprived blacks of political rights except in 'homelands' – modest tracts of poor land. Whites were guaranteed exclusive ownership of most of the country's best land, and most blacks, with no right of residence outside homelands few had ever seen, found themselves foreigners in their own country, obliged to carry passes at all times in a police state.

The African National Congress (ANC), the main black political organization, was banned, and black opposition was brutally suppressed. South Africa's racial policies led to increasing isolation from the rest of the world.

Changing demographic patterns (blacks were increasingly outnumbering whites) combined with international sanctions made apartheid unsupportable. The 1989 election of liberal Nationalist President F. W. de Klerk brought dramatic change. Veteran ANC leader Nelson Mandela was released from jail to the negotiating table, and in 1991 de Klerk announced his intention to dismantle the entire structure of apartheid. In 1992, an all-white referendum gave him a mandate to move quickly towards a multiracial democratic system. The first multiracial elections were held in April 1994, after which all internal boundaries were changed and the homelands abolished. A new constitution was adopted in 1996.

The development of minerals and urban complexes in South Africa caused an even greater divergence between black and white. The African farmers gained little from the mineral boom. With taxes to pay, they had little alternative but to seek employment in the mines or on European-owned farms. Migrant labour became the normal way of life for many men, while agriculture in black areas stagnated. Groups of Africans took up urban life, living in communities set apart from the white settlements. These townships, with their rudimentary housing often supplemented by shanty dwellings and without any real services, mushroomed during World War II and left South Africa with a major housing problem in the late 1940s. Nowhere was this problem greater than in Johannesburg where it was solved by building a vast complex of brick boxes called SOWETO, which stood for South-Western Townships. The contrast between the prosperity of blacks and whites increased rapidly.

At the start of World War II, opinion was divided as to whether South Africa should remain neutral or support Britain. The pro-British General Smuts triumphed. He became prime minister and South African forces served in Ethiopia, northern Africa and Europe. During the war, Daniel Malan, a supporter of Afrikaner nationalism, reorganized the National Party. The Nationalists came to power in 1948, with Malan as prime minister, and introduced the policy of apartheid. The African National Congress, which had been founded in 1912, became the leading black opposition group. Opposition to South Africa's segregationist policies mounted around the world. Stung by criticism from Britain and other Commonwealth members, South Africa became a republic and withdrew from the Commonwealth in 1961. In 1966, the United Nations voted to end South Africa's control over South West Africa, though it was not until 1990 that the territory finally became independent as Namibia.

In response to continuing opposition, South Africa repealed some apartheid laws and, in 1984, under a new constitution, a new three-house parliament was set up. The three houses were for whites, Coloureds and Asians, but there was still no provision for the black majority. In 1986, the European Community (now the European Union), the Commonwealth and the United States applied sanctions on South Africa, banning trade in certain areas. In 1989, F. W. de Klerk was elected president and in 1990 he released the banned ANC leader Nelson Mandela from prison.

In the early 1990s, more apartheid laws were repealed. The country began to prepare a new constitution giving all non-whites the right to vote, though progress towards majority rule was marred by fighting between the Zulu-dominated Inkatha Freedom Party and the ANC. Elections held in 1994 resulted in victory for the ANC and Nelson Mandela became president. Mandela advocated reconciliation between whites and non-whites, and his government sought to alleviate the poverty of Africans in the townships. The slow rate of progress disappointed many as did other problems, including an increase in crime and the continuing massive gap in living standards between the whites and the blacks. However, in 1999, following the retirement of Nelson Mandela, his successor, Thabo Mbeki, led the African National Congress to an overwhelming electoral victory.

Economy

South Africa is Africa's most developed country. However, most of the black people – rural and urban – are poor with low standards of living. Natural resources include diamonds and gold, which formed the basis of its economy from the late 19th century. Today, South Africa ranks first in the world in gold production and fifth in diamond production. South Africa also produces coal, chromite, copper, iron ore, manganese, platinum, phosphate rock, silver, uranium and vanadium. Mining and manufacturing are the most valuable economic activities and gold, metals and metal products, and gem diamonds are the chief exports.

Manufactures include chemicals, processed food, iron and steel, machinery, motor vehicles and textiles. The main industrial areas lie in and around the cities of Cape Town, Durban, Johannesburg, Port Elizabeth and Pretoria. Investment in South African mining and manufacturing declined in the 1980s, but foreign companies began to invest again following political changes which brought apartheid to an end.

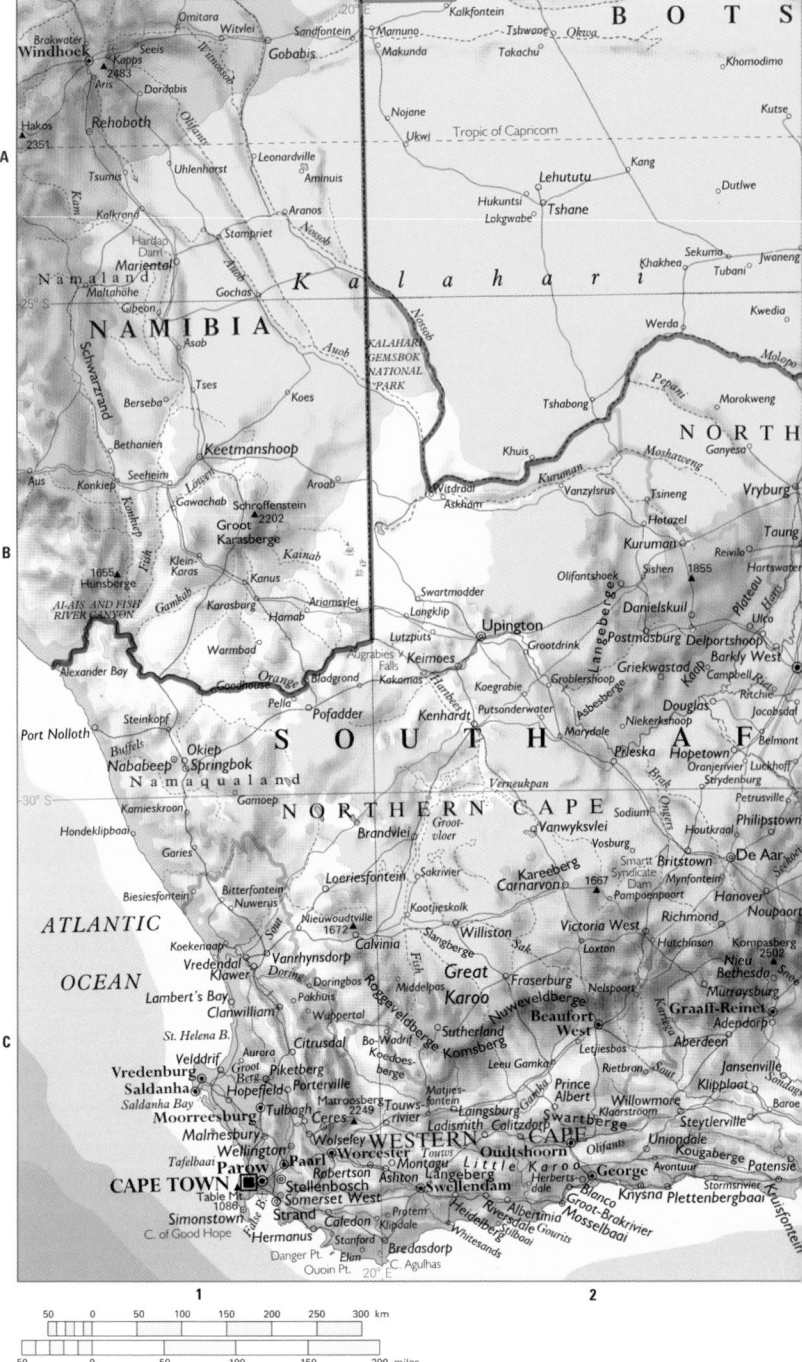

Farmland is limited by the aridity of many areas, but the country produces most of the food it needs and food products make up around 7% of South Africa's exports. Major crops include apples, grapes (for wine-making), maize, oranges, pineapples, sugar cane, tobacco and wheat. Sheep-rearing is important on land which is unfit for arable farming. Other livestock products include beef, dairy products, eggs and milk.

AREA	Coloured 9%,
1,219,916 sq km	Asian 2%
[470,566 sq mls]	**LANGUAGES**
POPULATION	Afrikaans, English,
42,835,000	Ndebele, North Sotho,
CAPITAL (POPULATION)	South Sotho, Swazi,
Cape Town (legislative,	Tsonga, Tswana,
2,350,000); Pretoria	Venda, Xhosa, Zulu (all official)
(administrative, 1,080,000);	**RELIGIONS**
Bloemfontein (judiciary, 300,000)	Christianity 68%,
GOVERNMENT	Hinduism 1%,
Multiparty republic	Islam 1%
ETHNIC GROUPS	**CURRENCY**
Black 76%, White 13%,	Rand = 100 cents

SOUTH AFRICA / LESOTHO

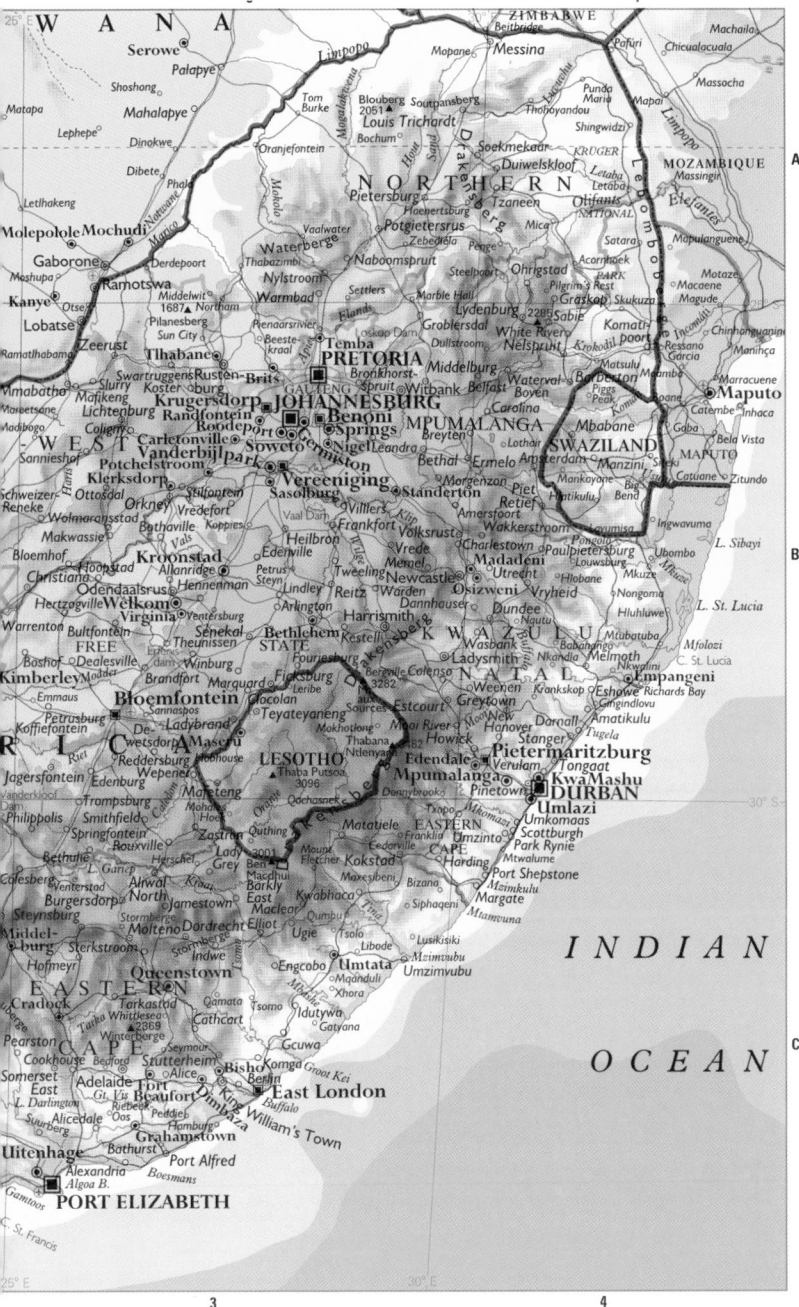

South Africa: Arable land 10.1% Permanent crops 0.67% Permanent grassland 66.6% Forest 6.72%

The country finally became independent in 1966 as the Kingdom of Lesotho, with Moshoeshoe II, great-grandson of Moshoeshoe I, as its king. Since independence, Lesotho has suffered instability. The military seized power in 1986 and stripped Moshoeshoe II of his powers in 1990, installing his son, Letsie III, as monarch. After elections in 1993, Moshoeshoe II was restored to office in 1995. But after his death in a car crash in 1996, Letsie III again became king. In 1998, an army revolt, following an election in which the ruling party won 79 out of the 80 seats, caused much damage to the economy, despite the intervention of a South African force intended to maintain order.

Economy

Lesotho is a 'low-income' developing country, which lacks natural resources. Agriculture, light manufacturing and money sent home by Basotho working abroad, mainly in the mines of South Africa, are the main sources of income.

AREA	ETHNIC GROUPS
30,350 sq km	Sotho 99%
[11,718 sq mls]	LANGUAGES
POPULATION	Sesotho and English (both official)
2,090,000	RELIGIONS
CAPITAL (POPULATION)	Christianity 93%
Maseru	(Roman Catholic 44%),
(130,000)	traditional beliefs 6%
GOVERNMENT	CURRENCY
Constitutional monarchy	Loti = 100 lisente

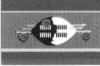

SWAZILAND

Geography and Climate

The Kingdom of Swaziland is a small, landlocked country in southern Africa. The country has four regions which run north–south. In the west, the Highveld, with an average height of 1,200 m [3,937 ft], makes up 30% of Swaziland. The Middleveld, between 350 m and 1,000 m [1,148–3,281 ft], covers 28% of the country. The Lowveld, with an average height of 270 m [886 ft], covers another 33%. The Lebombo Mountains reach 800 m [2,600 ft] along the eastern border.

The Lowveld is almost tropical, with an average temperature of 22°C [72°F] and low rainfall. The altitude moderates the climate in the west of the country.

History and Politics

In 1894, Britain and the Boers of South Africa placed Swaziland under the control of the South African Republic (the Transvaal). But at the end of the Anglo-Boer War (1899–1902), Britain took control of the country. In 1968, when Swaziland became fully independent as a constitutional monarchy, the head of state was King Sobhuza II, who died in 1982 after a reign of 82 years. In 1983, his son, Prince Makhosetive (born 1968), was chosen as his heir. In 1986, he was installed as King Mswati III. In 1993, Swaziland held its first-ever multiparty elections.

Economy

The World Bank classifies Swaziland as a 'lower-middle-income' developing country. Agriculture employs 74% of the people, and farm products and processed foods are the leading exports. Many farmers live at subsistence level. Swaziland is heavily dependent on South Africa and the two countries are linked through a customs union.

AREA	ETHNIC GROUPS
17,360 sq km [6,703 sq mls]	Swazi 84%, Zulu 10%
POPULATION	LANGUAGES
966,000	Siswati and English (both official)
CAPITAL (POPULATION)	RELIGIONS
Mbabane (42,000)	Christianity 77%,
GOVERNMENT	CURRENCY
Monarchy	Lilangeni = 100 cents

LESOTHO

Geography and Climate

The Kingdom of Lesotho is a landlocked country, enclosed by South Africa. The land is very mountainous, rising to 3,096 m [10,115 ft] in the north-east. The Drakensberg Range covers most of the country.

The climate is affected by the altitude, because most of the country lies above 1,500 m [4,921 ft]. Maseru experiences warm summers, but the temperatures fall below freezing in the winter. The mountains are colder. Rainfall varies, averaging around 700 mm [28 in].

History and Politics

The Basotho nation was founded in the 1820s by King Moshoeshoe I, who united various groups fleeing from tribal wars in southern Africa. Britain made the area a protectorate in 1868 and, in 1871, placed it under the British Cape Colony in South Africa. However, in 1884, Basutoland, as the area was called, was reconstituted as a British protectorate, where whites were not allowed to own land.

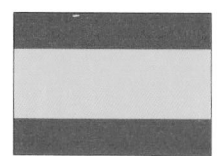

SPAIN

EUROPE

The colours on the Spanish flag date back to those used by the old kingdom of Aragon in the 12th century. The present design, in which the central yellow stripe is twice as wide as each of the red stripes, was adopted in 1938, during the Civil War.

Geography

The Kingdom of Spain is the second largest country in Western Europe after France. It shares the Iberian Peninsula with Portugal. A plateau, called the Meseta, covers most of Spain. Much of the Meseta is flat, but it is crossed by several mountain ranges, called sierras.

The northern highlands include the Cantabrian Mountains (Cordillera Cantabrica) and the high Pyrenees, which form Spain's border with France. But Mulhacén, the highest peak on the Spanish mainland, is in the Sierra Nevada in the south-east. Spain also contains fertile coastal plains. Other lowlands are the Ebro River Basin in the north-east and the Guadalquivir River Basin in the south-west. Spain also includes the Balearic Islands (Islas Baleares) in the Mediterranean Sea and the Canary Islands off the north-west coast of Africa. Tenerife in the Canary Islands contains Pico de Teide, Spain's highest peak at 3,718 m [12,918 ft].

Gibraltar

Local rock carvings demonstrate that Gibraltar has been inhabited since Neolithic times. Greeks and Romans also settled here, but the first sure date for colonization is AD 711 when Tariq ibn Zaid, a Berber chieftain, occupied it. Although taken over by Spaniards for a short while during the 14th century, it remained Moorish until 1462. An Anglo–Dutch naval force captured it in 1704 and it was formally recognized as a British possession at the Treaty of Utrecht in 1713. In spite of long sieges and assaults – not to mention pressure from Spain – it has remained British ever since, becoming a strategically vital naval dockyard and air base.

The Rock, as it is popularly known, guards the north-eastern end of the Strait of Gibraltar. It is 6.5 sq km [2.5 sq mls] in area and occupies a narrow peninsula, consisting largely of a ridge thrusting south along the eastern side of Algeciras Bay, terminating in the 30 m [100 ft] cliffs of Europa Point. The topography prohibits cultivation and the Gibraltarians rely on the port, the ship-repairing yards, the military and air bases, and on tourism for their livelihood.

The 28,051 Gibraltarians are of British, Spanish, Maltese, Portuguese and Genoan descent. Though bilingual in Spanish and English, they remain staunchly pro-British. In 1966, following a long-standing claim, the Spanish government called on Britain to give 'substantial sovereignty' of Gibraltar to Spain and closed the border (1.2 km [0.74 sq mls]) to all but pedestrian traffic. In a 1967 referendum the residents voted to remain under British control, and in 1969 they were granted the status of a self-governing dependency.

Spain closed the frontier completely, preventing thousands of Spaniards from reaching their daily work. The border was reopened fully by Spain in 1985. In 2000, Britain and Spain agreed that Gibraltarian identity cards would be recognized for the first time throughout the European Union, that police co-operation would be increased, and that Gibraltarian banks and financial institutions would be able to export their services through the EU. However, the major question of Gibraltar's final status remained unresolved.

Climate

Spain has perhaps the widest range of climate in Western Europe. One of the most striking contrasts is between the humid north and north-west, where winds from the Atlantic bring mild, wet weather throughout the year, and the mainly arid remainder of the country. Droughts are common in much of Spain, though they are occasionally interrupted by sudden thunderstorms.

The Meseta, removed from the influence of the sea, has a continental climate, with hot summers and cold winters, when frosts often occur and snow blankets the mountain ranges that rise above the plateau surface. By contrast, the Mediterranean coastlands and the Balearic Islands have mild, moist winters. Summers along the

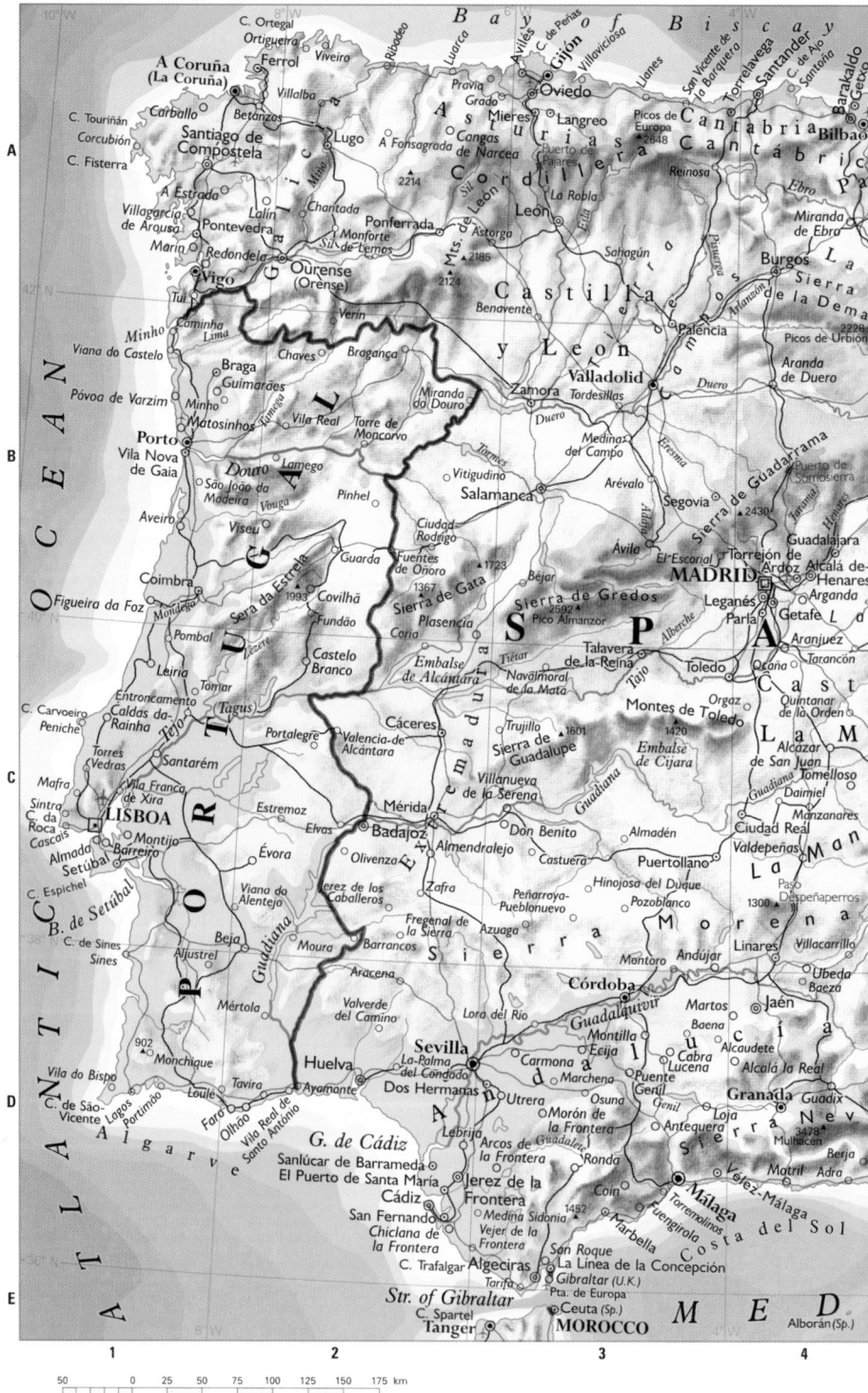

Mediterranean coast are hot and dry – ideal for tourists in search of sun and sea. The Canary Islands, with their mild to warm weather throughout the year, are another popular tourist area.

Vegetation

Spain's vegetation falls into three broad categories: forest, matorral and steppe. The forests are today mainly confined to the rainier north and north-west, with beech and deciduous oak being common. Towards the drier south and east, Mediterranean pines and evergreen oaks take over, and the forests resemble open parkland. Widespread clearance of natural vegetation for fuel and cultivation, together with overgrazing, have turned large areas into matorral, a Mediterranean scrub like the French *maquis*. This low bush growth, often of aromatic evergreen plants, may be dominated over large tracts by one species. Hence, *romillares* consist predominantly of rosemary, *tomillares* of thyme, and *retamales* of broom. Where soils are thin and drought is prevalent, matorral gives way to steppe, mainly of alfalfa and esparto.

History

About 5,000 years ago, Spain was inhabited by farming people called Iberians. Some historians believe the Basques in northern Spain may be descendants of these people. Around 3,000 years ago, Phoenicians from the eastern Mediterranean reached the Iberian Peninsula and began to establish trading colonies, some on the sites of modern cities, such as Cádiz and Málaga. Celtic peoples arrived later from the north, while Greeks reached the east coast of Spain around 600 BC.

In the 5th century BC, Carthaginians conquered much of Spain, but after the Second Punic War (218–201 BC), the Iberian Peninsula gradually came under Roman rule. The Romans made the peninsula a Roman province called *Hispania* and the Spanish name for Spain, *España*, is derived from this Latin word. The Romans left numerous monuments to their rule which can still be seen today.

During the 5th century AD, Germanic forces attacked the Iberian Peninsula, helping to bring about the final collapse of the Roman Empire in 476. By 573, the Visigoths had conquered the entire peninsula, including what is now Portugal, and they ruled until the early 8th century. In 711, Muslim Moors invaded from North Africa and, by 718, they had taken the entire peninsula apart from some mountain areas in the far north. The Moors introduced their culture and scholarship, which was far ahead of that of Europe at that time. They built superb mosques and palaces, some of which still stand today. However, in the 11th century, the country began to divide into many small Moorish kingdoms, leaving them open to attack by the Christian kingdoms in the north, while Portugal broke away from Spain in the 11th and 12th centuries.

By the late 13th century, Muslim power was confined to the Kingdom of Granada in the south. The rest of Spain was ruled by the Christian kingdoms of Aragon, Navarre and, the most powerful of all, Castile. In 1469, Prince Ferdinand of Aragon married Princess Isabella of Castile. When Ferdinand became king of Aragon in 1479, the kingdoms united. Ferdinand and Isabella started the Spanish Inquisition which persecuted Jews, Muslims and other non-Roman Catholics. In 1492, Ferdinand's forces captured the last Muslim stronghold of Granada and, in 1512, the Kingdom of Navarre was taken by Ferdinand. This completed the union of Spain.

In 1492, Christopher Columbus was sent by Ferdinand and Isabella on an expedition that opened up the Americas. By the mid-16th century, Spain was a great world power. At its peak, Spain controlled much of Central and South America, parts of Africa and the Philippines in Asia, but its power soon began to decline as a series of wars weakened its economy. A major disaster occurred in 1588, when King Philip II sent a fleet, the Armada, to conquer England, but the English navy and bad weather destroyed half of the Spanish ships. In the early 19th century, Spain lost all its American colonies, except for Cuba and Puerto Rico. However, these latter territories, together with the Philippines, were lost in the Spanish-American War of 1898. All that remained of Spain's empire were a few small territories in Africa.

Despite being neutral during World War I, Spain was one of Europe's poorest countries in the 1920s. A military government was established in 1923 and King Alfonso III allowed General Miguel Primo de Rivera, the prime minister, to rule as a dictator. After Primo de Rivera was forced to resign in 1930, Alfonso called for city elections. Republican candidates scored such a major victory in these elections that he left the country, though he did not renounce his claim to the throne. The republicans took over the government and called for parliamentary elections which were held in June 1931. In December, the elected Cortes (parliament) adopted a new democratic constitution. The new government faced many problems, both economic and political.

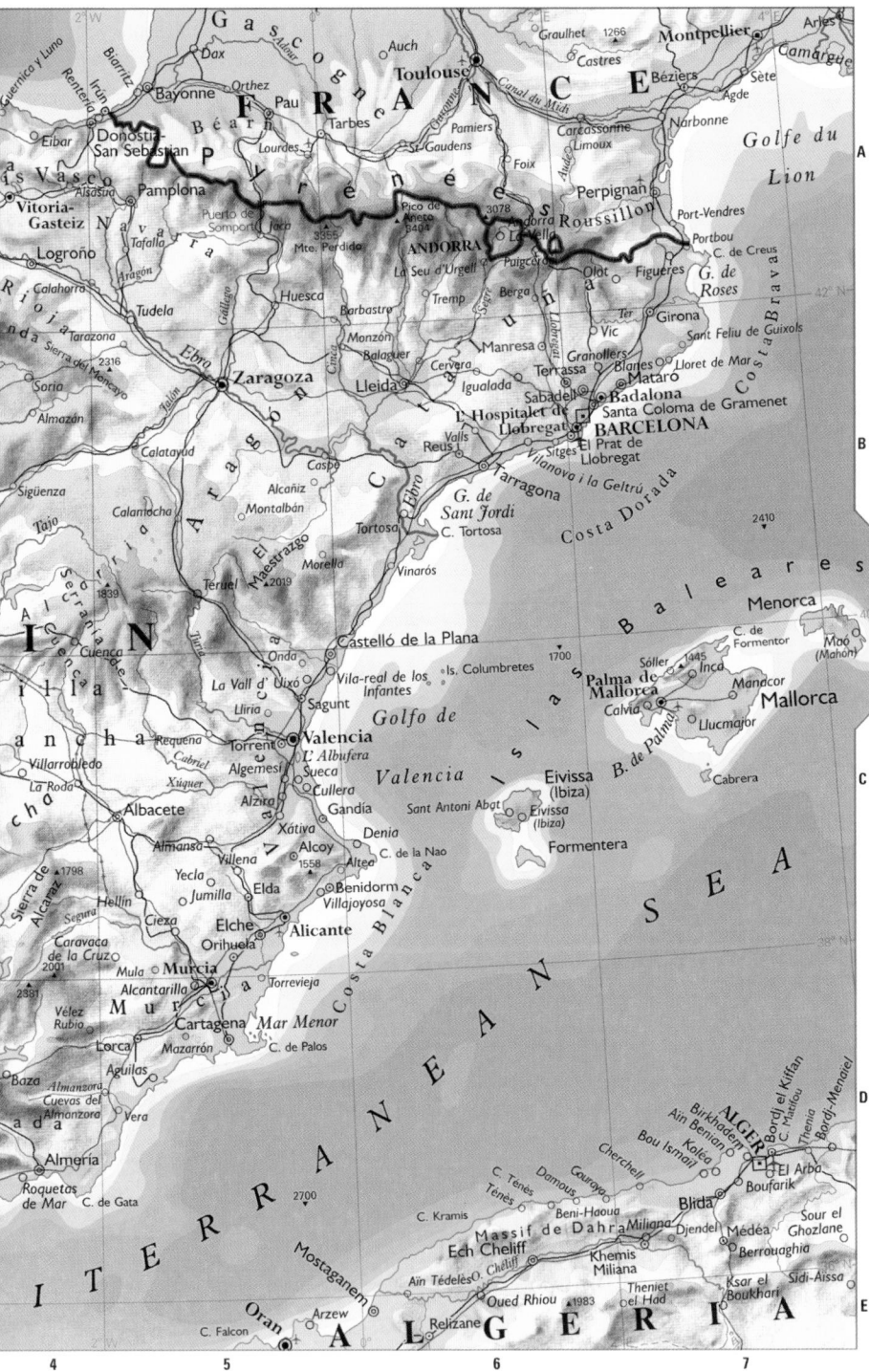

Arable land 31.3% Permanent crops 9.05%
Permanent grassland 21.4% Forest 32.3%

Deep political differences existed between the monarchists and the republicans, and also between the republicans themselves. In a highly charged situation, Spanish forces in Morocco launched a rebellion in 1936. In October of that year, the rebel Nationalists chose General Francisco Franco (1892–1975) as their commander and, supported by the Falange (Spain's fascist party), the Nationalists defeated the government forces in 1939. Franco became the dictator of Spain, ruling much like the Axis dictators, though technically the country was a monarchy. During World War II, Spain was officially neutral.

Politics

The revival of Spain's shattered economy began in the 1950s through the growth of manufacturing industries and tourism. As standards of living rose, people began to demand more freedom, while people in several regions agitated for self-government or full independence. After Franco died in 1975, the monarchy was restored and Juan Carlos, grandson of Alfonso III, became king. In 1976, the ban on political parties was lifted and, in 1977, elections were held. A new constitution making Spain a parliamentary democracy, with the king as head of state, came into effect in December 1978.

From the late 1970s, Spain began to tackle the problem of its regions. In 1980, a regional parliament with a considerable degree of autonomy was set up in the Basque Country (called *Euskadi* in Basque and *Pais Vasco* in Spanish). Similar parliaments were initiated in Catalonia (Cataluña) in the north-east and Galicia in the north-west. All of these regions have their own languages and cultures. While regional devolution was welcomed in Catalonia and Galicia, it did not end the terrorist campaign of the Basque separatist movement, the *Euskadi ta Askatasuna* (ETA). ETA announced an indefinite cease-fire in September 1998, but the truce was ended in December 1999 when talks failed to produce immediate results.

The return to democracy led to rapid economic growth and, in 1986, Felipe Gonzalez, prime minister and leader of the Socialist Workers' Party, took Spain into the European Community. However, after 13 years in office, the socialist government was defeated in 1996

by the conservative Popular Party. José Maria Aznar López became prime minister, heading a minority government, beholden in parliament to the Catalan nationalists. The Aznar government maintained the socialists' commitment to adopting the euro, the single European currency, on 1 January 1999, and in March 2000 Aznar's Popular Party won a second term by a landslide.

Economy

Since the 1950s, Spain has been transformed from a poor country, dependent on agriculture, into a fairly prosperous industrial nation. It has the fifth largest economy in the European Union, though its per capita gross national product, at US $14,510 in 1997, is relatively modest, exceeding only the per capita GNPs of Greece and Portugal.

By 1996, agriculture employed only 8% of the workforce. About two-thirds of the land is used for farming, including pasture, though productivity is low because of poor soils and the arid climate. Spain has about 20 million sheep, mainly of the native merino type which produces a fine fleece. Areas too steep for sheep are grazed by goats, while cattle are mainly restricted to regions with ample grass and water, as in the north. Pigs are also raised in the northern cattle districts.

Major crops include grapes for wine-making, olives and wheat, while maize is grown in wetter areas, and citrus fruits and vegetables in areas where irrigation is possible. Spain is the world's leading olive oil producer and ranks third among wine producers. In dry areas, barley, oats and rye, grown for fodder, replace wheat. Rice is important – Spain ranks second to Italy among European rice producers. Spain also outstrips other European countries in citrus fruit production, while industrial crops include cotton, hemp, flax and sugar beet.

Spain has some high-grade iron ore in the north, but the country generally lacks mineral resources. Small deposits of oil exist, though Spain is heavily dependent on imported oil. However, Spain is the world's leading producer of mercury, which accounted for 37% of the world production in 1995.

Manufactures include cars, chemicals, clothing, electronic goods, processed food, metal goods, steel and textiles. The leading manufacturing centres are Barcelona, Bilbao and Madrid. Tourism accounts for a tenth of the gross domestic product – in 1996 around 62 million tourists visited Spain. Also important to the economy are the foreigners who come to stay permanently or for much of the year. Spain's chief exports are transport equipment, farm products and machinery. France, Germany, Italy and the United Kingdom are Spain's major trading partners.

Regions of Spain

AREA	Catalan 16%, Galician 8%,
504,780 sq km	Basque 2%
[194,896 sq mls]	**LANGUAGES**
POPULATION	Castilian Spanish (official),
39,134,000	Catalan, Galician, Basque
CAPITAL (POPULATION)	**RELIGIONS**
Madrid (3,041,000)	Christianity
GOVERNMENT	(Roman Catholic 97%)
Constitutional monarchy	**CURRENCY**
ETHNIC GROUPS	Euro; Peseta
Castilian Spanish 72%,	= 100 céntimos

ANDORRA

Andorra is a tiny mini-state that is sandwiched between France and Spain. It is a co-principality and lies high in the Pyrenees Mountains. Most Andorrans live in the six valleys (the Valls) that drain into the River Valira.

Andorra experiences cold and fairly dry winters. The summers are a little rainier, but they are pleasantly cool.

Tourism remains Andorra's chief activity in both the winter, for winter sports, and in the summer. There is some farming in the valleys

and tobacco is the main crop. Cattle and sheep are grazed on the mountain slopes.

AREA	CAPITAL
453 sq km [175 sq mls]	Andorra La Vella
POPULATION	**CURRENCY**
75,000	Euro; French franc; peseta

Geography

The Democratic Socialist Republic of Sri Lanka is a beautiful island nation. Often called the 'pearl of the Indian Ocean', it was once part of the ancient continent of Gondwanaland. It lies on the same continental shelf as India, being separated from its neighbour by the shallow Palk Strait. Most of the land is low-lying but, in the south-central part of Sri Lanka, the land rises to a mountain massif. The nation's highest peak is Pidurutalagala, which reaches 2,524 m [8,281 ft] above sea level. The nearby Adam's Peak, at 2,243 m [7,359 ft], is a place of pilgrimage. The south-west is also mountainous, with long ridges.

Around the south-central highlands are broad plains, while the Jaffna Peninsula in the far north is made of limestone. The coastline is varied. Cliffs overlook the sea in the south-west, while lagoons line the coast in many other areas.

Climate

The western part of Sri Lanka experiences a wet equatorial climate. Temperatures are high and the rainfall is heavy. The wettest months are May and October, marking the advance and the retreat of the summer monsoon. Eastern Sri Lanka is drier than the west.

Vegetation

Forests cover nearly two-fifths of the land in Sri Lanka, with open grasslands in the eastern highlands. Farmland, including pasture, covers another two-fifths of the country.

History

The ancestors of the Sinhalese people probably came from northern India and settled on the island around 2,400 years ago. They pushed the Veddahs, descendants of the earliest inhabitants, into the interior. The Sinhalese founded the city of Anuradhapura, which was their centre from the 3rd century BC to the 10th century AD.

Tamils arrived around 2,100 years ago and the early history of Ceylon, as the island was known, was concerned with a struggle between the Sinhalese and the Tamils. Victory for the Tamils led the Sinhalese to move south.

Politics

From the early 16th century, Ceylon was ruled successively by the Portuguese, Dutch and British. Independence was achieved in 1948 and the country was renamed Sri Lanka in 1972.

After independence, rivalries between the two main ethnic groups, the Sinhalese and Tamils, marred progress. In the 1950s, the government made Sinhala the official language. Following protests, the prime minister made provisions for Tamil to be used in some areas. In 1959, the prime minister was assassinated by a Sinhalese extremist and he was succeeded by Sirimavo Bandanaraike, who became the world's first woman prime minister.

Conflict between Tamils and Sinhalese continued in the 1970s and 1980s. In 1987, India helped to engineer a cease-fire. Indian troops arrived to enforce the agreement. They withdrew in 1990 after failing to subdue the main guerrilla group, the Tamil Tigers, who wanted to set up an independent Tamil homeland in northern Sri Lanka. In 1993, the country's president, Ranasinghe Premadasa, was assassinated by a suspected Tamil separatist. A cease-fire was signed on 1 May 1993, but fighting soon broke out again. In 1995, government forces captured Jaffna, the stronghold of the 'Liberation Tigers of the Tamil Eelam' (LTTE). But the bombing of the Temple of the Tooth in Kandy in 1998 created great outrage among the Sinhalese Buddhists, who believe that the temple's treasured tooth belonged to the Buddha.

The bombing led to rioting and provoked President Chandrika Kumaratunga to ban the LTTE. These events led to some of the fiercest fighting in the civil war, including several suicide bombings. The government lost most of the gains it had made in the mid-1990s

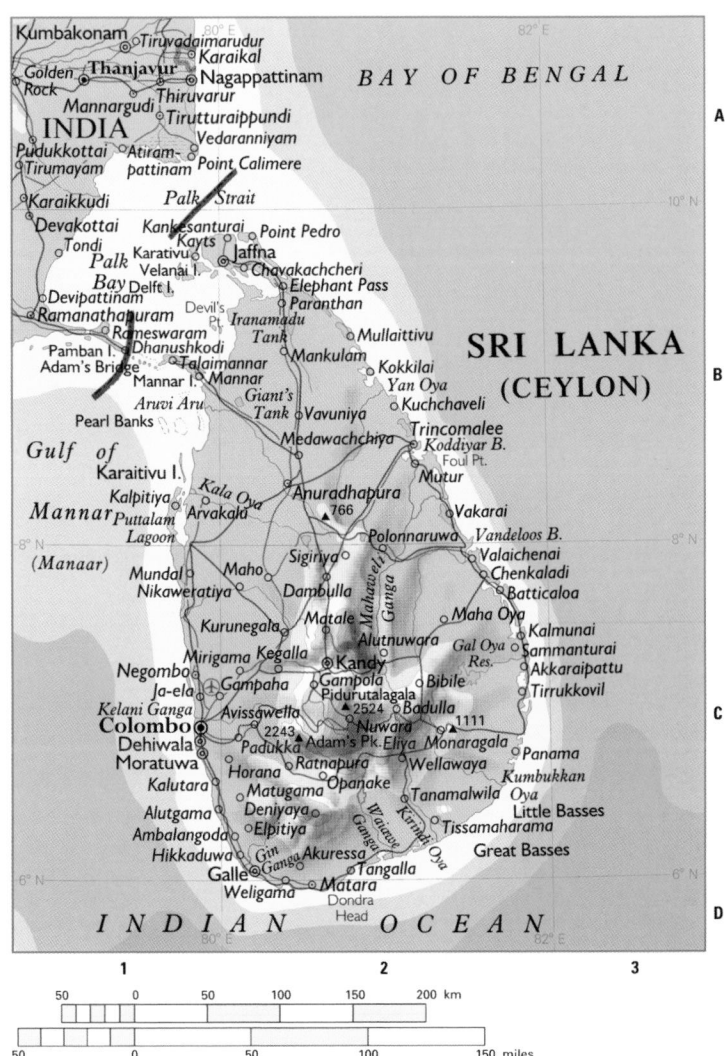

and, in December 1999, Kumaratunga herself was injured in a suicide bomb attack in her last election rally in Colombo. She went on to be re-elected president for a second term. By 1999, an estimated 60,000 people had died in the conflict, which had also badly damaged the tourist industry.

Economy

The World Bank classifies Sri Lanka as a 'low-income' developing country. Agriculture employs around a third of the workforce and coconuts, rubber and tea are the cash crops. Rice is the chief food crop. Cattle, water buffalo and goats are the chief farm animals, while fish provide another source of protein. Manufacturing is concerned mainly with processing agricultural products and producing textiles. The country's leading exports are clothing and accessories, gemstones, tea and natural rubber.

AREA	Sri Lankan Moor 7%
65,610 sq km [25,332 sq mls]	**LANGUAGES**
POPULATION	Sinhala and Tamil
18,934,000	(both official)
CAPITAL (POPULATION)	**RELIGIONS**
Colombo (1,863,000)	Buddhism 69%, Hinduism 16%,
GOVERNMENT	Islam 8%, Christianity 7%
Multiparty republic	**CURRENCY**
ETHNIC GROUPS	Sri Lankan rupee
Sinhalese 74%, Tamil 18%,	= 100 cents

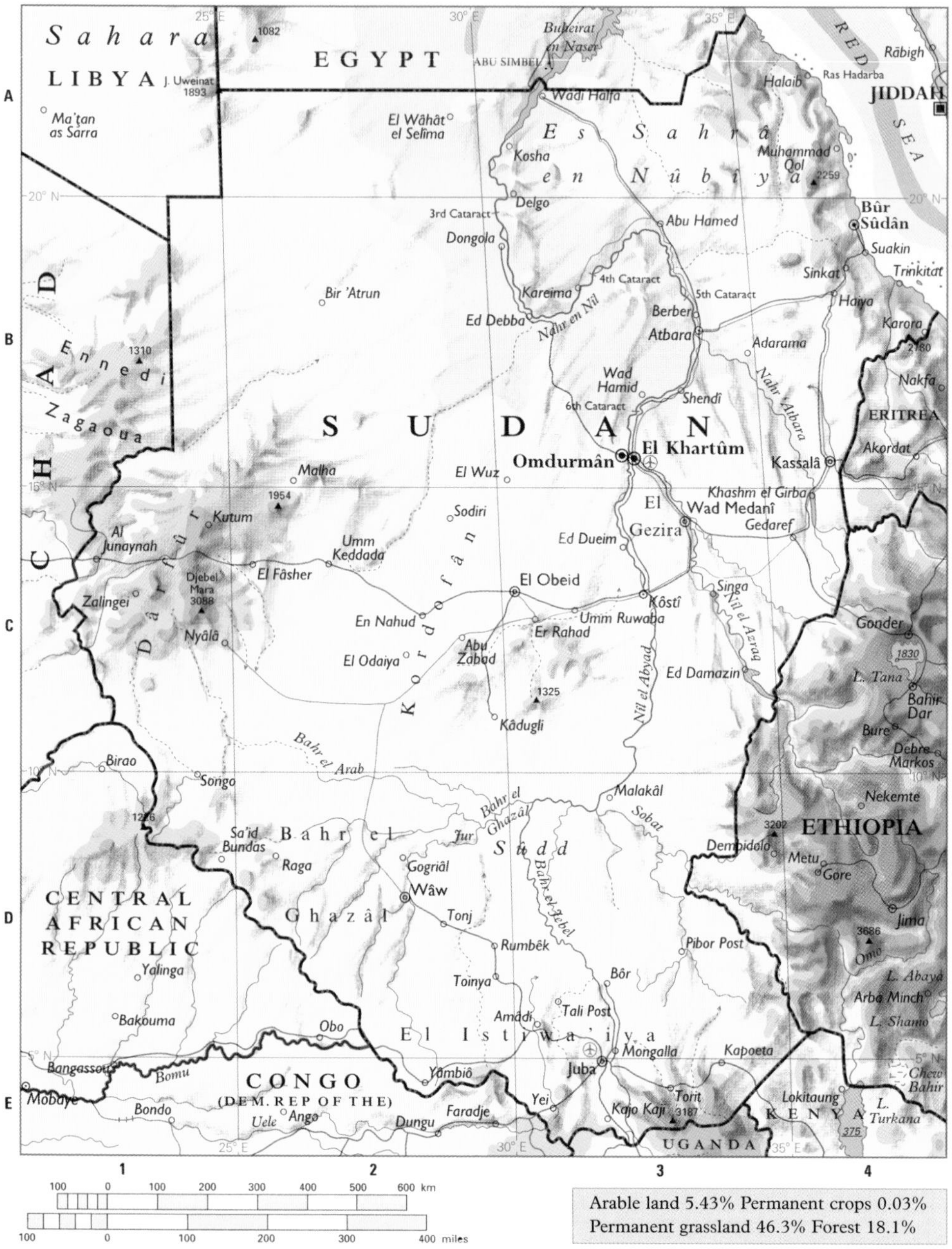

History

One of the earliest civilizations in the Nile region of northern Sudan was Nubia, which came under Ancient Egypt around 4,000 years ago. Another Nubian civilization, called Kush, developed from about 1000 BC, finally collapsing in AD 350. Christianity was introduced to northern Sudan in the 6th century, but Islam later became the dominant religion. In the 19th century, Egypt gradually took over Sudan. In 1881, a Muslim religious teacher, the Mahdi ('divinely appointed guide'), led an uprising. Britain and Egypt put the rebellion down in 1898. In 1899, they agreed to rule Sudan jointly as a condominium.

Politics

After Sudan's independence in 1952, the black Africans in the south, who were either Christians or followers of traditional beliefs, feared domination by the Muslim northerners. For example, they objected to the government declaring that Arabic was the only official language. In 1964, civil war broke out and continued until 1972, when the south was given regional self-government, though executive power was still vested in the military government in Khartoum.

In 1983, the government established Islamic law throughout the country. This sparked further conflict when the Sudan People's Liberation Army in the south launched attacks on government positions. Fighting continued and food shortages and the plight of refugees added to Sudan's difficulties, attracting global attention and humanitarian aid. In 1998, the government announced that it accepted, in principle, the holding of a referendum on the possible secession of the south, though definitions of what constituted the south varied.

Economy

The World Bank classifies Sudan as a 'low-income' economy. Agriculture employs 62% of the population. The leading crop is cotton. Other crops include groundnuts, gum arabic, millet, sesame, sorghum and sugar cane, while many people raise livestock. Minerals include chromium, gold, gypsum and oil. Manufacturing industries process foods and produce such things as cement, fertilizers and textiles. The main exports are cotton, gum arabic and sesame seeds.

Arable land 5.43% Permanent crops 0.03%
Permanent grassland 46.3% Forest 18.1%

Geography and Climate

The Republic of Sudan is the largest country in Africa. From north to south, it spans a vast area extending from the arid Sahara in the north to the wet equatorial region in the south. The land is mostly flat, with the highest mountains in the far south.

Northern Sudan is hot and arid. The centre has an average annual rainfall of 100 mm to 510 mm [4–32 in], while the tropical south has between 810 mm and 1,400 mm [32–55 in] of rain per year.

SUDAN (KHARTOUM)

Sudan extends from the Sahara Desert almost to the Equator, and the climate changes from desert to equatorial as the influence of the intertropical rainbelt increases southwards. At Khartoum, rain falls during the summer months when the rainbelt is at its most northerly extent. The rain may be squally and accompanied by dust storms called 'haboobs'. There is a large daily range of temperature and summer days are very hot.

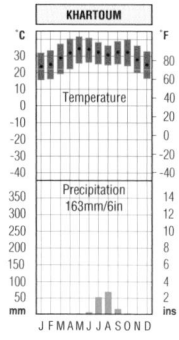

AREA	Nuba 8%, Beja 6%,
2,505,810 sq km [967,493 sq mls]	Nuer 5%, Azande 3%
POPULATION	**LANGUAGES**
33,551,000	Arabic (official), Nubian, Dinka
CAPITAL (POPULATION)	**RELIGIONS**
Khartoum (El Khartûm, 925,000)	Islam 73%, traditional beliefs
GOVERNMENT	17%, Christianity (Roman
Military regime	Catholic 4%, Protestant 2%)
ETHNIC GROUPS	**CURRENCY**
Sudanese Arab 49%, Dinka 12%,	Dinar = 10 Sudanese pounds

SURINAM – SEE GUYANA, PAGE 115;
SWAZILAND – SEE SOUTH AFRICA, PAGES 203–205

SWEDEN

Sweden's flag was adopted in 1906, though it had been in use since the time of King Gustavus Vasa (reigned 1523–60). This king won many victories for Sweden and laid the foundations of the modern nation. The colours on the flag come from a coat of arms dating from 1364.

Geography

The Kingdom of Sweden is the largest of the countries of Scandinavia in both area and population. It shares the Scandinavian Peninsula with Norway. The western part of the country, along the border with Norway, is mountainous. The highest point is Kebnekaise, which reaches 2,117 m [6,946 ft] in the north-west.

Sweden's share of the Scandinavian Peninsula is less mountainous than that of Norway. The northern half of the country forms part of the Baltic, or Fenno-Scandian Shield, a stable block of ancient granites and gneisses which extends around the head of the Gulf of Bothnia into Finland. The shield land is an area of low plateaux which rise gradually to the west. This part of Sweden contains most of the country's rich mineral wealth.

South of the plateaux is a belt of lowlands between the capital city, Stockholm, and the second city, Göteborg (Gothenburg). These lowlands contain several large lakes, the chief of which are Mälaren, near Stockholm, and the larger Vättern and Vänern. The lakes are all that is left of a strait, which during the last Ice Age connected the Baltic with the Kattegat. Now linked by canals, the lakes form an important waterway across Sweden. South of the lakes is a low plateau, sloping gently down to the small lowland area of Skåne (Scania). The scenery has been greatly shaped by ice action and some of the most fertile soils were formed from material deposited on the beds of glacial lakes.

Climate

The two main factors that influence the climate are the northerly latitude and high mountains and plateaux of Norway that cut Sweden off from the mild influences of the Atlantic in the west. However, the Gulf Stream warms the southern coastlands, but continental influences take over in the north. The February temperature in the central lowlands is just below freezing, but in the north it is −15°C [5°F].

Precipitation is low throughout Sweden, but lies as snow for more than six months in the north. The Baltic Sea is usually frozen for at least five months, but ice is rare on the western coast. In summer there is little difference between the north and south. Most areas have an average temperature range between 15°C and 20°C [59–68°F].

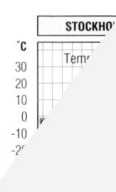

SWEDEN (STOCKHOLM)

Stockholm, in the central lowlands, has cold winters though they are not as long as those in the north. The precipitation is light and the wettest seasons are the summer and autumn. During winter, snow falls on an average of 60 days. Summers are relatively warm, with plenty of sunshine.

Vegetation

Extensive coniferou
south, the origin
cleared for agri
opportunity f
is farmland
spruce, of
of woo

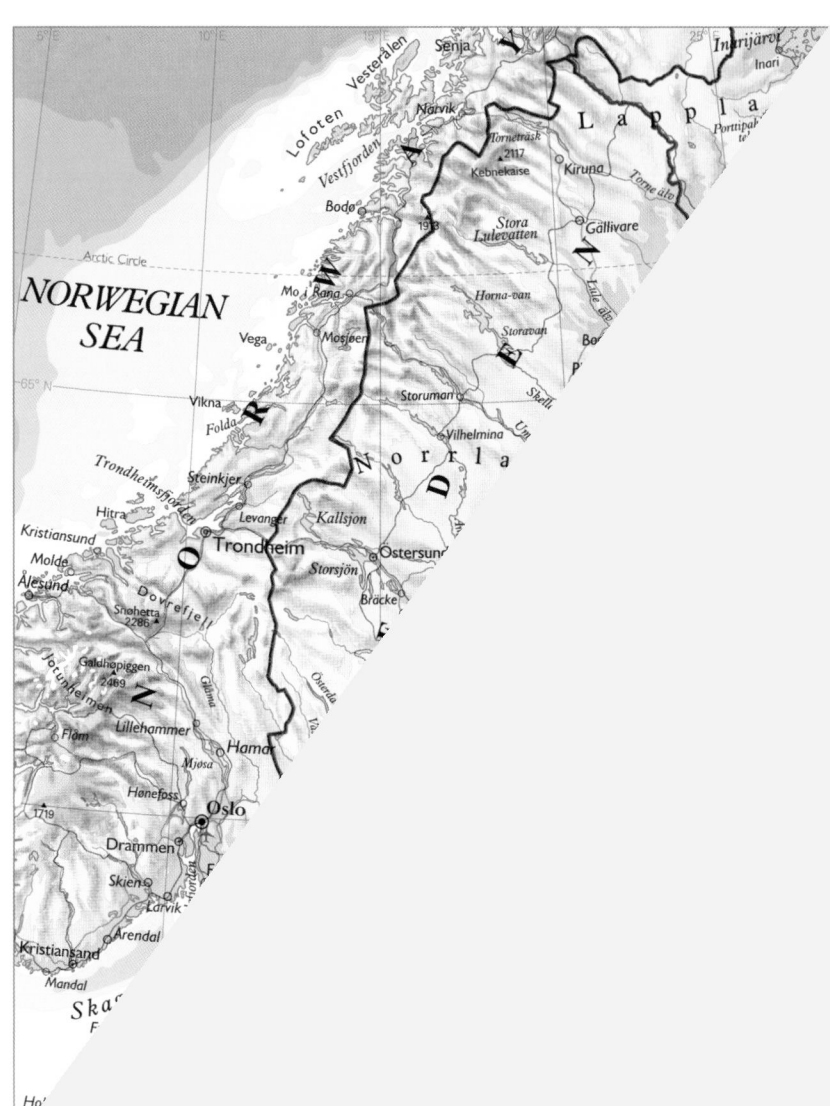

Germany on Sweden's affairs, turned to Queen Margaret of Denmark and Norway for help. The Germans were defeated in 1389 and, in 1397, Sweden, Denmark and Norway were united by a treaty called the Union of Kalmar. However, in 1523, Sweden defeated the Danes and, under Gustavus Vasa, a Swedish noble, Sweden broke away from the union and Gustavus Vasa was crowned as Gustavus I. Gustavus encouraged followers of Martin Luther to spread their ideas, and, by 1540, Lutheranism became the official religion and it remains so to this day.

From the late 16th century, Sweden became involved in a series of wars, during which it gained territory around the Baltic Ocean. King Gustavus Adolf (Gustav II Adolf) won victories for Sweden and the Protestant cause in the Thirty Years' War (1618–48), and, in 1658, Sweden forced Denmark to give up its provinces on the Swedish mainland. By the early 18th century, Sweden was a major European power. But, in 1709, following defeat at the hands of Tsar Peter the Great at the battle of Poltava in the Ukraine, east-south-east of Kiev, a coalition of Russia, Poland and Denmark forced Sweden to give up most of its European possessions.

More wars in the early 19th century, when Swedes fought against the armies of Napoleon, led to Sweden losing Finland to Russia in 1809, though it gained Norway from Denmark in 1814. The 19th century saw great social and economic changes. A fast-increasing population caused emigration, especially to the United States, but the exodus of people was halted by industrialization. By the late 19th century, Sweden was a major industrial nation. With industrialization came demands for political and social reform, and the Social Democratic Party was set up in 1889 to improve the conditions of workers. In June 1905, Norway's parliament voted for independence from Sweden. Sweden almost went to war, but finally acceded to Norway's secession in September 1905. Sweden was neutral in both World Wars.

Politics

The Swedes, who have avoided war or occupation for nearly two centuries, have achieved a high standard of living that is the envy of most other European countries. It has the highest percentage figure for public spending in the OECD (Organization for Economic Co-operation and Development), with more than 70% of the national budget going on one of the widest ranging welfare programmes in the world. In turn, the tax burden is the world's highest, and some Swedes believe that the 'soft' yet paternalistic approach has led to over-government, depersonalization and uniformity. They also argued that the maintenance of the welfare state had practically halted economic growth and was making Sweden less competitive in world markets.

The elections of September 1991 saw the end of the Social Democratic government, which had been in power for six years since 1932, with voters swinging towards parties advocating lower taxes. Other attractive policies appeared to include curbs on immigration and diversion of Third World aid (Sweden spends well above the OECD per capita average each year) to the Baltic states newly independent from the Soviet Union. Though the conservative-led government's austerity measures helped the Social Democrats return to power in 1994, they, too, were advocating economic stringency. The Social Democrats also emerged as the largest single party in the 1998 elections, though their support was at its lowest for 70 years and the prime minister, Göran Persson, was forced to form a minority government.

Other changes were also in the wind. A founder member of EFTA (European Free Trade Association), Sweden nevertheless applied for membership of the European Economic Community in 1991, finally joining the European Union in 1985 following a referendum. However, along with Denmark, Greece and the United Kingdom, it did not adopt the euro, the EU's single currency, on 1 January 1999.

Sweden remains a key nation in Scandinavia. With its long experience and stability, its wide industrial base built on efficiency and quality, together with its strategically central position and relatively large population, it can claim to be the most important power among the Nordic nations. While maintaining its reputation for neutrality, it has played an important part in world affairs and has acted as a negotiator in international disputes.

While some believe that Sweden's biggest problems are of its own

Åland

Swedish settlers colonized various coastal tracts of Finland from the 12th century onwards, and the 6.5% of the Finnish population who are Swedish-speaking include the 25,102 people of Åland. This group of more than 6,500 islands is situated between the two countries at the entrance to the Gulf of Bothnia, about 40 km [25 mls] off the coast of Sweden. Most of the islands are empty of people, but more than 100 of the islands are inhabited. The largest island in the group, which is also called Åland, contains the capital and chief port of Mariehamn (Maarianhamina) as well as the highest point, Orrdalsklint, which reaches 129 m [423 ft]. The south-eastern part of this island is a rich agricultural region, while the north contains rugged granite scenery.

Although the inhabitants voted to secede to Sweden in a 1917 referendum, the result was annulled in 1921 by the League of Nations for strategic reasons, and Åland (as Ahvenanmaa) remained a Finnish province. However, the islands were granted considerable autonomy and still enjoy a large degree of 'home rule' with their own flag, postage stamps and representation at the annual assembly of the Nordic Council.

Boasting many important relics of the Stone, Iron and Bronze Ages, together with Viking graveyards and many medieval churches, the province's income derives mainly from fishing, farming and, increasingly, tourism.

making, it is possible that it will be vulnerable to forces beyond its control. Like its neighbours, Sweden suffers from acid rain generated by Germany and United Kingdom that kills its forests. Also, after the 1986 disaster at Chernobyl (Chornobyl) in the Ukraine, Sweden was forced to reconsider its electricity-generating programme, which, at that time, was more than 40% dependent on nuclear power stations.

Economy

Sweden is a highly developed country, with a per capita gross national product of US $26,220 in 1997. In 1995, farming accounted for 2.4% of the gross domestic product, as compared with 24% from manufacturing. Cereal crops, potatoes, sugar beet and vegetables are grown for human consumption in Skåne and in central Sweden, but the greatest area of cultivated land is given over to the production of fodder crops for cattle and sheep. Dairy farming is important. Many farmers have left the land, attracted by the higher wages and lifestyles in the towns.

The country has created a high standard of living based on industry. Despite that, apart from its large iron ore deposits, it has to import many essential fuels and minerals. Most iron ore obtained from mines at Kiruna and Gällivare in Arctic Sweden is exported via Narvik in Norway or from Luleå to Germany. Development of hydroelectricity has made up for the lack of oil and coal. Sweden is famous for high-quality engineering products, such as ball bearings, agricultural machines, motor vehicles, ships and aircraft. Sweden also has a major forestry industry. In 1996, a decision was taken to decommission all Sweden's nuclear power stations. This was one of the boldest and most expensive environmental pledges ever made by a government.

Sweden's chief exports are machinery and transport equipment, paper products, chemicals and iron and steel products. The country's main trading partners are Germany, the United Kingdom, Norway, the United States and Denmark.

AREA	ETHNIC GROUPS
449,960 sq km	Swedish 91%, Finnish 3%
[173,730 sq mls]	LANGUAGES
POPULATION	Swedish (official), Finnish
8,887,000	RELIGIONS
CAPITAL (POPULATION)	Christianity
Stockholm	(Lutheran 89%,
(1,553,000)	Roman Catholic 2%)
GOVERNMENT	CURRENCY
Constitutional monarchy	Swedish krona = 100 öre

SWITZERLAND

Switzerland has used this square flag since 1848, though the white cross on the red shield has been Switzerland's emblem since the 14th century. The flag of the International Red Cross, which is based in Geneva, was derived from this flag.

Geography

The Swiss Confederation is a landlocked country in Western Europe. Much of the land is mountainous. The Jura Mountains lie along Switzerland's western border with France, while the Swiss Alps make up about 60% of the country in the south and east. Four-fifths of the people of Switzerland live on the fertile Swiss Plateau, which contains most of Switzerland's large cities.

Climate

The climate of Switzerland varies greatly according to the height of the land. The plateau region has a central European climate with warm summers, but cold and snowy winters. Rain occurs all through the year. The rainiest months are in summer.

History and Politics

In 1291, three small cantons (states) united to defend their freedom against the Habsburg rulers of the Holy Roman Empire. They were Schwyz, Uri and Unterwalden, and they called the confederation 'Switzerland'. In the 14th century, Switzerland defeated Austria in three wars of independence. But after a defeat by the French in 1515, the Swiss adopted a policy of neutrality.

In 1815, the Congress of Vienna expanded Switzerland to 22 cantons and guaranteed its neutrality. Switzerland's 23rd canton, Jura, was created in 1979 from part of Bern. Neutrality combined with the vigour of its people have made Switzerland prosperous. In 1993, the Swiss voted against joining the European Union. In 1999, the right-wing People's Party, which called for curbs on immigration, made sweeping gains in national elections. But a centrist coalition continued in office.

Economy

Although lacking in natural resources, Switzerland is a wealthy, industrialized country. Many workers are highly skilled. Major products include chemicals, electrical equipment, machinery and machine tools, precision instruments, processed food, watches and textiles. Farmers produce about three-fifths of the country's food – the rest is imported. Livestock raising, especially dairy farming, is the chief agricultural activity. Crops include fruits, potatoes and wheat. Tourism and banking are also important. Swiss banks attract investors from all over the world.

Switzerland: Arable land 10.4% Permanent crops 0.61% Permanent grassland 29% Forest 31.7%

AREA	Italian 8%, Yugoslav 3%,
41,290 sq km [15,942 sq mls]	Spanish 2%, Romansch 1%
POPULATION	**LANGUAGES**
7,260,000	French, German, Italian,
CAPITAL (POPULATION)	Romansch (all official)
Bern (324,000)	**RELIGIONS**
GOVERNMENT	Christianity (Roman Catholic
Federal republic	46%, Protestant 40%)
ETHNIC GROUPS	**CURRENCY**
German 64%, French 19%,	Swiss franc = 100 centimes

LIECHTENSTEIN

The Principality of Liechtenstein is sandwiched between Switzerland and Austria, where the Rhine cuts its way out of the Alpine chains. The capital, Vaduz, is situated on the Oberland Plateau above the fields and meadows of the Rhine Valley. The climate is relatively mild and the average annual precipitation is about 890 mm [35 in].

Liechtenstein, whose people speak a German dialect, became independent within the Holy Roman Empire in 1719. Since then, it has escaped incorporation into any of Europe's larger nations. It has a tradition of neutrality and has not been involved in a war since 1866. In 1919, Liechtenstein severed its contacts with Austria. Since 1923, it has been in customs and currency union with Switzerland, which also provides overseas representation. Although many Swiss regard it as their 27th canton, it retains full sovereignty in other spheres.

While Liechtenstein is best known abroad for its postage stamps – an important source of income – it is a haven for international companies, attracted by the low taxation and the strictest (most secretive) banking codes in the world. Since World War II, there has been an impressive growth in specialized manufacturing – the product of a mixture of Swiss engineers, Austrian technicians, Italian workers and international capital investment. Another source of income comes from tourists who are intrigued by this miniature state and its royal castle.

AREA	**CAPITAL**
157 sq km [61 sq mls]	Vaduz
POPULATION	**CURRENCY**
32,000	Swiss franc = 100 centimes

SYRIA

Syria has used this flag since 1980. The colours are those used by the Pan-Arab movement. This flag is the one that was used by the United Arab Republic between 1958 and 1961, when Syria was linked with Egypt and North Yemen.

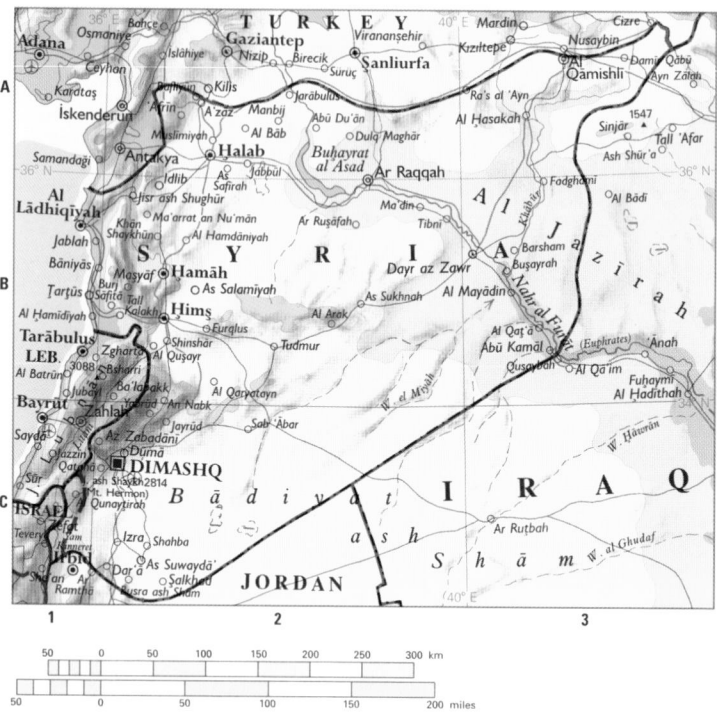

Geography

The Syrian Arab Republic is a country in south-western Asia. The narrow coastal plain is overlooked by a low mountain range which runs north–south. Another range, the Jabal ash Sharqi, runs along the border with Lebanon. South of this range is a region called the Golan Heights. Israel has occupied this region since 1967. East of the mountains, the bulk of Syria consists of fertile valleys, grassy plains and large sandy deserts. This region contains the valley of the River Euphrates (Nahr al Furat).

Climate

The coast has a Mediterranean climate, with dry, warm summers and wet, mild winters. The low mountains cut off Damascus from the sea. It has less rainfall than the coastal areas and becomes drier to the east.

SYRIA (DAMASCUS)

Damascus is isolated from the maritime influence of the Mediterranean by the Lebanon Mountains. Rainfall is lighter here than on the coast. Winter becomes colder further to the east, and frost and snow are common. Frosts can occur at Damascus between November and March. On the higher mountains, patches of snow lie all year. Summers are hot and dry with a large diurnal range of temperature of up to 20°C [36°F].

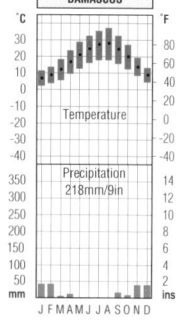

History

In early times, Syria lay at the crossroads of Asia, Africa and Europe. As a result, it is rich in historic sites from a wide range of periods. The earliest known settlers were Semites who arrived around 3,500 years ago. They set up city-states, such as Ebla, which existed between about 2700 and 2200 BC. The people of Ebla used clay tablets inscribed in cuneiform, an ancient system of writing developed by the Sumer people of Mesopotamia. Later conquerors of the area included the Akkadians, Canaanites, Phoenicians, Amorites, Aramaeans and the Hebrews, who introduced monotheism. The Assyrians occupied the area from 732 BC until 612 BC, when the Babylonians took over. The ancient Persians conquered the Babylonians in 539 BC, but the armies of Alexander the Great swept into the region in 331 BC, introducing Greek culture in their wake. The Romans took over in 64 BC, and Syria remained under Roman law for nearly 700 years.

Christianity became the state religion of Syria in the 4th century AD, but, in 636, Muslims from Arabia invaded the region. Islam gradually replaced Christianity as the main religion, and Arabic became the chief language. From 661, Damascus became the capital of a vast Muslim empire which was ruled by the Ummayad Dynasty. But the Abbasid Dynasty took over in 750 and the centre of power passed to Baghdad. From the late 11th century, Crusaders sought to win the Holy Land from the Muslims. But the Crusaders were unsuccessful in their aim because Saladin, a Muslim ruler of Egypt, defeated the Crusaders and ruled most of the area by the end of the 12th century.

The Mameluke Dynasty of Egypt ruled Syria from 1260–1516, when the region became part of the huge Turkish Ottoman Empire. During World War I, Syrians and other Arabs fought alongside British forces and overthrew the Turks.

Politics

Following World War I, Greater Syria was divided into Syria, which was later divided into Syria and Lebanon, and Palestine, which later became Palestine and Transjordan. France was mandated by the League of Nations to govern Syria and Lebanon. France developed the region's economy, but nationalist Syrians yearned for independence.

Syria became fully independent from France in 1946 and many Syrians wanted to re-create Greater Syria. But the partition of Palestine and the creation of Israel in 1947 led to the first Arab-Israeli war, when Syria and other Arab nations failed to defeat Israeli forces. In 1949, a military coup established a military regime, starting a long period of revolts and changes of government. In 1967, in the third Arab-Israeli war (known as the Six-Day War), Syria lost the strategically important Golan Heights.

In 1970, Lieutenant-General Hafez al Assad led a military revolt, becoming Syria's president in 1971. His repressive but stable regime attracted much Western criticism and was heavily reliant on Arab aid. But, Syria's anti-Iraq stance in the 1991 Gulf War, and the involvement of about 20,000 Syrian troops in the conflict, greatly improved its standing in the West. In the mid-1990s, Syria had talks with Israel over the future of the Golan Heights. Negotiations were suspended after the election of Binyamin Netanyahu's right-wing government in Israel in 1996. The election of the left-wing Ehud Barak as Israel's prime minister in 1999 held out new hopes for a peace settlement.

Economy

The World Bank classifies Syria as a 'lower-middle-income' developing country. But it has great potential for development. Its main resources are oil, hydroelectricity from the dam at Lake Assad (Buburut al Asad), and fertile land. Agriculture employs about 26% of the population and accounts for around 27% of the total economic production. Crops include barley, cotton, fruits, sugar beet, tobacco and wheat. Sheep are the most important livestock, followed by goats and cattle. Oil is the chief mineral product, and phosphates are mined to make fertilizers. Manufacturing is increasing, especially the production of textiles and processed farm products. Syria's leading export is oil, followed by vegetables and fruits.

AREA	**ETHNIC GROUPS**
185,180 sq km [71,498 sq mls]	Arab 89%, Kurd 6%
POPULATION	**LANGUAGES**
16,673,000	Arabic (official)
CAPITAL (POPULATION)	**RELIGIONS**
Damascus (Dimashq, 2,230,000)	Islam 90%, Christianity 9%
GOVERNMENT	**CURRENCY**
Multiparty republic	Syrian pound = 100 piastres

TAIWAN

In 1928, the Chinese Nationalists adopted this design as China's national flag and used it in the long struggle against Mao Zedong's Communist army. When the nationalists were forced to retreat to Taiwan in 1949, their flag went with them.

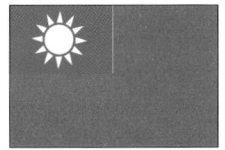

Geography

Taiwan, formerly known as Formosa, is an island about 140 km [87 mls] off the south coast of mainland China. The country also administers a number of islands close to the mainland. They include Quemoy (Jinmen) and Matsu (Mazu). High mountain ranges, extending the length of the island, occupy the central and eastern regions, and only a quarter of the island's surface is used for agriculture. The highest peak is Yü San (Morrison Mountain), reaching 3,997 m [13,113 ft] above sea level. Several peaks in the central ranges rise to more than 3,000 m [10,000 ft], and carry dense forests of broadleaved evergreen trees, such as camphor and Chinese cork oak. Above 1,500 m [5,000 ft], conifers, such as pine, larch and cedar, dominate. In the east, where the mountains often drop steeply down to the sea, the short rivers have cut deep gorges. The western slopes are more gentle.

Climate

Taiwan has a tropical monsoon climate. The average annual rainfall almost everywhere exceeds 2,000 mm [79 in]. From July to September, the island is often hit by typhoons. Humidity is high in summer, when the heat may become oppressive.

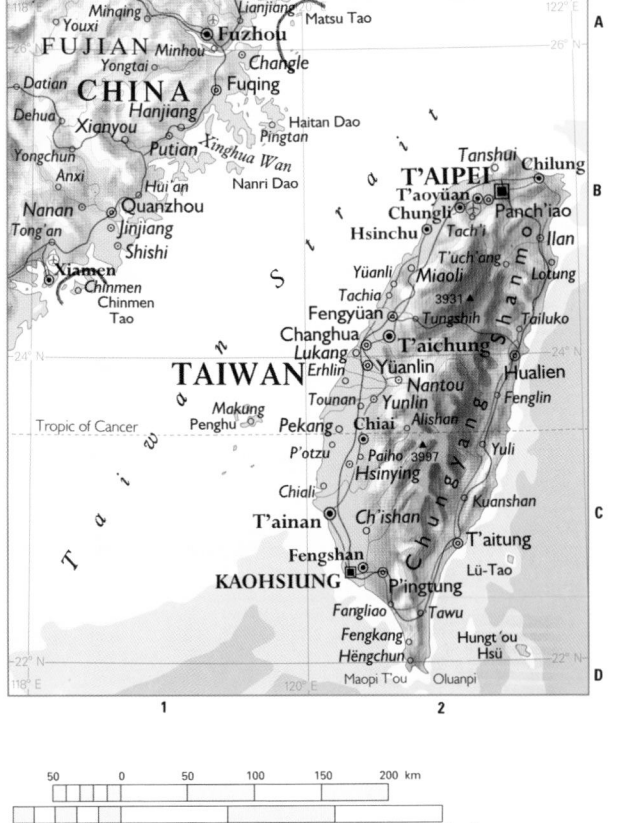

TAIWAN (TAIPEI)

Taiwan lies on the tropic line, but as the central island range reaches over 3,000 m [10,000 ft] at many points, it bears snow during winter. In Taipei night temperatures fall below 20°C [68°F] from October to March, but may reach over 30°C [86°F] in the day from June to September. Rainfall is heavy, falling mainly in the summer. Sunshine levels in the north are low – under 3 hours per day from December to March and only over 7 hours in July and August. The summer heat, when temperatures soar to 38°C [100°F], may be oppressive due to the high humidity.

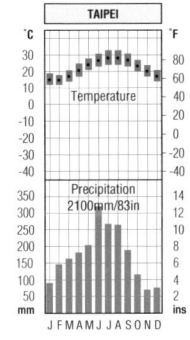

History

Chinese settlers arrived in Taiwan from the 7th century AD, displacing the Aboriginal people, but large settlements were not established until the 17th century. The Portuguese first reached the island in 1590. They named the island Formosa (meaning 'beautiful island'), but did not settle there. The Dutch occupied a trading port in 1624, but they were driven out in 1661 by refugees from the deposed Ming Dynasty on the mainland. A Ming official tried to use the island as a base for attacking the Manchu Dynasty, but the Manchus took the island in 1683 and incorporated it into what is now Fujian province.

The Manchus settled the island in the late 18th century and, by the mid-19th century, the population had increased to about 2,500,000. The island had become a major producer of sugar and rice, which were exported to the mainland. In 1886, the island became a Chinese province and Taipei became its capital in 1894. However, in 1895, Taiwan was ceded to Japan following the Chinese-Japanese War. Japan used the island as a source of food crops and, from the 1930s, they developed manufacturing industries based on hydroelectricity.

Politics

In 1945, the Japanese army surrendered Taiwan to General Chiang Kai-shek's Nationalist Chinese government. Following victories by Mao Zedong's Communists, about 2 million Nationalists, together with their leader, fled the mainland to Taiwan in the two years before 1949, when the People's Republic of China was proclaimed. The influx was met with hostility by the 8 million Taiwanese, and the new regime, the 'Republic of China', was imposed with force. Boosted by help from the United States, Chiang's government set about ambitious programmes for land reform and industrial expansion and, by 1980, Taiwan had become one of the top 20 industrial nations. Economic development was accompanied by a marked rise in living standards.

Nevertheless, Taiwan remained politically isolated and it lost its seat in the United Nations to Communist China in 1971. It was then abandoned diplomatically by the United States in 1979, when the US switched its recognition to mainland China. However, as economic progress continued, the authoritarian regime in Taiwan lifted martial law in 1987. In 1988, a native Taiwanese became president and in 1991 the country's first general election was held.

However, China continued to regard Taiwan as a Chinese province and, in 1999, tension developed when the Taiwanese President Lee Teng-hui stated that relations between China and Taiwan should be on a 'special state-by-state' basis. This angered the Chinese President Jiang Zemin, whose 'one-nation' policy was based on the concept that China and Taiwan should be regarded as one country with two equal governments. Tension mounted in March 2000, when Taiwan's opposition leader, Chen Shi-bian, was elected president. Chen had expressed a pro-independence stance and this had led to threats of a Chinese invasion should Taiwan attempt to declare itself a separate state.

Economy

The economy depends on manufacturing and trade. Manufactures include electronic goods, footwear and clothing, ships and television sets. The western coastal plains produce large rice crops. Other products include bananas, pineapples, sugar cane, sweet potatoes and tea. The growth of the economy has been a huge success story, and, despite the regional recession in 1997–8, the economy continues to grow.

AREA	mainland Chinese 14%
36,000 sq km [13,900 sq mls]	**LANGUAGES**
POPULATION	Mandarin (official),
21,908,000	Min, Hakka
CAPITAL (POPULATION)	**RELIGIONS**
Taipei (T'aipei, 2,653,000)	Buddhist 43%,
GOVERNMENT	Taoist and Confucian 49%
Unitary multiparty republic	**CURRENCY**
ETHNIC GROUPS	New Taiwan dollar
Taiwanese (Han Chinese) 84%,	= 100 cents

Tajikistan's flag was adopted in 1993. It replaced the flag used during the Communist period which showed a hammer and sickle. The new flag shows an unusual gold crown under an arc of seven stars on the central white band.

Arable land 5.83% Permanent crops 0.28%
Permanent grassland 25.2% Forest 3.82%

Arab armies conquered the area in the mid-7th century and introduced Islam, which remains the chief religion today. The region was later ruled by various Turkic tribes and later by the Mongols, led by Genghis Khan. Turkic peoples, called Uzbeks, ruled the area from the 16th to the 19th centuries.

Russia conquered parts of Tajikistan in the late 19th century and, by 1920, Russia took complete control. In 1924, Tajikistan became part of the Uzbek Soviet Socialist Republic. However, in 1929, it was expanded, taking in some areas that were populated by Uzbeks, becoming the Tajik Soviet Socialist Republic.

While the Soviet Union began to introduce reforms in the 1980s, many Tajiks demanded freedom. In 1989, the Tajik government made Tajik the official language instead of Russian and, in 1990, it stated that its local laws overruled Soviet laws. Tajikistan became fully independent in 1991, following the break-up of the Soviet Union. As the poorest of the ex-Soviet republics, Tajikistan faced many problems in trying to introduce a free-market system.

Geography and Climate

The Republic of Tajikistan is one of the five central Asian republics that formed part of the former Soviet Union. Only 7% of the land is below 1,000 m [3,280 ft], while almost all of eastern Tajikistan is above 3,000 m [9,840 ft]. The highest point is Communism Peak (Pik Kommunizma), which reaches 7,495 m [24,590 ft]. The main ranges are the westwards extension of the Tian Shan Range in the north and the snow-capped Pamirs (Pamir) in the south-east. Earthquakes are common throughout the country.

Tajikistan has an extreme continental climate. Summers are hot and dry in the lower valleys, and winters are long and bitterly cold in the mountains.

In 1992, civil war broke out between the government, which was run by former Communists, and an alliance of democrats and Islamic forces. The government maintained control, but it relied heavily on aid from the Commonwealth of Independent States, the organization through which most of the former Soviet republics kept in touch. Presidential elections in 1994 resulted in victory for Imomali Rakhmonov, though the Islamic opposition did not recognize the result. A cease-fire was signed in December 1996. Further agreements in 1997 provided for the opposition to have 30% of the ministerial posts in the government. But many small groups excluded from the agreement continued to undermine the peace process through a series of killings and military actions. In 1999, Rakhmonov was re-elected president.

TAJIKISTAN (DUSHANBE)

Dushanbe lies in a cotton-growing valley at the foot of the Gissar Range (Khrebet Gissarskiy). The city's sheltered position moderates temperatures during winter, while the summer heat is mitigated by cool breezes from the mountains to the north-east. The average annual rainfall is low, giving Dushanbe a desert climate. The majority of the scant rainfall occurs during the winter and spring.

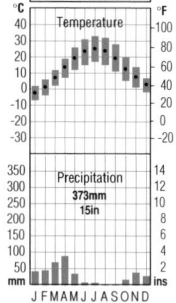

Economy

The World Bank classifies Tajikistan as a 'low-income' developing country. Agriculture is the main activity and cotton is the chief product. Other crops include fruits, grains and vegetables. The country has large hydroelectric power resources and it produces aluminium.

AREA	Russian 8%, Tatar,
143,100 sq km [55,520 sq mls]	Kyrgyz, Ukrainian,
POPULATION	German
6,020,000	**LANGUAGES**
CAPITAL (POPULATION)	Tajik (official), Uzbek,
Dushanbe (524,000)	Russian
GOVERNMENT	**RELIGIONS**
Transitional democracy	Islam
ETHNIC GROUPS	**CURRENCY**
Tajik 62%, Uzbek 24%,	Tajik rouble = 100 tanga

History and Politics

The ancestors of the people of Tajikistan were Persians who had settled in the area about 2,500 years ago. The area was conquered many times. Early invaders were the Persians in the 6th century BC and the Macedonian Greeks led by Alexander the Great in 331 BC. From 323 BC, the area was split into several independent states.

TANZANIA

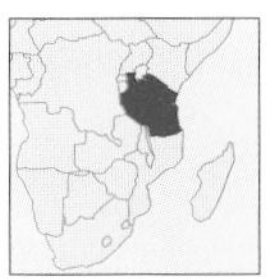

Tanzania's flag was adopted in 1964 when mainland Tanganyika joined with the island nation of Zanzibar to form the United Republic of Tanzania. The green represents agriculture and the yellow minerals. The black represents the people, while the blue symbolizes Zanzibar.

Geography

The United Republic of Tanzania consists of the former mainland country of Tanganyika and the island nation of Zanzibar, which also includes the island of Pemba. Behind a narrow coastal plain, the majority of Tanzania is a plateau lying between 900 m and 1,500 m [2,950–4,920 ft]. The plateau is broken by arms of the Great African Rift Valley. The western arm contains lakes Nyasa (also called Malawi) and Tanganyika, while the eastern arm contains the strongly alkaline Lake Natron, together with lakes Eyasi and Manyara. Lake Victoria occupies a shallow depression in the plateau and it is not situated within the Rift Valley. Kilimanjaro, the highest peak, is an extinct volcano. At 5,895 m [19,340 ft], it is also Africa's highest mountain. Zanzibar and Pemba are coral islands.

Climate

The coast has a hot and humid climate, with the greatest rainfall in April and May. The inland plateaux and mountains are cooler and less humid. The Rift Valley is hot, but Mount Kilimanjaro is permanently covered by snow and ice.

TANZANIA (DAR ES SALAAM)

In East Africa the winds blow mainly parallel to the coast and rainfall is lower than in many equatorial regions. The heaviest rain falls in April and May, when the intertropical rainbelt moves north. It is followed by the south-east trades which have lost much moisture over the mountains of Madagascar before reaching East Africa.

History

Around 2,000 years ago, Arabs, Persians and even Chinese probably traded along the Tanzanian coast, and the old cities and ruins testify to its importance. Arab traders often intermarried with local people and the Arab-African people produced the distinctive Arab-Swahili culture. The Portuguese took control of coastal trade in the early 16th century, but the Arabs regained control in the 17th century. In 1698, Arabs from Oman took control of Zanzibar. From this base, they developed inland trade, bringing gold, ivory and slaves from the interior. During the 19th century, European explorers and missionaries were active, mapping the country and striving to stop the slave trade.

Politics

Mainland Tanganyika became a German territory in the 1880s, while Zanzibar (including Pemba) became a British protectorate in 1890. The Germans introduced a system of forced labour to develop plantations. This led to a major rebellion in 1905, which was put down with great brutality. Britain gained control of Tanganyika in World War I and was granted a mandate to rule it by the League of Nations. Tanganyika won its independence in 1961, followed by Zanzibar in 1963. In 1964, Tanganyika and Zanzibar united to form the United Republic of Tanzania. The country's first president, Julius Nyerere, pursued socialist policies of self-help (called *ujamaa* in Swahili). While many of its social reforms were successful, the country failed to make economic progress. Nyerere resigned as president in 1985, though he remained influential until his death in 1999. His successors, Ali Hassan Mwinyi, who served from 1985 until 1995, and Benjamin Mkapa, pursued more liberal economic policies.

Arable land 3.40% Permanent crops 0.57% Forest 38.1%

Economy

Tanzania is one of the world's poorest countries. Although crops are grown on only 5% of the land, agriculture employs 85% of the people. Most farmers grow only enough to feed their families. Food crops include bananas, cassava, maize, millet, rice and vegetables. Export crops include coffee, cotton, cashew nuts, tea and tobacco. Other crops grown for export include cloves, coconuts and sisal. Some farmers raise animals, but sleeping sickness and drought restrict the areas for livestock farming. Diamonds and other gems are mined, together with some coal and gold. Industry is mostly small-scale. Manufactures include processed food, fertilizers, petroleum products and textiles.

Tourism is increasing. Tanzania has beautiful beaches, but its main attractions are its magnificent national parks and reserves, including the celebrated Serengeti and the Ngorongoro Crater. These are renowned for their wildlife and are among the world's finest. Tanzania also contains a major archaeological site, Olduvai Gorge, west of the Serengeti. Here, in 1964, the British archaeologist and anthropologist, Louis Leakey, discovered the remains of ancient human-like creatures.

AREA	Hehet and Bena 7%,
945,090 sq km [364,899 sq mls]	Makonde 6%, Haya 6%
POPULATION	**LANGUAGES**
30,609,000	Swahili and English (both official)
CAPITAL (POPULATION)	**RELIGIONS**
Dodoma (204,000)	Christianity (mostly Roman
GOVERNMENT	Catholic) 34%, Islam 33%
Multiparty republic	(99% in Zanzibar), traditional
ETHNIC GROUPS	beliefs and others 33%
Nyamwezi and Sukuma 21%,	**CURRENCY**
Swahili 9%,	Tanzanian shilling = 100 cents

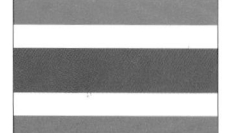

Thailand's flag was adopted in 1917. In the late 19th century, it featured a white elephant on a plain red flag. In 1916, white stripes were introduced above and below the elephant, but in 1917 the elephant was dropped and a central blue band was added.

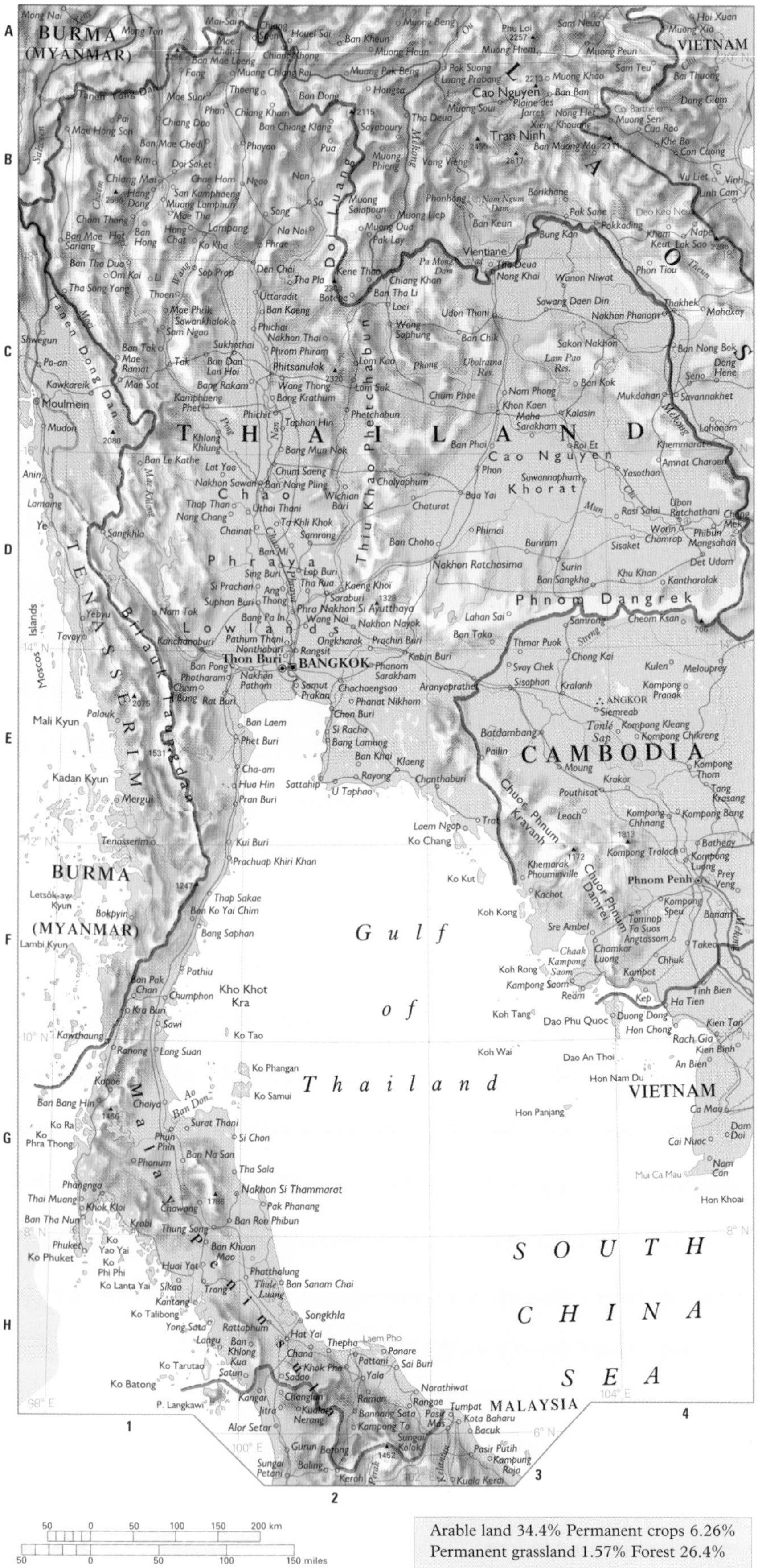

Geography

The Kingdom of Thailand is one of the ten countries in South-east Asia. The highest land occurs in the north, where Doi Inthanon, the highest peak, reaches 2,595 m [8,514 ft]. The Khorat Plateau, in the north-east, makes up about 30% of the country and is the most heavily populated part of Thailand. In the south, Thailand shares the finger-like Malay Peninsula with Burma and Malaysia.

Climate

Thailand has a tropical climate. Monsoon winds from the south-west bring heavy rains between the months of May and October. The rainfall in Bangkok is lower than in many other parts of South-east Asia, because mountains shelter the central plains from the rain-bearing winds.

History and Politics

The first Thai state was set up in the 13th century. By 1350, it included most of what is now Thailand. European contact began in the early 16th century. But, in the late 17th century, the Thais, fearing interference in their affairs, forced all Europeans to leave. This policy continued for 150 years. In 1782, a Thai General, Chao Phraya Chakkri, became king, founding a dynasty which continues today. The country became known as Siam, and Bangkok became its capital. From the mid-19th century, contacts with the West were restored.

In World War I, Siam supported the Allies against Germany and Austria-Hungary. But in 1941, the country was conquered by Japan and became its ally. But, after the end of World War II, it became an ally of the United States.

Economy

Since 1967, when Thailand became a member of ASEAN (Association of South-east Asian Nations), its economy has grown, especially its manufacturing and service industries. However, in 1997, it suffered recession along with other eastern Asian countries.

Despite its rapid progress, the World Bank classifies the country as a 'lower-middle-income' developing country. Manufactures, including food products, machinery, timber products and textiles, are exported, but agriculture still employs two-thirds of the people. Rice is the main food, while other major crops include cassava, cotton, maize, pineapples, rubber, sugar cane and tobacco. Thailand also mines tin and other minerals, and tourism is a major source of income.

AREA	Malay 4%,
513,120 sq km	Khmer 3%
[198,116 sq mls]	**LANGUAGES**
POPULATION	Thai (official),
60,037,000	Chinese, Malay
CAPITAL (POPULATION)	**RELIGIONS**
Bangkok (5,876,000)	Buddhism 94%,
GOVERNMENT	Islam 4%,
Constitutional monarchy	Christianity 1%
ETHNIC GROUPS	**CURRENCY**
Thai 80%, Chinese 12%,	Thai baht = 100 satang

Arable land 34.4% Permanent crops 6.26%
Permanent grassland 1.57% Forest 26.4%

TOGO – SEE BENIN, PAGE 54; TONGA – SEE PACIFIC OCEAN, PAGES 174–178; TRINIDAD AND TOBAGO – SEE CARIBBEAN SEA, PAGES 71–76; TRISTAN DA CUNHA – SEE ATLANTIC OCEAN, PAGES 41–43

TUNISIA

Tunisia's flag originated in about 1835 when the country was officially under Turkish rule. It became the national flag in 1956, when Tunisia became independent from France. The flag contains two traditional symbols of Islam, the crescent and the star.

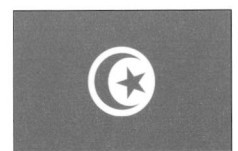

Geography and Climate

The Republic of Tunisia is the smallest country in North Africa. The mountains in the north are an eastwards and comparatively low extension of the Atlas Mountains.

To the north and east of the mountains lie fertile plains, especially between Sfax, Tunis and Bizerte. South of the mountains lie broad plateaux which descend towards the south. This low-lying region contains a large salt pan, called the Chott Djerid, and part of the Sahara.

Northern Tunisia has a Mediterranean climate, with dry summers, and mild winters with a moderate rainfall. The average yearly rainfall decreases towards the south, which forms part of the Sahara.

TUNISIA (TUNIS)

Although most rain in Tunisia falls during winter when the region is affected by low pressure, prevailing north-easterly winds from the sea in summer result in a shorter dry season than is found in many parts of the Mediterranean basin. Rain falls on a few days during summer. The influence of the sea also helps to moderate extremes of temperature, and though mostly sunny, summer days are seldom oppressive, humidity being low.

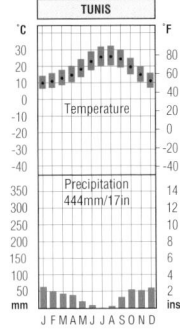

History and Politics

Tunisia has come under the influence of a succession of cultures, each of which has left its mark on the country, giving Tunisia a distinct identity and a long tradition of urban life. The Phoenicians began the Carthaginian Empire in Tunisia around 1100 BC and, according to legend, the colony of Carthage was established in 814 BC on a site near present-day Tunis. At its peak, Carthage controlled large areas in the eastern Mediterranean but, following the three Punic Wars with Rome, Carthage was destroyed in 146 BC. The Romans ruled the area for 600 years until the Vandals defeated the Romans in AD 439. The Vandals were finally conquered by the Byzantines. Arabs reached the area in the mid-7th century, introducing Islam and the Arabic language. In 1547, Tunisia came under the rule of the Turkish Ottoman Empire.

In 1881, France established a protectorate over Tunisia and ruled the country until 1956. Tunisian aspirations were felt before World War I, but it was not until 1934 that Habib Bourguiba founded the first effective opposition group, the Neo-Destour (New Constitution) Party, which was renamed the Socialist Destour Party in 1964, and is now known as the Constitutional Assembly. Tunisia supported the Allies during World War II and it was the scene of much fierce fighting. Following independence, the new parliament abolished the monarchy and declared Tunisia to be a republic in 1957. The nationalist leader, Habib Bourguiba, became president.

In 1975, Bourguiba was elected president for life. His government introduced many reforms, including votes for women. But problems arose from the government's successes. For example, the establishment of a national school system led to a very rapid increase in the number of educated people who were unable to find jobs that measured up to their qualifications. The growth of tourism, which provided a valuable source of foreign currency, also led to fears that Western influences might undermine traditional Muslim values. Finally, the prime minister, Zine el Abidine Ben Ali, removed Bourguiba from office in 1987 and succeeded him as president. He was elected president in 1989 and 1994, and his party dominated the Chamber of Deputies, though some seats were reserved for opposition parties whatever their proportion of the popular vote. But he faced opposition from Islamic fundamentalists. Occasional violence and the suppression of human rights, including the banning of al-Nahda, the main Islamic party, marred his presidency. However, Islamic fundamentalism in Tunisia did not prove to be anything like as effective as in Algeria.

Economy

The World Bank classifies Tunisia as a 'middle-income' developing country. Its main natural resources are oil and phosphates. Agriculture employs 22% of the people. Chief crops are barley, citrus fruits, dates, grapes, olives, sugar beet, tomatoes and wheat. Sheep are the most important livestock, but goats and cattle are also raised. Tourism has grown considerably. The number of tourists in 1996 approached 4 million, most of whom came from Europe.

Since independence, new industries and tourism have transformed a number of coastal towns, though the interior, by comparison, has been neglected. Major manufactures include cement, flour, phosphoric acid, processed food and steel. Exports include clothing and accessories, machinery and electrical products, oil and phosphates. An important stimulus to the economy was the signing of a free-trade agreement with the European Union in 1995. Tunisia became the first Arab country on the Mediterranean to sign such an agreement.

AREA	**ETHNIC GROUPS**
163,610 sq km [63,170 sq mls]	Arab 98%, Berber 1%, French
POPULATION	**LANGUAGES**
9,380,000	Arabic (official), French
CAPITAL (POPULATION)	**RELIGIONS**
Tunis (1,827,000)	Islam 99%
GOVERNMENT	**CURRENCY**
Multiparty republic	Dinar = 1,000 millimes

Turkey's flag was adopted when the Republic of Turkey was established in 1923. The crescent moon and the five-pointed star are traditional symbols of Islam. They were used on earlier Turkish flags used by the Turkish Ottoman Empire.

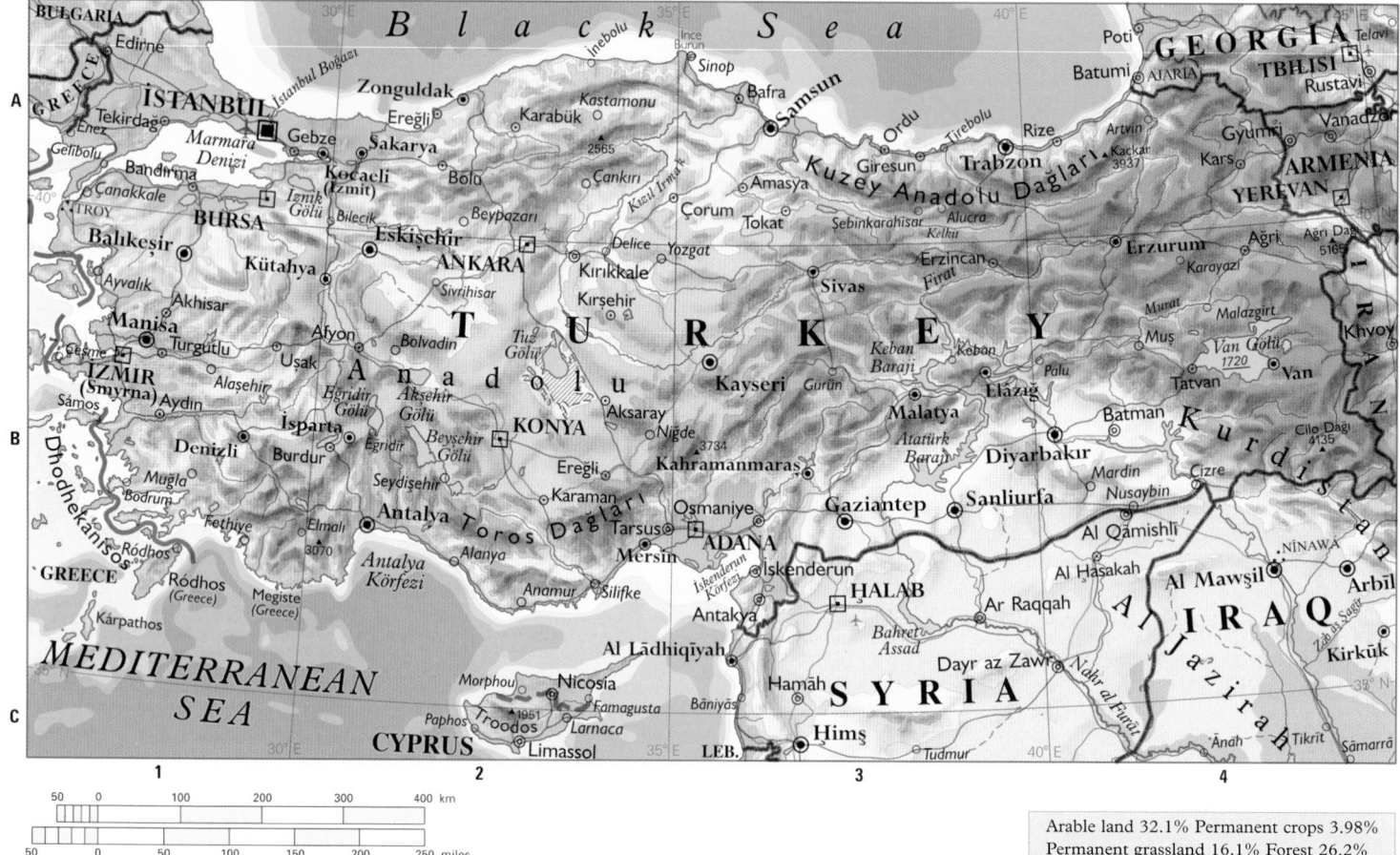

Arable land 32.1% Permanent crops 3.98%
Permanent grassland 16.1% Forest 26.2%

Geography and Climate

The Republic of Turkey lies in two continents. The European section lies west of a waterway between the Black and Mediterranean seas. This waterway consists of the Bosporus, on which the city of Istanbul stands, the Sea of Marmara and a narrow strait called the Dardanelles. European Turkey, also called Thrace, is a fertile, hilly region. Most of the Asian part of Turkey consists of plateaux and mountains, which rise to 5,165 m [16,945 ft] at Mount Ararat (Agri Dagi) near the border with Armenia.

Central Turkey has a dry climate, with hot, sunny summers and cold winters. The driest part of the central plateau lies south of the city of Ankara, around Lake Tuz. Western Turkey has a Mediterranean climate, while the Black Sea coast has cooler summers.

History and Politics

In AD 330, the Roman Empire moved its capital to Byzantium, which it renamed Constantinople. Constantinople became the capital of the East Roman (or Byzantine) Empire in 395. Muslim Seljuk Turks from central Asia invaded Anatolia in the 11th century. In the 14th century, another group of Turks, the Ottomans, conquered the area. In 1435, the Ottoman Turks took Constantinople, which they called Istanbul.

The Ottoman Turks built up a large empire which finally collapsed during World War I (1914–18). In 1923, Turkey became a republic. Its leader Mustafa Kemal, or Atatürk ('father of the Turks'), launched policies to modernize and secularize the country.

Since the 1940s, Turkey has sought to strengthen its ties with Western powers. It joined NATO (North Atlantic Treaty Organization) in 1951 and applied to join the European Economic Community in 1987. But Turkey's conflict with Greece, together with its invasion of northern Cyprus in 1974, have led many Europeans to treat Turkey's aspirations with caution. Political instability, military coups, conflict with Kurdish

nationalists in eastern Turkey and concern about the country's record on human rights are other problems. Turkey has enjoyed democracy since 1983, though, in 1998, the government banned the Islamist Welfare Party, accusing it of violating secular principles. In 1999, the Muslim Virtue Party (successor to Islamist Welfare Party) lost ground. The largest numbers of parliamentary seats were won by the ruling Democratic Left Party and the far-right Nationalist Action Party. Together, they formed a coalition government.

Economy

The World Bank classifies Turkey as a 'lower-middle-income' developing country. Agriculture employs 47% of the people, and barley, cotton, fruits, maize, tobacco and wheat are major crops. Livestock farming is important and wool is a leading product.

Turkey produces chromium, but manufacturing is the chief activity. Manufactures include processed farm products and textiles, cars, fertilizers, iron and steel, machinery, metal products and paper products. More than 9 million tourists visited Turkey in 1998. However, in 1999, tourism was threatened by Kurdish bombings in Ankara and Istanbul.

AREA	**ETHNIC GROUPS**
779,450 sq km	Turkish 86%,
[300,946 sq mls]	Kurdish 11%,
POPULATION	Arab 2%
64,568,000	**LANGUAGES**
CAPITAL (POPULATION)	Turkish (official), Kurdish
Ankara	**RELIGIONS**
(3,028,000)	Islam 99%
GOVERNMENT	**CURRENCY**
Multiparty republic	Turkish lira = 100 kurus

TURKMENISTAN

Turkmenistan's flag was adopted in 1992. It incorporates a typical Turkmen carpet design. The crescent is a symbol of Islam, while the five stars and the five elements in the carpet represent the traditional tribal groups of Turkmenistan.

Geography

The Republic of Turkmenistan is one of five central Asian republics which once formed part of the Soviet Union. Most of the land is low-lying, with mountains on the southern and south-western borders.

In the west lies the salty Caspian Sea. A depression called the Kara Bogaz Gol (Garabogazköl) Bay contains the country's lowest point. Most of the country is arid and Asia's largest sand desert, the Garagum, covers 80% of the country.

Climate

Turkmenistan has a continental climate, with average annual rainfall varying from 80 mm [3 in] in the desert to 300 mm [12 in] in the mountains. Summers are hot but temperatures during winter drop below freezing.

History

Russia took over in the 1870s. After the Russian Revolution, the area came under Communist rule and, in 1924, it became the Turkmen Soviet Socialist Republic. Communists controlled all aspects of life.

Politics

During the 1980s, the Soviet Union introduced reforms, and the Turkmen demanded more freedom. In 1990, the Turkmen government stated that its laws overruled Soviet laws. In 1991, Turkmenistan became independent after the break-up of the Soviet Union, but kept ties with Russia through the Commonwealth of Independent States (CIS).

In 1992, Turkmenistan adopted a new constitution, allowing for political parties, providing that they were not ethnic or religious in character. However, Turkmenistan remained a one-party state and, in 1992, Saparmurad Niyazov, the former Communist and now Democratic Party leader, was the only candidate. In 1994, 99.5% of voters in a referendum were in favour of prolonging his term of office to 2002.

Economy

Faced with numerous economic problems, Turkmenistan joined the Economic Co-operation Organization which was set up in 1985 by Iran, Pakistan and Turkey. The World Bank classifies Turkmenistan as a 'lower-middle-income' country. The chief resources are oil and natural gas, but agriculture is important. The chief crop, which is grown on irrigated land, is cotton. Grains and vegetables are also important.

AREA
488,100 sq km
[188,450 sq mls]
POPULATION
4,298,000
CAPITAL (POPULATION)
Ashgabat (407,000)
GOVERNMENT
Single-party republic

ETHNIC GROUPS
Turkmen 72%, Russian 10%,
Uzbek 9%, Kazak 3%, Tatar
LANGUAGES
Turkmen (official), Russian
RELIGIONS
Islam
CURRENCY
Manat = 100 tenesi

UZBEKISTAN

The Republic of Uzbekistan is one of five republics in Central Asia which were once part of the Soviet Union. Plains cover most of western Uzbekistan, with highlands in the east. The main rivers drain into the Aral Sea. Most of the country is desert.

Uzbekistan has a continental climate. Winters are cold, but temperatures soar in the summer. The west is extremely arid.

After the Russian Revolution of 1917, Communists took over, setting up the Uzbek Soviet Socialist Republic in 1924. In the late 1980s, people demanded more freedom and, in 1990, the government stated that its laws overruled those of the Soviet Union. Uzbekistan became independent in 1991, but retained links with Russia through the Commonwealth of Independent States. Islam Karimov, leader of the People's Democratic Party (formerly the Communist Party), was elected president in December 1991. In 1992–3, many opposition

leaders were arrested because the government said that they threatened national stability. In 1994–5, the PDP won victories in national elections and, in 1995, a referendum extended Karimov's term in office until 2000.

The World Bank classifies Uzbekistan as a 'lower-middle-income' developing country. Uzbekistan produces coal, copper, gold and oil.

AREA
447,400 sq km [172,740 sq mls]
POPULATION
23,784,000

CAPITAL (POPULATION)
Tashkent (Toshkent, 2,106,000)
CURRENCY
Som = 100 tyiyn

TURKS AND CAICOS ISLANDS – SEE CARIBBEAN SEA, PAGES 71–76;
TUVALU – SEE PACIFIC OCEAN, PAGES 174–178

The flag used by the party that won the first national election was adopted as the national flag when Uganda became independent from Britain in 1962. The black represents the people, the yellow the sun, and the red brotherhood. The crested crane is the country's emblem.

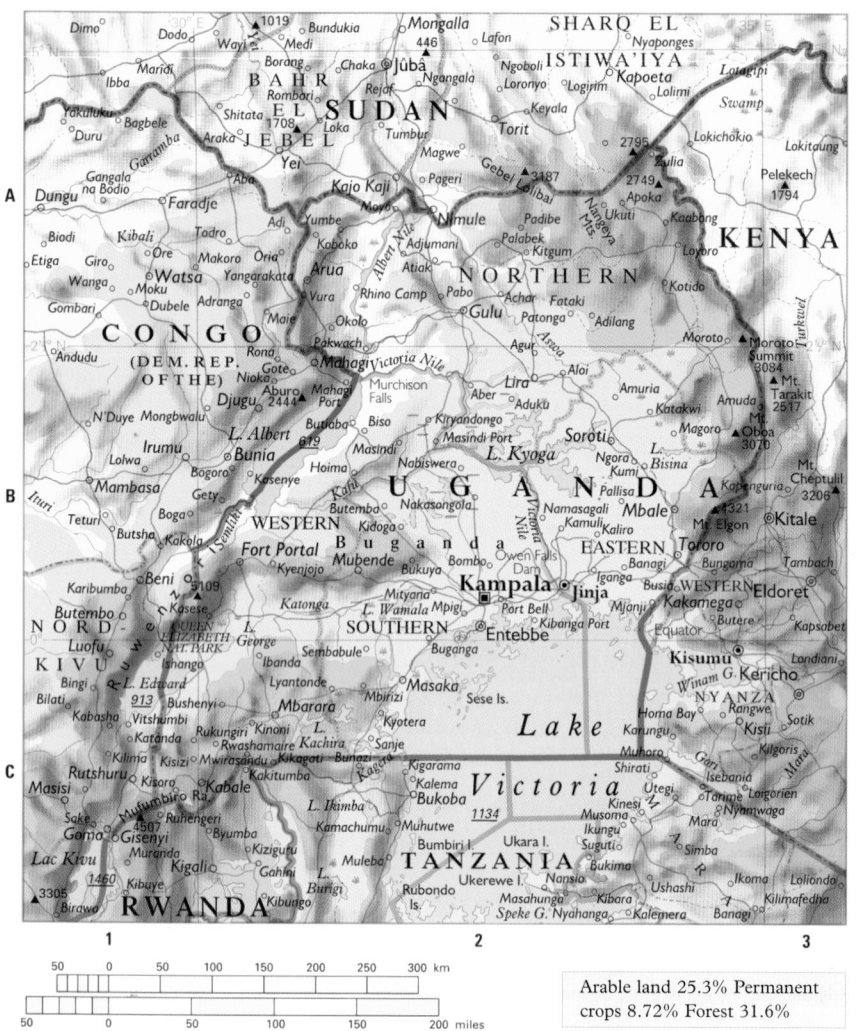

Arable land 25.3% Permanent crops 8.72% Forest 31.6%

Geography

The Republic of Uganda is a landlocked country on the East African Plateau. It contains part of Lake Victoria, Africa's largest lake and a source of the River Nile, which occupies a shallow depression in the plateau. The plateau varies in height from about 1,500 m [4,921 ft] in the south to 900 m [2,953 ft] in the north. The highest mountain is Margherita Peak, which reaches 5,109 m [16,762 ft] in the Ruwenzori Range in the south-west. Other mountains, including Mount Elgon at 4,321 m [14,177 ft], rise along Uganda's eastern border. Part of the Great African Rift Valley, which contains lakes Edward and Albert, lie in western Uganda. The landscapes range from rainforests in the south, through savanna in the centre, to semi-desert in the north.

Climate

The Equator runs through Uganda and the country is warm throughout the year, though the high altitude moderates the

temperature. The wettest regions are the lands to the north of Lake Victoria, and the western mountains, especially the high Ruwenzori Range. Much of Uganda has two rainy seasons, but these merge into one, with a distinctive dry season, in the centre and north.

History and Politics

Little is known of the early history of Uganda. When Europeans first reached the area in the 19th century, many of the people were organized in kingdoms, the most powerful of which was Buganda, the home of the Baganda people. Britain took over the country between 1894 and 1914, and ruled it until independence in 1962.

In 1967, Uganda became a republic and Buganda's Kabaka (king), Sir Edward Mutesa II, was made president. Tensions between the Kabaka and the prime minister, Apollo Milton Obote, led to the dismissal of Kabaka in 1966. Obote also abolished the traditional kingdoms, including Buganda. Obote was overthrown in 1971 by an army group led by General Idi Amin Dada. Amin ruled as a dictator. He forced most of the Asians living in Uganda to leave the country and had many of his opponents killed.

In 1978, a border dispute between Uganda and Tanzania led Tanzanian troops to enter Uganda. With help from Ugandan opponents of Amin, they overthrew Amin's government. In 1980, Obote led his party to victory in the national elections. But after charges of fraud, Obote's opponents began guerrilla warfare. A military group overthrew Obote in 1985, but strife continued until 1986, when Yoweri Museveni's National Resistance Movement seized power. In 1993, Museveni restored the traditional kingdoms, including Buganda where a new Kabaka was crowned. Museveni also held national elections in 1994 but political parties were not permitted. Museveni was elected president in 1996.

In the late 1990s, Uganda faced a huge drain on its economy in containing rebels in the north and west. Another factor was Uganda's support for the rebel forces which overthrew President Mobutu of Zaïre and, later, for the rebels who battled to remove Mobutu's successor, Laurent Kabila.

Economy

By 1991 Uganda was among the world's five poorest countries. Stability was restored under President Museveni and the economy expanded. But, confidence in the country's development was shaken in 1998, when Uganda sent troops into the Democratic Republic of the Congo to oppose Museveni's erstwhile protégé, Laurent Kabila.

Agriculture dominates the economy, employing 80% of the people. Food crops include bananas, cassava, maize, millet, sorghum and sweet potatoes, while the chief cash crops are coffee, cotton, sugar cane and tea. The only important metal is copper. The Owen Falls Dam at Jinja, on the outlet of Lake Victoria, produces cheap electricity.

UGANDA (KAMPALA)

The northern shores of Lake Victoria are the rainiest tracts of East Africa due to the moisture they receive. Temperatures are uniform throughout the year, but are moderated by altitude. There is a double maximum of rainfall, the heaviest rains occurring after the midday sun is at its hottest around the equinoxes. Much of the rain falls in thunderstorms which move northwards from the lake by day.

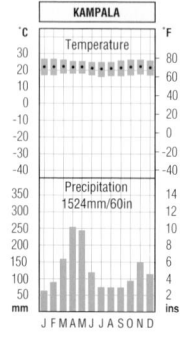

KAMPALA

AREA	Bagisu 7%, Bachiga 7%,
235,880 sq km [91,073 sq mls]	Lango 6%, Acholi 5%
POPULATION	**LANGUAGES**
22,167,000	English and Swahili
CAPITAL (POPULATION)	(both official)
Kampala (773,000)	**RELIGIONS**
GOVERNMENT	Christianity (Roman Catholic
Republic in transition	40%, Protestant 29%),
ETHNIC GROUPS	traditional beliefs 18%, Islam 7%
Baganda 18%, Banyoro 14%,	**CURRENCY**
Teso 9%, Banyan 8%, Basoga 8%,	Uganda shilling = 100 cents

UKRAINE

Ukraine's flag was first used between 1918 and 1922. It was readopted in September 1991. The colours were first used in 1848. They are heraldic in origin and were first used on the coat of arms of one of the Ukrainian kingdoms in the Middle Ages.

Geography

Ukraine is the second largest country in Europe after Russia. It was formerly part of the Soviet Union, which split apart in 1991. This mostly flat country faces the Black Sea in the south. The Crimean Peninsula includes a highland region overlooking Yalta. The highest point of the country is in the eastern Carpathian Mountains which extend into the Slovak Republic and Romania. The most extensive land region is the central plateau which descends to the north to the Dnipro (Dnieper)-Pripet Lowlands. A low plateau occupies the north-east.

Climate

Ukraine has warm summers, but the winters are cold, becoming more severe from west to east. In the summer, the east of the country is often warmer than the west. The heaviest rainfall occurs in the summer.

Vegetation

Woodland with such trees as ash, oak and pine grows in the north, while pine forests swathe the slopes of the Carpathians and Crimean mountains. Grassy steppe once covered central Ukraine, but much of the steppe is now farmed.

Arable land 57.5% Permanent crops 1.84%
Permanent grassland 13% Forest 17.9%

History

In the 9th century AD, a group of people, called the East Slavs, founded a civilization called Kievan Rus, with its capital at Kiev (Kyyiv). Russians took over the area in 980 and the region became prosperous. In the 13th century, Mongol armies ravaged the area. Later, the region was split into small kingdoms and large areas fell under foreign rule. In the 17th and 18th centuries, parts of Ukraine came under Polish and Russian rule. But Russia gained most of Ukraine in the late 18th century, although Austria held an area in the west, called Galicia. In 1917, following the Bolshevik Revolution, the Ukrainians set up an independent, non-Communist republic.

Austrian Ukraine declared itself a republic in 1918 and the two parts joined together. In 1919, however, Ukrainian Communists set up a second government and proclaimed the country a Soviet Socialist Republic. The Communists ultimately triumphed and, during 1922, Ukraine became one of the four original republics that formed the Soviet Union.

Millions of people died in the 1930s as the result of Soviet policies. Millions more died during the Nazi occupation between 1941 and 1944. In 1945, the Soviet Union added to Ukraine areas that were formerly in Czechoslovakia, Poland and Romania.

Politics

In the 1980s, Ukrainian people demanded more say over their affairs. The country finally became independent when the Soviet Union broke up in 1991. Ukraine continued to work with Russia through the Commonwealth of Independent States. But Ukraine differed with Russia on some issues, including control over Crimea. In 1999, a treaty ratifying Ukraine's present boundaries failed to get the approval of Russia's upper house.

A former Communist, Leonid Kravchuk was elected president in 1991. He was defeated in 1994 by Leonid Kuchma, the prime minister. A new constitution was adopted in 1996, declaring Ukraine to be a democratic, unitary state and guaranteeing civil rights, including the right to private ownership. Kuchma was re-elected in 1999, defeating the Communist Party leader, Petro Symonenko, who had campaigned for the restoration of the Soviet Union and cutting all links with NATO.

Economy

The World Bank classifies Ukraine as a 'lower-middle-income' economy. Agriculture is important. Crops include wheat and sugar beet, which are the major exports, together with barley, maize, potatoes, sunflowers and tobacco. Livestock rearing and fishing are also important industries.

Manufacturing is the chief economic activity. Major manufactures include iron and steel, machinery and vehicles. The country has large coalfields. The country imports oil and natural gas, though it has hydroelectric and nuclear power stations. In 1986, an accident at the Chernobyl (Chornobyl) nuclear power plant caused widespread nuclear radiation.

AREA
603,700 sq km
[233,100 sq mls]
POPULATION
50,125,000
CAPITAL (POPULATION)
Kiev
(Kyyiv, 2,630,000)
GOVERNMENT
Multiparty republic
ETHNIC GROUPS
Ukrainian 73%,
Russian 22%, Jewish 1%,
Belarussian 1%,
Moldovan, Bulgarian,
Polish
LANGUAGES
Ukrainian (official),
Russian
RELIGIONS
Christianity (mostly
Ukrainian Orthodox)
CURRENCY
Hryvna

UNITED ARAB EMIRATES – SEE GULF STATES, PAGES 113–114

The flag of the United Kingdom was officially adopted in 1801. The first Union flag, combining the cross of St George (England) and St Andrew (Scotland), dates back from 1603. In 1801, the cross of St Patrick, Ireland's emblem, was added to form the present flag.

Geography

The United Kingdom is a union of four countries: England, Northern Ireland, Scotland and Wales. The islands are confusingly named. Great Britain, the largest island in Europe, was named to distinguish it from Little Britain (Brittany, in France), and includes England, Scotland and Wales. Ireland was once a kingdom, but is currently divided into the Province of Northern Ireland, under the British Crown, and the Republic of Ireland. Great Britain, Northern Ireland and many island groups from the Scillies to the Shetlands, together make up the United Kingdom of Great Britain and Northern Ireland, commonly known as the UK. Even isolated Rockall, far out in the Atlantic Ocean, is part of the UK, but the Isle of Man (see page 228) and the Channel Islands (see page 227) are separate if direct dependencies of the Crown, with a degree of political autonomy and their own taxation systems.

Visitors to England are often amazed at the variety of the landscape. Complex folding, volcanic upheavals and eruptions, glacial planing and changes of sea level have all left their marks on the present landscape. Upland regions include the Pennines which extend southwards from Northumberland to the Trent. The Pennines is a region of rolling hills, plateaux and beautiful valleys known as 'dales'. Two outliers of the Pennines are the Forest of Rossendale, north of Manchester, and the Forest of Bowland in northern Lancashire. Lowlands border the uplands to the east and west. The Eden Valley separates the northern Pennines from Cumbria, which includes the Lake District. This scenic mountain region contains England's highest peak, Scafell Pike, which reaches 978 m [3,210 ft]. Exmoor in the south-west is a sandstone upland, while Dartmoor is a mainly granite area with many prominent tors. Elsewhere are isolated hills, small by world standards, but dramatic against the small-scale background of Britain, as shown by the Malvern Hills of Worcester and the Wrekin, near Shrewsbury.

The English lowland contains chalk downlands, familiar to visitors who enter England through Dover or Folkestone as the white cliffs. These are the exposed edges of the North and South Downs. The North Downs extend westwards to the Hampshire Downs. There is also a northwards extension through the Berkshire and Marlborough Downs to the Chilterns, and then north again into East Anglia to disappear under the edge of the fens near Cambridge. Chalk appears again in the wolds of Lincolnshire and Yorkshire, emerging at Flamborough Head.

Older limestones form the Cotswold Hills and the rolling hills of Leicestershire, the Lincoln and, finally, the North York Moors. England's main rivers are the Thames, Severn, the fenland Ouse, the Trent and the Great Yorkshire Ouse.

Wales is mainly hilly and mountainous. The best known of its highland areas is Snowdonia, a national park which contains Snowdon, the highest mountain in Wales at 1,085 m [3,560 ft]. There are also fine upland areas in central Wales, with the Brecon Beacons in the south. However, most of the people live in the industrialized area of South Wales, which includes the mining villages of Glamorgan.

More than half of Scotland's area lies in the Highlands and Islands which are bounded by a line drawn from Stonehaven, south of Aberdeen, to the mouth of the Clyde. This region is divided into two by the Great Glen, which extends from Fort William to Inverness and includes three lochs – Lochy, Oich and Ness – linked by the Caledonian Canal. The north-western part of the Highlands has fine scenery, as also do the Inner and Outer Hebrides. East of the Great Glen is a richer country, flanked on the east by the lowlands around Aberdeen. Ben Nevis, at 1,342 m [4,401 ft], dominating the town of Fort William in the Great Glen, is the highest peak in the British Isles. In the far north lie the Orkneys and the Shetlands. South of the Highlands and Islands is Scotland's Central Valley, which contains several rolling uplands, Clydeside, the country's greatest industrial area, and Edinburgh, which stands on splendid volcanic ridges. Though less spectacular than the Highlands, the Southern Uplands

contain beautiful hills, rolling moorlands and rich valleys. The Tweed, with its numerous tributaries, provides sheltered valleys for farming.

Northern Ireland is a land of rolling plains and low mountains. Its highest mountain is Slieve Donard, which reaches 852 m [2,796 ft] in the Mourne Mountains in the south-east. Other scenic features include Lough Neagh, the largest lake in the British Isles which has an area of 396 sq km [153 sq mls], and Giant's Causeway, a spectacular area of basalt columns formed from an ancient lava flow, north of Coleraine.

Climate

The UK has a mild climate, influenced by the warm Gulf Stream which flows across the Atlantic from the Gulf of Mexico, then past the British Isles. Moist winds from the south-west bring rain, which diminishes from west to east. Winds from the east and north bring cold conditions in winter. The weather is markedly changeable, because of the common occurrence of depressions with their associated fronts.

UNITED KINGDOM – LONDON

South-east England, sheltered from the ocean to the west, is one of the driest parts of the UK. Although rainfall varies little all year, greater evaporation creates a deficit between May and August. London has a small annual temperature range. Its record low is −10°C [14°F] and record high 34°C [93°F]. London creates its own local climate and nights are warmer than those in surrounding regions.

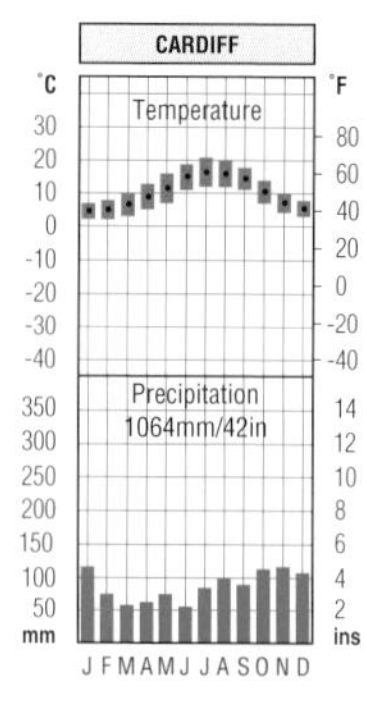

CARDIFF

Winter temperatures are not too cold: averages for December to February are 5°C [41°F]. The averages of the lowest in these months is −4°C to −2°C [25–28°F]. Averages from May to October are over 10°C [50°F], and from June to August 15°C [59°F] plus. Frost and snow-days are among the lowest in the country. Rainfall at 1,000 mm [39 in] is average, falling in all months with a winter peak, and falling on about 180 days per year.

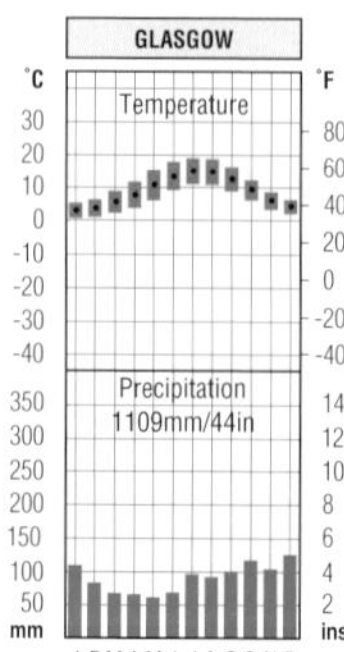

GLASGOW

Glasgow has a maritime climate with mild winters, cool summers, and well-distributed rainfall with an autumn maximum. The Clyde Valley is more sheltered than the estuary where Greenock receives more than 1,500 mm [590 in] of rain annually. At Glasgow rain falls on about 200 days per year. It averages about 3–5 hours of sunshine per day compared to 4–5 hours in the south.

Vegetation

Human activity has greatly modified the landscape and only small patches of the original woodland have survived. The ancient forests, dominated by oak, were cleared to make way for farmland, but forest clearance in marginal areas for grazing has led to the development of moorland and heathland. Moorlands and heathlands now cover about a third of the UK. In lowland Britain, the dominant plant of the heathland is the common heather, whose purple colour adorns the autumn countryside. Most of the former larger mammals which lived in the forests have become extinct.

UNITED KINGDOM

ATLANTIC OCEAN

Shetland Is.
Unst
Yell
Fetlar
Foula
Mainland
Lerwick

Fair Isle

Orkney Is.
Westray
Sanday
Stronsay
Mainland
Kirkwall
Hoy
South
Ronaldsay
Pentland Firth

C. Wrath
Thurso
Wick
Helmsdale
Lewis
Stornoway
Golspie
Lairg
789
Harris
Ullapool
Tain
Invergordon
Dingwall
Nairn
Elgin
Buckie
Banff
Fraserburgh
North West Highlands
North Minch
Outer Hebrides
St. Kilda
530
North
Uist
Benbecula
South Uist
Skye
Portree
L. Ness
Inverness
Aviemore
Huntly
Inverurie
Peterhead
Aberdeen
SCOTLAND
Grampian Mts.
Rhum
Eigg
Mallaig
Fort William
Ben Nevis
1342
1311
Ballater
Stonehaven
Barra
Coll
Tiree
Tobermory
1214
Forfar
Arbroath
Montrose
Mull
Oban
L. Lomond
Perth
St. Andrews
Dundee
238
Colonsay
973
Stirling
Dunfermline
Kirkcaldy
Dunbar
Jura
Greenock
Glasgow
Edinburgh
Islay
Paisley
East Kilbride
Hamilton
Berwick-upon-Tweed
Arran
Irvine
Kilmarnock
840
Galashiels
816
Alnwick
Campbeltown
Ayr
Southern Uplands
Jedburgh
Cheviot Hills
Malin Hd.
Buncrana
Coleraine
Girvan
Dumfries
Hawick
Aran I.
Letterkenny
Londonderry
Ballymena
Larne
North Channel
Stranraer
Kirkcudbright
Annan
Hexham
Newcastle-upon-Tyne
Lifford
Omagh
Antrim
Bangor
Firth of Clyde
Mull of Galloway
Carlisle
893
Gateshead
South Shields
Sunderland
Donegal
U l s t e r
NORTHERN IRELAND
Lough Neagh
Belfast
Whitehaven
Workington
Durham
Hartlepool
Redcar
Bundoran
Lower L. Erne
Enniskillen
Portadown
Lurgan
Lisburn
Douglas
I. of Man
Cumbrian Mts.
Darlington
Middlesbrough
Stockton-on-Tees
Ballina
Sligo
Clones
Armagh
Newry
UNITED
Barrow-in-Furness
Lancaster
Scarborough
Achill I.
L. Conn
Leitrim
Cavan
Castleblayney
Dundalk
KINGDOM
Blackpool
Harrogate
York
Bridlington
Castlebar
Roscommon
Longford
Ceanannus Mor
Drogheda
IRISH
Preston
Keighley
Burnley
Leeds
Beverley
Kingston upon Hull
Westport
Lough Mask
Connemara
Athlone
Lough Ree
Mullingar
Boyne
SEA
Blackburn
Bradford
Halifax
Huddersfield
Barnsley
Scunthorpe
Grimsby
Galway B.
Lough Corrib
Galway
Ballinasloe
Tullamore
Liffey
Anglesey
Holyhead
Liverpool
Manchester
Bolton
Oldham
Stockport
Doncaster
Rotherham
Sheffield
Louth
Aran Is.
Lough Derg
Ennis
Nenagh
Thurles
Kilkenny
928
Carlow
Wicklow Mts.
Arklow
Bangor
Colwyn Bay
Chester
Warrington
Chesterfield
Crewe
Mansfield
Lincoln
Skegness
Limerick
IRELAND
1085
Wrexham
Stoke-on-Trent
Derby
Nottingham
Boston
The Wash
Cromer
Listowel
Tralee
Tipperary
Clonmel
Carrick-on-Suir
Wexford
Rosslare
Pwllheli
Snowdon
Cambrian Mts.
Shrewsbury
Telford
Stafford
ENGLAND
Granthan
Trent
King's Lynn
Norwich
Great Yarmouth
Lowestoft
953
Dingle
Killarney
Mallow
Blackwater
Dungarvan
Cardigan Bay
Aberystwyth
Welshpool
Wolverhampton
Nuneaton
Leicester
Corby
Peterborough
Thetford
Carrantoohill
1041
Macgillycuddy's Reeks
Bandon
Youghal
BIRMINGHAM
Coventry
Rugby
Royal Leamington Spa
Northampton
Bedford
Cambridge
Bury St. Edmunds
Ipswich
Valencia
Bantry
Kinsale
Cork
Cobh
99
St. George's Channel
Carmarthen
Brecon
886
WALES
Worcester
Hereford
Redditch
Gloucester
Cheltenham
Oxford
Milton Keynes
Hemel Hempstead
Stevenage
Harlow
Colchester
Harwich
Felixstowe
36
C. Clear
Fishguard
Haverfordwest
Milford Haven
Pembroke
Merthyr Tydfil
Neath
Cwmbran
Newport
Cotswold Hills
High Wycombe
Luton
Watford
Basildon
Southend-on-Sea
CELTIC
Llanelli
Swansea
Rhondda
Cardiff
Bristol
Bath
Swindon
Newbury
Reading
LONDON
Slough
Chatham
Canterbury
Margate
Zeebrugge
Oostende
BELGIUM
Brugge
SEA
Port Talbot
Barry
Weston-super-Mare
Salisbury
Basingstoke
Guildford
Reigate
Maidstone
Ashford
Folkestone
Dunkerque
Tourcoing
Lille
Barnstaple
Exmoor
Taunton
Yeovil
Winchester
Crawley
Hastings
Str. of Dover
Calais
Gris-Nez
Boulogne
Béthune
Bude
618
Dartmoor
Exeter
Exmouth
Weymouth
Bournemouth
Poole
Southampton
Fareham
Havant
Portsmouth
Isle of Wight
Brighton
Worthing
Eastbourne
sur-Mer
Le Touquet-Paris-Plage
33
Bruay-la-Buissiere
Lens
Newquay
Truro
St. Austell
Torbay
Newport
English Channel
Le Tréport
Amiens
Noyon
Land's End
Penzance
Falmouth
Plymouth
Abbeville
Dieppe
FRANCE
Isles of Scilly
C. de la Hague
Pte. de Barfleur
Fécamp
Alderney

NORTH SEA

N O R T H
S E A

16

Penn ines

1224

316

60° N
58° N
56° N
54° N
52° N
50° N

10° W
8° W
6° W
4° W
2° W
0°
2° E
4° E

50 0 25 50 75 100 125 150 175 km

50 0 25 50 75 100 125 miles

Arable land 24.6% Permanent crops 0.19%
Permanent grassland 45.9% Forest 10.3%

North Sea Oil

The discovery of gas and oil in the North Sea in the 1960s transformed Britain from an oil importer into the world's fifth largest exporter within a decade. Gas from the new fields rapidly replaced coal gas in the British energy system, and by 1981 the country was self-sufficient in oil. In the peak production year of 1986, the British sector of the North Sea produced 141.8 million tonnes of crude oil, accounting for over 20% of UK export earnings. In 1996, the UK was the ninth largest producer of crude oil, producing 3.9% of the world total with a total production of 130 million tonnes. There were also important new discoveries west of Shetland in 1994, while the Foinaven and Schiehallion fields could account for 30% of the UK's known reserves. In 1998, a record 204 offshore fields were in operation. Of these fields, 109 were producing oil, 16 condensates (a lighter form of oil) and 79 were producing gas.

Up to the end of 1988, oil fields on the UK continental shelf had produced a cumulative total of 2,202 million tonnes, while the known continental-shelf reserves were estimated at about 1,800 million tonnes. The fields with the largest production totals are Forties, Brent, Ninian and Piper. The largest onshore oilfield is at Wytch Farm, Dorset. The search for new reserves continues. In 1998, production began at 12 new offshore oilfields, while 24 new development projects were approved.

In taxes and royalties, oil and natural gas from the North Sea gave an immense fillip to British government revenues. There was much discussion as to the best use for this windfall money, which is likely to taper away during the early part of the 21st century before vanishing altogether, but it certainly helped to finance substantial cuts in taxation.

The sight of North Sea oil wealth flowing south to the government treasury in London also provoked nationalist resentment in Scotland, off whose coast most of the oil rigs (and much of the gas) are situated.

History

The isolation of the United Kingdom from mainland Europe has made a major impact on its history. The narrow seas separating the British Isles from mainland Europe have served the islanders well against casual invasion, while Britons in turn sailed to explore and exploit the rest of the world. Despite insularity, Britons are of mixed stock.

Early immigrants – land-hungry farmers from the mainland – were often refugees from tribal warfare and unrest. The Belgic tribesmen escaping from Imperial Rome, the Romans themselves, whose troops included Macedonian, Spanish and probably North African mercenaries, the Angles, Saxons, Jutes, Danes and Normans all brought genetic variety. So too did the Huguenots, Sephardic and Ashkenazim Jews, and Dutch, French and German businessmen who followed them. Latterly, the waves of immigrants have included Belarussians, Poles, Italians, Ukrainians and Czechs, most of whom, like their predecessors, fugitives from European wars, overcrowding and intolerance.

During the 19th century, Britain often took in skilled European immigrants through the front door, while steadily losing her own sons and daughters – Scots and Irish peasants in particular – through the back. Most recent arrivals in Britain are immigrants from crowded and impoverished corners of the British Empire, notably the Caribbean, India and Pakistan, while a new wave of immigration in the 1990s led to an influx of refugees from war-torn former Yugoslavia, the Somali Republic, Sri Lanka and elsewhere.

The recorded history of the area that is now the United Kingdom began with the Roman conquest in 55 BC. Yet human habitation goes back to around 250,000 BC, the start of the Palaeolithic Period (Old Stone Age). The Mesolithic Period began around 8000 BC, at the end of the last phase of the Ice Age. In 5000 BC, rising sea levels finally cut the islands off from mainland Europe through the formation of the English Channel and the North Sea.

Shortly before 4000 BC, the Neolithic (New Stone Age) Period began. The Neolithic marked the introduction of a much more sophisticated farming culture. The Neolithic Period was followed by the Bronze Age and the Iron Age. Towards the end of the Bronze Age, when new immigrants introduced metal-working skills, the first of a succession of waves of Celtic immigrants reached the shores of Britain. Their language displaced earlier languages and it is the ancestor of Gaelic, Irish, Cornish, Manx and Welsh. Around 700 BC, more Celtic immigrants arrived who were skilled in the use of iron to make weapons and tools. In the first century BC, the Belgae, the advanced Celtic tribes, reached southern Britain from France. They built large settlements that became the basis for Britain's first towns.

When the Romans arrived in *Britannia* (the Roman name for Britain), they found a society divided into tribal communities ruled by kings or queens. However, after Julius Caesar's conquests in 55 and 54 BC, the Romans withdrew and did not return until AD 43, when Emperor Claudius captured the southern part of Britain and ruled it for more than 350 years. They built towns, roads, country villas and defensive sites, including Hadrian's Wall, the ruins of which today testify to their civilizing influence.

Christianity was introduced by the Romans and, by the 4th century, the Christian church was established in Britain. The withdrawal of the Romans in the early 5th century heralded the start of a period, often called the Dark Ages, which continued until the Norman Conquest in 1066. It was a period when Anglo-Saxon and Jutish raiders established settlements, displacing the Romanized Celts, many of whom moved northwards into Scotland and westwards into Wales. The small Anglo-Saxon kingdoms gradually merged into larger powers and, eventually, Wessex came to be the major force. From the late 8th century, Wessex resisted the Danish Viking warriors who began to raid Britain. However, the Danes also founded towns and developed trade with countries beyond the North Sea. By 1013, the Danes had conquered most of England and, in 1016, Canute, king of Denmark and Norway, also became king of England.

The Norman Duke William of Normandy, who was later crowned William I, defeated Harold II at Hastings in 1066. The Norman victory, the last successful invasion of Britain, marked the start of the Norman Conquest, during which the Normans gradually extended their rule, building great castles and churches. French became the language of the English court and nobles for the following 300 years, and the English kings ruled large areas in France until the mid-15th century.

Wales, a Celtic stronghold, was conquered in 1282, but Welsh nationalism remained powerful, leading to an unsuccessful rebellion at the beginning of the 15th century. It was the Tudor Dynasty (1485–1603), which was of Welsh origin, that was instrumental (during the reign of Henry VIII) in uniting Wales with England through the Acts of Union of 1536 and 1542, so beginning the evolution of the modern UK.

The Romans never conquered Scotland. During the Middle Ages, wars were fought between Scotland and England and, despite some defeats, the victory of Robert the Bruce over Edward II at the battle of Bannockburn in 1314 ensured the survival of the Scottish kings. The two kingdoms were finally united when Elizabeth I of England was succeeded in 1603 by James VI of Scotland, who became James I of England. However, Scotland and England remained separate territories, apart from a short period of enforced unification under Oliver Cromwell, until 1707, when the Act of Union formally united England (and Wales) with Scotland as the United Kingdom of Great Britain. In the 12th century, Ireland came under the influence of Norman nobles, and relations between England and Ireland gradually became closer. The Act of Union of 1801 created the United Kingdom of Great Britain and Ireland. But following the partition of Ireland in 1922 into the mainly Roman Catholic Irish Free State, and the predominantly Protestant Northern Ireland, this became the United Kingdom of Great Britain and Northern Ireland.

The modern history of the United Kingdom began in the 18th century, with the development of the British Empire, including Canada and India. Despite the loss of its 13 North American colonies, which became the core of the United States as the result of the War of Independence (1775–83), it gained new territories, such as Australia. The existence of the British colonies acquired between the early 17th century and the later 18th century stimulated commerce and trade. The slave trade became important, bringing great wealth to the seaport traders of Bristol and Liverpool. The slave trade was finally abolished throughout the British Empire in 1833.

The 18th century also saw another major development that put Britain at the forefront of technology. This was the start of the Industrial Revolution, whose innovations were to change the world. The 19th century saw the Victorian Age, named after Queen Victoria, who reigned from 1837 until 1901. This was a period of huge economic progress, with iron production increasing by six times between 1833 and 1865. Britain became the 'workshop of the world', and the world's top manufacturing nation. Industrial progress was accompanied by rapid population growth. At the time of the Act of Union in 1707, some 6 million English and Welsh joined about 1 million Scots. By 1801, the first national census revealed that there were 8.9 million people in England and Wales and 1.6 million in Scotland. By 1821, the total British population was 21 million. By 1851, it had risen to 31 million, with the populations of the cities and towns growing at a fast rate. The growing economy was accompanied by a second phase of colonization in the 19th and early 20th centuries, when the British Empire reached its height. Britain's colonies provided raw materials, such as cotton, sugar and tobacco, while they were major markets for Britain's manufactured goods, including textiles and clothing.

However, towards the end of the 19th century, Britain began to face growing competition when countries, such as France, Germany and the United States, became major industrial and trading economies. In the early 19th century, Britain could no longer rely on its policy of 'splendid isolation'. Instead, to maintain its defences, it entered into alliances with other major powers. World War I was fought between the Allies, including Britain, France and the United States, and the Central Powers, including Germany, Austria-Hungary, the Ottoman Empire and Bulgaria. By 1918, the Allies were triumphant, but the war had sapped Britain's economy, shaking its position as a world power.

The inter-war world economic recession created further problems and, by 1932, about 3 million people in the United Kingdom were unemployed. World War II proved an even greater drain on the economy of the UK and, at the end of the war, the United States and the Soviet Union had emerged as the world's two great super-powers.

Politics

A landslide for the Labour Party in 1945 led to many social changes that still affect politics in Britain today. Although the government faced many difficulties in seeking to restore the war-shattered economy, it set up a welfare state, with a social security system that provided welfare for people 'from the cradle to the grave'. The government also recognized the high costs of maintaining the British Empire in the face of growing nationalism and, in 1947, British India was partitioned, creating two new independent nations – India and Pakistan. Sri Lanka (then Ceylon) became independent in 1948, as also did Myanmar (then Burma).

In place of the British Empire, Britain retained much influence in the world through the Commonwealth of Nations, whose original members were Australia, Britain, Canada, Ireland, New Zealand, Newfoundland and South Africa. This policy was continued by the Conservative Party, which won office in 1951 and governed until 1964. During that time, Cyprus, Ghana, Kenya, Malaysia, Malta, Nigeria, Sudan, Tanganyika (now Tanzania), Trinidad and Tobago and Uganda all became independent. Because of the orderly way in which the British Empire broke up, most of the former colonies joined the Commonwealth when they became independent and, by 1999, the membership stood at 54.

While the UK was breaking up the British Empire, several Western European nations were setting up organizations to increase co-operation between them. At first, Britain wanted to stay out of these new organizations, fearing that it might lose some of its independence and reduce the importance of its partnerships with the Commonwealth of Nations and the United States. In the 1950s, it refused to join the ECSC (European Steel and Coal Community), EURATOM (European Atomic Energy Community) and, most significantly, the EEC (European Economic Community). Instead, in 1960, it helped to set up EFTA (European Free Trade Association) with six other

nations. However, EFTA's performance was modest by comparison with the EEC. In 1963, Britain's request to join the EEC was rejected, largely because it was opposed by the French President Charles De Gaulle, who was suspicious about 'Anglo-Saxon' motives.

The United Kingdom finally joined the EEC in 1973, though a strong body of opinion still feared that the development of a federal Europe would jeopardize British sovereignty. Membership was endorsed by a referendum in 1975, but, at the turn of the century, Britons were still debating whether it was advisable for Britain to adopt the euro, the single European currency which 11 of the 15 European Union members had adopted on 1 January 1999.

Another domestic issue of great importance involves the status of Northern Ireland. Since the 1960s, Northern Ireland has been the scene of conflict between the Protestant majority, who favour continuing union with the UK, and the Roman Catholic minority, many of whom are republicans who would like to see Ireland reunified. British troops were sent to the province in 1969 to control violence between the communities and, at various times, Britain has imposed direct rule over Northern Ireland. In 1998, the 'Good Friday' agreement held out hope for the future, when unionists and nationalists agreed that Northern Ireland would remain part of the United Kingdom, until a majority of its people voted in favour of a change. The agreement also allowed Ireland to play a part in the affairs of the north, while the republic amended its constitution to remove all claims to Northern Ireland. A Northern Ireland Assembly was set up to handle local affairs, though it was suspended in 2000 when the IRA (Irish Republican Army) failed to surrender their weapons.

Other problems have arisen in Scotland and Wales, where many nationalists, concerned about maintaining their own cultures, favoured self-government or even, in Scotland, independence. Before 1999, Scotland and Wales were directly ruled by the British parliament in London. But, in 1997, following the landslide victory of the Labour Party under Tony Blair, 74% of the people of Scotland and 50.3% of the people of Wales voted in favour of setting up local assemblies.

The Scottish parliament, which is responsible for local affairs and

The Channel Islands

Lying 16 to 48 km [10–30 mls] from the Cotentin Peninsula on the French mainland, the Channel Islands, known in French as Les Iles Normandes, or Les Iles Anglo-Normandes, are a British dependency and not officially part of the United Kingdom, covering an area of only 200 sq km [78 sq mls].

The largest island is Jersey, whose chief town is St Helier. Jersey covers an area of 115 sq km [45 sq mls] and has 85,100 inhabitants. The second largest island is Guernsey, whose chief town is St Peter Port. Guernsey covers an area of 78 sq km [30 sq mls] and has 58,600 people. The other islands, including Alderney, Brechou, Great Sark, Little Sark, Herm, Jethou and Lihou, are dependencies of Guernsey. Together they have a population of less than 3,000. The islands have a mild climate, which, together with fine scenery and beautiful vegetation, attracts tourists. Average temperatures in January and February, the coldest months, are 6°C [43°F].

The only part of the Duchy of Normandy retained by the English Crown after 1204, and the only part of Britain occupied by the Germans in World War II, the islands have their own legal system and government, with lower taxation than that of Britain. This, combined with a favourable climate and fine coastal scenery, has attracted a considerable number of wealthy residents, notably retired people, and established Jersey and Guernsey as offshore financial centres.

The main produce is agricultural, especially early potatoes, tomatoes and flowers for export to Britain, and the country-side has a vast number of glasshouses. Jersey and Guernsey cattle are famous breeds, introduced to several countries. Holiday-makers visit the islands in large numbers during the summer months, travelling by air or by various passenger boats, particularly from Weymouth. English is the official language, but French is widely spoken.

has limited powers to raise or reduce taxes, and the Welsh Assembly, which has no powers over taxation, met for the first time in 1999. Devolution has caused concern among those who fear that it might lead to the break-up of the United Kingdom. Devolution has also focused attention on the question of nationality, especially in England, where there has been discussion about what it means to be English.

Other political issues in Britain involve the future of the welfare state. While most people favour top-quality and free welfare services, they tend to vote for parties which advocate low taxation. The high cost of welfare services is a matter of political controversy that seems likely to continue well into the 21st century. There is also concern about the changing economy, with a decline in traditional manufacturing and the growth of service industries, both of which affect employment. Another issue is immigration and the fear that economic migrants entering the UK will lessen the job opportunities of the indigenous workforce.

Other issues are concerned with Britain's status in the world. Though no longer a top world power, the UK continues to play an important role in world affairs, both diplomatically and militarily. In 1982, the reoccupation of the Falkland Islands, after it had been invaded by Argentina, brought popularity to the then Conservative Party prime minister, Margaret Thatcher. However, others were concerned at the cost and morality of other British military operations in Iraq during the Gulf War of 1991 and in Kosovo, Yugoslavia, in 1999.

Economy

The United Kingdom has the world's fifth largest economy, after Japan, the United States, Germany and France. In 1996, agriculture contributed 1.8% of the gross domestic product, as compared with 24% from manufacturing and mining. Of the service industries, tourism is a long-term growth sector. The number of tourists reached more than 25 million in 1998, while tourism and related activities employed 1,780,000 people. London and its historic buildings and cultural institutions is the UK's most popular tourist centre, while the City of London's finance and insurance businesses have made the capital one of the world's leading financial cities.

The United Kingdom has to import about a third of the food it needs, but its farming techniques are modern and scientific, and yields are high. Between 1973 and 1998, agricultural productivity increased by more than 40%, which was largely the result of the declining number of people working on farms, now barely 1% of the country's workforce. The declining proportion of people employed on farms is an inevitable result of agricultural rationalization and improvements in farming methods. Those who deplore this trend might reflect that, though farming formerly employed many more people, it supported them at little more than subsistence level. About two-thirds of all farmland is owner-occupied; the rest is tenanted or rented.

Soils vary from the rich soils of lowland England, such as the fenlands of eastern England, to the poor ones of highland Britain, where grazing is the chief activity. Dairy farms or beef and sheep farms are found mainly in the upland and moorland parts of Northern Ireland, Scotland, Wales and south-western England. Cattle and sheep farming

make up about 42% of the value of Britain's total agricultural output. Pigs and poultry are also important, particularly in East Anglia, north-eastern Scotland and Yorkshire.

Arable farming is important in eastern and central-southern England, and also in eastern Scotland. Major crops include barley, oats, oilseed rape, potatoes, sugar beet and, most important of all, wheat. Eastern England produces most of the country's barley, sugar beet and wheat, while large-scale potato and vegetable production occurs in all areas where the soils are fertile. Mixed farming is common, but its character varies, with an emphasis on livestock in the wetter highlands, and an emphasis on crops in the lowlands. Local products include the hops of Kent and Hereford, the apples of Worcester, and the fine wools that are major products on the chalk downlands. Market gardening and small-scale dairy farming has also developed around almost every major settlement, taking advantage of the ready market close at hand.

Fishing is a major industry and the UK is one of the largest fishing countries in the European Union. Important catches include cod, haddock, mackerel, plaice, pollock, eel and whiting. In 1998, the fishing fleet included over 7,600 registered vessels, including 270 deep-sea vessels, while professional fishermen numbered about 14,000. Though the UK imports about 85% of its timber and wood products, forestry remains important, especially in Scotland, where woodland covers nearly 16% of the land, and Wales, where 12% of the land is forested.

The UK is a leading producer of petroleum, natural gas and coal, together with such non-energy minerals as china clay, potash and salt. The oil and gas come mainly from wells in the North Sea. Although coal still supplies a considerable proportion of the country's primary energy needs, the coal industry has declined in the last 50 years, because of competition with other energy sources. However, in early 1999, the UK had 41 underground mines and 59 opencast mines. Coal and iron ore reserves were the basis of the Industrial Revolution of the 18th century and the industrial growth of the 19th century, which together resulted in major changes in the landscapes of northern and central England, southern Wales and west-central Scotland.

Like coal, the steel industry has encountered stiff competition from the Far East and elsewhere, but steel production remains important, especially in southern Wales and northern England. The car industry, which depends on steel, has declined since the 1970s and, today, the country imports more cars than it exports. The UK also imports much steel, because its plentiful iron ore reserves are mostly low quality.

Competition from overseas had led the UK to diversify its manufacturing sector so that, today, it produces a wide variety of products. The UK is a major producer of heavy machinery for use in agriculture, manufacturing and mining, together with aircraft, space satellites and armaments. Another important group of products are made by the electronics industries, including television equipment, fibre-optic communications and radar devices. Other major industrial sectors include the chemical industry, producing pharmaceuticals, industrial chemicals and plastics, and the textile industry.

The economy of the UK is dependent on trade and the country ranks fifth in the world in the total value of its overseas trade. The country's leading exports are machinery and transport equipment, vehicles, chemicals, petroleum and petroleum products, textiles and paper and paper board. The country's top trading partners are Germany, the United States, France and the Netherlands. Also important are other fellow members of the European Union, namely Belgium-Luxembourg, Italy, Ireland and Spain. Japan is another major source of imports for the United Kingdom.

Isle of Man

Covering 590 sq km [227 sq mls], the Isle of Man sits in the Irish Sea almost equidistant from County Down and Cumbria, but nearer Galloway in Scotland. The uplands, pierced by the corridor valley from Douglas to Peel, extend from Ramsey to Port Erin. The population is about 71,700. The climate is temperate.

The first inhabitants of the island were Celts and the almost extinct Manx language is Celtic. English control began in 1406 and the island became a British Crown Possession in 1828. Mainly agricultural, the island is now largely dependent on tourism, especially during the TT (Tourist Trophy) motorcycle races each summer. Douglas, the capital, contains over a third of the population. The Isle of Man remains a dependency and is not part of the United Kingdom. It has its own legislative assembly (Court of Tynwald), legal system and tax controls.

AREA
243,368 sq km [94,202 sq mls]

POPULATION
58,970,000

CAPITAL (POPULATION)
London (8,089,000)

GOVERNMENT
Constitutional monarchy

ETHNIC GROUPS
White 94%, Asian Indian 1%, Pakistani 1%, West Indian 1%

LANGUAGES
English (official), Welsh, Gaelic

RELIGIONS
Christianity (Anglican 57%, Roman Catholic 13%, Presbyterian 7%, Methodist 4%, Baptist 1%), Islam 1%, Judaism, Hinduism, Sikhism

CURRENCY
Pound sterling = 100 pence

UNITED STATES OF AMERICA

This flag, known as the 'Stars and Stripes', has had the same basic design since 1777, during the War of Independence. The 13 stripes represent the 13 original colonies in the eastern United States. The 50 stars represent the 50 states of the Union.

Geography

The United States of America is the world's fourth largest country in area and the third largest in population. It contains 50 states, 48 of which lie between Canada and Mexico, plus Alaska in north-western North America and Hawaii, a group of volcanic islands in the North Pacific Ocean. Geographically, the main part (of the 48 states) can be divided into three main regions: the east, including the Appalachian Mountains and the eastern coastal plains; the centre, including the Mississippi Basin and the broad prairie plains; and the west, including the Rocky Mountains and the Pacific coastlands.

Eastern United States is crossed by a band of low, folded mountains which long formed a barrier to settlers. In the north are the Adirondacks, a southern extension of the ancient granite shield of Canada. The Appalachian Mountains, which extend from Maine to Alabama, are younger than the Adirondacks, but much older than the Rockies. They separate the Atlantic coastlands from the Great Lakes and the low plateaux of Ohio, Kentucky and Tennessee. In the north-east, the fertile, wooded six New England states made early settlers feel at home. To the south, the coastal plain widens, to be split by the drowned estuaries of the Susquehanna and Potomac Rivers draining into Chesapeake Bay. From Virginia to Florida, smaller rivers drain eastwards, across a broader plain, many of them entering coastal sounds with offshore bars and islands. In New York State, a major spillway cuts through the mountains between the Adirondacks and the Appalachians, linking the Great Lakes with the Hudson River Valley and the Atlantic Ocean. This is the line of the famous Erie Canal route, the most used of several that gave early settlers access to the Ohio country beyond the mountains. Other routes led to Pittsburgh and, through the southern Appalachians, into Tennessee. Central Ohio, Indiana and Illinois are rolling uplands and plains, smoothed by glaciation in the north, but more rugged in the south, and drained by the Ohio River.

The central states extend from the Dakotas to Texas. Within 1,400 km [875 mls] from the Mississippi to the foothills of the Rockies, the land rises almost 3,000 m [9,850 ft], though the slope is often imperceptible. From the Gulf of Mexico to Minnesota and the Dakotas, the rise is even less noticeable, but the landscape is occasionally relieved by uplands, such as the Ozarks of northern Arkansas. Westwards from the Mississippi, it grows progressively drier. The plains are crossed by a series of long, wide rivers that drain off the Rockies. They include the Missouri, the Platte, the Arkansas, the Canadian and the Red. In contrast to the Ohio, the rivers of the central United States provided little help to settlers moving westwards, due to seasonal variations in flow and the effort required to move upstream when floods gave them depth.

The western United States, for so long the final frontier of a youthful, expanding nation, is still the goal of thousands of immigrants each year and the holiday dream of many more. Topographically, the west is a land of high ranges divided by high plateaux and deep valleys. The highest mountains – the Rockies – form a spectacular eastern flank. The southern Rockies of Colorado and New Mexico, remnants of an ancient granite plateau, are carved by weathering into ranges of impressive peaks. Colorado alone has more than 1,000 peaks of 3,000 m [10,000 ft]. The central Rocky Mountains, towering over western Wyoming, Idaho and Montana, include a number of snow-capped peaks of more than 4,000 m [13,000 ft]. West of the Rockies, beyond the dry plateau scrublands of Arizona, Utah and Nevada, a double chain of mountains runs parallel to the coast from Mexico to Canada. In the south, they form the desert landscape on either side of the Gulf of California. At Los Angeles, they merge, parting again to form the Sierra Nevada and the Coastal Ranges that face each other across the Great Valley of central California. They rejoin in the Klamath Mountains, then continue north on either side of a broad valley – to the west as a lowly coastal chain, to the east as the imposing volcanic Cascade Range.

Climate

The climates of the United States vary greatly, ranging from the Arctic conditions in northern Alaska, where average temperatures plummet to −13°C [9°F], to the intense heat of Death Valley. Death Valley holds the record for the highest shade temperature ever recorded in the United States, namely 57°C [134°F].

New England, the Middle Atlantic States and the Midwest have cold winters and warm summers. By contrast, the southern states have long, hot summers and mild, wet winters. In the central United States, a lack of topographical features bars the northwards movement of hot, moist air from the Gulf of Mexico, and in winter the southwards movement of dry, cold air from the Arctic. These air masses produce contrasts of climate, exacerbated by storms, blizzards and tornadoes.

Parts of California have a pleasant Mediterranean-type climate, but the mountains of the west are much cooler and wetter. The central plains are arid, while deserts occur in parts of the west and south-west.

USA – NEW YORK CITY

New York City's average winter temperature is just above freezing. Temperatures lower than −20°C [−4°F] have been recorded from December to February, while the daily high from May to August is above 20°C [68°F], with temperatures of 35°C to 40°C [95–104°F] having been recorded. Rain and snow are uniform all year, with rain falling on a third of the days. Sunshine totals average 6–9 hours daily from March to October.

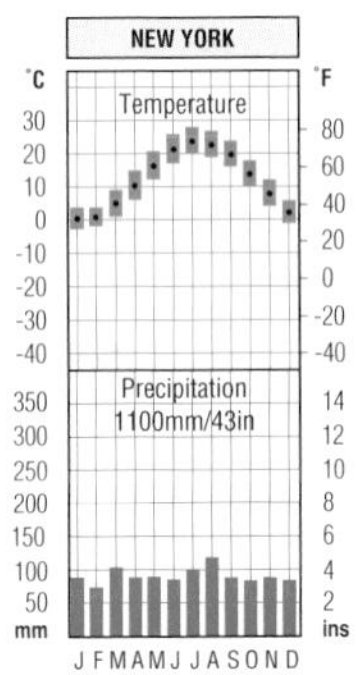

CHICAGO

To the east of the Rockies, the US is isolated from the influence of the Pacific. Here, it experiences very similar extremes to central Eurasia, but the edges of the Great Lakes are warmer in winter and cooler in summer than elsewhere. Temperatures of −20°C [−4°F] have been recorded between the months of December and February. Rainfall is uniform, with a summer maximum. Winter snowfall averages 1,000 mm [40 in].

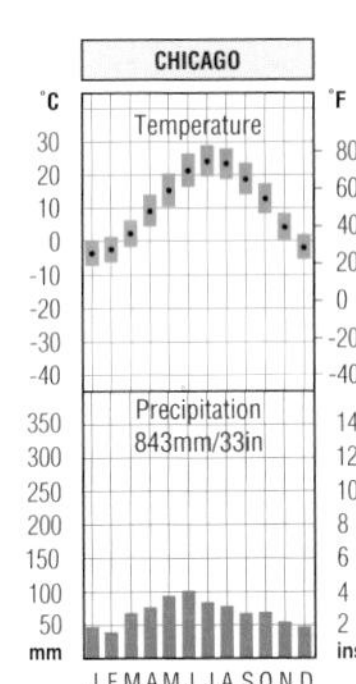

MIAMI

The Florida peninsula experiences the warmest winters of the US mainland, with a winter rainfall minimum. The lowest-ever recorded temperature is 1°C [34°F]. The summer is very hot and humid with prevailing southerly winds and thundery rain. Hurricanes may occur during late summer and they partially account for the high rainfall levels in September and October. Daily sunshine amounts average 7.5–9 hours.

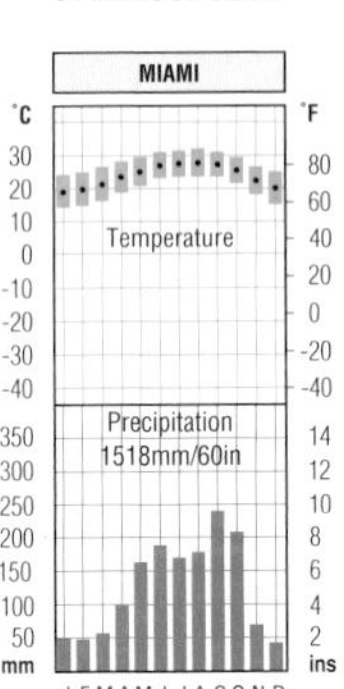

HOUSTON

Southern Texas experiences high rainfall levels throughout the year. During summer, the prevailing winds are from the south-east, and during winter from the north-east. In winter, very cold air from Canada may penetrate as far south as the Gulf, causing a sharp fall in temperature, and in autumn the region may be affected by hurricanes. Many degrees of frost can be recorded between the months of November and March.

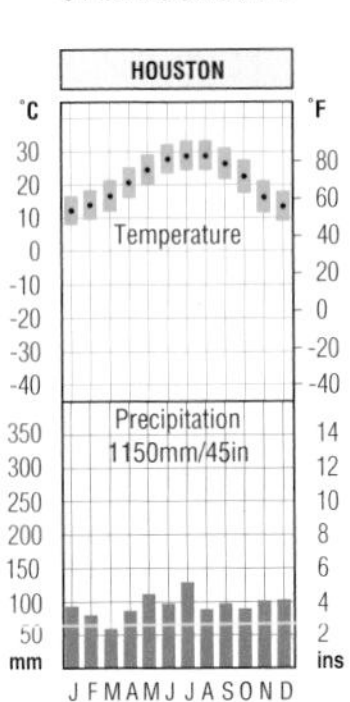

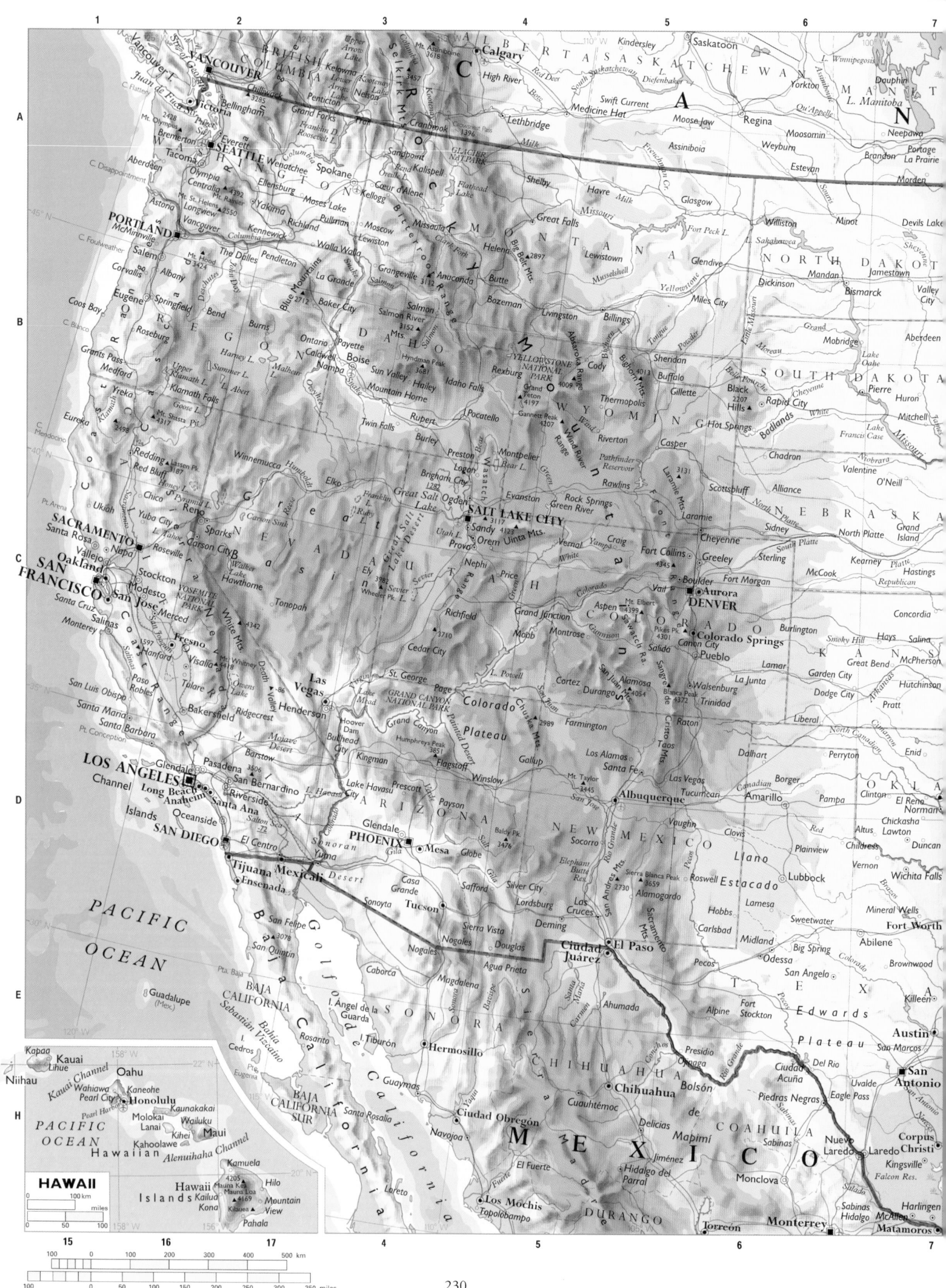

BRITISH COLUMBIA
ALBERTA
SASKATCHEWAN
MANITOBA
CANADA
WASHINGTON
OREGON
IDAHO
MONTANA
WYOMING
NORTH DAKOTA
SOUTH DAKOTA
NEBRASKA
KANSAS
NEVADA
UTAH
COLORADO
ARIZONA
NEW MEXICO
TEXAS
OKLA
CALIFORNIA
BAJA CALIFORNIA
BAJA CALIFORNIA SUR
SONORA
CHIHUAHUA
COAHUILA
DURANGO
MEXICO
PACIFIC OCEAN
ROCKY MTS.
Great Basin
Colorado Plateau
Llano Estacado
Edwards Plateau
Bolsón de Mapimí
Sierra Madre
Golfo de California
Great Salt Lake
Coast Ranges
Sierra Nevada
Cascade Range
YELLOWSTONE NATIONAL PARK
GRAND CANYON NATIONAL PARK
YOSEMITE NATIONAL PARK
GLACIER NAT.PARK
VANCOUVER
Victoria
SEATTLE
Tacoma
Olympia
Spokane
PORTLAND
Salem
Eugene
Boise
Calgary
Lethbridge
Medicine Hat
Moose Jaw
Regina
Great Falls
Helena
Billings
Bismarck
Cheyenne
SALT LAKE CITY
DENVER
Colorado Springs
Albuquerque
Santa Fe
El Paso
Ciudad Juárez
Tucson
PHOENIX
Las Vegas
Reno
SACRAMENTO
SAN FRANCISCO
Oakland
San Jose
Fresno
LOS ANGELES
SAN DIEGO
Tijuana
Mexicali
Hermosillo
Chihuahua
Monterrey
Torreón
San Antonio
Austin
Fort Worth
Lubbock
Amarillo
Matamoros
HAWAII
Kauai
Niihau
Oahu
Honolulu
Molokai
Lanai
Maui
Kahoolawe
Hawaii
Hawaiian Islands
Hilo
Mauna Kea
Mauna Loa
PACIFIC OCEAN
100 km
miles
0 50 100
100 0 100 200 300 400 500 km
100 0 50 100 150 200 250 300 350 miles

UNITED STATES OF AMERICA

8
9
10
11
12
13
A
B
C
D
E
F
Lake Winnipeg
Winnipeg
Lake of the Woods
Kenora
Dryden
Sioux Lookout
Lake Nipigon
Nipigon
Geraldton
Nakina
Hearst
Moosonee
Cochrane
Timmins
Kirkland Lake
Rouyn-Noranda
Amos
Chibougamau
Roberval
Jonquière
Chicoutimi
Alma
Baie-Comeau
Matane
Rimouski
Rivière-du-Loup
Edmundston
NEW BRUNSWICK
Fort Kent
Caribou
Presque Isle
Houlton
Millinocket
La Tuque
Québec
Shawinigan
Trois-Rivières
Joliette
Drummondville
Sherbrooke
MONTRÉAL
Mont-Laurier
Ottawa
Hull
Pembroke
Sudbury
North Bay
Huntsville
Sault Ste. Marie
Wawa
Marathon
Thunder Bay
Lake Superior
Fort Frances
International Falls
Grafton
Thief River Falls
Grand Forks
Bemidji
Hibbing
Virginia
Duluth
Superior
Two Harbors
Houghton
Marquette
Ishpeming
Iron Mountain
Escanaba
Manistique
Petoskey
Alpena
Traverse City
Manitoulin I.
Parry Sound
Georgian Bay
Orillia
Peterborough
Kingston
Barrie
Owen Sound
Oshawa
TORONTO
Kitchener
Hamilton
London
Lake Huron
Lake Michigan
Lake Ontario
Lake Erie
MINNESOTA
Moorhead
Fargo
Fergus Falls
Brainerd
Mille Lacs L.
St. Cloud
Coon Rapids
MINNEAPOLIS
ST. PAUL
Willmar
Watertown
Brookings
Owatonna
Mankato
Rochester
Austin
Albert Lea
Mason City
Charles City
Madison
Sioux Falls
Worthington
Spencer
Cherokee
Fort Dodge
Sioux City
Yankton
Norfolk
Columbus
Omaha
Council Bluffs
Lincoln
Red Oak
Creston
Des Moines
Ames
Iowa City
Waterloo
Cedar Rapids
Dubuque
Davenport
Ottumwa
IOWA
WISCONSIN
Winona
La Crosse
Eau Claire
Red Wing
Wausau
Stevens Point
Green Bay
Appleton
Oshkosh
Manitowoc
Sheboygan
Madison
MILWAUKEE
Racine
Kenosha
Janesville
Rockford
Elgin
CHICAGO
Aurora
Joliet
Gary
South Bend
Elkhart
Kankakee
Rock Island
Galesburg
Burlington
Peoria
Bloomington
Champaign
Springfield
Decatur
Danville
Mattoon
Effingham
ILLINOIS
Midwest
Lafayette
Kokomo
Marion
Muncie
INDIANAPOLIS
Richmond
Terre Haute
Bloomington
Columbus
INDIANA
Grand Rapids
Lansing
Muskegon
Ludington
Manistee
Cadillac
Midland
Saginaw
Bay City
Flint
Port Huron
Battle Creek
Kalamazoo
Jackson
Ann Arbor
DETROIT
Windsor
Toledo
Sandusky
Fort Wayne
Findlay
Lima
Marion
Mansfield
Canton
Akron
Youngstown
CLEVELAND
Ashtabula
Erie
OHIO
COLUMBUS
Dayton
Springfield
Zanesville
CINCINNATI
Wheeling
PITTSBURGH
Johnstown
Altoona
Oil City
Warren
Jamestown
Bradford
Elmira
BUFFALO
Niagara Falls
Rochester
Syracuse
Oswego
Watertown
Ithaca
Binghamton
Utica
Schenectady
Albany
Troy
Glens Falls
Adirondack Mts.
Ogdensburg
Plattsburgh
Burlington
Montpelier
VERMONT
Rutland
Catskill Mts.
Poughkeepsie
Scranton
Wilkes-Barre
Williamsport
PENNSYLVANIA
Harrisburg
Allentown
Reading
Lancaster
Newark
Paterson
Trenton
PHILADELPHIA
NEW YORK
Yonkers
Long I.
Bridgeport
New Haven
HARTFORD
Springfield
Worcester
Providence
Fall River
New Bedford
Martha's Vineyard
Nantucket
C. Cod
BOSTON
Lowell
Lawrence
Manchester
Nashua
Concord
NEW HAMPSHIRE
White Mts.
Portland
Lewiston
Augusta
Waterville
Bangor
Belfast
Penobscot Bay
Brunswick
Farmington
Berlin
Granby
MAINE
Atlantic City
Dover
Wilmington
BALTIMORE
Annapolis
WASHINGTON D.C.
Frederick
Cumberland
Morgantown
Clarksburg
Elkins
Parkersburg
Portsmouth
Huntington
Charleston
WEST VIRGINIA
Beckley
Bluefield
Harrisonburg
Charlottesville
Richmond
Lynchburg
Petersburg
Roanoke
Danville
Radford
Pulaski
Newport News
Norfolk
Virginia Beach
Elizabeth City
Albemarle Sd.
Pamlico Sd.
C. Hatteras
Salisbury
Delaware B.
Chesapeake Bay
Rocky Mount
Durham
Raleigh
Greensboro
Winston-Salem
Hickory
Greenville
Goldsboro
New Bern
Jacksonville
Onslow Bay
Wilmington
C. Fear
Fayetteville
NORTH CAROLINA
CHARLOTTE
Asheville
Spartanburg
Greenville
Rock Hill
Anderson
Columbia
Florence
Sumter
Myrtle Beach
Long Bay
Georgetown
SOUTH CAROLINA
Orangeburg
Charleston
Savannah
Statesboro
Augusta
Athens
ATLANTA
Roswell
Gainesville
Rome
Macon
Columbus
Dublin
GEORGIA
Albany
Cordele
Douglas
Waycross
Brunswick
Tifton
Valdosta
Thomasville
Tallahassee
Lake City
Jacksonville
St. Augustine
Gainesville
Ocala
Daytona Beach
Deltona
C. Canaveral
Orlando
Melbourne
Palm Bay
Fort Pierce
Lakeland
TAMPA
Clearwater
St. Petersburg
Tampa B.
Sarasota
Charlotte Harbor
Cape Coral
Fort Myers
Naples
L. Okeechobee
West Palm Beach
Fort Lauderdale
MIAMI
Florida Bay
Florida Keys
Key West
C. Sable
Straits of Florida
Grand Bahama I.
Freeport
Little Abaco I.
Great Abaco I.
N.E. Providence Channel
N.W. Providence Channel
BAHAMAS
Eleuthera I.
Nassau
New Providence I.
Cat I.
Exuma Sound
Great Exuma I.
Andros I.
Long I.
ATLANTIC OCEAN
Apalachee B.
Panama City
Pensacola
C. San Blas
Apalachicola
Dothan
Andalusia
Troy
Montgomery
Selma
Auburn
Tuscaloosa
Birmingham
Anniston
Gadsden
Huntsville
Decatur
Florence
ALABAMA
Demopolis
Mobile
Biloxi
Gulfport
Hattiesburg
Laurel
Meridian
Jackson
Vicksburg
Natchez
Yazoo City
MISSISSIPPI
Greenwood
Greenville
Cleveland
Clarksdale
Oxford
Tupelo
Columbus
Corinth
Memphis
Jackson
Dyersburg
Columbia
Chattanooga
Knoxville
Oak Ridge
Johnson City
Kingsport
Athens
Murfreesboro
Nashville
Clarksville
TENNESSEE
Hopkinsville
Bowling Green
Paducah
Mayfield
Middlesboro
Somerset
Hazard
Lexington
Frankfort
Richmond
Louisville
Owensboro
Evansville
Henderson
Danville
KENTUCKY
Vincennes
Mount Vernon
Marion
Carbondale
Cape Girardeau
Poplar Bluff
Blytheville
Jonesboro
Paragould
East St. Louis
ST. LOUIS
Alton
Hannibal
Quincy
Columbia
Jefferson City
MISSOURI
Sedalia
L. of the Ozarks
Rolla
Lebanon
Springfield
Ozark Plateau
Joplin
Kirksville
Chillicothe
St. Joseph
Maryville
KANSAS CITY
Leavenworth
Lawrence
Topeka
Manhattan
Beatrice
Emporia
Newton
Wichita
Fort Scott
Nevada
Parsons
Pittsburg
Arkansas City
Bartlesville
Ponca City
Stillwater
Tulsa
Muskogee
Oklahoma City
Shawnee
McAlester
Fort Smith
Fayetteville
Boston Mts.
West Plains
Russellville
Conway
Newport
Little Rock
Ouachita Mts.
Hot Springs
Stuttgart
Pine Bluff
Camden
El Dorado
Texarkana
Hope
ARKANSAS
Ardmore
Durant
Paris
Sherman
Denton
DALLAS
Arlington
Marshall
Longview
Tyler
Shreveport
Monroe
Corsicana
Waco
Palestine
Nacogdoches
Lufkin
Toledo Bend Res.
Natchitoches
Alexandria
De Ridder
Temple
Huntsville
Bryan
LOUISIANA
Baton Rouge
Lake Charles
Beaumont
Lafayette
New Iberia
Port Arthur
HOUSTON
Pasadena
Galveston
Victoria
Freeport
Port Lavaca
Matagorda I.
Aransas Pass
Padre I.
Laguna Madre
Brownsville
Rio Grande
NEW ORLEANS
L. Pontchartrain
Bogalusa
Houma
Morgan City
Atchafalaya B.
Marsh I.
Breton Sd.
Mississippi River Delta
GULF OF MEXICO
Appalachian Mts.
Cumberland Plateau
95° W
90° W
85° W
75° W
70° W
45° N
40° N
35° N
30° N
25° N

DENVER

Denver is situated at an altitude of over 1,500 m [5,000 ft]. Winters are very chilly but summers are pleasantly warm. The daily temperature range is high: January experiences an average temperature of 6°C [43°F], with a night-time average of −10°C [14°F]. Rainfall is low, with a maximum in April and May, rain falling on ten days in any month. Sunshine levels are high with an average of over 6 hours a day in all months, with over 9 hours in the summer months.

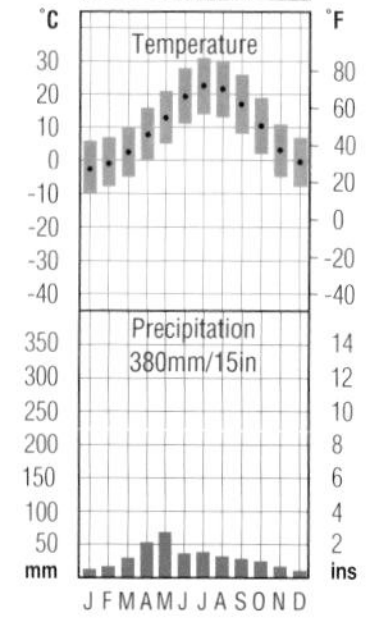

HONOLULU

Hawaii is cooled by the moisture-laden north-east trade winds. Temperatures remain high throughout the year, ranging from 22°C [72°F] to 26°C [79°F]. Rainfall varies greatly throughout the islands. Mt Waialeale on Kauai experiences a rainfall of 12,000 mm [472 in], while Puako on the leeward side of Hawaii receives less than 250 mm [10 in]. The lofty volcanoes, Mauna Kea and Mauna Loa, are frequently snow-covered.

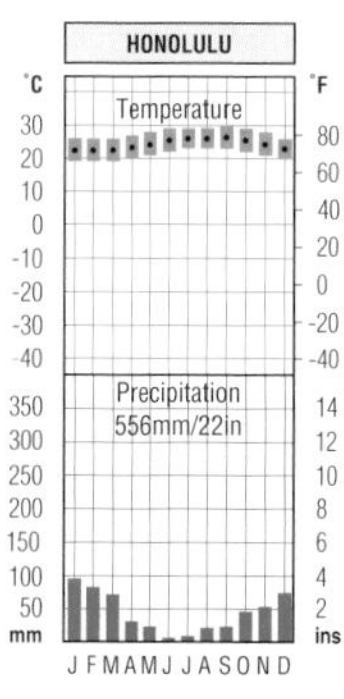

ANCHORAGE

The climate of southern Alaska is drier and more extreme than is expected from its maritime position. From November to May, winds are mainly easterly and winters are very cold, although ports remain ice-free. During the summer months, south-westerly winds increase in frequency, giving a late summer rainfall maximum. Northwards, beyond the Alaskan Range, it is drier and bitterly cold during the winter months.

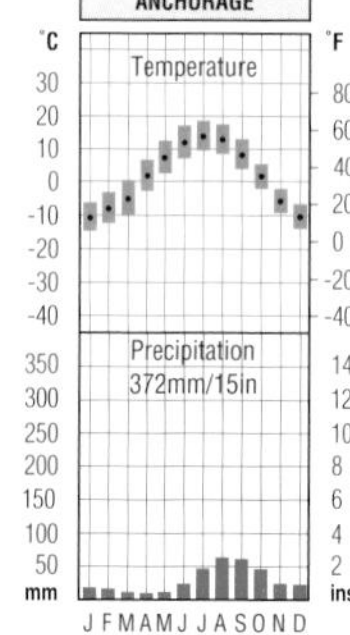

Vegetation

The original vegetation in the eastern United States was broadleaf deciduous forest of oak, ash, beech and maple, merging northwards into yellow birch, hemlock and pine. In the drier Midwest, woodlands turned to open country. Patchy grasslands covered northern Indiana and southern Illinois. In central Illinois, forests grew along most watercourses, with prairie bluestem grasses on the drier land between. Mixed oak, pine and tulip trees dominated in the southern Appalachians. Pines covered the coastal plains to the south and east, with bald cypress in northern Florida. Spruce blanketed the highlands from northern Maine to the Adirondacks, while spruce, tamarack and balsam fir covered the high Appalachians. Most of the original forest is now gone, but enough is left to leave the mountains a blaze of colour each autumn.

West of the margins of the Mississippi, tall bluestem prairie grasses once extended from the Canadian border to southern Texas. Trees grow only along watercourses – cottonwood and willow in the north, merging into oak and hickory further south. Westwards, the prairie grasslands thinned to the bunch grass and needle grass of the Great Plains in a belt from central North Dakota to western Oklahoma. West of about 100°W meridian, a variety of short grasses stretched from Montana and the Dakotas southwards to north-west Texas. In the far south, low xerophytic shrubs indicated increasing aridity.

Vegetation types in the west range from deserts in the south-west to the rain-soaked forests of Washington State in the north-west. Rising from cactus-and-sagebrush desert in the south-west, the lower slopes of the southern Rockies carry grey pinon pines and juniper scrub, with spruce, firs and pines above. Gnarled bristlecone pines, some 3,000 or more years old, grow at the timberline. Between the ranges, 'parks' of mixed forest and grassland support deer and other game in summer grazing. To the north lies the Wyoming Basin, where herds of bison once grazed. The Rockies are ecologically fascinating, with their forests, grasslands, alpine tundras and marshes. Here tourists may see bison, wapiti, mule, black and brown bears and beavers.

History

The first people in North America, the ancestors of the Native Americans (or American Indians) arrived from Asia around 15,000 or, according to some scholars, as much as 40,000 years ago. Gradually, they migrated south through North, Central and South America. Another group of migrants from Asia, the Inuit (also called Eskimos), crossed over into northern North America around 6,000 years ago, but they stayed in the far north, around the Arctic Circle. The Vikings were probably the first Europeans to reach North America, probably Newfoundland in Canada, around 1,000 years ago. However, European exploration proper did not begin until Christopher Columbus, an Italian navigator sailing for Spain, reached the Caribbean in 1492.

Spain was active in taking over Mexico, Central and much of South America, but in the north it was Britain and France that supplied the earliest explorers and fur traders. Spain founded the first permanent English settlement in what is now the United States – St Augustine, Florida. Spain also established missions in parts of the west and south. But of much greater significance was the first permanent settlement established in 1607 in Jamestown in what became the colony of Virginia. This was followed in 1620 by the arrival of the Pilgrims at Plymouth Colony, the second permanent English settlement in North America. These and subsequent settlements eventually developed into a string of colonies which, by the mid-18th century, stretched down the eastern seaboard from Maine to Georgia. Most of the settlers came from Britain. However, the colonies attracted other people from western Europe, while African slaves made up about 20% of the total population.

The mid-18th century saw a breakdown in relations with Britain and, on 19 April 1775, the Revolutionary War began. During the war, on 4 July 1776, the colonists declared their independence by adopting the Declaration of Independence and creating a new nation, the United States of America. The last major battle in the Revolutionary War took place in 1781, when the Americans defeated the British at Yorktown, Virginia. The war officially ended in 1783 with the signing of the Treaty of Paris. Washington D.C. became the national capital in 1800 and the nation almost doubled in size with the acquisition of the Louisiana Purchase in 1803. The early 19th century also saw a westwards expansion, as settlers crossed the mountains in the east and moved into the interior. In 1848, victory in the Mexican War gave the United States vast new territories in the west, extending from Texas to the Pacific. In the mid-19th century, disputes between the North and South (the Confederacy) came to a head over the issue of slavery in the new territories and states. This led to the Civil War (1861–5) during which, on 1 January 1863, President Abraham Lincoln signed the Emancipation Proclamation, proclaiming the freedom of all slaves in all parts of the Confederacy that were still in rebellion against the Union.

The 19th century saw a flood of immigrants into the country through the ports of Boston, New York City, Philadelphia and Baltimore. Many stayed to swell the cities while others moved into the interior to set up farms to feed the city masses. Railways spread over the booming farmlands, linking producer and consumer. Huge manufacturing cities, vast markets in their own right, developed along the Great Lakes as people continued to arrive – first from abroad, but latterly from the countryside – when mechanization threw people off the land into the cities and their factories. Between the late 18th and 19th centuries, the Ohio country passed from Native American-occupied forests and plains into mechanized farmlands of unparalleled efficiency. It became the granary of the Western world and it also spawned some of its greatest and wealthiest industrial cities. However, while the north boomed, the south-eastern states became over-dependent on cotton and they remained outside the mainstream of American prosperity. Today, although prosperity has spread through the east, the densest populations are still in the north-east, while the south-east remains comparatively rural. However, this pattern has been changing recently as the 'Sun Belt' in the southern United States, especially Florida, has attracted people looking for retirement homes.

The central states were formerly occupied by more than 30 major groups of Native Americans. Some, including the Mandan, Omaha and Kansa along the Missouri River, were settled farmers. Others, includ-

UNITED STATES OF AMERICA

ing the Blackfoot, Crow, Arapaho, Kiowa and Comanche, were nomads who lived on the drier western plains, hunting buffalo. European influence revolutionized their lives. By 1800, the horse, introduced from the south by the Spaniards, made the Indian population mobile as never before. The trappers and traders from the east brought firearms and this made the mounted Native Americans over-efficient at hunting, rapidly depleting their food supply. Behind the traders came the settlers, who killed off the buffalo and crowded in other Native peoples whom they had driven from their homelands in the south-east. As railways, cattle trails and the fences of ranchers crossed the old hunting grounds, the Native American farmers and hunters lost their traditional lands. By the late 19th century, the plains settlement was virtually complete.

The coming of railways after the Civil War not only doomed the remnant Native American societies, but it also introduced long and often bitter competition between different types of European farming. The dry prairies and steppe, which once supported the buffalo, could just as well support herds of cattle, raised to feed the eastern cities. The range lands also often became crop farms. But over-grazing and cultivation made the soil vulnerable to soil deterioration and erosion. With their markets in the East and in Europe, the plains farmers were caught in a vice between the dessication of their farms and the boom and slump of their markets. By the 1930s, agricultural depression led to massive foreclosing on mortgaged lands. When the dust storms of eroded topsoil came, the people were driven away – the 'Okies' of Woody Guthrie and John Steinbeck who fled to California. Much farmed land subsequently reverted to ranching. Farming prospects improved in the 1930s when the New Deal brought better price structures. New approaches to farming practices and widespread irrigation transformed the plains. Nevertheless, these areas are marginal to semi-desert and remain susceptible to periodic changes in precipitation over a wide area. Coupled with worldwide fluctuations in the cereals market, on which Midwestern farmers depend heavily, farming on the plains remains risky.

The Native American cultures of the western United States included hunting, fishing, seed gathering and primitive irrigation farming. Some groups were nomadic, while others lived in mostly small, scattered communities. The first European settlers, who spread northwards from New Spain (Mexico) in the 1760s, made little impact on their ways of life. But their forts and missions, including San Diego, Los Angeles and San Francisco, attracted later settlers who were more exploitative. From the 1840s, pressures increased with the arrival of land-hungry Americans, both by sea and along wagon trails from the east. Some of the immigrants were adventurers attracted by gold rushes. The Oregon coast, though visited by Spanish, British and Russian mariners in search of furs from the 16th century onwards, was first settled by American fur traders in 1811. Immigration began during the 1830s – the famous Oregon Trail across Wyoming and Idaho from the Mississippi coming into full use during the 1840s. After the establishment of the 49th parallel as the boundary with Canada, Oregon Territory (including Washington, Idaho and part of Montana) became part of the United States. Here, in the north-west, many battles were fought before the Native Americans were subdued and confined to reserves. Today, the wagon trails are major highways, the staging posts, mission stations and isolated forts transformed into cities. Gold mining, once the only kind of mining that mattered, has given way to the exploitation of a dozen lesser metals, from copper to molybdenum. Fish canning, food processing, electronics and aerospace are major sources of employment. The movie industry is based in Los Angeles, but this vast urban cluster now has a broad economy based on high-technology industries. The mountain states – once far behind in economic development – have caught up with the rest of the country. But the enduring beauty of the western mountains remains.

Politics

The United States has long played a leading role in industrial, economic, social and technological innovation, creating problems through sheer ebullience, and solving them – more or less – through inventiveness, enterprise, and with huge, wealth-bringing resources of energy and raw materials. The majority of Americans continue to enjoy one of

the world's highest material standards of living and the country continues to produce a highly skilled, literate and imaginative population. Yet at the same time, the country faces many problems. One concerns the maintenance of social cohesion as the composition of American society changes. Another is the issue of poverty and the low standards of living of a sizeable underclass of poor and inadequately educated people, many of whom are members of ethnic minorities. Other associated problems include crime, drug addiction and racial conflict.

The United States has one of the most diverse populations of any country in the world. Until about 1860, the population, with the exception of the Native Americans and the southern African Americans, was made up largely of immigrants of British and Irish origin, with small numbers of Spaniards and French. However, after the Civil War, increasing numbers of immigrants arrived from the countries of central and south-eastern Europe, including Italy, the Balkans, Poland, Scandinavia and Russia. This vast influx of Europeans, numbering about 30 million between 1860 and 1920, was vastly different in culture and language from the established population. More recently, the country has received lesser influxes of Japanese, Chinese, Filipinos, Cubans, Puerto Ricans, and large numbers of Mexicans, many of them illegal immigrants. Although strong influences and pressures towards Americanization still exist, members of these groups have tended to maintain their own culture, establishing social and cultural enclaves within American society.

Although the nation has never adopted an official language, English was readily adopted by most immigrants in the late 19th and early 20th century, because they sought acceptance in the 'melting pot' that makes up the United States. However, many of the recent Hispanic immigrants persist in speaking Spanish, which has become the country's second language. Many Americans are concerned about this trend towards 'cultural pluralism' rather than integration through the 'melting pot'. For example, they argue that Hispanics who do not speak English are at a disadvantage in American society and believe that everyone should speak English, either as a first or second language. According to some population forecasts, today's white majority will be outnumbered by other ethnic groups in 2050. With a total projected population of 380 million, Hispanics are expected to number around 80 million by 2050, while African Americans will account for another

Alaska

Alaska became the 49th state of the United States in 1959, becoming the first new state for 47 years. It is the nation's largest state and more than twice the size of Texas, which ranks second in area. The Brooks Range and northern coastal plains lie above the Arctic Circle. South of the Brooks Range lie the Central Uplands and Lowlands which are drained by the Yukon River, while the Alaska Range, including Mount McKinley, the highest peak in North America, is in the south. In the south-west lie the Alaska Peninsula and the volcanic Aleutian Islands – southern Alaska forms part of the 'Pacific ring of fire'. The south-eastern 'panhandle', where the capital Juneau is situated, is a drowned fjordland backed by ice-capped mountains. Forests cover about a third of the state, while the interior tablelands are tundra-covered and rich in migrant birds and mammals.

Southern Alaska, where temperatures are moderated by winds blowing eastwards across the Japan Current, has a relatively mild climate, with heavy precipitation in the south-east. Central and northern Alaska are dry with cold winters.

The United States purchased Alaska from the Tsarist government of Russia in 1867 for US $7 million. It remained a territory for over 90 years. A gold rush in the 1880s stimulated later development of other mineral resources, including copper and oil. Today, Alaska has become a test of the nation's resolve to balance economic development and conservation – the country's six largest national parks are in Alaska. Tourism is a growing industry and more than a million visitors arrive every year. Food-processing, fish and petroleum products are the chief manufactured goods.

62 million. Such a rapid growth of these communities is seen by some as a threat to the majority.

From the 1890s, the United States developed into a world power, and it played a leading role in international affairs throughout the 20th century. It played a key role in World Wars I and II, after which it was one of the world's two superpowers – the other being the Soviet Union. After World War II, it assumed the leadership of the West during the Cold War. Following the break-up of the Soviet Union in 1991 and subsequent problems faced by Russia, it became the world's only superpower and an active player in the international arena. Closer to home, it seeks to enlarge its economic links with Canada and Mexico through NAFTA (North American Free Trade Agreement) and also with other countries in the Americas.

Economy

Stimulated by education, research and sophisticated machinery following the Civil War, agriculture developed into a highly mechanized industry. Only a generation after the pioneering days, farmers found themselves integrated into a complex economic system with such factors as mortgages, freight prices and world markets as crucial to their success as climate and soil.

To the east of the western mountains, farming was established in a zonal pattern which remains intact today, though much modified. This pattern reflects both the possibilities offered by the climate and the soils, and the inclinations and national origins of the farmers who first farmed the lands. In the north, from Minnesota to New England, lies a broad belt where dairy farming predominates, providing butter, cheese and milk for the industrial cities. Spring wheat is grown further west, where the climate is drier. The eastern and central states, from Nebraska to Ohio, form the famous Corn Belt – immensely productive land, formerly prairie and forest, where corn (maize) is the main crop. Now much extended by the development of new, more tolerant strains, maize production has spread into belts on either side. No longer principally a human food, except in the poorer areas of the south-east, maize is grown mainly for feeding to cattle and pigs. Soya beans, oats and other food and fodder crops grow in the Corn Belt, with wheat and dairy farming prominent on the northern border. The cities of the central United States are great trading centres, dependent on agriculture for their prosperity. But some cities, such as Chicago, have diversified to become major manufacturing centres. For example, Chicago is the main Midwestern focus of the iron and steel industry.

Southwards again, stretching from Oklahoma and Kansas to Virginia, is a belt of mixed farming where winter wheat and maize alternate as dominant cereals. In the warmer southern states lies the former Cotton Belt, where cotton and tobacco were once the chief products. Both crops are now concentrated into small, highly productive areas where mechanical handling is possible, while the bulk of the land is used for a wide variety of other crops from vegetables to fruit.

In the west, the long, bone-dry summers once made farming – even ranching – difficult in the central valley of California. But the peaks of the Sierra Nevada, with their thick snow cover in winter, now provide water for summer irrigation. Damming and water channelling have made the semi-deserts and dry rangelands bloom all over southern California, which now produces temperate and tropical fruits, vegetables, cotton and other thirsty crops in abundance, despite severe droughts from the late 1980s.

Agriculture now employs only 2.6% of the labour force. The western plains are the main centres of production. Much of the land farmed by the Pilgrim Fathers and other settlers is now built over, or has reverted to forest. By concentrating effort in this way, the United States has become a leading producer of meat, dairy products, soya beans, maize, oats, wheat, barley, cotton, sugar and many other crops.

The spread of prosperity generated new consumer industries to satisfy demands of a large middle class for ever-increasing standards of comfort. The United States became a pioneer of large-scale industrial production of everything from thumbtacks to motor vehicles. With almost every raw material available within its own boundaries, or readily gained through trading, its mining and extractive industries have been heavily exploited. For several generations, coal formed the main source of power. Anthracite from eastern Pennsylvania, good bituminous and coking coals from the Appalachians, Indiana, Illinois, Colorado and Utah are still in demand, and vast reserves remain.

Oil, first drilled in Pennsylvania in 1859, was subsequently found in several major fields underlying the Midwest, the eastern and central mountain states, the Gulf of Mexico, California and Alaska. Home consumption of petroleum products has grown steadily. Although the United States is a major producer, it is also by far the world's greatest consumer and has long been a net importer of oil. In the Gulf Coast states, the exploitation of oil in Oklahoma, Texas and Louisiana has shifted the former dependence on agriculture to the refining and petrochemical industries. Oil has transformed Dallas-Fort Worth into a major conurbation, while Denver has changed from a small railhead town into a wealthy state capital. Natural gas is also found in abundance, usually associated with oil. It is moved to the consumer areas through a network of pipes.

Hawaii

Hawaii, the 50th and youngest state of the United States, joined the Union on 21 August 1959. Situated in the mid-North Pacific Ocean, it consists of eight large islands and over 100 others which were formed as the Pacific plate moved across a 'hot spot', or source of heat, in the Earth's mantle. Currently, the hot spot is under the biggest island in the group, which is also called Hawaii. This island contains the extinct Mauna Kea, a huge volcano which measures 10,203 m [33,437 ft] from its base on the sea floor, though only 4,205 m [13,796 ft] is above sea level. Also on Hawaii is the intermittently active Mauna Loa and Kilauea, which provides spectacular displays when it erupts. The climate is warm throughout the year, with heaviest precipitation on the north-eastern sides of the islands. Dense rainforests grow in the fertile volcanic soils on the rainy parts of the islands.

The archipelago, which is part of Polynesia, was visited by the British Captain James Cook in 1778. Following his discovery, the islands became a port-of-call for trans-Pacific shipping and a wintering station for New England whalers. It retained its independence until it was annexed by the United States in 1898. The naval base of Pearl Harbor was of great strategic importance and the Japanese attack on the base on 7 December 1941 brought the United States into World War II. Today, only 2% of its people are full-blooded Polynesians, though another 13% are mainly of Hawaiian descent. The rest are of European, Chinese, Japanese, Korean and Filipino origin. About 75% live on Oahu, with 33% of the state's population living in Honolulu.

Agriculture, fishing and food processing are the main industries, but defence and tourism are important. Sugar cane and pineapples are the leading commercial crops. The island of Hawaii has large cattle ranches, while dairy products and eggs are important on Oahu, Maui and Kauai. Tourism contributes more than US $11 billion to the economy. Tourist attractions include two national parks, the Haleakala National Park on Maui and the Hawaii Volcanoes National Park on Hawaii. The National Memorial marks the spot where the USS *Arizona* was sunk by the Japanese in 1941.

AREA	African American 12%,
9,372,610 sq km	other races 8%
[3,618,765 sq mls]	**LANGUAGES**
POPULATION	English (official), Spanish,
270,290,000	more than 30 others
CAPITAL (POPULATION)	**RELIGIONS**
Washington, D.C.	Christianity (Protestant 53%,
(4,466,000)	Roman Catholic 26%, other
GOVERNMENT	Christian 8%), Islam 2%,
Federal republic	Judaism 2%
ETHNIC GROUPS	**CURRENCY**
White 80%,	US dollar = 100 cents

URUGUAY

Uruguay has used this flag since 1830. The nine stripes represent the nine provinces which formed the country when it became an independent republic in 1828. The colours and the May Sun had originally been used by Argentina during its struggle against Spanish rule.

Geography

The Eastern Republic of Uruguay, as Uruguay is officially known, is South America's second smallest independent nation after Surinam. The River Uruguay, which forms the country's western border, flows into the Río de la Plata (River Plate), a large estuary fringed with lagoons and sand dunes, which leads into the South Atlantic Ocean.

The land consists of low-lying plains and hills. The highest point lies south of Minas and is only 501 m [1,644 ft] above sea level. The main river in the interior is the Rio Negro.

Climate

Uruguay has a mild climate, with rain in every month, though droughts sometimes occur. Summers are pleasantly warm, especially near the coast. The weather remains relatively mild throughout the winter.

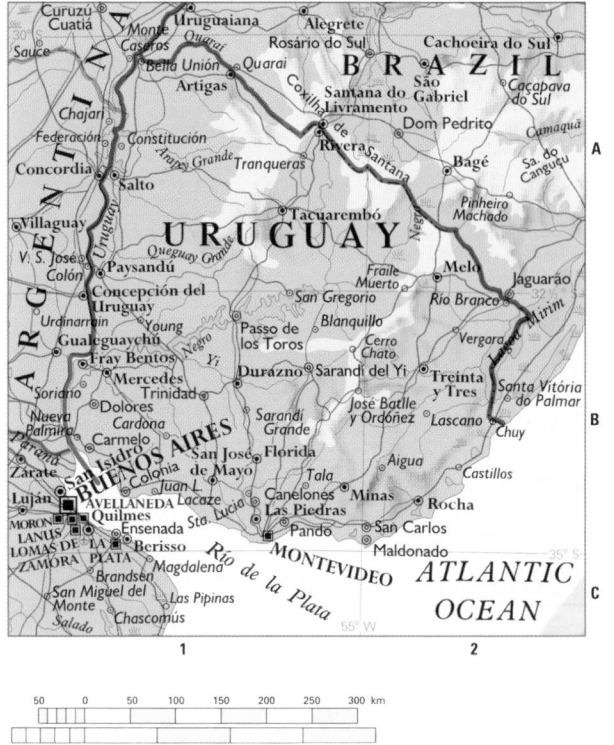

URUGUAY (MONTEVIDEO)

The plains around the estuary of the River Plate have an extremely uniform distribution of rainfall throughout the year. Much of this rain is associated with the advance of the cold air from the Southern Ocean, which may be accompanied by a *Pampero Sucio*. A Pampero Sucio is a violent squall with rain and thunder which is followed by cooler, sunny weather. Near to the ocean, the summers are pleasantly warm and the winters are not as cold than those at similar latitudes in the northern hemisphere.

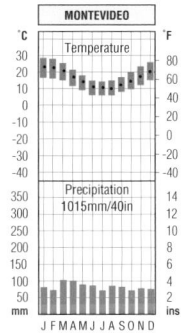

History

The first people of Uruguay were Amerindians. But the Amerindian population has largely disappeared. Many were killed by Europeans, some died of European diseases, while others fled into the interior. The majority of Uruguayans today are of European origin, though there are some mestizos (of mixed European and Amerindian descent).

The first European to arrive in Uruguay was a Spanish navigator, Juan Diaz de Solis, in 1516. But he and part of his crew were killed by the local Charrúa Amerindians when they went ashore. Few Europeans settled in the area until the late 17th century. In 1726, Spanish settlers founded Montevideo in order to prevent the Portuguese from gaining influence in the area. Uruguay was then little more than a buffer zone between the Portuguese territory to the north and Spanish territories to the west. By the late 18th century, Spaniards had settled on most of the country. Uruguay became part of a colony called the Viceroyalty of La Plata, which also included Argentina, Paraguay and parts of Bolivia, Brazil and Chile.

In 1820, Brazil annexed Uruguay, ending Spanish rule. In 1825, Uruguayans, supported by Argentina, began a struggle for independence. In 1828, Brazil and Argentina recognized Uruguay as an independent republic. Social and economic developments were slow in the 19th century, but, from 1903, governments made Uruguay a democratic and stable country. Since 1828, two political parties have dominated Uruguay. They are the Colorados (Liberals) and the Blancos (Conservatives).

Politics

During World War II, Uruguay prospered because of its export trade, especially in meat and wool. However, from the 1950s, economic problems caused unrest. Terrorist groups, notably the Tupumaros (Marxist urban guerrillas), carried out murders and kidnappings in the 1960s and early 1970s. In 1972, President Juan Maria Bordaberry declared war on the Tupumaros and the army crushed them. However, in 1973, the military seized power, suspended the constitution and ruled with great severity, committing major human rights abuses.

Military rule continued until 1984, when elections were held. General Gregorio Alvarez, who had been president since 1991, resigned and Julio Maria Sanguinetti, leader of the Colorado Party, became president in February 1985, leading a government of National Unity. He ordered the release of all political prisoners. In the 1990s, Uruguay faced problems in trying to rebuild its weakened economy and shoring up its democratic traditions. In 1991, Uruguay joined with Argentina, Brazil and Paraguay to form Mercosur, which aimed to create a common market. Mercosur's secretariat is in Montevideo.

Economy

Meat processing, pioneered at Fray Bentos in the 1860s, started a meat-and-hide export industry that established the nation's fortunes. Today, Uruguay is classed by the World Bank as an 'upper-middle-income' developing country. Although 90% of the population live in urban areas and agriculture employs 4% of the population, the economy depends on the exports of hides and leather goods, beef and wool. Main crops include maize, potatoes, rice, sugar beet and wheat.

The manufacturing sector concentrates on food processing and packing, though with a small domestic market, the economy has diversified into cement, chemicals, leather goods, textiles and steel. With inadequate supplies of fossil fuels, Uruguay depends largely on hydroelectric power for energy and it exports electricity to Argentina.

AREA	Mulatto or Black 6%
177,410 sq km [68,498 sq mls]	**LANGUAGES**
POPULATION	Spanish (official)
3,285,000	**RELIGIONS**
CAPITAL (POPULATION)	Christianity
Montevideo (1,326,000)	(Roman Catholic 66%,
GOVERNMENT	Protestant 2%),
Multiparty republic	Judaism 1%
ETHNIC GROUPS	**CURRENCY**
White 86%, Mestizo 8%,	Uruguay peso = 100 centésimos

UZBEKISTAN – SEE TURKMENISTAN, PAGE 221;

VANUATU – SEE PACIFIC OCEAN, PAGES 174–178;

VATICAN CITY – SEE ITALY, PAGES 131–133

235

VENEZUELA

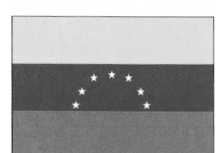

Venezuela's flag, adopted in 1954, has the same basic tricolour as the flags of Colombia and Ecuador. The colours were used by the Venezuelan patriot Francisco de Miranda. The seven stars represent the provinces in the Venezuelan Federation in 1811.

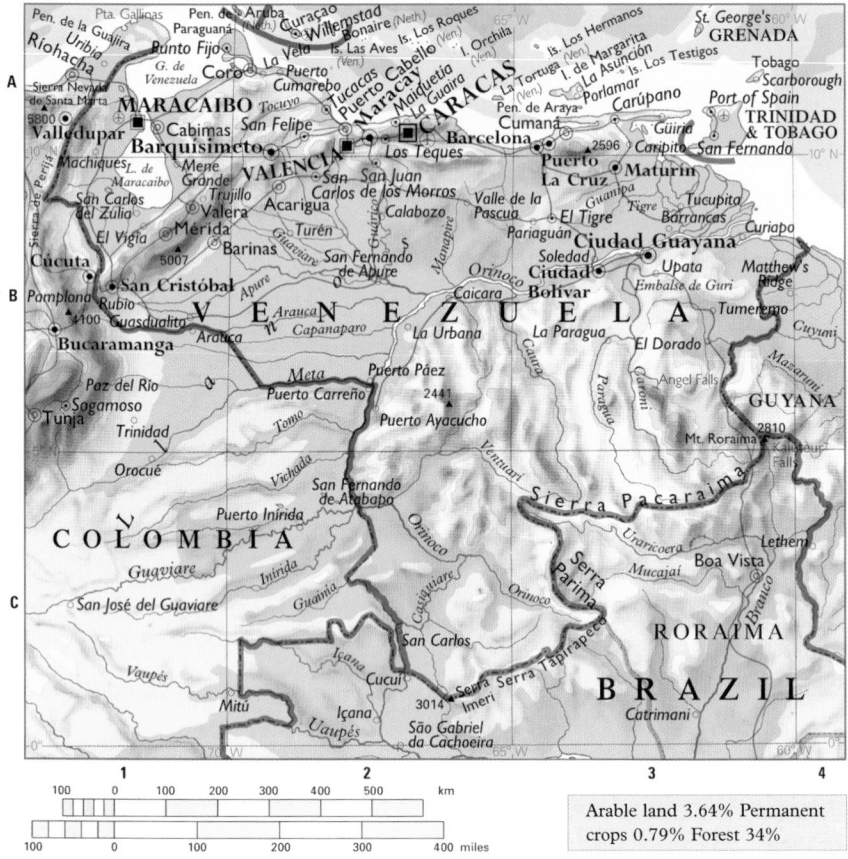

Arable land 3.64% Permanent
crops 0.79% Forest 34%

In the early 19th century, Spain's colonies in South America began their struggle for independence. The Venezuelan patriots Simón Bolívar and Francisco Miranda were prominent in the struggle. Venezuela was the first South American country to demand freedom and, in July 1811, it declared its independence, though Spaniards still held most of the country. The country did not become fully independent until 1821, after the Venezuelans had defeated the Spanish in a battle at Carabobo, near Valencia. In 1819, Venezuela became part of Gran Colombia, a republic led by Simón Bolívar that also included Colombia, Ecuador and Panama. Venezuela broke away from Gran Colombia in 1829 and a new constitution was drafted in 1830. The country's first president was General José Antonio Páez, one of the leaders of Venezuela's independence movement

Politics

The development of Venezuela in the 19th century and the first half of the 20th century was marred by instability, violence and periods of harsh dictatorial rule. However, the country has had elected governments since 1958. Venezuela has greatly benefited from its oil resources, which were first exploited in 1917. In 1960, Venezuela helped to form OPEC (the Organization of Petroleum Exporting Countries) and, in 1976, the government of Venezuela took control of the entire oil industry. Money from oil exports has helped Venezuela to raise living standards and diversify the economy.

Financial problems in the late 1990s led to the election of Hugo Chávez as president. Chávez, leader of the Patriotic Pole, a left-wing coalition, who had led an abortive military uprising in 1992, became president in February 1999. He announced that the country's official name would be changed to the Bolivarian Republic of Venezuela and held a referendum on a new constitution. This gave the president increased power over military and civilian institutions. Chávez argued that these powers were needed to counter corruption. His opponents argued that it created an elective dictatorship.

Economy

The World Bank classifies Venezuela as an 'upper-middle-income' developing country. Oil accounts for 80% of the exports. Other exports include bauxite and aluminium, iron ore and farm products. Agriculture employs 13% of the people. Cattle ranching is important and dairy cattle and poultry are also raised. Major crops include bananas, cassava, citrus fruits, coffee, maize, plantains, rice and sorghum. Most commercial crops are grown on large farms, but many people in remote areas farm small plots and produce barely enough to feed their families.

Manufacturing has increased greatly since the 1960s and industry now employs 25% of the population. The leading industry is petroleum refining, which is centred on Maracaibo. Other manufactures include aluminium, cement, processed food, steel and textiles.

Geography

The Republic of Venezuela, in northern South America, contains the Maracaibo Lowlands in the west. The lowlands surround the oil-rich Lake Maracaibo (L. de Maracaibo). Arms of the Andes Mountains enclose the lowlands and extend across most of northern Venezuela. Between the northern mountains and the scenic Guiana Highlands in the south-east, where the Angel Falls are found, lie the *llanos* (tropical grasslands), a low-lying region drained by the River Orinoco and its tributaries. The Orinoco is Venezuela's longest river.

Climate

Venezuela has a tropical climate. Temperatures are high throughout the year on the lowlands, though the mountains are much cooler. The rainfall is heaviest in the mountains. But much of the country has a marked dry season between December and April.

VENEZUELA (CARACAS)

Venezuela experiences little variation in temperature from month to month, but there are marked wet and dry seasons, the rain falling from May to November. The north-east trade winds leave little rain in the coastal lowlands, but the total increases when they hit the mountains. The monthly temperature of Caracas is between 19°C and 22°C [66–72°F], but this is much lower on the higher land. Some northern Andean peaks have permanent snow.

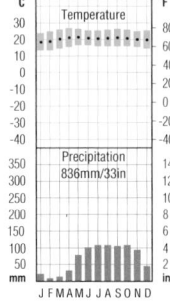

History

The Arawak and Carib Amerindians were the main inhabitants of Venezuela before the arrival of Europeans. The first European to arrive was Christopher Columbus, who sighted the area in 1498. Spaniards began to settle in the early 16th century, but economic development was slow.

AREA	**ETHNIC GROUPS**
912,050 sq km	Mestizo 67%, White 21%,
[352,143 sq mls]	Black 10%, Amerindian 2%
POPULATION	**LANGUAGES**
22,803,000	Spanish (official), Goajiro
CAPITAL (POPULATION)	**RELIGIONS**
Caracas	Christianity
(2,784,000)	(Roman Catholic 94%)
GOVERNMENT	**CURRENCY**
Federal republic	Bolívar = 100 céntimos

Vietnam's flag was first used by forces led by the Communist Ho Chi Minh during the liberation struggle against Japan in World War II (1939–45). It became the flag of North Vietnam in 1945 and it was retained when North and South Vietnam were reunited in 1975.

Geography and Climate

The Socialist Republic of Vietnam occupies an S-shaped strip of land facing the South China Sea in South-east Asia. The coastal plains include two densely populated, fertile river delta areas. The Red (Hong) Delta faces the Gulf of Tonkin in the north, while the Mekong Delta is in the south. Inland are thinly populated highland regions, including the Annam Cordillera (Chaîne Annamitique), which forms much of the boundary with Cambodia. The highlands in the north-west extend into Laos and China.

Vietnam has a tropical climate, though the drier months of January to March are cooler than the wet, hot summer months, when monsoon winds blow from the south-west. Typhoons sometimes hit the coast, causing much damage.

History and Politics

China dominated Vietnam for a thousand years before AD 939, when a Vietnamese state was founded. The French took over the area between the 1850s and 1880s. They ruled Vietnam as part of French Indo-China, which also included Cambodia and Laos.

Japan conquered Vietnam during World War II (1939–45). In 1946, war broke out between a nationalist group, the Vietminh, and the French colonial government. France withdrew in 1954 and Vietnam was divided into a Communist North Vietnam, led by the Vietminh leader Ho Chi Minh, and a non-Communist South.

A force called the Viet Cong rebelled against South Vietnam's government in 1957 and a war began, which gradually increased in intensity. The United States aided the South, but after it withdrew in 1975, South Vietnam surrendered. In 1976, the united Vietnam became a Socialist Republic.

Vietnamese troops intervened in Cambodia in 1978 to defeat the Communist Khmer Rouge government, but it withdrew its troops in 1989. In the 1990s, Vietnam began to introduce reforms. In 1995, relations with the US were normalized when the US opened an embassy in Hanoi.

Economy

The World Bank classifies Vietnam as a 'low-income' developing country. Agriculture employs 67% of the population and the main food crop is rice. Other products include maize and sweet potatoes, while commercial crops include bananas, coffee, groundnuts, rubber, soya beans and tea. Fishing is also important. Northern Vietnam has most of the country's natural resources, including coal. The country also produces chromium, oil (which was discovered off the south coast in 1986), phosphates and tin. Manufactures include cement, fertilizers, processed food, machinery, steel and textiles. The main exports are farm products and handicrafts, coal, minerals, oil and seafood.

AREA	Tho (Tay), Chinese (Hoa),
331,689 sq km	Tai, Khmer, Muong, Nung
[128,065 sq mls]	**LANGUAGES**
POPULATION	Vietnamese (official),
76,236,000	Chinese
CAPITAL (POPULATION)	**RELIGIONS**
Hanoi (3,056,000)	Buddhism 55%,
GOVERNMENT	Christianity (Roman
Socialist republic	Catholic 7%)
ETHNIC GROUPS	**CURRENCY**
Vietnamese 87%,	Dong = 10 hao = 100 xu

Arable land 18.1% Permanent crops 3.33%
Permanent grassland 1.01% Forest 29.6%

VIRGIN ISLANDS, UK AND US – SEE CARIBBEAN SEA, PAGES 71–76;
WALLIS AND FUTUNA ISLANDS – SEE PACIFIC OCEAN, PAGES 174–178;
WESTERN SAHARA – SEE MOROCCO, PAGE 161

Yemen's flag was adopted in 1990 when the Yemen Arab Republic (or North Yemen) united with the People's Democratic Republic of Yemen (or South Yemen). This simple flag is a tricolour of red, white and black, colours associated with the Pan-Arab movement.

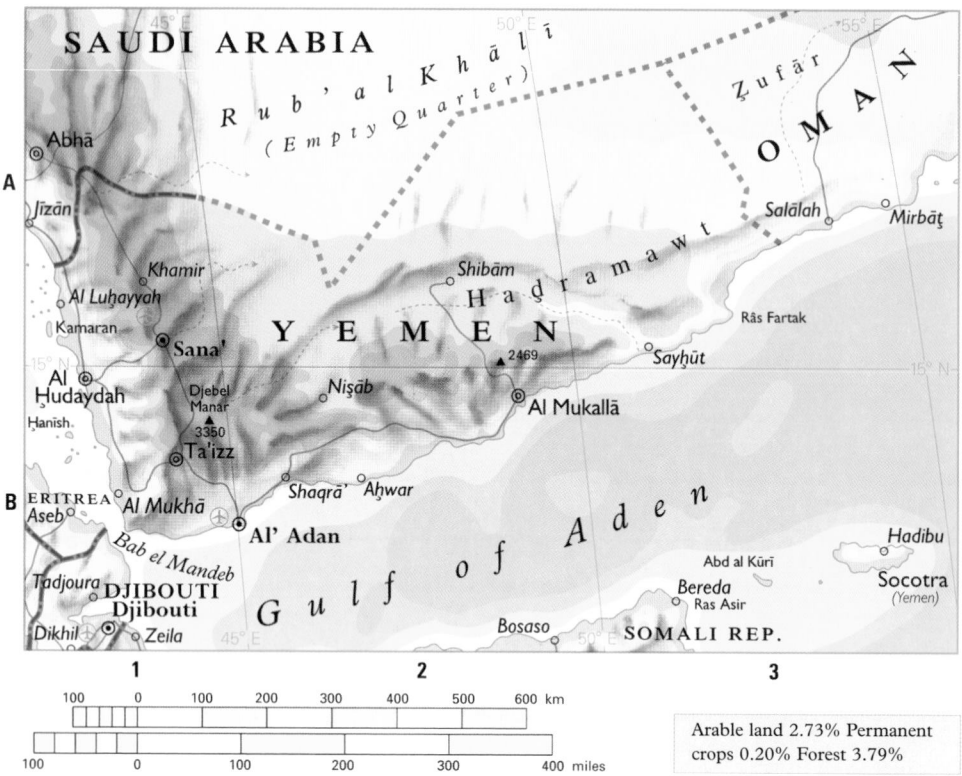

100   0   100   200   300   400   500   600 km

100   0   100   200   300   400 miles

Arable land 2.73% Permanent crops 0.20% Forest 3.79%

Geography and Climate

The Republic of Yemen faces the Red Sea and the Gulf of Aden in the south-western corner of the Arabian Peninsula. Behind the narrow coastal plain along the Red Sea, the land rises to a mountain region called High Yemen. Beyond the mountains, the land slopes down towards the Rub' al Khali Desert. Other mountains rise behind the coastal plain along the Gulf of Aden. To the east lies a fertile valley called the Hadramaut.

The climate in San'a is moderated by its altidtude. Temperatures are much lower than in Aden (Al' Adan), which is at sea level. In summer, south-west monsoon winds bring thunderstorms. But most of Yemen is arid. The south coasts are particularly hot and humid, especially from June to September.

YEMEN – SAN'A

San'a lies at over 2,000 m [6,500 ft], on the eastern side of the Yemen highlands. Temperatures are much lower than at sea level and the diurnal range is very large (over 20°C [36°F] in winter), frost occurring in winter. In August, the south-west monsoon brings heavy thunderstorms. As in Ethiopia, across the Red Sea, minor rains occur in spring. The western side of the mountains, famous for coffee plantations, is wetter and cloudier.

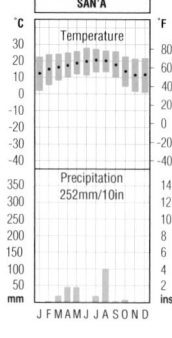

ADEN

Aden (Al' Adan) is situated on the southern coast of Yemen. Temperatures here are uniformly high through the year, and are higher than the temperatures elsewhere in the country. During January, an average of 24°C [75°F] is experienced. During July, this figure rises to 32°C [90°F]. Average annual rainfall in the north of Yemen is 508 mm [20 in]. In coastal areas, rainfall is very low with an annual average of just 46 mm [1.8 in].

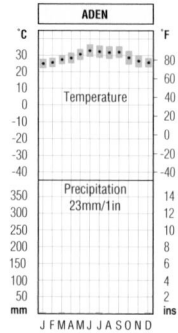

Vegetation

Palm trees grow on the coastline, while such plants as euphorbias, acacias and eucalyptus flourish in the interior. Thorn shrubs and mountain pasture are found in mountain areas. Inland lies barren desert.

History

From aound 1400 BC, Yemen lay on an important trading route, with frankincense, pearls and spices being the major commodities. But its prosperity declined in the 4th century AD, when it became divided between warring groups.

Islam was introduced during the 7th century by the son-in-law of the Prophet Muhammad. From 897, the country was ruled by a Muslim leader. In 1517, the area was taken over by the Turkish Ottoman Empire and remained under Turkish rule for the next 400 years.

Politics

After World War I, northern Yemen, which had been ruled by Turkey, began to evolve into a separate state from the south, where Britain was in control. Britain withdrew in 1967 and a left-wing government then took power in the south. In North Yemen, the monarchy was abolished in 1962 and the country became a republic.

Clashes occurred between the traditionalist Yemen Arab Republic in the north and the formerly British Marxist People's Democratic Republic of Yemen. But, in 1990, the two Yemens merged to form one country. The marrying of the needs of the two parts of Yemen has proved difficult. In May 1994, civil war erupted, with President Saleh, a northerner, attempting to remove the vice-president (a southerner). The war ended in July 1994, following the capture of Aden by government forces. In 1995, Yemen resolved border disputes with Oman and Saudi Arabia, but clashed with Eritrea over uninhabited islands in the Red Sea. In 1998–9, militants in the Aden-Abyan Islamic Army sought to destabilize the country, with kidnappings of tourists and bombings.

Economy

The World Bank classifies Yemen as a 'low-income' developing country. Agriculture employs up to 63% of the people. Herders raise sheep and other animals, while farmers grow such crops as barley, fruits, wheat and vegetables in highland valleys and around oases. Cash crops include coffee and cotton.

Imported oil is refined at Aden and petroleum extraction began in the north-west in the 1980s. Handicrafts, leather goods and textiles are manufactured. Remittances from Yemenis abroad are a major source of revenue.

AREA	ETHNIC GROUPS
527,970 sq km	Arab 96%,
[203,849 sq mls]	Somali 1%
POPULATION	**LANGUAGES**
16,388,000	Arabic
CAPITAL (POPULATION)	(official)
San'a	**RELIGIONS**
(Sana', 972,000)	Islam
GOVERNMENT	**CURRENCY**
Multiparty republic	Rial = 100 fils

YUGOSLAVIA

Yugoslavia's flag was adopted in 1992. Yugoslavia now consists of two republics (Serbia and Montenegro) which were formerly part of the socialist Federal People's Republic of Yugoslavia, which also included Bosnia-Herzegovina, Croatia, Macedonia and Slovenia.

Geography

The Federal Republic of Yugoslavia consists of Serbia and Montenegro, two of the six republics which made up the former country of Yugoslavia until it broke up in 1991 and 1992. Behind the short coastline along the Adriatic Sea lies a mountainous region, including the Dinaric Alps and part of the Balkan Mountains. The Pannonian Plains make up northern Yugoslavia.

Climate

The climate varies between the coast, which has a mild, Mediterranean climate, and inland highland areas where the climate is more continental. The highlands have cold, snowy winters. The Pannonian Plains have hot, arid summers, with heavy rains in spring and autumn.

History

People who became known as the South Slavs began to move into the region around 1,500 years ago. Each group, including the Serbs and Croats, founded its own state. But, by the 15th century, foreign countries controlled the region. Serbia and Montenegro were under the Turkish Ottoman Empire.

During the 19th century, many Slavs worked for independence and Slavic unity. In 1914, Austria-Hungary declared war on Serbia, blaming it for the assassination of Archduke Francis Ferdinand of Austria-Hungary. This led to World War I and the defeat of Austria-Hungary. In 1918, the South Slavs united in the Kingdom of the Serbs, Croats and Slovenes, which consisted of Bosnia-Herzegovina, Croatia, Dalmatia, Montenegro, Serbia and Slovenia. In 1929, King Alexander abolished the constitution and renamed the country Yugoslavia. Ruling as a dictator until he was assassinated in 1934, he sought to enforce the use of one language, Serbo-Croatian, and he created new political divisions that failed to acknowledge the historic boundaries determined by the ethnic groups. Hence, the unity of the new state was under constant threat from nationalist and ethnic tensions. The country's troubled history had so stirred the peoples of the region that there was no area that did not contain at least one aggrieved or distrusted minority. In the inter-war period, Yugoslavia was virtually a 'Greater Serbia' and, after the Germans invaded in 1941, Yugoslavs fought the Germans and themselves. The Communist-led partisans of Josip Broz Tito (a Croat) emerged victorious in 1945.

Politics

From 1945, the Communists controlled the country, which was called the Federal People's Republic of Yugoslavia. But after Tito's death in 1980, the country faced many problems. In 1990, non-Communist parties were permitted and non-Communists won majorities in elections in all but Serbia and Montenegro, where Socialists (former (Communists) won control. Yugoslavia split apart in 1991–2 with Bosnia-Herzegovina, Croatia, Macedonia and Slovenia proclaiming their independence. The two remaining republics of Serbia and Montenegro became the new Yugoslavia.

Fighting broke out in Croatia and Bosnia-Herzegovina as rival groups struggled for power. In 1992, the United Nations withdrew recognition of Yugoslavia because of its failure to halt atrocities committed by Serbs living in Croatia and Bosnia-Herzegovina. In 1995, Yugoslavia took part in talks that led to the Dayton Peace Accord, but it had problems of its own as international sanctions struck the war-ravaged economy. In 1998, the fragility of the region was again highlighted, in Kosovo, a former autonomous region in southern Serbia where most people are Albanian-speaking Muslims. In 1998, Serbians forced Muslim Albanians to leave their homes, but they were opposed by the Kosovo Liberation Army (KLA), which took over large areas. The Serbs hit back and thousands of civilians fled for their lives.

In March 1999, after attempts to find an agreement had failed, NATO forces intervened by launching aerial attacks on administrative

Arable land 27.5%
Forest 36.7%

and industrial targets in Kosovo and Serbia. Russia, opposed to the air strikes, held talks with the Yugoslav President Slobodan Milosevic, and US President Clinton. While bombings continued, Serbian forces stepped up attacks on Albanian-speaking villages, forcibly expelling the people who fled into Albania and Macedonia. The NATO offensive ended in June, when Serbian troops withdrew from Kosovo. The KLA was disbanded in September 1999, but UN peace-keepers were unable to prevent some reprisals by ethnic Albanians against ethnic Serbs.

Another problem facing Yugoslavia is the status of Montenegro, where many people favour a looser association with Serbia, or even independence. In late 1999, concerned at the weakness of the Yugoslav dinar, Montenegro made the German mark legal tender alongside the dinar.

Economy

Under Communist rule, manufacturing became important in Yugoslavia. But in the early 1990s, the World Bank classified the country as a 'lower-middle-income' economy. Its resources include bauxite, coal, copper and other metals, together with oil and natural gas. Manufactures include aluminium, machinery, plastics, steel, textiles and vehicles. Chief exports are manufactures, but agriculture remains important. Crops include fruits, maize, potatoes, tobacco and wheat.

AREA
102,170 sq km [39,449 sq mls]
POPULATION
10,500,000
CAPITAL (POPULATION)
Belgrade (Beograd, 1,137,000)
GOVERNMENT
Federal republic
ETHNIC GROUPS
Serb 62%, Albanian 17%,
Montenegrin 5%, Hungarian, Muslim, Croat
LANGUAGES
Serbo-Croat (official), Albanian
RELIGIONS
Christianity (mainly Serbian Orthodox), Islam
CURRENCY
Yugoslav new dinar = 100 paras

Zambia's flag was adopted when the country became independent from Britain in 1964. The colours are those of the United Nationalist Independence Party, which led the struggle against Britain and ruled until 1991. The flying eagle represents freedom.

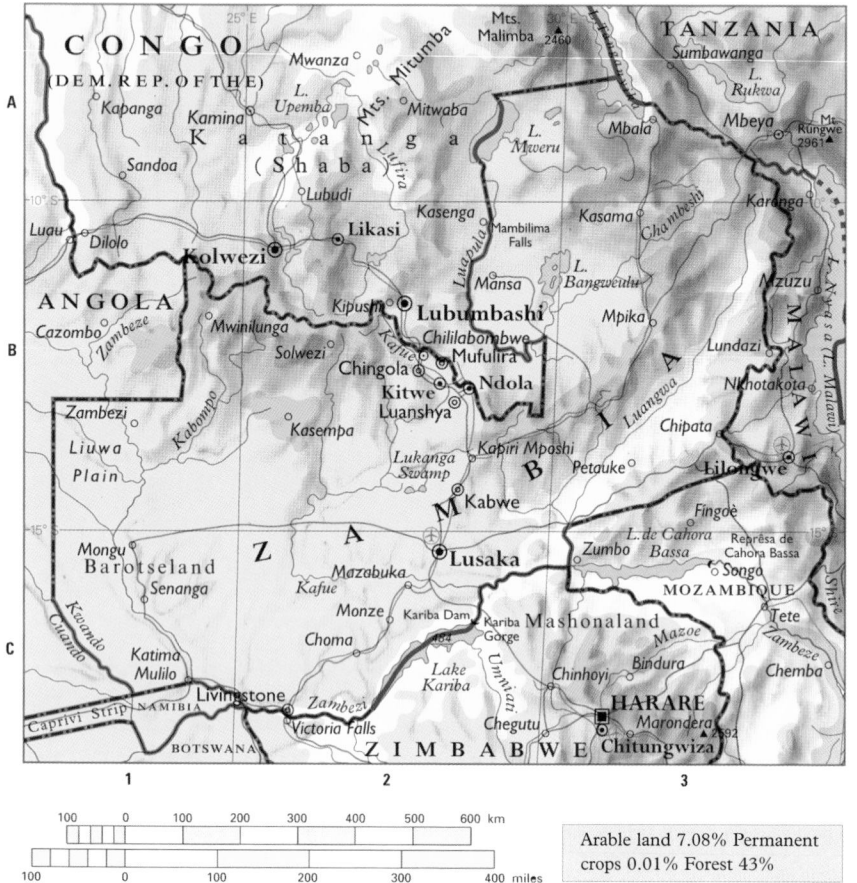

Arable land 7.08% Permanent crops 0.01% Forest 43%

Geography

The Republic of Zambia is a landlocked country in southern Africa. The country lies on the plateau that makes up most of southern Africa. Much of the land is between 900 m and 1,500 m [2,950–4,920 ft] above sea level. The Muchinga Mountains in the north-east rise above this flat land.

Lakes include Bangweulu, which is entirely within Zambia, together with parts of lakes Mweru and Tanganyika in the north. Most of the land is drained by the Zambezi and its two main tributaries, the Kafue and Luangwa. Lake Kariba, dammed in 1961 and the second largest artificial lake in Africa, occupies part of the Zambezi Valley. Zambia shares Lake Kariba and the Victoria Falls with Zimbabwe.

Climate

Zambia lies in the tropics, although temperatures are moderated by the altitude. The rainy season runs from between November and March, when the rivers sometimes flood. Northern Zambia is the wettest region of the country. The average annual rainfall ranges from about 1,300 mm [51 in] in the north down to 510 mm to 760 mm [20–30 in] in the south.

ZAMBIA (LUSAKA)

Lusaka is situated in the south-east of the country near to Lake Kariba. Temperatures are generally uniformly hot throughout the year. The average temperature in January reaches 21.1°C [70°F], while an average temperature of 16.1°C [61°F] has been recorded in July. There is a marked maximum of rainfall between November and March. The annual average amount of rainfall at Lusaka is 836 mm [33 in].

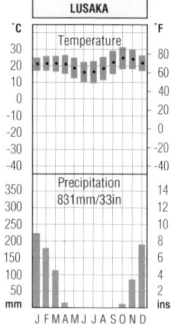

History

European contact with Zambia began in the 19th century, when the explorer David Livingstone crossed the River Zambezi. In the 1890s, the British South Africa Company, set up by Cecil Rhodes (1853–1902), the British financier and statesman, made treaties with local chiefs and gradually took over the area. In 1911, the Company named the area Northern Rhodesia. In 1924, Britain took over the government of the country and the discovery of copper led to a large influx of Europeans in the late 1920s.

Following World War II, the majority of Europeans living in Zambia wanted greater control of their government and some favoured a merger with their southern neighbour, Southern Rhodesia (now Zimbabwe). In 1953, Britain set up a federation of Northern Rhodesia, Southern Rhodesia and Nyasaland (now Malawi). Local Africans opposed the setting up of the federation. They argued that it concentrated power in the hands of the white minority in Southern Rhodesia. Their opposition proved effective and the federation was dissolved in 1963. In 1964, Northern Rhodesia became an independent nation called Zambia.

Politics

The leading opponent of British rule, Kenneth Kaunda, became president of Zambia in 1964. His government enjoyed reasonable income until copper prices crashed in the mid-1970s, but his collectivist policies failed to diversify the economy and neglected agriculture. In 1972, he declared the United Nationalist Independence Party (UNIP) the only legal party, and it was nearly 20 years before the country returned to democracy. Under a new constitution, adopted in 1990, elections were held in 1991 in which Kaunda was trounced by Frederick Chiluba of the Movement for Multiparty Democracy (MMD) – Kaunda's first challenger in the post-colonial period. In 1999, Kaunda, who remained politically active, was declared stateless by a high-court ruling. The ruling stated that Kaunda was born in Zambia of Malawian parentage, but because he had never properly renounced his Malawian nationality, he was neither Zambian nor Malawian.

Economy

Copper is the leading export, accounting for 90% of Zambia's total exports in 1990. Zambia also produces cobalt, lead, zinc and various gemstones, but the country's dependence on minerals has created problems, especially when prices fluctuate. Agriculture employs 69% of the people, as compared with 4% in mining and manufacturing. Major food crops include cassava, fruits and vegetables, maize, millet and sorghum, while cash crops include coffee, sugar cane and tobacco. The Copperbelt, centred on Kitwe, is the main urban region, while Lusaka, provides the other major growth pole. Rural–urban migration has increased since 1964, but work is scarce. The production of copper products is the leading industrial activity. Other manufactures include beverages, processed food, iron and steel, textiles and tobacco.

AREA	**ETHNIC GROUPS**
752,614 sq km	Bemba 36%, Maravi (Nyanja)
[290,586 sq mls]	18%, Tonga 15%
POPULATION	**LANGUAGES**
9,461,000	English (official), Bemba, Nyanja
CAPITAL (POPULATION)	**RELIGIONS**
Lusaka	Christianity 68%,
(982,000)	traditional beliefs 27%
GOVERNMENT	**CURRENCY**
Multiparty republic	Kwacha = 100 ngwee

ZIMBABWE

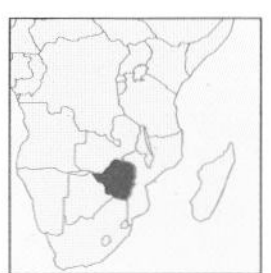

Zimbabwe's flag, adopted in 1980, is based on the colours used by the ruling Zimbabwe African National Union Patriotic Front. Within the white triangle is the Great Zimbabwe soapstone bird, the national emblem. The red star symbolizes the party's socialist policies.

Geography

The Republic of Zimbabwe is a landlocked country in southern Africa. Most of the country lies on a high plateau between the Zambezi and Limpopo Rivers between 900 m and 1,500 m [2,950–4,920 ft] above sea level. The main land feature is the High Veld, a ridge that crosses Zimbabwe from north-east to south-west. Bordering the High Veld is the Middle Veld, the country's largest region. Below 900 m [2,950 ft] is the Low Veld. The country's highest point is Mount Inyangani, which reaches 2,593 m [8,507 ft] near the Mozambique border. Zimbabwe's best-known physical feature, Victoria Falls, is in the north-east. The Falls are shared with Zambia, as too is the artificial Lake Kariba which is also on the River Zambezi.

Climate

During the summer the weather is hot and wet. But in the winter, daily temperatures can vary greatly. Frosts have been recorded between June and August. The climate varies according to the altitude. The Low Veld is much warmer and drier than the High Veld.

ZIMBABWE (HARARE)

Harare has a large diurnal range of temperature, particularly in the winter, and is cooler than lowlands at the same latitude. The summer rains are brought by south-easterly winds from the Indian Ocean, usually preceded by isolated thundery outbreaks which extend the rainy season from October to March.

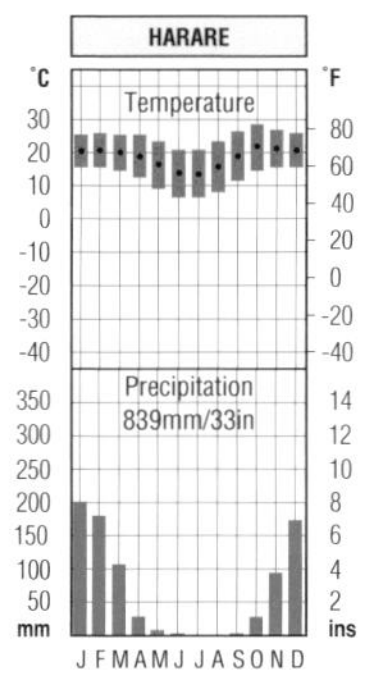

Arable land 7.11% Permanent crops 0.33%
Permanent grassland 44.3% Forest 23%

History

The Shona people were dominant in the region about 1,000 years ago. They built the Great Zimbabwe, a city of stone buildings. Under the statesman Cecil Rhodes (1853–1902), the British South Africa Company occupied the area in the 1890s, after obtaining mineral rights from local chiefs. The area was named Rhodesia and later Southern Rhodesia. It became a self-governing British colony in 1923. Between 1953 and 1963, Southern and Northern Rhodesia (now Zambia) were joined to Nyasaland (Malawi) in the Central African Federation.

Politics

In 1965, the European government of Southern Rhodesia (then called Rhodesia) declared their country independent. However, Britain refused to accept this declaration. Finally, after a civil war, the country became legally independent in 1980. After independence, rivalries between the Shona and Ndebele people threatened its stability. But order was restored when the Shona prime minister, Robert Mugabe, brought his Ndebele rivals into his government. In 1987, Mugabe became the country's executive president and, in 1991, the government renounced its Marxist ideology. In 1990, the state of emergency that had lasted since 1965 was allowed to lapse – three months after Mugabe had secured a landslide election victory. He was subsequently re-elected president in 1996.

In the late 1990s, Mugabe threatened to seize white-owned farms without paying compensation to owners. His announcement caused much disquiet among white farmers. The plan was eventually modified when the International Monetary Fund (IMF) threatened to withdraw a loan to Zimbabwe. However, the situation became increasingly dangerous during early 2000 when the landless 'war veterans' began to occupy white-owned farms, resulting in deaths and destruction.

Economy

The World Bank classifies Zimbabwe as a 'low-income' economy. However, its economy has become significantly more diverse since the 1960s, having evolved to virtual self-sufficiency during the days of international sanctions between 1965 and 1980. After independence, the economy underwent a surge in most sectors, with successful agrarian policies and the exploitation of the country's mineral resources. However, a fast-growing population continues to exert pressure both on land and resources of all kinds.

Agriculture employs approximately 30% of the people. Maize is the chief food crop, while cash crops include cotton, sugar and tobacco. Cattle ranching is another important activity. Gold, asbestos, chromium and nickel are mined and the country also has some coal and iron ore. Manufactures include beverages, chemicals, iron and steel, metal products, processed food, textiles and tobacco. Major exports include tobacco, gold, other metals, cotton and asbestos.

AREA	other Bantu-speaking
390,579 sq km	Africans 11%, White 2%
[150,873 sq mls]	**LANGUAGES**
POPULATION	English (official),
11,044,000	Shona,
CAPITAL (POPULATION)	Ndebele,
Harare	Nyanja
(1,189,000)	**RELIGIONS**
GOVERNMENT	Christianity 45%,
Multiparty republic	traditional beliefs 40%
ETHNIC GROUPS	**CURRENCY**
Shona 71%, Ndebele 16%,	Zimbabwe dollar = 100 cents

INDEX TO
COUNTRY MAPS

How to use the index

The index contains the names of all the principal places and features shown on the country maps. Each name is followed by an additional entry in italics giving the country or region within which it is located. The alphabetical order of names composed of two or more words is governed primarily by the first word and then by the second. This is an example of the rule:

Bac Quang, *Vietnam* **237 A2**
Bacan, Kepuluan, *Indonesia* **125 C7**
Bacarra, *Phil.* **184 B4**
Bacău, *Romania* **188 B4**
Bach Long Vi, Dao, *Vietnam* **237 B3**

Physical features composed of a proper name (Erie) and a description (Lake) are positioned alphabetically by the proper name. The description is positioned after the proper name and is usually abbreviated:

Erie, L., *N. Amer.* **14 E11**

Where a description forms part of a settlement or administrative name however, it is always written in full and put in its true alphabetic position:

Mount Isa, *Australia* **45 D6**

Names beginning with M' and Mc are indexed as if they were spelled Mac. Names beginning St. are alphabetised under Saint, but Sankt, Sint, Sant', Santa and San are all spelt in full and are alphabetised accordingly. If the same place name occurs two or more times in the index and all are in the same country, each is followed by the name of the administrative subdivision in which it is located.

The number in bold type which follows each name in the index refers to the number of the page where the map showing that feature or place will be found.

The letter and figure which are in bold type immediately after the page number give the grid square on the map page, within which the feature is situated. The letter represents the latitude and the figure the longitude.

In some cases the feature itself may fall within the specified square, while the name is outside. This is usually the case only with features which are larger than a grid square.

Rivers are indexed to their mouths or confluences, and carry the symbol ⌣ after their names. A solid square ■ follows the name of a country, while an open square □ refers to a first order administrative area.

The maps and index use the local spellings for most place names, that is the name by which a place or feature is known within the country in which it occurs:

Roma
's-Gravenhage

In the index the English form used in the text is cross-referenced to the local spelling:

Rome = Roma
Hague, The = 's-Gravenhage

Spellings of names generally agree with the rules of the U.S. Board on Geographic Names and the Permanent Committee on Geographical Names. Where languages do not use Roman alphabets certain rules are used to transcribe them into the Roman alphabet. These rules are based largely on pronunciation.

How to pronounce place names

English-speaking people usually have no difficulty in reading and pronouncing correctly English place names. However, foreign place name pronunciations may present many problems. Such problems can be minimised by following some simple rules. However, these rules cannot be applied to all situations, and there will be many exceptions.

1. In general, stress each syllable equally, unless your experience suggests otherwise.
2. Pronounce the letter 'a' as a broad 'a' as in 'arm'.
3. Pronounce the letter 'e' as a short 'e' as in 'elm'.
4. Pronounce the letter 'i' as a cross between a short 'i' and long 'e', as the two 'i's in 'California'.
5. Pronounce the letter 'o' as an intermediate 'o' as in 'soft'.
6. Pronounce the letter 'u' as an intermediate 'u' as in 'sure'.
7. Pronounce consonants hard, except in the Romance-language areas where 'g's are likely to be pronounced softly like 'j' in 'jam'; 'j' itself may be pronounced as 'y'; and 'x's may be pronounced as 'h'.
8. For names in mainland China, pronounce 'q' like the 'ch' in 'chin', 'x' like the 'sh' in 'she', 'zh' like the 'j' in 'jam', and 'z' as if it were spelled 'dz'. In general pronounce 'a' as in 'father', 'e' as in 'but', 'i' as in 'keep', 'o' as in 'or', and 'u' as in 'rule'.

Moreover, English has no diacritical marks (accent and pronunciation signs), although some languages do. The following is a brief and general guide to the pronunciation of those most frequently used in the principal Western European languages.

		Pronunciation as in
French	é	day and shows that the e is to be pronounced; e.g. Orléans.
	è	mare
	î	used over any vowel and does not affect pronunciation; shows contraction of the name, usually omission of 's' following a vowel.
	ç	's' before 'a', 'o' and 'u'.
	ë, ï, ü	over 'e', 'i' and 'u' when they are used with another vowel and shows that each is to be pronounced.
German	ä	fate
	ö	fur
	ü	no English equivalent; like French 'tu'
Italian	à, é	over vowels and indicates stress.
Portuguese	ã, õ	vowels pronounced nasally.
	ç	boss
	á	shows stress
	ô	shows that a vowel has an 'i' or 'u' sound combined with it.
Spanish	ñ	canyon
	ü	pronounced as w and separately from adjoining vowels.
	á	usually indicates that this is a stressed vowel.

Abbreviations

A.C.T. – Australian Capital Territory
A.R. – Autonomous Region
Afghan. – Afghanistan
Ala. – Alabama
Alta. – Alberta
Amer. – America(n)
Arch. – Archipelago
Ariz. – Arizona
Ark. – Arkansas
Atl. Oc. – Atlantic Ocean
B. – Baie, Bahía, Bay, Bucht, Bugt
B.C. – British Columbia
Bangla. – Bangladesh
Barr. – Barrage
Bos.-H. – Bosnia-Herzegovina
C. – Cabo, Cap, Cape, Coast
C.A.R. – Central African Republic
C. Prov. – Cape Province
Calif. – California
Cat. – Catarata
Cent. – Central
Chan. – Channel
Colo. – Colorado
Conn. – Connecticut
Cord. – Cordillera
Cr. – Creek
Czech. – Czech Republic
D.C. – District of Columbia
Del. – Delaware
Dem. – Democratic
Dep. – Dependency
Des. – Desert
Dét. – Détroit
Dist. – District
Dj. – Djebel
Domin. – Dominica
Dom. Rep. – Dominican Republic
E. – East

E. Salv. – El Salvador
Eq. Guin. – Equatorial Guinea
Est. – Estrecho
Falk. Is. – Falkland Is.
Fd. – Fjord
Fla. – Florida
Fr. – French
G. – Golfe, Golfo, Gulf, Guba, Gebel
Ga. – Georgia
Gt. – Great, Greater
Guinea-Biss. – Guinea-Bissau
H.K. – Hong Kong
H.P. – Himachal Pradesh
Hants. – Hampshire
Harb. – Harbor, Harbour
Hd. – Head
Hts. – Heights
I.(s). – Île, Ilha, Insel, Isla, Island, Isle
Ill. – Illinois
Ind. – Indiana
Ind. Oc. – Indian Ocean
Ivory C. – Ivory Coast
J. – Jabal, Jebel
Jaz. – Jazīrah
Junc. – Junction
K. – Kap, Kapp
Kans. – Kansas
Kep. – Kepulauan
Ky. – Kentucky
L. – Lac, Lacul, Lago, Lagoa, Lake, Limni, Loch, Lough
La. – Louisiana
Ld. – Land
Liech. – Liechtenstein
Lux. – Luxembourg
Mad. P. – Madhya Pradesh

Madag. – Madagascar
Man. – Manitoba
Mass. – Massachusetts
Md. – Maryland
Me. – Maine
Medit. S. – Mediterranean Sea
Mich. – Michigan
Minn. – Minnesota
Miss. – Mississippi
Mo. – Missouri
Mont. – Montana
Mozam. – Mozambique
Mt.(s) – Mont, Montaña, Mountain
Mte. – Monte
Mti. – Monti
N. – Nord, Norte, North, Northern, Nouveau
N.B. – New Brunswick
N.C. – North Carolina
N. Cal. – New Caledonia
N. Dak. – North Dakota
N.H. – New Hampshire
N.I. – North Island
N.J. – New Jersey
N. Mex. – New Mexico
N.S. – Nova Scotia
N.S.W. – New South Wales
N.W.T. – North West Territory
N.Y. – New York
N.Z. – New Zealand
Nat. – National
Nebr. – Nebraska
Neths. – Netherlands
Nev. – Nevada
Nfld. – Newfoundland
Nic. – Nicaragua
O. – Oued, Ouadi
Occ. – Occidentale

Okla. – Oklahoma
Ont. – Ontario
Or. – Orientale
Oreg. – Oregon
Os. – Ostrov
Oz. – Ozero
P. – Pass, Passo, Pasul, Pulau
P.E.I. – Prince Edward Island
Pa. – Pennsylvania
Pac. Oc. – Pacific Ocean
Papua N.G. – Papua New Guinea
Pass. – Passage
Pen. – Peninsula, Péninsule
Phil. – Philippines
Pk. – Peak
Plat. – Plateau
Prov. – Province, Provincial
Pt. – Point
Pta. – Ponta, Punta
Pte. – Pointe
Qué. – Québec
Queens. – Queensland
R. – Rio, River
R.I. – Rhode Island
Ra. – Range
Raj. – Rajasthan
Récr. – Récréatif
Reg. – Region
Rep. – Republic
Res. – Reserve, Reservoir
Rhld-Pfz. – Rheinland-Pfalz
S. – South, Southern, Sur
Si. Arabia – Saudi Arabia
S.C. – South Carolina
S. Dak. – South Dakota
S.I. – South Island
S. Leone – Sierra Leone
Sa. – Serra, Sierra

Sask. – Saskatchewan
Scot. – Scotland
Sd. – Sound
Sev. – Severnaya
Sib. – Siberia
Sprs. – Springs
St. – Saint
Sta. – Santa
Ste. – Sainte
Sto. – Santo
Str. – Strait, Stretto
Switz. – Switzerland
Tas. – Tasmania
Tenn. – Tennessee
Terr. – Territory, Territoire
Tex. – Texas
Tg. – Tanjung
Trin. & Tob. – Trinidad & Tobago
U.A.E. – United Arab Emirates
U.K. – United Kingdom
U.S.A. – United States of America
Ut. P. – Uttar Pradesh
Va. – Virginia
Vdkhr. – Vodokhranilishche
Vdskh. – Vodoskhovyshche
Vf. – Vírful
Vic. – Victoria
Vol. – Volcano
Vt. – Vermont
W. – Wadi, West
W. Va. – West Virginia
Wall. & F. Is. – Wallis and Futuna Is.
Wash. – Washington
Wis. – Wisconsin
Wlkp. – Wielkopolski
Wyo. – Wyoming
Yorks. – Yorkshire
Yug. – Yugoslavia

243

Amanab

Amanab, *Papua N. G.* 181 B1
Amangeldy, *Kazakstan* 140 A3
Amapá, *Brazil* 58 A3
Amapá □, *Brazil* 58 A3
Amarillo, *U.S.A.* 230 C6
Amaro, Mte., *Italy* 133 C5
Amassama, *Nigeria* 170 B2
Amasya □, *Turkey* 220 A3
Amatikulu, *S. Africa* 205 B4
Amau, *Papua N. G.* 181 F5
Amay, *Belgium* 52 B4
Amazon →, *S. Amer.* 20 D5
Amazonas □, *Brazil* 58 B2
Ambahakily, *Madag.* 152 C1
Ambahita, *Madag.* 152 C2
Ambala, *India* 118 A2
Ambalangoda, *Sri Lanka* 209 C2
Ambalavao, *Madag.* 152 C2
Ambam, *Cameroon* 65 C2
Ambanja, *Madag.* 152 A2
Ambararata, *Madag.* 152 B2
Ambarchik, *Russia* 191 C16
Ambarijeby, *Madag.* 152 A2
Ambaro, Helodranon', *Madag.* 152 A2
Ambato, *Ecuador* 94 B2
Ambato, *Madag.* 152 A2
Ambato Boeny, *Madag.* 152 B2
Ambatofinandrahana, *Madag.* 152 C2
Ambatolampy, *Madag.* 152 B2
Ambatomainty, *Madag.* 152 B2
Ambatomanoina, *Madag.* 152 B2
Ambatondrazaka, *Madag.* 152 B2
Ambatosoratra, *Madag.* 152 B2
Ambenja, *Madag.* 152 B2
Amberg, *Germany* 106 D3
Ambergris Cay, *Belize* 111 B2
Ambergris Cay, *Turks & Caicos* 76 B2
Amberley, *N.Z.* 167 E4
Ambilobé, *Madag.* 152 A2
Ambinanindrano, *Madag.* 152 C2
Ambinanitelo, *Madag.* 152 B2
Ambinda, *Madag.* 152 B2
Ambitle I., *Papua N. G.* 181 C7
Ambo, *Peru* 183 C2
Amboahangy, *Madag.* 152 C2
Ambodifototra, *Madag.* 152 B2
Ambodilazana, *Madag.* 152 B2
Ambodiriana, *Madag.* 152 B2
Ambohidratrimo, *Madag.* 152 B2
Ambohidray, *Madag.* 152 B2
Ambohimahamasina, *Madag.* 152 C2
Ambohimahasoa, *Madag.* 152 C2
Ambohimanga, *Madag.* 152 C2
Ambohimitombo, *Madag.* 152 C2
Ambohitra, *Madag.* 152 A2
Amboise, *France* 100 C4
Ambon, *Indonesia* 125 C7
Ambondro, *Madag.* 152 D2
Amboseli, L., *Kenya* 141 B2
Ambositra, *Madag.* 152 C2
Ambovombe, *Madag.* 152 D2
Ambriz, *Angola* 37 A1
Ambrym, *Vanuatu* 178 B2
Ambunti, *Papua N. G.* 181 C2
Amderma, *Russia* 190 C6
Ameca, *Mexico* 158 C4
Ameland, *Neths.* 165 A3
American Samoa ■, *Pac. Oc.* 177 B2
Amersfoort, *Neths.* 165 B3
Amersfoort, *S. Africa* 205 B3
Ames, *U.S.A.* 231 B8
Amga, *Russia* 191 C13
Amga →, *Russia* 191 C13
Amgu, *Russia* 191 E13
Amgun →, *Russia* 191 D13
Amherst, *Canada* 67 E10
Amiata, Mte., *Italy* 132 C3
Amiens, *France* 101 B5
Amindivi Is., *India* 123 A2
Amirante Is., *Seychelles* 10 K9
'Ammān, *Jordan* 139 B1
Ammassalik = Tasiilaq, *Greenland* 43 C5
Amnat Charoen, *Thailand* 218 D4
Amorgós, *Greece* 109 C4
Amos, *Canada* 67 E9
Amoy = Xiamen, *China* 81 D5
Ampanavoana, *Madag.* 152 B3
Ampangalana, Lakandranon', *Madag.* 152 C2
Ampanihy, *Madag.* 152 C1
Amparafaravola, *Madag.* 152 B2
Ampasinambo, *Madag.* 152 C2
Ampasindava, Helodranon', *Madag.* 152 A2
Ampasindava, Saikanosy, *Madag.* 152 A2
Ampenan, *Indonesia* 124 D5
Amper, *Nigeria* 170 B2
Amper →, *Germany* 106 D3
Ampombiantambo, *Madag.* 152 A2
Ampotaka, *Madag.* 152 D1
Ampoza, *Madag.* 152 C1
Amravati, *India* 118 B2
Amritsar, *India* 118 A2
Amsterdam, *Neths.* 165 B2
Amsterdam, I. = Nouvelle-Amsterdam, I., *Ind. Oc.* 3 F13
Amstetten, *Austria* 49 A4
Amudarya →, *Uzbekistan* 221 B2
Amund Ringnes I., *Canada* 67 B7
Amundsen Gulf, *Canada* 66 B4
Amuntai, *Indonesia* 124 C5
Amur →, *Russia* 191 D14
Amurang, *Indonesia* 125 B6
Amuri Pass, *N.Z.* 167 E4
Amursk, *Russia* 191 D13
Amyderya = Amudarya →, *Uzbekistan* 221 B2
An Bien, *Vietnam* 237 H2
An Hoa, *Vietnam* 237 E4
An Nabatīyah at Tahta, *Lebanon* 147 B1
An Nabk, *Syria* 214 B2
An Nafūd, *Si. Arabia* 10 G8
An Najaf, *Iraq* 126 B3
An Nāṣirīyah, *Iraq* 126 C3
An Nhon, *Vietnam* 237 F4
An Thoi, Dao, *Vietnam* 237 H2
An Uaimh, *Ireland* 128 C5
Anabar →, *Russia* 191 B11
Anaconda, *U.S.A.* 230 A4
Anacuao, Mt., *Phil.* 184 C4
Anadolu, *Turkey* 220 B2
Anadyr, *Russia* 191 C17
Anadyr →, *Russia* 191 C17
Anadyrskiy Zaliv, *Russia* 191 C18
'Ānah, *Iraq* 126 B2
Anaheim, *U.S.A.* 230 D3
Anaklia, *Georgia* 104 A2
Analalava, *Madag.* 152 A2
Analavoka, *Madag.* 152 C2
Anambas, Kepulauan, *Indonesia* 124 B3
Anambas Is. = Anambas, Kepulauan, *Indonesia* 124 B3
Anambra □, *Nigeria* 170 B2
Anamur, *Turkey* 220 B2
Anan, *Japan* 136 G4
Ananyevo, *Kyrgyzstan* 144 A5
Anār, *Iran* 127 C5
Anārak, *Iran* 127 B5
Anatolia = Anadolu, *Turkey* 220 B2
Anatsogno, *Madag.* 152 C1
Añatuya, *Argentina* 38 A2
Anbyŏn, *N. Korea* 142 C2
Anchorage, *U.S.A.* 15 C5
Ancohuma, Nevada, *Bolivia* 55 B1
Ancón, *Peru* 183 C2
Ancona, *Italy* 133 C4
Ancud, *Chile* 79 D1
Ancud, G. de, *Chile* 79 D1
Andaingo, *Madag.* 152 B2
Andalgalá, *Argentina* 38 A2
Andalucía □, *Spain* 206 D3
Andalusia = Andalucía □, *Spain* 206 D3
Andalusia, *U.S.A.* 231 D9
Andaman Is., *Ind. Oc.* 10 H13
Andapa, *Madag.* 152 A2
Andenne, *Belgium* 52 B4
Andermatt, *Switz.* 213 B3
Anderson, *U.S.A.* 231 D10
Anderson →, *Canada* 66 C4
Andes, Cord. de los, *S. Amer.* 20 G3
Andhra Pradesh □, *India* 118 C2
Andijon, *Uzbekistan* 221 B6
Andikíthira, *Greece* 109 D3
Andilamena, *Madag.* 152 B2
Andizhan = Andijon, *Uzbekistan* 221 B6
Andkhvoy, *Afghan.* 34 A2
Andoany, *Madag.* 152 A2
Andong, *S. Korea* 142 D3
Andorra ■, *Europe* 207
Andorra La Vella, *Andorra* 207 A6
Andradina, *Brazil* 58 D3
Andrahary, Mt., *Madag.* 152 A2
Andramasina, *Madag.* 152 B2
Andranopasy, *Madag.* 152 C1
Andranovory, *Madag.* 152 C1
Ándria, *Italy* 133 D6
Andriamena, *Madag.* 152 B2
Andriandampy, *Madag.* 152 C2
Andriba, *Madag.* 152 B2
Androka, *Madag.* 152 C1
Andropov = Rybinsk, *Russia* 190 D3
Ándros, *Greece* 109 C4
Andros I., *Bahamas* 71 A1
Andújar, *Spain* 206 C3
Andulo, *Angola* 37 B2
Anegada I., *Br. Virgin Is.* 76 A3
Anécho, *Togo* 54 D2
Aneityum, *Vanuatu* 178 C2
Aneto, Pico de, *Spain* 207 A6
Ang Mo Kio, *Singapore* 199 A3
Ang Thong, *Thailand* 218 D2
Angara →, *Russia* 191 D9
Angara-Débou, *Benin* 54 B3
Angarsk, *Russia* 191 D10
Ånge, *Sweden* 211 B3
Ángel, Salto = Angel Falls, *Venezuela* 236 B3
Angel Falls, *Venezuela* 236 B3
Angeles, *Phil.* 184 D4
Ångermanälven →, *Sweden* 211 B3
Angers, *France* 100 C3
Angkor, *Cambodia* 64 B1
Anglesey, *U.K.* 224 E4
Anglisidhes, *Cyprus* 91 B2
Angmagssalik = Tasiilaq, *Greenland* 43 C5
Ango, *Dem. Rep. of the Congo* 86 B4
Angoche, *Mozam.* 162 B2
Angola ■, *Africa* 37
Angoram, *Papua N. G.* 181 C3
Angoulême, *France* 100 D4
Angoumois, *France* 100 D3
Angren, *Uzbekistan* 221 B5
Angtassom, *Cambodia* 64 C2
Anguilla ■, *W. Indies* 71
Angwa →, *Zimbabwe* 241 A2
Anholt, *Denmark* 93 A3
Anhui □, *China* 81 C5
Anhwei = Anhui □, *China* 81 C5
Anié, *Togo* 54 D2
Anivorano, *Madag.* 152 B2
Anjou, *France* 100 C3
Anjouan, *Comoros Is.* 123 B2
Anjozorobe, *Madag.* 152 B2
Anju, *N. Korea* 142 C1
Anka, *Nigeria* 170 A2
Ankaboa, Tanjona, *Madag.* 152 C1
Ankang, *China* 81 C4
Ankara, *Turkey* 220 B2
Ankaramena, *Madag.* 152 C2
Ankasakasa, *Madag.* 152 B1
Ankavandra, *Madag.* 152 B2
Ankazoabo, *Madag.* 152 C1
Ankazobe, *Madag.* 152 B2
Ankilimalinika, *Madag.* 152 C1
Ankilizato, *Madag.* 152 C2
Ankisabe, *Madag.* 152 B2
Ankororoka, *Madag.* 152 D2
Anmyŏn-do, *S. Korea* 142 D2
Ann Arbor, *U.S.A.* 231 B10
Annaba, *Algeria* 36 A4
Annalee →, *Ireland* 128 B4
Annam, *Vietnam* 237 E4
Annan, *U.K.* 224 D5
Annanberg, *Papua N. G.* 181 C3
Annapolis, *U.S.A.* 231 C11
Annecy, *France* 101 D7
Anning, *China* 80 D4
Anniston, *U.S.A.* 231 D9
Annobón, *Atl. Oc.* 4 G4
Annotto Bay, *Jamaica* 74 A3
Anorotsangana, *Madag.* 152 A2
Anosibe, *Madag.* 152 B2
Anoumaba, *Ivory C.* 134 B2
Anqing, *China* 81 C5
Ansbach, *Germany* 106 D3
Anse-à-Veau, *Haiti* 73 B2
Anse Boileau, *Seychelles* 123 B1
Anse Rouge, *Haiti* 73 B2
Anse Royale, *Seychelles* 123 B2
Anshan, *China* 81 B6
Anshun, *China* 80 D4
Anson B., *Australia* 44 B5
Ansongo, *Mali* 156 B4
Ansudu, *Indonesia* 125 C9
Antabamba, *Peru* 183 C3
Antakya, *Turkey* 220 B3
Antalaha, *Madag.* 152 A3
Antalya, *Turkey* 220 B2
Antalya Körfezi, *Turkey* 220 B2
Antambohobe, *Madag.* 152 C2
Antanambao-Manampotsy, *Madag.* 152 B2
Antanambe, *Madag.* 152 B2
Antananarivo, *Madag.* 152 B2
Antananarivo □, *Madag.* 152 B2
Antanifotsy, *Madag.* 152 B2
Antanimbaribe, *Madag.* 152 C1
Antanimora, *Madag.* 152 C2
Antarctica 32
Antelope, *Zimbabwe* 241 B1
Antequera, *Spain* 206 D3
Antevamena, *Madag.* 152 C1
Anti Atlas, *Morocco* 161 C4
Anti-Lebanon = Ash Sharqi, Al Jabal, *Lebanon* 147 B2
Antibes, *France* 101 E7
Anticosti, Î. d', *Canada* 67 E10
Antigonish, *Canada* 67 E10
Antigua, *W. Indies* 71 B2
Antigua & Barbuda ■, *W. Indies* 71
Antilla, *Cuba* 90 B2
Antioquia, *Colombia* 85 B1
Antoetra, *Madag.* 152 C2
Antofagasta, *Chile* 79 B1
Antongila, Helodrano, *Madag.* 152 B2
Antonibé, *Madag.* 152 B2
Antonibé, Presqu'île d', *Madag.* 152 A2
Antrim, *U.K.* 224 D3
Antsakabary, *Madag.* 152 B2
Antsalova, *Madag.* 152 B1
Antsenavolo, *Madag.* 152 C2
Antsiafabositra, *Madag.* 152 B2
Antsirabe, *Antanarivo, Madag.* 152 B2
Antsirabe, *Antsiranana, Madag.* 152 A2
Antsirabe, *Mahajanga, Madag.* 152 B2
Antsiranana, *Madag.* 152 A2
Antsiranana □, *Madag.* 152 A2
Antsohihy, *Madag.* 152 A2
Antsohimbondrona Seranana, *Madag.* 152 A2
Antwerp = Antwerpen, *Belgium* 52 A3
Antwerpen, *Belgium* 52 A3
Antwerpen □, *Belgium* 52 A3
Anukur, C., *Papua N. G.* 181 D5
Anuradhapura, *Sri Lanka* 209 B2
Anvers = Antwerpen, *Belgium* 52 A3
Anxi, *China* 80 B3
Anxious B., *Australia* 44 F5
Anyama, *Ivory C.* 134 B2
Anyang, *China* 81 C5
Anzhero-Sudzhensk, *Russia* 190 D8
Ánzio, *Italy* 132 D4
Aoba, *Vanuatu* 178 B2
Aoga-Shima, *Japan* 136 G6
Aola, *Solomon Is.* 178 A2
Aomen = Macau □, *China* 81 D5
Aomori, *Japan* 136 C7
Aoraki Mount Cook, *N.Z.* 167 E3
Aosta, *Italy* 132 B1
Aouk, Bahr →, *C.A.R.* 77 B3
Aouk, Bahr →, *Chad* 78 D2
Aoukâr, *Mauritania* 157 C3
Aozou, *Chad* 78 A2
Apalachee B., *U.S.A.* 231 E10
Apam, *Ghana* 108 B2
Apapa, *Nigeria* 170 B1
Apaporis →, *Colombia* 85 D3
Aparri, *Phil.* 184 B4
Apatity, *Russia* 190 C3
Apeldoorn, *Neths.* 165 B3
Apennines = Appennini, *Italy* 132 B3
Apia, *Samoa* 177 A2
Apies →, *S. Africa* 205 B3
Aplao, *Peru* 183 D3
Apolo, *Bolivia* 55 A1
Apostle Is., *U.S.A.* 231 A8
Apostolos Andreas, C., *Cyprus* 91 A3
Apoteri, *Guyana* 115 B2
Appalachian Mts., *U.S.A.* 231 C11
Appennini, *Italy* 132 B3
Appenzell-Ausser Rhoden □, *Switz.* 213 A4
Appenzell-Inner Rhoden □, *Switz.* 213 A4
Approuague →, *Fr. Guiana* 115 B3
April →, *Papua N. G.* 181 C2
Aprília, *Italy* 132 D4
Apure →, *Venezuela* 236 B2
Apurimac →, *Peru* 183 C3
Aqaba = Al 'Aqabah, *Jordan* 139 B1
Āqcheh, *Afghan.* 34 A2
Aqmola = Astana, *Kazakstan* 140 A4
'Aqrah, *Iraq* 126 A2
Aqtaū, *Kazakstan* 140 B2
Aqtöbe, *Kazakstan* 140 A2
Aquin, *Haiti* 73 B2
Aquitain, Bassin, *France* 100 D3
Aqviligjuaq = Pelly Bay, *Canada* 67 C8
Ar Rachidiya = Er Rachidia, *Morocco* 161 B5
Ar Ramādī, *Iraq* 126 B2
Ar Raqqah, *Syria* 214 B2
Ar Rifā'ī, *Iraq* 126 C3
Ar Riyāḍ, *Si. Arabia* 196 C4
Ar Ruṣāfah, *Syria* 214 B2
Ar Ruṭbah, *Iraq* 126 B2
Ara, *India* 118 B3
'Arab, Bahr el →, *Sudan* 210 D2
Arab, Khalîg el, *Egypt* 95 A1
Arabia, *Asia* 10 G8
Arabian Desert = Es Sahrâ' Esh Sharqîya, *Egypt* 95 B2
Arabian Gulf = Gulf, The, *Asia* 10 G9
Arabian Sea, *Ind. Oc.* 10 H10
Aracaju, *Brazil* 58 C5
Aracati, *Brazil* 58 B5
Araçatuba, *Brazil* 58 D3
Aracena, *Spain* 206 D2
Aračinovo, *Macedonia* 151 A2
Araçuaí, *Brazil* 58 C4
'Arad, *Israel* 130 C2
Arad, *Romania* 188 B1
Arada, *Chad* 78 C3
Aradhippou, *Cyprus* 91 B2
Arafura Sea, *E. Indies* 10 K17
Aragats, *Armenia* 40 A2
Aragón □, *Spain* 207 B5
Aragón →, *Spain* 207 A5
Araguacema, *Brazil* 58 B4
Araguaia →, *Brazil* 58 B4
Araguari, *Brazil* 58 C4
Arak, *Algeria* 36 C3
Arāk, *Iran* 126 B4
Arakan Coast, *Burma* 63 F3
Arakan Yoma, *Burma* 63 F3
Aral, *Kazakstan* 140 B3
Aral Sea, *Asia* 10 E9
Aral Tengizi = Aral Sea, *Asia* 10 E9
Aralsk = Aral, *Kazakstan* 140 B3
Aralskoye More = Aral Sea, *Asia* 10 E9
Aramac, *Australia* 45 D8
Aramia →, *Papua N. G.* 181 D2
Aran I., *Ireland* 128 A3
Aran Is., *Ireland* 128 C2
Aranda de Duero, *Spain* 206 B4
Aranjuez, *Spain* 206 B4
Aransas Pass, *U.S.A.* 231 E7
Aranyaprathet, *Thailand* 218 E3
Arapey Grande →, *Uruguay* 235 A1
Arapiraca, *Brazil* 58 C4
Araraquara, *Brazil* 58 D4
Ararat, *Armenia* 40 B2
Ararat, *Australia* 45 G7
Ararat, Mt. = Ağrı Dağı, *Turkey* 220 B4
Araripe, Chapada do, *Brazil* 58 B5
Arauca, *Colombia* 85 B2
Arauca →, *Venezuela* 236 B2
Arawe Is., *Papua N. G.* 181 D5
Araya, Pen. de, *Venezuela* 236 A3
Arba Minch, *Ethiopia* 98 C2
Árbatax, *Italy* 132 E2
Arbīl, *Iraq* 126 A3
Arbroath, *U.K.* 224 C5
Arcachon, *France* 100 D3
Archangel = Arkhangelsk, *Russia* 190 C4
Archenu, J., *Chad* 78 A3
Archers Post, *Kenya* 141 A2
Arcos de la Frontera, *Spain* 206 D3
Arctic Bay, *Canada* 67 B8
Arctic Red River = Tsiigehtchic, *Canada* 66 C3
Arda →, *Bulgaria* 61 C3
Ardabīl, *Iran* 126 A4
Ardee, *Ireland* 128 C5
Ardennes, *Belgium* 28 F6
Arderin, *Ireland* 128 C4
Ardestān, *Iran* 127 B5
Ardmore, *U.S.A.* 231 D7
Arecibo, *Puerto Rico* 75 A2
Arena, Pt., *U.S.A.* 230 C2
Arendal, *Norway* 172 D2
Arenillas, *Ecuador* 94 C1
Arequipa, *Peru* 183 D3
Arévalo, *Spain* 206 B3
Arezzo, *Italy* 132 C3
Arganda, *Spain* 206 B4
Argentan, *France* 100 B3
Argentário, Mte., *Italy* 132 C3
Argentina ■, *S. Amer.* 38
Argentino, L., *Argentina* 38 D1
Argeş →, *Romania* 188 C4
Argolikós Kólpos, *Greece* 109 C3
Árgos, *Greece* 109 C3
Argostólion, *Greece* 109 B2
Argun →, *Russia* 191 D12
Argungu, *Nigeria* 170 A1
Århus, *Denmark* 93 A3
Ariana, *Tunisia* 219 A2
Aribinda, *Burkina Faso* 62 A2
Arica, *Chile* 79 A1
Arica, *Colombia* 85 D2
Arid, C., *Australia* 44 F3
Arida, *Japan* 136 F4
Aride, *Seychelles* 123 A2
Arima, *Trin. & Tob.* 76 C2
Arinos →, *Brazil* 20 E5
Aripo, Mt., *Trin. & Tob.* 76 C2
Aripuanã →, *Brazil* 58 B2
Arîsh, W. el →, *Egypt* 95 A2
Arivonimamo, *Madag.* 152 B2
Arizona □, *U.S.A.* 230 D4
Arjona, *Colombia* 85 A1
Arka, *Russia* 191 C14
Arkalyk = Arqalyk, *Kazakstan* 140 A3
Arkansas □, *U.S.A.* 231 D8
Arkansas →, *U.S.A.* 231 D8
Arkansas City, *U.S.A.* 231 C7
Arkhangelsk, *Russia* 190 C4
Arklow, *Ireland* 128 D5
Arkticheskiy, Mys, *Russia* 191 A9
Arlanzón →, *Spain* 206 A3
Arlbergpass, *Austria* 49 B2
Arles, *France* 101 E6
Arlington, *S. Africa* 205 B3
Arlit, *Niger* 169 B2
Arlon, *Belgium* 52 C4
Arly, *Burkina Faso* 62 C3
Armagh, *U.K.* 224 D3
Armavir, *Russia* 190 E4
Armenia, *Colombia* 85 C1
Armenia ■, *Asia* 40
Armidale, *Australia* 45 F9
Arnarfjörður, *Iceland* 117 B2
Arnaud →, *Canada* 67 D10
Arnauti, C., *Cyprus* 91 A1
Arnhem, *Neths.* 165 C3
Arnhem, C., *Australia* 45 B6
Arnhem B., *Australia* 45 B6
Arnhem Land, *Australia* 44 B5
Arno →, *Italy* 132 C3
Arnsberg, *Germany* 106 C2
Arochuku, *Nigeria* 170 B2
Aroroy, *Phil.* 184 E5
Arqalyk, *Kazakstan* 140 A3
Arrah = Ara, *India* 118 B3
Arrah, *Ivory C.* 134 B2
Arran, *U.K.* 224 D4
Arras, *France* 101 A5
Arrecife, *Canary Is.* 42 B2
Arrée, Mts. d', *France* 100 B2
Arrow, L., *Ireland* 128 B3
Arrowtown, *N.Z.* 167 F2
Árta, *Greece* 109 B2
Arteche, *Phil.* 184 E6
Artem = Artyom, *Azerbaijan* 40 A5
Artemovsk, *Russia* 191 D9
Artemovsk, *Ukraine* 223 B4
Artesia = Mosomane, *Botswana* 57 B2
Arthington, *Liberia* 148 B1
Arthur's Pass, *N.Z.* 167 E3
Arthur's Town, *Bahamas* 71 A2
Artigas, *Uruguay* 235 A1
Artik, *Armenia* 40 A1
Artois, *France* 101 A5
Artvin, *Turkey* 220 A4
Artyom, *Azerbaijan* 40 A5
Aru, Kepulauan, *Indonesia* 125 D8
Aru Is. = Aru, Kepulauan, *Indonesia* 125 D8
Arua, *Uganda* 222 A2
Aruanã, *Brazil* 58 C3
Aruba ■, *W. Indies* 74
Arunachal Pradesh □, *India* 118 B4
Arusha, *Tanzania* 217 A3
Aruvi →, *Sri Lanka* 209 B1
Aruwimi →, *Dem. Rep. of the Congo* 86 B3
Arvakalu, *Sri Lanka* 209 B1
Arxan, *China* 81 B5
Arys, *Kazakstan* 140 B3
Arzamas, *Russia* 190 D4
As Safirah, *Syria* 214 A2
As Salamiyah, *Syria* 214 B2
As Samāwah, *Iraq* 126 C3
As Sohar = Ṣuḥār, *Oman* 113 B3
As Sukhnah, *Syria* 214 B2
As Sulaymānīyah, *Iraq* 126 B3
As Sulayyil, *Si. Arabia* 196 C4
As Suwaydā', *Syria* 214 C2
As Şuwayrah, *Iraq* 126 B3
Asaba, *Nigeria* 170 B2
Asad, Buḥayrat al, *Syria* 214 B2
Asafo, *Ghana* 108 B1
Asahi-Gawa →, *Japan* 136 F3
Asahigawa, *Japan* 136 B8
Asamankese, *Ghana* 108 B2
Asansol, *India* 118 B3
Asau, *Samoa* 177 A1
Asbesberg, *S. Africa* 204 B2
Ascension I., *Atl. Oc.* 4 G2
Aschaffenburg, *Germany* 106 D2

Bradford

Berwick-upon-Tweed, U.K. 224 D5
Besalampy, Madag. 152 B1
Besançon, France 101 C7
Besar, Indonesia 124 C5
Beshenkovichi, Belarus 51 B4
Bessarabiya, Moldova 188 B5
Bessarabka = Basarabeasca, Moldova 188 B5
Bet She'an, Israel 130 B2
Bet Shemesh, Israel 130 C2
Betafo, Madag. 152 B2
Betanzos, Spain 206 A1
Bétaré Oya, Cameroon 65 B2
Betatao, Madag. 152 B2
Bétérou, Benin 54 C3
Bethal, S. Africa 205 B3
Bethel, Montserrat 74 A2
Bethlehem, S. Africa 205 B3
Bethulie, S. Africa 205 C3
Béthune, France 101 A5
Betioky, Madag. 152 C1
Betong, Thailand 218 J2
Betroka, Madag. 152 C2
Betsiboka →, Madag. 152 B2
Betung, Malaysia 154 B4
Beurkia, Chad 78 B2
Beveren, Belgium 52 A3
Beverley, Australia 44 F2
Beverley, U.K. 224 E6
Bevoalavo, Madag. 152 D1
Bex, Switz. 213 B2
Beyin, Ghana 108 B1
Beyla, Guinea 112 B3
Beyneu, Kazakstan 140 B2
Beypazarı, Turkey 220 A2
Beyşehir Gölü, Turkey 220 B2
Béziers, France 101 E5
Bezwada = Vijayawada, India 118 C3
Bhagalpur, India 118 B3
Bhamo, Burma 63 C4
Bharat = India ■, Asia 118
Bhaunagar = Bhavnagar, India 118 B2
Bhavnagar, India 118 B2
Bhima →, India 118 C2
Bhola, Bangla. 50 C3
Bhopal, India 118 B2
Bhubaneshwar, India 118 B3
Bhuj, India 118 B1
Bhutan ■, Asia 164
Biafra, B. of = Bonny, Bight of, Africa 4 F4
Biak, Indonesia 125 C9
Biała Podlaska, Poland 186 B5
Białogard, Poland 186 A1
Białystok, Poland 186 B5
Biankouma, Ivory C. 134 B1
Biaro, Indonesia 125 B7
Biarritz, France 100 E3
Biasca, Switz. 213 B3
Biba, Egypt 95 B2
Bibai, Japan 136 B7
Bibane, Bahiret el, Tunisia 219 B2
Bibassé, Gabon 103 A2
Biberach, Germany 106 D2
Bibi, Papua N. G. 181 C4
Bibiani, Ghana 108 B1
Bibile, Sri Lanka 209 C2
Bicaj, Albania 35 B2
Bichvinta, Georgia 104 A2
Bida, Nigeria 170 B2
Bidzar, Cameroon 65 B2
Bié, Planalto de, Angola 37 B2
Biel, Switz. 213 A2
Bielefeld, Germany 106 B2
Bielersee, Switz. 213 A2
Biella, Italy 132 B2
Bielsk Podlaski, Poland 186 B5
Bielsko-Biała, Poland 186 D3
Bien Hoa, Vietnam 237 G3
Bienne = Biel, Switz. 213 A2
Bienville, L., Canada 67 D9
Biesiesfontein, S. Africa 204 C1
Bifoum, Gabon 103 B2
Big Belt Mts., U.S.A. 230 A4
Big Bend, Swaziland 205 B4
Big Horn Mts. = Bighorn Mts., U.S.A. 230 B5
Big Sioux →, U.S.A. 231 B7
Big Spring, U.S.A. 230 D6
Big Trout L., Canada 67 D8
Biggar, Canada 66 D6
Bighorn →, U.S.A. 230 A5
Bighorn Mts., U.S.A. 230 B5
Bignona, Senegal 198 B1
Bihać, Bos.-H. 56 A1
Bihar □, India 118 B3
Bihor, Munţii, Romania 188 B2
Bijagós, Arquipélago dos, Guinea-Biss. 112 A1
Bijapur, India 118 C2
Bījār, Iran 126 B3
Bijeljina, Bos.-H. 56 A3
Bikaner, India 118 B2
Bikfayyā, Lebanon 147 B1
Bikin, Russia 191 E13
Bikita, Zimbabwe 241 B2
Bikoué, Cameroon 65 C2
Bila Tserkva, Ukraine 223 B3
Bilanga, Burkina Faso 62 B2
Bilaspur, India 118 B3
Biläsuvar, Azerbaijan 40 B4
Bilauk Taungdan, Thailand 218 E1
Bilbao, Spain 206 A4
Bilbo = Bilbao, Spain 206 A4
Bíldudalur, Iceland 117 B2
Bilecik, Turkey 220 A2
Bilhorod-Dnistrovskyy, Ukraine 223 B3
Bilibino, Russia 191 C16
Bilisht, Albania 35 C3
Billings, U.S.A. 230 A5
Billiton Is. = Belitung, Indonesia 124 C3
Bilma, Niger 169 B3
Biloela, Australia 45 D9
Biloxi, U.S.A. 231 D9
Biltine, Chad 78 C3
Bima, Indonesia 125 D5
Bimban, Egypt 95 C2
Bimbila, Ghana 108 B3
Bimbo, C.A.R. 77 C2
Bimini Is., Bahamas 71 A1
Bin Yauri, Nigeria 170 A1
Binalbagan, Phil. 184 F5
Binālūd, Kūh-e, Iran 127 A6
Binatang = Bintangor, Malaysia 154 B4
Binche, Belgium 52 B3
Binder, Chad 78 D1
Bindura, Zimbabwe 241 A2
Bingerville, Ivory C. 134 B2
Binghamton, U.S.A. 231 B11
Binh Dinh = An Nhon, Vietnam 237 F4
Binh Khe, Vietnam 237 F4
Binh Son, Vietnam 237 E4
Bini Erde, Chad 78 A2
Binjai, Indonesia 124 B3
Binji, Nigeria 170 A1
Binongko, Indonesia 125 D6
Bintan, Indonesia 124 B2
Bintangor, Malaysia 154 B4
Bintulu, Malaysia 154 B4
Bintuni, Indonesia 125 C8
Binzert = Bizerte, Tunisia 219 A1
Bioko, Eq. Guin. 103 A1
Bipindi, Cameroon 65 C2
Bîr Abu Hashim, Egypt 95 C2
Bîr Abu Minqar, Egypt 95 B1
Bir Aouine, Tunisia 219 B1
Bîr 'Asal, Egypt 95 B2
Bir Atrun, Sudan 210 B2
Bîr Diqnash, Egypt 95 A1
Bîr el Basur, Egypt 95 B1
Bîr el Gellaz, Egypt 95 A1
Bîr el Shaqqa, Egypt 95 A1
Bîr Fuad, Egypt 95 A1
Bir Gara, Chad 78 C2
Bîr Haimur, Egypt 95 C2
Bîr Kanayis, Egypt 95 C2
Bîr Kerawein, Egypt 95 B1
Bîr Maql, Egypt 95 C2
Bîr Misaha, Egypt 95 C1
Bîr Mogreïn, Mauritania 157 A2
Bîr Murr, Egypt 95 C2
Bîr Nakheila, Egypt 95 C2
Bîr Qatrani, Egypt 95 A1
Bîr Ranga, Egypt 95 C3
Bîr Sahara, Egypt 95 C1
Bîr Seiyâla, Egypt 95 B2
Bîr Shalatein, Egypt 95 C3
Bîr Shebb, Egypt 95 C1
Bîr Shût, Egypt 95 C3
Bîr Terfawi, Egypt 95 C1
Bîr Umm Qubûr, Egypt 95 C2
Bîr Ungât, Egypt 95 C2
Bîr Zeidûn, Egypt 95 B2
Biramféro, Guinea 112 A3
Birao, C.A.R. 77 B3
Birdsville, Australia 45 E6
Birein, Israel 130 D1
Bireuen, Indonesia 124 A1
Birifo, Gambia 198 B2
Birini, C.A.R. 77 B3
Birket Fatmé, Chad 78 C2
Birket Qârûn, Egypt 95 B2
Bîrlad = Bârlad, Romania 188 B4
Birmingham, U.K. 224 E6
Birmingham, U.S.A. 231 D9
Birni Nkonni, Niger 169 C2
Birnin Gwari, Nigeria 170 A2
Birnin Kebbi, Nigeria 170 A1
Birnin Kudu, Nigeria 170 A2
Birobidzhan, Russia 191 E13
Birougou, Mts., Gabon 103 B3
Birr, Ireland 128 C4
Birsk, Russia 190 D5
Biržai, Lithuania 150 A3
Birzebbugga, Malta 91 B2
Bisa, Indonesia 125 C7
Biscay, B. of, Atl. Oc. 28 F4
Bishkek, Kyrgyzstan 144 A4
Bisho, S. Africa 205 C3
Bisina, L., Uganda 222 B2
Biskra, Algeria 36 B4
Bismarck, U.S.A. 230 A6
Bismarck Arch., Papua N. G. 181 B6
Bismarck Ra., Papua N. G. 181 C3
Bismarck Sea, Papua N. G. 181 C4
Biso, Uganda 222 B2
Bissagos = Bijagós, Arquipélago dos, Guinea-Biss. 112 A1
Bissau, Guinea-Biss. 112 A1
Bissaula, Nigeria 170 B3
Bissikrima, Guinea 112 A2
Bissorã, Guinea-Biss. 112 A1
Bistriţa, Romania 188 B3
Bistriţa →, Romania 188 B4
Bita →, C.A.R. 77 B3
Bitam, Gabon 103 A2
Bitkine, Chad 78 C2
Bitola, Macedonia 151 B2
Bitolj = Bitola, Macedonia 151 B2
Bitter L. = Buheirat-Murrat-el-Kubra, Egypt 95 A2
Bitterfontein, S. Africa 204 C1
Bitterroot Range, U.S.A. 230 A4
Bittou, Burkina Faso 62 C2
Biu, Nigeria 170 A3
Biwa-Ko, Japan 136 F5
Biysk, Russia 190 D8
Bizana, S. Africa 205 C3
Bizen, Japan 136 F4
Bizerte, Tunisia 219 A1
Bjargtangar, Iceland 117 B1
Bjelovar, Croatia 89 B3
Black = Da →, Vietnam 237 B2
Black Forest = Schwarzwald, Germany 106 D2
Black Hd., Ireland 128 C2
Black Hills, U.S.A. 230 B6
Black Range, U.S.A. 230 D5
Black River, Jamaica 74 A2
Black Rock, Barbados 72 B1
Black Sea, Eurasia 28 G12
Blackall, Australia 45 D8
Blackball, N.Z. 167 E3
Blackburn, U.K. 224 E5
Blackpool, U.K. 224 E5
Blacksod B., Ireland 128 B1
Blackstone Ra., Australia 44 E4
Blackwater →, Meath, Ireland 128 C4
Blackwater →, Waterford, Ireland 128 D4
Blackwood, C., Papua N. G. 181 D3
Blagoevgrad, Bulgaria 61 B1
Blagoveshchensk, Russia 191 D12
Blair Athol, Australia 45 D8
Blanc, C., Tunisia 219 A1
Blanc, Mont, Alps 28 F7
Blanca, B., Argentina 38 B2
Blanca Peak, U.S.A. 230 C5
Blanche, L., S. Austral., Australia 45 E6
Blanche, L., W. Austral., Australia 44 D3
Blanchisseuse, Trin. & Tob. 76 C2
Blanco, S. Africa 204 C2
Blanco, C., Costa Rica 88 B1
Blanco, C., U.S.A. 230 B2
Blanda →, Iceland 117 B3
Blanes, Spain 207 B7
Blankenberge, Belgium 52 A2
Blanquillo, Uruguay 235 B1
Blantyre, Malawi 153 C2
Blarney, Ireland 128 E3
Blåvands Huk, Denmark 93 B2
Blaze, Pt., Australia 44 B5
Blenheim, N.Z. 167 D4
Blida, Algeria 36 A3
Bligh Sound, N.Z. 167 F1
Bligh Water, Fiji 175 A1
Blinisht, Albania 35 B1
Blitar, Indonesia 124 D4
Blitta, Togo 54 C2
Bloemfontein, S. Africa 205 B3
Bloemhof, S. Africa 205 B3
Blois, France 100 C4
Blönduós, Iceland 117 B3
Bloody Foreland, Ireland 128 A3
Bloomington, Ill., U.S.A. 231 B9
Bloomington, Ind., U.S.A. 231 C9
Blouberg, S. Africa 205 A3
Blowing Point, Anguilla 71 A1
Blowing Rock, Anguilla 71 A1
Blue Hills, Turks & Caicos 76 B1
Blue Mountain Pk., Jamaica 74 A3
Blue Mountains, The, Jamaica 74 A3
Blue Mts., U.S.A. 230 A3
Blue Mud B., Australia 45 B6
Blue Nile = Nîl el Azraq →, Sudan 210 B3
Blue Ridge Mts., U.S.A. 231 C10
Bluefield, U.S.A. 231 C10
Bluefields, Nic. 111 C3
Bluff, N.Z. 167 G2
Blumenau, Brazil 58 D4
Bo, S. Leone 148 A1
Bo Duc, Vietnam 237 G3
Bo Hai, China 81 C5
Boa Vista, Brazil 58 A2
Boa Vista, C. Verde Is. 42 A2
Boac, Phil. 184 E4
Boali, C.A.R. 77 C2
Boang I., Papua N. G. 181 B7
Bobo-Dioulasso, Burkina Faso 62 C2
Bobonaza →, Ecuador 94 C3
Bóbr →, Poland 186 B1
Bobraomby, Tanjon' i, Madag. 152 A2
Bobruysk = Babruysk, Belarus 51 C4
Boca Grande, Trin. & Tob. 76 C1
Bocanda, Ivory C. 134 B2
Bocaranga, C.A.R. 77 B2
Bocas del Toro, Panama 88 B2
Bochnia, Poland 186 D4
Bochum, Germany 106 C1
Boda, C.A.R. 77 C2
Bodaybo, Russia 191 D11
Bode Sadu, Nigeria 170 B1
Boden, Sweden 211 A4
Bodinga, Nigeria 170 A2
Bodø, Norway 172 B3
Bodoupa, C.A.R. 77 B2
Bodrichi, Chad 78 B2
Bodrog →, Hungary 116 A3
Bodrum, Turkey 220 B1
Boende, Dem. Rep. of the Congo 86 C3
Boesmans →, S. Africa 205 C3
Boffa, Guinea 112 A2
Bogalusa, U.S.A. 231 D9
Bogan →, Australia 45 E8
Bogandé, Burkina Faso 62 B2
Bogangolo, C.A.R. 77 B2
Boggeragh Mts., Ireland 128 D3
Bogia, Papua N. G. 181 C3
Bogo, Phil. 184 F6
Bogor, Indonesia 124 D3
Bogoso, Ghana 108 B1
Bogotá, Colombia 85 C2
Bogotol, Russia 190 D8
Bogou, Togo 54 B2
Bogra, Bangla. 50 B2
Boguchany, Russia 191 D9
Bohemian Forest = Böhmerwald, Germany 106 D4
Böhmerwald, Germany 106 D4
Bohol □, Phil. 184 G6
Bohongou, Burkina Faso 62 B3
Boi, Nigeria 170 B2
Boileau, C., Australia 44 C3
Boise, U.S.A. 230 B3
Bojador C., W. Sahara 161 C3
Bojana →, Albania 35 B1
Bojnūrd, Iran 127 A6
Bojonegoro, Indonesia 124 D4
Boju, Nigeria 170 B2
Bokala, Ivory C. 134 B2
Bokani, Nigeria 170 B2
Boké, Guinea 112 A2
Bokkos, Nigeria 170 B2
Bokolo, Gabon 103 B2
Bökönbaev, Kyrgyzstan 144 A5
Bokoro, Chad 78 C2
Bokpyin, Burma 63 K5
Boku, Papua N. G. 181 D8
Bol, Chad 78 C1
Bolama, Guinea-Biss. 112 A1
Bolan Pass, Pakistan 179 E4
Bolbec, France 100 B4
Bole, China 80 B2
Bole, Ghana 108 B1
Bolesławiec, Poland 186 C1
Bolgatanga, Ghana 108 A2
Bolinao, Phil. 184 C3
Bolívar □, Ecuador 94 B2
Bolivia ■, S. Amer. 55
Bolivian Plateau, S. Amer. 20 E3
Bolobo, Dem. Rep. of the Congo 86 C2
Bologna, Italy 132 B3
Bologoye, Russia 190 D3
Bolong, Chad 78 C2
Boloven, Cao Nguyen, Laos 145 E4
Bolsena, L. di, Italy 132 C3
Bolshevik, Ostrov, Russia 191 B10
Bolshoi Kavkas = Caucasus Mountains, Eurasia 28 G14
Bolshoy Anyuy →, Russia 191 C16
Bolshoy Begichev, Ostrov, Russia 191 B11
Bolshoy Lyakhovskiy, Ostrov, Russia 191 B14
Bolsward, Neths. 165 A3
Boltigen, Switz. 213 B2
Bolton, U.K. 224 E5
Bolu, Turkey 220 A2
Bolubolu, Papua N. G. 181 E6
Bolungavík, Iceland 117 A2
Bolvadin, Turkey 220 B2
Bolzano, Italy 132 A3
Boma, Dem. Rep. of the Congo 86 D1
Bombala, Australia 45 G8
Bombardopolis, Haiti 73 B2
Bombay = Mumbai, India 118 C2
Bomboma, Dem. Rep. of the Congo 86 B2
Bomboyo, Chad 78 C2
Bomi Hills, Liberia 148 B1
Bomu →, C.A.R. 77 C3
Bon, C., Tunisia 219 A2
Bon Acceuil, Mauritius 123 B2
Bon Sar Pa, Vietnam 237 F3
Bonaire, Neth. Ant. 74 A2
Bonao, Dom. Rep. 72 B2
Bonaparte Arch., Australia 44 B3
Bonavista, Canada 67 E11
Bondo, Dem. Rep. of the Congo 86 B3
Bondoukou, Ivory C. 134 B2
Bone, Teluk, Indonesia 125 C6
Bonerate, Indonesia 125 D6
Bonerate, Kepulauan, Indonesia 125 D6
Bong Son = Hoai Nhon, Vietnam 237 E4
Bongabong, Phil. 184 E4
Bongor, Chad 78 C2
Bongouanou, Ivory C. 134 B2
Bonifacio, France 101 F8
Bonifacio, Bouches de, Medit. S. 132 D2
Bonin Is., Pac. Oc. 10 G18
Bonn, Germany 106 C1
Bonnie Rock, Australia 44 F2
Bonny, Nigeria 170 C2
Bonny →, Nigeria 170 C2
Bonny, Bight of, Africa 4 F4
Bonoi, Indonesia 125 C9
Bontang, Indonesia 124 B5
Bonthe, S. Leone 148 B1
Bontoc, Phil. 184 C4
Bonyeri, Ghana 108 B1
Boola, Guinea 112 B3
Boothia, Gulf of, Canada 67 B8
Boothia Pen., Canada 66 B7
Booué, Gabon 103 B2
Boquete, Panama 88 B2
Bor, Serbia, Yug. 239 B3
Bôr, Sudan 210 D3
Bor Döbö, Kyrgyzstan 144 C3
Bor Mashash, Israel 130 C1
Borås, Sweden 211 C2
Borāzjān, Iran 126 C4
Borborema, Planalto da, Brazil 20 D7
Bordeaux, France 100 D3
Borden I., Canada 67 B5
Borden Pen., Canada 67 B8
Bordertown, Australia 45 G7
Borðeyri, Iceland 117 B3
Bordj Bourguiba, Tunisia 219 B2
Bordj Fly Ste. Marie, Algeria 36 C2
Bordj-in-Eker, Algeria 36 D4
Bordj Omar Driss, Algeria 36 C4
Borgarfjörður, Iceland 117 B7
Borgarnes, Iceland 117 B3
Borger, Neths. 165 B4
Borger, U.S.A. 230 C6
Borhoyn Tal, Mongolia 160 B4
Bori, Nigeria 170 C2
Borikhane, Laos 145 C2
Borisoglebsk, Russia 190 D4
Borisov = Barysaw, Belarus 51 B4
Borja, Peru 183 A2
Borjomi, Georgia 104 B3
Borkou, Chad 78 B2
Borkum, Germany 106 B1
Borneo, E. Indies 10 J15
Bornholm, Denmark 93 B5
Borno □, Nigeria 170 A3
Bornu Yassa, Nigeria 170 A3
Borogontsy, Russia 191 C13
Boromo, Burkina Faso 62 C2
Borongan, Phil. 184 F6
Borotangba Mts., C.A.R. 77 B4
Borotou, Ivory C. 134 B1
Borroloola, Australia 45 C6
Borşa, Romania 188 B3
Borūjerd, Iran 126 B4
Borzhomi = Borjomi, Georgia 104 B3
Borzya, Russia 191 D11
Bosa, Italy 132 D2
Bosanska Gradiška, Bos.-H. 56 A2
Bosaso, Somali Rep. 202 A2
Bosavi, Mt., Papua N. G. 181 D2
Boshof, S. Africa 205 B3
Boshrūyeh, Iran 127 B6
Bosna →, Bos.-H. 56 A3
Bosna i Hercegovina = Bosnia-Herzegovina ■, Europe 56
Bosnia-Herzegovina ■, Europe 56
Bosnik, Indonesia 125 C9
Bosobolo, Dem. Rep. of the Congo 86 B2
Bosporus = İstanbul Boğazı, Turkey 220 A1
Bossangoa, C.A.R. 77 B2
Bossembélé, C.A.R. 77 B2
Bossemtélé, C.A.R. 77 B2
Bosso, Niger 169 C3
Bosten Hu, China 80 B2
Boston, U.K. 224 E6
Boston, U.S.A. 231 B12
Botene, Laos 145 D1
Bothaville, S. Africa 205 B3
Bothnia, G. of, Europe 28 C9
Botletle →, Botswana 57 B1
Botoşani, Romania 188 B4
Botou, Burkina Faso 62 B3
Botro, Ivory C. 134 B1
Botswana ■, Africa 57
Bottle Creek, Turks & Caicos 76 B2
Bou Salem, Tunisia 219 A1
Bouaflé, Ivory C. 134 B1
Bouaké, Ivory C. 134 B1
Bouar, C.A.R. 77 B2
Bouârfa, Morocco 161 B5
Bouca, C.A.R. 77 B2
Bougainville, C., Australia 44 B4
Bougainville I., Papua N. G. 181 D8
Bougie = Bejaïa, Algeria 36 A4
Bougouni, Mali 156 C2
Bouillon, Belgium 52 C4
Boukombé, Benin 54 B2
Boulder, U.S.A. 230 B5
Boulder Dam = Hoover Dam, U.S.A. 230 C4
Boulembo, Gabon 103 B3
Boulia, Australia 45 D6
Boulogne-sur-Mer, France 101 A4
Boulou →, C.A.R. 77 B3
Boulsa, Burkina Faso 62 B2
Boultoum, Niger 169 C3
Boumba →, Cameroon 65 C2
Boumbé →, C.A.R. 77 C2
Boun Neua, Laos 145 B1
Boun Tai, Laos 145 B1
Bouna, Ivory C. 134 B2
Boundgi, Gabon 103 B2
Boundiali, Ivory C. 134 B1
Boungou →, C.A.R. 77 B3
Bourail, N. Cal. 176 A2
Bourbonnais, France 101 C5
Bourem, Mali 156 B3
Bourg-en-Bresse, France 101 C6
Bourg-St-Maurice, France 101 D7
Bourges, France 101 C5
Bourgogne, France 101 C6
Bourke, Australia 45 F8
Bournemouth, U.K. 224 F6
Bouroum, Burkina Faso 62 B2
Boussé, Burkina Faso 62 B2
Bousso, Chad 78 C2
Boussouma, Burkina Faso 62 B2
Bouvet I. = Bouvetøya, Antarctica 3 G10
Bouvetøya, Antarctica 3 G10
Bow →, Canada 66 D5
Bowen, Australia 45 D8
Bowling Green, U.S.A. 231 C9
Bowling Green, C., Australia 45 C8
Bowral, Australia 45 F9
Bowutu Mts., Papua N. G. 181 D4
Boxmeer, Neths. 165 C3
Boxtel, Neths. 165 C3
Boyle, Ireland 128 C3
Boyne →, Ireland 128 C5
Boyoma, Chutes, Dem. Rep. of the Congo 4 F6
Boyuibe, Bolivia 55 B2
Boze, Papua N. G. 181 E2
Bozeman, U.S.A. 230 A4
Bozen = Bolzano, Italy 132 A3
Bozoum, C.A.R. 77 B2
Bra, Italy 132 B1
Brabant □, Belgium 52 B3
Brač, Croatia 89 C3
Bracciano, L. di, Italy 132 C4
Brach, Libya 149 B2
Bräcke, Sweden 211 B3
Brad, Romania 188 B2
Bradenton, U.S.A. 231 E10
Bradford, U.K. 224 E6

Dodoma

Cullera, Spain 207 C5
Culver, Pt., Australia 44 F3
Culverden, N.Z. 167 E4
Cumaná, Venezuela 236 A3
Cumberland, U.S.A. 231 C11
Cumberland →, U.S.A. 231 C9
Cumberland Is., Australia 45 D8
Cumberland Pen., Canada 67 C10
Cumberland Plateau, U.S.A. 231 C10
Cumberland Sd., Canada 67 C10
Cumbrian Mts., U.K. 224 D5
Cunene →, Angola 37 C1
Cúneo, Italy 132 B1
Cunnamulla, Australia 45 E8
Cunupia, Trin. & Tob. 76 C2
Cupica, G. de, Colombia 85 B1
Curaçao, Neth. Ant. 74 A2
Curaray →, Peru 183 A3
Curepipe, Mauritius 123 B2
Curiapo, Venezuela 236 B3
Curicó, Chile 79 C1
Curieuse, Seychelles 123 A2
Curitiba, Brazil 58 D4
Curral Velho, C. Verde Is. 42 B2
Curtea de Argeş, Romania 188 C3
Curtis I., Australia 45 D9
Curup, Indonesia 124 C2
Cuttack, India 118 B3
Cuvier I., N.Z. 167 B5
Cuxhaven, Germany 106 B2
Cuyabeno, Ecuador 94 B3
Cuyapo, Phil. 184 D4
Cuyo, Phil. 184 F4
Cuyo East Pass, Phil. 184 F4
Cuyo West Pass, Phil. 184 F4
Cuyuni →, Guyana 115 A2
Cuzco, Bolivia 55 C1
Cuzco, Peru 183 C3
Cwmbran, U.K. 224 F5
Cyangugu, Rwanda 195 B1
Cyclades = Kikládhes, Greece 109 C4
Cyprus ■, Asia 91
Cyrenaica, Libya 149 B4
Czech Rep. ■, Europe 92
Częstochowa, Poland 186 C3

D

Da →, Vietnam 237 B2
Da Hinggan Ling, China 81 B6
Da Lat, Vietnam 237 G4
Da Nang, Vietnam 237 D4
Da Qaidam, China 80 C3
Daba Shan, China 81 C4
Dabai, Nigeria 170 A2
Dabakala, Ivory C. 134 B2
Dabo = Pasirkuning, Indonesia 124 C2
Dabola, Guinea 112 A2
Dabou, Ivory C. 134 B2
Daboya, Ghana 108 B2
Dacca = Dhaka, Bangla. 50 C3
Dacca = Dhaka □, Bangla. 50 B3
Dachau, Germany 106 D3
Dadanawa, Guyana 115 B2
Dadiya, Nigeria 170 B3
Dadu, Pakistan 179 F4
Daet, Phil. 184 D5
Dagana, Senegal 198 A1
Dagestan □, Russia 190 E4
Daghestan Republic = Dagestan □, Russia 190 E4
Dağlıq Qarabağ = Nagorno-Karabakh, Azerbaijan 40 B3
Dagö = Hiiumaa, Estonia 97 B2
Dagua, Papua N. G. 181 B2
Dagupan, Phil. 184 C4
Dahab, Egypt 95 B2
Dahlak Kebir, Eritrea 98 A3
Dahomey = Benin ■, Africa 54
Dahra, Senegal 198 A1
Dai Hao, Vietnam 237 C3
Dai-Sen, Japan 136 F3
Daingean, Ireland 128 C4
Daiō-Misaki, Japan 136 F5
Dairût, Egypt 95 B2
Daisetsu-Zan, Japan 136 B8
Dajarra, Australia 45 D6
Dak Dam, Cambodia 64 B3
Dak Nhe, Vietnam 237 E3
Dak Pek, Vietnam 237 E3
Dak Song, Vietnam 237 F3
Dak Sui, Vietnam 237 E3
Dakar, Senegal 198 B1
Dakhla, W. Sahara 161 D2
Dakhla, El Wâhât el-, Egypt 95 B1
Dakingari, Nigeria 170 A1
Đakovica, Kosovo, Yug. 239 C2
Dalaba, Guinea 112 A2
Dalälven, Sweden 211 B3
Dalandzadgad, Mongolia 160 B3
Dālbandīn, Pakistan 179 E3
Dalby, Australia 45 E9
Dalga, Egypt 95 B2
Dalhart, U.S.A. 230 C6
Dali, China 80 D4
Dalian, China 81 C6
Daliang Shan, China 80 D4
Däliyat el Karmel, Israel 130 B2
Dallas, U.S.A. 231 D7
Dalmacija, Croatia 89 C3
Dalmatia = Dalmacija, Croatia 89 C3
Dalnegorsk, Russia 191 E13
Dalnerechensk, Russia 191 E13
Daloa, Ivory C. 134 B1
Dalupiri I., Phil. 184 B4
Dalvík, Iceland 117 B4
Daly →, Australia 44 B5
Daly Waters, Australia 44 C5
Dam Doi, Vietnam 237 H2
Dam Ha, Vietnam 237 B3
Damanhûr, Egypt 95 A2
Damar, Indonesia 125 D7
Damara, C.A.R. 77 C2
Damaraland, Namibia 163 A1
Damascus = Dimashq, Syria 214 C2
Damaturu, Nigeria 170 A3
Damāvand, Iran 127 B5
Damāvand, Qolleh-ye, Iran 127 B5
Damba, Angola 37 A2
Dâmboviţa →, Romania 188 C4
Dambulla, Sri Lanka 209 C2
Dame Marie, Haiti 73 B1
Dame Marie, Cap, Haiti 73 B1
Dāmghān, Iran 127 A5
Damiel, Spain 206 C4
Damietta = Dumyât, Egypt 95 A2
Damīr Qābū, Syria 214 A3
Dampier, Australia 44 D2
Dampier, Selat, Indonesia 125 C8
Dampier Arch., Australia 44 D2
Dampier Str., Papua N. G. 181 C5
Damrei, Chuor Phnum, Cambodia 64 C1
Dan-Gulbi, Nigeria 170 A2
Dana, Indonesia 125 D6
Danakil Desert, Ethiopia 98 B3
Danané, Ivory C. 134 B1
Danao, Phil. 184 F6
Danau Poso, Indonesia 125 C6
Dandeldhura, Nepal 164 B2
Dandong, China 81 B6
Dangara, Tajikistan 216 B2
Danger Pt., S. Africa 204 C1
Dangla Shan = Tanggula Shan, China 80 C3
Dangora, Nigeria 170 A2
Dangouadougou, Burkina Faso 62 C2
Dangrek, Phnom, Thailand 218 D4
Dani, Burkina Faso 62 B2
Danielskuil, S. Africa 204 B2
Danissa, Kenya 141 A3
Danja, Nigeria 170 A2
Dankalwa, Nigeria 170 A3
Dankama, Nigeria 170 A2
Dannevirke, N.Z. 167 D6
Dannhauser, S. Africa 205 B4
Dante, Somali Rep. 202 A3
Danube →, Austria 28 F11
Danville, Ill., U.S.A. 231 B9
Danville, Ky., U.S.A. 231 C10
Danville, Va., U.S.A. 231 C11
Danzig = Gdańsk, Poland 186 A3
Daoukro, Ivory C. 134 B2
Dapaong, Togo 54 B2
Dapchi, Nigeria 170 A3
Dapitan, Phil. 184 G5
Dar Banda, Africa 4 F6
Dar el Beida = Casablanca, Morocco 161 B4
Dar es Salaam, Tanzania 217 B3
Dar Rounga, C.A.R. 77 B3
Dar'ā, Syria 214 C2
Dārāb, Iran 127 C5
Darai Hills, Papua N. G. 181 D2
Daraina, Madag. 152 A2
Daraj, Libya 149 A2
Daraut Kurgan = Daroot-Korgan, Kyrgyzstan 144 C3
Daraw, Egypt 95 C2
Darazo, Nigeria 170 A3
Darband, Pakistan 179 B7
Darbhanga, India 118 B3
Dardanelles, Turkey 28 G11
Dārfūr, Sudan 210 C1
Dargai, Pakistan 179 B6
Dargaville, N.Z. 167 A4
Darién, G. del, Colombia 85 B1
Darjeeling = Darjiling, India 118 B3
Darjiling, India 118 B3
Darling →, Australia 45 F7
Darling Ra., Australia 44 F2
Darlington, U.K. 224 D6
Darlington, L., S. Africa 205 C3
Darłowo, Poland 186 A2
Darmstadt, Germany 106 D2
Darnah, Libya 149 A4
Darnall, S. Africa 205 B4
Darnley B., Canada 66 C4
Daroot-Korgan, Kyrgyzstan 144 C3
Darou-Mousti, Senegal 198 A1
Dartmoor, U.K. 224 F5
Dartmouth, Canada 67 E10
Daru, Papua N. G. 181 E2
Darwendale, Zimbabwe 241 A2
Darwin, Australia 44 B5
Daryoi Amu = Amudarya →, Uzbekistan 221 B2
Dashen, Ras, Ethiopia 98 B2
Dashhowuz, Turkmenistan 221 B2
Dashkesan = Daşkäsän, Azerbaijan 40 A2
Dashköpri, Turkmenistan 221 C3
Dasht →, Pakistan 179 G1
Daşkäsän, Azerbaijan 40 A2
Dassa, Benin 54 D3
Datong, China 81 B5
Datu, Tanjung, Indonesia 124 B3
Datu Piang, Phil. 184 H6
Datuk, Tanjong = Datu, Tanjung, Indonesia 124 B3
Daugava →, Latvia 146 B3
Daugavpils, Latvia 146 C4
Daule, Ecuador 94 B2
Daule →, Ecuador 94 B2
Dauphin, Canada 66 D6
Dauphiné, France 101 D6
Daura, Borno, Nigeria 170 A3
Daura, Katsina, Nigeria 170 A2
Däväçi, Azerbaijan 40 A4
Davangere, India 118 C2
Davao, Phil. 184 H6
Davao G., Phil. 184 H6
Dāvar Panāh, Iran 127 D7
Davenport, U.S.A. 231 B8
David, Panama 88 B2
David Gorodok = Davyd Haradok, Belarus 51 C3
Davis Str., N. Amer. 14 C14
Davo →, Ivory C. 134 B1
Davos, Switz. 213 B4
Davyd Haradok, Belarus 51 C3
Dawaki, Bauchi, Nigeria 170 B2
Dawaki, Kano, Nigeria 170 A2
Dawei, Burma 63 H5
Dawros Hd., Ireland 128 B3
Dawson, Canada 66 C3
Dawson →, Australia 45 D8
Dawson Creek, Canada 66 D4
Dax, France 100 E3
Daxian, China 81 C4
Daxue Shan, China 80 C4
Dayr az Zawr, Syria 214 B3
Dayton, U.S.A. 231 C10
Daytona Beach, U.S.A. 231 E10
De Aar, S. Africa 204 C2
De Grey, Australia 44 D2
De Haan, Belgium 52 A2
De Panne, Belgium 52 A1
De Ridder, U.S.A. 231 D8
Dead Sea, Asia 10 F7
Deadman's Cay, Bahamas 71 B2
Dealesville, S. Africa 205 B3
Dease →, Canada 66 D4
Dease Lake, Canada 66 D3
Death Valley, U.S.A. 230 C3
Deba Habe, Nigeria 170 A3
Debar, Macedonia 151 B1
Debe, Trin. & Tob. 76 D2
Dębica, Poland 186 C4
Deboyne Is., Papua N. G. 181 F7
Debre Markos, Ethiopia 98 B2
Debre Tabor, Ethiopia 98 B2
Debre Zeyit, Ethiopia 98 C2
Debrecen, Hungary 116 B3
Decatur, Ala., U.S.A. 231 D9
Decatur, Ill., U.S.A. 231 C9
Deccan, India 118 C2
Deception B., Papua N. G. 181 D3
Děčín, Czech Rep. 92 A2
Dedéagach = Alexandroúpolis, Greece 109 A4
Dédougou, Burkina Faso 62 B2
Dedza, Malawi 153 B1
Dee →, U.K. 224 C5
Deer Lake, Canada 67 E11
Deerdepoort, S. Africa 205 A3
Degema, Nigeria 170 C2
Deggendorf, Germany 106 D4
Deh Bīd, Iran 127 C5
Déhane, Cameroon 65 C2
Dehibat, Tunisia 219 B2
Dehiwala, Sri Lanka 209 C1
Dehra Dun, India 118 A2
Deinze, Belgium 52 B2
Dej, Romania 188 B2
Deka →, Zimbabwe 241 A1
Dekese, Dem. Rep. of the Congo 86 C3
Dekoa, C.A.R. 77 B2
Del Rio, U.S.A. 230 E6
Delareyville, S. Africa 205 B3
Delaware □, U.S.A. 231 C11
Delaware B., U.S.A. 231 C12
Delčevo, Macedonia 151 B3
Delémont, Switz. 213 A2
Delft, Neths. 165 B2
Delft I., Sri Lanka 209 B1
Delfzijl, Neths. 165 A4
Delgado, C., Mozam. 162 A3
Delgo, Sudan 210 A3
Delhi, India 118 B2
Delice, Turkey 220 B2
Délices, Domin. 73 B2
Delicias, Mexico 158 B3
Déline, Canada 66 C4
Delmenhorst, Germany 106 B2
Delonga, Ostrova, Russia 191 B14
Delportshoop, S. Africa 204 B2
Delta □, Nigeria 170 B2
Delvinë, Albania 35 D2
Demanda, Sierra de la, Spain 206 A4
Demavand = Damāvand, Iran 127 B5
Dembidolo, Ethiopia 98 C1
Demer →, Belgium 52 B3
Deming, U.S.A. 230 D5
Demopolis, U.S.A. 231 D9
Dempo, Indonesia 124 C2
Den Burg, Neths. 165 A2
Den Chai, Thailand 218 C2
Den Haag = 's-Gravenhage, Neths. 165 B2
Den Helder, Neths. 165 B2
Den Oever, Neths. 165 B3
Dendang, Indonesia 124 C3
Dendé, Gabon 103 B2
Dendermonde, Belgium 52 A3
Deng Deng, Cameroon 65 B2
Denge, Nigeria 170 A2
Dengi, Nigeria 170 B2
Denham, Australia 44 E1
Denham, Mt., Jamaica 74 A2
Denham Ra., Australia 45 D8
Denia, Spain 207 C6
Deniliquin, Australia 45 G7
Denis, Gabon 103 A1
Deniyaya, Sri Lanka 209 C2
Denizli, Turkey 220 B1
Denmark, Australia 44 F2
Denmark ■, Europe 93
Denmark Str., Atl. Oc. 14 C17
Dennery, St. Lucia 75 B2
Denpasar, Indonesia 124 D5
Denton, U.S.A. 231 D7
D'Entrecasteaux, Pt., Australia 44 F2
D'Entrecasteaux Is., Papua N. G. 181 E6
Denu, Ghana 108 B3
Denver, U.S.A. 230 C5
Deosai Mts., Pakistan 179 B8
Deputatskiy, Russia 191 C13
Dera Ghazi Khan, Pakistan 179 D6
Dera Ismail Khan, Pakistan 179 D6
Derbent, Russia 190 E4
Derby, Australia 44 C3
Derby, U.K. 224 E6
Derg, L., Ireland 128 D3
Derry = Londonderry, U.K. 224 D3
Derryveagh Mts., Ireland 128 B3
Des Moines, U.S.A. 231 B8
Des Moines →, U.S.A. 231 B8
Desaguadero →, Bolivia 55 B1
Deschutes →, U.S.A. 230 A2
Dese, Ethiopia 98 B2
Deseado →, Argentina 38 C2
Desertas, Is., Madeira 43 B2
Desna →, Ukraine 223 A3
Desolación, I., Chile 79 E1
Despeñaperros, Paso, Spain 206 C4
Dessau, Germany 106 C4
Dessye = Dese, Ethiopia 98 B2
Det Udom, Thailand 218 D4
Dete, Zimbabwe 241 A1
Detmold, Germany 106 C2
Detroit, U.S.A. 231 B10
Deurne, Neths. 165 C3
Deutsche Bucht, Germany 106 A2
Deva, Romania 188 C2
Deventer, Neths. 165 B4
Devils Lake, U.S.A. 230 A7
Devil's Pt., Sri Lanka 209 B2
Devoll →, Albania 35 C2
Devon I., Canada 67 B8
Devonport, Australia 45 H8
Devonport, N.Z. 167 B5
Dewetsdorp, S. Africa 205 B3
Dewey, Puerto Rico 75 A3
Deyhūk, Iran 127 B6
Deyyer, Iran 127 D4
Dezfūl, Iran 126 B4
Dezhneva, Mys, Russia 191 C18
Dhaka, Bangla. 50 C3
Dhaka □, Bangla. 50 B3
Dhali, Cyprus 91 A2
Dhangarhi, Nepal 164 B2
Dhankuta, Nepal 164 C5
Dharwad, India 118 C2
Dhaulagiri, Nepal 164 B3
Dheftera, Cyprus 91 A2
Dherinia, Cyprus 91 A2
Dhiarrizos →, Cyprus 91 B1
Dhíkti Óros, Greece 109 D4
Dhírfis = Dhírfis Óros, Greece 109 B3
Dhírfis Óros, Greece 109 B3
Dhodhekánisos, Greece 109 C5
Dhule, India 118 B2
Di Linh, Vietnam 237 G4
Di Linh, Cao Nguyen, Vietnam 237 G4
Diabakania, Guinea 112 A2
Diablotin, Morne, Domin. 73 A2
Diafarabé, Mali 156 C3
Dialakoto, Senegal 198 B2
Diamantina, Brazil 58 C4
Diamantina →, Australia 45 E6
Diamantino, Brazil 58 C3
Dianra, Ivory C. 134 B1
Diapaga, Burkina Faso 62 B3
Diapangou, Burkina Faso 62 B3
Diariguila, Guinea 112 A2
Dibaya-Lubue, Dem. Rep. of the Congo 86 C2
Dibete, Botswana 57 B2
Dibrugarh, India 118 B4
Dickinson, U.S.A. 230 A6
Dickson = Dikson, Russia 190 B8
Didiéni, Mali 156 C2
Diébougou, Burkina Faso 62 C2
Diecke, Guinea 112 B3
Diefenbaker, L., Canada 66 D6
Diego Garcia, Ind. Oc. 3 E13
Diekirch, Lux. 52 C5
Diembéring, Senegal 198 B1
Dien Ban, Vietnam 237 E4
Dien Bien, Vietnam 237 B1
Dien Khanh, Vietnam 237 F4
Dieppe, France 100 B4
Dieppe Bay Town, St. Kitts & Nevis 75 A1
Diest, Belgium 52 B4
Dietikon, Switz. 213 A3
Dif, Somali Rep. 202 C1
Differdange, Lux. 52 C4
Digby, Canada 67 E10
Dighinala, Bangla. 50 C4
Digne-les-Bains, France 101 D7
Digos, Phil. 184 H6
Digranes, Iceland 117 A6
Digul →, Indonesia 125 D9
Dijlah, Nahr = Tigris →, Asia 10 F8
Dijon, France 101 C6
Dikhil, Djibouti 202 A1
Dikkil = Dikhil, Djibouti 202 A1
Dikodougou, Ivory C. 134 B1
Diksmuide, Belgium 52 A1
Dikson, Russia 190 B8
Dikwa, Nigeria 170 A3
Dila, Ethiopia 98 C2
Dili, E. Timor 125 D7
Dilijan, Armenia 40 A2
Dilizhan = Dilijan, Armenia 40 A2
Dilolo, Dem. Rep. of the Congo 86 E3
Dimashq, Syria 214 C2
Dimbaza, S. Africa 205 C3
Dimbokro, Ivory C. 134 B2
Dîmboviţa = Dâmboviţa →, Romania 188 C4
Dimitrovgrad, Bulgaria 61 B2
Dimitrovo = Pernik, Bulgaria 61 B1
Dimona, Israel 130 C2
Dinagat, Phil. 184 F6
Dinajpur, Bangla. 50 B2
Dinan, France 100 B2
Dinant, Belgium 52 B3
Dīnār, Kūh-e, Iran 127 C4
Dinara Planina, Croatia 89 C3
Dinard, France 100 B2
Dinaric Alps = Dinara Planina, Croatia 89 C3
Dingalan, Phil. 184 D4
Dingle, Ireland 128 D1
Dingle B., Ireland 128 D1
Dinguiraye, Guinea 112 A2
Dingwall, U.K. 224 C4
Dinh, Mui, Vietnam 237 G4
Dinh Lap, Vietnam 237 B3
Dinokwe, Botswana 57 B2
Diona, Chad 78 B3
Diouloulou, Senegal 198 B1
Diourbel, Senegal 198 B1
Dipolog, Phil. 184 G5
Dir, Pakistan 179 B6
Dire Dawa, Ethiopia 98 C3
Dirk Hartog I., Australia 44 E1
Dirranbandi, Australia 45 E8
Disappointment, C., U.S.A. 230 A2
Disappointment, L., Australia 44 D3
Disaster B., Australia 45 G8
Discovery B., Australia 45 G7
Disentis Muster, Switz. 213 B3
Dishna, Egypt 95 B2
Disina, Nigeria 170 A2
Disko = Qeqertarsuaq, Greenland 43 C4
Disko Bugt, Greenland 43 C4
Disna = Dzisna →, Belarus 51 B4
Disteghil Sar, Pakistan 179 A8
Distrito Federal □, Brazil 58 C4
Disûq, Egypt 95 A2
Divichi = Däväçi, Azerbaijan 40 A4
Divjake, Albania 35 C1
Divo, Ivory C. 134 B1
Diyarbakır, Turkey 220 B4
Djadié →, Gabon 103 A3
Djakarta = Jakarta, Indonesia 124 D3
Djambala, Congo 86 C1
Djanet, Algeria 36 D4
Djaul I., Papua N. G. 181 B6
Djawa = Jawa, Indonesia 124 D4
Djebiniana, Tunisia 219 A2
Djédaa, Chad 78 C2
Djelfa, Algeria 36 B3
Djema, C.A.R. 77 B4
Djember, Chad 78 C2
Djeneïene, Tunisia 219 B2
Djerba, Tunisia 219 B2
Djerba, I. de, Tunisia 219 B2
Djeréme →, Cameroon 65 B2
Djerid, Chott, Tunisia 219 B1
Djiba, Gabon 103 B3
Djibo, Burkina Faso 62 A2
Djibouti, Djibouti 202 A1
Djibouti ■, Africa 202
Djohong, Cameroon 65 B2
Djolu, Dem. Rep. of the Congo 86 B3
Djouab →, Gabon 103 A3
Djougou, Benin 54 C2
Djoum, Cameroon 65 C2
Djouna, Chad 78 C3
Djourab, Erg du, Chad 78 B2
Djúpivogur, Iceland 117 B6
Dmitriya Lapteva, Proliv, Russia 191 B14
Dnepr → = Dnipro →, Ukraine 223 B3
Dneprodzerzhinsk = Dniprodzerzhynsk, Ukraine 223 B3
Dnepropetrovsk = Dnipropetrovsk, Ukraine 223 B4
Dnestr = Dniester →, Europe 28 F11
Dnestrovski = Belgorod, Russia 190 D3
Dnieper = Dnipro →, Ukraine 223 B3
Dniester →, Europe 28 F11
Dnipro →, Ukraine 223 B3
Dniprodzerzhynsk, Ukraine 223 B3
Dnipropetrovsk, Ukraine 223 B4
Dnister = Dniester →, Europe 28 F11
Dnyapro = Dnipro →, Ukraine 223 B3
Doan Hung, Vietnam 237 B2
Doany, Madag. 152 A2
Doba, Chad 78 D2
Dobele, Latvia 146 B2
Doberai, Jazirah, Indonesia 125 C8
Dobo, Indonesia 125 D8
Doboj, Bos.-H. 56 A3
Dobreta-Turnu Severin, Romania 188 C2
Dobrich, Bulgaria 61 B3
Dobrush, Belarus 51 C5
Doc, Mui, Vietnam 237 D3
Dodecanese = Dhodhekánisos, Greece 109 C5
Dodge City, U.S.A. 230 C6
Dodoma, Tanzania 217 B3

Johnston, L.

I

I-n-Gall, *Niger* 169 B2
Iakora, *Madag.* 152 C2
Ialibu, *Papua N. G.* 181 D2
Ialomiţa →, *Romania* 188 C4
Iaşi, *Romania* 188 B4
Iba, *Phil.* 184 D4
Ibadan, *Nigeria* 170 B1
Ibagué, *Colombia* 85 C1
Iballë, *Albania* 35 A2
Ibar →, *Serbia, Yug.* 239 C2
Ibarra, *Ecuador* 94 A2
Iberian Peninsula, *Europe* 28 G4
Ibi, *Nigeria* 170 B2
Ibiapaba, Sa. da, *Brazil* 58 B4
Ibiza = Eivissa, *Spain* 207 C6
Ibonma, *Indonesia* 125 C8
Ibrāhīm →, *Lebanon* 147 A1
Ibshawâi, *Egypt* 95 B2
Ibu, *Indonesia* 125 B7
Ibusuki, *Japan* 136 H2
Ica, *Peru* 183 C2
Içà →, *Brazil* 58 B2
Icacos Pt., *Trin. & Tob.* 76 D1
Içel = Mersin, *Turkey* 220 B2
Iceland ■, *Europe* 117
Ich'ang = Yichang, *China* 81 C5
Ichihara, *Japan* 136 F7
Ichikawa, *Japan* 136 F6
Ichilo →, *Bolivia* 55 B2
Ichinohe, *Japan* 136 C7
Ichinomiya, *Japan* 136 F5
Ichinoseki, *Japan* 136 D7
Idah, *Nigeria* 170 B2
Idaho □, *U.S.A.* 230 B4
Idaho Falls, *U.S.A.* 230 B4
Idar-Oberstein, *Germany* 106 D1
Idfû, *Egypt* 95 C2
Ídhi Óros, *Greece* 109 D4
Ídhra, *Greece* 109 C3
Idi, *Indonesia* 124 A1
Idiofa, *Dem. Rep. of the Congo* 86 C2
Idlib, *Syria* 214 B2
Idutywa, *S. Africa* 205 C3
Ieper, *Belgium* 52 B1
Ierápetra, *Greece* 109 D4
Iesi, *Italy* 133 C4
Ifakara, *Tanzania* 217 B3
Ifanadiana, *Madag.* 152 C2
Ife, *Nigeria* 170 B1
Ifon, *Nigeria* 170 B2
Iforas, Adrar des, *Mali* 156 B4
Iganga, *Uganda* 222 B2
Igarka, *Russia* 190 C8
Igbetti, *Nigeria* 170 B1
Igbo-Ora, *Nigeria* 170 B1
Igboho, *Nigeria* 170 B1
Igbor, *Nigeria* 170 B2
Iglésias, *Italy* 132 E2
Igloolik, *Canada* 67 C8
Igluligaarjuk, *Canada* 67 C7
Iglulik = Igloolik, *Canada* 67 C8
'Igma, Gebel el, *Egypt* 95 B2
Igoumenítsa, *Greece* 109 B2
Iguaçu →, *Brazil* 58 D3
Iguaçu, Cat. del, *Brazil* 58 D3
Iguaçu Falls = Iguaçu, Cat. del, *Brazil* 58 D3
Iguala, *Mexico* 158 D5
Igualada, *Spain* 207 B6
Iguassu = Iguaçu →, *Brazil* 58 D3
Iguatu, *Brazil* 58 B5
Iguéla, *Gabon* 103 B1
Iguéla, Lagune, *Gabon* 103 B1
Iharana, *Madag.* 152 A3
Ihavandiffulu Atoll, *Maldives* 123 B1
Ihiala, *Nigeria* 170 B2
Ihosy, *Madag.* 152 C2
Ihotry, Farihy, *Madag.* 152 C1
Ihu, *Papua N. G.* 181 D3
Ihugh, *Nigeria* 170 B2
Iida, *Japan* 136 F5
Iisalmi, *Finland* 99 B3
Iiyama, *Japan* 136 E6
Iizuka, *Japan* 136 G2
Ijebu-Igbo, *Nigeria* 170 B1
Ijebu-Ode, *Nigeria* 170 B1
IJmuiden, *Neths.* 165 B2
IJssel →, *Neths.* 165 B3
IJsselmeer, *Neths.* 165 B3
Ikalamavony, *Madag.* 152 C2
Ikale, *Nigeria* 170 B2
Ikaluktutiak, *Canada* 66 C6
Ikang, *Nigeria* 170 C2
Ikara, *Nigeria* 170 A2
Ikare, *Nigeria* 170 B2
Ikaría, *Greece* 109 C5
Ikeda, *Japan* 136 F3
Ikeja, *Nigeria* 170 B1
Ikela, *Dem. Rep. of the Congo* 86 C3
Ikerre-Ekiti, *Nigeria* 170 B2
Iki, *Japan* 136 G1
Ikire, *Nigeria* 170 B1
Ikom, *Nigeria* 170 B2
Ikongo, *Madag.* 152 C2
Ikopa →, *Madag.* 152 B2
Ikot Ekpene, *Nigeria* 170 B2
Ikurun, *Nigeria* 170 B1
Ila, *Nigeria* 170 B1
Ilagan, *Phil.* 184 C4
Ilaka, *Madag.* 152 B2
Īlām, *Iran* 126 B3
Ilan, *Taiwan* 215 B2
Ilanskiy, *Russia* 191 D9
Ilaro, *Nigeria* 170 B1
Iława, *Poland* 186 B3
Île-de-France □, *France* 101 B5
Ilebo, *Dem. Rep. of the Congo* 86 C3
Ilek, *Russia* 190 D5
Ilero, *Nigeria* 170 B1
Ilesha, *Kwara, Nigeria* 170 B1
Ilesha, *Oyo, Nigeria* 170 B1
Ilfracombe, *Australia* 45 D7
Ilhéus, *Brazil* 58 C5
Ili →, *Kazakstan* 140 B4
Ilichevsk, *Azerbaijan* 40 B2
Iligan, *Phil.* 184 G6
Iligan Bay, *Phil.* 184 G6
Ilin I., *Phil.* 184 E4
Illampu = Ancohuma, Nevada, *Bolivia* 55 B1
Illana B., *Phil.* 184 H5
Illapel, *Chile* 79 C1
Iller →, *Germany* 106 D3
Illimani, Nevado, *Bolivia* 55 B1
Illinois □, *U.S.A.* 231 B9
Illinois →, *U.S.A.* 231 C8
Illium = Troy, *Turkey* 220 B1
Illizi, *Algeria* 36 C4
Ilo, *Peru* 183 D3
Ilobu, *Nigeria* 170 B1
Iloilo, *Phil.* 184 F5
Ilora, *Nigeria* 170 B1
Ilorin, *Nigeria* 170 B1
Ilwaki, *Indonesia* 125 D7
Imabari, *Japan* 136 F3
Imaloto →, *Madag.* 152 C2
Imandra, Ozero, *Russia* 190 C3
Imanombo, *Madag.* 152 C2
Imari, *Japan* 136 G1
Imatra, *Finland* 99 B3
Imbabura □, *Ecuador* 94 A2
imeni 26 Bakinskikh Komissarov = Neftçala, *Azerbaijan* 40 B4
imeni 26 Bakinskikh Komissarov, *Turkmenistan* 221 C1
Imerimandroso, *Madag.* 152 B2
Imi, *Ethiopia* 98 C3
Imishly = Imişli, *Azerbaijan* 40 B4
Imişli, *Azerbaijan* 40 B4
Imo □, *Nigeria* 170 B2
Imo →, *Nigeria* 170 C2
Ímola, *Italy* 132 B3
Imperatriz, *Brazil* 58 B4
Impéria, *Italy* 132 C2
Impfondo, *Congo* 86 B2
Imphal, *India* 118 B4
In Salah, *Algeria* 36 C3
Ina, *Japan* 136 F5
Inangahua Junction, *N.Z.* 167 D3
Inanwatan, *Indonesia* 125 C8
Iñapari, *Peru* 183 C4
Inari, *Finland* 99 A3
Inarijärvi, *Finland* 99 A3
Inawashiro-Ko, *Japan* 136 E7
Inca, *Spain* 207 C7
İnce Burun, *Turkey* 220 A2
Inch'ŏn, *S. Korea* 142 D2
Incomáti →, *Mozam.* 162 D1
Indalsälven →, *Sweden* 211 B3
Indaw, *Burma* 63 C4
Independence Fjord, *Greenland* 43 A5
India ■, *Asia* 118
Indian Ocean 122
Indiana □, *U.S.A.* 231 C9
Indianapolis, *U.S.A.* 231 C9
Indigirka →, *Russia* 191 B14
Indo-China, *Asia* 10 H14
Indonesia ■, *Asia* 124
Indore, *India* 118 B2
Indravati →, *India* 118 C3
Indre →, *France* 100 C4
Indus →, *Pakistan* 179 G4
İnebolu, *Turkey* 220 A2
Ingapirca, *Ecuador* 94 C2
Ingham, *Australia* 45 C8
Inglewood, *N.Z.* 167 C5
Ingólfshöfði, *Iceland* 117 C5
Ingolstadt, *Germany* 106 D3
Ingore, *Guinea-Biss.* 112 A1
Ingulec = Inhulec, *Ukraine* 223 B3
Inguri → = Enguri →, *Georgia* 104 A2
Ingushetia □, *Russia* 190 E4
Ingwavuma, *S. Africa* 205 B4
Inhambane, *Mozam.* 162 C2
Inharrime, *Mozam.* 162 C2
Inhulec, *Ukraine* 223 B3
Ining = Yining, *China* 80 B2
Inírida →, *Colombia* 85 C3
Inishbofin, *Ireland* 128 C1
Inisheer, *Ireland* 128 C2
Inishfree B., *Ireland* 128 A3
Inishkea North, *Ireland* 128 B1
Inishkea South, *Ireland* 128 B1
Inishmaan, *Ireland* 128 C2
Inishmore, *Ireland* 128 C2
Inishowen Pen., *Ireland* 128 A4
Inishshark, *Ireland* 128 C1
Inishturk, *Ireland* 128 C1
Inishvickillane, *Ireland* 128 D1
Injune, *Australia* 45 E8
Inland Sea = Setonaikai, *Japan* 136 F3
Inle L., *Burma* 63 E4
Inn →, *Austria* 49 A3
Inner Hebrides, *U.K.* 224 C3
Inner Mongolia = Nei Monggol Zizhiqu □, *China* 81 B5
Innisfail, *Australia* 45 C8
In'noshima, *Japan* 136 F3
Innsbruck, *Austria* 49 B2
Inny →, *Ireland* 128 C4
Inongo, *Dem. Rep. of the Congo* 86 C2
Inoucdjouac = Inukjuak, *Canada* 67 D9
Inowrocław, *Poland* 186 B3
Inpundong, *N. Korea* 142 B2
Insein, *Burma* 63 G4
Inta, *Russia* 190 C5
Interlaken, *Switz.* 213 B2
Inukjuak, *Canada* 67 D9
Inuvik, *Canada* 66 C3
Invercargill, *N.Z.* 167 G2
Inverell, *Australia* 45 E9
Invergordon, *U.K.* 224 C4
Inverness, *U.K.* 224 C4
Inverurie, *U.K.* 224 C5
Investigator Group, *Australia* 44 F5
Investigator Str., *Australia* 45 G6
Inya, *Russia* 190 D8
Inyanga, *Zimbabwe* 241 A2
Inyangani, *Zimbabwe* 241 A2
Inyantue, *Zimbabwe* 241 A1
Inza, *Russia* 190 D4
Ioánnina, *Greece* 109 B2
Iokea, *Papua N. G.* 181 E4
Ioma, *Papua N. G.* 181 E4
Ionian Is. = Iónioi Nísoi, *Greece* 109 B2
Ionian Sea, *Medit. S.* 28 H9
Iónioi Nísoi, *Greece* 109 B2
Íos, *Greece* 109 C4
Iowa □, *U.S.A.* 231 B8
Iowa City, *U.S.A.* 231 B8
Ipiales, *Colombia* 85 C1
Ipin = Yibin, *China* 80 D4
Ipoh, *Malaysia* 154 B2
Ippy, *C.A.R.* 77 B3
Ipswich, *Australia* 45 E9
Ipswich, *U.K.* 224 E7
Iqaluit, *Canada* 67 C10
Iquique, *Chile* 79 B1
Iquitos, *Peru* 183 A3
Iracoubo, *Fr. Guiana* 115 A3
Iráklion, *Greece* 109 D4
Iran ■, *Asia* 126
Iran, Gunung-Gunung, *Malaysia* 154 B4
Iran, Plateau of, *Asia* 10 F9
Iran Ra. = Iran, Gunung-Gunung, *Malaysia* 154 B4
Iranamadu Tank, *Sri Lanka* 209 B2
Īrānshahr, *Iran* 127 D7
Irapuato, *Mexico* 158 C4
Iraq ■, *Asia* 126
Irbid, *Jordan* 139 A1
Ireland ■, *Europe* 128
Ireland I., *Bermuda* 42 B2
Irele, *Nigeria* 170 B2
Irhyangdong, *N. Korea* 142 B3
Iri, *S. Korea* 142 E2
Irian Jaya □, *Indonesia* 125 C9
Iriba, *Chad* 78 B3
Irié, *Guinea* 112 B3
Iriga, *Phil.* 184 E5
Iringa, *Tanzania* 217 B3
Irish Sea, *U.K.* 224 E4
Irkeshtam = Erkech-Tam, *Kyrgyzstan* 144 C3
Irkutsk, *Russia* 191 D10
Irō-Zaki, *Japan* 136 F6
Iron Knob, *Australia* 45 F6
Iron Mountain, *U.S.A.* 231 A9
Ironwood, *U.S.A.* 231 A8
Irosin, *Phil.* 184 E6
Irrawaddy □, *Burma* 63 G3
Irrawaddy →, *Burma* 63 H3
Irrawaddy, Mouths of the, *Burma* 63 H3
Irtysh →, *Russia* 190 C6
Irún, *Spain* 207 A5
Irunea = Pamplona, *Spain* 207 A5
Irvine, *U.K.* 224 D4
Isa, *Nigeria* 170 A2
Isaac →, *Australia* 45 D8
Isabela, *Phil.* 184 H5
Isabela, *Puerto Rico* 75 A1
Ísafjarðardjúp, *Iceland* 117 A2
Ísafjörður, *Iceland* 117 A2
Isahaya, *Japan* 136 G2
Isanlu Makutu, *Nigeria* 170 B2
Isar →, *Germany* 106 D4
Íschia, *Italy* 133 D4
Ise, *Japan* 136 F5
Ise-Wan, *Japan* 136 F5
Isère →, *France* 101 D6
Isérnia, *Italy* 133 D5
Iseyin, *Nigeria* 170 B1
Isfahan = Eşfahān, *Iran* 127 B4
Isfana, *Kyrgyzstan* 144 C1
Isfara, *Tajikistan* 216 A3
Ishëm, *Albania* 35 B1
Ishikari-Gawa →, *Japan* 136 B7
Ishikari-Sammyaku, *Japan* 136 B8
Ishikari-Wan, *Japan* 136 B7
Ishim, *Russia* 190 D6
Ishim →, *Russia* 190 D7
Ishinomaki, *Japan* 136 D7
Ishioka, *Japan* 136 E7
Ishkashim, *Tajikistan* 216 C3
Ishkuman, *Pakistan* 179 A7
Ishpeming, *U.S.A.* 231 A9
Isil Kul, *Russia* 190 D7
Isiolo, *Kenya* 141 A2
Isiro, *Dem. Rep. of the Congo* 86 B4
Iskandar, *Uzbekistan* 221 B5
İskenderun, *Turkey* 220 B3
İskenderun Körfezi, *Turkey* 220 B3
Iski-Naukat = Eski-Nookat, *Kyrgyzstan* 144 B3
Iskŭr →, *Bulgaria* 61 B2
Islamabad, *Pakistan* 179 C7
Island Harbour, *Anguilla* 71 A1
Island L., *Canada* 66 D7
Islands, B. of, *N.Z.* 167 A5
Islay, *U.K.* 224 D3
Isle →, *France* 100 D3
Isle of Wight □, *U.K.* 224 F6
Isle Royale, *U.S.A.* 231 A9
Ismail = Izmayil, *Ukraine* 223 B2
Ismâ'iliya, *Egypt* 95 A2
Isna, *Egypt* 95 B2
Isoanala, *Madag.* 152 C2
Isparta, *Turkey* 220 B2
Íspica, *Italy* 133 F5
Israel ■, *Asia* 130
Issia, *Ivory C.* 134 B1
Issoire, *France* 101 D5
Issyk-Kul = Balykchy, *Kyrgyzstan* 144 A5
Issyk-Kul, Ozero = Ysyk-Köl, *Kyrgyzstan* 144 A5
İstanbul, *Turkey* 220 A1
İstanbul Boğazı, *Turkey* 220 A1
Istiaía, *Greece* 109 B3
Istra, *Croatia* 89 B2
Istres, *France* 101 E6
Istria = Istra, *Croatia* 89 B2
Itabira, *Brazil* 58 C4
Itabuna, *Brazil* 58 C5
Itacoatiara, *Brazil* 58 B3
Itajaí, *Brazil* 58 D4
Italy ■, *Europe* 132
Itampolo, *Madag.* 152 C1
Itandrano, *Madag.* 152 C2
Itapicuru →, *Brazil* 58 C5
Itbayat, *Phil.* 184 A4
Ithaca = Itháki, *Greece* 109 B2
Ithaca, *U.S.A.* 231 B11
Itháki, *Greece* 109 B2
Itō, *Japan* 136 F6
Itoigawa, *Japan* 136 E5
Itonamas →, *Bolivia* 55 A2
Itsa, *Egypt* 95 B2
Itu, *Nigeria* 170 B2
Iturup, Ostrov, *Russia* 191 E14
Itzehoe, *Germany* 106 B2
Ivahona, *Madag.* 152 C2
Ivanava, *Belarus* 51 C2
Ivanhoe, *Australia* 45 F7
Ivano-Frankivsk, *Ukraine* 223 B1
Ivano-Frankovsk = Ivano-Frankivsk, *Ukraine* 223 B1
Ivanovka, *Kyrgyzstan* 144 A4
Ivanovo = Ivanava, *Belarus* 51 C2
Ivanovo, *Russia* 190 D4
Ivato, *Madag.* 152 C2
Ivatsevichy, *Belarus* 51 C2
Ivindo →, *Gabon* 103 B3
Ivohibe, *Madag.* 152 C2
Ivory Coast ■, *Africa* 134
Ivrea, *Italy* 132 B1
Ivujivik, *Canada* 67 C9
Ivy, *Barbados* 72 B1
Iwaizumi, *Japan* 136 D7
Iwaki, *Japan* 136 E7
Iwakuni, *Japan* 136 F3
Iwamizawa, *Japan* 136 B7
Iwanai, *Japan* 136 B7
Iwata, *Japan* 136 F5
Iwate-San, *Japan* 136 D7
Iwo, *Nigeria* 170 B1
Ixiamas, *Bolivia* 55 A1
Ixopo, *S. Africa* 205 C4
Iyo, *Japan* 136 G3
Izhevsk, *Russia* 190 D5
Izmayil, *Ukraine* 223 B2
İzmir, *Turkey* 220 B1
İzmit = Kocaeli, *Turkey* 220 A1
İznik Gölü, *Turkey* 220 A1
Izra, *Syria* 214 C2
Izu-Shotō, *Japan* 136 F7
Izumi-Sano, *Japan* 136 F4
Izumo, *Japan* 136 F3

J

Ja-ela, *Sri Lanka* 209 C1
Jabalpur, *India* 118 B2
Jabbūl, *Syria* 214 A2
Jablah, *Syria* 214 B2
Jablonec nad Nisou, *Czech Rep.* 92 A2
Jaboatão, *Brazil* 58 B5
Jaca, *Spain* 207 A5
Jackson, *Barbados* 72 B1
Jackson, *Mich., U.S.A.* 231 B10
Jackson, *Miss., U.S.A.* 231 D8
Jackson, *Tenn., U.S.A.* 231 C9
Jackson B., *N.Z.* 167 E2
Jacksons, *N.Z.* 167 E3
Jacksonville, *U.S.A.* 231 D10
Jacmel, *Haiti* 73 B2
Jacobabad, *Pakistan* 179 E5
Jacqueville, *Ivory C.* 134 B2
Jadotville = Likasi, *Dem. Rep. of the Congo* 86 E4
Jaén, *Peru* 183 B2
Jaén, *Spain* 206 D4
Jaffa = Tel Aviv-Yafo, *Israel* 130 B1
Jaffna, *Sri Lanka* 209 B2
Jagdalpur, *India* 118 C3
Jagersfontein, *S. Africa* 205 B3
Jagodina, *Serbia, Yug.* 239 C2
Jagüey Grande, *Cuba* 90 A1
Jahrom, *Iran* 127 C5
Jailolo, *Indonesia* 125 B7
Jailolo, Selat, *Indonesia* 125 B7
Jaipur, *India* 118 B2
Jakarta, *Indonesia* 124 D3
Jakupica, *Macedonia* 151 B2
Jalal-Abad, *Kyrgyzstan* 144 B3
Jalālābād, *Afghan.* 34 B3
Jalapa Enríquez, *Mexico* 158 D5
Jalingo, *Nigeria* 170 B3
Jalna, *India* 118 C2
Jalón →, *Spain* 207 B5
Jamaari, *Nigeria* 170 A2
Jamaica ■, *W. Indies* 74
Jamalpur, *Bangla.* 50 B2
Jambi, *Indonesia* 124 C2
Jambi □, *Indonesia* 124 C2
James →, *U.S.A.* 231 B7
James B., *Canada* 67 D9
Jamestown, *Australia* 45 F6
Jamestown, *S. Africa* 205 C3
Jamestown, *N. Dak., U.S.A.* 230 A7
Jamestown, *N.Y., U.S.A.* 231 B11
Jammu, *India* 118 A2
Jammu & Kashmir □, *India* 118 A2
Jamnagar, *India* 118 B2
Jamshedpur, *India* 118 B3
Jan Mayen, *Arctic* 32 B6
Jand, *Pakistan* 179 C7
Jandaq, *Iran* 127 B5
Janesville, *U.S.A.* 231 B9
Janga, *Ghana* 108 A2
Jangy-Bazar, *Kyrgyzstan* 144 B2
Jangy-Jol, *Kyrgyzstan* 144 B3
Janjina, *Madag.* 152 C2
Januária, *Brazil* 58 C4
Japan ■, *Asia* 136
Japan, Sea of, *Asia* 10 E17
Japan Trench, *Pac. Oc.* 10 F18
Japen = Yapen, *Indonesia* 125 C9
Japurá →, *Brazil* 58 B2
Jaqué, *Panama* 88 B3
Jarābulus, *Syria* 214 A2
Jarama →, *Spain* 206 B4
Jardines de la Reina, Arch. de los, *Cuba* 90 B2
Jargalant = Hovd, *Mongolia* 160 B2
Jari →, *Brazil* 58 B3
Jarosław, *Poland* 186 C5
Jarres, Plaine des, *Laos* 145 C2
Jāsk, *Iran* 127 D6
Jasło, *Poland* 186 D4
Jason Is., *Falk. Is.* 43 A1
Jasper, *Canada* 66 D5
Jászberény, *Hungary* 116 B2
Jatibarang, *Indonesia* 124 D3
Jatinegara, *Indonesia* 124 D3
Játiva = Xátiva, *Spain* 207 C5
Jauja, *Peru* 183 C2
Jaunpur, *India* 118 B3
Java = Jawa, *Indonesia* 124 D4
Java Barat □, *Indonesia* 124 D3
Java Sea, *Indonesia* 124 C3
Java Tengah □, *Indonesia* 124 D4
Java Timur □, *Indonesia* 124 D4
Javhlant = Ulyasutay, *Mongolia* 160 B2
Jawa, *Indonesia* 124 D4
Jaya, Puncak, *Indonesia* 125 C9
Jayapura, *Indonesia* 125 C10
Jayawijaya, Pegunungan, *Indonesia* 125 D9
Jayrūd, *Syria* 214 C2
Jazzīn, *Lebanon* 147 B1
Jean Rabel, *Haiti* 73 B2
Jeanette, Ostrov = Zhannetty, Ostrov, *Russia* 191 B15
Jebba, *Nigeria* 170 B1
Jebel, Bahr el →, *Sudan* 210 D3
Jedburgh, *U.K.* 224 D5
Jedda = Jiddah, *Si. Arabia* 196 C2
Jędrzejów, *Poland* 186 C4
Jega, *Nigeria* 170 A1
Jēkabpils, *Latvia* 146 B3
Jelenia Góra, *Poland* 186 C1
Jelgava, *Latvia* 146 B2
Jember, *Indonesia* 124 D4
Jembongan, *Malaysia* 154 A5
Jena, *Germany* 106 C3
Jendouba, *Tunisia* 219 A1
Jequié, *Brazil* 58 C4
Jequitinhonha →, *Brazil* 58 C5
Jérémie, *Haiti* 73 B1
Jerez de la Frontera, *Spain* 206 D2
Jerez de los Caballeros, *Spain* 206 C2
Jerid, Chott = Djerid, Chott, *Tunisia* 219 B1
Jersey, *U.K.* 100 B2
Jersey City, *U.S.A.* 231 B12
Jerusalem, *Israel* 130 C2
Jervis B., *Australia* 45 G9
Jesi = Iesi, *Italy* 133 C4
Jesselton = Kota Kinabalu, *Malaysia* 154 A5
Jessore, *Bangla.* 50 C2
Jhal Jhao, *Pakistan* 179 F3
Jhang Maghiana, *Pakistan* 179 D7
Jhansi, *India* 118 B2
Jhelum, *Pakistan* 179 C7
Jhelum →, *Pakistan* 179 D7
Jiamusi, *China* 81 B7
Ji'an, *China* 81 D5
Jiangmen, *China* 81 D5
Jiangsu □, *China* 81 C6
Jiangxi □, *China* 81 D5
Jiaxing, *China* 81 C6
Jiayi = Chiai, *Taiwan* 215 C2
Jibiya, *Nigeria* 170 A2
Jibuti = Djibouti ■, *Africa* 202
Jicarón, I., *Panama* 88 B2
Jiddah, *Si. Arabia* 196 C2
Jigawa □, *Nigeria* 170 A2
Jihlava, *Czech Rep.* 92 B2
Jihlava →, *Czech Rep.* 92 B3
Jijiga, *Ethiopia* 98 C3
Jikamshi, *Nigeria* 170 A2
Jilin, *China* 81 B6
Jilong = Chilung, *Taiwan* 215 B2
Jima, *Ethiopia* 98 C2
Jiménez, *Mexico* 158 B4
Jinan, *China* 81 C5
Jindřichův Hradec, *Czech Rep.* 92 B2
Jingdezhen, *China* 81 D5
Jinggu, *China* 80 D4
Jinhua, *China* 81 D5
Jining, *Nei Monggol Zizhiqu, China* 81 B5
Jining, *Shandong, China* 81 C5
Jinja, *Uganda* 222 B2
Jinjini, *Ghana* 108 B1
Jinnah Barrage, *Pakistan* 179 C6
Jinzhou, *China* 81 B6
Jipijapa, *Ecuador* 94 B1
Jisr ash Shughūr, *Syria* 214 B2
Jiu →, *Romania* 188 C2
Jiujiang, *China* 81 D5
Jixi, *China* 81 B7
Jīzān, *Si. Arabia* 196 D3
Jizō-Zaki, *Japan* 136 F3
Jizzakh, *Uzbekistan* 221 B4
Joal Fadiout, *Senegal* 198 B1
João Pessoa, *Brazil* 58 B5
Jodhpur, *India* 118 B2
Joensuu, *Finland* 99 B3
Jōetsu, *Japan* 136 E6
Jõgeva, *Estonia* 97 B4
Jogjakarta = Yogyakarta, *Indonesia* 124 D4
Johannesburg, *S. Africa* 205 B3
John Crow Mts., *Jamaica* 74 A2
John Day →, *U.S.A.* 230 A2
Johnson City, *U.S.A.* 231 C10
Johnston, L., *Australia* 44 F3

M

Mashonaland East

Magarida, *Papua N. G.* 181 F5
Magburaka, *S. Leone* 148 A1
Magdalen Is. = Madeleine, Îs. de la, *Canada* 67 E10
Magdalena, *Bolivia* 55 A2
Magdalena →, *Colombia* 85 A2
Magdeburg, *Germany* 106 B3
Magelang, *Indonesia* 124 D4
Magellan's Str. = Magallanes, Estrecho de, *Chile* 79 E1
Maggia →, *Switz.* 213 B3
Maggiore, Lago, *Italy* 132 B2
Maggotty, *Jamaica* 74 A2
Maghâgha, *Egypt* 95 B2
Magistralnyy, *Russia* 191 D10
Magnetic Pole (North) = North Magnetic Pole, *Canada* 67 B6
Magnitogorsk, *Russia* 190 D5
Magoro, *Uganda* 222 B2
Magosa = Famagusta, *Cyprus* 91 A2
Mağusa = Famagusta, *Cyprus* 91 A2
Magwe, *Burma* 63 E3
Maha Oya, *Sri Lanka* 209 C2
Maha Sarakham, *Thailand* 218 C3
Mahābād, *Iran* 126 A3
Mahabo, *Madag.* 152 C1
Mahajamba →, *Madag.* 152 B2
Mahajamba, Helodranon' i, *Madag.* 152 B2
Mahajanga, *Madag.* 152 B2
Mahajanga □, *Madag.* 152 B2
Mahajilo →, *Madag.* 152 B2
Mahakam →, *Indonesia* 124 C5
Mahalapye, *Botswana* 57 B2
Maḩallāt, *Iran* 126 B4
Mahanoro, *Madag.* 152 B2
Maharashtra □, *India* 118 B2
Maharès, *Tunisia* 219 B2
Mahasoa, *Madag.* 152 C2
Mahasolo, *Madag.* 152 B2
Mahavavy →, *Madag.* 152 B2
Mahaweli Ganga →, *Sri Lanka* 209 B2
Mahaxay, *Laos* 145 D3
Mahdia, *Tunisia* 219 A2
Mahé, *Seychelles* 123 B1
Mahebourg, *Mauritius* 123 B2
Mahenge, *Tanzania* 217 B3
Maheno, *N.Z.* 167 F3
Mahia Pen., *N.Z.* 167 C6
Mahilyow, *Belarus* 51 C5
Maho, *Sri Lanka* 209 C2
Mahón = Maó, *Spain* 207 C8
Mahoua, *Chad* 78 C2
Mahuta, *Nigeria* 170 A1
Mai-Ndombe, L., *Dem. Rep. of the Congo* 86 C2
Mai-Sai, *Thailand* 218 A1
Maidstone, *U.K.* 224 F7
Maiduguri, *Nigeria* 170 A3
Maigatari, *Nigeria* 170 A2
Maigo, *Phil.* 184 G5
Maijdi, *Bangla.* 50 C3
Main →, *Germany* 106 C2
Main Ridge, *Trin. & Tob.* 76 A5
Maine, *France* 100 C3
Maine □, *U.S.A.* 231 A13
Maine →, *Ireland* 128 D2
Maingkwan, *Burma* 63 B4
Mainit, L., *Phil.* 184 G6
Mainland, *Orkney, U.K.* 224 B5
Mainland, *Shet., U.K.* 224 A6
Maintirano, *Madag.* 152 B1
Mainz, *Germany* 106 C2
Maio, *C. Verde Is.* 42 B2
Maiquetía, *Venezuela* 236 A2
Maisí, *Cuba* 90 B3
Maisí, Pta. de, *Cuba* 90 B3
Maitland, *Australia* 45 F9
Maiyema, *Nigeria* 170 A1
Maizuru, *Japan* 136 F4
Majene, *Indonesia* 125 C5
Majorca = Mallorca, *Spain* 207 C7
Maka, *Senegal* 198 B2
Makaha, *Zimbabwe* 241 A2
Makak, *Cameroon* 65 C2
Makakou, *Gabon* 103 B3
Makalamabedi, *Botswana* 57 B1
Makale, *Indonesia* 125 C5
Makamba, *Burundi* 195 C1
Makarikari = Makgadikgadi Salt Pans, *Botswana* 57 B2
Makarovo, *Russia* 191 D10
Makasar = Ujung Pandang, *Indonesia* 125 D5
Makasar, Selat, *Indonesia* 125 C5
Makasar, Str. of = Makasar, Selat, *Indonesia* 125 C5
Makat, *Kazakstan* 140 B2
Makedhonía □, *Greece* 109 A3
Makedonija = Macedonia ■, *Europe* 151
Makeni, *S. Leone* 148 A1
Makeyevka = Makiyivka, *Ukraine* 223 B4
Makgadikgadi Salt Pans, *Botswana* 57 B2
Makhachkala, *Russia* 190 E4
Makharadze = Ozurgeti, *Georgia* 104 B2
Makian, *Indonesia* 125 B7
Makindu, *Kenya* 141 B2
Makinsk, *Kazakstan* 140 A4
Makiyivka, *Ukraine* 223 B4
Makkah, *Si. Arabia* 196 C2
Makó, *Hungary* 116 B3
Mako, *Senegal* 198 B2
Makok, *Gabon* 103 B1
Makokou, *Gabon* 103 A3
Makran Coast Range, *Pakistan* 179 G3
Maktar, *Tunisia* 219 A1
Mākū, *Iran* 126 A3
Makunda, *Botswana* 57 B1
Makung, *Taiwan* 215 C1
Makurazaki, *Japan* 136 H2
Makurdi, *Nigeria* 170 B2
Makwassie, *S. Africa* 205 B3
Makwiro, *Zimbabwe* 241 A2
Mal B., *Ireland* 128 D2
Mala, Pta., *Panama* 88 B2
Malabang, *Phil.* 184 H6
Malabar Coast, *India* 118 C2
Malabo = Rey Malabo, *Eq. Guin.* 103 A1
Malabon, *Phil.* 184 D4
Malabu, *Nigeria* 170 B3
Malacca, Str. of, *Indonesia* 124 B2
Maladzyechna, *Belarus* 51 B3
Málaga, *Spain* 206 D3
Malagasy Rep. = Madagascar ■, *Africa* 152
Malahide, *Ireland* 128 C5
Malaimbandy, *Madag.* 152 C2
Malaita, *Solomon Is.* 178 A2
Malakâl, *Sudan* 210 D3
Malakand, *Pakistan* 179 B6
Malakula, *Vanuatu* 178 B2
Malalaua, *Papua N. G.* 181 E4
Malam, *Chad* 78 C3
Malamala, *Indonesia* 125 C6
Malang, *Indonesia* 124 D4
Malanje, *Angola* 37 A2
Mälaren, *Sweden* 211 C3
Malaryta, *Belarus* 51 D2
Malatya, *Turkey* 220 B3
Malawi ■, *Africa* 153
Malawi, L. = Nyasa, L., *Africa* 4 H7
Malay Pen., *Asia* 10 J14
Malaybalay, *Phil.* 184 G6
Malāyer, *Iran* 126 B4
Malaysia ■, *Asia* 154
Malazgirt, *Turkey* 220 B4
Malbork, *Poland* 186 B3
Malcolm, *Australia* 44 E3
Maldegem, *Belgium* 52 A2
Malden I., *Kiribati* 176 B5
Maldives ■, *Ind. Oc.* 123
Maldonado, *Uruguay* 235 B2
Malé, *Maldives* 123 C2
Malé Atoll, *Maldives* 123 C2
Malé Karpaty, *Slovak Rep.* 200 A1
Maléa, Ákra, *Greece* 109 C3
Malema, *Mozam.* 162 A2
Malendok I., *Papua N. G.* 181 B7
Malha, *Sudan* 210 B2
Malheur L., *U.S.A.* 230 B3
Mali, *Guinea* 112 A2
Mali ■, *Africa* 156
Mali →, *Burma* 63 C4
Mali Kyun, *Burma* 63 J5
Maliku, *Indonesia* 125 C6
Malili, *Indonesia* 125 C6
Malimba, Mts., *Dem. Rep. of the Congo* 86 D4
Malin Hd., *Ireland* 128 A4
Malin Pen., *Ireland* 128 A4
Malindi, *Kenya* 141 B3
Malines = Mechelen, *Belgium* 52 A3
Malino, *Indonesia* 125 B6
Maliq, *Albania* 35 C2
Mallacoota Inlet, *Australia* 45 G8
Mallaig, *U.K.* 224 C4
Mallawi, *Egypt* 95 B2
Mallembe, *Gabon* 103 B2
Mallicolo = Malakula, *Vanuatu* 178 B2
Mallorca, *Spain* 207 C7
Mallow, *Ireland* 128 D3
Malmédy, *Belgium* 52 B5
Malmesbury, *S. Africa* 204 C1
Malmö, *Sweden* 211 C2
Malo, *Vanuatu* 178 B2
Malombe L., *Malawi* 153 B2
Malosmadulu Atoll, *Maldives* 123 B2
Malpelo, I. de, *Colombia* 85 C0
Malta ■, *Europe* 91
Maltahöhe, *Namibia* 163 B2
Malu'a, *Solomon Is.* 178 A2
Maluku, *Indonesia* 125 C7
Maluku □, *Indonesia* 125 C7
Maluku Sea = Molucca Sea, *Indonesia* 125 C6
Malumfashi, *Nigeria* 170 A2
Maluwe, *Ghana* 108 B1
Malvinas, Is. = Falkland Is. □, *Atl. Oc.* 43
Malyy Lyakhovskiy, Ostrov, *Russia* 191 B14
Mama, *Russia* 191 D11
Mamasa, *Indonesia* 125 C5
Mamberamo →, *Indonesia* 125 C9
Mambéré →, *C.A.R.* 77 C2
Mambilima Falls, *Zambia* 240 B2
Mambrui, *Kenya* 141 B3
Mamburao, *Phil.* 184 E4
Mamfé, *Cameroon* 65 B1
Mamoré →, *Bolivia* 55 A1
Mamou, *Guinea* 112 A2
Mamoudzou, *Mayotte* 123 B2
Mampatá, *Guinea-Biss.* 112 A2
Mampikony, *Madag.* 152 B2
Mampong, *Ghana* 108 B2
Mamuju, *Indonesia* 125 C5
Mamuno, *Botswana* 57 B1
Mamuras, *Albania* 35 B1
Man, *Ivory C.* 134 B1
Man, I. of, *U.K.* 224 D4
Man Na, *Burma* 63 D4
Mana →, *Fr. Guiana* 115 A3
Manaar, G. of = Mannar, G. of, *Asia* 10 J11
Manabí □, *Ecuador* 94 B1
Manacor, *Spain* 207 C7
Manado, *Indonesia* 125 B6
Managua, *Nic.* 111 C2
Manakara, *Madag.* 152 C2
Manam I., *Papua N. G.* 181 C3
Manama = Al Manāmah, *Bahrain* 113 A2
Manambao →, *Madag.* 152 B1
Manambato, *Madag.* 152 A2
Manambolo →, *Madag.* 152 B1
Manambolosy, *Madag.* 152 B2
Mananara, *Madag.* 152 B2
Mananara →, *Madag.* 152 C2
Mananjary, *Madag.* 152 C2
Manantenina, *Madag.* 152 C2
Manaos = Manaus, *Brazil* 58 B3
Manapire →, *Venezuela* 236 B2
Manapouri, *N.Z.* 167 F1
Manapouri, L., *N.Z.* 167 F1
Manār, Jabal, *Yemen* 238 B1
Manaravolo, *Madag.* 152 C2
Manas, *China* 80 B2
Manas, Gora, *Kyrgyzstan* 144 A2
Manatí, *Puerto Rico* 75 A2
Manau, *Papua N. G.* 181 E4
Manaung, *Burma* 63 F2
Manaus, *Brazil* 58 B3
Manay, *Phil.* 184 H7
Manbij, *Syria* 214 A2
Manchegorsk, *Russia* 190 C3
Manchester, *U.K.* 224 E5
Manchester, *U.S.A.* 231 B12
Manchurian Plain, *China* 10 E16
Mand →, *Iran* 127 C5
Mandabé, *Madag.* 152 C1
Mandal, *Norway* 172 D2
Mandala, Puncak, *Indonesia* 125 C10
Mandalay, *Burma* 63 E4
Mandale = Mandalay, *Burma* 63 E4
Mandalī, *Iraq* 126 B3
Mandan, *U.S.A.* 230 A6
Mandaon, *Phil.* 184 E5
Mandar, Teluk, *Indonesia* 125 C5
Mandaue, *Phil.* 184 F5
Mandera, *Kenya* 141 A3
Mandeville, *Jamaica* 74 A2
Mandiana, *Guinea* 112 A3
Mandimba, *Mozam.* 162 A2
Mandioli, *Indonesia* 125 C7
Mandoto, *Madag.* 152 B2
Mandrare →, *Madag.* 152 D2
Mandritsara, *Madag.* 152 B2
Mandronarivo, *Madag.* 152 C2
Mandsaur, *India* 118 B2
Mandurah, *Australia* 44 F2
Mané, *Burkina Faso* 62 B2
Manengouba, Mts., *Cameroon* 65 C1
Manera, *Madag.* 152 C1
Manfalût, *Egypt* 95 B2
Manfredónia, *Italy* 133 D5
Manga, *Burkina Faso* 62 C2
Mangalia, *Romania* 188 D5
Mangalmé, *Chad* 78 C2
Mangalore, *India* 118 C2
Mangaweka, *N.Z.* 167 C5
Manggar, *Indonesia* 124 C3
Manggawitu, *Indonesia* 125 C8
Mangindrano, *Madag.* 152 A2
Mangkalihat, Tanjung, *Indonesia* 125 B5
Mangla Dam, *Pakistan* 179 C7
Mangnai, *China* 80 C3
Mango, *Togo* 54 B2
Mangoche, *Malawi* 153 B2
Mangoky →, *Madag.* 152 C1
Mangole, *Indonesia* 125 C6
Mangonui, *N.Z.* 167 A4
Mangoro →, *Madag.* 152 B2
Mangueigne, *Chad* 78 C3
Mangyshlak Poluostrov, *Kazakstan* 140 B2
Manhattan, *U.S.A.* 231 C7
Mania →, *Madag.* 152 B2
Manica, *Mozam.* 162 B1
Manicaland □, *Zimbabwe* 241 A2
Manicoré, *Brazil* 58 B2
Manicouagan →, *Canada* 67 E10
Manicouagan, Rés., *Canada* 67 D10
Manila, *Phil.* 184 D4
Manila B., *Phil.* 184 D4
Maninian, *Ivory C.* 134 A1
Manipur □, *India* 118 B4
Manipur →, *Burma* 63 D3
Manisa, *Turkey* 220 B1
Manistee, *U.S.A.* 231 B9
Manistique, *U.S.A.* 231 A9
Manitoba □, *Canada* 66 D7
Manitoba, L., *Canada* 66 D7
Manitoulin I., *Canada* 67 E8
Manitowoc, *U.S.A.* 231 B9
Manizales, *Colombia* 85 B1
Manja, *Madag.* 152 C1
Manjakandriana, *Madag.* 152 B2
Manjhand, *Pakistan* 179 G5
Manjimup, *Australia* 44 F2
Mankato, *U.S.A.* 231 B8
Mankayane, *Swaziland* 205 B4
Mankim, *Cameroon* 65 B3
Mankono, *Ivory C.* 134 B1
Mankulam, *Sri Lanka* 209 B2
Manna, *Indonesia* 124 C2
Mannar, *Sri Lanka* 209 B1
Mannar, G. of, *Asia* 10 J11
Mannar I., *Sri Lanka* 209 B1
Mannheim, *Germany* 106 D2
Manning, *Canada* 66 D5
Mano, *S. Leone* 148 A1
Mano →, *Liberia* 148 B1
Mano River, *Liberia* 148 B1
Manokwari, *Indonesia* 125 C8
Manombo, *Madag.* 152 C1
Manono, *Dem. Rep. of the Congo* 86 D4
Manosque, *France* 101 E6
Manp'o, *N. Korea* 142 B2
Manpojin = Manp'o, *N. Korea* 142 B2
Manresa, *Spain* 207 B6
Mansa, *Zambia* 240 B2
Mansel I., *Canada* 67 C9
Mansfield, *U.K.* 224 E6
Mansfield, *U.S.A.* 231 B10
Mansoa, *Guinea-Biss.* 112 A1
Manta, *Ecuador* 94 B1
Manta, B. de, *Ecuador* 94 B1
Mantalingajan, Mt., *Phil.* 184 G2
Mantes-la-Jolie, *France* 101 B4
Mantiqueira, Serra da, *Brazil* 20 F6
Mántova, *Italy* 132 B3
Mantua = Mántova, *Italy* 132 B3
Manu, *Peru* 183 C3
Manu →, *Peru* 183 C3
Manua Is., *Amer. Samoa* 177 B3
Manui, *Indonesia* 125 C6
Manukau, *N.Z.* 167 B5
Manuripi →, *Bolivia* 55 A1
Manus I., *Papua N. G.* 181 B4
Manych →, *Russia* 28 F14
Manzai, *Pakistan* 179 C6
Manzala, Bahra el, *Egypt* 95 A2
Manzanares, *Spain* 206 C4
Manzanillo, *Cuba* 90 B2
Manzanillo, *Mexico* 158 D4
Manzanillo, Pta., *Panama* 88 B3
Manzhouli, *China* 81 B5
Manzini, *Swaziland* 205 B4
Mao, *Chad* 78 C2
Mao, *Dom. Rep.* 72 B2
Maó, *Spain* 207 C8
Maoke, Pegunungan, *Indonesia* 125 C9
Maoming, *China* 81 D5
Mapam Yumco, *China* 80 C2
Mapfongui, *Gabon* 103 B3
Mapia, Kepulauan, *Indonesia* 125 B8
Maprik, *Papua N. G.* 181 B2
Maputo, *Mozam.* 162 D1
Maputo, B. de, *Mozam.* 4 J7
Maquela do Zombo, *Angola* 37 A2
Maquinchao, *Argentina* 38 C2
Mar, Serra do, *Brazil* 20 F6
Mar Chiquita, L., *Argentina* 38 B2
Mar del Plata, *Argentina* 38 B3
Mar Menor, *Spain* 207 D5
Marabá, *Brazil* 58 B4
Maracá, I. de, *Brazil* 58 A3
Maracaibo, *Venezuela* 236 A1
Maracaibo, L. de, *Venezuela* 236 B1
Maracay, *Venezuela* 236 A2
Maradi, *Niger* 169 C2
Marāgheh, *Iran* 126 A3
Marajó, I. de, *Brazil* 58 B4
Maralal, *Kenya* 141 A2
Maralinga, *Australia* 44 F5
Marampa, *S. Leone* 148 A1
Marand, *Iran* 126 A3
Maranhão = São Luís, *Brazil* 58 B4
Maranhão □, *Brazil* 58 B4
Maranoa →, *Australia* 45 E8
Marañón →, *Peru* 183 A3
Marão, *Mozam.* 162 C1
Maraş = Kahramanmaraş, *Turkey* 220 B3
Marathasa □, *Cyprus* 91 B1
Marathóvouno, *Cyprus* 91 A2
Maratua, *Indonesia* 125 B5
Maravari, *Solomon Is.* 178 A1
Marawi City, *Phil.* 184 H6
Marbella, *Spain* 206 D3
Marble Bar, *Australia* 44 D2
Marburg, *Germany* 106 C2
Marche, *France* 100 C4
Marche-en-Famenne, *Belgium* 52 B4
Marchena, *Spain* 206 D3
Mardan, *Pakistan* 179 B7
Mardin, *Turkey* 220 B4
Maré, I., *N. Cal.* 176 A4
Mareeba, *Australia* 45 C8
Mareetsane, *S. Africa* 205 B3
Marek = Stanke Dimitrov, *Bulgaria* 61 B1
Marenyi, *Kenya* 141 B2
Marerano, *Madag.* 152 C1
Marfa Pt., *Malta* 91 B1
Margarita, I. de, *Venezuela* 236 A3
Margate, *S. Africa* 205 C4
Margate, *U.K.* 224 F7
Marghilon = Margilan, *Uzbekistan* 221 B5
Margilan, *Uzbekistan* 221 B5
Margosatubig, *Phil.* 184 H5
Mārgow, Dasht-e, *Afghan.* 34 C1
Mari, *Papua N. G.* 181 E1
Mari El □, *Russia* 190 D4
Mari Republic = Mari El □, *Russia* 190 D4
Maria I., *Australia* 45 B6
Maria van Diemen, C., *N.Z.* 167 A4
Mariakani, *Kenya* 141 B2
Mariana Trench, *Pac. Oc.* 10 H18
Marianao, *Cuba* 90 A1
Mariato, Punta, *Panama* 88 B2
Maribor, *Slovenia* 201 A2
Marie-Galante, *Guadeloupe* 73 C2
Mariecourt = Kangiqsujuaq, *Canada* 67 C9
Mariembourg, *Belgium* 52 B3
Mariental, *Namibia* 163 B2
Mariga →, *Nigeria* 170 A2
Marigot, *Domin.* 73 A2
Marihatag, *Phil.* 184 G7
Mariinsk, *Russia* 190 D8
Marijampolė, *Lithuania* 150 B2
Marília, *Brazil* 58 D4
Marín, *Spain* 206 A1
Marion, *Ill., U.S.A.* 231 C9
Marion, *Ind., U.S.A.* 231 B9
Marion, *Ohio, U.S.A.* 231 B10
Mariscal Estigarribia, *Paraguay* 182 B1
Maritsa = Évros →, *Greece* 109 A4
Mariupol, *Ukraine* 223 B4
Marīvān, *Iran* 126 B3
Marj 'Uyūn, *Lebanon* 147 B1
Markazī □, *Iran* 126 B4
Markham →, *Papua N. G.* 181 D4
Markounda, *C.A.R.* 77 B2
Markovo, *Russia* 191 C16
Markoye, *Burkina Faso* 62 A3
Marmara, Sea of = Marmara Denizi, *Turkey* 220 A1
Marmara Denizi, *Turkey* 220 A1
Marmolada, Mte., *Italy* 132 A3
Marne →, *France* 101 B5
Marneuli, *Georgia* 104 B4
Maro, *Chad* 78 D2
Maroala, *Madag.* 152 B2
Maroantsetra, *Madag.* 152 B2
Marofandilia, *Madag.* 152 C1
Marolambo, *Madag.* 152 C2
Maromandia, *Madag.* 152 A2
Marondera, *Zimbabwe* 241 A2
Maroni →, *Fr. Guiana* 115 A3
Marosakoa, *Madag.* 152 B2
Maroseranana, *Madag.* 152 B2
Marotandrano, *Madag.* 152 B2
Marotaolano, *Madag.* 152 A2
Maroua, *Cameroon* 65 A2
Marovato, *Madag.* 152 B2
Marovoay, *Madag.* 152 B2
Marquard, *S. Africa* 205 B3
Marquesas Is. = Marquises, Is., *Pac. Oc.* 2 E3
Marquette, *U.S.A.* 231 A9
Marquis, *St. Lucia* 75 A2
Marquises, Is., *Pac. Oc.* 2 E3
Marra, Djebel, *Sudan* 210 C1
Marrakech, *Morocco* 161 B4
Marree, *Australia* 45 E6
Marrupa, *Mozam.* 162 A2
Marsá 'Alam, *Egypt* 95 B2
Marsá Matrûh, *Egypt* 95 A1
Marsabit, *Kenya* 141 A2
Marsala, *Italy* 132 F4
Marsalforn, *Malta* 91 A1
Marseille, *France* 101 E6
Marseilles = Marseille, *France* 101 E6
Marsh Harbour, *Bahamas* 71 A1
Marsh I., *U.S.A.* 231 E8
Marshall, *Liberia* 148 B1
Marshall, *U.S.A.* 231 D8
Marshall Bennett Is., *Papua N. G.* 181 E6
Marshall Is. ■, *Pac. Oc.* 3 D18
Marshbrook, *Zimbabwe* 241 A2
Martaban, *Burma* 63 G4
Martaban, G. of, *Burma* 63 G4
Martapura, *Kalimantan, Indonesia* 124 C4
Martapura, *Sumatera, Indonesia* 124 C2
Marte, *Nigeria* 170 A3
Martelange, *Belgium* 52 C4
Martha's Vineyard, *U.S.A.* 231 B12
Martigny, *Switz.* 213 B2
Martigues, *France* 101 E6
Martin, *Slovak Rep.* 200 A2
Martina Franca, *Italy* 133 D6
Martinborough, *N.Z.* 167 D5
Martinique ■, *W. Indies* 74
Martin's Bay, *Barbados* 72 B2
Marton, *N.Z.* 167 D5
Martos, *Spain* 206 D4
Martuni, *Armenia* 40 A2
Maru, *Nigeria* 170 A2
Marudi, *Malaysia* 154 B4
Ma'ruf, *Afghan.* 34 C2
Marugame, *Japan* 136 F3
Marui = Pagwi, *Papua N. G.* 181 C2
Mary, *Turkmenistan* 221 C3
Maryborough = Port Laoise, *Ireland* 128 C4
Maryborough, *Queens., Australia* 45 E9
Maryborough, *Vic., Australia* 45 G7
Maryland □, *U.S.A.* 231 C11
Maryland Junction, *Zimbabwe* 241 A2
Marystown, *Canada* 67 E11
Marzūq, *Libya* 149 B2
Masaka, *Uganda* 222 C2
Masalembo, Kepulauan, *Indonesia* 124 D4
Masalima, Kepulauan, *Indonesia* 124 D5
Masallı, *Azerbaijan* 40 B4
Masamba, *Indonesia* 125 C6
Masan, *S. Korea* 142 E3
Masandam, Ra's, *Oman* 113 A3
Masasi, *Tanzania* 217 C3
Masaya, *Nic.* 111 C2
Masba, *Nigeria* 170 A3
Masbate, *Phil.* 184 E5
Mascara, *Algeria* 36 A3
Masela, *Indonesia* 125 D7
Maseru, *Lesotho* 205 B3
Mashaba, *Zimbabwe* 241 B2
Mashegu, *Nigeria* 170 B2
Mashhad, *Iran* 127 A6
Mashi, *Nigeria* 170 A2
Māshkel, Hāmūn-i-, *Pakistan* 179 E2
Mashki Chāh, *Pakistan* 179 E2
Mashonaland Central □, *Zimbabwe* 241 A2
Mashonaland East □, *Zimbabwe* 241 A2

Mashonaland West

Mashonaland West □, Zimbabwe 241 A1
Mashtaga = Maştağa, Azerbaijan 40 A5
Masindi, Uganda 222 B2
Masindi Port, Uganda 222 B2
Maşīrah, Oman 113 B3
Maşīrah, Khalīj, Oman 113 B3
Masjed Soleyman, Iran 126 C4
Mask, L., Ireland 128 C2
Masoala, Tanjon' i, Madag. 152 B3
Masoarivo, Madag. 152 B1
Masohi = Amahai, Indonesia 125 C7
Masomeloka, Madag. 152 C2
Mason City, U.S.A. 231 B8
Masqat, Oman 113 B3
Massa, Italy 132 B3
Massachusetts □, U.S.A. 231 B12
Massaguet, Chad 78 C2
Massakory, Chad 78 C2
Massangena, Mozam. 162 C1
Massango, Angola 37 A2
Massawa = Mitsiwa, Eritrea 98 A2
Massénya, Chad 78 C2
Massif Central, France 101 D5
Massima, Gabon 103 B2
Massinga, Mozam. 162 C2
Massouka, Gabon 103 B1
Maştağa, Azerbaijan 40 A5
Mastanli = Momchilgrad, Bulgaria 61 C2
Masterton, N.Z. 167 D5
Mastuj, Pakistan 179 A7
Mastung, Pakistan 179 E4
Masty, Belarus 51 C2
Masuda, Japan 136 F2
Masvingo, Zimbabwe 241 B2
Masvingo □, Zimbabwe 241 B2
Maşyāf, Syria 214 B2
Mat →, Albania 35 B1
Matabeleland North □, Zimbabwe 241 A1
Matabeleland South □, Zimbabwe 241 B1
Matadi, Dem. Rep. of the Congo 86 D1
Matagalpa, Nic. 111 C2
Matagami, Canada 67 E9
Matagami, L., Canada 67 E9
Matagorda I., U.S.A. 231 E7
Matak, Indonesia 124 B3
Matale, Sri Lanka 209 C2
Matam, Senegal 198 A2
Matamoros, Coahuila, Mexico 158 B4
Matamoros, Tamaulipas, Mexico 158 B5
Ma'ṭan as Sarra, Libya 149 C4
Matane, Canada 67 E10
Matanzas, Cuba 90 A1
Matapa, Botswana 57 B1
Matapan, C. = Taínaron, Ákra, Greece 109 C3
Matara, Sri Lanka 209 D2
Mataram, Indonesia 124 D5
Matarani, Peru 183 D3
Mataranka, Australia 44 B5
Mataró, Spain 207 B7
Matatiele, S. Africa 205 C3
Mataura, N.Z. 167 G2
Matehuala, Mexico 158 C4
Mateke Hills, Zimbabwe 241 B2
Matelot, Trin. & Tob. 76 C2
Matera, Italy 133 D6
Matetsi, Zimbabwe 241 A1
Mateur, Tunisia 219 A1
Mathráki, Greece 109 B1
Mathura, India 118 B2
Mati, Phil. 184 H7
Matiakoali, Burkina Faso 62 B3
Matima, Botswana 57 B1
Matiri Ra., N.Z. 167 D4
Matjiesfontein, S. Africa 204 C2
Matlamanyane, Botswana 57 A2
Matmata, Tunisia 219 B1
Mato Grosso □, Brazil 58 C3
Mato Grosso, Planalto do, Brazil 58 C3
Mato Grosso do Sul □, Brazil 58 C3
Matochkin Shar, Russia 190 B5
Matong, Papua N. G. 181 C6
Matopo Hills, Zimbabwe 241 B1
Matopos, Zimbabwe 241 B1
Matosinhos, Portugal 187 B1
Matroosberg, S. Africa 204 C1
Maṭruḥ, Oman 113 B3
Matsena, Nigeria 170 A3
Matsu Tao, Taiwan 215 B2
Matsue, Japan 136 F3
Matsumae, Japan 136 C7
Matsumoto, Japan 136 E6
Matsusaka, Japan 136 F5
Matsuura, Japan 136 G1
Matsuyama, Japan 136 G3
Mattagami →, Canada 67 D8
Mattancheri, India 118 D2
Matterhorn, Switz. 213 C2
Matthew Town, Bahamas 71 B2
Matthew's Ridge, Guyana 115 A1
Mattō, Japan 136 E5
Matucana, Peru 183 C2
Matugama, Sri Lanka 209 C2
Matuka, Papua N. G. 181 C3
Matura, Trin. & Tob. 76 C2
Matura B., Trin. & Tob. 76 C2
Maturín, Venezuela 236 B3
Mau Escarpment, Kenya 141 B2
Maubeuge, France 101 A6
Maudin Sun, Burma 63 H3
Maulamyaing = Moulmein, Burma 63 G4
Maumere, Indonesia 125 D6
Maun, Botswana 57 B1
Maungmagan Kyunzu, Burma 63 H4
Maurice, L., Australia 44 E5
Mauritania ■, Africa 157
Mauritius ■, Ind. Oc. 123
Mavrovë, Albania 35 C1
Mavuradonha Mts., Zimbabwe 241 A2
Mawk Mai, Burma 63 E4
Mawlaik, Burma 63 D3
Mawlamyine = Moulmein, Burma 63 G4
Maxesibeni, S. Africa 205 C3
May Pen, Jamaica 74 B2
May River, Papua N. G. 181 C1
Maya →, Russia 191 D13
Mayaguana, Bahamas 71 B2
Mayagüez, Puerto Rico 75 A1
Mayarí, Cuba 90 B2
Mayaro B., Trin. & Tob. 76 D3
Mayenne →, France 100 C3
Mayfield, U.S.A. 231 C9
Maykop, Russia 190 E4
Mayli-Say = Mayluu-Suu, Kyrgyzstan 144 B3
Mayluu-Suu, Kyrgyzstan 144 B3
Maymak, Kyrgyzstan 144 A2
Maymyo, Burma 63 D4
Maynooth, Ireland 128 C5
Mayo, Canada 66 C3
Mayo, Trin. & Tob. 76 D2
Mayo □, Ireland 128 C2
Mayo Daga, Nigeria 170 B3
Mayo Faran, Nigeria 170 B3
Mayon Volcano, Phil. 184 E5
Mayor I., N.Z. 167 B6
Mayotte, Ind. Oc. 123 B2
Mayraira Pt., Phil. 184 B4
Mayu, Indonesia 125 B7
Mayumba, Gabon 103 B2
Mayya, Russia 191 C13
Mazabuka, Zambia 240 C2
Mazagán = El Jadida, Morocco 161 B4
Mazán, Peru 183 A3
Māzandarān □, Iran 127 A5
Mazār-e Sharīf, Afghan. 34 A2
Mazara del Vallo, Italy 132 F4
Mazarrón, Spain 207 D5
Mazaruni →, Guyana 115 A2
Mazatlán, Mexico 158 C3
Mažeikiai, Lithuania 150 A2
Māzhān, Iran 127 B6
Mazīnān, Iran 127 A6
Mazoe →, Mozam. 162 B1
Mazowe, Zimbabwe 241 A2
Mazurian Lakes = Mazurski, Pojezierze, Poland 186 B4
Mazurski, Pojezierze, Poland 186 B4
Mazyr, Belarus 51 C4
Mbaba, Senegal 198 B1
Mbabane, Swaziland 205 B4
Mbaéré →, C.A.R. 77 C2
M'bahiakro, Ivory C. 134 B2
Mbaïki, C.A.R. 77 C2
Mbakana, Mt. de, Cameroon 65 B3
Mbala, Zambia 240 A3
Mbalabala, Zimbabwe 241 B1
Mbale, Uganda 222 B2
Mbali →, C.A.R. 77 C2
Mbalmayo, Cameroon 65 C2
Mbam →, Cameroon 65 C2
Mbandaka, Dem. Rep. of the Congo 86 B2
Mbanga, Cameroon 65 C1
M'Banio, Lagune, Gabon 103 B2
Mbanza Congo, Angola 37 A1
Mbanza Ngungu, Dem. Rep. of the Congo 86 D1
Mbarara, Uganda 222 C2
Mbari →, C.A.R. 77 C3
Mbashe →, S. Africa 205 C3
Mbatto, Ivory C. 134 B2
Mbe, Eq. Guin. 103 A1
Mbengué, Gabon 103 B2
Mbengui, Gabon 103 B2
Mbéré →, Cameroon 65 B3
Mberengwa, Zimbabwe 241 B1
Mberengwa, Mt., Zimbabwe 241 B1
Mberubu, Nigeria 170 B2
Mbeya, Tanzania 217 B2
Mbigou, Gabon 103 B2
Mbini □, Eq. Guin. 103 A2
Mboki, C.A.R. 77 B4
M'bonge, Cameroon 65 C1
Mboro, Senegal 198 A1
Mboua, Cameroon 65 B2
M'boukou Res., Cameroon 65 B2
Mboune, Senegal 198 B2
Mbour, Senegal 198 B1
Mbrés, C.A.R. 77 B2
Mbuji-Mayi, Dem. Rep. of the Congo 86 D3
M'bwat, Cameroon 65 B2
Mchinji, Malawi 153 B1
Mead, L., U.S.A. 230 C4
Meadow Lake, Canada 66 D6
Meath □, Ireland 128 C5
Meaux, France 101 B5
Mebechi-Gawa →, Japan 136 C7
Mecca = Makkah, Si. Arabia 196 C2
Mechelen, Belgium 52 A3
Mecheria, Algeria 36 B2
Mecklenburg, Germany 106 B3
Mecklenburger Bucht, Germany 106 A3
Medan, Indonesia 124 B1
Medawachchiya, Sri Lanka 209 B2
Médéa, Algeria 36 A3
Médégué, Gabon 103 A2
Medellín, Colombia 85 B1
Medemblik, Neths. 165 B3
Médenine, Tunisia 219 B2
Medford, U.S.A. 230 B2
Medgidia, Romania 188 C5
Mediaş, Romania 188 B3
Medicine Hat, Canada 66 E5
Medina = Al Madīnah, Si. Arabia 196 C2
Medina del Campo, Spain 206 B3
Medina Sidonia, Spain 206 D3
Mediterranean Sea, Europe 4 C4
Medjerda, O. →, Tunisia 219 A2
Médoc, France 100 D3
Médouneu, Gabon 103 A2
Medvezhi, Ostrava, Russia 191 B16
Medvezhyegorsk, Russia 190 C3
Medžitlija, Macedonia 151 C2
Meekatharra, Australia 44 E2
Meerut, India 118 B2
Mega, Ethiopia 98 D2
Mégara, Greece 109 C3
Meghalaya □, India 118 B4
Meharry, Mt., Australia 44 D2
Meiganga, Cameroon 65 B2
Meighen I., Canada 67 A6
Meiktila, Burma 63 E3
Meiringen, Switz. 213 B3
Meissen, Germany 106 C4
Meizhou, China 81 D5
Mejillones, Chile 79 B1
Mékambo, Gabon 103 A3
Mekele, Ethiopia 98 B2
Mekhtar, Pakistan 179 D5
Meknès, Morocco 161 B4
Meko, Nigeria 170 B1
Mekong →, Asia 10 H14
Mekongga, Indonesia 125 C6
Mekrou →, Benin 54 A3
Mekvari = Kür →, Azerbaijan 40 B4
Melaka, Malaysia 154 B2
Melalap, Malaysia 154 A5
Melbourne, Australia 45 G8
Mélé, C.A.R. 77 B3
Mélèzes →, Canada 67 D9
Melfi, Chad 78 C2
Melfort, Canada 66 D6
Melfort, Zimbabwe 241 A2
Melitopol, Ukraine 223 B4
Melk, Austria 49 A4
Mellègue, O. →, Tunisia 219 A1
Mellieha, Malta 91 B1
Melo, Uruguay 235 B2
Melolo, Indonesia 125 D6
Melouprey, Cambodia 64 B2
Melun, France 101 B5
Melville, Canada 66 D6
Melville, C., Australia 45 B7
Melville I., Australia 44 B5
Melville I., Canada 67 B5
Melville Pen., Canada 67 C8
Memaliaj, Albania 35 C1
Memboro, Indonesia 125 D5
Memel = Klaipėda, Lithuania 150 B1
Memel, S. Africa 205 B3
Memmingen, Germany 106 E3
Mempawah, Indonesia 124 B3
Memphis, U.S.A. 231 C9
Ménaka, Mali 156 B4
Menan = Chao Phraya →, Thailand 218 E2
Menarandra →, Madag. 152 D1
Mendawai →, Indonesia 124 C4
Mende, France 101 D5
Mendi, Papua N. G. 181 D2
Mendocino, C., U.S.A. 230 B2
Mendoza, Argentina 38 B2
Mene Grande, Venezuela 236 B1
Menen, Belgium 52 B2
Menggala, Indonesia 124 C3
Mengzi, China 80 D4
Menin = Menen, Belgium 52 B2
Menindee, Australia 45 F7
Menominee, U.S.A. 231 A9
Menongue, Angola 37 B2
Menorca, Spain 207 C8
Mentawai, Kepulauan, Indonesia 124 C1
Menton, France 101 E7
Mentrie, Haiti 73 A2
Menyamya, Papua N. G. 181 D3
Menzel-Bourguiba, Tunisia 219 A1
Menzel-Chaker, Tunisia 219 B2
Menzel-Temime, Tunisia 219 A2
Menzies, Australia 44 E3
Me'ona, Israel 130 A2
Meppel, Neths. 165 B4
Merabéllou, Kólpos, Greece 109 D4
Merai, Papua N. G. 181 C7
Merak, Indonesia 124 D3
Meran = Merano, Italy 132 A3
Merano, Italy 132 A3
Merauke, Indonesia 125 D10
Merca, Somali Rep. 202 C1
Merced, U.S.A. 230 C2
Mercedes, Corrientes, Argentina 38 A3
Mercedes, San Luis, Argentina 38 B2
Mercedes, Uruguay 235 B1
Mercer, N.Z. 167 B5
Mercy C., Canada 67 C10
Meredith, C., Falk. Is. 43 B1
Mergui, Burma 63 J5
Mergui Arch. = Myeik Kyunzu, Burma 63 K4
Mérida, Mexico 158 C7
Mérida, Spain 206 C2
Mérida, Venezuela 236 B1
Mérida, Cord. de, Venezuela 236 B1
Meridian, U.S.A. 231 D9
Mérinaghène, Senegal 198 A1
Meringa, Nigeria 170 A3
Merredin, Australia 44 F2
Merrill, U.S.A. 231 A9
Merritt, Canada 66 D4
Mersch, Lux. 52 C5
Merseburg, Germany 106 C3
Mersin, Turkey 220 B2
Mersing, Malaysia 154 B2
Merthyr Tydfil, U.K. 224 F5
Mértola, Portugal 187 D2
Meru, Kenya 141 A2
Meru, Tanzania 217 A3
Mesa, U.S.A. 230 D4
Mesaoria □, Cyprus 91 A2
Meshed = Mashhad, Iran 127 A6
Mesocco, Switz. 213 B4
Mesolóngion, Greece 109 B2
Mesopotamia = Al Jazirah, Iraq 126 B2
Messaad, Algeria 36 B3
Méssaména, Cameroon 65 C2
Messina, Italy 133 E5
Messina, S. Africa 205 A4
Messina, Str. di, Italy 133 F5
Messíni, Greece 109 C3
Messiniakós Kólpos, Greece 109 C3
Mesta →, Bulgaria 61 C2
Meta →, S. Amer. 20 C4
Meta Incognita Peninsula, Canada 67 C10
Methven, N.Z. 167 E3
Metlaoui, Tunisia 219 B1
Metlik, Papua N. G. 181 C7
Metu, Ethiopia 98 C2
Metz, France 101 B7
Meulaboh, Indonesia 124 B1
Meureudu, Indonesia 124 A1
Meuse →, Europe 28 E6
Mexiana, I., Brazil 58 B4
Mexicali, Mexico 158 A1
Mexican Plateau, Mexico 14 G9
México, Mexico 158 D5
Mexico ■, Cent. Amer. 158
Mexico, G. of, Cent. Amer. 14 G10
Meymaneh, Afghan. 34 B2
Meyo, Cameroon 65 C2
Mezen, Russia 190 C4
Mezen →, Russia 190 C4
Mézenc, Mt., France 101 D6
Mezhdurechenskiy, Russia 190 D6
Mezőkövesd, Hungary 116 B3
Mezőtúr, Hungary 116 B3
Mfolozi →, S. Africa 205 B4
Mhlaba Hills, Zimbabwe 241 A2
Miami, U.S.A. 231 E10
Mīāndowāb, Iran 126 A3
Miandrivazo, Madag. 152 B2
Mīāneh, Iran 126 A3
Mianwali, Pakistan 179 C6
Miaoli, Taiwan 215 B2
Miarinarivo, Antananarivo, Madag. 152 B2
Miarinarivo, Toamasina, Madag. 152 B2
Miariravaratra, Madag. 152 C2
Miass, Russia 190 D6
Mica, S. Africa 205 A4
Michael, Mt., Papua N. G. 181 D3
Michalovce, Slovak Rep. 200 A3
Michigan □, U.S.A. 231 B9
Michigan, L., U.S.A. 231 B9
Michika, Nigeria 170 A3
Michurin, Bulgaria 61 B3
Michurinsk, Russia 190 D4
Micoud, St. Lucia 75 B2
Micronesia, Federated States of ■, Pac. Oc. 3 D17
Midai, Indonesia 124 B3
Middelburg, Neths. 165 C1
Middelburg, Eastern Cape, S. Africa 205 C3
Middelburg, Mpumalanga, S. Africa 205 B3
Middelpos, S. Africa 204 C2
Middelwit, S. Africa 205 A3
Middle East, Asia 10 F7
Middlesbrough, U.K. 224 D6
Midi, Canal du →, France 100 E4
Midland, Mich., U.S.A. 231 B10
Midland, Tex., U.S.A. 230 D6
Midlands □, Zimbabwe 241 A1
Midleton, Ireland 128 E3
Midongy, Tangorombohitr' i, Madag. 152 C2
Midongy Atsimo, Madag. 152 C2
Midsayap, Phil. 184 H6
Midway Is., Pac. Oc. 2 C1
Midzŏr, Bulgaria 61 B1
Międzychód, Poland 186 B1
Międzyrzec Podlaski, Poland 186 C5
Mielec, Poland 186 C4
Miercurea-Ciuc, Romania 188 B3
Mieres, Spain 206 A3
Mifraz Hefa, Israel 130 B2
Mihara, Japan 136 F3
Mikha-Tskhakaya = Senaki, Georgia 104 A3
Mikhaylovgrad = Montana, Bulgaria 61 B1
Mikhaylovka, Kyrgyzstan 144 A6
Míkonos, Greece 109 C4
Miladummadulu Atoll, Maldives 123 B2
Milagro, Ecuador 94 B2
Milagros, Phil. 184 E5
Milan = Milano, Italy 132 B2
Milano, Italy 132 B2
Milanoa, Madag. 152 A2
Milazzo, Italy 133 E5
Mildura, Australia 45 F7
Miles, Australia 45 E9
Miles City, U.S.A. 230 A5
Milford Haven, U.K. 224 F4
Milford Sd., N.Z. 167 F1
Milḥ, Baḥr al, Iraq 126 B2
Milk →, U.S.A. 230 A5
Millau, France 101 D5
Millennium I. = Caroline I., Kiribati 176 B5
Millicent, Australia 45 G7
Milltown Malbay, Ireland 128 D2
Mílos, Greece 109 C4
Milot, Albania 35 B1
Milton, N.Z. 167 G2
Milton Keynes, U.K. 224 E6
Miltou, Chad 78 C2
Milwaukee, U.S.A. 231 B9
Mim, Ghana 108 B1
Mimongo, Gabon 103 B2
Min Jiang →, Fujian, China 81 D5
Min Jiang →, Sichuan, China 80 D4
Minamata, Japan 136 G2
Minas, Uruguay 235 B1
Minas Gerais □, Brazil 58 C4
Minatitlán, Mexico 158 D6
Minbu, Burma 63 E3
Mindanao, Phil. 184 H6
Mindanao Trench, Pac. Oc. 10 H16
Mindelo, C. Verde Is. 42 A1
Minden, Germany 106 B2
Mindiptana, Indonesia 125 D10
Mindoro, Phil. 184 E4
Mindoro Str., Phil. 184 E4
Mindourou, Cameroon 65 C2
Mine, Japan 136 F2
Mineral Wells, U.S.A. 230 D7
Ming-Kush, Kyrgyzstan 144 B4
Mingäçevir, Azerbaijan 40 A3
Mingäçevir Su Anbarı, Azerbaijan 40 A3
Mingala, C.A.R. 77 B3
Mingechaur = Mingäçevir, Azerbaijan 40 A3
Mingechaurskoye Vdkhr. = Mingäçevir Su Anbarı, Azerbaijan 40 A3
Mingin, Burma 63 D3
Mingteke Daban = Mintaka Pass, Pakistan 179 A8
Minho = Miño →, Spain 206 A2
Minho, Portugal 187 B1
Minigwal, L., Australia 44 E3
Minj, Papua N. G. 181 C3
Minkebé, Gabon 103 A3
Minna, Nigeria 170 B2
Minneapolis, U.S.A. 231 B8
Minnesota □, U.S.A. 231 A8
Mino, Japan 136 F5
Miño →, Spain 206 A2
Minorca = Menorca, Spain 207 C8
Minot, U.S.A. 230 A6
Minsk, Belarus 51 C3
Mińsk Mazowiecki, Poland 186 B4
Mintaka Pass, Pakistan 179 A8
Minto, L., Canada 67 D9
Mintoum, Gabon 103 A3
Minûf, Egypt 95 A2
Minusinsk, Russia 191 D9
Minvoul, Gabon 103 A3
Mira, Italy 132 B4
Miram Shah, Pakistan 179 C6
Miramichi, Canada 67 E10
Miranda de Ebro, Spain 206 A4
Miranda do Douro, Portugal 187 B2
Mirango, Malawi 153 B1
Miras, Albania 35 C2
Mirbāṭ, Oman 113 C2
Mirear, Egypt 95 C3
Mirebalais, Haiti 73 B2
Miri, Malaysia 154 B4
Mirigama, Sri Lanka 209 C2
Mirnyy, Russia 191 C11
Mirpur Khas, Pakistan 179 G5
Miryang, S. Korea 142 E3
Mirzaani, Georgia 104 B5
Mirzapur, India 118 B3
Mirzapur-cum-Vindhyachal = Mirzapur, India 118 B3
Misawa, Japan 136 C7
Mishan, China 81 B7
Mishbih, Gebel, Egypt 95 C2
Mishima, Japan 136 F6
Misima I., Papua N. G. 181 F7
Miski, E. →, Chad 78 B2
Miskolc, Hungary 116 A3
Misool, Indonesia 125 C8
Mişrātah, Libya 149 A3
Missinaibi →, Canada 67 D8
Missirah, Senegal 198 B1
Mississippi □, U.S.A. 231 D9
Mississippi →, U.S.A. 231 E9
Mississippi River Delta, U.S.A. 231 E9
Missoula, U.S.A. 230 A4
Missouri □, U.S.A. 231 C8
Missouri →, U.S.A. 231 C8
Mistassini, L., Canada 67 D9
Misurata = Mişrātah, Libya 149 A3
Mît Ghamr, Egypt 95 A2
Mitchell, Australia 45 E8
Mitchell, U.S.A. 230 B7
Mitchell →, Australia 45 C7
Mitchelstown, Ireland 128 D3
Mitilíni, Greece 109 B5
Mito, Japan 136 E7
Mitra Mt., Eq. Guin. 103 A1
Mitrovica = Kosovska Mitrovica, Kosovo, Yug. 239 C2
Mitsang, Gabon 103 A3
Mitsinjo, Madag. 152 B2
Mitsiwa, Eritrea 98 A2
Mitsukaidō, Japan 136 E6
Mittimatalik = Pond Inlet, Canada 67 B9
Mitú, Colombia 85 C2
Mitumba, Mts., Dem. Rep. of the Congo 86 D4
Mitwaba, Dem. Rep. of the Congo 86 D4
Mityana, Uganda 222 B2
Mitzic, Gabon 103 A2
Miyāh, W. el →, Egypt 95 C2
Miyāh, W. el →, Syria 214 B2
Miyake-Jima, Japan 136 F6

Ondo □, Nigeria 170 B2
Öndverðarnes, Iceland 117 B1
Onega, Russia 190 C3
Onega →, Russia 28 C13
Onega, L. = Onezhskoye Ozero, Russia 190 C3
O'Neill, U.S.A. 230 B7
Onekotan, Ostrov, Russia 191 E15
Oneşti, Romania 188 B4
Onezhskoye Ozero, Russia 190 C3
Ongarue, N.Z. 167 C5
Ongers →, S. Africa 204 C2
Ongjin, N. Korea 142 D1
Ongkharak, Thailand 218 D2
Ongouendjo, Gabon 103 B1
Oni, Georgia 104 A3
Onilahy →, Madag. 152 C1
Onitsha, Nigeria 170 B2
Onoda, Japan 136 F2
Onpyŏng-ni, S. Korea 142 F2
Onslow, Australia 44 D2
Onslow B., U.S.A. 231 D11
Ontake-San, Japan 136 F5
Ontario, U.S.A. 230 B3
Ontario □, Canada 67 E8
Ontario, L., N. Amer. 14 E12
Oodnadatta, Australia 45 E6
Ooldea, Australia 44 F5
Oost-Vlaanderen □, Belgium 52 A2
Oostende, Belgium 52 A1
Oosterhout, Neths. 165 C2
Oosterschelde →, Neths. 165 C2
Oosterwolde, Neths. 165 B4
Opala, Dem. Rep. of the Congo 86 C3
Opanake, Sri Lanka 209 C2
Opava, Czech Rep. 92 B3
Ophthalmia Ra., Australia 44 D2
Opi, Nigeria 170 B2
Opobo, Nigeria 170 C2
Opol, Phil. 184 G6
Opole, Poland 186 C2
Oporto = Porto, Portugal 187 B1
Opotiki, N.Z. 167 C6
Opua, N.Z. 167 A5
Opunake, N.Z. 167 C4
Ora, Cyprus 91 B2
Oradea, Romania 188 B1
Öræfajökull, Iceland 117 B5
Oral = Zhayyq →, Kazakstan 140 B2
Oral, Kazakstan 140 A2
Oran, Algeria 36 A2
Orange, Australia 45 F8
Orange, France 101 D6
Orange →, S. Africa 204 B1
Orange, C., Brazil 58 A3
Orange Free State = Free State □, S. Africa 205 B3
Orangeburg, U.S.A. 231 D10
Orango, Guinea-Biss. 112 A1
Orani, Phil. 184 D4
Oranienburg, Germany 106 B4
Oranje = Orange →, S. Africa 204 B1
Oranje Vrystaat = Free State □, S. Africa 205 B3
Oranjerivier, S. Africa 204 B2
Oranjestad, Aruba 74 A1
Oras, Phil. 184 E6
Oraşul Stalin = Braşov, Romania 188 C3
Orbe, Switz. 213 B1
Orbetello, Italy 132 C3
Orbost, Australia 45 G8
Orchila, I., Venezuela 236 A2
Ord →, Australia 44 C4
Ord, Mt., Australia 44 C4
Ordos = Mu Us Shamo, China 81 C4
Ordu, Turkey 220 A3
Ordubad, Azerbaijan 40 B3
Ordzhonikidze = Vladikavkaz, Russia 190 E4
Ordzhonikidzeabad = Kofarnikhon, Tajikistan 216 B2
Ore Mts. = Erzgebirge, Germany 106 C4
Örebro, Sweden 211 C3
Oregon □, U.S.A. 230 B2
Orel, Russia 190 D3
Orem, U.S.A. 230 B4
Orenburg, Russia 190 D5
Orense = Ourense, Spain 206 A2
Orepuki, N.Z. 167 G1
Orestiás, Greece 109 A5
Orgaz, Spain 206 C4
Orgeyev = Orhei, Moldova 188 B5
Orhei, Moldova 188 B5
Orhon Gol →, Mongolia 160 A3
Oriental, Cordillera, Colombia 85 B2
Oriental, Cordillera, Dom. Rep. 72 B3
Orihuela, Spain 207 C5
Orikum, Albania 35 C1
Orinoco →, Venezuela 236 B3
Orissa □, India 118 C3
Orissaare, Estonia 97 B2
Oristano, Italy 132 E2
Oristano, G. di, Italy 132 E2
Orizaba, Mexico 158 D5
Orkney, S. Africa 205 B3
Orkney Is., U.K. 224 B5
Orlando, U.S.A. 231 E10
Orléanais, France 101 C5
Orléans, France 101 C4
Orlovka, Kyrgyzstan 144 A4
Ormara, Pakistan 179 G3
Ormoc, Phil. 184 F6
Ormond, N.Z. 167 C6
Örnsköldsvik, Sweden 211 B3
Oro, N. Korea 142 B2
Orocué, Colombia 85 C2
Orodara, Burkina Faso 62 C2
Orodo, Nigeria 170 B2
Orol Dengizi = Aral Sea, Asia 10 E9
Oron, Nigeria 170 C2
Oroquieta, Phil. 184 G5
Orosháza, Hungary 116 B3
Orotukan, Russia 191 C15
Orsha, Belarus 51 B5
Orsk, Russia 190 D5
Orşova, Romania 188 C2
Ortegal, C., Spain 206 A2
Orthez, France 100 E3
Ortigueira, Spain 206 A2
Ortles, Italy 132 A3
Orto-Tokoy, Kyrgyzstan 144 A5
Ortoire →, Trin. & Tob. 76 D2
Ortón →, Bolivia 55 A1
Orūmīyeh, Iran 126 A3
Orūmīyeh, Daryācheh-ye, Iran 126 A3
Oruro, Bolivia 55 B1
Oruzgān □, Afghan. 34 B2
Orvieto, Italy 132 C4
Oryakhovo, Bulgaria 61 B1
Osa, Pen. de, Costa Rica 88 B2
Ōsaka, Japan 136 F4
Osan, S. Korea 142 D2
Ösel = Saaremaa, Estonia 97 B2
Osh, Kyrgyzstan 144 B3
Oshakati, Namibia 163 A2
Oshawa, Canada 67 E9
Oshmyany = Ashmyany, Belarus 51 B2
Oshogbo, Nigeria 170 B1
Oshwe, Dem. Rep. of the Congo 86 C2
Osi, Nigeria 170 B2
Osijek, Croatia 89 B4
Osintorf, Belarus 51 B5
Osipenko = Berdyansk, Ukraine 223 B4
Osipovichi = Asipovichy, Belarus 51 C4
Osizweni, S. Africa 205 B4
Oskaloosa, U.S.A. 231 B8
Oskarshamn, Sweden 211 C3
Öskemen, Kazakstan 140 B5
Oslo, Norway 172 D3
Oslob, Phil. 184 G5
Oslofjorden, Norway 172 D3
Osmaniye, Turkey 220 B3
Osnabrück, Germany 106 B2
Osogovska Planina, Macedonia 151 A3
Osorno, Chile 79 D1
Osprey Reef, Australia 45 B8
Oss, Neths. 165 C3
Ossa, Mt., Australia 45 H8
Óssa, Óros, Greece 109 B3
Osse →, Nigeria 170 B2
Ossora, Russia 191 D16
Ostend = Oostende, Belgium 52 A1
Österdalälven, Sweden 211 B2
Östersund, Sweden 211 B2
Ostfriesische Inseln, Germany 106 B1
Ostrava, Czech Rep. 92 B4
Ostróda, Poland 186 B3
Ostrołęka, Poland 186 B4
Ostrów Mazowiecka, Poland 186 B4
Ostrów Wielkopolski, Poland 186 C2
Ostrowiec-Świętokrzyski, Poland 186 C4
Ostuni, Italy 133 D6
Osum →, Albania 35 C2
Osun □, Nigeria 170 B1
Osuna, Spain 206 D3
Oswego, U.S.A. 231 B11
Oświęcim, Poland 186 C3
Otago □, N.Z. 167 F2
Otago Harbour, N.Z. 167 F3
Otaheite B., Trin. & Tob. 76 D1
Ōtake, Japan 136 F3
Otaki, N.Z. 167 D5
Otaru, Japan 136 B7
Otaru-Wan = Ishikari-Wan, Japan 136 B7
Otavalo, Ecuador 94 A2
Otjiwarongo, Namibia 163 B2
Ötmök, Kyrgyzstan 144 A3
Otoineppu, Japan 136 A8
Otorohanga, N.Z. 167 C5
Otranto, Italy 133 D7
Otranto, C. d', Italy 133 D7
Otranto, Str. of, Italy 133 D7
Otse, S. Africa 205 B3
Otsu, Japan 136 F4
Ōtsuki, Japan 136 F6
Ottawa = Outaouais →, Canada 67 E9
Ottawa, Canada 67 E9
Ottawa Is., Canada 67 D8
Ottélé, Cameroon 65 C2
Ottilien Reef, Papua N. G. 181 C5
Otto Beit Bridge, Zimbabwe 241 A1
Ottosdal, S. Africa 205 B3
Ottumwa, U.S.A. 231 B8
Otu, Nigeria 170 B1
Otukpa, Nigeria 170 B2
Oturkpo, Nigeria 170 B2
Otway, C., Australia 45 G7
Otwock, Poland 186 B4
Ou →, Laos 145 B2
Ou Neua, Laos 145 A1
Ou-Sammyaku, Japan 136 D7
Ouachita →, U.S.A. 231 D8
Ouachita Mts., U.S.A. 231 D8
Ouadda, C.A.R. 77 B3
Ouagadougou, Burkina Faso 62 B2
Ouagam, Chad 78 C1
Ouaham →, C.A.R. 77 B2
Ouahigouya, Burkina Faso 62 B2
Ouahran = Oran, Algeria 36 A2
Ouallene, Algeria 36 D3
Ouanda Djallé, C.A.R. 77 B3
Ouandago, C.A.R. 77 B2
Ouandjia, Bahr →, C.A.R. 77 B3
Ouango, C.A.R. 77 C3
Ouantonou, C.A.R. 77 B2
Ouargaye, Burkina Faso 62 C3
Ouargla, Algeria 36 B4
Ouarkoye, Burkina Faso 62 B2
Ouarra →, C.A.R. 77 B3
Ouarzazate, Morocco 161 B4
Ouatere, C.A.R. 77 B2
Oubangi →, Dem. Rep. of the Congo 86 C2
Ouddorp, Neths. 165 C1
Oude Rijn →, Neths. 165 B2
Oudenaarde, Belgium 52 B2
Oudtshoorn, S. Africa 204 C2
Ouégoa, N. Cal. 176 A2
Oueita, Chad 78 B3
Ouellé, Ivory C. 134 B2
Ouéme →, Benin 54 D3
Ouessa, Burkina Faso 62 C2
Ouessant, Î. d', France 100 B1
Ouesso, Congo 86 B2
Ouezzane, Morocco 161 B4
Ougarou, Burkina Faso 62 B3
Oughterard, Ireland 128 C2
Ouhan →, Chad 78 D2
Ouidah, Benin 54 D3
Oujda, Morocco 161 B5
Ouli, Cameroon 65 B2
Oulou, Bahr →, C.A.R. 77 B3
Oulu, Finland 99 A3
Oulujärvi, Finland 99 B3
Oulujoki →, Finland 99 A3
Oum Chalouba, Chad 78 B3
Oum Hadjer, Chad 78 C2
Oum Hadjer, O. →, Chad 78 B3
Oumé, Ivory C. 134 B1
Ounianga Kébir, Chad 78 B3
Ounianga Sérir, Chad 78 B3
Our →, Lux. 52 C5
Ourense, Spain 206 A2
Ouro Prêto, Brazil 58 D4
Ouro Sogui, Senegal 198 A2
Oursi, Burkina Faso 62 A2
Ourthe →, Belgium 52 B4
Outaouais →, Canada 67 E9
Outer Hebrides, U.K. 224 C3
Outjo, Namibia 163 B2
Ouvéa, I., N. Cal. 176 A3
Ouyen, Australia 45 G7
Ovalle, Chile 79 C1
Ovamboland, Namibia 163 A2
Overflakkee, Neths. 165 C2
Overijssel □, Neths. 165 B4
Oviedo, Spain 206 A3
Oviši, Latvia 146 B1
Ovoro, Nigeria 170 B2
Owaka, N.Z. 167 G2
Owambo = Ovamboland, Namibia 163 A2
Owase, Japan 136 F5
Owatonna, U.S.A. 231 B8
Owbeh, Afghan. 34 B1
Owen Falls Dam, Uganda B2
Owen Sound, Canada 67 E8
Owen Stanley Ra., Papua N. G. 181 E4
Owendo, Gabon 103 A1
Owens L., U.S.A. 230 C3
Owensboro, U.S.A. 231 C9
Owerri, Nigeria 170 B2
Owo, Nigeria 170 B2
Owyhee →, U.S.A. 230 B3
Ox Mts. = Slieve Gamph, Ireland 128 B3
Öxarfjörður, Iceland 117 A5
Oxford, N.Z. 167 E4
Oxford, U.K. 224 F6
Oxus = Amudarya →, Uzbekistan 221 B2
Oy-Tal, Kyrgyzstan 144 B4
Oya, Malaysia 154 B4
Oyama, Japan 136 E6
Oyem, Gabon 103 A2
Oymyakon, Russia 191 C14
Oyo, Nigeria 170 B1
Oyo □, Nigeria 170 B1
Ōyūbari, Japan 136 B8
Ozamiz, Phil. 184 G5
Ozark Plateau, U.S.A. 231 C8
Ozarks, L. of the, U.S.A. 231 C8
Ózd, Hungary 116 A3
Özgön, Kyrgyzstan 144 B3
Ozurgeti, Georgia 104 B2

P

Pa, Burkina Faso 62 C2
Pa-an, Burma 63 G4
Pa Mong Dam, Thailand 218 C3
Paamiut, Greenland 43 C4
Paarl, S. Africa 204 C1
Pab Hills, Pakistan 179 F4
Pabianice, Poland 186 C3
Pabna, Bangla. 50 B2
Pabo, Uganda 222 A2
Pacaraima, Sa., S. Amer. 20 C4
Pacasmayo, Peru 183 B2
Pachitea →, Peru 183 B3
Pachuca, Mexico 158 C5
Pacific Ocean, Pac. Oc. 174
Padaido, Kepulauan, Indonesia 125 C9
Padang, Indonesia 124 C2
Padangpanjang, Indonesia 124 C2
Padangsidempuan, Indonesia 124 B1
Paderborn, Germany 106 C2
Pádova, Italy 132 B3
Padre I., U.S.A. 231 E7
Padre Las Casas, Dom. Rep. 72 B2
Padua = Pádova, Italy 132 B3
Paducah, U.S.A. 231 C9
Padukka, Sri Lanka 209 C2
Paengnyŏng-do, S. Korea 142 D1
Paeroa, N.Z. 167 B5
Pag, Croatia 89 B2
Paga, Gabon 103 B2
Paga, Ghana 108 A2
Pagadian, Phil. 184 H5
Pagai Selatan, Pulau, Indonesia 124 C2
Pagai Utara, Pulau, Indonesia 124 C2
Pagalu = Annobón, Atl. Oc. 4 G4
Pagastikós Kólpos, Greece 109 B3
Pagatan, Indonesia 124 C5
Page, U.S.A. 230 C4
Pagei, Papua N. G. 181 B1
Pago Pago, Amer. Samoa 177 B2
Pagua B., Domin. 73 A2
Pagwi, Papua N. G. 181 C2
Pahiatua, N.Z. 167 D5
Pai, Thailand 218 B1
Paide, Estonia 97 B3
Paiho, Taiwan 215 C2
Päijänne, Finland 99 B3
Pailin, Cambodia 64 B1
Painan, Indonesia 124 C2
Paint Hills = Wemindji, Canada 67 D9
Painted Desert, U.S.A. 230 C4
País Vasco □, Spain 207 A4
Paisley, U.K. 224 D4
Paita, Peru 183 B1
Pajares, Puerto de, Spain 206 A3
Pak Lay, Laos 145 C1
Pak Phanang, Thailand 218 G2
Pak Sane, Laos 145 C2
Pak Song, Laos 145 E4
Pak Suong, Laos 145 C2
Pakhuis, S. Africa 204 C1
Pakistan ■, Asia 179
Pakkading, Laos 145 C2
Pakokku, Burma 63 E3
Paktīā □, Afghan. 34 B3
Pakwach, Uganda 222 B2
Pakxe, Laos 145 E3
Pala, Chad 78 D2
Palabek, Uganda 222 A2
Palagruža, Croatia 89 C3
Palana, Russia 191 D15
Palanan, Phil. 184 C5
Palanan Pt., Phil. 184 C5
Palanga, Lithuania 150 B1
Palangkaraya, Indonesia 124 C4
Palanpur, India 118 B2
Palapye, Botswana 57 B2
Palatka, Russia 191 C15
Palau ■, Pac. Oc. 3 D16
Palauk, Burma 63 J5
Palawan, Phil. 184 G3
Paldiski, Estonia 97 A3
Paleleh, Indonesia 125 B6
Palembang, Indonesia 124 C2
Palencia, Spain 206 A3
Paleometokho, Cyprus 91 A2
Palermo, Italy 133 E4
Palestine, U.S.A. 231 D7
Paletwa, Burma 63 E2
Palghat, India 118 C2
Palioúrion, Ákra, Greece 109 B3
Paliseul, Belgium 52 C4
Palk Strait, Asia 10 H12
Palla Road = Dinokwe, Botswana 57 B2
Pallanza = Verbánia, Italy 132 B2
Pallës, Bishti i, Albania 35 B1
Pallisa, Uganda 222 B2
Palm Is., Australia 45 C8
Palma, B. de, Spain 207 C7
Palma de Mallorca, Spain 207 C7
Palma Soriano, Cuba 90 B2
Palmas, C., Liberia 148 C2
Pálmas, G. di, Italy 132 E2
Palmer →, Australia 44 D5
Palmerston, N.Z. 167 F3
Palmerston, C., Australia 45 D8
Palmerston North, N.Z. 167 D5
Palmi, Italy 133 E5
Palmira, Colombia 85 C1
Palmyra = Tudmur, Syria 214 B2
Palmyra Is., Pac. Oc. 176 A4
Palo Seco, Trin. & Tob. 76 D1
Palompon, Phil. 184 F6
Palopo, Indonesia 125 C6
Palos, C. de, Spain 207 D5
Palu, Indonesia 125 C5
Palu, Turkey 220 B4
Paluke, Liberia 148 B2
Pama, Burkina Faso 62 C3
Pama →, C.A.R. 77 C2
Pamiers, France 101 E4
Pamir, Tajikistan 216 C4
Pamir →, Tajikistan 216 C4
Pamlico Sd., U.S.A. 231 C11
Pampa, U.S.A. 230 C6
Pampanua, Indonesia 125 C6
Pampas, Argentina 38 B2
Pampas, Peru 183 C3
Pamplona, Colombia 85 B2
Pamplona, Spain 207 A5
Pampoenpoort, S. Africa 204 C2
Panabo, Phil. 184 H6
Panaitan, Indonesia 124 D3
Panaji, India 118 C2
Panamá, Panama 88 B3
Panama, Sri Lanka 209 C2
Panama ■, Cent. Amer. 88
Panamá, G. de, Panama 88 B3
Panama Canal, Panama 88 B3
Panama City, U.S.A. 231 D9
Panão, Peru 183 B2
Panaon I., Phil. 184 F6
Panare, Thailand 218 H2
Panay, Phil. 184 F5
Pančevo, Serbia, Yug. 239 B2
Panch'iao, Taiwan 215 B2
Pandan, Antique, Phil. 184 F5
Pandan, Catanduanes, Phil. 184 D6
Pando, Uruguay 235 B1
Pandora, Costa Rica 88 B2
Panevėžys, Lithuania 150 B3
Panfilov, Kazakstan 140 B5
Pang-Long, Burma 63 D5
Pang-Yang, Burma 63 D5
Pangalanes, Canal des = Ampangalana, Lakandranon', Madag. 152 C2
Pangani, Tanzania 217 B3
Pangfou = Bengbu, China 81 C5
Pangkajene, Indonesia 125 C5
Pangkalanbrandan, Indonesia 124 B1
Pangkalanbuun, Indonesia 124 C4
Pangkalpinang, Indonesia 124 C3
Pangnirtung, Canada 67 C10
Panguna, Papua N. G. 181 D8
Pangutaran Group, Phil. 184 H4
Panié, Mt., N. Cal. 176 A2
Panj = Pyandzh, Tajikistan 216 C2
Panjakent = Pendzhikent, Tajikistan 216 B1
Panjang, Hon, Vietnam 237 H1
Panjgur, Pakistan 179 F3
Panji Poyon, Tajikistan 216 C2
Panjim = Panaji, India 118 C2
Panjinad Barrage, Pakistan 179 E6
Pankshin, Nigeria 170 B2
Panmunjŏm, N. Korea 142 D2
Pannirtuuq = Pangnirtung, Canada 67 C10
Pano Lefkara, Cyprus 91 B2
Pano Panayia, Cyprus 91 B1
Pantar, Indonesia 125 D6
Pante Macassar, E. Timor 125 D6
Pantelleria, Italy 132 F3
Panyam, Nigeria 170 B2
Paola, Malta 91 B2
Paoting = Baoding, China 81 C5
Paot'ou = Baotou, China 81 B5
Paoua, C.A.R. 77 B2
Pápa, Hungary 116 B1
Papagayo, G. de, Costa Rica 88 A1
Papakura, N.Z. 167 B5
Papantla, Mexico 158 C5
Papar, Malaysia 154 A5
Paphos, Cyprus 91 B1
Papien Chiang = Da →, Vietnam 237 B2
Papoutsa, Cyprus 91 B2
Papua, G. of, Papua N. G. 181 E3
Papua New Guinea ■, Oceania 181
Papun, Burma 63 F4
Pará = Belém, Brazil 58 B4
Pará □, Brazil 58 B3
Paraburdoo, Australia 44 D2
Paracale, Phil. 184 D5
Parado, Indonesia 125 D5
Paragould, U.S.A. 231 C8
Paragua →, Venezuela 236 B3
Paraguaçu →, Brazil 58 C5
Paraguaná, Pen. de, Venezuela 236 A2
Paraguarí, Paraguay 182 C2
Paraguay ■, S. Amer. 182
Paraguay →, Paraguay 182 C2
Paraíba = João Pessoa, Brazil 58 B5
Paraíba □, Brazil 58 B5
Parakou, Benin 54 C3
Paralimni, Cyprus 91 A2
Parama I., Papua N. G. 181 E2
Paramaribo, Surinam 115 A2
Paramushir, Ostrov, Russia 191 D15
Paran →, Israel 130 D2
Paraná, Argentina 38 B2
Paraná □, Brazil 58 D3
Paraná →, Argentina 38 B3
Paranaguá, Brazil 58 D4
Paranaíba →, Brazil 58 D3
Paranapanema →, Brazil 58 D3
Paranas, Phil. 184 F6
Parang, Phil. 184 J4
Parângul Mare, Vf., Romania 188 C2
Paranthan, Sri Lanka 209 B2
Paraparaumu, N.Z. 167 D5
Parchim, Germany 106 B3
Pardes Hanna-Karkur, Israel 130 B1
Pardubice, Czech Rep. 92 A2
Parecis, Serra dos, Brazil 58 C3
Paren, Russia 191 C16
Parepare, Indonesia 125 C5
Párga, Greece 109 B2
Paria, Gulf of, Trin. & Tob. 76 D1
Pariaguán, Venezuela 236 B3
Parigi, Indonesia 125 C6
Parika, Guyana 115 A2
Parima, Serra, Brazil 58 A2
Parinari, Peru 183 A3
Pariñas, Pta., S. Amer. 20 D2
Parintins, Brazil 58 B3
Pariparit Kyun, Burma 63 H2
Paris, France 101 B5
Paris, U.S.A. 231 D7
Park Rynie, S. Africa 205 C4
Parkersburg, U.S.A. 231 C10
Parkes, Australia 45 F8
Parkhar, Tajikistan 216 C2
Parla, Spain 206 B4
Parma, Italy 132 B3
Parnaíba, Brazil 58 B4
Parnaíba →, Brazil 58 B4
Parnassós, Greece 109 B3
Pärnu, Estonia 97 B3
Paroo →, Australia 45 F7
Páros, Greece 109 C4
Parry Is., Canada 67 B6
Parry Sound, Canada 67 E9
Parsons, U.S.A. 231 C7
Partinico, Italy 133 E4
Paru →, Brazil 58 B3
Parvān □, Afghan. 34 B3
Parys, S. Africa 205 B3

Sailolof

Ransiki, *Indonesia* 125 C8
Rantabe, *Madag.* 152 B2
Rantauprapat, *Indonesia* 124 B1
Rantemario, *Indonesia* 125 C5
Rapallo, *Italy* 132 B2
Rāpch, *Iran* 127 D6
Raper, C., *Canada* 67 C10
Rapid City, *U.S.A.* 230 B6
Rapla, *Estonia* 97 A3
Rapu Rapu I., *Phil.* 184 E6
Ra's al 'Ayn, *Syria* 214 A3
Ra's al Khaymah, *U.A.E.* 113 A3
Ras Ghârib, *Egypt* 95 B2
Ras Mallap, *Egypt* 95 B2
Raseiniai, *Lithuania* 150 B2
Rashîd, *Egypt* 95 A2
Rashîd, Masabb, *Egypt* 95 A2
Rasht, *Iran* 126 A4
Rasi Salai, *Thailand* 218 D4
Rason L., *Australia* 44 E3
Rat Buri, *Thailand* 218 E1
Rath Luirc, *Ireland* 128 D3
Rathdrum, *Ireland* 128 D5
Rathenow, *Germany* 106 B4
Rathkeale, *Ireland* 128 D3
Rathmelton, *Ireland* 128 A4
Ratibor = Racibórz, *Poland* 186 C3
Ratnapura, *Sri Lanka* 209 C2
Raton, *U.S.A.* 230 C6
Rattaphum, *Thailand* 218 H2
Raufarhöfn, *Iceland* 117 A6
Raukumara Ra., *N.Z.* 167 C6
Rauma, *Finland* 99 B2
Raurkela, *India* 118 B3
Rausu-Dake, *Japan* 136 A9
Rava-Ruska, *Poland* 186 C5
Rava Russkaya = Rava-Ruska, *Poland* 186 C5
Rāvar, *Iran* 127 C6
Ravenna, *Italy* 132 B4
Ravensburg, *Germany* 106 E2
Ravenshoe, *Australia* 45 C8
Ravensthorpe, *Australia* 44 F3
Ravi →, *Pakistan* 179 D6
Rawalpindi, *Pakistan* 179 C7
Rawāndūz, *Iraq* 126 A3
Rawene, *N.Z.* 167 A4
Rawlinna, *Australia* 44 F4
Rawlins, *U.S.A.* 230 B5
Rawlinson Ra., *Australia* 44 D4
Rawson, *Argentina* 38 C2
Ray, C., *Canada* 67 E11
Raychikhinsk, *Russia* 191 E12
Raymond, C., *Haiti* 73 B2
Rayong, *Thailand* 218 E2
Raz, Pte. du, *France* 100 C1
Razgrad, *Bulgaria* 61 B3
Razim, Lacul, *Romania* 188 C5
Ré, Î. de, *France* 100 C3
Reading, *U.K.* 224 F6
Reading, *U.S.A.* 231 B11
Ream, *Cambodia* 64 C1
Rebi, *Indonesia* 125 D8
Rebiana, Sahrâ', *Libya* 149 C4
Rebun-Tō, *Japan* 136 A7
Recherche, Arch. of the, *Australia* 44 F3
Rechytsa, *Belarus* 51 C5
Recife, *Brazil* 58 B5
Recife, *Seychelles* 123 B2
Reconquista, *Argentina* 38 A3
Red →, *U.S.A.* 231 D8
Red Bluff, *U.S.A.* 230 B2
Red Deer, *Canada* 66 D5
Red Lake, *Canada* 66 D7
Red Oak, *U.S.A.* 231 B7
Red Sea, *Asia* 4 D7
Red Tower Pass = Turnu Roşu, P., *Romania* 188 C3
Red Wing, *U.S.A.* 231 B8
Redang, *Malaysia* 154 A2
Redange, *Lux.* 52 C4
Redcar, *U.K.* 224 D6
Reddersburg, *S. Africa* 205 B3
Redding, *U.S.A.* 230 B2
Redditch, *U.K.* 224 E6
Redhead, *Trin. & Tob.* 76 C3
Redon, *France* 100 C2
Redondela, *Spain* 206 A1
Ree, L., *Ireland* 128 C3
Reefton, *N.Z.* 167 E3
Reese →, *U.S.A.* 230 B3
Regensburg, *Germany* 106 D4
Reggâne = Zaouiet Reggâne, *Algeria* 36 C3
Réggio di Calábria, *Italy* 133 E5
Réggio nell'Emília, *Italy* 132 B3
Reghin, *Romania* 188 B3
Regina, *Canada* 66 D6
Rehoboth, *Namibia* 163 B2
Rehovot, *Israel* 130 C1
Reichenbach, *Germany* 106 C4
Reigate, *U.K.* 224 F6
Reims, *France* 101 B6
Reina Adelaida, Arch., *Chile* 79 E1
Reindeer L., *Canada* 66 D6
Reinga, C., *N.Z.* 167 A4
Reinosa, *Spain* 206 A3
Reitz, *S. Africa* 205 B3
Reivilo, *S. Africa* 204 B2
Remedios, *Panama* 88 B2
Remeshk, *Iran* 127 D6
Remich, *Lux.* 52 C5
Rendsburg, *Germany* 106 A2
Rengat, *Indonesia* 124 C2
Renmark, *Australia* 45 F7
Renner Springs, *Australia* 44 C5
Rennes, *France* 100 B3
Reno, *U.S.A.* 230 C3
Reno →, *Italy* 132 B4
Rentería, *Spain* 207 A5
Réo, *Burkina Faso* 62 B2
Republican →, *U.S.A.* 231 C7
Repulse Bay, *Canada* 67 C8
Requena, *Peru* 183 B3
Requena, *Spain* 207 C5
Resen, *Macedonia* 151 B2
Resht = Rasht, *Iran* 126 A4
Resistencia, *Argentina* 38 A3
Reşiţa, *Romania* 188 C1
Resolute, *Canada* 67 B7
Resolution I., *Canada* 67 C10
Resolution I., *N.Z.* 167 F1
Réthímnon, *Greece* 109 D4
Retiche, Alpi, *Switz.* 213 B5
Réunion ■, *Ind. Oc.* 123
Reus, *Spain* 207 B6
Reutlingen, *Germany* 106 D2
Reval = Tallinn, *Estonia* 97 A3
Revelstoke, *Canada* 66 D5
Reventazón, *Peru* 183 B1
Revillagigedo, Is. de, *Pac. Oc.* 14 H8
Revolyutsii, Pik, *Tajikistan* 216 B4
Revolyutsiya, Qullai = Revolyutsii, Pik, *Tajikistan* 216 B4
Rexburg, *U.S.A.* 230 B4
Rey, I. del, *Panama* 88 B3
Rey, Mayo →, *Cameroon* 65 B2
Rey, Rio-del-→, *Cameroon* 65 C1
Rey Bouba, *Cameroon* 65 B2
Rey Malabo, *Eq. Guin.* 103 A1
Reyðarfjörður, *Iceland* 117 B6
Reykjahlið, *Iceland* 117 B5
Reykjanes, *Iceland* 117 C2
Reykjavík, *Iceland* 117 B3
Reynolds Ra., *Australia* 44 D5
Reynosa, *Mexico* 158 B5
Rēzekne, *Latvia* 146 B4
Rhein = Rhine →, *Europe* 28 E7
Rhein-Main-Donau-Kanal, *Germany* 106 D3
Rheine, *Germany* 106 B1
Rheinland-Pfalz □, *Germany* 106 C1
Rhin = Rhine →, *Europe* 28 E7
Rhine →, *Europe* 28 E7
Rhineland-Palatinate = Rheinland-Pfalz □, *Germany* 106 C1
Rhinelander, *U.S.A.* 231 A9
Rhino Camp, *Uganda* 222 A2
Rhir, Cap, *Morocco* 161 B4
Rhode Island □, *U.S.A.* 231 B12
Rhodes = Ródhos, *Greece* 109 C6
Rhodesia = Zimbabwe ■, *Africa* 241
Rhodope Mts. = Rhodopi Planina, *Bulgaria* 61 C2
Rhodopi Planina, *Bulgaria* 61 C2
Rhön, *Germany* 106 C2
Rhondda, *U.K.* 224 F5
Rhône →, *France* 101 E6
Rhum, *U.K.* 224 C3
Ri-Aba, *Eq. Guin.* 103 A1
Riau □, *Indonesia* 124 C2
Riau, Kepulauan, *Indonesia* 124 B2
Riau Arch. = Riau, Kepulauan, *Indonesia* 124 B2
Ribadeo, *Spain* 206 A2
Ribado, *Nigeria* 170 B3
Ribao, *Cameroon* 65 B2
Ribe, *Denmark* 93 B2
Ribeira Brava, *Madeira* 43 B1
Ribeira Grande, *C. Verde Is.* 42 A1
Ribeirão Prêto, *Brazil* 58 D4
Riberalta, *Bolivia* 55 A1
Riccarton, *N.Z.* 167 E4
Richard Toll, *Senegal* 198 A1
Richards Bay, *S. Africa* 205 B4
Richfield, *U.S.A.* 230 C4
Richland, *U.S.A.* 230 A3
Richmond, *Australia* 45 D7
Richmond, *N.Z.* 167 D4
Richmond, *Ind., U.S.A.* 231 C10
Richmond, *Ky., U.S.A.* 231 C10
Richmond, *Va., U.S.A.* 231 C11
Ridder = Leninogorsk, *Kazakstan* 140 A5
Ridgecrest, *U.S.A.* 230 C3
Riebeek-Oos, *S. Africa* 205 C3
Ried, *Austria* 49 A3
Riesa, *Germany* 106 C4
Riet →, *S. Africa* 204 B2
Rietbron, *S. Africa* 204 C2
Rieti, *Italy* 133 C4
Rift Valley □, *Kenya* 141 A2
Rig Rig, *Chad* 78 C1
Rīga, *Latvia* 146 B3
Riga, G. of, *Latvia* 146 B2
Rigacikun, *Nigeria* 170 A2
Rīgas Jūras Līcis = Riga, G. of, *Latvia* 146 B2
Rīgestān, *Afghan.* 34 C2
Rigolet, *Canada* 67 D11
Rijau, *Nigeria* 170 A2
Rijeka, *Croatia* 89 B2
Rijssen, *Neths.* 165 B4
Rikuzentakada, *Japan* 136 D7
Rima →, *Nigeria* 170 A2
Rimi, *Nigeria* 170 A2
Rímini, *Italy* 132 B4
Rimouski, *Canada* 67 E10
Rinca, *Indonesia* 125 D5
Ringim, *Nigeria* 170 A2
Ringkøbing, *Denmark* 93 A2
Rinjani, *Indonesia* 124 D5
Rio Benito, *Eq. Guin.* 103 A1
Rio Branco, *Brazil* 58 B2
Río Branco, *Uruguay* 235 B2
Rio Claro, *Brazil* 58 D4
Rio Claro, *Trin. & Tob.* 76 D2
Río Cuarto, *Argentina* 38 B2
Rio de Janeiro, *Brazil* 58 D4
Rio de Janeiro □, *Brazil* 58 D4
Río Gallegos, *Argentina* 38 D2
Rio Grande = Grande, Rio →, *U.S.A.* 231 E7
Rio Grande, *Brazil* 58 E3
Río Grande de Santiago →, *Mexico* 158 C3
Rio Grande do Norte □, *Brazil* 58 B5
Rio Grande do Sul □, *Brazil* 58 D3
Río Hato, *Panama* 88 B2
Río Mulatos, *Bolivia* 55 B1
Río Muni = Mbini □, *Eq. Guin.* 103 A2
Ríobamba, *Ecuador* 94 B2
Ríohacha, *Colombia* 85 A2
Rioni →, *Georgia* 104 A2
Ríosucio, *Colombia* 85 B1
Rishiri-Tō, *Japan* 136 A7
Rishon le Ziyyon, *Israel* 130 C1
Riti, *Nigeria* 170 B2
Riva del Garda, *Italy* 132 B3
River Cess, *Liberia* 148 B2
Rivera, *Uruguay* 235 A1
Rivers □, *Nigeria* 170 C2
Riversdale, *S. Africa* 204 C2
Riverside, *U.S.A.* 230 D3
Riverton, *N.Z.* 167 G2
Riverton, *U.S.A.* 230 B5
Riviera di Levante, *Italy* 132 B2
Riviera di Ponente, *Italy* 132 B2
Rivière-du-Loup, *Canada* 67 E10
Rivière-Pilote, *Martinique* 74 B2
Rivne, *Ukraine* 223 A2
Rívoli, *Italy* 132 B1
Riyadh = Ar Riyāḍ, *Si. Arabia* 196 C4
Rize, *Turkey* 220 A4
Rizokarpaso, *Cyprus* 91 A3
Rizzuto, C., *Italy* 133 E6
Road Town, *Br. Virgin Is.* 76 B2
Roanne, *France* 101 C6
Roanoke, *U.S.A.* 231 C11
Roanoke →, *U.S.A.* 231 C11
Robertson, *S. Africa* 204 C1
Robertsport, *Liberia* 148 B1
Roberval, *Canada* 67 E9
Robeson Chan., *Greenland* 43 A3
Robinson Ra., *Australia* 44 E2
Roboré, *Bolivia* 55 B3
Robson, Mt., *Canada* 66 D5
Roca, C. da, *Portugal* 187 C1
Rocha, *Uruguay* 235 B2
Rochefort, *Belgium* 52 B4
Rochefort, *France* 100 D3
Rochester, *Minn., U.S.A.* 231 B8
Rochester, *N.Y., U.S.A.* 231 B11
Rock Hill, *U.S.A.* 231 D10
Rock Island, *U.S.A.* 231 B8
Rock Sound, *Bahamas* 71 A1
Rock Springs, *U.S.A.* 230 B5
Rockall, *Atl. Oc.* 28 D3
Rockford, *U.S.A.* 231 B9
Rockhampton, *Australia* 45 D9
Rockly B., *Trin. & Tob.* 76 B5
Rocky Mount, *U.S.A.* 231 C11
Rocky Mts., *N. Amer.* 14 D7
Rod, *Pakistan* 179 E2
Rødbyhavn, *Denmark* 93 B3
Rodez, *France* 101 D5
Ródhos, *Greece* 109 C6
Rodney, C., *N.Z.* 167 B5
Rodonit, Kepi i, *Albania* 35 B1
Rodriguez, *Ind. Oc.* 3 E13
Roebourne, *Australia* 44 D2
Roebuck B., *Australia* 44 C3
Roermond, *Neths.* 165 C4
Roes Welcome Sd., *Canada* 67 C8
Roeselare, *Belgium* 52 B2
Rogachev = Ragachow, *Belarus* 51 C5
Rogagua, L., *Bolivia* 55 A1
Roggeveldberge, *S. Africa* 204 C2
Rogoaguado, L., *Bolivia* 55 A1
Rohri, *Pakistan* 179 F5
Roi Et, *Thailand* 218 C3
Roja, *Latvia* 146 B2
Rojo, C., *Mexico* 158 C5
Rokan →, *Indonesia* 124 B2
Rokel →, *S. Leone* 148 A1
Rokiškis, *Lithuania* 150 B3
Rolla, *U.S.A.* 231 C8
Roma, *Australia* 45 E8
Roma, *Italy* 132 D4
Romaine →, *Canada* 67 D10
Roman, *Romania* 188 B4
Romang, *Indonesia* 125 D7
Români, *Egypt* 95 A2
Romania ■, *Europe* 188
Romano, Cayo, *Cuba* 90 B2
Romanovka = Basarabeasca, *Moldova* 188 B5
Romans-sur-Isère, *France* 101 D6
Romanshorn, *Switz.* 213 A4
Romblon, *Phil.* 184 E5
Rome = Roma, *Italy* 132 D4
Rome, *U.S.A.* 231 D9
Rømø, *Denmark* 93 B2
Romont, *Switz.* 213 B1
Romorantin-Lanthenay, *France* 101 C4
Ron, *Vietnam* 237 D3
Roncador, Serra do, *Brazil* 58 C3
Ronda, *Spain* 206 D3
Rondônia □, *Brazil* 58 C2
Rong, Koh, *Cambodia* 64 C1
Ronge, L. la, *Canada* 66 D6
Rønne, *Denmark* 93 B5
Ronse, *Belgium* 52 B2
Roodepoort, *S. Africa* 205 B3
Roosendaal, *Neths.* 165 C2
Roosevelt →, *Brazil* 20 D4
Roper →, *Australia* 44 B5
Roquetas de Mar, *Spain* 207 D4
Roraima □, *Brazil* 58 A2
Roraima, Mt., *Venezuela* 236 B3
Rorschach, *Switz.* 213 A4
Rosalie, *Domin.* 73 B2
Rosario, *Argentina* 38 B2
Rosario, *Mexico* 158 C3
Rosario, *Paraguay* 182 B2
Rosario de la Frontera, *Argentina* 38 A2
Roscommon, *Ireland* 128 C3
Roscommon □, *Ireland* 128 C3
Roscrea, *Ireland* 128 D4
Rose Belle, *Mauritius* 123 B2
Rose Hill, *Mauritius* 123 B1
Roseau, *Domin.* 73 B2
Roseburg, *U.S.A.* 230 B2
Rosenheim, *Germany* 106 E4
Roses, G. de, *Spain* 207 A7
Rosetown, *Canada* 66 D6
Rosetta = Rashîd, *Egypt* 95 A2
Roseville, *U.S.A.* 230 C2
Roshtqala, *Tajikistan* 216 C3
Rosignano Maríttimo, *Italy* 132 C3
Rosignol, *Guyana* 115 A2
Roşiori de Vede, *Romania* 188 C3
Roskilde, *Denmark* 93 B4
Roskovec, *Albania* 35 C1
Roslavl, *Russia* 190 D3
Rosmead, *S. Africa* 205 C3
Ross, *N.Z.* 167 E3
Ross River, *Canada* 66 C3
Rossan Pt., *Ireland* 128 B3
Rossano, *Italy* 133 E6
Rossel I., *Papua N. G.* 181 F8
Rosses, The, *Ireland* 128 A3
Rosslare, *Ireland* 128 D5
Rosso, *Mauritania* 157 C1
Rossosh, *Russia* 190 D3
Rostock, *Germany* 106 A4
Rostov, *Russia* 190 E3
Roswell, *U.S.A.* 230 D6
Rotherham, *U.K.* 224 E6
Roti, *Indonesia* 125 D6
Roto, *Australia* 45 F8
Rotondo Mte., *France* 101 E8
Rotoroa, L., *N.Z.* 167 D4
Rotorua, *N.Z.* 167 C6
Rotorua, L., *N.Z.* 167 C6
Rotterdam, *Neths.* 165 C2
Rottumeroog, *Neths.* 165 A4
Rottweil, *Germany* 106 D2
Roubaix, *France* 101 A5
Rouen, *France* 100 B4
Round Mt., *Australia* 45 F9
Roussillon, *France* 101 E5
Rouxville, *S. Africa* 205 C3
Rouyn-Noranda, *Canada* 67 E9
Rovaniemi, *Finland* 99 A3
Rovereto, *Italy* 132 B3
Rovigo, *Italy* 132 B3
Rovinj, *Croatia* 89 B1
Rovno = Rivne, *Ukraine* 223 A2
Rovuma = Ruvuma →, *Tanzania* 217 C4
Rowley Shoals, *Australia* 44 C2
Roxa, *Guinea-Biss.* 112 A1
Roxas, *Capiz, Phil.* 184 F5
Roxas, *Isabela, Phil.* 184 C4
Roxas, *Mind. Or., Phil.* 184 E4
Roxborough, *Trin. & Tob.* 76 B5
Roxburgh, *N.Z.* 167 F2
Royal Canal, *Ireland* 128 C4
Royal Leamington Spa, *U.K.* 224 E6
Royan, *France* 100 D3
Rrëshen, *Albania* 35 B1
Rrogozhine, *Albania* 35 B1
Ruahine Ra., *N.Z.* 167 C6
Ruapehu, *N.Z.* 167 C5
Ruapuke I., *N.Z.* 167 G2
Rub' al Khālī, *Si. Arabia* 196 D4
Rubik, *Albania* 35 B1
Rubino, *Ivory C.* 134 B2
Rubio, *Venezuela* 236 B1
Rubtsovsk, *Russia* 190 D8
Ruby L., *U.S.A.* 230 B3
Rudnyy, *Kazakstan* 140 A3
Rudolfa, Ostrov, *Russia* 190 A5
Rufiji →, *Tanzania* 217 B3
Rufisque, *Senegal* 198 B1
Rugby, *U.K.* 224 E6
Rügen, *Germany* 106 A4
Ruhengeri, *Rwanda* 195 A1
Ruhnu, *Estonia* 97 C2
Ruhr →, *Germany* 106 C1
Rujen, *Macedonia* 151 A3
Ruki →, *Dem. Rep. of the Congo* 86 C2
Rukwa, L., *Tanzania* 217 B2
Rum = Rhum, *U.K.* 224 C3
Rum Cay, *Bahamas* 71 B2
Rum Jungle, *Australia* 44 B5
Rumania = Romania ■, *Europe* 188
Rumbêk, *Sudan* 210 D2
Rumia, *Poland* 186 A3
Rumoi, *Japan* 136 B7
Rumonge, *Burundi* 195 B1
Rumuruti, *Kenya* 141 A2
Runanga, *N.Z.* 167 E3
Runaway, C., *N.Z.* 167 B6
Runaway Bay, *Jamaica* 74 A2
Rundu, *Namibia* 163 A2
Rungwe, *Tanzania* 4 G7
Rungwe, Mt., *Tanzania* 217 B2
Runka, *Nigeria* 170 A2
Ruoqiang, *China* 80 C2
Rupat, *Indonesia* 124 B2
Rupert, *U.S.A.* 230 B4
Rupert →, *Canada* 67 D9
Rupert House = Waskaganish, *Canada* 67 D9
Rurrenabaque, *Bolivia* 55 A1
Rusambo, *Zimbabwe* 241 A2
Rusape, *Zimbabwe* 241 A2
Ruschuk = Ruse, *Bulgaria* 61 B3
Ruse, *Bulgaria* 61 B3
Rush, *Ireland* 128 C5
Rushon, *Tajikistan* 216 C3
Russellville, *U.S.A.* 231 C8
Russia ■, *Eurasia* 190
Rustavi, *Georgia* 104 B4
Rustenburg, *S. Africa* 205 B3
Rutana, *Burundi* 195 B2
Ruteng, *Indonesia* 125 D6
Ruvuma →, *Tanzania* 217 C4
Ruwenzori, *Africa* 4 F6
Ruya →, *Zimbabwe* 241 A2
Ruyigi, *Burundi* 195 B2
Ružomberok, *Slovak Rep.* 200 A2
Rwanda ■, *Africa* 195
Ryazan, *Russia* 190 D3
Rybache = Rybachye, *Kazakstan* 140 B5
Rybachye = Balykchy, *Kyrgyzstan* 144 A5
Rybachye, *Kazakstan* 140 B5
Rybinsk, *Russia* 190 D3
Rybinsk Res., *Russia* 28 D13
Rybnitsa = Râbniţa, *Moldova* 188 B5
Ryōtsu, *Japan* 136 D6
Rypin, *Poland* 186 B3
Ryūgasaki, *Japan* 136 F7
Ryūkyū Is. = Ryūkyū-rettō, *Japan* 10 G16
Ryūkyū-rettō, *Japan* 10 G16
Rzeszów, *Poland* 186 C4
Rzhev, *Russia* 190 D3

S

Sa, *Thailand* 218 B2
Sa Dec, *Vietnam* 237 G2
Sa'ādatābād, *Iran* 127 C5
Saale →, *Germany* 106 C3
Saalfeld, *Germany* 106 C3
Saane →, *Switz.* 213 A2
Saarbrücken, *Germany* 106 D1
Saaremaa, *Estonia* 97 B2
Sab 'Ābar, *Syria* 214 C2
Šabac, *Serbia, Yug.* 239 B1
Sabadell, *Spain* 207 B7
Sabah □, *Malaysia* 154 A5
Sabalān, Kūhhā-ye, *Iran* 126 A3
Sabalana, Kepulauan, *Indonesia* 125 D5
Sábana de la Mar, *Dom. Rep.* 72 B3
Sábanalarga, *Colombia* 85 A2
Sabang, *Indonesia* 124 A1
Saberania, *Indonesia* 125 C9
Sabhah, *Libya* 149 B2
Sabie, *S. Africa* 205 B4
Sabinas, *Mexico* 158 B4
Sabinas Hidalgo, *Mexico* 158 B4
Sabine →, *U.S.A.* 231 E8
Sabirabad, *Azerbaijan* 40 A4
Sabka, *Chad* 78 B2
Sablayan, *Phil.* 184 E4
Sable, C., *Canada* 67 E10
Sable, C., *U.S.A.* 231 E10
Sable I., *Canada* 67 E11
Sable I., *Papua N. G.* 181 B8
Sabou, *Burkina Faso* 62 B2
Sabria, *Tunisia* 219 B1
Sabulubbek, *Indonesia* 124 C1
Sabzevār, *Iran* 127 A6
Sabzvārān, *Iran* 127 C6
Săcele, *Romania* 188 C3
Sachkhere, *Georgia* 104 A3
Sachsen □, *Germany* 106 C4
Sachsen-Anhalt □, *Germany* 106 C4
Sacramento, *U.S.A.* 230 C2
Sacramento →, *U.S.A.* 230 C2
Sacramento Mts., *U.S.A.* 230 D5
Sada-Misaki, *Japan* 136 G3
Sadao, *Thailand* 218 H2
Sadd el Aali, *Egypt* 95 C2
Sade, *Nigeria* 170 A3
Sado, *Japan* 136 E6
Sadon, *Burma* 63 C4
Sæby, *Denmark* 93 A3
Safaga, *Egypt* 95 B2
Safata B., *Samoa* 177 B2
Safford, *U.S.A.* 230 D5
Safi, *Morocco* 161 B4
Safia, *Papua N. G.* 181 E5
Safīd Kūh, *Afghan.* 34 B1
Safune, *Samoa* 177 A1
Sag Sag, *Papua N. G.* 181 C5
Saga, *Japan* 136 G2
Sagae, *Japan* 136 D7
Sagar, *India* 118 C2
Sagay, *Phil.* 184 F5
Sagleipie, *Liberia* 148 B2
Saglouc = Salluit, *Canada* 67 C9
Sagŏ-ri, *S. Korea* 142 E2
Sagua la Grande, *Cuba* 90 A1
Sagunt, *Spain* 207 C5
Sagunto = Sagunt, *Spain* 207 C5
Sahagún, *Spain* 206 A3
Sahamandrevo, *Madag.* 152 C2
Sahand, Kūh-e, *Iran* 126 A3
Sahara, *Africa* 4 D3
Saharan Atlas = Saharien, Atlas, *Algeria* 36 B3
Saharanpur, *India* 118 B2
Saharien, Atlas, *Algeria* 36 B3
Sahasinaka, *Madag.* 152 C2
Sahiwal, *Pakistan* 179 D7
Sai Buri, *Thailand* 218 H2
Sa'id Bundas, *Sudan* 210 D1
Sa'īdābād, *Iran* 127 C5
Sa'īdīyeh, *Iran* 126 A4
Saidor, *Papua N. G.* 181 C4
Saidpur, *Bangla.* 50 B2
Saidu, *Pakistan* 179 B7
Saigon = Thanh Pho Ho Chi Minh, *Vietnam* 237 G3
Saijō, *Japan* 136 G3
Saikanosy Masoala, *Madag.* 152 B3
Saiki, *Japan* 136 G2
Sailolof, *Indonesia* 125 C8

WORLD MAPS

SETTLEMENTS

■ PARIS　　　■ Berne　　　◉ Livorno　　　◎ Brugge　　　◎ Algeciras　　　○ *Frejus*　　　○ *Oberammergau*　　　○ Thira

Settlement symbols and type styles vary according to the scale of each map and indicate the importance
of towns on the map rather than specific population figures

∴ Ruins or Archæological Sites　　　　˅ Wells in Desert

ADMINISTRATION

———— International Boundaries

– – – – · International Boundaries
(Undefined or Disputed)

··········· Internal Boundaries

National Parks

Country Names
NICARAGUA

Administrative
Area Names

KENT

CALABRIA

International boundaries show the *de facto* situation where there are rival claims to territory

COMMUNICATIONS

———— Principal Roads

———— Other Roads

–|–··–|– Road Tunnels

⋈ Passes

⊕ Airfields

———— Principal Railways

– –·– – Railways
Under Construction

———— Other Railways

–|–··–|– Railway Tunnels

········ Principal Canals

PHYSICAL FEATURES

——— Perennial Streams

– –·– – Intermittent Streams

⬭ Perennial Lakes

⬭ Intermittent Lakes

Swamps and Marshes

Permanent Ice
and Glaciers

▲ 8848 Elevations in metres

▼ 8500 Sea Depths in metres

1134 Height of Lake Surface
Above Sea Level in metres

Projection: *Hammer Equal Area*

10 11 12 13 14 15 16 17 18

20 40 60 80 100 120 140 160 180 80

A R C T I C   O C E A N

Svalbard (Nor.)

an

Barents   Sea   Novaya   Zemlya   Kara Sea   Severnaya Zemlya   Laptev Sea   New Siberian Is.   East Siberian Sea   Wrangel I.   A

Murmansk   Salekhard   Norilsk   Verkhoyansk   Arctic Circle

Arkhangelsk   R U S S I A   Yakutsk   Magadan   Bering Sea   B

NORWAY SWEDEN FINLAND   Yenisey   Ob   L. Baikal   Sea of Okhotsk   Petropavlovsk-Kamchatskiy

Oslo   Helsinki   St. Petersburg   Perm   Yekaterinburg   Tomsk   Krasnoyarsk   Okhotsk   Sakhalin   International Date Line

Stockholm EST.   Volga   Kazan   Chelyabinsk   Omsk   Novosibirsk   Irkutsk   Ulan Ude   Komsomolsk

Copenhagen LATVIA   MOSCOW   Samara   Astana   Barnaul   Khabarovsk

DENMARK LITH.   Saratov   Qaraghandy   Ulan Bator   Harbin   Vladivostok   Sapporo

mburg NETH. POLAND BELARUS   Minsk   KAZAKSTAN   MONGOLIA   Changchun   SHENYANG   NORTH KOREA   JAPAN

sterdam Berlin GERMANY   Warsaw   Kiev   Volgograd   Aral Sea   Ürümqi   BEIJING TIANJIN   Pyongyang   SEOUL   TÔKYÔ

Brussels CZECH   Prague   UKRAINE   L. Balkhash   Almaty   Bishkek   CHINA   Dalian   SOUTH KOREA   Osaka   PACIFIC

PARIS LUX. Vienna SLOVAK   Budapest   Odessa   Caspian Sea   UZBEKISTAN   KYRGYZSTAN   Lanzhou   Taiyuan   Kitakyushu

AUSTRIA HUNG.   Bucharest   Black Sea   GEORGIA   Baku   Tashkent   TAJIKISTAN   Xi'an   Nanjing   OCEAN

Milan SLOV. ROMANIA   Belgrade   Tbilisi   ARM. AZER.   Samarkand   Dushanbe   Hwang Ho   SHANGHAI

arseilles ITALY CRO.   Sofia BULGARIA   Yerevan   TURKMENISTAN   Chengdu   Wuhan   East China Sea   C

Rome   MAC.   Istanbul   Ankara   Tabriz   Ashkhabad   AFGHANISTAN   CHONGQING   Ryukyu Is.

rcelona Naples   GREECE   TURKEY   İzmir   TEHRÂN   Mashhad   Kâbul   TIBET   Lhasa   GUANGZHOU   Taipei   TAIWAN

Sardinia   Athens   CYPRUS   SYRIA   Damascus   Baghdad   Esfahân   Islamabad   Lahore   DELHI   Kunming   Fuzhou

Algiers   Tunis   MALTA   Beirut   LEB.   Amman   IRAQ IRAN   PAKISTAN   New Delhi   NEPAL   Katmandu BHU.   Hanoi   HONG KONG

TUNISIA   Crete   Mediterranean Sea   ISR. JORDAN   KUWAIT   Shirâz   Kanpur   BANGLA-DESH   BURMA   Hainan

Tripoli   Benghazi   Alexandria   CAIRO   Jerusalem   The Gulf   BAHRAIN QATAR   Riyadh   Abu Dhabi   KARACHI   Ahmadabad   INDIA   CALCUTTA DACCA MYANMAR   South China Sea   MANILA   D

CRIA   LIBYA   EGYPT   Aswân   U.A.E.   Muscat   Nagpur   Bay of   Rangoon   Vientiane   VIET-   PHILIPPINES

SAUDI   Mecca   Red Sea   OMAN   Arabian Sea   MUMBAI (Bombay)   Bengal   BANGKOK   NAM

NIGER   CHAD   Omdurmân   ARABIA   Sana'   YEMEN   Hyderabad   CHENNAI (Madras)   THAILAND   Andaman Is. (India)   Phnom Penh   Ho Chi Minh City

Niamey   L. Chad   Khartoum   ERITREA   Asmara   Aden   G. of Aden   Socotra (Yemen)   Bangalore   SRI LANKA   Nicobar Is. (India)   Yap   FEDERATED STATES   MARSHALL IS.

NIGERIA   Kano   Ndjamena   SUDAN   DJIBOUTI   Addis Ababa   SOMALI   Lakshadweep Is. (India)   Colombo   Truk   Pohnpei   OF MICRONESIA

Abuja   CENTRAL   ETHIOPIA   REP.   MALDIVES   PALAU   Caroline Is.

Ibadan   CAMEROON AFRICAN   Bangui   L. Turkana   Mogadishu   Medan   Kuala Lumpur   SABAH   Gilbert I.

Lagos   Douala   REP.   UGANDA   KENYA   PEN. MALAYSIA   BRUNEI   NAURU KIRIBATI

EQUATORIAL   Yaoundé   Kisangani   Kampala   Nairobi   MALAYSIA   Borneo   IRIAN   New

nea GUINEA   Libreville GABON   CONGO   Victoria   Equator   INDONESIA   JAYA   Ireland

SÃO TOMÉ   Brazzaville DEM. REP. OF THE   RWANDA   Mombasa   SEYCHELLES   Chagos Arch. (U.K.)   Palembang   Banjarmasin   Ujung Pandang   PAPUA   New

& PRÍNCIPE   CONGO   Kinshasa   BURUNDI   Zanzibar   Amirante Is.   Diego Garcia   JAKARTA   NEW   Britain

Luanda   Kananga   Bujumbura   Dodoma   Dar es Salaam   Bandung   Surabaya   GUINEA   SOLOMON

CABINDA   TANZANIA   Lake Tanganyika   INDIAN   Java   Timor   Arafura Sea   Port   IS.

(Angola)   ANGOLA   Lubumbashi   L. Nyasa   Aldabra Is.   Agalega Is.   OCEAN   Moresby   Santa Cruz I.

Benguela   ZAMBIA   Lilongwe   COMOROS   Mayotte (Fr.)   Cocos Is. (Austral.)   Christmas I. (Austral.)   C. York   Darwin   E

Lusaka   MALAWI   MADAGASCAR   Cargados Carajos   VANUATU

Windhoek   NAMIBIA   ZIMBABWE MOZAMBIQUE   Harare   Rodriguez I.   MAURITIUS   Tropic of Capricorn   Cairns   NEW   FIJI

Bulawayo   Mozambique Channel   Antananarivo   RÉUNION (Fr.)   Port Hedland   Townsville   CALEDONIA (Fr.)   Suva

BOTSWANA   Gaborone   Pretoria   Alice Springs   Rockhampton

Johannesburg   SWAZILAND   AUSTRALIA

SOUTH   LESOTHO   Maputo   Geraldton   Kalgoorlie-Boulder   Brisbane

Cape Town   AFRICA   Durban   Amsterdam I. (Fr.)   Perth   Great   Adelaide   Newcastle   Lord Howe I. (Austral.)   F

C. of Good Hope   Port Elizabeth   St. Paul (Fr.)   Fremantle   Australian   Sydney   Norfolk I. (Austral.)

Bight   Canberra   Auckland   North I.

Prince Edward Is. (S. Africa)   Crozet Is. (Fr.)   Melbourne   Tasman   NEW   Wellington

Kerguelen (Fr.)   Tasmania   Sea   ZEALAND

Bouvet I. (Nor.)   McDonald Is. (Austral.)   Heard I. (Austral.)   Hobart   Christchurch   South I.

OUTHERN   OCEAN   Stewart I.   Dunedin   G

Antarctic Circle   Campbell I. (Austral.)   Auckland Is. (N.Z.)

c   t   i   c   a   H

East from Greenwich   20   40   60   80   100   120   140   160   180   80

10 11 12 13 14 15 16 17 18

Hanoi ◉ Capital Cities

4 ARCTIC OCEAN 1:35 000 000

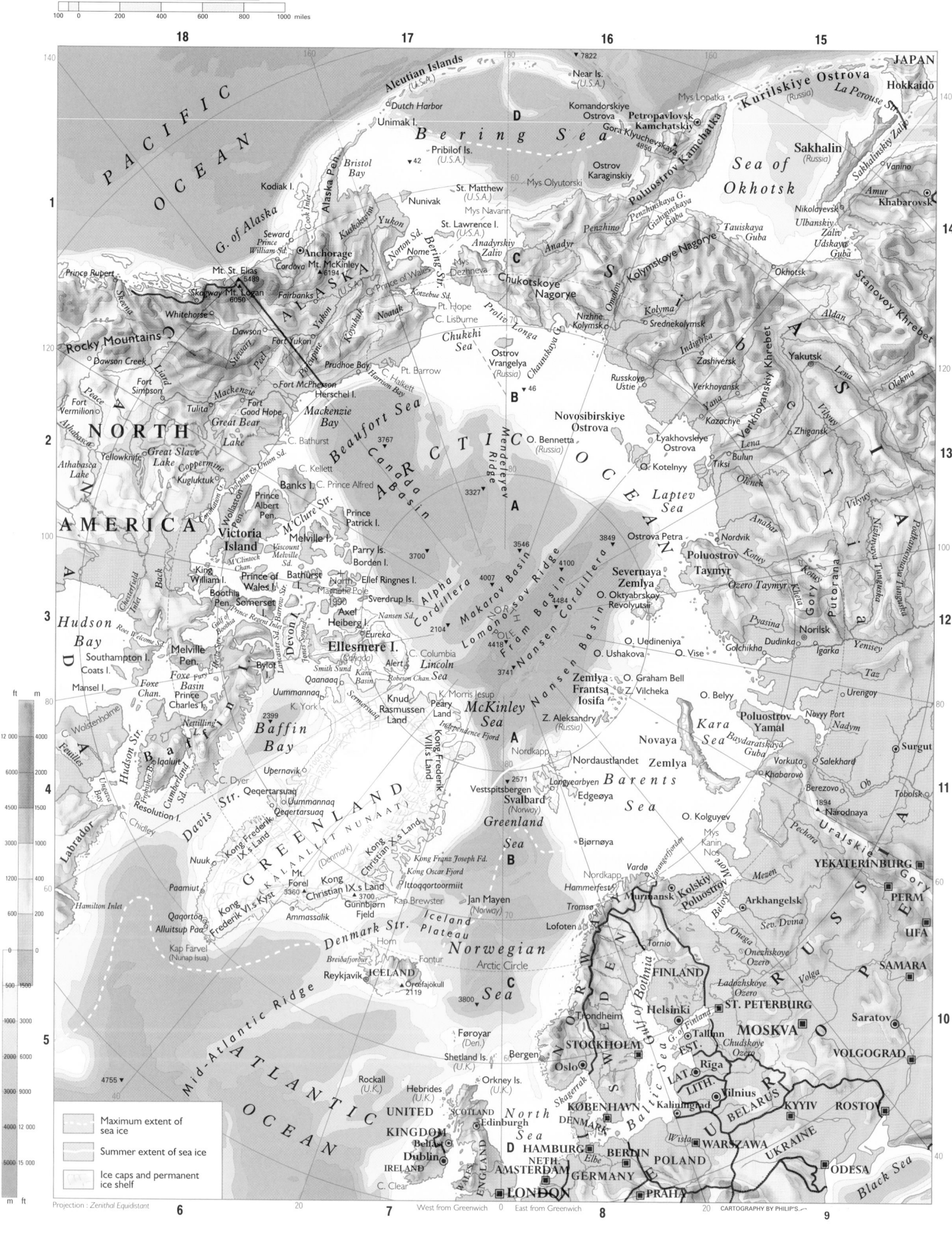

100 0 200 400 600 800 1000 1200 1400 km
100 0 200 400 600 800 1000 miles
PACIFIC OCEAN
Aleutian Islands (U.S.A.)
Dutch Harbor
Unimak I.
Bering Sea
Pribilof Is. (U.S.A.)
Near Is. (U.S.A.)
Komandorskiye Ostrova
Petropavlovsk Kamchatskiy
Poluostrov Kamchatka
Kurilskiye Ostrova (Russia)
JAPAN
Hokkaido
La Perouse Str.
Sakhalin (Russia)
Sea of Okhotsk
Khabarovsk
Bristol Bay
Kodiak I.
G. of Alaska
Alaska Pen.
Anchorage
Mt. McKinley 6194
Mt. St. Elias 5489
Mt. Logan 6050
ALASKA (U.S.A.)
Nunivak
St. Matthew (U.S.A.)
St. Lawrence I. (U.S.A.)
Bering Str.
Nome
Anadyrskiy Zaliv
Chukotskoye Nagorye
Kolymskoye Nagorye
Okhotsk
Stanovoy Khrebet
Prince Rupert
Rocky Mountains
Whitehorse
Dawson
Fairbanks
Chukchi Sea
Ostrov Vrangelya (Russia)
Pt. Barrow
Prudhoe Bay
Beaufort Sea
Mackenzie Bay
Herschel I.
Fort McPherson
Great Bear Lake
Great Slave Lake
Yellowknife
NORTH AMERICA
Banks I.
Victoria Island
Melville I.
Prince Patrick I.
Parry Is.
Ellef Ringnes I.
Axel Heiberg I.
Ellesmere I. (Canada)
Devon I.
Somerset I.
King William I.
Boothia Pen.
Hudson Bay
Southampton I.
Coats I.
Mansel I.
Foxe Basin
Baffin Bay
Baffin I.
Iqaluit
Hudson Str.
Labrador
Davis Str.
Qaanaaq
Upernavik
Nuuk
Paamiut
Qaqortoq
Kap Farvel (Nunap Isua)
GREENLAND (Denmark)
KALAALLIT NUNAAT
Ammassalik
Denmark Str.
ICELAND
Reykjavík
Jan Mayen (Norway)
Greenland Sea
Norwegian Sea
Arctic Circle
Svalbard (Norway)
Longyearbyen
Nordaustlandet
Barents Sea
Bjørnøya
Zemlya Frantsa Iosifa
Novaya Zemlya
Kara Sea
Severnaya Zemlya
Laptev Sea
Novosibirskiye Ostrova
ARCTIC OCEAN
Canada Basin
Alpha Cordillera
Makarov Basin
Lomonosov Ridge
Fram Basin
Nansen Basin
Nansen Cordillera
Mendeleyev Ridge
NORTH POLE
North Magnetic Pole
McKinley Sea
Lincoln Sea
Peary Land
Poluostrov Taymyr
Norilsk
Yakutsk
Verkhoyanskiy Khrebet
ASIA
Poluostrov Yamal
Vorkuta
Murmansk
Kolskiy Poluostrov
Arkhangelsk
YEKATERINBURG
PERM
UFA
SAMARA
MOSKVA
ST. PETERBURG
FINLAND
Helsinki
NORWAY
SWEDEN
STOCKHOLM
Oslo
Trondheim
Gulf of Bothnia
Tallinn
Riga
Vilnius
BELARUS
UKRAINE
KYYIV
ODESA
ROSTOV
VOLGOGRAD
Black Sea
POLAND
WARSZAWA
GERMANY
BERLIN
HAMBURG
KØBENHAVN
DENMARK
North Sea
Føroyar (Den.)
Shetland Is. (U.K.)
Orkney Is. (U.K.)
Bergen
Rockall (U.K.)
Hebrides (U.K.)
UNITED KINGDOM
Edinburgh
Belfast
Dublin
IRELAND
LONDON
AMSTERDAM
PRAHA
Mid-Atlantic Ridge
ATLANTIC OCEAN
Maximum extent of sea ice
Summer extent of sea ice
Ice caps and permanent ice shelf
Projection : Zenithal Equidistant
West from Greenwich
East from Greenwich
CARTOGRAPHY BY PHILIP'S

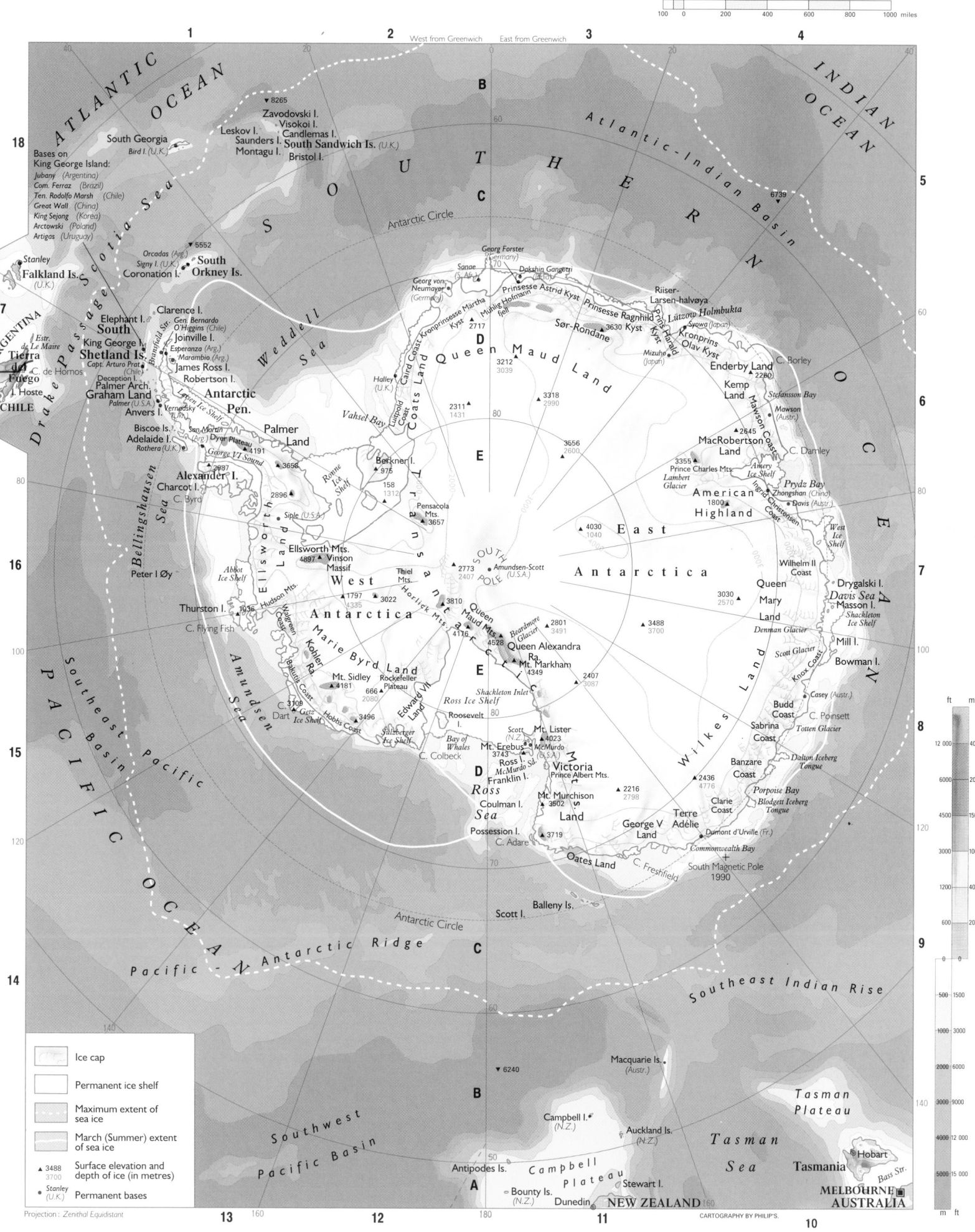

ATLANTIC OCEAN

INDIAN OCEAN

SOUTHERN

Atlantic-Indian Basin

▼ 8265

Zavodovski I.

Leskov I.   Visokoi I.
Saunders I. Candlemas I.
Montagu I.   **South Sandwich Is.** (U.K.)
             Bristol I.

South Georgia
Bird I. (U.K.)

Bases on
King George Island:
Jubany   (Argentina)
Com. Ferraz (Brazil)
Ten. Rodolfo Marsh (Chile)
Great Wall (China)
King Sejong (Korea)
Arctowski (Poland)
Artigas (Uruguay)

Antarctic Circle

Georg Forster
(Germany)

Sanae Dakshin Gangotri
(India)

Georg von
Neumayer
(Germany)

Prinsesse Astrid Kyst   Riiser-
Kronprinsesse Märtha   Larsen-halvøya
Kyst Mühlig Hofmann   Prinsesse Ragnhild
fjell 2717   Kyst Lützow Holmbukta
      Prinsesse Martha   Prins Harald Syowa (Japan)
      Kyst   Kyst Kronprins
Queen Maud Land   Olav Kyst

Orcadas (Arg.) ▼ 5552
Signy I. (U.K.) South
Coronation I.   **Orkney Is.**

Stanley
Falkland Is.
(U.K.)

ARGENTINA

Estr.
de Le Maire

C. de Hornos

Tierra
del
Fuego
I. Hoste

CHILE

Clarence I.
Elephant I. Gen. Bernardo
South   O'Higgins (Chile)
King George I. Joinville I.
Shetland Is. Esperanza (Arg.)
Capt. Arturo Prat Marambio (Arg.)
(Chile) James Ross I.
Deception I. Robertson I.
Antarctic
Pen.

Palmer Arch.
Graham Land Larsen Ice Shelf
Palmer (U.S.A.) Vernadsky (U.K.)
Anvers I. San Martin (Arg.)

Biscoe Is. Dyer Plateau
Adelaide I. 4191
Rothera (U.K.) George VI Sound
             3656

Charcot I. 2987 2896

C. Byrd

Siple (U.S.A.)

Peter I Øy

Thurston I. 936

C. Flying Fish

Abbot Ice Shelf

Hudson Mts.

Ellsworth Mts.
4897 Vinson
Massif

1797 3022
4335

West
Antarctica

Marie Byrd
Land

Kohler Ra.

Mt. Sidley
4181

Rockefeller
Plateau
666 2080

C. 3109
Dart

Getz
Ice Shelf

Hobbs Coast
3496

Sulzberger
Ice Shelf

Edward VII
Land

C. Colbeck

Bay of
Whales

Roosevelt I.

Ross Ice Shelf

Scott
(N.Z.)

Mt. Erebus
3743
Ross I.
McMurdo (U.S.A.)
McMurdo Sd.

Mt. Lister
4023

Franklin I.

Victoria
Prince Albert Mts.

Coulman I.

Mt. Murchison
3502

Possession I.

C. Adare 3719

Weddell
Sea

Halley
(U.K.)

Vahsel Bay

Luitpold
Coast

Coats Land

Caird Coast

Berkner I.
975

Ronne
Ice Shelf

158 1312

Pensacola
Mts.
3657

2773 3810
2407

South
POLE

Amundsen-Scott
(U.S.A.)

Thiel
Mts.

4528 4116

Queen
Maud Mts.

Horlick Mts.

Beardmore
Glacier

2801
3491

Queen Alexandra
Ra.
Mt. Markham
4349

Shackleton Inlet

2407
3087

3212
3039

3318
2990

3656
2600

4030
1040

East
Antarctica

3030
2570

3488
3700

2216
2798

Queen Maud Land

Enderby Land

C. Borley

Kemp
Land

Stefansson Bay

Mawson
(Austr.)

Mizuho
(Japan)

MacRobertson
Land

C. Darnley

3355 2645
Prince Charles Mts. Amery
Lambert Ice Shelf
Glacier

American
Highland
1800

Zhongshan
(China)

Prydz Bay
Davis (Austr.)

Ingrid
Christensen
Coast

West
Ice Shelf

Wilhelm II
Coast

Queen
Mary
Land

Drygalski I.

Davis Sea
Masson I.

Shackleton
Ice Shelf

Denman Glacier

Scott Glacier

Mill I.

Knox Coast

Casey (Austr.)

Bowman I.

Budd
Coast

Sabrina
Coast

Totten Glacier

Banzare
Coast

Dalton Iceberg
Tongue

Clarie
Coast

Porpoise Bay
Blodgett Iceberg
Tongue

Terre
Adélie

George V
Land

Dumont d'Urville (Fr.)

Commonwealth Bay
South Magnetic Pole
1990

2436
4776

Wilkes

Land

Oates Land

C. Freshfield

Scott I.

Balleny Is.

Antarctic Circle

Pacific-Antarctic Ridge

Southeast Indian Rise

▼ 6240

Macquarie Is.
(Austr.)

Tasman
Plateau

Tasman
Sea

Tasmania

Hobart

Bass Str.

Campbell I.
(N.Z.)

Auckland Is.
(N.Z.)

MELBOURNE
AUSTRALIA

Antipodes Is.

Bounty Is.
(N.Z.)

Campbell
Plateau

Stewart I.

Dunedin **NEW ZEALAND**

Southwest
Pacific Basin

PACIFIC OCEAN

Southeast Pacific Basin

Bellingshausen
Sea

Amundsen Sea

Drake Passage

Scotia Sea

ATLANTIC OCEAN

West from Greenwich
East from Greenwich

Ice cap

Permanent ice shelf

Maximum extent of
sea ice

March (Summer) extent
of sea ice

▲ 3488   Surface elevation and
  3700   depth of ice (in metres)

• Stanley Permanent bases
  (U.K.)

Projection: Zenithal Equidistant

CARTOGRAPHY BY PHILIP'S.

ft m

12 000 4000

6000   2000

4500   1500

3000   1000

1200   400

600   200

0   0

500   1500

1000   3000

2000   6000

3000   9000

4000   12 000

5000   15 000

m ft

Norwegian claim	45°E - 20°W	French claim	136°E - 142°E	British claim	80°W - 20°W
Australian claims	45°E - 136°E	New Zealand claim	160°E - 150°W	Argentine claim	74°W - 53°W
	142°E - 160°E	Chilean claim	90°W - 53°W		

EUROPE : Physical 1:20 000 000

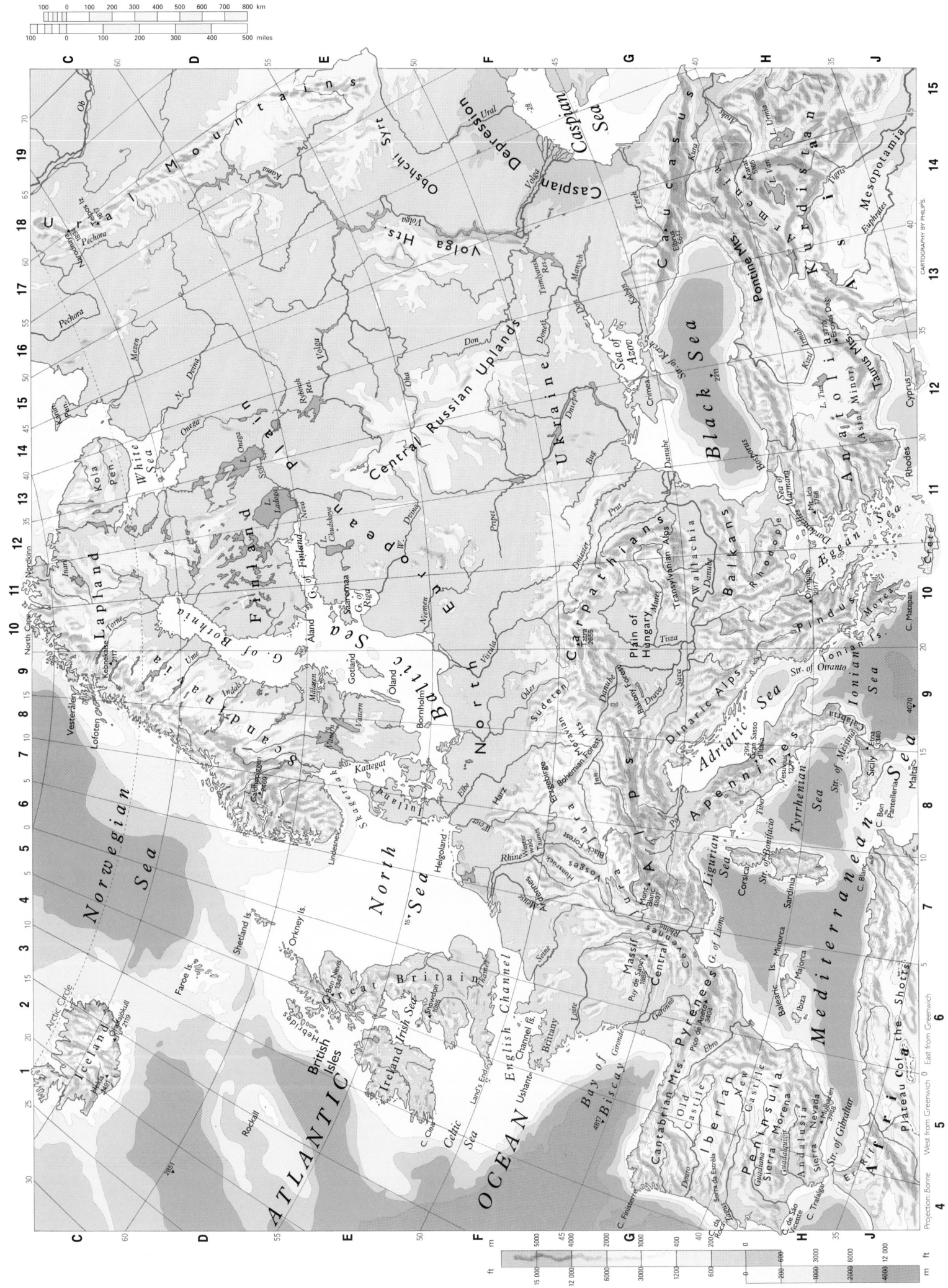

km
miles
Norwegian Sea
North Sea
ATLANTIC OCEAN
Bay of Biscay
Celtic Sea
English Channel
Irish Sea
Baltic Sea
G. of Bothnia
G. of Finland
G. of Riga
White Sea
Caspian Sea
Caspian Depression
Black Sea
Sea of Azov
Sea of Marmara
Ægean Sea
Ionian Sea
Adriatic Sea
Tyrrhenian Sea
Ligurian Sea
Mediterranean Sea
Str. of Gibraltar
Str. of Otranto
Str. of Messina
Str. of Bonifacio
Str. of Kerch
G. of Lions
Skagerrak
Kattegat
Iceland
Faroe Is.
Shetland Is.
Orkney Is.
Hebrides
British Isles
Great Britain
Ireland
Channel Is.
Brittany
Iberian Peninsula
Old Castile
New Castile
Andalusia
Pyrenees
Cantabrian Mts.
Sierra Morena
Sierra Nevada
Massif Central
Cevennes
Alps
Jura
Vosges
Black Forest
Ardennes
Harz
Erzgebirge
Bohemian Forest
Moravian Hts.
Sudeten
Carpathians
Transylvanian Alps
Plain of Hungary
Wallachia
Balkans
Rhodope
Pindus
Dinaric Alps
Apennines
Corsica
Sardinia
Sicily
Malta
Crete
Cyprus
Rhodes
Balearic Is.
Majorca
Minorca
Ibiza
Jutland
Scandinavia
Lapland
Finland
Kola Pen.
Kanin Pen.
North Cape
Nordkinn
Lofoten
Vesterålen
Gotland
Öland
Bornholm
Saaremaa
Åland
North European Plain
Central Russian Uplands
Ukraine
Crimea
Volga Hts.
Obshchi Syrt
Ural Mountains
Caucasus
Anatolia (Asia Minor)
Pontine Mts.
Taurus Mts.
Armenia
Kurdistan
Asia
Mesopotamia
Rif
Plateau of the Shotts
Africa
Volga
Don
Dnieper
Danube
Rhine
Elbe
Oder
Vistula
Seine
Loire
Rhône
Po
Ebro
Tagus
Guadalquivir
Pechora
Mezen
N. Dvina
Onega
Kama
Ural
Oka
Donets
Prut
Bug
Pripet
Niemen
Tisza
Drava
Sava
Mures
Tiber
Thames
Garonne
Gironde
Douro
Guadiana
L. Ladoga
L. Onega
L. Chudskoye
Vänern
Vättern
Mälaren
Rybinsk Res.
Tsimlyansk Res.
Mont Blanc 4807
Gran Sasso d'Italia 2914
Etna 3340
Vesuvius 1277
Olympus 2917
Mt. Ida 1766
Elbrus 5642
Ararat 5165
Pico de Aneto 3404
Mulhacén 3478
Galdhøpiggen 2469
Kebnekaise 2117
Snowdon 1085
Ben Nevis 1344
Tatra 2655
Puy de Sancy 1886
Land's End
Ushant
C. Finisterre
C. Clear
C. Matapan
C. Bon
C. Blanc
C. Trafalgar
C. da Roca
C. de São Vicente
Lindesnes
Helgoland
Rockall
Arctic Circle
Projection: Bonne
West from Greenwich
East from Greenwich
CARTOGRAPHY BY PHILIPS
m
ft

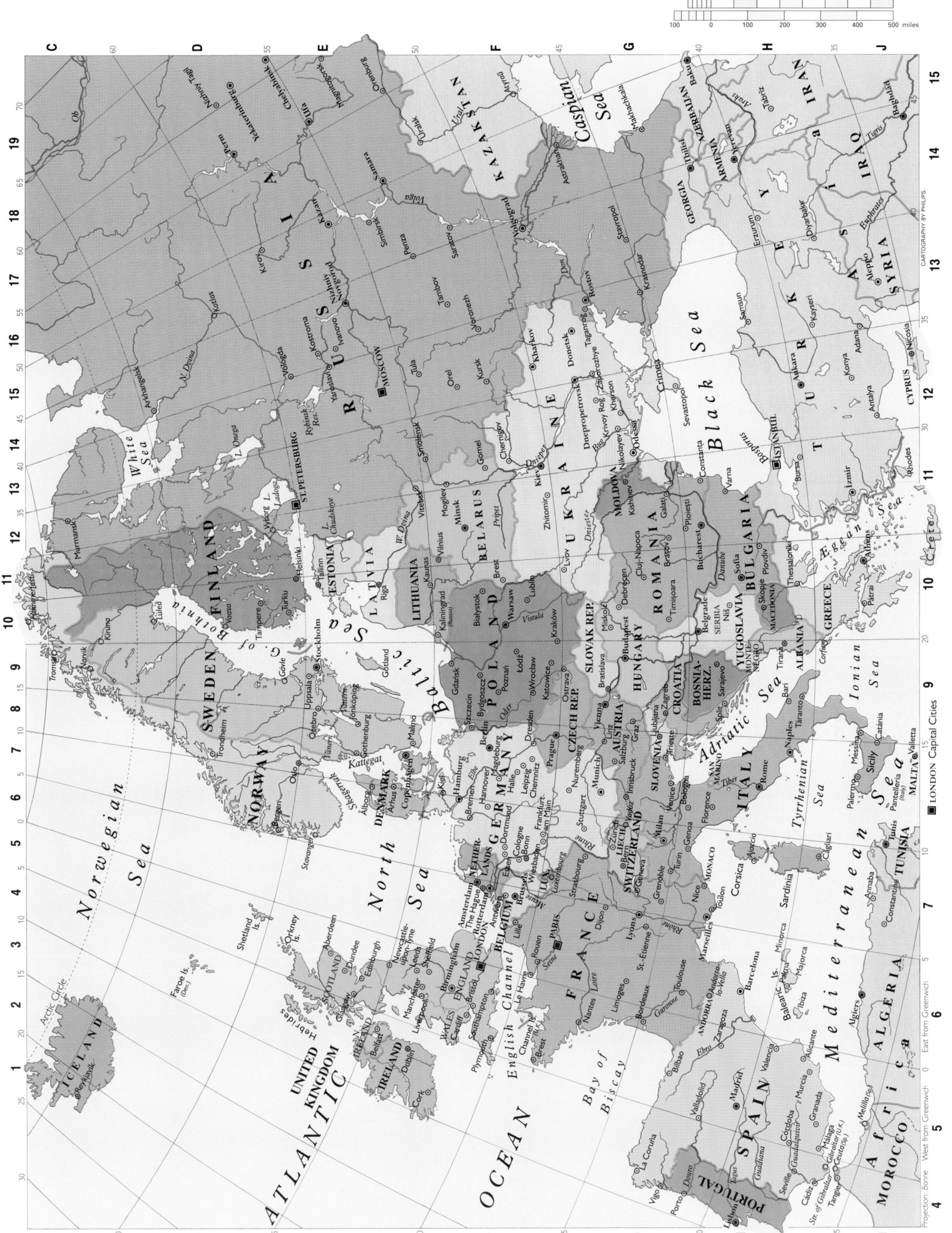
0 100 200 300 400 500 600 700 800 km
0 100 200 300 400 500 miles
ICELAND
Reykjavík
Arctic Circle
Faroe Is. (Den.)
Shetland Is.
Orkney Is.
Hebrides
UNITED KINGDOM
SCOTLAND
ENGLAND
WALES
LONDON
IRELAND
N. IRELAND
Dublin
Belfast
ATLANTIC
OCEAN
Norwegian Sea
North Sea
English Channel
Channel Is. (U.K.)
Bay of Biscay
NORWAY
Oslo
Bergen
Stavanger
Trondheim
Narvik
Tromsø
SWEDEN
Stockholm
Gothenburg
Malmö
Uppsala
Gävle
Kiruna
Luleå
FINLAND
Helsinki
Tampere
Turku
Vaasa
G. of Bothnia
Baltic Sea
Gotland
Kattegat
Skagerrak
DENMARK
Copenhagen
Århus
Ålborg
ESTONIA
Tallinn
LATVIA
Riga
LITHUANIA
Vilnius
Kaunas
Kaliningrad (Russia)
BELARUS
Minsk
Brest
Gomel
POLAND
Warsaw
Gdańsk
Poznań
Łódź
Kraków
Wrocław
GERMANY
Berlin
Hamburg
Munich
Frankfurt am Main
NETHERLANDS
Amsterdam
The Hague
Rotterdam
BELGIUM
Brussels
LUX.
FRANCE
PARIS
Lyons
Marseilles
Bordeaux
Toulouse
Nantes
SWITZERLAND
Bern
Zürich
Geneva
LIECH.
AUSTRIA
Vienna
CZECH REP.
Prague
SLOVAK REP.
Bratislava
HUNGARY
Budapest
SLOVENIA
Ljubljana
CROATIA
Zagreb
BOSNIA-HERZ.
Sarajevo
YUGOSLAVIA
SERBIA
MONTENEGRO
Belgrade
ALBANIA
Tirana
MACEDONIA
Skopje
GREECE
Athens
Thessaloniki
Crete
Ægean Sea
Ionian Sea
Adriatic Sea
Tyrrhenian Sea
Mediterranean Sea
ITALY
Rome
Milan
Naples
Sicily
Sardinia
Corsica
MALTA
Valletta
SAN MARINO
MONACO
ANDORRA
SPAIN
Madrid
Barcelona
Valencia
Seville
Balearic Is.
PORTUGAL
Lisbon
Porto
Str. of Gibraltar
Gibraltar (U.K.)
Ceuta (Sp.)
Melilla (Sp.)
MOROCCO
ALGERIA
Algiers
TUNISIA
Tunis
Africa
ROMANIA
Bucharest
MOLDOVA
Kishinev
BULGARIA
Sofia
Varna
UKRAINE
Kiev
Odessa
Kharkov
Crimea
Black Sea
TURKEY
Istanbul
Ankara
Bosporus
CYPRUS
Nicosia
SYRIA
IRAQ
Baghdad
IRAN
GEORGIA
Tbilisi
ARMENIA
Yerevan
AZERBAIJAN
Baku
Caspian Sea
KAZAKSTAN
RUSSIA
MOSCOW
ST. PETERSBURG
Nizhniy Novgorod
Volgograd
Samara
Kazan
Perm
Yekaterinburg
Arkhangelsk
Murmansk
White Sea
L. Ladoga
L. Onega
Volga
Ob
LONDON Capital Cities
Projection: Bonne
East from Greenwich
West from Greenwich
CARTOGRAPHY BY PHILIPS

SCANDINAVIA 1:5 000 000

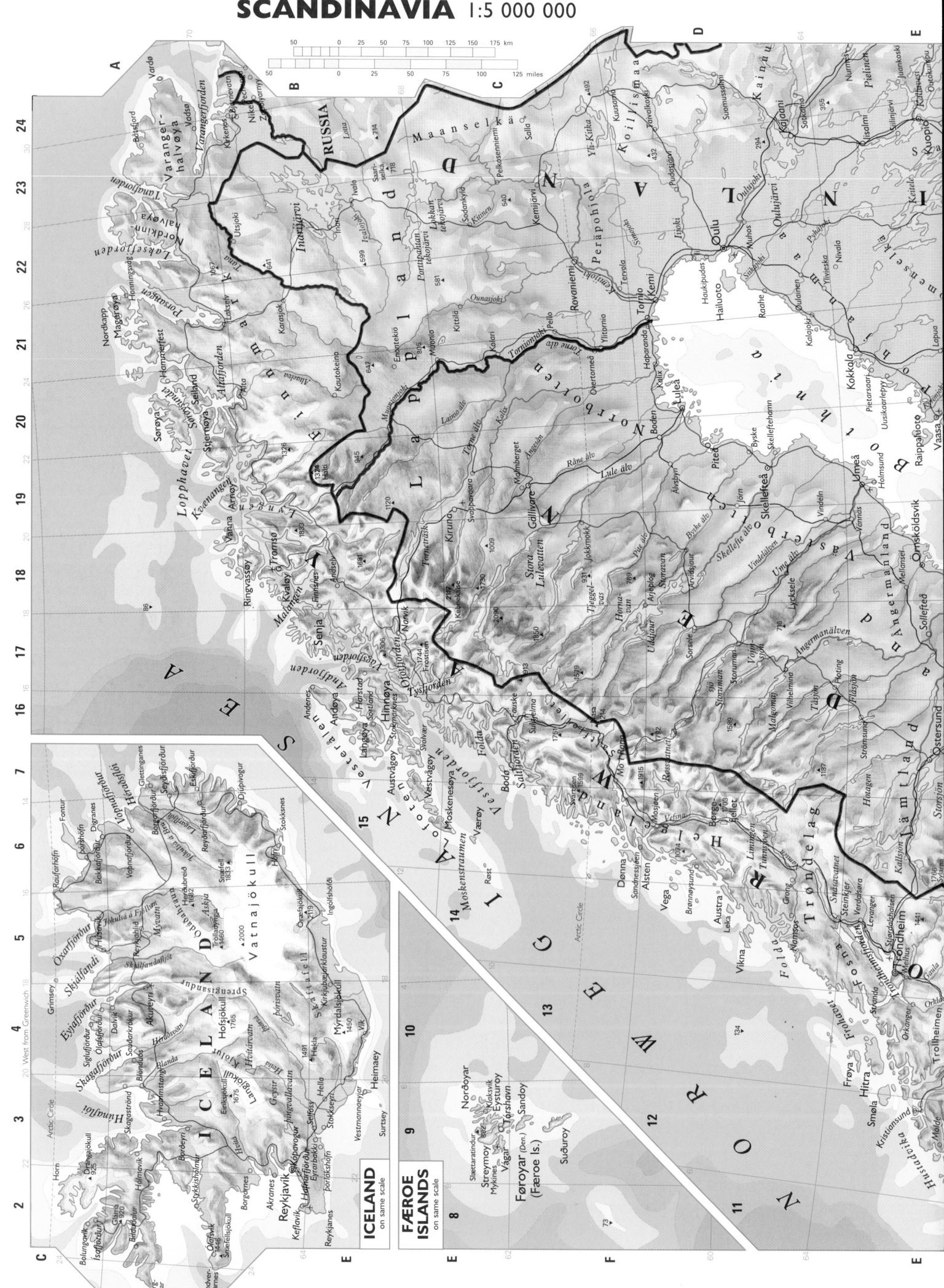
RUSSIA
ICELAND
on same scale
FÆROE
ISLANDS
on same scale
ICELAND
Vatnajökull
Reykjavík
Føroyar (Den.)
(Færoe Is.)
Tórshavn
NORWEGIAN SEA
Lofoten
Vesterålen
Lapland
Finnmark
Norrbotten
Västerbotten
Ångermanland
Jämtland
Trøndelag
Gulf of Bothnia
Tromsø
Narvik
Bodø
Trondheim
Kiruna
Luleå
Oulu
Umeå
Kemi
Tornio
Haparanda
Kuopio
Vaasa
Östersund
Rovaniemi
Hammerfest
Nordkapp
Arctic Circle
West from Greenwich

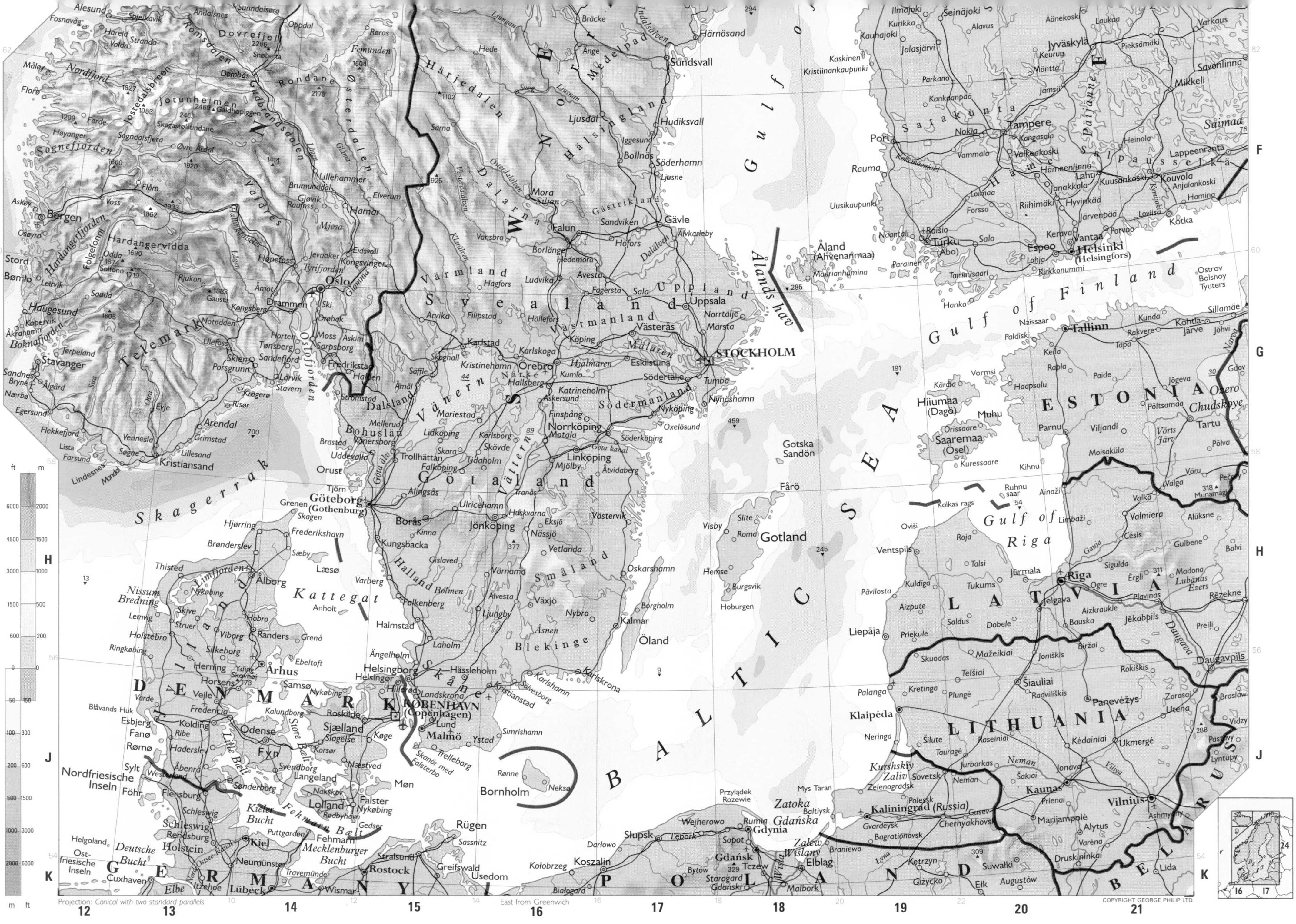

Major regions and seas

FINLAND · **ESTONIA** · **LATVIA** · **LITHUANIA** · **RUSSIA** · **POLAND** · **GERMANY** · **DENMARK** · **NORWAY** · **SWEDEN**

Gulf of Finland · Gulf of Riga · Gulf of Bothnia · BALTIC SEA · Kattegat · Skagerrak · Ålands hav

Suomi · Pohjanmaa · Pirkanmaa · Savonia · Lappeenranta · Uppland · Västmanland · Södermanland · Närke · Dalarna · Härjedalen · Hälsingland · Gästrikland · Värmland · Dalsland · Bohuslän · Västergötland · Östergötland · Gotland · Öland · Småland · Halland · Skåne · Blekinge · Götaland · Svealand · Valdres · Gudbrandsdalen · Österdalen · Hardangervidda · Jotunheimen · Dovrefjell · Rondane · Telemark · Sjælland · Lolland · Falster · Fyn · Møn · Langeland · Rügen · Usedom · Bornholm · Hiiumaa (Dago) · Saaremaa (Ösel) · Muhu · Åland (Ahvenanmaa)

Selected cities and towns

Finland: Helsinki (Helsingfors) · Espoo · Tampere · Turku (Åbo) · Lahti · Kouvola · Kotka · Hämeenlinna · Pori · Rauma · Vaasa · Jyväskylä · Mikkeli · Savonlinna · Lappeenranta · Kuopio · Kokkola · Seinäjoki · Riihimäki · Salo · Lohja · Rovaniemi area names

Estonia: Tallinn · Tartu · Narva · Pärnu · Viljandi · Rakvere · Paide · Haapsalu · Kuressaare

Latvia: Riga · Jelgava · Daugavpils · Ventspils · Liepāja · Jūrmala · Valmiera · Cēsis · Rēzekne · Jēkabpils · Tukums · Sigulda · Ogre

Lithuania: Vilnius · Kaunas · Klaipėda · Šiauliai · Panevėžys · Alytus · Marijampolė · Ukmergė · Kėdainiai · Utena · Telšiai · Tauragė · Mažeikiai · Plungė · Kretinga

Russia (Kaliningrad): Kaliningrad (Russia) · Sovetsk · Chernyakhovsk · Baltiysk · Zelenogradsk · Gvardeysk · Bagrationovsk

Poland: Gdańsk · Gdynia · Sopot · Elbląg · Malbork · Słupsk · Koszalin · Kołobrzeg · Tczew · Starogard Gdański · Bytów · Lębork · Wejherowo · Braniewo

Sweden: STOCKHOLM · Uppsala · Västerås · Örebro · Norrköping · Linköping · Jönköping · Gävle · Sundsvall · Härnösand · Hudiksvall · Söderhamn · Falun · Borlänge · Mora · Karlstad · Sundsvall · Eskilstuna · Nyköping · Katrineholm · Motala · Mjölby · Vetlanda · Växjö · Kalmar · Karlskrona · Karlshamn · Kristianstad · Hässleholm · Helsingborg · Malmö · Lund · Landskrona · Trelleborg · Ystad · Halmstad · Varberg · Göteborg (Gothenburg) · Borås · Trollhättan · Uddevalla · Lidköping · Skövde · Mariestad · Visby · Ronneby · Nässjö · Oskarshamn · Västervik · Ängelholm

Norway: Oslo · Bergen · Stavanger · Kristiansand · Drammen · Fredrikstad · Sarpsborg · Sandefjord · Tønsberg · Skien · Porsgrunn · Arendal · Hamar · Lillehammer · Ålesund · Molde · Flekkefjord · Mandal · Haugesund · Kongsvinger · Elverum · Røros

Denmark: KØBENHAVN (Copenhagen) · Århus · Ålborg · Odense · Esbjerg · Randers · Kolding · Vejle · Horsens · Roskilde · Helsingør · Hjørring · Frederikshavn · Silkeborg · Viborg · Herning · Ribe · Slagelse · Nykøbing · Korsør · Svendborg · Nakskov · Holstebro · Skagen

Germany: Kiel · Lübeck · Rostock · Stralsund · Greifswald · Flensburg · Neumünster · Schleswig · Rendsburg · Cuxhaven · Wismar · Travemünde · Sassnitz · Fehmarn · Nordfriesische Inseln · Ostfriesische Inseln · Helgoland

Legend / scale

Projection: Conical with two standard parallels
East from Greenwich
COPYRIGHT GEORGE PHILIP LTD.

ft · m
6000 · 2000
4500 · 1500
3000 · 1000
1500 · 500
600 · 200
0 · 0
50–150
100–300
200–600
400–1500
2000–3000
6000–6000
m · ft

Grid references: F · G · H · J · K · 9 · 12 · 13 · 14 · 15 · 16 · 17 · 18 · 19 · 20 · 21 · 22 · 24

ENGLAND AND WALES 1:2 000 000

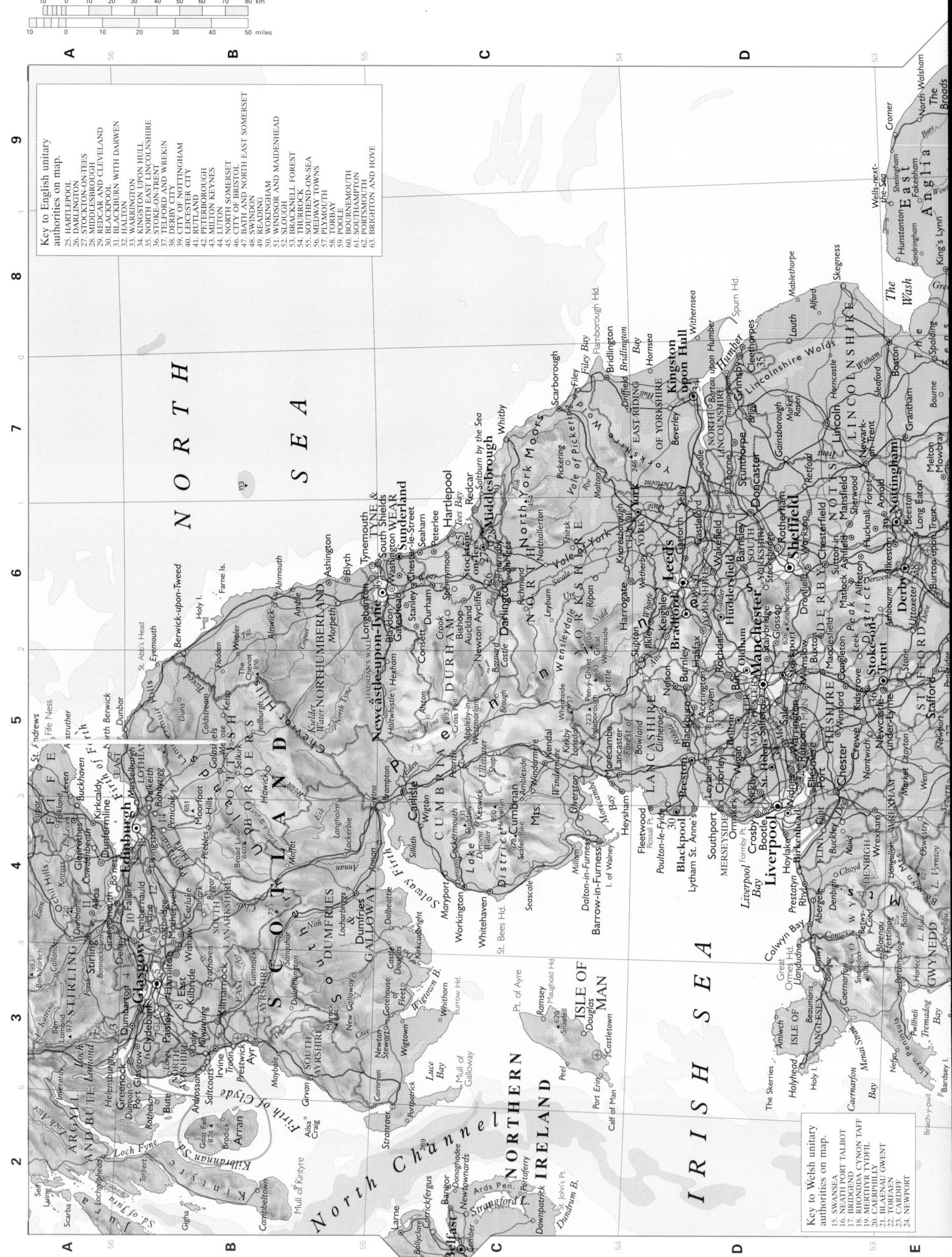

10 0 10 20 30 40 50 60 70 80 km
10 0 10 20 30 40 50 miles
Key to English unitary authorities on map.
25. HARTLEPOOL
26. DARLINGTON
27. STOCKTON-ON-TEES
28. MIDDLESBROUGH
29. REDCAR AND CLEVELAND
30. BLACKPOOL
31. BLACKBURN WITH DARWEN
32. HALTON
33. WARRINGTON
34. KINGSTON UPON HULL
35. NORTH EAST LINCOLNSHIRE
36. STOKE-ON-TRENT
37. TELFORD AND WREKIN
38. DERBY CITY
39. CITY OF NOTTINGHAM
40. LEICESTER CITY
41. RUTLAND
42. PETERBOROUGH
43. MILTON KEYNES
44. LUTON
45. NORTH SOMERSET
46. CITY OF BRISTOL
47. BATH AND NORTH EAST SOMERSET
48. SWINDON
49. READING
50. WOKINGHAM
51. WINDSOR AND MAIDENHEAD
52. SLOUGH
53. BRACKNELL FOREST
54. THURROCK
55. SOUTHEND-ON-SEA
56. MEDWAY TOWNS
57. PLYMOUTH
58. TORBAY
59. POOLE
60. BOURNEMOUTH
61. SOUTHAMPTON
62. PORTSMOUTH
63. BRIGHTON AND HOVE
Key to Welsh unitary authorities on map.
15. SWANSEA
16. NEATH PORT TALBOT
17. BRIDGEND
18. RHONDDA CYNON TAFF
19. MERTHYR TYDFIL
20. CAERPHILLY
21. BLAENAU GWENT
22. TORFAEN
23. CARDIFF
24. NEWPORT
NORTH SEA
IRISH SEA
North Channel
NORTHERN IRELAND
ISLE OF MAN
SCOTLAND

Map of southern England, Wales, the Channel Islands and northern France.

ENGLAND

WALES

FRANCE · NORMANDIE · HAUTE-NORMANDIE · SEINE-MARITIME · MANCHE · CALVADOS

LONDON · BIRMINGHAM · BRISTOL · Cardiff · Plymouth · Portsmouth · Southampton · Bournemouth · Brighton · Hove

NORFOLK · SUFFOLK · ESSEX · HERTS · BUCKS · BERKSHIRE · OXFORD · GLOUCS · WILTSHIRE · HAMPSHIRE · SURREY · WEST SUSSEX · EAST SUSSEX · KENT · DORSET · SOMERSET · DEVON · CORNWALL · WORCESTER · WARWICK · NORTHAMPTON · CAMBRIDGE · CEREDIGION · POWYS · PEMBROKESHIRE · CARMARTHENSHIRE · GLAMORGAN · HEREFORD · SHROPSHIRE · NORTHANTS · LEICESTER

ENGLISH CHANNEL · LA MANCHE · Bristol Channel · Cardigan Bay · Lyme Bay · Strait of Dover · Baie de la Seine · Baie de la Somme

CHANNEL ISLANDS (U.K.) · Jersey · Guernsey · Alderney · Sark · Herm · St. Helier · St. Peter Port

ISLE OF WIGHT · Newport · Ryde · Cowes · The Needles

Isles of Scilly
On same scale
St. Mary's · Tresco

Rouen · Le Havre · Caen · Cherbourg · Dieppe · Évreux · Lisieux · Bayeux · Calais · Boulogne-sur-Mer

East from Greenwich · West from Greenwich

Projection: Lambert's Conformal Conic

COPYRIGHT GEORGE PHILIP LTD.

ft m
3000 1000
1500 500
600 200
300 100
0
150
300
600
m ft

Grid references: E F G H · 1 2 3 4 5 6 7 8 9 · 50 51 52

10 0 10 20 30 40 50 60 70 80 km
10 0 10 20 30 40 50 miles

Key to Scottish unitary authorities on map
1. CITY OF ABERDEEN
2. DUNDEE CITY
3. WEST DUNBARTONSHIRE
4. EAST DUNBARTONSHIRE
5. CITY OF GLASGOW
6. INVERCLYDE
7. RENFREWSHIRE
8. EAST RENFREWSHIRE
9. NORTH LANARKSHIRE
10. FALKIRK
11. CLACKMANNANSHIRE
12. WEST LOTHIAN
13. CITY OF EDINBURGH
14. MIDLOTHIAN

ORKNEY IS.
On same scale
ORKNEY

SHETLAND IS.
On same scale
SHETLAND

Projection : Lambert's Conformal Conic
West from Greenwich
COPYRIGHT GEORGE PHILIP LTD.

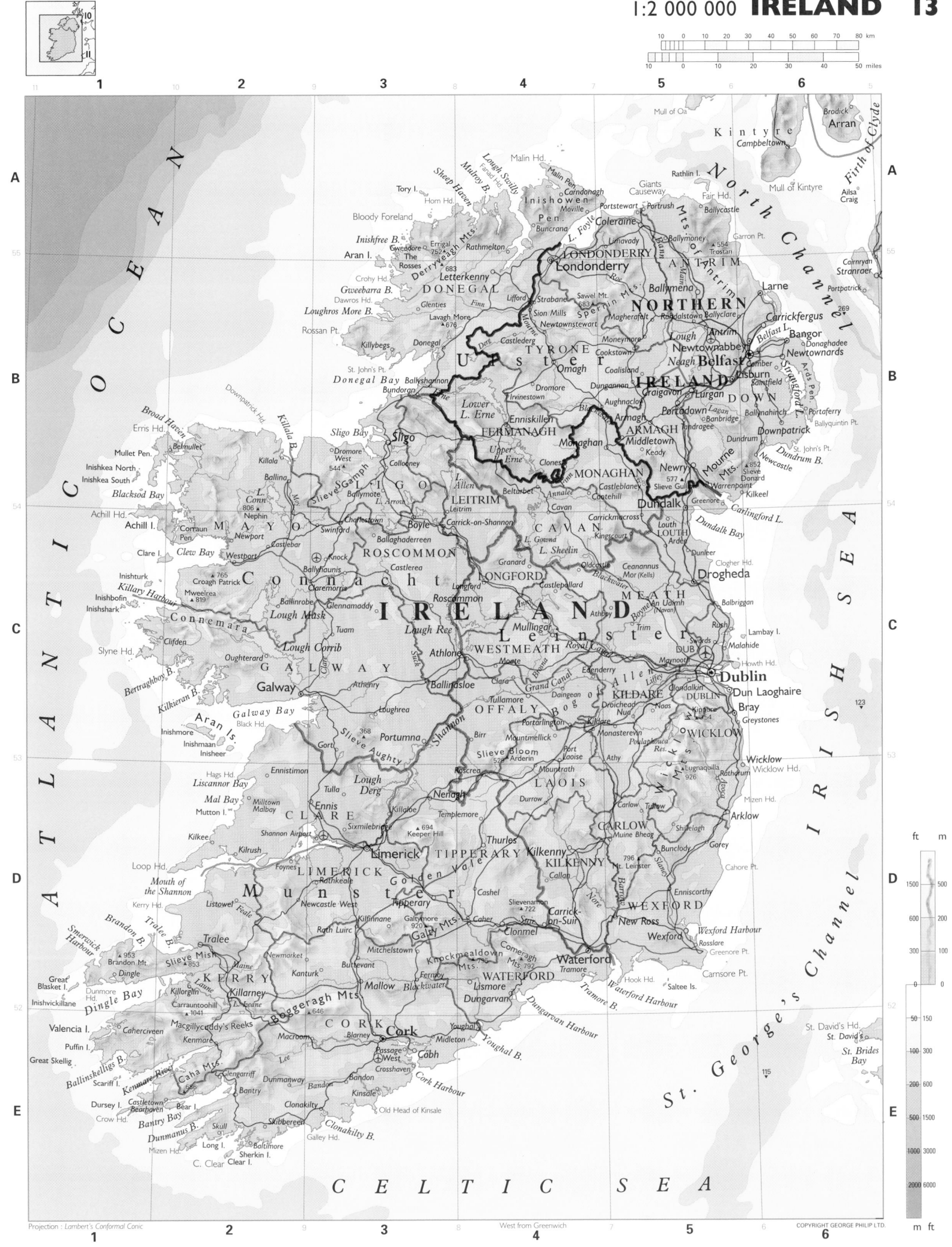

10 0 10 20 30 40 50 60 70 80 km
10 0   10   20   30   40 50 miles

1   **2**   **3**   **4**   **5**   **6**

ft m

A T L A N T I C   O C E A N

Mull of Oa

K i n t y r e

Brodick
Arran

Campbeltown

Firth of Clyde

Mull of Kintyre

Malin Hd.
Tory I.   Lough Swilly   Carndonagh
Horn Hd.   Fanad Hd.   Moville   Rathlin I.
Sheep Haven   *I n i s h o w e n*   Portstewart Portrush   Fair Hd.   *Ailsa*
Malin   *P e n.*   Buncrana   Coleraine   Giants   Ballycastle   Craig
Bloody Foreland   L. Foyle   Causeway

Inishfree B.   Gweedore   Errigal 752   Rathmullan   Limavady   *Cairnryan*
Aran I.   The   683   Letterkenny   **LONDONDERRY**   Ballymoney   554   *Stranraer*
Rosses   Derryveagh Mts   Lifford Strabane   Londonderry   Trostan   Garron Pt.   269
Crohy Hd.   683   *D O N E G A L*   Sion Mills   *A N T R I M*   *M t s.   o f*
Gweebarra B.   Glenties   Sawel Mt.   Magherafelt   Ballymena   Larne
Dawros Hd.   Lavagh More   Finn   **NORTHERN**   Roadstown Ballyclare   Portpatrick
Loughros More B.   676   *U l s t e r*   Newtownstewart   Lough   Antrim   Carrickfergus
Rossan Pt.   Killybegs   *T Y R O N E*   Moneymore   Newtownabbey   Bangor
Killala   Donegal   Omagh   Cookstown   Neagh **Belfast**   Donaghadee
D o n e g a l   B a y   Ballyshannon   Coalisland   *D O W N*   Newtownards
Bundoran   Dungannon   Craigavon   Lisburn   Comber
St. John's Pt.   *Lower*   Irvinestown   Lurgan   Strangford L.   Ards Pen.
L. Erne   Enniskillen   Armagh   Portadown   Lagan   Ballynahinch   Portaferry
Broad Haven   Downpatrick Hd.   *F E R M A N A G H*   Banbridge   Downpatrick
Erris Hd.   Killala B.   *Upper*   **ARMAGH**   Dundrum   Ballyquintin Pt.
Mullet Pen.   Belmullet   *Erne*   Monaghan   Keady   Dundrum B.
Inishkea North   Ballina   Clones   Middletown   Newry   852   St. John's Pt.
Inishkea South   544   Colloney   **MONAGHAN**   577   Slieve   Newcastle
Blacksod Bay   Dromore   Sligo   Beltarbet   Castleblaney   Slieve Gull   Donard   *Mourne*
West   *S L I G O*   L.   Annalee   Coatehill   Warrenpoint   Kilkeel   *Mts.*
Achill Hd.   Moy   Allen   *L E I T R I M*   Cavan   Carrickmacross   Greenore   Carlingford L.
Achill I.   L.   Slieve Gamph   Leitrim   **Dundalk**   Louth
Conn   806   Nephin   Ballymote   L. Arrow   *C A V A N*   Kingscourt   Louth   Dundalk Bay
Corraun   Charlestown   Boyle   Carrick-on-Shannon   L. Gowna   Oldcastle   **LOUTH**   Dunleer   Clogher Hd.
Pen.   *M A Y O*   Swinford   Ballaghaderreen   L. Sheelin   Ceanannus   Ardee
Clare I.   Newport   Castlebar   **ROSCOMMON**   Granard   Mor (Kells)   Blackwater   **Drogheda**
Clew Bay   Westport   Knock   Castlerea   **LONGFORD**   Castlepollard   *M E A T H*   Balbriggan
Inishturk   765   Ballyhaunis   Longford   Boyne   Navan   Rush
Killary Harbour   Croagh Patrick   *C o n n a c h t*   Claremorris   Roscommon   *W E S T M E A T H*   Trim   Lambay I.
Inishbofin   Mweelrea   819   Ballinrobe   Lough Ree   Mullingar   Royal Canal   Malahide
Inishshark   Glennamaddy   Athlone   Moate   Swords   Howth Hd.
Lough Mask   Tuam   **IRELAND**   *L e i n s t e r*   Edenderry   Maynooth   **DUBLIN**
Slyne Hd.   *C o n n e m a r a*   Oughterard   Lough Corrib   Lough   Clara   Allen   Bog   **Dublin**
Clifden   *G A L W A Y*   Athenry   Ballinasloe   Daingean   Naas   Dun Laoghaire
Bertraghboy B.   Galway   Loughrea   *O F F A L Y*   Tullamore   Nas   **KILDARE**   DUBLIN   Bray
Kilkieran B.   **Galway**   Birr   Portarlington   Kildare   Kippure   Greystones
Galway Bay   Black Hd.   Gort   368   Portumna   Shannon   Slieve Bloom   Mountmellick   Port   Monasterevin   54   **WICKLOW**
Aran Is.   Inishmore   Slieve Aughty   Roscrea   Slieve Bloom   Arderin   Laoise   Athy   Poulaphouca   123
Inishmaan   520   Mountrath   Res.   Wicklow
Inisheer   Ennistimon   Lough   Nenagh   Durrow   Lugnaquilla   Wicklow Hd.
Hags Hd.   Derg   *L A O I S*   926   Rathdrum
Liscannor Bay   Tulla   Killaloe   Templemore   Carlow   Tullow   Mizen Hd.
Mal Bay   Ennis   Thurles   **CARLOW**   Arklow
Mutton I.   694   Sixmilebridge   Kilkenny   Muine Bheag   Shillelagh   Gorey
C L A R E   Keeper Hill   796   Bunclody
Kilkee   Shannon Airport   *T I P P E R A R Y*   **KILKENNY**   Mt. Leinster   Cahore Pt.
Kilrush   Limerick   Kilkenny   Callan   Enniscorthy
Loop Hd.   **Limerick**   *Golden Vale*   Clara   *W E X F O R D*
Mouth of   Rathkeale   Tipperary   Cashel   Barrow   New Ross   Wexford Harbour
the Shannon   Foynes   *L I M E R I C K*   Slievenamon   722   Carrick-   **Wexford**   Rosslare
Kerry Hd.   Listowel   Newcastle West   Galtymore   on-Suir   Nore   Greenore Pt.
953   Tralee B.   Feale   Kilfinnane   920   Caher   Clonmel   Wexford Harbour   Carnsore Pt.
Brandon B.   Tralee   Galty Mts   Comeragh   Waterford   Saltee Is.
Smerwick   Brandon Mt.   Maine   Rath Luirc   Mitchelstown   Knockmealdown   Mts   792   Tramore   Hook Hd.   St. David's Hd.
Harbour   Slieve Mish   Newmarket   Mts.   **WATERFORD**   St. David's
Great   853   Kanturk   Buttevant   Fermoy   Lismore   Tramore Bay   St. Brides
Blasket I.   Dingle   Anne   Mallow   Blackwater   Dungarvan   Youghal B.   Bay
Dunmore   Killorglin   *K E R R Y*   Dungarvan Harbour   115
Hd.   Killarney   Boggeragh Mts   646   Youghal
Inishvickillane   Dingle Bay   Carrauntoohill   L. Leane   *C O R K*   Midleton   St. George's Channel
1041   Macgillycuddy's Reeks   Macroom   Blarney   **Cork**   Cobh
Valencia I.   Cahirciveen   Kenmare   Lee   Crosshaven
Puffin I.   Caha Mts   Glengarriff   Bandon   Bandon   Cork Harbour
Great Skellig   Ballinskelligs B.   Kenmare River   656   Dunmanway   Kinsale   Old Head of Kinsale
Scariff I.   Castletown   Bear   Bantry   Clonakilty
Dursey I.   Bearhaven   I.   Bantry Bay   Skibbereen   Clonakilty B.
Crow Hd.   Dunmanus B.   Skull   Long I.   Galley Hd.
Mizen Hd.   Baltimore   Sherkin I.
C. Clear   Clear I.

C E L T I C   S E A

N O R T H   C h a n n e l

I R I S H   S E A

Projection : Lambert's Conformal Conic

West from Greenwich

COPYRIGHT GEORGE PHILIP LTD.

m ft

1500   500
600   200
300   100
0   0
50   150
100   300
200   600
500   1500
1000   3000
2000   6000
m ft

ATLANTIC OCEAN
NORTH SEA
CELTIC SEA
IRISH SEA
English Channel
St. George's Channel
Bristol Channel
North Channel
Firth of Clyde
Moray Firth
Pentland Firth
North Minch
The Wash
Str. of Dover
Cardigan Bay
Galway B.
Shetland Is.
Yell
Unst
Fetlar
Mainland
Lerwick
Foula
Fair Isle
Orkney Is.
Westray
Sanday
Stronsay
Kirkwall
Hoy
South Ronaldsay
C. Wrath
Thurso
Wick
Helmsdale
Lairg
Golspie
Tain
Invergordon
Dingwall
Ullapool
Outer Hebrides
Inner Hebrides
Lewis
Stornoway
Harris
North Uist
Benbecula
South Uist
Barra
St. Kilda
Skye
Portree
Rhum
Eigg
Coll
Tiree
Mull
Tobermory
Oban
Colonsay
Jura
Islay
Arran
Mallaig
Fort William
Ben Nevis
North West Highlands
Grampian Mts.
SCOTLAND
Inverness
L. Ness
Nairn
Elgin
Buckie
Banff
Fraserburgh
Peterhead
Huntly
Inverurie
Aberdeen
Stonehaven
Aviemore
Ballater
Montrose
Arbroath
Forfar
Dundee
Perth
St. Andrews
Glenrothes
Kirkcaldy
Dunfermline
L. Lomond
Stirling
Dunbar
Edinburgh
Glasgow
Greenock
Paisley
Hamilton
East Kilbride
Irvine
Kilmarnock
Ayr
Campbeltown
Girvan
Stranraer
Kirkcudbright
Dumfries
Annan
Southern Uplands
Galashiels
Jedburgh
Hawick
Cheviot Hills
Berwick-upon-Tweed
Alnwick
Newcastle-upon-Tyne
South Shields
Sunderland
Hexham
Gateshead
Durham
Hartlepool
Redcar
Middlesbrough
Stockton-on-Tees
Darlington
Scarborough
Bridlington
Carlisle
Workington
Whitehaven
Cumbrian Mts.
Pennines
Barrow-in-Furness
Lancaster
Douglas
I. of Man
Mull of Galloway
UNITED KINGDOM
Harrogate
York
Beverley
Kingston upon Hull
Leeds
Bradford
Keighley
Blackpool
Preston
Burnley
Blackburn
Halifax
Huddersfield
Scunthorpe
Grimsby
Humber
Bolton
Barnsley
Doncaster
Rotherham
Manchester
Oldham
Liverpool
Warrington
Stockport
Sheffield
Chesterfield
Lincoln
Louth
Skegness
Anglesey
Holyhead
Bangor
Colwyn Bay
Chester
Crewe
Wrexham
Snowdon
Mansfield
Nottingham
Derby
Stoke on Trent
Stafford
Boston
Grantham
Cromer
King's Lynn
Norwich
Great Yarmouth
Lowestoft
Pwllheli
Shrewsbury
Telford
Welshpool
Cambrian Mts.
Aberystwyth
ENGLAND
Nuneaton
Leicester
Corby
Peterborough
Thetford
Wolverhampton
BIRMINGHAM
Coventry
Rugby
Ely
Bury St. Edmunds
Northampton
Cambridge
Ipswich
Felixstowe
Harwich
Colchester
Redditch
Worcester
Royal Leamington Spa
Bedford
Milton Keynes
Stevenage
Hereford
WALES
Fishguard
Carmarthen
Haverfordwest
Milford Haven
Pembroke
Brecon
Merthyr Tydfil
Neath
Llanelli
Swansea
Port Talbot
Rhondda
Barry
Cardiff
Cwmbran
Newport
Cheltenham
Gloucester
Cotswold Hills
Oxford
Hemel Hempstead
Luton
Harlow
Chelmsford
High Wycombe
Watford
Basildon
Southend-on-Sea
Slough
Thames
LONDON
Swindon
Bristol
Bath
Newbury
Reading
Basingstoke
Reigate
Chatham
Margate
Maidstone
Canterbury
Dover
Ashford
Folkestone
Guildford
Crawley
Hastings
Weston-super-Mare
Exmoor
Barnstaple
Taunton
Yeovil
Salisbury
Winchester
Fareham
Havant
Southampton
Brighton
Worthing
Eastbourne
Portsmouth
Isle of Wight
Bournemouth
Poole
Newport
Weymouth
Bude
Exeter
Dartmoor
Exmouth
Torbay
Newquay
Truro
St. Austell
Plymouth
Falmouth
Penzance
Land's End
Isles of Scilly
Malin Hd.
Aran I.
Buncrana
Letterkenny
Coleraine
Londonderry
Ballymena
Larne
NORTHERN IRELAND
Lifford
Donegal
Ulster
Lough Neagh
Antrim
Bangor
Belfast
Omagh
Lower L. Erne
Portadown
Lisburn
Lurgan
Enniskillen
Armagh
Newry
Clones
Bundoran
Sligo
Ballina
Achill I.
L. Conn
Castlebar
Leitrim
Cavan
Castleblaney
Dundalk
Drogheda
Connacht
Westport
Roscommon
Longford
Ceanannus Mor
Lough Mask
Connemara
Lough Corrib
Lough Ree
Mullingar
Boyne
Athlone
Dublin
Dun Laoghaire
Bray
Galway
Ballinasloe
Tullamore
Liffey
Aran Is.
IRELAND
Birr
Lough Derg
Port Laoise
Athy
Wicklow Mts.
Arklow
Ennis
Nenagh
Kilrush
Limerick
Thurles
Carlow
Kilkenny
Shannon
Listowel
Tipperary
Munster
Leinster
Tralee
Clonmel
Carrick-on-Suir
Wexford
Rosslare
Dingle
Carrantoohill
Killarney
Mallow
Waterford
Blackwater
Dungarvan
Valentia I.
Macgillycuddy's Reeks
Cork
Cobh
Youghal
Bantry
Bandon
Kinsale
C. Clear
C. de la Hague
Alderney
Pte. de Barfleur
Cherbourg
Valognes
Cotentin
Guernsey
St. Peter Port
Sark
Channel Is. (U.K.)
Jersey
St. Helier
Bayeux
Caen
Lisieux
Trouville-sur-Mer
Le Havre
Bolbec
Fécamp
Pays de Caux
Rouen
Elbeuf
Seine
Dieppe
Le Tréport
Abbeville
Amiens
Picardie
FRANCE
Somme
St-Quentin
Cambrai
Valenciennes
Lens
Béthune
Bruay-la-Buissière
Lille
Villeneuve-d'Ascq
Tournai
St-Omer
Boulogne-sur-Mer
Le Touquet-Paris-Plage
C. Gris-Nez
Calais
Dunkerque
Flandre
BELGIUM
BRUSSEL (Bruxelles)
Tourcoing
Gent
Mechelen
Brugge
Oostende
Zeebrugge
Antwerpen
Vlissingen
Dordrecht
ROTTERDAM
Hoek van Holland
's-Gravenhage (Den Haag)
NETHERLANDS
Haarlem
Alkmaar
Den Helder
Texel
Askøy
Bergen
Osøyro
Stord
Bømlo
Leirvik
NORWAY
Haugesund
Kopervik
Åkrahamn
Boknafjorden
Stavanger
Sandnes
Bryne
Nærbø
1224
316
789
1182
1342
1311
1214
973
840
816
893
978
636
1085
886
926
953
1041
618
238
16
36
33
99
ft
m
3000
1000
1500
500
600
200
0
50
150
100
300
200
600
500
1500
1000
3000
2000
6000
Projection: Conical with two standard parallels
East from Greenwich
West from Greenwich
COPYRIGHT GEORGE PHILIP LTD.

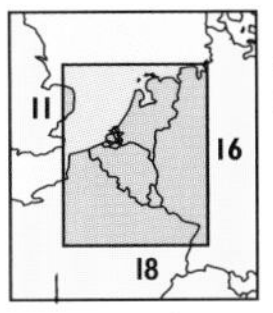

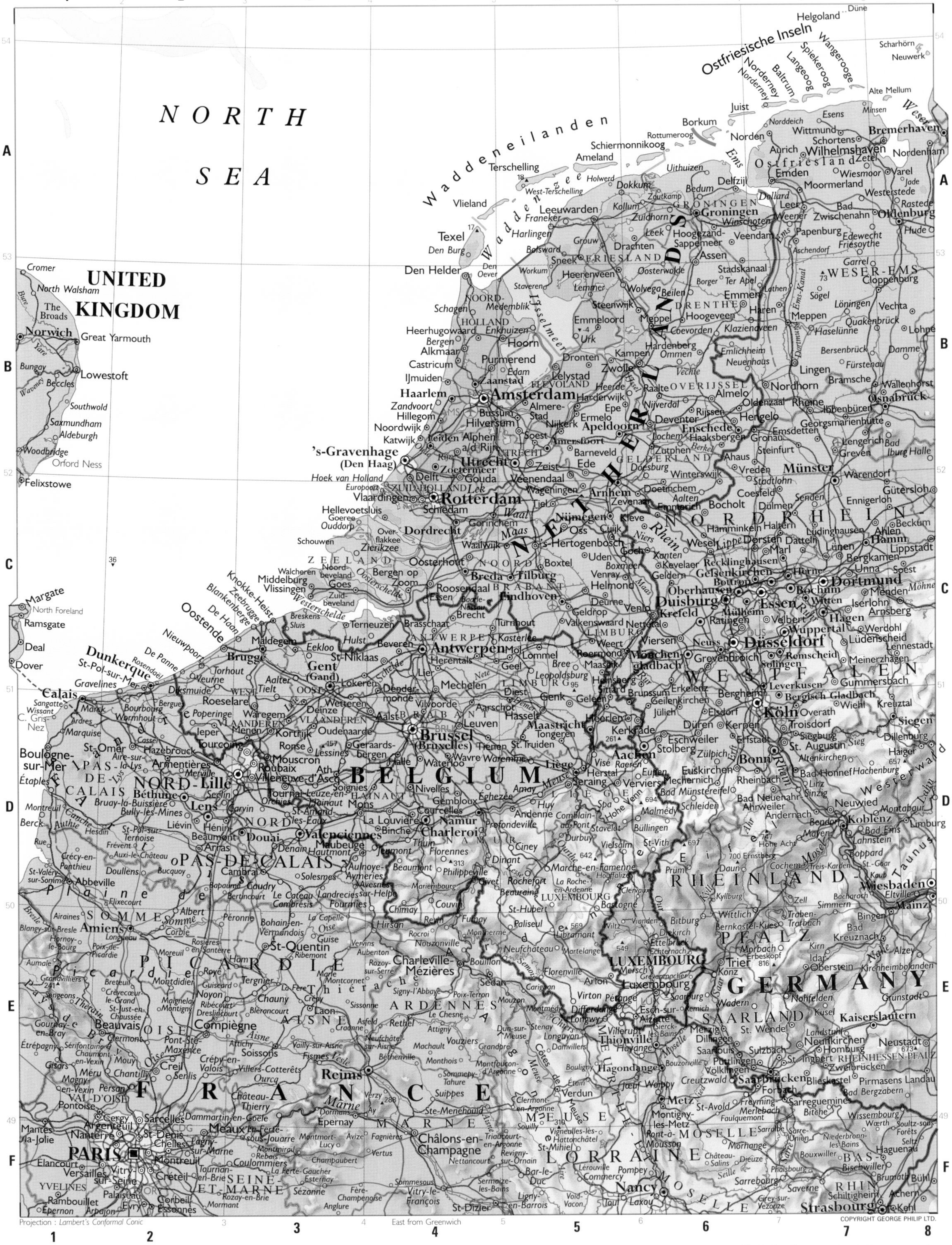

10 0 10 20 30 40 50 60 70 80 90 km
10 0 10 20 30 40 50 60 miles

NORTH SEA

UNITED KINGDOM

Cromer
North Walsham
The Broads
Norwich   Great Yarmouth
Bungay   Lowestoft
Beccles   Southwold
Saxmundham   Aldeburgh
Woodbridge   Orford Ness
Felixstowe
Margate
North Foreland
Ramsgate
Deal
Dover
Calais
Sangatte
Wissant
C. Gris Nez

Helgoland   Düne
Ostfriesische Inseln   Scharhörn   Neuwerk
Wangerooge   Alte Mellum
Spiekeroog
Langeoog
Baltrum
Norderney
Juist   Minsen   Esens
Borkum   Norddeich   Bremerhaven   Nordenham
Rottumeroog   Norden   Wittmund   Wilhelmshaven
Ameland   Uithuizen   Aurich   Schortens   Wiesmoor   Varel
Schiermonnikoog   Emden   Westerstede
Terschelling   Dokkum   Bedum   Ostfriesland   Papenburg   Edewecht   Friesoythe   Oldenburg
West-Terschelling   Holwerd   Groningen   Leer   Zwischenahn   Bad   Hude
Vlieland   Leeuwarden   Kollum   Zoutkamp   Dollard   Rastede
Texel   Franeker   Grou   Drachten   Assen   Löningen   Vechta
Den Burg   Harlingen   Bolsward   FRIESLAND   Oosterwolde   Wolvega   Borger   Ter Apel   Cloppenburg   Damme
Den Helder   Sneek   Heerenveen   Lemmer   Stadskanaal   Meppen   Quakenbrück   Lohne
Schagen   Noord-Medemblik   Steenwijk   DRENTHE   Haselünne   Bramsche   Wallenhorst
Heerhugowaard   Enkhuizen   Emmeloord   Hoogeveen   Haren   Lingen   Nordhorn   Osnabrück
Bergen   Hoorn   Urk   Coevorden   Klazienaveen   Bersenbrück   Fürstenau
Alkmaar   Dronten   Hardenberg   Emlichheim   Neuenhaus   Georgsmarienhütte
Castricum   Lelystad   Kampen   Ommen   Ootmarsum   Ibbenbüren   Greven   Warendorf
IJmuiden   Edam   Zwolle   Raalte   OVERIJSSEL   Almelo   Rheine   Iburg   Halle
Haarlem   Purmerend   FLEVOLAND   Heerde   Nijverdal   Hengelo   Emsdetten   Gütersloh
Zandvoort   Zaanstad   Amsterdam   Harderwijk   Epe   Deventer   Rijssen   Enschede   Gronau   Steinfurt   Münster
Hillegom   Bussum   Almere-Stad   Ermelo   Apeldoorn   Zutphen   Haaksbergen   Ahaus   Stadtlohn
Noordwijk   Hilversum   Nijkerk   Lochem   Vreden   Coesfeld   Ennigerloh
Katwijk   Leiden   Soest   Amersfoort   Barneveld   Berkel   Winterswijk   Dülmen   Beckum
's-Gravenhage (Den Haag)   Alphen a/d Rijn   UTRECHT   Zeist   Ede   GELDERLAND   Doetinchem   Aalten   Bocholt   Haltern   Hamm
Delft   Zoetermeer   Utrecht   Veenendaal   Wageningen   Arnhem   Zevenaar   Emmerich   Borken   Lüdinghausen   Ahlen   Lippstadt
Hoek van Holland   Gouda   Lek   Tiel   Kleve   Rhein   Doesburg   NORDRHEIN   Dorsten   Datteln   Bergkamen   Soest
Europoort   ZUID-HOLLAND   Nijmegen   Cuijk   Niers   Xanten   Wesel   Lippe   Recklinghausen   Unna   Möhne
Vlaardingen   Rotterdam   Waal   's-Hertogenbosch   Boxmeer   Geldern   Kevelaer   Gelsenkirchen   Bottrop   Herne   Arnsberg
Schiedam   Maas   Uden   Venray   Straelen   Krefeld   Oberhausen   Essen   Bochum   Witten   Iserlohn
Hellevoetsluis   Dordrecht   Oosterhout   NOORD   Boxtel   Helmond   Venlo   Mülheim   Duisburg   Dortmund
Ouddorp   Schouwen   Waalwijk   BRABANT   Eindhoven   Deurne   Nettetal   Viersen   Neuss   WESTFALEN   Hagen   Werdohl
Overflakkee   Breda   Tilburg   Geldrop   Weert   Mönchengladbach   Ratingen   Wuppertal   Lüdenscheid   Lennestadt
Goeree   ZEELAND   Roosendaal   Essen   Brecht   Valkenswaard   Nederweert   Grevenbroich   Düsseldorf   Remscheid   Meinerzhagen
Middelburg   Bergen op Zoom   Turnhout   Kasterlee   LIMBURG   Erkelenz   Bergisch Gladbach   Gummersbach
Vlissingen   Oosterschelde   Brasschaat   ANTWERPEN   Lommel   Roermond   Geilenkirchen   Leverkusen   Overath   Wiehl
Knokke-Heist   Zuid-beveland   Breskens   Hulst   Beveren   Antwerpen   Herentals   Bree   Brüggen   Jülich   Köln   Siegen
Zeebrugge   Sluis   St-Niklaas   Lier   Leopoldsburg   Maaseik   Brunssum   Bergheim   Troisdorf   Dillenburg
Blankenberge   Eekloo   Lokeren   Nete   Diest   Hasselt   Sittard   Heerlen   Düren   Kerpen   Bonn   Haiger
De Haan   Maldegem   Dender   Mechelen   Aarschot   LIMBURG   Genk   Kerkrade   Elsdorf   Bad Honnef   Hachenburg
Oostende   Torhout   Aalter   Wetteren   Vilvoorde   Leuven   Tienen   Tongeren   Maastricht   Aachen   Euskirchen   Altenkirchen
Nieuwpoort   Brugge   Tielt   Deinze   Aalst   BRABANT   Brussel (Bruxelles)   St. Truiden   Eschweiler   Stolberg   Zülpich   St. Augustin   Westerwald
De Panne   Gent (Gand)   Oudenaarde   Halle   Waterloo   Waremme   Liège   Visé   Raeren   Mechernich   Rheinbach   Siegen
Diksmuide   Roeselare   OOST   Ronse   Geraardsbergen   Nivelles   Gembloux   Andenne   Huy   Seraing   Verviers   Eupen   Bad Münstereifel   Neuwied
Veurne   Waregem   VLAANDEREN   Wavre   Combain   Spa   Venn   Malmedy   Schleiden   Ahrweiler   Andernach   Koblenz
Poperinge   Izegem   Kortrijk   Courcelles   Namur   Amay   Verviers   Bad Neuenahr   Sinzig
Ieper   WEST   Menen   Aulnoye   Binche   NAMUR   Durbuy   St-Vith   Mayen   Bad Ems   Lahnstein
Cassel   VLAANDEREN   Mouscron   Ath   Charleroi   Florennes   Marche-en-Famenne   RHEINLAND   Prüm   Daun   Cochem   Boppard   St-Goar
Dunkerque   Hazebrouck   Tourcoing   Leuze-en-Hainaut   Mons   Thuin   Dinant   LUXEMBOURG   Bastogne   Kyllburg   Traben-Trarbach   Bingen
St-Pol-sur-Mer   Armentières   Tournai   Villeneuve-d'Ascq   Beaumont   Philippeville   Rochefort   Beauraing   Bitburg   Bernkastel-Kues   Simmern   Bacharach   Mainz
Gravelines   Merville   Lille   Roubaix   HAINAUT   La Louvière   Jemeppe   Marienbourg   La Roche-en-Ardenne   Houffalize   Wittlich   Kirchheimbolanden
Bourbourg   Béthune   Seclin   Orchies   Cambrai   Chimay   Revin   Fumay   St-Hubert   RHEINLAND   Wiltz   Diekirch   Idar-Oberstein   Alzey
Bergues   DE   Lens   NORD   Douai   Maubeuge   Hirson   Couvin   Paliseul   PFALZ   Ettelbrück   Morbach   Bad Kreuznach
Wormhout   CALAIS   Liévin   Denain   Valenciennes   Jeumont   St-Quentin   Neufchâteau   LUXEMBOURG   Wadern   Kirn   Bad Bergzabern
Marquise   Bruay-la-Buissière   Bully-les-Mines   Les Eaux   La Capelle   Florenville   Martelange   Trier   SAARLAND   Neunkirchen   Oberstein
Boulogne-sur-Mer   Arras   Bapaume   Guise   Charleville-Mézières   Arlon   Pétange   Saarlouis   St. Wendel   Kaiserslautern
Étaples   Bruay   Cambrésis   Vervins   Bouillon   Luxembourg   Saarburg   Dillingen   RHEINHESSEN-PFALZ
Berck   Hesdin   Le Cateau   Landrecies-sur-Helpe   Rethel   Sedan   Carignan   Differdange   Esch-sur-Alzette   Homburg   Landstuhl   Neustadt
Montreuil   Frévent   Fourmies   Laon   Attigny   Vouziers   Longwy   Thionville   Saarbrücken   Landau
Doullens   Solesmes   Aymeries   Le Chesne   Mouzon   Esch   Creutzwald   Saargemünd   Wissembourg
Airaines   Albert   Péronne   Bohain-en-Vermandois   Oise   Reims   Suippes   Ste-Menehould   en-Argonne   Pont-à-MOSELLE   Haguenau
Amiens   SOMME   Corbie   Guiscard   Guise   Marle   Vervins   Épernay   MEUSE   Montigny-lès-Metz   Faulquemont   Morhange   Bitche   Bas-Rhin
Poix-de-Picardie   Rozières-en-Santerre   Chauny   Crépy   Marne   Dormans   Verdun   Metz   St-Avold   Merlebach   Sarreguemines
PICARDIE   Moreuil   Noyon   Ribécourt   Sissonne   Fère-en-Tardenois   Châlons-en-Champagne   Vigneulles-lès   LORRAINE   Sarralbe   Saverne   Strasbourg
Breteuil   Montdidier   Compiègne   Craonne   Fismes   Vertus   Triaucourt   Ligny-en-Barrois   Bouxwiller
SOMME   Montdidier   Guiscard   Soissons   Fère-Champenoise   St-Mihiel   Pompey   Morhange   Brumath   Achern
Beauvais   OISE   Pont-Ste-Maxence   Vailly-sur-Aisne   Sézanne   Sommesous   Bar-le-Duc   Toul   Nancy   Sélestat
Méru   Crépy-en-Valois   Soissons   Ourcq   Château-Thierry   Revigny   Vaucouleurs   Lunéville   Kehl
Chantilly   Senlis   Villers-Cotterêts   Reims   Marne   Esternay   Sézanne   MARNE   Anglure   St-Dizier
Creil   Dammartin-en-Goële   Meaux   La Ferté-sous-Jouarre   Coulommiers   La Ferté-Gaucher   Fère-Champenoise
Persan   Cergy   Sarcelles   St-Denis   Chelles   Lagny   Rozay-en-Brie   Provins
FRANCE   Pontoise   Argenteuil   Nanterre   PARIS   Montreuil   Créteil   Tournan-en-Brie   SEINE-ET-MARNE
Mantes-la-Jolie   Versailles   Vitry-sur-Seine   Corbeil-Essonnes   Mormant
YVELINES   Elancourt   Palaiseau   Brie-Comte-Robert
Rambouillet   Arpajon

Projection: Lambert's Conformal Conic   East from Greenwich   COPYRIGHT GEORGE PHILIP LTD.

Underlined towns give their name to the administrative area in which they stand.

NORTH SEA
BALTIC SEA
ADRIATIC SEA
Golfo di Génova
Golfo di Venézia
UNITED KINGDOM
NETHERLANDS
BELGIUM
LUXEMBOURG
DENMARK
GERMANY
FRANCE
SWITZERLAND
LIECHTENSTEIN
AUSTRIA
CZECH R.
SLOVENIA
ITALY
MONACO
SAN MARINO
AMSTERDAM
's-Gravenhage (Den Haag)
ROTTERDAM
BRUSSEL (Bruxelles)
PARIS
HAMBURG
BERLIN
PRAHA (Prague)
MÜNCHEN (Munich)
Zürich
Frankfurt
Köln (Cologne)
Hannover
Bremen
Leipzig
Dresden
Stuttgart
Nürnberg
Wien
Ljubljana
MILANO
TORINO (Turin)
Venézia (Venice)
Firenze (Florence)
Genova
LYON
MARSEILLE
Projection: Conical with two standard parallels

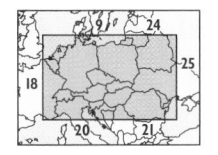

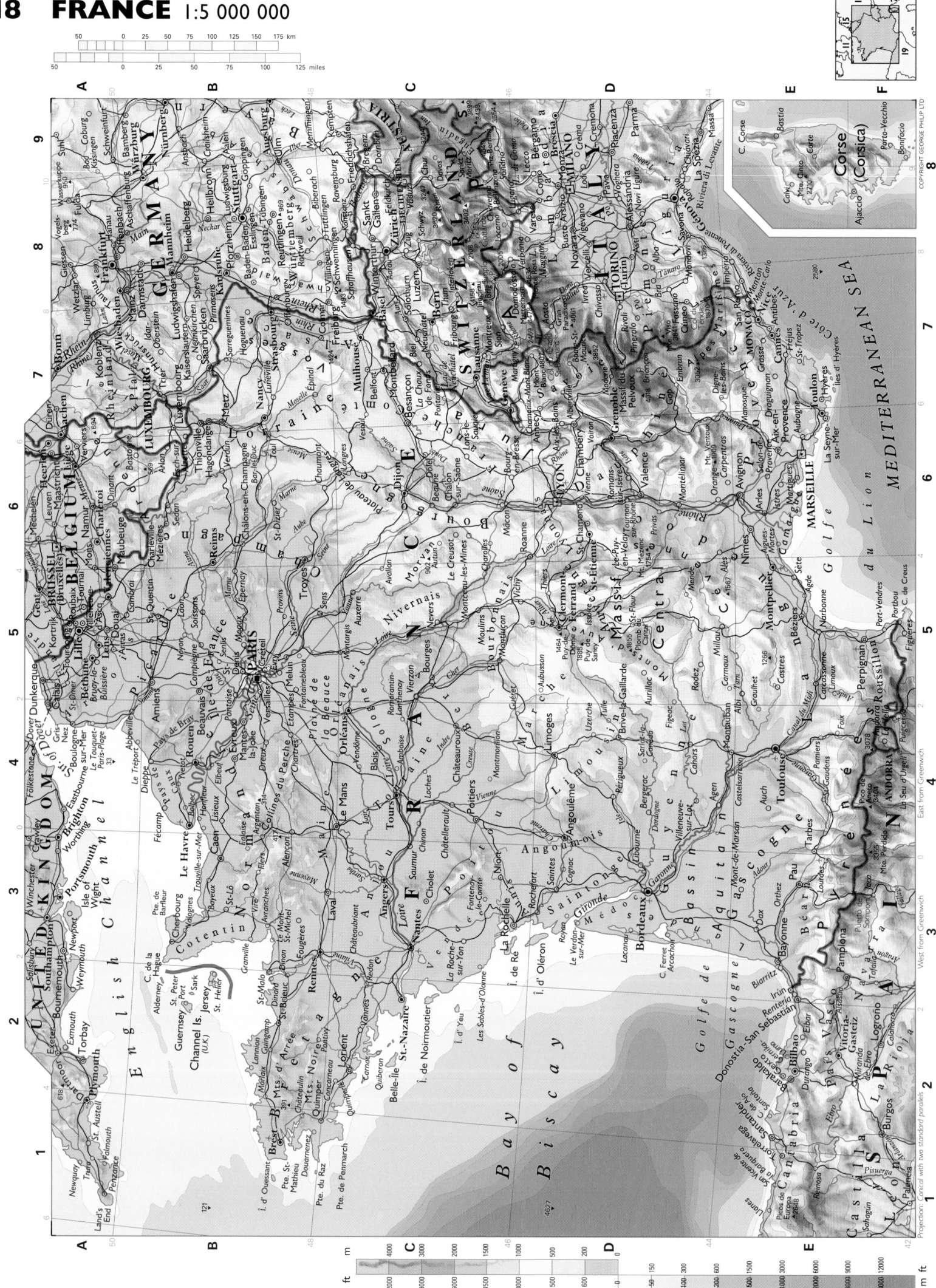

Corse (Corsica)

MEDITERRANEAN SEA

UNITED KINGDOM

GERMANY

BELGIUM

LUXEMBOURG

SWITZERLAND

AUSTRIA

ITALY

PARIS

FRANCE

MARSEILLE

SPAIN

ANDORRA

Bay of Biscay

English Channel

Golfe de Gascogne

Golfe du Lion

Projection: Conical with two standard parallels

East from Greenwich

West from Greenwich

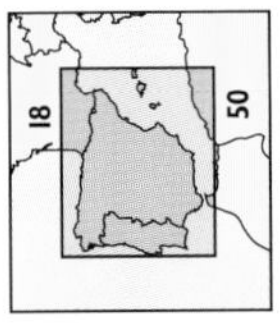

50   0   25   50   75   100   125   150   175 km
50   0   25   50   75   100 miles

COPYRIGHT GEORGE PHILIP LTD

SPAIN

PORTUGAL

FRANCE

MOROCCO

ALGERIA

MADRID

Barcelona

Valencia

Sevilla

Zaragoza

Málaga

Murcia

Lisboa

Porto

Bilbao

Toulouse

Montpellier

Béziers

Narbonne

Perpignan

ANDORRA

Pamplona

San Sebastián

Donostia

Vitoria-Gasteiz

Logroño

Burgos

Valladolid

León

Oviedo

Gijón

Santander

A Coruña (La Coruña)

Santiago de Compostela

Pontevedra

Vigo

Ourense (Orense)

Lugo

Ponferrada

Salamanca

Zamora

Ávila

Segovia

Guadalajara

Cuenca

Albacete

Ciudad Real

Córdoba

Jaén

Granada

Almería

Cartagena

Alicante

Elche

Gandia

Castelló de la Plana

Tarragona

Lleida

Huesca

Girona

Figueres

Cáceres

Badajoz

Mérida

Huelva

Cádiz

Gibraltar (U.K.)

Algeciras

Tanger

Tetouan

Ceuta (Sp.)

Melilla (Sp.)

Oran

Palma de Mallorca

Mallorca

Menorca

Eivissa (Ibiza)

Formentera

Cabrera

MEDITERRANEAN SEA

ATLANTIC OCEAN

B a l e a r e s

Golfe du Lion

G. de Cádiz

Str. of Gibraltar

Projection: Conical with two standard parallels

West from Greenwich   0   East from Greenwich

ft   m
6000 2000
4500 1500
3000 1000
1500 500
600 200
     0
-150 -50
-300 -100
-600 -200
-2000 -600
-6000 -2000
-9000 -3000
-12000 -4000
m ft

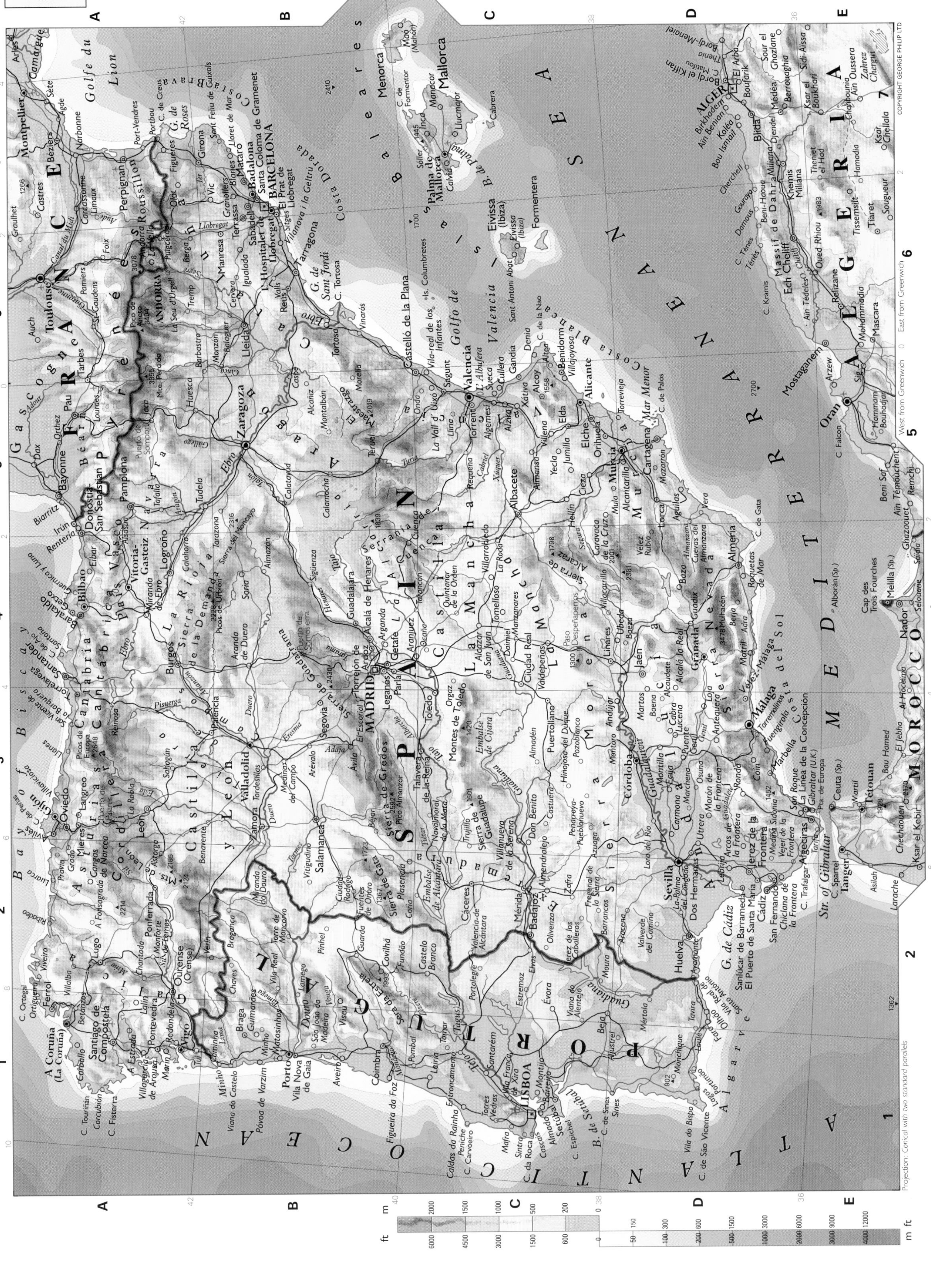

 1:5 000 000

SWITZERLAND
AUSTRIA
SLOVENIA
CROATIA
FRANCE
MONACO
SAN MARINO
VATICAN CITY
ALGERIA
TUNISIA
MALTA
LIGURIAN SEA
TYRRHENIAN SEA
ADRIATIC SEA
MEDITER
Golfo di Génova
Golfo di Venézia
Corse
Sardegna
MILANO
TORINO (Turin)
Venézia (Venice)
Génova
Firenze (Florence)
ROMA
NÁPOLI
Palermo
Tunis
Zagreb
Ljubljana
Trieste
Bologna
Bari
Cágliari
Valletta
Projection: Conical with two standard parallels

8 9 10 11 12 13

HUNGARY
ROMANIA
UKRAINE
YUGOSLAVIA
BOSNIA-HERZEGOVINA
SERBIA
MONTENEGRO
Kosovo
MACEDONIA
ALBANIA
BULGARIA
GREECE
TURKEY

BEOGRAD (Belgrade)
BUCUREŞTI (Bucharest)
SOFIYA
Skopje
Tiranë
Sarajevo
Podgorica
Thessaloníki
ATHÍNAI (Athens)
İSTANBUL
İZMIR (Smyrna)

BLACK SEA
IONIAN SEA
MEDITERRANEAN SEA
AEGEAN SEA
Marmara Denizi (Sea of Marmara)
Str. of Otranto

Transilvania
Carpaţii Meridionali
Walachia
Dobrogea
Stara Planina
Rhodopi Planina
Makedhonia
Thrace
Pindhos Óros
Pelopónnisos
Kikládhes
Dhodhekánisos
Kríti
Voríai Sporádhes

B C D E F G

East from Greenwich

8 9 10 11 12 13

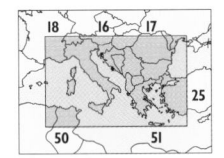

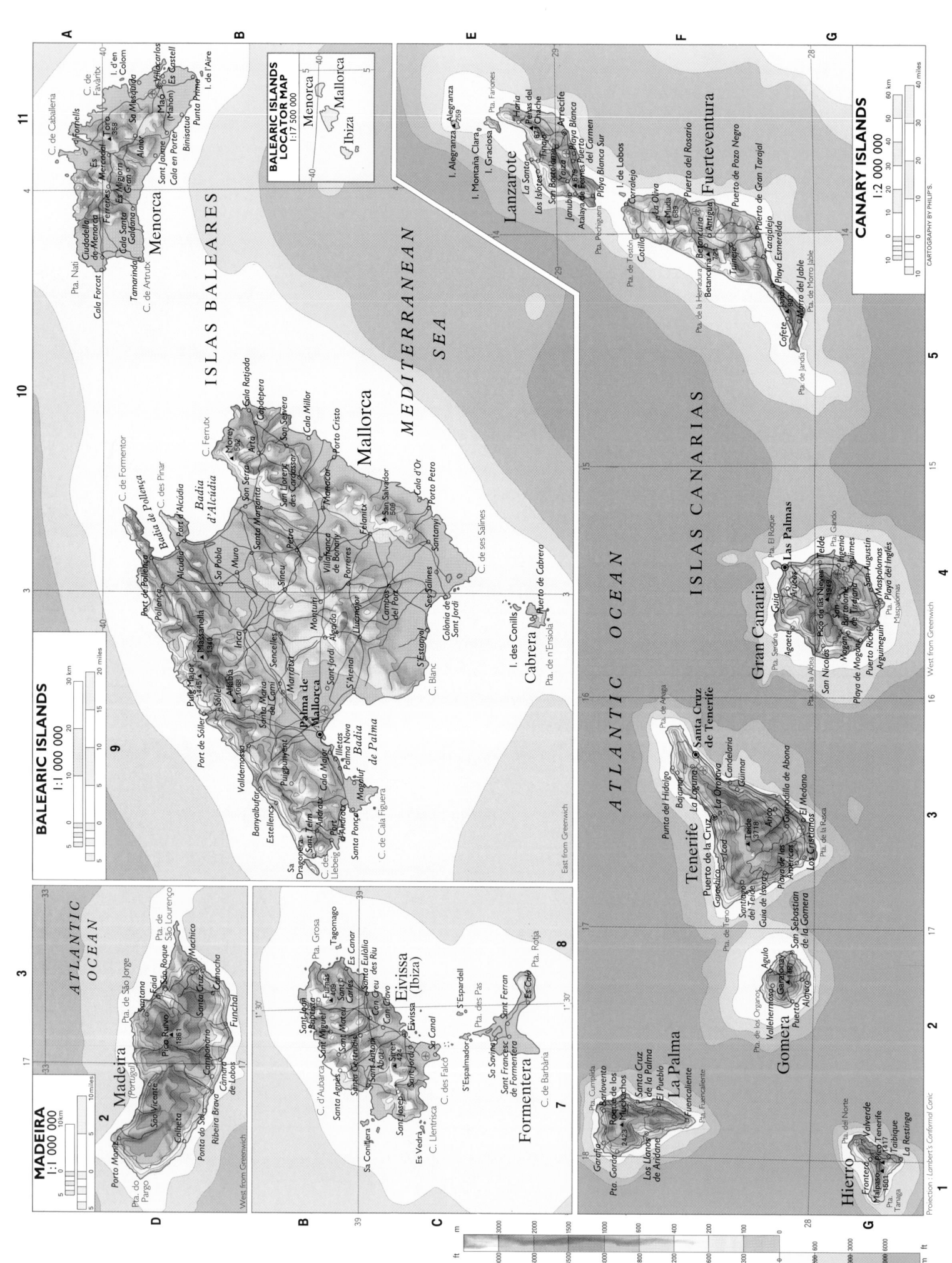

ISLAS BALEARES

Menorca

C. de Caballeria
Fornells
I. d'en Colom
C. de Favàritx
Es Mercadal
Toro 358
Sa Mesquida
Villacarlos
Es Castell
Punta Prima
I. de l'Aire
Maó (Mahón)
Alaior
Es Migjorn Gran
Sant Jaume
Cala en Porter
Binissalem
Ferreries
Cala Santa Galdana
Ciudadella de Menorca
Es
Pta. Nati
Cala Forcat
Tamarinda
C. de Artrutx

Mallorca

C. de Formentor
C. de Pollença
Badia de Pollença
Port de Pollença
C. des Pinar
Pollença
Alcúdia
Port d'Alcúdia
Badia d'Alcúdia
Sa Pobla
Muro
Santa Margarita
Petra
Son Serra
Capdepera
Cala Ratjada
Son Servera
Arta
Cala Millor
Son Llorenç des Cardassar
Porto Cristo
Manacor
Son Macià
Felanitx
San Salvador 509
Cala d'Or
Porto Petro
Santanyi
C. de ses Salines
S'Estanyol
Ses Salines
Colonia de Sant Jordi
C. Blanc
Campos del Port
Llucmajor
Porreres
Vilafranca de Bonany
Sineu
Sencelles
Inca
Selva
Massanella 1340
Puig Major 1445
1445
Son Sardina
Santa Maria del Camí
Alaró
Lloseta 1063
Sóller
Port de Sóller
Valldemossa
Banyalbufar
Estellencs
Puigpunyent
Marratxí
Sant Jordi
S'Arenal
Palma de Mallorca
Algaida
Montuiri
Badia de Palma
Magaluf
Palma Nova
Illetas
Cala Major
Santa Ponça
Port d'Andratx
Sant Telm
Sa Dragonera
C. de Cala Figuera
Banyalbufar
Andratx

Cabrera
I. des Conills
Pta. de n'Ensiola
Puerto de Cabrera

MEDITERRANEAN SEA

ISLAS BALEARES

ISLAS CANARIAS

BALEARIC ISLANDS LOCATOR MAP
1:17 500 000
Menorca
Mallorca
Ibiza

Lanzarote
Alegranza 289
I. Alegranza
I. Montaña Clara
I. Graciosa
Pta. Fariones
Haria
Peñas del Chache 671
Arrecife
La Santa
Los Islotes
San Bartolomé
Tinajo
Playa Blanca
Puerto del Carmen
Yaiza
Janubio
Atalaya de Femés
Playa Blanca Sur
I. de Lobos
Corralejo
Pta. Pechiguera

Fuerteventura
La Oliva
La Muda 689
Muda
Betancuria 724
d'Antigua
Puerto del Rosario
Pto. del Rosario
Puerto de Gran Tarajal
Tarajalejo
Playa Esmeralda
Morro del Jable
Pta. de Morro Jable
Cofete
Jandía
Pta. de Jandía
Cotillo
Pta. de Tostón
Pta. de la Herradura
Tuineje

ATLANTIC OCEAN

Gran Canaria
Pta. El Roque
Las Palmas
Telde
Pta. Gando
Arucas
Gáldar
Ingenio
Guia
Pico de las Nieves 1949
San Bartolomé de Tirajana
Agüimes
San Agustín
Mogán
Puerto Rico
Playa del Inglés
Maspalomas
Puerto de Mogán
Arguineguín
San Nicolás
Pta. de la Aldea
Agaete
Pta. Sardina

Tenerife
Pta. de Anaga
Santa Cruz de Tenerife
La Laguna
Tacoronte
La Orotava
Candelaria
Güímar
Tejina
Bajamar
Punta del Hidalgo
Puerto de la Cruz
Garachico
Icod
Teide 3718
Arico
Granadilla de Abona
El Médano
Playa de las Américas
Los Cristianos
Pta. de la Rasca
Guia de Isora
Santiago del Teide
Adeje
Pta. de Teno

Gomera
Pta. de los Organos
Agulo
Vallehermoso
Hermigua
San Sebastián de la Gomera
Garajonay 1487
Chipude
Alajero
Playa de Santiago
Valle Gran Rey
Pta. de la Aldea

La Palma
Pta. Cumplida
Barlovento
Roque de los Muchachos 2423
Santa Cruz de la Palma
Los Llanos de Aridane
El Pueblo
Garafía
Pta. Gorda
Fuencaliente
Pta. Fuencaliente

Hierro
Pta. del Norte
Valverde
Frontera
Malpaso 1501
Pico de Tenerife 1417
Taibique
La Restinga
Pta. Tanaja

ISLAS CANARIAS

CANARY ISLANDS
1:2 000 000

ATLANTIC OCEAN

Madeira (Portugal)
Porto Moniz
Pta. de São Jorge
Pta. do São Lourenço
Santana
Faial
São Roque
Machico
São Vicente
Pico Ruivo 1861
Seixal
Santa Cruz
Camacha
Ribeira Brava
Campanário
Câmara de Lobos
Funchal
Encumeada
Eira do Serrado
Curral das Freiras
Ponta do Sol
Calheta
Pta. do Pargo
Porto do Moniz
I. de Lobos

Eivissa (Ibiza)
Pta. Grosa
Tagomago
Pta. de Tagomago
Es Canar
Santa Eulària des Riu
Sant Carles
Can Clavo
Sant Joan de Labritja
Puig d'en Fita 409
Sant Miquel
Sant Mateu
Sant Antoni
Sant Antoni de Portmany
Sant Rafel
Santa Agnès
Santa Gertrudis
Sant Josep
Eivissa
Sant Jordi
Ses Salines
Es Vedrà
C. d'Aubarca
Sa Conillera
C. Llentrisca

Formentera
S'Espalmador
S'Espardell
Sa Savina
Sant Francesc de Formentera
Es Caló
Sant Ferran
Pta. des Pas
C. des Falcó
C. de Barbària
Pta. Roja

BALEARIC ISLANDS
1:1 000 000

MADEIRA
1:1 000 000

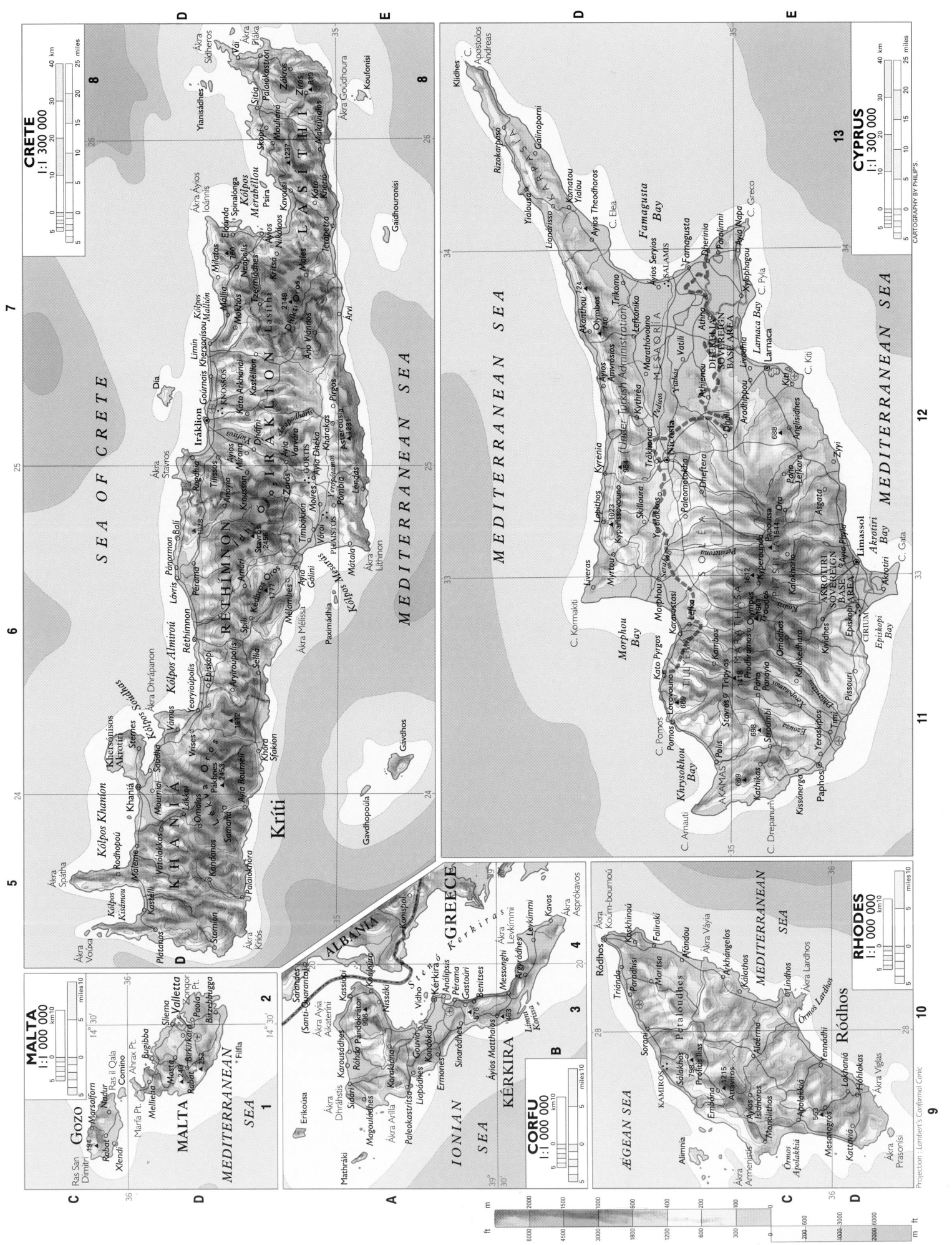
CRETE
1:1 300 000
SEA OF CRETE
MEDITERRANEAN SEA
Kríti
KHANIÁ
RÉTHÍMNON
IRÁKLION
LASÍTHI
Khaniá
Iráklion
Réthímnon
CYPRUS
1:1 300 000
MEDITERRANEAN SEA
Nicosia
Limassol
Larnaca
Famagusta
Paphos
Kyrenia
Morphou Bay
Famagusta Bay
(Under Turkish Administration)
MALTA
1:1 000 000
Gozo
MALTA
Valletta
MEDITERRANEAN SEA
CORFU
1:1 000 000
IONIAN SEA
KÉRKIRA
ALBANIA
GREECE
Kérkira
RHODES
1:1 000 000
ÆGEAN SEA
MEDITERRANEAN SEA
Ródhos
CARTOGRAPHY BY PHILIP'S
Projection : Lambert's Conformal Conic

24 EASTERN EUROPE AND TURKEY 1:10 000 000

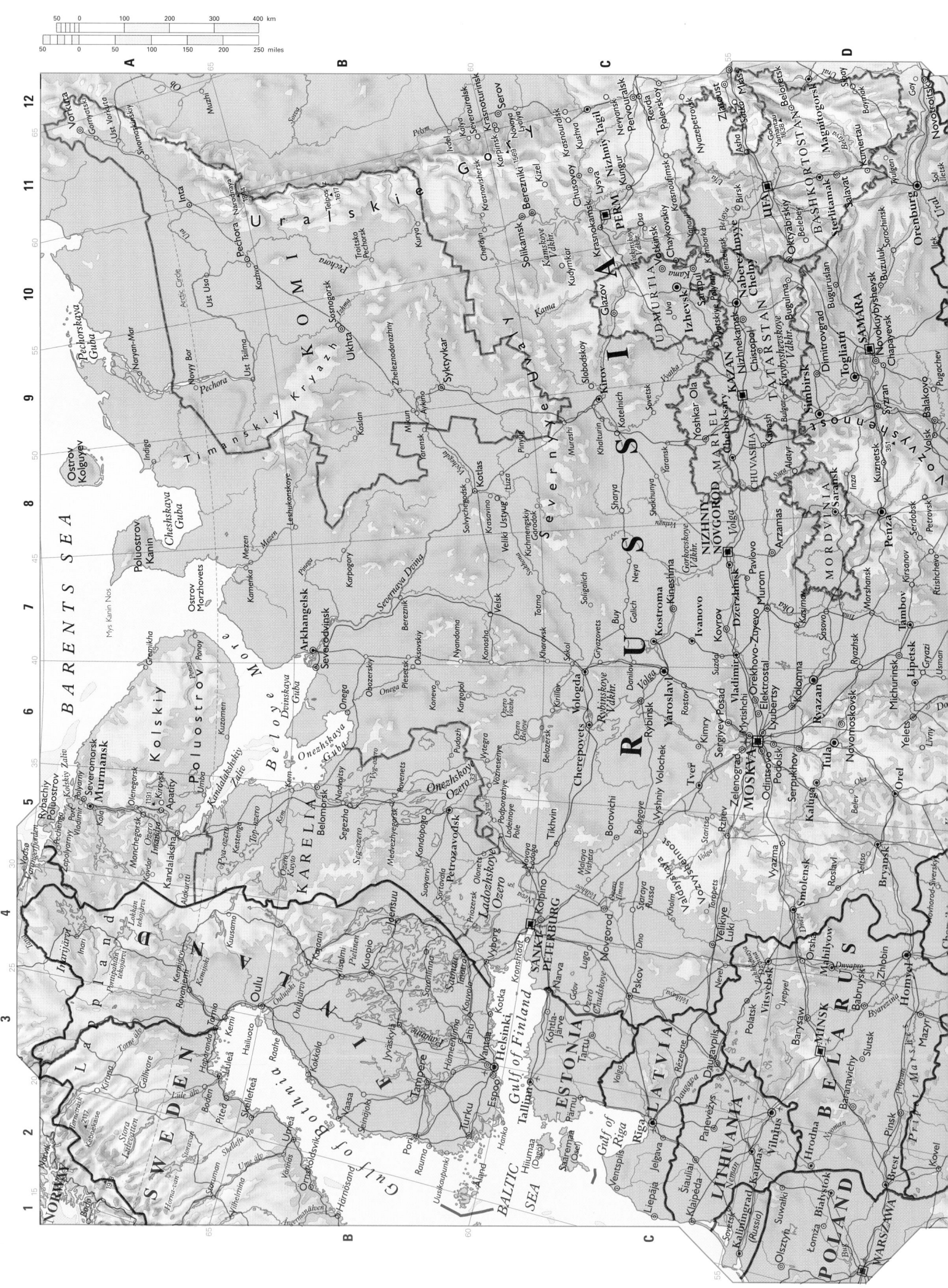
50 0 100 200 300 400 km
50 0 50 100 150 200 250 miles
BARENTS SEA
Beloye More
Gulf of Bothnia
Gulf of Finland
Gulf of Riga
BALTIC SEA
RUSSIA
KOMI
KARELIA
FINLAND
SWEDEN
NORWAY
ESTONIA
LATVIA
LITHUANIA
BELARUS
POLAND
UDMURTIA
TATARSTAN
BASHKORTOSTAN
CHUVASHIA
MORDVINIA
MARI EL
Lappland
Kolskiy Poluostrov
Timanskiy Kryazh
Uralskie Gory
Severnyye Uvaly
Vozvyshennost
Ostrov Kolguyev
Poluostrov Kanin
Cheshskaya Guba
Pechorskaya Guba
Onezhskaya Guba
Dvinskaya Guba
Kandalakshskiy Zaliv
Ladozhskoye Ozero
Onezhskoye Ozero
Rybinskoye Vdkhr.
Arctic Circle
MOSKVA
SANKT-PETERBURG
Helsinki
Tallinn
Riga
Vilnius
MINSK
WARSZAWA
Murmansk
Arkhangelsk
Severodvinsk
Vologda
Yaroslavl
Kostroma
Ivanovo
Vladimir
Ryazan
Tula
Kaluga
Smolensk
Tver
Novgorod
Pskov
NIZHNIY NOVGOROD
KAZAN
UFA
PERM
SAMARA
Saransk
Penza
Tambov
Lipetsk
Orenburg
Izhevsk
Kirov
Syktyvkar
Ukhta
Kotlas
Pechora
Inta
Vorkuta
Petrozavodsk
Oulu
Tampere
Turku
Kaliningrad (Russia)

ft	m
12 000	4000
9000	3000
6000	2000
4500	1500
3000	1000
1500	500
600	200
0	0
600	200
1500	500
3000	1000
6000	2000

Projection: Conical with two standard parallels

East from Greenwich

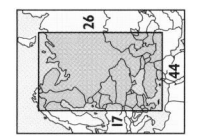

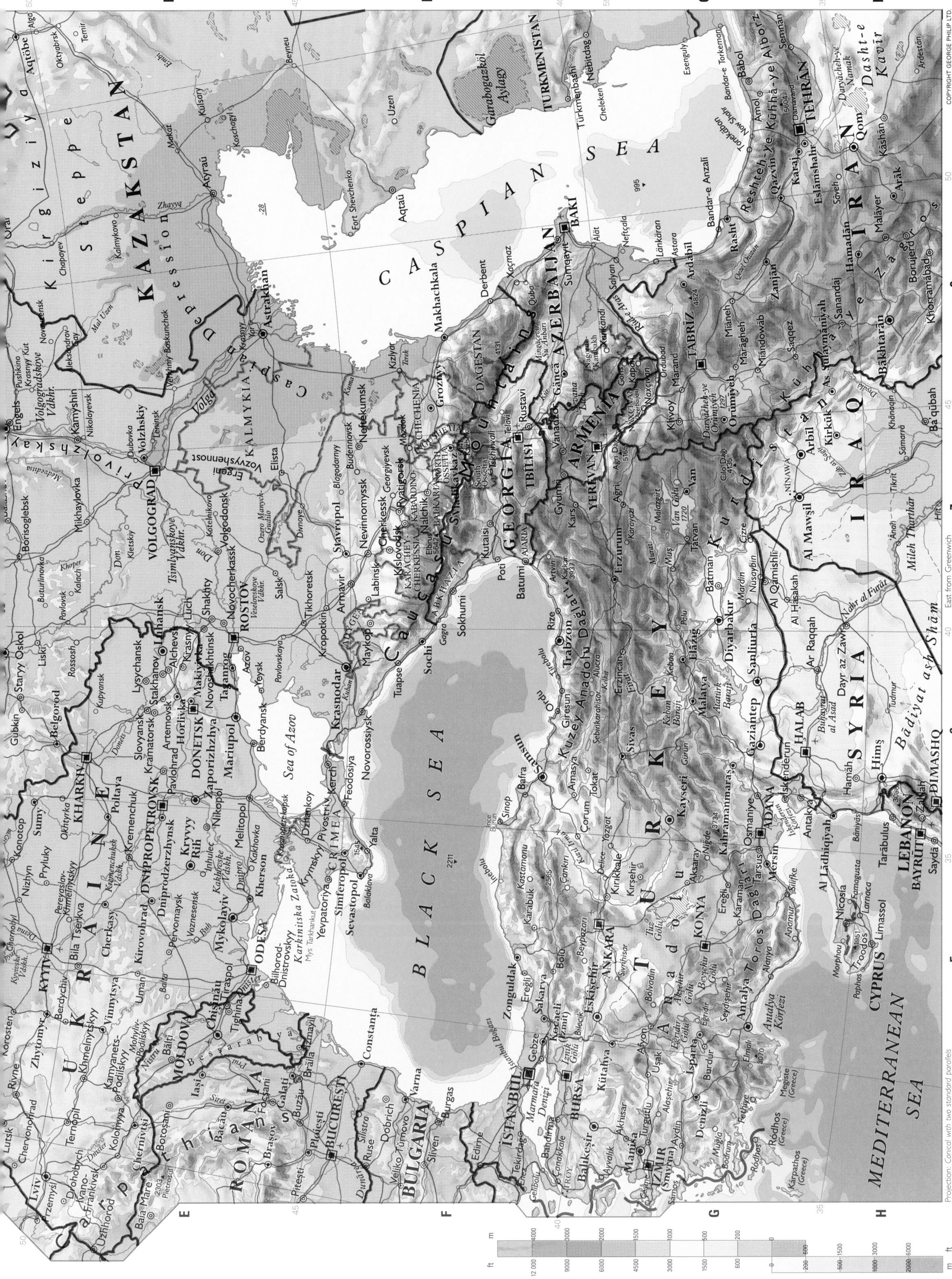

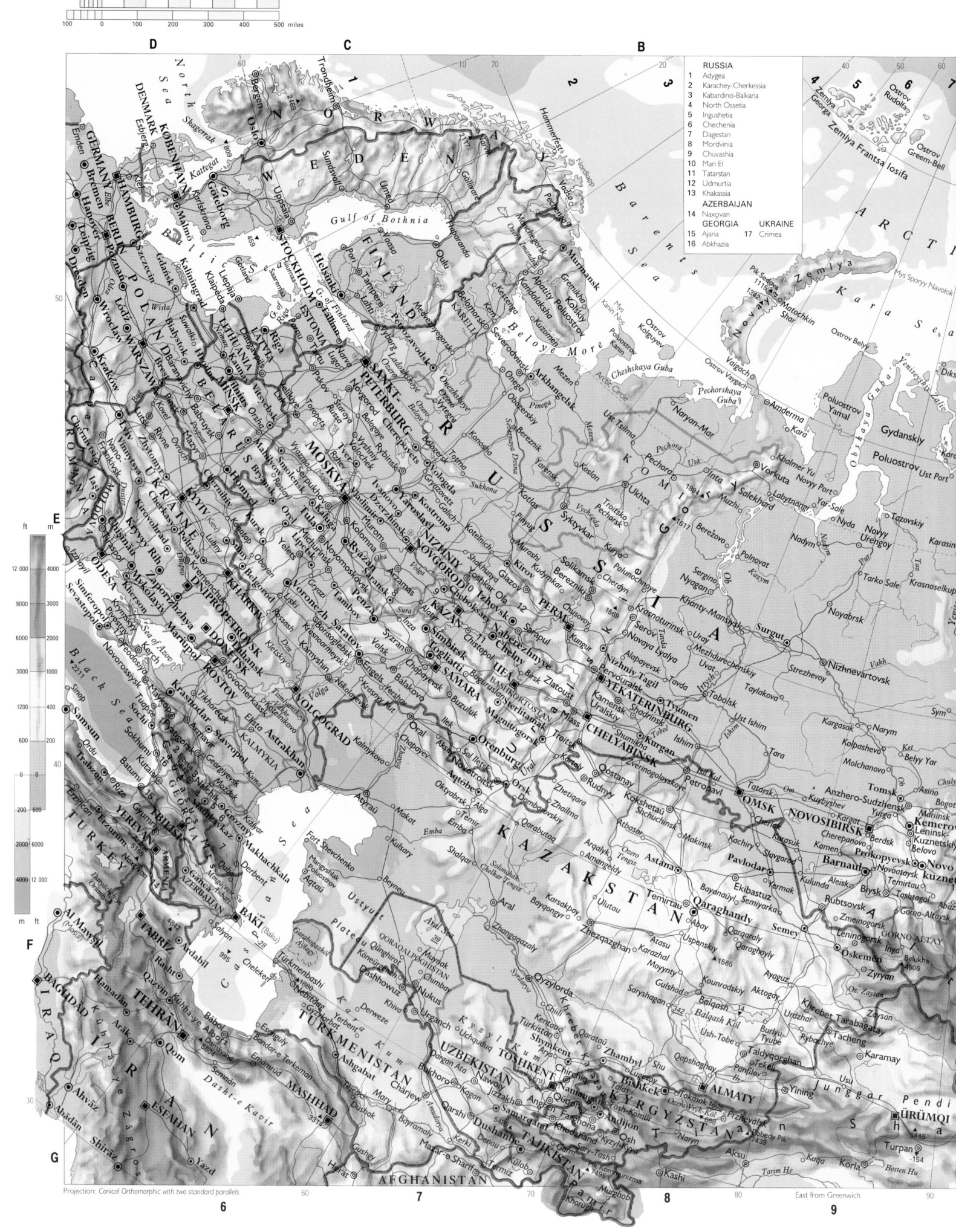

RUSSIA
1 Adygea
2 Karachey-Cherkessia
3 Kabardino-Balkaria
4 North Ossetia
5 Ingushetia
6 Chechenia
7 Dagestan
8 Mordvinia
9 Chuvashia
10 Mari El
11 Tatarstan
12 Udmurtia
13 Khakassia

AZERBAIJAN
14 Naxçivan

GEORGIA   UKRAINE
15 Ajaria   17 Crimea
16 Abkhazia

Projection: Conical Orthomorphic with two standard parallels

East from Greenwich

A   B   C

OCEAN

Laptev Sea

East Siberian Sea

Bering Sea

R   U   S   S   I   A

Khrebet Cherskogo

Kolymskoye Nagorye

Koryakskoye Nagorye

Sredinnyy Khrebet

Poluostrov Kamchatka

Sea of Okhotsk

Yablonovyy Khrebet

Stanovoy Khrebet

Khrebet Dzhugdzur

Sakhalin

Khrebet Sikhote Alin

Kurilskiye Ostrova

Sea of Japan

MONGOLIA

Ulaanbaatar

Gobi

CHINA

Dongbei

BEIJING

QIQIHAR

HARBIN

CHANGCHUN

JILIN

SHENYANG

ANSHAN

FUSHUN

DALIAN

NORTH KOREA

PYONGYANG

SOUTH KOREA

SOUL

PUSAN

JAPAN

SAPPORO

Hokkaidō

Honshū

OSAKA

Krasnoyarsk

Irkutsk

Bratsk

Ulan Ude

Khabarovsk

Komsomolsk

Vladivostok

Yakutsk

Magadan

Norilsk

COPYRIGHT GEORGE PHILIP LTD.

CARTOGRAPHY BY PHILIP'S

Projection: Bonne 30

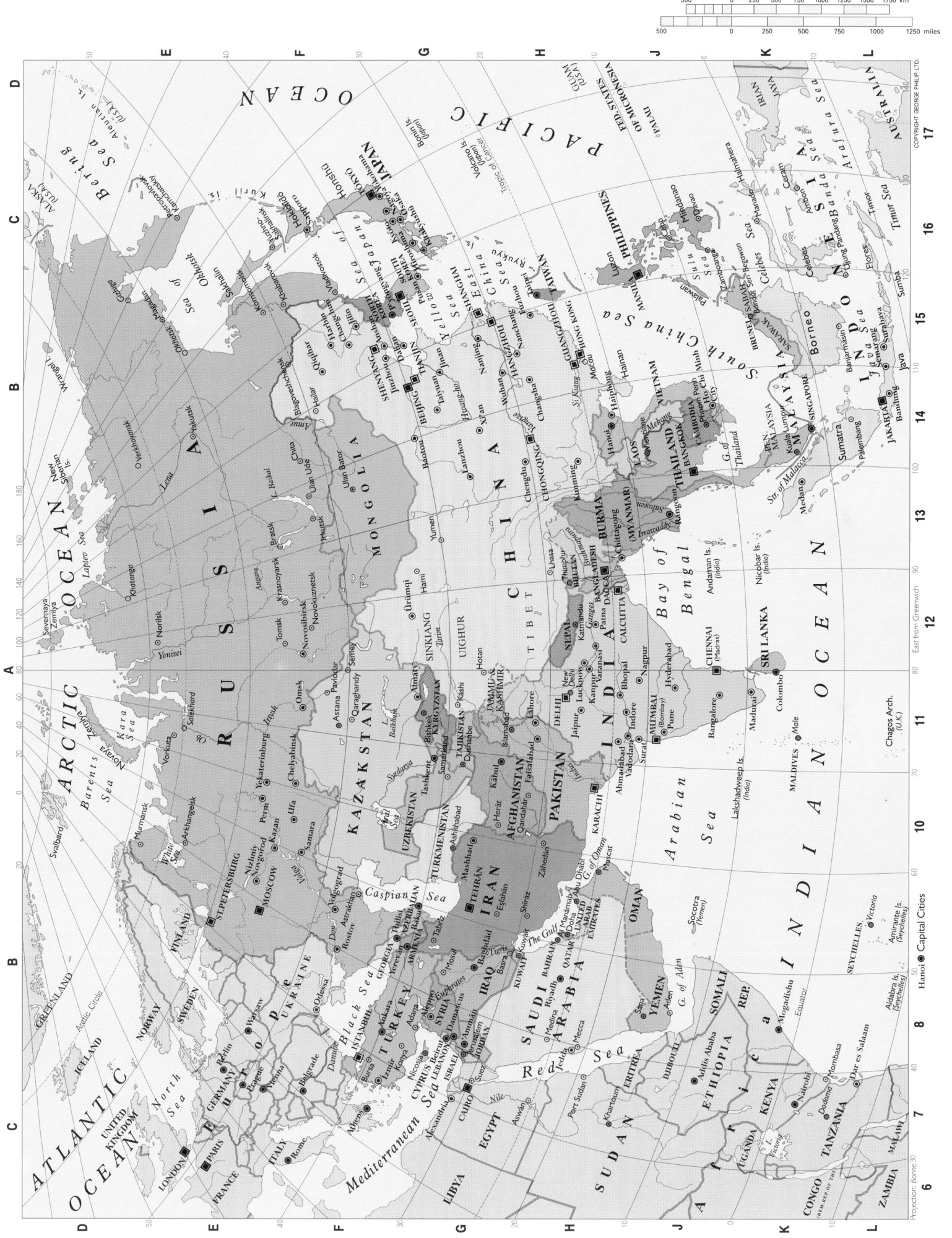
500 0 250 500 750 1000 1250 1500 1750 km
500 0 250 500 750 1000 1250 miles
ARCTIC OCEAN
PACIFIC OCEAN
INDIAN OCEAN
ATLANTIC OCEAN
R U S S I A
C H I N A
M O N G O L I A
K A Z A K S T A N
I N D I A
I N D O N E S I A
JAPAN
PHILIPPINES
THAILAND
VIETNAM
LAOS
CAMBODIA
BURMA (MYANMAR)
BANGLADESH
NEPAL
BHUTAN
SRI LANKA
PAKISTAN
AFGHANISTAN
IRAN
IRAQ
TURKEY
SYRIA
JORDAN
SAUDI ARABIA
YEMEN
OMAN
UZBEKISTAN
TURKMENISTAN
KYRGYZSTAN
TAJIKISTAN
TAIWAN
MALAYSIA
SINGAPORE
BRUNEI
NORTH KOREA
SOUTH KOREA
Bay of Bengal
Arabian Sea
South China Sea
East China Sea
Sea of Japan
Sea of Okhotsk
Bering Sea
Caspian Sea
Black Sea
Red Sea
Mediterranean Sea
Hanoi ● Capital Cities
Projection: Bonne 30
East from Greenwich
COPYRIGHT GEORGE PHILIP LTD.

JAPAN 1:5 000 000

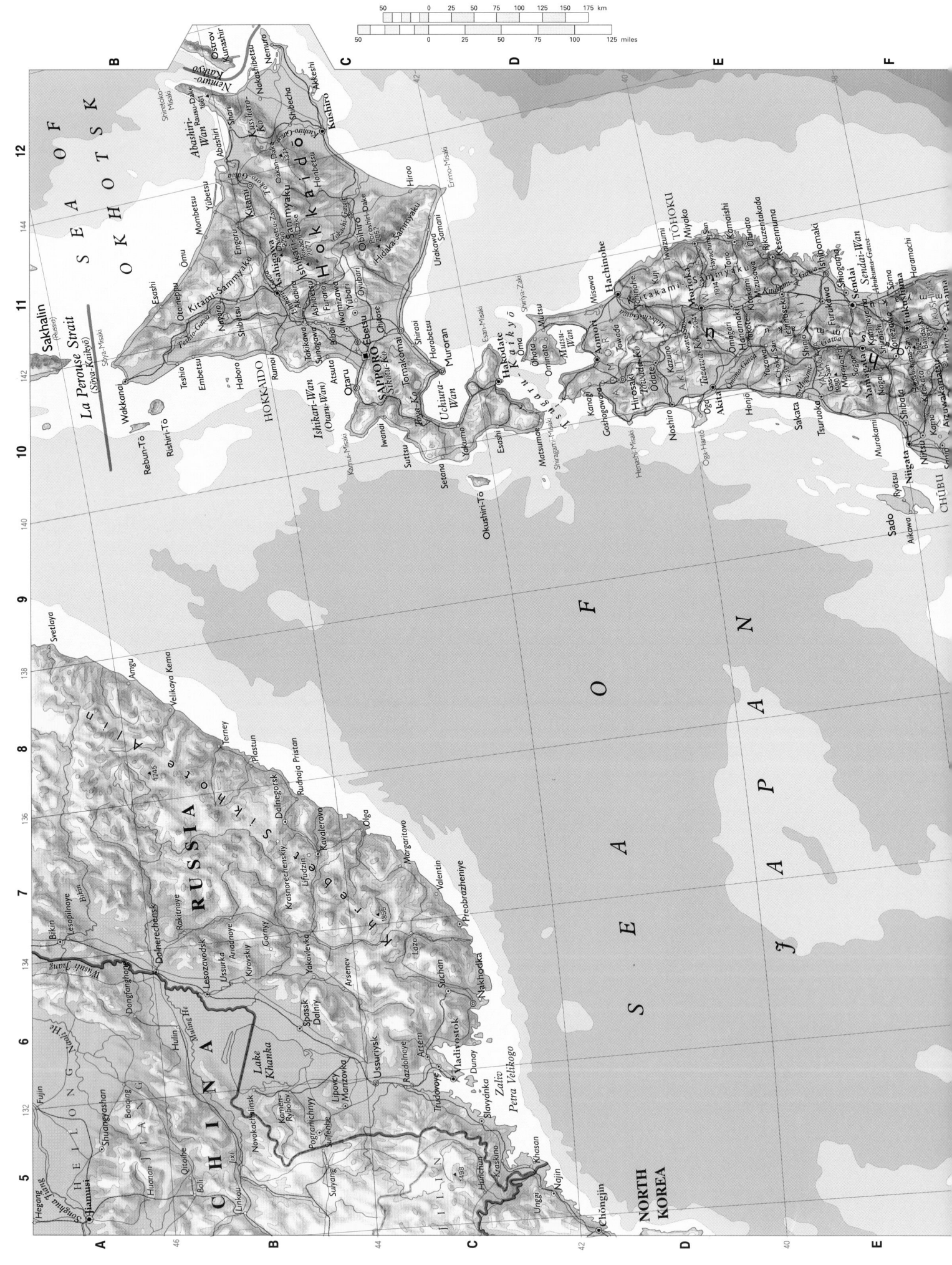

50 0 25 50 75 100 125 150 175 km
50 0 25 50 75 100 125 miles
SEA OF OKHOTSK
SEA OF JAPAN
La Perouse Strait (Sōya-Kaikyō)
Sakhalin (Russia)
Hokkaidō
HOKKAIDO
SAPPORO
Otaru
Ebetsu
Asahigawa
Kitami
Abashiri
Kushiro
Obihiro
Muroran
Hakodate
Tsugaru-Kaikyō
Wakkanai
Rebun-Tō
Rishiri-Tō
Okushiri-Tō
Ishikari-Wan (Otaru-Wan)
Uchiura-Wan
Mutsu-Wan
Nemuro
Nemuro-Kaikyō
Ostrov Kunashir
Aomori
Hachinohe
Morioka
Akita
Hirosaki
Sendai
Sendai-Wan
Yamagata
Niigata
Sado
TŌHOKU
CHŪBU
RUSSIA
CHINA
NORTH KOREA
Khrebet Sikhote Alin
Lake Khanka
Vladivostok
Nakhodka
Ussuriysk
Zaliv Petra Velikogo
Svetlaya
Terney
Plastun
Dalnegorsk
Olga
Valentin
Preobrazheniye
Dalnerechensk
Lesozavodsk
Spassk Dalniy
Artem
Jiamusi
Chŏngjin
Najin
Khasan
Hunchun

JAPAN

PACIFIC OCEAN

SOUTH KOREA

Korea Strait

Ullŭng-do (S. Korea)

Tok-do

Oki-Shotō

Tsushima

Izu-Shotō

Nansei-shotō

Ōsumi-Kaikyō

Ōsumi-Shotō

Tokara-Rettō

Satsunan-Shotō

CHŪGOKU

SHIKOKU

KINKI

KANTŌ

KYŪSHŪ

TOKYO

KAWASAKI

YOKOHAMA

NAGOYA

KYOTO

OSAKA

KOBE

HIROSHIMA

KITAKYŪSHŪ

FUKUOKA

RYUKYU ISLANDS

on same scale

EAST CHINA SEA

PACIFIC OCEAN

Nansei-shotō (Ryukyu Is.)

Sakashima-Guntō

Yaeyama-Rettō

Miyako-Rettō

Senkaku-Shotō

Okinawa-Guntō

Amami-Guntō

Amami-Ō-Shima

Okinawa-Jima

Naha

Koza

Projection: *Conical with two standard parallels*

East from Greenwich

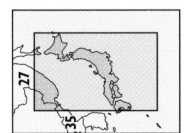

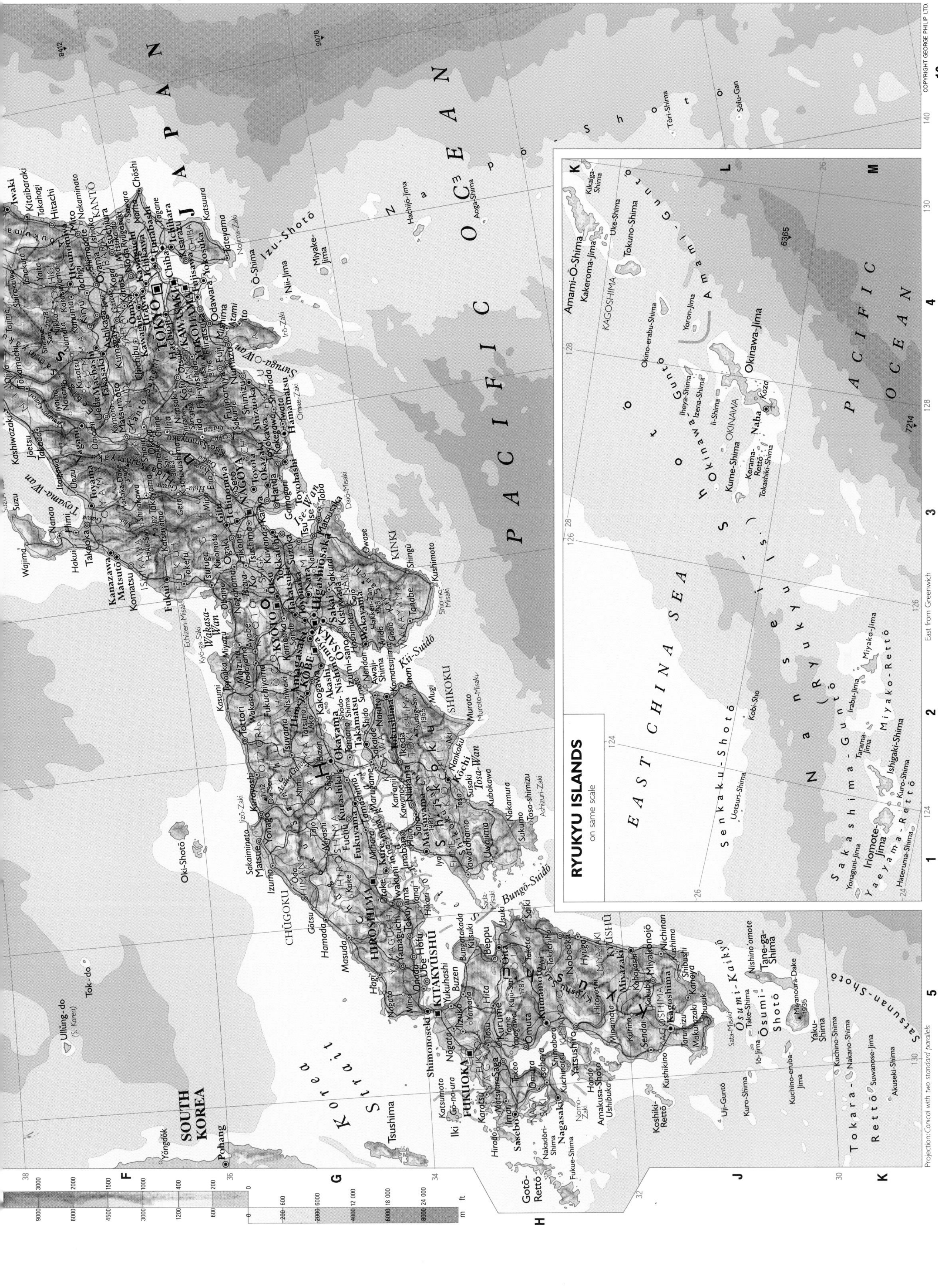

1 2 3 4 5

KAZAKSTAN

Qaraghandy Rubtsovsk Gorno-Altaysk **RUSSIA** Cheremkhovo
Karsakpay Semey Leninogorsk Angarsk Irkutsk
Zhezqazghan Qarqaraly Oskemen Belukha Munku-Sardyk 2491 Babushk
Moyynty Zyryan Ulaangom Hatgal Hövsgöl 455
4506 Tannu Ola Nuur Atanban

B 342 Balqash Köl Tarbagatay Uvs Nuur Hangayn Nuruu Ulaanbaatar
Shu Taldyqorghan Tacheng Har Us Nuur Shara Erdenet
Ala Tau Karamay Altay Tsetserleg Dzuumod
Balqash Qapshaghay Bole Junggar Pendi Bayanhongor
Shu Bishkek Yining Usu Manas **MONGO**
Zhambyl ALMATY Ili Shan Altay
KYRGYZSTAN Qapshaghay Bögeni URUMQI Qitai Barkol Kazak Zizhixian Dalandzadgad
Naryn Wensu Turpan 5445 Hami 4925
Pik Pobedy 7439 Turpan Hami 154
Andijon Tian Yanqi Aydingkol Hu
40 Aksu Kuqa Bosten Hu Kuruktag Gaxun Nur Linhe
Kashi Artux Korla **N** E
Kongur Shan 7719 Shule Tarim He Lop Nur Ximiao G
Muztagh-Ata 7546 Shache Tarim Pendi Ruoqiang Dunhuang Anxi Wuhai 251
Taxkorgan **XINJIANG UYGUR ZIZHIQU** Qiemo Qarqan He Altun Shan Yumen Jiayuguan Qilian Shan Zhangye Shandan
Tajik Zizhixian Yecheng **(SINKIANG)** Alxa Zuoqi Pingl
Pishan Taklamakan Mangnai Da Qaidam Jinchang Yinchuan NINGXIA
Karakoram Hotan Shamo Qaidam Pendi Tianjun Wuwei HUIZU
K2 8611 Yutian Ayakkum Hu Tart Har Hu ZIZHIQU
Nanga Parbat 8126 **JAMMU &** Wuluk'omushih Ling 7723 Hoh Xil Shan Golmud Qinghai Hu 3205 Xining Baiyin

C **KASHMIR** Kun-lun Shan Dulan Minhe **LANZHOU**
Srinagar Leh Da Qaidam Gonghe Linxia Dingxi Yongchang
Indus **XIZANG** Qinghai Guyuan
HIMACHAL Rutog **ZIZHIQU** Gyaring Hu 4237 Ngoring Hu Maqen Pinglian
PRADESH Kamet 7756 **(TIBET)** Bayan Har Shan 6094 Huang He Min Xian Tianshui Baoji
Dehra Dun Nanda Devi 7817 Mapam Yumco Tanggula (Dangla) Shan Yushu Songpan Wudu Qinli
Burang Siling Co 4495 Amdo Qamdo Garzê Min Jiang Hanzhong 3667
Meerut Moradabad Zhongba Nam Co 4627 Nagqu Yalong Guangyuan **C**
30 Dhaulagiri 8172 Xainza Nyainqentanglha Shan Markam Daxue Shan Mianyang Daxian **SI**
Delhi Annapurna 8078 Lhasa Shaluli Shan Deyang Santai Nanchong
New Delhi Bareilly Manaslu Lhaze Xigazê Yarlung Zangbo Jiang Namcha Barwa 7756 Bomi 7556 **CHENGDU** Ya'an Hechuan
Aligarh **NEPAL** Ngomring Yamzho Yumco Zhongdian Gongga Shan Leshan Neijiang **CHON**
Agra Mt Everest 8848 Kanchenjunga Pagri 6881 Zayü Wutongqiao Zigong **SI**
Katmandu Makalu 8598 Thimphu **BHUTAN** Dibrugarh Yibin Fuzhou
KANPUR **LUCKNOW** Gorakhpur 8481 Punakha **ARUNACHAL PRADESH** Nu Jiang Zhongdian Yuxing Jiang
Gwalior **PRADESH** Darbhanga Biratnagar Sadiya Yibin Zhaotong **GUIZH** Zunyi Meit
D Jhansi Allahabad Kod Bihar Brahmaputra Patkai Bum Xichang **GUIYAN**
Sagar PATNA Gauhati Tezpur **KACHIN** Lijiang Dukou Huize Lupanshui Anshun Duyu
INDIA VARANASI **ASSAM** 341 Myitkyina Dali Xiaguan Dongchuan **GUA**
Jabalpur BIHAR Gaya Khasi Hills **NAGALAND** Tengchong Xiangyun Anning Zhanyi Hechi
MADHYA PRADESH Rajshahi **MEGHALAYA** Imphal 3824 Bhamo Baoshan Chuxiong **KUNMING** Xingyi
Tropic of Cancer **BANGLADESH** Silchar **MANIPUR** Luxi Yuxi Chengjiang Hongshui Bose
Ranchi Asansol Berhampore **DHAKA** **BURMA** Lashio Shiping Jinggu Wenshan **GUA**
Raipur Barddhaman WEST Narayanganj Mandalay Kaiyuan Menzi **ZHU**
NAGPUR Jamshedpur Bilaspur Haora Khulna Monywa Shwebo Gejiu Nanning
Chanda **ORISSA** BENGAL CALCUTTA **CHITTAGONG** Myingyan Pingxiang **ZI**
Indravati Baleshwar BAY OF **(MYANMAR)** 3053 Hekou **VIETNAM** Hechi
20 Cuttack BENGAL Akyab Mandalay Shan 3143 **HANOI** Hong Gai
E Warangal Vizianagaram Myingyan Pegu Yoma Taunggyi Luang Prabang **HAIPHON**
Brahmapur Yamethin Yoma Nam Dinh
VISHAKHAPATNAM Irrawaddy Chiang Mai Mekong **LAOS** G. of Tonkin
Toungoo **THAILAND (SIAM)** 3143 Ho Binh

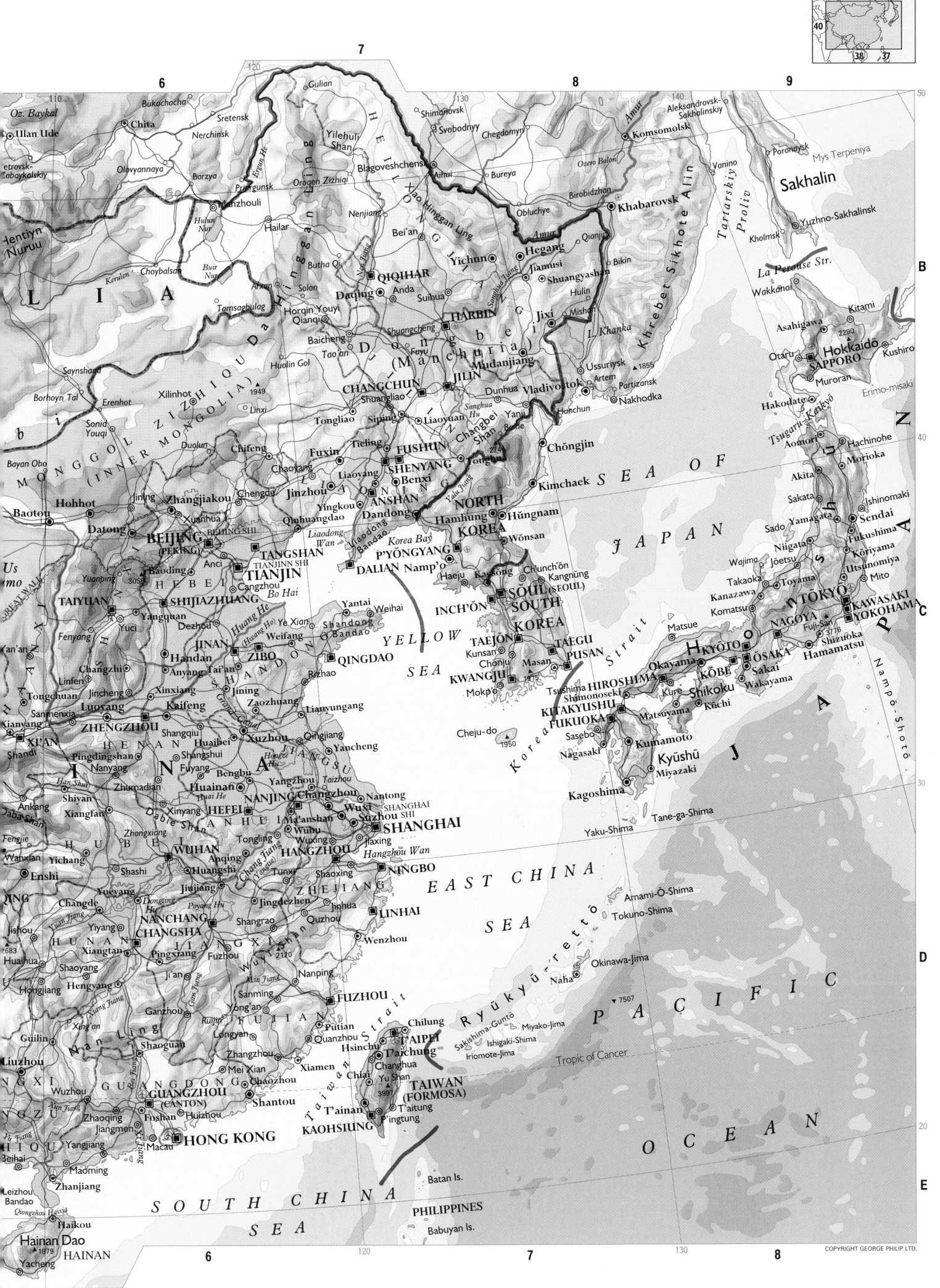

Oz. Baykal
Ulan Ude
etrovsk-Zabaykalskiy
Chita
Bukachacha
Nerchinsk
Sretensk
Gulian
Shimanovsk
Svobodnyy
Chegdomyn
Aleksandrovsk-Sakhalinskiy
Komsomolsk
Poronaysk
Mys Terpeniya
Sakhalin

Hentiyn Nuruu
Borzya
Olovyannaya
Manzhouli
Priargunsk
Oroqen Zizhiqi
Blagoveshchensk
Aihui
Bureya
Obluchye
Birobidzhan
Khabarovsk
Vanino
Yuzhno-Sakhalinsk
Kholmsk

Choybalsan
Hailar
Hulun Nur
Buir Nur
Nenjiang
Yichun
Hegang
Jiamusi
Bikin
Hulin
Wakkanai
La Perouse Str.

L I A
Tamsagbulag
Arxan
Solon
Butha Qi
QIQIHAR
Anda
Suihua
Shuangyashan
Mishan
L. Khanka
Asahigawa
Kitami
Hokkaidō
SAPPORO
Kushiro

Saynshand
Horqin Youyi Qianqi
Daqing
HARBIN
Jixi
Ussuriysk
Artem
1855
Otaru
Muroran
Erimo-misaki

Borhoyn Tal
Xilinhot
Baicheng
Tao'an
Fuyu
JILIN
Mudanjiang
Dunhua
Vladivostok
Nakhodka
Hakodate
Aomori
Hachinohe

Erenhot
Sonid Youqi
Linxi
Huolin Gol
CHANGCHUN
Shuangliao
Changbei Shan
Yanji
Tumen
Hunchun
Tsugaru-Kaikyō
Morioka

Bayan Bob
Duolun
Chifeng
Tongliao
Siping
Liaoyuan
Chǒngjin
SEA OF
Akita
Ishinomaki
Sendai

Hohhot
Zhangjiakou
Chengde
Fuxin
Tieling
FUSHUN
Tonghua
Kimchaek
Sakata
Yamagata
Fukushima

Baotou
Jining
Xuanhua
Chaoyang
Liaoyang
SHENYANG
Benxi
Hamhung
Hŭngnam
Wajima
Niigata
Kōriyama

Datong
Yuanping
Jinzhou
Yingkou
ANSHAN
NORTH
KOREA
Wǒnsan
JAPAN
Jōetsu
Utsunomiya

BEIJING
(PEKING)
Baoding
Qinhuangdao
Dandong
P'YŎNGYANG
Takaoka
Toyama
Mito

TANGSHAN
Anci
DALIAN
Namp'o
Haeju
Kaesong
Ch'unch'ǒn
Kanazawa
Komatsu
TOKYO
KAWASAKI
YOKOHAMA

TIANJIN
Cangzhou
Bo Hai
Yantai
Weihai
INCH'ǑN
SŎUL (SEOUL)
Matsue
NAGOYA
Fuji-San
Shizuoka

SHIJIAZHUANG
Yangquan
Dezhou
Ye Xian
SOUTH
KOREA
KYŌTO
ŌSAKA
Hamamatsu

TAIYUAN
Yuci
JINAN
Weifang
TAEJǑN
TAEGU
OKAYAMA
KŌBE
Sakai
Wakayama

Fenyang
Handan
Tai'an
ZIBO
QINGDAO
Kunsan
Chŏnju
PUSAN
HIROSHIMA
Kure
Shikoku

Changzhi
Anyang
Rizhao
KWANGJU
Masan
Tsushima
KITAKYUSHU
Matsuyama
Kōchi

Jincheng
Xinxiang
Jining
Mokp'o
FUKUOKA
Shimonoseki

YELLOW
SEA
Cheju-do
1950
Sasebo
Kumamoto
Kyūshū

ZHENGZHOU
Kaifeng
Zaozhuang
Lianyungang
Korea Strait
Nagasaki
Miyazaki

XI'AN
Shangqiu
Huaibei
Xuzhou
Qingjiang
Yancheng
Kagoshima
Tane-ga-Shima

Pingdingshan
Nanyang
Shangshui
Fuyang
Huainan
Yangzhou
Taizhou
Nantong
SHANGHAI
Yaku-Shima

NANJING
Changzhou
Wuxi
Suzhou SHI
EAST CHINA
SEA

HEFEI
Ma'anshan
Wuhu
Wuxing
HANGZHOU
Hangzhou Wan

WUHAN
Anqing
Tongling
Jiaxing
NINGBO
Shaoxing
Amami-Ō-Shima
Tokuno-Shima

Huangshi
Jiujiang
Jingdezhen
Jinhua
LINHAI
Tane-ga-Shima

NANCHANG
CHANGSHA
Shangrao
Quzhou
Wenzhou
Okinawa-Jima
Naha

Xiangtan
Pingxiang
Wuyi Shan
2120
Nanping
RYŪKYŪ-rettō
PACIFIC
7507

FUZHOU
Sanming
Putian
Quanzhou
Hsinchu
Chilung
Sakishima-Guntō
Miyako-Jima
Ishigaki-Shima
Tropic of Cancer

GUANGZHOU
(CANTON)
Longyan
Zhangzhou
Xiamen
TAIPEI
T'aichung
Changhua
Yu Shan
3997
Iriomote-Jima

Shaoguan
Mei Xian
Chaozhou
Shantou
TAIWAN
(FORMOSA)
T'ainan
T'aitung
P'ingtung

HONG KONG
Macau
KAOHSIUNG
Taiwan Strait
OCEAN

Hainan Dao
1879
HAINAN
Yacheng
Haikou
SOUTH CHINA
SEA
Batan Is.
PHILIPPINES
Babuyan Is.

COPYRIGHT GEORGE PHILIP LTD.

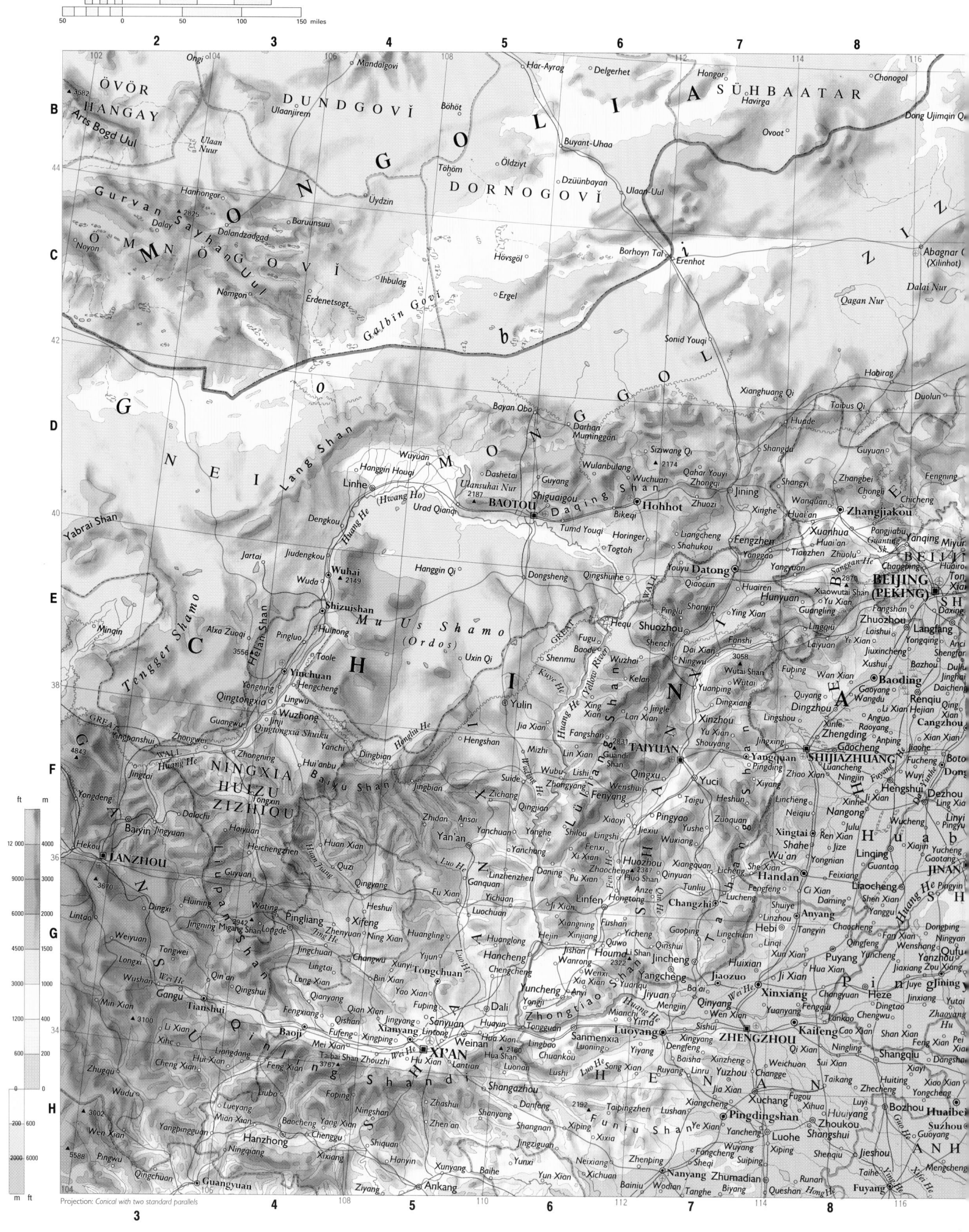

Projection: Conical with two standard parallels

9 10 11 12 13 14 15 16

B C D E F G H

Horqin Youyi Qianqi (Ulanhot)
Zhenlai
HARBIN
Bin Xian
Baicheng
Da'an
Maoxing
Zhaoyuan
Shuangcheng
Acheng
Yanshou
Linkou
Jixi
Turiy Rog
Ozero Khanka
Tuquan
Taonan
Anguang
Changchunling
HEILONGJIANG
Shangzhi
Hulingol
Hulin He
Qagan Nur
Qian Gorlos
Fuyu
Lalin
Yimianpo
Hengdaohezi
Muling
Maqiaohe
Xiachengzi
Pogranichnyy
Sanchahe
Yushu
Wuchang
Mudanjiang
Beitaolaizhao
Qian'an
Shenjingzi
Kaoshan
Shanhetun
Zhangguangcai Ling
1690
Hailin
Muling
Suiyang
Suifenhe
RUSSIA
Tongyu
Nong'an
Dehui
Shulan
Ning'an
Golenki
Dongning
Beizhengzhen
Zhanyu
Fulongquan
Jiutai
Changling
Gangyao
Wulajie
Dongjingcheng
Ussuriysk
1949
Jarud Qi
Xinkai He
Horqin Zuoyi Zhongqi
Maolin
CHANGCHUN
Huaidezhen
JILIN
Jiaohe
Xinzhan
Emu
Jingpo Hu
Chunyang
Luozigou
Razdolnoye
Tavrichanka
Artem
Vladivostok
Bairin Zuoqi
Kailu
Tongliao
Fanjiatun
Huangsongdian
Dunhua
Daxinggou
Shixian
Tumen Jiang
Songhua Hu
Shuangliao
Dongliao He
Shuangyang
Gongzhuling
Wangqing
Tumen
Hunchun
Slavyanka
Linxi
2029
Hexigten Qi
Bairin Youqi
Xiliao He
Lishu
Yitong
Mingyuegue
Yanji
Namyang
Siping
Panshi
Huadian
Longjing
Kraskino
Posyet
Xar Moron He
Jargalang
Bamiancheng
Liaoyuan
Huifa He
Manchuria
Erdao Jiang
Antu
Helong
Changbai Shan
Hoeamdong
Ongniud Qi
Laoha He
Wutonghaolai
Kangping
Zhangwu
Xifeng
Dongfeng
Huinan
Baishan
Baihe
1677
Hoeryong
Unggi
Sosura
2020
Hure Qi
Xiawa
Liu He
Faku
Tiefa
Kaiyuan
Meihekou
Jingyu
Fusong
Musan
Najin
WALL
Liao He
Shanchengzhen
Liuhe
Puryong
Pugodong
Chifeng
Fuxin
WILLOW
Zhangwu
Tieling
Qingyuan
Paektu-san
2744
Hupyongdong
Nanam
Chongjin
Kyongsong
Heishui
Xinlitun
Xinmin
Hunjiang
Linjiang
Chunggang-up
2541
Hachon
Chuuronjang
Weichang
Beipiao
Qinghemen
SHENYANG
FUSHUN
Dongbei
Xinbin
Tonghua
Changbai
Irhyangdong
Ondaejin
Heishan
1885
Ningcheng
Liaozhong
Qinghecheng
Huch'ang
Kosan-dong
Hyesan
Chaoyang
Yi Xian
Beizhen
Goubangzi
Liaoyang
Benxi
Inpundong
Hapsu
Simpungdong
Daling He
THE
LIAONING
Huanren
1845
Manp'o
Kapsan
Kilchu
Longhua
Lingyuan
Jinzhou
Panjin
Anping
Tianshifu
ANSHAN
Ji'an
Kanggye
Pujon-chosuji
Pungsan
Kosongni
Musudan
Kimch'aek (Songjin)
Chengde
Pingquan
Jinxi
Tianzhuangtai
Niuzhuang
Haicheng
Lianshanguan
Hun Jiang
Yalu Jiang
Kuup-tong
2522
Ch'ail-bong
Pujon-chosuji
Kwangdaeri
Tanch'on
Luanne
Luanping
Liugou
Jianchang
Huludao
Shangbancheng
Kuancheng
Xingcheng
Liaodong
Yingkou
Dashiqiao
Supung Shuiku
Kuandian
Ch'osan
Pyoktong
Changjin-chosuji
Changjin
Changhungni
Pukch'ong
Sinch'ang
Sohori
Koin-dong
Sinhung
Sinpo
Xinglong
Shuangshanzi
Suizhong
Xiongyuecheng
Gaizhou
Xiuyan
Fengcheng
Cao He
Sakchu
Taegwan
NORTH
Oro
Hongwon
Jianchangying
Wanfu
1131
Dandong
Uiju
Sinuiju
Pukchin
Kusong
Kujang
Hamhung
Hungnam
SEA OF
Zunhua
Buyun Shan
Gushan
Donggou
Yongamp'o
Chongju
Pakch'on
Tokch'on
KOREA
Tongch'on-ni
Tongjoson Man
Fengrun
Lulong
Funing
Qinhuangdao
Wan
Anju
Sunch'on
Yonghung
Yutian
Baodi
Luan Xian
Liaodong Bandao
Sonch'on
Kowon
Munch'on
Wonsan
TANGSHAN
TIANJIN SHI
Changli
Luan He
Wafangdian
Zhuanghe
Sukch'on
Sinchang-ni
Anbyon
Kojo
JAPAN
Leting
Pulandian
Pikou
Sunan
Songch'on
Kangdong
Tongyang
Wuqing
Hangu
Jingliuqing
TIANJIN
Jin Xian
P'YONGYANG
Chunghwa
Koksan
Singosan
Hoeyang
Kosong
Tanggu
Dagu
Lushun
DALIAN
Korea Bay
Namp'o
Songnim
Suan
Sepo-ri
1638
Changdo-ri
Kansong
Chiha-ri
Pyonggang
Sokch'o
Yangyang
Oikou
Bo Hai
Cho-do
Sariwon
Chaeryong
Sinmak
Nam-ch'on
Kumhwa
Ch'orwon
Hwach'on-chosuji
1578
Chumunjin
Miaodao Qundao
Changyon
Sinch'on
Kumch'on
Haeju
Kaesong
Panmunjom
Ch'unch'on
Kangnung
Huanghua
Uijongbu
Hongch'on
Ongjin
Yonan
Munsan
Paengnyong-do
Samch'ok
Ullung-do
Yanshan
Kanghwa
SOUL
Puch'on
Songnam
Hoengsong
Chongson
Qingyun
Wudi
Zhanhua
Huang He
Penglai
Longkou
Daxindian
Yantai
INCH'ON
Anyang
Wonju
Yongwol
Ulchin
Huimin
Laizhou
Huang Xian
Weihai
Ansan
Suwon
Ich'on
Yoju
Chech'on
Deping
Kenli
Dongying Wan
Muping
Chengshan Jiao
Osan
Ch'ungju
Yongju
Shanghe
Binzhou
Zhaoyuan
Fushan
Qixia
Wendeng
P'yongt'aek
Qingcheng
Gaoyuan
Laizhou
923
Rongcheng
Sosan
Ch'onan
SOUTH
Yech'on
Guangrao
Shouguang
Shandong Bandao
Chongju
Andong
Yongdok
Huantai
Linzi
Changyi
Pingdu
Laiyang
Rushan
Nanhuang
Shidao
Hongsong
Yesan
KOREA
Uisong
Zhoucun
ZIBO
Yidu
Weifang
Laixi
Haiyang
Kongju
TAEJON
Sangju
Sonsan
Chongha
P'ohang
Anmyon-do
Taech'on-ni
Nonsan
Kimch'on
Kumi
Fangzi
Lancun
Kanggyong
Yongdong
Yongch'on
Changgi-Ap
Tai Shan
1524
Boshan
Linqu
Anqiu
Gaomi
Jimo
Chengyang
Iri
Waegwan
TAEGU
Kyongju
Laiwu
1108
Zhucheng
Jiaozhou
Kunsan
Chonju
Tai'an
QINGDAO
Kimje
Kochang
Koryong
Ch'ongdo
Miryang
Ulsan
Jiaozhou Wan
Puan
Hamyang
Xintai
Chongup
Chii-san
Sishui
Mengyin
Yishui
Wulian
HUANG HAI
Namwon
Chinju
Masan
Kimhae
Tongnae
Sago-ri
Tamyang
1915
Yi He
Liangcheng
PUSAN
Pingyi
Ju Xian
Songjong-ni
KWANGJU
Ch'angwon
Hadong
Samch'onp'o
Rizhao
(Yellow Sea)
Naju
Tangtou
Shijiusuo
Sunch'on
Ch'ungmu
Sasuna
Andongwei
Posong
Polgyo-ri
Yosu
Fei Xian
Mokp'o
Saka
Tsushima
Tengzhou
Linyi
Haizhou Wan
Changhung
Korea Strait
Ganyu
Huksan-chedo
Haenam
Izuhara
Teng Xian
Zaozhuang
Lianyungang
Chindo
Weishan
Tancheng
Lianyungang
Haizhou
Hanzhuang
Jiawang
Pizhou
Chenjiagang
Iki
Weishan Hu
Guanyun
Xinyi
Xiangshui
Karatsu
Xuzhou
Yaowan
Guannan
Imari
Suqian
Shuyang
Binhai
Cheju
Cheju-do
JAPAN
Shuanggou
Onpyong-ni
Sasebo
Suining
Lianshui
Funing
Hallim
Halla-san
1950
Kashima
Sheyang
Taejong
Omura
Da Yunhe
Mosulpo
Sogwipo
Isahaya
Lingbi
Huaiyin
Huai'an
Nakadori-Shima
Hongze Hu
Yancheng
Guzhen
Suzhou
Baoying
Grand Canal
Nagasaki
Wuhe
Liuzhuang
Kuchinotsu
Fukue-Shima
Huaiyuan
Bengbu
Fengyang
Gaoyou Hu
Xinghua
Dongtai

118 120 122 124 126 128 130 132
44 42 40 38 36 34

9 10 11 12 13 14 15

East from Greenwich

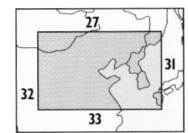

INDONESIA AND THE PHILIPPINES 1:12 500 000

BURMA (MYANMAR)
RANGOON (YANGON)
THAILAND
BANGKOK
LAOS
VIETNAM
CAMBODIA
Phnom Penh (Phnum Penh)
PHANH BHO HO CHI MINH
Gulf of Thailand
ANDAMAN SEA
SOUTH CHINA SEA
MALAYSIA
PENINSULAR MALAYSIA
KUALA LUMPUR
SINGAPORE
BRUNEI
SARAWAK
SABAH
Strait of Malacca
MEDAN
INDONESIA
PALEMBANG
JAKARTA
BANDUNG
SEMARANG
SURABAYA
Borneo
KALIMANTAN
Greater Sunda Islands
JAVA SEA
INDIAN OCEAN
Java Trench
Jawa (Java)
Projection: Mercator
East from Greenwich

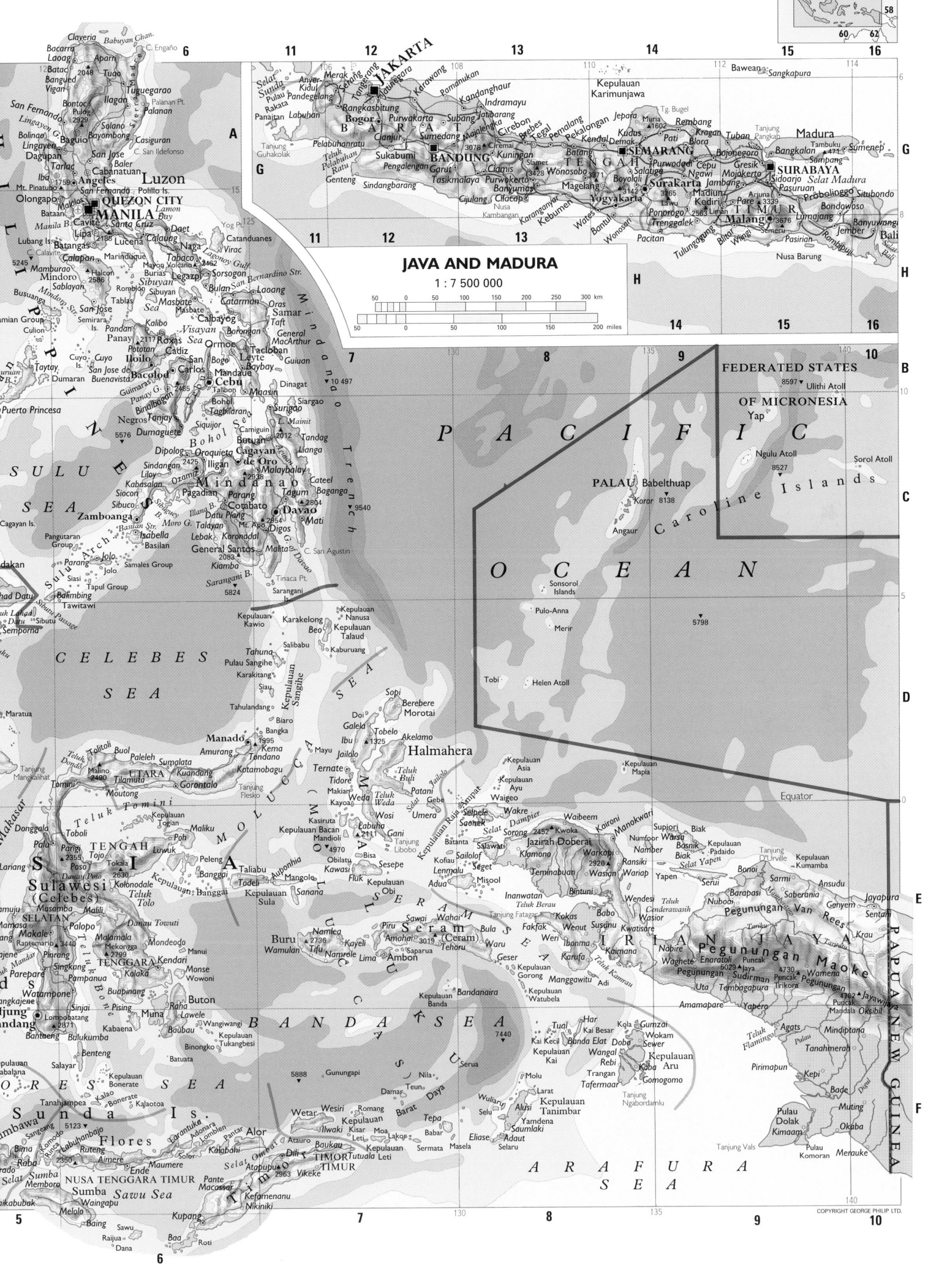

JAVA AND MADURA
1 : 7 500 000
JAKARTA
Bogor
BANDUNG
SEMARANG
SURABAYA
Surakarta
Yogyakarta
Malang
Madura
Kepulauan Karimunjawa
Bawean
Cirebon
Sukabumi
Kediri
Madiun
Jember
Banyuwangi
Bali
Nusa Barung
Selat Sunda
Selat Madura
PACIFIC OCEAN
FEDERATED STATES OF MICRONESIA
Caroline Islands
Yap
Ulithi Atoll
Ngulu Atoll
Sorol Atoll
PALAU
Babelthuap
Koror
Angaur
Sonsorol Islands
Pulo-Anna
Merir
Tobi
Helen Atoll
Mindanao Trench
PHILIPPINES
Luzon
QUEZON CITY
MANILA
Mindoro
Samar
Leyte
Panay
Negros
Cebu
Bohol
Mindanao
Davao
Zamboanga
Cagayan de Oro
General Santos
Palawan
Puerto Princesa
SULU SEA
Sulu Arch.
CELEBES SEA
Sulawesi (Celebes)
Manado
Ujung Pandang
Halmahera
Ternate
Morotai
MOLUCCA SEA
Buru
Seram (Ceram)
Ambon
BANDA SEA
Kepulauan Aru
Kepulauan Tanimbar
ARAFURA SEA
IRIAN JAYA
Pegunungan Maoke
Puncak Jaya
Jayapura
Merauke
PAPUA NEW GUINEA
Flores
Sumba
Sawu Sea
Timor
Kupang
Dili
Alor
Wetar
FLORES SEA
Sunda Is.
Equator
COPYRIGHT GEORGE PHILIP LTD.

50 0 50 100 150 200 km
50 0 50 100 150 miles

G. of Tonkin

HAINAN

GUANGXI ZHUANGZU ZIZHIQU

GUANGDONG

YUNNAN

BURMA (MYANMAR)

SHAN

KAYAH

KAWTHULE

TENASSERIM

THAILAND

LAOS

Chaîne Annamitique

VIETNAM

CAMBODIA

HANOI
Haiphong
Haikou
RANGOON
Mandalay
BANGKOK
Vientiane
Da Nang
Hue
Phnom Dangrek
ANGKOR
Tonlé Sap
Mekong
Lancang Jiang
Salween
Chao Phraya
Nan
Ping
Tenasserim
Bilauk Taungdan
Tanen Dong Dan
Moscos Islands

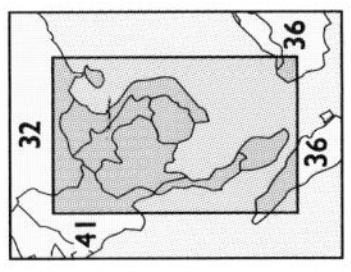

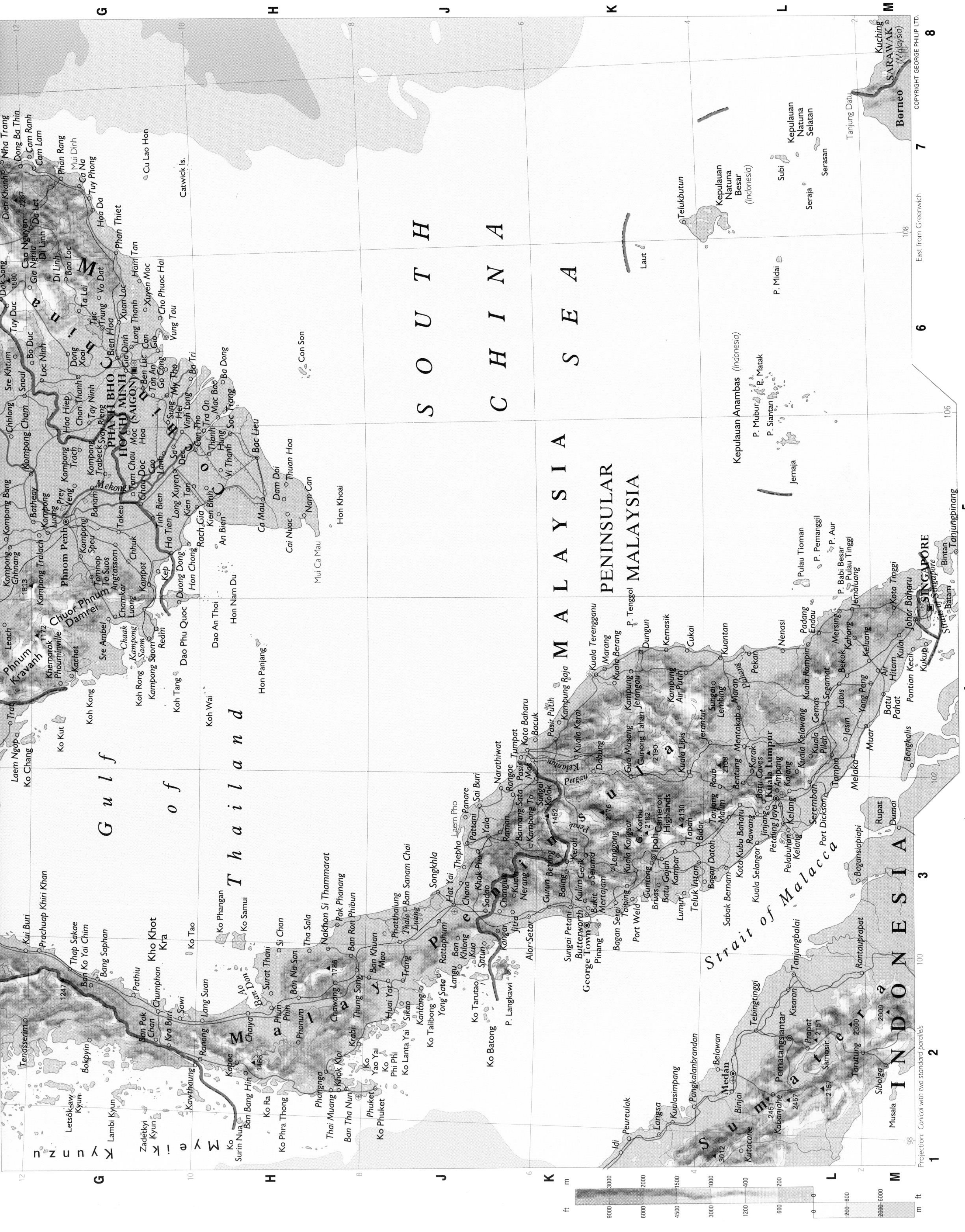

SOUTH

CHINA

SEA

MALAYSIA

PENINSULAR
MALAYSIA

G u l f

o f

T h a i l a n d

Gulf of Thailand

Strait of Malacca

INDONESIA

SARAWAK
(Malaysia)

Borneo

Kepulauan Natuna
Besar
(Indonesia)

Kepulauan Natuna
Selatan

Subi

Seraja

Serasan

Telukbutun

Laut

P. Midai

Kepulauan Anambas (Indonesia)

P. Mubur
P. Matak
P. Siantan

Jemaja

Tanjung Datu

East from Greenwich

COPYRIGHT GEORGE PHILIP LTD.

Kuching

M b u . i

Nha Trang
Dong Ba Thin
Cam Ranh
Cam Lam
Phan Rang
Ca Na
Mui Dinh
Tuy Phong
Hoa Da
Phan Thiet
Phan Tan
Ham Tan
Xuyen Moc
Cho Phuoc Hai
Ba Ria
Vung Tau

Catwick Is.

Cu Lao Hon

Da Lat
Di Linh
Di Linh
Ta Lai
Tuc Trung
Vo Dat

Dien Khanh
Cao Nguyen 2287
Gia Nghia 1580
Dak Song

Con Son

Dong
Xoai
Loc Ninh
Bu Dop
Sre Khtum
Snoul
Chlong
Kompong Cham
Kompong Speu
Tay Ninh
Hoa Hiep
Chon Thanh
Bien Hoa
Gia Dinh
Xuan Loc
Xuan Thanh
Long Thanh

PHAN BHO
HO CHI MINH
(SAIGON)

Trabeck Svay Rieng
Tan An
Go Cong
Ben Luc
Can Giuoc
Vinh Te
My Tho
Ba Tri
Sung Hei
Tra On
Mac Bac
Ba Dong

Mekong

Kompong
Thom

Kompong Chhnang

Phnom Penh

Kompong Trabach

Kampong
Tralach

Kompong
Prey Veng

Bareng

Takeo

Chau Doc
Sa Dec
Vinh Long
Soc Trang
Bac Lieu

Long Xuyen
Cao Lanh
Kien Tan
Kien Binh
Rach Gia
An Bien
Ca Mau

Can Tho
Thanh
Phu

Vi Thanh
Thuan Hoa
Dam Doi

Nam Can

Cai Nuoc
Hon Khoai

Mui Ca Mau

Tinh Bien

Ha Tien

Kep

Duong Dong

Hon Chong

Dao Phu Quoc

Dao An Thoi

Hon Nam Du

Hon Panjang

Chuor Phnum
Damrei

Phnum
Kravanh

Leach

Trat
Laem Ngop
Ko Chang
Ko Kut

Chaak
Sre Ambel
Kampong
Saom

Redim

Koh Rong
Kampong Som

Koh Tang

Koh Wai

Ko Kong
Koh Kong

Khemarak
1472
Phoumiville

Kachat
Chamkar
Luong

1813

Chhuk
Karpot

Kompong
Trach

Tonnop
To Suos

Angtassom

Baham

Luong

1247

Kui Buri
Prachuap Khiri Khan
Thap Sakae
Bang Saphan
Chumphon
Lang Suan

Ban Pak
Chan
Kra Buri
Ban Na San

Pathiu
Ao

Ban Dm

Surat Thani

Ban Don

Si Chon
Nakhon Si Thammarat

Ban Ron Phibun

Tha Sala

Pak Phanang

Phatthalung

Ban Sanam Chai

Luang

Thale
Luang

Ban Na Muang

Khuan Khanun

Phibun

Ranong

Kho Khot
Kra

Ko Tao

Ko Phangan

Ko Samui

Ko Phaluai

Chaiya

M a l a y

Thung Song

Huai Yot

Sikao

Trang

Yong Sata

Ko Talibong

Ko Lanta Yai

Ko Tarutao

Ko Batong

P. Langkawi

Perlis

Songkhla

Hat Yai
Chana
Thepha

Sadao

Na Thawi

Laem Pho

Thepha

Rattaphum

Sateng

Yala

Betong

Pattani
Sai Buri
Panare

Rangae
Narathiwat

Tumpat
Rantau Panjang
Kota Baharu
Pasir Mas
Pasir
Putih

Tanah
Merah
Kuala Krai
Gua Musang
Kuala Kerai

Dabong

Gunong Tahan
2190

Kampong
Raja

Kuala Terengganu

Marang
Kuala Berang
Dungun
Kemasik
Cukai

Kuantan

Pekan

Nenasi

Endau
Mersing

Kuala Rompin
Bekok
Kluang

Pulau Tioman

P. Tengol

P. Tinggi
P. Babi Besar
Pulau Tinggi
Padang
Endau

P. Aur
P. Pemanggil

Kukup
Pontian Kecil

Johor Baharu
SINGAPORE

Kota Tinggi

Kulai

Air Hitam
Batu Pahat

Muar

Melaka

Tampin
Segamat
Labis
Yong Peng

Jasin

Keluang

Kuala
Pilah

Bahau
Rompin

Gemas

Tampin
Seremban

Port Dickson

Kuala Kubu Baharu
Kajang
Kuala Kelawang
Kuala Kangsar

Petaling Jaya
Kelang
Port Kelang
Pelabuhan
Kelang

Bentung
Raub
Bentong
Karak
Tanjong
Malim

Batu Caves
Kuala Lumpur
Batu
Kampong

Cameron
Highlands
2130

Tapah
Teluk Intan

Bagan Datoh

Sabak Bernam

Sungai Besar

Bukit
Mertajam
George Town
Pinang
Butterworth
Sungai Petani

Alor Setar

Kangar
Kua
Satun
Kuala Kedah
Jitra
Changlun

Langu

Yong Sata

Kulim
Selama
Gurun
Baling
Kroh
Gerik
Kuala
Nerang
Kuala
Ketil

Perak
Pergau

Kampong Sato
Bamrang Sato
Kampong To

1452

Grik

2192
G. Korbu

Ipoh
Kuala
Kangsar

Batu Gajah
Kampar

Lenggong
Guntong

Brlids
Lurnut

Kampar

Bagan Serai
Port Weld
Taiping
Bagan Serai

S e l a t o r

P e n i n s u l a r

M a l a y s i a

Tenasserim

Letsok-aw
Kyun

Zadetkyi
Kyun

Bokpyin

Lambi Kyun

Kawthaung

Ko Surin Nua

Kra Buri

Ban Bang Hin

Kapoe

1456

Phangnga

Ban Tha Nun

Khok Kloi

Thai Muang

Ko Phuket

Ko Phra Thong

Ko Ra

Ko Yao Yai
Phi Phi
Ko Lanta Yai

Krabi

B u r m a

K y u n z u n

M y e i k

n z u n

K y u n

Projection: Conical with two standard parallels

Medan
Binjai
2451
Kutacane
2457
3012
Kabanjahe
Prapat
2151
Pematangsiantar
Tanjungbalai
Rantauprapat

Tebingtinggi
Kisaran

Belawan

2300
Toba
Samosir
2009
2150

Sibolga
Tarutung

Pangkalanbrandan

Kualasimpang
Langsa

Peureulak
Idi

Musala

S u m a t e r a

Bagansiapiapi

Bengkalis

Dumai

Rupat

Pangkalpinang

Bintan
Tanjungpinang
Batam
Selat
Tebrau

Kuala

Pakanbaru

K r a u

ft
m
9000
6000
4500
3000
1500
600
200
0
200 - 600
2000-6000
ft

m
3000
2000
1500
1000
400
200
600

SARAWAK

50 0 100 200 300 400 km
50 0 50 100 150 200 250 miles
TURKMENISTAN
AFGHANISTAN
IRAN
PAKISTAN
INDIA
SRI LANKA
ARABIAN SEA
Hindu Kush
Karakoram
JAMMU & KASHMIR
HERAT
HELMAND
ZABOL
QANDAHAR
GHAZNI
KABUL
NORTH WEST FRONTIER
PUNJAB
HARYANA
HIMACHAL PRADESH
RAJASTHAN
GUJARAT
MADHYA PRADESH
MAHARASHTRA
ANDHRA PRADESH
KARNATAKA
TAMIL NADU
KERALA
DADRA AND NAGAR HAVELI
BALUCHISTAN
SIND
Thar Desert
Great Indian Desert
Rann of Kachchh
Gulf of Kachchh
Gulf of Khambhat
Gulf of Mannar
Palk Strait
Adam's Bridge
Mouths of the Indus
Makran Coast Range
Central Makran Range
Siahan Range
Kirthar Range
Toba Kakar
Sulaiman Range
Vindhya Range
Satpura Range
Western Ghats
Eastern Ghats
Malabar Coast
Coromandel Coast
Indus
Kabul
Herat
Qandahar
Quetta
Peshawar
Rawalpindi
Islamabad
Srinagar
LAHORE
FAISALABAD
Multan
Amritsar
DELHI
New Delhi
KARACHI
Hyderabad
Jaipur
Agra
Ahmadabad
Surat
MUMBAI (BOMBAY)
Pune (Poona)
Nagpur
HYDERABAD
Bangalore
Chennai (Madras)
Mysore
Madurai
Colombo
Kandy
Tropic of Cancer
Continuation Southwards on same scale
Projection: Conical with two standard parallels

B

34

C

32

D

XINJIANG

UYGUR

Kunlun Shan

Huh Xil Shan

QINGHAI

Bayan Har Shan

Gyaring Hu

Ngoring Hu

Dogai Coring

Yushu

Dainkog

C H I N A

Nangqen

Garntog

Garzê

Baiyü

Xinlong

SICHUAN

Tanggula (Dangla) Shan

5180

Tanggula Shankou

Baqên

Dêngqên

Qamdo

Litang

Yajiang

Nganglong Kangri

7315

X I Z A N G

Tanggula

(T i b e t)

Kangri

Siling Co

Nagqu

Lhorong

Nu Jiang (Salween)

Zhaxizê

Ningjing

Yidun

Gongbo gyamda

7756

Gamba

(Tsangpo)

La'nga Co

Mapam Yumco

Gangdise Shan

Ombu

Coqên

Tangra Yumco

Gyaring Ca

Xainza

Nam Co

Nyainqentanglha Shan

Lhari

Lhinzub

7088

Lhasa

Maquan He (Tsangpo)

Xigazê

Gyangzê

Yarlung Zangbo Jiang

Nang Xian

Riga

Jido

Mainkung

Muli Zangzu Zizhixian

E

30

28

ARUNACHAL

Simikot

Mugu

Namco Shankou

4944

7059

Zhongba

Saga

Xixabangma Feng 8013

Lhazê

Comai

Cona

Towong

Nizamghat

Minutang

Hkakabo Razi Thala Lu

Zizhixian

Zhongdian

Weixi

6500

Lijiang

F

Baitadi

Dandeldhura

Silgarhi Doti

Jumla

Dhangarhi

Nepalganj

N E P A L

Dhaulagiri 8172

Mustang

Muktinath

Gurkha

Nuwakot

Maquan He

5602

Nyalam

Dinggyê

7314

Gamba

7554

Thunkar

Towong

Tongsa Dzong

Kangto 7089

Rupa

North Lakhimpur

Dibrugarh

Tinsukia

PRADESH

Dum Dumao Ghat

Minutang

Putao 3072

Jipangan Pass

Chaukan Pass

Lawngtlai Pit

6291

2432

KACHIN

Bumhpa Bum 3411

Yunlong

Jianchuan

Changning

G

26

TAR

Lakhimpur

Jarwa

Nautanwa

Balrampur

Gonda

Basti

Dhankuta

Darjiling

Mt Everest 8848

Kanchenjunga 8598

SIKKIM

Thimphu

Gangtok

BHUTAN

Tagg Dzong

Jayanti

Balipara

Tezpur

Dergaon

Jorhat

Sibsagar

Pakhui Bum

Kawngtit

Hukawng Valley

Mokokchung

NAGALAND

Maingkwan

Mogaung

Homalin

Singkaling Hkamti

3424

Myitkyina

2424

Mong Nai

Bhamo

Longling

YUNNAN

Tengchong

Baoshan

H

Lucknow

Unnao

Rae Bareli

Fatehpur

Allahabad

Faizabad

Gorakhpur

Deoria

Siwan

Gorakhpur

Chhapra

Deoria

Bettiah

Motihari

Darbhanga

Raxaul

Sitamarhi

Nirmali

Kishanganj

Saidpur

Dinajpur

Koch Bihar

Rangpur

Alipur

Duar

Siliguri

Cherrapunji

Tura

MEGHALAYA 1961

Mohanganj

Mymensingh

Barpeta

Mangaldai

Gauhati

Nowgong

W BENGAL

ASSAM

Brahmaputra

Rangia

Shillong

Sylhet

Barak R

Haflong

Manenglong

Imphal

MANIPUR

Churachandpur

Ukhrul

Barail Range

Silchar

Tamenglong

Tamu

Indaw

Katha

Shwegu

Wuntha

Tigyaing

Shweli

2299

Kunlong

Mong Yai

Namtu

Lashio

Mogok

Gokteik

Madaya

Mandalay

Pang-Yang

Pang-Long

Hsenwi

2693

Mong Hsu

Mong Pawk

Mong Wa

J

24

22

Manikpur

Mirzapur

Rewa 690

Burwa

Umaria

Shahdol

Anuppur

Mandla 1127

VARANASI

Ghazipur

Sasaram

Gaya

Aurangabad

Dudhi

Chirmiri 1225

Bharatpur

Patna

Bihar

Jamalpur

Bhagalpur

Monghyr

Bankipore

BIHAR

Hazaribag

Giridih

Dhanbad

Barhi

Gomoh

Jahanabad

Deoghar

Rampur Hat

Siuri

Baharampur

Asansol

Ranaganj

Katihar

Purnia

Bogra

Rajshahi

Kushtia

Pabna

Ingraj Bazar

Dinajpur

B A N G L A D E S H

Phulbari

Jamalpur

Tangail

Narayanganj

Comilla

DHAKA

Bhairab Bazar

Brahmanbaria

Agartala

TRIPURA

Sairang

MIZORAM 2157

Aizawl

Lunglei

Churachandpur

Tiddim

Kyauktaw

Falam

Haka

Mingin

Shwebo

Monywa

Sagaing

Budalin

Alon

Yinmabin

Kyaukse

Mong Kung

Mong Yang

Keng Tung

SHAN

H

Chirmiri 1225

Ambikapur

Chakradharpur

Ghatsila

Raurkela

Gua

Barddhaman

Bankura

Durgapur

Purulia

Ranchi

Lohardaga

Ramgarh

Krishnanagar

Kharagpur

Haldia

Medinipur

Shrirampur

Barakpur

Bhatpara

Khulna

Jessore

Madaripur

Faridpur

Barisal

Bhola I.

Maijdi

Noakhali

Chittagong

Dohazari

CHIN

Victoria Taungdeik 3053

Kanpetlet

Pauk

Pakokku

Myingyan

Meiktila

Thazi

Yamethin

Pyinmana

Taunggyi 2519

Heho

Lai-kaw

Mong Noi

Mong Ton

Muang Chiang Rai

J

22

BENGAL

Jamshedpur

Haora

CALCUTTA

Diamond Harbour

Port Canning

The Sundarbans

Lakshmikantapur

Contai

Hatia

Patuakhali

Cox's Bazar

Paletwa

ARAKAN

Sandoway

Kyaukpyu

Ramree I.

Taungup

Cheduba I.

BURMA

(MYANMAR)

Minbu

Magwe

Thayetmyo

Prome

Yenangyaung

MAGWE

Pyu

Madauk

KAYAH

Bawlake

Toungoo

Pyinmana

2620

Loikaw

2576

Muang Lamphun

Chiang Mai

Lampang

THAILAND

K

20

18

Bilaspur

Raigarh

Kharsia

Sarangarh

Sambalpur

Keonjhargarh

Baleshwar

Bhadrakh

Kendrapara

Paradip

Balangir

Sonepur

Titlagarh 1001

Bhawanipatna

Berhampur

Chatrapur

ORISSA

Hirakud Dam

Talcher

Dhenkanal

Cuttack

Bhubaneshwar

Puri

Chilka L.

Braumani

Mahanadi

Tangup

Sittwe (Akyab)

Arakan Coast

Myanaung

Letpadan

Tharrawaddy

Henzada

Bassein

Myaungmya

Ma-ubin

Gwa

RANGOON

PEGU

Pegu

Thaton

Kyongbyo

Yandoon

Rangon

Martaban

G. of Martaban

Moulmein

Amherst

TENASSERIM

Pa-an

Taninthayi

Ye

L

16

14

K A R N A T A K A

Bhamragarh

Indravati

Jagdalpur

Raygada

Bastar

Jeypore

Salur 1240

Parvatipuram

Bobbili

Tekkali

Srikakulam

Vizianagaram

Northern Circars

Konta

Kottagudem

Anakapalle

Vishakhapatnam

1680

Pithapuram

Kakinada

Godavari Point

Rajahmundry

Iluru

Vijayawada

Narsapur

Tenali

Machilipatnam

Bastar

1501

Bastar

BAY OF BENGAL

Cox's Bazar

Mouths of the Ganges

Hooghly R

Subarnarekha

Mahanadi

Chilka L.

1187

Preparis North Channel

Pariparit Kyun (Burma)

Preparis South Channel

Koko Kyunzu (Burma)

Maudin Sun

Mouths of the Irrawaddy

Kalegauk I.

Lamaing

Moscos Is.

Maungmagan Is.

Natkyizin

Nam Tok

Yebyu

Sangkhla

Buri

Tavoy 2070

Launglon Bok

TENASSERIM

Tanen Tong Dan

Mae Hong Son

Tak

M

INDIAN OCEAN

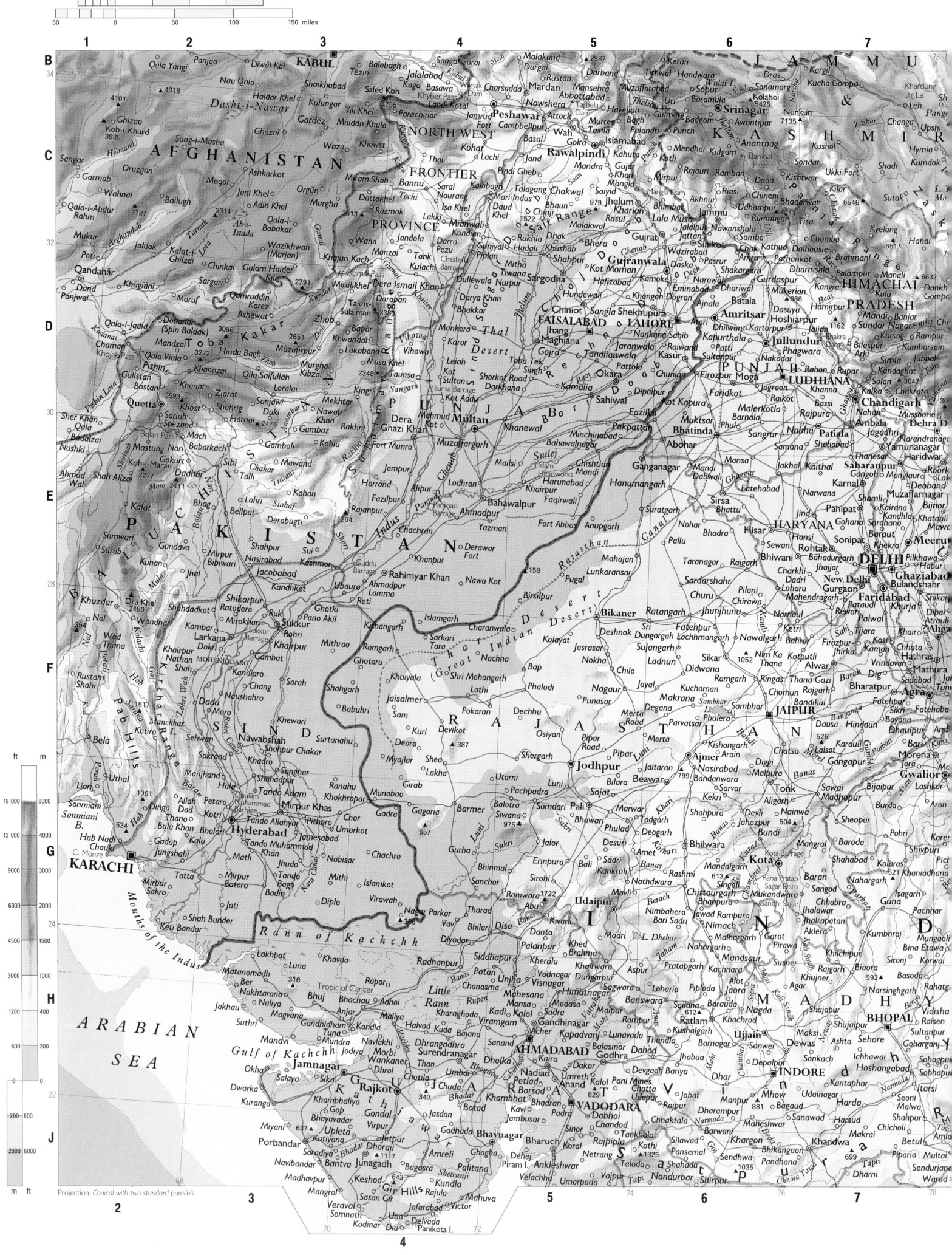

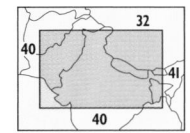

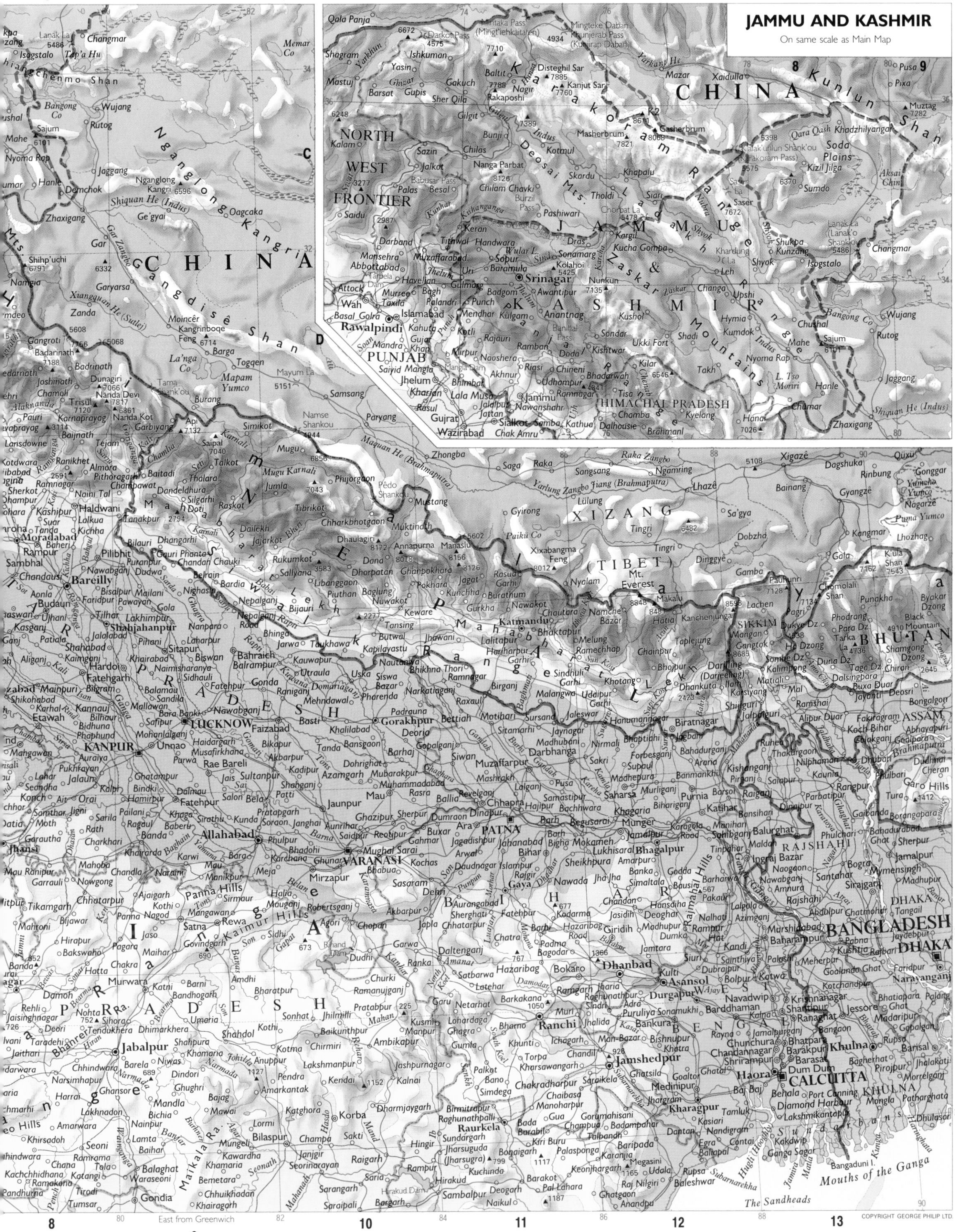

JAMMU AND KASHMIR
On same scale as Main Map

THE MIDDLE EAST 1:7 000 000

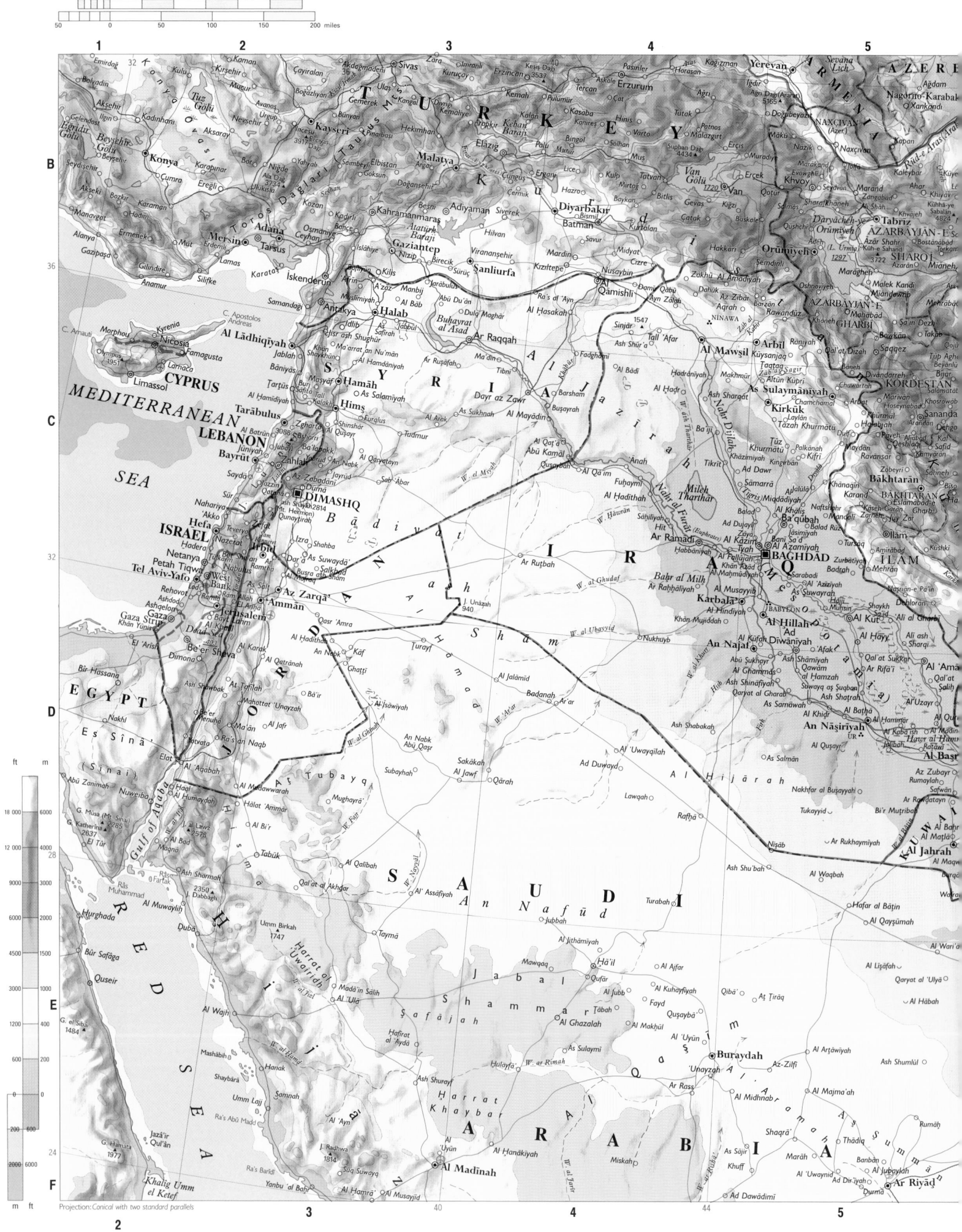

50 0 50 100 150 200 250 300 km
50 0 50 100 150 200 miles
1 2 3 4 5
B C D E F
T U R K E Y
ARMENIA
AZERBAIJAN
CYPRUS
MEDITERRANEAN SEA
LEBANON
ISRAEL
SYRIA
JORDAN
IRAQ
EGYPT
KUWAIT
SAUDI ARABIA
RED SEA
Es Sînâ' (Sinai)
Gulf of Aqaba
Bādiyat ash Shām
An Nafūd
Jabal Shammar
Al Hijārah
Al Jazīrah
Harrat Khaybar
Toros Dağları
Taurus Mts.
Kurdistan
Konya
Kayseri
Adana
Mersin
Tarsus
Gaziantep
Şanlıurfa
Malatya
Elazığ
Diyarbakır
Erzurum
Sivas
Van
Yerevan
Tabrīz
Orūmīyeh
Nicosia
Limassol
Famagusta
Larnaca
Kyrenia
Ḩalab
Al Lādhiqīyah
Ḩamāh
Ḩimş
Ar Raqqah
Dayr az Zawr
Al Qāmishlī
Al Ḩasakah
Ṭarābulus
Bayrūt
DIMASHQ
Ḩefa
Tel Aviv-Yafo
Jerusalem
Gaza
Be'er Sheva
'Ammān
Az Zarqā'
Irbid
Al 'Aqabah
Al Mawşil
Arbīl
Kirkūk
As Sulaymānīyah
BAGHDAD
Karbalā'
An Najaf
Al Ḩillah
Ad Dīwānīyah
An Nāşirīyah
Al Kūt
Al Başrah
Ar Ramādī
Bakhtarān
Ilām
Tabūk
Ḩā'il
Buraydah
Al Madīnah
Ar Riyāḑ
Al Jawf
Sakākah
Ar Ruţbah
Al Jahrah
ft m
18 000 6000
12 000 4000
9000 3000
6000 2000
4500 1500
3000 1000
1200 400
600 200
0 0
200 600
2000 6000
m ft
Projection: Conical with two standard parallels

CASPIAN SEA

TURKMENISTAN

Kara Kum

Kopet Dagh

IRAN

Dasht-e Kavir

Dasht-e Lut

AFGHANISTAN

PAKISTAN

THE GULF

Gulf of Oman

UNITED ARAB EMIRATES

OMAN

QATAR

BAHRAIN

East from Greenwich

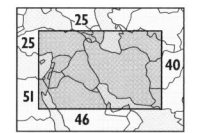

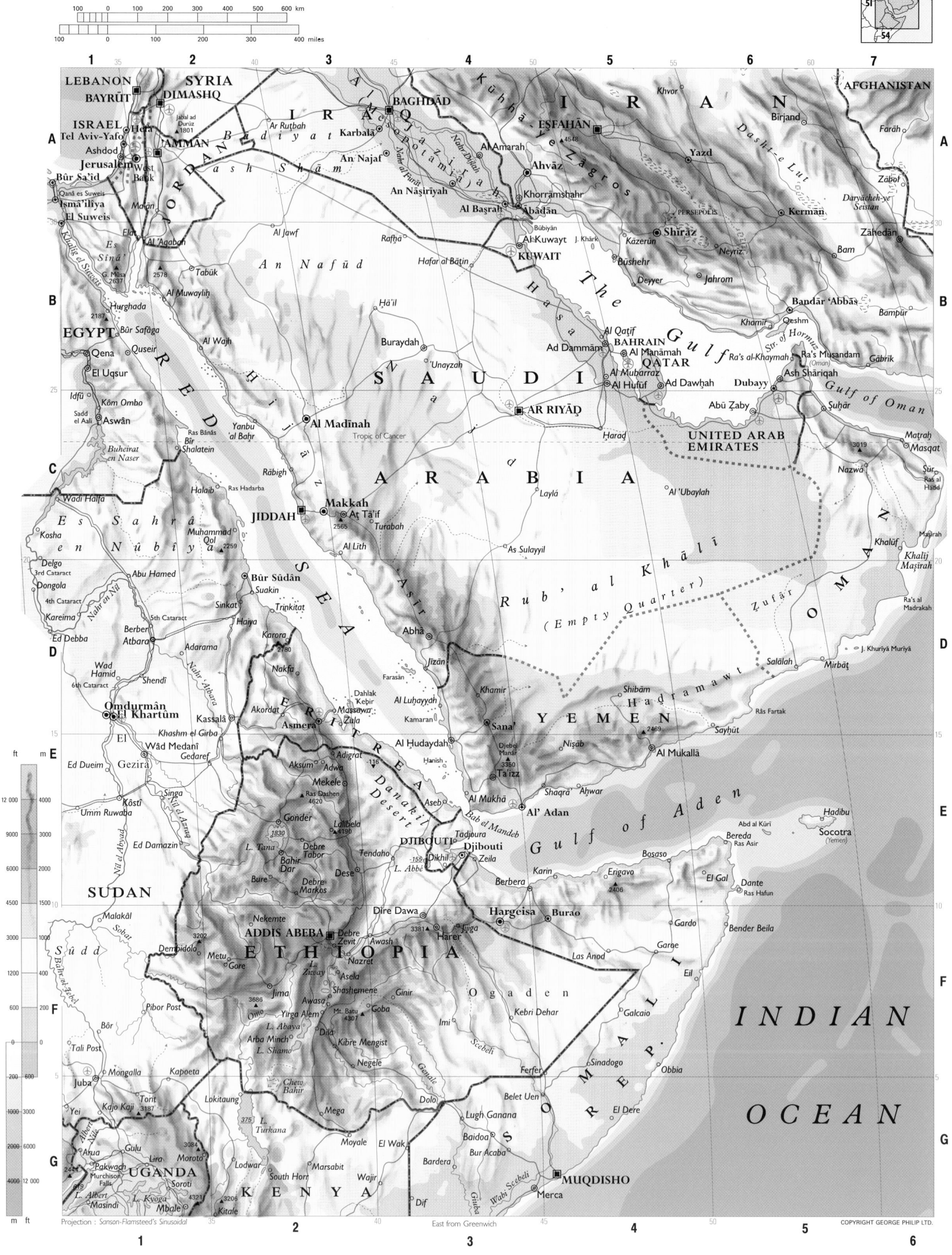

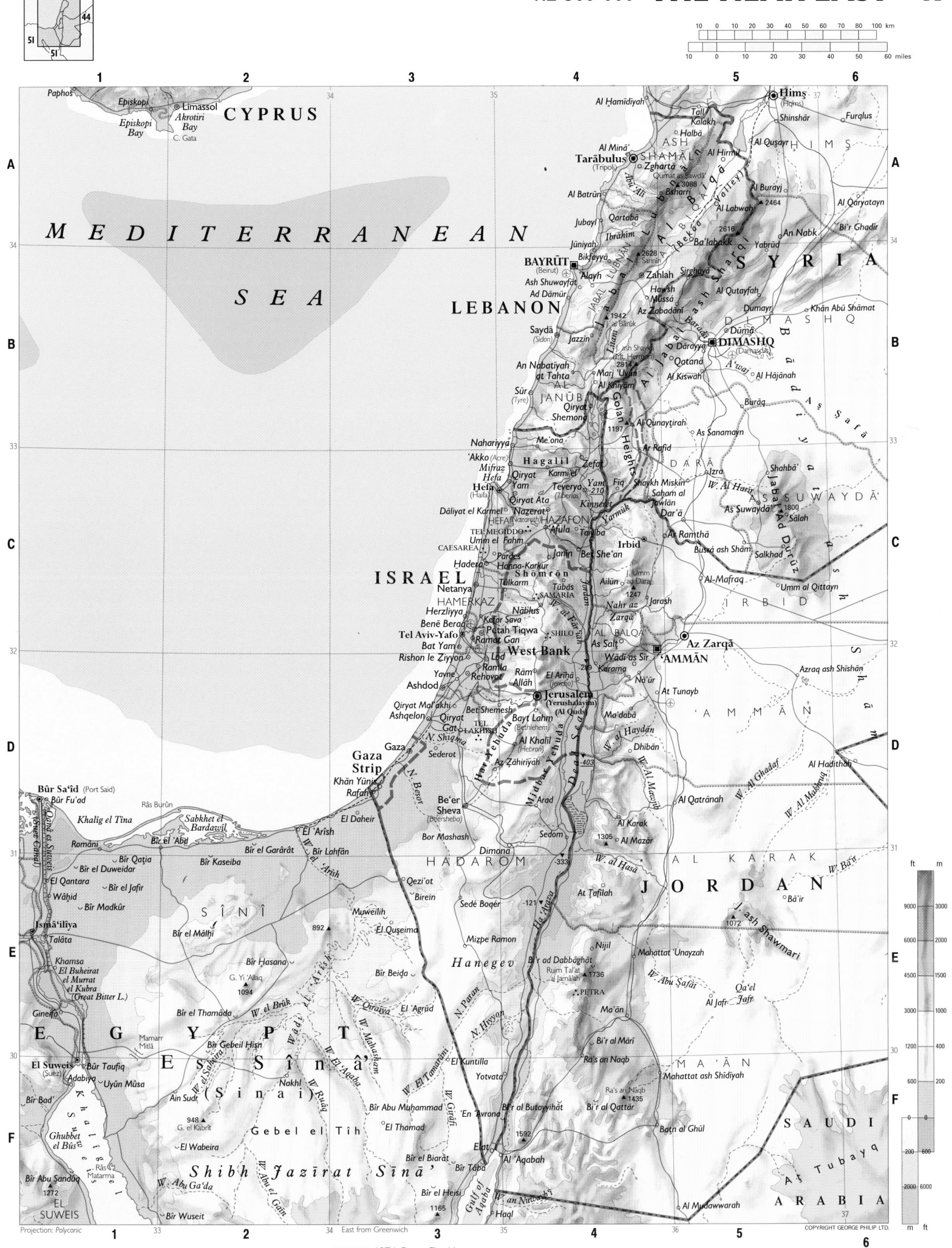

10 0 10 20 30 40 50 60 70 80 90 100 km
10 0 10 20 30 40 50 60 miles

CYPRUS

Paphos
Episkopi
Episkopi Bay
Akrotiri
Limassol
C. Gata

M E D I T E R R A N E A N

S E A

Al Hamidiyah
Tall Kalakh
Shinshār
Furqlus
Hims (Homs)

ASH SHAMĀL
Halbā
Al Hirmil
Al Qusayr
H I M S
Al Minā'
Tarābulus (Tripoli)
Zgharta
Qurnat as Sawdā' ▲3088
Al Batrūn
Al Burayj
Al Qaryatayn
Jubayl
Qartabā
Ibrāhīm
2616
An Nabk
Bi'r Ghadir
Jūniyah
Bikfayyā
2628 Sannin
Ba'labakk
Yabrūd
2464

S Y R I A

BAYRŪT (Beirut)
'Alayh
Zahlah
Sirghāyā
Khān Abū Shāmat
Ash Shuwayfāt
Ad Dāmūr
Hawsh Mūssá
Al Qutayfah
1942 al Bārūk
Az Zabadāni
Dumayr
Dūmā
DIMASHQ
Saydā (Sidon)
Jazzin
ash Shayk (Mt. Hermon) 2814
Darayyā
DIMASHQ (Damascus)
Qatanā

LEBANON
An Nabatīyah at Tahta
Sūr (Tyre)
Marj 'Uyūn
Al Khiyām
Al Kiswah
A'waj
Al Hājānah
Buráq
Al Qunaytirah
As Sanamayn
Burāq

AL JANŪB
Qiryat Shemona
Golan Heights
1197
Ar Rafid
DARĀ
Izra
Shahbā
AS SUWAYDĀ
W. Al Harir
As Suwaydā 1800
Sāleh

Nahariyya
Me'ona
Shaykh Miskin
Hagalil
'Akko (Acre)
Zefat
Karmi'el
Yam
Mifraz Hefa
Qiryat Yam
Teverya
Sahem al Jawlān
Dar'ā
Busrá ash Shām
Salkhad
Umm al Qittayn
Hefa (Haifa)
Qiryat Ata
Yam (Tiberias) -210
Kinneret
Yarmūk
J. ad Duruz

Dāliyat el Karmel
Nazerat (Nazareth)
HAZAFON
Afula
Taiyba
Irbid
Ar Ramthā
TEL MEGIDDO
Umm el Fahm
Bet She'an
Ailūn
Umm ad Daraj
Al-Mafraq
Umm al Qittayn
CAESAREA
Pardes Hanna-Karkur
Jānin
Shōmrōn
SAMARIA
1247
Jarash
IRBID

ISRAEL
Hadera
Tulkarm
Tūbās
Nahr az Zarqā
Netanya
HAMERKAZ
Nāblus
W. al Fār'ah
Jordan
Herzliyya
Benē Beraq
Kafar Sava
SHILO
As Salt
Az Zarqā
AL BALQĀ
Tel Aviv-Yafo
Petah Tiqwa
Ramat Gan
West Bank
Wādi as Sir
AMMĀN
Bat Yam
Rishon le Ziyyon
Lōd
Ram Allāh
239
Karama
Na'ūr
Azraq ash Shishān
Yavne
Ramla
Rehovot
El Arīha (Jericho)
'A M M Ā N

Ashdod
Qiryat Mal'akhi
Jerusalem (Yerushalayim) (Al Quds)
At Tunayb
Ashqelon
Bet Shemesh
Bayt Lahm (Bethlehem)
Ma'daba
Gat
Qiryat
TEL LAKHISH
N. Shiqma
Al Khalīl (Hebron)
W. al Haydān
Gaza
Sederot
Az Zāhirīyah
Dhibān

Gaza Strip
Khān Yūnis
Rafah
N. Besor
403
W. al Ghadaf
Al Hadithah
Bûr Sa'id (Port Said)
Bûr Fu'ad
Rās Burūn
Be'er Sheva (Beersheba)
Arad
Al Karak
W. al Maçuib

Khalig el Tîna
Sabkhet el Bardawîl
El Daheir
Bor Mashash
Sedom
AL KARAK
Qanā es Suweis
Romāni
El 'Arîsh
Dimona
1305
Al Mazār
W. al Hasā
El Qantara
Bîr el 'Abd
Bîr el Garârât
Bîr Lahfân
HADAROM
-333
JORDAN
Wâhid
Bîr Qaţia
Bîr Kaseiba
W. el 'Arîsh
Bā'ir
Bîr el Duweidar
Ismâ'ilîya
Talâta
Bîr el Jafir
Qezi'ot
Birein
At Tafilah

Khamsa
El Buheirat el Murrat el Kubra (Great Bitter L.)
Bîr Madkûr
Muweilih
Sedé Boqér
-121
J. ash Shawmari
1072
Gineifa
S Î N Î
El Quseima
Mizpe Ramon
Nijil
Mahattat 'Unayzah
El Suweis (Suez)
Bûr Taufiq
892
Bîr Hasana
Ha negev
Rujm Tal'at al Jamâ'ah 1736
Qa'el Jafr
Adabiya
Uyûn Mûsa
G. Yi 'Allaq 1094
Bîr Beiđa
Abu Şafāt
Bîr Bad'
Mamarr Mitlâ
Bîr el Thamâda
W. el Brûk
W. Qiraiya
El 'Agrûd
N. Paran
N. Hiyyon
PETRA
Ma'ān
E G Y P T
E S S Î N Â'
(S i n a i)
Ain Sudr
Nakhl
W. el Ruâd
W. Mahashim
El Kuntilla
Yotvata
Ra's an Naqb
MA'ĀN
Ghubbet el Bûs
Bîr Gebeil Hisn
948
Gebel el Tîh
El Thamad
'En 'Avrona
1435
Mahattat ash Shidiyah
Bîr Abu Sandûq
1272
G. el Kabrît
El Wabeira
Bîr Abu Muhammad
Girâfi
Bi'r al Butayhât
Bi'r al Qattar
Batn al Ghūl
SAUDI
Râs Matarma
Shibh Jazîrat Sînâ'
W. Abu Ga'da
Bîr el Biarât
1592
ARABIA
EL SUWEIS
W. Wuseit
1165
W. an Nveish
Al Aqabah
Haql
Al Mudawwarah
At Tubayq

Elat
Gulf of Aqaba
Bîr Tâba

▄▄▄ 1974 Cease Fire Lines

ft m
9000 3000
6000 2000
4500 1500
3000 1000
1200 400
600 200
0 0
200 600
2000 6000
m ft

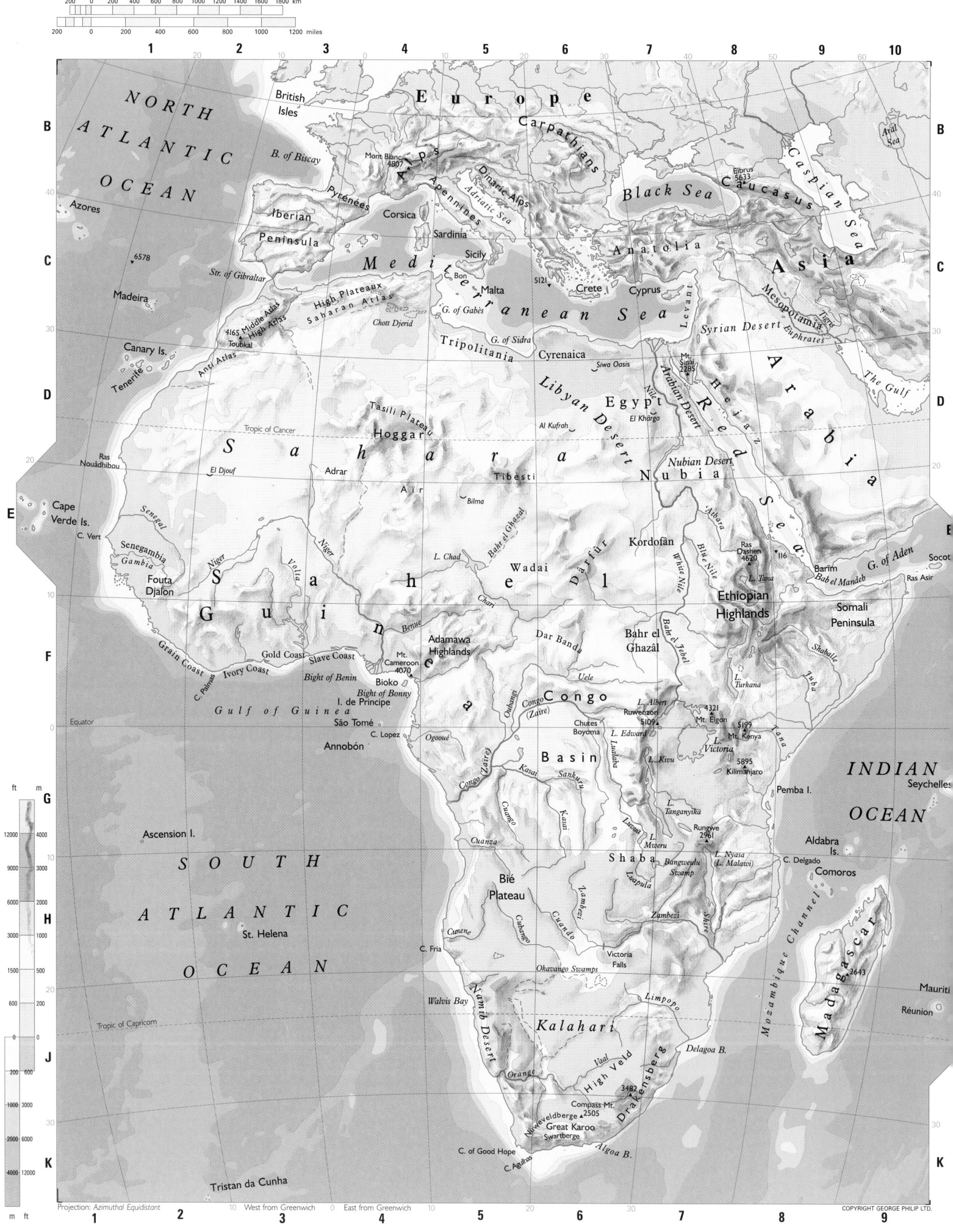
NORTH ATLANTIC OCEAN
Europe
British Isles
B. of Biscay
Alps
Mont Blanc 4807
Carpathians
Dinaric Alps
Apennines
Adriatic Sea
Pyrénées
Corsica
Sardinia
Sicily
Iberian Peninsula
Azores
Madeira
Str. of Gibraltar
Mediterranean Sea
Black Sea
Caucasus
Elbrus 5633
Caspian Sea
Aral Sea
Anatolia
Cyprus
Crete
Malta
C. Bon
G. of Gabès
G. of Sidra
Asia
Mesopotamia
Tigris
Euphrates
Syrian Desert
Levant
Arabia
The Gulf
Hejaz
Red Sea
Mt. Sinai 2285
High Plateaux
Saharan Atlas
Chott Djerid
Middle Atlas
High Atlas
4165 Toubkal
Anti Atlas
Canary Is.
Tenerife
Tripolitania
Cyrenaica
Siwa Oasis
Libyan Desert
Egypt
El Kharga
Al Kufrah
Nile
Arabian Desert
Nubian Desert
Nubia
Tasili Plateau
Hoggar
Sahara
Tropic of Cancer
Ras Nouâdhibou
El Djouf
Adrar
Aïr
Bilma
Tibesti
Cape Verde Is.
C. Vert
Senegal
Senegambia
Gambia
Fouta Djalon
Niger
Volta
Sahel
L. Chad
Bahr el Ghazal
Wadai
Darfur
Kordofân
White Nile
Blue Nile
Atbara
Ras Dashen 4620
L. Tana
Ethiopian Highlands
Barim
Bab el Mandeb
G. of Aden
Ras Asir
Somali Peninsula
Shaballe
Juba
Guinea
Chari
Benue
Grain Coast
Ivory Coast
Gold Coast
Slave Coast
Bight of Benin
Bight of Bonny
C. Palmas
Adamawa Highlands
Mt. Cameroon 4070
Bioko
I. de Principe
São Tomé
C. Lopez
Annobón
Gulf of Guinea
Equator
Dar Banda
Bahr el Ghazâl
Bahr el Jebel
Uele
L. Turkana
Congo Basin
Congo (Zaïre)
Oubangi
Ogooué
Chutes Boyoma
L. Albert
Ruwenzori 5109
L. Edward
Lualaba
L. Kivu
4321 Mt. Elgon
5199 Mt. Kenya
L. Victoria
5895 Kilimanjaro
Tana
Pemba I.
INDIAN OCEAN
Seychelles
Kasai
Sankuru
Cuango
L. Tanganyika
Lukuga
Rungwe 2961
Cuanza
L. Mweru
Shaba
Bangweulu Swamp
Luapula
L. Nyasa (L. Malawi)
C. Delgado
Aldabra Is.
Comoros
Bié Plateau
Zambezi
Shire
Cunene
Cubango
Cuando
C. Fria
Victoria Falls
Okavango Swamps
Mozambique Channel
Madagascar
2643
Mauriti
Réunion
Walvis Bay
Namib Desert
Kalahari
Limpopo
Tropic of Capricorn
Vaal
High Veld
Drakensberg
3482
Delagoa B.
Orange
Compass Mt.
Nieuveldberge 2505
Great Karoo
Swartberge
Algoa B.
C. of Good Hope
C. Agulhas
Ascension I.
SOUTH ATLANTIC OCEAN
St. Helena
Tristan da Cunha
6578
5121
116
Projection: Azimuthal Equidistant
West from Greenwich
East from Greenwich

200 0 200 400 600 800 1000 1200 1400 1600 1800 km

200 0 200 400 600 800 1000 1200 miles

NORTH

ATLANTIC

OCEAN

Azores
(Port.)

Madeira
(Port.)

Canary Is.
(Sp.)

PE VERDE IS.

Praia

RUSSIA

UKRAINE

KAZAKSTAN

UNITED
KINGDOM
LONDON

NETH.
BELG.

GERMANY

POLAND

Warsaw

Kiev

Volgograd

Aral
Sea

FRANCE

B. of Biscay

SWITZ.

Prague
CZECH REP.
Vienna
AUSTRIA
SLOVAK REP.
HUNGARY
CROATIA
BOS.
HERZ.
YUG.

ROMANIA

BULGARIA

Odessa

GEORGIA
ARM.
AZER.
Baku

TURKMEN.

Caspian Sea

SPAIN

Madrid

Lisbon

PORTUGAL

Corsica

Rome

ITALY

Sardinia

Adriatic Sea

ALB.

MAC.

GREECE

Athens

Sicily

Crete

CYPRUS

TURKEY

Ankara

Black Sea

Mosul

Aleppo

SYRIA

Tigris

Baghdad

Esfahan

TEHRAN

IRAN

Algiers

Annaba

Constantine

Tunis

MALTA

Tripoli

Misratah

Benghazi

Rabat
Tetouan
Casablanca
Fès
MOROCCO
Marrakesh

Mediterranean Sea

TUNISIA

Chott Djerid

ALGERIA

In Salah

Sahara

LIBYA

Marzuq

Al Jawf

Alexandria
Port Said
CAIRO
El Faiyum
Suez
EGYPT
Asyut

ISRAEL
JORDAN

Tel Aviv-
Jaffa
Jerusalem
Damascus
LEB.

Syrian Desert

IRAQ

Basra
KUWAIT

SAUDI

ARABIA

BAHRAIN
QATAR
The Gulf

Riyadh

El Aaiún

Dakhla

WESTERN SAHARA

Fdérik

Tropic of Cancer

Ras
Nouâdhibou

MAURITANIA

Nouakchott

St-Louis
C. Vert
Dakar
SENEGAL
GAMBIA
Banjul
GUINEA-
BISSAU
Bissau

Senegal

Tombouctou

MALI

Bámako

NIGER

Agadès

Niamey

BURKINA
Ouagadougou
FASO
Bobo-
Dioulasso

Niger

CHAD

L. Chad

Kano

Maiduguri

Abéché

Ndjamena

Chari

Aswân

Wadi Halfa

Port Sudan

Red Sea

Atbara

Omdurman
Khartoum
Wad Medani

SUDAN

El Fâsher

El Obeid

Athara

Medina

Mecca

Jedda

YEMEN

G. of Aden

Socotra
(Yemen)

Ras Asir

Mesewa

Asmera

ERITREA

DJIBOUTI

Djibouti

Berbera

GUINEA

Conakry

Freetown

SIERRA
LEONE

Monrovia

LIBERIA

IVORY
COAST

Bouaké

Yamoussoukro

Abidjan

GHANA

Kumasi

Sekondi-
Takoradi

Accra

TOGO

Lomé
Porto
Novo

BENIN

Ibadan

Lagos

NIGERIA

Abuja

Enugu

Benue

Port
Harcourt

Bight of Benin

CAMEROON

Douala

Malabo

Yaoundé

Bangui

CENTRAL

AFRICAN REP.

Wau

Bahr el Jebel

Malakâl

White Nile

Blue Nile

L. Tana

Addis Ababa

Harer

ETHIOPIA

Shabelle

SOMALI REP.

Mogadishu

Kismayu

EQUATORIAL
GUINEA

SÃO TOMÉ & PRINCIPE

Libreville

C. Lopez

GABON

Annobón

Equator

Gulf of Guinea

CONGO

Congo
(Zaïre)

Kasai

Ubangui

Mbandaka

Kisangani

CONGO

(DEM. REP. OF THE)

Brazzaville

Kinshasa

Matadi

Pointe-Noire

CABINDA
(Angola)

Kananga

RWANDA
Kigali
BURUNDI
Bujumbura

L. Albert

L. Edward
L.
Kivu

UGANDA

Kampala

L.
Victoria

Kisumu

Nairobi

KENYA

Mombasa

Tana

Juba

L. Turkana

INDIAN

OCEAN

SEYCHELLES

SOUTH

ATLANTIC

OCEAN

Ascension I.
(U.K.)

St. Helena
(U.K.)

Luanda

Lobito

Huambo

Namibe

C. Fria

ANGOLA

Cuanza

Cunene

Cubango

Kasai

TANZANIA

Dodoma

L. Tanganyika

Zanzibar

Dar es Salaam

Kalemie

L.
Mweru

Likasi

Lubumbashi

L. Malawi

L.

ZAMBIA

Ndola

Lusaka

Livingstone

Lilongwe

Blantyre

MALAWI

Zambezi

Moçambique

C. Delgado

Aldabra
Is.

COMOROS
Moroni

Mayotte
(Fr.)

Antsiranana

Mahajanga

Toamasina

MADAGASCAR

MAURITIUS
Port
Louis

Réunion
(Fr.)

NAMIBIA

Windhoek

Tropic of Capricorn

Okavango

BOTSWANA

Gaborone

Limpopo

ZIMBABWE

Harare

Bulawayo

Beira

MOZAMBIQUE

Mozambique Channel

Fianarantsoa

Antananarivo

Johannesburg

Pretoria

Maputo

Mbabane SWAZ.

LESOTHO
Maseru

Durban

Vaal

Orange

Kimberley

SOUTH AFRICA

Cape Town

C. of Good Hope

C. Agulhas

East
London

Port
Elizabeth

Tristan da Cunha
(U.K.)

ATLANTIC OCEAN
Azores (Port.)
Madeira (Port.)
Funchal
Porto Santo
Islas Canarias (Sp.)
Santa Cruz de Tenerife
Las Palmas
Gran Canaria
Tenerife
Lanzarote
Arrecife
Fuerteventura
La Palma
Gomera
Hierro
SPAIN
Cádiz
Málaga
Almería
Str. of Gibraltar
Gibraltar (U.K.)
Ceuta (Sp.)
Melilla (Sp.)
Tanger
Tétouan
Al Hoceïma
Nador
Oujda
Ksar el Kebir
Ouezzane
Kenitra
Salé
Rabat
Fès
Taza
Meknès
Khemisset
Mohammedia
CASABLANCA
El Jadida
Khouribga
Settat
Safi
Ras Beddouza
Beni Mellal
Marrakech
Essaouira
MOROCCO
Moyen Atlas
Haut Atlas
Anti Atlas
Dj. Toubkal 4165
Taroudannt
Ouarzazate
Ar Rachidiya
Bouârfa
Figuig
Béchar
Abadla
C. Rhir
Agadir
2359
Ifni
Goulimine
Tan-tan
C. Juby
Tarfaya
El Aaiún
Smara
Bu Craa
C. Bojador
WESTERN SAHARA
Dakhla
Tindouf
Aïn Ben Tili
Bir Mogreïn
Zouîrât
Fdérik
Tropic of Cancer
Râs Nouâdhibou
Nouâdhibou
Atâr
Chinguetti
Adrar
Akjoujt
Râs Timirist
MAURITANIA
Rachid
Tidjikja
Nouakchott
Aoukâr
Aleg
Rosso
Kaédi
Kiffa
'Ayoûn el 'Atroûs
Néma
St. Louis
Dagana
Matam
Louga
Linguère
Mboro
Thiès
Tivaouane
C. Vert
DAKAR
SENEGAL
Kaolack
Banjul
GAMBIA
Georgetown
Tambacounda
Sédhiou
Ziguinchor
GUINEA BISSAU
Bissau
Arq. dos Bijagós
Gaoual
Fouta Djalon
Labé
GUINEA
Dalaba
Kindia
Mamou
Dabola
Faranah
C. Verga
Dubréka
Conakry
Kabala
1948
SIERRA LEONE
Port Loko
Freetown
Yonibana
Bo
Sherbro I.
Bonthe
Sulima
Kenema
Pendembu
Monrovia
LIBERIA
Buchanan
River Cess
Grain Coast
Harper
C. Palmas
Gbarnga
Sanniquellie
Nzérékoré
Macenta
Kissidougou
Kankan
Fabala
Siguiri
Bafoulabé
Kayes
Bakel
Sélibabi
Nioro du Sahel
Nara
Kita
Satadougou
Bamako
Bougouni
Sikasso
Ségou
Diafarabé
Mopti
Didiéni
San
MALI
Hombori
Tombouctou
Niger
Bourem
Gao
Ansongo
Ménaka
Kidal
Tessalit
Adrar des Iforas
598
El Djouf
Taoudenni
Erg Chech
Erg Iguidi
Chegga
Tanezrouft
Sahara
ALGERIA
Alger
Blida
Médéa
Tizi-Ouzou
Bejaia
Skikda
Annaba
Sétif
Constantine
Batna
Tébessa
Khenchela
M'sila
Chott el Hodna
Biskra
Chott Melrhir
Touggourt
El Oued
Tozeur
Djelfa
Messad
Laghouat
Aflou
Chott ech Chergui
Saharien Atlas
El Bayadh
Mecheria
2235
Aïn-Sefra
Ghardaïa
Berriane
Ouargla
Hassi Messaoud
Oran
Mostaganem
Ech Cheliff
Mascara
Tiaret
Sidi-bel-Abbès
Tlemcen
Maghreb
Grand Erg Occidental
Grand Erg Oriental
El Goléa
Kerzaz
Timimoun
Plateau du Tademaït
Bordj Fly Ste. Marie
Zaouiet Reggane
In Salah
Ohanet
Bordj Omar Driss
Illizi
Tassili n Ajjer
2158
Djanet
Arak
Ouallene
Bordj-in-Eker
Ahaggar
Tahat 2918
Tamanrasset
Ténéré
Arlit
Iférouâne
Aïr
1900
Agadez
I-n-Gall
NIGER
Tahoua
Tanout
Zinder
Filingué
Niamey
Dosso
Birni Nkonni
Famalé
Dori
BURKINA FASO
Ouagadougou
Koudougou
Tougan
Kaya
Fada-n-Gourma
Bobo-Dioulasso
Gaoua
Tingréla
Botou
Gaya
Kandi
Dapaong
Mango
Natitingou
Bembéréké
Parakou
BENIN
TOGO
Sokodé
Savalou
Lomé
Porto-Novo
Cotonou
Abomey
Slave Coast
Bight of Benin
GHANA
Bawku
Tumu
Black Volta
Savelugu
Tamale
Salaga
Bole
Wenchi
Lake Volta
Kumasi
Obuasi
Asamankese
Koforidua
Tema
Accra
Cape Coast
Sekondi-Takoradi
Tarkwa
Axim
C. Three Points
Gold Coast
Kintampo
Berekum
Abengourou
Bondoukou
Bouna
Kong
Ferkéssédougou
Korhogo
Odienné
Boundiali
Koro
Man
Séguéla
Katiola
Bouaké
L. de Kossou
Bouaflé
Yamoussoukro
Daloa
Danané
IVORY COAST
Gagnoa
Adzopé
Agboville
Lakota
Divo
Sassandra
ABIDJAN
Grand Bassam
San Pédro
Tabou
Ivory Coast
Tapeta
Sokoto
Maradi
Katsina
Birnin Kebbi
Gusau
Jega
Gumel
Hadejia
Kano
Azare
Funtua
Bena
Zaria
Kaduna
Shanga
Kontagora
Kainji Res.
Bauchi
Jos
Minna
Kafanchan
Shendam
NIGERIA
Bida
Abuja
Keffi
Lafia
Baro
Benue
Makurdi
Wukari
Lokoja
Ilorin
Offa
Shaki
Ogbomosho
Oyo
Oshogbo
Ikare
Iwo
Ilesha
Owo
IBADAN
Ife
Abeokuta
Akure
Ijebu-Ode
LAGOS
Benin City
Enugu
Otukpo
Sapele
Onitsha
Warri
Aba
Uyo
Burutu
Calabar
Port Harcourt
Bamenda
Bafoussam
Kumba
Mt. Cameroun 4070
Limbe
Douala
Rey Malabo
Bioko
2850
Projection : Sanson-Flamsteed's Sinusoidal
West from Greenwich
East from Greenwich

8 9 10 11 12 13 14

A B C D E F G H

MEDITERRANEAN SEA
GREECE
TURKEY
CYPRUS
SYRIA
LEBANON
ISRAEL
JORDAN
IRAQ
MALTA
LIBYA
EGYPT
SAUDI ARABIA
RED SEA
SUDAN
CHAD
ERITREA
ETHIOPIA
CENTRAL AFRICAN REPUBLIC
CAMEROON
TUNIS
Tarābulus
EL QÂHIRA
EL GIZA
EL ISKANDARÎYA
Jerusalem
BAYRŪT
DIMASHQ
'AMMĀN
Nicosia
Valletta
Sicilia
Kríti
Iráklion
Ródhos
Antalya
ADANA
HALAB
Banghāzī
Misrātah
Sabhah
Aswân
Asyût
Wadi Halfa
Bûr Sûdân
Omdurmân
El Khartûm
El Obeid
Ndjamena
Abéché
Bangui
Yaoundé
Juba
Wâw
Tibesti
Borkou
Ennedi
Dârfûr
Kordofân
Cyrenaica
Tripolitania
Fezzan
Sahrâ' Lîbîya
Sahrâ' Rebiana
Es Sahrâ en Nûbîya
Bahr el Ghazâl
El Istiwa'iya
Lac Tchad
Nahr en Nîl
Nîl el Abyad
Nîl el Azraq

COPYRIGHT GEORGE PHILIP LTD.

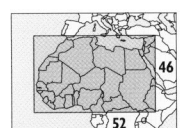

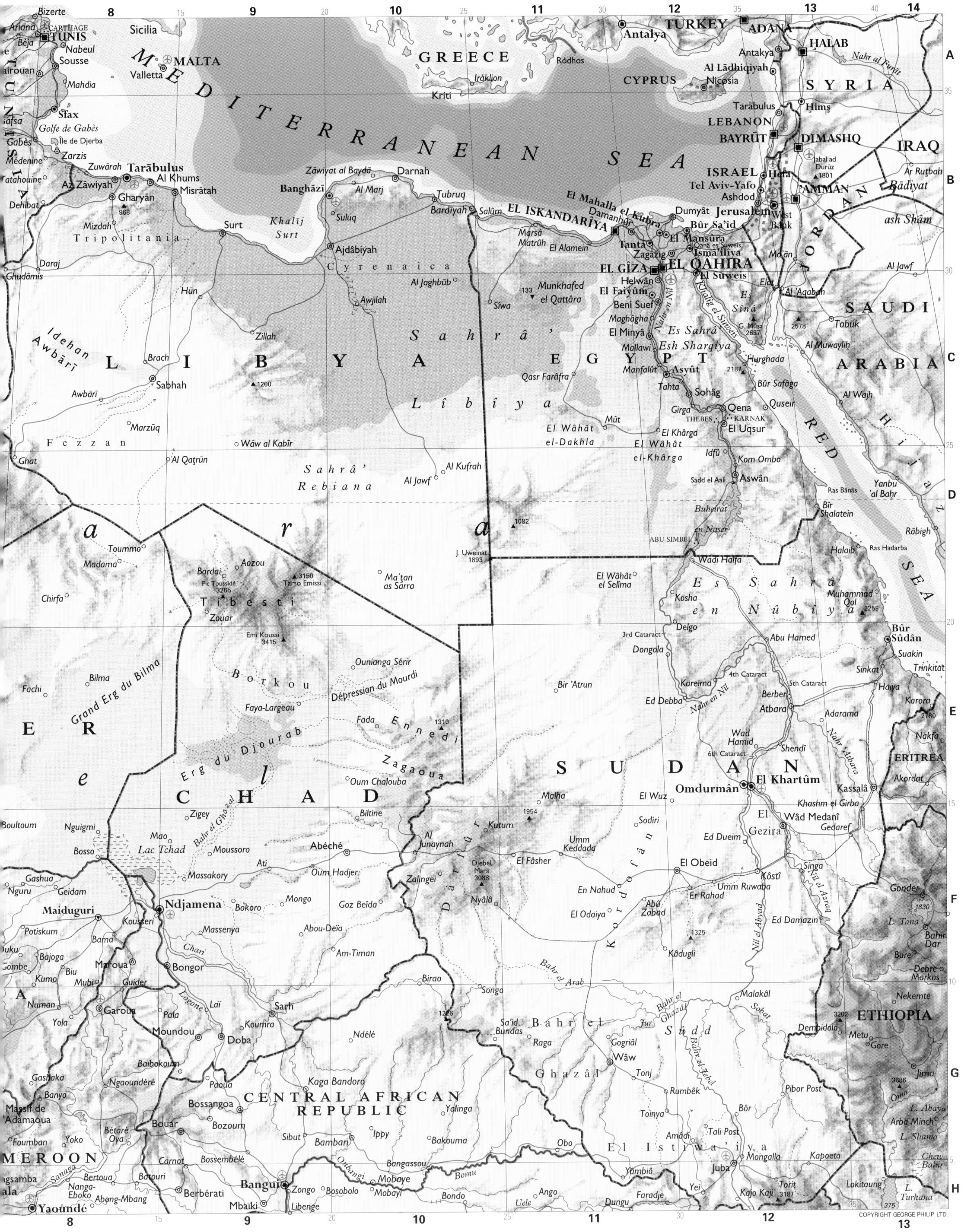

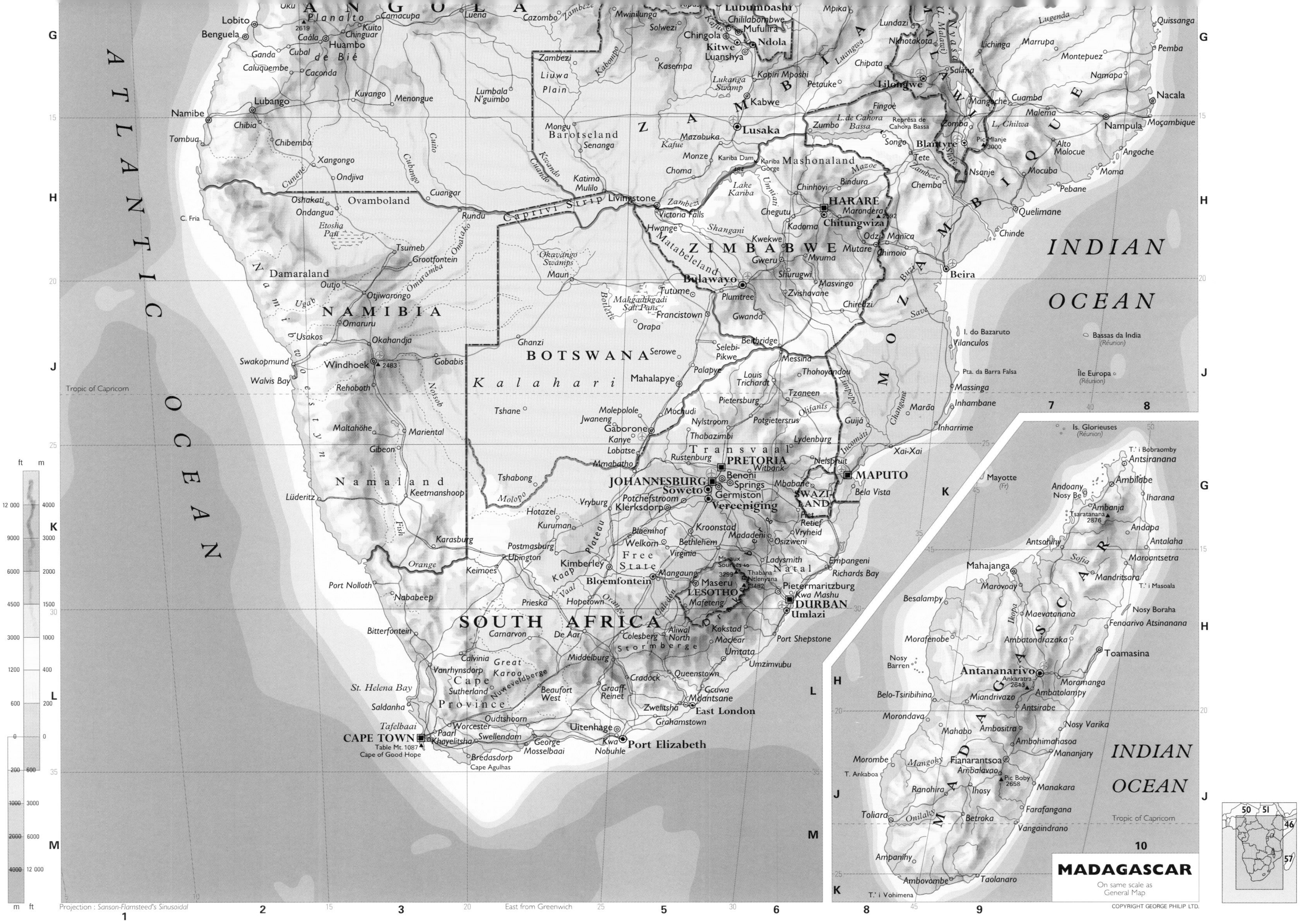

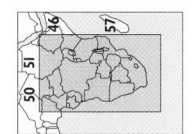

53

MADAGASCAR

On same scale as
General Map

COPYRIGHT GEORGE PHILIP LTD.

INDIAN OCEAN

ATLANTIC OCEAN

SOUTH AFRICA

NAMIBIA

BOTSWANA

ZIMBABWE

ANGOLA

ZAMBIA

MOZAMBIQUE

MALAWI

Tropic of Capricorn

East from Greenwich

Projection: Sanson-Flamsteed's Sinusoidal

EAST AFRICA 1:8 000 000

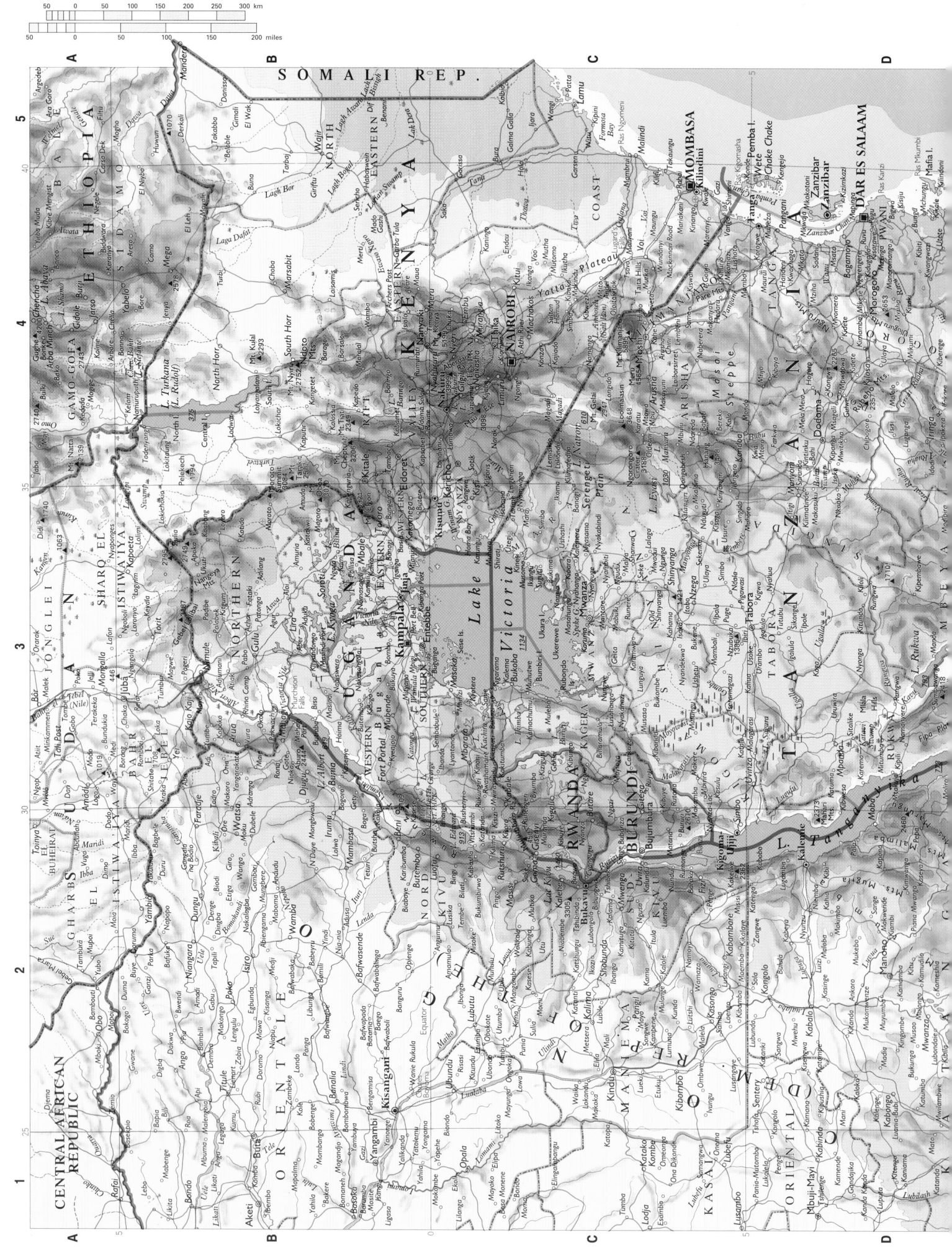
50 0 50 100 150 200 250 300 km
50 0 50 100 150 200 miles
SOMALI REP.
ETHIOPIA
KENYA
UGANDA
TANZANIA
RWANDA
BURUNDI
CENTRAL AFRICAN REPUBLIC
Lake Victoria
L. Turkana (L. Rudolf)
L. Tanganyika
NAIROBI
MOMBASA
DAR ES SALAAM
Zanzibar
Kampala
Kisangani
Juba

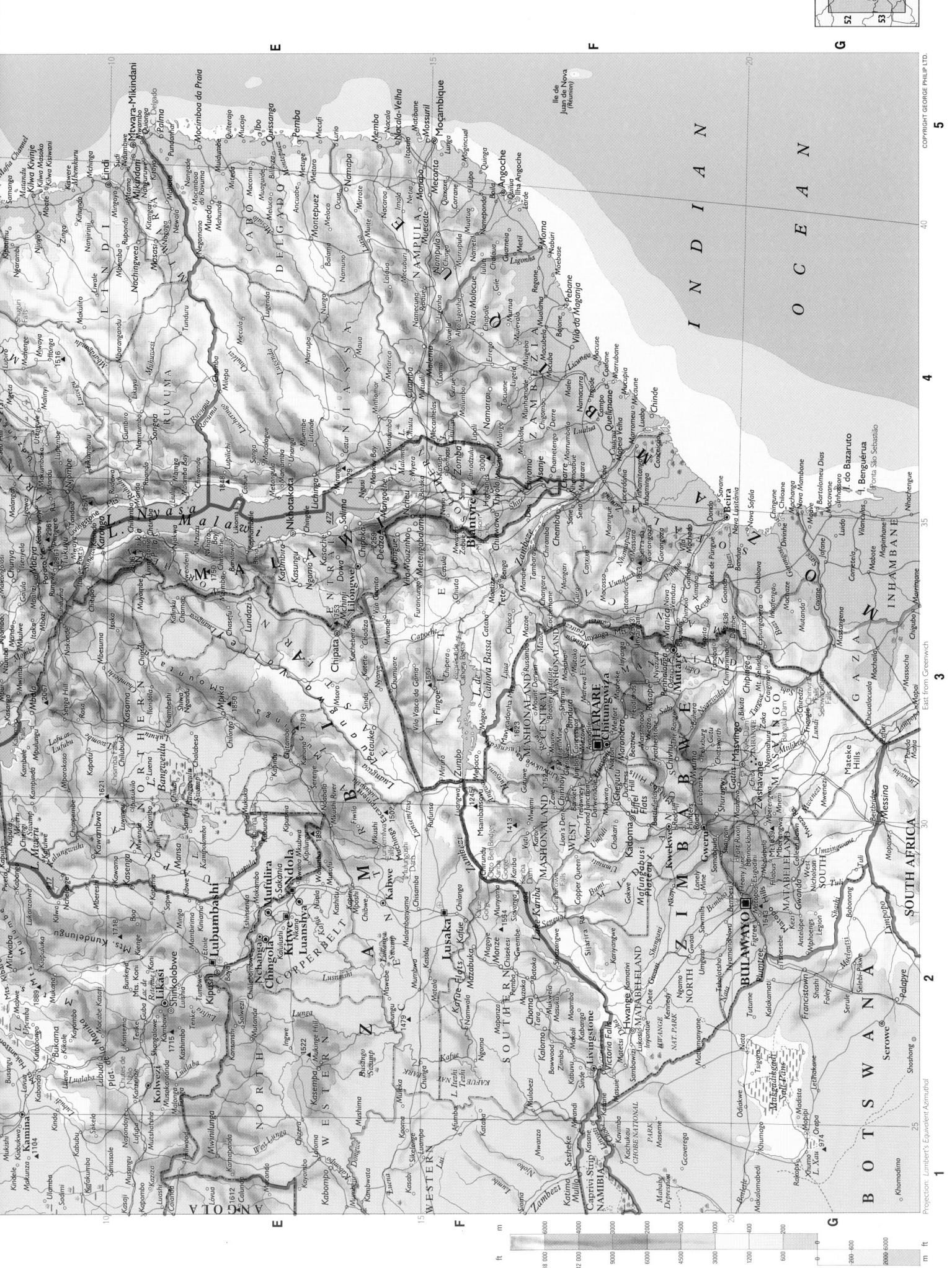

INDIAN

OCEAN

East from Greenwich

Projection: Lambert's Equivalent Azimuthal

SOUTHERN AFRICA 1:8 000 000

ZAMBIA
ANGOLA
CUNENE
CUANDO CUBANGO
WESTERN
SOUTH
NAMIBIA
BOTSWANA
SOUTH AFRICA
NORTH WEST
NORTHERN CAPE
WESTERN CAPE
EASTERN CAPE
ATLANTIC
OCEAN
Ovambolando
Etosha Pan
Damaraland
Namaland
Kalahari
Okavango Swamps
Makgadikgadi Salt Pans
Caprivi Strip
Namaqualand
Great Karoo
Tropic of Capricorn
Windhoek
Walvisbaai
Swakopmund
Lüderitz
Keetmanshoop
Rehoboth
Tsumeb
Grootfontein
Otjiwarongo
Outjo
Okahandja
Gobabis
Mariental
Maun
Serowe
Molepolole
Gaborone
Mochudi
Kanye
Lobatse
Ramotswa
Livingstone
Victoria Falls
Hwange
Upington
Kimberley
Bloemfontein
Welkom
Kroonstad
Klerksdorp
Potchefstroom
Vryburg
Kuruman
Springbok
Port Nolloth
De Aar
Beaufort West
Oudtshoorn
George
Knysna
Uitenhage
Grahamstown
Port Alfred
Queenstown
Cradock
Graaff-Reinet
Worcester
Paarl
Stellenbosch
Wellington
Malmesbury
Moorreesburg
Saldanha
Vredenburg
Parow
CAPE TOWN
PORT ELIZABETH
Mossel Baai
Plettenberg Baai
Swellendam
Hermanus
Simonstown
C. of Good Hope
C. Agulhas
Projection: Lambert's Equivalent Azimuthal

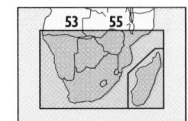

MADAGASCAR

On same scale as General Map

COPYRIGHT GEORGE PHILIP LTD.

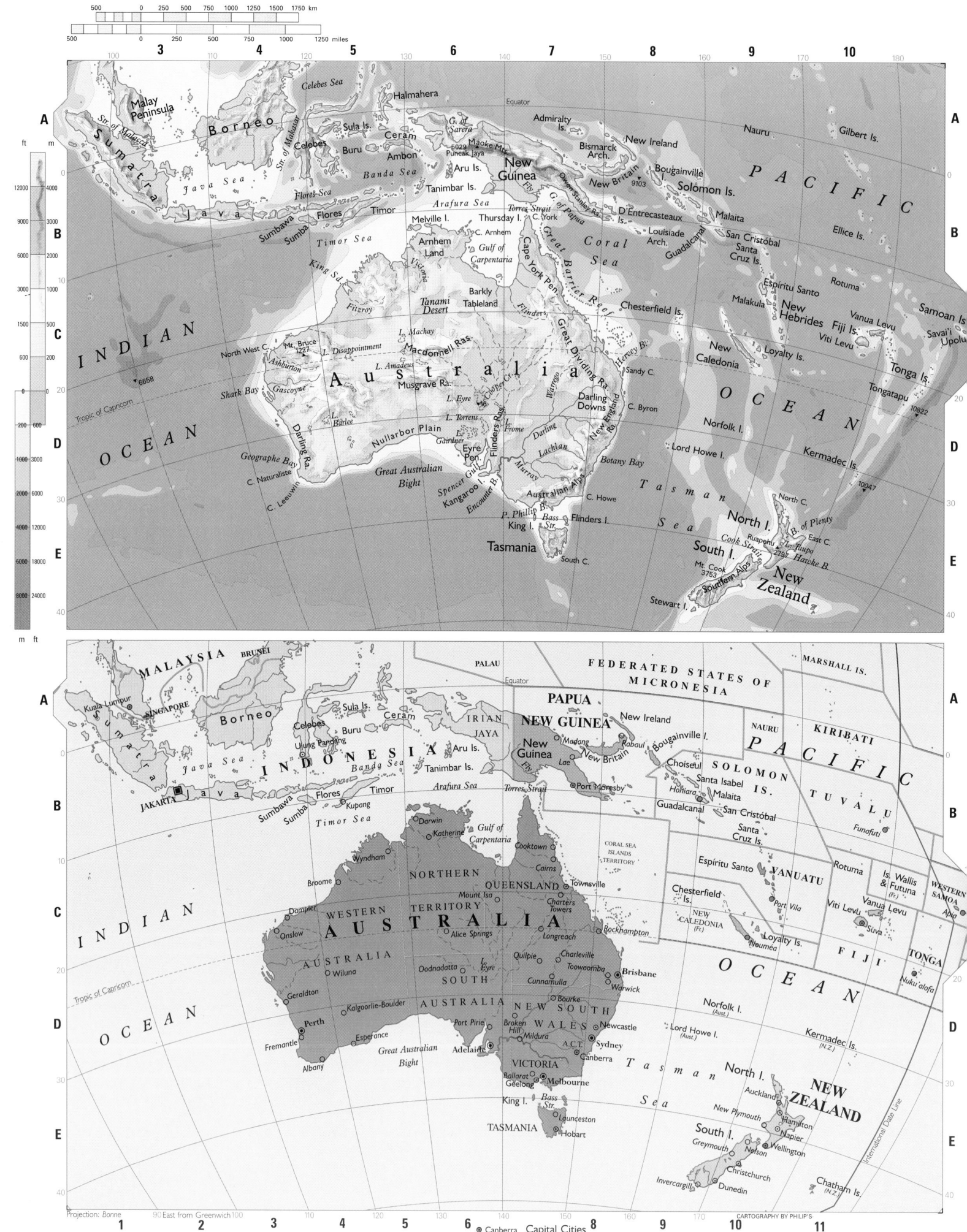

Physical map (top):

500 0 250 500 750 1000 1250 1500 1750 km
500 0 250 500 750 1000 1250 miles

3   4   5   6   7   8   9   10

ft m

12000 4000
9000 3000
6000 2000
3000 1000
1500 500
600 200
0 0
200 600
1000 3000
2000 6000
4000 12000
6000 18000
8000 24000

Celebes Sea
Malay Peninsula
Borneo
Sula Is.
Ceram
Halmahera
Equator
Admiralty Is.
Nauru
Gilbert Is.
Sumatra
Str. of Malacca
Str. of Macassar
Celebes
Buru
Ambon
6029 Puncak Jaya
Maoke Mts.
New Ireland
Bismarck Arch.
PACIFIC
Java Sea
Str. of Celebes
Aru Is.
New Guinea
New Britain 9103
Bougainville
Solomon Is.
Malaita
Ellice Is.
Java
Flores Sea
Banda Sea
Tanimbar Is.
Arafura Sea
Fly
Owen Stanley Ra.
D'Entrecasteaux
San Cristóbal
Santa Cruz Is.
Rotuma
Sumbawa
Sumba
Flores
Timor
Timor Sea
Melville I.
Thursday I.
C. York
Torres Strait
G. of Papua
Louisiade Arch.
Guadalcanal
Espíritu Santo
Samoan Is.
Arnhem Land
C. Arnhem
Cape York Pen.
Coral Sea
Malakula
New Hebrides
Fiji Is.
Vanua Levu
Savai'i
Upolu
King Sd.
Victoria
Gulf of Carpentaria
Great Barrier Reef
Chesterfield Is.
Viti Levu
INDIAN
Tanami Desert
Barkly Tableland
Flinders
Great Dividing Ra.
New Caledonia
Loyalty Is.
Tonga Is.
Fitzroy
North West C.
Mt. Bruce 1227
L. Disappointment
Macdonnell Ras.
L. Mackay
Hervey B.
Sandy C.
Tongatapu 10822
Ashburton
L. Amadeus
Australia
Musgrave Ra.
Cooper Cr.
Warrego
Darling Downs
C. Byron
OCEAN
Shark Bay
Gascoyne
6658
L. Eyre
Norfolk I.
OCEAN
Darling Ra.
L. Torrens
L. Barlee
Gairdner
Flinders Ras.
L. Frome
Darling
New England
Lord Howe I.
Kermadec Is.
Geographe Bay
Nullarbor Plain
Eyre Pen.
Lachlan
Murray
Botany Bay
10047
C. Naturaliste
Great Australian Bight
Spencer Gulf
Kangaroo I.
Encounter B.
Australian Alps
Tasman
North C.
C. Leeuwin
P. Phillip B.
Bass Str.
C. Howe
Sea
North I.
B. of Plenty
East C.
Ruapehu 2797 L. Taupo
Hawke B.
King I.
Flinders I.
Tasmania
South C.
South I.
Mt. Cook 3753
Southern Alps
New Zealand
Stewart I.
Tropic of Capricorn

Political map (bottom):

m ft

MALAYSIA
BRUNEI
PALAU
FEDERATED STATES OF MICRONESIA
MARSHALL IS.
Kuala Lumpur
SINGAPORE
Borneo
Sula Is.
Ceram
PAPUA NEW GUINEA
New Ireland
Equator
NAURU
KIRIBATI
Sumatra
Celebes
Buru
IRIAN JAYA
Aru Is.
New Guinea
Madang
Rabaul
New Britain
Bougainville
PACIFIC
Ujung Pandang
INDONESIA
Tanimbar Is.
Lae
Fly
Choiseul
SOLOMON IS.
Java Sea
Banda Sea
Santa Isabel
TUVALU
JAKARTA
Java
Arafura Sea
Torres Strait
Port Moresby
Honiara
Malaita
Sumbawa
Kupang
Flores
Timor
San Cristóbal
Funafuti
Sumba
Timor Sea
Darwin
Gulf of Carpentaria
Santa Cruz Is.
Katherine
Espíritu Santo
VANUATU
Rotuma
Is. Wallis & Futuna (Fr.)
WESTERN SAMOA
Wyndham
Cooktown
CORAL SEA ISLANDS TERRITORY
Broome
Cairns
Chesterfield Is.
Port Vila
Viti Levu
Apia
NORTHERN
Townsville
NEW CALEDONIA (Fr.)
Dampier
QUEENSLAND
Mount Isa
Charters Towers
Loyalty Is.
Onslow
WESTERN
TERRITORY
Nouméa
Silva
FIJI
INDIAN
AUSTRALIA
Alice Springs
Longreach
Rockhampton
OCEAN
Quilpie
Charleville
TONGA
Wiluna
Oodnadatta
L. Eyre
Toowoomba
Geraldton
SOUTH
Cunnamulla
Brisbane
Nuku'alofa
Tropic of Capricorn
Kalgoorlie-Boulder
AUSTRALIA
Bourke
Warwick
Norfolk I. (Aust.)
Perth
Port Pirie
NEW SOUTH
Lord Howe I. (Aust.)
Kermadec Is. (N.Z.)
Fremantle
Esperance
Broken Hill
Mildura
WALES
Newcastle
OCEAN
Albany
Great Australian Bight
Adelaide
A.C.T.
Sydney
Canberra
North I.
VICTORIA
Ballarat
Geelong
Melbourne
Tasman
Auckland
NEW ZEALAND
King I.
Bass Str.
Sea
New Plymouth
Hamilton
Napier
TASMANIA
Launceston
South I.
Wellington
Hobart
Greymouth
Nelson
Invercargill
Christchurch
Chatham Is. (N.Z.)
Dunedin
International Date Line

Projection: Bonne   90 East from Greenwich 100

1   2   3   4   5   6   7   8   9   10   11

Canberra Capital Cities

CARTOGRAPHY BY PHILIP'S

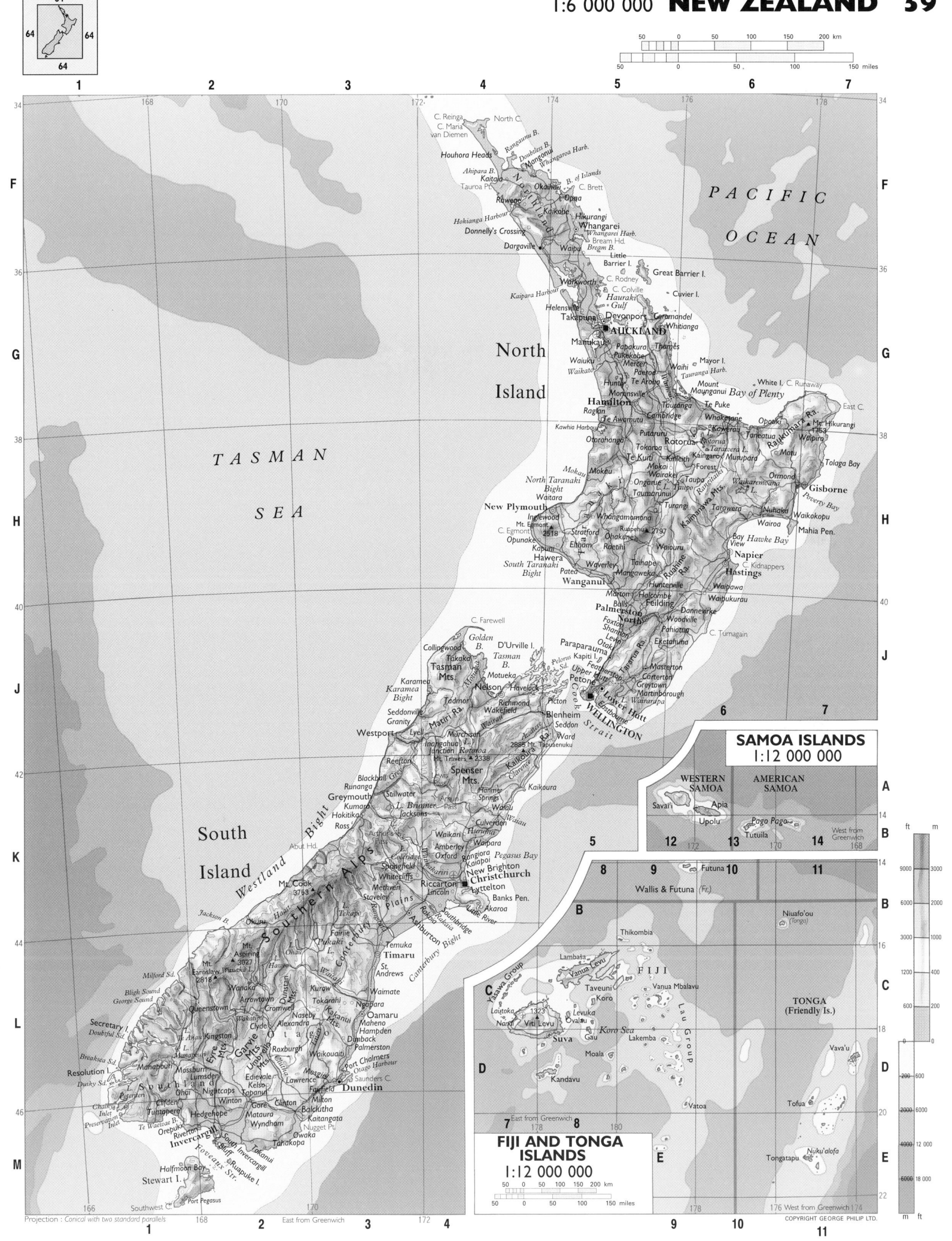

64
64   64
64

50   0   50   100   150   200 km
50   0   50   100   150 miles

PACIFIC

OCEAN

C. Reinga
C. Maria
van Diemen
North C.
Rangaunu B.
Houhora Heads
Doubless B.
Mangonui
Whangaroa Harb.
Ahipara B.
Kaitaia
Tauroa Pt.
Okahau
C. Brett
Rawene
Opua
B. of Islands
Hokianga Harbour
Kaikohe
Hikurangi
Donnelly's Crossing
Whangarei
Whangarei Harb.
Dargaville
Bream Hd.
Waipu
Bream B.
Little
Barrier I.
Great Barrier I.
Warkworth
C. Rodney
Helensville
C. Colville
Cuvier I.
Kaipara Harbour
Hauraki
Gulf
Coromandel
Takapuna
Devonport
Whitianga
AUCKLAND
Manukau
Papakura
Thames
Mayor I.
Waiuku
Pukekohe
Mercer
Waihi
C. Runaway
Waikato
Huntly
Te Aroha
Mount
Maunganui
White I.
Te Awamutu
Morrinsville
Tauranga
Bay of Plenty
Hamilton
Cambridge
Tauranga Harb.
Te Puke
Whakatane
East C.
Raglan
Putaruru
Rotorua
Kawerau
Opotiki
Kawhia Harbour
Otorohanga
Rotorua L.
Te Kuiti
Kinleith
Taranga Ra.
Mt. Hikurangi
Mokau
Tarawera L.
Forest
Kaingaroa
Murupara
Waipiro
Mokau
Waikite
Taupo
Tokoroa
Motu
North Taranaki
Bight
Ongarue
L. Taupo
Ruatahuna Mts.
Tolaga Bay
Waitara
Kaimanawa Mts.
Ormond
New Plymouth
Whangamomona
Taumarunui
Turangi
Waikaremoana L.
Gisborne
Inglewood
Mt. Egmont
Ruapehu
2797
Targewa
Nuhaka
Poverty Bay
C. Egmont
2518
Stratford
Ohakune
Waiouru
Waikokopu
Opunake
Eltham
Raetihi
Ruahine Ra.
Mahia Pen.
Kapuni
Tahape
Wairoa
Hawera
Waverley
Mangaweka
Napier
South Taranaki
Patea
Hunterville
Hastings
Bight
Wanganui
Marton
Halcombe
Waipawa
Bulls
Feilding
Dannevirke
Waipukurau
Palmerston
North
Woodville
C. Turnagain
Foxton
Pahiatua
Shannon
Levin
Ekatahuna
North
Island

TASMAN

SEA

C. Farewell
Golden
B.
D'Urville I.
Paraparaumu
Collingwood
Tasman
B.
Kapiti I.
Takaka
Motueka
Featherston
Tasman
Mts.
Nelson
Pelorus Sd.
Upper
Hutt
Carterton
Karamea
Havelock
Petone
Greytown
Karamea
Richmond
Martinborough
Bight
Tadmor
Wakefield
Lower Hutt
Wairarapa L.
Seddonville
Picton
WELLINGTON
Granity
Murchison
Blenheim
Westport
Lyell
Inangahua
Rotoroa L.
Seddon
Junction
2885 Mt. Tapuaenuku
Ward
Reefton
L. Travers 2338
Clarence
Kaikoura
Blackball
Spenser
Mts.
Runanga
Hanmer
Springs
Kaikoura
Greymouth
Stillwater
Kumara
L. Brunner
Culverden
Hokitika
Jacksons
Arthur's
Hurunui
Ross
Pass
Waiau
Waikari
Waipara
Amberley
Coleridge
Oxford
Rangiora
Whitecliffs
Springfield
Kaiapoi
South
Pegasus Bay
Methven
New Brighton
Island
Staveley
Rakaia
Christchurch
Mt. Cook
Riccarton
3753
Lincoln
Lyttelton
Ashburton
Banks Pen.
Akaroa
Westland Bight
Lake Ellesmere
Abut Hd.
Jackson B.
Tekapo
Okuru
Haast
Rakaia
Ashburton Bight
Mt.
Fairlie
Southern Alps
Aspiring
Pukaki
3027
L.
Temuka
Milford Sd.
Earnslaw
Ohau
St.
Timaru
2816
L.
Andrews
Bligh Sound
Wanaka I.
Canterbury Bight
George Sound
Wanaka
Hawea
Waimate
Queenstown
Arrowtown
Kurow
Cromwell
Tokarahi
Ngapara
Secretary I.
Wakatipu
Naseby
Oamaru
Doubtful Sd.
L.
Alexandra
Maheno
Te Anau
Kingston
Roxburgh
Hampden
Dunback
Resolution I.
Manapouri
Mossburn
Edievale
Palmerston
Dusky Sd.
Lumsden
Kelso
Port Chalmers
Breaksea Sd.
Nightcaps
Mosgiel
Otago Harbour
Te Waewae B.
Riverton
Lawrence
Saunders Pt.
Orepuki
Fairfield
Preservation Inlet
Otautau
Clinton
Dunedin
Waikouaiti
Winton
Gore
Milton
Chalky
Inlet
Tuatapere
Hedgehope
Balclutha
Clifden
Mataura
Kaitangata
Invercargill
Wyndham
Nugget Pt.
Bluff Invercargill
Tokanui
Oraka
Foveaux Str.
Ruapuke I.
Halfmoon Bay
Southwest C.
Stewart I.
Port Pegasus

Projection : Conical with two standard parallels

SAMOA ISLANDS
1:12 000 000

WESTERN
SAMOA
AMERICAN
SAMOA
Savai'i
Apia
Pago Pago
Upolu
Tutuila
West from
Greenwich

FIJI AND TONGA
ISLANDS
1:12 000 000

50 0 50 100 150 200 km
50 0 50 100 150 miles

Niuafo'ou
(Tonga)
Thikombia
Lambasa
Vanua Levu
FIJI
Yasawa Group
Taveuni
Vanua Mbalavu
Koro
Lautoka
Levuka
1323
Ovalau
Viti Levu
Lau Group
Nandi
Gau
Koro Sea
TONGA
Suva
Lakemba
(Friendly Is.)
Moala
Vava'u
Kandavu
Vatoa
Tofua
Tongatapu
Nuku'alofa

East from Greenwich
West from Greenwich

ft   m

9000   3000

6000   2000

3000   1000

1200   400

600   200

0   0

200   600

2000   6000

4000   12 000

6000   18 000

m   ft

NORTHERN TERRITORY

INDONESIA

TIMOR SEA

INDIAN OCEAN

Timor

Kupang

Sumba
Sumbawa
Bali
Lombok
Waingapu
Waikabubak
Savu
Roti
Semau
Dana
Raijua
Melolo
Boing

Tanami Desert

Great Sandy Desert

Gibson Desert

Darwin

Bathurst I.
Melville I.

Kimberley

Bonaparte Archipelago

King Leopold Ranges

Joseph Bonaparte Gulf

Hamersley Range

Broome

Port Hedland

Karratha

Exmouth Gulf

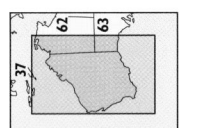

WESTERN AUSTRALIA

SOUTH AUSTRALIA

Great Victoria Desert

Gibson Desert

Nullarbor Plain

Hampton Tableland

Great Australian Bight

SOUTHERN OCEAN

INDIAN OCEAN

PERTH
Fremantle
Kwinana
Rockingham
Mandurah
Bunbury
Busselton
Albany
Esperance
Kalgoorlie-Boulder
Geraldton
Carnarvon

Petermann Ranges
Musgrave Ranges
Everard Ranges
Ayers Rock 868
Mt. Olga 1069
Mt. Woodroffe 1440
Mt. Morris 1387

Ernest Giles Ra.
L. Carnegie
L. Wells
L. Carey
L. Yeo
L. Minigwal
L. Throssell
L. Raeside
L. Austin
L. Moore
L. Barlee
L. Lefroy
L. Cowan
L. Dundas

Projection: Bonne

COPYRIGHT GEORGE PHILIP LTD.

East from Greenwich

ft
12 000
6000
4000
2000
600
0

m
3000
1200
600
400
200
0

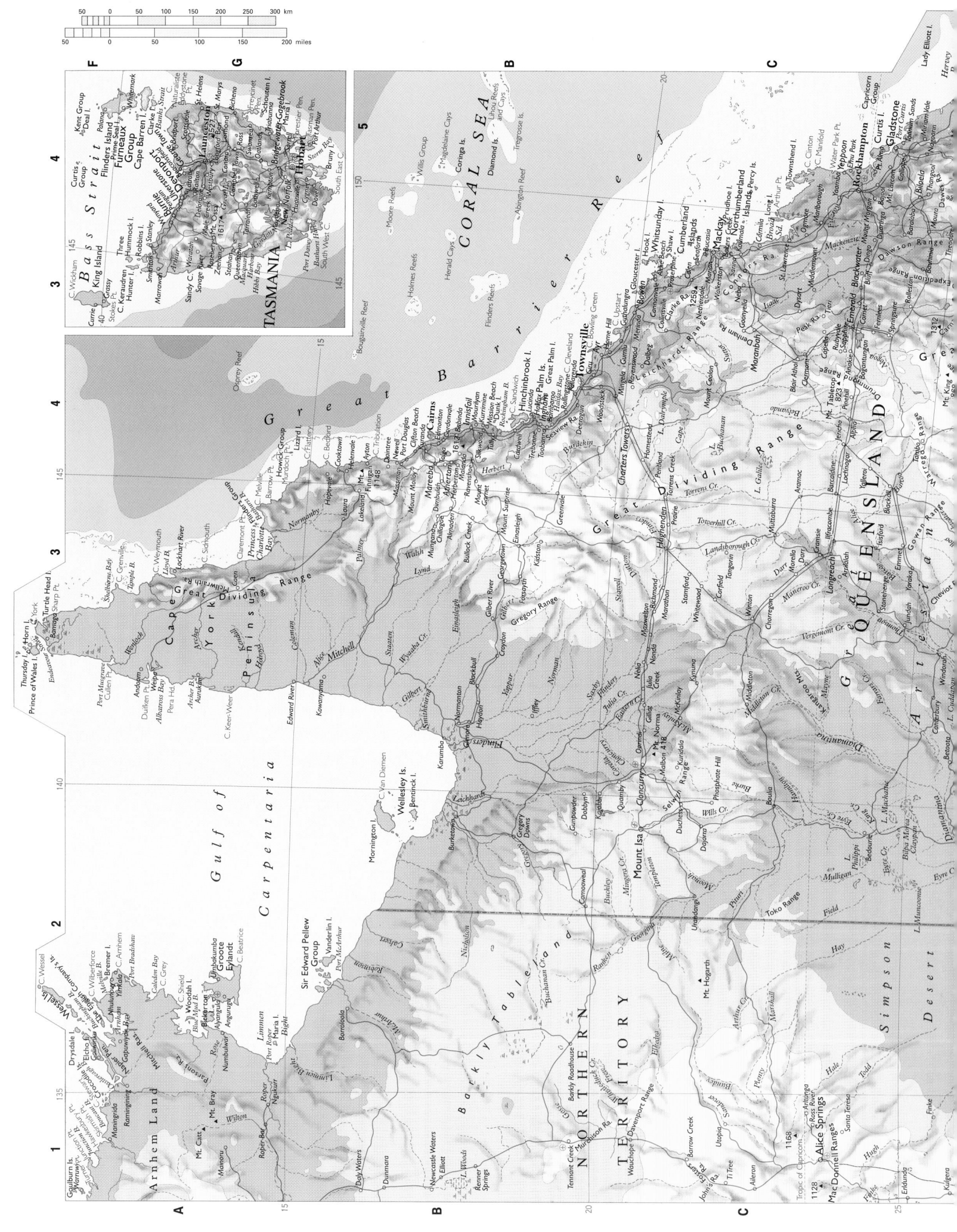

TASMANIA

Bass Strait

CORAL SEA

Great Barrier Reef

Gulf of Carpentaria

QUEENSLAND

NORTHERN TERRITORY

Great Dividing Range

Great Artesian Basin

Arnhem Land

Simpson Desert

Barkly Tableland

SOUTH AUSTRALIA
NEW SOUTH WALES
VICTORIA
SOUTHERN OCEAN
TASMAN SEA
Bass Strait
SYDNEY
CANBERRA
MELBOURNE
ADELAIDE
BRISBANE
Gold Coast
Tweed Heads
Newcastle
Wollongong
Geelong
Ballarat
Bendigo
Broken Hill
Mildura
Dubbo
Tamworth
Wagga Wagga
Albury-Wodonga
Port Augusta
Port Pirie
Whyalla
Port Lincoln
Mount Gambier
Warrnambool
Toowoomba
Ipswich
Coffs Harbour
Port Macquarie
Lake Eyre (North)
Lake Torrens
Lake Gairdner
Lake Frome
Kangaroo I.
King Island
Flinders Island
Furneaux Group
Dividing Range
Grey Range
Darling Downs
Darling
Murray
Spencer Gulf
Eyre Peninsula
Gippsland
Projection: Bonne
East from Greenwich
COPYRIGHT, GEORGE PHILIP LTD.
ft
m
4500
3000
1200
600
0
200
2000
4000
1500
1000
400
200
0
600
6000
12 000

RUSSIA

MOSKVA
Yekaterinburg
Tomsk
Novosibirsk
Ob
Lena
Irkutsk
Oz. Baykal
Chita
Okhotsk
Sea of Okhotsk
Poluostrov Kamchatka
Komandorskiye Ostrova (Russia)
Bering Sea
Near Is. (U.S.A.)
Andreanof (U.S.A.)
Volga
Astana (Aqmola)
Semey
Blagoveshchensk
Amur
Khabarovsk
Sakhalin
Petropavlovsk-Kamchatskiy
Aleutia
7822
Aleutian Trench

KAZAKSTAN
Aral Sea
Balqash Köl
Almaty
Ulaanbaatar
Harbin
La Pérouse Str.
Kurilskiye Ostrova (Russia)
Kuril Trench

MONGOLIA
Changchun
SHENYANG
Vladivostok
Sapporo
Hakodate
10,542

Toshkent
KYRGYZSTAN
Ürümqi
BEIJING
TIANJIN
Taiyuan
NORTH KOREA
SOUL
SOUTH KOREA
Sea of Japan
Sendai
Emperor Seamount Chain

TAJIKISTAN
AFGHANISTAN
Kabul
Srinagar
PAKISTAN
Lahore
DELHI
Kanpur

CHINA
Lanzhou
Xi'an
Nanjing
Dalian
Qingdao
Yellow Sea
Kyōto
Nagoya
Osaka
Kyūshū
Shikoku
TOKYO
Yokohama
JAPAN
Fuji-San 3776
10,554
Japan Trench

XIZANG
Kunlun Shan
Lhasa
8848 Mt. Everest
CHONGQING
Wuhan
Changsha
SHANGHAI
HANGZHOU
East China Sea
Ogasawara Gunto (Japan)
Midway Is. (U.S.A.)

Himalaya
NEPAL
Ganga
Brahmaputra
Chang
Kunming
Fuzhou
Taipei
Ryūkyū-rettō (Japan)
Kazan-Rettō (Japan)
Minami-Tori-Shima (Japan)
Lisianski I. (U.S.A.)

BANGLADESH
CALCUTTA
DHAKA
Mandalay
BURMA
Irrawaddy
GUANGZHOU
HONG KONG
Macau
TAIWAN
Necker Ridge
Wake I. (U.S.A.)

INDIA
Hyderabad
Salween
Hanoi
Hainan
C. Engano
Luzon
Paracel Is.
MANILA
NORTHERN MARIANAS (U.S.A.)
Saipan
MARSHALL IS.
Bikini
Enewetak Atoll

Bay of Bengal
Rangoon
THAILAND
BANGKOK
Mekong
LAOS
South China Sea
Mindoro
Samar
Palawan
PHILIPPINES
GUAM (U.S.A.)
11,022
Mariana Trench
Micronesia
Caroline Is.
Yap
Truk
Dalap-Uliga-Darrit
Jaluit I.

CHENNAI (Madras)
Andaman Is. (India)
CAMBODIA
Phnom Penh
Phanh Bho Ho Chi Minh
G. of Thailand
10,497
Sulu Sea
Mindanao
Mindanao Trench
Koror
Palikir
Pohnpei
Butaritari

SRI LANKA
Nicobar Is. (India)
MALAYSIA
Sea
4101
SABAH
Celebes Sea
Maluku
KOROR
PALAU
Melan
FEDERATED STATES OF MICRONESIA
Tarawa
Gilbert Is.
Banaba
Howland I. (U.S.A.)
Baker I. (U.S.A.)

Colombo
Kuala Lumpur
PEN. MALAYSIA
BRUNEI
SARAWAK
Borneo
Sulawesi
Buru
Seram
NAURU
Phoenix Is.
Abarirngi
Enderbury

SINGAPORE
Sumatera
INDONESIA
Halmahera
Puncak Jaya 5029
IRIAN JAYA
PAPUA NEW GUINEA
Admiralty Is.
Bismarck Arch.
New Ireland
New Guinea
KIRIBATI

Palembang
Ujung Pandang
Banda Sea
7440
New Britain
Bougainville
Rabaul
SOLOMON IS.
Fongafale
TUVALU
Tokelau Is. (N.Z.)

Java Sea
JAKARTA
Flores Sea
Surabaya
Jawa
Bali
Sumbawa
Sumba
Flores
Timor
Lae
Port Moresby
Honiara
Guadalcanal
Santa Cruz I.
9165
Rotuma
Is. Wallis & Futuna (Fr.)
WESTERN SAMOA
Apia

Cocos Is. (Austral.)
Christmas I. (Austral.)
Java Trench
Selat Sunda
Arafura Sea
Torres Strait
C. York
Louisiade Arch.
Coral Sea
Espíritu Santo
Port Vila
Vanua Levu
Viti Levu
Suva
FIJI
Nuku'alofa

INDIAN
C. Arnhem
Darwin
Gulf of Carpentaria
Cairns
VANUATU
Is. Chesterfield
5670
NEW CALEDONIA (Fr.)
Noumea
Is. Loyauté
TONGA
10,822
Tonga Trench

OCEAN
Broome
North West C.
AUSTRALIA
Alice Springs
Mount Isa
Townsville
Rockhampton
Norfolk I. (Austral.)
Lord Howe I. (Austral.)
Kermadec Is. (N.Z.)
Kermadec Trench
10,047

Geraldton
L. Eyre
Brisbane
Great Dividing Ra.
Darling

Perth
Great Australian Bight
Albany
Adelaide
Murray
Canberra
Sydney
Mt. Kosciuszko 2237
Tasman Sea
NEW ZEALAND
Auckland
Cook Strait
Wellington

Nouvelle Amsterdam (Fr.)
I. St. Paul (Fr.)
Melbourne
Bass Str.
Tasmania
Hobart
Mt. Cook 3753
Christchurch
Chatham I. (N.Z.)
Dunedin
Invercargill
Bounty Is. (N.Z.)

Is. Crozet (Fr.)
Mid-Indian Ridge
Antipodes Is. (N.Z.)
Auckland Is. (N.Z.)
Campbell I. (N.Z.)

Kerguelen (Fr.)
Macquarie I. (Austral.)

Heard I. (Austral.)

Projection: Mollweide's Homolographic
East from Greenwich

ft | m
12 000 | 4000
9000 | 3000
6000 | 2000
3000 | 1000
1500 | 500
600 | 200
0 | 0
200 | 600
1000 | 3000
2000 | 6000
4000 | 12 000
6000 | 18 000
8000 | 24 000
m | ft

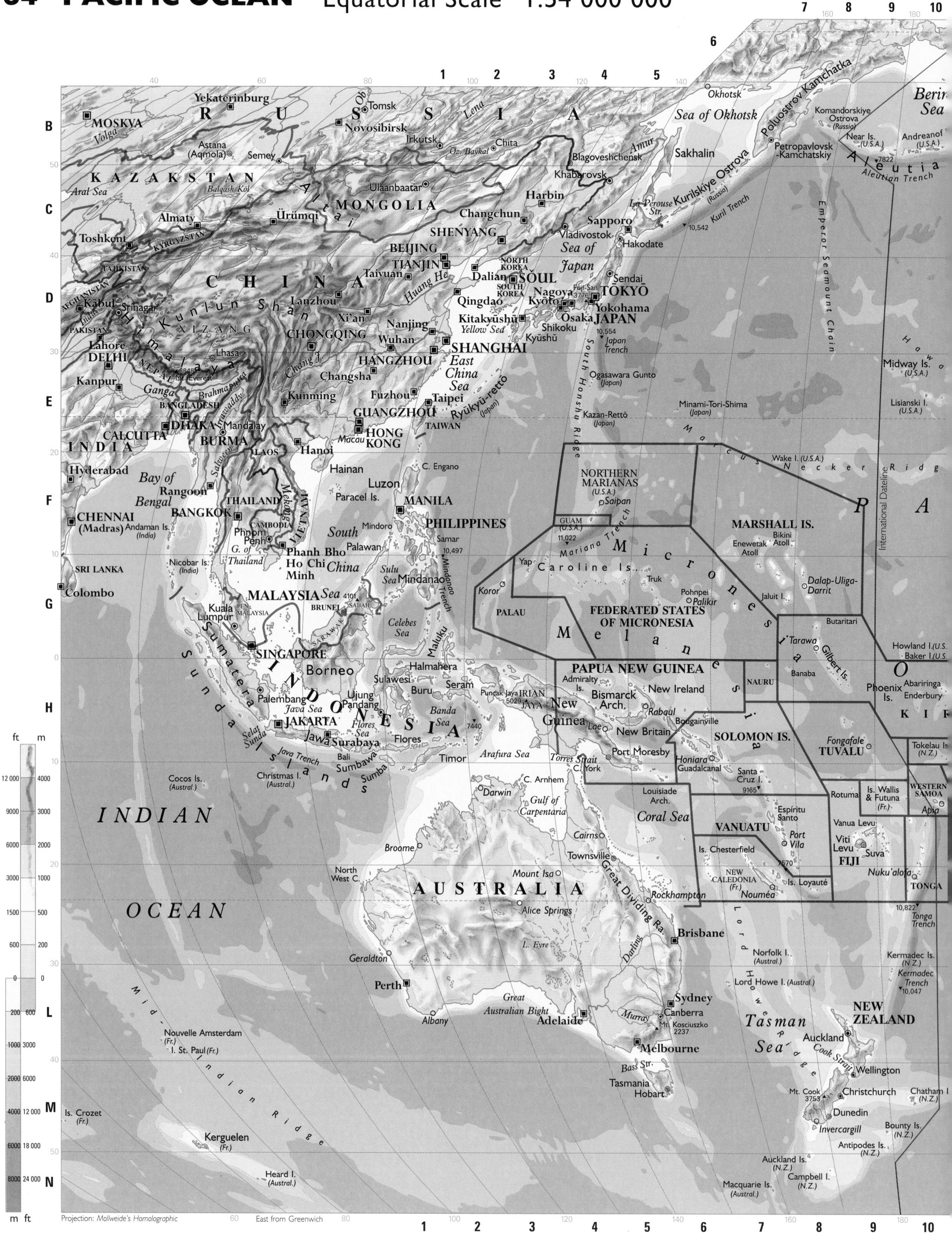

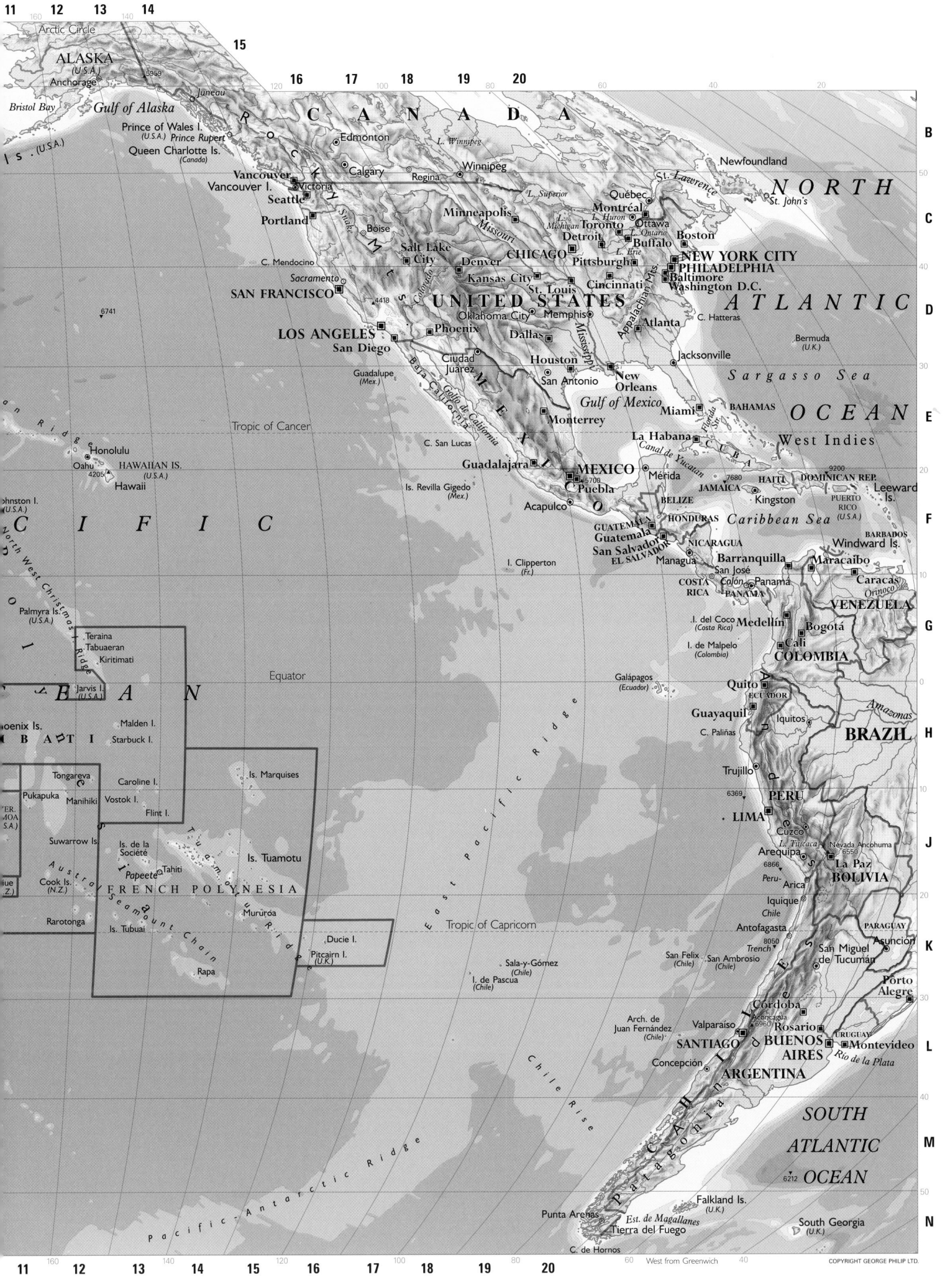

Arctic Circle

11 **12** **13** **14**
15

ALASKA
(U.S.A.)
Anchorage

Bristol Bay

Gulf of Alaska
Juneau

Prince of Wales I.
(U.S.A.) Prince Rupert
Queen Charlotte Is.
(Canada)

16 **17** **18** **19** **20**

C A N A D A

Edmonton

B

L. Winnipeg

Newfoundland

Vancouver
Vancouver I.
Victoria
Seattle

Calgary
Regina

Winnipeg

Quebec
Montréal

St. Lawrence

St. John's

N O R T H

C

Portland

Boise

Minneapolis

Missouri

L. Superior

L. Huron

Ottawa
Toronto
Detroit
Buffalo
L. Ontario
L. Erie

Boston

C. Mendocino

Salt Lake
City

Denver

CHICAGO

Pittsburgh

Cincinnati

NEW YORK CITY
PHILADELPHIA
Baltimore
Washington D.C.

A T L A N T I C

D

Sacramento

SAN FRANCISCO

6741

4418

Kansas City

UNITED STATES

Oklahoma City

St. Louis

Memphis

Appalachian Mts.

C. Hatteras

LOS ANGELES
San Diego

Phoenix

Dallas

Houston

San Antonio

New
Orleans

Jacksonville

Bermuda
(U.K.)

Sargasso Sea

Ciudad
Juarez

Guadalupe
(Mex.)

Gulf of California

Baja California

Mississippi

Gulf of Mexico
Miami

BAHAMAS

O C E A N

E

Tropic of Cancer

Monterrey

Honolulu
Oahu
4205
Hawaii

HAWAIIAN IS.

C. San Lucas

M E X I C O

La Habana

Canal de Yucatán

CUBA

West Indies

6741

Is. Revilla Gigedo
(Mex.)

Guadalajara
5700

MEXICO
Puebla

Mérida

JAMAICA

7680

Kingston

9200

HAITI
DOMINICAN REP.

PUERTO
RICO
(U.S.A.)

Leeward
Is.

johnston I.
(U.S.A.)

C I F I C

Acapulco

BELIZE

GUATEMALA
Guatemala
San Salvador
EL SALVADOR

HONDURAS

NICARAGUA

Caribbean Sea

BARBADOS

Windward Is.

F

I. Clipperton
(Fr.)

Managua

San José

COSTA
RICA

Colón
PANAMA

Barranquilla

Panama

Maracaibo

Caracas

Orinoco

VENEZUELA

Palmyra Is.
(U.S.A.)

North West Christmas Ridge

I. del Coco
(Costa Rica)

Medellín

Bogotá

G

Teraina
Tabuaeran
Kiritimati

Cali

COLOMBIA

I. de Malpelo
(Colombia)

Jarvis I.
(U.S.A.)

Equator

Galápagos
(Ecuador)

Quito

ECUADOR

B A N

Guayaquil

Iquitos

Amazonas

hoenix Is.

Malden I.

C. Palinas

BRAZIL

H

Tongareva

Caroline I.

Starbuck I.

Pukapuka
Manihiki

Vostok I.

Trujillo

ER.
MOA
S.A.)

Flint I.

6369

PERU

J

Suwarrow Is.

Is. Marquises

Cuzco

LIMA

Is. de la
Société
Papeete Tahiti

Tuamotu

L. Titicaca
Arequipa
6866
Peru-
Arica

Nevada Ancohuma
6550

La Paz

ue
Z.)

Cook Is.
(N.Z.)

F R E N C H   P O L Y N E S I A

Is. Tuamotu

Austral Seamount Chain

East Pacific Ridge

BOLIVIA

Rarotonga

Is. Tubuai

Mururoa

Iquique
Chile

Tropic of Capricorn

Antofagasta

PARAGUAY

K

Rapa

Ducie I.

Pitcairn I.
(U.K.)

Sala-y-Gómez
(Chile)

San Felix
(Chile)

San Ambrosio
(Chile)

8050
Trench

San Miguel
de Tucumán

Asunción

Pôrto
Alegre

I. de Pascua
(Chile)

Córdoba

Aconcagua
6960

Valparaíso
Rosario

URUGUAY

Arch. de
Juan Fernández
(Chile)

SANTIAGO

BUENOS
AIRES

Montevideo

Río de la Plata

L

Concepción

ARGENTINA

SOUTH

M

Chile Rise

ATLANTIC

Pacific Antarctic Ridge

6212

OCEAN

N

Punta Arenas

Falkland Is.
(U.K.)

South Georgia
(U.K.)

Est. de Magallanes
Tierra del Fuego

C. de Hornos

West from Greenwich

11 **12** **13** **14** **15** **16** **17** **18** **19** **20**

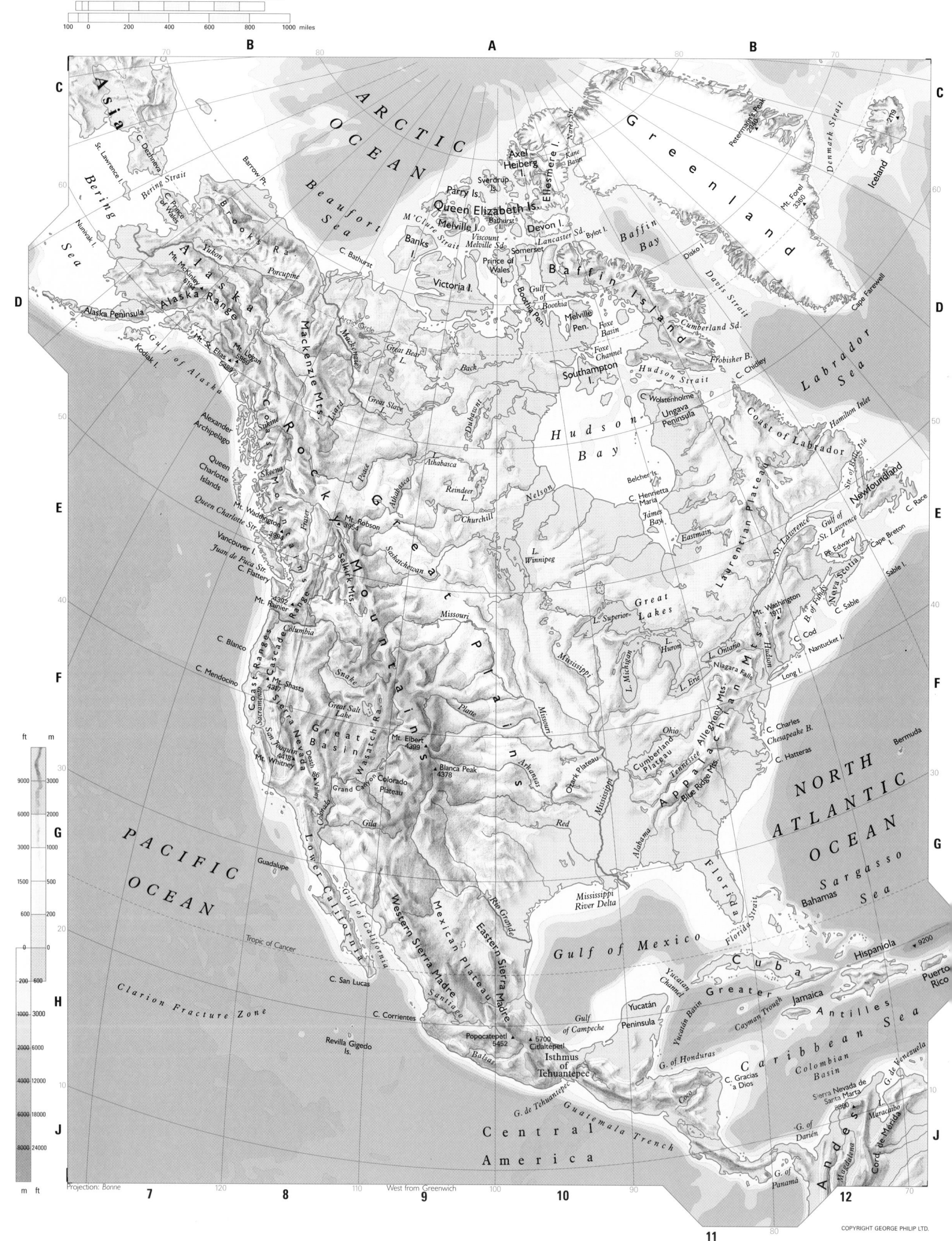

Projection: Bonne

West from Greenwich

COPYRIGHT GEORGE PHILIP LTD.

100 0 200 400 600 800 1000 1200 1400 km

100 0 200 400 600 800 1000 miles

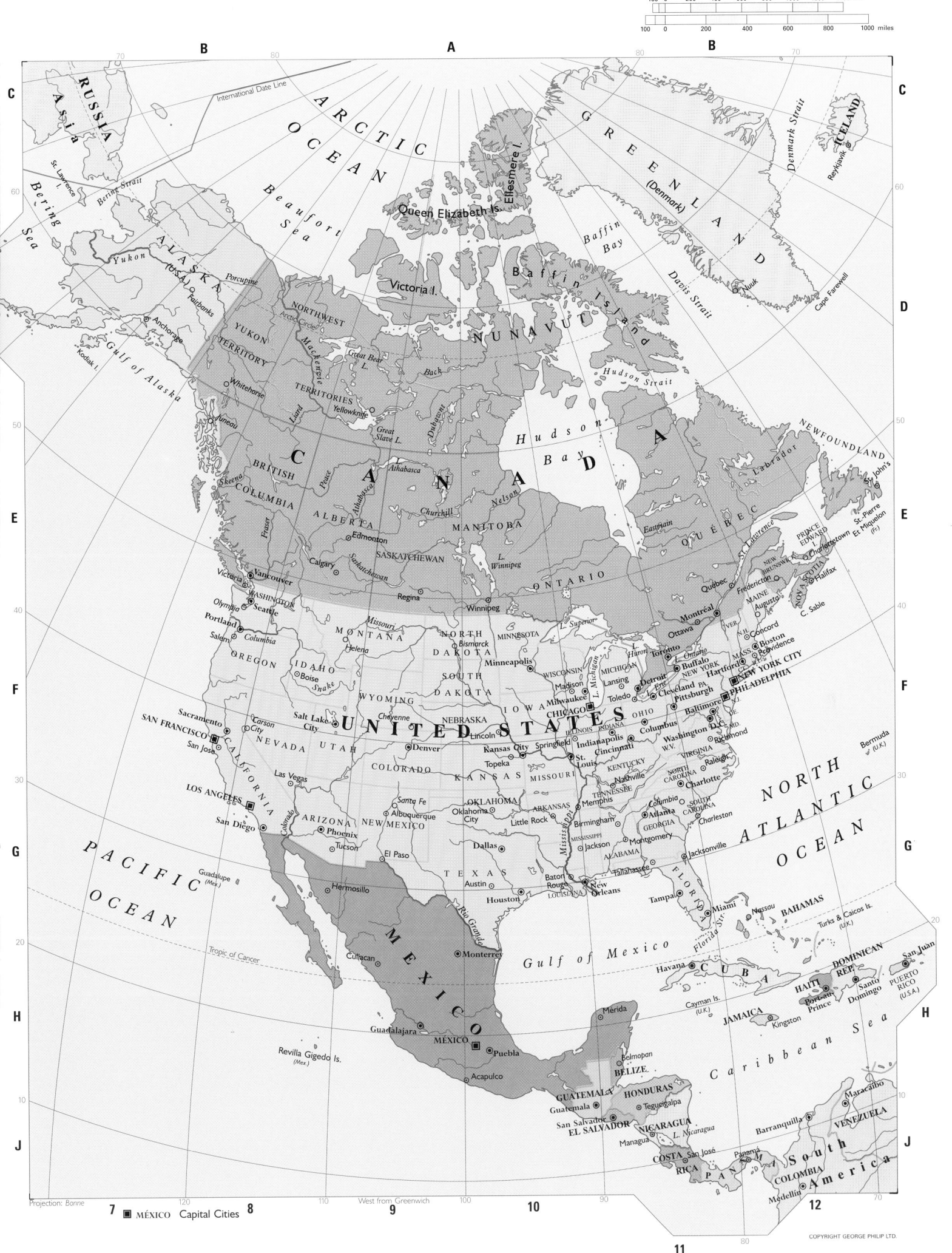

C RUSSIA
Asia
Bering Strait
Bering Sea
St. Lawrence I.
Kodiak I.

ARCTIC OCEAN

Beaufort Sea

International Date Line

Queen Elizabeth Is.

Ellesmere I.

GREENLAND
(Denmark)
Denmark Strait
ICELAND
Reykjavik

Baffin Bay

Nuuk
Cape Farewell

ALASKA
(USA)
Yukon
Fairbanks
Anchorage
Porcupine

Victoria I.

Baffin Island

NORTHWEST

Whitehorse

YUKON TERRITORY

Arctic Circle

Mackenzie

Great Bear L.

NUNAVUT

Davis Strait

Juneau

TERRITORIES
Yellowknife
Liard
Great Slave L.

Back

Dubawnt

Hudson Strait

NEWFOUNDLAND
Labrador

BRITISH COLUMBIA

Peace

Athabasca

CANADA

Hudson Bay

St. John's

Skeena
Fraser

ALBERTA
Athabasca

SASKATCHEWAN

Churchill
Nelson

MANITOBA

L. Winnipeg

Eastmain

QUÉBEC

St-Pierre Et Miquelon (Fr.)

Victoria
Vancouver
Edmonton
Calgary
Saskatchewan

Regina

Winnipeg

ONTARIO

Québec

PRINCE EDWARD
Charlottetown
NEW BRUNSWICK
Fredericton
NOVA SCOTIA
Halifax
C. Sable

Olympia
Seattle
WASHINGTON
Portland
Salem
OREGON
Columbia

Missouri

MONTANA
Helena

IDAHO
Boise
Snake

NORTH DAKOTA
Bismarck

SOUTH DAKOTA

MINNESOTA
Minneapolis

WISCONSIN
Madison

L. Superior

Ottawa
Montréal
VER.
N.H. Concord
Boston
MASS. Providence
Hartford
NEW YORK CITY

Toronto
L. Ontario
Buffalo
MICHIGAN
Lansing
Detroit
Erie
Cleveland
Pittsburgh
PA.
NEW YORK
PHILADELPHIA
MAINE
Augusta

L. Huron

L. Michigan

Sacramento
San Francisco
San Jose
NEVADA
Carson City
Salt Lake City
UTAH

WYOMING

Cheyenne

NEBRASKA
Lincoln

IOWA

ILLINOIS
CHICAGO

Milwaukee

Toledo
OHIO
Columbus
INDIANA
Indianapolis
Cincinnati
W.V.
Washington
D.C.
Baltimore
MD.
Richmond
VIRGINIA

UNITED STATES

CALIFORNIA
Las Vegas
LOS ANGELES
San Diego

COLORADO
Denver

KANSAS
Topeka

Kansas City
MISSOURI
St. Louis
Springfield

KENTUCKY
Nashville
TENNESSEE
NORTH CAROLINA
Charlotte
Raleigh

Santa Fe
Albuquerque
ARIZONA
Phoenix
Tucson
NEW MEXICO

OKLAHOMA
Oklahoma City
ARKANSAS
Little Rock
Memphis

Colorado

El Paso

Dallas

Mississippi

Birmingham
GEORGIA
Atlanta
Montgomery
ALABAMA
MISS.
Jackson

SOUTH CAROLINA
Columbia
Charleston

El Paso

TEXAS
Austin
Houston

Baton Rouge
New Orleans
LOUISIANA
Jacksonville
FLORIDA
Tallahassee

NORTH ATLANTIC OCEAN

Bermuda
(U.K.)

PACIFIC OCEAN

Guadalupe
(Mex.)

Tropic of Cancer

Hermosillo

Culiacan

MEXICO

Rio Grande

Monterrey

Tampa
Miami

Gulf of Mexico

Havana
CUBA

Nassau
BAHAMAS
Florida Str.

Cayman Is.
(U.K.)

Turks & Caicos Is.
(U.K.)

DOMINICAN REP.
San Juan
PUERTO RICO
(U.S.A.)

HAITI
Port-au-Prince
Santo Domingo

Revilla Gigedo Is.
(Mex.)

Guadalajara
MÉXICO
Puebla
Acapulco

Mérida

BELIZE
Belmopan

GUATEMALA
Guatemala
San Salvador
EL SALVADOR

HONDURAS
Tegucigalpa
NICARAGUA
L. Nicaragua
Managua

JAMAICA
Kingston

Caribbean Sea

Maracaibo
VENEZUELA
Barranquilla

COSTA RICA
San José
PANAMA
Panamá

COLOMBIA
Medellín

South America

CANADA 1:15 000 000

0 100 200 300 400 500 600 km
0 100 200 300 400 miles
PACIFIC OCEAN
ALASKA
YUKON TERRITORY
NORTHWEST TERRITORIES
BRITISH COLUMBIA
ALBERTA
SASKATCHEWAN
MANITOBA
WASHINGTON
MONTANA
NORTH DAKOTA
SOUTH DAKOTA
NEBRASKA
MINNESOTA
IOWA
UNITED STATES
Rocky Mountains
Mackenzie Mountains
Selwyn Mts.
Cassiar Mountains
Coast Mountains
Columbia Mountains
St. Elias Mts.
Wrangell Mts.
Selkirk Mts.
Victoria Island
Banks Island
Prince Albert Pen.
Prince of Wales I.
Boothia Peninsula
King William I.
Amundsen Gulf
Coronation Gulf
Queen Maud Gulf
Viscount Melville Sound
M'Clintock Channel
Great Bear L.
Great Slave L.
Lake Athabasca
Reindeer Lake
Lake Winnipeg
L. Winnipegosis
L. Manitoba
Alexander Archipelago
Queen Charlotte Is.
Vancouver I.
Anchorage
Whitehorse
Yellowknife
Edmonton
Calgary
Vancouver
Victoria
Seattle
Regina
Saskatoon
Winnipeg
Minneapolis
Omaha
Juneau
Inuvik
Dawson
Prince George
Prince Rupert
Kamloops
Spokane
Fort McMurray
Churchill
Projection : Bonne
ALASKA
1:30 000 000
0 100 200 300 400 500 600 km
0 100 200 300 400 miles
CHUKCHI SEA
BERING SEA
GULF OF ALASKA
PACIFIC OCEAN
Brooks Range
Alaska Range
Mt. McKinley 6194
Alaska Peninsula
Aleutian Is.
Kodiak I.
West from Greenwich
ft m
9000 3000
6000 2000
4500 1500
3000 1000
1200 400
600 200
0 0
200 600
2000 6000
4000 12 000
m ft

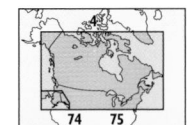

74 75

11 12 13 14 15 16

B

60

Devon I.
Lancaster Sound
Arctic Bay
Brodeur
Peninsula
Borden Pen.
Bylot I.
Pond Inlet
Clyde River
C. Adair
Baffin Bay
2136
1890
Eclipse
Nunavik
Uummannaq
Qeqertarsuaq
Qeqertarsuaq
Ilulissat
Qasigiannguit
G R E E N L A N D
(KALAALLIT NUNAAT)
(Denmark)
2850 Kong Frederik VI's Kyst
Ammassalik
Qaqortoq
Ikateq
Kuujjuarapik

B a f f i n   I s l a n d
Fury and Hecla Str.
Igloolik
Sanirajak
Prince Charles I.
Air Force I.
C. Raper
Home B.
Qikiqtarjuaq
Cumberland Peninsula
2591
Pangnirtung
Hoare B.
Mercy C.
Cumberland Sd.
D a v i s   S t r a i t
Sisimiut
Kangerlussuaq
Maniitsoq
Nuuk
Paamiut
Qeqertarsuatsiaat
Arsuk
Nanortalik

A T L A N T I C

Simpson Pen.
Pelly Bay
Melville
Peninsula
Committee B.
Foxe
Basin
Foxe Pen.
Amadjuak
Meta Incognita Peninsula
Iqaluit
Hall Peninsula
Kimmirut
Frobisher Bay
Resolution I.

C

N U N A V U T
C. Dorchester
Southampton I.
Salliq
Bell Pen.
Nottingham I.
Salisbury I.
H u d s o n   S t r a i t
Ivujivik
Salluit
Quaqtaq
Akpatok I.
C. Chidley

50

Rae Isthmus
Repulse Bay
Roes Welcome Sd.
Coats I.
Mansel I.
Kangiqsujuaq
P é n i n s u l e
d ' U n g a v a
Puvirnittuq
Kangirsuk
Arnaud
Ungava Bay
Kangiqsualujjuaq
Hebron
Nain
Hopedale
C. Harrison
Rigolet
Cartwright
Port Hope Simpson
Belle Isle

L a b r a d o r   S e a
3809

Ottawa Is.
257
H u d s o n
B a y
Sleeper Is.
King George Is.
Baker's Dozen Is.
Belcher Is.
C. Henrietta Maria
Inukjuak
L. à l'Eau Claire
L. Payne
L. Minto
Schefferville
Petitsikapau L.
Esker
Smallwood Res.
Labrador
North West River
Happy Valley
Goose Bay
Churchill Falls
Churchill
St-Augustin
Str. of Belle Isle
St. Anthony
C. Bauld

D

Big Trout L.
Tatnam
Peawanuck
Winisk
Severn
Attawapiskat
Pte. Louis XIV
A
Chisasibi
La Grande
Kanaaupscow
Rés. de Caniapiscau
Labrador City
Fermont
Ashuanipi
Gagnon
Q U É B E C
1135
Baie-Comeau
Port-Cartier
Sept-Îles
Havre-St-Pierre
Natashquan
Natashquan
Romaine
Î. d'Anticosti
Deer Lake
Corner Brook
Baie Verte
Grand Falls
N e w f o u n d l a n d
Twillingate
Gander
Bonavista
Carbonear
St. John's
C. Race
Placentia
Notre Dame B.
St-Pierre et Miquelon (Fr)

D

O N T A R I O
L. St. Joseph
Albany
Fort Albany
Attawapiskat
Moosonee
Akimiski I.
J a m e s   B a y
Wemindji
Eastmain
Eastmain
Waskaganish
Rupert
Charlton I.
L. Albanel
L. Bienville
Rés. Gouin
L. Mistassini
Chibougamau
Matagami
L. Matagami
L. Evans
Opinaca
Caniapiscau
Kaniapiskau
Koksoak
Feuilles
Baleine
George
N E W F O U N D L A N D
Moisie
Manicouagan
Manicouagan
Rés.
St. Lawrence
Matane
Pén. de Gaspé
Gaspé
Île de la Madeleine
Cabot Str.
Cape Breton I.
Glace Bay
Sydney
Port Hawkesbury
Antigonish
New Glasgow

L. Nipigon
Nipigon
Geraldton
Marathon
Oba
Kapuskasing
Hearst
Cochrane
Timmins
Iroquois Falls
Kirkland Lake
Rouyn-Noranda
Val-d'Or
Amos
Chapleau
New Liskeard
Chicoutimi
Jonquière
Roberval
Dolbeau
St-Félicien
La Tuque
Shawinigan
Trois-Rivières
1190
Québec
Lévis
Thetford Mines
Rivière-du-Loup
Edmundston
Grand Falls
N E W   B R U N S W I C K
Miramichi
Bathurst
Campbellton
Moncton
Amherst
Truro
N O V A   S C O T I A
Halifax
Dartmouth
Bridgewater
Liverpool

Thunder Bay
Lake Superior
Houghton 183
Ironwood
Marquette
M I C H I G A N
Escanaba
Menominee
Rhinelander
Wausau
W I S C O N S I N
Green Bay
Appleton
Sheboygan
Madison
MILWAUKEE
Racine
Kenosha
Rockford
CHICAGO
ILLINOIS
Gary
INDIANA
South Bend
Toledo
OHIO
DETROIT
CLEVELAND
Windsor
Sarnia
London
Flint
Lansing
Grand Rapids
Saginaw
Cadillac
Traverse City
Petoskey
Manistee
Manistique
Sault Ste. Marie
Sault Ste. Marie
Elliot Lake
Sudbury
North Bay
Parry Sound
Barrie
Owen Sound
Georgian Bay
Lake Huron
Manitoulin I.
Wawa
Huntsville
Pembroke
Peterborough
Oshawa
TORONTO
Hamilton
Kitchener
Niagara Falls
BUFFALO
L. Ontario
Rochester
Syracuse
Albany
N E W   Y O R K
Binghamton
Elmira
Jamestown
L. Erie
Scranton
Allentown
Trenton
PENNSYLVANIA
Erie
New Haven
Bridgeport
Newark
N.J.
NEW YORK
HARTFORD
CONN.
Springfield
Providence
R.I.
BOSTON
MASS.
Manchester
Concord
NEW HAMPSHIRE
Montpelier
VERMONT
Burlington
Ottawa
Cornwall
Kingston
Belleville
MONTREAL
Hull
Granby
St-Hyacinthe
Sherbrooke
Lewiston
Augusta
Portland
C. Cod
MAINE
Bangor
Fredericton
Saint John
B. of Fundy
Digby
Yarmouth
C. Sable

E

40

Lake Michigan
L. St. Clair

Outaouais
Champlain

West from Greenwich
COPYRIGHT GEORGE PHILIP LTD.

90 80 70 60

11 12 13 14

EASTERN CANADA 1:7 000 000

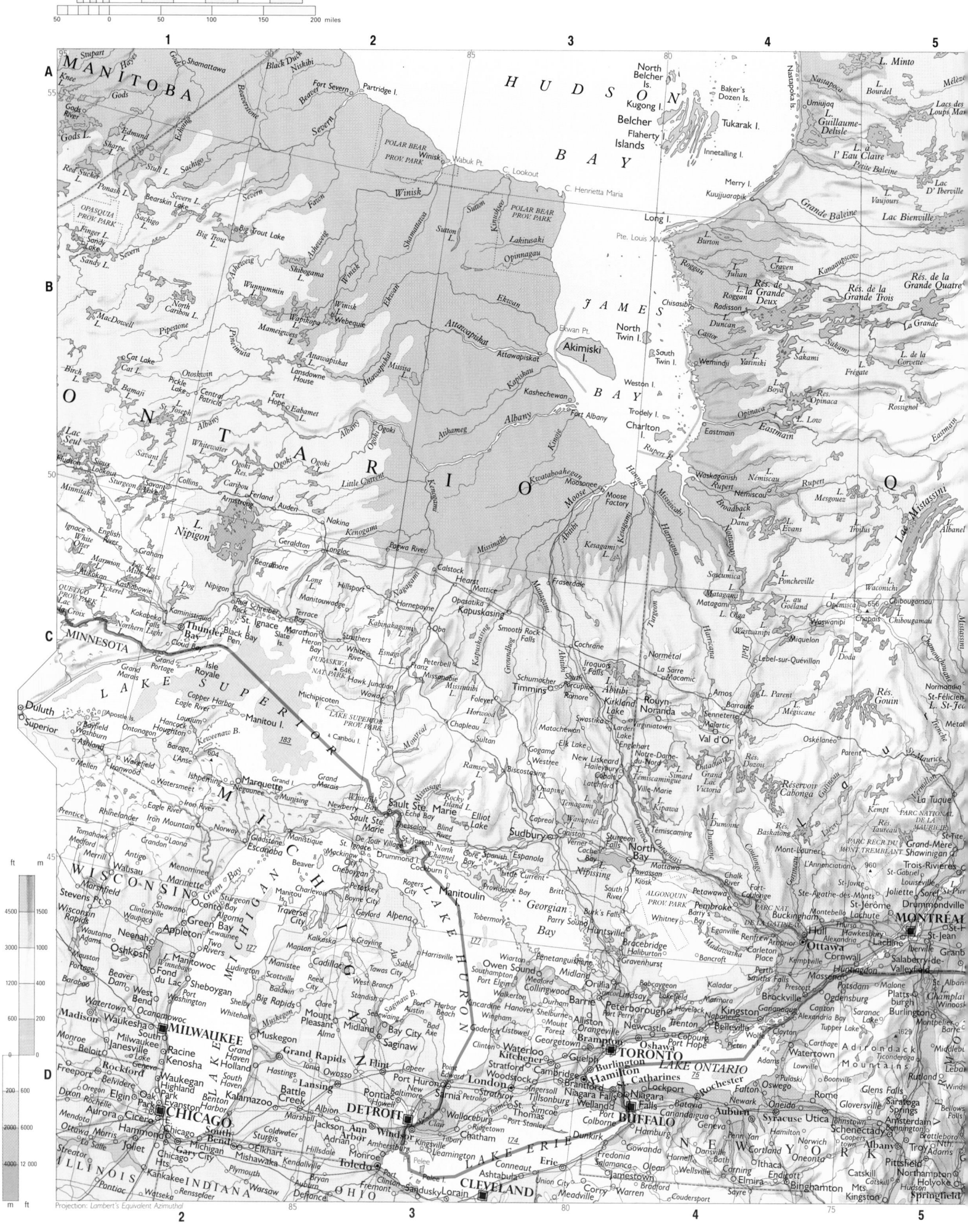
50 0 50 100 150 200 250 300 km
50 0 50 100 150 200 miles
HUDSON BAY
JAMES BAY
MANITOBA
ONTARIO
MINNESOTA
WISCONSIN
MICHIGAN
ILLINOIS
INDIANA
OHIO
NEW YORK
LAKE SUPERIOR
LAKE MICHIGAN
LAKE HURON
LAKE ERIE
LAKE ONTARIO
Belcher Islands
Akimiski I.
L. Nipigon
Georgian Bay
Manitoulin
Lac Mistassini
Thunder Bay
Sault Ste. Marie
Sudbury
Timmins
Moosonee
North Bay
Ottawa
MONTRÉAL
TORONTO
Hamilton
London
Kingston
DETROIT
CHICAGO
MILWAUKEE
CLEVELAND
BUFFALO
Duluth
Green Bay
Grand Rapids
Lansing
Toledo
Rochester
Syracuse
Albany
POLAR BEAR PROV. PARK
ALGONQUIN PROV. PARK
LAKE SUPERIOR PROV. PARK
Projection: Lambert's Equivalent Azimuthal

6 7 8 9

A B C D

LABRADOR SEA

Labrador

NEWFOUNDLAND

QUÉBEC

Newfoundland

South Aulatsivik I.
Paul I.
Nain
Voisey B.
Tunungayualok I.
Nunaksaluk I.
Kogaluk
Mistastin L.
Davis Inlet
Big Bay
Hopedale
Kaipokok B.
Aillik
Makkovik
Adlavik Is.
C. Harrison
Postville
Holton
Indian Harbour
Groswater B.
Rigolet
Hamilton Inlet
North River
Cartwright
Table B.
Black Tickle
Island of Ponds
Sandwich B.
Mealy Mts.
1128
Paradise River
Square Islands
Charlottetown
Williams harbour
Alexis
Port Hope Simpson
Battle Harbour
St. Lewis
Mary's Harbour
Lodge Bay
Belle Isle
Red Bay
L'Anse au Loup
L'Anse aux Meadows
St. Anthony
Str. of Belle Isle
Forteau
Blanc-Sablon
Rivière St-Paul
St-Paul
St-Augustin
Hare B.
Groais I.
St. Barbe
Roddickton
Englee
Bell I.
Port au Choix
Hawke's Bay
Harbour Deep
White B.
Horse Is.
C. St. John
La Scie
Baie Verte
Notre Dame B.
Fogo
Fogo I.
Twillingate
Musgrave Harbour
Long Range Mts.
Daniel's Harbour
Jackson's Arm
Springdale
GROS MORNE NAT. PARK
Rocky Harbour
Norris Point
Trout River
Deer Lake
South Brook
Lewisporte
Wesleyville
Bonavista B.
C. Bonavista
Bonavista
Catalina
Botwood
Bishop's Falls
Glenwood
Gander
Gambo
Badger
Grand Falls-Windsor
B. of Islands
Pasadena
Corner Brook
814
Buchans
Red Indian L.
Maelpaeg Res.
Glovertown
TERRA NOVA NAT. PARK
Port Blandford
Trinity
Trinity B.
Old Perlican
Conception B.
Clarenville
381
Heart's Content
Carbonear
Wabana
Torbay
St. John's
Mt. Pearl
Harbour Grace
Bay Roberts
Port au Port B.
Stephenville
St. George's
Victoria L.
Jeddore L.
Petit Jardin
C. St. George
St. George's B.
St. David's
South Branch
Great Codroy
St. Andrew's
C. Ray
Channel-Port aux Basques
Rose Blanche
Isle aux Morts
Granite L.
Grey
St. Alban's
Terrenceville
Fortune B.
Belleoram
Harbour Breton
François
Burgeo
Holyrood
Whitless Bay
Argentia
Placentia
Avalon Peninsula
Ferryland
Trepassey
Placentia B.
St. Bride's
St. Mary's B.
C. Pine
C. Race
Grand Bank
Marystown
Burin
Fortune
St. Lawrence
C. St. Mary's
Miquelon
Langlade
St.-Pierre
ST.-PIERRE ET MIQUELON (France)
Cabot Strait
St. Paul I.
Cape North

L. le Moyne
Caniapiscau
Baleine
George
L. de la Hutte Sauvage
Fraser
L. Nachicapau
L. Chakonipau
L. Otelnuk
Wheeler
L. Champdoré
L. Tudor
Mistinibi
610
Du Gué
Delay
L. Châteauguay
Sérigny
Sable
L. Wakuach
L. Whitegull
Harp L.
Attikamagen L.
Schefferville
Kanairiktok
Naskaupi
Seal L.
Petitsikapau L.
Menihek
Smallwood Reservoir
Nipishish L.
Grand L.
L. Melville
L. Néret
Rés. de Caniapiscau
Esker
North West River
Goose
Happy Valley-Goose Bay
Twin Falls
Churchill Falls
Churchill
L. Bermen
Ossokmanuan L.
Winokapau L.
Minipi L.
L. Damas
Nitchequon
Shabogamo L.
L. Opiscotéo
Labrador City
Wabush
L. Joseph
Atikonak L.
Natashquan
Little Mecatina
L. Nichicun
L. Naococane
Fermont
Ashuanipi L.
Burnt L.
Petit Mécatina
St-Augustin
1135
Manicouagan
Petit Lac Manicouagan
Gagnon
Rés. Manicouagan
Moisie
Ste-Marguerite
Romaine
Aguanus
Nabisipi
Natashquan
Olomane
Musquaro L.
L. Plétipi
1048
Magpie
L. Magpie
St-Jean
Île du Petit Mécatina
Harrington Harbour
L. Manitou
Kegaska
Romaine
Sheldrake
Mingan
Havre-St-Pierre
Natashquan
Péribonca
L. Manouane
Outardes
L. Walker
Clarke City
Moisie
Sept-Îles
Port-Cartier
Mistassini
L. Péribonca
Bersimis
Sainte-Anne
Rivière-Pentecôte
Rés. Pipmuacan
Pte. de l'Ouest
Port-Menier
Dét. de Jacques-Cartier
Î. d'Anticosti
Pte. Heath
Dét. d'Honguedo
Pte. du Sud-Ouest
Pte. du Sud
Baie Trinité
Pte. des Monts
Godbout
Baie Comeau
Chute-aux-Outardes
Grande-Vallée
Cap-Chat
Ste-Anne-des-Monts
Mont-Louis
1268
Mt. Jacques-Cartier
PARC DE CONSERVATION DE LA GASPÉSIE
Chic-Chocs
Mts.
Rivière-au-Renard
C. de Gaspé
Gaspé
Betsiamites
Forestville
Matane
Mont-Joli
Sayabec
Amqui
Pén. de Gaspé
Percé
Grande-Rivière
Chandler
GULF OF ST. LAWRENCE
572
Dolbeau
Mistassini
Roberval
Alma
Chicoutimi
Jonquière
Saguenay
La Baie
Les Escoumins
Rimouski
Causapscal
New Richmond
Bonaventure
Paspébiac
Miscou I.
Î. Brion
Tadoussac
Petite Saguenay
Lac Bouchette
Bic
Trois-Pistoles
St-Siméon
La Malbaie
Baie-St-Paul
PARC PROV. GRANDS JARDINS
1190
PARC PROV. DE LA JACQUES-CARTIER
St. Lawrence
Rivière-du-Loup
Cabano
Matapedia
Atholville
Campbellton
Dalhousie
Chaleur Bay
Lamèque
Shippegan
Caraquet
Tracadie-Sheila
Îs. de la Madeleine
Grande-Entrée
Fatima
Cap-aux-Meules
Madeleine (Québec)
Havre-Aubert
St. Pascal
Dégelis
Kedgwick
St. Quentin
Mt. Carleton
820
Bathurst
Edmundston
La Pocatière
Fort Kent
St. Leonard
Grand Falls
Van Buren
Neguac
Miramichi B.
Miramichi
North Cape
Tignish
Alberton
PRINCE EDWARD ISLAND
Pleasant Bay
CAPE BRETON HIGHLANDS NAT. PARK
Ingonish
532
St. Ann's B.
Sydney Mines
New Waterford
Chéticamp
Glace Bay
Cape Breton Island
Beaupré
Î. d'Orléans
Québec
Lévis
Donnaconna
Montmagny
St-Jean-Port-Joli
Eagle Lake
Plaster Rock
Perth-Andover
NEW BRUNSWICK
Newcastle
Rogersville
Richibucto
Kensington
St. Peters
East Pt.
Souris
Summerside
Borden
Charlottetown
Inverness
N. Sydney
Sydney
Louisbourg
Bras d'Or L.
La Pérade
Charny
St-Pamphile
Caribou
Presque Isle
Ashland
Buctouche
Doaktown
St. Antoine
Shediac
Cape Tormentine
Montague
Georgetown
Port Hood
Deschaillons
Cap-de-la-Madeleine
Plessisville
Beauceville
St-Georges
Hartland
Woodstock
Houlton
Minto
Grand L.
Moncton
Chipman
Petitcodiac
Murray Hr.
Northumberland Str.
Hawkesbury
St. Peters
I. Madame
Chedabucto B.
Canso
Victoriaville
Thetford Mines
Chamberlain L.
Chesuncook L.
Patten
St. John
Oromocto
Fredericton
Sackville
Amherst
Springhill
New Glasgow
Stellarton
Pictou
Antigonish
Mulgrave
Sherbrooke
Asbestos
Lac-Mégantic
Moosehead L.
Millinocket
Fredericton Junc.
Sussex
Hampton
Parrsboro
Rothesay
Chignecto B.
Minas Basin
Truro
Stewiacke
NOVA SCOTIA
Upper Musquodoboit
Jackman
East Angus
Sherbrooke
Magog
Coaticook
Greenville
Lincoln
MAINE
St. Stephen
St. George
Saint John
Kentville
Windsor
Enfield
Sheet Harbour
Musquodoboit Harbour
ATLANTIC OCEAN
Dover-Foxcroft
Calais
Eastport
Blacks Hr.
Grand Manan I.
Bay of Fundy
Bridgetown
Middleton
Annapolis Royal
Digby
Middle Sackville
Dartmouth
Halifax
Bingham
Moosehead-meguntic L.
Old Town
Brewer
Bangor
Machias
Newport
Island Pond
Skowhegan
Waterville
Ellsworth
KEJIMKUJIK NAT. PARK
Mahone Bay
Lunenburg
Sable I. (Nova Scotia)
Berlin
Rumford
St. Johnsbury
Augusta
Belfast
Bar Harbor
Mount Desert I.
Weymouth
Rossignol L.
Milton
Bridgewater
Liverpool
Norway
Auburn
Lewiston
Camden
Rockland
Brunswick
Bath
St. Mary's Bay
Conway
Sebago L.
Yarmouth
Wedgeport
Shelburne
Lockeport
Portland
Clark's Harbour
C. Sable
Hanover
Laconia
Sanford
Saco
Biddeford
Rochester
Concord
Dover
Portsmouth
Keene
Manchester
Nashua
Haverhill
Fitchburg
Lawrence
Gloucester
Greenfield
Lowell
Lynn
Newton
BOSTON
Quincy
Brockton
C. Cod
Worcester
Woonsocket
NEW HAMPSHIRE
MASS.
UNITED STATES

55 50 45

70 65 60 55 50

West from Greenwich

6 7 8

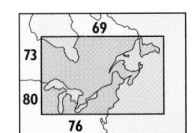

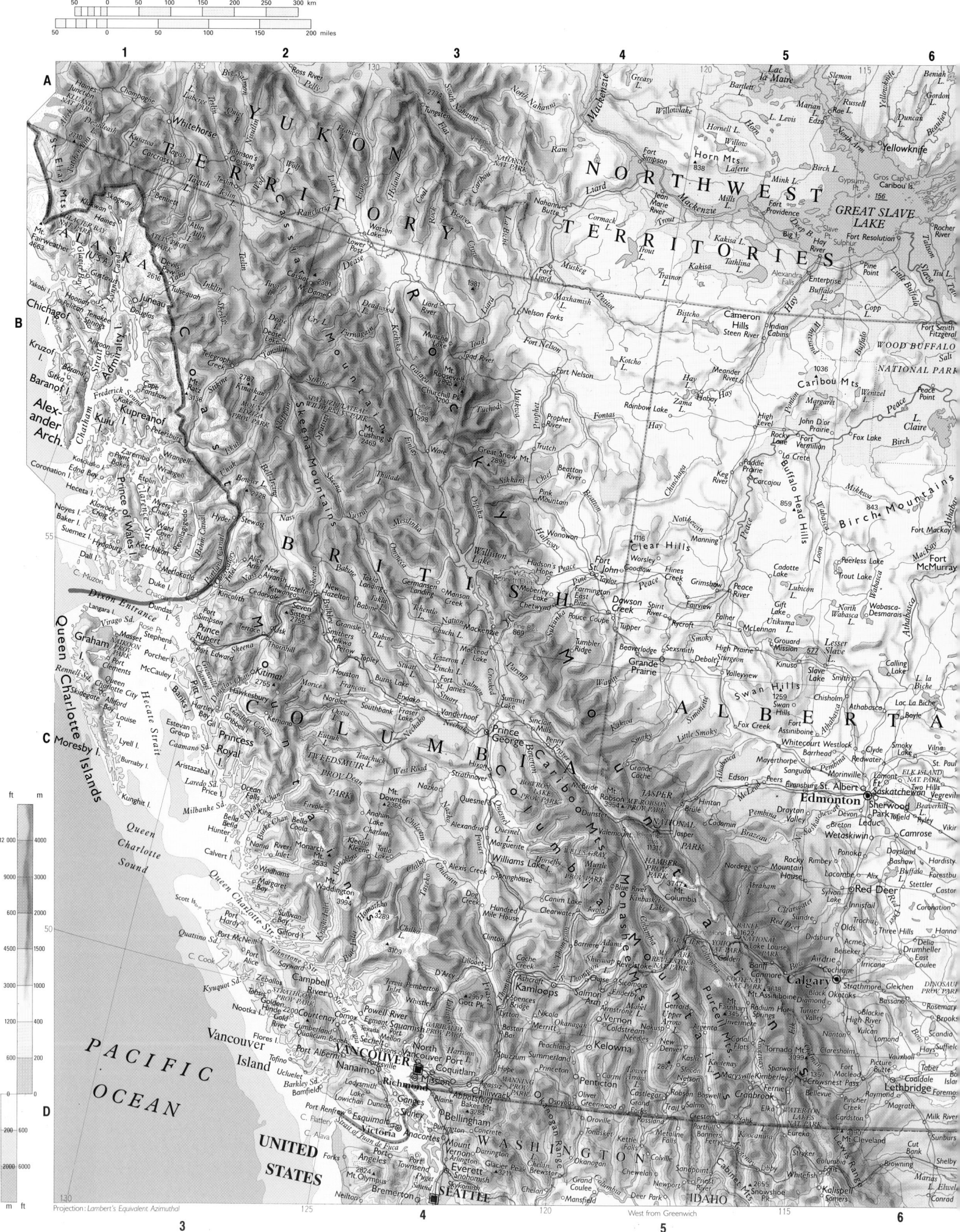

km
miles
YUKON TERRITORY
NORTHWEST TERRITORIES
BRITISH COLUMBIA
ALBERTA
ALASKA (U.S.A.)
WASHINGTON
IDAHO
UNITED STATES
PACIFIC OCEAN
GREAT SLAVE LAKE
WOOD BUFFALO NATIONAL PARK
Queen Charlotte Sound
Queen Charlotte Islands
Vancouver Island
Alexander Arch.
Chichagof I.
Baranof I.
Kupreanof I.
Prince of Wales I.
Dixon Entrance
Hecate Strait
Coast Mountains
Skeena Mountains
Cassiar Mountains
Rocky Mountains
Cariboo Mts.
Monashee Mts.
Columbia Mts.
Selkirk Mts.
Purcell Mts.
Caribou Mts.
Birch Mountains
Swan Hills
Clear Hills
Horn Mts.
Whitehorse
Yellowknife
Juneau
Prince Rupert
Prince George
Kamloops
Kelowna
VANCOUVER
Victoria
SEATTLE
Edmonton
Calgary
Red Deer
Lethbridge
Grande Prairie
Peace River
Dawson Creek
Fort St. John
Fort Nelson
Projection: Lambert's Equivalent Azimuthal
West from Greenwich

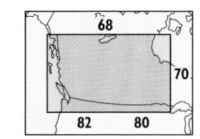

A

B

C

D

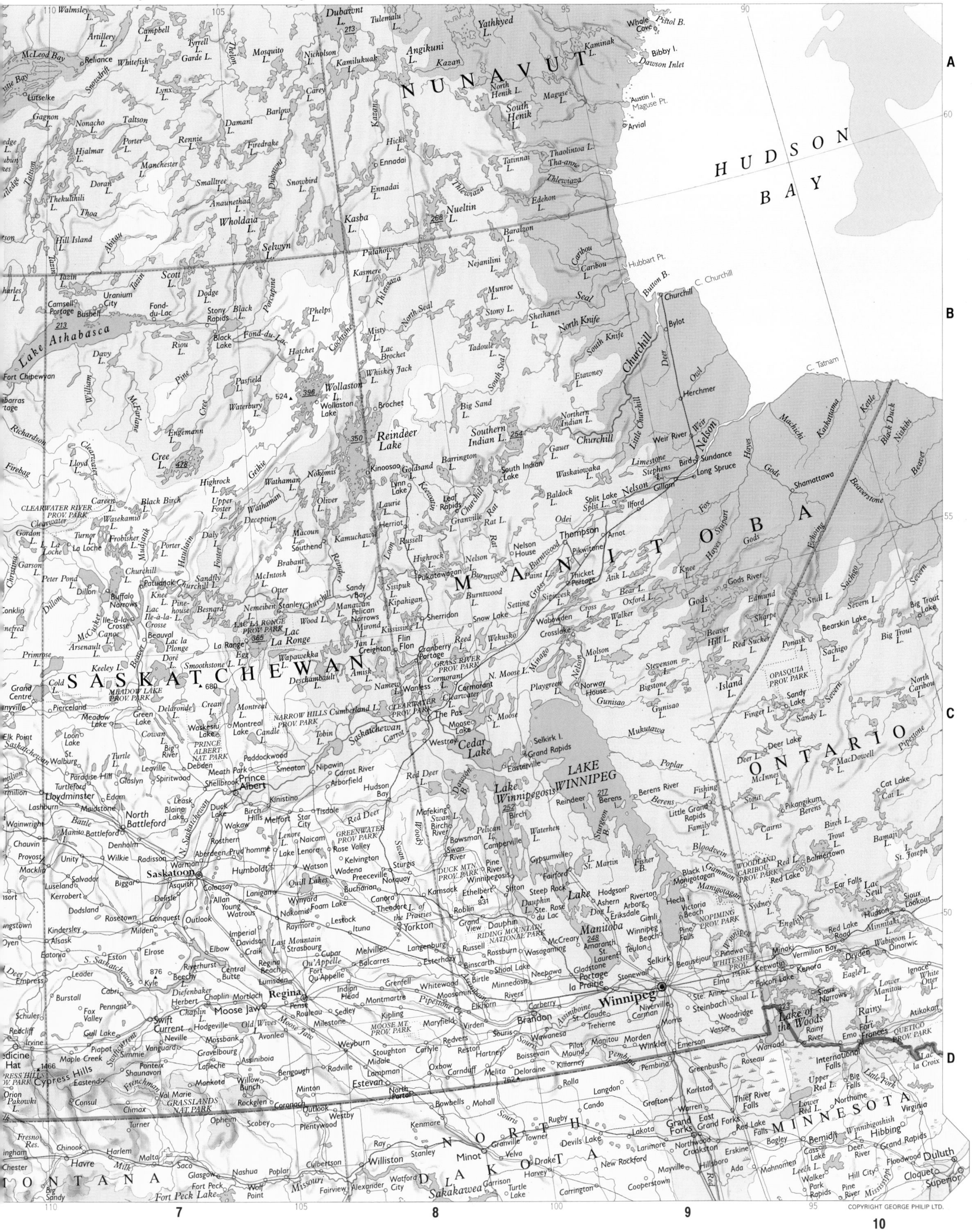

7   8   9   10   11

NUNAVUT

HUDSON BAY

MANITOBA

SASKATCHEWAN

ONTARIO

MINNESOTA

NORTH DAKOTA

MONTANA

Lake Athabasca

Reindeer Lake

Wollaston L.

LAKE WINNIPEG

Lake Winnipegosis

Cedar Lake

Lake of the Woods

Churchill

Winnipeg

Regina

Saskatoon

Prince Albert

Moose Jaw

Brandon

Thompson

The Pas

Flin Flon

La Ronge

Swift Current

Medicine Hat

Lloydminster

North Battleford

Dauphin

Portage la Prairie

Selkirk

Kenora

Dryden

Grand Forks

Minot

Williston

Duluth

Superior

RIDING MOUNTAIN NATIONAL PARK

PRINCE ALBERT NAT. PARK

GRASSLANDS NAT. PARK

CYPRESS HILLS PROV. PARK

QUETICO PROV. PARK

LA RONGE PROV. PARK

GRASS RIVER PROV. PARK

CLEARWATER RIVER PROV. PARK

MEADOW LAKE PROV. PARK

NARROW HILLS PROV. PARK

GREENWATER PROV. PARK

DUCK MTN. PROV. PARK

MOOSE MT. PROV. PARK

WOODLAND CARIBOU PROV. PARK

NOPIMING PROV. PARK

WHITESHELL PROV. PARK

OPASQUIA PROV. PARK

UNITED STATES 1:12 000 000

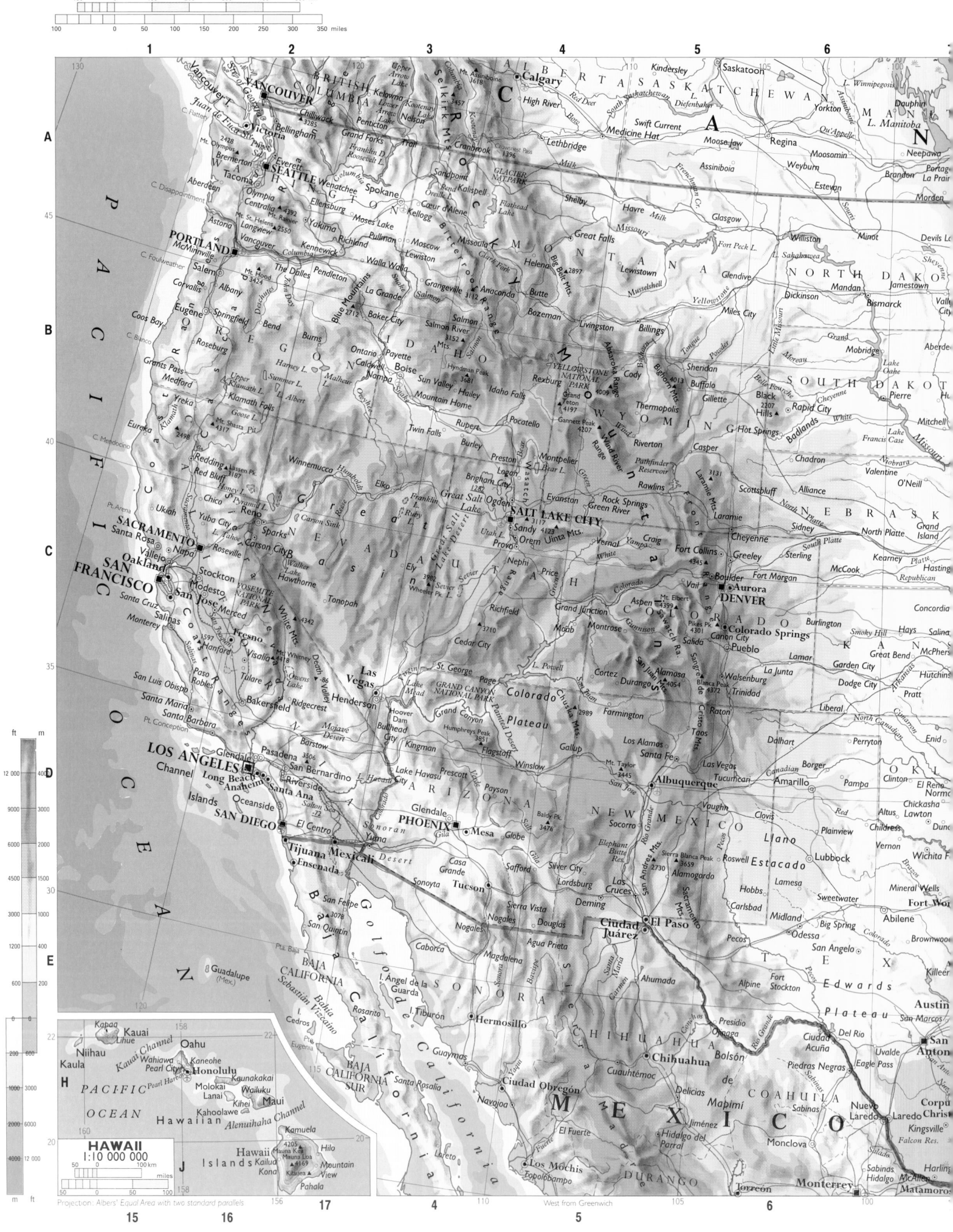

1 2 3 4 5 6
A B C D E H J
15 16 17 4 5 6
BRITISH COLUMBIA
ALBERTA
SASKATCHEWAN
CANADA
VANCOUVER
Victoria
Calgary
Saskatoon
Regina
Lethbridge
Medicine Hat
Swift Current
Moose Jaw
SEATTLE
Tacoma
Olympia
Spokane
Yakima
PORTLAND
Salem
Eugene
Boise
Idaho Falls
Pocatello
Helena
Great Falls
Billings
Butte
Missoula
MONTANA
WYOMING
IDAHO
OREGON
NEVADA
UTAH
COLORADO
ARIZONA
NEW MEXICO
NORTH DAKOTA
SOUTH DAKOTA
NEBRASKA
KANSAS
TEXAS
MEXICO
PACIFIC OCEAN
Bismarck
Pierre
Rapid City
Cheyenne
Casper
SALT LAKE CITY
Ogden
Provo
Great Salt Lake
Reno
Carson City
SACRAMENTO
SAN FRANCISCO
Oakland
San Jose
Fresno
Bakersfield
LOS ANGELES
SAN DIEGO
Las Vegas
PHOENIX
Tucson
Albuquerque
Santa Fe
El Paso
Ciudad Juárez
DENVER
Colorado Springs
Pueblo
Amarillo
Lubbock
Hermosillo
Chihuahua
Tijuana
Mexicali
Yellowstone National Park
Grand Canyon National Park
Great Basin
Colorado Plateau
Rocky Mountains
Llano Estacado
Edwards Plateau
Baja California
Golfo de California
HAWAII
1:10 000 000
Kauai
Oahu
Honolulu
Molokai
Maui
Lanai
Hawaii
Hilo
Projection: Albers' Equal Area with two standard parallels
West from Greenwich

68
69
86
87

8 9 10 11 12 13
A
B
C
D
E
F
CANADA
Lake Winnipeg
Lake Superior
Lake Michigan
Lake Huron
Lake Erie
Lake Ontario
MINNEAPOLIS
ST. PAUL
MILWAUKEE
CHICAGO
DETROIT
TORONTO
BUFFALO
CLEVELAND
MONTREAL
Ottawa
Québec
BOSTON
HARTFORD
NEW YORK
PHILADELPHIA
BALTIMORE
WASHINGTON D.C.
PITTSBURGH
COLUMBUS
INDIANAPOLIS
CINCINNATI
KANSAS CITY
ST. LOUIS
Memphis
Nashville
CHARLOTTE
ATLANTA
Birmingham
DALLAS
HOUSTON
NEW ORLEANS
Jacksonville
TAMPA
MIAMI
BAHAMAS
ATLANTIC OCEAN
GULF OF MEXICO
Straits of Florida
95 90 85 80 75
45 40 35 30 25
8 9 10 11 12

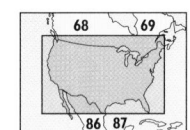

EASTERN UNITED STATES 1:6 000 000

50 0 50 100 150 200 km
50 0 50 100 150 miles
NEW YORK CITY
PHILADELPHIA
BALTIMORE
WASHINGTON D.C.
BOSTON
HARTFORD
MONTRÉAL
Québec
Ottawa
TORONTO
BUFFALO
PITTSBURGH
CLEVELAND
DETROIT
COLUMBUS
CINCINNATI
INDIANAPOLIS
CHICAGO
MILWAUKEE
LAKE ONTARIO
LAKE ERIE
LAKE HURON
LAKE MICHIGAN
LAKE SUPERIOR
Georgian Bay
Chesapeake Bay
Delaware Bay
ONTARIO
QUÉBEC
NEW YORK
PENNSYLVANIA
OHIO
INDIANA
MICHIGAN
WISCONSIN
ILLINOIS
KENTUCKY
WEST VIRGINIA
VIRGINIA
MARYLAND
DELAWARE
NEW JERSEY
VERMONT
NEW HAMPSHIRE
MASS.

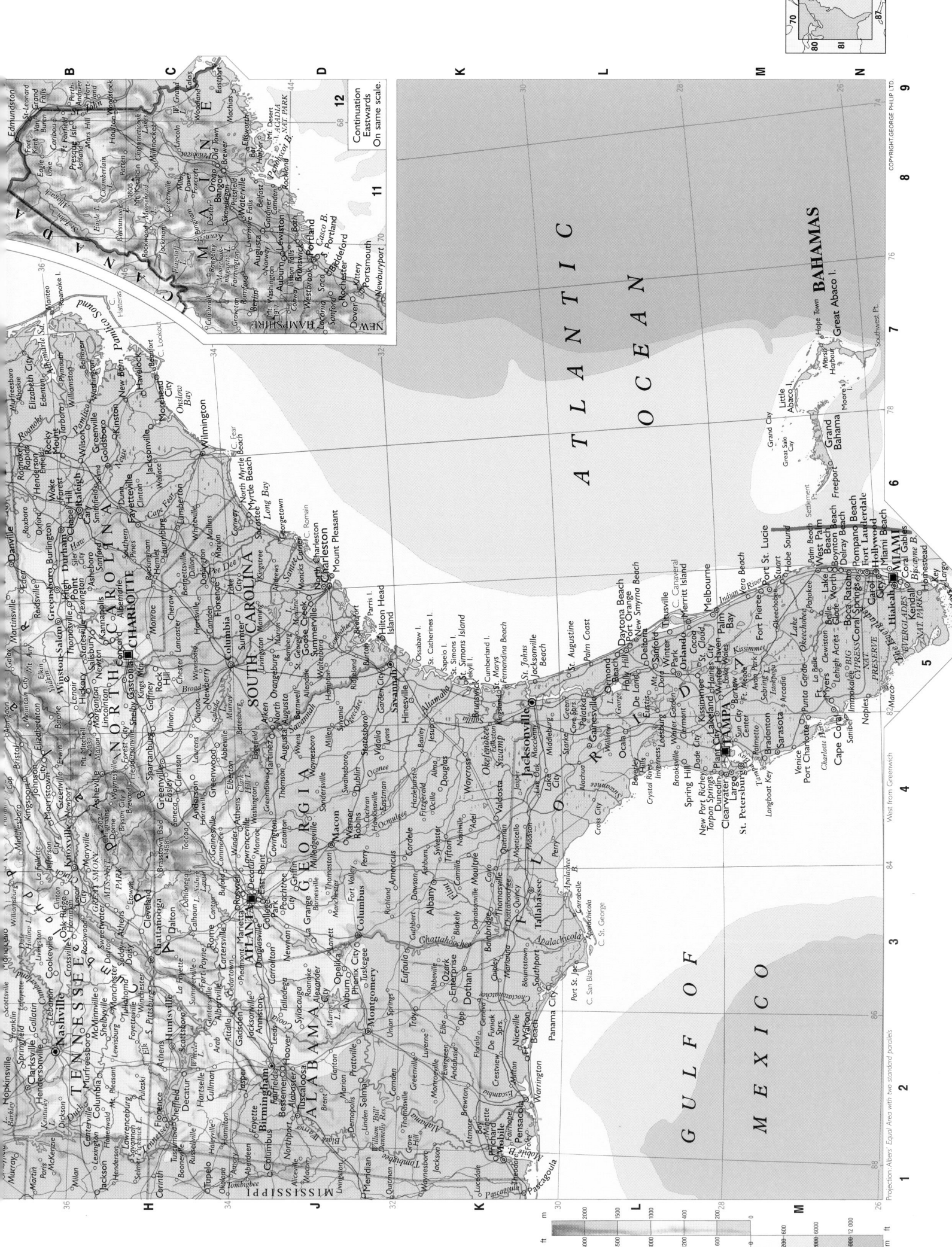

Continuation Eastwards
On same scale.

ATLANTIC OCEAN

GULF OF MEXICO

BAHAMAS

Projection: Albers' Equal Area with two standard parallels

COPYRIGHT GEORGE PHILIP LTD.

West from Greenwich

10 0 10 20 30 40 50 60 70 80 90 km
10 0 10 20 30 40 50 60 miles
Georgian Bay
Lucas Channel
Bruce Peninsula
LAKE HURON
176
208
Thunder Bay
Nottawasaga Bay
L. Simcoe
L. Muskoka
LAKE ONTARIO
75
LAKE ERIE
174
Long Pt.
64
Long Point Bay
L. St. Clair
MICHIGAN
OHIO
PENNSYLVANIA
NEW
CANADA
ONTARIO
Allegheny Plateau
Allegheny Mountains
Tussey Mountains
Tuscarora Mts.
TORONTO
Mississauga
Brampton
Oakville
Burlington
Hamilton
St. Catharines
Niagara Falls
Welland
Port Colborne
Fort Erie
BUFFALO
Lackawanna
Barrie
Orillia
Owen Sound
Kitchener
Waterloo
Guelph
Cambridge
Brantford
London
St. Thomas
Sarnia
Port Huron
Chatham
Windsor
DETROIT
Oshawa
Whitby
Ajax
Markham
Peterborough
Belleville
Rochester
Irondequoit
Erie
Jamestown
Olean
CLEVELAND
Lakewood
Euclid
Cleveland Heights
Parma
Lorain
Elyria
Akron
Canton
Youngstown
Warren
PITTSBURGH
Penn Hills
Altoona
State College
Johnstown
Steubenville
Wheeling
Projection: Bonne

QUÉBEC

VERMONT

NEW HAMPSHIRE

MAINE

MASSACHUSETTS

RHODE ISLAND

CONNECTICUT

NEW YORK

NEW JERSEY

ATLANTIC OCEAN

West from Greenwich

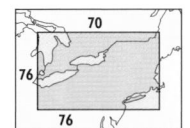

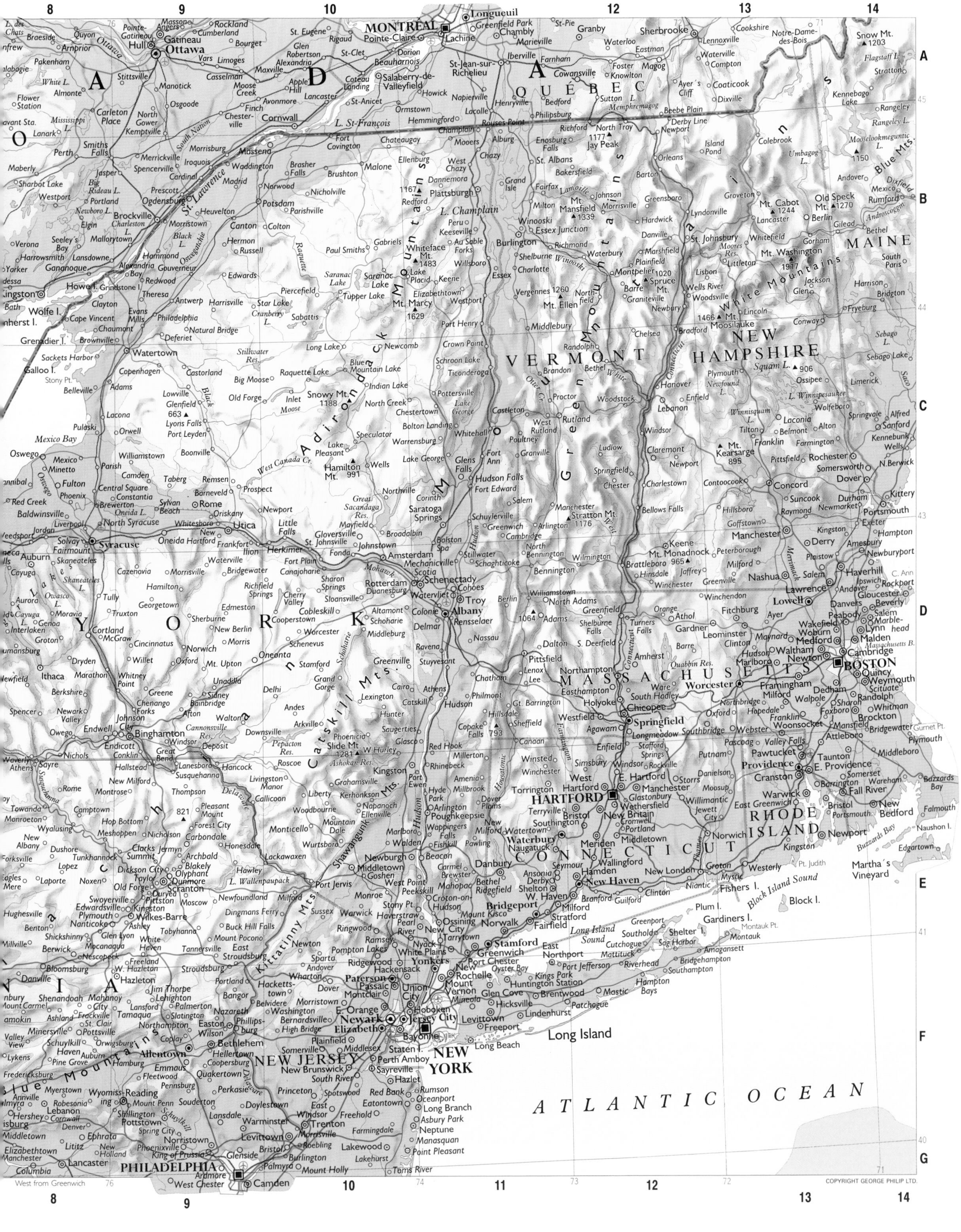

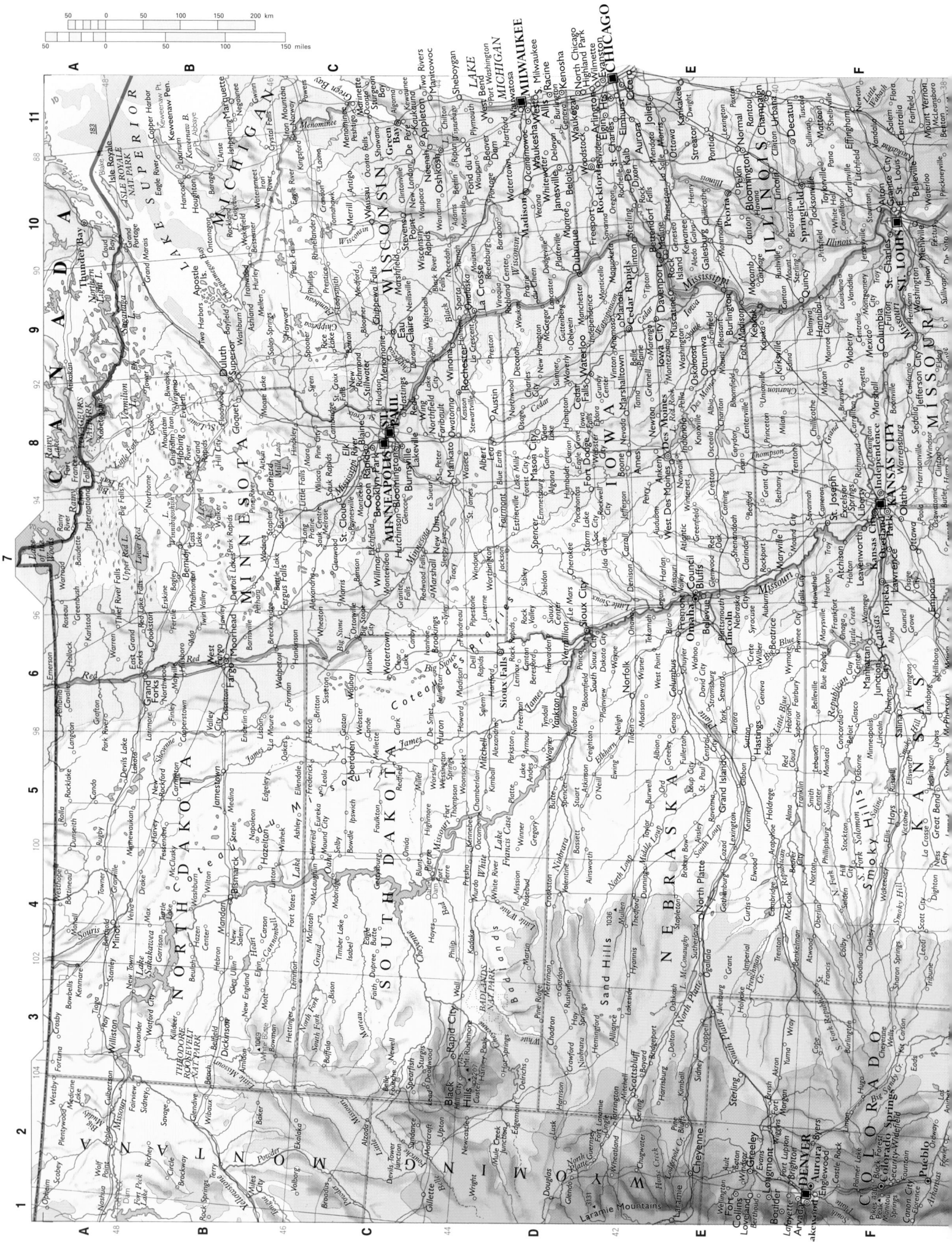
50 0 50 100 150 200 km
50 0 50 100 150 miles
CANADA
NORTH DAKOTA
SOUTH DAKOTA
NEBRASKA
KANSAS
MINNESOTA
IOWA
WISCONSIN
ILLINOIS
MISSOURI
MONTANA
WYOMING
COLORADO
LAKE SUPERIOR
LAKE MICHIGAN
MILWAUKEE
CHICAGO
MINNEAPOLIS
ST. PAUL
KANSAS CITY
ST. LOUIS
DENVER
Omaha
Des Moines
Sioux Falls
Bismarck
Fargo
Duluth
Madison
Lincoln
Topeka
Cheyenne
Sand Hills
Black Hills
Smoky Hills
Badlands
Laramie Mountains
Coteau des Prairies
Missouri
Mississippi
Platte
Red

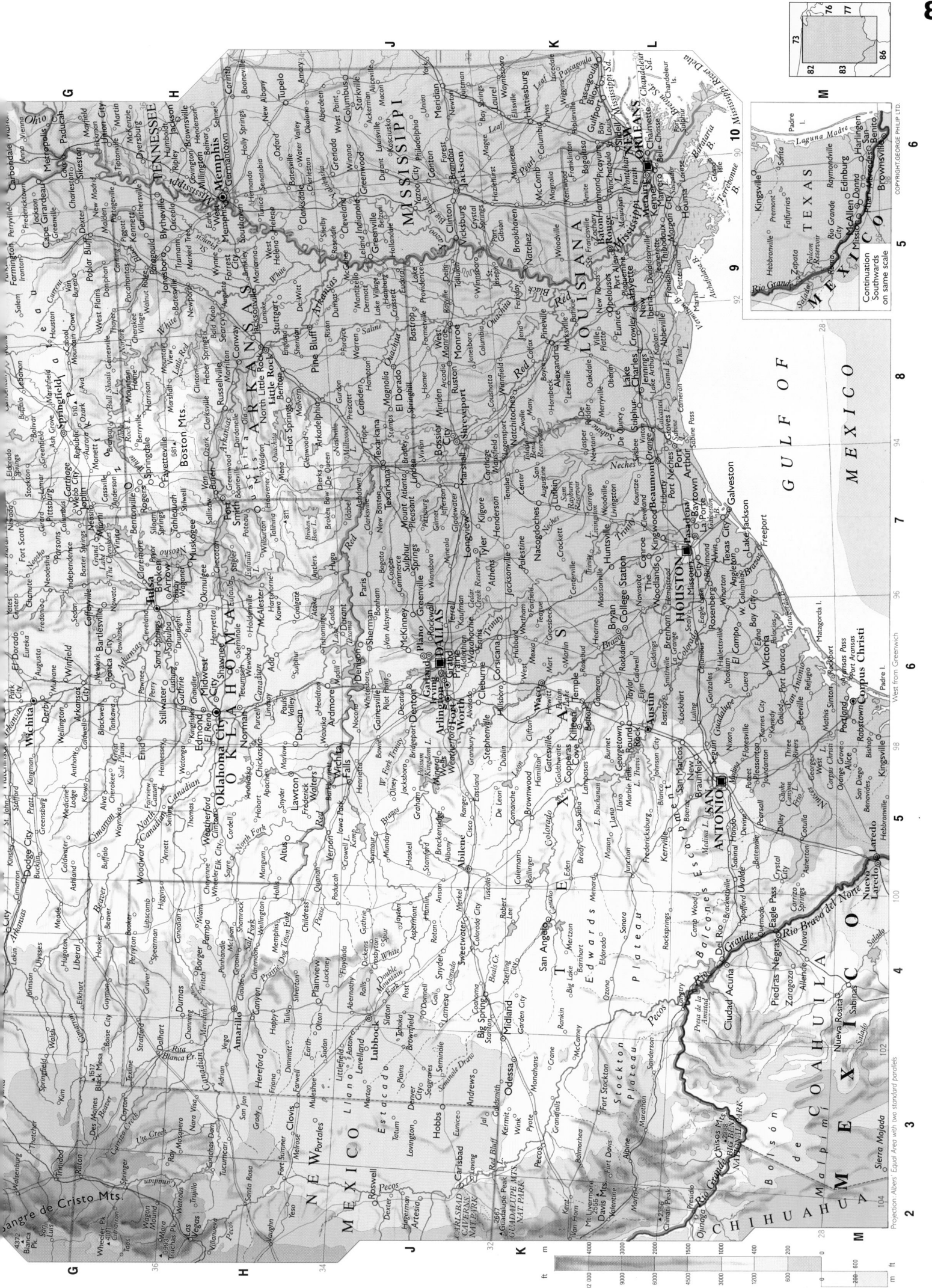
OKLAHOMA
ARKANSAS
TEXAS
LOUISIANA
MISSISSIPPI
TENNESSEE
NEW MEXICO
MEXICO
COAHUILA
CHIHUAHUA
GULF OF MEXICO
Ozark Plateau
Ouachita Mts.
Boston Mts.
Sangre de Cristo Mts.
Llano Estacado
Edwards Plateau
Stockton Plateau
Balcones Escarpment
Bolsón de Mapimí
Sierra Mojada
Chisos Mts.
BIG BEND NATIONAL PARK
GUADALUPE MTS. NAT. PARK
CARLSBAD CAVERNS NAT. PARK
Davis Mts.
Wichita
Tulsa
Oklahoma City
Dallas
Fort Worth
Arlington
Houston
San Antonio
Austin
Memphis
Little Rock
Shreveport
New Orleans
Baton Rouge
Jackson
Lubbock
Amarillo
Abilene
Midland
Odessa
Corpus Christi
Laredo
Galveston
Beaumont
Waco
Springfield
Mississippi
Red
Arkansas
Canadian
Brazos
Colorado
Pecos
Rio Grande
Sabine
Ouachita
White
Mississippi River Delta
TEXAS
MEXICO
Continuation Southwards on same scale
Kingsville
Brownsville
McAllen
Harlingen
Laguna Madre
Padre I.
73
76
77
82
83
86
Projection: Albers' Equal Area with two standard parallels
West from Greenwich
COPYRIGHT GEORGE PHILIP LTD.
ft
m
12 000
9000
6000
4500
3000
1200
600
0
200
4000
3000
2000
1500
1000
400
200
0
600
G
H
J
K
L
M
2
3
4
5
6
7
8
9
10

50 0 50 100 150 200 km
50 0 50 100 150 miles
BRITISH COLUMBIA
ALBERTA
SASKATCHEWAN
WASHINGTON
OREGON
IDAHO
MONTANA
WYOMING
NEVADA
UTAH
VANCOUVER
SEATTLE
PORTLAND
SACRAMENTO
SALT LAKE CITY
Spokane
Boise
Helena
Billings
Great Falls
Missoula
Butte
Salem
Eugene
Bend
Reno
Pocatello
Idaho Falls
Ogden
Casper
Laramie
Great Salt Lake
Great Salt Lake Desert
Bighorn Mountains
Absaroka Range
Salmon River Mountains
Sawtooth Range
Blue Mountains
Cascade Range
Rocky Mountains
Uinta Mountains
Medicine Bow Mts.
Columbia Basin
Olympic Mts.
Strait of Juan de Fuca
Puget Sound
Lethbridge
Medicine Hat
Swift Current
Cranbrook
Kalispell
Lewiston
Walla Walla
Yakima
Tacoma
Olympia
Bellingham
Medford
Klamath Falls
Redding
Elko
Twin Falls
Rock Springs
Provo

PACIFIC OCEAN
BAJA CALIFORNIA
Golfo de California
ARIZONA
NEW MEXICO
COLORADO
TEXAS
SONORA
CHIHUAHUA
MEXICO
LOS ANGELES
SAN DIEGO
PHOENIX
Tucson
Albuquerque
El Paso
Ciudad Juárez
Hermosillo
Chihuahua
Mexicali
Tijuana
Las Vegas
Colorado Plateau
Sangre de Cristo Mts.
San Juan Mts.
Sacramento Mts.
Mojave Desert
Sonoran Desert
Desierto de Altar
Death Valley
Grand Canyon
Channel Is.
Isla Guadalupe (Mexico)
West from Greenwich
Projection: Albers' Equal Area with two standard parallels
COPYRIGHT.GEORGE PHILIP LTD.

10 0 10 20 30 40 50 60 70 80 90 km

10 0 10 20 30 40 50 60 miles

82 83 86

H J K L M

N E V A D A

A R I Z O N A

C A L I F O R N I A

M E X I C O

BAJA CALIFORNIA

P A C I F I C O C E A N

M o j a v e D e s e r t

Sonoran Desert

Channel Islands

Las Vegas
Henderson
North Las Vegas
Boulder City
Lake Mead
Meadow Valley Wash
Overton
Logandale
Moapa
Jumbo Pk. 1757
LAKE MEAD NATIONAL RECREATION AREA
Hoover Dam
Colorado
Lake Mohave
Mt. Tipton 2179
Chloride
Kingman
Davis Dam
Bullhead City
Riviera
Oatman
Laughlin
Searchlight
Nelson
Alunite
Arden
Sloan
Jean
McCullough Mt. 2142
Potosi Mt. 2504
Goodsprings
Charleston Peak
Mt. Charleston 3633
Pahrump
Indian Springs
Mercury
Johnnie
Lathrop Wells
Death Valley Junction
Shoshone
Tecopa
Kingston Pk. 2232
Sandy Valley
Nipton
Mountain Pass 1442
Valley Wells
MOJAVE NATIONAL RESERVE
Cima
Providence Mts.
Essex
Needles
Topock
Yucca
Lake Havasu City
Lake Havasu
Parker Dam
Parker
Alamo Crossing
Signal
Wenden
Salome
Hope
Bouse
Vicksburg
Quartzsite
Poston
Vidal Junction
Vidal
Rice
Colorado River Aqueduct
Sonoran 1315
Signal Pk. 1487
Ehrenberg
Blythe
Ripley
Midland
Palo Verde
Cibola
Imperial Dam
Yuma
Winterhaven
Ogilby
Glamis
Chocolate Mts.
Desert Center
Eagle Mountain
Danby L.
Cadiz L.
Cadiz
Amboy
Bristol L.
Bagdad
Ludlow
Soda Lake
Baker
Silver Lake
Avawatz Mts. 1876
Amargosa Range
Pyramid Pk. 2043
Death Valley
Amargosa
DEATH VALLEY NATIONAL MONUMENT
Stovepipe Wells
Panamint Ra.
Telescope Pk. 3366
Wildrose
Panamint Springs
Darwin
Coso Pk. 2487
Coso Junction
Little Lake
Olancha
Olancha Pk. 3695
Searles L.
Argus Pk. 2800
Trona
Westend
China Lake
Ridgecrest
Johannesburg
Red Mountain
Atolia
Randsburg
Cantil
California City
Boron
Rogers L.
Edwards
Mojave
Rosamond
Fort Irwin
Newberry Springs
Yermo
Barstow
Daggett
Lenwood
Helendale
Hi Vista
Oro Grande
Adelanto
Victorville
Apple Valley
Lucerne Valley
Hesperia
Twentynine Palms
Old Dale
JOSHUA TREE NATIONAL PARK
Joshua Tree
Yucca Valley
Morongo Valley
San Bernardino Mts.
Big Bear Lake
Big Bear City
San Gorgonio Mt. 3505
Fawnskin
Crestline
San Bernardino
Redlands
Loma Linda
Banning
Desert Hot Springs
Cabazon
San Jacinto 3293
Palm Springs
Palm Desert
Indio
Coachella
Mecca
Toro Pk. 2637
Coachella Canal
Niland
Calipatria
Salton City
Salton Sea -72
Oasis
Westmorland
Brawley
Imperial Valley
Imperial
Holtville
El Centro
Heber
Calexico
Mexicali
Midway Wells
Plaster City
Mount Signal
San Felipe
Borrego Springs
Coyote Wells
Agua Caliente Springs
La Rumorosa
Mount Laguna
Jacumba
Tecate
El Compadre
Valle de las Palmas
Pine Valley
Alpine
Granite Mt. 1717
Julian
Santa Ysabel
Ramona
Anza
Mountain Center
Aguanga
Hemet
San Jacinto
Moreno Valley
Riverside
Perris
Sun City
Temecula
Lake Elsinore
Murrieta
Pala
Pauma Valley
Valley Center
Escondido
Poway
San Marcos
Vista
Oceanside
Bonsall
Fallbrook
Santa Margarita
Mission Viejo
San Juan Capistrano
San Clemente
San Onofre
Laguna Beach
Irvine
Costa Mesa
Santa Ana
Orange
Corona
Norco
Chino
Pomona
Fontana
Rancho Cucamonga
Ontario
Claremont
Mt. San Antonio 3068
San Gabriel Mts.
Wrightwood
Pinon Hills
Pearblossom
Palmdale
Lancaster
Lake Hughes
Fairmont
Santa Clarita
San Fernando
Glendale
Pasadena
Alhambra
Azusa
El Monte
W. Covina
Diamond Bar
Fullerton
Anaheim
Whittier
Buena Park
Garden Grove
Huntington Beach
Newport Beach
Long Beach
Norwalk
Downey
Compton
Carson
Torrance
Inglewood
Redondo Beach
Palos Verdes Estates
Pt. Palos Verdes
Santa Monica
Beverly Hills
Burbank
LOS ANGELES
Malibu
Thousand Oaks
Simi Valley
Moorpark
Camarillo
Oxnard
Port Hueneme
Ventura
Santa Paula
Fillmore
Ojai
Oak View
Carpinteria
Montecito
Santa Barbara
Goleta
Isla Vista
SANTA MONICA MTS. NAT. REC. AREA
Santa Barbara Channel
San Pedro Channel
Santa Catalina I.
Avalon
San Clemente I.
Santa Barbara I.
San Nicolas I.
Santa Cruz I.
Santa Rosa I.
San Miguel I.
CHANNEL ISLANDS NATIONAL PARK
Pt. Conception
Pt. Arguello
Jalama
Lompoc
Vandenberg
Surf
Gaviota
Buellton
Solvang
Santa Ynez
Los Olivos
Los Alamos
Santa Maria
Orcutt
Casmalia
Guadalupe
Oceano
Grover City
Pismo Beach
Avila Beach
Arroyo Grande
Nipomo
Huasna
Twitchell Reservoir
Garey
San Luis Obispo
Pozo
San Rafael Mts.
San Rafael Mt. 2010
McPherson Pk. 1792
Mt. Pinos 2692
Ventucopa
New Cuyama
Maricopa
Taft
Ford City
Tupman
Buttonwillow
McKittrick
Blackwells Corner
Temblor Range
Simmler
Stauffer
Lebec
Gorman
1275
Wheeler Ridge
Tehachapi Mts.
Tehachapi
Cummings Mt. 2363
Arvin
Lamont
Keene
Caliente
Monolith
Los Angeles Aqueduct
Bakersfield
Hillcrest Center
Oildale
Famosa
McFarland
Delano
Woody
Alta Sierra
Lake Isabella
Kernville
Fountain Springs
California Hot Springs
Johnsondale
Sirretta Pk. 3035
Onyx
Inyokern
Freeman
Wasco
Shafter
Greenfield
Buena Vista L.
Pond
Kern
Leucadia
Encinitas
Cardiff-by-the-Sea
Del Mar
Carlsbad
Gulf of Santa Catalina
La Mesa
Santee
Lakeside
El Cajon
Spring Valley
Lemon Grove
National City
SAN DIEGO
Coronado
Chula Vista
Imperial Beach
Tijuana
Agua Caliente
Las Palmas
Is. los Coronados
Rosarito
Pta. Descanso
El Descanso
Misión
Guadalupe

West from Greenwich

Projection: Bonne

m 4000 3000 2000 1500 1000 400 200 0
ft 12 000 9000 6000 4500 3000 1200 600 0

m 0 200 2000
ft 0 600 6000

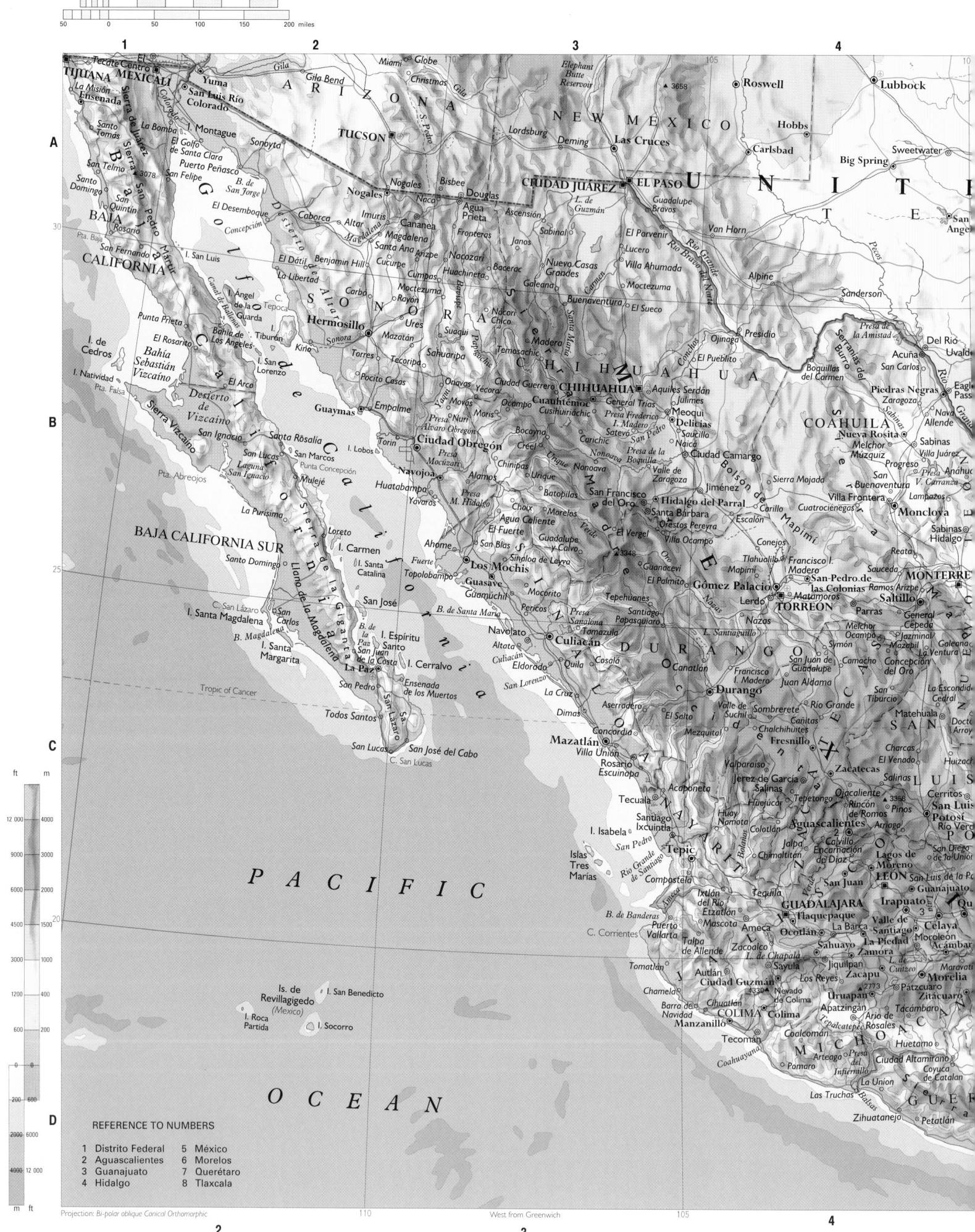

REFERENCE TO NUMBERS

1 Distrito Federal
2 Aguascalientes
3 Guanajuato
4 Hidalgo
5 México
6 Morelos
7 Querétaro
8 Tlaxcala

Projection: Bi-polar oblique Conical Orthomorphic

West from Greenwich

5 6 7 8

A B C D E

UNITED STATES
TEXAS
ARKANSAS
LOUISIANA
MISSISSIPPI
ALABAMA
GEORGIA
FLORIDA

Wichita Falls
Denison
Sherman
Paris
Hope
Camden
Texarkana
El Dorado
Greenville
Tuscaloosa
Opelika
Columbus
McRae
Denton
Greenville
Possum Kingdom Res.
Brazos
FORT WORTH
DALLAS
Marshall
Longview
Monroe
Vicksburg
Jackson
Meridian
Selma
Phenix City
Montgomery
Americus
Cordele
Albany
Tifton
Troy
Waycross
Ranger
Abilene
Cleburne
Tyler
Shreveport
Tallulah
Hillsboro
Corsicana
Palestine
Toledo Bend Res.
Natchez
Laurel
Hattiesburg
Flomaton
Dothan
Jim Woodruff Res.
Valdosta
Chattahoochee
Tallahassee
Brownwood
Waco
Nacogdoches
Lufkin
Sam Rayburn Reservoir
Jewett
Alexandria
McComb
MOBILE
Pensacola
Panama City
Lake City
Temple
Huntsville
Bryan
Baton Rouge
Hammond
Bogalusa
Biloxi
Gulfport
Apalachee Bay
Navasota
Austin
Beaumont
Lake Charles
Lafayette
L. Pontchartrain
NEW ORLEANS
Breton Sd.
Mobile Bay
C. San Blas
Suwannee
HOUSTON
Port Arthur
Atchafalaya Bay
Terrebonne Bay
Mississippi River Delta
Galveston
Rosenberg
SAN ANTONIO
Victoria
Guadalupe
Clearwater
Dilley
Nueces
Alice
Corpus Christi
Kingsville
Laredo
Nuevo Laredo
Zapata
Presa Falcón
Laguna Madre
Camargo
McAllen
Harlingen
Brownsville
Reynosa
Matamoros
Presa M.R. Gomez
China
Valle Hermoso
Santa Teresa
Laguna Madre
Montemorelos
Mendez
San Fernando
Linares
Villagrán
Hidalgo
Santander Jiménez
TAMAULIPAS
Zaragoza
La Pesca
Soto la Marina
Ciudad Victoria
Sierra de Tamaulipas
Llera
Aldama
Pta. Jerez
Ocampo
Ciudad Mante
Altamira
Ciudad Madero
Tampico
Ciudad de Valles
Pánuco
L. de Tamiahua
C. Rojo
Ozuluama
Tempoal
Tantoyuca
Tamazunchale
Chicontepec
Tuxpan
Poza Rica
Papantla
Zimapán
Zacualtipán
San Juan del Río
Huichapan
Pachuca
Huauchinango
Nautla
Misantla
Tulancingo
Teziutlán
Jalapa Enríquez
Zempoala
Tula
Zumpango
El Oro
MÉXICO
Apizaco
Veracruz
Toluca
Tlaxcala
PUEBLA
Citlaltépetl 5700
Córdoba
Orizaba
Amecameca
Popocatépetl 5452
Tenango
Cuernavaca
Alvarado
Tlacotalpan
San Andrés Tuxtla
Tehuacán
Cosamaloapan
VERACRUZ
Izúcar de Matamoros
Tres Valles
Acayucan
Coatzacoalcos
Minatitlán
Chilac
Ajalpan
Iguala
Acatlán
Huautla de Jiménez
Presa Miguel Alemán
San Juan Bautista Valle Nacional
Istmo de Tehuantepec
Jesús Carranza
Huajuapan de Leon
Asunción Nochixtlán
Chilapa
Chilpancingo
Silacayoapan
Sierra Madre del Sur
Tlaxiaco
Oaxaca
Tlacolula
Tierra Colorada
OAXACA
Ayutla
Ometepec
Ocotlán
San Jerónimo Taviche
Ejutla
Acapulco
Pinotepa Nacional
Miahuatlán
Tehuantepec
Juchitán
Salina Cruz
Jamiltepec
Tututepec
San Pedro Mixtepec
Pochutla
Puerto Escondido
Puerto Ángel
Punta Maldonado
Golfo de Tehuantepec
Mar Muerto
Arriaga
Tonalá
Matías Romero
Ixtepec
Tuxtla Gutiérrez
CHIAPAS
Chiapa de Corzo
San Cristóbal de las Casas
La Independencia
Comitán
Pijijiapan
Mapastepec
Puerto Arista
Motozintla
Huixtla
Tapachula
Coatepeque
Retalhuleu
La Concordia
Sierra Madre
Presa Netzahualcóyotl
Raudales de Malpaso
Copainalá
Ocosingo
Simojovel
Teapa
Palenque
Villahermosa
Macuspana
Cárdenas
TABASCO
La Venta
Paraíso
Comalcalco
Frontera
Palizada
Ciudad del Carmen
L. de Términos
CAMPECHE
Balancán
Tenosique
Usumacinta
Lacantún
Salinas
Champotón
Chenkán
Campeche
Edzná
Hopelchén
Tenabo
Bolonchenticul
Matamoros
Concepción
Maxcanú
Ticul
Uxmal
Tekax
Peto
Mayapán
Sotuta
Chichén Itzá
Mérida
Dzibilchaltún
Progreso
Motul
Temax
Izamal
Espita
Tizimín
Valladolid
YUCATÁN
Dzilam de Bravo
Pta. Yalkubul
Río Lagartos
El Cuyo
C. Catoche
Cancún
Puerto Juárez
Puerto Morelos
Cozumel
Isla Cozumel
Vigía Chico
B. de la Ascensión
B. del Espíritu Santo
Felipe Carrillo Puerto
QUINTANA ROO
Bacalar
Chetumal
B. de Chetumal
Banco Chinchorro
Corozal
Orange Walk
Hondo
Ambergris Cay
Belize City
BELIZE
Turneffe Is.
Belmopan
Dangriga
Benque Viejo
Maya Mts.
Monkey River
San Antonio
Punta Gorda
Uaxactún
Tikal
San Ignacio
L. Petén Itzá
La Libertad
Flores
San Luis
GUATEMALA
Cuchumatanes
Cobán
Sebol
L. de Izabal
Huehuetenango
Sierra de las Minas
Totonicapán
Sololá
Quetzaltenango
San Marcos
Tajumulco 4220
3993
Utatlán
Antigua
Mazatenango
GUATEMALA
Amatitlán
Jalapa
Chiquimula
Zacapa
Gualán
Livingston
Puerto Barrios
Golfo de Honduras
Santa Bárbara
Santa Rosa de Copán
L. de Yojoa
Comayagua
Tegucigalpa
HONDURAS
San Pedro Sula
El Progreso
Tela
Arenal
Yoro
Olanchito
Juticalpa
Catacamas
Patuca
Sulaco
Danlí
Yuscarán
La Paz
La Esperanza
Is. de la Bahía
Roatán
Puerto Castilla
Trujillo
Iriona
Balfate
Savá
Motagua
GULF OF MEXICO
Golfo de Campeche
Canal de Yucatán
Tropic of Cancer
I. Desterrada
I. Pérez (Mexico)
CUBA
La Esperanza
Guane
La Fé
C. San Antonio
C. Corrientes
SAN LUIS POTOSÍ
Cárdenas
Ciudad Valles
Querétaro
GUERRERO
Taxco
Teloloapan
Balsas
3703
Tecpan de Galeana
Benítez
3139
Papagayo
Verde
Trinidad
Mixteca

100 95 90 85
30 25 20 15

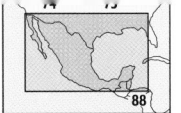

1:8 000 000

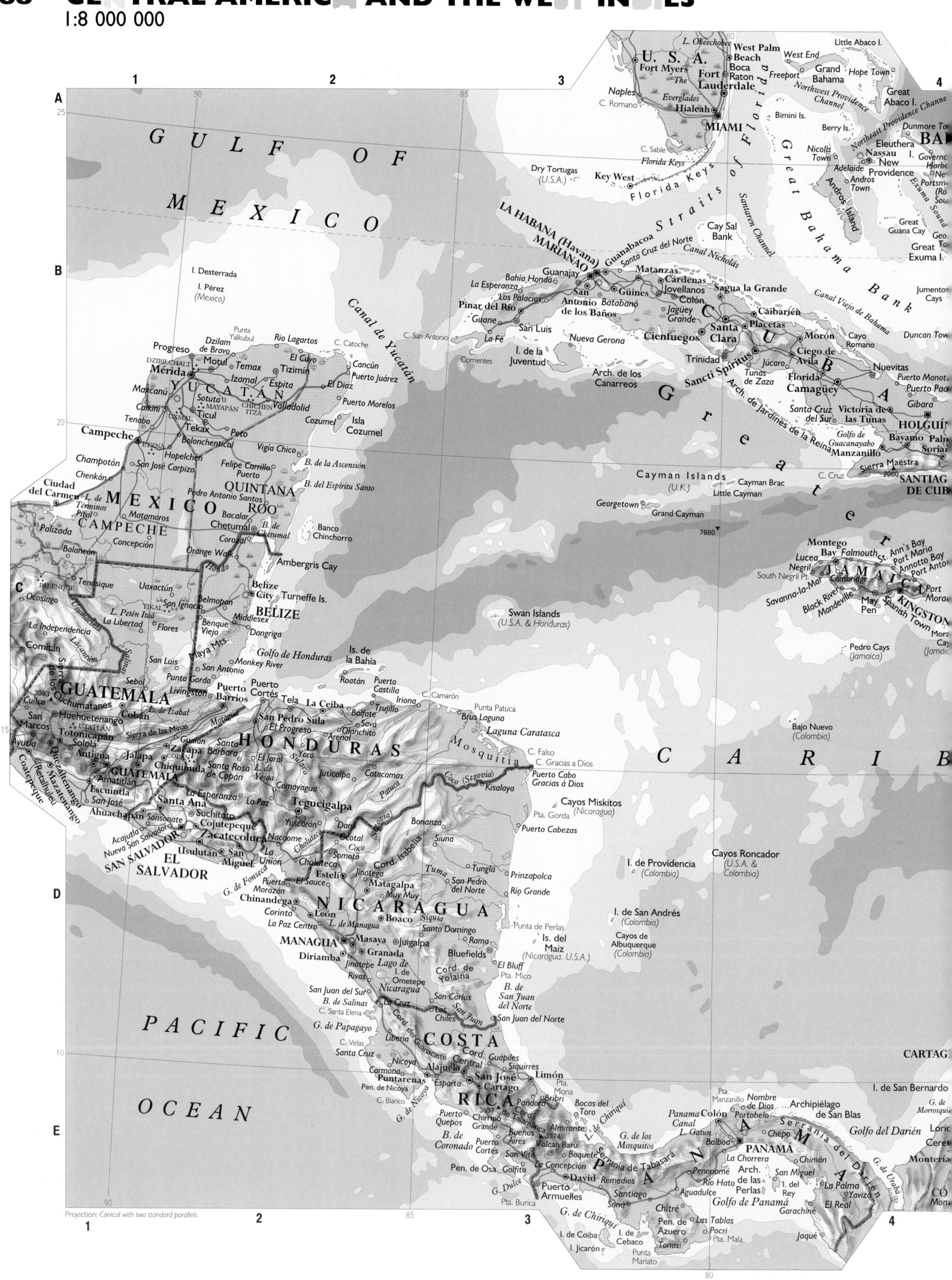

GULF OF MEXICO
MEXICO
YUCATÁN
CAMPECHE
QUINTANA ROO
BELIZE
GUATEMALA
HONDURAS
EL SALVADOR
SAN SALVADOR
NICARAGUA
MANAGUA
COSTA RICA
PANAMÁ
CUBA
JAMAICA
KINGSTON
LA HABANA (Havana)
MARIANAO
U. S. A.
MIAMI
Fort Myers
Fort Lauderdale
West Palm Beach
Boca Raton
Hialeah
Naples
C. Romano
The Everglades
C. Sable
Florida Keys
Key West
Dry Tortugas (U.S.A.)
Straits of Florida
Canal Nicholás
Cay Sal Bank
Santaren Channel
Great Bahama Bank
Grand Bahama
Freeport
West End
Little Abaco I.
Great Abaco I.
Hope Town
Northwest Providence Channel
Northeast Providence Channel
Bimini Is.
Berry Is.
Eleuthera I.
Nassau
New Providence
Andros Island
Andros Town
Nicolls Town
Adelaide
Great Guana Cay
Great Exuma I.
Exuma Sound
Jumentos Cays
Canal Viejo de Bahama
Duncan Town
Guanabacoa
Santa Cruz del Norte
Matanzas
Cárdenas
Jovellanos
Colón
Güines
Batabanó
San Antonio de los Baños
Guanajay
Bahía Honda
La Esperanza
Los Palacios
Pinar del Río
Guane
La Fé
San Luis
C. San Antonio
C. Corrientes
I. de la Juventud
Nueva Gerona
Arch. de los Canarreos
Sagua la Grande
Caibarién
Jagüey Grande
Santa Clara
Placetas
Cienfuegos
Trinidad
Sancti Spíritus
Júcaro
Tunas de Zaza
Morón
Cayo Romano
Ciego de Avila
Florida
Camagüey
Nuevitas
Puerto Manatí
Puerto Padre
Gibara
Santa Cruz del Sur
Victoria de las Tunas
HOLGUÍN
Golfo de Guacanayabo
Bayamo
Manzanillo
Sierra Maestra
2000
C. Cruz
SANTIAGO DE CUBA
Arch. de Jardines de la Reina
Greater
Cayman Islands (U.K.)
Cayman Brac
Little Cayman
Georgetown
Grand Cayman
7680
Montego Bay
Lucea
Negril
South Negril Pt.
Falmouth
St. Ann's Bay
Port Maria
Annotto Bay
Port Antonio
Savanna-la-Mar
Black River
Cambridge
Mandeville
May Pen
Spanish Town
Pedro Cays (Jamaica)
Swan Islands (U.S.A. & Honduras)
Bajo Nuevo (Colombia)
C A R I B
I. Desterrada
I. Pérez (Mexico)
Canal de Yucatán
Punta Yalkubul
Progreso
Dzilam de Bravo
Río Lagartos
C. Catoche
DZIBILCHALTÚN
Mérida
Motul
Temax
Tizimín
El Cuyo
Cancún
Puerto Juárez
Izamal
Espita
El Diaz
Maxcanú
Sotuta
MAYAPÁN
CHICHEN ITZÁ
Valladolid
Puerto Morelos
Calkiní
Ticul
UXMAL
Tekax
Cozumel
Isla Cozumel
Tenabo
Campeche
EDZNA
Peto
Bolonchenticul
Vigía Chico
Champotón
Hopelchén
San José Carpizo
Felipe Carrillo Puerto
B. de la Ascensión
B. del Espíritu Santo
Chenkán
Ciudad del Carmen
L. de Términos
Pedro Antonio Santos
Matamoros
Pital
Bacalar
Chetumal
B. de Chetumal
Banco Chinchorro
Palizada
Concepción
Corozal
Orange Walk
Hondo
Ambergris Cay
Balancán
PALENQUE
Tenosique
Uaxactún
Belize City
Turneffe Is.
San Ignacio
Belmopan
Ocosingo
L. Petén Itzá
TIKAL
La Libertad
Flores
Benque Viejo
Middlesex
Dangriga
La Independencia
Usumacinta
Lacantún
Comitán
Salinas
Maya Mts.
San Luis
Golfo de Honduras
Monkey River
San Antonio
Punta Gorda
Is. de la Bahía
Roatán
Sierra de los Cuchumatanes
3993
Cuilco
Sebol
Livingston
Puerto Barrios
Puerto Cortés
Tela
La Ceiba
Puerto Castilla
Trujillo
Iriona
C. Camarón
Punta Patuca
Brus Laguna
Laguna Caratasca
Huehuetenango
Cobán
L. de Izabal
San Pedro Sula
El Progreso
Balfate
Savá
Olanchito
Arenal
San Marcos
Totonicapán
UTATLÁN
Sierra de las Minas
Motagua
Yoro
Mosquitia
C. Falso
C. Gracias a Dios
Puerto Cabo Gracias á Dios
Coco (Segovia)
Kisalaya
Ayutla
Sololá
Antigua
Guatemala
Guastatoya
Zacapa
Santa Bárbara
El Jaral
L. de Yojoa
Juticalpa
Catacamas
Coatepeque
Quezaltenango
Mazatenango
Retalhuleu
Amatitlán
Jalapa
COPÁN
Chiquimula
Santa Rosa de Copán
Escuintla
La Esperanza
Comayagua
Patuca
San José
Santa Ana
La Paz
Tegucigalpa
Cayos Miskitos (Nicaragua)
Pta. Gorda
Ahuachapán
Sonsonate
Suchitoto
Cojutepeque
Yuscarán
Danlí
Bonanza
Puerto Cabezas
Acajutla
Nueva San Salvador
Zacatecoluca
Nacaome
Ocotal
Siuna
Usulután
San Miguel
La Unión
Choluteca
Somoto
Coco
Cord. Isabella
Tungla
Prinzapolca
Río Grande
Tuma
San Pedro del Norte
G. de Fonseca
Puerto Morazán
El Sauce
Estelí
Jinotega
Matagalpa
Muy Muy
Chinandega
Corinto
León
La Paz Centro
L. de Managua
Boaco
Siquia
Santo Domingo
Punta de Perlas
Is. del Maíz (Nicaragua, U.S.A.)
Masaya
Juigalpa
Rama
Diriamba
Granada
Bluefields
El Bluff
Pta. Mico
Jinotepe
Lago de Nicaragua
I. de Ometepe
Cord. de Yolaina
B. de San Juan del Norte
Rivas
San Juan del Sur
B. de Salinas
C. Santa Elena
La Cruz
San Carlos
Los Chiles
San Juan
San Juan del Norte
G. de Papagayo
C. Velas
Santa Cruz
Liberia
Cord. de Guanacaste
Nicoya
Cord. Central
Guápiles
Siquirres
Limón
Pen. de Nicoya
Carmona
Puntarenas
Esparza
Alajuela
San José
Cartago
Pta. Mona
C. Blanco
G. de Nicoya
Puerto Quepos
Chirripó Grande
3837
Cord. de Talamanca
Bribri
Pandora
Bocas del Toro
Almirante
L. de Chiriquí
3374
B. de Coronado
Puerto Cortés
Buenos Aires
Volcán Barú
Boquete
San Vito
La Concepción
Golfito
Pen. de Osa
G. Dulce
Pta. Burica
Puerto Armuelles
David
Remedios
G. de Chiriquí
I. de Coiba
I. Jicarón
I. de Cebaco
Punta Mariato
G. de los Mosquitos
Serranía de Tabasará
Santiago
Soná
Chitré
Pen. de Azuero
Tonosí
Las Tablas
Pocrí
Pta. Mala
Pta. Manzanillo
Nombre de Dios
Portobelo
Colón
Panama Canal
L. Gatún
Archipiélago de San Blas
Serranía del Darién
Chepo
Balboa
PANAMÁ
La Chorrera
Chimán
Penonomé
Río Hato
Aguadulce
Arch. de las Perlas
San Miguel
I. del Rey
Golfo de Panamá
La Palma
Yaviza
El Real
Garachiné
Jaqué
Golfo del Darién
G. de Urabá
I. de San Bernardo
G. de Morrosquillo
CARTAGENA
I. de Providencia (Colombia)
Cayos Roncador (U.S.A. & Colombia)
I. de San Andrés (Colombia)
Cayos de Albuquerque (Colombia)
PACIFIC OCEAN
Projection: Conical with two standard parallels

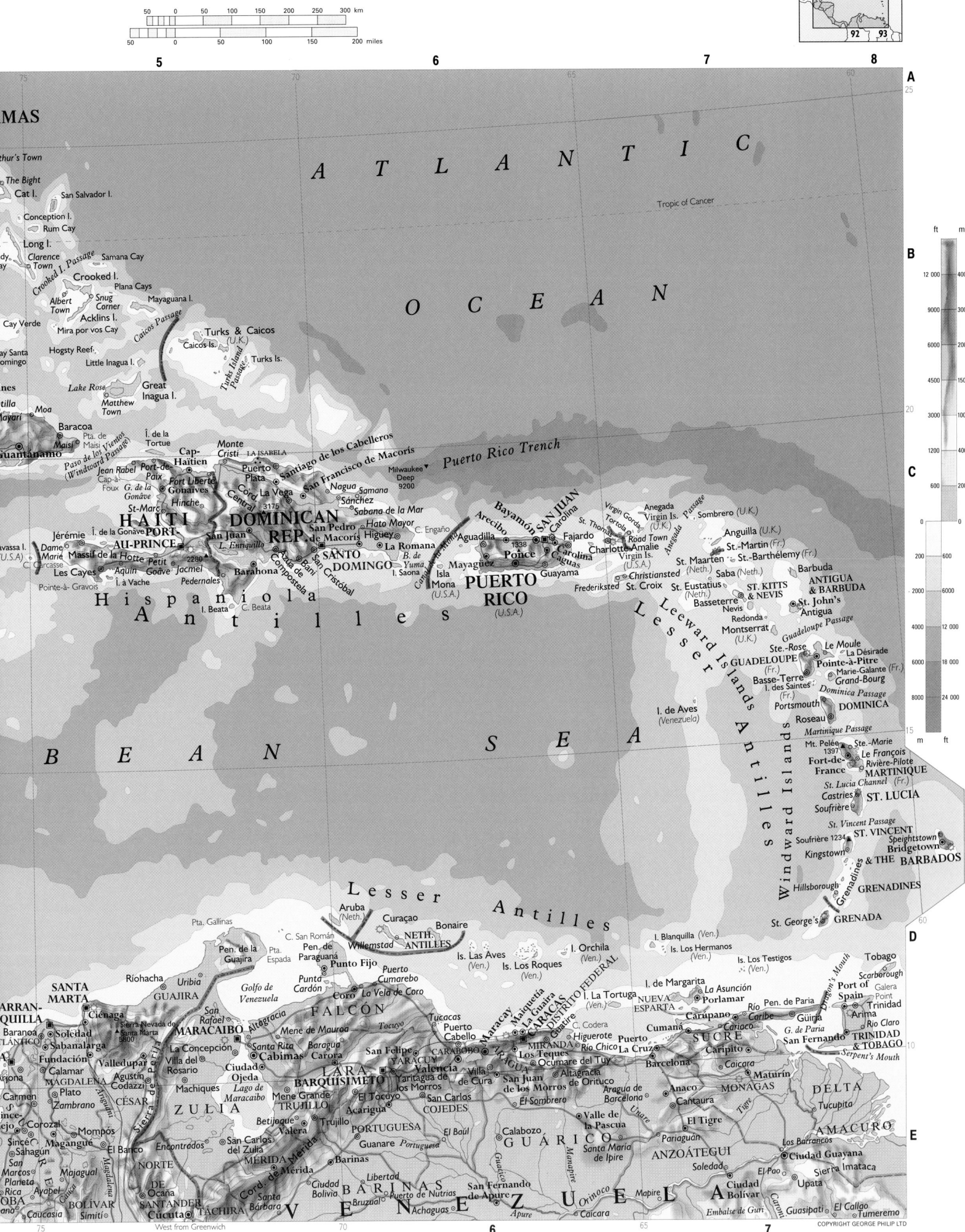
50 0 50 100 150 200 250 300 km
50 0 50 100 150 200 miles
ATLANTIC
OCEAN
Tropic of Cancer
Puerto Rico Trench
Milwaukee Deep 9200
Hispaniola
Antilles
Lesser Antilles
Leeward Islands
Windward Islands
BEAN SEA
HAITI
PORT-AU-PRINCE
DOMINICAN REP.
SANTO DOMINGO
PUERTO RICO (U.S.A.)
SAN JUAN
Turks & Caicos (U.K.)
Turks Island Passage
Caicos Passage
Crooked I. Passage
Paso de los Vientos (Windward Passage)
Canal de la Mona
Anegada Passage
Guadeloupe Passage
Dominica Passage
Martinique Passage
St. Lucia Channel
St. Vincent Passage
Great Inagua I.
Little Inagua I.
Mayaguana I.
Acklins I.
Crooked I.
Long I.
Cat I.
San Salvador I.
Conception I.
Rum Cay
Samana Cay
Plana Cays
Baracoa
Guantánamo
Moa
Cap-Haïtien
Port-de-Paix
Gonaïves
Jérémie
Les Cayes
Jacmel
Santiago de los Caballeros
San Francisco de Macorís
Puerto Plata
La Vega
San Pedro de Macorís
La Romana
Higüey
Barahona
Isla Mona (U.S.A.)
Aguadilla
Arecibo
Bayamón
Mayagüez
Ponce
Caguas
Carolina
Fajardo
Guayama
Charlotte Amalie
Virgin Is. (U.S.A.)
Virgin Is. (U.K.)
Road Town
Anegada
Sombrero (U.K.)
Anguilla (U.K.)
St.-Martin (Fr.)
St.-Barthélemy (Fr.)
St. Maarten (Neth.)
Saba (Neth.)
St. Eustatius (Neth.)
Christiansted
St. Croix
Frederiksted
ST. KITTS & NEVIS
Basseterre
Nevis
Redonda
Montserrat (U.K.)
Barbuda
ANTIGUA & BARBUDA
St. John's
Antigua
GUADELOUPE (Fr.)
Pointe-à-Pitre
Basse-Terre
Marie-Galante (Fr.)
La Désirade
DOMINICA
Roseau
Portsmouth
I. de Aves (Venezuela)
MARTINIQUE (Fr.)
Fort-de-France
Mt. Pelée 1397
ST. LUCIA
Castries
Soufrière
ST. VINCENT & THE GRENADINES
Kingstown
BARBADOS
Bridgetown
Speightstown
Hillsborough
GRENADA
St. George's
Grenadines
Aruba (Neth.)
Curaçao
Bonaire
NETH. ANTILLES
Willemstad
Is. Las Aves (Ven.)
Is. Los Roques (Ven.)
I. Orchila (Ven.)
I. Blanquilla (Ven.)
Is. Los Hermanos (Ven.)
Is. Los Testigos (Ven.)
I. de Margarita
I. La Tortuga (Ven.)
Tobago
Scarborough
Port of Spain
TRINIDAD & TOBAGO
Serpent's Mouth
Dragon's Mouth
Pta. Gallinas
Pen. de la Guajira
Pen. de Paraguaná
Golfo de Venezuela
Lago de Maracaibo
MARACAIBO
Cabimas
Punto Fijo
Coro
BARQUISIMETO
Valencia
Maracay
CARACAS
La Guaira
Barcelona
Cumaná
Carúpano
Maturín
Ciudad Guayana
Ciudad Bolívar
Mérida
Barinas
SANTA MARTA
BARRANQUILLA
Valledupar
Cúcuta
Orinoco
V E N E Z U E L A
West from Greenwich

100 0 200 400 600 800 1000 1200 1400 km
100 0 200 400 600 800 1000 miles

1 2 3 4 5 6 7

ft m

12000 4000
9000 3000
6000 2000
3000 1000
1500 500
600 200
0 0
200 600
1000 3000
2000 6000
4000 12000
6000 18000
8000 24000

m ft

Projection: Lambert's Azimuthal Equal Area

CARTOGRAPHY BY PHILIP'S

A

Tropic of Cancer

NORTH ATLANTIC OCEAN

Gulf of Campeche
Yucatán Peninsula
Yucatán Channel
Cuba
Greater Antilles
Turks & Caicos Is.
Hispaniola
9200
Puerto Rico
Jamaica
G. de Honduras
Isthmus of Tehuantepec
Guatemala Trench
C. Gracias a Dios
Coco
L. Nicaragua
Panama Canal
Guadeloupe
Dominica
Martinique
St. Lucia
St. Vincent
Barbados
Grenada
Tobago
Trinidad
Lesser Antilles
Caribbean Sea
I. Margarita

B

C

C. de la Aguja
Sierra Nevada de Santa Marta 5800
L. Maracaibo
Gulf of Darién
Panama Canal
Gulf of Panamá
Cordillera Occidental
Cordillera Central
Cordillera Oriental
Cord. de Mérida
Llanos
Meta
Orinoco
Guiana Highlands
Mt. Roraima 2810
Sierra Pacaraima
Caroní
Cuyuní
Essequibo
Serra Tumucumaque
C. Orange

C. de San Francisco
Cotopaxi 5897
Chimborazo 6267
Guaviare
Caquetá
Negro
Branco
Equator
Marajó I.

Galapagos Is.
G. of Guayaquil
Pta. Pariñas
Pta. Negra
Napo
Putumayo
Japurá
Amazon
Amazon
Tocantins
C. de São Roque

D

Marañón
Juruá
Purus
Madeira
Tapajós
Xingu
Araguaia
Parnaíba
São Francisco
Plat. of Borborema
Ucayali
Huascarán 6768
Selvas
Aripuanã
Roosevelt
Teles Pires
Arinos

E

Chincha Alta
Chile Peru Trench
L. Titicaca
Bolivian Plateau
Nevada Ancohuma 6550
L. de Poopó
Madre de Dios
Beni
Mamoré
Guaporé
Plateau of Mato Grosso
Brazilian Highlands
Abrolhos Bank

PACIFIC OCEAN

F

Tropic of Capricorn
San Félix
San Ambrosio
Atacama Desert
8050
Cerro Ojos del Salado 6863
Gran Chaco
Pilcomayo
Paraguay
Paraná
Iguaçu Falls
Uruguay
Serra da Mantiqueira 2890
Pico da Bandeira
Serra do Mar
C. Frio

Salinas Grandes
Salado
Entre Ríos

G

Arch. de Juan Fernández
Mt. Aconcagua 6960
Sierra de Córdoba
L. Mar Chiquita
Pampas
Río de la Plata
L. dos Patos

SOUTH ATLANTIC OCEAN

Colorado
Negro
Bahía Blanca
G. San Matías
Valdés Peninsula 40

H

Chile Rise
Chiloé I.
Chonos Archipelago
Taitao Peninsula
Gulf of Penas
Wellington I.
Madre de Dios I.
Magellan's Str.
Santa Inés I.
Canal Cockburn
Canal Beagle
C. Horn
Tierra del Fuego
Staten I.
Chubut
Mte. San Valentín 4058
Patagonia
Gulf of San Jorge
Argentine Basin
6212
West Falkland
East Falkland
Falkland Is.
South Georgia

30 West from Greenwich 50
60

1 2 3 4 5 6 7

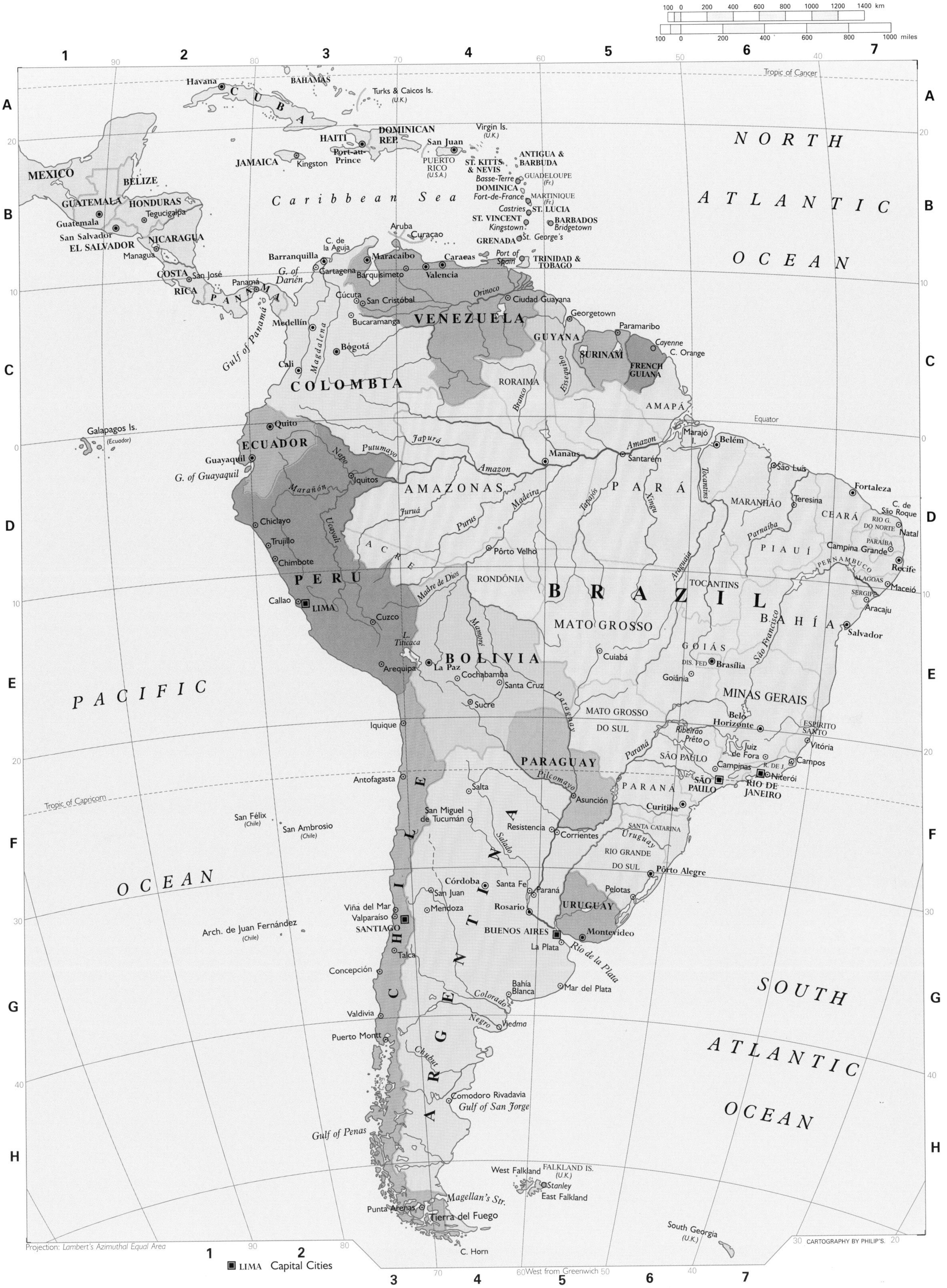

100 0 200 400 600 800 1000 1200 1400 km

100 0 200 400 600 800 1000 miles

1 90 **2** 80 **3** 70 **4** 60 **5** 50 **6** 40 **7**

Tropic of Cancer

A

Havana
BAHAMAS
Turks & Caicos Is.
(U.K.)

C U B A

NORTH

B

MEXICO
BELIZE
GUATEMALA
HONDURAS
Guatemala
Tegucigalpa
San Salvador
EL SALVADOR
NICARAGUA
Managua

JAMAICA
Kingston
HAITI
Port-au-Prince
DOMINICAN
REP.
San Juan
Virgin Is.
(U.K.)
PUERTO
RICO
(U.S.A.)

ST. KITTS
& NEVIS
Basse-Terre
DOMINICA
Fort-de-France
Castries
ST. VINCENT
Kingstown
GRENADA
St. George's

ANTIGUA &
BARBUDA
GUADELOUPE
(Fr.)
MARTINIQUE
(Fr.)
ST. LUCIA
BARBADOS
Bridgetown

ATLANTIC

Caribbean Sea

C

COSTA
RICA
San José
Panamá

P A N A M A

Gulf of Panama

G. of Darién

Barranquilla
Cartagena
C. de
la Aguja
Aruba
Curaçao
Maracaibo
Barquisimeto
Valencia
Caracas
Port of
Spain
TRINIDAD &
TOBAGO

Cúcuta
San Cristóbal
Medellín
Bucaramanga
Bogotá
Cali

Magdalena

VENEZUELA
Orinoco
Ciudad Guayana
Georgetown
Paramaribo
Cayenne
C. Orange

COLOMBIA
GUYANA
SURINAM
FRENCH
GUIANA

RORAIMA

AMAPÁ

OCEAN

D

Galapagos Is.
(Ecuador)

Quito
ECUADOR
Guayaquil
G. of Guayaquil
Iquitos

Napo
Putumayo
Japurá
Marañón
AMAZONAS
Amazon
Juruá
Purus
Madeira

Manaus
Santarém
Marajó
I.
Belém
São Luís

Amazon

PARÁ

Tapajós
Xingu
Tocantins

MARANHÃO
Teresina
Fortaleza
C. de
São Roque
Natal
CEARÁ
RIO G.
DO NORTE

Equator

Chiclayo
Trujillo
Chimbote

Ucayali
A C R E

Madre de Dios
Pôrto Velho
RONDÔNIA

Parnaíba
PIAUÍ
PARAÍBA
Campina Grande
Recife
PERNAMBUCO

PERU
Callao
LIMA
Cuzco

B R A Z I L

TOCANTINS
ALAGOAS
Maceió
SERGIPE
Aracaju

E

*L.
Titicaca*
Arequipa
La Paz
Cochabamba
Santa Cruz
BOLIVIA
Sucre

Mamoré

MATO GROSSO
Cuiabá

GOIÁS
DIS. FED
Goiânia
Brasília
BAHÍA

São Francisco
Salvador

MINAS GERAIS
Belo
Horizonte
ESPIRITO
SANTO
Vitória

PACIFIC

Iquique

MATO GROSSO
DO SUL

Paraguay
Paraná

Ribeirão
Prêto
SÃO PAULO
Campinas
Juiz
de Fora
R. DE J.
Campos

F

Antofagasta

Pilcomayo
PARAGUAY
Asunción

Salta

San Miguel
de Tucumán
Resistencia
Corrientes

Salado

A R G E N T I N A

SÃO
PAULO
RIO DE
JANEIRO
Niterói

PARANÁ
Curitiba
SANTA CATARINA
Uruguay
RIO GRANDE
DO SUL
Pôrto Alegre

San Félix
(Chile)
San Ambrosio
(Chile)

OCEAN

G

Arch. de Juan Fernández
(Chile)

Córdoba
San Juan
Mendoza
Viña del Mar
Valparaíso
SANTIAGO
Talca

Santa Fe
Paraná
Rosario
BUENOS AIRES
La Plata

Pelotas
URUGUAY
Montevideo
Río de la Plata

C H I L E

SOUTH

Concepción
Valdivia
Puerto Montt
Bahía
Blanca
Mar del Plata

Colorado
Negro
Viedma

ATLANTIC

H

Chubut

Comodoro Rivadavia
Gulf of San Jorge

Gulf of Penas

West Falkland
FALKLAND IS.
(U.K.)
Stanley
East Falkland

OCEAN

Punta Arenas
Magellan's Str.
Tierra del Fuego
C. Horn

South Georgia
(U.K.)

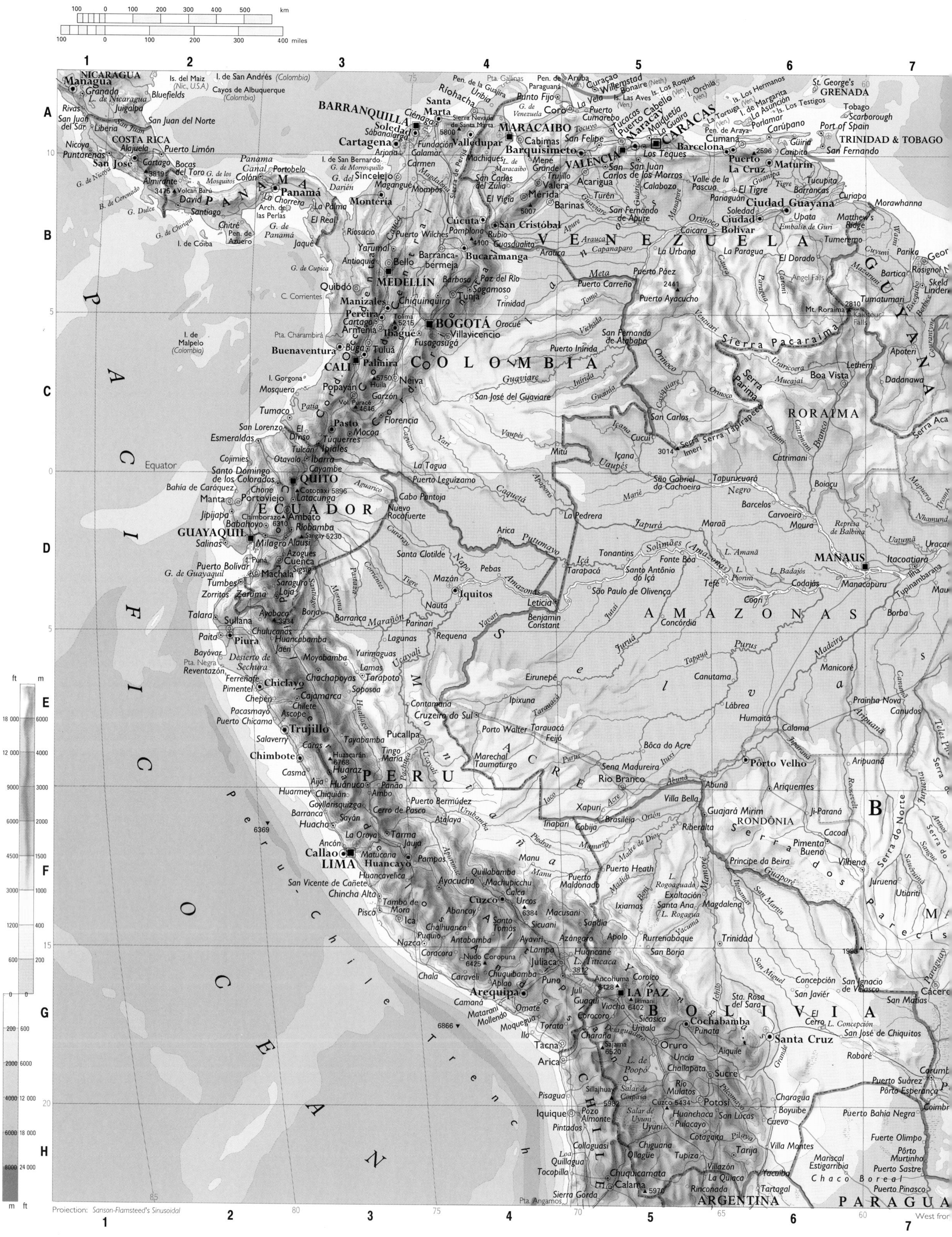

100 0 100 200 300 400 500 km
100 0 100 200 300 400 miles

1 2 3 4 5 6 7

NICARAGUA
Managua
L. de Nicaragua
Juigalpa
Bluefields
Is. del Maiz (Nic., U.S.A.)
I. de San Andrés (Colombia)
Cayos de Albuquerque (Colombia)

Pen. de la Guajira Pta. Gallinas
Pen. de Paraguaná Aruba (Neth) Curaçao Willemstad Bonaire (Neth)
Riohacha Uribia Punto Fijo La Vela Is. Las Aves (Ven) Los Roques La Orchila (Ven) St. George's GRENADA
Santa Marta Coro Cumarebo Tucacas Puerto Cabello Maiquetía La Tortuga (Ven) I. de Margarita Los Testigos Tobago Scarborough
BARRANQUILLA Ciénaga G. de Venezuela San Felipe CARACAS Barcelona La Asunción Porlamar Port of Spain
Sierra Nevada de Santa Marta 5800 Maracaibo Cabimas Naracay Los Teques Cumaná Pen. de Araya (Ven) Carúpano Güiria TRINIDAD & TOBAGO
Cartagena Soledad Sabanalarga Valledupar MARACAIBO Barquisimeto VALENCIA San Juan de los Morros Valle de la Pascua El Tigre Tigre Maturín San Fernando
Arjona Calamar Machiques Trujillo Carlos de los Morros Calabozo Pariaguán Ciudad Guayana Tucupita Curiapo Morawhanna
Carmen Fundación G. de Maracaibo Mene Grande Valera Acarigua Turén San Fernando de Apure Orinoco Ciudad Bolívar Upata Matthew's Ridge
Sincelejo Magangué El Vigía Mérida Barinas 5007 2596 Embalse de Guri Barrancas
G. del Darién Mompós 5007 San Cristóbal Apure Caicara La Urbana La Paragua Tumeremo Guyuni Parika Geor

A

Panamá Panama Canal Portobelo Colón Montería Cúcuta Pamplona Rubio ARAUCA Capanaparo Puerto Páez El Dorado GUYANA
PANAMA La Chorrera El Real Riosucio Puerto Wilches Guasdualito Meta Puerto Carreño 2441 Angel Falls Bartica Skeld Linden
David Santiago La Palma Yarumal Barranca-bermeja Toma Puerto Ayacucho Serra Parima Boa Vista Lethem Resignol
Chitré Pen. de Azuero Jaqué Antioquia Bello Barbosa Paz del Río Mt. Roraima 2810 Tumatumari Apoteri
I. de Coiba G. de Panamá G. de Cupica MEDELLÍN Chiquinquirá Sogamoso Sierra Pacaraima Serra Aca

B

C. Corrientes Manizales Tunja Trinidad Meta San Fernando de Atabapo RORAIMA
Quibdó Pereira Tolima 5215 BOGOTÁ Orocué Vichada San Carlos Serra Parima Dadanawa
Cartago Armenia Ibagué Villavicencio Inírida Mucajaí Catrimani
Buenaventura Buga Tuluá Fusagasugá Puerto Inírida Guainía 3014 Serra Tapirapecó
CALI Palmira COLOMBIA Guaviare Orinoco Içana Catrimani Serra Aca

C

I. Gorgona Popayán Huila 5750 Neiva Guaviare Castiquiare São Gabriel da Cachoeira Boiaçu
Mosquera Vol. Puracé 4646 Garzón San José del Guaviare Cucuí Içana Negro Uatumã
Tumaco Pasto Florencia Yarí Mitú Uaupés Maré Barcelos Carvoeiro Moura Represa de Balbina
San Lorenzo El Diviso Mocoa Caquetá Apaporis Tapurucuará Japurá Maraã MANAUS Itacoatiara
Esmeraldas Túquerres Ipiales Putumayo La Tagua Puerto Leguízamo L. Amanã Manacapuru Ilna
Cojimies Tulcán Otavalo Ibarra Cayambe Nuevo Rocafuerte Arica La Pedrera Santo Antônio do Içá Tefé L. Piorini Codajás Uracá
Equator Santo Domingo de los Colorados QUITO Aguarico Cabo Pantoja Içá Tonantins SOLIMÕES (AMAZONAS) São Paulo de Olivença Codajás Tupinambarana Borba

D

Bahía de Caráquez Chone Latacunga Cotopaxi 5896 Santa Clotilde Napo Mazán Pebas Tarapacá Fonte Boa AMAZONAS Tupinambarana
Manta Portoviejo Ambato Chimborazo 6310 Riobamba Curaray Mazán Iquitos Leticia Concórdia Manicoré
Jipijapa ECUADOR Sangay 5230 Tigre Nauta Benjamin Constant Juruá Purus Madeira
GUAYAQUIL Babahoyo Nuevo Yavari Requena Içá Jutaí Tapauá Canutama Manicoré
Salinas Milagro Alausi Parinari Ucayali Yavari Juruá e Lábrea Aripuanã Prainha Nova

D/E

Puerto Bolívar Azogues Cuenca Sígsig Lagunas Yurimaguas Eirunepé Humaitá Canudos
G. de Guayaquil Machala Saraguro Moyobamba Tarapoto Ipixuna Boca do Acre Calama Aripuanã
Tumbes Zorritos Zarumá Loja Lamas Saposoa Contamana Tarauacá Feijó Sena Madureira Humaitá
I. Puná Ayabaca 3934 Borja Chachapoyas Cruzeiro do Sul Porto Walter Tarauacá Bôca do Acre Humaitá
Talara Sullana Chulucanas Huancabamba Jaén Cajamarca Chilete Marechal Taumaturgo Rio Branco Abunã Pôrto Velho Aripuanã

E/F

Paita Piura Huancabamba Chiclayo Ferreñafe Pimentel Chepén Huallaga Pucallpa Rio Branco Abuná Ariquemes Ji-Paraná Cacoal
Pta. Negra Desierto de Sechura Pacasmayo Ascope Chilete Tayabamba Tingo María Villa Bella RONDÔNIA Pimenta Bueno Vilhena
Bayóvar Reventazón Puerto Chicama Trujillo Caras Huascarán 6768 Huánuco Panão Cobija Guajará Mirim Riberalta Príncipe da Beira
Salaverry Chimbote Casma Huaraz Aija Chiquián Cerro de Pasco Urubamba Xapuri Brasiléia Ortón B
Huarmey Goyllarisquizga Ambo Puerto Bermúdez Atalaya Iñapari Puerto Heath Magdalena Concepción

F

6369 Barranca Sayán La Oroya Tarma Manu Puerto Maldonado L. Rogoaguado Santa Ana San Borja San Ignacio de Velasco
Huacho PERU Jauja Pampas Apurímac Manu Exaltación L. Rogagua Santa Rosa del Sara San Matías
Ancón Matucana Huancayo Ayacucho Machupicchu Calca Urcos Sicuani Apolo Rurrenabaque Trinidad Concepción
Callao LIMA Huancavelica Quillabamba CUZCO 6384 Macusani Sandia Azángaro Juliaca Coroico Santa Cruz
San Vicente de Cañete Chincha Alta Tambo de Mora Ica Abancay Santo Tomás Chalhuanca Ayaviri L. Titicaca 3812 Ancohuma 6520 Cochabamba Roboré

G

Pisco Nazca Puquio Antabamba Nudo Coropuna 6425 Sicuani Lampa Huancané LA PAZ Illimani Sta. Rosa del Sará San José de Chiquitos
Coracora Chuquibamba Aplao Puno Juli Viacha 6402 Punata Oruro Cerro L. Concepción Puerto Suárez
Chala Caravelí Camaná AREQUIPA Omate Coroico Sicasica Aiquile Pôrto Esperanza
Matarani Mollendo Torata Desaguadero Umala Challapata Sucre Puerto Bahía Negra

G/H

6866 Moquegua Ilo Tacna L. Poopó Charaña Challapata Río Mulatos Charagua Coimb
Arica Pozo Almonte Guaqui 5980 Oruro Sillajhuay Huanchaca San Lucas Boyuibe Puerto Pinasco
Pisagua Iquique Salar de Coipasa Uncía Salar de Uyuni Potosí Tupiza Villa Montes Fuerte Olimpo
Pintados Cuzco 5434 Pulacayo Cotagaita Camiri Pôrto Murtinho
Collaguasi Ollagüe Ollagua Quillagua Tarija Mariscal Estigarribia Pôrto Sastre
Loa Tocopilla Chuquicamata Calama 5970 Rinconada La Quiaca Yacuíba Tartagal Chaco Boreal
Sierra Gorda Pta. Angamos ARGENTINA PARAGUAY

H

PACIFIC OCEAN

Peru-Chile Trench

BOLIVIA

CHILE

VENEZUELA

COSTA RICA San José Cartago Puerto Limón Liberia Puntarenas Nicoya Rivas San Juan del Sur

G. de los Mosquitos 3476 Volcán Barú 3819 Almirante Bocas del Toro G. de Nicoya G. de Chiriquí G. Dulce B. de Coronado

Projection: Sanson-Flamsteed's Sinusoidal

ft m
18 000 6000
12 000 4000
9000 3000
6000 2000
4500 1500
3000 1000
1200 400
600 200
0 0
200 600
2000 6000
4000 12 000
6000 18 000
8000 24 000
m ft

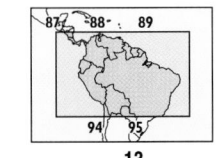

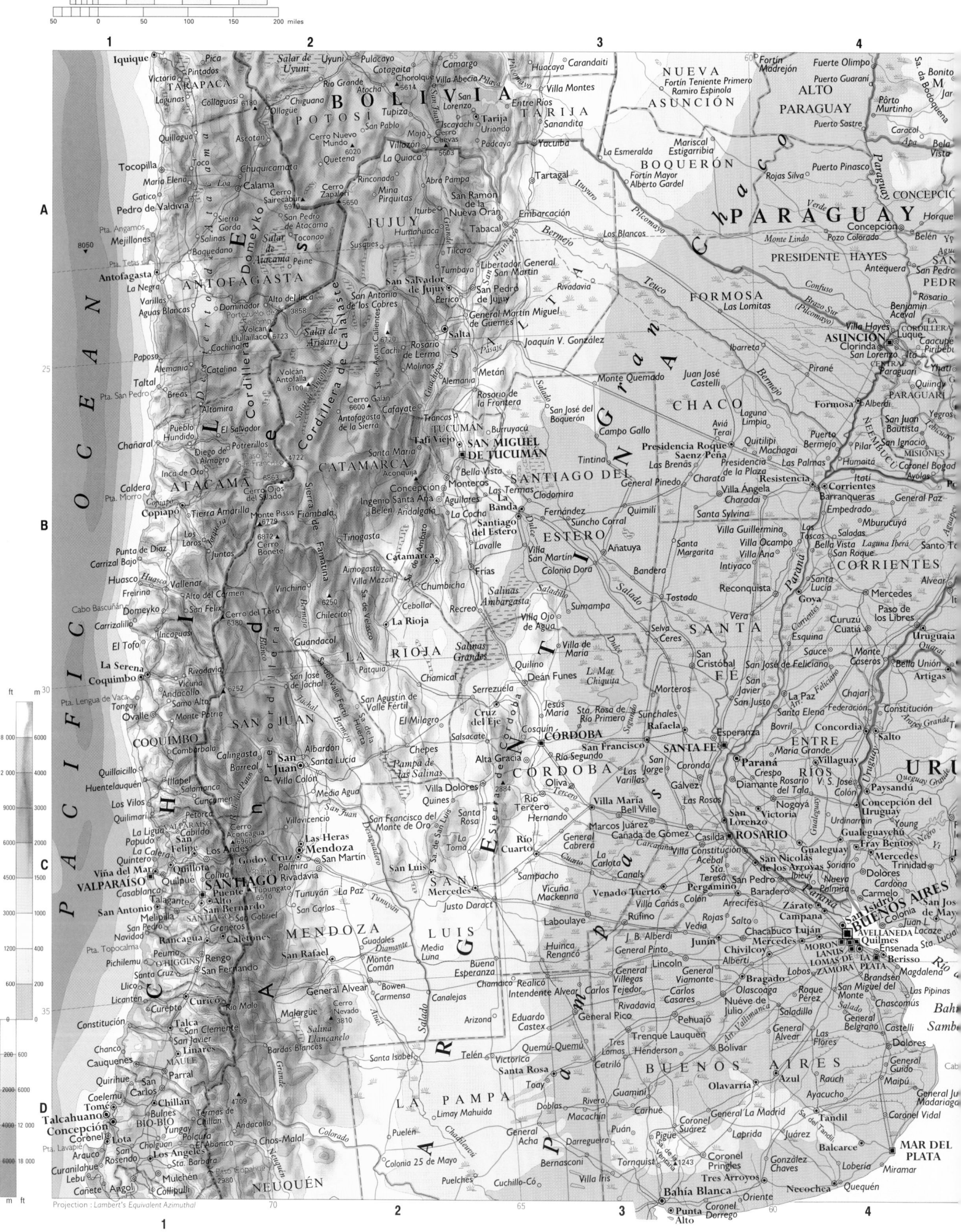
PACIFIC OCEAN
BOLIVIA
PARAGUAY
CHILE
ARGENTINA
Gran Chaco
Pampas
Andes
BUENOS AIRES
SANTIAGO
ASUNCIÓN
VALPARAÍSO
CÓRDOBA
ROSARIO
Mendoza
SAN MIGUEL DE TUCUMÁN
SANTA FE
Antofagasta
Iquique
Concepción
Mar del Plata
Bahía Blanca
Projection : Lambert's Equivalent Azimuthal

92
93
96
5
6
7
A
B
C
D
BELO HORIZONTE
Nova Lima
Itabirito
Vitória
Vila Velha
Guarapari
Congonhas
Conselheiro Lafaiete
Ouro Prêto
Ponte Nova
Pico da Bandeira 2890
Itaquari
Castelo
Cachoeiro de Itapemirim
Oliveira
Campo Belo
São João del Rei
Ubá
Carangola
Muriaé
Alegre
Barbacena
Cataguases
Itaperuna
Leopoldina
Cambuci
Guarus
CAMPOS
Cabo de São Tomé
Juiz de Fora
Três Rios
Além Paraíba
RIO DE JANEIRO
Barra do Piraí
Nova Friburgo
Petrópolis
Macaé
DUQUE DE CAXIAS
SÃO GONÇALO
NITERÓI
RIO DE JANEIRO
Cabo Frio
La. de Araruama
Tropic of Capricorn
Volta Redonda
Barra Mansa
NOVA IGUAÇU
Angra dos Reis
Ilha Grande
Baía da Ilha Grande
Pta. de Juatinga
Itajubá
2787
Cruzeiro
Guaratinguetá
Taubaté
São José dos C.
Jacareí
Moji das Cruzes
SANTO ANDRÉ
SÃO PAULO
São Bernardo do Campo
São Vicente
SANTOS
Guarujá
Ilha de São Sebastião
Pta. de Boi
Itanhaém
Três Pontas
Lavras
Varginha
Três Corações
Alfenas
Poços de Caldas
Pouso Alegre
Ouro Fino
Bragança Paulista
Mogi-Mirim
Americana
Jundiaí
Itu
Sorocaba
CAMPINAS
Piracicaba
Limeira
Rio Claro
São Carlos
Araraquara
São João da Boa Vista
Araras
Pinhal
Mococa
Casa Branca
Guaxupé
Passos
São Sebastião do Paraíso
Batatais
Ribeirão Prêto
Jaboticabal
Bebedouro
Olímpia
São José do Rio Prêto
Mirassol
Catanduva
Taquaritinga
Novo Horizonte
Penápolis
Lins
Birigui
Araçatuba
Andradina
Três Lagoas
Xavantina
Mirandópolis
Panorama
Adamantina
Presidente Epitácio
Santo Anastácio
SÃO PAULO
Tupã
Marília
Garça
Bariri
Jaú
Bauru
Pirajuí
Presidente Prudente
Martinópolis
Rancharia
Paraguaçu Paulista
Assis
Santa Cruz do Rio Pardo
Botucatu
Tatuí
Itapetininga
Avaré
Ourinhos
Cambará
Cornélio Procópio
Jacarèzinho
Joaquim Távora
Itaporanga
Itapeva
Itararé
Jaguariaíva
Apiaí
Registro
Iguape
Juquiá
Ilha Comprida
Ilha do Cardoso
Paranapiacaba
Londrina
Rolândia
Arapongas
Apucarana
Maringá
Ibaiti
Tibagi
Castro
Ponta Grossa
Palmeira
CURITIBA
1889
Antonina
Paranaguá
Matinhos
Guaratuba
Joinville
São Francisco do Sul
Rio Negro
Mafra
Lapa
Irati
São Mateus do Sul
União da Vitória
Pôrto União
Caçador
Blumenau
Itajaí
Brusque
Santa Cecília
SANTA CATARINA
Curitibanos
Rio do Sul
São José
Ilha de Santa Catarina
Florianópolis
Lajes
1808
Laguna
Cabo Santa Marta Grande
Tubarão
Criciúma
Araranguá
Torres
Campos Novos
Lagoa Vermelha
Vacaria
São Joaquim
Bento Gonçalves
Caxias do Sul
Nôvo Hamburgo
Taquara
São Leopoldo
Canoas
Osorio
PÔRTO ALEGRE
Viamão
Montenegro
Rio Pardo
Santa Cruz do Sul
Cachoeira do Sul
Santa Maria
Encantadas
Tapes
Camaquã
Mostardas
São Lourenço do Sul
Canguçu
Pelotas
Lagoa dos Patos
São José do Norte
Rio Grande
Jaguarão
Lagoa Mirim
Lagoa Mangueira
Santa Vitória do Palmar
Chuy
Castillos
Rocha
San Carlos
Maldonado
MONTEVIDEO
Plata
Pando
Minas
Aigua
Lascano
José Batlle y Ordóñez
Treinta y Tres
Cerro Chato
Vergara
Río Branco
Melo
Fraile Muerto
San Gregorio
Blanquillo
Sarandí del Yí
Tacuarembó
Rivera
Santana do Livramento
Dom Pedrito
Bagé
Pinheiro Machado
Caçapava do Sul
São Gabriel
Alegrete
Santiago
São Borja
São Luís Gonzaga
Santo Ângelo
Cruz Alta
Guaporé
Passo Fundo
Carazinho
Palmeira das Missões
Erechim
Frederico Westphalen
Chapecó
Joaçaba
Xanxerê
1340
São Miguel do Oeste
Palmas
Clevelândia
Pato Branco
Francisco Beltrão
Guarapuava
Laranjeiras do Sul
Prudentópolis
Medianeira
Foz do Iguaçu
Cascavel
Toledo
Ciudad del Este
Hernandarias
Encarnación
Posadas
Oberá
Leandro N. Alem
San Javier
Santa Rosa
Apóstoles
MISIONES
Umuarama
Cianorte
Cruzeiro do Oeste
Goio-Erê
Campo Mourão
PARANÁ
BRAZIL
Paranavaí
Nova Esperança
Mandaguari
Pitanga
Ubiratã
Cândido de Abreu
Guaíra
Mundo Novo
Salto del Guairá
Porto Mendes
Represa de Itaipu
Amambai
Naviraí
Ponta Porã
Pedro Juan Caballero
Dourados
Rio Brilhante
Maracaju
Nova Alvorada do Sul
Nova Andradina
Ivinhema
MATO GROSSO DO SUL
Sidrolândia
Nioaque
Pôrto São José
Centenário do Sul
Rosana
Porecatu
Sertanópolis
ATLANTIC OCEAN
5304
West from Greenwich
55
50
45
40
25
30
35
COPYRIGHT GEORGE PHILIP LTD

5

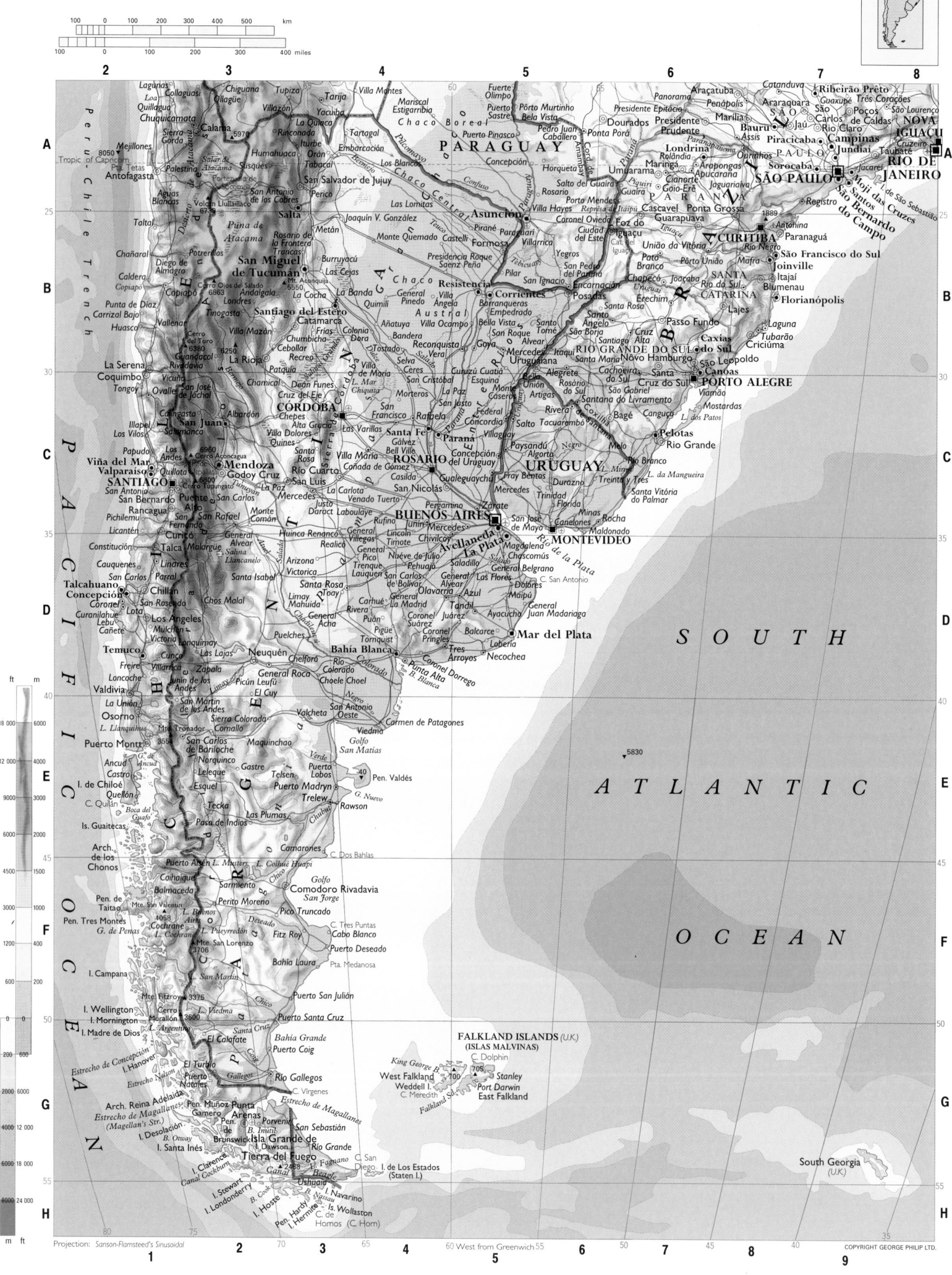

km
100 0 100 200 300 400 500

100 0 100 200 300
miles 400

ft   m

18 000 6000

12 000 4000

9000   3000

6000   2000

4500   1500

3000   1000

1200   400

600   200

0   0

200   600

2000   6000

4000   12 000

6000   18 000

8000   24 000

m   ft

Projection: Sanson-Flamsteed's Sinusoidal

60 West from Greenwich 55

COPYRIGHT GEORGE PHILIP LTD.

PARAGUAY

BRASIL

PARANÁ

SANTA CATARINA

RIO GRANDE DO SUL

URUGUAY

SÃO PAULO

RIO DE JANEIRO

CURITIBA

PORTO ALEGRE

MONTEVIDEO

BUENOS AIRES

CÓRDOBA

ROSARIO

SANTIAGO

MENDOZA

ARGENTINA

CHILE

PATAGONIA

PACIFIC OCEAN

SOUTH ATLANTIC OCEAN

FALKLAND ISLANDS (U.K.)
(ISLAS MALVINAS)

South Georgia (U.K.)

Tierra del Fuego

Tropic of Capricorn

Peru-Chile Trench

INDEX

The index contains the names of all the principal places and features shown on the World Maps. Each name is followed by an additional entry in italics giving the country or region within which it is located. The alphabetical order of names composed of two or more words is governed primarily by the first word and then by the second. This is an example of the rule:

Mīr Kūh, *Iran* . . . . **45 E8** 26 22N 58 55 E
Mīr Shahdād, *Iran* . . . . **45 E8** 26 15N 58 29 E
Mira, *Italy* . . . . **20 B5** 45 26N 12 8 E
Mira por vos Cay, *Bahamas* . **89 B5** 22 9N 74 30 W
Miraj, *India* . . . . **40 L9** 16 50N 74 45 E

Physical features composed of a proper name (Erie) and a description (Lake) are positioned alphabetically by the proper name. The description is positioned after the proper name and is usually abbreviated:

Erie, L., *N. Amer.* . . . . **78 D4** 42 15N 81 0 W

Where a description forms part of a settlement or administrative name however, it is always written in full and put in its true alphabetic position:

Mount Morris, *U.S.A.* . . . . . **78 D7** 42 44N 77 52 W

Names beginning with M' and Mc are indexed as if they were spelled Mac. Names beginning St. are alphabetised under Saint, but Sankt, Sint, Sant', Santa and San are all spelt in full and are alphabetised accordingly. If the same place name occurs two or more times in the index and all are in the same country, each is followed by the name of the administrative subdivision in which it is located. The names are placed in the alphabetical order of the subdivisions. For example:

Jackson, *Ky., U.S.A.* . . . . **76 G4** 37 33N 83 23 W
Jackson, *Mich., U.S.A.* . . . . . **76 D3** 42 15N 84 24 W
Jackson, *Minn., U.S.A.* . . . . . **80 D7** 43 37N 95 1 W

The number in bold type which follows each name in the index refers to the number of the map page where that feature or place will be found. This is usually the largest scale at which the place or feature appears.

The letter and figure which are in bold type immediately after the page number give the grid square on the map page, within which the feature is situated. The letter represents the latitude and the figure the longitude.

In some cases the feature itself may fall within the specified square, while the name is outside. This is usually the case only with features which are larger than a grid square.

For a more precise location the geographical coordinates which follow the letter/figure references give the latitude and the longitude of each place. The first set of figures represent the latitude which is the distance north or south of the Equator measured as an angle at the centre of the earth. The Equator is latitude 0°, the North Pole is 90°N, and the South Pole 90°S.

The second set of figures represent the longitude, which is the distance East or West of the prime meridian, which runs through Greenwich, England. Longitude is also measured as an angle at the centre of the earth and is given East or West of the prime meridian, from 0° to 180° in either direction.

The unit of measurement for latitude and longitude is the degree, which is subdivided into 60 minutes. Each index entry states the position of a place in degrees and minutes, a space being left between the degrees and the minutes.

The latitude is followed by N(orth) or S(outh) and the longitude by E(ast) or W(est).

Rivers are indexed to their mouths or confluences, and carry the symbol → after their names. A solid square ■ follows the name of a country, while an open square □ refers to a first order administrative area.

Abbreviations used in the index

A.C.T. – Australian Capital Territory
Afghan. – Afghanistan
Ala. – Alabama
Alta. – Alberta
Amer. – America(n)
Arch. – Archipelago
Ariz. – Arizona
Ark. – Arkansas
Atl. Oc. – Atlantic Ocean
B. – Baie, Bahía, Bay, Bucht, Bugt
B.C. – British Columbia
Bangla. – Bangladesh
Barr. – Barrage
Bos.-H. – Bosnia-Herzegovina
C. – Cabo, Cap, Cape, Coast
C.A.R. – Central African Republic
C. Prov. – Cape Province
Calif. – California
Cent. – Central
Chan. – Channel
Colo. – Colorado
Conn. – Connecticut
Cord. – Cordillera
Cr. – Creek
Czech. – Czech Republic
D.C. – District of Columbia
Del. – Delaware
Dep. – Dependency
Des. – Desert
Dist. – District
Dj. – Djebel
Domin. – Dominica
Dom. Rep. – Dominican Republic
E. – East

E. Salv. – El Salvador
Eq. Guin. – Equatorial Guinea
Fla. – Florida
Falk. Is. – Falkland Is.
G. – Golfe, Golfo, Gulf, Guba, Gebel
Ga. – Georgia
Gt. – Great, Greater
Guinea-Biss. – Guinea-Bissau
H.K. – Hong Kong
H.P. – Himachal Pradesh
Hants. – Hampshire
Harb. – Harbor, Harbour
Hd. – Head
Hts. – Heights
I.(s). – Île, Ilha, Insel, Isla, Island, Isle
Ill. – Illinois
Ind. – Indiana
Ind. Oc. – Indian Ocean
Ivory C. – Ivory Coast
J. – Jabal, Jebel, Jazira
Junc. – Junction
K. – Kap, Kapp
Kans. – Kansas
Kep. – Kepulauan
Ky. – Kentucky
L. – Lac, Lacul, Lago, Lagoa, Lake, Limni, Loch, Lough
La. – Louisiana
Liech. – Liechtenstein
Lux. – Luxembourg
Mad. P. – Madhya Pradesh
Madag. – Madagascar
Man. – Manitoba
Mass. – Massachusetts

Md. – Maryland
Me. – Maine
Medit. S. – Mediterranean Sea
Mich. – Michigan
Minn. – Minnesota
Miss. – Mississippi
Mo. – Missouri
Mont. – Montana
Mozam. – Mozambique
Mt.(e) – Mont, Monte, Monti, Montaña, Mountain
N. – Nord, Norte, North, Northern, Nouveau
N.B. – New Brunswick
N.C. – North Carolina
N. Cal. – New Caledonia
N. Dak. – North Dakota
N.H. – New Hampshire
N.I. – North Island
N.J. – New Jersey
N. Mex. – New Mexico
N.S. – Nova Scotia
N.S.W. – New South Wales
N.W.T. – North West Territory
N.Y. – New York
N.Z. – New Zealand
Nebr. – Nebraska
Neths. – Netherlands
Nev. – Nevada
Nfld. – Newfoundland
Nic. – Nicaragua
O. – Oued, Ouadi
Occ. – Occidentale
Okla. – Oklahoma
Ont. – Ontario
Or. – Orientale

Oreg. – Oregon
Os. – Ostrov
Oz. – Ozero
P. – Pass, Passo, Pasul, Pulau
P.E.I. – Prince Edward Island
Pa. – Pennsylvania
Pac. Oc. – Pacific Ocean
Papua N.G. – Papua New Guinea
Pass. – Passage
Pen. – Peninsula, Péninsule
Phil. – Philippines
Pk. – Park, Peak
Plat. – Plateau
Prov. – Province, Provincial
Pt. – Point
Pta. – Ponta, Punta
Pte. – Pointe
Qué. – Québec
Queens. – Queensland
R. – Rio, River
R.I. – Rhode Island
Ra.(s). – Range(s)
Raj. – Rajasthan
Reg. – Region
Rep. – Republic
Res. – Reserve, Reservoir
S. – San, South, Sea
Si. Arabia – Saudi Arabia
S.C. – South Carolina
S. Dak. – South Dakota
S.I. – South Island
S. Leone – Sierra Leone
Sa. – Serra, Sierra
Sask. – Saskatchewan
Scot. – Scotland
Sd. – Sound

Sev. – Severnaya
Sib. – Siberia
Sprs. – Springs
St. – Saint
Sta. – Santa, Station
Ste. – Sainte
Sto. – Santo
Str. – Strait, Stretto
Switz. – Switzerland
Tas. – Tasmania
Tenn. – Tennessee
Tex. – Texas
Tg. – Tanjung
Trin. & Tob. – Trinidad & Tobago
U.A.E. – United Arab Emirates
U.K. – United Kingdom
U.S.A. – United States of America
Ut. P. – Uttar Pradesh
Va. – Virginia
Vdkhr. – Vodokhranilishche
Vf. – Vîrful
Vic. – Victoria
Vol. – Volcano
Vt. – Vermont
W. – Wadi, West
W. Va. – West Virginia
Wash. – Washington
Wis. – Wisconsin
Wlkp. – Wielkopolski
Wyo. – Wyoming
Yorks. – Yorkshire
Yug. – Yugoslavia

A

Amadeus, L.

Al Fallūjah, Iraq 44 C4 33 20N 43 55 E
Al Fāw, Iraq 45 D6 30 0N 48 30 E
Al Fujayrah, U.A.E. 45 E8 25 7N 56 18 E
Al Ghadaf, W. →, Jordan 47 D5 31 26N 36 43 E
Al Ghammās, Iraq 44 D5 31 45N 44 37 E
Al Ghazālah, Si. Arabia 44 E4 26 48N 41 19 E
Al Hābah, Si. Arabia 44 E5 27 10N 47 0 E
Al Ḥadīthah, Iraq 44 C4 34 0N 41 13 E
Al Ḥadīthah, Si. Arabia 47 D6 31 28N 37 8 E
Al Ḥaḍr, Iraq 44 C4 35 35N 42 44 E
Al Ḥājānah, Syria 47 B5 33 20N 36 33 E
Al Hajar al Gharbi, Oman 45 E8 24 10N 56 15 E
Al Hāmad, Si. Arabia 44 D3 31 30N 39 30 E
Al Hamdānīyah, Syria 44 C3 35 25N 36 50 E
Al Ḥamīdīyah, Syria 47 A4 34 42N 35 57 E
Al Ḥammār, Iraq 44 D5 30 57N 46 51 E
Al Ḥamrā', Si. Arabia 44 E3 24 2N 38 55 E
Al Ḥanākīyah, Si. Arabia 44 E4 24 51N 40 31 E
Al Harīr, W. →, Syria 47 C4 32 44N 35 59 E
Al Ḥasā, W. →, Jordan 47 D4 31 4N 35 29 E
Al Ḥasakah, Syria 44 B4 36 35N 40 45 E
Al Haydān, W. →, Jordan 47 D4 31 29N 35 34 E
Al Ḥayy, Iraq 44 C5 32 5N 46 5 E
Al Ḥijarah, Asia 44 D4 30 0N 44 0 E
Al Ḥillah, Iraq 44 C5 32 30N 44 25 E
Al Hindīyah, Iraq 44 C5 32 30N 44 10 E
Al Hirmil, Lebanon 47 A5 34 26N 36 24 E
Al Hoceïma, Morocco 50 A5 35 8N 3 58W
Al Ḥudaydah, Yemen 46 E3 14 50N 43 0 E
Al Hufūf, Si. Arabia 45 E6 25 25N 49 45 E
Al Ḥumaydah, Si. Arabia 44 D2 29 14N 34 56 E
Al Ḥunayy, Si. Arabia 45 E6 25 58N 48 45 E
Al Īsāwīyah, Si. Arabia 44 D3 30 43N 37 59 E
Al Jafr, Jordan 47 E5 30 18N 36 14 E
Al Jāfūrah, Si. Arabia 45 E7 25 0N 50 15 E
Al Jaghbūb, Libya 51 C10 29 42N 24 38 E
Al Jahrah, Kuwait 44 D5 29 25N 47 40 E
Al Jalāmīd, Si. Arabia 44 D3 31 20N 40 6 E
Al Jamalīyah, Qatar 45 E6 25 37N 51 5 E
Al Janūb □, Lebanon 47 B4 33 20N 35 20 E
Al Jawf, Libya 51 D10 24 10N 23 24 E
Al Jawf, Si. Arabia 44 D3 29 55N 39 40 E
Al Jazirah, Iraq 44 C5 33 30N 44 0 E
Al Jithāmīyah, Si. Arabia 44 E4 27 41N 41 43 E
Al Jubayl, Si. Arabia 45 E6 27 0N 49 50 E
Al Jubaylah, Si. Arabia 44 E5 24 55N 46 25 E
Al Jubb, Si. Arabia 44 E4 27 11N 42 17 E
Al Junaynah, Sudan 51 F10 13 27N 22 45 E
Al Kabā'ish, Iraq 44 D5 30 58N 47 0 E
Al Karak, Jordan 47 D4 31 11N 35 42 E
Al Karak □, Jordan 47 E5 31 0N 36 0 E
Al Kāzim Tyah, Iraq 44 C5 33 22N 44 12 E
Al Khābūra, Oman 45 F8 23 57N 57 5 E
Al Khafji, Si. Arabia 45 E6 28 24N 48 29 E
Al Khalīl, West Bank 47 D4 31 32N 35 6 E
Al Khāliş, Iraq 44 C5 33 49N 44 32 E
Al Kharsānīyah, Si. Arabia 45 E6 27 13N 49 18 E
Al Khaşab, Oman 45 E8 26 14N 56 15 E
Al Khawr, Qatar 45 E6 25 41N 51 30 E
Al Khiḍr, Iraq 44 D5 31 12N 45 33 E
Al Khiyām, Lebanon 47 B4 33 20N 35 36 E
Al Khums, Libya 51 B8 32 40N 14 17 E
Al Kiswah, Syria 47 B5 33 23N 36 14 E
Al Kūfah, Iraq 44 C5 32 2N 44 24 E
Al Kufrah, Libya 51 D10 24 17N 23 15 E
Al Kuhayfīyah, Si. Arabia 44 E4 27 12N 43 3 E
Al Kūt, Iraq 44 C5 32 30N 46 0 E
Al Kuwayt, Kuwait 44 D5 29 30N 48 0 E
Al Labwah, Lebanon 47 A5 34 11N 36 20 E
Al Lādhiqīyah, Syria 44 C2 35 30N 35 45 E
Al Līth, Si. Arabia 46 C3 20 9N 40 15 E
Al Liwā', Oman 45 E8 24 31N 56 36 E
Al Luḥayyah, Yemen 46 D3 15 45N 42 40 E
Al Madīnah, Iraq 44 D5 30 57N 47 16 E
Al Madīnah, Si. Arabia 46 C2 24 35N 39 52 E
Al Mafraq, Jordan 47 C5 32 17N 36 14 E
Al Maḥmūdīyah, Iraq 44 C5 33 3N 44 21 E
Al Majma'ah, Si. Arabia 44 E5 25 57N 45 22 E
Al Makhruq, W. →, Jordan 47 D6 31 28N 37 0 E
Al Makḥūl, Si. Arabia 44 E4 26 37N 42 39 E
Al Manāmah, Bahrain 45 E6 26 10N 50 30 E
Al Maqwa', Kuwait 44 D5 29 10N 47 59 E
Al Marj, Libya 51 B10 32 25N 20 30 E
Al Maṭlā, Kuwait 44 D5 29 24N 47 40 E
Al Mawjib, W. →, Jordan 47 D4 31 28N 35 36 E
Al Mawşil, Iraq 44 B4 36 15N 43 5 E
Al Mayādin, Syria 44 C4 35 1N 40 27 E
Al Mazār, Jordan 47 D4 31 4N 35 41 E
Al Midhnab, Si. Arabia 44 E5 25 50N 44 18 E
Al Minā', Lebanon 47 A4 34 24N 35 49 E
Al Miqdādīyah, Iraq 44 C5 34 0N 45 0 E
Al Mubarraz, Si. Arabia 45 E6 25 30N 49 40 E
Al Mudawwarah, Jordan 47 F5 29 19N 36 0 E
Al Mughayrā', U.A.E. 45 E7 24 5N 53 32 E
Al Muḥarraq, Bahrain 45 E6 26 15N 50 40 E
Al Mukallā, Yemen 46 E4 14 33N 49 2 E
Al Mukhā, Yemen 46 E3 13 18N 43 15 E
Al Musayjīd, Si. Arabia 44 E3 24 5N 39 5 E
Al Musayyib, Iraq 44 C5 32 49N 44 20 E
Al Muwayliḥ, Si. Arabia 44 E2 27 40N 35 30 E
Al Qā'im, Iraq 44 C4 34 21N 41 7 E
Al Qalībah, Si. Arabia 44 D3 28 24N 37 42 E
Al Qāmishli, Syria 44 B4 37 10N 41 10 E
Al Qaryatayn, Syria 47 A6 34 12N 37 13 E
Al Qaşīm, Si. Arabia 44 E4 26 0N 43 0 E
Al Qaţ'ā, Syria 44 C4 34 40N 40 48 E
Al Qaţīf, Si. Arabia 45 E6 26 35N 50 0 E
Al Qatrānah, Jordan 47 D5 31 12N 36 6 E
Al Qaţrūn, Libya 51 D9 24 56N 15 3 E
Al Qayşūmah, Si. Arabia 44 D5 28 20N 46 7 E
Al Quds = Jerusalem, Israel 47 D4 31 47N 35 10 E
Al Qunayţirah, Syria 47 C4 32 55N 35 45 E
Al Qurnah, Iraq 44 D5 31 1N 47 25 E
Al Quşayr, Iraq 44 D5 30 39N 45 50 E
Al Quşayr, Syria 47 A5 34 31N 36 34 E
Al Qutayfah, Syria 47 B5 33 44N 36 36 E
Al 'Ubaylah, Si. Arabia 46 C5 21 59N 50 57 E
Al 'Udaylīyah, Si. Arabia 45 E6 25 8N 49 18 E
Al 'Ulā, Si. Arabia 44 E3 26 35N 38 0 E
Al 'Uqayr, Si. Arabia 45 E6 25 40N 50 15 E
Al 'Uthmānīyah, Si. Arabia 45 E6 25 5N 49 22 E
Al 'Uwaynid, Si. Arabia 44 E5 24 50N 46 0 E
Al 'Uwayqīlah, Si. Arabia 44 D4 30 30N 42 10 E
Al 'Uyūn, Ḥijāz, Si. Arabia 44 E3 24 33N 39 35 E
Al 'Uyūn, Najd, Si. Arabia 44 E4 26 30N 43 50 E
Al 'Uzayr, Iraq 44 D5 31 19N 47 25 E
Al Wajh, Si. Arabia 44 E3 26 10N 36 30 E
Al Wakrah, Qatar 45 E6 25 10N 51 40 E
Al Wannān, Si. Arabia 45 E6 26 55N 48 24 E
Al Waqbah, Si. Arabia 44 D5 28 48N 45 33 E
Al Wari'āh, Si. Arabia 44 E5 27 51N 47 25 E
Al Wusayl, Qatar 45 E6 25 29N 51 29 E
Ala Dağ, Turkey 44 B2 37 44N 35 9 E
Ala Tau Shankou = Dzungarian Gates, Kazakstan 32 B3 45 0N 82 0 E
Alabama □, U.S.A. 77 J2 33 0N 87 0W
Alabama →, U.S.A. 77 K2 31 8N 87 57W
Alabaster, U.S.A. 77 J2 33 15N 86 49W
Alaçam Dağları, Turkey 21 E13 39 18N 28 49 E
Alachua, U.S.A. 77 L4 29 47N 82 30W
Alaérma, Greece 23 C9 36 9N 27 57 E
Alagoa Grande, Brazil 93 E11 7 3S 35 35W
Alagoas □, Brazil 93 E11 9 0S 36 0W
Alagoinhas, Brazil 93 F11 12 7S 38 20W
Alaior, Spain 22 B11 39 57N 4 8 E
Alajero, Canary Is. 22 F2 28 3N 17 13W
Alajuela, Costa Rica 88 D3 10 2N 84 8W
Alakamisy, Madag. 57 C8 21 19S 47 14 E
Alaknanda →, India 43 D8 30 8N 78 36 E
Alakurtti, Russia 24 A5 67 0N 30 30 E
Alamarvdasht, Iran 45 E7 27 37N 52 59 E
Alameda, Calif., U.S.A. 84 H4 37 46N 122 15W
Alameda, N. Mex., U.S.A. 83 J10 35 11N 106 37W
Alamo, U.S.A. 85 J11 37 22N 115 10W
Alamo Crossing, U.S.A. 85 L13 34 16N 113 33W
Alamogordo, U.S.A. 83 K11 32 54N 105 57W
Alamos, Mexico 86 B3 27 0N 109 0W
Alamosa, U.S.A. 83 H11 37 28N 105 52W
Åland, Finland 9 F19 60 15N 20 0 E
Ålands hav, Sweden 9 F18 60 0N 19 30 E
Alandur, India 40 N12 13 0N 80 15 E
Alania = North Ossetia □, Russia 25 F7 43 30N 44 30 E
Alanya, Turkey 25 G5 36 38N 32 0 E
Alaotra, Farihin', Madag. 57 B8 17 30S 48 30 E
Alapayevsk, Russia 26 D7 57 52N 61 42 E
Alaşehir, Turkey 21 E13 38 23N 28 30 E
Alaska □, U.S.A. 68 B5 64 0N 154 0W
Alaska, G. of, Pac. Oc. 68 C5 58 0N 145 0W
Alaska Peninsula, U.S.A. 68 C4 56 0N 159 0W
Alaska Range, U.S.A. 68 B4 62 50N 151 0W
Älät, Azerbaijan 25 G8 39 58N 49 25 E
Alatyr, Russia 24 D8 54 55N 46 35 E
Alausi, Ecuador 92 D3 2 0S 78 50W
Alava, C., U.S.A. 82 B1 48 10N 124 44W
Alavus, Finland 9 E20 62 35N 23 36 E
Alawoona, Australia 63 E3 34 45S 140 30 E
'Alayh, Lebanon 47 B4 33 46N 35 33 E
Alba, Italy 18 D8 44 42N 8 2 E
Alba-Iulia, Romania 17 E12 46 8N 23 39 E
Albacete, Spain 19 C5 39 0N 1 50W
Albacutya, L., Australia 63 F3 35 45S 141 58 E
Albanel, L., Canada 70 B5 50 55N 73 12W
Albania ■, Europe 21 D9 41 0N 20 0 E
Albany, Australia 61 G2 35 1S 117 58 E
Albany, Ga., U.S.A. 77 K3 31 35N 84 10W
Albany, N.Y., U.S.A. 79 D11 42 39N 73 45W
Albany, Oreg., U.S.A. 82 D2 44 38N 123 6W
Albany, Tex., U.S.A. 81 J5 32 44N 99 18W
Albany →, Canada 70 B3 52 17N 81 31W
Albardón, Argentina 94 C2 31 20S 68 30W
Albatross B., Australia 62 A3 12 45S 141 30 E
Albemarle, U.S.A. 77 H5 35 21N 80 11W
Albemarle Sd., U.S.A. 77 H7 36 5N 76 0W
Alberche →, Spain 19 C3 39 58N 4 46W
Alberdi, Paraguay 94 B4 26 14S 58 20W
Albert, L., Australia 63 F2 35 30S 139 10 E
Albert Edward Ra., Australia 60 C4 18 17S 127 57 E
Albert L., Africa 54 B3 1 30N 31 0 E
Albert Lea, U.S.A. 80 D8 43 39N 93 22W
Albert Nile →, Uganda 54 B3 3 36N 32 2 E
Albert Town, Bahamas 89 B5 22 37N 74 33W
Alberta □, Canada 72 C6 54 40N 115 0W
Alberti, Argentina 94 D3 35 1S 60 16W
Albertinia, S. Africa 56 E3 34 11S 21 34 E
Alberton, Canada 71 C7 46 50N 64 0W
Albertville = Kalemie, Dem. Rep. of the Congo 54 D2 5 55S 29 9 E
Albertville, France 18 D7 45 40N 6 22 E
Albertville, U.S.A. 77 H2 34 16N 86 13W
Albi, France 18 E5 43 56N 2 9 E
Albia, U.S.A. 80 E8 41 2N 92 48W
Albina, Surinam 93 B8 5 37N 54 15W
Albina, Ponta, Angola 56 B1 15 52S 11 44 E
Albion, Mich., U.S.A. 76 D3 42 15N 84 45W
Albion, Nebr., U.S.A. 80 E6 41 42N 98 0W
Albion, Pa., U.S.A. 78 E4 41 53N 80 22W
Alborán, Medit. S. 19 E4 35 57N 3 0W
Ålborg, Denmark 9 H13 57 2N 9 54 E
Alborz, Reshteh-ye Kūhhā-ye, Iran 45 C7 36 0N 52 0 E
Albuquerque, U.S.A. 83 J10 35 5N 106 39W
Albuquerque, Cayos de, Caribbean 88 D3 12 10N 81 50W
Alburg, U.S.A. 79 B11 44 59N 73 18W
Albury-Wodonga, Australia 63 F4 36 3S 146 56 E
Alcalá de Henares, Spain 19 B4 40 28N 3 22W
Alcalá la Real, Spain 19 D4 37 27N 3 57W
Álcamo, Italy 20 F5 37 59N 12 55 E
Alcaníz, Spain 19 B5 41 2N 0 8W
Alcântara, Brazil 93 D10 2 20S 44 30W
Alcántara, Embalse de, Spain 19 C2 39 44N 6 50W
Alcantarilla, Spain 19 D5 37 59N 1 12W
Alcaraz, Sierra de, Spain 19 C4 38 40N 2 20W
Alcaudete, Spain 19 D3 37 35N 4 5W
Alcázar de San Juan, Spain 19 C4 39 24N 3 12W
Alchevsk, Ukraine 25 E6 48 30N 38 45 E
Alcira = Alzira, Spain 19 C5 39 9N 0 30W
Alcova, U.S.A. 82 E10 42 34N 106 43W
Alcoy, Spain 19 C5 38 43N 0 30W
Alcúdia, Spain 22 B10 39 51N 3 7 E
Alcúdia, B. d', Spain 22 B10 39 47N 3 15 E
Aldabra Is., Seychelles 49 G8 9 22S 46 28 E
Aldama, Mexico 87 C5 23 0N 98 4W
Aldan, Russia 27 D13 58 40N 125 30 E
Aldan →, Russia 27 C13 63 28N 129 35 E
Aldea, Pta. de la, Canary Is. 22 G4 28 0N 15 50W
Aldeburgh, U.K. 11 E9 52 10N 1 37 E
Alder Pk., U.S.A. 84 K5 35 53N 121 22W
Alderney, U.K. 11 H5 49 42N 2 11W
Aldershot, U.K. 11 F7 51 15N 0 44W
Aledo, U.S.A. 80 E9 41 12N 90 45W
Aleg, Mauritania 50 E3 17 3N 13 55W
Alegranza, Canary Is. 22 E6 29 23N 13 32W
Alegranza, I., Canary Is. 22 E6 29 23N 13 32W
Alegre, Brazil 95 A7 20 50S 41 30W
Alegrete, Brazil 95 B4 29 40S 56 0W
Aleisk, Russia 26 D9 52 40N 83 0 E
Aleksandriya = Oleksandriya, Ukraine 17 C14 50 37N 26 19 E
Aleksandrov Gay, Russia 25 D8 50 9N 48 34 E
Aleksandrovsk-Sakhalinskiy, Russia 27 D15 50 50N 142 20 E
Além Paraíba, Brazil 95 A7 21 52S 42 41W
Alemania, Argentina 94 B2 25 40S 65 30W
Alemania, Chile 94 B2 25 10S 69 55W
Alençon, France 18 B4 48 27N 0 4 E
Alenquer, Brazil 93 D8 1 56S 54 46W
Alenuihaha Channel, U.S.A. 74 H17 20 30N 156 0W
Aleppo = Ḥalab, Syria 44 B3 36 10N 37 15 E
Alès, France 18 D6 44 9N 4 5 E
Alessándria, Italy 18 D8 44 54N 8 37 E
Ålesund, Norway 9 E12 62 28N 6 12 E
Aleutian Is., Pac. Oc. 68 C2 52 0N 175 0W
Aleutian Trench, Pac. Oc. 64 C10 48 0N 180 0 E
Alexander, U.S.A. 80 B3 47 51N 103 39W
Alexander, Mt., Australia 61 E3 28 58S 120 16 E
Alexander Arch., U.S.A. 68 C6 56 0N 136 0W
Alexander Bay, S. Africa 56 D2 28 40S 16 30 E
Alexander City, U.S.A. 77 J3 32 56N 85 58W
Alexander I., Antarctica 5 C17 69 0S 70 0W
Alexandra, Australia 63 F4 37 8S 145 40 E
Alexandra, N.Z. 59 L2 45 14S 169 25 E
Alexandra Falls, Canada 72 A5 60 29N 116 18W
Alexandria = El Iskandarîya, Egypt 51 B11 31 13N 29 58 E
Alexandria, B.C., Canada 72 C4 52 35N 122 27W
Alexandria, Ont., Canada 79 A10 45 19N 74 38W
Alexandria, Romania 17 G13 43 57N 25 24 E
Alexandria, S. Africa 56 E4 33 38S 26 28 E
Alexandria, U.K. 12 F4 55 59N 4 35W
Alexandria, La., U.S.A. 81 K8 31 18N 92 27W
Alexandria, Minn., U.S.A. 80 C7 45 53N 95 22W
Alexandria, S. Dak., U.S.A. 80 D6 43 39N 97 47W
Alexandria, Va., U.S.A. 76 F7 38 48N 77 3W
Alexandria Bay, U.S.A. 79 B9 44 20N 75 55W
Alexandrina, L., Australia 63 F2 35 25S 139 10 E
Alexandroúpolis, Greece 21 D11 40 50N 25 54 E
Alexis →, Canada 71 B8 52 33N 56 8W
Alexis Creek, Canada 72 C4 52 10N 123 20W
Alfabia, Spain 22 B9 39 44N 2 44 E
Alfenas, Brazil 95 A6 21 20S 46 10W
Alford, Aberds., U.K. 12 D6 57 14N 2 41W
Alford, Lincs., U.K. 10 D8 53 15N 0 10 E
Alfred, Maine, U.S.A. 79 C14 43 29N 70 43W
Alfred, N.Y., U.S.A. 78 D7 42 16N 77 48W
Alfreton, U.K. 10 D6 53 6N 1 24W
Alga, Kazakstan 25 E10 49 53N 57 20 E
Algaida, Spain 22 B9 39 33N 2 53 E
Ålgård, Norway 9 G11 58 46N 5 53 E
Algarve, Portugal 19 D1 36 58N 8 20W
Algeciras, Spain 19 D3 36 9N 5 28W
Algemesí, Spain 19 C5 39 11N 0 27W
Alger, Algeria 50 A6 36 42N 3 8 E
Algeria ■, Africa 50 C6 28 30N 2 0 E
Alghero, Italy 20 D3 40 33N 8 19 E
Algiers = Alger, Algeria 50 A6 36 42N 3 8 E
Algoa B., S. Africa 56 E4 33 50S 25 45 E
Algoma, U.S.A. 76 C2 44 36N 87 26W
Algona, U.S.A. 80 D7 43 4N 94 14W
Algonac, U.S.A. 78 D2 42 37N 82 32W
Algonquin Prov. Park, Canada 70 C4 45 50N 78 30W
Algorta, Uruguay 96 C5 32 25S 57 23W
Alhambra, U.S.A. 85 L8 34 8N 118 6W
Alhucemas = Al Hoceïma, Morocco 50 A5 35 8N 3 58W
'Alī al Gharbī, Iraq 44 C5 32 30N 46 45 E
Alī ash Sharqī, Iraq 44 C5 32 7N 46 44 E
'Alī Khēl, Afghan. 42 C3 33 57N 69 43 E
Alī Shāh, Iran 44 B5 38 9N 45 50 E
'Alīābād, Khorāsān, Iran 45 C8 32 30N 57 30 E
'Alīābād, Kordestān, Iran 44 C5 35 4N 46 58 E
'Alīābād, Yazd, Iran 45 D7 31 41N 53 49 E
Aliağa, Turkey 21 E12 38 47N 26 59 E
Aliákmon →, Greece 21 D10 40 30N 22 36 E
Alicante, Spain 19 C5 38 23N 0 30W
Alice, S. Africa 56 E4 32 48S 26 55 E
Alice, U.S.A. 81 M5 27 45N 98 5W
Alice →, Queens., Australia 62 C3 24 2S 144 50 E
Alice →, Queens., Australia 62 B3 15 35S 142 20 E
Alice Arm, Canada 72 B3 55 29N 129 31W
Alice Springs, Australia 62 C1 23 40S 133 50 E
Alicedale, S. Africa 56 E4 33 15S 26 4 E
Aliceville, U.S.A. 77 J1 33 8N 88 9W
Aliganj, India 43 F8 27 30N 79 10 E
Aligarh, Raj., India 42 G7 25 55N 76 15 E
Aligarh, Ut. P., India 42 F8 27 55N 78 10 E
Alīgūdarz, Iran 45 C6 33 25N 49 45 E
Alimnía, Greece 23 C9 36 16N 27 43 E
Alingsås, Sweden 9 H15 57 56N 12 31 E
Alipur, Pakistan 42 E4 29 25N 70 55 E
Alipur Duar, India 41 F16 26 30N 89 35 E
Aliquippa, U.S.A. 78 F4 40 37N 80 15W
Alitus = Alytus, Lithuania 9 J21 54 24N 24 3 E
Aliwal North, S. Africa 56 E4 30 45S 26 45 E
Alix, Canada 72 C6 52 24N 113 11W
Aljustrel, Portugal 19 D1 37 55N 8 10W
Alkmaar, Neths. 15 B4 52 37N 4 45 E
All American Canal, U.S.A. 83 K6 32 45N 115 15W
Allagash →, U.S.A. 77 B11 47 5N 69 3W
Allah Dad, Pakistan 42 G2 25 38N 67 34 E
Allahabad, India 43 G9 25 25N 81 58 E
Allan, Canada 73 C7 51 53N 106 4W
Allanmyo, Burma 41 K19 19 30N 95 17 E
Allanridge, S. Africa 56 D4 27 45S 26 40 E
Allegany, U.S.A. 78 D6 42 6N 78 30W
Allegheny →, U.S.A. 78 F5 40 27N 80 1W
Allegheny Mts., U.S.A. 76 G6 38 15N 80 10W
Allegheny Reservoir, U.S.A. 78 E6 41 50N 79 0W
Allen, Bog of, Ireland 13 C5 53 15N 7 0W
Allen, L., Ireland 13 B3 54 8N 8 4W
Allendale, U.S.A. 77 J5 33 1N 81 18W
Allende, Mexico 86 B4 28 20N 100 50W
Allentown, U.S.A. 79 F9 40 37N 75 29W
Alleppey, India 40 Q10 9 30N 76 28 E
Aller →, Germany 16 B5 52 56N 9 12 E
Alliance, Nebr., U.S.A. 80 D3 42 6N 102 52W
Alliance, Ohio, U.S.A. 78 F3 40 55N 81 6W
Allier →, France 18 C5 46 57N 3 4 E
Alliford Bay, Canada 72 C2 53 12N 131 58W
Alliston, Canada 78 B5 44 9N 79 52W
Alloa, U.K. 12 E5 56 7N 3 47W
Allora, Australia 63 D5 28 2S 152 0 E
Alluitsup Paa = Sydprøven, Greenland 4 C5 60 30N 45 35W
Alma, Canada 71 C5 48 35N 71 40W
Alma, Ga., U.S.A. 77 K4 31 33N 82 28W
Alma, Kans., U.S.A. 80 F6 39 1N 96 17W
Alma, Mich., U.S.A. 76 D3 43 23N 84 39W
Alma, Nebr., U.S.A. 80 E5 40 6N 99 22W
Alma Ata = Almaty, Kazakstan 26 E8 43 15N 76 57 E
Almada, Portugal 19 C1 38 40N 9 9W
Almaden, Australia 62 B3 17 22S 144 40 E
Almadén, Spain 19 C3 38 49N 4 52W
Almanor, L., U.S.A. 82 F3 40 14N 121 9W
Almansa, Spain 19 C5 38 51N 1 5W
Almanzor, Pico, Spain 19 B3 40 15N 5 18W
Almanzora →, Spain 19 D5 37 14N 1 46W
Almaty, Kazakstan 26 E8 43 15N 76 57 E
Almazán, Spain 19 B4 41 30N 2 30W
Almeirim, Brazil 93 D8 1 30S 52 34W
Almelo, Neths. 15 B6 52 22N 6 42 E
Almendralejo, Spain 19 C2 38 41N 6 26W
Almere-Stad, Neths. 15 B5 52 20N 5 15 E
Almería, Spain 19 D4 36 52N 2 27W
Almirante, Panama 88 E3 9 10N 82 30W
Almiroú, Kólpos, Greece 23 D6 35 23N 24 20 E
Almond, U.S.A. 78 D7 42 19N 77 44W
Almont, U.S.A. 78 D1 42 55N 83 3W
Almonte, Canada 79 A8 45 14N 76 12W
Almora, India 43 E8 29 38N 79 40 E
Alness, U.K. 12 D4 57 41N 4 16W
Alnmouth, U.K. 10 B6 55 24N 1 37W
Alnwick, U.K. 10 B6 55 24N 1 42W
Aloi, Uganda 54 B3 2 16N 33 10 E
Alon, Burma 41 H19 22 12N 95 5 E
Alor, Indonesia 37 F6 8 15S 124 30 E
Alor Setar, Malaysia 39 J3 6 7N 100 22 E
Alot, India 42 H6 23 56N 75 40 E
Aloysius, Mt., Australia 61 E4 26 0S 128 38 E
Alpaugh, U.S.A. 84 K7 35 53N 119 29W
Alpena, U.S.A. 76 C4 45 4N 83 27W
Alpha, Australia 62 C4 23 39S 146 37 E
Alphen aan den Rijn, Neths. 15 B4 52 7N 4 40 E
Alpine, Ariz., U.S.A. 83 K9 33 51N 109 9W
Alpine, Calif., U.S.A. 85 N10 32 50N 116 46W
Alpine, Tex., U.S.A. 81 K3 30 22N 103 40W
Alps, Europe 18 C8 46 30N 9 30 E
Alsace, France 18 B7 48 15N 7 25 E
Alsask, Canada 73 C7 51 21N 109 59W
Alsasua, Spain 19 A4 42 54N 2 10W
Alsek →, U.S.A. 72 B1 59 10N 138 12W
Alsten, Norway 8 D15 65 58N 12 40 E
Alston, U.K. 10 C5 54 49N 2 25W
Alta, Norway 8 B20 69 57N 23 10 E
Alta Gracia, Argentina 94 C3 31 40S 64 30W
Alta Sierra, U.S.A. 85 K8 35 42N 118 33W
Altaelva →, Norway 8 B20 69 54N 23 17 E
Altafjorden, Norway 8 A20 70 5N 23 5 E
Altai = Aerhtai Shan, Mongolia 32 B4 46 40N 92 45 E
Altamaha →, U.S.A. 77 K5 31 20N 81 20W
Altamira, Brazil 93 D8 3 12S 52 10W
Altamira, Chile 94 B2 25 47S 69 51W
Altamira, Mexico 87 C5 22 24N 97 55W
Altamont, U.S.A. 79 D10 42 43N 74 3W
Altamura, Italy 20 D7 40 49N 16 33 E
Altanbulag, Mongolia 32 A5 50 16N 106 30 E
Altar, Mexico 86 A2 30 40N 111 50W
Altar, Desierto de, Mexico 86 B2 30 10N 112 0W
Altata, Mexico 86 C3 24 30N 108 0W
Altavista, U.S.A. 76 G6 37 6N 79 17W
Altay, China 32 B3 47 48N 88 10 E
Altea, Spain 19 C5 38 38N 0 2W
Altiplano = Bolivian Plateau, S. Amer. 90 E4 20 0S 67 30W
Alto Araguaia, Brazil 93 G8 17 15S 53 20W
Alto Cuchumatanes = Cuchumatanes, Sierra de los, Guatemala 88 C1 15 35N 91 25W
Alto del Carmen, Chile 94 B1 28 46S 70 30W
Alto del Inca, Chile 94 A2 24 10S 68 10W
Alto Ligonha, Mozam. 55 F4 15 30S 38 11 E
Alto Molocue, Mozam. 55 F4 15 50S 37 35 E
Alto Paraguay □, Paraguay 94 A4 21 0S 58 30W
Alto Paraná □, Paraguay 95 B5 25 30S 54 50W
Alton, Canada 78 C4 43 54N 80 5W
Alton, U.K. 11 F7 51 9N 0 59W
Alton, Ill., U.S.A. 80 F9 38 53N 90 11W
Alton, N.H., U.S.A. 79 C13 43 27N 71 13W
Altoona, U.S.A. 78 F6 40 31N 78 24W
Altūn Kūprī, Iraq 44 C5 35 45N 44 9 E
Altun Shan, China 32 C3 38 30N 88 0 E
Alturas, U.S.A. 82 F3 41 29N 120 32W
Altus, U.S.A. 81 H5 34 38N 99 20W
Alucra, Turkey 25 F6 40 22N 38 47 E
Alūksne, Latvia 9 H22 57 24N 27 3 E
Alunite, U.S.A. 85 K12 35 59N 114 55W
Alusi, Indonesia 37 F8 7 35S 131 40 E
Alva, U.S.A. 81 G5 36 48N 98 40W
Alvarado, Mexico 87 D5 18 40N 95 50W
Alvarado, U.S.A. 81 J6 32 24N 97 13W
Alvaro Obregón, Presa, Mexico 86 B3 27 55N 109 52W
Alvear, Argentina 94 B4 29 5S 56 30W
Alvesta, Sweden 9 H16 56 54N 14 35 E
Alvin, U.S.A. 81 L7 29 26N 95 15W
Alvinston, Canada 78 D3 42 49N 81 52W
Älvkarleby, Sweden 9 F17 60 34N 17 26 E
Alvord Desert, U.S.A. 82 E4 42 30N 118 25W
Älvsbyn, Sweden 8 D19 65 40N 21 0 E
Alwar, India 42 F7 27 38N 76 34 E
Alxa Zuoqi, China 34 E3 38 50N 105 40 E
Alyangula, Australia 62 A2 13 55S 136 30 E
Alyata = Älät, Azerbaijan 25 G8 39 58N 49 25 E
Alyth, U.K. 12 E5 56 38N 3 13W
Alytus, Lithuania 9 J21 54 24N 24 3 E
Alzada, U.S.A. 80 C2 45 2N 104 25W
Alzira, Spain 19 C5 39 9N 0 30W
Am-Timan, Chad 51 F10 11 0N 20 10 E
Amadeus, L., Australia 61 D5 24 54S 131 0 E

Amadi

Amadi, *Dem. Rep. of the Congo* . **54 B2** 3 40N 26 40 E
Amâdi, *Sudan* . **51 G12** 5 29N 30 25 E
Amadjuak L., *Canada* . **69 B12** 65 0N 71 8W
Amagansett, *U.S.A.* . **79 F12** 40 59N 72 9W
Amagasaki, *Japan* . **31 G7** 34 42N 135 20 E
Amahai, *Indonesia* . **37 E7** 3 20S 128 55 E
Amakusa-Shotō, *Japan* . **31 H5** 32 15N 130 10 E
Åmål, *Sweden* . **9 G15** 59 3N 12 42 E
Amaliás, *Greece* . **21 F9** 37 47N 21 22 E
Amalner, *India* . **40 J9** 21 5N 75 5 E
Amamapare, *Indonesia* . **37 E9** 4 53S 136 38 E
Amambaí, *Brazil* . **95 A4** 23 5S 55 13W
Amambaí →, *Brazil* . **95 A5** 23 22S 53 56W
Amambay □, *Paraguay* . **95 A4** 23 0S 56 0W
Amambay, Cordillera de, *S. Amer.* . **95 A4** 23 0S 55 45W
Amami-Guntō, *Japan* . **31 L4** 27 16N 129 21 E
Amami-Ō-Shima, *Japan* . **31 L4** 28 0N 129 0 E
Amaná, L., *Brazil* . **92 D6** 2 35S 64 40W
Amanat →, *India* . **43 G11** 24 7N 84 4 E
Amanda Park, *U.S.A.* . **84 C3** 47 28N 123 55W
Amangeldy, *Kazakstan* . **26 D7** 50 10N 65 10 E
Amapá, *Brazil* . **93 C8** 2 5N 50 50W
Amapá □, *Brazil* . **93 C8** 1 40N 52 0W
Amarante, *Brazil* . **93 E10** 6 14S 42 50W
Amaranth, *Canada* . **73 C9** 50 36N 98 43W
Amargosa →, *U.S.A.* . **85 J10** 36 14N 116 51W
Amargosa Range, *U.S.A.* . **85 J10** 36 20N 116 45W
Amári, *Greece* . **23 D6** 35 13N 24 40 E
Amarillo, *U.S.A.* . **81 H4** 35 13N 101 50W
Amarkantak, *India* . **43 H9** 22 40N 81 45 E
Amaro, Mte., *Italy* . **20 C6** 42 5N 14 5 E
Amarpur, *India* . **43 G12** 25 5N 87 0 E
Amarwara, *India* . **43 H8** 22 18N 79 10 E
Amasya □, *Turkey* . **25 F6** 40 40N 35 50 E
Amata, *Australia* . **61 E5** 26 9S 131 9 E
Amatikulu, *S. Africa* . **57 D5** 29 3S 31 33 E
Amatitlán, *Guatemala* . **88 D1** 14 29N 90 38W
Amay, *Belgium* . **15 D5** 50 33N 5 19 E
Amazon = Amazonas →, *S. Amer.* . **93 D9** 0 5S 50 0W
Amazonas □, *Brazil* . **92 E6** 5 0S 65 0W
Amazonas →, *S. Amer.* . **93 D9** 0 5S 50 0W
Ambah, *India* . **42 F8** 26 43N 78 13 E
Ambahakily, *Madag.* . **57 C7** 21 36S 43 41 E
Ambala, *India* . **42 D7** 30 23N 76 56 E
Ambalavao, *Madag.* . **57 C8** 21 50S 46 56 E
Ambanja, *Madag.* . **57 A8** 13 40S 48 27 E
Ambarchik, *Russia* . **27 C17** 69 40N 162 20 E
Ambarijeby, *Madag.* . **57 A8** 14 56S 47 41 E
Ambaro, Helodranon', *Madag.* . **57 A8** 13 23S 48 38 E
Ambato, *Ecuador* . **92 D3** 1 5S 78 42W
Ambato, Sierra de, *Argentina* . **94 B2** 28 25S 66 10W
Ambato Boeny, *Madag.* . **57 B8** 16 28S 46 43 E
Ambatofinandrahana, *Madag.* . **57 C8** 20 33S 46 48 E
Ambatolampy, *Madag.* . **57 B8** 19 20S 47 35 E
Ambatondrazaka, *Madag.* . **57 B8** 17 55S 48 28 E
Ambatosoratra, *Madag.* . **57 B8** 17 37S 48 31 E
Ambenja, *Madag.* . **57 B8** 15 17S 46 58 E
Amberg, *Germany* . **16 D6** 49 26N 11 52 E
Ambergris Cay, *Belize* . **87 D7** 18 0N 88 0W
Amberley, *N.Z.* . **59 K4** 43 9S 172 44 E
Ambikapur, *India* . **43 H10** 23 15N 83 15 E
Ambilobé, *Madag.* . **57 A8** 13 10S 49 3 E
Ambinanindrano, *Madag.* . **57 C8** 20 5S 48 23 E
Amble, *U.K.* . **10 B6** 55 20N 1 36W
Ambleside, *U.K.* . **10 C5** 54 26N 2 58W
Ambo, *Peru* . **92 F3** 10 5S 76 10W
Ambodifototra, *Madag.* . **57 B8** 16 59S 49 52 E
Ambodilazana, *Madag.* . **57 B8** 18 6S 49 10 E
Ambohimahasoa, *Madag.* . **57 C8** 21 7S 47 13 E
Ambohimanga, *Madag.* . **57 C8** 20 52S 47 36 E
Ambohitra, *Madag.* . **57 A8** 12 30S 49 10 E
Amboise, *France* . **18 C4** 47 24N 1 2 E
Ambon, *Indonesia* . **37 E7** 3 35S 128 20 E
Amboseli, L., *Kenya* . **54 C4** 2 40S 37 10 E
Ambositra, *Madag.* . **57 C8** 20 31S 47 25 E
Ambovombe, *Madag.* . **57 D8** 25 11S 46 5 E
Amboy, *U.S.A.* . **85 L11** 34 33N 115 45W
Amboyna Cay, *S. China Sea* **36 C4** 7 50N 112 50 E
Ambridge, *U.S.A.* . **78 F4** 40 36N 80 14W
Ambriz, *Angola* . **52 F2** 7 48S 13 8 E
Amchitka I., *U.S.A.* . **68 C1** 51 32N 179 0 E
Amderma, *Russia* . **26 C7** 69 45N 61 30 E
Amdhi, *India* . **43 H9** 23 51N 81 27 E
Ameca, *Mexico* . **86 C4** 20 30N 104 0W
Ameca →, *Mexico* . **86 C3** 20 40N 105 15W
Amecameca, *Mexico* . **87 D5** 19 7N 98 46W
Ameland, *Neths.* . **15 A5** 53 27N 5 45 E
Amenia, *U.S.A.* . **79 E11** 41 51N 73 33W
American Falls, *U.S.A.* . **82 E7** 42 47N 112 51W
American Falls Reservoir, *U.S.A.* . **82 E7** 42 47N 112 52W
American Fork, *U.S.A.* . **82 F8** 40 23N 111 48W
American Highland, *Antarctica* . **5 D6** 73 0S 75 0 E
American Samoa ■, *Pac. Oc.* . **59 B13** 14 20S 170 40W
Americana, *Brazil* . **95 A6** 22 45S 47 20W
Americus, *U.S.A.* . **77 K3** 32 4N 84 14W
Amersfoort, *Neths.* . **15 B5** 52 9N 5 23 E
Amersfoort, *S. Africa* . **57 D4** 26 59S 29 53 E
Amery Ice Shelf, *Antarctica* **5 C6** 69 30S 72 0 E
Ames, *U.S.A.* . **80 E8** 42 2N 93 37W
Amesbury, *U.S.A.* . **79 D14** 42 51N 70 56W
Amet, *India* . **42 G5** 25 18N 73 56 E
Amga, *Russia* . **27 C14** 60 50N 132 0 E
Amga →, *Russia* . **27 C14** 62 38N 134 32 E
Amgu, *Russia* . **27 E14** 45 45N 137 15 E
Amgun →, *Russia* . **27 D14** 52 56N 139 38 E
Amherst, *Burma* . **41 L20** 16 2N 97 20 E
Amherst, *Canada* . **71 C7** 45 48N 64 8W
Amherst, *Mass., U.S.A.* . **79 D12** 42 23N 72 31W
Amherst, *N.Y., U.S.A.* . **78 D6** 42 59N 78 48W
Amherst, *Ohio, U.S.A.* . **78 E2** 41 24N 82 14W
Amherst I., *Canada* . **79 B8** 44 8N 76 43W
Amherstburg, *Canada* . **70 D3** 42 6N 83 6W
Amiata, Mte., *Italy* . **20 C4** 42 53N 11 37 E
Amidon, *U.S.A.* . **80 B3** 46 29N 103 19W
Amiens, *France* . **18 B5** 49 54N 2 16 E
Amīrābād, *Iran* . **44 C5** 33 20N 46 16 E
Amirante Is., *Seychelles* . **28 K9** 6 0S 53 0 E
Amisk L., *Canada* . **73 C8** 54 35N 102 15W
Amistad, Presa de la, *Mexico* . **86 B4** 29 24N 101 0W
Amite, *U.S.A.* . **81 K9** 30 44N 90 30W
Amla, *India* . **42 J8** 21 56N 78 7 E
Amlia I., *U.S.A.* . **68 C2** 52 4N 173 30W
Amlwch, *U.K.* . **10 D3** 53 24N 4 20W
'Ammān, *Jordan* . **47 D4** 31 57N 35 52 E
'Ammān □, *Jordan* . **47 D5** 31 40N 36 30 E
Ammanford, *U.K.* . **11 F4** 51 48N 3 59W
Ammassalik = Angmagssalik, *Greenland* **4 C6** 65 40N 37 20W
Ammon, *U.S.A.* . **82 E8** 43 28N 111 58W
Amnat Charoen, *Thailand* . **38 E5** 15 51N 104 38 E
Amnura, *Bangla.* . **43 G13** 24 37N 88 25 E
Āmol, *Iran* . **45 B7** 36 23N 52 20 E
Amorgós, *Greece* . **21 F11** 36 50N 25 57 E
Amory, *U.S.A.* . **77 J1** 33 59N 88 29W
Amos, *Canada* . **70 C4** 48 35N 78 5W
Åmot, *Norway* . **9 G13** 59 57N 9 54 E
Amoy = Xiamen, *China* . **33 D6** 24 25N 118 4 E
Ampang, *Malaysia* . **39 L3** 3 8N 101 45 E
Ampanihy, *Madag.* . **57 C7** 24 40S 44 45 E
Ampasindava, Helodranon', *Madag.* . **57 A8** 13 40S 48 15 E
Ampasindava, Saikanosy, *Madag.* . **57 A8** 13 42S 47 55 E
Ampenan, *Indonesia* . **36 F5** 8 35S 116 13 E
Amper →, *Germany* . **16 D6** 48 29N 11 55 E
Ampotaka, *Madag.* . **57 D7** 25 3S 44 41 E
Ampoza, *Madag.* . **57 C7** 22 20S 44 44 E
Amqui, *Canada* . **71 C6** 48 28N 67 27W
Amravati, *India* . **40 J10** 20 55N 77 45 E
Amreli, *India* . **42 J4** 21 35N 71 17 E
Amritsar, *India* . **42 D6** 31 35N 74 57 E
Amroha, *India* . **43 E8** 28 53N 78 30 E
Amsterdam, *Neths.* . **15 B4** 52 23N 4 54 E
Amsterdam, *U.S.A.* . **79 D10** 42 56N 74 11W
Amsterdam, I., *Ind. Oc.* . **3 F13** 38 30S 77 30 E
Amstetten, *Austria* . **16 D8** 48 7N 14 51 E
Amudarya →, *Uzbekistan* **26 E6** 43 58N 59 34 E
Amundsen Gulf, *Canada* . **68 A7** 71 0N 124 0W
Amundsen Sea, *Antarctica* . **5 D15** 72 0S 115 0W
Amuntai, *Indonesia* . **36 E5** 2 28S 115 25 E
Amur →, *Russia* . **27 D15** 52 56N 141 10 E
Amurang, *Indonesia* . **37 D6** 1 5N 124 40 E
Amuri Pass, *N.Z.* . **59 K4** 42 31S 172 11 E
Amursk, *Russia* . **27 D14** 50 14N 136 54 E
Amyderya = Amudarya →, *Uzbekistan* . **26 E6** 43 58N 59 34 E
An Bien, *Vietnam* . **39 H5** 9 45N 105 0 E
An Hoa, *Vietnam* . **38 E7** 15 40N 108 5 E
An Nabatīyah at Tahta, *Lebanon* . **47 B4** 33 23N 35 27 E
An Nabk, *Si. Arabia* . **44 D3** 31 20N 37 20 E
An Nabk, *Syria* . **47 A5** 34 2N 36 44 E
An Nabk Abū Qaşr, *Si. Arabia* . **44 D3** 30 21N 38 34 E
An Nafūd, *Si. Arabia* . **44 D4** 28 15N 41 0 E
An Najaf, *Iraq* . **44 C5** 32 3N 44 15 E
An Nāşirīyah, *Iraq* . **44 D5** 31 0N 46 15 E
An Nhon, *Vietnam* . **38 F7** 13 55N 109 7 E
An Nu'ayrīyah, *Si. Arabia* . **45 E6** 27 30N 48 30 E
An Nuwaybi', W. →, *Si. Arabia* . **47 F3** 29 18N 34 57 E
An Thoi, Dao, *Vietnam* . **39 H5** 9 58N 104 0 E
An Uaimh, *Ireland* . **13 C5** 53 39N 6 41W
Anabar →, *Russia* . **27 B12** 73 8N 113 36 E
'Anabtā, *West Bank* . **47 C4** 32 19N 35 7 E
Anaconda, *U.S.A.* . **82 C7** 46 8N 112 57W
Anacortes, *U.S.A.* . **84 B4** 48 30N 122 37W
Anadarko, *U.S.A.* . **81 H5** 35 4N 98 15W
Anadolu, *Turkey* . **25 G5** 39 0N 30 0 E
Anadyr, *Russia* . **27 C18** 64 35N 177 20 E
Anadyr →, *Russia* . **27 C18** 64 55N 176 5 E
Anadyrskiy Zaliv, *Russia* . **27 C19** 64 0N 180 0 E
Anaga, Pta. de, *Canary Is.* . **22 F3** 28 34N 16 9W
'Ānah, *Iraq* . **44 C4** 34 25N 42 0 E
Anaheim, *U.S.A.* . **85 M9** 33 50N 117 55W
Anahim Lake, *Canada* . **72 C3** 52 28N 125 18W
Anáhuac, *Mexico* . **86 B4** 27 14N 100 9W
Anakapalle, *India* . **41 L13** 17 42N 83 6 E
Anakie, *Australia* . **62 C4** 23 32S 147 45 E
Analalava, *Madag.* . **57 A8** 14 35S 48 0 E
Análipsis, *Greece* . **23 A3** 39 36N 19 55 E
Anambar →, *Pakistan* . **42 D3** 30 15N 68 50 E
Anambas, Kepulauan, *Indonesia* . **39 L6** 3 20N 106 30 E
Anambas Is. = Anambas, Kepulauan, *Indonesia* . **39 L6** 3 20N 106 30 E
Anamosa, *U.S.A.* . **80 D9** 42 7N 91 17W
Anamur, *Turkey* . **25 G5** 36 8N 32 58 E
Anan, *Japan* . **31 H7** 33 54N 134 40 E
Anand, *India* . **42 H5** 22 32N 72 59 E
Anantnag, *India* . **43 C6** 33 45N 75 10 E
Ananyiv, *Ukraine* . **17 E15** 47 44N 29 58 E
Anapodháris →, *Greece* . **23 E7** 34 59N 25 20 E
Anápolis, *Brazil* . **93 G9** 16 15S 48 50W
Anapu →, *Brazil* . **93 D8** 1 53S 50 53W
Anār, *Iran* . **45 D7** 30 55N 55 13 E
Anārak, *Iran* . **45 C7** 33 25N 53 40 E
Anas →, *India* . **42 H5** 23 26N 74 0 E
Anatolia = Anadolu, *Turkey* **25 G5** 39 0N 30 0 E
Anatsogno, *Madag.* . **57 C7** 23 33S 43 46 E
Añatuya, *Argentina* . **94 B3** 28 20S 62 50W
Anaunethad L., *Canada* . **73 A8** 60 55N 104 25W
Anbyŏn, *N. Korea* . **35 E14** 39 1N 127 35 E
Ancaster, *Canada* . **78 C5** 43 13N 79 59W
Anchor Bay, *U.S.A.* . **84 G3** 38 48N 123 34W
Anchorage, *U.S.A.* . **68 B5** 61 13N 149 54W
Anci, *China* . **34 E9** 39 20N 116 40 E
Ancohuma, Nevada, *Bolivia* **92 G5** 16 0S 68 50W
Ancón, *Peru* . **92 F3** 11 50S 77 10W
Ancona, *Italy* . **20 C5** 43 38N 13 30 E
Ancud, *Chile* . **96 E2** 42 0S 73 50W
Ancud, G. de, *Chile* . **96 E2** 42 0S 73 0W
Anda, *China* . **33 B7** 46 24N 125 19 E
Andacollo, *Argentina* . **94 D1** 37 10S 70 42W
Andacollo, *Chile* . **94 C1** 30 14S 71 6W
Andalgalá, *Argentina* . **94 B2** 27 40S 66 30W
Åndalsnes, *Norway* . **9 E12** 62 35N 7 43 E
Andalucía □, *Spain* . **19 D3** 37 35N 5 0W
Andalusia = Andalucía □, *Spain* . **19 D3** 37 35N 5 0W
Andalusia, *U.S.A.* . **77 K2** 31 18N 86 29W
Andaman Is., *Ind. Oc.* . **28 H13** 12 30N 92 30 E
Andaman Sea, *Ind. Oc.* . **36 B1** 13 0N 96 0 E
Andamooka Opal Fields, *Australia* . **63 E2** 30 27S 137 9 E
Andapa, *Madag.* . **57 A8** 14 39S 49 39 E
Andara, *Namibia* . **56 B3** 18 2S 21 9 E
Andenes, *Norway* . **8 B17** 69 19N 16 18 E
Andenne, *Belgium* . **15 D5** 50 28N 5 5 E
Anderson, *Alaska, U.S.A.* . **68 B5** 64 25N 149 15W
Anderson, *Calif., U.S.A.* . **82 F2** 40 27N 122 18W
Anderson, *Ind., U.S.A.* . **76 E3** 40 10N 85 41W
Anderson, *Mo., U.S.A.* . **81 G7** 36 39N 94 27W
Anderson, *S.C., U.S.A.* . **77 H4** 34 31N 82 39W
Anderson →, *Canada* . **68 B7** 69 42N 129 0W
Andes, *U.S.A.* . **79 D10** 42 12N 74 47W
Andes, Cord. de los, *S. Amer.* . **92 H5** 20 0S 68 0W
Andfjorden, *Norway* . **8 B17** 69 10N 16 20 E
Andhra Pradesh □, *India* . **40 L11** 18 0N 79 0 E
Andijon, *Uzbekistan* . **26 E8** 41 10N 72 15 E
Andikíthira, *Greece* . **21 G10** 35 52N 23 15 E
Andīmeshk, *Iran* . **45 C6** 32 27N 48 21 E
Andizhan = Andijon, *Uzbekistan* . **26 E8** 41 10N 72 15 E
Andoany, *Madag.* . **57 A8** 13 25S 48 16 E
Andong, *S. Korea* . **35 F15** 36 40N 128 43 E
Andongwei, *China* . **35 G10** 35 6N 119 20 E
Andoom, *Australia* . **62 A3** 12 25S 141 53 E
Andorra ■, *Europe* . **18 E4** 42 30N 1 30 E
Andorra La Vella, *Andorra* . **18 E4** 42 31N 1 32 E
Andover, *U.K.* . **11 F6** 51 12N 1 29W
Andover, *Maine, U.S.A.* . **79 B14** 44 38N 70 45W
Andover, *Mass., U.S.A.* . **79 D13** 42 40N 71 8W
Andover, *N.J., U.S.A.* . **79 F10** 40 59N 74 45W
Andover, *N.Y., U.S.A.* . **78 D7** 42 10N 77 48W
Andover, *Ohio, U.S.A.* . **78 E4** 41 36N 80 34W
Andøya, *Norway* . **8 B16** 69 10N 15 50 E
Andradina, *Brazil* . **93 H8** 20 54S 51 23W
Andrahary, Mt., *Madag.* . **57 A8** 13 37S 49 17 E
Andramasina, *Madag.* . **57 B8** 19 11S 47 35 E
Andranopasy, *Madag.* . **57 C7** 21 17S 43 44 E
Andratx, *Spain* . **22 B9** 39 39N 2 25 E
Andreanof Is., *U.S.A.* . **68 C2** 51 30N 176 0W
Andrews, *S.C., U.S.A.* . **77 J6** 33 27N 79 34W
Andrews, *Tex., U.S.A.* . **81 J3** 32 19N 102 33W
Ándria, *Italy* . **20 D7** 41 13N 16 17 E
Andriba, *Madag.* . **57 B8** 17 30S 46 58 E
Androka, *Madag.* . **57 C7** 24 58S 44 2 E
Andropov = Rybinsk, *Russia* **24 C6** 58 5N 38 50 E
Ándros, *Greece* . **21 F11** 37 50N 24 57 E
Andros I., *Bahamas* . **88 B4** 24 30N 78 0W
Andros Town, *Bahamas* . **88 B4** 24 43N 77 47W
Androscoggin →, *U.S.A.* . **79 C14** 43 58N 70 0W
Andselv, *Norway* . **8 B18** 69 4N 18 34 E
Andújar, *Spain* . **19 C3** 38 3N 4 5W
Andulo, *Angola* . **52 G3** 11 25S 16 45 E
Anegada I., *Virgin Is.* . **89 C7** 18 45N 64 20W
Anegada Passage, *W. Indies* **89 C7** 18 15N 63 45W
Aneto, Pico de, *Spain* . **19 A6** 42 37N 0 40 E
Ang Thong, *Thailand* . **38 E3** 14 35N 100 31 E
Angamos, Punta, *Chile* . **94 A1** 23 1S 70 32W
Angara →, *Russia* . **27 D10** 58 5N 94 20 E
Angarsk, *Russia* . **27 D11** 52 30N 104 0 E
Angas Hills, *Australia* . **60 D4** 23 0S 127 50 E
Angaston, *Australia* . **63 E2** 34 30S 139 8 E
Angaur I., *Pac. Oc.* . **37 C8** 6 54N 134 9 E
Ånge, *Sweden* . **9 E16** 62 31N 15 35 E
Ángel, Salto = Angel Falls, *Venezuela* . **92 B6** 5 57N 62 30W
Ángel de la Guarda, I., *Mexico* . **86 B2** 29 30N 113 30W
Angel Falls, *Venezuela* . **92 B6** 5 57N 62 30W
Angeles, *Phil.* . **37 A6** 15 9N 120 33 E
Ängelholm, *Sweden* . **9 H15** 56 15N 12 58 E
Angels Camp, *U.S.A.* . **84 G6** 38 4N 120 32W
Ångermanälven →, *Sweden* . **8 E17** 62 40N 18 0 E
Ångermanland, *Sweden* . **8 E18** 63 36N 17 45 E
Angers, *Canada* . **79 A9** 45 31N 75 29W
Angers, *France* . **18 C3** 47 30N 0 35W
Ängesån →, *Sweden* . **8 C20** 66 16N 22 47 E
Angikuni L., *Canada* . **73 A9** 62 0N 100 0W
Angkor, *Cambodia* . **38 F4** 13 22N 103 50 E
Anglesey, *U.K.* . **10 D3** 53 17N 4 20W
Anglesey, Isle of □, *U.K.* . **10 D3** 53 16N 4 18W
Angleton, *U.S.A.* . **81 L7** 29 10N 95 26W
Anglisidhes, *Cyprus* . **23 E12** 34 51N 33 27 E
Angmagssalik, *Greenland* . **4 C6** 65 40N 37 20W
Ango, *Dem. Rep. of the Congo* . **54 B2** 4 10N 26 5 E
Angoche, *Mozam.* . **55 F4** 16 8S 39 55 E
Angoche, I., *Mozam.* . **55 F4** 16 20S 39 50 E
Angol, *Chile* . **94 D1** 37 56S 72 45W
Angola, *Ind., U.S.A.* . **76 E3** 41 38N 85 0W
Angola, *N.Y., U.S.A.* . **78 D5** 42 38N 79 2W
Angola ■, *Africa* . **53 G3** 12 0S 18 0 E
Angoulême, *France* . **18 D4** 45 39N 0 10 E
Angoumois, *France* . **18 D3** 45 50N 0 25 E
Angra dos Reis, *Brazil* . **95 A7** 23 0S 44 10W
Angren, *Uzbekistan* . **26 E8** 41 1N 70 12 E
Angtassom, *Cambodia* . **39 G5** 11 1N 104 41 E
Angu, *Dem. Rep. of the Congo* . **54 B1** 3 25N 24 28 E
Anguang, *China* . **35 B12** 45 15N 123 45 E
Anguilla ■, *W. Indies* . **89 C7** 18 14N 63 5W
Anguo, *China* . **34 E8** 38 28N 115 15 E
Angurugu, *Australia* . **62 A2** 14 0S 136 25 E
Angus □, *U.K.* . **12 E6** 56 46N 2 56W
Anhanduí →, *Brazil* . **95 A5** 21 46S 52 9W
Anholt, *Denmark* . **9 H14** 56 42N 11 33 E
Anhui □, *China* . **33 C6** 32 0N 117 0 E
Anhwei = Anhui □, *China* . **33 C6** 32 0N 117 0 E
Anichab, *Namibia* . **56 C1** 21 0S 14 46 E
Animas →, *U.S.A.* . **83 H9** 36 43N 108 13W
Anivorano, *Madag.* . **57 B8** 18 44S 48 58 E
Anjalankoski, *Finland* . **9 F22** 60 45N 26 51 E
Anjar, *India* . **42 H4** 23 6N 70 10 E
Anjidiv I., *India* . **40 M9** 14 40N 74 10 E
Anjou, *France* . **18 C3** 47 20N 0 15W
Anjozorobe, *Madag.* . **57 B8** 18 22S 47 52 E
Anju, *N. Korea* . **35 E13** 39 36N 125 40 E
Ankaboa, Tanjon, *Madag.* . **57 C7** 21 58S 43 20 E
Ankang, *China* . **34 H5** 32 40N 109 1 E
Ankara, *Turkey* . **25 G5** 39 57N 32 54 E
Ankaramena, *Madag.* . **57 C8** 21 57S 46 39 E
Ankaratra, *Madag.* . **53 H9** 19 25S 47 12 E
Ankazoabo, *Madag.* . **57 C7** 22 18S 44 31 E
Ankazobe, *Madag.* . **57 B8** 18 20S 47 10 E
Ankeny, *U.S.A.* . **80 E8** 41 44N 93 36W
Ankisabe, *Madag.* . **57 B8** 19 17S 46 29 E
Ankoro, *Dem. Rep. of the Congo* . **54 D2** 6 45S 26 55 E
Anmyŏn-do, *S. Korea* . **35 F14** 36 25N 126 25 E
Ann, C., *U.S.A.* . **79 D14** 42 38N 70 35W
Ann Arbor, *U.S.A.* . **76 D4** 42 17N 83 45W
Anna, *U.S.A.* . **81 G10** 37 28N 89 15W
Annaba, *Algeria* . **50 A7** 36 50N 7 46 E
Annalee →, *Ireland* . **13 B4** 54 2N 7 24W
Annam, *Vietnam* . **38 E7** 16 0N 108 0 E
Annamitique, Chaîne, *Asia* **38 D6** 17 0N 106 0 E
Annan, *U.K.* . **12 G5** 54 59N 3 16W
Annan →, *U.K.* . **12 G5** 54 58N 3 16W
Annapolis, *U.S.A.* . **76 F7** 38 59N 76 30W
Annapolis Royal, *Canada* . **71 D6** 44 44N 65 32W
Annapurna, *Nepal* . **43 E10** 28 34N 83 50 E
Annean, L., *Australia* . **61 E2** 26 54S 118 14 E
Annecy, *France* . **18 D7** 45 55N 6 8 E
Anning, *China* . **32 D5** 24 55N 102 26 E
Anniston, *U.S.A.* . **77 J3** 33 39N 85 50W
Annobón, *Atl. Oc.* . **49 G4** 1 25S 5 36 E
Annotto Bay, *Jamaica* . **88 C4** 18 17N 76 45W
Annville, *U.S.A.* . **79 F8** 40 20N 76 31W
Áno Viánnos, *Greece* . **23 D7** 35 2N 25 21 E
Anorotsangana, *Madag.* . **57 A8** 13 56S 47 55 E
Anóyia, *Greece* . **23 D6** 35 16N 24 52 E
Anping, *Hebei, China* . **34 E8** 38 15N 115 30 E
Anping, *Liaoning, China* . **35 D12** 41 5N 123 30 E
Anqing, *China* . **33 C6** 30 30N 117 3 E
Anqiu, *China* . **35 F10** 36 25N 119 10 E
Ansai, *China* . **34 F5** 36 50N 109 20 E
Ansbach, *Germany* . **16 D6** 49 28N 10 34 E
Anshan, *China* . **35 D12** 41 5N 122 58 E
Anshun, *China* . **32 D5** 26 18N 105 57 E
Ansley, *U.S.A.* . **80 E5** 41 18N 99 23W
Anson, *U.S.A.* . **81 J5** 32 45N 99 54W
Anson B., *Australia* . **60 B5** 13 20S 130 6 E
Ansongo, *Mali* . **50 E6** 15 25N 0 35 E
Ansonia, *U.S.A.* . **79 E11** 41 21N 73 5W
Anstruther, *U.K.* . **12 E6** 56 14N 2 41W
Ansudu, *Indonesia* . **37 E9** 2 11S 139 22 E
Antabamba, *Peru* . **92 F4** 14 40S 73 0W
Antakya, *Turkey* . **25 G6** 36 14N 36 10 E
Antalaha, *Madag.* . **57 A9** 14 57S 50 20 E
Antalya, *Turkey* . **25 G5** 36 52N 30 45 E
Antalya Körfezi, *Turkey* . **25 G5** 36 15N 31 30 E
Antananarivo, *Madag.* . **57 B8** 18 55S 47 31 E
Antananarivo □, *Madag.* . **57 B8** 19 0S 47 0 E
Antanimbaribe, *Madag.* . **57 C7** 21 30S 44 48 E
Antarctic Pen., *Antarctica* . **5 C18** 67 0S 60 0W
Antarctica . **5 E3** 90 0S 0 0 E
Antelope, *Zimbabwe* . **55 G2** 21 2S 28 31 E
Antequera, *Paraguay* . **94 A4** 24 8S 57 7W
Antequera, *Spain* . **19 D3** 37 5N 4 33W
Antero, Mt., *U.S.A.* . **83 G10** 38 41N 106 15W
Anthony, *Kans., U.S.A.* . **81 G5** 37 9N 98 2W
Anthony, *N. Mex., U.S.A.* . **83 K10** 32 0N 106 36W
Anti Atlas, *Morocco* . **50 C4** 30 0N 8 30W
Anti-Lebanon = Ash Sharqi, Al Jabal, *Lebanon* . **47 B5** 33 40N 36 10 E
Antibes, *France* . **18 E7** 43 34N 7 6 E
Anticosti, Î. d', *Canada* . **71 C7** 49 30N 63 0W
Antigo, *U.S.A.* . **80 C10** 45 9N 89 9W
Antigonish, *Canada* . **71 C7** 45 38N 61 58W
Antigua, *Canary Is.* . **22 F5** 28 24N 14 1W
Antigua, *W. Indies* . **89 C7** 17 0N 61 50W
Antigua & Barbuda ■, *W. Indies* . **89 C7** 17 20N 61 48W
Antigua Guatemala, *Guatemala* . **88 D1** 14 34N 90 41W
Antilla, *Cuba* . **88 B4** 20 40N 75 50W
Antilles = West Indies, *Cent. Amer.* . **89 D7** 15 0N 65 0W
Antioch, *U.S.A.* . **84 G5** 38 1N 121 48W
Antioquia, *Colombia* . **92 B3** 6 40N 75 55W
Antipodes Is., *Pac. Oc.* . **64 M9** 49 45S 178 40 E
Antlers, *U.S.A.* . **81 H7** 34 14N 95 37W
Antofagasta, *Chile* . **94 A1** 23 50S 70 30W
Antofagasta □, *Chile* . **94 A2** 24 0S 69 0W
Antofagasta de la Sierra, *Argentina* . **94 B2** 26 5S 67 20W
Antofalla, *Argentina* . **94 B2** 25 30S 68 5W
Antofalla, Salar de, *Argentina* . **94 B2** 25 40S 67 45W
Anton, *U.S.A.* . **81 J3** 33 49N 102 10W
Antongila, Helodrano, *Madag.* . **57 B8** 15 30S 49 50 E
Antonibé, *Madag.* . **57 B8** 15 7S 47 24 E
Antonibé, Presqu'île d', *Madag.* . **57 A8** 14 55S 47 20 E
Antonina, *Brazil* . **95 B6** 25 26S 48 42W
Antrim, *U.K.* . **13 B5** 54 43N 6 14W
Antrim, *U.S.A.* . **78 F3** 40 7N 81 21W
Antrim □, *U.K.* . **13 B5** 54 56N 6 25W
Antrim, Mts. of, *U.K.* . **13 A5** 55 3N 6 14W
Antrim Plateau, *Australia* . **60 C4** 18 8S 128 20 E
Antsalova, *Madag.* . **57 B7** 18 40S 44 37 E
Antsirabe, *Madag.* . **57 B8** 19 55S 47 2 E
Antsiranana, *Madag.* . **57 A8** 12 25S 49 20 E
Antsohihy, *Madag.* . **57 A8** 14 50S 47 59 E
Antsohimbondrona Seranana, *Madag.* . **57 A8** 13 7S 48 48 E
Antu, *China* . **35 C15** 42 30N 128 20 E
Antwerp = Antwerpen, *Belgium* . **15 C4** 51 13N 4 25 E
Antwerp, *U.S.A.* . **79 B9** 44 12N 75 37W
Antwerpen, *Belgium* . **15 C4** 51 13N 4 25 E
Antwerpen □, *Belgium* . **15 C4** 51 15N 4 40 E
Anupgarh, *India* . **42 E5** 29 10N 73 10 E
Anuppur, *India* . **43 H9** 23 6N 81 41 E
Anuradhapura, *Sri Lanka* . **40 Q12** 8 22N 80 28 E
Anveh, *Iran* . **45 E7** 27 23N 54 11 E
Anvers = Antwerpen, *Belgium* . **15 C4** 51 13N 4 25 E
Anvers I., *Antarctica* . **5 C17** 64 30S 63 40W
Anxi, *China* . **32 B4** 40 30N 95 43 E
Anxious B., *Australia* . **63 E1** 33 24S 134 45 E
Anyang, *China* . **34 F8** 36 5N 114 21 E
Anyer-Kidul, *Indonesia* . **37 G11** 6 4S 105 53 E
Anyi, *China* . **34 G6** 35 2N 111 2 E
Anza, *U.S.A.* . **85 M10** 33 35N 116 39W
Anze, *China* . **34 F7** 36 10N 112 12 E
Anzhero-Sudzhensk, *Russia* **26 D9** 56 10N 86 0 E
Ánzio, *Italy* . **20 D5** 41 27N 12 37 E
Aoga-Shima, *Japan* . **31 H9** 32 28N 139 46 E
Aomen = Macau, *China* . **33 D6** 22 16N 113 35 E
Aomori, *Japan* . **30 D10** 40 45N 140 45 E

Asmara

Aomori □, *Japan* **30 D10** 40 45N 140 40 E
Aonla, *India* **43 E8** 28 16N 79 11 E
Aosta, *Italy* **18 D7** 45 45N 7 20 E
Aouker, *Mauritania* **50 E4** 17 40N 10 0W
Aozou, *Chad* **51 D9** 21 45N 17 28 E
Apa →, *S. Amer.* **94 A4** 22 6S 58 2W
Apache, *U.S.A.* **81 H5** 34 54N 98 22W
Apache Junction, *U.S.A.* **83 K8** 33 25N 111 33W
Apalachee B., *U.S.A.* **77 L4** 30 0N 84 0W
Apalachicola, *U.S.A.* **77 L3** 29 43N 84 59W
Apalachicola →, *U.S.A.* **77 L3** 29 43N 84 58W
Apaporis →, *Colombia* **92 D5** 1 23S 69 25W
Aparri, *Phil.* **37 A6** 18 22N 121 38 E
Apatity, *Russia* **24 A5** 67 34N 33 22 E
Apatzingán, *Mexico* **86 D4** 19 0N 102 20W
Apeldoorn, *Neths.* **15 B5** 52 13N 5 57 E
Apennines = Appennini, *Italy* **20 B4** 44 0N 10 0 E
Apia, *W. Samoa* **59 A13** 13 50S 171 50W
Apiacás, Serra dos, *Brazil* **92 E7** 9 50S 57 0W
Apizaco, *Mexico* **87 D5** 19 26N 98 9W
Aplao, *Peru* **92 G4** 16 0S 72 40W
Apo, Mt., *Phil.* **37 C7** 6 53N 125 14 E
Apolakkiá, *Greece* **23 C9** 36 5N 27 48 E
Apolakkiá, Órmos, *Greece* **23 C9** 36 5N 27 45 E
Apollo Bay, *Australia* **63 F3** 38 45S 143 40 E
Apolo, *Bolivia* **92 F5** 14 30S 68 30W
Aporé →, *Brazil* **93 G8** 19 27S 50 57W
Apostle Is., *U.S.A.* **80 B9** 47 0N 90 40W
Apóstoles, *Argentina* **95 B4** 28 0S 56 0W
Apostolos Andreas, C., *Cyprus* **23 D13** 35 42N 34 35 E
Apoteri, *Guyana* **92 C7** 4 2N 58 32W
Appalachian Mts., *U.S.A.* **76 G6** 38 0N 80 0W
Appennini, *Italy* **20 B4** 44 0N 10 0 E
Apple Hill, *Canada* **79 A10** 45 13N 74 46W
Apple Valley, *U.S.A.* **85 L9** 34 32N 117 14W
Appleby-in-Westmorland, *U.K.* **10 C5** 54 35N 2 29W
Appleton, *U.S.A.* **76 C1** 44 16N 88 25W
Approuague →, *Fr. Guiana* **93 C8** 4 30N 51 57W
Aprília, *Italy* **20 D5** 41 36N 12 39 E
Apsley, *Canada* **78 B6** 44 45N 78 6W
Apucarana, *Brazil* **95 A5** 23 55S 51 33W
Apure →, *Venezuela* **92 B5** 7 37N 66 25W
Apurimac →, *Peru* **92 F4** 12 17S 73 56W
Āqā Jarī, *Iran* **45 D6** 30 42N 49 50 E
Aqaba = Al 'Aqabah, *Jordan* **47 F4** 29 31N 35 0 E
Aqaba, G. of, *Red Sea* **44 D2** 28 15N 33 20 E
'Aqabah, Khalīj al = Aqaba, G. of, *Red Sea* **44 D2** 28 15N 33 20 E
'Aqdā, *Iran* **45 C7** 32 26N 53 37 E
Aqmola = Astana, *Kazakstan* **26 D8** 51 10N 71 30 E
Aqrah, *Iraq* **44 B4** 36 46N 43 45 E
Aqtaū, *Kazakstan* **26 E6** 43 39N 51 12 E
Aqtöbe, *Kazakstan* **25 D10** 50 17N 57 10 E
Aquidauana, *Brazil* **93 H7** 20 30S 55 50W
Aquiles Serdán, *Mexico* **86 B3** 28 37N 105 54W
Aquin, *Haiti* **89 C5** 18 16N 73 24W
Aquitain, Bassin, *France* **18 D3** 44 0N 0 30W
Ar Rachidiya, *Morocco* **50 B5** 31 58N 4 20W
Ar Rafid, *Syria* **47 C4** 32 57N 35 52 E
Ar Raḥḥālīyah, *Iraq* **44 C4** 32 44N 43 23 E
Ar Ramādī, *Iraq* **44 C4** 33 25N 43 20 E
Ar Ramthā, *Jordan* **47 C5** 32 34N 36 0 E
Ar Raqqah, *Syria* **44 C3** 35 59N 39 8 E
Ar Rass, *Si. Arabia* **44 E4** 25 50N 43 40 E
Ar Rifā'ī, *Iraq* **44 D5** 31 50N 46 10 E
Ar Riyāḍ, *Si. Arabia* **46 C4** 24 41N 46 42 E
Ar Ru'ays, *Qatar* **45 E6** 26 8N 51 12 E
Ar Rukhaymīyah, *Iraq* **44 D5** 29 22N 45 38 E
Ar Ruqayyidah, *Si. Arabia* **45 E6** 25 21N 49 34 E
Ar Ruṣāfah, *Syria* **44 C3** 35 45N 38 49 E
Ar Ruṭbah, *Iraq* **44 C4** 33 0N 40 15 E
Ara, *India* **43 G11** 25 35N 84 32 E
Arab, *U.S.A.* **77 H2** 34 19N 86 30W
'Arab, Bahr el →, *Sudan* **51 G11** 9 0N 29 30 E
'Arabābād, *Iran* **45 C8** 33 2N 57 41 E
Arabia, *Asia* **28 G8** 25 0N 45 0 E
Arabian Desert = Es Sahrâ' Esh Sharqîya, *Egypt* **51 C12** 27 30N 32 30 E
Arabian Gulf = Gulf, The, *Asia* **45 E6** 27 0N 50 0 E
Arabian Sea, *Ind. Oc.* **29 H10** 16 0N 65 0 E
Aracaju, *Brazil* **93 F11** 10 55S 37 4W
Aracati, *Brazil* **93 D11** 4 30S 37 44W
Araçatuba, *Brazil* **95 A5** 21 10S 50 30W
Aracena, *Spain* **19 D2** 37 53N 6 38W
Araçuai, *Brazil* **93 G10** 16 52S 42 4W
'Arad, *Israel* **47 D4** 31 15N 35 12 E
Arad, *Romania* **17 E11** 46 10N 21 20 E
Arādān, *Iran* **45 C7** 35 21N 52 30 E
Aradhippou, *Cyprus* **23 E12** 34 57N 33 36 E
Arafura Sea, *E. Indies* **37 F9** 9 0S 135 0 E
Aragón □, *Spain* **19 B5** 41 25N 0 40W
Aragón →, *Spain* **19 A5** 42 13N 1 44W
Araguacema, *Brazil* **93 E9** 8 50S 49 20W
Araguaia →, *Brazil* **93 E9** 5 21S 48 41W
Araguaína, *Brazil* **93 E9** 7 12S 48 12W
Araguari, *Brazil* **93 G9** 18 38S 48 11W
Araguari →, *Brazil* **93 C9** 1 15N 49 55W
Arain, *India* **42 F6** 26 27N 75 2 E
Arak, *Algeria* **50 C6** 25 20N 3 45 E
Arāk, *Iran* **45 C6** 34 0N 49 40 E
Arakan Coast, *Burma* **41 K19** 19 0N 94 0 E
Arakan Yoma, *Burma* **41 K19** 20 0N 94 40 E
Araks = Aras, Rūd-e →, *Azerbaijan* **44 B5** 40 5N 48 29 E
Aral, *Kazakstan* **26 E7** 46 41N 61 45 E
Aral Sea, *Asia* **26 E7** 44 30N 60 0 E
Aral Tengizi = Aral Sea, *Asia* **26 E7** 44 30N 60 0 E
Aralsk = Aral, *Kazakstan* **26 E7** 46 41N 61 45 E
Aralskoye More = Aral Sea, *Asia* **26 E7** 44 30N 60 0 E
Aramac, *Australia* **62 C4** 22 58S 145 14 E
Aran I., *Ireland* **13 A3** 55 0N 8 30W
Aran Is., *Ireland* **13 C2** 53 6N 9 38W
Aranda de Duero, *Spain* **19 B4** 41 39N 3 42W
Arandān, *Iran* **44 C5** 35 23N 46 55 E
Aranjuez, *Spain* **19 B4** 40 1N 3 40W
Aranos, *Namibia* **56 C2** 24 9S 19 7 E
Aransas Pass, *U.S.A.* **81 M6** 27 55N 97 9W
Aranyaprathet, *Thailand* **38 F4** 13 41N 102 30 E
Arapahoe, *U.S.A.* **80 E5** 40 18N 99 54W
Arapey Grande →, *Uruguay* **94 C4** 30 55S 57 49W
Arapgir, *Turkey* **44 B3** 39 5N 38 30 E
Arapiraca, *Brazil* **93 E11** 9 45S 36 39W
Arapongas, *Brazil* **95 A5** 23 29S 51 28W
Ar'ar, *Si. Arabia* **44 D4** 30 59N 41 2 E
Araranguá, *Brazil* **95 B6** 29 0S 49 30W
Araraquara, *Brazil* **93 H9** 21 50S 48 0W
Ararás, Serra das, *Brazil* **95 B5** 25 0S 53 10W
Ararat, *Australia* **63 F3** 37 16S 143 0 E
Ararat, Mt. = Ağrı Dağı, *Turkey* **25 G7** 39 50N 44 15 E
Araria, *India* **43 F12** 26 9N 87 33 E
Araripe, Chapada do, *Brazil* **93 E11** 7 20S 40 0W
Araruama, L. de, *Brazil* **95 A7** 22 53S 42 12W
Aras, Rūd-e →, *Azerbaijan* **44 B5** 40 5N 48 29 E
Arauca, *Colombia* **92 B4** 7 0N 70 40W
Arauca →, *Venezuela* **92 B5** 7 24N 66 35W
Arauco, *Chile* **94 D1** 37 16S 73 25W
Araxá, *Brazil* **93 G9** 19 35S 46 55W
Araya, Pen. de, *Venezuela* **92 A6** 10 40N 64 0W
Arba Minch, *Ethiopia* **46 F2** 6 0N 37 30 E
Arbat, *Iraq* **44 C5** 35 25N 45 35 E
Árbatax, *Italy* **20 E3** 39 56N 9 42 E
Arbīl, *Iraq* **44 B5** 36 15N 44 5 E
Arborfield, *Canada* **73 C8** 53 6N 103 39W
Arborg, *Canada* **73 C9** 50 54N 97 13W
Arbroath, *U.K.* **12 E6** 56 34N 2 35W
Arbuckle, *U.S.A.* **84 F4** 39 1N 122 3W
Arcachon, *France* **18 D3** 44 40N 1 10W
Arcade, *Calif., U.S.A.* **85 L8** 34 2N 118 15W
Arcade, *N.Y., U.S.A.* **78 D6** 42 32N 78 25W
Arcadia, *Fla., U.S.A.* **77 M5** 27 13N 81 52W
Arcadia, *La., U.S.A.* **81 J8** 32 33N 92 55W
Arcadia, *Pa., U.S.A.* **78 F6** 40 47N 78 51W
Arcata, *U.S.A.* **82 F1** 40 52N 124 5W
Archangel = Arkhangelsk, *Russia* **24 B7** 64 38N 40 36 E
Archbald, *U.S.A.* **79 E9** 41 30N 75 32W
Archer →, *Australia* **62 A3** 13 28S 141 41 E
Archer B., *Australia* **62 A3** 13 20S 141 30 E
Archers Post, *Kenya* **54 B4** 0 35N 37 35 E
Arches National Park, *U.S.A.* **83 G9** 38 45N 109 25W
Arckaringa Cr. →, *Australia* **63 D2** 28 10S 135 22 E
Arco, *U.S.A.* **82 E7** 43 38N 113 18W
Arcos de la Frontera, *Spain* **19 D3** 36 45N 5 49W
Arcot, *India* **40 N11** 12 53N 79 20 E
Arctic Bay, *Canada* **69 A11** 73 1N 85 7W
Arctic Ocean, *Arctic* **4 B18** 78 0N 160 0W
Arctic Red River = Tsiigehtchic, *Canada* **68 B6** 67 15N 134 0W
Arda →, *Bulgaria* **21 D12** 41 40N 26 30 E
Ardabīl, *Iran* **45 B6** 38 15N 48 18 E
Ardakān = Sepīdān, *Iran* **45 D7** 30 20N 52 5 E
Ardakān, *Iran* **45 C7** 32 19N 53 59 E
Ardee, *Ireland* **13 C5** 53 52N 6 33W
Arden, *Canada* **78 B8** 44 43N 76 56W
Arden, *Calif., U.S.A.* **84 G5** 38 36N 121 33W
Arden, *Nev., U.S.A.* **85 J11** 36 1N 115 14W
Ardenne, *Belgium* **16 D3** 49 50N 5 5 E
Ardennes = Ardenne, *Belgium* **16 D3** 49 50N 5 5 E
Arderin, *Ireland* **13 C4** 53 2N 7 39W
Ardestān, *Iran* **45 C7** 33 20N 52 25 E
Ardivachar Pt., *U.K.* **12 D1** 57 23N 7 26W
Ardlethan, *Australia* **63 E4** 34 22S 146 53 E
Ardmore, *Okla., U.S.A.* **81 H6** 34 10N 97 8W
Ardmore, *Pa., U.S.A.* **79 G9** 39 58N 75 18W
Ardnamurchan, Pt. of, *U.K.* **12 E2** 56 43N 6 14W
Ardnave Pt., *U.K.* **12 F2** 55 53N 6 20W
Ardrossan, *Australia* **63 E2** 34 26S 137 53 E
Ardrossan, *U.K.* **12 F4** 55 39N 4 49W
Ards Pen., *U.K.* **13 B6** 54 33N 5 34W
Arecibo, *Puerto Rico* **89 C6** 18 29N 66 43W
Areia Branca, *Brazil* **93 E11** 5 0S 37 0W
Arena, Pt., *U.S.A.* **84 G3** 38 57N 123 44W
Arenal, *Honduras* **88 C2** 15 21N 86 50W
Arendal, *Norway* **9 G13** 58 28N 8 46 E
Arequipa, *Peru* **92 G4** 16 20S 71 30W
Arévalo, *Spain* **19 B3** 41 3N 4 43W
Arezzo, *Italy* **20 C4** 43 25N 11 53 E
Arga, *Turkey* **44 B3** 38 21N 37 59 E
Arganda, *Spain* **19 B4** 40 19N 3 26W
Argenta, *Canada* **72 C5** 50 11N 116 56W
Argentan, *France* **18 B3** 48 45N 0 1W
Argentário, Mte., *Italy* **20 C4** 42 24N 11 9 E
Argentia, *Canada* **71 C9** 47 18N 53 58W
Argentina ■, *S. Amer.* **96 D3** 35 0S 66 0W
Argentino Is., *Antarctica* **5 C17** 66 0S 64 0W
Argentino, L., *Argentina* **96 G2** 50 10S 73 0W
Argeş →, *Romania* **17 F14** 44 5N 26 38 E
Arghandab →, *Afghan.* **42 D1** 31 30N 64 15 E
Argolikós Kólpos, *Greece* **21 F10** 37 20N 22 52 E
Árgos, *Greece* **21 F10** 37 40N 22 43 E
Argostólion, *Greece* **21 E9** 38 12N 20 33 E
Arguello, Pt., *U.S.A.* **85 L6** 34 35N 120 39W
Arguineguín, *Canary Is.* **22 G4** 27 46N 15 41W
Argun →, *Russia* **27 D13** 53 20N 121 28 E
Argus Pk., *U.S.A.* **85 K9** 35 52N 117 26W
Argyle, L., *Australia* **60 C4** 16 20S 128 40 E
Argyll & Bute □, *U.K.* **12 E3** 56 13N 5 28W
Århus, *Denmark* **9 H14** 56 8N 10 11 E
Ariadnoye, *Russia* **30 B7** 45 8N 134 25 E
Ariamsvlei, *Namibia* **56 D2** 28 9S 19 51 E
Ariana, *Tunisia* **51 A7** 36 52N 10 12 E
Arica, *Chile* **92 G4** 18 32S 70 20W
Arica, *Colombia* **92 D4** 2 0S 71 50W
Arico, *Canary Is.* **22 F3** 28 9N 16 29W
Arid, C., *Australia* **61 F3** 34 1S 123 10 E
Arida, *Japan* **31 G7** 34 5N 135 8 E
Arílla, Ákra, *Greece* **23 A3** 39 43N 19 39 E
Arima, *Trin. & Tob.* **89 D7** 10 38N 61 17W
Arinos →, *Brazil* **92 F7** 10 25S 58 20W
Ario de Rosales, *Mexico* **86 D4** 19 12N 102 0W
Aripuanã, *Brazil* **92 E6** 9 25S 60 30W
Aripuanã →, *Brazil* **92 E6** 5 7S 60 25W
Ariquemes, *Brazil* **92 E6** 9 55S 63 6W
Arisaig, *U.K.* **12 E3** 56 55N 5 51W
Aristazabal I., *Canada* **72 C3** 52 40N 129 10W
Arivonimamo, *Madag.* **57 B8** 19 1S 47 11 E
Arizaro, Salar de, *Argentina* **94 A2** 24 40S 67 50W
Arizona, *Argentina* **94 D2** 35 45S 65 25W
Arizona □, *U.S.A.* **83 J8** 34 0N 112 0W
Arizpe, *Mexico* **86 A2** 30 20N 110 11W
Arjeplog, *Sweden* **8 D18** 66 3N 18 2 E
Arjona, *Colombia* **92 A3** 10 14N 75 22W
Arjuna, *Indonesia* **37 G15** 7 49S 112 34 E
Arka, *Russia* **27 C15** 60 15N 142 0 E
Arkadelphia, *U.S.A.* **81 H8** 34 7N 93 4W
Arkaig, L., *U.K.* **12 E3** 56 59N 5 10W
Arkalyk = Arqalyk, *Kazakstan* **26 D7** 50 13N 66 50 E
Arkansas □, *U.S.A.* **81 H8** 35 0N 92 30W
Arkansas →, *U.S.A.* **81 J9** 33 47N 91 4W
Arkansas City, *U.S.A.* **81 G6** 37 4N 97 2W
Arkaroola, *Australia* **63 E2** 30 20S 139 22 E
Arkhángelos, *Greece* **23 C10** 36 13N 28 7 E
Arkhangelsk, *Russia* **24 B7** 64 38N 40 36 E
Arki, *India* **42 D7** 31 9N 76 58 E
Arklow, *Ireland* **13 D5** 52 48N 6 10W
Arkport, *U.S.A.* **78 D7** 42 24N 77 42W
Arkticheskiy, Mys, *Russia* **27 A10** 81 10N 95 0 E
Arkville, *U.S.A.* **79 D10** 42 9N 74 37W
Arlanzón →, *Spain* **19 A3** 42 3N 4 17W
Arlbergpass, *Austria* **16 E6** 47 9N 10 12 E
Arles, *France* **18 E6** 43 41N 4 40 E
Arlington, *S. Africa* **57 D4** 28 1S 27 53 E
Arlington, *N.Y., U.S.A.* **79 E11** 41 42N 73 54W
Arlington, *Oreg., U.S.A.* **82 D3** 45 43N 120 12W
Arlington, *S. Dak., U.S.A.* **80 C6** 44 22N 97 8W
Arlington, *Tex., U.S.A.* **81 J6** 32 44N 97 7W
Arlington, *Va., U.S.A.* **76 F7** 38 53N 77 7W
Arlington, *Vt., U.S.A.* **79 C11** 43 5N 73 9W
Arlington, *Wash., U.S.A.* **84 B4** 48 12N 122 8W
Arlington Heights, *U.S.A.* **76 D2** 42 5N 87 59W
Arlit, *Niger* **50 E7** 19 0N 7 38 E
Arlon, *Belgium* **15 E5** 49 42N 5 49 E
Arltunga, *Australia* **62 C1** 23 26S 134 41 E
Armagh, *U.K.* **13 B5** 54 21N 6 39W
Armagh □, *U.K.* **13 B5** 54 18N 6 37W
Armavir, *Russia* **25 E7** 45 2N 41 7 E
Armenia, *Colombia* **92 C3** 4 35N 75 45W
Armenia ■, *Asia* **25 F7** 40 20N 45 0 E
Armenistís, Ákra, *Greece* **23 C9** 36 8N 27 42 E
Armidale, *Australia* **63 E5** 30 30S 151 40 E
Armour, *U.S.A.* **80 D5** 43 19N 98 21W
Armstrong, *B.C., Canada* **72 C5** 50 25N 119 10W
Armstrong, *Ont., Canada* **70 B2** 50 18N 89 4W
Arnarfjörður, *Iceland* **8 D2** 65 48N 23 40W
Arnaud →, *Canada* **69 C13** 60 0N 70 0W
Arnauti, C., *Cyprus* **23 D11** 35 6N 32 17 E
Arnett, *U.S.A.* **81 G5** 36 8N 99 46W
Arnhem, *Neths.* **15 C5** 51 58N 5 55 E
Arnhem, C., *Australia* **62 A2** 12 20S 137 30 E
Arnhem B., *Australia* **62 A2** 12 20S 136 10 E
Arnhem Land, *Australia* **62 A1** 13 10S 134 30 E
Arno →, *Italy* **20 C4** 43 41N 10 17 E
Arno Bay, *Australia* **63 E2** 33 54S 136 34 E
Arnold, *U.K.* **10 D6** 53 1N 1 7W
Arnold, *U.S.A.* **84 G6** 38 15N 120 20W
Arnot, *Canada* **73 B9** 55 56N 96 41W
Arnøy, *Norway* **8 A19** 70 9N 20 40 E
Arnprior, *Canada* **79 A8** 45 26N 76 21W
Arnsberg, *Germany* **16 C5** 51 24N 8 5 E
Aroab, *Namibia* **56 D2** 26 41S 19 39 E
Aron, *India* **42 G6** 25 57N 77 56 E
Arqalyk, *Kazakstan* **26 D7** 50 13N 66 50 E
Arrah = Ara, *India* **43 G11** 25 35N 84 32 E
Arran, *U.K.* **12 F3** 55 34N 5 12W
Arras, *France* **18 A5** 50 17N 2 46 E
Arrecife, *Canary Is.* **22 F6** 28 57N 13 37W
Arrecifes, *Argentina* **94 C3** 34 6S 60 9W
Arrée, Mts. d', *France* **18 B2** 48 26N 3 55W
Arriaga, *Chiapas, Mexico* **87 D6** 16 15N 93 52W
Arriaga, *San Luis Potosí, Mexico* **86 C4** 21 55N 101 23W
Arrilalah, *Australia* **62 C3** 23 43S 143 54 E
Arrino, *Australia* **61 E2** 29 30S 115 40 E
Arrow, L., *Ireland* **13 B3** 54 3N 8 19W
Arrowhead, L., *U.S.A.* **85 L9** 34 16N 117 10W
Arrowtown, *N.Z.* **59 L2** 44 57S 168 50 E
Arroyo Grande, *U.S.A.* **85 K6** 35 7N 120 35W
Ars, *Iran* **44 B5** 37 9N 47 46 E
Arsenault L., *Canada* **73 B7** 55 6N 108 32W
Arsenev, *Russia* **30 B6** 44 10N 133 15 E
Árta, *Greece* **21 E9** 39 8N 21 2 E
Artà, *Spain* **22 B10** 39 41N 3 21 E
Arteaga, *Mexico* **86 D4** 18 50N 102 20W
Artem, *Russia* **30 C6** 43 22N 132 13 E
Artemovsk, *Russia* **27 D10** 54 45N 93 35 E
Artemovsk, *Ukraine* **25 E6** 48 35N 38 0 E
Artesia = Mosomane, *Botswana* **56 C4** 24 2S 26 19 E
Artesia, *U.S.A.* **81 J2** 32 51N 104 24W
Arthur, *Canada* **78 C4** 43 50N 80 32W
Arthur →, *Australia* **62 G3** 41 2S 144 40 E
Arthur Cr. →, *Australia* **62 C2** 22 30S 136 25 E
Arthur Pt., *Australia* **62 C5** 22 7S 150 3 E
Arthur River, *Australia* **61 F2** 33 20S 117 2 E
Arthur's Pass, *N.Z.* **59 K3** 42 54S 171 35 E
Arthur's Town, *Bahamas* **89 B4** 24 38N 75 42W
Artigas, *Uruguay* **94 C4** 30 20S 56 30W
Artillery L., *Canada* **73 A7** 63 9N 107 52W
Artois, *France* **18 A5** 50 20N 2 30 E
Artrutx, C. de, *Spain* **22 B10** 39 55N 3 49 E
Artsyz, *Ukraine* **17 E15** 46 4N 29 26 E
Artvin, *Turkey* **25 F7** 41 14N 41 44 E
Aru, Kepulauan, *Indonesia* **37 F8** 6 0S 134 30 E
Aru Is. = Aru, Kepulauan, *Indonesia* **37 F8** 6 0S 134 30 E
Arua, *Uganda* **54 B3** 3 1N 30 58 E
Aruanã, *Brazil* **93 F8** 14 54S 51 10W
Aruba ■, *W. Indies* **89 D6** 12 30N 70 0W
Arucas, *Canary Is.* **22 F4** 28 7N 15 32W
Arun →, *Nepal* **43 F12** 26 55N 87 10 E
Arun →, *U.K.* **11 G7** 50 49N 0 33W
Arunachal Pradesh □, *India* **41 F19** 28 0N 95 0 E
Arusha, *Tanzania* **54 C4** 3 20S 36 40 E
Arusha □, *Tanzania* **54 C4** 4 0S 36 30 E
Arusha Chini, *Tanzania* **54 C4** 3 32S 37 20 E
Aruwimi →, *Dem. Rep. of the Congo* **54 B1** 1 13N 23 36 E
Arvada, *Colo., U.S.A.* **80 F2** 39 48N 105 5W
Arvada, *Wyo., U.S.A.* **82 D10** 44 39N 106 8W
Árvi, *Greece* **23 E7** 34 59N 25 28 E
Arviat, *Canada* **73 A10** 61 6N 93 59W
Arvidsjaur, *Sweden* **8 D18** 65 35N 19 10 E
Arvika, *Sweden* **9 G15** 59 40N 12 36 E
Arvin, *U.S.A.* **85 K8** 35 12N 118 50W
Arwal, *India* **43 G11** 25 15N 84 41 E
Arxan, *China* **33 B6** 47 11N 119 57 E
Aryirádhes, *Greece* **23 B3** 39 27N 19 58 E
Aryiroúpolis, *Greece* **23 D6** 35 17N 24 20 E
Arys, *Kazakstan* **26 E7** 42 26N 68 48 E
Arzamas, *Russia* **24 C7** 55 27N 43 55 E
Aş Şadr, *U.A.E.* **45 E7** 24 40N 54 41 E
Aş Şafā, *Syria* **47 B6** 33 10N 37 0 E
As Saffānīyah, *Si. Arabia* **45 E6** 27 55N 48 50 E
As Safirah, *Syria* **44 B3** 36 5N 37 21 E
Aş Şahm, *Oman* **45 E8** 24 10N 56 53 E
As Sājir, *Si. Arabia* **44 E5** 25 11N 44 36 E
As Salamīyah, *Syria* **44 C3** 35 1N 37 2 E
As Salmān, *Iraq* **44 D5** 30 30N 44 32 E
As Salṭ, *Jordan* **47 C4** 32 2N 35 43 E
As Sal'w'a, *Qatar* **45 E6** 24 23N 50 50 E
As Samāwah, *Iraq* **44 D5** 31 15N 45 15 E
As Sanamayn, *Syria* **47 B5** 33 3N 36 10 E
As Sohar = Şuḥār, *Oman* **45 E8** 24 20N 56 40 E
As Sukhnah, *Syria* **44 C3** 34 52N 38 52 E
As Sulaymānīyah, *Iraq* **44 C5** 35 35N 45 29 E
As Sulaymī, *Si. Arabia* **44 E4** 26 17N 41 21 E
As Sulayyil, *Si. Arabia* **46 C4** 20 27N 45 34 E
As Summān, *Si. Arabia* **44 E5** 25 0N 47 0 E
As Suwaydā', *Syria* **47 C5** 32 40N 36 30 E
As Suwaydā' □, *Syria* **47 C5** 32 45N 36 45 E
As Suwayq, *Oman* **45 F8** 23 51N 57 26 E
As Şuwayrah, *Iraq* **44 C5** 32 55N 45 0 E
Asab, *Namibia* **56 D2** 25 30S 18 0 E
Asad, Buḥayrat al, *Syria* **44 C3** 36 0N 38 15 E
Asahi-Gawa →, *Japan* **31 G6** 34 36N 133 58 E
Asahigawa, *Japan* **30 C11** 43 46N 142 22 E
Asamankese, *Ghana* **50 G5** 5 50N 0 40W
Asan →, *India* **43 F8** 26 37N 78 24 E
Asansol, *India* **43 H12** 23 40N 87 1 E
Asbesberge, *S. Africa* **56 D3** 29 0S 23 0 E
Asbestos, *Canada* **71 C5** 45 47N 71 58W
Asbury Park, *U.S.A.* **79 F10** 40 13N 74 1W
Ascensión, *Mexico* **86 A3** 31 6N 107 59W
Ascensión, B. de la, *Mexico* **87 D7** 19 50N 87 20W
Ascension I., *Atl. Oc.* **49 G2** 8 0S 14 15W
Aschaffenburg, *Germany* **16 D5** 49 58N 9 6 E
Aschersleben, *Germany* **16 C6** 51 45N 11 29 E
Ascoli Piceno, *Italy* **20 C5** 42 51N 13 34 E
Ascope, *Peru* **92 E3** 7 46S 79 8W
Ascotán, *Chile* **94 A2** 21 45S 68 17W
Aseb, *Eritrea* **46 E3** 13 0N 42 40 E
Asela, *Ethiopia* **46 F2** 8 0N 39 0 E
Asenovgrad, *Bulgaria* **21 C11** 42 1N 24 51 E
Aserradero, *Mexico* **86 C3** 23 40N 105 43W
Asgata, *Cyprus* **23 E12** 34 46N 33 15 E
Ash Fork, *U.S.A.* **83 J7** 35 13N 112 29W
Ash Grove, *U.S.A.* **81 G8** 37 19N 93 35W
Ash Shabakah, *Iraq* **44 D4** 30 49N 43 39 E
Ash Shamāl □, *Lebanon* **47 A5** 34 25N 36 0 E
Ash Shāmīyah, *Iraq* **44 D5** 31 55N 44 35 E
Ash Shāriqah, *U.A.E.* **45 E7** 25 23N 55 26 E
Ash Sharmah, *Si. Arabia* **44 D2** 28 1N 35 16 E
Ash Sharqāṭ, *Iraq* **44 C4** 35 27N 43 16 E
Ash Sharqi, Al Jabal, *Lebanon* **47 B5** 33 40N 36 10 E
Ash Shaṭrah, *Iraq* **44 D5** 31 30N 46 10 E
Ash Shawbak, *Jordan* **44 D2** 30 32N 35 34 E
Ash Shawmari, J., *Jordan* **47 E5** 30 35N 36 35 E
Ash Shināfīyah, *Iraq* **44 D5** 31 35N 44 39 E
Ash Shu'bah, *Si. Arabia* **44 D5** 28 54N 44 44 E
Ash Shumlūl, *Si. Arabia* **44 E5** 26 31N 47 20 E
Ash Shūr'a, *Iraq* **44 C4** 35 58N 43 13 E
Ash Shurayf, *Si. Arabia* **44 E3** 25 43N 39 14 E
Ash Shuwayfāt, *Lebanon* **47 B4** 33 45N 35 30 E
Asha, *Russia* **24 D10** 55 0N 57 16 E
Ashau, *Vietnam* **38 D6** 16 6N 107 22 E
Ashbourne, *U.K.* **10 D6** 53 2N 1 43W
Ashburn, *U.S.A.* **77 K4** 31 43N 83 39W
Ashburton, *N.Z.* **59 K3** 43 53S 171 48 E
Ashburton →, *Australia* **60 D1** 21 40S 114 56 E
Ashcroft, *Canada* **72 C4** 50 40N 121 20W
Ashdod, *Israel* **47 D3** 31 49N 34 35 E
Ashdown, *U.S.A.* **81 J7** 33 40N 94 8W
Asheboro, *U.S.A.* **77 H6** 35 43N 79 49W
Ashern, *Canada* **73 C9** 51 11N 98 21W
Asherton, *U.S.A.* **81 L5** 28 27N 99 46W
Asheville, *U.S.A.* **77 H4** 35 36N 82 33W
Ashewat, *Pakistan* **42 D3** 31 22N 68 32 E
Asheweig →, *Canada* **70 B2** 54 17N 87 12W
Ashford, *Australia* **63 D5** 29 15S 151 3 E
Ashford, *U.K.* **11 F8** 51 8N 0 53 E
Ashgabat, *Turkmenistan* **26 F6** 38 0N 57 50 E
Ashibetsu, *Japan* **30 C11** 43 31N 142 11 E
Ashikaga, *Japan* **31 F9** 36 28N 139 29 E
Ashington, *U.K.* **10 B6** 55 11N 1 33W
Ashizuri-Zaki, *Japan* **31 H6** 32 44N 133 0 E
Ashkarkot, *Afghan.* **42 C2** 33 3N 67 58 E
Ashkhabad = Ashgabat, *Turkmenistan* **26 F6** 38 0N 57 50 E
Āshkhāneh, *Iran* **45 B8** 37 26N 56 55 E
Ashland, *Kans., U.S.A.* **81 G5** 37 11N 99 46W
Ashland, *Ky., U.S.A.* **76 F4** 38 28N 82 38W
Ashland, *Mont., U.S.A.* **82 D10** 45 36N 106 16W
Ashland, *Ohio, U.S.A.* **78 F2** 40 52N 82 19W
Ashland, *Oreg., U.S.A.* **82 E2** 42 12N 122 43W
Ashland, *Pa., U.S.A.* **79 F8** 40 45N 76 22W
Ashland, *Va., U.S.A.* **76 G7** 37 46N 77 29W
Ashland, *Wis., U.S.A.* **80 B9** 46 35N 90 53W
Ashley, *N. Dak., U.S.A.* **80 B5** 46 2N 99 22W
Ashley, *Pa., U.S.A.* **79 E9** 41 12N 75 55W
Ashmore Reef, *Australia* **60 B3** 12 14S 123 5 E
Ashmyany, *Belarus* **9 J21** 54 26N 25 52 E
Ashokan Reservoir, *U.S.A.* **79 E10** 41 56N 74 13W
Ashqelon, *Israel* **47 D3** 31 42N 34 35 E
Ashta, *India* **42 H7** 23 1N 76 43 E
Ashtabula, *U.S.A.* **78 E4** 41 52N 80 47W
Ashton, *S. Africa* **56 E3** 33 50S 20 5 E
Ashton, *U.S.A.* **82 D8** 44 4N 111 27W
Ashuanipi, L., *Canada* **71 B6** 52 45N 66 15W
Ashville, *U.S.A.* **78 F6** 40 34N 78 33W
Asia **28 E11** 45 0N 75 0 E
Asia, Kepulauan, *Indonesia* **37 D8** 1 0N 131 13 E
Āsīā Bak, *Iran* **45 C6** 35 19N 50 30 E
Asifabad, *India* **40 K11** 19 20N 79 24 E
Asinara, *Italy* **20 D3** 41 4N 8 16 E
Asinara, G. dell', *Italy* **20 D3** 41 0N 8 30 E
Asino, *Russia* **26 D9** 57 0N 86 0 E
Asipovichy, *Belarus* **17 B15** 53 19N 28 33 E
'Asīr □, *Si. Arabia* **46 D3** 18 40N 42 30 E
Asir, Ras, *Somali Rep.* **46 E5** 11 55N 51 10 E
Askersund, *Sweden* **9 G16** 58 53N 14 55 E
Askham, *S. Africa* **56 D3** 26 59S 20 47 E
Askim, *Norway* **9 G14** 59 35N 11 10 E
Askja, *Iceland* **8 D5** 65 3N 16 48W
Askøy, *Norway* **9 F11** 60 29N 5 10 E
Asmara = Asmera, *Eritrea* **46 D2** 15 19N 38 55 E

Asmera

Asmera, Eritrea 46 D2 15 19N 38 55 E
Åsnen, Sweden 9 H16 56 37N 14 45 E
Aspen, U.S.A. 83 G10 39 11N 106 49W
Aspermont, U.S.A. 81 J4 33 8N 100 14W
Aspiring, Mt., N.Z. 59 L2 44 23S 168 46 E
Asprókavos, Ákra, Greece 23 B4 39 21N 20 6 E
Aspur, India 42 H6 23 58N 74 7 E
Asquith, Canada 73 C7 52 8N 107 13W
Assam □, India 41 G18 26 0N 93 0 E
Asse, Belgium 15 D4 50 24N 4 10 E
Assen, Neths. 15 A6 53 0N 6 35 E
Assiniboia, Canada 73 D7 49 40N 105 59W
Assiniboine →, Canada 73 D9 49 53N 97 8W
Assiniboine, Mt., Canada 72 C5 50 52N 115 39W
Assis, Brazil 95 A5 22 40S 50 20W
Assisi, Italy 20 C5 43 4N 12 37 E
Assynt, L., U.K. 12 C3 58 10N 5 3W
Astana, Kazakstan 26 D8 51 10N 71 30 E
Āstāneh, Iran 45 B6 37 17N 49 59 E
Astara, Azerbaijan 25 G8 38 30N 48 50 E
Asteroúsia, Greece 23 E7 34 59N 25 3 E
Asti, Italy 18 D8 44 54N 8 12 E
Astipálaia, Greece 21 F12 36 32N 26 22 E
Astorga, Spain 19 A2 42 29N 6 8W
Astoria, U.S.A. 84 D3 46 11N 123 50W
Astrakhan, Russia 25 E8 46 25N 48 5 E
Asturias □, Spain 19 A3 43 15N 6 0W
Asunción, Paraguay 94 B4 25 10S 57 30W
Asunción Nochixtlán, Mexico 87 D5 17 28N 97 14W
Aswa →, Uganda 54 B3 3 43N 31 55 E
Aswân, Egypt 51 D12 24 4N 32 57 E
Aswân High Dam = Sadd el Aali, Egypt 51 D12 23 54N 32 54 E
Asyût, Egypt 51 C12 27 11N 31 4 E
At Ṭafilah, Jordan 47 E4 30 45N 35 30 E
Aṭ Ṭā'if, Si. Arabia 46 C3 21 5N 40 27 E
Aṭ Ṭirāq, Si. Arabia 44 E5 27 19N 44 33 E
Aṭ Tubayq, Si. Arabia 44 D3 29 30N 37 0 E
Atacama □, Chile 94 B2 27 30S 70 0W
Atacama, Desierto de, Chile 94 A2 24 0S 69 20W
Atacama, Salar de, Chile 94 A2 23 30S 68 20W
Atalaya, Peru 92 F4 10 45S 73 50W
Atalaya de Femes, Canary Is. 22 F6 28 56N 13 47W
Atami, Japan 31 G9 35 5N 139 4 E
Atapupu, Indonesia 37 F6 9 0S 124 51 E
Atâr, Mauritania 50 D3 20 30N 13 5W
Atari, Pakistan 42 D6 30 56N 74 2 E
Atascadero, U.S.A. 84 K6 35 29N 120 40W
Atasu, Kazakstan 26 E8 48 30N 71 0 E
Atatürk Barajı, Turkey 25 G6 37 28N 38 30 E
Atauro, Indonesia 37 F7 8 10S 125 30 E
Atbara, Sudan 51 E12 17 42N 33 59 E
'Atbara →, Sudan 51 E12 17 40N 33 56 E
Atbasar, Kazakstan 26 D7 51 48N 68 20 E
Atchafalaya B., U.S.A. 81 L9 29 25N 91 25W
Atchison, U.S.A. 80 F7 39 34N 95 7W
Āteshān, Iran 45 C7 35 35N 52 37 E
Ath, Belgium 15 D3 50 38N 3 47 E
Athabasca, Canada 72 C6 54 45N 113 20W
Athabasca →, Canada 73 B6 58 40N 110 50W
Athabasca, L., Canada 73 B7 59 15N 109 15W
Athboy, Ireland 13 C5 53 37N 6 56W
Athenry, Ireland 13 C3 53 18N 8 44W
Athens = Athínai, Greece 21 F10 37 58N 23 46 E
Athens, Ala., U.S.A. 77 H2 34 48N 86 58W
Athens, Ga., U.S.A. 77 J4 33 57N 83 23W
Athens, N.Y., U.S.A. 79 D11 42 16N 73 49W
Athens, Ohio, U.S.A. 76 F4 39 20N 82 6W
Athens, Pa., U.S.A. 79 E8 41 57N 76 31W
Athens, Tenn., U.S.A. 77 H3 35 27N 84 36W
Athens, Tex., U.S.A. 81 J7 32 12N 95 51W
Atherley, Canada 78 B5 44 37N 79 20W
Atherton, Australia 62 B4 17 17S 145 30 E
Athienou, Cyprus 23 D12 35 3N 33 32 E
Athínai, Greece 21 F10 37 58N 23 46 E
Athlone, Ireland 13 C4 53 25N 7 56W
Athna, Cyprus 23 D12 35 3N 33 47 E
Athol, U.S.A. 79 D12 42 36N 72 14W
Atholl, Forest of, U.K. 12 E5 56 51N 3 50W
Atholville, Canada 71 C6 47 59N 66 43W
Áthos, Greece 21 D11 40 9N 24 22 E
Athy, Ireland 13 C5 53 0N 7 0W
Ati, Chad 51 F9 13 13N 18 20 E
Atiak, Uganda 54 B3 3 12N 32 2 E
Atik L., Canada 73 B9 55 15N 96 0W
Atikameg →, Canada 70 B3 52 30N 82 46W
Atikokan, Canada 70 C1 48 45N 91 37W
Atikonak L., Canada 71 B7 52 40N 64 32W
Atka, Russia 27 C16 60 50N 151 48 E
Atka I., U.S.A. 68 C2 52 7N 174 30W
Atkinson, U.S.A. 80 D5 42 32N 98 59W
Atlanta, Ga., U.S.A. 77 J3 33 45N 84 23W
Atlanta, Tex., U.S.A. 81 J7 33 7N 94 10W
Atlantic, U.S.A. 80 E7 41 24N 95 1W
Atlantic City, U.S.A. 76 F8 39 21N 74 27W
Atlantic Ocean 2 E9 0 0 20 0W
Atlas Mts. = Haut Atlas, Morocco 50 B4 32 30N 5 0W
Atlin, Canada 72 B2 59 31N 133 41W
Atlin, L., Canada 72 B2 59 26N 133 45W
Atlin Prov. Park, Canada 72 B2 59 10N 134 30W
Atmore, U.S.A. 77 K2 31 2N 87 29W
Atoka, U.S.A. 81 H6 34 23N 96 8W
Atolia, U.S.A. 85 K9 35 19N 117 37W
Atrai →, Bangla. 43 G13 24 7N 89 22 E
Atrak = Atrek →, Turkmenistan 45 B8 37 35N 53 58 E
Atrauli, India 42 E8 28 2N 78 20 E
Atrek →, Turkmenistan 45 B8 37 35N 53 58 E
Atsuta, Japan 30 C10 43 24N 141 26 E
Attalla, U.S.A. 77 H2 34 1N 86 6W
Attapu, Laos 38 E6 14 48N 106 50 E
Attáviros, Greece 23 C9 36 12N 27 50 E
Attawapiskat, Canada 70 B3 52 56N 82 24W
Attawapiskat →, Canada 70 B3 52 57N 82 18W
Attawapiskat L., Canada 70 B2 52 18N 87 54W
Attica, Ind., U.S.A. 76 E2 40 18N 87 15W
Attica, Ohio, U.S.A. 78 E2 41 4N 82 53W
Attikamagen L., Canada 71 B6 55 0N 66 30W
Attleboro, U.S.A. 79 E13 41 57N 71 17W
Attock, Pakistan 42 C5 33 52N 72 20 E
Attopeu = Attapu, Laos 38 E6 14 48N 106 50 E
Attu I., U.S.A. 68 C1 52 55N 172 55 E
Attur, India 40 P11 11 35N 78 30 E
Atuel →, Argentina 94 D2 36 17S 66 50W
Åtvidaberg, Sweden 9 G17 58 12N 16 0 E
Atwater, U.S.A. 84 H6 37 21N 120 37W
Atwood, Canada 78 C3 43 40N 81 1W
Atwood, U.S.A. 80 F4 39 48N 101 3W
Atyraū, Kazakstan 25 E9 47 5N 52 0 E
Au Sable, U.S.A. 78 B1 44 25N 83 20W
Au Sable →, U.S.A. 76 C4 44 25N 83 20W
Au Sable Forks, U.S.A. 79 B11 44 27N 73 41W
Au Sable Pt., U.S.A. 78 B1 44 20N 83 20W
Aubagne, France 18 E6 43 17N 5 37 E
Aubarca, C. d', Spain 22 B7 39 4N 1 22 E
Aube →, France 18 B5 48 34N 3 43 E
Auberry, U.S.A. 84 H7 37 7N 119 29W
Auburn, Ala., U.S.A. 77 J3 32 36N 85 29W
Auburn, Calif., U.S.A. 84 G5 38 54N 121 4W
Auburn, Ind., U.S.A. 76 E3 41 22N 85 4W
Auburn, Maine, U.S.A. 77 C10 44 6N 70 14W
Auburn, N.Y., U.S.A. 79 D8 42 56N 76 34W
Auburn, Nebr., U.S.A. 80 E7 40 23N 95 51W
Auburn, Pa., U.S.A. 79 F8 40 36N 76 6W
Auburn, Wash., U.S.A. 84 C4 47 18N 122 14W
Auburn Ra., Australia 63 D5 25 15S 150 30 E
Aubusson, France 18 D5 45 57N 2 11 E
Auch, France 18 E4 43 39N 0 36 E
Auckland, N.Z. 59 G5 36 52S 174 46 E
Auckland Is., Pac. Oc. 64 N8 50 40S 166 5 E
Aude →, France 18 E5 43 13N 3 14 E
Auden, Canada 70 B2 50 14N 87 53W
Audubon, U.S.A. 80 E7 41 43N 94 56W
Augathella, Australia 63 D4 25 48S 146 35 E
Aughnacloy, U.K. 13 B5 54 25N 6 59W
Augrabies Falls, S. Africa 56 D3 28 35S 20 20 E
Augsburg, Germany 16 D6 48 25N 10 52 E
Augusta, Australia 61 F2 34 19S 115 9 E
Augusta, Italy 20 F6 37 13N 15 13 E
Augusta, Ark., U.S.A. 81 H9 35 17N 91 22W
Augusta, Ga., U.S.A. 77 J5 33 28N 81 58W
Augusta, Kans., U.S.A. 81 G6 37 41N 96 59W
Augusta, Maine, U.S.A. 69 D13 44 19N 69 47W
Augusta, Mont., U.S.A. 82 C7 47 30N 112 24W
Augustów, Poland 17 B12 53 51N 23 0 E
Augustus, Mt., Australia 61 D2 24 20S 116 50 E
Augustus I., Australia 60 C3 15 20S 124 30 E
Aukum, U.S.A. 84 G6 38 34N 120 43W
Auld, L., Australia 60 D3 22 25S 123 50 E
Ault, U.S.A. 80 E2 40 35N 104 44W
Aunis, France 18 C3 46 5N 0 50W
Auponhia, Indonesia 37 E7 1 58S 125 27 E
Aur, Pulau, Malaysia 39 L5 2 35N 104 10 E
Auraiya, India 43 F8 26 28N 79 33 E
Aurangabad, Bihar, India 43 G11 24 45N 84 18 E
Aurangabad, Maharashtra, India 40 K9 19 50N 75 23 E
Aurich, Germany 16 B4 53 28N 7 28 E
Aurillac, France 18 D5 44 55N 2 26 E
Aurora, Canada 78 C5 44 0N 79 28W
Aurora, S. Africa 56 E2 32 40S 18 29 E
Aurora, Colo., U.S.A. 80 F2 39 44N 104 52W
Aurora, Ill., U.S.A. 76 E1 41 45N 88 19W
Aurora, Mo., U.S.A. 81 G8 36 58N 93 43W
Aurora, N.Y., U.S.A. 79 D8 42 45N 76 42W
Aurora, Nebr., U.S.A. 80 E6 40 52N 98 0W
Aurora, Ohio, U.S.A. 78 E3 41 21N 81 20W
Aurukun, Australia 62 A3 13 20S 141 45 E
Aus, Namibia 56 D2 26 35S 16 12 E
Ausable →, Canada 78 C3 43 19N 81 46W
Auschwitz = Oświęcim, Poland 17 C10 50 2N 19 11 E
Austin, Minn., U.S.A. 80 D8 43 40N 92 58W
Austin, Nev., U.S.A. 82 G5 39 30N 117 4W
Austin, Pa., U.S.A. 78 E6 41 38N 78 6W
Austin, Tex., U.S.A. 81 K6 30 17N 97 45W
Austin, L., Australia 61 E2 27 40S 118 0 E
Austin I., Canada 73 A10 61 10N 94 0W
Austra, Norway 8 D14 65 8N 11 55 E
Austral Is. = Tubuai Is., Pac. Oc. 65 K13 25 0S 150 0W
Austral Seamount Chain, Pac. Oc. 65 K13 24 0S 150 0W
Australia ■, Oceania 64 K5 23 0S 135 0 E
Australian Capital Territory □, Australia 63 F4 35 30S 149 0 E
Australind, Australia 61 F2 33 17S 115 42 E
Austria ■, Europe 16 E8 47 0N 14 0 E
Austvågøy, Norway 8 B16 68 20N 14 40 E
Autlán, Mexico 86 D4 19 40N 104 30W
Autun, France 18 C6 46 58N 4 17 E
Auvergne, France 18 D5 45 20N 3 15 E
Auvergne, Mts. d', France 18 D5 45 20N 2 55 E
Auxerre, France 18 C5 47 48N 3 32 E
Ava, U.S.A. 81 G8 36 57N 92 40W
Avallon, France 18 C5 47 30N 3 53 E
Avalon, U.S.A. 85 M8 33 21N 118 20W
Avalon Pen., Canada 71 C9 47 30N 53 20W
Avanos, Turkey 44 B2 38 43N 34 51 E
Avaré, Brazil 95 A6 23 4S 48 58W
Avawatz Mts., U.S.A. 85 K10 35 40N 116 30W
Aveiro, Brazil 93 D7 3 10S 55 5W
Aveiro, Portugal 19 B1 40 37N 8 38W
Āvej, Iran 45 C6 35 40N 49 15 E
Avellaneda, Argentina 94 C4 34 50S 58 10W
Avellino, Italy 20 D6 40 54N 14 47 E
Avenal, U.S.A. 84 K6 36 0N 120 8W
Aversa, Italy 20 D6 40 58N 14 12 E
Avery, U.S.A. 82 C6 47 15N 115 49W
Aves, Is. las, Venezuela 89 D6 12 0N 67 30W
Avesta, Sweden 9 F17 60 9N 16 10 E
Avezzano, Italy 20 C5 42 2N 13 25 E
Aviá Terai, Argentina 94 B3 26 45S 60 50W
Aviemore, U.K. 12 D5 57 12N 3 50W
Avignon, France 18 E6 43 57N 4 50 E
Ávila, Spain 19 B3 40 39N 4 43W
Avila Beach, U.S.A. 85 K6 35 11N 120 44W
Avilés, Spain 19 A3 43 35N 5 57W
Avis, U.S.A. 78 E7 41 11N 77 19W
Avoca, U.S.A. 78 D7 42 25N 77 25W
Avoca →, Australia 63 F3 35 40S 143 43 E
Avoca →, Ireland 13 D5 52 48N 6 10W
Avola, Canada 72 C5 51 45N 119 19W
Avola, Italy 20 F6 36 56N 15 7 E
Avon, U.S.A. 78 D7 42 55N 77 45W
Avon →, Australia 61 F2 31 40S 116 7 E
Avon →, Bristol, U.K. 11 F5 51 29N 2 41W
Avon →, Dorset, U.K. 11 G6 50 44N 1 46W
Avon →, Warks., U.K. 11 E5 52 0N 2 8W
Avon Park, U.S.A. 77 M5 27 36N 81 31W
Avondale, Zimbabwe 55 F3 17 43S 30 58 E
Avonlea, Canada 73 D8 50 0N 105 0W
Avonmore, Canada 79 A10 45 10N 74 58W
Avranches, France 18 B3 48 40N 1 20W
A'waj →, Syria 47 B5 33 23N 36 20 E
Awaji-Shima, Japan 31 G7 34 30N 134 50 E
'Awālī, Bahrain 45 E6 26 0N 50 30 E
Awantipur, India 43 C6 33 55N 75 3 E
Awasa, Ethiopia 46 F2 7 3N 38 28 E
Awash, Ethiopia 46 F3 9 1N 40 10 E
Awatere →, N.Z. 59 J5 41 37S 174 10 E
Awbārī, Libya 51 C8 26 46N 12 57 E
Awe, L., U.K. 12 E3 56 17N 5 16W
Awjilah, Libya 51 C10 29 8N 21 7 E
Axe →, U.K. 11 F5 50 42N 3 4W
Axel Heiberg I., Canada 4 B3 80 0N 90 0W
Axim, Ghana 50 H5 4 51N 2 15W
Axiós →, Greece 21 D10 40 57N 22 35 E
Axminster, U.K. 11 G4 50 46N 3 0W
Ayabaca, Peru 92 D3 4 40S 79 53W
Ayabe, Japan 31 G7 35 20N 135 20 E
Ayacucho, Argentina 94 D4 37 5S 58 20W
Ayacucho, Peru 92 F4 13 0S 74 0W
Ayaguz, Kazakstan 26 E9 48 10N 80 10 E
Ayamonte, Spain 19 D2 37 12N 7 24W
Ayan, Russia 27 D14 56 30N 138 16 E
Ayaviri, Peru 92 F4 14 50S 70 35W
Aydın, Turkey 21 F12 37 51N 27 51 E
Aydin □, Turkey 25 G4 37 50N 28 0 E
Ayer, U.S.A. 79 D13 42 34N 71 35W
Ayer's Cliff, Canada 79 A12 45 10N 72 3W
Ayers Rock, Australia 61 E5 25 23S 131 5 E
Ayia Aikaterini, Ákra, Greece 23 A3 39 50N 19 50 E
Ayia Dhéka, Greece 23 D6 35 3N 24 58 E
Ayia Gálini, Greece 23 D6 35 6N 24 41 E
Ayia Napa, Cyprus 23 E13 34 59N 34 0 E
Ayia Phyla, Cyprus 23 E12 34 43N 33 1 E
Ayia Varvára, Greece 23 D7 35 8N 25 1 E
Áyios Amvrósios, Cyprus 23 D12 35 20N 33 35 E
Áyios Evstrátios, Greece 21 E11 39 34N 24 58 E
Áyios Ioánnis, Ákra, Greece 23 D7 35 20N 25 40 E
Áyios Isidhoros, Greece 23 C9 36 9N 27 51 E
Áyios Matthaios, Greece 23 B3 39 30N 19 47 E
Áyios Nikólaos, Greece 23 D7 35 11N 25 41 E
Áyios Seryios, Cyprus 23 D12 35 12N 33 53 E
Áyios Theodhoros, Cyprus 23 D13 35 22N 34 1 E
Aykino, Russia 24 B8 62 15N 49 56 E
Aylesbury, U.K. 11 F7 51 49N 0 49W
Aylmer, Canada 78 D4 42 46N 80 59W
Aylmer, L., Canada 68 B8 64 0N 110 8W
'Ayn, Wādī al, Oman 45 F7 22 15N 55 28 E
Ayn Dār, Si. Arabia 45 E7 25 55N 49 10 E
Ayn Zālah, Iraq 44 B4 36 45N 42 35 E
Ayolas, Paraguay 94 B4 27 10S 56 59W
Ayon, Ostrov, Russia 27 C17 69 50N 169 0 E
'Ayoûn el 'Atroûs, Mauritania 50 E4 16 40N 9 37W
Ayr, Australia 62 B4 19 35S 147 25 E
Ayr, Canada 78 C4 43 17N 80 27W
Ayr, U.K. 12 F4 55 28N 4 38W
Ayr →, U.K. 12 F4 55 28N 4 38W
Ayre, Pt. of, U.K. 10 C3 54 25N 4 21W
Ayton, Australia 62 B4 15 56S 145 22 E
Aytos, Bulgaria 21 C12 42 42N 27 16 E
Ayu, Kepulauan, Indonesia 37 D8 0 35N 131 5 E
Ayutla, Guatemala 88 D1 14 40N 92 10W
Ayutla, Mexico 87 D5 16 58N 99 17W
Ayvacık, Turkey 21 E12 39 36N 26 24 E
Ayvalık, Turkey 21 E12 39 20N 26 46 E
Az Zabadānī, Syria 47 B5 33 43N 36 5 E
Az Zāhirīyah, West Bank 47 D3 31 25N 34 58 E
Az Zahrān, Si. Arabia 45 E6 26 10N 50 7 E
Az Zarqā, Jordan 47 C5 32 5N 36 4 E
Az Zarqā', U.A.E. 45 E7 24 53N 53 4 E
Az Zāwiyah, Libya 51 B8 32 52N 12 56 E
Az Zībār, Iraq 44 B5 36 52N 44 4 E
Az-Zilfī, Si. Arabia 44 E5 26 12N 44 52 E
Az Zubayr, Iraq 44 D5 30 26N 47 40 E
Azamgarh, India 43 F10 26 5N 83 13 E
Azangaro, Peru 92 F4 14 55S 70 13W
Āzār Shahr, Iran 44 B5 37 45N 45 59 E
Azarān, Iran 44 B5 37 25N 47 16 E
Azärbayjan = Azerbaijan ■, Asia 25 F8 40 20N 48 0 E
Āzarbāyjān-e Gharbī □, Iran 44 B5 37 0N 44 30 E
Āzarbāyjān-e Sharqī □, Iran 44 B5 37 20N 47 0 E
Azare, Nigeria 50 F8 11 55N 10 10 E
A'zāz, Syria 44 B3 36 36N 37 4 E
Azbine = Aïr, Niger 50 E7 18 30N 8 0 E
Azerbaijan ■, Asia 25 F8 40 20N 48 0 E
Azerbaijchan = Azerbaijan ■, Asia 25 F8 40 20N 48 0 E
Azimganj, India 43 G13 24 14N 88 16 E
Azogues, Ecuador 92 D3 2 35S 78 0W
Azores, Atl. Oc. 50 A1 38 44N 29 0W
Azov, Russia 25 E6 47 3N 39 25 E
Azov, Sea of, Europe 25 E6 46 0N 36 30 E
Azovskoye More = Azov, Sea of, Europe 25 E6 46 0N 36 30 E
Azraq ash Shīshān, Jordan 47 D5 31 50N 36 49 E
Aztec, U.S.A. 83 H10 36 49N 107 59W
Azúa de Compostela, Dom. Rep. 89 C5 18 25N 70 44W
Azuaga, Spain 19 C3 38 16N 5 39W
Azuero, Pen. de, Panama 88 E3 7 30N 80 30W
Azul, Argentina 94 D4 36 42S 59 43W
Azusa, U.S.A. 85 L9 34 8N 117 52W

B

Ba Don, Vietnam 38 D6 17 45N 106 26 E
Ba Dong, Vietnam 39 H6 9 40N 106 33 E
Ba Ngoi = Cam Lam, Vietnam 39 G7 11 54N 109 10 E
Ba Tri, Vietnam 39 G6 10 2N 106 36 E
Ba Xian = Bazhou, China 34 E9 39 8N 116 22 E
Baa, Indonesia 37 F6 10 50S 123 0 E
Baarle-Nassau, Belgium 15 C4 51 27N 4 56 E
Bab el Mandeb, Red Sea 46 E3 12 35N 43 25 E
Baba Burnu, Turkey 21 E12 39 29N 26 2 E
Bābā Kalū, Iran 45 D6 30 7N 50 49 E
Babadag, Romania 17 F15 44 53N 28 44 E
Babadayhan, Turkmenistan 26 F7 37 42N 60 23 E
Babaeski, Turkey 21 D12 41 26N 27 6 E
Babahoyo, Ecuador 92 D3 1 40S 79 30W
Babai = Sarju →, India 43 F9 27 21N 81 23 E
Babar, Indonesia 37 F7 8 0S 129 30 E
Babar, Pakistan 42 D3 31 7N 69 32 E
Babarkach, Pakistan 42 E3 29 45N 68 0 E
Babb, U.S.A. 82 B7 48 51N 113 27W
Babelthuap, Pac. Oc. 37 C8 7 30N 134 30 E
Baberu, India 43 G9 25 33N 80 43 E
Babi Besar, Pulau, Malaysia 39 L4 2 25N 103 59 E
Babinda, Australia 62 B4 17 20S 145 56 E
Babine, Canada 72 B3 55 22N 126 37W
Babine →, Canada 72 B3 55 45N 127 44W
Babine L., Canada 72 C3 54 48N 126 0W
Babo, Indonesia 37 E8 2 30S 133 30 E
Bābol, Iran 45 B7 36 40N 52 50 E
Bābol Sar, Iran 45 B7 36 45N 52 45 E
Babruysk, Belarus 17 B15 53 10N 29 15 E
Babuhri, India 42 F3 26 49N 69 43 E
Babusar Pass, Pakistan 43 B5 35 12N 73 59 E
Babuyan Chan., Phil. 37 A6 18 40N 121 30 E
Babylon, Iraq 44 C5 32 34N 44 22 E
Bac Lieu, Vietnam 39 H5 9 17N 105 43 E
Bac Phan, Vietnam 38 B5 22 0N 105 0 E
Bacabal, Brazil 93 D10 4 15S 44 45W
Bacalar, Mexico 87 D7 18 50N 87 27W
Bacan, Kepulauan, Indonesia 37 E7 0 35S 127 30 E
Bacarra, Phil. 37 A6 18 15N 120 37 E
Bacău, Romania 17 E14 46 35N 26 55 E
Bacerac, Mexico 86 A3 30 18N 108 50W
Bach Long Vi, Dao, Vietnam 38 B6 20 10N 107 40 E
Bachelina, Russia 26 D7 57 45N 67 20 E
Bachhwara, India 43 G11 25 35N 85 54 E
Back →, Canada 68 B9 65 10N 104 0W
Bacolod, Phil. 37 B6 10 40N 122 57 E
Bacuk, Malaysia 39 J4 6 4N 102 25 E
Bād, Iran 45 C7 33 41N 52 1 E
Bad →, U.S.A. 80 C4 44 21N 100 22W
Bad Axe, U.S.A. 78 C2 43 48N 83 0W
Bad Ischl, Austria 16 E7 47 44N 13 38 E
Bad Kissingen, Germany 16 C6 50 11N 10 4 E
Bad Lands, U.S.A. 80 D3 43 40N 102 10W
Bada Barabil, India 43 H11 22 7N 85 24 E
Badagara, India 40 P9 11 35N 75 40 E
Badajós, L., Brazil 92 D6 3 15S 62 50W
Badajoz, Spain 19 C2 38 50N 6 59W
Badalona, Spain 19 B7 41 26N 2 15 E
Badalzai, Afghan. 42 E1 29 50N 65 35 E
Badampahar, India 41 H15 22 10N 86 10 E
Badanah, Si. Arabia 44 D4 30 58N 41 30 E
Badarinath, India 43 D8 30 45N 79 30 E
Badas, Kepulauan, Indonesia 36 D3 0 45N 107 5 E
Baddo →, Pakistan 40 F4 28 0N 64 20 E
Bade, Indonesia 37 F9 7 10S 139 35 E
Baden, Austria 16 D9 48 1N 16 13 E
Baden, U.S.A. 78 F4 40 38N 80 14W
Baden-Baden, Germany 16 D5 48 44N 8 13 E
Baden-Württemberg □, Germany 16 D5 48 20N 8 40 E
Badgastein, Austria 16 E7 47 7N 13 9 E
Badger, Canada 71 C8 49 0N 56 4W
Badger, U.S.A. 84 J7 36 38N 119 1W
Bādghīsāt □, Afghan. 40 B3 35 0N 63 0 E
Badgom, India 43 B6 34 1N 74 45 E
Badin, Pakistan 42 G3 24 38N 68 54 E
Badlands National Park, U.S.A. 80 D3 43 38N 102 56W
Badrah, Iraq 44 C5 33 6N 45 58 E
Badrinath, India 43 D8 30 44N 79 29 E
Badulla, Sri Lanka 40 R12 7 1N 81 7 E
Baena, Spain 19 D3 37 37N 4 20W
Baeza, Spain 19 D4 37 57N 3 25W
Baffin B., Canada 4 B4 72 0N 64 0W
Baffin I., Canada 69 B12 68 0N 75 0W
Bafing →, Mali 50 F3 13 49N 10 50W
Bafliyūn, Syria 44 B3 36 37N 36 59 E
Bafoulabé, Mali 50 F3 13 50N 10 55W
Bafoussam, Cameroon 52 C2 5 28N 10 25 E
Bāfq, Iran 45 D7 31 40N 55 25 E
Bafra, Turkey 25 F6 41 34N 35 54 E
Bāft, Iran 45 D8 29 15N 56 38 E
Bafwasende, Dem. Rep. of the Congo 54 B2 1 3N 27 5 E
Bagamoyo, Tanzania 54 D4 6 28S 38 55 E
Bagan Datoh, Malaysia 39 L3 3 59N 100 47 E
Bagan Serai, Malaysia 39 K3 5 1N 100 32 E
Baganga, Phil. 37 C7 7 34N 126 33 E
Bagani, Namibia 56 B3 18 7S 21 41 E
Bagansiapiapi, Indonesia 36 D2 2 12N 100 50 E
Bagasra, India 42 J4 21 30N 71 0 E
Bagaud, India 42 H6 22 19N 75 53 E
Bagdad, U.S.A. 85 L11 34 35N 115 53W
Bagdarin, Russia 27 D12 54 26N 113 36 E
Bagé, Brazil 95 C5 31 20S 54 15W
Bagenalstown = Muine Bheag, Ireland 13 D5 52 42N 6 58W
Baggs, U.S.A. 82 F10 41 2N 107 39W
Bagh, Pakistan 43 C5 33 59N 73 45 E
Baghain →, India 43 G9 25 32N 81 1 E
Baghdād, Iraq 44 C5 33 20N 44 30 E
Bagheria, Italy 20 E5 38 5N 13 30 E
Baghlān, Afghan. 40 A6 36 12N 69 0 E
Bagley, U.S.A. 80 B7 47 32N 95 24W
Bagodar, India 43 G11 24 5N 85 52 E
Bagrationovsk, Russia 9 J19 54 23N 20 39 E
Baguio, Phil. 37 A6 16 26N 120 34 E
Bah, India 43 F8 26 53N 78 36 E
Bahadurganj, India 43 F12 26 16N 87 49 E
Bahadurgarh, India 42 E7 28 40N 76 57 E
Bahama, Canal Viejo de, W. Indies 88 B4 22 10N 77 30W
Bahamas ■, N. Amer. 89 B5 24 0N 75 0W
Baharampur, India 43 G13 24 2N 88 27 E
Bahawalnagar, Pakistan 42 E5 30 0N 73 15 E
Bahawalpur, Pakistan 42 E4 29 24N 71 40 E
Baheri, India 43 E8 28 45N 79 34 E
Bahgul →, India 43 F8 27 45N 79 36 E
Bahi, Tanzania 54 D4 5 58S 35 21 E
Bahi Swamp, Tanzania 54 D4 6 10S 35 0 E
Bahia = Salvador, Brazil 93 F11 13 0S 38 30W
Bahia □, Brazil 93 F10 12 0S 42 0W
Bahía, Is. de la, Honduras 88 C2 16 45N 86 15W
Bahía Blanca, Argentina 94 D3 38 35S 62 13W
Bahía de Caráquez, Ecuador 92 D2 0 40S 80 27W
Bahía Honda, Cuba 88 B3 22 54N 83 10W
Bahía Laura, Argentina 96 F3 48 10S 66 30W
Bahía Negra, Paraguay 92 H7 20 5S 58 5W

103

Big Timber

Belfast, Maine, U.S.A. 77 C11 44 26N 69 1W
Belfast, N.Y., U.S.A. 78 D6 42 21N 78 7W
Belfast L., U.K. 13 B6 54 40N 5 50W
Belfield, U.S.A. 80 B3 46 53N 103 12W
Belfort, France 18 C7 47 38N 6 50 E
Belfry, U.S.A. 82 D9 45 9N 109 1W
Belgaum, India 40 M9 15 55N 74 35 E
Belgium ■, Europe 15 D4 50 30N 5 0 E
Belgorod, Russia 25 D6 50 35N 36 35 E
Belgorod-Dnestrovskiy = Bilhorod-Dnistrovskyy, Ukraine 25 E5 46 11N 30 23 E
Belgrade = Beograd, Serbia, Yug. 21 B9 44 50N 20 37 E
Belgrade, U.S.A. 82 D8 45 47N 111 11W
Belhaven, U.S.A. 77 H7 35 33N 76 37W
Beli Drim →, Europe 21 C9 42 6N 20 25 E
Belinyu, Indonesia 36 E3 1 35S 105 50 E
Beliton Is. = Belitung, Indonesia 36 E3 3 10S 107 50 E
Belitung, Indonesia 36 E3 3 10S 107 50 E
Belize ■, Cent. Amer. 87 D7 17 0N 88 30W
Belize City, Belize 87 D7 17 25N 88 0W
Belkovskiy, Ostrov, Russia 27 B14 75 32N 135 44 E
Bell →, Canada 70 C4 49 48N 77 38W
Bell I., Canada 71 B8 50 46N 55 35W
Bell-Irving →, Canada 72 B3 56 12N 129 5W
Bell Peninsula, Canada 69 B11 63 50N 82 0W
Bell Ville, Argentina 94 C3 32 40S 62 40W
Bella Bella, Canada 72 C3 52 10N 128 10W
Bella Coola, Canada 72 C3 52 25N 126 40W
Bella Unión, Uruguay 94 C4 30 15S 57 40W
Bella Vista, Corrientes, Argentina 94 B4 28 33S 59 0W
Bella Vista, Tucuman, Argentina 94 B2 27 10S 65 25W
Bellaire, U.S.A. 78 F4 40 1N 80 45W
Bellary, India 40 M10 15 10N 76 56 E
Bellata, Australia 63 D4 29 53S 149 46 E
Belle-Chasse, U.S.A. 81 L10 29 51N 89 59W
Belle Fourche, U.S.A. 80 C3 44 40N 103 51W
Belle Fourche →, U.S.A. 80 C3 44 26N 102 18W
Belle Glade, U.S.A. 77 M5 26 41N 80 40W
Belle-Île, France 18 C2 47 20N 3 10W
Belle Isle, Canada 71 B8 51 57N 55 25W
Belle Isle, Str. of, Canada 71 B8 51 30N 56 30W
Belle Plaine, U.S.A. 80 E8 41 54N 92 17W
Bellefontaine, U.S.A. 76 E4 40 22N 83 46W
Bellefonte, U.S.A. 78 F7 40 55N 77 47W
Belleoram, Canada 71 C8 47 31N 55 25W
Belleville, Canada 78 B7 44 10N 77 23W
Belleville, Ill., U.S.A. 80 F10 38 31N 89 59W
Belleville, Kans., U.S.A. 80 F6 39 50N 97 38W
Belleville, N.Y., U.S.A. 79 C8 43 46N 76 10W
Bellevue, Canada 72 D6 49 35N 114 22W
Bellevue, Idaho, U.S.A. 82 E6 43 28N 114 16W
Bellevue, Nebr., U.S.A. 80 E7 41 8N 95 53W
Bellevue, Ohio, U.S.A. 78 E2 41 17N 82 51W
Bellevue, Wash., U.S.A. 84 C4 47 37N 122 12W
Bellin = Kangirsuk, Canada 69 C13 60 0N 70 0W
Bellingen, Australia 63 E5 30 25S 152 50 E
Bellingham, U.S.A. 68 D7 48 46N 122 29W
Bellingshausen Sea, Antarctica 5 C17 66 0S 80 0W
Bellinzona, Switz. 18 C8 46 11N 9 1 E
Bello, Colombia 92 B3 6 20N 75 33W
Bellows Falls, U.S.A. 79 C12 43 8N 72 27W
Bellpat, Pakistan 42 E3 29 0N 68 5 E
Belluno, Italy 20 A5 46 9N 12 13 E
Bellwood, U.S.A. 78 F6 40 36N 78 20W
Belmont, Canada 78 D3 42 53N 81 5W
Belmont, S. Africa 56 D3 29 28S 24 22 E
Belmont, U.S.A. 78 D6 42 14N 78 2W
Belmonte, Brazil 93 G11 16 0S 39 0W
Belmopan, Belize 87 D7 17 18N 88 30W
Belmullet, Ireland 13 B2 54 14N 9 58W
Belo Horizonte, Brazil 93 G10 19 55S 43 56W
Belo-sur-Mer, Madag. 57 C7 20 42S 44 0 E
Belo-Tsiribihina, Madag. 57 B7 19 40S 44 30 E
Belogorsk, Russia 27 D13 51 0N 128 20 E
Beloha, Madag. 57 D8 25 10S 45 3 E
Beloit, Kans., U.S.A. 80 F5 39 28N 98 6W
Beloit, Wis., U.S.A. 80 D10 42 31N 89 2W
Belokorovichi, Ukraine 17 C15 51 7N 28 2 E
Belomorsk, Russia 24 B5 64 35N 34 54 E
Belonia, India 41 H17 23 15N 91 30 E
Beloretsk, Russia 24 D10 53 58N 58 24 E
Belorussia = Belarus ■, Europe 17 B14 53 30N 27 0 E
Belovo, Russia 26 D9 54 30N 86 0 E
Beloye, Ozero, Russia 24 B6 60 10N 37 35 E
Beloye More, Russia 24 A6 66 30N 38 0 E
Belozersk, Russia 24 B6 60 1N 37 45 E
Belpre, U.S.A. 76 F5 39 17N 81 34W
Belrain, India 43 E9 28 23N 80 55 E
Belt, U.S.A. 82 C8 47 23N 110 55W
Beltana, Australia 63 E2 30 48S 138 25 E
Belterra, Brazil 93 D8 2 45S 55 0W
Belton, U.S.A. 81 K6 31 3N 97 28W
Belton L., U.S.A. 81 K6 31 8N 97 32W
Beltsy = Bălţi, Moldova 17 E14 47 48N 27 58 E
Belturbet, Ireland 13 B4 54 6N 7 26W
Belukha, Russia 26 E9 49 50N 86 50 E
Beluran, Malaysia 36 C5 5 48N 117 35 E
Belvidere, Ill., U.S.A. 80 D10 42 15N 88 50W
Belvidere, N.J., U.S.A. 79 F9 40 50N 75 5W
Belyando →, Australia 62 C4 21 38S 146 50 E
Belyy, Ostrov, Russia 26 B8 73 30N 71 0 E
Belyy Yar, Russia 26 D9 58 26N 84 39 E
Belzoni, U.S.A. 81 J9 33 11N 90 29W
Bemaraha, Lembalemban' i, Madag. 57 B7 18 40S 44 45 E
Bemarivo, Madag. 57 C7 21 45S 44 45 E
Bemarivo →, Madag. 57 B8 15 27S 47 40 E
Bemavo, Madag. 57 C8 21 33S 45 25 E
Bembéréke, Benin 50 F6 10 11N 2 43 E
Bembesi, Zimbabwe 55 G2 20 0S 28 58 E
Bembesi →, Zimbabwe 55 F2 18 57S 27 47 E
Bemetara, India 43 J9 21 42N 81 32 E
Bemidji, U.S.A. 80 B7 47 28N 94 53W
Ben, Iran 45 C6 32 32N 50 45 E
Ben Cruachan, U.K. 12 E3 56 26N 5 8W
Ben Dearg, U.K. 12 D4 57 47N 4 56W
Ben Hope, U.K. 12 C4 58 25N 4 36W
Ben Lawers, U.K. 12 E4 56 32N 4 14W
Ben Lomond, N.S.W., Australia 63 E5 30 1S 151 43 E
Ben Lomond, Tas., Australia 62 G4 41 38S 147 42 E
Ben Lomond, U.K. 12 E4 56 11N 4 38W
Ben Luc, Vietnam 39 G6 10 39N 106 29 E
Ben Macdhui, U.K. 12 D5 57 4N 3 40W
Ben Mhor, U.K. 12 D1 57 15N 7 18W
Ben More, Arg. & Bute, U.K. 12 E2 56 26N 6 1W
Ben More, Stirl., U.K. 12 E4 56 23N 4 32W
Ben More Assynt, U.K. 12 C4 58 8N 4 52W
Ben Nevis, U.K. 12 E3 56 48N 5 1W
Ben Quang, Vietnam 38 D6 17 3N 106 55 E
Ben Vorlich, U.K. 12 E4 56 21N 4 14W
Ben Wyvis, U.K. 12 D4 57 40N 4 35W
Bena, Nigeria 50 F7 11 20N 5 50 E
Benalla, Australia 63 F4 36 30S 146 0 E
Benares = Varanasi, India 43 G10 25 22N 83 0 E
Benavente, Spain 19 A3 42 2N 5 43W
Benavides, U.S.A. 81 M5 27 36N 98 25W
Benbecula, U.K. 12 D1 57 26N 7 21W
Benbonyathe, Australia 63 E2 30 25S 139 11 E
Bend, U.S.A. 82 D3 44 4N 121 19W
Bendemeer, Australia 63 E5 30 53S 151 8 E
Bender Beila, Somali Rep. 46 F5 9 30N 50 48 E
Bendery = Tighina, Moldova 17 E15 46 50N 29 30 E
Bendigo, Australia 63 F3 36 40S 144 15 E
Benē Beraq, Israel 47 C3 32 6N 34 51 E
Benenitra, Madag. 57 C8 23 27S 45 5 E
Benevento, Italy 20 D6 41 8N 14 45 E
Benga, Mozam. 55 F3 16 11S 33 40 E
Bengal, Bay of, Ind. Oc. 41 M17 15 0N 90 0 E
Bengbu, China 35 H9 32 58N 117 20 E
Benghazi = Banghāzī, Libya 51 B10 32 11N 20 3 E
Bengkalis, Indonesia 36 D2 1 30N 102 10 E
Bengkulu, Indonesia 36 E2 3 50S 102 12 E
Bengkulu □, Indonesia 36 E2 3 48S 102 16 E
Bengough, Canada 73 D7 49 25N 105 10W
Benguela, Angola 53 G2 12 37S 13 25 E
Benguérua, I., Mozam. 57 C6 21 58S 35 28 E
Beni, Dem. Rep. of the Congo 54 B2 0 30N 29 27 E
Beni →, Bolivia 92 F5 10 23S 65 24W
Beni Mellal, Morocco 50 B4 32 21N 6 21W
Beni Suef, Egypt 51 C12 29 5N 31 6 E
Beniah L., Canada 72 A6 63 23N 112 17W
Benicia, U.S.A. 84 G4 38 3N 122 9W
Benidorm, Spain 19 C5 38 33N 0 9W
Benin ■, Africa 50 G6 10 0N 2 0 E
Benin, Bight of, W. Afr. 50 H6 5 0N 3 0 E
Benin City, Nigeria 50 G7 6 20N 5 31 E
Benitses, Greece 23 A3 39 32N 19 55 E
Benjamin Aceval, Paraguay 94 A4 24 58S 57 34W
Benjamin Constant, Brazil 92 D4 4 40S 70 15W
Benjamin Hill, Mexico 86 A2 30 10N 111 10W
Benkelman, U.S.A. 80 E4 40 3N 101 32W
Bennett, Canada 72 B2 59 56N 134 53W
Bennett, L., Australia 60 D5 22 50S 131 2 E
Bennetta, Ostrov, Russia 27 B15 76 21N 148 56 E
Bennettsville, U.S.A. 77 H6 34 37N 79 41W
Bennington, N.H., U.S.A. 79 D11 43 0N 71 55W
Bennington, Vt., U.S.A. 79 D11 42 53N 73 12W
Benoni, S. Africa 57 D4 26 11S 28 18 E
Benque Viejo, Belize 87 D7 17 5N 89 8W
Benson, Ariz., U.S.A. 83 L8 31 58N 110 18W
Benson, Minn., U.S.A. 80 C7 45 19N 95 36W
Bent, Iran 45 E8 26 20N 59 31 E
Benteng, Indonesia 37 F6 6 10S 120 30 E
Bentinck I., Australia 62 B2 17 3S 139 35 E
Bento Gonçalves, Brazil 95 B5 29 10S 51 31W
Benton, Ark., U.S.A. 81 H8 34 34N 92 35W
Benton, Calif., U.S.A. 84 H8 37 48N 118 32W
Benton, Ill., U.S.A. 80 G10 38 0N 88 55W
Benton, Pa., U.S.A. 79 E8 41 12N 76 23W
Benton Harbor, U.S.A. 76 D2 42 6N 86 27W
Bentonville, U.S.A. 81 G7 36 22N 94 13W
Bentung, Malaysia 39 L3 3 31N 101 55 E
Benue →, Nigeria 50 G7 7 48N 6 46 E
Benxi, China 35 D12 41 20N 123 48 E
Beo, Indonesia 37 D7 4 25N 126 50 E
Beograd, Serbia, Yug. 21 B9 44 50N 20 37 E
Beppu, Japan 31 H5 33 15N 131 30 E
Beqaa Valley = Al Biqā, Lebanon 47 A5 34 10N 36 10 E
Ber Mota, India 42 H3 23 27N 68 34 E
Berach →, India 42 G6 25 15N 75 2 E
Berati, Albania 21 D8 40 43N 19 59 E
Berau, Teluk, Indonesia 37 E8 2 30S 132 30 E
Berber, Sudan 51 E12 18 0N 34 0 E
Berbera, Somali Rep. 46 E4 10 30N 45 2 E
Berbérati, C.A.R. 52 D3 4 15N 15 40 E
Berbice →, Guyana 92 B7 6 20N 57 32W
Berdichev = Berdychiv, Ukraine 17 D15 49 57N 28 30 E
Berdsk, Russia 26 D9 54 47N 83 2 E
Berdyansk, Ukraine 25 E6 46 45N 36 50 E
Berdychiv, Ukraine 17 D15 49 57N 28 30 E
Berea, U.S.A. 76 G3 37 34N 84 17W
Berebere, Indonesia 37 D7 2 25N 128 45 E
Bereda, Somali Rep. 46 E5 11 45N 51 0 E
Berehove, Ukraine 17 D12 48 15N 22 35 E
Berekum, Ghana 50 G5 7 29N 2 34W
Berens →, Canada 73 C9 52 25N 97 2W
Berens I., Canada 73 C9 52 18N 97 18W
Berens River, Canada 73 C9 52 25N 97 0W
Beresford, U.S.A. 80 D6 43 5N 96 47W
Berestechko, Ukraine 17 C13 50 22N 25 5 E
Berevo, Mahajanga, Madag. 57 B7 17 14S 44 17 E
Berevo, Toliara, Madag. 57 B7 19 44S 44 58 E
Bereza, Belarus 17 B13 52 31N 24 51 E
Berezhany, Ukraine 17 D13 49 26N 24 58 E
Berezina = Byarezina →, Belarus 17 B16 52 33N 30 14 E
Bereznik, Russia 24 B7 62 51N 42 40 E
Berezniki, Russia 24 C10 59 24N 56 46 E
Berezovo, Russia 26 C7 64 0N 65 0 E
Berga, Spain 19 A6 42 6N 1 48 E
Bergama, Turkey 21 E12 39 8N 27 11 E
Bérgamo, Italy 18 D8 45 41N 9 43 E
Bergen, Neths. 15 B4 52 40N 4 43 E
Bergen, Norway 9 F11 60 20N 5 20 E
Bergen, U.S.A. 78 C7 43 5N 77 57W
Bergen op Zoom, Neths. 15 C4 51 28N 4 18 E
Bergerac, France 18 D4 44 51N 0 30 E
Bergholz, U.S.A. 78 F4 40 31N 80 53W
Bergisch Gladbach, Germany 15 D7 50 59N 7 8 E
Bergville, S. Africa 57 D4 28 52S 29 18 E
Berhala, Selat, Indonesia 36 E2 1 0S 104 15 E
Berhampore = Baharampur, India 43 G13 24 2N 88 27 E
Berhampur = Brahmapur, India 41 K14 19 15N 84 54 E
Bering Sea, Pac. Oc. 68 C1 58 0N 171 0 E
Bering Strait, Pac. Oc. 68 B3 65 30N 169 0W
Beringovskiy, Russia 27 C18 63 3N 179 19 E
Berisso, Argentina 94 C4 34 56S 57 50W
Berja, Spain 19 D4 36 50N 2 56W
Berkeley, U.S.A. 84 H4 37 52N 122 16W
Berkner I., Antarctica 5 D18 79 30S 50 0W
Berkshire, U.S.A. 79 D8 42 19N 76 11W
Berkshire Downs, U.K. 11 F6 51 33N 1 29W
Berlin, Germany 16 B7 52 30N 13 25 E
Berlin, Md., U.S.A. 76 F8 38 20N 75 13W
Berlin, N.H., U.S.A. 79 B13 44 28N 71 11W
Berlin, N.Y., U.S.A. 79 D11 42 42N 73 23W
Berlin, Wis., U.S.A. 76 D1 43 58N 88 57W
Berlin L., U.S.A. 78 E4 41 3N 81 0W
Bermejo →, Formosa, Argentina 94 B4 26 51S 58 23W
Bermejo →, San Juan, Argentina 94 C2 32 30S 67 30W
Bermen, L., Canada 71 B6 53 35N 68 55W
Bermuda ■, Atl. Oc. 66 F13 32 45N 65 0W
Bern, Switz. 18 C7 46 57N 7 28 E
Bernalillo, U.S.A. 83 J10 35 18N 106 33W
Bernardo de Irigoyen, Argentina 95 B5 26 15S 53 40W
Bernardo O'Higgins □, Chile 94 C1 34 15S 70 45W
Bernardsville, U.S.A. 79 F10 40 43N 74 34W
Bernasconi, Argentina 94 D3 37 55S 63 44W
Bernburg, Germany 16 C6 51 47N 11 44 E
Berne = Bern, Switz. 18 C7 46 57N 7 28 E
Berneray, U.K. 12 D1 57 43N 7 11W
Bernier I., Australia 61 D1 24 50S 113 12 E
Bernina, Piz, Switz. 18 C8 46 20N 9 54 E
Beroroha, Madag. 57 C8 21 40S 45 10 E
Beroun, Czech Rep. 16 D8 49 57N 14 5 E
Berri, Australia 63 E3 34 14S 140 35 E
Berriane, Algeria 50 B6 32 50N 3 46 E
Berrigan, Australia 63 F4 35 38S 145 49 E
Berry, Australia 63 E5 34 46S 150 43 E
Berry, France 18 C5 46 50N 2 0 E
Berry Is., Bahamas 88 A4 25 40N 77 50W
Berryessa L., U.S.A. 84 G4 38 31N 122 6W
Berryville, U.S.A. 81 G8 36 22N 93 34W
Bershad, Ukraine 17 D15 48 22N 29 31 E
Berthold, U.S.A. 80 A4 48 19N 101 44W
Berthoud, U.S.A. 80 E2 40 19N 105 5W
Bertoua, Cameroon 52 D2 4 30N 13 45 E
Bertraghboy B., Ireland 13 C2 53 22N 9 54W
Berwick, U.S.A. 79 E8 41 3N 76 14W
Berwick-upon-Tweed, U.K. 10 B6 55 46N 2 0W
Berwyn Mts., U.K. 10 E4 52 54N 3 26W
Besal, Pakistan 43 B5 35 4N 73 56 E
Besalampy, Madag. 57 B7 16 43S 44 29 E
Besançon, France 18 C7 47 15N 6 2 E
Besar, Indonesia 36 E5 2 40S 116 0 E
Besnard L., Canada 73 B7 55 25N 106 0W
Besni, Turkey 44 B3 37 41N 37 52 E
Besor, N. →, Egypt 47 D3 31 28N 34 22 E
Bessarabiya, Moldova 17 E15 47 0N 28 10 E
Bessarabka = Basarabeasca, Moldova 17 E15 46 21N 28 58 E
Bessemer, Ala., U.S.A. 77 J2 33 24N 86 58W
Bessemer, Mich., U.S.A. 80 B9 46 29N 90 3W
Bessemer, Pa., U.S.A. 78 F4 40 59N 80 30W
Beswick, Australia 60 B5 14 34S 132 53 E
Bet She'an, Israel 47 C4 32 30N 35 30 E
Bet Shemesh, Israel 47 D4 31 44N 35 0 E
Betafo, Madag. 57 B8 19 50S 46 51 E
Betancuria, Canary Is. 22 F5 28 25N 14 3W
Betanzos, Spain 19 A1 43 15N 8 12W
Bétaré Oya, Cameroon 52 C2 5 40N 14 5 E
Bethal, S. Africa 57 D4 26 27S 29 28 E
Bethanien, Namibia 56 D2 26 31S 17 8 E
Bethany, Canada 78 B6 44 11N 78 34W
Bethany, U.S.A. 80 E7 40 16N 94 2W
Bethel, Alaska, U.S.A. 68 B3 60 48N 161 45W
Bethel, Conn., U.S.A. 79 E11 41 22N 73 25W
Bethel, Maine, U.S.A. 79 B14 44 25N 70 47W
Bethel, Vt., U.S.A. 79 C12 43 50N 72 38W
Bethel Park, U.S.A. 78 F4 40 20N 80 1W
Bethlehem = Bayt Lahm, West Bank 47 D4 31 43N 35 12 E
Bethlehem, S. Africa 57 D4 28 14S 28 18 E
Bethlehem, U.S.A. 79 F9 40 37N 75 23W
Bethulie, S. Africa 56 E4 30 30S 25 59 E
Béthune, France 18 A5 50 30N 2 38 E
Betioky, Madag. 57 C7 23 48S 44 20 E
Betong, Thailand 39 K3 5 45N 101 5 E
Betoota, Australia 62 D3 25 45S 140 42 E
Betroka, Madag. 57 C8 23 16S 46 0 E
Betsiamites, Canada 71 C6 48 56N 68 40W
Betsiamites →, Canada 71 C6 48 56N 68 38W
Betsiboka →, Madag. 57 B8 16 3S 46 36 E
Bettendorf, U.S.A. 80 E9 41 32N 90 30W
Bettiah, India 43 F11 26 48N 84 33 E
Betul, India 40 J10 21 58N 77 59 E
Betung, Malaysia 36 D4 1 24N 111 31 E
Betws-y-Coed, U.K. 10 D4 53 5N 3 48W
Beulah, Mich., U.S.A. 76 C2 44 38N 86 6W
Beulah, N. Dak., U.S.A. 80 B4 47 16N 101 47W
Beveren, Belgium 15 C4 51 12N 4 16 E
Beverley, Australia 61 F2 32 9S 116 56 E
Beverley, U.K. 10 D7 53 51N 0 26W
Beverley Hills, U.S.A. 77 L4 28 56N 82 28W
Beverly, U.S.A. 79 D14 42 33N 70 53W
Beverly Hills, U.S.A. 85 L8 34 4N 118 25W
Bewas →, India 43 H8 23 59N 79 21 E
Bexhill, U.K. 11 G8 50 51N 0 29 E
Beyānlū, Iran 44 C5 36 0N 47 51 E
Beyneu, Kazakstan 25 E10 45 18N 55 9 E
Beypazarı, Turkey 25 F5 40 10N 31 56 E
Beyşehir Gölü, Turkey 25 G5 37 41N 31 33 E
Béziers, France 18 E5 43 20N 3 12 E
Bezwada = Vijayawada, India 41 L12 16 31N 80 39 E
Bhabua, India 43 G10 25 3N 83 37 E
Bhachau, India 40 H7 23 20N 70 16 E
Bhadar →, Gujarat, India 42 H5 22 17N 72 20 E
Bhadar →, Gujarat, India 42 J3 21 27N 69 47 E
Bhadarwah, India 43 C6 32 58N 75 46 E
Bhadohi, India 43 G10 25 25N 82 34 E
Bhadra, India 42 E6 29 8N 75 14 E
Bhadrakh, India 41 J15 21 10N 86 30 E
Bhadran, India 42 H5 22 19N 72 6 E
Bhadravati, India 40 N9 13 49N 75 40 E
Bhag, Pakistan 42 E2 29 2N 67 49 E
Bhagalpur, India 43 G12 25 10N 87 0 E
Bhagirathi →, Ut. P., India 43 D8 30 8N 78 35 E
Bhagirathi →, W. Bengal, India 43 H13 23 25N 88 23 E
Bhakkar, Pakistan 42 D4 31 40N 71 5 E
Bhakra Dam, India 42 D7 31 30N 76 45 E
Bhamo, Burma 41 G20 24 15N 97 15 E
Bhandara, India 40 J11 21 5N 79 42 E
Bhanpura, India 42 G6 24 31N 75 44 E
Bhanrer Ra., India 43 H8 23 40N 79 45 E
Bhaptiahi, India 43 F12 26 19N 86 44 E
Bharat = India ■, Asia 40 K11 20 0N 78 0 E
Bharatpur, Mad. P., India 43 H9 23 44N 81 46 E
Bharatpur, Raj., India 42 F7 27 15N 77 30 E
Bharno, India 43 H11 23 14N 84 53 E
Bhatinda, India 42 D6 30 15N 74 57 E
Bhatpara, India 43 H13 22 50N 88 25 E
Bhattu, India 42 E6 29 36N 75 19 E
Bhaun, Pakistan 42 C5 32 55N 72 40 E
Bhaunagar = Bhavnagar, India 40 J8 21 45N 72 10 E
Bhavnagar, India 40 J8 21 45N 72 10 E
Bhawanipatna, India 41 K12 19 55N 80 10 E
Bhawari, India 42 G5 25 42N 73 4 E
Bhayavadar, India 42 J4 21 51N 70 15 E
Bhera, Pakistan 42 C5 32 29N 72 57 E
Bhikangaon, India 42 J6 21 52N 75 57 E
Bhilsa = Vidisha, India 42 H7 23 28N 77 53 E
Bhilwara, India 42 G6 25 25N 74 38 E
Bhima →, India 40 L10 16 25N 77 17 E
Bhimavaram, India 41 L12 16 30N 81 30 E
Bhimbar, Pakistan 43 C6 32 59N 74 3 E
Bhind, India 43 F8 26 30N 78 46 E
Bhinga, India 43 F9 27 43N 81 56 E
Bhinmal, India 42 G5 25 0N 72 15 E
Bhiwandi, India 40 K8 19 20N 73 0 E
Bhiwani, India 42 E7 28 50N 76 9 E
Bhogava →, India 42 H5 22 26N 72 20 E
Bhola, Bangla. 41 H17 22 45N 90 35 E
Bholari, Pakistan 42 G3 25 19N 68 13 E
Bhopal, India 42 H7 23 20N 77 30 E
Bhubaneshwar, India 41 J14 20 15N 85 50 E
Bhuj, India 42 H3 23 15N 69 49 E
Bhusaval, India 40 J9 21 3N 75 46 E
Bhutan ■, Asia 41 F17 27 25N 90 30 E
Biafra, B. of = Bonny, Bight of, Africa 52 D1 3 30N 9 20 E
Biak, Indonesia 37 E9 1 10S 136 6 E
Biała Podlaska, Poland 17 B12 52 4N 23 6 E
Białogard, Poland 16 A8 54 2N 15 58 E
Białystok, Poland 17 B12 53 10N 23 10 E
Biaora, India 42 H7 23 56N 76 56 E
Bīārjmand, Iran 45 B7 36 6N 55 53 E
Biaro, Indonesia 37 D7 2 5N 125 26 E
Biarritz, France 18 E3 43 29N 1 33W
Bibai, Japan 30 C10 43 19N 141 52 E
Bibby I., Canada 73 A10 61 55N 93 0W
Biberach, Germany 16 D5 48 5N 9 47 E
Bibungwa, Dem. Rep. of the Congo 54 C2 2 40S 28 15 E
Bic, Canada 71 C6 48 20N 68 41W
Bicester, U.K. 11 F6 51 54N 1 9W
Bicheno, Australia 62 G4 41 52S 148 18 E
Bichia, India 43 H9 22 27N 80 42 E
Bickerton I., Australia 62 A2 13 45S 136 10 E
Bida, Nigeria 50 G7 9 3N 5 58 E
Bidar, India 40 L10 17 55N 77 35 E
Biddeford, U.S.A. 77 D10 43 30N 70 28W
Bideford, U.K. 11 F3 51 1N 4 13W
Bideford Bay, U.K. 11 F3 51 5N 4 20W
Bidhuna, India 43 F8 26 49N 79 31 E
Bidor, Malaysia 39 K3 4 6N 101 15 E
Bié, Planalto de, Angola 53 G3 12 0S 16 0 E
Bieber, U.S.A. 82 F3 41 7N 121 8W
Biel, Switz. 18 C7 47 8N 7 14 E
Bielefeld, Germany 16 B5 52 1N 8 33 E
Biella, Italy 18 D8 45 34N 8 3 E
Bielsk Podlaski, Poland 17 B12 52 47N 23 12 E
Bielsko-Biała, Poland 17 D10 49 50N 19 2 E
Bien Hoa, Vietnam 39 G6 10 57N 106 49 E
Bienne = Biel, Switz. 18 C7 47 8N 7 14 E
Bienville, L., Canada 70 A5 55 5N 72 40W
Biesiesfontein, S. Africa 56 E2 30 57S 17 58 E
Big →, Canada 71 B8 54 50N 58 55W
Big B., Canada 71 A7 55 43N 60 35W
Big Bear City, U.S.A. 85 L10 34 16N 116 51W
Big Bear Lake, U.S.A. 85 L10 34 15N 116 56W
Big Belt Mts., U.S.A. 82 C8 46 30N 111 25W
Big Bend, Swaziland 57 D5 26 50S 31 58 E
Big Bend National Park, U.S.A. 81 L3 29 20N 103 5W
Big Black →, U.S.A. 81 K9 32 3N 91 4W
Big Blue →, U.S.A. 80 F6 39 35N 96 34W
Big Creek, U.S.A. 84 H7 37 11N 119 14W
Big Cypress National Preserve, U.S.A. 77 M5 26 0N 81 10W
Big Cypress Swamp, U.S.A. 77 M5 26 12N 81 10W
Big Falls, U.S.A. 80 A8 48 12N 93 48W
Big Fork →, U.S.A. 80 A8 48 31N 93 43W
Big Horn Mts. = Bighorn Mts., U.S.A. 82 D10 44 30N 107 30W
Big I., Canada 72 A5 61 7N 116 45W
Big Lake, U.S.A. 81 K4 31 12N 101 28W
Big Moose, U.S.A. 79 C10 43 49N 74 58W
Big Muddy Cr. →, U.S.A. 80 A2 48 8N 104 36W
Big Pine, U.S.A. 84 H8 37 10N 118 17W
Big Piney, U.S.A. 82 E8 42 32N 110 7W
Big Rapids, U.S.A. 76 D3 43 42N 85 29W
Big Rideau L., Canada 79 B8 44 40N 76 15W
Big River, Canada 73 C7 53 50N 107 0W
Big Run, U.S.A. 78 F6 40 57N 78 55W
Big Sable Pt., U.S.A. 76 C2 44 3N 86 1W
Big Salmon →, Canada 72 A2 61 52N 134 55W
Big Sand L., Canada 73 B9 57 45N 99 45W
Big Sandy, U.S.A. 82 B8 48 11N 110 7W
Big Sandy →, U.S.A. 76 F4 38 25N 82 36W
Big Sandy Cr. →, U.S.A. 80 F3 38 7N 102 29W
Big Sioux →, U.S.A. 80 D6 42 29N 96 27W
Big Spring, U.S.A. 81 J4 32 15N 101 28W
Big Stone City, U.S.A. 80 C6 45 18N 96 28W
Big Stone Gap, U.S.A. 77 G4 36 52N 82 47W
Big Stone L., U.S.A. 80 C6 45 30N 96 35W
Big Sur, U.S.A. 84 J5 36 15N 121 48W
Big Timber, U.S.A. 82 D9 45 50N 109 57W

Broad

Bolton, *U.K.* **10 D5** 53 35N 2 26W
Bolton Landing, *U.S.A.* **79 C11** 43 32N 73 35W
Bolu, *Turkey* **25 F5** 40 45N 31 35 E
Bolungavík, *Iceland* **8 C2** 66 9N 23 15W
Bolvadin, *Turkey* **25 G5** 38 45N 31 4 E
Bolzano, *Italy* **20 A4** 46 31N 11 22 E
Bom Jesus da Lapa, *Brazil* **93 F10** 13 15S 43 25W
Boma, *Dem. Rep. of the Congo* **52 F2** 5 50S 13 4 E
Bombala, *Australia* **63 F4** 36 56S 149 15 E
Bombay = Mumbai, *India* **40 K8** 18 55N 72 50 E
Bomboma, *Dem. Rep. of the Congo* **52 D3** 2 25N 18 55 E
Bombombwa, *Dem. Rep. of the Congo* **54 B2** 1 40N 25 40 E
Bomili, *Dem. Rep. of the Congo* **54 B2** 1 45N 27 5 E
Bømlo, *Norway* **9 G11** 59 37N 5 13 E
Bomokandi →, *Dem. Rep. of the Congo* **54 B2** 3 39N 26 8 E
Bomu →, *C.A.R.* **52 D4** 4 40N 22 30 E
Bon, C., *Tunisia* **48 C5** 37 1N 11 2 E
Bon Sar Pa, *Vietnam* **38 F6** 12 24N 107 35 E
Bonaigarh, *India* **43 J11** 21 50N 84 57 E
Bonaire, *Neth. Ant.* **89 D6** 12 10N 68 15W
Bonang, *Australia* **63 F4** 37 11S 148 41 E
Bonanza, *Nic.* **88 D3** 13 54N 84 35W
Bonaparte Arch., *Australia* **60 B3** 14 0S 124 30 E
Bonaventure, *Canada* **71 C6** 48 5N 65 32W
Bonavista, *Canada* **71 C9** 48 40N 53 5W
Bonavista, C., *Canada* **71 C9** 48 42N 53 5W
Bonavista B., *Canada* **71 C9** 48 45N 53 25W
Bondo, *Dem. Rep. of the Congo* **54 B1** 3 55N 23 53 E
Bondoukou, *Ivory C.* **50 G5** 8 2N 2 47W
Bondowoso, *Indonesia* **37 G15** 7 55S 113 49 E
Bone, Teluk, *Indonesia* **37 E6** 4 10S 120 50 E
Bonerate, *Indonesia* **37 F6** 7 25S 121 5 E
Bonerate, Kepulauan, *Indonesia* **37 F6** 6 30S 121 10 E
Bo'ness, *U.K.* **12 E5** 56 1N 3 37W
Bonete, Cerro, *Argentina* **94 B2** 27 55S 68 40W
Bong Son = Hoai Nhon, *Vietnam* **38 E7** 14 28N 109 1 E
Bongor, *Chad* **51 F9** 10 35N 15 20 E
Bonham, *U.S.A.* **81 J6** 33 35N 96 11W
Bonifacio, *France* **18 F8** 41 24N 9 10 E
Bonifacio, Bouches de, *Medit. S.* **20 D3** 41 12N 9 15 E
Bonin Is. = Ogasawara Gunto, *Pac. Oc.* **28 G18** 27 0N 142 0 E
Bonn, *Germany* **16 C4** 50 46N 7 6 E
Bonne Terre, *U.S.A.* **81 G9** 37 55N 90 33W
Bonners Ferry, *U.S.A.* **82 B5** 48 42N 116 19W
Bonney, L., *Australia* **63 F3** 37 50S 140 20 E
Bonnie Rock, *Australia* **61 F2** 30 29S 118 22 E
Bonny, Bight of, *Africa* **52 D1** 3 30N 9 20 E
Bonnyrigg, *U.K.* **12 F5** 55 53N 3 6W
Bonnyville, *Canada* **73 C6** 54 20N 110 45W
Bonoi, *Indonesia* **37 E9** 1 45S 137 41 E
Bonsall, *U.S.A.* **85 M9** 33 16N 117 14W
Bontang, *Indonesia* **36 D5** 0 10N 117 30 E
Bonthe, *S. Leone* **50 G3** 7 30N 12 33W
Bontoc, *Phil.* **37 A6** 17 7N 120 58 E
Bonython Ra., *Australia* **60 D4** 23 40S 128 45 E
Bookabie, *Australia* **61 F5** 31 50S 132 41 E
Booker, *U.S.A.* **81 G4** 36 27N 100 32W
Booligal, *Australia* **63 E3** 33 58S 144 53 E
Boonah, *Australia* **63 D5** 27 58S 152 41 E
Boone, *Iowa, U.S.A.* **80 D8** 42 4N 93 53W
Boone, *N.C., U.S.A.* **77 G5** 36 13N 81 41W
Booneville, *Ark., U.S.A.* **81 H8** 35 8N 93 55W
Booneville, *Miss., U.S.A.* **77 H1** 34 39N 88 34W
Boonville, *Calif., U.S.A.* **84 F3** 39 1N 123 22W
Boonville, *Ind., U.S.A.* **76 F2** 38 3N 87 16W
Boonville, *Mo., U.S.A.* **80 F8** 38 58N 92 44W
Boonville, *N.Y., U.S.A.* **79 C9** 43 29N 75 20W
Boorindal, *Australia* **63 E4** 30 22S 146 11 E
Boorowa, *Australia* **63 E4** 34 28S 148 44 E
Boothia, Gulf of, *Canada* **69 A11** 71 0N 90 0W
Boothia Pen., *Canada* **68 A10** 71 0N 94 0W
Bootle, *U.K.* **10 D4** 53 28N 3 1W
Booué, *Gabon* **52 E2** 0 5S 11 55 E
Boquete, *Panama* **88 E3** 8 46N 82 27W
Boquilla, Presa de la, *Mexico* **86 B3** 27 40N 105 30W
Boquillas del Carmen, *Mexico* **86 B4** 29 17N 102 53W
Bor, *Serbia, Yug.* **21 B10** 44 5N 22 7 E
Bôr, *Sudan* **51 G12** 6 10N 31 40 E
Bor Mashash, *Israel* **47 D3** 31 7N 34 50 E
Borah Peak, *U.S.A.* **82 D7** 44 8N 113 47W
Borås, *Sweden* **9 H15** 57 43N 12 56 E
Borāzjān, *Iran* **45 D6** 29 22N 51 10 E
Borba, *Brazil* **92 D7** 4 12S 59 34W
Borborema, Planalto da, *Brazil* **90 D7** 7 0S 37 0W
Bord Khūn-e Now, *Iran* **45 D6** 28 3N 51 28 E
Borda, C., *Australia* **63 F2** 35 45S 136 34 E
Bordeaux, *France* **18 D3** 44 50N 0 36W
Borden, *Australia* **61 F2** 34 3S 118 12 E
Borden, *Canada* **71 C7** 46 18N 63 47W
Borden I., *Canada* **4 B2** 78 30N 111 30W
Borden Pen., *Canada* **69 A11** 73 0N 83 0W
Borders = Scottish Borders □, *U.K.* **12 F6** 55 35N 2 50W
Bordertown, *Australia* **63 F3** 36 19S 140 45 E
Borðeyri, *Iceland* **8 D3** 65 12N 21 6W
Bordj Fly Ste. Marie, *Algeria* **50 C5** 27 19N 2 32W
Bordj-in-Eker, *Algeria* **50 D7** 24 9N 5 3 E
Bordj Omar Driss, *Algeria* **50 C7** 28 10N 6 40 E
Borehamwood, *U.K.* **11 F7** 51 40N 0 15W
Borgå = Porvoo, *Finland* **9 F21** 60 24N 25 40 E
Borgarfjörður, *Iceland* **8 D7** 65 31N 13 49W
Borgarnes, *Iceland* **8 D3** 64 32N 21 55W
Børgefjellet, *Norway* **8 D15** 65 20N 13 45 E
Borger, *Neths.* **15 B6** 52 54N 6 44 E
Borger, *U.S.A.* **81 H4** 35 39N 101 24W
Borgholm, *Sweden* **9 H17** 56 52N 16 39 E
Borhoyn Tal, *Mongolia* **34 C6** 43 50N 111 58 E
Borikhane, *Laos* **38 C4** 18 33N 103 43 E
Borisoglebsk, *Russia* **25 D7** 51 27N 42 5 E
Borisov = Barysaw, *Belarus* **17 A15** 54 17N 28 28 E
Borja, *Peru* **92 D3** 4 20S 77 40W
Borkou, *Chad* **51 E9** 18 15N 18 50 E
Borkum, *Germany* **16 B4** 53 34N 6 40 E
Borlänge, *Sweden* **9 F16** 60 29N 15 26 E
Borley, C., *Antarctica* **5 C5** 66 15S 52 30 E
Borneo, *E. Indies* **36 D5** 1 0N 115 0 E
Bornholm, *Denmark* **9 J16** 55 10N 15 0 E
Borogontsy, *Russia* **27 C14** 62 42N 131 8 E
Boron, *U.S.A.* **85 L9** 35 0N 117 39W
Borongan, *Phil.* **37 B7** 11 37N 125 26 E
Borovichi, *Russia* **24 C5** 58 25N 33 55 E
Borrego Springs, *U.S.A.* **85 M10** 33 15N 116 23W
Borroloola, *Australia* **62 B2** 16 4S 136 17 E
Borşa, *Romania* **17 E13** 47 41N 24 50 E
Borsad, *India* **42 H5** 22 25N 72 54 E
Borth, *U.K.* **11 E3** 52 29N 4 2W
Borūjerd, *Iran* **45 C6** 33 55N 48 50 E
Boryslav, *Ukraine* **17 D12** 49 18N 23 28 E
Borzya, *Russia* **27 D12** 50 24N 116 31 E
Bosa, *Italy* **20 D3** 40 18N 8 30 E
Bosanska Gradiška, *Bos.-H.* **20 B7** 45 10N 17 15 E
Bosaso, *Somali Rep.* **46 E4** 11 12N 49 18 E
Boscastle, *U.K.* **11 G3** 50 41N 4 42W
Boshan, *China* **35 F9** 36 28N 117 49 E
Boshof, *S. Africa* **56 D4** 28 31S 25 13 E
Boshrūyeh, *Iran* **45 C8** 33 50N 57 30 E
Bosna →, *Bos.-H.* **21 B8** 45 4N 18 29 E
Bosna i Hercegovina = Bosnia-Herzegovina ■, *Europe* **20 B7** 44 0N 18 0 E
Bosnia-Herzegovina ■, *Europe* **20 B7** 44 0N 18 0 E
Bosnik, *Indonesia* **37 E9** 1 5S 136 10 E
Bosobolo, *Dem. Rep. of the Congo* **52 D3** 4 15N 19 50 E
Bosporus = İstanbul Boğazı, *Turkey* **21 D13** 41 10N 29 10 E
Bosque Farms, *U.S.A.* **83 J10** 34 53N 106 40W
Bossangoa, *C.A.R.* **52 C3** 6 35N 17 30 E
Bossier City, *U.S.A.* **81 J8** 32 31N 93 44W
Bosso, *Niger* **51 F8** 13 43N 13 19 E
Bostan, *Pakistan* **42 D2** 30 26N 67 2 E
Bostānābād, *Iran* **44 B5** 37 50N 46 50 E
Bosten Hu, *China* **32 B3** 41 55N 87 40 E
Boston, *U.K.* **10 E7** 52 59N 0 2W
Boston, *U.S.A.* **79 D13** 42 22N 71 4W
Boston Bar, *Canada* **72 D4** 49 52N 121 30W
Boston Mts., *U.S.A.* **81 H8** 35 42N 93 15W
Boswell, *Canada* **72 D5** 49 28N 116 45W
Boswell, *U.S.A.* **78 F5** 40 10N 79 2W
Botad, *India* **42 H4** 22 15N 71 40 E
Botene, *Laos* **38 D3** 17 35N 101 12 E
Bothaville, *S. Africa* **56 D4** 27 23S 26 34 E
Bothnia, G. of, *Europe* **8 E19** 63 0N 20 15 E
Bothwell, *Australia* **62 G4** 42 20S 147 1 E
Bothwell, *Canada* **78 D3** 42 38N 81 52W
Botletle →, *Botswana* **56 C3** 20 10S 23 15 E
Botoşani, *Romania* **17 E14** 47 42N 26 41 E
Botou, *Burkina Faso* **50 F6** 12 40N 2 3 E
Botswana ■, *Africa* **56 C3** 22 0S 24 0 E
Bottineau, *U.S.A.* **80 A4** 48 50N 100 27W
Bottrop, *Germany* **15 C6** 51 31N 6 58 E
Botucatu, *Brazil* **95 A6** 22 55S 48 30W
Botwood, *Canada* **71 C8** 49 6N 55 23W
Bouaflé, *Ivory C.* **50 G4** 7 1N 5 47W
Bouaké, *Ivory C.* **50 G4** 7 40N 5 2W
Bouar, *C.A.R.* **52 C3** 6 0N 15 40 E
Bouârfa, *Morocco* **50 B5** 32 32N 1 58W
Boucaut B., *Australia* **62 A1** 12 0S 134 25 E
Bougainville, C., *Australia* **60 B4** 13 57S 126 4 E
Bougainville I., *Papua N. G.* **64 H7** 6 0S 155 0 E
Bougainville Reef, *Australia* **62 B4** 15 30S 147 5 E
Bougie = Bejaia, *Algeria* **50 A7** 36 42N 5 2 E
Bougouni, *Mali* **50 F4** 11 30N 7 20W
Bouillon, *Belgium* **15 E5** 49 44N 5 3 E
Boulder, *Colo., U.S.A.* **80 E2** 40 1N 105 17W
Boulder, *Mont., U.S.A.* **82 C7** 46 14N 112 7W
Boulder City, *U.S.A.* **85 K12** 35 59N 114 50W
Boulder Creek, *U.S.A.* **84 H4** 37 7N 122 7W
Boulder Dam = Hoover Dam, *U.S.A.* **85 K12** 36 1N 114 44W
Boulia, *Australia* **62 C2** 22 52S 139 51 E
Boulogne-sur-Mer, *France* **18 A4** 50 42N 1 36 E
Boultoum, *Niger* **51 F8** 14 45N 10 25 E
Boun Neua, *Laos* **38 B3** 21 38N 101 54 E
Boun Tai, *Laos* **38 B3** 21 23N 101 58 E
Bouna, *Ivory C.* **50 G5** 9 10N 3 0W
Boundary Peak, *U.S.A.* **84 H8** 37 51N 118 21W
Boundiali, *Ivory C.* **50 G4** 9 30N 6 20W
Bountiful, *U.S.A.* **82 F8** 40 53N 111 53W
Bounty Is., *Pac. Oc.* **64 M9** 48 0S 178 30 E
Bourbonnais, *France* **18 C5** 46 28N 3 0 E
Bourdel L., *Canada* **70 A5** 56 43N 74 10W
Bourem, *Mali* **50 E5** 17 0N 0 24W
Bourg-en-Bresse, *France* **18 C6** 46 13N 5 12 E
Bourg-St-Maurice, *France* **18 D7** 45 35N 6 46 E
Bourges, *France* **18 C5** 47 9N 2 25 E
Bourget, *Canada* **79 A9** 45 26N 75 9W
Bourgogne, *France* **18 C6** 47 0N 4 50 E
Bourke, *Australia* **63 E4** 30 8S 145 55 E
Bourne, *U.K.* **10 E7** 52 47N 0 22W
Bournemouth, *U.K.* **11 G6** 50 43N 1 52W
Bournemouth □, *U.K.* **11 G6** 50 43N 1 52W
Bouse, *U.S.A.* **85 M13** 33 56N 114 0W
Bouvet I. = Bouvetøya, *Antarctica* **3 G10** 54 26S 3 24 E
Bouvetøya, *Antarctica* **3 G10** 54 26S 3 24 E
Bovill, *U.S.A.* **82 C5** 46 51N 116 24W
Bovril, *Argentina* **94 C4** 31 21S 59 26W
Bow →, *Canada* **72 C6** 49 57N 111 41W
Bow Island, *Canada* **72 D6** 49 50N 111 23W
Bowbells, *U.S.A.* **80 A3** 48 48N 102 15W
Bowdle, *U.S.A.* **80 C5** 45 27N 99 39W
Bowelling, *Australia* **61 F2** 33 25S 116 30 E
Bowen, *Argentina* **94 D2** 35 0S 67 31W
Bowen, *Australia* **62 C4** 20 0S 148 16 E
Bowen Mts., *Australia* **63 F4** 37 0S 147 50 E
Bowie, *Ariz., U.S.A.* **83 K9** 32 19N 109 29W
Bowie, *Tex., U.S.A.* **81 J6** 33 34N 97 51W
Bowkān, *Iran* **44 B5** 36 31N 46 12 E
Bowland, Forest of, *U.K.* **10 D5** 54 0N 2 30W
Bowling Green, *Ky., U.S.A.* **76 G2** 36 59N 86 27W
Bowling Green, *Ohio, U.S.A.* **76 E4** 41 23N 83 39W
Bowling Green, C., *Australia* **62 B4** 19 19S 147 25 E
Bowman, *U.S.A.* **80 B3** 46 11N 103 24W
Bowman I., *Antarctica* **5 C8** 65 0S 104 0 E
Bowmanville, *Canada* **78 C6** 43 55N 78 41W
Bowmore, *U.K.* **12 F2** 55 45N 6 17W
Bowral, *Australia* **63 E5** 34 26S 150 27 E
Bowraville, *Australia* **63 E5** 30 37S 152 52 E
Bowron →, *Canada* **72 C4** 54 3N 121 50W
Bowron Lake Prov. Park, *Canada* **72 C4** 53 10N 121 5W
Bowser L., *Canada* **72 B3** 56 30N 129 30W
Bowsman, *Canada* **73 C8** 52 14N 101 12W
Bowwood, *Zambia* **55 F2** 17 5S 26 20 E
Box Cr. →, *Australia* **63 E3** 34 10S 143 50 E
Boxmeer, *Neths.* **15 C5** 51 38N 5 56 E
Boxtel, *Neths.* **15 C5** 51 36N 5 20 E
Boyce, *U.S.A.* **81 K8** 31 23N 92 40W
Boyd L., *Canada* **70 B4** 52 46N 76 42W
Boyle, *Canada* **72 C6** 54 35N 112 49W
Boyle, *Ireland* **13 C3** 53 59N 8 18W
Boyne →, *Ireland* **13 C5** 53 43N 6 15W
Boyne City, *U.S.A.* **76 C3** 45 13N 85 1W
Boynton Beach, *U.S.A.* **77 M5** 26 32N 80 4W
Boyolali, *Indonesia* **37 G14** 7 32S 110 35 E
Boyoma, Chutes, *Dem. Rep. of the Congo* **54 B2** 0 35N 25 23 E
Boysen Reservoir, *U.S.A.* **82 E9** 43 25N 108 11W
Boyuibe, *Bolivia* **92 G6** 20 25S 63 17W
Boyup Brook, *Australia* **61 F2** 33 50S 116 23 E
Boz Dağları, *Turkey* **21 E13** 38 20N 28 0 E
Bozburun, *Turkey* **21 F13** 36 43N 28 4 E
Bozcaada, *Turkey* **21 E12** 39 49N 26 3 E
Bozdoğan, *Turkey* **21 F13** 37 40N 28 17 E
Bozeman, *U.S.A.* **82 D8** 45 41N 111 2W
Bozen = Bolzano, *Italy* **20 A4** 46 31N 11 22 E
Bozhou, *China* **34 H8** 33 55N 115 41 E
Bozoum, *C.A.R.* **52 C3** 6 25N 16 35 E
Bra, *Italy* **18 D7** 44 42N 7 51 E
Brabant □, *Belgium* **15 D4** 50 46N 4 30 E
Brabant L., *Canada* **73 B8** 55 58N 103 43W
Brač, *Croatia* **20 C7** 43 20N 16 40 E
Bracadale, L., *U.K.* **12 D2** 57 20N 6 30W
Bracciano, L. di, *Italy* **20 C5** 42 7N 12 14 E
Bracebridge, *Canada* **78 A5** 45 2N 79 19W
Brach, *Libya* **51 C8** 27 31N 14 20 E
Bräcke, *Sweden* **9 E16** 62 45N 15 26 E
Brackettville, *U.S.A.* **81 L4** 29 19N 100 25W
Bracknell, *U.K.* **11 F7** 51 25N 0 43W
Bracknell Forest □, *U.K.* **11 F7** 51 25N 0 44W
Brad, *Romania* **17 E12** 46 10N 22 50 E
Bradenton, *U.S.A.* **77 M4** 27 30N 82 34W
Bradford, *Canada* **78 B5** 44 7N 79 34W
Bradford, *U.K.* **10 D6** 53 47N 1 45W
Bradford, *Pa., U.S.A.* **78 E6** 41 58N 78 38W
Bradford, *Vt., U.S.A.* **79 C12** 43 59N 72 9W
Bradley, *Ark., U.S.A.* **81 J8** 33 6N 93 39W
Bradley, *Calif., U.S.A.* **84 K6** 35 52N 120 48W
Bradley Institute, *Zimbabwe* **55 F3** 17 7S 31 25 E
Brady, *U.S.A.* **81 K5** 31 9N 99 20W
Braemar, *U.K.* **12 D5** 57 0N 3 23W
Braeside, *Canada* **79 A8** 45 28N 76 24W
Braga, *Portugal* **19 B1** 41 35N 8 25W
Bragado, *Argentina* **94 D3** 35 2S 60 27W
Bragança, *Brazil* **93 D9** 1 0S 47 2W
Bragança, *Portugal* **19 B2** 41 48N 6 50W
Bragança Paulista, *Brazil* **95 A6** 22 55S 46 32W
Brahmanbaria, *Bangla.* **41 H17** 23 58N 91 15 E
Brahmani →, *India* **41 J15** 20 39N 86 46 E
Brahmapur, *India* **41 K14** 19 15N 84 54 E
Brahmaputra →, *India* **43 H13** 23 58N 89 50 E
Braich-y-pwll, *U.K.* **10 E3** 52 47N 4 46W
Braidwood, *Australia* **63 F4** 35 27S 149 49 E
Brăila, *Romania* **17 F14** 45 19N 27 59 E
Brainerd, *U.S.A.* **80 B7** 46 22N 94 12W
Braintree, *U.K.* **11 F8** 51 53N 0 34 E
Braintree, *U.S.A.* **79 D14** 42 13N 71 0W
Brak →, *S. Africa* **56 D3** 29 35S 22 55 E
Brakwater, *Namibia* **56 C2** 22 28S 17 3 E
Brampton, *Canada* **78 C5** 43 45N 79 45W
Brampton, *U.K.* **10 C5** 54 57N 2 44W
Branco →, *Brazil* **92 D6** 1 20S 61 50W
Brandenburg = Neubrandenburg, *Germany* **16 B7** 53 33N 13 15 E
Brandenburg, *Germany* **16 B7** 52 25N 12 33 E
Brandenburg □, *Germany* **16 B6** 52 50N 13 0 E
Brandfort, *S. Africa* **56 D4** 28 40S 26 30 E
Brandon, *Canada* **73 D9** 49 50N 99 57W
Brandon, *U.S.A.* **79 C11** 43 48N 73 4W
Brandon B., *Ireland* **13 D1** 52 17N 10 8W
Brandon Mt., *Ireland* **13 D1** 52 15N 10 15W
Brandsen, *Argentina* **94 D4** 35 10S 58 15W
Brandvlei, *S. Africa* **56 E3** 30 25S 20 30 E
Branford, *U.S.A.* **79 E12** 41 17N 72 49W
Braniewo, *Poland* **17 A10** 54 25N 19 50 E
Bransfield Str., *Antarctica* **5 C18** 63 0S 59 0W
Branson, *U.S.A.* **81 G8** 36 39N 93 13W
Brantford, *Canada* **78 C4** 43 10N 80 15W
Bras d'Or L., *Canada* **71 C7** 45 50N 60 50W
Brasher Falls, *U.S.A.* **79 B10** 44 49N 74 47W
Brasil, Planalto, *Brazil* **90 E6** 18 0S 46 30W
Brasiléia, *Brazil* **92 F5** 11 0S 68 45W
Brasília, *Brazil* **93 G9** 15 47S 47 55W
Brasília Legal, *Brazil* **93 D7** 3 49S 55 36W
Braslaw, *Belarus* **9 J22** 55 38N 27 0 E
Braşov, *Romania* **17 F13** 45 38N 25 35 E
Brasschaat, *Belgium* **15 C4** 51 19N 4 27 E
Brassey, Banjaran, *Malaysia* **36 D5** 5 0N 117 15 E
Brassey Ra., *Australia* **61 E3** 25 8S 122 15 E
Brasstown Bald, *U.S.A.* **77 H4** 34 53N 83 49W
Brastad, *Sweden* **9 G14** 58 23N 11 30 E
Bratislava, *Slovak Rep.* **17 D9** 48 10N 17 7 E
Bratsk, *Russia* **27 D11** 56 10N 101 30 E
Brattleboro, *U.S.A.* **79 D12** 42 51N 72 34W
Braunau, *Austria* **16 D7** 48 15N 13 3 E
Braunschweig, *Germany* **16 B6** 52 15N 10 31 E
Braunton, *U.K.* **11 F3** 51 7N 4 10W
Bravo del Norte, Rio = Grande, Rio →, *U.S.A.* **81 N6** 25 58N 97 9W
Brawley, *U.S.A.* **85 N11** 32 59N 115 31W
Bray, *Ireland* **13 C5** 53 13N 6 7W
Bray, Mt., *Australia* **62 A1** 14 0S 134 30 E
Bray, Pays de, *France* **18 B4** 49 46N 1 26 E
Brazeau →, *Canada* **72 C5** 52 55N 115 14W
Brazil, *U.S.A.* **76 F2** 39 32N 87 8W
Brazil ■, *S. Amer.* **93 F9** 12 0S 50 0W
Brazilian Highlands = Brasil, Planalto, *Brazil* **90 E6** 18 0S 46 30W
Brazo Sur →, *S. Amer.* **94 B4** 25 21S 57 42W
Brazos →, *U.S.A.* **81 L7** 28 53N 95 23W
Brazzaville, *Congo* **52 E3** 4 9S 15 12 E
Brčko, *Bos.-H.* **21 B8** 44 54N 18 46 E
Breaden, L., *Australia* **61 E4** 25 51S 125 28 E
Breaksea Sd., *N.Z.* **59 L1** 45 35S 166 35 E
Bream B., *N.Z.* **59 F5** 35 56S 174 28 E
Bream Hd., *N.Z.* **59 F5** 35 51S 174 36 E
Breas, *Chile* **94 B1** 25 29S 70 24W
Brebes, *Indonesia* **37 G13** 6 52S 109 3 E
Brechin, *Canada* **78 B5** 44 32N 79 10W
Brechin, *U.K.* **12 E6** 56 44N 2 39W
Brecht, *Belgium* **15 C4** 51 21N 4 38 E
Breckenridge, *Colo., U.S.A.* **82 G10** 39 29N 106 3W
Breckenridge, *Minn., U.S.A.* **80 B6** 46 16N 96 35W
Breckenridge, *Tex., U.S.A.* **81 J5** 32 45N 98 54W
Breckland, *U.K.* **11 E8** 52 30N 0 40 E
Brecon, *U.K.* **11 F4** 51 57N 3 23W
Brecon Beacons, *U.K.* **11 F4** 51 53N 3 26W
Breda, *Neths.* **15 C4** 51 35N 4 45 E
Bredasdorp, *S. Africa* **56 E3** 34 33S 20 2 E
Bree, *Belgium* **15 C5** 51 8N 5 35 E
Bregenz, *Austria* **16 E5** 47 30N 9 45 E
Breiðafjörður, *Iceland* **8 D2** 65 15N 23 15W
Brejo, *Brazil* **93 D10** 3 41S 42 47W
Bremen, *Germany* **16 B5** 53 4N 8 47 E
Bremer Bay, *Australia* **61 F2** 34 21S 119 20 E
Bremer I., *Australia* **62 A2** 12 5S 136 45 E
Bremerhaven, *Germany* **16 B5** 53 33N 8 36 E
Bremerton, *U.S.A.* **84 C4** 47 34N 122 38W
Brenham, *U.S.A.* **81 K6** 30 10N 96 24W
Brennerpass, *Austria* **16 E6** 47 2N 11 30 E
Brent, *U.S.A.* **77 J2** 32 56N 87 10W
Brentwood, *U.K.* **11 F8** 51 37N 0 19 E
Brentwood, *Calif., U.S.A.* **84 H5** 37 56N 121 42W
Brentwood, *N.Y., U.S.A.* **79 F11** 40 47N 73 15W
Bréscia, *Italy* **18 D9** 45 33N 10 15 E
Breskens, *Neths.* **15 C3** 51 23N 3 33 E
Breslau = Wrocław, *Poland* **17 C9** 51 5N 17 5 E
Bressanone, *Italy* **20 A4** 46 43N 11 39 E
Bressay, *U.K.* **12 A7** 60 9N 1 6W
Brest, *Belarus* **17 B12** 52 10N 23 40 E
Brest, *France* **18 B1** 48 24N 4 31W
Brest-Litovsk = Brest, *Belarus* **17 B12** 52 10N 23 40 E
Bretagne, *France* **18 B2** 48 10N 3 0W
Breton, *Canada* **72 C6** 53 7N 114 28W
Breton Sd., *U.S.A.* **81 L10** 29 35N 89 15W
Brett, C., *N.Z.* **59 F5** 35 10S 174 20 E
Brevard, *U.S.A.* **77 H4** 35 14N 82 44W
Breves, *Brazil* **93 D8** 1 40S 50 29W
Brewarrina, *Australia* **63 E4** 30 0S 146 51 E
Brewer, *U.S.A.* **77 C11** 44 48N 68 46W
Brewer, Mt., *U.S.A.* **84 J8** 36 44N 118 28W
Brewster, *N.Y., U.S.A.* **79 E11** 41 23N 73 37W
Brewster, *Ohio, U.S.A.* **78 F3** 40 43N 81 36W
Brewster, *Wash., U.S.A.* **82 B4** 48 6N 119 47W
Brewster, Kap, *Greenland* **4 B6** 70 7N 22 0W
Brewton, *U.S.A.* **77 K2** 31 7N 87 4W
Breyten, *S. Africa* **57 D5** 26 16S 30 0 E
Brezhnev = Naberezhnyye Chelny, *Russia* **24 C9** 55 42N 52 19 E
Briançon, *France* **18 D7** 44 54N 6 39 E
Bribie I., *Australia* **63 D5** 27 0S 153 10 E
Bribri, *Costa Rica* **88 E3** 9 38N 82 50W
Bridgehampton, *U.S.A.* **79 F12** 40 56N 72 19W
Bridgend, *U.K.* **11 F4** 51 30N 3 34W
Bridgend □, *U.K.* **11 F4** 51 36N 3 36W
Bridgeport, *Calif., U.S.A.* **84 G7** 38 15N 119 14W
Bridgeport, *Conn., U.S.A.* **79 E11** 41 11N 73 12W
Bridgeport, *Nebr., U.S.A.* **80 E3** 41 40N 103 6W
Bridgeport, *Tex., U.S.A.* **81 J6** 33 13N 97 45W
Bridger, *U.S.A.* **82 D9** 45 18N 108 55W
Bridgeton, *U.S.A.* **76 F8** 39 26N 75 14W
Bridgetown, *Australia* **61 F2** 33 58S 116 7 E
Bridgetown, *Barbados* **89 D8** 13 5N 59 30W
Bridgetown, *Canada* **71 D6** 44 55N 65 18W
Bridgewater, *Canada* **71 D7** 44 25N 64 31W
Bridgewater, *Mass., U.S.A.* **79 E14** 41 59N 70 58W
Bridgewater, *N.Y., U.S.A.* **79 D9** 42 53N 75 15W
Bridgewater, C., *Australia* **63 F3** 38 23S 141 23 E
Bridgewater-Gagebrook, *Australia* **62 G4** 42 44S 147 14 E
Bridgnorth, *U.K.* **11 E5** 52 32N 2 25W
Bridgton, *U.S.A.* **79 B14** 44 3N 70 42W
Bridgwater, *U.K.* **11 F5** 51 8N 2 59W
Bridgwater B., *U.K.* **11 F4** 51 15N 3 15W
Bridlington, *U.K.* **10 C7** 54 5N 0 12W
Bridlington B., *U.K.* **10 C7** 54 4N 0 10W
Bridport, *Australia* **62 G4** 40 59S 147 23 E
Bridport, *U.K.* **11 G5** 50 44N 2 45W
Brig, *Switz.* **18 C7** 46 18N 7 59 E
Brigg, *U.K.* **10 D7** 53 34N 0 28W
Brigham City, *U.S.A.* **82 F7** 41 31N 112 1W
Bright, *Australia* **63 F4** 36 42S 146 56 E
Brighton, *Australia* **63 F2** 35 5S 138 30 E
Brighton, *Canada* **78 B7** 44 2N 77 44W
Brighton, *U.K.* **11 G7** 50 49N 0 7W
Brighton, *Colo., U.S.A.* **80 F2** 39 59N 104 49W
Brighton, *N.Y., U.S.A.* **78 C7** 43 8N 77 34W
Brilliant, *U.S.A.* **78 F4** 40 15N 80 39W
Brindisi, *Italy* **21 D7** 40 39N 17 55 E
Brinkley, *U.S.A.* **81 H9** 34 53N 91 12W
Brinnon, *U.S.A.* **84 C4** 47 41N 122 54W
Brion, I., *Canada* **71 C7** 47 46N 61 26W
Brisbane, *Australia* **63 D5** 27 25S 153 2 E
Brisbane →, *Australia* **63 D5** 27 24S 153 9 E
Bristol, *U.K.* **11 F5** 51 26N 2 35W
Bristol, *Conn., U.S.A.* **79 E12** 41 40N 72 57W
Bristol, *Pa., U.S.A.* **79 F10** 40 6N 74 51W
Bristol, *R.I., U.S.A.* **79 E13** 41 40N 71 16W
Bristol, *Tenn., U.S.A.* **77 G4** 36 36N 82 11W
Bristol, City of □, *U.K.* **11 F5** 51 27N 2 36W
Bristol B., *U.S.A.* **68 C4** 58 0N 160 0W
Bristol Channel, *U.K.* **11 F3** 51 18N 4 30W
Bristol I., *Antarctica* **5 B1** 58 45S 28 0W
Bristol L., *U.S.A.* **83 J5** 34 23N 116 50W
Bristow, *U.S.A.* **81 H6** 35 50N 96 23W
Britain = Great Britain, *Europe* **6 E5** 54 0N 2 15W
British Columbia □, *Canada* **72 C3** 55 0N 125 15W
British Indian Ocean Terr. = Chagos Arch., *Ind. Oc.* **29 K11** 6 0S 72 0 E
British Isles, *Europe* **6 E5** 54 0N 4 0W
Brits, *S. Africa* **57 D4** 25 37S 27 48 E
Britstown, *S. Africa* **56 E3** 30 37S 23 30 E
Britt, *Canada* **70 C3** 45 46N 80 34W
Brittany = Bretagne, *France* **18 B2** 48 10N 3 0W
Britton, *U.S.A.* **80 C6** 45 48N 97 45W
Brive-la-Gaillarde, *France* **18 D4** 45 10N 1 32 E
Brixen = Bressanone, *Italy* **20 A4** 46 43N 11 39 E
Brixham, *U.K.* **11 G4** 50 23N 3 31W
Brno, *Czech Rep.* **17 D9** 49 10N 16 35 E
Broad →, *U.S.A.* **77 J5** 34 1N 81 4W

Cárdenas

Cabora Bassa Dam = Cahora Bassa, Represêa de, Mozam. 55 F3 15 20S 32 50 E
Caborca, Mexico 86 A2 30 40N 112 10W
Cabot, Mt., U.S.A. 79 B13 44 30N 71 25W
Cabot Hd., Canada 78 A3 45 14N 81 17W
Cabot Str., Canada 71 C8 47 15N 59 40W
Cabra, Spain 19 D3 37 30N 4 28W
Cabrera, Spain 22 B9 39 8N 2 57 E
Cabri, Canada 73 C7 50 35N 108 25W
Cabriel →, Spain 19 C5 39 14N 1 3W
Caçador, Brazil 95 B5 26 47S 51 0W
Čačak, Serbia, Yug. 21 C9 43 54N 20 20 E
Caçapava do Sul, Brazil 95 C5 30 30S 53 30W
Cáceres, Brazil 92 G7 16 5S 57 40W
Cáceres, Spain 19 C2 39 26N 6 23W
Cache Bay, Canada 70 C4 46 22N 80 0W
Cache Cr. →, U.S.A. 84 G5 38 42N 121 42W
Cache Creek, Canada 72 C4 50 48N 121 19W
Cachi, Argentina 94 B2 25 5S 66 10W
Cachimbo, Serra do, Brazil 93 E7 9 30S 55 30W
Cachinal de la Sierra, Chile 94 A2 24 58S 69 32W
Cachoeira, Brazil 93 F11 12 30S 39 0W
Cachoeira de Itapemirim, Brazil 95 A7 20 51S 41 7W
Cachoeira do Sul, Brazil 95 C5 30 3S 52 53W
Cacoal, Brazil 92 F6 11 32S 61 18W
Cacólo, Angola 52 G3 10 9S 19 21 E
Caconda, Angola 53 G3 13 48S 15 8 E
Caddo, U.S.A. 81 H6 34 7N 96 16W
Cader Idris, U.K. 11 E4 52 42N 3 53W
Cadereyta, Mexico 86 B5 25 36N 100 0W
Cadibarrawirracanna, L., Australia 63 D2 28 52S 135 27 E
Cadillac, U.S.A. 76 C3 44 15N 85 24W
Cadiz, Phil. 37 B6 10 57N 123 15 E
Cádiz, Spain 19 D2 36 30N 6 20W
Cadiz, Calif., U.S.A. 85 L11 34 30N 115 28W
Cadiz, Ohio, U.S.A. 78 F4 40 22N 81 0W
Cádiz, G. de, Spain 19 D2 36 40N 7 0W
Cadiz L., U.S.A. 83 J6 34 18N 115 24W
Cadney Park, Australia 63 D1 27 55S 134 3 E
Cadomin, Canada 72 C5 53 2N 117 20W
Cadotte Lake, Canada 72 B5 56 26N 116 23W
Cadoux, Australia 61 F2 30 46S 117 7 E
Caen, France 18 B3 49 10N 0 22W
Caernarfon, U.K. 10 D3 53 8N 4 16W
Caernarfon B., U.K. 10 D3 53 4N 4 40W
Caernarvon = Caernarfon, U.K. 10 D3 53 8N 4 16W
Caerphilly, U.K. 11 F4 51 35N 3 13W
Caerphilly □, U.K. 11 F4 51 37N 3 12W
Caesarea, Israel 47 C3 32 30N 34 53 E
Caetité, Brazil 93 F10 13 50S 42 32W
Cafayate, Argentina 94 B2 26 2S 66 0W
Cafu, Angola 56 B2 16 30S 15 8 E
Cagayan de Oro, Phil. 37 C6 8 30N 124 40 E
Cagayan Is., Phil. 37 C5 9 40N 121 16 E
Cágliari, Italy 20 E3 39 13N 9 7 E
Cágliari, G. di, Italy 20 E3 39 8N 9 11 E
Caguán →, Colombia 92 D4 0 8S 74 18W
Caguas, Puerto Rico 89 C6 18 14N 66 2W
Caha Mts., Ireland 13 E2 51 45N 9 40W
Cahama, Angola 56 B1 16 17S 14 19 E
Caher, Ireland 13 D4 52 22N 7 56W
Caherciveen, Ireland 13 E1 51 56N 10 14W
Cahora Bassa, Represêa de, Mozam. 55 F3 15 20S 32 50 E
Cahore Pt., Ireland 13 D5 52 33N 6 12W
Cahors, France 18 D4 44 27N 1 27 E
Cahul, Moldova 17 F15 45 50N 28 15 E
Cai Nuoc, Vietnam 39 H5 8 56N 105 1 E
Caia, Mozam. 55 F4 17 51S 35 24 E
Caianda, Angola 55 E1 11 2S 23 31 E
Caibarién, Cuba 88 B4 22 30N 79 30W
Caicara, Venezuela 92 B5 7 38N 66 10W
Caicó, Brazil 93 E11 6 20S 37 0W
Caicos Is., W. Indies 89 B5 21 40N 71 40W
Caicos Passage, W. Indies 89 B5 22 45N 72 45W
Caird Coast, Antarctica 5 D1 75 0S 25 0W
Cairn Gorm, U.K. 12 D5 57 7N 3 39W
Cairngorm Mts., U.K. 12 D5 57 6N 3 42W
Cairnryan, U.K. 12 G3 54 59N 5 1W
Cairns, Australia 62 B4 16 57S 145 45 E
Cairns L., Canada 73 C10 51 42N 94 30W
Cairo = El Qâhira, Egypt 51 B12 30 1N 31 14 E
Cairo, Ga., U.S.A. 77 K3 30 52N 84 13W
Cairo, Ill., U.S.A. 81 G10 37 0N 89 11W
Cairo, N.Y., U.S.A. 79 D11 42 18N 74 0W
Caithness, Ord of, U.K. 12 C5 58 8N 3 36W
Cajamarca, Peru 92 E3 7 5S 78 28W
Cajàzeiras, Brazil 93 E11 6 52S 38 30W
Cala d'Or, Spain 22 B10 39 23N 3 14 E
Cala en Porter, Spain 22 B11 39 52N 4 8 E
Cala Figuera, C. de, Spain 22 B9 39 27N 2 31 E
Cala Forcat, Spain 22 B10 40 0N 3 47 E
Cala Major, Spain 22 B9 39 33N 2 37 E
Cala Mezquida = Sa Mesquida, Spain 22 B11 39 55N 4 16 E
Cala Millor, Spain 22 B10 39 35N 3 22 E
Cala Ratjada, Spain 22 B10 39 43N 3 27 E
Cala Santa Galdana, Spain 22 B10 39 56N 3 58 E
Calabar, Nigeria 50 H7 4 57N 8 20 E
Calabogie, Canada 79 A8 45 18N 76 43W
Calabozo, Venezuela 92 B5 9 0N 67 28W
Calábria □, Italy 20 E7 39 0N 16 30 E
Calafate, Argentina 96 G2 50 19S 72 15W
Calahorra, Spain 19 A5 42 18N 1 59W
Calais, France 18 A4 50 57N 1 56 E
Calais, U.S.A. 77 C12 45 11N 67 17W
Calalaste, Cord. de, Argentina 94 B2 25 0S 67 0W
Calama, Brazil 92 E6 8 0S 62 50W
Calama, Chile 94 A2 22 30S 68 55W
Calamar, Colombia 92 A4 10 15N 74 55W
Calamian Group, Phil. 37 B5 11 50N 119 55 E
Calamocha, Spain 19 B5 40 50N 1 17W
Calang, Indonesia 36 D1 4 37N 95 37 E
Calapan, Phil. 37 B6 13 25N 121 7 E
Călăraşi, Romania 17 F14 44 12N 27 20 E
Calatayud, Spain 19 B5 41 20N 1 40W
Calauag, Phil. 37 B6 13 55N 122 15 E
Calavite, C., Phil. 37 B6 13 26N 120 20 E
Calbayog, Phil. 37 B6 12 4N 124 38 E
Calca, Peru 92 F4 13 22S 72 0W
Calcasieu L., U.S.A. 81 L8 29 55N 93 18W
Calcutta, India 43 H13 22 36N 88 24 E
Calcutta, U.S.A. 78 F4 40 40N 80 34W
Caldas da Rainha, Portugal 19 C1 39 24N 9 8W
Calder →, U.K. 10 D6 53 44N 1 22W
Caldera, Chile 94 B1 27 5S 70 55W
Caldwell, Idaho, U.S.A. 82 E5 43 40N 116 41W
Caldwell, Kans., U.S.A. 81 G6 37 2N 97 37W
Caldwell, Tex., U.S.A. 81 K6 30 32N 96 42W
Caledon, S. Africa 56 E2 34 14S 19 26 E
Caledon →, S. Africa 56 E4 30 31S 26 5 E
Caledon B., Australia 62 A2 12 45S 137 0 E
Caledonia, Canada 78 C5 43 7N 79 58W
Caledonia, U.S.A. 78 D7 42 58N 77 51W
Calemba, Angola 56 B2 16 0S 15 44 E
Calen, Australia 62 C4 20 56S 148 48 E
Caletones, Chile 94 C1 34 6S 70 27W
Calexico, U.S.A. 85 N11 32 40N 115 30W
Calf of Man, U.K. 10 C3 54 3N 4 48W
Calgary, Canada 72 C6 51 0N 114 10W
Calheta, Madeira 22 D2 32 44N 17 11W
Calhoun, U.S.A. 77 H3 34 30N 84 57W
Cali, Colombia 92 C3 3 25N 76 35W
Calicut, India 40 P9 11 15N 75 43 E
Caliente, U.S.A. 83 H6 37 37N 114 31W
California, Mo., U.S.A. 80 F8 38 38N 92 34W
California, Pa., U.S.A. 78 F5 40 4N 79 54W
California □, U.S.A. 84 H7 37 30N 119 30W
California, Baja, Mexico 86 A1 32 10N 115 12W
California, Baja, T.N. = Baja California □, Mexico 86 B2 30 0N 115 0W
California, Baja, T.S. = Baja California Sur □, Mexico 86 B2 25 50N 111 50W
California, G. de, Mexico 86 B2 27 0N 111 0W
California City, U.S.A. 85 K9 35 10N 117 55W
California Hot Springs, U.S.A. 85 K8 35 51N 118 41W
Calingasta, Argentina 94 C2 31 15S 69 30W
Calipatria, U.S.A. 85 M11 33 8N 115 31W
Calistoga, U.S.A. 84 G4 38 35N 122 35W
Calitzdorp, S. Africa 56 E3 33 33S 21 42 E
Callabonna, L., Australia 63 D3 29 40S 140 5 E
Callan, Ireland 13 D4 52 32N 7 24W
Callander, U.K. 12 E4 56 15N 4 13W
Callao, Peru 92 F3 12 0S 77 0W
Calles, Mexico 87 C5 23 2N 98 42W
Callicoon, U.S.A. 79 E9 41 46N 75 3W
Calling Lake, Canada 72 B6 55 15N 113 12W
Calliope, Australia 62 C5 24 0S 151 16 E
Calne, U.K. 11 F6 51 26N 2 0W
Calola, Angola 56 B2 16 25S 17 48 E
Caloundra, Australia 63 D5 26 45S 153 10 E
Calpella, U.S.A. 84 F3 39 14N 123 12W
Calpine, U.S.A. 84 F6 39 40N 120 27W
Calstock, Canada 70 C3 49 47N 84 9W
Caltagirone, Italy 20 F6 37 14N 14 31 E
Caltanissetta, Italy 20 F6 37 29N 14 4 E
Calulo, Angola 52 G2 10 1S 14 56 E
Caluquembe, Angola 53 G2 13 47S 14 44 E
Calvert →, Australia 62 B2 16 17S 137 44 E
Calvert I., Canada 72 C3 51 30N 128 0W
Calvert Ra., Australia 60 D3 24 0S 122 30 E
Calvi, France 18 E8 42 34N 8 45 E
Calviá, Spain 19 C7 39 34N 2 31 E
Calvillo, Mexico 86 C4 21 51N 102 43W
Calvinia, S. Africa 56 E2 31 28S 19 45 E
Calwa, U.S.A. 84 J7 36 42N 119 46W
Cam →, U.K. 11 E8 52 21N 0 16 E
Cam Lam, Vietnam 39 G7 11 54N 109 10 E
Cam Ranh, Vietnam 39 G7 11 54N 109 12 E
Cam Xuyen, Vietnam 38 C6 18 15N 106 0 E
Camabatela, Angola 52 F3 8 20S 15 26 E
Camacha, Madeira 22 D3 32 41N 16 49W
Camacho, Mexico 86 C4 24 25N 102 18W
Camacupa, Angola 53 G3 11 58S 17 22 E
Camagüey, Cuba 88 B4 21 20N 78 0W
Camaná, Peru 92 G4 16 30S 72 50W
Camanche Reservoir, U.S.A. 84 G6 38 14N 121 1W
Camaquã, Brazil 95 C5 30 51S 51 49W
Camaquã →, Brazil 95 C5 31 17S 51 47W
Câmara de Lobos, Madeira 22 D3 32 39N 16 59W
Camargo, Mexico 87 B5 26 19N 98 50W
Camargue, France 18 E6 43 34N 4 34 E
Camarillo, U.S.A. 85 L7 34 13N 119 2W
Camarón, C., Honduras 88 C2 16 0N 85 5W
Camarones, Argentina 96 E3 44 50S 65 40W
Camas, U.S.A. 84 E4 45 35N 122 24W
Camas Valley, U.S.A. 82 E2 43 2N 123 40W
Camballin, Australia 60 C3 17 59S 124 12 E
Cambará, Brazil 95 A5 23 2S 50 5W
Cambay = Khambhat, India 42 H5 22 23N 72 33 E
Cambay, G. of = Khambhat, G. of, India 40 J8 20 45N 72 30 E
Cambodia ■, Asia 38 F5 12 15N 105 0 E
Camborne, U.K. 11 G2 50 12N 5 19W
Cambrai, France 18 A5 50 11N 3 14 E
Cambria, U.S.A. 84 K5 35 34N 121 5W
Cambrian Mts., U.K. 11 E4 52 3N 3 57W
Cambridge, Canada 78 C4 43 23N 80 15W
Cambridge, Jamaica 88 C4 18 18N 77 54W
Cambridge, N.Z. 59 G5 37 54S 175 29 E
Cambridge, U.K. 11 E8 52 12N 0 8 E
Cambridge, Mass., U.S.A. 79 D13 42 22N 71 6W
Cambridge, Md., U.S.A. 75 C11 38 34N 76 5W
Cambridge, Minn., U.S.A. 80 C8 45 34N 93 13W
Cambridge, N.Y., U.S.A. 79 C11 43 2N 73 22W
Cambridge, Nebr., U.S.A. 80 E4 40 17N 100 10W
Cambridge, Ohio, U.S.A. 78 F3 40 2N 81 35W
Cambridge Bay = Ikaluktutiak, Canada 68 B9 69 10N 105 0W
Cambridge G., Australia 60 B4 14 55S 128 15 E
Cambridge Springs, U.S.A. 78 E4 41 48N 80 4W
Cambridgeshire □, U.K. 11 E7 52 25N 0 7W
Cambuci, Brazil 95 A7 21 35S 41 55W
Cambundi-Catembo, Angola 52 G3 10 10S 17 35 E
Camden, Ala., U.S.A. 77 K2 31 59N 87 17W
Camden, Ark., U.S.A. 81 J8 33 35N 92 50W
Camden, Maine, U.S.A. 77 C11 44 13N 69 4W
Camden, N.J., U.S.A. 79 G9 39 56N 75 7W
Camden, N.Y., U.S.A. 79 C9 43 20N 75 45W
Camden, S.C., U.S.A. 77 H5 34 16N 80 36W
Camden Sd., Australia 60 C3 15 27S 124 25 E
Camdenton, U.S.A. 81 F8 38 1N 92 45W
Cameron, Ariz., U.S.A. 83 J8 35 53N 111 25W
Cameron, La., U.S.A. 81 L8 29 48N 93 20W
Cameron, Mo., U.S.A. 80 F7 39 44N 94 14W
Cameron, Tex., U.S.A. 81 K6 30 51N 96 59W
Cameron Highlands, Malaysia 39 K3 4 27N 101 22 E
Cameron Hills, Canada 72 B5 59 48N 118 0W
Cameroon ■, Africa 52 C2 6 0N 12 30 E
Cameroun, Mt., Cameroon 52 D1 4 13N 9 10 E
Cametá, Brazil 93 D9 2 12S 49 30W
Camiguin I., Phil. 37 C6 18 56N 121 55 E
Camilla, U.S.A. 77 K3 31 14N 84 12W
Caminha, Portugal 19 B1 41 50N 8 50W
Camino, U.S.A. 84 G6 38 44N 120 41W
Camira Creek, Australia 63 D5 29 15S 152 58 E
Cammal, U.S.A. 78 E7 41 24N 77 28W
Camocim, Brazil 93 D10 2 55S 40 50W
Camooweal, Australia 62 B2 19 56S 138 7 E
Camopi, Fr. Guiana 93 C8 3 12N 52 17W
Camp Borden, Canada 78 B5 44 18N 79 56W
Camp Hill, U.S.A. 78 F8 40 14N 76 55W
Camp Nelson, U.S.A. 85 J8 36 8N 118 39W
Camp Pendleton, U.S.A. 85 M9 33 16N 117 23W
Camp Verde, U.S.A. 83 J8 34 34N 111 51W
Camp Wood, U.S.A. 81 L5 29 40N 100 1W
Campana, Argentina 94 C4 34 10S 58 55W
Campana, I., Chile 96 F1 48 20S 75 20W
Campanário, Madeira 22 D2 32 39N 17 2W
Campánia □, Italy 20 D6 41 0N 14 30 E
Campbell, S. Africa 56 D3 28 48S 23 44 E
Campbell, Calif., U.S.A. 84 H5 37 17N 121 57W
Campbell, Ohio, U.S.A. 78 E4 41 5N 80 37W
Campbell I., Pac. Oc. 64 N8 52 30S 169 0 E
Campbell L., Canada 73 A7 63 14N 106 55W
Campbell River, Canada 72 C3 50 5N 125 20W
Campbell Town, Australia 62 G4 41 52S 147 30 E
Campbellford, Canada 78 B7 44 18N 77 48W
Campbellpur, Pakistan 42 C5 33 46N 72 26 E
Campbellsville, U.S.A. 76 G3 37 21N 85 20W
Campbellton, Canada 71 C6 47 57N 66 43W
Campbelltown, Australia 63 E5 34 4S 150 49 E
Campbeltown, U.K. 12 F3 55 26N 5 36W
Campeche, Mexico 87 D6 19 50N 90 32W
Campeche □, Mexico 87 D6 19 50N 90 32W
Campeche, Golfo de, Mexico 87 D6 19 30N 93 0W
Camperdown, Australia 63 F3 38 14S 143 9 E
Camperville, Canada 73 C8 51 59N 100 9W
Câmpina, Romania 17 F13 45 10N 25 45 E
Campina Grande, Brazil 93 E11 7 20S 35 47W
Campinas, Brazil 95 A6 22 50S 47 0W
Campo Grande, Brazil 93 H8 20 25S 54 40W
Campo Maíor, Brazil 93 D10 4 50S 42 12W
Campo Mourão, Brazil 95 A5 24 3S 52 22W
Campobasso, Italy 20 D6 41 34N 14 39 E
Campos, Brazil 95 A7 21 50S 41 20W
Campos Belos, Brazil 93 F9 13 10S 47 3W
Campos del Puerto, Spain 22 B10 39 26N 3 1 E
Campos Novos, Brazil 95 B5 27 21S 51 50W
Camptonville, U.S.A. 84 F5 39 27N 121 3W
Camptown, U.S.A. 79 E8 41 44N 76 14W
Câmpulung, Romania 17 F13 45 17N 25 3 E
Camrose, Canada 72 C6 53 0N 112 50W
Camsell Portage, Canada 73 B7 59 37N 109 15W
Çan, Turkey 21 D12 40 2N 27 3 E
Can Clavo, Spain 22 C7 38 57N 1 27 E
Can Creu, Spain 22 C7 38 58N 1 28 E
Can Gio, Vietnam 39 G6 10 25N 106 58 E
Can Tho, Vietnam 39 G5 10 2N 105 46 E
Canaan, U.S.A. 79 D11 42 2N 73 20W
Canada ■, N. Amer. 68 C10 60 0N 100 0W
Cañada de Gómez, Argentina 94 C3 32 40S 61 30W
Canadian, U.S.A. 81 H4 35 55N 100 23W
Canadian →, U.S.A. 81 H7 35 28N 95 3W
Canajoharie, U.S.A. 79 D10 42 54N 74 35W
Çanakkale, Turkey 21 D12 40 8N 26 24 E
Çanakkale Boğazı, Turkey 21 D12 40 17N 26 32 E
Canal Flats, Canada 72 C5 50 10N 115 48W
Canalejas, Argentina 94 D2 35 15S 66 34W
Canals, Argentina 94 C3 33 35S 62 53W
Canandaigua, U.S.A. 78 D7 42 54N 77 17W
Canandaigua L., U.S.A. 78 D7 42 47N 77 19W
Cananea, Mexico 86 A2 31 0N 110 20W
Canarias, Is., Atl. Oc. 22 F4 28 30N 16 0W
Canarreos, Arch. de los, Cuba 88 B3 21 35N 81 40W
Canary Is. = Canarias, Is., Atl. Oc. 22 F4 28 30N 16 0W
Canaseraga, U.S.A. 78 D7 42 27N 77 45W
Canatlán, Mexico 86 C4 24 31N 104 47W
Canaveral, C., U.S.A. 77 L5 28 27N 80 32W
Canavieiras, Brazil 93 G11 15 39S 39 0W
Canberra, Australia 63 F4 35 15S 149 8 E
Canby, Calif., U.S.A. 82 F3 41 27N 120 52W
Canby, Minn., U.S.A. 80 C6 44 43N 96 16W
Canby, Oreg., U.S.A. 84 E4 45 16N 122 42W
Cancún, Mexico 87 C7 21 8N 86 44W
Candelaria, Argentina 95 B4 27 29S 55 44W
Candelaria, Canary Is. 22 F3 28 22N 16 22W
Candelo, Australia 63 F4 36 47S 149 43 E
Candia = Iráklion, Greece 23 D7 35 20N 25 12 E
Candle L., Canada 73 C7 53 50N 105 18W
Candlemas I., Antarctica 5 B1 57 3S 26 40W
Cando, U.S.A. 80 A5 48 32N 99 12W
Canea = Khaniá, Greece 23 D6 35 30N 24 4 E
Canelones, Uruguay 95 C4 34 32S 56 17W
Cañete, Chile 94 D1 37 50S 73 30W
Cañete, Peru 92 F3 13 8S 76 30W
Cangas de Narcea, Spain 19 A2 43 10N 6 32W
Canguaretama, Brazil 93 E11 6 20S 35 5W
Canguçu, Brazil 95 C5 31 22S 52 43W
Canguçu, Serra do, Brazil 95 C5 31 20S 52 40W
Cangzhou, China 34 E9 38 19N 116 52 E
Caniapiscau →, Canada 71 A6 56 40N 69 30W
Caniapiscau Rés. de, Canada 71 B6 54 10N 69 55W
Canicattì, Italy 20 F5 37 21N 13 51 E
Canim Lake, Canada 72 C4 51 47N 120 54W
Canindeyu □, Paraguay 95 A5 24 10S 55 0W
Canisteo, U.S.A. 78 D7 42 16N 77 36W
Canisteo →, U.S.A. 78 D7 42 7N 77 8W
Cañitas, Mexico 86 C4 23 36N 102 43W
Çankırı, Turkey 25 F5 40 40N 33 37 E
Cankuzo, Burundi 54 C3 3 10S 30 31 E
Canmore, Canada 72 C5 51 7N 115 18W
Cann River, Australia 63 F4 37 35S 149 7 E
Canna, U.K. 12 D2 57 3N 6 33W
Cannanore, India 40 P9 11 53N 75 27 E
Cannes, France 18 E7 43 32N 7 1 E
Canning Town = Port Canning, India 43 H13 22 23N 88 40 E
Cannington, Canada 78 B5 44 20N 79 2W
Cannock, U.K. 11 E5 52 41N 2 1W
Cannon Ball →, U.S.A. 80 B4 46 20N 100 38W
Cannondale Mt., Australia 62 D4 25 13S 148 57 E
Cannonsville Reservoir, U.S.A. 79 D9 42 4N 75 22W
Cannonvale, Australia 62 C4 20 17S 148 43 E
Canoas, Brazil 95 B5 29 56S 51 11W
Canoe L., Canada 73 B7 55 10N 108 15W
Canon City, U.S.A. 80 F2 38 27N 105 14W
Canora, Canada 73 C8 51 40N 102 30W
Canowindra, Australia 63 E4 33 35S 148 38 E
Canso, Canada 71 C7 45 20N 61 0W
Cantabria □, Spain 19 A4 43 10N 4 0W
Cantabrian Mts. = Cantábrica, Cordillera, Spain 19 A3 43 0N 5 10W
Cantábrica, Cordillera, Spain 19 A3 43 0N 5 10W
Cantal, Plomb du, France 18 D5 45 3N 2 45 E
Canterbury, Australia 62 D3 25 23S 141 53 E
Canterbury, U.K. 11 F9 51 16N 1 6 E
Canterbury □, N.Z. 59 K3 43 45S 171 19 E
Canterbury Bight, N.Z. 59 L3 44 16S 171 55 E
Canterbury Plains, N.Z. 59 K3 43 55S 171 22 E
Cantil, U.S.A. 85 K9 35 18N 117 58W
Canton = Guangzhou, China 33 D6 23 5N 113 10 E
Canton, Ga., U.S.A. 77 H3 34 14N 84 29W
Canton, Ill., U.S.A. 80 E9 40 33N 90 2W
Canton, Miss., U.S.A. 81 J9 32 37N 90 2W
Canton, Mo., U.S.A. 80 E9 40 8N 91 32W
Canton, N.Y., U.S.A. 79 B9 44 36N 75 10W
Canton, Ohio, U.S.A. 78 F3 40 48N 81 23W
Canton, Pa., U.S.A. 78 E8 41 39N 76 51W
Canton, S. Dak., U.S.A. 80 D6 43 18N 96 35W
Canton L., U.S.A. 81 G5 36 6N 98 35W
Canudos, Brazil 92 E7 7 13S 58 5W
Canumã →, Brazil 92 D7 3 55S 59 10W
Canutama, Brazil 92 E6 6 30S 64 20W
Canutillo, U.S.A. 83 L10 31 55N 106 36W
Canvey, U.K. 11 F8 51 31N 0 37 E
Canyon, U.S.A. 81 H4 34 59N 101 55W
Canyonlands National Park, U.S.A. 83 G9 38 15N 110 0W
Canyonville, U.S.A. 82 E2 42 56N 123 17W
Cao He →, China 35 D13 40 10N 124 32 E
Cao Lanh, Vietnam 39 G5 10 27N 105 38 E
Cao Xian, China 34 G8 34 50N 115 35 E
Cap-aux-Meules, Canada 71 C7 47 23N 61 52W
Cap-Chat, Canada 71 C6 49 6N 66 40W
Cap-de-la-Madeleine, Canada 70 C5 46 22N 72 31W
Cap-Haïtien, Haiti 89 C5 19 40N 72 20W
Capac, U.S.A. 78 C2 43 1N 82 56W
Capanaparo →, Venezuela 92 B5 7 1N 67 7W
Cape →, Australia 62 C4 20 59S 146 51 E
Cape Barren I., Australia 62 G4 40 25S 148 15 E
Cape Breton Highlands Nat. Park, Canada 71 C7 46 50N 60 40W
Cape Breton I., Canada 71 C7 46 0N 60 30W
Cape Charles, U.S.A. 76 G8 37 16N 76 1W
Cape Coast, Ghana 50 G5 5 5N 1 15W
Cape Coral, U.S.A. 77 M5 26 33N 81 57W
Cape Dorset, Canada 69 B12 64 14N 76 32W
Cape Fear →, U.S.A. 77 H6 33 53N 78 1W
Cape Girardeau, U.S.A. 81 G10 37 19N 89 32W
Cape May, U.S.A. 76 F8 38 56N 74 56W
Cape May Point, U.S.A. 75 C12 38 56N 74 58W
Cape Province □, S. Africa 53 L3 32 0S 23 0 E
Cape Tormentine, Canada 71 C7 46 8N 63 47W
Cape Town, S. Africa 56 E2 33 55S 18 22 E
Cape Verde Is. ■, Atl. Oc. 49 E1 17 10N 25 20W
Cape Vincent, U.S.A. 79 B8 44 8N 76 20W
Cape York Peninsula, Australia 62 A3 12 0S 142 30 E
Capela, Brazil 93 F11 10 30S 37 0W
Capella, Australia 62 C4 23 2S 148 1 E
Capenda Camulemba, Angola 52 F3 9 24S 18 27 E
Capim →, Brazil 93 D9 1 40S 47 47W
Capitan, U.S.A. 83 K11 33 35N 105 35W
Capitol Reef National Park, U.S.A. 83 G8 38 15N 111 10W
Capitola, U.S.A. 84 J5 36 59N 121 57W
Capoche →, Mozam. 55 F3 15 35S 33 0 E
Capraia, Italy 18 E8 43 2N 9 50 E
Capreol, Canada 70 C3 46 43N 80 56W
Capri, Italy 20 D6 40 33N 14 14 E
Capricorn Group, Australia 62 C5 23 30S 151 55 E
Capricorn Ra., Australia 60 D2 23 20S 116 50 E
Caprivi Strip, Namibia 56 B3 18 0S 23 0 E
Captain's Flat, Australia 63 F4 35 35S 149 27 E
Caquetá →, Colombia 92 D5 1 15S 69 15W
Caracal, Romania 17 F13 44 8N 24 22 E
Caracas, Venezuela 92 A5 10 30N 66 55W
Caracol, Brazil 94 A4 22 18S 57 1W
Caracol, Piauí, Brazil 93 E10 9 15S 43 22W
Carajas, Brazil 93 E8 6 5S 50 23W
Carajás, Serra dos, Brazil 93 E8 6 0S 51 30W
Carangola, Brazil 95 A7 20 44S 42 5W
Caransebeş, Romania 17 F12 45 28N 22 18 E
Caraquet, Canada 71 C6 47 48N 64 57W
Caras, Peru 92 E3 9 3S 77 47W
Caratasca, L., Honduras 88 C3 15 20N 83 40W
Caratinga, Brazil 93 G10 19 50S 42 10W
Caraúbas, Brazil 93 E11 5 43S 37 33W
Caravaca = Caravaca de la Cruz, Spain 19 C5 38 8N 1 52W
Caravaca de la Cruz, Spain 19 C5 38 8N 1 52W
Caravelas, Brazil 93 G11 17 45S 39 15W
Caraveli, Peru 92 G4 15 45S 73 25W
Caràzinho, Brazil 95 B5 28 16S 52 46W
Carballo, Spain 19 A1 43 13N 8 41W
Carberry, Canada 73 D9 49 50N 99 25W
Carbó, Mexico 86 B2 29 42N 110 58W
Carbonara, C., Italy 20 E3 39 6N 9 31 E
Carbondale, Colo., U.S.A. 82 G10 39 24N 107 13W
Carbondale, Ill., U.S.A. 81 G10 37 44N 89 13W
Carbondale, Pa., U.S.A. 79 E9 41 35N 75 30W
Carbonear, Canada 71 C9 47 42N 53 13W
Carbónia, Italy 20 E3 39 10N 8 30 E
Carcajou, Canada 72 B5 57 47N 117 6W
Carcarana →, Argentina 94 C3 32 27S 60 48W
Carcasse, C., Haiti 89 C5 18 30N 74 28W
Carcassonne, France 18 E5 43 13N 2 20 E
Carcross, Canada 72 A2 60 13N 134 45W
Cardamon Hills, India 40 Q10 9 30N 77 15 E
Cárdenas, Cuba 88 B3 23 0N 81 30W
Cárdenas, San Luis Potosí, Mexico 87 C5 22 0N 99 41W

Chinchilla

Chamical, Argentina 94 C2 30 22S 66 27W
Chamkar Luong, Cambodia 39 G4 11 0N 103 45 E
Chamoli, India 43 D8 30 24N 79 21 E
Chamonix-Mont Blanc, France 18 D7 45 55N 6 51 E
Chamouchouane —►, Canada 70 C5 48 37N 72 20W
Champa, India 43 H10 22 2N 82 43 E
Champagne, Canada 72 A1 60 49N 136 30W
Champagne, France 18 B6 48 40N 4 20 E
Champaign, U.S.A. 76 E1 40 7N 88 15W
Champassak, Laos 38 E5 14 53N 105 52 E
Champawat, India 43 E9 29 20N 80 6 E
Champdoré, L., Canada 71 A6 55 55N 65 49W
Champion, U.S.A. 78 E4 41 19N 80 51W
Champlain, U.S.A. 79 B11 44 59N 73 27W
Champlain, L., U.S.A. 79 B11 44 40N 73 20W
Champotón, Mexico 87 D6 19 20N 90 50W
Champua, India 43 H11 22 5N 85 40 E
Chana, Thailand 39 J3 6 55N 100 44 E
Chañaral, Chile 94 B1 26 23S 70 40W
Chanārān, Iran 45 B8 36 39N 59 6 E
Chanasma, India 42 H5 23 44N 72 5 E
Chanco, Chile 94 D1 35 44S 72 32W
Chand, India 43 J8 21 57N 79 7 E
Chandan, India 43 G12 24 38N 86 40 E
Chandan Chauki, India 43 E9 28 33N 80 47 E
Chandannagar, India 43 H13 22 52N 88 24 E
Chandausi, India 43 E8 28 27N 78 49 E
Chandeleur Is., U.S.A. 81 L10 29 55N 88 57W
Chandeleur Sd., U.S.A. 81 L10 29 55N 89 0W
Chandigarh, India 42 D7 30 43N 76 47 E
Chandil, India 43 H12 22 58N 86 3 E
Chandler, Australia 63 D1 27 0S 133 19 E
Chandler, Canada 71 C7 48 18N 64 46W
Chandler, Ariz., U.S.A. 83 K8 33 18N 111 50W
Chandler, Okla., U.S.A. 81 H6 35 42N 96 53W
Chandod, India 42 J5 21 59N 73 28 E
Chandpur, Bangla. 41 H17 23 8N 90 45 E
Chandrapur, India 40 K11 19 57N 79 25 E
Chānf, Iran 45 E9 26 38N 60 29 E
Chang, Pakistan 42 F3 26 59N 68 30 E
Chang, Ko, Thailand 39 G4 12 0N 102 23 E
Ch'ang Chiang = Chang Jiang —►, China 33 C7 31 48N 121 10 E
Chang Jiang —►, China 33 C7 31 48N 121 10 E
Changa, India 43 C7 33 53N 77 35 E
Changanacheri, India 40 Q10 9 25N 76 31 E
Changane —►, Mozam. 57 C5 24 30S 33 30 E
Changbai, China 35 D15 41 25N 128 5 E
Changbai Shan, China 35 C15 42 20N 129 0 E
Changchiak'ou = Zhangjiakou, China 34 D8 40 48N 114 55 E
Ch'angchou = Changzhou, China 33 C6 31 47N 119 58 E
Changchun, China 35 C13 43 57N 125 17 E
Changchunling, China 35 B13 45 18N 125 27 E
Changde, China 33 D6 29 4N 111 35 E
Changdo-ri, N. Korea 35 E14 38 30N 127 40 E
Changhai = Shanghai, China 33 C7 31 15N 121 26 E
Changhua, Taiwan 33 D7 24 2N 120 30 E
Changhŭng, S. Korea 35 G14 34 41N 126 52 E
Changhŭngni, N. Korea 35 D15 40 24N 128 19 E
Changjiang, China 38 C7 19 20N 108 55 E
Changjin, N. Korea 35 D14 40 23N 127 15 E
Changjin-chŏsuji, N. Korea 35 D14 40 30N 127 15 E
Changli, China 35 E10 39 40N 119 13 E
Changling, China 35 B12 44 20N 123 58 E
Changlun, Malaysia 39 J3 6 25N 100 26 E
Changping, China 34 D9 40 14N 116 12 E
Changsha, China 33 D6 28 12N 113 0 E
Changwu, China 34 G4 35 10N 107 45 E
Changyi, China 35 F10 36 40N 119 30 E
Changyŏn, N. Korea 35 E13 38 15N 125 6 E
Changyuan, China 34 G8 35 15N 114 42 E
Changzhi, China 34 F7 36 10N 113 6 E
Changzhou, China 33 C6 31 47N 119 58 E
Chanhanga, Angola 56 B1 16 0S 14 8 E
Channapatna, India 40 N10 12 40N 77 15 E
Channel Is., U.K. 11 H5 49 19N 2 24W
Channel Is., U.S.A. 85 M7 33 40N 119 15W
Channel Islands National Park, U.S.A. 85 M8 33 30N 119 0W
Channel-Port aux Basques, Canada 71 C8 47 30N 59 9W
Channel Tunnel, Europe 11 F9 51 0N 1 30 E
Channing, U.S.A. 81 H3 35 41N 102 20W
Chantada, Spain 19 A2 42 36N 7 46W
Chanthaburi, Thailand 38 F4 12 38N 102 12 E
Chantrey Inlet, Canada 68 B10 67 48N 96 20W
Chanute, U.S.A. 81 G7 37 41N 95 27W
Chao Phraya —►, Thailand 38 F3 13 32N 100 36 E
Chao Phraya Lowlands, Thailand 38 E3 15 30N 100 0 E
Chaocheng, China 34 F8 36 4N 115 37 E
Chaoyang, China 35 D11 41 35N 120 22 E
Chaozhou, China 33 D6 23 42N 116 32 E
Chapais, Canada 70 C5 49 47N 74 51W
Chapala, Mozam. 55 F4 15 50S 37 35 E
Chapala, L. de, Mexico 86 C4 20 10N 103 20W
Chapayev, Kazakstan 25 D9 50 25N 51 10 E
Chapayevsk, Russia 24 D8 53 0N 49 40 E
Chapecó, Brazil 95 B5 27 14S 52 41W
Chapel Hill, U.S.A. 77 H6 35 55N 79 4W
Chapleau, Canada 70 C3 47 50N 83 24W
Chaplin, Canada 73 C7 50 28N 106 40W
Chaplin L., Canada 73 C7 50 22N 106 36W
Chappell, U.S.A. 80 E3 41 6N 102 28W
Chapra = Chhapra, India 43 G11 25 48N 84 44 E
Chara, Russia 27 D12 56 54N 118 20 E
Charadai, Argentina 94 B4 27 35S 59 55W
Charagua, Bolivia 92 G6 19 45S 63 10W
Charambirá, Punta, Colombia 92 C3 4 16N 77 32W
Charaña, Bolivia 92 G5 17 30S 69 25W
Charanwala, India 42 F5 27 51N 72 10 E
Charata, Argentina 94 B3 27 13S 61 14W
Charcas, Mexico 86 C4 23 10N 101 20W
Chard, U.K. 11 G5 50 52N 2 58W
Chardon, U.S.A. 78 E3 41 35N 81 12W
Chardzhou = Chärjew, Turkmenistan 26 F7 39 6N 63 34 E
Charente —►, France 18 D3 45 57N 1 5W
Chari —►, Chad 51 F8 12 58N 14 31 E
Chārīkār, Afghan. 40 B6 35 0N 69 10 E
Chariton —►, U.S.A. 80 F8 39 19N 92 58W
Chärjew, Turkmenistan 26 F7 39 6N 63 34 E
Charkhari, India 43 G8 25 24N 79 45 E
Charkhi Dadri, India 42 E7 28 37N 76 17 E
Charleroi, Belgium 15 D4 50 24N 4 27 E
Charleroi, U.S.A. 78 F5 40 9N 79 57W
Charles, C., U.S.A. 76 G8 37 7N 75 58W
Charles City, U.S.A. 80 D8 43 4N 92 41W
Charles L., Canada 73 B6 59 50N 110 33W
Charles Town, U.S.A. 76 F7 39 17N 77 52W
Charleston, Ill., U.S.A. 76 F1 39 30N 88 10W
Charleston, Miss., U.S.A. 81 H9 34 1N 90 4W
Charleston, Mo., U.S.A. 81 G10 36 55N 89 21W
Charleston, S.C., U.S.A. 77 J6 32 46N 79 56W
Charleston, W. Va., U.S.A. 76 F5 38 21N 81 38W
Charleston L., Canada 79 B9 44 32N 76 0W
Charleston Peak, U.S.A. 85 J11 36 16N 115 42W
Charlestown, Ireland 13 C3 53 58N 8 48W
Charlestown, S. Africa 57 D4 27 26S 29 53 E
Charlestown, Ind., U.S.A. 76 F3 38 27N 85 40W
Charlestown, N.H., U.S.A. 79 C12 43 14N 72 25W
Charleville = Rath Luirc, Ireland 13 D3 52 21N 8 40W
Charleville, Australia 63 D4 26 24S 146 15 E
Charleville-Mézières, France 18 B6 49 44N 4 40 E
Charlevoix, U.S.A. 76 C3 45 19N 85 16W
Charlotte, Mich., U.S.A. 76 D3 42 34N 84 50W
Charlotte, N.C., U.S.A. 77 H5 35 13N 80 51W
Charlotte, Vt., U.S.A. 79 B11 44 19N 73 14W
Charlotte Amalie, Virgin Is. 89 C7 18 21N 64 56W
Charlotte Harbor, U.S.A. 77 M4 26 50N 82 10W
Charlotte L., Canada 72 C3 52 12N 125 19W
Charlottesville, U.S.A. 76 F6 38 2N 78 30W
Charlottetown, Nfld., Canada 71 B8 52 46N 56 7W
Charlottetown, P.E.I., Canada 71 C7 46 14N 63 8W
Charlton, Australia 63 F3 36 16S 143 24 E
Charlton, U.S.A. 80 E8 40 59N 93 20W
Charlton I., Canada 70 B4 52 0N 79 20W
Charny, Canada 71 C5 46 43N 71 15W
Charolles, France 18 C6 46 27N 4 16 E
Charre, Mozam. 55 F4 17 13S 35 10 E
Charsadda, Pakistan 42 B4 34 7N 71 45 E
Charters Towers, Australia 62 C4 20 5S 146 13 E
Chartres, France 18 B4 48 29N 1 30 E
Chascomús, Argentina 94 D4 35 30S 58 0W
Chasefu, Zambia 55 E3 11 55S 33 8 E
Chashma Barrage, Pakistan 42 C4 32 27N 71 20 E
Chāt, Iran 45 B7 37 59N 55 16 E
Châteaubriant, France 18 C3 47 43N 1 23W
Chateaugay, U.S.A. 79 B10 44 56N 74 5W
Châteauguay, L., Canada 71 A5 56 26N 70 3W
Châteaulin, France 18 B1 48 11N 4 8W
Châteauroux, France 18 C4 46 50N 1 40 E
Châtellerault, France 18 C4 46 50N 0 30 E
Chatham = Miramichi, Canada 71 C6 47 2N 65 28W
Chatham, Canada 78 D2 42 24N 82 11W
Chatham, U.K. 11 F8 51 22N 0 32 E
Chatham, U.S.A. 79 D11 42 21N 73 36W
Chatham Is., Pac. Oc. 64 M10 44 0S 176 40W
Chatmohar, Bangla. 43 G13 24 15N 89 15 E
Chatra, India 43 G11 24 12N 84 56 E
Chatrapur, India 41 K14 19 22N 85 2 E
Chats, L. des, Canada 79 A8 45 30N 76 20W
Chatsu, India 42 F6 26 36N 75 57 E
Chatsworth, Canada 78 B4 44 27N 80 54W
Chatsworth, Zimbabwe 55 F3 19 38S 31 13 E
Chattahoochee, U.S.A. 77 K3 30 42N 84 51W
Chattahoochee —►, U.S.A. 77 K3 30 54N 84 57W
Chattanooga, U.S.A. 77 H3 35 3N 85 19W
Chatteris, U.K. 11 E8 52 28N 0 2 E
Chaturat, Thailand 38 E3 15 40N 101 51 E
Chau Doc, Vietnam 39 G5 10 42N 105 7 E
Chauk, Burma 41 J19 20 53N 94 49 E
Chaukan La, Burma 41 F20 27 0N 97 15 E
Chaumont, France 18 B6 48 7N 5 8 E
Chaumont, U.S.A. 79 B8 44 4N 76 8W
Chautauqua L., U.S.A. 78 D5 42 10N 79 24W
Chauvin, Canada 73 C6 52 45N 110 10W
Chaves, Brazil 93 D9 0 15S 49 55W
Chaves, Portugal 19 B2 41 45N 7 32W
Chawang, Thailand 39 H2 8 25N 99 30 E
Chaykovskiy, Russia 24 C9 56 47N 54 9 E
Chazy, U.S.A. 79 B11 44 53N 73 26W
Cheb, Czech Rep. 16 C7 50 9N 12 28 E
Cheboksary, Russia 24 C8 56 8N 47 12 E
Cheboygan, U.S.A. 76 C3 45 39N 84 29W
Chech, Erg, Africa 50 D5 25 0N 2 15W
Chechenia □, Russia 25 F8 43 30N 45 29 E
Checheno-Ingush Republic = Chechenia □, Russia 25 F8 43 30N 45 29 E
Chechnya = Chechenia □, Russia 25 F8 43 30N 45 29 E
Chech'ŏn, S. Korea 35 F15 37 8N 128 12 E
Checotah, U.S.A. 81 H7 35 28N 95 31W
Chedabucto B., Canada 71 C7 45 25N 61 8W
Cheduba I., Burma 41 K18 18 45N 93 40 E
Cheepie, Australia 63 D4 26 33S 145 1 E
Chegdomyn, Russia 27 D14 51 7N 133 1 E
Chegga, Mauritania 50 C4 25 27N 5 40W
Chegutu, Zimbabwe 55 F3 18 10S 30 14 E
Chehalis, U.S.A. 84 D4 46 40N 122 58W
Chehalis —►, U.S.A. 84 D3 46 57N 123 50W
Cheju do, S. Korea 35 H14 33 29N 126 34 E
Chekiang = Zhejiang □, China 33 D7 29 0N 120 0 E
Chela, Sa. da, Angola 56 B1 16 20S 13 20 E
Chelan, U.S.A. 82 C4 47 51N 120 1W
Chelan, L., U.S.A. 82 B3 48 11N 120 30W
Cheleken, Turkmenistan 25 G9 39 34N 53 16 E
Cheleken Yarymadasy, Turkmenistan 45 B7 39 30N 53 15 E
Chelforó, Argentina 96 D3 39 0S 66 33W
Chelkar = Shalqar, Kazakstan 26 E6 47 48N 59 39 E
Chelkar Tengiz, Solonchak, Kazakstan 26 E7 48 5N 63 7 E
Chełm, Poland 17 C12 51 8N 23 30 E
Chełmno, Poland 17 B10 53 20N 18 30 E
Chelmsford, U.K. 11 F8 51 44N 0 29 E
Chelsea, U.S.A. 79 C12 43 59N 72 27W
Cheltenham, U.K. 11 F5 51 54N 2 4W
Chelyabinsk, Russia 26 D7 55 10N 61 24 E
Chelyuskin, C., Russia 28 B14 77 30N 103 0 E
Chemainus, Canada 84 B3 48 55N 123 42W
Chemba, Mozam. 53 H6 17 9S 34 53 E
Chemnitz, Germany 16 C7 50 51N 12 54 E
Chemult, U.S.A. 82 E3 43 14N 121 47W
Chen, Gora, Russia 27 C15 65 16N 141 50 E
Chenab —►, Pakistan 42 D4 30 23N 71 2 E
Chenango Forks, U.S.A. 79 D9 42 15N 75 51W
Cheney, U.S.A. 82 C5 47 30N 117 35W
Cheng Xian, China 34 H3 33 43N 105 42 E
Chengcheng, China 34 G5 35 8N 109 56 E
Chengchou = Zhengzhou, China 34 G7 34 45N 113 34 E
Chengde, China 35 D9 40 59N 117 58 E
Chengdu, China 32 C5 30 38N 104 2 E
Chenggu, China 34 H4 33 10N 107 21 E
Chengjiang, China 32 D5 24 39N 103 0 E
Ch'engmai, China 38 C7 19 50N 109 58 E
Ch'engtu = Chengdu, China 32 C5 30 38N 104 2 E
Chengwu, China 34 G8 34 58N 115 50 E
Chengyang, China 35 F11 36 18N 120 21 E
Chenjiagang, China 35 G10 34 23N 119 47 E
Chenkán, Mexico 87 D6 19 8N 90 58W
Chennai, India 40 N12 13 8N 80 19 E
Cheo Reo, Vietnam 36 B3 13 25N 108 28 E
Cheom Ksan, Cambodia 38 E5 14 13N 104 56 E
Chepén, Peru 92 E3 7 15S 79 23W
Chepes, Argentina 94 C2 31 20S 66 35W
Chepo, Panama 88 E4 9 10N 79 6W
Chepstow, U.K. 11 F5 51 38N 2 41W
Cheptulil, Mt., Kenya 54 B4 1 25N 35 35 E
Chequamegon B., U.S.A. 80 B9 46 40N 90 30W
Cher —►, France 18 C4 47 21N 0 29 E
Cheraw, U.S.A. 77 H6 34 42N 79 53W
Cherbourg, France 18 B3 49 39N 1 40W
Cherdyn, Russia 24 B10 60 24N 56 29 E
Cheremkhovo, Russia 27 D11 53 8N 103 1 E
Cherepanovo, Russia 26 D9 54 15N 83 30 E
Cherepovets, Russia 24 C6 59 5N 37 55 E
Chergui, Chott ech, Algeria 50 B6 34 21N 0 25 E
Cherikov = Cherykaw, Belarus 17 B16 53 32N 31 20 E
Cherkasy, Ukraine 25 E5 49 27N 32 4 E
Cherkessk, Russia 25 F7 44 15N 42 5 E
Cherlak, Russia 26 D8 54 15N 74 55 E
Chernaya, Russia 27 B9 70 30N 89 10 E
Chernigov = Chernihiv, Ukraine 24 D5 51 28N 31 20 E
Chernihiv, Ukraine 24 D5 51 28N 31 20 E
Chernivtsi, Ukraine 17 D13 48 15N 25 52 E
Chernobyl = Chornobyl, Ukraine 17 C16 51 20N 30 15 E
Chernogorsk, Russia 27 D10 53 49N 91 18 E
Chernovtsy = Chernivtsi, Ukraine 17 D13 48 15N 25 52 E
Chernyakhovsk, Russia 9 J19 54 36N 21 48 E
Chernysheyskiy, Russia 27 C12 63 0N 112 30 E
Cherokee, Iowa, U.S.A. 80 D7 42 45N 95 33W
Cherokee, Okla., U.S.A. 81 G5 36 45N 98 21W
Cherokee Village, U.S.A. 81 G9 36 17N 91 30W
Cherokees, Grand Lake O' The, U.S.A. 81 G7 36 28N 95 2W
Cherrapunji, India 41 G17 25 17N 91 47 E
Cherry Valley, Calif., U.S.A. 85 M10 33 59N 116 57W
Cherry Valley, N.Y., U.S.A. 79 D10 42 48N 74 45W
Cherskiy, Russia 27 C17 68 45N 161 18 E
Cherskogo Khrebet, Russia 27 C15 65 0N 143 0 E
Cherven, Belarus 17 B15 53 45N 28 28 E
Chervonohrad, Ukraine 17 C13 50 25N 24 10 E
Cherwell —►, U.K. 11 F6 51 44N 1 14W
Cherykaw, Belarus 17 B16 53 32N 31 20 E
Chesapeake, U.S.A. 76 G7 36 50N 76 17W
Chesapeake B., U.S.A. 76 G7 38 0N 76 10W
Cheshire □, U.K. 10 D5 53 14N 2 30W
Cheshskaya Guba, Russia 24 A8 67 20N 47 0 E
Cheshunt, U.K. 11 F7 51 43N 0 1W
Chesil Beach, U.K. 11 G5 50 37N 2 33W
Chesley, Canada 78 B3 44 17N 81 5W
Chester, U.K. 10 D5 53 12N 2 53W
Chester, Calif., U.S.A. 82 F3 40 19N 121 14W
Chester, Ill., U.S.A. 81 G10 37 55N 89 49W
Chester, Mont., U.S.A. 82 B8 48 31N 110 58W
Chester, Pa., U.S.A. 76 F8 39 51N 75 22W
Chester, S.C., U.S.A. 77 H5 34 43N 81 12W
Chester, Vt., U.S.A. 79 C12 43 16N 72 36W
Chester, W. Va., U.S.A. 78 F4 40 37N 80 34W
Chester-le-Street, U.K. 10 C6 54 51N 1 34W
Chesterfield, U.K. 10 D6 53 15N 1 25W
Chesterfield, Is., N. Cal. 64 J7 19 52S 158 15 E
Chesterfield Inlet, Canada 68 B10 63 30N 90 45W
Chesterton Ra., Australia 63 D4 25 30S 147 27 E
Chestertown, U.S.A. 79 C11 43 40N 73 48W
Chesterville, Canada 79 A9 45 6N 75 14W
Chestnut Ridge, U.S.A. 78 F5 40 20N 79 10W
Chesuncook L., U.S.A. 77 C11 46 0N 69 21W
Chéticamp, Canada 71 C7 46 37N 60 59W
Chetumal, Mexico 87 D7 18 30N 88 20W
Chetumal, B. de, Mexico 87 D7 18 40N 88 10W
Chetwynd, Canada 72 B4 55 45N 121 36W
Cheviot, The, U.K. 10 B5 55 29N 2 9W
Cheviot Hills, U.K. 10 B5 55 20N 2 30W
Cheviot Ra., Australia 62 D3 25 20S 143 45 E
Chew Bahir, Ethiopia 46 G2 4 40N 36 50 E
Chewelah, U.S.A. 82 B5 48 17N 117 43W
Cheyenne, Okla., U.S.A. 81 H5 35 37N 99 40W
Cheyenne, Wyo., U.S.A. 80 E2 41 8N 104 49W
Cheyenne —►, U.S.A. 80 C4 44 41N 101 18W
Cheyenne Wells, U.S.A. 80 F3 38 49N 102 21W
Cheyne B., Australia 61 F2 34 35S 118 50 E
Chhabra, India 42 G7 24 40N 76 54 E
Chhaktala, India 42 H6 22 6N 74 11 E
Chhapra, India 43 G11 25 48N 84 44 E
Chhata, India 42 F7 27 42N 77 30 E
Chhatarpur, Bihar, India 43 G11 24 23N 84 11 E
Chhatarpur, Mad. P., India 43 G8 24 55N 79 35 E
Chhep, Cambodia 38 F5 13 45N 105 24 E
Chhindwara, Mad. P., India 43 H8 23 3N 79 29 E
Chhindwara, Mad. P., India 43 H8 22 2N 78 59 E
Chhlong, Cambodia 39 F5 12 15N 105 58 E
Chhota Tawa —►, India 42 H7 22 14N 76 36 E
Chhoti Kali Sindh —►, India 42 G6 24 2N 75 31 E
Chhuikhadan, India 43 J9 21 32N 80 59 E
Chhuk, Cambodia 39 G5 10 46N 104 28 E
Chi —►, Thailand 38 E5 15 11N 104 43 E
Chiai, Taiwan 33 D7 23 29N 120 25 E
Chiamboni, Somali Rep. 52 E8 1 39S 41 35 E
Chiamussu = Jiamusi, China 33 B8 46 40N 130 26 E
Chiang Dao, Thailand 38 C2 19 22N 98 58 E
Chiang Kham, Thailand 38 C3 19 32N 100 18 E
Chiang Khan, Thailand 38 D3 17 52N 101 36 E
Chiang Mai, Thailand 38 C2 18 47N 98 59 E
Chiang Rai, Thailand 38 C2 19 52N 99 50 E
Chiapa —►, Mexico 87 D6 16 42N 93 0W
Chiapa de Corzo, Mexico 87 D6 16 42N 93 0W
Chiapas □, Mexico 87 D6 17 0N 92 45W
Chiautla, Mexico 87 D5 18 18N 98 34W
Chiávari, Italy 18 D8 44 19N 9 19 E
Chiavenna, Italy 18 C8 46 19N 9 24 E
Chiba, Japan 31 G10 35 30N 140 7 E
Chiba □, Japan 31 G10 35 30N 140 20 E
Chibabava, Mozam. 57 C5 20 17S 33 35 E
Chibemba, Cunene, Angola 53 H2 15 48S 14 8 E
Chibemba, Huila, Angola 56 B2 16 20S 15 20 E
Chibia, Angola 53 H2 15 10S 13 42 E
Chibougamau, Canada 70 C5 49 56N 74 24W
Chibougamau L., Canada 70 C5 49 50N 74 20W
Chic-Chocs, Mts., Canada 71 C6 48 55N 66 0W
Chicacole = Srikakulam, India 41 K13 18 14N 83 58 E
Chicago, U.S.A. 76 E2 41 53N 87 38W
Chicago Heights, U.S.A. 76 E2 41 30N 87 38W
Chichagof I., U.S.A. 68 C6 57 30N 135 30W
Chichén-Itzá, Mexico 87 C7 20 40N 88 36W
Chicheng, China 34 D8 40 55N 115 55 E
Chichester, U.K. 11 G7 50 50N 0 47W
Chichester Ra., Australia 60 D2 22 12S 119 15 E
Chichibu, Japan 31 F9 36 5N 139 10 E
Ch'ich'ihaerh = Qiqihar, China 27 E13 47 26N 124 0 E
Chicholi, India 42 H8 22 1N 77 40 E
Chickasha, U.S.A. 81 H6 35 3N 97 58W
Chiclana de la Frontera, Spain 19 D2 36 26N 6 9W
Chiclayo, Peru 92 E3 6 42S 79 50W
Chico, U.S.A. 84 F5 39 44N 121 50W
Chico —►, Chubut, Argentina 96 E3 44 0S 67 0W
Chico —►, Santa Cruz, Argentina 96 G3 50 0S 68 30W
Chicomo, Mozam. 57 C5 24 31S 34 6 E
Chicontepec, Mexico 87 C5 20 58N 98 10W
Chicopee, U.S.A. 79 D12 42 9N 72 37W
Chicoutimi, Canada 71 C5 48 28N 71 5W
Chicualacuala, Mozam. 57 C5 22 6S 31 42 E
Chidambaram, India 40 P11 11 20N 79 45 E
Chidenguele, Mozam. 57 C5 24 55S 34 11 E
Chidley, C., Canada 69 B13 60 23N 64 26W
Chiede, Angola 56 B2 17 15S 16 22 E
Chiefs Pt., Canada 78 B3 44 41N 81 18W
Chiem Hoa, Vietnam 38 A5 22 12N 105 17 E
Chiemsee, Germany 16 E7 47 53N 12 28 E
Chiengi, Zambia 55 D2 8 45S 29 10 E
Chiengmai = Chiang Mai, Thailand 38 C2 18 47N 98 59 E
Chiese —►, Italy 18 D9 45 8N 10 25 E
Chieti, Italy 20 C6 42 21N 14 10 E
Chifeng, China 35 C10 42 18N 118 58 E
Chignecto B., Canada 71 C7 45 30N 64 40W
Chiguana, Bolivia 94 A2 21 0S 67 58W
Chigwell, U.K. 11 F8 51 37N 0 5 E
Chiha-ri, N. Korea 35 E14 38 40N 126 30 E
Chihli, G. of = Bo Hai, China 35 E10 39 0N 119 0 E
Chihuahua, Mexico 86 B3 28 40N 106 3W
Chihuahua □, Mexico 86 B3 28 40N 106 3W
Chiili, Kazakstan 26 E7 44 20N 66 15 E
Chik Bollapur, India 40 N10 13 25N 77 45 E
Chikmagalur, India 40 N9 13 15N 75 45 E
Chikwawa, Malawi 55 F3 16 2S 34 50 E
Chilac, Mexico 87 D5 18 20N 97 24W
Chilam Chavki, Pakistan 43 B6 35 5N 75 5 E
Chilanga, Zambia 55 F2 15 33S 28 16 E
Chilapa, Mexico 87 D5 17 40N 99 11W
Chilas, Pakistan 43 B6 35 25N 74 5 E
Chilaw, Sri Lanka 40 R11 7 30N 79 50 E
Chilcotin —►, Canada 72 C4 51 44N 122 23W
Childers, Australia 63 D5 25 15S 152 17 E
Childress, U.S.A. 81 H4 34 25N 100 13W
Chile ■, S. Amer. 96 D2 35 0S 72 0W
Chile Rise, Pac. Oc. 65 L18 38 0S 92 0W
Chilecito, Argentina 94 B2 29 10S 67 30W
Chilete, Peru 92 E3 7 10S 78 50W
Chililabombwe, Zambia 55 E2 12 18S 27 43 E
Chilin = Jilin, China 35 C14 43 44N 126 30 E
Chilka L., India 41 K14 19 40N 85 25 E
Chilko —►, Canada 72 C4 52 0N 123 40W
Chilko L., Canada 72 C4 51 20N 124 10W
Chillagoe, Australia 62 B3 17 7S 144 33 E
Chillán, Chile 94 D1 36 40S 72 10W
Chillicothe, Ill., U.S.A. 80 E10 40 55N 89 29W
Chillicothe, Mo., U.S.A. 80 F8 39 48N 93 33W
Chillicothe, Ohio, U.S.A. 76 F4 39 20N 82 59W
Chilliwack, Canada 72 D4 49 10N 121 54W
Chilo, India 42 F5 27 25N 73 32 E
Chiloane, I., Mozam. 57 C5 20 40S 34 55 E
Chiloé, I. de, Chile 96 E2 42 30S 73 50W
Chilpancingo, Mexico 87 D5 17 30N 99 30W
Chiltern Hills, U.K. 11 F7 51 40N 0 53W
Chilton, U.S.A. 76 C1 44 2N 88 10W
Chilubi, Zambia 55 E2 11 5S 29 58 E
Chilubula, Zambia 55 E3 10 14S 30 51 E
Chilumba, Malawi 55 E3 10 28S 34 12 E
Chilung, Taiwan 33 D7 25 3N 121 45 E
Chilwa, L., Malawi 55 F4 15 15S 35 40 E
Chimaltitán, Mexico 86 C4 21 46N 103 50W
Chimán, Panama 88 E4 8 45N 78 40W
Chimay, Belgium 15 D4 50 3N 4 20 E
Chimayo, U.S.A. 83 H11 36 0N 105 56W
Chimbay, Uzbekistan 26 E6 42 57N 59 47 E
Chimborazo, Ecuador 92 D3 1 29S 78 55W
Chimbote, Peru 92 E3 9 0S 78 35W
Chimkent = Shymkent, Kazakstan 26 E7 42 18N 69 36 E
Chimoio, Mozam. 55 F3 19 4S 33 30 E
Chimpembe, Zambia 55 D2 9 31S 29 33 E
Chin □, Burma 41 J18 22 0N 93 0 E
Chin Ling Shan = Qinling Shandi, China 34 H5 33 50N 108 10 E
China, Mexico 87 B5 25 40N 99 20W
China ■, Asia 33 D6 30 0N 110 0 E
China Lake, U.S.A. 85 K9 35 44N 117 37W
Chinan = Jinan, China 34 F9 36 38N 117 1 E
Chinandega, Nic. 88 D2 12 35N 87 12W
Chinati Peak, U.S.A. 81 L2 29 57N 104 29W
Chincha Alta, Peru 92 F3 13 25S 76 7W
Chinchaga —►, Canada 72 B5 58 53N 118 20W
Chinchilla, Australia 63 D5 26 45S 150 38 E

Corrientes

Corrientes □, *Argentina* 94 B4 28 0S 57 0W
Corrientes —►, *Argentina* 94 C4 30 42S 59 38W
Corrientes —►, *Peru* 92 D4 3 43S 74 35W
Corrientes, C., *Colombia* 92 B3 5 30N 77 34W
Corrientes, C., *Cuba* 88 B3 21 43N 84 30W
Corrientes, C., *Mexico* 86 C3 20 25N 105 42W
Corrigan, *U.S.A.* 81 K7 31 0N 94 52W
Corrigin, *Australia* 61 F2 32 20S 117 53 E
Corry, *U.S.A.* 78 E5 41 55N 79 39W
Corryong, *Australia* 63 F4 36 12S 147 53 E
Corse, *France* 18 F8 42 0N 9 0 E
Corse, C., *France* 18 E8 43 1N 9 25 E
Corsica = Corse, *France* 18 F8 42 0N 9 0 E
Corsicana, *U.S.A.* 81 J6 32 6N 96 28W
Corte, *France* 18 E8 42 19N 9 11 E
Cortez, *U.S.A.* 83 H9 37 21N 108 35W
Cortland, *N.Y., U.S.A.* 79 D8 42 36N 76 11W
Cortland, *Ohio, U.S.A.* 78 E4 41 20N 80 44W
Çorum, *Turkey* 25 F5 40 30N 34 57 E
Corumbá, *Brazil* 92 G7 19 0S 57 30W
Corunna = A Coruña, *Spain* 19 A1 43 20N 8 25W
Corvallis, *U.S.A.* 82 D2 44 34N 123 16W
Corvette, L. de la, *Canada* 70 B5 53 25N 74 3W
Corydon, *U.S.A.* 80 E8 40 46N 93 19W
Cosalá, *Mexico* 86 C3 24 28N 106 40W
Cosamaloapan, *Mexico* 87 D5 18 23N 95 50W
Cosenza, *Italy* 20 E7 39 18N 16 15 E
Coshocton, *U.S.A.* 78 F3 40 16N 81 51W
Cosmo Newberry, *Australia* 61 E3 28 0S 122 54 E
Coso Junction, *U.S.A.* 85 J9 36 3N 117 57W
Coso Pk., *U.S.A.* 85 J9 36 13N 117 44W
Cosquín, *Argentina* 94 C3 31 15S 64 30W
Costa Blanca, *Spain* 19 C5 38 25N 0 10W
Costa Brava, *Spain* 19 B7 41 30N 3 0 E
Costa del Sol, *Spain* 19 D3 36 30N 4 30W
Costa Dorada, *Spain* 19 B6 41 12N 1 15 E
Costa Mesa, *U.S.A.* 85 M9 33 38N 117 55W
Costa Rica ■, *Cent. Amer.* 88 E3 10 0N 84 0W
Cosumnes —►, *U.S.A.* 84 G5 38 16N 121 26W
Cotabato, *Phil.* 37 C6 7 14N 124 15 E
Cotagaita, *Bolivia* 94 A2 20 45S 65 40W
Côte d'Azur, *France* 18 E7 43 25N 7 10 E
Côte-d'Ivoire = Ivory Coast ■, *Africa* 50 G4 7 30N 5 0W
Coteau des Prairies, *U.S.A.* 80 C6 45 20N 97 50W
Coteau du Missouri, *U.S.A.* 80 B4 47 0N 100 0W
Coteau Landing, *Canada* 79 A10 45 15N 74 13W
Cotentin, *France* 18 B3 49 15N 1 30W
Cotillo, *Canary Is.* 22 F5 28 41N 14 1W
Cotonou, *Benin* 50 G6 6 20N 2 25 E
Cotopaxi, *Ecuador* 92 D3 0 40S 78 30W
Cotswold Hills, *U.K.* 11 F5 51 42N 2 10W
Cottage Grove, *U.S.A.* 82 E2 43 48N 123 3W
Cottbus, *Germany* 16 C8 51 45N 14 20 E
Cottonwood, *U.S.A.* 83 J7 34 45N 112 1W
Cotulla, *U.S.A.* 81 L5 28 26N 99 14W
Coudersport, *U.S.A.* 78 E6 41 46N 78 1W
Couedic, C. du, *Australia* 63 F2 36 5S 136 40 E
Coulee City, *U.S.A.* 82 C4 47 37N 119 17W
Coulman I., *Antarctica* 5 D11 73 35S 170 0 E
Coulonge —►, *Canada* 70 C4 45 52N 76 46W
Coulterville, *U.S.A.* 84 H6 37 43N 120 12W
Council, *U.S.A.* 82 D5 44 44N 116 26W
Council Bluffs, *U.S.A.* 80 E7 41 16N 95 52W
Council Grove, *U.S.A.* 80 F6 38 40N 96 29W
Coupeville, *U.S.A.* 84 B4 48 13N 122 41W
Courantyne —►, *S. Amer.* 92 B7 5 55N 57 5W
Courcelles, *Belgium* 15 D4 50 28N 4 22 E
Courtenay, *Canada* 72 D4 49 45N 125 0W
Courtland, *U.S.A.* 84 G5 38 20N 121 34W
Courtrai = Kortrijk, *Belgium* 15 D3 50 50N 3 17 E
Courtright, *Canada* 78 D2 42 49N 82 28W
Coushatta, *U.S.A.* 81 J8 32 1N 93 21W
Coutts Crossing, *Australia* 63 D5 29 49S 152 55 E
Couvin, *Belgium* 15 D4 50 3N 4 29 E
Cove I., *Canada* 78 A3 45 17N 81 44W
Coventry, *U.K.* 11 E6 52 25N 1 28W
Covilhã, *Portugal* 19 B2 40 17N 7 31W
Covington, *Ga., U.S.A.* 77 J4 33 36N 83 51W
Covington, *Ky., U.S.A.* 76 F3 39 5N 84 31W
Covington, *Okla., U.S.A.* 81 G6 36 18N 97 35W
Covington, *Tenn., U.S.A.* 81 H10 35 34N 89 39W
Covington, *Va., U.S.A.* 76 G5 37 47N 79 59W
Cowal, L., *Australia* 63 E4 33 40S 147 25 E
Cowan, L., *Australia* 61 F3 31 45S 121 45 E
Cowan L., *Canada* 73 C7 54 0N 107 15W
Cowangie, *Australia* 63 F3 35 12S 141 26 E
Cowansville, *Canada* 79 A12 45 14N 72 46W
Coward Springs, *Australia* 63 D2 29 24S 136 49 E
Cowcowing Lakes, *Australia* 61 F2 30 55S 117 20 E
Cowdenbeath, *U.K.* 12 E5 56 7N 3 21W
Cowell, *Australia* 63 E2 33 39S 136 56 E
Cowes, *U.K.* 11 G6 50 45N 1 18W
Cowichan L., *Canada* 84 B2 48 53N 124 17W
Cowlitz —►, *U.S.A.* 84 D4 46 6N 122 55W
Cowra, *Australia* 63 E4 33 49S 148 42 E
Coxilha Grande, *Brazil* 95 B5 28 18S 51 30W
Coxim, *Brazil* 93 G8 18 30S 54 55W
Cox's Bazar, *Bangla.* 41 J17 21 26N 91 59 E
Coyote Wells, *U.S.A.* 85 N11 32 44N 115 58W
Coyuca de Benítez, *Mexico* 87 D4 17 1N 100 8W
Coyuca de Catalan, *Mexico* 86 D4 18 18N 100 41W
Cozad, *U.S.A.* 80 E5 40 52N 99 59W
Cozumel, *Mexico* 87 C7 20 31N 86 55W
Cozumel, Isla, *Mexico* 87 C7 20 30N 86 40W
Cracow = Kraków, *Poland* 17 C10 50 4N 19 57 E
Cracow, *Australia* 63 D5 25 17S 150 17 E
Cradock, *Australia* 63 E2 32 6S 138 31 E
Cradock, *S. Africa* 56 E4 32 8S 25 36 E
Craig, *U.S.A.* 82 F10 40 31N 107 33W
Craigavon, *U.K.* 13 B5 54 27N 6 23W
Craigmore, *Zimbabwe* 55 G3 20 28S 32 50 E
Craik, *Canada* 73 C7 51 3N 105 49W
Crailsheim, *Germany* 16 D6 49 8N 10 5 E
Craiova, *Romania* 17 F12 44 21N 23 48 E
Cramsie, *Australia* 62 C3 23 20S 144 15 E
Cranberry L., *U.S.A.* 79 B10 44 11N 74 50W
Cranberry Portage, *Canada* 73 C8 54 35N 101 23W
Cranbrook, *Australia* 61 F2 34 18S 117 33 E
Cranbrook, *Canada* 72 D5 49 30N 115 46W
Crandon, *U.S.A.* 80 C10 45 34N 88 54W
Crane, *Oreg., U.S.A.* 82 E4 43 25N 118 35W
Crane, *Tex., U.S.A.* 81 K3 31 24N 102 21W
Cranston, *U.S.A.* 79 E13 41 47N 71 26W
Crater L., *U.S.A.* 82 E2 42 56N 122 6W
Crater Lake National Park, *U.S.A.* 82 E2 42 55N 122 10W
Crateús, *Brazil* 93 E10 5 10S 40 39W
Crato, *Brazil* 93 E11 7 10S 39 25W
Craven, L., *Canada* 70 B4 54 20N 76 56W
Crawford, *U.S.A.* 80 D3 42 41N 103 25W
Crawfordsville, *U.S.A.* 76 E2 40 2N 86 54W
Crawley, *U.K.* 11 F7 51 7N 0 11W
Crazy Mts., *U.S.A.* 82 C8 46 12N 110 20W
Crean L., *Canada* 73 C7 54 5N 106 9W
Crediton, *Canada* 78 C3 43 17N 81 33W
Cree —►, *Canada* 73 B7 58 57N 105 47W
Cree —►, *U.K.* 12 G4 54 55N 4 25W
Cree L., *Canada* 73 B7 57 30N 106 30W
Creede, *U.S.A.* 83 H10 37 51N 106 56W
Creekside, *U.S.A.* 78 F5 40 40N 79 11W
Creel, *Mexico* 86 B3 27 45N 107 38W
Creemore, *Canada* 78 B4 44 19N 80 6W
Creighton, *Canada* 73 C8 54 45N 101 54W
Creighton, *U.S.A.* 80 D6 42 28N 97 54W
Crema, *Italy* 18 D8 45 22N 9 41 E
Cremona, *Italy* 18 D9 45 7N 10 2 E
Cres, *Croatia* 16 F8 44 58N 14 25 E
Crescent City, *U.S.A.* 82 F1 41 45N 124 12W
Crespo, *Argentina* 94 C3 32 2S 60 19W
Cresson, *U.S.A.* 78 F6 40 28N 78 36W
Crestline, *Calif., U.S.A.* 85 L9 34 14N 117 18W
Crestline, *Ohio, U.S.A.* 78 F2 40 47N 82 44W
Creston, *Canada* 72 D5 49 10N 116 31W
Creston, *Calif., U.S.A.* 84 K6 35 32N 120 33W
Creston, *Iowa, U.S.A.* 80 E7 41 4N 94 22W
Crestview, *Calif., U.S.A.* 84 H8 37 46N 118 58W
Crestview, *Fla., U.S.A.* 77 K2 30 46N 86 34W
Crete = Kríti, *Greece* 23 D7 35 15N 25 0 E
Crete, *U.S.A.* 80 E6 40 38N 96 58W
Créteil, *France* 18 B5 48 47N 2 28 E
Creus, C. de, *Spain* 19 A7 42 20N 3 19 E
Creuse —►, *France* 18 C4 47 0N 0 34 E
Crewe, *U.K.* 10 D5 53 6N 2 26W
Crewkerne, *U.K.* 11 G5 50 53N 2 48W
Criciúma, *Brazil* 95 B6 28 40S 49 23W
Crieff, *U.K.* 12 E5 56 22N 3 50W
Crimea □, *Ukraine* 25 E5 45 30N 33 10 E
Crimean Pen. = Krymskyy Pivostriv, *Ukraine* 25 F5 45 0N 34 0 E
Crişul Alb —►, *Romania* 17 E11 46 42N 21 17 E
Crişul Negru —►, *Romania* 17 E11 46 42N 21 16 E
Crna —►, *Macedonia* 21 D9 41 33N 21 59 E
Crna Gora = Montenegro □, *Yugoslavia* 21 C8 42 40N 19 20 E
Crna Gora, *Macedonia* 21 C9 42 10N 21 30 E
Crna Reka = Crna —►, *Macedonia* 21 D9 41 33N 21 59 E
Croagh Patrick, *Ireland* 13 C2 53 46N 9 40W
Croatia ■, *Europe* 16 F9 45 20N 16 0 E
Crocker, Banjaran, *Malaysia* 36 C5 5 40N 116 30 E
Crockett, *U.S.A.* 81 K7 31 19N 95 27W
Crocodile = Krokodil —►, *Mozam.* 57 D5 25 14S 32 18 E
Crocodile Is., *Australia* 62 A1 12 3S 134 58 E
Crohy Hd., *Ireland* 13 B3 54 55N 8 26W
Croix, L. La, *Canada* 70 C1 48 20N 92 15W
Croker, C., *Australia* 60 B5 10 58S 132 35 E
Croker, C., *Canada* 78 B4 44 58N 80 59W
Croker I., *Australia* 60 B5 11 12S 132 32 E
Cromarty, *U.K.* 12 D4 57 40N 4 2W
Cromer, *U.K.* 10 E9 52 56N 1 17 E
Cromwell, *N.Z.* 59 L2 45 3S 169 14 E
Cromwell, *U.S.A.* 79 E12 41 36N 72 39W
Crook, *U.K.* 10 C6 54 43N 1 45W
Crooked —►, *Canada* 72 C4 54 50N 122 54W
Crooked —►, *U.S.A.* 82 D3 44 32N 121 16W
Crooked I., *Bahamas* 89 B5 22 50N 74 10W
Crooked Island Passage, *Bahamas* 89 B5 23 0N 74 30W
Crookston, *Minn., U.S.A.* 80 B6 47 47N 96 37W
Crookston, *Nebr., U.S.A.* 80 D4 42 56N 100 45W
Crookwell, *Australia* 63 E4 34 28S 149 24 E
Crosby, *U.K.* 10 D4 53 30N 3 3W
Crosby, *U.S.A.* 78 E6 41 45N 78 23W
Crosbyton, *U.S.A.* 81 J4 33 40N 101 14W
Cross City, *U.S.A.* 77 L4 29 38N 83 7W
Cross Fell, *U.K.* 10 C5 54 43N 2 28W
Cross L., *Canada* 73 C9 54 45N 97 30W
Cross Lake, *Canada* 73 C9 54 37N 97 47W
Cross Sound, *U.S.A.* 68 C6 58 0N 135 0W
Crossett, *U.S.A.* 81 J9 33 8N 91 58W
Crosshaven, *Ireland* 13 E3 51 47N 8 17W
Crossville, *U.S.A.* 77 G3 35 57N 85 2W
Croswell, *U.S.A.* 78 C2 43 16N 82 37W
Croton-on-Hudson, *U.S.A.* 79 E11 41 12N 73 55W
Crotone, *Italy* 20 E7 39 5N 17 8 E
Crow —►, *Canada* 72 B4 59 41N 124 20W
Crow Agency, *U.S.A.* 82 D10 45 36N 107 28W
Crow Hd., *Ireland* 13 E1 51 35N 10 9W
Crowell, *U.S.A.* 81 J5 33 59N 99 43W
Crowley, *U.S.A.* 81 K8 30 13N 92 22W
Crowley, L., *U.S.A.* 84 H8 37 35N 118 42W
Crown Point, *Ind., U.S.A.* 76 E2 41 25N 87 22W
Crown Point, *N.Y., U.S.A.* 79 C11 43 57N 73 26W
Crownpoint, *U.S.A.* 83 J9 35 41N 108 9W
Crows Landing, *U.S.A.* 84 H5 37 23N 121 6W
Crows Nest, *Australia* 63 D5 27 16S 152 4 E
Crowsnest Pass, *Canada* 72 D6 49 40N 114 40W
Croydon, *Australia* 62 B3 18 13S 142 14 E
Croydon, *U.K.* 11 F7 51 22N 0 5W
Crozet Is., *Ind. Oc.* 3 G12 46 27S 52 0 E
Cruz, C., *Cuba* 88 C4 19 50N 77 50W
Cruz Alta, *Brazil* 95 B5 28 45S 53 40W
Cruz del Eje, *Argentina* 94 C3 30 45S 64 50W
Cruzeiro, *Brazil* 95 A7 22 33S 45 0W
Cruzeiro do Oeste, *Brazil* 95 A5 23 46S 53 4W
Cruzeiro do Sul, *Brazil* 92 E4 7 35S 72 35W
Cry L., *Canada* 72 B3 58 45N 129 0W
Crystal Bay, *U.S.A.* 84 F7 39 15N 120 0W
Crystal Brook, *Australia* 63 E2 33 21S 138 12 E
Crystal City, *U.S.A.* 81 L5 28 41N 99 50W
Crystal Falls, *U.S.A.* 76 B1 46 5N 88 20W
Crystal River, *U.S.A.* 77 L4 28 54N 82 35W
Crystal Springs, *U.S.A.* 81 K9 31 59N 90 21W
Csongrád, *Hungary* 17 E11 46 43N 20 12 E
Cu Lao Hon, *Vietnam* 39 G7 10 54N 108 18 E
Cua Rao, *Vietnam* 38 C5 19 16N 104 27 E
Cuácua —►, *Mozam.* 55 F4 17 54S 37 0 E
Cuamato, *Angola* 56 B2 17 2S 15 7 E
Cuamba, *Mozam.* 55 E4 14 45S 36 22 E
Cuando —►, *Angola* 53 H4 17 30S 23 15 E
Cuando Cubango □, *Angola* 56 B3 16 25S 20 0 E
Cuangar, *Angola* 56 B2 17 36S 18 39 E
Cuanza —►, *Angola* 52 F2 9 2S 13 30 E
Cuarto —►, *Argentina* 94 C3 33 25S 63 2W
Cuatrociénegas, *Mexico* 86 B4 26 59N 102 5W
Cuauhtémoc, *Mexico* 86 B3 28 25N 106 52W
Cuba, *N. Mex., U.S.A.* 83 J10 36 1N 107 4W
Cuba, *N.Y., U.S.A.* 78 D6 42 13N 78 17W
Cuba ■, *W. Indies* 88 B4 22 0N 79 0W
Cubal, *Angola* 53 G2 12 26S 14 3 E
Cubango —►, *Africa* 56 B3 18 50S 22 25 E
Cuchumatanes, Sierra de los, *Guatemala* 88 C1 15 35N 91 25W
Cuckfield, *U.K.* 11 F7 51 1N 0 8W
Cucuí, *Brazil* 92 C5 1 12N 66 50W
Cucurpe, *Mexico* 86 A2 30 20N 110 43W
Cúcuta, *Colombia* 92 B4 7 54N 72 31W
Cuddalore, *India* 40 P11 11 46N 79 45 E
Cuddapah, *India* 40 M11 14 30N 78 47 E
Cuddapah, L., *Australia* 62 D3 25 45S 141 26 E
Cue, *Australia* 61 E2 27 25S 117 54 E
Cuenca, *Ecuador* 92 D3 2 50S 79 9W
Cuenca, *Spain* 19 B4 40 5N 2 10W
Cuenca, Serranía de, *Spain* 19 C5 39 55N 1 50W
Cuernavaca, *Mexico* 87 D5 18 55N 99 15W
Cuero, *U.S.A.* 81 L6 29 6N 97 17W
Cuevas del Almanzora, *Spain* 19 D5 37 18N 1 58W
Cuevo, *Bolivia* 92 H6 20 15S 63 30W
Cuiabá, *Brazil* 93 G7 15 30S 56 0W
Cuiabá —►, *Brazil* 93 G7 17 5S 56 36W
Cuijk, *Neths.* 15 C5 51 44N 5 50 E
Cuilco, *Guatemala* 88 C1 15 24N 91 58W
Cuillin Hills, *U.K.* 12 D2 57 13N 6 15W
Cuillin Sd., *U.K.* 12 D2 57 4N 6 20W
Cuito —►, *Angola* 56 B3 18 1S 20 48 E
Cuitzeo, L. de, *Mexico* 86 D4 19 55N 101 5W
Cukai, *Malaysia* 39 K4 4 13N 103 25 E
Culbertson, *U.S.A.* 80 A2 48 9N 104 31W
Culcairn, *Australia* 63 F4 35 41S 147 3 E
Culgoa —►, *Australia* 63 D4 29 56S 146 20 E
Culiacán, *Mexico* 86 C3 24 50N 107 23W
Culiacán —►, *Mexico* 86 C3 24 30N 107 42W
Culion, *Phil.* 37 B6 11 54N 119 58 E
Cullarin Ra., *Australia* 63 E4 34 30S 149 30 E
Cullen, *U.K.* 12 D6 57 42N 2 49W
Cullen Pt., *Australia* 62 A3 11 57S 141 54 E
Cullera, *Spain* 19 C5 39 9N 0 17W
Cullman, *U.S.A.* 77 H2 34 11N 86 51W
Culpeper, *U.S.A.* 76 F7 38 30N 78 0W
Culuene —►, *Brazil* 93 F8 12 56S 52 51W
Culver, Pt., *Australia* 61 F3 32 54S 124 43 E
Culverden, *N.Z.* 59 K4 42 47S 172 49 E
Cumaná, *Venezuela* 92 A6 10 30N 64 5W
Cumberland, *B.C., Canada* 72 D4 49 40N 125 0W
Cumberland, *Ont., Canada* 79 A9 45 29N 75 24W
Cumberland, *U.S.A.* 76 F6 39 39N 78 46W
Cumberland —►, *U.S.A.* 77 G2 36 15N 87 0W
Cumberland, L., *U.S.A.* 77 G3 36 57N 84 55W
Cumberland I., *U.S.A.* 77 K5 30 50N 81 25W
Cumberland Is., *Australia* 62 C4 20 35S 149 10 E
Cumberland L., *Canada* 73 C8 54 3N 102 18W
Cumberland Pen., *Canada* 69 B13 67 0N 64 0W
Cumberland Plateau, *U.S.A.* 77 H3 36 0N 85 0W
Cumberland Sd., *Canada* 69 B13 65 30N 66 0W
Cumbernauld, *U.K.* 12 F5 55 57N 3 58W
Cumborah, *Australia* 63 D4 29 40S 147 45 E
Cumbria □, *U.K.* 10 C5 54 42N 2 52W
Cumbrian Mts., *U.K.* 10 C5 54 30N 3 0W
Cumbum, *India* 40 M11 15 40N 79 10 E
Cuminá —►, *Brazil* 93 D7 1 30S 56 0W
Cummings Mt., *U.S.A.* 85 K8 35 2N 118 34W
Cummins, *Australia* 63 E2 34 16S 135 43 E
Cumnock, *Australia* 63 E4 32 59S 148 46 E
Cumnock, *U.K.* 12 F4 55 28N 4 17W
Cumpas, *Mexico* 86 B3 30 0N 109 48W
Cumplida, Pta., *Canary Is.* 22 F2 28 50N 17 48W
Cunco, *Chile* 96 D2 38 55S 72 2W
Cuncumén, *Chile* 94 C1 31 53S 70 38W
Cunderdin, *Australia* 61 F2 31 37S 117 12 E
Cunene —►, *Angola* 56 B1 17 20S 11 50 E
Cúneo, *Italy* 18 D7 44 23N 7 32 E
Çüngüş, *Turkey* 44 B3 38 13N 39 17 E
Cunillera, I. = Sa Conillera, *Spain* 22 C7 38 59N 1 13 E
Cunnamulla, *Australia* 63 D4 28 2S 145 38 E
Cupar, *Canada* 73 C8 50 57N 104 10W
Cupar, *U.K.* 12 E5 56 19N 3 1W
Cupica, G. de, *Colombia* 92 B3 6 25N 77 30W
Curaçao, *Neth. Ant.* 89 D6 12 10N 69 0W
Curanilahue, *Chile* 94 D1 37 29S 73 28W
Curaray —►, *Peru* 92 D4 2 20S 74 5W
Curepto, *Chile* 94 D1 35 8S 72 1W
Curiapo, *Venezuela* 92 B6 8 33N 61 5W
Curicó, *Chile* 94 C1 34 55S 71 20W
Curitiba, *Brazil* 95 B6 25 20S 49 10W
Curitibanos, *Brazil* 95 B5 27 18S 50 36W
Currabubula, *Australia* 63 E5 31 16S 150 44 E
Currais Novos, *Brazil* 93 E11 6 13S 36 30W
Curralinho, *Brazil* 93 D9 1 45S 49 46W
Currant, *U.S.A.* 82 G6 38 51N 115 32W
Current —►, *U.S.A.* 81 G9 36 15N 90 55W
Currie, *Australia* 62 F3 39 56S 143 53 E
Currie, *U.S.A.* 82 F6 40 16N 114 45W
Curtea de Argeş, *Romania* 17 F13 45 12N 24 42 E
Curtis, *U.S.A.* 80 E4 40 38N 100 31W
Curtis Group, *Australia* 62 F4 39 30S 146 37 E
Curtis I., *Australia* 62 C5 23 35S 151 10 E
Curuápanema —►, *Brazil* 93 D7 2 25S 55 2W
Curuçá, *Brazil* 93 D9 0 43S 47 50W
Curuguaty, *Paraguay* 95 A4 24 31S 55 42W
Curup, *Indonesia* 36 E2 4 26S 102 13 E
Cururupu, *Brazil* 93 D10 1 50S 44 50W
Curuzú Cuatiá, *Argentina* 94 B4 29 50S 58 5W
Curvelo, *Brazil* 93 G10 18 45S 44 27W
Cushing, *U.S.A.* 81 H6 35 59N 96 46W
Cushing, Mt., *Canada* 72 B3 57 35N 126 57W
Cusihuiriáchic, *Mexico* 86 B3 28 10N 106 50W
Custer, *U.S.A.* 80 D3 43 46N 103 36W
Cut Bank, *U.S.A.* 82 B7 48 38N 112 20W
Cutchogue, *U.S.A.* 79 E12 41 1N 72 30W
Cuthbert, *U.S.A.* 77 K3 31 46N 84 48W
Cutler, *U.S.A.* 84 J7 36 31N 119 17W
Cuttaburra —►, *Australia* 63 D3 29 43S 144 22 E
Cuttack, *India* 41 J14 20 25N 85 57 E
Cuvier, C., *Australia* 61 D1 23 14S 113 22 E
Cuvier I., *N.Z.* 59 G5 36 27S 175 50 E
Cuxhaven, *Germany* 16 B5 53 51N 8 41 E
Cuyahoga Falls, *U.S.A.* 78 E3 41 8N 81 29W
Cuyo, *Phil.* 37 B6 10 50N 121 5 E
Cuyuni —►, *Guyana* 92 B7 6 23N 58 41W
Cuzco, *Bolivia* 92 H5 20 0S 66 50W
Cuzco, *Peru* 92 F4 13 32S 72 0W
Cwmbran, *U.K.* 11 F4 51 39N 3 2W
Cyangugu, *Rwanda* 54 C2 2 29S 28 54 E
Cyclades = Kikládhes, *Greece* 21 F11 37 0N 24 30 E
Cygnet, *Australia* 62 G4 43 8S 147 1 E
Cynthiana, *U.S.A.* 76 F3 38 23N 84 18W
Cypress Hills, *Canada* 73 D7 49 40N 109 30W
Cypress Hills Prov. Park, *Canada* 73 D7 49 40N 109 30W
Cyprus ■, *Asia* 23 E12 35 0N 33 0 E
Cyrenaica, *Libya* 51 C10 27 0N 23 0 E
Czar, *Canada* 73 C6 52 27N 110 50W
Czech Rep. ■, *Europe* 16 D8 50 0N 15 0 E
Częstochowa, *Poland* 17 C10 50 49N 19 7 E

D

Da Hinggan Ling, *China* 33 B7 48 0N 121 0 E
Da Lat, *Vietnam* 39 G7 11 56N 108 25 E
Da Nang, *Vietnam* 38 D7 16 4N 108 13 E
Da Qaidam, *China* 32 C4 37 50N 95 15 E
Da Yunhe —►, *China* 35 G11 34 25N 120 5 E
Da'an, *China* 35 B13 45 30N 124 7 E
Daba Shan, *China* 33 C5 32 0N 109 0 E
Dabbagh, Jabal, *Si. Arabia* 44 E2 27 52N 35 45 E
Dabhoi, *India* 42 H5 22 10N 73 20 E
Dabo = Pasirkuning, *Indonesia* 36 E2 0 30S 104 33 E
Dabola, *Guinea* 50 F3 10 50N 11 5W
Dabung, *Malaysia* 39 K4 5 23N 102 1 E
Dacca = Dhaka, *Bangla.* 43 H14 23 43N 90 26 E
Dacca = Dhaka □, *Bangla.* 43 G14 24 25N 90 25 E
Dachau, *Germany* 16 D6 48 15N 11 26 E
Dadanawa, *Guyana* 92 C7 2 50N 59 30W
Dade City, *U.S.A.* 77 L4 28 22N 82 11W
Dadhar, *Pakistan* 42 E2 29 28N 67 39 E
Dadra & Nagar Haveli □, *India* 40 J8 20 5N 73 0 E
Dadri = Charkhi Dadri, *India* 42 E7 28 37N 76 17 E
Dadu, *Pakistan* 42 F2 26 45N 67 45 E
Daet, *Phil.* 37 B6 14 2N 122 55 E
Dagana, *Senegal* 50 E2 16 30N 15 35W
Dagestan □, *Russia* 25 F8 42 30N 47 0 E
Daggett, *U.S.A.* 85 L10 34 52N 116 52W
Daghestan Republic = Dagestan □, *Russia* 25 F8 42 30N 47 0 E
Dağlıq Qarabağ = Nagorno-Karabakh, *Azerbaijan* 25 F8 39 55N 46 45 E
Dagö = Hiiumaa, *Estonia* 9 G20 58 50N 22 45 E
Dagu, *China* 35 E9 38 59N 117 40 E
Dagupan, *Phil.* 37 A6 16 3N 120 20 E
Daguragu, *Australia* 60 C5 17 33S 130 30 E
Dahlak Kebir, *Eritrea* 46 D3 15 50N 40 10 E
Dahlonega, *U.S.A.* 77 H4 34 32N 83 59W
Dahod, *India* 42 H6 22 50N 74 15 E
Dahomey = Benin ■, *Africa* 50 G6 10 0N 2 0 E
Dahūk, *Iraq* 44 B3 36 50N 43 1 E
Dai Hao, *Vietnam* 38 C6 18 1N 106 25 E
Dai-Sen, *Japan* 31 G6 35 22N 133 32 E
Dai Xian, *China* 34 E7 39 4N 112 58 E
Daicheng, *China* 34 E9 38 42N 116 38 E
Daingean, *Ireland* 13 C4 53 18N 7 17W
Daintree, *Australia* 62 B4 16 20S 145 20 E
Daiō-Misaki, *Japan* 31 G8 34 15N 136 45 E
Daisetsu-Zan, *Japan* 30 C11 43 30N 142 57 E
Dajarra, *Australia* 62 C2 21 42S 139 30 E
Dak Dam, *Cambodia* 38 F6 12 20N 107 21 E
Dak Nhe, *Vietnam* 38 E6 15 28N 107 48 E
Dak Pek, *Vietnam* 38 E6 15 4N 107 44 E
Dak Song, *Vietnam* 39 F6 12 19N 107 35 E
Dak Sui, *Vietnam* 38 E6 14 55N 107 43 E
Dakar, *Senegal* 50 F2 14 34N 17 29W
Dakhla, *W. Sahara* 50 D2 23 50N 15 53W
Dakhla, El Wâhât el-, *Egypt* 51 C11 25 30N 28 50 E
Dakor, *India* 42 H5 22 45N 73 11 E
Dakota City, *U.S.A.* 80 D6 42 25N 96 25W
Đakovica, *Yugoslavia* 21 C9 42 22N 20 26 E
Dalachi, *China* 34 F3 36 48N 105 0 E
Dalai Nur, *China* 34 C9 43 20N 116 45 E
Dālaki, *Iran* 45 D6 29 26N 51 17 E
Dalälven, *Sweden* 9 F17 60 12N 16 43 E
Dalaman —►, *Turkey* 21 F13 36 41N 28 43 E
Dalandzadgad, *Mongolia* 34 C3 43 27N 104 30 E
Dalap-Uliga-Darrit, *Marshall Is.* 64 G9 7 7N 171 24 E
Dalarna, *Sweden* 9 F16 61 0N 14 0 E
Dālbandīn, *Pakistan* 40 E4 29 0N 64 23 E
Dalbeattie, *U.K.* 12 G5 54 56N 3 50W
Dalbeg, *Australia* 62 C4 20 16S 147 18 E
Dalby, *Australia* 63 D5 27 10S 151 17 E
Dale City, *U.S.A.* 76 F7 38 38N 77 18W
Dale Hollow L., *U.S.A.* 77 G3 36 32N 85 27W
Dalgān, *Iran* 45 E8 27 31N 59 19 E
Dalhart, *U.S.A.* 81 G3 36 4N 102 31W
Dalhousie, *Canada* 71 C6 48 5N 66 26W
Dalhousie, *India* 42 C6 32 38N 75 58 E
Dali, *Shaanxi, China* 34 G5 34 48N 109 58 E
Dali, *Yunnan, China* 32 D5 25 40N 100 10 E
Dalian, *China* 35 E11 38 50N 121 40 E
Daliang Shan, *China* 32 D5 28 0N 102 45 E
Daling He —►, *China* 35 D11 40 55N 121 40 E
Dāliyat el Karmel, *Israel* 47 C4 32 43N 35 2 E
Dalkeith, *U.K.* 12 F5 55 54N 3 4W
Dallas, *Oreg., U.S.A.* 82 D2 44 55N 123 19W
Dallas, *Tex., U.S.A.* 81 J6 32 47N 96 49W
Dalmā, *U.A.E.* 45 E7 24 30N 52 20 E
Dalmacija, *Croatia* 20 C7 43 20N 17 0 E
Dalmas, L., *Canada* 71 B5 53 30N 71 50W
Dalmatia = Dalmacija, *Croatia* 20 C7 43 20N 17 0 E
Dalmau, *India* 43 F9 26 4N 81 2 E
Dalmellington, *U.K.* 12 F4 55 19N 4 23W
Dalnegorsk, *Russia* 27 E14 44 32N 135 33 E
Dalnerechensk, *Russia* 27 E14 45 50N 133 40 E
Daloa, *Ivory C.* 50 G4 7 0N 6 30W
Dalry, *U.K.* 12 F4 55 42N 4 43W
Dalrymple, L., *Australia* 62 C4 20 40S 147 0 E
Dalsland, *Sweden* 9 G14 58 50N 12 15 E
Daltenganj, *India* 43 H11 24 0N 84 4 E
Dalton, *Ga., U.S.A.* 77 H3 34 46N 84 58W

Eddystone Pt.

Dowerin, Australia 61 F2 31 12S 117 2 E
Dowgha'i, Iran 45 B8 36 54N 58 32 E
Dowlatābād, Iran 45 D8 28 20N 56 40 E
Down □, U.K. 13 B5 54 23N 6 2W
Downey, Calif., U.S.A. 85 M8 33 56N 118 7W
Downey, Idaho, U.S.A. 82 E7 42 26N 112 7W
Downham Market, U.K. 11 E8 52 37N 0 23 E
Downieville, U.S.A. 84 F6 39 34N 120 50W
Downpatrick, U.K. 13 B6 54 20N 5 43W
Downpatrick Hd., Ireland 13 B2 54 20N 9 21W
Downsville, U.S.A. 79 D10 42 5N 74 50W
Downton, Mt., Canada 72 C4 52 42N 124 52W
Dowsārī, Iran 45 D8 28 25N 57 59 E
Doyle, U.S.A. 84 E6 40 2N 120 6W
Doylestown, U.S.A. 79 F9 40 21N 75 10W
Dozois, Rés., Canada 70 C4 47 30N 77 5W
Dra Khel, Pakistan 42 F2 27 58N 66 45 E
Drachten, Neths. 15 A6 53 7N 6 5 E
Drăgăşani, Romania 17 F13 44 39N 24 17 E
Dragichyn, Belarus 17 B13 52 15N 25 8 E
Dragoman, Prokhod, Bulgaria 21 C10 42 58N 22 53 E
Draguignan, France 18 E7 43 32N 6 27 E
Drain, U.S.A. 82 E2 43 40N 123 19W
Drake, U.S.A. 80 B4 47 55N 100 23W
Drake Passage, S. Ocean 5 B17 58 0S 68 0W
Drakensberg, S. Africa 57 E4 31 0S 28 0 E
Dráma, Greece 21 D11 41 9N 24 10 E
Drammen, Norway 9 G14 59 42N 10 12 E
Drangajökull, Iceland 8 C2 66 9N 22 15W
Dras, India 43 B6 34 25N 75 48 E
Drau = Drava →, Croatia 21 B8 45 33N 18 55 E
Drava →, Croatia 21 B8 45 33N 18 55 E
Drayton Valley, Canada 72 C6 53 12N 114 58W
Drenthe □, Neths. 15 B6 52 52N 6 40 E
Drepanum, C., Cyprus 23 E11 34 54N 32 19 E
Dresden, Canada 78 D2 42 35N 82 11W
Dresden, Germany 16 C7 51 3N 13 44 E
Dreux, France 18 B4 48 44N 1 23 E
Driffield, U.K. 10 C7 54 0N 0 26W
Driftwood, U.S.A. 78 E6 41 20N 78 8W
Driggs, U.S.A. 82 E8 43 44N 111 6W
Drina →, Bos.-H. 21 B8 44 53N 19 21 E
Drini →, Albania 21 C8 42 1N 19 38 E
Drøbak, Norway 9 G14 59 39N 10 39 E
Drochia, Moldova 17 D14 48 2N 27 48 E
Drogheda, Ireland 13 C5 53 43N 6 22W
Drogichin = Dragichyn, Belarus 17 B13 52 15N 25 8 E
Drogobych = Drohobych, Ukraine 17 D12 49 20N 23 30 E
Drohobych, Ukraine 17 D12 49 20N 23 30 E
Droichead Atha = Drogheda, Ireland 13 C5 53 43N 6 22W
Droichead Nua, Ireland 13 C5 53 11N 6 48W
Droitwich, U.K. 11 E5 52 16N 2 8W
Dromedary, C., Australia 63 F5 36 17S 150 10 E
Dromore, U.K. 13 B4 54 31N 7 28W
Dromore West, Ireland 13 B3 54 15N 8 52W
Dronfield, U.K. 10 D6 53 19N 1 27W
Dronten, Neths. 15 B5 52 32N 5 43 E
Drumbo, Canada 78 C4 43 16N 80 35W
Drumheller, Canada 72 C6 51 25N 112 40W
Drummond, U.S.A. 82 C7 46 40N 113 9W
Drummond I., U.S.A. 76 C4 46 1N 83 39W
Drummond Pt., Australia 63 E2 34 9S 135 16 E
Drummond Ra., Australia 62 C4 23 45S 147 10 E
Drummondville, Canada 70 C5 45 55N 72 25W
Drumright, U.S.A. 81 H6 35 59N 96 36W
Druskininkai, Lithuania 9 J20 54 3N 23 58 E
Drut →, Belarus 17 B16 53 8N 30 5 E
Druzhina, Russia 27 C15 68 14N 145 18 E
Dry Tortugas, U.S.A. 88 B3 24 38N 82 55W
Dryden, Canada 73 D10 49 47N 92 50W
Dryden, U.S.A. 79 D8 42 30N 76 18W
Drygalski I., Antarctica 5 C7 66 0S 92 0 E
Drysdale →, Australia 60 B4 13 59S 126 51 E
Drysdale I., Australia 62 A2 11 41S 136 0 E
Du Bois, U.S.A. 78 E6 41 8N 78 46W
Du Gué →, Canada 70 A5 57 21N 70 45W
Du Quoin, U.S.A. 80 G10 38 1N 89 14W
Duanesburg, U.S.A. 79 D10 42 45N 74 11W
Duaringa, Australia 62 C4 23 42S 149 42 E
Ḍubā, Si. Arabia 44 E2 27 10N 35 40 E
Dubai = Dubayy, U.A.E. 45 E7 25 18N 55 20 E
Dubăsari, Moldova 17 E15 47 15N 29 10 E
Dubăsari Vdkhr., Moldova 17 E15 47 30N 29 0 E
Dubawnt →, Canada 73 A8 64 33N 100 6W
Dubawnt, L., Canada 73 A8 63 4N 101 42W
Dubayy, U.A.E. 45 E7 25 18N 55 20 E
Dubbo, Australia 63 E4 32 11S 148 35 E
Dubele, Dem. Rep. of the Congo 54 B2 2 56N 29 35 E
Dublin, Ireland 13 C5 53 21N 6 15W
Dublin, Ga., U.S.A. 77 J4 32 32N 82 54W
Dublin, Tex., U.S.A. 81 J5 32 5N 98 21W
Dublin □, Ireland 13 C5 53 24N 6 20W
Dubno, Ukraine 17 C13 50 25N 25 45 E
Dubois, U.S.A. 82 D7 44 10N 112 14W
Dubossary = Dubăsari, Moldova 17 E15 47 15N 29 10 E
Dubossary Vdkhr. = Dubăsari Vdkhr., Moldova 17 E15 47 30N 29 0 E
Dubovka, Russia 25 E7 49 5N 44 50 E
Dubrajpur, India 43 H12 23 48N 87 25 E
Dubréka, Guinea 50 G3 9 46N 13 31W
Dubrovitsa = Dubrovytsya, Ukraine 17 C14 51 31N 26 35 E
Dubrovnik, Croatia 21 C8 42 39N 18 6 E
Dubrovytsya, Ukraine 17 C14 51 31N 26 35 E
Dubuque, U.S.A. 80 D9 42 30N 90 41W
Duchesne, U.S.A. 82 F8 40 10N 110 24W
Duchess, Australia 62 C2 21 20S 139 50 E
Ducie I., Pac. Oc. 65 K15 24 40S 124 48W
Duck →, U.S.A. 77 G2 36 2N 87 52W
Duck Cr. →, Australia 60 D2 22 37S 116 53 E
Duck Lake, Canada 73 C7 52 50N 106 16W
Duck Mountain Prov. Park, Canada 73 C8 51 45N 101 0W
Duckwall, Mt., U.S.A. 84 H6 37 58N 120 7W
Dudhi, India 41 G13 24 15N 83 10 E
Dudinka, Russia 27 C9 69 30N 86 13 E
Dudley, U.K. 11 E5 52 31N 2 5W
Dudwa, India 43 E9 28 30N 80 41 E
Duero = Douro →, Europe 19 B1 41 8N 8 40W
Dufftown, U.K. 12 D5 57 27N 3 8W
Dugi Otok, Croatia 16 G8 44 0N 15 3 E
Duifken Pt., Australia 62 A3 12 33S 141 38 E
Duisburg, Germany 16 C4 51 26N 6 45 E
Duiwelskloof, S. Africa 57 C5 23 42S 30 10 E
Dūkdamīn, Iran 45 C8 35 59N 57 43 E
Dukelský Průsmyk, Slovak Rep. 17 D11 49 25N 21 42 E
Dukhān, Qatar 45 E6 25 25N 50 50 E
Duki, Pakistan 40 D6 30 14N 68 25 E
Duku, Nigeria 51 F8 10 43N 10 43 E
Dulce, U.S.A. 83 H10 36 56N 107 0W
Dulce →, Argentina 94 C3 30 32S 62 33W
Dulce, G., Costa Rica 88 E3 8 40N 83 20W
Dulf, Iraq 44 C5 35 7N 45 51 E
Dulit, Banjaran, Malaysia 36 D4 3 15N 114 30 E
Duliu, China 34 E9 39 2N 116 55 E
Dullewala, Pakistan 42 D4 31 50N 71 25 E
Dulq Maghār, Syria 44 B3 36 22N 38 39 E
Duluth, U.S.A. 80 B8 46 47N 92 6W
Dum Dum, India 43 H13 22 39N 88 33 E
Dum Duma, India 41 F19 27 40N 95 40 E
Dūmā, Syria 47 B5 33 34N 36 24 E
Dumaguete, Phil. 37 C6 9 17N 123 15 E
Dumai, Indonesia 36 D2 1 35N 101 28 E
Dumaran, Phil. 37 B5 10 33N 119 50 E
Dumas, Ark., U.S.A. 81 J9 33 53N 91 29W
Dumas, Tex., U.S.A. 81 H4 35 52N 101 58W
Ḍumayr, Syria 47 B5 33 39N 36 42 E
Dumbarton, U.K. 12 F4 55 57N 4 33W
Dumbleyung, Australia 61 F2 33 17S 117 42 E
Dumfries, U.K. 12 F5 55 4N 3 37W
Dumfries & Galloway □, U.K. 12 F5 55 9N 3 58W
Dumka, India 43 G12 24 12N 87 15 E
Dumoine →, Canada 70 C4 46 13N 77 51W
Dumoine, L., Canada 70 C4 46 55N 77 55W
Dumraon, India 43 G11 25 33N 84 8 E
Dumyât, Egypt 51 B12 31 24N 31 48 E
Dún Dealgan = Dundalk, Ireland 13 B5 54 1N 6 24W
Dun Laoghaire, Ireland 13 C5 53 17N 6 8W
Duna = Dunărea →, Europe 17 F15 45 20N 29 40 E
Dunagiri, India 43 D8 30 31N 79 52 E
Dunaj = Dunărea →, Europe 17 F15 45 20N 29 40 E
Dunakeszi, Hungary 17 E10 47 37N 19 8 E
Dunărea →, Europe 17 F15 45 20N 29 40 E
Dunaújváros, Hungary 17 E10 46 58N 18 57 E
Dunav = Dunărea →, Europe 17 F15 45 20N 29 40 E
Dunay, Russia 30 C6 42 52N 132 22 E
Dunback, N.Z. 59 L3 45 23S 170 36 E
Dunbar, U.K. 12 E6 56 0N 2 31W
Dunblane, U.K. 12 E5 56 11N 3 58W
Duncan, Canada 72 D4 48 45N 123 40W
Duncan, Ariz., U.S.A. 83 K9 32 43N 109 6W
Duncan, Okla., U.S.A. 81 H6 34 30N 97 57W
Duncan, L., Canada 70 B4 53 29N 77 58W
Duncan L., Canada 72 A6 62 51N 113 58W
Duncan Town, Bahamas 88 B4 22 15N 75 45W
Duncannon, U.S.A. 78 F7 40 23N 77 2W
Duncansby Head, U.K. 12 C5 58 38N 3 1W
Duncansville, U.S.A. 78 F6 40 25N 78 26W
Dundalk, Canada 78 B4 44 10N 80 24W
Dundalk, Ireland 13 B5 54 1N 6 24W
Dundalk, U.S.A. 76 F7 39 16N 76 32W
Dundalk Bay, Ireland 13 C5 53 55N 6 15W
Dundas, Canada 78 C5 43 17N 79 59W
Dundas, L., Australia 61 F3 32 35S 121 50 E
Dundas I., Canada 72 C2 54 30N 130 50W
Dundas Str., Australia 60 B5 11 15S 131 35 E
Dundee, S. Africa 57 D5 28 11S 30 15 E
Dundee, U.K. 12 E6 56 28N 2 59W
Dundee, U.S.A. 78 D8 42 32N 76 59W
Dundee City □, U.K. 12 E6 56 30N 2 58W
Dundgovĭ □, Mongolia 34 B4 45 10N 106 0 E
Dundrum, U.K. 13 B6 54 16N 5 52W
Dundrum B., U.K. 13 B6 54 13N 5 47W
Dunedin, N.Z. 59 L3 45 50S 170 33 E
Dunedin, U.S.A. 77 L4 28 1N 82 47W
Dunedoo, Australia 63 E4 32 0S 149 25 E
Dunfermline, U.K. 12 E5 56 5N 3 27W
Dungannon, Canada 78 C3 43 51N 81 36W
Dungannon, U.K. 13 B5 54 31N 6 46W
Dungarpur, India 42 H5 23 52N 73 45 E
Dungarvan, Ireland 13 D4 52 5N 7 37W
Dungarvan Harbour, Ireland 13 D4 52 4N 7 35W
Dungeness, U.K. 11 G8 50 54N 0 59 E
Dungo, L. do, Angola 56 B2 17 15S 19 0 E
Dungog, Australia 63 E5 32 22S 151 46 E
Dungu, Dem. Rep. of the Congo 54 B2 3 40N 28 32 E
Dungun, Malaysia 39 K4 4 45N 103 25 E
Dunhua, China 35 C15 43 20N 128 14 E
Dunhuang, China 32 B4 40 8N 94 36 E
Dunk I., Australia 62 B4 17 59S 146 29 E
Dunkeld, Australia 63 E4 33 25S 149 29 E
Dunkeld, U.K. 12 E5 56 34N 3 35W
Dunkerque, France 18 A5 51 2N 2 20 E
Dunkery Beacon, U.K. 11 F4 51 9N 3 36W
Dunkirk = Dunkerque, France 18 A5 51 2N 2 20 E
Dunkirk, U.S.A. 78 D5 42 29N 79 20W
Dúnleary = Dun Laoghaire, Ireland 13 C5 53 17N 6 8W
Dunleer, Ireland 13 C5 53 50N 6 24W
Dunmanus B., Ireland 13 E2 51 31N 9 50W
Dunmanway, Ireland 13 E2 51 43N 9 6W
Dunmara, Australia 62 B1 16 42S 133 25 E
Dunmore, U.S.A. 79 E9 41 25N 75 38W
Dunmore Hd., Ireland 13 D1 52 10N 10 35W
Dunmore Town, Bahamas 88 A4 25 30N 76 39W
Dunn, U.S.A. 77 H6 35 19N 78 37W
Dunnet Hd., U.K. 12 C5 58 40N 3 21W
Dunning, U.S.A. 80 E4 41 50N 100 6W
Dunnville, Canada 78 D5 42 54N 79 36W
Dunolly, Australia 63 F3 36 51S 143 44 E
Dunoon, U.K. 12 F4 55 57N 4 56W
Dunphy, U.S.A. 82 F5 40 42N 116 31W
Duns, U.K. 12 F6 55 47N 2 20W
Dunseith, U.S.A. 80 A4 48 50N 100 3W
Dunsmuir, U.S.A. 82 F2 41 13N 122 16W
Dunstable, U.K. 11 F7 51 53N 0 32W
Dunstan Mts., N.Z. 59 L2 44 53S 169 35 E
Dunster, Canada 72 C5 53 8N 119 50W
Dunvegan L., Canada 73 A7 60 8N 107 10W
Duolun, China 34 C9 42 12N 116 28 E
Duong Dong, Vietnam 39 G4 10 13N 103 58 E
Dupree, U.S.A. 80 C4 45 4N 101 35W
Dupuyer, U.S.A. 82 B7 48 13N 112 30W
Duque de Caxias, Brazil 95 A7 22 45S 43 19W
Durack →, Australia 60 C4 15 33S 127 52 E
Durack Ra., Australia 60 C4 16 50S 127 40 E
Durance →, France 18 E6 43 55N 4 45 E
Durand, U.S.A. 80 C9 44 38N 91 58W
Durango, Mexico 86 C4 24 3N 104 39W
Durango, U.S.A. 83 H10 37 16N 107 53W
Durango □, Mexico 86 C4 25 0N 105 0W
Durant, Miss., U.S.A. 81 J10 33 4N 89 51W
Durant, Okla., U.S.A. 81 J6 33 59N 96 25W
Durazno, Uruguay 94 C4 33 25S 56 31W
Durazzo = Durrësi, Albania 21 D8 41 19N 19 28 E
Durban, S. Africa 57 D5 29 49S 31 1 E
Durbuy, Belgium 15 D5 50 21N 5 28 E
Düren, Germany 16 C4 50 48N 6 29 E
Durg, India 41 J12 21 15N 81 22 E
Durgapur, India 43 H12 23 30N 87 20 E
Durham, Canada 78 B4 44 10N 80 49W
Durham, U.K. 10 C6 54 47N 1 34W
Durham, Calif., U.S.A. 84 F5 39 39N 121 48W
Durham, N.C., U.S.A. 77 H6 35 59N 78 54W
Durham, N.H., U.S.A. 79 C14 43 8N 70 56W
Durham □, U.K. 10 C6 54 42N 1 45W
Ḍurmā, Si. Arabia 44 E5 24 37N 46 8 E
Durmitor, Montenegro, Yug. 21 C8 43 10N 19 0 E
Durness, U.K. 12 C4 58 34N 4 45W
Durrësi, Albania 21 D8 41 19N 19 28 E
Durrow, Ireland 13 D4 52 51N 7 24W
Dursey I., Ireland 13 E1 51 36N 10 12W
Dursunbey, Turkey 21 E13 39 35N 28 37 E
Duru, Dem. Rep. of the Congo 54 B2 4 14N 28 50 E
Durūz, Jabal ad, Jordan 47 C5 32 35N 36 40 E
D'Urville, Tanjung, Indonesia 37 E9 1 28S 137 54 E
D'Urville I., N.Z. 59 J4 40 50S 173 55 E
Duryea, U.S.A. 79 E9 41 20N 75 45W
Dushak, Turkmenistan 26 F7 37 13N 60 1 E
Dushanbe, Tajikistan 26 F7 38 33N 68 48 E
Dushore, U.S.A. 79 E8 41 31N 76 24W
Dusky Sd., N.Z. 59 L1 45 47S 166 30 E
Dussejour, C., Australia 60 B4 14 45S 128 13 E
Düsseldorf, Germany 16 C4 51 14N 6 47 E
Dutch Harbor, U.S.A. 68 C3 53 53N 166 32W
Dutlwe, Botswana 56 C3 23 58S 23 46 E
Dutton, Canada 78 D3 42 39N 81 30W
Dutton →, Australia 62 C3 20 44S 143 10 E
Duwayhin, Khawr, U.A.E. 45 E6 24 20N 51 25 E
Duyun, China 32 D5 26 18N 107 29 E
Duzdab = Zāhedān, Iran 45 D9 29 30N 60 50 E
Dvina, Severnaya →, Russia 24 B7 64 32N 40 30 E
Dvinsk = Daugavpils, Latvia 9 J22 55 53N 26 32 E
Dvinskaya Guba, Russia 24 B6 65 0N 39 0 E
Dwarka, India 42 H3 22 18N 69 8 E
Dwellingup, Australia 61 F2 32 43S 116 4 E
Dwight, Canada 78 A5 45 20N 79 1W
Dwight, U.S.A. 76 E1 41 5N 88 26W
Dyatlovo = Dzyatlava, Belarus 17 B13 53 28N 25 28 E
Dyce, U.K. 12 D6 57 13N 2 12W
Dyer, C., Canada 69 B13 66 40N 61 0W
Dyer Bay, Canada 78 A3 45 10N 81 20W
Dyer Plateau, Antarctica 5 D17 70 45S 65 30W
Dyersburg, U.S.A. 81 G10 36 3N 89 23W
Dyfi →, U.K. 11 E3 52 32N 4 3W
Dymer, Ukraine 17 C16 50 47N 30 18 E
Dysart, Australia 62 C4 22 32S 148 23 E
Dzamin Üüd = Borhoyn Tal, Mongolia 34 C6 43 50N 111 58 E
Dzerzhinsk, Russia 24 C7 56 14N 43 30 E
Dzhalinda, Russia 27 D13 53 26N 124 0 E
Dzhambul = Zhambyl, Kazakstan 26 E8 42 54N 71 22 E
Dzhankoy, Ukraine 25 E5 45 40N 34 20 E
Dzhezkazgan = Zhezqazghan, Kazakstan 26 E7 47 44N 67 40 E
Dzhizak = Jizzakh, Uzbekistan 26 E7 40 6N 67 50 E
Dzhugdzur, Khrebet, Russia 27 D14 57 30N 138 0 E
Dzhungarskiye Vorota = Dzungarian Gates, Kazakstan 32 B3 45 0N 82 0 E
Działdowo, Poland 17 B11 53 15N 20 15 E
Dzibilchaltun, Mexico 87 C7 21 5N 89 36W
Dzierzoniów, Poland 17 C9 50 45N 16 39 E
Dzilam de Bravo, Mexico 87 C7 21 24N 88 53W
Dzungaria = Junggar Pendi, China 32 B3 44 30N 86 0 E
Dzungarian Gates, Kazakstan 32 B3 45 0N 82 0 E
Dzuumod, Mongolia 32 B5 47 45N 106 58 E
Dzyarzhynsk, Belarus 17 B14 53 40N 27 1 E
Dzyatlava, Belarus 17 B13 53 28N 25 28 E

E

Eabamet L., Canada 70 B2 51 30N 87 46W
Eads, U.S.A. 80 F3 38 29N 102 47W
Eagar, U.S.A. 83 J9 34 6N 109 17W
Eagle, Alaska, U.S.A. 68 B5 64 47N 141 12W
Eagle, Colo., U.S.A. 82 G10 39 39N 106 50W
Eagle →, Canada 71 B8 53 36N 57 26W
Eagle Butte, U.S.A. 80 C4 45 0N 101 10W
Eagle Grove, U.S.A. 80 D8 42 40N 93 54W
Eagle L., Canada 73 D10 49 42N 93 13W
Eagle L., Calif., U.S.A. 82 F3 40 39N 120 45W
Eagle L., Maine, U.S.A. 77 B11 46 20N 69 22W
Eagle Lake, Canada 78 A6 45 8N 78 29W
Eagle Lake, Maine, U.S.A. 77 B11 47 3N 68 36W
Eagle Lake, Tex., U.S.A. 81 L6 29 35N 96 20W
Eagle Mountain, U.S.A. 85 M11 33 49N 115 27W
Eagle Nest, U.S.A. 83 H11 36 33N 105 16W
Eagle Pass, U.S.A. 81 L4 28 43N 100 30W
Eagle Pk., U.S.A. 84 G7 38 10N 119 25W
Eagle Pt., Australia 60 C3 16 11S 124 23 E
Eagle River, Mich., U.S.A. 76 B1 47 24N 88 18W
Eagle River, Wis., U.S.A. 80 C10 45 55N 89 15W
Eaglehawk, Australia 63 F3 36 44S 144 15 E
Eagles Mere, U.S.A. 79 E8 41 25N 76 33W
Ealing, U.K. 11 F7 51 31N 0 20W
Ear Falls, Canada 73 C10 50 38N 93 13W
Earle, U.S.A. 81 H9 35 16N 90 28W
Earlimart, U.S.A. 85 K7 35 53N 119 16W
Earn →, U.K. 12 E5 56 21N 3 18W
Earn, L., U.K. 12 E4 56 23N 4 13W
Earnslaw, Mt., N.Z. 59 L2 44 32S 168 27 E
Earth, U.S.A. 81 H3 34 14N 102 24W
Easley, U.S.A. 77 H4 34 50N 82 36W
East Anglia, U.K. 10 E9 52 30N 1 0 E
East Angus, Canada 71 C5 45 30N 71 40W
East Aurora, U.S.A. 78 D6 42 46N 78 37W
East Ayrshire □, U.K. 12 F4 55 26N 4 11W
East Bengal, Bangla. 41 H17 24 0N 90 0 E
East Beskids = Vychodné Beskydy, Europe 17 D11 49 20N 22 0 E
East Brady, U.S.A. 78 F5 40 59N 79 36W
East C., N.Z. 59 G7 37 42S 178 35 E
East Chicago, U.S.A. 76 E2 41 38N 87 27W
East China Sea, Asia 33 D7 30 0N 126 0 E
East Coulee, Canada 72 C6 51 23N 112 27W
East Dereham, U.K. 11 E8 52 41N 0 57 E
East Dunbartonshire □, U.K. 12 F4 55 57N 4 13W
East Falkland, Falk. Is. 96 G5 51 30S 58 30W
East Grand Forks, U.S.A. 80 B6 47 56N 97 1W
East Greenwich, U.S.A. 79 E13 41 40N 71 27W
East Grinstead, U.K. 11 F8 51 7N 0 0 E
East Hartford, U.S.A. 79 E12 41 46N 72 39W
East Helena, U.S.A. 82 C8 46 35N 111 56W
East Indies, Asia 28 K15 0 0 120 0 E
East Kilbride, U.K. 12 F4 55 47N 4 11W
East Lansing, U.S.A. 76 D3 42 44N 84 29W
East Liverpool, U.S.A. 78 F4 40 37N 80 35W
East London, S. Africa 57 E4 33 0S 27 55 E
East Lothian □, U.K. 12 F6 55 58N 2 44W
East Main = Eastmain, Canada 70 B4 52 10N 78 30W
East Northport, U.S.A. 79 F11 40 53N 73 20W
East Orange, U.S.A. 79 F10 40 46N 74 13W
East Pacific Ridge, Pac. Oc. 65 J17 15 0S 110 0W
East Palestine, U.S.A. 78 F4 40 50N 80 33W
East Pine, Canada 72 B4 55 48N 120 12W
East Point, U.S.A. 77 J3 33 41N 84 27W
East Providence, U.S.A. 79 E13 41 49N 71 23W
East Pt., Canada 71 C7 46 27N 61 58W
East Renfrewshire □, U.K. 12 F4 55 46N 4 21W
East Retford = Retford, U.K. 10 D7 53 19N 0 56W
East Riding of Yorkshire □, U.K. 10 D7 53 55N 0 30W
East Rochester, U.S.A. 78 C7 43 7N 77 29W
East St. Louis, U.S.A. 80 F9 38 37N 90 9W
East Schelde = Oosterschelde →, Neths. 15 C4 51 33N 4 0 E
East Siberian Sea, Russia 27 B17 73 0N 160 0 E
East Stroudsburg, U.S.A. 79 E9 41 1N 75 11W
East Sussex □, U.K. 11 G8 50 56N 0 19 E
East Tawas, U.S.A. 76 C4 44 17N 83 29W
East Timor = Timor Timur □, Indonesia 37 F7 9 0S 125 0 E
East Toorale, Australia 63 E4 30 27S 145 28 E
East Walker →, U.S.A. 84 G7 38 52N 119 10W
East Windsor, U.S.A. 79 F10 40 17N 74 34W
Eastbourne, N.Z. 59 J5 41 19S 174 55 E
Eastbourne, U.K. 11 G8 50 46N 0 18 E
Eastend, Canada 73 D7 49 32N 108 50W
Easter I. = Pascua, I. de, Pac. Oc. 65 K17 27 0S 109 0W
Eastern □, Kenya 54 C4 0 0 38 30 E
Eastern □, Uganda 54 B3 1 50N 33 45 E
Eastern Cape □, S. Africa 56 E4 32 0S 26 0 E
Eastern Cr. →, Australia 62 C3 20 40S 141 35 E
Eastern Ghats, India 40 N11 14 0N 78 50 E
Eastern Group = Lau Group, Fiji 59 C9 17 0S 178 30W
Eastern Group, Australia 61 F3 33 30S 124 30 E
Eastern Transvaal = Mpumalanga □, S. Africa 57 B5 26 0S 30 0 E
Easterville, Canada 73 C9 53 8N 99 49W
Easthampton, U.S.A. 79 D12 42 16N 72 40W
Eastlake, U.S.A. 78 E3 41 40N 81 26W
Eastland, U.S.A. 81 J5 32 24N 98 49W
Eastleigh, U.K. 11 G6 50 58N 1 21W
Eastmain, Canada 70 B4 52 10N 78 30W
Eastmain →, Canada 70 B4 52 27N 78 26W
Eastman, Canada 79 A12 45 18N 72 19W
Eastman, U.S.A. 77 J4 32 12N 83 11W
Easton, Md., U.S.A. 76 F7 38 47N 76 5W
Easton, Pa., U.S.A. 79 F9 40 41N 75 13W
Easton, Wash., U.S.A. 84 C5 47 14N 121 11W
Eastpointe, U.S.A. 78 D2 42 27N 82 56W
Eastport, U.S.A. 77 C12 44 56N 67 0W
Eastsound, U.S.A. 84 B4 48 42N 122 55W
Eaton, U.S.A. 80 E2 40 32N 104 42W
Eatonia, Canada 73 C7 51 13N 109 25W
Eatonton, U.S.A. 77 J4 33 20N 83 23W
Eatontown, U.S.A. 79 F10 40 19N 74 4W
Eatonville, U.S.A. 84 D4 46 52N 122 16W
Eau Claire, U.S.A. 80 C9 44 49N 91 30W
Eau Claire, L. à l', Canada 70 A5 56 10N 74 25W
Ebbw Vale, U.K. 11 F4 51 46N 3 12W
Ebeltoft, Denmark 9 H14 56 12N 10 41 E
Ebensburg, U.S.A. 78 F6 40 29N 78 44W
Eberswalde-Finow, Germany 16 B7 52 50N 13 49 E
Ebetsu, Japan 30 C10 43 7N 141 34 E
Ebolowa, Cameroon 52 D2 2 55N 11 10 E
Ebro →, Spain 19 B6 40 43N 0 54 E
Eceabat, Turkey 21 D12 40 11N 26 21 E
Ech Cheliff, Algeria 50 A6 36 10N 1 20 E
Echigo-Sammyaku, Japan 31 F9 36 50N 139 50 E
Echizen-Misaki, Japan 31 G7 35 59N 135 57 E
Echo Bay, N.W.T., Canada 68 B8 66 5N 117 55W
Echo Bay, Ont., Canada 70 C3 46 29N 84 4W
Echoing →, Canada 70 B1 55 51N 92 5W
Echternach, Lux. 15 E6 49 49N 6 25 E
Echuca, Australia 63 F3 36 10S 144 20 E
Ecija, Spain 19 D3 37 30N 5 10W
Eclipse Is., Australia 60 B4 13 54S 126 19 E
Eclipse Sd., Canada 69 A11 72 38N 79 0W
Ecuador ■, S. Amer. 92 D3 2 0S 78 0W
Ed Damazin, Sudan 51 F12 11 46N 34 21 E
Ed Debba, Sudan 51 E12 18 0N 30 51 E
Ed Dueim, Sudan 51 F12 14 0N 32 10 E
Edam, Canada 73 C7 53 11N 108 46W
Edam, Neths. 15 B5 52 31N 5 3 E
Eday, U.K. 12 B6 59 11N 2 47W
Eddrachillis B., U.K. 12 C3 58 17N 5 14W
Eddystone Pt., Australia 62 G4 40 59S 148 20 E

Ede, *Neths.* **15 B5** 52 4N 5 40 E
Edehon L., *Canada* **73 A9** 60 25N 97 15W
Eden, *Australia* **63 F4** 37 3S 149 55 E
Eden, *N.C., U.S.A.* **77 G6** 36 29N 79 53W
Eden, *N.Y., U.S.A.* **78 D6** 42 39N 78 55W
Eden, *Tex., U.S.A.* **81 K5** 31 13N 99 51W
Eden ➝, *U.K.* **10 C4** 54 57N 3 1W
Edenburg, *S. Africa* **56 D4** 29 43S 25 58 E
Edendale, *S. Africa* **57 D5** 29 39S 30 18 E
Edenderry, *Ireland* **13 C4** 53 21N 7 4W
Edenhope, *Australia* **63 F3** 37 4S 141 19 E
Edenton, *U.S.A.* **77 G7** 36 4N 76 39W
Edenville, *S. Africa* **57 D4** 27 37S 27 34 E
Eder ➝, *Germany* **16 C5** 51 12N 9 28 E
Edgar, *U.S.A.* **80 E6** 40 22N 97 58W
Edgartown, *U.S.A.* **79 E14** 41 23N 70 31W
Edge Hill, *U.K.* **11 E6** 52 8N 1 26W
Edgefield, *U.S.A.* **77 J5** 33 47N 81 56W
Edgeley, *U.S.A.* **80 B5** 46 22N 98 43W
Edgemont, *U.S.A.* **80 D3** 43 18N 103 50W
Edgeøya, *Svalbard* **4 B9** 77 45N 22 30 E
Édhessa, *Greece* **21 D10** 40 48N 22 5 E
Edievale, *N.Z.* **59 L2** 45 49S 169 22 E
Edina, *U.S.A.* **80 E8** 40 10N 92 11W
Edinboro, *U.S.A.* **78 E4** 41 52N 80 8W
Edinburg, *U.S.A.* **81 M5** 26 18N 98 10W
Edinburgh, *U.K.* **12 F5** 55 57N 3 13W
Edineţ, *Moldova* **17 D14** 48 9N 27 18 E
Edirne, *Turkey* **21 D12** 41 40N 26 34 E
Edison, *U.S.A.* **84 B4** 48 33N 122 27W
Edithburgh, *Australia* **63 F2** 35 5S 137 43 E
Edmeston, *U.S.A.* **79 D9** 42 42N 75 15W
Edmond, *U.S.A.* **81 H6** 35 39N 97 29W
Edmonds, *U.S.A.* **84 C4** 47 49N 122 23W
Edmonton, *Australia* **62 B4** 17 2S 145 46 E
Edmonton, *Canada* **72 C6** 53 30N 113 30W
Edmund L., *Canada* **70 B1** 54 45N 93 17W
Edmundston, *Canada* **71 C6** 47 23N 68 20W
Edna, *U.S.A.* **81 L6** 28 59N 96 39W
Edremit, *Turkey* **21 E12** 39 34N 27 0 E
Edremit Körfezi, *Turkey* **21 E12** 39 30N 26 45 E
Edson, *Canada* **72 C5** 53 35N 116 28W
Eduardo Castex, *Argentina* **94 D3** 35 50S 64 18W
Edward ➝, *Australia* **63 F3** 35 5S 143 30 E
Edward, L., *Africa* **54 C2** 0 25S 29 40 E
Edward River, *Australia* **62 A3** 14 59S 141 26 E
Edward VII Land, *Antarctica* **5 E13** 80 0S 150 0W
Edwards, *Calif., U.S.A.* **85 L9** 34 55N 117 51W
Edwards, *N.Y., U.S.A.* **79 B9** 44 20N 75 15W
Edwards Air Force Base, *U.S.A.* **85 L9** 34 50N 117 40W
Edwards Plateau, *U.S.A.* **81 K4** 30 45N 101 20W
Edwardsville, *U.S.A.* **79 E9** 41 15N 75 56W
Edzo, *Canada* **72 A5** 62 49N 116 4W
Eeklo, *Belgium* **15 C3** 51 11N 3 33 E
Effingham, *U.S.A.* **76 F1** 39 7N 88 33W
Égadi, Ísole, *Italy* **20 F5** 37 55N 12 16 E
Egan Range, *U.S.A.* **82 G6** 39 35N 114 55W
Eganville, *Canada* **78 A7** 45 32N 77 5W
Eger = Cheb, *Czech Rep.* **16 C7** 50 9N 12 28 E
Eger, *Hungary* **17 E11** 47 53N 20 27 E
Egersund, *Norway* **9 G12** 58 26N 6 1 E
Egg L., *Canada* **73 B7** 55 5N 105 30W
Éghezée, *Belgium* **15 D4** 50 35N 4 55 E
Egmont, *Canada* **72 D4** 49 45N 123 56W
Egmont, C., *N.Z.* **59 H4** 39 16S 173 45 E
Egmont, Mt., *N.Z.* **59 H5** 39 17S 174 5 E
Egra, *India* **43 J12** 21 54N 87 32 E
Eğridir, *Turkey* **25 G5** 37 52N 30 51 E
Eğridir Gölü, *Turkey* **25 G5** 37 53N 30 50 E
Egvekinot, *Russia* **27 C19** 66 19N 179 50W
Egypt ■, *Africa* **51 C12** 28 0N 31 0 E
Ehime □, *Japan* **31 H6** 33 30N 132 40 E
Ehrenberg, *U.S.A.* **85 M12** 33 36N 114 31W
Eibar, *Spain* **19 A4** 43 11N 2 28W
Eidsvold, *Australia* **63 D5** 25 25S 151 12 E
Eidsvoll, *Norway* **9 F14** 60 19N 11 14 E
Eifel, *Germany* **16 C4** 50 15N 6 50 E
Eiffel Flats, *Zimbabwe* **55 F3** 18 20S 30 0 E
Eigg, *U.K.* **12 E2** 56 54N 6 10W
Eighty Mile Beach, *Australia* **60 C3** 19 30S 120 40 E
Eil, *Somali Rep.* **46 F4** 8 0N 49 50 E
Eil, L., *U.K.* **12 E3** 56 51N 5 16W
Eildon, *Australia* **63 F4** 37 14S 145 55 E
Eildon, L., *Australia* **63 F4** 37 10S 146 0 E
Einasleigh, *Australia* **62 B3** 18 32S 144 5 E
Einasleigh ➝, *Australia* **62 B3** 17 30S 142 17 E
Eindhoven, *Neths.* **15 C5** 51 26N 5 28 E
Eire = Ireland ■, *Europe* **13 C4** 53 50N 7 52W
Eiríksjökull, *Iceland* **8 D3** 64 46N 20 24W
Eirunepé, *Brazil* **92 E5** 6 35S 69 53W
Eisenach, *Germany* **16 C6** 50 58N 10 19 E
Eisenerz, *Austria* **16 E8** 47 32N 14 54 E
Eivissa, *Spain* **22 C7** 38 54N 1 26 E
Ejutla, *Mexico* **87 D5** 16 34N 96 44W
Ekalaka, *U.S.A.* **80 C2** 45 53N 104 33W
Eketahuna, *N.Z.* **59 J5** 40 38S 175 43 E
Ekibastuz, *Kazakstan* **26 D8** 51 50N 75 10 E
Ekoli, *Dem. Rep. of the Congo* **54 C1** 0 23S 24 13 E
Eksjö, *Sweden* **9 H16** 57 40N 14 58 E
Ekwan ➝, *Canada* **70 B3** 53 12N 82 15W
Ekwan Pt., *Canada* **70 B3** 53 16N 82 7W
El Aaiún, *W. Sahara* **50 C3** 27 9N 13 12W
El Abanico, *Chile* **94 D1** 37 20S 71 31W
El 'Agrûd, *Egypt* **47 E3** 30 14N 34 24 E
El Alamein, *Egypt* **51 B11** 30 48N 28 58 E
El 'Aqaba, W. ➝, *Egypt* **47 E2** 30 7N 33 54 E
El Arihã, *West Bank* **47 D4** 31 52N 35 27 E
El 'Arîsh, *Egypt* **47 D2** 31 8N 33 50 E
El 'Arîsh, W. ➝, *Egypt* **47 D2** 31 8N 33 47 E
El Asnam = Ech Cheliff, *Algeria* **50 A6** 36 10N 1 20 E
El Bayadh, *Algeria* **50 B6** 33 40N 1 1 E
El Bluff, *Nic.* **88 D3** 11 59N 83 40W
El Brûk, W. ➝, *Egypt* **47 E2** 30 15N 33 50 E
El Cajon, *U.S.A.* **85 N10** 32 48N 116 58W
El Campo, *U.S.A.* **81 L6** 29 12N 96 16W
El Centro, *U.S.A.* **85 N11** 32 48N 115 34W
El Cerro, *Bolivia* **92 G6** 17 30S 61 40W
El Compadre, *Mexico* **85 N10** 32 20N 116 14W
El Cuy, *Argentina* **96 D3** 39 55S 68 25W
El Cuyo, *Mexico* **87 C7** 21 30N 87 40W
El Daheir, *Egypt* **47 D3** 31 13N 34 10 E
El Dátil, *Mexico* **86 B2** 30 7N 112 15W
El Dere, *Somali Rep.* **46 G4** 3 50N 47 8 E
El Descanso, *Mexico* **85 N10** 32 12N 116 58W
El Desemboque, *Mexico* **86 A2** 30 30N 112 57W
El Diviso, *Colombia* **92 C3** 1 22N 78 14W
El Djouf, *Mauritania* **50 D4** 20 0N 9 0W
El Dorado, *Ark., U.S.A.* **81 J8** 33 12N 92 40W
El Dorado, *Kans., U.S.A.* **81 G6** 37 49N 96 52W
El Dorado, *Venezuela* **92 B6** 6 55N 61 37W
El Escorial, *Spain* **19 B3** 40 35N 4 7W
El Faiyûm, *Egypt* **51 C12** 29 19N 30 50 E
El Fâsher, *Sudan* **51 F11** 13 33N 25 26 E
El Ferrol = Ferrol, *Spain* **19 A1** 43 29N 8 15W
El Fuerte, *Mexico* **86 B3** 26 30N 108 40W
El Gal, *Somali Rep.* **46 E5** 10 58N 50 20 E
El Geneina = Al Junaynah, *Sudan* **51 F10** 13 27N 22 45 E
El Gîza, *Egypt* **51 C12** 30 0N 31 10 E
El Goléa, *Algeria* **50 B6** 30 30N 2 50 E
El Iskandarîya, *Egypt* **51 B11** 31 13N 29 58 E
El Istiwa'iya, *Sudan* **51 G11** 5 0N 28 0 E
El Jadida, *Morocco* **50 B4** 33 11N 8 17W
El Jardal, *Honduras* **88 D2** 14 54N 88 50W
El Kabrît, G., *Egypt* **47 F2** 29 42N 33 16 E
El Khârga, *Egypt* **51 C12** 25 30N 30 33 E
El Khartûm, *Sudan* **51 E12** 15 31N 32 35 E
El Kuntilla, *Egypt* **47 E3** 30 1N 34 45 E
El Maestrazgo, *Spain* **19 B5** 40 30N 0 25W
El Mahalla el Kubra, *Egypt* **51 B12** 31 0N 31 0 E
El Mansûra, *Egypt* **51 B12** 31 0N 31 19 E
El Medano, *Canary Is.* **22 F3** 28 3N 16 32W
El Milagro, *Argentina* **94 C2** 30 59S 65 59W
El Minyâ, *Egypt* **51 C12** 28 7N 30 33 E
El Monte, *U.S.A.* **85 L8** 34 4N 118 1W
El Obeid, *Sudan* **51 F12** 13 8N 30 10 E
El Odaiya, *Sudan* **51 F11** 12 8N 28 12 E
El Oro, *Mexico* **87 D4** 19 48N 100 8W
El Oued, *Algeria* **50 B7** 33 20N 6 58 E
El Palmito, Presa, *Mexico* **86 B3** 25 40N 105 30W
El Paso, *U.S.A.* **83 L10** 31 45N 106 29W
El Paso Robles, *U.S.A.* **84 K6** 35 38N 120 41W
El Portal, *U.S.A.* **84 H7** 37 41N 119 47W
El Porvenir, *Mexico* **86 A3** 31 15N 105 51W
El Prat de Llobregat, *Spain* **19 B7** 41 18N 2 3 E
El Progreso, *Honduras* **88 C2** 15 26N 87 51W
El Pueblito, *Mexico* **86 B3** 29 3N 105 4W
El Pueblo, *Canary Is.* **22 F2** 28 36N 17 47W
El Puerto de Santa María, *Spain* **19 D2** 36 36N 6 13W
El Qâhira, *Egypt* **51 B12** 30 1N 31 14 E
El Qantara, *Egypt* **47 E1** 30 51N 32 20 E
El Quseima, *Egypt* **47 E3** 30 40N 34 15 E
El Real, *Panama* **92 B3** 8 0N 77 40W
El Reno, *U.S.A.* **81 H6** 35 32N 97 57W
El Rio, *U.S.A.* **85 L7** 34 14N 119 10W
El Roque, Pta., *Canary Is.* **22 F4** 28 10N 15 25W
El Rosarito, *Mexico* **86 B2** 28 38N 114 4W
El Saheira, W. ➝, *Egypt* **47 E2** 30 5N 33 25 E
El Salto, *Mexico* **86 C3** 23 47N 105 22W
El Salvador ■, *Cent. Amer.* **88 D2** 13 50N 89 0W
El Sauce, *Nic.* **88 D2** 13 0N 86 40W
El Sueco, *Mexico* **86 B3** 29 54N 106 24W
El Suweis, *Egypt* **51 C12** 29 58N 32 31 E
El Tamarâni, W. ➝, *Egypt* **47 E3** 30 7N 34 43 E
El Thamad, *Egypt* **47 F3** 29 40N 34 28 E
El Tigre, *Venezuela* **92 B6** 8 44N 64 15W
El Tîh, Gebal, *Egypt* **47 F2** 29 40N 33 50 E
El Tîna, Khalîg, *Egypt* **47 D1** 31 10N 32 40 E
El Tofo, *Chile* **94 B1** 29 22S 71 18W
El Tránsito, *Chile* **94 B1** 28 52S 70 17W
El Tûr, *Egypt* **44 D2** 28 14N 33 36 E
El Turbio, *Argentina* **96 G2** 51 45S 72 5W
El Uqsur, *Egypt* **51 C12** 25 41N 32 38 E
El Venado, *Mexico* **86 C4** 22 56N 101 10W
El Vergel, *Mexico* **86 B3** 26 28N 106 22W
El Vigía, *Venezuela* **92 B4** 8 38N 71 39W
El Wabeira, *Egypt* **47 F2** 29 34N 33 6 E
El Wak, *Kenya* **54 B5** 2 49N 40 56 E
El Wuz, *Sudan* **51 E12** 15 5N 30 7 E
Elat, *Israel* **47 F3** 29 30N 34 56 E
Elâzığ, *Turkey* **25 G6** 38 37N 39 14 E
Elba, *Italy* **20 C4** 42 46N 10 17 E
Elba, *U.S.A.* **77 K2** 31 25N 86 4W
Elbasani, *Albania* **21 D9** 41 9N 20 9 E
Elbe, *U.S.A.* **84 D4** 46 45N 122 10W
Elbe ➝, *Europe* **16 B5** 53 50N 9 0 E
Elbert, Mt., *U.S.A.* **83 G10** 39 7N 106 27W
Elberton, *U.S.A.* **77 H4** 34 7N 82 52W
Elbeuf, *France* **18 B4** 49 17N 1 2 E
Elbidtan, *Turkey* **44 B3** 38 13N 37 12 E
Elbing = Elbląg, *Poland* **17 A10** 54 10N 19 25 E
Elbląg, *Poland* **17 A10** 54 10N 19 25 E
Elbow, *Canada* **73 C7** 51 7N 106 35W
Elbrus, *Asia* **25 F7** 43 21N 42 30 E
Elburz Mts. = Alborz, Reshteh-ye Kūhhā-ye, *Iran* **45 C7** 36 0N 52 0 E
Elche, *Spain* **19 C5** 38 15N 0 42W
Elcho I., *Australia* **62 A2** 11 55S 135 45 E
Elda, *Spain* **19 C5** 38 29N 0 47W
Elde ➝, *Germany* **16 B6** 53 7N 11 15 E
Eldon, *Mo., U.S.A.* **80 F8** 38 21N 92 35W
Eldon, *Wash., U.S.A.* **84 C3** 47 33N 123 3W
Eldora, *U.S.A.* **80 D8** 42 22N 93 5W
Eldorado, *Argentina* **95 B5** 26 28S 54 43W
Eldorado, *Canada* **78 B7** 44 35N 77 31W
Eldorado, *Mexico* **86 C3** 24 20N 107 22W
Eldorado, *Ill., U.S.A.* **76 G1** 37 49N 88 26W
Eldorado, *Tex., U.S.A.* **81 K4** 30 52N 100 36W
Eldorado Springs, *U.S.A.* **81 G8** 37 52N 94 1W
Eldoret, *Kenya* **54 B4** 0 30N 35 17 E
Eldred, *U.S.A.* **78 E6** 41 58N 78 23W
Elea, C., *Cyprus* **23 D13** 35 19N 34 4 E
Eleanora, Pk., *Australia* **61 F3** 32 57S 121 9 E
Electra, *U.S.A.* **74 D7** 34 2N 98 55W
Elefantes ➝, *Mozam.* **57 C5** 24 10S 32 40 E
Elektrostal, *Russia* **24 C6** 55 41N 38 32 E
Elephant Butte Reservoir, *U.S.A.* **83 K10** 33 9N 107 11W
Elephant I., *Antarctica* **5 C18** 61 0S 55 0W
Eleuthera, *Bahamas* **88 B4** 25 0N 76 20W
Elgin, *Canada* **79 B8** 44 36N 76 13W
Elgin, *U.K.* **12 D5** 57 39N 3 19W
Elgin, *Ill., U.S.A.* **76 D1** 42 2N 88 17W
Elgin, *N. Dak., U.S.A.* **80 B4** 46 24N 101 51W
Elgin, *Oreg., U.S.A.* **82 D5** 45 34N 117 55W
Elgin, *Tex., U.S.A.* **81 K6** 30 21N 97 22W
Elgon, Mt., *Africa* **54 B3** 1 10N 34 30 E
Eliase, *Indonesia* **37 F8** 8 21S 130 48 E
Elim, *S. Africa* **56 E2** 34 35S 19 45 E
Elisabethville = Lubumbashi, *Dem. Rep. of the Congo* **55 E2** 11 40S 27 28 E
Elista, *Russia* **25 E7** 46 16N 44 14 E
Elizabeth, *Australia* **63 E2** 34 42S 138 41 E
Elizabeth, *N.J., U.S.A.* **79 F10** 40 39N 74 13W
Elizabeth, *N.J., U.S.A.* **79 F10** 40 40N 74 13W
Elizabeth City, *U.S.A.* **77 G7** 36 18N 76 14W
Elizabethton, *U.S.A.* **77 G4** 36 21N 82 13W
Elizabethtown, *Ky., U.S.A.* **76 G3** 37 42N 85 52W
Elizabethtown, *N.Y., U.S.A.* **79 B11** 44 13N 73 36W
Elizabethtown, *Pa., U.S.A.* **79 F8** 40 9N 76 36W
Ełk, *Poland* **17 B12** 53 50N 22 21 E
Elk ➝, *Canada* **72 C5** 49 11N 115 14W
Elk ➝, *U.S.A.* **77 H2** 34 46N 87 16W
Elk City, *U.S.A.* **81 H5** 35 25N 99 25W
Elk Creek, *U.S.A.* **84 F4** 39 36N 122 32W
Elk Grove, *U.S.A.* **84 G5** 38 25N 121 22W
Elk Island Nat. Park, *Canada* **72 C6** 53 35N 112 59W
Elk Lake, *Canada* **70 C3** 47 40N 80 25W
Elk Point, *Canada* **73 C6** 53 54N 110 55W
Elk River, *Idaho, U.S.A.* **82 C5** 46 47N 116 11W
Elk River, *Minn., U.S.A.* **80 C8** 45 18N 93 35W
Elkedra ➝, *Australia* **62 C2** 21 8S 136 22 E
Elkhart, *Ind., U.S.A.* **76 E3** 41 41N 85 58W
Elkhart, *Kans., U.S.A.* **81 G4** 37 0N 101 54W
Elkhorn, *Canada* **73 D8** 49 59N 101 14W
Elkhorn ➝, *U.S.A.* **80 E6** 41 8N 96 19W
Elkhovo, *Bulgaria* **21 C12** 42 10N 26 35 E
Elkin, *U.S.A.* **77 G5** 36 15N 80 51W
Elkins, *U.S.A.* **76 F6** 38 55N 79 51W
Elkland, *U.S.A.* **78 E7** 41 59N 77 19W
Elko, *Canada* **72 D5** 49 20N 115 10W
Elko, *U.S.A.* **82 F6** 40 50N 115 46W
Elkton, *U.S.A.* **78 C1** 43 49N 83 11W
Ell, L., *Australia* **61 E4** 29 13S 127 46 E
Ellef Ringnes I., *Canada* **4 B2** 78 30N 102 2W
Ellen, Mt., *U.S.A.* **79 B12** 44 9N 72 56W
Ellenburg, *U.S.A.* **79 B11** 44 54N 73 48W
Ellendale, *U.S.A.* **80 B5** 46 0N 98 32W
Ellensburg, *U.S.A.* **82 C3** 46 59N 120 34W
Ellenville, *U.S.A.* **79 E10** 41 43N 74 24W
Ellery, Mt., *Australia* **63 F4** 37 28S 148 47 E
Ellesmere, L., *N.Z.* **59 M4** 47 47S 172 28 E
Ellesmere I., *Canada* **4 B4** 79 30N 80 0W
Ellesmere Port, *U.K.* **10 D5** 53 17N 2 54W
Ellice Is. = Tuvalu ■, *Pac. Oc.* **64 H9** 8 0S 178 0 E
Ellicottville, *U.S.A.* **78 D6** 42 17N 78 40W
Elliot, *Australia* **62 B1** 17 33S 133 32 E
Elliot, *S. Africa* **57 E4** 31 22S 27 48 E
Elliot Lake, *Canada* **70 C3** 46 25N 82 35W
Elliotdale = Xhora, *S. Africa* **57 E4** 31 55S 28 38 E
Ellis, *U.S.A.* **80 F5** 38 56N 99 34W
Elliston, *Australia* **63 E1** 33 39S 134 53 E
Ellisville, *U.S.A.* **81 K10** 31 36N 89 12W
Ellon, *U.K.* **12 D6** 57 22N 2 4W
Ellore = Eluru, *India* **41 L12** 16 48N 81 8 E
Ellsworth, *Kans., U.S.A.* **80 F5** 38 44N 98 14W
Ellsworth, *Maine, U.S.A.* **77 C11** 44 33N 68 25W
Ellsworth Land, *Antarctica* **5 D16** 76 0S 89 0W
Ellsworth Mts., *Antarctica* **5 D16** 78 30S 85 0W
Ellwood City, *U.S.A.* **78 F4** 40 52N 80 17W
Elma, *Canada* **73 D9** 49 52N 95 55W
Elma, *U.S.A.* **84 D3** 47 0N 123 25W
Elmalı, *Turkey* **25 G4** 36 44N 29 56 E
Elmhurst, *U.S.A.* **76 E2** 41 53N 87 56W
Elmira, *Canada* **78 C4** 43 36N 80 33W
Elmira, *U.S.A.* **78 D8** 42 6N 76 48W
Elmira Heights, *U.S.A.* **78 D8** 42 8N 76 50W
Elmore, *Australia* **63 F3** 36 30S 144 37 E
Elmore, *U.S.A.* **85 M11** 33 7N 115 49W
Elmshorn, *Germany* **16 B5** 53 43N 9 40 E
Elmvale, *Canada* **78 B5** 44 35N 79 52W
Elora, *Canada* **78 C4** 43 41N 80 26W
Eloúnda, *Greece* **23 D7** 35 16N 25 42 E
Eloy, *U.S.A.* **83 K8** 32 45N 111 33W
Elrose, *Canada* **73 C7** 51 12N 108 0W
Elsie, *U.S.A.* **84 E3** 45 52N 123 36W
Elsinore = Helsingør, *Denmark* **9 H15** 56 2N 12 35 E
Eltham, *N.Z.* **59 H5** 39 26S 174 19 E
Eluru, *India* **41 L12** 16 48N 81 8 E
Elvas, *Portugal* **19 C2** 38 50N 7 10W
Elverum, *Norway* **9 F14** 60 53N 11 34 E
Elvire ➝, *Australia* **60 C4** 17 51S 128 11 E
Elvire, Mt., *Australia* **61 E2** 29 22S 119 36 E
Elwell, L., *U.S.A.* **82 B8** 48 22N 111 17W
Elwood, *Ind., U.S.A.* **76 E3** 40 17N 85 50W
Elwood, *Nebr., U.S.A.* **80 E5** 40 36N 99 52W
Elx = Elche, *Spain* **19 C5** 38 15N 0 42W
Ely, *U.K.* **11 E8** 52 24N 0 16 E
Ely, *Minn., U.S.A.* **80 B9** 47 55N 91 51W
Ely, *Nev., U.S.A.* **82 G6** 39 15N 114 54W
Elyria, *U.S.A.* **78 E2** 41 22N 82 7W
Emāmrūd, *Iran* **45 B7** 36 30N 55 0 E
Emba, *Kazakstan* **26 E6** 48 50N 58 8 E
Emba ➝, *Kazakstan* **25 E9** 46 55N 53 28 E
Embarcación, *Argentina* **94 A3** 23 10S 64 0W
Embarras Portage, *Canada* **73 B6** 58 27N 111 28W
Embetsu, *Japan* **30 B10** 44 44N 141 47 E
Embi = Emba, *Kazakstan* **26 E6** 48 50N 58 8 E
Embi = Emba ➝, *Kazakstan* **25 E9** 46 55N 53 28 E
Embóna, *Greece* **23 C9** 36 13N 27 51 E
Embrun, *France* **18 D7** 44 34N 6 30 E
Embu, *Kenya* **54 C4** 0 32S 37 38 E
Emden, *Germany* **16 B4** 53 21N 7 12 E
Emerald, *Australia* **62 C4** 23 32S 148 10 E
Emerson, *Canada* **73 D9** 49 0N 97 10W
Emet, *Turkey* **21 E13** 39 20N 29 15 E
Emi Koussi, *Chad* **51 E9** 19 45N 18 55 E
Eminabad, *Pakistan* **42 C6** 32 2N 74 8 E
Emine, Nos, *Bulgaria* **21 C12** 42 40N 27 56 E
Emlenton, *U.S.A.* **78 E5** 41 11N 79 43W
Emmaus, *U.S.A.* **79 F9** 40 32N 75 30W
Emmeloord, *Neths.* **15 B5** 52 44N 5 46 E
Emmen, *Neths.* **15 B6** 52 48N 6 57 E
Emmet, *Australia* **62 C3** 24 45S 144 30 E
Emmetsburg, *U.S.A.* **80 D7** 43 7N 94 41W
Emmett, *Idaho, U.S.A.* **82 E5** 43 52N 116 30W
Emmett, *Mich., U.S.A.* **78 D2** 42 59N 82 46W
Emmonak, *U.S.A.* **68 B3** 62 46N 164 30W
Emo, *Canada* **73 D10** 48 38N 93 50W
Empalme, *Mexico* **86 B2** 28 1N 110 49W
Empangeni, *S. Africa* **57 D5** 28 50S 31 52 E
Empedrado, *Argentina* **94 B4** 28 0S 58 46W
Emperor Seamount Chain, *Pac. Oc.* **64 D9** 40 0N 170 0 E
Emporia, *Kans., U.S.A.* **80 F6** 38 25N 96 11W
Emporia, *Va., U.S.A.* **77 G7** 36 42N 77 32W
Emporium, *U.S.A.* **78 E6** 41 31N 78 14W
Empress, *Canada* **73 C7** 50 57N 110 0W
Empty Quarter = Rub' al Khālī, *Si. Arabia* **46 D4** 18 0N 48 0 E
Ems ➝, *Germany* **16 B4** 53 20N 7 12 E
Emsdale, *Canada* **78 A5** 45 32N 79 19W
Emu, *China* **35 C15** 43 40N 128 6 E
Emu Park, *Australia* **62 C5** 23 13S 150 50 E
'En 'Avrona, *Israel* **47 F4** 29 43N 35 0 E
En Nahud, *Sudan* **51 F11** 12 45N 28 25 E
Ena, *Japan* **31 G8** 35 25N 137 25 E
Enana, *Namibia* **56 B2** 17 30S 16 23 E
Enaratoli, *Indonesia* **37 E9** 3 55S 136 21 E
Enard B., *U.K.* **12 C3** 58 5N 5 20W
Enare = Inarijärvi, *Finland* **8 B22** 69 0N 28 0 E
Encampment, *U.S.A.* **82 F10** 41 12N 106 47W
Encantadas, Serra, *Brazil* **95 C5** 30 40S 53 0W
Encarnación, *Paraguay* **95 B4** 27 15S 55 50W
Encarnación de Diaz, *Mexico* **86 C4** 21 30N 102 13W
Encinitas, *U.S.A.* **85 M9** 33 3N 117 17W
Encino, *U.S.A.* **83 J11** 34 39N 105 28W
Encounter B., *Australia* **63 F2** 35 45S 138 45 E
Endako, *Canada* **72 C3** 54 6N 125 2W
Ende, *Indonesia* **37 F6** 8 45S 121 40 E
Endeavour Str., *Australia* **62 A3** 10 45S 142 0 E
Enderbury I., *Kiribati* **64 H10** 3 8S 171 5W
Enderby, *Canada* **72 C5** 50 35N 119 10W
Enderby I., *Australia* **60 D2** 20 35S 116 30 E
Enderby Land, *Antarctica* **5 C5** 66 0S 53 0 E
Enderlin, *U.S.A.* **80 B6** 46 38N 97 36W
Endicott, *U.S.A.* **79 D8** 42 6N 76 4W
Endwell, *U.S.A.* **79 D8** 42 6N 76 2W
Endyalgout I., *Australia* **60 B5** 11 40S 132 35 E
Eneabba, *Australia* **61 E2** 29 49S 115 16 E
Enewetak Atoll, *Marshall Is.* **64 F8** 11 30N 162 15 E
Enez, *Turkey* **21 D12** 40 45N 26 5 E
Enfield, *Canada* **71 D7** 44 56N 63 32W
Enfield, *Conn., U.S.A.* **79 E12** 41 58N 72 36W
Enfield, *N.H., U.S.A.* **79 C12** 43 39N 72 9W
Engadin, *Switz.* **18 C9** 46 45N 10 10 E
Engaño, C., *Dom. Rep.* **89 C6** 18 30N 68 20W
Engaño, C., *Phil.* **37 A6** 18 35N 122 23 E
Engaru, *Japan* **30 B11** 44 3N 143 31 E
Engcobo, *S. Africa* **57 E4** 31 37S 28 0 E
Engels, *Russia* **25 D8** 51 28N 46 6 E
Engemann L., *Canada* **73 B7** 58 0N 106 55W
Enggano, *Indonesia* **36 F2** 5 20S 102 40 E
England, *U.S.A.* **81 H9** 34 33N 91 58W
England □, *U.K.* **10 D7** 53 0N 2 0W
Englee, *Canada* **71 B8** 50 45N 56 5W
Englehart, *Canada* **70 C4** 47 49N 79 52W
Englewood, *U.S.A.* **80 F2** 39 39N 104 59W
English ➝, *Canada* **73 C10** 50 35N 93 30W
English Bazar = Ingraj Bazar, *India* **43 G13** 24 58N 88 10 E
English Channel, *Europe* **11 G6** 50 0N 2 0W
English River, *Canada* **70 C1** 49 14N 91 0W
Enid, *U.S.A.* **81 G6** 36 24N 97 53W
Enkhuizen, *Neths.* **15 B5** 52 42N 5 17 E
Enna, *Italy* **20 F6** 37 34N 14 16 E
Ennadai, *Canada* **73 A8** 61 8N 100 53W
Ennadai L., *Canada* **73 A8** 61 0N 101 0W
Ennedi, *Chad* **51 E10** 17 15N 22 0 E
Enngonia, *Australia* **63 D4** 29 21S 145 50 E
Ennis, *Ireland* **13 D3** 52 51N 8 59W
Ennis, *Mont., U.S.A.* **82 D8** 45 21N 111 44W
Ennis, *Tex., U.S.A.* **81 J6** 32 20N 96 38W
Enniscorthy, *Ireland* **13 D5** 52 30N 6 34W
Enniskillen, *U.K.* **13 B4** 54 21N 7 39W
Ennistimon, *Ireland* **13 D2** 52 57N 9 17W
Enns ➝, *Austria* **16 D8** 48 14N 14 32 E
Enontekiö, *Finland* **8 B20** 68 23N 23 37 E
Enosburg Falls, *U.S.A.* **79 B12** 44 55N 72 48W
Enriquillo, L., *Dom. Rep.* **89 C5** 18 20N 72 5W
Enschede, *Neths.* **15 B6** 52 13N 6 53 E
Ensenada, *Argentina* **94 C4** 34 55S 57 55W
Ensenada, *Mexico* **86 A1** 31 50N 116 50W
Ensenada de los Muertos, *Mexico* **86 C2** 23 59N 109 50W
Ensiola, Pta. de n', *Spain* **22 B9** 39 7N 2 55 E
Entebbe, *Uganda* **54 B3** 0 4N 32 28 E
Enterprise, *Canada* **72 A5** 60 47N 115 45W
Enterprise, *Ala., U.S.A.* **77 K3** 31 19N 85 51W
Enterprise, *Oreg., U.S.A.* **82 D5** 45 25N 117 17W
Entre Ríos, *Bolivia* **94 A3** 21 30S 64 25W
Entre Ríos □, *Argentina* **94 C4** 30 30S 58 30W
Entroncamento, *Portugal* **19 C1** 39 28N 8 28W
Enugu, *Nigeria* **50 G7** 6 20N 7 30 E
Enumclaw, *U.S.A.* **84 C5** 47 12N 121 59W
Eólie, Ís., *Italy* **20 E6** 38 30N 14 57 E
Epe, *Neths.* **15 B5** 52 21N 5 59 E
Épernay, *France* **18 B5** 49 3N 3 56 E
Ephesus, *Turkey* **21 F12** 37 55N 27 22 E
Ephraim, *U.S.A.* **82 G8** 39 22N 111 35W
Ephrata, *Pa., U.S.A.* **79 F8** 40 11N 76 11W
Ephrata, *Wash., U.S.A.* **82 C4** 47 19N 119 33W
Épinal, *France* **18 B7** 48 10N 6 27 E
Episkopi, *Cyprus* **23 E11** 34 40N 32 54 E
Episkopi, *Greece* **23 D6** 35 20N 24 20 E
Episkopi Bay, *Cyprus* **23 E11** 34 35N 32 50 E
Epsom, *U.K.* **11 F7** 51 19N 0 16W
Epukiro, *Namibia* **56 C2** 21 40S 19 9 E
Equatorial Guinea ■, *Africa* **52 D1** 2 0N 8 0 E
Er Rahad, *Sudan* **51 F12** 12 45N 30 32 E
Er Rif, *Morocco* **50 A5** 35 1N 4 1W
Erāwadī Myit = Irrawaddy ➝, *Burma* **41 M19** 15 50N 95 6 E
Erbil = Arbīl, *Iraq* **44 B5** 36 15N 44 5 E
Erçek, *Turkey* **44 B4** 38 39N 43 36 E
Erciyaş Dağı, *Turkey* **25 G6** 38 30N 35 30 E
Érd, *Hungary* **17 E10** 47 22N 18 56 E
Erdao Jiang ➝, *China* **35 C14** 43 0N 127 0 E
Erdek, *Turkey* **21 D12** 40 23N 27 47 E
Erdene = Ulaan-Uul, *Mongolia* **34 B6** 44 13N 111 10 E
Erdenetsogt, *Mongolia* **34 C4** 42 55N 106 5 E
Erebus, Mt., *Antarctica* **5 D11** 77 35S 167 0 E
Erechim, *Brazil* **95 B5** 27 35S 52 15W
Ereğli, *Konya, Turkey* **25 G5** 37 31N 34 4 E
Ereğli, *Zonguldak, Turkey* **25 F5** 41 15N 31 24 E
Erenhot, *China* **34 C7** 43 48N 112 2 E
Eresma ➝, *Spain* **19 B3** 41 26N 4 45W
Erewadi Myitwanya, *Burma* **41 M19** 15 30N 95 0 E

Feldkirch

Erfenisdam, S. Africa 56 D4 28 30S 26 50 E
Erfurt, Germany 16 C6 50 58N 11 2 E
Erg Iguidi, Africa 50 C4 27 0N 7 0 E
Ergani, Turkey 44 B3 38 17N 39 49 E
Ergel, Mongolia 34 C5 43 8N 109 5 E
Ergeni Vozvyshennost, Russia 25 E7 47 0N 44 0 E
Ērgli, Latvia 9 H21 56 54N 25 38 E
Eriboll, L., U.K. 12 C4 58 30N 4 42W
Érice, Italy 20 E5 38 2N 12 35 E
Erie, U.S.A. 78 D4 42 8N 80 5W
Erie, L., N. Amer. 78 D4 42 15N 81 0W
Erie Canal, U.S.A. 78 C7 43 5N 78 43W
Erieau, Canada 78 D3 42 16N 81 57W
Erigavo, Somali Rep. 46 E4 10 35N 47 20 E
Erikoúsa, Greece 23 A3 39 53N 19 34 E
Eriksdale, Canada 73 C9 50 52N 98 7W
Erimanthos, Greece 21 F9 37 57N 21 50 E
Erimo-misaki, Japan 30 D11 41 50N 143 15 E
Erinpura, India 42 G5 25 9N 73 3 E
Eriskay, U.K. 12 D1 57 4N 7 18W
Eritrea ■, Africa 46 D2 14 0N 38 30 E
Erlangen, Germany 16 D6 49 36N 11 0 E
Erldunda, Australia 62 D1 25 14S 133 12 E
Ermelo, Neths. 15 B5 52 18N 5 35 E
Ermelo, S. Africa 57 D4 26 31S 29 59 E
Ermenek, Turkey 44 B2 36 38N 33 0 E
Ermones, Greece 23 A3 39 37N 19 46 E
Ermoúpolis = Síros, Greece 21 F11 37 28N 24 57 E
Ernakulam = Cochin, India 40 Q10 9 59N 76 22 E
Erne →, Ireland 13 B3 54 30N 8 16W
Erne, Lower L., U.K. 13 B4 54 28N 7 47W
Erne, Upper L., U.K. 13 B4 54 14N 7 32W
Ernest Giles Ra., Australia 61 E3 27 0S 123 45 E
Erode, India 40 P10 11 24N 77 45 E
Eromanga, Australia 63 D3 26 40S 143 11 E
Erongo, Namibia 56 C2 21 39S 15 58 E
Erramala Hills, India 40 M11 15 30N 78 15 E
Errigal, Ireland 13 A3 55 2N 8 6W
Erris Hd., Ireland 13 B1 54 19N 10 0W
Erskine, U.S.A. 80 B7 47 40N 96 0W
Ertis = Irtysh →, Russia 26 C7 61 4N 68 52 E
Erwin, U.S.A. 77 G4 36 9N 82 25W
Erzgebirge, Germany 16 C7 50 27N 12 55 E
Erzin, Russia 27 D10 50 15N 95 10 E
Erzincan, Turkey 25 G6 39 46N 39 30 E
Erzurum, Turkey 25 G7 39 57N 41 15 E
Es Caló, Spain 22 C8 38 40N 1 30 E
Es Canar, Spain 22 B8 39 2N 1 36 E
Es Mercadal, Spain 22 B11 39 59N 4 5 E
Es Migjorn Gran, Spain 22 B11 39 57N 4 3 E
Es Sahrâ' Esh Sharqîya, Egypt 51 C12 27 30N 32 30 E
Es Sînâ', Egypt 47 F3 29 0N 34 0 E
Es Vedrà, Spain 22 C7 38 52N 1 12 E
Esambo, Dem. Rep. of the Congo 54 C1 3 48S 23 30 E
Esan-Misaki, Japan 30 D10 41 40N 141 10 E
Esashi, Hokkaidō, Japan 30 B11 44 56N 142 35 E
Esashi, Hokkaidō, Japan 30 D10 41 52N 140 7 E
Esbjerg, Denmark 9 J13 55 29N 8 29 E
Escalante, U.S.A. 83 H8 37 47N 111 36W
Escalante →, U.S.A. 83 H8 37 24N 110 57W
Escalón, Mexico 86 B4 26 46N 104 20W
Escambia →, U.S.A. 77 K2 30 32N 87 11W
Escanaba, U.S.A. 76 C2 45 45N 87 4W
Esch-sur-Alzette, Lux. 18 B6 49 32N 6 0 E
Escondido, U.S.A. 85 M9 33 7N 117 5W
Escuinapa, Mexico 86 C3 22 50N 105 50W
Escuintla, Guatemala 88 D1 14 20N 90 48W
Esenguly, Turkmenistan 26 F6 37 37N 53 59 E
Eşfahān, Iran 45 C6 32 39N 51 43 E
Eşfahān □, Iran 45 C6 32 50N 51 50 E
Esfarāyen, Iran 45 B8 37 4N 57 30 E
Esfideh, Iran 45 C8 33 39N 59 46 E
Esh Sham = Dimashq, Syria 47 B5 33 30N 36 18 E
Esha Ness, U.K. 12 A7 60 29N 1 38W
Esher, U.K. 11 F7 51 21N 0 20W
Eshowe, S. Africa 57 D5 28 50S 31 30 E
Esil = Ishim →, Russia 26 D8 57 45N 71 10 E
Esk →, Cumb., U.K. 12 G5 54 58N 3 2W
Esk →, N. Yorks., U.K. 10 C7 54 30N 0 37W
Eskān, Iran 45 E9 26 48N 63 9 E
Esker, Canada 71 B6 53 53N 66 25W
Eskifjörður, Iceland 8 D7 65 3N 13 55W
Eskilstuna, Sweden 9 G17 59 22N 16 32 E
Eskimo Pt., Canada 68 B10 61 10N 94 15W
Eskişehir, Turkey 25 G5 39 50N 30 30 E
Esla →, Spain 19 B2 41 29N 6 3W
Eslāmābād-e Gharb, Iran 44 C5 34 10N 46 30 E
Eslāmshahr, Iran 45 C6 35 40N 51 10 E
Eşme, Turkey 21 E13 38 23N 28 58 E
Esmeraldas, Ecuador 92 C3 1 0N 79 40W
Esnagi L., Canada 70 C3 48 36N 84 33W
Espanola, Canada 70 C3 46 15N 81 46W
Espanola, U.S.A. 83 H10 35 59N 106 5W
Esparta, Costa Rica 88 E3 9 59N 84 40W
Esperance, Australia 61 F3 33 45S 121 55 E
Esperance B., Australia 61 F3 33 48S 121 55 E
Esperanza, Argentina 94 C3 31 29S 61 3W
Espichel, C., Portugal 19 C1 38 22N 9 16W
Espigão, Serra do, Brazil 95 B5 26 35S 50 30W
Espinazo, Sierra del = Espinhaço, Serra do, Brazil 93 G10 17 30S 43 30W
Espinhaço, Serra do, Brazil 93 G10 17 30S 43 30W
Espinilho, Serra do, Brazil 95 B5 28 30S 55 0W
Espírito Santo □, Brazil 93 H10 20 0S 40 45W
Espíritu Santo, Vanuatu 64 J8 15 15S 166 50 E
Espíritu Santo, B. del, Mexico 87 D7 19 15N 87 0W
Espíritu Santo, I., Mexico 86 C2 24 30N 110 23W
Espita, Mexico 87 C7 21 1N 88 19W
Espoo, Finland 9 F21 60 12N 24 40 E
Espungabera, Mozam. 57 C5 20 29S 32 45 E
Esquel, Argentina 96 E2 42 55S 71 20W
Esquimalt, Canada 72 D4 48 26N 123 25W
Esquina, Argentina 94 C4 30 0S 59 30W
Essaouira, Morocco 50 B4 31 32N 9 42W
Essebie, Dem. Rep. of the Congo 54 B3 2 58N 30 40 E
Essen, Belgium 15 C4 51 28N 4 28 E
Essen, Germany 16 C4 51 28N 7 2 E
Essendon, Mt., Australia 61 E3 25 0S 120 29 E
Essequibo →, Guyana 92 B7 6 50N 58 30W
Essex, Canada 78 D2 42 10N 82 49W
Essex, Calif., U.S.A. 85 L11 34 44N 115 15W
Essex, N.Y., U.S.A. 79 B11 44 19N 73 21W
Essex □, U.K. 11 F8 51 54N 0 27 E
Essex Junction, U.S.A. 79 B11 44 29N 73 7W
Esslingen, Germany 16 D5 48 44N 9 18 E
Estados, I. de Los, Argentina 96 G4 54 40S 64 30W
Eşţahbānāt, Iran 45 D7 29 8N 54 4 E
Estância, Brazil 93 F11 11 16S 37 26W
Estancia, U.S.A. 83 J10 34 46N 106 4W
Estārm, Iran 45 D8 28 21N 58 21 E
Estcourt, S. Africa 57 D4 29 0S 29 53 E
Estelí, Nic. 88 D2 13 9N 86 22W
Estellencs, Spain 22 B9 39 39N 2 29 E
Esterhazy, Canada 73 C8 50 37N 102 5W
Estevan, Canada 73 D8 49 10N 102 59W
Estevan Group, Canada 72 C3 53 3N 129 38W
Estherville, U.S.A. 80 D7 43 24N 94 50W
Eston, Canada 73 C7 51 8N 108 40W
Estonia ■, Europe 9 G21 58 30N 25 30 E
Estreito, Brazil 93 E9 6 32S 47 25W
Estrela, Serra da, Portugal 19 B2 40 10N 7 45W
Estremoz, Portugal 19 C2 38 51N 7 39W
Estrondo, Serra do, Brazil 93 E9 7 20S 48 0W
Esztergom, Hungary 17 E10 47 47N 18 44 E
Etah, India 43 F8 27 35N 78 40 E
Étampes, France 18 B5 48 26N 2 10 E
Etanga, Namibia 56 B1 17 55S 13 0 E
Etawah, India 43 F8 26 48N 79 6 E
Etawney L., Canada 73 B9 57 50N 96 50W
Ethel, U.S.A. 84 D4 46 32N 122 46W
Ethelbert, Canada 73 C8 51 32N 100 25W
Ethiopia ■, Africa 46 F3 8 0N 40 0 E
Ethiopian Highlands, Ethiopia 28 J7 10 0N 37 0 E
Etive, L., U.K. 12 E3 56 29N 5 10W
Etna, Italy 20 F6 37 50N 14 55 E
Etoile, Dem. Rep. of the Congo 55 E2 11 33S 27 30 E
Etosha Pan, Namibia 56 B2 18 40S 16 30 E
Etowah, U.S.A. 77 H3 35 20N 84 32W
Ettelbruck, Lux. 15 E6 49 51N 6 5 E
Ettrick Water →, U.K. 12 F6 55 31N 2 55W
Etuku, Dem. Rep. of the Congo 54 C2 3 42S 25 45 E
Etzatlán, Mexico 86 C4 20 48N 104 5W
Etzná, Mexico 87 D6 19 35N 90 15W
Euboea = Évvoia, Greece 21 E11 38 30N 24 0 E
Eucla, Australia 61 F4 31 41S 128 52 E
Euclid, U.S.A. 78 E3 41 34N 81 32W
Eucumbene, L., Australia 63 F4 36 2S 148 40 E
Eudora, U.S.A. 81 J9 33 7N 91 16W
Eufaula, Ala., U.S.A. 77 K3 31 54N 85 9W
Eufaula, Okla., U.S.A. 81 H7 35 17N 95 35W
Eufaula L., U.S.A. 81 H7 35 18N 95 21W
Eugene, U.S.A. 82 E2 44 5N 123 4W
Eugowra, Australia 63 E4 33 22S 148 24 E
Eulo, Australia 63 D4 28 10S 145 3 E
Eunice, La., U.S.A. 81 K8 30 30N 92 25W
Eunice, N. Mex., U.S.A. 81 J3 32 26N 103 10W
Eupen, Belgium 15 D6 50 37N 6 3 E
Euphrates = Furāt, Nahr al →, Asia 44 D5 31 0N 47 25 E
Eureka, Canada 4 B3 80 0N 85 56W
Eureka, Calif., U.S.A. 82 F1 40 47N 124 9W
Eureka, Kans., U.S.A. 81 G6 37 49N 96 17W
Eureka, Mont., U.S.A. 82 B6 48 53N 115 3W
Eureka, Nev., U.S.A. 82 G5 39 31N 115 58W
Eureka, S. Dak., U.S.A. 80 C5 45 46N 99 38W
Eureka, Mt., Australia 61 E3 26 35S 121 35 E
Euroa, Australia 63 F4 36 44S 145 35 E
Europa, Île, Ind. Oc. 53 J8 22 20S 40 22 E
Europa, Picos de, Spain 19 A3 43 10N 4 49W
Europa, Pta. de, Gib. 19 D3 36 3N 5 21W
Europe 6 E10 50 0N 20 0 E
Europoort, Neths. 15 C4 51 57N 4 10 E
Eustis, U.S.A. 77 L5 28 51N 81 41W
Euston, Australia 63 E3 34 30S 142 46 E
Eutsuk L., Canada 72 C3 53 20N 126 45W
Evale, Angola 56 B2 16 33S 15 44 E
Evans, U.S.A. 80 E2 40 23N 104 41W
Evans, L., Canada 70 B4 50 50N 77 0W
Evans City, U.S.A. 78 F4 40 46N 80 4W
Evans Head, Australia 63 D5 29 7S 153 27 E
Evans Mills, U.S.A. 79 B9 44 6N 75 48W
Evansburg, Canada 72 C5 53 36N 114 59W
Evanston, Ill., U.S.A. 76 E2 42 3N 87 41W
Evanston, Wyo., U.S.A. 82 F8 41 16N 110 58W
Evansville, U.S.A. 76 G2 37 58N 87 35W
Evaz, Iran 45 E7 27 46N 53 59 E
Eveleth, U.S.A. 80 B8 47 28N 92 32W
Evensk, Russia 27 C16 62 12N 159 30 E
Everard, L., Australia 63 E2 31 30S 135 0 E
Everard Ranges, Australia 61 E5 27 5S 132 28 E
Everest, Mt., Nepal 43 E12 28 5N 86 58 E
Everett, Pa., U.S.A. 78 F6 40 1N 78 23W
Everett, Wash., U.S.A. 84 C4 47 59N 122 12W
Everglades, The, U.S.A. 77 N5 25 50N 81 0W
Everglades National Park, U.S.A. 77 N5 25 30N 81 0W
Evergreen, Ala., U.S.A. 77 K2 31 26N 86 57W
Evergreen, Mont., U.S.A. 82 B6 48 9N 114 13W
Evesham, U.K. 11 E6 52 6N 1 56W
Evje, Norway 9 G12 58 36N 7 51 E
Évora, Portugal 19 C2 38 33N 7 57W
Evowghlī, Iran 44 B5 38 43N 45 13 E
Évreux, France 18 B4 49 3N 1 8 E
Évros →, Bulgaria 21 D12 41 40N 26 34 E
Évry, France 18 B5 48 38N 2 27 E
Évvoia, Greece 21 E11 38 30N 24 0 E
Ewe, L., U.K. 12 D3 57 49N 5 38W
Ewing, U.S.A. 80 D5 42 16N 98 21W
Ewo, Congo 52 E2 0 48S 14 45 E
Exaltación, Bolivia 92 F5 13 10S 65 20W
Excelsior Springs, U.S.A. 80 F7 39 20N 94 13W
Exe →, U.K. 11 G4 50 41N 3 29W
Exeter, Canada 78 C3 43 21N 81 29W
Exeter, U.K. 11 G4 50 43N 3 31W
Exeter, Calif., U.S.A. 84 J7 36 18N 119 9W
Exeter, N.H., U.S.A. 79 D14 42 59N 70 57W
Exmoor, U.K. 11 F4 51 12N 3 45W
Exmouth, Australia 60 D1 21 54S 114 10 E
Exmouth, U.K. 11 G4 50 37N 3 25W
Exmouth G., Australia 60 D1 22 15S 114 15 E
Expedition Ra., Australia 62 C4 24 30S 149 12 E
Extremadura □, Spain 19 C2 39 30N 6 5W
Exuma Sound, Bahamas 88 B4 24 30N 76 20W
Eyasi, L., Tanzania 54 C4 3 30S 35 0 E
Eye Pen., U.K. 12 C2 58 13N 6 10W
Eyemouth, U.K. 12 F6 55 52N 2 5W
Eyjafjörður, Iceland 8 C4 66 15N 18 30W
Eyre (North), L., Australia 63 D2 28 30S 137 20 E
Eyre (South), L., Australia 63 D2 29 18S 137 25 E
Eyre Mts., N.Z. 59 L2 45 25S 168 25 E
Eyre Pen., Australia 63 E2 33 30S 136 17 E
Eysturoy, Færoe Is. 8 E9 62 13N 6 54W
Eyvānkī, Iran 45 C6 35 24N 51 56 E
Ezine, Turkey 21 E12 39 48N 26 20 E
Ezouza →, Cyprus 23 E11 34 44N 32 27 E

F

F.Y.R.O.M. = Macedonia ■, Europe 21 D9 41 53N 21 40 E
Fabala, Guinea 50 G4 9 44N 9 5W
Fabens, U.S.A. 83 L10 31 30N 106 10W
Fabriano, Italy 20 C5 43 20N 12 54 E
Fachi, Niger 51 E8 18 6N 11 34 E
Fada, Chad 51 E10 17 13N 21 34 E
Fada-n-Gourma, Burkina Faso 50 F6 12 10N 0 30 E
Faddeyevskiy, Ostrov, Russia 27 B15 76 0N 144 0 E
Fadghāmī, Syria 44 C4 35 53N 40 52 E
Faenza, Italy 20 B4 44 17N 11 53 E
Færoe Is. = Føroyar, Atl. Oc. 8 F9 62 0N 7 0W
Făgăras, Romania 17 F13 45 48N 24 58 E
Fagersta, Sweden 9 F16 60 1N 15 46 E
Fagnano, L., Argentina 96 G3 54 30S 68 0W
Fahlīān, Iran 45 D6 30 11N 51 28 E
Fahraj, Kermān, Iran 45 D8 29 0N 59 0 E
Fahraj, Yazd, Iran 45 D7 31 46N 54 36 E
Faial, Madeira 22 D3 32 47N 16 53W
Fair Haven, U.S.A. 76 D9 43 36N 73 16W
Fair Hd., U.K. 13 A5 55 14N 6 9W
Fair Oaks, U.S.A. 84 G5 38 39N 121 16W
Fairbanks, U.S.A. 68 B5 64 51N 147 43W
Fairbury, U.S.A. 80 E6 40 8N 97 11W
Fairfax, U.S.A. 79 B11 44 40N 73 1W
Fairfield, Ala., U.S.A. 77 J2 33 29N 86 55W
Fairfield, Calif., U.S.A. 84 G4 38 15N 122 3W
Fairfield, Conn., U.S.A. 79 E11 41 9N 73 16W
Fairfield, Idaho, U.S.A. 82 E6 43 21N 114 44W
Fairfield, Ill., U.S.A. 76 F1 38 23N 88 22W
Fairfield, Iowa, U.S.A. 80 E9 40 56N 91 57W
Fairfield, Tex., U.S.A. 81 K7 31 44N 96 10W
Fairford, Canada 73 C9 51 37N 98 38W
Fairhope, U.S.A. 77 K2 30 31N 87 54W
Fairlie, N.Z. 59 L3 44 5S 170 49 E
Fairmead, U.S.A. 84 H6 37 5N 120 10W
Fairmont, Minn., U.S.A. 80 D7 43 39N 94 28W
Fairmont, W. Va., U.S.A. 76 F5 39 29N 80 9W
Fairmount, Calif., U.S.A. 85 L8 34 45N 118 26W
Fairmount, N.Y., U.S.A. 79 C8 43 5N 76 12W
Fairplay, U.S.A. 83 G11 39 15N 106 2W
Fairport, U.S.A. 78 C7 43 6N 77 27W
Fairport Harbor, U.S.A. 78 E3 41 45N 81 17W
Fairview, Canada 72 B5 56 5N 118 25W
Fairview, Mont., U.S.A. 80 B2 47 51N 104 3W
Fairview, Okla., U.S.A. 81 G5 36 16N 98 29W
Fairweather, Mt., U.S.A. 72 B1 58 55N 137 32W
Faisalabad, Pakistan 42 D5 31 30N 73 5 E
Faith, U.S.A. 80 C3 45 2N 102 2W
Faizabad, India 43 F10 26 45N 82 10 E
Fajardo, Puerto Rico 89 C6 18 20N 65 39W
Fajr, Wādī, Si. Arabia 44 D3 29 10N 38 10 E
Fakenham, U.K. 10 E8 52 51N 0 51 E
Fakfak, Indonesia 37 E8 3 0S 132 15 E
Faku, China 35 C12 42 32N 123 21 E
Falaise, France 18 B3 48 54N 0 12W
Falaise, Mui, Vietnam 38 C5 19 6N 105 45 E
Falam, Burma 41 H18 23 0N 93 45 E
Falcó, C. des, Spain 22 C7 38 50N 1 23 E
Falcón, Presa, Mexico 87 B5 26 35N 99 10W
Falcon Lake, Canada 73 D9 49 42N 95 15W
Falcon Reservoir, U.S.A. 81 M5 26 34N 99 10W
Falconara Marittima, Italy 20 C5 43 37N 13 24 E
Falcone, C. del, Italy 20 D3 40 58N 8 12 E
Falconer, U.S.A. 78 D5 42 7N 79 13W
Faleshty = Făleşti, Moldova 17 E14 47 32N 27 44 E
Făleşti, Moldova 17 E14 47 32N 27 44 E
Falfurrias, U.S.A. 81 M5 27 14N 98 9W
Falher, Canada 72 B5 55 44N 117 15W
Falirakí, Greece 23 C10 36 22N 28 12 E
Falkenberg, Sweden 9 H15 56 54N 12 30 E
Falkirk, U.K. 12 F5 56 0N 3 47W
Falkirk □, U.K. 12 F5 55 58N 3 49W
Falkland, U.K. 12 E5 56 16N 3 12W
Falkland Is. □, Atl. Oc. 96 G5 51 30S 59 0W
Falkland Sd., Falk. Is. 96 G5 52 0S 60 0W
Falköping, Sweden 9 G15 58 12N 13 33 E
Fall River, U.S.A. 79 E13 41 43N 71 10W
Fallbrook, U.S.A. 85 M9 33 23N 117 15W
Fallon, U.S.A. 82 G4 39 28N 118 47W
Falls City, U.S.A. 80 E7 40 3N 95 36W
Falls Creek, U.S.A. 78 E6 41 9N 78 48W
Falmouth, Jamaica 88 C4 18 30N 77 40W
Falmouth, U.K. 11 G2 50 9N 5 5W
Falmouth, U.S.A. 79 E14 41 33N 70 37W
Falsa, Pta., Mexico 86 B1 27 51N 115 3W
False B., S. Africa 56 E2 34 15S 18 40 E
Falso, C., Honduras 88 C3 15 12N 83 21W
Falster, Denmark 9 J14 54 45N 11 55 E
Falsterbo, Sweden 9 J15 55 23N 12 50 E
Fălticeni, Romania 17 E14 47 21N 26 20 E
Falun, Sweden 9 F16 60 37N 15 37 E
Famagusta, Cyprus 23 D12 35 8N 33 55 E
Famagusta Bay, Cyprus 23 D13 35 15N 34 0 E
Famalé, Niger 50 F6 14 33N 1 5 E
Famatina, Sierra de, Argentina 94 B2 27 30S 68 0W
Family L., Canada 73 C9 51 54N 95 27W
Famoso, U.S.A. 85 K7 35 37N 119 12W
Fan Xian, China 34 G8 35 55N 115 38 E
Fanad Hd., Ireland 13 A4 55 17N 7 38W
Fandriana, Madag. 57 C8 20 14S 47 21 E
Fangcheng, China 34 H7 33 18N 112 59 E
Fangshan, China 34 E6 38 3N 111 25 E
Fangzi, China 35 F10 36 33N 119 10 E
Fanjiatun, China 35 C13 43 40N 125 15 E
Fannich, L., U.K. 12 D4 57 38N 4 59W
Fannūj, Iran 45 E8 26 35N 59 38 E
Fanø, Denmark 9 J13 55 25N 8 25 E
Fano, Italy 20 C5 43 50N 13 1 E
Fanshi, China 34 E7 39 12N 113 20 E
Fao = Al Fāw, Iraq 45 D6 30 0N 48 30 E
Faqirwali, Pakistan 42 E5 29 27N 73 0 E
Faradje, Dem. Rep. of the Congo 54 B2 3 50N 29 45 E
Farafangana, Madag. 57 C8 22 49S 47 50 E
Farāh, Afghan. 40 C3 32 20N 62 7 E
Farāh □, Afghan. 40 C3 32 25N 62 10 E
Farahalana, Madag. 57 A9 14 26S 50 10 E
Faranah, Guinea 50 F3 10 3N 10 45W
Farasān, Jazā'ir, Si. Arabia 46 D3 16 45N 41 55 E
Farasan Is. = Farasān, Jazā'ir, Si. Arabia 46 D3 16 45N 41 55 E
Faratsiho, Madag. 57 B8 19 24S 46 57 E
Fareham, U.K. 11 G6 50 51N 1 11W
Farewell, C., N.Z. 59 J4 40 29S 172 43 E
Farewell C. = Farvel, Kap, Greenland 4 D5 59 48N 43 55W
Farghona, Uzbekistan 26 E8 40 23N 71 19 E
Fargo, U.S.A. 80 B6 46 53N 96 48W
Fār'iah, W. al →, West Bank 47 C4 32 12N 35 27 E
Faribault, U.S.A. 80 C8 44 18N 93 16W
Faridabad, India 42 E6 28 26N 77 19 E
Faridkot, India 42 D6 30 44N 74 45 E
Faridpur, Bangla. 43 H13 23 15N 89 55 E
Faridpur, India 43 E8 28 13N 79 33 E
Farīmān, Iran 45 C8 35 40N 59 49 E
Farina, Australia 63 E2 30 3S 138 15 E
Fariones, Pta., Canary Is. 22 E6 29 13N 13 28W
Farmerville, U.S.A. 81 J8 32 47N 92 24W
Farmingdale, U.S.A. 79 F10 40 12N 74 10W
Farmington, Canada 72 B4 55 54N 120 30W
Farmington, Calif., U.S.A. 84 H6 37 55N 120 59W
Farmington, Maine, U.S.A. 77 C10 44 40N 70 9W
Farmington, Mo., U.S.A. 81 G9 37 47N 90 25W
Farmington, N.H., U.S.A. 79 C13 43 24N 71 4W
Farmington, N. Mex., U.S.A. 83 H9 36 44N 108 12W
Farmington, Utah, U.S.A. 82 F8 41 0N 111 12W
Farmington →, U.S.A. 79 E12 41 51N 72 38W
Farmville, U.S.A. 76 G6 37 18N 78 24W
Farne Is., U.K. 10 B6 55 38N 1 37W
Farnham, Canada 79 A12 45 17N 72 59W
Farnham, Mt., Canada 72 C5 50 29N 116 30W
Faro, Brazil 93 D7 2 10S 56 39W
Faro, Canada 68 B6 62 11N 133 22W
Faro, Portugal 19 D2 37 2N 7 55W
Fårö, Sweden 9 H18 57 55N 19 5 E
Farquhar, C., Australia 61 D1 23 50S 113 36 E
Farrars Cr. →, Australia 62 D3 25 35S 140 43 E
Farrāshband, Iran 45 D7 28 57N 52 5 E
Farrell, U.S.A. 78 E4 41 13N 80 30W
Farrokhī, Iran 45 C8 33 50N 59 31 E
Farruch, C. = Ferrutx, C., Spain 22 B10 39 47N 3 21 E
Farrukhabad-cum-Fatehgarh, India 40 F11 27 30N 79 32 E
Fārs □, Iran 45 D7 29 30N 55 0 E
Fársala, Greece 21 E10 39 17N 22 23 E
Farson, U.S.A. 82 E9 42 6N 109 27W
Farsund, Norway 9 G12 58 5N 6 55 E
Fartak, Râs, Si. Arabia 44 D2 28 5N 34 34 E
Fartak, Ra's, Yemen 46 D5 15 38N 52 15 E
Fartura, Serra da, Brazil 95 B5 26 21S 52 52W
Fārūj, Iran 45 B8 37 14N 58 14 E
Farvel, Kap, Greenland 4 D5 59 48N 43 55W
Farwell, U.S.A. 81 H3 34 23N 103 2W
Fasā, Iran 45 D7 29 0N 53 39 E
Fasano, Italy 20 D7 40 50N 17 22 E
Fastiv, Ukraine 17 C15 50 7N 29 57 E
Fastov = Fastiv, Ukraine 17 C15 50 7N 29 57 E
Fatagar, Tanjung, Indonesia 37 E8 2 46S 131 57 E
Fatehabad, Haryana, India 42 E6 29 31N 75 27 E
Fatehabad, Ut. P., India 42 F8 27 1N 78 19 E
Fatehgarh, India 43 F8 27 25N 79 35 E
Fatehpur, Bihar, India 43 G11 24 38N 85 14 E
Fatehpur, Raj., India 42 F6 28 0N 74 40 E
Fatehpur, Ut. P., India 43 G9 25 56N 81 13 E
Fatehpur, Ut. P., India 43 F9 27 10N 81 13 E
Fatehpur Sikri, India 42 F6 27 6N 77 40 E
Fatima, Canada 71 C7 47 24N 61 53W
Faulkton, U.S.A. 80 C5 45 2N 99 8W
Faure I., Australia 61 E1 25 52S 113 50 E
Fauresmith, S. Africa 56 D4 29 44S 25 17 E
Fauske, Norway 8 C16 67 17N 15 25 E
Favara, Italy 20 F5 37 19N 13 39 E
Favāritx, C. de, Spain 22 B11 40 0N 4 15 E
Favignana, Italy 20 F5 37 56N 12 20 E
Fawcett, Pt., Australia 60 B5 11 46S 130 2 E
Fawn →, Canada 70 A2 55 20N 87 35W
Fawnskin, U.S.A. 85 L10 34 16N 116 56W
Faxaflói, Iceland 8 D2 64 29N 23 0W
Faya-Largeau, Chad 51 E9 17 58N 19 6 E
Fayd, Si. Arabia 44 E4 27 1N 42 52 E
Fayette, Ala., U.S.A. 77 J2 33 41N 87 50W
Fayette, Mo., U.S.A. 80 F8 39 9N 92 41W
Fayetteville, Ark., U.S.A. 81 G7 36 4N 94 10W
Fayetteville, N.C., U.S.A. 77 H6 35 3N 78 53W
Fayetteville, Tenn., U.S.A. 77 H2 35 9N 86 34W
Fazilka, India 42 D6 30 27N 74 2 E
Fazilpur, Pakistan 42 E4 29 18N 70 29 E
Fdérik, Mauritania 50 D3 22 40N 12 45W
Feale →, Ireland 13 D2 52 27N 9 37W
Fear, C., U.S.A. 77 J7 33 50N 77 58W
Feather →, U.S.A. 82 G3 38 47N 121 36W
Feather Falls, U.S.A. 84 F5 39 36N 121 16W
Featherston, N.Z. 59 J5 41 6S 175 20 E
Featherstone, Zimbabwe 55 F3 18 42S 30 55 E
Fécamp, France 18 B4 49 45N 0 22 E
Fedala = Mohammedia, Morocco 50 B4 33 44N 7 21W
Federación, Argentina 94 C4 31 0S 57 55W
Féderal, Argentina 96 C5 30 57S 58 48W
Federal Way, U.S.A. 84 C4 47 18N 122 19W
Fedeshkūh, Iran 45 D7 28 49N 53 50 E
Fehmarn, Germany 16 A6 54 27N 11 7 E
Fehmarn Bælt, Europe 9 J14 54 35N 11 20 E
Fehmarn Belt = Fehmarn Bælt, Europe 9 J14 54 35N 11 20 E
Fei Xian, China 35 G9 35 18N 117 59 E
Feijó, Brazil 92 E4 8 9S 70 21W
Feilding, N.Z. 59 J5 40 13S 175 35 E
Feira de Santana, Brazil 93 F11 12 15S 38 57W
Feixiang, China 34 F8 36 30N 114 45 E
Felanitx, Spain 22 B10 39 28N 3 9 E
Feldkirch, Austria 16 E5 47 15N 9 37 E

Felipe Carrillo Puerto

Felipe Carrillo Puerto, Mexico 87 D7 19 38N 88 3W
Felixstowe, U.K. 11 F9 51 58N 1 23 E
Felton, U.S.A. 84 H4 37 3N 122 4W
Femer Bælt = Fehmarn Bælt, Europe 9 J14 54 35N 11 20 E
Femunden, Norway 9 E14 62 10N 11 53 E
Fen He →, China 34 G6 35 36N 110 42 E
Fenelon Falls, Canada 78 B6 44 32N 78 45W
Feng Xian, Jiangsu, China 34 G9 34 43N 116 35 E
Feng Xian, Shaanxi, China 34 H4 33 54N 106 40 E
Fengcheng, China 35 D13 40 28N 124 5 E
Fengfeng, China 34 F8 36 28N 114 8 E
Fengjie, China 33 C5 31 5N 109 36 E
Fengning, China 34 D9 41 10N 116 33 E
Fengqiu, China 34 G8 35 2N 114 25 E
Fengrun, China 35 E10 39 48N 118 8 E
Fengtai, China 34 E9 39 50N 116 18 E
Fengxiang, China 34 G4 34 29N 107 25 E
Fengyang, China 35 H9 32 51N 117 29 E
Fengzhen, China 34 D7 40 25N 113 2 E
Fenoarivo Afovoany, Madag. 57 B8 18 26S 46 34 E
Fenoarivo Atsinanana, Madag. 57 B8 17 22S 49 25 E
Fens, The, U.K. 10 E7 52 38N 0 2W
Fenton, U.S.A. 76 D4 42 48N 83 42W
Fenxi, China 34 F6 36 40N 111 31 E
Fenyang, China 34 F6 37 18N 111 48 E
Feodosiya, Ukraine 25 E6 45 2N 35 16 E
Ferdows, Iran 45 C8 33 58N 58 2 E
Ferfer, Somali Rep. 46 F4 5 4N 45 9 E
Fergana = Farghona, Uzbekistan 26 E8 40 23N 71 19 E
Fergus, Canada 78 C4 43 43N 80 24W
Fergus Falls, U.S.A. 80 B6 46 17N 96 4W
Ferkéssédougou, Ivory C. 50 G4 9 35N 5 6W
Ferland, Canada 70 B2 50 19N 88 27W
Fermanagh □, U.K. 13 B4 54 21N 7 40W
Fermo, Italy 20 C5 43 9N 13 43 E
Fermont, Canada 71 B6 52 47N 67 5W
Fermont, Qué., Canada 69 C13 50 28N 67 29W
Fermoy, Ireland 13 D3 52 9N 8 16W
Fernández, Argentina 94 B3 27 55S 63 50W
Fernandina Beach, U.S.A. 77 K5 30 40N 81 27W
Fernando de Noronha, Brazil 93 D12 4 0S 33 10W
Fernando Póo = Bioko, Eq. Guin. 52 D1 3 30N 8 40 E
Ferndale, U.S.A. 84 B4 48 51N 122 36W
Fernie, Canada 72 D5 49 30N 115 5W
Fernlees, Australia 62 C4 23 51S 148 7 E
Fernley, U.S.A. 82 G4 39 36N 119 15W
Ferozepore = Firozpur, India 42 D6 30 55N 74 40 E
Ferrara, Italy 20 B4 44 50N 11 35 E
Ferreñafe, Peru 92 E3 6 42S 79 50W
Ferrerías, Spain 22 B11 39 59N 4 1 E
Ferret, C., France 18 D3 44 38N 1 15W
Ferriday, U.S.A. 81 K9 31 38N 91 33W
Ferrol, Spain 19 A1 43 29N 8 15W
Ferron, U.S.A. 83 G8 39 5N 111 8W
Ferrutx, C., Spain 22 B10 39 47N 3 21 E
Ferryland, Canada 71 C9 47 2N 52 53W
Fertile, U.S.A. 80 B6 47 32N 96 17W
Fès, Morocco 50 B5 34 0N 5 0W
Fessenden, U.S.A. 80 B5 47 39N 99 38W
Festus, U.S.A. 80 F9 38 13N 90 24W
Feteşti, Romania 17 F14 44 22N 27 51 E
Fethiye, Turkey 25 G4 36 36N 29 6 E
Fetlar, U.K. 12 A8 60 36N 0 52W
Feuilles →, Canada 69 C12 58 47N 70 4W
Fez = Fès, Morocco 50 B5 34 0N 5 0W
Fezzan, Libya 51 C8 27 0N 13 0 E
Fiambalá, Argentina 94 B2 27 45S 67 37W
Fianarantsoa, Madag. 57 C8 21 26S 47 5 E
Fianarantsoa □, Madag. 57 B8 19 30S 47 0 E
Ficksburg, S. Africa 57 D4 28 51S 27 53 E
Field →, Australia 62 C2 23 48S 138 0 E
Field I., Australia 60 B5 12 5S 132 23 E
Fieri, Albania 21 D8 40 43N 19 33 E
Fife □, U.K. 12 E5 56 16N 3 1W
Fife Ness, U.K. 12 E6 56 17N 2 35W
Fifth Cataract, Sudan 51 E12 18 23N 33 47 E
Figeac, France 18 D5 44 37N 2 2 E
Figtree, Zimbabwe 55 G2 20 22S 28 20 E
Figueira da Foz, Portugal 19 B1 40 7N 8 54W
Figueres, Spain 19 A7 42 18N 2 58 E
Figuig, Morocco 50 B5 32 5N 1 11W
Fihaonana, Madag. 57 B8 18 36S 47 12 E
Fiherenana, Madag. 57 B8 18 29S 48 24 E
Fiherenana →, Madag. 57 C7 23 19S 43 37 E
Fiji ■, Pac. Oc. 59 C8 17 20S 179 0 E
Filey, U.K. 10 C7 54 12N 0 18W
Filey B., U.K. 10 C7 54 12N 0 15W
Filfla, Malta 23 D1 35 47N 14 24 E
Filiatrá, Greece 21 F9 37 9N 21 35 E
Filingué, Niger 50 F6 14 21N 3 22 E
Filipstad, Sweden 9 G16 59 43N 14 9 E
Fillmore, Calif., U.S.A. 85 L8 34 24N 118 55W
Fillmore, Utah, U.S.A. 83 G7 38 58N 112 20W
Finch, Canada 79 A9 45 11N 75 7W
Findhorn →, U.K. 12 D5 57 38N 3 38W
Findlay, U.S.A. 76 E4 41 2N 83 39W
Finger L., Canada 70 B1 53 33N 93 30W
Finger Lakes, U.S.A. 79 D8 42 40N 76 30W
Fingoè, Mozam. 55 E3 14 55S 31 50 E
Finisterre, C. = Fisterra, C., Spain 19 A1 42 50N 9 19W
Finke, Australia 62 D1 25 34S 134 35 E
Finland ■, Europe 8 E22 63 0N 27 0 E
Finland, G. of, Europe 9 G21 60 0N 26 0 E
Finlay →, Canada 72 B3 57 0N 125 10W
Finley, Australia 63 F4 35 38S 145 35 E
Finley, U.S.A. 80 B6 47 31N 97 50W
Finn →, Ireland 13 B4 54 51N 7 28W
Finnigan, Mt., Australia 62 B4 15 49S 145 17 E
Finniss, C., Australia 63 E1 33 8S 134 51 E
Finnmark, Norway 8 B20 69 37N 23 57 E
Finnsnes, Norway 8 B18 69 14N 18 0 E
Finspång, Sweden 9 G16 58 43N 15 47 E
Fiora →, Italy 20 C4 42 20N 11 34 E
Fiq, Syria 47 C4 32 46N 35 41 E
Firat = Furāt, Nahr al →, Asia 44 D5 31 0N 47 25 E
Firebag →, Canada 73 B6 57 45N 111 21W
Firebaugh, U.S.A. 84 J6 36 52N 120 27W
Firedrake L., Canada 73 A8 61 25N 104 30W
Firenze, Italy 20 C4 43 46N 11 15 E
Firk →, Iraq 44 D5 30 59N 44 34 E
Firozabad, India 43 F8 27 10N 78 25 E
Firozpur, India 42 D6 30 55N 74 40 E
Firozpur-Jhirka, India 42 F7 27 48N 76 57 E
Fīrūzābād, Iran 45 D7 28 52N 52 35 E
Fīrūzkūh, Iran 45 C7 35 50N 52 50 E
Firvale, Canada 72 C3 52 27N 126 13W
Fish →, Namibia 56 D2 28 7S 17 10 E
Fish →, S. Africa 56 E3 31 30S 20 16 E
Fisher, Australia 61 F5 30 30S 131 0 E
Fisher B., Canada 73 C9 51 35N 97 13W
Fishers I., U.S.A. 79 E13 41 15N 72 0W
Fishguard, U.K. 11 E3 52 0N 4 58W
Fishing L., Canada 73 C9 52 10N 95 24W
Fishkill, U.S.A. 79 E11 41 32N 73 53W
Fisterra, C., Spain 19 A1 42 50N 9 19W
Fitchburg, U.S.A. 79 D13 42 35N 71 48W
Fitz Roy, Argentina 96 F3 47 0S 67 0W
Fitzgerald, Canada 72 B6 59 51N 111 36W
Fitzgerald, U.S.A. 77 K4 31 43N 83 15W
Fitzmaurice →, Australia 60 B5 14 45S 130 5 E
Fitzroy →, Queens., Australia 62 C5 23 32S 150 52 E
Fitzroy →, W. Austral., Australia 60 C3 17 31S 123 35 E
Fitzroy, Mte., Argentina 96 F2 49 17S 73 5W
Fitzroy Crossing, Australia 60 C4 18 9S 125 38 E
Fitzwilliam I., Canada 78 A3 45 30N 81 45W
Fiume = Rijeka, Croatia 16 F8 45 20N 14 21 E
Five Points, U.S.A. 84 J6 36 26N 120 6W
Fizi, Dem. Rep. of the Congo 54 C2 4 17S 28 55 E
Flagstaff, U.S.A. 83 J8 35 12N 111 39W
Flagstaff L., Maine, U.S.A. 77 C10 45 12N 70 19W
Flagstaff L., Maine, U.S.A. 79 A14 45 12N 70 18W
Flaherty I., Canada 70 A4 56 15N 79 15W
Flåm, Norway 9 F12 60 50N 7 7 E
Flambeau →, U.S.A. 80 C9 45 18N 91 14W
Flamborough Hd., U.K. 10 C7 54 7N 0 5W
Flaming Gorge Reservoir, U.S.A. 82 F9 41 10N 109 25W
Flamingo, Teluk, Indonesia 37 F9 5 30S 138 0 E
Flanders = Flandre, Europe 18 A5 50 50N 2 30 E
Flandre, Europe 18 A5 50 50N 2 30 E
Flandre Occidentale = West-Vlaanderen □, Belgium 15 D2 51 0N 3 0 E
Flandre Orientale = Oost-Vlaanderen □, Belgium 15 C3 51 5N 3 50 E
Flandreau, U.S.A. 80 C6 44 3N 96 36W
Flanigan, U.S.A. 84 E7 40 10N 119 53W
Flannan Is., U.K. 12 C1 58 9N 7 52W
Flåsjön, Sweden 8 D16 64 5N 15 40 E
Flat →, Canada 72 A3 61 33N 125 18W
Flathead L., U.S.A. 82 C7 47 51N 114 8W
Flattery, C., Australia 62 A4 14 58S 145 21 E
Flattery, C., U.S.A. 84 B2 48 23N 124 29W
Flatwoods, U.S.A. 76 F4 38 31N 82 43W
Fleetwood, U.K. 10 D4 53 55N 3 1W
Fleetwood, U.S.A. 79 F9 40 27N 75 49W
Flekkefjord, Norway 9 G12 58 18N 6 39 E
Flemington, U.S.A. 78 E7 41 7N 77 28W
Flensburg, Germany 16 A5 54 47N 9 27 E
Flers, France 18 B3 48 47N 0 33W
Flesherton, Canada 78 B4 44 16N 80 33W
Flesko, Tanjung, Indonesia 37 D6 0 29N 124 30 E
Fleurieu Pen., Australia 63 F2 35 40S 138 5 E
Flevoland □, Neths. 15 B5 52 30N 5 30 E
Flin Flon, Canada 73 C8 54 46N 101 53W
Flinders →, Australia 62 B3 17 36S 140 36 E
Flinders B., Australia 61 F2 34 19S 115 19 E
Flinders Group, Australia 62 A3 14 11S 144 15 E
Flinders I., S. Austral., Australia 63 E1 33 44S 134 41 E
Flinders I., Tas., Australia 62 G4 40 0S 148 0 E
Flinders Ranges, Australia 63 E2 31 30S 138 30 E
Flinders Reefs, Australia 62 B4 17 37S 148 31 E
Flint, U.K. 10 D4 53 15N 3 8W
Flint, U.S.A. 76 D4 43 1N 83 41W
Flint →, U.S.A. 77 K3 30 57N 84 34W
Flint I., Kiribati 65 J12 11 26S 151 48W
Flintshire □, U.K. 10 D4 53 17N 3 17W
Flodden, U.K. 10 B5 55 37N 2 8W
Floodwood, U.S.A. 80 B8 46 55N 92 55W
Flora, U.S.A. 76 F1 38 40N 88 29W
Florala, U.S.A. 77 K2 31 0N 86 20W
Florence = Firenze, Italy 20 C4 43 46N 11 15 E
Florence, Ala., U.S.A. 77 H2 34 48N 87 41W
Florence, Ariz., U.S.A. 83 K8 33 2N 111 23W
Florence, Colo., U.S.A. 80 F2 38 23N 105 8W
Florence, Oreg., U.S.A. 82 E1 43 58N 124 7W
Florence, S.C., U.S.A. 77 H6 34 12N 79 46W
Florence, L., Australia 63 D2 28 53S 138 9 E
Florencia, Colombia 92 1 36N 75 36W
Florennes, Belgium 15 D4 50 15N 4 35 E
Florenville, Belgium 15 E5 49 40N 5 19 E
Flores, Guatemala 88 C2 16 59N 89 50W
Flores, Indonesia 37 F6 8 35S 121 0 E
Flores I., Canada 72 D3 49 20N 126 10W
Flores Sea, Indonesia 37 F6 6 30S 120 0 E
Floreşti, Moldova 17 E15 47 53N 28 17 E
Floresville, U.S.A. 81 L5 29 8N 98 10W
Floriano, Brazil 93 E10 6 50S 43 0W
Florianópolis, Brazil 95 B6 27 30S 48 30W
Florida, Cuba 88 B4 21 32N 78 14W
Florida, Uruguay 95 C4 34 7S 56 10W
Florida □, U.S.A. 77 L5 28 0N 82 0W
Florida, Straits of, U.S.A. 88 B4 25 0N 80 0W
Florida B., U.S.A. 88 B3 25 0N 80 45W
Florida Keys, U.S.A. 77 N5 24 40N 81 0W
Flórina, Greece 21 D9 40 48N 21 26 E
Florø, Norway 9 F11 61 35N 5 1 E
Flower Station, Canada 79 A8 45 10N 76 41W
Flowerpot I., Canada 78 A3 45 18N 81 38W
Floydada, U.S.A. 81 J4 33 59N 101 20W
Fluk, Indonesia 37 E7 1 42S 127 44 E
Flushing = Vlissingen, Neths. 15 C3 51 26N 3 34 E
Flying Fish, C., Antarctica 5 D15 72 6S 102 29W
Foam Lake, Canada 73 C8 51 40N 103 32W
Foça, Turkey 21 E12 38 39N 26 46 E
Focşani, Romania 17 F14 45 41N 27 15 E
Fóggia, Italy 20 D6 41 27N 15 34 E
Fogo, Canada 71 C9 49 43N 54 17W
Fogo I., Canada 71 C9 49 40N 54 5W
Föhr, Germany 16 A5 54 43N 8 30 E
Foix, France 18 E4 42 58N 1 38 E
Folda, Nord-Trøndelag, Norway 8 D14 64 32N 10 30 E
Folda, Nordland, Norway 8 C16 67 38N 14 50 E
Foley, U.S.A. 77 K2 30 24N 87 41W
Foleyet, Canada 70 C3 48 15N 82 25W
Folgefonni, Norway 9 F12 60 3N 6 23 E
Foligno, Italy 20 C5 42 57N 12 42 E
Folkestone, U.K. 11 F9 51 5N 1 12 E
Folkston, U.S.A. 77 K5 30 50N 82 0W
Follansbee, U.S.A. 78 F4 40 19N 80 35W
Folsom L., U.S.A. 84 G5 38 42N 121 9W
Fond-du-Lac, Canada 73 B7 59 19N 107 12W
Fond du Lac, U.S.A. 80 D10 43 47N 88 27W
Fond-du-Lac →, Canada 73 B7 59 17N 106 0W
Fonda, U.S.A. 79 D10 42 57N 74 22W
Fondi, Italy 20 D5 41 21N 13 25 E
Fongafale, Tuvalu 64 H9 8 31S 179 13 E
Fonsagrada = A Fonsagrada, Spain 19 A2 43 8N 7 4W
Fonseca, G. de, Cent. Amer. 88 D2 13 10N 87 40W
Fontainebleau, France 18 B5 48 24N 2 40 E
Fontana, U.S.A. 85 L9 34 6N 117 26W
Fontas →, Canada 72 B4 58 14N 121 48W
Fonte Boa, Brazil 92 D5 2 33S 66 0W
Fontenay-le-Comte, France 18 C3 46 28N 0 48W
Fontenelle Reservoir, U.S.A. 82 E8 42 1N 110 3W
Fontur, Iceland 8 C6 66 23N 14 32W
Foochow = Fuzhou, China 33 D6 26 5N 119 16 E
Foping, China 34 H5 33 41N 108 0 E
Forbes, Australia 63 E4 33 22S 148 0 E
Forbesganj, India 43 F12 26 17N 87 18 E
Ford City, Calif., U.S.A. 85 K7 35 9N 119 27W
Ford City, Pa., U.S.A. 78 F5 40 46N 79 32W
Førde, Norway 9 F11 61 27N 5 53 E
Ford's Bridge, Australia 63 D4 29 41S 145 29 E
Fordyce, U.S.A. 81 J8 33 49N 92 25W
Forel, Mt., Greenland 4 C6 66 52N 36 55W
Foremost, Canada 72 D6 49 26N 111 34W
Forest, Canada 78 C3 43 6N 82 0W
Forest, U.S.A. 81 J10 32 22N 89 29W
Forest City, Iowa, U.S.A. 80 D8 43 16N 93 39W
Forest City, N.C., U.S.A. 77 H5 35 20N 81 52W
Forest City, Pa., U.S.A. 79 E9 41 39N 75 28W
Forest Grove, U.S.A. 84 E3 45 31N 123 7W
Forestburg, Canada 72 C6 52 35N 112 1W
Foresthill, U.S.A. 84 F6 39 1N 120 49W
Forestier Pen., Australia 62 G4 43 0S 148 0 E
Forestville, Canada 71 C6 48 48N 69 2W
Forestville, Calif., U.S.A. 84 G4 38 28N 122 54W
Forestville, N.Y., U.S.A. 78 D5 42 28N 79 10W
Forfar, U.K. 12 E6 56 39N 2 53W
Forks, U.S.A. 84 C2 47 57N 124 23W
Forksville, U.S.A. 79 E8 41 29N 76 35W
Forlì, Italy 20 B5 44 13N 12 3 E
Forman, U.S.A. 80 B6 46 7N 97 38W
Formby Pt., U.K. 10 D4 53 33N 3 6W
Formentera, Spain 22 C7 38 43N 1 27 E
Formentor, C. de, Spain 22 B10 39 58N 3 13 E
Former Yugoslav Republic of Macedonia = Macedonia ■, Europe 21 D9 41 53N 21 40 E
Fórmia, Italy 20 D5 41 15N 13 37 E
Formosa = Taiwan ■, Asia 33 D7 23 30N 121 0 E
Formosa, Argentina 94 B4 26 15S 58 10W
Formosa, Brazil 93 G9 15 32S 47 20W
Formosa □, Argentina 94 B4 25 0S 60 0W
Formosa, Serra, Brazil 93 F8 12 0S 55 0W
Formosa Bay, Kenya 54 C5 2 40S 40 20 E
Fornells, Spain 22 A11 40 3N 4 7 E
Føroyar, Atl. Oc. 8 F9 62 0N 7 0W
Forres, U.K. 12 D5 57 37N 3 37W
Forrest, Australia 61 F4 30 51S 128 6 E
Forrest, Mt., Australia 61 D4 24 48S 127 45 E
Forrest City, U.S.A. 81 H9 35 1N 90 47W
Forsayth, Australia 62 B3 18 33S 143 34 E
Forssa, Finland 9 F20 60 49N 23 38 E
Forst, Germany 16 C8 51 45N 14 37 E
Forsyth, U.S.A. 82 C10 46 16N 106 41W
Fort Abbas, Pakistan 42 E5 29 12N 72 52 E
Fort Albany, Canada 70 B3 52 15N 81 35W
Fort Ann, U.S.A. 79 C11 43 25N 73 30W
Fort Assiniboine, Canada 72 C6 54 20N 114 45W
Fort Augustus, U.K. 12 D4 57 9N 4 42W
Fort Beaufort, S. Africa 56 E4 32 46S 26 40 E
Fort Benton, U.S.A. 82 C8 47 49N 110 40W
Fort Bragg, U.S.A. 82 G2 39 26N 123 48W
Fort Bridger, U.S.A. 82 F8 41 19N 110 23W
Fort Chipewyan, Canada 73 B6 58 42N 111 8W
Fort Collins, U.S.A. 80 E2 40 35N 105 5W
Fort-Coulonge, Canada 70 C4 45 50N 76 45W
Fort Covington, U.S.A. 79 B10 44 59N 74 29W
Fort Davis, U.S.A. 81 K3 30 35N 103 54W
Fort-de-France, Martinique 89 D7 14 36N 61 2W
Fort Defiance, U.S.A. 83 J9 35 45N 109 5W
Fort Dodge, U.S.A. 80 D7 42 30N 94 11W
Fort Edward, U.S.A. 79 C11 43 16N 73 35W
Fort Erie, Canada 78 D6 42 54N 78 56W
Fort Fairfield, U.S.A. 77 B12 46 46N 67 50W
Fort Frances, Canada 73 D10 48 36N 93 24W
Fort Garland, U.S.A. 83 H11 37 26N 105 26W
Fort George = Chisasibi, Canada 70 B4 53 50N 79 0W
Fort Good-Hope, Canada 68 B7 66 14N 128 40W
Fort Hancock, U.S.A. 83 L11 31 18N 105 51W
Fort Hertz = Putao, Burma 41 F20 27 28N 97 30 E
Fort Hope, Canada 70 B2 51 30N 88 0W
Fort Irwin, U.S.A. 85 K10 35 16N 116 34W
Fort Jameson = Chipata, Zambia 55 E3 13 38S 32 28 E
Fort Kent, U.S.A. 77 B11 47 15N 68 36W
Fort Klamath, U.S.A. 82 E3 42 42N 122 0W
Fort-Lamy = Ndjamena, Chad 51 F8 12 10N 14 59 E
Fort Laramie, U.S.A. 80 D2 42 13N 104 31W
Fort Lauderdale, U.S.A. 77 M5 26 7N 80 8W
Fort Liard, Canada 72 A4 60 14N 123 30W
Fort Liberté, Haiti 89 C5 19 42N 71 51W
Fort Lupton, U.S.A. 80 E2 40 5N 104 49W
Fort Mackay, Canada 72 B6 57 12N 111 41W
Fort Macleod, Canada 72 D6 49 45N 113 30W
Fort McMurray, Canada 72 B6 56 44N 111 7W
Fort McPherson, Canada 68 B6 67 30N 134 55W
Fort Madison, U.S.A. 80 E9 40 38N 91 27W
Fort Meade, U.S.A. 77 M5 27 45N 81 48W
Fort Morgan, U.S.A. 80 E3 40 15N 103 48W
Fort Munro, Pakistan 42 E3 29 54N 69 58 E
Fort Myers, U.S.A. 77 M5 26 39N 81 52W
Fort Nelson, Canada 72 B4 58 50N 122 44W
Fort Nelson →, Canada 72 B4 59 32N 124 0W
Fort Norman = Tulita, Canada 68 B7 64 57N 125 30W
Fort Payne, U.S.A. 77 H3 34 26N 85 43W
Fort Peck, U.S.A. 82 B10 48 1N 106 27W
Fort Peck Dam, U.S.A. 82 C10 48 0N 106 26W
Fort Peck L., U.S.A. 82 C10 48 0N 106 26W
Fort Pierce, U.S.A. 77 M5 27 27N 80 20W
Fort Pierre, U.S.A. 80 C4 44 21N 100 22W
Fort Plain, U.S.A. 79 D10 42 56N 74 37W
Fort Portal, Uganda 54 B3 0 40N 30 20 E
Fort Providence, Canada 72 A5 61 3N 117 40W
Fort Qu'Appelle, Canada 73 C8 50 45N 103 50W
Fort Resolution, Canada 72 A6 61 10N 113 40W
Fort Rixon, Zimbabwe 55 G2 20 2S 29 17 E
Fort Rosebery = Mansa, Zambia 55 E2 11 13S 28 55 E
Fort Ross, U.S.A. 84 G3 38 32N 123 13W
Fort Rousset = Owando, Congo 52 E3 0 29S 15 55 E
Fort Rupert = Waskaganish, Canada 70 B4 51 30N 78 40W
Fort St. James, Canada 72 C4 54 30N 124 10W
Fort St. John, Canada 72 B4 56 15N 120 50W
Fort Sandeman = Zhob, Pakistan 42 D3 31 20N 69 31 E
Fort Saskatchewan, Canada 72 C6 53 40N 113 15W
Fort Scott, U.S.A. 81 G7 37 50N 94 42W
Fort Severn, Canada 70 A2 56 0N 87 40W
Fort Shevchenko, Kazakstan 25 F9 44 35N 50 23 E
Fort Simpson, Canada 72 A4 61 45N 121 15W
Fort Smith, Canada 72 B6 60 0N 111 51W
Fort Smith, U.S.A. 81 H7 35 23N 94 25W
Fort Stockton, U.S.A. 81 K3 30 53N 102 53W
Fort Sumner, U.S.A. 81 H2 34 28N 104 15W
Fort Thompson, U.S.A. 80 C5 44 3N 99 26W
Fort Trinquet = Bir Mogreïn, Mauritania 50 C3 25 10N 11 25W
Fort Valley, U.S.A. 77 J4 32 33N 83 53W
Fort Vermilion, Canada 72 B5 58 24N 116 0W
Fort Walton Beach, U.S.A. 77 K2 30 25N 86 36W
Fort Wayne, U.S.A. 76 E3 41 4N 85 9W
Fort William, U.K. 12 E3 56 49N 5 7W
Fort Worth, U.S.A. 81 J6 32 45N 97 18W
Fort Yates, U.S.A. 80 B4 46 5N 100 38W
Fort Yukon, U.S.A. 68 B5 66 34N 145 16W
Fortaleza, Brazil 93 D11 3 45S 38 35W
Forteau, Canada 71 B8 51 28N 56 58W
Fortescue →, Australia 60 D2 21 0S 116 4 E
Forth →, U.K. 12 E5 56 9N 3 50W
Forth, Firth of, U.K. 12 E6 56 5N 2 55W
Fortrose, U.K. 12 D4 57 35N 4 9W
Fortuna, Calif., U.S.A. 82 F1 40 36N 124 9W
Fortuna, N. Dak., U.S.A. 80 A3 48 55N 103 47W
Fortune, Canada 71 C8 47 4N 55 50W
Fortune B., Canada 71 C8 47 30N 55 22W
Forūr, Iran 45 E7 26 17N 54 32 E
Foshan, China 33 D6 23 4N 113 5 E
Fosna, Norway 8 E14 63 50N 10 20 E
Fosnavåg, Norway 9 E11 62 22N 5 38 E
Fossano, Italy 18 D7 44 33N 7 43 E
Fossil, U.S.A. 82 D3 45 0N 120 9W
Foster, Australia 63 F4 38 40S 146 15 E
Foster, Canada 79 A12 45 17N 72 30W
Foster →, Canada 73 B7 55 47N 105 49W
Fosters Ra., Australia 62 C1 21 35S 133 48 E
Fostoria, U.S.A. 76 E4 41 10N 83 25W
Fougères, France 18 B3 48 21N 1 14W
Foul Pt., Sri Lanka 40 Q12 8 35N 81 18 E
Foula, U.K. 12 A6 60 10N 2 5W
Foulness I., U.K. 11 F8 51 36N 0 55 E
Foulpointe, Madag. 57 B8 17 41S 49 31 E
Foulweather, C., U.S.A. 74 B2 44 50N 124 5W
Foumban, Cameroon 52 C2 5 45N 10 50 E
Fountain, U.S.A. 80 F2 38 41N 104 42W
Fountain Springs, U.S.A. 85 K8 35 54N 118 51W
Fouriesburg, S. Africa 56 D4 28 38S 28 14 E
Foúrnoi, Greece 21 F12 37 36N 26 32 E
Fourth Cataract, Sudan 51 E12 18 47N 32 3 E
Fouta Djalon, Guinea 50 F3 11 20N 12 10W
Foux, Cap-à-, Haiti 89 C5 19 43N 73 27W
Foveaux Str., N.Z. 59 M2 46 42S 168 10 E
Fowey, U.K. 11 G3 50 20N 4 39W
Fowler, Calif., U.S.A. 84 J7 36 38N 119 41W
Fowler, Colo., U.S.A. 80 F3 38 8N 104 2W
Fowlers B., Australia 61 F5 31 59S 132 34 E
Fowman, Iran 45 B6 37 13N 49 19 E
Fox →, Canada 73 B10 56 3N 93 18W
Fox Creek, Canada 72 C5 54 24N 116 48W
Fox Lake, Canada 72 B6 58 28N 114 31W
Fox Valley, Canada 73 C7 50 30N 109 25W
Foxboro, U.S.A. 79 D13 42 4N 71 16W
Foxe Basin, Canada 69 B12 66 0N 77 0W
Foxe Chan., Canada 69 B12 65 0N 80 0W
Foxe Pen., Canada 69 B12 65 0N 76 0W
Foxton, N.Z. 59 J5 40 29S 175 18 E
Foyle, Lough, U.K. 13 A4 55 7N 7 4W
Foynes, Ireland 13 D2 52 37N 9 7W
Fóz do Cunene, Angola 56 B1 17 15S 11 48 E
Foz do Iguaçu, Brazil 95 B5 25 30S 54 30W
Frackville, U.S.A. 79 F8 40 47N 76 14W
Fraile Muerto, Uruguay 95 C5 32 31S 54 32W
Framingham, U.S.A. 79 D13 42 17N 71 25W
Franca, Brazil 93 H9 20 33S 47 30W
Francavilla Fontana, Italy 21 D7 40 32N 17 35 E
France ■, Europe 18 C5 47 0N 3 0 E
Frances, Australia 63 F3 36 41S 140 55 E
Frances →, Canada 72 A3 60 16N 129 10W
Frances L., Canada 72 A3 61 23N 129 30W
Franceville, Gabon 52 E2 1 40S 13 32 E
Franche-Comté, France 18 C6 46 50N 5 55 E
Francis Case, L., U.S.A. 80 D5 43 4N 98 34W
Francisco Beltrão, Brazil 95 B5 26 5S 53 4W
Francisco I. Madero, Coahuila, Mexico 86 B4 25 48N 103 18W
Francisco I. Madero, Durango, Mexico 86 C4 24 32N 104 22W
Francistown, Botswana 57 C4 21 7S 27 33 E
François, Canada 71 C8 47 35N 56 45W
François L., Canada 72 C3 54 0N 125 30W
Franeker, Neths. 15 A5 53 12N 5 33 E
Frankford, Canada 78 B7 44 12N 77 36W
Frankfort, S. Africa 57 D4 27 17S 28 30 E
Frankfort, Ind., U.S.A. 76 E2 40 17N 86 31W
Frankfort, Kans., U.S.A. 80 F6 39 42N 96 25W
Frankfort, Ky., U.S.A. 76 F3 38 12N 84 52W
Frankfort, N.Y., U.S.A. 79 C9 43 2N 75 4W

Gatton

Frankfurt, Brandenburg, Germany **16 B8** 52 20N 14 32 E
Frankfurt, Hessen, Germany **16 C5** 50 7N 8 41 E
Fränkische Alb, Germany **16 D6** 49 10N 11 23 E
Frankland →, Australia **61 G2** 35 0S 116 48 E
Franklin, Ky., U.S.A. **77 G2** 36 43N 86 35W
Franklin, La., U.S.A. **81 L9** 29 48N 91 30W
Franklin, Mass., U.S.A. **79 D13** 42 5N 71 24W
Franklin, N.H., U.S.A. **79 C13** 43 27N 71 39W
Franklin, Nebr., U.S.A. **80 E5** 40 6N 98 57W
Franklin, Pa., U.S.A. **78 E5** 41 24N 79 50W
Franklin, Va., U.S.A. **77 G7** 36 41N 76 56W
Franklin, W. Va., U.S.A. **76 F6** 38 39N 79 20W
Franklin B., Canada **68 B7** 69 45N 126 0W
Franklin D. Roosevelt L., U.S.A. **82 B4** 48 18N 118 9W
Franklin I., Antarctica **5 D11** 76 10S 168 30 E
Franklin L., U.S.A. **82 F6** 40 25N 115 22W
Franklin Mts., Canada **68 B7** 65 0N 125 0W
Franklin Str., Canada **68 A10** 72 0N 96 0W
Franklinton, U.S.A. **81 K9** 30 51N 90 9W
Franklinville, U.S.A. **78 D6** 42 20N 78 27W
Franks Pk., U.S.A. **82 E9** 43 58N 109 18W
Frankston, Australia **63 F4** 38 8S 145 8 E
Frantsa Iosifa, Zemlya, Russia **26 A6** 82 0N 55 0 E
Franz, Canada **70 C3** 48 25N 84 30W
Franz Josef Land = Frantsa Iosifa, Zemlya, Russia **26 A6** 82 0N 55 0 E
Fraser, U.S.A. **78 D2** 42 32N 82 57W
Fraser →, B.C., Canada **72 D4** 49 7N 123 11W
Fraser →, Nfld., Canada **71 A7** 56 39N 62 10W
Fraser, Mt., Australia **61 E2** 25 35S 118 20 E
Fraser I., Australia **63 D5** 25 15S 153 10 E
Fraser Lake, Canada **72 C4** 54 0N 124 50W
Fraserburg, S. Africa **56 E3** 31 55S 21 30 E
Fraserburgh, U.K. **12 D6** 57 42N 2 1W
Fraserdale, Canada **70 C3** 49 55N 81 37W
Fray Bentos, Uruguay **94 C4** 33 10S 58 15W
Fredericia, Denmark **9 J13** 55 34N 9 45 E
Frederick, Md., U.S.A. **76 F7** 39 25N 77 25W
Frederick, Okla., U.S.A. **81 H5** 34 23N 99 1W
Frederick, S. Dak., U.S.A. **80 C5** 45 50N 98 31W
Fredericksburg, Pa., U.S.A. **79 F8** 40 27N 76 26W
Fredericksburg, Tex., U.S.A. **81 K5** 30 16N 98 52W
Fredericksburg, Va., U.S.A. **76 F7** 38 18N 77 28W
Fredericktown, Mo., U.S.A. **81 G9** 37 34N 90 18W
Fredericktown, Ohio, U.S.A. **78 F2** 40 29N 82 33W
Frederico I. Madero, Presa, Mexico **86 B3** 28 7N 105 40W
Frederico Westphalen, Brazil **95 B5** 27 22S 53 24W
Fredericton, Canada **71 C6** 45 57N 66 40W
Fredericton Junction, Canada **71 C6** 45 41N 66 40W
Frederikshåb, Greenland **4 C5** 62 0N 49 43W
Frederikshavn, Denmark **9 H14** 57 28N 10 31 E
Frederiksted, Virgin Is. **89 C7** 17 43N 64 53W
Fredonia, Ariz., U.S.A. **83 H7** 36 57N 112 32W
Fredonia, Kans., U.S.A. **81 G7** 37 32N 95 49W
Fredonia, N.Y., U.S.A. **78 D5** 42 26N 79 20W
Fredrikstad, Norway **9 G14** 59 13N 10 57 E
Free State □, S. Africa **56 D4** 28 30S 27 0 E
Freehold, U.S.A. **79 F10** 40 16N 74 17W
Freel Peak, U.S.A. **84 G7** 38 52N 119 54W
Freeland, U.S.A. **79 E9** 41 1N 75 54W
Freels, C., Canada **71 C9** 49 15N 53 30W
Freeman, Calif., U.S.A. **85 K9** 35 35N 117 53W
Freeman, S. Dak., U.S.A. **80 D6** 43 21N 97 26W
Freeport, Bahamas **88 A4** 26 30N 78 47W
Freeport, Ill., U.S.A. **80 D10** 42 17N 89 36W
Freeport, N.Y., U.S.A. **79 F11** 40 39N 73 35W
Freeport, Ohio, U.S.A. **78 F3** 40 12N 81 15W
Freeport, Pa., U.S.A. **78 F5** 40 41N 79 41W
Freeport, Tex., U.S.A. **81 L7** 28 57N 95 21W
Freetown, S. Leone **50 G3** 8 30N 13 17W
Frégate, L., Canada **70 B5** 53 15N 74 45W
Fregenal de la Sierra, Spain **19 C2** 38 10N 6 39W
Freibourg = Fribourg, Switz. **18 C7** 46 49N 7 9 E
Freiburg, Germany **16 E4** 47 59N 7 51 E
Freire, Chile **96 D2** 38 54S 72 38W
Freirina, Chile **94 B1** 28 30S 71 10W
Freising, Germany **16 D6** 48 24N 11 45 E
Freistadt, Austria **16 D8** 48 30N 14 30 E
Fréjus, France **18 E7** 43 25N 6 44 E
Fremantle, Australia **61 F2** 32 7S 115 47 E
Fremont, Calif., U.S.A. **84 H4** 37 32N 121 57W
Fremont, Mich., U.S.A. **76 D3** 43 28N 85 57W
Fremont, Nebr., U.S.A. **80 E6** 41 26N 96 30W
Fremont, Ohio, U.S.A. **76 E4** 41 21N 83 7W
Fremont →, U.S.A. **83 G8** 38 24N 110 42W
French Camp, U.S.A. **84 H5** 37 53N 121 16W
French Creek →, U.S.A. **78 E5** 41 24N 79 50W
French Guiana ■, S. Amer. **93 C8** 4 0N 53 0W
French Pass, N.Z. **59 J4** 40 55S 173 55 E
French Polynesia ■, Pac. Oc. **65 K13** 20 0S 145 0W
Frenchman Cr. →, N. Amer. **82 B10** 48 31N 107 10W
Frenchman Cr. →, U.S.A. **80 E4** 40 14N 100 50W
Fresco →, Brazil **93 E8** 7 15S 51 30W
Freshfield, C., Antarctica **5 C10** 68 25S 151 10 E
Fresnillo, Mexico **86 C4** 23 10N 103 0W
Fresno, U.S.A. **84 J7** 36 44N 119 47W
Fresno Reservoir, U.S.A. **82 B9** 48 36N 109 57W
Frew →, Australia **62 C2** 20 0S 135 38 E
Frewsburg, U.S.A. **78 D5** 42 3N 79 10W
Freycinet Pen., Australia **62 G4** 42 10S 148 25 E
Fria, C., Namibia **56 B1** 18 0S 12 0 E
Friant, U.S.A. **84 J7** 36 59N 119 43W
Frías, Argentina **94 B2** 28 40S 65 5W
Fribourg, Switz. **18 C7** 46 49N 7 9 E
Friday Harbor, U.S.A. **84 B3** 48 32N 123 1W
Friedens, U.S.A. **78 F6** 40 3N 78 59W
Friedrichshafen, Germany **16 E5** 47 39N 9 30 E
Friendly Is. = Tonga ■, Pac. Oc. **59 D11** 19 50S 174 30W
Friendship, U.S.A. **78 D6** 42 12N 78 8W
Friesland □, Neths. **15 A5** 53 5N 5 50 E
Frio →, U.S.A. **81 L5** 28 26N 98 11W
Frio, C., Brazil **90 F6** 22 50S 41 50W
Friona, U.S.A. **81 H3** 34 38N 102 43W
Fritch, U.S.A. **81 H4** 35 38N 101 36W
Frobisher B., Canada **69 B13** 62 30N 66 0W
Frobisher Bay = Iqaluit, Canada **69 B13** 63 44N 68 31W
Frobisher L., Canada **73 B7** 56 20N 108 15W
Frohavet, Norway **8 E13** 64 0N 9 30 E
Frome, U.K. **11 F5** 51 14N 2 19W
Frome →, U.K. **11 G5** 50 41N 2 6W
Frome, L., Australia **63 E2** 30 45S 139 45 E
Front Range, U.S.A. **74 C5** 40 25N 105 45W
Front Royal, U.S.A. **76 F6** 38 55N 78 12W
Frontera, Canary Is. **22 G2** 27 47N 17 59W
Frontera, Mexico **87 D6** 18 30N 92 40W
Fronteras, Mexico **86 A3** 30 56N 109 31W
Frosinone, Italy **20 D5** 41 38N 13 19 E
Frostburg, U.S.A. **76 F6** 39 39N 78 56W
Frostisen, Norway **8 B17** 68 14N 17 10 E
Frøya, Norway **8 E13** 63 43N 8 40 E
Frunze = Bishkek, Kyrgyzstan **26 E8** 42 54N 74 46 E
Frutal, Brazil **93 H9** 20 0S 49 0W
Frýdek-Místek, Czech Rep. **17 D10** 49 40N 18 20 E
Fryeburg, U.S.A. **79 B14** 44 1N 70 59W
Fu Xian = Wafangdian, China **35 E11** 39 38N 121 58 E
Fu Xian, China **34 G5** 36 0N 109 20 E
Fucheng, China **34 F9** 37 50N 116 10 E
Fuchou = Fuzhou, China **33 D6** 26 5N 119 16 E
Fuchū, Japan **31 G6** 34 34N 133 14 E
Fuencaliente, Canary Is. **22 F2** 28 28N 17 50W
Fuencaliente, Pta., Canary Is. **22 F2** 28 27N 17 51W
Fuengirola, Spain **19 D3** 36 32N 4 41W
Fuentes de Oñoro, Spain **19 B2** 40 33N 6 52W
Fuerte →, Mexico **86 B3** 25 50N 109 25W
Fuerte Olimpo, Paraguay **94 A4** 21 0S 57 51W
Fuerteventura, Canary Is. **22 F6** 28 30N 14 0W
Fufeng, China **34 G5** 34 22N 108 0 E
Fugou, China **34 G8** 34 3N 114 25 E
Fugu, China **34 E6** 39 2N 111 3 E
Fuhai, China **32 B3** 47 2N 87 25 E
Fuḩaymī, Iraq **44 C4** 34 16N 42 10 E
Fuji, Japan **31 G9** 35 9N 138 39 E
Fuji-San, Japan **31 G9** 35 22N 138 44 E
Fuji-yoshida, Japan **31 G9** 35 30N 138 46 E
Fujian □, China **33 D6** 26 0N 118 0 E
Fujinomiya, Japan **31 G9** 35 10N 138 40 E
Fujisawa, Japan **31 G9** 35 22N 139 29 E
Fujiyama, Mt. = Fuji-San, Japan **31 G9** 35 22N 138 44 E
Fukien = Fujian □, China **33 D6** 26 0N 118 0 E
Fukuchiyama, Japan **31 G7** 35 19N 135 9 E
Fukue-Shima, Japan **31 H4** 32 40N 128 45 E
Fukui, Japan **31 F8** 36 5N 136 10 E
Fukui □, Japan **31 G8** 36 0N 136 12 E
Fukuoka, Japan **31 H5** 33 39N 130 21 E
Fukuoka □, Japan **31 H5** 33 30N 131 0 E
Fukushima, Japan **30 F10** 37 44N 140 28 E
Fukushima □, Japan **30 F10** 37 30N 140 15 E
Fukuyama, Japan **31 G6** 34 35N 133 20 E
Fulda, Germany **16 C5** 50 32N 9 40 E
Fulda →, Germany **16 C5** 51 25N 9 39 E
Fulford Harbour, Canada **84 B3** 48 47N 123 27W
Fullerton, Calif., U.S.A. **85 M9** 33 53N 117 56W
Fullerton, Nebr., U.S.A. **80 E6** 41 22N 97 58W
Fulongquan, China **35 B13** 44 20N 124 42 E
Fulton, Mo., U.S.A. **80 F9** 38 52N 91 57W
Fulton, N.Y., U.S.A. **79 C8** 43 19N 76 25W
Funabashi, Japan **31 G10** 35 45N 140 0 E
Funchal, Madeira **22 D3** 32 38N 16 54W
Fundación, Colombia **92 A4** 10 31N 74 11W
Fundão, Portugal **19 B2** 40 8N 7 30W
Fundy, B. of, Canada **71 D6** 45 0N 66 0W
Funing, Hebei, China **35 E10** 39 53N 119 12 E
Funing, Jiangsu, China **35 H10** 33 45N 119 50 E
Funiu Shan, China **34 H7** 33 30N 112 20 E
Funtua, Nigeria **50 F7** 11 30N 7 18 E
Fuping, Hebei, China **34 E8** 38 48N 114 12 E
Fuping, Shaanxi, China **34 G5** 34 42N 109 10 E
Furano, Japan **30 C11** 43 21N 142 23 E
Furāt, Nahr al →, Asia **44 D5** 31 0N 47 25 E
Fūrg, Iran **45 D7** 28 18N 55 13 E
Furnás, Spain **22 B8** 39 3N 1 32 E
Furnas, Reprêsa de, Brazil **95 A6** 20 50S 45 30W
Furneaux Group, Australia **62 G4** 40 10S 147 50 E
Furqlus, Syria **47 A6** 34 36N 37 8 E
Fürstenwalde, Germany **16 B8** 52 22N 14 3 E
Fürth, Germany **16 D6** 49 28N 10 59 E
Furukawa, Japan **30 E10** 38 34N 140 58 E
Fury and Hecla Str., Canada **69 B11** 69 56N 84 0W
Fusagasuga, Colombia **92 C4** 4 21N 74 22W
Fushan, Shandong, China **35 F11** 37 30N 121 15 E
Fushan, Shanxi, China **34 G6** 35 58N 111 51 E
Fushun, China **35 D12** 41 50N 123 56 E
Fusong, China **35 C14** 42 20N 127 15 E
Futuna, Wall. & F. Is. **59 B8** 14 25S 178 20 E
Fuxin, China **35 C11** 42 5N 121 48 E
Fuyang, China **34 H8** 33 0N 115 48 E
Fuyang He →, China **34 E9** 38 12N 117 0 E
Fuyu, China **35 B13** 45 12N 124 43 E
Fuzhou, China **33 D6** 26 5N 119 16 E
Fylde, U.K. **10 D5** 53 50N 2 58W
Fyn, Denmark **9 J14** 55 20N 10 30 E
Fyne, L., U.K. **12 F3** 55 59N 5 23W

G

Gabela, Angola **52 G2** 11 0S 14 24 E
Gabès, Tunisia **51 B8** 33 53N 10 2 E
Gabès, G. de, Tunisia **51 B8** 34 0N 10 30 E
Gabon ■, Africa **52 E2** 0 10S 10 0 E
Gaborone, Botswana **56 C4** 24 45S 25 57 E
Gabriels, U.S.A. **79 B10** 44 26N 74 12W
Gābrīk, Iran **45 E8** 25 44N 58 28 E
Gabrovo, Bulgaria **21 C11** 42 52N 25 19 E
Gāch Sār, Iran **45 B6** 36 7N 51 19 E
Gachsārān, Iran **45 D6** 30 15N 50 45 E
Gadag, India **40 M9** 15 30N 75 45 E
Gadap, Pakistan **42 G2** 25 5N 67 28 E
Gadarwara, India **43 H8** 22 50N 78 50 E
Gadhada, India **42 J4** 22 0N 71 35 E
Gadra, Pakistan **42 G4** 25 40N 70 38 E
Gadsden, U.S.A. **77 H3** 34 1N 86 1W
Gadwal, India **40 L10** 16 10N 77 50 E
Gaffney, U.S.A. **77 H5** 35 5N 81 39W
Gafsa, Tunisia **50 B7** 34 24N 8 43 E
Gagaria, India **42 G4** 25 43N 70 46 E
Gagnoa, Ivory C. **50 G4** 6 56N 5 16W
Gagnon, Canada **71 B6** 51 50N 68 5W
Gagnon, L., Canada **73 A6** 62 3N 110 27W
Gahini, Rwanda **54 C3** 1 50S 30 30 E
Gahmar, India **43 G10** 25 27N 83 49 E
Gai Xian = Gaizhou, China **35 D12** 40 22N 122 20 E
Gaïdhouronísi, Greece **23 E7** 34 53N 25 41 E
Gail, U.S.A. **81 J4** 32 46N 101 27W
Gaillimh = Galway, Ireland **13 C2** 53 17N 9 3W
Gaines, U.S.A. **78 E7** 41 46N 77 35W
Gainesville, Fla., U.S.A. **77 L4** 29 40N 82 20W
Gainesville, Ga., U.S.A. **77 H4** 34 18N 83 50W
Gainesville, Mo., U.S.A. **81 G8** 36 36N 92 26W
Gainesville, Tex., U.S.A. **81 J6** 33 38N 97 8W
Gainsborough, U.K. **10 D7** 53 24N 0 46W
Gairdner, L., Australia **63 E2** 31 30S 136 0 E
Gairloch, L., U.K. **12 D3** 57 43N 5 45W
Gaizhou, China **35 D12** 40 22N 122 20 E
Gaj →, Pakistan **42 F2** 26 26N 67 21 E
Gakuch, Pakistan **43 A5** 36 7N 73 45 E
Galán, Cerro, Argentina **94 B2** 25 55S 66 52W
Galana →, Kenya **54 C5** 3 9S 40 8 E
Galápagos, Pac. Oc. **90 D1** 0 0 91 0W
Galashiels, U.K. **12 F6** 55 37N 2 49W
Galaţi, Romania **17 F15** 45 27N 28 2 E
Galatina, Italy **21 D8** 40 10N 18 10 E
Galax, U.S.A. **77 G5** 36 40N 80 56W
Galcaio, Somali Rep. **46 F4** 6 30N 47 30 E
Galdhøpiggen, Norway **9 F12** 61 38N 8 18 E
Galeana, Mexico **86 C4** 24 50N 100 4W
Galeana, Nuevo León, Mexico **86 A3** 24 50N 100 4W
Galela, Indonesia **37 D7** 1 50N 127 49 E
Galena, U.S.A. **68 B4** 64 44N 156 56W
Galera Point, Trin. & Tob. **89 D7** 10 8N 61 0W
Galesburg, U.S.A. **80 E9** 40 57N 90 22W
Galeton, U.S.A. **78 E7** 41 44N 77 39W
Galich, Russia **24 C7** 58 22N 42 24 E
Galicia □, Spain **19 A2** 42 43N 7 45W
Galilee = Hagalil, Israel **47 C4** 32 53N 35 18 E
Galilee, L., Australia **62 C4** 22 20S 145 50 E
Galilee, Sea of = Yam Kinneret, Israel **47 C4** 32 45N 35 35 E
Galinoporni, Cyprus **23 D13** 35 31N 34 18 E
Galion, U.S.A. **78 F2** 40 44N 82 47W
Galiuro Mts., U.S.A. **83 K8** 32 30N 110 20W
Galiwinku, Australia **62 A2** 12 2S 135 34 E
Gallan Hd., U.K. **12 C1** 58 15N 7 2W
Gallatin, U.S.A. **77 G2** 36 24N 86 27W
Galle, Sri Lanka **40 R12** 6 5N 80 10 E
Gállego →, Spain **19 B5** 41 39N 0 51W
Gallegos →, Argentina **96 G3** 51 35S 69 0W
Galley Hd., Ireland **13 E3** 51 32N 8 55W
Gallinas, Pta., Colombia **92 A4** 12 28N 71 40W
Gallipoli = Gelibolu, Turkey **21 D12** 40 28N 26 43 E
Gallipoli, Italy **21 D8** 40 3N 17 58 E
Gallipolis, U.S.A. **76 F4** 38 49N 82 12W
Gällivare, Sweden **8 C19** 67 9N 20 40 E
Galloo I., U.S.A. **79 C8** 43 55N 76 25W
Galloway, U.K. **12 F4** 55 1N 4 29W
Galloway, Mull of, U.K. **12 G4** 54 39N 4 52W
Gallup, U.S.A. **83 J9** 35 32N 108 45W
Galoya, Sri Lanka **40 Q12** 8 10N 80 55 E
Galt, U.S.A. **84 G5** 38 15N 121 18W
Galty Mts., Ireland **13 D3** 52 22N 8 10W
Galtymore, Ireland **13 D3** 52 21N 8 11W
Galva, U.S.A. **80 E9** 41 10N 90 3W
Galveston, U.S.A. **81 L7** 29 18N 94 48W
Galveston B., U.S.A. **81 L7** 29 36N 94 50W
Gálvez, Argentina **94 C3** 32 0S 61 14W
Galway, Ireland **13 C2** 53 17N 9 3W
Galway □, Ireland **13 C2** 53 22N 9 1W
Galway B., Ireland **13 C2** 53 13N 9 10W
Gam →, Vietnam **38 B5** 21 55N 105 12 E
Gamagori, Japan **31 G8** 34 50N 137 14 E
Gambat, Pakistan **42 F3** 27 17N 68 26 E
Gambhir →, India **42 F6** 26 58N 77 27 E
Gambia ■, W. Afr. **50 F2** 13 25N 16 0W
Gambia →, W. Afr. **50 F2** 13 28N 16 34W
Gambier, U.S.A. **78 F2** 40 22N 82 23W
Gambier, C., Australia **60 B5** 11 56S 130 57 E
Gambier Is., Australia **63 F2** 35 3S 136 30 E
Gambo, Canada **71 C9** 48 47N 54 13W
Gamboli, Pakistan **42 E3** 29 53N 68 24 E
Gamboma, Congo **52 E3** 1 55S 15 52 E
Gamlakarleby = Kokkola, Finland **8 E20** 63 50N 23 8 E
Gammon →, Canada **73 C9** 51 24N 95 44W
Gan Jiang →, China **33 D6** 29 15N 116 0 E
Ganado, U.S.A. **83 J9** 35 43N 109 33W
Gananoque, Canada **79 B8** 44 20N 76 10W
Ganāveh, Iran **45 D6** 29 35N 50 35 E
Gäncä, Azerbaijan **25 F8** 40 45N 46 20 E
Gancheng, China **38 C7** 18 51N 108 37 E
Gand = Gent, Belgium **15 C3** 51 2N 3 42 E
Ganda, Angola **53 G2** 13 3S 14 35 E
Gandajika, Dem. Rep. of the Congo **52 F4** 6 45S 23 57 E
Gandak →, India **43 G11** 25 39N 85 13 E
Gandava, Pakistan **42 E2** 28 32N 67 32 E
Gander, Canada **71 C9** 48 58N 54 35W
Gander L., Canada **71 C9** 48 58N 54 35W
Ganderowe Falls, Zimbabwe **55 F2** 17 20S 29 10 E
Gandhi Sagar, India **42 G6** 24 40N 75 40 E
Gandhinagar, India **42 H5** 23 15N 72 45 E
Gandía, Spain **19 C5** 38 58N 0 9W
Gando, Pta., Canary Is. **22 G4** 27 55N 15 22W
Ganedidalem = Gani, Indonesia **37 E7** 0 48S 128 14 E
Ganga →, India **43 H14** 23 20N 90 30 E
Ganga Sagar, India **43 J13** 21 38N 88 5 E
Gangan →, India **43 E8** 28 38N 78 58 E
Ganganagar, India **42 E5** 29 56N 73 56 E
Gangapur, India **42 F7** 26 32N 76 49 E
Gangaw, Burma **41 H19** 22 5N 94 5 E
Gangdisê Shan, China **41 D12** 31 20N 81 0 E
Ganges = Ganga →, India **43 H14** 23 20N 90 30 E
Ganges, Canada **72 D4** 48 51N 123 31W
Ganges, Mouths of the, India **43 J14** 21 30N 90 0 E
Gangoh, India **42 E7** 29 46N 77 18 E
Gangroti, India **43 D8** 30 50N 79 10 E
Gangtok, India **41 F16** 27 20N 88 37 E
Gangu, China **34 G3** 34 40N 105 15 E
Gangyao, China **35 B14** 44 12N 126 37 E
Gani, Indonesia **37 E7** 0 48S 128 14 E
Ganj, India **43 F8** 27 45N 78 57 E
Gannett Peak, U.S.A. **82 E9** 43 11N 109 39W
Ganquan, China **34 F5** 36 20N 109 20 E
Gansu □, China **34 G3** 36 0N 104 0 E
Ganta, Liberia **50 G4** 7 15N 8 59W
Gantheaume, C., Australia **63 F2** 36 4S 137 32 E
Gantheaume B., Australia **61 E1** 27 40S 114 10 E
Gantsevichi = Hantsavichy, Belarus **17 B14** 52 49N 26 30 E
Ganyem = Genyem, Indonesia **37 E10** 2 46S 140 12 E
Ganyu, China **35 G10** 34 50N 119 8 E
Ganzhou, China **33 D6** 25 51N 114 56 E
Gao, Mali **50 E5** 16 15N 0 5W
Gaomi, China **35 F10** 36 20N 119 42 E
Gaoping, China **34 G7** 35 45N 112 55 E
Gaotang, China **34 F9** 36 50N 116 15 E
Gaoua, Burkina Faso **50 F5** 10 20N 3 8W
Gaoual, Guinea **50 F3** 11 45N 13 25W
Gaoxiong = Kaohsiung, Taiwan **33 D7** 22 35N 120 16 E
Gaoyang, China **34 E8** 38 40N 115 45 E
Gaoyou Hu, China **35 H10** 32 45N 119 20 E
Gaoyuan, China **35 F9** 37 8N 117 58 E
Gap, France **18 D7** 44 33N 6 5 E
Gapat →, India **43 G10** 24 30N 82 28 E
Gapuwiyak, Australia **62 A2** 12 25S 135 43 E
Gar, China **32 C2** 32 10N 79 58 E
Garabogazköl Aylagy, Turkmenistan **25 F9** 41 0N 53 30 E
Garachico, Canary Is. **22 F3** 28 22N 16 46W
Garachiné, Panama **88 E4** 8 0N 78 12W
Garafia, Canary Is. **22 F2** 28 48N 17 57W
Garah, Australia **63 D4** 29 5S 149 38 E
Garajonay, Canary Is. **22 F2** 28 7N 17 14W
Garanhuns, Brazil **93 E11** 8 50S 36 30W
Garautha, India **43 G8** 25 34N 79 18 E
Garba Tula, Kenya **54 B4** 0 30N 38 32 E
Garberville, U.S.A. **82 F2** 40 6N 123 48W
Garbiyang, India **43 D9** 30 8N 80 54 E
Garda, L. di, Italy **20 B4** 45 40N 10 41 E
Garde L., Canada **73 A7** 62 50N 106 13W
Garden City, Ga., U.S.A. **77 J5** 32 6N 81 9W
Garden City, Kans., U.S.A. **81 G4** 37 58N 100 53W
Garden City, Tex., U.S.A. **81 K4** 31 52N 101 29W
Garden Grove, U.S.A. **85 M9** 33 47N 117 55W
Gardēz, Afghan. **42 C3** 33 37N 69 9 E
Gardiner, Maine, U.S.A. **77 C11** 44 14N 69 47W
Gardiner, Mont., U.S.A. **82 D8** 45 2N 110 22W
Gardiners I., U.S.A. **79 E12** 41 6N 72 6W
Gardner, U.S.A. **79 D13** 42 34N 71 59W
Gardner Canal, Canada **72 C3** 53 27N 128 8W
Gardnerville, U.S.A. **84 G7** 38 56N 119 45W
Gardo, Somali Rep. **46 F4** 9 30N 49 6 E
Garey, U.S.A. **85 L6** 34 53N 120 19W
Garfield, U.S.A. **82 C5** 47 1N 117 9W
Garforth, U.K. **10 D6** 53 47N 1 24W
Gargano, Mte., Italy **20 D6** 41 43N 15 43 E
Garibaldi Prov. Park, Canada **72 D4** 49 50N 122 40W
Garies, S. Africa **56 E2** 30 32S 17 59 E
Garigliano →, Italy **20 D5** 41 13N 13 45 E
Garissa, Kenya **54 C4** 0 25S 39 40 E
Garland, Tex., U.S.A. **81 J6** 32 55N 96 38W
Garland, Utah, U.S.A. **82 F7** 41 47N 112 10W
Garm, Tajikistan **26 F8** 39 0N 70 20 E
Garmāb, Iran **45 C8** 35 25N 56 45 E
Garmisch-Partenkirchen, Germany **16 E6** 47 30N 11 6 E
Garmsār, Iran **45 C7** 35 20N 52 25 E
Garner, U.S.A. **80 D8** 43 6N 93 36W
Garnett, U.S.A. **80 F7** 38 17N 95 14W
Garo Hills, India **43 G14** 25 30N 90 30 E
Garoe, Somali Rep. **46 F4** 8 25N 48 33 E
Garonne →, France **18 D3** 45 2N 0 36W
Garot, India **42 G6** 24 19N 75 41 E
Garoua, Cameroon **51 G8** 9 19N 13 21 E
Garrauli, India **43 G8** 25 5N 79 22 E
Garrison, Mont., U.S.A. **82 C7** 46 31N 112 49W
Garrison, N. Dak., U.S.A. **80 B4** 47 40N 101 25W
Garrison Res. = Sakakawea, L., U.S.A. **80 B4** 47 30N 101 25W
Garron Pt., U.K. **13 A6** 55 3N 5 59W
Garry →, U.K. **12 E5** 56 44N 3 47W
Garry, L., Canada **68 B9** 65 58N 100 18W
Garsen, Kenya **54 C5** 2 20S 40 5 E
Garson L., Canada **73 B6** 56 19N 110 2W
Garu, India **43 H11** 23 40N 84 14 E
Garub, Namibia **56 D2** 26 37S 16 0 E
Garut, Indonesia **37 G12** 7 14S 107 53 E
Garvie Mts., N.Z. **59 L2** 45 30S 168 50 E
Garwa = Garoua, Cameroon **51 G8** 9 19N 13 21 E
Garwa, India **43 G10** 24 11N 83 47 E
Gary, U.S.A. **76 E2** 41 36N 87 20W
Garzê, China **32 C5** 31 38N 100 1 E
Garzón, Colombia **92 C3** 2 10N 75 40W
Gas-San, Japan **30 E10** 38 32N 140 1 E
Gasan Kuli = Esenguly, Turkmenistan **26 F6** 37 37N 53 59 E
Gascogne, France **18 E4** 43 45N 0 20 E
Gascogne, G. de, Europe **18 D2** 44 0N 2 0W
Gascony = Gascogne, France **18 E4** 43 45N 0 20 E
Gascoyne →, Australia **61 D1** 24 52S 113 37 E
Gascoyne Junction, Australia **61 E2** 25 2S 115 17 E
Gashaka, Nigeria **51 G8** 7 20N 11 29 E
Gasherbrum, Pakistan **43 B7** 35 40N 76 40 E
Gashua, Nigeria **51 F8** 12 54N 11 0 E
Gaspé, Canada **71 C7** 48 52N 64 30W
Gaspé, C. de, Canada **71 C7** 48 48N 64 7W
Gaspé, Pén. de, Canada **71 C6** 48 45N 65 40W
Gaspésie, Parc de Conservation de la, Canada **71 C6** 48 55N 65 50W
Gasteiz = Vitoria-Gasteiz, Spain **19 A4** 42 50N 2 41W
Gastonia, U.S.A. **77 H5** 35 16N 81 11W
Gastre, Argentina **96 E3** 42 20S 69 15W
Gata, C., Cyprus **23 E12** 34 34N 33 2 E
Gata, C. de, Spain **19 D4** 36 41N 2 13W
Gata, Sierra de, Spain **19 B2** 40 20N 6 45W
Gataga →, Canada **72 B3** 58 35N 126 59W
Gatehouse of Fleet, U.K. **12 G4** 54 53N 4 12W
Gates, U.S.A. **78 C7** 43 9N 77 42W
Gateshead, U.K. **10 C6** 54 57N 1 35W
Gatesville, U.S.A. **81 K6** 31 26N 97 45W
Gaths, Zimbabwe **55 G3** 20 2S 30 32 E
Gatico, Chile **94 A1** 22 29S 70 20W
Gatineau, Canada **79 A9** 45 29N 75 38W
Gatineau →, Canada **70 C4** 45 27N 75 42W
Gatineau, Parc Nat. de la, Canada **70 C4** 45 40N 76 0W
Gatton, Australia **63 D5** 27 32S 152 17 E

Grenadines

Goldsworthy, *Australia* .... **60 D2** 20 21 S 119 30 E
Goldthwaite, *U.S.A.* **81 K5** 31 27N 98 34W
Goleniów, *Poland* .... **16 B8** 53 35N 14 50 E
Golestānak, *Iran* .... **45 D7** 30 36N 54 14 E
Goleta, *U.S.A.* **85 L7** 34 27N 119 50W
Golfito, *Costa Rica* **88 E3** 8 41N 83 5W
Golfo Aranci, *Italy* .... **20 D3** 40 59N 9 38 E
Goliad, *U.S.A.* **81 L6** 28 40N 97 23W
Golpāyegān, *Iran* .... **45 C6** 33 27N 50 18 E
Golra, *Pakistan* .... **42 C5** 33 37N 72 56 E
Golspie, *U.K.* **12 D5** 57 58N 3 59W
Goma, *Dem. Rep. of the Congo* . **54 C2** 1 37S 29 10 E
Gomal Pass, *Pakistan* ..... **42 D3** 31 56N 69 20 E
Gomati →, *India* .... **43 G10** 25 32N 83 11 E
Gombari, *Dem. Rep. of the Congo* . **54 B2** 2 45N 29 3 E
Gombe, *Nigeria* .... **51 F8** 10 19N 11 2 E
Gombe →, *Tanzania* ..... **54 C3** 4 38S 31 40 E
Gomel = Homyel, *Belarus* . **17 B16** 52 28N 31 0 E
Gomera, *Canary Is.* **22 F2** 28 7N 17 14W
Gómez Palacio, *Mexico* ... **86 B4** 25 40N 104 0W
Gomīshān, *Iran* .... **45 B7** 37 4N 54 6 E
Gomogomo, *Indonesia* .... **37 F8** 6 39S 134 43 E
Gomoh, *India* .... **41 H15** 23 52N 86 10 E
Gompa = Ganta, *Liberia* .. **50 G4** 7 15N 8 59W
Gonābād, *Iran* .... **45 C8** 34 15N 58 45 E
Gonaïves, *Haiti* **89 C5** 19 20N 72 42W
Gonâve, G. de la, *Haiti* ... **89 C5** 19 29N 72 42W
Gonâve, I. de la, *Haiti* ... **89 C5** 18 45N 73 0W
Gonbad-e Kāvūs, *Iran* .... **45 B7** 37 20N 55 25 E
Gonda, *India* .... **43 F9** 27 9N 81 58 E
Gondal, *India* .... **42 J4** 21 58N 70 52 E
Gonder, *Ethiopia* .... **46 E2** 12 39N 37 30 E
Gondia, *India* .... **40 J12** 21 23N 80 10 E
Gondola, *Mozam.* .... **55 F3** 19 10S 33 37 E
Gönen, *Turkey* .... **21 D12** 40 6N 27 39 E
Gonghe, *China* .... **32 C5** 36 18N 100 32 E
Gongolgon, *Australia* ..... **63 E4** 30 21S 146 54 E
Gongzhuling, *China* ...... **35 C13** 43 30N 124 40 E
Gonzales, *Calif., U.S.A.* ... **84 J5** 36 30N 121 26W
Gonzales, *Tex., U.S.A.* **81 L6** 29 30N 97 27W
González Chaves, *Argentina* **94 D3** 38 2S 60 5W
Good Hope, C. of, *S. Africa* **56 E2** 34 24S 18 30 E
Gooderham, *Canada* **78 B6** 44 54N 78 21W
Gooding, *U.S.A.* **82 E6** 42 56N 114 43W
Goodland, *U.S.A.* **80 F4** 39 21N 101 43W
Goodlow, *Canada* **72 B4** 56 20N 120 8W
Goodooga, *Australia* ...... **63 D4** 29 3S 147 28 E
Goodsprings, *U.S.A.* **85 K11** 35 49N 115 27W
Goole, *U.K.* **10 D7** 53 42N 0 53W
Goolgowi, *Australia* ...... **63 E4** 33 58S 145 41 E
Goolwa, *Australia* .... **63 F2** 35 30S 138 47 E
Goomalling, *Australia* ..... **61 F2** 31 15S 116 49 E
Goomeri, *Australia* .... **63 D5** 26 12S 152 6 E
Goonda, *Mozam.* .... **55 F3** 19 48S 33 57 E
Goondiwindi, *Australia* ... **63 D5** 28 30S 150 21 E
Goongarrie, L., *Australia* ... **61 F3** 30 3S 121 9 E
Goonyella, *Australia* ..... **62 C4** 21 47S 147 58 E
Goose →, *Canada* **71 B7** 53 20N 60 35W
Goose Creek, *U.S.A.* **77 J5** 32 59N 80 2W
Goose L., *U.S.A.* **82 F3** 41 56N 120 26W
Gop, *India* .... **40 H6** 22 5N 69 50 E
Gopalganj, *India* .... **43 F11** 26 28N 84 30 E
Göppingen, *Germany* ..... **16 D5** 48 42N 9 39 E
Gorakhpur, *India* .... **43 F10** 26 47N 83 23 E
Goražde, *Bos.-H.* .... **21 C8** 43 38N 18 58 E
Gorda, *U.S.A.* **84 K5** 35 53N 121 26W
Gorda, Pta., *Canary Is.* **22 F2** 28 45N 18 0W
Gorda, Pta., *Nic.* **88 D3** 14 20N 83 10W
Gordan B., *Australia* ...... **60 B5** 11 35S 130 10 E
Gordon, *U.S.A.* **80 D3** 42 48N 102 12W
Gordon →, *Australia* .... **62 G4** 42 27S 145 30 E
Gordon L., *Alta., Canada* .. **73 B6** 56 30N 110 25W
Gordon L., *N.W.T., Canada* **72 A6** 63 5N 113 11W
Gordonvale, *Australia* ..... **62 B4** 17 5S 145 50 E
Gore, *Ethiopia* .... **46 F2** 8 12N 35 32 E
Gore, *N.Z.* .... **59 M2** 46 5S 168 58 E
Gore Bay, *Canada* **70 C3** 45 57N 82 28W
Gorey, *Ireland* **13 D5** 52 41N 6 18W
Gorg, *Iran* .... **45 D8** 29 29N 59 43 E
Gorgān, *Iran* .... **45 B7** 36 50N 54 29 E
Gorgona, I., *Colombia* **92 C3** 3 0N 78 10W
Gorham, *U.S.A.* **79 B13** 44 23N 71 10W
Goriganga →, *India* ..... **43 E9** 29 45N 80 23 E
Gorinchem, *Neths.* .... **15 C4** 51 50N 4 59 E
Goris, *Armenia* .... **25 G8** 39 31N 46 22 E
Gorízia, *Italy* .... **20 B5** 45 56N 13 37 E
Gorki = Nizhniy Novgorod, *Russia* .... **24 C7** 56 20N 44 0 E
Gorkiy = Nizhniy Novgorod, *Russia* .... **24 C7** 56 20N 44 0 E
Gorkovskoye Vdkhr., *Russia* **24 C7** 57 2N 43 4 E
Görlitz, *Germany* .... **16 C8** 51 9N 14 58 E
Gorlovka = Horlivka, *Ukraine* .... **25 E6** 48 19N 38 5 E
Gorman, *U.S.A.* **85 L8** 34 47N 118 51W
Gorna Dzhumayo = Blagoevgrad, *Bulgaria* .. **21 C10** 42 2N 23 5 E
Gorna Oryakhovitsa, *Bulgaria* .... **21 C11** 43 7N 25 40 E
Gorno-Altay □, *Russia* .... **26 D9** 51 0N 86 0 E
Gorno-Altaysk, *Russia* .... **26 D9** 51 50N 86 5 E
Gornyatski, *Russia* .... **24 A11** 67 32N 64 3 E
Gornyy, *Russia* .... **30 B6** 44 57N 133 59 E
Gorodenka = Horodenka, *Ukraine* .... **17 D13** 48 41N 25 29 E
Gorodok = Horodok, *Ukraine* .... **17 D12** 49 46N 23 32 E
Gorokhov = Horokhiv, *Ukraine* .... **17 C13** 50 30N 24 45 E
Goromonzi, *Zimbabwe* .... **55 F3** 17 52S 31 22 E
Gorong, Kepulauan, *Indonesia* .... **37 E8** 3 59S 131 25 E
Gorongose →, *Mozam.* .. **57 C5** 20 30S 34 40 E
Gorongoza, *Mozam.* ...... **55 F3** 18 44S 34 2 E
Gorongoza, Sa. da, *Mozam.* **55 F3** 18 27S 34 2 E
Gorontalo, *Indonesia* ..... **37 D6** 0 35N 123 5 E
Gort, *Ireland* **13 C3** 53 3N 8 49W
Gortis, *Greece* .... **23 D6** 35 4N 24 58 E
Gorzów Wielkopolski, *Poland* .... **16 B8** 52 43N 15 15 E
Gosford, *Australia* .... **63 E5** 33 23S 151 18 E
Goshen, *Calif., U.S.A.* **84 J7** 36 21N 119 25W
Goshen, *Ind., U.S.A.* **76 E3** 41 35N 85 50W
Goshen, *N.Y., U.S.A.* **79 E10** 41 24N 74 20W
Goshogawara, *Japan* ..... **30 D10** 40 48N 140 27 E
Goslar, *Germany* .... **16 C6** 51 54N 10 25 E
Gospič, *Croatia* .... **16 F8** 44 35N 15 23 E
Gosport, *U.K.* **11 G6** 50 48N 1 9W
Gosse →, *Australia* ..... **62 B1** 19 32S 134 37 E
Göta älv →, *Sweden* .... **9 H14** 57 42N 11 54 E
Göta kanal, *Sweden* ...... **9 G16** 58 30N 15 58 E
Götaland, *Sweden* .... **9 G15** 57 30N 14 30 E
Göteborg, *Sweden* .... **9 H14** 57 43N 11 59 E
Gotha, *Germany* .... **16 C6** 50 56N 10 42 E
Gothenburg = Göteborg, *Sweden* .... **9 H14** 57 43N 11 59 E
Gothenburg, *U.S.A.* **80 E4** 40 56N 100 10W
Gotland, *Sweden* .... **9 H18** 57 30N 18 33 E
Gotō-Rettō, *Japan* .... **31 H4** 32 55N 129 5 E
Gotska Sandön, *Sweden* .. **9 G18** 58 24N 19 15 E
Gōtsu, *Japan* .... **31 G6** 35 0N 132 14 E
Gott Pk., *Canada* **72 C4** 50 18N 122 16W
Göttingen, *Germany* ...... **16 C5** 51 31N 9 55 E
Gottwaldov = Zlin, *Czech Rep.* .... **17 D9** 49 14N 17 40 E
Goubangzi, *China* .... **35 D11** 41 20N 121 52 E
Gouda, *Neths.* .... **15 B4** 52 1N 4 42 E
Goúdhoura, Ákra, *Greece* . **23 E8** 34 59N 26 6 E
Gough I., *Atl. Oc.* **2 G9** 40 10S 9 45W
Gouin, Rés., *Canada* **70 C5** 48 35N 74 40W
Goulburn, *Australia* ...... **63 E4** 34 44S 149 44 E
Goulburn Is., *Australia* .... **62 A1** 11 40S 133 20 E
Goulimine, *Morocco* **50 C3** 28 56N 10 0W
Gourits →, *S. Africa* .... **56 E3** 34 21S 21 52 E
Goúrnais, *Greece* .... **23 D7** 35 19N 25 16 E
Gouverneur, *U.S.A.* **79 B9** 44 20N 75 28W
Gouviá, *Greece* .... **23 A3** 39 39N 19 50 E
Governador Valadares, *Brazil* **93 G10** 18 15S 41 57W
Governor's Harbour, *Bahamas* **88 A4** 25 10N 76 14W
Govindgarh, *India* .... **43 G9** 24 23N 81 18 E
Gowan Ra., *Australia* ..... **62 D4** 25 0S 145 0 E
Gowanda, *U.S.A.* **78 D6** 42 28N 78 56W
Gowd-e Zirreh, *Afghan.* .... **40 E3** 29 45N 62 0 E
Gower, *U.K.* **11 F3** 51 35N 4 10W
Gowna, L., *Ireland* **13 C4** 53 51N 7 34W
Goya, *Argentina* **94 B4** 29 10S 59 10W
Goyder Lagoon, *Australia* . **63 D2** 27 3S 138 58 E
Goyllarisquisga, *Peru* **92 F3** 10 31S 76 24W
Goz Beïda, *Chad* .... **51 F10** 12 10N 21 20 E
Gozo, *Malta* .... **23 C1** 36 3N 14 13 E
Graaff-Reinet, *S. Africa* .... **56 E3** 32 13S 24 32 E
Gračac, *Croatia* .... **16 F8** 44 18N 15 57 E
Gracias a Dios, C., *Honduras* **88 D3** 15 0N 83 10W
Graciosa, I., *Canary Is.* **22 E6** 29 15N 13 32W
Grado, *Spain* **19 A2** 43 23N 6 4W
Grady, *U.S.A.* **81 H3** 34 49N 103 19W
Grafham Water, *U.K.* **11 E7** 52 19N 0 18W
Grafton, *Australia* .... **63 D5** 29 38S 152 58 E
Grafton, *N. Dak., U.S.A.* ... **80 A6** 48 25N 97 25W
Grafton, *W. Va., U.S.A.* **76 F5** 39 21N 80 2W
Graham, *Canada* **70 C1** 49 20N 90 30W
Graham, *U.S.A.* **81 J5** 33 6N 98 35W
Graham, Mt., *U.S.A.* **83 K9** 32 42N 109 52W
Graham Bell, Ostrov = Greem-Bell, Ostrov, *Russia* .... **26 A7** 81 0N 62 0 E
Graham I., *B.C., Canada* ... **72 C2** 53 40N 132 30W
Graham I., *N.W.T., Canada* **68 C6** 77 25N 90 30W
Graham Land, *Antarctica* .. **5 C17** 65 0S 64 0W
Grahamstown, *S. Africa* ... **56 E4** 33 19S 26 31 E
Grahamsville, *U.S.A.* **79 E10** 41 51N 74 33W
Grain Coast, *W. Afr.* **50 H3** 4 20N 10 0W
Grajaú, *Brazil* **93 E9** 5 50S 46 4W
Grajaú →, *Brazil* **93 D10** 3 41S 44 48W
Grampian, *U.S.A.* **78 F6** 40 58N 78 37W
Grampian Highlands = Grampian Mts., *U.K.* **12 E5** 56 50N 4 0W
Grampian Mts., *U.K.* **12 E5** 56 50N 4 0W
Grampians, The, *Australia* . **63 F3** 37 0S 142 20 E
Gran Canaria, *Canary Is.* .. **22 G4** 27 55N 15 35W
Gran Chaco, *S. Amer.* **94 B3** 25 0S 61 0W
Gran Paradiso, *Italy* ...... **18 D7** 45 33N 7 17 E
Gran Sasso d'Itália, *Italy* .. **20 C5** 42 27N 13 42 E
Granada, *Nic.* **88 D2** 11 58N 86 0W
Granada, *Spain* **19 D4** 37 10N 3 35W
Granada, *U.S.A.* **81 F3** 38 4N 102 19W
Granadilla de Abona, *Canary Is.* **22 F3** 28 7N 16 33W
Granard, *Ireland* **13 C4** 53 47N 7 30W
Granbury, *U.S.A.* **81 J6** 32 27N 97 47W
Granby, *Canada* **79 A12** 45 25N 72 45W
Granby, *U.S.A.* **82 F11** 40 5N 105 56W
Grand →, *Canada* **78 D5** 42 51N 79 34W
Grand →, *Mo., U.S.A.* **80 F8** 39 23N 93 7W
Grand →, *S. Dak., U.S.A.* . **80 C4** 45 40N 100 45W
Grand Bahama, *Bahamas* . **88 A4** 26 40N 78 30W
Grand Bank, *Canada* **71 C8** 47 6N 55 48W
Grand Bassam, *Ivory C.* ... **50 G5** 5 10N 3 49W
Grand-Bourg, *Guadeloupe* . **89 C7** 15 53N 61 19W
Grand Canal = Yun Ho →, *China* .... **35 E9** 39 10N 117 10 E
Grand Canyon, *U.S.A.* **83 H7** 36 3N 112 9W
Grand Canyon National Park, *U.S.A.* **83 H7** 36 15N 112 30W
Grand Cayman, *Cayman Is.* **88 C3** 19 20N 81 20W
Grand Centre, *Canada* **73 C6** 54 25N 110 13W
Grand Coulee, *U.S.A.* **82 C4** 47 57N 119 0W
Grand Coulee Dam, *U.S.A.* **82 C4** 47 57N 118 59W
Grand Erg du Bilma, *Niger* **51 E8** 18 30N 14 0 E
Grand Erg Occidental, *Algeria* .... **50 B6** 30 20N 1 0 E
Grand Erg Oriental, *Algeria* **50 B7** 30 0N 6 30 E
Grand Falls, *Canada* **71 C6** 47 3N 67 44W
Grand Falls-Windsor, *Canada* **71 C8** 48 56N 55 40W
Grand Forks, *Canada* **72 D5** 49 0N 118 30W
Grand Forks, *U.S.A.* **80 B6** 47 55N 97 3W
Grand Gorge, *U.S.A.* **79 D10** 42 21N 74 29W
Grand Haven, *U.S.A.* **76 D2** 43 4N 86 13W
Grand I., *Mich., U.S.A.* **76 B2** 46 31N 86 40W
Grand I., *N.Y., U.S.A.* **78 D6** 43 0N 78 58W
Grand Island, *U.S.A.* **80 E5** 40 55N 98 21W
Grand Isle, *La., U.S.A.* **81 L9** 29 14N 90 0W
Grand Isle, *Vt., U.S.A.* **79 B11** 44 43N 73 18W
Grand Junction, *U.S.A.* ... **83 G9** 39 4N 108 33W
Grand L., *N.B., Canada* **71 C6** 45 57N 66 7W
Grand L., *Nfld., Canada* **71 C8** 49 0N 57 30W
Grand L., *Nfld., Canada* **71 B7** 53 40N 60 30W
Grand L., *U.S.A.* **81 L8** 29 55N 92 47W
Grand Lake, *U.S.A.* **82 F11** 40 15N 105 49W
Grand Manan I., *Canada* .. **71 D6** 44 45N 66 52W
Grand Marais, *Canada* **80 B9** 47 45N 90 25W
Grand Marais, *U.S.A.* **76 B3** 46 40N 85 59W
Grand-Mère, *Canada* **70 C5** 46 36N 72 40W
Grand Prairie, *U.S.A.* **81 J6** 32 47N 97 0W
Grand Rapids, *Canada* **73 C9** 53 12N 99 19W
Grand Rapids, *Mich., U.S.A.* **76 D2** 42 58N 85 40W
Grand Rapids, *Minn., U.S.A.* **80 B8** 47 14N 93 31W
Grand St-Bernard, Col du, *Europe* .... **18 D7** 45 50N 7 10 E
Grand Teton, *U.S.A.* **82 E8** 43 54N 111 50W
Grand Teton National Park, *U.S.A.* **82 D8** 43 50N 110 50W
Grand Union Canal, *U.K.* .. **11 E7** 52 7N 0 53W
Grand View, *Canada* **73 C8** 51 10N 100 42W
Grande →, *Jujuy, Argentina* **94 A2** 24 20S 65 2W
Grande →, *Mendoza, Argentina* **94 D2** 36 52S 69 45W
Grande →, *Bolivia* **92 G6** 15 51S 64 39W
Grande →, *Bahia, Brazil* . **93 F10** 11 30S 44 30W
Grande →, *Minas Gerais, Brazil* **93 H8** 20 6S 51 4W
Grande, B., *Argentina* **96 G3** 50 30S 68 20W
Grande, Rio →, *U.S.A.* **81 N6** 25 58N 97 9W
Grande Baleine, R. de la →, *Canada* **70 A4** 55 16N 77 47W
Grande Cache, *Canada* **72 C5** 53 53N 119 8W
Grande-Entrée, *Canada* ... **71 C7** 47 30N 61 40W
Grande Prairie, *Canada* ... **72 B5** 55 10N 118 50W
Grande-Rivière, *Canada* ... **71 C7** 48 26N 64 30W
Grande-Vallée, *Canada* ... **71 C6** 49 14N 65 8W
Grandfalls, *U.S.A.* **81 K3** 31 20N 102 51W
Grandview, *U.S.A.* **82 C4** 46 15N 119 54W
Graneros, *Chile* **94 C1** 34 5S 70 45W
Grangemouth, *U.K.* **12 E5** 56 1N 3 42W
Granger, *U.S.A.* **82 F9** 41 35N 109 58W
Grangeville, *U.S.A.* **82 D5** 45 56N 116 7W
Granisle, *Canada* **72 C3** 54 53N 126 13W
Granite City, *U.S.A.* **80 F9** 38 42N 90 9W
Granite Falls, *U.S.A.* **80 C7** 44 49N 95 33W
Granite L., *Canada* **71 C8** 48 8N 57 5W
Granite Mt., *U.S.A.* **85 M10** 33 5N 116 28W
Granite Pk., *U.S.A.* **82 D9** 45 10N 109 48W
Graniteville, *U.S.A.* **79 B12** 44 8N 72 29W
Granity, *N.Z.* .... **59 J3** 41 39S 171 51 E
Granja, *Brazil* **93 D10** 3 7S 40 50W
Granollers, *Spain* .... **19 B7** 41 39N 2 18 E
Grant, *U.S.A.* **80 E4** 40 53N 101 42W
Grant, Mt., *U.S.A.* **82 G4** 38 34N 118 48W
Grant City, *U.S.A.* **80 E7** 40 29N 94 25W
Grant I., *Australia* .... **60 B5** 11 10S 132 52 E
Grant Range, *U.S.A.* **83 G6** 38 30N 115 25W
Grantham, *U.K.* **10 E7** 52 55N 0 38W
Grantown-on-Spey, *U.K.* .. **12 D5** 57 20N 3 36W
Grants, *U.S.A.* **83 J10** 35 9N 107 52W
Grants Pass, *U.S.A.* **82 E2** 42 26N 123 19W
Grantsville, *U.S.A.* **82 F7** 40 36N 112 28W
Granville, *France* **18 B3** 48 50N 1 35W
Granville, *N. Dak., U.S.A.* .. **80 A4** 48 16N 100 47W
Granville, *N.Y., U.S.A.* **79 C11** 43 24N 73 16W
Granville, *Ohio, U.S.A.* **78 F2** 40 4N 82 31W
Granville L., *Canada* **73 B8** 56 18N 100 30W
Graskop, *S. Africa* .... **57 C5** 24 56S 30 49 E
Grass →, *Canada* **73 B9** 56 3N 96 33W
Grass Range, *U.S.A.* **82 C9** 47 0N 109 0W
Grass River Prov. Park, *Canada* **73 C8** 54 40N 100 50W
Grass Valley, *Calif., U.S.A.* . **84 F6** 39 13N 121 4W
Grass Valley, *Oreg., U.S.A.* **82 D3** 45 22N 120 47W
Grasse, *France* .... **18 E7** 43 38N 6 56 E
Grassflat, *U.S.A.* **78 F6** 41 0N 78 6W
Grasslands Nat. Park, *Canada* **73 D7** 49 11N 107 38W
Grassy, *Australia* .... **62 G3** 40 3S 144 5 E
Graulhet, *France* .... **18 E4** 43 45N 1 59 E
Gravelbourg, *Canada* **73 D7** 49 50N 106 35W
's-Gravenhage, *Neths.* .... **15 B4** 52 7N 4 17 E
Gravenhurst, *Canada* **78 B5** 44 52N 79 20W
Gravesend, *Australia* ..... **63 D5** 29 35S 150 20 E
Gravesend, *U.K.* .... **11 F8** 51 26N 0 22 E
Gravois, Pointe-à-, *Haiti* .. **89 C5** 18 15N 73 56W
Grayling, *U.S.A.* **76 C3** 44 40N 84 43W
Grays Harbor, *U.S.A.* **82 C1** 46 59N 124 1W
Grays L., *U.S.A.* **82 E8** 43 4N 111 26W
Grays River, *U.S.A.* **84 D3** 46 21N 123 37W
Graz, *Austria* .... **16 E8** 47 4N 15 27 E
Greasy L., *Canada* **72 A4** 62 55N 122 12W
Great Abaco I., *Bahamas* .. **88 A4** 26 25N 77 10W
Great Artesian Basin, *Australia* .... **62 C3** 23 0S 144 0 E
Great Australian Bight, *Australia* .... **61 F5** 33 30S 130 0 E
Great Bahama Bank, *Bahamas* **88 B4** 23 15N 78 0W
Great Barrier I., *N.Z.* ..... **59 G5** 36 11S 175 25 E
Great Barrier Reef, *Australia* **62 B4** 18 0S 146 50 E
Great Barrington, *U.S.A.* .. **79 D11** 42 12N 73 22W
Great Basin, *U.S.A.* **82 G5** 40 0N 117 0W
Great Basin Nat. Park, *U.S.A.* **82 G6** 38 55N 114 14W
Great Bear →, *Canada* .. **68 B7** 65 0N 124 0W
Great Bear L., *Canada* **68 B8** 65 30N 120 0W
Great Belt = Store Bælt, *Denmark* .... **9 J14** 55 20N 11 0 E
Great Bend, *Kans., U.S.A.* . **80 F5** 38 22N 98 46W
Great Bend, *Pa., U.S.A.* ... **79 E9** 41 58N 75 45W
Great Blasket I., *Ireland* ... **13 D1** 52 6N 10 32W
Great Britain, *Europe* **6 E5** 54 0N 2 15W
Great Codroy, *Canada* **71 C8** 47 51N 59 16W
Great Dividing Ra., *Australia* **62 C4** 23 0S 146 0 E
Great Driffield = Driffield, *U.K.* **10 C7** 54 0N 0 26W
Great Exuma I., *Bahamas* . **88 B4** 23 30N 75 50W
Great Falls, *U.S.A.* **82 C8** 47 30N 111 17W
Great Fish = Groot Vis →, *S. Africa* .... **56 E4** 33 28S 27 5 E
Great Guana Cay, *Bahamas* **88 B4** 24 0N 76 20W
Great Inagua I., *Bahamas* .. **89 B5** 21 0N 73 20W
Great Indian Desert = Thar Desert, *India* .... **42 F5** 28 0N 72 0 E
Great Karoo, *S. Africa* .... **56 E3** 31 55S 21 0 E
Great Lake, *Australia* ..... **62 G4** 41 50S 146 40 E
Great Lakes, *N. Amer.* **66 E11** 46 0N 84 0W
Great Malvern, *U.K.* **11 E5** 52 7N 2 18W
Great Miami →, *U.S.A.* .. **76 F3** 39 20N 84 40W
Great Ormes Head, *U.K.* ... **10 D4** 53 20N 3 52W
Great Ouse →, *U.K.* ..... **10 E8** 52 48N 0 21 E
Great Palm I., *Australia* ... **62 B4** 18 45S 146 40 E
Great Plains, *N. Amer.* **74 A6** 47 0N 105 0W
Great Ruaha →, *Tanzania* **54 D4** 7 56S 37 52 E
Great Sacandaga Res., *U.S.A.* **79 C10** 43 6N 74 16W
Great Saint Bernard Pass = Grand St-Bernard, Col du, *Europe* .... **18 D7** 45 50N 7 10 E
Great Salt L., *U.S.A.* **82 F7** 41 15N 112 40W
Great Salt Lake Desert, *U.S.A.* **82 F7** 40 50N 113 30W
Great Salt Plains L., *U.S.A.* **81 G5** 36 45N 98 8W
Great Sandy Desert, *Australia* .... **60 D3** 21 0S 124 0 E
Great Sangi = Sangihe, Pulau, *Indonesia* ..... **37 D7** 3 45N 125 30 E
Great Skellig, *Ireland* **13 E1** 51 47N 10 33W
Great Slave L., *Canada* **72 A5** 61 23N 115 38W
Great Smoky Mts. Nat. Park, *U.S.A.* **77 H4** 35 40N 83 40W
Great Snow Mt., *Canada* .. **72 B4** 57 26N 124 0W
Great Stour = Stour →, *U.K.* .... **11 F9** 51 18N 1 22 E
Great Victoria Desert, *Australia* .... **61 E4** 29 30S 126 30 E
Great Wall, *China* .... **34 E5** 38 30N 109 30 E
Great Whernside, *U.K.* **10 C6** 54 10N 1 58W
Great Yarmouth, *U.K.* ..... **11 E9** 52 37N 1 44 E
Greater Antilles, *W. Indies* . **89 C5** 17 40N 74 0W
Greater London □, *U.K.* ... **11 F7** 51 31N 0 6W
Greater Manchester □, *U.K.* **10 D5** 53 30N 2 15W
Greater Sunda Is., *Indonesia* **36 F4** 7 0S 112 0 E
Greco, C., *Cyprus* .... **23 E13** 34 57N 34 5 E
Gredos, Sierra de, *Spain* .. **19 B3** 40 20N 5 0W
Greece, *U.S.A.* **78 C7** 43 13N 77 41W
Greece ■, *Europe* .... **21 E9** 40 0N 23 0 E
Greeley, *Colo., U.S.A.* **80 E2** 40 25N 104 42W
Greeley, *Nebr., U.S.A.* **80 E5** 41 33N 98 32W
Greem-Bell, Ostrov, *Russia* **26 A7** 81 0N 62 0 E
Green, *U.S.A.* **82 E2** 43 9N 123 22W
Green →, *Ky., U.S.A.* **76 G2** 37 54N 87 30W
Green →, *Utah, U.S.A.* ... **83 G9** 38 11N 109 53W
Green B., *U.S.A.* **76 C2** 45 0N 87 30W
Green Bay, *U.S.A.* **76 C2** 44 31N 88 0W
Green C., *Australia* .... **63 F5** 37 13S 150 1 E
Green Cove Springs, *U.S.A.* **77 L5** 29 59N 81 42W
Green Lake, *Canada* **73 C7** 54 17N 107 47W
Green Mts., *U.S.A.* **79 C12** 43 45N 72 45W
Green River, *Utah, U.S.A.* .. **83 G8** 38 59N 110 10W
Green River, *Wyo., U.S.A.* . **82 F9** 41 32N 109 28W
Green Valley, *U.S.A.* **83 L8** 31 52N 110 56W
Greenbank, *U.S.A.* **84 B4** 48 6N 122 34W
Greenbush, *Mich., U.S.A.* .. **78 B1** 44 35N 83 19W
Greenbush, *Minn., U.S.A.* .. **80 A6** 48 42N 96 11W
Greencastle, *U.S.A.* **76 F2** 39 38N 86 52W
Greene, *U.S.A.* **79 D9** 42 20N 75 46W
Greenfield, *Calif., U.S.A.* .. **84 J5** 36 19N 121 15W
Greenfield, *Calif., U.S.A.* .. **85 K8** 35 15N 119 0W
Greenfield, *Ind., U.S.A.* ... **76 F3** 39 47N 85 46W
Greenfield, *Iowa, U.S.A.* .. **80 E7** 41 18N 94 28W
Greenfield, *Mass., U.S.A.* .. **79 D12** 42 35N 72 36W
Greenfield, *Mo., U.S.A.* ... **81 G8** 37 25N 93 51W
Greenfield Park, *Canada* ... **79 A11** 45 29N 73 29W
Greenland ■, *N. Amer.* **4 C5** 66 0N 45 0W
Greenland Sea, *Arctic* **4 B7** 73 0N 10 0W
Greenock, *U.K.* **12 F4** 55 57N 4 46W
Greenore, *Ireland* **13 B5** 54 2N 6 8W
Greenore Pt., *Ireland* **13 D5** 52 14N 6 19W
Greenough, *Australia* ..... **61 E1** 28 58S 114 43 E
Greenough →, *Australia* . **61 E1** 28 51S 114 38 E
Greenough Pt., *Canada* ... **78 B3** 44 58N 81 26W
Greenport, *U.S.A.* **79 E12** 41 6N 72 22W
Greensboro, *Ga., U.S.A.* ... **77 J4** 33 35N 83 11W
Greensboro, *N.C., U.S.A.* .. **77 G6** 36 4N 79 48W
Greensboro, *Vt., U.S.A.* ... **79 B12** 44 36N 72 18W
Greensburg, *Ind., U.S.A.* .. **76 F3** 39 20N 85 29W
Greensburg, *Kans., U.S.A.* . **81 G5** 37 36N 99 18W
Greensburg, *Pa., U.S.A.* ... **78 F5** 40 18N 79 33W
Greenstone Pt., *U.K.* **12 D3** 57 55N 5 37W
Greenvale, *Australia* ...... **62 B4** 18 59S 145 7 E
Greenville, *Ala., U.S.A.* ... **77 K2** 31 50N 86 38W
Greenville, *Calif., U.S.A.* .. **84 E6** 40 8N 120 57W
Greenville, *Maine, U.S.A.* . **77 C11** 45 28N 69 35W
Greenville, *Mich., U.S.A.* .. **76 D3** 43 11N 85 15W
Greenville, *Miss., U.S.A.* .. **81 J9** 33 24N 91 4W
Greenville, *Mo., U.S.A.* ... **81 G9** 37 8N 90 27W
Greenville, *N.C., U.S.A.* ... **77 H7** 35 37N 77 23W
Greenville, *N.H., U.S.A.* ... **79 D13** 42 46N 71 49W
Greenville, *N.Y., U.S.A.* ... **79 D10** 42 25N 74 1W
Greenville, *Ohio, U.S.A.* .. **76 E3** 40 6N 84 38W
Greenville, *Pa., U.S.A.* ... **78 E4** 41 24N 80 23W
Greenville, *S.C., U.S.A.* ... **77 H4** 34 51N 82 24W
Greenville, *Tenn., U.S.A.* .. **77 G4** 36 13N 82 51W
Greenville, *Tex., U.S.A.* ... **81 J6** 33 8N 96 7W
Greenwater Lake Prov. Park, *Canada* **73 C8** 52 32N 103 30W
Greenwich, *U.K.* .... **11 F8** 51 29N 0 1 E
Greenwich, *Conn., U.S.A.* . **79 E11** 41 2N 73 38W
Greenwich, *N.Y., U.S.A.* ... **79 C11** 43 5N 73 30W
Greenwich, *Ohio, U.S.A.* .. **78 E2** 41 2N 82 31W
Greenwood, *Canada* **72 D5** 49 10N 118 40W
Greenwood, *Ark., U.S.A.* .. **81 H7** 35 13N 94 16W
Greenwood, *Ind., U.S.A.* .. **76 F2** 39 37N 86 7W
Greenwood, *Miss., U.S.A.* . **81 J9** 33 31N 90 11W
Greenwood, *S.C., U.S.A.* .. **77 H4** 34 12N 82 10W
Greenwood, Mt., *Australia* . **60 B5** 13 48S 130 4 E
Gregory, *U.S.A.* **80 D5** 43 14N 99 20W
Gregory →, *Australia* ... **62 B2** 17 53S 139 17 E
Gregory, L., *S. Austral., Australia* .... **63 D2** 28 55S 139 0 E
Gregory, L., *W. Austral., Australia* .... **61 E2** 25 38S 119 58 E
Gregory Downs, *Australia* . **62 B2** 18 35S 138 45 E
Gregory L., *Australia* ..... **60 D4** 20 0S 127 40 E
Gregory Ra., *Queens., Australia* .... **62 B3** 19 30S 143 40 E
Gregory Ra., *W. Austral., Australia* .... **60 D3** 21 20S 121 12 E
Greifswald, *Germany* ..... **16 A7** 54 5N 13 23 E
Greiz, *Germany* .... **16 C7** 50 39N 12 10 E
Gremikha, *Russia* .... **24 A6** 67 59N 39 47 E
Grenå, *Denmark* .... **9 H14** 56 25N 10 53 E
Grenada, *U.S.A.* **81 J10** 33 47N 89 49W
Grenada ■, *W. Indies* **89 D7** 12 10N 61 40W
Grenadier I., *U.S.A.* **79 B8** 44 3N 76 22W
Grenadines, *W. Indies* **89 D7** 12 40N 61 20W

Grenen

Grenen, *Denmark* **9 H14** 57 44N 10 40 E
Grenfell, *Australia* **63 E4** 33 52S 148 8 E
Grenfell, *Canada* **73 C8** 50 30N 102 56W
Grenoble, *France* **18 D6** 45 12N 5 42 E
Grenville, C., *Australia* **62 A3** 12 0S 143 13 E
Grenville Chan., *Canada* **72 C3** 53 40N 129 46W
Gresham, *U.S.A.* **84 E4** 45 30N 122 26W
Gresik, *Indonesia* **37 G15** 7 13S 112 38 E
Gretna, *U.K.* **12 F5** 55 0N 3 3W
Grevenmacher, *Lux.* **15 E6** 49 41N 6 26 E
Grey →, *Canada* **71 C8** 47 34N 57 6W
Grey →, *N.Z.* **59 K3** 42 27S 171 12 E
Grey, C., *Australia* **62 A2** 13 0S 136 35 E
Grey Ra., *Australia* **63 D3** 27 0S 143 30 E
Greybull, *U.S.A.* **82 D9** 44 30N 108 3W
Greymouth, *N.Z.* **59 K3** 42 29S 171 13 E
Greystones, *Ireland* **13 C5** 53 9N 6 5W
Greytown, *N.Z.* **59 J5** 41 5S 175 29 E
Greytown, *S. Africa* **57 D5** 29 1S 30 36 E
Gribbell I., *Canada* **72 C3** 53 23N 129 0W
Gridley, *U.S.A.* **84 F5** 39 22N 121 42W
Griekwastad, *S. Africa* **56 D3** 28 49S 23 15 E
Griffin, *U.S.A.* **77 J3** 33 15N 84 16W
Griffith, *Australia* **63 E4** 34 18S 146 2 E
Griffith, *Canada* **78 A7** 45 15N 77 10W
Griffith I., *Canada* **78 B4** 44 50N 80 55W
Grimaylov = Hrymayliv, *Ukraine* **17 D14** 49 20N 26 5 E
Grimes, *U.S.A.* **84 F5** 39 4N 121 54W
Grimsay, *U.K.* **12 D1** 57 29N 7 14W
Grimsby, *Canada* **78 C5** 43 12N 79 34W
Grimsby, *U.K.* **10 D7** 53 34N 0 5W
Grímsey, *Iceland* **8 C5** 66 33N 17 58W
Grimshaw, *Canada* **72 B5** 56 10N 117 40W
Grimstad, *Norway* **9 G13** 58 20N 8 35 E
Grindstone I., *Canada* **79 B8** 44 43N 76 14W
Grinnell, *U.S.A.* **80 E8** 41 45N 92 43W
Gris-Nez, C., *France* **18 A4** 50 52N 1 35 E
Groais I., *Canada* **71 B8** 50 55N 55 35W
Groblersdal, *S. Africa* **57 D4** 25 15S 29 25 E
Grodno = Hrodna, *Belarus* **17 B12** 53 42N 23 52 E
Grodzyanka = Hrodzyanka, *Belarus* **17 B15** 53 31N 28 42 E
Groesbeck, *U.S.A.* **81 K6** 31 31N 96 31W
Grójec, *Poland* **17 C11** 51 50N 20 58 E
Grong, *Norway* **8 D15** 64 25N 12 8 E
Groningen, *Neths.* **15 A6** 53 15N 6 35 E
Groningen □, *Neths.* **15 A6** 53 16N 6 40 E
Groom, *U.S.A.* **81 H4** 35 12N 101 6W
Groot →, *S. Africa* **56 E3** 33 45S 24 36 E
Groot Berg →, *S. Africa* **56 E2** 32 47S 18 8 E
Groot-Brakrivier, *S. Africa* **56 E3** 34 2S 22 18 E
Groot-Kei →, *S. Africa* **57 E4** 32 41S 28 22 E
Groot Vis →, *S. Africa* **56 E4** 33 28S 27 5 E
Groote Eylandt, *Australia* **62 A2** 14 0S 136 40 E
Grootfontein, *Namibia* **56 B2** 19 31S 18 6 E
Grootlaagte →, *Africa* **56 C3** 20 55S 21 27 E
Grootvloer, *S. Africa* **56 E3** 30 0S 20 40 E
Gros C., *Canada* **72 A6** 61 59N 113 32W
Gros Morne Nat. Park, *Canada* **71 C8** 49 40N 57 50W
Grossa, Pta., *Spain* **22 B8** 39 6N 1 36 E
Grosser Arber, *Germany* **16 D7** 49 6N 13 8 E
Grosseto, *Italy* **20 C4** 42 46N 11 8 E
Grossglockner, *Austria* **16 E7** 47 5N 12 40 E
Groswater B., *Canada* **71 B8** 54 20N 57 40W
Groton, *Conn., U.S.A.* **79 E12** 41 21N 72 5W
Groton, *N.Y., U.S.A.* **79 D8** 42 36N 76 22W
Groton, *S. Dak., U.S.A.* **80 C5** 45 27N 98 6W
Grouard Mission, *Canada* **72 B5** 55 33N 116 9W
Groundhog →, *Canada* **70 C3** 48 45N 82 58W
Grouw, *Neths.* **15 A5** 53 5N 5 51 E
Grove City, *U.S.A.* **78 E4** 41 10N 80 5W
Grove Hill, *U.S.A.* **77 K2** 31 42N 87 47W
Groveland, *U.S.A.* **84 H6** 37 50N 120 14W
Grover City, *U.S.A.* **85 K6** 35 7N 120 37W
Groves, *U.S.A.* **81 L8** 29 57N 93 54W
Groveton, *U.S.A.* **79 B13** 44 36N 71 31W
Groznyy, *Russia* **25 F8** 43 20N 45 45 E
Grudziądz, *Poland* **17 B10** 53 30N 18 47 E
Gruinard B., *U.K.* **12 D3** 57 56N 5 35W
Grundy Center, *U.S.A.* **80 D8** 42 22N 92 47W
Gruver, *U.S.A.* **81 G4** 36 16N 101 24W
Gryazi, *Russia* **24 D6** 52 30N 39 58 E
Gryazovets, *Russia* **24 C7** 58 50N 40 10 E
Gua, *India* **41 H14** 22 18N 85 20 E
Gua Musang, *Malaysia* **39 K3** 4 53N 101 58 E
Guacanayabo, G. de, *Cuba* **88 B4** 20 40N 77 20W
Guachípas →, *Argentina* **94 B2** 25 40S 65 30W
Guadalajara, *Mexico* **86 C4** 20 40N 103 20W
Guadalajara, *Spain* **19 B4** 40 37N 3 12W
Guadalcanal, *Solomon Is.* **64 H8** 9 32S 160 12 E
Guadales, *Argentina* **94 C2** 34 30S 67 55W
Guadalete →, *Spain* **19 D2** 36 35N 6 13W
Guadalquivir →, *Spain* **19 D2** 36 47N 6 22W
Guadalupe = Guadeloupe ■, *W. Indies* **89 C7** 16 20N 61 40W
Guadalupe, *Mexico* **85 N10** 32 4N 116 32W
Guadalupe, *U.S.A.* **85 L6** 34 59N 120 33W
Guadalupe →, *Mexico* **85 N10** 32 6N 116 51W
Guadalupe →, *U.S.A.* **81 L6** 28 27N 96 47W
Guadalupe, Sierra de, *Spain* **19 C3** 39 28N 5 30W
Guadalupe Bravos, *Mexico* **86 A3** 31 20N 106 10W
Guadalupe I., *Pac. Oc.* **66 G8** 29 0N 118 50W
Guadalupe Mts. Nat. Park, *U.S.A.* **81 K2** 32 0N 104 30W
Guadalupe Peak, *U.S.A.* **81 K2** 31 50N 104 52W
Guadalupe y Calvo, *Mexico* **86 B3** 26 6N 106 58W
Guadarrama, Sierra de, *Spain* **19 B4** 41 0N 4 0W
Guadeloupe ■, *W. Indies* **89 C7** 16 20N 61 40W
Guadeloupe Passage, *W. Indies* **89 C7** 16 50N 62 15W
Guadiana →, *Portugal* **19 D2** 37 14N 7 22W
Guadix, *Spain* **19 D4** 37 18N 3 11W
Guafo, Boca del, *Chile* **96 E2** 43 35S 74 0W
Guainía →, *Colombia* **92 C5** 2 1N 67 7W
Guaíra, *Brazil* **95 A5** 24 5S 54 10W
Guaira □, *Paraguay* **94 B4** 25 45S 56 30W
Guaitecas, Is., *Chile* **96 E2** 44 0S 74 30W
Guajará-Mirim, *Brazil* **92 F5** 10 50S 65 20W
Guajira, Pen. de la, *Colombia* **92 A4** 12 0N 72 0W
Gualán, *Guatemala* **88 C2** 15 8N 89 22W
Gualeguay, *Argentina* **94 C4** 33 10S 59 14W
Gualeguaychú, *Argentina* **94 C4** 33 3S 59 31W
Gualequay →, *Argentina* **94 C4** 33 19S 59 39W
Guam ■, *Pac. Oc.* **64 F6** 13 27N 144 45 E
Guamini, *Argentina* **94 D3** 37 1S 62 28W
Guamúchil, *Mexico* **86 B3** 25 25N 108 3W
Guanabacoa, *Cuba* **88 B3** 23 8N 82 18W
Guanacaste, Cordillera del, *Costa Rica* **88 D2** 10 40N 85 4W
Guanaceví, *Mexico* **86 B3** 25 40N 106 0W
Guanahani = San Salvador I., *Bahamas* **89 B5** 24 0N 74 40W
Guanajay, *Cuba* **88 B3** 22 56N 82 42W
Guanajuato, *Mexico* **86 C4** 21 0N 101 20W
Guanajuato □, *Mexico* **86 C4** 20 40N 101 20W
Guandacol, *Argentina* **94 B2** 29 30S 68 40W
Guane, *Cuba* **88 B3** 22 10N 84 7W
Guangdong □, *China* **33 D6** 23 0N 113 0 E
Guangling, *China* **34 E8** 39 47N 114 22 E
Guangrao, *China* **35 F10** 37 5N 118 25 E
Guangwu, *China* **34 F3** 37 48N 105 57 E
Guangxi Zhuangzu Zizhiqu □, *China* **33 D5** 24 0N 109 0 E
Guangzhou, *China* **33 D6** 23 5N 113 10 E
Guanipa →, *Venezuela* **92 B6** 9 56N 62 26W
Guannan, *China* **35 G10** 34 8N 119 21 E
Guantánamo, *Cuba* **89 B4** 20 10N 75 14W
Guantao, *China* **34 F8** 36 42N 115 25 E
Guanyun, *China* **35 G10** 34 20N 119 18 E
Guápiles, *Costa Rica* **88 D3** 10 10N 83 46W
Guaporé, *Brazil* **95 B5** 28 51S 51 54W
Guaporé →, *Brazil* **92 F5** 11 55S 65 4W
Guaqui, *Bolivia* **92 G5** 16 41S 68 54W
Guarapari, *Brazil* **95 A7** 20 40S 40 30W
Guarapuava, *Brazil* **95 B5** 25 20S 51 30W
Guaratinguetá, *Brazil* **95 A6** 22 49S 45 9W
Guaratuba, *Brazil* **95 B6** 25 53S 48 38W
Guarda, *Portugal* **19 B2** 40 32N 7 20W
Guardafui, C. = Asir, Ras, *Somali Rep.* **46 E5** 11 55N 51 10 E
Guárico □, *Venezuela* **92 B5** 8 40N 66 35W
Guarujá, *Brazil* **95 A6** 24 2S 46 25W
Guarus, *Brazil* **95 A7** 21 44S 41 20W
Guasave, *Mexico* **86 B3** 25 34N 108 27W
Guasdualito, *Venezuela* **92 B4** 7 15N 70 44W
Guatemala, *Guatemala* **88 D1** 14 40N 90 22W
Guatemala ■, *Cent. Amer.* **88 C1** 15 40N 90 30W
Guaviare →, *Colombia* **92 C5** 4 3N 67 44W
Guaxupé, *Brazil* **95 A6** 21 10S 47 5W
Guayama, *Puerto Rico* **89 C6** 17 59N 66 7W
Guayaquil, *Ecuador* **92 D3** 2 15S 79 52W
Guayaquil, G. de, *Ecuador* **92 D2** 3 10S 81 0W
Guaymas, *Mexico* **86 B2** 27 59N 110 54W
Guba, *Dem. Rep. of the Congo* **55 E2** 10 38S 26 27 E
Gubkin, *Russia* **25 D6** 51 17N 37 32 E
Gudbrandsdalen, *Norway* **9 F14** 61 33N 10 10 E
Guddu Barrage, *Pakistan* **40 E6** 28 30N 69 50 E
Gudivada, *India* **41 L12** 16 30N 81 3 E
Gudur, *India* **40 M11** 14 12N 79 55 E
Guecho = Getxo, *Spain* **19 A4** 43 21N 2 59W
Guelph, *Canada* **78 C4** 43 35N 80 20W
Guéret, *France* **18 C4** 46 11N 1 51 E
Guerneville, *U.S.A.* **84 G4** 38 30N 123 0W
Guernica = Gernika-Lumo, *Spain* **19 A4** 43 19N 2 40W
Guernsey, *U.K.* **11 H5** 49 26N 2 35W
Guernsey, *U.S.A.* **80 D2** 42 19N 104 45W
Guerrero □, *Mexico* **87 D5** 17 30N 100 0W
Gügher, *Iran* **45 D8** 29 28N 56 27 E
Guhakolak, Tanjung, *Indonesia* **37 G11** 6 50S 105 14 E
Guia, *Canary Is.* **22 F4** 28 8N 15 38W
Guia de Isora, *Canary Is.* **22 F3** 28 12N 16 46W
Guia Lopes da Laguna, *Brazil* **95 A4** 21 26S 56 7W
Guiana, *S. Amer.* **90 C4** 5 10N 60 40W
Guider, *Cameroon* **51 G8** 9 56N 13 57 E
Guidónia-Montecélio, *Italy* **20 C5** 42 1N 12 45 E
Guijá, *Mozam.* **57 C5** 24 27S 33 0 E
Guildford, *U.K.* **11 F7** 51 14N 0 34W
Guilford, *U.S.A.* **79 E12** 41 17N 72 41W
Guilin, *China* **33 D6** 25 18N 110 15 E
Guillaume-Delisle L., *Canada* **70 A4** 56 15N 76 17W
Güímar, *Canary Is.* **22 F3** 28 18N 16 24W
Guimarães, *Portugal* **19 B1** 41 28N 8 24W
Guimaras, *Phil.* **37 B6** 10 35N 122 37 E
Guinda, *U.S.A.* **84 G4** 38 50N 122 12W
Guinea, *Africa* **48 F4** 8 0N 8 0 E
Guinea ■, *W. Afr.* **50 F3** 10 20N 11 30W
Guinea, Gulf of, *Atl. Oc.* **48 F4** 3 0N 2 30 E
Guinea-Bissau ■, *Africa* **50 F3** 12 0N 15 0W
Güines, *Cuba* **88 B3** 22 50N 82 0W
Guingamp, *France* **18 B2** 48 34N 3 10W
Güiria, *Venezuela* **92 A6** 10 32N 62 18W
Guiuan, *Phil.* **37 B7** 11 5N 125 55 E
Guiyang, *China* **32 D5** 26 32N 106 40 E
Guizhou □, *China* **32 D5** 27 0N 107 0 E
Gujar Khan, *Pakistan* **42 C5** 33 16N 73 19 E
Gujarat □, *India* **42 H4** 23 20N 71 0 E
Gujranwala, *Pakistan* **42 C6** 32 10N 74 12 E
Gujrat, *Pakistan* **42 C6** 32 40N 74 2 E
Gulargambone, *Australia* **63 E4** 31 20S 148 30 E
Gulbarga, *India* **40 L10** 17 20N 76 50 E
Gulbene, *Latvia* **9 H22** 57 8N 26 52 E
Gulf, The, *Asia* **45 E6** 27 0N 50 0 E
Gulfport, *U.S.A.* **81 K10** 30 22N 89 6W
Gulgong, *Australia* **63 E4** 32 20S 149 49 E
Gulistan, *Pakistan* **42 D2** 30 30N 66 35 E
Gull Lake, *Canada* **73 C7** 50 10N 108 29W
Güllük, *Turkey* **21 F12** 37 14N 27 35 E
Gulmarg, *India* **43 B6** 34 3N 74 25 E
Gulshad, *Kazakstan* **26 E8** 46 45N 74 25 E
Gulu, *Uganda* **54 B3** 2 48N 32 17 E
Gulwe, *Tanzania* **54 D4** 6 30S 36 25 E
Gumal →, *Pakistan* **42 D4** 31 40N 71 50 E
Gumbaz, *Pakistan* **42 D3** 30 2N 69 0 E
Gumel, *Nigeria* **50 F7** 12 39N 9 22 E
Gumla, *India* **43 H11** 23 3N 84 33 E
Gumlu, *Australia* **62 B4** 19 53S 147 41 E
Gumma □, *Japan* **31 F9** 36 30N 138 20 E
Gumzai, *Indonesia* **37 F8** 5 28S 134 42 E
Guna, *India* **42 G7** 24 40N 77 19 E
Gunisao →, *Canada* **73 C9** 53 56N 97 53W
Gunisao L., *Canada* **73 C9** 53 33N 96 15W
Gunjyal, *Pakistan* **42 C4** 32 20N 71 55 E
Gunnbjørn Fjeld, *Greenland* **4 C6** 68 55N 29 47W
Gunnedah, *Australia* **63 E5** 30 59S 150 15 E
Gunnewin, *Australia* **63 D4** 25 59S 148 33 E
Gunningbar Cr. →, *Australia* **63 E4** 31 14S 147 6 E
Gunnison, *Colo., U.S.A.* **83 G10** 38 33N 106 56W
Gunnison, *Utah, U.S.A.* **82 G8** 39 9N 111 49W
Gunnison →, *U.S.A.* **83 G9** 39 4N 108 35W
Gunpowder, *Australia* **62 B2** 19 42S 139 22 E
Guntakal, *India* **40 M10** 15 11N 77 27 E
Guntersville, *U.S.A.* **77 H2** 34 21N 86 18W
Guntong, *Malaysia* **39 K3** 4 36N 101 3 E
Guntur, *India* **41 L12** 16 23N 80 30 E
Gunungapi, *Indonesia* **37 F7** 6 45S 126 30 E
Gunungsitoli, *Indonesia* **36 D1** 1 15N 97 30 E
Gunza, *Angola* **52 G2** 10 50S 13 50 E
Guo He →, *China* **35 H9** 32 59N 117 10 E
Guoyang, *China* **34 H9** 33 32N 116 12 E
Gupis, *Pakistan* **43 A5** 36 15N 73 20 E
Gurdaspur, *India* **42 C6** 32 5N 75 31 E
Gurdon, *U.S.A.* **81 J8** 33 55N 93 9W
Gurgaon, *India* **42 E7** 28 27N 77 1 E
Gurgueia →, *Brazil* **93 E10** 6 50S 43 24W
Gurha, *India* **42 G4** 25 12N 71 39 E
Guri, Embalse de, *Venezuela* **92 B6** 7 50N 62 52W
Gurkha, *Nepal* **43 E11** 28 5N 84 40 E
Gurley, *Australia* **63 D4** 29 45S 149 48 E
Gurnet Point, *U.S.A.* **79 D14** 42 1N 70 34W
Gurué, *Mozam.* **55 F4** 15 25S 36 58 E
Gurun, *Malaysia* **39 K3** 5 49N 100 27 E
Gürün, *Turkey* **25 G6** 38 43N 37 15 E
Gurupá, *Brazil* **93 D8** 1 25S 51 35W
Gurupá, I. Grande de, *Brazil* **93 D8** 1 25S 51 45W
Gurupi, *Brazil* **93 F9** 11 43S 49 4W
Gurupi →, *Brazil* **93 D9** 1 13S 46 6W
Guryev = Atyraū, *Kazakstan* **25 E9** 47 5N 52 0 E
Gusau, *Nigeria* **50 F7** 12 12N 6 40 E
Gusev, *Russia* **9 J20** 54 35N 22 10 E
Gushan, *China* **35 E12** 39 50N 123 35 E
Gushgy, *Turkmenistan* **26 F7** 35 20N 62 18 E
Gusinoozersk, *Russia* **27 D11** 51 16N 106 27 E
Gustavus, *U.S.A.* **72 B1** 58 25N 135 44W
Gustine, *U.S.A.* **84 H6** 37 16N 121 0W
Güstrow, *Germany* **16 B7** 53 47N 12 10 E
Gütersloh, *Germany* **16 C5** 51 54N 8 24 E
Gutha, *Australia* **61 E2** 28 58S 115 55 E
Guthalungra, *Australia* **62 B4** 19 52S 147 50 E
Guthrie, *Okla., U.S.A.* **81 H6** 35 53N 97 25W
Guthrie, *Tex., U.S.A.* **81 J4** 33 37N 100 19W
Guttenberg, *U.S.A.* **80 D9** 42 47N 91 6W
Guyana ■, *S. Amer.* **92 C7** 5 0N 59 0W
Guyane française = French Guiana ■, *S. Amer.* **93 C8** 4 0N 53 0W
Guyang, *China* **34 D6** 41 0N 110 5 E
Guyenne, *France* **18 D4** 44 30N 0 40 E
Guymon, *U.S.A.* **81 G4** 36 41N 101 29W
Guyra, *Australia* **63 E5** 30 15S 151 40 E
Guyuan, *Hebei, China* **34 D8** 41 37N 115 40 E
Guyuan, *Ningxia Huizu, China* **34 G4** 36 0N 106 20 E
Guzhen, *China* **35 H9** 33 22N 117 18 E
Guzmán, L. de, *Mexico* **86 A3** 31 25N 107 25W
Gvardeysk, *Russia* **9 J19** 54 39N 21 5 E
Gwa, *Burma* **41 L19** 17 36N 94 34 E
Gwaai, *Zimbabwe* **55 F2** 19 15S 27 45 E
Gwabegar, *Australia* **63 E4** 30 31S 149 0 E
Gwādar, *Pakistan* **40 G3** 25 10N 62 18 E
Gwalior, *India* **42 F8** 26 12N 78 10 E
Gwanda, *Zimbabwe* **55 G2** 20 55S 29 0 E
Gwane, *Dem. Rep. of the Congo* **54 B2** 4 45N 25 48 E
Gweebarra B., *Ireland* **13 B3** 54 51N 8 23W
Gweedore, *Ireland* **13 A3** 55 3N 8 13W
Gweru, *Zimbabwe* **55 F2** 19 28S 29 45 E
Gwinn, *U.S.A.* **76 B2** 46 19N 87 27W
Gwydir →, *Australia* **63 D4** 29 27S 149 48 E
Gwynedd □, *U.K.* **10 E3** 52 52N 4 10W
Gyandzha = Gäncä, *Azerbaijan* **25 F8** 40 45N 46 20 E
Gyaring Hu, *China* **32 C4** 34 50N 97 40 E
Gydanskiy Poluostrov, *Russia* **26 C8** 70 0N 78 0 E
Gympie, *Australia* **63 D5** 26 11S 152 38 E
Gyöngyös, *Hungary* **17 E10** 47 48N 19 56 E
Győr, *Hungary* **17 E9** 47 41N 17 40 E
Gypsum Pt., *Canada* **72 A6** 61 53N 114 35W
Gypsumville, *Canada* **73 C9** 51 45N 98 40W
Gyula, *Hungary* **17 E11** 46 38N 21 17 E
Gyumri, *Armenia* **25 F7** 40 47N 43 50 E
Gyzylarbat, *Turkmenistan* **26 F6** 39 4N 56 23 E
Gyzyletrek, *Turkmenistan* **45 B7** 37 36N 54 46 E

H

Ha 'Arava →, *Israel* **47 E4** 30 50N 35 20 E
Ha Tien, *Vietnam* **39 G5** 10 23N 104 29 E
Ha Tinh, *Vietnam* **38 C5** 18 20N 105 54 E
Ha Trung, *Vietnam* **38 C5** 19 58N 105 50 E
Haaksbergen, *Neths.* **15 B6** 52 9N 6 45 E
Haapsalu, *Estonia* **9 G20** 58 56N 23 30 E
Haarlem, *Neths.* **15 B4** 52 23N 4 39 E
Haast →, *N.Z.* **59 K2** 43 50S 169 2 E
Haast Bluff, *Australia* **60 D5** 23 22S 132 0 E
Hab →, *Pakistan* **42 G3** 24 53N 66 41 E
Hab Nadi Chauki, *Pakistan* **42 G2** 25 0N 66 50 E
Habaswein, *Kenya* **54 B4** 1 2N 39 30 E
Habay, *Canada* **72 B5** 58 50N 118 44W
Ḥabbānīyah, *Iraq* **44 C4** 33 17N 43 29 E
Haboro, *Japan* **30 B10** 44 22N 141 42 E
Ḥabshān, *U.A.E.* **45 F7** 23 50N 53 37 E
Hachijō-Jima, *Japan* **31 H9** 33 5N 139 45 E
Hachinohe, *Japan* **30 D10** 40 30N 141 29 E
Hachiōji, *Japan* **31 G9** 35 40N 139 20 E
Hachŏn, *N. Korea* **35 D15** 41 29N 129 2 E
Hackensack, *U.S.A.* **79 F10** 40 53N 74 3W
Hackettstown, *U.S.A.* **79 F10** 40 51N 74 50W
Hadali, *Pakistan* **42 C5** 32 16N 72 11 E
Hadarba, Ras, *Sudan* **51 D13** 22 4N 36 51 E
Hadarom □, *Israel* **47 E4** 31 0N 35 0 E
Hadd, Ra's al, *Oman* **46 C6** 22 35N 59 50 E
Hadejia, *Nigeria* **50 F7** 12 30N 10 5 E
Ḥadera, *Israel* **47 C3** 32 27N 34 55 E
Ḥadera, N. →, *Israel* **47 C3** 32 28N 34 52 E
Haderslev, *Denmark* **9 J13** 55 15N 9 30 E
Hadhramaut = Ḥaḍramawt, *Yemen* **46 D4** 15 30N 49 30 E
Hadibu, *Yemen* **46 E5** 12 39N 54 2 E
Hadong, *S. Korea* **35 G14** 35 5N 127 44 E
Ḥaḍramawt, *Yemen* **46 D4** 15 30N 49 30 E
Ḥadrānīyah, *Iraq* **44 C4** 35 38N 43 14 E
Hadrian's Wall, *U.K.* **10 B5** 55 0N 2 30W
Haeju, *N. Korea* **35 E13** 38 3N 125 45 E
Haenam, *S. Korea* **35 G14** 34 34N 126 35 E
Haerhpin = Harbin, *China* **35 B14** 45 48N 126 40 E
Hafar al Bāṭin, *Si. Arabia* **44 D5** 28 32N 45 52 E
Ḥafirat al 'Aydā, *Si. Arabia* **44 E3** 26 26N 39 12 E
Ḥafit, *Oman* **45 F7** 23 59N 55 49 E
Ḥafit, Jabal, *Oman* **45 E7** 24 3N 55 46 E
Hafizabad, *Pakistan* **42 C5** 32 5N 73 40 E
Haflong, *India* **41 G18** 25 10N 93 5 E
Hafnarfjörður, *Iceland* **8 D3** 64 4N 21 57W
Haft Gel, *Iran* **45 D6** 31 30N 49 32 E
Hafun, Ras, *Somali Rep.* **46 E5** 10 29N 51 30 E
Hagalil, *Israel* **47 C4** 32 53N 35 18 E
Hagen, *Germany* **16 C4** 51 21N 7 27 E
Hagerman, *U.S.A.* **81 J2** 33 7N 104 20W
Hagerstown, *U.S.A.* **76 F7** 39 39N 77 43W
Hagersville, *Canada* **78 D4** 42 58N 80 3W
Hagfors, *Sweden* **9 F15** 60 3N 13 45 E
Hagi, *Japan* **31 G5** 34 30N 131 22 E
Hagolan, *Syria* **47 C4** 33 0N 35 45 E
Hagondange, *France* **18 B7** 49 16N 6 11 E
Hags Hd., *Ireland* **13 D2** 52 57N 9 28W
Hague, C. de la, *France* **18 B3** 49 44N 1 56W
Hague, The = 's-Gravenhage, *Neths.* **15 B4** 52 7N 4 17 E
Haguenau, *France* **18 B7** 48 49N 7 47 E
Haicheng, *China* **35 D12** 40 50N 122 45 E
Haidar Khel, *Afghan.* **42 C3** 33 58N 68 38 E
Haidargarh, *India* **43 F9** 26 37N 81 22 E
Haifa = Ḥefa, *Israel* **47 C4** 32 46N 35 0 E
Haikou, *China* **33 D6** 20 1N 110 16 E
Ḥā'il, *Si. Arabia* **44 E4** 27 28N 41 45 E
Hailar, *China* **33 B6** 49 10N 119 38 E
Hailey, *U.S.A.* **82 E6** 43 31N 114 19W
Haileybury, *Canada* **70 C4** 47 30N 79 38W
Hailin, *China* **35 B15** 44 37N 129 30 E
Hailong, *China* **35 C13** 42 32N 125 40 E
Hailuoto, *Finland* **8 D21** 65 3N 24 45 E
Hainan □, *China* **33 E5** 19 0N 109 30 E
Hainaut □, *Belgium* **15 D4** 50 30N 4 0 E
Haines, *Alaska, U.S.A.* **72 B1** 59 14N 135 26W
Haines, *Oreg., U.S.A.* **82 D5** 44 55N 117 56W
Haines City, *U.S.A.* **77 L5** 28 7N 81 38W
Haines Junction, *Canada* **72 A1** 60 45N 137 30W
Haiphong, *Vietnam* **32 D5** 20 47N 106 41 E
Haiti ■, *W. Indies* **89 C5** 19 0N 72 30W
Haiya, *Sudan* **51 E13** 18 20N 36 21 E
Haiyang, *China* **35 F11** 36 47N 121 9 E
Haiyuan, *China* **34 F3** 36 35N 105 52 E
Haizhou, *China* **35 G10** 34 37N 119 7 E
Haizhou Wan, *China* **35 G10** 34 50N 119 20 E
Hajdúböszörmény, *Hungary* **17 E11** 47 40N 21 30 E
Hajipur, *India* **43 G11** 25 45N 85 13 E
Ḥājjī Muḥsin, *Iraq* **44 C5** 32 35N 45 29 E
Ḥājjīābād, *Iran* **45 D7** 28 19N 55 55 E
Ḥājjīābād-e Zarrīn, *Iran* **45 C7** 33 9N 54 51 E
Hajnówka, *Poland* **17 B12** 52 47N 23 35 E
Hakansson, Mts., *Dem. Rep. of the Congo* **55 D2** 8 40S 25 45 E
Hakkâri, *Turkey* **44 B4** 37 34N 43 44 E
Hakken-Zan, *Japan* **31 G7** 34 10N 135 54 E
Hakodate, *Japan* **30 D10** 41 45N 140 44 E
Haku-San, *Japan* **31 F8** 36 9N 136 46 E
Hakui, *Japan* **31 F8** 36 53N 136 47 E
Hala, *Pakistan* **40 G6** 25 43N 68 20 E
Ḥalab, *Syria* **44 B3** 36 10N 37 15 E
Ḥalabjah, *Iraq* **44 C5** 35 10N 45 58 E
Halaib, *Sudan* **51 D13** 22 12N 36 30 E
Hālat 'Ammār, *Si. Arabia* **44 D3** 29 10N 36 4 E
Halbā, *Lebanon* **47 A5** 34 34N 36 6 E
Halberstadt, *Germany* **16 C6** 51 54N 11 3 E
Halcombe, *N.Z.* **59 J5** 40 8S 175 30 E
Halcon, *Phil.* **37 B6** 13 0N 121 30 E
Halden, *Norway* **9 G14** 59 9N 11 23 E
Haldia, *India* **41 H16** 22 5N 88 3 E
Haldwani, *India* **43 E8** 29 31N 79 30 E
Hale →, *Australia* **62 C2** 24 56S 135 53 E
Haleakala Crater, *U.S.A.* **74 H16** 20 43N 156 16W
Halesowen, *U.K.* **11 E5** 52 27N 2 3W
Haleyville, *U.S.A.* **77 H2** 34 14N 87 37W
Halfway →, *Canada* **72 B4** 56 12N 121 32W
Halia, *India* **43 G10** 24 50N 82 19 E
Haliburton, *Canada* **78 A6** 45 3N 78 30W
Halifax, *Australia* **62 B4** 18 32S 146 22 E
Halifax, *Canada* **71 D7** 44 38N 63 35W
Halifax, *U.K.* **10 D6** 53 43N 1 52W
Halifax, *U.S.A.* **78 F8** 40 25N 76 55W
Halifax B., *Australia* **62 B4** 18 50S 147 0 E
Halifax I., *Namibia* **56 D2** 26 38S 15 4 E
Halīl →, *Iran* **45 E8** 27 40N 58 30 E
Halkirk, *U.K.* **12 C5** 58 30N 3 29W
Hall Beach = Sanirajak, *Canada* **69 B11** 68 46N 81 12W
Hall Pen., *Canada* **69 B13** 63 30N 66 0W
Hall Pt., *Australia* **60 C3** 15 40S 124 23 E
Halland, *Sweden* **9 H15** 57 8N 12 47 E
Halle, *Belgium* **15 D4** 50 44N 4 13 E
Halle, *Germany* **16 C6** 51 30N 11 56 E
Hällefors, *Sweden* **9 G16** 59 47N 14 31 E
Hallett, *Australia* **63 E2** 33 25S 138 55 E
Hallettsville, *U.S.A.* **81 L6** 29 27N 96 57W
Hallim, *S. Korea* **35 H14** 33 24N 126 15 E
Hallingdalselvi →, *Norway* **9 F13** 60 23N 9 35 E
Halls Creek, *Australia* **60 C4** 18 16S 127 38 E
Hallsberg, *Sweden* **9 G16** 59 5N 15 7 E
Hallstead, *U.S.A.* **79 E9** 41 58N 75 45W
Halmahera, *Indonesia* **37 D7** 0 40N 128 0 E
Halmstad, *Sweden* **9 H15** 56 41N 12 52 E
Hälsingborg = Helsingborg, *Sweden* **9 H15** 56 3N 12 42 E
Hälsingland, *Sweden* **9 F16** 61 40N 16 5 E
Halstead, *U.K.* **11 F8** 51 57N 0 40 E
Halti, *Finland* **8 B19** 69 17N 21 18 E
Halton □, *U.K.* **10 D5** 53 22N 2 45W
Haltwhistle, *U.K.* **10 C5** 54 58N 2 26W
Ḥalul, *Qatar* **45 E7** 25 40N 52 40 E
Halvad, *India* **42 H4** 23 1N 71 11 E
Ḥalvān, *Iran* **45 C8** 33 57N 56 15 E
Ham Tan, *Vietnam* **39 G6** 10 40N 107 45 E
Ham Yen, *Vietnam* **38 A5** 22 4N 105 3 E
Hamab, *Namibia* **56 D2** 28 7S 19 16 E
Hamada, *Japan* **31 G6** 34 56N 132 4 E
Hamadān, *Iran* **45 C6** 34 52N 48 32 E

Henryville

Hamadān □, *Iran* 45 C6 35 0N 49 0 E
Hamāh, *Syria* 44 C3 35 5N 36 40 E
Hamamatsu, *Japan* 31 G8 34 45N 137 45 E
Hamar, *Norway* 9 F14 60 48N 11 7 E
Hamâta, Gebel, *Egypt* 44 E2 24 17N 35 0 E
Hambantota, *Sri Lanka* 40 R12 6 10N 81 10 E
Hamber Prov. Park, *Canada* 72 C5 52 20N 118 0W
Hamburg, *Germany* 16 B5 53 33N 9 59 E
Hamburg, *Ark., U.S.A.* 81 J9 33 14N 91 48W
Hamburg, *N.Y., U.S.A.* 78 D6 42 43N 78 50W
Hamburg, *Pa., U.S.A.* 79 F9 40 33N 75 59W
Ḥamḍ, W. al –►, *Si. Arabia* 44 E3 24 55N 36 20 E
Hamden, *U.S.A.* 79 E12 41 23N 72 54W
Häme, *Finland* 9 F20 61 38N 25 10 E
Hämeenlinna, *Finland* 9 F21 61 0N 24 28 E
Hamelin Pool, *Australia* 61 E1 26 22S 114 20 E
Hameln, *Germany* 16 B5 52 6N 9 21 E
Hamerkaz □, *Israel* 47 C3 32 15N 34 55 E
Hamersley Ra., *Australia* 60 D2 22 0S 117 45 E
Hamhung, *N. Korea* 35 E14 39 54N 127 30 E
Hami, *China* 32 B4 42 55N 93 25 E
Hamilton, *Australia* 63 F3 37 45S 142 2 E
Hamilton, *Canada* 78 C5 43 15N 79 50W
Hamilton, *N.Z.* 59 G5 37 47S 175 19 E
Hamilton, *U.K.* 12 F4 55 46N 4 2W
Hamilton, *Ala., U.S.A.* 77 H1 34 9N 87 59W
Hamilton, *Mont., U.S.A.* 82 C6 46 15N 114 10W
Hamilton, *N.Y., U.S.A.* 79 D9 42 50N 75 33W
Hamilton, *Ohio, U.S.A.* 76 F3 39 24N 84 34W
Hamilton, *Tex., U.S.A.* 81 K5 31 42N 98 7W
Hamilton –►, *Australia* 62 C2 23 30S 139 47 E
Hamilton City, *U.S.A.* 84 F4 39 45N 122 1W
Hamilton Inlet, *Canada* 71 B8 54 0N 57 30W
Hamilton Mt., *U.S.A.* 79 C10 43 25N 74 22W
Hamina, *Finland* 9 F22 60 34N 27 12 E
Hamirpur, *H.P., India* 42 D7 31 41N 76 31 E
Hamirpur, *Ut. P., India* 43 G9 25 57N 80 9 E
Hamlet, *U.S.A.* 77 H6 34 53N 79 42W
Hamley Bridge, *Australia* 63 E2 34 17S 138 35 E
Hamlin = Hameln, *Germany* 16 B5 52 6N 9 21 E
Hamlin, *N.Y., U.S.A.* 78 C7 43 17N 77 55W
Hamlin, *Tex., U.S.A.* 81 J4 32 53N 100 8W
Hamm, *Germany* 16 C4 51 40N 7 50 E
Ḥammār, Hawr al, *Iraq* 44 D5 30 50N 47 10 E
Hammerfest, *Norway* 8 A20 70 39N 23 41 E
Hammond, *Ind., U.S.A.* 76 E2 41 38N 87 30W
Hammond, *La., U.S.A.* 81 K9 30 30N 90 28W
Hammond, *N.Y., U.S.A.* 79 B9 44 27N 75 42W
Hammondsport, *U.S.A.* 78 D7 42 25N 77 13W
Hammonton, *U.S.A.* 76 F8 39 39N 74 48W
Hampden, *N.Z.* 59 L3 45 18S 170 50 E
Hampshire □, *U.K.* 11 F6 51 7N 1 23W
Hampshire Downs, *U.K.* 11 F6 51 15N 1 10W
Hampton, *N.B., Canada* 71 C6 45 32N 65 51W
Hampton, *Ont., Canada* 78 C6 43 58N 78 45W
Hampton, *Ark., U.S.A.* 81 J8 33 32N 92 28W
Hampton, *Iowa, U.S.A.* 80 D8 42 45N 93 13W
Hampton, *N.H., U.S.A.* 79 D14 42 57N 70 50W
Hampton, *S.C., U.S.A.* 77 J5 32 52N 81 7W
Hampton, *Va., U.S.A.* 76 G7 37 2N 76 21W
Hampton Bays, *U.S.A.* 79 F12 40 53N 72 30W
Hampton Tableland, *Australia* 61 F4 32 0S 127 0 E
Hamyang, *S. Korea* 35 G14 35 32N 127 42 E
Han Pijesak, *Bos.-H.* 21 B8 44 5N 18 57 E
Hana, *U.S.A.* 74 H17 20 45N 155 59W
Hanak, *Si. Arabia* 44 E3 25 32N 37 0 E
Hanamaki, *Japan* 30 E10 39 23N 141 7 E
Hanang, *Tanzania* 54 C4 4 30S 35 25 E
Hanau, *Germany* 16 C5 50 7N 8 56 E
Hanbogd = Ihbulag, *Mongolia* 34 C4 43 11N 107 10 E
Hancheng, *China* 34 G6 35 31N 110 25 E
Hancock, *Mich., U.S.A.* 80 B10 47 8N 88 35W
Hancock, *N.Y., U.S.A.* 79 E9 41 57N 75 17W
Handa, *Japan* 31 G8 34 53N 136 55 E
Handan, *China* 34 F8 36 35N 114 28 E
Handeni, *Tanzania* 54 D4 5 25S 38 2 E
Handwara, *India* 43 B6 34 21N 74 20 E
Hanegev, *Israel* 47 E4 30 50N 35 0 E
Hanford, *U.S.A.* 84 J7 36 20N 119 39W
Hang Chat, *Thailand* 38 C2 18 20N 99 21 E
Hang Dong, *Thailand* 38 C2 18 41N 98 55 E
Hangang –►, *S. Korea* 35 F14 37 50N 126 30 E
Hangayn Nuruu, *Mongolia* 32 B4 47 30N 99 0 E
Hangchou = Hangzhou, *China* 33 C7 30 18N 120 11 E
Hanggin Houqi, *China* 34 D4 40 58N 107 4 E
Hanggin Qi, *China* 34 E5 39 52N 108 50 E
Hangu, *China* 35 E9 39 18N 117 53 E
Hangzhou, *China* 33 C7 30 18N 120 11 E
Hangzhou Wan, *China* 33 C7 30 15N 120 45 E
Hanhongor, *Mongolia* 34 C3 43 55N 104 28 E
Ḥanīdh, *Si. Arabia* 45 E6 26 35N 48 38 E
Ḥanīsh, *Yemen* 46 E3 13 45N 42 46 E
Hankinson, *U.S.A.* 80 B6 46 4N 96 54W
Hanko, *Finland* 9 G20 59 50N 22 57 E
Hanksville, *U.S.A.* 83 G8 38 22N 110 43W
Hanle, *India* 43 C8 32 42N 79 4 E
Hanmer Springs, *N.Z.* 59 K4 42 32S 172 50 E
Hann –►, *Australia* 60 C4 17 26S 126 17 E
Hann, Mt., *Australia* 60 C4 15 45S 126 0 E
Hanna, *Canada* 72 C6 51 40N 111 54W
Hanna, *U.S.A.* 82 F10 41 52N 106 34W
Hannah B., *Canada* 70 B4 51 40N 80 0W
Hannibal, *Mo., U.S.A.* 80 F9 39 42N 91 22W
Hannibal, *N.Y., U.S.A.* 79 C8 43 19N 76 35W
Hannover, *Germany* 16 B5 52 22N 9 46 E
Hanoi, *Vietnam* 32 D5 21 5N 105 55 E
Hanover = Hannover, *Germany* 16 B5 52 22N 9 46 E
Hanover, *Canada* 78 B3 44 9N 81 2W
Hanover, *S. Africa* 56 E3 31 4S 24 29 E
Hanover, *N.H., U.S.A.* 79 C12 43 42N 72 17W
Hanover, *Ohio, U.S.A.* 78 F2 40 4N 82 16W
Hanover, *Pa., U.S.A.* 76 F7 39 48N 76 59W
Hanover, I., *Chile* 96 G2 51 0S 74 50W
Hansdiha, *India* 43 G12 24 36N 87 5 E
Hansi, *India* 42 E6 29 10N 75 57 E
Hanson, L., *Australia* 63 E2 31 0S 136 15 E
Hantsavichy, *Belarus* 17 B14 52 49N 26 30 E
Hanumangarh, *India* 42 E6 29 35N 74 19 E
Hanzhong, *China* 34 H4 33 10N 107 1 E
Hanzhuang, *China* 35 G9 34 33N 117 23 E
Haora, *India* 43 H13 22 37N 88 20 E
Haparanda, *Sweden* 8 D21 65 52N 24 8 E
Happy, *U.S.A.* 81 H4 34 45N 101 52W
Happy Camp, *U.S.A.* 82 F2 41 48N 123 23W
Happy Valley-Goose Bay, *Canada* 71 B7 53 15N 60 20W
Hapsu, *N. Korea* 35 D15 41 13N 128 51 E
Hapur, *India* 42 E7 28 45N 77 45 E
Ḥaql, *Si. Arabia* 47 F3 29 10N 34 58 E
Har, *Indonesia* 37 F8 5 16S 133 14 E
Har-Ayrag, *Mongolia* 34 B5 45 47N 109 16 E
Har Hu, *China* 32 C4 38 20N 97 38 E
Har Us Nuur, *Mongolia* 32 B4 48 0N 92 0 E
Har Yehuda, *Israel* 47 D3 31 35N 34 57 E
Ḥaraḍ, *Si. Arabia* 46 C4 24 22N 49 0 E
Haranomachi, *Japan* 30 F10 37 38N 140 58 E
Harare, *Zimbabwe* 55 F3 17 43S 31 2 E
Harbin, *China* 35 B14 45 48N 126 40 E
Harbor Beach, *U.S.A.* 78 C2 43 51N 82 39W
Harbour Breton, *Canada* 71 C8 47 29N 55 50W
Harbour Deep, *Canada* 71 B8 50 25N 56 32W
Harda, *India* 42 H7 22 27N 77 5 E
Hardangerfjorden, *Norway* 9 F12 60 5N 6 0 E
Hardangervidda, *Norway* 9 F12 60 7N 7 20 E
Hardap Dam, *Namibia* 56 C2 24 32S 17 50 E
Hardenberg, *Neths.* 15 B6 52 34N 6 37 E
Harderwijk, *Neths.* 15 B5 52 21N 5 38 E
Hardey –►, *Australia* 60 D2 22 45S 116 8 E
Hardin, *U.S.A.* 82 D10 45 44N 107 37W
Harding, *S. Africa* 57 E4 30 35S 29 55 E
Harding Ra., *Australia* 60 C3 16 17S 124 55 E
Hardisty, *Canada* 72 C6 52 40N 111 18W
Hardoi, *India* 43 F9 27 26N 80 6 E
Hardwar = Haridwar, *India* 42 E8 29 58N 78 9 E
Hardwick, *U.S.A.* 79 B12 44 30N 72 22W
Hardy, Pen., *Chile* 96 H3 55 30S 68 20W
Hare B., *Canada* 71 B8 51 15N 55 45W
Hareid, *Norway* 9 E12 62 22N 6 1 E
Harer, *Ethiopia* 46 F3 9 20N 42 8 E
Hargeisa, *Somali Rep.* 46 F3 9 30N 44 2 E
Hari –►, *Indonesia* 36 E2 1 16S 104 5 E
Haria, *Canary Is.* 22 E6 29 8N 13 32W
Haridwar, *India* 42 E8 29 58N 78 9 E
Harim, Jabal al, *Oman* 45 E8 25 58N 56 14 E
Haringhata –►, *Bangla.* 41 J16 22 0N 89 58 E
Harīrūd –►, *Asia* 40 A2 37 24N 60 38 E
Härjedalen, *Sweden* 9 E15 62 22N 13 5 E
Harlan, *Iowa, U.S.A.* 80 E7 41 39N 95 19W
Harlan, *Ky., U.S.A.* 77 G4 36 51N 83 19W
Harlech, *U.K.* 10 E3 52 52N 4 6W
Harlem, *U.S.A.* 82 B9 48 32N 108 47W
Harlingen, *Neths.* 15 A5 53 11N 5 25 E
Harlingen, *U.S.A.* 81 M6 26 12N 97 42W
Harlow, *U.K.* 11 F8 51 46N 0 8 E
Harlowton, *U.S.A.* 82 C9 46 26N 109 50W
Harnai, *Pakistan* 42 D2 30 6N 67 56 E
Harney Basin, *U.S.A.* 82 E4 43 30N 119 0W
Harney L., *U.S.A.* 82 E4 43 14N 119 8W
Harney Peak, *U.S.A.* 80 D3 43 52N 103 32W
Härnösand, *Sweden* 9 E17 62 38N 17 55 E
Haroldswick, *U.K.* 12 A8 60 48N 0 50W
Harp L., *Canada* 71 A7 55 5N 61 50W
Harper, *Liberia* 50 H4 4 25N 7 43W
Harrai, *India* 43 H8 22 37N 79 13 E
Harrand, *Pakistan* 42 E4 29 28N 70 3 E
Harricana –►, *Canada* 70 B4 50 56N 79 32W
Harriman, *U.S.A.* 77 H3 35 56N 84 33W
Harrington Harbour, *Canada* 71 B8 50 31N 59 30W
Harris, *U.K.* 12 D2 57 50N 6 55W
Harris, Sd. of, *U.K.* 12 D1 57 44N 7 6W
Harris L., *Australia* 63 E2 31 10S 135 10 E
Harris Pt., *Canada* 78 C2 43 6N 82 9W
Harrisburg, *Ill., U.S.A.* 81 G10 37 44N 88 32W
Harrisburg, *Nebr., U.S.A.* 80 E3 41 33N 103 44W
Harrisburg, *Pa., U.S.A.* 78 F8 40 16N 76 53W
Harrismith, *S. Africa* 57 D4 28 15S 29 8 E
Harrison, *Ark., U.S.A.* 81 G8 36 14N 93 7W
Harrison, *Maine, U.S.A.* 79 B14 44 7N 70 39W
Harrison, *Nebr., U.S.A.* 80 D3 42 41N 103 53W
Harrison, C., *Canada* 71 B8 54 55N 57 55W
Harrison L., *Canada* 72 D4 49 33N 121 50W
Harrisonburg, *U.S.A.* 76 F6 38 27N 78 52W
Harrisonville, *U.S.A.* 80 F7 38 39N 94 21W
Harriston, *Canada* 78 C4 43 57N 80 53W
Harrisville, *Mich., U.S.A.* 78 B1 44 39N 83 17W
Harrisville, *N.Y., U.S.A.* 79 B9 44 9N 75 19W
Harrisville, *Pa., U.S.A.* 78 E5 41 8N 80 0W
Harrodsburg, *U.S.A.* 76 G3 37 46N 84 51W
Harrogate, *U.K.* 10 C6 54 0N 1 33W
Harrow, *U.K.* 11 F7 51 35N 0 21W
Harrowsmith, *Canada* 79 B8 44 24N 76 40W
Harry S. Truman Reservoir, *U.S.A.* 80 F7 38 16N 93 24W
Harsin, *Iran* 44 C5 34 18N 47 33 E
Harstad, *Norway* 8 B17 68 48N 16 30 E
Harsud, *India* 42 H7 22 6N 76 44 E
Hart, *U.S.A.* 76 D2 43 42N 86 22W
Hart, L., *Australia* 63 E2 31 10S 136 25 E
Hartbees –►, *S. Africa* 56 D3 28 45S 20 32 E
Hartford, *Conn., U.S.A.* 79 E12 41 46N 72 41W
Hartford, *Ky., U.S.A.* 76 G2 37 27N 86 55W
Hartford, *S. Dak., U.S.A.* 80 D6 43 38N 96 57W
Hartford, *Wis., U.S.A.* 80 D10 43 19N 88 22W
Hartford City, *U.S.A.* 76 E3 40 27N 85 22W
Hartland, *Canada* 71 C6 46 20N 67 32W
Hartland Pt., *U.K.* 11 F3 51 1N 4 32W
Hartlepool, *U.K.* 10 C6 54 42N 1 13W
Hartlepool □, *U.K.* 10 C6 54 42N 1 17W
Hartley Bay, *Canada* 72 C3 53 25N 129 15W
Hartmannberge, *Namibia* 56 B1 17 0S 13 0 E
Hartney, *Canada* 73 D8 49 30N 100 35W
Harts –►, *S. Africa* 56 D3 28 24S 24 17 E
Hartselle, *U.S.A.* 77 H2 34 27N 86 56W
Hartshorne, *U.S.A.* 81 H7 34 51N 95 34W
Hartstown, *U.S.A.* 78 E4 41 33N 80 23W
Hartsville, *U.S.A.* 77 H5 34 23N 80 4W
Hartwell, *U.S.A.* 77 H4 34 21N 82 56W
Harunabad, *Pakistan* 42 E5 29 35N 73 8 E
Harvand, *Iran* 45 D7 28 25N 55 43 E
Harvey, *Australia* 61 F2 33 5S 115 54 E
Harvey, *Ill., U.S.A.* 76 E2 41 36N 87 50W
Harvey, *N. Dak., U.S.A.* 80 B5 47 47N 99 56W
Harwich, *U.K.* 11 F9 51 56N 1 17 E
Haryana □, *India* 42 E7 29 0N 76 10 E
Haryn –►, *Belarus* 17 B14 52 7N 27 17 E
Harz, *Germany* 16 C6 51 38N 10 44 E
Hasa □, *Si. Arabia* 45 E6 25 50N 49 0 E
Ḥasanābād, *Iran* 45 C7 32 8N 52 44 E
Hasdo –►, *India* 43 J10 21 44N 82 44 E
Hashimoto, *Japan* 31 G7 34 19N 135 37 E
Hashtjerd, *Iran* 45 C6 35 52N 50 40 E
Haskell, *U.S.A.* 81 J5 33 10N 99 44W
Haslemere, *U.K.* 11 F7 51 5N 0 43W
Hasselt, *Belgium* 15 D5 50 56N 5 21 E
Hassi Messaoud, *Algeria* 50 B7 31 51N 6 1 E
Hässleholm, *Sweden* 9 H15 56 10N 13 46 E
Hastings, *N.Z.* 59 H6 39 39S 176 52 E
Hastings, *U.K.* 11 G8 50 51N 0 35 E
Hastings, *Mich., U.S.A.* 76 D3 42 39N 85 17W
Hastings, *Minn., U.S.A.* 80 C8 44 44N 92 51W
Hastings, *Nebr., U.S.A.* 80 E5 40 35N 98 23W
Hastings Ra., *Australia* 63 E5 31 15S 152 14 E
Hat Yai, *Thailand* 39 J3 7 1N 100 27 E
Hatanbulag = Ergel, *Mongolia* 34 C5 43 8N 109 5 E
Hatay = Antalya, *Turkey* 25 G5 36 52N 30 45 E
Hatch, *U.S.A.* 83 K10 32 40N 107 9W
Hatchet L., *Canada* 73 B8 58 36N 103 40W
Hateruma-Shima, *Japan* 31 M1 24 3N 123 47 E
Hatfield P.O., *Australia* 63 E3 33 54S 143 49 E
Hatgal, *Mongolia* 32 A5 50 26N 100 9 E
Hathras, *India* 42 F8 27 36N 78 6 E
Hatia, *Bangla.* 41 H17 22 30N 91 5 E
Hato Mayor, *Dom. Rep.* 89 C6 18 46N 69 15W
Hatta, *India* 43 G8 24 7N 79 36 E
Hattah, *Australia* 63 E3 34 48S 142 17 E
Hatteras, C., *U.S.A.* 77 H8 35 14N 75 32W
Hattiesburg, *U.S.A.* 81 K10 31 20N 89 17W
Hatvan, *Hungary* 17 E10 47 40N 19 45 E
Hau Bon = Cheo Reo, *Vietnam* 36 B3 13 25N 108 28 E
Hau Duc, *Vietnam* 38 E7 15 20N 108 13 E
Haugesund, *Norway* 9 G11 59 23N 5 13 E
Haukipudas, *Finland* 8 D21 65 12N 25 20 E
Haultain –►, *Canada* 73 B7 55 51N 106 46W
Hauraki G., *N.Z.* 59 G5 36 35S 175 5 E
Haut Atlas, *Morocco* 50 B4 32 30N 5 0W
Haut-Zaïre = Orientale □, *Dem. Rep. of the Congo* 54 B2 2 20N 26 0 E
Hautes Fagnes = Hohe Venn, *Belgium* 15 D6 50 30N 6 5 E
Hauts Plateaux, *Algeria* 48 C4 35 0N 1 0 E
Havana = La Habana, *Cuba* 88 B3 23 8N 82 22W
Havana, *U.S.A.* 80 E9 40 18N 90 4W
Havant, *U.K.* 11 G7 50 51N 0 58W
Havasu, L., *U.S.A.* 85 L12 34 18N 114 28W
Havel –►, *Germany* 16 B7 52 50N 12 3 E
Havelian, *Pakistan* 42 B5 34 2N 73 10 E
Havelock, *Canada* 78 B7 44 26N 77 53W
Havelock, *N.Z.* 59 J4 41 17S 173 48 E
Havelock, *U.S.A.* 77 H7 34 53N 76 54W
Haverfordwest, *U.K.* 11 F3 51 48N 4 58W
Haverhill, *U.S.A.* 79 D13 42 47N 71 5W
Haverstraw, *U.S.A.* 79 E11 41 12N 73 58W
Havirga, *Mongolia* 34 B7 45 41N 113 5 E
Havířov, *Czech.* 17 D10 49 46N 18 20 E
Havlíčkův Brod, *Czech Rep.* 16 D8 49 36N 15 33 E
Havre, *U.S.A.* 82 B9 48 33N 109 41W
Havre-Aubert, *Canada* 71 C7 47 12N 61 56W
Havre-St.-Pierre, *Canada* 71 B7 50 18N 63 33W
Haw –►, *U.S.A.* 77 H6 35 36N 79 3W
Hawaii □, *U.S.A.* 74 H16 19 30N 156 30W
Hawaii I., *Pac. Oc.* 74 J17 20 0N 155 0W
Hawaiian Is., *Pac. Oc.* 74 H17 20 30N 156 0W
Hawaiian Ridge, *Pac. Oc.* 65 E11 24 0N 165 0W
Hawarden, *U.S.A.* 80 D6 43 0N 96 29W
Hawea, L., *N.Z.* 59 L2 44 28S 169 19 E
Hawera, *N.Z.* 59 H5 39 35S 174 19 E
Hawick, *U.K.* 12 F6 55 26N 2 47W
Hawk Junction, *Canada* 70 C3 48 5N 84 38W
Hawke B., *N.Z.* 59 H6 39 25S 177 20 E
Hawker, *Australia* 63 E2 31 59S 138 22 E
Hawkesbury, *Canada* 70 C5 45 37N 74 37W
Hawkesbury I., *Canada* 72 C3 53 37N 129 3W
Hawkesbury Pt., *Australia* 62 A1 11 55S 134 5 E
Hawkinsville, *U.S.A.* 77 J4 32 17N 83 28W
Hawley, *Minn., U.S.A.* 80 B6 46 53N 96 19W
Hawley, *Pa., U.S.A.* 79 E9 41 28N 75 11W
Ḥawrān, W. –►, *Iraq* 44 C4 33 58N 42 34 E
Hawsh Mūssá, *Lebanon* 47 B4 33 45N 35 55 E
Hawthorne, *U.S.A.* 82 G4 38 32N 118 38W
Hay, *Australia* 63 E3 34 30S 144 51 E
Hay –►, *Australia* 62 C2 24 50S 138 0 E
Hay –►, *Canada* 72 A5 60 50N 116 26W
Hay, C., *Australia* 60 B4 14 5S 129 29 E
Hay I., *Canada* 78 B4 44 53N 80 58W
Hay L., *Canada* 72 B5 58 50N 118 50W
Hay-on-Wye, *U.K.* 11 E4 52 5N 3 8W
Hay River, *Canada* 72 A5 60 51N 115 44W
Hay Springs, *U.S.A.* 80 D3 42 41N 102 41W
Haya = Tehoru, *Indonesia* 37 E7 3 19S 129 37 E
Hayachine-San, *Japan* 30 E10 39 34N 141 29 E
Hayden, *U.S.A.* 82 F10 40 30N 107 16W
Haydon, *Australia* 62 B3 18 0S 141 30 E
Hayes, *U.S.A.* 80 C4 44 23N 101 1W
Hayes –►, *Canada* 70 A1 57 3N 92 12W
Hayes Creek, *Australia* 60 B5 13 43S 131 22 E
Hayle, *U.K.* 11 G2 50 11N 5 26W
Hayling I., *U.K.* 11 G7 50 48N 0 59W
Hayrabolu, *Turkey* 21 D12 41 12N 27 5 E
Hays, *Canada* 72 C6 50 6N 111 48W
Hays, *U.S.A.* 80 F5 38 53N 99 20W
Haysyn, *Ukraine* 17 D15 48 57N 29 25 E
Hayvoron, *Ukraine* 17 D15 48 22N 29 52 E
Hayward, *Calif., U.S.A.* 84 H4 37 40N 122 5W
Hayward, *Wis., U.S.A.* 80 B9 46 1N 91 29W
Haywards Heath, *U.K.* 11 G7 51 0N 0 5W
Haẓafon □, *Israel* 47 C4 32 40N 35 20 E
Hazārān, Kūh-e, *Iran* 45 D8 29 35N 57 20 E
Hazard, *U.S.A.* 76 G4 37 15N 83 12W
Hazaribag, *India* 43 H11 23 58N 85 26 E
Hazaribag Road, *India* 43 G11 24 12N 85 57 E
Hazelton, *Canada* 72 B3 55 20N 127 42W
Hazelton, *U.S.A.* 80 B4 46 29N 100 17W
Hazen, *U.S.A.* 80 B4 47 18N 101 38W
Hazlehurst, *Ga., U.S.A.* 77 K4 31 52N 82 36W
Hazlehurst, *Miss., U.S.A.* 81 K9 31 52N 90 24W
Hazlet, *U.S.A.* 79 F10 40 25N 74 12W
Hazleton, *U.S.A.* 79 F9 40 57N 75 59W
Hazlett, L., *Australia* 60 D4 21 30S 128 48 E
Hazro, *Turkey* 44 B4 38 15N 40 47 E
Head of Bight, *Australia* 61 F5 31 30S 131 25 E
Headlands, *Zimbabwe* 55 F3 18 15S 32 2 E
Healdsburg, *U.S.A.* 84 G4 38 37N 122 52W
Healdton, *U.S.A.* 81 H6 34 14N 97 29W
Healesville, *Australia* 63 F4 37 35S 145 30 E
Heard I., *Ind. Oc.* 3 G13 53 0S 74 0 E
Hearne, *U.S.A.* 81 K6 30 53N 96 36W
Hearst, *Canada* 70 C3 49 40N 83 41W
Heart –►, *U.S.A.* 80 B4 46 46N 100 50W
Heart's Content, *Canada* 71 C9 47 54N 53 27W
Heath Pt., *Canada* 71 C7 49 8N 61 40W
Heavener, *U.S.A.* 81 H7 34 53N 94 36W
Hebbronville, *U.S.A.* 81 M5 27 18N 98 41W
Hebei □, *China* 34 E9 39 0N 116 0 E
Hebel, *Australia* 63 D4 28 58S 147 47 E
Heber, *U.S.A.* 85 N11 32 44N 115 32W
Heber City, *U.S.A.* 82 F8 40 31N 111 25W
Heber Springs, *U.S.A.* 81 H9 35 30N 92 2W
Hebert, *Canada* 73 C7 50 30N 107 10W
Hebgen L., *U.S.A.* 82 D8 44 52N 111 20W
Hebi, *China* 34 G8 35 57N 114 7 E
Hebrides, *U.K.* 6 D4 57 30N 7 0W
Hebron = Al Khalīl, *West Bank* 47 D4 31 32N 35 6 E
Hebron, *Canada* 69 C13 58 5N 62 30W
Hebron, *N. Dak., U.S.A.* 80 B3 46 54N 102 3W
Hebron, *Nebr., U.S.A.* 80 E6 40 10N 97 35W
Hecate Str., *Canada* 72 C2 53 10N 130 30W
Heceta I., *U.S.A.* 72 B2 55 46N 133 40W
Hechi, *China* 32 D5 24 40N 108 2 E
Hechuan, *China* 32 C5 30 2N 106 12 E
Hecla, *U.S.A.* 80 C5 45 53N 98 9W
Hecla I., *Canada* 73 C9 51 10N 96 43W
Hede, *Sweden* 9 E15 62 23N 13 30 E
Hedemora, *Sweden* 9 F16 60 18N 15 58 E
Heerde, *Neths.* 15 B6 52 24N 6 2 E
Heerenveen, *Neths.* 15 B5 52 57N 5 55 E
Heerhugowaard, *Neths.* 15 B4 52 40N 4 51 E
Heerlen, *Neths.* 18 A6 50 55N 5 58 E
Ḥefa, *Israel* 47 C4 32 46N 35 0 E
Ḥefa □, *Israel* 47 C4 32 40N 35 0 E
Hefei, *China* 33 C6 31 52N 117 18 E
Hegang, *China* 33 B8 47 20N 130 19 E
Heichengzhen, *China* 34 F4 36 24N 106 3 E
Heidelberg, *Germany* 16 D5 49 24N 8 42 E
Heidelberg, *S. Africa* 56 E3 34 6S 20 59 E
Heilbron, *S. Africa* 57 D4 27 16S 27 59 E
Heilbronn, *Germany* 16 D5 49 9N 9 13 E
Heilongjiang □, *China* 33 B7 48 0N 126 0 E
Heilunkiang = Heilongjiang □, *China* 33 B7 48 0N 126 0 E
Heimaey, *Iceland* 8 E3 63 26N 20 17W
Heinola, *Finland* 9 F22 61 13N 26 2 E
Heinze Is., *Burma* 41 M20 14 25N 97 45 E
Heishan, *China* 35 D12 41 40N 122 5 E
Heishui, *China* 35 C10 42 8N 119 30 E
Hejaz = Ḥijāz □, *Si. Arabia* 46 C3 24 0N 40 0 E
Hejian, *China* 34 E9 38 25N 116 5 E
Hejin, *China* 34 G6 35 35N 110 42 E
Hekimhan, *Turkey* 44 B3 38 50N 37 55 E
Hekla, *Iceland* 8 E4 63 56N 19 35W
Hekou, *China* 32 D5 22 30N 103 59 E
Helan Shan, *China* 34 E3 38 30N 105 55 E
Helen Atoll, *Pac. Oc.* 37 D8 2 40N 132 0 E
Helena, *Ark., U.S.A.* 81 H9 34 32N 90 36W
Helena, *Mont., U.S.A.* 82 C7 46 36N 112 2W
Helendale, *U.S.A.* 85 L9 34 44N 117 19W
Helensburgh, *U.K.* 12 E4 56 1N 4 43W
Helensville, *N.Z.* 59 G5 36 41S 174 29 E
Helenvale, *Australia* 62 B4 15 43S 145 14 E
Helgeland, *Norway* 8 C15 66 7N 13 29 E
Helgoland, *Germany* 16 A4 54 10N 7 53 E
Heligoland = Helgoland, *Germany* 16 A4 54 10N 7 53 E
Heligoland B. = Deutsche Bucht, *Germany* 16 A5 54 15N 8 0 E
Hella, *Iceland* 8 E3 63 50N 20 24W
Hellertown, *U.S.A.* 79 F9 40 35N 75 21W
Hellespont = Çanakkale Boğazı, *Turkey* 21 D12 40 17N 26 32 E
Hellevoetsluis, *Neths.* 15 C4 51 50N 4 8 E
Hellín, *Spain* 19 C5 38 31N 1 40W
Helmand □, *Afghan.* 40 D4 31 20N 64 0 E
Helmand –►, *Afghan.* 40 D2 31 12N 61 34 E
Helmond, *Neths.* 15 C5 51 29N 5 41 E
Helmsdale, *U.K.* 12 C5 58 7N 3 39W
Helmsdale –►, *U.K.* 12 C5 58 7N 3 40W
Helong, *China* 35 C15 42 40N 129 0 E
Helper, *U.S.A.* 82 G8 39 41N 110 51W
Helsingborg, *Sweden* 9 H15 56 3N 12 42 E
Helsingfors = Helsinki, *Finland* 9 F21 60 15N 25 3 E
Helsingør, *Denmark* 9 H15 56 2N 12 35 E
Helsinki, *Finland* 9 F21 60 15N 25 3 E
Helston, *U.K.* 11 G2 50 6N 5 17W
Helvellyn, *U.K.* 10 C4 54 32N 3 1W
Helwân, *Egypt* 51 C12 29 50N 31 20 E
Hemel Hempstead, *U.K.* 11 F7 51 44N 0 28W
Hemet, *U.S.A.* 85 M10 33 45N 116 58W
Hemingford, *U.S.A.* 80 D3 42 19N 103 4W
Hemmingford, *Canada* 79 A11 45 3N 73 35W
Hempstead, *U.S.A.* 81 K6 30 6N 96 5W
Hemse, *Sweden* 9 H18 57 15N 18 22 E
Henan □, *China* 34 H8 34 0N 114 0 E
Henares –►, *Spain* 19 B4 40 24N 3 30W
Henashi-Misaki, *Japan* 30 D9 40 37N 139 51 E
Henderson, *Argentina* 94 D3 36 18S 61 43W
Henderson, *Ky., U.S.A.* 76 G2 37 50N 87 35W
Henderson, *N.C., U.S.A.* 77 G6 36 20N 78 25W
Henderson, *Nev., U.S.A.* 85 J12 36 2N 114 59W
Henderson, *Tenn., U.S.A.* 77 H1 35 26N 88 38W
Henderson, *Tex., U.S.A.* 81 J7 32 9N 94 48W
Hendersonville, *N.C., U.S.A.* 77 H4 35 19N 82 28W
Hendersonville, *Tenn., U.S.A.* 77 G2 36 18N 86 37W
Hendījān, *Iran* 45 D6 30 14N 49 43 E
Hendorābī, *Iran* 45 E7 26 40N 53 37 E
Hengcheng, *China* 34 E4 38 18N 106 28 E
Hengdaohezi, *China* 35 B15 44 52N 129 0 E
Hengelo, *Neths.* 15 B6 52 16N 6 48 E
Hengshan, *China* 34 F5 37 58N 109 5 E
Hengshui, *China* 34 F8 37 41N 115 40 E
Hengyang, *China* 33 D6 26 52N 112 33 E
Henlopen, C., *U.S.A.* 76 F8 38 48N 75 6W
Hennenman, *S. Africa* 56 D4 27 59S 27 1 E
Hennessey, *U.S.A.* 81 G6 36 6N 97 54W
Henrietta, *U.S.A.* 81 J5 33 49N 98 12W
Henrietta, Ostrov = Genriyetty, Ostrov, *Russia* 27 B16 77 6N 156 30 E
Henrietta Maria, C., *Canada* 70 A3 55 9N 82 20W
Henry, *U.S.A.* 80 E10 41 7N 89 22W
Henryetta, *U.S.A.* 81 H7 35 27N 95 59W
Henryville, *Canada* 79 A11 45 8N 73 11W

Indore

Indore, India 42 H6 22 42N 75 53 E
Indramayu, Indonesia 37 G13 6 20S 108 19 E
Indravati →, India 41 K12 19 20N 80 20 E
Indre →, France 18 C4 47 16N 0 11 E
Indulkana, Australia 63 D1 26 58S 133 5 E
Indus →, Pakistan 42 G2 24 20N 67 47 E
Indus, Mouth of the, Pakistan 42 H3 24 0N 68 0 E
İnebolu, Turkey 25 F5 41 55N 33 40 E
Infiernillo, Presa del, Mexico 86 D4 18 9N 102 0W
Ingenio, Canary Is. 22 G4 27 55N 15 26W
Ingenio Santa Ana, Argentina 94 B2 27 25S 65 40W
Ingersoll, Canada 78 C4 43 4N 80 55W
Ingham, Australia 62 B4 18 43S 146 10 E
Ingleborough, U.K. 10 C5 54 10N 2 22W
Inglewood, Queens., Australia 63 D5 28 25S 151 2 E
Inglewood, Vic., Australia 63 F3 36 29S 143 53 E
Inglewood, N.Z. 59 H5 39 9S 174 14 E
Inglewood, U.S.A. 85 M8 33 58N 118 21W
Ingólfshöfði, Iceland 8 E5 63 48N 16 39W
Ingolstadt, Germany 16 D6 48 46N 11 26 E
Ingomar, U.S.A. 82 C10 46 35N 107 23W
Ingonish, Canada 71 C7 46 42N 60 18W
Ingraj Bazar, India 43 G13 24 58N 88 10 E
Ingrid Christensen Coast, Antarctica 5 C6 69 30S 76 0 E
Ingulec = Inhulec, Ukraine 25 E5 47 42N 33 14 E
Ingushetia □, Russia 25 E8 43 20N 44 50 E
Ingwavuma, S. Africa 57 D5 27 9S 31 59 E
Inhaca, I., Mozam. 57 D5 26 1S 32 57 E
Inhafenga, Mozam. 57 C5 20 36S 33 53 E
Inhambane, Mozam. 57 C6 23 54S 35 30 E
Inhambane □, Mozam. 57 C5 22 30S 34 20 E
Inhaminga, Mozam. 55 F4 18 26S 35 0 E
Inharrime, Mozam. 57 C6 24 30S 35 0 E
Inharrime →, Mozam. 57 C6 24 30S 35 0 E
Inhulec, Ukraine 25 E5 47 42N 33 14 E
Ining = Yining, China 26 E9 43 58N 81 10 E
Inírida →, Colombia 92 C5 3 55N 67 52W
Inishbofin, Ireland 13 C1 53 37N 10 13W
Inisheer, Ireland 13 C2 53 3N 9 32W
Inishfree B., Ireland 13 A3 55 4N 8 23W
Inishkea North, Ireland 13 B1 54 9N 10 11W
Inishkea South, Ireland 13 B1 54 7N 10 12W
Inishmaan, Ireland 13 C2 53 5N 9 35W
Inishmore, Ireland 13 C2 53 8N 9 45W
Inishowen Pen., Ireland 13 A4 55 14N 7 15W
Inishshark, Ireland 13 C1 53 37N 10 16W
Inishturk, Ireland 13 C1 53 42N 10 7W
Inishvickillane, Ireland 13 D1 52 3N 10 37W
Injune, Australia 63 D4 25 53S 148 32 E
Inklin →, Canada 72 B2 58 50N 133 10W
Inle L., Burma 41 J20 20 30N 96 58 E
Inlet, U.S.A. 79 C10 43 45N 74 48W
Inn →, Austria 16 D7 48 35N 13 28 E
Innamincka, Australia 63 D3 27 44S 140 46 E
Inner Hebrides, U.K. 12 E2 57 0N 6 30W
Inner Mongolia = Nei Monggol Zizhiqu □, China 34 D7 42 0N 112 0 E
Inner Sound, U.K. 12 D3 57 30N 5 55W
Innerkip, Canada 78 C4 43 13N 80 42W
Innetalling I., Canada 70 A4 56 0N 79 0W
Innisfail, Australia 62 B4 17 33S 146 5 E
Innisfail, Canada 72 C6 52 0N 113 57W
In'no-shima, Japan 31 G6 34 19N 133 10 E
Innsbruck, Austria 16 E6 47 16N 11 23 E
Inny →, Ireland 13 C4 53 30N 7 50W
Inongo, Dem. Rep. of the Congo 52 E3 1 55S 18 30 E
Inoucdjouac = Inukjuak, Canada 69 C12 58 25N 78 15W
Inowrocław, Poland 17 B10 52 50N 18 12 E
Inpundong, N. Korea 35 D14 41 25N 126 34 E
Inscription, C., Australia 61 E1 25 29S 112 59 E
Insein, Burma 41 L20 16 50N 96 5 E
Inta, Russia 24 A11 66 5N 60 8 E
Intendente Alvear, Argentina 94 D3 35 12S 63 32W
Interlaken, Switz. 18 C7 46 41N 7 50 E
Interlaken, U.S.A. 79 D8 42 37N 76 44W
International Falls, U.S.A. 80 A8 48 36N 93 25W
Intiyaco, Argentina 94 B3 28 43S 60 5W
Inukjuak, Canada 69 C12 58 25N 78 15W
Inútil, B., Chile 96 G2 53 30S 70 15W
Inuvik, Canada 68 B6 68 16N 133 40W
Inveraray, U.K. 12 E3 56 14N 5 5W
Inverbervie, U.K. 12 E6 56 51N 2 17W
Invercargill, N.Z. 59 M2 46 24S 168 24 E
Inverclyde □, U.K. 12 F4 55 55N 4 49W
Inverell, Australia 63 D5 29 45S 151 8 E
Invergordon, U.K. 12 D4 57 41N 4 10W
Inverloch, Australia 63 F4 38 38S 145 45 E
Invermere, Canada 72 C5 50 30N 116 2W
Inverness, Canada 71 C7 46 15N 61 19W
Inverness, U.K. 12 D4 57 29N 4 13W
Inverness, U.S.A. 77 L4 28 50N 82 20W
Inverurie, U.K. 12 D6 57 17N 2 23W
Investigator Group, Australia 63 E1 34 45S 134 20 E
Investigator Str., Australia 63 F2 35 30S 137 0 E
Inya, Russia 26 D9 50 28N 86 37 E
Inyanga, Zimbabwe 55 F3 18 12S 32 40 E
Inyangani, Zimbabwe 55 F3 18 5S 32 50 E
Inyantue, Zimbabwe 55 F2 18 30S 26 40 E
Inyo Mts., U.S.A. 84 J9 36 40N 118 0W
Inyokern, U.S.A. 85 K9 35 39N 117 49W
Inza, Russia 24 D8 53 55N 46 25 E
Iō-Jima, Japan 31 J5 30 48N 130 18 E
Ioánnina, Greece 21 E9 39 42N 20 47 E
Iola, U.S.A. 81 G7 37 55N 95 24W
Iona, U.K. 12 E2 56 20N 6 25W
Ione, U.S.A. 84 G6 38 21N 120 56W
Ionia, U.S.A. 76 D3 42 59N 85 4W
Ionian Is. = Iónioi Nísoi, Greece 21 E9 38 40N 20 0 E
Ionian Sea, Medit. S. 21 E7 37 30N 17 30 E
Iónioi Nísoi, Greece 21 E9 38 40N 20 0 E
Íos, Greece 21 F11 36 41N 25 20 E
Iowa □, U.S.A. 80 D8 42 18N 93 30W
Iowa →, U.S.A. 80 E9 41 10N 91 1W
Iowa City, U.S.A. 80 E9 41 40N 91 32W
Iowa Falls, U.S.A. 80 D8 42 31N 93 16W
Iowa Park, U.S.A. 81 J5 33 57N 98 40W
Ipala, Tanzania 54 C3 4 30S 32 52 E
Ipameri, Brazil 93 G9 17 44S 48 9W
Ipatinga, Brazil 93 G10 19 32S 42 30W
Ipiales, Colombia 92 C3 0 50N 77 37W
Ipin = Yibin, China 32 D5 28 45N 104 32 E
Ipixuna, Brazil 92 E4 7 0S 71 40W
Ipoh, Malaysia 39 K3 4 35N 101 5 E
Ippy, C.A.R. 52 C4 6 5N 21 7 E
Ipsala, Turkey 21 D12 40 55N 26 23 E
Ipswich, Australia 63 D5 27 35S 152 40 E
Ipswich, U.K. 11 E9 52 4N 1 10 E
Ipswich, Mass., U.S.A. 79 D14 42 41N 70 50W
Ipswich, S. Dak., U.S.A. 80 C5 45 27N 99 2W
Ipu, Brazil 93 D10 4 23S 40 44W
Iqaluit, Canada 69 B13 63 44N 68 31W
Iquique, Chile 92 H4 20 19S 70 5W
Iquitos, Peru 92 D4 3 45S 73 10W
Irabu-Jima, Japan 31 M2 24 50N 125 10 E
Iracoubo, Fr. Guiana 93 B8 5 30N 53 10W
Īrafshān, Iran 45 E9 26 42N 61 56 E
Iráklion, Greece 23 D7 35 20N 25 12 E
Iráklion □, Greece 23 D7 35 10N 25 10 E
Irala, Paraguay 95 B5 25 55S 54 35W
Iran ■, Asia 45 C7 33 0N 53 0 E
Iran, Gunung-Gunung, Malaysia 36 D4 2 20N 114 50 E
Iran, Plateau of, Asia 28 F9 32 0N 55 0 E
Iran Ra. = Iran, Gunung-Gunung, Malaysia 36 D4 2 20N 114 50 E
Īrānshahr, Iran 45 E9 27 15N 60 40 E
Irapuato, Mexico 86 C4 20 40N 101 30W
Iraq ■, Asia 44 C5 33 0N 44 0 E
Irati, Brazil 95 B5 25 25S 50 38W
Irbid, Jordan 47 C4 32 35N 35 48 E
Irbid □, Jordan 47 C5 32 15N 36 35 E
Ireland ■, Europe 13 C4 53 50N 7 52W
Irhyangdong, N. Korea 35 D15 41 15N 129 30 E
Iri, S. Korea 35 G14 35 59N 127 0 E
Irian Jaya □, Indonesia 37 E9 4 0S 137 0 E
Iringa, Tanzania 54 D4 7 48S 35 43 E
Iringa □, Tanzania 54 D4 7 48S 35 43 E
Iriomote-Jima, Japan 31 M1 24 19N 123 48 E
Iriona, Honduras 88 C2 15 57N 85 11W
Iriri →, Brazil 93 D8 3 52S 52 37W
Irish Republic ■, Europe 13 C3 53 0N 8 0W
Irish Sea, U.K. 10 D3 53 38N 4 48W
Irkutsk, Russia 27 D11 52 18N 104 20 E
Irma, Canada 73 C6 52 55N 111 14W
Irō-Zaki, Japan 31 G9 34 36N 138 51 E
Iron Baron, Australia 63 E2 32 58S 137 11 E
Iron Gate = Portile de Fier, Europe 17 F12 44 44N 22 30 E
Iron Knob, Australia 63 E2 32 46S 137 8 E
Iron Mountain, U.S.A. 76 C1 45 49N 88 4W
Iron River, U.S.A. 80 B10 46 6N 88 39W
Irondequoit, U.S.A. 78 C7 43 13N 77 35W
Ironstone Kopje, Botswana 56 D3 25 17S 24 5 E
Ironton, Mo., U.S.A. 81 G9 37 36N 90 38W
Ironton, Ohio, U.S.A. 76 F4 38 32N 82 41W
Ironwood, U.S.A. 80 B9 46 27N 90 9W
Iroquois, Canada 79 B9 44 51N 75 19W
Iroquois Falls, Canada 70 C3 48 46N 80 41W
Irpin, Ukraine 17 C16 50 30N 30 15 E
Irrara Cr. →, Australia 63 D4 29 35S 145 31 E
Irrawaddy □, Burma 41 L19 17 0N 95 0 E
Irrawaddy →, Burma 41 M19 15 50N 95 6 E
Irricana, Canada 72 C6 51 19N 113 37W
Irtysh →, Russia 26 C7 61 4N 68 52 E
Irumu, Dem. Rep. of the Congo 54 B2 1 32N 29 53 E
Irún, Spain 19 A5 43 20N 1 52W
Irunea = Pamplona, Spain 19 A5 42 48N 1 38W
Irvine, Canada 73 D6 49 57N 110 16W
Irvine, U.K. 12 F4 55 37N 4 41W
Irvine, Calif., U.S.A. 85 M9 33 41N 117 46W
Irvine, Ky., U.S.A. 76 G4 37 42N 83 58W
Irvinestown, U.K. 13 B4 54 28N 7 39W
Irving, U.S.A. 81 J6 32 49N 96 56W
Irvona, U.S.A. 78 F6 40 46N 78 33W
Irwin →, Australia 61 E1 29 15S 114 54 E
Irymple, Australia 63 E3 34 14S 142 8 E
Isa Khel, Pakistan 42 C4 32 41N 71 17 E
Isaac →, Australia 62 C4 22 55S 149 20 E
Isabel, U.S.A. 80 C4 45 24N 101 26W
Isabela, I., Mexico 86 C3 21 51N 105 55W
Isabella, Cord., Nic. 88 D2 13 30N 85 25W
Isabella, Phil. 37 C6 6 40N 122 10 E
Isabella Ra., Australia 60 D3 21 0S 121 4 E
Ísafjarðardjúp, Iceland 8 C2 66 10N 23 0W
Ísafjörður, Iceland 8 C2 66 5N 23 9W
Isagarh, India 42 G7 24 48N 77 51 E
Isahaya, Japan 31 H5 32 52N 130 2 E
Isaka, Tanzania 54 C3 3 56S 32 59 E
Isan →, India 43 F9 26 51N 80 7 E
Isana = Içana →, Brazil 92 C5 0 26N 67 19W
Isar →, Germany 16 D7 48 48N 12 57 E
Ischia, Italy 20 D5 40 44N 13 57 E
Isdell →, Australia 60 C3 16 27S 124 51 E
Ise, Japan 31 G8 34 25N 136 45 E
Ise-Wan, Japan 31 G8 34 43N 136 43 E
Iseramagazi, Tanzania 54 C3 4 37S 32 10 E
Isère →, France 18 D6 44 59N 4 51 E
Isérnia, Italy 20 D6 41 36N 14 14 E
Isfahan = Eşfahān, Iran 45 C6 32 39N 51 43 E
Ishigaki-Shima, Japan 31 M2 24 20N 124 10 E
Ishikari-Gawa →, Japan 30 C10 43 15N 141 23 E
Ishikari-Sammyaku, Japan 30 C11 43 30N 143 0 E
Ishikari-Wan, Japan 30 C10 43 25N 141 1 E
Ishikawa □, Japan 31 F8 36 30N 136 30 E
Ishim, Russia 26 D7 56 10N 69 30 E
Ishim →, Russia 26 D8 57 45N 71 10 E
Ishinomaki, Japan 30 E10 38 32N 141 20 E
Ishioka, Japan 31 F10 36 11N 140 16 E
Ishkuman, Pakistan 43 A5 36 30N 73 50 E
Ishpeming, U.S.A. 76 B2 46 29N 87 40W
Isil Kul, Russia 26 D8 54 55N 71 16 E
Isiolo, Kenya 54 B4 0 24N 37 33 E
Isiro, Dem. Rep. of the Congo 54 B2 2 53N 27 40 E
Isisford, Australia 62 C3 24 15S 144 21 E
İskenderun, Turkey 25 G6 36 32N 36 10 E
İskenderun Körfezi, Turkey 25 G6 36 40N 35 50 E
Iskŭr →, Bulgaria 21 C11 43 45N 24 25 E
Iskut →, Canada 72 B2 56 45N 131 49W
Isla →, U.K. 12 E5 56 32N 3 20W
Isla Vista, U.S.A. 85 L7 34 25N 119 53W
Islam Headworks, Pakistan 42 E5 29 49N 72 33 E
Islamabad, Pakistan 42 C5 33 40N 73 10 E
Islamgarh, Pakistan 42 F4 27 51N 70 48 E
Islamkot, Pakistan 42 G4 24 42N 70 13 E
Islampur, India 43 G11 25 9N 85 12 E
Island L., Canada 73 C10 53 47N 94 25W
Island Lagoon, Australia 63 E2 31 30S 136 40 E
Island Pond, U.S.A. 79 B13 44 49N 71 53W
Islands, B. of, Canada 71 C8 49 11N 58 15W
Islay, U.K. 12 F2 55 46N 6 10W
Isle →, France 18 D3 44 55N 0 15W
Isle aux Morts, Canada 71 C8 47 35N 59 0W
Isle of Wight □, U.K. 11 G6 50 41N 1 17W
Isle Royale, U.S.A. 80 B10 48 0N 88 54W
Isle Royale National Park, U.S.A. 80 B10 48 0N 88 55W
Isleton, U.S.A. 84 G5 38 10N 121 37W
Ismail = Izmayil, Ukraine 17 F15 45 22N 28 46 E
Ismâ'ilîya, Egypt 51 B12 30 37N 32 18 E
Isogstalo, India 43 B8 34 15N 78 46 E
Isparta, Turkey 25 G5 37 47N 30 30 E
Ispica, Italy 20 F6 36 47N 14 55 E
Israel ■, Asia 47 D3 32 0N 34 50 E
Issoire, France 18 D5 45 32N 3 15 E
Issyk-Kul = Ysyk-Köl, Kyrgyzstan 28 E11 42 26N 76 12 E
Issyk-Kul, Ozero = Ysyk-Köl, Ozero, Kyrgyzstan 26 E8 42 25N 77 15 E
İstanbul, Turkey 21 D13 41 0N 29 0 E
İstanbul Boğazı, Turkey 21 D13 41 10N 29 10 E
Istiaía, Greece 21 E10 38 57N 23 9 E
Istokpoga, L., U.S.A. 77 M5 27 23N 81 17W
Istra, Croatia 16 F7 45 10N 14 0 E
Istres, France 18 E6 43 31N 4 59 E
Istria = Istra, Croatia 16 F7 45 10N 14 0 E
Itá, Paraguay 94 B4 25 29S 57 21W
Itaberaba, Brazil 93 F10 12 32S 40 18W
Itabira, Brazil 93 G10 19 37S 43 13W
Itabirito, Brazil 95 A7 20 15S 43 48W
Itabuna, Brazil 93 F11 14 48S 39 16W
Itacaunas →, Brazil 93 E9 5 21S 49 8W
Itacoatiara, Brazil 92 D7 3 8S 58 25W
Itaipú, Represa de, Brazil 95 B5 25 30S 54 30W
Itaituba, Brazil 93 D7 4 10S 55 50W
Itajaí, Brazil 95 B6 27 50S 48 39W
Itajubá, Brazil 95 A6 22 24S 45 30W
Itaka, Tanzania 55 D3 8 50S 32 49 E
Italy ■, Europe 20 C5 42 0N 13 0 E
Itamaraju, Brazil 93 G11 17 5S 39 31W
Itampolo, Madag. 57 C7 24 41S 43 57 E
Itapecuru-Mirim, Brazil 93 D10 3 24S 44 20W
Itaperuna, Brazil 95 A7 21 10S 41 54W
Itapetininga, Brazil 95 A6 23 36S 48 7W
Itapeva, Brazil 95 A6 23 59S 48 59W
Itapicuru →, Bahia, Brazil 93 F11 11 47S 37 32W
Itapicuru →, Maranhão, Brazil 93 D10 2 52S 44 12W
Itapipoca, Brazil 93 D11 3 30S 39 35W
Itapuá □, Paraguay 95 B4 26 40S 55 40W
Itaquari, Brazil 95 A7 20 20S 40 25W
Itaquí, Brazil 94 B4 29 8S 56 30W
Itararé, Brazil 95 A6 24 6S 49 23W
Itarsi, India 42 H7 22 36N 77 51 E
Itati, Argentina 94 B4 27 16S 58 15W
Itchen →, U.K. 11 G6 50 55N 1 22W
Itezhi Tezhi, L., Zambia 55 F2 15 30S 25 30 E
Ithaca = Itháki, Greece 21 E9 38 25N 20 40 E
Ithaca, U.S.A. 79 D8 42 27N 76 30W
Itháki, Greece 21 E9 38 25N 20 40 E
Itiquira →, Brazil 93 G7 17 18S 56 44W
Ito, Japan 31 G9 34 58N 139 5 E
Ito Aba I., S. China Sea 36 B4 10 23N 114 21 E
Itoigawa, Japan 31 F8 37 2N 137 51 E
Itonamas →, Bolivia 92 F6 12 28S 64 24W
Ittoqqortoormiit = Scoresbysund, Greenland 4 B6 70 20N 23 0W
Itu, Brazil 95 A6 23 17S 47 15W
Ituiutaba, Brazil 93 G9 19 0S 49 25W
Itumbiara, Brazil 93 G9 18 20S 49 10W
Ituna, Canada 73 C8 51 10N 103 24W
Itunge Port, Tanzania 55 D3 9 40S 33 55 E
Iturbe, Argentina 94 A2 23 0S 65 25W
Ituri →, Dem. Rep. of the Congo 54 B2 1 40N 27 1 E
Iturup, Ostrov, Russia 27 E15 45 0N 148 0 E
Ituxi →, Brazil 92 E6 7 18S 64 51W
Ituyuro →, Argentina 94 A3 22 40S 63 50W
Itzehoe, Germany 16 B5 53 55N 9 31 E
Ivaí →, Brazil 95 A5 23 18S 53 42W
Ivalo, Finland 8 B22 68 38N 27 35 E
Ivalojoki →, Finland 8 B22 68 40N 27 40 E
Ivanava, Belarus 17 B13 52 7N 25 29 E
Ivanhoe, Australia 63 E3 32 56S 144 20 E
Ivanhoe, Calif., U.S.A. 84 J7 36 23N 119 13W
Ivanhoe, Minn., U.S.A. 80 C6 44 28N 96 15W
Ivano-Frankivsk, Ukraine 17 D13 48 40N 24 40 E
Ivano-Frankovsk = Ivano-Frankivsk, Ukraine 17 D13 48 40N 24 40 E
Ivanovo = Ivanava, Belarus 17 B13 52 7N 25 29 E
Ivanovo, Russia 24 C7 57 5N 41 0 E
Ivato, Madag. 57 C8 20 37S 47 10 E
Ivatsevichy, Belarus 17 B13 52 43N 25 21 E
Ivdel, Russia 24 B11 60 42N 60 24 E
Ivindo →, Gabon 52 D2 0 9S 12 9 E
Ivinheima →, Brazil 95 A5 23 14S 53 42W
Ivinhema, Brazil 95 A5 22 10S 53 37W
Ivohibe, Madag. 57 C8 22 31S 46 57 E
Ivory Coast, Africa 50 H4 5 0N 5 0W
Ivory Coast ■, Africa 50 G4 7 30N 5 0W
Ivrea, Italy 18 D7 45 28N 7 52 E
Ivujivik, Canada 69 B12 62 24N 77 55W
Ivybridge, U.K. 11 G4 50 23N 3 56W
Iwaizumi, Japan 30 E10 39 50N 141 45 E
Iwaki, Japan 31 F10 37 3N 140 55 E
Iwakuni, Japan 31 G6 34 15N 132 8 E
Iwamizawa, Japan 30 C10 43 12N 141 46 E
Iwanai, Japan 30 C10 42 58N 140 30 E
Iwata, Japan 31 G8 34 42N 137 51 E
Iwate □, Japan 30 E10 39 30N 141 30 E
Iwate-San, Japan 30 E10 39 51N 141 0 E
Iwo, Nigeria 50 G6 7 39N 4 9 E
Ixiamas, Bolivia 92 F5 13 50S 68 5W
Ixopo, S. Africa 57 E5 30 11S 30 5 E
Ixtepec, Mexico 87 D5 16 32N 95 10W
Ixtlán del Río, Mexico 86 C4 21 5N 104 21W
Iyo, Japan 31 H6 33 45N 132 45 E
Izabal, L. de, Guatemala 88 C2 15 30N 89 10W
Izamal, Mexico 87 C7 20 56N 89 1W
Izena-Shima, Japan 31 L3 26 56N 127 56 E
Izhevsk, Russia 24 C9 56 51N 53 14 E
Izhma →, Russia 24 A9 65 19N 52 54 E
Izmayil, Ukraine 17 F15 45 22N 28 46 E
İzmir, Turkey 21 E12 38 25N 27 8 E
İzmit = Kocaeli, Turkey 25 F4 40 45N 29 50 E
İznik Gölü, Turkey 21 D13 40 27N 29 30 E
Izra, Syria 47 C5 32 51N 36 15 E
Izu-Shotō, Japan 31 G10 34 30N 140 0 E
Izúcar de Matamoros, Mexico 87 D5 18 36N 98 28W
Izumi-sano, Japan 31 G7 34 23N 135 18 E
Izumo, Japan 31 G6 35 20N 132 46 E
Izyaslav, Ukraine 17 C14 50 5N 26 50 E

J

Jabalpur, India 43 H8 23 9N 79 58 E
Jabbūl, Syria 44 B3 36 4N 37 30 E
Jabiru, Australia 60 B5 12 40S 132 53 E
Jablah, Syria 44 C3 35 20N 36 0 E
Jablonec nad Nisou, Czech Rep. 16 C8 50 43N 15 10 E
Jaboatão, Brazil 93 E11 8 7S 35 1W
Jaboticabal, Brazil 95 A6 21 15S 48 17W
Jaca, Spain 19 A5 42 35N 0 33W
Jacareí, Brazil 95 A6 23 20S 46 0W
Jacarèzinho, Brazil 95 A6 23 5S 49 58W
Jackman, U.S.A. 77 C10 45 35N 70 17W
Jacksboro, U.S.A. 81 J5 33 14N 98 15W
Jackson, Ala., U.S.A. 77 K2 31 31N 87 53W
Jackson, Calif., U.S.A. 84 G6 38 21N 120 46W
Jackson, Ky., U.S.A. 76 G4 37 33N 83 23W
Jackson, Mich., U.S.A. 76 D3 42 15N 84 24W
Jackson, Minn., U.S.A. 80 D7 43 37N 95 1W
Jackson, Miss., U.S.A. 81 J9 32 18N 90 12W
Jackson, Mo., U.S.A. 81 G10 37 23N 89 40W
Jackson, N.H., U.S.A. 79 B13 44 10N 71 11W
Jackson, Ohio, U.S.A. 76 F4 39 3N 82 39W
Jackson, Tenn., U.S.A. 77 H1 35 37N 88 49W
Jackson, Wyo., U.S.A. 82 E8 43 29N 110 46W
Jackson B., N.Z. 59 K2 43 58S 168 42 E
Jackson L., U.S.A. 82 E8 43 52N 110 36W
Jacksons, N.Z. 59 K3 42 46S 171 32 E
Jackson's Arm, Canada 71 C8 49 52N 56 47W
Jacksonville, Ala., U.S.A. 77 J3 33 49N 85 46W
Jacksonville, Ark., U.S.A. 81 H8 34 52N 92 7W
Jacksonville, Calif., U.S.A. 84 H6 37 52N 120 24W
Jacksonville, Fla., U.S.A. 77 K5 30 20N 81 39W
Jacksonville, Ill., U.S.A. 80 F9 39 44N 90 14W
Jacksonville, N.C., U.S.A. 77 H7 34 45N 77 26W
Jacksonville, Tex., U.S.A. 81 K7 31 58N 95 17W
Jacksonville Beach, U.S.A. 77 K5 30 17N 81 24W
Jacmel, Haiti 89 C5 18 14N 72 32W
Jacob Lake, U.S.A. 83 H7 36 43N 112 13W
Jacobabad, Pakistan 42 E3 28 20N 68 29 E
Jacobina, Brazil 93 F10 11 11S 40 30W
Jacques Cartier, Dét. de, Canada 71 C7 50 0N 63 30W
Jacques-Cartier, Mt., Canada 71 C6 48 57N 66 0W
Jacques Cartier, Parc Prov., Canada 71 C5 47 15N 71 33W
Jacuí →, Brazil 95 C5 30 2S 51 15W
Jacumba, U.S.A. 85 N10 32 37N 116 11W
Jacundá →, Brazil 93 D8 1 57S 50 26W
Jadotville = Likasi, Dem. Rep. of the Congo 55 E2 10 55S 26 48 E
Jaén, Peru 92 E3 5 25S 78 40W
Jaén, Spain 19 D4 37 44N 3 43W
Jafarabad, India 42 J4 20 52N 71 22 E
Jaffa = Tel Aviv-Yafo, Israel 47 C3 32 4N 34 48 E
Jaffa, C., Australia 63 F2 36 58S 139 40 E
Jaffna, Sri Lanka 40 Q12 9 45N 80 2 E
Jaffrey, U.S.A. 79 D12 42 49N 72 2W
Jagadhri, India 42 D7 30 10N 77 20 E
Jagadishpur, India 43 G11 25 30N 84 21 E
Jagdalpur, India 41 K13 19 3N 82 0 E
Jagersfontein, S. Africa 56 D4 29 44S 25 27 E
Jaghīn →, Iran 45 E8 27 17N 57 13 E
Jagodina, Serbia, Yug. 21 C9 44 5N 21 15 E
Jagraon, India 40 D9 30 50N 75 25 E
Jagtial, India 40 K11 18 50N 79 0 E
Jaguariaíva, Brazil 95 A6 24 10S 49 50W
Jaguaribe →, Brazil 93 D11 4 25S 37 45W
Jagüey Grande, Cuba 88 B3 22 35N 81 7W
Jahanabad, India 43 G11 25 13N 84 59 E
Jahazpur, India 42 G6 25 37N 75 17 E
Jahrom, Iran 45 D7 28 30N 53 31 E
Jaijon, India 42 D7 31 21N 76 9 E
Jailolo, Indonesia 37 D7 1 5N 127 30 E
Jailolo, Selat, Indonesia 37 D7 0 5N 129 5 E
Jaipur, India 42 F6 27 0N 75 50 E
Jais, India 43 F9 26 15N 81 32 E
Jaisalmer, India 42 F4 26 55N 70 54 E
Jaisinghnagar, India 43 H8 23 38N 78 34 E
Jaitaran, India 42 F5 26 12N 73 56 E
Jaithari, India 43 H8 23 14N 78 37 E
Jājarm, Iran 45 B8 36 58N 56 27 E
Jakam →, India 42 H6 23 54N 74 13 E
Jakarta, Indonesia 37 G12 6 9S 106 49 E
Jakhal, India 42 E6 29 48N 75 50 E
Jakhau, India 42 H3 23 13N 68 43 E
Jakobstad = Pietarsaari, Finland 8 E20 63 40N 22 43 E
Jal, U.S.A. 81 J3 32 7N 103 12W
Jalalabad, Afghan. 42 B4 34 30N 70 29 E
Jalalabad, India 43 F8 27 41N 79 42 E
Jalalpur Jattan, Pakistan 42 C6 32 38N 74 11 E
Jalama, U.S.A. 85 L6 34 29N 120 29W
Jalapa, Guatemala 88 D2 14 39N 89 59W
Jalapa Enríquez, Mexico 87 D5 19 32N 96 55W
Jalasjärvi, Finland 9 E20 62 29N 22 47 E
Jalaun, India 43 F8 26 8N 79 25 E
Jaldhaka →, Bangla. 43 F13 26 16N 89 16 E
Jalesar, India 42 F8 27 29N 78 19 E
Jaleswar, Nepal 43 F11 26 38N 85 48 E
Jalgaon, Maharashtra, India 40 J10 21 2N 76 31 E
Jalgaon, Maharashtra, India 40 J9 21 0N 75 42 E
Jalībah, Iraq 44 D5 30 35N 46 32 E
Jalisco □, Mexico 86 D4 20 20N 104 0W
Jalkot, Pakistan 43 B5 35 14N 73 24 E
Jalna, India 40 K9 19 48N 75 38 E
Jalón →, Spain 19 B5 41 47N 1 4W
Jalor, India 42 G5 25 21N 72 37 E
Jalpa, Mexico 86 C4 21 38N 102 58W
Jalpaiguri, India 41 F16 26 32N 88 46 E
Jaluit I., Marshall Is. 64 G8 6 0N 169 30 E

Juruena

Jalūlā, *Iraq* 44 C5 34 16N 45 10 E
Jamaica ■, *W. Indies* 88 C4 18 10N 77 30W
Jamalpur, *Bangla.* 41 G16 24 52N 89 56 E
Jamalpur, *India* 43 G12 25 18N 86 28 E
Jamalpurganj, *India* 43 H13 23 2N 87 59 E
Jamanxim →, *Brazil* 93 D7 4 43S 56 18W
Jambi, *Indonesia* 36 E2 1 38S 103 30 E
Jambi □, *Indonesia* 36 E2 1 30S 102 30 E
Jambusar, *India* 42 H5 22 3N 72 51 E
James →, *S. Dak., U.S.A.* 80 D6 42 52N 97 18W
James →, *Va., U.S.A.* 76 G7 36 56N 76 27W
James B., *Canada* 70 B3 54 0N 80 0W
James Ranges, *Australia* 60 D5 24 10S 132 30 E
James Ross I., *Antarctica* 5 C18 63 58S 57 50W
Jamesabad, *Pakistan* 42 G3 25 17N 69 15 E
Jamestown, *Australia* 63 E2 33 10S 138 32 E
Jamestown, *S. Africa* 56 E4 31 6S 26 45 E
Jamestown, *N. Dak., U.S.A.* 80 B5 46 54N 98 42W
Jamestown, *N.Y., U.S.A.* 78 D5 42 6N 79 14W
Jamestown, *Pa., U.S.A.* 78 E4 41 29N 80 27W
Jamīlābād, *Iran* 45 C6 34 24N 48 28 E
Jamiltepec, *Mexico* 87 D5 16 17N 97 49W
Jamira →, *India* 43 J13 21 35N 88 28 E
Jamkhandi, *India* 40 L9 16 30N 75 15 E
Jammu, *India* 42 C6 32 43N 74 54 E
Jammu & Kashmir □, *India* 43 B7 34 25N 77 0 E
Jamnagar, *India* 42 H4 22 30N 70 6 E
Jamni →, *India* 43 G8 25 13N 78 35 E
Jampur, *Pakistan* 42 E4 29 39N 70 40 E
Jamrud, *Pakistan* 42 C4 33 59N 71 24 E
Jämsä, *Finland* 9 F21 61 53N 25 10 E
Jamshedpur, *India* 43 H12 22 44N 86 12 E
Jamtara, *India* 43 H12 23 59N 86 49 E
Jämtland, *Sweden* 8 E15 63 31N 14 0 E
Jan L., *Canada* 73 C8 54 56N 102 55W
Jan Mayen, *Arctic* 4 B7 71 0N 9 0W
Janakkala, *Finland* 9 F21 60 54N 24 36 E
Janaúba, *Brazil* 93 G10 15 48S 43 19W
Jand, *Pakistan* 42 C5 33 30N 72 6 E
Jandaq, *Iran* 45 C7 34 3N 54 22 E
Jandia, *Canary Is.* 22 F5 28 6N 14 21W
Jandia, Pta. de, *Canary Is.* 22 F5 28 3N 14 31W
Jandola, *Pakistan* 42 C4 32 20N 70 9 E
Jandowae, *Australia* 63 D5 26 45S 151 7 E
Janesville, *U.S.A.* 80 D10 42 41N 89 1W
Janghai, *India* 43 G10 25 33N 82 19 E
Janin, *West Bank* 47 C4 32 28N 35 18 E
Janjgir, *India* 43 J10 22 1N 82 34 E
Janos, *Mexico* 86 A3 30 45N 108 10W
Januária, *Brazil* 93 G10 15 25S 44 25W
Janubio, *Canary Is.* 22 F6 28 56N 13 50W
Jaora, *India* 42 H6 23 40N 75 10 E
Japan ■, *Asia* 31 G8 36 0N 136 0 E
Japan, Sea of, *Asia* 30 E7 40 0N 135 0 E
Japan Trench, *Pac. Oc.* 28 F18 32 0N 142 0 E
Japen = Yapen, *Indonesia* 37 E9 1 50S 136 0 E
Japla, *India* 43 G11 24 33N 84 1 E
Japurá →, *Brazil* 92 D5 3 8S 65 46W
Jaquarão, *Brazil* 95 C5 32 34S 53 23W
Jaqué, *Panama* 88 E4 7 27N 78 8W
Jarābulus, *Syria* 44 B3 36 49N 38 1 E
Jarama →, *Spain* 19 B4 40 24N 3 32W
Jaranwala, *Pakistan* 42 D5 31 15N 73 26 E
Jarash, *Jordan* 47 C4 32 17N 35 54 E
Jardim, *Brazil* 94 A4 21 28S 56 2W
Jardines de la Reina, Arch. de los, *Cuba* 88 B4 20 50N 78 50W
Jargalang, *China* 35 C12 43 5N 122 55 E
Jargalant = Hovd, *Mongolia* 32 B4 48 2N 91 37 E
Jari →, *Brazil* 93 D8 1 9S 51 54W
Jarīr, W. al →, *Si. Arabia* 44 E4 25 38N 42 30 E
Jarosław, *Poland* 17 C12 50 2N 22 42 E
Jarrahdale, *Australia* 61 F2 32 24S 116 5 E
Jarrahi →, *Iran* 45 D6 30 49N 48 48 E
Jarres, Plaine des, *Laos* 38 C4 19 27N 103 10 E
Jartai, *China* 34 E3 39 45N 105 48 E
Jarud Qi, *China* 35 B11 44 28N 120 50 E
Järvenpää, *Finland* 9 F21 60 29N 25 5 E
Jarvis, *Canada* 78 D4 42 53N 80 6W
Jarvis I., *Pac. Oc.* 65 H12 0 15S 159 55W
Jarwa, *India* 43 F10 27 38N 82 30 E
Jasdan, *India* 42 H4 22 2N 71 12 E
Jashpurnagar, *India* 43 H11 22 54N 84 9 E
Jasidih, *India* 43 G12 24 31N 86 39 E
Jāsimīyah, *Iraq* 44 C5 33 45N 44 41 E
Jasin, *Malaysia* 39 L4 2 20N 102 26 E
Jāsk, *Iran* 45 E8 25 38N 57 45 E
Jasło, *Poland* 17 D11 49 45N 21 30 E
Jaso, *India* 43 G9 24 30N 80 29 E
Jasper, *Alta., Canada* 72 C5 52 55N 118 5W
Jasper, *Ont., Canada* 79 B9 44 52N 75 57W
Jasper, *Ala., U.S.A.* 77 J2 33 50N 87 17W
Jasper, *Fla., U.S.A.* 77 K4 30 31N 82 57W
Jasper, *Ind., U.S.A.* 76 F2 38 24N 86 56W
Jasper, *Tex., U.S.A.* 81 K8 30 56N 94 1W
Jasper Nat. Park, *Canada* 72 C5 52 50N 118 8W
Jasrasar, *India* 42 F5 27 43N 73 49 E
Jászberény, *Hungary* 17 E10 47 30N 19 55 E
Jataí, *Brazil* 93 G8 17 58S 51 48W
Jati, *Pakistan* 42 G3 24 20N 68 19 E
Jatibarang, *Indonesia* 37 G13 6 28S 108 18 E
Jatinegara, *Indonesia* 37 G12 6 13S 106 52 E
Játiva = Xátiva, *Spain* 19 C5 38 59N 0 32W
Jaú, *Brazil* 95 A6 22 10S 48 30W
Jauja, *Peru* 92 F3 11 45S 75 15W
Jaunpur, *India* 43 G10 25 46N 82 44 E
Java = Jawa, *Indonesia* 37 G14 7 0S 110 0 E
Java Barat □, *Indonesia* 37 G12 7 0S 107 0 E
Java Sea, *Indonesia* 36 E3 4 35S 107 15 E
Java Tengah □, *Indonesia* 37 G14 7 0S 110 0 E
Java Timur □, *Indonesia* 37 G15 8 0S 113 0 E
Java Trench, *Ind. Oc.* 36 F3 9 0S 105 0 E
Javhlant = Uliastay, *Mongolia* 32 B4 47 56N 97 28 E
Jawa, *Indonesia* 37 G14 7 0S 110 0 E
Jawad, *India* 42 G6 24 36N 74 51 E
Jay Peak, *U.S.A.* 79 B12 44 55N 72 32W
Jaya, Puncak, *Indonesia* 37 E9 3 57S 137 17 E
Jayanti, *India* 41 F16 26 45N 89 40 E
Jayapura, *Indonesia* 37 E10 2 28S 140 38 E
Jayawijaya, Pegunungan, *Indonesia* 37 F9 5 0S 139 0 E
Jaynagar, *India* 41 F15 26 43N 86 9 E
Jayrūd, *Syria* 44 C3 33 49N 36 44 E
Jayton, *U.S.A.* 81 J4 33 15N 100 34W
Jāz Mūrīān, Hāmūn-e, *Iran* 45 E8 27 20N 58 55 E
Jazīreh-ye Shīf, *Iran* 45 D6 29 4N 50 54 E
Jazminal, *Mexico* 86 C4 24 56N 101 25W
Jazzīn, *Lebanon* 47 B4 33 31N 35 35 E
Jean, *U.S.A.* 85 K11 35 47N 115 20W
Jean Marie River, *Canada* 72 A4 61 32N 120 38W
Jean Rabel, *Haiti* 89 C5 19 50N 73 5W
Jeanerette, *U.S.A.* 81 L9 29 55N 91 40W
Jeanette, Ostrov = Zhannetty, Ostrov, *Russia* 27 B16 76 43N 158 0 E
Jeannette, *U.S.A.* 78 F5 40 20N 79 36W
Jebāl Bārez, Kūh-e, *Iran* 45 D8 28 30N 58 20 E
Jebel, Bahr el →, *Sudan* 51 G12 9 30N 30 25 E
Jedburgh, *U.K.* 12 F6 55 29N 2 33W
Jedda = Jiddah, *Si. Arabia* 46 C2 21 29N 39 10 E
Jeddore L., *Canada* 71 C8 48 3N 55 55W
Jędrzejów, *Poland* 17 C11 50 35N 20 15 E
Jefferson, *Iowa, U.S.A.* 80 D7 42 1N 94 23W
Jefferson, *Ohio, U.S.A.* 78 E4 41 44N 80 46W
Jefferson, *Tex., U.S.A.* 81 J7 32 46N 94 21W
Jefferson, Mt., *Nev., U.S.A.* 82 G5 38 51N 117 0W
Jefferson, Mt., *Oreg., U.S.A.* 82 D3 44 41N 121 48W
Jefferson City, *Mo., U.S.A.* 80 F8 38 34N 92 10W
Jefferson City, *Tenn., U.S.A.* 77 G4 36 7N 83 30W
Jeffersontown, *U.S.A.* 76 F3 38 12N 85 35W
Jeffersonville, *U.S.A.* 76 F3 38 17N 85 44W
Jeffrey City, *U.S.A.* 82 E10 42 30N 107 49W
Jega, *Nigeria* 50 F6 12 15N 4 23 E
Jēkabpils, *Latvia* 9 H21 56 29N 25 57 E
Jekyll I., *U.S.A.* 77 K5 31 4N 81 25W
Jelenia Góra, *Poland* 16 C8 50 50N 15 45 E
Jelgava, *Latvia* 9 H20 56 41N 23 49 E
Jemaja, *Indonesia* 39 L5 3 5N 105 45 E
Jemaluang, *Malaysia* 39 L4 2 16N 103 52 E
Jember, *Indonesia* 37 H15 8 11S 113 41 E
Jembongan, *Malaysia* 36 C5 6 45N 117 20 E
Jena, *Germany* 16 C6 50 54N 11 35 E
Jena, *U.S.A.* 81 K8 31 41N 92 8W
Jenkins, *U.S.A.* 76 G4 37 10N 82 38W
Jenner, *U.S.A.* 84 G3 38 27N 123 7W
Jennings, *U.S.A.* 81 K8 30 13N 92 40W
Jepara, *Indonesia* 37 G14 7 40S 109 14 E
Jeparit, *Australia* 63 F3 36 8S 142 1 E
Jequié, *Brazil* 93 F10 13 51S 40 5W
Jequitinhonha, *Brazil* 93 G10 16 30S 41 0W
Jequitinhonha →, *Brazil* 93 G11 15 51S 38 53W
Jerantut, *Malaysia* 39 L4 3 56N 102 22 E
Jérémie, *Haiti* 89 C5 18 40N 74 10W
Jerez, Punta, *Mexico* 87 C5 22 58N 97 40W
Jerez de García Salinas, *Mexico* 86 C4 22 39N 103 0W
Jerez de la Frontera, *Spain* 19 D2 36 41N 6 7W
Jerez de los Caballeros, *Spain* 19 C2 38 20N 6 45W
Jericho = El Arīḥā, *West Bank* 47 D4 31 52N 35 27 E
Jericho, *Australia* 62 C4 23 38S 146 6 E
Jerilderie, *Australia* 63 F4 35 20S 145 41 E
Jermyn, *U.S.A.* 79 E9 41 31N 75 31W
Jerome, *U.S.A.* 82 E6 42 44N 114 31W
Jerramungup, *Australia* 61 F2 33 55S 118 55 E
Jersey, *U.K.* 11 H5 49 11N 2 7W
Jersey City, *U.S.A.* 79 F10 40 44N 74 4W
Jersey Shore, *U.S.A.* 78 E7 41 12N 77 15W
Jerseyville, *U.S.A.* 80 F9 39 7N 90 20W
Jerusalem, *Israel* 47 D4 31 47N 35 10 E
Jervis B., *Australia* 63 F5 35 8S 150 46 E
Jervis Inlet, *Canada* 72 C4 50 0N 123 57W
Jesselton = Kota Kinabalu, *Malaysia* 36 C5 6 0N 116 4 E
Jessore, *Bangla.* 41 H16 23 10N 89 10 E
Jesup, *U.S.A.* 77 K5 31 36N 81 53W
Jesús Carranza, *Mexico* 87 D5 17 28N 95 1W
Jesús María, *Argentina* 94 C3 30 59S 64 5W
Jetmore, *U.S.A.* 81 F5 38 4N 99 54W
Jetpur, *India* 42 J4 21 45N 70 10 E
Jevnaker, *Norway* 9 F14 60 15N 10 26 E
Jewett, *U.S.A.* 78 F3 40 22N 81 2W
Jewett City, *U.S.A.* 79 E13 41 36N 72 0W
Jeyḥūnābād, *Iran* 45 C6 34 58N 48 59 E
Jeypore, *India* 41 K13 18 50N 82 38 E
Jha Jha, *India* 43 G12 24 46N 86 22 E
Jhabua, *India* 42 H6 22 46N 74 36 E
Jhajjar, *India* 42 E7 28 37N 76 42 E
Jhal, *Pakistan* 42 E2 28 17N 67 27 E
Jhal Jhao, *Pakistan* 40 F4 26 20N 65 35 E
Jhalawar, *India* 42 G7 24 40N 76 10 E
Jhalida, *India* 43 H11 23 22N 85 58 E
Jhalrapatan, *India* 42 G7 24 33N 76 10 E
Jhang Maghiana, *Pakistan* 42 D5 31 15N 72 22 E
Jhansi, *India* 43 G8 25 30N 78 36 E
Jhargram, *India* 43 H12 22 27N 86 59 E
Jharia, *India* 43 H12 23 45N 86 26 E
Jharsuguda, *India* 41 J14 21 56N 84 5 E
Jhelum, *Pakistan* 42 C5 33 0N 73 45 E
Jhelum →, *Pakistan* 42 D5 31 20N 72 10 E
Jhilmilli, *India* 43 H10 23 24N 82 51 E
Jhudo, *Pakistan* 42 G3 24 58N 69 18 E
Jhunjhunu, *India* 42 E6 28 10N 75 30 E
Ji-Paraná, *Brazil* 92 F6 10 52S 62 57W
Ji Xian, *Hebei, China* 34 F8 37 35N 115 30 E
Ji Xian, *Henan, China* 34 G8 35 22N 114 5 E
Ji Xian, *Shanxi, China* 34 F6 36 7N 110 40 E
Jia Xian, *Henan, China* 34 H7 33 59N 113 12 E
Jia Xian, *Shaanxi, China* 34 E6 38 12N 110 28 E
Jiamusi, *China* 33 B8 46 40N 130 26 E
Ji'an, *Jiangxi, China* 33 D6 27 6N 114 59 E
Ji'an, *Jilin, China* 35 D14 41 5N 126 10 E
Jianchang, *China* 35 D11 40 55N 120 35 E
Jianchangying, *China* 35 D10 40 10N 118 50 E
Jiangcheng, *China* 32 D5 22 36N 101 52 E
Jiangmen, *China* 33 D6 22 32N 113 0 E
Jiangsu □, *China* 35 H11 33 0N 120 0 E
Jiangxi □, *China* 33 D6 27 30N 116 0 E
Jiao Xian = Jiaozhou, *China* 35 F11 36 18N 120 1 E
Jiaohe, *Hebei, China* 34 E9 38 2N 116 20 E
Jiaohe, *Jilin, China* 35 C14 43 40N 127 22 E
Jiaozhou, *China* 35 F11 36 18N 120 1 E
Jiaozhou Wan, *China* 35 F11 36 5N 120 10 E
Jiaozuo, *China* 34 G7 35 16N 113 12 E
Jiawang, *China* 35 G9 34 28N 117 26 E
Jiaxiang, *China* 34 G9 35 25N 116 20 E
Jiaxing, *China* 33 C7 30 49N 120 45 E
Jiayi = Chiai, *Taiwan* 33 D7 23 29N 120 25 E
Jibuti = Djibouti ■, *Africa* 46 E3 12 0N 43 0 E
Jicarón, I., *Panama* 88 E3 7 10N 81 50W
Jiddah, *Si. Arabia* 46 C2 21 29N 39 10 E
Jido, *India* 41 E19 29 2N 94 58 E
Jieshou, *China* 34 H8 33 18N 115 22 E
Jiexiu, *China* 34 F6 37 2N 111 55 E
Jiggalong, *Australia* 60 D3 23 21S 120 47 E
Jigni, *India* 43 G8 25 45N 79 25 E
Jihlava, *Czech Rep.* 16 D8 49 28N 15 35 E
Jihlava →, *Czech Rep.* 17 D9 48 55N 16 36 E
Jijiga, *Ethiopia* 46 F3 9 20N 42 50 E
Jilin, *China* 35 C14 43 44N 126 30 E
Jilin □, *China* 35 C14 44 0N 127 0 E
Jilong = Chilung, *Taiwan* 33 D7 25 3N 121 45 E
Jim Thorpe, *U.S.A.* 79 F9 40 52N 75 44W
Jima, *Ethiopia* 46 F2 7 40N 36 47 E
Jiménez, *Mexico* 86 B4 27 10N 104 54W
Jimo, *China* 35 F11 36 23N 120 30 E
Jin Xian = Jinzhou, *China* 34 E8 38 2N 115 2 E
Jin Xian, *China* 35 E11 38 55N 121 42 E
Jinan, *China* 34 F9 36 38N 117 1 E
Jincheng, *China* 34 G7 35 29N 112 50 E
Jind, *India* 42 E7 29 19N 76 22 E
Jindabyne, *Australia* 63 F4 36 25S 148 35 E
Jindřichův Hradec, *Czech Rep.* 16 D8 49 10N 15 2 E
Jing He →, *China* 34 G5 34 27N 109 4 E
Jingbian, *China* 34 F5 37 20N 108 30 E
Jingchuan, *China* 34 G4 35 20N 107 20 E
Jingdezhen, *China* 33 D6 29 20N 117 11 E
Jinggu, *China* 32 D5 23 35N 100 41 E
Jinghai, *China* 34 E9 38 55N 116 55 E
Jingle, *China* 34 E6 38 20N 111 55 E
Jingning, *China* 34 G3 35 30N 105 43 E
Jingpo Hu, *China* 35 C15 43 55N 128 55 E
Jingtai, *China* 34 F3 37 10N 104 6 E
Jingxing, *China* 34 E8 38 2N 114 8 E
Jingyang, *China* 34 G5 34 30N 108 50 E
Jingyu, *China* 35 C14 42 25N 126 45 E
Jingyuan, *China* 34 F3 36 30N 104 40 E
Jingziguan, *China* 34 H6 33 15N 111 0 E
Jinhua, *China* 33 D6 29 8N 119 38 E
Jining, *Nei Mongol Zizhiqu, China* 34 D7 41 5N 113 0 E
Jining, *Shandong, China* 34 G9 35 22N 116 34 E
Jinja, *Uganda* 54 B3 0 25N 33 12 E
Jinjang, *Malaysia* 39 L3 3 13N 101 39 E
Jinji, *China* 34 F4 37 58N 106 8 E
Jinnah Barrage, *Pakistan* 40 C7 32 58N 71 33 E
Jinotega, *Nic.* 88 D2 13 6N 85 59W
Jinotepe, *Nic.* 88 D2 11 50N 86 10W
Jinsha Jiang →, *China* 32 D5 28 50N 104 36 E
Jinxi, *China* 35 D11 40 52N 120 50 E
Jinxiang, *China* 34 G9 35 5N 116 22 E
Jinzhou, *Hebei, China* 34 E8 38 2N 115 2 E
Jinzhou, *Liaoning, China* 35 D11 41 5N 121 3 E
Jiparaná →, *Brazil* 92 E6 8 3S 62 52W
Jipijapa, *Ecuador* 92 D2 1 0S 80 40W
Jiquilpan, *Mexico* 86 D4 19 57N 102 42W
Jishan, *China* 34 G6 35 34N 110 58 E
Jisr ash Shughūr, *Syria* 44 C3 35 49N 36 18 E
Jitarning, *Australia* 61 F2 32 48S 117 57 E
Jitra, *Malaysia* 39 J3 6 16N 100 25 E
Jiu →, *Romania* 17 F12 43 47N 23 48 E
Jiudengkou, *China* 34 E4 39 56N 106 40 E
Jiujiang, *China* 33 D6 29 42N 115 58 E
Jiutai, *China* 35 B13 44 10N 125 50 E
Jiuxiangcheng, *China* 34 H8 33 12N 114 50 E
Jiuxincheng, *China* 34 E8 39 17N 115 59 E
Jixi, *China* 35 B16 45 20N 130 50 E
Jiyang, *China* 35 F9 37 0N 117 12 E
Jiyuan, *China* 34 G7 35 7N 112 57 E
Jīzān, *Si. Arabia* 46 D3 17 0N 42 20 E
Jize, *China* 34 F8 36 54N 114 56 E
Jīzl, Wādī al, *Si. Arabia* 44 E3 25 39N 38 25 E
Jizō-Zaki, *Japan* 31 G6 35 34N 133 20 E
Jizzakh, *Uzbekistan* 26 E7 40 6N 67 50 E
Joaçaba, *Brazil* 95 B5 27 5S 51 31W
João Pessoa, *Brazil* 93 E12 7 10S 34 52W
Joaquín V. González, *Argentina* 94 B3 25 10S 64 0W
Jobat, *India* 42 H6 22 25N 74 34 E
Jodhpur, *India* 42 F5 26 23N 73 8 E
Jodiya, *India* 42 H4 22 42N 70 18 E
Joensuu, *Finland* 24 B4 62 37N 29 49 E
Jōetsu, *Japan* 31 F9 37 12N 138 10 E
Jofane, *Mozam.* 57 C5 21 15S 34 18 E
Jogbani, *India* 43 F12 26 25N 87 15 E
Jõgeva, *Estonia* 9 G22 58 45N 26 24 E
Jogjakarta = Yogyakarta, *Indonesia* 37 G14 7 49S 110 22 E
Johannesburg, *S. Africa* 57 D4 26 10S 28 2 E
Johannesburg, *U.S.A.* 85 K9 35 22N 117 38W
Johilla →, *India* 43 H9 23 37N 81 14 E
John Day, *U.S.A.* 82 D4 44 25N 118 57W
John Day →, *U.S.A.* 82 D3 45 44N 120 39W
John D'Or Prairie, *Canada* 72 B5 58 30N 115 8W
John H. Kerr Reservoir, *U.S.A.* 77 G6 36 36N 78 18W
John o' Groats, *U.K.* 12 C5 58 38N 3 4W
Johnnie, *U.S.A.* 85 J10 36 25N 116 5W
John's Ra., *Australia* 62 C1 21 55S 133 23 E
Johnson, *Kans., U.S.A.* 81 G4 37 34N 101 45W
Johnson, *Vt., U.S.A.* 79 B12 44 38N 72 41W
Johnson City, *N.Y., U.S.A.* 79 D9 42 7N 75 58W
Johnson City, *Tenn., U.S.A.* 77 G4 36 19N 82 21W
Johnson City, *Tex., U.S.A.* 81 K5 30 17N 98 25W
Johnsonburg, *U.S.A.* 78 E6 41 29N 78 41W
Johnsondale, *U.S.A.* 85 K8 35 58N 118 32W
Johnson's Crossing, *Canada* 72 A2 60 29N 133 18W
Johnston, L., *Australia* 61 F3 32 25S 120 30 E
Johnston Falls = Mambilima Falls, *Zambia* 55 E2 10 31S 28 45 E
Johnston I., *Pac. Oc.* 65 F11 17 10N 169 8W
Johnstone Str., *Canada* 72 C3 50 28N 126 0W
Johnstown, *N.Y., U.S.A.* 79 C10 43 0N 74 22W
Johnstown, *Ohio, U.S.A.* 78 F2 40 9N 82 41W
Johnstown, *Pa., U.S.A.* 78 F6 40 20N 78 55W
Johor Baharu, *Malaysia* 39 M4 1 28N 103 46 E
Jõhvi, *Estonia* 9 G22 59 22N 27 27 E
Joinville, *Brazil* 95 B6 26 15S 48 55W
Joinville I., *Antarctica* 5 C18 65 0S 55 30W
Jojutla, *Mexico* 87 D5 18 37N 99 11W
Jokkmokk, *Sweden* 8 C18 66 35N 19 50 E
Jökulsá á Bru →, *Iceland* 8 D6 65 40N 14 16W
Jökulsá á Fjöllum →, *Iceland* 8 C5 66 10N 16 30W
Jolfā, *Āzarbājān-e Sharqī, Iran* 44 B5 38 57N 45 38 E
Jolfā, *Eşfahan, Iran* 45 C6 32 58N 51 37 E
Joliet, *U.S.A.* 76 E1 41 32N 88 5W
Joliette, *Canada* 70 C5 46 3N 73 24W
Jolo, *Phil.* 37 C6 6 0N 121 0 E
Jolon, *U.S.A.* 84 K5 35 58N 121 9W
Jombang, *Indonesia* 37 G15 7 33S 112 14 E
Jonava, *Lithuania* 9 J21 55 8N 24 12 E
Jones Sound, *Canada* 4 B3 76 0N 85 0W
Jonesboro, *Ark., U.S.A.* 81 H9 35 50N 90 42W
Jonesboro, *La., U.S.A.* 81 J8 32 15N 92 43W
Joniškis, *Lithuania* 9 H20 56 13N 23 35 E
Jönköping, *Sweden* 9 H16 57 45N 14 8 E
Jonquière, *Canada* 71 C5 48 27N 71 14W
Joplin, *U.S.A.* 81 G7 37 6N 94 31W
Jora, *India* 42 F6 26 20N 77 49 E
Jordan, *Mont., U.S.A.* 82 C10 47 19N 106 55W
Jordan, *N.Y., U.S.A.* 79 C8 43 4N 76 29W
Jordan ■, *Asia* 47 E5 31 0N 36 0 E
Jordan →, *Asia* 47 D4 31 48N 35 32 E
Jordan Valley, *U.S.A.* 82 E5 42 59N 117 3W
Jorhat, *India* 41 F19 26 45N 94 12 E
Jörn, *Sweden* 8 D19 65 4N 20 1 E
Jorong, *Indonesia* 36 E4 3 58S 114 56 E
Jørpeland, *Norway* 9 G11 59 3N 6 1 E
Jorquera →, *Chile* 94 B2 28 3S 69 58W
Jos, *Nigeria* 50 G7 9 53N 8 51 E
José Batlle y Ordóñez, *Uruguay* 95 C4 33 20S 55 10W
Joseph, L., *Nfld., Canada* 71 B6 52 45N 65 18W
Joseph, L., *Ont., Canada* 78 A5 45 10N 79 44W
Joseph Bonaparte G., *Australia* 60 B4 14 35S 128 50 E
Joshinath, *India* 43 D8 30 34N 79 34 E
Joshua Tree, *U.S.A.* 85 L10 34 8N 116 19W
Joshua Tree National Park, *U.S.A.* 85 M10 33 55N 116 0W
Jostedalsbreen, *Norway* 9 F12 61 40N 6 59 E
Jotunheimen, *Norway* 9 F13 61 35N 8 25 E
Jourdanton, *U.S.A.* 81 L5 28 55N 98 33W
Jovellanos, *Cuba* 88 B3 22 40N 81 10W
Ju Xian, *China* 35 F10 36 35N 118 20 E
Juan Aldama, *Mexico* 86 C4 24 20N 103 23W
Juan Bautista Alberdi, *Argentina* 94 C3 34 26S 61 48W
Juan de Fuca Str., *Canada* 84 B3 48 15N 124 0W
Juan de Nova, *Ind. Oc.* 57 B7 17 3S 43 45 E
Juan Fernández, Arch. de, *Pac. Oc.* 90 G2 33 50S 80 0W
Juan José Castelli, *Argentina* 94 B3 25 27S 60 57W
Juan L. Lacaze, *Uruguay* 94 C4 34 26S 57 25W
Juankoski, *Finland* 8 E23 63 3N 28 19 E
Juárez, *Argentina* 94 D4 37 40S 59 43W
Juárez, *Mexico* 85 N11 32 20N 115 57W
Juárez, Sierra de, *Mexico* 86 A1 32 0N 116 0W
Juàzeiro, *Brazil* 93 E10 9 30S 40 30W
Juàzeiro do Norte, *Brazil* 93 E11 7 10S 39 18W
Juba, *Sudan* 51 H12 4 50N 31 35 E
Jubayl, *Lebanon* 47 A4 34 5N 35 39 E
Jubbah, *Si. Arabia* 44 D4 28 2N 40 56 E
Jubbal, *India* 42 D7 31 5N 77 40 E
Jubbulpore = Jabalpur, *India* 43 H8 23 9N 79 58 E
Jubilee L., *Australia* 61 E4 29 0S 126 50 E
Juby, C., *Morocco* 50 C3 28 0N 12 59W
Júcar = Xúquer →, *Spain* 19 C5 39 5N 0 10W
Júcaro, *Cuba* 88 B4 21 37N 78 51W
Juchitán, *Mexico* 87 D5 16 27N 95 5W
Judaea = Har Yehuda, *Israel* 47 D3 31 35N 34 57 E
Judith →, *U.S.A.* 82 C9 47 44N 109 39W
Judith, Pt., *U.S.A.* 79 E13 41 22N 71 29W
Judith Gap, *U.S.A.* 82 C9 46 41N 109 45W
Jugoslavia = Yugoslavia ■, *Europe* 21 B9 43 20N 20 0 E
Juigalpa, *Nic.* 88 D2 12 6N 85 26W
Juiz de Fora, *Brazil* 95 A7 21 43S 43 19W
Jujuy □, *Argentina* 94 A2 23 20S 65 40W
Julesburg, *U.S.A.* 80 E3 40 59N 102 16W
Juli, *Peru* 92 G5 16 10S 69 25W
Julia Cr. →, *Australia* 62 C3 20 0S 141 11 E
Julia Creek, *Australia* 62 C3 20 39S 141 44 E
Juliaca, *Peru* 92 G4 15 25S 70 10W
Julian, *U.S.A.* 85 M10 33 4N 116 38W
Julian L., *Canada* 70 B4 54 25N 77 57W
Julianatop, *Surinam* 93 C7 3 40N 56 30W
Julianehåb, *Greenland* 4 C5 60 43N 46 0W
Julimes, *Mexico* 86 B3 28 25N 105 27W
Jullundur, *India* 42 D6 31 20N 75 40 E
Julu, *China* 34 F8 37 15N 115 2 E
Jumbo, *Zimbabwe* 55 F3 17 30S 30 58 E
Jumbo Pk., *U.S.A.* 85 J12 36 12N 114 11W
Jumentos Cays, *Bahamas* 88 B4 23 0N 75 40W
Jumilla, *Spain* 19 C5 38 28N 1 19W
Jumla, *Nepal* 43 E10 29 15N 82 13 E
Jumna = Yamuna →, *India* 43 G9 25 30N 81 53 E
Junagadh, *India* 42 J4 21 30N 70 30 E
Junction, *Tex., U.S.A.* 81 K5 30 29N 99 46W
Junction, *Utah, U.S.A.* 83 G7 38 14N 112 13W
Junction B., *Australia* 62 A1 11 52S 133 55 E
Junction City, *Kans., U.S.A.* 80 F6 39 2N 96 50W
Junction City, *Oreg., U.S.A.* 82 D2 44 13N 123 12W
Junction Pt., *Australia* 62 A1 11 45S 133 50 E
Jundah, *Australia* 62 C3 24 46S 143 2 E
Jundiaí, *Brazil* 95 A6 24 30S 47 0W
Juneau, *U.S.A.* 72 B2 58 18N 134 25W
Junee, *Australia* 63 E4 34 53S 147 35 E
Jungfrau, *Switz.* 18 C7 46 32N 7 58 E
Junggar Pendi, *China* 32 B3 44 30N 86 0 E
Jungshahi, *Pakistan* 42 G2 24 52N 67 44 E
Juniata →, *U.S.A.* 78 F7 40 30N 77 40W
Junín, *Argentina* 94 C3 34 33S 60 57W
Junín de los Andes, *Argentina* 96 D2 39 45S 71 0W
Jūniyah, *Lebanon* 47 B4 33 59N 35 38 E
Juntas, *Chile* 94 B2 28 24S 69 58W
Juntura, *U.S.A.* 82 E4 43 45N 118 5W
Jur, Nahr el →, *Sudan* 51 G11 8 45N 29 15 E
Jura = Jura, Mts. du, *Europe* 18 C7 46 40N 6 5 E
Jura = Schwäbische Alb, *Germany* 16 D5 48 20N 9 30 E
Jura, *U.K.* 12 F3 56 0N 5 50W
Jura, Mts. du, *Europe* 18 C7 46 40N 6 5 E
Jura, Sd. of, *U.K.* 12 F3 55 57N 5 45W
Jurbarkas, *Lithuania* 9 J20 55 4N 22 46 E
Jurien, *Australia* 61 F2 30 18S 115 2 E
Jūrmala, *Latvia* 9 H20 56 58N 23 34 E
Juruá →, *Brazil* 92 D5 2 37S 65 44W
Juruena, *Brazil* 92 F7 13 0S 58 10W

Juruena

Juruena →, *Brazil* **92 E7** 7 20S 58 3W
Juruti, *Brazil* **93 D7** 2 9S 56 4W
Justo Daract, *Argentina* . . . **94 C2** 33 52S 65 12W
Jutaí →, *Brazil* **92 D5** 2 43S 66 57W
Juticalpa, *Honduras* **88 D2** 14 40N 86 12W
Jutland = Jylland, *Denmark* **9 H13** 56 25N 9 30 E
Juventud, I. de la, *Cuba* . . . **88 B3** 21 40N 82 40W
Juwain, *Afghan.* . . . . **40 D2** 31 45N 61 30 E
Jūy Zar, *Iran* . . . . **44 C5** 33 50N 46 18 E
Juye, *China* . . . . **34 G9** 35 22N 116 5 E
Jwaneng, *Botswana* . . . . . . **53 J4** 24 45S 24 50 E
Jylland, *Denmark* . . . . **9 H13** 56 25N 9 30 E
Jyväskylä, *Finland* . . . . **9 E21** 62 14N 25 50 E

K

K2, *Pakistan* . . . . **43 B7** 35 58N 76 32 E
Kaap Plateau, *S. Africa* . . . . **56 D3** 28 30S 24 0 E
Kaapkruis, *Namibia* . . . . **56 C1** 21 55S 13 57 E
Kaapstad = Cape Town, *S. Africa* . . . . **56 E2** 33 55S 18 22 E
Kabaena, *Indonesia* . . . . . . **37 F6** 5 15S 122 0 E
Kabala, *S. Leone* **50 G3** 9 38N 11 37W
Kabale, *Uganda* . . . . **54 C3** 1 15S 30 0 E
Kabalo, *Dem. Rep. of the Congo* . **54 D2** 6 0S 27 0 E
Kabambare, *Dem. Rep. of the Congo* . **54 C2** 4 41S 27 39 E
Kabango, *Dem. Rep. of the Congo* . **55 D2** 8 35S 28 30 E
Kabanjahe, *Indonesia* . . . . . **36 D1** 3 6N 98 30 E
Kabardino-Balkar Republic = Kabardino-Balkaria □, *Russia* . . . . **25 F7** 43 30N 43 30 E
Kabardino-Balkaria □, *Russia* . . . . **25 F7** 43 30N 43 30 E
Kabarega Falls = Murchison Falls, *Uganda* . . . . **54 B3** 2 15N 31 30 E
Kabasalan, *Phil.* . . . . **37 C6** 7 47N 122 44 E
Kabetogama, *U.S.A.* **80 A8** 48 28N 92 59W
Kabin Buri, *Thailand* . . . . . . **38 F3** 13 57N 101 43 E
Kabinakagami L., *Canada* . . **70 C3** 48 54N 84 25W
Kabinda, *Dem. Rep. of the Congo* . **52 F4** 6 19S 24 20 E
Kabompo, *Zambia* . . . . **55 E1** 13 36S 24 14 E
Kabompo →, *Zambia* . . . . **53 G4** 14 10S 23 11 E
Kabondo, *Dem. Rep. of the Congo* . **55 D2** 8 58S 25 40 E
Kabongo, *Dem. Rep. of the Congo* . **54 D2** 7 22S 25 33 E
Kabūd Gonbad, *Iran* . . . . . . **45 B8** 37 5N 59 45 E
Kābul, *Afghan.* . . . . **42 B3** 34 28N 69 11 E
Kābul □, *Afghan.* . . . . **40 B6** 34 30N 69 0 E
Kabul →, *Pakistan* . . . . . . **42 C5** 33 55N 72 14 E
Kabunga, *Dem. Rep. of the Congo* . **54 C2** 1 38S 28 3 E
Kaburuang, *Indonesia* . . . . **37 D7** 3 50N 126 30 E
Kabwe, *Zambia* . . . . **55 E2** 14 30S 28 29 E
Kachchh, Gulf of, *India* . . . . **42 H3** 22 50N 69 15 E
Kachchh, Rann of, *India* . . . **42 H4** 24 0N 70 0 E
Kachchhidhana, *India* . . . . . **43 J8** 21 44N 78 46 E
Kachebera, *Zambia* . . . . **55 E3** 13 50S 32 50 E
Kachin □, *Burma* . . . . **41 G20** 26 0N 97 30 E
Kachira, L., *Uganda* . . . . . . **54 C3** 0 40S 31 7 E
Kachiry, *Kazakstan* . . . . **26 D8** 53 10N 75 50 E
Kachnara, *India* . . . . **42 H6** 23 50N 75 6 E
Kachot, *Cambodia* . . . . **39 G4** 11 30N 103 3 E
Kaçkar, *Turkey* . . . . **25 F7** 40 45N 41 10 E
Kadan Kyun, *Burma* . . . . . . **38 F2** 12 30N 98 20 E
Kadanai →, *Afghan.* . . . . . . **42 D1** 31 22N 65 45 E
Kadi, *India* . . . . **42 H5** 23 18N 72 23 E
Kadina, *Australia* . . . . **63 E2** 33 55S 137 43 E
Kadipur, *India* . . . . **43 F10** 26 10N 82 23 E
Kadirli, *Turkey* . . . . **44 B3** 37 23N 36 5 E
Kadiyevka = Stakhanov, *Ukraine* . . . . **25 E6** 48 35N 38 40 E
Kadoka, *U.S.A.* **80 D4** 43 50N 101 31W
Kadoma, *Zimbabwe* . . . . **55 F2** 18 20S 29 52 E
Kâdugli, *Sudan* . . . . **51 F11** 11 0N 29 45 E
Kaduna, *Nigeria* . . . . **50 F7** 10 30N 7 21 E
Kaédi, *Mauritania* **50 E3** 16 9N 13 28W
Kaeng Khoi, *Thailand* . . . . . **38 E3** 14 35N 101 0 E
Kaesŏng, *N. Korea* . . . . **35 F14** 37 58N 126 35 E
Kāf, *Si. Arabia* . . . . **44 D3** 31 25N 37 29 E
Kafan = Kapan, *Armenia* . . **25 G8** 39 18N 46 27 E
Kafanchan, *Nigeria* . . . . **50 G7** 9 40N 8 20 E
Kafinda, *Zambia* . . . . **55 E3** 12 32S 30 20 E
Kafirévs, Ákra, *Greece* . . . . **21 E11** 38 9N 24 38 E
Kafue, *Zambia* . . . . **55 F2** 15 46S 28 9 E
Kafue →, *Zambia* . . . . **53 H5** 15 30S 29 0 E
Kafue Flats, *Zambia* . . . . . . **55 F2** 15 40S 27 25 E
Kafue Nat. Park, *Zambia* . . . **55 F2** 15 0S 25 30 E
Kafulwe, *Zambia* . . . . **55 D2** 9 0S 29 1 E
Kaga, *Afghan.* . . . . **42 B4** 34 14N 70 10 E
Kaga Bandoro, *C.A.R.* . . . . . **52 C3** 7 0N 19 10 E
Kagan, *Uzbekistan* . . . . **26 F7** 39 43N 64 33 E
Kagawa □, *Japan* . . . . **31 G7** 34 15N 134 0 E
Kagera □, *Tanzania* . . . . . . **54 C3** 2 0S 31 30 E
Kagera →, *Uganda* . . . . **54 C3** 0 57S 31 47 E
Kağızman, *Turkey* . . . . **44 A4** 40 5N 43 10 E
Kagoshima, *Japan* . . . . **31 J5** 31 35N 130 33 E
Kagoshima □, *Japan* . . . . . **31 J5** 31 30N 130 30 E
Kagul = Cahul, *Moldova* . . **17 F15** 45 50N 28 15 E
Kahak, *Iran* . . . . **45 B6** 36 6N 49 46 E
Kahama, *Tanzania* . . . . **54 C3** 4 8S 32 30 E
Kahan, *Pakistan* . . . . **42 E3** 29 18N 68 54 E
Kahang, *Malaysia* . . . . **39 L4** 2 12N 103 32 E
Kahayan →, *Indonesia* . . . . **36 E4** 3 40S 114 0 E
Kahe, *Tanzania* . . . . **54 C4** 3 30S 37 25 E
Kahnūj, *Iran* . . . . **45 E8** 27 55N 57 40 E
Kahoka, *U.S.A.* **80 E9** 40 25N 91 44W
Kahoolawe, *U.S.A.* **74 H16** 20 33N 156 37W
Kahramanmaraş, *Turkey* . . **25 G6** 37 37N 36 53 E
Kahuta, *Pakistan* . . . . **42 C5** 33 35N 73 24 E
Kai, Kepulauan, *Indonesia* . **37 F8** 5 55S 132 45 E
Kai Besar, *Indonesia* . . . . . . **37 F8** 5 35S 133 0 E
Kai Is. = Kai, Kepulauan, *Indonesia* . . . . **37 F8** 5 55S 132 45 E
Kai Kecil, *Indonesia* . . . . . . **37 F8** 5 45S 132 40 E
Kaiapoi, *N.Z.* . . . . **59 K4** 43 24S 172 40 E
Kaieteur Falls, *Guyana* **92 B7** 5 1N 59 10W
Kaifeng, *China* . . . . **34 G8** 34 48N 114 21 E
Kaikohe, *N.Z.* . . . . **59 F4** 35 25S 173 49 E
Kaikoura, *N.Z.* . . . . **59 K4** 42 25S 173 43 E
Kaikoura Ra., *N.Z.* . . . . **59 J4** 41 59S 173 41 E
Kailu, *China* . . . . **35 C11** 43 38N 121 18 E
Kailua Kona, *U.S.A.* **74 J17** 19 39N 155 59W
Kaimana, *Indonesia* . . . . . . **37 E8** 3 39S 133 45 E
Kaimanawa Mts., *N.Z.* . . . . **59 H5** 39 15S 175 56 E
Kaimganj, *India* . . . . **43 F8** 27 33N 79 24 E
Kaimur Hills, *India* . . . . **43 G10** 24 30N 82 0 E
Kaingaroa Forest, *N.Z.* . . . . **59 H6** 38 24S 176 30 E
Kainji Res., *Nigeria* . . . . **50 F6** 10 1N 4 40 E
Kainuu, *Finland* . . . . **8 D23** 64 30N 29 7 E
Kaipara Harbour, *N.Z.* . . . . . **59 G5** 36 25S 174 14 E
Kaipokok B., *Canada* **71 B8** 54 54N 59 47W
Kaira, *India* . . . . **42 H5** 22 45N 72 50 E
Kairana, *India* . . . . **42 E7** 29 24N 77 15 E
Kaironi, *Indonesia* . . . . **37 E8** 0 47S 133 40 E
Kairouan, *Tunisia* . . . . **51 A8** 35 45N 10 5 E
Kaiserslautern, *Germany* . . **16 D4** 49 26N 7 45 E
Kaitaia, *N.Z.* . . . . **59 F4** 35 8S 173 17 E
Kaitangata, *N.Z.* . . . . **59 M2** 46 17S 169 51 E
Kaithal, *India* . . . . **42 E7** 29 48N 76 26 E
Kaitu →, *Pakistan* . . . . **42 C4** 33 10N 70 30 E
Kaiwi Channel, *U.S.A.* **74 H16** 21 15N 157 30W
Kaiyuan, *China* . . . . **35 C13** 42 28N 124 1 E
Kajaani, *Finland* . . . . **8 D22** 64 17N 27 46 E
Kajabbi, *Australia* . . . . **62 C3** 20 0S 140 1 E
Kajana = Kajaani, *Finland* . **8 D22** 64 17N 27 46 E
Kajang, *Malaysia* . . . . **39 L3** 2 59N 101 48 E
Kajiado, *Kenya* . . . . **54 C4** 1 53S 36 48 E
Kajo Kaji, *Sudan* . . . . **51 H12** 3 58N 31 40 E
Kakabeka Falls, *Canada* . . . **70 C2** 48 24N 89 37W
Kakadu Nat. Park, *Australia* **60 B5** 12 30S 132 5 E
Kakamas, *S. Africa* . . . . **56 D3** 28 45S 20 33 E
Kakamega, *Kenya* . . . . **54 B3** 0 20N 34 46 E
Kakanui Mts., *N.Z.* . . . . **59 L3** 45 10S 170 30 E
Kakdwip, *India* . . . . **43 J13** 21 53N 88 11 E
Kake, *Japan* . . . . **31 G6** 34 36N 132 19 E
Kake, *U.S.A.* **72 B2** 56 59N 133 57W
Kakegawa, *Japan* . . . . **31 G9** 34 45N 138 1 E
Kakeroma-Jima, *Japan* . . . . **31 K4** 28 8N 129 14 E
Kakhovka, *Ukraine* . . . . **25 E5** 46 45N 33 30 E
Kakhovske Vdskh., *Ukraine* . **25 E5** 47 5N 34 0 E
Kakinada, *India* . . . . **41 L13** 16 57N 82 11 E
Kakisa →, *Canada* **72 A5** 61 3N 118 10W
Kakisa L., *Canada* **72 A5** 60 56N 117 43W
Kakogawa, *Japan* . . . . **31 G7** 34 46N 134 51 E
Kakwa →, *Canada* **72 C5** 54 37N 118 28W
Kāl Gūsheh, *Iran* . . . . **45 D8** 30 59N 58 12 E
Kal Safīd, *Iran* . . . . **44 C5** 34 52N 47 23 E
Kalabagh, *Pakistan* . . . . **42 C4** 33 0N 71 28 E
Kalabahi, *Indonesia* . . . . **37 F6** 8 13S 124 31 E
Kalach, *Russia* . . . . **25 D7** 50 22N 41 0 E
Kaladan →, *Burma* . . . . **41 J18** 20 20N 93 5 E
Kaladar, *Canada* **78 B7** 44 37N 77 5W
Kalahari, *Africa* . . . . **56 C3** 24 0S 21 30 E
Kalahari Gemsbok Nat. Park, *S. Africa* . . . . **56 D3** 25 30S 20 30 E
Kalajoki, *Finland* . . . . **8 D20** 64 12N 24 10 E
Kālak, *Iran* . . . . **45 E8** 25 29N 59 22 E
Kalakamati, *Botswana* . . . . . **57 C4** 20 40S 27 25 E
Kalakan, *Russia* . . . . **27 D12** 55 15N 116 45 E
K'alak'unlun Shank'ou, *Pakistan* . . . . **43 B7** 35 33N 77 46 E
Kalam, *Pakistan* . . . . **43 B5** 35 34N 72 30 E
Kalama, *Dem. Rep. of the Congo* . **54 C2** 2 52S 28 35 E
Kalama, *U.S.A.* **84 E4** 46 1N 122 51W
Kalámai, *Greece* . . . . **21 F10** 37 3N 22 10 E
Kalamata = Kalámai, *Greece* **21 F10** 37 3N 22 10 E
Kalamazoo, *U.S.A.* **76 D3** 42 17N 85 35W
Kalamazoo →, *U.S.A.* **76 D2** 42 40N 86 10W
Kalambo Falls, *Tanzania* . . . **55 D3** 8 37S 31 35 E
Kalan, *Turkey* . . . . **44 B3** 39 7N 39 32 E
Kalannie, *Australia* . . . . **61 F2** 30 22S 117 5 E
Kalāntarī, *Iran* . . . . **45 C7** 32 10N 54 8 E
Kalao, *Indonesia* . . . . **37 F6** 7 21S 121 0 E
Kalaotoa, *Indonesia* . . . . **37 F6** 7 20S 121 50 E
Kalasin, *Thailand* . . . . **38 D4** 16 26N 103 30 E
Kalat, *Pakistan* . . . . **40 E5** 29 8N 66 31 E
Kalāteh, *Iran* . . . . **45 B7** 36 33N 55 41 E
Kalāteh-ye Ganj, *Iran* . . . . . **45 E8** 27 31N 57 55 E
Kalbarri, *Australia* . . . . **61 E1** 27 40S 114 10 E
Kalce, *Slovenia* . . . . **16 F8** 45 54N 14 13 E
Kale, *Turkey* . . . . **21 F13** 37 27N 28 49 E
Kalegauk Kyun, *Burma* . . . . **41 M20** 15 33N 97 35 E
Kalehe, *Dem. Rep. of the Congo* . **54 C2** 2 6S 28 50 E
Kalema, *Tanzania* . . . . **54 C3** 1 12S 31 55 E
Kalemie, *Dem. Rep. of the Congo* . **54 D2** 5 55S 29 9 E
Kalewa, *Burma* . . . . **41 H19** 23 10N 94 15 E
Kaleybar, *Iran* . . . . **44 B5** 38 47N 47 2 E
Kalgan = Zhangjiakou, *China* . . . . **34 D8** 40 48N 114 55 E
Kalgoorlie-Boulder, *Australia* **61 F3** 30 40S 121 22 E
Kali →, *India* . . . . **43 F8** 27 6N 79 55 E
Kali Sindh →, *India* . . . . . . **42 G6** 25 32N 76 17 E
Kaliakra, Nos, *Bulgaria* . . . . **21 C13** 43 21N 28 30 E
Kalianda, *Indonesia* . . . . **36 F3** 5 50S 105 45 E
Kalibo, *Phil.* . . . . **37 B6** 11 43N 122 22 E
Kalima, *Dem. Rep. of the Congo* . **54 C2** 2 33S 26 32 E
Kalimantan □, *Indonesia* . . . **36 E4** 0 0 114 0 E
Kalimantan Barat □, *Indonesia* . . . . **36 E4** 0 0 110 30 E
Kalimantan Selatan □, *Indonesia* . . . . **36 E5** 2 30S 115 30 E
Kalimantan Tengah □, *Indonesia* . . . . **36 E4** 2 0S 113 30 E
Kalimantan Timur □, *Indonesia* . . . . **36 D5** 1 30N 116 30 E
Kálimnos, *Greece* . . . . **21 F12** 37 0N 27 0 E
Kalimpong, *India* . . . . **43 F13** 27 4N 88 35 E
Kalinin = Tver, *Russia* . . . . **24 C6** 56 55N 35 55 E
Kaliningrad, *Russia* . . . . **9 J19** 54 42N 20 32 E
Kalinkavichy, *Belarus* . . . . . **17 B15** 52 12N 29 20 E
Kalinkovichi = Kalinkavichy, *Belarus* . . . . **17 B15** 52 12N 29 20 E
Kaliro, *Uganda* . . . . **54 B3** 0 56N 33 30 E
Kalispell, *U.S.A.* **82 B6** 48 12N 114 19W
Kalisz, *Poland* . . . . **17 C10** 51 45N 18 8 E
Kaliua, *Tanzania* . . . . **54 D3** 5 5S 31 48 E
Kalix, *Sweden* . . . . **8 D20** 65 53N 23 12 E
Kalix →, *Sweden* . . . . **8 D20** 65 50N 23 11 E
Kalka, *India* . . . . **42 D7** 30 46N 76 57 E
Kalkarindji, *Australia* . . . . . . **60 C5** 17 30S 130 47 E
Kalkaska, *U.S.A.* **76 C3** 44 44N 85 11W
Kalkfeld, *Namibia* . . . . **56 C2** 20 57S 16 14 E
Kalkfontein, *Botswana* . . . . **56 C3** 22 4S 20 57 E
Kalkrand, *Namibia* . . . . **56 C2** 24 1S 17 35 E
Kallavesi, *Finland* . . . . **8 E22** 62 58N 27 30 E
Kallsjön, *Sweden* . . . . **8 E15** 63 38N 13 0 E
Kalmar, *Sweden* . . . . **9 H17** 56 40N 16 20 E
Kalmyk Republic = Kalmykia □, *Russia* . . . . . **25 E8** 46 5N 46 1 E
Kalmykia □, *Russia* . . . . **25 E8** 46 5N 46 1 E
Kalmykovo, *Kazakstan* . . . . **25 E9** 49 0N 51 47 E
Kalna, *India* . . . . **43 H13** 23 13N 88 25 E
Kalnai, *India* . . . . **43 H10** 22 46N 83 30 E
Kalocsa, *Hungary* . . . . **17 E10** 46 32N 19 0 E
Kalokhorio, *Cyprus* . . . . **23 E12** 34 51N 33 2 E
Kaloko, *Dem. Rep. of the Congo* . **54 D2** 6 47S 25 48 E
Kalol, *Gujarat, India* . . . . . . **42 H5** 22 37N 73 31 E
Kalol, *Gujarat, India* . . . . . . **42 H5** 23 15N 72 33 E
Kalomo, *Zambia* . . . . **55 F2** 17 0S 26 30 E
Kalpi, *India* . . . . **43 F8** 26 8N 79 47 E
Kalu, *Pakistan* . . . . **42 G2** 25 5N 67 39 E
Kaluga, *Russia* . . . . **24 D6** 54 35N 36 10 E
Kalulushi, *Zambia* . . . . **55 E2** 12 50S 28 3 E
Kalundborg, *Denmark* . . . . . **9 J14** 55 41N 11 5 E
Kalush, *Ukraine* . . . . **17 D13** 49 3N 24 23 E
Kalutara, *Sri Lanka* . . . . **40 R12** 6 35N 80 0 E
Kalya, *Russia* . . . . **24 B10** 60 15N 59 59 E
Kama, *Dem. Rep. of the Congo* . **54 C2** 3 30S 27 5 E
Kama →, *Russia* . . . . **24 C9** 55 45N 52 0 E
Kamachumu, *Tanzania* . . . . . **54 C3** 1 37S 31 37 E
Kamaishi, *Japan* . . . . **30 E10** 39 16N 141 53 E
Kamalia, *Pakistan* . . . . **42 D5** 30 44N 72 42 E
Kaman, *India* . . . . **42 F6** 27 39N 77 16 E
Kamapanda, *Zambia* . . . . . . **55 E1** 12 5S 24 0 E
Kamaran, *Yemen* . . . . **46 D3** 15 21N 42 35 E
Kamativi, *Zimbabwe* . . . . . . **55 F2** 18 15S 27 27 E
Kambalda, *Australia* . . . . . . **61 F3** 31 10S 121 37 E
Kambar, *Pakistan* . . . . **42 F3** 27 37N 68 1 E
Kambarka, *Russia* . . . . **24 C9** 56 15N 54 11 E
Kambolé, *Zambia* . . . . **55 D3** 8 47S 30 48 E
Kambos, *Cyprus* . . . . **23 D11** 35 2N 32 44 E
Kambove, *Dem. Rep. of the Congo* . **55 E2** 10 51S 26 33 E
Kamchatka, Poluostrov, *Russia* . . . . **27 D17** 57 0N 160 0 E
Kamchatka Pen. = Kamchatka, Poluostrov, *Russia* . . . . **27 D17** 57 0N 160 0 E
Kamchiya →, *Bulgaria* . . . **21 C12** 43 4N 27 44 E
Kamen, *Russia* . . . . **26 D9** 53 50N 81 30 E
Kamen-Rybolov, *Russia* . . . **30 B6** 44 46N 132 2 E
Kamenjak, Rt., *Croatia* . . . . **16 F7** 44 47N 13 55 E
Kamenka, *Russia* . . . . **24 A7** 65 58N 44 0 E
Kamenka Bugskaya = Kamyanka-Buzka, *Ukraine* **17 C13** 50 8N 24 16 E
Kamensk Uralskiy, *Russia* . . **26 D7** 56 25N 62 2 E
Kamenskoye, *Russia* . . . . . . **27 C17** 62 45N 165 30 E
Kameoka, *Japan* . . . . **31 G7** 35 0N 135 35 E
Kamiah, *U.S.A.* **82 C5** 46 14N 116 2W
Kamieskroon, *S. Africa* . . . . **56 E2** 30 9S 17 56 E
Kamilukuak, L., *Canada* **73 A8** 62 22N 101 40W
Kamin-Kashyrskyy, *Ukraine* **17 C13** 51 39N 24 56 E
Kamina, *Dem. Rep. of the Congo* . **55 D2** 8 45S 25 0 E
Kaminak L., *Canada* **73 A10** 62 10N 95 0W
Kaministiquia, *Canada* **70 C1** 48 32N 89 35W
Kaminoyama, *Japan* . . . . **30 E10** 38 9N 140 17 E
Kamiros, *Greece* . . . . **23 C9** 36 20N 27 56 E
Kamituga, *Dem. Rep. of the Congo* . **54 C2** 3 2S 28 10 E
Kamla →, *India* . . . . **43 G12** 25 35N 86 36 E
Kamloops, *Canada* **72 C4** 50 40N 120 20W
Kamo, *Japan* . . . . **30 F9** 37 39N 139 3 E
Kamoke, *Pakistan* . . . . **42 C6** 32 4N 74 4 E
Kampala, *Uganda* . . . . **54 B3** 0 20N 32 30 E
Kampang Chhnang, *Cambodia* . . . . **39 F5** 12 20N 104 35 E
Kampar, *Malaysia* . . . . **39 K3** 4 18N 101 9 E
Kampar →, *Indonesia* . . . . . **36 D2** 0 30N 103 8 E
Kampen, *Neths.* . . . . **15 B5** 52 33N 5 53 E
Kampene, *Dem. Rep. of the Congo* . **52 E5** 3 36S 26 40 E
Kamphaeng Phet, *Thailand* . **38 D2** 16 28N 99 30 E
Kampolombo, L., *Zambia* . . . **55 E2** 11 37S 29 42 E
Kampong Saom, *Cambodia* . **39 G4** 10 38N 103 30 E
Kampong Saom, Chaak, *Cambodia* . . . . **36 B2** 10 45N 103 30 E
Kampong Saom, Chaak, *Cambodia* . . . . **39 G4** 10 50N 103 32 E
Kampong To, *Thailand* . . . . . **39 J3** 6 3N 101 13 E
Kampot, *Cambodia* . . . . **39 G5** 10 36N 104 10 E
Kampuchea = Cambodia ■, *Asia* . . . . **38 F5** 12 15N 105 0 E
Kampung Air Putih, *Malaysia* . . . . **39 K4** 4 15N 103 10 E
Kampung Jerangau, *Malaysia* . . . . **39 K4** 4 50N 103 10 E
Kampung Raja, *Malaysia* . . . **39 K4** 5 45N 102 35 E
Kampungbaru = Tolitoli, *Indonesia* . . . . **37 D6** 1 5N 120 50 E
Kamrau, Teluk, *Indonesia* . . **37 E8** 3 30S 133 36 E
Kamsack, *Canada* **73 C8** 51 34N 101 54W
Kamskoye Vdkhr., *Russia* . . **24 C10** 58 41N 56 7 E
Kamuchawie L., *Canada* **73 B8** 56 18N 101 59W
Kamuela, *U.S.A.* **74 H17** 20 1N 155 41W
Kamui-Misaki, *Japan* . . . . . . **30 C10** 43 20N 140 21 E
Kamyanets-Podilskyy, *Ukraine* . . . . **17 D14** 48 45N 26 40 E
Kamyanka-Buzka, *Ukraine* . . **17 C13** 50 8N 24 16 E
Kāmyārān, *Iran* . . . . **44 C5** 34 47N 46 56 E
Kamyshin, *Russia* . . . . **25 D8** 50 10N 45 24 E
Kanaaupscow, *Canada* **70 B4** 54 2N 76 30W
Kanaaupscow →, *Canada* . . **69 C12** 53 39N 77 9W
Kanab, *U.S.A.* **83 H7** 37 3N 112 32W
Kanab →, *U.S.A.* **83 H7** 36 24N 112 38W
Kanagi, *Japan* . . . . **30 D10** 40 54N 140 27 E
Kanairiktok →, *Canada* . . . **71 A7** 55 2N 60 18W
Kananga, *Dem. Rep. of the Congo* . **52 F4** 5 55S 22 18 E
Kanash, *Russia* . . . . **24 C8** 55 30N 47 32 E
Kanaskat, *U.S.A.* **84 C5** 47 19N 121 54W
Kanastraíon, Ákra = Paliouríon, Ákra, *Greece* . **21 E10** 39 57N 23 45 E
Kanawha →, *U.S.A.* **76 F4** 38 50N 82 9W
Kanazawa, *Japan* . . . . **31 F8** 36 30N 136 38 E
Kanchanaburi, *Thailand* . . . . **38 E2** 14 2N 99 31 E
Kanchenjunga, *Nepal* . . . . . **43 F13** 27 50N 88 10 E
Kanchipuram, *India* . . . . **40 N11** 12 52N 79 45 E
Kandaghat, *India* . . . . **42 D7** 30 59N 77 7 E
Kandahar = Qandahār, *Afghan.* . . . . **40 D4** 31 32N 65 30 E
Kandalaksha, *Russia* . . . . . . **24 A5** 67 9N 32 30 E
Kandalakshkiy Zaliv, *Russia* **24 A6** 66 0N 35 0 E
Kandalu, *Afghan.* . . . . **40 E3** 29 55N 63 20 E
Kandangan, *Indonesia* . . . . . **36 E5** 2 50S 115 20 E
Kandanghaur, *Indonesia* . . . **37 G13** 6 21S 108 6 E
Kandanos, *Greece* . . . . **23 D5** 35 19N 23 44 E
Kandhkot, *Pakistan* . . . . **42 E3** 28 16N 69 8 E
Kandhla, *India* . . . . **42 E7** 29 18N 77 19 E
Kandi, *Benin* . . . . **50 F6** 11 7N 2 55 E
Kandi, *India* . . . . **43 H13** 23 58N 88 5 E
Kandiaro, *Pakistan* . . . . **42 F3** 27 4N 68 13 E
Kandla, *India* . . . . **42 H4** 23 0N 70 10 E
Kandos, *Australia* . . . . **63 E4** 32 45S 149 58 E
Kandy, *Sri Lanka* . . . . **40 R12** 7 18N 80 43 E
Kane, *U.S.A.* **78 E6** 41 40N 78 49W
Kane Basin, *Greenland* **4 B4** 79 1N 70 0W
Kaneohe, *U.S.A.* **74 H16** 21 25N 157 48W
Kangān, *Fārs, Iran* . . . . **45 E7** 27 50N 52 3 E
Kangān, *Hormozgān, Iran* . . **45 E8** 25 48N 57 28 E
Kangar, *Malaysia* . . . . **39 J3** 6 27N 100 12 E
Kangaroo I., *Australia* . . . . . **63 F2** 35 45S 137 0 E
Kangaroo Mts., *Australia* . . **62 C3** 23 29S 141 51 E
Kangasala, *Finland* . . . . **9 F21** 61 28N 24 4 E
Kangāvar, *Iran* . . . . **45 C6** 34 40N 48 0 E
Kangdong, *N. Korea* . . . . . . **35 E14** 39 9N 126 5 E
Kangean, Kepulauan, *Indonesia* . . . . **36 F5** 6 55S 115 23 E
Kangean Is. = Kangean, Kepulauan, *Indonesia* . . . . **36 F5** 6 55S 115 23 E
Kanggye, *N. Korea* . . . . **35 D14** 41 0N 126 35 E
Kanggyŏng, *S. Korea* . . . . . **35 F14** 36 10N 127 0 E
Kanghwa, *S. Korea* . . . . **35 F14** 37 45N 126 30 E
Kangiqsualujjuaq, *Canada* . **69 C13** 58 30N 65 59W
Kangiqsujuaq, *Canada* **69 B12** 61 30N 72 0W
Kangirsuk, *Canada* **69 C13** 60 0N 70 0W
Kangnŭng, *S. Korea* . . . . . . **35 F15** 37 45N 128 54 E
Kangping, *China* . . . . **35 C12** 42 43N 123 18 E
Kangra, *India* . . . . **42 C7** 32 6N 76 16 E
Kangto, *India* . . . . **41 F18** 27 50N 92 35 E
Kanhar →, *India* . . . . **43 G10** 24 28N 83 8 E
Kaniama, *Dem. Rep. of the Congo* . **54 D1** 7 30S 24 12 E
Kaniapiskau = Caniapiscau →, *Canada* **71 A6** 56 40N 69 30W
Kaniapiskau, Res. = Caniapiscau Rés. de, *Canada* **71 B6** 54 10N 69 55W
Kanin, Poluostrov, *Russia* . **24 A8** 68 0N 45 0 E
Kanin Nos, Mys, *Russia* . . . **24 A7** 68 39N 43 32 E
Kanin Pen. = Kanin, Poluostrov, *Russia* . . . . . . **24 A8** 68 0N 45 0 E
Kaniva, *Australia* . . . . **63 F3** 36 22S 141 18 E
Kanjut Sar, *Pakistan* . . . . . . **43 A6** 36 7N 75 25 E
Kankaanpää, *Finland* . . . . . **9 F20** 61 44N 22 50 E
Kankakee, *U.S.A.* **76 E2** 41 7N 87 52W
Kankakee →, *U.S.A.* **76 E1** 41 23N 88 15W
Kankan, *Guinea* **50 F4** 10 23N 9 15W
Kankendy = Xankändi, *Azerbaijan* . . . . **25 G8** 39 52N 46 49 E
Kanker, *India* . . . . **41 J12** 20 10N 81 40 E
Kankroli, *India* . . . . **42 G5** 25 4N 73 53 E
Kannapolis, *U.S.A.* **77 H5** 35 30N 80 37W
Kannauj, *India* . . . . **43 F8** 27 3N 79 56 E
Kannod, *India* . . . . **40 H10** 22 45N 76 40 E
Kano, *Nigeria* . . . . **50 F7** 12 2N 8 30 E
Kan'onji, *Japan* . . . . **31 G6** 34 7N 133 39 E
Kanowit, *Malaysia* . . . . **36 D4** 2 14N 112 20 E
Kanoya, *Japan* . . . . **31 J5** 31 25N 130 50 E
Kanpetlet, *Burma* . . . . **41 J18** 21 10N 93 59 E
Kanpur, *India* . . . . **43 F9** 26 28N 80 20 E
Kansas □, *U.S.A.* **80 F6** 38 30N 99 0W
Kansas →, *U.S.A.* **80 F7** 39 7N 94 37W
Kansas City, *Kans., U.S.A.* . . **80 F7** 39 7N 94 38W
Kansas City, *Mo., U.S.A.* . . . **80 F7** 39 6N 94 35W
Kansenia, *Dem. Rep. of the Congo* . **55 E2** 10 20S 26 0 E
Kansk, *Russia* . . . . **27 D10** 56 20N 95 37 E
Kansŏng, *S. Korea* . . . . **35 E15** 38 24N 128 30 E
Kansu = Gansu □, *China* . . **34 G3** 36 0N 104 0 E
Kantaphor, *India* . . . . **42 H7** 22 35N 76 34 E
Kantharalak, *Thailand* . . . . . **38 E5** 14 39N 104 39 E
Kantli →, *India* . . . . **42 E6** 28 20N 75 30 E
Kantō □, *Japan* . . . . **31 F9** 36 15N 139 30 E
Kantō-Sanchi, *Japan* . . . . . . **31 G9** 35 59N 138 50 E
Kanturk, *Ireland* **13 D3** 52 11N 8 54W
Kanuma, *Japan* . . . . **31 F9** 36 34N 139 42 E
Kanus, *Namibia* . . . . **56 D2** 27 50S 18 39 E
Kanye, *Botswana* . . . . **56 C4** 24 55S 25 28 E
Kanzenze, *Dem. Rep. of the Congo* . **55 E2** 10 30S 25 12 E
Kanzi, Ras, *Tanzania* . . . . . . **54 D4** 7 1S 39 33 E
Kaohsiung, *Taiwan* . . . . **33 D7** 22 35N 120 16 E
Kaokoveld, *Namibia* . . . . **56 B1** 19 15S 14 30 E
Kaolack, *Senegal* **50 F2** 14 5N 16 8W
Kaoshan, *China* . . . . **35 B13** 44 38N 124 50 E
Kapaa, *U.S.A.* **74 G15** 22 5N 159 19W
Kapadvanj, *India* . . . . **42 H5** 23 5N 73 0 E
Kapan, *Armenia* . . . . **25 G8** 39 18N 46 27 E
Kapanga, *Dem. Rep. of the Congo* . **52 F4** 8 30S 22 40 E
Kapchagai = Qapshaghay, *Kazakstan* . . . . **26 E8** 43 51N 77 14 E
Kapela = Velika Kapela, *Croatia* . . . . **16 F8** 45 10N 15 5 E
Kapema, *Dem. Rep. of the Congo* . **55 E2** 10 45S 28 22 E
Kapfenberg, *Austria* . . . . **16 E8** 47 26N 15 18 E
Kapiri Mposhi, *Zambia* . . . . **55 E2** 13 59S 28 43 E
Kapiskau →, *Canada* **70 B3** 52 47N 81 55W
Kapit, *Malaysia* . . . . **36 D4** 2 0N 112 55 E
Kapiti I., *N.Z.* . . . . **59 J5** 40 50S 174 56 E
Kaplan, *U.S.A.* **81 K8** 30 0N 92 17W
Kapoe, *Thailand* . . . . **39 H2** 9 34N 98 32 E
Kapoeta, *Sudan* . . . . **51 H12** 4 50N 33 35 E
Kaposvár, *Hungary* . . . . **17 E9** 46 25N 17 47 E
Kapowsin, *U.S.A.* **84 D4** 46 59N 122 13W
Kapps, *Namibia* . . . . **56 C2** 22 32S 17 18 E
Kapsan, *N. Korea* . . . . **35 D15** 41 4N 128 19 E
Kapsukas = Marijampole, *Lithuania* . . . . **9 J20** 54 33N 23 19 E
Kapuas →, *Indonesia* . . . . . **36 E3** 0 25S 109 20 E
Kapuas Hulu, Pegunungan, *Malaysia* . . . . **36 D4** 1 30N 113 30 E

Kentucky L.

Kapuas Hulu Ra. = Kapuas Hulu, Pegunungan, Malaysia 36 D4 1 30N 113 30 E
Kapulo, Dem. Rep. of the Congo 55 D2 8 18S 29 15 E
Kapunda, Australia 63 E2 34 20S 138 56 E
Kapuni, N.Z. 59 H5 39 29S 174 8 E
Kapurthala, India 42 D6 31 23N 75 25 E
Kapuskasing, Canada 70 C3 49 25N 82 30W
Kapuskasing —►, Canada 70 C3 49 49N 82 0W
Kaputar, Australia 63 E5 30 15S 150 10 E
Kaputir, Kenya 54 B4 2 5N 35 28 E
Kara, Russia 26 C7 69 10N 65 0 E
Kara Bogaz Gol, Zaliv = Garabogazköl Aylagy, Turkmenistan 25 F9 41 0N 53 30 E
Kara Kalpak Republic = Karakalpakstan □, Uzbekistan 26 E6 43 0N 58 0 E
Kara Kum, Turkmenistan 26 F7 39 30N 60 0 E
Kara Sea, Russia 26 B8 75 0N 70 0 E
Karabiğa, Turkey 21 D12 40 23N 27 17 E
Karabük, Turkey 25 F5 41 12N 32 37 E
Karaburun, Turkey 21 E12 38 41N 26 28 E
Karabutak = Qarabutaq, Kazakstan 26 E7 49 59N 60 14 E
Karacabey, Turkey 21 D13 40 12N 28 21 E
Karacasu, Turkey 21 F13 37 43N 28 35 E
Karachey-Cherkessia □, Russia 25 F7 43 40N 41 30 E
Karachi, Pakistan 42 G2 24 53N 67 0 E
Karad, India 40 L9 17 15N 74 10 E
Karaganda = Qaraghandy, Kazakstan 26 E8 49 50N 73 10 E
Karagayly, Kazakstan 26 E8 49 26N 76 0 E
Karaginskiy, Ostrov, Russia 27 D17 58 45N 164 0 E
Karagiye, Vpadina, Kazakstan 25 F9 43 27N 51 45 E
Karagiye Depression = Karagiye, Vpadina, Kazakstan 25 F9 43 27N 51 45 E
Karagola Road, India 43 G12 25 29N 87 23 E
Karaikal, India 40 P11 10 59N 79 50 E
Karaikkudi, India 40 P11 10 5N 78 45 E
Karaj, Iran 45 C6 35 48N 51 0 E
Karak, Malaysia 39 L4 3 25N 102 2 E
Karakalpakstan □, Uzbekistan 26 E6 43 0N 58 0 E
Karakelong, Indonesia 37 D7 4 35N 126 50 E
Karakitang, Indonesia 37 D7 3 14N 125 28 E
Karaklis = Vanadzor, Armenia 25 F7 40 48N 44 30 E
Karakoram Pass, Pakistan 43 B7 35 33N 77 50 E
Karakoram Ra., Pakistan 43 B7 35 30N 77 0 E
Karalon, Russia 27 D12 57 5N 115 50 E
Karama, Jordan 47 D4 31 57N 35 35 E
Karaman, Turkey 25 G5 37 14N 33 13 E
Karamay, China 32 B3 45 30N 84 58 E
Karambu, Indonesia 36 E5 3 53S 116 6 E
Karamea Bight, N.Z. 59 J3 41 22S 171 40 E
Karamnasa —►, India 43 G10 25 31N 83 52 E
Karand, Iran 44 C5 34 16N 46 15 E
Karanganyar, Indonesia 37 G13 7 38S 109 37 E
Karanjia, India 43 J11 21 47N 85 58 E
Karasburg, Namibia 56 D2 28 0S 18 44 E
Karasino, Russia 26 C9 66 50N 86 50 E
Karasjok, Norway 8 B21 69 27N 25 30 E
Karasuk, Russia 26 D8 53 44N 78 2 E
Karasuyama, Japan 31 F10 36 39N 140 9 E
Karatau = Qarataū, Kazakstan 26 E8 43 10N 70 28 E
Karatau, Khrebet, Kazakstan 26 E7 43 30N 69 30 E
Karatsu, Japan 31 H5 33 26N 129 58 E
Karaul, Russia 26 B9 70 6N 82 15 E
Karauli, India 42 F7 26 30N 77 4 E
Karavostasi, Cyprus 23 D11 35 8N 32 50 E
Karawang, Indonesia 37 G12 6 30S 107 15 E
Karawanken, Europe 16 E8 46 30N 14 40 E
Karayazı, Turkey 25 G7 39 41N 42 9 E
Karazhal, Kazakstan 26 E8 48 2N 70 49 E
Karbalā', Iraq 44 C5 32 36N 44 3 E
Karcag, Hungary 17 E11 47 19N 20 57 E
Karcha —►, Pakistan 43 B7 34 45N 76 10 E
Karchana, India 43 G9 25 17N 81 56 E
Kardhítsa, Greece 21 E9 39 23N 21 54 E
Kärdla, Estonia 9 G20 58 50N 22 40 E
Kareeberge, S. Africa 56 E3 30 59S 21 50 E
Kareha —►, India 43 G12 25 44N 86 21 E
Kareima, Sudan 51 E12 18 30N 31 49 E
Karelia □, Russia 24 A5 65 30N 32 30 E
Karelian Republic = Karelia □, Russia 24 A5 65 30N 32 30 E
Karera, India 42 G8 25 32N 78 9 E
Karevāndar, Iran 45 E9 27 53N 60 44 E
Kargasok, Russia 26 D9 59 3N 80 53 E
Kargat, Russia 26 D9 55 10N 80 15 E
Kargil, India 43 B7 34 32N 76 12 E
Kargopol, Russia 24 B6 61 30N 38 58 E
Karhal, India 43 F8 27 1N 78 57 E
Karīān, Iran 45 E8 26 57N 57 14 E
Kariba, Zimbabwe 55 F2 16 28S 28 50 E
Kariba, L., Zimbabwe 55 F2 16 40S 28 25 E
Kariba Dam, Zimbabwe 55 F2 16 30S 28 35 E
Kariba Gorge, Zambia 55 F2 16 30S 28 50 E
Karibib, Namibia 56 C2 22 0S 15 56 E
Karimata, Kepulauan, Indonesia 36 E3 1 25S 109 0 E
Karimata, Selat, Indonesia 36 E3 2 0S 108 40 E
Karimata Is. = Karimata, Kepulauan, Indonesia 36 E3 1 25S 109 0 E
Karimnagar, India 40 K11 18 26N 79 10 E
Karimunjawa, Kepulauan, Indonesia 36 F4 5 50S 110 30 E
Karin, Somali Rep. 46 E4 10 50N 45 52 E
Karīt, Iran 45 C8 33 29N 56 55 E
Kariya, Japan 31 G8 34 58N 137 1 E
Karkaralinsk = Qarqaraly, Kazakstan 26 E8 49 26N 75 30 E
Karkheh —►, Iran 44 D5 31 2N 47 29 E
Karkinitska Zatoka, Ukraine 25 E5 45 56N 33 0 E
Karkinitskiy Zaliv = Karkinitska Zatoka, Ukraine 25 E5 45 56N 33 0 E
Karl-Marx-Stadt = Chemnitz, Germany 16 C7 50 51N 12 54 E
Karlovac, Croatia 16 F8 45 31N 15 36 E
Karlovo, Bulgaria 21 C11 42 38N 24 47 E
Karlovy Vary, Czech Rep. 16 C7 50 13N 12 51 E
Karlsbad = Karlovy Vary, Czech Rep. 16 C7 50 13N 12 51 E
Karlsborg, Sweden 9 G16 58 33N 14 33 E
Karlshamn, Sweden 9 H16 56 10N 14 51 E
Karlskoga, Sweden 9 G16 59 28N 14 33 E
Karlskrona, Sweden 9 H16 56 10N 15 35 E
Karlsruhe, Germany 16 D5 49 0N 8 23 E
Karlstad, Sweden 9 G15 59 23N 13 30 E
Karlstad, U.S.A. 80 A6 48 35N 96 31W
Karmi'el, Israel 47 C4 32 55N 35 18 E
Karnak, Egypt 51 C12 25 43N 32 39 E
Karnal, India 42 E7 29 42N 77 2 E
Karnali —►, Nepal 43 E9 28 45N 81 16 E
Karnaphuli Res., Bangla. 41 H18 22 40N 92 20 E
Karnaprayag, India 43 D8 30 16N 79 15 E
Karnataka □, India 40 N10 13 15N 77 0 E
Karnes City, U.S.A. 81 L6 28 53N 97 54W
Karnische Alpen, Europe 16 E7 46 36N 13 0 E
Kärnten □, Austria 16 E8 46 52N 13 30 E
Karoi, Zimbabwe 55 F2 16 48S 29 45 E
Karonga, Malawi 55 D3 9 57S 33 55 E
Karoonda, Australia 63 F2 35 1S 139 59 E
Karor, Pakistan 42 D4 31 15N 70 59 E
Karora, Sudan 51 E13 17 44N 38 15 E
Karpasia □, Cyprus 23 D13 35 32N 34 15 E
Kárpathos, Greece 21 G12 35 37N 27 10 E
Karpinsk, Russia 24 C11 59 45N 60 1 E
Karpogory, Russia 24 B7 64 0N 44 27 E
Karpuz Burnu = Apostolos Andreas, C., Cyprus 23 D13 35 42N 34 35 E
Karratha, Australia 60 D2 20 53S 116 40 E
Kars, Turkey 25 F7 40 40N 43 5 E
Karsakpay, Kazakstan 26 E7 47 55N 66 40 E
Karshi = Qarshi, Uzbekistan 26 F7 38 53N 65 48 E
Karsiyang, India 43 F13 26 56N 88 18 E
Karsog, India 42 D7 31 23N 77 12 E
Kartaly, Russia 26 D7 53 3N 60 40 E
Kartapur, India 42 D6 31 27N 75 32 E
Karthaus, U.S.A. 78 E6 41 8N 78 9W
Karufa, Indonesia 37 E8 3 50S 133 20 E
Karumba, Australia 62 B3 17 31S 140 50 E
Karumo, Tanzania 54 C3 2 25S 32 50 E
Karumwa, Tanzania 54 C3 3 12S 32 38 E
Kārūn —►, Iran 45 D6 30 26N 48 10 E
Karungu, Kenya 54 C3 0 50S 34 10 E
Karviná, Czech Rep. 17 D10 49 53N 18 31 E
Karwan —►, India 42 F8 27 26N 78 4 E
Karwar, India 40 M9 14 55N 74 13 E
Karwi, India 43 G9 25 12N 80 57 E
Kasache, Malawi 55 E3 13 25S 34 20 E
Kasai —►, Dem. Rep. of the Congo 52 E3 3 30S 16 10 E
Kasaï-Oriental □, Dem. Rep. of the Congo 54 D1 5 0S 24 30 E
Kasaji, Dem. Rep. of the Congo 55 E1 10 25S 23 27 E
Kasama, Zambia 55 E3 10 16S 31 9 E
Kasan-dong, N. Korea 35 D14 41 18N 126 55 E
Kasane, Namibia 56 B3 17 34S 24 50 E
Kasanga, Tanzania 55 D3 8 30S 31 10 E
Kasaragod, India 40 N9 12 30N 74 58 E
Kasba L., Canada 73 A8 60 20N 102 10W
Kāseh Garān, Iran 44 C5 34 5N 46 2 E
Kasempa, Zambia 55 E2 13 30S 25 44 E
Kasenga, Dem. Rep. of the Congo 55 E2 10 20S 28 45 E
Kasese, Uganda 54 B3 0 13N 30 3 E
Kasewa, Zambia 55 E2 14 28S 28 53 E
Kasganj, India 43 F8 27 48N 78 42 E
Kashabowie, Canada 70 C1 48 40N 90 26W
Kashaf, Iran 45 C9 35 58N 61 7 E
Kāshān, Iran 45 C6 34 5N 51 30 E
Kashechewan, Canada 70 B3 52 18N 81 37W
Kashi, China 32 C2 39 30N 76 2 E
Kashimbo, Dem. Rep. of the Congo 55 E2 11 12S 26 19 E
Kashipur, India 43 E8 29 15N 79 0 E
Kashiwazaki, Japan 31 F9 37 22N 138 33 E
Kashk-e Kohneh, Afghan. 40 B3 34 55N 62 30 E
Kashkū'īyeh, Iran 45 D7 30 31N 55 40 E
Kāshmar, Iran 45 C8 35 16N 58 26 E
Kashmir, Asia 43 C7 34 0N 76 0 E
Kashmor, Pakistan 42 E3 28 28N 69 32 E
Kashun Noerh = Gaxun Nur, China 32 B5 42 22N 100 30 E
Kasiari, India 43 H12 22 8N 87 14 E
Kasimov, Russia 24 D7 54 55N 41 20 E
Kasinge, Dem. Rep. of the Congo 54 D2 6 15S 26 58 E
Kasiruta, Indonesia 37 E7 0 25S 127 12 E
Kaskaskia —►, U.S.A. 80 G10 37 58N 89 57W
Kaskattama —►, Canada 73 B10 57 3N 90 4W
Kaskinen, Finland 9 E19 62 22N 21 15 E
Kaslo, Canada 72 D5 49 55N 116 55W
Kasmere L., Canada 73 B8 59 34N 101 10W
Kasongo, Dem. Rep. of the Congo 54 C2 4 30S 26 33 E
Kasongo Lunda, Dem. Rep. of the Congo 52 F3 6 35S 16 49 E
Kásos, Greece 21 G12 35 20N 26 55 E
Kassalâ, Sudan 51 E13 15 30N 36 0 E
Kassel, Germany 16 C5 51 18N 9 26 E
Kassiópi, Greece 23 A3 39 48N 19 53 E
Kasson, U.S.A. 80 C8 44 2N 92 45W
Kastamonu, Turkey 25 F5 41 25N 33 43 E
Kastélli, Greece 23 D5 35 29N 23 38 E
Kastéllion, Greece 23 D7 35 12N 25 20 E
Kasterlee, Belgium 15 C4 51 15N 4 59 E
Kastoría, Greece 21 D9 40 30N 21 19 E
Kasulu, Tanzania 54 C3 4 37S 30 5 E
Kasumi, Japan 31 G7 35 38N 134 38 E
Kasungu, Malawi 55 E3 13 0S 33 29 E
Kasur, Pakistan 42 D6 31 5N 74 25 E
Kataba, Zambia 55 F2 16 5S 25 10 E
Katahdin, Mt., U.S.A. 77 C11 45 54N 68 56W
Katako Kombe, Dem. Rep. of the Congo 54 C1 3 25S 24 20 E
Katale, Tanzania 54 C3 4 52S 31 7 E
Katanda, Katanga, Dem. Rep. of the Congo 54 D1 7 52S 24 13 E
Katanda, Nord-Kivu, Dem. Rep. of the Congo 54 C2 0 55S 29 21 E
Katanga □, Dem. Rep. of the Congo 54 D2 8 0S 25 0 E
Katangi, India 40 J11 21 56N 79 50 E
Katanning, Australia 61 F2 33 40S 117 33 E
Katavi Swamp, Tanzania 54 D3 6 50S 31 10 E
Kateríni, Greece 21 D10 40 18N 22 37 E
Katghora, India 43 H10 22 30N 82 33 E
Katha, Burma 41 G20 24 10N 96 30 E
Kathrîna, Gebel, Egypt 44 D2 28 30N 33 57 E
Katherine, Australia 60 B5 14 27S 132 20 E
Katherine Gorge, Australia 60 B5 14 18S 132 28 E
Kathi, India 42 J6 21 47N 74 3 E
Kathiawar, India 42 H4 22 20N 71 0 E
Kathikas, Cyprus 23 E11 34 55N 32 25 E
Kathua, India 42 C6 32 23N 75 34 E
Katihar, India 43 G12 25 34N 87 36 E
Katima Mulilo, Zambia 56 B3 17 28S 24 13 E
Katimbira, Malawi 55 E3 12 40S 34 0 E
Katingan = Mendawai —►, Indonesia 36 E4 3 30S 113 0 E
Katiola, Ivory C. 50 G4 8 10N 5 10W
Katmandu, Nepal 43 F11 27 45N 85 20 E
Katni, India 43 H9 23 51N 80 24 E
Káto Arkhánai, Greece 23 D7 35 15N 25 10 E
Káto Khorió, Greece 23 D7 35 3N 25 47 E
Kato Pyrgos, Cyprus 23 D11 35 11N 32 41 E
Katompe, Dem. Rep. of the Congo 54 D2 6 2S 26 23 E
Katonga —►, Uganda 54 B3 0 34N 31 50 E
Katoomba, Australia 63 E5 33 41S 150 19 E
Katowice, Poland 17 C10 50 17N 19 5 E
Katrine, L., U.K. 12 E4 56 15N 4 30W
Katrineholm, Sweden 9 G17 59 9N 16 12 E
Katsepe, Madag. 57 B8 15 45S 46 15 E
Katsina, Nigeria 50 F7 13 0N 7 32 E
Katsumoto, Japan 31 H4 33 51N 129 42 E
Katsuura, Japan 31 G10 35 10N 140 20 E
Katsuyama, Japan 31 F8 36 3N 136 30 E
Kattaviá, Greece 23 D9 35 57N 27 46 E
Kattegat, Denmark 9 H14 56 40N 11 20 E
Katumba, Dem. Rep. of the Congo 54 D2 7 40S 25 17 E
Katungu, Kenya 54 C5 2 55S 40 3 E
Katwa, India 43 H13 23 30N 88 5 E
Katwijk, Neths. 15 B4 52 12N 4 24 E
Kauai, U.S.A. 74 H15 22 3N 159 30W
Kauai Channel, U.S.A. 74 H15 21 45N 158 50W
Kaufman, U.S.A. 81 J6 32 35N 96 19W
Kauhajoki, Finland 9 E20 62 25N 22 10 E
Kaukauna, U.S.A. 76 C1 44 17N 88 17W
Kaukauveld, Namibia 56 C3 20 0S 20 15 E
Kaunakakai, U.S.A. 74 H16 21 6N 157 1W
Kaunas, Lithuania 9 J20 54 54N 23 54 E
Kaunia, Bangla. 43 G13 25 46N 89 26 E
Kautokeino, Norway 8 B20 69 0N 23 4 E
Kauwapur, India 43 F10 27 31N 82 18 E
Kavacha, Russia 27 C17 60 16N 169 51 E
Kavalerovo, Russia 30 B7 44 15N 135 4 E
Kavali, India 40 M12 14 55N 80 1 E
Kavála, Greece 21 D11 40 57N 24 28 E
Kavār, Iran 45 D7 29 11N 52 44 E
Kavi, India 42 H5 22 12N 72 38 E
Kavir, Dasht-e, Iran 45 C7 34 30N 55 0 E
Kavos, Greece 23 B4 39 23N 20 3 E
Kaw, Fr. Guiana 93 C8 4 30N 52 15W
Kawagama L., Canada 78 A6 45 18N 78 45W
Kawagoe, Japan 31 G9 35 55N 139 29 E
Kawaguchi, Japan 31 G9 35 52N 139 45 E
Kawaihae, U.S.A. 74 H17 20 3N 155 50W
Kawambwa, Zambia 55 D2 9 48S 29 3 E
Kawanoe, Japan 31 G6 34 1N 133 34 E
Kawardha, India 43 J9 22 0N 81 17 E
Kawasaki, Japan 31 G9 35 35N 139 42 E
Kawasi, Indonesia 37 E7 1 38S 127 28 E
Kawerau, N.Z. 59 H6 38 7S 176 42 E
Kawhia Harbour, N.Z. 59 H5 38 5S 174 51 E
Kawio, Kepulauan, Indonesia 37 D7 4 30N 125 30 E
Kawnro, Burma 41 H21 22 48N 99 8 E
Kawthaung, Burma 39 H2 10 5N 98 36 E
Kawthoolei = Kawthule □, Burma 41 L20 18 0N 97 30 E
Kawthule □, Burma 41 L20 18 0N 97 30 E
Kaya, Burkina Faso 50 F5 13 4N 1 10W
Kayah □, Burma 41 K20 19 15N 97 15 E
Kayan —►, Indonesia 36 D5 2 55N 117 35 E
Kaycee, U.S.A. 82 E10 43 43N 106 38W
Kayeli, Indonesia 37 E7 3 20S 127 10 E
Kayenta, U.S.A. 83 H8 36 44N 110 15W
Kayes, Mali 50 F3 14 25N 11 30W
Kayin = Kawthule □, Burma 41 L20 18 0N 97 30 E
Kayoa, Indonesia 37 D7 0 1N 127 28 E
Kayomba, Zambia 55 E1 13 11S 24 2 E
Kayseri, Turkey 25 G6 38 45N 35 30 E
Kaysville, U.S.A. 82 F8 41 2N 111 56W
Kazachye, Russia 27 B14 70 52N 135 58 E
Kazakstan ■, Asia 26 E8 50 0N 70 0 E
Kazan, Russia 24 C8 55 50N 49 10 E
Kazan —►, Canada 73 A9 64 3N 95 35W
Kazan-Rettō, Pac. Oc. 64 E6 25 0N 141 0 E
Kazanlŭk, Bulgaria 21 C11 42 38N 25 20 E
Kazatin = Kozyatyn, Ukraine 17 D15 49 45N 28 50 E
Kāzerūn, Iran 45 D6 29 38N 51 40 E
Kazi Magomed = Qazimämmäd, Azerbaijan 45 A6 40 3N 49 0 E
Kazuno, Japan 30 D10 40 10N 140 45 E
Kazym —►, Russia 26 C7 63 54N 65 50 E
Kéa, Greece 21 F11 37 35N 24 22 E
Keady, U.K. 13 B5 54 15N 6 42W
Kearney, U.S.A. 80 E5 40 42N 99 5W
Kearny, U.S.A. 83 K8 33 3N 110 55W
Kearsarge, Mt., U.S.A. 79 C13 43 22N 71 50W
Keban, Turkey 25 G6 38 50N 38 50 E
Keban Baraji, Turkey 25 G6 38 41N 38 33 E
Kebnekaise, Sweden 8 C18 67 53N 18 33 E
Kebri Dehar, Ethiopia 46 F3 6 45N 44 17 E
Kebumen, Indonesia 37 G13 7 42S 109 40 E
Kechika —►, Canada 72 B3 59 41N 127 12W
Kecskemét, Hungary 17 E10 46 57N 19 42 E
Kėdainiai, Lithuania 9 J21 55 15N 24 2 E
Kedarnath, India 43 D8 30 44N 79 4 E
Kedgwick, Canada 71 C6 47 40N 67 20W
Kédhros Óros, Greece 23 D6 35 11N 24 37 E
Kedia Hill, Botswana 56 C3 21 28S 24 37 E
Kediri, Indonesia 37 G15 7 51S 112 1 E
Keeler, U.S.A. 84 J9 36 29N 117 52W
Keeley L., Canada 73 C7 54 54N 108 8W
Keeling Is. = Cocos Is., Ind. Oc. 64 J1 12 10S 96 55 E
Keelung = Chilung, Taiwan 33 D7 25 3N 121 45 E
Keene, Canada 78 B6 44 15N 78 10W
Keene, Calif., U.S.A. 85 K8 35 13N 118 33W
Keene, N.H., U.S.A. 79 D12 42 56N 72 17W
Keene, N.Y., U.S.A. 79 B11 44 16N 73 46W
Keeper Hill, Ireland 13 D3 52 45N 8 16W
Keer-Weer, C., Australia 62 A3 14 0S 141 32 E
Keeseville, U.S.A. 79 B11 44 29N 73 30W
Keetmanshoop, Namibia 56 D2 26 35S 18 8 E
Keewatin, Canada 73 D10 49 46N 94 34W
Keewatin —►, Canada 73 B8 56 29N 100 46W
Kefallinía, Greece 21 E9 38 20N 20 30 E
Kefamenanu, Indonesia 37 F6 9 28S 124 29 E
Kefar Sava, Israel 47 C3 32 11N 34 54 E
Keffi, Nigeria 50 G7 8 55N 7 43 E
Keflavík, Iceland 8 D2 64 2N 22 35W
Keg River, Canada 72 B5 57 54N 117 55W
Kegaska, Canada 71 B7 50 9N 61 18W
Keighley, U.K. 10 D6 53 52N 1 54W
Keila, Estonia 9 G21 59 18N 24 25 E
Keimoes, S. Africa 56 D3 28 41S 20 59 E
Keitele, Finland 8 E22 63 10N 26 20 E
Keith, Australia 63 F3 36 6S 140 20 E
Keith, U.K. 12 D6 57 32N 2 57W
Keizer, U.S.A. 82 D2 44 57N 123 1W
Kejimkujik Nat. Park, Canada 71 D6 44 25N 65 25W
Kejser Franz Joseph Fjord = Kong Franz Joseph Fd., Greenland 4 B6 73 30N 24 30W
Kekri, India 42 G6 26 0N 75 10 E
Kelan, China 34 E6 38 43N 111 31 E
Kelang, Malaysia 39 L3 3 2N 101 26 E
Kelantan —►, Malaysia 39 J4 6 13N 102 14 E
Kelkit —►, Turkey 25 F6 40 45N 36 32 E
Kellerberrin, Australia 61 F2 31 36S 117 38 E
Kellett, C., Canada 4 B1 72 0N 126 0W
Kelleys I., U.S.A. 78 E2 41 36N 82 42W
Kellogg, U.S.A. 82 C5 47 32N 116 7W
Kells = Ceanannus Mor, Ireland 13 C5 53 44N 6 53W
Kelokedhara, Cyprus 23 E11 34 48N 32 39 E
Kelowna, Canada 72 D5 49 50N 119 25W
Kelseyville, U.S.A. 84 G4 38 59N 122 50W
Kelso, N.Z. 59 L2 45 54S 169 15 E
Kelso, U.K. 12 F6 55 36N 2 26W
Kelso, U.S.A. 84 D4 46 9N 122 54W
Keluang, Malaysia 39 L4 2 3N 103 18 E
Kelvington, Canada 73 C8 52 10N 103 30W
Kem, Russia 24 B5 65 0N 34 38 E
Kem —►, Russia 24 B5 64 57N 34 41 E
Kema, Indonesia 37 D7 1 22N 125 8 E
Kemah, Turkey 44 B3 39 32N 39 5 E
Kemaman, Malaysia 36 D2 4 12N 103 18 E
Kemano, Canada 72 C3 53 35N 128 0W
Kemasik, Malaysia 39 K4 4 25N 103 27 E
Kemerovo, Russia 26 D9 55 20N 86 5 E
Kemi, Finland 8 D21 65 44N 24 34 E
Kemi älv = Kemijoki —►, Finland 8 D21 65 47N 24 32 E
Kemijärvi, Finland 8 C22 66 43N 27 22 E
Kemijoki —►, Finland 8 D21 65 47N 24 32 E
Kemmerer, U.S.A. 82 F8 41 48N 110 32W
Kemmuna = Comino, Malta 23 C1 36 2N 14 20 E
Kemp, L., U.S.A. 81 J5 33 46N 99 9W
Kemp Land, Antarctica 5 C5 69 0S 55 0 E
Kempsey, Australia 63 E5 31 1S 152 50 E
Kempt, L., Canada 70 C5 47 25N 74 22W
Kempten, Germany 16 E6 47 45N 10 17 E
Kempton, Australia 62 G4 42 31S 147 12 E
Kemptville, Canada 79 B9 45 0N 75 38W
Ken —►, India 43 G9 25 13N 80 27 E
Kenai, U.S.A. 68 B4 60 33N 151 16W
Kendai, India 43 H10 22 45N 82 37 E
Kendal, Indonesia 37 G14 6 56S 110 14 E
Kendal, U.K. 10 C5 54 20N 2 44W
Kendall, Australia 63 E5 31 35S 152 44 E
Kendall, U.S.A. 77 N5 25 41N 80 19W
Kendall —►, Australia 62 A3 14 4S 141 35 E
Kendallville, U.S.A. 76 E3 41 27N 85 16W
Kendari, Indonesia 37 E6 3 50S 122 30 E
Kendawangan, Indonesia 36 E4 2 32S 110 17 E
Kendrapara, India 41 J15 20 35N 86 30 E
Kendrew, S. Africa 56 E3 32 32S 24 30 E
Kene Thao, Laos 38 D3 17 44N 101 10 E
Kenedy, U.S.A. 81 L6 28 49N 97 51W
Kenema, S. Leone 50 G3 7 50N 11 14W
Keng Kok, Laos 38 D5 16 26N 105 12 E
Keng Tawng, Burma 41 J21 20 45N 98 18 E
Keng Tung, Burma 41 J21 21 0N 99 30 E
Kenge, Dem. Rep. of the Congo 52 E3 4 50S 17 4 E
Kengeja, Tanzania 54 D4 5 26S 39 45 E
Kenhardt, S. Africa 56 D3 29 19S 21 12 E
Kenitra, Morocco 50 B4 34 15N 6 40W
Kenli, China 35 F10 37 30N 118 20 E
Kenmare, Ireland 13 E2 51 53N 9 36W
Kenmare, U.S.A. 80 A3 48 41N 102 5W
Kenmare River, Ireland 13 E2 51 48N 9 51W
Kennebago Lake, U.S.A. 79 A14 45 4N 70 40W
Kennebec, U.S.A. 80 D5 43 54N 99 52W
Kennebec —►, U.S.A. 77 D11 43 45N 69 46W
Kennebunk, U.S.A. 79 C14 43 23N 70 33W
Kennedy, Zimbabwe 55 F2 18 52S 27 10 E
Kennedy Ra., Australia 61 D2 24 45S 115 10 E
Kennedy Taungdeik, Burma 41 H18 23 15N 93 45 E
Kenner, U.S.A. 81 L9 29 59N 90 15W
Kennet —►, U.K. 11 F7 51 27N 0 57W
Kenneth Ra., Australia 61 D2 23 50S 117 8 E
Kennett, U.S.A. 81 G9 36 14N 90 3W
Kennewick, U.S.A. 82 C4 46 12N 119 7W
Kenogami —►, Canada 70 B3 51 6N 84 28W
Kenora, Canada 73 D10 49 47N 94 29W
Kenosha, U.S.A. 76 D2 42 35N 87 49W
Kensington, Canada 71 C7 46 28N 63 34W
Kent, Ohio, U.S.A. 78 E3 41 9N 81 22W
Kent, Tex., U.S.A. 81 K2 31 4N 104 13W
Kent, Wash., U.S.A. 84 C4 47 23N 122 14W
Kent □, U.K. 11 F8 51 12N 0 40 E
Kent Group, Australia 62 F4 39 30S 147 20 E
Kent Pen., Canada 68 B9 68 30N 107 0W
Kentau, Kazakstan 26 E7 43 32N 68 36 E
Kentland, U.S.A. 76 E2 40 46N 87 27W
Kenton, U.S.A. 76 E4 40 39N 83 37W
Kentucky □, U.S.A. 76 G3 37 0N 84 0W
Kentucky —►, U.S.A. 76 F3 38 41N 85 11W
Kentucky L., U.S.A. 77 G2 37 1N 88 16W

Kościan

Kinsale, Old Hd. of, Ireland 13 E3 51 37N 8 33W
Kinsha = Chang Jiang →, China 33 C7 31 48N 121 10 E
Kinshasa, Dem. Rep. of the Congo 52 E3 4 20S 15 15 E
Kinsley, U.S.A. 81 G5 37 55N 99 25W
Kinsman, U.S.A. 78 E4 41 26N 80 35W
Kinston, U.S.A. 77 H7 35 16N 77 35W
Kintore Ra., Australia 60 D4 23 15S 128 47 E
Kintyre, U.K. 12 F3 55 30N 5 35W
Kintyre, Mull of, U.K. 12 F3 55 17N 5 47W
Kinushseo →, Canada 70 A3 55 15N 83 45W
Kinuso, Canada 72 B5 55 20N 115 25W
Kinyangiri, Tanzania 54 C3 4 25S 34 37 E
Kinzua, U.S.A. 78 E6 41 52N 78 58W
Kinzua Dam, U.S.A. 78 E6 41 53N 79 0W
Kiosk, Canada 70 C4 46 6N 78 53W
Kiowa, Kans., U.S.A. 81 G5 37 1N 98 29W
Kiowa, Okla., U.S.A. 81 H7 34 43N 95 54W
Kipahigan L., Canada 73 B8 55 20N 101 55W
Kipanga, Tanzania 54 D4 6 15S 35 20 E
Kiparissia, Greece 21 F9 37 15N 21 40 E
Kiparissiakós Kólpos, Greece 21 F9 37 25N 21 25 E
Kipawa, L., Canada 70 C4 46 50N 79 0W
Kipembawe, Tanzania 54 D3 7 38S 33 27 E
Kipengere Ra., Tanzania 55 D3 9 12S 34 15 E
Kipili, Tanzania 54 D3 7 28S 30 32 E
Kipini, Kenya 54 C5 2 30S 40 32 E
Kipling, Canada 73 C8 50 6N 102 38W
Kippure, Ireland 13 C5 53 11N 6 21W
Kipushi, Dem. Rep. of the Congo 55 E2 11 48S 27 12 E
Kirensk, Russia 27 D11 57 50N 107 55 E
Kirghizia = Kyrgyzstan ■, Asia 26 E8 42 0N 75 0 E
Kirghizstan = Kyrgyzstan ■, Asia 26 E8 42 0N 75 0 E
Kirgiziya Steppe, Eurasia 25 E10 50 0N 55 0 E
Kiribati ■, Pac. Oc. 64 H10 5 0S 180 0 E
Kırıkkale, Turkey 25 G5 39 51N 33 32 E
Kirillov, Russia 24 C6 59 49N 38 24 E
Kirin = Jilin, China 35 C14 43 44N 126 30 E
Kiritimati, Kiribati 65 G12 1 58N 157 27W
Kirkby, U.K. 10 D5 53 30N 2 54W
Kirkby Lonsdale, U.K. 10 C5 54 12N 2 36W
Kirkcaldy, U.K. 12 E5 56 7N 3 9W
Kirkcudbright, U.K. 12 G4 54 50N 4 2W
Kirkee, India 40 K8 18 34N 73 56 E
Kirkenes, Norway 8 B23 69 40N 30 5 E
Kirkfield, Canada 78 B6 44 34N 78 59W
Kirkjubæjarklaustur, Iceland 8 E4 63 47N 18 4W
Kirkkonummi, Finland 9 F21 60 8N 24 26 E
Kirkland Lake, Canada 70 C3 48 9N 80 2W
Kırklareli, Turkey 21 D12 41 44N 27 15 E
Kirksville, U.S.A. 80 E8 40 12N 92 35W
Kirkūk, Iraq 44 C5 35 30N 44 21 E
Kirkwall, U.K. 12 C6 58 59N 2 58W
Kirkwood, S. Africa 56 E4 33 22S 25 15 E
Kirov, Russia 24 C8 58 35N 49 40 E
Kirovabad = Gäncä, Azerbaijan 25 F8 40 45N 46 20 E
Kirovakan = Vanadzor, Armenia 25 F7 40 48N 44 30 E
Kirovograd = Kirovohrad, Ukraine 25 E5 48 35N 32 20 E
Kirovohrad, Ukraine 25 E5 48 35N 32 20 E
Kirovsk = Babadayhan, Turkmenistan 26 F7 37 42N 60 23 E
Kirovsk, Russia 24 A5 67 32N 33 41 E
Kirovskiy, Kamchatka, Russia 27 D16 54 27N 155 42 E
Kirovskiy, Primorsk, Russia 30 B6 45 7N 133 30 E
Kirriemuir, U.K. 12 E5 56 41N 3 1W
Kirsanov, Russia 24 D7 52 35N 42 40 E
Kırşehir, Turkey 25 G5 39 14N 34 5 E
Kirthar Range, Pakistan 42 F2 27 0N 67 0 E
Kirtland, U.S.A. 83 H9 36 44N 108 21W
Kiruna, Sweden 8 C19 67 52N 20 15 E
Kirundu, Dem. Rep. of the Congo 54 C2 0 50S 25 35 E
Kiryū, Japan 31 F9 36 24N 139 20 E
Kisaga, Tanzania 54 C3 4 30S 34 23 E
Kisalaya, Nic. 88 D3 14 40N 84 3W
Kisámou, Kólpos, Greece 23 D5 35 30N 23 38 E
Kisanga, Dem. Rep. of the Congo 54 B2 2 30N 26 35 E
Kisangani, Dem. Rep. of the Congo 54 B2 0 35N 25 15 E
Kisar, Indonesia 37 F7 8 5S 127 10 E
Kisarawe, Tanzania 54 D4 6 53S 39 0 E
Kisarazu, Japan 31 G9 35 23N 139 55 E
Kishanganga →, Pakistan 43 B5 34 18N 73 28 E
Kishanganj, India 43 F13 26 3N 88 14 E
Kishangarh, Raj., India 42 F6 26 34N 74 52 E
Kishangarh, Raj., India 42 F4 27 50N 70 30 E
Kishinev = Chişinău, Moldova 17 E15 47 2N 28 50 E
Kishiwada, Japan 31 G7 34 28N 135 22 E
Kishtwar, India 43 C6 33 20N 75 48 E
Kisii, Kenya 54 C3 0 40S 34 45 E
Kisiju, Tanzania 54 D4 7 23S 39 19 E
Kisizi, Uganda 54 C2 1 0S 29 58 E
Kiskőrös, Hungary 17 E10 46 37N 19 20 E
Kiskunfélegyháza, Hungary 17 E10 46 42N 19 53 E
Kiskunhalas, Hungary 17 E10 46 28N 19 37 E
Kislovodsk, Russia 25 F7 43 50N 42 45 E
Kismayu = Chisimaio, Somali Rep. 49 G8 0 22S 42 32 E
Kiso-Gawa →, Japan 31 G8 35 20N 136 45 E
Kiso-Sammyaku, Japan 31 G8 35 45N 137 45 E
Kisofukushima, Japan 31 G8 35 52N 137 43 E
Kisoro, Uganda 54 C2 1 17S 29 48 E
Kissidougou, Guinea 50 G3 9 5N 10 5W
Kissimmee, U.S.A. 77 L5 28 18N 81 24W
Kissimmee →, U.S.A. 77 M5 27 9N 80 52W
Kississing L., Canada 73 B8 55 10N 101 20W
Kissónerga, Cyprus 23 E11 34 49N 32 24 E
Kisumu, Kenya 54 C3 0 3S 34 45 E
Kiswani, Tanzania 54 C4 4 5S 37 57 E
Kiswere, Tanzania 55 D4 9 27S 39 30 E
Kit Carson, U.S.A. 80 F3 38 46N 102 48W
Kita, Mali 50 F4 13 5N 9 25W
Kitaibaraki, Japan 31 F10 36 50N 140 45 E
Kitakami, Japan 30 E10 39 20N 141 10 E
Kitakami-Gawa →, Japan 30 E10 38 25N 141 19 E
Kitakami-Sammyaku, Japan 30 E10 39 30N 141 30 E
Kitakata, Japan 30 F9 37 39N 139 52 E
Kitakyūshū, Japan 31 H5 33 50N 130 50 E
Kitale, Kenya 54 B4 1 0N 35 0 E
Kitami, Japan 30 C11 43 48N 143 54 E
Kitami-Sammyaku, Japan 30 B11 44 22N 142 43 E
Kitangiri, L., Tanzania 54 C3 4 5S 34 20 E
Kitaya, Tanzania 55 E5 10 38S 40 8 E
Kitchener, Canada 78 C4 43 27N 80 29W
Kitega = Gitega, Burundi 54 C2 3 26S 29 56 E
Kitengo, Dem. Rep. of the Congo 54 D1 7 26S 24 8 E
Kitgum, Uganda 54 B3 3 17N 32 52 E
Kithira, Greece 21 F10 36 8N 23 0 E
Kithnos, Greece 21 F11 37 26N 24 27 E
Kiti, Cyprus 23 E12 34 50N 33 34 E
Kiti, C., Cyprus 23 E12 34 48N 33 36 E
Kitimat, Canada 72 C3 54 3N 128 38W
Kitinen →, Finland 8 C22 67 14N 27 27 E
Kitsuki, Japan 31 H5 33 25N 131 37 E
Kittakittaooloo, L., Australia 63 D2 28 3S 138 14 E
Kittanning, U.S.A. 78 F5 40 49N 79 31W
Kittatinny Mts., U.S.A. 79 F10 41 0N 75 0W
Kittery, U.S.A. 77 D10 43 5N 70 45W
Kittilä, Finland 8 C21 67 40N 24 51 E
Kitui, Kenya 54 C4 1 17S 38 0 E
Kitwanga, Canada 72 B3 55 6N 128 4W
Kitwe, Zambia 55 E2 12 54S 28 13 E
Kivarli, India 42 G5 24 33N 72 46 E
Kivertsi, Ukraine 17 C13 50 50N 25 28 E
Kividhes, Cyprus 23 E11 34 46N 32 51 E
Kivu, L., Dem. Rep. of the Congo 54 C2 1 48S 29 0 E
Kiyev = Kyyiv, Ukraine 17 C16 50 30N 30 28 E
Kiyevskoye Vdkhr. = Kyyivske Vdskh., Ukraine 17 C16 51 0N 30 25 E
Kizel, Russia 24 C10 59 3N 57 40 E
Kiziguru, Rwanda 54 C3 1 46S 30 23 E
Kızıl Irmak →, Turkey 25 F6 41 44N 35 58 E
Kizil Jilga, India 43 B8 35 26N 78 50 E
Kızıltepe, Turkey 44 B4 37 12N 40 35 E
Kizimkazi, Tanzania 54 D4 6 28S 39 30 E
Kizlyar, Russia 25 F8 43 51N 46 40 E
Kizyl-Arvat = Gyzylarbat, Turkmenistan 26 F6 39 4N 56 23 E
Kjölur, Iceland 8 D4 64 50N 19 25W
Kladno, Czech Rep. 16 C8 50 10N 14 7 E
Klaeng, Thailand 38 F3 12 47N 101 39 E
Klagenfurt, Austria 16 E8 46 38N 14 20 E
Klaipėda, Lithuania 9 J19 55 43N 21 10 E
Klaksvík, Færoe Is. 8 E9 62 14N 6 35W
Klamath →, U.S.A. 82 F1 41 33N 124 5W
Klamath Falls, U.S.A. 82 E3 42 13N 121 46W
Klamath Mts., U.S.A. 82 F2 41 20N 123 0W
Klamono, Indonesia 37 E8 1 8S 131 30 E
Klappan →, Canada 72 B3 58 0N 129 43W
Klarälven →, Sweden 9 G15 59 23N 13 32 E
Klatovy, Czech Rep. 16 D7 49 23N 13 18 E
Klawer, S. Africa 56 E2 31 44S 18 36 E
Klazienaveen, Neths. 15 B6 52 44N 7 0 E
Kleena Kleene, Canada 72 C4 52 0N 124 59W
Klein-Karas, Namibia 56 D2 27 33S 18 7 E
Klerksdorp, S. Africa 56 D4 26 53S 26 38 E
Kletsk = Klyetsk, Belarus 17 B14 53 5N 26 45 E
Kletskiy, Russia 25 E7 49 16N 43 11 E
Klickitat, U.S.A. 82 D3 45 49N 121 9W
Klickitat →, U.S.A. 84 E5 45 42N 121 17W
Klidhes, Cyprus 23 D13 35 42N 34 36 E
Klinaklini →, Canada 72 C3 51 21N 125 40W
Klipdale, S. Africa 56 E2 34 19S 19 57 E
Klipplaat, S. Africa 56 E3 33 1S 24 22 E
Kłodzko, Poland 17 C9 50 28N 16 38 E
Klouto, Togo 50 G6 6 57N 0 44 E
Kluane L., Canada 68 B6 61 15N 138 40W
Kluane Nat. Park, Canada 72 A1 60 45N 139 30W
Kluczbork, Poland 17 C10 50 58N 18 12 E
Klukwan, U.S.A. 72 B1 59 24N 135 54W
Klyetsk, Belarus 17 B14 53 5N 26 45 E
Klyuchevskaya, Gora, Russia 27 D17 55 50N 160 30 E
Knaresborough, U.K. 10 C6 54 1N 1 28W
Knee L., Man., Canada 70 A1 55 3N 94 45W
Knee L., Sask., Canada 73 B7 55 51N 107 0W
Knight Inlet, Canada 72 C3 50 45N 125 40W
Knighton, U.K. 11 E4 52 21N 3 3W
Knights Ferry, U.S.A. 84 H6 37 50N 120 40W
Knights Landing, U.S.A. 84 G5 38 48N 121 43W
Knob, C., Australia 61 F2 34 32S 119 16 E
Knock, Ireland 13 C3 53 48N 8 55W
Knockmealdown Mts., Ireland 13 D4 52 14N 7 56W
Knokke-Heist, Belgium 15 C3 51 21N 3 17 E
Knossós, Greece 23 D7 35 16N 25 10 E
Knowlton, Canada 79 A12 45 13N 72 31W
Knox, U.S.A. 76 E2 41 18N 86 37W
Knox Coast, Antarctica 5 C8 66 30S 108 0 E
Knoxville, Iowa, U.S.A. 80 E8 41 19N 93 6W
Knoxville, Pa., U.S.A. 78 E7 41 57N 77 27W
Knoxville, Tenn., U.S.A. 77 H4 35 58N 83 55W
Knysna, S. Africa 56 E3 34 2S 23 2 E
Ko Kha, Thailand 38 C2 18 11N 99 24 E
Koartac = Quaqtaq, Canada 69 B13 60 55N 69 40W
Koba, Indonesia 37 F8 6 37S 134 37 E
Kobarid, Slovenia 16 E7 46 15N 13 30 E
Kobayashi, Japan 31 J5 31 56N 130 59 E
Kobdo = Hovd, Mongolia 32 B4 48 2N 91 37 E
Kōbe, Japan 31 G7 34 45N 135 10 E
København, Denmark 9 J15 55 41N 12 34 E
Kōbi-Sho, Japan 31 M1 25 56N 123 41 E
Koblenz, Germany 16 C4 50 21N 7 36 E
Kobryn, Belarus 17 B13 52 15N 24 22 E
Kocaeli, Turkey 25 F4 40 45N 29 50 E
Kočani, Macedonia 21 D10 41 55N 22 25 E
Koch Bihar, India 41 F16 26 22N 89 29 E
Kochang, S. Korea 35 G14 35 41N 127 55 E
Kochas, India 43 G10 25 15N 83 56 E
Kōchi, Japan 31 H6 33 30N 133 35 E
Kōchi □, Japan 31 H6 33 40N 133 30 E
Kochiu = Gejiu, China 32 D5 23 20N 103 10 E
Kodarma, India 43 G11 24 28N 85 36 E
Kodiak, U.S.A. 68 C4 57 47N 152 24W
Kodiak I., U.S.A. 68 C4 57 30N 152 45W
Kodinar, India 42 J4 20 46N 70 46 E
Koes, Namibia 56 D2 26 0S 19 15 E
Koffiefontein, S. Africa 56 D4 29 30S 25 0 E
Kofiau, Indonesia 37 E7 1 11S 129 50 E
Koforidua, Ghana 50 G5 6 3N 0 17W
Kōfu, Japan 31 G9 35 40N 138 30 E
Koga, Japan 31 F9 36 11N 139 43 E
Kogaluk →, Canada 71 A7 56 12N 61 44W
Køge, Denmark 9 J15 55 27N 12 11 E
Koh-i-Bābā, Afghan. 40 B5 34 30N 67 0 E
Koh-i-Khurd, Afghan. 42 C1 33 30N 65 59 E
Koh-i-Maran, Pakistan 42 E2 29 18N 66 50 E
Kohat, Pakistan 42 C4 33 40N 71 29 E
Kohima, India 41 G19 25 35N 94 10 E
Kohkīlūyeh va Būyer Aḥmadi □, Iran 45 D6 31 30N 50 30 E
Kohler Ra., Antarctica 5 D15 77 0S 110 0W
Kohlu, Pakistan 42 E3 29 54N 69 15 E
Kohtla-Järve, Estonia 9 G22 59 20N 27 20 E
Koillismaa, Finland 8 D23 65 44N 28 36 E
Koin-dong, N. Korea 35 D14 40 28N 126 18 E
Kojō, N. Korea 35 E14 38 58N 127 58 E
Kojonup, Australia 61 F2 33 48S 117 10 E
Kojūr, Iran 45 B6 36 23N 51 43 E
Kokand = Qūqon, Uzbekistan 26 E8 40 30N 70 57 E
Kokas, Indonesia 37 E8 2 42S 132 26 E
Kokchetav = Kökshetaū, Kazakstan 26 D7 53 20N 69 25 E
Kokemäenjoki →, Finland 9 F19 61 32N 21 44 E
Kokkola, Finland 8 E20 63 50N 23 8 E
Koko Kyunzu, Burma 41 M18 14 10N 93 25 E
Kokomo, U.S.A. 76 E2 40 29N 86 8W
Koksan, N. Korea 35 E14 38 46N 126 40 E
Kökshetaū, Kazakstan 26 D7 53 20N 69 25 E
Koksoak →, Canada 69 C13 58 30N 68 10W
Kokstad, S. Africa 57 E4 30 32S 29 29 E
Kokubu, Japan 31 J5 31 44N 130 46 E
Kola, Indonesia 37 F8 5 35S 134 30 E
Kola, Russia 24 A5 68 45N 33 8 E
Kola Pen. = Kolskiy Poluostrov, Russia 24 A6 67 30N 38 0 E
Kolachi →, Pakistan 42 F2 27 8N 67 2 E
Kolahoi, India 43 B6 34 12N 75 22 E
Kolaka, Indonesia 37 E6 4 3S 121 46 E
Kolar, India 40 N11 13 12N 78 15 E
Kolar Gold Fields, India 40 N11 12 58N 78 16 E
Kolaras, India 42 G6 25 14N 77 36 E
Kolari, Finland 8 C20 67 20N 23 48 E
Kolayat, India 40 F8 27 50N 72 50 E
Kolchugino = Leninsk-Kuznetskiy, Russia 26 D9 54 44N 86 10 E
Kolding, Denmark 9 J13 55 30N 9 29 E
Kolepom = Dolak, Pulau, Indonesia 37 F9 8 0S 138 30 E
Kolguyev, Ostrov, Russia 24 A8 69 20N 48 30 E
Kolhapur, India 40 L9 16 43N 74 15 E
Kolín, Czech Rep. 16 C8 50 2N 15 9 E
Kolkas rags, Latvia 9 H20 57 46N 22 37 E
Kollum, Neths. 15 A6 53 17N 6 10 E
Kolmanskop, Namibia 56 D2 26 45S 15 14 E
Köln, Germany 16 C4 50 56N 6 57 E
Koło, Poland 17 B10 52 14N 18 40 E
Kołobrzeg, Poland 16 A8 54 10N 15 35 E
Kolomna, Russia 24 C6 55 8N 38 45 E
Kolomyya, Ukraine 17 D13 48 31N 25 2 E
Kolonodale, Indonesia 37 E6 2 3S 121 25 E
Kolosib, India 41 G18 24 15N 92 45 E
Kolpashevo, Russia 26 D9 58 20N 83 5 E
Kolpino, Russia 24 C5 59 44N 30 39 E
Kolskiy Poluostrov, Russia 24 A6 67 30N 38 0 E
Kolskiy Zaliv, Russia 24 A5 69 23N 34 0 E
Kolwezi, Dem. Rep. of the Congo 55 E2 10 40S 25 25 E
Kolyma →, Russia 27 C17 69 30N 161 0 E
Kolymskoye Nagorye, Russia 27 C16 63 0N 157 0 E
Kôm Ombo, Egypt 51 D12 24 25N 32 52 E
Komandorskiye Is. = Komandorskiye Ostrova, Russia 27 D17 55 0N 167 0 E
Komandorskiye Ostrova, Russia 27 D17 55 0N 167 0 E
Komárno, Slovak Rep. 17 E10 47 49N 18 5 E
Komatipoort, S. Africa 57 D5 25 25S 31 55 E
Komatou Yialou, Cyprus 23 D13 35 25N 34 8 E
Komatsu, Japan 31 F8 36 25N 136 30 E
Komatsujima, Japan 31 H7 34 0N 134 35 E
Komi □, Russia 24 B10 64 0N 55 0 E
Kommunarsk = Alchevsk, Ukraine 25 E6 48 30N 38 45 E
Kommunizma, Pik, Tajikistan 26 F8 39 0N 72 2 E
Komodo, Indonesia 37 F5 8 37S 119 20 E
Komoran, Pulau, Indonesia 37 F9 8 18S 138 45 E
Komoro, Japan 31 F9 36 19N 138 26 E
Komotini, Greece 21 D11 41 9N 25 26 E
Kompasberg, S. Africa 56 E3 31 45S 24 32 E
Kompong Bang, Cambodia 39 F5 12 24N 104 40 E
Kompong Cham, Cambodia 39 G5 12 0N 105 30 E
Kompong Chhnang = Kampang Chhnang, Cambodia 39 F5 12 20N 104 35 E
Kompong Chikreng, Cambodia 38 F5 13 5N 104 18 E
Kompong Kleang, Cambodia 38 F5 13 6N 104 8 E
Kompong Luong, Cambodia 39 G5 11 49N 104 48 E
Kompong Pranak, Cambodia 38 F5 13 35N 104 55 E
Kompong Som = Kampong Saom, Cambodia 39 G4 10 38N 103 30 E
Kompong Som, Chhung = Kampong Saom, Chaak, Cambodia 39 G4 10 50N 103 32 E
Kompong Speu, Cambodia 39 G5 11 26N 104 32 E
Kompong Sralao, Cambodia 38 E5 14 5N 105 46 E
Kompong Thom, Cambodia 38 F5 12 35N 104 51 E
Kompong Trabeck, Cambodia 38 F5 13 6N 105 14 E
Kompong Trabeck, Cambodia 39 G5 11 9N 105 28 E
Kompong Trach, Cambodia 39 G5 11 25N 105 48 E
Kompong Tralach, Cambodia 39 G5 11 54N 104 47 E
Komrat = Comrat, Moldova 17 E15 46 18N 28 40 E
Komsberg, S. Africa 56 E3 32 40S 20 45 E
Komsomolets, Ostrov, Russia 27 A10 80 30N 95 0 E
Komsomolsk, Russia 27 D14 50 30N 137 0 E
Kon Tum, Vietnam 38 E7 14 24N 108 0 E
Kon Tum, Plateau du, Vietnam 38 E7 14 30N 108 30 E
Konarhā □, Afghan. 40 B7 35 30N 71 3 E
Konārī, Iran 45 D6 28 13N 51 36 E
Konch, India 43 G8 26 0N 79 10 E
Konde, Tanzania 54 C4 4 57S 39 45 E
Kondinin, Australia 61 F2 32 34S 118 8 E
Kondoa, Tanzania 54 C4 4 55S 35 50 E
Kondókali, Greece 23 A3 39 38N 19 51 E
Kondopaga, Russia 24 B5 62 12N 34 17 E
Kondratyevo, Russia 27 D10 57 22N 98 15 E
Köneürgench, Turkmenistan 26 E6 42 19N 59 10 E
Konevo, Russia 24 B6 62 8N 39 20 E
Kong = Khong →, Cambodia 38 F5 13 32N 105 58 E
Kong, Ivory C. 50 G5 8 54N 4 36W
Kong, Koh, Cambodia 39 G4 11 20N 103 0 E
Kong Christian IX.s Land, Greenland 4 C6 68 0N 36 0W
Kong Christian X.s Land, Greenland 4 B6 74 0N 29 0W
Kong Franz Joseph Fd., Greenland 4 B6 73 30N 24 30W
Kong Frederik IX.s Land, Greenland 4 C5 67 0N 52 0W
Kong Frederik VI.s Kyst, Greenland 4 C5 63 0N 43 0W
Kong Frederik VIII.s Land, Greenland 4 B6 78 30N 26 0W
Kong Oscar Fjord, Greenland 4 B6 72 20N 24 0W
Kongju, S. Korea 35 F14 36 30N 127 0 E
Konglu, Burma 41 F20 27 13N 97 57 E
Kongolo, Kasai-Or., Dem. Rep. of the Congo 54 D1 5 26S 24 49 E
Kongolo, Katanga, Dem. Rep. of the Congo 54 D2 5 22S 27 0 E
Kongsberg, Norway 9 G13 59 39N 9 39 E
Kongsvinger, Norway 9 F15 60 12N 12 2 E
Kongwa, Tanzania 54 D4 6 11S 36 26 E
Koni, Dem. Rep. of the Congo 55 E2 10 40S 27 11 E
Koni, Mts., Dem. Rep. of the Congo 55 E2 10 36S 27 10 E
Königsberg = Kaliningrad, Russia 9 J19 54 42N 20 32 E
Konin, Poland 17 B10 52 12N 18 15 E
Konjic, Bos.-H. 21 C7 43 42N 17 58 E
Konkiep, Namibia 56 D2 26 49S 17 15 E
Konosha, Russia 24 B7 61 0N 40 5 E
Kōnosu, Japan 31 F9 36 3N 139 31 E
Konotop, Ukraine 25 D5 51 12N 33 7 E
Końskie, Poland 17 C11 51 15N 20 23 E
Konstanz, Germany 16 E5 47 40N 9 10 E
Kont, Iran 45 E9 26 55N 61 50 E
Kontagora, Nigeria 50 F7 10 23N 5 27 E
Konya, Turkey 25 G5 37 52N 32 35 E
Konza, Kenya 54 C4 1 45S 37 7 E
Koocanusa, L., Canada 82 B6 49 20N 115 15W
Kookynie, Australia 61 E3 29 17S 121 22 E
Koolyanobbing, Australia 61 F2 30 48S 119 36 E
Koonibba, Australia 63 E1 31 54S 133 25 E
Koorawatha, Australia 63 E4 34 2S 148 33 E
Koorda, Australia 61 F2 30 48S 117 35 E
Kooskia, U.S.A. 82 C6 46 9N 115 59W
Kootenay →, U.S.A. 72 D5 49 19N 117 39W
Kootenay L., Canada 72 D5 49 45N 116 50W
Kootenay Nat. Park, Canada 72 C5 51 0N 116 0W
Kootjieskolk, S. Africa 56 E3 31 15S 20 21 E
Kopaonik, Serbia, Yug. 21 C9 43 10N 20 50 E
Kópavogur, Iceland 8 D3 64 6N 21 55W
Koper, Slovenia 16 F7 45 31N 13 44 E
Kopervik, Norway 9 G11 59 17N 5 17 E
Kopet Dagh, Asia 45 B8 38 0N 58 0 E
Kopi, Australia 63 E2 33 24S 135 40 E
Köping, Sweden 9 G17 59 31N 16 3 E
Koppeh Dāgh = Kopet Dagh, Asia 45 B8 38 0N 58 0 E
Koppies, S. Africa 57 D4 27 20S 27 30 E
Koprivnica, Croatia 20 A7 46 12N 16 45 E
Kopychyntsi, Ukraine 17 D13 49 7N 25 58 E
Korab, Macedonia 21 D9 41 44N 20 40 E
Korakiána, Greece 23 A3 39 42N 19 45 E
Koral, India 42 J5 21 50N 73 12 E
Korba, India 43 H10 22 20N 82 45 E
Korbu, G., Malaysia 39 K3 4 41N 101 18 E
Korça, Albania 21 D9 40 37N 20 50 E
Korce = Korça, Albania 21 D9 40 37N 20 50 E
Korčula, Croatia 20 C7 42 56N 16 57 E
Kord Kūy, Iran 45 B7 36 48N 54 7 E
Kord Sheykh, Iran 45 D7 28 31N 52 53 E
Kordestān □, Iran 44 C5 36 0N 47 0 E
Kordofân, Sudan 51 F11 13 0N 29 0 E
Korea, North ■, Asia 35 E14 40 0N 127 0 E
Korea, South ■, Asia 35 G15 36 0N 128 0 E
Korea Bay, Korea 35 E13 39 0N 124 0 E
Korea Strait, Asia 35 H15 34 0N 129 30 E
Korets, Ukraine 17 C14 50 40N 27 5 E
Korhogo, Ivory C. 50 G4 9 29N 5 28W
Korinthiakós Kólpos, Greece 21 E10 38 16N 22 30 E
Kórinthos, Greece 21 F10 37 56N 22 55 E
Korissa, Límni, Greece 23 B3 39 27N 19 53 E
Kōriyama, Japan 30 F10 37 24N 140 23 E
Korla, China 32 B3 41 45N 86 4 E
Kormakiti, C., Cyprus 23 D11 35 23N 32 56 E
Korneshty = Corneşti, Moldova 17 E15 47 21N 28 1 E
Koro, Fiji 59 C8 17 19S 179 23 E
Koro, Ivory C. 50 G4 8 32N 7 30W
Koro Sea, Fiji 59 C9 17 30S 179 45W
Korogwe, Tanzania 54 D4 5 5S 38 25 E
Koronadal, Phil. 37 C6 6 12N 125 1 E
Koror, Palau 37 C8 7 20N 134 28 E
Körös →, Hungary 17 E11 46 43N 20 12 E
Korosten, Ukraine 17 C15 50 54N 28 36 E
Korostyshev, Ukraine 17 C15 50 19N 29 4 E
Korraraika, Helodranon' i, Madag. 57 B7 17 45S 43 57 E
Korsakov, Russia 27 E15 46 36N 142 42 E
Korshunovo, Russia 27 D12 58 37N 110 10 E
Korsør, Denmark 9 J14 55 20N 11 9 E
Kortrijk, Belgium 15 D3 50 50N 3 17 E
Korwai, India 42 G8 24 7N 78 5 E
Koryakskoye Nagorye, Russia 27 C18 61 0N 171 0 E
Koryŏng, S. Korea 35 G15 35 44N 128 15 E
Kos, Greece 21 F12 36 50N 27 15 E
Koschagyl, Kazakstan 25 E9 46 40N 54 0 E
Kościan, Poland 17 B9 52 5N 16 40 E

Lappeenranta

Lappeenranta, *Finland* **9 F23** 61 3N 28 12 E
Lappland, *Europe* **8 B21** 68 7N 24 0 E
Laprida, *Argentina* **94 D3** 37 34S 60 45W
Lapseki, *Turkey* **21 D12** 40 20N 26 41 E
Laptev Sea, *Russia* **27 B13** 76 0N 125 0 E
Lapua, *Finland* **8 E20** 62 58N 23 0 E
L'Áquila, *Italy* **20 C5** 42 22N 13 22 E
Lār, *Āzarbājān-e Sharqī, Iran* **44 B5** 38 30N 47 52 E
Lār, *Fārs, Iran* **45 E7** 27 40N 54 14 E
Laramie, *U.S.A.* **80 E2** 41 19N 105 35W
Laramie ~►, *U.S.A.* **82 F11** 42 13N 104 33W
Laramie Mts., *U.S.A.* **80 E2** 42 0N 105 30W
Laranjeiras do Sul, *Brazil* **95 B5** 25 23S 52 23W
Larantuka, *Indonesia* **37 F6** 8 21S 122 55 E
Larat, *Indonesia* **37 F8** 7 0S 132 0 E
Larde, *Mozam.* **55 F4** 16 28S 39 43 E
Larder Lake, *Canada* **70 C4** 48 5N 79 40W
Lardhos, Ákra = Líndhos, Ákra, *Greece* **23 C10** 36 4N 28 10 E
Lardhos, Órmos, *Greece* **23 C10** 36 4N 28 2 E
Laredo, *U.S.A.* **81 M5** 27 30N 99 30W
Laredo Sd., *Canada* **72 C3** 52 30N 128 53W
Largo, *U.S.A.* **77 M4** 27 55N 82 47W
Largs, *U.K.* **12 F4** 55 47N 4 52W
Lariang, *Indonesia* **37 E5** 1 26S 119 17 E
Larimore, *U.S.A.* **80 B6** 47 54N 97 38W
Lārīn, *Iran* **45 C7** 35 55N 52 19 E
Lárisa, *Greece* **21 E10** 39 36N 22 27 E
Larkana, *Pakistan* **42 F3** 27 32N 68 18 E
Larnaca, *Cyprus* **23 E12** 34 55N 33 38 E
Larnaca Bay, *Cyprus* **23 E12** 34 53N 33 45 E
Larne, *U.K.* **13 B6** 54 51N 5 51W
Larned, *U.S.A.* **80 F5** 38 11N 99 6W
Larose, *U.S.A.* **81 L9** 29 34N 90 23W
Larrimah, *Australia* **60 C5** 15 35S 133 12 E
Larsen Ice Shelf, *Antarctica* **5 C17** 67 0S 62 0W
Larvik, *Norway* **9 G14** 59 4N 10 2 E
Las Animas, *U.S.A.* **80 F3** 38 4N 103 13W
Las Anod, *Somali Rep.* **46 F4** 8 26N 47 19 E
Las Aves, Is., *W. Indies* **89 C7** 15 45N 63 55W
Las Brenãs, *Argentina* **94 B3** 27 5S 61 7W
Las Cejas, *Argentina* **96 B4** 26 53S 64 44W
Las Chimeneas, *Mexico* **85 N10** 32 8N 116 5W
Las Cruces, *U.S.A.* **83 K10** 32 19N 106 47W
Las Flores, *Argentina* **94 D4** 36 10S 59 7W
Las Heras, *Argentina* **94 C2** 32 51S 68 49W
Las Lajas, *Argentina* **96 D2** 38 30S 70 25W
Las Lomitas, *Argentina* **94 A3** 24 43S 60 35W
Las Palmas, *Argentina* **94 B4** 27 8S 58 45W
Las Palmas, *Canary Is.* **22 F4** 28 7N 15 26W
Las Palmas ~►, *Mexico* **85 N10** 32 26N 116 54W
Las Piedras, *Uruguay* **95 C4** 34 44S 56 14W
Las Pipinas, *Argentina* **94 D4** 35 30S 57 19W
Las Plumas, *Argentina* **96 E3** 43 40S 67 15W
Las Rosas, *Argentina* **94 C3** 32 30S 61 35W
Las Tablas, *Panama* **88 E3** 7 49N 80 14W
Las Termas, *Argentina* **94 B3** 27 29S 64 52W
Las Toscas, *Argentina* **94 B4** 28 21S 59 18W
Las Truchas, *Mexico* **86 D4** 17 57N 102 13W
Las Varillas, *Argentina* **94 C3** 31 50S 62 50W
Las Vegas, *N. Mex., U.S.A.* **83 J11** 35 36N 105 13W
Las Vegas, *Nev., U.S.A.* **85 J11** 36 10N 115 9W
Lascano, *Uruguay* **95 C5** 33 35S 54 12W
Lashburn, *Canada* **73 C7** 53 10N 109 40W
Lashio, *Burma* **41 H20** 22 56N 97 45 E
Lashkar, *India* **42 F8** 26 10N 78 10 E
Lasíthi, *Greece* **23 D7** 35 11N 25 31 E
Lasíthi □, *Greece* **23 D7** 35 5N 25 50 E
Lāsjerd, *Iran* **45 C7** 35 24N 53 4 E
Lassen Pk., *U.S.A.* **82 F3** 40 29N 121 31W
Lassen Volcanic National Park, *U.S.A.* **82 F3** 40 30N 121 20W
Last Mountain L., *Canada* **73 C7** 51 5N 105 14W
Lastchance Cr. ~►, *U.S.A.* **84 E5** 40 2N 121 15W
Lastoursville, *Gabon* **52 E2** 0 55S 12 38 E
Lastovo, *Croatia* **20 C7** 42 46N 16 55 E
Lat Yao, *Thailand* **38 E2** 15 45N 99 48 E
Latacunga, *Ecuador* **92 D3** 0 50S 78 35W
Latakia = Al Lādhiqīyah, *Syria* **44 C2** 35 30N 35 45 E
Latchford, *Canada* **70 C4** 47 20N 79 50W
Latehar, *India* **43 H11** 23 45N 84 30 E
Latham, *Australia* **61 E2** 29 44S 116 20 E
Lathi, *India* **42 F4** 27 43N 71 23 E
Lathrop Wells, *U.S.A.* **85 J10** 36 39N 116 24W
Latina, *Italy* **20 D5** 41 28N 12 52 E
Latium = Lazio □, *Italy* **20 C5** 42 10N 12 30 E
Laton, *U.S.A.* **84 J7** 36 26N 119 41W
Latouche Treville, C., *Australia* **60 C3** 18 27S 121 49 E
Latrobe, *Australia* **62 G4** 41 14S 146 30 E
Latrobe, *U.S.A.* **78 F5** 40 19N 79 23W
Latvia ■, *Europe* **9 H20** 56 50N 24 0 E
Lau Group, *Fiji* **59 C9** 17 0S 178 30W
Lauchhammer, *Germany* **16 C7** 51 29N 13 47 E
Laughlin, *U.S.A.* **83 J6** 35 8N 114 35W
Laukaa, *Finland* **9 E21** 62 24N 25 56 E
Launceston, *Australia* **62 G4** 41 24S 147 8 E
Launceston, *U.K.* **11 G3** 50 38N 4 22W
Laune ~►, *Ireland* **13 D2** 52 7N 9 47W
Launglon Bok, *Burma* **38 F1** 13 50N 97 54 E
Laura, *Australia* **62 B3** 15 32S 144 32 E
Laurel, *Miss., U.S.A.* **81 K10** 31 41N 89 8W
Laurel, *Mont., U.S.A.* **82 D9** 45 40N 108 46W
Laurencekirk, *U.K.* **12 E6** 56 50N 2 28W
Laurens, *U.S.A.* **77 H4** 34 30N 82 1W
Laurentian Plateau, *Canada* **71 B6** 52 0N 70 0W
Lauria, *Italy* **20 E6** 40 2N 15 50 E
Laurie L., *Canada* **73 B8** 56 35N 101 57W
Laurinburg, *U.S.A.* **77 H6** 34 47N 79 28W
Laurium, *U.S.A.* **76 B1** 47 14N 88 27W
Lausanne, *Switz.* **18 C7** 46 32N 6 38 E
Laut, *Indonesia* **39 K6** 4 45N 108 0 E
Laut, Pulau, *Indonesia* **36 E5** 3 40S 116 10 E
Laut Kecil, Kepulauan, *Indonesia* **36 E5** 4 45S 115 40 E
Lautoka, *Fiji* **59 C7** 17 37S 177 27 E
Lavagh More, *Ireland* **13 B3** 54 46N 8 6W
Laval, *France* **18 B3** 48 4N 0 48W
Lavalle, *Argentina* **94 B2** 28 15S 65 15W
Lavant Station, *Canada* **79 A8** 45 3N 76 42W
Lāvar Meydān, *Iran* **45 D7** 30 20N 54 30 E
Laverton, *Australia* **61 E3** 28 44S 122 29 E
Lavras, *Brazil* **95 A7** 21 20S 45 0W
Lávrion, *Greece* **21 F11** 37 40N 24 4 E
Lávris, *Greece* **23 D6** 35 25N 24 40 E
Lavumisa, *Swaziland* **57 D5** 27 20S 31 55 E
Lawas, *Malaysia* **36 D5** 4 55N 115 25 E
Lawele, *Indonesia* **37 F6** 5 16S 123 3 E
Lawng Pit, *Burma* **41 G20** 25 30N 97 25 E
Lawqah, *Si. Arabia* **44 D4** 29 49N 42 45 E
Lawrence, *N.Z.* **59 L2** 45 55S 169 41 E
Lawrence, *Kans., U.S.A.* **80 F7** 38 58N 95 14W
Lawrence, *Mass., U.S.A.* **79 D13** 42 43N 71 10W
Lawrenceburg, *Ind., U.S.A.* **76 F3** 39 6N 84 52W
Lawrenceburg, *Tenn., U.S.A.* **77 H2** 35 14N 87 20W
Lawrenceville, *Ga., U.S.A.* **77 J4** 33 57N 83 59W
Lawrenceville, *Pa., U.S.A.* **78 E7** 41 59N 77 8W
Laws, *U.S.A.* **84 H8** 37 24N 118 20W
Lawton, *U.S.A.* **81 H5** 34 37N 98 25W
Lawu, *Indonesia* **37 G14** 7 40S 111 13 E
Laxford, L., *U.K.* **12 C3** 58 24N 5 6W
Laylá, *Si. Arabia* **46 C4** 22 10N 46 40 E
Laylān, *Iraq* **44 C5** 35 18N 44 31 E
Layton, *U.S.A.* **82 F7** 41 4N 111 58W
Laytonville, *U.S.A.* **82 G2** 39 41N 123 29W
Lazio □, *Italy* **20 C5** 42 10N 12 30 E
Lazo, *Russia* **30 C6** 43 25N 133 55 E
Le Creusot, *France* **18 C6** 46 48N 4 24 E
Le François, *Martinique* **89 D7** 14 38N 60 57W
Le Havre, *France* **18 B4** 49 30N 0 5 E
Le Mans, *France* **18 C4** 48 0N 0 10 E
Le Mars, *U.S.A.* **80 D6** 42 47N 96 10W
Le Mont-St-Michel, *France* **18 B3** 48 40N 1 30W
Le Moule, *Guadeloupe* **89 C7** 16 20N 61 22W
Le Puy-en-Velay, *France* **18 D5** 45 3N 3 52 E
Le Sueur, *U.S.A.* **80 C8** 44 28N 93 55W
Le Thuy, *Vietnam* **38 D6** 17 14N 106 49 E
Le Touquet-Paris-Plage, *France* **18 A4** 50 30N 1 36 E
Le Tréport, *France* **18 A4** 50 3N 1 20 E
Le Verdon-sur-Mer, *France* **18 D3** 45 33N 1 4W
Lea ~►, *U.K.* **11 F8** 51 31N 0 1 E
Leach, *Cambodia* **39 F4** 12 21N 103 46 E
Lead, *U.S.A.* **80 C3** 44 21N 103 46W
Leader, *Canada* **73 C7** 50 50N 109 30W
Leadville, *U.S.A.* **83 G10** 39 15N 106 18W
Leaf ~►, *U.S.A.* **81 K10** 30 59N 88 44W
Leaf Rapids, *Canada* **73 B9** 56 30N 99 59W
Leamington, *Canada* **78 D2** 42 3N 82 36W
Leamington, *U.S.A.* **82 G7** 39 32N 112 17W
Leamington Spa = Royal Leamington Spa, *U.K.* **11 E6** 52 18N 1 31W
Leandro Norte Alem, *Argentina* **95 B4** 27 34S 55 15W
Leane, L., *Ireland* **13 D2** 52 2N 9 32W
Learmonth, *Australia* **60 D1** 22 13S 114 10 E
Leask, *Canada* **73 C7** 53 5N 106 45W
Leatherhead, *U.K.* **11 F7** 51 18N 0 20W
Leavenworth, *Kans., U.S.A.* **80 F7** 39 19N 94 55W
Leavenworth, *Wash., U.S.A.* **82 C3** 47 36N 120 40W
Lebak, *Phil.* **37 C6** 6 32N 124 5 E
Lebam, *U.S.A.* **84 D3** 46 34N 123 33W
Lebanon, *Ind., U.S.A.* **76 E2** 40 3N 86 28W
Lebanon, *Kans., U.S.A.* **80 F5** 39 49N 98 33W
Lebanon, *Ky., U.S.A.* **76 G3** 37 34N 85 15W
Lebanon, *Mo., U.S.A.* **81 G8** 37 41N 92 40W
Lebanon, *N.H., U.S.A.* **79 C12** 43 39N 72 15W
Lebanon, *Oreg., U.S.A.* **82 D2** 44 32N 122 55W
Lebanon, *Pa., U.S.A.* **79 F8** 40 20N 76 26W
Lebanon, *Tenn., U.S.A.* **77 G2** 36 12N 86 18W
Lebanon ■, *Asia* **47 B5** 34 0N 36 0 E
Lebec, *U.S.A.* **85 L8** 34 50N 118 52W
Lebel-sur-Quévillon, *Canada* **70 C4** 49 3N 76 59W
Lebomboberge, *S. Africa* **57 C5** 24 30S 32 0 E
Lębork, *Poland* **17 A9** 54 33N 17 46 E
Lebrija, *Spain* **19 D2** 36 53N 6 5W
Lebu, *Chile* **94 D1** 37 40S 73 47W
Lecce, *Italy* **21 D8** 40 23N 18 11 E
Lecco, *Italy* **18 D8** 45 51N 9 23 E
Lech ~►, *Germany* **16 D6** 48 43N 10 56 E
Lecontes Mills, *U.S.A.* **78 E6** 41 5N 78 17W
Łęczyca, *Poland* **17 B10** 52 5N 19 15 E
Ledong, *China* **38 C7** 18 41N 109 5 E
Leduc, *Canada* **72 C6** 53 15N 113 30W
Lee, *U.S.A.* **79 D11** 42 19N 73 15W
Lee ~►, *Ireland* **13 E3** 51 53N 8 56W
Lee Vining, *U.S.A.* **84 H7** 37 58N 119 7W
Leech L., *U.S.A.* **80 B7** 47 10N 94 24W
Leechburg, *U.S.A.* **78 F5** 40 37N 79 36W
Leeds, *U.K.* **10 D6** 53 48N 1 33W
Leeds, *U.S.A.* **77 J2** 33 33N 86 33W
Leek, *Neths.* **15 A6** 53 10N 6 24 E
Leek, *U.K.* **10 D5** 53 7N 2 1W
Leeman, *Australia* **61 E1** 29 57S 114 58 E
Leeper, *U.S.A.* **78 E5** 41 22N 79 18W
Leer, *Germany* **16 B4** 53 13N 7 26 E
Leesburg, *U.S.A.* **77 L5** 28 49N 81 53W
Leesville, *U.S.A.* **81 K8** 31 9N 93 16W
Leeton, *Australia* **63 E4** 34 33S 146 23 E
Leetonia, *U.S.A.* **78 F4** 40 53N 80 45W
Leeu Gamka, *S. Africa* **56 E3** 32 47S 21 59 E
Leeuwarden, *Neths.* **15 A5** 53 15N 5 48 E
Leeuwin, C., *Australia* **61 F2** 34 20S 115 9 E
Leeward Is., *Atl. Oc.* **89 C7** 16 30N 63 30W
Lefka, *Cyprus* **23 D11** 35 6N 32 51 E
Lefkoniko, *Cyprus* **23 D12** 35 18N 33 44 E
Lefroy, *Canada* **78 B5** 44 16N 79 34W
Lefroy, L., *Australia* **61 F3** 31 21S 121 40 E
Leganés, *Spain* **19 B4** 40 19N 3 45W
Legazpi, *Phil.* **37 B6** 13 10N 123 45 E
Legendre I., *Australia* **60 D2** 20 22S 116 55 E
Leghorn = Livorno, *Italy* **20 C4** 43 33N 10 19 E
Legionowo, *Poland* **17 B11** 52 25N 20 50 E
Legnago, *Italy* **20 B4** 45 11N 11 18 E
Legnica, *Poland* **16 C9** 51 12N 16 10 E
Leh, *India* **43 B7** 34 9N 77 35 E
Lehigh Acres, *U.S.A.* **77 M5** 26 36N 81 39W
Lehighton, *U.S.A.* **79 F9** 40 50N 75 43W
Lehututu, *Botswana* **56 C3** 23 54S 21 55 E
Leiah, *Pakistan* **42 D4** 30 58N 70 58 E
Leicester, *U.K.* **11 E6** 52 38N 1 8W
Leicester City □, *U.K.* **11 E6** 52 38N 1 8W
Leicestershire □, *U.K.* **11 E6** 52 41N 1 17W
Leichhardt ~►, *Australia* **62 B2** 17 35S 139 48 E
Leichhardt Ra., *Australia* **62 C4** 20 46S 147 40 E
Leiden, *Neths.* **15 B4** 52 9N 4 30 E
Leie ~►, *Belgium* **15 C3** 51 2N 3 45 E
Leigh Creek, *Australia* **63 E2** 30 38S 138 26 E
Leine ~►, *Germany* **16 B5** 52 43N 9 36 E
Leinster, *Australia* **61 E3** 27 51S 120 36 E
Leinster □, *Ireland* **13 C4** 53 3N 7 8W
Leinster, Mt., *Ireland* **13 D5** 52 37N 6 46W
Leipzig, *Germany* **16 C7** 51 18N 12 22 E
Leiria, *Portugal* **19 C1** 39 46N 8 53W
Leirvik, *Norway* **9 G11** 59 47N 5 28 E
Leisler, Mt., *Australia* **60 D4** 23 23S 129 20 E
Leith, *U.K.* **12 F5** 55 59N 3 11W
Leith Hill, *U.K.* **11 F7** 51 11N 0 22W
Leitrim, *Ireland* **13 B3** 54 0N 8 5W
Leitrim □, *Ireland* **13 B4** 54 8N 8 0W
Leizhou Bandao, *China* **33 D6** 21 0N 110 0 E
Lek ~►, *Neths.* **15 C4** 51 54N 4 35 E
Leka, *Norway* **8 D14** 65 5N 11 35 E
Lékva Óros, *Greece* **23 D6** 35 18N 24 3 E
Leland, *Mich., U.S.A.* **76 C3** 45 1N 85 45W
Leland, *Miss., U.S.A.* **81 J9** 33 24N 90 54W
Leleque, *Argentina* **96 E2** 42 28S 71 0W
Lelystad, *Neths.* **15 B5** 52 30N 5 25 E
Léman, L., *Europe* **18 C7** 46 26N 6 30 E
Lemera, *Dem. Rep. of the Congo* **54 C2** 3 0S 28 55 E
Lemhi Ra., *U.S.A.* **82 D7** 44 30N 113 30W
Lemmer, *Neths.* **15 B5** 52 51N 5 43 E
Lemmon, *U.S.A.* **80 C3** 45 57N 102 10W
Lemon Grove, *U.S.A.* **85 N9** 32 45N 117 2W
Lemoore, *U.S.A.* **84 J7** 36 18N 119 46W
Lemvig, *Denmark* **9 H13** 56 33N 8 20 E
Lena ~►, *Russia* **27 B13** 72 52N 126 40 E
Léndas, *Greece* **23 E6** 34 56N 24 56 E
Lendeh, *Iran* **45 D6** 30 58N 50 25 E
Lenggong, *Malaysia* **39 K3** 5 6N 100 58 E
Lengua de Vaca, Pta., *Chile* **94 C1** 30 14S 71 38W
Leninabad = Khudzhand, *Tajikistan* **26 E7** 40 17N 69 37 E
Leninakan = Gyumri, *Armenia* **25 F7** 40 47N 43 50 E
Leningrad = Sankt-Peterburg, *Russia* **24 C5** 59 55N 30 20 E
Leninogorsk, *Kazakstan* **26 D9** 50 20N 83 30 E
Leninsk, *Russia* **25 E8** 48 40N 45 15 E
Leninsk-Kuznetskiy, *Russia* **26 D9** 54 44N 86 10 E
Lenkoran = Länkäran, *Azerbaijan* **25 G8** 38 48N 48 52 E
Lenmalu, *Indonesia* **37 E8** 1 45S 130 15 E
Lennox, *U.S.A.* **80 D6** 43 21N 96 53W
Lennoxville, *Canada* **79 A13** 45 22N 71 51W
Lenoir, *U.S.A.* **77 H5** 35 55N 81 32W
Lenoir City, *U.S.A.* **77 H3** 35 48N 84 16W
Lenore L., *Canada* **73 C8** 52 30N 104 59W
Lenox, *U.S.A.* **79 D11** 42 22N 73 17W
Lens, *France* **18 A5** 50 26N 2 50 E
Lensk, *Russia* **27 C12** 60 48N 114 55 E
Lentini, *Italy* **20 F6** 37 17N 15 0 E
Lenwood, *U.S.A.* **85 L9** 34 53N 117 7W
Lenya, *Burma* **36 B1** 11 33N 98 57 E
Leoben, *Austria* **16 E8** 47 22N 15 5 E
Leodhas = Lewis, *U.K.* **12 C2** 58 9N 6 40W
Leola, *U.S.A.* **80 C5** 45 43N 98 56W
Leominster, *U.K.* **11 E5** 52 14N 2 43W
Leominster, *U.S.A.* **79 D13** 42 32N 71 46W
León, *Mexico* **86 C4** 21 7N 101 40W
León, *Nic.* **88 D2** 12 20N 86 51W
León, *Spain* **19 A3** 42 38N 5 34W
Leon, *U.S.A.* **80 E8** 40 44N 93 45W
Leon ~►, *U.S.A.* **81 K6** 31 14N 97 28W
León, Montes de, *Spain* **19 A2** 42 30N 6 18W
Leonardtown, *U.S.A.* **76 F7** 38 17N 76 38W
Leongatha, *Australia* **63 F4** 38 30S 145 58 E
Leonora, *Australia* **61 E3** 28 49S 121 19 E
Léopold II, Lac = Mai-Ndombe, L., *Dem. Rep. of the Congo* **52 E3** 2 0S 18 20 E
Leopoldina, *Brazil* **95 A7** 21 28S 42 40W
Leopoldsburg, *Belgium* **15 C5** 51 7N 5 13 E
Léopoldville = Kinshasa, *Dem. Rep. of the Congo* **52 E3** 4 20S 15 15 E
Leoti, *U.S.A.* **80 F4** 38 29N 101 21W
Leova, *Moldova* **17 E15** 46 28N 28 15 E
Leoville, *Canada* **73 C7** 53 39N 107 33W
Lepel = Lyepyel, *Belarus* **24 D4** 54 50N 28 40 E
Lépo, L. do, *Angola* **56 B2** 17 0S 19 0 E
Leppävirta, *Finland* **9 E22** 62 29N 27 46 E
Lerdo, *Mexico* **86 B4** 25 32N 103 32W
Leribe, *Lesotho* **57 D4** 28 51S 28 3 E
Lérida = Lleida, *Spain* **19 B6** 41 37N 0 39 E
Lerwick, *U.K.* **12 A7** 60 9N 1 9W
Les Cayes, *Haiti* **89 C5** 18 15N 73 46W
Les Sables-d'Olonne, *France* **18 C3** 46 30N 1 45W
Lesbos = Lésvos, *Greece* **21 E12** 39 10N 26 20 E
Leshan, *China* **32 D5** 29 33N 103 41 E
Leshukonskoye, *Russia* **24 B8** 64 54N 45 46 E
Leskov I., *Antarctica* **5 B1** 56 0S 28 0W
Leskovac, *Serbia, Yug.* **21 C9** 43 0N 21 58 E
Lesopilnoye, *Russia* **30 A7** 46 44N 134 20 E
Lesotho ■, *Africa* **57 D4** 29 40S 28 0 E
Lesozavodsk, *Russia* **27 E14** 45 30N 133 29 E
Lesse ~►, *Belgium* **15 D4** 50 15N 4 54 E
Lesser Antilles, *W. Indies* **89 D7** 15 0N 61 0W
Lesser Slave L., *Canada* **72 B5** 55 30N 115 25W
Lesser Sunda Is., *Indonesia* **37 F6** 7 0S 120 0 E
Lessines, *Belgium* **15 D3** 50 42N 3 50 E
Lester, *U.S.A.* **84 C5** 47 12N 121 29W
Lestock, *Canada* **73 C8** 51 19N 103 59W
Lesuer I., *Australia* **60 B4** 13 50S 127 17 E
Lésvos, *Greece* **21 E12** 39 10N 26 20 E
Leszno, *Poland* **17 C9** 51 50N 16 30 E
Letchworth, *U.K.* **11 F7** 51 59N 0 13W
Lethbridge, *Canada* **72 D6** 49 45N 112 45W
Lethem, *Guyana* **92 C7** 3 20N 59 50W
Leti, Kepulauan, *Indonesia* **37 F7** 8 10S 128 0 E
Leti Is. = Leti, Kepulauan, *Indonesia* **37 F7** 8 10S 128 0 E
Letiahau ~►, *Botswana* **56 C3** 21 16S 24 0 E
Leticia, *Colombia* **92 D5** 4 9S 70 0W
Leting, *China* **35 E10** 39 23N 118 55 E
Letjiesbos, *S. Africa* **56 E3** 32 34S 22 16 E
Letlhakeng, *Botswana* **56 C3** 24 0S 24 59 E
Letong, *Indonesia* **36 D3** 2 58N 105 42 E
Letpadan, *Burma* **41 L19** 17 45N 95 45 E
Letpan, *Burma* **41 K19** 19 28N 94 10 E
Letsôk-aw Kyun, *Burma* **39 G2** 11 30N 98 25 E
Letterkenny, *Ireland* **13 B4** 54 57N 7 45W
Leucadia, *U.S.A.* **85 M9** 33 4N 117 18W
Leuser, G., *Indonesia* **36 D1** 3 46N 97 12 E
Leuven, *Belgium* **15 D4** 50 52N 4 42 E
Leuze-en-Hainaut, *Belgium* **15 D3** 50 36N 3 37 E
Levádhia, *Greece* **21 E10** 38 27N 22 54 E
Levanger, *Norway* **8 E14** 63 45N 11 19 E
Levelland, *U.S.A.* **81 J3** 33 35N 102 23W
Leven, *U.K.* **12 E6** 56 12N 3 0W
Leven, L., *U.K.* **12 E5** 56 12N 3 22W
Leven, Toraka, *Madag.* **57 A8** 12 30S 47 45 E
Leveque C., *Australia* **60 C3** 16 20S 123 0 E
Levice, *Slovak Rep.* **17 D10** 48 13N 18 35 E
Levin, *N.Z.* **59 J5** 40 37S 175 18 E
Lévis, *Canada* **71 C5** 46 48N 71 9W
Levis, L., *Canada* **72 A5** 62 37N 117 58W
Levittown, *N.Y., U.S.A.* **79 F11** 40 44N 73 31W
Levittown, *Pa., U.S.A.* **79 F10** 40 9N 74 51W
Levkás, *Greece* **21 E9** 38 40N 20 43 E
Levkímmi, *Greece* **23 B4** 39 25N 20 3 E
Levkímmi, Ákra, *Greece* **23 B4** 39 29N 20 4 E
Levkôsia = Nicosia, *Cyprus* **23 D12** 35 10N 33 25 E
Levskigrad = Karlovo, *Bulgaria* **21 C11** 42 38N 24 47 E
Lewes, *U.K.* **11 G8** 50 52N 0 1 E
Lewes, *U.S.A.* **76 F8** 38 46N 75 9W
Lewis, *U.K.* **12 C2** 58 9N 6 40W
Lewis ~►, *U.S.A.* **84 E4** 45 51N 122 48W
Lewis, Butt of, *U.K.* **12 C2** 58 31N 6 16W
Lewis Ra., *Australia* **60 D4** 20 3S 128 50 E
Lewis Range, *U.S.A.* **82 C7** 48 5N 113 5W
Lewis Run, *U.S.A.* **78 E6** 41 52N 78 40W
Lewisburg, *Pa., U.S.A.* **78 F8** 40 58N 76 54W
Lewisburg, *Tenn., U.S.A.* **77 H2** 35 27N 86 48W
Lewisburg, *W. Va., U.S.A.* **76 G5** 37 48N 80 27W
Lewisporte, *Canada* **71 C8** 49 15N 55 3W
Lewiston, *Idaho, U.S.A.* **82 C5** 46 25N 117 1W
Lewiston, *Maine, U.S.A.* **77 C11** 44 6N 70 13W
Lewiston, *N.Y., U.S.A.* **78 C5** 43 11N 79 3W
Lewistown, *Mont., U.S.A.* **82 C9** 47 4N 109 26W
Lewistown, *Pa., U.S.A.* **78 F7** 40 36N 77 34W
Lexington, *Ill., U.S.A.* **80 E10** 40 39N 88 47W
Lexington, *Ky., U.S.A.* **76 F3** 38 3N 84 30W
Lexington, *Mich., U.S.A.* **78 C2** 43 16N 82 32W
Lexington, *Mo., U.S.A.* **80 F8** 39 11N 93 52W
Lexington, *N.C., U.S.A.* **77 H5** 35 49N 80 15W
Lexington, *N.Y., U.S.A.* **79 D10** 42 15N 74 22W
Lexington, *Nebr., U.S.A.* **80 E5** 40 47N 99 45W
Lexington, *Ohio, U.S.A.* **78 F2** 40 41N 82 35W
Lexington, *Tenn., U.S.A.* **77 H1** 35 39N 88 24W
Lexington, *Va., U.S.A.* **76 G6** 37 47N 79 27W
Lexington Park, *U.S.A.* **76 F7** 38 16N 76 27W
Leyburn, *U.K.* **10 C6** 54 19N 1 48W
Leyland, *U.K.* **10 D5** 53 42N 2 43W
Leyte, *Phil.* **37 B7** 11 0N 125 0 E
Lezha, *Albania* **21 D8** 41 47N 19 39 E
Lhasa, *China* **32 D4** 29 25N 90 58 E
Lhazê, *China* **32 D3** 29 5N 87 38 E
Lhokkruet, *Indonesia* **36 D1** 4 55N 95 24 E
Lhokseumawe, *Indonesia* **36 C1** 5 10N 97 10 E
L'Hospitalet de Llobregat, *Spain* **19 B7** 41 21N 2 6 E
Lhuntsi Dzong, *India* **41 F17** 27 39N 91 10 E
Li, *Thailand* **38 D2** 17 48N 98 57 E
Li Xian, *Gansu, China* **34 G3** 34 10N 105 5 E
Li Xian, *Hebei, China* **34 E8** 38 30N 115 35 E
Lianga, *Phil.* **37 C7** 8 38N 126 6 E
Liangcheng, *Nei Mongol Zizhiqu, China* **34 D7** 40 28N 112 25 E
Liangcheng, *Shandong, China* **35 G10** 35 32N 119 37 E
Liangdang, *China* **34 H4** 33 56N 106 18 E
Liangpran, *Indonesia* **36 D4** 1 4N 114 23 E
Lianshanguan, *China* **35 D12** 40 53N 123 43 E
Lianshui, *China* **35 H10** 33 42N 119 20 E
Lianyungang, *China* **35 G10** 34 40N 119 11 E
Liao He ~►, *China* **35 D11** 41 0N 121 50 E
Liaocheng, *China* **34 F8** 36 28N 115 58 E
Liaodong Bandao, *China* **35 E12** 40 0N 122 30 E
Liaodong Wan, *China* **35 D11** 40 20N 121 10 E
Liaoning □, *China* **35 D12** 41 40N 122 30 E
Liaoyang, *China* **35 D12** 41 15N 122 58 E
Liaoyuan, *China* **35 C13** 42 58N 125 2 E
Liaozhong, *China* **35 D12** 41 23N 122 50 E
Liard ~►, *Canada* **72 A4** 61 51N 121 18W
Liard River, *Canada* **72 B3** 59 25N 126 5W
Liari, *Pakistan* **42 G2** 25 37N 66 30 E
Libau = Liepāja, *Latvia* **9 H19** 56 30N 21 0 E
Libby, *U.S.A.* **82 B6** 48 23N 115 33W
Libenge, *Dem. Rep. of the Congo* **52 D3** 3 40N 18 55 E
Liberal, *U.S.A.* **81 G4** 37 3N 100 55W
Liberec, *Czech Rep.* **16 C8** 50 47N 15 7 E
Liberia, *Costa Rica* **88 D2** 10 40N 85 30W
Liberia ■, *W. Afr.* **50 G4** 6 30N 9 30W
Liberty, *Mo., U.S.A.* **80 F7** 39 15N 94 25W
Liberty, *N.Y., U.S.A.* **79 E10** 41 48N 74 45W
Liberty, *Pa., U.S.A.* **78 E7** 41 34N 77 6W
Liberty, *Tex., U.S.A.* **81 K7** 30 3N 94 48W
Lībīya, Sahrā', *Africa* **51 C10** 25 0N 25 0 E
Libobo, Tanjung, *Indonesia* **37 E7** 0 54S 128 28 E
Libode, *S. Africa* **57 E4** 31 33S 29 2 E
Libourne, *France* **18 D3** 44 55N 0 14W
Libramont, *Belgium* **15 E5** 49 55N 5 23 E
Libreville, *Gabon* **52 D1** 0 25N 9 26 E
Libya ■, *N. Afr.* **51 C9** 27 0N 17 0 E
Libyan Desert = Lībīya, Sahrā', *Africa* **51 C10** 25 0N 25 0 E
Licantén, *Chile* **94 D1** 35 55S 72 0W
Licata, *Italy* **20 F5** 37 6N 13 56 E
Licheng, *China* **34 F7** 36 28N 113 20 E
Lichfield, *U.K.* **11 E6** 52 41N 1 49W
Lichinga, *Mozam.* **55 E4** 13 13S 35 11 E
Lichtenburg, *S. Africa* **56 D4** 26 8S 26 8 E
Licking ~►, *U.S.A.* **76 F3** 39 6N 84 30W
Lida, *Belarus* **9 K21** 53 53N 25 15 E
Lidköping, *Sweden* **9 G15** 58 31N 13 7 E
Liebig, Mt., *Australia* **60 D5** 23 18S 131 22 E
Liechtenstein ■, *Europe* **18 C8** 47 8N 9 35 E
Liège, *Belgium* **15 D5** 50 38N 5 35 E
Liège □, *Belgium* **15 D5** 50 32N 5 35 E
Liegnitz = Legnica, *Poland* **16 C9** 51 12N 16 10 E
Lienart, *Dem. Rep. of the Congo* **54 B2** 3 3N 25 31 E
Lienyünchiangshih = Lianyungang, *China* **35 G10** 34 40N 119 11 E
Lienz, *Austria* **16 E7** 46 50N 12 46 E
Liepāja, *Latvia* **9 H19** 56 30N 21 0 E
Lier, *Belgium* **15 C4** 51 7N 4 34 E
Lièvre ~►, *Canada* **70 C4** 45 31N 75 26W
Liffey ~►, *Ireland* **13 C5** 53 21N 6 13W
Lifford, *Ireland* **13 B4** 54 51N 7 29W

Mallaig

McConaughy, L., *U.S.A.* **80 E4** 41 14N 101 40W
McCook, *U.S.A.* **80 E4** 40 12N 100 38W
McCreary, *Canada* **73 C9** 50 47N 99 29W
McCullough Mt., *U.S.A.* **85 K11** 35 35N 115 13W
McCusker →, *Canada* **73 B7** 55 32N 108 39W
McDame, *Canada* **72 B3** 59 44N 128 59W
McDermitt, *U.S.A.* **82 F5** 41 59N 117 43W
McDonald, *U.S.A.* **78 F4** 40 22N 80 14W
Macdonald, L., *Australia* **60 D4** 23 30S 129 0 E
McDonald Is., *Ind. Oc.* **3 G13** 53 0S 73 0 E
MacDonnell Ranges, *Australia* **60 D5** 23 40S 133 0 E
MacDowell L., *Canada* **70 B1** 52 15N 92 45W
Macduff, *U.K.* **12 D6** 57 40N 2 31W
Macedonia = Makedhonía □, *Greece* **21 D10** 40 39N 22 0 E
Macedonia, *U.S.A.* **78 E3** 41 19N 81 31W
Macedonia ■, *Europe* **21 D9** 41 53N 21 40 E
Maceió, *Brazil* **93 E11** 9 40S 35 41W
Macerata, *Italy* **20 C5** 43 18N 13 27 E
McFarland, *U.S.A.* **85 K7** 35 41N 119 14W
McFarlane →, *Canada* **73 B7** 59 12N 107 58W
Macfarlane, L., *Australia* **63 E2** 32 0S 136 40 E
McGehee, *U.S.A.* **81 J9** 33 38N 91 24W
McGill, *U.S.A.* **82 G6** 39 23N 114 47W
Macgillycuddy's Reeks, *Ireland* **13 E2** 51 58N 9 45W
McGraw, *U.S.A.* **79 D8** 42 36N 76 8W
McGregor, *U.S.A.* **80 D9** 43 1N 91 11W
McGregor Ra., *Australia* **63 D3** 27 0S 142 45 E
Mach, *Pakistan* **40 E5** 29 50N 67 20 E
Māch Kowr, *Iran* **45 E9** 25 48N 61 28 E
Machado = Jiparaná →, *Brazil* **92 E6** 8 3S 62 52W
Machagai, *Argentina* **94 B3** 26 56S 60 2W
Machakos, *Kenya* **54 C4** 1 30S 37 15 E
Machala, *Ecuador* **92 D3** 3 20S 79 57W
Machanga, *Mozam.* **57 C6** 20 59S 35 0 E
Machattie, L., *Australia* **62 C2** 24 50S 139 48 E
Machava, *Mozam.* **57 D5** 25 54S 32 28 E
Machece, *Mozam.* **55 F4** 19 15S 35 32 E
Machhu →, *India* **42 H4** 23 6N 70 46 E
Machias, *Maine, U.S.A.* **77 C12** 44 43N 67 28W
Machias, *N.Y., U.S.A.* **78 D6** 42 25N 78 30W
Machichi →, *Canada* **73 B10** 57 3N 92 6W
Machico, *Madeira* **22 D3** 32 43N 16 44W
Machilipatnam, *India* **41 L12** 16 12N 81 8 E
Machiques, *Venezuela* **92 A4** 10 4N 72 34W
Machupicchu, *Peru* **92 F4** 13 8S 72 30W
Machynlleth, *U.K.* **11 E4** 52 35N 3 50W
McIlwraith Ra., *Australia* **62 A3** 13 50S 143 20 E
McInnes L., *Canada* **73 C10** 52 13N 93 45W
McIntosh, *U.S.A.* **80 C4** 45 55N 101 21W
McIntosh L., *Canada* **73 B8** 55 45N 105 0W
Macintosh Ra., *Australia* **61 E4** 27 39S 125 32 E
Macintyre →, *Australia* **63 D5** 28 37S 150 47 E
Mackay, *Australia* **62 C4** 21 8S 149 11 E
Mackay, *U.S.A.* **82 E7** 43 55N 113 37W
MacKay →, *Canada* **72 B6** 57 10N 111 38W
Mackay, L., *Australia* **60 D4** 22 30S 129 0 E
McKay Ra., *Australia* **60 D3** 23 0S 122 30 E
McKeesport, *U.S.A.* **78 F5** 40 21N 79 52W
McKellar, *Canada* **78 A5** 45 30N 79 55W
McKenna, *U.S.A.* **84 D4** 46 56N 122 33W
Mackenzie, *Canada* **72 B4** 55 20N 123 5W
McKenzie, *U.S.A.* **77 G1** 36 8N 88 31W
Mackenzie →, *Australia* **62 C4** 23 38S 149 46 E
Mackenzie →, *Canada* **68 B6** 69 10N 134 20W
McKenzie →, *U.S.A.* **82 D2** 44 7N 123 6W
Mackenzie Bay, *Canada* **4 B1** 69 0N 137 30W
Mackenzie City = Linden, *Guyana* **92 B7** 6 0N 58 10W
Mackenzie Mts., *Canada* **68 B7** 64 0N 130 0W
Mackinaw City, *U.S.A.* **76 C3** 45 47N 84 44W
McKinlay, *Australia* **62 C3** 21 16S 141 18 E
McKinlay →, *Australia* **62 C3** 20 50S 141 28 E
McKinley, Mt., *U.S.A.* **68 B4** 63 4N 151 0W
McKinley Sea, *Arctic* **4 A7** 82 0N 0 0 E
McKinney, *U.S.A.* **81 J6** 33 12N 96 37W
Mackinnon Road, *Kenya* **54 C4** 3 40S 39 1 E
McKittrick, *U.S.A.* **85 K7** 35 18N 119 37W
Macklin, *Canada* **73 C7** 52 20N 109 56W
Macksville, *Australia* **63 E5** 30 40S 152 56 E
McLaughlin, *U.S.A.* **80 C4** 45 49N 100 49W
Maclean, *Australia* **63 D5** 29 26S 153 16 E
McLean, *U.S.A.* **81 H4** 35 14N 100 36W
McLeansboro, *U.S.A.* **80 F10** 38 6N 88 32W
Maclear, *S. Africa* **57 E4** 31 2S 28 23 E
Macleay →, *Australia* **63 E5** 30 56S 153 0 E
McLennan, *Canada* **72 B5** 55 42N 116 50W
McLeod →, *Canada* **72 C5** 54 9N 115 44W
MacLeod, B., *Canada* **73 A7** 62 53N 110 0W
McLeod, L., *Australia* **61 D1** 24 9S 113 47 E
MacLeod Lake, *Canada* **72 C4** 54 58N 123 0W
McLoughlin, Mt., *U.S.A.* **82 E2** 42 27N 122 19W
McMechen, *U.S.A.* **78 G4** 39 57N 80 44W
McMinnville, *Oreg., U.S.A.* **82 D2** 45 13N 123 12W
McMinnville, *Tenn., U.S.A.* **77 H3** 35 41N 85 46W
McMurdo Sd., *Antarctica* **5 D11** 77 0S 170 0 E
McMurray = Fort McMurray, *Canada* **72 B6** 56 44N 111 7W
McMurray, *U.S.A.* **84 B4** 48 19N 122 14W
Macodoene, *Mozam.* **57 C6** 23 32S 35 5 E
Macomb, *U.S.A.* **80 E9** 40 27N 90 40W
Mâcon, *France* **18 C6** 46 19N 4 50 E
Macon, *Ga., U.S.A.* **77 J4** 32 51N 83 38W
Macon, *Miss., U.S.A.* **77 J1** 33 7N 88 34W
Macon, *Mo., U.S.A.* **80 F8** 39 44N 92 28W
Macossa, *Mozam.* **55 F3** 17 55S 33 56 E
Macoun L., *Canada* **73 B8** 56 32N 103 40W
Macovane, *Mozam.* **57 C6** 21 30S 35 2 E
McPherson, *U.S.A.* **80 F6** 38 22N 97 40W
McPherson Pk., *U.S.A.* **85 L7** 34 53N 119 53W
McPherson Ra., *Australia* **63 D5** 28 15S 153 15 E
Macquarie →, *Australia* **63 E4** 30 5S 147 30 E
Macquarie Harbour, *Australia* **62 G4** 42 15S 145 23 E
Macquarie Is., *Pac. Oc.* **64 N7** 54 36S 158 55 E
MacRobertson Land, *Antarctica* **5 D6** 71 0S 64 0 E
Macroom, *Ireland* **13 E3** 51 54N 8 57W
MacTier, *Canada* **78 A5** 45 9N 79 46W
Macubela, *Mozam.* **55 F4** 16 53S 37 49 E
Macuiza, *Mozam.* **55 F3** 18 7S 34 29 E
Macusani, *Peru* **92 F4** 14 4S 70 29W
Macuse, *Mozam.* **55 F4** 17 45S 37 10 E
Macuspana, *Mexico* **87 D6** 17 46N 92 36W
Macusse, *Angola* **56 B3** 17 48S 20 23 E
Madadeni, *S. Africa* **57 D5** 27 43S 30 3 E
Madagascar ■, *Africa* **57 C8** 20 0S 47 0 E
Madā'in Sālih, *Si. Arabia* **44 E3** 26 46N 37 57 E
Madama, *Niger* **51 D8** 22 0N 13 40 E
Madame I., *Canada* **71 C7** 45 30N 60 58W
Madaripur, *Bangla.* **41 H17** 23 19N 90 15 E
Madauk, *Burma* **41 L20** 17 56N 96 52 E
Madawaska, *Canada* **78 A7** 45 30N 78 0W
Madawaska →, *Canada* **78 A8** 45 27N 76 21W
Madaya, *Burma* **41 H20** 22 12N 96 10 E
Maddalena, *Italy* **20 D3** 41 16N 9 23 E
Madeira, *Atl. Oc.* **22 D3** 32 50N 17 0W
Madeira →, *Brazil* **92 D7** 3 22S 58 45W
Madeleine, Îs. de la, *Canada* **71 C7** 47 30N 61 40W
Madera, *Mexico* **86 B3** 29 12N 108 7W
Madera, *Calif., U.S.A.* **84 J6** 36 57N 120 3W
Madera, *Pa., U.S.A.* **78 F6** 40 49N 78 26W
Madha, *India* **40 L9** 18 0N 75 30 E
Madhavpur, *India* **42 J3** 21 15N 69 58 E
Madhepura, *India* **43 F12** 26 11N 86 23 E
Madhubani, *India* **43 F12** 26 21N 86 7 E
Madhupur, *India* **43 G12** 24 16N 86 39 E
Madhya Pradesh □, *India* **42 J8** 22 50N 78 0 E
Madidi →, *Bolivia* **92 F5** 12 32S 66 52W
Madikeri, *India* **40 N9** 12 30N 75 45 E
Madill, *U.S.A.* **81 H6** 34 6N 96 46W
Madimba, *Dem. Rep. of the Congo* **52 E3** 4 58S 15 5 E
Ma'din, *Syria* **44 C3** 35 45N 39 36 E
Madingou, *Congo* **52 E2** 4 10S 13 33 E
Madirovalo, *Madag.* **57 B8** 16 26S 46 32 E
Madison, *Calif., U.S.A.* **84 G5** 38 41N 121 59W
Madison, *Fla., U.S.A.* **77 K4** 30 28N 83 25W
Madison, *Ind., U.S.A.* **76 F3** 38 44N 85 23W
Madison, *Nebr., U.S.A.* **80 E6** 41 50N 97 27W
Madison, *Ohio, U.S.A.* **78 E3** 41 46N 81 3W
Madison, *S. Dak., U.S.A.* **80 D6** 44 0N 97 7W
Madison, *Wis., U.S.A.* **80 D10** 43 4N 89 24W
Madison →, *U.S.A.* **82 D8** 45 56N 111 31W
Madison Heights, *U.S.A.* **76 G6** 37 25N 79 8W
Madisonville, *Ky., U.S.A.* **76 G2** 37 20N 87 30W
Madisonville, *Tex., U.S.A.* **81 K7** 30 57N 95 55W
Madista, *Botswana* **56 C4** 21 15S 25 6 E
Madiun, *Indonesia* **37 G14** 7 38S 111 32 E
Madoc, *Canada* **78 B7** 44 30N 77 28W
Madona, *Latvia* **9 H22** 56 53N 26 5 E
Madrakah, Ra's al, *Oman* **46 D6** 19 0N 57 50 E
Madras = Chennai, *India* **40 N12** 13 8N 80 19 E
Madras = Tamil Nadu □, *India* **40 P10** 11 0N 77 0 E
Madras, *U.S.A.* **82 D3** 44 38N 121 8W
Madre, L., *Mexico* **87 C5** 25 0N 97 30W
Madre, Laguna, *U.S.A.* **81 M6** 27 0N 97 30W
Madre, Sierra, *Phil.* **37 A6** 17 0N 122 0 E
Madre de Dios →, *Bolivia* **92 F5** 10 59S 66 8W
Madre de Dios, I., *Chile* **96 G1** 50 20S 75 10W
Madre del Sur, Sierra, *Mexico* **87 D5** 17 30N 100 0W
Madre Occidental, Sierra, *Mexico* **86 B3** 27 0N 107 0W
Madre Oriental, Sierra, *Mexico* **86 C5** 25 0N 100 0W
Madri, *India* **42 G5** 24 16N 73 32 E
Madrid, *Spain* **19 B4** 40 25N 3 45W
Madrid, *U.S.A.* **79 B9** 44 45N 75 8W
Madura, *Australia* **61 F4** 31 55S 127 0 E
Madura, *Indonesia* **37 G15** 7 30S 114 0 E
Madura, Selat, *Indonesia* **37 G15** 7 30S 113 20 E
Madurai, *India* **40 Q11** 9 55N 78 10 E
Madurantakam, *India* **40 N11** 12 30N 79 50 E
Mae Chan, *Thailand* **38 B2** 20 9N 99 52 E
Mae Hong Son, *Thailand* **38 C2** 19 16N 97 56 E
Mae Khlong →, *Thailand* **38 F3** 13 24N 100 0 E
Mae Phrik, *Thailand* **38 D2** 17 27N 99 7 E
Mae Ramat, *Thailand* **38 D2** 16 58N 98 31 E
Mae Rim, *Thailand* **38 C2** 18 54N 98 57 E
Mae Sot, *Thailand* **38 D2** 16 43N 98 34 E
Mae Suai, *Thailand* **38 C2** 19 39N 99 33 E
Mae Tha, *Thailand* **38 C2** 18 28N 99 8 E
Maebashi, *Japan* **31 F9** 36 24N 139 4 E
Maesteg, *U.K.* **11 F4** 51 36N 3 40W
Maestra, Sierra, *Cuba* **88 B4** 20 15N 77 0W
Maevatanana, *Madag.* **57 B8** 16 56S 46 49 E
Mafeking = Mafikeng, *S. Africa* **56 D4** 25 50S 25 38 E
Mafeking, *Canada* **73 C8** 52 40N 101 10W
Mafeteng, *Lesotho* **56 D4** 29 51S 27 15 E
Maffra, *Australia* **63 F4** 37 53S 146 58 E
Mafia I., *Tanzania* **54 D4** 7 45S 39 50 E
Mafikeng, *S. Africa* **56 D4** 25 50S 25 38 E
Mafra, *Brazil* **95 B6** 26 10S 49 55W
Mafra, *Portugal* **19 C1** 38 55N 9 20W
Mafungabusi Plateau, *Zimbabwe* **55 F2** 18 30S 29 8 E
Magadan, *Russia* **27 D16** 59 38N 150 50 E
Magadi, *Kenya* **54 C4** 1 54S 36 19 E
Magadi, L., *Kenya* **54 C4** 1 54S 36 19 E
Magaliesburg, *S. Africa* **57 D4** 26 0S 27 32 E
Magallanes, Estrecho de, *Chile* **96 G2** 52 30S 75 0W
Magangué, *Colombia* **92 B4** 9 14N 74 45W
Magdalen Is. = Madeleine, Îs. de la, *Canada* **71 C7** 47 30N 61 40W
Magdalena, *Argentina* **94 D4** 35 5S 57 30W
Magdalena, *Bolivia* **92 F6** 13 13S 63 57W
Magdalena, *Mexico* **86 A2** 30 50N 112 0W
Magdalena, *U.S.A.* **83 J10** 34 7N 107 15W
Magdalena →, *Colombia* **92 A4** 11 6N 74 51W
Magdalena →, *Mexico* **86 A2** 30 40N 112 25W
Magdalena, B., *Mexico* **86 C2** 24 30N 112 10W
Magdalena, Llano de la, *Mexico* **86 C2** 25 0N 111 30W
Magdeburg, *Germany* **16 B6** 52 7N 11 38 E
Magdelaine Cays, *Australia* **62 B5** 16 33S 150 18 E
Magee, *U.S.A.* **81 K10** 31 52N 89 44W
Magelang, *Indonesia* **37 G14** 7 29S 110 13 E
Magellan's Str. = Magallanes, Estrecho de, *Chile* **96 G2** 52 30S 75 0W
Magenta, L., *Australia* **61 F2** 33 30S 119 2 E
Magerøya, *Norway* **8 A21** 71 3N 25 40 E
Maggiore, Lago, *Italy* **18 D8** 45 57N 8 39 E
Maghâgha, *Egypt* **51 C12** 28 38N 30 50 E
Magherafelt, *U.K.* **13 B5** 54 45N 6 37W
Maghreb, *N. Afr.* **50 B5** 32 0N 4 0W
Magistralnyy, *Russia* **27 D11** 56 16N 107 36 E
Magnetic Pole (North) = North Magnetic Pole, *Canada* **4 B2** 77 58N 102 8W
Magnetic Pole (South) = South Magnetic Pole, *Antarctica* **5 C9** 64 8S 138 8 E
Magnitogorsk, *Russia* **24 D10** 53 27N 59 4 E
Magnolia, *Ark., U.S.A.* **81 J8** 33 16N 93 14W
Magnolia, *Miss., U.S.A.* **81 K9** 31 9N 90 28W
Magog, *Canada* **79 A12** 45 18N 72 9W
Magoro, *Uganda* **54 B3** 1 45N 34 12 E
Magosa = Famagusta, *Cyprus* **23 D12** 35 8N 33 55 E
Magouládhes, *Greece* **23 A3** 39 45N 19 42 E
Magoye, *Zambia* **55 F2** 16 1S 27 30 E
Magozal, *Mexico* **87 C5** 21 34N 97 59W
Magpie, L., *Canada* **71 B7** 51 0N 64 41W
Magrath, *Canada* **72 D6** 49 25N 112 50W
Maguarinho, C., *Brazil* **93 D9** 0 15S 48 30W
Mağusa = Famagusta, *Cyprus* **23 D12** 35 8N 33 55 E
Maguse L., *Canada* **73 A9** 61 40N 95 10W
Maguse Pt., *Canada* **73 A10** 61 20N 93 50W
Magvana, *India* **42 H3** 23 13N 69 22 E
Magwe, *Burma* **41 J19** 20 10N 95 0 E
Maha Sarakham, *Thailand* **38 D4** 16 12N 103 16 E
Mahābād, *Iran* **44 B5** 36 50N 45 45 E
Mahabharat Lekh, *Nepal* **43 E10** 28 30N 82 0 E
Mahabo, *Madag.* **57 C7** 20 23S 44 40 E
Mahadeo Hills, *India* **43 H8** 22 20N 78 30 E
Mahaffey, *U.S.A.* **78 F6** 40 53N 78 44W
Mahagi, *Dem. Rep. of the Congo* **54 B3** 2 20N 31 0 E
Mahajamba →, *Madag.* **57 B8** 15 33S 47 8 E
Mahajamba, Helodranon' i, *Madag.* **57 B8** 15 24S 47 5 E
Mahajan, *India* **42 E5** 28 48N 73 56 E
Mahajanga, *Madag.* **57 B8** 15 40S 46 25 E
Mahajanga □, *Madag.* **57 B8** 17 0S 47 0 E
Mahajilo →, *Madag.* **57 B8** 19 42S 45 22 E
Mahakam →, *Indonesia* **36 E5** 0 35S 117 17 E
Mahalapye, *Botswana* **56 C4** 23 1S 26 51 E
Maḩallāt, *Iran* **45 C6** 33 55N 50 30 E
Māhān, *Iran* **45 D8** 30 5N 57 18 E
Mahan →, *India* **43 H10** 23 30N 82 50 E
Mahanadi →, *India* **41 J15** 20 20N 86 25 E
Mahananda →, *India* **43 G12** 25 12N 87 52 E
Mahanoro, *Madag.* **57 B8** 19 54S 48 48 E
Mahanoy City, *U.S.A.* **79 F8** 40 49N 76 9W
Maharashtra □, *India* **40 J9** 20 30N 75 30 E
Mahari Mts., *Tanzania* **54 D3** 6 20S 30 0 E
Mahasham, W. →, *Egypt* **47 E3** 30 15N 34 10 E
Mahasolo, *Madag.* **57 B8** 19 7S 46 22 E
Mahattat ash Shīdīyah, *Jordan* **47 F4** 29 55N 35 55 E
Mahattat 'Unayzah, *Jordan* **47 E4** 30 30N 35 47 E
Mahaxay, *Laos* **38 D5** 17 22N 105 12 E
Mahbubnagar, *India* **40 L10** 16 45N 77 59 E
Maḩḑah, *Oman* **45 E7** 24 24N 55 59 E
Mahdia, *Tunisia* **51 A8** 35 28N 11 0 E
Mahe, *India* **43 C8** 33 10N 78 32 E
Mahendragarh, *India* **42 E7** 28 17N 76 14 E
Mahenge, *Tanzania* **55 D4** 8 45S 36 41 E
Maheno, *N.Z.* **59 L3** 45 10S 170 50 E
Mahesana, *India* **42 H5** 23 39N 72 26 E
Maheshwar, *India* **42 H6** 22 11N 75 35 E
Mahgawan, *India* **43 F8** 26 29N 78 37 E
Mahi →, *India* **42 H5** 22 15N 72 55 E
Mahia Pen., *N.Z.* **59 H6** 39 9S 177 55 E
Mahilyow, *Belarus* **17 B16** 53 55N 30 18 E
Mahmud Kot, *Pakistan* **42 D4** 30 16N 71 0 E
Mahnomen, *U.S.A.* **80 B7** 47 19N 95 58W
Mahoba, *India* **43 G8** 25 15N 79 55 E
Mahón = Maó, *Spain* **22 B11** 39 53N 4 16 E
Mahone Bay, *Canada* **71 D7** 44 30N 64 20W
Mahopac, *U.S.A.* **79 E11** 41 22N 73 45W
Mahuva, *India* **42 J4** 21 5N 71 48 E
Mai-Ndombe, L., *Dem. Rep. of the Congo* **52 E3** 2 0S 18 20 E
Mai-Sai, *Thailand* **38 B2** 20 20N 99 55 E
Maicurú →, *Brazil* **93 D8** 2 14S 54 17W
Maidan Khula, *Afghan.* **42 C3** 33 36N 69 50 E
Maidenhead, *U.K.* **11 F7** 51 31N 0 42W
Maidstone, *Canada* **73 C7** 53 5N 109 20W
Maidstone, *U.K.* **11 F8** 51 16N 0 32 E
Maiduguri, *Nigeria* **51 F8** 12 0N 13 20 E
Maihar, *India* **43 G9** 24 16N 80 45 E
Maijdi, *Bangla.* **41 H17** 22 48N 91 10 E
Maikala Ra., *India* **41 J12** 22 0N 81 0 E
Mailani, *India* **43 E9** 28 17N 80 21 E
Mailsi, *Pakistan* **42 E5** 29 48N 72 15 E
Main →, *Germany* **16 C5** 50 0N 8 18 E
Main →, *U.K.* **13 B5** 54 48N 6 18W
Maine, *France* **18 C3** 48 20N 0 15W
Maine □, *U.S.A.* **77 C11** 45 20N 69 0W
Maine →, *Ireland* **13 D2** 52 9N 9 45W
Maingkwan, *Burma* **41 F20** 26 15N 96 37 E
Mainit, L., *Phil.* **37 C7** 9 31N 125 30 E
Mainland, *Orkney, U.K.* **12 C5** 58 59N 3 8W
Mainland, *Shet., U.K.* **12 A7** 60 15N 1 22W
Mainoru, *Australia* **62 A1** 14 0S 134 6 E
Mainpuri, *India* **43 F8** 27 18N 79 4 E
Maintirano, *Madag.* **57 B7** 18 3S 44 1 E
Mainz, *Germany* **16 C5** 50 1N 8 14 E
Maipú, *Argentina* **94 D4** 36 52S 57 50W
Maiquetía, *Venezuela* **92 A5** 10 36N 66 57W
Mairabari, *India* **41 F18** 26 30N 92 22 E
Maisí, *Cuba* **89 B5** 20 17N 74 9W
Maisí, Pta. de, *Cuba* **89 B5** 20 10N 74 10W
Maitland, *N.S.W., Australia* **63 E5** 32 33S 151 36 E
Maitland, *S. Austral., Australia* **63 E2** 34 23S 137 40 E
Maitland →, *Canada* **78 C3** 43 45N 81 43W
Maiz, Is. del, *Nic.* **88 D3** 12 15N 83 4W
Maizuru, *Japan* **31 G7** 35 25N 135 22 E
Majalengka, *Indonesia* **37 G13** 6 50S 108 13 E
Majene, *Indonesia* **37 E5** 3 38S 118 57 E
Majorca = Mallorca, *Spain* **22 B10** 39 30N 3 0 E
Makale, *Indonesia* **37 E5** 3 6S 119 51 E
Makamba, *Burundi* **54 C2** 4 8S 29 49 E
Makarikari = Makgadikgadi Salt Pans, *Botswana* **56 C4** 20 40S 25 45 E
Makarovo, *Russia* **27 D11** 57 40N 107 45 E
Makasar = Ujung Pandang, *Indonesia* **37 F5** 5 10S 119 20 E
Makasar, Selat, *Indonesia* **37 E5** 1 0S 118 20 E
Makasar, Str. of = Makasar, Selat, *Indonesia* **37 E5** 1 0S 118 20 E
Makat, *Kazakstan* **25 E9** 47 39N 53 19 E
Makedhonía □, *Greece* **21 D10** 40 39N 22 0 E
Makedonija = Macedonia ■, *Europe* **21 D9** 41 53N 21 40 E
Makena, *U.S.A.* **74 H16** 20 39N 156 27W
Makeyevka = Makiyivka, *Ukraine* **25 E6** 48 0N 38 0 E
Makgadikgadi Salt Pans, *Botswana* **56 C4** 20 40S 25 45 E
Makhachkala, *Russia* **25 F8** 43 0N 47 30 E
Makhmūr, *Iraq* **44 C4** 35 46N 43 35 E
Makian, *Indonesia* **37 D7** 0 20N 127 20 E
Makindu, *Kenya* **54 C4** 2 18S 37 50 E
Makinsk, *Kazakstan* **26 D8** 52 37N 70 26 E
Makiyivka, *Ukraine* **25 E6** 48 0N 38 0 E
Makkah, *Si. Arabia* **46 C2** 21 30N 39 54 E
Makkovik, *Canada* **71 A8** 55 10N 59 10W
Makó, *Hungary* **17 E11** 46 14N 20 33 E
Makokou, *Gabon* **52 D2** 0 40N 12 50 E
Makongo, *Dem. Rep. of the Congo* **54 B2** 3 25N 26 17 E
Makoro, *Dem. Rep. of the Congo* **54 B2** 3 10N 29 59 E
Makrai, *India* **40 H10** 22 2N 77 0 E
Makran Coast Range, *Pakistan* **40 G4** 25 40N 64 0 E
Makrana, *India* **42 F6** 27 2N 74 46 E
Makriyialos, *Greece* **23 D7** 35 2N 25 59 E
Mākū, *Iran* **44 B5** 39 15N 44 31 E
Makunda, *Botswana* **56 C3** 22 30S 20 7 E
Makurazaki, *Japan* **31 J5** 31 15N 130 20 E
Makurdi, *Nigeria* **50 G7** 7 43N 8 35 E
Makūyeh, *Iran* **45 D7** 28 7N 53 9 E
Makwassie, *S. Africa* **56 D4** 27 17S 26 0 E
Mal B., *Ireland* **13 D2** 52 50N 9 30W
Mala, Pta., *Panama* **88 E3** 7 28N 80 2W
Malabar Coast, *India* **40 P9** 11 0N 75 0 E
Malabo = Rey Malabo, *Eq. Guin.* **52 D1** 3 45N 8 50 E
Malacca, Str. of, *Indonesia* **39 L3** 3 0N 101 0 E
Malad City, *U.S.A.* **82 E7** 42 12N 112 15W
Maladzyechna, *Belarus* **17 A14** 54 20N 26 50 E
Málaga, *Spain* **19 D3** 36 43N 4 23W
Malagarasi, *Tanzania* **54 D3** 5 5S 30 50 E
Malagarasi →, *Tanzania* **54 D2** 5 12S 29 47 E
Malagasy Rep. = Madagascar ■, *Africa* **57 C8** 20 0S 47 0 E
Malahide, *Ireland* **13 C5** 53 26N 6 9W
Malaimbandy, *Madag.* **57 C8** 20 20S 45 36 E
Malakâl, *Sudan* **51 G12** 9 33N 31 40 E
Malakand, *Pakistan* **42 B4** 34 40N 71 55 E
Malakwal, *Pakistan* **42 C5** 32 34N 73 13 E
Malamala, *Indonesia* **37 E6** 3 21S 120 55 E
Malanda, *Australia* **62 B4** 17 22S 145 35 E
Malang, *Indonesia* **37 G15** 7 59S 112 45 E
Malangen, *Norway* **8 B18** 69 24N 18 37 E
Malanje, *Angola* **52 F3** 9 36S 16 17 E
Mälaren, *Sweden* **9 G17** 59 30N 17 10 E
Malargüe, *Argentina* **94 D2** 35 32S 69 30W
Malartic, *Canada* **70 C4** 48 9N 78 9W
Malaryta, *Belarus* **17 C13** 51 50N 24 3 E
Malatya, *Turkey* **25 G6** 38 25N 38 20 E
Malawi ■, *Africa* **55 E3** 11 55S 34 0 E
Malawi, L. = Nyasa, L., *Africa* **55 E3** 12 30S 34 30 E
Malay Pen., *Asia* **39 J3** 7 25N 100 0 E
Malaya Vishera, *Russia* **24 C5** 58 55N 32 25 E
Malaybalay, *Phil.* **37 C7** 8 5N 125 7 E
Malāyer, *Iran* **45 C6** 34 19N 48 51 E
Malaysia ■, *Asia* **39 K4** 5 0N 110 0 E
Malazgirt, *Turkey* **25 G7** 39 10N 42 33 E
Malbon, *Australia* **62 C3** 21 5S 140 17 E
Malbooma, *Australia* **63 E1** 30 41S 134 11 E
Malbork, *Poland* **17 B10** 54 3N 19 1 E
Malcolm, *Australia* **61 E3** 28 51S 121 25 E
Malcolm, Pt., *Australia* **61 F3** 33 48S 123 45 E
Maldah, *India* **43 G13** 25 2N 88 9 E
Maldegem, *Belgium* **15 C3** 51 14N 3 26 E
Malden, *Mass., U.S.A.* **79 D13** 42 26N 71 4W
Malden, *Mo., U.S.A.* **81 G10** 36 34N 89 57W
Malden I., *Kiribati* **65 H12** 4 3S 155 1W
Maldives ■, *Ind. Oc.* **29 J11** 5 0N 73 0 E
Maldonado, *Uruguay* **95 C5** 34 59S 55 0W
Maldonado, Punta, *Mexico* **87 D5** 16 19N 98 35W
Malé, *Maldives* **29 J11** 4 0N 73 28 E
Malé Karpaty, *Slovak Rep.* **17 D9** 48 30N 17 20 E
Maléa, Ákra, *Greece* **21 F10** 36 28N 23 7 E
Malegaon, *India* **40 J9** 20 30N 74 38 E
Malei, *Mozam.* **55 F4** 17 12S 36 58 E
Malek Kandī, *Iran* **44 B5** 37 9N 46 6 E
Malela, *Dem. Rep. of the Congo* **54 C2** 4 22S 26 8 E
Malema, *Mozam.* **55 E4** 14 57S 37 20 E
Máleme, *Greece* **23 D5** 35 31N 23 49 E
Maleny, *Australia* **63 D5** 26 45S 152 52 E
Malerkotla, *India* **42 D6** 30 32N 75 58 E
Máles, *Greece* **23 D7** 35 6N 25 35 E
Malgomaj, *Sweden* **8 D17** 64 40N 16 30 E
Malha, *Sudan* **51 E11** 15 8N 25 10 E
Malhargarh, *India* **42 G6** 24 17N 74 59 E
Malheur →, *U.S.A.* **82 D5** 44 4N 116 59W
Malheur L., *U.S.A.* **82 E4** 43 20N 118 48W
Mali ■, *Africa* **50 E5** 17 0N 3 0W
Mali →, *Burma* **41 G20** 25 40N 97 40 E
Mali Kyun, *Burma* **38 F2** 13 0N 98 20 E
Malibu, *U.S.A.* **85 L8** 34 2N 118 41W
Maliku, *Indonesia* **37 E6** 0 39S 123 16 E
Malili, *Indonesia* **37 E6** 2 42S 121 6 E
Malimba, Mts., *Dem. Rep. of the Congo* **54 D2** 7 30S 29 30 E
Malin Hd., *Ireland* **13 A4** 55 23N 7 23W
Malin Pen., *Ireland* **13 A4** 55 20N 7 17W
Malindi, *Kenya* **54 C5** 3 12S 40 5 E
Malines = Mechelen, *Belgium* **15 C4** 51 2N 4 29 E
Malino, *Indonesia* **37 D6** 1 0N 121 0 E
Malinyi, *Tanzania* **55 D4** 8 56S 36 0 E
Malita, *Phil.* **37 C7** 6 19N 125 39 E
Maliwun, *Burma* **36 B1** 10 17N 98 40 E
Maliya, *India* **42 H4** 23 5N 70 46 E
Malkara, *Turkey* **21 D12** 40 53N 26 53 E
Mallacoota Inlet, *Australia* **63 F4** 37 34S 149 40 E
Mallaig, *U.K.* **12 D3** 57 0N 5 50W

Mallawan, *India* 43 F9 27 4N 80 12 E
Mallawi, *Egypt* 51 C12 27 44N 30 44 E
Mállia, *Greece* 23 D7 35 17N 25 32 E
Mallión, Kólpos, *Greece* 23 D7 35 19N 25 27 E
Mallorca, *Spain* 22 B10 39 30N 3 0 E
Mallorytown, *Canada* 79 B9 44 29N 75 53W
Mallow, *Ireland* 13 D3 52 8N 8 39W
Malmberget, *Sweden* 8 C19 67 11N 20 40 E
Malmédy, *Belgium* 15 D6 50 25N 6 2 E
Malmesbury, *S. Africa* 56 E2 33 28S 18 41 E
Malmö, *Sweden* 9 J15 55 36N 12 59 E
Malolos, *Phil.* 37 B6 14 50N 120 49 E
Malombe L., *Malawi* 55 E4 14 40S 35 15 E
Malone, *U.S.A.* 79 B10 44 51N 74 18W
Måløy, *Norway* 9 F11 61 57N 5 6 E
Malpaso, *Canary Is.* 22 G1 27 43N 18 3W
Malpelo, I. de, *Colombia* 92 C2 4 3N 81 35W
Malpur, *India* 42 H5 23 21N 73 27 E
Malpura, *India* 42 F6 26 17N 75 23 E
Malta, *Idaho, U.S.A.* 82 E7 42 18N 113 22W
Malta, *Mont., U.S.A.* 82 B10 48 21N 107 52W
Malta ■, *Europe* 23 D2 35 50N 14 30 E
Maltahöhe, *Namibia* 56 C2 24 55S 17 0 E
Malton, *Canada* 78 C5 43 42N 79 38W
Malton, *U.K.* 10 C7 54 8N 0 49W
Maluku, *Indonesia* 37 E7 1 0S 127 0 E
Maluku ◻, *Indonesia* 37 E7 3 0S 128 0 E
Maluku Sea = Molucca Sea, *Indonesia* 37 E6 2 0S 124 0 E
Malvan, *India* 40 L8 16 2N 73 30 E
Malvern, *U.S.A.* 81 H8 34 22N 92 49W
Malvern Hills, *U.K.* 11 E5 52 0N 2 19W
Malvinas, Is. = Falkland Is. ◻, *Atl. Oc.* 96 G5 51 30S 59 0W
Malya, *Tanzania* 54 C3 3 5S 33 38 E
Malyn, *Ukraine* 17 C15 50 46N 29 3 E
Malyy Lyakhovskiy, Ostrov, *Russia* 27 B15 74 7N 140 36 E
Mama, *Russia* 27 D12 58 18N 112 54 E
Mamanguape, *Brazil* 93 E11 6 50S 35 4W
Mamarr Mitlā, *Egypt* 47 E1 30 2N 32 54 E
Mamasa, *Indonesia* 37 E5 2 55S 119 20 E
Mambasa, *Dem. Rep. of the Congo* 54 B2 1 22N 29 3 E
Mamberamo →, *Indonesia* 37 E9 2 0S 137 50 E
Mambilima Falls, *Zambia* 55 E2 10 31S 28 45 E
Mambirima, *Dem. Rep. of the Congo* 55 E2 11 25S 27 33 E
Mambo, *Tanzania* 54 C4 4 52S 38 22 E
Mambrui, *Kenya* 54 C5 3 5S 40 5 E
Mamburao, *Phil.* 37 B6 13 13N 120 39 E
Mameigwess L., *Canada* 70 B2 52 35N 87 50W
Mammoth, *U.S.A.* 83 K8 32 43N 110 39W
Mammoth Cave National Park, *U.S.A.* 76 G3 37 8N 86 13W
Mamoré →, *Bolivia* 92 F5 10 23S 65 53W
Mamou, *Guinea* 50 F3 10 15N 12 0W
Mamuju, *Indonesia* 37 E5 2 41S 118 50 E
Man, *Ivory C.* 50 G4 7 30N 7 40W
Man, I. of, *U.K.* 10 C3 54 15N 4 30W
Man-Bazar, *India* 43 H12 23 4N 86 39 E
Man Na, *Burma* 41 H20 23 27N 97 19 E
Mana →, *Fr. Guiana* 93 B8 5 45N 53 55W
Manaar, G. of = Mannar, G. of, *Asia* 40 Q11 8 30N 79 0 E
Manacapuru, *Brazil* 92 D6 3 16S 60 37W
Manacor, *Spain* 22 B10 39 34N 3 13 E
Manado, *Indonesia* 37 D6 1 29N 124 51 E
Managua, *Nic.* 88 D2 12 6N 86 20W
Managua, L. de, *Nic.* 88 D2 12 20N 86 30W
Manakara, *Madag.* 57 C8 22 8S 48 1 E
Manali, *India* 42 C7 32 16N 77 10 E
Manama = Al Manāmah, *Bahrain* 45 E6 26 10N 50 30 E
Manambao →, *Madag.* 57 B7 17 35S 44 0 E
Manambato, *Madag.* 57 A8 13 43S 49 7 E
Manambolo →, *Madag.* 57 B7 19 18S 44 22 E
Manambolosy, *Madag.* 57 B8 16 2S 49 40 E
Mananara, *Madag.* 57 B8 16 10S 49 46 E
Mananara →, *Madag.* 57 C8 23 21S 47 42 E
Mananjary, *Madag.* 57 C8 21 13S 48 20 E
Manantenina, *Madag.* 57 C8 24 17S 47 19 E
Manaos = Manaus, *Brazil* 92 D7 3 0S 60 0W
Manapire →, *Venezuela* 92 B5 7 42N 66 7W
Manapouri, *N.Z.* 59 L1 45 34S 167 39 E
Manapouri, L., *N.Z.* 59 L1 45 32S 167 32 E
Manār, Jabal, *Yemen* 46 E3 14 2N 44 17 E
Manas, *China* 32 B3 44 17N 85 56 E
Manas →, *India* 41 F17 26 12N 90 40 E
Manaslu, *Nepal* 43 E11 28 33N 84 33 E
Manasquan, *U.S.A.* 79 F10 40 8N 74 3W
Manassa, *U.S.A.* 83 H11 37 11N 105 56W
Manaung, *Burma* 41 K18 18 45N 93 40 E
Manaus, *Brazil* 92 D7 3 0S 60 0W
Manawan L., *Canada* 73 B8 55 24N 103 14W
Manbij, *Syria* 44 B3 36 31N 37 57 E
Manchegorsk, *Russia* 26 C4 67 54N 32 58 E
Manchester, *U.K.* 10 D5 53 29N 2 12W
Manchester, *Calif., U.S.A.* 84 G3 38 58N 123 41W
Manchester, *Conn., U.S.A.* 79 E12 41 47N 72 31W
Manchester, *Ga., U.S.A.* 77 J3 32 51N 84 37W
Manchester, *Iowa, U.S.A.* 80 D9 42 29N 91 27W
Manchester, *Ky., U.S.A.* 76 G4 37 9N 83 46W
Manchester, *N.H., U.S.A.* 79 D13 42 59N 71 28W
Manchester, *N.Y., U.S.A.* 78 D7 42 56N 77 16W
Manchester, *Pa., U.S.A.* 79 F8 40 4N 76 43W
Manchester, *Tenn., U.S.A.* 77 H2 35 29N 86 5W
Manchester, *Vt., U.S.A.* 79 C11 43 10N 73 5W
Manchester L., *Canada* 73 A7 61 28N 107 29W
Manchhar L., *Pakistan* 42 F2 26 25N 67 39 E
Manchuria = Dongbei, *China* 35 D13 45 0N 125 0 E
Manchurian Plain, *China* 28 E16 47 0N 124 0 E
Mand →, *India* 43 J10 21 42N 83 15 E
Mand →, *Iran* 45 D7 28 20N 52 30 E
Manda, *Chunya, Tanzania* 54 D3 6 51S 32 29 E
Manda, *Ludewe, Tanzania* 55 E3 10 30S 34 40 E
Mandabé, *Madag.* 57 C7 21 0S 44 55 E
Mandaguari, *Brazil* 95 A5 23 32S 51 42W
Mandah = Töhöm, *Mongolia* 34 B5 44 27N 108 2 E
Mandal, *Norway* 9 G12 58 2N 7 25 E
Mandala, Puncak, *Indonesia* 37 E10 4 44S 140 20 E
Mandalay, *Burma* 41 J20 22 0N 96 4 E
Mandale = Mandalay, *Burma* 41 J20 22 0N 96 4 E
Mandalgarh, *India* 42 G6 25 12N 75 6 E
Mandalgovi, *Mongolia* 34 B4 45 45N 106 10 E
Mandalī, *Iraq* 44 C5 33 43N 45 28 E
Mandan, *U.S.A.* 80 B4 46 50N 100 54W
Mandar, Teluk, *Indonesia* 37 E5 3 35S 119 15 E
Mandaue, *Phil.* 37 B6 10 20N 123 56 E
Mandera, *Kenya* 54 B5 3 55N 41 53 E
Mandi, *India* 42 D7 31 39N 76 58 E
Mandi Dabwali, *India* 42 E6 29 58N 74 42 E
Mandimba, *Mozam.* 55 E4 14 20S 35 40 E
Mandioli, *Indonesia* 37 E7 0 40S 127 20 E
Mandla, *India* 43 H9 22 39N 80 30 E
Mandorah, *Australia* 60 B5 12 32S 130 42 E
Mandoto, *Madag.* 57 B8 19 34S 46 17 E
Mandra, *Pakistan* 42 C5 33 23N 73 12 E
Mandrare →, *Madag.* 57 D8 25 10S 46 30 E
Mandritsara, *Madag.* 57 B8 15 50S 48 49 E
Mandsaur, *India* 42 G6 24 3N 75 8 E
Mandurah, *Australia* 61 F2 32 36S 115 48 E
Mandvi, *India* 42 H3 22 51N 69 22 E
Mandya, *India* 40 N10 12 30N 77 0 E
Mandzai, *Pakistan* 42 D2 30 55N 67 6 E
Maneh, *Iran* 45 B8 37 39N 57 7 E
Maneroo Cr. →, *Australia* 62 C3 23 21S 143 53 E
Manfalût, *Egypt* 51 C12 27 20N 30 52 E
Manfredónia, *Italy* 20 D6 41 38N 15 55 E
Mangabeiras, Chapada das, *Brazil* 93 F9 10 0S 46 30W
Mangalia, *Romania* 17 G15 43 50N 28 35 E
Mangalore, *India* 40 N9 12 55N 74 47 E
Mangan, *India* 43 F13 27 31N 88 32 E
Mangaung, *S. Africa* 53 K5 29 10S 26 25 E
Mangawan, *India* 43 G9 24 41N 81 33 E
Mangaweka, *N.Z.* 59 H5 39 48S 175 47 E
Manggar, *Indonesia* 36 E3 2 50S 108 10 E
Manggawitu, *Indonesia* 37 E8 4 8S 133 32 E
Mangkalihat, Tanjung, *Indonesia* 37 D5 1 2N 118 59 E
Mangla, *Pakistan* 42 C5 33 7N 73 39 E
Mangla Dam, *Pakistan* 43 C5 33 9N 73 44 E
Manglaur, *India* 42 E7 29 44N 77 49 E
Mangnai, *China* 32 C4 37 52N 91 43 E
Mango, *Togo* 50 F6 10 20N 0 30 E
Mangoche, *Malawi* 55 E4 14 25S 35 16 E
Mangoky →, *Madag.* 57 C7 21 29S 43 41 E
Mangole, *Indonesia* 37 E6 1 50S 125 55 E
Mangombe, *Dem. Rep. of the Congo* 54 C2 1 20S 26 48 E
Mangonui, *N.Z.* 59 F4 35 1S 173 32 E
Mangrol, *Mad. P., India* 42 J4 21 7N 70 7 E
Mangrol, *Raj., India* 42 G6 25 20N 76 31 E
Mangueira, L. da, *Brazil* 95 C5 33 0S 52 50W
Mangum, *U.S.A.* 81 H5 34 53N 99 30W
Mangyshlak Poluostrov, *Kazakstan* 26 E6 44 30N 52 30 E
Manhattan, *U.S.A.* 80 F6 39 11N 96 35W
Manhiça, *Mozam.* 57 D5 25 23S 32 49 E
Mania →, *Madag.* 57 B8 19 42S 45 22 E
Manica, *Mozam.* 57 B5 18 58S 32 59 E
Manica e Sofala ◻, *Mozam.* 57 B5 19 10S 33 45 E
Manicaland ◻, *Zimbabwe* 55 F3 19 0S 32 30 E
Manicoré, *Brazil* 92 E6 5 48S 61 16W
Manicouagan →, *Canada* 71 C6 49 30N 68 30W
Manicouagan, Rés., *Canada* 71 B6 51 5N 68 40W
Maniema ◻, *Dem. Rep. of the Congo* 54 C2 3 0S 26 0 E
Manīfah, *Si. Arabia* 45 E6 27 44N 49 0 E
Manifold, C., *Australia* 62 C5 22 41S 150 50 E
Manigotagan, *Canada* 73 C9 51 6N 96 18W
Manigotagan →, *Canada* 73 C9 51 7N 96 20W
Manihari, *India* 43 G12 25 21N 87 38 E
Manihiki, *Cook Is.* 65 J11 10 24S 161 1W
Manika, Plateau de la, *Dem. Rep. of the Congo* 55 E2 10 0S 25 5 E
Manikpur, *India* 43 G9 25 4N 81 7 E
Manila, *Phil.* 37 B6 14 40N 121 3 E
Manila, *U.S.A.* 82 F9 40 59N 109 43W
Manila B., *Phil.* 37 B6 14 40N 120 35 E
Manilla, *Australia* 63 E5 30 45S 150 43 E
Maningrida, *Australia* 62 A1 12 3S 134 13 E
Manipur ◻, *India* 41 G19 25 0N 94 0 E
Manipur →, *Burma* 41 H19 23 45N 94 20 E
Manisa, *Turkey* 21 E12 38 38N 27 30 E
Manistee, *U.S.A.* 76 C2 44 15N 86 19W
Manistee →, *U.S.A.* 76 C2 44 15N 86 21W
Manistique, *U.S.A.* 76 C2 45 57N 86 15W
Manito L., *Canada* 73 C7 52 43N 109 43W
Manitoba ◻, *Canada* 73 B9 55 30N 97 0W
Manitoba, L., *Canada* 73 C9 51 0N 98 45W
Manitou, *Canada* 73 D9 49 15N 98 32W
Manitou, L., *Canada* 71 B6 50 55N 65 17W
Manitou Is., *U.S.A.* 76 C3 45 8N 86 0W
Manitou Springs, *U.S.A.* 80 F2 38 52N 104 55W
Manitoulin I., *Canada* 70 C3 45 40N 82 30W
Manitouwadge, *Canada* 70 C2 49 8N 85 48W
Manitowoc, *U.S.A.* 76 C2 44 5N 87 40W
Manizales, *Colombia* 92 B3 5 5N 75 32W
Manja, *Madag.* 57 C7 21 26S 44 20 E
Manjacaze, *Mozam.* 57 C5 24 45S 34 0 E
Manjakandriana, *Madag.* 57 B8 18 55S 47 47 E
Manjhand, *Pakistan* 42 G3 25 50N 68 10 E
Manjil, *Iran* 45 B6 36 46N 49 30 E
Manjimup, *Australia* 61 F2 34 15S 116 6 E
Manjra →, *India* 40 K10 18 49N 77 52 E
Mankato, *Kans., U.S.A.* 80 F5 39 47N 98 13W
Mankato, *Minn., U.S.A.* 80 C8 44 10N 94 0W
Mankayane, *Swaziland* 57 D5 26 40S 31 4 E
Mankera, *Pakistan* 42 D4 31 23N 71 26 E
Mankota, *Canada* 73 D7 49 25N 107 5W
Manlay = Üydzin, *Mongolia* 34 B4 44 9N 107 0 E
Manmad, *India* 40 J9 20 18N 74 28 E
Mann Ranges, *Australia* 61 E5 26 6S 130 5 E
Manna, *Indonesia* 36 E2 4 25S 102 55 E
Mannahill, *Australia* 63 E3 32 25S 140 0 E
Mannar, *Sri Lanka* 40 Q11 9 1N 79 54 E
Mannar, G. of, *Asia* 40 Q11 8 30N 79 0 E
Mannar I., *Sri Lanka* 40 Q11 9 5N 79 45 E
Mannheim, *Germany* 16 D5 49 29N 8 29 E
Manning, *Canada* 72 B5 56 53N 117 39W
Manning, *Oreg., U.S.A.* 84 E3 45 45N 123 13W
Manning, *S.C., U.S.A.* 77 J5 33 42N 80 13W
Manning Prov. Park, *Canada* 72 D4 49 5N 120 45W
Mannum, *Australia* 63 E2 34 50S 139 20 E
Manoharpur, *India* 43 H11 22 23N 85 12 E
Manokwari, *Indonesia* 37 E8 0 54S 134 0 E
Manombo, *Madag.* 57 C7 22 57S 43 28 E
Manono, *Dem. Rep. of the Congo* 54 D2 7 15S 27 25 E
Manosque, *France* 18 E6 43 49N 5 47 E
Manotick, *Canada* 79 A9 45 13N 75 41W
Manouane →, *Canada* 71 C5 49 30N 71 10W
Manouane, L., *Canada* 71 B5 50 45N 70 45W
Manp'o, *N. Korea* 35 D14 41 6N 126 24 E
Manpojin = Manp'o, *N. Korea* 35 D14 41 6N 126 24 E
Manpur, *Mad. P., India* 42 H6 22 26N 75 37 E
Manpur, *Mad. P., India* 43 H10 23 17N 83 35 E
Manresa, *Spain* 19 B6 41 48N 1 50 E
Mansa, *Gujarat, India* 42 H5 23 27N 72 45 E
Mansa, *Punjab, India* 42 E6 30 0N 75 27 E
Mansa, *Zambia* 55 E2 11 13S 28 55 E
Mansehra, *Pakistan* 42 B5 34 20N 73 15 E
Mansel I., *Canada* 69 B12 62 0N 80 0W
Mansfield, *Australia* 63 F4 37 4S 146 6 E
Mansfield, *U.K.* 10 D6 53 9N 1 11W
Mansfield, *La., U.S.A.* 81 J8 32 2N 93 43W
Mansfield, *Mass., U.S.A.* 79 D13 42 2N 71 13W
Mansfield, *Ohio, U.S.A.* 78 F2 40 45N 82 31W
Mansfield, *Pa., U.S.A.* 78 E7 41 48N 77 5W
Mansfield, Mt., *U.S.A.* 79 B12 44 33N 72 49W
Manson Creek, *Canada* 72 B4 55 37N 124 32W
Manta, *Ecuador* 92 D2 1 0S 80 40W
Mantalingajan, Mt., *Phil.* 36 C5 8 55N 117 45 E
Mantare, *Tanzania* 54 C3 2 42S 33 13 E
Manteca, *U.S.A.* 84 H5 37 48N 121 13W
Manteo, *U.S.A.* 77 H8 35 55N 75 40W
Mantes-la-Jolie, *France* 18 B4 48 58N 1 41 E
Manthani, *India* 40 K11 18 40N 79 35 E
Manti, *U.S.A.* 82 G8 39 16N 111 38W
Mantiqueira, Serra da, *Brazil* 95 A7 22 0S 44 0W
Manton, *U.S.A.* 76 C3 44 25N 85 24W
Mántova, *Italy* 20 B4 45 9N 10 48 E
Mänttä, *Finland* 9 E21 62 0N 24 40 E
Mantua = Mántova, *Italy* 20 B4 45 9N 10 48 E
Manu, *Peru* 92 F4 12 10S 70 51W
Manu →, *Peru* 92 F4 12 16S 70 55W
Manua Is., *Amer. Samoa* 59 B14 14 13S 169 35W
Manuel Alves →, *Brazil* 93 F9 11 19S 48 28W
Manui, *Indonesia* 37 E6 3 35S 123 5 E
Manuripi →, *Bolivia* 92 F5 11 6S 67 36W
Many, *U.S.A.* 81 K8 31 34N 93 29W
Manyara, L., *Tanzania* 54 C4 3 40S 35 50 E
Manych-Gudilo, Ozero, *Russia* 25 E7 46 24N 42 38 E
Manyonga →, *Tanzania* 54 C3 4 10S 34 15 E
Manyoni, *Tanzania* 54 D3 5 45S 34 55 E
Manzai, *Pakistan* 42 C4 32 12N 70 15 E
Manzanares, *Spain* 19 C4 39 2N 3 22W
Manzanillo, *Cuba* 88 B4 20 20N 77 31W
Manzanillo, *Mexico* 86 D4 19 0N 104 20W
Manzanillo, Pta., *Panama* 88 E4 9 30N 79 40W
Manzano Mts., *U.S.A.* 83 J10 34 40N 106 20W
Manzarīyeh, *Iran* 45 C6 34 53N 50 50 E
Manzhouli, *China* 33 B6 49 35N 117 25 E
Manzini, *Swaziland* 57 D5 26 30S 31 25 E
Mao, *Chad* 51 F9 14 4N 15 19 E
Maó, *Spain* 22 B11 39 53N 4 16 E
Maoke, Pegunungan, *Indonesia* 37 E9 3 40S 137 30 E
Maolin, *China* 35 C12 43 58N 123 30 E
Maoming, *China* 33 D6 21 50N 110 54 E
Maoxing, *China* 35 B13 45 28N 124 40 E
Mapam Yumco, *China* 32 C3 30 45N 81 28 E
Mapastepec, *Mexico* 87 D6 15 26N 92 54W
Mapia, Kepulauan, *Indonesia* 37 D8 0 50N 134 20 E
Mapimí, *Mexico* 86 B4 25 50N 103 50W
Mapimí, Bolsón de, *Mexico* 86 B4 27 30N 104 15W
Mapinga, *Tanzania* 54 D4 6 40S 39 12 E
Mapinhane, *Mozam.* 57 C6 22 20S 35 0 E
Maple Creek, *Canada* 73 D7 49 55N 109 29W
Maple Valley, *U.S.A.* 84 C4 47 25N 122 3W
Mapleton, *U.S.A.* 82 D2 44 2N 123 52W
Mapuera →, *Brazil* 92 D7 1 5S 57 2W
Maputo, *Mozam.* 57 D5 25 58S 32 32 E
Maputo, B. de, *Mozam.* 57 D5 25 50S 32 45 E
Maqiaohe, *China* 35 B16 44 40N 130 30 E
Maqnā, *Si. Arabia* 44 D2 28 25N 34 50 E
Maquela do Zombo, *Angola* 52 F3 6 0S 15 15 E
Maquinchao, *Argentina* 96 E3 41 15S 68 50W
Maquoketa, *U.S.A.* 80 D9 42 4N 90 40W
Mar, Serra do, *Brazil* 95 B6 25 30S 49 0W
Mar Chiquita, L., *Argentina* 94 C3 30 40S 62 50W
Mar del Plata, *Argentina* 94 D4 38 0S 57 30W
Mar Menor, *Spain* 19 D5 37 40N 0 45W
Mara, *Tanzania* 54 C3 1 30S 34 32 E
Mara ◻, *Tanzania* 54 C3 1 45S 34 20 E
Maraã, *Brazil* 92 D5 1 52S 65 25W
Marabá, *Brazil* 93 E9 5 20S 49 5W
Maracá, I. de, *Brazil* 93 C8 2 10N 50 30W
Maracaibo, *Venezuela* 92 A4 10 40N 71 37W
Maracaibo, L. de, *Venezuela* 92 B4 9 40N 71 30W
Maracaju, *Brazil* 95 A4 21 38S 55 9W
Maracay, *Venezuela* 92 A5 10 15N 67 28W
Maradi, *Niger* 50 F7 13 29N 7 20 E
Marāgheh, *Iran* 44 B5 37 30N 46 12 E
Marāh, *Si. Arabia* 44 E5 25 0N 45 35 E
Marajó, I. de, *Brazil* 93 D9 1 0S 49 30W
Marākand, *Iran* 44 B5 38 51N 45 16 E
Maralal, *Kenya* 54 B4 1 0N 36 38 E
Maralinga, *Australia* 61 F5 30 13S 131 32 E
Maran, *Malaysia* 39 L4 3 35N 102 45 E
Marana, *U.S.A.* 83 K8 32 27N 111 13W
Maranboy, *Australia* 60 B5 14 40S 132 39 E
Marand, *Iran* 44 B5 38 30N 45 45 E
Marang, *Malaysia* 39 K4 5 12N 103 13 E
Maranguape, *Brazil* 93 D11 3 55S 38 50W
Maranhão = São Luís, *Brazil* 93 D10 2 39S 44 15W
Maranhão ◻, *Brazil* 93 E9 5 0S 46 0W
Maranoa →, *Australia* 63 D4 27 50S 148 37 E
Marañón →, *Peru* 92 D4 4 30S 73 35W
Marão, *Mozam.* 57 C5 24 18S 34 2 E
Maraş = Kahramanmaraş, *Turkey* 25 G6 37 37N 36 53 E
Marathasa ◻, *Cyprus* 23 E11 34 59N 32 51 E
Marathon, *Australia* 62 C3 20 51S 143 32 E
Marathon, *Canada* 70 C2 48 44N 86 23W
Marathon, *N.Y., U.S.A.* 79 D8 42 26N 76 2W
Marathon, *N.Y., U.S.A.* 79 D8 42 27N 76 2W
Marathon, *Tex., U.S.A.* 81 K3 30 12N 103 15W
Marathóvouno, *Cyprus* 23 D12 35 13N 33 37 E
Maratua, *Indonesia* 37 D5 2 10N 118 35 E
Maravatío, *Mexico* 86 D4 19 51N 100 25W
Marāwih, *U.A.E.* 45 E7 24 18N 53 18 E
Marbella, *Spain* 19 D3 36 30N 4 57W
Marble Bar, *Australia* 60 D2 21 9S 119 44 E
Marble Falls, *U.S.A.* 81 K5 30 35N 98 16W
Marblehead, *U.S.A.* 79 D14 42 30N 70 51W
Marburg, *Germany* 16 C5 50 47N 8 46 E
March, *U.K.* 11 E8 52 33N 0 5 E
Marche, *France* 18 C4 46 5N 1 20 E
Marche-en-Famenne, *Belgium* 15 D5 50 14N 5 19 E
Marchena, *Spain* 19 D3 37 18N 5 23W
Marco, *U.S.A.* 77 N5 25 58N 81 44W
Marcos Juárez, *Argentina* 94 C3 32 42S 62 5W
Marcus I. = Minami-Tori-Shima, *Pac. Oc.* 64 E7 24 20N 153 58 E
Marcus Necker Ridge, *Pac. Oc.* 64 F9 20 0N 175 0 E
Marcy, Mt., *U.S.A.* 79 B11 44 7N 73 56W
Mardan, *Pakistan* 42 B5 34 20N 72 0 E
Mardin, *Turkey* 25 G7 37 20N 40 43 E
Maree, L., *U.K.* 12 D3 57 40N 5 26W
Mareeba, *Australia* 62 B4 16 59S 145 28 E
Marek = Stanke Dimitrov, *Bulgaria* 21 C10 42 17N 23 9 E
Marengo, *U.S.A.* 80 E8 41 48N 92 4W
Marenyi, *Kenya* 54 C4 4 22S 39 8 E
Marerano, *Madag.* 57 C7 21 23S 44 52 E
Marfa, *U.S.A.* 81 K2 30 19N 104 1W
Marfa Pt., *Malta* 23 D1 35 59N 14 19 E
Margaret →, *Australia* 60 C4 18 9S 125 41 E
Margaret Bay, *Canada* 72 C3 51 20N 127 35W
Margaret L., *Canada* 72 B5 58 56N 115 25W
Margaret River, *Australia* 61 F2 33 57S 115 4 E
Margarita, I. de, *Venezuela* 92 A6 11 0N 64 0W
Margaritovo, *Russia* 30 C7 43 25N 134 45 E
Margate, *S. Africa* 57 E5 30 50S 30 20 E
Margate, *U.K.* 11 F9 51 23N 1 23 E
Marguerite, *Canada* 72 C4 52 30N 122 25W
Mari El ◻, *Russia* 24 C8 56 30N 48 0 E
Mari Indus, *Pakistan* 42 C4 32 57N 71 34 E
Mari Republic = Mari El ◻, *Russia* 24 C8 56 30N 48 0 E
María Elena, *Chile* 94 A2 22 18S 69 40W
María Grande, *Argentina* 94 C4 31 45S 59 55W
Maria I., *N. Terr., Australia* 62 A2 14 52S 135 45 E
Maria I., *Tas., Australia* 62 G4 42 35S 148 0 E
Maria van Diemen, C., *N.Z.* 59 F4 34 29S 172 40 E
Mariakani, *Kenya* 54 C4 3 50S 39 27 E
Marian, *Australia* 62 C4 21 9S 148 57 E
Marian L., *Canada* 72 A5 63 0N 116 15W
Mariana Trench, *Pac. Oc.* 28 H18 13 0N 145 0 E
Marianao, *Cuba* 88 B3 23 8N 82 24W
Marianna, *Ark., U.S.A.* 81 H9 34 46N 90 46W
Marianna, *Fla., U.S.A.* 77 K3 30 46N 85 14W
Marias →, *U.S.A.* 82 C8 47 56N 110 30W
Mariato, Punta, *Panama* 88 E3 7 12N 80 52W
Maribor, *Slovenia* 16 E8 46 36N 15 40 E
Marico →, *Africa* 56 C4 23 35S 26 57 E
Maricopa, *Ariz., U.S.A.* 83 K7 33 4N 112 3W
Maricopa, *Calif., U.S.A.* 85 K7 35 4N 119 24W
Marié →, *Brazil* 92 D5 0 27S 66 26W
Marie Byrd Land, *Antarctica* 5 D14 79 30S 125 0W
Marie-Galante, *Guadeloupe* 89 C7 15 56N 61 16W
Mariecourt = Kangiqsujuaq, *Canada* 69 B12 61 30N 72 0W
Mariembourg, *Belgium* 15 D4 50 6N 4 31 E
Mariental, *Namibia* 56 C2 24 36S 18 0 E
Marienville, *U.S.A.* 78 E5 41 28N 79 8W
Mariestad, *Sweden* 9 G15 58 43N 13 50 E
Marietta, *Ga., U.S.A.* 77 J3 33 57N 84 33W
Marietta, *Ohio, U.S.A.* 76 F5 39 25N 81 27W
Marieville, *Canada* 79 A11 45 26N 73 10W
Mariinsk, *Russia* 26 D9 56 10N 87 20 E
Marijampole, *Lithuania* 9 J20 54 33N 23 19 E
Marília, *Brazil* 95 A6 22 13S 50 0W
Marín, *Spain* 19 A1 42 23N 8 42W
Marina, *U.S.A.* 84 J5 36 41N 121 48W
Marinduque, *Phil.* 37 B6 13 25N 122 0 E
Marinette, *U.S.A.* 76 C2 45 6N 87 38W
Maringá, *Brazil* 95 A5 23 26S 52 2W
Marion, *Ala., U.S.A.* 77 J2 32 38N 87 19W
Marion, *Ill., U.S.A.* 81 G10 37 44N 88 56W
Marion, *Ind., U.S.A.* 76 E3 40 32N 85 40W
Marion, *Iowa, U.S.A.* 80 D9 42 2N 91 36W
Marion, *Kans., U.S.A.* 80 F6 38 21N 97 1W
Marion, *N.C., U.S.A.* 77 H5 35 41N 82 1W
Marion, *Ohio, U.S.A.* 76 E4 40 35N 83 8W
Marion, *S.C., U.S.A.* 77 H6 34 11N 79 24W
Marion, *Va., U.S.A.* 77 G5 36 50N 81 31W
Marion, L., *U.S.A.* 77 J5 33 28N 80 10W
Mariposa, *U.S.A.* 84 H7 37 29N 119 58W
Mariscal Estigarribia, *Paraguay* 94 A3 22 3S 60 40W
Maritime Alps = Maritimes, Alpes, *Europe* 18 D7 44 10N 7 10 E
Maritimes, Alpes, *Europe* 18 D7 44 10N 7 10 E
Maritsa = Évros →, *Bulgaria* 21 D12 41 40N 26 34 E
Maritsá, *Greece* 23 C10 36 22N 28 8 E
Mariupol, *Ukraine* 25 E6 47 5N 37 31 E
Marīvān, *Iran* 44 C5 35 30N 46 25 E
Marj 'Uyūn, *Lebanon* 47 B4 33 20N 35 35 E
Markazī ◻, *Iran* 45 C6 35 0N 49 30 E
Markdale, *Canada* 78 B4 44 19N 80 39W
Marked Tree, *U.S.A.* 81 H9 35 32N 90 25W
Market Drayton, *U.K.* 10 E5 52 54N 2 29W
Market Harborough, *U.K.* 11 E7 52 29N 0 55W
Market Rasen, *U.K.* 10 D7 53 24N 0 20W
Markham, *Canada* 78 C5 43 52N 79 16W
Markham, Mt., *Antarctica* 5 E11 83 0S 164 0 E
Markleeville, *U.S.A.* 84 G7 38 42N 119 47W
Markovo, *Russia* 27 C17 64 40N 170 24 E
Marks, *Russia* 24 D8 51 45N 46 50 E
Marksville, *U.S.A.* 81 K8 31 8N 92 4W
Marla, *Australia* 63 D1 27 19S 133 33 E
Marlbank, *Canada* 78 B7 44 26N 77 6W
Marlboro, *Mass., U.S.A.* 79 D13 42 19N 71 33W
Marlboro, *N.Y., U.S.A.* 79 E11 41 36N 73 59W
Marlborough, *Australia* 62 C4 22 46S 149 52 E
Marlborough, *U.K.* 11 F6 51 25N 1 43W
Marlborough Downs, *U.K.* 11 F6 51 27N 1 53W
Marlin, *U.S.A.* 81 K6 31 18N 96 54W
Marlow, *U.S.A.* 81 H6 34 39N 97 58W
Marmagao, *India* 40 M8 15 25N 73 56 E
Marmara, *Turkey* 21 D12 40 35N 27 38 E

Mehndawal

Marmara, Sea of = Marmara Denizi, Turkey . 21 D13 40 45N 28 15 E
Marmara Denizi, Turkey ... 21 D13 40 45N 28 15 E
Marmaris, Turkey .... 21 F13 36 50N 28 14 E
Marmion, Mt., Australia ... 61 E2 29 16S 119 50 E
Marmion L., Canada 70 C1 48 55N 91 20W
Marmolada, Mte., Italy .... 20 A4 46 26N 11 51 E
Marmora, Canada 78 B7 44 28N 77 41W
Marne →, France .... 18 B5 48 48N 2 24 E
Maroala, Madag. .... 57 B8 15 23S 47 59 E
Maroantsetra, Madag. .... 57 B8 15 26S 49 44 E
Maromandia, Madag. ..... 57 A8 14 13S 48 5 E
Marondera, Zimbabwe ..... 55 F3 18 5S 31 42 E
Maroni →, Fr. Guiana ... 93 B8 5 30N 54 0W
Maroochydore, Australia .. 63 D5 26 29S 153 5 E
Maroona, Australia .... 63 F3 37 27S 142 54 E
Marosakoa, Madag. .... 57 B8 15 26S 46 38 E
Maroua, Cameroon .... 51 F8 10 40N 14 20 E
Marovoay, Madag. .... 57 B8 16 6S 46 39 E
Marquard, S. Africa ...... 56 D4 28 40S 27 28 E
Marquesas Is. = Marquises, Is., Pac. Oc. 65 H14 9 30S 140 0W
Marquette, U.S.A. 76 B2 46 33N 87 24W
Marquises, Is., Pac. Oc. 65 H14 9 30S 140 0W
Marra, Djebel, Sudan ..... 51 F10 13 10N 24 22 E
Marracuene, Mozam. ..... 57 D5 25 45S 32 35 E
Marrakech, Morocco 50 B4 31 9N 8 0W
Marrawah, Australia ...... 62 G3 40 55S 144 42 E
Marree, Australia .... 63 D2 29 39S 138 1 E
Marrero, U.S.A. 81 L9 29 54N 90 6W
Marrimane, Mozam. ...... 57 C5 22 58S 33 34 E
Marromeu, Mozam. ...... 57 B6 18 15S 36 25 E
Marrowie Cr. →, Australia 63 E4 33 23S 145 40 E
Marrubane, Mozam. ...... 55 F4 18 0S 37 0 E
Marrupa, Mozam. .... 55 E4 13 8S 37 30 E
Mars Hill, U.S.A. 77 B12 46 31N 67 52W
Marsá Matrûh, Egypt ..... 51 B11 31 19N 27 9 E
Marsabit, Kenya .... 54 B4 2 18N 38 0 E
Marsala, Italy .... 20 F5 37 48N 12 26 E
Marsalforn, Malta .... 23 C1 36 4N 14 15 E
Marsden, Australia .... 63 E4 33 47S 147 32 E
Marseille, France .... 18 E6 43 18N 5 23 E
Marseilles = Marseille, France .... 18 E6 43 18N 5 23 E
Marsh I., U.S.A. 81 L9 29 34N 91 53W
Marshall, Ark., U.S.A. 81 H8 35 55N 92 38W
Marshall, Mich., U.S.A. 76 D3 42 16N 84 58W
Marshall, Minn., U.S.A. ... 80 C7 44 25N 95 45W
Marshall, Mo., U.S.A. 80 F8 39 7N 93 12W
Marshall, Tex., U.S.A. 81 J7 32 33N 94 23W
Marshall →, Australia .... 62 C2 22 59S 136 59 E
Marshall Is. ■, Pac. Oc. .... 64 G9 9 0N 171 0 E
Marshalltown, U.S.A. 80 D8 42 3N 92 55W
Marshfield, Mo., U.S.A. ... 81 G8 37 15N 92 54W
Marshfield, Vt., U.S.A. 79 B12 44 20N 72 20W
Marshfield, Wis., U.S.A. ... 80 C9 44 40N 90 10W
Marshūn, Iran .... 45 B6 36 19N 49 23 E
Märsta, Sweden .... 9 G17 59 37N 17 52 E
Mart, U.S.A. 81 K6 31 33N 96 50W
Martaban, Burma .... 41 L20 16 30N 97 35 E
Martaban, G. of, Burma ... 41 L20 16 5N 96 30 E
Martapura, Kalimantan, Indonesia .... 36 E4 3 22S 114 47 E
Martapura, Sumatera, Indonesia .... 36 E2 4 19S 104 22 E
Martelange, Belgium ..... 15 E5 49 49N 5 43 E
Martha's Vineyard, U.S.A. . 79 E14 41 25N 70 38W
Martigny, Switz. .... 18 C7 46 6N 7 3 E
Martigues, France .... 18 E6 43 24N 5 4 E
Martin, Slovak Rep. ...... 17 D10 49 6N 18 58 E
Martin, S. Dak., U.S.A. 80 D4 43 11N 101 44W
Martin, Tenn., U.S.A. 81 G10 36 21N 88 51W
Martin L., U.S.A. 77 J3 32 41N 85 55W
Martina Franca, Italy ..... 20 D7 40 42N 17 20 E
Martinborough, N.Z. ..... 59 J5 41 14S 175 29 E
Martinez, Calif., U.S.A. 84 G4 38 1N 122 8W
Martinez, Ga., U.S.A. 77 J4 33 31N 82 4W
Martinique ■, W. Indies ... 89 D7 14 40N 61 0W
Martinique Passage, W. Indies 89 C7 15 15N 61 0W
Martinópolis, Brazil 95 A5 22 11S 51 12W
Martins Ferry, U.S.A. 78 F4 40 6N 80 44W
Martinsburg, Pa., U.S.A. ... 78 F6 40 19N 78 20W
Martinsburg, W. Va., U.S.A. 76 F7 39 27N 77 58W
Martinsville, Ind., U.S.A. .. 76 F2 39 26N 86 25W
Martinsville, Va., U.S.A. ... 77 G6 36 41N 79 52W
Marton, N.Z. .... 59 J5 40 4S 175 23 E
Martos, Spain 19 D4 37 44N 3 58W
Marudi, Malaysia .... 36 D4 4 11N 114 19 E
Ma'ruf, Afghan. .... 40 D5 31 30N 67 6 E
Marugame, Japan .... 31 G6 34 15N 133 40 E
Marunga, Angola .... 56 B3 17 28S 20 2 E
Marungu, Mts., Dem. Rep. of the Congo . 54 D3 7 30S 30 0 E
Marv Dasht, Iran .... 45 D7 29 50N 52 40 E
Marvast, Iran .... 45 D7 30 30N 54 15 E
Marvel Loch, Australia .... 61 F2 31 28S 119 29 E
Marwar, India .... 42 G5 25 43N 73 45 E
Mary, Turkmenistan ...... 26 F7 37 40N 61 50 E
Maryborough = Port Laoise, Ireland 13 C4 53 2N 7 18W
Maryborough, Queens., Australia .... 63 D5 25 31S 152 37 E
Maryborough, Vic., Australia 63 F3 37 0S 143 44 E
Maryfield, Canada 73 D8 49 50N 101 35W
Maryland □, U.S.A. 76 F7 39 0N 76 30W
Maryland Junction, Zimbabwe .... 55 F3 17 45S 30 31 E
Maryport, U.K. 10 C4 54 44N 3 28W
Mary's Harbour, Canada .. 71 B8 52 18N 55 51W
Marystown, Canada 71 C8 47 10N 55 10W
Marysville, Canada 72 D5 49 35N 116 0W
Marysville, Calif., U.S.A. ... 84 F5 39 9N 121 35W
Marysville, Kans., U.S.A. .. 80 F6 39 51N 96 39W
Marysville, Mich., U.S.A. .. 78 D2 42 54N 82 29W
Marysville, Ohio, U.S.A. ... 76 E4 40 14N 83 22W
Marysville, Wash., U.S.A. .. 84 B4 48 3N 122 11W
Maryville, Mo., U.S.A. 80 E7 40 21N 94 52W
Maryville, Tenn., U.S.A. ... 77 H4 35 46N 83 58W
Marzūq, Libya .... 51 C8 25 53N 13 57 E
Masahunga, Tanzania ..... 54 C3 2 6S 33 18 E
Masai Steppe, Tanzania ... 54 C4 4 30S 36 30 E
Masaka, Uganda .... 54 C3 0 21S 31 45 E
Masalembo, Kepulauan, Indonesia .... 36 F4 5 35S 114 30 E
Masalima, Kepulauan, Indonesia .... 36 F5 5 4S 117 5 E
Masamba, Indonesia ..... 37 E6 2 30S 120 15 E
Masan, S. Korea .... 35 G15 35 11N 128 32 E
Masandam, Ra's, Oman ... 45 E8 26 30N 56 30 E
Masasi, Tanzania .... 55 E4 10 45S 38 52 E
Masaya, Nic. 88 D2 12 0N 86 7W
Masbate, Phil. .... 37 B6 12 21N 123 36 E
Mascara, Algeria .... 50 A6 35 26N 0 6 E
Mascota, Mexico 86 C4 20 30N 104 50W
Masela, Indonesia .... 37 F7 8 9S 129 51 E
Maseru, Lesotho .... 56 D4 29 18S 27 30 E
Mashaba, Zimbabwe ..... 55 G3 20 2S 30 29 E
Mashābih, Si. Arabia ..... 44 E3 25 35N 36 30 E
Masherbrum, Pakistan .... 43 B7 35 38N 76 18 E
Mashhad, Iran .... 45 B8 36 20N 59 35 E
Mashīz, Iran .... 45 D8 29 56N 56 37 E
Mashkel, Hamun-i, Pakistan 40 E3 28 20N 62 56 E
Mashki Chāh, Pakistan .... 40 E3 29 5N 62 30 E
Mashonaland, Zimbabwe ... 53 H6 16 30S 31 0 E
Mashonaland Central □, Zimbabwe .... 57 B5 17 30S 31 0 E
Mashonaland East □, Zimbabwe .... 57 B5 18 0S 32 0 E
Mashonaland West □, Zimbabwe .... 57 B4 17 30S 29 30 E
Mashrakh, India .... 43 F11 26 7N 84 48 E
Masindi, Uganda .... 54 B3 1 40N 31 43 E
Masindi Port, Uganda ..... 54 B3 1 43N 32 2 E
Maşirah, Oman .... 46 C6 21 0N 58 50 E
Maşirah, Khalīj, Oman .... 46 C6 20 10N 58 10 E
Masisi, Dem. Rep. of the Congo . 54 C2 1 23S 28 49 E
Masjed Soleyman, Iran ... 45 D6 31 55N 49 18 E
Mask, L., Ireland 13 C2 53 36N 9 22W
Maskin, Oman .... 45 F8 23 30N 56 50 E
Masoala, Tanjon' i, Madag. 57 B9 15 59S 50 13 E
Masoarivo, Madag. .... 57 B7 19 3S 44 19 E
Masohi = Amahai, Indonesia .... 37 E7 3 20S 128 55 E
Masomeloka, Madag. ..... 57 C8 20 17S 48 37 E
Mason, Nev., U.S.A. 84 G7 38 56N 119 8W
Mason, Tex., U.S.A. 81 K5 30 45N 99 14W
Mason City, U.S.A. 80 D8 43 9N 93 12W
Maspalomas, Canary Is. ... 22 G4 27 46N 15 35W
Maspalomas, Pta., Canary Is. 22 G4 27 43N 15 36W
Masqat, Oman .... 46 C6 23 37N 58 36 E
Massa, Italy .... 18 D9 44 1N 10 9 E
Massachusetts □, U.S.A. .. 79 D13 42 30N 72 0W
Massachusetts B., U.S.A. .. 79 D14 42 20N 70 50W
Massakory, Chad .... 51 F9 13 0N 15 49 E
Massanella, Spain .... 22 B9 39 48N 2 51 E
Massangena, Mozam. ..... 57 C5 21 34S 33 0 E
Massango, Angola .... 52 F3 8 2S 16 21 E
Massawa = Mitsiwa, Eritrea 46 D2 15 35N 39 25 E
Massena, U.S.A. 79 B10 44 56N 74 54W
Massénya, Chad .... 51 F9 11 21N 16 9 E
Masset, Canada 72 C2 54 2N 132 10W
Massif Central, France .... 18 D5 44 55N 3 0 E
Massillon, U.S.A. 78 F3 40 48N 81 32W
Massinga, Mozam. .... 57 C6 23 15S 35 22 E
Masson, Canada 79 A9 45 32N 75 25W
Masson I., Antarctica ..... 5 C7 66 10S 93 20 E
Mastanli = Momchilgrad, Bulgaria .... 21 D11 41 33N 25 23 E
Masterton, N.Z. .... 59 J5 40 56S 175 39 E
Mastic, U.S.A. 79 F12 40 47N 72 54W
Mastuj, Pakistan .... 43 A5 36 20N 72 36 E
Mastung, Pakistan .... 40 E5 29 50N 66 56 E
Masty, Belarus .... 17 B13 53 27N 24 38 E
Masuda, Japan .... 31 G5 34 40N 131 51 E
Masvingo, Zimbabwe ..... 55 G3 20 8S 30 49 E
Masvingo □, Zimbabwe ... 55 G3 21 0S 31 30 E
Maşyāf, Syria .... 44 C3 35 4N 36 20 E
Matabeleland, Zimbabwe .. 53 H5 18 0S 27 0 E
Matabeleland North □, Zimbabwe .... 55 F2 19 0S 28 0 E
Matabeleland South □, Zimbabwe .... 55 G2 21 0S 29 0 E
Matachewan, Canada 70 C3 47 56N 80 39W
Matadi, Dem. Rep. of the Congo . 52 F2 5 52S 13 31 E
Matagalpa, Nic. 88 D2 13 0N 85 58W
Matagami, Canada 70 C4 49 45N 77 34W
Matagami, L., Canada 70 C4 49 50N 77 40W
Matagorda B., U.S.A. 81 L6 28 40N 96 0W
Matagorda I., U.S.A. 81 L6 28 15N 96 30W
Matak, Indonesia .... 39 L6 3 18N 106 16 E
Mátala, Greece .... 23 E6 34 59N 24 45 E
Matam, Senegal 50 E3 15 34N 13 17W
Matamoros, Campeche, Mexico 87 D6 18 50N 90 50W
Matamoros, Coahuila, Mexico 86 B4 25 33N 103 15W
Matamoros, Tamaulipas, Mexico 87 B5 25 50N 97 30W
Ma'ṭan as Sarra, Libya .... 51 D10 21 45N 22 0 E
Matandu →, Tanzania .... 55 D3 8 45S 34 19 E
Matane, Canada 71 C6 48 50N 67 33W
Matanomadh, India .... 42 H3 23 33N 68 57 E
Matanzas, Cuba 88 B3 23 0N 81 40W
Matapan, C. = Taínaron, Ákra, Greece .... 21 F10 36 22N 22 27 E
Matapédia, Canada 71 C6 48 0N 66 59W
Matara, Sri Lanka .... 40 S12 5 58N 80 30 E
Mataram, Indonesia ...... 36 F5 8 41S 116 10 E
Matarani, Peru 92 G4 17 0S 72 10W
Mataranka, Australia ..... 60 B5 14 55S 133 4 E
Matarma, Râs, Egypt ..... 47 E1 30 27N 32 44 E
Mataró, Spain .... 19 B7 41 32N 2 29 E
Matatiele, S. Africa .... 57 E4 30 20S 28 49 E
Mataura, N.Z. .... 59 M2 46 11S 168 51 E
Matehuala, Mexico 86 C4 23 40N 100 40W
Mateke Hills, Zimbabwe ... 55 G3 21 48S 31 0 E
Matera, Italy .... 20 D7 40 40N 16 36 E
Matetsi, Zimbabwe .... 55 F2 18 12S 26 0 E
Mathis, U.S.A. 81 L6 28 6N 97 50W
Mathráki, Greece .... 23 A3 39 48N 19 31 E
Mathura, India .... 42 F7 27 30N 77 40 E
Mati, Phil. .... 37 C7 6 55N 126 15 E
Matiali, India .... 43 F13 26 56N 88 49 E
Matías Romero, Mexico 87 D5 16 53N 95 2W
Matibane, Mozam. .... 55 E5 14 49S 40 45 E
Matima, Botswana .... 56 C3 20 15S 24 26 E
Matiri Ra., N.Z. .... 59 J4 41 38S 172 20 E
Matla →, India .... 43 J13 21 40N 88 40 E
Matli, Pakistan .... 42 G3 25 2N 68 39 E
Matlock, U.K. 10 D6 53 9N 1 33W
Mato Grosso □, Brazil 93 F8 14 0S 55 0W
Mato Grosso, Planalto do, Brazil 93 G8 15 0S 55 0W
Mato Grosso do Sul □, Brazil 93 G8 18 0S 55 0W
Matochkin Shar, Russia ... 26 B6 73 10N 56 40 E
Matopo Hills, Zimbabwe .. 55 G2 20 36S 28 20 E
Matopos, Zimbabwe ...... 55 G2 20 20S 28 29 E
Matosinhos, Portugal 19 B1 41 11N 8 42W
Maṭraḥ, Oman .... 46 C6 23 37N 58 30 E
Matsue, Japan .... 31 G6 35 25N 133 10 E
Matsumae, Japan .... 30 D10 41 26N 140 7 E
Matsumoto, Japan .... 31 F9 36 15N 138 0 E
Matsusaka, Japan .... 31 G8 34 34N 136 32 E
Matsutō, Japan .... 31 F8 36 31N 136 34 E
Matsuura, Japan .... 31 H4 33 20N 129 49 E
Matsuyama, Japan .... 31 H6 33 45N 132 45 E
Mattagami →, Canada ... 70 B3 50 43N 81 29W
Mattancheri, India .... 40 Q10 9 50N 76 15 E
Mattawa, Canada 70 C4 46 20N 78 45W
Matterhorn, Switz. .... 18 D7 45 58N 7 39 E
Matthew Town, Bahamas .. 89 B5 20 57N 73 40W
Matthew's Ridge, Guyana .. 92 B6 7 37N 60 10W
Mattice, Canada 70 C3 49 40N 83 20W
Mattituck, U.S.A. 79 F12 40 59N 72 32W
Mattoon, U.S.A. 76 F1 39 29N 88 23W
Matuba, Mozam. .... 57 C5 24 28S 32 49 E
Matucana, Peru 92 F3 11 55S 76 25W
Matūn = Khowst, Afghan. . 42 C3 33 22N 69 58 E
Maturín, Venezuela 92 B6 9 45N 63 11W
Mau, India .... 43 G10 25 56N 83 33 E
Mau, Mad. P., India ...... 43 F8 26 17N 78 41 E
Mau, Ut. P., India .... 43 G9 25 17N 81 23 E
Mau Escarpment, Kenya .. 54 C4 0 40S 36 0 E
Mau Ranipur, India .... 43 G8 25 16N 79 8 E
Maubeuge, France .... 18 A6 50 17N 3 57 E
Maud, Pt., Australia ...... 60 D1 23 6S 113 45 E
Maude, Australia .... 63 E3 34 29S 144 18 E
Maudin Sun, Burma ...... 41 M19 16 0N 94 30 E
Maués, Brazil 92 D7 3 20S 57 45W
Mauganj, India .... 41 G12 24 50N 81 55 E
Maughold Hd., U.K. 10 C3 54 18N 4 18W
Maui, U.S.A. 74 H16 20 48N 156 20W
Maulamyaing = Moulmein, Burma .... 41 L20 16 30N 97 40 E
Maule □, Chile 94 D1 36 5S 72 30W
Maumee, U.S.A. 76 E4 41 34N 83 39W
Maumee →, U.S.A. 76 E4 41 42N 83 28W
Maumere, Indonesia ...... 37 F6 8 38S 122 13 E
Maun, Botswana .... 56 C3 20 0S 23 26 E
Mauna Kea, U.S.A. 74 J17 19 50N 155 28W
Mauna Loa, U.S.A. 74 J17 19 30N 155 35W
Maungmagan Is., Burma .. 38 F1 14 0N 97 30 E
Maungmagan Kyunzu, Burma .... 41 N20 14 0N 97 48 E
Maupin, U.S.A. 82 D3 45 11N 121 5W
Maurepas, L., U.S.A. 81 K9 30 15N 90 30W
Maurice, L., Australia ..... 61 E5 29 30S 131 0 E
Mauricie, Parc Nat. de la, Canada 70 C5 46 45N 73 0W
Mauritania ■, Africa 50 E3 20 50N 10 0W
Mauritius ■, Ind. Oc. ..... 49 J9 20 0S 57 0 E
Mauston, U.S.A. 80 D9 43 48N 90 5W
Mavli, India .... 42 G5 24 45N 73 55 E
Mavuradonha Mts., Zimbabwe .... 55 F3 16 30S 31 30 E
Mawa, Dem. Rep. of the Congo . 54 B2 2 45N 26 40 E
Mawai, India .... 43 H9 22 30N 81 4 E
Mawana, India .... 42 E7 29 6N 77 58 E
Mawand, Pakistan .... 42 E3 29 33N 68 38 E
Mawk Mai, Burma .... 41 J20 20 14N 97 37 E
Mawlaik, Burma .... 41 H19 23 40N 94 26 E
Mawqaq, Si. Arabia ...... 44 E4 27 25N 41 8 E
Mawson Coast, Antarctica . 5 C6 68 30S 63 0 E
Max, U.S.A. 80 B4 47 49N 101 18W
Maxcanú, Mexico 87 C6 20 40N 92 0W
Maxesibeni, S. Africa ..... 57 E4 30 49S 29 23 E
Maxhamish L., Canada 72 B4 59 50N 123 17W
Maxixe, Mozam. .... 57 C6 23 54S 35 17 E
Maxville, Canada 79 A10 45 17N 74 51W
Maxwell, U.S.A. 84 F4 39 17N 122 11W
Maxwelton, Australia ..... 62 C3 20 43S 142 41 E
May, C., U.S.A. 76 F8 38 56N 74 58W
May Pen, Jamaica 88 C4 17 58N 77 15W
Maya →, Russia .... 27 D14 60 28N 134 28 E
Maya Mts., Belize 87 D7 16 30N 89 0W
Mayaguana, Bahamas 89 B5 22 30N 72 44W
Mayagüez, Puerto Rico 89 C6 18 12N 67 9W
Mayāmey, Iran .... 45 B7 36 24N 55 42 E
Mayanup, Australia ...... 61 F2 33 57S 116 27 E
Mayapan, Mexico 87 C7 20 30N 89 25W
Mayarí, Cuba 89 B4 20 40N 75 41W
Maybell, U.S.A. 82 F9 40 31N 108 5W
Maybole, U.K. 12 F4 55 21N 4 42W
Maydān, Iraq .... 44 C5 34 55N 45 37 E
Maydena, Australia ...... 62 G4 42 45S 146 30 E
Mayenne →, France 18 C3 47 30N 0 32W
Mayer, U.S.A. 83 J7 34 24N 112 14W
Mayerthorpe, Canada 72 C5 53 57N 115 8W
Mayfield, Ky., U.S.A. 77 G1 36 44N 88 38W
Mayfield, N.Y., U.S.A. 79 C10 43 6N 74 16W
Mayhill, U.S.A. 83 K11 32 53N 105 29W
Maykop, Russia .... 25 F7 44 35N 40 10 E
Maymyo, Burma .... 38 A1 22 2N 96 28 E
Maynard, Mass., U.S.A. ... 79 D13 42 26N 71 27W
Maynard, Wash., U.S.A. ... 84 C4 47 59N 122 55W
Maynard Hills, Australia ... 61 E2 28 28S 119 49 E
Mayne →, Australia ...... 62 C3 23 40S 141 55 E
Maynooth, Ireland 13 C5 53 23N 6 34W
Mayo, Canada 68 B6 63 38N 135 57W
Mayo □, Ireland 13 C2 53 53N 9 3W
Mayon Volcano, Phil. ..... 37 B6 13 15N 123 41 E
Mayor I., N.Z. .... 59 G6 37 16S 176 17 E
Mayotte, I., Mayotte ...... 53 G9 12 50S 45 10 E
Maysville, U.S.A. 76 F4 38 39N 83 46W
Mayu, Indonesia .... 37 D7 1 30N 126 30 E
Mayumba, Gabon .... 52 E2 3 25S 10 39 E
Mayville, N. Dak., U.S.A. ... 80 B6 47 30N 97 20W
Mayville, N.Y., U.S.A. 78 D5 42 15N 79 30W
Mayya, Russia .... 27 C14 61 44N 130 18 E
Mazabuka, Zambia .... 55 F2 15 52S 27 44 E
Mazagán = El Jadida, Morocco 50 B4 33 11N 8 17W
Mazagão, Brazil 93 D8 0 7S 51 16W
Mazán, Peru 92 D4 3 30S 73 0W
Māzandarān □, Iran ...... 45 B7 36 30N 52 0 E
Mazapil, Mexico 86 C4 24 38N 101 34W
Mazara del Vallo, Italy .... 20 F5 37 39N 12 35 E
Mazarrón, Spain 19 D5 37 38N 1 19W
Mazaruni →, Guyana 92 B7 6 25N 58 35W
Mazatán, Mexico 86 B2 29 0N 110 8W
Mazatenango, Guatemala . 88 D1 14 35N 91 30W
Mazatlán, Mexico 86 C3 23 13N 106 25W
Mažeikiai, Lithuania ...... 9 H20 56 20N 22 20 E
Māzhān, Iran .... 45 C8 32 30N 59 0 E
Mazīnān, Iran .... 45 B8 36 19N 56 56 E
Mazoe, Mozam. .... 55 F3 16 42S 33 7 E
Mazoe →, Mozam. ...... 55 F3 16 20S 33 30 E
Mazowe, Zimbabwe ...... 55 F3 17 28S 30 58 E
Mazurian Lakes = Mazurski, Pojezierze, Poland ...... 17 B11 53 50N 21 0 E
Mazurski, Pojezierze, Poland 17 B11 53 50N 21 0 E
Mazyr, Belarus .... 17 B15 51 59N 29 15 E
Mbabane, Swaziland ..... 57 D5 26 18S 31 6 E
Mbaïki, C.A.R. .... 52 D3 3 53N 18 1 E
Mbala, Zambia .... 55 D3 8 46S 31 24 E
Mbale, Uganda .... 54 B3 1 8N 34 12 E
Mbalmayo, Cameroon .... 52 D2 3 33N 11 33 E
Mbamba Bay, Tanzania ... 55 E3 11 13S 34 49 E
Mbandaka, Dem. Rep. of the Congo . 52 D3 0 1N 18 18 E
Mbanza Congo, Angola ... 52 F2 6 18S 14 16 E
Mbanza Ngungu, Dem. Rep. of the Congo . 52 F2 5 12S 14 53 E
Mbarara, Uganda .... 54 C3 0 35S 30 40 E
Mbashe →, S. Africa .... 57 E4 32 15S 28 54 E
Mbenkuru →, Tanzania ... 55 D4 9 25S 39 50 E
Mberengwa, Zimbabwe ... 55 G2 20 29S 29 57 E
Mberengwa, Mt., Zimbabwe 55 G2 20 37S 29 55 E
Mbesuma, Zambia .... 55 E3 10 0S 32 2 E
Mbeya, Tanzania .... 55 D3 8 54S 33 29 E
Mbeya □, Tanzania ...... 54 D3 8 15S 33 30 E
Mbinga, Tanzania .... 55 E4 10 50S 35 0 E
Mbini □, Eq. Guin. .... 52 D2 1 30N 10 0 E
Mbour, Senegal 50 F2 14 22N 16 54W
Mbuji-Mayi, Dem. Rep. of the Congo . 54 D1 6 9S 23 40 E
Mbulu, Tanzania .... 54 C4 3 45S 35 30 E
Mburucuyá, Argentina 94 B4 28 1S 58 14W
Mchinja, Tanzania .... 55 D4 9 44S 39 45 E
Mchinji, Malawi .... 55 E3 13 47S 32 58 E
Mdantsane, S. Africa ..... 53 L5 32 56S 27 46 E
Mead, L., U.S.A. 85 J12 36 1N 114 44W
Meade, U.S.A. 81 G4 37 17N 100 20W
Meadow Lake, Canada 73 C7 54 10N 108 26W
Meadow Lake Prov. Park, Canada 73 C7 54 27N 109 0W
Meadow Valley Wash →, U.S.A. 85 J12 36 40N 114 34W
Meadville, U.S.A. 78 E4 41 39N 80 9W
Meaford, Canada 78 B4 44 36N 80 35W
Mealy Mts., Canada 71 B8 53 10N 58 0W
Meander River, Canada ... 72 B5 59 2N 117 42W
Meares, C., U.S.A. 82 D2 45 37N 124 0W
Mearim →, Brazil 93 D10 3 4S 44 35W
Meath □, Ireland 13 C5 53 40N 6 57W
Meath Park, Canada 73 C7 53 27N 105 22W
Meaux, France .... 18 B5 48 58N 2 50 E
Mebechi-Gawa →, Japan 30 D10 40 31N 141 31 E
Mecanhelas, Mozam. ..... 55 F4 15 12S 35 54 E
Mecca = Makkah, Si. Arabia 46 C2 21 30N 39 54 E
Mecca, U.S.A. 85 M10 33 34N 116 5W
Mechanicsburg, U.S.A. 78 F8 40 13N 77 1W
Mechanicville, U.S.A. 79 D11 42 54N 73 41W
Mechelen, Belgium .... 15 C4 51 2N 4 29 E
Mecheria, Algeria 50 B5 33 35N 0 18W
Mecklenburg, Germany ... 16 B6 53 33N 11 40 E
Mecklenburger Bucht, Germany .... 16 A6 54 20N 11 40 E
Meconta, Mozam. .... 55 E4 14 59S 39 50 E
Medan, Indonesia .... 36 D1 3 40N 98 38 E
Medanosa, Pta., Argentina . 96 F3 48 8S 66 0W
Médéa, Algeria .... 50 A6 36 12N 2 50 E
Medellín, Colombia 92 B3 6 15N 75 35W
Medelpad, Sweden .... 9 E17 62 33N 16 30 E
Medemblik, Neths. .... 15 B5 52 46N 5 8 E
Medford, Mass., U.S.A. ... 79 D13 42 25N 71 7W
Medford, Oreg., U.S.A. ... 82 E2 42 19N 122 52W
Medford, Wis., U.S.A. 80 C9 45 9N 90 20W
Medgidia, Romania .... 17 F15 44 15N 28 19 E
Media Agua, Argentina 94 C2 31 58S 68 25W
Media Luna, Argentina 94 C2 34 45S 66 44W
Medianeira, Brazil 95 B5 25 17S 54 5W
Mediaş, Romania .... 17 E13 46 9N 24 22 E
Medicine Bow, U.S.A. 82 F10 41 54N 106 12W
Medicine Bow Pk., U.S.A. . 82 F10 41 21N 106 19W
Medicine Bow Ra., U.S.A. . 82 F10 41 10N 106 25W
Medicine Hat, Canada 73 D6 50 0N 110 45W
Medicine Lake, U.S.A. 80 A2 48 30N 104 30W
Medicine Lodge, U.S.A. ... 81 G5 37 17N 98 35W
Medina = Al Madīnah, Si. Arabia .... 46 C2 24 35N 39 52 E
Medina, N. Dak., U.S.A. ... 80 B5 46 54N 99 18W
Medina, N.Y., U.S.A. 78 C6 43 13N 78 23W
Medina, Ohio, U.S.A. 78 E3 41 8N 81 52W
Medina →, U.S.A. 81 L5 29 16N 98 29W
Medina del Campo, Spain . 19 B3 41 18N 4 55W
Medina L., U.S.A. 81 L5 29 32N 98 56W
Medina Sidonia, Spain 19 D3 36 28N 5 57W
Medinipur, India .... 43 H12 22 25N 87 21 E
Mediterranean Sea, Europe 6 H7 35 0N 15 0 E
Médoc, France 18 D3 45 10N 0 50W
Medveditsa →, Russia ... 25 E7 49 35N 42 41 E
Medvezhi, Ostrava, Russia . 27 B17 71 0N 161 0 E
Medvezhyegorsk, Russia .. 24 B5 63 0N 34 25 E
Medway →, U.K. .... 11 F8 51 27N 0 46 E
Medway Towns □, U.K. ... 11 F8 51 25N 0 32 E
Meekatharra, Australia .... 61 E2 26 32S 118 29 E
Meeker, U.S.A. 82 F10 40 2N 107 55W
Meelpaeg Res., Canada ... 71 C8 48 15N 56 33W
Meerut, India .... 42 E7 29 1N 77 42 E
Meeteetse, U.S.A. 82 D9 44 9N 108 52W
Mega, Ethiopia .... 46 G2 3 57N 38 19 E
Mégara, Greece .... 21 F10 37 58N 23 22 E
Megasini, India .... 43 J12 21 38N 86 21 E
Meghalaya □, India ...... 41 G17 25 50N 91 0 E
Mégiscane, L., Canada 70 C4 48 35N 75 55W
Meharry, Mt., Australia ... 60 D2 22 59S 118 35 E
Mehlville, U.S.A. 80 F9 38 30N 90 19W
Mehndawal, India .... 43 F10 26 58N 83 5 E

Mehr Jān

Montour Falls

Minigwal, L., *Australia* **61 E3** 29 31S 123 14 E
Minilya →, *Australia* **61 D1** 23 45S 114 0 E
Minilya Roadhouse, *Australia* **61 D1** 23 55S 114 0 E
Minipi L., *Canada* **71 B7** 52 25N 60 45W
Mink L., *Canada* **72 A5** 61 54N 117 40W
Minna, *Nigeria* **50 G7** 9 37N 6 30 E
Minneapolis, *Kans., U.S.A.* **80 F6** 39 8N 97 42W
Minneapolis, *Minn., U.S.A.* **80 C8** 44 59N 93 16W
Minnedosa, *Canada* **73 C9** 50 14N 99 50W
Minnesota □, *U.S.A.* **80 B8** 46 0N 94 15W
Minnesota →, *U.S.A.* **80 C8** 44 54N 93 9W
Minnewaukan, *U.S.A.* **80 A5** 48 4N 99 15W
Minnipa, *Australia* **63 E2** 32 51S 135 9 E
Minnitaki L., *Canada* **70 C1** 49 57N 92 10W
Mino, *Japan* **31 G8** 35 32N 136 55 E
Miño →, *Spain* **19 A2** 41 52N 8 40W
Minorca = Menorca, *Spain* **22 B11** 40 0N 4 0 E
Minot, *U.S.A.* **80 A4** 48 14N 101 18W
Minqin, *China* **34 E2** 38 38N 103 20 E
Minsk, *Belarus* **17 B14** 53 52N 27 30 E
Mińsk Mazowiecki, *Poland* **17 B11** 52 10N 21 33 E
Mintabie, *Australia* **63 D1** 27 15S 133 7 E
Mintaka Pass, *Pakistan* **43 A6** 37 0N 74 58 E
Minteke Daban = Mintaka Pass, *Pakistan* **43 A6** 37 0N 74 58 E
Minto, *Canada* **71 C6** 46 5N 66 5W
Minto, L., *Canada* **70 A5** 57 13N 75 0W
Minton, *Canada* **73 D8** 49 10N 104 35W
Minturn, *U.S.A.* **82 G10** 39 35N 106 26W
Minusinsk, *Russia* **27 D10** 53 43N 91 20 E
Minutang, *India* **41 E20** 28 15N 96 30 E
Miquelon, *Canada* **70 C4** 49 25N 76 27W
Miquelon, *St- P. & M.* **71 C8** 47 8N 56 22W
Mīr Kūh, *Iran* **45 E8** 26 22N 58 55 E
Mīr Shahdād, *Iran* **45 E8** 26 15N 58 29 E
Mira, *Italy* **20 B5** 45 26N 12 8 E
Mira por vos Cay, *Bahamas* **89 B5** 22 9N 74 30W
Miraj, *India* **40 L9** 16 50N 74 45 E
Miram Shah, *Pakistan* **42 C4** 33 0N 70 2 E
Miramar, *Argentina* **94 D4** 38 15S 57 50W
Miramar, *Mozam.* **57 C6** 23 50S 35 35 E
Miramichi, *Canada* **71 C6** 47 2N 65 28W
Miramichi B., *Canada* **71 C7** 47 15N 65 0W
Miranda, *Brazil* **93 H7** 20 10S 56 15W
Miranda →, *Brazil* **92 G7** 19 25S 57 20W
Miranda de Ebro, *Spain* **19 A4** 42 41N 2 57W
Miranda do Douro, *Portugal* **19 B2** 41 30N 6 16W
Mirandópolis, *Brazil* **95 A5** 21 9S 51 6W
Mirango, *Malawi* **55 E3** 13 32S 34 58 E
Mirassol, *Brazil* **95 A6** 20 46S 49 28W
Mirbāţ, *Oman* **46 D5** 17 0N 54 45 E
Miri, *Malaysia* **36 D4** 4 23N 113 59 E
Miriam Vale, *Australia* **62 C5** 24 20S 151 33 E
Mirim, L., *S. Amer.* **95 C5** 32 45S 52 50W
Mirnyy, *Russia* **27 C12** 62 33N 113 53 E
Mirokhan, *Pakistan* **42 F3** 27 46N 68 6 E
Mirond L., *Canada* **73 B8** 55 6N 102 47W
Mirpur, *Pakistan* **43 C5** 33 32N 73 56 E
Mirpur Batoro, *Pakistan* **42 G3** 24 44N 68 16 E
Mirpur Bibiwari, *Pakistan* **42 E2** 28 33N 67 44 E
Mirpur Khas, *Pakistan* **42 G3** 25 30N 69 0 E
Mirpur Sakro, *Pakistan* **42 G2** 24 33N 67 41 E
Mirtağ, *Turkey* **44 B4** 38 23N 41 56 E
Miryang, *S. Korea* **35 G15** 35 31N 128 44 E
Mirzapur, *India* **43 G10** 25 10N 82 34 E
Mirzapur-cum-Vindhyachal = Mirzapur, *India* **43 G10** 25 10N 82 34 E
Misantla, *Mexico* **87 D5** 19 56N 96 50W
Misawa, *Japan* **30 D10** 40 41N 141 24 E
Miscou I., *Canada* **71 C7** 47 57N 64 31W
Mish'āb, Ra's al, *Si. Arabia* **45 D6** 28 15N 48 43 E
Mishan, *China* **33 B8** 45 37N 131 48 E
Mishawaka, *U.S.A.* **76 E2** 41 40N 86 11W
Mishima, *Japan* **31 G9** 35 10N 138 52 E
Misión, *Mexico* **85 N10** 32 6N 116 53W
Misiones □, *Argentina* **95 B5** 27 0S 55 0W
Misiones □, *Paraguay* **94 B4** 27 0S 56 0W
Miskah, *Si. Arabia* **44 E4** 24 49N 42 56 E
Miskitos, Cayos, *Nic.* **88 D3** 14 26N 82 50W
Miskolc, *Hungary* **17 D11** 48 7N 20 50 E
Misoke, *Dem. Rep. of the Congo* **54 C2** 0 42S 28 2 E
Misool, *Indonesia* **37 E8** 1 52S 130 10 E
Misrātah, *Libya* **51 B9** 32 24N 15 3 E
Missanabie, *Canada* **70 C3** 48 20N 84 6W
Missinaibi →, *Canada* **70 B3** 50 43N 81 29W
Missinaibi L., *Canada* **70 C3** 48 23N 83 40W
Mission, *Canada* **72 D4** 49 10N 122 15W
Mission, *S. Dak., U.S.A.* **80 D4** 43 18N 100 39W
Mission, *Tex., U.S.A.* **81 M5** 26 13N 98 20W
Mission Beach, *Australia* **62 B4** 17 53S 146 6 E
Mission Viejo, *U.S.A.* **85 M9** 33 36N 117 40W
Missisa L., *Canada* **70 B2** 52 20N 85 7W
Missisicabi →, *Canada* **70 B4** 51 14N 79 31W
Mississagi →, *Canada* **70 C3** 46 15N 83 9W
Mississauga, *Canada* **78 C5** 43 32N 79 35W
Mississippi □, *U.S.A.* **81 J10** 33 0N 90 0W
Mississippi →, *U.S.A.* **81 L10** 29 9N 89 15W
Mississippi L., *Canada* **79 A8** 45 5N 76 10W
Mississippi River Delta, *U.S.A.* **81 L9** 29 10N 89 15W
Mississippi Sd., *U.S.A.* **81 K10** 30 20N 89 0W
Missoula, *U.S.A.* **82 C7** 46 52N 114 1W
Missouri □, *U.S.A.* **80 F8** 38 25N 92 30W
Missouri →, *U.S.A.* **80 F9** 38 49N 90 7W
Missouri City, *U.S.A.* **81 L7** 29 37N 95 32W
Missouri Valley, *U.S.A.* **80 E7** 41 34N 95 53W
Mist, *U.S.A.* **84 E3** 45 59N 123 15W
Mistassibi →, *Canada* **71 B5** 48 53N 72 13W
Mistassini, *Canada* **71 C5** 48 53N 72 12W
Mistassini →, *Canada* **71 C5** 48 42N 72 20W
Mistassini, L., *Canada* **70 B5** 51 0N 73 30W
Mistastin L., *Canada* **71 A7** 55 57N 63 20W
Mistinibi, L., *Canada* **71 A7** 55 56N 64 17W
Misty L., *Canada* **73 B8** 58 53N 101 40W
Misurata = Misrātah, *Libya* **51 B9** 32 24N 15 3 E
Mitchell, *Australia* **63 D4** 26 29S 147 58 E
Mitchell, *Canada* **78 C3** 43 28N 81 12W
Mitchell, *Nebr., U.S.A.* **80 E3** 41 57N 103 49W
Mitchell, *Oreg., U.S.A.* **82 D3** 44 34N 120 9W
Mitchell, *S. Dak., U.S.A.* **80 D6** 43 43N 98 2W
Mitchell →, *Australia* **62 B3** 15 12S 141 35 E
Mitchell, Mt., *U.S.A.* **77 H4** 35 46N 82 16W
Mitchell Ranges, *Australia* **62 A2** 12 49S 135 36 E
Mitchelstown, *Ireland* **13 D3** 52 15N 8 16W
Mitha Tiwana, *Pakistan* **42 C5** 32 13N 72 6 E
Mithi, *Pakistan* **42 G3** 24 44N 69 48 E
Mithrao, *Pakistan* **42 F3** 27 28N 69 40 E
Mitilíni, *Greece* **21 E12** 39 6N 26 35 E
Mito, *Japan* **31 F10** 36 20N 140 30 E
Mitrovica = Kosovska Mitrovica, *Serbia, Yug.* **21 C9** 42 54N 20 52 E
Mitsinjo, *Madag.* **57 B8** 16 1S 45 52 E
Mitsiwa, *Eritrea* **46 D2** 15 35N 39 25 E
Mitsukaidō, *Japan* **31 F9** 36 1N 139 59 E
Mittagong, *Australia* **63 E5** 34 28S 150 29 E
Mitú, *Colombia* **92 C4** 1 15N 70 13W
Mitumba, *Tanzania* **54 D3** 7 8S 31 2 E
Mitumba, Mts., *Dem. Rep. of the Congo* **54 D2** 7 0S 27 30 E
Mitwaba, *Dem. Rep. of the Congo* **55 D2** 8 2S 27 17 E
Mityana, *Uganda* **54 B3** 0 23N 32 2 E
Mixteco →, *Mexico* **87 D5** 18 11N 98 30W
Miyagi □, *Japan* **30 E10** 38 15N 140 45 E
Miyah, W. el →, *Syria* **44 C3** 34 44N 39 57 E
Miyake-Jima, *Japan* **31 G9** 34 5N 139 30 E
Miyako, *Japan* **30 E10** 39 40N 141 59 E
Miyako-Jima, *Japan* **31 M2** 24 45N 125 20 E
Miyako-Rettō, *Japan* **31 M2** 24 24N 125 0 E
Miyakonojō, *Japan* **31 J5** 31 40N 131 5 E
Miyani, *India* **42 J3** 21 50N 69 26 E
Miyanoura-Dake, *Japan* **31 J5** 30 20N 130 31 E
Miyazaki, *Japan* **31 J5** 31 56N 131 30 E
Miyazaki □, *Japan* **31 H5** 32 30N 131 30 E
Miyazu, *Japan* **31 G7** 35 35N 135 10 E
Miyet, Bahr el = Dead Sea, *Asia* **47 D4** 31 30N 35 30 E
Miyoshi, *Japan* **31 G6** 34 48N 132 51 E
Miyun, *China* **34 D9** 40 28N 116 50 E
Miyun Shuiku, *China* **35 D9** 40 30N 117 0 E
Mizdah, *Libya* **51 B8** 31 30N 13 0 E
Mizen Hd., *Cork, Ireland* **13 E2** 51 27N 9 50W
Mizen Hd., *Wick., Ireland* **13 D5** 52 51N 6 4W
Mizhi, *China* **34 F6** 37 47N 110 12 E
Mizoram □, *India* **41 H18** 23 30N 92 40 E
Mizpe Ramon, *Israel* **47 E3** 30 34N 34 49 E
Mizusawa, *Japan* **30 E10** 39 8N 141 8 E
Mjölby, *Sweden* **9 G16** 58 20N 15 10 E
Mjøsa, *Norway* **9 F14** 60 40N 11 0 E
Mkata, *Tanzania* **54 D4** 5 45S 38 20 E
Mkokotoni, *Tanzania* **54 D4** 5 55S 39 15 E
Mkomazi, *Tanzania* **54 C4** 4 40S 38 7 E
Mkomazi →, *S. Africa* **57 E5** 30 12S 30 50 E
Mkulwe, *Tanzania* **55 D3** 8 37S 32 20 E
Mkumbi, Ras, *Tanzania* **54 D4** 7 38S 39 55 E
Mkushi, *Zambia* **55 E2** 14 25S 29 15 E
Mkushi River, *Zambia* **55 E2** 13 32S 29 45 E
Mkuze, *S. Africa* **57 D5** 27 10S 32 0 E
Mladá Boleslav, *Czech Rep.* **16 C8** 50 27N 14 53 E
Mlala Hills, *Tanzania* **54 D3** 6 50S 31 40 E
Mlange = Mulanje, *Malawi* **55 F4** 16 2S 35 33 E
Mlanje, Pic, *Malawi* **53 H7** 15 57S 35 38 E
Mława, *Poland* **17 B11** 53 9N 20 25 E
Mljet, *Croatia* **20 C7** 42 43N 17 30 E
Mmabatho, *S. Africa* **56 D4** 25 49S 25 30 E
Mo i Rana, *Norway* **8 C16** 66 20N 14 7 E
Moa, *Cuba* **89 B4** 20 40N 74 56W
Moa, *Indonesia* **37 F7** 8 0S 128 0 E
Moab, *U.S.A.* **83 G9** 38 35N 109 33W
Moala, *Fiji* **59 D8** 18 36S 179 53 E
Moama, *Australia* **63 F3** 36 7S 144 46 E
Moapa, *U.S.A.* **85 J12** 36 40N 114 37W
Moate, *Ireland* **13 C4** 53 24N 7 44W
Moba, *Dem. Rep. of the Congo* **54 D2** 7 0S 29 48 E
Mobārakābād, *Iran* **45 D7** 28 24N 53 20 E
Mobaye, *C.A.R.* **52 D4** 4 25N 21 5 E
Mobayi, *Dem. Rep. of the Congo* **52 D4** 4 15N 21 8 E
Moberley Lake, *Canada* **72 B4** 55 50N 121 44W
Moberly, *U.S.A.* **80 F8** 39 25N 92 26W
Mobile, *U.S.A.* **77 K1** 30 41N 88 3W
Mobile B., *U.S.A.* **77 K2** 30 30N 88 0W
Mobridge, *U.S.A.* **80 C4** 45 32N 100 26W
Mobutu Sese Seko, L. = Albert L., *Africa* **54 B3** 1 30N 31 0 E
Moc Chau, *Vietnam* **38 B5** 20 50N 104 38 E
Moc Hoa, *Vietnam* **39 G5** 10 46N 105 56 E
Mocabe Kasari, *Dem. Rep. of the Congo* **55 D2** 9 58S 26 12 E
Moçambique, *Mozam.* **55 F5** 15 3S 40 42 E
Moçâmedes = Namibe, *Angola* **53 H2** 15 7S 12 11 E
Mocanaqua, *U.S.A.* **79 E8** 41 9N 76 8W
Mochudi, *Botswana* **56 C4** 24 27S 26 7 E
Mocimboa da Praia, *Mozam.* **55 E5** 11 25S 40 20 E
Moclips, *U.S.A.* **84 C2** 47 14N 124 13W
Mocoa, *Colombia* **92 C3** 1 7N 76 35W
Mococa, *Brazil* **95 A6** 21 28S 47 0W
Mocorito, *Mexico* **86 B3** 25 30N 107 53W
Moctezuma, *Mexico* **86 B3** 29 50N 109 0W
Moctezuma →, *Mexico* **87 C5** 21 59N 98 34W
Mocuba, *Mozam.* **55 F4** 16 54S 36 57 E
Mocúzari, Presa, *Mexico* **86 B3** 27 10N 109 10W
Modane, *France* **18 D7** 45 12N 6 40 E
Modasa, *India* **42 H5** 23 30N 73 21 E
Modder →, *S. Africa* **56 D3** 29 2S 24 37 E
Modderrivier, *S. Africa* **56 D3** 29 2S 24 38 E
Módena, *Italy* **20 B4** 44 40N 10 55 E
Modena, *U.S.A.* **83 H7** 37 48N 113 56W
Modesto, *U.S.A.* **84 H6** 37 39N 121 0W
Módica, *Italy* **20 F6** 36 52N 14 46 E
Moe, *Australia* **63 F4** 38 12S 146 19 E
Moebase, *Mozam.* **55 F4** 17 3S 38 41 E
Moengo, *Surinam* **93 B8** 5 45N 54 20W
Moffat, *U.K.* **12 F5** 55 21N 3 27W
Moga, *India* **42 D6** 30 48N 75 8 E
Mogadishu = Muqdisho, *Somali Rep.* **46 G4** 2 2N 45 25 E
Mogador = Essaouira, *Morocco* **50 B4** 31 32N 9 42W
Mogalakwena →, *S. Africa* **57 C4** 22 38S 28 40 E
Mogami-Gawa →, *Japan* **30 E10** 38 45N 140 0 E
Mogán, *Canary Is.* **22 G4** 27 53N 15 43W
Mogaung, *Burma* **41 G20** 25 20N 97 0 E
Mogi das Cruzes, *Brazil* **95 A6** 23 31S 46 11W
Mogi-Guaçu →, *Brazil* **95 A6** 20 53S 48 10W
Mogi-Mirim, *Brazil* **95 A6** 22 29S 47 0W
Mogilev = Mahilyow, *Belarus* **17 B16** 53 55N 30 18 E
Mogilev-Podolskiy = Mohyliv-Podilskyy, *Ukraine* **17 D14** 48 26N 27 48 E
Mogincual, *Mozam.* **55 F5** 15 35S 40 25 E
Mogocha, *Russia* **27 D12** 53 40N 119 50 E
Mogok, *Burma* **41 H20** 23 0N 96 40 E
Mogollon Rim, *U.S.A.* **83 J8** 34 10N 110 50W
Mogumber, *Australia* **61 F2** 31 2S 116 3 E
Mohács, *Hungary* **17 F10** 45 58N 18 41 E
Mohales Hoek, *Lesotho* **56 E4** 30 7S 27 26 E
Mohall, *U.S.A.* **80 A4** 48 46N 101 31W
Moḩammadābād, *Iran* **45 B8** 37 52N 59 5 E
Mohammedia, *Morocco* **50 B4** 33 44N 7 21W
Mohana →, *India* **43 G11** 24 43N 85 0 E
Mohanlalganj, *India* **43 F9** 26 41N 80 58 E
Mohave, L., *U.S.A.* **85 K12** 35 12N 114 34W
Mohawk →, *U.S.A.* **79 D11** 42 47N 73 41W
Mohenjodaro, *Pakistan* **42 F3** 27 19N 68 7 E
Mohicanville Reservoir, *U.S.A.* **78 F3** 40 45N 82 0W
Mohoro, *Tanzania* **54 D4** 8 6S 39 8 E
Mohyliv-Podilskyy, *Ukraine* **17 D14** 48 26N 27 48 E
Moidart, L., *U.K.* **12 E3** 56 47N 5 52W
Moira →, *Canada* **78 B7** 44 21N 77 24W
Moíres, *Greece* **23 D6** 35 4N 24 56 E
Moisaküla, *Estonia* **9 G21** 58 3N 25 12 E
Moisie, *Canada* **71 B6** 50 12N 66 1W
Moisie →, *Canada* **71 B6** 50 14N 66 5W
Mojave, *U.S.A.* **85 K8** 35 3N 118 10W
Mojave Desert, *U.S.A.* **85 L10** 35 0N 116 30W
Mojo, *Bolivia* **94 A2** 21 48S 65 33W
Mojokerto, *Indonesia* **37 G15** 7 28S 112 26 E
Mokai, *N.Z.* **59 H5** 38 32S 175 56 E
Mokambo, *Dem. Rep. of the Congo* **55 E2** 12 25S 28 20 E
Mokameh, *India* **43 G11** 25 24N 85 55 E
Mokelumne →, *U.S.A.* **84 G5** 38 13N 121 28W
Mokelumne Hill, *U.S.A.* **84 G6** 38 18N 120 43W
Mokhós, *Greece* **23 D7** 35 16N 25 27 E
Mokhotlong, *Lesotho* **57 D4** 29 22S 29 2 E
Mokokchung, *India* **41 F19** 26 15N 94 30 E
Mokp'o, *S. Korea* **35 G14** 34 50N 126 25 E
Mokra Gora, *Serbia, Yug.* **21 C9** 42 50N 20 30 E
Mol, *Belgium* **15 C5** 51 11N 5 5 E
Molchanovo, *Russia* **26 D9** 57 40N 83 50 E
Mold, *U.K.* **10 D4** 53 9N 3 8W
Moldavia = Moldova ■, *Europe* **17 E15** 47 0N 28 0 E
Molde, *Norway* **8 E12** 62 45N 7 9 E
Moldova ■, *Europe* **17 E15** 47 0N 28 0 E
Moldoveana, Vf., *Romania* **17 F13** 45 36N 24 45 E
Mole →, *U.K.* **11 F7** 51 24N 0 21W
Mole Creek, *Australia* **62 G4** 41 34S 146 24 E
Molepolole, *Botswana* **56 C4** 24 28S 25 28 E
Molfetta, *Italy* **20 D7** 41 12N 16 36 E
Moline, *U.S.A.* **80 E9** 41 30N 90 31W
Molinos, *Argentina* **94 B2** 25 28S 66 15W
Moliro, *Dem. Rep. of the Congo* **54 D3** 8 12S 30 30 E
Mollendo, *Peru* **92 G4** 17 0S 72 0W
Mollerin, L., *Australia* **61 F2** 30 30S 117 35 E
Molodechno = Maladzyechna, *Belarus* **17 A14** 54 20N 26 50 E
Molokai, *U.S.A.* **74 H16** 21 8N 157 0W
Molong, *Australia* **63 E4** 33 5S 148 54 E
Molopo →, *Africa* **56 D3** 27 30S 20 13 E
Molotov = Perm, *Russia* **24 C10** 58 0N 56 10 E
Molson L., *Canada* **73 C9** 54 22N 96 40W
Molteno, *S. Africa* **56 E4** 31 22S 26 22 E
Molu, *Indonesia* **37 F8** 6 45S 131 40 E
Molucca Sea, *Indonesia* **37 E6** 2 0S 124 0 E
Moluccas = Maluku, *Indonesia* **37 E7** 1 0S 127 0 E
Moma, *Dem. Rep. of the Congo* **54 C1** 1 35S 23 52 E
Moma, *Mozam.* **55 F4** 16 47S 39 4 E
Mombasa, *Kenya* **54 C4** 4 2S 39 43 E
Mombetsu, *Japan* **30 B11** 44 21N 143 22 E
Momchilgrad, *Bulgaria* **21 D11** 41 33N 25 23 E
Momi, *Dem. Rep. of the Congo* **54 C2** 1 42S 27 0 E
Mompós, *Colombia* **92 B4** 9 14N 74 26W
Møn, *Denmark* **9 J15** 54 57N 12 20 E
Mon →, *Burma* **41 J19** 20 25N 94 30 E
Mona, Canal de la, *W. Indies* **89 C6** 18 30N 67 45W
Mona, Isla, *Puerto Rico* **89 C6** 18 5N 67 54W
Mona, Pta., *Costa Rica* **88 E3** 9 37N 82 36W
Monaca, *U.S.A.* **78 F4** 40 41N 80 17W
Monaco ■, *Europe* **18 E7** 43 46N 7 23 E
Monadhliath Mts., *U.K.* **12 D4** 57 10N 4 4W
Monadnock, Mt., *U.S.A.* **79 D12** 42 52N 72 7W
Monaghan, *Ireland* **13 B5** 54 15N 6 57W
Monaghan □, *Ireland* **13 B5** 54 11N 6 56W
Monahans, *U.S.A.* **81 K3** 31 36N 102 54W
Monapo, *Mozam.* **55 E5** 14 56S 40 19 E
Monar, L., *U.K.* **12 D3** 57 26N 5 8W
Monarch Mt., *Canada* **72 C3** 51 55N 125 57W
Monashee Mts., *Canada* **72 C5** 51 0N 118 43W
Monasterevin, *Ireland* **13 C4** 53 8N 7 4W
Monastir = Bitola, *Macedonia* **21 D9** 41 1N 21 20 E
Moncayo, Sierra del, *Spain* **19 B5** 41 48N 1 50W
Monchegorsk, *Russia* **24 A5** 67 54N 32 58 E
Mönchengladbach, *Germany* **16 C4** 51 11N 6 27 E
Monchique, *Portugal* **19 D1** 37 19N 8 38W
Moncks Corner, *U.S.A.* **77 J5** 33 12N 80 1W
Monclova, *Mexico* **86 B4** 26 50N 101 30W
Moncton, *Canada* **71 C7** 46 7N 64 51W
Mondego →, *Portugal* **19 B1** 40 9N 8 52W
Mondeodo, *Indonesia* **37 E6** 3 34S 122 9 E
Mondovì, *Italy* **18 D7** 44 23N 7 49 E
Mondrain I., *Australia* **61 F3** 34 9S 122 14 E
Monessen, *U.S.A.* **78 F5** 40 9N 79 54W
Monett, *U.S.A.* **81 G8** 36 55N 93 55W
Moneymore, *U.K.* **13 B5** 54 41N 6 40W
Monforte de Lemos, *Spain* **19 A2** 42 31N 7 33W
Mong Hsu, *Burma* **41 J21** 21 54N 98 30 E
Mong Kung, *Burma* **41 J20** 21 35N 97 35 E
Mong Nai, *Burma* **41 J20** 20 32N 97 46 E
Mong Pawk, *Burma* **41 H21** 22 4N 99 16 E
Mong Ton, *Burma* **41 J21** 20 17N 98 45 E
Mong Wa, *Burma* **41 J22** 21 26N 100 27 E
Mong Yai, *Burma* **41 H21** 22 21N 98 3 E
Mongalla, *Sudan* **51 G12** 5 8N 31 42 E
Mongers, L., *Australia* **61 E2** 29 25S 117 5 E
Monghyr = Munger, *India* **43 G12** 25 23N 86 30 E
Mongibello = Etna, *Italy* **20 F6** 37 50N 14 55 E
Mongo, *Chad* **51 F9** 12 14N 18 43 E
Mongolia ■, *Asia* **27 E10** 47 0N 103 0 E
Mongu, *Zambia* **53 H4** 15 16S 23 12 E
Môngua, *Angola* **56 B2** 16 43S 15 20 E
Monifieth, *U.K.* **12 E6** 56 30N 2 48W
Monkey Bay, *Malawi* **55 E4** 14 7S 35 1 E
Monkey Mia, *Australia* **61 E1** 25 48S 113 43 E
Monkey River, *Belize* **87 D7** 16 22N 88 29W
Monkoto, *Dem. Rep. of the Congo* **52 E4** 1 38S 20 35 E
Monkton, *Canada* **78 C3** 43 35N 81 5W
Monmouth, *U.K.* **11 F5** 51 48N 2 42W
Monmouth, *Ill., U.S.A.* **80 E9** 40 55N 90 39W
Monmouth, *Oreg., U.S.A.* **82 D2** 44 51N 123 14W
Monmouthshire □, *U.K.* **11 F5** 51 48N 2 54W
Mono L., *U.S.A.* **84 H7** 38 1N 119 1W
Monolith, *U.S.A.* **85 K8** 35 7N 118 22W
Monólithos, *Greece* **23 C9** 36 7N 27 45 E
Monongahela, *U.S.A.* **78 F5** 40 12N 79 56W
Monópoli, *Italy* **20 D7** 40 57N 17 18 E
Monroe, *Ga., U.S.A.* **77 J4** 33 47N 83 43W
Monroe, *La., U.S.A.* **81 J8** 32 30N 92 7W
Monroe, *Mich., U.S.A.* **76 E4** 41 55N 83 24W
Monroe, *N.C., U.S.A.* **77 H5** 34 59N 80 33W
Monroe, *N.Y., U.S.A.* **79 E10** 41 20N 74 11W
Monroe, *Utah, U.S.A.* **83 G7** 38 38N 112 7W
Monroe, *Wash., U.S.A.* **84 C5** 47 51N 121 58W
Monroe, *Wis., U.S.A.* **80 D10** 42 36N 89 38W
Monroe City, *U.S.A.* **80 F9** 39 39N 91 44W
Monroeton, *U.S.A.* **79 E8** 41 43N 76 29W
Monroeville, *Ala., U.S.A.* **77 K2** 31 31N 87 20W
Monroeville, *Pa., U.S.A.* **78 F5** 40 26N 79 45W
Monrovia, *Liberia* **50 G3** 6 18N 10 47W
Mons, *Belgium* **15 D3** 50 27N 3 58 E
Monse, *Indonesia* **37 E6** 4 0S 123 10 E
Mont-de-Marsan, *France* **18 E3** 43 54N 0 31W
Mont-Joli, *Canada* **71 C6** 48 37N 68 10W
Mont-Laurier, *Canada* **70 C4** 46 35N 75 30W
Mont-Louis, *Canada* **71 C6** 49 15N 65 44W
Mont-St-Michel, Le = Le Mont-St-Michel, *France* **18 B3** 48 40N 1 30W
Mont Tremblant, Parc Recr. du, *Canada* **70 C5** 46 30N 74 30W
Montagu, *S. Africa* **56 E3** 33 45S 20 8 E
Montagu I., *Antarctica* **5 B1** 58 25S 26 20W
Montague, *Canada* **71 C7** 46 10N 62 39W
Montague, I., *Mexico* **86 A2** 31 40N 114 56W
Montague Ra., *Australia* **61 E2** 27 15S 119 30 E
Montague Sd., *Australia* **60 B4** 14 28S 125 20 E
Montalbán, *Spain* **19 B5** 40 50N 0 45W
Montalvo, *U.S.A.* **85 L7** 34 15N 119 12W
Montana, *Bulgaria* **21 C10** 43 27N 23 16 E
Montaña, *Peru* **92 E4** 6 0S 73 0W
Montana □, *U.S.A.* **82 C9** 47 0N 110 0W
Montaña Clara, I., *Canary Is.* **22 E6** 29 17N 13 33W
Montargis, *France* **18 C5** 47 59N 2 43 E
Montauban, *France* **18 D4** 44 2N 1 21 E
Montauk, *U.S.A.* **79 E13** 41 3N 71 57W
Montauk Pt., *U.S.A.* **79 E13** 41 4N 71 52W
Montbéliard, *France* **18 C7** 47 31N 6 48 E
Montceau-les-Mines, *France* **18 C6** 46 40N 4 23 E
Montclair, *U.S.A.* **79 F10** 40 49N 74 13W
Monte Albán, *Mexico* **87 D5** 17 2N 96 45W
Monte Alegre, *Brazil* **93 D8** 2 0S 54 0W
Monte Azul, *Brazil* **93 G10** 15 9S 42 53W
Monte Bello Is., *Australia* **60 D2** 20 30S 115 45 E
Monte-Carlo, *Monaco* **18 E7** 43 46N 7 23 E
Monte Caseros, *Argentina* **94 C4** 30 10S 57 50W
Monte Comán, *Argentina* **94 C2** 34 40S 67 53W
Monte Cristi, *Dom. Rep.* **89 C5** 19 52N 71 39W
Monte Lindo →, *Paraguay* **94 A4** 23 56S 57 12W
Monte Patria, *Chile* **94 C1** 30 42S 70 58W
Monte Quemado, *Argentina* **94 B3** 25 53S 62 41W
Monte Rio, *U.S.A.* **84 G4** 38 28N 123 0W
Monte Santu, C. di, *Italy* **20 D3** 40 5N 9 44 E
Monte Vista, *U.S.A.* **83 H10** 37 35N 106 9W
Monteagudo, *Argentina* **95 B5** 27 14S 54 8W
Montebello, *Canada* **70 C5** 45 40N 74 55W
Montecito, *U.S.A.* **85 L7** 34 26N 119 40W
Montecristo, *Italy* **20 C4** 42 20N 10 19 E
Montego Bay, *Jamaica* **88 C4** 18 30N 78 0W
Montélimar, *France* **18 D6** 44 33N 4 45 E
Montello, *U.S.A.* **80 D10** 43 48N 89 20W
Montemorelos, *Mexico* **87 B5** 25 11N 99 42W
Montenegro, *Brazil* **95 B5** 29 39S 51 29W
Montenegro □, *Yugoslavia* **21 C8** 42 40N 19 20 E
Montepuez, *Mozam.* **55 E4** 13 8S 38 59 E
Montepuez →, *Mozam.* **55 E5** 12 32S 40 27 E
Monterey, *U.S.A.* **84 J5** 36 37N 121 55W
Monterey B., *U.S.A.* **84 J5** 36 45N 122 0W
Montería, *Colombia* **92 B3** 8 46N 75 53W
Monteros, *Argentina* **94 B2** 27 11S 65 30W
Monterrey, *Mexico* **86 B4** 25 40N 100 30W
Montes Claros, *Brazil* **93 G10** 16 30S 43 50W
Montesano, *U.S.A.* **84 D3** 46 59N 123 36W
Montesilvano, *Italy* **20 C6** 42 29N 14 8 E
Montevideo, *Uruguay* **95 C4** 34 50S 56 11W
Montevideo, *U.S.A.* **80 C7** 44 57N 95 43W
Montezuma, *U.S.A.* **80 E8** 41 35N 92 32W
Montgomery = Sahiwal, *Pakistan* **42 D5** 30 45N 73 8 E
Montgomery, *U.K.* **11 E4** 52 34N 3 8W
Montgomery, *Ala., U.S.A.* **77 J2** 32 23N 86 19W
Montgomery, *Pa., U.S.A.* **78 E8** 41 10N 76 53W
Montgomery, *W. Va., U.S.A.* **76 F5** 38 11N 81 19W
Montgomery City, *U.S.A.* **80 F9** 38 59N 91 30W
Monticello, *Ark., U.S.A.* **81 J9** 33 38N 91 47W
Monticello, *Fla., U.S.A.* **77 K4** 30 33N 83 52W
Monticello, *Ind., U.S.A.* **76 E2** 40 45N 86 46W
Monticello, *Iowa, U.S.A.* **80 D9** 42 15N 91 12W
Monticello, *Ky., U.S.A.* **77 G3** 36 50N 84 51W
Monticello, *Minn., U.S.A.* **80 C8** 45 18N 93 48W
Monticello, *Miss., U.S.A.* **81 K9** 31 33N 90 7W
Monticello, *N.Y., U.S.A.* **79 E10** 41 39N 74 42W
Monticello, *Utah, U.S.A.* **83 H9** 37 52N 109 21W
Montijo, *Portugal* **19 C1** 38 41N 8 54W
Montilla, *Spain* **19 D3** 37 36N 4 40W
Montluçon, *France* **18 C5** 46 22N 2 36 E
Montmagny, *Canada* **71 C5** 46 58N 70 34W
Montmartre, *Canada* **73 C8** 50 14N 103 27W
Montmorillon, *France* **18 C4** 46 26N 0 50 E
Monto, *Australia* **62 C5** 24 52S 151 6 E
Montoro, *Spain* **19 C3** 38 1N 4 27W
Montour Falls, *U.S.A.* **78 D8** 42 21N 76 51W

Montoursville

Montoursville, *U.S.A.* **78 E8** 41 15N 76 55W
Montpelier, *Idaho, U.S.A.* .. **82 E8** 42 19N 111 18W
Montpelier, *Vt., U.S.A.* **79 B12** 44 16N 72 35W
Montpellier, *France* .... **18 E5** 43 37N 3 52 E
Montréal, *Canada* **79 A11** 45 31N 73 34W
Montreal →, *Canada* **70 C3** 47 14N 84 39W
Montreal L., *Canada* **73 C7** 54 20N 105 45W
Montreal Lake, *Canada* **73 C7** 54 3N 105 46W
Montreux, *Switz.* .... **18 C7** 46 26N 6 55 E
Montrose, *U.K.* **12 E6** 56 44N 2 27W
Montrose, *Colo., U.S.A.* ... **83 G10** 38 29N 107 53W
Montrose, *Pa., U.S.A.* **79 E9** 41 50N 75 53W
Monts, Pte. des, *Canada* .. **71 C6** 49 20N 67 12W
Montserrat ■, *W. Indies* ... **89 C7** 16 40N 62 10W
Montuiri, *Spain* .... **22 B9** 39 34N 2 59 E
Monywa, *Burma* .... **41 H19** 22 7N 95 11 E
Monza, *Italy* .... **18 D8** 45 35N 9 16 E
Monze, *Zambia* .... **55 F2** 16 17S 27 29 E
Monze, C., *Pakistan* .... **42 G2** 24 47N 66 37 E
Monzón, *Spain* .... **19 B6** 41 52N 0 10 E
Mooers, *U.S.A.* **79 B11** 44 58N 73 35W
Mooi River, *S. Africa* ..... **57 D4** 29 13S 29 50 E
Moonah →, *Australia* .... **62 C2** 22 3S 138 33 E
Moonda, L., *Australia* .... **62 D3** 25 52S 140 25 E
Moonie, *Australia* .... **63 D5** 27 46S 150 20 E
Moonie →, *Australia* .... **63 D4** 29 19S 148 43 E
Moonta, *Australia* .... **63 E2** 34 6S 137 32 E
Moora, *Australia* .... **61 F2** 30 37S 115 58 E
Moorcroft, *U.S.A.* **80 C2** 44 16N 104 57W
Moore →, *Australia* ..... **61 F2** 31 22S 115 30 E
Moore, L., *Australia* ..... **61 E2** 29 50S 117 35 E
Moore Park, *Australia* .... **62 C5** 24 43S 152 17 E
Moore Reefs, *Australia* .... **62 B4** 16 0S 149 5 E
Moorefield, *U.S.A.* **76 F6** 39 5N 78 59W
Moores Res., *U.S.A.* **79 B13** 44 45N 71 50W
Moorfoot Hills, *U.K.* **12 F5** 55 44N 3 8W
Moorhead, *U.S.A.* **80 B6** 46 53N 96 45W
Moorpark, *U.S.A.* **85 L8** 34 17N 118 53W
Moorreesburg, *S. Africa* ... **56 E2** 33 6S 18 38 E
Moose →, *Canada* **70 B3** 51 20N 80 25W
Moose →, *U.S.A.* **79 C9** 43 38N 75 24W
Moose Creek, *Canada* **79 A10** 45 15N 74 58W
Moose Factory, *Canada* **70 B3** 51 16N 80 32W
Moose Jaw, *Canada* **73 C7** 50 24N 105 30W
Moose Jaw →, *Canada* .. **73 C7** 50 34N 105 18W
Moose Lake, *Canada* **73 C8** 53 43N 100 20W
Moose Lake, *U.S.A.* **80 B8** 46 27N 92 46W
Moose Mountain Prov. Park,
Canada **73 D8** 49 48N 102 25W
Moosehead L., *U.S.A.* **77 C11** 45 38N 69 40W
Mooselookmeguntic L.,
U.S.A. **77 C10** 44 55N 70 49W
Moosilauke, Mt., *U.S.A.* ... **79 B13** 44 3N 71 40W
Moosomin, *Canada* **73 C8** 50 9N 101 40W
Moosonee, *Canada* **70 B3** 51 17N 80 39W
Moosup, *U.S.A.* **79 E13** 41 43N 71 53W
Mopeia Velha, *Mozam.* .... **55 F4** 17 30S 35 40 E
Mopipi, *Botswana* .... **56 C3** 21 6S 24 55 E
Mopoi, *C.A.R.* .... **54 A2** 5 6N 26 54 E
Mopti, *Mali* **50 F5** 14 30N 4 0W
Moqor, *Afghan.* .... **42 C2** 32 50N 67 42 E
Moquegua, *Peru* **92 G4** 17 15S 70 46W
Mora, *Sweden* .... **9 F16** 61 2N 14 38 E
Mora, *Minn., U.S.A.* **80 C8** 45 53N 93 18W
Mora, *N. Mex., U.S.A.* **83 J11** 35 58N 105 20W
Mora →, *U.S.A.* **81 H2** 35 35N 104 25W
Moradabad, *India* .... **43 E8** 28 50N 78 50 E
Morafenobe, *Madag.* ..... **57 B7** 17 50S 44 53 E
Moramanga, *Madag.* ..... **57 B8** 18 56S 48 12 E
Moran, *Kans., U.S.A.* **81 G7** 37 55N 95 10W
Moran, *Wyo., U.S.A.* **82 E8** 43 53N 110 37W
Moranbah, *Australia* ..... **62 C4** 22 1S 148 6 E
Morant Cays, *Jamaica* **88 C4** 17 22N 76 0W
Morant Pt., *Jamaica* **88 C4** 17 55N 76 12W
Morar, *India* .... **42 F8** 26 14N 78 14 E
Morar, L., *U.K.* **12 E3** 56 57N 5 40W
Moratuwa, *Sri Lanka* ..... **40 R11** 6 45N 79 55 E
Morava →, *Serbia, Yug.* . **21 B9** 44 36N 21 4 E
Morava →, *Slovak Rep.* .. **17 D9** 48 10N 16 59 E
Moravia, *U.S.A.* **79 D8** 42 43N 76 25W
Moravian Hts. =
Českomoravská
Vrchovina, *Czech Rep.* .. **16 D8** 49 30N 15 40 E
Morawa, *Australia* .... **61 E2** 29 13S 116 0 E
Morawhanna, *Guyana* **92 B7** 8 30N 59 40W
Moray □, *U.K.* **12 D5** 57 31N 3 18W
Moray Firth, *U.K.* **12 D5** 57 40N 3 52W
Morbi, *India* .... **42 H4** 22 50N 70 42 E
Morden, *Canada* **73 D9** 49 15N 98 10W
Mordovian Republic =
Mordvinia □, *Russia* .... **24 D7** 54 20N 44 30 E
Mordvinia □, *Russia* ..... **24 D7** 54 20N 44 30 E
Morea, *Greece* .... **6 H10** 37 45N 22 10 E
Moreau →, *U.S.A.* **80 C4** 45 18N 100 43W
Morecambe, *U.K.* **10 C5** 54 5N 2 52W
Morecambe B., *U.K.* **10 C5** 54 7N 3 0W
Moree, *Australia* .... **63 D4** 29 28S 149 54 E
Morehead, *U.S.A.* **76 F4** 38 11N 83 26W
Morehead City, *U.S.A.* **77 H7** 34 43N 76 43W
Morel →, *India* .... **42 F7** 26 13N 76 36 E
Morelia, *Mexico* **86 D4** 19 42N 101 7W
Morella, *Australia* .... **62 C3** 23 0S 143 52 E
Morella, *Spain* **19 B5** 40 35N 0 5W
Morelos, *Mexico* **86 B3** 26 42N 107 40W
Morelos □, *Mexico* **87 D5** 18 40N 99 10W
Morena, *India* .... **42 F8** 26 30N 78 4 E
Morena, Sierra, *Spain* **19 C3** 38 20N 4 0W
Moreno Valley, *U.S.A.* **85 M10** 33 56N 117 15W
Moresby I., *Canada* **72 C2** 52 30N 131 40W
Moreton I., *Australia* ..... **63 D5** 27 10S 153 25 E
Morey, *Spain* .... **22 B10** 39 44N 3 20 E
Morgan, *U.S.A.* **82 F8** 41 2N 111 41W
Morgan City, *U.S.A.* **81 L9** 29 42N 91 12W
Morgan Hill, *U.S.A.* **84 H5** 37 8N 121 39W
Morganfield, *U.S.A.* **76 G2** 37 41N 87 55W
Morganton, *U.S.A.* **77 H5** 35 45N 81 41W
Morgantown, *U.S.A.* **76 F6** 39 38N 79 57W
Morgenzon, *S. Africa* ..... **57 D4** 26 45S 29 36 E
Morghak, *Iran* .... **45 D8** 29 7N 57 54 E
Morhar →, *India* .... **43 G11** 25 29N 85 11 E
Moriarty, *U.S.A.* **83 J10** 34 59N 106 3W
Morice L., *Canada* **72 C3** 53 50N 127 40W
Morinville, *Canada* **72 C6** 53 49N 113 41W
Morioka, *Japan* .... **30 E10** 39 45N 141 8 E
Moris, *Mexico* **86 B3** 28 8N 108 32W
Morlaix, *France* **18 B2** 48 36N 3 52W
Mornington, *Australia* .... **63 F4** 38 15S 145 5 E
Mornington, I., *Chile* **96 F1** 49 50S 75 30W
Mornington I., *Australia* ... **62 B2** 16 30S 139 30 E
Moro, *Pakistan* .... **42 F2** 26 40N 68 0 E
Moro →, *Pakistan* ...... **42 E2** 29 42N 67 22 E
Moro G., *Phil.* .... **37 C6** 6 30N 123 0 E
Morocco ■, *N. Afr.* **50 B4** 32 0N 5 50W
Morogoro, *Tanzania* ...... **54 D4** 6 50S 37 40 E
Morogoro □, *Tanzania* .... **54 D4** 8 0S 37 0 E
Moroleón, *Mexico* **86 C4** 20 8N 101 32W
Morombe, *Madag.* .... **57 C7** 21 45S 43 22 E
Moron, *Argentina* **94 C4** 34 39S 58 37W
Morón, *Cuba* **88 B4** 22 8N 78 39W
Morón de la Frontera, *Spain* **19 D3** 37 6N 5 28W
Morona →, *Peru* **92 D3** 4 40S 77 10W
Morondava, *Madag.* ...... **57 C7** 20 17S 44 17 E
Morongo Valley, *U.S.A.* ... **85 L10** 34 3N 116 37W
Moroni, *Comoros Is.* ...... **49 H8** 11 40S 43 16 E
Moroni, *U.S.A.* **82 G8** 39 32N 111 35W
Morotai, *Indonesia* .... **37 D7** 2 10N 128 30 E
Moroto, *Uganda* .... **54 B3** 2 28N 34 42 E
Moroto Summit, *Kenya* .... **54 B3** 2 30N 34 43 E
Morpeth, *U.K.* **10 B6** 55 10N 1 41W
Morphou, *Cyprus* .... **23 D11** 35 12N 32 59 E
Morphou Bay, *Cyprus* .... **23 D11** 35 15N 32 50 E
Morrilton, *U.S.A.* **81 H8** 35 9N 92 44W
Morrinhos, *Brazil* **93 G9** 17 45S 49 10W
Morrinsville, *N.Z.* .... **59 G5** 37 40S 175 32 E
Morris, *Canada* **73 D9** 49 25N 97 22W
Morris, *Minn., U.S.A.* **80 C7** 45 35N 95 55W
Morris, *N.Y., U.S.A.* **79 D9** 42 33N 75 15W
Morris, *Pa., U.S.A.* **78 E7** 41 35N 77 17W
Morris, Mt., *Australia* .... **61 E5** 26 9S 131 4 E
Morrisburg, *Canada* **79 B9** 44 55N 75 7W
Morristown, *Ariz., U.S.A.* .. **83 K7** 33 51N 112 37W
Morristown, *N.J., U.S.A.* .. **79 F10** 40 48N 74 29W
Morristown, *N.Y., U.S.A.* .. **79 B9** 44 35N 75 39W
Morristown, *Tenn., U.S.A.* . **77 G4** 36 13N 83 18W
Morrisville, *N.Y., U.S.A.* ... **79 D9** 42 53N 75 35W
Morrisville, *Pa., U.S.A.* **79 F10** 40 13N 74 47W
Morrisville, *Vt., U.S.A.* **79 B12** 44 34N 72 36W
Morro, Pta., *Chile* **94 B1** 27 6S 71 0W
Morro Bay, *U.S.A.* **84 K6** 35 22N 120 51W
Morro del Jable, *Canary Is.* **22 F5** 28 3N 14 23W
Morro Jable, Pta. de,
Canary Is. **22 F5** 28 2N 14 20W
Morrosquillo, G. de,
Colombia **88 E4** 9 35N 75 40W
Morrumbene, *Mozam.* .... **57 C6** 23 31S 35 16 E
Morshansk, *Russia* ...... **24 D7** 53 28N 41 50 E
Morteros, *Argentina* **94 C3** 30 50S 62 0W
Mortlach, *Canada* **73 C7** 50 27N 106 4W
Mortlake, *Australia* ...... **63 F3** 38 5S 142 50 E
Morton, *Tex., U.S.A.* **81 J3** 33 44N 102 46W
Morton, *Wash., U.S.A.* **84 D4** 46 34N 122 17W
Morundah, *Australia* ..... **63 E4** 34 57S 146 19 E
Moruya, *Australia* .... **63 F5** 35 58S 150 3 E
Morvan, *France* .... **18 C6** 47 5N 4 3 E
Morven, *Australia* .... **63 D4** 26 22S 147 5 E
Morvern, *U.K.* **12 E3** 56 38N 5 44W
Morwell, *Australia* .... **63 F4** 38 10S 146 22 E
Morzhovets, Ostrov, *Russia* **24 A7** 66 44N 42 35 E
Moscos Is. = Maungmagan
Is., *Burma* .... **38 F1** 14 0N 97 30 E
Moscow = Moskva, *Russia* **24 C6** 55 45N 37 35 E
Moscow, *Idaho, U.S.A.* **82 C5** 46 44N 117 0W
Moscow, *Pa., U.S.A.* **79 E9** 41 20N 75 31W
Mosel →, *Europe* .... **18 A7** 50 22N 7 36 E
Moselle = Mosel →,
Europe .... **18 A7** 50 22N 7 36 E
Moses Lake, *U.S.A.* **82 C4** 47 8N 119 17W
Mosgiel, *N.Z.* .... **59 L3** 45 53S 170 21 E
Moshi, *Tanzania* .... **54 C4** 3 22S 37 18 E
Moshupa, *Botswana* ...... **56 C4** 24 46S 25 29 E
Mosjøen, *Norway* .... **8 D15** 65 51N 13 12 E
Moskenesøya, *Norway* .... **8 C15** 67 58N 13 0 E
Moskenstraumen, *Norway* . **8 C15** 67 47N 12 45 E
Moskva, *Russia* .... **24 C6** 55 45N 37 35 E
Mosomane, *Botswana* .... **56 C4** 24 2S 26 19 E
Moson-magyaróvár,
Hungary .... **17 E9** 47 52N 17 18 E
Mosquera, *Colombia* **92 C3** 2 35N 78 24W
Mosquero, *U.S.A.* **81 H3** 35 47N 103 58W
Mosquitia, *Honduras* **88 C3** 15 20N 84 10W
Mosquito Coast =
Mosquitia, *Honduras* **88 C3** 15 20N 84 10W
Mosquito Creek L., *U.S.A.* . **78 E4** 41 18N 80 46W
Mosquito L., *Canada* **73 A8** 62 35N 103 20W
Mosquitos, G. de los,
Panama **88 E3** 9 15N 81 10W
Moss, *Norway* .... **9 G14** 59 27N 10 40 E
Moss Vale, *Australia* ..... **63 E5** 34 32S 150 25 E
Mossbank, *Canada* **73 D7** 49 56N 105 56W
Mossburn, *N.Z.* .... **59 L2** 45 41S 168 15 E
Mosselbaai, *S. Africa* ..... **56 E3** 34 11S 22 8 E
Mossendjo, *Congo* .... **52 E2** 2 55S 12 42 E
Mossgiel, *Australia* ...... **63 E3** 33 15S 144 5 E
Mossman, *Australia* ...... **62 B4** 16 21S 145 15 E
Mossoró, *Brazil* **93 E11** 5 10S 37 15W
Mossuril, *Mozam.* .... **55 E5** 14 58S 40 42 E
Most, *Czech Rep.* .... **16 C7** 50 31N 13 38 E
Mosta, *Malta* .... **23 D1** 35 54N 14 24 E
Moşţafáābād, *Iran* .... **45 C7** 33 39N 54 53 E
Mostaganem, *Algeria* ..... **50 A6** 35 54N 0 5 E
Mostar, *Bos.-H.* .... **21 C7** 43 22N 17 50 E
Mostardas, *Brazil* **95 C5** 31 2S 50 51W
Mostiska = Mostyska,
Ukraine .... **17 D12** 49 48N 23 4 E
Mosty = Masty, *Belarus* ... **17 B13** 53 27N 24 38 E
Mostyska, *Ukraine* .... **17 D12** 49 48N 23 4 E
Mosul = Al Mawşil, *Iraq* .. **44 B4** 36 15N 43 5 E
Mosŭlpo, *S. Korea* .... **35 H14** 33 20N 126 17 E
Motagua →, *Guatemala* . **88 C2** 15 44N 88 14W
Motala, *Sweden* .... **9 G16** 58 32N 15 1 E
Moth, *India* .... **43 G8** 25 43N 78 57 E
Motherwell, *U.K.* **12 F5** 55 47N 3 58W
Motihari, *India* .... **43 F11** 26 30N 84 55 E
Motozintla de Mendoza,
Mexico **87 D6** 15 21N 92 14W
Motril, *Spain* **19 D4** 36 31N 3 37W
Mott, *U.S.A.* **80 B3** 46 23N 102 20W
Motueka, *N.Z.* .... **59 J4** 41 7S 173 1 E
Motueka →, *N.Z.* .... **59 J4** 41 5S 173 1 E
Motul, *Mexico* **87 C7** 21 0N 89 20W
Mouchalagane →, *Canada* **71 B6** 50 56N 68 41W
Moúdhros, *Greece* .... **21 E11** 39 50N 25 18 E
Mouila, *Gabon* .... **52 E2** 1 50S 11 0 E
Moulamein, *Australia* ..... **63 F3** 35 3S 144 1 E
Moulianá, *Greece* .... **23 D7** 35 10N 25 59 E
Moulins, *France* .... **18 C5** 46 35N 3 19 E
Moulmein, *Burma* .... **41 L20** 16 30N 97 40 E
Moulouya, O. →, *Morocco* **50 B5** 35 5N 2 25W
Moultrie, *U.S.A.* **77 K4** 31 11N 83 47W
Moultrie, L., *U.S.A.* **77 J5** 33 20N 80 5W
Mound City, *Mo., U.S.A.* .. **80 E7** 40 7N 95 14W
Mound City, *S. Dak., U.S.A.* **80 C4** 45 44N 100 4W
Moundou, *Chad* .... **51 G9** 8 40N 16 10 E
Moundsville, *U.S.A.* **78 G4** 39 55N 80 44W
Moung, *Cambodia* .... **38 F4** 12 46N 103 27 E
Mount Airy, *U.S.A.* **77 G5** 36 31N 80 37W
Mount Albert, *Canada* **78 B5** 44 8N 79 19W
Mount Barker, *S. Austral.,*
Australia .... **63 F2** 35 5S 138 52 E
Mount Barker, *W. Austral.,*
Australia .... **61 F2** 34 38S 117 40 E
Mount Beauty, *Australia* .. **63 F4** 36 47S 147 10 E
Mount Brydges, *Canada* ... **78 D3** 42 54N 81 29W
Mount Burr, *Australia* ..... **63 F3** 37 34S 140 26 E
Mount Carmel, *Ill., U.S.A.* . **76 F2** 38 25N 87 46W
Mount Carmel, *Pa., U.S.A.* . **79 F8** 40 47N 76 24W
Mount Charleston, *U.S.A.* . **85 J11** 36 16N 115 37W
Mount Clemens, *U.S.A.* ... **78 D2** 42 35N 82 53W
Mount Coolon, *Australia* .. **62 C4** 21 25S 147 25 E
Mount Darwin, *Zimbabwe* . **55 F3** 16 47S 31 38 E
Mount Desert I., *U.S.A.* ... **77 C11** 44 21N 68 20W
Mount Dora, *U.S.A.* **77 L5** 28 48N 81 38W
Mount Edziza Prov. Park,
Canada **72 B2** 57 30N 130 45W
Mount Fletcher, *S. Africa* .. **57 E4** 30 40S 28 30 E
Mount Forest, *Canada* **78 C4** 43 59N 80 43W
Mount Gambier, *Australia* . **63 F3** 37 50S 140 46 E
Mount Garnet, *Australia* ... **62 B4** 17 37S 145 6 E
Mount Holly, *U.S.A.* **79 G10** 39 59N 74 47W
Mount Holly Springs, *U.S.A.* **78 F7** 40 7N 77 12W
Mount Hope, *N.S.W.,*
Australia .... **63 E4** 32 51S 145 51 E
Mount Hope, *S. Austral.,*
Australia .... **63 E2** 34 7S 135 23 E
Mount Isa, *Australia* ...... **62 C2** 20 42S 139 26 E
Mount Jewett, *U.S.A.* **78 E6** 41 44N 78 39W
Mount Kisco, *U.S.A.* **79 E11** 41 12N 73 44W
Mount Laguna, *U.S.A.* **85 N10** 32 52N 116 25W
Mount Larcom, *Australia* .. **62 C5** 23 48S 150 59 E
Mount Lofty Ra., *Australia* . **63 E2** 34 35S 139 5 E
Mount Magnet, *Australia* .. **61 E2** 28 2S 117 47 E
Mount Maunganui, *N.Z.* ... **59 G6** 37 40S 176 14 E
Mount Molloy, *Australia* .. **62 B4** 16 42S 145 20 E
Mount Morgan, *Australia* .. **62 C5** 23 40S 150 25 E
Mount Morris, *U.S.A.* **78 D7** 42 44N 77 52W
Mount Pearl, *Canada* **71 C9** 47 31N 52 47W
Mount Penn, *U.S.A.* **79 F9** 40 20N 75 54W
Mount Perry, *Australia* .... **63 D5** 25 13S 151 42 E
Mount Pleasant, *Iowa,*
U.S.A. **80 E9** 40 58N 91 33W
Mount Pleasant, *Mich.,*
U.S.A. **76 D3** 43 36N 84 46W
Mount Pleasant, *Pa., U.S.A.* **78 F5** 40 9N 79 33W
Mount Pleasant, *S.C., U.S.A.* **77 J6** 32 47N 79 52W
Mount Pleasant, *Tenn.,*
U.S.A. **77 H2** 35 32N 87 12W
Mount Pleasant, *Tex., U.S.A.* **81 J7** 33 9N 94 58W
Mount Pleasant, *Utah,*
U.S.A. **82 G8** 39 33N 111 27W
Mount Pocono, *U.S.A.* **79 E9** 41 7N 75 22W
Mount Rainier Nat. Park,
U.S.A. **84 D5** 46 55N 121 50W
Mount Revelstoke Nat. Park,
Canada **72 C5** 51 5N 118 30W
Mount Robson Prov. Park,
Canada **72 C5** 53 0N 119 0W
Mount Shasta, *U.S.A.* **82 F2** 41 19N 122 19W
Mount Signal, *U.S.A.* **85 N11** 32 39N 115 37W
Mount Sterling, *Ill., U.S.A.* . **80 F9** 39 59N 90 45W
Mount Sterling, *Ky., U.S.A.* **76 F4** 38 4N 83 56W
Mount Surprise, *Australia* . **62 B3** 18 10S 144 17 E
Mount Union, *U.S.A.* **78 F7** 40 23N 77 53W
Mount Upton, *U.S.A.* **79 D9** 42 26N 75 23W
Mount Vernon, *Ill., U.S.A.* . **76 F1** 38 19N 88 55W
Mount Vernon, *Ind., U.S.A.* **80 F10** 38 17N 88 57W
Mount Vernon, *N.Y., U.S.A.* **79 F11** 40 55N 73 50W
Mount Vernon, *Ohio, U.S.A.* **78 F2** 40 23N 82 29W
Mount Vernon, *Wash.,*
U.S.A. **84 B4** 48 25N 122 20W
Mountain Ash, *U.K.* **11 F4** 51 40N 3 23W
Mountain Center, *U.S.A.* .. **85 M10** 33 42N 116 44W
Mountain City, *Nev., U.S.A.* **82 F6** 41 50N 115 58W
Mountain City, *Tenn., U.S.A.* **77 G5** 36 29N 81 48W
Mountain Dale, *U.S.A.* **79 E10** 41 41N 74 32W
Mountain Grove, *U.S.A.* ... **81 G8** 37 8N 92 16W
Mountain Home, *Ark.,*
U.S.A. **81 G8** 36 20N 92 23W
Mountain Home, *Idaho,*
U.S.A. **82 E6** 43 8N 115 41W
Mountain Iron, *U.S.A.* **80 B8** 47 32N 92 37W
Mountain Pass, *U.S.A.* **85 K11** 35 29N 115 35W
Mountain View, *Ark., U.S.A.* **81 H8** 35 52N 92 7W
Mountain View, *Calif.,*
U.S.A. **84 H4** 37 23N 122 5W
Mountain View, *Hawaii,*
U.S.A. **74 J17** 19 33N 155 7W
Mountainair, *U.S.A.* **83 J10** 34 31N 106 15W
Mountlake Terrace, *U.S.A.* . **84 C4** 47 47N 122 19W
Mountmellick, *Ireland* **13 C4** 53 7N 7 20W
Mountrath, *Ireland* **13 D4** 53 0N 7 28W
Moura, *Australia* .... **62 C4** 24 35S 149 58 E
Moura, *Brazil* **92 D6** 1 32S 61 38W
Moura, *Portugal* **19 C2** 38 7N 7 30W
Mourdi, Dépression du,
Chad .... **51 E10** 18 10N 23 0 E
Mourilyan, *Australia* ..... **62 B4** 17 35S 146 3 E
Mourne →, *U.K.* **13 B4** 54 52N 7 26W
Mourne Mts., *U.K.* **13 B5** 54 10N 6 0W
Mourniaí, *Greece* .... **23 D6** 35 29N 24 1 E
Mournies = Mourniaí,
Greece .... **23 D6** 35 29N 24 1 E
Mouscron, *Belgium* ...... **15 D3** 50 45N 3 12 E
Moussoro, *Chad* .... **51 F9** 13 41N 16 35 E
Moutohara, *N.Z.* .... **59 H6** 38 27S 177 32 E
Moutong, *Indonesia* ...... **37 D6** 0 28N 121 13 E
Movas, *Mexico* **86 B3** 28 10N 109 25W
Moville, *Ireland* **13 A4** 55 11N 7 3W
Mowandjum, *Australia* .... **60 C3** 17 22S 123 40 E
Moy →, *Ireland* **13 B2** 54 8N 9 8W
Moyale, *Kenya* .... **54 B4** 3 30N 39 0 E
Moyen Atlas, *Morocco* **50 B4** 33 0N 5 0W
Moyne, L. le, *Canada* **71 A6** 56 45N 68 47W
Moyo, *Indonesia* .... **36 F5** 8 10S 117 40 E
Moyobamba, *Peru* **92 E3** 6 0S 77 0W
Moyyero →, *Russia* ..... **27 C11** 68 44N 103 42 E
Moyynty, *Kazakstan* ...... **26 E8** 47 10N 73 18 E
Mozambique =
Moçambique, *Mozam.* .. **55 F5** 15 3S 40 42 E
Mozambique ■, *Africa* .... **55 F4** 19 0S 35 0 E
Mozambique Chan., *Africa* . **57 B7** 17 30S 42 30 E
Mozdok, *Russia* .... **25 F7** 43 45N 44 48 E
Mozdūrān, *Iran* .... **45 B9** 36 9N 60 35 E
Mozhnābād, *Iran* .... **45 C9** 34 7N 60 6 E
Mozyr = Mazyr, *Belarus* ... **17 B15** 51 59N 29 15 E
Mpanda, *Tanzania* .... **54 D3** 6 23S 31 1 E
Mpika, *Zambia* .... **55 E3** 11 51S 31 25 E
Mpulungu, *Zambia* .... **55 D3** 8 51S 31 5 E
Mpumalanga, *S. Africa* .... **57 D5** 29 50S 30 33 E
Mpumalanga □, *S. Africa* . **57 B5** 26 0S 30 0 E
Mpwapwa, *Tanzania* ...... **54 D4** 6 23S 36 30 E
Msambansovu, *Zimbabwe* . **55 F3** 15 50S 30 3 E
M'sila →, *Algeria* .... **50 A6** 35 30N 4 29 E
Msoro, *Zambia* .... **55 E3** 13 35S 31 50 E
Mstislavl = Mstsislaw,
Belarus .... **17 A16** 54 0N 31 50 E
Mstsislaw, *Belarus* .... **17 A16** 54 0N 31 50 E
Mtama, *Tanzania* .... **55 E4** 10 17S 39 21 E
Mtilikwe →, *Zimbabwe* .. **55 G3** 21 9S 31 30 E
Mtubatuba, *S. Africa* ..... **57 D5** 28 30S 32 8 E
Mtwara-Mikindani, *Tanzania* **55 E5** 10 20S 40 20 E
Mu Gia, Deo, *Vietnam* .... **38 D5** 17 40N 105 47 E
Mu Us Shamo, *China* ..... **34 E5** 39 0N 109 0 E
Muang Chiang Rai = Chiang
Rai, *Thailand* .... **38 C2** 19 52N 99 50 E
Muang Khong, *Laos* ...... **38 E5** 14 7N 105 51 E
Muang Khong, *Laos* ...... **36 B3** 14 5N 105 52 E
Muang Lamphun, *Thailand* **38 C2** 18 40N 99 2 E
Muar, *Malaysia* .... **39 L4** 2 3N 102 34 E
Muarabungo, *Indonesia* ... **36 E2** 1 28S 102 52 E
Muaraenim, *Indonesia* .... **36 E2** 3 40S 103 50 E
Muarajuloi, *Indonesia* .... **36 E4** 0 12S 114 3 E
Muarakaman, *Indonesia* ... **36 E5** 0 2S 116 45 E
Muaratebo, *Indonesia* .... **36 E2** 1 30S 102 26 E
Muaratembesi, *Indonesia* .. **36 E2** 1 42S 103 8 E
Muaratewe, *Indonesia* .... **36 E4** 0 58S 114 52 E
Mubarakpur, *India* .... **43 F10** 26 6N 83 18 E
Mubarraz = Al Mubarraz,
Si. Arabia .... **45 E6** 25 30N 49 40 E
Mubende, *Uganda* .... **54 B3** 0 33N 31 22 E
Mubi, *Nigeria* .... **51 F8** 10 18N 13 16 E
Mubur, Pulau, *Indonesia* .. **39 L6** 3 20N 106 12 E
Mucajaí →, *Brazil* **92 C6** 2 25N 60 52W
Muchachos, Roque de los,
Canary Is. **22 F2** 28 44N 17 52W
Muchinga Mts., *Zambia* ... **55 E3** 11 30S 31 30 E
Muck, *U.K.* **12 E2** 56 50N 6 15W
Muckadilla, *Australia* ..... **63 D4** 26 35S 148 23 E
Mucuri, *Brazil* **93 G11** 18 0S 39 36W
Mucusso, *Angola* .... **56 B3** 18 1S 21 25 E
Muda, *Canary Is.* **22 F6** 28 34N 13 57W
Mudanjiang, *China* ...... **35 B15** 44 38N 129 30 E
Mudanya, *Turkey* .... **21 D13** 40 25N 28 50 E
Muddy Cr. →, *U.S.A.* **83 H8** 38 24N 110 42W
Mudgee, *Australia* .... **63 E4** 32 32S 149 31 E
Mudjatik →, *Canada* **73 B7** 56 1N 107 36W
Muecate, *Mozam.* .... **55 E4** 14 55S 39 40 E
Mueda, *Mozam.* .... **55 E4** 11 36S 39 28 E
Mueller Ra., *Australia* .... **60 C4** 18 18S 126 46 E
Muende, *Mozam.* .... **55 E3** 14 28S 33 0 E
Muerto, Mar, *Mexico* **87 D6** 16 10N 94 10W
Mufulira, *Zambia* .... **55 E2** 12 32S 28 15 E
Mufumbiro Range, *Africa* .. **54 C2** 1 25S 29 30 E
Mughal Sarai, *India* ...... **43 G10** 25 18N 83 7 E
Mughayrā', *Si. Arabia* .... **44 D3** 29 17N 37 41 E
Mugi, *Japan* .... **31 H7** 33 40N 134 25 E
Mugila, Mts.,
Dem. Rep. of the Congo . **54 D2** 7 0S 28 50 E
Muğla, *Turkey* .... **21 F13** 37 15N 28 22 E
Mugu, *Nepal* .... **43 E10** 29 45N 82 30 E
Muhammad, Râs, *Egypt* ... **44 E2** 27 44N 34 16 E
Muhammad Qol, *Sudan* ... **51 D13** 20 53N 37 9 E
Muhammadabad, *India* .... **43 F10** 26 4N 83 25 E
Muhesi →, *Tanzania* .... **54 D4** 7 0S 35 20 E
Mühlhausen, *Germany* .... **16 C6** 51 12N 10 27 E
Mühlig Hofmann fjell,
Antarctica .... **5 D3** 72 30S 5 0 E
Muhos, *Finland* .... **8 D22** 64 47N 25 59 E
Muhu, *Estonia* .... **9 G20** 58 36N 23 11 E
Muhutwe, *Tanzania* ...... **54 C3** 1 35S 31 45 E
Muine Bheag, *Ireland* **13 D5** 52 42N 6 58W
Muir, L., *Australia* .... **61 F2** 34 30S 116 40 E
Mukacheve, *Ukraine* ...... **17 D12** 48 27N 22 45 E
Mukachevo = Mukacheve,
Ukraine .... **17 D12** 48 27N 22 45 E
Mukah, *Malaysia* .... **36 D4** 2 55N 112 5 E
Mukandwara, *India* ...... **42 G6** 24 49N 75 59 E
Mukdahan, *Thailand* ..... **38 D5** 16 32N 104 43 E
Mukden = Shenyang, *China* **35 D12** 41 48N 123 27 E
Mukerian, *India* .... **42 D6** 31 57N 75 37 E
Mukhtuya = Lensk, *Russia* **27 C12** 60 48N 114 55 E
Mukinbudin, *Australia* .... **61 F2** 30 55S 118 5 E
Mukishi,
Dem. Rep. of the Congo . **55 D1** 8 30S 24 44 E
Mukomuko, *Indonesia* .... **36 E2** 2 30S 101 10 E
Mukomwenze,
Dem. Rep. of the Congo . **54 D2** 6 49S 27 15 E
Muktsar, *India* .... **42 D6** 30 30N 74 30 E
Mukur = Moqor, *Afghan.* .. **42 C2** 32 50N 67 42 E
Mukutawa →, *Canada* **73 C9** 53 10N 97 24W
Mukwela, *Zambia* .... **55 F2** 17 0S 26 40 E
Mula, *Spain* **19 C5** 38 3N 1 33W
Mula →, *Pakistan* ...... **42 F2** 27 57N 67 36 E
Mulange,
Dem. Rep. of the Congo . **54 C2** 3 40S 27 10 E
Mulanje, *Malawi* .... **55 F4** 16 2S 35 33 E
Mulchén, *Chile* **94 D1** 37 45S 72 20W
Mulde →, *Germany* ...... **16 C7** 51 53N 12 15 E
Mule Creek Junction, *U.S.A.* **80 D2** 43 19N 104 8W
Muleba, *Tanzania* .... **54 C3** 1 50S 31 37 E
Mulejé, *Mexico* **86 B2** 26 53N 112 1W
Muleshoe, *U.S.A.* **81 H3** 34 13N 102 43W
Mulgrave, *Canada* **71 C7** 45 38N 61 31W
Mulhacén, *Spain* **19 D4** 37 4N 3 20W
Mülheim, *Germany* ...... **33 C6** 51 25N 6 54 E

Nanching

Mulhouse, France 18 C7 47 40N 7 20 E
Muling, China 35 B16 44 35N 130 10 E
Mull, U.K. 12 E3 56 25N 5 56W
Mull, Sound of, U.K. 12 E3 56 30N 5 50W
Mullaittivu, Sri Lanka 40 Q12 9 15N 80 49 E
Mullen, U.S.A. 80 D4 42 3N 101 1W
Mullens, U.S.A. 76 G5 37 35N 81 23W
Muller, Pegunungan, Indonesia 36 D4 0 30N 113 30 E
Mullet Pen., Ireland 13 B1 54 13N 10 2W
Mullewa, Australia 61 E2 28 29S 115 30 E
Mulligan →, Australia 62 D2 25 0S 139 0 E
Mullingar, Ireland 13 C4 53 31N 7 21W
Mullins, U.S.A. 77 H6 34 12N 79 15W
Mullumbimby, Australia 63 D5 28 30S 153 30 E
Mulobezi, Zambia 55 F2 16 45S 25 7 E
Mulroy B., Ireland 13 A4 55 15N 7 46W
Multan, Pakistan 42 D4 30 15N 71 36 E
Mulumbe, Mts., Dem. Rep. of the Congo 55 D2 8 40S 27 30 E
Mulungushi Dam, Zambia 55 E2 14 48S 28 48 E
Mulvane, U.S.A. 81 G6 37 29N 97 15W
Mumbai, India 40 K8 18 55N 72 50 E
Mumbwa, Zambia 55 F2 15 0S 27 0 E
Mun →, Thailand 38 E5 15 19N 105 30 E
Muna, Indonesia 37 F6 5 0S 122 30 E
Munabao, India 42 G4 25 45N 70 17 E
Munamagi, Estonia 9 H22 57 43N 27 4 E
München, Germany 16 D6 48 8N 11 34 E
Munchen-Gladbach = Mönchengladbach, Germany 16 C4 51 11N 6 27 E
Muncho Lake, Canada 72 B3 59 0N 125 50W
Munch'ŏn, N. Korea 35 E14 39 14N 127 19 E
Muncie, U.S.A. 76 E3 40 12N 85 23W
Muncoonie, L., Australia 62 D2 25 12S 138 40 E
Mundabbera, Australia 63 D5 25 36S 151 18 E
Munday, U.S.A. 81 J5 33 27N 99 38W
Münden, Germany 16 C5 51 25N 9 38 E
Mundiwindi, Australia 60 D3 23 47S 120 9 E
Mundo Novo, Brazil 93 F10 11 50S 40 29W
Mundra, India 42 H3 22 54N 69 48 E
Mundrabilla, Australia 61 F4 31 52S 127 51 E
Mungallala, Australia 63 D4 26 28S 147 34 E
Mungallala Cr. →, Australia 63 D4 28 53S 147 5 E
Mungana, Australia 62 B3 17 8S 144 27 E
Mungaoli, India 42 G8 24 24N 78 7 E
Mungari, Mozam. 55 F3 17 12S 33 30 E
Mungbere, Dem. Rep. of the Congo 54 B2 2 36N 28 28 E
Mungeli, India 43 H9 22 4N 81 41 E
Munger, India 43 G12 25 23N 86 30 E
Munich = München, Germany 16 D6 48 8N 11 34 E
Munising, U.S.A. 76 B2 46 25N 86 40W
Munku-Sardyk, Russia 27 D11 51 45N 100 20 E
Muñoz Gamero, Pen., Chile 96 G2 52 30S 73 5W
Munroe L., Canada 73 B9 59 13N 98 35W
Munsan, S. Korea 35 F14 37 51N 126 48 E
Münster, Germany 16 C4 51 58N 7 37 E
Munster □, Ireland 13 D3 52 18N 8 44W
Muntadgin, Australia 61 F2 31 45S 118 33 E
Muntok, Indonesia 36 E3 2 5S 105 10 E
Munyama, Zambia 55 F2 16 5S 28 31 E
Muong Et, Laos 38 B5 20 49N 104 1 E
Muong Hiem, Laos 38 B4 20 5N 103 22 E
Muong Kau, Laos 38 E5 15 6N 105 47 E
Muong Khao, Laos 38 C4 19 38N 103 32 E
Muong Liep, Laos 38 C3 18 29N 101 40 E
Muong May, Laos 38 E6 14 49N 106 56 E
Muong Nong, Laos 38 D6 16 22N 106 30 E
Muong Oua, Laos 38 C3 18 18N 101 20 E
Muong Phalane, Laos 38 D5 16 39N 105 34 E
Muong Phieng, Laos 38 C3 19 6N 101 32 E
Muong Phine, Laos 38 D6 16 32N 106 2 E
Muong Saiapoun, Laos 38 C3 18 24N 101 31 E
Muong Sen, Vietnam 38 C5 19 24N 104 8 E
Muong Soui, Laos 38 C4 19 33N 102 52 E
Muong Xia, Vietnam 38 B5 20 19N 104 50 E
Muonio, Finland 8 C20 67 57N 23 40 E
Muonionjoki →, Finland 8 C20 67 11N 23 34 E
Muping, China 35 F11 37 22N 121 36 E
Muqdisho, Somali Rep. 46 G4 2 2N 45 25 E
Mur →, Austria 17 E9 46 18N 16 52 E
Murakami, Japan 30 E9 38 14N 139 29 E
Murallón, Cerro, Chile 96 F2 49 48S 73 30W
Muranda, Rwanda 54 C2 1 52S 29 20 E
Murang'a, Kenya 54 C4 0 45S 37 9 E
Murashi, Russia 24 C8 59 30N 49 0 E
Murat →, Turkey 25 G7 38 46N 40 0 E
Muratlı, Turkey 21 D12 41 10N 27 29 E
Murayama, Japan 30 E10 38 30N 140 25 E
Murban, U.A.E. 45 F7 23 50N 53 45 E
Murchison →, Australia 61 E1 27 45S 114 0 E
Murchison, Mt., Antarctica 5 D11 73 0S 168 0 E
Murchison Falls, Uganda 54 B3 2 15N 31 30 E
Murchison Ra., Australia 62 C1 20 0S 134 10 E
Murchison Rapids, Malawi 55 F3 15 55S 34 35 E
Murcia, Spain 19 D5 38 5N 1 10W
Murcia □, Spain 19 D5 37 50N 1 30W
Murdo, U.S.A. 80 D4 43 53N 100 43W
Murdoch Pt., Australia 62 A3 14 37S 144 55 E
Mureş →, Romania 17 E11 46 15N 20 13 E
Mureşul = Mureş →, Romania 17 E11 46 15N 20 13 E
Murfreesboro, N.C., U.S.A. 77 G7 36 27N 77 6W
Murfreesboro, Tenn., U.S.A. 77 H2 35 51N 86 24W
Murgab = Murghob, Tajikistan 26 F8 38 10N 74 2 E
Murgab →, Turkmenistan 45 B9 38 18N 61 12 E
Murgenella, Australia 60 B5 11 34S 132 56 E
Murgha Kibzai, Pakistan 42 D3 30 44N 69 25 E
Murghob, Tajikistan 26 F8 38 10N 74 2 E
Murgon, Australia 63 D5 26 15S 151 54 E
Muri, India 43 H11 23 22N 85 52 E
Muria, Indonesia 37 G14 6 36S 110 53 E
Muriaé, Brazil 95 A7 21 8S 42 23W
Muriel Mine, Zimbabwe 55 F3 17 14S 30 40 E
Müritz, Germany 16 B7 53 25N 12 42 E
Murka, Kenya 54 C4 3 27S 38 0 E
Murliganj, India 43 G12 25 54N 86 59 E
Murmansk, Russia 24 A5 68 57N 33 10 E
Muro, Spain 22 B10 39 44N 3 3 E
Murom, Russia 24 C7 55 35N 42 3 E
Muroran, Japan 30 C10 42 25N 141 0 E
Muroto, Japan 31 H7 33 18N 134 9 E
Muroto-Misaki, Japan 31 H7 33 15N 134 10 E
Murphy, U.S.A. 82 E5 43 13N 116 33W
Murphys, U.S.A. 84 G6 38 8N 120 28W
Murray, Ky., U.S.A. 77 G1 36 37N 88 19W
Murray, Utah, U.S.A. 82 F8 40 40N 111 53W
Murray →, Australia 63 F2 35 20S 139 22 E
Murray, L., U.S.A. 77 H5 34 3N 81 13W
Murray Bridge, Australia 63 F2 35 6S 139 14 E
Murray Harbour, Canada 71 C7 46 0N 62 28W
Murraysburg, S. Africa 56 E3 31 58S 23 47 E
Murree, Pakistan 42 C5 33 56N 73 28 E
Murrieta, U.S.A. 85 M9 33 33N 117 13W
Murrumbidgee →, Australia 63 E3 34 43S 143 12 E
Murrumburrah, Australia 63 E4 34 32S 148 22 E
Murrurundi, Australia 63 E5 31 42S 150 51 E
Murshidabad, India 43 G13 24 11N 88 19 E
Murtle L., Canada 72 C5 52 8N 119 38W
Murtoa, Australia 63 F3 36 35S 142 28 E
Murungu, Tanzania 54 C3 4 12S 31 10 E
Mururoa, Pac. Oc. 65 K14 21 52S 138 55W
Murwara, India 43 H9 23 46N 80 28 E
Murwillumbah, Australia 63 D5 28 18S 153 27 E
Mürzzuschlag, Austria 16 E8 47 36N 15 41 E
Muş, Turkey 25 G7 38 45N 41 30 E
Mûsa, Gebel, Egypt 44 D2 28 33N 33 59 E
Musa Khel, Pakistan 42 D3 30 59N 69 52 E
Mūsá Qal'eh, Afghan. 40 C4 32 20N 64 50 E
Musaffargarh, Pakistan 40 D7 30 10N 71 10 E
Musafirkhana, India 43 F9 26 22N 81 48 E
Musala, Bulgaria 21 C10 42 13N 23 37 E
Musala, Indonesia 36 D1 1 41N 98 28 E
Musan, N. Korea 35 C15 42 12N 129 12 E
Musangu, Dem. Rep. of the Congo 55 E1 10 28S 23 55 E
Musasa, Tanzania 54 C3 3 25S 31 30 E
Musay'īd, Qatar 45 E6 25 0N 51 33 E
Muscat = Masqat, Oman 46 C6 23 37N 58 36 E
Muscat & Oman = Oman ■, Asia 46 C6 23 0N 58 0 E
Muscatine, U.S.A. 80 E9 41 25N 91 3W
Musgrave Harbour, Canada 71 C9 49 27N 53 58W
Musgrave Ranges, Australia 61 E5 26 0S 132 0 E
Mushie, Dem. Rep. of the Congo 52 E3 2 56S 16 55 E
Musi →, Indonesia 36 E2 2 20S 104 56 E
Muskeg →, Canada 72 A4 60 20N 123 20W
Muskegon, U.S.A. 76 D2 43 14N 86 16W
Muskegon →, U.S.A. 76 D2 43 14N 86 21W
Muskegon Heights, U.S.A. 76 D2 43 12N 86 16W
Muskogee, U.S.A. 81 H7 35 45N 95 22W
Muskoka, L., Canada 78 B5 45 0N 79 25W
Muskwa →, Canada 72 B4 58 47N 122 48W
Muslīmiyah, Syria 44 B3 36 19N 37 12 E
Musofu, Zambia 55 E2 13 30S 29 0 E
Musoma, Tanzania 54 C3 1 30S 33 48 E
Musquaro, L., Canada 71 B7 50 38N 61 5W
Musquodoboit Harbour, Canada 71 D7 44 50N 63 9W
Musselburgh, U.K. 12 F5 55 57N 3 2W
Musselshell →, U.S.A. 82 C10 47 21N 107 57W
Mussoorie, India 42 D8 30 27N 78 6 E
Mussuco, Angola 56 B2 17 2S 19 3 E
Mustafakemalpaşa, Turkey 21 D13 40 2N 28 24 E
Mustang, Nepal 43 E10 29 10N 83 55 E
Musters, L., Argentina 96 F3 45 20S 69 25W
Musudan, N. Korea 35 D15 40 50N 129 43 E
Muswellbrook, Australia 63 E5 32 16S 150 56 E
Mût, Egypt 51 C11 25 28N 28 58 E
Mut, Turkey 44 B2 36 40N 33 28 E
Mutanda, Mozam. 57 C5 21 0S 33 34 E
Mutanda, Zambia 55 E2 12 24S 26 13 E
Mutare, Zimbabwe 55 F3 18 58S 32 38 E
Muting, Indonesia 37 F10 7 23S 140 20 E
Mutoray, Russia 27 C11 60 56N 101 0 E
Mutshatsha, Dem. Rep. of the Congo 55 E1 10 35S 24 20 E
Mutsu, Japan 30 D10 41 5N 140 55 E
Mutsu-Wan, Japan 30 D10 41 5N 140 55 E
Muttaburra, Australia 62 C3 22 38S 144 29 E
Mutton I., Ireland 13 D2 52 49N 9 32W
Mutuáli, Mozam. 55 E4 14 55S 37 0 E
Muweilih, Egypt 47 E3 30 42N 34 19 E
Muy Muy, Nic. 88 D2 12 39N 85 36W
Muyinga, Burundi 54 C3 3 14S 30 33 E
Muynak, Uzbekistan 26 E6 43 44N 59 10 E
Muzaffarabad, Pakistan 43 B5 34 25N 73 30 E
Muzaffargarh, Pakistan 42 D4 30 5N 71 14 E
Muzaffarnagar, India 42 E7 29 26N 77 40 E
Muzaffarpur, India 43 F11 26 7N 85 23 E
Muzafirpur, Pakistan 42 D3 30 58N 69 9 E
Muzhi, Russia 24 A11 65 25N 64 40 E
Mvuma, Zimbabwe 55 F3 19 16S 30 30 E
Mvurwi, Zimbabwe 55 F3 17 0S 30 57 E
Mwadui, Tanzania 54 C3 3 26S 33 32 E
Mwambo, Tanzania 55 E5 10 30S 40 22 E
Mwandi, Zambia 55 F1 17 30S 24 51 E
Mwanza, Dem. Rep. of the Congo 54 D2 7 55S 26 43 E
Mwanza, Tanzania 54 C3 2 30S 32 58 E
Mwanza, Zambia 55 F1 16 58S 24 28 E
Mwanza □, Tanzania 54 C3 2 0S 33 0 E
Mwaya, Tanzania 55 D3 9 32S 33 55 E
Mweelrea, Ireland 13 C2 53 39N 9 49W
Mweka, Dem. Rep. of the Congo 52 E4 4 50S 21 34 E
Mwene-Ditu, Dem. Rep. of the Congo 52 F4 6 35S 22 27 E
Mwenezi, Zimbabwe 55 G3 21 15S 30 48 E
Mwenezi →, Mozam. 55 G3 22 40S 31 50 E
Mwenga, Dem. Rep. of the Congo 54 C2 3 1S 28 28 E
Mweru, L., Zambia 55 D2 9 0S 28 40 E
Mweza Range, Zimbabwe 55 G3 21 0S 30 0 E
Mwilambwe, Dem. Rep. of the Congo 54 D2 8 7S 25 5 E
Mwimbi, Tanzania 55 D3 8 38S 31 39 E
Mwinilunga, Zambia 55 E1 11 43S 24 25 E
My Tho, Vietnam 39 G6 10 29N 106 23 E
Myajlar, India 42 F4 26 15N 70 20 E
Myanaung, Burma 41 K19 18 18N 95 22 E
Myanmar = Burma ■, Asia 41 J20 21 0N 96 30 E
Myaungmya, Burma 41 L19 16 30N 94 40 E
Mycenæ, Greece 21 F10 37 39N 22 52 E
Myeik Kyunzu, Burma 39 G1 11 30N 97 30 E
Myers Chuck, U.S.A. 72 B2 55 44N 132 11W
Myerstown, U.S.A. 79 F8 40 22N 76 19W
Myingyan, Burma 41 J19 21 30N 95 20 E
Myitkyina, Burma 41 G20 25 24N 97 26 E
Mykines, Færoe Is. 8 E9 62 7N 7 35W
Mykolayiv, Ukraine 25 E5 46 58N 32 0 E
Mymensingh, Bangla. 41 G17 24 45N 90 24 E
Mynydd Du, U.K. 11 F4 51 52N 3 50W
Mýrdalsjökull, Iceland 8 E4 63 40N 19 6W
Myrtle Beach, U.S.A. 77 J6 33 42N 78 53W
Myrtle Creek, U.S.A. 82 E2 43 1N 123 17W
Myrtle Point, U.S.A. 82 E1 43 4N 124 8W
Myrtou, Cyprus 23 D12 35 18N 33 4 E
Mysia, Turkey 21 E12 39 50N 27 0 E
Mysore = Karnataka □, India 40 N10 13 15N 77 0 E
Mysore, India 40 N10 12 17N 76 41 E
Mystic, U.S.A. 79 E13 41 21N 71 58W
Myszków, Poland 17 C10 50 45N 19 22 E
Mytishchi, Russia 24 C6 55 50N 37 50 E
Mývatn, Iceland 8 D5 65 36N 17 0W
Mzimba, Malawi 55 E3 11 55S 33 39 E
Mzimkulu →, S. Africa 57 E5 30 44S 30 28 E
Mzimvubu →, S. Africa 57 E4 31 38S 29 33 E
Mzuzu, Malawi 55 E3 11 30S 33 55 E

N

Na Hearadh = Harris, U.K. 12 D2 57 50N 6 55W
Na Noi, Thailand 38 C3 18 19N 100 43 E
Na Phao, Laos 38 D5 17 35N 105 44 E
Na San, Vietnam 38 B5 21 12N 104 2 E
Naab →, Germany 16 D6 49 1N 12 2 E
Naantali, Finland 9 F19 60 29N 22 2 E
Naas, Ireland 13 C5 53 12N 6 40W
Nababiep, S. Africa 56 D2 29 36S 17 46 E
Nabadwip = Navadwip, India 43 H13 23 34N 88 20 E
Nabari, Japan 31 G8 34 37N 136 5 E
Nabawa, Australia 61 E1 28 30S 114 48 E
Nabberu, L., Australia 61 E3 25 50S 120 30 E
Naberezhnyye Chelny, Russia 24 C9 55 42N 52 19 E
Nabeul, Tunisia 51 A8 36 30N 10 44 E
Nabha, India 42 D7 30 26N 76 14 E
Nabīd, Iran 45 D8 29 40N 57 38 E
Nabire, Indonesia 37 E9 3 15S 135 26 E
Nabisar, Pakistan 42 G3 25 8N 69 40 E
Nabisipi →, Canada 71 B7 50 14N 62 13W
Nabiswera, Uganda 54 B3 1 27N 32 15 E
Nablus = Nābulus, West Bank 47 C4 32 14N 35 15 E
Naboomspruit, S. Africa 57 C4 24 32S 28 40 E
Nābulus, West Bank 47 C4 32 14N 35 15 E
Nacala, Mozam. 55 E5 14 31S 40 34 E
Nacala-Velha, Mozam. 55 E5 14 32S 40 34 E
Nacaome, Honduras 88 D2 13 31N 87 30W
Nacaroa, Mozam. 55 E4 14 22S 39 56 E
Naches, U.S.A. 82 C3 46 44N 120 42W
Naches →, U.S.A. 84 D6 46 38N 120 31W
Nachicapau, L., Canada 71 A6 56 40N 68 5W
Nachingwea, Tanzania 55 E4 10 23S 38 49 E
Nachna, India 42 F4 27 34N 71 41 E
Nacimiento L., U.S.A. 84 K6 35 46N 120 53W
Naco, Mexico 86 A3 31 20N 109 56W
Nacogdoches, U.S.A. 81 K7 31 36N 94 39W
Nácori Chico, Mexico 86 B3 29 39N 109 1W
Nacozari, Mexico 86 A3 30 24N 109 39W
Nadiad, India 42 H5 22 41N 72 56 E
Nador, Morocco 50 B5 35 14N 2 58W
Nadur, Malta 23 C1 36 2N 14 17 E
Nadūshan, Iran 45 C7 32 2N 53 35 E
Nadvirna, Ukraine 17 D13 48 37N 24 30 E
Nadvoitsy, Russia 24 B5 63 52N 34 14 E
Nadvornaya = Nadvirna, Ukraine 17 D13 48 37N 24 30 E
Nadym, Russia 26 C8 65 35N 72 42 E
Nadym →, Russia 26 C8 66 12N 72 0 E
Nærbø, Norway 9 G11 58 40N 5 39 E
Næstved, Denmark 9 J14 55 13N 11 44 E
Naft-e Safīd, Iran 45 D6 31 40N 49 17 E
Naftshahr, Iran 44 C5 34 0N 45 30 E
Nafud Desert = An Nafūd, Si. Arabia 44 D4 28 15N 41 0 E
Naga, Phil. 37 B6 13 38N 123 15 E
Nagahama, Japan 31 G8 35 23N 136 16 E
Nagai, Japan 30 E10 38 6N 140 2 E
Nagaland □, India 41 G19 26 0N 94 30 E
Nagano, Japan 31 F9 36 40N 138 10 E
Nagano □, Japan 31 F9 36 15N 138 0 E
Nagaoka, Japan 31 F9 37 27N 138 51 E
Nagappattinam, India 40 P11 10 46N 79 51 E
Nagar →, Bangla. 43 G13 24 27N 89 12 E
Nagar Parkar, Pakistan 42 G4 24 28N 70 46 E
Nagasaki, Japan 31 H4 32 47N 129 50 E
Nagasaki □, Japan 31 H4 32 50N 129 40 E
Nagato, Japan 31 G5 34 19N 131 5 E
Nagaur, India 42 F5 27 15N 73 45 E
Nagda, India 42 H6 23 27N 75 25 E
Nagercoil, India 40 Q10 8 12N 77 26 E
Nagina, India 43 E8 29 30N 78 30 E
Nagineh, Iran 45 C8 34 20N 57 15 E
Nagir, Pakistan 43 A6 36 12N 74 42 E
Nagod, India 43 G9 24 34N 80 36 E
Nagoorin, Australia 62 C5 24 17S 151 15 E
Nagorno-Karabakh, Azerbaijan 25 F8 39 55N 46 45 E
Nagornyy, Russia 27 D13 55 58N 124 57 E
Nagoya, Japan 31 G8 35 10N 136 50 E
Nagpur, India 40 J11 21 8N 79 10 E
Nagua, Dom. Rep. 89 C6 19 23N 69 50W
Nagykanizsa, Hungary 17 E9 46 28N 17 0 E
Nagykörös, Hungary 17 E10 47 5N 19 48 E
Naha, Japan 31 L3 26 13N 127 42 E
Nahan, India 42 D7 30 33N 77 18 E
Nahanni Butte, Canada 72 A4 61 2N 123 31W
Nahanni Nat. Park, Canada 72 A4 61 15N 125 0W
Nahargarh, Mad. P., India 42 G6 24 10N 75 14 E
Nahargarh, Raj., India 42 G7 24 55N 76 50 E
Nahariyya, Israel 44 C2 33 1N 35 5 E
Nahāvand, Iran 45 C6 34 10N 48 22 E
Naicá, Mexico 86 B3 27 53N 105 31W
Naicam, Canada 73 C8 52 30N 104 30W
Naikoon Prov. Park, Canada 72 C2 53 55N 131 55W
Naimisharanya, India 43 F9 27 21N 80 30 E
Nain, Canada 71 A7 56 34N 61 40W
Nā'īn, Iran 45 C7 32 54N 53 0 E
Naini Tal, India 43 E8 29 30N 79 30 E
Nainpur, India 40 H12 22 30N 80 10 E
Nainwa, India 42 G6 25 46N 75 51 E
Nairn, U.K. 12 D5 57 35N 3 53W
Nairobi, Kenya 54 C4 1 17S 36 48 E
Naissaar, Estonia 9 G21 59 34N 24 29 E
Naivasha, Kenya 54 C4 0 40S 36 30 E
Naivasha, L., Kenya 54 C4 0 48S 36 20 E
Najafābād, Iran 45 C6 32 40N 51 15 E
Najd, Si. Arabia 46 B3 26 30N 42 0 E
Najibabad, India 42 E8 29 40N 78 20 E
Najin, N. Korea 35 C16 42 12N 130 15 E
Najmah, Si. Arabia 45 E6 26 42N 50 6 E
Naju, S. Korea 35 G14 35 3N 126 43 E
Nakadōri-Shima, Japan 31 H4 32 57N 129 4 E
Nakalagba, Dem. Rep. of the Congo 54 B2 2 50N 27 58 E
Nakaminato, Japan 31 F10 36 21N 140 36 E
Nakamura, Japan 31 H6 32 59N 132 56 E
Nakano, Japan 31 F9 36 45N 138 22 E
Nakano-Shima, Japan 31 K4 29 51N 129 52 E
Nakashibetsu, Japan 30 C12 43 33N 144 59 E
Nakfa, Eritrea 46 D2 16 40N 38 32 E
Nakhfar al Buşayyah, Iraq 44 D5 30 0N 46 10 E
Nakhichevan = Naxçıvan, Azerbaijan 25 G8 39 12N 45 15 E
Nakhichevan Republic = Naxçıvan □, Azerbaijan 25 G8 39 25N 45 26 E
Nakhl, Egypt 47 F2 29 55N 33 43 E
Nakhl-e Taqī, Iran 45 E7 27 28N 52 36 E
Nakhodka, Russia 27 E14 42 53N 132 54 E
Nakhon Nayok, Thailand 38 E3 14 12N 101 13 E
Nakhon Pathom, Thailand 38 F3 13 49N 100 3 E
Nakhon Phanom, Thailand 38 D5 17 23N 104 43 E
Nakhon Ratchasima, Thailand 38 E4 14 59N 102 12 E
Nakhon Sawan, Thailand 38 E3 15 35N 100 10 E
Nakhon Si Thammarat, Thailand 39 H3 8 29N 100 0 E
Nakhon Thai, Thailand 38 D3 17 5N 100 44 E
Nakhtarana, India 42 H3 23 20N 69 15 E
Nakina, Canada 70 B2 50 10N 86 40W
Nakodar, India 42 D6 31 8N 75 31 E
Nakskov, Denmark 9 J14 54 50N 11 8 E
Naktong →, S. Korea 35 G15 35 7N 128 57 E
Nakuru, Kenya 54 C4 0 15S 36 4 E
Nakuru, L., Kenya 54 C4 0 23S 36 5 E
Nakusp, Canada 72 C5 50 20N 117 45W
Nal, Pakistan 42 F2 27 40N 66 12 E
Nal →, Pakistan 42 G1 25 20N 65 30 E
Nalchik, Russia 25 F7 43 30N 43 33 E
Nalgonda, India 40 L11 17 6N 79 15 E
Nalhati, India 43 G12 24 17N 87 52 E
Naliya, India 42 H3 23 16N 68 50 E
Nallamalai Hills, India 40 M11 15 30N 78 50 E
Nam Can, Vietnam 39 H5 8 46N 104 59 E
Nam-ch'on, N. Korea 35 E14 38 15N 126 26 E
Nam Co, China 32 C4 30 30N 90 45 E
Nam Du, Hon, Vietnam 39 H5 9 41N 104 21 E
Nam Ngum Dam, Laos 38 C4 18 35N 102 34 E
Nam-Phan = Cochin China, Vietnam 39 G6 10 30N 106 0 E
Nam Phong, Thailand 38 D4 16 42N 102 52 E
Nam Tok, Thailand 38 E2 14 21N 99 4 E
Namacunde, Angola 56 B2 17 18S 15 50 E
Namacurra, Mozam. 57 B6 17 30S 36 50 E
Namak, Daryācheh-ye, Iran 45 C7 34 30N 52 0 E
Namak, Kavir-e, Iran 45 C8 34 30N 57 30 E
Namakzār, Daryācheh-ye, Iran 45 C9 34 0N 60 30 E
Namaland, Namibia 56 C2 26 0S 17 0 E
Namangan, Uzbekistan 26 E8 41 0N 71 40 E
Namapa, Mozam. 55 E4 13 43S 39 50 E
Namaqualand, S. Africa 56 E2 30 0S 17 25 E
Namasagali, Uganda 54 B3 1 2N 33 0 E
Namber, Indonesia 37 E8 1 2S 134 49 E
Nambour, Australia 63 D5 26 32S 152 58 E
Nambucca Heads, Australia 63 E5 30 37S 153 0 E
Namcha Barwa, China 32 D4 29 40N 95 10 E
Namche Bazar, Nepal 43 F12 27 51N 86 47 E
Namchonjŏm = Nam-ch'on, N. Korea 35 E14 38 15N 126 26 E
Namecunda, Mozam. 55 E4 14 54S 37 37 E
Nameponda, Mozam. 55 F4 15 50S 39 50 E
Nametil, Mozam. 55 F4 15 40S 39 21 E
Namew L., Canada 73 C8 54 14N 101 56W
Namgia, India 43 D8 31 48N 78 40 E
Namib Desert = Namibwoestyn, Namibia 56 C2 22 30S 15 0 E
Namibe, Angola 53 H2 15 7S 12 11 E
Namibe □, Angola 56 B1 16 35S 12 30 E
Namibia ■, Africa 56 C2 22 0S 18 9 E
Namibwoestyn, Namibia 56 C2 22 30S 15 0 E
Namlea, Indonesia 37 E7 3 18S 127 5 E
Namoi →, Australia 63 E4 30 12S 149 30 E
Nampa, U.S.A. 82 E5 43 34N 116 34W
Namp'o, N. Korea 35 E13 38 52N 125 10 E
Nampō-Shotō, Japan 31 J10 32 0N 140 0 E
Nampula, Mozam. 55 F4 15 6S 39 15 E
Namrole, Indonesia 37 E7 3 46S 126 46 E
Namse Shankou, China 41 E13 30 0N 82 25 E
Namsen →, Norway 8 D14 64 28N 11 37 E
Namsos, Norway 8 D14 64 29N 11 30 E
Namtsy, Russia 27 C13 62 43N 129 37 E
Namtu, Burma 41 H20 23 5N 97 28 E
Namtumbo, Tanzania 55 E4 10 30S 36 4 E
Namu, Canada 72 C3 51 52N 127 50W
Namur, Belgium 15 D4 50 27N 4 52 E
Namur □, Belgium 15 D4 50 17N 5 0 E
Namutoni, Namibia 56 B2 18 49S 16 55 E
Namwala, Zambia 55 F2 15 44S 26 30 E
Namwŏn, S. Korea 35 G14 35 23N 127 23 E
Nan, Thailand 38 C3 18 48N 100 46 E
Nan →, Thailand 38 E3 15 42N 100 9 E
Nan-ch'ang = Nanchang, China 33 D6 28 42N 115 55 E
Nanaimo, Canada 72 D4 49 10N 124 0W
Nanam, N. Korea 35 D15 41 44N 129 40 E
Nanango, Australia 63 D5 26 40S 152 0 E
Nanao, Japan 31 F8 37 0N 137 0 E
Nanchang, China 33 D6 28 42N 115 55 E
Nanching = Nanjing, China 33 C6 32 2N 118 47 E

Nanchong

Nanchong, *China* . . . . **32 C5** 30 43N 106 2 E
Nancy, *France* . . . . **18 B7** 48 42N 6 12 E
Nanda Devi, *India* . . . . **43 D8** 30 23N 79 59 E
Nanda Kot, *India* . . . . **43 D9** 30 17N 80 5 E
Nandan, *Japan* . . . . **31 G7** 34 10N 134 42 E
Nanded, *India* . . . . **40 K10** 19 10N 77 20 E
Nandewar Ra., *Australia* . . **63 E5** 30 15S 150 35 E
Nandi, *Fiji* . . . . **59 C7** 17 42S 177 20 E
Nandigram, *India* . . . . **43 H12** 22 1N 87 58 E
Nandurbar, *India* . . . . **40 J9** 21 20N 74 15 E
Nandyal, *India* . . . . **40 M11** 15 30N 78 30 E
Nanga-Eboko, *Cameroon* . . **52 D2** 4 41N 12 22 E
Nanga Parbat, *Pakistan* . . . **43 B6** 35 10N 74 35 E
Nangade, *Mozam.* . . . . **55 E4** 11 5S 39 36 E
Nangapinoh, *Indonesia* . . . . **36 E4** 0 20S 111 44 E
Nangarhār □, *Afghan.* . . . . **40 B7** 34 20N 70 0 E
Nangatayap, *Indonesia* . . . . **36 E4** 1 32S 110 34 E
Nangeya Mts., *Uganda* . . . . **54 B3** 3 30N 33 30 E
Nangong, *China* . . . . **34 F8** 37 23N 115 22 E
Nanhuang, *China* . . . . **35 F11** 36 58N 121 48 E
Nanjeko, *Zambia* . . . . **55 F1** 15 31S 23 30 E
Nanjing, *China* . . . . **33 C6** 32 2N 118 47 E
Nanjirinji, *Tanzania* . . . . **55 D4** 9 41S 39 5 E
Nankana Sahib, *Pakistan* . . **42 D5** 31 27N 73 38 E
Nanking = Nanjing, *China* . **33 C6** 32 2N 118 47 E
Nankoku, *Japan* . . . . **31 H6** 33 39N 133 44 E
Nanning, *China* . . . . **32 D5** 22 48N 108 20 E
Nannup, *Australia* . . . . **61 F2** 33 59S 115 48 E
Nanpara, *India* . . . . **43 F9** 27 52N 81 33 E
Nanpi, *China* . . . . **34 E9** 38 2N 116 45 E
Nanping, *China* . . . . **33 D6** 26 38N 118 10 E
Nanripe, *Mozam.* . . . . **55 E4** 13 52S 38 52 E
Nansei-Shotō = Ryūkyū-
rettō, *Japan* . . . . **31 M3** 26 0N 126 0 E
Nansen Sd., *Canada* **4 A3** 81 0N 91 0W
Nanshan I., *S. China Sea* . . **36 B5** 10 45N 115 49 E
Nansio, *Tanzania* . . . . **54 C3** 2 3S 33 4 E
Nantes, *France* **18 C3** 47 12N 1 33W
Nanticoke, *U.S.A.* **79 E8** 41 12N 76 0W
Nanton, *Canada* **72 C6** 50 21N 113 46W
Nantong, *China* . . . . **33 C7** 32 1N 120 52 E
Nantucket I., *U.S.A.* **76 E10** 41 16N 70 5W
Nantwich, *U.K.* **10 D5** 53 4N 2 31W
Nanty Glo, *U.S.A.* **78 F6** 40 28N 78 50W
Nanuque, *Brazil* **93 G10** 17 50S 40 21W
Nanusa, Kepulauan,
Indonesia . . . . **37 D7** 4 45N 127 1 E
Nanutarra Roadhouse,
Australia . . . . **60 D2** 22 32S 115 30 E
Nanyang, *China* . . . . **34 H7** 33 11N 112 30 E
Nanyuan, *China* . . . . **34 E9** 39 44N 116 22 E
Nanyuki, *Kenya* . . . . **54 B4** 0 2N 37 4 E
Nao, C. de la, *Spain* . . . . . . **19 C6** 38 44N 0 14 E
Naococane, L., *Canada* **71 B5** 52 50N 70 45W
Napa, *U.S.A.* **84 G4** 38 18N 122 17W
Napa →, *U.S.A.* **84 G4** 38 10N 122 19W
Napanee, *Canada* **78 B8** 44 15N 77 0W
Napanoch, *U.S.A.* **79 E10** 41 44N 74 22W
Nape, *Laos* . . . . **38 C5** 18 18N 105 6 E
Nape Pass = Keo Neua,
Deo, *Vietnam* . . . . **38 C5** 18 23N 105 10 E
Napier, *N.Z.* . . . . **59 H6** 39 30S 176 56 E
Napier Broome B., *Australia* **60 B4** 14 2S 126 37 E
Napier Pen., *Australia* . . . . **62 A2** 12 4S 135 43 E
Napierville, *Canada* **79 A11** 45 11N 73 25W
Naples = Nápoli, *Italy* . . . . **20 D6** 40 50N 14 15 E
Naples, *U.S.A.* **77 M5** 26 8N 81 48W
Napo →, *Peru* **92 D4** 3 20S 72 40W
Napoleon, *N. Dak., U.S.A.* . . **80 B5** 46 30N 99 46W
Napoleon, *Ohio, U.S.A.* **76 E3** 41 23N 84 8W
Nápoli, *Italy* . . . . **20 D6** 40 50N 14 15 E
Napopo,
Dem. Rep. of the Congo . **54 B2** 4 15N 28 0 E
Naqqāsh, *Iran* . . . . **45 C6** 35 40N 49 6 E
Nara, *Japan* . . . . **31 G7** 34 40N 135 49 E
Nara, *Mali* **50 E4** 15 10N 7 20W
Nara □, *Japan* . . . . **31 G8** 34 30N 136 0 E
Nara Canal, *Pakistan* . . . . . . **42 G3** 24 30N 69 20 E
Nara Visa, *U.S.A.* **81 H3** 35 37N 103 6W
Naracoorte, *Australia* . . . . . . **63 F3** 36 58S 140 45 E
Naradhan, *Australia* . . . . **63 E4** 33 34S 146 17 E
Naraini, *India* . . . . **43 G9** 25 11N 80 29 E
Narasapur, *India* . . . . **41 L12** 16 26N 81 40 E
Narathiwat, *Thailand* . . . . . . **39 J3** 6 30N 101 48 E
Narayanganj, *Bangla.* . . . . . **41 H17** 23 40N 90 33 E
Narayanpet, *India* . . . . **40 L10** 16 45N 77 30 E
Narbonne, *France* . . . . **18 E5** 43 11N 3 0 E
Nardīn, *Iran* . . . . **45 B7** 37 3N 55 59 E
Nardò, *Italy* . . . . **21 D8** 40 11N 18 2 E
Narembeen, *Australia* . . . . . **61 F2** 32 7S 118 24 E
Narendranagar, *India* . . . . . **42 D8** 30 10N 78 18 E
Nares Str., *Arctic* **66 A13** 80 0N 70 0W
Naretha, *Australia* . . . . **61 F3** 31 0S 124 45 E
Narew →, *Poland* . . . . **17 B11** 52 26N 20 41 E
Nari →, *Pakistan* . . . . **42 F2** 28 0N 67 40 E
Narin, *Afghan.* . . . . **40 A6** 36 5N 69 0 E
Narindra, Helodranon' i,
Madag. . . . . **57 A8** 14 55S 47 30 E
Narita, *Japan* . . . . **31 G10** 35 47N 140 19 E
Narmada →, *India* . . . . **42 J5** 21 38N 72 36 E
Narmland, *Sweden* . . . . **9 F15** 60 0N 13 30 E
Narnaul, *India* . . . . **42 E7** 28 5N 76 11 E
Narodnaya, *Russia* . . . . **24 A10** 65 5N 59 58 E
Narok, *Kenya* . . . . **54 C4** 1 55S 35 52 E
Narooma, *Australia* . . . . **63 F5** 36 14S 150 4 E
Narowal, *Pakistan* . . . . **42 C6** 32 6N 74 52 E
Narrabri, *Australia* . . . . **63 E4** 30 19S 149 46 E
Narran →, *Australia* . . . . . . **63 D4** 28 37S 148 12 E
Narrandera, *Australia* . . . . . **63 E4** 34 42S 146 31 E
Narrogin, *Australia* . . . . **61 F2** 32 58S 117 14 E
Narromine, *Australia* . . . . . . **63 E4** 32 12S 148 12 E
Narrow Hills Prov. Park,
Canada **73 C8** 54 0N 104 37W
Narsimhapur, *India* . . . . **43 H8** 22 54N 79 14 E
Narsinghgarh, *India* . . . . . . **42 H7** 23 45N 76 40 E
Naruto, *Japan* . . . . **31 G7** 34 11N 134 37 E
Narva, *Estonia* . . . . **24 C4** 59 23N 28 12 E
Narva →, *Russia* . . . . **9 G22** 59 27N 28 2 E
Narvik, *Norway* . . . . **8 B17** 68 28N 17 26 E
Narwana, *India* . . . . **42 E7** 29 39N 76 6 E
Naryan-Mar, *Russia* . . . . . . **24 A9** 67 42N 53 12 E
Narym, *Russia* . . . . **26 D9** 59 0N 81 30 E
Naryn, *Kyrgyzstan* . . . . **26 E8** 41 26N 75 58 E
Nasa, *Norway* . . . . **8 C16** 66 29N 15 23 E
Naseby, *N.Z.* . . . . **59 L3** 45 1S 170 10 E
Naselle, *U.S.A.* **84 D3** 46 22N 123 49W
Naser, Buheirat en, *Egypt* . **51 D12** 23 0N 32 30 E
Nashua, *Mont., U.S.A.* **82 B10** 48 8N 106 22W
Nashua, *N.H., U.S.A.* **79 D13** 42 45N 71 28W
Nashville, *Ark., U.S.A.* **81 J8** 33 57N 93 51W
Nashville, *Ga., U.S.A.* **77 K4** 31 12N 83 15W
Nashville, *Tenn., U.S.A.* . . . **77 G2** 36 10N 86 47W
Nasik, *India* . . . . **40 K8** 19 58N 73 50 E
Nasirabad, *India* . . . . **42 F6** 26 15N 74 45 E
Nasirabad, *Pakistan* . . . . . . **42 E3** 28 23N 68 24 E
Naskaupi →, *Canada* **71 B7** 53 47N 60 51W
Naşrābād, *Iran* . . . . **45 C6** 34 8N 51 26 E
Naşriān-e Pā'īn, *Iran* . . . . . . **44 C5** 32 52N 46 52 E
Nass →, *Canada* **72 C3** 55 0N 129 40W
Nassau, *Bahamas* **88 A4** 25 5N 77 20W
Nassau, *U.S.A.* **79 D11** 42 31N 73 37W
Nassau, B., *Chile* **96 H3** 55 20S 68 0W
Nasser, L. = Naser, Buheirat
en, *Egypt* . . . . **51 D12** 23 0N 32 30 E
Nasser City = Kôm Ombo,
Egypt . . . . **51 D12** 24 25N 32 52 E
Nässjö, *Sweden* . . . . **9 H16** 57 39N 14 42 E
Nastapoka →, *Canada* . . . **70 A4** 56 55N 76 33W
Nastapoka, Is., *Canada* . . . **70 A4** 56 55N 76 50W
Nata, *Botswana* . . . . **56 C4** 20 12S 26 12 E
Natal, *Brazil* **93 E11** 5 47S 35 13W
Natal, *Indonesia* . . . . **36 D1** 0 35N 99 7 E
Natal □, *S. Africa* . . . . **53 K6** 28 30S 30 30 E
Naţanz, *Iran* . . . . **45 C6** 33 30N 51 55 E
Natashquan, *Canada* **71 B7** 50 14N 61 46W
Natashquan →, *Canada* . . **71 B7** 50 7N 61 50W
Natchez, *U.S.A.* **81 K9** 31 34N 91 24W
Natchitoches, *U.S.A.* **81 K8** 31 46N 93 5W
Nathalia, *Australia* . . . . **63 F4** 36 1S 145 13 E
Nathdwara, *India* . . . . **42 G5** 24 55N 73 50 E
Nati, Pta., *Spain* . . . . **22 A10** 40 3N 3 50 E
Natimuk, *Australia* . . . . **63 F3** 36 42S 142 0 E
Nation →, *Canada* **72 B4** 55 30N 123 32W
National City, *U.S.A.* **85 N9** 32 41N 117 6W
Natitingou, *Benin* . . . . **50 F6** 10 20N 1 26 E
Natividad, I., *Mexico* **86 B1** 27 50N 115 10W
Natkyizin, *Burma* . . . . **38 E1** 14 57N 97 59 E
Natron, L., *Tanzania* . . . . . . **54 C4** 2 20S 36 0 E
Natrona Heights, *U.S.A.* . . . **78 F5** 40 37N 79 44W
Natuna Besar, Kepulauan,
Indonesia . . . . **39 L7** 4 0N 108 15 E
Natuna Is. = Natuna Besar,
Kepulauan, *Indonesia* . . . **39 L7** 4 0N 108 15 E
Natuna Selatan, Kepulauan,
Indonesia . . . . **39 L7** 2 45N 109 0 E
Natural Bridge, *U.S.A.* **79 B9** 44 5N 75 30W
Naturaliste, C., *Australia* . . **62 G4** 40 50S 148 15 E
Nau Qala, *Afghan.* . . . . **42 B3** 34 5N 68 5 E
Naugatuck, *U.S.A.* **79 E11** 41 30N 73 3W
Naumburg, *Germany* . . . . . . **16 C6** 51 9N 11 47 E
Nā'ūr at Tunayb, *Jordan* . . **47 D4** 31 48N 35 57 E
Nauru ■, *Pac. Oc.* . . . . **64 H8** 1 0S 166 0 E
Naushahra = Nowshera,
Pakistan . . . . **40 C8** 34 0N 72 0 E
Naushahro, *Pakistan* . . . . . . **42 F3** 26 50N 68 7 E
Naushon I., *U.S.A.* **79 E14** 41 29N 70 45W
Nauta, *Peru* **92 D4** 4 31S 73 35W
Nautanwa, *India* . . . . **41 F13** 27 20N 83 25 E
Nautla, *Mexico* **87 C5** 20 20N 96 50W
Nava, *Mexico* **86 B4** 28 25N 100 46W
Navadwip, *India* . . . . **43 H13** 23 34N 88 20 E
Navahrudak, *Belarus* . . . . . **17 B13** 53 40N 25 50 E
Navajo Reservoir, *U.S.A.* . . **83 H10** 36 48N 107 36W
Navalmoral de la Mata,
Spain **19 C3** 39 52N 5 33W
Navan = An Uaimh, *Ireland* **13 C5** 53 39N 6 41W
Navarino, I., *Chile* **96 H3** 55 0S 67 40W
Navarra □, *Spain* **19 A5** 42 40N 1 40W
Navarre, *U.S.A.* **78 F3** 40 43N 81 31W
Navarro →, *U.S.A.* **84 F3** 39 11N 123 45W
Navasota, *U.S.A.* **81 K6** 30 23N 96 5W
Navassa I., *W. Indies* **89 C5** 18 30N 75 0W
Naver →, *U.K.* **12 C4** 58 32N 4 14W
Navibandar, *India* . . . . **42 J3** 21 26N 69 48 E
Navidad, *Chile* **94 C1** 33 57S 71 50W
Navirai, *Brazil* **95 A5** 23 8S 54 13W
Navlakhi, *India* . . . . **42 H4** 22 58N 70 28 E
Năvodari, *Romania* . . . . **17 F15** 44 19N 28 36 E
Navoi = Nawoiy, *Uzbekistan* **26 E7** 40 9N 65 22 E
Navojoa, *Mexico* **86 B3** 27 0N 109 30W
Navolato, *Mexico* **86 C3** 24 47N 107 42W
Návpaktos, *Greece* . . . . **21 E9** 38 24N 21 50 E
Návplion, *Greece* . . . . **21 F10** 37 33N 22 50 E
Navsari, *India* . . . . **40 J8** 20 57N 72 59 E
Nawa Kot, *Pakistan* . . . . . . **42 E4** 28 21N 71 24 E
Nawab Khan, *Pakistan* . . . . **42 D3** 30 17N 69 12 E
Nawabganj, *Ut. P., India* . . **43 F9** 26 56N 81 14 E
Nawabganj, *Ut. P., India* . . **43 E8** 28 32N 79 40 E
Nawabshah, *Pakistan* . . . . . **42 F3** 26 15N 68 25 E
Nawada, *India* . . . . **43 G11** 24 50N 85 33 E
Nawakot, *Nepal* . . . . **43 F11** 27 55N 85 10 E
Nawalgarh, *India* . . . . **42 F6** 27 50N 75 15 E
Nawanshahr, *India* . . . . **43 C6** 32 33N 74 48 E
Nawoiy, *Uzbekistan* . . . . . . **26 E7** 40 9N 65 22 E
Naxçıvan, *Azerbaijan* . . . . . **25 G8** 39 12N 45 15 E
Naxçıvan □, *Azerbaijan* . . . **25 G8** 39 25N 45 26 E
Náxos, *Greece* . . . . **21 F11** 37 8N 25 25 E
Nay, Mui, *Vietnam* . . . . **36 B3** 12 55N 109 23 E
Nāy Band, *Būshehr, Iran* . . **45 E7** 27 20N 52 40 E
Nāy Band, *Khorāsān, Iran* . . **45 C8** 32 20N 57 34 E
Nayakhan, *Russia* . . . . **27 C16** 61 56N 159 0 E
Nayarit □, *Mexico* **86 C4** 22 0N 105 0W
Nayoro, *Japan* . . . . **30 B11** 44 21N 142 28 E
Nayyāl, W. →, *Si. Arabia* . **44 D3** 28 35N 39 4 E
Nazaré, *Brazil* **93 F11** 13 2S 39 0W
Nazareth = Nazerat, *Israel* . **47 C4** 32 42N 35 17 E
Nazareth, *U.S.A.* **79 F9** 40 44N 75 19W
Nazas, *Mexico* **86 B4** 25 10N 104 6W
Nazas →, *Mexico* **86 B4** 25 35N 103 25W
Nazca, *Peru* **92 F4** 14 50S 74 57W
Naze, The, *U.K.* . . . . **11 F9** 51 53N 1 18 E
Nazerat, *Israel* . . . . **47 C4** 32 42N 35 17 E
Nāzik, *Iran* . . . . **44 B5** 39 1N 45 4 E
Nazilli, *Turkey* . . . . **21 F13** 37 55N 28 15 E
Nazir Hat, *Bangla.* . . . . **41 H17** 22 35N 91 49 E
Nazko, *Canada* **72 C4** 53 1N 123 37W
Nazko →, *Canada* **72 C4** 53 7N 123 34W
Nazret, *Ethiopia* . . . . **46 F2** 8 32N 39 22 E
Nazwá, *Oman* . . . . **46 C6** 22 56N 57 32 E
Nchanga, *Zambia* . . . . **55 E2** 12 30S 27 49 E
Ncheu, *Malawi* . . . . **55 E3** 14 50S 34 47 E
Ndala, *Tanzania* . . . . **54 C3** 4 45S 33 15 E
Ndalatando, *Angola* . . . . . . **52 F2** 9 12S 14 48 E
Ndareda, *Tanzania* . . . . **54 C4** 4 12S 35 30 E
Ndélé, *C.A.R.* . . . . **52 C4** 8 25N 20 36 E
Ndjamena, *Chad* . . . . **51 F8** 12 10N 14 59 E
Ndola, *Zambia* . . . . **55 E2** 13 0S 28 34 E
Ndoto Mts., *Kenya* . . . . **54 B4** 2 0N 37 0 E
Nduguti, *Tanzania* . . . . **54 C3** 4 18S 34 41 E
Neagh, Lough, *U.K.* **13 B5** 54 37N 6 25W
Neah Bay, *U.S.A.* **84 B2** 48 22N 124 37W
Neale, L., *Australia* . . . . **60 D5** 24 15S 130 0 E
Neápolis, *Greece* . . . . **23 D7** 35 15N 25 37 E
Near Is., *U.S.A.* . . . . **68 C1** 52 30N 174 0 E
Neath, *U.K.* **11 F4** 51 39N 3 48W
Neath Port Talbot □, *U.K.* . . **11 F4** 51 42N 3 45W
Nebine Cr. →, *Australia* . . **63 D4** 29 27S 146 56 E
Nebitdag, *Turkmenistan* . . . **25 G9** 39 30N 54 22 E
Nebo, *Australia* . . . . **62 C4** 21 42S 148 42 E
Nebraska □, *U.S.A.* **80 E5** 41 30N 99 30W
Nebraska City, *U.S.A.* **80 E7** 40 41N 95 52W
Nébrodi, Monti, *Italy* . . . . . **20 F6** 37 54N 14 35 E
Necedah, *U.S.A.* **80 C9** 44 2N 90 4W
Nechako →, *Canada* **72 C4** 53 30N 122 44W
Neches →, *U.S.A.* **81 L8** 29 58N 93 51W
Neckar →, *Germany* . . . . . . **16 D5** 49 27N 8 29 E
Necochea, *Argentina* **94 D4** 38 30S 58 50W
Needles, *Canada* **72 D5** 49 53N 118 7W
Needles, *U.S.A.* **85 L12** 34 51N 114 37W
Needles, The, *U.K.* **11 G6** 50 39N 1 35W
Ñeembucú □, *Paraguay* . . . **94 B4** 27 0S 58 0W
Neemuch = Nimach, *India* . **42 G6** 24 30N 74 56 E
Neenah, *U.S.A.* **76 C1** 44 11N 88 28W
Neepawa, *Canada* **73 C9** 50 15N 99 30W
Neftçala, *Azerbaijan* . . . . . . **25 G8** 39 19N 49 12 E
Neftekumsk, *Russia* . . . . . . **25 F7** 44 46N 44 50 E
Nefyn, *U.K.* **10 E3** 52 56N 4 31W
Negapatam =
Nagappattinam, *India* . . . **40 P11** 10 46N 79 51 E
Negaunee, *U.S.A.* **76 B2** 46 30N 87 36W
Negele, *Ethiopia* . . . . **46 F2** 5 20N 39 36 E
Negev Desert = Hanegev,
Israel . . . . **47 E4** 30 50N 35 0 E
Negombo, *Sri Lanka* . . . . . . **40 R11** 7 12N 79 50 E
Negotin, *Serbia, Yug.* . . . . . **21 B10** 44 16N 22 37 E
Negra, Pta., *Peru* **92 E2** 6 6S 81 10W
Negrais, C. = Maudin Sun,
Burma . . . . **41 M19** 16 0N 94 30 E
Negril, *Jamaica* **88 C4** 18 22N 78 20W
Negro →, *Argentina* **96 E4** 41 2S 62 47W
Negro →, *Brazil* **92 D7** 3 0S 60 0W
Negro →, *Uruguay* **95 C4** 33 24S 58 22W
Negros, *Phil.* . . . . **37 C6** 9 30N 122 40 E
Neguac, *Canada* **71 C6** 47 15N 65 5W
Nehalem →, *U.S.A.* **84 E3** 45 40N 123 56W
Nehāvand, *Iran* . . . . **45 C6** 35 56N 49 31 E
Nehbandān, *Iran* . . . . **45 D9** 31 35N 60 5 E
Nei Monggol Zizhiqu □,
China . . . . **34 D7** 42 0N 112 0 E
Neijiang, *China* . . . . **32 D5** 29 35N 104 55 E
Neillsville, *U.S.A.* **80 C9** 44 34N 90 36W
Neilton, *U.S.A.* **82 C2** 47 25N 123 53W
Neiqiu, *China* . . . . **34 F8** 37 15N 114 30 E
Neiva, *Colombia* **92 C3** 2 56N 75 18W
Neixiang, *China* . . . . **34 H6** 33 10N 111 52 E
Nejanilini L., *Canada* **73 B9** 59 33N 97 48W
Nejd = Najd, *Si. Arabia* . . . **46 B3** 26 30N 42 0 E
Nekā, *Iran* . . . . **45 B7** 36 39N 53 19 E
Nekemte, *Ethiopia* . . . . **46 F2** 9 4N 36 30 E
Neksø, *Denmark* . . . . **9 J16** 55 4N 15 8 E
Nelia, *Australia* . . . . **62 C3** 20 39S 142 12 E
Neligh, *U.S.A.* **80 D5** 42 8N 98 2W
Nelkan, *Russia* . . . . **27 D14** 57 40N 136 4 E
Nellore, *India* . . . . **40 M11** 14 27N 79 59 E
Nelson, *Canada* **72 D5** 49 30N 117 20W
Nelson, *N.Z.* . . . . **59 J4** 41 18S 173 16 E
Nelson, *U.K.* **10 D5** 53 50N 2 13W
Nelson, *Ariz., U.S.A.* **83 J7** 35 31N 113 19W
Nelson, *Nev., U.S.A.* **85 K12** 35 42N 114 50W
Nelson →, *Canada* **73 C9** 54 33N 98 2W
Nelson, C., *Australia* . . . . . . **63 F3** 38 26S 141 32 E
Nelson, Estrecho, *Chile* . . . **96 G2** 51 30S 75 0W
Nelson Bay, *Australia* . . . . . **63 E5** 32 43S 152 9 E
Nelson Forks, *Canada* **72 B4** 59 30N 124 0W
Nelson House, *Canada* **73 B9** 55 47N 98 51W
Nelson L., *Canada* **73 B8** 55 48N 100 7W
Nelspoort, *S. Africa* . . . . **56 E3** 32 7S 23 0 E
Nelspruit, *S. Africa* . . . . **57 D5** 25 29S 30 59 E
Néma, *Mauritania* **50 E4** 16 40N 7 15W
Neman, *Russia* . . . . **9 J20** 55 2N 22 2 E
Neman →, *Lithuania* . . . . . . **9 J20** 55 25N 21 10 E
Nemeiben L., *Canada* **73 B7** 55 20N 105 20W
Némiscau, *Canada* **70 B4** 51 18N 76 54W
Némiscau, L., *Canada* **70 B4** 51 25N 76 40W
Nemunas = Neman →,
Lithuania . . . . **9 J20** 55 25N 21 10 E
Nemuro, *Japan* . . . . **30 C12** 43 20N 145 35 E
Nemuro-Kaikyō, *Japan* . . . . **30 C12** 43 30N 145 30 E
Nen Jiang →, *China* . . . . . . **35 B13** 45 28N 124 30 E
Nenagh, *Ireland* **13 D3** 52 52N 8 11W
Nenasi, *Malaysia* . . . . **39 L4** 3 9N 103 23 E
Nene →, *U.K.* . . . . **11 E8** 52 49N 0 11 E
Nenjiang, *China* . . . . **33 B7** 49 10N 125 10 E
Neno, *Malawi* . . . . **55 F3** 15 25S 34 40 E
Neodesha, *U.S.A.* **81 G7** 37 25N 95 41W
Neosho, *U.S.A.* **81 G7** 36 52N 94 22W
Neosho →, *U.S.A.* **81 H7** 36 48N 95 18W
Nepal ■, *Asia* . . . . **43 F11** 28 0N 84 30 E
Nepalganj, *Nepal* . . . . **43 E9** 28 5N 81 40 E
Nepalganj Road, *India* . . . . **43 E9** 28 1N 81 41 E
Nephi, *U.S.A.* **82 G8** 39 43N 111 50W
Nephin, *Ireland* **13 B2** 54 1N 9 22W
Neptune, *U.S.A.* **79 F10** 40 13N 74 2W
Nerang, *Australia* . . . . **63 D5** 27 58S 153 20 E
Nerchinsk, *Russia* . . . . **27 D12** 52 0N 116 39 E
Néret, L., *Canada* **71 B5** 54 45N 70 44W
Neretva →, *Croatia* . . . . **21 C7** 43 1N 17 27 E
Neringa, *Lithuania* . . . . **9 J19** 55 20N 21 5 E
Neryungri, *Russia* . . . . **27 D13** 57 38N 124 28 E
Nescopeck, *U.S.A.* **79 E8** 41 3N 76 12W
Ness, L., *U.K.* **12 D4** 57 15N 4 32W
Ness City, *U.S.A.* **80 F5** 38 27N 99 54W
Nesterov, *Poland* . . . . **17 C12** 50 4N 23 58 E
Nesvizh = Nyasvizh, *Belarus* **17 B14** 53 14N 26 38 E
Netanya, *Israel* . . . . **47 C3** 32 20N 34 51 E
Netarhat, *India* . . . . **43 H11** 23 29N 84 16 E
Nete →, *Belgium* . . . . **15 C4** 51 7N 4 14 E
Netherdale, *Australia* . . . . . **62 C4** 21 10S 148 33 E
Netherlands ■, *Europe* . . . . **15 C5** 52 0N 5 30 E
Netherlands Antilles ■,
W. Indies **92 A5** 12 15N 69 0W
Netrang, *India* . . . . **42 J5** 21 39N 73 21 E
Nettilling L., *Canada* **69 B12** 66 30N 71 0W
Netzahualcoyotl, Presa,
Mexico **87 D6** 17 10N 93 30W
Neubrandenburg, *Germany* **16 B7** 53 33N 13 15 E
Neuchâtel, *Switz.* . . . . **18 C7** 47 0N 6 55 E
Neuchâtel, Lac de, *Switz.* . . **18 C7** 46 53N 6 50 E
Neufchâteau, *Belgium* . . . . **15 E5** 49 50N 5 25 E
Neumünster, *Germany* . . . . **16 A5** 54 4N 9 58 E
Neunkirchen, *Germany* . . . . **16 D4** 49 20N 7 9 E
Neuquén, *Argentina* **96 D3** 38 55S 68 0W
Neuquén □, *Argentina* **94 D2** 38 0S 69 50W
Neuruppin, *Germany* . . . . . . **16 B7** 52 55N 12 48 E
Neuse →, *U.S.A.* **77 H7** 35 6N 76 29W
Neusiedler See, *Austria* . . . **17 E9** 47 50N 16 47 E
Neustrelitz, *Germany* . . . . . . **16 B7** 53 21N 13 4 E
Neva →, *Russia* . . . . **24 C5** 59 50N 30 30 E
Nevada, *Iowa, U.S.A.* **80 D8** 42 1N 93 27W
Nevada, *Mo., U.S.A.* **81 G7** 37 51N 94 22W
Nevada □, *U.S.A.* **82 G5** 39 0N 117 0W
Nevada, Sierra, *Spain* **19 D4** 37 3N 3 15W
Nevada, Sierra, *U.S.A.* **82 G3** 39 0N 120 30W
Nevada City, *U.S.A.* **84 F6** 39 16N 121 1W
Nevado, Cerro, *Argentina* . . **94 D2** 35 30S 68 32W
Nevel, *Russia* . . . . **24 C4** 56 0N 29 55 E
Nevers, *France* . . . . **18 C5** 47 0N 3 9 E
Nevertire, *Australia* . . . . **63 E4** 31 50S 147 44 E
Neville, *Canada* **73 D7** 49 58N 107 39W
Nevinnomyssk, *Russia* . . . . **25 F7** 44 40N 42 0 E
Nevis, *W. Indies* **89 C7** 17 0N 62 30W
Nevşehir, *Turkey* . . . . **44 B2** 38 33N 34 40 E
Nevyansk, *Russia* . . . . **24 C11** 57 30N 60 13 E
New →, *U.S.A.* **76 F5** 38 10N 81 12W
New Aiyansh, *Canada* **72 B3** 55 12N 129 4W
New Albany, *Ind., U.S.A.* . . **76 F3** 38 18N 85 49W
New Albany, *Miss., U.S.A.* . **81 H10** 34 29N 89 0W
New Albany, *Pa., U.S.A.* . . . **79 E8** 41 36N 76 27W
New Amsterdam, *Guyana* . . **92 B7** 6 15N 57 36W
New Angledool, *Australia* . . **63 D4** 29 5S 147 55 E
New Baltimore, *U.S.A.* **78 D2** 42 41N 82 44W
New Bedford, *U.S.A.* **79 E14** 41 38N 70 56W
New Berlin, *N.Y., U.S.A.* . . . **79 D9** 42 37N 75 20W
New Berlin, *Pa., U.S.A.* **78 F8** 40 50N 76 57W
New Bern, *U.S.A.* **77 H7** 35 7N 77 3W
New Bethlehem, *U.S.A.* **78 F5** 41 0N 79 20W
New Bloomfield, *U.S.A.* **78 F7** 40 25N 77 11W
New Boston, *U.S.A.* **81 J7** 33 28N 94 25W
New Braunfels, *U.S.A.* **81 L5** 29 42N 98 8W
New Brighton, *N.Z.* . . . . **59 K4** 43 29S 172 43 E
New Brighton, *U.S.A.* **78 F4** 40 42N 80 19W
New Britain, *Papua N. G.* . . **64 H7** 5 50S 150 20 E
New Britain, *U.S.A.* **79 E12** 41 40N 72 47W
New Brunswick, *U.S.A.* **79 F10** 40 30N 74 27W
New Brunswick □, *Canada* **71 C6** 46 50N 66 30W
New Caledonia ■, *Pac. Oc.* **64 K8** 21 0S 165 0 E
New Castile = Castilla-La
Mancha □, *Spain* **19 C4** 39 30N 3 30W
New Castle, *Ind., U.S.A.* . . . **76 F3** 39 55N 85 22W
New Castle, *Pa., U.S.A.* . . . **78 F4** 41 0N 80 21W
New City, *U.S.A.* **79 E11** 41 9N 73 59W
New Concord, *U.S.A.* **78 G3** 39 59N 81 54W
New Cumberland, *U.S.A.* . . **78 F4** 40 30N 80 36W
New Cuyama, *U.S.A.* **85 L7** 34 57N 119 38W
New Delhi, *India* . . . . **42 E7** 28 37N 77 13 E
New Denver, *Canada* **72 D5** 50 0N 117 25W
New Don Pedro Reservoir,
U.S.A. **84 H6** 37 43N 120 24W
New England, *U.S.A.* **80 B3** 46 32N 102 52W
New England Ra., *Australia* **63 E5** 30 20S 151 45 E
New Forest, *U.K.* **11 G6** 50 53N 1 34W
New Galloway, *U.K.* **12 F4** 55 5N 4 9W
New Glasgow, *Canada* **71 C7** 45 35N 62 36W
New Guinea, *Oceania* . . . . . **28 K17** 4 0S 136 0 E
New Hamburg, *Canada* **78 C4** 43 23N 80 42W
New Hampshire □, *U.S.A.* . **79 C13** 44 0N 71 30W
New Hampton, *U.S.A.* **80 D8** 43 3N 92 19W
New Hanover, *S. Africa* . . . . **57 D5** 29 22S 30 31 E
New Hartford, *U.S.A.* **79 C9** 43 4N 75 18W
New Haven, *Conn., U.S.A.* . **79 E12** 41 18N 72 55W
New Haven, *Mich., U.S.A.* . . **78 D2** 42 44N 82 48W
New Hazelton, *Canada* **72 B3** 55 20N 127 30W
New Hebrides = Vanuatu ■,
Pac. Oc. . . . . **64 J8** 15 0S 168 0 E
New Holland, *U.S.A.* **79 F8** 40 6N 76 5W
New Iberia, *U.S.A.* **81 K9** 30 1N 91 49W
New Ireland, *Papua N. G.* . . **64 H7** 3 20S 151 50 E
New Jersey □, *U.S.A.* **76 E8** 40 0N 74 30W
New Kensington, *U.S.A.* . . . **78 F5** 40 34N 79 46W
New Lexington, *U.S.A.* **76 F4** 39 43N 82 13W
New Liskeard, *Canada* **70 C4** 47 31N 79 41W
New London, *Conn., U.S.A.* **79 E12** 41 22N 72 6W
New London, *Ohio, U.S.A.* . **78 E2** 41 5N 82 24W
New London, *Wis., U.S.A.* . . **80 C10** 44 23N 88 45W
New Madrid, *U.S.A.* **81 G10** 36 36N 89 32W
New Martinsville, *U.S.A.* . . **76 F5** 39 39N 80 52W
New Meadows, *U.S.A.* **82 D5** 44 58N 116 18W
New Melones L., *U.S.A.* . . . **84 H6** 37 57N 120 31W
New Mexico □, *U.S.A.* **83 J10** 34 30N 106 0W
New Milford, *Conn., U.S.A.* **79 E11** 41 35N 73 25W
New Milford, *Pa., U.S.A.* . . . **79 E9** 41 52N 75 44W
New Norcia, *Australia* . . . . . **61 F2** 30 57S 116 13 E
New Norfolk, *Australia* . . . . **62 G4** 42 46S 147 2 E
New Orleans, *U.S.A.* **81 L9** 29 58N 90 4W
New Philadelphia, *U.S.A.* . . **78 F3** 40 30N 81 27W
New Plymouth, *N.Z.* . . . . . . **59 H5** 39 4S 174 5 E
New Plymouth, *U.S.A.* **82 E5** 43 58N 116 49W
New Port Richey, *U.S.A.* . . . **77 L4** 28 16N 82 43W
New Providence, *Bahamas* **88 A4** 25 25N 78 35W
New Quay, *U.K.* **11 E3** 52 13N 4 21W
New Radnor, *U.K.* **11 E4** 52 15N 3 9W
New Richmond, *Canada* . . . **71 C6** 48 15N 65 45W
New Richmond, *U.S.A.* **80 C8** 45 7N 92 32W
New Roads, *U.S.A.* **81 K9** 30 42N 91 26W
New Rochelle, *U.S.A.* **79 F11** 40 55N 73 47W
New Rockford, *U.S.A.* **80 B5** 47 41N 99 8W
New Romney, *U.K.* . . . . **11 G8** 50 59N 0 57 E
New Ross, *Ireland* **13 D5** 52 23N 6 57W
New Salem, *U.S.A.* **80 B4** 46 51N 101 25W
New Scone, *U.K.* **12 E5** 56 25N 3 24W
New Siberian I. = Novaya
Sibir, Ostrov, *Russia* . . . . **27 B16** 75 10N 150 0 E
New Siberian Is. =
Novosibirskiye Ostrova,
Russia . . . . **27 B15** 75 0N 142 0 E

North Knife

New Smyrna Beach, U.S.A. 77 L5 29 1N 80 56W
New South Wales □, Australia 63 E4 33 0S 146 0 E
New Town, U.S.A. 80 B3 47 59N 102 30W
New Tredegar, U.K. 11 F4 51 44N 3 16W
New Ulm, U.S.A. 80 C7 44 19N 94 28W
New Waterford, Canada 71 C7 46 13N 60 4W
New Westminster, Canada 84 A4 49 13N 122 55W
New York, U.S.A. 79 F11 40 45N 74 0W
New York □, U.S.A. 79 D9 43 0N 75 0W
New York Mts., U.S.A. 83 J6 35 0N 115 20W
New Zealand ■, Oceania 59 J6 40 0S 176 0 E
Newaj →, India 42 G7 24 24N 76 49 E
Newala, Tanzania 55 E4 10 58S 39 18 E
Newark, Del., U.S.A. 76 F8 39 41N 75 46W
Newark, N.J., U.S.A. 79 F10 40 44N 74 10W
Newark, N.Y., U.S.A. 78 C7 43 3N 77 6W
Newark, Ohio, U.S.A. 78 F2 40 3N 82 24W
Newark-on-Trent, U.K. 10 D7 53 5N 0 48W
Newark Valley, U.S.A. 79 D8 42 14N 76 11W
Newberg, U.S.A. 82 D2 45 18N 122 58W
Newberry, Mich., U.S.A. 76 B3 46 21N 85 30W
Newberry, S.C., U.S.A. 77 H5 34 17N 81 37W
Newberry Springs, U.S.A. 85 L10 34 50N 116 41W
Newboro L., Canada 79 B8 44 38N 76 20W
Newbridge = Droichead Nua, Ireland 13 C5 53 11N 6 48W
Newburgh, Canada 78 B8 44 19N 76 52W
Newburgh, U.S.A. 79 E10 41 30N 74 1W
Newbury, U.K. 11 F6 51 24N 1 20W
Newbury, N.H., U.S.A. 79 B12 43 19N 72 3W
Newbury, Vt., U.S.A. 79 B12 44 5N 72 4W
Newburyport, U.S.A. 77 D10 42 49N 70 53W
Newcastle, Australia 63 E5 33 0S 151 46 E
Newcastle, N.B., Canada 71 C6 47 1N 65 38W
Newcastle, Ont., Canada 70 D4 43 55N 78 35W
Newcastle, S. Africa 57 D4 27 45S 29 58 E
Newcastle, U.K. 13 B6 54 13N 5 54W
Newcastle, Calif., U.S.A. 84 G5 38 53N 121 8W
Newcastle, Wyo., U.S.A. 80 D2 43 50N 104 11W
Newcastle Emlyn, U.K. 11 E3 52 2N 4 28W
Newcastle Ra., Australia 60 C5 15 45S 130 15 E
Newcastle-under-Lyme, U.K. 10 D5 53 1N 2 14W
Newcastle-upon-Tyne, U.K. 10 C6 54 58N 1 36W
Newcastle Waters, Australia 62 B1 17 30S 133 28 E
Newcastle West, Ireland 13 D2 52 27N 9 3W
Newcomb, U.S.A. 79 C10 43 58N 74 10W
Newcomerstown, U.S.A. 78 F3 40 16N 81 36W
Newdegate, Australia 61 F2 33 6S 119 0 E
Newell, Australia 62 B4 16 20S 145 16 E
Newell, U.S.A. 80 C3 44 43N 103 25W
Newfane, U.S.A. 78 C6 43 17N 78 43W
Newfield, U.S.A. 79 D8 42 18N 76 33W
Newfound L., U.S.A. 79 C13 43 40N 71 47W
Newfoundland, N. Amer. 66 E14 49 0N 55 0W
Newfoundland, U.S.A. 79 E9 41 18N 75 19W
Newfoundland □, Canada 71 B8 53 0N 58 0W
Newhall, U.S.A. 85 L8 34 23N 118 32W
Newhaven, U.K. 11 G8 50 47N 0 3 E
Newkirk, U.S.A. 81 G6 36 53N 97 3W
Newlyn, U.K. 11 G2 50 6N 5 34W
Newman, Australia 60 D2 23 18S 119 45 E
Newman, U.S.A. 84 H5 37 19N 121 1W
Newmarket, Canada 78 B5 44 3N 79 28W
Newmarket, Ireland 13 D2 52 13N 9 0W
Newmarket, U.K. 11 E8 52 15N 0 25 E
Newmarket, N.H., U.S.A. 79 C14 43 4N 70 56W
Newmarket, N.H., U.S.A. 79 C14 43 5N 70 56W
Newnan, U.S.A. 77 J3 33 23N 84 48W
Newport, Ireland 13 C2 53 53N 9 33W
Newport, I. of W., U.K. 11 G6 50 42N 1 17W
Newport, Newp., U.K. 11 F5 51 35N 3 0W
Newport, Ark., U.S.A. 81 H9 35 37N 91 16W
Newport, Ky., U.S.A. 76 F3 39 5N 84 30W
Newport, N.H., U.S.A. 79 C12 43 22N 72 10W
Newport, N.Y., U.S.A. 79 C9 43 11N 75 1W
Newport, Oreg., U.S.A. 82 D1 44 39N 124 3W
Newport, Pa., U.S.A. 78 F7 40 29N 77 8W
Newport, R.I., U.S.A. 79 E13 41 29N 71 19W
Newport, Tenn., U.S.A. 77 H4 35 58N 83 11W
Newport, Vt., U.S.A. 79 B12 44 56N 72 13W
Newport, Wash., U.S.A. 82 B5 48 11N 117 3W
Newport □, U.K. 11 F4 51 33N 3 1W
Newport Beach, U.S.A. 85 M9 33 37N 117 56W
Newport News, U.S.A. 76 G7 36 59N 76 25W
Newport Pagnell, U.K. 11 E7 52 5N 0 43W
Newquay, U.K. 11 G2 50 25N 5 6W
Newry, U.K. 13 B5 54 11N 6 21W
Newton, Ill., U.S.A. 80 F10 38 59N 88 10W
Newton, Iowa, U.S.A. 80 E8 41 42N 93 3W
Newton, Kans., U.S.A. 81 F6 38 3N 97 21W
Newton, Mass., U.S.A. 79 D13 42 21N 71 12W
Newton, Miss., U.S.A. 81 J10 32 19N 89 10W
Newton, N.C., U.S.A. 77 H5 35 40N 81 13W
Newton, N.J., U.S.A. 79 E10 41 3N 74 45W
Newton, Tex., U.S.A. 81 K8 30 51N 93 46W
Newton Abbot, U.K. 11 G4 50 32N 3 37W
Newton Aycliffe, U.K. 10 C6 54 37N 1 34W
Newton Falls, U.S.A. 78 E4 41 11N 80 59W
Newton Stewart, U.K. 12 G4 54 57N 4 30W
Newtonmore, U.K. 12 D4 57 4N 4 8W
Newtown, U.K. 11 E4 52 31N 3 19W
Newtownabbey, U.K. 13 B6 54 40N 5 56W
Newtownards, U.K. 13 B6 54 36N 5 42W
Newtownbarry = Bunclody, Ireland 13 D5 52 39N 6 40W
Newtownstewart, U.K. 13 B4 54 43N 7 23W
Newville, U.S.A. 78 F7 40 10N 77 24W
Neya, Russia 24 C7 58 21N 43 49 E
Neyrīz, Iran 45 D7 29 15N 54 19 E
Neyshābūr, Iran 45 B8 36 10N 58 50 E
Nezhin = Nizhyn, Ukraine 25 D5 51 5N 31 55 E
Nezperce, U.S.A. 82 C5 46 14N 116 14W
Ngabang, Indonesia 36 D3 0 23N 109 55 E
Ngabordamlu, Tanjung, Indonesia 37 F8 6 56S 134 11 E
N'Gage, Angola 52 F3 7 46S 15 16 E
Ngami Depression, Botswana 56 C3 20 30S 22 46 E
Ngamo, Zimbabwe 55 F2 19 3S 27 32 E
Nganglong Kangri, China 41 C12 33 0N 81 0 E
Ngao, Thailand 38 C2 18 46N 99 59 E
Ngaoundéré, Cameroon 52 C2 7 15N 13 35 E
Ngapara, N.Z. 59 L3 44 57S 170 46 E
Ngara, Tanzania 54 C3 2 29S 30 40 E
Ngawi, Indonesia 37 G14 7 24S 111 26 E
Ngoma, Malawi 55 E3 13 8S 33 45 E
Ngomahura, Zimbabwe 55 G3 20 26S 30 43 E
Ngomba, Tanzania 55 D3 8 20S 32 53 E
Ngoring Hu, China 32 C4 34 55N 97 5 E
Ngorongoro, Tanzania 54 C4 3 11S 35 32 E
Ngozi, Burundi 54 C2 2 54S 29 50 E
Ngudu, Tanzania 54 C3 2 58S 33 25 E
Nguigmi, Niger 51 F8 14 20N 13 20 E
Nguiu, Australia 60 B5 11 46S 130 38 E
Ngukurr, Australia 62 A1 14 44S 134 44 E
Ngulu Atoll, Pac. Oc. 37 C9 8 0N 137 30 E
Ngunga, Tanzania 54 C3 3 37S 33 37 E
Nguru, Nigeria 51 F8 12 56N 10 29 E
Nguru Mts., Tanzania 54 D4 6 0S 37 30 E
Nha Trang, Vietnam 39 F7 12 16N 109 10 E
Nhacoongo, Mozam. 57 C6 24 18S 35 14 E
Nhamaabué, Mozam. 55 F4 17 25S 35 5 E
Nhamundá →, Brazil 93 D7 2 12S 56 41W
Nhangutazi, L., Mozam. 57 C5 24 0S 34 30 E
Nhill, Australia 63 F3 36 18S 141 40 E
Nhulunbuy, Australia 62 A2 12 10S 137 20 E
Nia-nia, Dem. Rep. of the Congo 54 B2 1 30N 27 40 E
Niagara Falls, Canada 78 C5 43 7N 79 5W
Niagara Falls, U.S.A. 78 C6 43 5N 79 4W
Niagara-on-the-Lake, Canada 78 C5 43 15N 79 4W
Niah, Malaysia 36 D4 3 58N 113 46 E
Niamey, Niger 50 F6 13 27N 2 6 E
Niangara, Dem. Rep. of the Congo 54 B2 3 42N 27 50 E
Niantic, U.S.A. 79 E12 41 20N 72 11W
Nias, Indonesia 36 D1 1 0N 97 30 E
Niassa □, Mozam. 55 E4 13 30S 36 0 E
Nibāk, Si. Arabia 45 E7 24 25N 50 50 E
Nicaragua ■, Cent. Amer. 88 D2 11 40N 85 30W
Nicaragua, L. de, Nic. 88 D2 12 0N 85 30W
Nicastro, Italy 20 E7 38 59N 16 19 E
Nice, France 18 E7 43 42N 7 14 E
Niceville, U.S.A. 77 K2 30 31N 86 30W
Nichicun, L., Canada 71 B5 53 5N 71 0W
Nichinan, Japan 31 J5 31 38N 131 23 E
Nicholás, Canal, W. Indies 88 B3 23 30N 80 5W
Nicholasville, U.S.A. 76 G3 37 53N 84 34W
Nichols, U.S.A. 79 D8 42 1N 76 22W
Nicholson, Australia 60 C4 18 2S 128 54 E
Nicholson, U.S.A. 79 E9 41 37N 75 47W
Nicholson →, Australia 62 B2 17 31S 139 36 E
Nicholson L., Canada 73 A8 62 40N 102 40W
Nicholson Ra., Australia 61 E2 27 15S 116 45 E
Nicholville, U.S.A. 79 B10 44 41N 74 39W
Nicobar Is., Ind. Oc. 28 J13 9 0N 93 0 E
Nicola, Canada 72 C4 50 12N 120 40W
Nicolls Town, Bahamas 88 A4 25 8N 78 0W
Nicosia, Cyprus 23 D12 35 10N 33 25 E
Nicoya, Costa Rica 88 D2 10 9N 85 27W
Nicoya, G. de, Costa Rica 88 E3 10 0N 85 0W
Nicoya, Pen. de, Costa Rica 88 E2 9 45N 85 40W
Nidd →, U.K. 10 D6 53 59N 1 23W
Niedersachsen □, Germany 16 B5 52 50N 9 0 E
Niekerkshoop, S. Africa 56 D3 29 19S 22 51 E
Niemba, Dem. Rep. of the Congo 54 D2 5 58S 28 24 E
Niemen = Neman →, Lithuania 9 J20 55 25N 21 10 E
Nienburg, Germany 16 B5 52 39N 9 13 E
Nieu Bethesda, S. Africa 56 E3 31 51S 24 34 E
Nieuw Amsterdam, Surinam 93 B7 5 53N 55 5W
Nieuw Nickerie, Surinam 93 B7 6 0N 56 59W
Nieuwoudtville, S. Africa 56 E2 31 23S 19 7 E
Nieuwpoort, Belgium 15 C2 51 8N 2 45 E
Nieves, Pico de las, Canary Is. 22 G4 27 57N 15 35W
Niğde, Turkey 25 G5 37 58N 34 40 E
Nigel, S. Africa 57 D4 26 27S 28 25 E
Niger ■, W. Afr. 50 E7 17 30N 10 0 E
Niger →, W. Afr. 50 G7 5 33N 6 33 E
Nigeria ■, W. Afr. 50 G7 8 30N 8 0 E
Nighasin, India 43 E9 28 14N 80 52 E
Nightcaps, N.Z. 59 L2 45 57S 168 2 E
Nii-Jima, Japan 31 G9 34 20N 139 15 E
Niigata, Japan 30 F9 37 58N 139 0 E
Niigata □, Japan 31 F9 37 15N 138 45 E
Niihama, Japan 31 H6 33 55N 133 16 E
Niihau, U.S.A. 74 H14 21 54N 160 9W
Niimi, Japan 31 G6 34 59N 133 28 E
Niitsu, Japan 30 F9 37 48N 139 7 E
Nijil, Jordan 47 E4 30 32N 35 33 E
Nijkerk, Neths. 15 B5 52 13N 5 30 E
Nijmegen, Neths. 15 C5 51 50N 5 52 E
Nijverdal, Neths. 15 B6 52 22N 6 28 E
Nīk Pey, Iran 45 B6 36 50N 48 10 E
Nikiniki, Indonesia 37 F6 9 49S 124 30 E
Nikkō, Japan 31 F9 36 45N 139 35 E
Nikolayev = Mykolayiv, Ukraine 25 E5 46 58N 32 0 E
Nikolayevsk, Russia 25 E8 50 0N 45 35 E
Nikolayevsk-na-Amur, Russia 27 D15 53 8N 140 44 E
Nikolskoye, Russia 27 D17 55 12N 166 0 E
Nikopol, Ukraine 25 E5 47 35N 34 25 E
Nīkshahr, Iran 45 E9 26 15N 60 10 E
Nikšić, Montenegro, Yug. 21 C8 42 50N 18 57 E
Nîl, Nahr en →, Africa 51 B12 30 10N 31 6 E
Nîl el Abyad →, Sudan 51 E12 15 38N 32 31 E
Nîl el Azraq →, Sudan 51 E12 15 38N 32 31 E
Nila, Indonesia 37 F7 6 44S 129 31 E
Niland, U.S.A. 85 M11 33 14N 115 31W
Nile = Nîl, Nahr en →, Africa 51 B12 30 10N 31 6 E
Niles, Mich., U.S.A. 76 E2 41 50N 86 15W
Niles, Ohio, U.S.A. 78 E4 41 11N 80 46W
Nim Ka Thana, India 42 F6 27 44N 75 48 E
Nimach, India 42 G6 24 30N 74 56 E
Nimbahera, India 42 G6 24 37N 74 45 E
Nîmes, France 18 E6 43 50N 4 23 E
Nimfaíon, Ákra = Pínnes, Ákra, Greece 21 D11 40 5N 24 20 E
Nimmitabel, Australia 63 F4 36 29S 149 15 E
Ninawá, Iraq 44 B4 36 25N 43 10 E
Nindigully, Australia 63 D4 28 21S 148 50 E
Nineveh = Nīnawá, Iraq 44 B4 36 25N 43 10 E
Ning Xian, China 34 G4 35 30N 107 58 E
Ning'an, China 35 B15 44 22N 129 20 E
Ningbo, China 33 D7 29 51N 121 28 E
Ningcheng, China 35 D10 41 32N 119 53 E
Ningjin, China 34 F8 37 35N 114 57 E
Ningjing Shan, China 32 D4 30 0N 98 20 E
Ningling, China 34 G8 34 25N 115 22 E
Ningpo = Ningbo, China 33 D7 29 51N 121 28 E
Ningqiang, China 34 H4 32 47N 106 15 E
Ningshan, China 34 H5 33 21N 108 21 E
Ningsia Hui A.R. = Ningxia Huizu Zizhiqu □, China 34 F4 38 0N 106 0 E
Ningwu, China 34 E7 39 0N 112 18 E
Ningxia Huizu Zizhiqu □, China 34 F4 38 0N 106 0 E
Ningyang, China 34 G9 35 47N 116 45 E
Ninh Giang, Vietnam 38 B6 20 44N 106 24 E
Ninh Hoa, Vietnam 38 F7 12 30N 109 7 E
Ninh Ma, Vietnam 38 F7 12 48N 109 21 E
Ninove, Belgium 15 D4 50 51N 4 2 E
Nioaque, Brazil 95 A4 21 5S 55 50W
Niobrara, U.S.A. 80 D6 42 45N 98 2W
Niobrara →, U.S.A. 80 D6 42 46N 98 3W
Nioro du Sahel, Mali 50 E4 15 15N 9 30W
Niort, France 18 C3 46 19N 0 29W
Nipawin, Canada 73 C8 53 20N 104 0W
Nipigon, Canada 70 C2 49 0N 88 17W
Nipigon, L., Canada 70 C2 49 50N 88 30W
Nipishish L., Canada 71 B7 54 12N 60 45W
Nipissing, L., Canada 70 C4 46 20N 80 0W
Nipomo, U.S.A. 85 K6 35 3N 120 29W
Nipton, U.S.A. 85 K11 35 28N 115 16W
Niquelândia, Brazil 93 F9 14 33S 48 23W
Nīr, Iran 44 B5 38 2N 47 59 E
Nirasaki, Japan 31 G9 35 42N 138 27 E
Nirmal, India 40 K11 19 3N 78 20 E
Nirmali, India 43 F12 26 20N 86 35 E
Niš, Serbia, Yug. 21 C9 43 19N 21 58 E
Nişāb, Si. Arabia 44 D5 29 11N 44 43 E
Nişāb, Yemen 46 E4 14 25N 46 29 E
Nishinomiya, Japan 31 G7 34 45N 135 20 E
Nishin'omote, Japan 31 J5 30 43N 130 59 E
Nishiwaki, Japan 31 G7 34 59N 134 58 E
Niskibi →, Canada 70 A2 56 29N 88 9W
Nisqually →, U.S.A. 84 C4 47 6N 122 42W
Nissáki, Greece 23 A3 39 43N 19 52 E
Nissum Bredning, Denmark 9 H13 56 40N 8 20 E
Nistru = Dnister →, Europe 17 E16 46 18N 30 17 E
Nisutlin →, Canada 72 A2 60 14N 132 34W
Nitchequon, Canada 71 B5 53 10N 70 58W
Niterói, Brazil 95 A7 22 52S 43 0W
Nith →, Canada 78 C4 43 12N 80 23W
Nith →, U.K. 12 F5 55 14N 3 33W
Nitra, Slovak Rep. 17 D10 48 19N 18 4 E
Nitra →, Slovak Rep. 17 E10 47 46N 18 10 E
Niuafo'ou, Tonga 59 B11 15 30S 175 58W
Niue, Cook Is. 65 J11 19 2S 169 54W
Niut, Indonesia 36 D4 0 55N 110 6 E
Niuzhuang, China 35 D12 40 58N 122 28 E
Nivala, Finland 8 E21 63 56N 24 57 E
Nivelles, Belgium 15 D4 50 35N 4 20 E
Nivernais, France 18 C5 47 15N 3 30 E
Niwas, India 43 H9 23 3N 80 26 E
Nixon, U.S.A. 81 L6 29 16N 97 46W
Nizamabad, India 40 K11 18 45N 78 7 E
Nizamghat, India 41 E19 28 20N 95 45 E
Nizhne Kolymsk, Russia 27 C17 68 34N 160 55 E
Nizhnekamsk, Russia 24 C9 55 38N 51 49 E
Nizhneudinsk, Russia 27 D10 54 54N 99 3 E
Nizhnevartovsk, Russia 26 C8 60 56N 76 38 E
Nizhniy Novgorod, Russia 24 C7 56 20N 44 0 E
Nizhniy Tagil, Russia 24 C10 57 55N 59 57 E
Nizhyn, Ukraine 25 D5 51 5N 31 55 E
Nizip, Turkey 44 B3 37 5N 37 50 E
Nizké Tatry, Slovak Rep. 17 D10 48 55N 19 30 E
Njakwa, Malawi 55 E3 11 1S 33 56 E
Njanji, Zambia 55 E3 14 25S 31 46 E
Njinjo, Tanzania 55 D4 8 48S 38 54 E
Njombe, Tanzania 55 D3 9 20S 34 50 E
Njombe →, Tanzania 54 D4 6 56S 35 6 E
Nkana, Zambia 55 E2 12 50S 28 8 E
Nkayi, Zimbabwe 55 F2 19 41S 29 20 E
Nkhotakota, Malawi 55 E3 12 56S 34 15 E
Nkongsamba, Cameroon 52 D1 4 55N 9 55 E
Nkurenkuru, Namibia 56 B2 17 42S 18 32 E
Nmai →, Burma 41 G20 25 30N 97 25 E
Noakhali = Maijdi, Bangla. 41 H17 22 48N 91 10 E
Nobel, Canada 78 A4 45 25N 80 6W
Nobeoka, Japan 31 H5 32 36N 131 41 E
Noblesville, U.S.A. 76 E3 40 3N 86 1W
Nocera Inferiore, Italy 20 D6 40 44N 14 38 E
Nocona, U.S.A. 81 J6 33 47N 97 44W
Noda, Japan 31 G9 35 56N 139 52 E
Nogales, Mexico 86 A2 31 20N 110 56W
Nogales, U.S.A. 83 L8 31 20N 110 56W
Nōgata, Japan 31 H5 33 48N 130 44 E
Noggerup, Australia 61 F2 33 32S 116 5 E
Noginsk, Russia 27 C10 64 30N 90 50 E
Nogoa →, Australia 62 C4 23 40S 147 55 E
Nogoyá, Argentina 94 C4 32 24S 59 48W
Nohar, India 42 E6 29 11N 74 49 E
Nohta, India 43 H8 23 40N 79 34 E
Noire, Mts., France 18 B2 48 7N 3 28W
Noirmoutier, Î. de, France 18 C2 46 58N 2 10W
Nojane, Botswana 56 C3 23 15S 20 14 E
Nojima-Zaki, Japan 31 G9 34 54N 139 53 E
Nok Kundi, Pakistan 40 E3 28 50N 62 45 E
Nokaneng, Botswana 56 B3 19 40S 22 17 E
Nokia, Finland 9 F20 61 30N 23 30 E
Nokomis, Canada 73 C8 51 35N 105 0W
Nokomis L., Canada 73 B8 57 0N 103 0W
Nola, C.A.R. 52 D3 3 35N 16 4 E
Noma Omuramba →, Namibia 56 B3 18 52S 20 53 E
Nombre de Dios, Panama 88 E4 9 34N 79 28W
Nome, U.S.A. 68 B3 64 30N 165 25W
Nomo-Zaki, Japan 31 H4 32 35N 129 44 E
Nonacho L., Canada 73 A7 61 42N 109 40W
Nonda, Australia 62 C3 20 40S 142 28 E
Nong Chang, Thailand 38 E2 15 23N 99 51 E
Nong Het, Laos 38 C4 19 29N 103 59 E
Nong Khai, Thailand 38 D4 17 50N 102 46 E
Nong'an, China 35 B13 44 25N 125 5 E
Nongoma, S. Africa 57 D5 27 58S 31 35 E
Nonoava, Mexico 86 B3 27 28N 106 44W
Nonoava →, Mexico 86 B3 27 29N 106 45W
Nonthaburi, Thailand 38 F3 13 51N 100 34 E
Noonamah, Australia 60 B5 12 40S 131 4 E
Noord Brabant □, Neths. 15 C5 51 40N 5 0 E
Noord Holland □, Neths. 15 B4 52 30N 4 45 E
Noordbeveland, Neths. 15 C3 51 35N 3 50 E
Noordoostpolder, Neths. 15 B5 52 45N 5 45 E
Noordwijk, Neths. 15 B4 52 14N 4 26 E
Nootka I., Canada 72 D3 49 32N 126 42W
Nopiming Prov. Park, Canada 73 C9 50 30N 95 37W
Noralee, Canada 72 C3 53 59N 126 26W
Noranda = Rouyn-Noranda, Canada 70 C4 48 20N 79 0W
Norco, U.S.A. 85 M9 33 56N 117 33W
Nord-Kivu □, Dem. Rep. of the Congo 54 C2 1 0S 29 0 E
Nord-Ostsee-Kanal, Germany 16 A5 54 12N 9 32 E
Nordaustlandet, Svalbard 4 B9 79 14N 23 0 E
Nordegg, Canada 72 C5 52 29N 116 5W
Norderney, Germany 16 B4 53 42N 7 9 E
Norderstedt, Germany 16 B5 53 42N 10 1 E
Nordfjord, Norway 9 F11 61 55N 5 30 E
Nordfriesische Inseln, Germany 16 A5 54 40N 8 20 E
Nordhausen, Germany 16 C6 51 30N 10 47 E
Norðoyar, Færoe Is. 8 E9 62 17N 6 35W
Nordkapp, Norway 8 A21 71 10N 25 50 E
Nordkapp, Svalbard 4 A9 80 31N 20 0 E
Nordkinn = Kinnarodden, Norway 6 A11 71 8N 27 40 E
Nordkinn-halvøya, Norway 8 A22 70 55N 27 40 E
Nordrhein-Westfalen □, Germany 16 C4 51 45N 7 30 E
Nordvik, Russia 27 B12 74 2N 111 32 E
Nore →, Ireland 13 D4 52 25N 6 58W
Norfolk, Nebr., U.S.A. 80 D6 42 2N 97 25W
Norfolk, Va., U.S.A. 76 G7 36 51N 76 17W
Norfolk □, U.K. 11 E8 52 39N 0 54 E
Norfolk I., Pac. Oc. 64 K8 28 58S 168 3 E
Norfork L., U.S.A. 81 G8 36 15N 92 14W
Norilsk, Russia 27 C9 69 20N 88 6 E
Norma, Mt., Australia 62 C3 20 55S 140 42 E
Normal, U.S.A. 80 E10 40 31N 88 59W
Norman, U.S.A. 81 H6 35 13N 97 26W
Norman →, Australia 62 B3 19 18S 141 51 E
Norman Wells, Canada 68 B7 65 17N 126 51W
Normanby →, Australia 62 A3 14 23S 144 10 E
Normandie, France 18 B4 48 45N 0 10 E
Normandin, Canada 70 C5 48 49N 72 31W
Normandy = Normandie, France 18 B4 48 45N 0 10 E
Normanhurst, Mt., Australia 61 E3 25 4S 122 30 E
Normanton, Australia 62 B3 17 40S 141 10 E
Normétal, Canada 70 C4 49 0N 79 22W
Norquay, Canada 73 C8 51 53N 102 5W
Norquinco, Argentina 96 E2 41 51S 70 55W
Norrbotten □, Sweden 8 C19 66 30N 22 30 E
Norris Point, Canada 71 C8 49 31N 57 53W
Norristown, U.S.A. 79 F9 40 7N 75 21W
Norrköping, Sweden 9 G17 58 37N 16 11 E
Norrland, Sweden 9 E16 62 15N 15 45 E
Norrtälje, Sweden 9 G18 59 46N 18 42 E
Norseman, Australia 61 F3 32 8S 121 43 E
Norsk, Russia 27 D14 52 30N 130 5 E
Norte, Pta. del, Canary Is. 22 G2 27 51N 17 57W
Norte, Serra do, Brazil 92 11 20S 59 0W
North, C., Canada 71 C7 47 2N 60 20W
North Adams, U.S.A. 79 D11 42 42N 73 7W
North Arm, Canada 72 A5 62 0N 114 30W
North Augusta, U.S.A. 77 J5 33 30N 81 59W
North Ayrshire □, U.K. 12 F4 55 45N 4 44W
North Bass I., U.S.A. 78 E2 41 43N 82 49W
North Battleford, Canada 73 C7 52 50N 108 17W
North Bay, Canada 70 C4 46 20N 79 30W
North Belcher Is., Canada 70 A4 56 50N 79 50W
North Bend, Oreg., U.S.A. 82 E1 43 24N 124 14W
North Bend, Pa., U.S.A. 78 E7 41 20N 77 42W
North Bend, Wash., U.S.A. 84 C5 47 30N 121 47W
North Bennington, U.S.A. 79 D11 42 56N 73 15W
North Berwick, U.K. 12 E6 56 4N 2 42W
North Berwick, U.S.A. 79 C14 43 18N 70 44W
North C., Canada 71 C7 47 5N 64 0W
North C., N.Z. 59 F4 34 23S 173 4 E
North Canadian →, U.S.A. 81 H7 35 16N 95 31W
North Canton, U.S.A. 78 F3 40 53N 81 24W
North Cape = Nordkapp, Norway 8 A21 71 10N 25 50 E
North Cape = Nordkapp, Svalbard 4 A9 80 31N 20 0 E
North Caribou L., Canada 70 B1 52 50N 90 40W
North Carolina □, U.S.A. 77 H6 35 30N 80 0W
North Cascades National Park, U.S.A. 82 B3 48 45N 121 10W
North Channel, Canada 70 C3 46 0N 83 0W
North Channel, U.K. 12 F3 55 13N 5 52W
North Charleston, U.S.A. 77 J6 32 53N 79 58W
North Chicago, U.S.A. 76 D2 42 19N 87 51W
North Creek, U.S.A. 79 C11 43 41N 73 59W
North Dakota □, U.S.A. 80 B5 47 30N 100 15W
North Downs, U.K. 11 F8 51 19N 0 21 E
North East, U.S.A. 78 D5 42 13N 79 50W
North East Frontier Agency = Arunachal Pradesh □, India 41 F19 28 0N 95 0 E
North East Lincolnshire □, U.K. 10 D7 53 34N 0 2W
North Eastern □, Kenya 54 B5 1 30N 40 0 E
North Esk →, U.K. 12 E6 56 46N 2 24W
North European Plain, Europe 6 E10 55 0N 25 0 E
North Foreland, U.K. 11 F9 51 22N 1 28 E
North Fork, U.S.A. 84 H7 37 14N 119 21W
North Fork American →, U.S.A. 84 G5 38 57N 120 59W
North Fork Feather →, U.S.A. 84 F5 38 33N 121 30W
North Fork Grand →, U.S.A. 80 C3 45 47N 102 16W
North Fork Red →, U.S.A. 81 H5 34 24N 99 14W
North Frisian Is. = Nordfriesische Inseln, Germany 16 A5 54 40N 8 20 E
North Gower, Canada 79 A9 45 8N 75 43W
North Hd., Australia 61 F1 30 14S 114 59 E
North Henik L., Canada 73 A9 61 45N 97 40W
North Highlands, U.S.A. 84 G5 38 40N 121 23W
North Horr, Kenya 54 B4 3 20N 37 8 E
North I., Kenya 54 B4 4 5N 36 5 E
North I., N.Z. 59 H5 38 0S 175 0 E
North Kingsville, U.S.A. 78 E4 41 54N 80 42W
North Knife →, Canada 73 B10 58 53N 94 45W

Oshkosh

Ofotfjorden, Norway 8 B17 68 27N 17 0 E
Ofunato, Japan 30 E10 39 4N 141 43 E
Oga, Japan 30 E9 39 55N 139 50 E
Oga-Hantō, Japan 30 E9 39 58N 139 47 E
Ogaden, Ethiopia 46 F3 7 30N 45 30 E
Ōgaki, Japan 31 G8 35 21N 136 37 E
Ogallala, U.S.A. 80 E4 41 8N 101 43W
Ogasawara Gunto, Pac. Oc. 28 G18 27 0N 142 0 E
Ogbomosho, Nigeria 50 G6 8 1N 4 11 E
Ogden, U.S.A. 82 F7 41 13N 111 58W
Ogdensburg, U.S.A. 79 B9 44 42N 75 30W
Ogeechee →, U.S.A. 77 K5 31 50N 81 3W
Ogilby, U.S.A. 85 N12 32 49N 114 50W
Oglio →, Italy 20 B4 45 2N 10 39 E
Ogmore, Australia 62 C4 22 37S 149 35 E
Ogoki, Canada 70 B2 51 38N 85 58W
Ogoki →, Canada 70 B2 51 38N 85 57W
Ogoki L., Canada 70 B2 50 50N 87 10W
Ogoki Res., Canada 70 B2 50 45N 88 15W
Ogooué →, Gabon 52 E1 1 0S 9 0 E
Ogowe = Ogooué →, Gabon 52 E1 1 0S 9 0 E
Ogre, Latvia 9 H21 56 49N 24 36 E
Ogurchinskiy, Ostrov, Turkmenistan 45 B7 38 55N 53 2 E
Ohai, N.Z. 59 L2 45 55S 168 0 E
Ohakune, N.Z. 59 H5 39 24S 175 24 E
Ohata, Japan 30 D10 41 24N 141 10 E
Ohau, L., N.Z. 59 L2 44 15S 169 53 E
Ohio □, U.S.A. 78 F2 40 15N 82 45W
Ohio →, U.S.A. 76 G1 36 59N 89 8W
Ohře →, Czech Rep. 16 C8 50 30N 14 10 E
Ohrid, Macedonia 21 D9 41 8N 20 52 E
Ohridsko Jezero, Macedonia 21 D9 41 8N 20 52 E
Ohrigstad, S. Africa 57 C5 24 39S 30 36 E
Oiapoque, Brazil 93 3 50N 51 50W
Oikou, China 35 E9 38 35N 117 42 E
Oil City, U.S.A. 78 E5 41 26N 79 42W
Oil Springs, Canada 78 D2 42 47N 82 7W
Oildale, U.S.A. 85 K7 35 25N 119 1W
Oise →, France 18 B5 49 0N 2 4 E
Ōita, Japan 31 H5 33 14N 131 36 E
Ōita □, Japan 31 H5 33 15N 131 30 E
Oiticica, Brazil 93 E10 5 3S 41 5W
Ojacaliente, Mexico 86 C4 22 34N 102 15W
Ojai, U.S.A. 85 L7 34 27N 119 15W
Ojinaga, Mexico 86 B4 29 34N 104 25W
Ojiya, Japan 31 F9 37 18N 138 48 E
Ojos del Salado, Cerro, Argentina 94 B2 27 0S 68 40W
Oka →, Russia 24 C7 56 20N 43 59 E
Okaba, Indonesia 37 F9 8 6S 139 42 E
Okahandja, Namibia 56 C2 22 0S 16 59 E
Okahukura, N.Z. 59 H5 38 48S 175 14 E
Okanagan L., Canada 72 D5 50 0N 119 30W
Okanogan, U.S.A. 82 B4 48 22N 119 35W
Okanogan →, U.S.A. 82 B4 48 6N 119 44W
Okaputa, Namibia 56 C2 20 5S 17 0 E
Okara, Pakistan 42 D5 30 50N 73 31 E
Okarito, N.Z. 59 K3 43 15S 170 9 E
Okaukuejo, Namibia 56 B2 19 10S 16 0 E
Okavango Swamps, Botswana 56 B3 18 45S 22 45 E
Okaya, Japan 31 F9 36 5N 138 10 E
Okayama, Japan 31 G6 34 40N 133 54 E
Okayama □, Japan 31 G6 35 0N 133 50 E
Okazaki, Japan 31 G8 34 57N 137 10 E
Okeechobee, U.S.A. 77 M5 27 15N 80 50W
Okeechobee, L., U.S.A. 77 M5 27 0N 80 50W
Okefenokee Swamp, U.S.A. 77 K4 30 40N 82 20W
Okehampton, U.K. 11 G4 50 44N 4 0W
Okha, India 42 H3 22 27N 69 4 E
Okha, Russia 27 D15 53 40N 143 0 E
Okhotsk, Russia 27 D15 59 20N 143 10 E
Okhotsk, Sea of, Asia 27 D15 55 0N 145 0 E
Okhotskiy Perevoz, Russia 27 C14 61 52N 135 35 E
Okhtyrka, Ukraine 25 D5 50 25N 35 0 E
Oki-Shotō, Japan 31 F6 36 5N 133 15 E
Okiep, S. Africa 56 D2 29 39S 17 53 E
Okinawa □, Japan 31 L4 26 40N 128 0 E
Okinawa-Guntō, Japan 31 L4 26 40N 128 0 E
Okinawa-Jima, Japan 31 L4 26 32N 128 0 E
Okino-erabu-Shima, Japan 31 L4 27 21N 128 33 E
Oklahoma □, U.S.A. 81 H6 35 20N 97 30W
Oklahoma City, U.S.A. 81 H6 35 30N 97 30W
Okmulgee, U.S.A. 81 H7 35 37N 95 58W
Oknitsa = Ocniţa, Moldova 17 D14 48 25N 27 30 E
Okolo, Uganda 54 B3 2 37N 31 8 E
Okolona, U.S.A. 81 J10 34 0N 88 45W
Okotoks, Canada 72 C6 50 43N 113 58W
Oksibil, Indonesia 37 E10 4 59S 140 35 E
Oksovskiy, Russia 24 B6 62 33N 39 57 E
Oktabrsk = Oktyabrsk, Kazakstan 25 E10 49 28N 57 25 E
Oktyabrsk, Kazakstan 25 E10 49 28N 57 25 E
Oktyabrskiy = Aktsyabrski, Belarus 17 B15 52 38N 28 53 E
Oktyabrskiy, Russia 24 D9 54 28N 53 28 E
Oktyabrskoy Revolyutsii, Ostrov, Russia 27 B10 79 30N 97 0 E
Okuru, N.Z. 59 K2 43 55S 168 55 E
Okushiri-Tō, Japan 30 C9 42 15N 139 30 E
Okwa →, Botswana 56 C3 22 30S 23 0 E
Ola, U.S.A. 81 H8 35 2N 93 13W
Ólafsfjörður, Iceland 8 C4 66 4N 18 39W
Ólafsvík, Iceland 8 D2 64 53N 23 43W
Olancha, U.S.A. 85 J8 36 17N 118 1W
Olancha Pk., U.S.A. 85 J8 36 15N 118 7W
Olanchito, Honduras 88 C2 15 30N 86 30W
Öland, Sweden 9 H17 56 45N 16 38 E
Olary, Australia 63 E3 32 18S 140 19 E
Olascoaga, Argentina 94 D3 35 15S 60 39W
Olathe, U.S.A. 80 F7 38 53N 94 49W
Olavarría, Argentina 94 D3 36 55S 60 20W
Oława, Poland 17 C9 50 57N 17 20 E
Ólbia, Italy 20 D3 40 55N 9 31 E
Olcott, U.S.A. 78 C6 43 20N 78 42W
Old Bahama Chan. = Bahama, Canal Viejo de, W. Indies 88 B4 22 10N 77 30W
Old Baldy Pk. = San Antonio, Mt., U.S.A. 85 L9 34 17N 117 38W
Old Castile = Castilla y Leon □, Spain 19 B3 42 0N 5 0W
Old Crow, Canada 68 B6 67 30N 139 55W
Old Dale, U.S.A. 85 L11 34 8N 115 47W
Old Forge, N.Y., U.S.A. 79 C10 43 43N 74 58W
Old Forge, Pa., U.S.A. 79 E9 41 22N 75 45W
Old Perlican, Canada 71 C9 48 5N 53 1W
Old Shinyanga, Tanzania 54 C3 3 33S 33 27 E
Old Speck Mt., U.S.A. 79 B14 44 34N 70 57W
Old Town, U.S.A. 77 C11 44 56N 68 39W
Old Washington, U.S.A. 78 F3 40 2N 81 27W
Old Wives L., Canada 73 C7 50 5N 106 0W
Oldbury, U.K. 11 F5 51 38N 2 33W
Oldcastle, Ireland 13 C4 53 46N 7 10W
Oldeani, Tanzania 54 C4 3 22S 35 35 E
Oldenburg, Germany 16 B5 53 9N 8 13 E
Oldenzaal, Neths. 15 B6 52 19N 6 53 E
Oldham, U.K. 10 D5 53 33N 2 7W
Oldman →, Canada 72 D6 49 57N 111 42W
Oldmeldrum, U.K. 12 D6 57 20N 2 19W
Olds, Canada 72 C6 51 50N 114 10W
Oldziyt, Mongolia 34 B5 44 40N 109 1 E
Olean, U.S.A. 78 D6 42 5N 78 26W
Olekma →, Russia 27 C13 60 22N 120 42 E
Olekminsk, Russia 27 C13 60 25N 120 30 E
Oleksandriya, Ukraine 17 C14 50 37N 26 19 E
Olema, U.S.A. 84 G4 38 3N 122 47W
Olenegorsk, Russia 24 A5 68 9N 33 18 E
Olenek, Russia 27 C12 68 28N 112 18 E
Olenek →, Russia 27 B13 73 0N 120 10 E
Oléron, Î. d', France 18 D3 45 55N 1 15W
Oleśnica, Poland 17 C9 51 13N 17 22 E
Olevsk, Ukraine 17 C14 51 12N 27 39 E
Olga, Russia 27 E14 43 50N 135 14 E
Olga, L., Canada 70 C4 49 47N 77 15W
Olga, Mt., Australia 61 E5 25 20S 130 50 E
Olhão, Portugal 19 D2 37 3N 7 48W
Olifants →, Africa 57 C5 23 57S 31 58 E
Olifantshoek, S. Africa 56 D3 27 57S 22 42 E
Ólimbos, Óros, Greece 21 D10 40 6N 22 23 E
Olímpia, Brazil 95 A6 20 44S 48 54W
Olinda, Brazil 93 E12 8 1S 34 51W
Oliva, Argentina 94 C3 32 0S 63 38W
Olivehurst, U.S.A. 84 F5 39 6N 121 34W
Olivenza, Spain 19 C2 38 41N 7 9W
Oliver, Canada 72 D5 49 13N 119 37W
Oliver L., Canada 73 B8 56 56N 103 22W
Ollagüe, Chile 94 A2 21 15S 68 10W
Olney, Ill., U.S.A. 76 F1 38 44N 88 5W
Olney, Tex., U.S.A. 81 J5 33 22N 98 45W
Olomane →, Canada 71 B7 50 14N 60 37W
Olomouc, Czech Rep. 17 D9 49 38N 17 12 E
Olonets, Russia 24 B5 61 0N 32 54 E
Olongapo, Phil. 37 B6 14 50N 120 18 E
Olot, Spain 19 A7 42 11N 2 30 E
Olovyannaya, Russia 27 D12 50 58N 115 35 E
Oloy →, Russia 27 C16 66 29N 159 29 E
Olsztyn, Poland 17 B11 53 48N 20 29 E
Olt →, Romania 17 G13 43 43N 24 51 E
Olteniţa, Romania 17 F14 44 7N 26 42 E
Olton, U.S.A. 81 H3 34 11N 102 8W
Olymbos, Cyprus 23 D12 35 21N 33 45 E
Olympia, Greece 21 F9 37 39N 21 39 E
Olympia, U.S.A. 84 D4 47 3N 122 53W
Olympic Dam, Australia 63 E2 30 30S 136 55 E
Olympic Mts., U.S.A. 84 C3 47 55N 123 45W
Olympic Nat. Park, U.S.A. 84 C3 47 48N 123 30W
Olympus, Cyprus 23 E11 34 56N 32 52 E
Olympus, Mt. = Ólimbos, Óros, Greece 21 D10 40 6N 22 23 E
Olympus, Mt. = Uludağ, Turkey 21 D13 40 4N 29 13 E
Olympus, Mt., U.S.A. 84 C3 47 48N 123 43W
Olyphant, U.S.A. 79 E9 41 27N 75 36W
Om →, Russia 26 D8 54 59N 73 22 E
Om Koi, Thailand 38 D2 17 48N 98 22 E
Ōma, Japan 30 D10 41 45N 141 5 E
Ōmachi, Japan 31 F8 36 30N 137 50 E
Omae-Zaki, Japan 31 G9 34 36N 138 14 E
Ōmagari, Japan 30 E10 39 27N 140 29 E
Omagh, U.K. 13 B4 54 36N 7 19W
Omagh □, U.K. 13 B4 54 35N 7 15W
Omaha, U.S.A. 80 E7 41 17N 95 58W
Omak, U.S.A. 82 B4 48 25N 119 31W
Omalos, Greece 23 D5 35 19N 23 55 E
Oman ■, Asia 46 C6 23 0N 58 0 E
Oman, G. of, Asia 45 E8 24 30N 58 30 E
Omaruru, Namibia 56 C2 21 26S 16 0 E
Omaruru →, Namibia 56 C1 22 7S 14 15 E
Omate, Peru 92 G4 16 45S 71 0W
Ombai, Selat, Indonesia 37 F6 8 30S 124 50 E
Omboué, Gabon 52 E1 1 35S 9 15 E
Ombrone →, Italy 20 C4 42 42N 11 5 E
Omdurmân, Sudan 51 E12 15 40N 32 28 E
Omemee, Canada 78 B6 44 18N 78 33W
Omeo, Australia 63 F4 37 6S 147 36 E
Omeonga, Dem. Rep. of the Congo 54 C1 3 40S 24 22 E
Ometepe, I. de, Nic. 88 D2 11 32N 85 35W
Ometepec, Mexico 87 D5 16 39N 98 23W
Ominato, Japan 30 D10 41 17N 141 10 E
Omineca →, Canada 72 B4 56 3N 124 16W
Omitara, Namibia 56 C2 22 16S 18 2 E
Ōmiya, Japan 31 G9 35 54N 139 38 E
Ommen, Neths. 15 B6 52 31N 6 26 E
Ömnögovĭ □, Mongolia 34 C3 43 15N 104 0 E
Omo →, Ethiopia 46 F2 6 25N 36 10 E
Omodhos, Cyprus 23 E11 34 51N 32 48 E
Omolon →, Russia 27 C16 68 42N 158 36 E
Omono-Gawa →, Japan 30 E10 39 46N 140 3 E
Omsk, Russia 26 D8 55 0N 73 12 E
Omsukchan, Russia 27 C16 62 32N 155 48 E
Ōmu, Japan 30 B11 44 34N 142 58 E
Omul, Vf., Romania 17 F13 45 27N 25 29 E
Ōmura, Japan 31 H4 32 56N 129 57 E
Omuramba Omatako →, Namibia 53 H4 17 45S 20 25 E
Ōmuta, Japan 31 H5 33 5N 130 26 E
Onaga, U.S.A. 80 F6 39 29N 96 10W
Onalaska, U.S.A. 80 D9 43 53N 91 14W
Onancock, U.S.A. 76 G8 37 43N 75 45W
Onang, Indonesia 37 E5 3 2S 118 49 E
Onaping L., Canada 70 C3 47 3N 81 30W
Onavas, Mexico 86 B3 28 28N 109 30W
Onawa, U.S.A. 80 D6 42 2N 96 6W
Oncócua, Angola 56 B1 16 30S 13 25 E
Onda, Spain 19 C5 39 55N 0 17W
Ondaejin, N. Korea 35 D15 41 34N 129 40 E
Ondangua, Namibia 56 B2 17 57S 16 4 E
Ondjiva, Angola 56 B2 16 48S 15 50 E
Öndörshil, Mongolia 34 B5 45 13N 108 5 E
Öndverðarnes, Iceland 8 D1 64 52N 24 0W
One Tree, Australia 63 E3 34 11S 144 43 E
Onega, Russia 24 B6 64 0N 38 10 E
Onega →, Russia 24 B6 63 58N 38 2 E
Onega, G. of = Onezhskaya Guba, Russia 24 B6 64 24N 36 38 E
Onega, L. = Onezhskoye Ozero, Russia 24 B6 61 44N 35 22 E
Onehunga, N.Z. 59 G5 36 55S 174 48 E
Oneida, U.S.A. 79 C9 43 6N 75 39W
Oneida L., U.S.A. 79 C9 43 12N 75 54W
O'Neill, U.S.A. 80 D5 42 27N 98 39W
Onekotan, Ostrov, Russia 27 E16 49 25N 154 45 E
Onema, Dem. Rep. of the Congo 54 C1 4 35S 24 30 E
Oneonta, U.S.A. 79 D9 42 27N 75 4W
Oneşti, Romania 17 E14 46 15N 26 45 E
Onezhskaya Guba, Russia 24 B6 64 24N 36 38 E
Onezhskoye Ozero, Russia 24 B6 61 44N 35 22 E
Ongarue, N.Z. 59 H5 38 42S 175 19 E
Ongerup, Australia 61 F2 33 58S 118 28 E
Ongjin, N. Korea 35 F13 37 56N 125 21 E
Ongkharak, Thailand 38 E3 14 8N 101 1 E
Ongniud Qi, China 35 C10 43 0N 118 38 E
Ongoka, Dem. Rep. of the Congo 54 C2 1 20S 26 0 E
Ongole, India 40 M12 15 33N 80 2 E
Ongon = Havirga, Mongolia 34 B7 45 41N 113 5 E
Onida, U.S.A. 80 C4 44 42N 100 4W
Onilahy →, Madag. 57 C7 23 34S 43 45 E
Onitsha, Nigeria 50 G7 6 6N 6 42 E
Onoda, Japan 31 G5 34 2N 131 25 E
Onpyŏng-ni, S. Korea 35 H14 33 25N 126 55 E
Onslow, Australia 60 D2 21 40S 115 12 E
Onslow B., U.S.A. 77 H7 34 20N 77 15W
Ontake-San, Japan 31 G8 35 53N 137 29 E
Ontario, Calif., U.S.A. 85 L9 34 4N 117 39W
Ontario, Oreg., U.S.A. 82 D5 44 2N 116 58W
Ontario □, Canada 70 B2 48 0N 83 0W
Ontario, L., N. Amer. 75 B11 43 20N 78 0W
Ontonagon, U.S.A. 80 B10 46 52N 89 19W
Onyx, U.S.A. 85 K8 35 41N 118 14W
Oodnadatta, Australia 63 D2 27 33S 135 30 E
Ooldea, Australia 61 F5 30 27S 131 50 E
Oombulgurri, Australia 60 C4 15 15S 127 45 E
Oorindi, Australia 62 C3 20 40S 141 1 E
Oost-Vlaanderen □, Belgium 15 C3 51 5N 3 50 E
Oostende, Belgium 15 C2 51 15N 2 54 E
Oosterhout, Neths. 15 C4 51 39N 4 47 E
Oosterschelde →, Neths. 15 C4 51 33N 4 0 E
Oosterwolde, Neths. 15 B6 53 0N 6 17 E
Ootacamund = Udagamandalam, India 40 P10 11 30N 76 44 E
Ootsa L., Canada 72 C3 53 50N 126 2W
Opala, Dem. Rep. of the Congo 54 C1 0 40S 24 20 E
Opanake, Sri Lanka 40 R12 6 35N 80 40 E
Opasatika, Canada 70 C3 49 30N 82 50W
Opasquia Prov. Park, Canada 70 B1 53 33N 93 5W
Opava, Czech Rep. 17 D9 49 57N 17 58 E
Opelika, U.S.A. 77 J3 32 39N 85 23W
Opelousas, U.S.A. 81 K8 30 32N 92 5W
Opémisca, L., Canada 70 C5 49 56N 74 52W
Opheim, U.S.A. 82 B10 48 51N 106 24W
Ophthalmia Ra., Australia 60 D2 23 15S 119 30 E
Opinaca →, Canada 70 B4 52 15N 78 2W
Opinaca, Rés., Canada 70 B4 52 39N 76 20W
Opinnagau →, Canada 70 B3 54 12N 82 25W
Opiscoteo, L., Canada 71 B6 53 10N 68 10W
Opole, Poland 17 C9 50 42N 17 58 E
Oporto = Porto, Portugal 19 B1 41 8N 8 40W
Opotiki, N.Z. 59 H6 38 1S 177 19 E
Opp, U.S.A. 77 K2 31 17N 86 16W
Oppdal, Norway 9 E13 62 35N 9 41 E
Opportunity, U.S.A. 82 C5 47 39N 117 15W
Opua, N.Z. 59 F5 35 19S 174 9 E
Opunake, N.Z. 59 H4 39 26S 173 52 E
Ora, Cyprus 23 E12 34 51N 33 12 E
Oracle, U.S.A. 83 K8 32 37N 110 46W
Oradea, Romania 17 E11 47 2N 21 58 E
Öræfajökull, Iceland 8 D5 64 2N 16 39W
Orai, India 43 G8 25 58N 79 30 E
Oral = Zhayyq →, Kazakstan 25 E9 47 0N 51 48 E
Oral, Kazakstan 25 D9 51 20N 51 20 E
Oran, Algeria 50 A5 35 45N 0 39W
Orange, Australia 63 E4 33 15S 149 7 E
Orange, France 18 D6 44 8N 4 47 E
Orange, Calif., U.S.A. 85 M9 33 47N 117 51W
Orange, Mass., U.S.A. 79 D12 42 35N 72 19W
Orange, Tex., U.S.A. 81 K8 30 6N 93 44W
Orange, Va., U.S.A. 76 F6 38 15N 78 7W
Orange →, S. Africa 56 D2 28 41S 16 28 E
Orange, C., Brazil 93 C8 4 20N 51 30W
Orange Cove, U.S.A. 84 J7 36 38N 119 19W
Orange Free State = Free State □, S. Africa 56 D4 28 30S 27 0 E
Orange Grove, U.S.A. 81 M6 27 58N 97 56W
Orange Walk, Belize 87 D7 18 6N 88 33W
Orangeburg, U.S.A. 77 J5 33 30N 80 52W
Orangeville, Canada 78 C4 43 55N 80 5W
Oranienburg, Germany 16 B7 52 45N 13 14 E
Oranje = Orange →, S. Africa 56 D2 28 41S 16 28 E
Oranje Vrystaat = Free State □, S. Africa 56 D4 28 30S 27 0 E
Oranjemund, Namibia 56 D2 28 38S 16 29 E
Oranjerivier, S. Africa 56 D3 29 40S 24 12 E
Orapa, Botswana 53 J5 21 15S 25 30 E
Oras, Phil. 37 B7 12 9N 125 28 E
Oraşul Stalin = Braşov, Romania 17 F13 45 38N 25 35 E
Orbetello, Italy 20 C4 42 27N 11 13 E
Orbisonia, U.S.A. 78 F7 40 15N 77 54W
Orbost, Australia 63 F4 37 40S 148 29 E
Orcas I., U.S.A. 84 B4 48 42N 122 56W
Orchard City, U.S.A. 83 G10 38 50N 107 58W
Orchila, I., Venezuela 89 D6 11 48N 66 10W
Orcutt, U.S.A. 85 L6 34 52N 120 27W
Ord, U.S.A. 80 E5 41 36N 98 56W
Ord →, Australia 60 C4 15 33S 128 15 E
Ord, Mt., Australia 60 C4 17 20S 125 34 E
Orderville, U.S.A. 83 H7 37 17N 112 38W
Ordos = Mu Us Shamo, China 34 E5 39 0N 109 0 E
Ordu, Turkey 25 F6 40 55N 37 53 E
Ordway, U.S.A. 80 F3 38 13N 103 46W
Ordzhonikidze = Vladikavkaz, Russia 25 F7 43 0N 44 35 E
Ore, Dem. Rep. of the Congo 54 B2 3 17N 29 30 E
Ore Mts. = Erzgebirge, Germany 16 C7 50 27N 12 55 E
Örebro, Sweden 9 G16 59 20N 15 18 E
Oregon, U.S.A. 80 D10 42 1N 89 20W
Oregon □, U.S.A. 82 E3 44 0N 121 0W
Oregon City, U.S.A. 84 E4 45 21N 122 36W
Orekhovo-Zuyevo, Russia 24 C6 55 50N 38 55 E
Orel, Russia 24 D6 52 57N 36 3 E
Orem, U.S.A. 74 B4 40 19N 111 42W
Ören, Turkey 21 F12 37 3N 27 57 E
Orenburg, Russia 24 D10 51 45N 55 6 E
Orense = Ourense, Spain 19 A2 42 19N 7 55W
Orepuki, N.Z. 59 M1 46 19S 167 46 E
Orestiás, Greece 21 D12 41 30N 26 33 E
Orestos Pereyra, Mexico 86 B3 26 31N 105 40W
Orford Ness, U.K. 11 E9 52 5N 1 35 E
Organos, Pta. de los, Canary Is. 22 F2 28 12N 17 17W
Orgaz, Spain 19 C4 39 39N 3 53W
Orgeyev = Orhei, Moldova 17 E15 47 24N 28 50 E
Orhaneli, Turkey 21 E13 39 54N 28 59 E
Orhangazi, Turkey 21 D13 40 29N 29 18 E
Orhei, Moldova 17 E15 47 24N 28 50 E
Orhon Gol →, Mongolia 32 A5 50 21N 106 0 E
Oriental, Cordillera, Colombia 92 B4 6 0N 73 0W
Orientale □, Dem. Rep. of the Congo 54 B2 2 20N 26 0 E
Oriente, Argentina 94 D3 38 44S 60 37W
Orihuela, Spain 19 C5 38 7N 0 55W
Orillia, Canada 78 B5 44 40N 79 24W
Orinoco →, Venezuela 92 B6 9 15N 61 30W
Orion, Canada 73 D6 49 27N 110 49W
Oriskany, U.S.A. 79 C9 43 10N 75 20W
Orissa □, India 41 K14 20 0N 84 0 E
Orissaare, Estonia 9 G20 58 34N 23 5 E
Oristano, Italy 20 E3 39 54N 8 36 E
Oristano, G. di, Italy 20 E3 39 50N 8 29 E
Orizaba, Mexico 87 D5 18 51N 97 6W
Orkanger, Norway 8 E13 63 18N 9 52 E
Orkla →, Norway 8 E13 63 18N 9 51 E
Orkney, S. Africa 56 D4 26 58S 26 40 E
Orkney □, U.K. 12 B5 59 2N 3 13W
Orkney Is., U.K. 12 B6 59 0N 3 0W
Orland, U.S.A. 84 F4 39 45N 122 12W
Orlando, U.S.A. 77 L5 28 33N 81 23W
Orléanais, France 18 C5 48 0N 2 0 E
Orléans, France 18 C4 47 54N 1 52 E
Orleans, U.S.A. 79 B12 44 49N 72 12W
Orléans, I. d', Canada 71 C5 46 54N 70 58W
Ormara, Pakistan 40 G4 25 16N 64 33 E
Ormoc, Phil. 37 B6 11 0N 124 37 E
Ormond, N.Z. 59 H6 38 33S 177 56 E
Ormond Beach, U.S.A. 77 L5 29 17N 81 3W
Ormskirk, U.K. 10 D5 53 35N 2 54W
Ormstown, Canada 79 A11 45 8N 74 0W
Örnsköldsvik, Sweden 8 E18 63 17N 18 40 E
Oro, N. Korea 35 D14 40 1N 127 27 E
Oro →, Mexico 86 B3 25 35N 105 2W
Oro Grande, U.S.A. 85 L9 34 36N 117 20W
Oro Valley, U.S.A. 83 K8 32 26N 110 58W
Orocué, Colombia 92 C4 4 48N 71 20W
Orofino, U.S.A. 82 C5 46 29N 116 15W
Orol Dengizi = Aral Sea, Asia 26 E7 44 30N 60 0 E
Oromocto, Canada 71 C6 45 54N 66 29W
Orono, Canada 78 C6 43 59N 78 37W
Orono, U.S.A. 77 C11 44 53N 68 40W
Oronsay, U.K. 12 E2 56 1N 6 15W
Oroqen Zizhiqi, China 33 A7 50 34N 123 43 E
Oroquieta, Phil. 37 C6 8 32N 123 44 E
Orosháza, Hungary 17 E11 46 32N 20 42 E
Orotukan, Russia 27 C16 62 16N 151 42 E
Oroville, Calif., U.S.A. 84 F5 39 31N 121 33W
Oroville, Wash., U.S.A. 82 B4 48 56N 119 26W
Oroville, L., U.S.A. 84 F5 39 33N 121 29W
Orroroo, Australia 63 E2 32 43S 138 38 E
Orrville, U.S.A. 78 F3 40 50N 81 46W
Orsha, Belarus 24 D5 54 30N 30 25 E
Orsk, Russia 26 D6 51 12N 58 34 E
Orşova, Romania 17 F12 44 41N 22 25 E
Ortaca, Turkey 21 F13 36 49N 28 45 E
Ortegal, C., Spain 19 A2 43 43N 7 52W
Orthez, France 18 E3 43 29N 0 48W
Ortigueira, Spain 19 A2 43 40N 7 50W
Orting, U.S.A. 84 C4 47 6N 122 12W
Ortles, Italy 18 C9 46 31N 10 33 E
Ortón →, Bolivia 92 F5 10 50S 67 0W
Ortonville, U.S.A. 80 C6 45 19N 96 27W
Orūmīyeh, Iran 44 B5 37 40N 45 0 E
Orūmīyeh, Daryācheh-ye, Iran 44 B5 37 50N 45 30 E
Oruro, Bolivia 92 G5 18 0S 67 9W
Orust, Sweden 9 G14 58 10N 11 40 E
Oruzgān □, Afghan. 40 C5 33 30N 66 0 E
Orvieto, Italy 20 C5 42 43N 12 7 E
Orwell, N.Y., U.S.A. 79 C9 43 35N 75 50W
Orwell, Ohio, U.S.A. 78 E4 41 32N 80 52W
Orwell →, U.K. 11 F9 51 59N 1 18 E
Orwigsburg, U.S.A. 79 F8 40 38N 76 6W
Oryakhovo, Bulgaria 21 C10 43 40N 23 57 E
Osa, Russia 24 C10 57 17N 55 26 E
Osa, Pen. de, Costa Rica 88 E3 8 0N 84 0W
Osage, U.S.A. 80 D8 43 17N 92 49W
Osage →, U.S.A. 80 F9 38 35N 91 57W
Osage City, U.S.A. 80 F7 38 38N 95 50W
Ōsaka, Japan 31 G7 34 40N 135 30 E
Osan, S. Korea 35 F14 37 11N 127 4 E
Osawatomie, U.S.A. 80 F7 38 31N 94 57W
Osborne, U.S.A. 80 F5 39 26N 98 42W
Osceola, Ark., U.S.A. 81 H10 35 42N 89 58W
Osceola, Iowa, U.S.A. 80 E8 41 2N 93 46W
Oscoda, U.S.A. 78 B1 44 26N 83 20W
Ösel = Saaremaa, Estonia 9 G20 58 30N 22 30 E
Osgoode, Canada 79 A9 45 8N 75 36W
Osh, Kyrgyzstan 26 E8 40 37N 72 49 E
Oshakati, Namibia 53 H3 17 45S 15 40 E
Oshawa, Canada 78 C6 43 50N 78 50W
Oshkosh, Nebr., U.S.A. 80 E3 41 24N 102 21W
Oshkosh, Wis., U.S.A. 80 C10 44 1N 88 33W

P

151

Posse

Posse, *Brazil* **93 F9** 14 4S 46 18W
Possession I., *Antarctica* **5 D11** 72 4S 172 0 E
Possum Kingdom L., *U.S.A.* **81 J5** 32 52N 98 26W
Post, *U.S.A.* **81 J4** 33 12N 101 23W
Post Falls, *U.S.A.* **82 C5** 47 43N 116 57W
Postavy = Pastavy, *Belarus* **9 J22** 55 4N 26 50 E
Poste-de-la-Baleine = Kuujjuarapik, *Canada* **70 A4** 55 20N 77 35W
Postmasburg, *S. Africa* **56 D3** 28 18S 23 5 E
Postojna, *Slovenia* **16 F8** 45 46N 14 12 E
Poston, *U.S.A.* **85 M12** 34 0N 114 24W
Postville, *Canada* **71 B8** 54 54N 59 47W
Potchefstroom, *S. Africa* **56 D4** 26 41S 27 7 E
Poteau, *U.S.A.* **81 H7** 35 3N 94 37W
Poteet, *U.S.A.* **81 L5** 29 2N 98 35W
Potenza, *Italy* **20 D6** 40 38N 15 48 E
Poteriteri, L., *N.Z.* **59 M1** 46 5S 167 10 E
Potgietersrus, *S. Africa* **57 C4** 24 10S 28 55 E
Poti, *Georgia* **25 F7** 42 10N 41 38 E
Potiskum, *Nigeria* **51 F8** 11 39N 11 2 E
Potomac →, *U.S.A.* **76 G7** 38 0N 76 23W
Potosí, *Bolivia* **92 G5** 19 38S 65 50W
Potosi Mt., *U.S.A.* **85 K11** 35 57N 115 29W
Pototan, *Phil.* **37 B6** 10 54N 122 38 E
Potrerillos, *Chile* **94 B2** 26 30S 69 30W
Potsdam, *Germany* **16 B7** 52 25N 13 4 E
Potsdam, *U.S.A.* **79 B10** 44 40N 74 59W
Pottersville, *U.S.A.* **79 C11** 43 43N 73 50W
Pottstown, *U.S.A.* **79 F9** 40 15N 75 39W
Pottsville, *U.S.A.* **79 F8** 40 41N 76 12W
Pottuvil, *Sri Lanka* **40 R12** 6 55N 81 50 E
Pouce Coupé, *Canada* **72 B4** 55 40N 120 10W
Poughkeepsie, *U.S.A.* **79 E11** 41 42N 73 56W
Poulaphouca Res., *Ireland* **13 C5** 53 8N 6 30W
Poulsbo, *U.S.A.* **84 C4** 47 44N 122 39W
Poultney, *U.S.A.* **79 C11** 43 31N 73 14W
Poulton-le-Fylde, *U.K.* **10 D5** 53 51N 2 58W
Pouso Alegre, *Brazil* **95 A6** 22 14S 45 57W
Pouthisat, *Cambodia* **38 F4** 12 34N 103 50 E
Považská Bystrica, *Slovak Rep.* **17 D10** 49 8N 18 27 E
Povenets, *Russia* **24 B5** 62 50N 34 50 E
Poverty B., *N.Z.* **59 H7** 38 43S 178 2 E
Póvoa de Varzim, *Portugal* **19 B1** 41 25N 8 46W
Povungnituk = Puvirnituq, *Canada* **69 B12** 60 2N 77 10W
Powassan, *Canada* **70 C4** 46 5N 79 25W
Poway, *U.S.A.* **85 N9** 32 58N 117 2W
Powder →, *U.S.A.* **80 B2** 46 45N 105 26W
Powder River, *U.S.A.* **82 E10** 43 2N 106 59W
Powell, *U.S.A.* **82 D9** 44 45N 108 46W
Powell, L., *U.S.A.* **83 H8** 36 57N 111 29W
Powell River, *Canada* **72 D4** 49 50N 124 35W
Powers, *U.S.A.* **76 C2** 45 41N 87 32W
Powys □, *U.K.* **11 E4** 52 20N 3 20W
Poyang Hu, *China* **33 D6** 29 5N 116 20 E
Poyarkovo, *Russia* **27 E13** 49 36N 128 41 E
Poza Rica, *Mexico* **87 C5** 20 33N 97 27W
Požarevac, *Serbia, Yug.* **21 B9** 44 35N 21 18 E
Poznań, *Poland* **17 B9** 52 25N 16 55 E
Pozo, *U.S.A.* **85 K6** 35 20N 120 24W
Pozo Almonte, *Chile* **92 H5** 20 10S 69 50W
Pozo Colorado, *Paraguay* **94 A4** 23 30S 58 45W
Pozoblanco, *Spain* **19 C3** 38 23N 4 51W
Pozzuoli, *Italy* **20 D6** 40 49N 14 7 E
Prachin Buri, *Thailand* **38 F3** 14 0N 101 25 E
Prachuap Khiri Khan, *Thailand* **39 G2** 11 49N 99 48 E
Prado, *Brazil* **93 G11** 17 20S 39 13W
Prague = Praha, *Czech Rep.* **16 C8** 50 5N 14 22 E
Praha, *Czech Rep.* **16 C8** 50 5N 14 22 E
Praia, *C. Verde Is.* **49 E1** 14 55N 23 30W
Prainha, *Amazonas, Brazil* **92 E6** 7 10S 60 30W
Prainha, *Pará, Brazil* **93 D8** 1 45S 53 30W
Prairie, *Australia* **62 C3** 20 50S 144 35 E
Prairie City, *U.S.A.* **82 D4** 44 28N 118 43W
Prairie Dog Town Fork →, *U.S.A.* **81 H5** 34 30N 99 23W
Prairie du Chien, *U.S.A.* **80 D9** 43 3N 91 9W
Prairies, L. of the, *Canada* **73 C8** 51 16N 101 32W
Pran Buri, *Thailand* **38 F2** 12 23N 99 55 E
Prapat, *Indonesia* **36 D1** 2 41N 98 58 E
Prasonísi, Ákra, *Greece* **23 D9** 35 42N 27 46 E
Prata, *Brazil* **93 G9** 19 25S 48 54W
Pratabpur, *India* **43 H10** 23 28N 83 15 E
Pratapgarh, *Raj., India* **42 G6** 24 2N 74 40 E
Pratapgarh, *Ut. P., India* **43 G9** 25 56N 81 59 E
Prato, *Italy* **20 C4** 43 53N 11 6 E
Pratt, *U.S.A.* **81 G5** 37 39N 98 44W
Prattville, *U.S.A.* **77 J2** 32 28N 86 29W
Pravia, *Spain* **19 A2** 43 30N 6 12W
Praya, *Indonesia* **36 F5** 8 39S 116 17 E
Precordillera, *Argentina* **94 C2** 30 0S 69 1W
Preeceville, *Canada* **73 C8** 51 57N 102 40W
Preiļi, *Latvia* **9 H22** 56 18N 26 43 E
Premont, *U.S.A.* **81 M5** 27 22N 98 7W
Prentice, *U.S.A.* **80 C9** 45 33N 90 17W
Preobrazheniye, *Russia* **30 C6** 42 54N 133 54 E
Preparis North Channel, *Ind. Oc.* **41 M18** 15 12N 93 40 E
Preparis South Channel, *Ind. Oc.* **41 M18** 14 36N 93 40 E
Přerov, *Czech Rep.* **17 D9** 49 28N 17 27 E
Prescott, *Canada* **79 B9** 44 45N 75 30W
Prescott, *Ariz., U.S.A.* **83 J7** 34 33N 112 28W
Prescott, *Ark., U.S.A.* **81 J8** 33 48N 93 23W
Prescott Valley, *U.S.A.* **83 J7** 34 40N 112 18W
Preservation Inlet, *N.Z.* **59 M1** 46 8S 166 35 E
Presho, *U.S.A.* **80 D4** 43 54N 100 3W
Presidencia de la Plaza, *Argentina* **94 B4** 27 0S 59 50W
Presidencia Roque Saenz Peña, *Argentina* **94 B3** 26 45S 60 30W
Presidente Epitácio, *Brazil* **93 H8** 21 56S 52 6W
Presidente Hayes □, *Paraguay* **94 A4** 24 0S 59 0W
Presidente Prudente, *Brazil* **95 A5** 22 5S 51 25W
Presidio, *Mexico* **86 B4** 29 29N 104 23W
Presidio, *U.S.A.* **81 L2** 29 34N 104 22W
Prešov, *Slovak Rep.* **17 D11** 49 0N 21 15 E
Prespa, L. = Prespansko Jezero, *Macedonia* **21 D9** 40 55N 21 0 E
Prespansko Jezero, *Macedonia* **21 D9** 40 55N 21 0 E
Presque I., *U.S.A.* **78 D4** 42 9N 80 6W
Presque Isle, *U.S.A.* **77 B12** 46 41N 68 1W
Prestatyn, *U.K.* **10 D4** 53 20N 3 24W
Presteigne, *U.K.* **11 E5** 52 17N 3 0W
Preston, *Canada* **78 C4** 43 23N 80 21W
Preston, *U.K.* **10 D5** 53 46N 2 42W
Preston, *Idaho, U.S.A.* **82 E8** 42 6N 111 53W
Preston, *Minn., U.S.A.* **80 D8** 43 40N 92 5W
Preston, C., *Australia* **60 D2** 20 51S 116 12 E
Prestonburg, *U.S.A.* **76 G4** 37 39N 82 46W
Prestwick, *U.K.* **12 F4** 55 29N 4 37W
Pretoria, *S. Africa* **57 D4** 25 44S 28 12 E
Préveza, *Greece* **21 E9** 38 57N 20 47 E
Prey Veng, *Cambodia* **39 G5** 11 35N 105 29 E
Pribilof Is., *U.S.A.* **68 C2** 57 0N 170 0W
Příbram, *Czech Rep.* **16 D8** 49 41N 14 2 E
Price, *U.S.A.* **82 G8** 39 36N 110 49W
Price I., *Canada* **72 C3** 52 23N 128 41W
Prichard, *U.S.A.* **77 K1** 30 44N 88 5W
Priekule, *Latvia* **9 H19** 56 26N 21 35 E
Prienai, *Lithuania* **9 J20** 54 38N 23 57 E
Prieska, *S. Africa* **56 D3** 29 40S 22 42 E
Priest L., *U.S.A.* **82 B5** 48 35N 116 52W
Priest River, *U.S.A.* **82 B5** 48 10N 116 54W
Priest Valley, *U.S.A.* **84 J6** 36 10N 120 39W
Prievidza, *Slovak Rep.* **17 D10** 48 46N 18 36 E
Prikaspiyskaya Nizmennost = Caspian Depression, *Eurasia* **25 E8** 47 0N 48 0 E
Prilep, *Macedonia* **21 D9** 41 21N 21 32 E
Priluki = Pryluky, *Ukraine* **25 D5** 50 30N 32 24 E
Prime Seal I., *Australia* **62 G4** 40 3S 147 43 E
Primrose L., *Canada* **73 C7** 54 55N 109 45W
Prince Albert, *Canada* **73 C7** 53 15N 105 50W
Prince Albert, *S. Africa* **56 E3** 33 12S 22 2 E
Prince Albert Mts., *Antarctica* **5 D11** 76 0S 161 30 E
Prince Albert Nat. Park, *Canada* **73 C7** 54 0N 106 25W
Prince Albert Pen., *Canada* **68 A8** 72 30N 116 0W
Prince Albert Sd., *Canada* **68 A8** 70 25N 115 0W
Prince Alfred, C., *Canada* **4 B1** 74 20N 124 40W
Prince Charles I., *Canada* **69 B12** 67 47N 76 12W
Prince Charles Mts., *Antarctica* **5 D6** 72 0S 67 0 E
Prince Edward I. □, *Canada* **71 C7** 46 20N 63 20W
Prince Edward Is., *Ind. Oc.* **3 G11** 46 35S 38 0 E
Prince Edward Pt., *Canada* **78 C8** 43 56N 76 52W
Prince George, *Canada* **72 C4** 53 55N 122 50W
Prince of Wales, C., *U.S.A.* **66 C3** 65 36N 168 5W
Prince of Wales I., *Australia* **62 A3** 10 40S 142 10 E
Prince of Wales I., *Canada* **68 A10** 73 0N 99 0W
Prince of Wales I., *U.S.A.* **68 C6** 55 47N 132 50W
Prince Patrick I., *Canada* **4 B2** 77 0N 120 0W
Prince Regent Inlet, *Canada* **4 B3** 73 0N 90 0W
Prince Rupert, *Canada* **72 C2** 54 20N 130 20W
Princess Charlotte B., *Australia* **62 A3** 14 25S 144 0 E
Princess May Ranges, *Australia* **60 C4** 15 30S 125 30 E
Princess Royal I., *Canada* **72 C3** 53 0N 128 40W
Princeton, *Canada* **72 D4** 49 27N 120 30W
Princeton, *Calif., U.S.A.* **84 F4** 39 24N 122 1W
Princeton, *Ill., U.S.A.* **80 E10** 41 23N 89 28W
Princeton, *Ind., U.S.A.* **76 F2** 38 21N 87 34W
Princeton, *Ky., U.S.A.* **76 G2** 37 7N 87 53W
Princeton, *Mo., U.S.A.* **80 E8** 40 24N 93 35W
Princeton, *N.J., U.S.A.* **79 F10** 40 21N 74 39W
Princeton, *W. Va., U.S.A.* **76 G5** 37 22N 81 6W
Principe, I. de, *Atl. Oc.* **48 F4** 1 37N 7 27 E
Principe da Beira, *Brazil* **92 F6** 12 20S 64 30W
Prineville, *U.S.A.* **82 D3** 44 18N 120 51W
Prins Harald Kyst, *Antarctica* **5 D4** 70 0S 35 1 E
Prinsesse Astrid Kyst, *Antarctica* **5 D3** 70 45S 12 30 E
Prinsesse Ragnhild Kyst, *Antarctica* **5 D4** 70 15S 27 30 E
Prinzapolca, *Nic.* **88 D3** 13 20N 83 35W
Priozersk, *Russia* **24 B5** 61 2N 30 7 E
Pripet = Prypyat →, *Europe* **17 C16** 51 20N 30 15 E
Pripet Marshes, *Europe* **17 B15** 52 10N 28 10 E
Pripyat Marshes = Pripet Marshes, *Europe* **17 B15** 52 10N 28 10 E
Pripyats = Prypyat →, *Europe* **17 C16** 51 20N 30 15 E
Priština, *Yugoslavia* **21 C9** 42 40N 21 13 E
Privas, *France* **18 D6** 44 45N 4 37 E
Privolzhskaya Vozvyshennost, *Russia* **25 D8** 51 0N 46 0 E
Prizren, *Yugoslavia* **21 C9** 42 13N 20 45 E
Probolinggo, *Indonesia* **37 G15** 7 46S 113 13 E
Proctor, *U.S.A.* **79 C11** 43 40N 73 2W
Proddatur, *India* **40 M11** 14 45N 78 30 E
Prodhromos, *Cyprus* **23 E11** 34 57N 32 50 E
Profítis Ilías, *Greece* **23 C9** 36 17N 27 56 E
Profondeville, *Belgium* **15 D4** 50 23N 4 52 E
Progreso, *Mexico* **87 C7** 21 20N 89 40W
Progreso, *Yucatán, Mexico* **86 B4** 21 17N 89 40W
Prokopyevsk, *Russia* **26 D9** 54 0N 86 45 E
Prokuplje, *Serbia, Yug.* **21 C9** 43 16N 21 36 E
Prome = Pyè, *Burma* **41 K19** 18 49N 95 13 E
Prophet →, *Canada* **72 B4** 58 48N 122 40W
Prophet River, *Canada* **72 B4** 58 6N 122 43W
Propriá, *Brazil* **93 F11** 10 13S 36 51W
Proserpine, *Australia* **62 C4** 20 21S 148 36 E
Prosna →, *Poland* **17 B9** 52 6N 17 44 E
Prospect, *U.S.A.* **79 C9** 43 18N 75 9W
Prosser, *U.S.A.* **82 C4** 46 12N 119 46W
Prostějov, *Czech Rep.* **17 D9** 49 30N 17 9 E
Proston, *Australia* **63 D5** 26 8S 151 32 E
Provence, *France* **18 E6** 43 40N 5 46 E
Providence, *Ky., U.S.A.* **76 G2** 37 24N 87 46W
Providence, *R.I., U.S.A.* **79 E13** 41 49N 71 24W
Providence Bay, *Canada* **70 C3** 45 41N 82 15W
Providence Mts., *U.S.A.* **85 K11** 35 10N 115 15W
Providencia, I. de, *Colombia* **88 D3** 13 25N 81 26W
Provideniya, *Russia* **27 C19** 64 23N 173 18W
Provins, *France* **18 B5** 48 33N 3 15 E
Provo, *U.S.A.* **82 F8** 40 14N 111 39W
Provost, *Canada* **73 C6** 52 25N 110 20W
Prudhoe Bay, *U.S.A.* **68 A5** 70 18N 148 22W
Prudhoe I., *Australia* **62 C4** 21 19S 149 41 E
Prud'homme, *Canada* **73 C7** 52 20N 105 54W
Pruszków, *Poland* **17 B11** 52 9N 20 49 E
Prut →, *Romania* **17 F15** 45 28N 28 10 E
Pruzhany, *Belarus* **17 B13** 52 33N 24 28 E
Prydz B., *Antarctica* **5 C6** 69 0S 74 0 E
Pryluky, *Ukraine* **25 D5** 50 30N 32 24 E
Pryor, *U.S.A.* **81 G7** 36 19N 95 19W
Prypyat →, *Europe* **17 C16** 51 20N 30 15 E
Przemyśl, *Poland* **17 D12** 49 50N 22 45 E
Przhevalsk, *Kyrgyzstan* **26 E8** 42 30N 78 20 E
Psará, *Greece* **21 E11** 38 37N 25 38 E
Psira, *Greece* **23 D7** 35 12N 25 52 E
Pskov, *Russia* **24 C4** 57 50N 28 25 E
Pskovskoye, Ozero, *Russia* **9 H22** 58 0N 27 58 E
Ptich = Ptsich →, *Belarus* **17 B15** 52 9N 28 52 E
Ptolemaís, *Greece* **21 D9** 40 30N 21 43 E
Ptsich →, *Belarus* **17 B15** 52 9N 28 52 E
Pu Xian, *China* **34 F6** 36 24N 111 6 E
Pua, *Thailand* **38 C3** 19 11N 100 55 E
Puán, *Argentina* **94 D3** 37 30S 62 45W
Puan, *S. Korea* **35 G14** 35 44N 126 44 E
Pucallpa, *Peru* **92 E4** 8 25S 74 30W
Pudasjärvi, *Finland* **8 D22** 65 23N 26 53 E
Pudozh, *Russia* **24 B6** 61 48N 36 32 E
Pudukkottai, *India* **40 P11** 10 28N 78 47 E
Puebla, *Mexico* **87 D5** 19 3N 98 12W
Puebla □, *Mexico* **87 D5** 18 30N 98 0W
Pueblo, *U.S.A.* **80 F2** 38 16N 104 37W
Pueblo Hundido, *Chile* **94 B1** 26 20S 70 5W
Puelches, *Argentina* **94 D2** 38 5S 65 51W
Puelén, *Argentina* **94 D2** 37 32S 67 38W
Puente Alto, *Chile* **94 C1** 33 32S 70 35W
Puente-Genil, *Spain* **19 D3** 37 22N 4 47W
Puerco →, *U.S.A.* **83 J10** 34 22N 107 50W
Puerto, *Canary Is.* **22 F2** 28 5N 17 20W
Puerto Aisén, *Chile* **96 F2** 45 27S 73 0W
Puerto Ángel, *Mexico* **87 D5** 15 40N 96 29W
Puerto Arista, *Mexico* **87 D6** 15 56N 93 48W
Puerto Armuelles, *Panama* **88 E3** 8 20N 82 51W
Puerto Ayacucho, *Venezuela* **92 B5** 5 40N 67 35W
Puerto Barrios, *Guatemala* **88 C2** 15 40N 88 32W
Puerto Bermejo, *Argentina* **94 B4** 26 55S 58 34W
Puerto Bermúdez, *Peru* **92 F4** 10 20S 74 58W
Puerto Bolívar, *Ecuador* **92 D3** 3 19S 79 55W
Puerto Cabello, *Venezuela* **92 A5** 10 28N 68 1W
Puerto Cabezas, *Nic.* **88 D3** 14 0N 83 30W
Puerto Cabo Gracias á Dios, *Nic.* **88 D3** 15 0N 83 10W
Puerto Carreño, *Colombia* **92 B5** 6 12N 67 22W
Puerto Castilla, *Honduras* **88 C2** 16 0N 86 0W
Puerto Chicama, *Peru* **92 E3** 7 45S 79 20W
Puerto Coig, *Argentina* **96 G3** 50 54S 69 15W
Puerto Cortés, *Costa Rica* **88 E3** 8 55N 84 0W
Puerto Cortés, *Honduras* **88 C2** 15 51N 88 0W
Puerto Cumarebo, *Venezuela* **92 A5** 11 29N 69 30W
Puerto de Alcudia = Port d'Alcúdia, *Spain* **22 B10** 39 50N 3 7 E
Puerto de Andraitx, *Spain* **22 B9** 39 32N 2 23 E
Puerto de Cabrera, *Spain* **22 B9** 39 8N 2 56 E
Puerto de Gran Tarajal, *Canary Is.* **22 F5** 28 13N 14 1W
Puerto de la Cruz, *Canary Is.* **22 F3** 28 24N 16 32W
Puerto de Pozo Negro, *Canary Is.* **22 F6** 28 19N 13 55W
Puerto de Sóller = Port de Sóller, *Spain* **22 B9** 39 48N 2 42 E
Puerto del Carmen, *Canary Is.* **22 F6** 28 55N 13 38W
Puerto del Rosario, *Canary Is.* **22 F6** 28 30N 13 52W
Puerto Deseado, *Argentina* **96 F3** 47 55S 66 0W
Puerto Escondido, *Mexico* **87 D5** 15 50N 97 3W
Puerto Heath, *Bolivia* **92 F5** 12 34S 68 39W
Puerto Inírida, *Colombia* **92 C5** 3 53N 67 52W
Puerto Juárez, *Mexico* **87 C7** 21 11N 86 49W
Puerto La Cruz, *Venezuela* **92 A6** 10 13N 64 38W
Puerto Leguízamo, *Colombia* **92 D4** 0 12S 74 46W
Puerto Limón, *Colombia* **92 C4** 3 23N 73 30W
Puerto Lobos, *Argentina* **96 E3** 42 0S 65 3W
Puerto Madryn, *Argentina* **96 E3** 42 48S 65 4W
Puerto Maldonado, *Peru* **92 F5** 12 30S 69 10W
Puerto Manotí, *Cuba* **88 B4** 21 22N 76 50W
Puerto Montt, *Chile* **96 E2** 41 28S 73 0W
Puerto Morazán, *Nic.* **88 D2** 12 51N 87 11W
Puerto Morelos, *Mexico* **87 C7** 20 49N 86 52W
Puerto Natales, *Chile* **96 G2** 51 45S 72 15W
Puerto Padre, *Cuba* **88 B4** 21 13N 76 35W
Puerto Páez, *Venezuela* **92 B5** 6 13N 67 28W
Puerto Peñasco, *Mexico* **86 A2** 31 20N 113 33W
Puerto Pinasco, *Paraguay* **94 A4** 22 36S 57 50W
Puerto Plata, *Dom. Rep.* **89 C5** 19 48N 70 45W
Puerto Pollensa = Port de Pollença, *Spain* **22 B10** 39 54N 3 4 E
Puerto Princesa, *Phil.* **37 C5** 9 46N 118 45 E
Puerto Quepos, *Costa Rica* **88 E3** 9 29N 84 6W
Puerto Rico, *Canary Is.* **22 G4** 27 47N 15 42W
Puerto Rico ■, *W. Indies* **89 C6** 18 15N 66 45W
Puerto Rico Trench, *Atl. Oc.* **89 C6** 19 50N 66 0W
Puerto San Julián, *Argentina* **96 F3** 49 18S 67 43W
Puerto Sastre, *Paraguay* **94 A4** 22 2S 57 55W
Puerto Suárez, *Bolivia* **92 G7** 18 58S 57 52W
Puerto Vallarta, *Mexico* **86 C3** 20 36N 105 15W
Puerto Wilches, *Colombia* **92 B4** 7 21N 73 54W
Puertollano, *Spain* **19 C3** 38 43N 4 7W
Pueyrredón, L., *Argentina* **96 F2** 47 20S 72 0W
Puffin I., *Ireland* **13 E1** 51 50N 10 24W
Pugachev, *Russia* **24 D8** 52 0N 48 49 E
Pugal, *India* **42 E5** 28 30N 72 48 E
Puge, *Tanzania* **54 C3** 4 45S 33 11 E
Puget Sound, *U.S.A.* **82 C2** 47 50N 122 30W
Pugŏdong, *N. Korea* **35 C16** 42 5N 130 0 E
Pugu, *Tanzania* **54 D4** 6 55S 39 4 E
Pūgūnzī, *Iran* **45 E8** 25 49N 59 10 E
Puig Major, *Spain* **22 B9** 39 48N 2 47 E
Puigcerdà, *Spain* **19 A6** 42 24N 1 50 E
Puigpunyent, *Spain* **22 B9** 39 38N 2 32 E
Pujon-chŏsuji, *N. Korea* **35 D14** 40 35N 127 35 E
Pukaki L., *N.Z.* **59 L3** 44 4S 170 1 E
Pukapuka, *Cook Is.* **65 J11** 10 53S 165 49W
Pukaskwa Nat. Park, *Canada* **70 C2** 48 20N 86 0W
Pukatawagan, *Canada* **73 B8** 55 45N 101 20W
Pukchin, *N. Korea* **35 D13** 40 12N 125 45 E
Pukch'ŏng, *N. Korea* **35 D15** 40 14N 128 10 E
Pukekohe, *N.Z.* **59 G5** 37 12S 174 55 E
Pukhrayan, *India* **43 F8** 26 14N 79 51 E
Pula, *Croatia* **16 F7** 44 54N 13 57 E
Pulacayo, *Bolivia* **92 H5** 20 25S 66 41W
Pulandian, *China* **35 E11** 39 25N 121 58 E
Pularumpi, *Australia* **60 B5** 11 24S 130 26 E
Pulaski, *N.Y., U.S.A.* **79 C8** 43 34N 76 8W
Pulaski, *Tenn., U.S.A.* **77 H2** 35 12N 87 2W
Pulaski, *Va., U.S.A.* **76 G5** 37 3N 80 47W
Pulau →, *Indonesia* **37 F9** 5 50S 138 15 E
Puławy, *Poland* **17 C11** 51 23N 21 59 E
Pulga, *U.S.A.* **84 F5** 39 48N 121 29W
Pulicat L., *India* **40 N12** 13 40N 80 15 E
Pullman, *U.S.A.* **82 C5** 46 44N 117 10W
Pulo-Anna, *Pac. Oc.* **37 D8** 4 30N 132 5 E
Pulog, *Phil.* **37 A6** 16 40N 120 50 E
Pultusk, *Poland* **17 B11** 52 43N 21 6 E
Pumlumon Fawr, *U.K.* **11 E4** 52 28N 3 46W
Puná, I., *Ecuador* **92 D2** 2 55S 80 5W
Punakha, *Bhutan* **41 F16** 27 42N 89 52 E
Punasar, *India* **42 F5** 27 6N 73 6 E
Punata, *Bolivia* **92 G5** 17 32S 65 50W
Punch, *India* **43 C6** 33 48N 74 4 E
Punch →, *Pakistan* **42 C5** 33 12N 73 40 E
Pune, *India* **40 K8** 18 29N 73 57 E
P'ungsan, *N. Korea* **35 D15** 40 50N 128 9 E
Pungue, Ponte de, *Mozam.* **55 F3** 19 0S 34 0 E
Punjab □, *India* **42 D7** 31 0N 76 0 E
Punjab □, *Pakistan* **42 E6** 32 0N 74 30 E
Puno, *Peru* **92 G4** 15 55S 70 3W
Punpun →, *India* **43 G11** 25 31N 85 18 E
Punta Alta, *Argentina* **96 D4** 38 53S 62 4W
Punta Arenas, *Chile* **96 G2** 53 10S 71 0W
Punta de Díaz, *Chile* **94 B1** 28 0S 70 45W
Punta Gorda, *Belize* **87 D7** 16 10N 88 45W
Punta Gorda, *U.S.A.* **77 M5** 26 56N 82 3W
Punta Prieta, *Mexico* **86 B2** 28 58N 114 17W
Punta Prima, *Spain* **22 B11** 39 48N 4 16 E
Puntarenas, *Costa Rica* **88 E3** 10 0N 84 50W
Punto Fijo, *Venezuela* **92 A4** 11 50N 70 13W
Punxsatawney, *U.S.A.* **78 F6** 40 57N 78 59W
Puquio, *Peru* **92 F4** 14 45S 74 10W
Pur →, *Russia* **26 C8** 67 31N 77 55 E
Purace, Vol., *Colombia* **92 C3** 2 21N 76 23W
Puralia = Puruliya, *India* **43 H12** 23 17N 86 24 E
Puranpur, *India* **43 E9** 28 31N 80 9 E
Purbeck, Isle of, *U.K.* **11 G6** 50 39N 1 59W
Purcell, *U.S.A.* **81 H6** 35 1N 97 22W
Purcell Mts., *Canada* **72 D5** 49 55N 116 15W
Puri, *India* **41 K14** 19 50N 85 58 E
Purmerend, *Neths.* **15 B4** 52 32N 4 58 E
Purnia, *India* **43 G12** 25 45N 87 31 E
Pursat = Pouthisat, *Cambodia* **38 F4** 12 34N 103 50 E
Purukcahu, *Indonesia* **36 E4** 0 35S 114 35 E
Puruliya, *India* **43 H12** 23 17N 86 24 E
Purus →, *Brazil* **92 D6** 3 42S 61 28W
Purvis, *U.S.A.* **81 K10** 31 9N 89 25W
Purwa, *India* **43 F9** 26 28N 80 47 E
Purwakarta, *Indonesia* **37 G12** 6 35S 107 29 E
Purwodadi, *Indonesia* **37 G14** 7 7S 110 55 E
Purwokerto, *Indonesia* **37 G13** 7 25S 109 14 E
Puryŏng, *N. Korea* **35 C15** 42 5N 129 43 E
Pusa, *India* **43 G11** 25 59N 85 41 E
Pusan, *S. Korea* **35 G15** 35 5N 129 0 E
Pushkino, *Russia* **25 D8** 51 16N 47 0 E
Putahow L., *Canada* **73 B8** 59 54N 100 40W
Putao, *Burma* **41 F20** 27 28N 97 30 E
Putaruru, *N.Z.* **59 H5** 38 2S 175 50 E
Puthein Myit →, *Burma* **41 M19** 15 56N 94 18 E
Putignano, *Italy* **20 D7** 40 51N 17 7 E
Puting, Tanjung, *Indonesia* **36 E4** 3 31S 111 46 E
Putnam, *U.S.A.* **79 E13** 41 55N 71 55W
Putorana, Gory, *Russia* **27 C10** 69 0N 95 0 E
Puttalam, *Sri Lanka* **40 Q11** 8 1N 79 55 E
Puttgarden, *Germany* **16 A6** 54 30N 11 10 E
Putumayo →, *S. Amer.* **92 D5** 3 7S 67 58W
Putussibau, *Indonesia* **36 D4** 0 50N 112 56 E
Puvirnituq, *Canada* **69 B12** 60 2N 77 10W
Puy-de-Dôme, *France* **18 D5** 45 46N 2 57 E
Puyallup, *U.S.A.* **84 C4** 47 12N 122 18W
Puyang, *China* **34 G8** 35 40N 115 1 E
Pūzeh Rīg, *Iran* **45 E8** 27 20N 58 40 E
Pwani □, *Tanzania* **54 D4** 7 0S 39 0 E
Pweto, *Dem. Rep. of the Congo* **55 D2** 8 25S 28 51 E
Pwllheli, *U.K.* **10 E3** 52 53N 4 25W
Pya-ozero, *Russia* **24 A5** 66 5N 30 58 E
Pyapon, *Burma* **41 L19** 16 20N 95 40 E
Pyasina →, *Russia* **27 B9** 73 30N 87 0 E
Pyatigorsk, *Russia* **25 F7** 44 2N 43 6 E
Pyè, *Burma* **41 K19** 18 49N 95 13 E
Pyetrikaw, *Belarus* **17 B15** 52 11N 28 29 E
Pyhäjoki, *Finland* **8 D21** 64 28N 24 14 E
Pyinmana, *Burma* **41 K20** 19 45N 96 12 E
Pyla, C., *Cyprus* **23 E12** 34 56N 33 51 E
Pymatuning Reservoir, *U.S.A.* **78 E4** 41 30N 80 28W
Pyŏktong, *N. Korea* **35 D13** 40 50N 125 50 E
Pyŏnggang, *N. Korea* **35 E14** 38 24N 127 17 E
P'yŏngt'aek, *S. Korea* **35 F14** 37 1N 127 4 E
P'yŏngyang, *N. Korea* **35 E13** 39 0N 125 30 E
Pyote, *U.S.A.* **81 K3** 31 32N 103 8W
Pyramid L., *U.S.A.* **82 G4** 40 1N 119 35W
Pyramid Pk., *U.S.A.* **85 J10** 36 25N 116 37W
Pyrénées, *Europe* **18 E4** 42 45N 0 18 E
Pyu, *Burma* **41 K20** 18 30N 96 28 E

Q

Qaanaaq = Thule, *Greenland* **4 B4** 77 40N 69 0W
Qachasnek, *S. Africa* **57 E4** 30 6S 28 42 E
Qa'el Jafr, *Jordan* **47 E5** 30 20N 36 25 E
Qa'emābād, *Iran* **45 D9** 31 44N 60 2 E
Qā'emshahr, *Iran* **45 B7** 36 30N 52 53 E
Qagan Nur, *China* **34 C8** 43 30N 114 55 E
Qahar Youyi Zhongqi, *China* **34 D7** 41 12N 112 40 E
Qahremānshahr = Bākhtarān, *Iran* **44 C5** 34 23N 47 0 E
Qaidam Pendi, *China* **32 C4** 37 0N 95 0 E
Qajarīyeh, *Iran* **45 D6** 31 1N 48 22 E
Qala, Ras il, *Malta* **23 C1** 36 1N 14 20 E
Qala-i-Jadid = Spīn Búldak, *Afghan.* **42 D2** 31 1N 66 25 E
Qala Viala, *Pakistan* **42 D2** 30 49N 67 17 E
Qala Yangi, *Afghan.* **42 B2** 34 20N 66 30 E

Râs Timirist

Qal'at al Akhḍar, Si. Arabia 44 E3 28 0N 37 10 E
Qal'at Dīzah, Iraq 44 B5 36 11N 45 7 E
Qal'at Ṣaliḥ, Iraq 44 D5 31 31N 47 16 E
Qal'at Sukkar, Iraq 44 D5 31 51N 46 5 E
Qal'eh Shaharak, Afghan. 40 B4 34 10N 64 20 E
Qamdo, China 32 C4 31 15N 97 6 E
Qamruddin Karez, Pakistan 42 D3 31 45N 68 20 E
Qandahār, Afghan. 40 D4 31 32N 65 30 E
Qandahār □, Afghan. 40 D4 31 0N 65 0 E
Qapān, Iran 45 B7 37 40N 55 47 E
Qapshaghay, Kazakstan 26 E8 43 51N 77 14 E
Qaqortoq = Julianehåb,
Greenland 4 C5 60 43N 46 0W
Qara Qash →, India 43 B8 35 0N 78 30 E
Qarabutaq, Kazakstan 26 E7 49 59N 60 14 E
Qaraghandy, Kazakstan 26 E8 49 50N 73 10 E
Qārah, Si. Arabia 44 D4 29 55N 40 3 E
Qarataū, Kazakstan 26 E8 43 10N 70 28 E
Qareh →, Iran 44 B5 39 25N 47 22 E
Qareh Tekān, Iran 45 B6 36 38N 49 29 E
Qarqan He →, China 32 C3 39 30N 88 30 E
Qarqaraly, Kazakstan 26 E8 49 26N 75 30 E
Qarshi, Uzbekistan 26 F7 38 53N 65 48 E
Qartabā, Lebanon 47 A4 34 4N 35 50 E
Qaryat al Gharab, Iraq 44 D5 31 27N 44 48 E
Qaryat al 'Ulyā, Si. Arabia 44 E5 27 33N 47 42 E
Qasr 'Amra, Jordan 44 D3 31 48N 36 35 E
Qaṣr-e Qand, Iran 45 E9 26 15N 60 45 E
Qasr Farâfra, Egypt 51 C11 27 0N 28 1 E
Qatanā, Syria 47 B5 33 26N 36 4 E
Qatar ■, Asia 45 E6 25 30N 51 15 E
Qatlīsh, Iran 45 B8 37 50N 57 19 E
Qattâra, Munkhafed el,
Egypt 51 C11 29 30N 27 30 E
Qattâra Depression =
Qattâra, Munkhafed el,
Egypt 51 C11 29 30N 27 30 E
Qawām al Ḥamzah, Iraq 44 D5 31 43N 44 58 E
Qāyen, Iran 45 C8 33 40N 59 10 E
Qazaqstan = Kazakstan ■,
Asia 26 E8 50 0N 70 0 E
Qazimämmäd, Azerbaijan 45 A6 40 3N 49 0 E
Qazvin, Iran 45 B6 36 15N 50 0 E
Qena, Egypt 51 C12 26 10N 32 43 E
Qeqertarsuaq = Disko,
Greenland 4 C5 69 45N 53 30W
Qeqertarsuaq = Godhavn,
Greenland 4 C5 69 15N 53 38W
Qeshlāq, Iran 44 C5 34 55N 46 28 E
Qeshm, Iran 45 E8 26 55N 56 10 E
Qeys, Iran 45 E7 26 32N 53 58 E
Qezel Owzen →, Iran 45 B6 36 45N 49 22 E
Qezi'ot, Israel 47 E3 30 52N 34 26 E
Qi Xian, China 34 G8 34 40N 114 48 E
Qian Gorlos, China 35 B13 45 5N 124 42 E
Qian Xian, China 34 G5 34 31N 108 15 E
Qianyang, China 34 G4 34 40N 107 8 E
Qibā', Si. Arabia 44 E5 27 24N 44 20 E
Qikiqtarjuaq, Canada 69 B13 67 33N 63 0W
Qila Safed, Pakistan 40 E2 29 0N 61 30 E
Qila Saifullāh, Pakistan 42 D3 30 45N 68 17 E
Qilian Shan, China 32 C4 38 30N 96 0 E
Qin He →, China 34 G7 35 1N 113 22 E
Qin Ling = Qinling Shandi,
China 34 H5 33 50N 108 10 E
Qin'an, China 34 G3 34 48N 105 40 E
Qing Xian, China 34 E9 38 35N 116 45 E
Qingcheng, China 35 F9 37 15N 117 40 E
Qingdao, China 35 F11 36 5N 120 20 E
Qingfeng, China 34 G8 35 52N 115 8 E
Qinghai □, China 32 C4 36 0N 98 0 E
Qinghai Hu, China 32 C5 36 40N 100 10 E
Qinghecheng, China 35 D13 41 28N 124 15 E
Qinghemen, China 35 D11 41 48N 121 25 E
Qingjian, China 34 F6 37 8N 110 8 E
Qingjiang = Huaiyin, China 35 H10 33 30N 119 2 E
Qingshui, China 34 G4 34 48N 106 8 E
Qingshuihe, China 34 E6 39 55N 111 35 E
Qingtongxia Shuiku, China 34 F3 37 50N 105 58 E
Qingxu, China 34 F7 37 34N 112 22 E
Qingyang, China 34 F4 36 2N 107 55 E
Qingyuan, China 35 C13 42 10N 124 55 E
Qingyun, China 35 F9 37 45N 117 20 E
Qinhuangdao, China 35 E10 39 56N 119 30 E
Qinling Shandi, China 34 H5 33 50N 108 10 E
Qinshui, China 34 G7 35 40N 112 8 E
Qinyang = Jiyuan, China 34 G7 35 7N 112 57 E
Qinyuan, China 34 F7 36 29N 112 20 E
Qinzhou, China 32 D5 21 58N 108 38 E
Qionghai, China 38 C8 19 15N 110 26 E
Qiongzhou Haixia, China 38 B8 20 10N 110 15 E
Qiqihar, China 27 E13 47 26N 124 0 E
Qiraîya, W. →, Egypt 47 E3 30 27N 34 0 E
Qiryat Ata, Israel 47 C4 32 47N 35 6 E
Qiryat Gat, Israel 47 D3 31 32N 34 46 E
Qiryat Mal'akhi, Israel 47 D3 31 44N 34 44 E
Qiryat Shemona, Israel 47 B4 33 13N 35 35 E
Qiryat Yam, Israel 47 C4 32 51N 35 4 E
Qishan, China 34 G4 34 25N 107 38 E
Qitai, China 32 B3 44 2N 89 35 E
Qixia, China 35 F11 37 17N 120 52 E
Qızılağac Körfäzi, Azerbaijan 45 B6 39 9N 49 0 E
Qojūr, Iran 44 B5 36 12N 47 55 E
Qom, Iran 45 C6 34 40N 51 0 E
Qomolangma Feng =
Everest, Mt., Nepal 43 E12 28 5N 86 58 E
Qomsheh, Iran 45 D6 32 0N 51 55 E
Qostanay, Kazakstan 26 D7 53 10N 63 35 E
Quabbin Reservoir, U.S.A. 79 D12 42 20N 72 20W
Quairading, Australia 61 F2 32 0S 117 21 E
Quakertown, U.S.A. 79 F9 40 26N 75 21W
Qualicum Beach, Canada 72 D4 49 22N 124 26W
Quambatook, Australia 63 F3 35 49S 143 34 E
Quambone, Australia 63 E4 30 57S 147 53 E
Quamby, Australia 62 C3 20 22S 140 17 E
Quan Long = Ca Mau,
Vietnam 39 H5 9 7N 105 8 E
Quanah, U.S.A. 81 H5 34 18N 99 44W
Quang Ngai, Vietnam 38 E7 15 13N 108 58 E
Quang Tri, Vietnam 38 D6 16 45N 107 13 E
Quantock Hills, U.K. 11 F4 51 8N 3 10W
Quanzhou, China 33 D6 24 55N 118 34 E
Qu'Appelle, Canada 73 C8 50 33N 103 53W
Quaqtaq, Canada 69 B13 60 55N 69 40W
Quaraí, Brazil 94 C4 30 15S 56 20W
Quartu Sant'Élena, Italy 20 E3 39 15N 9 10 E
Quartzsite, U.S.A. 85 M12 33 40N 114 13W
Quatsino Sd., Canada 72 C3 50 25N 127 58W
Quba, Azerbaijan 25 F8 41 21N 48 32 E
Qūchān, Iran 45 B8 37 10N 58 27 E
Queanbeyan, Australia 63 F4 35 17S 149 14 E
Québec, Canada 71 C5 46 52N 71 13W
Québec □, Canada 71 C6 48 0N 74 0W
Queen Alexandra Ra.,
Antarctica 5 E11 85 0S 170 0 E
Queen Charlotte City,
Canada 72 C2 53 15N 132 2W
Queen Charlotte Is., Canada 72 C2 53 20N 132 10W
Queen Charlotte Sd.,
Canada 72 C3 51 0N 128 0W
Queen Charlotte Strait,
Canada 72 C3 50 45N 127 10W
Queen Elizabeth Is., Canada 66 B10 76 0N 95 0W
Queen Elizabeth Nat. Park,
Uganda 54 C3 0 0 30 0 E
Queen Mary Land,
Antarctica 5 D7 70 0S 95 0 E
Queen Maud G., Canada 68 B9 68 15N 102 30W
Queen Maud Land,
Antarctica 5 D3 72 30S 12 0 E
Queen Maud Mts.,
Antarctica 5 E13 86 0S 160 0W
Queens Chan., Australia 60 C4 15 0S 129 30 E
Queenscliff, Australia 63 F3 38 16S 144 39 E
Queensland □, Australia 62 C3 22 0S 142 0 E
Queenstown, Australia 62 G4 42 4S 145 35 E
Queenstown, N.Z. 59 L2 45 1S 168 40 E
Queenstown, S. Africa 56 E4 31 52S 26 52 E
Queets, U.S.A. 84 C2 47 32N 124 20W
Queguay Grande →,
Uruguay 94 C4 32 9S 58 9W
Queimadas, Brazil 93 F11 11 0S 39 38W
Quelimane, Mozam. 55 F4 17 53S 36 58 E
Quellón, Chile 96 E2 43 7S 73 37W
Quelpart = Cheju do,
S. Korea 35 H14 33 29N 126 34 E
Quemado, N. Mex., U.S.A. 83 J9 34 20N 108 30W
Quemado, Tex., U.S.A. 81 L4 28 58N 100 35W
Quemú-Quemú, Argentina 94 D3 36 3S 63 36W
Quequén, Argentina 94 D4 38 30S 58 30W
Querétaro, Mexico 86 C4 20 36N 100 23W
Querétaro □, Mexico 86 C5 20 30N 100 0W
Queshan, China 34 H8 32 55N 114 2 E
Quesnel, Canada 72 C4 53 0N 122 30W
Quesnel →, Canada 72 C4 52 58N 122 29W
Quesnel L., Canada 72 C4 52 30N 121 20W
Questa, U.S.A. 83 H11 36 42N 105 36W
Quetico Prov. Park, Canada 70 C1 48 30N 91 45W
Quetta, Pakistan 42 D2 30 15N 66 55 E
Quezaltenango, Guatemala 88 D1 14 50N 91 30W
Quezon City, Phil. 37 B6 14 38N 121 0 E
Qufār, Si. Arabia 44 E4 27 26N 41 37 E
Qui Nhon, Vietnam 38 F7 13 40N 109 13 E
Quibaxe, Angola 52 F2 8 24S 14 27 E
Quibdo, Colombia 92 B3 5 42N 76 40W
Quiberon, France 18 C2 47 29N 3 9W
Quiet L., Canada 72 A2 61 5N 133 5W
Quiindy, Paraguay 94 B4 25 58S 57 14W
Quila, Mexico 86 C3 24 23N 107 13W
Quilán, C., Chile 96 E2 43 15S 74 30W
Quilcene, U.S.A. 84 C4 47 49N 122 53W
Quilimarí, Chile 94 C1 32 5S 71 30W
Quilino, Argentina 94 C3 30 14S 64 29W
Quill Lakes, Canada 73 C8 51 55N 104 13W
Quillabamba, Peru 92 F4 12 50S 72 50W
Quillagua, Chile 94 A2 21 40S 69 40W
Quillaicillo, Chile 94 C1 31 17S 71 40W
Quillota, Chile 94 C1 32 54S 71 16W
Quilmes, Argentina 94 C4 34 43S 58 15W
Quilon, India 40 Q10 8 50N 76 38 E
Quilpie, Australia 63 D3 26 35S 144 11 E
Quilpué, Chile 94 C1 33 5S 71 33W
Quilua, Mozam. 55 F4 16 17S 39 54 E
Quimilí, Argentina 94 B3 27 40S 62 30W
Quimper, France 18 B1 48 0N 4 9W
Quimperlé, France 18 C2 47 53N 3 33W
Quinault →, U.S.A. 84 C2 47 21N 124 18W
Quincy, Calif., U.S.A. 84 F6 39 56N 120 57W
Quincy, Fla., U.S.A. 77 K3 30 35N 84 34W
Quincy, Ill., U.S.A. 80 F9 39 56N 91 23W
Quincy, Mass., U.S.A. 79 D14 42 15N 71 0W
Quincy, Wash., U.S.A. 82 C4 47 22N 119 56W
Quines, Argentina 94 C2 32 13S 65 48W
Quinga, Mozam. 55 F5 15 49S 40 15 E
Quinns Rocks, Australia 61 F2 31 40S 115 42 E
Quintana Roo □, Mexico 87 D7 19 0N 88 0W
Quintanar de la Orden,
Spain 19 C4 39 36N 3 5W
Quintero, Chile 94 C1 32 45S 71 30W
Quirihue, Chile 94 D1 36 15S 72 35W
Quirindi, Australia 63 E5 31 28S 150 40 E
Quirinópolis, Brazil 93 G8 18 32S 50 30W
Quissanga, Mozam. 55 E5 12 24S 40 28 E
Quitilipi, Argentina 94 B3 26 50S 60 13W
Quitman, U.S.A. 77 K4 30 47N 83 34W
Quito, Ecuador 92 D3 0 15S 78 35W
Quixadá, Brazil 93 D11 4 55S 39 0W
Quixaxe, Mozam. 55 F5 15 17S 40 4 E
Qul'ân, Jazâ'ir, Egypt 44 E2 24 22N 35 31 E
Qumbu, S. Africa 57 E4 31 10S 28 48 E
Quneitra, Syria 47 B4 33 7N 35 48 E
Qŭnghirot, Uzbekistan 26 E6 43 6N 58 54 E
Quoin I., Australia 60 B4 14 54S 129 32 E
Quoin Pt., S. Africa 56 E2 34 46S 19 37 E
Quorn, Australia 63 E2 32 25S 138 5 E
Qŭqon, Uzbekistan 26 E8 40 30N 70 57 E
Qurnat as Sawdā', Lebanon 47 A5 34 18N 36 6 E
Quṣaybā', Si. Arabia 44 E4 26 53N 43 35 E
Qusaybah, Iraq 44 C4 34 24N 40 59 E
Quseir, Egypt 44 E2 26 7N 34 16 E
Qūshchī, Iran 44 B5 37 59N 45 3 E
Quthing, Lesotho 57 E4 30 25S 27 36 E
Qūṭīābād, Iran 45 C6 35 47N 48 30 E
Quwo, China 34 G6 35 38N 111 25 E
Quyang, China 34 E8 38 35N 114 40 E
Quynh Nhai, Vietnam 38 B4 21 49N 103 33 E
Quyon, Canada 79 A8 45 31N 76 14W
Quzhou, China 33 D6 28 57N 118 54 E
Quzi, China 34 F4 36 20N 107 20 E
Qyzylorda, Kazakstan 26 E7 44 48N 65 28 E

R

Ra, Ko, Thailand 39 H2 9 13N 98 16 E
Raahe, Finland 8 D21 64 40N 24 28 E
Raalte, Neths. 15 B6 52 23N 6 16 E
Raasay, U.K. 12 D2 57 25N 6 4W
Raasay, Sd. of, U.K. 12 D2 57 30N 6 8W
Raba, Indonesia 37 F5 8 36S 118 55 E
Rába →, Hungary 17 E9 47 38N 17 38 E
Rabai, Kenya 54 C4 3 50S 39 31 E
Rabat, Malta 23 D1 35 53N 14 25 E
Rabat, Morocco 50 B4 34 2N 6 48W
Rabaul, Papua N. G. 64 H7 4 24S 152 18 E
Rābigh, Si. Arabia 46 C2 22 50N 39 5 E
Râbniţa, Moldova 17 E15 47 45N 29 0 E
Rābor, Iran 45 D8 29 17N 56 55 E
Race, C., Canada 71 C9 46 40N 53 5W
Rach Gia, Vietnam 39 G5 10 5N 105 5 E
Rachid, Mauritania 50 E3 18 48N 11 41W
Racibórz, Poland 17 C10 50 7N 18 18 E
Racine, U.S.A. 76 D2 42 41N 87 51W
Rackerby, U.S.A. 84 F5 39 26N 121 22W
Radama, Nosy, Madag. 57 A8 14 0S 47 47 E
Radama, Saikanosy, Madag. 57 A8 14 16S 47 53 E
Rădăuţi, Romania 17 E13 47 50N 25 59 E
Radcliff, U.S.A. 76 G3 37 51N 85 57W
Radekhiv, Ukraine 17 C13 50 25N 24 32 E
Radekhov = Radekhiv,
Ukraine 17 C13 50 25N 24 32 E
Radford, U.S.A. 76 G5 37 8N 80 34W
Radhanpur, India 42 H4 23 50N 71 38 E
Radhwa, Jabal, Si. Arabia 44 E3 24 34N 38 18 E
Radisson, Canada 70 B4 53 47N 77 37W
Radisson, Sask., Canada 73 C7 52 30N 107 20W
Radium Hot Springs,
Canada 72 C5 50 35N 116 2W
Radnor Forest, U.K. 11 E4 52 17N 3 10W
Radom, Poland 17 C11 51 23N 21 12 E
Radomsko, Poland 17 C10 51 5N 19 28 E
Radomyshl, Ukraine 17 C15 50 30N 29 12 E
Radstock, C., Australia 63 E1 33 12S 134 20 E
Radviliškis, Lithuania 9 J20 55 49N 23 33 E
Radville, Canada 73 D8 49 30N 104 15W
Rae, Canada 72 A5 62 50N 116 3W
Rae Bareli, India 43 F9 26 18N 81 20 E
Rae Isthmus, Canada 69 B11 66 40N 87 30W
Raeren, Belgium 15 D6 50 41N 6 7 E
Raeside, L., Australia 61 E3 29 20S 122 0 E
Raetihi, N.Z. 59 H5 39 25S 175 17 E
Rafaela, Argentina 94 C3 31 10S 61 30W
Rafah, Gaza Strip 47 D3 31 18N 34 14 E
Rafai, C.A.R. 54 B1 4 59N 23 58 E
Rafḥā, Si. Arabia 44 D4 29 35N 43 35 E
Rafsanjān, Iran 45 D8 30 30N 56 5 E
Raft Pt., Australia 60 C3 16 4S 124 26 E
Raga, Sudan 51 G11 8 28N 25 41 E
Ragachow, Belarus 17 B16 53 8N 30 5 E
Ragama, Sri Lanka 40 R11 7 0N 79 50 E
Ragged, Mt., Australia 61 F3 33 27S 123 25 E
Raghunathpalli, India 43 H11 22 14N 84 48 E
Raghunathpur, India 43 H12 23 33N 86 40 E
Raglan, N.Z. 59 G5 37 55S 174 55 E
Ragusa, Italy 20 F6 36 55N 14 44 E
Raha, Indonesia 37 E6 4 55S 123 0 E
Rahaeng = Tak, Thailand 38 D2 16 52N 99 8 E
Rahatgarh, India 43 H8 23 47N 78 22 E
Raḥimah, Si. Arabia 45 E6 26 42N 50 4 E
Rahimyar Khan, Pakistan 42 E4 28 30N 70 25 E
Rāhjerd, Iran 45 C6 34 22N 50 22 E
Rahon, India 42 D7 31 3N 76 7 E
Raichur, India 40 L10 16 10N 77 20 E
Raiganj, India 43 G13 25 37N 88 10 E
Raigarh, India 41 J13 21 56N 83 25 E
Raijua, Indonesia 37 F6 10 37S 121 36 E
Raikot, India 42 D6 30 41N 75 42 E
Railton, Australia 62 G4 41 25S 146 28 E
Rainbow Lake, Canada 72 B5 58 30N 119 23W
Rainier, U.S.A. 84 D4 46 53N 122 41W
Rainier, Mt., U.S.A. 84 D5 46 52N 121 46W
Rainy L., Canada 73 D10 48 42N 93 10W
Rainy River, Canada 73 D10 48 43N 94 29W
Raippaluoto, Finland 8 E19 63 13N 21 14 E
Raipur, India 41 J12 21 17N 81 45 E
Raisen, India 42 H8 23 20N 77 48 E
Raisio, Finland 9 F20 60 28N 22 11 E
Raj Nandgaon, India 41 J12 21 5N 81 5 E
Raj Nilgiri, India 43 J12 21 28N 86 46 E
Raja, Ujung, Indonesia 36 D1 3 40N 96 25 E
Raja Ampat, Kepulauan,
Indonesia 37 E8 0 30S 130 0 E
Rajahmundry, India 41 L12 17 1N 81 48 E
Rajang →, Malaysia 36 D4 2 30N 112 0 E
Rajanpur, Pakistan 42 E4 29 6N 70 19 E
Rajapalaiyam, India 40 Q10 9 25N 77 35 E
Rajasthan □, India 42 F5 26 45N 73 30 E
Rajasthan Canal, India 42 F5 28 0N 72 0 E
Rajauri, India 43 C6 33 25N 74 21 E
Rajgarh, Mad. P., India 42 G7 24 2N 76 45 E
Rajgarh, Raj., India 42 F7 27 14N 76 38 E
Rajgarh, Raj., India 42 E6 28 40N 75 25 E
Rajgir, India 43 G11 25 2N 85 25 E
Rajkot, India 42 H4 22 15N 70 56 E
Rajmahal Hills, India 43 G12 24 30N 87 30 E
Rajpipla, India 40 J8 21 50N 73 30 E
Rajpur, India 42 H6 22 18N 74 21 E
Rajpura, India 42 D7 30 25N 76 32 E
Rajshahi, Bangla. 41 G16 24 22N 88 39 E
Rajshahi □, Bangla. 43 G13 25 0N 89 0 E
Rajula, India 42 J4 21 3N 71 26 E
Rakaia, N.Z. 59 K4 43 45S 172 1 E
Rakaia →, N.Z. 59 K4 43 36S 172 15 E
Rakan, Ra's, Qatar 45 E6 26 10N 51 20 E
Rakaposhi, Pakistan 43 A6 36 10N 74 25 E
Rakata, Pulau, Indonesia 36 F3 6 10S 105 20 E
Rakhiv, Ukraine 17 D13 48 3N 24 12 E
Rakhni, Pakistan 42 D3 30 4N 69 56 E
Rakhni →, Pakistan 42 E3 29 31N 69 36 E
Rakitnoye, Russia 30 B7 45 36N 134 17 E
Rakops, Botswana 56 C3 21 1S 24 28 E
Rakvere, Estonia 9 G22 59 20N 26 25 E
Raleigh, U.S.A. 77 H6 35 47N 78 39W
Raleigh B., U.S.A. 75 D11 34 50N 76 15W
Ralls, U.S.A. 81 J4 33 41N 101 24W
Ralston, U.S.A. 78 E8 41 30N 76 57W
Ram →, Canada 72 A4 62 1N 123 41W
Rām Allāh, West Bank 47 D4 31 55N 35 10 E
Ram Hd., Australia 63 F4 37 47S 149 30 E
Rama, Nic. 88 D3 12 9N 84 15W
Ramakona, India 43 J8 21 43N 78 50 E
Raman, Thailand 39 J3 6 29N 101 18 E
Ramanathapuram, India 40 Q11 9 25N 78 55 E
Ramanetaka, B. de, Madag. 57 A8 14 13S 47 52 E
Ramanujganj, India 43 H10 23 48N 83 42 E
Ramat Gan, Israel 47 C3 32 4N 34 48 E
Ramatlhabama, S. Africa 56 D4 25 37S 25 33 E
Ramban, India 43 C6 33 14N 75 12 E
Rambipuji, Indonesia 37 H15 8 12S 113 37 E
Ramechhap, Nepal 43 F12 27 25N 86 10 E
Ramganga →, India 43 F8 27 5N 79 58 E
Ramgarh, Bihar, India 43 H11 23 40N 85 35 E
Ramgarh, Raj., India 42 F6 27 16N 75 14 E
Ramgarh, Raj., India 42 F4 27 30N 70 36 E
Rāmhormoz, Iran 45 D6 31 15N 49 35 E
Ramīān, Iran 45 B7 37 3N 55 16 E
Ramingining, Australia 62 A2 12 19S 135 3 E
Ramla, Israel 47 D3 31 55N 34 52 E
Ramnad =
Ramanathapuram, India 40 Q11 9 25N 78 55 E
Ramnagar, India 43 E8 29 24N 79 7 E
Ramnagar,
Jammu & Kashmir, India 43 C6 32 47N 75 18 E
Râmnicu Sărat, Romania 17 F14 45 26N 27 3 E
Râmnicu Vâlcea, Romania 17 F13 45 9N 24 21 E
Ramona, U.S.A. 85 M10 33 2N 116 52W
Ramore, Canada 70 C3 48 30N 80 25W
Ramotswa, Botswana 56 C4 24 50S 25 52 E
Rampur, H.P., India 42 D7 31 26N 77 43 E
Rampur, Mad. P., India 42 H5 23 25N 73 53 E
Rampur, Ut. P., India 43 E8 28 50N 79 5 E
Rampur Hat, India 43 G12 24 10N 87 50 E
Rampura, India 42 G6 24 30N 75 27 E
Ramrama Tola, India 43 J8 21 52N 79 55 E
Ramree I. = Ramree Kyun,
Burma 41 K19 19 0N 94 0 E
Ramree Kyun, Burma 41 K19 19 0N 94 0 E
Rāmsar, Iran 45 B6 36 53N 50 41 E
Ramsey, U.K. 10 C3 54 20N 4 22W
Ramsey, U.S.A. 79 E10 41 4N 74 9W
Ramsey L., Canada 70 C3 47 13N 82 15W
Ramsgate, U.K. 11 F9 51 20N 1 25 E
Ramtek, India 40 J11 21 20N 79 15 E
Rana Pratap Sagar Dam,
India 42 G6 24 58N 75 38 E
Ranaghat, India 43 H13 23 15N 88 35 E
Ranahu, Pakistan 42 G3 25 55N 69 45 E
Ranau, Malaysia 36 C5 6 2N 116 40 E
Rancagua, Chile 94 C1 34 10S 70 50W
Rancheria →, Canada 72 A3 60 13N 129 7W
Ranchester, U.S.A. 82 D10 44 54N 107 10W
Ranchi, India 43 H11 23 19N 85 27 E
Rancho Cucamonga, U.S.A. 85 L9 34 10N 117 30W
Randalstown, U.K. 13 B5 54 45N 6 19W
Randers, Denmark 9 H14 56 29N 10 1 E
Randfontein, S. Africa 57 D4 26 8S 27 45 E
Randle, U.S.A. 84 D5 46 32N 121 57W
Randolph, Mass., U.S.A. 79 D13 42 10N 71 2W
Randolph, N.Y., U.S.A. 78 D6 42 10N 78 59W
Randolph, Utah, U.S.A. 82 F8 41 40N 111 11W
Randolph, Vt., U.S.A. 79 C12 43 55N 72 40W
Randsburg, U.S.A. 85 K9 35 22N 117 39W
Råne älv →, Sweden 8 D20 65 50N 22 20 E
Rangae, Thailand 39 J3 6 19N 101 44 E
Rangaunu B., N.Z. 59 F4 34 51S 173 15 E
Rangeley, U.S.A. 79 B14 44 58N 70 39W
Rangeley L., U.S.A. 79 B14 44 55N 70 43W
Rangely, U.S.A. 82 F9 40 5N 108 48W
Ranger, U.S.A. 81 J5 32 28N 98 41W
Rangia, India 41 F17 26 28N 91 38 E
Rangiora, N.Z. 59 K4 43 19S 172 36 E
Rangitaiki →, N.Z. 59 G6 37 54S 176 49 E
Rangitata →, N.Z. 59 K3 43 45S 171 15 E
Rangkasbitung, Indonesia 37 G12 6 21S 106 15 E
Rangon →, Burma 41 L20 16 28N 96 40 E
Rangoon, Burma 41 L20 16 45N 96 20 E
Rangpur, Bangla. 41 G16 25 42N 89 22 E
Rangsit, Thailand 38 F3 13 59N 100 37 E
Ranibennur, India 40 M9 14 35N 75 30 E
Raniganj, Ut. P., India 43 F9 27 3N 82 13 E
Raniganj, W. Bengal, India 41 H15 23 40N 87 5 E
Ranikhet, India 43 E8 29 39N 79 25 E
Raniwara, India 40 G8 24 50N 72 10 E
Rāniyah, Iraq 44 B5 36 15N 44 53 E
Ranka, India 43 H10 23 59N 83 47 E
Ranken →, Australia 62 C2 20 31S 137 36 E
Rankin, U.S.A. 81 K4 31 13N 101 56W
Rankin Inlet, Canada 68 B10 62 30N 93 0W
Rankins Springs, Australia 63 E4 33 49S 146 14 E
Rannoch, L., U.K. 12 E4 56 41N 4 20W
Rannoch Moor, U.K. 12 E4 56 38N 4 48W
Ranobe, Helodranon' i,
Madag. 57 C7 23 3S 43 33 E
Ranohira, Madag. 57 C8 22 29S 45 24 E
Ranomafana, Toamasina,
Madag. 57 B8 18 57S 48 50 E
Ranomafana, Toliara,
Madag. 57 C8 24 34S 47 0 E
Ranong, Thailand 39 H2 9 56N 98 40 E
Rānsa, Iran 45 C6 33 39N 48 18 E
Ransiki, Indonesia 37 E8 1 30S 134 10 E
Rantauprapat, Indonesia 36 D1 2 15N 99 50 E
Rantemario, Indonesia 37 E5 3 15S 119 57 E
Rantoul, U.S.A. 76 E1 40 19N 88 9W
Raoyang, China 34 E8 38 15N 115 45 E
Rapa, Pac. Oc. 65 K13 27 35S 144 20W
Rapallo, Italy 18 D8 44 21N 9 14 E
Rapar, India 42 H4 23 34N 70 38 E
Rāpch, Iran 45 E8 25 40N 59 15 E
Raper, C., Canada 69 B13 69 44N 67 6W
Rapid City, U.S.A. 80 D3 44 5N 103 14W
Rapid River, U.S.A. 76 C2 45 55N 86 58W
Rapla, Estonia 9 G21 59 1N 24 52 E
Rapti →, India 43 F10 26 18N 83 41 E
Raquette →, U.S.A. 79 B10 45 0N 74 42W
Raquette Lake, U.S.A. 79 C10 43 49N 74 40W
Rarotonga, Cook Is. 65 K12 21 30S 160 0W
Ra's al 'Ayn, Syria 44 B4 36 45N 40 12 E
Ra's al Khaymah, U.A.E. 45 E8 25 50N 55 59 E
Ra's an Naqb, Jordan 47 F4 30 0N 35 29 E
Ras Dashen, Ethiopia 46 E2 13 8N 38 26 E
Râs Timirist, Mauritania 50 E2 19 21N 16 30W

Rasca, Pta. de la

Rasca, Pta. de la, *Canary Is.* **22 G3** 27 59N 16 41W
Raseiniai, *Lithuania* **9 J20** 55 25N 23 5 E
Rashmi, *India* **42 G6** 25 4N 74 22 E
Rasht, *Iran* **45 B6** 37 20N 49 40 E
Rasi Salai, *Thailand* **38 E5** 15 20N 104 9 E
Rason L., *Australia* **61 E3** 28 45S 124 25 E
Rasra, *India* **43 G10** 25 50N 83 50 E
Rasul, *Pakistan* **42 C5** 32 42N 73 34 E
Rat Buri, *Thailand* **38 F2** 13 30N 99 54 E
Rat Islands, *U.S.A.* **68 C1** 52 0N 178 0 E
Rat L., *Canada* **73 B9** 56 10N 99 40W
Ratangarh, *India* **42 E6** 28 5N 74 35 E
Raţāwī, *Iraq* **44 D5** 30 38N 47 13 E
Ratcatchers L., *Australia* **63 E3** 32 38S 143 10 E
Rath, *India* **43 G8** 25 36N 79 37 E
Rath Luirc, *Ireland* **13 D3** 52 21N 8 40W
Rathdrum, *Ireland* **13 D5** 52 56N 6 14W
Rathenow, *Germany* **16 B7** 52 37N 12 19 E
Rathkeale, *Ireland* **13 D3** 52 32N 8 56W
Rathlin I., *U.K.* **13 A5** 55 18N 6 14W
Rathmelton, *Ireland* **13 A4** 55 2N 7 38W
Ratibor = Racibórz, *Poland* **17 C10** 50 7N 18 18 E
Ratlam, *India* **42 H6** 23 20N 75 0 E
Ratnagiri, *India* **40 L8** 16 57N 73 18 E
Ratodero, *Pakistan* **42 F3** 27 48N 68 18 E
Raton, *U.S.A.* **81 G2** 36 54N 104 24W
Rattaphum, *Thailand* **39 J3** 7 8N 100 16 E
Rattray Hd., *U.K.* **12 D7** 57 38N 1 50W
Ratz, Mt., *Canada* **72 B2** 57 23N 132 12W
Raub, *Malaysia* **39 L3** 3 47N 101 52 E
Rauch, *Argentina* **94 D4** 36 45S 59 5W
Raudales de Malpaso, *Mexico* **87 D6** 17 30N 23 30W
Raufarhöfn, *Iceland* **8 C6** 66 27N 15 57W
Raufoss, *Norway* **9 F14** 60 44N 10 37 E
Raukumara Ra., *N.Z.* **59 H6** 38 5S 177 55 E
Rauma, *Finland* **9 F19** 61 10N 21 30 E
Raurkela, *India* **43 H11** 22 14N 84 50 E
Rausu-Dake, *Japan* **30 B12** 44 4N 145 7 E
Rava-Ruska, *Poland* **17 C12** 50 15N 23 42 E
Rava Russkaya = Rava-Ruska, *Poland* **17 C12** 50 15N 23 42 E
Ravalli, *U.S.A.* **82 C6** 47 17N 114 11W
Ravānsar, *Iran* **44 C5** 34 43N 46 40 E
Rāvar, *Iran* **45 D8** 31 20N 56 51 E
Ravena, *U.S.A.* **79 D11** 42 28N 73 49W
Ravenna, *Italy* **20 B5** 44 25N 12 12 E
Ravenna, *Nebr., U.S.A.* **80 E5** 41 1N 98 55W
Ravenna, *Ohio, U.S.A.* **78 E3** 41 9N 81 15W
Ravensburg, *Germany* **16 E5** 47 46N 9 36 E
Ravenshoe, *Australia* **62 B4** 17 37S 145 29 E
Ravensthorpe, *Australia* **61 F3** 33 35S 120 2 E
Ravenswood, *Australia* **62 C4** 20 6S 146 54 E
Ravenswood, *U.S.A.* **76 F5** 38 57N 81 46W
Ravi —►, *Pakistan* **42 D4** 30 35N 71 49 E
Rawalpindi, *Pakistan* **42 C5** 33 38N 73 8 E
Rawāndūz, *Iraq* **44 B5** 36 40N 44 30 E
Rawang, *Malaysia* **39 L3** 3 20N 101 35 E
Rawene, *N.Z.* **59 F4** 35 25S 173 32 E
Rawlinna, *Australia* **61 F4** 30 58S 125 28 E
Rawlins, *U.S.A.* **82 F10** 41 47N 107 14W
Rawlinson Ra., *Australia* **61 D4** 24 40S 128 30 E
Rawson, *Argentina* **96 E3** 43 15S 65 5W
Raxaul, *India* **43 F11** 26 59N 84 51 E
Ray, *U.S.A.* **80 A3** 48 21N 103 10W
Ray, C., *Canada* **71 C8** 47 33N 59 15W
Rayadurg, *India* **40 M10** 14 40N 76 50 E
Rayagada, *India* **41 K13** 19 15N 83 20 E
Raychikhinsk, *Russia* **27 E13** 49 46N 129 25 E
Rāyen, *Iran* **45 D8** 29 34N 57 26 E
Rayleigh, *U.K.* **11 F8** 51 36N 0 37 E
Raymond, *Canada* **72 D6** 49 30N 112 35W
Raymond, *Calif., U.S.A.* **84 H7** 37 13N 119 54W
Raymond, *N.H., U.S.A.* **79 C13** 43 2N 71 11W
Raymond, *Wash., U.S.A.* **84 D3** 46 41N 123 44W
Raymond Terrace, *Australia* **63 E5** 32 45S 151 44 E
Raymondville, *U.S.A.* **81 M6** 26 29N 97 47W
Raymore, *Canada* **73 C8** 51 25N 104 31W
Rayna, *India* **43 H12** 23 5N 87 54 E
Rayón, *Mexico* **86 B2** 29 43N 110 35W
Rayong, *Thailand* **38 F3** 12 40N 101 20 E
Rayville, *U.S.A.* **81 J9** 32 29N 91 46W
Raz, Pte. du, *France* **18 C1** 48 2N 4 47W
Razan, *Iran* **45 C6** 35 23N 49 2 E
Razdel'naya = Rozdilna, *Ukraine* **17 E16** 46 50N 30 2 E
Razdolnoye, *Russia* **30 C5** 43 30N 131 52 E
Razeh, *Iran* **45 C6** 32 47N 48 9 E
Razgrad, *Bulgaria* **21 C12** 43 33N 26 34 E
Razim, Lacul, *Romania* **17 F15** 44 50N 29 0 E
Razmak, *Pakistan* **42 C3** 32 45N 69 50 E
Ré, Î. de, *France* **18 C3** 46 12N 1 30W
Reading, *U.K.* **11 F7** 51 27N 0 58W
Reading, *U.S.A.* **79 F9** 40 20N 75 56W
Reading □, *U.K.* **11 F7** 51 27N 0 58W
Realicó, *Argentina* **94 D3** 35 0S 64 15W
Ream, *Cambodia* **39 G4** 10 34N 103 39 E
Reata, *Mexico* **86 B4** 26 8N 101 5W
Reay Forest, *U.K.* **12 C4** 58 22N 4 55W
Rebi, *Indonesia* **37 F8** 6 23S 134 7 E
Rebiana, *Libya* **51 D10** 24 12N 22 10 E
Rebun-Tō, *Japan* **30 B10** 45 23N 141 2 E
Recherche, Arch. of the, *Australia* **61 F3** 34 15S 122 50 E
Rechna Doab, *Pakistan* **42 D5** 31 35N 73 30 E
Rechytsa, *Belarus* **17 B16** 52 21N 30 24 E
Recife, *Brazil* **93 E12** 8 0S 35 0W
Recklinghausen, *Germany* **15 C7** 51 37N 7 12 E
Reconquista, *Argentina* **94 B4** 29 10S 59 45W
Recreo, *Argentina* **94 B2** 29 25S 65 10W
Red —►, *La., U.S.A.* **81 K9** 31 1N 91 45W
Red —►, *N. Dak., U.S.A.* **68 C10** 49 0N 97 15W
Red Bank, *U.S.A.* **79 F10** 40 21N 74 5W
Red Bay, *Canada* **71 B8** 51 44N 56 25W
Red Bluff, *U.S.A.* **82 F2** 40 11N 122 15W
Red Bluff L., *U.S.A.* **81 K3** 31 54N 103 55W
Red Cliffs, *Australia* **63 E3** 34 19S 142 11 E
Red Cloud, *U.S.A.* **80 E5** 40 5N 98 32W
Red Creek, *U.S.A.* **79 C8** 43 14N 76 45W
Red Deer, *Canada* **72 C6** 52 20N 113 50W
Red Deer —►, *Alta., Canada* **73 C7** 50 58N 110 0W
Red Deer —►, *Man., Canada* **73 C8** 52 53N 101 1W
Red Deer L., *Canada* **73 C8** 52 55N 101 20W
Red Hook, *U.S.A.* **79 E11** 41 55N 73 53W
Red Indian L., *Canada* **71 C8** 48 35N 57 0W
Red L., *Canada* **73 C10** 51 3N 93 49W
Red Lake, *Canada* **73 C10** 51 3N 93 49W
Red Lake Falls, *U.S.A.* **80 B6** 47 53N 96 16W
Red Lake Road, *Canada* **73 C10** 49 59N 93 25W
Red Lodge, *U.S.A.* **82 D9** 45 11N 109 15W
Red Mountain, *U.S.A.* **85 K9** 35 37N 117 38W
Red Oak, *U.S.A.* **80 E7** 41 1N 95 14W
Red Rock, *Canada* **70 C2** 48 55N 88 15W
Red Rock, L., *U.S.A.* **80 E8** 41 22N 92 59W
Red Rocks Pt., *Australia* **61 F4** 32 13S 127 32 E
Red Sea, *Asia* **46 C2** 25 0N 36 0 E
Red Slate Mt., *U.S.A.* **84 H8** 37 31N 118 52W
Red Sucker L., *Canada* **70 B1** 54 9N 93 40W
Red Tower Pass = Turnu Roşu, P., *Romania* **17 F13** 45 33N 24 17 E
Red Wing, *U.S.A.* **80 C8** 44 34N 92 31W
Redang, *Malaysia* **36 C2** 5 49N 103 2 E
Redange, *Lux.* **15 E5** 49 46N 5 52 E
Redcar, *U.K.* **10 C6** 54 37N 1 4W
Redcar & Cleveland □, *U.K.* **10 C7** 54 29N 1 0W
Redcliff, *Canada* **73 C6** 50 10N 110 50W
Redcliffe, *Australia* **63 D5** 27 12S 153 0 E
Redcliffe, Mt., *Australia* **61 E3** 28 30S 121 30 E
Reddersburg, *S. Africa* **56 D4** 29 41S 26 10 E
Redding, *U.S.A.* **82 F2** 40 35N 122 24W
Redditch, *U.K.* **11 E6** 52 18N 1 55W
Redfield, *U.S.A.* **80 C5** 44 53N 98 31W
Redford, *U.S.A.* **79 B11** 44 38N 73 48W
Redlands, *U.S.A.* **85 M9** 34 4N 117 11W
Redmond, *Oreg., U.S.A.* **82 D3** 44 17N 121 11W
Redmond, *Wash., U.S.A.* **84 C4** 47 41N 122 7W
Redon, *France* **18 C2** 47 40N 2 6W
Redonda, *Antigua* **89 C7** 16 58N 62 19W
Redondela, *Spain* **19 A1** 42 15N 8 38W
Redondo Beach, *U.S.A.* **85 M8** 33 50N 118 23W
Redruth, *U.K.* **11 G2** 50 14N 5 14W
Redvers, *Canada* **73 D8** 49 35N 101 40W
Redwater, *Canada* **72 C6** 53 55N 113 6W
Redwood, *U.S.A.* **79 B9** 44 18N 75 48W
Redwood City, *U.S.A.* **84 H4** 37 30N 122 15W
Redwood Falls, *U.S.A.* **80 C7** 44 32N 95 7W
Redwood National Park, *U.S.A.* **82 F1** 41 40N 124 5W
Ree, L., *Ireland* **13 C3** 53 35N 8 0W
Reed, L., *Canada* **73 C8** 54 38N 100 30W
Reed City, *U.S.A.* **76 D3** 43 53N 85 31W
Reedley, *U.S.A.* **84 J7** 36 36N 119 27W
Reedsburg, *U.S.A.* **80 D9** 43 32N 90 0W
Reedsport, *U.S.A.* **82 E1** 43 42N 124 6W
Reedsville, *U.S.A.* **78 F7** 40 39N 77 35W
Reefton, *N.Z.* **59 K3** 42 6S 171 51 E
Reese —►, *U.S.A.* **82 F5** 40 48N 117 4W
Refugio, *U.S.A.* **81 L6** 28 18N 97 17W
Regensburg, *Germany* **16 D7** 49 1N 12 6 E
Réggio di Calábria, *Italy* **20 E6** 38 6N 15 39 E
Réggio nell'Emília, *Italy* **20 B4** 44 43N 10 36 E
Reghin, *Romania* **17 E13** 46 46N 24 42 E
Regina, *Canada* **73 C8** 50 27N 104 35W
Regina Beach, *Canada* **73 C8** 50 47N 105 0W
Registro, *Brazil* **95 A6** 24 29S 47 49W
Rehar —►, *India* **43 H10** 23 55N 82 40 E
Rehli, *India* **43 H8** 23 38N 79 5 E
Rehoboth, *Namibia* **56 C2** 23 15S 17 4 E
Rehovot, *Israel* **47 D3** 31 54N 34 48 E
Reichenbach, *Germany* **16 C7** 50 37N 12 17 E
Reid, *Australia* **61 F4** 30 49S 128 26 E
Reidsville, *U.S.A.* **77 G6** 36 21N 79 40W
Reigate, *U.K.* **11 F7** 51 14N 0 12W
Reims, *France* **18 B6** 49 15N 4 1 E
Reina Adelaida, Arch., *Chile* **96 G2** 52 20S 74 0W
Reindeer —►, *Canada* **73 B8** 55 36N 103 11W
Reindeer I., *Canada* **73 C9** 52 30N 98 0W
Reindeer L., *Canada* **73 B8** 57 15N 102 15W
Reinga, C., *N.Z.* **59 F4** 34 25S 172 43 E
Reinosa, *Spain* **19 A3** 43 2N 4 15W
Reitz, *S. Africa* **57 D4** 27 48S 28 29 E
Reivilo, *S. Africa* **56 D3** 27 36S 24 8 E
Reliance, *Canada* **73 A7** 63 0N 109 20W
Remarkable, Mt., *Australia* **63 E2** 32 48S 138 10 E
Rembang, *Indonesia* **37 G14** 6 42S 111 21 E
Remedios, *Panama* **88 E3** 8 15N 81 50W
Remeshk, *Iran* **45 E8** 26 55N 58 50 E
Remich, *Lux.* **15 E6** 49 32N 6 22 E
Remscheid, *Germany* **15 C7** 51 11N 7 12 E
Ren Xian, *China* **34 F8** 37 8N 114 40 E
Rendsburg, *Germany* **16 A5** 54 17N 9 39 E
Renfrew, *Canada* **79 A8** 45 30N 76 40W
Renfrewshire □, *U.K.* **12 F4** 55 49N 4 38W
Rengat, *Indonesia* **36 E2** 0 30S 102 45 E
Rengo, *Chile* **94 C1** 34 24S 70 50W
Reni, *Ukraine* **17 F15** 45 28N 28 15 E
Renmark, *Australia* **63 E3** 34 11S 140 43 E
Rennell Sd., *Canada* **72 C2** 53 23N 132 35W
Renner Springs, *Australia* **62 B1** 18 20S 133 47 E
Rennes, *France* **18 B3** 48 7N 1 41W
Rennie L., *Canada* **73 A7** 61 32N 105 35W
Reno, *U.S.A.* **84 F7** 39 31N 119 48W
Reno —►, *Italy* **20 B5** 44 38N 12 16 E
Renovo, *U.S.A.* **78 E7** 41 20N 77 45W
Renqiu, *China* **34 E9** 38 43N 116 5 E
Rensselaer, *Ind., U.S.A.* **76 E2** 40 57N 87 9W
Rensselaer, *N.Y., U.S.A.* **79 D11** 42 38N 73 45W
Rentería, *Spain* **19 A5** 43 19N 1 54W
Renton, *U.S.A.* **84 C4** 47 29N 122 12W
Reotipur, *India* **43 G10** 25 33N 83 45 E
Republic, *Mo., U.S.A.* **81 G8** 37 7N 93 29W
Republic, *Wash., U.S.A.* **82 B4** 48 39N 118 44W
Republican —►, *U.S.A.* **80 F6** 39 4N 96 48W
Repulse Bay, *Canada* **69 B11** 66 30N 86 30W
Requena, *Peru* **92 E4** 5 5S 73 52W
Requena, *Spain* **19 C5** 39 30N 1 4W
Reşadiye = Datça, *Turkey* **21 F12** 36 46N 27 40 E
Reserve, *U.S.A.* **83 K9** 33 43N 108 45W
Resht = Rasht, *Iran* **45 B6** 37 20N 49 40 E
Resistencia, *Argentina* **94 B4** 27 30S 59 0W
Reşiţa, *Romania* **17 F11** 45 18N 21 53 E
Resolution I., *Canada* **69 B13** 61 30N 65 0W
Resolution I., *N.Z.* **59 L1** 45 40S 166 40 E
Ressano Garcia, *Mozam.* **57 D5** 25 25S 32 0 E
Reston, *Canada* **73 D8** 49 33N 101 6W
Retalhuleu, *Guatemala* **88 D1** 14 33N 91 46W
Retenue, L. de, *Dem. Rep. of the Congo* **55 E2** 11 0S 27 0 E
Retford, *U.K.* **10 D7** 53 19N 0 56W
Réthímnon, *Greece* **23 D6** 35 18N 24 30 E
Réthímnon □, *Greece* **23 D6** 35 23N 24 28 E
Reti, *Pakistan* **42 E3** 28 5N 69 48 E
Réunion ■, *Ind. Oc.* **49 J9** 21 0S 56 0 E
Reus, *Spain* **19 B6** 41 10N 1 5 E
Reutlingen, *Germany* **16 D5** 48 29N 9 12 E
Reval = Tallinn, *Estonia* **9 G21** 59 22N 24 48 E
Revda, *Russia* **24 C10** 56 48N 59 57 E
Revelganj, *India* **43 G11** 25 50N 84 40 E
Revelstoke, *Canada* **72 C5** 51 0N 118 10W
Reventazón, *Peru* **92 E2** 6 10S 80 58W
Revillagigedo, Is. de, *Pac. Oc.* **86 D2** 18 40N 112 0W
Revuè —►, *Mozam.* **55 F3** 19 50S 34 0 E
Rewa, *India* **43 G9** 24 33N 81 25 E
Rewari, *India* **42 E7** 28 15N 76 40 E
Rexburg, *U.S.A.* **82 E8** 43 49N 111 47W
Rey, *Iran* **45 C6** 35 35N 51 25 E
Rey, I. del, *Panama* **88 E4** 8 20N 78 30W
Rey Malabo, *Eq. Guin.* **52 D1** 3 45N 8 50 E
Reyðarfjörður, *Iceland* **8 D6** 65 2N 14 13W
Reyes, Pt., *U.S.A.* **84 H3** 38 0N 123 0W
Reykjahlið, *Iceland* **8 D5** 65 40N 16 55W
Reykjanes, *Iceland* **8 E2** 63 48N 22 40W
Reykjavík, *Iceland* **8 D3** 64 10N 21 57W
Reynolds Ra., *Australia* **60 D5** 22 30S 133 0 E
Reynoldsville, *U.S.A.* **78 E6** 41 5N 78 58W
Reynosa, *Mexico* **87 B5** 26 5N 98 18W
Rēzekne, *Latvia* **9 H22** 56 30N 27 17 E
Rezvān, *Iran* **45 E8** 27 34N 56 6 E
Rhayader, *U.K.* **11 E4** 52 18N 3 29W
Rhein —►, *Europe* **15 C6** 51 52N 6 2 E
Rhein-Main-Donau-Kanal, *Germany* **16 D6** 49 15N 11 15 E
Rheine, *Germany* **16 B4** 52 17N 7 26 E
Rheinland-Pfalz □, *Germany* **16 C4** 50 0N 7 0 E
Rhin = Rhein —►, *Europe* **15 C6** 51 52N 6 2 E
Rhine = Rhein —►, *Europe* **15 C6** 51 52N 6 2 E
Rhinebeck, *U.S.A.* **79 E11** 41 56N 73 55W
Rhineland-Palatinate = Rheinland-Pfalz □, *Germany* **16 C4** 50 0N 7 0 E
Rhinelander, *U.S.A.* **80 C10** 45 38N 89 25W
Rhinns Pt., *U.K.* **12 F2** 55 40N 6 29W
Rhino Camp, *Uganda* **54 B3** 3 0N 31 22 E
Rhir, Cap, *Morocco* **50 B4** 30 38N 9 54W
Rhode Island □, *U.S.A.* **79 E13** 41 40N 71 30W
Rhodes = Ródhos, *Greece* **23 C10** 36 15N 28 10 E
Rhodesia = Zimbabwe ■, *Africa* **55 F3** 19 0S 30 0 E
Rhodope Mts. = Rhodopi Planina, *Bulgaria* **21 D11** 41 40N 24 20 E
Rhodopi Planina, *Bulgaria* **21 D11** 41 40N 24 20 E
Rhön = Rhön, *Germany* **16 C5** 50 24N 9 58 E
Rhön, *Germany* **16 C5** 50 24N 9 58 E
Rhondda, *U.K.* **11 F4** 51 39N 3 31W
Rhondda Cynon Taff □, *U.K.* **11 F4** 51 42N 3 27W
Rhône —►, *France* **18 E6** 43 28N 4 42 E
Rhum, *U.K.* **12 E2** 57 0N 6 20W
Rhyl, *U.K.* **10 D4** 53 20N 3 29W
Riachão, *Brazil* **93 E9** 7 20S 46 37W
Riasi, *India* **43 C6** 33 10N 74 50 E
Riau □, *Indonesia* **36 E2** 0 0 102 35 E
Riau, Kepulauan, *Indonesia* **36 D2** 0 30N 104 20 E
Riau Arch. = Riau, Kepulauan, *Indonesia* **36 D2** 0 30N 104 20 E
Ribadeo, *Spain* **19 A2** 43 35N 7 5W
Ribas do Rio Pardo, *Brazil* **93 H8** 20 27S 53 46W
Ribble —►, *U.K.* **10 D5** 53 52N 2 25W
Ribe, *Denmark* **9 J13** 55 19N 8 44 E
Ribeira Brava, *Madeira* **22 D2** 32 41N 17 4W
Ribeirão Prêto, *Brazil* **95 A6** 21 10S 47 50W
Riberalta, *Bolivia* **92 F5** 11 0S 66 0W
Riccarton, *N.Z.* **59 K4** 43 32S 172 37 E
Rice, *U.S.A.* **85 L12** 34 5N 114 51W
Rice L., *Canada* **78 B6** 44 12N 78 10W
Rice Lake, *U.S.A.* **80 C9** 45 30N 91 44W
Rich, C., *Canada* **78 B4** 44 43N 80 38W
Richards Bay, *S. Africa* **57 D5** 28 48S 32 6 E
Richardson —►, *Canada* **73 B6** 58 25N 111 14W
Richardson Lakes, *U.S.A.* **76 C10** 44 46N 70 58W
Richardson Springs, *U.S.A.* **84 F5** 39 51N 121 46W
Riche, C., *Australia* **61 F2** 34 36S 118 47 E
Richey, *U.S.A.* **80 B2** 47 39N 105 4W
Richfield, *U.S.A.* **83 G8** 38 46N 112 5W
Richfield Springs, *U.S.A.* **79 D10** 42 51N 74 59W
Richford, *U.S.A.* **79 B12** 45 0N 72 40W
Richibucto, *Canada* **71 C7** 46 42N 64 54W
Richland, *Ga., U.S.A.* **77 J3** 32 5N 84 40W
Richland, *Wash., U.S.A.* **82 C4** 46 17N 119 18W
Richland Center, *U.S.A.* **80 D9** 43 21N 90 23W
Richlands, *U.S.A.* **76 G5** 37 6N 81 48W
Richmond, *Australia* **62 C3** 20 43S 143 8 E
Richmond, *N.Z.* **59 J4** 41 20S 173 12 E
Richmond, *U.K.* **10 C6** 54 25N 1 43W
Richmond, *Calif., U.S.A.* **84 H4** 37 56N 122 21W
Richmond, *Ind., U.S.A.* **76 F3** 39 50N 84 53W
Richmond, *Ky., U.S.A.* **76 G3** 37 45N 84 18W
Richmond, *Mich., U.S.A.* **78 D2** 42 49N 82 45W
Richmond, *Mo., U.S.A.* **80 F8** 39 17N 93 58W
Richmond, *Tex., U.S.A.* **81 L7** 29 35N 95 46W
Richmond, *Utah, U.S.A.* **82 F8** 41 56N 111 48W
Richmond, *Va., U.S.A.* **76 G7** 37 33N 77 27W
Richmond, *Vt., U.S.A.* **79 B12** 44 24N 72 59W
Richmond Hill, *Canada* **78 C5** 43 52N 79 27W
Richmond Ra., *Australia* **63 D5** 29 0S 152 45 E
Richwood, *U.S.A.* **76 F5** 38 14N 80 32W
Ridder = Leninogorsk, *Kazakstan* **26 D9** 50 20N 83 30 E
Riddlesburg, *U.S.A.* **78 F6** 40 9N 78 15W
Ridgecrest, *U.S.A.* **85 K9** 35 38N 117 40W
Ridgefield, *Conn., U.S.A.* **79 E11** 41 17N 73 30W
Ridgefield, *Wash., U.S.A.* **84 E4** 45 49N 122 45W
Ridgeland, *U.S.A.* **77 J5** 32 29N 80 59W
Ridgetown, *Canada* **78 D3** 42 26N 81 52W
Ridgewood, *U.S.A.* **79 F10** 40 59N 74 7W
Ridgway, *U.S.A.* **78 E6** 41 25N 78 44W
Riding Mountain Nat. Park, *Canada* **73 C9** 50 50N 100 0W
Ridley, Mt., *Australia* **61 F3** 33 12S 122 7 E
Ried, *Austria* **16 D7** 48 14N 13 30 E
Riesa, *Germany* **16 C7** 51 17N 13 17 E
Riet —►, *S. Africa* **56 D3** 29 0S 23 54 E
Rieti, *Italy* **20 C5** 42 24N 12 51 E
Riffe L., *U.S.A.* **84 D4** 46 32N 122 26W
Rifle, *U.S.A.* **82 G10** 39 32N 107 47W
Rift Valley □, *Kenya* **54 B4** 0 20N 36 0 E
Rīga, *Latvia* **9 H21** 56 53N 24 8 E
Riga, G. of, *Latvia* **9 H20** 57 40N 23 45 E
Rīgān, *Iran* **45 D8** 28 37N 58 58 E
Rīgas Jūras Līcis = Riga, G. of, *Latvia* **9 H20** 57 40N 23 45 E
Rigaud, *Canada* **79 A10** 45 29N 74 18W
Rigby, *U.S.A.* **82 E8** 43 40N 111 55W
Rīgestān □, *Afghan.* **40 D4** 30 15N 65 0 E
Riggins, *U.S.A.* **82 D5** 45 25N 116 19W
Rigolet, *Canada* **71 B8** 54 10N 58 23W
Rihand Dam, *India* **43 G10** 24 9N 83 2 E
Riihimäki, *Finland* **9 F21** 60 45N 24 48 E
Riiser-Larsen-halvøya, *Antarctica* **5 C4** 68 0S 35 0 E
Rijeka, *Croatia* **16 F8** 45 20N 14 21 E
Rijssen, *Neths.* **15 B6** 52 19N 6 31 E
Rikuzentakada, *Japan* **30 E10** 39 0N 141 40 E
Riley, *U.S.A.* **82 E4** 43 32N 119 28W
Rimah, Wadi ar —►, *Si. Arabia* **44 E4** 26 5N 41 30 E
Rimbey, *Canada* **72 C6** 52 35N 114 15W
Rimersburg, *U.S.A.* **78 E5** 41 3N 79 30W
Rímini, *Italy* **20 B5** 44 3N 12 33 E
Rimouski, *Canada* **71 C6** 48 27N 68 30W
Rimrock, *U.S.A.* **84 D5** 46 38N 121 10W
Rinca, *Indonesia* **37 F5** 8 45S 119 35 E
Rincón de Romos, *Mexico* **86 C4** 22 14N 102 18W
Rinconada, *Argentina* **94 A2** 22 26S 66 10W
Rind —►, *India* **43 G9** 25 53N 80 33 E
Ringas, *India* **42 F6** 27 21N 75 34 E
Ringkøbing, *Denmark* **9 H13** 56 5N 8 15 E
Ringvassøy, *Norway* **8 B18** 69 56N 19 15 E
Ringwood, *U.S.A.* **79 E10** 41 7N 74 15W
Rinjani, *Indonesia* **36 F5** 8 24S 116 28 E
Rio Branco, *Brazil* **92 E5** 9 58S 67 49W
Río Branco, *Uruguay* **95 C5** 32 40S 53 40W
Río Bravo del Norte —►, *Mexico* **87 B5** 25 57N 97 9W
Rio Brilhante, *Brazil* **95 A5** 21 48S 54 33W
Rio Claro, *Brazil* **95 A6** 22 19S 47 35W
Rio Claro, *Trin. & Tob.* **89 D7** 10 20N 61 25W
Río Colorado, *Argentina* **96 D4** 39 0S 64 0W
Río Cuarto, *Argentina* **94 C3** 33 10S 64 25W
Rio das Pedras, *Mozam.* **57 C6** 23 8S 35 28 E
Rio de Janeiro, *Brazil* **95 A7** 23 0S 43 12W
Rio de Janeiro □, *Brazil* **95 A7** 22 50S 43 0W
Rio do Sul, *Brazil* **95 B6** 27 13S 49 37W
Río Gallegos, *Argentina* **96 G3** 51 35S 69 15W
Rio Grande = Grande, Rio —►, *U.S.A.* **81 N6** 25 58N 97 9W
Río Grande, *Argentina* **96 G3** 53 50S 67 45W
Rio Grande, *Brazil* **95 C5** 32 0S 52 20W
Río Grande, *Mexico* **86 C4** 23 50N 103 2W
Río Grande, *Nic.* **88 D3** 12 54N 83 33W
Rio Grande City, *U.S.A.* **81 M5** 26 23N 98 49W
Río Grande de Santiago —►, *Mexico* **86 C3** 21 36N 105 26W
Rio Grande del Norte —►, *N. Amer.* **75 E7** 26 0N 97 0W
Rio Grande do Norte □, *Brazil* **93 E11** 5 40S 36 0W
Rio Grande do Sul □, *Brazil* **95 C5** 30 0S 53 0W
Río Hato, *Panama* **88 E3** 8 22N 80 10W
Río Lagartos, *Mexico* **87 C7** 21 36N 88 10W
Rio Largo, *Brazil* **93 E11** 9 28S 35 50W
Río Mulatos, *Bolivia* **92 G5** 19 40S 66 50W
Río Muni = Mbini □, *Eq. Guin.* **52 D2** 1 30N 10 0 E
Rio Negro, *Brazil* **95 B6** 26 0S 49 55W
Rio Pardo, *Brazil* **95 C5** 30 0S 52 30W
Rio Rancho, *U.S.A.* **83 J10** 35 14N 106 38W
Río Segundo, *Argentina* **94 C3** 31 40S 63 59W
Río Tercero, *Argentina* **94 C3** 32 15S 64 8W
Rio Verde, *Brazil* **93 G8** 17 50S 51 0W
Río Verde, *Mexico* **87 C5** 21 56N 99 59W
Rio Vista, *U.S.A.* **84 G5** 38 10N 121 42W
Riobamba, *Ecuador* **92 D3** 1 50S 78 45W
Ríohacha, *Colombia* **92 A4** 11 33N 72 55W
Riosucio, *Colombia* **92 B3** 7 27N 77 7W
Riou L., *Canada* **73 B7** 59 7N 106 25W
Ripley, *Canada* **78 B3** 44 4N 81 35W
Ripley, *Calif., U.S.A.* **85 M12** 33 32N 114 39W
Ripley, *N.Y., U.S.A.* **78 D5** 42 16N 79 43W
Ripley, *Tenn., U.S.A.* **81 H10** 35 45N 89 32W
Ripley, *W. Va., U.S.A.* **76 F5** 38 49N 81 43W
Ripon, *U.K.* **10 C6** 54 9N 1 31W
Ripon, *Calif., U.S.A.* **84 H5** 37 44N 121 7W
Ripon, *Wis., U.S.A.* **76 D1** 43 51N 88 50W
Rishā', W. ar —►, *Si. Arabia* **44 E5** 25 33N 44 5 E
Rishiri-Tō, *Japan* **30 B10** 45 11N 141 15 E
Rishon le Ziyyon, *Israel* **47 D3** 31 58N 34 48 E
Rison, *U.S.A.* **81 J8** 33 58N 92 11W
Risør, *Norway* **9 G13** 58 43N 9 13 E
Rita Blanca Cr. —►, *U.S.A.* **81 H3** 35 40N 102 29W
Ritter, Mt., *U.S.A.* **84 H7** 37 41N 119 12W
Rittman, *U.S.A.* **78 F3** 40 58N 81 47W
Ritzville, *U.S.A.* **82 C4** 47 8N 118 23W
Riva del Garda, *Italy* **20 B4** 45 53N 10 50 E
Rivadavia, *Buenos Aires, Argentina* **94 D3** 35 29S 62 59W
Rivadavia, *Mendoza, Argentina* **94 C2** 33 13S 68 30W
Rivadavia, *Salta, Argentina* **94 A3** 24 5S 62 54W
Rivadavia, *Chile* **94 B1** 29 57S 70 35W
Rivas, *Nic.* **88 D2** 11 30N 85 50W
River Cess, *Liberia* **50 G4** 5 30N 9 32W
River Jordan, *Canada* **84 B2** 48 26N 124 3W
Rivera, *Argentina* **94 D3** 37 12S 63 14W
Rivera, *Uruguay* **95 C4** 31 0S 55 50W
Riverbank, *U.S.A.* **84 H6** 37 44N 120 56W
Riverdale, *U.S.A.* **84 J7** 36 26N 119 52W
Riverhead, *U.S.A.* **79 F12** 40 55N 72 40W
Riverhurst, *Canada* **73 C7** 50 55N 106 50W
Rivers, *Canada* **73 C8** 50 2N 100 14W
Rivers Inlet, *Canada* **72 C3** 51 42N 127 15W
Riversdale, *S. Africa* **56 E3** 34 7S 21 15 E
Riverside, *U.S.A.* **85 M9** 33 59N 117 22W
Riverton, *Australia* **63 E2** 34 10S 138 46 E
Riverton, *Canada* **73 C9** 51 1N 97 0W
Riverton, *N.Z.* **59 M2** 46 21S 168 0 E
Riverton, *U.S.A.* **82 E9** 43 2N 108 23W
Riverton Heights, *U.S.A.* **84 C4** 47 28N 122 17W
Riviera, *U.S.A.* **85 K12** 35 4N 114 35W
Riviera di Levante, *Italy* **18 D8** 44 15N 9 30 E
Riviera di Ponente, *Italy* **18 D8** 44 10N 8 20 E
Rivière-au-Renard, *Canada* **71 C7** 48 59N 64 23W
Rivière-du-Loup, *Canada* **71 C6** 47 50N 69 30W
Rivière-Pentecôte, *Canada* **71 C6** 49 57N 67 1W

Rzhev

Rivière-Pilote, *Martinique* **89 D7** 14 26N 60 53W
Rivière St. Paul, *Canada* **71 B8** 51 28N 57 45W
Rivne, *Ukraine* **17 C14** 50 40N 26 10 E
Rivoli, *Italy* **18 D7** 45 3N 7 31 E
Rivoli B., *Australia* **63 F3** 37 32S 140 3 E
Riyadh = Ar Riyāḍ,
Si. Arabia **46 C4** 24 41N 46 42 E
Rize, *Turkey* **25 F7** 41 0N 40 30 E
Rizhao, *China* **35 G10** 35 25N 119 30 E
Rizokarpaso, *Cyprus* **23 D13** 35 36N 34 23 E
Rizzuto, C., *Italy* **20 E7** 38 53N 17 5 E
Rjukan, *Norway* **9 G13** 59 54N 8 33 E
Road Town, *Virgin Is.* **89 C7** 18 27N 64 37W
Roan Plateau, *U.S.A.* **82 G9** 39 20N 109 20W
Roanne, *France* **18 C6** 46 3N 4 4 E
Roanoke, *Ala., U.S.A.* **77 J3** 33 9N 85 22W
Roanoke, *Va., U.S.A.* **76 G6** 37 16N 79 56W
Roanoke →, *U.S.A.* **77 H7** 35 57N 76 42W
Roanoke I., *U.S.A.* **77 H8** 35 55N 75 40W
Roanoke Rapids, *U.S.A.* **77 G7** 36 28N 77 40W
Roatán, *Honduras* **88 C2** 16 18N 86 35W
Robāt Sang, *Iran* **45 C8** 35 35N 59 10 E
Robbins I., *Australia* **62 G4** 40 42S 145 0 E
Robe, *Australia* **63 F2** 37 11S 139 45 E
Robe →, *Australia* **60 D2** 21 42S 116 15 E
Robert Lee, *U.S.A.* **81 K4** 31 54N 100 29W
Robertsdale, *U.S.A.* **78 F6** 40 11N 78 6W
Robertsganj, *India* **43 G10** 24 44N 83 4 E
Robertson, *S. Africa* **56 E2** 33 46S 19 50 E
Robertson I., *Antarctica* **5 C18** 65 15S 59 30W
Robertson Ra., *Australia* **60 D3** 23 15S 121 0 E
Robertstown, *Australia* **63 E2** 33 58S 139 5 E
Roberval, *Canada* **71 C5** 48 32N 72 15W
Robeson Chan., *Greenland* **4 A4** 82 0N 61 30W
Robesonia, *U.S.A.* **79 F8** 40 21N 76 8W
Robinson, *U.S.A.* **76 F2** 39 0N 87 44W
Robinson →, *Australia* **62 B2** 16 3S 137 16 E
Robinson Ra., *Australia* **61 E2** 25 40S 119 0 E
Robinvale, *Australia* **63 E3** 34 40S 142 45 E
Roblin, *Canada* **73 C8** 51 14N 101 21W
Roboré, *Bolivia* **92 G7** 18 10S 59 45W
Robson, *Canada* **72 D5** 49 20N 117 41W
Robson, Mt., *Canada* **72 C5** 53 10N 119 10W
Robstown, *U.S.A.* **81 M6** 27 47N 97 40W
Roca, C. da, *Portugal* **19 C1** 38 40N 9 31W
Roca Partida, I., *Mexico* **86 D2** 19 1N 112 2W
Rocas, I., *Brazil* **93 D12** 4 0S 34 1W
Rocha, *Uruguay* **95 C5** 34 30S 54 25W
Rochdale, *U.K.* **10 D5** 53 38N 2 9W
Rochefort, *Belgium* **15 D5** 50 9N 5 12 E
Rochefort, *France* **18 D3** 45 56N 0 57W
Rochelle, *U.S.A.* **80 E10** 41 56N 89 4W
Rocher River, *Canada* **72 A6** 61 23N 112 44W
Rochester, *U.K.* **11 F8** 51 23N 0 31 E
Rochester, *Ind., U.S.A.* **76 E2** 41 4N 86 13W
Rochester, *Minn., U.S.A.* **80 C8** 44 1N 92 28W
Rochester, *N.H., U.S.A.* **79 C14** 43 18N 70 59W
Rochester, *N.Y., U.S.A.* **78 C7** 43 10N 77 37W
Rock →, *Canada* **72 A3** 60 7N 127 7W
Rock Creek, *U.S.A.* **78 E4** 41 40N 80 52W
Rock Falls, *U.S.A.* **80 E10** 41 47N 89 41W
Rock Hill, *U.S.A.* **77 H5** 34 56N 81 1W
Rock Island, *U.S.A.* **80 E9** 41 30N 90 34W
Rock Rapids, *U.S.A.* **80 D6** 43 26N 96 10W
Rock Sound, *Bahamas* **88 B4** 24 54N 76 12W
Rock Springs, *Mont., U.S.A.* **82 C10** 46 49N 106 15W
Rock Springs, *Wyo., U.S.A.* **82 F9** 41 35N 109 14W
Rock Valley, *U.S.A.* **80 D6** 43 12N 96 18W
Rockall, *Atl. Oc.* **6 D3** 57 37N 13 42W
Rockdale, *Tex., U.S.A.* **81 K6** 30 39N 97 0W
Rockdale, *Wash., U.S.A.* **84 C5** 47 22N 121 28W
Rockefeller Plateau,
Antarctica **5 E14** 80 0S 140 0W
Rockford, *U.S.A.* **80 D10** 42 16N 89 6W
Rockglen, *Canada* **73 D7** 49 11N 105 57W
Rockhampton, *Australia* **62 C5** 23 22S 150 32 E
Rockingham, *Australia* **61 F2** 32 15S 115 38 E
Rockingham, *U.S.A.* **77 H6** 34 57N 79 46W
Rockingham B., *Australia* **62 B4** 18 5S 146 10 E
Rocklake, *U.S.A.* **80 A5** 48 47N 99 15W
Rockland, *Canada* **79 A9** 45 33N 75 17W
Rockland, *Idaho, U.S.A.* **82 E7** 42 34N 112 53W
Rockland, *Maine, U.S.A.* **77 C11** 44 6N 69 7W
Rockland, *Mich., U.S.A.* **80 B10** 46 44N 89 11W
Rocklin, *U.S.A.* **84 G5** 38 48N 121 14W
Rockport, *Mass., U.S.A.* **79 D14** 42 39N 70 37W
Rockport, *Mo., U.S.A.* **80 E7** 40 25N 95 31W
Rockport, *Tex., U.S.A.* **81 L6** 28 2N 97 3W
Rocksprings, *U.S.A.* **81 K4** 30 1N 100 13W
Rockville, *Conn., U.S.A.* **79 E12** 41 52N 72 28W
Rockville, *Md., U.S.A.* **76 F7** 39 5N 77 9W
Rockwall, *U.S.A.* **81 J6** 32 56N 96 28W
Rockwell City, *U.S.A.* **80 D7** 42 24N 94 38W
Rockwood, *Canada* **78 C4** 43 37N 80 8W
Rockwood, *Maine, U.S.A.* **77 C11** 45 41N 69 45W
Rockwood, *Tenn., U.S.A.* **77 H3** 35 52N 84 41W
Rocky Ford, *U.S.A.* **80 F3** 38 3N 103 43W
Rocky Gully, *Australia* **61 F2** 34 30S 116 57 E
Rocky Harbour, *Canada* **71 C8** 49 36N 57 55W
Rocky Island L., *Canada* **70 C3** 46 55N 83 0W
Rocky Lane, *Canada* **72 B5** 58 31N 116 22W
Rocky Mount, *U.S.A.* **77 H7** 35 57N 77 48W
Rocky Mountain House,
Canada **72 C6** 52 22N 114 55W
Rocky Mountain National
Park, *U.S.A.* **82 F11** 40 25N 105 45W
Rocky Mts., *N. Amer.* **74 C5** 49 0N 115 0W
Rod, *Pakistan* **40 E3** 28 10N 63 5 E
Rødbyhavn, *Denmark* **9 J14** 54 39N 11 22 E
Roddickton, *Canada* **71 B8** 50 51N 56 8W
Rodez, *France* **18 D5** 44 21N 2 33 E
Rodhopoú, *Greece* **23 D5** 35 34N 23 45 E
Ródhos, *Greece* **23 C10** 36 15N 28 10 E
Rodney, *Canada* **78 D3** 42 34N 81 41W
Rodney, C., *N.Z.* **59 G5** 36 17S 174 50 E
Rodriguez, *Ind. Oc.* **3 E13** 19 45S 63 20 E
Roe →, *U.K.* **13 A5** 55 6N 6 59W
Roebling, *U.S.A.* **79 F10** 40 7N 74 47W
Roebourne, *Australia* **60 D2** 20 44S 117 9 E
Roebuck B., *Australia* **60 C3** 18 5S 122 20 E
Roermond, *Neths.* **15 C6** 51 12N 6 0 E
Roes Welcome Sd., *Canada* **69 B11** 65 0N 87 0W
Roeselare, *Belgium* **15 D3** 50 57N 3 7 E
Rogachev = Ragachow,
Belarus **17 B16** 53 8N 30 5 E
Rogagua, L., *Bolivia* **92 F5** 13 43S 66 50W
Rogatyn, *Ukraine* **17 D13** 49 24N 24 36 E
Rogdhia, *Greece* **23 D7** 35 22N 25 1 E
Rogers, *U.S.A.* **81 G7** 36 20N 94 7W
Rogers City, *U.S.A.* **76 C4** 45 25N 83 49W
Rogersville, *Canada* **71 C6** 46 44N 65 26W
Roggan →, *Canada* **70 B4** 54 24N 79 25W
Roggan L., *Canada* **70 B4** 54 8N 77 50W
Roggeveldberge, *S. Africa* **56 E3** 32 10S 20 10 E
Rogoaguado, L., *Bolivia* **92 F5** 13 0S 65 30W
Rogue →, *U.S.A.* **82 E1** 42 26N 124 26W
Róhda, *Greece* **23 A3** 39 48N 19 46 E
Rohnert Park, *U.S.A.* **84 G4** 38 16N 122 40W
Rohri, *Pakistan* **42 F3** 27 45N 68 51 E
Rohri Canal, *Pakistan* **42 F3** 26 15N 68 27 E
Rohtak, *India* **42 E7** 28 55N 76 43 E
Roi Et, *Thailand* **38 D4** 16 4N 103 40 E
Roja, *Latvia* **9 H20** 57 29N 22 43 E
Rojas, *Argentina* **94 C3** 34 10S 60 45W
Rojo, C., *Mexico* **87 C5** 21 33N 97 20W
Rokan →, *Indonesia* **36 D2** 2 0N 100 50 E
Rokiškis, *Lithuania* **9 J21** 55 55N 25 35 E
Rolândia, *Brazil* **95 A5** 23 18S 51 23W
Rolla, *U.S.A.* **81 G9** 37 57N 91 46W
Rolleston, *Australia* **62 C4** 24 28S 148 35 E
Rollingstone, *Australia* **62 B4** 19 2S 146 24 E
Roma, *Australia* **63 D4** 26 32S 148 49 E
Roma, *Italy* **20 D5** 41 54N 12 29 E
Roma, *Sweden* **9 H18** 57 32N 18 26 E
Roma, *U.S.A.* **81 M5** 26 25N 99 1W
Romain C., *U.S.A.* **77 J6** 33 0N 79 22W
Romaine, *Canada* **71 B7** 50 13N 60 40W
Romaine →, *Canada* **71 B7** 50 18N 63 47W
Roman, *Romania* **17 E14** 46 57N 26 55 E
Romang, *Indonesia* **37 F7** 7 30S 127 20 E
Romani, *Egypt* **47 E1** 30 59N 32 38 E
Romania ■, *Europe* **17 F12** 46 0N 25 0 E
Romano, Cayo, *Cuba* **88 B4** 22 0N 77 30W
Romanovka =
Basarabeasca, *Moldova* **17 E15** 46 21N 28 58 E
Romans-sur-Isère, *France* **18 D6** 45 3N 5 3 E
Romblon, *Phil.* **37 B6** 12 33N 122 17 E
Rome = Roma, *Italy* **20 D5** 41 54N 12 29 E
Rome, *Ga., U.S.A.* **77 H3** 34 15N 85 10W
Rome, *N.Y., U.S.A.* **79 C9** 43 13N 75 27W
Rome, *Pa., U.S.A.* **79 E8** 41 51N 76 21W
Romney, *U.S.A.* **76 F6** 39 21N 78 45W
Romney Marsh, *U.K.* **11 F8** 51 2N 0 54 E
Rømø, *Denmark* **9 J13** 55 10N 8 30 E
Romorantin-Lanthenay,
France **18 C4** 47 21N 1 45 E
Romsdalen, *Norway* **9 E12** 62 25N 7 52 E
Romsey, *U.K.* **11 G6** 51 0N 1 29W
Ron, *Vietnam* **38 D6** 17 53N 106 27 E
Rona, *U.K.* **12 D3** 57 34N 5 59W
Ronan, *U.S.A.* **82 C6** 47 32N 114 6W
Roncador, Cayos, *Caribbean* **88 D3** 13 32N 80 4W
Roncador, Serra do, *Brazil* **93 F8** 12 30S 52 30W
Ronda, *Spain* **19 D3** 36 46N 5 12W
Rondane, *Norway* **9 F13** 61 57N 9 50 E
Rondônia □, *Brazil* **92 F6** 11 0S 63 0W
Rondonópolis, *Brazil* **93 G8** 16 28S 54 38W
Rong, Koh, *Cambodia* **39 G4** 10 45N 103 15 E
Ronge, L. la, *Canada* **73 B7** 55 6N 105 17W
Rønne, *Denmark* **9 J16** 55 6N 14 43 E
Ronne Ice Shelf, *Antarctica* **5 D18** 78 0S 60 0W
Ronsard, C., *Australia* **61 D1** 24 46S 113 10 E
Ronse, *Belgium* **15 D3** 50 45N 3 35 E
Roodepoort, *S. Africa* **57 D4** 26 11S 27 54 E
Roof Butte, *U.S.A.* **83 H9** 36 28N 109 5W
Roorkee, *India* **42 E7** 29 52N 77 59 E
Roosendaal, *Neths.* **15 C4** 51 32N 4 29 E
Roosevelt, *U.S.A.* **82 F8** 40 18N 109 59W
Roosevelt →, *Brazil* **92 E6** 7 35S 60 20W
Roosevelt, Mt., *Canada* **72 B3** 58 26N 125 20W
Roosevelt I., *Antarctica* **5 D12** 79 30S 162 0W
Roper →, *Australia* **62 A2** 14 43S 135 27 E
Roper Bar, *Australia* **62 A1** 14 44S 134 44 E
Roque Pérez, *Argentina* **94 D4** 35 25S 59 24W
Roquetas de Mar, *Spain* **19 D4** 36 46N 2 36W
Roraima □, *Brazil* **92 C6** 2 0N 61 30W
Roraima, Mt., *Venezuela* **92 B6** 5 10N 60 40W
Røros, *Norway* **9 E14** 62 35N 11 23 E
Rosa, *Zambia* **55 D3** 9 33S 31 15 E
Rosa, L., *Bahamas* **89 B5** 21 0N 73 30W
Rosa, Monte, *Europe* **18 D7** 45 57N 7 53 E
Rosalia, *U.S.A.* **82 C5** 47 14N 117 22W
Rosamond, *U.S.A.* **85 L8** 34 52N 118 10W
Rosario, *Argentina* **94 C3** 33 0S 60 40W
Rosário, *Brazil* **93 D10** 3 0S 44 15W
Rosario, *Baja Calif., Mexico* **86 B1** 30 0N 115 50W
Rosario, *Sinaloa, Mexico* **86 C3** 23 0N 105 52W
Rosario, *Paraguay* **94 A4** 24 30S 57 35W
Rosario de la Frontera,
Argentina **94 B3** 25 50S 65 0W
Rosario de Lerma, *Argentina* **94 A2** 24 59S 65 35W
Rosario del Tala, *Argentina* **94 C4** 32 20S 59 10W
Rosário do Sul, *Brazil* **95 C5** 30 15S 54 55W
Rosarito, *Mexico* **85 N9** 32 18N 117 4W
Roscoe, *U.S.A.* **79 E10** 41 56N 74 55W
Roscommon, *Ireland* **13 C3** 53 38N 8 11W
Roscommon □, *Ireland* **13 C3** 53 49N 8 23W
Roscrea, *Ireland* **13 D4** 52 57N 7 49W
Rose →, *Australia* **62 A2** 14 16S 135 45 E
Rose Blanche, *Canada* **71 C8** 47 38N 58 45W
Rose Pt., *Canada* **72 C2** 54 11N 131 39W
Rose Valley, *Canada* **73 C8** 52 19N 103 49W
Roseau, *Domin.* **89 C7** 15 20N 61 24W
Roseau, *U.S.A.* **80 A7** 48 51N 95 46W
Rosebery, *Australia* **62 G4** 41 46S 145 33 E
Rosebud, *S. Dak., U.S.A.* **80 D4** 43 14N 100 51W
Rosebud, *Tex., U.S.A.* **81 K6** 31 4N 96 59W
Roseburg, *U.S.A.* **82 E2** 43 13N 123 20W
Rosedale, *U.S.A.* **81 J9** 33 51N 91 2W
Roseland, *U.S.A.* **84 G4** 38 25N 122 43W
Rosemary, *Canada* **72 C6** 50 46N 112 5W
Rosenberg, *U.S.A.* **81 L7** 29 34N 95 49W
Rosenheim, *Germany* **16 E7** 47 51N 12 7 E
Roses, G. de, *Spain* **19 A7** 42 10N 3 15 E
Rosetown, *Canada* **73 C7** 51 35N 107 59W
Roseville, *Calif., U.S.A.* **84 G5** 38 45N 121 17W
Roseville, *Mich., U.S.A.* **78 D2** 42 30N 82 56W
Rosewood, *Australia* **63 D5** 27 38S 152 36 E
Roshkhvār, *Iran* **45 C8** 34 58N 59 37 E
Rosignano Marittimo, *Italy* **20 C4** 43 24N 10 28 E
Rosignol, *Guyana* **92 B7** 6 15N 57 30W
Roşiori-de-Vede, *Romania* **17 F13** 44 7N 24 59 E
Roskilde, *Denmark* **9 J15** 55 38N 12 3 E
Roslavl, *Russia* **24 D5** 53 57N 32 55 E
Rosmead, *S. Africa* **56 E4** 31 29S 25 8 E
Ross, *Australia* **62 G4** 42 2S 147 30 E
Ross, *N.Z.* **59 K3** 42 53S 170 49 E
Ross I., *Antarctica* **5 D11** 77 30S 168 0 E
Ross Ice Shelf, *Antarctica* **5 E12** 80 0S 180 0 E
Ross L., *U.S.A.* **82 B3** 48 44N 121 4W
Ross-on-Wye, *U.K.* **11 F5** 51 54N 2 34W
Ross River, *Australia* **62 C1** 23 44S 134 30 E
Ross River, *Canada* **72 A2** 62 30N 131 30W
Ross Sea, *Antarctica* **5 D11** 74 0S 178 0 E
Rossall Pt., *U.K.* **10 D4** 53 55N 3 3W
Rossan Pt., *Ireland* **13 B3** 54 42N 8 47W
Rossano, *Italy* **20 E7** 39 36N 16 39 E
Rossburn, *Canada* **73 C8** 50 40N 100 49W
Rosseau, *Canada* **78 A5** 45 16N 79 39W
Rosseau L., *Canada* **78 A5** 45 10N 79 35W
Rosses, The, *Ireland* **13 A3** 55 2N 8 20W
Rossignol, L., *Canada* **70 B5** 52 43N 73 40W
Rossignol Res., *Canada* **71 D6** 44 12N 65 10W
Rossland, *Canada* **72 D5** 49 6N 117 50W
Rosslare, *Ireland* **13 D5** 52 17N 6 24W
Rosso, *Mauritania* **50 E2** 16 40N 15 45W
Rossosh, *Russia* **25 D6** 50 15N 39 28 E
Røssvatnet, *Norway* **8 D16** 65 45N 14 5 E
Røst, *Norway* **8 C15** 67 32N 12 0 E
Rosthern, *Canada* **73 C7** 52 40N 106 20W
Rostock, *Germany* **16 A7** 54 5N 12 8 E
Rostov, *Don, Russia* **25 E6** 47 15N 39 45 E
Rostov, *Yaroslavl, Russia* **24 C6** 57 14N 39 25 E
Roswell, *Ga., U.S.A.* **77 H3** 34 2N 84 22W
Roswell, *N. Mex., U.S.A.* **81 J2** 33 24N 104 32W
Rotan, *U.S.A.* **81 J4** 32 51N 100 28W
Rother →, *U.K.* **11 G8** 50 59N 0 45 E
Rotherham, *U.K.* **10 D6** 53 26N 1 20W
Rothes, *U.K.* **12 D5** 57 32N 3 13W
Rothesay, *Canada* **71 C6** 45 23N 66 0W
Rothesay, *U.K.* **12 F3** 55 50N 5 3W
Roti, *Indonesia* **37 F6** 10 50S 123 0 E
Roto, *Australia* **63 E4** 33 0S 145 30 E
Rotondo Mte., *France* **18 E8** 42 14N 9 8 E
Rotoroa, L., *N.Z.* **59 J4** 41 55S 172 39 E
Rotorua, *N.Z.* **59 H6** 38 9S 176 16 E
Rotorua, L., *N.Z.* **59 H6** 38 5S 176 18 E
Rotterdam, *Neths.* **15 C4** 51 55N 4 30 E
Rotterdam, *U.S.A.* **79 D10** 42 48N 74 1W
Rottnest I., *Australia* **61 F2** 32 0S 115 27 E
Rottumeroog, *Neths.* **15 A6** 53 33N 6 34 E
Rottweil, *Germany* **16 D5** 48 9N 8 37 E
Rotuma, *Fiji* **64 J9** 12 25S 177 5 E
Roubaix, *France* **18 A5** 50 40N 3 10 E
Rouen, *France* **18 B4** 49 27N 1 4 E
Rouleau, *Canada* **73 C8** 50 10N 104 56W
Round Mountain, *U.S.A.* **82 G5** 38 43N 117 4W
Round Mt., *Australia* **63 E5** 30 26S 152 16 E
Round Rock, *U.S.A.* **81 K6** 30 31N 97 41W
Roundup, *U.S.A.* **82 C9** 46 27N 108 33W
Rousay, *U.K.* **12 B5** 59 10N 3 2W
Rouses Point, *U.S.A.* **79 B11** 44 59N 73 22W
Rouseville, *U.S.A.* **78 E5** 41 28N 79 42W
Roussillon, *France* **18 E5** 42 30N 2 35 E
Rouxville, *S. Africa* **56 E4** 30 25S 26 50 E
Rouyn-Noranda, *Canada* **70 C4** 48 20N 79 0W
Rovaniemi, *Finland* **8 C21** 66 29N 25 41 E
Rovereto, *Italy* **20 B4** 45 53N 11 3 E
Rovigo, *Italy* **20 B4** 45 4N 11 47 E
Rovinj, *Croatia* **16 F7** 45 5N 13 40 E
Rovno = Rivne, *Ukraine* **17 C14** 50 40N 26 10 E
Rovuma = Ruvuma →,
Tanzania **55 E5** 10 29S 40 28 E
Row'ān, *Iran* **45 C6** 35 8N 48 51 E
Rowena, *Australia* **63 D4** 29 48S 148 55 E
Rowley Shoals, *Australia* **60 C2** 17 30S 119 0 E
Roxas, *Phil.* **37 B6** 11 36N 122 49 E
Roxboro, *U.S.A.* **77 G6** 36 24N 78 59W
Roxburgh, *N.Z.* **59 L2** 45 33S 169 19 E
Roxbury, *U.S.A.* **78 F7** 40 6N 77 39W
Roy, *Mont., U.S.A.* **82 C9** 47 20N 108 58W
Roy, *N. Mex., U.S.A.* **81 H2** 35 57N 104 12W
Roy, *Utah, U.S.A.* **82 F7** 41 10N 112 2W
Royal Canal, *Ireland* **13 C4** 53 30N 7 13W
Royal Leamington Spa, *U.K.* **11 E6** 52 18N 1 31W
Royal Tunbridge Wells, *U.K.* **11 F8** 51 7N 0 16 E
Royan, *France* **18 D3** 45 37N 1 2W
Royston, *U.K.* **11 E7** 52 3N 0 0 E
Rozdilna, *Ukraine* **17 E16** 46 50N 30 2 E
Rozhyshche, *Ukraine* **17 C13** 50 54N 25 15 E
Rtishchevo, *Russia* **24 C7** 52 18N 43 46 E
Ruacaná, *Angola* **56 B1** 17 20S 14 12 E
Ruahine Ra., *N.Z.* **59 H6** 39 55S 176 2 E
Ruapehu, *N.Z.* **59 H5** 39 17S 175 35 E
Ruapuke I., *N.Z.* **59 M2** 46 46S 168 31 E
Ruâq, W. →, *Egypt* **47 F2** 30 0N 33 49 E
Rub' al Khālī, *Si. Arabia* **46 D4** 18 0N 48 0 E
Rubeho Mts., *Tanzania* **54 D4** 6 50S 36 25 E
Rubh a' Mhail, *U.K.* **12 F2** 55 56N 6 8W
Rubha Hunish, *U.K.* **12 D2** 57 42N 6 20W
Rubha Robhanais = Lewis,
Butt of, *U.K.* **12 C2** 58 31N 6 16W
Rubicon →, *U.S.A.* **84 G5** 38 53N 121 4W
Rubio, *Venezuela* **92 B4** 7 43N 72 22W
Rubtsovsk, *Russia* **26 D9** 51 30N 81 10 E
Ruby L., *U.S.A.* **82 F6** 40 10N 115 28W
Ruby Mts., *U.S.A.* **82 F6** 40 30N 115 20W
Rubyvale, *Australia* **62 C4** 23 25S 147 42 E
Rūd Sar, *Iran* **45 B6** 37 8N 50 18 E
Rudall, *Australia* **63 E2** 33 43S 136 17 E
Rudall →, *Australia* **60 D3** 22 34S 122 13 E
Rudewa, *Tanzania* **55 E3** 10 7S 34 40 E
Rudnyy, *Kazakstan* **26 D7** 52 57N 63 7 E
Rudolfa, Ostrov, *Russia* **26 A6** 81 45N 58 30 E
Rudyard, *U.S.A.* **76 B3** 46 14N 84 36W
Rufiji →, *Tanzania* **54 D4** 7 50S 39 15 E
Rufino, *Argentina* **94 C3** 34 20S 62 50W
Rufunsa, *Zambia* **55 F2** 15 4S 29 34 E
Rugby, *U.K.* **11 E6** 52 23N 1 16W
Rugby, *U.S.A.* **80 A5** 48 22N 100 0W
Rügen, *Germany* **16 A7** 54 22N 13 24 E
Ruhengeri, *Rwanda* **54 C2** 1 30S 29 36 E
Ruhnu, *Estonia* **9 H20** 57 48N 23 15 E
Ruhr →, *Germany* **16 C4** 51 27N 6 43 E
Ruhuhu →, *Tanzania* **55 E3** 10 31S 34 34 E
Ruidoso, *U.S.A.* **83 K11** 33 20N 105 41W
Ruivo, Pico, *Madeira* **22 D3** 32 45N 16 56W
Rujm Tal'at al Jamā'ah,
Jordan **47 E4** 30 24N 35 30 E
Ruk, *Pakistan* **42 F3** 27 50N 68 42 E
Rukhla, *Pakistan* **42 C4** 32 27N 71 57 E
Ruki →,
Dem. Rep. of the Congo **52 E3** 0 5N 18 17 E
Rukwa □, *Tanzania* **54 D3** 7 0S 31 30 E
Rukwa, L., *Tanzania* **54 D3** 8 0S 32 20 E
Rulhieres, C., *Australia* **60 B4** 13 56S 127 22 E
Rum = Rhum, *U.K.* **12 E2** 57 0N 6 20W
Rum Cay, *Bahamas* **89 B5** 23 40N 74 58W
Rum Jungle, *Australia* **60 B5** 13 0S 130 59 E
Rumāḥ, *Si. Arabia* **44 E5** 25 29N 47 10 E
Rumania = Romania ■,
Europe **17 F12** 46 0N 25 0 E
Rumaylah, *Iraq* **44 D5** 30 47N 47 37 E
Rumbêk, *Sudan* **51 G11** 6 54N 29 37 E
Rumford, *U.S.A.* **77 C10** 44 33N 70 33W
Rumia, *Poland* **17 A10** 54 37N 18 25 E
Rumoi, *Japan* **30 C10** 43 56N 141 39 E
Rumonge, *Burundi* **54 C2** 3 59S 29 26 E
Rumson, *U.S.A.* **79 F11** 40 23N 74 0W
Rumuruti, *Kenya* **54 B4** 0 17N 36 32 E
Runan, *China* **34 H8** 33 0N 114 30 E
Runanga, *N.Z.* **59 K3** 42 25S 171 15 E
Runaway, C., *N.Z.* **59 G6** 37 32S 177 59 E
Runcorn, *U.K.* **10 D5** 53 21N 2 44W
Rundu, *Namibia* **53 H3** 17 52S 19 43 E
Rungwa, *Tanzania* **54 D3** 6 55S 33 32 E
Rungwa →, *Tanzania* **54 D3** 7 36S 31 50 E
Rungwe, *Tanzania* **55 D3** 9 11S 33 32 E
Rungwe, Mt., *Tanzania* **52 F6** 9 8S 33 40 E
Runton Ra., *Australia* **60 D3** 23 31S 123 6 E
Ruoqiang, *China* **32 C3** 38 55N 88 10 E
Rupa, *India* **41 F18** 27 15N 92 21 E
Rupar, *India* **42 D7** 31 2N 76 38 E
Rupat, *Indonesia* **36 D2** 1 45N 101 40 E
Rupen →, *India* **42 H4** 23 28N 71 31 E
Rupert, *U.S.A.* **82 E7** 42 37N 113 41W
Rupert →, *Canada* **70 B4** 51 29N 78 45W
Rupert B., *Canada* **70 B4** 51 35N 79 0W
Rupert House =
Waskaganish, *Canada* **70 B4** 51 30N 78 40W
Rupsa, *India* **43 J12** 21 37N 87 1 E
Rurrenabaque, *Bolivia* **92 F5** 14 30S 67 32W
Rusambo, *Zimbabwe* **55 F3** 16 30S 32 4 E
Rusape, *Zimbabwe* **55 F3** 18 35S 32 8 E
Ruschuk = Ruse, *Bulgaria* **21 C12** 43 48N 25 59 E
Ruse, *Bulgaria* **21 C12** 43 48N 25 59 E
Rush, *Ireland* **13 C5** 53 31N 6 6W
Rushan, *China* **35 F11** 36 56N 121 30 E
Rushden, *U.K.* **11 E7** 52 18N 0 35W
Rushmore, Mt., *U.S.A.* **80 D3** 43 53N 103 28W
Rushville, *Ill., U.S.A.* **80 E9** 40 7N 90 34W
Rushville, *Ind., U.S.A.* **76 F3** 39 37N 85 27W
Rushville, *Nebr., U.S.A.* **80 D3** 42 43N 102 28W
Russas, *Brazil* **93 D11** 4 55S 37 50W
Russell, *Canada* **73 C8** 50 50N 101 20W
Russell, *Kans., U.S.A.* **80 F5** 38 54N 98 52W
Russell, *N.Y., U.S.A.* **79 B9** 44 27N 75 9W
Russell, *Pa., U.S.A.* **78 E5** 41 56N 79 8W
Russell L., *Man., Canada* **73 B8** 56 15N 101 30W
Russell L., *N.W.T., Canada* **72 A5** 63 5N 115 44W
Russellkonda, *India* **41 K14** 19 57N 84 42 E
Russellville, *Ala., U.S.A.* **77 H2** 34 30N 87 44W
Russellville, *Ark., U.S.A.* **81 H8** 35 17N 93 8W
Russellville, *Ky., U.S.A.* **77 G2** 36 51N 86 53W
Russia ■, *Eurasia* **27 C11** 62 0N 105 0 E
Russian →, *U.S.A.* **84 G3** 38 27N 123 8W
Russkoye Ustie, *Russia* **4 B15** 71 0N 149 0 E
Rustam, *Pakistan* **42 B5** 34 25N 72 13 E
Rustam Shahr, *Pakistan* **42 F2** 26 58N 66 6 E
Rustavi, *Georgia* **25 F8** 41 30N 45 0 E
Rustenburg, *S. Africa* **56 D4** 25 41S 27 14 E
Ruston, *U.S.A.* **81 J8** 32 32N 92 38W
Rutana, *Burundi* **54 C3** 3 55S 30 0 E
Ruteng, *Indonesia* **37 F6** 8 35S 120 30 E
Ruth, *U.S.A.* **78 C2** 43 42N 82 45W
Rutherford, *U.S.A.* **84 G4** 38 26N 122 24W
Rutland, *U.S.A.* **79 C12** 43 37N 72 58W
Rutland □, *U.K.* **11 E7** 52 38N 0 40W
Rutland Water, *U.K.* **11 E7** 52 39N 0 38W
Rutledge →, *Canada* **73 A6** 61 4N 112 0W
Rutledge L., *Canada* **73 A6** 61 33N 110 47W
Rutshuru,
Dem. Rep. of the Congo **54 C2** 1 13S 29 25 E
Ruvu, *Tanzania* **54 D4** 6 49S 38 43 E
Ruvu →, *Tanzania* **54 D4** 6 23S 38 52 E
Ruvuma □, *Tanzania* **55 E4** 10 20S 36 0 E
Ruvuma →, *Tanzania* **55 E5** 10 29S 40 28 E
Ruwais, *U.A.E.* **45 E7** 24 5N 52 50 E
Ruwenzori, *Africa* **54 B2** 0 30N 29 55 E
Ruyigi, *Burundi* **54 C3** 3 29S 30 15 E
Ružomberok, *Slovak Rep.* **17 D10** 49 3N 19 17 E
Rwanda ■, *Africa* **54 C3** 2 0S 30 0 E
Ryan, L., *U.K.* **12 G3** 55 0N 5 2W
Ryazan, *Russia* **24 D6** 54 40N 39 40 E
Ryazhsk, *Russia* **24 D7** 53 45N 40 3 E
Rybache = Rybachye,
Kazakstan **26 E9** 46 40N 81 20 E
Rybachiy Poluostrov, *Russia* **24 A5** 69 43N 32 0 E
Rybachye = Ysyk-Köl,
Kyrgyzstan **28 E11** 42 26N 76 12 E
Rybachye, *Kazakstan* **26 E9** 46 40N 81 20 E
Rybinsk, *Russia* **24 C6** 58 5N 38 50 E
Rybinskoye Vdkhr., *Russia* **24 C6** 58 30N 38 25 E
Rybnitsa = Râbniţa,
Moldova **17 E15** 47 45N 29 0 E
Rycroft, *Canada* **72 B5** 55 45N 118 40W
Ryde, *U.K.* **11 G6** 50 43N 1 9W
Ryderwood, *U.S.A.* **84 D3** 46 23N 123 3W
Rye, *U.K.* **11 G8** 50 57N 0 45 E
Rye →, *U.K.* **10 C7** 54 11N 0 44W
Rye Bay, *U.K.* **11 G8** 50 52N 0 49 E
Rye Patch Reservoir, *U.S.A.* **82 F4** 40 28N 118 19W
Ryegate, *U.S.A.* **82 C9** 46 18N 109 15W
Ryley, *Canada* **72 C6** 53 17N 112 26W
Rylstone, *Australia* **63 E4** 32 46S 149 58 E
Ryōtsu, *Japan* **30 E9** 38 5N 138 26 E
Rypin, *Poland* **17 B10** 53 3N 19 25 E
Ryūgasaki, *Japan* **31 G10** 35 54N 140 11 E
Ryūkyū Is. = Ryūkyū-rettō,
Japan **31 M3** 26 0N 126 0 E
Ryūkyū-rettō, *Japan* **31 M3** 26 0N 126 0 E
Rzeszów, *Poland* **17 C11** 50 5N 21 58 E
Rzhev, *Russia* **24 C5** 56 20N 34 20 E

Sánchez

Sánchez, *Dom. Rep.* **89 C6** 19 15N 69 36W
Sanchor, *India* .... **42 G4** 24 45N 71 55 E
Sancti Spíritus, *Cuba* **88 B4** 21 52N 79 33W
Sancy, Puy de, *France* .... **18 D5** 45 32N 2 50 E
Sand →, *S. Africa* ...... **57 C5** 22 25S 30 5 E
Sand Hills, *U.S.A.* **80 D4** 42 10N 101 30W
Sand Springs, *U.S.A.* **81 G6** 36 9N 96 7W
Sanda, *Japan* .... **31 G7** 34 53N 135 14 E
Sandakan, *Malaysia* ...... **36 C5** 5 53N 118 4 E
Sandan = Sambor,
Cambodia .... **38 F6** 12 46N 106 0 E
Sandanski, *Bulgaria* ...... **21 D10** 41 35N 23 16 E
Sanday, *U.K.* **12 B6** 59 16N 2 31W
Sandefjord, *Norway* ...... **9 G14** 59 10N 10 15 E
Sanders, *U.S.A.* **83 J9** 35 13N 109 20W
Sanderson, *U.S.A.* **81 K3** 30 9N 102 24W
Sandersville, *U.S.A.* **77 J4** 32 59N 82 48W
Sandfire Roadhouse,
Australia .... **60 C3** 19 45S 121 15 E
Sandfly L., *Canada* **73 B7** 55 43N 106 6W
Sandía, *Peru* **92 F5** 14 10S 69 30W
Sandila, *India* .... **43 F9** 27 5N 80 31 E
Sandnes, *Norway* .... **9 G11** 58 50N 5 45 E
Sandnessjøen, *Norway* ... **8 C15** 66 2N 12 38 E
Sandoa,
Dem. Rep. of the Congo . **52 F4** 9 41S 23 0 E
Sandomierz, *Poland* ..... **17 C11** 50 40N 21 43 E
Sandover →, *Australia* ... **62 C2** 21 43S 136 32 E
Sandoway, *Burma* .... **41 K19** 18 20N 94 30 E
Sandoy, *Fœroe Is.* **8 F9** 61 52N 6 46W
Sandpoint, *U.S.A.* **82 B5** 48 17N 116 33W
Sandray, *U.K.* **12 E1** 56 53N 7 31W
Sandringham, *U.K.* .... **10 E8** 52 51N 0 31 E
Sandstone, *Australia* ..... **61 E2** 27 59S 119 16 E
Sandusky, *Mich., U.S.A.* ... **78 C2** 43 25N 82 50W
Sandusky, *Ohio, U.S.A.* ... **78 E2** 41 27N 82 42W
Sandviken, *Sweden* ...... **9 F17** 60 38N 16 46 E
Sandwich, C., *Australia* ... **62 B4** 18 14S 146 18 E
Sandwich B., *Canada* **71 B8** 53 40N 57 15W
Sandwich B., *Namibia* .... **56 C1** 23 25S 14 20 E
Sandwip Chan., *Bangla.* ... **41 H17** 22 35N 91 35 E
Sandy, *Oreg., U.S.A.* **84 E4** 45 24N 122 16W
Sandy, *Pa., U.S.A.* **78 E6** 41 6N 78 46W
Sandy, *Utah, U.S.A.* **82 F8** 40 35N 111 50W
Sandy Bay, *Canada* **73 B8** 55 31N 102 19W
Sandy Bight, *Australia* .... **61 F3** 33 50S 123 20 E
Sandy C., *Queens., Australia* **62 C5** 24 42S 153 15 E
Sandy C., *Tas., Australia* .. **62 G3** 41 25S 144 45 E
Sandy Cay, *Bahamas* **89 B4** 23 13N 75 18W
Sandy Cr. →, *U.S.A.* **82 F9** 41 51N 109 47W
Sandy L., *Canada* **70 B1** 53 2N 93 0W
Sandy Lake, *Canada* **70 B1** 53 0N 93 15W
Sandy Valley, *U.S.A.* **85 K11** 35 49N 115 36W
Sanford, *Fla., U.S.A.* **77 L5** 28 48N 81 16W
Sanford, *Maine, U.S.A.* **77 D10** 43 27N 70 47W
Sanford, *N.C., U.S.A.* **77 H6** 35 29N 79 10W
Sanford →, *Australia* .... **61 E2** 27 22S 115 53 E
Sanford, Mt., *U.S.A.* **68 B5** 62 13N 144 8W
Sang-i-Masha, *Afghan.* .... **42 C2** 33 8N 67 27 E
Sanga, *Mozam.* .... **55 E4** 12 22S 35 21 E
Sanga →, *Congo* .... **52 E3** 1 5S 17 0 E
Sangamner, *India* .... **40 K9** 19 37N 74 15 E
Sangar, *Afghan.* .... **42 C1** 32 56N 65 30 E
Sangar, *Russia* .... **27 C13** 64 2N 127 31 E
Sangar Sarai, *Afghan.* .... **42 B4** 34 27N 70 35 E
Sangarh →, *Pakistan* .... **42 D4** 30 43N 70 44 E
Sangay, *Ecuador* **92 D3** 2 0S 78 20W
Sange,
Dem. Rep. of the Congo . **54 D2** 6 58S 28 21 E
Sangeang, *Indonesia* ..... **37 F5** 8 12S 119 6 E
Sanger, *U.S.A.* **84 J7** 36 42N 119 33W
Sangerhausen, *Germany* .. **16 C6** 51 28N 11 18 E
Sanggan He →, *China* .... **34 E9** 38 12N 117 15 E
Sanggau, *Indonesia* ...... **36 D4** 0 5N 110 30 E
Sanghar, *Pakistan* .... **42 F3** 26 2N 68 57 E
Sangihe, Kepulauan,
Indonesia .... **37 D7** 3 0N 126 0 E
Sangihe, Pulau, *Indonesia* . **37 D7** 3 45N 125 30 E
Sangju, *S. Korea* .... **35 F15** 36 25N 128 10 E
Sangkapura, *Indonesia* ... **36 F4** 5 52S 112 40 E
Sangkhla, *Thailand* .... **38 E2** 14 57N 98 28 E
Sangkulirang, *Indonesia* .. **36 D5** 0 59N 117 58 E
Sangla, *Pakistan* .... **42 D5** 31 43N 73 23 E
Sangli, *India* .... **40 L9** 16 55N 74 33 E
Sangmélima, *Cameroon* .. **52 D2** 2 57N 12 1 E
Sangod, *India* .... **42 G7** 24 55N 76 17 E
Sangre de Cristo Mts.,
U.S.A. **81 G2** 37 30N 105 20W
Sangrur, *India* .... **42 D6** 30 14N 75 50 E
Sangudo, *Canada* **72 C6** 53 50N 114 54W
Sangue →, *Brazil* **92 F7** 11 1S 58 39W
Sanibel, *U.S.A.* **77 M4** 26 26N 82 1W
Sanirajak, *Canada* **69 B11** 68 46N 81 12W
Sanjawi, *Pakistan* .... **42 D3** 30 17N 68 21 E
Sanje, *Uganda* .... **54 C3** 0 49S 31 30 E
Sanjo, *Japan* .... **30 F9** 37 37N 138 57 E
Sankh →, *India* .... **43 H11** 22 15N 84 48 E
Sankt Gallen, *Switz.* ..... **18 C8** 47 26N 9 22 E
Sankt Moritz, *Switz.* ..... **18 C8** 46 30N 9 50 E
Sankt-Peterburg, *Russia* .. **24 C5** 59 55N 30 20 E
Sankt Pölten, *Austria* ..... **16 D8** 48 12N 15 38 E
Sankuru →,
Dem. Rep. of the Congo . **52 E4** 4 17S 20 25 E
Sanliurfa, *Turkey* .... **25 G6** 37 12N 38 50 E
Sanlúcar de Barrameda,
Spain **19 D2** 36 46N 6 21W
Sanmenxia, *China* .... **34 G6** 34 47N 111 12 E
Sanming, *China* .... **33 D6** 26 15N 117 40 E
Sannaspos, *S. Africa* ..... **56 D4** 29 6S 26 34 E
Sannicandro Gargánico,
Italy .... **20 D6** 41 50N 15 34 E
Sânnicolau Mare, *Romania* **17 E11** 46 5N 20 39 E
Sannieshof, *S. Africa* ..... **56 D4** 26 30S 25 47 E
Sannīn, J., *Lebanon* ...... **47 B4** 33 57N 35 52 E
Sanniquellie, *Liberia* **50 G4** 7 19N 8 38W
Sanok, *Poland* .... **17 D12** 49 35N 22 10 E
Sanquhar, *U.K.* **12 F5** 55 22N 3 54W
Sant Antoni Abat, *Spain* .. **22 C7** 38 59N 1 19 E
Sant Carles, *Spain* .... **22 B8** 39 3N 1 34 E
Sant Feliu de Guíxols, *Spain* **19 B7** 41 45N 3 1 E
Sant Ferran, *Spain* ...... **22 C7** 38 42N 1 28 E
Sant Francesc de
Formentera, *Spain* ...... **22 C7** 38 42N 1 26 E
Sant Jaume, *Spain* ...... **22 B11** 39 54N 4 4 E
Sant Joan Baptista, *Spain* . **22 B8** 39 5N 1 31 E
Sant Jordi, *Spain* .... **22 B9** 39 33N 2 46 E
Sant Jordi, G. de, *Spain* ... **19 B6** 40 53N 1 2 E
Sant Llorenç des Cardassar,
Spain .... **22 B10** 39 37N 3 17 E
Sant Mateu, *Spain* .... **22 B7** 39 3N 1 23 E
Sant Miquel, *Spain* .... **22 B7** 39 3N 1 26 E
Sant Telm, *Spain* .... **22 B9** 39 35N 2 21 E
Santa Agnés, *Spain* ...... **22 B7** 39 3N 1 21 E
Santa Ana, *Bolivia* **92 F5** 13 50S 65 40W
Santa Ana, *El Salv.* **88 D2** 14 0N 89 31W
Santa Ana, *Mexico* **86 A2** 30 31N 111 8W
Santa Ana, *U.S.A.* **85 M9** 33 46N 117 52W
Sant' Antioco, *Italy* ...... **20 E3** 39 4N 8 27 E
Santa Barbara, *Chile* **94 D1** 37 40S 72 1W
Santa Barbara, *Honduras* .. **88 D2** 14 53N 88 14W
Santa Bárbara, *Mexico* **86 B3** 26 48N 105 50W
Santa Barbara, *U.S.A.* **85 L7** 34 25N 119 42W
Santa Barbara Channel,
U.S.A. **85 L7** 34 15N 120 0W
Santa Barbara I., *U.S.A.* ... **85 M7** 33 29N 119 2W
Santa Catalina, Gulf of,
U.S.A. **85 N9** 33 10N 117 50W
Santa Catalina, I., *Mexico* . **86 B2** 25 40N 110 50W
Santa Catalina I., *U.S.A.* ... **85 M8** 33 23N 118 25W
Santa Catarina □, *Brazil* ... **95 B6** 27 25S 48 30W
Santa Catarina, I. de, *Brazil* **95 B6** 27 30S 48 40W
Santa Cecília, *Brazil* **95 B5** 26 56S 50 18W
Santa Clara, *Cuba* **88 B4** 22 20N 80 0W
Santa Clara, *Calif., U.S.A.* . **84 H5** 37 21N 121 57W
Santa Clara, *Utah, U.S.A.* .. **83 H7** 37 8N 113 39W
Santa Clara, El Golfo de,
Mexico **86 A2** 31 42N 114 30W
Santa Clara de Olimar,
Uruguay **95 C5** 32 50S 54 54W
Santa Clarita, *U.S.A.* **85 L8** 34 24N 118 30W
Santa Clotilde, *Peru* **92 D4** 2 33S 73 45W
Santa Coloma de Gramenet,
Spain .... **19 B7** 41 27N 2 13 E
Santa Cruz, *Argentina* **96 G3** 50 0S 68 32W
Santa Cruz, *Bolivia* **92 G6** 17 43S 63 10W
Santa Cruz, *Chile* **94 C1** 34 38S 71 27W
Santa Cruz, *Costa Rica* **88 D2** 10 15N 85 35W
Santa Cruz, *Madeira* **22 D3** 32 42N 16 46W
Santa Cruz, *Phil.* .... **37 B6** 14 20N 121 24 E
Santa Cruz, *U.S.A.* **84 J4** 36 58N 122 1W
Santa Cruz →, *Argentina* . **96 G3** 50 10S 68 20W
Santa Cruz de la Palma,
Canary Is. **22 F2** 28 41N 17 46W
Santa Cruz de Tenerife,
Canary Is. **22 F3** 28 28N 16 15W
Santa Cruz del Norte, *Cuba* **88 B3** 23 9N 81 55W
Santa Cruz del Sur, *Cuba* .. **88 B4** 20 44N 78 0W
Santa Cruz do Rio Pardo,
Brazil **95 A6** 22 54S 49 37W
Santa Cruz do Sul, *Brazil* .. **95 B5** 29 42S 52 25W
Santa Cruz I., *U.S.A.* **85 M7** 34 1N 119 43W
Santa Cruz Is., *Solomon Is.* **64 J8** 10 30S 166 0 E
Santa Domingo, Cay,
Bahamas **88 B4** 21 25N 75 15W
Santa Elena, *Argentina* **94 C4** 30 58S 59 47W
Santa Elena, C., *Costa Rica* **88 D2** 10 54N 85 56W
Santa Eulàlia des Riu, *Spain* **22 C8** 38 59N 1 32 E
Santa Fe, *Argentina* **94 C3** 31 35S 60 41W
Santa Fe, *U.S.A.* **83 J11** 35 41N 105 57W
Santa Fé □, *Argentina* **94 C3** 31 50S 60 55W
Santa Fé do Sul, *Brazil* **93 H8** 20 13S 50 56W
Santa Filomena, *Brazil* **93 E9** 9 6S 45 50W
Santa Gertrudis, *Spain* .... **22 C7** 39 0N 1 26 E
Santa Inês, *Brazil* **93 F11** 13 17S 39 48W
Santa Inés, I., *Chile* **96 G2** 54 0S 73 0W
Santa Isabel = Rey Malabo,
Eq. Guin. .... **52 D1** 3 45N 8 50 E
Santa Isabel, *Argentina* ... **94 D2** 36 10S 66 54W
Santa Isabel do Morro,
Brazil **93 F8** 11 34S 50 40W
Santa Lucía, *Corrientes,*
Argentina **94 B4** 28 58S 59 5W
Santa Lucía, *San Juan,*
Argentina **94 C2** 31 30S 68 30W
Santa Lucía, *Uruguay* **94 C4** 34 27S 56 24W
Santa Lucia Range, *U.S.A.* . **84 K5** 36 0N 121 20W
Santa Magdalena, I., *Mexico* **86 C2** 24 40N 112 15W
Santa Margarita, *Argentina* **94 D3** 38 28S 61 35W
Santa Margarita, *Spain* ... **22 B10** 39 42N 3 6 E
Santa Margarita, *U.S.A.* ... **84 K6** 35 23N 120 37W
Santa Margarita →, *U.S.A.* **85 M9** 33 13N 117 23W
Santa Margarita, I., *Mexico* **86 C2** 24 30N 111 50W
Santa María, *Argentina* ... **94 B2** 26 40S 66 0W
Santa Maria, *Brazil* **95 B5** 29 40S 53 48W
Santa Maria, *U.S.A.* **85 L6** 34 57N 120 26W
Santa María →, *Mexico* ... **86 A3** 31 0N 107 14W
Santa María, B. de, *Mexico* **86 B3** 25 10N 108 40W
Santa Maria da Vitória,
Brazil **93 F10** 13 24S 44 12W
Santa Maria del Camí, *Spain* **22 B9** 39 38N 2 47 E
Santa Maria di Léuca, C.,
Italy .... **21 E8** 39 47N 18 22 E
Santa Marta, *Colombia* **92 A4** 11 15N 74 13W
Santa Marta, Sierra Nevada
de, *Colombia* **92 A4** 10 55N 73 50W
Santa Marta Grande, C.,
Brazil **95 B6** 28 43S 48 50W
Santa Maura = Levkás,
Greece .... **21 E9** 38 40N 20 43 E
Santa Monica, *U.S.A.* **85 M8** 34 1N 118 29W
Santa Paula, *U.S.A.* **85 L7** 34 21N 119 4W
Santa Ponsa, *Spain* ...... **22 B9** 39 30N 2 28 E
Santa Rita, *U.S.A.* **83 K10** 32 48N 108 4W
Santa Rosa, *La Pampa,*
Argentina **94 D3** 36 40S 64 17W
Santa Rosa, *San Luis,*
Argentina **94 C2** 32 21S 65 10W
Santa Rosa, *Brazil* **95 B5** 27 52S 54 29W
Santa Rosa, *Calif., U.S.A.* .. **84 G4** 38 26N 122 43W
Santa Rosa, *N. Mex., U.S.A.* **81 H2** 34 57N 104 41W
Santa Rosa de Copán,
Honduras **88 D2** 14 47N 88 46W
Santa Rosa de Río Primero,
Argentina **94 C3** 31 8S 63 20W
Santa Rosa del Sara, *Bolivia* **92 G6** 17 7S 63 35W
Santa Rosa I., *U.S.A.* **85 M6** 33 58N 120 6W
Santa Rosa Range, *U.S.A.* . **82 F5** 41 45N 117 40W
Santa Rosalía, *Mexico* **86 B2** 27 20N 112 20W
Santa Sylvina, *Argentina* .. **94 B3** 27 50S 61 10W
Santa Tecla = Nueva San
Salvador, *El Salv.* **88 D2** 13 40N 89 18W
Santa Teresa, *Argentina* ... **94 C3** 33 25S 60 47W
Santa Teresa, *Australia* ... **62 C1** 24 8S 134 22 E
Santa Teresa, *Mexico* **87 B5** 25 17N 97 51W
Santa Vitória do Palmar,
Brazil **95 C5** 33 32S 53 25W
Santa Ynez, *U.S.A.* **85 L6** 34 37N 120 5W
Santa Ynez →, *U.S.A.* **85 L6** 35 41N 120 36W
Santa Ynez Mts., *U.S.A.* ... **85 L6** 34 30N 120 0W
Santa Ysabel, *U.S.A.* **85 M10** 33 7N 116 40W
Santai, *China* .... **32 C5** 31 5N 104 58 E
Santana, *Madeira* **22 D3** 32 48N 16 52W
Santana, Coxilha de, *Brazil* **95 C4** 30 50S 55 35W
Santana do Livramento,
Brazil **95 C4** 30 55S 55 30W
Santander, *Spain* **19 A4** 43 27N 3 51W
Santander Jiménez, *Mexico* **87 C5** 24 11N 98 29W
Santanyí, *Spain* .... **22 B10** 39 20N 3 5 E
Santaquin, *U.S.A.* **82 G8** 39 59N 111 47W
Santarém, *Brazil* **93 D8** 2 25S 54 42W
Santarém, *Portugal* **19 C1** 39 12N 8 42W
Santaren Channel, *W. Indies* **88 B4** 24 0N 79 30W
Santee, *U.S.A.* **85 N10** 32 50N 116 58W
Santee →, *U.S.A.* **77 J6** 33 7N 79 17W
Santiago, *Brazil* **95 B5** 29 11S 54 52W
Santiago, *Chile* **94 C1** 33 24S 70 40W
Santiago, *Panama* **88 E3** 8 0N 81 0W
Santiago □, *Chile* **94 C1** 33 30S 70 50W
Santiago →, *Mexico* **66 G9** 25 11N 105 26W
Santiago →, *Peru* **92 D3** 4 27S 77 38W
Santiago de Compostela,
Spain **19 A1** 42 52N 8 37W
Santiago de Cuba, *Cuba* .. **88 C4** 20 0N 75 49W
Santiago de los Cabelleros,
Dom. Rep. **89 C5** 19 30N 70 40W
Santiago del Estero,
Argentina **94 B3** 27 50S 64 15W
Santiago del Estero □,
Argentina **94 B3** 27 40S 63 15W
Santiago del Teide,
Canary Is. **22 F3** 28 17N 16 48W
Santiago Ixcuintla, *Mexico* . **86 C3** 21 50N 105 11W
Santiago Papasquiaro,
Mexico **86 C3** 25 0N 105 20W
Santiaguillo, L. de, *Mexico* **86 C4** 24 50N 104 50W
Santo Amaro, *Brazil* **93 F11** 12 30S 38 43W
Santo Anastácio, *Brazil* ... **95 A5** 21 58S 51 39W
Santo André, *Brazil* **95 A6** 23 39S 46 29W
Santo Ângelo, *Brazil* **95 B5** 28 15S 54 15W
Santo Antônio do Içá, *Brazil* **92 D5** 3 5S 67 57W
Santo Antônio do Leverger,
Brazil **93 G7** 15 52S 56 5W
Santo Domingo, *Dom. Rep.* **89 C6** 18 30N 69 59W
Santo Domingo, *Baja Calif.,*
Mexico **86 A1** 30 43N 116 2W
Santo Domingo,
Baja Calif. S., Mexico ... **86 B2** 25 32N 112 2W
Santo Domingo, *Nic.* **88 D3** 12 14N 84 59W
Santo Domingo de los
Colorados, *Ecuador* **92 D3** 0 15S 79 9W
Santo Domingo Pueblo,
U.S.A. **83 J10** 35 31N 106 22W
Santo Tomás, *Mexico* **86 A1** 31 33N 116 24W
Santo Tomás, *Peru* **92 F4** 14 26S 72 8W
Santo Tomé, *Argentina* ... **95 B4** 28 40S 56 5W
Santo Tomé de Guayana =
Ciudad Guayana,
Venezuela **92 B6** 8 0N 62 30W
Santoña, *Spain* **19 A4** 43 29N 3 27W
Santorini = Thíra, *Greece* . **21 F11** 36 23N 25 27 E
Santos, *Brazil* **95 A6** 24 0S 46 20W
Santos Dumont, *Brazil* **95 A7** 22 55S 43 10W
Sanwer, *India* .... **42 H6** 22 59N 75 50 E
Sanyuan, *China* .... **34 G5** 34 35N 108 58 E
São Bernardo do Campo,
Brazil **95 A6** 23 45S 46 34W
São Borja, *Brazil* **95 B4** 28 39S 56 0W
São Carlos, *Brazil* **95 A6** 22 0S 47 50W
São Cristóvão, *Brazil* **93 F11** 11 1S 37 15W
São Domingos, *Brazil* **93 F9** 13 25S 46 19W
São Francisco, *Brazil* **93 G10** 16 0S 44 50W
São Francisco →, *Brazil* .. **93 F11** 10 30S 36 24W
São Francisco do Sul, *Brazil* **95 B6** 26 15S 48 36W
São Gabriel, *Brazil* **95 C5** 30 20S 54 20W
São Gonçalo, *Brazil* **95 A7** 22 48S 43 5W
Sao Hill, *Tanzania* .... **55 D4** 8 20S 35 12 E
São João da Boa Vista,
Brazil **95 A6** 22 0S 46 52W
São João da Madeira,
Portugal **19 B1** 40 54N 8 30W
São João del Rei, *Brazil* ... **95 A7** 21 8S 44 15W
São João do Araguaia,
Brazil **93 E9** 5 23S 48 46W
São João do Piauí, *Brazil* .. **93 E10** 8 21S 42 15W
São Joaquim, *Brazil* **95 B6** 28 18S 49 56W
São Jorge, Pta. de, *Madeira* **22 D3** 32 50N 16 53W
São José, *Brazil* **95 B5** 27 38S 48 39W
São José do Norte, *Brazil* . **95 C5** 32 1S 52 3W
São José do Rio Prêto,
Brazil **95 A6** 20 50S 49 20W
São José dos Campos,
Brazil **95 A6** 23 7S 45 52W
São Leopoldo, *Brazil* **95 B5** 29 50S 51 10W
São Lourenço, *Brazil* **95 A6** 22 7S 45 3W
São Lourenço →, *Brazil* .. **93 G7** 17 53S 57 27W
São Lourenço, Pta. de,
Madeira **22 D3** 32 44N 16 39W
São Lourenço do Sul, *Brazil* **95 C5** 31 22S 51 58W
São Luís, *Brazil* **93 D10** 2 39S 44 15W
São Luís Gonzaga, *Brazil* .. **95 B5** 28 25S 55 0W
São Marcos →, *Brazil* **93 G9** 18 15S 47 37W
São Marcos, B. de, *Brazil* .. **93 D10** 2 0S 44 0W
São Mateus, *Brazil* **93 G11** 18 44S 39 50W
São Mateus do Sul, *Brazil* . **95 B5** 25 52S 50 23W
São Miguel do Oeste, *Brazil* **95 B5** 26 45S 53 34W
São Paulo, *Brazil* **95 A6** 23 32S 46 37W
São Paulo □, *Brazil* **95 A6** 22 0S 49 0W
São Paulo, I., *Atl. Oc.* **2 D8** 0 50N 31 40W
São Paulo de Olivença,
Brazil **92 D5** 3 27S 68 48W
São Roque, *Madeira* **22 D3** 32 46N 16 48W
São Roque, C. de, *Brazil* .. **93 E11** 5 30S 35 16W
São Sebastião, I. de, *Brazil* **95 A6** 23 50S 45 18W
São Sebastião do Paraíso,
Brazil **95 A6** 20 54S 46 59W
São Tomé, *Atl. Oc.* ...... **48 F4** 0 10N 6 39 E
São Tomé, C. de, *Brazil* ... **95 A7** 22 0S 40 59W
São Tomé & Principe ■,
Africa .... **49 F4** 0 12N 6 39 E
São Vicente, *Brazil* **95 A6** 23 57S 46 23W
São Vicente, *Madeira* **22 D2** 32 48N 17 3W
São Vicente, C. de, *Portugal* **19 D1** 37 0N 9 0W
Saona, I., *Dom. Rep.* **89 C6** 18 10N 68 40W
Saône →, *France* .... **18 D6** 45 44N 4 50 E
Saonek, *Indonesia* .... **37 E8** 0 22S 130 55 E
Saparua, *Indonesia* ...... **37 E7** 3 33S 128 40 E
Sapele, *Nigeria* .... **50 G7** 5 50N 5 40 E
Sapelo I., *U.S.A.* **77 K5** 31 25N 81 12W
Saposoa, *Peru* **92 E3** 6 55S 76 45W
Sapphire, *Australia* ...... **62 C4** 23 28S 147 43 E
Sappho, *U.S.A.* **84 B2** 48 4N 124 16W
Sapporo, *Japan* .... **30 C10** 43 0N 141 21 E
Sapulpa, *U.S.A.* **81 H6** 35 59N 96 5W
Saqqez, *Iran* .... **44 B5** 36 15N 46 20 E
Sar Dasht, *Iran* .... **45 C6** 32 32N 48 52 E
Sar Gachīneh, *Iran* ...... **45 D6** 30 31N 51 31 E
Sar Planina, *Macedonia* ... **21 C9** 42 0N 21 0 E
Sara Buri = Saraburi,
Thailand .... **38 E3** 14 30N 100 55 E
Sarāb, *Iran* .... **44 B5** 37 55N 47 40 E
Sarabadi, *Iraq* .... **44 C5** 33 1N 44 48 E
Saraburi, *Thailand* ...... **38 E3** 14 30N 100 55 E
Sarada →, *India* .... **41 F12** 27 21N 81 23 E
Saradiya, *India* .... **42 J4** 21 34N 70 2 E
Saragossa = Zaragoza,
Spain **19 B5** 41 39N 0 53W
Saraguro, *Ecuador* **92 D3** 3 35S 79 16W
Sarai Naurang, *Pakistan* ... **42 C4** 32 50N 70 47 E
Saraikela, *India* .... **43 H11** 22 42N 85 56 E
Sarajevo, *Bos.-H.* .... **21 C8** 43 52N 18 26 E
Sarakhs, *Turkmenistan* .... **45 B9** 36 32N 61 13 E
Saran, Gunung, *Indonesia* . **36 E4** 0 30S 111 25 E
Saranac L., *U.S.A.* **79 B10** 44 20N 74 10W
Saranac Lake, *U.S.A.* **79 B10** 44 20N 74 8W
Saranda, *Tanzania* ...... **54 D3** 5 45S 34 59 E
Sarandí del Yi, *Uruguay* ... **95 C4** 33 18S 55 38W
Sarandí Grande, *Uruguay* . **94 C4** 33 44S 56 20W
Sarangani B., *Phil.* .... **37 C7** 6 0N 125 13 E
Sarangani Is., *Phil.* .... **37 C7** 5 25N 125 25 E
Sarangarh, *India* .... **41 J13** 21 30N 83 5 E
Saransk, *Russia* .... **24 D8** 54 10N 45 10 E
Sarapul, *Russia* .... **24 C9** 56 28N 53 48 E
Sarasota, *U.S.A.* **77 M4** 27 20N 82 32W
Saratoga, *Calif., U.S.A.* **84 H4** 37 16N 122 2W
Saratoga, *Wyo., U.S.A.* **82 F10** 41 27N 106 49W
Saratoga Springs, *U.S.A.* .. **79 C11** 43 5N 73 47W
Saratok, *Malaysia* .... **36 D4** 1 55N 111 17 E
Saratov, *Russia* .... **25 D8** 51 30N 46 2 E
Saravane, *Laos* .... **38 E6** 15 43N 106 25 E
Sarawak □, *Malaysia* ..... **36 D4** 2 0N 113 0 E
Saray, *Turkey* .... **21 D12** 41 26N 27 55 E
Sarayköy, *Turkey* .... **21 F13** 37 55N 28 54 E
Sarbāz, *Iran* .... **45 E9** 26 38N 61 19 E
Sarbīsheh, *Iran* .... **45 C8** 32 30N 59 40 E
Sarda = Sarada →, *India* **41 F12** 27 21N 81 23 E
Sardarshahr, *India* .... **42 E6** 28 30N 74 29 E
Sardegna □, *Italy* .... **20 D3** 40 0N 9 0 E
Sardhana, *India* .... **42 E7** 29 9N 77 39 E
Sardina, Pta., *Canary Is.* ... **22 F4** 28 9N 15 44W
Sardinia = Sardegna □,
Italy .... **20 D3** 40 0N 9 0 E
Sardis, *Turkey* .... **21 E12** 38 28N 28 2 E
Sārdūīyeh = Dar Mazār, *Iran* **45 D8** 29 14N 57 20 E
S'Arenal, *Spain* .... **22 B9** 39 30N 2 45 E
Sargasso Sea, *Atl. Oc.* **66 G13** 27 0N 72 0W
Sargodha, *Pakistan* ...... **42 C5** 32 10N 72 40 E
Sarh, *Chad* .... **51 G9** 9 5N 18 23 E
Sārī, *Iran* .... **45 B7** 36 30N 53 4 E
Saria, *India* .... **43 J10** 21 38N 83 22 E
Sariab, *Pakistan* .... **42 D2** 30 6N 66 59 E
Sarıgöl, *Turkey* .... **21 E13** 38 14N 28 41 E
Sarikei, *Malaysia* .... **36 D4** 2 8N 111 30 E
Sarila, *India* .... **43 G8** 25 46N 79 41 E
Sarina, *Australia* .... **62 C4** 21 22S 149 13 E
Sarita, *U.S.A.* **81 M6** 27 13N 97 47W
Sariwŏn, *N. Korea* .... **35 E13** 38 31N 125 46 E
Sarju →, *India* .... **43 F9** 27 21N 81 23 E
Sark, *U.K.* **11 H5** 49 25N 2 22W
Sarkari Tala, *India* .... **42 F4** 27 39N 70 52 E
Şarköy, *Turkey* .... **21 D12** 40 36N 27 6 E
Sarlat-la-Canéda, *France* .. **18 D4** 44 54N 1 13 E
Sarmi, *Indonesia* .... **37 E9** 1 49S 138 44 E
Sarmiento, *Argentina* **96 F3** 45 35S 69 5W
Särna, *Sweden* .... **9 F15** 61 41N 13 8 E
Sarnia, *Canada* **78 D2** 42 58N 82 23W
Sarolangun, *Indonesia* .... **36 E2** 2 19S 102 42 E
Saronikós Kólpos, *Greece* . **21 F10** 37 45N 23 45 E
Saros Körfezi, *Turkey* ..... **21 D12** 40 30N 26 15 E
Sarpsborg, *Norway* ...... **9 G14** 59 16N 11 7 E
Sarre = Saar →, *Europe* . **18 B7** 49 41N 6 32 E
Sarreguemines, *France* ... **18 B7** 49 5N 7 4 E
Sarthe →, *France* **18 C3** 47 33N 0 31W
Saruna →, *Pakistan* ..... **42 F2** 26 31N 67 7 E
Sarvar, *India* .... **42 F6** 26 4N 75 0 E
Sarvestān, *Iran* .... **45 D7** 29 20N 53 10 E
Sary-Tash, *Kyrgyzstan* .... **26 F8** 39 44N 73 15 E
Saryshagan, *Kazakstan* .... **26 E8** 46 12N 73 38 E
Sasan Gir, *India* .... **42 J4** 21 10N 70 36 E
Sasaram, *India* .... **43 G11** 24 57N 84 5 E
Sasebo, *Japan* .... **31 H4** 33 10N 129 43 E
Saser, *India* .... **43 B7** 34 50N 77 50 E
Saskatchewan □, *Canada* . **73 C7** 54 40N 106 0W
Saskatchewan →, *Canada* **73 C8** 53 37N 100 40W
Saskatoon, *Canada* **73 C7** 52 10N 106 38W
Saskylakh, *Russia* .... **27 B12** 71 55N 114 1 E
Sasolburg, *S. Africa* ...... **57 D4** 26 46S 27 49 E
Sasovo, *Russia* .... **24 D7** 54 25N 41 55 E
Sassandra, *Ivory C.* **50 H4** 4 55N 6 8W
Sassandra →, *Ivory C.* ... **50 H4** 4 58N 6 5W
Sássari, *Italy* .... **20 D3** 40 43N 8 34 E
Sassnitz, *Germany* ...... **16 A7** 54 29N 13 39 E
Sassuolo, *Italy* .... **20 B4** 44 33N 10 47 E
Sasumua Dam, *Kenya* .... **54 C4** 0 45S 36 40 E
Sasyk, Ozero, *Ukraine* .... **17 F15** 45 45N 29 20 E
Sata-Misaki, *Japan* ...... **31 J5** 31 0N 130 40 E
Satadougou, *Mali* **50 F3** 12 25N 11 25W
Satakunta, *Finland* ...... **9 F20** 61 45N 23 0 E
Satara, *India* .... **40 L8** 17 44N 73 58 E
Satbarwa, *India* .... **43 H11** 23 55N 84 16 E
Satevó, *Mexico* **86 B3** 27 57N 106 7W
Satilla →, *U.S.A.* **77 K5** 30 59N 81 29W
Satka, *Russia* .... **24 C10** 55 3N 59 1 E
Satmala Hills, *India* ...... **40 J9** 20 15N 74 40 E
Satna, *India* .... **43 G9** 24 35N 80 50 E
Sátoraljaújhely, *Hungary* .. **17 D11** 48 25N 21 41 E

Shadyside

Satpura Ra., *India* **40 J10** 21 25N 76 10 E
Satsuna-Shotō, *Japan* **31 K5** 30 0N 130 0 E
Sattahip, *Thailand* **38 F3** 12 41N 100 54 E
Satu Mare, *Romania* **17 E12** 47 46N 22 55 E
Satui, *Indonesia* **36 E5** 3 50S 115 27 E
Satun, *Thailand* **39 J3** 6 43N 100 2 E
Saturnina →, *Brazil* **92 F7** 12 15S 58 10W
Sauce, *Argentina* **94 C4** 30 5S 58 46W
Sauceda, *Mexico* **86 B4** 25 55N 101 18W
Saucillo, *Mexico* **86 B3** 28 1N 105 17W
Sauda, *Norway* **9 G12** 59 40N 6 20 E
Sauðarkrókur, *Iceland* **8 D4** 65 45N 19 40W
Saudi Arabia ■, *Asia* **46 B3** 26 0N 44 0 E
Sauerland, *Germany* **16 C4** 51 12N 7 59 E
Saugeen →, *Canada* **78 B3** 44 30N 81 22W
Saugerties, *U.S.A.* **79 D11** 42 5N 73 57W
Saugus, *U.S.A.* **85 L8** 34 25N 118 32W
Sauk Centre, *U.S.A.* **80 C7** 45 44N 94 57W
Sauk Rapids, *U.S.A.* **80 C7** 45 35N 94 10W
Sault Ste. Marie, *Canada* **70 C3** 46 30N 84 20W
Sault Ste. Marie, *U.S.A.* **69 D11** 46 30N 84 21W
Saumlaki, *Indonesia* **37 F8** 7 55S 131 20 E
Saumur, *France* **18 C3** 47 15N 0 5W
Saunders C., *N.Z.* **59 L3** 45 53S 170 45 E
Saunders I., *Antarctica* **5 B1** 57 48S 26 28W
Saunders Point, *Australia* **61 E4** 27 52S 125 38 E
Saurimo, *Angola* **52 F4** 9 40S 20 12 E
Sausalito, *U.S.A.* **84 H4** 37 51N 122 29W
Savá, *Honduras* **88 C2** 15 32N 86 15W
Sava →, *Serbia, Yug.* **21 B9** 44 50N 20 26 E
Savage, *U.S.A.* **80 B2** 47 27N 104 21W
Savage I. = Niue, *Cook Is.* **65 J11** 19 2S 169 54W
Savage River, *Australia* **62 G4** 41 31S 145 14 E
Savai'i, *W. Samoa* **59 A12** 13 28S 172 24W
Savalou, *Benin* **50 G6** 7 57N 1 58 E
Savane, *Mozam.* **55 F4** 19 37S 35 8 E
Savanna, *U.S.A.* **80 D9** 42 5N 90 8W
Savanna-la-Mar, *Jamaica* **88 C4** 18 10N 78 10W
Savannah, *Ga., U.S.A.* **77 J5** 32 5N 81 6W
Savannah, *Mo., U.S.A.* **80 F7** 39 56N 94 50W
Savannah, *Tenn., U.S.A.* **77 H1** 35 14N 88 15W
Savannah →, *U.S.A.* **77 J5** 32 2N 80 53W
Savannakhet, *Laos* **38 D5** 16 30N 104 49 E
Savant L., *Canada* **70 B1** 50 16N 90 44W
Savant Lake, *Canada* **70 B1** 50 14N 90 40W
Savanur, *India* **40 M9** 14 59N 75 21 E
Save →, *Mozam.* **57 C5** 21 16S 34 0 E
Sāveh, *Iran* **45 C6** 35 2N 50 20 E
Savelugu, *Ghana* **50 G5** 9 38N 0 54W
Savo, *Finland* **8 E22** 62 45N 27 30 E
Savoie □, *France* **18 D7** 45 26N 6 25 E
Savona, *Italy* **18 D8** 44 17N 8 30 E
Savona, *U.S.A.* **78 D7** 42 17N 77 13W
Savonlinna, *Finland* **24 B4** 61 52N 28 53 E
Savoy = Savoie □, *France* **18 D7** 45 26N 6 25 E
Savur, *Turkey* **44 B4** 37 34N 40 53 E
Sawahlunto, *Indonesia* **36 E2** 0 40S 100 52 E
Sawai, *Indonesia* **37 E7** 3 0S 129 5 E
Sawai Madhopur, *India* **42 G7** 26 0N 76 25 E
Sawang Daen Din, *Thailand* **38 D4** 17 28N 103 28 E
Sawankhalok, *Thailand* **38 D2** 17 19N 99 50 E
Sawara, *Japan* **31 G10** 35 55N 140 30 E
Sawatch Range, *U.S.A.* **83 G10** 38 30N 106 30W
Sawel Mt., *U.K.* **13 B4** 54 50N 7 2W
Sawi, *Thailand* **39 G2** 10 14N 99 5 E
Sawmills, *Zimbabwe* **55 F2** 19 30S 28 2 E
Sawtooth Range, *U.S.A.* **82 E6** 44 3N 114 58W
Sawu, *Indonesia* **37 F6** 10 35S 121 50 E
Sawu Sea, *Indonesia* **37 F6** 9 30S 121 50 E
Saxby →, *Australia* **62 B3** 18 25S 140 53 E
Saxmundham, *U.K.* **11 E9** 52 13N 1 30 E
Saxony = Sachsen □, *Germany* **16 C7** 50 55N 13 10 E
Saxony, Lower = Niedersachsen □, *Germany* **16 B5** 52 50N 9 0 E
Saxton, *U.S.A.* **78 F6** 40 13N 78 15W
Sayabec, *Canada* **71 C6** 48 35N 67 41W
Sayaboury, *Laos* **38 C3** 19 15N 101 45 E
Sayán, *Peru* **92 F3** 11 8S 77 12W
Sayan, Vostochnyy, *Russia* **27 D10** 54 0N 96 0 E
Sayan, Zapadnyy, *Russia* **27 D10** 52 30N 94 0 E
Saydā, *Lebanon* **47 B4** 33 35N 35 25 E
Sayhandulaan = Oldziyt, *Mongolia* **34 B5** 44 40N 109 1 E
Sayḥūt, *Yemen* **46 D5** 15 12N 51 10 E
Saynshand, *Mongolia* **34 B6** 44 55N 110 11 E
Sayre, *Okla., U.S.A.* **81 H5** 35 18N 99 38W
Sayre, *Pa., U.S.A.* **79 E8** 41 59N 76 32W
Sayreville, *U.S.A.* **79 F10** 40 28N 74 22W
Sayula, *Mexico* **86 D4** 19 50N 103 40W
Sayward, *Canada* **72 C3** 50 21N 125 55W
Sazanit, *Albania* **21 D8** 40 30N 19 20 E
Sázava →, *Czech Rep.* **16 D8** 49 53N 14 24 E
Sazin, *Pakistan* **43 B5** 35 35N 73 30 E
Scafell Pike, *U.K.* **10 C4** 54 27N 3 14W
Scalloway, *U.K.* **12 A7** 60 9N 1 17W
Scalpay, *U.K.* **12 D3** 57 18N 6 0W
Scandia, *Canada* **72 C6** 50 20N 112 0W
Scandicci, *Italy* **20 C4** 43 45N 11 11 E
Scandinavia, *Europe* **6 C8** 64 0N 12 0 E
Scapa Flow, *U.K.* **12 C5** 58 53N 3 3W
Scappoose, *U.S.A.* **84 E4** 45 45N 122 53W
Scarba, *U.K.* **12 E3** 56 11N 5 43W
Scarborough, *Trin. & Tob.* **89 D7** 11 11N 60 42W
Scarborough, *U.K.* **10 C7** 54 17N 0 24W
Scariff I., *Ireland* **13 E1** 51 44N 10 15W
Scarp, *U.K.* **12 C1** 58 1N 7 8W
Scebeli, Wabi →, *Somali Rep.* **46 G3** 2 0N 44 0 E
Schaffhausen, *Switz.* **18 C8** 47 42N 8 39 E
Schagen, *Neths.* **15 B4** 52 49N 4 48 E
Schaghticoke, *U.S.A.* **79 D11** 42 54N 73 35W
Schefferville, *Canada* **71 B6** 54 48N 66 50W
Schelde →, *Belgium* **15 C4** 51 15N 4 16 E
Schell Creek Ra., *U.S.A.* **82 G6** 39 15N 114 30W
Schellsburg, *U.S.A.* **78 F6** 40 3N 78 39W
Schenectady, *U.S.A.* **79 D11** 42 49N 73 57W
Schenevus, *U.S.A.* **79 D10** 42 33N 74 50W
Schiedam, *Neths.* **15 C4** 51 55N 4 25 E
Schiermonnikoog, *Neths.* **15 A6** 53 30N 6 15 E
Schio, *Italy* **20 B4** 45 43N 11 21 E
Schleswig, *Germany* **16 A5** 54 31N 9 34 E
Schleswig-Holstein □, *Germany* **16 A5** 54 30N 9 30 E
Schoharie, *U.S.A.* **79 D10** 42 40N 74 19W
Schoharie →, *U.S.A.* **79 D10** 42 57N 74 18W
Scholls, *U.S.A.* **84 E4** 45 24N 122 56W
Schouten I., *Australia* **62 G4** 42 20S 148 20 E
Schouten Is. = Supiori, *Indonesia* **37 E9** 1 0S 136 0 E
Schouwen, *Neths.* **15 C3** 51 43N 3 45 E
Schreiber, *Canada* **70 C2** 48 45N 87 20W
Schroon Lake, *U.S.A.* **79 C11** 43 50N 73 46W
Schuler, *Canada* **73 C6** 50 20N 110 6W
Schumacher, *Canada* **70 C3** 48 30N 81 16W
Schurz, *U.S.A.* **82 G4** 38 57N 118 49W
Schuyler, *U.S.A.* **80 E6** 41 27N 97 4W
Schuylerville, *U.S.A.* **79 C11** 43 6N 73 35W
Schuylkill →, *U.S.A.* **79 G9** 39 53N 75 12W
Schuylkill Haven, *U.S.A.* **79 F8** 40 37N 76 11W
Schwäbische Alb, *Germany* **16 D5** 48 20N 9 30 E
Schwaner, Pegunungan, *Indonesia* **36 E4** 1 0S 112 30 E
Schwarzwald, *Germany* **16 D5** 48 30N 8 20 E
Schwedt, *Germany* **16 B8** 53 3N 14 16 E
Schweinfurt, *Germany* **16 C6** 50 3N 10 14 E
Schweizer-Reneke, *S. Africa* **56 D4** 27 11S 25 18 E
Schwenningen = Villingen-Schwenningen, *Germany* **16 D5** 48 3N 8 26 E
Schwerin, *Germany* **16 B6** 53 36N 11 22 E
Schwyz, *Switz.* **18 C8** 47 2N 8 39 E
Sciacca, *Italy* **20 F5** 37 31N 13 3 E
Scilla, *Italy* **20 E6** 38 15N 15 43 E
Scilly, Isles of, *U.K.* **11 H1** 49 56N 6 22W
Scioto →, *U.S.A.* **76 F4** 38 44N 83 1W
Scituate, *U.S.A.* **79 D14** 42 12N 70 44W
Scobey, *U.S.A.* **80 A2** 48 47N 105 25W
Scone, *Australia* **63 E5** 32 5S 150 52 E
Scoresbysund, *Greenland* **4 B6** 70 20N 23 0W
Scotia, *Calif., U.S.A.* **82 F1** 40 29N 124 6W
Scotia, *N.Y., U.S.A.* **79 D11** 42 50N 73 58W
Scotia Sea, *Antarctica* **5 B18** 56 5S 56 0W
Scotland, *Canada* **78 C4** 43 1N 80 22W
Scotland □, *U.K.* **12 E5** 57 0N 4 0W
Scott, C., *Australia* **60 B4** 13 30S 129 49 E
Scott City, *U.S.A.* **80 F4** 38 29N 100 54W
Scott Glacier, *Antarctica* **5 C8** 66 15S 100 5 E
Scott I., *Antarctica* **5 C11** 67 0S 179 0 E
Scott Is., *Canada* **72 C3** 50 48N 128 40W
Scott L., *Canada* **73 B7** 59 55N 106 18W
Scott Reef, *Australia* **60 B3** 14 0S 121 50 E
Scottburgh, *S. Africa* **57 E5** 30 15S 30 47 E
Scottdale, *U.S.A.* **78 F5** 40 6N 79 35W
Scottish Borders □, *U.K.* **12 F6** 55 35N 2 50W
Scottsbluff, *U.S.A.* **80 E3** 41 52N 103 40W
Scottsboro, *U.S.A.* **77 H3** 34 40N 86 2W
Scottsburg, *U.S.A.* **76 F3** 38 41N 85 47W
Scottsdale, *Australia* **62 G4** 41 9S 147 31 E
Scottsdale, *U.S.A.* **83 K7** 33 29N 111 56W
Scottsville, *Ky., U.S.A.* **77 G2** 36 45N 86 11W
Scottsville, *N.Y., U.S.A.* **78 C7** 43 2N 77 47W
Scottville, *U.S.A.* **76 D2** 43 58N 86 17W
Scranton, *U.S.A.* **79 E9** 41 25N 75 40W
Scugog, L., *Canada* **78 B6** 44 10N 78 55W
Scunthorpe, *U.K.* **10 D7** 53 36N 0 39W
Seabrook, L., *Australia* **61 F2** 30 55S 119 40 E
Seaford, *U.K.* **11 G8** 50 47N 0 7 E
Seaford, *U.S.A.* **76 F8** 38 39N 75 37W
Seaforth, *Australia* **62 C4** 20 55S 148 57 E
Seaforth, *Canada* **78 C3** 43 35N 81 25W
Seaforth, L., *U.K.* **12 D2** 57 52N 6 36W
Seagraves, *U.S.A.* **81 J3** 32 57N 102 34W
Seaham, *U.K.* **10 C6** 54 50N 1 20W
Seal →, *Canada* **73 B10** 59 4N 94 48W
Seal L., *Canada* **71 B7** 54 20N 61 30W
Sealy, *U.S.A.* **81 L6** 29 47N 96 9W
Searchlight, *U.S.A.* **85 K12** 35 28N 114 55W
Searcy, *U.S.A.* **81 H9** 35 15N 91 44W
Searles L., *U.S.A.* **85 K9** 35 44N 117 21W
Seascale, *U.K.* **10 C4** 54 24N 3 29W
Seaside, *Calif., U.S.A.* **84 J5** 36 37N 121 50W
Seaside, *Oreg., U.S.A.* **84 E3** 46 0N 123 56W
Seaspray, *Australia* **63 F4** 38 25S 147 15 E
Seattle, *U.S.A.* **84 C4** 47 36N 122 20W
Seaview Ra., *Australia* **62 B4** 18 40S 145 45 E
Sebago L., *U.S.A.* **79 C14** 43 52N 70 34W
Sebago Lake, *U.S.A.* **79 C14** 43 51N 70 34W
Sebastián Vizcaíno, B., *Mexico* **86 B2** 28 0N 114 30W
Sebastopol = Sevastopol, *Ukraine* **25 F5** 44 35N 33 30 E
Sebastopol, *U.S.A.* **84 G4** 38 24N 122 49W
Sebewaing, *U.S.A.* **76 D4** 43 44N 83 27W
Sebha = Sabhah, *Libya* **51 C8** 27 9N 14 29 E
Şebinkarahisar, *Turkey* **25 F6** 40 22N 38 28 E
Sebring, *Fla., U.S.A.* **77 M5** 27 30N 81 27W
Sebring, *Ohio, U.S.A.* **78 F3** 40 55N 81 2W
Sebringville, *Canada* **78 C3** 43 24N 81 4W
Sebta = Ceuta, *N. Afr.* **19 E3** 35 52N 5 18W
Sebuku, *Indonesia* **36 E5** 3 30S 116 25 E
Sebuku, Teluk, *Malaysia* **36 D5** 4 0N 118 10 E
Sechelt, *Canada* **72 D4** 49 25N 123 42W
Sechura, Desierto de, *Peru* **92 E2** 6 0S 80 30W
Secretary I., *N.Z.* **59 L1** 45 15S 166 56 E
Secunderabad, *India* **40 L11** 17 28N 78 30 E
Security-Widefield, *U.S.A.* **80 F2** 38 45N 104 45W
Sedalia, *U.S.A.* **80 F8** 38 42N 93 14W
Sedan, *France* **18 B6** 49 43N 4 57 E
Sedan, *U.S.A.* **81 G6** 37 8N 96 11W
Seddon, *N.Z.* **59 J5** 41 40S 174 7 E
Seddonville, *N.Z.* **59 J4** 41 33S 172 1 E
Sedé Boqér, *Israel* **47 E3** 30 52N 34 47 E
Sedeh, *Fārs, Iran* **45 D7** 30 45N 52 11 E
Sedeh, *Khorāsān, Iran* **45 C8** 33 20N 59 14 E
Sederot, *Israel* **47 D3** 31 32N 34 37 E
Sédhiou, *Senegal* **50 F2** 12 44N 15 30W
Sedley, *Canada* **73 C8** 50 10N 104 0W
Sedona, *U.S.A.* **83 J8** 34 52N 111 46W
Sedova, Pik, *Russia* **26 B6** 73 29N 54 58 E
Sedro Woolley, *U.S.A.* **84 B4** 48 30N 122 14W
Seeheim, *Namibia* **56 D2** 26 50S 17 45 E
Seekoei →, *S. Africa* **56 E4** 30 18S 25 1 E
Seeley's Bay, *Canada* **79 B8** 44 29N 76 14W
Seferihisar, *Turkey* **21 E12** 38 10N 26 50 E
Seg-ozero, *Russia* **24 B5** 63 20N 33 46 E
Segamat, *Malaysia* **39 L4** 2 30N 102 50 E
Segesta, *Italy* **20 F5** 37 56N 12 50 E
Seget, *Indonesia* **37 E8** 1 24S 130 58 E
Segezha, *Russia* **24 B5** 63 44N 34 19 E
Ségou, *Mali* **50 F4** 13 30N 6 16W
Segovia = Coco →, *Cent. Amer.* **88 D3** 15 0N 83 8W
Segovia, *Spain* **19 B3** 40 57N 4 10W
Segre →, *Spain* **19 B6** 41 40N 0 43 E
Séguéla, *Ivory C.* **50 G4** 7 55N 6 40W
Seguin, *U.S.A.* **81 L6** 29 34N 97 58W
Segundo →, *Argentina* **94 C3** 30 53S 62 44W
Segura →, *Spain* **19 C5** 38 3N 0 44W
Seh Konj, Kūh-e, *Iran* **45 D8** 30 6N 57 30 E
Seh Qal'eh, *Iran* **45 C8** 33 40N 58 24 E
Sehitwa, *Botswana* **56 C3** 20 30S 22 30 E
Sehore, *India* **42 H7** 23 10N 77 5 E
Sehwan, *Pakistan* **42 F2** 26 28N 67 53 E
Seil, *U.K.* **12 E3** 56 18N 5 38W
Seiland, *Norway* **8 A20** 70 25N 23 15 E
Seiling, *U.S.A.* **81 G5** 36 9N 98 56W
Seinäjoki, *Finland* **9 E20** 62 40N 22 51 E
Seine →, *France* **18 B4** 49 26N 0 26 E
Sekayu, *Indonesia* **36 E2** 2 51S 103 51 E
Seke, *Tanzania* **54 C3** 3 20S 33 31 E
Sekenke, *Tanzania* **54 C3** 4 18S 34 11 E
Sekondi-Takoradi, *Ghana* **50 H5** 4 58N 1 45W
Sekuma, *Botswana* **56 C3** 24 36S 23 50 E
Selah, *U.S.A.* **82 C3** 46 39N 120 32W
Selama, *Malaysia* **39 K3** 5 12N 100 42 E
Selaru, *Indonesia* **37 F8** 8 9S 131 0 E
Selby, *U.K.* **10 D6** 53 47N 1 5W
Selby, *U.S.A.* **80 C4** 45 31N 100 2W
Selçuk, *Turkey* **21 F12** 37 56N 27 22 E
Selden, *U.S.A.* **80 F4** 39 33N 100 34W
Sele →, *Italy* **20 D6** 40 29N 14 56 E
Selebi-Pikwe, *Botswana* **57 C4** 21 58S 27 48 E
Selemdzha →, *Russia* **27 D13** 51 42N 128 53 E
Selenga = Selenge Mörön →, *Asia* **32 A5** 52 16N 106 16 E
Selenge Mörön →, *Asia* **32 A5** 52 16N 106 16 E
Seletan, Tanjung, *Indonesia* **36 E4** 4 10S 114 40 E
Sélibabi, *Mauritania* **50 E3** 15 10N 12 15W
Seligman, *U.S.A.* **83 J7** 35 20N 112 53W
Selîma, El Wâhât el, *Sudan* **51 D11** 21 22N 29 19 E
Selinda Spillway, *Botswana* **56 B3** 18 35S 23 10 E
Selinsgrove, *U.S.A.* **78 F8** 40 48N 76 52W
Selkirk, *Canada* **73 C9** 50 10N 96 55W
Selkirk, *U.K.* **12 F6** 55 33N 2 50W
Selkirk I., *Canada* **73 C9** 53 20N 99 6W
Selkirk Mts., *Canada* **68 C8** 51 15N 117 40W
Selliá, *Greece* **23 D6** 35 12N 24 23 E
Sells, *U.S.A.* **83 L8** 31 55N 111 53W
Selma, *Ala., U.S.A.* **77 J2** 32 25N 87 1W
Selma, *Calif., U.S.A.* **84 J7** 36 34N 119 37W
Selma, *N.C., U.S.A.* **77 H6** 35 32N 78 17W
Selmer, *U.S.A.* **77 H1** 35 10N 88 36W
Selowandoma Falls, *Zimbabwe* **55 G3** 21 15S 31 50 E
Selpele, *Indonesia* **37 E8** 0 1S 130 5 E
Selsey Bill, *U.K.* **11 G7** 50 43N 0 47W
Seltso, *Russia* **24 D5** 53 22N 34 4 E
Selu, *Indonesia* **37 F8** 7 32S 130 55 E
Selva, *Argentina* **94 B3** 29 50S 62 0W
Selvas, *Brazil* **92 E5** 6 30S 67 0W
Selwyn L., *Canada* **73 B8** 60 0N 104 30W
Selwyn Mts., *Canada* **68 B6** 63 0N 130 0W
Selwyn Ra., *Australia* **62 C3** 21 10S 140 0 E
Semani →, *Albania* **21 D8** 40 47N 19 30 E
Semarang, *Indonesia* **37 G14** 7 0S 110 26 E
Sembabule, *Uganda* **54 C3** 0 4S 31 25 E
Semeru, *Indonesia* **37 H15** 8 4S 112 55 E
Semey, *Kazakstan* **26 D9** 50 30N 80 10 E
Seminoe Reservoir, *U.S.A.* **82 F10** 42 9N 106 55W
Seminole, *Okla., U.S.A.* **81 H6** 35 14N 96 41W
Seminole, *Tex., U.S.A.* **81 J3** 32 43N 102 39W
Seminole Draw →, *U.S.A.* **81 J3** 32 27N 102 20W
Semipalatinsk = Semey, *Kazakstan* **26 D9** 50 30N 80 10 E
Semirara Is., *Phil.* **37 B6** 12 0N 121 20 E
Semitau, *Indonesia* **36 D4** 0 29N 111 57 E
Semiyarka, *Kazakstan* **26 D8** 50 55N 78 23 E
Semiyarskoye = Semiyarka, *Kazakstan* **26 D8** 50 55N 78 23 E
Semmering P., *Austria* **16 E8** 47 41N 15 45 E
Semnān, *Iran* **45 C7** 35 40N 53 23 E
Semnān □, *Iran* **45 C7** 36 0N 54 0 E
Semporna, *Malaysia* **37 D5** 4 30N 118 33 E
Semuda, *Indonesia* **36 E4** 2 51S 112 58 E
Sen →, *Cambodia* **36 B3** 13 45N 105 12 E
Senā, *Iran* **45 D6** 28 27N 51 36 E
Sena, *Mozam.* **55 F4** 17 25S 35 0 E
Sena Madureira, *Brazil* **92 E5** 9 5S 68 45W
Senador Pompeu, *Brazil* **93 E11** 5 40S 39 20W
Senanga, *Zambia* **56 B3** 16 2S 23 14 E
Senatobia, *U.S.A.* **81 H10** 34 37N 89 58W
Sencelles, *Spain* **22 B9** 39 39N 2 54 E
Sendai, *Kagoshima, Japan* **31 J5** 31 50N 130 20 E
Sendai, *Miyagi, Japan* **30 E10** 38 15N 140 53 E
Sendai-Wan, *Japan* **30 E10** 38 15N 141 0 E
Sendhwa, *India* **42 J6** 21 41N 75 6 E
Seneca, *U.S.A.* **77 H4** 34 41N 82 57W
Seneca Falls, *U.S.A.* **79 D8** 42 55N 76 48W
Seneca L., *U.S.A.* **78 D8** 42 40N 76 54W
Senecaville L., *U.S.A.* **78 G3** 39 55N 81 25W
Senegal ■, *W. Afr.* **50 F3** 14 30N 14 30W
Senegal →, *W. Afr.* **50 E2** 15 48N 16 32W
Senegambia, *Africa* **48 E2** 12 45N 12 0W
Senekal, *S. Africa* **57 D4** 28 20S 27 36 E
Senga Hill, *Zambia* **55 D3** 9 19S 31 11 E
Senge Khambab = Indus →, *Pakistan* **42 G2** 24 20N 67 47 E
Sengua →, *Zimbabwe* **55 F2** 17 7S 28 5 E
Senhor-do-Bonfim, *Brazil* **93 F10** 10 30S 40 10W
Senigállia, *Italy* **20 C5** 43 43N 13 13 E
Senj, *Croatia* **16 F8** 45 0N 14 58 E
Senja, *Norway* **8 B17** 69 25N 17 30 E
Senkaku-Shotō, *Japan* **31 L1** 25 45N 124 0 E
Senlis, *France* **18 B5** 49 13N 2 35 E
Senmonorom, *Cambodia* **38 F6** 12 27N 107 12 E
Senneterre, *Canada* **70 C4** 48 25N 77 15W
Seno, *Laos* **38 D5** 16 35N 104 50 E
Sens, *France* **18 B5** 48 11N 3 15 E
Senta, *Serbia, Yug.* **21 B9** 45 55N 20 3 E
Sentani, *Indonesia* **37 E10** 2 36S 140 37 E
Sentery, *Dem. Rep. of the Congo* **54 D2** 5 17S 25 42 E
Sentinel, *U.S.A.* **83 K7** 32 52N 113 13W
Seo de Urgel = La Seu d'Urgell, *Spain* **19 A6** 42 22N 1 23 E
Seohara, *India* **43 E8** 29 15N 78 33 E
Seonath →, *India* **43 J10** 21 44N 82 28 E
Seondha, *India* **43 F8** 26 9N 78 48 E
Seoni, *India* **43 H8** 22 5N 79 30 E
Seoni Malwa, *India* **42 H8** 22 27N 77 28 E
Seoul = Sŏul, *S. Korea* **35 F14** 37 31N 126 58 E
Sepīdān, *Iran* **45 D7** 30 20N 52 5 E
Sepo-ri, *N. Korea* **35 E14** 38 57N 127 25 E
Sepone, *Laos* **38 D6** 16 45N 106 13 E
Sept-Îles, *Canada* **71 B6** 50 13N 66 22W
Sequim, *U.S.A.* **84 B3** 48 5N 123 6W
Sequoia National Park, *U.S.A.* **84 J8** 36 30N 118 30W
Seraing, *Belgium* **15 D5** 50 35N 5 32 E
Seraja, *Indonesia* **39 L7** 2 41N 108 35 E
Serakhis →, *Cyprus* **23 D11** 35 13N 32 55 E
Seram, *Indonesia* **37 E7** 3 10S 129 0 E
Seram Sea, *Indonesia* **37 E7** 2 30S 128 30 E
Serang, *Indonesia* **37 G12** 6 8S 106 10 E
Serasan, *Indonesia* **39 L7** 2 29N 109 4 E
Serbia □, *Yugoslavia* **21 C9** 43 30N 21 0 E
Serdobsk, *Russia* **24 D7** 52 28N 44 10 E
Seremban, *Malaysia* **39 L3** 2 43N 101 53 E
Serengeti Plain, *Tanzania* **54 C4** 2 40S 35 0 E
Serenje, *Zambia* **55 E3** 13 14S 30 15 E
Sereth = Siret →, *Romania* **17 F14** 45 24N 28 1 E
Sergino, *Russia* **26 C7** 62 25N 65 12 E
Sergipe □, *Brazil* **93 F11** 10 30S 37 30W
Sergiyev Posad, *Russia* **24 C6** 56 20N 38 10 E
Seria, *Brunei* **36 D4** 4 37N 114 23 E
Serian, *Malaysia* **36 D4** 1 10N 110 31 E
Seribu, Kepulauan, *Indonesia* **36 F3** 5 36S 106 33 E
Sérifos, *Greece* **21 F11** 37 9N 24 30 E
Sérigny →, *Canada* **71 A6** 56 47N 66 0W
Seringapatam Reef, *Australia* **60 B3** 13 38S 122 5 E
Sermata, *Indonesia* **37 F7** 8 15S 128 50 E
Serov, *Russia* **24 C11** 59 29N 60 35 E
Serowe, *Botswana* **56 C4** 22 25S 26 43 E
Serpentine Lakes, *Australia* **61 E4** 28 30S 129 10 E
Serpukhov, *Russia* **24 D6** 54 55N 37 28 E
Serra do Navio, *Brazil* **93 C8** 0 59N 52 3W
Sérrai, *Greece* **21 D10** 41 5N 23 31 E
Serrezuela, *Argentina* **94 C2** 30 40S 65 20W
Serrinha, *Brazil* **93 F11** 11 39S 39 0W
Sertanópolis, *Brazil* **95 A5** 23 4S 51 2W
Serua, *Indonesia* **37 F8** 6 18S 130 1 E
Serui, *Indonesia* **37 E9** 1 53S 136 10 E
Serule, *Botswana* **56 C4** 21 57S 27 20 E
Sese Is., *Uganda* **54 C3** 0 20S 32 20 E
Sesepe, *Indonesia* **37 E7** 1 30S 127 59 E
Sesfontein, *Namibia* **56 B1** 19 7S 13 39 E
Sesheke, *Zambia* **56 B3** 17 29S 24 13 E
S'Espalmador, *Spain* **22 C7** 38 47N 1 26 E
S'Espardell, *Spain* **22 C7** 38 48N 1 29 E
S'Estanyol, *Spain* **22 B9** 39 22N 2 54 E
Setana, *Japan* **30 C9** 42 26N 139 51 E
Sète, *France* **18 E5** 43 25N 3 42 E
Sete Lagôas, *Brazil* **93 G10** 19 27S 44 16W
Sétif, *Algeria* **50 A7** 36 9N 5 26 E
Seto, *Japan* **31 G8** 35 14N 137 6 E
Setonaikai, *Japan* **31 G6** 34 20N 133 30 E
Settat, *Morocco* **50 B4** 33 0N 7 40W
Setting L., *Canada* **73 C9** 55 0N 98 38W
Settle, *U.K.* **10 C5** 54 5N 2 16W
Settlement Pt., *Bahamas* **77 M6** 26 40N 79 0W
Setúbal, *Portugal* **19 C1** 38 30N 8 58W
Setúbal, B. de, *Portugal* **19 C1** 38 40N 8 56W
Seul, Lac, *Canada* **68 C10** 50 20N 92 30W
Sevan, Ozero = Sevana Lich, *Armenia* **25 F8** 40 30N 45 20 E
Sevana Lich, *Armenia* **25 F8** 40 30N 45 20 E
Sevastopol, *Ukraine* **25 F5** 44 35N 33 30 E
Seven Sisters, *Canada* **72 C3** 54 56N 128 10W
Severn →, *Canada* **70 A2** 56 2N 87 36W
Severn →, *U.K.* **11 F5** 51 35N 2 40W
Severn L., *Canada* **70 B1** 53 54N 90 48W
Severnaya Zemlya, *Russia* **27 B11** 79 0N 100 0 E
Severnyye Uvaly, *Russia* **24 C8** 60 0N 50 0 E
Severo-Kurilsk, *Russia* **27 D16** 50 40N 156 8 E
Severo-Yeniseyskiy, *Russia* **27 C10** 60 22N 93 1 E
Severodvinsk, *Russia* **24 B6** 64 27N 39 58 E
Severomorsk, *Russia* **24 A5** 69 5N 33 27 E
Severouralsk, *Russia* **24 B10** 60 9N 59 57 E
Sevier, *U.S.A.* **83 G7** 38 39N 112 11W
Sevier →, *U.S.A.* **83 G7** 39 4N 113 6W
Sevier Desert, *U.S.A.* **82 G7** 39 40N 112 45W
Sevier L., *U.S.A.* **82 G7** 38 54N 113 9W
Sevilla, *Spain* **19 D2** 37 23N 5 58W
Seville = Sevilla, *Spain* **19 D2** 37 23N 5 58W
Sevlievo, *Bulgaria* **21 C11** 43 2N 25 6 E
Sewani, *India* **42 E6** 28 58N 75 39 E
Seward, *Alaska, U.S.A.* **68 B5** 60 7N 149 27W
Seward, *Nebr., U.S.A.* **80 E6** 40 55N 97 6W
Seward, *Pa., U.S.A.* **78 F5** 40 25N 79 1W
Seward Peninsula, *U.S.A.* **68 B3** 65 30N 166 0W
Sewell, *Chile* **94 C1** 34 10S 70 23W
Sewer, *Indonesia* **37 F8** 5 53S 134 40 E
Sewickley, *U.S.A.* **78 F4** 40 32N 80 12W
Sexsmith, *Canada* **72 B5** 55 21N 118 47W
Seychelles ■, *Ind. Oc.* **29 K9** 5 0S 56 0 E
Seyðisfjörður, *Iceland* **8 D6** 65 16N 13 57W
Seydişehir, *Turkey* **25 G5** 37 25N 31 51 E
Seydvān, *Iran* **44 B5** 38 34N 45 2 E
Seyhan →, *Turkey* **44 B2** 36 43N 34 53 E
Seym →, *Ukraine* **25 D5** 51 27N 32 34 E
Seymour, *Australia* **63 F4** 37 0S 145 10 E
Seymour, *S. Africa* **57 E4** 32 33S 26 46 E
Seymour, *Conn., U.S.A.* **79 E11** 41 24N 73 4W
Seymour, *Ind., U.S.A.* **76 F3** 38 58N 85 53W
Seymour, *Tex., U.S.A.* **81 J5** 33 35N 99 16W
Sfântu Gheorghe, *Romania* **17 F13** 45 52N 25 48 E
Sfax, *Tunisia* **51 B8** 34 49N 10 48 E
Shaanxi □, *China* **34 G5** 35 0N 109 0 E
Shaba = Katanga □, *Dem. Rep. of the Congo* **54 D2** 8 0S 25 0 E
Shabogamo L., *Canada* **71 B6** 53 15N 66 30W
Shabunda, *Dem. Rep. of the Congo* **54 C2** 2 40S 27 16 E
Shache, *China* **32 C2** 38 20N 77 10 E
Shackleton Ice Shelf, *Antarctica* **5 C8** 66 0S 100 0 E
Shackleton Inlet, *Antarctica* **5 E11** 83 0S 160 0 E
Shādegān, *Iran* **45 D6** 30 40N 48 38 E
Shadi, *India* **43 C7** 33 24N 77 14 E
Shadrinsk, *Russia* **26 D7** 56 5N 63 32 E
Shadyside, *U.S.A.* **78 G4** 39 58N 80 45W

Shafter

Shafter, *U.S.A.* **85 K7** 35 30N 119 16W
Shaftesbury, *U.K.* **11 F5** 51 0N 2 11W
Shagram, *Pakistan* **43 A5** 36 24N 72 20 E
Shah Alizai, *Pakistan* **42 E2** 29 25N 66 33 E
Shah Bunder, *Pakistan* **42 G2** 24 13N 67 56 E
Shahabad, *Punjab, India* **42 D7** 30 10N 76 55 E
Shahabad, *Raj., India* **42 G7** 25 15N 77 11 E
Shahabad, *Ut. P., India* **43 F8** 27 36N 79 56 E
Shahadpur, *Pakistan* **42 G3** 25 55N 68 35 E
Shahba, *Syria* **47 C5** 32 52N 36 38 E
Shahdād, *Iran* **45 D8** 30 30N 57 40 E
Shahdād, Namakzār-e, *Iran* **45 D8** 30 20N 58 20 E
Shahdadkot, *Pakistan* **42 F2** 27 50N 67 55 E
Shahdol, *India* **43 H9** 23 19N 81 26 E
Shahe, *China* **34 F8** 37 0N 114 32 E
Shahganj, *India* **43 F10** 26 3N 82 44 E
Shahgarh, *India* **40 F6** 27 15N 69 50 E
Shahjahanpur, *India* **43 F8** 27 54N 79 57 E
Shahpur, *India* **42 H7** 22 12N 77 58 E
Shahpur, *Baluchistan, Pakistan* **42 E3** 28 46N 68 27 E
Shahpur, *Punjab, Pakistan* **42 C5** 32 17N 72 26 E
Shahpur Chakar, *Pakistan* **42 F3** 26 9N 68 39 E
Shahpura, *Mad. P., India* **43 H9** 23 10N 80 45 E
Shahpura, *Raj., India* **42 G6** 25 38N 74 56 E
Shahr-e Bābak, *Iran* **45 D7** 30 7N 55 9 E
Shahr-e Kord, *Iran* **45 C6** 32 15N 50 55 E
Shāhrakht, *Iran* **45 C9** 33 38N 60 16 E
Shahrig, *Pakistan* **42 D2** 30 15N 67 40 E
Shahukou, *China* **34 D7** 40 20N 112 18 E
Shaikhabad, *Afghan.* **42 B3** 34 2N 68 45 E
Shajapur, *India* **42 H7** 23 27N 76 21 E
Shakargarh, *Pakistan* **42 C6** 32 17N 75 10 E
Shakawe, *Botswana* **56 B3** 18 28S 21 49 E
Shaker Heights, *U.S.A.* **78 E3** 41 29N 81 32W
Shakhty, *Russia* **25 E7** 47 40N 40 16 E
Shakhunya, *Russia* **24 C8** 57 40N 46 46 E
Shaki, *Nigeria* **50 G6** 8 41N 3 21 E
Shallow Lake, *Canada* **78 B3** 44 36N 81 5W
Shalqar, *Kazakstan* **26 E6** 47 48N 59 39 E
Shaluli Shan, *China* **32 C4** 30 40N 99 55 E
Shām, *Iran* **45 E8** 26 39N 57 21 E
Shām, Bādiyat ash, *Asia* **44 C3** 32 0N 40 0 E
Shamâl Kordofân □, *Sudan* **48 E6** 15 0N 30 0 E
Shamattawa, *Canada* **70 A1** 55 51N 92 5W
Shamattawa →, *Canada* **70 A2** 55 1N 85 23W
Shamīl, *Iran* **45 E8** 27 30N 56 55 E
Shāmkūh, *Iran* **45 C8** 35 47N 57 50 E
Shamli, *India* **42 E7** 29 32N 77 18 E
Shammar, Jabal, *Si. Arabia* **44 E4** 27 40N 41 0 E
Shamo = Gobi, *Asia* **34 C6** 44 0N 110 0 E
Shamo, L., *Ethiopia* **46 F2** 5 45N 37 30 E
Shamokin, *U.S.A.* **79 F8** 40 47N 76 34W
Shamrock, *U.S.A.* **81 H4** 35 13N 100 15W
Shamva, *Zimbabwe* **55 F3** 17 20S 31 32 E
Shan □, *Burma* **41 J21** 21 30N 98 30 E
Shan Xian, *China* **34 G9** 34 50N 116 5 E
Shanchengzhen, *China* **35 C13** 42 20N 125 20 E
Shāndak, *Iran* **45 D9** 28 28N 60 27 E
Shandon, *U.S.A.* **84 K6** 35 39N 120 23W
Shandong □, *China* **35 G10** 36 0N 118 0 E
Shandong Bandao, *China* **35 F11** 37 0N 121 0 E
Shang Xian = Shangzhou, *China* **34 H5** 33 50N 109 58 E
Shanga, *Nigeria* **50 F6** 11 12N 4 33 E
Shangalowe, *Dem. Rep. of the Congo* **55 E2** 10 50S 26 30 E
Shangani →, *Zimbabwe* **55 F2** 18 41S 27 10 E
Shangbancheng, *China* **35 D10** 40 50N 118 1 E
Shangdu, *China* **34 D7** 41 30N 113 30 E
Shanghai, *China* **33 C7** 31 15N 121 26 E
Shanghe, *China* **35 F9** 37 20N 117 10 E
Shangnan, *China* **34 H6** 33 32N 110 50 E
Shangqiu, *China* **34 G8** 34 26N 115 36 E
Shangrao, *China* **33 D6** 28 25N 117 59 E
Shangshui, *China* **34 H8** 33 42N 114 35 E
Shangzhi, *China* **35 B14** 45 22N 127 56 E
Shangzhou, *China* **34 H5** 33 50N 109 58 E
Shanhetun, *China* **35 B14** 44 33N 127 15 E
Shannon, *N.Z.* **59 J5** 40 33S 175 25 E
Shannon →, *Ireland* **13 D2** 52 35N 9 30W
Shannon, Mouth of the, *Ireland* **13 D2** 52 30N 9 55W
Shannon Airport, *Ireland* **13 D3** 52 42N 8 57W
Shansi = Shanxi □, *China* **34 F7** 37 0N 112 0 E
Shantar, Ostrov Bolshoy, *Russia* **27 D14** 55 9N 137 40 E
Shantipur, *India* **43 H13** 23 17N 88 25 E
Shantou, *China* **33 D6** 23 18N 116 40 E
Shantung = Shandong □, *China* **35 G10** 36 0N 118 0 E
Shanxi □, *China* **34 F7** 37 0N 112 0 E
Shanyang, *China* **34 H5** 33 31N 109 55 E
Shanyin, *China* **34 E7** 39 25N 112 56 E
Shaoguan, *China* **33 D6** 24 48N 113 35 E
Shaoxing, *China* **33 D7** 30 0N 120 35 E
Shaoyang, *China* **33 D6** 27 14N 111 25 E
Shap, *U.K.* **10 C5** 54 32N 2 40W
Shapinsay, *U.K.* **12 B6** 59 3N 2 51W
Shaqra', *Si. Arabia* **44 E5** 25 15N 45 16 E
Shaqrā', *Yemen* **46 E4** 13 22N 45 44 E
Sharafkhāneh, *Iran* **44 B5** 38 11N 45 29 E
Sharbot Lake, *Canada* **79 B8** 44 46N 76 41W
Shari, *Japan* **30 C12** 43 55N 144 40 E
Sharjah = Ash Shāriqah, *U.A.E.* **45 E7** 25 23N 55 26 E
Shark B., *Australia* **61 E1** 25 30S 113 32 E
Sharon, *Mass., U.S.A.* **79 D13** 42 7N 71 11W
Sharon, *Pa., U.S.A.* **78 E4** 41 14N 80 31W
Sharon Springs, *Kans., U.S.A.* **80 F4** 38 54N 101 45W
Sharon Springs, *N.Y., U.S.A.* **79 D10** 42 48N 74 37W
Sharp Pt., *Australia* **62 A3** 10 58S 142 43 E
Sharpe L., *Canada* **70 B1** 54 24N 93 40W
Sharpsville, *U.S.A.* **78 E4** 41 15N 80 29W
Sharya, *Russia* **24 C8** 58 22N 45 20 E
Shashemene, *Ethiopia* **46 F2** 7 13N 38 33 E
Shashi, *Botswana* **57 C4** 21 15S 27 27 E
Shashi, *China* **33 C6** 30 25N 112 14 E
Shashi →, *Africa* **55 G2** 21 14S 29 20 E
Shasta, Mt., *U.S.A.* **82 F2** 41 25N 122 12W
Shasta L., *U.S.A.* **82 F2** 40 43N 122 25W
Shatt al'Arab →, *Iraq* **45 D6** 29 57N 48 34 E
Shaunavon, *Canada* **73 D7** 49 35N 108 25W
Shaver L., *U.S.A.* **84 H7** 37 9N 119 18W
Shaw →, *Australia* **60 D2** 20 21S 119 17 E
Shaw I., *Australia* **62 C4** 20 30S 149 2 E
Shawanaga, *Canada* **78 A4** 45 31N 80 17W
Shawangunk Mts., *U.S.A.* **79 E10** 41 35N 74 30W
Shawano, *U.S.A.* **76 C1** 44 47N 88 36W
Shawinigan, *Canada* **70 C5** 46 35N 72 50W
Shawnee, *U.S.A.* **81 H6** 35 20N 96 55W
Shay Gap, *Australia* **60 D3** 20 30S 120 10 E
Shaybārā, *Si. Arabia* **44 E3** 25 26N 36 47 E
Shaykh, J. ash, *Lebanon* **47 B4** 33 25N 35 50 E
Shaykh Miskīn, *Syria* **47 C5** 32 49N 36 9 E
Shaykh Sa'īd, *Iraq* **44 C5** 32 34N 46 17 E
Shcherbakov = Rybinsk, *Russia* **24 C6** 58 5N 38 50 E
Shchuchinsk, *Kazakstan* **26 D8** 52 56N 70 12 E
She Xian, *China* **34 F7** 36 30N 113 40 E
Shebele = Scebeli, Wabi →, *Somali Rep.* **46 G3** 2 0N 44 0 E
Sheboygan, *U.S.A.* **76 D2** 43 46N 87 45W
Shediac, *Canada* **71 C7** 46 14N 64 32W
Sheelin, L., *Ireland* **13 C4** 53 48N 7 20W
Sheep Haven, *Ireland* **13 A4** 55 11N 7 52W
Sheerness, *U.K.* **11 F8** 51 26N 0 47 E
Sheet Harbour, *Canada* **71 D7** 44 56N 62 31W
Sheffield, *U.K.* **10 D6** 53 23N 1 28W
Sheffield, *Ala., U.S.A.* **77 H2** 34 46N 87 41W
Sheffield, *Mass., U.S.A.* **79 D11** 42 5N 73 21W
Sheffield, *Pa., U.S.A.* **78 E5** 41 42N 79 3W
Sheikhpura, *India* **43 G11** 25 9N 85 53 E
Shekhupura, *Pakistan* **42 D5** 31 42N 73 58 E
Shelburne, *N.S., Canada* **71 D6** 43 47N 65 20W
Shelburne, *Ont., Canada* **78 B4** 44 4N 80 15W
Shelburne, *Vt., U.S.A.* **79 B11** 44 22N 73 13W
Shelburne, *Vt., U.S.A.* **79 B11** 44 23N 73 14W
Shelburne B., *Australia* **62 A3** 11 50S 142 50 E
Shelburne Falls, *U.S.A.* **79 D12** 42 36N 72 45W
Shelby, *Mich., U.S.A.* **76 D2** 43 37N 86 22W
Shelby, *Miss., U.S.A.* **81 J9** 33 57N 90 46W
Shelby, *Mont., U.S.A.* **82 B8** 48 30N 111 51W
Shelby, *N.C., U.S.A.* **77 H5** 35 17N 81 32W
Shelby, *Ohio, U.S.A.* **78 F2** 40 53N 82 40W
Shelbyville, *Ill., U.S.A.* **80 F10** 39 24N 88 48W
Shelbyville, *Ind., U.S.A.* **76 F3** 39 31N 85 47W
Shelbyville, *Ky., U.S.A.* **76 F3** 38 13N 85 14W
Shelbyville, *Tenn., U.S.A.* **77 H2** 35 29N 86 28W
Sheldon, *U.S.A.* **80 D7** 43 11N 95 51W
Sheldrake, *Canada* **71 B7** 50 20N 64 51W
Shelikhova, Zaliv, *Russia* **27 D16** 59 30N 157 0 E
Shell Lakes, *Australia* **61 E4** 29 20S 127 30 E
Shellbrook, *Canada* **73 C7** 53 13N 106 24W
Shellharbour, *Australia* **63 E5** 34 31S 150 51 E
Shelter I, *U.S.A.* **79 E12** 41 5N 72 21W
Shelton, *Conn., U.S.A.* **79 E11** 41 19N 73 5W
Shelton, *Wash., U.S.A.* **84 C3** 47 13N 123 6W
Shen Xian, *China* **34 F8** 36 15N 115 40 E
Shenandoah, *Iowa, U.S.A.* **80 E7** 40 46N 95 22W
Shenandoah, *Pa., U.S.A.* **79 F8** 40 49N 76 12W
Shenandoah, *Va., U.S.A.* **76 F6** 38 29N 78 37W
Shenandoah →, *U.S.A.* **76 F7** 39 19N 77 44W
Shenandoah National Park, *U.S.A.* **76 F6** 38 35N 78 22W
Shenchi, *China* **34 E7** 39 8N 112 10 E
Shendam, *Nigeria* **50 G7** 8 49N 9 30 E
Shendī, *Sudan* **51 E12** 16 46N 33 22 E
Shengfang, *China* **34 E9** 39 3N 116 42 E
Shenjingzi, *China* **35 B13** 44 40N 124 30 E
Shenmu, *China* **34 E6** 38 50N 110 29 E
Shenqiu, *China* **34 H8** 33 25N 115 5 E
Shenqiucheng, *China* **34 H8** 33 24N 115 2 E
Shensi = Shaanxi □, *China* **34 G5** 35 0N 109 0 E
Shenyang, *China* **35 D12** 41 48N 123 27 E
Sheo, *India* **42 F4** 26 11N 71 15 E
Sheopur Kalan, *India* **40 G10** 25 40N 76 40 E
Shepetivka, *Ukraine* **17 C14** 50 10N 27 10 E
Shepetovka = Shepetivka, *Ukraine* **17 C14** 50 10N 27 10 E
Shepparton, *Australia* **63 F4** 36 23S 145 26 E
Sheppey, I. of, *U.K.* **11 F8** 51 25N 0 48 E
Shepton Mallet, *U.K.* **11 F5** 51 11N 2 33W
Sheqi, *China* **34 H7** 33 12N 112 57 E
Sher Qila, *Pakistan* **43 A6** 36 7N 74 2 E
Sherborne, *U.K.* **11 G5** 50 57N 2 31W
Sherbro I., *S. Leone* **50 G3** 7 30N 12 40W
Sherbrooke, *Canada* **71 C7** 45 8N 61 59W
Sherbrooke, *Qué., Canada* **79 A13** 45 28N 71 57W
Sherburne, *U.S.A.* **79 D9** 42 41N 75 30W
Shergarh, *India* **42 F5** 26 20N 72 18 E
Sherghati, *India* **43 G11** 24 34N 84 47 E
Sheridan, *Ark., U.S.A.* **81 H8** 34 19N 92 24W
Sheridan, *Wyo., U.S.A.* **82 D10** 44 48N 106 58W
Sheringham, *U.K.* **10 E9** 52 56N 1 13 E
Sherkin I., *Ireland* **13 E2** 51 28N 9 26W
Sherkot, *India* **43 E8** 29 22N 78 35 E
Sherman, *U.S.A.* **81 J6** 33 40N 96 35W
Sherpur, *India* **43 G10** 25 34N 83 47 E
Sherridon, *Canada* **73 B8** 55 8N 101 5W
Sherwood Forest, *U.K.* **10 D6** 53 6N 1 7W
Sherwood Park, *Canada* **72 C6** 53 31N 113 19W
Sheslay →, *Canada* **72 B2** 58 48N 132 5W
Shethanei L., *Canada* **73 B9** 58 48N 97 50W
Shetland □, *U.K.* **12 A7** 60 30N 1 30W
Shetland Is., *U.K.* **12 A7** 60 30N 1 30W
Shetrunji →, *India* **42 J5** 21 19N 72 7 E
Sheyenne →, *U.S.A.* **80 B6** 47 2N 96 50W
Shibām, *Yemen* **46 D4** 16 0N 48 36 E
Shibata, *Japan* **30 F9** 37 57N 139 20 E
Shibecha, *Japan* **30 C12** 43 17N 144 36 E
Shibetsu, *Japan* **30 B11** 44 10N 142 23 E
Shibogama L., *Canada* **70 B2** 53 35N 88 15W
Shibushi, *Japan* **31 J5** 31 25N 131 8 E
Shickshinny, *U.S.A.* **79 E8** 41 9N 76 9W
Shickshock Mts. = Chic-Chocs, Mts., *Canada* **71 C6** 48 55N 66 0W
Shidao, *China* **35 F12** 36 50N 122 25 E
Shido, *Japan* **31 G7** 34 19N 134 10 E
Shiel, L., *U.K.* **12 E3** 56 48N 5 34W
Shield, C., *Australia* **62 A2** 13 20S 136 20 E
Shiga □, *Japan* **31 G8** 35 20N 136 0 E
Shiguaigou, *China* **34 D6** 40 52N 110 15 E
Shihchiachuangi = Shijiazhuang, *China* **34 E8** 38 2N 114 28 E
Shijiazhuang, *China* **34 E8** 38 2N 114 28 E
Shikarpur, *India* **42 E8** 28 17N 78 7 E
Shikarpur, *Pakistan* **42 F3** 27 57N 68 39 E
Shikohabad, *India* **43 F8** 27 6N 78 36 E
Shikoku □, *Japan* **31 H6** 33 30N 133 30 E
Shikoku-Sanchi, *Japan* **31 H6** 33 30N 133 30 E
Shiliguri, *India* **41 F16** 26 45N 88 25 E
Shilka, *Russia* **27 D12** 52 0N 115 55 E
Shilka →, *Russia* **27 D13** 53 20N 121 26 E
Shillelagh, *Ireland* **13 D5** 52 45N 6 32W
Shillington, *U.S.A.* **79 F9** 40 18N 75 58W
Shillong, *India* **41 G17** 25 35N 91 53 E
Shilo, *West Bank* **47 C4** 32 4N 35 18 E
Shilou, *China* **34 F6** 37 0N 110 48 E
Shimabara, *Japan* **31 H5** 32 48N 130 20 E
Shimada, *Japan* **31 G9** 34 49N 138 10 E
Shimane □, *Japan* **31 G6** 35 0N 132 30 E
Shimanovsk, *Russia* **27 D13** 52 15N 127 30 E
Shimizu, *Japan* **31 G9** 35 0N 138 30 E
Shimodate, *Japan* **31 F9** 36 20N 139 55 E
Shimoga, *India* **40 N9** 13 57N 75 32 E
Shimoni, *Kenya* **54 C4** 4 38S 39 20 E
Shimonoseki, *Japan* **31 H5** 33 58N 130 55 E
Shimpuru Rapids, *Angola* **56 B2** 17 45S 19 55 E
Shin, L., *U.K.* **12 C4** 58 5N 4 30W
Shinano-Gawa →, *Japan* **31 F9** 36 50N 138 30 E
Shināş, *Oman* **45 E8** 24 46N 56 28 E
Shīndand, *Afghan.* **40 C3** 33 12N 62 8 E
Shinglehouse, *U.S.A.* **78 E6** 41 58N 78 12W
Shingū, *Japan* **31 H7** 33 40N 135 55 E
Shinjō, *Japan* **30 E10** 38 46N 140 18 E
Shinshār, *Syria* **47 A5** 34 36N 36 43 E
Shinyanga, *Tanzania* **54 C3** 3 45S 33 27 E
Shinyanga □, *Tanzania* **54 C3** 3 50S 34 0 E
Shio-no-Misaki, *Japan* **31 H7** 33 25N 135 45 E
Shiogama, *Japan* **30 E10** 38 19N 141 1 E
Shiojiri, *Japan* **31 F8** 36 6N 137 58 E
Shipchenski Prokhod, *Bulgaria* **21 C11** 42 45N 25 15 E
Shiping, *China* **32 D5** 23 45N 102 23 E
Shipki La, *India* **40 D11** 31 45N 78 40 E
Shippegan, *Canada* **71 C7** 47 45N 64 45W
Shippensburg, *U.S.A.* **78 F7** 40 3N 77 31W
Shippenville, *U.S.A.* **78 E5** 41 15N 79 28W
Shiprock, *U.S.A.* **83 H9** 36 47N 108 41W
Shiqma, N. →, *Israel* **47 D3** 31 37N 34 30 E
Shiquan, *China* **34 H5** 33 5N 108 15 E
Shiquan He = Indus →, *Pakistan* **42 G2** 24 20N 67 47 E
Shīr Kūh, *Iran* **45 D7** 31 39N 54 3 E
Shiragami-Misaki, *Japan* **30 D10** 41 24N 140 12 E
Shirakawa, *Fukushima, Japan* **31 F10** 37 7N 140 13 E
Shirakawa, *Gifu, Japan* **31 F8** 36 17N 136 56 E
Shirane-San, *Gumma, Japan* **31 F9** 36 48N 139 22 E
Shirane-San, *Yamanashi, Japan* **31 G9** 35 42N 138 9 E
Shiraoi, *Japan* **30 C10** 42 33N 141 21 E
Shīrāz, *Iran* **45 D7** 29 42N 52 30 E
Shire →, *Africa* **55 F4** 17 42S 35 19 E
Shiretoko-Misaki, *Japan* **30 B12** 44 21N 145 20 E
Shirinab →, *Pakistan* **42 D2** 30 15N 66 28 E
Shiriya-Zaki, *Japan* **30 D10** 41 25N 141 30 E
Shiroishi, *Japan* **30 F10** 38 0N 140 37 E
Shīrvān, *Iran* **45 B8** 37 30N 57 50 E
Shirwa, L. = Chilwa, L., *Malawi* **55 F4** 15 15S 35 40 E
Shivpuri, *India* **42 G7** 25 26N 77 42 E
Shixian, *China* **35 C15** 43 5N 129 50 E
Shizuishan, *China* **34 E4** 39 15N 106 50 E
Shizuoka, *Japan* **31 G9** 34 57N 138 24 E
Shizuoka □, *Japan* **31 G9** 35 15N 138 40 E
Shklov = Shklow, *Belarus* **17 A16** 54 16N 30 15 E
Shklow, *Belarus* **17 A16** 54 16N 30 15 E
Shkoder = Shkodra, *Albania* **21 C8** 42 4N 19 32 E
Shkodra, *Albania* **21 C8** 42 4N 19 32 E
Shkumbini →, *Albania* **21 D8** 41 2N 19 31 E
Shmidta, Ostrov, *Russia* **27 A10** 81 0N 91 0 E
Shō-Gawa →, *Japan* **31 F8** 36 47N 137 4 E
Shoal L., *Canada* **73 D9** 49 33N 95 1W
Shoal Lake, *Canada* **73 C8** 50 30N 100 35W
Shōdo-Shima, *Japan* **31 G7** 34 30N 134 15 E
Sholapur = Solapur, *India* **40 L9** 17 43N 75 56 E
Shologontsy, *Russia* **27 C12** 66 13N 114 0 E
Shōmrōn, *West Bank* **47 C4** 32 15N 35 13 E
Shoreham by Sea, *U.K.* **11 G7** 50 50N 0 16W
Shori →, *Pakistan* **42 E3** 28 29N 69 44 E
Shorkot Road, *Pakistan* **42 D5** 30 47N 72 15 E
Shoshone, *Calif., U.S.A.* **85 K10** 35 58N 116 16W
Shoshone, *Idaho, U.S.A.* **82 E6** 42 56N 114 25W
Shoshone L., *U.S.A.* **82 D8** 44 22N 110 43W
Shoshone Mts., *U.S.A.* **82 G5** 39 20N 117 25W
Shoshong, *Botswana* **56 C4** 22 56S 26 31 E
Shoshoni, *U.S.A.* **82 E9** 43 14N 108 7W
Shouguang, *China* **35 F10** 37 52N 118 45 E
Shouyang, *China* **34 F7** 37 54N 113 8 E
Show Low, *U.S.A.* **83 J9** 34 15N 110 2W
Shreveport, *U.S.A.* **81 J8** 32 31N 93 45W
Shrewsbury, *U.K.* **11 E5** 52 43N 2 45W
Shri Mohangarh, *India* **42 F4** 27 17N 71 18 E
Shrirampur, *India* **43 H13** 22 44N 88 21 E
Shropshire □, *U.K.* **11 E5** 52 36N 2 45W
Shu, *Kazakstan* **26 E8** 43 36N 73 42 E
Shu →, *Kazakstan* **28 E10** 45 0N 67 44 E
Shuangcheng, *China* **35 B14** 45 20N 126 15 E
Shuanggou, *China* **35 G9** 34 2N 117 30 E
Shuangliao, *China* **35 C12** 43 29N 123 30 E
Shuangshanzi, *China* **35 D10** 40 20N 119 8 E
Shuangyang, *China* **35 C13** 43 28N 125 40 E
Shuangyashan, *China* **33 B8** 46 28N 131 5 E
Shuguri Falls, *Tanzania* **55 D4** 8 33S 37 22 E
Shuiye, *China* **34 F8** 36 7N 114 8 E
Shujalpur, *India* **42 H7** 23 18N 76 46 E
Shukpa Kunzang, *India* **43 B8** 34 22N 78 22 E
Shulan, *China* **35 B14** 44 28N 127 0 E
Shule, *China* **32 C2** 39 25N 76 3 E
Shumagin Is., *U.S.A.* **68 C4** 55 7N 160 30W
Shumen, *Bulgaria* **21 C12** 43 18N 26 55 E
Shumikha, *Russia* **26 D7** 55 10N 63 15 E
Shuo Xian = Shuozhou, *China* **34 E7** 39 20N 112 33 E
Shuozhou, *China* **34 E7** 39 20N 112 33 E
Shūr →, *Fārs, Iran* **45 D7** 28 30N 55 0 E
Shūr →, *Kermān, Iran* **45 D8** 30 52N 57 37 E
Shūr →, *Yazd, Iran* **45 D7** 31 45N 55 15 E
Shūr Āb, *Iran* **45 C6** 34 23N 51 11 E
Shūr Gaz, *Iran* **45 D8** 29 10N 59 20 E
Shūrāb, *Iran* **45 C8** 33 43N 56 29 E
Shūrjestān, *Iran* **45 D7** 31 24N 52 25 E
Shurugwi, *Zimbabwe* **55 F3** 19 40S 30 0 E
Shūsf, *Iran* **45 D9** 31 50N 60 5 E
Shūshtar, *Iran* **45 D6** 32 0N 48 50 E
Shuswap L., *Canada* **72 C5** 50 55N 119 3W
Shuyang, *China* **35 G10** 34 10N 118 42 E
Shūzū, *Iran* **45 D7** 29 52N 54 30 E
Shwebo, *Burma* **41 H19** 22 30N 95 45 E
Shwegu, *Burma* **41 G20** 24 15N 96 26 E
Shweli →, *Burma* **41 H20** 23 45N 96 45 E
Shymkent, *Kazakstan* **26 E7** 42 18N 69 36 E
Shyok, *India* **43 B8** 34 13N 78 12 E
Shyok →, *Pakistan* **43 B6** 35 13N 75 53 E
Si Chon, *Thailand* **39 H2** 9 0N 99 54 E
Si Kiang = Xi Jiang →, *China* **33 D6** 22 5N 113 20 E
Si-ngan = Xi'an, *China* **34 G5** 34 15N 109 0 E
Si Prachan, *Thailand* **38 E3** 14 37N 100 9 E
Si Racha, *Thailand* **38 F3** 13 10N 100 48 E
Si Xian, *China* **35 H9** 33 30N 117 50 E
Siahaf →, *Pakistan* **42 E3** 29 3N 68 57 E
Siahan Range, *Pakistan* **40 F4** 27 30N 64 40 E
Siaksriindrapura, *Indonesia* **36 D2** 0 51N 102 0 E
Sialkot, *Pakistan* **42 C6** 32 32N 74 30 E
Siam = Thailand ■, *Asia* **38 E4** 16 0N 102 0 E
Sian = Xi'an, *China* **34 G5** 34 15N 109 0 E
Siantan, *Indonesia* **36 D3** 3 10N 106 15 E
Siāreh, *Iran* **45 D9** 28 5N 60 14 E
Siargao, *Phil.* **37 C7** 9 52N 126 3 E
Siari, *Pakistan* **43 B7** 34 55N 76 40 E
Siasi, *Phil.* **37 C6** 5 34N 120 50 E
Siau, *Indonesia* **37 D7** 2 50N 125 25 E
Šiauliai, *Lithuania* **9 J20** 55 56N 23 15 E
Sibâi, Gebel el, *Egypt* **44 E2** 25 45N 34 10 E
Sibay, *Russia* **24 D10** 52 42N 58 39 E
Sibayi, L., *S. Africa* **57 D5** 27 20S 32 45 E
Šibenik, *Croatia* **20 C6** 43 48N 15 54 E
Siberia, *Russia* **4 D13** 60 0N 100 0 E
Siberut, *Indonesia* **36 E1** 1 30S 99 0 E
Sibi, *Pakistan* **42 E2** 29 30N 67 54 E
Sibil = Oksibil, *Indonesia* **37 E10** 4 59S 140 35 E
Sibiti, *Congo* **52 E2** 3 38S 13 19 E
Sibiu, *Romania* **17 F13** 45 45N 24 9 E
Sibley, *U.S.A.* **80 D7** 43 24N 95 45W
Sibolga, *Indonesia* **36 D1** 1 42N 98 45 E
Sibsagar, *India* **41 F19** 27 0N 94 36 E
Sibu, *Malaysia* **36 D4** 2 18N 111 49 E
Sibuco, *Phil.* **37 C6** 7 20N 122 10 E
Sibuguey B., *Phil.* **37 C6** 7 50N 122 45 E
Sibut, *C.A.R.* **52 C3** 5 46N 19 10 E
Sibutu, *Phil.* **37 D5** 4 45N 119 30 E
Sibutu Passage, *E. Indies* **37 D6** 4 50N 120 0 E
Sibuyan, *Phil.* **37 B6** 12 25N 122 40 E
Sibuyan Sea, *Phil.* **37 B6** 12 30N 122 20 E
Sicamous, *Canada* **72 C5** 50 49N 119 0W
Siccus →, *Australia* **63 E2** 31 26S 139 30 E
Sichuan □, *China* **32 C5** 31 0N 104 0 E
Sicilia, *Italy* **20 F6** 37 30N 14 30 E
Sicily = Sicilia, *Italy* **20 F6** 37 30N 14 30 E
Sicuani, *Peru* **92 F4** 14 21S 71 10W
Sidári, *Greece* **23 A3** 39 47N 19 41 E
Siddhapur, *India* **42 H5** 23 56N 72 25 E
Siddipet, *India* **40 K11** 18 5N 78 51 E
Sidhauli, *India* **43 F9** 27 17N 80 50 E
Sidheros, Ákra, *Greece* **23 D8** 35 19N 26 19 E
Sidhi, *India* **43 G9** 24 25N 81 53 E
Sidi-bel-Abbès, *Algeria* **50 A5** 35 13N 0 39W
Sidlaw Hills, *U.K.* **12 E5** 56 32N 3 2W
Sidley, Mt., *Antarctica* **5 D14** 77 2S 126 2W
Sidmouth, *U.K.* **11 G4** 50 40N 3 15W
Sidmouth, C., *Australia* **62 A3** 13 25S 143 36 E
Sidney, *Canada* **72 D4** 48 39N 123 24W
Sidney, *Mont., U.S.A.* **80 B2** 47 43N 104 9W
Sidney, *N.Y., U.S.A.* **79 D9** 42 19N 75 24W
Sidney, *Nebr., U.S.A.* **80 E3** 41 8N 102 59W
Sidney, *Ohio, U.S.A.* **76 E3** 40 17N 84 9W
Sidney Lanier L., *U.S.A.* **77 H4** 34 10N 84 4W
Sidoarjo, *Indonesia* **37 G15** 7 27S 112 43 E
Sidon = Saydā, *Lebanon* **47 B4** 33 35N 35 25 E
Sidra, G. of = Surt, Khalīj, *Libya* **51 B9** 31 40N 18 30 E
Siedlce, *Poland* **17 B12** 52 10N 22 20 E
Sieg →, *Germany* **16 C4** 50 46N 7 6 E
Siegen, *Germany* **16 C5** 50 51N 8 0 E
Siem Pang, *Cambodia* **38 E6** 14 7N 106 23 E
Siem Reap = Siemreab, *Cambodia* **38 F4** 13 20N 103 52 E
Siemreab, *Cambodia* **38 F4** 13 20N 103 52 E
Siena, *Italy* **20 C4** 43 19N 11 21 E
Sieradz, *Poland* **17 C10** 51 37N 18 41 E
Sierra Blanca, *U.S.A.* **83 L11** 31 11N 105 22W
Sierra Blanca Peak, *U.S.A.* **83 K11** 33 23N 105 49W
Sierra City, *U.S.A.* **84 F6** 39 34N 120 38W
Sierra Colorada, *Argentina* **96 E3** 40 35S 67 50W
Sierra Gorda, *Chile* **94 A2** 22 50S 69 15W
Sierra Leone ■, *W. Afr.* **50 G3** 9 0N 12 0W
Sierra Madre, *Mexico* **87 D6** 16 0N 93 0W
Sierra Mojada, *Mexico* **86 B4** 27 19N 103 42W
Sierra Nevada, *U.S.A.* **84 H8** 37 30N 119 0W
Sierra Vista, *U.S.A.* **83 L8** 31 33N 110 18W
Sierraville, *U.S.A.* **84 F6** 39 36N 120 22W
Sífnos, *Greece* **21 F11** 37 0N 24 45 E
Sifton, *Canada* **73 C8** 51 21N 100 8W
Sifton Pass, *Canada* **72 B3** 57 52N 126 15W
Sighetu-Marmaţiei, *Romania* **17 E12** 47 57N 23 52 E
Sighişoara, *Romania* **17 E13** 46 12N 24 50 E
Sigli, *Indonesia* **36 C1** 5 25N 96 0 E
Siglufjörður, *Iceland* **8 C4** 66 12N 18 55W
Signal, *U.S.A.* **85 L13** 34 30N 113 38W
Signal Pk., *U.S.A.* **85 M12** 33 20N 114 2W
Sigsig, *Ecuador* **92 D3** 3 0S 78 50W
Sigüenza, *Spain* **19 B4** 41 3N 2 40W
Siguiri, *Guinea* **50 F4** 11 31N 9 10W
Sigulda, *Latvia* **9 H21** 57 10N 24 55 E
Sihanoukville = Kampong Saom, *Cambodia* **39 G4** 10 38N 103 30 E
Sihora, *India* **43 H9** 23 29N 80 6 E
Siikajoki →, *Finland* **8 D21** 64 50N 24 43 E
Siilinjärvi, *Finland* **8 E22** 63 4N 27 39 E
Sijarira Ra., *Zimbabwe* **55 F2** 17 36S 27 45 E
Sika, *India* **42 H3** 22 26N 69 47 E
Sikao, *Thailand* **39 J2** 7 34N 99 21 E
Sikar, *India* **42 F6** 27 33N 75 10 E
Sikasso, *Mali* **50 F4** 11 18N 5 35W
Sikeston, *U.S.A.* **81 G10** 36 53N 89 35W
Sikhote Alin, Khrebet, *Russia* **27 E14** 45 0N 136 0 E
Sikhote Alin Ra. = Sikhote Alin, Khrebet, *Russia* **27 E14** 45 0N 136 0 E

Sursar

Staten, I. = Estados, I. de Los, *Argentina* 96 G4 54 40S 64 30W
Staten I., *U.S.A.* 79 F10 40 35N 74 9W
Statesboro, *U.S.A.* 77 J5 32 27N 81 47W
Statesville, *U.S.A.* 77 H5 35 47N 80 53W
Stauffer, *U.S.A.* 85 L7 34 45N 119 3W
Staunton, *Ill., U.S.A.* 80 F10 39 1N 89 47W
Staunton, *Va., U.S.A.* 76 F6 38 9N 79 4W
Stavanger, *Norway* 9 G11 58 57N 5 40 E
Staveley, *N.Z.* 59 K3 43 40S 171 32 E
Stavelot, *Belgium* 15 D5 50 23N 5 55 E
Stavern, *Norway* 9 G14 59 0N 10 1 E
Stavoren, *Neths.* 15 B5 52 53N 5 22 E
Stavropol, *Russia* 25 E7 45 5N 42 0 E
Stavros, *Cyprus* 23 D11 35 1N 32 38 E
Stavrós, *Greece* 23 D6 35 12N 24 45 E
Stavros, Ákra, *Greece* 23 D6 35 26N 24 58 E
Stawell, *Australia* 63 F3 37 5S 142 47 E
Stawell →, *Australia* 62 C3 20 20S 142 55 E
Stayner, *Canada* 78 B4 44 25N 80 5W
Stayton, *U.S.A.* 82 D2 44 48N 122 48W
Steamboat Springs, *U.S.A.* 82 F10 40 29N 106 50W
Steele, *U.S.A.* 80 B5 46 51N 99 55W
Steelton, *U.S.A.* 78 F8 40 14N 76 50W
Steen River, *Canada* 72 B5 59 40N 117 12W
Steenkool = Bintuni, *Indonesia* 37 E8 2 7S 133 32 E
Steens Mt., *U.S.A.* 82 E4 42 35N 118 40W
Steenwijk, *Neths.* 15 B6 52 47N 6 7 E
Steep Pt., *Australia* 61 E1 26 8S 113 8 E
Steep Rock, *Canada* 73 C9 51 30N 98 48W
Stefanie L. = Chew Bahir, *Ethiopia* 46 G2 4 40N 36 50 E
Stefansson Bay, *Antarctica* 5 C5 67 20S 59 8 E
Steiermark □, *Austria* 16 E8 47 26N 15 0 E
Steilacoom, *U.S.A.* 84 C4 47 10N 122 36W
Steinbach, *Canada* 73 D9 49 32N 96 40W
Steinkjer, *Norway* 8 D14 64 1N 11 31 E
Steinkopf, *S. Africa* 56 D2 29 18S 17 43 E
Stellarton, *Canada* 71 C7 45 32N 62 30W
Stellenbosch, *S. Africa* 56 E2 33 58S 18 50 E
Stendal, *Germany* 16 B6 52 36N 11 53 E
Steornabhaigh = Stornoway, *U.K.* 12 C2 58 13N 6 23W
Stepanakert = Xankändi, *Azerbaijan* 25 G8 39 52N 46 49 E
Stephens Creek, *Australia* 63 E3 31 50S 141 30 E
Stephens I., *Canada* 72 C2 54 10N 130 45W
Stephens L., *Canada* 73 B9 56 32N 95 0W
Stephenville, *Canada* 71 C8 48 31N 58 35W
Stephenville, *U.S.A.* 81 J5 32 13N 98 12W
Stepnoi = Elista, *Russia* 25 E7 46 16N 44 14 E
Steppe, *Asia* 28 D9 50 0N 50 0 E
Sterkstroom, *S. Africa* 56 E4 31 32S 26 32 E
Sterling, *Colo., U.S.A.* 80 E3 40 37N 103 13W
Sterling, *Ill., U.S.A.* 80 E10 41 48N 89 42W
Sterling, *Kans., U.S.A.* 80 F5 38 13N 98 12W
Sterling City, *U.S.A.* 81 K4 31 51N 101 0W
Sterling Heights, *U.S.A.* 76 D4 42 35N 83 0W
Sterling Run, *U.S.A.* 78 E6 41 25N 78 12W
Sterlitamak, *Russia* 24 D10 53 40N 56 0 E
Stérnes, *Greece* 23 D6 35 30N 24 9 E
Stettin = Szczecin, *Poland* 16 B8 53 27N 14 27 E
Stettiner Haff, *Germany* 16 B8 53 47N 14 15 E
Stettler, *Canada* 72 C6 52 19N 112 40W
Steubenville, *U.S.A.* 78 F4 40 22N 80 37W
Stevenage, *U.K.* 11 F7 51 55N 0 13W
Stevens Point, *U.S.A.* 80 C10 44 31N 89 34W
Stevenson, *U.S.A.* 84 E5 45 42N 121 53W
Stevenson L., *Canada* 73 C9 53 55N 96 0W
Stevensville, *U.S.A.* 82 C6 46 30N 114 5W
Stewart, *B.C., Canada* 72 B3 55 56N 129 57W
Stewart, *N.W.T., Canada* 68 B6 63 19N 139 26W
Stewart, *U.S.A.* 84 F7 39 5N 119 46W
Stewart, C., *Australia* 62 A1 11 57S 134 56 E
Stewart, I., *Chile* 96 G2 54 50S 71 15W
Stewart I., *N.Z.* 59 M1 46 58S 167 54 E
Stewarts Point, *U.S.A.* 84 G3 38 39N 123 24W
Stewartville, *U.S.A.* 80 D8 43 51N 92 29W
Stewiacke, *Canada* 71 C7 45 9N 63 22W
Steynsburg, *S. Africa* 56 E4 31 15S 25 49 E
Steyr, *Austria* 16 D8 48 3N 14 25 E
Steytlerville, *S. Africa* 56 E3 33 17S 24 19 E
Stigler, *U.S.A.* 81 H7 35 15N 95 8W
Stikine →, *Canada* 72 B2 56 40N 132 30W
Stilfontein, *S. Africa* 56 D4 26 51S 26 50 E
Stillwater, *N.Z.* 59 K3 42 27S 171 20 E
Stillwater, *Minn., U.S.A.* 80 C8 45 3N 92 49W
Stillwater, *N.Y., U.S.A.* 79 D11 42 55N 73 41W
Stillwater, *Okla., U.S.A.* 81 G6 36 7N 97 4W
Stillwater Range, *U.S.A.* 82 G4 39 50N 118 5W
Stillwater Reservoir, *U.S.A.* 79 C9 43 54N 75 3W
Stilwell, *U.S.A.* 81 H7 35 49N 94 38W
Štip, *Macedonia* 21 D10 41 42N 22 10 E
Stirling, *Canada* 78 B7 44 18N 77 33W
Stirling, *U.K.* 12 E5 56 8N 3 57W
Stirling □, *U.K.* 12 E4 56 12N 4 18W
Stirling Ra., *Australia* 61 F2 34 23S 118 0 E
Stittsville, *Canada* 79 A9 45 15N 75 55W
Stjernøya, *Norway* 8 A20 70 20N 22 40 E
Stjørdalshalsen, *Norway* 8 E14 63 29N 10 51 E
Stockerau, *Austria* 16 D9 48 24N 16 12 E
Stockholm, *Sweden* 9 G18 59 20N 18 3 E
Stockport, *U.K.* 10 D5 53 25N 2 9W
Stocksbridge, *U.K.* 10 D6 53 29N 1 35W
Stockton, *Calif., U.S.A.* 84 H5 37 58N 121 17W
Stockton, *Kans., U.S.A.* 80 F5 39 26N 99 16W
Stockton, *Mo., U.S.A.* 81 G8 37 42N 93 48W
Stockton-on-Tees, *U.K.* 10 C6 54 35N 1 19W
Stockton-on-Tees □, *U.K.* 10 C6 54 35N 1 19W
Stockton Plateau, *U.S.A.* 81 K3 30 30N 102 30W
Stoeng Treng, *Cambodia* 38 F5 13 31N 105 58 E
Stoer, Pt. of, *U.K.* 12 C3 58 16N 5 23W
Stoke-on-Trent, *U.K.* 10 D5 53 1N 2 11W
Stoke-on-Trent □, *U.K.* 10 D5 53 1N 2 11W
Stokes Pt., *Australia* 62 G3 40 10S 143 56 E
Stokes Ra., *Australia* 60 C5 15 50S 130 50 E
Stokksnes, *Iceland* 8 D6 64 14N 14 58W
Stokmarknes, *Norway* 8 B16 68 34N 14 54 E
Stolac, *Bos.-H.* 21 C7 43 5N 17 59 E
Stolbovoy, Ostrov, *Russia* 27 D17 74 44N 135 14 E
Stolbtsy = Stowbtsy, *Belarus* 17 B14 53 30N 26 43 E
Stolin, *Belarus* 17 C14 51 53N 26 50 E
Stomion, *Greece* 23 D5 35 21N 23 32 E
Stone, *U.K.* 10 E5 52 55N 2 9W
Stoneboro, *U.S.A.* 78 E4 41 20N 80 7W
Stonehaven, *U.K.* 12 E6 56 59N 2 12W
Stonehenge, *Australia* 62 C3 24 22S 143 17 E
Stonehenge, *U.K.* 11 F6 51 9N 1 45W
Stonewall, *Canada* 73 C9 50 10N 97 19W
Stony L., *Man., Canada* 73 B9 58 51N 98 40W
Stony L., *Ont., Canada* 78 B6 44 30N 78 5W
Stony Point, *U.S.A.* 79 E11 41 14N 73 59W
Stony Pt., *U.S.A.* 79 C8 43 50N 76 18W
Stony Rapids, *Canada* 73 B7 59 16N 105 50W
Stony Tunguska = Tunguska, Podkamennaya →, *Russia* 27 C10 61 50N 90 13 E
Stonyford, *U.S.A.* 84 F4 39 23N 122 33W
Stora Lulevatten, *Sweden* 8 C18 67 10N 19 30 E
Storavan, *Sweden* 8 D18 65 45N 18 10 E
Stord, *Norway* 9 G11 59 52N 5 23 E
Store Bælt, *Denmark* 9 J14 55 20N 11 0 E
Storm B., *Australia* 62 G4 43 10S 147 30 E
Storm Lake, *U.S.A.* 80 D7 42 39N 95 13W
Stormberge, *S. Africa* 56 E4 31 16S 26 17 E
Stormsrivier, *S. Africa* 56 E3 33 59S 23 52 E
Stornoway, *U.K.* 12 C2 58 13N 6 23W
Storozhinets = Storozhynets, *Ukraine* 17 D13 48 14N 25 45 E
Storozhynets, *Ukraine* 17 D13 48 14N 25 45 E
Storrs, *U.S.A.* 79 E12 41 49N 72 15W
Storsjön, *Sweden* 8 E16 63 9N 14 30 E
Storuman, *Sweden* 8 D17 65 5N 17 10 E
Storuman, sjö, *Sweden* 8 D17 65 13N 16 50 E
Stouffville, *Canada* 78 C5 43 58N 79 15W
Stoughton, *Canada* 73 D8 49 40N 103 0W
Stour →, *Dorset, U.K.* 11 G6 50 43N 1 47W
Stour →, *Kent, U.K.* 11 F9 51 18N 1 22 E
Stour →, *Suffolk, U.K.* 11 F9 51 57N 1 4 E
Stourbridge, *U.K.* 11 E5 52 28N 2 8W
Stout L., *Canada* 73 C10 52 0N 94 40W
Stove Pipe Wells Village, *U.S.A.* 85 J9 36 35N 117 11W
Stow, *U.S.A.* 78 E3 41 10N 81 27W
Stowbtsy, *Belarus* 17 B14 53 30N 26 43 E
Stowmarket, *U.K.* 11 E9 52 12N 1 0 E
Strabane, *U.K.* 13 B4 54 50N 7 27W
Strahan, *Australia* 62 G4 42 9S 145 20 E
Stralsund, *Germany* 16 A7 54 18N 13 4 E
Strand, *S. Africa* 56 E2 34 9S 18 48 E
Stranda, *Møre og Romsdal, Norway* 9 E12 62 19N 6 58 E
Stranda, *Nord-Trøndelag, Norway* 8 E14 63 33N 10 14 E
Strangford L., *U.K.* 13 B6 54 30N 5 37W
Stranraer, *U.K.* 12 G3 54 54N 5 1W
Strasbourg, *Canada* 73 C8 51 4N 104 55W
Strasbourg, *France* 18 B7 48 35N 7 42 E
Stratford, *Canada* 78 C4 43 23N 81 0W
Stratford, *N.Z.* 59 H5 39 20S 174 19 E
Stratford, *Calif., U.S.A.* 84 J7 36 11N 119 49W
Stratford, *Conn., U.S.A.* 79 E11 41 12N 73 8W
Stratford, *Tex., U.S.A.* 81 G3 36 20N 102 4W
Stratford-upon-Avon, *U.K.* 11 E6 52 12N 1 42W
Strath Spey, *U.K.* 12 D5 57 9N 3 49W
Strathalbyn, *Australia* 63 F2 35 13S 138 53 E
Strathaven, *U.K.* 12 F4 55 40N 4 5W
Strathcona Prov. Park, *Canada* 72 D3 49 38N 125 40W
Strathmore, *Canada* 72 C6 51 5N 113 18W
Strathmore, *U.K.* 12 E5 56 37N 3 7W
Strathmore, *U.S.A.* 84 J7 36 9N 119 4W
Strathnaver, *Canada* 72 C4 53 20N 122 33W
Strathpeffer, *U.K.* 12 D4 57 35N 4 32W
Strathroy, *Canada* 78 D3 42 58N 81 38W
Strathy Pt., *U.K.* 12 C4 58 36N 4 1W
Strattanville, *U.S.A.* 78 E5 41 12N 79 19W
Stratton, *U.S.A.* 79 A14 45 8N 70 26W
Stratton Mt., *U.S.A.* 79 C12 43 4N 72 55W
Straubing, *Germany* 16 D7 48 52N 12 34 E
Straumnes, *Iceland* 8 C2 66 26N 23 8W
Strawberry →, *U.S.A.* 82 F8 40 10N 110 24W
Streaky B., *Australia* 63 E1 32 48S 134 13 E
Streaky Bay, *Australia* 63 E1 32 51S 134 18 E
Streator, *U.S.A.* 80 E10 41 8N 88 50W
Streetsboro, *U.S.A.* 78 E3 41 14N 81 21W
Streetsville, *Canada* 78 C5 43 35N 79 42W
Strelka, *Russia* 27 D10 58 5N 93 3 E
Streng →, *Cambodia* 38 F4 13 12N 103 37 E
Streymoy, *Færoe Is.* 8 E9 62 8N 7 5W
Strezhevoy, *Russia* 26 C8 60 42N 77 34 E
Strimón →, *Greece* 21 D10 40 46N 23 51 E
Strimonikós Kólpos, *Greece* 21 D11 40 33N 24 0 E
Stroma, *U.K.* 12 C5 58 41N 3 7W
Strómboli, *Italy* 20 E6 38 47N 15 13 E
Stromeferry, *U.K.* 12 D3 57 21N 5 33W
Stromness, *U.K.* 12 C5 58 58N 3 17W
Stromsburg, *U.S.A.* 80 E6 41 7N 97 36W
Strömstad, *Sweden* 9 G14 58 56N 11 10 E
Strömsund, *Sweden* 8 E16 63 51N 15 33 E
Strongsville, *U.S.A.* 78 E3 41 19N 81 50W
Stronsay, *U.K.* 12 B6 59 7N 2 35W
Stroud, *U.K.* 11 F5 51 45N 2 13W
Stroud Road, *Australia* 63 E5 32 18S 151 57 E
Stroudsburg, *U.S.A.* 79 F9 40 59N 75 12W
Stroumbi, *Cyprus* 23 E11 34 53N 32 29 E
Struer, *Denmark* 9 H13 56 30N 8 35 E
Strumica, *Macedonia* 21 D10 41 28N 22 41 E
Struthers, *Canada* 70 C2 48 41N 85 51W
Struthers, *U.S.A.* 78 E4 41 4N 80 39W
Stryker, *U.S.A.* 82 B6 48 41N 114 46W
Stryy, *Ukraine* 17 D12 49 16N 23 48 E
Strzelecki Cr. →, *Australia* 63 D2 29 37S 139 59 E
Stuart, *Fla., U.S.A.* 77 M5 27 12N 80 15W
Stuart, *Nebr., U.S.A.* 80 D5 42 36N 99 8W
Stuart →, *Canada* 72 C4 54 0N 123 35W
Stuart Bluff Ra., *Australia* 60 D5 22 50S 131 52 E
Stuart L., *Canada* 72 C4 54 30N 124 30W
Stuart Ra., *Australia* 63 D1 29 10S 134 56 E
Stull, L., *Canada* 70 B1 54 24N 92 34W
Stung Treng = Stoeng Treng, *Cambodia* 38 F5 13 31N 105 58 E
Stupart →, *Canada* 70 A1 56 0N 93 25W
Sturgeon B., *Canada* 73 C9 52 0N 97 50W
Sturgeon Bay, *U.S.A.* 76 C2 44 50N 87 23W
Sturgeon Falls, *Canada* 70 C4 46 25N 79 57W
Sturgeon L., *Alta., Canada* 72 B5 55 6N 117 32W
Sturgeon L., *Ont., Canada* 70 C1 50 0N 90 45W
Sturgeon L., *Ont., Canada* 78 B6 44 28N 78 43W
Sturgis, *Canada* 73 C8 51 56N 102 36W
Sturgis, *Mich., U.S.A.* 76 E3 41 48N 85 25W
Sturgis, *S. Dak., U.S.A.* 80 C3 44 25N 103 31W
Sturt Cr. →, *Australia* 60 C4 19 8S 127 50 E
Stutterheim, *S. Africa* 56 E4 32 33S 27 28 E
Stuttgart, *Germany* 16 D5 48 48N 9 11 E
Stuttgart, *U.S.A.* 81 H9 34 30N 91 33W
Stuyvesant, *U.S.A.* 79 D11 42 23N 73 45W
Stykkishólmur, *Iceland* 8 D2 65 2N 22 40W
Styria = Steiermark □, *Austria* 16 E8 47 26N 15 0 E
Su Xian = Suzhou, *China* 34 H9 33 41N 116 59 E
Suakin, *Sudan* 51 E13 19 8N 37 20 E
Suan, *N. Korea* 35 E14 38 42N 126 22 E
Suaqui, *Mexico* 86 B3 29 12N 109 41W
Suar, *India* 43 E8 29 2N 79 3 E
Subang, *Indonesia* 37 G12 6 34S 107 45 E
Subansiri →, *India* 41 F18 26 48N 93 50 E
Subarnarekha →, *India* 43 H12 22 34N 87 24 E
Subayhah, *Si. Arabia* 44 D3 30 2N 38 50 E
Subi, *Indonesia* 39 L7 2 58N 108 50 E
Subotica, *Serbia, Yug.* 21 A8 46 6N 19 39 E
Suceava, *Romania* 17 E14 47 38N 26 16 E
Suchan, *Russia* 30 C6 43 8N 133 9 E
Suchitoto, *El Salv.* 88 D2 13 56N 89 0W
Suchou = Suzhou, *China* 33 C7 31 19N 120 38 E
Süchow = Xuzhou, *China* 35 G9 34 18N 117 10 E
Suck →, *Ireland* 13 C3 53 17N 8 3W
Sucre, *Bolivia* 92 G5 19 0S 65 15W
Sucuriú →, *Brazil* 93 H8 20 47S 51 38W
Sud, Pte. du, *Canada* 71 C7 49 3N 62 14W
Sud-Kivu □, *Dem. Rep. of the Congo* 54 C2 3 30S 28 0 E
Sud-Ouest, Pte. du, *Canada* 71 C7 49 23N 63 36W
Sudan, *U.S.A.* 81 H3 34 4N 102 32W
Sudan ■, *Africa* 51 E11 15 0N 30 0 E
Sudbury, *Canada* 70 C3 46 30N 81 0W
Sudbury, *U.K.* 11 E8 52 2N 0 45 E
Sûdd, *Sudan* 51 G12 8 20N 30 0 E
Sudeten Mts. = Sudety, *Europe* 17 C9 50 20N 16 45 E
Sudety, *Europe* 17 C9 50 20N 16 45 E
Suðuroy, *Færoe Is.* 8 F9 61 32N 6 50W
Sudi, *Tanzania* 55 E4 10 11S 39 57 E
Sudirman, Pegunungan, *Indonesia* 37 E9 4 30S 137 0 E
Sueca, *Spain* 19 C5 39 12N 0 21W
Suemez I., *U.S.A.* 72 B2 55 15N 133 20W
Suez = El Suweis, *Egypt* 51 C12 29 58N 32 31 E
Suez, G. of = Suweis, Khalîg el, *Egypt* 51 C12 28 40N 33 0 E
Suez Canal = Suweis, Qanâ es, *Egypt* 51 B12 31 0N 32 20 E
Suffield, *Canada* 72 C6 50 12N 111 10W
Suffolk, *U.S.A.* 76 G7 36 44N 76 35W
Suffolk □, *U.K.* 11 E9 52 16N 1 0 E
Sugargrove, *U.S.A.* 78 E5 41 59N 79 21W
Sugarive →, *India* 43 F12 26 16N 86 24 E
Sugluk = Salluit, *Canada* 69 B12 62 14N 75 38W
Şuḩār, *Oman* 45 E8 24 20N 56 40 E
Sühbaatar □, *Mongolia* 34 B8 45 30N 114 0 E
Suhl, *Germany* 16 C6 50 36N 10 42 E
Sui, *Pakistan* 42 E3 28 37N 69 19 E
Sui Xian, *China* 34 G8 34 25N 115 2 E
Suide, *China* 34 F6 37 30N 110 12 E
Suifenhe, *China* 35 B16 44 25N 131 10 E
Suihua, *China* 33 B7 46 32N 126 55 E
Suining, *China* 35 H9 33 56N 117 58 E
Suiping, *China* 34 H7 33 10N 113 59 E
Suir →, *Ireland* 13 D4 52 16N 7 9W
Suisun City, *U.S.A.* 84 G4 38 15N 122 2W
Suiyang, *China* 35 B16 44 30N 130 56 E
Suizhong, *China* 35 D11 40 21N 120 20 E
Sujangarh, *India* 42 F6 27 42N 74 31 E
Sukabumi, *Indonesia* 37 G12 6 56S 106 50 E
Sukadana, *Indonesia* 36 E4 1 10S 110 0 E
Sukagawa, *Japan* 31 F10 37 17N 140 23 E
Sukaraja, *Indonesia* 36 E4 2 28S 110 25 E
Sukarnapura = Jayapura, *Indonesia* 37 E10 2 28S 140 38 E
Sukch'ŏn, *N. Korea* 35 E13 39 22N 125 35 E
Sukhona →, *Russia* 24 C6 61 15N 46 39 E
Sukhothai, *Thailand* 38 D2 17 1N 99 49 E
Sukhumi = Sokhumi, *Georgia* 25 F7 43 0N 41 0 E
Sukkur, *Pakistan* 42 F3 27 42N 68 54 E
Sukkur Barrage, *Pakistan* 42 F3 27 40N 68 50 E
Sukri →, *India* 42 G4 25 4N 71 43 E
Sukumo, *Japan* 31 H6 32 56N 132 44 E
Sukunka →, *Canada* 72 B4 55 45N 121 15W
Sula, Kepulauan, *Indonesia* 37 E7 1 45S 125 0 E
Sulaco →, *Honduras* 88 C2 15 2N 87 44W
Sulaiman Range, *Pakistan* 42 D3 30 30N 69 50 E
Sūlār, *Iran* 45 D6 31 53N 51 54 E
Sulawesi □, *Indonesia* 37 E6 2 0S 120 0 E
Sulawesi Sea = Celebes Sea, *Indonesia* 37 D6 3 0N 123 0 E
Sulawesi Selatan □, *Indonesia* 37 E6 2 30S 120 0 E
Sulawesi Utara □, *Indonesia* 37 D6 1 0N 122 30 E
Sulima, *S. Leone* 50 G3 6 58N 11 32W
Sulina, *Romania* 17 F15 45 10N 29 40 E
Sulitjelma, *Norway* 8 C17 67 9N 16 3 E
Sullana, *Peru* 92 D2 4 52S 80 39W
Sullivan, *Ill., U.S.A.* 80 F10 39 36N 88 37W
Sullivan, *Ind., U.S.A.* 76 F2 39 6N 87 24W
Sullivan, *Mo., U.S.A.* 80 F9 38 13N 91 10W
Sullivan Bay, *Canada* 72 C3 50 55N 126 50W
Sullivan I. = Lambi Kyun, *Burma* 39 G2 10 50N 98 20 E
Sulphur, *La., U.S.A.* 81 K8 30 14N 93 23W
Sulphur, *Okla., U.S.A.* 81 H6 34 31N 96 58W
Sulphur Pt., *Canada* 72 A6 60 56N 114 48W
Sulphur Springs, *U.S.A.* 81 J7 33 8N 95 36W
Sultan, *Canada* 70 C3 47 36N 82 47W
Sultan, *U.S.A.* 84 C5 47 52N 121 49W
Sultanpur, *India* 43 F10 26 18N 82 4 E
Sultanpur, *Mad. P., India* 42 H8 23 9N 77 56 E
Sultanpur, *Punjab, India* 42 D6 31 13N 75 11 E
Sulu Arch., *Phil.* 37 C6 6 0N 121 0 E
Sulu Sea, *E. Indies* 37 C6 8 0N 120 0 E
Suluq, *Libya* 51 B10 31 44N 20 14 E
Sulzberger Ice Shelf, *Antarctica* 5 D10 78 0S 150 0 E
Sumalata, *Indonesia* 37 D6 1 0N 122 31 E
Sumampa, *Argentina* 94 B3 29 25S 63 29W
Sumatera □, *Indonesia* 36 D2 0 40N 100 20 E
Sumatera Barat □, *Indonesia* 36 E2 1 0S 101 0 E
Sumatera Utara □, *Indonesia* 36 D1 2 30N 98 0 E
Sumatra = Sumatera □, *Indonesia* 36 D2 0 40N 100 20 E
Sumba, *Indonesia* 37 F5 9 45S 119 35 E
Sumba, Selat, *Indonesia* 37 F5 9 0S 118 40 E
Sumbawa, *Indonesia* 36 F5 8 26S 117 30 E
Sumbawa Besar, *Indonesia* 36 F5 8 30S 117 26 E
Sumbawanga □, *Tanzania* 52 F6 8 0S 31 30 E
Sumbe, *Angola* 52 G2 11 10S 13 48 E
Sumburgh Hd., *U.K.* 12 B7 59 52N 1 17W
Sumdeo, *India* 43 D8 31 26N 78 44 E
Sumdo, *India* 43 B8 35 6N 78 41 E
Sumedang, *Indonesia* 37 G12 6 52S 107 55 E
Šumen = Shumen, *Bulgaria* 21 C12 43 18N 26 55 E
Sumenep, *Indonesia* 37 G15 7 1S 113 52 E
Sumgait = Sumqayıt, *Azerbaijan* 25 F8 40 34N 49 38 E
Summer L., *U.S.A.* 82 E3 42 50N 120 45W
Summerland, *Canada* 72 D5 49 32N 119 41W
Summerside, *Canada* 71 C7 46 24N 63 47W
Summersville, *U.S.A.* 76 F5 38 17N 80 51W
Summerville, *Ga., U.S.A.* 77 H3 34 29N 85 21W
Summerville, *S.C., U.S.A.* 77 J5 33 1N 80 11W
Summit Lake, *Canada* 72 C4 54 20N 122 40W
Summit Peak, *U.S.A.* 83 H10 37 21N 106 42W
Sumner, *Iowa, U.S.A.* 80 D8 42 51N 92 6W
Sumner, *Wash., U.S.A.* 84 C4 47 12N 122 14W
Sumoto, *Japan* 31 G7 34 21N 134 54 E
Šumperk, *Czech Rep.* 17 D9 49 59N 16 59 E
Sumqayıt, *Azerbaijan* 25 F8 40 34N 49 38 E
Sumter, *U.S.A.* 77 J5 33 55N 80 21W
Sumy, *Ukraine* 25 D5 50 57N 34 50 E
Sun City, *Ariz., U.S.A.* 83 K7 33 36N 112 17W
Sun City, *Calif., U.S.A.* 85 M9 33 42N 117 11W
Sun City Center, *U.S.A.* 77 M4 27 43N 82 18W
Sun Lakes, *U.S.A.* 83 K8 33 10N 111 52W
Sun Valley, *U.S.A.* 82 E6 43 42N 114 21W
Sunagawa, *Japan* 30 C10 43 29N 141 55 E
Sunan, *N. Korea* 35 E13 39 15N 125 40 E
Sunart, L., *U.K.* 12 E3 56 42N 5 43W
Sunburst, *U.S.A.* 82 B8 48 53N 111 55W
Sunbury, *Australia* 63 F3 37 35S 144 44 E
Sunbury, *U.S.A.* 79 F8 40 52N 76 48W
Sunchales, *Argentina* 94 C3 30 58S 61 35W
Suncho Corral, *Argentina* 94 B3 27 55S 63 27W
Sunch'ŏn, *S. Korea* 35 G14 34 52N 127 31 E
Suncook, *U.S.A.* 79 C13 43 8N 71 27W
Sunda, Selat, *Indonesia* 36 F3 6 20S 105 30 E
Sunda Is., *Indonesia* 28 K14 5 0S 105 0 E
Sunda Str. = Sunda, Selat, *Indonesia* 36 F3 6 20S 105 30 E
Sundance, *Canada* 73 B10 56 32N 94 4W
Sundance, *U.S.A.* 80 C2 44 24N 104 23W
Sundar Nagar, *India* 42 D7 31 32N 76 53 E
Sundarbans, The, *Asia* 41 J16 22 0N 89 0 E
Sundargarh, *India* 41 H14 22 4N 84 5 E
Sundays = Sondags →, *S. Africa* 56 E4 33 44S 25 51 E
Sunderland, *Canada* 78 B5 44 16N 79 4W
Sunderland, *U.K.* 10 C6 54 55N 1 23W
Sundre, *Canada* 72 C6 51 49N 114 38W
Sundsvall, *Sweden* 9 E17 62 23N 17 17 E
Sung Hei, *Vietnam* 39 G6 10 20N 106 2 E
Sungai Kolok, *Thailand* 39 J3 6 2N 101 58 E
Sungai Lembing, *Malaysia* 39 L4 3 55N 103 3 E
Sungai Petani, *Malaysia* 39 K3 5 37N 100 30 E
Sungaigerong, *Indonesia* 36 E2 2 59S 104 52 E
Sungailiat, *Indonesia* 36 E3 1 51S 106 8 E
Sungaipenuh, *Indonesia* 36 E2 2 1S 101 20 E
Sungari = Songhua Jiang →, *China* 33 B8 47 45N 132 30 E
Sunghua Chiang = Songhua Jiang →, *China* 33 B8 47 45N 132 30 E
Sunland Park, *U.S.A.* 83 L10 31 50N 106 40W
Sunndalsøra, *Norway* 9 E13 62 40N 8 33 E
Sunnyside, *U.S.A.* 82 C3 46 20N 120 0W
Sunnyvale, *U.S.A.* 84 H4 37 23N 122 2W
Suntar, *Russia* 27 C12 62 15N 117 30 E
Suomenselkä, *Finland* 8 E21 62 52N 24 0 E
Suomussalmi, *Finland* 8 D23 64 54N 29 10 E
Suoyarvi, *Russia* 24 B5 62 3N 32 20 E
Supai, *U.S.A.* 83 H7 36 15N 112 41W
Supaul, *India* 43 F12 26 10N 86 40 E
Superior, *Ariz., U.S.A.* 83 K8 33 18N 111 6W
Superior, *Mont., U.S.A.* 82 C6 47 12N 114 53W
Superior, *Nebr., U.S.A.* 80 E5 40 1N 98 4W
Superior, *Wis., U.S.A.* 80 B8 46 44N 92 6W
Superior, L., *N. Amer.* 70 C2 47 0N 87 0W
Suphan Buri, *Thailand* 38 E3 14 14N 100 10 E
Suphan Dağı, *Turkey* 44 B4 38 54N 42 48 E
Supiori, *Indonesia* 37 E9 1 0S 136 0 E
Supung Shuiku, *China* 35 D13 40 35N 124 50 E
Sūq Suwayq, *Si. Arabia* 44 E3 24 23N 38 27 E
Suqian, *China* 35 H10 33 54N 118 8 E
Sūr, *Lebanon* 47 B4 33 19N 35 16 E
Sūr, *Oman* 46 C6 22 34N 59 32 E
Sur, Pt., *U.S.A.* 84 J5 36 18N 121 54W
Sura →, *Russia* 24 C8 56 6N 46 0 E
Surab, *Pakistan* 42 E2 28 25N 66 15 E
Surabaja = Surabaya, *Indonesia* 37 G15 7 17S 112 45 E
Surabaya, *Indonesia* 37 G15 7 17S 112 45 E
Surakarta, *Indonesia* 37 G14 7 35S 110 48 E
Surat, *Australia* 63 D4 27 10S 149 6 E
Surat, *India* 40 J8 21 12N 72 55 E
Surat Thani, *Thailand* 39 H2 9 6N 99 20 E
Suratgarh, *India* 42 E5 29 18N 73 55 E
Surendranagar, *India* 42 H4 22 45N 71 40 E
Surf, *U.S.A.* 85 L6 34 41N 120 36W
Surgut, *Russia* 26 C8 61 14N 73 20 E
Suriapet, *India* 40 L11 17 10N 79 40 E
Surigao, *Phil.* 37 C7 9 47N 125 29 E
Surin, *Thailand* 38 E4 14 50N 103 34 E
Surin Nua, Ko, *Thailand* 39 H1 9 30N 97 55 E
Surinam ■, *S. Amer.* 93 C7 4 0N 56 0W
Suriname = Surinam ■, *S. Amer.* 93 C7 4 0N 56 0W
Suriname →, *Surinam* 93 B7 5 50N 55 15W
Sūrmaq, *Iran* 45 D7 31 3N 52 48 E
Surrey □, *U.K.* 11 F7 51 15N 0 31W
Sursand, *India* 43 F11 26 39N 85 43 E
Sursar →, *India* 43 F12 26 14N 87 3 E

T

Tha Sala

Tanout, *Niger* **50 F7** 14 50N 8 55 E
Tanta, *Egypt* **51 B12** 30 45N 30 57 E
Tantoyuca, *Mexico* **87 C5** 21 21N 98 10W
Tantung = Dandong, *China* **35 D13** 40 10N 124 20 E
Tanunda, *Australia* **63 E2** 34 30S 139 0 E
Tanzania ■, *Africa* **54 D3** 6 0S 34 0 E
Tanzilla →, *Canada* **72 B2** 58 8N 130 43W
Tao, Ko, *Thailand* **39 G2** 10 5N 99 52 E
Tao'an = Taonan, *China* **35 B12** 45 22N 122 40 E
Tao'er He →, *China* **35 B13** 45 45N 124 5 E
Taolanaro, *Madag.* **57 D8** 25 2S 47 0 E
Taole, *China* **34 E4** 38 48N 106 40 E
Taonan, *China* **35 B12** 45 22N 122 40 E
Taos, *U.S.A.* **83 H11** 36 24N 105 35W
Taoudenni, *Mali* **50 D5** 22 40N 3 55W
Tapa, *Estonia* **9 G21** 59 15N 25 50 E
Tapa Shan = Daba Shan, *China* **33 C5** 32 0N 109 0 E
Tapachula, *Mexico* **87 E6** 14 54N 92 17W
Tapah, *Malaysia* **39 K3** 4 12N 101 15 E
Tapajós →, *Brazil* **93 D8** 2 24S 54 41W
Tapaktuan, *Indonesia* **36 D1** 3 15N 97 10 E
Tapanahoni →, *Surinam* **93 C8** 4 20N 54 25W
Tapanui, *N.Z.* **59 L2** 45 56S 169 18 E
Tapauá →, *Brazil* **92 E6** 5 40S 64 21W
Tapes, *Brazil* **95 C5** 30 40S 51 23W
Tapeta, *Liberia* **50 G4** 6 29N 8 52W
Taphan Hin, *Thailand* **38 D3** 16 13N 100 26 E
Tapirapecó, Serra, *Venezuela* **92 C6** 1 10N 65 0W
Tapuaenuku, Mt., *N.Z.* **59 K4** 42 0S 173 39 E
Tapul Group, *Phil.* **37 C6** 5 35N 120 50 E
Tapurucuará, *Brazil* **92 D5** 0 24S 65 2W
Taqtaq, *Iraq* **44 C5** 35 53N 44 35 E
Taquara, *Brazil* **95 B5** 29 36S 50 46W
Taquari →, *Brazil* **92 G7** 19 15S 57 17W
Tara, *Australia* **63 D5** 27 17S 150 31 E
Tara, *Canada* **78 B3** 44 28N 81 9W
Tara, *Russia* **26 D8** 56 55N 74 24 E
Tara, *Zambia* **55 F2** 16 58S 26 45 E
Tara →, *Montenegro, Yug.* **21 C8** 43 21N 18 51 E
Tarabagatay, Khrebet, *Kazakstan* **26 E9** 48 0N 83 0 E
Tarābulus, *Lebanon* **47 A4** 34 31N 35 50 E
Tarābulus, *Libya* **51 B8** 32 49N 13 7 E
Taradehi, *India* **43 H8** 23 18N 79 21 E
Tarajalejo, *Canary Is.* **22 F5** 28 12N 14 7W
Tarakan, *Indonesia* **36 D5** 3 20N 117 35 E
Tarakit, Mt., *Kenya* **54 B4** 2 2N 35 10 E
Tarama-Jima, *Japan* **31 M2** 24 39N 124 42 E
Taran, Mys, *Russia* **9 J18** 54 56N 19 59 E
Taranagar, *India* **42 E6** 28 43N 74 50 E
Taranaki □, *N.Z.* **59 H5** 39 25S 174 30 E
Tarancón, *Spain* **19 B4** 40 1N 3 0W
Taranga Hill, *India* **40 H8** 24 0N 72 40 E
Taransay, *U.K.* **12 D1** 57 54N 7 0W
Táranto, *Italy* **20 D7** 40 28N 17 14 E
Táranto, G. di, *Italy* **20 D7** 40 8N 17 20 E
Tarapacá, *Colombia* **92 D5** 2 56S 69 46W
Tarapacá □, *Chile* **94 A2** 20 45S 69 30W
Tarapoto, *Peru* **92 E3** 6 30S 76 20W
Tararua Ra., *N.Z.* **59 J5** 40 45S 175 25 E
Tarashcha, *Ukraine* **17 D16** 49 30N 30 31 E
Tarauacá, *Brazil* **92 E4** 8 6S 70 48W
Tarauacá →, *Brazil* **92 E5** 6 42S 69 48W
Tarawa, *Kiribati* **64 G9** 1 30N 173 0 E
Tarawera, *N.Z.* **59 H6** 39 2S 176 36 E
Tarawera L., *N.Z.* **59 H6** 38 13S 176 27 E
Tarazona, *Spain* **19 B5** 41 55N 1 43W
Tarbat Ness, *U.K.* **12 D5** 57 52N 3 47W
Tarbela Dam, *Pakistan* **42 B5** 34 8N 72 52 E
Tarbert, *Arg. & Bute, U.K.* **12 F3** 55 52N 5 25W
Tarbert, *W. Isles, U.K.* **12 D2** 57 54N 6 49W
Tarbes, *France* **18 E4** 43 15N 0 3 E
Tarboro, *U.S.A.* **77 H7** 35 54N 77 32W
Tarcoola, *Australia* **63 E1** 30 44S 134 36 E
Tarcoon, *Australia* **63 E4** 30 15S 146 43 E
Taree, *Australia* **63 E5** 31 50S 152 30 E
Tarfaya, *Morocco* **50 C3** 27 55N 12 55W
Târgovişte, *Romania* **17 F13** 44 55N 25 27 E
Târgu-Jiu, *Romania* **17 F12** 45 5N 23 19 E
Târgu Mureş, *Romania* **17 E13** 46 31N 24 38 E
Tarif, *U.A.E.* **45 E7** 24 3N 53 46 E
Tarifa, *Spain* **19 D3** 36 1N 5 36W
Tarija, *Bolivia* **94 A3** 21 30S 64 40W
Tarija □, *Bolivia* **94 A3** 21 30S 63 30W
Tariku →, *Indonesia* **37 E9** 2 55S 138 26 E
Tarim Basin = Tarim Pendi, *China* **32 B3** 40 0N 84 0 E
Tarim He →, *China* **32 C3** 39 30N 88 30 E
Tarim Pendi, *China* **32 B3** 40 0N 84 0 E
Taritatu →, *Indonesia* **37 E9** 2 54S 138 27 E
Tarka →, *S. Africa* **56 E4** 32 10S 26 0 E
Tarkastad, *S. Africa* **56 E4** 32 0S 26 16 E
Tarkhankut, Mys, *Ukraine* **25 E5** 45 25N 32 30 E
Tarko Sale, *Russia* **26 C8** 64 55N 77 50 E
Tarkwa, *Ghana* **50 G5** 5 20N 2 0W
Tarlac, *Phil.* **37 A6** 15 29N 120 35 E
Tarma, *Peru* **92 F3** 11 25S 75 45W
Tarn →, *France* **18 E4** 44 5N 1 6 E
Târnăveni, *Romania* **17 E13** 46 19N 24 13 E
Tarnobrzeg, *Poland* **17 C11** 50 35N 21 41 E
Tarnów, *Poland* **17 C11** 50 3N 21 0 E
Tarnowskie Góry, *Poland* **17 C10** 50 27N 18 54 E
Tarom, *Iran* **45 D7** 28 11N 55 46 E
Taroom, *Australia* **63 D4** 25 36S 149 48 E
Taroudannt, *Morocco* **50 B4** 30 30N 8 52W
Tarpon Springs, *U.S.A.* **77 L4** 28 9N 82 45W
Tarragona, *Spain* **19 B6** 41 5N 1 17 E
Tarraleah, *Australia* **62 G4** 42 17S 146 26 E
Tarrasa = Terrassa, *Spain* **19 B7** 41 34N 2 1 E
Tarrytown, *U.S.A.* **79 E11** 41 4N 73 52W
Tarshiha = Me'ona, *Israel* **47 B4** 33 1N 35 15 E
Tarso Emissi, *Chad* **51 D9** 21 27N 18 36 E
Tarsus, *Turkey* **25 G5** 36 58N 34 55 E
Tartagal, *Argentina* **94 A3** 22 30S 63 50W
Tartu, *Estonia* **9 G22** 58 20N 26 44 E
Tartūs, *Syria* **44 C2** 34 55N 35 55 E
Tarumizu, *Japan* **31 J5** 31 29N 130 42 E
Tarutao, Ko, *Thailand* **39 J2** 6 33N 99 40 E
Tarutung, *Indonesia* **36 D1** 2 0N 98 54 E
Taseko →, *Canada* **72 C4** 52 8N 123 45W
Tash-Kömür, *Kyrgyzstan* **26 E8** 41 40N 72 10 E
Tash-Kumyr = Tash-Kömür, *Kyrgyzstan* **26 E8** 41 40N 72 10 E
Tashauz = Dashhowuz, *Turkmenistan* **26 E6** 41 49N 59 58 E
Tashi Chho Dzong = Thimphu, *Bhutan* **41 F16** 27 31N 89 45 E
Tashk, Daryācheh-ye, *Iran* **45 D7** 29 45N 53 35 E
Tashkent = Toshkent, *Uzbekistan* **26 E7** 41 20N 69 10 E
Tashtagol, *Russia* **26 D9** 52 47N 87 53 E
Tasikmalaya, *Indonesia* **37 G13** 7 18S 108 12 E
Tåsjön, *Sweden* **8 D16** 64 15N 15 40 E
Taskan, *Russia* **27 C16** 62 59N 150 20 E
Tasman B., *N.Z.* **59 J4** 40 59S 173 25 E
Tasman Mts., *N.Z.* **59 J4** 41 3S 172 25 E
Tasman Pen., *Australia* **62 G4** 43 10S 148 0 E
Tasman Sea, *Pac. Oc.* **64 L8** 36 0S 160 0 E
Tasmania □, *Australia* **62 G4** 42 0S 146 30 E
Tassili n'Ajjer, *Algeria* **50 C7** 25 47N 8 1 E
Tatabánya, *Hungary* **17 E10** 47 32N 18 25 E
Tatahouine, *Tunisia* **51 B8** 32 56N 10 27 E
Tatar Republic = Tatarstan □, *Russia* **24 C9** 55 30N 51 30 E
Tatarbunary, *Ukraine* **17 F15** 45 50N 29 39 E
Tatarsk, *Russia* **26 D8** 55 14N 76 0 E
Tatarstan □, *Russia* **24 C9** 55 30N 51 30 E
Tateyama, *Japan* **31 G9** 35 0N 139 50 E
Tathlina L., *Canada* **72 A5** 60 33N 117 39W
Tathra, *Australia* **63 F4** 36 44S 149 59 E
Tati →, *India* **40 J8** 21 8N 72 41 E
Tatinnai L., *Canada* **73 A9** 60 55N 97 40W
Tatla L., *Canada* **72 C4** 52 0N 124 20W
Tatnam, C., *Canada* **73 B10** 57 16N 91 0W
Tatra = Tatry, *Slovak Rep.* **17 D11** 49 20N 20 0 E
Tatry, *Slovak Rep.* **17 D11** 49 20N 20 0 E
Tatshenshini →, *Canada* **72 B1** 59 28N 137 45W
Tatsuno, *Japan* **31 G7** 34 52N 134 33 E
Tatta, *Pakistan* **42 G2** 24 42N 67 55 E
Tatuī, *Brazil* **95 A6** 23 25S 47 53W
Tatum, *U.S.A.* **81 J3** 33 16N 103 19W
Tat'ung = Datong, *China* **34 D7** 40 6N 113 18 E
Tatvan, *Turkey* **25 G7** 38 31N 42 15 E
Taubaté, *Brazil* **95 A6** 23 0S 45 36W
Tauern, *Austria* **16 E7** 47 15N 12 40 E
Taumarunui, *N.Z.* **59 H5** 38 53S 175 15 E
Taumaturgo, *Brazil* **92 E4** 8 54S 72 51W
Taung, *S. Africa* **56 D3** 27 33S 24 47 E
Taungdwingyi, *Burma* **41 J19** 20 1N 95 40 E
Taunggyi, *Burma* **41 J20** 20 50N 97 0 E
Taungup, *Burma* **41 K19** 18 51N 94 14 E
Taungup Pass, *Burma* **41 K19** 18 40N 94 45 E
Taungup Taunggya, *Burma* **41 K18** 18 20N 93 40 E
Taunsa, *Pakistan* **42 D4** 30 42N 70 39 E
Taunsa Barrage, *Pakistan* **42 D4** 30 42N 70 50 E
Taunton, *U.K.* **11 F4** 51 1N 3 5W
Taunton, *U.S.A.* **79 E13** 41 54N 71 6W
Taunus, *Germany* **16 C5** 50 13N 8 34 E
Taupo, *N.Z.* **59 H6** 38 41S 176 7 E
Taupo, L., *N.Z.* **59 H5** 38 46S 175 55 E
Tauragė, *Lithuania* **9 J20** 55 14N 22 16 E
Tauranga, *N.Z.* **59 G6** 37 42S 176 11 E
Tauranga Harb., *N.Z.* **59 G6** 37 30S 176 5 E
Taureau, Rés., *Canada* **70 C5** 46 46N 73 50W
Taurianova, *Italy* **20 E7** 38 21N 16 1 E
Taurus Mts. = Toros Dağları, *Turkey* **25 G5** 37 0N 32 30 E
Tavda, *Russia* **26 D7** 58 7N 65 8 E
Tavda →, *Russia* **26 D7** 57 47N 67 18 E
Taveta, *Tanzania* **54 C4** 3 23S 37 37 E
Taveuni, *Fiji* **59 C9** 16 51S 179 58W
Tavira, *Portugal* **19 D2** 37 8N 7 40W
Tavistock, *Canada* **78 C4** 43 19N 80 50W
Tavistock, *U.K.* **11 G3** 50 33N 4 9W
Tavoy = Dawei, *Burma* **38 E2** 14 2N 98 12 E
Taw →, *U.K.* **11 F3** 51 4N 4 4W
Tawa →, *India* **42 H8** 22 48N 77 48 E
Tawas City, *U.S.A.* **76 C4** 44 16N 83 31W
Tawau, *Malaysia* **36 D5** 4 20N 117 55 E
Tawitawi, *Phil.* **37 C6** 5 10N 120 0 E
Taxco de Alarcón, *Mexico* **87 D5** 18 33N 99 36W
Taxila, *Pakistan* **42 C5** 33 42N 72 52 E
Tay →, *U.K.* **12 E5** 56 37N 3 38W
Tay, Firth of, *U.K.* **12 E5** 56 25N 3 8W
Tay, L., *Australia* **61 F3** 32 55S 120 48 E
Tay, L., *U.K.* **12 E4** 56 32N 4 8W
Tay Ninh, *Vietnam* **39 G6** 11 20N 106 5 E
Tayabamba, *Peru* **92 E3** 8 15S 77 16W
Taylakova, *Russia* **26 D8** 59 13N 74 0 E
Taylakovy = Taylakova, *Russia* **26 D8** 59 13N 74 0 E
Taylor, *Canada* **72 B4** 56 13N 120 40W
Taylor, *Nebr., U.S.A.* **80 E5** 41 46N 99 23W
Taylor, *Pa., U.S.A.* **79 E9** 41 23N 75 43W
Taylor, *Tex., U.S.A.* **81 K6** 30 34N 97 25W
Taylor, Mt., *U.S.A.* **83 J10** 35 14N 107 37W
Taylorville, *U.S.A.* **80 F10** 39 33N 89 18W
Taymā, *Si. Arabia* **44 E3** 27 35N 38 45 E
Taymyr, Oz., *Russia* **27 B11** 74 20N 102 0 E
Taymyr, Poluostrov, *Russia* **27 B11** 75 0N 100 0 E
Tayport, *U.K.* **12 E6** 56 27N 2 52W
Tayshet, *Russia* **27 D10** 55 58N 98 1 E
Taytay, *Phil.* **37 B5** 10 45N 119 30 E
Taz →, *Russia* **26 C8** 67 32N 78 40 E
Taza, *Morocco* **50 B5** 34 16N 4 6W
Tāzah Khurmātū, *Iraq* **44 C5** 35 18N 44 20 E
Tazawa-Ko, *Japan* **30 E10** 39 43N 140 40 E
Tazin, *Canada* **73 B7** 59 48N 109 55W
Tazin L., *Canada* **73 B7** 59 44N 108 42W
Tazovskiy, *Russia* **26 C8** 67 30N 78 44 E
Tbilisi, *Georgia* **25 F7** 41 43N 44 50 E
Tchad = Chad ■, *Africa* **51 F8** 15 0N 17 15 E
Tchad, L., *Chad* **51 F8** 13 30N 14 30 E
Tch'eng-tou = Chengdu, *China* **32 C5** 30 38N 104 2 E
Tchentlo L., *Canada* **72 B4** 55 15N 125 0W
Tchibanga, *Gabon* **52 E2** 2 45S 11 0 E
Tch'ong-k'ing = Chongqing, *China* **32 D5** 29 35N 106 25 E
Tczew, *Poland* **17 A10** 54 8N 18 50 E
Te Anau, L., *N.Z.* **59 L1** 45 15S 167 45 E
Te Aroha, *N.Z.* **59 G5** 37 32S 175 44 E
Te Awamutu, *N.Z.* **59 H5** 38 1S 175 20 E
Te Kuiti, *N.Z.* **59 H5** 38 20S 175 11 E
Te Puke, *N.Z.* **59 G6** 37 46S 176 22 E
Te Waewae B., *N.Z.* **59 M1** 46 13S 167 33 E
Teague, *U.S.A.* **81 K6** 31 38N 96 17W
Teapa, *Mexico* **87 D6** 18 35N 92 56W
Tebakang, *Malaysia* **36 D4** 1 6N 110 30 E
Tébessa, *Algeria* **50 A7** 35 22N 8 8 E
Tebicuary →, *Paraguay* **94 B4** 26 36S 58 16W
Tebingtinggi, *Indonesia* **36 D1** 3 20N 99 9 E
Tebintingii, *Indonesia* **36 E2** 1 0N 102 45 E
Tecate, *Mexico* **85 N10** 32 34N 116 38W
Tecka, *Argentina* **96 E2** 43 29S 70 48W
Tecomán, *Mexico* **86 D4** 18 55N 103 53W
Tecopa, *U.S.A.* **85 K10** 35 51N 116 13W
Tecoripa, *Mexico* **86 B3** 28 37N 109 57W
Tecuala, *Mexico* **86 C3** 22 23N 105 27W
Tecuci, *Romania* **17 F14** 45 51N 27 27 E
Tecumseh, *Canada* **78 D2** 42 19N 82 54W
Tecumseh, *Mich., U.S.A.* **76 D4** 42 0N 83 57W
Tecumseh, *Okla., U.S.A.* **81 H6** 35 15N 96 56W
Tedzhen = Tejen, *Turkmenistan* **26 F7** 37 23N 60 31 E
Tees →, *U.K.* **10 C6** 54 37N 1 10W
Tees B., *U.K.* **10 C6** 54 40N 1 9W
Teeswater, *Canada* **78 C3** 43 59N 81 17W
Tefé, *Brazil* **92 D6** 3 25S 64 50W
Tegal, *Indonesia* **37 G13** 6 52S 109 8 E
Tegid, L. = Bala, L., *U.K.* **10 E4** 52 53N 3 37W
Tegucigalpa, *Honduras* **88 D2** 14 5N 87 14W
Tehachapi, *U.S.A.* **85 K8** 35 8N 118 27W
Tehachapi Mts., *U.S.A.* **85 L8** 35 0N 118 30W
Tehoru, *Indonesia* **37 E7** 3 19S 129 37 E
Tehrān, *Iran* **45 C6** 35 44N 51 30 E
Tehri, *India* **43 D8** 30 23N 78 29 E
Tehuacán, *Mexico* **87 D5** 18 30N 97 30W
Tehuantepec, *Mexico* **87 D5** 16 21N 95 13W
Tehuantepec, G. de, *Mexico* **87 D5** 15 50N 95 12W
Tehuantepec, Istmo de, *Mexico* **87 D6** 17 0N 94 30W
Teide, *Canary Is.* **22 F3** 28 15N 16 38W
Teifi →, *U.K.* **11 E3** 52 5N 4 41W
Teign →, *U.K.* **11 G4** 50 32N 3 32W
Teignmouth, *U.K.* **11 G4** 50 33N 3 31W
Tejam, *India* **43 E9** 29 57N 80 11 E
Tejen, *Turkmenistan* **26 F7** 37 23N 60 31 E
Tejen →, *Turkmenistan* **45 B9** 37 24N 60 38 E
Tejo →, *Europe* **19 C1** 38 40N 9 24W
Tejon Pass, *U.S.A.* **85 L8** 34 49N 118 53W
Tekamah, *U.S.A.* **80 E6** 41 47N 96 13W
Tekapo, L., *N.Z.* **59 K3** 43 53S 170 33 E
Tekax, *Mexico* **87 C7** 20 11N 89 18W
Tekeli, *Kazakstan* **26 E8** 44 50N 79 0 E
Tekirdağ, *Turkey* **21 D12** 40 58N 27 30 E
Tekkali, *India* **41 K14** 18 37N 84 15 E
Tekoa, *U.S.A.* **82 C5** 47 14N 117 4W
Tel Aviv-Yafo, *Israel* **47 C3** 32 4N 34 48 E
Tel Lakhish, *Israel* **47 D3** 31 34N 34 51 E
Tel Megiddo, *Israel* **47 C4** 32 35N 35 11 E
Tela, *Honduras* **88 C2** 15 40N 87 28W
Telanaipura = Jambi, *Indonesia* **36 E2** 1 38S 103 30 E
Telavi, *Georgia* **25 F8** 42 0N 45 30 E
Telde, *Canary Is.* **22 G4** 27 59N 15 25W
Telegraph Creek, *Canada* **72 B2** 58 0N 131 10W
Telekhany = Tsyelyakhany, *Belarus* **17 B13** 52 30N 25 46 E
Telemark, *Norway* **9 G12** 59 15N 7 40 E
Telén, *Argentina* **94 D2** 36 15S 65 31W
Teleng, *Iran* **45 E9** 25 47N 61 3 E
Teles Pires →, *Brazil* **92 E7** 7 21S 58 3W
Telescope Pk., *U.S.A.* **85 J9** 36 10N 117 5W
Telfer Mine, *Australia* **60 C3** 21 40S 122 12 E
Telford, *U.K.* **11 E5** 52 40N 2 27W
Telford and Wrekin □, *U.K.* **10 E5** 52 45N 2 27W
Telkwa, *Canada* **72 C3** 54 41N 127 5W
Tell City, *U.S.A.* **76 G2** 37 57N 86 46W
Tellicherry, *India* **40 P9** 11 45N 75 30 E
Telluride, *U.S.A.* **83 H10** 37 56N 107 49W
Teloloapán, *Mexico* **87 D5** 18 21N 99 51W
Telpos Iz, *Russia* **24 B10** 63 16N 59 13 E
Telsen, *Argentina* **96 E3** 42 30S 66 50W
Telšiai, *Lithuania* **9 H20** 55 59N 22 14 E
Teluk Anson = Teluk Intan, *Malaysia* **39 K3** 4 3N 101 0 E
Teluk Betung = Tanjungkarang Telukbetung, *Indonesia* **36 F3** 5 20S 105 10 E
Teluk Intan, *Malaysia* **39 K3** 4 3N 101 0 E
Telukbutun, *Indonesia* **39 K7** 4 13N 108 12 E
Telukdalem, *Indonesia* **36 D1** 0 33N 97 50 E
Tema, *Ghana* **50 G5** 5 41N 0 0 E
Temax, *Mexico* **87 C7** 21 10N 88 50W
Temba, *S. Africa* **57 D4** 25 20S 28 17 E
Tembagapura, *Indonesia* **37 E9** 4 20S 137 0 E
Tembe, *Dem. Rep. of the Congo* **54 C2** 0 16S 28 14 E
Temblor Range, *U.S.A.* **85 K7** 35 20N 119 50W
Teme →, *U.K.* **11 E5** 52 11N 2 13W
Temecula, *U.S.A.* **85 M9** 33 30N 117 9W
Temerloh, *Malaysia* **36 D2** 3 27N 102 25 E
Teminabuan, *Indonesia* **37 E8** 1 26S 132 1 E
Temir, *Kazakstan* **25 E10** 49 1N 57 14 E
Temirtau, *Kazakstan* **26 D8** 50 5N 72 56 E
Temirtau, *Russia* **26 D9** 53 10N 87 30 E
Temiscamie →, *Canada* **71 B5** 50 59N 73 5W
Témiscaming, *Canada* **70 C4** 46 44N 79 5W
Témiscamingue, L., *Canada* **70 C4** 47 10N 79 25W
Temosachic, *Mexico* **86 B3** 28 58N 107 50W
Tempe, *U.S.A.* **83 K8** 33 25N 111 56W
Tempiute, *U.S.A.* **84 H11** 37 39N 115 38W
Temple, *U.S.A.* **81 K6** 31 6N 97 21W
Temple B., *Australia* **62 A3** 12 15S 143 3 E
Templemore, *Ireland* **13 D4** 52 47N 7 51W
Templeton, *U.S.A.* **84 K6** 35 33N 120 42W
Templeton →, *Australia* **62 C2** 21 0S 138 40 E
Tempoal, *Mexico* **87 C5** 21 31N 98 23W
Temuco, *Chile* **96 D2** 38 45S 72 40W
Temuka, *N.Z.* **59 L3** 44 14S 171 17 E
Tenabo, *Mexico* **87 C6** 20 2N 90 12W
Tenaha, *U.S.A.* **81 K7** 31 57N 94 15W
Tenakee Springs, *U.S.A.* **72 B1** 57 47N 135 13W
Tenali, *India* **40 L12** 16 15N 80 35 E
Tenancingo, *Mexico* **87 D5** 19 0N 99 33W
Tenango, *Mexico* **87 D5** 19 7N 99 33W
Tenasserim, *Burma* **39 F2** 12 6N 99 3 E
Tenasserim □, *Burma* **38 F2** 14 0N 98 30 E
Tenby, *U.K.* **11 F3** 51 40N 4 42W
Tenda, Colle di, *France* **18 D7** 44 7N 7 36 E
Tendaho, *Ethiopia* **46 E3** 11 48N 40 54 E
Tendukhera, *India* **43 H8** 23 24N 79 33 E
Ténéré, *Niger* **50 E7** 19 0N 10 30 E
Tenerife, *Canary Is.* **22 F3** 28 15N 16 35W
Tenerife, Pico, *Canary Is.* **22 G1** 27 43N 18 1W
Teng Xian, *China* **35 G9** 35 5N 117 10 E
Tengah □, *Indonesia* **37 E6** 2 0S 122 0 E
Tengah, Kepulauan, *Indonesia* **36 F5** 7 5S 118 15 E
Tengchong, *China* **32 D4** 25 0N 98 28 E
Tengchowfu = Penglai, *China* **35 F11** 37 48N 120 42 E
Tenggara □, *Indonesia* **37 E6** 3 0S 122 0 E
Tenggarong, *Indonesia* **36 E5** 0 24S 116 58 E
Tenggol, Pulau, *Malaysia* **39 K4** 4 48N 103 41 E
Tengiz, Ozero, *Kazakstan* **26 D7** 50 30N 69 0 E
Tenino, *U.S.A.* **84 D4** 46 51N 122 51W
Tenkasi, *India* **40 Q10** 8 55N 77 20 E
Tenke, *Katanga, Dem. Rep. of the Congo* **55 E2** 11 22S 26 40 E
Tenke, *Katanga, Dem. Rep. of the Congo* **55 E2** 10 32S 26 7 E
Tennant Creek, *Australia* **62 B1** 19 30S 134 15 E
Tennessee □, *U.S.A.* **77 H2** 36 0N 86 30W
Tennessee →, *U.S.A.* **76 G1** 37 4N 88 34W
Teno, Pta. de, *Canary Is.* **22 F3** 28 21N 16 55W
Tenom, *Malaysia* **36 C5** 5 4N 115 57 E
Tenosique, *Mexico* **87 D6** 17 30N 91 24W
Tenryū-Gawa →, *Japan* **31 G8** 35 39N 137 48 E
Tenterden, *U.K.* **11 F8** 51 4N 0 42 E
Tenterfield, *Australia* **63 D5** 29 0S 152 0 E
Teófilo Otoni, *Brazil* **93 G10** 17 50S 41 30W
Tepa, *Indonesia* **37 F7** 7 52S 129 31 E
Tepalcatepec →, *Mexico* **86 D4** 18 35N 101 59W
Tepehuanes, *Mexico* **86 B3** 25 21N 105 44W
Tepetongo, *Mexico* **86 C4** 22 28N 103 9W
Tepic, *Mexico* **86 C4** 21 30N 104 54W
Teplice, *Czech Rep.* **16 C7** 50 40N 13 48 E
Tepoca, C., *Mexico* **86 A2** 30 20N 112 25W
Tequila, *Mexico* **86 C4** 20 54N 103 47W
Ter →, *Spain* **19 A7** 42 2N 3 12 E
Ter Apel, *Neths.* **15 B7** 52 53N 7 5 E
Teraina, *Kiribati* **65 G11** 4 43N 160 25W
Téramo, *Italy* **20 C5** 42 39N 13 42 E
Terang, *Australia* **63 F3** 38 15S 142 55 E
Tercero →, *Argentina* **94 C3** 32 58S 61 47W
Terebovlya, *Ukraine* **17 D13** 49 18N 25 44 E
Terek →, *Russia* **25 F8** 44 0N 47 30 E
Teresina, *Brazil* **93 E10** 5 9S 42 45W
Terewah, L., *Australia* **63 D4** 29 52S 147 35 E
Teridgerie Cr. →, *Australia* **63 E4** 30 25S 148 50 E
Termez = Termiz, *Uzbekistan* **26 F7** 37 15N 67 15 E
Términi Imerese, *Italy* **20 F5** 37 59N 13 42 E
Términos, L. de, *Mexico* **87 D6** 18 35N 91 30W
Termiz, *Uzbekistan* **26 F7** 37 15N 67 15 E
Térmoli, *Italy* **20 C6** 42 0N 15 0 E
Ternate, *Indonesia* **37 D7** 0 45N 127 25 E
Terneuzen, *Neths.* **15 C3** 51 20N 3 50 E
Terney, *Russia* **27 E14** 45 3N 136 37 E
Terni, *Italy* **20 C5** 42 34N 12 37 E
Ternopil, *Ukraine* **17 D13** 49 30N 25 40 E
Ternopol = Ternopil, *Ukraine* **17 D13** 49 30N 25 40 E
Terowie, *Australia* **63 E2** 33 8S 138 55 E
Terra Bella, *U.S.A.* **85 K7** 35 58N 119 3W
Terra Nova Nat. Park, *Canada* **71 C9** 48 33N 53 55W
Terrace, *Canada* **72 C3** 54 30N 128 35W
Terrace Bay, *Canada* **70 C2** 48 47N 87 5W
Terracina, *Italy* **20 D5** 41 17N 13 15 E
Terralba, *Italy* **20 E3** 39 43N 8 39 E
Terranova = Ólbia, *Italy* **20 D3** 40 55N 9 31 E
Terrassa, *Spain* **19 B7** 41 34N 2 1 E
Terre Haute, *U.S.A.* **76 F2** 39 28N 87 25W
Terrebonne B., *U.S.A.* **81 L9** 29 5N 90 35W
Terrell, *U.S.A.* **81 J6** 32 44N 96 17W
Terrenceville, *Canada* **71 C9** 47 40N 54 44W
Terry, *U.S.A.* **80 B2** 46 47N 105 19W
Terryville, *U.S.A.* **79 E11** 41 41N 73 3W
Terschelling, *Neths.* **15 A5** 53 25N 5 20 E
Teruel, *Spain* **19 B5** 40 22N 1 8W
Tervola, *Finland* **8 C21** 66 6N 24 49 E
Teryaweyna L., *Australia* **63 E3** 32 18S 143 22 E
Teshio, *Japan* **30 B10** 44 53N 141 44 E
Teshio-Gawa →, *Japan* **30 B10** 44 53N 141 45 E
Tesiyn Gol →, *Mongolia* **32 A4** 50 40N 93 20 E
Teslin, *Canada* **72 A2** 60 10N 132 43W
Teslin →, *Canada* **72 A2** 61 34N 134 35W
Teslin L., *Canada* **72 A2** 60 15N 132 57W
Tessalit, *Mali* **50 D6** 20 12N 1 0 E
Test →, *U.K.* **11 G6** 50 56N 1 29W
Testigos, Is. Las, *Venezuela* **89 D7** 11 23N 63 7W
Tetachuck L., *Canada* **72 C3** 53 18N 125 55W
Tetas, Pta., *Chile* **94 A1** 23 31S 70 38W
Tete, *Mozam.* **55 F3** 16 13S 33 33 E
Tete □, *Mozam.* **55 F3** 15 15S 32 40 E
Teterev →, *Ukraine* **17 C16** 51 1N 30 5 E
Teteven, *Bulgaria* **21 C11** 42 58N 24 17 E
Tethul →, *Canada* **72 A6** 60 35N 112 12W
Tetiyev, *Ukraine* **17 D15** 49 22N 29 38 E
Teton →, *U.S.A.* **82 C8** 47 56N 110 31W
Tétouan, *Morocco* **50 A4** 35 35N 5 21W
Tetovo, *Macedonia* **21 C9** 42 1N 20 59 E
Teuco →, *Argentina* **94 B3** 25 35S 60 11W
Teulon, *Canada* **73 C9** 50 23N 97 16W
Teun, *Indonesia* **37 F7** 6 59S 129 8 E
Teutoburger Wald, *Germany* **16 B5** 52 5N 8 22 E
Tevere →, *Italy* **20 D5** 41 44N 12 14 E
Teverya, *Israel* **47 C4** 32 47N 35 32 E
Teviot →, *U.K.* **12 F6** 55 29N 2 38W
Tewantin, *Australia* **63 D5** 26 27S 153 3 E
Tewkesbury, *U.K.* **11 F5** 51 59N 2 9W
Texada I., *Canada* **72 D4** 49 40N 124 25W
Texarkana, *Ark., U.S.A.* **81 J8** 33 26N 94 2W
Texarkana, *Tex., U.S.A.* **81 J7** 33 26N 94 3W
Texas, *Australia* **63 D5** 28 49S 151 9 E
Texas □, *U.S.A.* **81 K5** 31 40N 98 30W
Texas City, *U.S.A.* **81 L7** 29 24N 94 54W
Texel, *Neths.* **15 A4** 53 5N 4 50 E
Texline, *U.S.A.* **81 G3** 36 23N 103 2W
Texoma, L., *U.S.A.* **81 J6** 33 50N 96 34W
Tezin, *Afghan.* **42 B3** 34 24N 69 30 E
Teziutlán, *Mexico* **87 D5** 19 50N 97 22W
Tezpur, *India* **41 F18** 26 40N 92 45 E
Tezzeron L., *Canada* **72 C4** 54 43N 124 30W
Tha-anne →, *Canada* **73 A10** 60 31N 94 37W
Tha Deua, *Laos* **38 D4** 17 57N 102 53 E
Tha Deua, *Laos* **38 C3** 19 26N 101 50 E
Tha Pla, *Thailand* **38 D3** 17 48N 100 32 E
Tha Rua, *Thailand* **38 E3** 14 34N 100 44 E
Tha Sala, *Thailand* **39 H2** 8 40N 99 56 E

Tha Song Yang

Tha Song Yang, *Thailand* . **38 D1** 17 34N 97 55 E
Thaba Putsoa, *Lesotho* .... **57 D4** 29 45S 28 0 E
Thabana Ntlenyana, *Lesotho* **57 D4** 29 30S 29 16 E
Thabazimbi, *S. Africa* ..... **57 C4** 24 40S 27 21 E
Thādiq, *Si. Arabia* .... **44 E5** 25 18N 45 52 E
Thai Muang, *Thailand* .... **39 H2** 8 24N 98 16 E
Thailand ■, *Asia* .... **38 E4** 16 0N 102 0 E
Thailand, G. of, *Asia* ...... **39 G3** 11 30N 101 0 E
Thakhek, *Laos* .... **38 D5** 17 25N 104 45 E
Thal, *Pakistan* .... **42 C4** 33 28N 70 33 E
Thal Desert, *Pakistan* ..... **42 D4** 31 10N 71 30 E
Thala La, *Burma* .... **41 E20** 28 25N 97 23 E
Thalabarivat, *Cambodia* ... **38 F5** 13 33N 105 57 E
Thallon, *Australia* .... **63 D4** 28 39S 148 49 E
Thames, *N.Z.* .... **59 G5** 37 7S 175 34 E
Thames →, *Canada* **78 D2** 42 20N 82 25W
Thames →, *U.K.* .... **11 F8** 51 29N 0 34 E
Thames →, *U.S.A.* **79 E12** 41 18N 72 5W
Thames Estuary, *U.K.* ..... **11 F8** 51 29N 0 52 E
Thamesford, *Canada* **78 C4** 43 4N 81 0W
Thamesville, *Canada* **78 D3** 42 33N 81 59W
Than, *India* .... **42 H4** 22 34N 71 11 E
Than Uyen, *Vietnam* ...... **38 B4** 22 0N 103 54 E
Thana Gazi, *India* .... **42 F7** 27 25N 76 19 E
Thandla, *India* .... **42 H6** 23 0N 74 34 E
Thane, *India* .... **40 K8** 19 12N 72 59 E
Thanesar, *India* .... **42 D7** 30 1N 76 52 E
Thanet, I. of, *U.K.* .... **11 F9** 51 21N 1 20 E
Thangool, *Australia* ...... **62 C5** 24 38S 150 42 E
Thanh Hoa, *Vietnam* ...... **38 C5** 19 48N 105 46 E
Thanh Hung, *Vietnam* .... **39 H5** 9 55N 105 43 E
Thanh Pho Ho Chi Minh = Phanh Bho Ho Chi Minh, *Vietnam* .... **39 G6** 10 58N 106 40 E
Thanh Thuy, *Vietnam* ..... **38 A5** 22 55N 104 51 E
Thanjavur, *India* .... **40 P11** 10 48N 79 12 E
Thano Bula Khan, *Pakistan* **42 G2** 25 22N 67 50 E
Thaolinta L., *Canada* **73 A9** 61 30N 96 25W
Thap Sakae, *Thailand* ..... **39 G2** 11 30N 99 37 E
Thap Than, *Thailand* ...... **38 E2** 15 27N 99 54 E
Thar Desert, *India* .... **42 F5** 28 0N 72 0 E
Tharad, *India* .... **42 G4** 24 30N 71 44 E
Thargomindah, *Australia* .. **63 D3** 27 58S 143 46 E
Tharrawaddy, *Burma* ..... **41 L19** 17 38N 95 48 E
Tharthār, Mileh, *Iraq* ...... **44 C4** 34 0N 43 15 E
Tharthār, W. ath →, *Iraq* . **44 C4** 33 59N 43 12 E
Thásos, *Greece* .... **21 D11** 40 40N 24 40 E
Thatcher, *Ariz., U.S.A.* **83 K9** 32 51N 109 46W
Thatcher, *Colo., U.S.A.* **81 G2** 37 33N 104 7W
Thaton, *Burma* .... **41 L20** 16 55N 97 22 E
Thaungdut, *Burma* .... **41 G19** 24 30N 94 40 E
Thayer, *U.S.A.* **81 G9** 36 31N 91 33W
Thayetmyo, *Burma* .... **41 K19** 19 20N 95 10 E
Thazi, *Burma* .... **41 J20** 21 0N 96 5 E
The Alberga →, *Australia* **63 D2** 27 6S 135 33 E
The Bight, *Bahamas* **89 B4** 24 19N 75 24W
The Coorong, *Australia* .... **63 F2** 35 50S 139 20 E
The Dalles, *U.S.A.* **82 D3** 45 36N 121 10W
The English Company's Is., *Australia* .... **62 A2** 11 50S 136 32 E
The Frome →, *Australia* . **63 D2** 29 8S 137 54 E
The Great Divide = Great Dividing Ra., *Australia* .. **62 C4** 23 0S 146 0 E
The Hague = 's-Gravenhage, *Neths.* .... **15 B4** 52 7N 4 17 E
The Hamilton →, *Australia* **63 D2** 26 40S 135 19 E
The Macumba →, *Australia* .... **63 D2** 27 52S 137 12 E
The Neales →, *Australia* . **63 D2** 28 8S 136 47 E
The Officer →, *Australia* . **61 E5** 27 46S 132 30 E
The Pas, *Canada* **73 C8** 53 45N 101 15W
The Range, *Zimbabwe* .... **55 F3** 19 2S 31 2 E
The Rock, *Australia* ...... **63 F4** 35 15S 147 2 E
The Salt L., *Australia* ..... **63 E3** 30 6S 142 8 E
The Sandheads, *India* ..... **43 J13** 21 10N 88 20 E
The Stevenson →, *Australia* .... **63 D2** 27 6S 135 33 E
The Warburton →, *Australia* .... **63 D2** 28 4S 137 28 E
The Woodlands, *U.S.A.* **81 K7** 30 9N 95 27W
Thebes = Thívai, *Greece* .. **21 E10** 38 19N 23 19 E
Thebes, *Egypt* .... **51 C12** 25 40N 32 35 E
Thedford, *Canada* **78 C3** 43 9N 81 51W
Thedford, *U.S.A.* **80 E4** 41 59N 100 35W
Theebine, *Australia* .... **63 D5** 25 57S 152 34 E
Thekulthili L., *Canada* **73 A7** 61 3N 110 0W
Thelon →, *Canada* **73 A8** 62 35N 104 3W
Theodore, *Australia* ...... **62 C5** 24 55S 150 3 E
Theodore, *Canada* **73 C8** 51 26N 102 55W
Theodore, *U.S.A.* **77 K1** 30 33N 88 10W
Theodore Roosevelt National Memorial Park, *U.S.A.* **80 B3** 47 0N 103 25W
Theodore Roosevelt Res., *U.S.A.* **83 K8** 33 46N 111 0W
Thepha, *Thailand* .... **39 J3** 6 52N 100 58 E
Theresa, *U.S.A.* **79 B9** 44 13N 75 48W
Thermaïkós Kólpos, *Greece* **21 D10** 40 15N 22 45 E
Thermopolis, *U.S.A.* **82 E9** 43 39N 108 13W
Thermopylae P., *Greece* ... **21 E10** 38 48N 22 35 E
Thessalon, *Canada* **70 C3** 46 20N 83 30W
Thessaloníki, *Greece* ...... **21 D10** 40 38N 22 58 E
Thessaloniki, Gulf of = Thermaïkós Kólpos, *Greece* .... **21 D10** 40 15N 22 45 E
Thetford, *U.K.* .... **11 E8** 52 25N 0 45 E
Thetford Mines, *Canada* ... **71 C5** 46 8N 71 18W
Theun →, *Laos* .... **38 C5** 18 19N 104 0 E
Theunissen, *S. Africa* ..... **56 D4** 28 26S 26 43 E
Thevenard, *Australia* ..... **63 E1** 32 9S 133 38 E
Thibodaux, *U.S.A.* **81 L9** 29 48N 90 49W
Thicket Portage, *Canada* .. **73 B9** 55 19N 97 42W
Thief River Falls, *U.S.A.* ... **80 A6** 48 7N 96 10W
Thiel Mts., *Antarctica* **5 E16** 85 15S 91 0W
Thiers, *France* .... **18 D5** 45 52N 3 33 E
Thiès, *Senegal* **50 F2** 14 50N 16 51W
Thika, *Kenya* .... **54 C4** 1 1S 37 5 E
Thikombia, *Fiji* **59 B9** 15 44S 179 55W
Thimphu, *Bhutan* .... **41 F16** 27 31N 89 45 E
þingvallavatn, *Iceland* **8 D3** 64 11N 21 9W
Thionville, *France* .... **18 B7** 49 20N 6 10 E
Thíra, *Greece* .... **21 F11** 36 23N 25 27 E
Third Cataract, *Sudan* ..... **51 E12** 19 42N 30 20 E
Thirsk, *U.K.* **10 C6** 54 14N 1 19W
Thisted, *Denmark* .... **9 H13** 56 58N 8 40 E
Thistle I., *Australia* .... **63 F2** 35 0S 136 8 E
Thívai, *Greece* .... **21 E10** 38 19N 23 19 E
þjórsá →, *Iceland* **8 E3** 63 47N 20 48W
Thlewiaza →, *Man., Canada* **73 B8** 59 43N 100 5W
Thlewiaza →, *N.W.T., Canada* **73 A10** 60 29N 94 40W
Thmar Puok, *Cambodia* ... **38 F4** 13 57N 103 4 E
Tho Vinh, *Vietnam* .... **38 C5** 19 16N 105 42 E
Thoa →, *Canada* **73 A7** 60 31N 109 47W
Thoen, *Thailand* .... **38 D2** 17 43N 99 12 E
Thoeng, *Thailand* .... **38 C3** 19 41N 100 12 E
Thohoyandou, *S. Africa* ... **53 J6** 22 58S 30 29 E
Tholdi, *Pakistan* .... **43 B7** 35 5N 76 6 E
Thomas, *U.S.A.* **81 H5** 35 45N 98 45W
Thomas, L., *Australia* ..... **63 D2** 26 4S 137 58 E
Thomaston, *U.S.A.* **77 J3** 32 53N 84 20W
Thomasville, *Ala., U.S.A.* .. **77 K2** 31 55N 87 44W
Thomasville, *Ga., U.S.A.* .. **77 K4** 30 50N 83 59W
Thomasville, *N.C., U.S.A.* .. **77 H5** 35 53N 80 5W
Thompson, *Canada* **73 B9** 55 45N 97 52W
Thompson, *U.S.A.* **79 E9** 41 52N 75 31W
Thompson →, *Canada* .. **72 C4** 50 15N 121 24W
Thompson →, *U.S.A.* **80 F8** 39 46N 93 37W
Thompson Falls, *U.S.A.* ... **82 C6** 47 36N 115 21W
Thompson Pk., *U.S.A.* **82 F2** 41 0N 123 0W
Thompson Springs, *U.S.A.* **83 G9** 38 58N 109 43W
Thompsontown, *U.S.A.* ... **78 F7** 40 33N 77 14W
Thomson, *U.S.A.* **77 J4** 33 28N 82 30W
Thomson →, *Australia* ... **62 C3** 25 11S 142 53 E
Thomson's Falls = Nyahururu, *Kenya* ...... **54 B4** 0 2N 36 27 E
þórisvatn, *Iceland* **8 D4** 64 20N 18 55W
Thornaby on Tees, *U.K.* **10 C6** 54 33N 1 18W
Thornbury, *Canada* **78 B4** 44 34N 80 26W
Thorne, *U.K.* **10 D7** 53 37N 0 57W
Thornhill, *Canada* **72 C3** 54 31N 128 32W
Thorold, *Canada* **78 C5** 43 7N 79 12W
þórshöfn, *Iceland* **8 C6** 66 12N 15 20W
Thouin, C., *Australia* ...... **60 D2** 20 20S 118 10 E
Thousand Oaks, *U.S.A.* **85 L8** 34 10N 118 50W
Thrace, *Turkey* .... **21 D12** 41 0N 27 0 E
Three Forks, *U.S.A.* **82 D8** 45 54N 111 33W
Three Hills, *Canada* **72 C6** 51 43N 113 15W
Three Hummock I., *Australia* **62 G3** 40 25S 144 55 E
Three Points, C., *Ghana* **50 H5** 4 42N 2 6W
Three Rivers, *Calif., U.S.A.* . **84 J8** 36 26N 118 54W
Three Rivers, *Tex., U.S.A.* .. **81 L5** 28 28N 98 11W
Three Sisters, *U.S.A.* **82 D3** 44 4N 121 51W
Three Springs, *Australia* .. **61 E2** 29 32S 115 45 E
Throssell, L., *Australia* .... **61 E3** 27 33S 124 10 E
Throssell Ra., *Australia* .... **60 D3** 22 3S 121 43 E
Thuan Hoa, *Vietnam* ...... **39 H5** 8 58N 105 30 E
Thubun Lakes, *Canada* **73 A6** 61 30N 112 0W
Thuin, *Belgium* .... **15 D4** 50 20N 4 17 E
Thule, *Greenland* **4 B4** 77 40N 69 0W
Thun, *Switz.* .... **18 C7** 46 45N 7 38 E
Thunder B., *U.S.A.* **78 B1** 45 0N 83 20W
Thunder Bay, *Canada* **70 C2** 48 20N 89 15W
Thung Song, *Thailand* .... **39 H2** 8 10N 99 40 E
Thunkar, *Bhutan* .... **41 F17** 27 55N 91 0 E
Thuong Tra, *Vietnam* ..... **38 D6** 16 2N 107 42 E
Thüringer Wald, *Germany* . **16 C6** 50 35N 11 0 E
Thurles, *Ireland* **13 D4** 52 41N 7 49W
Thurrock □, *U.K.* .... **11 F8** 51 31N 0 23 E
Thursday I., *Australia* ..... **62 A3** 10 30S 142 3 E
Thurso, *Canada* **70 C4** 45 36N 75 15W
Thurso, *U.K.* **12 C5** 58 36N 3 32W
Thurso →, *U.K.* **12 C5** 58 36N 3 32W
Thurston I., *Antarctica* **5 D16** 72 0S 100 0W
Thutade L., *Canada* **72 B3** 57 0N 126 55W
Thyolo, *Malawi* .... **55 F4** 16 7S 35 5 E
Thysville = Mbanza Ngungu, *Dem. Rep. of the Congo* . **52 F2** 5 12S 14 53 E
Ti Tree, *Australia* .... **62 C1** 22 5S 133 22 E
Tian Shan, *Asia* .... **32 B3** 42 0N 76 0 E
Tianjin, *China* .... **35 E9** 39 8N 117 10 E
Tianshui, *China* .... **34 G3** 34 32N 105 40 E
Tianzhen, *China* .... **34 D8** 40 24N 114 5 E
Tianzhuangtai, *China* ..... **35 D12** 40 43N 122 5 E
Tiaret, *Algeria* .... **50 A6** 35 20N 1 21 E
Tibagi, *Brazil* **95 A5** 24 30S 50 24W
Tibagi →, *Brazil* **95 A5** 22 47S 51 1W
Tiber = Tevere →, *Italy* .. **20 D5** 41 44N 12 14 E
Tiberias = Teverya, *Israel* . **47 C4** 32 47N 35 32 E
Tiberias, L. = Yam Kinneret, *Israel* .... **47 C4** 32 45N 35 35 E
Tibesti, *Chad* .... **51 D9** 21 0N 17 30 E
Tibet = Xizang Zizhiqu □, *China* .... **32 C3** 32 0N 88 0 E
Tibet, Plateau of, *Asia* .... **28 F12** 32 0N 86 0 E
Tibnī, *Syria* .... **44 C3** 35 36N 39 50 E
Tibooburra, *Australia* ..... **63 D3** 29 26S 142 1 E
Tiburón, I., *Mexico* **86 B2** 29 0N 112 30W
Ticino →, *Italy* .... **18 D8** 45 9N 9 14 E
Ticonderoga, *U.S.A.* **79 C11** 43 51N 73 26W
Ticul, *Mexico* **87 C7** 20 20N 89 31W
Tidaholm, *Sweden* .... **9 G15** 58 12N 13 58 E
Tiddim, *Burma* .... **41 H18** 23 28N 93 45 E
Tidioute, *U.S.A.* **78 E5** 41 41N 79 24W
Tidjikja, *Mauritania* **50 E3** 18 29N 11 35W
Tidore, *Indonesia* .... **37 D7** 0 40N 127 25 E
Tiel, *Neths.* .... **15 C5** 51 53N 5 26 E
Tieling, *China* .... **35 C12** 42 20N 123 55 E
Tielt, *Belgium* .... **15 C3** 51 0N 3 20 E
Tien Shan = Tian Shan, *Asia* .... **32 B3** 42 0N 76 0 E
Tien-tsin = Tianjin, *China* . **35 E9** 39 8N 117 10 E
Tien Yen, *Vietnam* .... **38 B6** 21 20N 107 24 E
T'ienching = Tianjin, *China* **35 E9** 39 8N 117 10 E
Tienen, *Belgium* .... **15 D4** 50 48N 4 57 E
Tientsin = Tianjin, *China* .. **35 E9** 39 8N 117 10 E
Tieri, *Australia* .... **62 C4** 23 2S 148 21 E
Tierra Amarilla, *Chile* **94 B1** 27 28S 70 18W
Tierra Amarilla, *U.S.A.* **83 H10** 36 42N 106 33W
Tierra Colorada, *Mexico* ... **87 D5** 17 10N 99 35W
Tierra de Campos, *Spain* .. **19 A3** 42 10N 4 50W
Tierra del Fuego, I. Gr. de, *Argentina* **96 G3** 54 0S 69 0W
Tiétar →, *Spain* **19 C3** 39 50N 6 1W
Tieté →, *Brazil* **95 A5** 20 40S 51 35W
Tiffin, *U.S.A.* **76 E4** 41 7N 83 11W
Tiflis = Tbilisi, *Georgia* .... **25 F7** 41 43N 44 50 E
Tifton, *U.S.A.* **77 K4** 31 27N 83 31W
Tifu, *Indonesia* .... **37 E7** 3 39S 126 24 E
Tighina, *Moldova* .... **17 E15** 46 50N 29 30 E
Tigil, *Russia* .... **27 D16** 57 49N 158 40 E
Tignish, *Canada* **71 C7** 46 58N 64 2W
Tigre →, *Peru* **92 D4** 4 30S 74 10W
Tigre →, *Venezuela* **92 B6** 9 20N 62 30W
Tigris = Dijlah, Nahr →, *Asia* .... **44 D5** 31 0N 47 25 E
Tigyaing, *Burma* .... **41 H20** 23 45N 96 10 E
Tījara, *India* .... **42 F7** 27 56N 76 31 E
Tijuana, *Mexico* **85 N9** 32 30N 117 10W
Tikal, *Guatemala* **88 C2** 17 13N 89 24W
Tikamgarh, *India* .... **43 G8** 24 44N 78 50 E
Tikhoretsk, *Russia* .... **25 E7** 45 56N 40 5 E
Tikhvin, *Russia* .... **24 C5** 59 35N 33 30 E
Tikrīt, *Iraq* .... **44 C4** 34 35N 43 37 E
Tiksi, *Russia* .... **27 B13** 71 40N 128 45 E
Tilamuta, *Indonesia* ...... **37 D6** 0 32N 122 23 E
Tilburg, *Neths.* .... **15 C5** 51 31N 5 6 E
Tilbury, *Canada* **78 D2** 42 17N 82 23W
Tilbury, *U.K.* .... **11 F8** 51 27N 0 22 E
Tilcara, *Argentina* **94 A2** 23 36S 65 23W
Tilden, *U.S.A.* **80 D6** 42 3N 97 50W
Tilhar, *India* .... **43 F8** 28 0N 79 45 E
Tilichiki, *Russia* .... **27 C17** 60 27N 166 5 E
Tílissos, *Greece* .... **23 D7** 35 20N 25 1 E
Till →, *U.K.* **10 B5** 55 41N 2 13W
Tillamook, *U.S.A.* **82 D2** 45 27N 123 51W
Tillsonburg, *Canada* **78 D4** 42 53N 80 44W
Tillyeria □, *Cyprus* .... **23 D11** 35 6N 32 40 E
Tílos, *Greece* .... **21 F12** 36 27N 27 27 E
Tilpa, *Australia* .... **63 E3** 30 57S 144 24 E
Tilsit = Sovetsk, *Russia* ... **9 J19** 55 6N 21 50 E
Tilt →, *U.K.* **12 E5** 56 46N 3 51W
Tilton, *U.S.A.* **79 C13** 43 27N 71 36W
Tiltonsville, *U.S.A.* **78 F4** 40 10N 80 41W
Timagami, L., *Canada* **70 C3** 47 0N 80 10W
Timanskiy Kryazh, *Russia* . **24 A9** 65 58N 50 5 E
Timaru, *N.Z.* .... **59 L3** 44 23S 171 14 E
Timau, *Kenya* .... **54 B4** 0 4N 37 15 E
Timbákion, *Greece* .... **23 D6** 35 4N 24 45 E
Timber Creek, *Australia* ... **60 C5** 15 40S 130 29 E
Timber Lake, *U.S.A.* **80 C4** 45 26N 101 5W
Timber Mt., *U.S.A.* **84 H10** 37 6N 116 28W
Timbuktu = Tombouctou, *Mali* **50 E5** 16 50N 3 0W
Timi, *Cyprus* .... **23 E11** 34 44N 32 31 E
Timimoun, *Algeria* .... **50 C6** 29 14N 0 16 E
Timişoara, *Romania* ...... **17 F11** 45 43N 21 15 E
Timmins, *Canada* **70 C3** 48 28N 81 25W
Timok →, *Serbia, Yug.* .... **21 B10** 44 10N 22 40 E
Timor, *Indonesia* .... **37 F7** 9 0S 125 0 E
Timor Sea, *Ind. Oc.* .... **60 B4** 12 0S 127 0 E
Timor Timur □, *Indonesia* . **37 F7** 9 0S 125 0 E
Tin Can Bay, *Australia* .... **63 D5** 25 56S 153 0 E
Tin Mt., *U.S.A.* **84 J9** 36 50N 117 10W
Tinaca Pt., *Phil.* .... **37 C7** 5 30N 125 25 E
Tinajo, *Canary Is.* **22 E6** 29 4N 13 42W
Tindal, *Australia* .... **60 B5** 14 31S 132 22 E
Tindouf, *Algeria* **50 C4** 27 42N 8 10W
Tinggi, Pulau, *Malaysia* ... **39 L5** 2 18N 104 7 E
Tingo Maria, *Peru* **92 E3** 9 10S 75 54W
Tingrela, *Ivory C.* **50 F4** 10 27N 6 25W
Tinh Bien, *Vietnam* .... **39 G5** 10 36N 104 57 E
Tinnevelly = Tirunelveli, *India* .... **40 Q10** 8 45N 77 45 E
Tinogasta, *Argentina* **94 B2** 28 5S 67 32W
Tínos, *Greece* .... **21 F11** 37 33N 25 8 E
Tinpahar, *India* .... **43 G12** 24 59N 87 44 E
Tintina, *Argentina* **94 B3** 27 2S 62 45W
Tintinara, *Australia* ...... **63 F3** 35 48S 140 2 E
Tioga, *N. Dak., U.S.A.* **80 A3** 48 23N 102 56W
Tioga, *Pa., U.S.A.* **78 E7** 41 55N 77 8W
Tioman, Pulau, *Malaysia* .. **39 L5** 2 50N 104 10 E
Tionesta, *U.S.A.* **78 E5** 41 30N 79 28W
Tipongpani, *India* .... **41 F19** 27 20N 95 55 E
Tipperary, *Ireland* **13 D3** 52 28N 8 10W
Tipperary □, *Ireland* **13 D4** 52 37N 7 55W
Tipton, *Calif., U.S.A.* **84 J7** 36 4N 119 19W
Tipton, *Iowa, U.S.A.* **80 E9** 41 46N 91 8W
Tipton Mt., *U.S.A.* **85 K12** 35 32N 114 12W
Tiptonville, *U.S.A.* **81 G10** 36 23N 89 29W
Tīrān, *Iran* .... **45 C6** 32 45N 51 8 E
Tirana, *Albania* .... **21 D8** 41 18N 19 49 E
Tiranë = Tirana, *Albania* .. **21 D8** 41 18N 19 49 E
Tiraspol, *Moldova* .... **17 E15** 46 55N 29 35 E
Tire, *Turkey* .... **21 E12** 38 5N 27 45 E
Tirebolu, *Turkey* .... **25 F6** 40 58N 38 45 E
Tiree, *U.K.* **12 E2** 56 31N 6 55W
Tiree, Passage of, *U.K.* **12 E2** 56 30N 6 30W
Tîrgovişte = Târgovişte, *Romania* .... **17 F13** 44 55N 25 27 E
Tîrgu-Jiu = Târgu-Jiu, *Romania* .... **17 F12** 45 5N 23 19 E
Tîrgu Mureş = Târgu Mureş, *Romania* .... **17 E13** 46 31N 24 38 E
Tirich Mir, *Pakistan* .... **40 A7** 36 15N 71 55 E
Tírnavos, *Greece* .... **21 E10** 39 45N 22 18 E
Tirodi, *India* .... **40 J11** 21 40N 79 44 E
Tirol □, *Austria* .... **16 E6** 47 3N 10 43 E
Tirso →, *Italy* .... **20 E3** 39 53N 8 32 E
Tiruchchirappalli, *India* .... **40 P11** 10 45N 78 45 E
Tirunelveli, *India* .... **40 Q10** 8 45N 77 45 E
Tirupati, *India* .... **40 N11** 13 39N 79 25 E
Tiruppur, *India* .... **40 P10** 11 5N 77 22 E
Tiruvannamalai, *India* ..... **40 N11** 12 15N 79 5 E
Tisa, *India* .... **42 C7** 32 50N 76 9 E
Tisa →, *Serbia, Yug.* ..... **21 B9** 45 15N 20 17 E
Tisdale, *Canada* **73 C8** 52 50N 104 0W
Tishomingo, *U.S.A.* **81 H6** 34 14N 96 41W
Tisza = Tisa →, *Serbia, Yug.* .... **21 B9** 45 15N 20 17 E
Tit-Ary, *Russia* .... **27 B13** 71 55N 127 2 E
Tithwal, *Pakistan* .... **43 B5** 34 21N 73 50 E
Titicaca, L., *S. Amer.* **92 G5** 15 30S 69 30W
Titograd = Podgorica, *Montenegro, Yug.* ...... **21 C8** 42 30N 19 19 E
Titule, *Dem. Rep. of the Congo* . **54 B2** 3 15N 25 31 E
Titusville, *Fla., U.S.A.* **77 L5** 28 37N 80 49W
Titusville, *Pa., U.S.A.* **78 E5** 41 38N 79 41W
Tivaouane, *Senegal* **50 F2** 14 56N 16 45W
Tiverton, *U.K.* **11 G4** 50 54N 3 29W
Tívoli, *Italy* .... **20 D5** 41 58N 12 45 E
Tizi-Ouzou, *Algeria* ...... **50 A6** 36 42N 4 3 E
Tizimín, *Mexico* **87 C7** 21 0N 88 1W
Tjeggelvas, *Sweden* ...... **8 C17** 66 37N 17 45 E
Tjirebon = Cirebon, *Indonesia* .... **37 G13** 6 45S 108 32 E
Tjörn, *Sweden* .... **9 G14** 58 0N 11 35 E
Tlacotalpan, *Mexico* **87 D5** 18 37N 95 40W
Tlahualilo, *Mexico* **86 B4** 26 20N 103 30W
Tlaquepaque, *Mexico* **86 C4** 20 39N 103 19W
Tlaxcala, *Mexico* **87 D5** 19 20N 98 14W
Tlaxcala □, *Mexico* **87 D5** 19 30N 98 20W
Tlaxiaco, *Mexico* **87 D5** 17 18N 97 40W
Tlemcen, *Algeria* **50 B5** 34 52N 1 21W
To Bong, *Vietnam* .... **38 F7** 12 45N 109 16 E
Toad →, *Canada* **72 B4** 59 25N 124 57W
Toad River, *Canada* **72 B3** 58 51N 125 14W
Toamasina, *Madag.* .... **57 B8** 18 10S 49 25 E
Toamasina □, *Madag.* .... **57 B8** 18 0S 49 0 E
Toay, *Argentina* **94 D3** 36 43S 64 38W
Toba, *Japan* .... **31 G8** 34 30N 136 51 E
Toba, Danau, *Indonesia* ... **36 D1** 2 30N 97 30 E
Toba Kakar, *Pakistan* ..... **42 D3** 31 30N 69 0 E
Toba Tek Singh, *Pakistan* .. **42 D5** 30 55N 72 25 E
Tobago, *W. Indies* **89 D7** 11 10N 60 30W
Tobelo, *Indonesia* .... **37 D7** 1 45N 127 56 E
Tobermory, *Canada* **78 A3** 45 12N 81 40W
Tobermory, *U.K.* **12 E2** 56 38N 6 5W
Tobi, *Pac. Oc.* .... **37 D8** 2 40N 131 10 E
Tobin, *U.S.A.* **84 F5** 39 55N 121 19W
Tobin, L., *Australia* ...... **60 D4** 21 45S 125 49 E
Tobin L., *Canada* **73 C8** 53 35N 103 30W
Toboali, *Indonesia* .... **36 E3** 3 0S 106 25 E
Tobol →, *Russia* .... **26 D7** 58 10N 68 12 E
Toboli, *Indonesia* .... **37 E6** 0 38S 120 5 E
Tobolsk, *Russia* .... **26 D7** 58 15N 68 10 E
Tobruk = Tubruq, *Libya* ... **51 B10** 32 7N 23 55 E
Tobyhanna, *U.S.A.* **79 E9** 41 11N 75 25W
Tobyl = Tobol →, *Russia* **26 D7** 58 10N 68 12 E
Tocantinópolis, *Brazil* **93 E9** 6 20S 47 25W
Tocantins □, *Brazil* **93 F9** 10 0S 48 0W
Tocantins →, *Brazil* **93 D9** 1 45S 49 10W
Toccoa, *U.S.A.* **77 H4** 34 35N 83 19W
Tochi →, *Pakistan* .... **42 C4** 32 49N 70 41 E
Tochigi, *Japan* .... **31 F9** 36 25N 139 45 E
Tochigi □, *Japan* .... **31 F9** 36 45N 139 45 E
Toconao, *Chile* **94 A2** 23 11S 68 1W
Tocopilla, *Chile* **94 A1** 22 5S 70 10W
Tocumwal, *Australia* ...... **63 F4** 35 51S 145 31 E
Tocuyo →, *Venezuela* **92 A5** 11 3N 68 23W
Todd →, *Australia* ...... **62 C2** 24 52S 135 48 E
Todeli, *Indonesia* .... **37 E6** 1 38S 124 34 E
Todenyang, *Kenya* .... **54 B4** 4 35N 35 56 E
Todgarh, *India* .... **42 G5** 25 42N 73 58 E
Todos os Santos, B. de, *Brazil* **93 F11** 12 48S 38 38W
Todos Santos, *Mexico* **86 C2** 23 27N 110 13W
Toe Hd., *U.K.* **12 D1** 57 50N 7 8W
Tofield, *Canada* **72 C6** 53 25N 112 40W
Tofino, *Canada* **72 D3** 49 11N 125 55W
Tofua, *Tonga* **59 D11** 19 45S 175 5W
Tōgane, *Japan* .... **31 G10** 35 33N 140 22 E
Togian, Kepulauan, *Indonesia* .... **37 E6** 0 20S 121 50 E
Togliatti, *Russia* .... **24 D8** 53 32N 49 24 E
Togo ■, *W. Afr.* .... **50 G6** 8 30N 1 35 E
Togtoh, *China* .... **34 D6** 40 15N 111 10 E
Tōhoku □, *Japan* .... **30 E10** 39 50N 141 45 E
Töhöm, *Mongolia* .... **34 B5** 44 27N 108 2 E
Toinya, *Sudan* .... **51 G11** 6 17N 29 46 E
Toiyabe Range, *U.S.A.* **82 G5** 39 30N 117 0W
Tojikiston = Tajikistan ■, *Asia* .... **26 F8** 38 30N 70 0 E
Tojo, *Indonesia* .... **37 E6** 1 20S 121 15 E
Tōjō, *Japan* .... **31 G6** 34 53N 133 16 E
Tok, *U.S.A.* **68 B5** 63 20N 142 59W
Tok-do, *Japan* .... **31 F5** 37 15N 131 52 E
Tokachi-Dake, *Japan* ..... **30 C11** 43 17N 142 5 E
Tokachi-Gawa →, *Japan* . **30 C11** 42 44N 143 42 E
Tokala, *Indonesia* .... **37 E6** 1 30S 121 40 E
Tōkamachi, *Japan* .... **31 F9** 37 8N 138 43 E
Tokanui, *N.Z.* .... **59 M2** 46 34S 168 56 E
Tokara-Rettō, *Japan* ...... **31 K4** 29 37N 129 43 E
Tokarahi, *N.Z.* .... **59 L3** 44 56S 170 39 E
Tokashiki-Shima, *Japan* ... **31 L3** 26 11N 127 21 E
Tokat □, *Turkey* .... **25 F6** 40 15N 36 30 E
Tŏkch'ŏn, *N. Korea* ...... **35 E14** 39 45N 126 18 E
Tokeland, *U.S.A.* **84 D3** 46 42N 123 59W
Tokelau Is., *Pac. Oc.* **64 H10** 9 0S 171 45W
Tokmak, *Kyrgyzstan* ...... **26 E8** 42 49N 75 15 E
Toko Ra., *Australia* .... **62 C2** 23 5S 138 20 E
Tokoro-Gawa →, *Japan* .. **30 B12** 44 7N 144 5 E
Tokuno-Shima, *Japan* ..... **31 L4** 27 56N 128 55 E
Tokushima, *Japan* .... **31 G7** 34 4N 134 34 E
Tokushima □, *Japan* ..... **31 H7** 33 55N 134 0 E
Tokuyama, *Japan* .... **31 G5** 34 3N 131 50 E
Tōkyō, *Japan* .... **31 G9** 35 45N 139 45 E
Tolaga Bay, *N.Z.* .... **59 H7** 38 21S 178 20 E
Tolbukhin = Dobrich, *Bulgaria* .... **21 C12** 43 37N 27 49 E
Toledo, *Brazil* **95 A5** 24 44S 53 45W
Toledo, *Spain* **19 C3** 39 50N 4 2W
Toledo, *Ohio, U.S.A.* **76 E4** 41 39N 83 33W
Toledo, *Oreg., U.S.A.* **82 D2** 44 37N 123 56W
Toledo, *Wash., U.S.A.* **82 C2** 46 26N 122 51W
Toledo, Montes de, *Spain* . **19 C3** 39 33N 4 20W
Toledo Bend Reservoir, *U.S.A.* **81 K8** 31 11N 93 34W
Tolga, *Australia* .... **62 B4** 17 15S 145 29 E
Toliara, *Madag.* .... **57 C7** 23 21S 43 40 E
Toliara □, *Madag.* .... **57 C8** 21 0S 45 0 E
Tolima, *Colombia* **92 C3** 4 40N 75 19W
Tolitoli, *Indonesia* .... **37 D6** 1 5N 120 50 E
Tollhouse, *U.S.A.* **84 H7** 37 1N 119 24W
Tolo, Teluk, *Indonesia* .... **37 E6** 2 20S 122 10 E
Toluca, *Mexico* **87 D5** 19 20N 99 40W
Tom Burke, *S. Africa* ..... **57 C4** 23 5S 28 0 E
Tom Price, *Australia* ...... **60 D2** 22 40S 117 48 E
Tomah, *U.S.A.* **80 D9** 43 59N 90 30W
Tomahawk, *U.S.A.* **80 C10** 45 28N 89 44W
Tomakomai, *Japan* .... **30 C10** 42 38N 141 36 E
Tomales, *U.S.A.* **84 G4** 38 15N 122 53W
Tomales B., *U.S.A.* **84 G3** 38 15N 123 58W
Tomar, *Portugal* **19 C1** 39 36N 8 25W
Tomaszów Mazowiecki, *Poland* .... **17 C10** 51 30N 20 2 E
Tomatlán, *Mexico* **86 D3** 19 56N 105 15W
Tombador, Serra do, *Brazil* **92 F7** 12 0S 58 0W
Tombigbee →, *U.S.A.* **77 K2** 31 8N 87 57W
Tombouctou, *Mali* **50 E5** 16 50N 3 0W
Tombstone, *U.S.A.* **83 L8** 31 43N 110 4W
Tombua, *Angola* .... **56 B1** 15 55S 11 55 E

Tukuyu

Tukuyu, *Tanzania* **55 D3** 9 17S 33 35 E
Tula, *Hidalgo, Mexico* **87 C5** 20 5N 99 20W
Tula, *Tamaulipas, Mexico* **87 C5** 23 0N 99 40W
Tula, *Russia* **24 D6** 54 13N 37 38 E
Tulancingo, *Mexico* **87 C5** 20 5N 99 22W
Tulare, *U.S.A.* **84 J7** 36 13N 119 21W
Tulare Lake Bed, *U.S.A.* **84 K7** 36 0N 119 48W
Tularosa, *U.S.A.* **83 K10** 33 5N 106 1W
Tulbagh, *S. Africa* **56 E2** 33 16S 19 6 E
Tulcán, *Ecuador* **92 C3** 0 48N 77 43W
Tulcea, *Romania* **17 F15** 45 13N 28 46 E
Tulchyn, *Ukraine* **17 D15** 48 41N 28 49 E
Tūleh, *Iran* **45 C7** 34 35N 52 33 E
Tulemalu L., *Canada* **73 A9** 62 58N 99 25W
Tuli, *Zimbabwe* **55 G2** 21 58S 29 13 E
Tulia, *U.S.A.* **81 H4** 34 32N 101 46W
Tulita, *Canada* **68 B7** 64 57N 125 30W
Ţūlkarm, *West Bank* **47 C4** 32 19N 35 2 E
Tulla, *Ireland* **13 D3** 52 53N 8 46W
Tullahoma, *U.S.A.* **77 H2** 35 22N 86 13W
Tullamore, *Australia* **63 E4** 32 39S 147 36 E
Tullamore, *Ireland* **13 C4** 53 16N 7 31W
Tulle, *France* **18 D4** 45 16N 1 46 E
Tullow, *Ireland* **13 D5** 52 49N 6 45W
Tully, *Australia* **62 B4** 17 56S 145 55 E
Tully, *U.S.A.* **79 D8** 42 48N 76 7W
Tulsa, *U.S.A.* **81 G7** 36 10N 95 55W
Tulsequah, *Canada* **72 B2** 58 39N 133 35W
Tulua, *Colombia* **92 C3** 4 6N 76 11W
Tulun, *Russia* **27 D11** 54 32N 100 35 E
Tulungagung, *Indonesia* **37 H14** 8 5S 111 54 E
Tuma →, *Nic.* **88 D3** 13 6N 84 35W
Tumaco, *Colombia* **92 C3** 1 50N 78 45W
Tumatumari, *Guyana* **92 B7** 5 20N 58 55W
Tumba, *Sweden* **9 G17** 59 12N 17 48 E
Tumba, L.,
Dem. Rep. of the Congo **52 E3** 0 50S 18 0 E
Tumbarumba, *Australia* **63 F4** 35 44S 148 0 E
Tumbaya, *Argentina* **94 A2** 23 50S 65 26W
Tumbes, *Peru* **92 D2** 3 37S 80 27W
Tumbwe,
Dem. Rep. of the Congo **55 E2** 11 25S 27 15 E
Tumby Bay, *Australia* **63 E2** 34 21S 136 8 E
Tumd Youqi, *China* **34 D6** 40 30N 110 30 E
Tumen, *China* **35 C15** 43 0N 129 50 E
Tumen Jiang →, *China* **35 C16** 42 20N 130 35 E
Tumeremo, *Venezuela* **92 B6** 7 18N 61 30W
Tumkur, *India* **40 N10** 13 18N 77 6 E
Tump, *Pakistan* **40 F3** 26 7N 62 16 E
Tumpat, *Malaysia* **39 J4** 6 11N 102 10 E
Tumu, *Ghana* **50 F5** 10 56N 1 56W
Tumucumaque, Serra, *Brazil* **93 C8** 2 0N 55 0W
Tumut, *Australia* **63 F4** 35 16S 148 13 E
Tumwater, *U.S.A.* **84 C4** 47 1N 122 54W
Tuna, *India* **42 H4** 22 59N 70 5 E
Tunas de Zaza, *Cuba* **88 B4** 21 39N 79 34W
Tunbridge Wells = Royal
Tunbridge Wells, *U.K.* **11 F8** 51 7N 0 16 E
Tuncurry-Forster, *Australia* **63 E5** 32 17S 152 29 E
Tundla, *India* **42 F8** 27 12N 78 17 E
Tunduru, *Tanzania* **55 E4** 11 8S 37 25 E
Tundzha →, *Bulgaria* **21 C11** 41 40N 26 35 E
Tunga Pass, *India* **41 E19** 29 0N 94 14 E
Tungabhadra →, *India* **40 M11** 15 57N 78 15 E
Tungla, *Nic.* **88 D3** 13 24N 84 21W
Tungsten, *Canada* **72 A3** 61 57N 128 16W
Tunguska, Nizhnyaya →,
Russia **27 C9** 65 48N 88 4 E
Tunguska,
Podkamennaya →,
Russia **27 C10** 61 50N 90 13 E
Tunica, *U.S.A.* **81 H9** 34 41N 90 23W
Tunis, *Tunisia* **51 A8** 36 50N 10 11 E
Tunisia ■, *Africa* **51 A7** 33 30N 9 10 E
Tunja, *Colombia* **92 B4** 5 33N 73 25W
Tunkhannock, *U.S.A.* **79 E9** 41 32N 75 57W
Tunliu, *China* **34 F7** 36 13N 112 52 E
Tunnsjøen, *Norway* **8 D15** 64 45N 13 25 E
Tunungayualok I., *Canada* **71 A7** 56 0N 61 0W
Tunuyán, *Argentina* **94 C2** 33 35S 69 0W
Tunuyán →, *Argentina* **94 C2** 33 33S 67 30W
Tuolumne, *U.S.A.* **84 H6** 37 58N 120 15W
Tuolumne →, *U.S.A.* **84 H5** 37 36N 121 13W
Tūp Āghāj, *Iran* **44 B5** 36 3N 47 50 E
Tupã, *Brazil* **95 A5** 21 57S 50 28W
Tupelo, *U.S.A.* **77 H1** 34 16N 88 43W
Tupinambaranas, *Brazil* **92 D7** 3 0S 58 0W
Tupiza, *Bolivia* **94 A2** 21 30S 65 40W
Tupman, *U.S.A.* **85 K7** 35 18N 119 21W
Tupper, *Canada* **72 B4** 55 32N 120 1W
Tupper Lake, *U.S.A.* **79 B10** 44 14N 74 28W
Tupungato, Cerro, *S. Amer.* **94 C2** 33 15S 69 50W
Tuquan, *China* **35 B11** 45 18N 121 38 E
Túquerres, *Colombia* **92 C3** 1 5N 77 37W
Tura, *Russia* **27 C11** 64 20N 100 17 E
Turabah, *Si. Arabia* **46 C3** 28 20N 43 15 E
Tūrān, *Iran* **45 C8** 35 39N 56 42 E
Turan, *Russia* **27 D10** 51 55N 95 0 E
Ţurayf, *Si. Arabia* **44 D3** 31 41N 38 39 E
Turda, *Romania* **17 E12** 46 34N 23 47 E
Turek, *Poland* **17 B10** 52 3N 18 30 E
Turen, *Venezuela* **92 B5** 9 17N 69 6W
Turfan = Turpan, *China* **32 B3** 43 58N 89 10 E
Turfan Depression = Turpan
Hami, *China* **28 E12** 42 40N 89 25 E
Turgeon →, *Canada* **70 C4** 50 0N 78 56W
Tŭrgovishte, *Bulgaria* **21 C12** 43 17N 26 38 E
Turgutlu, *Turkey* **21 E12** 38 30N 27 43 E
Turia →, *Spain* **19 C5** 39 27N 0 19W
Turiaçu, *Brazil* **93 D9** 1 40S 45 19W
Turiaçu →, *Brazil* **93 D9** 1 36S 45 19W
Turin = Torino, *Italy* **18 D7** 45 3N 7 40 E
Turkana, L., *Africa* **54 B4** 3 30N 36 5 E
Turkestan = Türkistan,
Kazakstan **26 E7** 43 17N 68 16 E
Turkey ■, *Eurasia* **25 G6** 39 0N 36 0 E
Turkey Creek, *Australia* **60 C4** 17 2S 128 12 E
Türkistan, *Kazakstan* **26 E7** 43 17N 68 16 E
Türkmenbashi,
Turkmenistan **25 G9** 40 5N 53 5 E
Turkmenistan ■, *Asia* **26 F6** 39 0N 59 0 E
Turks & Caicos Is. ■,
W. Indies **89 B5** 21 20N 71 20W
Turks Island Passage,
W. Indies **89 B5** 21 30N 71 30W
Turku, *Finland* **9 F20** 60 30N 22 19 E
Turkwel →, *Kenya* **54 B4** 3 6N 36 6 E
Turlock, *U.S.A.* **84 H6** 37 30N 120 51W
Turnagain →, *Canada* **72 B3** 59 12N 127 35W
Turnagain, C., *N.Z.* **59 J6** 40 28S 176 38 E
Turneffe Is., *Belize* **87 D7** 17 20N 87 50W
Turner, *U.S.A.* **82 B9** 48 51N 108 24W
Turner Pt., *Australia* **62 A1** 11 47S 133 32 E
Turner Valley, *Canada* **72 C6** 50 40N 114 17W
Turners Falls, *U.S.A.* **79 D12** 42 36N 72 33W
Turnhout, *Belgium* **15 C4** 51 19N 4 57 E
Turnor L., *Canada* **73 B7** 56 35N 108 35W
Tŭrnovo = Veliko Tŭrnovo,
Bulgaria **21 C11** 43 5N 25 41 E
Turnu Măgurele, *Romania* **17 G13** 43 46N 24 56 E
Turnu Roşu, P., *Romania* **17 F13** 45 33N 24 17 E
Turpan, *China* **32 B3** 43 58N 89 10 E
Turpan Hami, *China* **28 E12** 42 40N 89 25 E
Turriff, *U.K.* **12 D6** 57 32N 2 27W
Tursāq, *Iraq* **44 C5** 33 27N 45 47 E
Turtle Head I., *Australia* **62 A3** 10 56S 142 37 E
Turtle L., *Canada* **73 C7** 53 36N 108 38W
Turtle Lake, *U.S.A.* **80 B4** 47 31N 100 53W
Turtleford, *Canada* **73 C7** 53 23N 108 57W
Turukhansk, *Russia* **27 C9** 65 21N 88 5 E
Tuscaloosa, *U.S.A.* **77 J2** 33 12N 87 34W
Tuscany = Toscana □, *Italy* **20 C4** 43 25N 11 0 E
Tuscarawas →, *U.S.A.* **78 F3** 40 24N 81 25W
Tuscarora Mt., *U.S.A.* **78 F7** 40 55N 77 55W
Tuscola, *Ill., U.S.A.* **76 F1** 39 48N 88 17W
Tuscola, *Tex., U.S.A.* **81 J5** 32 12N 99 48W
Tuscumbia, *U.S.A.* **77 H2** 34 44N 87 42W
Tuskegee, *U.S.A.* **77 J3** 32 25N 85 42W
Tustin, *U.S.A.* **85 M9** 33 44N 117 49W
Tuticorin, *India* **40 Q11** 8 50N 78 12 E
Tutóia, *Brazil* **93 D10** 2 45S 42 20W
Tutong, *Brunei* **36 D4** 4 47N 114 40 E
Tutrakan, *Bulgaria* **21 B12** 44 2N 26 40 E
Tuttle Creek L., *U.S.A.* **80 F6** 39 22N 96 40W
Tuttlingen, *Germany* **16 E5** 47 58N 8 48 E
Tutuala, *Indonesia* **37 F7** 8 25S 127 15 E
Tutuila, *Amer. Samoa* **59 B13** 14 19S 170 50W
Tutume, *Botswana* **53 J5** 20 30S 27 5 E
Tututepec, *Mexico* **87 D5** 16 9N 97 38W
Tuva □, *Russia* **27 D10** 51 30N 95 0 E
Tuvalu ■, *Pac. Oc.* **64 H9** 8 0S 178 0 E
Tuxpan, *Mexico* **87 C5** 20 58N 97 23W
Tuxtla Gutiérrez, *Mexico* **87 D6** 16 50N 93 10W
Tuy = Tui, *Spain* **19 A1** 42 3N 8 39W
Tuy An, *Vietnam* **38 F7** 13 17N 109 16 E
Tuy Duc, *Vietnam* **39 F6** 12 15N 107 27 E
Tuy Hoa, *Vietnam* **38 F7** 13 5N 109 10 E
Tuy Phong, *Vietnam* **39 G7** 11 14N 108 43 E
Tuya L., *Canada* **72 B2** 59 7N 130 35W
Tuyen Hoa, *Vietnam* **38 D6** 17 50N 106 10 E
Tūysarkān, *Iran* **45 C6** 34 33N 48 27 E
Tuz Gölü, *Turkey* **25 G5** 38 42N 33 18 E
Ţūz Khurmātū, *Iraq* **44 C5** 34 56N 44 38 E
Tuzla, *Bos.-H.* **21 B8** 44 34N 18 41 E
Tver, *Russia* **24 C6** 56 55N 35 55 E
Twain, *U.S.A.* **84 E5** 40 1N 121 3W
Twain Harte, *U.S.A.* **84 G6** 38 2N 120 14W
Tweed, *Canada* **78 B7** 44 29N 77 19W
Tweed →, *U.K.* **12 F6** 55 45N 2 0W
Tweed Heads, *Australia* **63 D5** 28 10S 153 31 E
Tweedsmuir Prov. Park,
Canada **72 C3** 53 0N 126 20W
Twentynine Palms, *U.S.A.* **85 L10** 34 8N 116 3W
Twillingate, *Canada* **71 C9** 49 42N 54 45W
Twin Bridges, *U.S.A.* **82 D7** 45 33N 112 20W
Twin Falls, *Canada* **71 B7** 53 30N 64 32W
Twin Falls, *U.S.A.* **82 E6** 42 34N 114 28W
Twin Valley, *U.S.A.* **80 B6** 47 16N 96 16W
Twinsburg, *U.S.A.* **78 E3** 41 18N 81 26W
Twitchell Reservoir, *U.S.A.* **85 L6** 34 59N 120 19W
Two Harbors, *U.S.A.* **80 B9** 47 2N 91 40W
Two Hills, *Canada* **72 C6** 53 43N 111 52W
Two Rivers, *U.S.A.* **76 C2** 44 9N 87 34W
Two Rocks, *Australia* **61 F2** 31 30S 115 35 E
Twofold B., *Australia* **63 F4** 37 8S 149 59 E
Tyachiv, *Ukraine* **17 D12** 48 1N 23 35 E
Tychy, *Poland* **17 C10** 50 9N 18 59 E
Tyler, *U.S.A.* **75 D7** 32 18N 95 17W
Tyler, *Minn., U.S.A.* **80 C6** 44 18N 96 8W
Tyler, *Tex., U.S.A.* **81 J7** 32 21N 95 18W
Tynda, *Russia* **27 D13** 55 10N 124 43 E
Tyndall, *U.S.A.* **80 D6** 43 0N 97 50W
Tyne →, *U.K.* **10 C6** 54 59N 1 32W
Tyne & Wear □, *U.K.* **10 B6** 55 6N 1 17W
Tynemouth, *U.K.* **10 B6** 55 1N 1 26W
Tyre = Sūr, *Lebanon* **47 B4** 33 19N 35 16 E
Tyrifjorden, *Norway* **9 F14** 60 2N 10 8 E
Tyrol = Tirol □, *Austria* **16 E6** 47 3N 10 43 E
Tyrone, *U.S.A.* **78 F6** 40 40N 78 14W
Tyrone □, *U.K.* **13 B4** 54 38N 7 11W
Tyrrell →, *Australia* **63 F3** 35 26S 142 51 E
Tyrrell, L., *Australia* **63 F3** 35 20S 142 50 E
Tyrrell L., *Canada* **73 A7** 63 7N 105 27W
Tyrrhenian Sea, *Medit. S.* **20 E5** 40 0N 12 30 E
Tysfjorden, *Norway* **8 B17** 68 7N 16 25 E
Tyulgan, *Russia* **24 D10** 52 22N 56 12 E
Tyumen, *Russia* **26 D7** 57 11N 65 29 E
Tywi →, *U.K.* **11 F3** 51 48N 4 21W
Tywyn, *U.K.* **11 E3** 52 35N 4 5W
Tzaneen, *S. Africa* **57 C5** 23 47S 30 9 E
Tzermiádhes, *Greece* **23 D7** 35 12N 25 29 E
Tzukong = Zigong, *China* **32 D5** 29 15N 104 48 E

U

U Taphao, *Thailand* **38 F3** 12 35N 101 0 E
U.S.A. = United States of
America ■, *N. Amer.* **74 C7** 37 0N 96 0W
Uatumã →, *Brazil* **92 D7** 2 26S 57 37W
Uaupés, *Brazil* **92 D5** 0 8S 67 5W
Uaupés →, *Brazil* **92 C5** 0 2N 67 16W
Uaxactún, *Guatemala* **88 C2** 17 25N 89 29W
Ubá, *Brazil* **95 A7** 21 8S 43 0W
Ubaitaba, *Brazil* **93 F11** 14 18S 39 20W
Ubangi = Oubangi →,
Dem. Rep. of the Congo **52 E3** 0 30S 17 50 E
Ubauro, *Pakistan* **42 E3** 28 15N 69 45 E
Ubayyiḍ, W. al →, *Iraq* **44 C4** 32 34N 43 48 E
Ube, *Japan* **31 H5** 33 56N 131 15 E
Úbeda, *Spain* **19 C4** 38 3N 3 23W
Uberaba, *Brazil* **93 G9** 19 50S 47 55W
Uberlândia, *Brazil* **93 G9** 19 0S 48 20W
Ubolratna Res., *Thailand* **38 D4** 16 45N 102 30 E
Ubombo, *S. Africa* **57 D5** 27 31S 32 4 E
Ubon Ratchathani, *Thailand* **38 E5** 15 15N 104 50 E
Ubondo,
Dem. Rep. of the Congo **54 C2** 0 55S 25 42 E
Ubort →, *Belarus* **17 B15** 52 6N 28 30 E
Ubundu,
Dem. Rep. of the Congo **54 C2** 0 22S 25 30 E
Ucayali →, *Peru* **92 D4** 4 30S 73 30W
Uchiura-Wan, *Japan* **30 C10** 42 25N 140 40 E
Uchquduq, *Uzbekistan* **26 E7** 41 50N 62 50 E
Uchur →, *Russia* **27 D14** 58 48N 130 35 E
Ucluelet, *Canada* **72 D3** 48 57N 125 32W
Uda →, *Russia* **27 D14** 54 42N 135 14 E
Udagamandalam, *India* **40 P10** 11 30N 76 44 E
Udainagar, *India* **42 H7** 22 33N 76 13 E
Udaipur, *India* **42 G5** 24 36N 73 44 E
Udaipur Garhi, *Nepal* **43 F12** 27 0N 86 35 E
Udala, *India* **43 J12** 21 35N 86 34 E
Uddevalla, *Sweden* **9 G14** 58 21N 11 55 E
Uddjaur, *Sweden* **8 D17** 65 56N 17 49 E
Uden, *Neths.* **15 C5** 51 40N 5 37 E
Udgir, *India* **40 K10** 18 25N 77 5 E
Udhampur, *India* **43 C6** 33 0N 75 5 E
Údine, *Italy* **20 A5** 46 3N 13 14 E
Udmurtia □, *Russia* **24 C9** 57 30N 52 30 E
Udon Thani, *Thailand* **38 D4** 17 29N 102 46 E
Udupi, *India* **40 N9** 13 25N 74 42 E
Udzungwa Range, *Tanzania* **55 D4** 9 30S 35 10 E
Ueda, *Japan* **31 F9** 36 24N 138 16 E
Uedineniya, Os., *Russia* **4 B12** 78 0N 85 0 E
Uele →,
Dem. Rep. of the Congo **52 D4** 3 45N 24 45 E
Uelen, *Russia* **27 C19** 66 10N 170 0W
Uelzen, *Germany* **16 B6** 52 57N 10 32 E
Ufa, *Russia* **24 D10** 54 45N 55 55 E
Ufa →, *Russia* **24 D10** 54 40N 56 0 E
Ugab →, *Namibia* **56 C1** 20 55S 13 30 E
Ugalla →, *Tanzania* **54 D3** 5 8S 30 42 E
Uganda ■, *Africa* **54 B3** 2 0N 32 0 E
Ugie, *S. Africa* **57 E4** 31 10S 28 13 E
Uglegorsk, *Russia* **27 E15** 49 5N 142 2 E
Ugljan, *Croatia* **16 F8** 44 12N 15 10 E
Uhrichsville, *U.S.A.* **78 F3** 40 24N 81 21W
Uibhist a Deas = South
Uist, *U.K.* **12 D1** 57 20N 7 15W
Uibhist a Tuath = North
Uist, *U.K.* **12 D1** 57 40N 7 15W
Uig, *U.K.* **12 D2** 57 35N 6 21W
Uíge, *Angola* **52 F2** 7 30S 14 40 E
Uijŏngbu, *S. Korea* **35 F14** 37 48N 127 0 E
Ŭiju, *N. Korea* **35 D13** 40 15N 124 35 E
Uinta Mts., *U.S.A.* **82 F8** 40 45N 110 30W
Uitenhage, *S. Africa* **56 E4** 33 40S 25 28 E
Uithuizen, *Neths.* **15 A6** 53 24N 6 41 E
Ujh →, *India* **42 C6** 32 10N 75 18 E
Ujhani, *India* **43 F8** 28 0N 79 6 E
Uji-guntō, *Japan* **31 J4** 31 15N 129 25 E
Ujjain, *India* **42 H6** 23 9N 75 43 E
Ujung Pandang, *Indonesia* **37 F5** 5 10S 119 20 E
Uka, *Russia* **27 D17** 57 50N 162 0 E
Ukara I., *Tanzania* **54 C3** 1 50S 33 0 E
Uke-Shima, *Japan* **31 K4** 28 2N 129 14 E
Ukerewe I., *Tanzania* **54 C3** 2 0S 33 0 E
Ukhrul, *India* **41 G19** 25 10N 94 25 E
Ukhta, *Russia* **24 B9** 63 34N 53 41 E
Ukiah, *U.S.A.* **84 F3** 39 9N 123 13W
Ukki Fort, *India* **43 C7** 33 28N 76 54 E
Ukmergė, *Lithuania* **9 J21** 55 15N 24 45 E
Ukraine ■, *Europe* **25 E5** 49 0N 32 0 E
Uku, *Angola* **53 G2** 11 24S 14 22 E
Ukwi, *Botswana* **56 C3** 23 29S 20 30 E
Ulaan-Uul, *Mongolia* **34 B6** 44 13N 111 10 E
Ulaanbaatar, *Mongolia* **27 E11** 47 55N 106 53 E
Ulaangom, *Mongolia* **32 A4** 50 5N 92 10 E
Ulaanjirem, *Mongolia* **34 B3** 45 5N 105 30 E
Ulamba,
Dem. Rep. of the Congo **55 D1** 9 3S 23 38 E
Ulan Bator = Ulaanbaatar,
Mongolia **27 E11** 47 55N 106 53 E
Ulan Ude, *Russia* **27 D11** 51 45N 107 40 E
Ulaya, *Morogoro, Tanzania* **54 D4** 7 3S 36 55 E
Ulaya, *Tabora, Tanzania* **54 C3** 4 25S 33 30 E
Ulcinj, *Montenegro, Yug.* **21 D8** 41 58N 19 10 E
Ulco, *S. Africa* **56 D3** 28 21S 24 15 E
Ulefoss, *Norway* **9 G13** 59 17N 9 16 E
Ulhasnagar, *India* **40 K8** 19 15N 73 10 E
Uliastay, *Mongolia* **32 B4** 47 56N 97 28 E
Ulithi Atoll, *Pac. Oc.* **37 B9** 10 0N 139 30 E
Ulladulla, *Australia* **63 F5** 35 21S 150 29 E
Ullapool, *U.K.* **12 D3** 57 54N 5 9W
Ullswater, *U.K.* **10 C5** 54 34N 2 52W
Ullŭng-do, *S. Korea* **31 F5** 37 30N 130 30 E
Ulm, *Germany* **16 D5** 48 23N 9 58 E
Ulmarra, *Australia* **63 D5** 29 37S 153 4 E
Ulonguè, *Mozam.* **55 E3** 14 37S 34 19 E
Ulricehamn, *Sweden* **9 H15** 57 46N 13 26 E
Ulsan, *S. Korea* **35 G15** 35 20N 129 15 E
Ulsta, *U.K.* **12 A7** 60 30N 1 9W
Ulster □, *U.K.* **13 B5** 54 35N 6 30W
Ulubat Gölü, *Turkey* **21 D13** 40 9N 28 35 E
Uludağ, *Turkey* **21 D13** 40 4N 29 13 E
Uluguru Mts., *Tanzania* **54 D4** 7 15S 37 40 E
Ulungur He →, *China* **32 B3** 47 1N 87 24 E
Uluru = Ayers Rock,
Australia **61 E5** 25 23S 131 5 E
Uluru Nat. Park, *Australia* **61 E5** 25 15S 131 20 E
Ulutau, *Kazakstan* **26 E7** 48 39N 67 1 E
Ulva, *U.K.* **12 E2** 56 29N 6 13W
Ulverston, *U.K.* **10 C4** 54 13N 3 5W
Ulverstone, *Australia* **62 G4** 41 11S 146 11 E
Ulya, *Russia* **27 D15** 59 10N 142 0 E
Ulyanovsk = Simbirsk,
Russia **24 D8** 54 20N 48 25 E
Ulyasutay = Uliastay,
Mongolia **32 B4** 47 56N 97 28 E
Ulysses, *U.S.A.* **81 G4** 37 35N 101 22W
Umala, *Bolivia* **92 G5** 17 25S 68 5W
Uman, *Ukraine* **17 D16** 48 40N 30 12 E
Umaria, *India* **41 H12** 23 35N 80 50 E
Umarkot, *Pakistan* **40 G6** 25 15N 69 40 E
Umarpada, *India* **42 J5** 21 27N 73 30 E
Umatilla, *U.S.A.* **82 D4** 45 55N 119 21W
Umba, *Russia* **24 A5** 66 42N 34 11 E
Umbagog L., *U.S.A.* **79 B13** 44 46N 71 3W
Umbakumba, *Australia* **62 A2** 13 47S 136 50 E
Umbrella Mts., *N.Z.* **59 L2** 45 35S 169 5 E
Ume älv →, *Sweden* **8 E19** 63 45N 20 20 E
Umeå, *Sweden* **8 E19** 63 45N 20 20 E
Umera, *Indonesia* **37 E7** 0 12S 129 37 E
Umfuli →, *Zimbabwe* **55 F2** 17 30S 29 23 E
Umgusa, *Zimbabwe* **55 F2** 19 29S 27 52 E
Umkomaas, *S. Africa* **57 E5** 30 13S 30 48 E
Umlazi, *S. Africa* **53 L6** 29 59S 30 54 E
Umm ad Daraj, J., *Jordan* **47 C4** 32 18N 35 48 E
Umm al Qaywayn, *U.A.E.* **45 E7** 25 30N 55 35 E
Umm al Qittayn, *Jordan* **47 C5** 32 18N 36 40 E
Umm Bāb, *Qatar* **45 E6** 25 12N 50 48 E
Umm el Fahm, *Israel* **47 C4** 32 31N 35 9 E
Umm Keddada, *Sudan* **51 F11** 13 36N 26 42 E
Umm Lajj, *Si. Arabia* **44 E3** 25 0N 37 23 E
Umm Ruwaba, *Sudan* **51 F12** 12 50N 31 20 E
Umnak I., *U.S.A.* **68 C3** 53 15N 168 20W
Umniati →, *Zimbabwe* **55 F2** 16 49S 28 45 E
Umpqua →, *U.S.A.* **82 E1** 43 40N 124 12W
Umreth, *India* **42 H5** 22 41N 73 4 E
Umtata, *S. Africa* **57 E4** 31 36S 28 49 E
Umuarama, *Brazil* **95 A5** 23 45S 53 20W
Umvukwe Ra., *Zimbabwe* **55 F3** 16 45S 30 45 E
Umzimvubu = Port St.
Johns, *S. Africa* **57 E4** 31 38S 29 33 E
Umzingwane →,
Zimbabwe **55 G2** 22 12S 29 56 E
Umzinto, *S. Africa* **57 E5** 30 15S 30 45 E
Una, *India* **42 J4** 20 46N 71 8 E
Una →, *Bos.-H.* **16 F9** 45 0N 16 20 E
Unadilla, *U.S.A.* **79 D9** 42 20N 75 19W
Unalakleet, *U.S.A.* **68 B3** 63 52N 160 47W
Unalaska, *U.S.A.* **68 C3** 53 53N 166 32W
Unalaska I., *U.S.A.* **68 C3** 53 35N 166 50W
'Unayzah, *Si. Arabia* **44 E4** 26 6N 43 58 E
'Unāzah, J., *Asia* **44 C3** 32 12N 39 18 E
Uncía, *Bolivia* **92 G5** 18 25S 66 40W
Uncompahgre Peak, *U.S.A.* **83 G10** 38 4N 107 28W
Uncompahgre Plateau,
U.S.A. **83 G9** 38 20N 108 15W
Underbool, *Australia* **63 F3** 35 10S 141 51 E
Ungarie, *Australia* **63 E4** 33 38S 146 56 E
Ungarra, *Australia* **63 E2** 34 12S 136 2 E
Ungava, Pén. d', *Canada* **69 C12** 60 0N 74 0W
Ungava B., *Canada* **69 C13** 59 30N 67 30W
Ungeny = Ungheni,
Moldova **17 E14** 47 11N 27 51 E
Unggi, *N. Korea* **35 C16** 42 16N 130 28 E
Ungheni, *Moldova* **17 E14** 47 11N 27 51 E
União da Vitória, *Brazil* **95 B5** 26 13S 51 5W
Unimak I., *U.S.A.* **68 C3** 54 45N 164 0W
Union, *Miss., U.S.A.* **81 J10** 32 34N 89 7W
Union, *Mo., U.S.A.* **80 F9** 38 27N 91 0W
Union, *S.C., U.S.A.* **77 H5** 34 43N 81 37W
Union City, *Calif., U.S.A.* **84 H4** 37 36N 122 1W
Union City, *N.J., U.S.A.* **79 F10** 40 45N 74 2W
Union City, *Pa., U.S.A.* **78 E5** 41 54N 79 51W
Union City, *Tenn., U.S.A.* **81 G10** 36 26N 89 3W
Union Gap, *U.S.A.* **82 C3** 46 33N 120 28W
Union Springs, *U.S.A.* **77 J3** 32 9N 85 43W
Uniondale, *S. Africa* **56 E3** 33 39S 23 7 E
Uniontown, *U.S.A.* **76 F6** 39 54N 79 44W
Unionville, *U.S.A.* **80 E8** 40 29N 93 1W
United Arab Emirates ■,
Asia **45 F7** 23 50N 54 0 E
United Kingdom ■, *Europe* **7 E5** 53 0N 2 0W
United States of America ■,
N. Amer. **74 C7** 37 0N 96 0W
Unity, *Canada* **73 C7** 52 30N 109 5W
University Park, *U.S.A.* **83 K10** 32 17N 106 45W
Unjha, *India* **42 H5** 23 46N 72 24 E
Unnao, *India* **43 F9** 26 35N 80 30 E
Unst, *U.K.* **12 A8** 60 44N 0 53W
Unuk →, *Canada* **72 B2** 56 5N 131 3W
Uozu, *Japan* **31 F8** 36 48N 137 24 E
Upata, *Venezuela* **92 B6** 8 1N 62 24W
Upemba, L.,
Dem. Rep. of the Congo **55 D2** 8 30S 26 20 E
Upernavik, *Greenland* **4 B5** 72 49N 56 20W
Upington, *S. Africa* **56 D3** 28 25S 21 15 E
Upleta, *India* **42 J4** 21 46N 70 16 E
Upolu, *W. Samoa* **59 A13** 13 58S 172 0W
Upper Alkali L., *U.S.A.* **82 F3** 41 47N 120 8W
Upper Arrow L., *Canada* **72 C5** 50 30N 117 50W
Upper Foster L., *Canada* **73 B7** 56 47N 105 20W
Upper Hutt, *N.Z.* **59 J5** 41 8S 175 5 E
Upper Klamath L., *U.S.A.* **82 E3** 42 25N 121 55W
Upper Lake, *U.S.A.* **84 F4** 39 10N 122 54W
Upper Musquodoboit,
Canada **71 C7** 45 10N 62 58W
Upper Red L., *U.S.A.* **80 A7** 48 8N 94 45W
Upper Sandusky, *U.S.A.* **76 E4** 40 50N 83 17W
Upper Volta = Burkina
Faso ■, *Africa* **50 F5** 12 0N 1 0W
Uppland, *Sweden* **9 F17** 59 59N 17 48 E
Uppsala, *Sweden* **9 G17** 59 53N 17 38 E
Upshi, *India* **43 C7** 33 48N 77 52 E
Upstart, C., *Australia* **62 B4** 19 41S 147 45 E
Upton, *U.S.A.* **80 C2** 44 6N 104 38W
Ur, *Iraq* **44 D5** 30 55N 46 25 E
Urad Qianqi, *China* **34 D5** 40 40N 108 30 E
Urakawa, *Japan* **30 C11** 42 9N 142 47 E
Ural = Zhayyq →,
Kazakstan **25 E9** 47 0N 51 48 E
Ural, *Australia* **63 E4** 33 21S 146 12 E
Ural Mts. = Uralskie Gory,
Eurasia **24 C10** 60 0N 59 0 E
Uralla, *Australia* **63 E5** 30 37S 151 29 E
Uralsk = Oral, *Kazakstan* **25 D9** 51 20N 51 20 E
Uralskie Gory, *Eurasia* **24 C10** 60 0N 59 0 E
Urambo, *Tanzania* **54 D3** 5 4S 32 0 E
Urana, *Australia* **63 F4** 35 15S 146 21 E
Urandangi, *Australia* **62 C2** 21 32S 138 14 E
Uranium City, *Canada* **73 B7** 59 34N 108 37W
Uraricoera →, *Brazil* **92 C6** 3 2N 60 30W
Urawa, *Japan* **31 G9** 35 50N 139 40 E
Uray, *Russia* **26 C7** 60 5N 65 15 E
'Uray'irah, *Si. Arabia* **45 E6** 25 57N 48 53 E
Urbana, *Ill., U.S.A.* **76 E1** 40 7N 88 12W
Urbana, *Ohio, U.S.A.* **76 E4** 40 7N 83 45W
Urbino, *Italy* **20 C5** 43 43N 12 38 E
Urbión, Picos de, *Spain* **19 A4** 42 1N 2 52W
Urcos, *Peru* **92 F4** 13 40S 71 38W

Vesterålen

Urdinarrain, *Argentina* 94 C4 32 37S 58 52W
Urdzhar, *Kazakstan* 26 E9 47 5N 81 38 E
Ure →, *U.K.* 10 C6 54 5N 1 20W
Ures, *Mexico* 86 B2 29 30N 110 30W
Urfa = Sanliurfa, *Turkey* 25 G6 37 12N 38 50 E
Urganch, *Uzbekistan* 26 E7 41 40N 60 41 E
Urgench = Urganch, *Uzbekistan* 26 E7 41 40N 60 41 E
Ürgüp, *Turkey* 44 B2 38 38N 34 56 E
Uri, *India* 43 B6 34 8N 74 2 E
Uribia, *Colombia* 92 A4 11 43N 72 16W
Uriondo, *Bolivia* 94 A3 21 41S 64 41W
Urique, *Mexico* 86 B3 27 13N 107 55W
Urique →, *Mexico* 86 B3 26 29N 107 58W
Urk, *Neths.* 15 B5 52 39N 5 36 E
Urla, *Turkey* 21 E12 38 20N 26 47 E
Urmia = Orūmīyeh, *Iran* 44 B5 37 40N 45 0 E
Urmia, L. = Orūmīyeh, Daryācheh-ye, *Iran* 44 B5 37 50N 45 30 E
Uroševac, *Yugoslavia* 21 C9 42 23N 21 10 E
Uruaçu, *Brazil* 93 F9 14 30S 49 10W
Uruapan, *Mexico* 86 D4 19 30N 102 0W
Urubamba →, *Peru* 92 F4 10 43S 73 48W
Uruçara, *Brazil* 92 D7 2 20S 57 50W
Uruçuí, *Brazil* 93 E10 7 20S 44 28W
Uruguai →, *Brazil* 95 B5 26 0S 53 30W
Uruguaiana, *Brazil* 94 B4 29 50S 57 0W
Uruguay ■, *S. Amer.* 94 C4 32 30S 56 30W
Uruguay →, *S. Amer.* 94 C4 34 12S 58 18W
Urumchi = Ürümqi, *China* 26 E9 43 45N 87 45 E
Ürümqi, *China* 26 E9 43 45N 87 45 E
Urup, Ostrov, *Russia* 27 E16 46 0N 151 0 E
Usa →, *Russia* 24 A10 66 16N 59 49 E
Uşak, *Turkey* 25 G4 38 43N 29 28 E
Usakos, *Namibia* 56 C2 21 54S 15 31 E
Usedom, *Germany* 16 B8 53 55N 14 2 E
Useless Loop, *Australia* 61 E1 26 8S 113 23 E
Ush-Tobe, *Kazakstan* 26 E8 45 16N 78 0 E
Ushakova, Ostrov, *Russia* 4 A12 82 0N 80 0 E
Ushant = Ouessant, Î. d', *France* 18 B1 48 28N 5 6W
Ushashi, *Tanzania* 54 C3 1 59S 33 57 E
Ushibuka, *Japan* 31 H5 32 11N 130 1 E
Ushuaia, *Argentina* 96 G3 54 50S 68 23W
Ushumun, *Russia* 27 D13 52 47N 126 32 E
Usk, *Canada* 72 C3 54 38N 128 26W
Usk →, *U.K.* 11 F5 51 33N 2 58W
Uska, *India* 43 F10 27 12N 83 7 E
Usman, *Russia* 24 D6 52 5N 39 48 E
Usoke, *Tanzania* 54 D3 5 8S 32 24 E
Usolye Sibirskoye, *Russia* 27 D11 52 48N 103 40 E
Uspallata, P. de, *Argentina* 94 C2 32 37S 69 22W
Uspenskiy, *Kazakstan* 26 E8 48 41N 72 43 E
Ussuri →, *Asia* 30 A7 48 27N 135 0 E
Ussuriysk, *Russia* 27 E14 43 48N 131 59 E
Ussurka, *Russia* 30 B6 45 12N 133 31 E
Ust-Aldan = Batamay, *Russia* 27 C13 63 30N 129 15 E
Ust Amginskoye = Khandyga, *Russia* 27 C14 62 42N 135 35 E
Ust-Bolsheretsk, *Russia* 27 D16 52 50N 156 15 E
Ust Chaun, *Russia* 27 C18 68 47N 170 30 E
Ust Ilimpeya = Yukta, *Russia* 27 C11 63 26N 105 42 E
Ust-Ilimsk, *Russia* 27 D11 58 3N 102 39 E
Ust Ishim, *Russia* 26 D8 57 45N 71 10 E
Ust-Kamchatsk, *Russia* 27 D17 56 10N 162 28 E
Ust-Kamenogorsk = Öskemen, *Kazakstan* 26 E9 50 0N 82 36 E
Ust Khayryuzovo, *Russia* 27 D16 57 15N 156 45 E
Ust-Kut, *Russia* 27 D11 56 50N 105 42 E
Ust Kuyga, *Russia* 27 B14 70 1N 135 43 E
Ust Maya, *Russia* 27 C14 60 30N 134 28 E
Ust-Mil, *Russia* 27 D14 59 40N 133 11 E
Ust-Nera, *Russia* 27 C15 64 35N 143 15 E
Ust-Nyukzha, *Russia* 27 D13 56 34N 121 37 E
Ust Olenek, *Russia* 27 B12 73 0N 120 5 E
Ust-Omchug, *Russia* 27 C15 61 9N 149 38 E
Ust Port, *Russia* 26 C9 69 40N 84 26 E
Ust Tsilma, *Russia* 24 A9 65 28N 52 11 E
Ust Urt = Ustyurt Plateau, *Asia* 26 E6 44 0N 55 0 E
Ust Usa, *Russia* 24 A10 66 2N 56 57 E
Ust Vorkuta, *Russia* 24 A11 67 24N 64 0 E
Ústí nad Labem, *Czech Rep.* 16 C8 50 41N 14 3 E
Ústica, *Italy* 20 E5 38 42N 13 11 E
Ustinov = Izhevsk, *Russia* 24 C9 56 51N 53 14 E
Ustyurt Plateau, *Asia* 26 E6 44 0N 55 0 E
Usu, *China* 32 B3 44 27N 84 40 E
Usuki, *Japan* 31 H5 33 8N 131 49 E
Usulután, *El Salv.* 88 D2 13 25N 88 28W
Usumacinta →, *Mexico* 87 D6 17 0N 91 0W
Usumbura = Bujumbura, *Burundi* 54 C2 3 16S 29 18 E
Usure, *Tanzania* 54 C3 4 40S 34 22 E
Uta, *Indonesia* 37 E9 4 33S 136 0 E
Utah □, *U.S.A.* 82 G8 39 20N 111 30W
Utah L., *U.S.A.* 82 F8 40 10N 111 58W
Utarni, *India* 42 F4 26 5N 71 58 E
Utatlan, *Guatemala* 88 C1 15 2N 91 11W
Ute Creek →, *U.S.A.* 81 H3 35 21N 103 50W
Utena, *Lithuania* 9 J21 55 27N 25 40 E
Utete, *Tanzania* 54 D4 8 0S 38 45 E
Uthai Thani, *Thailand* 38 E3 15 22N 100 3 E
Uthal, *Pakistan* 42 G2 25 44N 66 40 E
Utiariti, *Brazil* 92 F7 13 0S 58 10W
Utica, *N.Y., U.S.A.* 79 C9 43 6N 75 14W
Utica, *Ohio, U.S.A.* 78 F2 40 14N 82 27W
Utikuma L., *Canada* 72 B5 55 50N 115 30W
Utopia, *Australia* 62 C1 22 14S 134 33 E
Utraula, *India* 43 F10 27 19N 82 25 E
Utrecht, *Neths.* 15 B5 52 5N 5 8 E
Utrecht, *S. Africa* 57 D5 27 38S 30 20 E
Utrecht □, *Neths.* 15 B5 52 6N 5 7 E
Utrera, *Spain* 19 D3 37 12N 5 48W
Utsjoki, *Finland* 8 B22 69 51N 26 59 E
Utsunomiya, *Japan* 31 F9 36 30N 139 50 E
Uttar Pradesh □, *India* 43 F9 27 0N 80 0 E
Uttaradit, *Thailand* 38 D3 17 36N 100 5 E
Uttoxeter, *U.K.* 10 E6 52 54N 1 52W
Ummannarsuaq = Farvel, Kap, *Greenland* 4 D5 59 48N 43 55W
Uusikaarlepyy, *Finland* 8 E20 63 32N 22 31 E
Uusikaupunki, *Finland* 9 F19 60 47N 21 25 E
Uva, *Russia* 24 C9 56 59N 52 13 E
Uvalde, *U.S.A.* 81 L5 29 13N 99 47W
Uvat, *Russia* 26 D7 59 5N 68 50 E
Uvinza, *Tanzania* 54 D3 5 5S 30 24 E
Uvira, *Dem. Rep. of the Congo* 54 C2 3 22S 29 3 E
Uvs Nuur, *Mongolia* 32 A4 50 20N 92 30 E
'Uwairidh, Harrat al, *Si. Arabia* 44 E3 26 50N 38 0 E
Uwajima, *Japan* 31 H6 33 10N 132 35 E
Uweinat, Jebel, *Sudan* 51 D10 21 54N 24 58 E
Uxbridge, *Canada* 78 B5 44 6N 79 7W
Uxin Qi, *China* 34 E5 38 50N 109 5 E
Uxmal, *Mexico* 87 C7 20 22N 89 46W
Üydzin, *Mongolia* 34 B4 44 9N 107 0 E
Uyo, *Nigeria* 50 G7 5 1N 7 53 E
Uyûn Mûsa, *Egypt* 47 F1 29 53N 32 40 E
Uyuni, *Bolivia* 92 H5 20 28S 66 47W
Uzbekistan ■, *Asia* 26 E7 41 30N 65 0 E
Uzen, *Kazakstan* 25 F9 43 29N 52 54 E
Uzen, Mal →, *Kazakstan* 25 E8 49 4N 49 44 E
Uzerche, *France* 18 D4 45 25N 1 34 E
Uzh →, *Ukraine* 17 C16 51 15N 30 12 E
Uzhgorod = Uzhhorod, *Ukraine* 17 D12 48 36N 22 18 E
Uzhhorod, *Ukraine* 17 D12 48 36N 22 18 E
Užice, *Serbia, Yug.* 21 C8 43 55N 19 50 E
Uzunköprü, *Turkey* 21 D12 41 16N 26 43 E

V

Vaal →, *S. Africa* 56 D3 29 4S 23 38 E
Vaal Dam, *S. Africa* 57 D4 27 0S 28 14 E
Vaalwater, *S. Africa* 57 C4 24 15S 28 8 E
Vaasa, *Finland* 8 E19 63 6N 21 38 E
Vác, *Hungary* 17 E10 47 49N 19 10 E
Vacaria, *Brazil* 95 B5 28 31S 50 52W
Vacaville, *U.S.A.* 84 G5 38 21N 121 59W
Vach = Vakh →, *Russia* 26 C8 60 45N 76 45 E
Vache, Î. à, *Haiti* 89 C5 18 2N 73 35W
Vadnagar, *India* 42 H5 23 47N 72 40 E
Vadodara, *India* 42 H5 22 20N 73 10 E
Vadsø, *Norway* 8 A23 70 3N 29 50 E
Vaduz, *Liech.* 18 C8 47 8N 9 31 E
Værøy, *Norway* 8 C15 67 40N 12 40 E
Vágar, *Færoe Is.* 8 E9 62 5N 7 15W
Vågsfjorden, *Norway* 8 B17 68 50N 16 50 E
Váh →, *Slovak Rep.* 17 D9 47 43N 18 7 E
Vahsel B., *Antarctica* 5 D1 75 0S 35 0W
Vaï, *Greece* 23 D8 35 15N 26 18 E
Vaigach, *Russia* 26 B6 70 10N 59 0 E
Vail, *U.S.A.* 74 C5 39 40N 106 20W
Vaisali →, *India* 43 F8 26 28N 78 53 E
Vakh →, *Russia* 26 C8 60 45N 76 45 E
Val-d'Or, *Canada* 70 C4 48 7N 77 47W
Val Marie, *Canada* 73 D7 49 15N 107 45W
Valahia, *Romania* 17 F13 44 35N 25 0 E
Valandovo, *Macedonia* 21 D10 41 19N 22 34 E
Valcheta, *Argentina* 96 E3 40 40S 66 8W
Valdayskaya Vozvyshennost, *Russia* 24 C5 57 0N 33 30 E
Valdepeñas, *Spain* 19 C4 38 43N 3 25W
Valdés, Pen., *Argentina* 96 E4 42 30S 63 45W
Valdez, *U.S.A.* 68 B5 61 7N 146 16W
Valdivia, *Chile* 96 D2 39 50S 73 14W
Valdosta, *U.S.A.* 77 K4 30 50N 83 17W
Valdres, *Norway* 9 F13 61 5N 9 5 E
Vale, *U.S.A.* 82 E5 43 59N 117 15W
Vale of Glamorgan □, *U.K.* 11 F4 51 28N 3 25W
Valemount, *Canada* 72 C5 52 50N 119 15W
Valença, *Brazil* 93 F11 13 20S 39 5W
Valença do Piaui, *Brazil* 93 E10 6 20S 41 45W
Valence, *France* 18 D6 44 57N 4 54 E
Valencia, *Spain* 19 C5 39 27N 0 23W
Valencia, *U.S.A.* 83 J10 34 48N 106 43W
Valencia, *Venezuela* 92 A5 10 11N 68 0W
Valencia □, *Spain* 19 C5 39 20N 0 40W
Valencia, G. de, *Spain* 19 C6 39 30N 0 20 E
Valencia de Alcántara, *Spain* 19 C2 39 25N 7 14W
Valencia I., *Ireland* 13 E1 51 54N 10 22W
Valenciennes, *France* 18 A5 50 20N 3 34 E
Valentim, Sa. do, *Brazil* 93 E10 6 0S 43 30W
Valentin, *Russia* 30 C7 43 8N 134 17 E
Valentine, *Nebr., U.S.A.* 74 B6 42 52N 100 33W
Valentine, *Tex., U.S.A.* 81 K2 30 35N 104 30W
Valera, *Venezuela* 92 B4 9 19N 70 37W
Valga, *Estonia* 9 H22 57 47N 26 2 E
Valier, *U.S.A.* 82 B7 48 18N 112 16W
Valjevo, *Serbia, Yug.* 21 B8 44 18N 19 53 E
Valka, *Latvia* 9 H21 57 42N 25 57 E
Valkeakoski, *Finland* 9 F20 61 16N 24 2 E
Valkenswaard, *Neths.* 15 C5 51 21N 5 29 E
Vall de Uxó = La Vall d'Uixó, *Spain* 19 C5 39 49N 0 15W
Valladolid, *Mexico* 87 C7 20 40N 88 11W
Valladolid, *Spain* 19 B3 41 38N 4 43W
Valldemossa, *Spain* 22 B9 39 43N 2 37 E
Valle de la Pascua, *Venezuela* 92 B5 9 13N 66 0W
Valle de las Palmas, *Mexico* 85 N10 32 20N 116 43W
Valle de Santiago, *Mexico* 86 C4 20 25N 101 15W
Valle de Suchil, *Mexico* 86 C4 23 38N 103 55W
Valle de Zaragoza, *Mexico* 86 B3 27 28N 105 49W
Valle Fértil, Sierra del, *Argentina* 94 C2 30 20S 68 0W
Valle Hermoso, *Mexico* 87 B5 25 35N 97 40W
Valledupar, *Colombia* 92 A4 10 29N 73 15W
Vallehermoso, *Canary Is.* 22 F2 28 10N 17 15W
Vallejo, *U.S.A.* 84 G4 38 7N 122 14W
Vallenar, *Chile* 94 B1 28 30S 70 50W
Valletta, *Malta* 23 D2 35 54N 14 31 E
Valley Center, *U.S.A.* 85 M9 33 13N 117 2W
Valley City, *U.S.A.* 80 B6 46 55N 98 0W
Valley Falls, *Oreg., U.S.A.* 82 E3 42 29N 120 17W
Valley Falls, *R.I., U.S.A.* 79 E13 41 54N 71 24W
Valley Springs, *U.S.A.* 84 G6 38 12N 120 50W
Valley View, *U.S.A.* 79 F8 40 39N 76 33W
Valley Wells, *U.S.A.* 85 K11 35 27N 115 46W
Valleyview, *Canada* 72 B5 55 5N 117 17W
Vallimanca, Arroyo, *Argentina* 94 D4 35 40S 59 10W
Valls, *Spain* 19 B6 41 18N 1 15 E
Valmiera, *Latvia* 9 H21 57 37N 25 29 E
Valognes, *France* 18 B3 49 30N 1 28W
Valona = Vlóra, *Albania* 21 D8 40 32N 19 28 E
Valozhyn, *Belarus* 17 A14 54 3N 26 30 E
Valparaíso, *Chile* 94 C1 33 2S 71 40W
Valparaíso, *Mexico* 86 C4 22 50N 103 32W
Valparaiso, *U.S.A.* 76 E2 41 28N 87 4W
Valparaíso □, *Chile* 94 C1 33 2S 71 40W
Vals →, *S. Africa* 56 D4 27 23S 26 30 E
Vals, Tanjung, *Indonesia* 37 F9 8 26S 137 25 E
Valsad, *India* 40 J8 20 40N 72 58 E
Valverde, *Canary Is.* 22 G2 27 48N 17 55W
Valverde del Camino, *Spain* 19 D2 37 35N 6 47W
Vammala, *Finland* 9 F20 61 20N 22 54 E
Vámos, *Greece* 23 D6 35 24N 24 13 E
Van, *Turkey* 25 G7 38 30N 43 20 E
Van, L. = Van Gölü, *Turkey* 25 G7 38 30N 43 0 E
Van Alstyne, *U.S.A.* 81 J6 33 25N 96 35W
Van Blommestein Meer, *Surinam* 93 C7 4 45N 55 5W
Van Buren, *Canada* 71 C6 47 10N 67 55W
Van Buren, *Ark., U.S.A.* 81 H7 35 26N 94 21W
Van Buren, *Maine, U.S.A.* 77 B11 47 10N 67 58W
Van Buren, *Mo., U.S.A.* 81 G9 37 0N 91 1W
Van Canh, *Vietnam* 38 F7 13 37N 109 0 E
Van Diemen, C., *N. Terr., Australia* 60 B5 11 9S 130 24 E
Van Diemen, C., *Queens., Australia* 62 B2 16 30S 139 46 E
Van Diemen G., *Australia* 60 B5 11 45S 132 0 E
Van Gölü, *Turkey* 25 G7 38 30N 43 0 E
Van Horn, *U.S.A.* 81 K2 31 3N 104 50W
Van Ninh, *Vietnam* 38 F7 12 42N 109 14 E
Van Rees, Pegunungan, *Indonesia* 37 E9 2 35S 138 15 E
Van Wert, *U.S.A.* 76 E3 40 52N 84 35W
Vanadzor, *Armenia* 25 F7 40 48N 44 30 E
Vanavara, *Russia* 27 C11 60 22N 102 16 E
Vancouver, *Canada* 72 D4 49 15N 123 10W
Vancouver, *U.S.A.* 84 E4 45 38N 122 40W
Vancouver, C., *Australia* 61 G2 35 2S 118 11 E
Vancouver I., *Canada* 72 D3 49 50N 126 0W
Vandalia, *Ill., U.S.A.* 80 F10 38 58N 89 6W
Vandalia, *Mo., U.S.A.* 80 F9 39 19N 91 29W
Vandenburg, *U.S.A.* 85 L6 34 35N 120 33W
Vanderbijlpark, *S. Africa* 57 D4 26 42S 27 54 E
Vandergrift, *U.S.A.* 78 F5 40 36N 79 34W
Vanderhoof, *Canada* 72 C4 54 0N 124 0W
Vanderkloof Dam, *S. Africa* 56 E3 30 4S 24 40 E
Vanderlin I., *Australia* 62 B2 15 44S 137 2 E
Vänern, *Sweden* 9 G15 58 47N 13 30 E
Vänersborg, *Sweden* 9 G15 58 26N 12 19 E
Vang Vieng, *Laos* 38 C4 18 58N 102 32 E
Vanga, *Kenya* 54 C4 4 35S 39 12 E
Vangaindrano, *Madag.* 57 C8 23 21S 47 36 E
Vanguard, *Canada* 73 D7 49 55N 107 20W
Vanino, *Russia* 27 E15 48 50N 140 5 E
Vanna, *Norway* 8 A18 70 6N 19 50 E
Vännäs, *Sweden* 8 E18 63 58N 19 48 E
Vannes, *France* 18 C2 47 40N 2 47W
Vanrhynsdorp, *S. Africa* 56 E2 31 36S 18 44 E
Vansbro, *Sweden* 9 F16 60 32N 14 15 E
Vansittart B., *Australia* 60 B4 14 3S 126 17 E
Vantaa, *Finland* 9 F21 60 18N 24 58 E
Vanua Levu, *Fiji* 59 C8 16 33S 179 15 E
Vanua Mbalavu, *Fiji* 59 C9 17 40S 178 57W
Vanuatu ■, *Pac. Oc.* 64 J8 15 0S 168 0 E
Vanwyksvlei, *S. Africa* 56 E3 30 18S 21 49 E
Vanzylsrus, *S. Africa* 56 D3 26 52S 22 4 E
Vapnyarka, *Ukraine* 17 D15 48 32N 28 45 E
Varanasi, *India* 43 G10 25 22N 83 0 E
Varanger-halvøya, *Norway* 8 A23 70 25N 29 30 E
Varangerfjorden, *Norway* 8 A23 70 3N 29 25 E
Varaždin, *Croatia* 16 E9 46 20N 16 20 E
Varberg, *Sweden* 9 H15 57 6N 12 20 E
Vardar = Axiós →, *Greece* 21 D10 40 57N 22 35 E
Varde, *Denmark* 9 J13 55 38N 8 29 E
Vardø, *Norway* 8 A24 70 23N 31 5 E
Varella, Mui, *Vietnam* 38 F7 12 54N 109 26 E
Varena, *Lithuania* 9 J21 54 12N 24 30 E
Varese, *Italy* 18 D8 45 48N 8 50 E
Varginha, *Brazil* 95 A6 21 33S 45 25W
Varillas, *Chile* 94 A1 24 0S 70 10W
Varkaus, *Finland* 9 E22 62 19N 27 50 E
Varna, *Bulgaria* 21 C12 43 13N 27 56 E
Värnamo, *Sweden* 9 H16 57 10N 14 3 E
Vars, *Canada* 79 A9 45 21N 75 21W
Varysburg, *U.S.A.* 78 D6 42 46N 78 19W
Varzaneh, *Iran* 45 C7 32 25N 52 40 E
Vasa Barris →, *Brazil* 93 F11 11 10S 37 10W
Vascongadas = País Vasco □, *Spain* 19 A4 42 50N 2 45W
Vasht = Khāsh, *Iran* 40 E2 28 15N 61 15 E
Vasilevichi, *Belarus* 17 B15 52 15N 29 50 E
Vasilkov = Vasylkiv, *Ukraine* 17 C16 50 7N 30 15 E
Vaslui, *Romania* 17 E14 46 38N 27 42 E
Vassar, *Canada* 73 D9 49 10N 95 55W
Vassar, *U.S.A.* 76 D4 43 22N 83 35W
Västerås, *Sweden* 9 G17 59 37N 16 38 E
Västerbotten, *Sweden* 8 D18 64 36N 20 4 E
Västerdalälven →, *Sweden* 9 F16 60 30N 14 7 E
Västervik, *Sweden* 9 H17 57 43N 16 33 E
Västmanland, *Sweden* 9 G16 59 45N 16 20 E
Vasto, *Italy* 20 C6 42 8N 14 40 E
Vasylkiv, *Ukraine* 17 C16 50 7N 30 15 E
Vatersay, *U.K.* 12 E1 56 55N 7 32W
Vatican City ■, *Europe* 20 D5 41 54N 12 27 E
Vatili, *Cyprus* 23 D12 35 6N 33 40 E
Vatnajökull, *Iceland* 8 D5 64 30N 16 48W
Vatoa, *Fiji* 59 D9 19 50S 178 13W
Vatólakkos, *Greece* 23 D5 35 27N 23 53 E
Vatoloha, *Madag.* 57 B8 17 52S 47 48 E
Vatomandry, *Madag.* 57 B8 19 20S 48 59 E
Vatra-Dornei, *Romania* 17 E13 47 22N 25 22 E
Vatrak →, *India* 42 H5 23 9N 73 2 E
Vättern, *Sweden* 9 G16 58 25N 14 30 E
Vaughn, *Mont., U.S.A.* 82 C8 47 33N 111 33W
Vaughn, *N. Mex., U.S.A.* 83 J11 34 36N 105 13W
Vaujours L., *Canada* 70 A5 55 27N 74 15W
Vaupés = Uaupés →, *Brazil* 92 C5 0 2N 67 16W
Vaupes □, *Colombia* 92 C4 1 0N 71 0W
Vauxhall, *Canada* 72 C6 50 5N 112 9W
Vav, *India* 42 G4 24 22N 71 31 E
Vava'u, *Tonga* 59 D12 18 36S 174 0W
Vawkavysk, *Belarus* 17 B13 53 9N 24 30 E
Växjö, *Sweden* 9 H16 56 52N 14 50 E
Vaygach, Ostrov, *Russia* 26 C7 70 0N 60 0 E
Váyia, Ákra, *Greece* 23 C10 36 15N 28 11 E
Vechte →, *Neths.* 15 B6 52 34N 6 6 E
Vedea →, *Romania* 17 G13 43 42N 25 41 E
Vedia, *Argentina* 94 C3 34 30S 61 31W
Veendam, *Neths.* 15 A6 53 5N 6 52 E
Veenendaal, *Neths.* 15 B5 52 2N 5 34 E
Vefsna →, *Norway* 8 D15 65 48N 13 10 E
Vega, *Norway* 8 D14 65 40N 11 55 E
Vega, *U.S.A.* 81 H3 35 15N 102 26W
Vegreville, *Canada* 72 C6 53 30N 112 5W
Vejer de la Frontera, *Spain* 19 D3 36 15N 5 59W
Vejle, *Denmark* 9 J13 55 43N 9 30 E
Velas, C., *Costa Rica* 88 D2 10 21N 85 52W
Velasco, Sierra de, *Argentina* 94 B2 29 20S 67 10W
Velddrif, *S. Africa* 56 E2 32 42S 18 11 E
Velebit Planina, *Croatia* 16 F8 44 50N 15 20 E
Veles, *Macedonia* 21 D9 41 46N 21 47 E
Vélez-Málaga, *Spain* 19 D3 36 48N 4 5W
Vélez Rubio, *Spain* 19 D4 37 41N 2 5W
Velhas →, *Brazil* 93 G10 17 13S 44 49W
Velika Kapela, *Croatia* 16 F8 45 10N 15 5 E
Velikaya →, *Russia* 24 C4 57 48N 28 10 E
Velikaya Kema, *Russia* 30 B8 45 30N 137 12 E
Veliki Ustyug, *Russia* 24 B8 60 47N 46 20 E
Velikiye Luki, *Russia* 24 C5 56 25N 30 32 E
Veliko Tŭrnovo, *Bulgaria* 21 C11 43 5N 25 41 E
Velikonda Range, *India* 40 M11 14 45N 79 10 E
Velletri, *Italy* 20 D5 41 41N 12 47 E
Vellore, *India* 40 N11 12 57N 79 10 E
Velsk, *Russia* 24 B7 61 10N 42 5 E
Velva, *U.S.A.* 80 A4 48 4N 100 56W
Venado Tuerto, *Argentina* 94 C3 33 50S 62 0W
Vendée □, *France* 18 C3 46 50N 1 35W
Vendôme, *France* 18 C4 47 47N 1 3 E
Venézia, *Italy* 20 B5 45 27N 12 21 E
Venézia, G. di, *Italy* 20 B5 45 15N 13 0 E
Venezuela ■, *S. Amer.* 92 B5 8 0N 66 0W
Venezuela, G. de, *Venezuela* 92 A4 11 30N 71 0W
Vengurla, *India* 40 M8 15 53N 73 45 E
Venice = Venézia, *Italy* 20 B5 45 27N 12 21 E
Venice, *U.S.A.* 77 M4 27 6N 82 27W
Venkatapuram, *India* 41 K12 18 20N 80 30 E
Venlo, *Neths.* 15 C6 51 22N 6 11 E
Vennesla, *Norway* 9 G12 58 15N 7 59 E
Venray, *Neths.* 15 C6 51 31N 6 0 E
Ventana, Punta de la, *Mexico* 86 C3 24 4N 109 48W
Ventana, Sa. de la, *Argentina* 94 D3 38 0S 62 30W
Ventersburg, *S. Africa* 56 D4 28 7S 27 9 E
Venterstad, *S. Africa* 56 E4 30 47S 25 48 E
Ventnor, *U.K.* 11 G6 50 36N 1 12W
Ventotène, *Italy* 20 D5 40 47N 13 25 E
Ventoux, Mt., *France* 18 D6 44 10N 5 17 E
Ventspils, *Latvia* 9 H19 57 25N 21 32 E
Ventuari →, *Venezuela* 92 C5 3 58N 67 2W
Ventucopa, *U.S.A.* 85 L7 34 50N 119 29W
Ventura, *U.S.A.* 85 L7 34 17N 119 18W
Venus B., *Australia* 63 F4 38 40S 145 42 E
Vera, *Argentina* 94 B3 29 30S 60 20W
Vera, *Spain* 19 D5 37 15N 1 51W
Veracruz, *Mexico* 87 D5 19 10N 96 10W
Veracruz □, *Mexico* 87 D5 19 0N 96 15W
Veraval, *India* 42 J4 20 53N 70 27 E
Verbánia, *Italy* 18 D8 45 56N 8 33 E
Vercelli, *Italy* 18 D8 45 19N 8 25 E
Verdalsøra, *Norway* 8 E14 63 48N 11 30 E
Verde →, *Argentina* 96 E3 41 56S 65 5W
Verde →, *Goiás, Brazil* 93 G8 18 1S 50 14W
Verde →, *Mato Grosso do Sul, Brazil* 93 H8 21 25S 52 20W
Verde →, *Chihuahua, Mexico* 86 B3 26 29N 107 58W
Verde →, *Oaxaca, Mexico* 87 D5 15 59N 97 50W
Verde →, *Veracruz, Mexico* 86 C4 21 10N 102 50W
Verde →, *Paraguay* 94 A4 23 9S 57 37W
Verde →, *U.S.A.* 74 D4 33 33N 111 40W
Verde, Cay, *Bahamas* 88 B4 23 0N 75 5W
Verden, *Germany* 16 B5 52 55N 9 14 E
Verdi, *U.S.A.* 84 F7 39 31N 119 59W
Verdun, *France* 18 B6 49 9N 5 24 E
Vereeniging, *S. Africa* 57 D4 26 38S 27 57 E
Verga, C., *Guinea* 50 F3 10 30N 14 10W
Vergara, *Uruguay* 95 C5 32 56S 53 57W
Vergemont Cr. →, *Australia* 62 C3 24 16S 143 16 E
Vergennes, *U.S.A.* 79 B11 44 10N 73 15W
Verín, *Spain* 19 B2 41 57N 7 27W
Verkhnevilyuysk, *Russia* 27 C13 63 27N 120 18 E
Verkhniy Baskunchak, *Russia* 25 E8 48 14N 46 44 E
Verkhoyansk, *Russia* 27 C14 67 35N 133 25 E
Verkhoyansk Ra. = Verkhoyanskiy Khrebet, *Russia* 27 C13 66 0N 129 0 E
Verkhoyanskiy Khrebet, *Russia* 27 C13 66 0N 129 0 E
Vermilion, *Canada* 73 C6 53 20N 110 50W
Vermilion, *U.S.A.* 78 E2 41 25N 82 22W
Vermilion →, *Alta., Canada* 73 C6 53 22N 110 51W
Vermilion →, *Qué., Canada* 70 C5 47 38N 72 56W
Vermilion, B., *U.S.A.* 81 L9 29 45N 91 55W
Vermilion Bay, *Canada* 73 D10 49 51N 93 34W
Vermilion L., *U.S.A.* 80 B8 47 53N 92 26W
Vermillion, *U.S.A.* 80 D6 42 47N 96 56W
Vermont □, *U.S.A.* 79 C12 44 0N 73 0W
Vernal, *U.S.A.* 82 F9 40 27N 109 32W
Vernalis, *U.S.A.* 84 H5 37 36N 121 17W
Verner, *Canada* 70 C3 46 25N 80 8W
Verneukpan, *S. Africa* 56 E3 30 0S 21 0 E
Vernon, *Canada* 72 C5 50 20N 119 15W
Vernon, *U.S.A.* 81 H5 34 9N 99 17W
Vernonia, *U.S.A.* 84 E3 45 52N 123 11W
Vero Beach, *U.S.A.* 77 M5 27 38N 80 24W
Véroia, *Greece* 21 D10 40 34N 22 12 E
Verona, *Canada* 79 B8 44 29N 76 42W
Verona, *Italy* 20 B4 45 27N 10 59 E
Verona, *U.S.A.* 80 D10 42 59N 89 32W
Versailles, *France* 18 B5 48 48N 2 8 E
Vert, C., *Senegal* 50 F2 14 45N 17 30W
Verulam, *S. Africa* 57 D5 29 38S 31 2 E
Verviers, *Belgium* 15 D5 50 37N 5 52 E
Veselovskoye Vdkhr., *Russia* 25 E7 46 58N 41 25 E
Vesoul, *France* 18 C7 47 40N 6 11 E
Vesterålen, *Norway* 8 B16 68 45N 15 0 E

Vestfjorden

Vestfjorden, *Norway* **8 C15** 67 55N 14 0 E
Vestmannaeyjar, *Iceland* **8 E3** 63 27N 20 15W
Vestspitsbergen, *Svalbard* **4 B8** 78 40N 17 0 E
Vestvågøy, *Norway* **8 B15** 68 18N 13 50 E
Vesuvio, *Italy* **20 D6** 40 49N 14 26 E
Vesuvius, Mt. = Vesuvio, *Italy* **20 D6** 40 49N 14 26 E
Veszprém, *Hungary* **17 E9** 47 8N 17 57 E
Vetlanda, *Sweden* **9 H16** 57 24N 15 3 E
Vetlugu →, *Russia* **24 C8** 56 36N 46 4 E
Vettore, Mte., *Italy* **20 C5** 42 49N 13 16 E
Veurne, *Belgium* **15 C2** 51 5N 2 40 E
Veys, *Iran* **45 D6** 31 30N 49 0 E
Vezhen, *Bulgaria* **21 C11** 42 50N 24 20 E
Vi Thanh, *Vietnam* **39 H5** 9 42N 105 26 E
Viacha, *Bolivia* **92 G5** 16 39S 68 18W
Viamão, *Brazil* **95 C5** 30 5S 51 0W
Viana, *Brazil* **93 D10** 3 13S 44 55W
Viana do Alentejo, *Portugal* **19 C2** 38 17N 7 59W
Viana do Castelo, *Portugal* **19 B1** 41 42N 8 50W
Vianden, *Lux.* **15 E6** 49 56N 6 12 E
Vianópolis, *Brazil* **93 G9** 16 40S 48 35W
Viaréggio, *Italy* **20 C4** 43 52N 10 14 E
Vibo Valéntia, *Italy* **20 E7** 38 40N 16 6 E
Viborg, *Denmark* **9 H13** 56 27N 9 23 E
Vic, *Spain* **19 B7** 41 58N 2 19 E
Vicenza, *Italy* **20 B4** 45 33N 11 33 E
Vich = Vic, *Spain* **19 B7** 41 58N 2 19 E
Vichada →, *Colombia* **92 C5** 4 55N 67 50W
Vichy, *France* **18 C5** 46 9N 3 26 E
Vicksburg, *Ariz., U.S.A.* **85 M13** 33 45N 113 45W
Vicksburg, *Miss., U.S.A.* **81 J9** 32 21N 90 53W
Victor, *India* **42 J4** 21 0N 71 30 E
Victor, *U.S.A.* **78 D7** 42 58N 77 24W
Victor Harbor, *Australia* **63 F2** 35 30S 138 37 E
Victoria = Labuan, *Malaysia* **36 C5** 5 20N 115 14 E
Victoria, *Argentina* **94 C3** 32 40S 60 10W
Victoria, *Canada* **72 D4** 48 30N 123 25W
Victoria, *Chile* **96 D2** 38 13S 72 20W
Victoria, *Malta* **23 C1** 36 2N 14 14 E
Victoria, *Kans., U.S.A.* **80 F5** 38 52N 99 9W
Victoria, *Tex., U.S.A.* **81 L6** 28 48N 97 0W
Victoria □, *Australia* **63 F3** 37 0S 144 0 E
Victoria →, *Australia* **60 C4** 15 10S 129 40 E
Victoria, Grand L., *Canada* **70 C4** 47 31N 77 30W
Victoria, L., *Africa* **54 C3** 1 0S 33 0 E
Victoria, L., *Australia* **63 E3** 33 57S 141 15 E
Victoria Beach, *Canada* **73 C9** 50 40N 96 35W
Victoria de Durango = Durango, *Mexico* **86 C4** 24 3N 104 39W
Victoria de las Tunas, *Cuba* **88 B4** 20 58N 76 59W
Victoria Falls, *Zimbabwe* **55 F2** 17 58S 25 52 E
Victoria Harbour, *Canada* **78 B5** 44 45N 79 45W
Victoria I., *Canada* **68 A8** 71 0N 111 0W
Victoria L., *Canada* **71 C8** 48 20N 57 27W
Victoria Ld., *Antarctica* **5 D11** 75 0S 160 0 E
Victoria Nile →, *Uganda* **54 B3** 2 14N 31 26 E
Victoria River, *Australia* **60 C5** 16 25S 131 0 E
Victoria Str., *Canada* **68 B9** 69 30N 100 0W
Victoria Taungdeik, *Burma* **41 J18** 21 15N 93 55 E
Victoria West, *S. Africa* **56 E3** 31 25S 23 4 E
Victoriaville, *Canada* **71 C5** 46 4N 71 56W
Victorica, *Argentina* **94 D2** 36 20S 65 30W
Victorville, *U.S.A.* **85 L9** 34 32N 117 18W
Vicuña, *Chile* **94 C1** 30 0S 70 50W
Vicuña Mackenna, *Argentina* **94 C3** 33 53S 64 25W
Vidal, *U.S.A.* **85 L12** 34 7N 114 31W
Vidal Junction, *U.S.A.* **85 L12** 34 11N 114 34W
Vidalia, *U.S.A.* **77 J4** 32 13N 82 25W
Vidho, *Greece* **23 A3** 39 38N 19 55 E
Vidin, *Bulgaria* **21 C10** 43 59N 22 50 E
Vidisha, *India* **42 H7** 23 28N 77 53 E
Vidzy, *Belarus* **9 J22** 55 23N 26 37 E
Viedma, *Argentina* **96 E4** 40 50S 63 0W
Viedma, L., *Argentina* **96 F2** 49 30S 72 30W
Vielsalm, *Belgium* **15 D5** 50 17N 5 54 E
Vienna = Wien, *Austria* **16 D9** 48 12N 16 22 E
Vienna, *Ill., U.S.A.* **81 G10** 37 25N 88 54W
Vienna, *Mo., U.S.A.* **80 F9** 38 11N 91 57W
Vienne, *France* **18 D6** 45 31N 4 53 E
Vienne →, *France* **18 C4** 47 13N 0 5 E
Vientiane, *Laos* **38 D4** 17 58N 102 36 E
Vientos, Paso de los, *Caribbean* **89 C5** 20 0N 74 0W
Vierzon, *France* **18 C5** 47 13N 2 5 E
Vietnam ■, *Asia* **38 C6** 19 0N 106 0 E
Vigan, *Phil.* **37 A6** 17 35N 120 28 E
Vigévano, *Italy* **18 D8** 45 19N 8 51 E
Vigia, *Brazil* **93 D9** 0 50S 48 5W
Vigía Chico, *Mexico* **87 D7** 19 46N 87 35W
Víglas, Ákra, *Greece* **23 D9** 35 54N 27 51 E
Vigo, *Spain* **19 A1** 42 12N 8 41W
Vihowa, *Pakistan* **42 D4** 31 8N 70 30 E
Vihowa →, *Pakistan* **42 D4** 31 8N 70 41 E
Vijayawada, *India* **41 L12** 16 31N 80 39 E
Vik, *Iceland* **8 E4** 63 25N 19 1W
Vikeke, *Indonesia* **37 F7** 8 52S 126 23 E
Viking, *Canada* **72 C6** 53 7N 111 50W
Vikna, *Norway* **8 D14** 64 55N 10 58 E
Vila da Maganja, *Mozam.* **55 F4** 17 18S 37 30 E
Vila de João Belo = Xai-Xai, *Mozam.* **57 D5** 25 6S 33 31 E
Vila do Bispo, *Portugal* **19 D1** 37 5N 8 53W
Vila do Chibuto, *Mozam.* **57 C5** 24 40S 33 33 E
Vila Franca de Xira, *Portugal* **19 C1** 38 57N 8 59W
Vila Gamito, *Mozam.* **55 E3** 14 12S 33 0 E
Vila Gomes da Costa, *Mozam.* **57 C5** 24 20S 33 37 E
Vila Machado, *Mozam.* **55 F3** 19 15S 34 14 E
Vila Mouzinho, *Mozam.* **55 E3** 14 48S 34 25 E
Vila Nova de Gaia, *Portugal* **19 B1** 41 8N 8 37W
Vila Real, *Portugal* **19 B2** 41 17N 7 48W
Vila-real de los Infantes, *Spain* **19 C5** 39 55N 0 3W
Vila Real de Santo António, *Portugal* **19 D2** 37 10N 7 28W
Vila Vasco da Gama, *Mozam.* **55 E3** 14 54S 32 14 E
Vila Velha, *Brazil* **95 A7** 20 20S 40 17W
Vilagarcía de Arousa, *Spain* **19 A1** 42 34N 8 46W
Vilaine →, *France* **18 C2** 47 30N 2 27W
Vilanandro, Tanjona, *Madag.* **57 B7** 16 11S 44 27 E
Vilanculos, *Mozam.* **57 C6** 22 1S 35 17 E
Vilanova i la Geltrú, *Spain* **19 B6** 41 13N 1 40 E
Vileyka, *Belarus* **17 A14** 54 30N 26 53 E
Vilhelmina, *Sweden* **8 D17** 64 35N 16 39 E
Vilhena, *Brazil* **92 F6** 12 40S 60 5W
Viliga, *Russia* **27 C16** 61 36N 156 56 E
Viliya →, *Lithuania* **9 J21** 55 8N 24 16 E
Viljandi, *Estonia* **9 G21** 58 28N 25 30 E
Vilkitskogo, Proliv, *Russia* **27 B11** 78 0N 103 0 E
Vilkovo = Vylkove, *Ukraine* **17 F15** 45 28N 29 32 E
Villa Abecia, *Bolivia* **94 A2** 21 0S 68 18W
Villa Ahumada, *Mexico* **86 A3** 30 38N 106 30W
Villa Ana, *Argentina* **94 B4** 28 28S 59 40W
Villa Ángela, *Argentina* **94 B3** 27 34S 60 45W
Villa Bella, *Bolivia* **92 F5** 10 25S 65 22W
Villa Bens = Tarfaya, *Morocco* **50 C3** 27 55N 12 55W
Villa Cañás, *Argentina* **94 C3** 34 0S 61 35W
Villa Cisneros = Dakhla, *W. Sahara* **50 D2** 23 50N 15 53W
Villa Colón, *Argentina* **94 C2** 31 38S 68 20W
Villa Constitución, *Argentina* **94 C3** 33 15S 60 20W
Villa de María, *Argentina* **94 B3** 29 55S 63 43W
Villa Dolores, *Argentina* **94 C2** 31 58S 65 15W
Villa Frontera, *Mexico* **86 B4** 26 56N 101 27W
Villa Guillermina, *Argentina* **94 B4** 28 15S 59 29W
Villa Hayes, *Paraguay* **94 B4** 25 5S 57 20W
Villa Iris, *Argentina* **94 D3** 38 12S 63 12W
Villa Juárez, *Mexico* **86 B4** 27 37N 100 44W
Villa María, *Argentina* **94 C3** 32 20S 63 10W
Villa Mazán, *Argentina* **94 B2** 28 40S 66 30W
Villa Montes, *Bolivia* **94 A3** 21 10S 63 30W
Villa Ocampo, *Argentina* **94 B4** 28 30S 59 20W
Villa Ocampo, *Mexico* **86 B3** 26 29N 105 30W
Villa Ojo de Agua, *Argentina* **94 B3** 29 30S 63 44W
Villa San José, *Argentina* **94 C4** 32 12S 58 15W
Villa San Martín, *Argentina* **94 B3** 28 15S 64 9W
Villa Unión, *Mexico* **86 C3** 23 12N 106 14W
Villacarlos, *Spain* **22 B11** 39 53N 4 17 E
Villacarrillo, *Spain* **19 C4** 38 7N 3 3W
Villach, *Austria* **16 E7** 46 37N 13 51 E
Villafranca de los Caballeros, *Spain* **22 B10** 39 34N 3 25 E
Villagrán, *Mexico* **87 C5** 24 29N 99 29W
Villaguay, *Argentina* **94 C4** 32 0S 59 0W
Villahermosa, *Mexico* **87 D6** 17 59N 92 55W
Villajoyosa, *Spain* **19 C5** 38 30N 0 12W
Villalba, *Spain* **19 A2** 43 26N 7 40W
Villanueva, *U.S.A.* **81 H2** 35 16N 105 22W
Villanueva de la Serena, *Spain* **19 C3** 38 59N 5 50W
Villanueva y Geltrú = Vilanova i la Geltrú, *Spain* **19 B6** 41 13N 1 40 E
Villarreal = Vila-real de los Infantes, *Spain* **19 C5** 39 55N 0 3W
Villarrica, *Chile* **96 D2** 39 15S 72 15W
Villarrica, *Paraguay* **94 B4** 25 40S 56 30W
Villarrobledo, *Spain* **19 C4** 39 18N 2 36W
Villavicencio, *Argentina* **94 C2** 32 28S 69 0W
Villavicencio, *Colombia* **92 C4** 4 9N 73 37W
Villaviciosa, *Spain* **19 A3** 43 32N 5 27W
Villazón, *Bolivia* **94 A2** 22 0S 65 35W
Ville-Marie, *Canada* **70 C4** 47 20N 79 30W
Ville Platte, *U.S.A.* **81 K8** 30 41N 92 17W
Villena, *Spain* **19 C5** 38 39N 0 52W
Villeneuve-d'Ascq, *France* **18 A5** 50 38N 3 9 E
Villeneuve-sur-Lot, *France* **18 D4** 44 24N 0 42 E
Villiers, *S. Africa* **57 D4** 27 2S 28 36 E
Villingen-Schwenningen, *Germany* **16 D5** 48 3N 8 26 E
Vilna, *Canada* **72 C6** 54 7N 111 55W
Vilnius, *Lithuania* **9 J21** 54 38N 25 19 E
Vilvoorde, *Belgium* **15 D4** 50 56N 4 26 E
Vilyuy →, *Russia* **27 C13** 64 24N 126 26 E
Vilyuysk, *Russia* **27 C13** 63 40N 121 35 E
Viña del Mar, *Chile* **94 C1** 33 0S 71 30W
Vinarós, *Spain* **19 B6** 40 30N 0 27 E
Vincennes, *U.S.A.* **76 F2** 38 41N 87 32W
Vincent, *U.S.A.* **85 L8** 34 33N 118 11W
Vinchina, *Argentina* **94 B2** 28 45S 68 15W
Vindelälven →, *Sweden* **8 E18** 63 55N 19 50 E
Vindeln, *Sweden* **8 D18** 64 12N 19 43 E
Vindhya Ra., *India* **42 H7** 22 50N 77 0 E
Vineland, *U.S.A.* **76 F8** 39 29N 75 2W
Vinh, *Vietnam* **38 C5** 18 45N 105 38 E
Vinh Linh, *Vietnam* **38 D6** 17 4N 107 2 E
Vinh Long, *Vietnam* **39 G5** 10 16N 105 57 E
Vinita, *U.S.A.* **81 G7** 36 39N 95 9W
Vinkovci, *Croatia* **21 B8** 45 19N 18 48 E
Vinnitsa = Vinnytsya, *Ukraine* **17 D15** 49 15N 28 30 E
Vinnytsya, *Ukraine* **17 D15** 49 15N 28 30 E
Vinton, *Calif., U.S.A.* **84 F6** 39 48N 120 10W
Vinton, *Iowa, U.S.A.* **80 D8** 42 10N 92 1W
Vinton, *La., U.S.A.* **81 K8** 30 11N 93 35W
Virac, *Phil.* **37 B6** 13 30N 124 20 E
Virachei, *Cambodia* **38 F6** 13 59N 106 49 E
Virago Sd., *Canada* **72 C2** 54 0N 132 30W
Viramgam, *India* **42 H5** 23 5N 72 0 E
Viranşehir, *Turkey* **44 B3** 37 13N 39 45 E
Virawah, *Pakistan* **42 G4** 24 31N 70 46 E
Virden, *Canada* **73 D8** 49 50N 100 56W
Vire, *France* **18 B3** 48 50N 0 53W
Virgenes, C., *Argentina* **96 G3** 52 19S 68 21W
Virgin →, *U.S.A.* **83 H6** 36 28N 114 21W
Virgin Gorda, *Virgin Is.* **89 C7** 18 30N 64 26W
Virgin Is. (British) ■, *W. Indies* **89 C7** 18 30N 64 30W
Virgin Is. (U.S.) ■, *W. Indies* **89 C7** 18 20N 65 0W
Virginia, *S. Africa* **56 D4** 28 8S 26 55 E
Virginia, *U.S.A.* **80 B8** 47 31N 92 32W
Virginia □, *U.S.A.* **76 G7** 37 30N 78 45W
Virginia Beach, *U.S.A.* **76 G8** 36 51N 75 59W
Virginia City, *Mont., U.S.A.* **82 D8** 45 18N 111 56W
Virginia City, *Nev., U.S.A.* **84 F7** 39 19N 119 39W
Virginia Falls, *Canada* **72 A3** 61 38N 125 42W
Virginiatown, *Canada* **70 C4** 48 9N 79 36W
Viroqua, *U.S.A.* **80 D9** 43 34N 90 53W
Virovitica, *Croatia* **20 B7** 45 51N 17 21 E
Virpur, *India* **42 J4** 21 51N 70 42 E
Virton, *Belgium* **15 E5** 49 35N 5 32 E
Virudunagar, *India* **40 Q10** 9 30N 77 58 E
Vis, *Croatia* **20 C7** 43 4N 16 10 E
Visalia, *U.S.A.* **84 J7** 36 20N 119 18W
Visayan Sea, *Phil.* **37 B6** 11 30N 123 30 E
Visby, *Sweden* **9 H18** 57 37N 18 18 E
Viscount Melville Sd., *Canada* **4 B2** 74 10N 108 0W
Visé, *Belgium* **15 D5** 50 44N 5 41 E
Višegrad, *Bos.-H.* **21 C8** 43 47N 19 17 E
Viseu, *Brazil* **93 D9** 1 10S 46 5W
Viseu, *Portugal* **19 B2** 40 40N 7 55W
Vishakhapatnam, *India* **41 L13** 17 45N 83 20 E
Visnagar, *India* **42 H5** 23 45N 72 32 E
Viso, Mte., *Italy* **18 D7** 44 38N 7 5 E
Visokoi I., *Antarctica* **5 B1** 56 43S 27 15W
Vista, *U.S.A.* **85 M9** 33 12N 117 14W
Vistula = Wisła →, *Poland* **17 A10** 54 22N 18 55 E
Vitebsk = Vitsyebsk, *Belarus* **24 C5** 55 10N 30 15 E
Viterbo, *Italy* **20 C5** 42 25N 12 6 E
Viti Levu, *Fiji* **59 C7** 17 30S 177 30 E
Vitigudino, *Spain* **19 B2** 41 1N 6 26W
Vitim, *Russia* **27 D12** 59 28N 112 35 E
Vitim →, *Russia* **27 D12** 59 26N 112 34 E
Vitória, *Brazil* **93 H10** 20 20S 40 22W
Vitória da Conquista, *Brazil* **93 F10** 14 51S 40 51W
Vitória de São Antão, *Brazil* **93 E11** 8 10S 35 20W
Vitoria-Gasteiz, *Spain* **19 A4** 42 50N 2 41W
Vitsyebsk, *Belarus* **24 C5** 55 10N 30 15 E
Vittória, *Italy* **20 F6** 36 57N 14 32 E
Vittório Véneto, *Italy* **20 B5** 45 59N 12 18 E
Viveiro, *Spain* **19 A2** 43 39N 7 38W
Vivian, *U.S.A.* **81 J8** 32 53N 93 59W
Vizcaíno, Desierto de, *Mexico* **86 B2** 27 40N 113 50W
Vizcaíno, Sierra, *Mexico* **86 B2** 27 30N 114 0W
Vize, *Turkey* **21 D12** 41 34N 27 45 E
Vizianagaram, *India* **41 K13** 18 6N 83 30 E
Vjosa →, *Albania* **21 D8** 40 37N 19 24 E
Vlaardingen, *Neths.* **15 C4** 51 55N 4 21 E
Vladikavkaz, *Russia* **25 F7** 43 0N 44 35 E
Vladimir, *Russia* **24 C7** 56 15N 40 30 E
Vladimir Volynskiy = Volodymyr-Volynskyy, *Ukraine* **17 C13** 50 50N 24 18 E
Vladivostok, *Russia* **27 E14** 43 10N 131 53 E
Vlieland, *Neths.* **15 A4** 53 16N 4 55 E
Vlissingen, *Neths.* **15 C3** 51 26N 3 34 E
Vlóra, *Albania* **21 D8** 40 32N 19 28 E
Vltava →, *Czech Rep.* **16 D8** 50 21N 14 30 E
Vo Dat, *Vietnam* **39 G6** 11 9N 107 31 E
Voe, *U.K.* **12 A7** 60 21N 1 16W
Vogelkop = Doberai, Jazirah, *Indonesia* **37 E8** 1 25S 133 0 E
Vogelsberg, *Germany* **16 C5** 50 31N 9 12 E
Voghera, *Italy* **18 D8** 44 59N 9 1 E
Vohibinany, *Madag.* **57 B8** 18 49S 49 4 E
Vohimarina = Iharana, *Madag.* **57 A9** 13 25S 50 0 E
Vohimena, Tanjon' i, *Madag.* **57 D8** 25 36S 45 8 E
Vohipeno, *Madag.* **57 C8** 22 22S 47 51 E
Voi, *Kenya* **54 C4** 3 25S 38 32 E
Voiron, *France* **18 D6** 45 22N 5 35 E
Voisey B., *Canada* **71 A7** 56 15N 61 50W
Vojmsjön, *Sweden* **8 D17** 64 55N 16 40 E
Vojvodina □, *Serbia, Yug.* **21 B9** 45 20N 20 0 E
Volborg, *U.S.A.* **80 C2** 45 51N 105 41W
Volcano Is. = Kazan-Rettō, *Pac. Oc.* **64 E6** 25 0N 141 0 E
Volda, *Norway* **9 E12** 62 9N 6 5 E
Volga →, *Russia* **25 E8** 46 0N 48 30 E
Volga Hts. = Privolzhskaya Vozvyshennost, *Russia* **25 D8** 51 0N 46 0 E
Volgodonsk, *Russia* **25 E7** 47 33N 42 5 E
Volgograd, *Russia* **25 E7** 48 40N 44 25 E
Volgogradskoye Vdkhr., *Russia* **25 E8** 50 0N 45 20 E
Volkhov →, *Russia* **24 B5** 60 8N 32 20 E
Volkovysk = Vawkavysk, *Belarus* **17 B13** 53 9N 24 30 E
Volksrust, *S. Africa* **57 D4** 27 24S 29 53 E
Volochanka, *Russia* **27 B10** 71 0N 94 28 E
Volodymyr-Volynskyy, *Ukraine* **17 C13** 50 50N 24 18 E
Vologda, *Russia* **24 C6** 59 10N 39 45 E
Vólos, *Greece* **21 E10** 39 24N 22 59 E
Volovets, *Ukraine* **17 D12** 48 43N 23 11 E
Volozhin = Valozhyn, *Belarus* **17 A14** 54 3N 26 30 E
Volsk, *Russia* **24 D8** 52 5N 47 22 E
Volta →, *Ghana* **48 F4** 5 46N 0 41 E
Volta, L., *Ghana* **50 G6** 7 30N 0 0 E
Volta Redonda, *Brazil* **95 A7** 22 31S 44 5W
Voltaire, C., *Australia* **60 B4** 14 16S 125 35 E
Volterra, *Italy* **20 C4** 43 24N 10 51 E
Volturno →, *Italy* **20 D5** 41 1N 13 55 E
Volzhskiy, *Russia* **25 E7** 48 56N 44 46 E
Vondrozo, *Madag.* **57 C8** 22 49S 47 20 E
Vopnafjörður, *Iceland* **8 D6** 65 45N 14 50W
Vóriai Sporádhes, *Greece* **21 E10** 39 15N 23 30 E
Vorkuta, *Russia* **24 A11** 67 48N 64 20 E
Vormsi, *Estonia* **9 G20** 59 1N 23 13 E
Voronezh, *Russia* **25 D6** 51 40N 39 10 E
Voroshilovgrad = Luhansk, *Ukraine* **25 E6** 48 38N 39 15 E
Voroshilovsk = Alchevsk, *Ukraine* **25 E6** 48 30N 38 45 E
Võrts Järv, *Estonia* **9 G22** 58 16N 26 3 E
Võru, *Estonia* **9 H22** 57 48N 26 54 E
Vosges, *France* **18 B7** 48 20N 7 10 E
Voss, *Norway* **9 F12** 60 38N 6 26 E
Vostok I., *Kiribati* **65 J12** 10 5S 152 23W
Votkinsk, *Russia* **24 C9** 57 0N 53 55 E
Votkinskoye Vdkhr., *Russia* **24 C10** 57 22N 55 12 E
Votsuri-Shima, *Japan* **31 M1** 25 45N 123 29 E
Vouga →, *Portugal* **19 B1** 40 41N 8 40W
Voúxa, Ákra, *Greece* **23 D5** 35 37N 23 32 E
Vozhe, Ozero, *Russia* **24 B6** 60 45N 39 0 E
Voznesensk, *Ukraine* **25 E5** 47 35N 31 21 E
Voznesenye, *Russia* **24 B6** 61 0N 35 28 E
Vrangelya, Ostrov, *Russia* **27 B19** 71 0N 180 0 E
Vranje, *Serbia, Yug.* **21 C9** 42 34N 21 54 E
Vratsa, *Bulgaria* **21 C10** 43 15N 23 30 E
Vrbas →, *Bos.-H.* **20 B7** 45 8N 17 29 E
Vrede, *S. Africa* **57 D4** 27 24S 29 6 E
Vredefort, *S. Africa* **56 D4** 27 0S 27 22 E
Vredenburg, *S. Africa* **56 E2** 32 56S 18 0 E
Vredendal, *S. Africa* **56 E2** 31 41S 18 35 E
Vrindavan, *India* **42 F7** 27 37N 77 40 E
Vrises, *Greece* **23 D6** 35 23N 24 13 E
Vršac, *Serbia, Yug.* **21 B9** 45 8N 21 20 E
Vryburg, *S. Africa* **56 D3** 26 55S 24 45 E
Vryheid, *S. Africa* **57 D5** 27 45S 30 47 E
Vu Liet, *Vietnam* **38 C5** 18 43N 105 23 E
Vukovar, *Croatia* **21 B8** 45 21N 18 59 E
Vulcan, *Canada* **72 C6** 50 25N 113 15W
Vulcan, *Romania* **17 F12** 45 23N 23 17 E
Vulcaneşti, *Moldova* **17 F15** 45 41N 28 18 E
Vulcano, *Italy* **20 E6** 38 24N 14 58 E
Vulkaneshty = Vulcaneşti, *Moldova* **17 F15** 45 41N 28 18 E
Vunduzi →, *Mozam.* **55 F3** 18 56S 34 1 E
Vung Tau, *Vietnam* **39 G6** 10 21N 107 4 E
Vyatka = Kirov, *Russia* **24 C8** 58 35N 49 40 E
Vyatka →, *Russia* **24 C9** 55 37N 51 28 E
Vyatskiye Polyany, *Russia* **24 C9** 56 14N 51 5 E
Vyazemskiy, *Russia* **27 E14** 47 32N 134 45 E
Vyazma, *Russia* **24 C5** 55 10N 34 15 E
Vyborg, *Russia* **24 B4** 60 43N 28 47 E
Vychegda →, *Russia* **24 B8** 61 18N 46 36 E
Vychodné Beskydy, *Europe* **17 D11** 49 20N 22 0 E
Vyg-ozero, *Russia* **24 B5** 63 47N 34 29 E
Vylkove, *Ukraine* **17 F15** 45 28N 29 32 E
Vynohradiv, *Ukraine* **17 D12** 48 9N 23 2 E
Vyrnwy, L., *U.K.* **10 E4** 52 48N 3 31W
Vyshniy Volochek, *Russia* **24 C5** 57 30N 34 30 E
Vyškov, *Czech Rep.* **17 D9** 49 17N 17 0 E
Vytegra, *Russia* **24 B6** 61 0N 36 27 E

W

W.A.C. Bennett Dam, *Canada* **72 B4** 56 2N 122 6W
Waal →, *Neths.* **15 C5** 51 37N 5 0 E
Waalwijk, *Neths.* **15 C5** 51 42N 5 4 E
Wabana, *Canada* **71 C9** 47 40N 53 0W
Wabasca →, *Canada* **72 B5** 58 22N 115 20W
Wabasca-Desmarais, *Canada* **72 B6** 55 57N 113 56W
Wabash, *U.S.A.* **76 E3** 40 48N 85 49W
Wabash →, *U.S.A.* **76 G1** 37 48N 88 2W
Wabigoon L., *Canada* **73 D10** 49 44N 92 44W
Wabowden, *Canada* **73 C9** 54 55N 98 38W
Wabuk Pt., *Canada* **70 A2** 55 20N 85 5W
Wabush, *Canada* **71 B6** 52 55N 66 52W
Waco, *U.S.A.* **81 K6** 31 33N 97 9W
Waconichi, L., *Canada* **70 B5** 50 8N 74 0W
Wad Hamid, *Sudan* **51 E12** 16 30N 32 45 E
Wâd Medanî, *Sudan* **51 F12** 14 28N 33 30 E
Wad Thana, *Pakistan* **42 F2** 27 22N 66 23 E
Wadai, *Africa* **48 E5** 12 0N 19 0 E
Wadayama, *Japan* **31 G7** 35 19N 134 52 E
Waddeneilanden, *Neths.* **15 A5** 53 20N 5 10 E
Waddenzee, *Neths.* **15 A5** 53 6N 5 10 E
Waddington, *U.S.A.* **79 B9** 44 52N 75 12W
Waddington, Mt., *Canada* **72 C3** 51 23N 125 15W
Waddy Pt., *Australia* **63 C5** 24 58S 153 21 E
Wadebridge, *U.K.* **11 G3** 50 31N 4 51W
Wadena, *Canada* **73 C8** 51 57N 103 47W
Wadena, *U.S.A.* **80 B7** 46 26N 95 8W
Wadeye, *Australia* **60 B4** 14 28S 129 52 E
Wadhams, *Canada* **72 C3** 51 30N 127 30W
Wādī as Sīr, *Jordan* **47 D4** 31 56N 35 49 E
Wadi Halfa, *Sudan* **51 D12** 21 53N 31 19 E
Wadsworth, *Nev., U.S.A.* **82 G4** 39 38N 119 17W
Wadsworth, *Ohio, U.S.A.* **78 E3** 41 2N 81 44W
Waegwan, *S. Korea* **35 G15** 35 59N 128 23 E
Wafangdian, *China* **35 E11** 39 38N 121 58 E
Wafrah, *Si. Arabia* **44 D5** 28 33N 47 56 E
Wageningen, *Neths.* **15 C5** 51 58N 5 40 E
Wager B., *Canada* **69 B11** 65 26N 88 40W
Wagga Wagga, *Australia* **63 F4** 35 7S 147 24 E
Waghete, *Indonesia* **37 E9** 4 10S 135 50 E
Wagin, *Australia* **61 F2** 33 17S 117 25 E
Wagner, *U.S.A.* **80 D5** 43 5N 98 18W
Wagon Mound, *U.S.A.* **81 G2** 36 1N 104 42W
Wagoner, *U.S.A.* **81 H7** 35 58N 95 22W
Wah, *Pakistan* **42 C5** 33 45N 72 40 E
Wahai, *Indonesia* **37 E7** 2 48S 129 35 E
Wahiawa, *U.S.A.* **74 H15** 21 30N 158 2W
Wâḥid, *Egypt* **47 E1** 30 48N 32 21 E
Wahnai, *Afghan.* **42 C1** 32 40N 65 50 E
Wahoo, *U.S.A.* **80 E6** 41 13N 96 37W
Wahpeton, *U.S.A.* **80 B6** 46 16N 96 36W
Wai, Koh, *Cambodia* **39 H4** 9 55N 102 55 E
Waiau →, *N.Z.* **59 K4** 42 47S 173 22 E
Waibeem, *Indonesia* **37 E8** 0 30S 132 59 E
Waigeo, *Indonesia* **37 E8** 0 20S 130 40 E
Waihi, *N.Z.* **59 G5** 37 23S 175 52 E
Waihou →, *N.Z.* **59 G5** 37 15S 175 40 E
Waika, *Dem. Rep. of the Congo* **54 C2** 2 22S 25 42 E
Waikabubak, *Indonesia* **37 F5** 9 45S 119 25 E
Waikari, *N.Z.* **59 K4** 42 58S 172 41 E
Waikato →, *N.Z.* **59 G5** 37 23S 174 43 E
Waikerie, *Australia* **63 E3** 34 9S 140 0 E
Waikokopu, *N.Z.* **59 H6** 39 3S 177 52 E
Waikouaiti, *N.Z.* **59 L3** 45 36S 170 41 E
Wailuku, *U.S.A.* **74 H16** 20 53N 156 30W
Waimakariri →, *N.Z.* **59 K4** 43 24S 172 42 E
Waimate, *N.Z.* **59 L3** 44 45S 171 3 E
Wainganga →, *India* **40 K11** 18 50N 79 55 E
Waingapu, *Indonesia* **37 F6** 9 35S 120 11 E
Waini →, *Guyana* **92 B7** 8 20N 59 50W
Wainwright, *Canada* **73 C6** 52 50N 110 50W
Waiouru, *N.Z.* **59 H5** 39 28S 175 41 E
Waipara, *N.Z.* **59 K4** 43 3S 172 46 E
Waipawa, *N.Z.* **59 H6** 39 56S 176 38 E
Waipiro, *N.Z.* **59 H7** 38 2S 178 22 E
Waipu, *N.Z.* **59 F5** 35 59S 174 29 E
Waipukurau, *N.Z.* **59 J6** 40 1S 176 33 E
Wairakei, *N.Z.* **59 H6** 38 37S 176 6 E
Wairarapa, L., *N.Z.* **59 J5** 41 14S 175 15 E
Wairoa, *N.Z.* **59 H6** 39 3S 177 25 E
Waitaki →, *N.Z.* **59 L3** 44 56S 171 7 E
Waitara, *N.Z.* **59 H5** 38 59S 174 15 E
Waitsburg, *U.S.A.* **82 C5** 46 16N 118 9W
Waiuku, *N.Z.* **59 G5** 37 15S 174 45 E
Wajima, *Japan* **31 F8** 37 30N 137 0 E
Wajir, *Kenya* **54 B5** 1 42N 40 5 E
Wakasa, *Japan* **31 G7** 35 20N 134 24 E
Wakasa-Wan, *Japan* **31 G7** 35 40N 135 30 E
Wakatipu, L., *N.Z.* **59 L2** 45 5S 168 33 E
Wakaw, *Canada* **73 C7** 52 39N 105 44W
Wakayama, *Japan* **31 G7** 34 15N 135 15 E
Wakayama □, *Japan* **31 H7** 33 50N 135 30 E
Wake Forest, *U.S.A.* **77 H6** 35 59N 78 30W

West Ice Shelf

Wake I., Pac. Oc. 64 F8 19 18N 166 36 E
WaKeeney, U.S.A. 80 F5 39 1N 99 53W
Wakefield, N.Z. 59 J4 41 24S 173 5 E
Wakefield, U.K. 10 D6 53 41N 1 29W
Wakefield, Mass., U.S.A. 79 D13 42 30N 71 4W
Wakefield, Mich., U.S.A. 80 B10 46 29N 89 56W
Wakema, Burma 41 L19 16 30N 95 11 E
Wakkanai, Japan 30 B10 45 28N 141 35 E
Wakkerstroom, S. Africa 57 D5 27 24S 30 10 E
Wakool, Australia 63 F3 35 28S 144 23 E
Wakool →, Australia 63 F3 35 5S 143 33 E
Wakre, Indonesia 37 E8 0 19S 131 5 E
Wakuach, L., Canada 71 A6 55 34N 67 32W
Walamba, Zambia 55 E2 13 30S 28 42 E
Wałbrzych, Poland 16 C9 50 45N 16 18 E
Walbury Hill, U.K. 11 F6 51 21N 1 28W
Walcha, Australia 63 E5 30 55S 151 31 E
Walcheren, Neths. 15 C3 51 30N 3 35 E
Walcott, U.S.A. 82 F10 41 46N 106 51W
Wałcz, Poland 16 B9 53 17N 16 27 E
Waldburg Ra., Australia 61 D2 24 40S 117 35 E
Walden, Colo., U.S.A. 82 F10 40 44N 106 17W
Walden, N.Y., U.S.A. 79 E10 41 34N 74 11W
Waldport, U.S.A. 82 D1 44 26N 124 4W
Waldron, U.S.A. 81 H7 34 54N 94 5W
Walebing, Australia 61 F2 30 41S 116 13 E
Wales □, U.K. 11 E3 52 19N 4 43W
Walgett, Australia 63 E4 30 0S 148 5 E
Walgreen Coast, Antarctica 5 D15 75 15S 105 0W
Walker, U.S.A. 80 B7 47 6N 94 35W
Walker, L., Canada 71 B6 50 20N 67 11W
Walker L., Canada 73 C9 54 42N 95 57W
Walker L., U.S.A. 82 G4 38 42N 118 43W
Walkerston, Australia 62 C4 21 11S 149 8 E
Walkerton, Canada 78 B3 44 10N 81 10W
Wall, U.S.A. 80 D3 44 0N 102 8W
Walla Walla, U.S.A. 82 C4 46 4N 118 20W
Wallace, Idaho, U.S.A. 82 C6 47 28N 115 56W
Wallace, N.C., U.S.A. 77 H7 34 44N 77 59W
Wallaceburg, Canada 78 D2 42 34N 82 23W
Wallachia = Valahia, Romania 17 F13 44 35N 25 0 E
Wallal, Australia 63 D4 26 32S 146 7 E
Wallam Cr. →, Australia 63 D4 28 40S 147 20 E
Wallambin, L., Australia 61 F2 30 57S 117 35 E
Wallan, Australia 63 F3 37 26S 144 59 E
Wallangarra, Australia 63 D5 28 56S 151 58 E
Wallaroo, Australia 63 E2 33 56S 137 39 E
Wallenpaupack, L., U.S.A. 79 E9 41 25N 75 15W
Wallingford, U.S.A. 79 E12 41 27N 72 50W
Wallis & Futuna, Is., Pac. Oc. 64 J10 13 18S 176 10W
Wallowa, U.S.A. 82 D5 45 34N 117 32W
Wallowa Mts., U.S.A. 82 D5 45 20N 117 30W
Walls, U.K. 12 A7 60 14N 1 33W
Wallula, U.S.A. 82 C4 46 5N 118 54W
Wallumbilla, Australia 63 D4 26 33S 149 9 E
Walmsley, L., Canada 73 A7 63 25N 108 36W
Walney, I. of, U.K. 10 C4 54 6N 3 15W
Walnut Creek, U.S.A. 84 H4 37 54N 122 4W
Walnut Ridge, U.S.A. 81 G9 36 4N 90 57W
Walpole, Australia 61 F2 34 58S 116 44 E
Walpole, U.S.A. 79 D13 42 9N 71 15W
Walsall, U.K. 11 E6 52 35N 1 58W
Walsenburg, U.S.A. 81 G2 37 38N 104 47W
Walsh, U.S.A. 81 G3 37 23N 102 17W
Walsh →, Australia 62 B3 16 31S 143 42 E
Walterboro, U.S.A. 77 J5 32 55N 80 40W
Walters, U.S.A. 81 H5 34 22N 98 19W
Waltham, U.S.A. 79 D13 42 23N 71 14W
Waltman, U.S.A. 82 E10 43 4N 107 12W
Walton, U.S.A. 79 D9 42 10N 75 8W
Walton-on-the-Naze, U.K. 11 F9 51 51N 1 17 E
Walvis Bay, Namibia 56 C1 23 0S 14 28 E
Walvisbaai = Walvis Bay, Namibia 56 C1 23 0S 14 28 E
Wamba, Dem. Rep. of the Congo 54 B2 2 10N 27 57 E
Wamba, Kenya 54 B4 0 58N 37 19 E
Wamego, U.S.A. 80 F6 39 12N 96 18W
Wamena, Indonesia 37 E9 4 4S 138 57 E
Wamsutter, U.S.A. 82 F9 41 40N 107 58W
Wamulan, Indonesia 37 E7 3 27S 126 7 E
Wan Xian, China 34 E8 38 47N 115 7 E
Wana, Pakistan 42 C3 32 20N 69 32 E
Wanaaring, Australia 63 D3 29 38S 144 9 E
Wanaka, N.Z. 59 L2 44 42S 169 9 E
Wanaka L., N.Z. 59 L2 44 33S 169 7 E
Wanapitei L., Canada 70 C3 46 45N 80 40W
Wandel Sea = McKinley Sea, Arctic 4 A7 82 0N 0 0 E
Wanderer, Zimbabwe 55 F3 19 36S 30 1 E
Wandhari, Pakistan 42 F2 27 42N 66 48 E
Wandoan, Australia 63 D4 26 5S 149 55 E
Wanfu, China 35 D12 40 8N 122 38 E
Wang →, Thailand 38 D2 17 8N 99 2 E
Wang Noi, Thailand 38 E3 14 13N 100 44 E
Wang Saphung, Thailand 38 D3 17 18N 101 46 E
Wang Thong, Thailand 38 D3 16 50N 100 26 E
Wanga, Dem. Rep. of the Congo 54 B2 2 58N 29 12 E
Wangal, Indonesia 37 F8 6 8S 134 9 E
Wanganella, Australia 63 F3 35 6S 144 49 E
Wanganui, N.Z. 59 H5 39 56S 175 3 E
Wangaratta, Australia 63 F4 36 21S 146 19 E
Wangary, Australia 63 E2 34 35S 135 29 E
Wangdu, China 34 E8 38 40N 115 7 E
Wangerooge, Germany 16 B4 53 47N 7 54 E
Wangi, Kenya 54 C5 1 58S 40 58 E
Wangiwangi, Indonesia 37 F6 5 22S 123 37 E
Wangqing, China 35 C15 43 12N 129 42 E
Wankaner, India 42 H4 22 35N 71 0 E
Wanless, Canada 73 C8 54 11N 101 21W
Wanning, Taiwan 38 C8 23 15N 121 17 E
Wanon Niwat, Thailand 38 D4 17 38N 103 46 E
Wanquan, China 34 D8 40 50N 114 40 E
Wanrong, China 34 G6 35 25N 110 50 E
Wantage, U.K. 11 F6 51 35N 1 25W
Wanxian, China 33 C5 30 42N 108 20 E
Wapakoneta, U.S.A. 76 E3 40 34N 84 12W
Wapato, U.S.A. 82 C3 46 27N 120 25W
Wapawekka L., Canada 73 C8 54 55N 104 40W
Wapikopa L., Canada 70 B2 52 56N 87 53W
Wapiti →, Canada 72 B5 55 5N 118 18W
Wappingers Falls, U.S.A. 79 E11 41 36N 73 55W
Wapsipinicon →, U.S.A. 80 E9 41 44N 90 19W
Warangal, India 40 L11 17 58N 79 35 E
Waraseoni, India 43 J9 21 45N 80 2 E
Waratah, Australia 62 G4 41 30S 145 30 E
Waratah B., Australia 63 F4 38 54S 146 5 E
Warburton, Vic., Australia 63 F4 37 47S 145 42 E
Warburton, W. Austral., Australia 61 E4 26 8S 126 35 E
Warburton Ra., Australia 61 E4 25 55S 126 28 E
Ward, N.Z. 59 J5 41 49S 174 11 E
Ward →, Australia 63 D4 26 28S 146 6 E
Ward Mt., U.S.A. 84 H8 37 12N 118 54W
Warden, S. Africa 57 D4 27 50S 29 0 E
Wardha, India 40 J11 20 45N 78 39 E
Wardha →, India 40 K11 19 57N 79 11 E
Ware, Canada 72 B3 57 26N 125 41W
Ware, U.S.A. 79 D12 42 16N 72 14W
Waregem, Belgium 15 D3 50 53N 3 27 E
Wareham, U.S.A. 79 E14 41 46N 70 43W
Waremme, Belgium 15 D5 50 43N 5 15 E
Warialda, Australia 63 D5 29 29S 150 33 E
Wariap, Indonesia 37 E8 1 30S 134 5 E
Warin Chamrap, Thailand 38 E5 15 12N 104 53 E
Warkopi, Indonesia 37 E8 1 12S 134 9 E
Warm Springs, U.S.A. 83 G5 38 10N 116 20W
Warman, Canada 73 C7 52 19N 106 30W
Warmbad, Namibia 56 D2 28 25S 18 42 E
Warmbad, S. Africa 57 C4 24 51S 28 19 E
Warminster, U.K. 11 F5 51 12N 2 10W
Warminster, U.S.A. 79 F9 40 12N 75 6W
Warner Mts., U.S.A. 82 F3 41 40N 120 15W
Warner Robins, U.S.A. 77 J4 32 37N 83 36W
Waroona, Australia 61 F2 32 50S 115 58 E
Warracknabeal, Australia 63 F3 36 9S 142 26 E
Warragul, Australia 63 F4 38 10S 145 58 E
Warrego →, Australia 63 E4 30 24S 145 21 E
Warrego Ra., Australia 62 C4 24 58S 146 0 E
Warren, Australia 63 E4 31 42S 147 51 E
Warren, Ark., U.S.A. 81 J8 33 37N 92 4W
Warren, Mich., U.S.A. 76 D4 42 30N 83 0W
Warren, Minn., U.S.A. 80 A6 48 12N 96 46W
Warren, Ohio, U.S.A. 78 E4 41 14N 80 49W
Warren, Pa., U.S.A. 78 E5 41 51N 79 9W
Warrenpoint, U.K. 13 B5 54 6N 6 15W
Warrensburg, Mo., U.S.A. 80 F8 38 46N 93 44W
Warrensburg, N.Y., U.S.A. 79 C11 43 29N 73 46W
Warrenton, S. Africa 56 D3 28 9S 24 47 E
Warrenton, U.S.A. 84 D3 46 10N 123 56W
Warri, Nigeria 50 G7 5 30N 5 41 E
Warrina, Australia 63 D2 28 12S 135 50 E
Warrington, U.K. 10 D5 53 24N 2 35W
Warrington, U.S.A. 77 K2 30 23N 87 17W
Warrington □, U.K. 10 D5 53 24N 2 35W
Warrnambool, Australia 63 F3 38 25S 142 30 E
Warroad, U.S.A. 80 A7 48 54N 95 19W
Warruwi, Australia 62 A1 11 36S 133 20 E
Warsa, Indonesia 37 E9 0 47S 135 55 E
Warsak Dam, Pakistan 42 B4 34 11N 71 19 E
Warsaw = Warszawa, Poland 17 B11 52 13N 21 0 E
Warsaw, Ind., U.S.A. 76 E3 41 14N 85 51W
Warsaw, N.Y., U.S.A. 78 D6 42 45N 78 8W
Warsaw, Ohio, U.S.A. 78 F3 40 20N 82 0W
Warszawa, Poland 17 B11 52 13N 21 0 E
Warta →, Poland 16 B8 52 35N 14 39 E
Warthe = Warta →, Poland 16 B8 52 35N 14 39 E
Waru, Indonesia 37 E8 3 30S 130 36 E
Warwick, Australia 63 D5 28 10S 152 1 E
Warwick, U.K. 11 E6 52 18N 1 35W
Warwick, N.Y., U.S.A. 79 E10 41 16N 74 22W
Warwick, R.I., U.S.A. 79 E13 41 42N 71 28W
Warwickshire □, U.K. 11 E6 52 14N 1 38W
Wasaga Beach, Canada 78 B4 44 31N 80 1W
Wasagaming, Canada 73 C9 50 39N 99 58W
Wasatch Ra., U.S.A. 82 F8 40 30N 111 15W
Wasbank, S. Africa 57 D5 28 15S 30 9 E
Wasco, Calif., U.S.A. 85 K7 35 36N 119 20W
Wasco, Oreg., U.S.A. 82 D3 45 36N 120 42W
Waseca, U.S.A. 80 C8 44 5N 93 30W
Wasekamio L., Canada 73 B7 56 45N 108 45W
Wash, The, U.K. 10 E8 52 58N 0 20 E
Washago, Canada 78 B5 44 45N 79 20W
Washburn, N. Dak., U.S.A. 80 B4 47 17N 101 2W
Washburn, Wis., U.S.A. 80 B9 46 40N 90 54W
Washim, India 40 J10 20 3N 77 0 E
Washington, U.K. 10 C6 54 55N 1 30W
Washington, D.C., U.S.A. 76 F7 38 54N 77 2W
Washington, Ga., U.S.A. 77 J4 33 44N 82 44W
Washington, Ind., U.S.A. 76 F2 38 40N 87 10W
Washington, Iowa, U.S.A. 80 E9 41 18N 91 42W
Washington, Mo., U.S.A. 80 F9 38 33N 91 1W
Washington, N.C., U.S.A. 77 H7 35 33N 77 3W
Washington, N.J., U.S.A. 79 F10 40 46N 74 59W
Washington, Pa., U.S.A. 78 F4 40 10N 80 15W
Washington, Utah, U.S.A. 83 H7 37 8N 113 31W
Washington □, U.S.A. 82 C3 47 30N 120 30W
Washington, Mt., U.S.A. 79 B13 44 16N 71 18W
Washington Court House, U.S.A. 76 F4 39 32N 83 26W
Washington I., U.S.A. 76 C2 45 23N 86 54W
Washougal, U.S.A. 84 E4 45 35N 122 21W
Wasian, Indonesia 37 E8 1 47S 133 19 E
Wasilla, U.S.A. 68 B5 61 35N 149 26W
Wasior, Indonesia 37 E8 2 43S 134 30 E
Waskaganish, Canada 70 B4 51 30N 78 40W
Waskaiowaka, L., Canada 73 B9 56 33N 96 23W
Waskesiu Lake, Canada 73 C7 53 55N 106 5W
Wasserkuppe, Germany 16 C5 50 29N 9 55 E
Waswanipi, Canada 70 C4 49 40N 76 29W
Waswanipi, L., Canada 70 C4 49 35N 76 40W
Watampone, Indonesia 37 E6 4 29S 120 25 E
Water Park Pt., Australia 62 C5 22 56S 150 47 E
Water Valley, U.S.A. 81 H10 34 10N 89 38W
Waterberge, S. Africa 57 C4 24 10S 28 0 E
Waterbury, Conn., U.S.A. 79 E11 41 33N 73 3W
Waterbury, Vt., U.S.A. 79 B12 44 20N 72 46W
Waterbury L., Canada 73 B8 58 10N 104 22W
Waterdown, Canada 78 C5 43 20N 79 53W
Waterford, Canada 78 D4 42 56N 80 17W
Waterford, Ireland 13 D4 52 15N 7 8W
Waterford, Calif., U.S.A. 84 H6 37 38N 120 46W
Waterford, Pa., U.S.A. 78 E5 41 57N 79 59W
Waterford □, Ireland 13 D4 52 10N 7 40W
Waterford Harbour, Ireland 13 D5 52 8N 6 58W
Waterhen L., Canada 73 C9 52 10N 99 40W
Waterloo, Belgium 15 D4 50 43N 4 25 E
Waterloo, Ont., Canada 78 C4 43 30N 80 32W
Waterloo, Qué., Canada 79 A12 45 22N 72 32W
Waterloo, Ill., U.S.A. 80 F9 38 20N 90 9W
Waterloo, Iowa, U.S.A. 80 D8 42 30N 92 21W
Waterloo, N.Y., U.S.A. 78 D8 42 54N 76 52W
Watersmeet, U.S.A. 80 B10 46 16N 89 11W
Waterton Nat. Park, U.S.A. 82 B7 48 45N 115 0W
Watertown, Conn., U.S.A. 79 E11 41 36N 73 7W
Watertown, N.Y., U.S.A. 79 C9 43 59N 75 55W
Watertown, S. Dak., U.S.A. 80 C6 44 54N 97 7W
Watertown, Wis., U.S.A. 80 D10 43 12N 88 43W
Waterval-Boven, S. Africa 57 D5 25 40S 30 18 E
Waterville, Canada 79 A13 45 16N 71 54W
Waterville, Maine, U.S.A. 77 C11 44 33N 69 38W
Waterville, N.Y., U.S.A. 79 D9 42 56N 75 23W
Waterville, Pa., U.S.A. 78 E7 41 19N 77 21W
Waterville, Wash., U.S.A. 82 C3 47 39N 120 4W
Watervliet, U.S.A. 79 D11 42 44N 73 42W
Wates, Indonesia 37 G14 7 51S 110 10 E
Watford, Canada 78 D3 42 57N 81 53W
Watford, U.K. 11 F7 51 40N 0 24W
Watford City, U.S.A. 80 B3 47 48N 103 17W
Wathaman →, Canada 73 B8 57 16N 102 59W
Wathaman L., Canada 73 B8 56 58N 103 44W
Watheroo, Australia 61 F2 30 15S 116 0 E
Wating, China 34 G4 35 40N 106 38 E
Watkins Glen, U.S.A. 78 D8 42 23N 76 52W
Watling I. = San Salvador I., Bahamas 89 B5 24 0N 74 40W
Watonga, U.S.A. 81 H5 35 51N 98 25W
Watrous, Canada 73 C7 51 40N 105 25W
Watrous, U.S.A. 81 H2 35 48N 104 59W
Watsa, Dem. Rep. of the Congo 54 B2 3 4N 29 30 E
Watseka, U.S.A. 76 E2 40 47N 87 44W
Watson, Australia 61 F5 30 29S 131 31 E
Watson, Canada 73 C8 52 10N 104 30W
Watson Lake, Canada 72 A3 60 6N 128 49W
Watsontown, U.S.A. 78 E8 41 5N 76 52W
Watsonville, U.S.A. 84 J5 36 55N 121 45W
Wattiwarriganna Cr. →, Australia 63 D2 28 57S 136 10 E
Watuata = Batuata, Indonesia 37 F6 6 12S 122 42 E
Watubela, Kepulauan, Indonesia 37 E8 4 28S 131 35 E
Watubela Is. = Watubela, Kepulauan, Indonesia 37 E8 4 28S 131 35 E
Wau, Sudan 49 F6 7 45N 28 1 E
Waubamik, Canada 78 A4 45 27N 80 1W
Waubay, U.S.A. 80 C6 45 20N 97 18W
Wauchope, N.S.W., Australia 63 E5 31 28S 152 45 E
Wauchope, N. Terr., Australia 62 C1 20 36S 134 15 E
Waukarlycarly, L., Australia 60 D3 21 18S 121 56 E
Waukegan, U.S.A. 75 B9 42 22N 87 50W
Waukesha, U.S.A. 76 D1 43 1N 88 14W
Waukon, U.S.A. 80 D9 43 16N 91 29W
Waupaca, U.S.A. 80 C10 44 21N 89 5W
Waupun, U.S.A. 80 D10 43 38N 88 44W
Waurika, U.S.A. 81 H6 34 10N 98 0W
Wausau, U.S.A. 80 C10 44 58N 89 38W
Wautoma, U.S.A. 80 C10 44 4N 89 18W
Wauwatosa, U.S.A. 76 D2 43 3N 88 0W
Waveney →, U.K. 11 E9 52 35N 1 39 E
Waverley, N.Z. 59 H5 39 46S 174 37 E
Waverly, Iowa, U.S.A. 80 D8 42 44N 92 29W
Waverly, N.Y., U.S.A. 79 E8 42 1N 76 32W
Wavre, Belgium 15 D4 50 43N 4 38 E
Wâw, Sudan 51 G11 7 45N 28 1 E
Wāw al Kabīr, Libya 51 C9 25 20N 16 43 E
Wawa, Canada 70 C3 47 59N 84 47W
Wawanesa, Canada 73 D9 49 36N 99 40W
Wawona, U.S.A. 84 H7 37 32N 119 39W
Waxahachie, U.S.A. 81 J6 32 24N 96 51W
Way, L., Australia 61 E3 26 45S 120 16 E
Waycross, U.S.A. 77 K4 31 13N 82 21W
Wayland, U.S.A. 78 D7 42 34N 77 35W
Wayne, Nebr., U.S.A. 80 D6 42 14N 97 1W
Wayne, W. Va., U.S.A. 76 F4 38 13N 82 27W
Waynesboro, Ga., U.S.A. 77 J4 33 6N 82 1W
Waynesboro, Miss., U.S.A. 77 K1 31 40N 88 39W
Waynesboro, Pa., U.S.A. 76 F7 39 45N 77 35W
Waynesboro, Va., U.S.A. 76 F6 38 4N 78 53W
Waynesburg, U.S.A. 76 F5 39 54N 80 11W
Waynesville, U.S.A. 77 H4 35 28N 82 58W
Waynoka, U.S.A. 81 G5 36 35N 98 53W
Wazirabad, Pakistan 42 C6 32 30N 74 8 E
We, Indonesia 36 C1 5 51N 95 18 E
Weald, The, U.K. 11 F8 51 4N 0 20 E
Wear →, U.K. 10 C6 54 55N 1 23W
Weatherford, Okla., U.S.A. 81 H5 35 32N 98 43W
Weatherford, Tex., U.S.A. 81 J6 32 46N 97 48W
Weaverville, U.S.A. 82 F2 40 44N 122 56W
Webb City, U.S.A. 81 G7 37 9N 94 28W
Webequie, Canada 70 B2 52 59N 87 21W
Webster, Mass., U.S.A. 79 D13 42 3N 71 53W
Webster, N.Y., U.S.A. 78 C7 43 13N 77 26W
Webster, S. Dak., U.S.A. 80 C6 45 20N 97 31W
Webster City, U.S.A. 80 D8 42 28N 93 49W
Webster Springs, U.S.A. 76 F5 38 29N 80 25W
Weda, Indonesia 37 D7 0 21N 127 50 E
Weda, Teluk, Indonesia 37 D7 0 30N 127 50 E
Weddell I., Falk. Is. 96 G4 51 50S 61 0W
Weddell Sea, Antarctica 5 D1 72 30S 40 0W
Wedderburn, Australia 63 F3 36 26S 143 33 E
Wedgeport, Canada 71 D6 43 44N 65 59W
Wedza, Zimbabwe 55 F3 18 40S 31 33 E
Wee Waa, Australia 63 E4 30 11S 149 26 E
Weed, U.S.A. 82 F2 41 25N 122 23W
Weed Heights, U.S.A. 84 G7 38 59N 119 13W
Weedsport, U.S.A. 79 C8 43 3N 76 35W
Weedville, U.S.A. 78 E6 41 17N 78 30W
Weenen, S. Africa 57 D5 28 48S 30 7 E
Weert, Neths. 15 C5 51 15N 5 43 E
Wei He →, Hebei, China 34 F8 36 10N 115 45 E
Wei He →, Shaanxi, China 34 G6 34 38N 110 15 E
Weichang, China 35 D9 41 58N 117 49 E
Weichuan, China 34 G7 34 20N 113 59 E
Weiden, Germany 16 D7 49 41N 12 10 E
Weifang, China 35 F10 36 44N 119 7 E
Weihai, China 35 F12 37 30N 122 6 E
Weimar, Germany 16 C6 50 58N 11 19 E
Weinan, China 34 G5 34 31N 109 29 E
Weipa, Australia 62 A3 12 40S 141 50 E
Weir →, Australia 63 D4 28 20S 149 50 E
Weir →, Canada 73 B10 56 54N 93 21W
Weir River, Canada 73 B10 56 49N 94 6W
Weirton, U.S.A. 78 F4 40 24N 80 35W
Weiser, U.S.A. 82 D5 44 10N 117 0W
Weishan, China 35 G9 34 47N 117 5 E
Weiyuan, China 34 G3 35 7N 104 10 E
Wejherowo, Poland 17 A10 54 35N 18 12 E
Wekusko L., Canada 73 C9 54 40N 99 50W
Welch, U.S.A. 76 G5 37 26N 81 35W
Welkom, S. Africa 56 D4 28 0S 26 46 E
Welland, Canada 78 D5 43 0N 79 15W
Welland →, U.K. 11 E7 52 51N 0 5W
Wellesley Is., Australia 62 B2 16 42S 139 30 E
Wellingborough, U.K. 11 E7 52 19N 0 41W
Wellington, Australia 63 E4 32 35S 148 59 E
Wellington, Canada 78 C7 43 57N 77 20W
Wellington, N.Z. 59 J5 41 19S 174 46 E
Wellington, S. Africa 56 E2 33 38S 19 1 E
Wellington, Somst., U.K. 11 G4 50 58N 3 13W
Wellington, Telford & Wrekin, U.K. 11 E5 52 42N 2 30W
Wellington, Colo., U.S.A. 80 E2 40 42N 105 0W
Wellington, Kans., U.S.A. 81 G6 37 16N 97 24W
Wellington, Nev., U.S.A. 84 G7 38 45N 119 23W
Wellington, Ohio, U.S.A. 78 E2 41 10N 82 13W
Wellington, Tex., U.S.A. 81 H4 34 51N 100 13W
Wellington, I., Chile 96 F2 49 30S 75 0W
Wellington, L., Australia 63 F4 38 6S 147 20 E
Wells, U.K. 11 F5 51 13N 2 39W
Wells, Maine, U.S.A. 79 C14 43 20N 70 35W
Wells, N.Y., U.S.A. 79 C10 43 24N 74 17W
Wells, Nev., U.S.A. 82 F6 41 7N 114 58W
Wells, L., Australia 61 E3 26 44S 123 15 E
Wells, Mt., Australia 60 C4 17 25S 127 8 E
Wells Gray Prov. Park, Canada 72 C4 52 30N 120 15W
Wells-next-the-Sea, U.K. 10 E8 52 57N 0 51 E
Wells River, U.S.A. 79 B12 44 9N 72 4W
Wellsboro, U.S.A. 78 E7 41 45N 77 18W
Wellsburg, U.S.A. 78 F4 40 16N 80 37W
Wellsville, N.Y., U.S.A. 78 D7 42 7N 77 57W
Wellsville, Ohio, U.S.A. 78 F4 40 36N 80 39W
Wellsville, Utah, U.S.A. 82 F8 41 38N 111 56W
Wellton, U.S.A. 83 K6 32 40N 114 8W
Wels, Austria 16 D8 48 9N 14 1 E
Welshpool, U.K. 11 E4 52 39N 3 8W
Welwyn Garden City, U.K. 11 F7 51 48N 0 12W
Wem, U.K. 10 E5 52 52N 2 44W
Wembere →, Tanzania 54 C3 4 10S 34 15 E
Wemindji, Canada 70 B4 53 0N 78 49W
Wen Xian, China 34 G7 34 55N 113 5 E
Wenatchee, U.S.A. 82 C3 47 25N 120 19W
Wenchang, China 38 C8 19 38N 110 42 E
Wenchi, Ghana 50 G5 7 46N 2 8W
Wenchow = Wenzhou, China 33 D7 28 0N 120 38 E
Wenden, U.S.A. 85 M13 33 49N 113 33W
Wendeng, China 35 F12 37 15N 122 5 E
Wendesi, Indonesia 37 E8 2 30S 134 17 E
Wendover, U.S.A. 82 F6 40 44N 114 2W
Wenlock →, Australia 62 A3 12 2S 141 55 E
Wenshan, China 32 D5 23 20N 104 18 E
Wenshang, China 34 G9 35 45N 116 30 E
Wenshui, China 34 F7 37 26N 112 1 E
Wensleydale, U.K. 10 C6 54 17N 2 0W
Wensu, China 32 B3 41 15N 80 10 E
Wensum →, U.K. 10 E8 52 40N 1 15 E
Wentworth, Australia 63 E3 34 2S 141 54 E
Wentzel L., Canada 72 B6 59 2N 114 28W
Wenut, Indonesia 37 E8 3 11S 133 19 E
Wenxi, China 34 G6 35 20N 111 10 E
Wenxian, China 34 H3 32 43N 104 36 E
Wenzhou, China 33 D7 28 0N 120 38 E
Weott, U.S.A. 82 F2 40 20N 123 55W
Wepener, S. Africa 56 D4 29 42S 27 3 E
Werda, Botswana 56 D3 25 24S 23 15 E
Weri, Indonesia 37 E8 3 10S 132 38 E
Werra →, Germany 16 C5 51 24N 9 39 E
Werrimull, Australia 63 E3 34 25S 141 38 E
Werris Creek, Australia 63 E5 31 18S 150 38 E
Weser →, Germany 16 B5 53 36N 8 28 E
Wesiri, Indonesia 37 F7 7 30S 126 30 E
Weslemkoon L., Canada 78 A7 45 2N 77 25W
Wesleyville, Canada 71 C9 49 8N 53 36W
Wesleyville, U.S.A. 78 D4 42 9N 80 0W
Wessel, C., Australia 62 A2 10 59S 136 46 E
Wessel Is., Australia 62 A2 11 10S 136 45 E
Wessington Springs, U.S.A. 80 C5 44 5N 98 34W
West, U.S.A. 81 K6 31 48N 97 6W
West →, U.S.A. 79 D12 42 52N 72 33W
West Baines →, Australia 60 C4 15 38S 129 59 E
West Bank □, Asia 47 C4 32 6N 35 13 E
West Bend, U.S.A. 76 D1 43 25N 88 11W
West Bengal □, India 43 H13 23 0N 88 0 E
West Berkshire □, U.K. 11 F6 51 25N 1 17W
West Beskids = Západné Beskydy, Europe 17 D10 49 30N 19 0 E
West Branch, U.S.A. 76 C3 44 17N 84 14W
West Branch Susquehanna →, U.S.A. 79 F8 40 53N 76 48W
West Bromwich, U.K. 11 E6 52 32N 1 59W
West Burra, U.K. 12 A7 60 5N 1 21W
West Canada Cr. →, U.S.A. 79 C10 43 1N 74 58W
West Cape Howe, Australia 61 G2 35 8S 117 36 E
West Chazy, U.S.A. 79 B11 44 49N 73 28W
West Chester, U.S.A. 79 G9 39 58N 75 36W
West Columbia, U.S.A. 81 L7 29 9N 95 39W
West Covina, U.S.A. 85 L9 34 4N 117 54W
West Des Moines, U.S.A. 80 E8 41 35N 93 43W
West Dunbartonshire □, U.K. 12 F4 55 59N 4 30W
West End, Bahamas 88 A4 26 41N 78 58W
West Falkland, Falk. Is. 96 G5 51 40S 60 0W
West Fargo, U.S.A. 80 B6 46 52N 96 54W
West Farmington, U.S.A. 78 E4 41 23N 80 58W
West Fjord = Vestfjorden, Norway 8 C15 67 55N 14 0 E
West Fork Trinity →, U.S.A. 81 J6 32 48N 96 54W
West Frankfort, U.S.A. 80 G10 37 54N 88 55W
West Hartford, U.S.A. 79 E12 41 45N 72 44W
West Haven, U.S.A. 79 E12 41 17N 72 57W
West Hazleton, U.S.A. 79 F9 40 58N 76 0W
West Helena, U.S.A. 81 H9 34 33N 90 38W
West Hurley, U.S.A. 79 E10 41 59N 74 7W
West Ice Shelf, Antarctica 5 C7 67 0S 85 0 E

West Indies

West Indies, *Cent. Amer.* **89 D7** 15 0N 65 0W
West Jordan, *U.S.A.* **82 F8** 40 36N 111 56W
West Lorne, *Canada* **78 D3** 42 36N 81 36W
West Lothian □, *U.K.* **12 F5** 55 54N 3 36W
West Lunga →, *Zambia* **55 E1** 13 6S 24 39 E
West Memphis, *U.S.A.* **81 H9** 35 9N 90 11W
West Midlands □, *U.K.* **11 E6** 52 26N 2 0W
West Mifflin, *U.S.A.* **78 F5** 40 22N 79 52W
West Milton, *U.S.A.* **78 E8** 41 1N 76 50W
West Monroe, *U.S.A.* **81 J8** 32 31N 92 9W
West Newton, *U.S.A.* **78 F5** 40 14N 79 46W
West Nicholson, *Zimbabwe* **55 G2** 21 2S 29 20 E
West Palm Beach, *U.S.A.* **77 M5** 26 43N 80 3W
West Plains, *U.S.A.* **81 G9** 36 44N 91 51W
West Point, *N.Y., U.S.A.* **79 E11** 41 24N 73 58W
West Point, *Nebr., U.S.A.* **80 E6** 41 51N 96 43W
West Point, *Va., U.S.A.* **76 G7** 37 32N 76 48W
West Pt. = Ouest, Pte. de l', *Canada* **71 C7** 49 52N 64 40W
West Pt., *Australia* **63 F2** 35 1S 135 56 E
West Road →, *Canada* **72 C4** 53 18N 122 53W
West Rutland, *U.S.A.* **75 B12** 43 38N 73 5W
West Schelde = Westerschelde →, *Neths.* **15 C3** 51 25N 3 25 E
West Seneca, *U.S.A.* **78 D6** 42 51N 78 48W
West Siberian Plain, *Russia* **28 C11** 62 0N 75 0 E
West Sussex □, *U.K.* **11 G7** 50 55N 0 30W
West-Terschelling, *Neths.* **15 A5** 53 22N 5 13 E
West Valley City, *U.S.A.* **82 F8** 40 42N 111 57W
West Virginia □, *U.S.A.* **76 F5** 38 45N 80 30W
West-Vlaanderen □, *Belgium* **15 D2** 51 0N 3 0 E
West Walker →, *U.S.A.* **84 G7** 38 54N 119 9W
West Wyalong, *Australia* **63 E4** 33 56S 147 10 E
West Yellowstone, *U.S.A.* **82 D8** 44 40N 111 6W
West Yorkshire □, *U.K.* **10 D6** 53 45N 1 40W
Westall Pt., *Australia* **63 E1** 32 55S 134 4 E
Westbrook, *U.S.A.* **77 D10** 43 41N 70 22W
Westbury, *Australia* **62 G4** 41 30S 146 51 E
Westby, *U.S.A.* **80 A2** 48 52N 104 3W
Westend, *U.S.A.* **85 K9** 35 42N 117 24W
Westerland, *Germany* **9 J13** 54 54N 8 17 E
Westerly, *U.S.A.* **79 E13** 41 22N 71 50W
Western □, *Kenya* **54 B3** 0 30N 34 30 E
Western □, *Uganda* **54 B3** 1 45N 31 30 E
Western □, *Zambia* **55 F1** 15 15S 24 30 E
Western Australia □, *Australia* **61 E2** 25 0S 118 0 E
Western Cape □, *S. Africa* **56 E3** 34 0S 20 0 E
Western Dvina = Daugava →, *Latvia* **9 H21** 57 4N 24 3 E
Western Ghats, *India* **40 N9** 14 0N 75 0 E
Western Isles □, *U.K.* **12 D1** 57 30N 7 10W
Western Sahara ■, *Africa* **50 D3** 25 0N 13 0W
Western Samoa ■, *Pac. Oc.* **59 B13** 14 0S 172 0W
Westernport, *U.S.A.* **76 F6** 39 29N 79 3W
Westerschelde →, *Neths.* **15 C3** 51 25N 3 25 E
Westerwald, *Germany* **16 C4** 50 38N 7 56 E
Westfield, *Mass., U.S.A.* **79 D12** 42 7N 72 45W
Westfield, *N.Y., U.S.A.* **78 D5** 42 20N 79 35W
Westfield, *Pa., U.S.A.* **78 E7** 41 55N 77 32W
Westhill, *U.K.* **12 D6** 57 9N 2 19W
Westhope, *U.S.A.* **80 A4** 48 55N 101 1W
Westland Bight, *N.Z.* **59 K3** 42 55S 170 5 E
Westlock, *Canada* **72 C6** 54 9N 113 55W
Westmar, *Australia* **63 D4** 27 55S 149 44 E
Westmeath □, *Ireland* **13 C4** 53 33N 7 34W
Westminster, *U.S.A.* **76 F7** 39 34N 76 59W
Westmont, *U.S.A.* **78 F6** 40 19N 78 58W
Westmorland, *U.S.A.* **85 M11** 33 2N 115 37W
Weston, *Oreg., U.S.A.* **82 D4** 45 49N 118 26W
Weston, *W. Va., U.S.A.* **76 F5** 39 2N 80 28W
Weston I., *Canada* **70 B4** 52 33N 79 36W
Weston-super-Mare, *U.K.* **11 F5** 51 21N 2 58W
Westover, *U.S.A.* **78 F6** 40 45N 78 40W
Westport, *Canada* **79 B8** 44 40N 76 25W
Westport, *Ireland* **13 C2** 53 48N 9 31W
Westport, *N.Z.* **59 J3** 41 46S 171 37 E
Westport, *N.Y., U.S.A.* **79 B11** 44 11N 73 26W
Westport, *Oreg., U.S.A.* **84 D3** 46 8N 123 23W
Westport, *Wash., U.S.A.* **84 D2** 46 53N 124 6W
Westray, *Canada* **73 C8** 53 36N 101 24W
Westray, *U.K.* **12 B5** 59 18N 3 0W
Westree, *Canada* **70 C3** 47 26N 81 34W
Westville, *U.S.A.* **84 F6** 39 8N 120 42W
Westwood, *U.S.A.* **82 F3** 40 18N 121 0W
Wetar, *Indonesia* **37 F7** 7 30S 126 30 E
Wetaskiwin, *Canada* **72 C6** 52 55N 113 24W
Wete, *Tanzania* **52 F7** 5 4S 39 43 E
Wetherby, *U.K.* **10 D6** 53 56N 1 23W
Wethersfield, *U.S.A.* **79 E12** 41 42N 72 40W
Wetteren, *Belgium* **15 D3** 51 0N 3 53 E
Wetzlar, *Germany* **16 C5** 50 32N 8 31 E
Wewoka, *U.S.A.* **81 H6** 35 9N 96 30W
Wexford, *Ireland* **13 D5** 52 20N 6 28W
Wexford □, *Ireland* **13 D5** 52 20N 6 25W
Wexford Harbour, *Ireland* **13 D5** 52 20N 6 25W
Weyburn, *Canada* **73 D8** 49 40N 103 50W
Weymouth, *Canada* **71 D6** 44 30N 66 1W
Weymouth, *U.K.* **11 G5** 50 37N 2 28W
Weymouth, *U.S.A.* **79 D14** 42 13N 70 58W
Weymouth, C., *Australia* **62 A3** 12 37S 143 27 E
Wha Ti, *Canada* **68 B8** 63 8N 117 16W
Whakatane, *N.Z.* **59 G6** 37 57S 177 1 E
Whale →, *Canada* **71 A6** 58 15N 67 40W
Whale Cove, *Canada* **73 A10** 62 11N 92 36W
Whales, B. of, *Antarctica* **5 D12** 78 0S 165 0W
Whalsay, *U.K.* **12 A8** 60 22N 0 59W
Whangamomona, *N.Z.* **59 H5** 39 8S 174 44 E
Whangarei, *N.Z.* **59 F5** 35 43S 174 21 E
Whangarei Harb., *N.Z.* **59 F5** 35 45S 174 28 E
Wharfe →, *U.K.* **10 D6** 53 51N 1 9W
Wharfedale, *U.K.* **10 C5** 54 6N 2 1W
Wharton, *N.J., U.S.A.* **79 F10** 40 54N 74 35W
Wharton, *Pa., U.S.A.* **78 E6** 41 31N 78 1W
Wharton, *Tex., U.S.A.* **81 L6** 29 19N 96 6W
Wheatland, *Calif., U.S.A.* **84 F5** 39 1N 121 25W
Wheatland, *Wyo., U.S.A.* **80 D2** 42 3N 104 58W
Wheatley, *Ont., Canada* **78 D2** 42 6N 82 27W
Wheatley, *Ont., Canada* **78 D2** 42 6N 82 27W
Wheaton, *Md., U.S.A.* **76 F7** 39 3N 77 3W
Wheaton, *Minn., U.S.A.* **80 C6** 45 48N 96 30W
Wheelbarrow Pk., *U.S.A.* **84 H10** 37 26N 116 5W
Wheeler, *Oreg., U.S.A.* **82 D2** 45 41N 123 53W
Wheeler, *Tex., U.S.A.* **81 H4** 35 27N 100 16W
Wheeler →, *Canada* **71 A6** 57 2N 67 13W
Wheeler L., *U.S.A.* **77 H2** 34 48N 87 23W
Wheeler Pk., *N. Mex., U.S.A.* **83 H11** 36 34N 105 25W
Wheeler Pk., *Nev., U.S.A.* **83 G6** 38 57N 114 15W
Wheeler Ridge, *U.S.A.* **85 L8** 35 0N 118 57W
Wheeling, *U.S.A.* **78 F4** 40 4N 80 43W
Whernside, *U.K.* **10 C5** 54 14N 2 24W
Whiskey Jack L., *Canada* **73 B8** 58 23N 101 55W
Whistleduck Cr. →, *Australia* **62 C2** 20 15S 135 18 E
Whistler, *Canada* **72 C4** 50 7N 122 58W
Whitby, *Canada* **78 C6** 43 52N 78 56W
Whitby, *U.K.* **10 C7** 54 29N 0 37W
White →, *Ark., U.S.A.* **81 J9** 33 57N 91 5W
White →, *Ind., U.S.A.* **76 F2** 38 25N 87 45W
White →, *S. Dak., U.S.A.* **80 D5** 43 42N 99 27W
White →, *Tex., U.S.A.* **81 J4** 33 14N 100 56W
White →, *Utah, U.S.A.* **82 F9** 40 4N 109 41W
White →, *Vt., U.S.A.* **79 C12** 43 37N 72 20W
White →, *Wash., U.S.A.* **84 C4** 47 12N 122 15W
White, L., *Australia* **60 D4** 21 9S 128 56 E
White B., *Canada* **71 C8** 50 0N 56 35W
White Bird, *U.S.A.* **82 D5** 45 46N 116 18W
White Butte, *U.S.A.* **80 B3** 46 23N 103 18W
White City, *U.S.A.* **82 E2** 42 26N 122 51W
White Cliffs, *Australia* **63 E3** 30 50S 143 10 E
White Hall, *U.S.A.* **80 F9** 39 26N 90 24W
White Haven, *U.S.A.* **79 E9** 41 4N 75 47W
White Horse, Vale of, *U.K.* **11 F6** 51 37N 1 30W
White I., *N.Z.* **59 G6** 37 30S 177 13 E
White L., *Canada* **79 A8** 45 18N 76 31W
White L., *U.S.A.* **81 L8** 29 44N 92 30W
White Mountain Peak, *U.S.A.* **83 G4** 37 38N 118 15W
White Mts., *Calif., U.S.A.* **84 H8** 37 30N 118 15W
White Mts., *N.H., U.S.A.* **75 B12** 44 15N 71 15W
White Mts., *N.H., U.S.A.* **76 C10** 44 10N 71 20W
White Nile = Nîl el Abyad →, *Sudan* **51 E12** 15 38N 32 31 E
White Otter L., *Canada* **70 C1** 49 5N 91 55W
White Pass, *U.S.A.* **84 D5** 46 38N 121 24W
White Plains, *U.S.A.* **79 E11** 41 2N 73 46W
White River, *Canada* **70 C2** 48 35N 85 20W
White River, *S. Africa* **57 D5** 25 20S 31 0 E
White River, *U.S.A.* **80 D4** 43 34N 100 45W
White Rock, *Canada* **84 A4** 49 2N 122 48W
White Russia = Belarus ■, *Europe* **17 B14** 53 30N 27 0 E
White Sea = Beloye More, *Russia* **24 A6** 66 30N 38 0 E
White Sulphur Springs, *Mont., U.S.A.* **82 C8** 46 33N 110 54W
White Sulphur Springs, *W. Va., U.S.A.* **76 G5** 37 48N 80 18W
White Swan, *U.S.A.* **84 D6** 46 23N 120 44W
Whitecliffs, *N.Z.* **59 K3** 43 26S 171 55 E
Whitecourt, *Canada* **72 C5** 54 10N 115 45W
Whiteface Mt., *U.S.A.* **79 B11** 44 22N 73 54W
Whitefield, *U.S.A.* **79 B13** 44 23N 71 37W
Whitefish, *U.S.A.* **82 B6** 48 25N 114 20W
Whitefish L., *Canada* **73 A7** 62 41N 106 48W
Whitefish Point, *U.S.A.* **76 B3** 46 45N 84 59W
Whitegull, L., *Canada* **71 A7** 55 27N 64 17W
Whitehall, *Mich., U.S.A.* **76 D2** 43 24N 86 21W
Whitehall, *Mont., U.S.A.* **82 D7** 45 52N 112 6W
Whitehall, *N.Y., U.S.A.* **79 C11** 43 33N 73 24W
Whitehall, *Wis., U.S.A.* **80 C9** 44 22N 91 19W
Whitehaven, *U.K.* **10 C4** 54 33N 3 35W
Whitehorse, *Canada* **72 A1** 60 43N 135 3W
Whitemark, *Australia* **62 G4** 40 7S 148 3 E
Whiteriver, *U.S.A.* **83 K9** 33 50N 109 58W
Whitesand →, *Canada* **72 A5** 60 9N 115 45W
Whitesboro, *N.Y., U.S.A.* **79 C9** 43 7N 75 18W
Whitesboro, *Tex., U.S.A.* **81 J6** 33 39N 96 54W
Whiteshell Prov. Park, *Canada* **73 D9** 50 0N 95 40W
Whitesville, *U.S.A.* **78 D7** 42 2N 77 46W
Whiteville, *U.S.A.* **77 H6** 34 20N 78 42W
Whitewater, *U.S.A.* **76 D1** 42 50N 88 44W
Whitewater Baldy, *U.S.A.* **83 K9** 33 20N 108 39W
Whitewater L., *Canada* **70 B2** 50 50N 89 10W
Whitewood, *Australia* **62 C3** 21 28S 143 30 E
Whitewood, *Canada* **73 C8** 50 20N 102 20W
Whithorn, *U.K.* **12 G4** 54 44N 4 26W
Whitianga, *N.Z.* **59 G5** 36 47S 175 41 E
Whitman, *U.S.A.* **79 D14** 42 5N 70 56W
Whitney, *Canada* **78 A6** 45 31N 78 14W
Whitney, Mt., *U.S.A.* **84 J8** 36 35N 118 18W
Whitney Point, *U.S.A.* **79 D9** 42 20N 75 58W
Whitstable, *U.K.* **11 F9** 51 21N 1 3 E
Whitsunday I., *Australia* **62 C4** 20 15S 149 4 E
Whittier, *U.S.A.* **85 M8** 33 58N 118 3W
Whittlesea, *Australia* **63 F4** 37 27S 145 9 E
Wholdaia L., *Canada* **73 A8** 60 43N 104 20W
Whyalla, *Australia* **63 E2** 33 2S 137 30 E
Wiarton, *Canada* **78 B3** 44 40N 81 10W
Wiay, *U.K.* **12 D1** 57 24N 7 13W
Wibaux, *U.S.A.* **80 B2** 46 59N 104 11W
Wichian Buri, *Thailand* **38 E3** 15 39N 101 7 E
Wichita, *U.S.A.* **81 G6** 37 42N 97 20W
Wichita Falls, *U.S.A.* **81 J5** 33 54N 98 30W
Wick, *U.K.* **12 C5** 58 26N 3 5W
Wicked Pt., *Canada* **78 C7** 43 52N 77 15W
Wickenburg, *U.S.A.* **83 K7** 33 58N 112 44W
Wickepin, *Australia* **61 F2** 32 50S 117 30 E
Wickham, *Australia* **60 D2** 20 42S 117 11 E
Wickham, C., *Australia* **62 F3** 39 35S 143 57 E
Wickliffe, *U.S.A.* **78 E3** 41 36N 81 28W
Wicklow, *Ireland* **13 D5** 52 59N 6 3W
Wicklow □, *Ireland* **13 D5** 52 57N 6 25W
Wicklow Hd., *Ireland* **13 D6** 52 58N 6 0W
Wicklow Mts., *Ireland* **13 C5** 52 58N 6 26W
Widgeegoara Cr. →, *Australia* **63 D4** 28 51S 146 34 E
Widgiemooltha, *Australia* **61 F3** 31 30S 121 34 E
Widnes, *U.K.* **10 D5** 53 23N 2 45W
Wieluń, *Poland* **17 C10** 51 15N 18 34 E
Wien, *Austria* **16 D9** 48 12N 16 22 E
Wiener Neustadt, *Austria* **16 E9** 47 49N 16 16 E
Wiesbaden, *Germany* **16 C5** 50 4N 8 14 E
Wigan, *U.K.* **10 D5** 53 33N 2 38W
Wiggins, *Colo., U.S.A.* **80 E2** 40 14N 104 4W
Wiggins, *Miss., U.S.A.* **81 K10** 30 51N 89 8W
Wight, I. of □, *U.K.* **11 G6** 50 40N 1 20W
Wigston, *U.K.* **11 E6** 52 35N 1 6W
Wigton, *U.K.* **10 C4** 54 50N 3 10W
Wigtown, *U.K.* **12 G4** 54 53N 4 27W
Wigtown B., *U.K.* **12 G4** 54 46N 4 15W
Wilber, *U.S.A.* **80 E6** 40 29N 96 58W
Wilberforce, *Canada* **78 A6** 45 2N 78 13W
Wilberforce, C., *Australia* **62 A2** 11 54S 136 35 E
Wilburton, *U.S.A.* **81 H7** 34 55N 95 19W
Wilcannia, *Australia* **63 E3** 31 30S 143 26 E
Wilcox, *U.S.A.* **78 E6** 41 35N 78 41W
Wildrose, *U.S.A.* **85 J9** 36 14N 117 11W
Wildspitze, *Austria* **16 E6** 46 53N 10 53 E
Wilge →, *S. Africa* **57 D4** 27 3S 28 20 E
Wilhelm II Coast, *Antarctica* **5 C7** 68 0S 90 0 E
Wilhelmshaven, *Germany* **16 B5** 53 31N 8 7 E
Wilhelmstal, *Namibia* **56 C2** 21 58S 16 21 E
Wilkes-Barre, *U.S.A.* **79 E9** 41 15N 75 53W
Wilkie, *Canada* **73 C7** 52 27N 108 42W
Wilkinsburg, *U.S.A.* **78 F5** 40 26N 79 53W
Wilkinson Lakes, *Australia* **61 E5** 29 40S 132 39 E
Willandra Creek →, *Australia* **63 E4** 33 22S 145 52 E
Willapa B., *U.S.A.* **82 C2** 46 40N 124 0W
Willapa Hills, *U.S.A.* **84 D3** 46 35N 123 25W
Willard, *N.Y., U.S.A.* **78 D8** 42 40N 76 50W
Willard, *Ohio, U.S.A.* **78 E2** 41 3N 82 44W
Willcox, *U.S.A.* **83 K9** 32 15N 109 50W
Willemstad, *Neth. Ant.* **89 D6** 12 5N 69 0W
Willet, *U.S.A.* **79 D9** 42 28N 75 55W
William →, *Canada* **73 B7** 59 8N 109 19W
William 'Bill' Dannely Res., *U.S.A.* **77 J2** 32 10N 87 10W
William Creek, *Australia* **63 D2** 28 58S 136 22 E
Williams, *Australia* **61 F2** 33 2S 116 52 E
Williams, *Ariz., U.S.A.* **83 J7** 35 15N 112 11W
Williams, *Calif., U.S.A.* **84 F4** 39 9N 122 9W
Williams Harbour, *Canada* **71 B8** 52 33N 55 47W
Williams Lake, *Canada* **72 C4** 52 10N 122 10W
Williamsburg, *Ky., U.S.A.* **77 G3** 36 44N 84 10W
Williamsburg, *Pa., U.S.A.* **78 F6** 40 28N 78 12W
Williamsburg, *Va., U.S.A.* **76 G7** 37 17N 76 44W
Williamson, *N.Y., U.S.A.* **78 C7** 43 14N 77 11W
Williamson, *W. Va., U.S.A.* **76 G4** 37 41N 82 17W
Williamsport, *U.S.A.* **78 E7** 41 15N 77 0W
Williamston, *U.S.A.* **77 H7** 35 51N 77 4W
Williamstown, *Australia* **63 F3** 37 51S 144 52 E
Williamstown, *Ky., U.S.A.* **76 F3** 38 38N 84 34W
Williamstown, *Mass., U.S.A.* **79 D11** 42 41N 73 12W
Williamstown, *N.Y., U.S.A.* **79 C9** 43 26N 75 53W
Willimantic, *U.S.A.* **79 E12** 41 43N 72 13W
Willingboro, *U.S.A.* **76 E8** 40 3N 74 54W
Willis Group, *Australia* **62 B5** 16 18S 150 0 E
Williston, *S. Africa* **56 E3** 31 20S 20 53 E
Williston, *Fla., U.S.A.* **77 L4** 29 23N 82 27W
Williston, *N. Dak., U.S.A.* **80 A3** 48 9N 103 37W
Williston L., *Canada* **72 B4** 56 0N 124 0W
Willits, *U.S.A.* **82 G2** 39 25N 123 21W
Willmar, *U.S.A.* **80 C7** 45 7N 95 3W
Willoughby, *U.S.A.* **78 E3** 41 39N 81 24W
Willow Bunch, *Canada* **73 D7** 49 20N 105 35W
Willow L., *Canada* **72 A5** 62 10N 119 8W
Willow Wall, The, *China* **35 C12** 42 10N 122 0 E
Willowick, *U.S.A.* **78 E3** 41 38N 81 28W
Willowlake →, *Canada* **72 A4** 62 42N 123 8W
Willowmore, *S. Africa* **56 E3** 33 15S 23 30 E
Willows, *U.S.A.* **84 F4** 39 31N 122 12W
Willowvale = Gatyana, *S. Africa* **57 E4** 32 16S 28 31 E
Wills, L., *Australia* **60 D4** 21 25S 128 51 E
Wills Cr. →, *Australia* **62 C3** 22 43S 140 2 E
Willsboro, *U.S.A.* **79 B11** 44 21N 73 24W
Willunga, *Australia* **63 F2** 35 15S 138 30 E
Wilmette, *U.S.A.* **76 D2** 42 5N 87 42W
Wilmington, *Australia* **63 E2** 32 39S 138 7 E
Wilmington, *Del., U.S.A.* **76 F8** 39 45N 75 33W
Wilmington, *N.C., U.S.A.* **77 H7** 34 14N 77 55W
Wilmington, *Ohio, U.S.A.* **76 F4** 39 27N 83 50W
Wilmington, *Vt., U.S.A.* **79 D12** 42 52N 72 52W
Wilmslow, *U.K.* **10 D5** 53 19N 2 13W
Wilpena →, *Australia* **63 E2** 31 25S 139 29 E
Wilsall, *U.S.A.* **82 D8** 45 59N 110 38W
Wilson, *N.C., U.S.A.* **77 H7** 35 44N 77 55W
Wilson, *N.Y., U.S.A.* **78 C6** 43 19N 78 50W
Wilson, *Pa., U.S.A.* **79 F9** 40 41N 75 15W
Wilson →, *Australia* **60 C4** 16 48S 128 16 E
Wilson Bluff, *Australia* **61 F4** 31 41S 129 0 E
Wilson Inlet, *Australia* **61 G2** 35 0S 117 22 E
Wilsons Promontory, *Australia* **63 F4** 38 55S 146 25 E
Wilton, *U.S.A.* **80 B4** 47 10N 100 47W
Wilton →, *Australia* **62 A1** 14 45S 134 33 E
Wiltshire □, *U.K.* **11 F6** 51 18N 1 53W
Wiltz, *Lux.* **15 E5** 49 57N 5 55 E
Wiluna, *Australia* **61 E3** 26 36S 120 14 E
Wimborne Minster, *U.K.* **11 G6** 50 48N 1 59W
Wimmera →, *Australia* **63 F3** 36 8S 141 56 E
Winam G., *Kenya* **54 C3** 0 20S 34 15 E
Winburg, *S. Africa* **56 D4** 28 30S 27 2 E
Winchendon, *U.S.A.* **79 D12** 42 41N 72 3W
Winchester, *U.K.* **11 F6** 51 4N 1 18W
Winchester, *Conn., U.S.A.* **79 E11** 41 53N 73 9W
Winchester, *Idaho, U.S.A.* **82 C5** 46 14N 116 38W
Winchester, *Ind., U.S.A.* **76 E3** 40 10N 84 59W
Winchester, *Ky., U.S.A.* **76 G3** 38 0N 84 11W
Winchester, *N.H., U.S.A.* **79 D12** 42 46N 72 23W
Winchester, *Nev., U.S.A.* **85 J11** 36 6N 115 10W
Winchester, *Tenn., U.S.A.* **77 H2** 35 11N 86 7W
Winchester, *Va., U.S.A.* **76 F6** 39 11N 78 10W
Wind →, *U.S.A.* **82 E9** 43 12N 108 12W
Wind River Range, *U.S.A.* **82 E9** 43 0N 109 30W
Windau = Ventspils, *Latvia* **9 H19** 57 25N 21 32 E
Windber, *U.S.A.* **78 F6** 40 14N 78 50W
Winder, *U.S.A.* **77 J4** 34 0N 83 45W
Windermere, *Cumb., U.K.* **10 C5** 54 23N 2 55W
Windermere, *Cumb., U.K.* **10 C5** 54 22N 2 56W
Windhoek, *Namibia* **56 C2** 22 35S 17 4 E
Windom, *U.S.A.* **80 D7** 43 52N 95 7W
Windorah, *Australia* **62 D3** 25 24S 142 36 E
Window Rock, *U.S.A.* **83 J9** 35 41N 109 3W
Windrush →, *U.K.* **11 F6** 51 43N 1 24W
Windsor, *Australia* **63 E5** 33 37S 150 50 E
Windsor, *N.S., Canada* **71 D7** 44 59N 64 5W
Windsor, *Ont., Canada* **78 D2** 42 18N 83 0W
Windsor, *U.K.* **11 F7** 51 29N 0 36W
Windsor, *Colo., U.S.A.* **80 E2** 40 29N 104 54W
Windsor, *Conn., U.S.A.* **79 E12** 41 50N 72 39W
Windsor, *Mo., U.S.A.* **80 F8** 38 32N 93 31W
Windsor, *N.Y., U.S.A.* **79 D9** 42 5N 75 37W
Windsor, *Vt., U.S.A.* **79 C12** 43 29N 72 24W
Windsor & Maidenhead □, *U.K.* **11 F7** 51 29N 0 40W
Windsorton, *S. Africa* **56 D3** 28 16S 24 44 E
Windward Is., *W. Indies* **89 D7** 13 0N 61 0W
Windward Passage = Vientos, Paso de los, *Caribbean* **89 C5** 20 0N 74 0W
Winefred L., *Canada* **73 B6** 55 30N 110 30W
Winfield, *U.S.A.* **81 G6** 37 15N 96 59W
Wingate Mts., *Australia* **60 B5** 14 25S 130 40 E
Wingham, *Australia* **63 E5** 31 48S 152 22 E
Wingham, *Canada* **78 C3** 43 55N 81 20W
Winisk, *Canada* **70 A2** 55 20N 85 15W
Winisk →, *Canada* **70 A2** 55 17N 85 5W
Winisk L., *Canada* **70 B2** 52 55N 87 22W
Wink, *U.S.A.* **81 K3** 31 45N 103 9W
Winkler, *Canada* **73 D9** 49 10N 97 56W
Winlock, *U.S.A.* **84 D4** 46 30N 122 56W
Winnebago, L., *U.S.A.* **76 D1** 44 0N 88 26W
Winnecke Cr. →, *Australia* **60 C5** 18 35S 131 34 E
Winnemucca, *U.S.A.* **82 F5** 40 58N 117 44W
Winnemucca L., *U.S.A.* **82 F4** 40 7N 119 21W
Winnett, *U.S.A.* **82 C9** 47 0N 108 21W
Winnfield, *U.S.A.* **81 K8** 31 56N 92 38W
Winnibigoshish, L., *U.S.A.* **80 B7** 47 27N 94 13W
Winnipeg, *Canada* **73 D9** 49 54N 97 9W
Winnipeg →, *Canada* **73 C9** 50 38N 96 19W
Winnipeg, L., *Canada* **73 C9** 52 0N 97 0W
Winnipeg Beach, *Canada* **73 C9** 50 30N 96 58W
Winnipegosis, *Canada* **73 C9** 51 39N 99 55W
Winnipegosis L., *Canada* **73 C9** 52 30N 100 0W
Winnipesaukee, L., *U.S.A.* **79 C13** 43 38N 71 21W
Winnisquam L., *U.S.A.* **79 C13** 43 33N 71 31W
Winnsboro, *La., U.S.A.* **81 J9** 32 10N 91 43W
Winnsboro, *S.C., U.S.A.* **77 H5** 34 23N 81 5W
Winnsboro, *Tex., U.S.A.* **81 J7** 32 58N 95 17W
Winokapau, L., *Canada* **71 B7** 53 15N 62 50W
Winona, *Minn., U.S.A.* **80 C9** 44 3N 91 39W
Winona, *Miss., U.S.A.* **81 J10** 33 29N 89 44W
Winooski, *U.S.A.* **79 B11** 44 29N 73 11W
Winooski →, *U.S.A.* **79 B11** 44 32N 73 17W
Winschoten, *Neths.* **15 A7** 53 9N 7 3 E
Winsford, *U.K.* **10 D5** 53 12N 2 31W
Winslow, *Ariz., U.S.A.* **83 J8** 35 2N 110 42W
Winslow, *Wash., U.S.A.* **84 C4** 47 38N 122 31W
Winsted, *U.S.A.* **79 E11** 41 55N 73 4W
Winston-Salem, *U.S.A.* **77 G5** 36 6N 80 15W
Winter Garden, *U.S.A.* **77 L5** 28 34N 81 35W
Winter Haven, *U.S.A.* **77 M5** 28 1N 81 44W
Winter Park, *U.S.A.* **77 L5** 28 36N 81 20W
Winterhaven, *U.S.A.* **85 N12** 32 47N 114 39W
Winters, *U.S.A.* **84 G5** 38 32N 121 58W
Wintersville, *U.S.A.* **78 F4** 40 23N 80 42W
Winterswijk, *Neths.* **15 C6** 51 58N 6 43 E
Winterthur, *Switz.* **18 C8** 47 30N 8 44 E
Winthrop, *U.S.A.* **82 B3** 48 28N 120 10W
Winton, *Australia* **62 C3** 22 24S 143 3 E
Winton, *N.Z.* **59 M2** 46 8S 168 20 E
Wirrulla, *Australia* **63 E1** 32 24S 134 31 E
Wisbech, *U.K.* **11 E8** 52 41N 0 9 E
Wisconsin □, *U.S.A.* **80 C10** 44 45N 89 30W
Wisconsin →, *U.S.A.* **80 D9** 43 0N 91 15W
Wisconsin Rapids, *U.S.A.* **80 C10** 44 23N 89 49W
Wisdom, *U.S.A.* **82 D7** 45 37N 113 27W
Wishaw, *U.K.* **12 F5** 55 46N 3 54W
Wishek, *U.S.A.* **80 B5** 46 16N 99 33W
Wisła →, *Poland* **17 A10** 54 22N 18 55 E
Wismar, *Germany* **16 B6** 53 54N 11 29 E
Wisner, *U.S.A.* **80 E6** 41 59N 96 55W
Witbank, *S. Africa* **57 D4** 25 51S 29 14 E
Witdraai, *S. Africa* **56 D3** 26 58S 20 48 E
Witham, *U.K.* **11 F8** 51 48N 0 40 E
Witham →, *U.K.* **10 E7** 52 59N 0 2W
Withernsea, *U.K.* **10 D8** 53 44N 0 1 E
Witney, *U.K.* **11 F6** 51 48N 1 28W
Witnossob →, *Namibia* **56 D3** 26 55S 20 37 E
Wittenberge, *Germany* **16 B6** 53 0N 11 45 E
Wittenoom, *Australia* **60 D2** 22 15S 118 20 E
Wkra →, *Poland* **17 B11** 52 27N 20 44 E
Wlingi, *Indonesia* **37 H15** 8 5S 112 25 E
Włocławek, *Poland* **17 B10** 52 40N 19 3 E
Włodawa, *Poland* **17 C12** 51 33N 23 31 E
Woburn, *U.S.A.* **79 D13** 42 29N 71 9W
Wodian, *China* **34 H7** 32 50N 112 35 E
Wokam, *Indonesia* **37 F8** 5 45S 134 28 E
Woking, *U.K.* **11 F7** 51 19N 0 34W
Wokingham □, *U.K.* **11 F7** 51 25N 0 51W
Wolf →, *Canada* **72 A2** 60 17N 132 33W
Wolf Creek, *U.S.A.* **82 C7** 47 0N 112 4W
Wolf L., *Canada* **72 A2** 60 24N 131 40W
Wolf Point, *U.S.A.* **80 A2** 48 5N 105 39W
Wolfe I., *Canada* **79 B8** 44 7N 76 20W
Wolfeboro, *U.S.A.* **79 C13** 43 35N 71 13W
Wolfsberg, *Austria* **16 E8** 46 50N 14 52 E
Wolfsburg, *Germany* **16 B6** 52 25N 10 48 E
Wolin, *Poland* **16 B8** 53 50N 14 37 E
Wollaston, Is., *Chile* **96 H3** 55 40S 67 30W
Wollaston L., *Canada* **73 B8** 58 7N 103 10W
Wollaston Lake, *Canada* **73 B8** 58 3N 103 33W
Wollaston Pen., *Canada* **68 B8** 69 30N 115 0W
Wollongong, *Australia* **63 E5** 34 25S 150 54 E
Wolmaransstad, *S. Africa* **56 D4** 27 12S 25 59 E
Wolseley, *S. Africa* **56 E2** 33 26S 19 7 E
Wolsey, *U.S.A.* **80 C5** 44 24N 98 28W
Wolstenholme, C., *Canada* **66 C12** 62 35N 77 30W
Wolvega, *Neths.* **15 B6** 52 52N 6 0 E
Wolverhampton, *U.K.* **11 E5** 52 35N 2 7W
Wondai, *Australia* **63 D5** 26 20S 151 49 E
Wongalarroo L., *Australia* **63 E3** 31 32S 144 0 E
Wongan Hills, *Australia* **61 F2** 30 51S 116 37 E
Wŏnju, *S. Korea* **35 F14** 37 22N 127 58 E
Wonosari, *Indonesia* **37 G14** 7 58S 110 36 E
Wonosobo, *Indonesia* **37 G13** 7 22S 109 54 E
Wonowon, *Canada* **72 B4** 56 44N 121 48W
Wŏnsan, *N. Korea* **35 E14** 39 11N 127 27 E
Wonthaggi, *Australia* **63 F4** 38 37S 145 37 E
Wood Buffalo Nat. Park, *Canada* **72 B6** 59 0N 113 41W
Wood Is., *Australia* **60 C3** 16 24S 123 19 E
Wood L., *Canada* **73 B8** 55 17N 103 17W
Woodah I., *Australia* **62 A2** 13 27S 136 10 E
Woodbourne, *U.S.A.* **79 E10** 41 46N 74 36W
Woodbridge, *Canada* **78 C5** 43 47N 79 36W
Woodbridge, *U.K.* **11 E9** 52 6N 1 20 E
Woodburn, *U.S.A.* **82 D2** 45 9N 122 51W
Woodenbong, *Australia* **63 D5** 28 24S 152 39 E